COMMERCIAL LAW

TEXT, CASES, AND MATERIALS

FOURTH EDITION

L S SEALY

S J Berwin Professor Emeritus of Corporate Law
University of Cambridge;
Barrister and Solicitor (New Zealand)

R J A HOOLEY

Professor of Law at King's College London;
Fellow of Fitzwilliam College, Cambridge;
Barrister of the Middle Temple

OXFORD
UNIVERSITY PRESS

OXFORD
UNIVERSITY PRESS

Great Clarendon Street, Oxford OX2 6DP

Oxford University Press is a department of the University of Oxford.
It furthers the University's objective of excellence in research, scholarship,
and education by publishing worldwide in

Oxford New York

Auckland Cape Town Dar es Salaam Hong Kong Karachi
Kuala Lumpur Madrid Melbourne Mexico City Nairobi
New Delhi Shanghai Taipei Toronto

With offices in

Argentina Austria Brazil Chile Czech Republic France Greece
Guatemala Hungary Italy Japan Poland Portugal Singapore
South Korea Switzerland Thailand Turkey Ukraine Vietnam

Oxford is a registered trade mark of Oxford University Press
in the UK and in certain other countries

Published in the United States
by Oxford University Press Inc., New York

© Oxford University Press 2009

British Library Cataloguing in Publication Data

Data available

Library of Congress Cataloging in Publication Data

Sealy, L. S.

Commercial law : text, cases, and materials / L. S. Sealy, R. J. A. Hooley.—4th ed.
p. cm.
Includes index.
ISBN 978–0–19–929903–4
1. Commercial law—Wales—Cases. 2. Commercial law—England.—Cases.
I. Hooley, Richard, Dr. II. Title.
KD1629.S43 2008
346.4207—dc22   2008021532

Typeset by Newgen Imaging Systems (P) Ltd., Chennai, India
Printed in Great Britain by Bell and Bain Ltd, Glasgow

ISBN 978–0–19–929903–4

20 19 18 17 16 15 14 13 12

For my parents
RH

COMMERCIAL LAW—
TEXT, CASES, AND MATERIALS

WITHDRAWN

PREFACE TO THE FOURTH EDITION

Our aim in writing the fourth edition of this book has been the same as it was for all previous editions: to provide students of commercial law with a book that combines extracts from the cases and other materials with a substantial commentary that helps put those extracts in context and questions their significance. We hope we have got somewhere near to achieving that goal.

The fourth edition takes account of scores of new cases and includes extracts from the most significant: *J & H Ritchie Ltd v Lloyd Ltd* (sale of goods); *Lonsdale v Howard & Hallam Ltd* (agency); *Architects of Wine Ltd v Barclays Bank plc* (cheques); *Barbados Trust Co v Bank of Zambia* and *Offer-Hoar v Larkstore Ltd* (assignment); *Re Spectrum Plus Ltd* (charges); *Marubeni Hong Kong and South China Ltd v Mongolian Government* (guarantees). New legislation has also impacted upon commercial law, including the Consumer Credit Act 2006, which amends the Consumer Credit Act 1974, and the Companies Act 2006, and we have assumed that these important statutes are fully in force whenever we have referred to them in the book. The chapter on trade finance has been rewritten to take account of the 2007 revision of the *Uniform Customs and Practice for Documentary Credits*, and the section of the book that deals with bills of exchange and banking incorporates references to the 2008 editions of the *Banking Code* and the *Business Banking Code*.

We are grateful to the many people who have provided us with advice and assistance. Our particular thanks go to our colleagues in Cambridge and beyond, to David Wills and the staff of the Squire Law Library, to Meera Patel, who provided valuable administrative assistance as the project drew to a close, to our publishers and, not least, to our families.

We have tried to state the law as it stood from sources available to us on 1 January 2008, although our publishers have kindly allowed us to incorporate some changes and new material at proof stage.

Len Sealy
Richard Hooley
Cambridge
May 2008

CONTENTS

PART I   INTRODUCTION

PART II THE LAW OF AGENCY

PART III DOMESTIC SALES LAW

PART IX PRINCIPLES OF INSURANCE LAW

PART X INSOLVENCY LAW

APPENDIX FORMS

ACKNOWLEDGEMENTS

Grateful acknowledgement is made to all the authors and publishers of copyright material which appears in this book, and in particular to the following for permission to reprint material from the sources indicated.

Extracts from *Law Commission Reports*, Committee Reports and other government papers are Crown copyright material and are reproduced under Class Licence Number C2006010631 with the permission of the Controller of OPSI and the Queen's Printer.

Association for Payment Clearing Services for tables from *UK Payments Statistics 2007*, copyright © APACS 2007. Note: APACS can accept no liability that may arise from any third party's reliance on these data.

Cambridge Law Journal and the authors for extracts from *Cambridge Law Journal*: Kevin Gray: 'Property in Thin Air', CLJ 252 (1991); and L S Sealy: '"Risk" in the Law of Sale', CLJ 225 (1972).

Canadian Bar Association for extract from G H L Fridman: 'The Demise of Watteau v Fenwick: Sign-o-Lite Ltd v Metropolitan Life Insurance Co' 70 *Canadian Bar Review* 329 (1991).

CCH Editions for extracts from *Commercial Law Cases* and *British Company Cases*.

Council for Law Reporting for New South Wales for extract from the *New South Wales Law Reports* (NSWLR) : *Grey v Australian Motorists and General Insurance Co Pty Ltd* [1976] 1 NSWLR 669, copyright © Council of Law Reporting for New South Wales 1994.

R Hooley for extract from 'Payment in a Cashless Society' in B A K Rider (ed): *The Realm of Company Law—A Collection of Papers in Honour of Professor Leonard Sealy* (1998).

HSBC Bank plc and Roger A Brown, Senior Legal Advisor, Group Legal Department, HSBC Holdings plc for the trade finance documentation used in the Appendix.

ICC Services Publications, 38 Cours Albert 1er, 75008 Paris, France, www.iccbooks.com, for article 14(a) and (b) from *Uniform Customs and Practice for Documentary Credits* (International Chamber of Commerce (ICC) Paris), copyright © ICC 2006. All rights reserved.

Incorporated Council of Law Reporting for extracts from the *Law Reports: Appeal Cases* (AC), *Chancery Division* (Ch), *King's Bench Division* (KB), *Queen's Bench Division* (QB), and *Weekly Law Reports* (WLR).

Informa Law for figures from Mario Giovanoli: 'Legal Issues Regarding Payment and Netting Systems' in J J Norton, C Reed and I Waldron (eds): *Cross-Border Electronic Banking* (1995); and for extracts from *Lloyd's Law Reports* (LLR).

Israel Law Review Association and the author for extract from A Barak: 'The Nature of the Negotiable Instrument', 18 *Israel LR* 49 (1983).

Law Book Co for extracts from *Commonwealth Law Reports* (CLR), © Law Book Co, part of Thomson Legal and Regulatory Ltd, http://thomson.co.au.

Monash University Law Review for extract from R Goode: 'The Codification of Commercial Law', 14 *Mon LR* 135 (1988).

Mohr Siebeck Verlag for extract from Tony Weir: 'The Common Law System' in *International Encyclopedia of Comparative Law, Vol II*, ch 2, Part III.

New Zealand Council for Law Reporting for extracts from the *New Zealand Law Reports* (NZLR).

Oxford University Press for extracts from Paul Finn: 'Fiduciary Law and the Modern Commercial World' in E McKendrick (ed): *Commercial Aspects of Trust and Fiduciary Obligations* (OUP, 1992); R Goode: 'Reflections on the Harmonization of Commercial Law' in R Cranston and R Goode (eds): *Commercial and Consumer Law—National and International Dimensions* (OUP, 1993); L Sealy and S Worthington: *Cases and Materials in Company Law* (8e, OUP, 2007); and from *Oxford Journal of Legal Studies*: E P Ellinger: 'Bank's liability for paying fraudulently issued cheques', 5 OJLS 293 (1985).

Reed Elsevier (UK) Ltd trading as LexisNexis Butterworths for extracts from Kevin J Gray: *Elements of Land Law* (1e, Butterworths, 1987); forms and documents used in the Appendix from *Encyclopedia of Forms and Precedents* (Reed Elsevier, 5e, 2002); and extracts from Law Reports: *Butterworths Company Law Cases* (BCLC) and *All ER*.

Standen Engineering Ltd for commercial invoice used in the Appendix.

Sweet and Maxwell Ltd for extracts from R Goode: 'Commercial Law in an International Environment: Towards the Next Millennium' in R Goode: *Commercial Law in the Next Millennium* (1998); F Oditah: *Legal Aspects of Receivables Financing* (1991); N E Palmer: *Bailment* (2e, 1991); *Snell's Equity* (30th edition, 2000); and *Bowstead & Reynolds on Agency* (18th edition); and for extracts from *Law Quarterly Review*: R M Goode: 'Ownership and Obligation in Commercial Transactions', 103 LQR 433 (1987); G McMeel: 'Philosophical Foundations of the Law of Agency', 116 LQR 387 (2000); Sir Peter Millett: 'Equity's place in the Law of Commerce', 114 LQR 21(1998); Severine Saintier: 'Final guidelines on compensation of commercial agents', 124 LQR 31 (2008); G Samuel: 'Civil and Commercial Law: A Distinction worth making', 102 LQR 569 (1986); and A Tettenborn: ' "Pay Now, Sue Later"—Direct Debits, Set-Off and Commercial Practice', 113 LQR 374, (1997); and from *Journal of Business Law*: Charles Debattista: 'The New UCP 600: Changes to the Tender of the Sellers Shipping Documents under Letters of Credit', JBL 329 (2007); R M Goode: 'Some Aspects of Factoring Law 1—The Acquisition of Rights and Receivables', JBL 240 (1982) and 'The Banker's Duty of Confidentiality', JBL 269 (1989); and C M Schmitthoff: 'The concept of Economic Law in England', JBL 309 (1966) and 'The codification of the Law of International Trade', JBL 34 (1985); and from Law Reports: *Professional Negligence Law Reports (PNLR)* and *Palmer's Company Cases (PCC)*.

TransCargo International UK Ltd for combined transport bill of lading used in the Appendix.

Wiley-Blackwell Publishing Ltd for extracts from *Modern Law Review*: G Battersby and A D Preston: 'The Concepts of "Property", "Title" and "Owner" used in the Sale of Goods

Act', 35 MLR 268 (1972); F E Dowrick: 'The Relationship of Principal Agent', 17 MLR 24 (1954); and R King: 'The Receiving Bank's Role in Credit Transfer Transactions', 45 MLR 369 (1982).

Every effort has been made to trace and contact copyright holders prior to publication but this has not been possible in every case. If notified, the publisher will undertake to rectify any errors or omissions at the earliest opportunity.

TABLE OF STATUTES

TABLE OF CASES

Page references printed in **bold** indicate where a case is set out.

M

PART I

INTRODUCTION

CHAPTER 1

AN INTRODUCTION TO COMMERCIAL LAW

1 THE NATURE OF COMMERCIAL LAW

What is commercial law? In the absence of any established legal definition of commercial law, writers on the subject have put forward various definitions of their own. These include the following:

'Commercial law' is an expression incapable of strict definition, but it is used to comprehend all that portion of the law of England which is more especially concerned with commerce, trade and business.

(HW Disney *The Elements of Commercial Law* (1931), p 1)

The object of commerce is to deal in merchandise and, if we adopt this criterion, commercial law can be defined as the special rules which apply to contracts for the sale of goods and to such contracts as are ancillary thereto, namely, contracts for the carriage and insurance of goods and contracts the main purpose of which is to finance the carrying out of contracts of sale.

(HC Gutteridge 'Contract and Commercial Law' (1935) 51 LQR 117)

Professor Sir Roy Goode, the leading academic commercial lawyer in the country, has described commercial law as 'that branch of law which is concerned with rights and duties arising from the supply of goods and services in the way of trade' (RM Goode *Commercial Law* (3rd edn, 2004), p 8).[1] This makes it a subject of wide compass, embracing many different areas of English law; a point made by Professor Goode in his 1997 Hamlyn Lectures when he said:

In my own perception commercial law represents the totality of the law's response to mercantile disputes. It encompasses all those principles, rules and statutory provisions, of whatever kind and from whatever source, which bear on the private law rights and obligations of parties to commercial transactions, whether between themselves or in their relationship with others.

   Thus commercial law draws for its sustenance on all the great streams of law that together make up the corpus of English jurisprudence, with the law of contract as its core, whilst equity acts now

---

[1] Roy Goode's work has had a profound impact on the way commercial law is taught and practised in this country. His enormous contribution to the development of the subject is reflected in a series of essays written by leading academics and practitioners to mark his retirement as Norton Rose Professor of English Law in the University of Oxford: see R Cranston (ed) *Making Commercial Law—Essays in Honour of Roy Goode* (1997). It is also reflected in the number of times his work is cited, and extracts from it appear, in this book! His textbook *Commercial Law*, first published in 1982, and now in its third edition (2004), is essential reading for every student of the subject.

as its handmaiden, now as the keeper of its conscience. The great judicial reformer Brougham was surely right to describe commercial law as 'far purer and free from defects than any other part of the system'.

(R Goode *Commercial Law in the Next Millennium* (1998), pp 8–9).

The thread running through these various definitions of commercial law is the mercantile nature of the subject. Commercial law *is* the law of commerce. It is concerned with commercial transactions, ie transactions in which both parties deal with each other in the course of business. The Late Payment of Commercial Debts (Interest) Act 1998 can be used to illustrate the point. According to its preamble, the Act makes 'provision with respect to interest on the late payment of certain debts arising under *commercial contracts* for the supply of goods and services; and for connected purposes' (emphasis added). The essence of a commercial contract caught by the Act can be gleaned from s 2(1) which provides that the Act 'applies to a contract for the supply of goods or services where the purchaser and the supplier are each acting in the course of a business, other than an excepted contract'. The paradigm commercial transaction is the sale and supply of goods by one merchant to another (but note that s 2(7) of the Late Payment of Commercial Debts (Interest) Act 1998 provides an extended definition of the term 'business' to include a profession and the activities of government departments or local or public authorities). However, there are many other types of commercial transaction, eg contracts for the carriage of goods, contracts for the insurance of goods, contracts for the finance of sale transactions, equipment leasing agreements, receivables financing arrangements and so on.

Many different spheres of commercial activity fall within the ambit of commercial law. It is not possible, nor desirable, to draw up an exhaustive list of the contents of the subject. Commercial law is a pragmatic and responsive subject which looks to facilitate the commercial practices of the business community. As those practices change and develop, often to accommodate new technology, the contents of commercial law may change and develop with them. A rigid definition of the scope of the subject would only inhibit this process.

'The Codification of Commercial Law' by R Goode

(1988) 14 Mon LR 135, pp 141–143

III WHAT SHOULD GO INTO A COMMERCIAL CODE?

On one view, this is simply another way of posing the question: what is commercial law? Some would even ask: does commercial law exist? Having taught the subject for nearly two decades I desperately hope it does! But what goes into it is another matter. For my purposes I shall treat commercial law as that body of law which governs commercial transactions, that is, agreements and arrangements between professionals for the provision and acquisition of goods, services and facilities in the way of trade. Commercial law as thus defined possesses four characteristics. It is based on transactions, not on institutions; it is concerned primarily with dealings between merchants, in the broad sense of professionals as opposed to consumers; it is centred on contract and on the usages of the market; and it is concerned with a large mass of transactions in which each participant is a regular player, so that the transactions are typical and in large measure repetitive and lend themselves to a substantial measure of standardised treatment. On this basis we would expect commercial law in the sense in which I have used it to exclude consumer law as a *lex specialis* involving non-professionals; to exclude for the most part obligations of a kind normally derived from non-contractual sources of law such as tort, equity, bankruptcy and trusts; and to exclude the law governing institutional structures such as partnerships, corporations, banks, insurance companies, and the like. This is not to say that these are unsuitable subjects for codification, merely that they do not belong in a *commercial* code, which is concerned with contracts and with the dynamics of goods and services moving in the stream of trade rather than with the general law of obligations and the statics of institutional structure and organisation . . .

(i) Types of transaction to be covered

Central to commercial law is that most common of contracts, the contract of sale, with its associated contracts of carriage, warehousing, insurance and finance. But the modern view of commercial law embodies a wider perspective, embracing equipment leasing, receivables financing, payment systems, personal property security, rights to investment securities, and a range of other commercial transactions not derived from a contract of sale. It is also necessary for a modern commercial code to accommodate new technology, in particular the teletransmission of trade and financial data, and new systems for clearing dealings in money, commodities and securities.

In deciding what items from a shopping list should be included in a commercial code, two points must be borne in mind. First, commercial law is not an abstraction, it is a tool for its users, whose needs will vary from place to place according to national practices, tradition and the level of sophistication of its business and financial institutions. No country should slavishly copy the sophisticated model represented by the American *Uniform Commercial Code,* which is designed for a country of fifty jurisdictions and some two hundred million inhabitants addicted to lawyers and litigation. Secondly, where the business community has codified trade usage this may make legislation both unnecessary and unhelpful. For example, there would seem little need to codify the law relating to documentary credits in view of the adoption around the world of the Uniform Customs and Practice.

(ii) The application of a commercial code to non-commercial transactions

While the emphasis of the *Uniform Commercial Code* is on commercial transactions, the draftsmen, preserving the common law tradition, made no attempt to exclude non-commercial contracts from its ambit. The formal separation of civil and commercial transactions to be found in some civil law systems has never been adopted by the common law and even those civil law jurisdictions that have it are said to have experienced difficulties. What the *Uniform Commercial Code* does do is to identify certain rules which apply solely to dealings between merchants and others which are restricted to transactions involving consumers. This is a sensible approach, for many of the Code rules are equally appropriate for commercial and non-commercial transactions, and little purpose is served by leaving the latter to remain governed by the vagaries of the common law.

(iii) Transactions omitted from the Uniform Commercial Code

Of some interest is the omission from the *Uniform Commercial Code* of major types of commercial transaction which one might expect to find covered in a code of this kind. Examples are guarantees, commercial agency, banking transactions (other than those relating to cheques) and insurance contracts. One explanation of the omission of these is that the function of the *Uniform Commercial Code* was seen not so much as codifying the commercial law in general but rather as bringing together in revised and integrated form those branches of commercial law which had already been codified in uniform laws prepared under the aegis of the National Conference of Commissions on Uniform State Laws. It may also be noted that, whether by accident or by design, the types of contract selected for inclusion in the code and its statutory predecessors are those which had been allowed to develop with the minimum interference of equity, whereas guarantees, agency, duties of bankers to customers and third parties and contracts of insurance are heavily underpinned by concepts of equitable obligation, reflecting the fact that the parties are involved not merely in a contract but in a continuing relationship and, moreover, a relationship attracting fiduciary duties. The Code, on the other hand, is concerned primarily with short-term, discrete contracts; it is not directed to on-going relationships, nor has it anything to say about the special problems of long-term contracts, problems which are relational, not purely contractual.

There is in my view no necessary reason why the rights and duties of the various parties arising from contracts of guarantee, commercial agency and the like should not be dealt with in a commercial code;

indeed, their inclusion would do much to dispel the widespread ignorance of these matters prevailing among lawyers as well as laymen . . . .

NOTES

1.   Although written with the specific purpose of stating what should go into a commercial code, this extract offers a sharp insight into the nature of commercial law generally. Unlike most civil law systems, and unlike the United States with its Uniform Commercial Code, English law has no comprehensive commercial code. Professor Goode advocates that there should be one. The issue is considered further below at pp 46–48.

2.   The American Uniform Commercial Code is a model statute sponsored by the National Conference of Commissioners on Uniform State Laws and the American Law Institute. The first official text of the UCC was approved by its sponsors and the American Bar Association in 1952 and it has been revised on several occasions since. The UCC has been fully adopted by all the United States except Louisiana (which has a civil law tradition). The stated purpose of the UCC is 'to simplify, clarify and modernize the law governing commercial transactions; to permit the continued expansion of commercial practices through custom usage and agreement of the parties; to make uniform the law among the various jurisdictions' (s 1–102(2)). It covers a wide range of commercial activity: sales (art 2); leases (art 2A); negotiable instruments (rev art 3); bank deposits and collections (art 4); wholesale wire transfers (art 4A); letters of credit (rev art 5); bulk transfers and bulk sales (rev art 6); warehouse receipts, bills of lading and other documents of title (art 7); investment securities (rev art 8); secured transactions (rev art 9). The UCC has been a great success. Much of the credit for this must go to the Code's chief architect, Professor Karl N Llewellyn. Professor Llewellyn's desire to avoid unnecessary theorisation and keep the Code as close to business reality as possible has made the UCC extremely workable.

3.   Professor Goode asks: does commercial law exist? His entertaining answer disguises the importance of the question. It is sometimes argued that commercial law consists of no more than a collection of distinct subjects (eg agency, sales, negotiable instruments, security) each possessing its own rules but with no common thread of principle running through them. If this is true, 'commercial law' is merely a label which is useful for gathering together diverse material with no obvious home of its own, so as to aid exposition on a lecture course or in a textbook, or for the better organisation of the business of the High Court of Justice (see the Civil Procedure Rules 1998, r 58.1 (2), set out below at p 11, defining the business suitable to be heard by the Commercial Court), but no more. On the other hand, if there are common principles running through the law's response to those spheres of commercial activity which fall within the ambit of 'commercial law', the subject gains an existence of its own. Those common principles may then be used for the better understanding of the subject and as important guides when facing new problems not previously the subject of judicial decisions. Professor Goode firmly believes that such unifying principles do exist (see the extract which appears below at pp 38–43). We agree with him, but note that those principles are not so easy to identify. There is no neat body of uniform rules unique to commercial transactions. Unlike most civil law systems, English common law does not make any formal distinction between commercial and non-commercial transactions (statute may do so, see, eg the Unfair Contract Terms Act 1977, ss 3, 6, 7; the Sale of Goods Act 1979, ss 14(2), 2(D), (3), 15A, 20(4), 32(4), 35(3), 48A–F; the Unfair Terms in Consumer Contracts

Regulations 1999 (SI 1999/2083), regs 3, 4; the Late Payment of Commercial Debts (Interest) Act 1998, s 2(1)), although there is some evidence that English judges do distinguish between commercial law and civil law generally when deciding cases. Compare the following extracts.

'The Common Law System' by Tony Weir in *International Encyclopedia of Comparative Law Vol II*, Ch 2, Part III, para 146

Resistance of judges and jurists.—Holdsworth (History V 147) said that 'the distinctive character of the rules of commercial law, and their adaptability to the ever changing needs of new commercial conditions, have caused them to preserve many characteristic features unknown in other departments of the common law'. This statement is, however, open to doubt. It has already been seen that the common law adapted increasingly slowly, when at all, to the changing needs and practices of commerce. Legislation was frequently called for and 'the necessity of such recourse . . . seems to argue a failure on the part of the lawyers to adjust to the views of commerce'. Furthermore, it is not at all clear that the rules of commercial law are really very different in substance from the rules of civil law. Some transactions, of course, will be entered only by merchants as, for example, marine insurance. But the rules of marine insurance, though different from those of land insurance, are surprisingly little different. Other transactions, such as sale of goods, are entered by merchants and private citizens alike. In such cases the common law studiously avoids making different rules for the two cases, although it may well be that the same rules are applied somewhat differently.

Indicative of the dislike of the judges for treating commercial law as special is their readiness to analogise from the commercial to the private sphere. The liability of the shipowner to the cargo-owner for damage to the goods is compared with the liability of the employer to the employee injured at work; whether a stevedore can claim the sea carrier's limitation of liability for damaging the cargo is related to whether a bus driver can claim his employer's immunity in a question with a passenger who falls off a bus.

In a difficult case concerning a time-voyage charterparty the House of Lords were pressed with the analogy of the consumer taking a car on hire-purchase; and of deviation from the contract by sea-carrier and dry-cleaner one judge said 'both are governed by and *only* by the general law relating to contracts' (judicial emphasis). The judges do not think of commercial law as a separate part of the law or they would not analogise so widely.

The same is true of jurists. Textbooks on the law of contract juxtapose, almost without comment, contracts in restraint of marriage and contracts in restraint of trade; both are treated simply as promises which are unenforceable on the grounds of public policy, and the distinction between civil law and commercial law is simply not perceived or, by not being mentioned, is actually obscured. More particularly, a decision of the Court of Appeal in 1906 has met with almost unanimous condemnation from academic writers. The Court decided that whereas a person was bound who carelessly permitted himself to be deceived into signing a negotiable instrument, subsequently negotiated, a person was not bound who similarly signed a non-negotiable instrument, it being supposed in both cases that the person signing the document believed himself to be signing a document of a quite different kind.

Writers think that the distinction between a negotiable instrument and a non-negotiable instrument is unsound. Yet almost any lawyer with a sense of the needs of commerce would find the distinction worth considering. Most significant of all indications that common lawyers do not consider commercial law as distinct from civil law is the fact that in English law the general part of contract is huge, and the differences between the specific types of contract always underplayed.

'Civil and Commercial Law: A Distinction Worth Making' by G Samuel
(1986) 102 LQR 569, pp 577–578

At first sight it is very easy to answer the question whether the common lawyer recognises the distinction between civil and commercial law. As Weir has observed, the 'phrase "commercial law" is by no means unknown to English lawyers or unused by them,' but 'if asked what it contrasted with rather than what it contained [the English lawyer] would have no answer at all.' No doubt, then, the academic could write a monograph on the topic and the practitioner would see an important procedural significance in cases which attracted the label; yet if either the academic or the practitioner was asked whether it would be of significance that the parties, or a party, to a property or contractual transaction fall(s) into the class of *commerçant* the likely response would be in the negative. However such a response might well have to be qualified on reflection. Despite Maine, it is not beneath the dignity of a modern court to link ownership with mercantile status nor to measure liability by reference to the 'commercial man' or 'men of business or professional men'; and legislation for some time now has been prepared to place a litigant (including the state) into a business class if his activities are of a certain kind. The status of a party, whether it is defined directly or indirectly, can have a bearing on the application and interpretation of private law rules.

Moreover the status test is, as the Continental lawyer will testify, only one approach. If one looks at the other test, that of the type of transaction, then the problem for the English lawyer becomes more acute: for although topics like contract and tort do not on the whole like formally to distinguish between the status of the parties, the fact that the relationship or transaction is a commercial one can be of great significance. This transaction approach is, not surprisingly, of relevance in legislation, particularly in legislation recognising consumer interests; yet the common law must by no means be overlooked. Thus in bailment relationships the fact that the bailment is a 'commercial one' can be of importance in the determination of a restitution claim for the bailee's expenses; and in the law of contract not only must 'commercial reality' be on occasions openly recognised as an aid to the inter-pretation and application of a rule like consideration but the fact that the contract itself is a mercantile one can have important implications with regard to implied terms or agency. Furthermore in the tort relationship of duty of care a business context is to be differentiated from the social gathering when the focus is upon advice given or statements made; and in deciding upon the validity of an assignment of a cause of action much will depend upon whether the assignee has 'a genuine commercial interest' in enforcing the claim. The fact, then, that the act or transaction is a 'commercial' or 'business' one in that it involves, say, a mercantile contract, a commercial interest or a business context may well have a direct bearing upon the outcome of some contract, tort and property cases.

NOTE

In *Re State of Norway's Application (No 1 & 2)* [1990] 1 AC 723, the House of Lords had to decide whether a Norwegian court's request for the oral examination of witnesses in England related to 'proceedings in any civil or commercial matter' under s 9(1) of the Evidence (Proceedings in Other Jurisdictions) Act 1975. Lord Goff, with whom all their Lordships agreed, had no doubt that the words in s 9(1) should be given their ordinary meaning, so that proceedings in any civil matter should include all proceedings other than criminal proceedings, and proceedings in any commercial matter should be treated as falling within proceedings in civil matters. This means that the distinction between commercial and non-commercial civil matters is meaningless for the purposes of interpreting s 9(1) of the 1975 Act. The case does not decide that the distinction is necessarily meaningless in another context.

2 THE FUNCTION OF COMMERCIAL LAW

In *Kum v Wah Tat Bank Ltd* [1971] 1 Lloyd's Rep 439 at 444, Lord Devlin stated that:

The function of the commercial law is to allow, so far as it can, commercial men to do business in the way they want to do it and not to require them to stick to forms that they may think to be outmoded. The common law is not bureaucratic.

This statement captures the fundamental purpose of commercial law: the facilitation of commercial transactions, ie transactions between parties dealing with each other in the course of business. This purpose generally underlies the reasoning of the judges in cases involving commercial disputes. As Lord Goff once wrote in an article analysing the objectives of the judges when interpreting commercial contracts ([1984] LMCLQ 382 at p 391):

Our only desire is to give sensible commercial effect to the transaction. We are there to help businessmen, not to hinder them: we are there to give effect to their transactions, not to frustrate them: we are there to oil the wheels of commerce, not to put a spanner in the works, or even grit in the oil.

Often the judges are simply giving their seal of approval to techniques developed by practising commercial lawyers who use the law as a 'malleable resource which can be used instrumentally to achieve their clients' ends' (R Cranston 'Doctrine and Practice in Commercial Law' in Ch 9 of K Hawkins (ed) *The Human Face of Law–Essays in Honour of Donald Harris* (1997), p 199). As Professor Cranston observes (ibid, pp 218–219):

The practising lawyers are the main creative element, reacting to the needs of their clients; the courts then respond to the devices which the lawyers develop, approving (with or without qualification) or disapproving. Importantly, common law courts have in the main approved—instead of being too concerned with elaborate edifices or logical consistency, common law courts have crafted doctrinal lines consistent with commercial needs in a largely pragmatic manner (eg R Chorley, 'Liberal Trends in Present-Day Commercial Law' (1940) 1 MLR 272).

This was the stance taken by Lord Hoffmann in *Re Bank of Credit and Commerce International SA (No 8)* [1998] AC 214, where the House of Lords had to consider whether it was legally possible for a bank to take an effective charge over its own customer's credit balance, a matter of common commercial practice, when he declared (at 228):

I think that the Courts should be very slow to declare a practice of the commercial community to be conceptually impossible.[2]

Lord Hoffmann, delivering a judgment with which all their Lordships agreed, went on to hold that there was no reason why a bank could not take a charge over its own customer's deposit. However, the decision has been criticised by no less than Professor Goode, usually a strong advocate of commercial realism injudicial decision making, as 'showing how a determined jurist can surmount apparently insuperable conceptual problems in order to arrive at what he perceives to be a sensible commercial result' (RM Goode *Commercial Law in the Next Millennium* (1998), p 69). The case highlights the tension that can exist when a court bends established legal doctrine, in this case the meaning of the concept of proprietary interest, to fit commercial needs (for further details, see below, p 1040).

---

[2] This echoes the famous dictum of Hammond J in *Commercial Factors Ltd v Maxwell Printing Ltd* [1994] NZLR 724 at 727 that good commercial law should follow good commercial practice.

Only in exceptional cases will the court relegate commercial needs to the back seat. This happened in *Hazell v Hammersmith and Fulham London Borough Council* [1992] 2 AC 1, where the House of Lords held that local authorities did not have the capacity to enter into swap transactions[3] with the result that such transactions concluded between banks and other financial institutions with local authorities were void *ab initio*.[4] The result of this decision was that the local authorities were allowed to walk away from the swap agreements they had freely entered into. Although swap transactions are normal everyday occurrences in the financial markets, and are recognised as a valuable mechanism for the effective management of debt, so far as their Lordships were concerned swaps were highly speculative in character and the ratepayers of Hammersmith and Fulham had to be protected from having public funds used in this way. The decision caused great concern in the City of London, and was condemned as damaging the City's reputation as a world financial centre, especially with foreign banks which had entered into swap transactions with local authorities in good faith. It may be best explained as a case of 'public law trumping commercial law' (R Cranston 'Doctrine and Practice in Commercial Law' in Ch 9 of K Hawkins (ed) *The Human Face—Essays in Honour of Donald Harris* (1997), p 217).

Businessmen have special needs. First, they demand that their agreements be upheld. Secondly, they require the decisions of the courts on commercial issues to be predictable so that they know where they stand. Thirdly, they need the law to be flexible enough to take account of their latest business practices. Fourthly, they want their disputes resolved quickly, inexpensively and effectively. Both in its substance and in its procedure commercial law attempts to facilitate commercial transactions by endeavouring to meet these special needs of the business community.

As to the first need (upholding commercial bargains), the courts adopt a non-interventionist approach with regard to commercial contracts. The judges work on the assumption that there is equality of bargaining power between commercial men. This assumption underpins two basic principles of commercial law: freedom of contract and sanctity of contract. As the late Professor Schmitthoff wrote ([1966] JBL 309 at p 315):

The basis of commercial law is the contractual principle of autonomy of the parties' will. Subject to the ultimate reservation of public policy, the parties are free to arrange their affairs as they like.

As to the second need (predictability of legal decisions on commercial issues), the courts have consistently promoted considerations of 'certainty', in the sense of predictability, of outcome over those of fairness and justice. In *Vallejo v Wheeler* (1774) 1 Cowp 143 at 153 Lord Mansfield said: 'In all mercantile transactions the great object should be certainty: and therefore, it is of more consequence that a rule be certain, than whether the rule is established one way or the other. Because speculators in trade then know what ground to go upon.' More recently, in *Mardorf Peach & Co Ltd v Attica Sea Carriers Corpn of Liberia, The Laconia* [1977] AC 850 at 878, Lord Salmon stated tersely that: 'Certainty is of primary importance in all commercial transactions.' Sometimes the courts forget this. The majority decision of the House of Lords in *Kleinwort Benson Ltd v Lincoln City Council* [1999] 2 AC 349, which

---

[3] There are various types of swap transactions, eg interest rate swaps, currency swaps etc. In its simplest form a swap involves 'an agreement between two parties by which each agrees to pay the other on a specified date or dates an amount calculated by reference to the interest which would have accrued over a given period on the same notional principal sum assuming different rates of interest are payable in each case' (*Hazell v Hammersmith and Fulham London Borough Council* [1990] 2 QB 697, 739–741, Div Ct).

[4] For a review of the swaps litigation and fallout following it, see E McKendrick 'Local Authorities and Swaps: Undermining the Market?' in Ch 9 of R Cranston (ed) *Making Commercial Law* (1997).

allows a payer to rely on the retrospective effect of a change in the law arising from a subsequent judicial decision to recover money paid decades earlier, on the ground that it was paid under a mistake, even though it was paid under a settled view of the law at that time, may be criticised for failing to take into account the fundamental principles of certainty and finality in commercial transactions. The same criticism can be made of *The Golden Victory* [2007] UKHL 12, [2007] 2 WLR 691, where a majority of the House of Lords ignored the usual rule that damages are assessed at the time of breach of contract and, applying the principle of 'fair compensation', held that there was an exception to this rule when subsequent events, known to the court, had reduced the value of the contractual rights in question. But the contract that had been repudiated in this case was a charterparty, a commercial contract par excellence, and we must agree with the powerful dissent of Lord Bingham who pointed out (at [1]) that 'the [majority's] decision undermines the quality of certainty which is a traditional strength and major selling point of English commercial law'.

Traditionally, the third need (flexibility to accommodate new commercial practices) has been met by judicial recognition of mercantile custom and usage. Courts take mercantile custom and usage into account when interpreting commercial contracts. However, not every trade custom and usage will be recognised by the courts, and the presence of a well drafted contract usually leaves little scope for reference to it (P Devlin (1951) 14 MLR 249 at 251). A trade custom or usage will not be received by the court unless it can be shown to be reasonable, to be consistent with the express terms of the contract and to be universally recognised in the trade as a binding custom (see below, p 24). This last requirement can often be difficult to prove. Where the courts are unable to take account of mercantile practice, so that the smooth operation of commercial transactions is being frustrated by the courts, Parliament may intervene to remedy the situation. For example, see the Carriage of Goods by Sea Act 1992, which avoids problems of privity of contract by allowing the buyer, sub-buyer or consignee of goods, as lawful holder of the bill of lading (or certain other documents commonly used in sea transport), the right to sue the carrier on the contract of carriage (see below, p 491). But contrast the stance taken by the Government after *Hazell v Hammersmith and Fulham London Borough Council* [1992] 2 AC 1 (above), when it refused to introduce retrospective legislation reversing the House of Lords' decision that swap transactions concluded by banks with local authorities were *ultra vires* the local authorities (perhaps venting its displeasure at the fact that the banks had assisted the local authorities to avoid Government controls on their expenditure).

The fourth need (speedy, inexpensive and efficient dispute resolution) is met, to a greater or lesser degree, by the practice and procedures of the Commercial Court and the availability of commercial arbitration. The Commercial Court has jurisdiction to try 'commercial claims', defined in r 58.1(2) of the Civil Procedure Rules 1998 to mean:

any claim arising out of the transaction of trade and commerce and includes any claim relating to: (a) a business document or contract, (b) the export or import of goods, (c) the carriage of goods by land, sea, air or pipeline, (d) the exploitation of oil and gas reserves or other natural resources, (e) insurance and re-insurance, (f) banking and financial services, (g) the operation of markets and exchanges, (h) the purchase and sale of commodities, (i) the construction of ships, (j) business agency, and (k) arbitration.

The Commercial Court is a separate court of the Queen's Bench Division of the High Court staffed by judges who are experienced arbiters of commercial disputes.[5] The rules of the

---

[5] It seems that one of the main reasons for establishing the Commercial List in 1875 was the outrage caused by the incompetence of Mr Justice JC Lawrence in his conduct of the trial in *Rose v Bank of Australasia* [1894] AC 687, a claim by a shipowner for general average contribution from cargo-owners. According to a note

Commercial Court are flexible and operate with the minimum of formality. The judges of the Commercial Court have developed procedures which meet the needs of Court users: eg injunctions to prevent defendants from disposing of their assets (a 'freezing injunction', formerly known as a *Mareva* injunction) and orders allowing seizure of evidence which might otherwise be destroyed (a 'search order', formerly known as an *Anton Piller* order— the jurisdiction for which can now be found in s 7 of the Civil Procedure Act 1997). Many of the procedures of the Commercial Court, together with efficient case management techniques developed by commercial court judges, were adopted by Lord Woolf in his blueprint for reform of civil litigation in general (*Access to Justice, Final Report,* July 1996), and have found their way into the Civil Procedure Rules 1998. For detailed guidance on the workings of the Commercial Court, see the *Admiralty and Commercial Court Guide* (7th edn, 2006), available via the Court Service website at www.courtservice.gov.uk. See also A Colman, *Commercial Court* (5th edn, 2000); R Cranston (2007) 26 CJQ 190.

Litigation can be slow and prove costly,[6] and it is generally thought that arbitration provides a quicker and cheaper alternative for dispute resolution. There are a number of other reasons why the parties to a commercial dispute may opt for arbitration as opposed to litigation: these include more flexible procedures, confidentiality, the availability of arbitrators who have personal experience of the trade in which the dispute has arisen, and the fact that there is only a limited right of appeal against arbitration awards thus ensuring that the dispute is not prolonged by a long appeal process. To ensure that arbitration continues to provide fair, speedy and cost effective resolution of disputes by an impartial tribunal, English arbitration law was overhauled by the Arbitration Act 1996, which reflects as far as possible the structure, language and spirit of the UNCITRAL Model Law on International Commercial Arbitration (1985). Unusually for English legislation, the Act contains a number of statements of general principles which reveal its philosophy. Section 1 of the Arbitration Act 1996 provides that:

The provisions of this Part are founded on the following principles and shall be construed accordingly—

(a) the object of arbitration is to obtain the fair resolution of disputes by an impartial tribunal without unnecessary delay or expense;

(b) the parties should be free to agree how their disputes are resolved, subject only to such safeguards as are necessary in the public interest;

(c) in matters governed by this Part the court should not intervene except as provided by this Part.

The Arbitration Act 1996 restates in clearer terms the previous legislation on arbitration, codifies principles established by recent case law and introduces a number of changes into the law. Two changes warrant special mention. First, the Act makes it even harder than it was before to appeal from an arbitration award (s 69). This has led Lord Saville, the chief

---

written by Sir Francis Mackinnon in the Law Quarterly Review ((1944) 60 LQR 323), Lawrence J was 'a stupid man, a very ill-equipped lawyer, and a bad judge' who 'knew as much about the principles of general average as a Hindoo about figure-skating'. The transcript of Lawrence J's judgment is reproduced in 'Mr Justice Lawrence: the 'True Begetter' of the English Commercial Court' by VV Veeder QC in (1994) 110 LQR 292.

[6] The Civil Justice Review published in 1988 records that trials estimated as lasting 2–4 weeks would take 3½ years before they could be heard by the Commercial Court, and trials estimated to last over 4 weeks would take over 4 years before they were heard. This sort of delay undermines the very *raison d'être* of the Commercial Court and led to the establishment, from 1990 onwards, of 'Mercantile Lists' in major regional centres, such as Liverpool, Manchester, Birmingham, Cardiff, Chester, Leeds, Newcastle and Bristol, to take pressure off the Commercial Court in London (there is also now a separate Mercantile Court in London which deals with claims of lesser value and complexity than come before the Commercial Court). See the Civil Procedure Rules 1998, Part 59 'Mercantile Courts'.

architect of the Act, to comment: 'This should, and is intended to, make successful applications for leave to appeal from an arbitration award very rare indeed' ([1997] LMCLQ 502,
509). Secondly, s 46(1)(b) allows the parties to authorise the arbitral tribunal to decide the
dispute 'in accordance with such other considerations as are agreed by them or determined
by the tribunal'. This enables the parties to agree that their disputes are to be decided in
accordance with 'equity clauses' (or arbitration *'ex aequo et bono'* or as *'aimable composi-
teur'*). Prior to the Arbitration Act 1996, there had been uncertainty as to whether such
clauses were valid under English law. One commentator has remarked that s 46(1)(b) 'is
extraordinarily bold, as it apparently allows invocation not only of standards such as equity,
but any criteria whatsoever, limited only by public policy' (F Davidson [1997] JBL 101, 121).
Finally, it should be noted that while the Act is intended to be a comprehensive statute, it is
not intended to be an exhaustive code. For example, a basic tenet of English arbitration law
is that, subject to certain exceptions, an arbitration is confidential, but this principle is not
to be found in the Act. The courts uphold the confidentiality of the arbitration as an implied
term of the contract to arbitrate (*Ali Shipping Corpn v Shipyard Trogir* [1998] 2 All ER 136,
CA; see also S Males [1998] LMCLQ 245).

Sir John Donaldson MR (later Lord Donaldson) once described the courts and the arbitrators respectively as the public and private sectors of the administration of justice industry
(*Bremer Vulkan Schiffbau und Maschinenfabrik v South India Shipping Corpn Ltd* [1981] AC
909 at 921). Both sectors of the industry have striven to meet the needs of the business community and in doing so have attracted many foreign litigants and arbitrants to have their
disputes resolved in this jurisdiction. Over 80% of all claims heard in the Commercial Court
have a claimant or defendant from outside the jurisdiction (*Report of the Commercial Court
and Admiralty Court 2005–2006*, p 2: available via www.hmcourts-service.gov.uk). This has
brought much needed revenue into the United Kingdom. It is estimated that litigation at the
Commercial Court brings in invisible earnings of some £800 million a year.

Potential litigants and arbitrants also have an array of alternative dispute resolution
('ADR') procedures available to them (eg conciliation, mediation, minitrials, early neutral
evaluation). Unlike litigation or arbitration, ADR processes are non-binding (which some
perceive as a disadvantage), but they tend to be more informal, flexible and cheaper that traditional dispute resolution machinery (clear advantages). ADR is particularly useful where
the parties to the dispute have a continuing relationship which would be placed in jeopardy
by the more hostile, adversarial, environment of litigation or arbitration. For some time the
Commercial Court has encouraged use of ADR procedures in appropriate cases, particularly
those cases which would be unduly costly or cumbersome to litigate before the court and
has even offered its own early neutral evaluation service since 1996. The Commercial Court
has been an innovator in this respect. But following Lord Woolf's proposals for reform of
the civil justice system, all courts are now enjoined, as part of 'active case management', to
encourage and facilitate the use of ADR where appropriate (Civil Procedure Rules 1998,
r 1.4). Parties and their lawyers might have to face uncomfortable costs consequences if they
turn down out of hand the chance of ADR (*Dunnett v Railtrack plc (in railway administration)* [2002] EWCA Civ 303, [2002] 2 All ER 850 at [14]–[15], per Brooke LJ). The issue turns
on whether the party that rejects ADR has acted 'unreasonably'. Failure to accede to the
court's suggestion is necessarily unreasonable (A Burrows (ed), *English Private Law*, 2nd
edn, 2007, para 22.95); failure to accede to the opponent's suggestion must be assessed against
guidance provided by the Court of Appeal in *Halsey v Milton Keynes General NHA Trust*
[2004] EWCA Civ 576, [2004] 1 WLR 3002, at [16]ff. The court may stay proceedings to allow
the use of ADR, either where the parties request it or where the court, of its own initiative,

considers it appropriate (r 26.4). In the Commercial Court it is rare for proceedings to be stayed. The normal practice is to adjourn the proceedings or to extend time limits or, more usually, to space out the case management timetable to allow a limited period during which ADR can be attempted (*Cable & Wireless plc v IBM United Kingdom Ltd* [2002] EWHC 2059 (Comm), [2002] 2 All ER (Comm) 1041 at [34], per Colman J).

QUESTIONS

1.　Why do you think that English commercial law has been so accommodating to the needs of the business community?

2.　Is there always equality of bargaining power between business enterprises?

3.　Why did Lord Saville intend to make successful applications for leave to appeal from arbitration awards 'very rare indeed'?

3　THE HISTORICAL DEVELOPMENT OF COMMERCIAL LAW [7]

(a)　The *lex mercatoria*

Modern commercial law has its roots in the *lex mercatoria* (law merchant) of the Middle Ages. During that period merchants would travel with their goods to fairs and markets across Europe. Their disputes would be settled by special local courts, such as the courts of the fairs and boroughs and the staple courts, where judge and jury would be merchants themselves. These merchant courts would decide cases quickly and apply the *lex mercatoria* as opposed to the local law.

The *lex mercatoria* was an international law of commerce. It was based on the general customs and practices of merchants which were common throughout Europe and was applied almost uniformly by the merchant courts in different countries. In England the *lex mercatoria* developed outside the common law and many of its principles differed from those of the common law (although some modern legal historians now dispute this, arguing instead that the *lex mercatoria* did not develop as a distinct body of substantive law but was 'an expeditious procedure especially adapted for the needs of men who could not tarry for the common law').[8] The *lex mercatoria* derived its authority from voluntary acceptance by the merchants whose conduct it sought to regulate. The *lex mercatoria* suited their needs. It emphasised freedom of contract and freedom of alienability of movable property. It was flexible enough to adapt to new mercantile practices. Most significantly of all, it was speed-ily administered by merchant courts which shunned legal technicalities and often decided cases *ex aequo et bono*. It was during this period that some of the most important features of modern commercial law were developed: the bill of exchange, the charterparty and the

---

[7]　For an excellent summary of the historical development of commercial law, see CM Schmitthoff *Commercial Law in a Changing Economic Climate* (2nd edn, 1981), Chs 1 and 2. See also Lord Irvine of Lairg LC 'The Law: An Engine for Trade' (2001) 64 MLR 333. For a detailed survey, see WS Holdsworth *A History of English Law,* Vol 1, pp 526–573; Vol 5, pp 60–154; Vol 8, pp 99–300.

[8]　See JH Baker 'The Law Merchant and the Common Law' (1979) 38 CLJ 295 at p 301; JS Rogers *The Early History of the Law of Bills and Notes* (1995), especially Ch 1.

bill of lading, the concepts of assignability and negotiability, the acceptance of stoppage in transit and general average.

(b) Incorporation of the *lex mercatoria* into the common law

In the fifteenth and sixteenth centuries most of the business of the merchant courts was taken over by the Court of Admiralty, which continued to recognise the *lex mercatoria*. But in the seventeenth century the commercial jurisdiction of the Admiralty Court was itself taken over by the common law courts. This was mainly due to the work of Sir Edward Coke. As the merchant courts were by then defunct, the common law courts captured most of the nation's mercantile litigation. In an attempt to keep that business the common law courts adopted some of the rules of the *lex mercatoria*. But it was not until the late seventeenth and eighteenth centuries that the *lex mercatoria* was fully incorporated into the common law. This was largely done through the work of Sir John Holt (Chief Justice from 1689 to 1710) and Lord Mansfield (Chief Justice from 1756 to 1788). Holt CJ was responsible for important developments in the law relating to negotiable instruments, bailment and agency. But he was too conservative in outlook to complete the process of incorporation of the *lex mercatoria* into the common law (eg see his judgment in *Clerke v Martin* (1702) 2 Ld Raym 757: below, p 522). It was left to Lord Mansfield to complete this task and earn himself the accolade of 'founder of the commercial law of this country' (*Lickbarrow v Mason* (1787) 2 Term Rep 63 at 73, per Buller J). As the late Professor Schmitthoff wrote:

…the reform which Lord Mansfield carried out when sitting with his special jurymen at Guildhall in London was ostensibly aimed at the simplification of commercial procedure but was, in fact, much more: its purpose was the creation of a body of substantive commercial law, logical, just, modern in character and at the same time in harmony with the principles of the common law. It was due to Lord Mansfield's genius that the harmonisation of commercial custom and the common law was carried out with an almost complete understanding of the requirements of the commercial community, and the fundamental principles of the old law and that that marriage of ideas proved acceptable to both merchants and lawyers.

(C M Schmitthoff 'International Business Law, A New Law Merchant' in
Current Law and Social Problems (1961), p 137)

(c) The age of commercial codification[9]

The development of commercial law through the common law led to a complex, and sometimes conflicting, mass of case law. In the nineteenth century there was a call for rationalisation of the law through codification. This process was achieved not by an all-embracing commercial code but through the codification of certain defined areas of commercial law. It resulted from the work of some exceptional draftsmen. Sir Mackenzie Chalmers drafted the Bills of Exchange Act 1882, the Sale of Goods Act 1893 and the Marine Insurance Act 1906. Sir Frederick Pollock drafted the Partnership Act 1890. All of these statutes remain in force today—though the Sale of Goods Act 1893 has been re-enacted with several amendments as the Sale of Goods Act 1979 (and the 1979 Act was itself amended in 1994,1995 and 2003, although it still retains most of the essential features of the 1893 Act). A fine testimony to the

[9]   HC Gutteridge 'Contract and Commercial Law' (1935) 51 LQR 91 at p 117.

work of these great draftsmen. For an historical account of the codification of commercial law in Victorian Britain, see A Rodgers (1992) 109 LQR 570.

(d) The rise of consumerism

The next great era of change came with the development of the welfare state after the Second World War. During this period there has been a move away from the principles of freedom and sanctity of contract (and the laissez-faire economics upon which those principles were based) which had dominated Victorian thinking,[10] towards those of social responsibility and the protection of the economically weaker against the economically stronger.[11] This change is reflected in the expansion of consumer protection legislation in recent years: see especially the Trade Descriptions Acts 1968 and 1972, the Unsolicited Goods and Services Act 1971, the Fair Trading Act 1973, the Supply of Goods (Implied Terms) Act 1973, the Consumer Credit Act 1974, the Unfair Contract Terms Act 1977, and the Consumer Protection Act 1987, together with a host of delegated legislation, often implementing EC consumer protection initiatives, including, most significantly, the Unfair Terms in Consumer Contracts Regulations 1999 (SI 1999/2083) and the Consumer Protection from Unfair Trading Regulations 2008 (SI 2008/1277) which implement EC Directive 2005/29 concerning unfair business-to-consumer commercial practices.

It is important to get some idea of the relationship between consumer law and commercial law (as defined at the start of this chapter). Some see consumer law as an application of general commercial law principles in a specific context, although greatly amended by special consumer legislation (see F Reynolds 'The Applicability of General Rules of Private Law to Consumer Disputes' in S Andermann et al (eds) *Law and the Weaker Party* (1982), Vol 2, pp 93–110). But the differences between the two seem much more fundamental than this approach suggests. Whereas commercial law is concerned with transactions in which both parties deal with each other in the course of business, consumer law is primarily concerned with transactions between ordinary individuals (consumers) and those who provide goods and services on a commercial basis. Whereas commercial law is based on the premise that businessmen are of roughly equal bargaining power, consumer law assumes that the consumer and business enterprise are economically unequal. Whilst commercial law is happy for businessmen to regulate their own affairs through mercantile usage, usage plays only a peripheral role in consumer transactions (a consumer may be bound by the reasonable usage of the market in which the business provider of goods or services deals, eg 'a man who employs a banker is bound by the usage of bankers' *Hare v Henty* (1861) 10 CBNS 65, 142 ER 374, 379). These fundamental differences in philosophy mean that whereas commercial law is non-interventionist and essentially pragmatic in nature, consumer law intrudes into contracts made between consumer and business supplier and is essentially an instrument of social policy.

To allow the principles of consumer law to intervene in commercial transactions would undermine the level of certainty that such transactions demand. It is certainly true to say that the legislature and courts have kept consumer law and international trade law separate, eg the statutory control of exemption clauses, under the Unfair Contract Terms Act 1977,

---

[10] See generally, PS Atiyah *The Rise and Fall of Freedom of Contract* (1979).
[11] Atiyah and Smith note that the principles of freedom of contract have been revitalised since 1980 because of the influence of a new generation of pro-market economists and economist-lawyers: see SA Smith, *Atiyah's Introduction to the Law of Contract* (6th edn, 2006), pp 16–20.

does not apply to contracts of insurance, contracts of marine salvage or towage, charterparties, contracts for the carriage of goods by sea, and international supply contracts (ss 1(2), 26; Sch 1). However, the same cannot always be said with regard to the relationship between consumer law and commercial law on the domestic level. Despite some legislative attempts to keep the two separate (eg ss 15A, 20(4) and 48A–F of the Sale of Goods Act 1979 draw a clear line between consumer sales and non-consumer sales), and the fact that the courts generally appear to keep the commercial or consumer nature of a dispute in mind when applying rules which do not formally distinguish between the two types of transaction (see above, p 8), there is evidence that the ambit of consumer law is expanding and that it threatens to draw within it some transactions which previously fell within the commercial domain. First, some consumer protection legislation applies as much to business enterprises as it does to private individuals, eg the Consumer Credit Act 1974 applies where credit is provided to a business, so long as it is an unincorporated business (but the Act does not apply where the credit exceeds £25,000 and it is provided wholly or predominately for business purposes). Secondly, the courts have been willing to expand the concept of 'consumer' to include within it a corporate business enterprise (see *R&B Customs Brokers Co Ltd v United Dominions Trust Ltd* [1988] 1 WLR 321, CA; *Feldarol Foundry plc v Hermes Leasing (London) Ltd* [2004] EWCA Civ 747; cf *Stevenson v Rogers* [1999] 1 All ER 613, CA). Thirdly, even the Sale of Goods Act 1979, drafted in its original form in 1893 with only merchants in mind, was amended in 1994 so as to eliminate the statutory implication that goods be of 'merchantable quality' and replace it with the consumer orientated requirement that they be of 'satisfactory quality' (see Sale of Goods Act 1979, s 14(2)–(2F): in March 2003, the Act was further amended by the Sale and Supply of Goods to Consumers Regulations 2002, SI 2002/3045, in order to provide additional remedies to consumers in accordance with EC Directive 1999/44 on certain aspects of the sale of consumer goods and associated guarantees, see below, p 385–386). There must be some cause for concern as to how far consumer protection principles should be allowed to intervene in purely mercantile arrangements. The interventionist approach of consumer protection legislation appears to be at odds with the essential needs of the business community (see, eg M Bridge (2003) 119 LQR 173, calling for separate legislation to deal with commercial sales and consumer sales).

Consumer protection law has developed into a subject worthy of study in its own right. We do not intend to deal with the subject in any detail in this book, although we shall refer to certain consumer protection measures which are covered in some commercial law textbooks and on certain commercial law courses: eg consumer credit and product liability. Those students who would like to study consumer protection law further are referred to the following books: C Scott and J Black *Cranston's Consumers and the Law* (3rd edn, 2000); D Oughton and J Lowry *Textbook on Consumer Law* (2nd edn, 2000); B Harvey and D Parry *The Law of Consumer Protection and Fair Trading* (6th edn, 2000).

(e) A new *lex mercatoria*?

In the seventeenth and eighteenth centuries the *lex mercatoria* was incorporated into the national laws of Europe. This meant that commercial law in England, and in other countries, lost much of its international character. However, in the second half of the twentieth century there has been a growing call for the harmonisation of the principles and rules of commercial law governing international transactions. (The extract which follows gives you some idea of the arguments for and against harmonisation.) This process of harmonisation has led to the development of what is now known as transnational commercial law (students of the subject are now well served by R Goode, H Kronke and E McKendrick's *Transnational Commercial Law: Text, Cases, and Materials* (2007)). Harmonisation of national commercial law has taken place in a number of ways (see generally, R Goode 'Reflections on the Harmonization of Commercial Law', Ch 1 in R Cranston and R Goode (eds) *Commercial and Consumer Law—National and International Dimensions* (1993)). First, there has been the work of bodies such as the Hague Conference on Private International Law, the International Institute for the Unification of Private Law (UNIDROIT), the United Nations Commission on Uniform Trade Law (UNCITRAL), the International Chamber of Commerce (ICC), the Council of Europe and the European Union. These bodies have sought to harmonise national laws relating to specific areas of international trade, including the international sale of goods, international factoring and financial leasing, international payment mechanisms, international shipping laws, international commercial arbitration, the assignment of receivables in international trade and international security interests in mobile equipment. Harmonisation has been achieved through a variety of mechanisms—conventions, model laws, uniform rules, codification of custom and usage or of trade terms, and model contracts. Secondly, there has been harmonisation through the uncodified international trade usage of merchants. Some scholars have argued that uncodified international trade usage constitutes a new *lex mercatoria*, ie an autonomous international set of principles and rules which govern international transactions without the need for their incorporation into a contract or the support of national laws. In a sense they are right, for at the heart of the *lex mercatoria* is the idea that the law is fashioned by the mercantile community. But uncodified international trade usage falls short of true *lex mercatoria* for it only has legal force by virtue of its express or implied incorporation into contract, or its reception into national law, or supranational law (eg EC law), through judicial recognition or legislation, and not simply by dint of its mere existence (as convincingly argued by Professor Goode in (1997) 46 ICLQ 1). Nevertheless, uncodified international trade practice remains important even when it has not reached the status of law. Professor Goode (2005) 54 ICLQ 539, 549, explains as follows:

As law the *lex mercatoria* consists of binding usage and depends in the last resort on recognition by national law. As observed practice the *lex mercatoria* is not dependent on external legal recognition at all, for it is not truly *lex*. It simply exists, and it is effective because business people in the relevant community perceive its observance as necessary to the fair and efficient conduct of business, so that the sanction for failure to follow the practice is not a legal sanction but opprobrium from fellow businessmen, their unwillingness to deal with the culprit and, in the last resort, expulsion from the relevant mercantile community. *Lex mercatoria* as practice is thus almost as potent as true law, and this is why it has been described by some leading scholars as operating at the periphery of the legal process and as soft law but not real law.

Thirdly, there has been both the conscious and unconscious borrowing of legal concepts from foreign law by judges in different countries. This has been described as 'judicial parallelism' (see R Goode *Commercial Law in the Next Millennium* (1998), pp 92–93). Fourthly, the work of scholars has also been influential in the development of transnational commercial law, especially the two different (though overlapping) groups of scholars who worked on the UNIDROIT *Principles of International Commercial Contracts* (1st edn, 1994; 2nd edn 2004) and the *Principles of European Contract Law* (Part I, 1995; Parts I and II, 2000; Part III, 2003) prepared by the Commission on European Contract Law. The former are designed for worldwide application, but are restricted to commercial contracts of an international character: the latter are designed for contracts within Europe, but cover contracts generally, whether domestic or international and whether commercial or non-commercial. Both sets of principles take the form of restatements similar to those prepared by the American Law

Institute in the US. Each set of principles not only sets out common rules and principles of law but also seeks to improve the law by identifying the best solutions to typical contract problems. Both embody approaches not currently found in English contract law, eg the duty of good faith and fair dealing (see generally, R Goode 'International Restatements of Contract and English Contract Law' in EZ Lomnicka and CGJ Morse (eds) *Contemporary Issues in Commercial Law—Essays in Honour of Professor AG Guest* (1997), pp 63–78). Although neither set of principles has the force of law (they represent 'soft law'), each is available to contracting parties for incorporation into their contracts, and each can be used by courts and tribunals when seeking the best solution to a contract problem or simply filling in gaps in existing international conventions. The UNIDROIT *Principles* have been particularly influential in the short time they have been around (see MJ Bonnell [1997] 1 Uniform Law Rev 34). Some have even suggested that these constitute a new kind of codified international *lex mercatoria* in the field of contract law (R Goode *Commercial Law in the Next Millennium* (1998), p 93; E McKendrick 'English Contract Law—A Rich Past, an Uncertain Future?' in MDA Freeman and ADE Lewis (eds) *Law and Opinion at the End of the Twentieth Century* (1997), p 58). The *Principles of European Contract Law* may at some future time form the basis for European legislation, including a possible European Code of Contracts (O Lando and H Beale *Principles of European Contract Law: Parts I and II* (2000), editorial introduction).

R Goode 'Reflections on the Harmonization of Commercial Law' in Ch 1 of R Cranston & R Goode (eds) *Commercial and Consumer Law—National and International Dimensions* (1993), pp 24–27

The advantages of harmonizing law relating to international transactions would seem fairly evident even to the layman. But given the reluctance of businessmen, their legal advisers, and their legislatures to modify their national law in favour or harmonization measures, it is perhaps worthwhile restating the advantages of harmonization. The harmonizing measure:

(1) may fill a legal vacuum by providing rules in a field where national law was previously non-existent or obscure;

(2) substitutes a single law for a proliferation of national laws and thus within the given field dispenses with the need to resort to conflict-of-laws rules and the opportunity these give for forum shopping;

(3) is usually available in several languages, official or unofficial, and is therefore more readily accessible than a national law;

(4) by reason of (1) and (2), facilitates conversance with its provisions and saves time and expense;

(5) provides a neutral law for parties to a contract neither of whom is willing to accept the law of the other's country;

(6) offers a legal regime more attuned to international transactions than domestic law, since it reflects the influence of many legal systems, whereas domestic law is focused on internal transactions and may thus be less accommodating on international dealings;

(7) operates as part of the law of each ratifying State, so that the courts of each such State take judicial notice of it and is established by legal argument, not by the expensive and time-consuming process of adducing expert evidence, often from a different jurisdiction;

(8) facilitates a common market.

Despite these manifold advantages it is often hard to persuade the commercial community even to take an interest in proposals for harmonization affecting their sphere of business, still less to give the proposals their support. Why is this so? Numerous reasons possessing varying degrees of persuasiveness are advanced.

Traditionally the first and principal line of attack is that existing domestic law is better or, if not better, is at least well known and understood. This may be true but presupposes that the law in question is the one which will govern the contract, whereas the reality is that for every contract governed by that law there will be another contract governed by a foreign law with which the party concerned may be unfamiliar, which is in a foreign language he does not understand, and which, when put to the test, may prove demonstrably inferior not only to his own law but to the proposed uniform law.

A second line of attack is that the proposed harmonizing measure is inadequate in scope. Thus the Vienna Sales Convention has been criticized for excluding questions relating to the validity of the contract of sale, the transfer of property, or the resolution of property disputes between the seller or buyer and a third party. The response of those engaged in the arduous labours which led to the conclusion of the Convention is no doubt not dissimilar to that of the scholar who writes a book on the doctrine of unconscionability in contract law and is then taken to task by a reviewer for his failure to cover breach and termination—in other words, for not writing a different book. Some limits have to be set to any project. How they are set is a difficult question to which I shall return, but those who decry as too narrow the scope of a Convention running to over a hundred Articles must surely embody the resuscitated spirit of Oliver Twist who will always cry for more.

Then, of course, there is the inevitable criticism of the drafting. If ever I get to Heaven (which my friends tell me is unlikely) one of my first requests will be to witness The Perfect Draft. Such a thing is certainly not to be found on this earth; yet those who pick to pieces the open texture or verbal infelicities of an international Convention rarely pause to consider how, when legislation prepared in a single legal system is generally so verbose, obscure, and generally badly drafted, one can reasonably expect more of the product of many hands drawn from widely differing legal systems with different cultures, legal structures, and methods of legal reasoning and decision-making, entailing maximum flexibility, co-operation, and compromise.

This is not to say that all criticism is unjustified. There are good Conventions and bad Conventions. The good ones are those which, for all their rough edges, are found to work and are widely used. The bad ones do not work and are rightly neglected. The Geneva Convention on Bills of Exchange is an example of an excellent Convention which has functioned extremely effectively and has been widely adopted. By contrast, the Uniform Law for International Sales, the forlorn predecessor of the Vienna Sales Convention, is an indifferent product which has not attracted support.

But behind the expressed reasons for antagonism or inertia in the face of proposals for harmonization lies a more fundamental consideration. It is human nature to be antipathetic to change. Let me render this more accurately. It is human nature to advocate change in someone else's affairs whilst vigorously opposing its necessity in one's own. The force of this NIMBY (Not in my backyard) approach, as it has become known in England, should not be underestimated. Few individuals or institutions are truly resistant to it. Even academics, who are supposed to embody the quintessence of detached assessment, somehow respond with a lack of enthusiasm when it is suggested that their own methods of teaching, research, or organization might benefit from review.

This inherent resistance to change is exacerbated by the low priority accorded by our law schools to the teaching of comparative law and, in England, by an unwillingness to grapple with foreign languages, itself both a cause and a consequence of English becoming the new lingua franca. If the harmonization process is to have any hope of acceleration it is essential for law schools to reduce their preoccupation with national law and their assumption of its superiority over other legal systems and to revert at least in some degree to the internationalism of medieval law teaching. It is primarily by the spreading of awareness of foreign legal systems among our students that we can hope to accelerate the process of harmonization and to produce practitioners and judges of the future prepared to look beyond the horizon of their own legal system. In his outstanding study of unification [*The International Unification of Private Law,* II Int Ency Comp Law, Ch 5, p 16] that great French comparativist the late Professor Réne David exposed the kernel of the matter with his customary elegance and felicity:

Legal theory suffocates within the frontiers of a State. Like all science its prosperity requires a cosmopolitan atmosphere; only schools of a low intellectual level can exist in a country with closed frontiers, training narrow-minded practitioners, mere pawns to carry out decrees of power. Universality is necessary to legal theory, and it is a factor favourable to the unification of law.

4 THE SOURCES OF COMMERCIAL LAW

(a) Contracts

The law of contract lies at the heart of commercial law. In the world of commerce, goods and services are supplied pursuant to the terms of contracts made between businessmen. Sometimes each term of the contract will have been individually negotiated by the parties. But in many cases there will have been little or no negotiation as to the precise terms of the agreement beyond those terms relating to subject matter and price. In such cases the parties prefer to use standard form contracts to embody their bargain and thereby save time and money that would otherwise have been spent on the negotiation of each term. So long as the standard form contract is made between businessmen, and not between an ordinary person and the business provider of goods and services, the courts are reluctant to interfere with the principles of freedom and sanctity of contract. This is particularly true of those standard form contracts drawn up by trade associations and adopted by their members, eg bills of lading, charterparties, policies of insurance and contracts of sale in the commodity markets. As Lord Diplock said in *Schroeder Music Publishing Co Ltd v Macaulay* [1974] 1 WLR 1308 at 1316: 'The standard clauses in these contracts have been settled over the years by negotiation by representatives of the commercial interests involved and have been widely adopted because experience has shown that they facilitate the conduct of trade.'

Some types of standard form contract have been the subject of detailed legal analysis. A jurisprudence has grown up around them giving many of their terms legally predictable meanings. Lord Goff has even gone so far as to suggest that those standard form contracts which are widely used throughout the world (eg the Lloyd's standard marine policy, the various forms of charterparty and commodity trade contracts) each form the basis of their own separate commercial code ([1993] JCL 1 at p 3). See also CM Schmitthoff (1968) 17 ICLQ 551 discussing the harmonisation of international trade law by means of standard form contracts.

The courts are often called upon to construe the terms of commercial contracts. Most cases before the Commercial Court turn on points of construction of such contracts. The task of the court is to discover the mutual intention of the parties as revealed by their written contract, which is the outward manifestation of that intention. In the past the courts took a literalist approach to construction; however, in recent years, mainly as a result of the speeches of Lord Wilberforce in *Prenn v Simmonds* [1971] 1 WLR 1381 and *Reardon Smith Ltd v Yngvar Hansen Tangen, The Diana Prosperity* [1976] 1 WLR 989, there has been a shift from strict construction of commercial instruments to what is now referred to as commercial (or common sense) construction of such documents. In *Mannai Investment Co Ltd v Eagle Star Life Assurance Co Ltd* [1997] AC 749 at 771, Lord Steyn explained that:

In determining the meaning of the language of a commercial contract, and unilateral contractual notices, the law therefore generally favours a commercially sensible construction. The reason for this approach is that a commercial construction is more likely to give effect to the intention of the parties. Words are therefore interpreted in the same way in which a reasonable commercial person would construe them. And the standard of the reasonable commercial person is hostile to technical interpretations and undue emphasis on niceties of language.

The principles by which contractual documents are nowadays construed were summarised by Lord Hoffmann in *Investors Compensation Scheme Ltd v West Bromwich Building Society* [1998] 1 All ER 98 at 114 as follows:

(1) Interpretation is the ascertainment of the meaning which the document would convey to a reasonable person having all the background knowledge which would reasonably have been available to the parties in the situation in which they were at the time of the contract.

(2) The background was famously referred to by Lord Wilberforce as the 'matrix of fact', but this phrase is, if anything, an understated description of what the background may include. Subject to the requirement that it should have been reasonably available to the parties, and to the exception to be mentioned next, it includes absolutely anything which would have affected the way in which the language of the document would have been understood by a reasonable man.

(3) The law excludes from the admissible background the previous negotiations of the parties and their declarations of subjective intent. They are admissible only in an action for rectification. The law makes this distinction for reasons of practical policy and, in this respect only, legal interpretation differs from the way we would interpret utterances in ordinary life. The boundaries of this exception are in some respects unclear. But this is not the occasion on which to explore them.

(4) The meaning which a document (or any other utterance) would convey to a reasonable man is not the same thing as the meaning of its words. The meaning of words is a matter of dictionaries and grammars; the meaning of the document is what the parties using those words against the relevant background would reasonably have been understood to mean. The background may not merely enable the reasonable man to choose between the possible meanings of words which are ambiguous but even (as occasionally happens in ordinary life) to conclude that the parties must, for whatever reason, have used the wrong words or syntax (see *Mannai Investment Co Ltd v Eagle Star Life Assurance Co Ltd* [1997] AC 749, [1997] 3 All ER 352).

(5) The 'rule' that words should be given their 'natural and ordinary meaning' reflects the commonsense proposition that we do not easily accept that people have made linguistic mistakes, particularly in formal documents. On the other hand, if one would nevertheless conclude from the background that something must have gone wrong with the language, the law does not require judges to attribute to the parties an intention which they plainly could not have had. Lord Diplock made this point more vigorously when he said in *Antaios Cia Naviera SA v Salen RederiernaAB, The Antaios* [1985] AC 191 at 201, [1984] 3 All ER 229 at 233:

'...if detailed semantic and syntactical analysis of words in a commercial contract is going to lead to a conclusion that flouts business common sense, it must be made to yield to business common sense.'

Lord Hoffmann's statement is important. It represents a further advance in the move away from the literal approach to contractual interpretation towards one based on a 'commercially sensible construction'. Thus, in *The Starsin* [2003] UKHL 12, [2004] 1 AC 715, the document in question was a bill of lading and it was appropriate to ask what meaning it would have conveyed to the merchants or bankers to whom it was addressed and who would rely on it in their dealings. However, Lord Hoffmann's statement has generated some criticism. The first criticism is that it leads to greater uncertainty because it extends the circumstances in which the courts can depart from the 'ordinary and natural meaning' of the words (see R Calnan, chapter 2 in A Burrows and E Peel (eds), *Contract Terms* (2007)). It is no longer necessary for there to be an ambiguity in the words used by the parties before the court can have regard to surrounding circumstances. Secondly, there is concern that Lord Hoffmann's approach will increase the cost and complexity of litigation because it allows the introduction of a very wide range of material when interpreting the contract (the 'matrix of fact'). Sir Christopher Staughton, a retired Lord Justice of Appeal, has been particularly vocal in his criticism of Lord Hoffmann's second principle of interpretation (see [1999] CLJ 303, 306–308, and his judgment in *Scottish Power plc v Britoil (Exploration) Ltd* [1997] 47 LS Gaz R 30). These criticisms have some merit but they have not won the day. Lord Hoffmann's statement has been cited on over 200 occasions and is now regularly applied by the courts (an observation made by Professor Ewan McKendrick in his excellent book, *Contract Law: Text, Cases and Materials* (2nd edn, 2005), at p 424: chapter 11, on the interpretation of contracts, is well worth reading in its entirety).

There are also limits to the range of material that can be examined by the courts for the purpose of constructing the matrix of fact. First, in *Bank of Credit and Commerce International SA v Ali* [2001] UKHL 8, [2002] 1 AC 251 at [39], Lord Hoffmann qualified his second principle in the following terms:

I did not think it necessary to emphasise that I meant anything which a reasonable man would have regarded as *relevant*. I was merely saying that there is no conceptual limit to what can be regarded as background. It is not, for example, confined to the factual background but can include the state of the law (as in cases in which one takes into account that the parties are unlikely to have intended to agree to something unlawful or legally ineffective) or proved common assumptions which were in fact quite mistaken ... I was certainly not encouraging a trawl through 'background' which could not have made a reasonable person think that the parties must have departed from conventional usage.

Secondly, it remains the case that evidence of pre-contractual negotiations and post-contractual conduct of the parties remain generally inadmissible (the arguments for and against greater liberalisation in this area are finely balanced and are reviewed by Professor Gerard McMeel in (2003) 119 LQR 272), and also by Lord Nicholls in (2005) 121 LQR 577, both advocating removal of the restriction). But where the contract contains words or phrases which have no obvious meaning in themselves, evidence of pre-contractual communications is admissible to show that the parties gave them a particular meaning (see *Proforce Recruit Ltd v The Rugby Group Ltd* [2006] EWCA Civ 69, 'preferred supplier status': criticised by A Berg (2006) 122 LQR 354). Thirdly, it must be emphasised that this approach to contract construction does not allow the court to rewrite the contract, especially a commercial contract, whenever it thinks it just to do so. In *Charter Reinsurance Co Ltd v Fagan* [1997] AC 313 at 388, Lord Mustill warned that:

There comes a point at which the court should remind itself that the task is to discover what the parties meant from what they have said, and that to force upon the words a meaning which they cannot fairly bear is to substitute for the bargain actually made one which the court believes could better have been philosophy of economic law is economic *dirigism,* ie, the idea that the paternalistic state may limit the autonomy of the parties' will in the public interest. Economic law should thus be placed between commercial law and administrative law; it shares with the former its concern with economic affairs and with the latter its governmental technique.

From this point of view, England has its fair share of economic law. Indeed, as state planning asserts itself in a constantly more consistent pattern, economic law develops into the discipline which reflects the transition to a planned and directed free market economy. Its importance is growing and full academic recognition cannot be withheld from it indefinitely.

What are the divisions of English economic law? This subject can be arranged into the law relating to:

1 financial regulation,
2 competitive economic regulation,
3 prices and incomes regulation, and
4 consumer protection regulation....

The Characteristics of English Economic Law

English economic law shows two characteristics. First, it has evolved the central concept of public interest and, secondly, its fabric is very different from that of other branches of law.

It has been pointed out elsewhere that, unlike public policy, the term 'public interest' does not carry an inherent element of opprobrium. 'The new concept of public interest is used to indicate the wide—and growing—area in which Parliament has regulated certain activities of private persons in the social and economic sphere because it considers such regulation to be desirable for the common weal.' The concept of public interest is thus a socio-political concept. In the legislation relating to restrictive trade practices and resale price maintenance the notion of public interest is clearly defined; it operates in this manner that certain restrictive trade arrangements are generally declared to be prohibited by Parliament as being contrary to the public interest but that the relevant enactments establish closely defined grounds on which those arrangements can be justified; these grounds are known as the 'gateways' to legality....

Secondly, the fabric of economic law is different from that of other branches of law. The normal technique of the legislator in commercial law is to place at the disposal of the parties certain legal institutions, to regulate their effect and to leave it to the parties to adopt the statutory scheme or to modify it as desired. Enactments pertaining to economic law are constructed differently. They are of mandatory rather than permissive character. They embody Governmental policy, and do so in considerable detail....The detailed incorporation of Government policy into statutes gives English economic law its peculiar flavour.

NOTES

1.   The City of London is one of the world's pre-eminent financial centres. The financial services industry in the UK is huge, accounting for one-fifth of the UK's GDP. The financial markets require effective regulation to protect their integrity and stability, as well as to control risk. Until recently, the provision of financial services was regulated by the Securities and Investment Board (the 'SIB') and a series of self-regulatory organisations operating under a scheme established by the Financial Services Act 1986. However, in May 1997 a new Labour Government announced the wholesale reform of the regulation of financial services. It immediately established the Financial Services Authority (the 'FSA') as the new single regulator of the whole of the financial services sector in the UK: banking, insurance and investment business all fall within its domain. The functions, responsibilities and powers of the FSA are contained in the Financial Services and Markets Act 2000, which came into

force on 1 December 2001. The Financial Services Act 1986 has been repealed; the SIB has been scrapped. Self-regulation has been replaced with a system of mandatory centralised regulation through the FSA. For further discussion of the functions of the FSA (in the context of bank regulation), see Chapter 17, section 1 below.

2.   The term 'economic law', as used by Professor Schmitthoff, must not be confused with what is called the law and economics movement which has become prominent in American and Canadian law schools. This movement focuses on the application of economic theory to matters of legal concern. It uses economic concepts of market incentives, utility maximisation and allocative efficiency to analyse legal institutions, concepts and rules, including those relevant to commercial law: see JS Ziegel 'What Can the Economic Analysis of Law Teach Commercial and Consumer Law Scholars?' in R Cranston and R Goode (eds) *Commercial and Consumer Law* (1993), Ch 12 and the literature footnoted therein.

(d) European Community law

The European Community (the EC) or European Union (the EU) was established by the EC Treaty, then known as the EEC Treaty, signed in Rome on 25 March 1957, which entered into force on 1 January 1958. It is currently made up of 27 member states including the United Kingdom (which joined the EC on 1 January 1973).

EC law is a separate legal system, distinct from, though closely linked to, the national legal systems of Member States (see generally TC Hartley *The Foundations of European Community Law* (6th edn, 2007), Pt 2). It has had a profound impact on UK law. Section 2(1) of the European Communities Act 1972 provides that directly effective EC law must be recognised and enforced in the UK. It is now well settled that where there is a conflict between directly effective EC law and national law, including Acts of Parliament, EC law prevails (*R v Secretary of State for Transport, ex p Factortame* [1990] 2 AC 85, HL).

So far as the commercial world is concerned, the influence of EC law has mainly been felt in the area of regulatory law, for example, there have been various EC Directives dealing with the harmonisation of bank regulation across Member States (see below, pp 601–602). By contrast, the EC has been relatively inactive in the area of private rights of those involved in commercial, as opposed to consumer, transactions. As Professor Goode observes (*Commercial Law in the Next Millennium* (1998), pp 88–89):

It is an interesting phenomenon that the impact of European Community law on the private rights of parties to commercial transactions, as opposed to transactions with consumers, has so far been almost negligible. If we leave on one side EC conventions of a general character, such as the Rome Convention on the law applicable to contractual obligations and the Brussels and related conventions on jurisdiction and the enforcement of judgments, it is hard to recall any measure of significance in the field of private commercial law other than the Directive on commercial agents, which certainly introduced concepts novel to English law, such as the non-excludable right of a commercial agent to compensation or an indemnity on termination of his agency. So what we have is mainly a public law superstructure which, outside commercial agency, has not so far been underpinned by any measures to harmonise, for example, the law of obligations or the law governing dealings in commercial assets.

Professor Goode believes (at p 89) that 'the European Union has been wise to exercise restraint in this regard, for there are other agencies whose remit is universal rather than regional and whose products are more focused on the private law of commercial transactions'. (We turn to the work of these agencies in the next section.) Nevertheless, on 13 July 2001, the European Commission issued a communication of European Contract law to the

Council and European Parliament. In February 2003, the Commission issued an 'Action Plan' in which it promised to produce a common frame of reference (CFR) containing common rules and terminology in the area of European contract law. In October 2004, the Commission issued a further Communication on a European Contract Law and the Revision of the Acquis: The Way Forward (COM (2004) 651 Final), in which the Commission states that it will 'pursue the elaboration of the CFR'. The development of a European Contract Law may be some way off but it remains firmly on the agenda.

(e) International conventions, model laws, uniform rules and uniform trade terms

We have already examined the various forces behind the harmonisation of international trade law (see above, pp 17–21). The two methods of harmonisation which have had the greatest impact are, on the one hand, international conventions and model laws, favoured by international intergovernmental bodies such as UNIDROIT and UNCITRAL (sometimes collectively, though inaccurately, referred to as 'international legislation': see CM Schmitthoff, *Commercial Law in a Changing Economic Climate* (2nd edn, 1981), p 22), and on the other hand, uniform rules and uniform trade terms, especially those promoted by the International Chamber of Commerce (ICC), a non-governmental body.

International conventions only have the force of law in England if incorporated into our national law by legislation. A convention must be incorporated in its entirety into domestic law, save for those parts of it covered by permitted reservations and declarations. Even then the convention may be 'voluntary' to the extent that the parties to a commercial transaction can exclude the operation of its provisions. Examples of harmonising conventions include the Vienna Convention on Contracts for the International Sale of Goods (1980) (see below, p 489), the Geneva Convention on Agency in the International Sale of Goods (1983) (see below, p 110), the UN Convention on International Bills of Exchange and International Promissory Notes (1988) (see below, p 769), the Ottawa Conventions on International Factoring and International Financial Leasing (1988) (see below, p 1072 and p 927), the UN Convention on Independent Guarantees and Standby Letters of Credit (1995) (see below, p 924) the UN Convention on the Assignment of Receivables in International Trade (2001) (see below, p 1072) and the Cape Town Convention on International Interests in Mobile Equipment (2001) (see below, p 1081). None of these conventions have been ratified by the UK (although there have been conventions on the carriage of goods by road, rail, sea and air which have been incorporated into the law of the UK). The current attitude against ratification is reflected in the words of Mr Justice (now Lord) Hobhouse who wrote in (1990) 106 LQR 530 at p 533, with specific reference to the Vienna Sales Convention, as follows:

These conventions are inevitably and confessedly drafted as multi-cultural compromises between different schemes of law. Consequently they will normally have less merit than most of the individual legal systems from which they have been derived. They lack coherence and consistency. They create problems about their scope. They introduce uncertainty where no uncertainty existed before. They probably deprive the law of those very features which enable it to be an effective tool for the use of international commerce.

For a point by point rebuttal of these, and other, criticisms made by Lord Hobhouse, see J Steyn (now Lord Steyn) 'A Kind of Esperanto?', in Ch 1 of PBH Birks (ed) *The Frontiers of Liability* (1994), Vol 2. More generally, see the extract from Professor Goode's paper 'Reflections on the Harmonization of Commercial Law' which appears above at pp 19–21.

The Vienna Sales Convention has been ratified by 70 states, but not the UK. Save for Japan, the Convention has been ratified by most of the world's other leading trading nations.

A model law has no legal force as such: it merely provides a model which a state can adopt in whole or in part, with or without amendment. A good example is the UNCITRAL Model Law on International Commercial Arbitration (1985). Although the UK did not adopt this model law in its entirety, it clearly influenced the way the Arbitration Act 1996 was drafted (see above, p 12).

Uniform rules and uniform trade terms only have the force of law when incorporated into a contract either expressly or by previous course of dealing or by custom or usage of the trade. Examples of such harmonising measures include the Incoterms (2000 Revision) (see below, p 489), the Uniform Rules for Demand Guarantees (1992) (see below, p 923), the Uniform Customs and Practice for Documentary Credits (2007 Revision) (see below, p 851), the Uniform Rules for Contract Bonds (1993) (see below, p 914), Uniform Rules for Collections (1995 Revision) (see below, p 848), and the Rules on International Standby Practices (1998) (see below, p 914), all of which have been sponsored by the ICC. Typically, uniform rules and uniform trade terms codify existing trade practice and usage.

QUESTION

In his Law Quarterly Review note (106 LQR 530), Lord Hobhouse distinguished between international conventions which establish international safety standards, recognise and protect intellectual property rights, and govern the rights and liability of carriers in international carriage, all of which he saw as having an important and valuable role to play in the commercial world, and those conventions, like the Vienna Sales Convention, which he disliked for 'seeking to legislate for the ordinary law governing the basic elements of commercial relationships'. Do you think Lord Hobhouse was right to make such a distinction? Can you draw any parallels with the way the European Union has legislated with regard to commercial law (see above)?

5 THE ROLE OF EQUITY IN COMMERCIAL LAW

Westdeutsche Landesbank Girozentrale v Islington London Borough Council
[1996] AC 669, House of Lords

Lord Browne-Wilkinson: ... My Lords, wise judges have often warned against the wholesale importation into commercial law of equitable principles inconsistent with the certainty and speed which are essential requirements for the orderly conduct of business affairs.

'Equity's Place in the Law of Commerce' by Sir Peter Millett
(1998) 114 LQR 214, 214–217

Equity's place in the law of commerce, long resisted by commercial lawyers, can no longer be denied. What they once opposed through excessive caution they now embrace with excessive enthusiasm. I propose to consider the reasons for this development, and then to examine the two principal concepts which equity deploys in the commercial field: the fiduciary duty and the constructive trust.

Even twenty years ago there was still a widely held belief, by no means confined to common lawyers, that equity had no place in the world of commerce. Businessmen need speed and certainty; these do not permit a detailed and leisurely examination of the parties' conduct. Commerce needs the kind of bright line rules which the common law provides and which equity abhors. Resistance to the intrusion of equity into the business world is justified by concern for the certainty and security of commercial transactions.[1] Such considerations led Lindley LJ over a century ago to give his well-known warning against the extension of the equitable doctrine of constructive notice to commercial transactions.[2] This is often repeated like a mantra. But it is inaccurate and its influence has been harmful. The purchase of land and the giving of a bank guarantee are both commercial transactions; yet the doctrine of constructive notice applies to both. In fact Lindley LJ was speaking of the doctrine of constructive notice as it was developed by the Court of Chancery in relation to land, with its many refinements and its insistence on a proper investigation of title in every case. This cannot be applied without modification to transactions where there is no recognised procedure for investigating title.[3] The principal modification[4] is to insist on the need to show that the circumstances were such as to put the transferee on inquiry; and in an ordinary commercial context this is very difficult to establish.[5]

While the purchaser of land and the bank which takes a guarantee are not immune from equity's intervention, however, they are not fiduciaries. This is not because the transactions in question are commercial; it is because the relationships to which they are parties are exclusively commercial. In Canada and Australia there has been a tendency to extend applications of equitable doctrines to commercial transactions through the concepts of constructive trust and fiduciary obligations more widely than we would do. But the pendulum is swinging back again, at least in Australia. The rejection of any fiduciary relationship by the High Court of Australia in an ordinary commercial distributorship agreement in *Hospital Products Ltd v United States Surgical Corpn*[6] marks a welcome insistence on principle. The situation in Canada is rather less satisfactory, perhaps because only lip service appears to have been paid to the valuable comment of Sopinka J that:

> Fiduciary duties should not be superimposed on . . . [c]ommon law duties to improve the nature or extent of the remedy.[7]

There has to be a proper import licence. Moreover, there is a different licence for each doctrine. In Australia Dawson J has warned of the:

> . . . undesirability of extending fiduciary duties to commercial relationships and the anomaly of imposing those duties where the parties are at arms' length from one another.[8]

If this warning is not observed then equity's place in the commercial world will be put at risk: it will be found to do more harm than good. When the question is concerned with the imposition of fiduciary duties, the distinction is not between commercial and non-commercial *transactions,* a distinction which Lehane has described as 'a red herring',[9] but between commercial and non- commercial *relationships.*

It is of course far too late to suppose that the body of law which owes its origin to family and friendship cannot be introduced into the market place without making some kind of category mistake.[10] It is no longer possible to dispute Sir Anthony Mason's extrajudicial observation that the concepts, doctrines, principles and remedies developed by the old Court of Chancery:

> . . . have extended beyond the old boundaries into new territory where no Lord Chancellor's foot has previously left its imprint . . . Equitable doctrines and reliefs have penetrated the citadels of business and commerce long thought, at least by common lawyers, to be immune from the intrusion of such principles.[11]

Three things have combined to bring about this development. First, there is the growing complexity and professionalism of commercial life which have accompanied the change from an industrial to a service economy and the growth of the financial services industry. Much commerce today is based on trust; on each side of a commercial arms' length transaction there are likely to be relationships of trust and confidence. As a result, the modern fiduciary is usually a professional. He expects to be paid for his services, and he expects to be liable (and to be covered by appropriate insurance) if he performs his duties negligently. The picture of the trustee or fiduciary as an old friend of the family who has gratuitously volunteered his services is long obsolete. Principles of equity designed to mitigate the severity of its rules as they bore on the well-meaning amateur are incongruous when applied to the paid professional.

We ought to stop repeating the inaccurate incantation that equity does not permit a trustee to profit from his trust. Of course it does. What it forbids is his making a *secret or uncovenanted* profit from his trust. We also need to reconsider the propriety of including the standard form of trustee exemption clause which exempts the trustee from liability for loss or damage not caused by his own dishonesty. The view is widely held that these clauses have gone too far, and that trustees who charge for their services and who, as professional men, would not dream of excluding liability for ordinary professional negligence, should not be able to rely on a trustee exemption clause which excludes liability for gross negligence. Jersey introduced a law in 1989 which denies effect to a trustee exemption clause which purports to absolve a trustee from liability for his own 'fraud, wilful misconduct or gross negligence'. The subject is presently under consideration in this country by the Trust Law Committee under the chairmanship of Sir John Vinelott and its proposals will be awaited with interest.

Secondly, there has never been a greater need to impose on those who engage in commerce the high standards of conduct which equity demands. The common law insists on honesty, diligence, and the due performance of contractual obligations. But equity insists on nobler and subtler qualities: loyalty, fidelity, integrity, respect for confidentiality, and the disinterested discharge of obligations of trust and confidence. It exacts higher standards than those of the market place, where the end justifies the means and the old virtues of loyalty, fidelity and responsibility are admired less than the idols of 'success, self-interest, wealth, winning and not getting caught'.[12] It is unrealistic to expect that employees can be given incentives through enormous bonuses without undermining their business ethics. It is hardly necessary to say more on this subject in a year in which we have seen employees in the financial services industry, enticed by the prospect of even larger bonuses, threaten not only to leave their employer for a competitor but to take their entire teams of junior staff with them; and in which we have seen a takeover bidder make use, possibly of stolen documents, but certainly of confidential information belonging to the target company, with major City firms apparently regarding such conduct as acceptable.

Thirdly, plaintiffs and their advisers have discovered the apparent advantages of alleging breach of trust or fiduciary duty, with the result that a statement of claim is considered to be seriously deficient if it does not contain inappropriate references to these concepts which are often scattered throughout the pleadings with complete abandon.

At first equity lawyers looked with disdain at their common law colleagues who were obviously using equitable concepts without any understanding of their proper scope. More recently, however, we have been challenged to define these expressions, and to our dismay have realised that we cannot agree on their meanings. We have been forced to re-examine our terminology and reconsider our own concepts. The process is a continuing one and is marked by considerable controversy. It has, however, been greatly assisted by a number of academic monographs on particular concepts as subrogation,[13] fiduciary obligations,[14] and constructive[15] and resulting trusts,[16] which are required reading for anyone seriously interested in the concepts on which the development of equity into the next century depends.

Footnotes

1 See *Scandinavian Trading Tanker Co AB v Flota Petrolera Ecuatoriana* [1983] QB 529 at pp 540–541 per Robert Goff J, approved by Lord Diplock [1983] 2 AC 694 at p 704.

2 *Manchester Trust v Furness, Withy & Co* [1895] 2 QB 539 at p 545.

3 See *El Ajou v Dollar Land Holdings plc* [1993] 3 All ER 717 at p 739; *Macmillan Inc v Bishopsgate Trust plc (No 3)* [1995] 1 WLR 978 at p 1000.

4 The consequences of a failure to make proper inquiry are also different. When there is a recognised procedure for investigating title, failure to make such investigation fixes a party with notice of what he would have discovered if he had done so. This cannot be applied without modification where there is no such procedure.

5 See *Sanders Bros v Maclean & Co* (1883) 11 QBD 327 at p 343 per Bowen LJ; *Barclays Bank plc v Quincecare Ltd* [1992] 4 All ER 363 at p 377 per Steyn J.

6 (1984) 156 CLR 41. The case contains a valuable, if inconclusive, discussion of the criteria which may be indicative of the fiduciary or non-fiduciary nature of the relationship.

7 *Norberg v Wynrib* [1992] 2 SCR 226 at p 312.

8 *Hospital Products Ltd v United States Surgical Corpn,* supra, at p 149.

9 See *Essays in Equity,* ed Finn (1985), p 104.

10 See Glover, *Commercial Equity: Fiduciary Relationships* (1995), p 4.

11 'The Place of Equity and Equitable Remedies in the Contemporary Common Law World' (1994) 110 LQR 238 at p 238.

12 Sacks, *The Politics of Hope* (1997), p 179.

13 Mitchell, *The Law of Subrogation* (1994).

14 Eg Finn, *Fiduciary Obligations* (1977).

15 Elias, *Explaining Constructive Trusts* (1990).

16 Chambers, *Resulting Trusts* (1997).

NOTES

1.   There are several reasons why a claimant might wish to assert breach of a fiduciary duty against a defendant. First, it may allow him to take advantage of more flexible equitable tracing rules. Secondly, it may enable him to assert a proprietary claim and thereby gain priority over other creditors in the event of the defendant's insolvency, or maintain a claim to profits. Thirdly, he may be able to benefit from more flexible rules as to recovery of compensation for loss and so avoid the common law rules of causation and remoteness of damages. Fourthly, there are more favourable limitation periods in equity than at common law.

2.   English courts have resisted the temptation to impose fiduciary obligations on parties to a purely commercial relationship who deal with each other at arm's length and can be expected to look after their own interests. There are various modern examples of this approach: see *Kelly v Cooper* [1993] AC 205, PC (below, p 212); *Re Stapylton Fletcher Ltd* [1994] 1 WLR 1181 (below, p 319); and *Re Goldcorp Exchange Ltd* [1995] 1 AC 74, PC (below, p 319). Where businessmen have defined their relationship in the terms of a contract freely negotiated between them, the courts should hesitate before interfering with their bargain. By the terms of their contract each party has accepted certain risks, including the risk of the other party's insolvency before completing performance of the contract, and the law should be slow to confer additional rights upon them through the medium of equitable intervention. This does not mean that a commercial relationship and a fiduciary relationship are mutually exclusive, but it does mean that it is necessary to show something more, in terms of a relationship of trust and confidence, influence or confidentiality, before a court will impose a fiduciary relationship on top of a commercial one. The imposition of a fiduciary relationship brings with it the obligation to act selflessly, something which is usually out of place in the adversarial world of commerce.

3.   Although Lord Browne-Wilkinson warned in the *Westdeutsche* case against the wholesale importation of equitable principles into the common law, we can see from the extract

from Sir Peter (now Lord) Millett's article that equity has the potential to play an important role in commerce. English courts may be slow to *impose* fiduciary obligations on parties to arm's length commercial transactions, but they are quick to give effect to fiduciary obligations which are *expressly intended* by the parties. In *Don King Productions Inc v Warren* [2000] Ch 291 at 317, the facts of which appear below at p 982, Lightman J referred to the warning of Lord Browne-Wilkinson in *Westdeutsche* and continued: There can however be no sustainable objection on these grounds to the recognition of a trust if the parties have manifested their intention to create it, *a fortiori* when this is necessary to achieve justice between the parties.' In that case the subject matter of the trust was a management and promotion contract made between a boxer and his manager, which, it was argued, could not be held on trust by the manager for his business partner because normal trust rules would have allowed the partner to interfere in the management of the contract and this was quite contrary to the personal nature of the contract. On appeal, the Court of Appeal dismissed this objection and held that although the benefit of the contract was held on trust, normal trust rules had to be modified in this context, so that the partner could not insist on rendering vicarious performance of the personal obligations arising under the contract ([2000] Ch 291 at 335–336). Their Lordships relied on the observations of Lord Browne-Wilkinson in *Target Holdings Ltd v Redferns* [1996] AC 421 at 435, when he said:

In my judgment it is in any event wrong to lift wholesale the detailed rules developed in the context of traditional trusts and then seek to apply them to trusts of quite a different kind. In the modern world the trust has become a valuable device in commercial and financial dealings. The fundamental principles of equity apply as much to such trusts as they do to the traditional trusts in relation to which those principles were originally formulated. But in my judgment it is important, if the trust is not to be rendered commercially useless, to distinguish between the basic principles of trust law and those specialist rules developed in relation to traditional trusts which are applicable only to such trusts and the rationale of which has no application to trusts of quite a different kind.

4.   There are numerous examples of parties to commercial and financial transactions intending to apply the doctrines of equity and trusts. In many cases the parties wish to take advantage of one particular aspect of the trust, namely the 'insolvency ring fence' which affords priority to claimants over general creditors of the defendant. Trusts are regularly used, for example, in the international financial markets (see, generally, D Hayton, H Piggott and J Benjamin [2002] JIBFL 23). In secured syndicated loans the security interest is invariably held by a trustee on behalf of the lenders. In international bond issues a trustee is appointed to safeguard the interests of the bondholders and to act on their behalf in policing and, if necessary, enforcing payment of the bonds. A global custodian may declare that it holds a pool of assets on trust, the terms of which are to meet the claims of the global custodian itself and for the client. The main feature of trusts used in commercial and financial arrangements is that the rights and duties of the parties are determined on the basis of the contractual documents. The contractual arrangements dominate the fiduciary concepts inherent in the trust. The risk with this approach is that the contract may strip the arrangement of the core features necessary for it to be characterised as a trust in the first place (described in *Armitage v Nurse* [1998] Ch 241, 253, as the 'irreducible core'). However, the English courts seem reluctant to recharacterise 'commercial trusts' in this way (see, eg *Citibank NA v MBIA Assurance SA* [2006] EWHC 3215 (Ch), noted by A Trukhtanov (2007) 123 LQR 342). The fear is that an interventionist approach would introduce an element of uncertainty which might undermine the predominant position of the City of London as a world financial market. Even the Law Commission has recently bowed to pressure from

the City and exempted commercial trusts from its very limited proposals for the introduction of a special disclosure regime for trustee exemption clauses (Law Com Report No 301, *Trustee Exemption Clauses*, 2006). On financial and commercial uses of trusts, see C Duffett (1992) JITCP 23–30, S Moerman (1999–2000) 6 Trusts and Trustees 21, AR Anderson and P O'Hagan (2000) JITCP 185 and chapters by D Hayton, J Langbein and D Waters in D Hayton (ed) *Modern International Developments in Trust Law* (1999).

5. The role of equity is particularly important where money is lent, or payment made for goods in advance of delivery, or goods supplied before payment, and the borrower, seller or purchaser, as the case may be, subsequently becomes insolvent before performing his side of the bargain. Any claim in contract, or for recovery of the price on a total failure of consideration, or in debt, is only a personal claim against the general assets of the insolvent person. As a personal claim it will abate with the claims of other creditors in the insolvency. On the other hand, if the payer or supplier can establish an equitable proprietary interest in the money paid or goods supplied, he will gain priority over other creditors in the insolvency. Thus, where the payer can show that the money paid is held by the recipient subject to a trust in his favour, the payer will be able to withdraw *his* assets from those available in the insolvency: see, eg *Barclays Bank Ltd v Quistclose Investments Ltd* [1970] AC 567 (money lent for a specified purpose held on trust for the lender when the purpose failed; the nature of the trust is explained in *Twinsectra Ltd v Yardley* [2002] UKHL 12, [2002] 2 AC 164, see, especially, Lord Millett at [77]–[102]); *Re Kayford Ltd* [1975] 1 WLR 279 (customers' pre-payments for goods held on trust in favour of the customers). Where goods are supplied before payment, the supplier may be able to rely upon a reservation of title clause to make the purchaser a trustee of the goods, their product, or the proceeds of their sale, until he is paid in full—a claim which may involve tracing in equity: see *Aluminium Industrie Vaassen BV v Romalpa Aluminium Ltd* [1976] 1 WLR 676, and those cases considered below at pp 452–470. See generally, W Goodhart and G Jones (1980) 43 MLR 489; R Goode (1987) 103 LQR 433 at pp 434–447.

6. In each case referred to in note 5 above, the claimant relied on his pre-existing right of property to bring a proprietary claim against the defendant. However, there are cases which suggest that, in appropriate circumstances, the English courts may create a trust or lien if the defendant's conduct is unconscionable and will not be deterred from doing so by the absence of a 'proprietary base'. There are dicta in a number of cases which tentatively suggest that an English court might recognise the remedial constructive trust which allows the court to grant, by way of remedy, a proprietary right to someone who, beforehand, had no proprietary right (see *Neste Oy v Lloyds Bank plc* [1983] 2 Lloyd's Rep 658 at 666, per Bingham J; *Metall und Rohstoff AG v Donaldson Lufkin & Jenrette Inc* [1990] 1 QB 391 at 479, CA; but contrast *A-G v Blake (Jonathan Cape Ltd, third party)* [1998] Ch 439 at 459, per Lord Woolf MR affirmed on other grounds [2001] 1 AC 268; *Re Polly Peck International plc (in administration) (No 2)* [1998] 3 All ER 812 at 831, per Nourse LJ; *Box v Barclays Bank plc* [1998] Lloyd's Rep Bank 185 at 200, per Ferris J). Significantly, in *Westdeutsche Landesbank Girozentrale v Islington London Borough Council* [1996] AC 669, Lord Browne-Wilkinson expressly left open the door to future recognition of the remedial constructive trust in English law. He remarked (at 716) that: The court by way of remedy might impose a constructive trust on a defendant who knowingly retains property of which the plaintiff has been unjustly deprived. Since the remedy can be tailored to the circumstances of the particular case, innocent third parties would not be prejudiced and restitutionary defences, such as change of position, are capable of being given effect.' Innocent third parties could include the defendant's secured and unsecured creditors. In *Re Polly Peck International plc (in administration) (No 2)* [1998] 3 All ER 812, the Court of Appeal refused to impose a remedial constructive trust over the assets of an insolvent company 'since the effect of the statutory scheme [contained in the Insolvency Act 1986] applicable on insolvency is to shut out a remedy which would, if available, have the effect of conferring a priority not accorded by the provisions of the statutory insolvency regime' (per Mummery LJ at 827). In any event, the immediate prospects of recognition of the remedial constructive trust in English law are not good. Lord Millett has stated extra-judicially that '[t]he remedial constructive trust has taken root in the United States and Canada: it is unlikely to do so in England or Australia' ((1998) 114 LQR 399). This reflects his earlier extra-judicial statement that such trusts are 'a counsel of despair which too readily concedes the impossibility of propounding a general rationale for the availability of proprietary remedies' ((1995–96) 6 King's College LJ 1, 19). This should not displease commercial lawyers for the remedial constructive trust would give the court a wide discretion to vary property rights whenever it considers it just to so and thereby introduce new and unwelcome risks into commercial dealings.

7.   The courts have traditionally opposed the application of the equitable standard of constructive notice to commercial transactions. As Lindley LJ stated forcefully in *Manchester Trust Ltd v Furness* [1895] 2 QB 539 at 545:

…as regards the extension of the equitable doctrines of constructive notice to commercial transactions, the Courts have always set their faces resolutely against it. The equitable doctrines of constructive notice are common enough in dealing with land and estates, with which the Court is familiar; but there have been repeated protests against the introduction into commercial transactions of anything like an extension of those doctrines, and the protest is founded on perfect good sense. In dealing with estates in land title is everything, and it can be leisurely investigated; in commercial transactions possession is everything, and there is no time to investigate title; and if we were to extend the doctrine of constructive notice to commercial transactions we should be doing infinite mischief and paralyzing the trade of the country

Lord Millett identifies the flaws in this approach (see extract above). He is right to do so. It has been convincingly argued by David Fox ([1998] CLJ 391) that constructive notice does not always require the same detailed level of inquiry that purchasers of land are expected to observe; on the contrary, the standard of inquiry varies from one transaction to another, and reasonable conduct must be measured against the standard practice of that business or trade. Fox continues (at 395):

Notice can be sensitive to the demands of commercial dealing where speed and security of transaction are important. Recent authority supports this more flexible view. The conduct of a bank receiving a deposit of misappropriated trust money should be measured against the standard of inquiry that could reasonably be expected of a banker not a purchaser of land. Likewise the facts that raise the duty of inquiry may differ from one kind of property transfer to another. Outside land transactions inquiries need not be made as a matter of routine. A commercial recipient may only be put on inquiry if the facts immediately known to him make it glaringly obvious that some impropriety is afoot.

6 PUBLIC LAW IN THE COMMERCIAL ARENA

A commercial lawyer cannot afford to ignore the impact of public law on commercial interests. Public law impacts on commercial interests in at least three different ways.

First, public bodies or local authorities may themselves enter into commercial transactions. Public authorities whose powers derive from statute are subject to the doctrine of *ultra vires,* which is designed to protect the public funds entrusted to such bodies. For example, in *Hazell v Hammersmith and Fulham London Borough Council* [1992] 2 AC 1, the House of Lords held that banks which entered into interest rate swaps with local authorities could not sue on their contracts when they were held to be *ultra vires* the local authorities. The effect of this decision, and others like it (eg *Credit Suisse v Allerdale Borough Council* [1997] QB 306; *Credit Suisse v Waltham Forest Borough Council* [1997] QB 362), caused considerable uncertainty amongst those financial institutions which dealt with local authorities. Fearing that this uncertainty would inhibit financial institutions from entering into commercial relationships with local authorities, the Government introduced legislation to provide them with reassurance and to facilitate the policy of encouraging the Private Finance Initiative (PFI), partnerships, and other contractual relationships between local authorities and the private sector. The Local Government (Contracts) Act 1997 applies to contracts by local authorities for the purposes of or in connection with the discharge of any of their functions which are intended to operate for a period of at least five years. Section 2 of the Act provides that where a local authority has issued a certificate stating it has power to enter into the contract, then the contract has effect 'as if the local authority had had power to enter into it (and exercised that power properly in entering into it)'. The contract may then only be challenged on the ground that the local authority had no power to enter into it through an application for judicial review or by audit review. Even if this challenge results in the contract being declared unlawful, the court still has power to allow it to continue (s 5) or to require the local authority to pay damages to the other contracting party (ss 6, 7).

Other public law principles may come into conflict with the fundamental principles of freedom and sanctity of contract which are so prized in the commercial world. In the case of public authorities the principle of freedom of contract is limited by legislation (see the Local Government Act 1988, s 17 and the Local Government Act 1999) and regulations implementing EC Directives on public sector contracts (see the Public Contracts Regulations 2006, SI 2006/5 and the Utilities Contracts Regulations 2006, SI 2006/6), as well as the general principles governing the exercise of discretionary powers. There are particularly rigid controls on advertising and tendering procedures (see, generally, S Arrowsmith *The Law of Public and Utilities Procurement* (2nd edn 2005)). The principle of sanctity of contract can come into conflict with the public law principle that a court will not enforce a term of a contract which has the effect of fettering a public body's statutory discretion (*Ayr Harbour Trustees v Oswald* (1883) 8 App Cas 623; *Yorke Corpn v Henry Leetham & Sons* [1924] 1 Ch 557).

Secondly, we have already seen how areas of commercial activity are regulated by statute or through the use of statutory powers (see above, p 25). This is particularly true of the financial markets, where it is vital to have regulation which is both predictable, so as to avoid uncertainty, and yet sufficiently flexible to accommodate new business products and practices (an important point made by R Goode in *Commercial Law in the Next Millennium* (1998), pp 44–52). Flexibility can be achieved by giving a regulator wide discretionary powers (eg the Financial Services Authority has wide power under the Financial Services and Markets Act 2000 and associated secondary legislation to refuse or revoke authorisation to carry on a deposit taking business: see below, p 597); but the price for this is the increased risk of arbitrary and unfair decisions. It is here that public law has a vital role to play through what has become known as 'commercial judicial review' (see, generally, J Black, P Muchlinski and P Walker (eds) *Commercial Regulation and Judicial Review* (1998)). The 'path-breaking decision' (per HWR Wade (1987) 103 LQR 323 at 327) was *R v Panel on Take-overs and Mergers, ex p Datafin plc* [1987] QB 815. There the Court of Appeal held that decisions of the take-over panel, a private body which monitored a code of rules, promulgated by itself, governing company take-overs and mergers, but which had neither statutory nor governmental powers, were susceptible to judicial review on the ground that the panel had wide *de facto* powers which it exercised in the public sphere. (Since May 2006 the panel and its rules have had statutory basis.) The case is important because it extends judicial review to regulatory bodies operating in the commercial sphere which do not exercise statutory or prerogative powers, although there must be a 'public element' and the body must not derive its power solely through consensual submission to its jurisdiction (*Datafin,* at 838). Thus, decisions of self-regulatory organisations set up under the (now repealed) Financial Services Act 1986 to regulate sectors of the financial markets (see, eg *R v Life Assurance Unit Trust Regulatory Authority, exp Ross* [1993] QB 17), and even those of the Stock Exchange (*R v International Stock Exchange of the United Kingdom and the Republic of Ireland Ltd, exp Else (1982) Ltd* [1993] QB 534), have been held to be amenable to judicial review (but contrast *R v Lloyd's of London, exp Briggs* [1993] 1 Lloyd's Rep 176, where the Court of Appeal held there could be no review of powers exercised by Lloyd's over its members when Lloyd's exercised those powers solely by virtue of a contractual agreement with its members). Furthermore, the Financial Services Authority, enthroned as the new super-regulator of the financial services industry under the Financial Services and Markets Act 2000, itself a private company but with statutory powers, is also subject to judicial review. However, the danger that arises through the extension of judicial review into the commercial sphere is that it causes uncertainty in the markets and delays commercial transactions as decisions of regulatory bodies are challenged in the courts. Sir John Donaldson MR identified the danger in *Datafin* (at 840), and stated that, save in a case of a breach of natural justice, judicial review in such cases should be 'historic rather than contemporaneous', with the court giving declaratory guidance as to future conduct and leaving existing decisions alone (at 842). In one exceptional case, the Court of Appeal relied, *inter alia*, on the need for finality and certainty in the financial markets, when justifying its decision to refuse relief against an *ultra vires* delegation of power to the chairman of the Monopoly and Mergers Commission (*R v Monopolies and Mergers Commission, ex p Argyll Group* [1986] 1 WLR 763).

Thirdly, it is likely that the Human Rights Act 1998 will have a significant impact upon commercial interests. The Act incorporates the European Convention for the Protection of Human Rights and Fundamental Freedoms into English law. It does this by three mechanisms. First, by requiring the courts to construe all legislation 'so far as it is possible to do so ... in a way which is compatible with the Convention rights' (s 3). Secondly, by introducing a procedure whereby the courts can declare legislation incompatible with the Convention rights, leaving it to Parliament to amend the legislation should it wish to do so (s 4). Thirdly, by making it unlawful for a public authority to act in a way which is incompatible with a Convention right (s 6(1)). The Act provides that a 'public authority' includes 'a court or tribunal' (s 6(3)). This means that the Convention will inevitably effect such matters as the exercise of judicial discretion, and the development of the common law (*Money Markets International Stockbrokers Ltd (in liquidation) v London Stock Exchange Ltd* [2002] 1 WLR 1150 at [139], per Neuberger J). The Act does not give private citizens a direct horizontal right of action against each other based on breach of the Convention rights (the Court of Appeal gave the Act direct horizontal effect in *McKennitt v Ash* [2006] EWCA Civ 1714, [2007] 3 WLR 194, but this goes against the weight of academic opinion and previous case law: see NA Moreham (2007) 123 LQR 373, 375–6), but it is inevitable that it will have an indirect horizontal effect in the manner in which courts and tribunals deal with proceedings between private parties and there is already evidence of this occurring (see, eg *Wilson v First National Trust Ltd (No 2)* [2003] UKHL 40, [2004] 1 AC 816; *Campbell v Mirror Group Newspapers Ltd* [2004] UKHL 22, [2004] 2 AC 457). The degree to which the Act affects legal relations between private individuals is controversial (see, eg at one extreme, HWR Wade (2000) 116 LQR 217, arguing for full horizontal effect, and at the other, R Buxton (2000) 116 LQR 48, denying that the Act creates private law rights, and for a view somewhere in between these two extremes, N Bamforth (2001) 117 LQR 34).

The provisions of the Convention of most relevance to the protection of commercial interests are: (a) the right to property (Protocol No 1, article 1: see, eg *Air Canada v United Kingdom* (1995) 20 EHRR 150, where Air Canada argued that the seizure of its commercial aircraft by HM Customs and Excise following the discovery of cannabis resin aboard the aircraft was a violation of the Convention); (b) the right of access to a court (an inherent element of the notion of a fair trial embodied in art 6(1)); (c) the right to a fair trial in relation to the determination of a person's civil rights and obligations or of any criminal charges brought against him (art 6, which offers particularly stringent protection in the case of criminal proceedings—it is well established that whether a matter is 'civil' or 'criminal' depends on objective tests and not simply on the classification of the domestic law—eg in *Saunders v United Kingdom* (1996) 23 EHRR 313, the European Court of Human Rights held that there had been an infringement of Mr Saunders' right not to incriminate himself where statements made by him under compulsion to Department of Trade and Industry inspectors were used extensively against him in subsequent criminal proceedings); (d) the right to freedom of expression (art 10); (e) the right to respect for privacy (art 8); and (f) the right of freedom of association (art 11) (see P Duffy 'The Protection of Commercial Interests Under the European Convention on Human Rights', in Ch 23 of R Cranston (ed) *Making Commercial Law—Essays in Honour of Roy Goode* (1997)).

7 THE PHILOSOPHY AND CONCEPTS OF COMMERCIAL LAW

'The Codification of Commercial Law' by R Goode
(1988) 14 Mon LR 135, pp 147–155

…*are* there concepts of commercial law? Or is commercial law no more than an aggregation of the different rules governing particular forms of commercial contract, with no linking themes of any kind? If this is the case, and if it is what we want, then a commercial code is not for us. I believe that commercial law does exist and that it embodies a philosophy, not always very coherent but nonetheless present, and fundamental concepts, not always very clearly articulated but nonetheless helping to implement that philosophy and to serve the needs of the business community. By the philosophy of commercial law I mean those underlying assumptions of fairness and utility which inform commercial law and run like a thread through its different branches. By concepts of commercial law I mean those principles of law, whether the common law or legislation, which are a particular response to the needs of the commercial community and thus apply with special vigour to commercial transactions, even though they are capable of application to non-commercial dealings.

VI THE PHILOSOPHY AND CONCEPTS OF COMMERCIAL LAW

The primary function of commercial law, in the sense in which I use that term, is to accommodate the legitimate practices and expectations of the business community in relation to their commercial dealings. This sounds much easier than it is. Business law reflects commercial life, and life is not simple. The law and the judges have to balance a range of competing values, the relative weight of which varies not only from one legal system to another but from one age to another within a single jurisdiction. Those who criticise the *Uniform Commercial Code* for appearing to face all ways at once are correct in the accusation but unfair in the criticism, for the Code does no more than reflect the fact that desirable objectives often pull in opposite directions and require conflicting treatments. The problem for the law maker is much the same as that confronting two consultants treating the same patient, one for diabetes which requires insulin and another for hypoglycaemia which reacts adversely to insulin.

1. The philosophy of commercial law

There would seem to me to be eight principles which together make up the philosophy of commercial law. They are:...

(a) Party autonomy

The general philosophy of the common law is that businessmen should be free to make their own law. A contract is a contract. A party is entitled to the benefit of his bargain and to the strict performance of conditions of the contract, whether they relate to the time of performance or the description or quality of what is to be tendered as performance. Only where contract terms are so restrictive, oppressive or otherwise incompatible with society's goals as to offend against the public interest should the courts intervene to curb the sanctity of contract. One reason for upholding contracts is a philosophical one, that of freedom under the law, including the freedom to fetter one's own freedom. Another is that the enforcement of contractual undertakings helps to promote security and predictability, a matter of some importance to the business world. Hence the *Uniform Commercial Code* makes it clear, in section I–102(2)(b) and (3), that freedom of contract is a principle of the Code. But freedom of contract cannot be absolute, and the Code itself contains numerous specific restrictions, as well as a general bar on contracting out of the obligations of good faith, diligence, reasonableness and care. The circumstances which are considered to justify legislative or judicial interference in the bargain of the parties to a commercial transaction vary widely according to the *mores* of the particular society, the familiarity of the judges with the problems of business life and the relative importance of a particular State as an international centre of commerce or finance.... The view in London, as I see it, may be broadly expressed in these terms: 'business life is rough and tough; if you can't take care of yourself or don't know what you're doing, you shouldn't get into it in the first place!' In other words, in a contest between contract and equity in a commercial dispute, contract wins almost every time; and I suspect that one reason why foreigners so frequently select English law, rather than Continental law, to govern their contracts and English courts to adjudicate their disputes is that they know where they stand on the law and can rely on judges experienced in commercial transactions to give effect to their understanding. Related to the contract/equity conflict is the tension between conflicting goals expressed in the opposing maxims of international law, *pacta sunt servanda* and *rebus sic stantibus*. It takes a great deal to persuade an English court that change of circumstances modifies or discharges even a long-term contract.

(b) Predictability

The business world attaches high importance to the predictability of judicial decisions on legal issues. The weight given by a legal system to the need for predictability compared with equity and flexibility will, of course, vary from jurisdiction to jurisdiction and will depend in no small measure on the volume of business and of dispute resolution a particular State has or wishes to attract. A reasonable degree of predictability is needed in the commercial world because so much planning and so many transactions, standardised or high in value, are undertaken on the basis that the courts will continue to follow the rules laid down in preceding cases. But every businessman and his lawyer knows that there are tides in judicial philosophy, that every action ultimately produces a reaction, that a form of liability denied by one generation of judges will be vigorously developed by the next . . . .

(c) Flexibility

Needless to say, the man of affairs wishes to have his cake and eat it; to be given predictability on the one hand and flexibility to accommodate new practices and developments on the other. Karl Llewellyn was acutely aware of the need to accommodate these opposing goals in the *Uniform Commercial Code;* and he sought, with a fair measure of success, to achieve that accommodation by building into the Code a range of flexible words and concepts to encourage the organic growth of Code law whilst trusting the courts to observe the general policies and philosophy of the Code as a whole. Thus we find references to 'the continued expansion of commercial practices through custom, usage and agreement of the parties' and to 'obligations of good faith, diligence, reasonableness and care' as well as the preservation of general principles of law and equity. In England the courts are on the whole very responsive to the needs of the business community and reluctant to deny recognition to the legal efficacy of commercial instruments and practices in widespread use. As in the Army, there are two opposing but equally effective techniques to avoid bringing disaster on your head from on high. One is to keep out of the way, proceed in stealth and hope that no one will know you are there, still less what you are doing. The other is the exact opposite, namely to promote your activities with a fanfare of trumpets, persuade the rest of the corps to join you and then defy the authorities to upset such a large number of people and such a huge volume of business by declaring it illegal! In the international markets the latter technique seems to work rather well, always so long as one does not come up against a rural judge whose main interests lie in equity and the avoidance of unconscionable bargains!

(d) Good faith

The attitude of the common law to the question of good faith in contracts is curiously ambivalent and is fashioned by English legal history. In civil law jurisdictions the duty of good faith is inherent not only in contractual but in pre-contractual relationships. Particularly vigorous is the general requirement of good faith embodied in section 242 of the German *Civil Code*, which has given rise to a mass of doctrine and jurisprudence and is widely applied. Section 1–203 of the *Uniform Commercial Code* provides that:

> Every contract or duty within this Act imposes an obligation of good faith in its performance or enforcement.

By contrast, good faith is not a general requirement of English law for the enforcement of *legal* rights or the exercise of *legal* remedies. A party can exercise a right to terminate a contract for breach even though it causes him no loss and his sole motive is to escape the consequences of a bad bargain; and a party able to perform a contract without need of the other party's co-operation can in general proceed with performance against the other party's wishes, and even when that party no longer has an interest in the performance, and then claim payment of the contract sum. Where good faith does surface in commercial transactions is in a priority dispute or where some equitable right or remedy is involved. It is surely high time that English law adopted a general principle of good faith and cast off its historical shackles.

(e) The encouragement of self-help

Compared to continental legal systems, the common law is remarkably indulgent towards self-help. Acceleration clauses can be invoked, contracts can be terminated or rescinded, goods repossessed, liens and rights of contractual set-off exercised, receivers and managers appointed and securities realised, all without any need for judicial approval, the only limiting factor (in the absence of special legislation) being that one must not commit a breach of the peace. There seems no pressure to modify this approach in relation to commercial transactions, nor, with the enormous pressure of work on courts all over the world, does a change seem particularly necessary or desirable. Civilised self-help has the advantages of speed, efficiency, flexibility and cheapness upon which the smooth functioning of business life so much depends.

(f) The facilitation of security aspects

As an aspect of the common law's attitude towards self-help, but also an independent characteristic, we may note that—again by comparison with continental systems—it is extremely favourable to the creation of security interests. Security can be taken over almost any kind of asset, tangible or intangible, usually with little or no formality; it can cover present and future property without the need for specific description; and it can secure present and future indebtedness. The creditor has the option of security by possession, ownership (mortgage) or mere charge. He has the facility of appointing a receiver over the entirety of a debtor company's assets, with full powers to take over and manage the company's business, without the creditor being in any way responsible for his receiver's acts or omissions so long as the creditor does not intervene in the conduct of the receivership. Moreover, one of the particular features of insolvency law is that it recognizes and protects interests created and perfected under non-insolvency rules, so that in general a security interest will be accepted as having priority over the claims of the general body of unsecured creditors in the debtor's bankruptcy or winding up.

One of the criticisms levelled against Article 9 was that it was *too* favourable to secured creditors and gave inadequate consideration to the claims of the general body of unsecured creditors. But the balance of the interests of secured and unsecured creditors is primarily a function of insolvency law, not of commercial law, for so long as the debtor is solvent the existence of security is of no moment to the unsecured creditor, who can take a judgment and enforce it by execution.

(g) The protection of vested rights

(h) The protection of innocent third parties

These two well established principles of commercial law do, of course, run in opposite directions. The first reflects a general feeling that an owner should not lose his property without fault; the second, that innocent buyers (including incumbrancers) should be protected against proprietary rights of which they have no notice, in order to ensure the free flow of goods in the stream of trade. Like most legal systems, English law faces both ways. Its starting position is the *nemo dat* principle but its *Sale of Goods Act* moves towards the civilian principle *possession vaut titre*. Third parties may also acquire overriding rights where the holder of a prior security interest has failed to perfect it by registration. No ordering of priorities can do justice in every case, but the position in English law has probably become more incoherent than under most legal systems. Certainly we would expect a commercial code to provide a reasonably rational balance between competing interests and one which, as under the *Uniform Commercial Code,* moves away from distinctions between legal and equitable interests. A rational law should seek to embody two principles: first, that no one should suffer loss or subordination of his rights without fault; secondly, that no one should be affected by a prior interest of which he has neither knowledge nor the means of acquiring knowledge. These two competing principles can be harmonised in some measure by registration requirements, which on the one hand provide the owner of an interest with a means of protecting it and on the other allow third parties to ignore a registrable interest which is unregistered. But we cannot prescribe registration of all real rights, and the problem then is to establish the general, or residuary, rule. For residuary cases I believe the interests of commerce require the civilian principle of *possession vaut titre* rather than the common law principle *nemo dat quod non habet.* A party who puts an article of commerce, tangible or intangible, into the stream of trade must take his chances. This is simply an application in the field of property rights of the policy that dictates that equity should be slow to interfere in commercial transactions.

2. The concepts of commercial law

(a) The concept of a market

As one would expect in a body of law concerned with dealings among merchants, the concept of a market is central to commercial law. By this is meant not necessarily a physical market in which traders strike bargains *in praesenti* on the floor of the market but a mechanism for bringing together substantial numbers of participants who deal in commodities, securities or money and who make a market by acting both as buyers and as sellers at prices determined by supply and demand. With the advent of telecommunications physical markets are steadily giving way to markets established by computer networks in which the participants are linked to each other and to a central system operated by the relevant exchange for striking bargains and displaying market prices. Commercial law is influenced by the concept of a market in a variety of ways. Parties dealing in a market are deemed to contract with reference to its established and reasonable customs and usages, which can have the effect of giving a special meaning to ordinary words, of importing rights and obligations not normally implied, of permitting tolerances in performance which would not be accepted in the general law of contract and of expanding or restricting remedies for a shortfall in performance, as where a small deficiency in quantity or quality is compensatable by an allowance against the price, to the exclusion of the remedy of termination of the contract. The market price is taken as the reference point in computing damages against a seller who fails to deliver or a buyer who fails to accept the subject-matter of the contract, and a party who reduces his loss by a subsequent sale at a higher price or a subsequent purchase at a lower price is not normally required to bring this saving into account, contrary to the normal contract rules as to mitigation of damages.

   The problem for commercial law is to define the manner in which a usage of the market is to be established, a matter that can be of great difficulty but on which much may turn....

(b) The importance of customs or usages of a trade or locality

Even without a market a court will recognize established customs or usages, such as those of a particular trade or locality, where the circumstances indicate that the parties were contracting by reference to the custom or usage. The enforceability of abstract payment undertakings is an important example to which I shall allude in more detail shortly.

(c) The importance of a course of dealing

Since traders are often concerned in a continuous and consistent course of dealing with each other, it is taken for granted that the usual terms apply, whether or not spelled out in the contract. Terms implied by a course of dealing are thus a fruitful source of implication into commercial contracts.

(d) The concept of negotiability

A key feature of commercial law is its recognition of the need for the ready marketability of commercial assets, in particular goods, money obligations and securities. Hence the development of documents of title and negotiable instruments and securities, the delivery of which (with any necessary indorsement) passes constructive possession (goods) or legal title (instruments and securities) to the underlying rights. Hence also the rule, confined to negotiable instruments, that a holder in due course acquires a title free from equities and defects in the title of his transferor. The concept of negotiability derives from the old law merchant and is a particular characteristic of commercial law. Its importance in facilitating dealings with goods in transit and with negotiable securities may be expected to decline as systems evolve for the paperless transfer of goods and securities, an evolution which the draftsman of a commercial code will have to be ready to accommodate. The same is true of negotiable instruments payable at sight or on demand, since these are payment documents rather than credit instruments and in relative terms are gradually giving way to electronic funds transfers. By contrast, term instruments may be expected to retain their vigour, since there seems no reasonable prospect of devising a commercially viable system for replicating electronically the negotiability of a paper document.

(e) The enforceability of abstract payment undertakings

General contract law requires a promise not made under seal to be supported by consideration if it is to be enforceable. But all kinds of legal magic can be worked by mercantile usage. It is generally accepted—though to this day there are no English decisions directly on the point—that certain types of payment undertaking become binding when communicated to the beneficiary, despite the absence of any consideration or any act of reliance on the part of the beneficiary. I refer in particular to the obligations of a bank issuing a documentary credit, a standby credit and a performance bond or guarantee. The contracts engendered by such undertakings are of a peculiar kind, since they are neither unilateral nor bilateral in the ordinary sense, they involve no acceptance of an offer and no consideration. Exactly what types of payment undertaking will be so enforced remains a matter of conjecture. Is this privileged status confined to undertakings by banks? And if so, which types of undertaking? The answer apparently lies in mercantile custom and usage, a force so powerful that it can sweep aside without argument what is generally considered to be a basic principle of contract law.

I hope I have demonstrated to your satisfaction that there *is* a philosophy of commercial law and there *are* concepts of commercial law which mark out commercial transactions for special treatment. Other concepts may suggest themselves as desirable, such as the irrevocability of firm offers in dealings between merchants. But my purpose is not to produce an exhaustive catalogue, simply to refute the notion still current in some circles that commercial law is merely an aggregation of rules governing particular classes of transaction with no common threads calling for an integrated codification.

NOTES

1.   When commercial people deal with each other, they usually do so in a spirit of trust and confidence. As Bowen LJ put it in *Sanders Bros v Maclean & Co* (1883) 11 QBD 327 at 343:

Credit, not distrust, is the basis of commercial dealing; mercantile genius consists principally in knowing whom to trust and with whom to deal, and commercial intercourse and communication is no more based on the supposition of fraud than it is on the supposition of forgery.

Yet English law knows no general doctrine of good faith (*Walford v Miles* [1992] 2 AC 128 at 138, per Lord Ackner). Under the common law a party may enforce his *legal* rights and exercise his *legal* remedies without regard to any general requirement of good faith: there is no rule against abuse of rights (see the dictum of Lord Reid in *White & Carter (Councils) Ltd v McGregor* [1962] AC 413, 430; and see also Lord Mustill [1985] LMCLQ 314, 323). Some academic commentators would like to change this by introducing a general principle of good faith into English contract law (see, eg R Brownsword (1994) 7 JCL 197, (1996) 49 CLP 111, and his *Contract Law: Themes for the Twenty-First Century* (2nd edn, 2006), Ch 5). Others question the need for such wholesale incorporation of a principle of good faith, preferring instead to rely on an incremental approach towards good faith principles. As Bingham LJ stated in *Interfoto Picture Library Ltd v Stiletto Visual Programmes Ltd* [1988] 1 All ER 348 at 352–353:

In many civil law systems, and perhaps in most legal systems outside the common law world, the law of obligations recognises and enforces an overriding principle that in making and carrying out contracts parties should act in good faith. This does not simply mean that they should not deceive each other, a principle which any legal system must recognise; its effect is most aptly conveyed by such metaphorical colloquialisms as 'playing fair', 'coming clean' or 'putting one's cards face upwards on the table'. It is in essence a principle of fair and open dealing…

English law has, characteristically, committed itself to no such overriding principle but has developed piecemeal solutions in response to demonstrated problems of unfairness. Many examples could be given. Thus equity has intervened to strike down unconscionable bargains. Parliament has stepped in to regulate the imposition of exemption clauses and the form of certain hire-purchase agreements. The common law also has made its contribution, by holding that certain classes of contract require the utmost good faith, by treating as irrecoverable what purport to be agreed estimates of damage but are in truth a disguised penalty for breach, and in many other ways.

There is no doubt that good faith plays an important role in priority disputes (eg the protection given to a good faith purchaser or incumbrancer) and also where *equitable* rights or remedies are involved (reflected in the general maxims of equity 'he who seeks equity must do equity' and 'he who comes to equity must come with clean hands'). However, there is a strong case for keeping a general principle of good faith out of the common law, especially in the case of commercial transactions (see RM Goode *Commercial Law in the Next Millennium* (1998), pp 19–20, who seems to have changed his mind on the issue, and also MG Bridge (1984) 9 Can Bus LJ 385). First, what do we mean by good faith? The concept seems impossible to define with any degree of precision (see the range of different attempts at definition in J Beatson and D Friedmann (eds) *Good Faith and Fault in Contract Law* (1995)). Good faith means different things in different jurisdictions and within different legal traditions (F Reynolds [2002] LMCLQ 182, 197; and see also *Director General of Fair Trading v First National Bank plc* [2001] UKHL 52, [2002] 1 AC 481 at [17], per Lord Bingham: The member states [of the European Union] have no common concept of fairness or good faith'.) Secondly, the uncertain scope of the concept would make it difficult to predict the outcome of legal disputes, something valued by the commercial community. Thirdly, a general concept of good faith seems unnecessary when there are a number of alternative mechanisms already available to the courts to regulate the conduct of negotiations and the performance of contracts. The following concepts can all be added to the list of regulatory mechanisms set out by Bingham LJ in *Interfoto v Stiletto*: election, estoppel, waiver, relief against forfeiture (although the House of Lords denied its application to a commercial contracts (a time charter) in *The Scaptrade* [1983] 2 AC 694, the door has recently been opened to the application of the doctrine outside proprietary or possessory interests so that the power to grant relief may be available in other commercial contracts, see *On Demand Information plc (in administrative receivership) v Michael Gerson (Finance) plc* [2002] UKHL 13, [2003] 1 AC 368 at [29], per Lord Millett: see below, p 69, the contra proferentem rule, the requirement that in exceptional cases an innocent party ought to accept a repudiation and mitigate his loss (*White & Carter (Councils) Ltd v McGregor* [1962] AC 413, HL; *Stocznia Gdanska SA v Latvian Shipping Co* [1996] 2 Lloyd's Rep 132,138–139, C A, a point not taken before the House of Lords, [1998] 1 WLR574), the willingness of the courts to imply a duty of co-operation on a contracting party in order to achieve a common goal of the contract (*Mackay v Dick* (1881)6 App Cas 251, 263, per Lord Blackburn; cf *North Sea Energy Holdings NV v Petroleum Authority of Thailand* [1999] 1 All ER (Comm) 173, 185–186, CA: held duty to co-operate negatived by terms of contract), and the control of a lender's discretion to vary interest rates in a mortgage agreement through an implied term that it was not to be exercised dishonestly, for an improper purpose, capriciously or so unreasonably that no reasonable lender would have acted in that way (*Paragon Finance plc v Nash* [2001] EWCA Civ 1466, [2002] 1 WLR 685, cf *Sterling Credit plc v Rahman* [2002] EWHC 3008 (Ch)). In one case, Winn LJ even went so far as to refer to a developing doctrine of 'fair conduct' between parties to commercial contracts (*Panchaud Frères SA v Etablissements General Grain Co* [1970] 1 Lloyd's Rep 53 at 59). This is certainly consistent with what Steyn J has described as 'the aim of our commercial law', namely 'to encourage fair dealing between the parties' (*CTN Cash and Carry Ltd v Gallaher Ltd* [1994] 4 All ER 714 at 719); although Lord Steyn (as he now is) does not think it necessary to introduce a general principle of good faith to achieve this goal, since the courts can be relied on to respect the reasonable expectation of the parties through other means (see Lord Steyn (1997) 113 LQR 433, 438–439; cf AF Mason (2000) 116 LQR 66 at 94: 'recognition of good faith and fair dealing concepts would bring greater coherence and unity to the varied array of principles which are presently available'). One such means is to uphold a duty to act in good faith in a particular respect when that duty has been made an express contractual term. Longmore LJ (obiter) recently expressed his willingness to uphold an obligation to negotiate in good faith when that obligation was an express term in a commercial contract drawn up with the benefit of professional legal advice (*Petromec Inc v Petroleo Brasiliero SA Petrobras (No 3)* [2005] EWCA Civ 891, [2006] 1 Lloyd's Rep 121 at [115]–[121]). Lord Bingham returned to the question of good faith in *Director General of Fair Trading v First National Bank plc*, above, where he observed (at [17]) that 'since Lord Mansfield was its champion, it is not a concept wholly unfamiliar to British lawyers'. This is undoubtedly true: for example, the duty of disclosure in insurance contracts can be traced back to the decision of Lord Mansfield in *Carter v Boehm* (1766) 3 Burr 1905. But this is merely one example of the English courts responding to a particular situation or relationship, it is not part of an overarching doctrine of good faith in English law.

A requirement of good faith does feature in some of the most important pieces of English commercial legislation, although here it emerges as a subjective standard of honesty rather than an objective one of fair dealing. Both the Bills of Exchange Act 1882 and the Sale of Goods Act 1979 demand the exercise of good faith before certain rights, particularly those rights protecting third party purchasers, can be acquired (see BEA, ss 12, 29(1), 30(2), 59(1), 60, 79(2), 80; SGA, ss 22–25, 47). Both statutes define good faith in terms of 'honesty in fact' (BEA, s 90; SGA, s 61(3)), although it is clear that wilfully turning a blind eye to one's own suspicions is evidence of dishonesty (*Jones v Gordon* (1877) 2 App Cas 616 at 629, per Lord Blackburn, see below, p 526; *London Joint Stock Bank v Simmons* [1892] AC 201 at 221, per Lord Herschell). See also the Factors Act 1889, ss 2(1), 8 and 9; the Marine Insurance Act 1906, s 17; the Cheques Act 1957, ss 1 and 4; the Hire- Purchase Act 1964, ss 27–29.

References in statutes to standards of good faith, particularly in the objective sense of fair dealing, are likely to increase with the harmonisation of commercial law in the European Union (see, eg EC Directive 1986/653 on Self-Employed Commercial Agents, arts 3(1) and 4(1), as implemented by the Commercial Agents (Council Directive) Regulations 1993, SI 1993/3053, regs 3(1) and 4(1)) and the harmonisation of world trade law (see, eg the Vienna Convention on Contracts for the International Sale of Goods (1980), art 7(1), not yet ratified by the UK). It comes as no surprise that art 1.7 of the UNIDROIT *Principles of International Commercial Contracts* (above, p 18), and also art 1.201(1) of the *Principles of European Contract Law* (above, p 18), prepared by the Commission on European Contract Law, demand that 'each party must act in accordance with good faith and fair dealing'. Furthermore, English courts have become familiar with the concept of good faith when using their powers under the Unfair Terms in Consumer Contracts Regulations 1999 (SI 1999/2083), which implements the EC Directive on Unfair Terms in Consumer Contracts (93/13), to police 'unfair terms' in consumer contracts (ie those terms which have not been individually negotiated and which 'contrary to the requirement of good faith causes a significant imbalance in the parties' rights and obligations arising under the contract to the detriment of the consumer': reg 5(1) of the Regulations, art 3(1) of the Directive). This imports an objective standard of good faith into English law and the English courts have been quick to recognise its origins in continental civil law (*Director General of Fair Trading v First National Bank plc* [2000] 1 WLR 99 at 109, Evans-Lombe J; [2000] QB 672 at 687, Peter Gibson J; [2001] UKHL 52, [2002] 1 AC 481 at [17], Lord Bingham, and at [36], Lord Steyn). There must be some chance that the courts will allow the influence of good faith to extend beyond consumer transactions covered by the Regulations and 'to percolate throughout our law of contract' (J Beatson [1997] CLJ 291 at 292, and also at (2001) 117 LQR 247, for the case that statute can influence the development of the common law).

2. Professor Goode returned to the subject of the influence of the concept of a market on the development of commercial law when delivering the 33rd Lionel Cohen lecture in 1990 (see R Goode (1990) 24 Israel Law Review 185, later published in [1991] LMCLQ 177). He argued (at 186; at 178) that:

...the needs and practices of the market are driving English contract and commercial law, in particular by forcing the evolution of new techniques for the creation and transfer of rights, by applying old concepts to new situations and by modifying and expanding rules of law both to accommodate legitimate business expectations and to protect the stability and integrity of the market.

The English courts have generally been good at doing this, but there have been some notable exceptions. We have already seen how the uncertainty created by the decision of the House of Lords in *Hazell v Hammersmith and Fulham London Borough Council* [1992] 2 AC 1 (above, p 10), the swaps case, seriously dented the City of London's reputation with foreign investors. This led directly to the Bank of England setting up the Legal Risk Review Committee and then, on the Committee's recommendation, the Financial Law Panel, and, in 2002, following on from the closure of the Financial Law Panel, the Financial Markets Law Committee, whose function is to identify issues of legal uncertainty in the framework of the wholesale financial markets which might give rise to material risks, and to consider how such issues can be addressed.

8   THE CODIFICATION OF COMMERCIAL LAW

You will have realised by reading this far that there have been calls for the codification of English commercial law. Those who make that call, such as Professor Goode, do not ask for codification along Victorian lines, where there were virtually no links between the codified statutes. On the contrary, the modern advocates of codification want a comprehensive commercial code along the lines of the American Uniform Commercial Code (UCC) (above, p 6). An English commercial code would embody 'a set of principles and main rules for a handful of key commercial transactions—sale, secured transactions, intermediated securities and electronic funds transfer, and perhaps agency and suretyship guarantees, together with a set of general provisions—that would be regularly reviewed and could be amended by some fast-track procedure' (R Goode (2007) 123 LQR 602, 605–606). Such a code would contain statements of principle and would not attempt to deal in detail with every problem that might arise in commerce.

The case for codification can be summarised as follows: it simplifies the law and makes it easily accessible; the process of codification highlights areas of weakness in the existing law; it enables the law to be modernised and reduces ambiguities and inconsistencies between statutes; it provides an integrated body of commercial law of which the various branches are linked by common concepts, a coherent philosophy and a consistent terminology. It is said that the net effect of commercial codification will be to improve the law and also produce savings in time, effort and money for those who must advise on it and comply with it. See generally, R Goode (1988) 14 Mon LR 135 at pp 137–140, upon which this summary is based (and also the extract from Professor Goode's 1997 Hamlyn Lecture 'Commercial Law in an International Environment: Towards the Next Millennium' which appears below at p 48). Professor Goode is not alone in calling for an English commercial code (see also Mrs Justice Arden [1997] CLJ 516, especially at pp 530–534).

Yet there has been no call for a commercial code from the vast majority of our commercial judges or practitioners (Lord Goff (1992) 5 JCL 1 at p 3; although Lord Goff has since declared that he has come 'to entertain new thoughts about codification' (1997) 46 ICLQ 745 at p 751). The opponents of such general codification say that it is unnecessary, inflexible and contrary to our common law tradition of responding to the changing needs of the business community as they arise. Furthermore, there is the perceived danger that codification will stifle the ability of judges to develop the law (but this has not occurred in Germany where there is a Civil Code (the BGB): see Lord Goff (1997) 46 ICLQ 745 at pp 751–752). Of course, those who see commercial law as an amalgam of distinct subjects, and who deny that there are any general principles of commercial law, see the whole process of general codification as meaningless.

As the next extract illustrates, there have been similar calls for wholesale codification of international trade law.

'The Codification of the Law of International Trade' by CM Schmitthoff
[1985] JBL 34, pp 41–43

...we have to consider whether the creation of a world code on international trade law—a task which, as I have already observed, undoubtedly would fall to UNCITRAL—would be beneficial and feasible. Three questions have here to be examined: what would be the purpose of such codification, what would be the method of it, and what would be the contents of such a code?

As regards the benefits of such codification, they would be, in my view, considerable. Probably the greatest benefit would be that such a code would offer countries in the course of development a compact package deal. If they adopt the code, they would at once have the most modern and comprehensive legal instrument for the conduct of their international business. Secondly, it would be possible to establish in a general part of such code certain principles which should apply to all international trade transactions. I am thinking here, eg of the obligation of good faith in the performance and enforcement of an international contract, as it is laid down in paragraph 1–203 of the American Uniform Commercial Code. Other equitable rules of the American Code's General Provisions may likewise be suitable for incorporation into a general part of a world code, eg those on severability of an invalid provision, or those on a liberal construction, according to the underlying purposes and policies, in this context, of international Conventions or other international instruments.

Further, a code of international trade law could deal with certain general questions which affect all international trade contracts, such as the effect of telecommunications and the determination of a universal unit of accounts for international conventions, ie the Special Drawing Rights of the World Bank. Lastly, the creation of a code on international trade law would emphasise the inherent unity of the work of UNCITRAL and other formulating agencies in their efforts to harmonise and unify the legal regulation of international trade on a worldwide basis. This inherent unit is not always clearly discernible in the present state of development as these organisations have often to deal with highly specialised topics of relatively small ambit.

As to the method of codification, little has to be said. It is obvious that the empirical method has to be adopted. The code would thus be nothing more than a technical legal instrument of consolidation.

As to its contents, the code would necessarily have to be built on existing measures of unification. It would have to include, in an integrated manner, the United Nations Conventions so far promulgated and other international measures widely accepted by the practice. It should not be limited to measures sponsored by UNCITRAL but should include suitable texts drafted by other formulating agencies and approved by UNCITRAL. But this may not be enough. A general part would have to be provided, bracketing together the substantive parts. In addition, some further specific subjects may have to be included in order to make the code comprehensive and workable in practice. I have indicated elsewhere what I would consider to be the substance of such a code. I said [CM Schmitthoff *Commercial Law in a Changing Economic Climate* (2nd edn, 1981), p 30]:

> If the Unidroit project on the Code of International Trade Law and the ICC scheme on trade usages are joined together with the United Nations Convention on Contracts for the International Sale of Goods, the ICC Uniform Customs and Practice on Documentary Credits and the Uniform Rules

for Collections, the United Nations Hamburg Rules on the Carriage of Goods by Sea, and the UNCITRAL Arbitration Rules, the basis of a world code on international trade is already laid. What has to be done, is to weld together these disjoined pieces of unification into a logical, integrated work and to supplement it by unifications which are still extant, such as the proposed uniform law on international bills of exchange and promissory notes, the regulation of the international contracts of forwarding and warehousing, and other relevant topics.

In the result, the creation of a uniform world code on international trade law would, in my view, serve a useful purpose and, having regard to the existing and planned unificatory measures, is a feasible proposition.

NOTE

Professor Schmitthoff is not referring to the piecemeal harmonisation of trade law that has already taken place via international conventions and codes. He is calling for a worldwide code of international trade. Like Professor Goode, he points to the American UCC as proof that such a code is not a Utopian goal. Such a code would create a new *lex mercatoria*.

QUESTION

Given the UK's past track record with regard to ratification of international conventions which seek to harmonise specific areas of international trade law (see above, p 28), would you expect the UK to be in the vanguard of states lobbying for a worldwide code as proposed by Professor Schmitthoff? (Try not to laugh too loud when answering this question!) If not, why not?

9 THE CHALLENGES FOR COMMERCIAL LAW IN THE TWENTY-FIRST CENTURY

'Commercial Law in an International Environment: Towards the Next Millennium', Ch 4 in *Commercial Law in the Next Millennium* by R Goode (1998), pp 96–104

What are the challenges for commercial law as we approach the 21st century? I have already referred to the importance of harmonisation, whether in the form of hard law, such as an international convention, or of contractually incorporated rules, such as those issued by the ICC, or of so-called soft law, as exemplified by the two international restatements of contract previously mentioned. In this concluding part of the final Hamlyn lecture I should like, first, to consider some of the legal implications of new technology, secondly, to comment on the changing approach to commercial dispute resolution, and, thirdly, to offer some more general reflections on the present shape of English commercial law.

Technological developments

In debates concerning the legal implications of an electronic business environment there is an unfortunate tendency to over-emphasise the technology and to assume that it automatically changes everything so far as legal relationships are concerned. This is a myth which I am anxious to dispel. Whether one is dealing with electronic funds transfer, the dematerialisation or immobilisation of securities or the use of electronic bills of lading, it is necessary to ask why, if the message is broadly the same, its legal significance should be affected by the medium through which it is sent. My heart warmed to a member of the audience at an International Bar Association gathering in Vienna some years ago who asked what, conceptually, was the difference between a funds transfer effected as the result of communication across the ether and the delivery of a sack of notes or gold carried over the shoulder from one place to another. This is a very perceptive question and one that needs to be addressed. Of course, it can be said that there are legal instruments, such as a bill of exchange or a bill of lading, which depend for their legal efficacy on a writing and a signature. The shipping conventions, for example, all refer to a signed bill of lading. But what is really at stake is an authenticated message, and modern legal definitions of writing and signature allow for any medium of communication and any proper system of authentication so long as the message is capable of being reproduced in tangible form.[11] Moreover, even where it is necessary to interpret international conventions as requiring a physical, signed document,[12] in most cases the desired effects of those conventions can be achieved by a contractual incorporation of the convention rules, which will thus apply as terms of the contract.

What, then, is so special about the medium? Why should electronic transmissions necessitate different rules of law? These questions are worth asking because in many cases we find the same rules apply to electronic transactions as to written ones. For example, the basic concepts of payment and the revocability of a payment instruction remain unchanged, though some tweaking of the rules is needed and this is usually achieved by rules of the clearing house. But computer technology does have an impact on legal rules and legal risk. Copyright issues have to be considered. Rules must be devised to govern the payment systems themselves, the rights and obligations of the parties and the allocation of risk where the system fails or is improperly accessed. The ease and speed with which large sums can be moved around the world in an electronic environment creates the potential for large-scale losses through fraud or system failure. There was a celebrated event many years ago in New York when a clearing bank appeared to become increasingly insolvent as the day drew to a close. It transpired that a computer, with the malignity of intent that characterised the last weeks of the master computer HAL in 2001, was debiting the bank with all its outflows but failing to credit it with its inflows. The problems was dealt with by deferring the daily settlement for a few hours, during which time the defect was rectified. But imagine the consequences if it had not been.

There are also public law implications of electronic trading, particularly in the field of regulation. Data protection has become in increasingly complex field; so also has the legal treatment of digital cash. Is a person who holds value in an electronic purse to be treated as a depositor for the purpose of the Banking Act because of his right to require the bank issuing the electronic value to redeem it? Probably not in most cases, but the issue continues to be debated. How is control to be exercised over regulated activities where these are conducted through the Internet? How are we to establish in which jurisdiction relevant acts have occurred? And what is the position if one of the ingredients of an offence is committed in this country and the other or others abroad? These are matters yet to be resolved; they add a new dimension to the task of the regulator.

The resolution of commercial disputes

So far tonight I have concentrated on substantive law. But as I have remarked earlier in this lecture series, the procedure for the resolution of commercial disputes is itself of vital importance. It is no use having legal rights if they cannot readily be enforced and if disputes cannot be fairly and expeditiously resolved. It is generally considered that our central courts—in particular the specialist Commercial Court and the more general courts of the Queen's Bench and Chancery Divisions—provide a good, often an excellent, service to commercial users. Even so, over time the delays and expense associated with litigation led to the growth of commercial arbitration. This was seen as fast, flexible, informal, private, relatively inexpensive and conducive to finality. This is still true of a considerable amount of arbitration, particularly in the commodities field. But it has to be said that much commercial arbitration has become almost indistinguishable from litigation. Arbitral proceedings, particularly with a three-person tribunal in an international arbitration, can be very protracted and a good deal more expensive than litigation. We do at least have the benefit of a modern Arbitration Act[13] ordered in a logical arrangement and expressed in plain English. The Act follows the spirit of the UNCITRAL Model Law more closely than had at one time been envisaged, though Scotland was still bolder in its adoption of the Model Law. Even so, there is much dissatisfaction with arbitration and a growing drift towards alternative dispute resolution methods, such as mediation and the min-trial. In the early days of ADR experienced arbitrators were inclined to be dismissive, taking the rather lofty view that it would no doubt work well enough in family disputes but would be quite unsuited to disputes of a commercial character. That view is increasingly seen as misplaced and ADR is growing. It is a great deal quicker and cheaper. Of course, it may not be successful, but most hearings appear to end in agreement. Of equal importance is the fact that ADR is designed to be non-confrontational, to expose the real reason, rather than the ostensible reason, for the parties' disagreement and to offer the prospects of continuance of their relationship instead of the acceptance of its breakdown. Moreover, because ADR is not fettered by legal rights and remedies and can facilitate non-legal forms of relief, such as the offer of a substitute contract to the aggrieved party or the resuscitation of an agreement that has been legally ended. What the commercial community has not yet fully appreciated is the importance of laying down procedures in advance at the contract stage by which principals not previously involved in the handling of the dispute and with the authority to negotiate are brought into discussions at an early stage with a view to avoiding a breakdown of the relationship rather than simply assuming the breakdown and alleviating it consequences. I have discussed this in more detail elsewhere.[14]

The present state of English commercial law

I have said that we need to become more outward-looking, more international in our approach to international conventions. But what of the internal state of English commercial law? How well placed are we to undertake the challenges of change as we enter the next millennium? Here I have to say that for many years now the judiciary seems to have been more attuned than the legislature to the need to keep abreast of legal thought and dynamics in the international community. The courts have shown an ever-increasing readiness to look to patterns of judicial lawmaking in other legal systems for solutions to help resolve complex issues of legal policy. Law, like friendship, has to be constantly cultivated and regularly renewed. When I visit other common law countries, and in particular Canada and the United States, I am immensely impressed with their concern to keep their commercial law up to date and with the enormous energy and legal creativity which their academic and practising lawyers bring to bear to modernise and keep under regular review their laws governing commercial transactions. Pride of place must go to the American Uniform Commercial Code. Admittedly this is powerfully driven by the need for harmonisation among 50 jurisdictions, a motive power we lack; but it is clear that the Americans take the health of their law very seriously indeed. And when I return to England I feel, as always, uplifted by the remarkably high standard in which our judiciary is held but depressed by the state of our statute book and by our inertia and complacent belief in the innate superiority of English commercial law. I believe that at the legislative level we have shamefully neglected our commercial law for as long as I can remember.

To test this, let us take a look at our principal commercial statutes. The Sale of Goods Act 1979 largely re-enacts the Sale of Goods Act 1893, which was brilliantly drafted by Sir Mackenzie Chalmers but is now 104 years old. A charge over goods by a company is registrable under section 395 of the Companies Act 1985 where, had it been given by an individual, it would have been registrable as a bill of sale. To find this out it is necessary to resort to the Bills of Sale Acts 1878 and 1882, which are among the most exquisitely technical ever to have been enacted and can be fully interpreted only by reading literally hundreds of reported cases. Our legislation dealing with factors and mercantile agents is itself 108 years old. What of our negotiable instruments law? We do not have a negotiable instruments law. What we have is a statute passed in 1882, another of Chalmers' outstanding pieces of legislation, which, however, has hardly been touched since it was passed and does not cover any of the newer forms of instrument. So we have no statutory provisions to make clear what is assumed in the market place (I believe correctly) that such instruments as certificates of deposit, floating rate notes and bearer bonds are negotiable despite any uncertainty as to the amount to be paid and despite the fact that some of these kinds of instrument are expressed to be subject to the terms of trust deeds and the power of trustees.

How is it that we feel able to embark on the 21st century with commercial law statutes passed in the 19th? How can we seriously expect to confront the problems of modern commerce with legislation enacted in the era of the steam coach, which had to be preceded by a man with a red flag; when the aeroplane, television, the computer and spacecraft were all in the future? Our version of a well-known aphorism is: if it's broken, don't fix it! And as if this were not bad enough, there are whole areas of the law relating to commercial transactions on which we have virtually no legislation whatsoever: nothing on funds transfers or payment systems, nothing on indirect holdings of immobilised securities, nothing on warehouse receipts and no up-to-date and integrated treatment of documents of title generally. And we are the world's leading financial centre! As so often in so many areas, when Parliament is inert it is the courts that have to come to the rescue; and it is only because of the commercial awareness of our judges and the high standing they enjoy with foreigners that we are able to manage. Surely it is not too much to ask that commercial law statutes be reviewed at least once every 25 years; and when more than a century has elapsed without significant change, we can reasonably assume that it is time to replace the entire legislation and begin again.

> 'Ah love! Could thou and I with Fate conspire
> To grasp this sorry Scheme of Things entire,
> Would not we shatter it to bits—and then
> Re-mould it nearer to the Heart's Desire!'[15]

My strong preference is for a commercial code of the kind so successfully adopted thoughout the United States. A commercial code has many advantages.[16] It gathers together in one place the rules governing the major forms of commercial transaction and thereby makes the law accessible both to lawyers and to laymen. At present we have to resort to textbooks. Helpful though they may be, they are no substitute for a code, for within a given subject they analyse each principle and rule separately, so that these are diffused across the entire work and are not available to the reader in one place as with the code.

A commercial code is also an exportable product. Even if not taken over in its entirety, it can provide the inspiration for a modern commercial law elsewhere and particularly in developing countries and those that have moved or are moving to a market economy. A code integrates what are at present a disparate collection of statutes, unconnected to each other, replacing them with provisions which cover the field as a whole, in which each part is linked to the others and which are bedded down on a set of general provisions governing all transactions to which the code applies. The very process of preparing a commercial code helps to expose the inadequacies and inconsistencies of the present law and provides an opportunity for commerce, industry and finance to identify weaknesses and to suggest what is needed to overcome them. There are other benefits. Transactions could be conducted more efficiently, legal rules would be much more susceptible to developing business needs than they are now and much time currently spent in digging for particles of commercial law and then arduously assembling them into a coherent principle would be saved.

The preparation of a code would involve several years of effort and a not inconsiderable expense; but that is the price to be paid for a quality product and it is surely a price worth paying. We continue to suffer from false economies in the shape of quick fixes that come unstuck, of half-baked legislation in other areas which has to be corrected, of a philosophy which counts nothing as worth doing unless it can be done quickly and produce an immediate return. But if industry does not shirk at devoting large sums of money and years of research to producing quality products, surely the lawmakers, for a fraction of the cost, can do the same. But if such a project is to succeed it must engage the interest and the involvement not only of academic and practising lawyers but of businessmen in industry, commerce and finance. They must be willing to join the lawyers in such an enterprise, to put their shoulders behind the wheel and, having helped to produce the modern legislation we so desperately need, to urge on government the importance of enacting it.

My final plea is for a greater academic commitment to commercial law. We need more, many more, academic lawyers in the field than we currently possess. Particularly do we need young scholars of an enquiring turn of mind, interested in the workings of commercial practice as well as the development of theory, who can advance the boundaries of knowledge and take our students forward into the next age of commercial law. They will find a warm welcome not only from their colleagues but from practitioners, who are only too happy to share their expertise, and from the judges, who from the House of Lords downwards have, in recent years in particular, been generous in acknowledging the contribution of scholarly writings to their decisions. The academic community is in turn indebted to Bench and Bar for reasoned arguments and judgments which form the basis of much of our teaching and research and which often possess such a combination of creative thinking and intellectual rigour as to make some of us wonder if it is not the members of the practising profession who are often the true scholars!

We have come a long way from the ancient caravan trade and the medieval market, from the runner and the carrier pigeon to instananeous global communication, from the longboat and the Phoenician round ship to the Japanese oil tanker, from dealings in physical assets to dealings in derivatives and other bundles of intangible rights. Yet the basis of our commerce remains as it was in early times: an organised, regulated market with an efficient clearing and settlement system, a procedure for the fair and expeditious resolution of disputes and a high degree of predictability of outcomes on issues of legal entitlement and obligation. It is a matter for some astonishment that although our legislation governing commercial transactions is archaic, foreigners continue to resort to English law and to English courts, while our own mercantile community remains able to structure agreements and relationships to produce almost any commercially desirable result, and to fashion new financial and commercial instruments, confident in the belief that these will be upheld and that the reasonable usages of merchants will be respected. But that is the genius of English commercial law.

Footnotes

11 See, for example, the 1988 Unidroit Convention on International Factoring, art. I(4)(b) (' "notice in writing" includes, but is not limited to, telegrams, telex and any other telecommunication capable of being reproduced in tangible form'); and the 1996 UNCITRAL Model Law on Electronic Commerce, art 6(1) ('Where the law requires information to be in writing, that requirement is met by a data message if the information contained therein is accessible so as to be usable for subsequent reference'). For a detailed study of the meanings and requirements of 'writing' and 'document' in English primary and subordinate legislation, see Chris Reed, *Digital Information Law* (1996), which examines the provisions in a wide variety of statutes and statutory instruments.

12 A requirement which could be conveniently overcome by ratification of the 1996 UNCITRAL Model Law on Electronic Commerce. See n 11 above.

13 Arbitration Act 1996.

14 'Dispute Resolution in the 21 st Century', the 1997 Alexander Lecture, delivered in the Old Hall, Lincoln's Inn on June 24, 1997 and reproduced in (1998) 64 *Arbitration 9*.

15 *The Rubáiyát of Omar Khayyam* (trans. Edward Fitzgerald), 1st edn, stanza 73.

16 For a full development of this thesis, see Roy Goode, 'The Codification of Commercial Law' (1986) 14 Monash Univ. L. Rev. 135. The Chairman of the Law Commission, Mrs Justice Arden, also stressed the advantages of codification in her 1997 COMBAR lecture, 'Time for an English Commercial Code?'.

NOTES

1.   Professor Goode identifies some of the legal challenges thrown up by electronic commerce. There are others. When and where is an electronic contract formed? Is an Internet service provider to face civil or criminal liability in respect of third party material carried over his network? Are those who have access to electronic records subject to a duty of confidentiality? These issues are being addressed at global, regional and national levels.

2.   In 1996, UNCITRAL adopted a Model Law on Electronic Commerce. Most countries which have dealt with or propose to deal with e-commerce have based their legislation on

or have at least purported to make it consistent with this Model Law (Law Com, op cit, para 2.1). In 2001, UNCITRAL also adopted a Model Law on Electronic Signatures.

3. In 1999, the European Union adopted a Directive 99/93 on a framework for electronic signatures ([2000] OJ LI3/12), and this was followed in 2000 by Directive 00/31 on certain legal aspects of information society services, in particular electronic commerce, in the Internal Market ([2000] OJ L178/1).

4. Implementation of the Electronic Signatures Directive in the UK has been through the Electronic Communications Act 2000 and the Electronic Signatures Regulations 2002, SI 2002/318. This establishes a legal framework for electronic signatures. Parts of the E-Commerce Directive has been implemented by the Electronic Commerce (EC Directive) Regulations 2002, SI 2002/ 2013, together with four statutory instruments relating to financial services. The Directive and the Regulations address three main areas: (a) liberalising the European Economic Area internal market in e-commerce services; (b) requiring providers of e-commerce services to incorporate certain features into their online ordering process and to provide particular information to users; and (c) defining the liability of online intermediaries such as Internet service providers (see, generally, G Smith and A Hand [2002] NLJ 1597).

5. In December 2001, the Law Commission published its Advice to Government entitled *Electronic Commerce: Formal Requirements in Commercial Transactions* (for a useful summary, see H Beale and L Griffiths [2002] LMCLQ 467). The Law Commission had considered whether law reform was required to prevent formal requirements in various commercial transactions hindering the development of electronic commerce. There was particular concern as to whether specific measures were needed to implement art 9 of the E-Commerce Directive, which requires that:

Member States shall ensure that their legal system allows contracts to be concluded by electronic means. Member States shall in particular ensure that the legal requirements applicable to the contractual process neither create obstacles for the use of electronic contracts nor result in such contracts being deprived of legal effectiveness and validity on account of their having been made electronically.

The Advice focused on the international sale and carriage of goods and the associated banking and insurance transactions. The Law Commission concluded (as summarised in Part 10 of the Advice) that:

- statutory requirements for 'writing' and a 'signature' were generally capable of being satisfied by e-mails (later confirmed by *J Pereira Fernandes SA v Mehta* [2006] EWHC 813, [2006] 1 WLR 1543: see below, p 1166) and by website trading (but not by Electronic Data Interchange);

- because English law seldom imposes such form requirements in a contractual context, it was only in very rare cases that the statute book conflicts with the obligations imposed by art 9 of the Electronic Commerce Directive;

- general reform of the statute book was not therefore required, and

- where particular statutory rules did conflict with the requirements of the E-Commerce Directive, an order under s 8 of the Electronic Communications Act 2000 could be used to make context-specific reform. Section 8 gives Ministers the authority to review statutes and related legislation that requires documents to be in writing and to amend them by way of secondary legislation 'in such manner as [the Minister] may think fit for the purpose of authorising or facilitating the use of electronic communications or electronic storage'.

6.   Consumers engaged in e-commerce require special protection. There is the ever- present fear of fraud and concern that privacy will be violated. Because these concerns could affect consumer confidence and reduce consumer participation in e-commerce, they have been addressed in the UK through legislation which implements various European Union initiatives. Thus, fraud is one of the issues addressed in both the Consumer Protection (Distance Selling) Regulations 2000, SI 2000/2334, implementing EC Directive 97/7 on the protection of consumers in respect of distance contracts for the supply of goods and (non-financial) services and the Financial Services (Distance Marketing) Regulations 2004, SI 2004/2095, implementing EC Directive 2002/65 concerning the distance marketing of consumer financial services (see below, p 838). The Data Protection Act 1998 bolsters the consumer's right to privacy, as do the Privacy and Electronic Communications (EC Directive) Regulations 2003, SI 2003/2426.

QUESTION

Why is it in the national interest for English law to keep up to date with, and reflect, modern trading practices?

CHAPTER 2
BASIC CONCEPTS OF PERSONAL PROPERTY

In this chapter, we shall examine some basic concepts of personal property law: the nature of personal property, the characteristics and significance of property rights, ownership, possession and bailment.[1] It is important to understand these concepts as commercial law is primarily concerned with dealings in personal property, eg the sale of goods, the issue and transfer of negotiable instruments and the factoring of debts.

1 THE DISTINCTION BETWEEN REAL AND PERSONAL PROPERTY

The common law distinguishes between real property and personal property. In general terms, real property is land and all things built on land. Personal property is all the property that is left after real property has been subtracted from the class of property taken as a whole. Personal property is, therefore, a residual class of property.

The reason for the division between real and personal property is historical. In the Middle Ages the common law allowed an owner who had been wrongfully dispossessed of his freehold land to bring an action, called a real action, to recover it. On the other hand, an owner of personal property (which, technically, includes leasehold interests in land) could not bring an action to recover it; he was restricted to a personal action for damages against the person who had wrongfully deprived him of his personal property. This procedural distinction still applies today, save that the courts now have a discretion to order delivery of goods back to their owner (Torts (Interference with Goods) Act 1977, s 3).

Leaving aside leasehold interests, which for practical purposes are interests in land, the law treats real and personal property differently. For example, specific performance will

---

[1] See generally, RM Goode *Commercial Law* (3rd edn, 2004) ('Goode'), Ch 2 (a masterly survey on which much that follows is based). For an excellent short commentary on the law of personal property, see MG Bridge *Personal Property Law* (3rd edn, 2002) ('Bridge'). Students are well-served with Sarah Worthington's *Personal Property Law: Text, Cases and Materials* (2000). For more detailed analysis, see Crossley Vaines *Personal Property* (5th edn, 1973) ('Crossley Vaines'); AP Bell *Modern Law of Personal Property in England and Ireland* (1989) ('Bell'). For a stimulating collection of essays dealing with many of the areas covered in this chapter, see N Palmer and E McKendrick (eds) *Interests in Goods* (2nd edn, 1998).

rarely be ordered when a buyer fails to deliver goods, whereas it is the usual remedy when a vendor fails to complete a contract for the sale of land; there are different rules for the creation and *inter vivos* transfer of interests in real property (where formalities are required) and personal property (where few formalities are required); and, as we have seen, whereas the wrongfully dispossessed owner of real property may recover it as a matter of course, the recovery of personal property is subject to the court's discretion. But why is real and personal property treated so differently? Professor Goode points to the different characteristics of the two types of property: land is generally immovable, relatively permanent, readily split into multiple interests, primarily acquired for use and not intended to circulate in the flow of trade; on the other hand, personal property moves freely in the world of commerce, usually has a relatively short life, has a primary value measured in money and does not readily lend itself to division into multiple interests (Goode, pp 29–31). He concludes:

...land is governed primarily by property law concepts, goods and choses in action by commercial law concepts; land law is concerned essentially with status, commercial law with obligations. But...many rules of property law apply equally well to land and chattels.

2 TYPES OF PERSONAL PROPERTY

Personal property may be divided into chattels real and chattels personal. Chattels real consist mainly of leasehold interests in land. Chattels personal are those items of personal property that are not chattels real. Chattels personal may themselves be divided into tangible movables (choses in possession) and intangible movables (choses in action): see *Colonial Bank v Whinney* (1885) 30 Ch D 261 at 285, per Fry LJ.

While tangible movables include goods and money, intangible movables encompass a broader spectrum of personal property ('choses in action' are defined in greater detail below at p 931). Intangible movables can be divided into documentary intangibles and pure intangibles. Documentary intangibles are documents that not only evidence an underlying right to money, goods or securities but also embody that right (considered further, in relation to negotiable instruments, below at pp 516–519). The distinguishing feature of a documentary intangible is that the right the document represents may be pledged or otherwise transferred simply by delivery of the document, together with any necessary indorsement. Examples of documentary intangibles include bills of lading, negotiable instruments, documentary letters of credit and policies of insurance. Pure intangibles are those choses in action that are not documentary intangibles. Examples of pure intangibles include debts, copyright and goodwill.

It should be noted that intellectual property rights such as copyright, patents, trademarks and related rights also fall under the heading of intangible personal property. However, intellectual property forms a subject in its own right and will not be considered further in this book. (Those interested in the subject should consult J Phillips and A Firth *An Introduction to Intellectual Property Law* (4th edn, 2001); WR Cornish and D Llewellyn *Intellectual Property* (6th edn, 2007).)

We have already noted that personal property is defined in negative terms, ie all property that is left after real property has been subtracted from the class of property taken as a whole. This means that anything that can be described as property, so long as it is not real property, is personal property. As Andrew Bell has observed: 'the list [of personal property] is an open-ended one: any novel phenomenon that is recognised as property will in practice be classified as personal property' (Bell, p 1). So, what is property?

3 WHAT IS PROPERTY?

Crossley Vaines on Personal Property
(5th edn, 1973) (eds E Tyler and N Palmer), p 3

'Property' is a word of different meanings. It may mean a thing owned (my watch or my house is 'my property'); it may mean ownership itself as when I speak of my 'property' in my watch which may pass to the person to whom I sell the watch before I actually hand the watch over or it may even mean an interest in a thing less than ownership but nevertheless conferring certain rights, as when we speak of the 'property' or 'special property' of a bailee in the thing bailed . . . In English law, therefore, 'property' comprehends tangibles and intangibles, movables and immovables; it means a tangible thing (land or chattel) itself, or rights in respect of that thing, or rights, such as a debt, in relation to which no tangible thing exists.

Elements of Land Law by K Gray
(1st edn, 1987), pp 8–14

THE MEANING OF PROPERTY

It is important at the outset to dispel one common lay notion concerning 'property'. Non-lawyers (and sometimes lawyers) speak loosely of property as the *thing* which is owned. While this usage is harmless enough in day-to-day speech, it has the effect of obscuring certain salient features of property as a legal phenomenon, for semantically 'property' is the condition of being 'proper' to (or belonging to) a particular person.

(1) Property is not a 'thing' but a 'relationship'

It was the philosopher, Jeremy Bentham, who had to remind lawyers that property is not a thing but a relationship. Bentham pointed out that 'in common speech in the phrase *the object of a man's property,* the words *the object of* are commonly left out; and by an ellipsis, which, violent as it is, is now become more familiar than the phrase at length, they have made that part of it which consists of the words *a man's property* perform the office of the whole.' More recently Professor Macpherson has drawn attention to the way in which, in the transition from the pre-capitalist world to the world of the exchange economy, the distinction between a right to a thing (ie the legal relation) and the thing itself, became blurred. 'The thing itself became, in common parlance, the property'.

(a) Potential multiplicity of competing users

At one level of analysis, then, 'property' is a relation between the owner and the thing (ie between a 'subject' and an 'object'). However, as has already been suggested, it is unreal to think simply in terms of 'the' owner of any particular thing. It is possible for conflicting claims to be brought by two or more 'subjects' in respect of the same 'object', and therefore the property lawyer is almost always concerned with the relative merits of different claims. In order to establish what belongs to, or is 'proper' to, any particular 'subject', he must first analyse the legal relations between a number of competing subjects vis à vis the same object. A further level of complexity arises because any particular 'object' of property may itself be capable of sustaining a wide variety of different (but not necessarily conflicting) claims. This is demonstrated most clearly in the case of land. Land may, for instance, be the object of a multiplicity of claims made simultaneously by an owner-occupier, a tenant, a building society, a neighbour who enjoys a right of way or restrictive covenant, or even by a spouse who has certain rights not to be evicted from the property.

(b) A network of 'property' relationships

In the ultimate analysis the law of property is concerned with entire networks of legal relationship existing between individuals in respect of things. 'Property' is thus the name given to the bundles of mutual rights and obligations which prevail between 'subjects' in respect of certain 'objects', and the study of property law accordingly becomes an inquiry into a variety of socially defined relationships and morally conditioned obligations. This relational view highlights certain characteristics of property which are essential to any real understanding of land law.

Professor Bruce Ackerman has spoken of the need to disabuse law students of their primitive lay notions regarding ownership. In the words of Ackerman, 'only the ignorant think it meaningful to talk about owning things free and clear of further obligation'. Instead of defining the relationship between a person and 'his' things, property law considers the 'way rights to use things may be parcelled out amongst a host of competing resource users'. Ackerman points out that each resource user is conceived as holding 'a bundle of rights vis à vis other potential users' and that the ways in which user rights may be legally packaged and distributed are 'wondrously diverse'. Ackerman concludes that

> it is probably never true that the law assigns to any single person the right to use any thing in absolutely *any* way he pleases. Hence, it risks serious confusion to identify any single individual as *the* owner of any particular thing. At best, this locution may sometimes serve as identifying the holder of that bundle of rights which contains a range of entitlements more numerous or more valuable than the bundle held by any other person with respect to the thing in question. Yet, like all shorthands, talk about 'the' property owner invites the fallacy of misplaced concreteness, of reification. Once one begins to think sloppily, it is all too easy to start thinking that 'the' property owner, by virtue of being 'the' property owner, must *necessarily* own a particular bundle of rights over a thing. And this is to commit the error that separates layman from lawyer. For the fact (or is it the law?) of the matter is that property is not a thing, but a set of legal relations between persons governing the use of things.

(2) Property is a dynamic relationship

If property is a relationship, it is a dynamic relationship; the content of the relationship is liable to change. The 'subjects' of property may differ from one social era to another. The 'objects' of property are likewise liable to fluctuate with the passage of time and the emergence of new economic conditions. Above all, the ideology of property is profoundly influenced by changing factors of social, political and economic philosophy.

(a) The changing 'subjects' of property

An element of social control is exercised over the property relation in every society, in that each social group to a greater or lesser extent determines for itself the categories of person who may be recognised as the potential 'subjects' of property. In some societies of the past various classes of labourer or serf (eg slaves) were excluded from legal competence as potential 'subjects' of property. Even until relatively recently in England, the married woman was deprived of capacity to hold a legal title in her own name. However, the present century has seen the 'emergence of a property-owning, particularly a real-property-mortgaged-to-a-building-society-owning, democracy.' The years of greater affluence following the World Wars brought about, in the words of Lord Wilberforce, 'the extension, beyond the paterfamilias, of rights of ownership, itself following from the diffusion of property and earning capacity.' Less obviously this diffusion of ownership rights has accentuated the demand that other kinds of right should be recognised as 'proprietary' rights on behalf of less advantaged social groups. Those, for instance, who are not owners of the homes in which they live may wish to assert that their occupation rights (eg as tenants) represent a proprietary status equivalent to that of the owner-occupier.

(b) The changing 'objects' of property

If the 'objects' of property are those resources to which social or economic value is generally attached, it is inevitable that over time variations of social interest and concern should alter the emphasis of the property relationship. There was, for instance, an age in which both wives and slaves were regarded as appropriate 'objects' of property. In medieval England the husband was viewed as enjoying proprietary rights in relation to his wife, her domestic services and her productive capacity. Much of the concern which generated this assessment of the spousal relationship was itself brought about by the supposed paramountcy of the need to ensure the devolution of property within a dynastic line of legitimate issue. However, the 'objects' of property are continually redefined by the prevalent social ethic, and today it is no longer acceptable that either wives or certain classes of labourer should be regarded as the 'objects' of a proprietary relation.

(i) *Transformation of material wealth* The 'objects' of property can, however, change in more subtle degrees. For centuries the most highly prized 'object' of property in the common law world was land. In the 19th century and early 20th century the phenomenon of the company share came close to dislodging land as the pre-eminent 'object' of commercial value, at a time when the bulk of ordinary men and women owned little of value other than perhaps the clothes which they wore. In the modern post-industrial society, however, with the diffusion of ownership amongst classes never before entitled, the traditional concept of a man's wealth has undergone yet another transformation. Nowadays a person's material substance is no longer related particularly to the ownership of tangible assets designed for enjoyment and consumption; it is more readily expressed in terms of intangible, non-assignable, and often non-survivable, claims of a largely personal nature. The things which today are of real value to the man in the street are assets like his job, his pension, and the right to undisturbed possession of his home. On the fringes of these new categories of property lie certain less well defined rights such as the right to education, the right to health and the right to a wholesome environment.

(ii) *The 'new property'* The changing concept of wealth in the modern world was classically described by Professor Charles Reich in a seminal law review article in 1964. Reich drew attention to the dramatic changes taking place in the nature and forms of wealth in industrial democratic societies. In particular, he pointed to the way in which government has begun to operate today as a major distributor of wealth in the form of welfare payments, salaries for those in public service, pensions for those who have retired from employment, and many other forms of licence, franchise, subsidy and fiscal benefit. As Reich indicated, 'today's distribution of largesse is on a vast, imperial scale.' Reich went on to argue that the principal forms of wealth for most people in our society are comprised in their employment or profession (and in various work-related benefits such as pensions) or in their dependency claims upon government (in the guise of social security payments). These forms of wealth, which for Reich were concerned essentially with income security, have become in fact the 'new property', and Reich's major thesis was that this 'new property' should be accorded the same standard of legal protection as had been accorded in the past to more traditional entitlements of private property. In his view, the goal of future development in this area must be to 'try to build an economic basis for liberty today—a Homestead Act for rootless twentieth century man. We must create a new property.'

The call for legal recognition of and protection for the 'new property' has intensified during the two decades since the publication of Reich's major article. In 1970, in its fundamentally significant decision in *Goldberg v Kelly,* the Supreme Court of the United States acknowledged the 'new property' to be deserving of constitutional protection. In the years following this decision, the prominence of the 'new property' has been accentuated by developments in other fields of law.

(iii) *The changing balance of family, work and government* The emergence of the 'new property' can also be placed in the historical context of a more general shift in the relative importance of family, work and government as determinants of social status and as sources of economic security. Today, in an age of liberal divorce and increasingly attenuated family ties, the primary source of economic security for the individual is no longer the family but rather the individual's employment or his dependency relationship with government....

(iv) *Residential security* The jurisprudence of the 'new property' has emerged largely in the context of the individual's rights in the fields of employment and social security. However, an object which lies more immediately within the ambit of a 'Homestead Act for rootless twentieth century man' is the general provision of security in the enjoyment of residential accommodation....

(c) The contemporary redefinition of 'property'

During the present century claims of social welfare have been increasingly recognised through interventionist legislation in the fields of social security, housing and employment protection. By according legal force to various kinds of 'security claim', this legislation has already gone some distance towards ensuring a more equitable distribution of the 'goods of life'. The security claims recognised in these areas broadly cover the kinds of interest which are comprised within the 'new property'. Thus the claim to security in employment is recognised, at least to some extent, by legislation which protects the individual employee from 'unfair dismissal'; the claim to residential security, by the Rent and Housing Acts and other statutory means; the claim to income security, by the vast range of legislation which underpins the social security system. Inherent in all these measures is a significant return to the idea of a 'status'. The individual receives the benefits of protective legislation, not because he has in any sense contracted or bargained to received them, but because he enjoys a defined 'status' which entitles him to some appropriate form of 'security'.

All these developments tend to suggest that, by operating effectively as an agent of distributive justice, the 'new property' has initiated a redefinition of the ideology of property. In the conventional analysis, the concept of property is essentially negative and exclusory: the traditional concept of a property right comprises the right to exclude all others from the use or enjoyment of some thing. The 'new property' comprises by contrast various kinds of claim *not* to be excluded from the use or enjoyment of some thing. Indeed it has been said that the idea of property is gradually being broadened to include a 'right to a kind of society or set of power relations which will enable the individual to live a fully human life.' At least in some incipient form, this perspective may indicate an intellectual shift away from the idea that property is a private right to exclude from personally owned resources, and may point instead towards a reappraisal of property as a public right of access to socially valued resources.

NOTE

Three important points emerge from the extract taken from Professor Gray's textbook on land law. These points are just as relevant to the commercial lawyer as they are to the (real) property lawyer. The points are:

(1) Property is not a thing but rather a set of legal relations existing between persons in respect of things (Ackerman would regard the editors of *Crossley Values* as guilty of 'sloppy thinking' because they define property, *inter alia*, as 'a thing owned').

(2) Property is a relative, not an absolute, concept. Two or more 'subjects' may have concurrent property rights in respect of the same 'object'. These rights may or may not conflict. For example, S sells goods to B1 and then sells the same goods to B2: rights of B1 and B2 conflict; O hires his car to H for a month: O's rights as owner do not conflict with H's rights as bailee. You should keep this point in mind, particularly when you study the basic principle *nemo dat quod non habet* and its exceptions (Chapter 9).

(3) Property is a dynamic relationship. Both the 'subjects' and 'objects' of property may change. Whether a person has property rights in respect of an object may be of great practical significance to the commercial lawyer. For example, is confidential information property? (*OBG Ltd v Allan* [2007] UKHL 21, [2007] 2 WLR 920 at [275], *per* Lord Walker: 'information, even if it is confidential, cannot properly be regarded as a form of property'; and see also P Kohler and N Palmer, 'Information as Property', Ch 1 in N

Palmer and E McKendrick (eds) *Interests in Goods* (2nd edn, 1998)). Is a debt a personal obligation, or property capable of being the subject of a charge by the creditor in favour of the debtor? (see below, pp 1036–1043).

4 WHAT ARE THE CHARACTERISTICS OF PROPERTY RIGHTS?

The commercial world has always been concerned with the buying and selling of commodities be they goods, ideas, debts or shares. To facilitate this process, the law has limited the number of property interests that can exist in relation to the commodity in question and ensured that each interest is clearly defined, easily discoverable by third parties and readily convertible into money (see, especially, *National Provincial Bank Ltd v Ainsworth* [1965] AC 1175 at 1247–1248, per Lord Wilberforce). However, as one commentator has put it, 'it is increasingly apparent that there is more to life than buying and selling, and that this is just as true of commercial life as it is of social and domestic life' (A Clarke (1997) 50 CLP 119 at 121). Commodities are bought and sold, but they can, for example, just as easily be made the subject of a bailment or security transaction. Put simply, commerce does sometimes require things simply to be bought and sold as commodities, in which case the first priority is free alienability, but at other times it requires us to do more complex things with them, and in those cases alienability is relatively unimportant' (Clarke, op cit, p 122). In the extract which follows Professor Gray is also critical of our preoccupation with alienability and searches for an alternative hallmark of 'property'

'Property in Thin Air' by K Gray
[1991] CLJ 252, pp 292–295

IV. 'PROPERTY' AS CONTROL OVER ACCESS

And so continues our search for the inner mystery of 'property'. Let us look back and see how far we have got since we started. There is no real likelihood that we have arrived at our destination, for the quest for the essential nature of 'property' has beguiled thinkers for many centuries. The essence of 'property' is indeed elusive. That is why, in a sense, we have tried to catch the concept by surprise by asking not 'What is property?' but rather 'What is not property?' We have started from the other end of the earth—both geographically and conceptually—and we have deliberately come by the direction which seemed least probable. But along the way we may have discovered something of value. We may have discovered the irreducible conditions which underlie any claim of 'property'.

The classic common law criteria of 'property' have tended to rest a twin emphasis on the assignability of the benefits inherent in a resource and on the relative permanence of those benefits if unassigned. Before a right can be admitted within the category of 'property' it must, according to Lord Wilberforce in *National Provincial Bank Ltd v Ainsworth,* be 'definable, identifiable by third parties, capable in its nature of assumption by third parties, and have some degree of permanence or stability'. This preoccupation with assignability of benefit and enforceability of burden doubtless owes much to the fact that the formative phases of the common law concept of property coincided with a remarkable culture of bargain and exchange. Non-transferable rights or rights which failed on transfer were simply not 'property'. Within the crucible of transfer lawyers affected to demarcate rights of 'property' from rights founded in contract and tort or, for that matter, from human rights and civil liberties. Only brief reflection is required in order to perceive the horrible circularity of such hallmarks of 'property'. If naively we ask which rights are proprietary, we are told that they are those rights which are assignable to and enforceable against third parties. When we then ask which rights these may be, we are told that they comprise, of course, the rights which are traditionally identified as 'proprietary'. 'Property' is 'property' because it is 'property': property status and proprietary consequence confuse each other in a deadening embrace of cause and effect.

Nor have the philosophers given significantly greater assistance in explaining the phenomenon of 'property'. Perhaps inevitably lawyers have concentrated their attention on locating the *ownership* of 'property', this task of identification assuming vital significance in a legal culture dominated by transfer and conveyance. By contrast philosophers have directed their efforts principally towards rationalising the *institution* of 'property'. While lawyers discuss who owns what, philosophers ask why anyone can legitimately claim to own anything. Justificatory theories of 'property' range diversely from appeals to the investment of labour or the existence of a social contract to arguments based upon first occupancy, utility or personhood. A pervasive influence in all philosophical thinking on 'property' is still the brooding omnipresence of John Locke. But Locke's concentration on original acquisition ill suits legal discourse in a modern world which is based on derivative acquisition and in which original acquisition (except perhaps in the area of intellectual property) is now virtually impossible. Even Locke himself cannot have believed that in late 17th century England the 'Commons' still contained many unappropriated acorns yet to be 'picket up under an Oak' or apples to be 'gathered from the Trees in the Wood', even if he did think that 'property' in such things was 'fixed' by the labour invested in their 'first gathering'. As Walton Hamilton noted much later, Locke's natural state is 'a curious affair, peopled with the Indians of North America and run by the scientific principles of his friend Sir Isaac Newton'.

In their respective preoccupations with resource allocation and institutional justification, lawyers and philosophers alike have largely failed to identify the characteristic hallmark of the common law notion of 'property'. If our own travels in search of 'property' have indicated one thing, it is that the criterion of 'excludability' gets us much closer to the core of 'property' than does the conventional legal emphasis on the assignability or enforceability of benefits. For 'property' resides not in consumption of benefits but in control over benefits. 'Property' is not about *enjoyment of access* but about *control over access*. 'Property' is the power-relation constituted by the state's endorsement of private claims to regulate the access of strangers to the benefits of particular resources. If, in respect of a given claimant and a given resource, the exercise of such regulatory control is physically impracticable or legally abortive or morally or socially undesirable, we say that such a claimant can assert no 'property' in that resource and for that matter can lose no 'property' in it either. Herein lies an important key to the 'propertiness' of property.

Here too lies the key to the divergent approaches evident in *Victoria Park Racing and Recreation Grounds Co Ltd v Taylor*. The minority in the High Court of Australia found a misappropriation of 'property' in the sheer fact that the defendants had diminished the plaintiff's *access* to the benefits of certain resources. By contrast the majority found that there has been no taking of 'property', precisely because the defendants' conduct could never in any event have deprived the plaintiff of *control over access* to those resources. For a variety of reasons the resources in dispute had remained at all times inherently non-excludable. The plaintiff might have enjoyed *access* to the benefits of the contested resources, but it never had a *control over access* which could be prejudiced by the actions of the defendants. The resources in issue could never have sustained any claim of 'property' by the plaintiff and could not now therefore support any allegation of loss or misappropriation. Whatever it was the defendants took— and they undeniably took something—they took none of the plaintiff's 'property'.

The concept of excludability thus takes us some way towards discovering a rationally defensible content in the term 'property'. The differentiation of excludable and non-excludable resources points up the irreducible elements which lie at the core of the 'property' notion. But these irreducibles, once isolated and identified, leave little if anything of value to be gathered from the traditional indicia of 'property'. The concept of excludability does not, of course, resolve entirely the issue of justice in holdings; it merely demarcates the categories of resource in which it is possible to claim 'property'. It sets outer limits on claims of 'property', but provides no criteria for justifying such claims on behalf of particular individuals—except to the extent that we accept the initially unpalatable (but historically attested) proposition that the sustained assertion of effective control over access to the benefits of a resource tends ultimately to be constitutive of 'property' in that resource. The precise allocation of 'property' in excludable resources is left to be determined—is indeed constantly formulated and reformulated—by various kinds of social and moral consensus over legitimate modes of acquisition and the relative priority of competing claims. This consensus is reinforced by a machinery of legal recognition and enforcement which thus adds or withholds the legitimacy of state sanction in relation to individual assertions of 'property'.

NOTES

1. In *Victoria Park Racing and Recreation Grounds Co Ltd v Taylor* (1937) 58 CLR 479, the owner of a racecourse applied for an injunction to stop the owner of neighbouring land, and a broadcasting company, from using a platform erected on the neighbouring land to watch horse races which took place at the racecourse and broadcasting a radio commentary of those races. The racecourse owner charged the public for admission to the course and his business had suffered because punters stayed at home, or in the local hostelry, to listen to the defendant's broadcasts. By a majority of 3:2 the High Court of Australia held that the defendants had committed no legal wrong. Although much of the discussion in the case was in terms of the law of nuisance, the central issue was whether the defendants had taken anything that might be regarded as the plaintiffs 'property'. The majority held that they had not because there could be no property in a spectacle such as a horse race. A spectacle, according to Latham CJ, 'cannot be owned in any ordinary sense of the word' (at 496; cf DF Libling (1978) 94 LQR 103 at p 106).

2. According to Professor Gray (op cit, p 268):

The primordial principle which emerges from the majority judgments in *Victoria Park Racing* is that a resource can be propertised only if it is 'excludable'. A resource is 'excludable' only if it is feasible for a legal person to exercise regulatory control over the access of strangers to the various benefits inherent in the resource.

In *Victoria Park Racing,* it was not reasonably practical to physically exclude the defendants from the benefits of the spectacle provided on the plaintiff's land.

3. A vast literature on the meaning of 'property', and the justification of private property, has been produced by lawyers, philosophers and political scientists: recent examples include J Waldron *The Right to Private Property* (1990); JE Penner *The Idea of Property in Law* (2000); JW Harris *Property and Justice* (2002). You are encouraged to read K Gray 'Equitable Property' (1994) 47(2) CLP 157.

QUESTIONS

1. A buys a car from B. Can A exclude others from the car? What if the car had been stolen by B and the true owner wants it back? Does A have 'property' in the car? The sale of goods by a non-owner is considered below in Chapter 9.

2. C owes £100 to D. Can D exclude others from the debt? If C erroneously pays the debt to E, the debt still exists and D continues to look to C for payment. Therefore, does D have 'property' in the debt?

5 TYPES OF PROPERTY RIGHTS

The common law recognises two types of property rights over personal property: (1) ownership, and (2) possession for a limited interest, including liens (below, p 1106) and rights arising under pledges (below, p 1091). All other rights exist only in equity, eg the rights of a beneficiary under a trust, mere charges (see below, p 1131), non-possessory liens (below, p 1138) and the mortgagor's right of redemption (below, p 1124). But an equitable interest must be distinguished from a 'mere equity', which is 'a personal power in one person to set aside, reduce or extinguish to his own advantage an asset held by another', eg the right to rescind a contract for fraud or misrepresentation, and so reacquire ownership of goods which passed under that contract; the right in equity to set off one money claim against another due on a separate account (Goode, p 27).

As a general rule, these rights display the two traditional characteristics of property rights: they are assignable and they are enforceable against third parties. But this may not always be the case. For example, in certain circumstances common law property rights may be overriden and equitable rights may be defeated by a bona fide purchaser for value without notice. This confirms what we have already noted, property rights are relative, not absolute.

6 THE SIGNIFICANCE OF PROPERTY RIGHTS

'Ownership and Obligation in Commercial Transactions' by RM Goode
(1987) 103 LQR 433, pp 433–435, 436–438

I INTRODUCTION

In common with other legal systems, English law sharply distinguishes property rights from mere personal rights to the delivery or transfer of an asset. I *own* property; I am *owed* performance of a transfer obligation. Ownership attracts several advantages, and some disadvantages, in law, and is frequently a condition precedent to the assertion of contractual rights. If I own an asset in the possession of another who becomes bankrupt, I can withdraw it from the reach of his creditors; if I am owed a purely personal obligation to transfer the asset to me I have no right to remove it from the common pool. As owner of a chattel I am entitled to a remedy in tort for negligence if it is carelessly damaged or destroyed by another. Ownership also carries with it a right to possession, where no one else has a better right, and is protected by the law of torts, in particular the tort of conversion. If I own goods, I bear the burden of accidental loss or damage. The transfer of ownership is in general a condition of the seller's right to sue for the price under a contract of sale of goods; and the acquisition of ownership is a prerequisite to certain statutory transfers of contractual rights, such as the transfer of the shipper's rights under a bill of lading to a consignee or indorsee under section 1 of the Bills of Lading Act 1855 [since replaced by section 2 of the Carriage of Goods by Sea Act 1992]....

II OWNERSHIP IN INSOLVENCY

(i) Practical importance of the question

In the commercial world the distinction between ownership of an asset and a purely personal right to acquire an asset, eg under a contract, is usually of little significance so long as the debtor is traceable and solvent, for the interest of a commercial creditor in the performance of a transfer undertaking is usually monetary rather than in ownership for its own sake, and if the debtor (using this term in the broad sense of an obligor) fails to deliver then the creditor can simply obtain what is due to him, either in cash or in kind, by suing for it and enforcing any resulting judgment.

It is upon the debtor's insolvency that the distinction between ownership and a personal right to an asset becomes of crucial significance, for it is a basic policy of insolvency law to adopt the non-bankruptcy ordering of rights and thus to respect proprietary rights held by another prior to the debtor's bankruptcy. Hence in principle the estate available for distribution among the general body of creditors is limited to the debtor's own assets. Owners and secured creditors can withdraw from the pool the assets they own or over which they have security, whilst unsecured creditors are left to prove in competition with each other for such crumbs as remain after proprietary rights, the expenses of the insolvency proceedings and the claims of preferential creditors have been satisfied.

It follows that the degree in which the law is willing to recognise rights as proprietary rather than merely personal is of great moment to unsecured creditors, for every extension of the concept of ownership erodes the debtor's estate and thus reduces the significance of the hallowed principle of pari passu distribution. Conversely, every condition precedent attached by the law to the acquisition of ownership represents a pitfall for the would-be investor and the would-be secured creditor who lays out his money in the expectation of receiving in exchange some proprietary interest in the debtor's patrimony....

(iii) The growth of equitable property rights

Property and obligation at law

The common law (in its narrow sense) sharply distinguished transfers of property from mere personal undertakings. A transfer from A to B had to relate to an existing asset in which A had a subsisting interest, and the transfer itself had to be in proper form. Except in the case of a contract for the sale of existing goods, where the agreement was effective by itself to transfer title, an agreement for transfer conferred no proprietary rights on the intended transferee even if he had parted with his money. A purported transfer by A to B of A's after-acquired property was at best a contract and could not of itself operate to vest the property in B even after A had acquired it; a new act of transfer was necessary after the acquisition. Similarly, a transfer by A to C to hold on trust for B conferred no interest on B, for the conveyance was not made to him.

These common law rules still apply in relation to the transfer of a legal title, save for the special case of contracts of sale of goods, in relation to which the Sale of Goods Act prescribes the automatic transfer of title to future goods upon their acquisition by the seller, if the parties so agree.

Property and obligation in equity

Under the influence of equity the distinction between property rights *in* an asset and personal rights *to* an asset became blurred. Acting on the basis that equity treats as done that which ought to be done, courts of equity came to regard an unperfected agreement to assign as an assignment which became perfected by payment of the consideration; they upheld the assignment of future property as effective on acquisition by the debtor without the need for any new act of transfer; they recognised the interest of the beneficiary under a passive trust as a proprietary interest; and they accorded proprietary status to the right of an owner of an asset to trace the products and proceeds of dispositions by the owner's bailee.

Even after all this the ingenuity of the equity lawyers was not exhausted. A person might succeed to a claim by assignment or by subrogation. Equity also came to recognise the existence of proprietary rights not in a specific asset but in a shifting fund of assets, as exemplified by the interest of the beneficiary under an active trust and of a debenture holder under a floating charge, and these interests became included in the category of proprietary rights having priority over the claims of unsecured creditors.

The development of the resulting trust and the constructive trust led to the recognition of proprietary rights in a variety of situations in which one person improperly held assets or benefits to which another had a better right. Among the events that have been held to attract these forms of trust are the payment of money for a purpose which has failed, the payment of money under a mistake of fact and the acquisition of an asset by the defendant from a third party, or the retention of such an asset, in breach of the defendant's fiduciary duty to the plaintiff.

Finally, even a 'mere equity,' such as a right to rescind (eg for fraud or misrepresentation) a contract under which the bankrupt acquired an asset can be asserted against his trustee, thus removing the asset from the general body of creditors even after the commencement of bankruptcy.

The result of this equitable development is that most obligations owed by B to A to transfer an asset to A are proprietary in nature rather than merely personal, though often A has a personal right to the asset running concurrently with his proprietary interest in it. It is unusual to find a situation in which B has a duty to make over to A an asset still in B's hands without A thereby enjoying equitable ownership of the asset. In equity, the obligation to transfer, whatever its source, is itself a transfer provided that the obligation is not merely contingent, the subject-matter is identifiable and the consideration is in due course paid. The one outstanding exception to this rule is the contract of sale of goods, where the buyer either acquires legal title or acquires nothing beyond a mere contract right. This exception reflects not only the universality of the contract of sale of goods, which makes it undesirable to complicate the contract by equitable ownership, but the fact that under a contract of sale title passes by agreement, and except where this is reserved to secure payment a seller who has not reached the stage of passing legal title usually intends to reserve a right to dispose of the goods elsewhere.

NOTES

1.   In *Leigh & Sillivan Ltd v Aliakmon Shipping Co Ltd, The Aliakmon* [1986] AC 785, a carrier contracted with sellers to ship steel coils which the sellers had sold to buyers. The goods were damaged during the voyage as a result of negligent stowage by the carrier. The damage occurred at a time when the risk in the goods, but not the property in them, had passed to the buyers. The buyers had no claim against the carrier under the contract of carriage as they were not a party to that contract (the Carriage of Goods by Sea Act 1992, s 2(1) would, however, now give the buyers a contractual right of action against the carrier: see below, p 491). The House of Lords held that the buyers also had no cause of action against the carrier in tort for negligence. Lord Brandon, with whose speech all their Lordships agreed, stated (at 809) that:

...there is a long line of authority for a principle of law that, in order to enable a person to claim in negligence for loss caused to him by reason of loss of or damage to property, he must have had either the legal ownership of or a possessory title to the property concerned at the time the loss or damage occurred, and it is not enough for him to have only had contractual rights in relation to such property which have been adversely affected by the loss of or damage to it.

2.   A property right binds third parties. However, there is a line of authority which suggests that, in certain circumstances, a personal right relating to personal property may do the same. In *De Mattos v Gibson* (1858) 4 De G & J 276, the owner of a ship entered into a charterparty. The owner subsequently mortgaged the vessel to a mortgagee who at all times was aware of the charterparty and its terms. The mortgagee sought to enforce his security and divert the ship to another port to sell it. The charterer applied for an injunction to prevent the mortgagee from doing anything which would interfere with the performance of the charterparty. Knight Bruce and Turner LJJ granted the charterer's application for an interlocutory injunction. Knight Bruce LJ said (at 282):

Reason and justice seem to prescribe that, at least as a general rule, where a man, by gift or purchase, acquires property from another, with knowledge of a previous contract, lawfully and for valuable consideration made by him with a third person, to use and employ the property for a particular purpose in a specified manner, the acquirer shall not, to the material damage of the third person, in opposition to the contract and inconsistently with it, use and employ the property in a manner not allowable to the giver or seller. This rule, applicable alike in general as I conceive to moveable and immoveable property, and recognized and adopted, as I apprehend, by the English law, may, like other general rules, be liable to exceptions arising from special circumstances; but I see at present no room for any exception in the instance before us.

At the full hearing Lord Chelmsford refused the injunction for other reasons.

The principle formulated by Knight Bruce LJ in *De Mattos v Gibson* was later applied by the Privy Council in *Lord Strathcona Steamship Co Ltd v Dominion Coal Co* [1926] AC 108 to restrain the purchaser of a ship from using it inconsistently with a time charter granted by the previous owner. The Privy Council drew an analogy with the rule in *Tulk v Moxhay* (1848) 2 Ph 774 relating to the use of land. However, the rule for covenants running with land requires the covenantee to have a proprietary interest in some adjacent land. A time (or voyage) charterer has no proprietary interest in the chartered vessel, but the Board got over that problem by declaring that the charterer had 'a plain interest' in the ship. This reasoning was rightly criticised by Diplock J in *Port Line Ltd v Ben Line Steamers Ltd* [19581 2 QB 146, who thought the *Strathcona* case wrongly decided.

In *Swiss Bank Corpn v Lloyds Bank Ltd* [1979] Ch 548 (revsd [1982] AC 584 on other grounds), Browne-Wilkinson J thought the *De Mattos* principle represented good law and explained it in terms of the equitable counterpart of the tort of knowing interference with contractual rights (which is wrong as the two are doctrinally distinct and subject to different requirements: see A Tettenborn [1982] CLJ 58 at 82–83). The *De Mattos* principle was relied on by Scott LJ in *Mac-Jordan Construction Ltd v Brookmount Erostin Ltd* [1992] BCLC 350, and also by Hoffmann J in *Law Debenture Trust Corpn plc v Ural Caspian Oil Corpn Ltd* [1993] 1 WLR 138 (affd on other grounds, [1995] Ch 152), who emphasised (at 144) that it 'permits no more than the grant of a negative injunction to restrain the third party from doing acts which would be inconsistent with performance of the contract by the original contracting party'. In neither cases was there argument as to the correctness of the principle.

The *De Mattos* principle is surrounded by confusion and uncertainty. Neither *De Mattos v Gibson* or the *Strathcona* case is authority for the general proposition that a purchaser of a chattel, even with actual notice, will be bound by covenants concerning its use previously entered into by his vendor (W Swadling The Proprietary Effect of a Hire of Goods', Ch 20 in N Palmer and E McKendrick (eds) *Interests in Goods* (2nd edn, 1998), p 504). The principle seems best restricted to 'the very special case of a ship under charterparty' (*Clore v Theatrical Properties Ltd* [1936] 3 All ER 483 at 490, per Lord Wright MR). Even then the better view is that the right of the charterer to an injunction to restrain use of the ship inconsistently with his charterparty arises only if the purchaser is liable for the tort of inducing his vendor to break his contract with the charterer (*Lumley v Gye* (1853) 2 E & B 216). Such liability depends on the purchaser intending to induce the breach (*OBG Ltd v Allan* [2007] UKHL 21, [2007] 2 WLR 920 at [8] and [62]). It follows that the purchaser must have actual knowledge (which includes deliberately shutting his eyes) not only of the existence of the contract but also of the term alleged to have been broken (at [39]–[41]). As the purchaser's liability is accessory in nature, it does not arise where no breach is induced (at [86], [129] and [248]). The tort of inducing a breach of contract can apply wherever the purchaser of a chattel (not just a ship) intends to (and does) induce a breach of his vendor's prior contractual undertaking to use the chattel in a particular way. The purchaser of the chattel may be restrained by injunction if he commits or threatens to commit the tort (see generally, A Tettenborn [1982] CLJ 58).

QUESTION

In *Re Bank of Credit and Commerce International SA (No 8)* [1998] AC 214 (see below, p 1040), where the House of Lords indicated that it was conceptually possible for a bank take a charge over its own indebtedness to one of its customers, Lord Hoffmann described a 'proprietary interest' in terms of anything which is binding on an assignee or a liquidator or trustee in bankruptcy (at 227). Was he right to do so? See R Goode (1998) 114 LQR 178 at 179.

7 OWNERSHIP

Honoré defines ownership 'as the *greatest possible interest in a thing which a mature system of law recognizes*' (AM Honoré 'Ownership' in AG Guest (edn) *Oxford Essays in Jurisprudence* (1961), p 108, his emphasis). Ownership carries with it a bundle of rights, and some obligations, which Honoré describes as the 'standard incidents of ownership' and which he lists (at p 113) as follows: 'the right to possess, the right to use, the right to manage, the right to the income of the thing, the right to the capital, the right to security, the rights or incidents of transmissibility and absence of term, the prohibition of harmful use, liability to execution, and the incident of residuarity'. For criticism of Honoré's analysis, see P Eleftheriadis (1996) 16 OJLS 31.

A person can be described as 'owner' even though all the listed incidents of ownership are not present. An individual may have the greatest possible interest in a thing, and be described as its owner, where lesser interests have been granted to others. Thus, if I lend you my car for a week, I have residual rights, and an absolute interest, in the car; you have special rights of possession as bailee, and a limited interest, in it (in fact, you would have a limited interest in the car if you took it under a pledge, lease, rental, or other form of bailment). At the end of the week your lesser rights revert back to me. This illustrates the residuary character of ownership. In essence ownership is the residue of legal rights in an asset left in a person after lesser rights have been granted to others (Honoré, pp 126–128).

(a) Legal and equitable ownership

Ownership may be legal or equitable. Legal and equitable ownership of a chattel may be vested in the same person. Alternatively, legal ownership may be vested in one person and equitable ownership vested in another, eg when A (legal owner) holds goods on trust for B (equitable owner). However, it is not possible for legal ownership of a chattel to be split and a smaller legal interest carved out of it: legal ownership must be transferred entire (which is why an *agreement* by which a chattel is let on lease or rental confers no legal—or equitable[2]—interest

---

[2]   The view of Browne-Wilkinson V-C in *Bristol Airport plc v Powdrill* [1990] Ch 744 at 759, that the right of a lessee to delivery of possession of an aircraft under a chattel lease constituted 'property' for the purposes of s 436 of the Insolvency Act 1986, on the ground that 'the "lessee" has at least an equitable right of some kind in that aircraft', cannot easily be reconciled with these basic principles of personal property law. See criticisms of RM Goode *Principles of Corporate Insolvency Law* (3rd edn, 2005), para 10–57.

on the lessee: only on taking delivery does the lessee acquire a limited legal interest in the chattel by virtue of his *possession)*[3] The only other absolute legal interest that may exist in a chattel at the same time as that of the true owner (the person with the best right to the chattel) is the independent legal interest of a person who holds possession of the chattel with the intention of asserting rights of ownership (who is also treated in law as an owner). In short, it is only possible for two *absolute* legal interests to exist in a chattel at the same time: the interests of the true owner and the interests of someone holding possession *animo domini*. By contrast, there is no limit to the number of equitable interests which may subsist in a chattel at any one time.

(b) Interest and title

A person's interest in an asset denotes the quantum of rights over it which he enjoys against other persons, though not necessarily against *all* other persons. His title measures the strength of the interest he enjoys in relation to others . . . .

(Goode, p 31)

Both the true owner of an asset and the person in possession of an asset *animo domini* have an independent legal *interest* in the asset. Each has title to the absolute interest in the asset and each may assert his interest against a third party, so long as the third party does not have a better title. However, as against each other, the true owner has an *absolute* (or indefeasible) title to the asset and the possessor only a *relative* title. The possessor may not assert his title against the true owner, nor anyone deriving title from him or acting with his authority. It is even possible for a third party to defend an action for wrongful interference brought by someone with a possessory title on the ground that the claimant is not the true owner, ie he may plead *jus tertii* (Torts (Interference with Goods) Act 1977, s 8(1): see below, pp 91–92).

The concept of relativity of title also applies to equitable interests. But it should be noted that an equitable interest is also liable to be overridden by a transfer of the legal interest to a bona fide purchaser for value without notice. See generally, David Fox, 'Relativity of Title at Law and in Equity' [2006] *CLJ* 330, and, especially, at pp 351–361, on the relativity of equitable titles.

(c) Co-ownership

Personal property may be the subject of co-ownership at law and in equity. Although legal ownership is indivisible, two or more persons may be the legal co-owners of a chattel as joint tenants or as tenants in common. For example, the courts have found it useful to rely on the concept of tenancy in common where chattels are mixed to form an indistinguishable mass (see, eg *Re Stapylton Fletcher Ltd* [1994] 1 WLR 1181, where a wine merchant segregated

---

[3] In *On Demand Information plc v Michael Gerson (Finance) plc* [2001] 1 WLR 155 at 171, Robert Walker LJ stated that:

Contractual rights which entitle the hirer to indefinite possession of chattels so long as the hire payments are duly made, and which qualify and limit the owner's general property in the chattels, cannot aptly be described as purely contractual rights.

This conclusion was 'in accordance with principle' according to Lord Millett (on appeal in the same case: [2002] UKHL 13, [2003] 1 AC 368 at para [29]).

But *On Demand* was a case concerning relief against forfeiture where the hirer had taken possession of the chattel and as such undoubtedly had a limited legal interest in the chattel by virtue of that possession.

wine purchased by customers from his own trading stock and stored it in composite stacks containing cases of wine sold to other customers. The judge held that the various customers owned the composite stacks as tenants in common. See also *Mercer v Craven Grain Storage Ltd* [1994] CLC 328, where farmers deposited grain with a grain storage company, allowing it to be mixed with grain deposited by other farmers. The House of Lords held that all the farmers were tenants in common of the commingled mass). Parliament has also used the concept of tenancy in common to provide a statutory solution to the problems faced by a pre-paying buyer who purchases a stated quantity of goods forming part of an identified bulk when the seller becomes insolvent before the contract quantity is separated from the bulk (see Sale of Goods Act 1979, ss 20A and 20B, inserted by the Sale of Goods (Amendment) Act 1995, considered further below at pp 320–321). It appears that legal co-ownership of a chose in action must be as joint tenants (*Re McKerrell, McKerrell v Gowans* [1912] 2 Ch 648 at 653). If the co-owners are joint tenants and one of them dies the deceased's share passes to the others by survivorship. In the case of tenants in common, the deceased's share forms part of his estate and passes under his will or on his intestacy. Where there is equitable co-ownership, including co-ownership of a chose in action, there is a presumption in favour of a tenancy in common (RM Goode *Proprietary Rights and Insolvency in Sales Transactions* (2nd edn, 1989), p 6).

8 ACQUISITION AND TRANSFER OF LEGAL AND EQUITABLE OWNERSHIP

(a) Legal ownership

Legal ownership may be acquired by any of the following means:

(1) By taking possession of an existing thing which does not have an owner, eg taking possession of a wild animal.

(2) By bringing a new thing into existence. This mode of acquisition of legal ownership is particularly relevant where goods are manufactured. Prima facie, the manufacturer will be the legal owner of the newly manufactured product. However, the position is complicated where the manufacturer has made the new product from material supplied under a contract of sale which reserves ownership of the material in the supplier until payment. Such reservation of title clauses may even purport to claim ownership of the finished product. Further difficulties arise where the finished product is manufactured from material supplied by different suppliers each relying on their own reservation of title clause to claim ownership of the finished product. These issues are fully explored below, at pp 452–470.

(3) By consensual transfer of a thing from the existing owner. Although consensual transfer may be by gift, the typical form of transfer in the commercial world is by sale. At common law there are strict rules controlling the transfer of ownership of personal property: the transferor must have legal title or a power to pass legal title, the transfer must be effected by the delivery of possession or by a grant (by deed in the case of a gift of a chattel, by word of mouth in the case of other transfers of a chattel), and there must be an intention to make a present, not future, transfer of ownership (see Goode, p 37; above,

pp 64–66). It is important to note that the common law does not normally give effect to an agreement to transfer after-acquired property (ie property which the transferor does not yet own or possess). There must be some new act of transfer after the property has been acquired by the transferor for the ownership to vest in the transferee (*Lunn v Thornton* (1845) 1 CB 379). Exceptionally, in the case of contracts for the sale of goods, ownership of future goods will automatically transfer to the buyer when those goods have been acquired by the seller, if the parties have so agreed (Sale of Goods Act 1979, s 2(5), (6)). Furthermore, property which does not yet exist, but which will grow out of existing property owned by the transferor, eg the right to receive sums payable in the future under an existing building contract, may be made the subject of a present transfer of legal ownership (see below, pp 937–939).

(4) By transfer which overrides the rights of the existing owner. The general rule is *nemo dat quod non habet*. However, there are exceptions to the *nemo dat* rule which allow A to transfer to B a good title to C's goods without the latter's consent. The rule and its exceptions are considered below in Chapter 9.

(5) By operation of law when goods become fixtures or accessions or through specification, confusion or commingling, see P Birks 'Mixtures' and H Bennett 'Attachment of Chattels to Land' in N Palmer and E McKendrick (eds) *Interests in Goods* (2nd edn, 1998), Chs 9 and 11 respectively.

(6) By operation of law on death or insolvency (see Bell, Chs 17, 18).

(b) Equitable ownership

Equitable ownership may be acquired by any one of the following means:

(1) by an agreement to transfer legal or equitable ownership;

(2) by a defective transfer of legal ownership;

(3) by a purported present transfer of an after-acquired asset;

(4) by declaration of trust: either the transferor of an asset declares himself to hold it on trust for the transferee, or the transferor instructs a third party to hold the asset on trust for the transferee;

(5) by a transfer made by someone who holds merely an equitable title.

Equitable ownership may be transferred by written assignment or declaration of trust (for the requirement of writing, see Law of Property Act 1925, s 53(1)(c): below, p 959).

It is because equity regards as done that which ought to have been done that the obligation to transfer an asset is treated in equity as a transfer (but an agreement for the sale of goods is an exception to this rule: *Re Wait* [1927] 1 Ch 606; although see now Sale of Goods Act 1979, ss 20A and 20B, which protects a prepaying buyer by other means, see below, pp 320–321). The conditions which must exist for such a transfer to operate are that the obligation is not merely contingent, the subject matter is identifiable and the consideration is in due course paid (see above, pp 65–66, and below, pp 1028–1032). If the consideration is not paid when the agreement to transfer is made, it seems that the intended transferee merely acquires an inchoate equitable interest at that time. The intended transferee cannot assert an inchoate interest against the intended transferor or third parties until he pays the price and converts that interest into full equitable ownership, which is deemed to relate back to the time the agreement was made (RM Goode (1987) 103 LQR 433 at p 437, fn; *Lysaght v*

Edwards (1876) 2 Ch D 499; *Rayner v Preston* (1881) 18 Ch D 1). Similarly, when there has been an agreement to transfer an after-acquired asset, the transferee has an inchoate interest which attaches to the asset when it is acquired by the transferor with effect from the date of the agreement (*Tailby v Official Receiver* (1888) 13 App Cas 523, HL: below, p 1029; *Re Lind* [1915] 2 Ch 345, CA).

Finally, it should be noted that legal ownership and equitable ownership may be transferred outright or by way of security. We shall examine the different legal consequences of transfer by way of security, compared to outright transfer, when we consider receivables financing in Chapter 23.

9 POSSESSION

An Essay on Possession in the Common Law by F Pollock and RS Wright (1888), pp 26–28

The Nature of Possession

Throughout our inquiry we have to bear in mind that the following elements are quite distinct in conception, and, though very often found in combination, are also separable and often separated in practice. They are

i.   Physical control, detention, or *de facto* possession. This, as an actual relation between a person and a thing, is matter of fact. Nevertheless questions which the Court must decide as matter of law arise as to the proof of the facts.

ii.   Legal possession, the state of being a possessor in the eye of the law.

This is a definite legal relation of the possessor to the thing possessed. In its most normal and obvious form, it coexists with the fact of physical control, and with other facts making the exercise of that control rightful. But it may exist either with or without detention, and either with or without a rightful origin.

A tailor sends to JS's house a coat which JS has ordered. JS puts on the coat, and then has both physical control and rightful possession in law.

JS takes off the coat and gives it to a servant to take back to the tailor for some alterations. Now the servant has physical control (in this connexion generally called 'custody' by our authorities) and JS still has the possession in law.

While the servant is going on his errand, Z assaults him and robs him of the coat. Z is not only physically master of the coat, but, so soon as he has complete control of it, he has possession in law, though a wrongful possession. To see what is left to JS we must look to the next head.

iii. Right to possess or to have legal possession. This includes the right to physical possession. It can exist apart from both physical and legal possession; it is, for example, that which remains to a rightful possessor immediately after he has been wrongfully dispossessed. It is a normal incident of ownership or property, and the name of 'property' is often given to it. Unlike possession itself, it is not necessarily exclusive. A may have the right to possess a thing as against B and every one else, while B has at the same time a right to possess it as against every one except A. So joint tenants have both single possession and a single joint right to possess, but tenants in common have a single possession with several rights to possess. When a person having right to possess a thing acquires the physical control of it, he necessarily acquires legal possession also.

Right to possess, when separated from possession, is often called 'constructive possession'. The correct use of the term would seem to be coextensive with and limited to those cases where a person entitled to possess is (or was) allowed the same remedies as if he had really been in possession. But it is also sometimes specially applied to the cases where the legal possession is with one person and the custody with his servant, or some other person for the time being in a like position; and sometimes it is extended to other cases where legal possession is separated from detention.

'Actual possession' as opposed to 'constructive possession' is in the same way an ambiguous term. It is most commonly used to signify physical control, with or without possession in law. 'Bare possession' is sometimes used with the same meaning. 'Lawful possession' means a legal possession which is also rightful or at least excusable; this may be consistent with a superior right to possess in some other person.

The whole terminology of the subject, however, is still very loose and unsettled in the books, and the reader cannot be too strongly warned that careful attention must in every case be paid to the context.

NOTES

1. In *United States of America and Republic of France v Dollfus Mieg et Cie SA and Bank of England* [1952] AC 582 at 605, Earl Jowitt observed that 'English law has never worked out a completely logical and exhaustive definition of possession'. As Andrew Bell explains (Bell, p 34):

The truth is that 'possession' has no single meaning: it is used in different senses in different contexts. This is perfectly reasonable, for the essence of possession is control, but the degree of control required for a particular rule will depend on the purpose of that rule. This flexibility has its price, however, the price of uncertainty.

Despite the fact that many eminent jurists have expended much energy developing various theories to explain the concept of possession (see, eg DR Harris 'The Concept of Possession in English Law' in *Oxford Essays in Jurisprudence* (ed AG Guest), Ch 4; and see generally, RWM Dias *Jurisprudence* (5th edn, 1985), Ch 13), the subject remains an enigma. It lacks even an agreed terminology to explain the various forms of possession. The warning given by Pollock and Wright at the end of the extract (above) remains as relevant today as it was in 1888.

2.   (i)   *De facto possession.* Physical control of a chattel may not create possession in law. To constitute possession in law, physical control must be coupled with an intention to exclude others. As Pollock and Wright observe (at p 20): 'Possession in fact, with the manifest intent of sole and exclusive dominion, always imports possession in law.' Control in fact may be acquired by taking physical possession of the chattel itself or possession of an object which gives physical control of the chattel, eg the key to the warehouse in which the chattel is stored (although possession of a key to a container or to a building has been variously described by the courts as giving 'actual', 'constructive' or 'symbolic' possession of the chattels contained therein: see below, pp 1093–1098). The degree of control necessary to acquire possession will be relative to the nature of the chattel. For example, in *The Tubantia* [1924] P 78, the plaintiffs carried out salvage work on a wreck lying in 100 feet of water in the North Sea. They had cut a hole into a hold, buoyed the wreck and recovered some of the cargo when the defendants, a rival salvage company, interrupted their work. Sir Henry Drake P held that the plaintiffs had possession of the wreck and were entitled to an injunction and damages against the defendants for trespass. Although the plaintiffs had only been able to work on the wreck for short periods, with long interruptions because of the weather, the President was satisfied that '[t]here was the use and occupation of which the subject matter was capable'. Finally, it should be noted that the degree of control needed to acquire possession may not have to be maintained for possession to continue (see, eg Bridge, p 18; Bell, pp 35–36). Once acquired, possession is deemed to continue unless it is acquired by someone else or it is abandoned (Harris, op cit, p 73).

(ii) *Legal possession.* In the examples given by Pollock and Wright, JS has legal possession of the coat when he has both ownership and physical control of it. JS maintains legal possession when he gives up physical control to his employee (servant). The employee does not acquire legal possession of the coat because although he has physical control (or custody) of it, he does not have the necessary intention to control. However, if the employee took possession of the coat for a limited interest of his own, eg holds the coat as bailee under a pledge, he would acquire legal possession of it. As possession is indivisible, JS would have lost legal possession to the employee taking possession for a limited interest. Similarly, Z, the thief, acquires legal possession of the coat, and JS loses such possession, when he steals it from the employee. However, Z holds possession with the intention of asserting ownership rights. Therefore, Z's possession *animo domini* gives him an absolute legal interest in and a relative title to the coat. In this final example, possession gives rise to legal ownership (see above, p 69).

(iii) *Right to possess or to have legal possession.* Where a bailee holds possession of a chattel for his own interest, eg asserting a right of lien or other limited interest, or rights of owner, the bailor maintains a right to possess but he does not have legal possession of the chattel. This is because possession is single and exclusive (per Pollock and Wright, op cit, p 20). Like ownership, possession is indivisible and can only be held and transferred entire. But where the bailee holds possession for the bailor's interest, ie he is a bailee at will holding the chattel to the bailor's order, the bailor and bailee will share legal possession. In such circumstances, the bailor may be said to have constructive possession of the chattel. Constructive possession is a legal concept; there is no such thing as equitable possession in English law.

Constructive possession may even operate in favour of a person with a mere possessory title. For example, in *Wilson v Lombank Ltd* [1963] 1 All ER 740, W purchased a car from someone who had no title to sell. W took the car to a garage for repairs. The repairs were completed but whilst the car was awaiting collection a representative of L Ltd (who were not the true owners of the car) removed it from the garage in error. Hinchcliffe J held that W was in possession of the car and could sue L Ltd for trespass. W had a possessory title to the car which the garage held as bailees at will. Therefore, W had constructive possession of the car when it was in the actual possession of the garage. See also *United States of America and Republic of France v Dollfus Mieg et Cie SA and Bank of England* [1952] AC 582 at 611, per Lord Porter.

3.   In cases of doubt over who has possession of property, eg when the property is on premises which are jointly occupied, the owner is presumed to be the person in possession of it (*Ramsay v Margrett* [1894] 2 QB 18; *French v Gething* [1922] 1 KB 236).

QUESTIONS

1.   B steals A's car. C steals the same car from B. Can B assert a possessory title against C and sue him in conversion? See *Costello v Chief Constable of Derbyshire Constabulary* [2001] EWCA Civ 381, [2001] 1 WLR 1437; *Webb v Chief Constable of Merseyside Police* [2000] QB 427, CA; *Parker v British Airways Board* [1982] QB 1004 at 1010, per Donaldson LJ; cf the Torts (Interference with Goods) Act 1977, s 8 (see below, pp 91–92), but s 8 is of no assistance where the third party with a better title than the claimant cannot be identified. What if controlled drugs and not a car that had been stolen in this question? See *Costello*, above at

[15], per Lightman J. For useful notes (on *Costello),* see J Getzler (2001) 117 LQR 565; D Fox [2002] CLJ 27; G Battersby (2002) 65 MLR 603.

2. In *Wilson v Lombank Ltd,* above, Hinchcliffe J held that the garage did not have a lien on the car. Why was this important to the eventual outcome of the case?

10 ATTORNMENT

Attornment is an important commercial application of the concept of constructive possession. Attornment is the process by which a person (the attornor) holding actual possession of a chattel for himself or another person (under the terms of a bailment), later undertakes to hold possession of the goods for someone else (the attornee). The attornor must give his undertaking *to the attornee* (*Godts v Rose* (1855) 17 CB 229; Sale of Goods Act 1979, s 29(4)) and, once given, the attornee is deemed to have constructive possession of the chattel. Attornment most frequently arises where goods sold by A to B are held by C, who is a warehouseman or carrier (but attornment may not involve a third party as where, for example, A retains possession of goods he has sold to B under a sale and leaseback arrangement, and A acknowledges that he holds the goods for B: see *Michael Gerson (Leasing) Ltd v Wilkinson* [2001] QB 514, CA, especially at [28], per Clarke LJ). C will attorn to B when he acknowledges, with A's assent, that he henceforth holds the goods for B. However, for attornment to take place the goods must be identified. Thus, where the goods sold by A to B form an unidentified part of a bulk held by C, the acknowledgment by C that he now holds the goods for B cannot operate as an attornment so as to give constructive possession to B, but it will estop C from denying that he holds the goods as described on behalf of B (*Re London Wine Co (Shippers) Ltd* [1986] PCC 121; *Maynegrain Pty Ltd v Compafina Bank* [1982] 2 NSWLR 141, Court of Appeal of New South Wales, noted by FMB Reynolds (1984) 4 Ox JLS 434; revsd on another ground (1984) 58 ALJR 389, PC—it is unlikely that ss 20A and 20B of the Sale of Goods Act 1979, introduced by the Sale of Goods (Amendment) Act 1985 (see below, pp 320–321), alters this basic rule in favour of a prepaying buyer of part of an identified bulk who thereby becomes an owner in common of the bulk, although the position is uncertain: see L Gullifer [1999] LMCLQ 93). This process is sometimes known as quasi-attornment (RM Goode *Proprietary Rights in Insolvency and Sales Transactions* (2nd edn, 1989), p 11). The essential difference between attornment and quasi-attornment is that attornment operates to give the attornee property rights in the goods, whereas an estoppel merely gives the 'attornee' a personal right of action in conversion if the 'attornor' fails to release to him, or his order, goods of the requisite description and quantity.

The possession of a document of title to goods held by a third party does not usually carry with it constructive possession of the goods themselves (*Dublin City Distillery Ltd v Doherty* [1914] AC 823: below, p 1097). Possession of the goods depends upon further attornment by the third party to the holder of the document of title. An important exception to this rule arises in the case of a bill of lading (see below, p 490), which is the only true document of title recognised at common law (*Official Assignee of Madras v Mercantile Bank of India* [1935] AC 53 at 59, per Lord Wright: below, p 1093). The holder of a bill of lading is deemed to have constructive, or more likely symbolic, possession of the goods referred to therein, so long as the bill of lading has been properly transferred to him by delivery or by delivery and indorsement as required (the case for symbolic, as opposed to constructive, possession has been persuasively argued by Michael Bools in his excellent book *The Bill of Lading: A Document of Title to Goods* (1997), Ch 7). No attornment is required after the transferee has received delivery of the bill of lading, so long as it was delivered to him with the *intention* that he is to be given constructive or symbolic possession of the goods (see *The Future Express* [1992] 2 Lloyd's Rep 79, 95–96, per HH Judge Diamond QC, approved on this point [1993] 2 Lloyd's Rep 542, 550, CA: it may be that delivery of the bill of lading carries with it a transferable attornment by the carrier, see *Borealis AB v Stargas Ltd, The Berge Sisar* [2001] UKHL 17, [2002] 2 AC 205 at [18], per Lord Hobhouse, although in *East West Corpn v DKBS 1912* [2003] EWCA Civ 83, [2003] 1 All ER (Comm) 525 at [42], Mance LJ described this as 'a difficult area'; see further RM Goode *Proprietary Rights in Insolvency and Sales Transactions* (2nd edn, 1989), pp 9–10; Bools, above, pp 153–156). On the other hand, a delivery warrant issued by a warehouseman or other bailee does require attornment of the warehouseman or other bailee before the transferee takes constructive possession of the goods referred to therein (*Farina v Home* (1846) 16 M &W 119). However, certain statutory documents of title are treated in the same way as a negotiable bill of lading, eg statutory dock and warehouse warrants.

11 TRANSFER OF POSSESSION

Although the transfer of possession of a chattel may be effected by unilateral assumption of possession (including theft) or by operation of law (on death or personal insolvency), the most common method is voluntary transfer effected by actual or constructive delivery. Actual delivery transfers actual possession of the chattel to the deliveree. Constructive delivery transfers control of the chattel to the deliveree, usually without giving him actual possession. Constructive delivery may take place in any one of the following ways:

(1) where a deliveror, being in actual possession of the chattel, agrees to hold it as bailee for the deliveree (*Michael Gerson (Leasing) Ltd v Wilkinson* [2001] QB 514, CA);

(2) where a third party, being in actual possession of the chattel as bailee for the deliveror, attorns to the deliveree with the deliveror's consent;

(3) where the deliveror agrees that the deliveree, who is already in actual possession of the chattel as bailee for the deliveror, shall continue to hold the chattel for himself (the deliveree has actual possession after constructive delivery);

(4) where the deliveror agrees that the deliveree, who is already holding custody of the chattel for the deliveror, shall continue to hold the chattel for himself (again, the deliveree has actual possession after constructive delivery);

(5) where the deliveror transfers a document of title to goods to the deliveree (but see above);

(6) where the seller of goods (the deliveror) transfers them to a carrier for the purpose of transmission to the buyer (the deliveree): Sale of Goods Act 1979, s 32(1);

(7) where the deliveror transfers to the deliveree an object giving physical control of the chattel, eg a key to the warehouse where the goods are stored (but see above, p 73).

Delivery is considered further below at pp 423–425. See also *Official Assignee of Madras v Mercantile Bank of India Ltd* [1935] AC 53 at 58–59, per Lord Wright: below, pp 1093–1094.

12 THE IMPORTANCE OF POSSESSION

Before considering the commercial importance of possession, it is worth making a few preliminary observations. First, possession is a legal concept, it has no counterpart in equity. An agreement to give possession does not create property rights in law or in equity. If a person fails to hand over possession at the contractually agreed time, the best the disappointed party can do is to sue for breach of contract. Secondly, possession is only relevant to chattels which are capable of physical possession. Goods, money and documentary intangibles are all capable of physical possession, but a pure intangible is not (and, hence, cannot be made the subject of an action in conversion: *OBG Ltd v Allan* [2007] UKHL 21, [2007] 2 WLR 920, but note the powerful dissents of Lord Nicholls at [220]–[237] and Baroness Hale at [308]–[317] on this issue: see S Green (2008) 71 MLR 114). It is uncertain whether a digitised product that exists only in an electronic format, often referred to as 'software', can be reduced to possession and be the subject of conversion (see S Green [2006] LMCLQ 568). Thirdly, where a changing fund of assets is given to one person to manage on behalf of another, the person for whom the assets are managed does not have a possessory or proprietary right to any particular component of the fund, unless he has and exercises a power to terminate the manager's authority and crystallise the fund (RM Goode (1976) 92 LQR 360 at p 384 and 528 at p 529; and see, generally, C Davis [2002] CLJ 423; R Nolan (2004) 120 LQR 108).

However, even in the light of these limitations, the concept of possession remains important for the following reasons:

(1) Possession is relevant to the acquisition of legal ownership, at least where a possessory title is claimed, and to the acquisition of other legal interests that depend on possession, eg the special property of bailees in general, and pledgees and lienees in particular (Bell, p 33).

(2) Possession is relevant to the transfer of legal ownership, eg as a gift. But the passing of property under a contract for the sale of goods does not depend on the delivery of possession (Sale of Goods Act 1979, s 18, rule 1: below, p 324). However, several exceptions to the *nemo dat* rule do turn on possession (eg Sale of Goods Act 1979, ss 24, 25: below, pp 377ff and 381ff).

(3) Possession is prima facie evidence of ownership (but see *Elliott v Kemp* (1840) 7 M & W 306).

(4) Possession is the basis for certain remedies (see, generally, N Palmer 'Possessory Title' in N Palmer and E McKendrick (eds) *Interests in Goods* (2nd edn, 1998), Ch 3). The claimant in an action for trespass to chattels must have been in possession, or had an immediate right to possession under a bailment at will, at the time of the interference alleged against the defendant (Crossley Vaines, p 23; cf Bridge, pp 51–52). The claimant in an action for conversion of chattels must, at the time of conversion, have either been in actual possession of them, or have had an immediate right to possession of them, and it does not matter whether the claimant acquired possession lawfully or unlawfully (*Costello v Chief Constable of Derbyshire Constabulary* [2001] EWCA Civ 381, [2001] 1 WLR 1437 at [31]). Therefore, a legal owner of a chattel who lacks actual possession, or a right to immediate possession, will not be able to sue in conversion (*Gordon v Harper* (1796) 7 Term Rep 9), but he may have an action in tort for any damage done to his reversionary interest in the chattel (*Mears v London & South Western Rly Co* (1862) 11 CBNS 850; *HSBC Rail (UK) Ltd v Network Rail Infrastructure Ltd* [2005] EWCA Civ 1437,

[2006] 1 All ER (Comm) 345; and see generally, A Tettenborn [1994] CLJ 326). Someone with only an equitable title or interest, eg a beneficiary under a trust, and no possessory title, cannot sue in conversion or claim in tort for reversionary damage (*MCC Proceeds Inc v Lehman Bros International (Europe)* [1998] 4 All ER 675, CA, adopting arguments made by A Tettenborn [1996] CLJ 36). The claimant in an action for negligence causing loss or damage to chattels must have had either legal ownership or a possessory title to the chattels at the time when the loss or damage occurred (*The Aliakmon* [1986] AC 785 at 809, per Lord Brandon). But see ss 7 and 8 of the Torts (Interference with Goods) Act 1977 which has, to a certain extent, reduced the importance of possessory title in tort: see below, pp 91–92.

(5) Possession may be relevant in cases of insolvency. Where the buyer of goods becomes insolvent, an unpaid seller may still be able to exercise a lien on the goods, despite property in the goods having passed to the buyer, if he retains possession of them, or a right to stop the goods in transit if they have not yet reached the buyer's possession (Sale of Goods Act 1979, ss 39–46).

Furthermore, where the buyer takes possession of goods under an agreement for sale, and the seller later becomes insolvent, the buyer has a right to retain possession of the goods and may complete the transaction by tendering the price (RM Goode *Proprietary Rights and Insolvency in Sales Transactions* (2nd edn, 1989), p 7).

13 BAILMENT[4]

We have already made a number of references to bailment in this chapter. But what is bailment? In their treatise *An Essay on Possession in the Common Law* (1888), Pollock and Wright wrote (at p 163):

…any person is to be considered as a bailee who otherwise than as a servant either receives possession of a thing from another or consents to receive or hold possession of a thing for another upon an undertaking with the other person either to keep and return or deliver to him the specific thing or to (convey and) apply the specific thing according to the directions antecedent or future of the other person.

Possession lies at the heart of bailment. In *Ashby v Tolhurst* [1937] 2 KB 242, the owner of a car left it in a private car park. He paid the attendant and received a ticket from him. Whilst the owner went about his business, the attendant allowed a thief to drive off in the car. The thief, who had neither the ticket nor the car key, had misled the attendant into believing that he was taking the car with the owner's permission. The owners of the car park admitted that the attendant had been negligent but, relying on an exclusion clause printed on the ticket, denied liability. The case then turned on whether the owners of the car park had become bailees of the car. Reversing the trial judge, the Court of Appeal held that the relationship between the parties was that of licensor and licensee, and not that of bailor and bailee. The

---

[4] What follows deals with certain aspects of the law of bailment. For more detailed coverage, see generally NE Palmer *Bailment* (2nd edn, 1991) ('Palmer'); Crossley Vaines, Ch 6; Bell, Ch 5. By contrast, see Gerard McMeel, 'The redundancy of bailment' [2003] LMCLQ 169, for the interesting, if somewhat heretical, view that bailment does not constitute an independent concept but is better explained in terms of general principles of contract, tort, unjust enrichment and property. See also G. S McBain, 'Modernising and Codifying the Law of Bailment' [2008] JBL 1.

car owner had merely been given permission to park in the car park, the owners of the car park had not received possession of the car.

But possession alone is not enough to create a bailment: two other conditions must also be fulfilled. First, the bailor must retain a superior interest in the chattel to that of the bailee. The bailee acquires a limited possessory interest in the chattel which is subordinate to the bailor's interest. This is reflected in the fact that at the end of the bailment the bailee must redeliver the chattel to the bailor or deal with it according to the bailor's instructions (*Wincanton Ltd v P & O Trans European Ltd* [2001] CLC 962 at [19], per Dyson LJ). However, in *Mercer v Craven Grain Storage Ltd* [1994] CLC 328, noted by L Smith (1995) 111 LQR 10, the House of Lords held, somewhat surprisingly, and with no consideration of the relevant authorities, that it is possible to have a bailment where the bailee is authorised to substitute other goods for those bailed: there a grain storage society was held to be the bailee of grain deposited by farmers, even though the grain delivered by any particular farmer was commingled, with the farmer's consent, with grain delivered by other framers creating an indistinguishable mass which was subject to continual additions and withdrawals). By contrast, where possession *and ownership* of the chattel are conveyed by the transferor to the transferee there can be no bailment (in *Mercer v Craven Grain Storage Ltd,* the agreement under which the farmers deposited grain with the storage society specified that 'the grain shall remain the property of the grower'). For example, the buyer of identified goods under a contract of sale would normally acquire ownership of the goods and not hold them as bailee for the seller (but where goods are delivered to the buyer 'on sale or return', the buyer is a mere bailee prior to the passing of property: see *Atari Corpn (UK) Ltd v Electronics Boutique Stores (UK) Ltd* [1998] QB 539, CA). However, where goods are sold subject to a reservation of title clause the buyer may hold them as bailee, even though he is given the power to sell the goods to a sub-buyer or use them himself in his own manufacturing process (*Clough Mill Ltd v Martin* [1985] 1 WLR 111 at 116, per Robert Goff LJ).

Secondly, the bailee must consent to take possession of the chattel for there to be a bailment. This raises the question whether 'involuntary bailments' are really bailments at all. Involuntary bailments arise where a person is in control of a chattel belonging to another without consenting to act as bailee, eg when goods are sent to the 'bailee's' premises by mistake (as in *AVX Ltd v EGM Solders Ltd* (1982) Times, 7 July). It is probably best to regard these cases as *sui generis*. Another difficult issue is whether the bailor must consent to the bailee having possession of the chattel. Traditionally, bailment has been explained on the basis of mutual consent (see, eg Pollock and Wright, op cit, p 163: above). However, in recent years the consensual theory of bailment has been challenged. It has been argued that it is the bailee's, not the bailor's, consent which matters, and that 'any person who voluntarily assumes possession of goods belonging to another will be held to owe at least the principal duties of the bailee at common law' (Palmer, p 37). This new theory has now been endorsed by the Privy Council in *The Pioneer Container* [1994] 2 AC 324, where the owners of cargo (bailors) were held to have consented to an exclusive jurisdiction clause in a contract concluded between the carrier (bailee) and a sub-carrier (sub-bailee) employed to carry the goods over the last stage of the voyage from Taiwan to Hong Kong. Lord Goff, delivering the advice of the Board, said (at 341):

In truth, at the root of this question lies a doctrinal dispute of a fundamental nature, which is epitomised in the question: is it a prerequisite of a bailment that the bailor should have consented to the bailee's possession of the goods? An affirmative answer to this question (which is the answer given by Bell, *Modern Law of Personal Property in England and Ireland,* at pp 88–89) leads to the conclusion that, if the owner seeks to hold a sub-bailee responsible to him as bailee, he has to accept all the terms of the sub-bailment, warts and all; for either he will have consented to the sub-bailment on those terms or, if not, he will (by holding the sub-bailee liable to him as bailee) be held to have ratified all the terms of the sub-bailment. A negative answer to the question is however supported by other writers, notably by Palmer, *Bailment,* at pp 31 et seq., where Professor Palmer cites a number of examples of bailment without the consent of the owner, and by Professor Tay in her article 'The Essence of Bailment: Contract, Agreement or Possession?' (1966) 5 Sydney Law Review 239. On this approach, a person who voluntarily takes another person's goods into his custody holds them as bailee of that person (the owner); and he can only invoke, for example, terms of a sub-bailment under which he received the goods from an intermediate bailee as qualifying or otherwise affecting his responsibility to the owner if the owner consented to them. It is the latter approach which, as their Lordships have explained, has been adopted by English law and, with English law, the law of Hong Kong.

Their Lordships wish to add that this conclusion, which flows from the decisions in *Morris v CW Martin & Sons Ltd* [1966] 1 QB 716 and the *Gilchrist Watt* case [1970] 1 WLR 1262, produces a result which in their opinion is both principled and just. They incline to the opinion that a sub-bailee can only be said for these purposes to have voluntarily taken into his possession the goods of another if he has sufficient notice that a person other than the bailee is interested in the goods so that it can properly be said that (in addition to his duties to the bailee) he has, by taking the goods into his custody, assumed towards that other person the responsibility for the goods which is characteristic of a bailee. This they believe to be the underlying principle. Moreover, their Lordships do not consider this principle to impose obligations on the sub-bailee which are onerous or unfair, once it is recognised that he can invoke against the owner terms of the sub-bailment which the owner has actually (expressly or impliedly) or even ostensibly authorised. In the last resort the sub-bailee may, if necessary and appropriate, be able to invoke against the bailee the principle of warranty of authority.

Mance LJ recently summarised the modern approach to bailment in the following terms: 'What is fundamental is not contract, but the *bailee's* consent…the essence of bailment is the bailee's voluntary possession of another's goods' (*East West Corpn v DKBS 1912* [2003] EWCA Civ 83, [2003] QB 1509 at [24] and [26]). However, as one leading commentator observes: 'In rejecting consensus as the basis of bailments, *The Pioneer Container* clearly moves the law of bailment away from the law of contract and towards the law of tort' (A Bell 'The Place of Bailment in the Modern Law of Obligations', ch 19 in N Palmer and E McKendrick (eds) *Interests in Goods* (2nd edn, 1998), p 471, although Bell stresses, at p 488, following an examination of obligations to which bailments give rise, that 'bailment is indeed an independent source of obligations and…in moving away from contract, bailment has not in the process been simply absorbed by the law of tort'). It has been held, applying *The Pioneer Container,* that there is no bailment if the bailee is wholly unaware of the existence of the bailor (*Marcq v Christie, Manson & Woods Ltd* [2003] EWCA Civ 731, [2004] QB 286: auctioneer takes possession of painting from X unaware that it has been stolen from Y, Court of Appeal held no bailor-bailee relationship between Y and auctioneer).

14 TYPES OF BAILMENT

Coggs v Bernard

(1703) 2 Ld Raym 909, Court of King's Bench

Holt CJ: …And there are six sorts of bailments. The first sort of bailment is, a bare naked bailment of goods, delivered by one man to another to keep for the use of the bailor; and this I call a depositum, and it is that sort of bailment which is mentioned in *Southcote's case* ((1601) Cro Eliz 815). The second sort is, when goods or chattels that are useful, are lent to a friend gratis, to be used by him; and this is called commodatum, because the thing is to be restored in specie. The third sort is, when goods are left with the bailee to be used by him for hire; this is called locatio et conductio, and the lender is called locator, and the borrower conductor. The fourth sort is, when goods or chattels are delivered to another as a pawn, to be a security to him for money borrowed of him by the bailor; and this is called in Latin vadium, and in English a pawn or a pledge. The fifth sort is when goods or chattels are delivered to be carried, or something is to be done about them for a reward to be paid by the person who delivers them to the bailee, who is to do the thing about them. The sixth sort is when there is a delivery of goods or chattels to somebody, who is to carry them, or do something about them gratis, without any rewards for such his work or carriage, which is this present case. I mention these things, not so much that they are all of them so necessary in order to maintain the proposition which is to be proved, as to clear the reason of the obligation, which is upon persons in cases of trust.

Bailment by N E Palmer (2nd edn, 1991), pp 124–125

Although there seems to have been no particular reason for the order in which these six varieties of bailment were enumerated, it cannot be denied that Holt CJ's descriptive classification corresponded with the major contemporary manifestations of the bailor-bailee relationship and proved markedly influential upon subsequent discussions of the subject. Even today, it is not easy to think of types of bailment that are not accommodated by his categorisation, and the broad sweep of his analysis is one which has been adopted, with certain refinements, in the present treatment of the subject. Nevertheless, Holt CJ's division is governed by a fundamentally consensual concept of bailment and by the most obvious social or commercial examples of that concept. It therefore pays no regard to the more hybrid or peripheral kinds of bailment and, by leaving them out altogether, suggests that they do not belong to the realm of bailment at all. Admittedly, this observation is based in part upon developments which have occurred since *Coggs v Bernard,* and is therefore a statement of Holt CJ's failure to foresee these developments rather than a criticism of his failure to observe them as a contemporary force. The fact remains that a large number of bailments, of a more or less orthodox character, are excluded from his classification. These include bailments by finding, bailments which arise upon a wrongful or mistaken seizure of property, 'mutual loans', bailments which arise when a landlord levies distress upon his tenant's goods or when a finance company calls in its security, bailments existing between an owner of goods and a sub-bailee, and bailments which, although redounding to the mutual benefit of the parties, are not the product of a direct bargain or do not involve a 'reward to be paid' from bailor to bailee or vice-versa. Nor is it clear that certain bailments of a more modern but conventional kind (such as the contract of hire-purchase, the conditional sale arising by virtue of a title retention clause, the issue of a ticket to a railway passenger on condition that he surrender it at the end of his journey, the custody of a will by the testator's solicitor, the delivery of a manuscript to a publisher, or the delivery of a tool to a workman in order that he can perform certain work with it) can find a place within the foregoing classification. Although it would be unfair to criticise Holt CJ's analysis merely for failing to be watertight or comprehensive, it seems that if the value of classification rests in the earmarking of variant obligations within a basic unitary concept, the analysis is not complete. By concentrating exclusively upon the kinds of bailment that arise from some privity or bargain inter parties, the learned Chief Justice's approach neglects the extended or constructive bailment; by concentrating upon the more conventional types of consensual bailment he neglects certain others which fall within the consensual definition; and by stressing only the elements of purpose and reward he discounts certain other criteria which may affect the obligations of the parties.

NOTES

1.   There have been numerous attempts to classify the various types of bailment (they are reviewed by Palmer, pp 125–131). But as Professor Palmer himself acknowledges 'no general pattern is entirely satisfactory' (Palmer, p 123). However, it is common practice amongst textbook writers to divide bailments into two categories: gratutitous bailments (eg where you lend this book to a friend to use without charge) and bailments for reward (eg ware-housing, carriage, hire, hire-purchase and pledge). In certain circumstances, it may also be important to ascertain whether the bailment is for a fixed term or is determinable at the will of the bailor (see below, p 92).

2.   Where there is a contract of bailment, as is usually the case, the contractual incidents will supplement those that arise out of the proprietary relationship of bailor and bailee. But there does not have to be a contract between the parties for one to become the bailee of the other. For example, where the bailor consents, the bailee may bail the chattel to another person, who becomes the sub-bailee of the original bailor even though there is no contract between them (*Morris v C W Martin & Sons Ltd* [1966] 1QB 716, CA; *The Pioneer Container* [1994] 2 AC 324, PC). Where there is a non-contractual bailment, the rights and duties of the bailor and the bailee *inter se* may be defined according to the general law of tort. However, it seems that bailment also gives rise to obligations which are independent of both contract and tort, and that there is such a thing as a cause of action in bailment (see *The Pioneer Container* [1994] 2 AC 324 at 343–344, per Lord Goff; Palmer, pp 44–63; A Bell 'The Place of Bailment in the Modern Law of Obligations', ch 19 in N Palmer and E McKendrick (eds) *Interests in Goods* (2nd edn, 1998); cf Bridge, p 34).

15   THE BAILEE'S LIABILITY

The bailee owes the bailor a duty to take reasonable care of the bailed chattel. This duty of care is central to their relationship. But does the standard of care required of the bailee vary according to whether the bailment is gratuitous or for reward?

Houghland v RR Low (Luxury Coaches) Ltd
[1962] 1 QB 694, Court of Appeal

Returning from a trip to Jersey, Mrs H and her husband boarded one of the defendants' coaches at Southampton. Their suitcase was loaded into the boot of the coach, which was locked by the driver. After completing part of the journey the coach stopped at Ternhill, Shropshire, for the passengers to take tea. After tea the driver was unable to restart the coach and so he called for a relief coach which arrived some three hours later. During this period the coach stood unattended in the dark. When the relief coach arrived the driver supervised the loading of the passengers' luggage into it. The unloading of the luggage from the first coach and its transfer to the relief coach was done by the passengers themselves without supervision. The boot of the relief coach was locked. The relief coach continued the journey stopping occasionally to allow passengers to disembark. When the coach arrived at its final destination, Hoy lake, Cheshire, Mrs H and her husband could not find their suitcase. Mrs H sued the defendants in detinue (unlawful detention) and for negligence.

Ormerod LJ: The judge, according to the note that we have of his judgment…found in the first place that the driver of the coach was a bailee of the suitcase, and that the bailment was a gratuitous bailment. I am not sure that there is any evidence for the latter finding; and indeed, I might well, I think, have come to a different conclusion....

The judge then found that it was probably at Ternhill that the suitcase was either taken or lost, and in the circumstances he decided that the defendants were liable to pay the plaintiff £82 10s 11d.

The objection made to the judgment, as I understand it, is that, as this was a gratuitous bailment, the high degree of negligence required, otherwise called gross negligence in some of the cases, has not been established; that the judge made no finding of negligence, and that, in the circumstances, the judgment should not stand. I am bound to say that I am not sure what is meant by the term 'gross negligence' which has been in use for a long time in cases of this kind. There is no doubt, of course, that it is a phrase which has been commonly used in cases of this sort since the time of *Coggs v Bernard,* when the distinction was made in a judgment of Lord Holt CJ ((1703) 2 Ld Raym 909,913) which has been frequently referred to and cited; but as we know from the judgment of Lord Chelmsford in *Giblin v McMullen* ((1868) LR 2 PC 317, 336) that it was said, after referring to the use of the term 'gross negligence' over a long period: 'At last, Lord Cranworth (then Baron Rolfe) in the case of *Wilson v Brett* ((1843) 11 M & W 113, 115) objected to it, saying that he "could see no difference between negligence and gross negligence; that it was the same thing, with the addition of a vituperative epithet." And this critical observation has been since approved of by other eminent judges.'

For my part, I have always found some difficulty in understanding just what was 'gross negligence,' because it appears to me that the standard of care required in a case of bailment, or any other type of case, is the standard demanded by the circumstances of that particular case. It seems to me that to try and put a bailment, for instance, into a watertight compartment—such as gratuitous bailment on the one hand, and bailment for reward on the other—is to overlook the fact that there might well be an infinite variety of cases, which might come into one or the other category. The question that we have to consider in a case of this kind, if it is necessary to consider negligence, is whether in the circumstances of this particular case a sufficient standard of care has been observed by the defendants or their servants.

First, I think, I should deal with the question of detinue. It has been admitted by Mr Somerset Jones on behalf of the defendants that this is a case where a prima facie case has been established by the plaintiff. If that be so, I find it difficult to appreciate that there can be any grounds for appeal. Mr Somerset Jones has endeavoured to establish, and he has done it by reference to authority, that to found a prima facie case is not sufficient—that there must, in addition, be affirmative evidence before the plaintiff can succeed. I am bound to say that is a doctrine which rather surprises me. If a prima facie case is once established, it is something which may be rebutted easily, but it can only be rebutted by evidence, and that is not present in this case; and therefore, the prima facie case having been established, still remains.

Supposing that the claim is one in detinue, then it would appear that once the bailment has been established, and once the failure of the bailee to hand over the articles in question has been proved, there is a prima facie case, and the plaintiff is entitled to recover, unless the defendant can establish to the satisfaction of the court a defence; and that, I think, is very clear from the words used by Bankes LJ in *Coldman v Hill* ([1919] 1 KB 443,449) in a passage that appears to me to be important in this case: 'I think the law still is that if a bailee is sued in detinue only, it is a good answer for him to say that the goods were stolen without any default on his part, as the general bailment laid in the declaration pledges the plaintiff to the proof of nothing except that the goods were in the defendant's hands and were wrongfully detained.' So far, so good, but it is, of course, in those circumstances for the defendants to establish affirmatively, not only that the goods were stolen, but that they were stolen without default on their part; in other words, that there was no negligence on their part in the care which they took of the goods.

Applying that principle here, Mr Somerset Jones has been at pains to point out that the judge has made no finding that these goods were in fact stolen. The only view that the judge has expressed on the point is: 'It is impossible to say what happened to this suitcase when it was lost on its journey,' and with that I am bound to agree. It was put on the coach at Southampton, and it was not in the boot of the relief coach when it arrived at Hoylake. The judge has come to the conclusion that, on the probabilities, and again I agree with him, something happened to that suitcase when the transfer took place at Ternhill, or when the coach was delayed for some considerable period of time there. There seems to be no doubt that for something like three hours in the darkness that coach remained there unattended.

In these circumstances, I find it difficult to appreciate what substance there is in the complaint made by Mr Somerset Jones that in this case the judge, in treating this as a case of detinue, was in error. But let us suppose for a moment that the issue here is an issue in negligence: then he admits, and I think properly admits, that there is a prima facie case against the defendants derived from the fact that the suitcase was found by the judge to have been put on the coach at Southampton, and was not on the second coach when it arrived at its destination at Hoylake. In those circumstances, it is for the defendants to adduce evidence which will rebut a presumption of negligence.

But the case goes further than that. The evidence is that when the first coach was at Ternhill, and when the relief coach arrived driven by the managing director of the defendants, and whilst he went for his tea, the luggage was transferred from the first coach to the relief coach, and this was done by being supervised at the relief coach end without any supervision of any kind at the first coach end; and anything might have happened to a suitcase being transferred from one coach to the other. The defendants had their managing director there, and it was not unreasonable to expect that he and the driver between them might have supervised the transfer of this luggage from one coach to another. That did not happen; the transfer took place in the manner described. There was no supervision of the baggage being taken from the first coach. The driver of the coach said that he trusted the passengers, and it may be he was justified in doing that. It may well be that the passengers were honest; but in the darkness of the night, who is to know that some suitcase was not stolen by someone who had nothing at all to do with that particular trip?

In the circumstances, I fail to see where the judge went wrong, and I would dismiss this appeal.

Willmer LJ: I agree, and there is not much that I wish to add. In my judgment, this appeal fails on the facts. In saying that I do not think that it makes any difference whether the case is put in detinue, or whether it is treated as an action on the case for negligence. Whichever be the correct approach, it has been admitted in argument that the plaintiff, by proving the delivery of the suitcase at Southampton and its non-return on the arrival of the coach at Hoylake, made out a prima facie case. That prima facie case stands unless and until it is rebutted. The burden was on the defendants to adduce evidence in rebuttal. They could discharge that burden by proving what in fact did happen to the suitcase, and by showing that what did happen happened without any default on their part. They certainly did not succeed in doing that, for the judge was left in the position that he simply did not know what did happen to the suitcase.

Alternatively, the defendants could discharge the burden upon them by showing that, although they could not put their finger on what actually did happen to the suitcase, nevertheless, whatever did occur occurred notwithstanding all reasonable care having been exercised by them throughout the whole of the journey. Clearly the judge was not satisfied that they had proved the exercise of any such degree of care throughout the whole of the journey. On the evidence, particularly having regard to his preference for the plaintiff's evidence as against that called for the defendants, it was plainly open to him to come to that conclusion. All we know is that, in relation to the stop at Ternhill, this coach was apparently standing deserted in the middle of the night for a period of three hours. When the relief coach arrived, and the time came to transfer the luggage, this was done apparently with only the one member of the defendants' staff supervising the reloading on the second coach, and with no supervision at all over the discharge of the luggage from the first coach. In those circumstances, it is only too clear that the defendants entirely failed to show that throughout the period, when they had this suitcase in their custody, they exercised reasonable care.

I, therefore, agree that this appeal must fail.

[Danckwerts LJ concurred.]

NOTES

1. The traditional approach has been for different standards of care to apply according to whether the bailment is for reward (bailee liable for ordinary negligence) or merely gratuitous (bailee only liable in the case of *gross* negligence). In *Houghland v RR Low (Luxury Coaches) Ltd* [1962] 1 QB 694, the Court of Appeal rejected the traditional approach and held that the same test applies to all types of bailment: the bailee's standard of care is that required by the circumstances of the particular case. Unfortunately, the issue cannot be treated as closed. Later in *Port Swettenham Authority v TG Wu & Co Sdn Bhd* [1979] AC 580, the Privy Council continued to distinguish between the standard of care expected of a bailee for reward and that expected of a gratuitous bailee; whilst in *The Winson* [1982] AC 939 at 960, Lord Diplock declared that the lower standard of care of a gratuitous bailee is 'too well known and too well-established to call for any citation of authority'. However, in *Sutcliffe v Chief Constable of West Yorkshire* [1996] RTR 86, the Court of Appeal followed the *Houghland* case, with Otton LJ making it clear (at 90) that 'no distinction is to be drawn between a gratuitous bailment and one for reward' (although Andrew Bell notes that no reference was made to the *Port Swettenham* case or *The Winson* in *Sutcliffe* 'and so there is still a need for a clear, authoritative resolution of this issue': A Bell 'The Place of Bailment in the Modern Law of Obligations', ch 19 in N Palmer and E McKendrick (eds) *Interests in Goods* (2nd edn, 1998), p 477).

2. Despite the stance taken by the Court of Appeal in *Houghland v RR Low (Luxury Coaches) Ltd,* there remain a number of other reasons for the courts to distinguish between contractual and gratuitous bailments.

First, the Supply of Goods and Services Act 1982 only applies to contractual bailments. The Act contains provisions relating to the bailee's duty of care (when the contract is for the supply of services in the course of business: s 13) and the bailor's obligations to the bailee (when the contract is for the hire of goods: ss 7–10).

Secondly, there may be contractual exemption clauses which exclude or limit the bailee's duties, subject to those controls contained in the Unfair Contract Terms Act 1977 and, where the bailor is a consumer, the Unfair Terms in Consumer Contracts Regulations 1999 (although where a bailment is gratuitous a disclaimer may prevent a tortious duty of care being imposed on the bailee: see *Halloway v Cuozzo* (9 February 1999, unreported), CA, where a gratuitous bailee who collected a football pools coupon from the bailor for submission to a pools promoter was able to rely on a disclaimer printed on the coupon to avoid liability when, by mistake, he failed to submit the bailor's winning coupon estimated to be worth at least £200,000). The position is more complicated in the case of a sub-bailment on terms; however, in *The Pioneer Container* [1994] 2 AC 324, the Privy Council held that a sub-bailee who knows that the goods are not the bailee's goods can rely on a term of the sub-bailment where the bailor has expressly or impliedly consented to that term or if the bailee has ostensible authority to include the term in the sub-bailment. The bailor may also be able to rely on some of the terms agreed between the bailee and the sub-bailee to increase the liability of the sub-bailee beyond that arising at common law. In *Sandeman Coprimar SA v Transitos y Transportes Integrates SL* [2003] EWCA Civ 113, [2003] QB 1270 at [62], the Court of Appeal held that 'where a bailor consents to and thereby authorises a sub-bailment on terms, all the terms agreed between the bailee and the sub-bailee, in so far as these are applicable to the relationship of the bailor and the sub-bailee, apply as between the bailor and the sub-bailee'. The Court of Appeal held that this was also likely to follow from the principles of the law of contract. Lord Phillips MR, delivering the judgment of the Court, continued (at [63]):

Where a bailee had the consent, and thus the authority, of the bailor to enter into a sub-bailment on particular terms and does so, and where those terms purport to govern the relationship not merely between the sub-bailee and the bailee, but between the sub-bailee and bailor, it seems to us that all the elements of a collateral contract binding the sub-bailee and the bailor will be present, for there will be privity, via the agency of the bailee, and no difficulty in identifying consideration, at least if the terms are capable of resulting in benefit to each of the parties.

The sub-bailee may also benefit from a 'Himalaya' clause in the main contract of bailment between the bailor and the bailee (such clauses extend immunity from liability to sub-contractors employed by the bailee, although much turns on the construction of the clause in question: see *The Mahkutai* [1996] AC 650, PC), But where the sub-bailee speaks for himself, eg by issuing a shipping note direct to the bailor, the terms of that note will take precedence where they are inconsistent with the terms of the Himalaya clause in the contract between the bailor and the bailee (*Lotus Cars Ltd v Southampton Cargo Handling plc* [2000] 2 All ER (Comm) 705 at [49], per Rix LJ). Until recently, the sub-bailee would have had to comply with the somewhat technical principles articulated by the Privy Council in *The Eurymedon* [1975] AC 154 and *The New York Star* [1981] 1 WLR 138 , in order to take advantage of a term in the contract between the bailor and the bailee. However, the Contracts (Rights of Third Parties) Act 1999 now offers the sub-bailee a much easier route to gain the protection of a Himalaya clause in the main contract of bailment, although alternative methods of relying on the clause still remain open to him.

Thirdly, the fact that the bailment is gratuitous may be relevant when assessing whether the bailee has exercised reasonable care 'in all the circumstances' (for the analogous situation of a gratuitous agent, see *Chaudhry v Prabhakar*[1989] 1 WLR 29, below, p 203). This last point seems consistent with the stance taken by the Court of Appeal in *Houghland* itself, namely that the bailee's standard of care is that required by the circumstances of the particular case.

3.   In certain circumstances, the bailee's liability for loss or damage to the bailed chattel may be strict. Strict liability generally arises as follows:

(1)   Where the bailee is a common carrier, unless the loss or damage to the goods is caused by an excepted peril, eg Act of God, inherent vice etc. However, strict liability may be avoided by contractual exemption clauses or by the assumption of the status of private carrier, and various statutes permit or prescribe ways by which liability may be excluded or limited: see, eg the Carriage of Goods by Air Act 1961, the Carriage of Goods by Sea Act 1971.

(2)   Where the bailee 'deviates' in the conduct of the bailment, eg by storing the chattel somewhere other than the place agreed (*Lilley v Doubleday* (1881) 7 QBD 510); or by entrusting the chattel without authority to a third person (*Edwards v Newland & Co* [1950] 2 KB 534); or by wrongfully refusing to return the chattel, or negligently failing to return it, when called upon to do so by the bailor at the end of the bailment (*Mitchell v Ealing London Borough Council* [1979] QB 1; or by carrying the chattel otherwise than by the agreed route, unless there is no causative link between the deviation and loss or damage to the chattel (*James Morrison & Co Ltd v Shaw, Savill and Albion Co Ltd* [1916] 2 KB 783). Deviation in the conduct of the bailment also has other consequences: it amounts to a repudiatory breach and gives the bailor an immediate right to possess the chattel; where the deviation is so serious as to amount to a blatant disregard of the bailor's interests, it may constitute conversion by the bailee (*Garnham, Harris and Elton Ltd v Alfred W Ellis (Transport) Ltd* [1967] 2 Lloyd's Rep 22); and the bailee will generally

lose the protection of any contractual exclusion clauses (*Gibaud v Great Eastern Rly Co* [1921] 2 KB 426; see also Bell, pp 115–118).

4.   Detinue was abolished by s 2(1) of the Torts (Interference with Goods) Act 1977. However, s 2(2) of the 1977 Act goes on to provide that: 'An action lies in conversion for loss or destruction of goods which a bailee has allowed to happen in breach of his duty to his bailor (that is to say it lies in a case which is not otherwise conversion, but would have been detinue before detinue was abolished).' This means that if the chattel has been lost or destroyed as a result of the bailee's breach of duty so that the bailee cannot redeliver it back to the bailor, the bailee will be liable to the bailor for breach of duty, breach of bailment (ie breach of the bailee's duty to redeliver) and conversion under s 2(2). By contrast, where the bailee delivers the chattel to the wrong person, the bailee will be held liable to the bailor even if the misdelivery was entirely innocent (*Devereux v Barclay* (1819) 2 B & Ald 702; but an involuntary bailee will only be liable for misdelivery if he acts negligently in making it: *Elvin and Powell Ltd v Plummer Roddis Ltd* (1933) 50 TLR 158, bailee acted reasonably and not held liable; contrast *Hiort v Bott* (1874) LR 9 Exch 86, bailee acted unreasonably and held liable).

5.   It is traditionally said that an 'involuntary bailee' will not be liable for mere negligence (*Howard v Harris* (1884) Cab & El 253: theatre manager not liable for loss of unsolicited script of play sent to him by playwright) and that his sole duty is to refrain from intentional destruction or damage of the goods (*Hiort v Bott* (1874) LR 9 Exch 86 at 90, per Bramwell B, *obiter),* unless they are of a noxious character when he may scrap them (*AVX Ltd v EGM Solders Ltd* (1982) Times, 7 July, per Staughton J: an unsatisfactory case which is best explained as one of 'involuntary bailment', see Palmer, pp 451–455). However, it has been persuasively argued by Professor Norman Palmer that an involuntary bailee of goods should owe a duty of care towards their owner, although the standard of care, which will vary according to what is reasonable in all the circumstances of the case, will generally be an undemanding one given that the involuntary bailee did not agree to have the goods in the first place (Palmer, pp 680–689). Sometimes, the 'involuntary bailee' may treat the goods as his own. In certain circumstances, the recipient of unsolicited goods may treat them as an unconditional gift from the sender (Consumer Protection (Distance Selling) Regulations 2000, SI 2000/2334, reg 24; previously the relevant provisions were contained in the Unsolicited Goods and Services Act 1971, s 1).

QUESTIONS

1.   Henry took his Rolex watch to Percy to be repaired. Percy agreed to repair the watch for a fee and told Henry to return and collect it the next day. Percy carried out the repair work, then locked the watch away in his safe and properly secured his workshop for the night. That night Toby, a thief, broke into Percy's workshop, forced the safe and stole Henry's watch. Will Percy be liable to Henry for this loss? Would your answer be different if Percy had been tricked into handing over the watch to Toby, who had falsely claimed to be Henry's butler and had produced a cleverly forged letter of authority from Henry to support his claim? Again, would it make any difference to your answer if Toby had executed his fraud some six months after Henry had delivered the watch to Percy and in the interim period Percy had constantly urged Henry to come and collect it?

2.   Electron plc, a manufacturer of electrical products, decides to stockpile certain electrical components which it fears will soon be in short supply. It arranges to store a large

consignment of these components in Secure Ltd's warehouse in Manchester. Electron pays all storage charges in advance and warns Secure to have the components ready for it to collect in six months' time. After the components are delivered to Secure's warehouse, Secure sells them to Transtech plc, another manufacturer of electrical products, and employs Cargo Ltd, a firm of carriers, to transport the components to Transtech's factory in Leeds. During the transit Cargo's lorry is blown over by freak hurricane-force winds on the Pennines. The lorry and its cargo of electrical components are completely destroyed. What rights, if any, does Electron have against Secure and/or Cargo? See the notes above and also *Hollins v Fowler* (1875) LR 7 HL 757 at 766–767; *Marcq v Christie, Manson & Woods Ltd* [2003] EWCA Civ 731, [2004] QB 286 at [53], CA.

16 BAILMENT AND THIRD PARTIES

The Winkfield

[1902] P 42, Court of Appeal

(The facts appear from Collins MR's judgment.)

Collins MR: This is an appeal from the order of Sir Francis Jeune dismissing a motion made on behalf of the Postmaster-General in the case of *The Winkfield.*

The question arises out of a collision which occurred on April 5, 1900, between the steamship *Mexican* and the steamship *Winkfield,* and which resulted in the loss of the former with a portion of the mails which she was carrying at the time.

The owners of the *Winkfield* under a decree limiting liability to £32,514 17s 10d paid that amount into court, and the claim in question was one by the Postmaster-General on behalf of himself and the Postmasters-General of Cape Colony and Natal to recover out of that sum the value of letters, parcels, etc, in his custody as bailee and lost on board the *Mexican.*

The case was dealt with by all parties in the Court below as a claim by a bailee who was under no liability to his bailor for the loss in question, as to which it was admitted that the authority of *Claridge v South Staffordshire Tramway Co* ([1892] 1 QB 422) was conclusive, and the President accordingly, without argument and in deference to that authority, dismissed the claim. The Postmaster-General now appeals.

The question for decision, therefore, is whether *Claridge's Case* was well decided. I emphasize this because it disposes of a point which was faintly suggested by the respondents, and which, if good, would distinguish *Claridge's Case,* namely, that the applicant was not himself in actual occupation of the things bailed at the time of the loss. This point was not taken below, and having regard to the course followed by all parties on the hearing of the motion, I think it is not open to the respondents to make it now, and I therefore deal with the case upon the footing upon which it was dealt with on the motion, namely, that it is covered by *Claridge's Case.* I assume, therefore, that the subject-matter of the bailment was in the custody of the Postmaster-General as bailee at the time of the accident. For the reasons which I am about to state I am of opinion that *Claridge's Case* was wrongly decided, and that the law is that in an action against a stranger for loss of goods caused by his negligence, the bailee in possession can recover the value of the goods, although he would have had a good answer to an action by the bailor for damages for the loss of the thing bailed.

It seems to me that the position, that possession is good against a wrongdoer and that the latter cannot set up the jus tertii unless he claims under it, is well established in our law, and really concludes this case against the respondents. As I shall shew presently, a long series of authorities establishes this in actions of trover and trespass at the suit of a possessor. And the principle being the same, it follows that he can equally recover the whole value of the goods in an action on the case for their loss through the tortious conduct of the defendant. I think it involves this also, that the wrongdoer who is not defending under the title of the bailor is quite unconcerned with what the rights are between the bailor and bailee, and must treat the possessor as the owner of the goods for all purposes quite irrespective of the rights and obligations as between him and the bailor.

I think this position is well established in our law, though it may be that reasons for its existence have been given in some of the cases which are not quite satisfactory. I think also that the obligation of the bailee to the bailor to account for what he has received in respect of the destruction or conversion of the thing bailed has been admitted so often in decided cases that it cannot now be questioned; and, further, I think it can be shewn that the right of the bailee to recover cannot be rested on the ground suggested in some of the cases, namely, that he was liable over to the bailor for the loss of the goods converted or destroyed. It cannot be denied that since the case of *Armory v Delamirie* ((1722) 1 Stra 505), not to mention earlier cases from the Year Books onward, a mere finder may recover against a wrongdoer the full value of the thing converted. That decision involves the principle that as between possessor and wrongdoer the presumption of law is, in the words of Lord Campbell in *Jeffries v Great Western Rly Co* ((1856) 5 E & B 802,806), 'that the person who has possession has the property.' In the same case he says: 'I am of opinion that the law is that a person possessed of goods as his property has a good title as against every stranger, and that one who takes them from him, having no title in himself, is a wrongdoer, and cannot defend himself by shewing that there was title in some third person, for *against a wrongdoer possession is title.* The law is so stated by the very learned annotator in his note to *Wilbraham v Snow* ((1670) 2 Wms Saund 47f).' Therefore it is not open to the defendant, being a wrongdoer, to inquire into the nature or limitation of the possessor's right, and unless it is competent for him to do so the question of his relation to, or liability towards, the true owner cannot come into the discussion at all; and, therefore, as between those two parties full damages have to be paid without any further inquiry. The extent of the liability of the finder to the true owner not being relevant to the discussion between him and the wrongdoer, the facts which would ascertain it would not have been admissible in evidence, and therefore the right of the finder to recover full damages cannot be made to depend upon the extent of his liability over to the true owner. To hold otherwise would, it seems to me, be in effect to permit a wrongdoer to set up a jus tertii under which he cannot claim. But, if this be the fact in the case of a finder, why should it not be equally the fact in the case of a bailee? Why, as against a wrongdoer, should the nature of the plaintiff's interest in the thing converted be any more relevant to the inquiry, and therefore admissible in evidence, than in the case of a finder? It seems to me that neither in one case nor the other ought it to be competent for the defendant to go into evidence on that matter.

[His Lordship then reviewed several cases showing that a bailee had an unqualified right to sue the wrongdoer. He continued:]

The ground of the decision in *Claridge's Case* was that the plaintiff in that case, being under no liability to his bailor, could recover no damages, and though for the reasons I have already given I think this position is untenable, it is necessary to follow it out a little further. There is no doubt that the reason given in *Heydon and Smith's Case* ((1610) 13 Co Rep 67 at 69)—and itself drawn from the Year Books—has been repeated in many subsequent cases. The words are these: 'Clearly, the bailee, or he who hath a special property, shall have a general action of trespass against a stranger, and shall recover all in damages because that he is chargeable over.'

It is now well established that the bailee is accountable, as stated in the passage cited and repeated in many subsequent cases. But whether the obligation to account was a condition of his right to sue, or only an incident arising upon his recovery of damages, is a very different question, though it was easy to confound one view with the other.

Holmes CJ in his admirable lectures on the Common Law, in the chapter devoted to bailments, traces the origin of the bailee's right to sue and recover the whole value of chattels converted, and arrives at the clear conclusion that the bailee's obligation to account arose from the fact that he was originally the only person who could sue, though afterwards by an extension, not perhaps quite logical, the right to sue was conceded to the bailor also. He says at p 167: 'At first the bailee was answerable to the owner because he was the only person who could sue; now it was said he could sue because he was answerable to the owner.' And again at p 170: 'The inverted explanation of Beaumanoir will be remembered, that the bailee could sue because he was answerable over, in place of the original rule that he was answerable over so strictly because only he could sue.' This inversion, as he points out, is traceable through the Year Books, and has survived into modern times, though, as he shews, it has not been acted upon. Pollock and Maitland's History of English Law, vol 2, p 170, puts the position thus:—'Perhaps we come nearest to historical truth if we say that between the two old rules there was no logical priority. The bailee had the action because he was liable, and was liable because he had the action.' It may be that in early times the obligation of the bailee to the bailor was absolute, that is to say, he was an insurer. But long after the decision of *Coggs v Bernard,* which classified the obligations of bailees, the bailee has, nevertheless, been allowed to recover full damages against a wrongdoer, where the facts would have afforded a complete answer for him against his bailor. The cases above cited are instances of this. In each of them the bailee would have had a good answer to an action by his bailor; for in none of them was it suggested that the act of the wrongdoer was traceable to negligence on the part of the bailee. I think, therefore, that the statement drawn, as I have said, from the Year Books may be explained, as Holmes CJ explains it, but whether that be the true view of it or not, it is clear that it has not been treated as law in our Courts.... Therefore, as I said at the outset, and as I think I have now shewn by authority, the root principle of the whole discussion is that, as against a wrongdoer, possession is title. The chattel that has been converted or damaged is deemed to be the chattel of the possessor and of no other, and therefore its loss or deterioration is his loss, and to him, if he demands it, it must be recouped. His obligation to account to the bailor is really not ad rem in the discussion. It only comes in after he has carried his legal position to its logical consequence against a wrongdoer, and serves to soothe a mind disconcerted by the notion that a person who is not himself the complete owner should be entitled to receive back the full value of the chattel converted or destroyed. There is no inconsistency between the two positions; the one is the complement of the other. As between bailee and stranger possession gives title—that is, not a limited interest, but absolute and complete ownership, and he is entitled to receive back a complete equivalent for the whole loss or deterioration of the thing itself. As between bailor and bailee the real interests of each must be inquired into, and, as the bailee has to account for the thing bailed, so he must account for that which has become its equivalent and now represents it. What he has received above his own interest he has received to the use of his bailor. The wrongdoer, having once paid full damages to the bailee, has an answer to any action by the bailor.

[Stirling and Mathew LJJ concurred.]

NOTES

1.   A bailee's possession is sufficient to meet the requirement that a claimant in an action for trespass, conversion or detinue (now abolished, but see above at p 87) must have been in possession of the chattel at the time of the interference alleged against the wrongdoer (the other prerequisites for a successful action based on these property torts are to be found in the standard tort textbooks, eg *Winfield & Jolowicz on Tort* (17th edn, 2006) (ed WVH Rogers), Ch 17). The bailee may also rely on his possession to bring an action against the wrongdoer in negligence. It has recently been confirmed by the Court of Appeal that a mere contractual right to enter into immediate possession is enough to sue in conversion (*Iran v Barakat Galleries Ltd* [2007] EWCA Civ 1374). Despite having only a limited interest in the chattel, the bailee is entitled, at common law, to recover the full market value of the chattel against the wrongdoer (*The Winkfield),* and also damages for consequential loss unless too remote (as to which, see *Kuwait Airways Corpn v Iraqi Airways Co (Nos 4 & 5)* [2002]

UKHL 19, [2002] 2 AC 883 at 1096–1098, HL). The same rule applies where the bailee sues the wrongdoer for breach of contract (*Tanenbaum v WJ Bell Paper Co Ltd* (1956) 4 DLR (2d) 177). In *The Jag Shakti* [1986] AC 337, the Privy Council even went so far as to apply *The Winkfield* to a bailee who had merely a right to immediate possession of the goods at the time of the wrong (criticised by Professor Palmer in Palmer, pp 342–351, and also in his essay 'Possessory Title', Ch 3 in N Palmer and E McKendrick (eds) *Interests in Goods* (2nd ed, 1998), pp 68–71).

But in three exceptional situations the wrongdoer may raise another person's superior title to the chattel as a defence against an action brought by the bailee. These are as follows:

(1) when the wrongdoer defends the action on behalf of, and with the authority of, the true owner;

(2) when the wrongdoing was committed with the authority of the true owner;

(3) when the wrongdoer has, since the time of the wrongdoing, become the owner of the goods.

2.   Having recovered in full from the wrongdoer, the bailee may subtract the value (if any) of his own interest, but he must pay the surplus to the bailor (*The Winkfield*). Although the bailee is sometimes described as holding the surplus on trust for the bailor, there appears to be no direct decision favouring a proprietary rather than a personal claim (Professor Palmer, citing by analogy *Mathew v TM Sutton Ltd* [1994] 4 All ER 793, where a pledgee was deemed to hold surplus sale proceeds on trust, submits that the bailor has an interest in proceeds of the bailee's claim equivalent to that which he had in the original goods and is an equitable owner of the fund: see N Palmer 'Possessory Title', Ch 3 in N Palmer and E McKendrick (eds) *Interests in Goods* (2nd edn, 1998), pp 67–68). Why do you think it matters whether the bailor has a proprietary or personal claim against the bailee?

3.   When the bailee recovers damages in full from the wrongdoer no action may later be maintained by the bailor, even if he would otherwise have a right of action to sue (*Nicolls v Bastard* (1835) 2 Cr M & R 659 at 660, per Parke B). Similarly, the bailee will be prevented from recovering against the wrongdoer if the bailor has already done so. Thus, in *O' Sullivan v Williams* [1992] 3 All ER 385, the owner of a car lent the vehicle to his girlfriend while he was on holiday. The car was damaged while in her possession. His successful claim for damages, based on his right to recover the car from the girlfriend at his will, was held by the Court of Appeal to preclude a second action by the girlfriend, even though she had possession of the car at the time it was damaged. You will be pleased to know that this incident did not stop the owner later marrying his girlfriend!

4.   *The Winkfield* must now be read in the light of ss 7 and 8 of the Torts (Interference with Goods) Act 1977 which allow a wrongdoer to join all claimants to an action for wrongful interference with goods (ie an action in tort) so that they may recover according to their actual interests and thus avoid double liability of the wrongdoer. Where all claimants are not joined to the action, s 7(3) imposes on a party with a possessory title the duty to account to another potential claimant 'to such an extent to avoid double liability'. Should the other claimant later bring his own claim, with the result that the wrongdoer pays twice, s 7(4) imposes a duty on that claimant to reimburse the wrongdoer to the extent of his unjust enrichment (which depends on him having also received payment from the first claimant). But this provision offers no additional benefit to a wrongdoer who has already paid the full value of the chattel to the bailee and has a complete defence at common law to any future action brought by the bailor. Section 8 allows the wrongdoer to set up a third party's superior title as a defence to the claimant's claim for wrongful interference (ie to plead *jus tertii),* although he can probably only do this if the person he claims to have a better title than the claimant is joined as a party to the action (*De Franco v Metropolitan Police Comr* (1987) Times, 8 May, per Lloyd LJ). It is even possible for the bailee to rely on s 8 and plead *jus tertii* against the bailor, something he cannot generally do at common law (but the common law rule still applies where the bailee is sued by his bailor for breach of contract or breach of bailment).

5.   Finally, it should be noted the bailor's right of action in trespass or conversion (including what was detinue) against a wrongdoer depends on the bailor having a right to immediate possession of the bailed chattel at the time of the wrongdoing. Where the bailment is at the will of the bailor he will have such a right (as in *O' Sullivan v Williams*, above). For example, where goods are entrusted to carriers, the general presumption is that the bailment is revocable at will, so that the bailor retains a right to immediate possession of the goods to enable him to pursue possessory remedies against persons injuring or interfering with the goods (*Transcontainer Express Ltd v Custodian Security Ltd* [1988] 1 Lloyd's Rep 128, CA). Similarly, the bailor retains a right to immediate possession of the goods where he transfers a bill of lading to a bank, named as consignee, to hold as his agent, whether or not the effect of that transfer was to confer on the bank a sufficient possessory interest for it to pursue claims in bailment (*East West Corpn v DKBS 1912* [2003] EWCA Civ 83, [2003] QB 1509 at [39], CA). But where the bailment is for a fixed term the bailor has no right to immediate possession, unless the bailee commits a wrongful act amounting to repudiation of the bailment, eg deviation in the conduct of the bailment (see above, p 86), or destroying the subject matter of the bailment (see below, p 1102), or the contract of bailment provides that the bailor has the immediate right to terminate the bailment for any breach of its terms (*North Central Wagon & Finance Co Ltd v Graham* [1950] 2 KB 7). Where the bailor does not have possession, or a right to immediate possession, of the bailed chattel, he may only sue the wrongdoer for damage to his reversionary interest, and where he has been fully compensated by the bailee he will have suffered no such damage (*HSBC Rail (UK) Ltd v Network Rail Infrastructure Ltd* [2005] EWCA Civ 1437, [2006] 1 All ER (Comm) 345: held no loss to bailor as bailed goods repaired or replaced by bailee).

PART II

THE LAW OF AGENCY

CHAPTER 3
INTRODUCTION

1 THE LEGAL CONCEPT OF AGENCY[1]

(a) Definitions of agency

Agency is the fiduciary relationship that arises when one person (a 'principal') manifests assent to another person (an 'agent') that the agent shall act on the principal's behalf and subject to the principal's control, and the agent manifests or otherwise consents so to act.

(American Restatement of the Law of Agency (3rd edn, 2006), para 1.01)

Agency is the fiduciary relationship which exists between two persons, one of whom expressly or impliedly manifests assent that the other should act on his behalf so as to affect his relations with third parties, and the other of whom similarly manifests assent so to act or so acts pursuant to the manifestation.

(Bowstead and Reynolds on Agency (18th edn, 2006), art 1 (1))

Agency is the relationship that exists between two persons when one, called the *agent,* is considered in law to represent the other, called the *principal,* in such a way as to be able to affect the principal's legal position in respect of strangers to the relationship by the making of contracts or the disposition of property.

(GHL Fridman The Law of Agency (7th edn, 1996), p 11)

NOTES

1. Any concise definition of the concept of agency must be treated with care. Striving for brevity, the definition is likely to be flawed by errors and omissions which may make it misleading. However, the definitions set out above do provide a starting point from which to begin our assessment of the theoretical basis of agency.

2. Various theories have been advanced to explain the concept of agency (they are reviewed in *Bowstead and Reynolds*, Ch 1). The definition provided in *Bowstead and Reynolds*, which is based on that given in the American *Restatement* (3rd edn 2006) focuses on the manifestation of assent to the agency by both the principal and the agent. In most cases the

---

[1] In this and the succeeding chapters dealing with the law of agency, the following abbreviations are used in referring to standard textbooks:

Bowstead and Reynolds: FMB Reynolds *Bowstead and Reynolds on Agency* (18th edn, 2006);
Fridman: GHL Fridman *The Law of Agency* (7th edn, 1996);
Markesinis and Munday: BS Markesinis and RJC Munday *An Outline of the Law of Agency* (4th edn, 1998).

principal agrees to the agent acting on his behalf and the agent agrees to do so. Such consensual agency is described in *Bowstead and Reynolds* as the 'paradigm case' (para 1–011). But the consent theory breaks down when we move away from the paradigm case. The theory fails to account for the fact that agency can also arise out of apparent authority (below, pp 117–128) irrespective of, and sometimes contrary to, the wishes of the parties (see, for example, *Boardman v Phipps* [1967] 2 AC 46, where the House of Lords held that an agency relationship existed even though there was no consent by the principal). Such cases can only be brought within the consent theory by a strained construction of the term 'consent' (cf *Bowstead and Reynolds,* para 1–013: 'the authority stems from the principal's objectively determined assent'; see also G McMeel (2000) 116 LQR 387, 392: 'qualified by the objective principle, the consent theory of agency is capable of explaining the majority of agency cases'). There is no consent where agency arises by operation of law, especially in cases of agency of necessity (below, pp 133–139). Furthermore, the consent theory turns the existence of an agency relationship into a question of fact (ie if there is consent, there is agency) when it is really a question of law (*Garnac Grain Co Inc v HMF Faure and Fairclough Ltd* [1968] AC 1130 at 1137, per Lord Pearson; see also *Fridman,* p 15 (and (1968) 84 LQR 224, 231) and *Markesinis and Munday,* pp 5–6 for contrasting interpretations of Lord Pearson's speech).

3.   Fridman's definition of agency is based on a power-liability analysis of the relationship between the principal and agent. The power-liability analysis focuses on the agent's power to alter the principal's *legal* relations with third parties (in particular by making contracts on behalf of the principal or by disposing of the principal's property) and the principal's consequent liability to have his relations so altered. The power-liability relationship of the principal and agent is best explained by Professor Dowrick in the next extract.

'The Relationship of Principal and Agent' by FE Dowrick
(1954) 17 MLR 24, pp 36–38

The essential characteristic of an agent is that he is invested with a legal power to alter his principal's legal relations with third persons: the principal is under a correlative liability to have his legal relations altered. It is submitted that this power-liability relation is the essence of the relationship of principal and agent. The rules which normally attach to the parties, the normal incidents of the relation, are ancillary to this power-liability relation. To satisfy principals' claims in a myriad of cases the judges have imposed on agents certain rules constituting safeguards against the abuse of their powers. To satisfy agents' claims for reimbursement the judges have granted certain rights to agents. But the parties, the best judges of their own interests, may exclude these normal incidents of the relation by their agreement. This power-liability relation, which, it is contended, is the nucleus of the relation of principal and agent, needs to be examined more closely. A power-liability relation is one of the fundamental legal relations. It exists between two persons, A and B, when A has the ability, conferred on him by law, by his own acts to alter B's legal relations. Agency is but one of the numerous kinds of power-liability relations recognised in our legal system. The distinctive feature of the agency power-liability relation is that the power of the one party to alter the legal relations of the other party is a reproduction of the power possessed by the latter to alter his own legal position. In other words, the power conferred by law on the agent is a facsimile of the principal's own power. This is to be inferred from the main principles of the law of agency, notably the following: when an agent acts on behalf of his principal in a legal transaction and uses the principal's name, the result in law is that the principal's legal position is altered but the agent himself drops out of the transaction: persons who are not themselves *sui juris* may nevertheless have the power to act as agents for persons who are: the power of an agent to bind his principal is limited to the power of the principal to bind himself: if the powers of the principal to alter his own legal relations are ended by his death, insanity, or bankruptcy, the agent's powers are terminated automatically . . . .

At this juncture it is tempting to define the relation of principal and agent as that existing between two legal persons, P and A, when A is invested with a legal power to alter P's legal relations which is a facsimile of the legal power possessed by P himself, and further to proceed to distinguish the relation from such other special legal relations as master-servant and trustee-beneficiary on the simple ground that in the latter relations this power-liability nexus is not essential But in common law special legal relations are not to be confined within the strait-jackets of definitions; *elegantia juris* may be achieved only at the expense of the dynamic element in our law. Moreover the distinctions between agency and these other special legal relations cannot be so sharply drawn. Suffice it to assert that in mid-twentieth-century English law the nucleus of the rules in the doctrine of principal and agent is this power-liability relation.

NOTES

1. The terms 'power' and 'authority' should not be confused. As Professor Dowrick has emphasised (op cit, p 37 fn):

A power is a legal concept: it connotes the ability of a person to alter legal relations by doing some act: an agent's power is such an ability existing in the eyes of the law. Authority is a matter of fact: it connotes that one person has given instructions or permission to another to act on his behalf. The legal attribute of an agent, his power, may be called into being by the fact that he has his principal's authority to act, but it may be called into being by other facts, such as the necessity of the case.

2. It is clear, therefore, that the principal cannot actually confer power on his agent. As Professor Montrose has explained ((1938) 16 Can Bar Rev 757 at p 761):

The term power . . . is a legal relation, one which exists by virtue of a legal rule. The power of an agent is not strictly conferred by the principal but by the law: the principal and agent do the acts which bring the rule into operation, as a result of which the agent acquires a power.

The legal rule will be brought into operation if the principal actually authorises the agent to do certain acts. Once the legal rule comes into operation the agent will be vested with power to affect the principal's legal relations with third parties. Even if the principal does not give the agent any authority, or the agent exceeds his authority, the legal rule may still be brought into operation and vest the agent with power. In such circumstances, public policy will determine the existence and extent of the agent's power to affect his principal's relations (see generally, WA Seavey (1920) 29 Yale LJ 859; and JL Montrose, op cit, p 761). For further jurisprudential discussion of the power-liability relation, see W H Hohfeld *Fundamental Legal Conceptions as Applied in Judicial Reasoning* (1923), pp 50–60; *Salmond on Jurisprudence* (12th edn, 1966), pp 22–231; RWM Dias, *Jurisprudence* (5th edn, 1985), pp 33–39.

3. Explaining agency in terms of a power-liability relationship appears to avoid the criticisms which we have already made of those definitions based on the consent of the parties (see above, p 96). However, the danger with an explanation which focuses on the agent's power to affect the principal's relations with third parties is that it shifts attention away from the *internal* relationship between the principal and agent to the *external* relationship between the principal and third party. It must always be remembered that agency is a triangular relationship between principal, agent and third party. The law of agency is as much concerned with the relationship between the principal and agent (eg the agent's right to remuneration or indemnity from the principal; the agent's fiduciary duties owed to the principal) as it is concerned with the relationship between the principal and third party. The triangular relationship between principal, agent and third party is highlighted in the next extract, taken from an article by Professor McMeel in which he subjects the power-liability analysis advanced by Professor Dowrick to penetrating criticism.

'Philosophical Foundations of the Law of Agency' by G McMeel
(2000) 116 LQR 387, pp 393–396

The seminal instance of 'power-liability' analysis is acknowledged to be Hohfeld in *Fundamental Legal Conceptions* which first appeared in 1913:

> . . . X has the power to create contractual obligations of various kinds. Agency cases are likewise instructive. By use of some metaphorical expression such as the Latin, *qui facit per alium, facit per se,* the true nature of agency relations is only too frequently obscured. The creation of the agency relation involves, inter alia, the grant of legal powers to the so-called agent, and the creation of correlative liabilities in the principal. That is to say, one party P has the power to create agency powers in another party A,—for example, the power to convey X's property, the power to impose (so-called) contractual obligations on P, the power to 'receive' title to property so that it shall vest in P, and so forth.

This discussion was contextualised in Hohfeld's conceptual critique of attempts to reduce most legal relationships simply to rights and duties. Instead, he proposed four categories of rights together with their jural correlatives and opposites. First, true *rights;* correlative: *duty;* opposite: no rights. Secondly, *privilege;* correlative: *no right;* opposite: duty. Thirdly, *power;* correlative: *liability;* opposite: disability. Fourthly, *immunity;* correlative: *disability;* opposite: liability. Further, Hohfeld suggests the nearest synonym for 'power' is '(legal) ability'. Note in the extract, Hohfeld first mentions the ability to enter into contracts. Prior to that he instanced the example of the power to dispose to one's own property.

It is clearly correct at this level of generality to classify agency reasoning as a species of legal power or ability. It was an important insight of Hart's jurisprudence that modern systems of law are constituted as much by power-conferring rules (both in the public and private spheres) as by duty-imposing norms. Such 'facilitative institutions' constitute a large segment of private law, not just contract and commercial law, but also corporate law, trusts and succession. In the particular context of agency, the deployment of conceptual tools such as 'power' and 'liability' merits close analysis. Note that Dorwick speaks of the agent having the power to affect the principal's legal relations, and the principal coming under a correlative liability to the third party. Contrast the earlier analysis of Hohfeld which more accurately captures the existence of two distinct legal powers. First, the *principal's power* to confer upon an agent the power to act upon his behalf. This results, in Pollock's graphic phrase, in the law recognising that ' . . . by agency the individual's legal personality is multiplied in space'. Note multiplication: nothing in agency doctrine forbids a principal from acting personally in respect of the business entrusted to the agent. Secondly and consequently, the *agent's power* to act upon the principal's behalf and to impose obligations on him *vis-a-vis* third parties, within the scope of his authority. Further, contrary to Dowrick's, but consistent with Hohfeld's formulation, there are two separate liabilities. First, the *principal's:* having conferred power upon the agent, he is subject to obligations and liabilities to third parties under the transactions thereby effected. Secondly, the *agent's:* if he chooses to act in accordance with the powers entrusted to him, he must do so in accordance with the legal consequences which attend agency. He must act with reasonable care and skill and he is subject to the stringency of the fiduciary regime. The first of these two distinct power-liability relationships is explicit in Hohfeld's formulation, and the second (it is submitted) is implicit in it.

Pursuing the critique of Dowrick's elision a little further it is submitted that, the true explanation of even simple legal phenomena may require complex analysis—a spider's web [of] conceptually distinct relations. Where there is a contractual regime between principal and agent, the agent may be bound to act and the principal bound to remunerate, yielding a relationship of the Hofeldian claim-rights and duties. To this framework must be added the claim-right/duty *vinculum juris* which results between principal and third party. Note that the triangular relationship involved in agency requires rejection of Dowrick's over-simplification . It is superseded by at least three logically distinct relationships. Whatever lip-service is paid to the (simplified) power-liability analysis, in practice textbooks do regard agency in this way. The details of the rules of the three sides of the triangular nexus—principal/agent; agent/contractor; contractor/principal—are analysed separately. Therefore, it is submitted, true Hohfeldian analysis yields a complex nexus of relationships at a conceptual level. Much modern agency theory fails to do justice to the Hohfeldian scheme.

So why the shift in emphasis between Hohfeld's and Dowrick's analysis? Hohfeld's discussion needs to be contextualised in his discussion of other 'facilitative institutions': agency is treated alongside the general ability to contract, and to dispose of property interests by acts of transmissive consent. The discussion is not directed to non-core instances of agency, such as apparent authority or agency of necessity, but seems to envisage only actual authority. Contrast Dowrick and other 'externalised theories' which are directed to incorporating the miscellaneous examples of non-standard doctrine into a single grand theory of agency. Therefore the double power-liability analysis of Hohfeld (which is only apt to cover consensual manifestations of agency) is transmuted into a single power-liability analysis. The agent is invested with power to affect the principal's legal relations. Therefore it is the task of jurists to enumerate the instances where the law recognises such power: there is no need to focus upon consensual instances. The principal, consequently, is under liability to any third parties who deal with the legally constituted agent: his consent is not conclusive of this legal determination. The reformulated power-liability analysis is seen has having three key strengths. First, it unites the various instances of agency into a single formulation which applies to each equally, without having to recognise any particular example (such as consensual agency) as the paradigm case. Secondly, it emphasises that the recognition of the relationship of agency is a matter of law, and not simply a determination of the facts. The answer to the legal question posed depends upon considerations of public policy generally, and is not simply focused upon consent. Thirdly, in contradistinction to the consensual model which concentrates upon the linear relationship between principal and agent, the power-liability model focuses upon the triangular configuration which is a hallmark of true agency. Rather than being attentive solely to the 'internal relationship' between principal and agent, consideration is paid to the 'external relationship' between principal/agent and contractor.

The strengths of the 'power-liability' analysis are clear, but weaknesses soon begin to surface. Is it not the case that the conceptual elegance of the resulting model is bought at the expense of under-elaboration of doctrine? Whether the agent is invested with power is treated as being a question of public policy. However once it is admitted that evidence of the principal's consent to the agent wielding power on his behalf is a sufficient public policy reason to recognise agency, there is serious danger of the 'power-liability' model collapsing into the qualified consensual approach. Further, by de-emphasising Hohfeld's 'power-to-invest-another-with-power' approach, the modern power-liability model overlooks the paradigm instance of responsibility, in favour of more marginal cases. Most significantly the refined model does not advert to the responsibilities of the agent in discharging the functions conferred upon him, such as duties of competence and fidelity. A favourite case with power-liability theorists, *Boardman v. Phipps,* where there was no consent (and no possibility of consent) to the actions of the 'self-appointed' agents, was concerned not with the liability of the principal, but the liability of the agent for breach of fiduciary duty. Therefore, like many simple models, the power-liability analysis only presents one perspective on a multi-dimensional phenomenon. This was inevitable when the aim of 'power-liability' theorists was to reduce agency relationships to the lowest common denominator.

NOTES

1.   McMeel (at p 396) considers that:

The danger of a modern 'power-liability' analysis of agency collapsing into a qualified consensual model, is not accidental. Its location on a slippery slope is inevitable and understandable once it is appreciated that the 'power-liability' and the 'consensual' model are not opposing accounts of the same legal doctrine. Rather they are examples of different types of legal theory. In truth, rather than being in opposition to one another, the two theories are readily reconcilable.

McMeel regards the 'power-liability' model as an example of 'ontological', 'conceptual' or 'descriptive' theorising, whereas he sees the 'consensual' model as a species of a 'normative', 'justificatory' or 'presumptive' analysis (see pp 396–399). In his view (expressed at p 398), '[n]othing in the "power-liability" analysis contradicts the "consensual model" and vice-versa'.

2.   McMeel places a 'qualified consent' model at the heart of his analysis of the nature of agency (at pp 400–401):

Modern contract law is at its core consensual, but is supplemented by principles which protect injurious reliance. Turning back to agency, it is submitted that a consensual model, supplemented by protection of misplaced reliance, can account for all the legally recognised instances of actual and apparent authority . . . With regard to other agency doctrines, ratification or *post hoc* authority can be regarded as a matter of commercial reality, recognising that authorisation as a matter of mercantile practice may not always be neatly contemporaneous with the initial transaction. Similarly, the agent's liability for breach of warranty of authority can be seen as an archetypal instance of legal protection for misplaced reliance upon the deed or words of others.

McMeel acknowledges that agency of necessity is more difficult to account for, but regards true agency of necessity (ie where the necessitous intervener creates contractual rights and obligations between principal and third party) as so rare 'that it seems misguided to distort the conceptual account of the nature of agency just in order to accommodate it' (at p 409).

3.   In response, it is submitted that while actual consent lies at the heart of most agency cases, this can just as readily be seen as one of several 'triggers' that activate the legal rule vesting the agent with power to affect the principal's legal relations with third parties. The power-liability theory embraces cases of actual consent and also what McMeel describes as cases involving 'protection of misplaced reliance'. We shall see (at pp 117–128) that in cases of apparent authority the principal may become exposed to contractual liabilities to a third party without the benefit of reciprocal rights (hence the need for ratification). This, it is submitted, is a public policy response to acts or omissions of the principal that are far removed from anything that can in reality (as opposed to by some legal fiction) be described as 'consent'. Even the objective principle when applied to contract formation allows both parties (including the party whose intentions have been objectively assessed) to enforce the resultant contract. Finally, it is submitted that the consent theory cannot stand on its own two feet: it requires support from at least two sources. The first is that it must be 'supplemented by the principle protecting misplaced reliance (or the policy favouring an objective reading of commercial communications)'; the second is that 'it is further supplemented by instances of policy motivated recognitions of agency' (McMeel, p 410).

(b)   Agency distinguished from other relationships

We have seen how Professor Dowrick distinguished agency from other power-liability relationships. But what are those other relationships?

Agency and trusts. Agents and trustees are similar in many ways. They can, for example, both affect the legal position of those persons with whose affairs they are dealing and are both accountable to their principals for any profits derived from their position. However, these similarities mask an important conceptual difference between the two institutions. Whereas an agent acts for another, a trustee holds property for another. This means that the beneficial owner of the property held in trust will usually be able to enforce his rights against the trustee on a proprietary basis, whereas a principal may only be able to enforce his rights against an agent on a personal basis (although the principal may have a proprietary remedy against an agent who has breached his fiduciary duties: see, eg *A-G for Hong Kong v Reid* [1994] 1 AC 324, PC). Furthermore, whereas an agent represents his principal to the outside world, the trustee does not represent the beneficiary and so cannot create contractual relations between that beneficiary and third parties. For further differences between agency and trusts, see *Fridman,* pp 23–27.

Finally, it is important to note that a normal principal and agent relationship does not of itself give rise to a trust relationship (*Kingscroft Insurance Co Ltd v HS Weavers (Underwriting) Agencies Ltd* [1993] 1 Lloyd's Rep 187 at 191, *per* Harman J). Whether there is a simultaneous trust relationship between the principal and agent will depend on the intentions of the parties, which are usually ascertained from the terms of the agency contract (see *Bowstead and Reynolds,* para 6–040).

Agency and bailment. Bailment occurs when there is the delivery or transfer of a chattel (or other item of personal property) by one person (the bailor) to another (the bailee) with a specific mandate which requires the identical item to be delivered up to the bailor or to be dealt with in a particular way by the bailee (see above, pp 78ff). There are two important features which distinguish agency and bailment; namely:

(1) the bailee merely exercises, with leave of the bailor, certain powers over the bailed property but, unlike the agent, the bailee does not represent the bailor; and

(2) the bailee cannot enter into contracts on the bailor's behalf, although he may have power to do things which are reasonably incidental to his use of the goods which he holds (eg to have the property repaired) and thereby make the bailor liable to a third party (see, for example, *Tappenden v Artus* [1964] 2 QB 185, below, p 1114).

Agency and sale. Consider the following scenarios:

(1) A asks B to acquire goods for him, and B is held to be A's agent. In these circumstances A will be privy to any contract B makes with his supplier, B will not be liable for failing to acquire the goods if he has used his best endeavours to do so, and B will not be liable if the goods prove defective so long as he exercised due care and skill in his purchase from the third party. On the other hand, if B agrees to obtain the goods and resell them to A there will be no privity between A and B's supplier, B will be absolutely liable to A if he does not obtain the goods, and B will also be liable to A for defects in the goods (under express terms of the contract of sale, or under terms implied by the Sale of Goods Act 1979, ss 13–15).

(2) C agrees to dispose of D's goods, and C is held to be D's agent. In these circumstances D will be privy to any contract of sale made by C with a third party, D (not C) will be liable to the third party on the contract of sale for defects in the goods, and if the third party pays C, who fails to account to D for the money, the third party will only be discharged if C was authorised to receive his payment. On the other hand, if C is held to have purchased the goods from D there will be no privity between D and the third party, C (not

D) will be liable to the third party on the contract of sale for defects in the goods, and the third party will be discharged if he pays C.

The importance of distinguishing between agency and sale is clear. But it may not always be easy to make the distinction. In the world of commerce the term 'agent' is often used without regard to its legal meaning (eg a car dealer may describe himself as the 'agent' of a particular manufacturer, but it is probably the case that he purchases the vehicles from the manufacturer and resells them to his own customers). However, the distinction can be made according to whether the 'agent' intended to act on his own behalf or on behalf of someone else. If the evidence shows that he intended to act on his own behalf he cannot be an agent, for an agency relationship can only arise when one person intends to act on behalf of another. Of particular relevance to this issue is the extent to which the 'agent' is accountable to the 'principal' for moneys received by him and also whether the resale price is fixed by the 'agent' or the 'principal'. But no single factor need be decisive of the issue and each case must be examined on its facts. Thus, in *AMB Imballaggi Plastici SRL v Pacflex Ltd* [1999] 2 All ER (Comm) 249, the Court of Appeal held that a price 'mark up' was a telling factor pointing to the conclusion that a party was not an agent but a principal and thus not a 'commercial agent' within reg 2(1) of the Commercial Agents (Council Directive) Regulations 1993 (see p 106, below). On the other hand, in *Mercantile International Group plc v Chuan Soon Huat Industrial Group Ltd* [2002] EWCA Civ 288, [2002] 1 All ER (Comm) 788, the Court of Appeal reached the opposite conclusion. There the claimant (agent) charged more to third parties than it confirmed to the defendant (principal). The mark up, whose amount was unknown to and uncontrolled by the defendant, was retained by the claimant, who received no other commission for its services. The Court of Appeal held that there was an agency relationship between the claimant and the defendant as there was documentation (agreed not to be a sham) which purported to describe the relationship between claimant, defendant and third parties in these terms. The Court held that the absence of such documentation in the *AMB* case distinguished that case from this. Rix LJ did note (at 791), however, that it was 'common ground that the word 'agent' can be carelessly and indiscriminately used, and that the test is ultimately one of substance rather than form'.

Agency, distributorship and franchising. When a manufacturer supplies goods to a distributor or a franchisee that person may be described as a 'selling agent' or 'exclusive agent' of the manufacturer. Often the distributor/franchisee will have agreed to promote the sale of the manufacturer's goods and be prohibited from selling goods of rival manufacturers (which may raise restraint of trade and UK and EC competition law issues: see below, pp 108–109). Yet, whatever the extent of the additional obligations the distributor/franchisee has contractually undertaken, the central relationship between the parties is usually one of sale not agency. This is because the distributor/franchisee will buy the goods from the manufacturer and resell them to his own customers. However, difficult issues of agency law are raised when the contract of sale between the manufacturer and the distributor/franchisee contain reservation of title clauses, which authorise the distributor/franchisee to sell the goods as agent for the manufacturer (see *Aluminium Industrie Vaassen BV v Romalpa Aluminium Ltd* [1976] 1 WLR 676, considered below at pp 452ff; FMB Reynolds (1978) 94 LQR 224, 235–238).

Agency, servants and independent contractors. As some servants (or employees) and some independent contractors have agency powers, whereas others do not, there may be little practical value in attempting to distinguish these persons from agents (see *Bowstead and Reynolds*, para 1–030; cf *Fridman*, pp 31–37). The issue tends to arise in the context of vicarious liability. The principle upon which vicarious liability depends is well-established: 'It is that the wrong of the servant or agent for which the master or principal is liable is one committed in the case of a servant in the course of his employment, and in the case of an agent in the course of his authority.' (*Crédit Lyonnais Bank Nederland NV v Export Credits Guarantee Department* [2000] 1 AC 486 at 494, per Lord Woolf MR, sitting in the House of Lords). Where an employee also acts as his employer's agent, there may be a question over whether the course of his employment is co-extensive with the course of his authority, actual or apparent. It seems likely that an employee who acts within the scope of his actual or apparent authority also acts within the course of his employment. However, it is possible to envisage situations where the agent acts outside the scope of his actual or apparent authority, but within the course of his employment. Is the employer to be held vicariously liable for his employee's torts in the latter case? The answer to this question depends on the nature of the tort (see especially *Armagas Ltd v Mundogas SA, The Ocean Frost* [1986] AC 717, CA and HL). In cases of deceit, or other torts where the claimant relies on a representation made by the employee, the employer will only be held vicariously liable where the employee acts within the scope of his actual or apparent authority. Thus in *Lloyd v Grace, Smith & Co* [1912] AC 716, a clerk, employed by a firm of solicitors, fraudulently persuaded a widow to transfer her property to him and was able to do this because of the position he had been placed in by his employer. The House of Lords held the firm of solicitors vicariously liable for the clerk's fraud on the ground that he had acted within the scope of his apparent authority. By contrast, in *Hornsby v Clark Kenneth Leventhal* [1998] PNLR 635, the Court of Appeal held that a firm of accountants was not vicariously liable for the fraud of their employee where the claimant had known that the business conducted by the employee in his employer's time, and on the employer's premises, was not the business of his employer. On the other hand, where the tort involves no reliance by the claimant upon a representation of the employee, eg those torts involving intentional or negligent physical acts by the employee, then the employer will be held vicariously liable where all the features of the wrong which were necessary to make the employee liable occurred in the course of his employment (*Crédit Lyonnais Bank Nederland NV v Export Credits Guarantee Department,* above).

Finally, it is important to note that the relationships between agency and (1) trusts, (2) bailment, (3) distributors/franchisees, (4) servants/independent contractors, are not mutually exclusive, eg a trustee *may* also have agency powers in appropriate circumstances, an agent *may* hold money or property as trustee or bailee. But the relationship between agency and sale is mutually exclusive; as the editor of *Bowstead and Reynolds* states (para 1–032): 'in respect of a particular transaction a person cannot be acting as agent if he is a buyer from or seller to his principal and vice versa'.

(c) Examples of types of agent

There are many different types of agent. They include:

(1) auctioneers, who are agents for the seller, but may also be agents for the buyer for certain purposes (*Hinde v Whitehouse* (1806) 7 East 558);

(2) directors, who are agents of the company when they act collectively as a Board of Directors (although the company's Articles of Association usually provide also for delegation of some or all of the Board's functions to individual directors);

(3) partners, who are agents of the firm and their other partners for the purpose of the business of the partnership (Partnership Act 1890, s 5); and

(4) solicitors and counsel, who are agents of their clients when, *inter alia*, they effect a com-
    promise of matters connected with, but not merely collateral to, the litigation in ques-
    tion (*Waugh v HB Clifford & Sons Ltd* [1982] Ch 374).

There are other types of 'agent' who may have little or no power to change their principal's
legal relations with third parties but nevertheless owe fiduciary obligations to their principal. Estate agents are an example of this type of agent, for their powers are extremely limited.
Whilst they may have power to make representations about the property (*Sorrell v Finch*
[1977] AC 728 at 753), they have no power to make a contract between their client and the
prospective purchaser, unless specifically authorised to do so (*Spiro v Lintern* [1973] 1 WLR
1002, where there was such authority). Such agents do not fit into the power-liability analysis
of agency outline by Professor Dowrick (above, pp 96–97) and have been described by one
commentator as 'anomalous' (*Fridman,* p 13 fn) and by another as 'incomplete' (*Bowstead
and Reynolds,* para 1–019).
    We shall now turn to those agents who play a particular role in commercial transactions.

Factors. The term 'factor' was used to a great extent in the nineteenth century and is now
important for the understanding of cases from that era. A factor was an agent who was given
possession or control of goods to be sold for his principal. He usually sold the goods in his
own name without disclosing the name of his principal (*Baring v Corrie* (1818) 2B& Aid
137), although he would remain a factor if he sold the goods in his principal's name (*Stevens
v Biller* (1883) 25 Ch D 31). Those who purchased goods from the factor could often rely on
his apparent authority to sell them, or his apparent ownership of them, to validate any disposition which had not been authorised by the factor's principal. But the term 'factor' is little
used in its traditional sense today (although see below, p 1026, for the term being used in a
different sense). The Factors Act 1889 introduced the term 'mercantile agent' to cover those
persons (including factors) who had a statutory power to make unauthorised dispositions
which would bind their principal (see below, p 364). It is now more important to identify a
person as a mercantile agent than it is to identify him as a factor. For a legal history of the
factor, see RJC Munday (1977) 6 Anglo-American LR 221.

Brokers. A broker is a negotiator who makes contracts between buyers and sellers of goods.
Unlike a factor, the broker is not given possession or control of the goods he sells and he may
not sell those goods in his own name (*Baring v Corrie,* above). But it should be noted that
there are other types of broker eg stockbroker, insurance broker and credit-broker (considered by *Fridman,* p 38).

Del credere agent. A *del credere* agent, in return for an extra commission, undertakes to
indemnify the principal should the principal suffer loss as a result of the failure of a customer, introduced by the agent, to pay the purchase price of the goods sold, when the price
is ascertained and due (*Morris v Cleasby* (1816) 4 M & S 566). A *del credere* agent can only be
made liable to pay the price of the goods on default or insolvency of the buyer; the principal
is not entitled to litigate with a *del credere* agent any disputes arising out of the performance
of the contract of sale made by the agent (*Thomas Gabriel & Sons v Churchill and Sim* [1914]
3 KB 1272). *Del credere* agents are of particular use to exporters who are uncertain of the
financial risks and creditworthiness of overseas buyers introduced by the agent. However,
the modern practice is for an exporter to rely on documentary credits (see below, p 849),
credit guarantees (see below, p 928) and confirmations (see immediately below) to secure
payment from overseas buyers.

Confirming houses. A confirming house usually acts as an agent for an overseas buyer who
wishes to import goods. As such the confirming house may do one of the following:

(1) purchase goods in the domestic market as agent for the overseas buyer and not itself become liable to the seller on the contract of sale;

(2) buy from the seller as principal and then resell to the overseas buyer;

(3) act as agent of the overseas buyer with regard to the contract of sale but also enter into a collateral contract with the seller whereby the confirming house agrees to be liable for the solvency of, and performance of the contract of sale by, the overseas buyer: this is known as 'confirmation' (see *Sobell Industries Ltd v Cory Bros & Co* [1955] 2 Lloyd's Rep 82); and

(4) purchase from the seller as principal and yet remain as an agent in relation to the overseas buyer (*Anglo-African Shipping Co of New York Inc v J Mortner Ltd* [1962] 1 Lloyd's Rep 610, may well be an example of this). For further discussion, see DJ Hill (1972) Journal of Maritime Law and Commerce 307.

Commission agents. A commission agent (sometimes called 'commission merchant') contracts with third parties as a principal in his own name, although all contracts will be made by the agent on behalf of his own principal. As a consequence, the commission agent creates privity of contract between himself and the third party (not between his principal and the third party), yet remains in an agency relationship with his own principal. Although this type of agency is well established in civil law countries (where it is called 'indirect representation'), it has not been generally recognised in English law (early recognition by Blackburn J in *Ireland v Livingston* (1872) LR 5 HL 395 and *Robinson v Mollett* (1875) LR 7 HL 802 has found little support in more recent cases: see *Bowstead and Reynolds,* para 1–021). One reason why this type of agency has not been assimilated into English law is that it does not sit easily, if at all, with the traditional agency theory that the hallmark of an agent is his power to alter the principal's legal relations with third parties and then drop out of the transaction himself. However, whilst English law has not been prepared to recognise a general category of 'commission agent' there is evidence from commercial practice that certain agents do enter into contracts with third parties as principals and yet remain in an agency relationship with their own principal (see example (4) under 'Confirming houses', above). The doctrine of undisclosed principal is analogous to the civil law contract of commission (where 'commission' refers to the entrusting of a task to the agent and not the method of payment), although, unlike a commission agent, the agent of an undisclosed principal makes his principal liable and entitled on the contract, subject to the rules of election and merger (FMB Reynolds (1978) 94 LQR 224, p 234). For a strong case in support of recognition of the commission agent in English law, see DJ Hill (1968) 31 MLR 623; see also [1964] JBL 304; [1967] JBL 122; cf *Fridman,* pp 30, 49–50).

(d) Agency law and the European Community

(i) Self-employed commercial agents

On 1 January 1994 the Commercial Agents (Council Directive) Regulations 1993 (SI 1993/3053, as amended), implementing EC Directive 86/653 on self-employed commercial agents, came into force. The EC Directive was drafted in response to a perceived need to protect self-employed commercial agents against exploitation by their principals. In *Page v Combined Shipping and Trading Co Ltd* [1997] 3 All ER 656, 660, Staughton LJ said that the preamble to the Directive suggested that 'commercial agents are a down-trodden race, and need and should be afforded protection against their principals' (although in *Lonsdale v Howard & Hallam Ltd* [2007] UKHL 32, [2007] 1 WLR 2055 at [19], Lord Hoffmann remarked that Staughton LJ's comment was made 'with more than a touch of irony' and constituted 'generalities which do not help one to decide what protection is sufficient to give effect to the policy of the Directive'). Through the terms of the Directive, and the implementing Regulations, commercial agents have been given protection against their principals in a way which treats them more as employees than as the independent contractors which most of them are. This represents a new departure for English law. Hitherto, English law has not singled out any particular category of agent for special protection: the common law rules as to the relationship between principal and agent being based on freedom of contract.

The Regulations govern the relations between commercial agents and their principals and, unless the parties have agreed that the agency agreement is to be governed by the law of another Member State, apply in relation to the activities of commercial agents in Great Britain (reg 1(2), (3)). Regulation l(3)(b) confirms that an agent who performs his duties outside Great Britain but within another Member State of the Euoropean Economic Area, under an agreement governed by English law, falls within the Regulations, provided the law of that other Member State implementing the Directive allows the parties to agree that the agency contract is to be governed by the law of a different Member State. The Regulations also have extra-territorial effect. In *Ingmar GB Ltd v Eaton Leonard Technologies Inc* Case C-381/98 [2001] 1 All ER (Comm) 329, an English agent conducted activities in the UK for a Californian principal under an agency contract which the parties expressly chose to be governed by Californian law. The English Court of Appeal asked the European Court of Justice for a preliminary ruling on whether the Regulations laid down mandatory rules which should apply regardless of the choice of law. The ECJ held that they do. The purpose of the Directive was to protect commercial agents on a uniform basis throughout the Community. 'It must therefore be held that it is essential for the Community legal order that a principal established in a non-member country, whose commercial agent carries on his activity within the Community, cannot evade those provisions by the simple expedient of a choice-of-law clause' (para 25). The rights given by the Directive must be applied whenever the commercial agent carries on business in a Member State, irrespective of the law chosen by the parties to govern their contract. For criticism of this decision, see Verhagen (2002) 51 ICLQ 135.

A commercial agent is defined in the Regulations as 'a self-employed intermediary who has continuing authority to negotiate the sale or purchase of goods on behalf of another person (the "principal"), or to negotiate and conclude the sale or purchase of goods on behalf of and in the name of that principal' (reg 2(1)). Several points emerge from this definition.

(1) The agent must be self-employed. This means that the agent must be what the common law would describe as an 'independent contractor'. Hence a company or a partnership can be a commercial agent (*Bell Electrical Ltd v Aweco Appliance Systems GmbH & Co KG* [2002] EWHC 872 (QB), [2002] CLC 1246 at [50], Elias J).

(2) The agent must have 'continuing authority'. This means that an agent appointed for a single transaction would fall outside the definition of a commercial agent. However, the European Court of Justice has recently held, in a preliminary ruling, that where a self-employed intermediary has authority to conclude a single contract, subsequently extended over several years, the condition in art 1(2) of the Directive (same definition of 'commercial agent' as found in reg 2(1)) that the authority be 'continuing' required that the principal should have conferred continuing authority on that intermediary to negotiate successive extensions to that contract; the mere fact that the intermediary maintained relations with

the principal throughout the contractual period was, in itself, insufficient to demonstrate such authority (*Poseidon Chartering BV v Marianne Zeeschip VOF*, Case C-3/04, [2006] 2 Lloyd's Rep 105). In *Light v Ty Europe Ltd* [2003] EWCA Civ 1238, [2004] 1 Lloyd's Rep 693, the Court of Appeal held that a sub-agent, who had contracted with the principal's agent and not with the principal himself, could have continuing authority to act for the principal and so fall within the definition of a commercial agent in reg 2(1), but that as there was no direct contractual relationship between them, the sub-agent could not rely on the rights and obligations laid down by the Regulations as against the principal. The decision may be criticised for failing to adopt a purposive approach to the construction of legislation which is based on a European Directive. The Court of Appeal left open the question whether a sub-agent could claim under the Regulations against the agent (Ward LJ was prepared to contemplate that he could). The problem for the sub-agent with this claim is that it may prove difficult to convince a court that he has continuing authority to negotiate sales on behalf of the agent as opposed to the real principal.

(3) The agent must have continuing authority to 'negotiate' on behalf of the principal. In *Parks v Esso Petroleum Co Ltd* (1999) 19 Tr LR 232, the Court of Appeal held that a person selling fuel under a licence at a self service petrol-station did not 'negotiate' with motorists who bought petrol, and hence was not a commercial agent, because he did not 'deal with, manage or conduct' (the Oxford English Dictionary definition of 'negotiate') the sales to motorists since he took no part in their choice and self-service and so did not provide any skill or consideration. The decision has been rightly criticised for its narrow interpretation of what is meant by negotiation (see S Sainter [2001] JBL 540). By contrast, the Irish High Court took a broader view of 'negotiate' in *Kenny v Ireland ROC Ltd* [2005] IEHC 241, where again the question was whether an agent who ran a self-service petrol station had authority to 'negotiate' on behalf of his principal. Clark J held the agent to be a commercial agent because he exercised a 'limited but not insignificant autonomy' over the way the forecourt and shop were run and in his relations with some suppliers. It seems that Mr Kenny had a higher degree of responsibility and autonomy than Mr Parks and so the two cases are distinguishable on that ground. However, Clark J went further and said (at [6.1]) that insofar as the decision in *Parks* was to be taken as implying that it was not possible for a person to be a commercial agent when that person exercised skill in attracting customers, but where the ultimate transaction was by self-service and payment, he would not find the judgment persuasive and would not follow it. There is evidence of this broader view now finding favour this side of the Irish sea. In *PJ Pipe & Valve Co v Audco India Ltd* [2005] EWHC 1904 (QB), [2006] Eu LR 368, Fulford J held that an agent who introduced customers to his principal, but had no authority to negotiate price or bind his principal to a sale agreement, was nevertheless a commercial agent because he contributed to the development of goodwill in his principal's business. This approach to the meaning of 'negotiate' is to be welcomed for it gives effect to the purpose of the legislation, which is to protect an agent who builds up business goodwill within a particular area for his principal (see further C Gardiner [2007] JBL 412, 414–420).

(4) A person who buys and sells as principal, and therefore acts on his own behalf and not on behalf of another, is not a commercial agent within the Regulations. A distributor purchasing goods from a manufacturer and selling the goods on at an increased price (the 'mark-up') is a good example of this (*AMB Imballaggi Plastici SRL v Pacflex Ltd* [1999] 2 All ER (Comm) 249, CA). But charging a mark-up is not always decisive of the issue; other factors, eg the contractual documentation, may indicate an agency relationship despite the

presence of a mark-up (*Mercantile International Group plc v Chuan Soon Huat Industrial Group Ltd* [2002] EWCA Civ 288, [2002] 1 All ER (Comm) 788, CA: see above, p 102).

A few commercial agents (ie those whose activities are unpaid, those who work on commodity exchanges and in commodity markets, and Crown Agents for Overseas Governments) are expressly excluded from the Regulations (reg 2(2)), and this exclusion also extends to anyone whose activities as a commercial agent are considered as *secondary* (reg 2(3), (4)). The Directive contemplates that the activities of the person as agent are secondary when they are not his primary activities as compared to the rest of his business. However, the Schedule to the Regulations seems to contemplate a different test involving only an assessment of the agent's arrangements with the principal and not a comparison with the agent's other business (which is how Morison J applied the test in *Tamarind International Ltd v Eastern Natural Gas (Retail) Ltd* [2000] CLC 1397). In *Crane v Sky In-Home Service Ltd* [2007] EWHC 66 (Ch), [2007] 2 All ER (Comm) 599, where the agent's activities (which related to the sale of Sky box packages) were held to be secondary, Briggs J (at [59]) considered that the Schedule was 'directed at distinguishing between a relationship where the agent develops goodwill ... which passes to the principal, and one where that does not happen'. The Court of Appeal has highlighted the (apparently unintentional) inconsistency between the Directive and the Schedule to the Regulations, and called for speedy amendment to bring the Regulations in line with the Directive (*AMB Imballaggi Plastici*, above); nevertheless, the UK's power to make special provision in the Schedule has recently been affirmed (*Crane*, above, at [41]). The Regulations contain a rebuttable presumption that the activities of mail order catalogue agents for consumer goods and consumer credit agents are secondary (Sch, para 5). But there is some uncertainty as to the burden of proof in general. A number of Scottish cases have placed the burden of proof on the person alleging that he is a commercial agent, but this was doubted by the English Court of Appeal in *Edwards v International Connection (UK) Ltd* [2006] EWCA Civ 662, where it is suggested that if a claimant can show that reg 2(1) applies to him it might be for the defendant to show that his activities are secondary within reg 2(4) and the Schedule.

The main effects of the Regulations will be referred to at appropriate points in the chapters which follow. At this stage, by way of summary, it should be noted that the Regulations cover such matters as the rights and duties of the principal and commercial agent (regs 3–5), remuneration of the commercial agent (regs 6–12), termination of the agency agreement (regs 13–16), the agent's right to an indemnity or compensation on termination of the agency agreement (regs 17–19), and restraint of trade clauses (reg 20). In many respects these provisions merely reflect the existing position at common law, although English lawyers will find the requirement that each party acts dutifully and *in good faith* towards the other somewhat unfamiliar (regs 3(1) and 4(1): see also above, p 00). However, the introduction of the agent's right to compensation on termination of his agency, above and beyond any claim he may have for damages for breach of contract by the principal, does mark a radical new departure from existing common law principles.

(ii) Competition law

Articles 81 and 82 of the EC Treaty (formerly numbered as arts 85 and 86 respectively until the Treaty of Amsterdam came into force on 1 May 1999) are the main European Community competition provisions. Article 81(1) prohibits, as incompatible with the common market, all agreements between undertakings that may affect trade between Member States and which have as their object or effect the prevention, restriction or distortion of competition within the common market. Article 82 prohibits, as incompatible with the common market, any abuse by one or more undertakings of a dominant position within the common market or a substantial part of it, in so far as it affects trade between Member States. The UK's Competition Act 1998 mirrors these provisions. It is beyond the scope of this book to consider the provisions of the EC Treaty that relate to competition, or the similar provisions in the Competition Act 1998 in any detail (see generally, R Whish *Competition Law* (5th edn, 2003); A Albors-Llorens *EC Competition Law and Policy* (2002), for detailed discussion).

Many agency agreements fall outside art 81(1). The European Commission's *Guidelines on Vertical Restraints* ([2000] OJ C 291/1) defines agency agreements as those that cover a situation where one person negotiates and/or concludes contracts on behalf of another for the purchase or sale of goods or services, by or from the principal (para 12). In the case of a 'genuine' agency agreement, Article 81 does not apply to the obligations imposed on the agent, but in the case of a 'non-genuine' agency agreement it may do. The factor which determines whether art 81(1) applies is 'the financial or commercial risk borne by the agent in relation to the activities for which he has been appointed as an agent by the principal' (para 13). In essence, the more the agent accepts risk the more likely it is that the agreement falls within art 81(1). However, even a 'genuine' agency agreement may be caught by art 81(1) where it contains non-compete provisions which could foreclose access to the market (para 19), or if it facilitates an anti-competitive agreement or concerted practice (para 20).

An agency agreement falling within art 81(1) may still be eligible for block exemption under Regulation 2790/99 on Vertical Agreements and Concerted Practices ([1999] OJ L 336/21). Regulation 2790/99 entered into force on 1 January 2000, and the block exemption conferred by it applies with effect from 1 June 2000. The Regulation replaced a series of earlier Regulations conferring block exemptions for exclusive distribution, exclusive purchasing and franchising agreements. Paragraph 13 of the *Guidelines* states that Regulation 2790/99 is capable of application to 'non-genuine' agency agreements. To come within the block exemption it would be necessary for the agency agreement to avoid the 'hard-core' restrictions set out in art 4 of the Regulation (ie certain types of severely anti-competitive restrictions such as minimum and resale prices, and certain types of territorial protection) and non-compete provisions of the kind set out in art 5 of the Regulation.

It used to be possible for the European Commission to grant individual exemption to a vertical agreement which infringed art 81(1) and was ineligible for block exemption under Regulation 2790/99. The agreement had to satisfy the terms of art 81(3), ie contribute to improving the production or distribution of goods or promote technical and economic progress, while allowing consumers a fair share of the resulting benefit. However, the system of notifying agreements to the Commission for individual exemption was abolished in May 2004 under Regulation 1/2003. Henceforth, national courts and national competition authorities are to apply the provisions of art 81(3) to vertical (and any other) agreements.

By reg 20 of the Commercial Agents (Council Directive) Regulations 1993 (above, p 105), a restraint of trade clause restricting the right of a commercial agent to act as such after termination of an agency contract will only be valid if, and to the extent that, it is in writing; it relates to the geographical area, or to both the group of customers and the geographical area, and to the kind of goods in respect of which the commercial agent has a right to act; it is reasonable from the point of view of the principal and the commercial agent and their common customers; and it does not apply for a period of more than two years after the termination of the agency contract. The restraint of trade clause would also be subject to the common law on restraint of trade agreements (as to which, see E Peel *Treitel's Law of Contract* (12th edn, 2007), paras 11-056ff): see reg 20(3).

(e) Harmonisation of agency law

To facilitate the unification of international trade law, a diplomatic conference held in Geneva in 1983, and attended by delegations from 58 countries, approved a Convention on Agency in the International Sale of Goods. The Convention, based on a draft prepared by the International Institute for the Unification of Private Law (UNIDROIT), supplements the rules contained in the 1980 Vienna Convention on Contracts for the International Sale of Goods (see below, p 489). Like the Vienna Convention, the Geneva Convention will enter into force when ratified by ten states (art 33(1)). Neither Convention has been ratified by the United Kingdom.

The Geneva Convention only applies where:

(1) the agent has authority or purports to have authority on behalf of the principal to conclude a contract for the sale of goods with a third party (art 1(1));

(2) the principal and the third party have their places of business in different states (art 2(1)); and

(3) the agent has his place of business in a contracting state or the rules of private international law lead to the application of the law of a contracting state (art 2(1)).

If the third party did not know, nor ought to have known, that the agent was acting as an agent, then the Convention will only apply if the agent and the third party had their places of business in different states and if the requirements of art 2(1) are satisfied (art 2(2)). Certain types of agency, eg the agency of a dealer on a stock, commodity or other exchange, fall outside the provisions of the Convention (art 3).

The Geneva Convention is concerned only with relations between the principal or agent on the one hand, and the third party on the other (art 1(3)). The Convention does not regulate the internal relationship between the principal and the agent. This omission, which was necessary to ensure the adoption of the Convention, may reduce the practical importance of the Geneva Convention (M J Bonell (1984) 32 *American Journal of Comparative Law* 717 at p 747). However, within its stated object, the Convention does represent an impressive attempt to assimilate the different common law and civil law rules of agency. For detailed analysis of the Geneva Convention, see M Evans [1984] Uniform Law Review 74; and Bonell, op cit, which contains a copy of the text of the Convention.

CHAPTER 4

CREATION OF AGENCY AND THE AUTHORITY OF THE AGENT

1 CREATION OF THE AGENCY RELATIONSHIP

The relationship of principal and agent may be created in any one of the following ways:

(1) by express or implied agreement between principal and agent;

(2) under the doctrine of apparent authority (see below, pp 117–128);

(3) by operation of law (see below, pp 133–139); and

(4) by ratification of the agent's acts by the principal (see below, pp 139–149).

Agency arising out of agreement will always be consensual but it need not be contractual. An agency may be gratuitous. Even in the commercial context the agency may not be contractual (although this is rare). As Coleman J said in *Yasuda Fire & Marine Insurance Co of Europe Ltd v Orion Marine Insurance Underwriting Agency Ltd* [1995] QB 174 at 185:

Although in modern commercial transactions agencies are almost invariably founded upon a contract between principal and agent, there is no necessity for such a contract to exist. It is sufficient if there is consent by the principal to the exercise by the agent of authority and consent by the agent to his exercising such authority on behalf of the principal.

The main differences between a purely consensual and a contractual agency are (1) the presence or absence of consideration, and (2) the fact that with a contractual agency the agent is usually under an *obligation* to carry out his functions and the principal is under a corresponding obligation to remunerate him. The agent's contractual right to remuneration must be distinguished from his right to an indemnity for loss and expense incurred in the execution of his duties. The right to an indemnity arises by operation of law irrespective of any agreement between the parties (see below, p 242).

The agreement between the principal and agent may be expressed orally, in writing or by deed (usually called a 'power of attorney'). In general, no formality is required and an agent may be appointed orally even when he is appointed to make a contract which has to be in writing or evidenced in writing, as with a contract for the purchase of land or a contract of guarantee (*Heard v Pilley* (1869) 4 Ch App 548). But there are some statutory exceptions to this rule (eg Law of Property Act 1925, ss 53(1), 54). Furthermore, if an agent is appointed to *execute* a deed, his appointment must be by deed (*Berkeley v Hardy* (1826) 5 B & C 355), unless the agent executes the deed in the presence of the principal (*Ball v Dunsterville* (1791) 4 Term Rep 313). But under s 1(1)(c) of the Law of Property (Miscellaneous Provisions) Act 1989 a deed is no longer required to authorise *delivery* of a deed. Under the Commercial Agents (Council Directive) Regulations 1993 (above, p 105), a commercial agent and his principal are each entitled to receive from the other, on request, a signed written statement of the terms of the agency contract, including any terms agreed after the creation of the agency contract (reg 13(1)). This does not mean that the agency contract must be in writing, but it does require each party to provide the other with a written record of its terms. This right may not be waived (reg 13(2)).

Alternatively, the agreement between the principal and agent may be implied from their conduct (see *Garnac Grain Co Inc v HMF Faure and Fairclough Ltd* [1968] AC 1130 at 1137, per Lord Pearson). For example, the consent of the principal may be implied from the fact that he appointed a person to a position in which he would usually act as agent for the person who appoints him (see *Pole v Leask* (1862) 33 LJ Ch 155 at 161–162). The principal may simply acquiesce in the acts of another, but consent will not be presumed merely from the principal's silence, unless other factors indicate that he acquiesced in the agency (*Burnside v Dayrell* (1849) 3 Exch 224). The consent of the agent may be inferred from the fact that he purports to act on behalf of the principal (*Roberts v Ogilby* (1821) 9 Price 269). But merely doing what the principal requests does not invariably result in an agency relationship. As Professor Powell has stated (*The Law of Agency* (2nd ed, 1961), p 297):

Suppose, for example, that A is about to buy for himself a racehorse called Saucy Sally and receives [an e-mail] from P: 'Buy Saucy Sally for me at £900.' Must it be supposed that A's subsequent purchase of the horse, even at £900, makes A P's agent with a liability to deliver the horse to P? Or that P's authorisation imposes on A any obligation to communicate to P his refusal to act as P's agent? If, therefore, the indication of A's consent is to be the performance of an act by A, that act must show unequivocally that A has consented to act as P's agent.

Finally, it should be noted that any person who is capable of consenting can act as an agent, even though he has only limited or no contractual capacity himself (although any contractual liability to his principal or a third party would depend on his contractual capacity). In general, the principal will only be bound by the contracts and acts of his agent if the principal has capacity to contract or to do the act himself (but see s 39(1) of the Companies Act 2006 for an example of an exception to this rule: 'the validity of an act done by a company shall not be called into question on the ground of lack of capacity by reason of anything in the company's constitution').

QUESTION

Adam writes to Bill asking him to purchase a particular Ming vase for him and promising to reimburse Bill the cost of the purchase. Before Bill receives the letter, he purchases the vase as a birthday present for Adam and gives it to him. The next day Bill receives Adam's letter and now seeks to recover the cost of the vase from him.

Advise Bill. Would it make any difference to your answer if Bill had bought the vase in anticipation of receiving instructions from Adam to do so, rather than as a present for him? See *Bowstead and Reynolds*, para 2–033.

2 AUTHORITY OF THE AGENT

The relationship between the 'power' and 'authority' of an agent was considered in the previous chapter (above, p 97). However, you will see from what appears below that the term 'authority' is not always used in its strict sense.

(a) Actual authority

Whether an agent has authority is a question of fact. If the principal has given prior consent to the agent acting on his behalf then the agent can be said to have 'actual' authority. Actual authority will be conferred on the agent by the principal under the terms of the agreement or contract between them. As Diplock LJ stated in *Freeman and Lockyer v Buckhurst Park Properties (Mangal) Ltd* [1964] 2 QB 480 at 502:

An 'actual' authority is a legal relationship between principal and agent created by a consensual agreement to which they alone are parties. Its scope is to be ascertained by applying ordinary principles of construction of contracts, including any proper implications from the express words used, the usages of the trade, or the business between the parties.

Ascertaining the scope of the agent's actual authority is important. As a general rule, only if the agent acts within the scope of his actual authority is he entitled to an indemnity from his principal (and the same applies to any remuneration due under a contract of agency). Moreover, if the agent acts outside his actual authority he may be liable to his principal for breach of contract (see below, p 202), or liable to a third party for breach of his implied warranty of authority (see below, pp 173–179). The position would be otherwise if the principal later adopted or ratified the agent's unauthorised actions (see below, pp 139–149 and 178).

(i) Express actual authority

Ireland v Livingston
(1872) LR 5 HL 395, House of Lords

Livingston wrote to Ireland asking him to ship 500 tons of sugar. The letter continued: 'Fifty tons more or less of no moment, if it enables you to get a suitable price.' Ireland shipped 400 tons in one vessel, presumably intending to ship the rest in another vessel. Livingston refused to accept the 400 tons and wrote to Ireland to cancel any further shipment. The House of Lords held that Livingston was bound to accept the sugar.

Lord Chelmsford: My Lords, the difference of opinion which has prevailed amongst the Judges in this case, shews that the order given to the Plaintiffs by the Defendant in his letter of the 25th of July, 1864 (upon which the question principally turns) is of doubtful construction; and this, in my mind, is a sufficient ground in itself for bringing me to the conclusion at which I have arrived....

Now it appears to me that if a principal gives an order to an agent in such uncertain terms as to be susceptible of two different meanings, and the agent *bona fide* adopts one of them and acts upon it, it is not competent to the principal to repudiate the act as unauthorized because he meant the order to be read in the other sense of which it is equally capable. It is a fair answer to such an attempt to disown the agents' authority to tell the principal that the departure from his intention was occasioned by his own fault, and that he should have given his order in clear and unambiguous terms. This view of the case will, in my opinion, dispense with the necessity of determining which is the more correct construction of the contract, that which was adopted unanimously by the Court of Queen's Bench, and by two of the Judges of the Exchequer Chamber, or that which the four other Judges of the Exchequer Chamber considered to be the right interpretation of it. It is sufficient for the justification of the Plaintiffs, that the meaning which they affixed to the order of the Defendant is, that which is sanctioned by so many learned Judges. It would be most unjust, after the Plaintiffs have honestly acted upon what they conceived to be the wishes of the Defendant, as expressed in his order, that he should be allowed to repudiate the whole transaction and throw the loss of it upon the Plaintiffs in order (as his correspondence shews) to escape from a speculation which had become a losing one in consequence of the market prices of sugars having fallen.

The short ground upon which I think the case may be disposed of, renders it unnecessary for me to express my opinion as to the proper interpretation of the letters upon which the Courts below have proceeded....

The Plaintiffs have construed the meaning of the Defendant's language in a manner for which there was a reasonable excuse, if not a complete justification, and with an honest desire to perform their duty to him, and have obeyed his order according to their understanding of its meaning.

[Lords Westbury and Colonsay delivered concurring opinions.]

NOTES

1. In *Woodhouse AC Israel Cocoa Ltd SA v Nigerian Produce Marketing Co Ltd* [1972] AC 741 at 772, Lord Salmon observed that 'in 1872 there were no means by which an agent, at the other end of the world, receiving ambiguous instructions, could communicate with his principal in London to clear up any doubt about their meaning before carrying out his duty to act upon them promptly'. But with the speed of modern communication methods it is unlikely that an agent would be deemed to have a reasonable excuse to adopt one interpretation of patently ambiguous instructions without first clarifying those instructions with his principal (*European Asian Bank AG v Punjab and Sind Bank (No 2)* [1983] 1 WLR 642 at 656, per Robert Goff LJ).

2. *Ireland v Livingston* was a case where the principal's instruction was conveyed to the agent in a letter. Where the authority of an agent is given by an instruction in a document not under seal, or has been given orally, it is construed liberally, with regard to the purpose of the agency and to the usages of trade or business (*Ashford Shire Council v Dependable Motors Pry Ltd* [1961] AC 336, PC). If the authority is contained in a deed, the usual strict rules of construction apply. In particular, this means that (1) authority will be limited to the purpose for which it was given (*Midland Bank Ltd v Reckitt* [1933] AC 1), and (2) general words of appointment will be restricted by other specific words which describe the particular acts the agent is authorised to perform (*Jacobs v Morris* [1902] 1 Ch 816). However, it should be noted that under s 10 of the Powers of Attorney Act 1971, if a general power of attorney is drawn up in the statutory form or in a similar manner and expressed to be made under the Act, it confers on the donee of the power authority to do on behalf of the donor, ie the principal, 'anything which he can lawfully do by an attorney'. Thus, if the words are unqualified, the agent's authority will only be restricted by any incapacity of his principal.

(ii) Implied actual authority

Hely-Hutchinson v Brayhead Ltd
[1968] 1 QB 549, Court of Appeal

Richards was the chairman of Brayhead. To the knowledge, and with the acquiescence, of Brayhead's board he also acted as the company's *de facto* managing director. Brayhead held shares in another company, Perdio Electronics Ltd. To encourage Hely-Hutchinson to inject funds into Perdio, Richards, in his capacity as chairman of Brayhead, wrote to him undertaking to indemnify him for any loss he might incur as a result of lending money to Perdio or guaranteeing any loan made to Perdio. In reliance on this undertaking Hely-Hutchinson advanced £45,000 to Perdio. Subsequently, Perdio went into liquidation and Hely-Hutchinson had to pay off a company loan which he had guaranteed. Hely-Hutchinson sought to recover that sum, and the £45,000 lent to Perdio, from Brayhead. He relied on the terms of Brayhead's letter of indemnity and this raised the question of Richards' authority to bind the company. Roskill J upheld the claim on the ground that Richards had ostensible or apparent authority to bind Brayhead. The Court of Appeal dismissed Brayhead's appeal on the ground that Richards had implied actual authority to bind Brayhead.

Lord Denning MR: I need not consider at length the law on the authority of an agent, actual, apparent, or ostensible. That has been done in the judgments of this court in *Freeman & Lockyer v Buckhurst Park Properties (Mangal) Ltd* ([1964] 2 QB 480). It is there shown that actual authority may be express or implied. It is *express* when it is given by express words, such as when a board of directors pass a resolution which authorises two of their number to sign cheques. It is *implied* when it is inferred from the conduct of the parties and the circumstances of the case, such as when the board of directors appoint one of their number to be managing director. They thereby impliedly authorise him to do all such things as fall within the usual scope of that office. Actual authority, express or implied, is binding as between the company and the agent, and also as between the company and others, whether they are within the company or outside it.

Ostensible or apparent authority is the authority of an agent as it *appears* to others. It often coincides with actual authority. Thus, when the board appoint one of their number to be managing director, they invest him not only with implied authority, but also with ostensible authority to do all such things as fall within the usual scope of that office. Other people who see him acting as managing director are entitled to assume that he has the usual authority of a managing director. But sometimes ostensible authority exceeds actual authority. For instance, when the board appoint the managing director, they may expressly limit his authority by saying he is not to order goods worth more than £500 without the sanction of the board. In that case his *actual* authority is subject to the £500 limitation, but his *ostensible* authority includes all the usual authority of a managing director. The company is bound by his ostensible authority in his dealings with those who do not know of the limitation. He may himself do the 'holding-out.' Thus, if he orders goods worth £1,000 and signs himself 'Managing Director for and on behalf of the company,' the company is bound to the other party who does not know of the £500 limitation, see *British Thomson-Houston Co Ltd v Federated European Bank Ltd* ([1932] 2 KB 176), which was quoted for this purpose by Pearson LJ in *Freeman & Lockyer* (at 499). Even if the other party happens himself to be a director of the company, nevertheless the company may be bound by the ostensible authority. Suppose the managing director orders £1,000 worth of goods from a new director who has just joined the company and does not know of the £500 limitation, not having studied the minute book, the company may yet be bound. Lord Simonds in *Morris v Kanssen* ([1946] AC 459 at 475–476), envisaged that sort of case, which was considered by Roskill J in the present case.

Apply these principles here. It is plain that Mr Richards had no express authority to enter into these two contracts on behalf of the company: nor had he any such authority implied from the nature of his office. He had been duly appointed chairman of the company but that office in itself did not carry with it authority to enter into these contracts without the sanction of the board. But I think he had authority implied from the conduct of the parties and the circumstances of the case. The judge did not rest his decision on implied authority, but I think his findings necessarily carry that consequence. The judge finds that Mr Richards acted as de facto managing director of Brayhead. He was the chief executive who made the final decision on any matter concerning finance. He often committed Brayhead to contracts without the knowledge of the board and reported the matter afterwards. The judge said:

> I have no doubt that Mr. Richards was, by virtue of his position as de facto managing director of Brayhead or, as perhaps one might more compendiously put it, as Brayhead's chief executive, the man who had, in Diplock LJ's words, 'actual authority to manage,' and he was acting as such when he signed those two documents.

And later he said:

> ...the board of Brayhead knew of and acquiesced in Mr. Richards acting as de facto managing director of Brayhead.

The judge held that Mr Richards had ostensible or apparent authority to make the contract, but I think his findings carry with it the necessary inference that he had also actual authority, such authority being implied from the circumstance that the board by their conduct over many months had acquiesced in his acting as their chief executive and committing Brayhead Ltd to contracts without the necessity of sanction from the board.

[Lords Wilberforce and Pearson delivered concurring judgments.]

NOTES

1. Implied actual authority may arise in any of the following forms:

(1) Incidental authority, ie an agent has implied actual authority to do everything necessary for, or ordinarily incidental to, the effective execution of his express authority in the usual way. For example, in one case an agent instructed to sell a house was held to have incidental authority to sign the agreement of sale (*Rosenbaum v Belson* [1900] 2 Ch 267) and, in another case, an agent employed to promote sales of his principal's goods was held to have incidental authority to enter into commission agreements with third parties (*SMC Electronics Ltd v Akhter Computers Ltd* [2001] 1 BCLC 433, CA). But an agent who is instructed to 'find a purchaser', not to 'sell', has no incidental authority to conclude a contract (*Earner v Sharp* (1874) LR 19 Eq 108). In each case the scope of the agent's incidental authority turned on construction of his express authority.

(2) Usual authority, ie an agent has implied actual authority to do what is usual in his trade, profession, or business for the purpose of carrying out his authority or anything necessary or incidental thereto. For example, if the board of directors appoint someone to be managing director 'they thereby impliedly authorise him to do all such things as fall within the usual scope of that office' (*Hely-Hutchinson v Brayhead Ltd*, above, p 115, per Lord Denning MR). A solicitor's authority to compromise litigation is a further example of this form of implied actual authority (*Waugh v HB Clifford & Sons Ltd* [1982] Ch 374, CA; see generally G Fridman (1987) 36 UNB LJ 9 at pp 24–40). For further examples, see *Bowstead and Reynolds*, paras 3–024 and 3–029.

(3) Customary authority, ie an agent has implied actual authority to act in accordance with the usages and customs of the particular place, market or business in which he is employed, so long as those usages or customs are reasonable and lawful. A usage or custom will be unreasonable if it is inconsistent with the instructions given by the principal to the agent, or with the nature of the principal and agent relationship itself. A principal will only be bound by an unreasonable usage or custom if he had actual notice of it at the time he conferred authority on the agent (*Robinson v Mollett* (1875) LR 7 HL 802). Whether an illegal usage or custom can bind a principal, who is aware of the illegality,

probably depends on the nature of the illegality (*Bowstead and Reynolds,* para 3–035). For the definition of 'usage', see *Cunliffe-Owen v Teather and Greenwood* [1967] 1 WLR 1421 at 1438–1439, per Ungoed-Thomas J; also see above, p 24.

(4) Implied actual authority may be inferred from the conduct of the parties and the circumstances of the case. For example, in *Hely-Hutchinson,* Lord Denning MR held that Richards' authority was to be 'implied from the conduct of the parties and the circumstances of the case' (above, p 115). It should be noted that, unlike the types of implied authority considered under paragraphs (1)–(3) above, the type of implied authority considered in this paragraph corresponds to the creation of an agency relationship by implied agreement (above, p 112).

2. An agent cannot have *actual* authority when he exceeds an express limit on his authority or when he does something which his principal has expressly prohibited. This means that the principal can prevent implied actual authority arising by expressly restricting his agent's authority. However, the principal will continue to be bound by prohibited acts of his agent if (1) those acts fall within the authority which an agent of that type would usually possess (usual authority), and (2) the third party dealing with the agent is not aware of restrictions which the principal has placed on the agent's authority. Here the agent's usual authority will not be a form of implied actual authority (because of the prohibition), rather it goes to invest the agent with apparent authority (see *First Energy (UK) Ltd v Hungarian International Bank Ltd* [1993] 2 Lloyd's Rep 194 at 201, per Steyn LJ; *AMB Generali Holding AG v SEB Trygg Liv Holding AB* [2005] EWCA Civ 1237, [2006] 1 WLR 2276 at [32], per Buxton LJ). To avoid terminological confusion, it is important to note that the expression 'usual authority' can be used in these two very different senses, and is probably best restricted to them (see RTH Stone [1993] JBL 325, 336–337). Unfortunately, as we shall soon discover, it can also be used in a third sense (below, p 128).

3. An agent has no actual authority to bind his principal when he acts fraudulently or in furtherance of his own interests (*Hopkins v TL Dallas Group Ltd* [2004] EWHC 1389 (Ch), [2005] 1 BCLC 543 at [89], Lightman J). An agent acting within the scope of his apparent authority may bind his principal when he acts fraudulently or in furtherance of his own interests (ibid). But where the person dealing with an agent knows or has reason to believe that the contract or transaction is not in the commercial interests of the agent's principal, it is likely to be very difficult for the person to assert with any creditability that he believed the agent had actual authority and lack of such belief will prevent him claiming the agent had apparent authority (*Criterion Properties plc v Stratford UK Properties LLC* [2004] UKHL 28, [2004] 1 WLR 1846 at [31], Lord Scott).

(b) Apparent authority

Rama Corpn Ltd v Proved Tin and General Investments Ltd

[1952] 2 QB 147, Queen's Bench Division

(The facts are irrelevant.)

Slade J: Ostensible or apparent authority . . . is merely a form of estoppel, indeed, it has been termed agency by estoppel, and you cannot call in aid an estoppel unless you have three ingredients: (i) a representation, (ii) reliance on the representation, and (iii) an alteration of your position resulting from such reliance.

Freeman & Lockyer v Buckhurst Park Properties (Mangal) Ltd
[1964] 2 QB 480, Court of Appeal

K and H formed the defendant company to purchase and resell a large estate. K and H, together with their nominees, were the directors of the company. The articles of association of the company contained a power to appoint a managing director but none was appointed. However, to the knowledge, and with the acquiescence, of the board, K acted as *de facto* managing director and entered into contracts on the company's behalf. On one occasion K employed a firm of architects to apply for planning permission to develop the estate and to do other work in that connection. K had no actual authority to do this and when the architects claimed their fees from the defendant company an issue arose as to whether K had apparent authority to bind it. The trial judge held that K had such apparent authority. The Court of Appeal dismissed the company's appeal from that decision.

Diplock LJ: ... We are concerned in the present case with the authority of an agent to create contractual rights and liabilities between his principal and a third party whom I will call 'the contractor.' This branch of the law has developed pragmatically rather than logically owing to the early history of the action of assumpsit and the consequent absence of a general jus quaesitum tertii in English law. But it is possible (and for the determination of this appeal I think it is desirable) to restate it upon a rational basis.

It is necessary at the outset to distinguish between an 'actual' authority of an agent on the one hand, and an 'apparent' or 'ostensible' authority on the other. Actual authority and apparent authority are quite independent of one another. Generally they co-exist and coincide, but either may exist without the other and their respective scopes may be different. As I shall endeavour to show, it is upon the apparent authority of the agent that the contractor normally relies in the ordinary course of business when entering into contracts.

An 'actual' authority is a legal relationship between principal and agent created by a consensual agreement to which they alone are parties. Its scope is to be ascertained by applying ordinary principles of construction of contracts, including any proper implications from the express words used, the usages of the trade, or the course of business between the parties. To this agreement the contractor is a stranger; he may be totally ignorant of the existence of any authority on the part of the agent. Nevertheless, if the agent does enter into a contract pursuant to the 'actual' authority, it does create contractual rights and liabilities between the principal and the contractor. It may be that this rule relating to 'undisclosed principals,' which is peculiar to English law, can be rationalised as avoiding circuity of action, for the principal could in equity compel the agent to lend his name in an action to enforce the contract against the contractor, and would at common law be liable to indemnify the agent in respect of the performance of the obligations assumed by the agent under the contract.

An 'apparent' or 'ostensible' authority, on the other hand, is a legal relationship between the principal and the contractor created by a representation, made by the principal to the contractor, intended to be and in fact acted upon by the contractor, that the agent has authority to enter on behalf of the principal into a contract of a kind within the scope of the 'apparent' authority, so as to render the principal liable to perform any obligations imposed upon him by such contract. To the relationship so created the agent is a stranger. He need not be (although he generally is) aware of the existence of the representation but he must not purport to make the agreement as principal himself. The representation, when acted upon by the contractor by entering into a contract with the agent, operates as an estoppel, preventing the principal from asserting that he is not bound by the contract. It is irrelevant whether the agent had actual authority to enter into the contract.

In ordinary business dealings the contractor at the time of entering into the contract can in the nature of things hardly ever rely on the 'actual' authority of the agent. His information as to the authority must be derived either from the principal or from the agent or from both, for they alone know what the agent's actual authority is. All that the contractor can know is what they tell him, which may or may not be true. In the ultimate analysis he relies either upon the representation of the principal, that is, apparent authority, or upon the representation of the agent, that is, warranty of authority.

The representation which creates 'apparent' authority may take a variety of forms of which the commonest is representation by conduct, that is, by permitting the agent to act in some way in the conduct of the principal's business with other persons. By so doing the principal represents to anyone who becomes aware that the agent is so acting that the agent has authority to enter on behalf of the principal into contracts with other persons of the kind which an agent so acting in the conduct of his principal's business has usually 'actual' authority to enter into.

In applying the law as I have endeavoured to summarise it to the case where the principal is not a natural person, but a fictitious person, namely, a corporation, two further factors arising from the legal characteristics of a corporation have to be borne in mind. The first is that the capacity of a corporation is limited by its constitution, that is, in the case of a company incorporated under the Companies Act, by its memorandum and articles of association; the second is that a corporation cannot do any act, and that includes making a representation, except through its agent.

[Diplock LJ examined certain aspects of the ultra vires and constructive notice doctrines—now repealed: see note 5 below—and continued:]

The second characteristic of a corporation, namely, that unlike a natural person it can only make a representation through an agent, has the consequence that in order to create an estoppel between the corporation and the contractor, the representation as to the authority of the agent which creates his 'apparent' authority must be made by some person or persons who have 'actual' authority from the corporation to make the representation. Such 'actual' authority may be conferred by the constitution of the corporation itself, as, for example, in the case of a company, upon the board of directors, or it may be conferred by those who under its constitution have the powers of management upon some other person to whom the constitution permits them to delegate authority to make representations of this kind. It follows that where the agent upon whose 'apparent' authority the contractor relies has no 'actual' authority from the corporation to enter into a particular kind of contract with the contractor on behalf of the corporation, the contractor cannot rely upon the agent's own representation as to his actual authority. He can rely only upon a representation by a person or persons who have actual authority to manage or conduct that part of the business of the corporation to which the contract relates.

The commonest form of representation by a principal creating an 'apparent' authority of an agent is by conduct, namely, by permitting the agent to act in the management or conduct of the principal's business. Thus, if in the case of a company the board of directors who have 'actual' authority under the memorandum and articles of association to manage the company's business permit the agent to act in the management or conduct of the company's business, they thereby represent to all persons dealing with such agent that he has authority to enter on behalf of the corporation into contracts of a kind which an agent authorised to do acts of the kind which he is in fact permitted to do usually enters into in the ordinary course of such business. The making of such a representation is itself an act of management of the company's business. Prima facie it falls within the 'actual' authority of the board of directors, and unless the memorandum or articles of the company either make such a contract ultra vires the company or prohibit the delegation of such authority to the agent,[1] the company is estopped from denying to anyone who has entered into a contract with the agent in reliance upon such 'apparent' authority that the agent had authority to contract on behalf of the company.

If the foregoing analysis of the relevant law is correct, it can be summarised by stating four conditions which must be fulfilled to entitle a contractor to enforce against a company a contract entered into on

---

[1] [These remarks must now be read in the light of s 40 of the Companies Act 2006: see note 5 below.]

behalf of the company by an agent who had no actual authority to do so. It must be shown:

(1) that a representation that the agent had authority to enter on behalf of the company into a contract of the kind sought to be enforced was made to the contractor;

(2) that such representation was made by a person or persons who had 'actual' authority to manage the business of the company either generally or in respect of those matters to which the contract relates;

(3) that he (the contractor) was induced by such representation to enter into the contract, that is, that he in fact relied upon it; and

(4) that under its memorandum or articles of association the company was not deprived of the capacity either to enter into a contract of the kind sought to be enforced or to delegate authority to enter into a contract of that kind to the agent.[2]

The confusion which, I venture to think, has sometimes crept into the cases is in my view due to a failure to distinguish between these four separate conditions, and in particular to keep steadfastly in mind (a) that the only 'actual' authority which is relevant is that of the persons making the representation relied upon, and (b) that the memorandum and articles of association of the company are always relevant (whether they are in fact known to the contractor or not) to the questions (i) whether condition (2) is fulfilled, and (ii) whether condition (4) is fulfilled, and (but only if they are in fact known to the contractor) may be relevant (iii) as part of the representation on which the contractor relied. . . .

In the present case the findings of fact by the county court judge are sufficient to satisfy the four conditions, and thus to establish that Kapoor had 'apparent' authority to enter into contracts on behalf of the company for their services in connection with the sale of the company's property, including the obtaining of development permission with respect to its use. The judge found that the board knew that Kapoor had throughout been acting as managing director in employing agents and taking other steps to find a purchaser. They permitted him to do so, and by such conduct represented that he had authority to enter into contracts of a kind which a managing director or an executive director responsible for finding a purchaser would in the normal course be authorised to enter into on behalf of the company. Condition (1) was thus fulfilled. The articles of association conferred full powers of management on the board. Condition (2) was thus fulfilled. The plaintiffs, finding Kapoor acting in relation to the company's property as he was authorised by the board to act, were induced to believe that he was authorised by the company to enter into contracts on behalf of the company for their services in connection with the sale of the company' s property, including the obtaining of development permission with respect to its use. Condition (3) was thus fulfilled. The articles of association, which contained powers for the board to delegate any of the functions of management to a managing director or to a single director, did not deprive the company of capacity to delegate authority to Kapoor, a director, to enter into contracts of that kind on behalf of the company. Condition (4) was thus fulfilled.

I think the judgment was right, and would dismiss the appeal.

[Willmer and Pearson LJJ delivered concurring judgments.]

NOTES

1.   Apparent authority can operate (a) to create authority where there was none before; (b) to enlarge an agent's actual authority; (c) to clothe an agent with authority where he would usually have actual authority but for the existence of a restriction unknown to the third party; and (d) to extend an agent's authority beyond termination of the agency relationship. An example of (a) is *Barrett v Deere* (1828) Mood & M 200, where A entered P's

---

[2]   [This fourth requirement is now irrelevant, in the light of the reforms mentioned in the preceding footnote, unless the 'contractor' cannot bring himself within s 40, eg because he was not dealing in good faith.]

counting house and acted as if entrusted with the conduct of P's business. Payment of a debt to A was held to be good payment to P because, although A was a stranger to P and not his agent, P allowed A to enter his business premises and appear to be responsible for the conduct of that business. An example of (b) is *First Energy (UK) Ltd v Hungarian International Bank Ltd* [1993] 2 Lloyd's Rep 194, where a senior regional manager of a bank was held to have had apparent authority to convey head office approval of a certain type of loan, when he had neither actual authority to grant that type of loan nor to convey head office approval of it (a difficult case, considered in detail below at p 125). An example of (c) is *Manchester Trust v Furness* [1895] 2 QB 539, where a charterparty provided that the ship's master, appointed by the owners, was to sign bills of lading as agent of the charterers only, but the owners were nevertheless held liable on a bill of lading signed by the master because the third party holder of the bill of lading, who was unaware of the restriction, was entitled to assume that the usual situation applied, namely that the master was the agent of the owner. An example of (d) is *AMB Generali Holding AG v SEB Trygg Liv Holding AB* [2005] EWCA Civ 1237, [2006] 1 WLR 2276, where H (the agent) resigned as a director of a company (the principal) but was held to have apparent authority to bind the company to arbitration proceedings after his resignation because of a general representation from his appointment as director that he had all the usual authority of the post, and also from specific representations by the company, the effect of which survived his resignation until the third party was put on notice of it, and no further representation by the company was needed for apparent authority to continue after revocation of the director's actual authority.

2. For the inter-relationship between implied actual authority and apparent authority, see *Hely-Hutchinson v Brayhead Ltd,* above, p 114; and *Waugh v HB Clifford & Sons Ltd* [1982] Ch 374, CA.

3. There has been some debate as to whether or not apparent authority is 'real' authority (see *Bowstead and Reynolds,* para 8–029 for references to the relevant literature). It has been submitted by some writers that, like actual authority, apparent authority is based on consent and is, therefore, real authority. These writers concentrate on the objective appearance of consent as manifested in the principal's representations and conduct (eg see M Conant (1968) Nebraska LR 678, 681–686; FMB Reynolds (1994) 110 LQR 21, 22; G McMeel (2000) 116 LQR 387, 407). However, the objective consent theory has not found favour with the English courts. Since the *Freeman and Lockyer* decision, the English courts have almost invariably referred to apparent authority as a form of estoppel (eg *Egyptian International Foreign Trade Co v Soplex Wholesale Supplies Ltd and PS Refson SL Co Ltd, The Raffaella* [1985] 2 Lloyd's Rep 36 at 41, CA; *Armagas Ltd v Mundogas SA* [1986] AC 717 at 777, HL; *Lloyds Bank plc v Independent Insurance Co Ltd* [2000] QB 110 at 121–122, CA; *AMB Generali Holdings AB v SEB Trygg Liv Holding AB* [2005] EWCA Civ 1237, [2006] 1 Lloyd's Rep 318 at [31]-[32], CA; *Ing Re (UK) Ltd v R & V Versicherung AG* [2006] EWHC 1544 (Comm), [2006] 2 All ER (Comm) 890 at [99], Toulson J). In *Homburg Houtimport BV v Agrosin Private Ltd* [2000] 1 Lloyd's Rep 85 at 95, Coleman J said that apparent authority was based on 'a substantially similar public policy foundation...as for estoppel by representation', namely 'unconscionability' (on appeal [2001] 1 Lloyd's Rep 437, CA, and [2003] UKHL 12, [2004] 1 AC 715, but without reference to this point). As such, apparent authority cannot be real authority, rather it creates the appearance of authority which, for policy reasons, the law recognises as giving the agent power to affect the legal relations of the principal (see above, p 97). For an interesting historical survey of how the basis of an agent's external authority changed from that of general authority, a form of actual authority derived from status, to that of apparent authority, in the form of a holding-out by the principal to the third party, as business practices changed in the nineteenth century, see I Brown [2006] JBL 391.

4.   Although this debate may appear somewhat academic, it does have practical significance. Some of the consequences of the agent having actual authority, as opposed to apparent authority, have already been considered (above, p 113). Furthermore, as a form of estoppel, apparent authority can only make the principal liable under any contract made by his agent, it cannot give the principal an independent cause of action unless he ratifies his agent's unauthorised act (although the editor of *Bowstead and Reynolds* submits, at para 8–031, that the principal should be able to make counterclaims and raise defences against any action brought against him by the third party on the unauthorised contract). If apparent authority was true authority the principal could sue and be sued on the contract (*Powell,* op cit, p 70; Conant, op cit, p 683).

5.   In *Freeman and Lockyer,* Diplock LJ considered how limitations in a company's constitution could affect the capacity of the company to do acts and the power of the board to delegate authority to an agent. (Prior to the coming into force of the relevant provisions of the Companies Act 2006, a company's constitution was made up of its memorandum of association and its articles of association, but under s 17 of the 2006 Act a company's constitution is now defined to include its articles of association and not its memorandum of association: see s 28 for companies formed under the old Companies Acts.) However, these comments must now be considered in the light of changes to the law made first in 1989, through amendment of the Companies Act 1985, and now to be found in the Companies Act 2006 which has repealed and replaced the 1985 Act. In most cases limitations on the company's capacity and on the board's power to delegate are no longer relevant. Section 39(1) of the Companies Act 2006 provides that 'the validity of an act done by a company shall not be called into question on the ground of lack of capacity by reason of anything in the company's constitution'. This provision effectively abolishes the *ultra vires* doctrine. Section 40(1) of the Companies Act 2006 extends the protection for third parties by providing that 'in favour of a person dealing with a company in good faith, the power of the directors to bind the company, or authorise others to do so, shall be deemed to be free of any limitation under the company's constitution'. Under s 40(2)(b)(i), a third party is not bound to enquire whether there is any limitation on the powers of the directors to bind the company or authorise others to do so; under s 40(2)(b)(ii), a third party is presumed to have acted in good faith unless the contrary is proved; and under s 40(2)(b)(iii), a third party shall not be deemed to have acted in bad faith merely because he actual knows that a transaction is beyond the directors' powers under the company's constitution. The net effect of these provisions is that the doctrine of constructive notice (whereby a person dealing with a company was deemed to have notice of that company's constitutional documents) has effectively been abolished. But the protection offered by s 40 is not intended to allow directors and their associates to take advantage of the company, and so s 41 alters the presumptions found in s 40 where a transaction is with a director or a person connect with a director. For further discussion of the rules relating to corporate capacity and the authority of a company's agents, see L Sealy and S Worthington, *Cases and Materials in Company Law* (8th edn, 2007), Ch 3.

The requirements for apparent authority were summarised by Slade J in the *Rama* case (above, p 117) as (i) representation, (ii) reliance, (iii) alteration of position.

(i) Representation

Egyptian International Foreign Trade Co v Soplex Wholesale Supplies Ltd and PS Refson & Co Ltd, The Raffaella

[1985] 2 Lloyd's Rep 36, Court of Appeal

The plaintiffs sued the defendant bank on a letter of guarantee signed solely by the bank's credit manager, Mr Booth. At the trial it was common ground that, under the bank's internal rules, Mr Booth did not have actual authority to bind the bank to the guarantee on his sole signature (although at the time he signed the guarantee Mr Booth had assured the plaintiffs representative that one signature was sufficient to do this). The trial judge, and the Court of Appeal, held that Mr Booth had apparent authority to bind the bank to the guarantee by virtue of his designation as credit manager and because of what the bank had permitted him to do in the past.

Browne-Wilkinson LJ: I have so far ignored the representation made by Mr Booth that 'in London one signature is sufficient'. Mr Stamler submitted that a principal cannot be held liable as a result of the agent holding himself out as possessing an authority he does not in fact possess: he relied on remarks to that effect in the *Freeman & Lockyer* case ([1964] 2 QB 480) at p 505, *A-G for Ceylon v Silva* [1953] 1 Lloyd's Rep 563, [1953] AC 461 at pp 571 and 479, *The British Bank of The Middle East case* ([1983] 2 Lloyd's Rep 9) and *Armagas Ltd v Mundogas SA* [1985] 1 Lloyd's Rep 1. As at present advised, I am not satisfied that the principle to be derived from those cases is as wide as Mr Stamler suggests: they were all cases or dicta dealing with the position where the agent had neither authority to enter into the transaction nor authority to make representations on behalf of the principal. It is obviously correct that an agent who has no actual or apparent authority either (a) to enter into a transaction or (b) to make representations as to the transaction cannot hold himself out as having authority to enter into the transaction so as to affect the principal's position. But, suppose a company confers actual or apparent authority on X to make representations and X erroneously represents to a third party that Y has authority to enter into a transaction; why should not such a representation be relied upon as part of the holding out of Y by the company? By parity of reasoning, if a company confers actual or apparent authority on A to make representations on the company's behalf but no actual authority on A to enter into the specific transaction, why should a representation made by A as to his authority not be capable of being relied on as one of the acts of holding out? There is substantial authority that it can be: see *British Thomson-Houston Co Ltd v Federated European Bank Ltd* [1932] 2 KB 176, especially at p 182 (where the only holding out was an erroneous representation by the agent that he was managing director); and the *Freeman & Lockyer* case per Lord Justice Pearson at p 499; *Hely-Hutchinson v Brayhead Ltd* [1968] 1 QB 549 per Lord Denning MR at p 593A-D. If, as I am inclined to think an agent with authority to make representations can make a representation that he has authority to enter into a transaction, then the Judge was entitled to hold, as he did, that Mr Booth, as the representative of Refson in charge of the transaction, had implied or apparent authority to make the representation that only one signature was required and that this representation was a relevant consideration in deciding whether Refson had held out Mr Booth as having authority to sign the undertaking. However, since it is not necessary to decide this point for the purposes of this appeal, I express no concluded view on it.

Kerr LJ: In this summary I have deliberately made no reference to one other matter concerning the letter of July 26, although Mr Sharobeem undoubtedly placed some reliance on it. This was Mr Booth's assurance, in answer to Mr Sharobeem's question, that he was authorized to sign the letter by himself. The recent decision of this Court in *Armagas Ltd v Mundogas SA* shows that, when a third party is aware that an agent has no actual authority to do a particular act, then the agent's untrue subsequent assurance that he has obtained the necessary authority cannot possibly invest him with any apparent authority for this purpose. In the argument before us this situation was aptly referred to as one where the agent is seeking to pull himself up by his own bootstraps. The present case is different, because it is conceded that the plaintiffs had no reason to doubt Mr Booth's authority at any point. Nevertheless, I would not, as at present advised, accept the argument of Mr Johnson QC that the plaintiffs derive some additional support from Mr Booth's assurance to Mr Sharobeem. As I see it, the issue as to Mr Booth's apparent authority must be resolved with the same result even if this question had not been asked and answered as it was, and I therefore prefer to leave this matter there.

[Lawton LJ delivered a concurring judgment.]

NOTES

1.   The representation that the agent has authority must be made by the principal and not by the agent himself (*A-G for Ceylon v Silva* [1953] AC 461 at 479, PC). As Lord Donaldson MR said in *United Bank of Kuwait v Hammoud* [1988] 1 **WLR** 1051 at 1066, 'it is trite law that an agent cannot ordinarily confer ostensible authority on himself. He cannot pull himself up by his own shoe laces.' However, the representation may be made by another (intermediate) agent with actual authority to make such a representation (*Bowstead and Reynolds*, para 8–021). Difficult questions arise as to whether an intermediate agent with no actual authority to make representations can nevertheless have apparent authority to make such representation. Similarly, can an agent have apparent authority to make representations about his own authority?

2.   In *Ing Re (UK) Ltd v R & V Versicherung AG* [2006] EWHC 1544 (Comm), [2006] 2 All ER (Comm) 870, Toulson J held (at [99]) that the doctrine of apparent authority was based on estoppel by representation and would apply where the principal (P) represented or caused to be represented to a third party (T) that an agent (A) had authority to act on P's behalf, and T dealt with A as P's agent on the faith of that representation. He continued (at [100]):

I accept that the same principle can also apply at one remove where T relies on a representation made by an agent having ostensible (but not actual) authority to make such a representation on behalf of P. Thus, where P represents or causes it to be represented to T that A1 has authority to represent to T that A2 has authority to act on P's behalf, and T deals with A2 as P's agent on the faith of such representations, P is bound by A2's acts to the same extent as if he had the authority which he was represented as having. The critical requirement is that A2's authority must be able to be traced back to the principal by a representation or chain of representations upon which T acted and whose authenticity P is estopped from denying by his representation through words or conduct. There is little case law on this variant of the doctrine, but I agree with the statement in Bowstead and Reynolds on Agency, 17th ed (2001) at para 8–021:

It seems correct in principle to say that an agent can have apparent authority to make representations as to the authority of other agents, provided that his own authority can finally be traced back to a representation by the principal or to a person with actual authority from the principal to make it.

In almost all cases the intermediate agent (A1) will have apparent authority because he has usual authority to do the act in question but his authority has been limited by his principal's secret reservation (*British Bank of the Middle East v Sun Life Assurance Co of Canada (UK) Ltd* [1983] 2 Lloyd's Rep 9, HL, is consistent with this view: see note 4 below). If an intermediate agent does not usually have authority to do the act, the third party would normally be put on inquiry should the intermediate agent represent that another agent is authorised to do it (see note 3 below).

3.   The same principles apply to the question whether an agent can ever make representations about his own authority. In principle, an agent can have apparent authority to make

representations as to his own authority (*The Raffaella, obiter,* above at p 123; *First Energy (UK) Ltd v Hungarian International Bank Ltd* [1993] 2 Lloyd's Rep 194; also *Canadian Laboratory Supplies Ltd v Engelhard Industries Ltd* (1979) 97 DLR (3d) 1 at 10, Supreme Court of Canada). But such cases will be extremely rare (*Suncorp Insurance and Finance v Milano Assicurazioni SpA* [1993] 2 Lloyd's Rep 225 at 232, per Waller J). Unless the agent would usually have authority to do the act in question, it will be very difficult for the third party to rely on a specific representation of the agent's authority to act, as the third party would normally have been put on enquiry as to the actual limitation on the agent's authority (*Fridman,* p 125). This point is illustrated by *Armagas Ltd v Mundogas SA* [1986] AC 717. In this case, the third party knew that the agent had no general authority to enter into the transaction in question. It was held by both the Court of Appeal and the House of Lords that, with this knowledge, the third party could not rely on the agent's representation of his own authority to enter into this particular transaction, even though the principal had employed the agent in a senior position in its organisation. With regard to any specific representation of authority made by the principal, Lord Keith stated that (at 777):

It must be a most unusual and peculiar case where an agent who is known to have no general authority to enter into transactions of a certain type can by reason of circumstances created by the principal reasonably be believed to have specific authority to enter into a particular transaction of that type. The facts in the present case fall far short of establishing such a situation.

4. *First Energy (UK) Ltd v Hungarian International Bank Ltd* [1993] 2 Lloyd's Rep 194 (noted by FMB Reynolds (1994) 110 LQR 21) was such an exceptional case. The senior manager in charge of the Manchester office of the defendant bank (as the plaintiff company's representative knew) had no actual authority to sanction a credit facility for the plaintiff. However, the senior manager wrote and signed (alone) a letter offering to provide the plaintiff with finance. He had no actual authority to do this either, as such a letter should have been signed by two bank officials. Nevertheless, the Court of Appeal held that the senior manager had apparent authority, by virtue of the usual authority associated with his position, to communicate such an offer on behalf of the bank—ie to inform the plaintiff that head office approval had been given for the offer to be made—and so the bank was bound. The Court of Appeal stressed that the decision was consistent with the reasonable expectations of the parties and that it was unrealistic to expect the plaintiff to have checked with the bank's head office as to whether an employee as senior as this manager had actually obtained necessary approval to make the offer. This decision may be contrasted with *British Bank of the Middle East v Sun Life Assurance Co of Canada (UK) Ltd* [1983] 2 Lloyd's Rep 9 (noted by J Collier [1984] CLJ 26), where the House of Lords held that a branch manager of an insurance company had no usual authority to represent to the plaintiff that a junior employee had actual authority to execute undertakings to pay money to the bank. The evidence was that all such undertakings were in practice executed by insurance companies at their head office. Whereas the plaintiff in *First Energy* could rely on the fact that the senior manager had usual authority to sign and send letters on the bank's behalf (the plaintiff being unaware of the bank's restriction on that authority), the plaintiff in *British Bank of the Middle East* could not do the same because of the limited nature of the branch manager's usual authority.

The protection of the third party is limited in this type of case to the extent of the usual authority of the agent, which is itself governed by what would normally be implied between principal and agent, something of which the third party may be quite ignorant, despite the fact that he may have acted reasonably. This may seem harsh on the third party (as the *British Bank of the Middle East* case illustrates), especially where he deals with an agent who is just one cog in a large impersonal corporate machine, when it is unreasonable to expect the third party to make intrusive inquiries about the agent's authority. This has led one commentator to suggest that 'there should be a realignment of the rules of apparent authority to focus attention primarily upon the *agent's* conduct, as seen from the third party's perspective, rather than the *principal's* conduct in creating the appearance of authority. The reasonable reliance of the third party on the apparent normality of the agent's acts should thus be dominant.' (I Brown [1995] JBL 360, 372). *Prima facie,* the *First Energy* decision seems to offer some support to this alternative approach: after all, Steyn LJ did stress in his judgment (at 196) that 'a theme that runs through our law of contract is that the reasonable expectations of honest men must be protected.' Yet his Lordship also emphasised (at 204) that he decided the case on 'orthodox principles', and the traditional requirements of representation and reliance also underpin the reasoning of Evans and Nourse LJJ, the two other member of the court. *First Energy* may be an exceptional case (in *Habton Farms v Nimmo* (25 January 2002, unreported) at [101], upheld on appeal [2003] EWCA Civ 68, [2004] QB 1, HH Judge Behrens recently described it as 'a very special case on its own facts'), but it is probably overly optimistic to herald it as the harbinger of a new approach to apparent authority.

5.　Other points to note about the representation are:

(1)　It can be express (oral or in writing); or implied from a course of dealing (eg in *Summers v Solomon* (1857) 7 E & B 879, P employed A to run his jewellery shop and regularly paid for jewellery ordered by A from TP for resale in the shop: held P liable to pay for jewellery ordered by A from TP after A had left P's employment since the previous course of dealings had led TP to believe that A had authority to pledge his credit and P had not informed TP that that authority had terminated); or implied from conduct, such as putting the agent in a position that carries with it usual authority (above, pp 116–117); or by entrusting the agent with the indicia of ownership of property (see below, p 353).

(2)　It must be made to the particular third party who deals with the agent, or to the public at large when it would be expected that members of the general public would be likely to deal with the agent (*Farquharson Bros & Co v King & Co* [1902] AC 325 at 341, per Lord Lindley).

(3)　It must be of fact and not of law (*Chapleo v Brunswick Permanent Building Society* (1881) 6 QBD 696). However, the distinction must now be reviewed in the light of *Kleinwort Benson Ltd v Lincoln City Council* [1999] 2 AC 349, where the House of Lords allowed recovery in restitution of money paid under mistake of law. The *Kleinwort Benson* decision has had an impact outside the law of restitution, so that a contract may be *void* for mistake of law or *rescinded* for a misrepresentation of law. It has been argued that it should not be applied to the present rule, which is concerned with the *creation* of contractual rights (see E Peel, *Treitel's Law of Contract*, 12th edn, 2007, para 16–022).

(4)　It must be that the 'agent' is authorised to act as agent and not as principal (see below, pp 129–130).

(5)　It must be made intentionally or, possibly, negligently (*Bowstead and Reynolds,* para 8–026; *Fridman,* p 118; *Markesinis and Munday,* p 46).

(ii) Reliance

The third party must have relied on the representation. There must be a causal connection between the representation and the third party's dealing with the agent. Furthermore, in cases of representation by negligence, the principal's breach of duty of care owed to the third party must be the proximate cause of his damage (*Swan v North British Australasian Co Ltd* (1863) 2 H & C 175).

The third party will not be able to say he relied on the representation if he knew, or ought to have known, of the restriction on the agent's authority. In the words of Nourse LJ in *Heinl v Jyske Bank* [1999] Lloyd's Rep Bank 511 at 521, 'the knowledge of the other party unclothes [the agent] of ostensible authority to contract on behalf of the principal'. In *Overbrooke Estates Ltd v Glencombe Properties Ltd* [1974] 1 WLR 1335, a purchaser of land at an auction failed to establish that the seller was bound by a misrepresentation relating to the property made by his agent (the auctioneer) before the sale. Before any contract was made, and before any representation was made, the purchaser had been in possession of the conditions of sale of the property which contained a clause to the effect that the auctioneer had no authority to give representations or warranties. Brightman J held that the purchaser 'knew, or ought to have known, that [the auctioneer] had no authority to make or give any representation or warranty in relation to this property'.

Contracts or transactions that appear to run against the commercial interests of the principal must be treated with particular caution by the third party. As Lord Scott warned in *Criterion Properties plc v Stratford UK Properties LLC* [2004] UKHL 28, [2004] 1 WLR 1846 at [31]: 'if a person dealing with an agent knows or has reason to believe that the contract or transaction is contrary to the commercial interests of the agent's principal, it is likely to be very difficult for the person to assert with any credibility that he believed the agent did have actual authority. Lack of such a belief would be fatal to a claim that the agent had apparent authority'. Thus, in *Hopkins v TL Dallas Group Ltd* [2004] EWHC 1379 (Ch), [2005] 1 BCLC 543, a director (A) signed letters of undertaking on behalf of his company (P), agreeing to pay sums totalling just under £1 million to another company (T), in discharge of indebtedness owed to T by a further company (X), a company with which P had no connection. Lightman J held that the transaction was not binding on P. First, A was held had to have no actual authority because he was acting contrary to his principal's interests (see above, p 117). Secondly, A was held to have had no apparent authority because the director acting for the company receiving the undertakings (T) knew that A was not acting in the interests of his company (P). Lightman J stated (at [96]) that, even if there was no actual knowledge of the breach of fiduciary duty by A, the director acting for the company to whom the undertakings were given (T) was 'on the clearest notice that the transactions were both abnormal and suspicious and required confirmation of their propriety and regularity'.

(iii) Alteration of position

Must the third party alter his position to his detriment? There are cases going either way (eg *Rama Corpn v Proved Tin and General Investments,* above at p 117, and *Freeman and Lockyer v Buckhurst Park (Mangal) Properties Ltd,* above at p 118 call simply for an alteration of position; *Farquharson Bros & Co v King & Co* [1902] AC 325, and *Norfolk County Council v Secretary of State for the Environment* [1973] 3 All ER 673, call for detrimental reliance). The need for detriment is consistent with the strict requirements of an estoppel, but in one of the more recent cases on apparent authority Gatehouse J held that '[t]he only detriment that has to be shown … is the entering into the contract': *The Tatra* [1990] 2 Lloyd's Rep 51 at 59.

(iv) Subsequent conduct of the principal

The principal may be bound by a contract, even though the requirements of apparent authority are not satisfied, if he is precluded by his *subsequent* conduct from denying that the contract was made on his behalf. In *Spiro v Lintern* [1973] 1 WLR 1002, a wife contracted to sell her husband's house. The wife had no actual authority to do this and, because she appeared to be the owner of the house (not her husband's agent), she had no apparent authority. However, after the contract was entered into the husband neither stated that his wife was acting without his authority nor indicated that he was not willing for the sale to proceed. On the contrary, the husband allowed the purchaser to incur various expenses with regard to the property. In an action for specific performance of the contract, the Court of Appeal held the husband was estopped from denying that his wife had authority to sell the house on his behalf. As Buckley LJ stated (at 1011):

If A sees B acting in the mistaken belief that A is under some binding obligation to him and in a manner consistent only with the existence of such an obligation, which would be to B's disadvantage if A were thereafter to deny the obligation, A is under a duty to B to disclose the non-existence of the supposed obligation.

Buckley LJ emphasised that detrimental reliance was necessary for this type of estoppel (contrast this with apparent authority, above) but held that the purchaser had acted to his detriment by incurring expenses.

There is a difference between the estoppel that operates in a case like *Spiro v Lintern* and the estoppel that operates in a case of apparent authority. It was identified by Mance LJ in *Baird Textiles Holdings Ltd v Marks and Spencer plc* [2001] EWCA Civ 274, [2002] 1 All ER (Comm) 737 at [90] as follows:

The doctrine of apparent or ostensible authority also rests on the ability of an estoppel to preclude a person (A) who has held out another person (B) as his agent to a third person (C) from denying the existence of such authority or therefore the validity of a contract purportedly made by B on A's behalf with C. A may also estop himself after the event from denying that B was acting as his agent in contracting with C: *Spiro v Lintern*. But in these situations there is either a purported or an actual legal relationship created by the conduct of B and C, to which A is estopped from denying that he is a party. In the former situation, he is estopped from denying the existence of a collateral condition of the validity of such relationship (authority). In the latter, he is estopped from denying that B was acting as his undisclosed agent in making an actual contract.

QUESTIONS

1.   In *Armagas Ltd v Mundogas SA* (above, p 125) would the third party have any remedy against the 'agent'?

2.   Philip, a businessman, employs Alice as his personal assistant. Alice has held similar posts with other employers and is told by Philip 'do for me what you have always done as a personal assistant for your previous employers, but never book me on a plane as I hate flying'. A few weeks later, forgetting Philip's restriction, Alice rings up EasiAir and books Philip on a flight to Manchester to attend an important business meeting which he would not have had time to attend unless he travelled by plane. When he finds out about the flight, Philip refuses to go and is now being sued by EasiAir for the cost of his ticket. Advise Philip. Would it make any difference if the person who dealt with the booking at EasiAir had dealt with Philip before and knew he hated flying?

(c) Usual authority

Watteau v Fenwick

[1893] 1 QB 346, Queen's Bench Division

(The facts appear from the judgment of Wills J.)

Lord Coleridge C J: The judgment which I am about to read has been written by my brother Wills, and I entirely concur in it.

Wills J: The plaintiff sues the defendants for the price of cigars supplied to the Victoria Hotel, Stockton-upon-Tees. The house was kept, not by the defendants, but by a person named Humble, whose name was over the door. The plaintiff gave credit to Humble, and to him alone, and had never heard of the defendants. The business, however, was really the defendants', and they had put Humble into it to manage it for them, and had forbidden him to buy cigars on credit. The cigars, however, were such as would usually be supplied to and dealt in at such an establishment. The learned county court judge held that the defendants were liable. I am of opinion that he was right.

There seems to be less of direct authority on the subject than one would expect. But I think that the Lord Chief Justice during the argument laid down the correct principle, viz, once it is established that the defendant was the real principal, the ordinary doctrine as to principal and agent applies—that the principal is liable for all the acts of the agent which are within the authority usually confided to an agent of that character, notwithstanding limitations, as between the principal and the agent, put upon that authority. It is said that it is only so where there has been a holding out of authority—which cannot be said of a case where the person supplying the goods knew nothing of the existence of a principal. But I do not think so. Otherwise, in every case of undisclosed principal, or at least in every case where the fact of there being a principal was undisclosed, the secret limitation of authority would prevail and defeat the action of the person dealing with the agent and then discovering that he was an agent and had a principal.

But in the case of a dormant partner it is clear law that no limitation of authority as between the dormant and active partner will avail the dormant partner as to things within the ordinary authority of a partner. The law of partnership is, on such a question, nothing but a branch of the general law of principal and agent, and it appears to me to be undisputed and conclusive on the point now under discussion.

The principle laid down by the Lord Chief Justice, and acted upon by the learned county court judge, appears to be identical with that enunciated in the judgments of Cockburn CJ and Mellor J in *Edmunds v Bushell* ((1865) LR 1 QB 97), the circumstances of which case, though not identical with those of the present, come very near to them. There was no holding out, as the plaintiff knew nothing of the defendant. I appreciate the distinction drawn by Mr Finlay in his argument, but the principle laid down in the judgments referred to, if correct, abundantly covers the present case. I cannot find that any doubt has ever been expressed that it is correct, and I think it is right, and that very mischievous consequences would often result if that principle were not upheld.

In my opinion this appeal ought to be dismissed with costs.

Appeal dismissed.

'The Demise of Watteau v Fenwick: Sign-O-Lite Ltd v Metropolitan Life Insurance Co' by GHL Fridman

(1991) 70 Can Bar Rev 329, pp 329–333

Introduction

In the law of agency the most difficult and controversial decision is that of Wills J in *Watteau v Fenwick*[1] It has been criticised by commentators[2] and distinguished or not followed by judges.[3] Several years ago an English judge described the case as puzzling, the argument for the plaintiff as fallacious, and the doctrine of the case as one that courts should be wary about following.[4]

The case concerned the liability of an undisclosed principal for unauthorised contracts entered into by the principal's agent....

The problem with this case is the logical one of saying that someone who is not known to be an agent can be regarded as having been held out by a principal as having an apparent authority, culled from what was usual or customary in the business in which the agent was engaged,[5] to contract in the way he did, although he lacked any actual authority to do so.[6] Since the doctrine of apparent authority is based upon a principal's holding out someone as his agent with authority to act on his, that is, the principal's behalf,[7] it is difficult to conceive of a case of undisclosed agency as involving the application of the doctrine of apparent authority. One who is not apparently an agent cannot logically be said to have been held out as having any authority at all, whether based on custom, what is usual, or otherwise. The only logical way in which such a conclusion can be reached is by starting from the premise that anyone who employs an agent and does not disclose that he is an agent, inferentially accepts liability for any and every transaction into which the undisclosed agent enters as long as such transaction has a connection with the business or other activity which has been entrusted to the undisclosed agent. The difficulty about this, however, from a practical, if not a logical point of view, is that it would expose the undisclosed principal to a potentially very wide, almost limitless liability for what the agent does. This might protect third parties transacting with the agent. It would mean that the principal has accepted a very great risk by employing an agent and allowing him to appear to be the principal.[8]

Not surprisingly other decisions have taken a contrary view of such a situation. They have held that the act of an undisclosed agent would not make an undisclosed principal liable, even where the act or acts in question related to the authority which, unknown to the third party, had been given to the agent.[9] These decisions hold that, if there has been a limitation placed on the agent's authority by the undisclosed principal, this will bind the third party dealing with the agent, even though the third party was unaware that he was dealing with an agent, and, therefore, was necessarily ignorant of any such limitations. What is surprising, however, is that no decision has firmly and decisively held that *Watteau v Fenwick* was wrong and should be discredited. Such a decision can now be found in the judgment of the British Columbia Court of Appeal in *Sign-O-Lite Plastics Ltd v Metropolitan Life Insurance Co.*[10]

Sign-O-Lite Plastics Ltd v Metropolitan Life Insurance Co

The facts in this case were as follows. In 1978 the plaintiff contracted with Calbax Properties Ltd for the renting of an electronic sign to be installed and maintained by the plaintiff at the Market Mall shopping centre in Calgary. This rental agreement was to last for 61 months. It contained a clause providing for automatic renewal for a further term of 60 months in the event that neither party communicated a contrary intention to the other, in writing, more than 30 days before the end of the first term. By virtue of that clause the agreement was renewed in 1984. Prior to that date, however, the defendant, in two stages, acquired ownership of the company which owned and controlled the shopping mall in which the sign was displayed. As part of this transaction the defendants agreed to assume the 1978 rental agreement between Calbax Properties Ltd and the plaintiff. When the defendant acquired ownership of the mall it was agreed with The Baxter Group Ltd that the latter should manage the mall as agent for the defendant. For that purpose the Baxter Group Ltd was given limited authority to enter into contracts on behalf of its principal, the defendants. The plaintiff knew nothing of the change of ownership of the mall. In other words the plaintiff was unaware of the existence of an undisclosed principal of The Baxter Group Ltd. In 1985, after the automatic renewal of the rental agreement in accordance with the original terms of 1978, The Baxter Group Ltd entered into a new rental agreement with the plaintiff intended by both parties to replace the original agreement. At that time the plaintiff believed, as it had every reason to believe, that it was dealing with a different corporate form of the same owner with which the plaintiff had originally contracted in 1978. The new agreement was one which The Baxter Group Ltd had not authority to contract. This was because (a) it did not disclose that The Baxter Group Ltd was acting as agent for the defendant, and (b) it did not provide for cancellation on 60 days' notice. As a result of various later transactions, which are not relevant to the problem in this case, the plaintiff eventually sued the defendant for damages for breach of contract, that is, the contract entered into in 1985 (not the original contract of 1978). At the trial the plaintiff was unsuccessful in establishing liability under the 1985 agreement, and was awarded damages on the 1978 contract. The defendant appealed and the plaintiff cross-appealed.

Two issues were before the court. The first was whether the defendant could be liable, as an undisclosed principal. This raised directly the question whether *Watteau v Fenwick* was good law and was part of the law in British Columbia. After considering the language of Wills J in *Watteau v Fenwick* and the subsequent case-law in which that decision had been rejected in Ontario[11] (as well as in Alberta[12]), Wood JA delivering the judgment of the court, declared that the reports he had researched were 'bereft of any hint that *Watteau v Fenwick* should be considered good law',[13] In view of the decisions to which reference has been made earlier, it is hardly a matter for surprise that Wood JA should have reached that conclusion.

Wills J had said in 1883 that once it was established that a defendant was a real principal, the ordinary doctrine as to principal and agent applied—that the principal was liable for all the acts of the agent that were within the authority usually confided to an agent of that character, notwithstanding limitations as between the principal and agent upon that authority.[14] In 1919 in *McLaughlin v Gentles*,[15] Hodgins J A of the Ontario Court of Appeal said:

> It seems to me to be straining the doctrine of ostensible agency or holding out to apply it in a case where the fact of agency and the holding out were unknown to the person dealing with the so-called agent at the time, and to permit that person, when he discovered that his purchaser was only an agent, to recover against the principal, on the theory that the latter was estopped from denying that he authorized the purchase. It appears to me that the fact that there was a limitation of authority is at least as important as the fact that the purchaser was an agent.

For reasons previously mentioned, the opinion of Hodgins JA is undoubtedly preferable to that of Wills J. But, as Wood JA said in the *Sign-O-Lite* case:[16]

> It is astonishing that, after all these years, an authority of such doubtful origin, and of such unanimously unfavourable reputation, should still be exhibiting signs of life and disturbing the peace of mind of trial judges.

It was time to end any uncertainty that might linger as to its proper place in the law of agency. He had no difficulty in concluding that the doctrine set out in *Watteau v Fenwick* was not part of the law of British Columbia. On that ground the plaintiff's cross-appeal failed: the defendant was not liable as an undisclosed principal on the 1985 contract.

Although this case dealt only with the law of British Columbia, it does not appear unreasonable to conclude, in light of this decision and the earlier Ontario cases referred to therein, that in common law Canada generally, whatever the state of the law in England, the doctrine of *Watteau v Fenwick* is defunct. It is to be hoped that the same will ultimately prove to be the situation in England. There is every indication that when the time comes for a court to do so, it will give the same short shrift to the decision of Wills J as it has now received at the hands of the British Columbia Court of Appeal.

Footnotes

1 [1893] 1 QB 346 (QBD).

2 FMB Reynolds [*Bowstead and Reynolds on Agency* (18th edn, 2006), paras 3–006, 8–079]; GHL Fridman, *Law of Agency* [(7th edn, 1996), pp 69–76]; R Powell *Law of Agency* (2nd edn, 1961), pp 75–78; SJ Stoljar *Law of Agency* (6th edn, 1990), pp 60–66; AL Goodhart and CJ Hamson, *Undisclosed Principals in Contract* (1932) 4 Camb LJ 320; JA Hornby *The Usual Authority of An Agent* [1961] Camb LJ 239.

3 *Miles v McIlwraith* (1883) 8 App Cas 120 (PC); *Becherer v Asher* (1896) 23 OAR 202 (Ont CA); *McLaughlin v Gentles* (1919) 51 DLR 383,46 OLR 477 (Ont App Div); *Massey Harris Co Ltd v Bond* [1930] 2 DLR 57, [1930] 1 WWR 72 (Alta SC). See also *Johnston v Reading* (1893) 9 TLR 200 (QBD); *Lloyd's Bank v Suisse Bankverein* (1912) 107 LT 309, aff'd (1913) 108 LT 143 (CA); *Jerome v Bentley* [1952] 2 All ER 114 (QBD); *International Paper Co v Spicer* (1906) 4 CLR 739 (Aust HC).

4 *Rhodian River Shipping Co SA v Halla Maritime Corp* [1984] 1 Lloyd's Rep 373, at pp 378–379 (QBD), per Bingham J. Curiously, this case was not referred to in the British Columbia decision that is now under discussion.

5 Bowstead, op cit, footnote 2, [paras 3–005–3–006]; Fridman, op cit, footnote 2, [pp 69–76, 122–128].
6 On actual authority see Bowstead, ibid, [paras 3–001—3–004]; Fridman, ibid, [pp 62–64].
7 See the authorities cited, supra, footnote 5.
8 It also seems to be rejected by the decision of the House of Lords in *Keighley Maxsted & Co v Durant* [1901] AC 240, on which see Bowstead, op cit, footnote 2, [para 2–061]; Fridman, op cit, footnote 2, [pp 89–90].
9 See, eg *McLaughlin v Gentles,* supra, footnote 3: cf *Keighley Maxsted & Co v Durant,* supra, footnote 8.
10 (1990) 73 DLR (4th) 541, 49 BCLR (2d) 183 (BCCA).
11 *McLaughlin v Gentles,* supra, footnote 3; *Massey Harris Co Ltd v Bond,* supra, footnote 3.
12 *Massey Harris Co Ltd v Bond,* ibid.
13 Supra, footnote 10, at pp 548 (DLR), 191 (BCLR).
14 *Watteau v Fenwick,* supra, footnote 1, at pp 348–349.
15 Supra, footnote 3, at pp 394–395 (DLR), 490 (OLR).
16 Supra, footnote 10, at pp 548 (DLR), 191 (BCLR).

NOTES

1.   A number of theories have been advanced in an attempt to explain *Watteau v Fenwick:* apparent authority (A L Goodhart and C J Hamson (1931) 4 CLJ 320 at 336; but see above for Fridman's response); 'inherent agency power' (*Restatement of the Law of Agency* (2nd edn, 1958), paras 8A, 140; but see M Conant (1968) 47 Nebraska LR 678, 686, and the concept is not used in the third edition of the *Restatement*, although art 2.06 retains a rule similar to the effect of *Watteau v Fenwick*); an independent type of usual authority (*Bowstead and Reynolds,* para 3–006; R Powell *Law of Agency* (2nd edn, 1961), p 78; but see also *Bowstead and Reynolds,* para 8–079); by analogy with the doctrine of vicarious liability in tort (E Peel *Treitel's Law of Contract* (12th edn, 2007), para 16–029; but see J Collier [1985] CLJ 363 at p 365); and as an extension of the doctrine of apparent ownership (M Conant, op cit, pp 687–688; but see J Hornby [1961] CLJ 239 at p 246). All these theories are open to criticism and none provides a satisfactory explanation of the case. If *Watteau v Fenwick* can be explained at all, it may be necessary to go outside the realm of agency and see it as an example of estoppel by conduct (but not of agency created by estoppel): 'what Fenwick represented by leaving Humble in charge was not that Humble was Fenwick's agent, but rather *that Humble and the owner of the Victoria Hotel (whoever that might he) were one and the same person.* By putting someone in charge of their business in such a way that he seemed to be the proprietor of it, they gave Watteau the impression that they, as owners of the hotel, were not a distinct legal entity from the person Watteau did business with.' (A Tettenborn [1998] CLJ 274, 279). Alternatively, it may be better simply to regard the decision as a product of its time, when the actual, general authority of a manager of a business was enough to make the principal responsible to a third party for his agent's acts, irrespective of internal restrictions on the agent's authority (see I Brown [2004] JBL 391, 407–412).

2.   Whatever the theoretical basis of the decision, it is submitted that there are good policy reasons against holding an undisclosed principal liable to a third party when the principal's agent exceeds his actual authority (contrast Collier, op cit, p 364, who describes *Watteau v Fenwick* as 'eminently just'). It must be remembered that *Watteau v Fenwick* places the undisclosed principal under a personal liability, it does not give him any right to sue the third party (*Bowstead and Reynolds,* para 8–079). Furthermore, because the agent exceeds his actual authority the principal cannot sue the third party under the doctrine of undisclosed principal (below, p 180); neither can he rely on ratification of the agent's acts, as an undisclosed principal cannot ratify (below, p 140). It seems unjust that the principal should have a liability without a right of action, especially when he never wished to be bound by such a contract in the first

place. However, by analogy with the doctrine of apparent authority, if the principal is sued on a contract made by his agent, he can probably make counterclaims as well as adduce defences, as opposed to suing on the contract of his own motion (see above, p 122). The issue remains undecided.

3.   Whatever the faults of the decision, *Watteau v Fenwick* has not been overruled in England. However, the limits of the case are clear. First, 'there should be an existing agency relationship, and the agent should be of such a character that it is possible to identify the 'usual' powers that such an agent will have' (RTH Stone [1993] JBL 325, 328). Identifying the 'usual' powers of any one category of agent may not be easy: 'late twentieth century business practices do not enable a facile classification of stereotypical agents with concomitant, standard authorities' (I Brown [1995] JBL 360, 367). Secondly, *Watteau v Fenwick* will not apply where the agent acts for himself and not for his principal (this is why *Kinahan & Co Ltd v Parry* [1910] 2 KB 389, where *Watteau v Fenwick* was followed, was reversed on appeal: [1911] 1 KB 459), or where the third party knows, or ought reasonably to know, of the restriction on the agent's authority (*Daun v Simmins* (1879) 41 LT 783, CA).

QUESTIONS

1.   In *Watteau v Fenwick,* could Watteau have sued Humble for the price of the cigars?

2.   Pippa appoints Audrey as her general manager for the purchase of houses in Leeds, instructing Audrey, however, not to disclose the existence of the agency, and not to purchase except on a surveyor's report. Audrey discloses her position to Tessa, withholding, however, the requirement of a surveyor's report and purchases houses in Leeds from Tessa as agent for Pippa without a surveyor's report. Is Pippa liable to Tessa for the price of the houses? See Montrose (1939) 17 Can Bar Rev 693 at pp 710–711; Hornby [1961] CLJ 239 at p 240 fn.

3.   Article 2.2.4 of the UNIDROIT *Principles of International Commercial Contracts* (2004) (see above, p 18) provides as follows:

(1) Where an agent acts within the scope of its authority and the third party neither knew nor ought to have known that the agent was acting as an agent, the acts of the agent shall affect only the relations between the agent and the third party.

(2) However, where such an agent, when contracting with the third party on behalf of a business, represents itself to be the owner of that business, the third party, upon discovery of the real owner of the business, may exercise also against the latter the rights it has against the agent.

What reason could there be for retaining the exception in art 2.2.4(2)? Can you think of an alternative way of protecting the third party in such circumstances? See *Bowstead and Reynolds*, para 8–079.

(d) Authority by operation of law

Agency of necessity

Bowstead and Reynolds on Agency

(18th edn, 2006), art 33

Doctrine of Agency of Necessity

(1) A person may have authority to act on behalf of another in certain cases where he is faced with an emergency in which the property or interests of that other are in imminent jeopardy and it becomes necessary, in order to preserve the property or interest, so to act.

(2) In some cases this authority may entitle him to affect his principal's legal position by making contracts or disposing of property. In others it may merely entitle him to reimbursement of expenses or indemnity against liabilities incurred in so acting, or to a defence against a claim that what he did was wrongful as against the person for whose benefit he acted.

China-Pacific SA v Food Corpn of India, The Winson
[1982] AC 939, House of Lords

The defendant cargo owner chartered a ship to carry wheat from the United States to Bombay. During the voyage the ship stranded on a reef. The ship's managing agents (in effect the ship's master) then entered into a Lloyd's Standard Form of Salvage Agreement No Cure—No Pay (known as the Lloyd's open form) with the plaintiffs, who were professional salvors. To assist the salvage operation, the salvors unloaded several parcels of wheat and shipped them to Manilla. To protect the wheat from deterioration, the salvors contracted with various depositaries to warehouse it at the salvors' expense. The salvors then looked to the cargo owner for reimbursement of these storage charges. Lloyd J held the cargo owner liable to reimburse the salvors but his decision was reversed by the Court of Appeal. The House of Lords upheld the salvors' appeal against the Court of Appeal's ruling and restored the judgment of Lloyd J.

Lord Diplock: Lloyd's open form is expressed by clause 16 to be signed by the master 'as agent for the vessel her cargo and freight and the respective owners thereof and binds each (but not the one for the other or himself personally) to the due performance thereof.' The legal nature of the relationship between the master and the owner of the cargo aboard the vessel in signing the agreement on the latter's behalf is often though not invariably an agency of necessity. It arises only when salvage services by a third party are necessary for the preservation of the cargo. Whether one person is entitled to act as agent of necessity for another person is relevant to the question whether circumstances exist which in law have the effect of conferring on him authority to create contractual rights and obligations between that other person and a third party that are directly enforceable by each against the other. It would, I think, be an aid to clarity of legal thinking if the use of the expression 'agent of necessity' were confined to contexts in which this was the question to be determined and not extended, as it often is, to cases where the only relevant question is whether a person who without obtaining instructions from the owner of goods incurs expense in taking steps that are reasonably necessary for their preservation is in law entitled to recover from the owner of the goods the reasonable expenses incurred by him in taking those steps. Its use in this wider sense may, I think, have led to some confusion in the instant case, since where reimbursement is the only relevant question all of those conditions that must be fulfilled in order to entitle one person to act on behalf of another in creating direct contractual relationships between that other person and a third party may not necessarily apply.

In the instant case it is not disputed that when the Lloyd's open form was signed on January 22,1975, the circumstances that existed at that time were such as entitled the master to enter into the agreement on the cargo owner's behalf as its agent of necessity. The rendering of salvage services under the Lloyd's open agreement does not usually involve the salvor's taking possession of the vessel or its cargo from the shipowner; the shipowner remains in possession of both ship and cargo while salvage services are being carried out by the salvors on the ship. But salvage services may involve the transfer of possession of cargo from the shipowner to the salvors, and will do so in a case of stranding as respects part of the cargo if it becomes necessary to lighten the vessel in order to refloat her. When, in the course of salvage operations cargo is off-loaded from the vessel by which the contract of carriage was being performed and conveyed separately from that vessel to a place of safety by means (in the instant case, barges) provided by the salvor, the direct relationship of bailor and bailee is created between cargo owner and salvor as soon as the cargo is loaded on vessels provided by the salvor to convey it to a place of safety; and all the mutual rights and duties attaching to that relationship at common law apply, save in so far as any of them are inconsistent with the express terms of the Lloyd's open agreement....

My Lords, in the courts below and in argument before your Lordships there has been some discussion as to whether on their obtaining possession of the cargo from the shipowner the relationship of the salvors to the cargo owner was that of bailee or sub-bailee. A sub-bailee is one to whom actual possession of goods is transferred by someone who is not himself the owner of the goods but has a present right to possession of them as bailee of the owner. In the instant case Lloyd J and the Court of Appeal were of the view that the salvors were bailees of the cargo owner, and this was, in my view also, plainly right. They would only be sub-bailees of the cargo owner if the contract to render salvage services to the cargo under Lloyd's open form had been signed by the master as agent for the shipowner only. This was plainly not the case. The contract was one under which the salvors' remuneration in respect of salvage services to the cargo was a liability of the cargo owner, not of the shipowner, and security for such remuneration could be required by the salvors to be given by the cargo owner alone; so the only consideration for salvage services rendered to the cargo by salvors under Lloyd's open form came from the cargo owner. The only sub-bailments involved in the instant case were those effected by the salvors themselves with the depositaries when they deposited the salved wheat for safe keeping at Manila....

Upon the assumption, whether correct or not, to which I have already referred as being that upon which this case has been argued throughout, that the salvage services which the salvors had contracted to render to the cargo owner came to an end as respects each parcel of salved wheat when it arrived at a place of safety in Manila Harbour, the legal relationship of bailor and bailee between cargo owner and salvors nevertheless continued to subsist until possession of the wheat was accepted by the cargo owner from the depositaries who had been the salvors' sub-bailees. Subject always to the question of the salvors' right to the provision of security before removal of the salved wheat from Manila, with which I shall deal separately later, the bailment which up to the conclusion of the salvage services had been a bailment for valuable consideration became a gratuitous bailment; and so long as that relationship of bailor and bailee continued to subsist the salvors, under the ordinary principles of the law of bailment too well known and too well-established to call for any citation of authority, owed a duty of care to the cargo owner to take such measures to preserve the salved wheat from deterioration by exposure to the elements as a man of ordinary prudence would take for the preservation of his own property. For any breach of such duty the bailee is liable to his bailor in damages for any diminution in value of the goods consequent upon his failure to take such measures; and if he fulfils that duty he has, in my view, a correlative right to charge the owner of the goods with the expenses reasonably incurred in doing so.

My Lords, as I have already said, there is not any direct authority as to the existence of this correlative right to reimbursement of expenses in the specific case of a salvor who retains possession of cargo after the salvage services rendered by him to that cargo have ended; but Lloyd J discerned what he considered to be helpful analogous applications of the principle of the bailee's right to reimbursement in *Cargo ex Argos* (1873) LR 5 PC 134, from which I have taken the expression 'correlative right,' and in *Great Northern Rly Co v Swaffield* (1874) LR 9 Exch 132. Both these were cases of carriage of goods in which the carrier/bailee was left in possession of the goods after the carriage contracted for had terminated. Steps necessary for the preservation of the goods were taken by the bailee in default of any instructions from owner/bailor to do otherwise. To these authorities I would add *Notara v Henderson* (1872) LR 7 QB 225, in which the bailee was held liable in damages for breach of his duty to take steps necessary for the preservation of the goods, and the Scots case of *Garriock v Walker* (1873) 1 R 100 in which the bailee recovered the expenses incurred by him in taking such steps. Although in both these cases, which involved carriage of goods by sea, the steps for the prevention of deterioration of the cargo needed to be taken before the contract voyage was completed, the significance of the Scots case is that the cargo owner was on the spot when the steps were taken by the carrier/bailee and did not acquiesce in them. Nevertheless, he took the benefit of them by taking delivery of the cargo thus preserved at the conclusion of the voyage.

In the instant case the cargo owner was kept informed of the salvors' intentions as to the storage of the salved wheat upon its arrival in Manila; it made no alternative proposals; it made no request to the salvors for delivery of any of the wheat after its arrival at Manila, and a request made by the salvors to the cargo owner through their solicitors on February 25,1975, after the arrival of the second of the six parcels, to take delivery of the parcels of salved wheat on arrival at Manila remained unanswered and uncomplied with until after notice of abandonment of the charter voyage had been received by the cargo owner from the shipowner.

The failure of the cargo owner as bailor to give any instructions to the salvors as its bailee although it was fully apprised of the need to store the salved wheat under cover on arrival at Manila if it was to be preserved from rapid deterioration was, in the view of Lloyd J, sufficient to attract the application of the principle to which I have referred above and to entitle the salvors to recover from the cargo owner their expenses in taking measures necessary for its preservation. For my part I think that in this he was right and the Court of Appeal, who took the contrary view, were wrong. It is, of course, true that in English law a mere stranger cannot compel an owner of goods to pay for a benefit bestowed upon him against his will; but this latter principle does not apply where there is a pre-existing legal relationship between the owner of the goods and the bestower of the benefit, such as that of bailor and bailee, which imposes upon the bestower of the benefit a legal duty of care in respect of the preservation of the goods that is owed by him to their owner.

In the Court of Appeal Megaw LJ, as I understand his judgment, with which Bridge and Cumming-Bruce LJJ expressed agreement, was of opinion that, in order to entitle the salvors to reimbursement of the expenses incurred by them in storing the salvaged wheat at Manila up to April 24,1975, they would have to show not only that, looked at objectively, the measures that they took were necessary to preserve it from rapid deterioration, but, in addition, that it was impossible for them to communicate with the cargo owner to obtain from him such instructions (if any) as he might want to give. My Lords, it may be that this would have been so if the question in the instant case had been whether the depositaries could have sued the cargo owner directly for their contractual storage charges on the ground that the cargo owner was party as principal to the contracts of storage made on its behalf by the salvors as its agents of necessity; for English law is economical in recognising situations that give rise to agency of necessity. In my view, inability to communicate with the owner of the goods is not a condition precedent to the bailee's own right to reimbursement of his expenses. The bailor's failure to give any instructions when apprised of the situation is sufficient.

So, on the cargo owner's main propositions of law in this appeal, I think it fails and that on these points the Court of Appeal was wrong in reversing Lloyd J.

Lord Simon of Glaisdale held that the salvors' right of reimbursement arose by implication from the Lloyd's open form agreement and from the common law of bailment. He continued:
Agency of necessity. Lloyd J decided in favour of the salvor on the further ground that he was the cargo owner's agent of necessity and as such entitled to reimbursement of the expenses in issue. The Court of Appeal held that there was no agency of necessity.

One of the ways in which an agency of necessity can arise is where A is in possession of goods the property of B, and an emergency arises which places those goods in imminent jeopardy: If A cannot obtain instructions from B as to how he should act in such circumstances, A is bound to take without authority such action in relation to the goods as B, as a prudent owner, would himself have taken in the circumstances. The relationship between A and B is then known as an 'agency of necessity,' A being the agent and B the principal. This was the situation described by Lloyd J and denied by the Court of Appeal.

Issues as to agency of necessity generally arise forensically when A enters into a contract with C in relation to the goods, the question being whether B is bound by that contract. The purely terminological suggestion that, in order to avoid confusion, 'agent of necessity' should be confined to such contractual situations does not involve that other relevant general incidents of agency are excluded from the relationship between A and B. In particular, if A incurs reasonable expenses in safeguarding B's goods in a situation of emergency, A is entitled to be reimbursed by B: . . .

To confine 'agent of necessity' terminologically to the contractual situations is justified by the fact that the law of bailment will often resolve any issue between alleged principal and agent of necessity, as it has done here. But sometimes the law of agency will be more useful: for example, if available here it would obviate any problem about the correlation of performance of a duty of care with a claim for reimbursement, since an agent is undoubtedly entitled to an indemnity for expenses incurred reasonably to benefit his principal.

However, I respectfully agree with the Court of Appeal [1981] QB 403,424 that:

> The relevant time, for the purpose of considering whether there was a necessity, or an emergency . . . is . . . the time when the existence of the supposed emergency became apparent. The emergency would be the arrival, or expected arrival, of salved cargo at Manila, with no arrangements for its off-loading or for its preservation in proper storage having been made or put in hand. There never was, so far as one can ascertain from the evidential matter here, such an emergency.

In addition to the factual difficulty in treating the case as one of agency of necessity, there are legal difficulties in the way of the salvor. For an agency of necessity to arise, the action taken must be necessary for the protection of the interests of the alleged principal, not of the agent; the alleged agent must have acted bona fide in the interests of the alleged principal: . . . The Court of Appeal [1981] QB 403, 425 held that the salvor's purpose in storing the salved cargo was to maintain his lien on it. This was assuredly at least in part the salvor's purpose. The law does not seem to have determined in this context what ensues where interests are manifold or motives mixed: it may well be that the court will look to the interest mainly served or to the dominant motive. In view of the opinion I have formed on the rights arising by implication from the Lloyd's open form and from the common law bailment, it is unnecessary to come to any conclusion on these issues.

[Lord Keith of Kinkel, Lord Roskill and Lord Brandon of Oakbrook concurred with Lord Diplock.]

NOTES

1. Traditionally, the courts have not distinguished between cases where an agent of necessity creates a contractual relationship between his principal and a third party and those where the agent of necessity simply seeks reimbursement from the principal, or looks to defend an action for wrongful interference with the principal's goods. However, the distinction was made by Lord Diplock in *The Winson* and we shall adopt it here (cf E Peel *Treitel's Law of Contract* (12th edn, 2007), para 16–041; A Burrows, *The Law of Restitution* (2nd edn, 2002), p 308).

2. (a) *True agents of necessity.* In such cases the agent has power to affect the legal relations of his principal. The agent may contract with third parties on behalf of his principal and he may dispose of his principal's property. The agent will have a defence if sued by his principal and he may be able to claim reimbursement from the principal for expenses incurred. However, agency of necessity will only arise if:

(1) it is impossible or impracticable for the agent to communicate with the principal (*Springer v Great Western Rly Co* [1921] 1 KB 257 at 265, per Bankes LJ)—improved

methods of communication in the modern commercial world mean that this requirement is now rarely met;

(2) the action is necessary for the benefit of the principal (*Prager v Blatspiel, Stamp and
Heacock Ltd* [1924] 1 KB 566 at 571, per McCardie J);

(3) the agent acts bona fide in the interests of the principal (*Prager v Blatspiel*, above, at
572);

(4) the action taken by the agent is reasonable and prudent (*F v West Berkshire Health
Authority* [1989] 2 All ER 545 at 566, per Lord Goff); and

(5) the principal has not given the agent express instructions to the contrary (see *Bowstead
and Reynolds*, para 4–005: 'this follows from the fact that [agency of necessity] does not
operate where the principal can be consulted. The inference is that the principal could
forbid the action at the time: if so, he can do so in advance.').

The traditional (possibly only) example of a true agent of necessity is the master of a ship
who acts in an emergency to save the ship or the cargo (*Hawtayne v Bourne* (1841) 7 M &
W 595 at 599, per Parke B). Sometimes it is possible to explain the master's agency in terms
of implied actual authority, eg when he signs a salvage contract on behalf of the shipowner
(*The Unique Mariner* [1978] 1 Lloyd's Rep 438). On other occasions it may only be possible
to explain the master's action in terms of necessity, eg in *The Choko Star* [1990] 1 Lloyd's
Rep 516 the Court of Appeal stressed that the ship's master had no implied actual authority
to sign a salvage agreement on behalf of cargo owners, but he could do so as an agent of
necessity (noted by RJC Munday [1991] LMCLQ 1; I Brown (1992) 55 MLR 414). But now
see the Merchant Shipping Act 1995, s 224(1), implementing art 6(2) of the International
Convention on Salvage of 1989, which gives the master wide powers, including the power to
sign a salvage contract for the cargo.

There has been considerable debate as to whether true agency of necessity is restricted
to cases of the carriage of goods by sea. For conflicting dicta, see *Prager v Blatspiel, Stamp
and Heacock Ltd* [1924] 1 KB 566 at 569–571, per McCardie J; and *Jebarav Ottoman Bank*
[1927] 2 KB 254 at 270–271, per Scrutton LJ. However, it has been established that agency
of necessity also extends to the carriage or storage of perishable goods or livestock on land
(*Great Northern Rly Co v Swaffield* (1874) LR 9 Exch 132; *Sachs v Miklos* [1948] 2 KB 23) and
there seems no reason why non-perishable goods should not be included in this category,
although such cases are likely to be rare. The dicta of Lord Simon in *The Winson* appears to
support this broader approach (above). See also ss 12, 13 and Sch 1 of the Torts (Interference
with Goods) Act 1977 (conferring a power of sale on bailees of goods in specified circumstances). Cf *Bowstead and Reynolds*, para 4–006 and *Fridman*, pp 142–143, who submit that
these non-maritime cases are more appropriately dealt with as part of the law of restitution,
ie under category (b) below.

3.   (b) *Agents who act for another in circumstances of necessity and seek reimbursement
or look to defend themselves against an action for interference with the principal's property.* *The Winson* provides an example of this type of agent. Lord Diplock did not think it
necessary that such an agent need comply with all the strict rules as apply to true agents of
necessity (above, p 133) and this view is supported by *Bowstead and Reynolds* (para 4–005).
Whether this type of agency is confined to situations where there it is a pre-existing relationship (contractual or otherwise) between the principal and agent is a difficult question
to answer. In *The Winson* such a relationship existed, ie that of bailor and bailee. It is really
a question for the law of restitution. English law has traditionally set itself against a general

principle (outside the law of maritime salvage) entitling a stranger who protects or benefits the property of another to seek reimbursement or claim a lien (see the classic dictum of Bowen LJ in *Flacke v Scottish Imperial Insurance Co* (1886) 34 Ch D 234, 248–249). The long established right of an acceptor of a bill of exchange for honour to seek reimbursement from the drawer would appear to be an exception to this general rule (Bills of Exchange Act 1882, s 68(5)). However, recent developments in the law of restitution indicate that a stranger who intervenes in an emergency will have a good claim if (a) there was a pressing emergency which compelled intervention without the property owner's authority; (b) he acted reasonably and in the best interests of the property owner; (c) he was not able to obtain the 'principal's' instructions; and (d) (possibly) he is a professional performing a professional service (see R Goff and G Jones *The Law of Restitution* (7th edn, 2007), para 17–013). In *Surrey Breakdown Ltd v Knight* [1999] RTR 84, Sir Christopher Staughton, speaking by way of *obiter dictum,* described this more flexible approach to the availability of a restitutionary claim as representing the modern law. In that case the police called in a garage to pull a stolen car out of a pond. The garage did so and later claimed the cost of this service, and subsequent storage charges, from the car's owner. The Court of Appeal rejected the claim on the ground that the facts of the case did not meet condition (a): there was no pressing emergency compelling intervention without the car owner's authority. For further reading, see *Goff and Jones,* above, Ch 17; A Burrows *The Law of Restitution* (2nd edn, 2002), Ch 9; G Virgo *Principles of the Law of Restitution* (2nd edn, 2002), Ch 11.

4.   The Mental Capacity Act 2005, ss 5–8, creates a statutory form of agency of necessity for mentally incapacitated persons (see *Bowstead and Reynolds,* para 4–012). It enables a person to intervene on behalf of a mentally incapacitated person to pledge that person's credit in connection with his care or treatment, and to use that person's money and/or seek indemnity in respect of acts done for that purpose. This regime does not affect the operation of a lasting power of attorney that may have been drawn up by the mentally incapacitated person before the incapacity arose.

QUESTION

'Agency by estoppel is really agency by operation of law' (*Fridman,* p 19). Discuss.

(e) Ratification

If a person (the 'agent') acts without authority, or exceeds his authority, his actions cannot bind the person (the 'principal') on whose behalf he purports to act. Subsequently, however, the principal may ratify the agent's acts. Ratification validates the agent's actions with effect from the time those actions took place. As Lord Sterndale MR stated in *Koenigsblatt v Sweet* [1923] 2 Ch 314 at 325: 'Ratification…is equivalent to an antecedent authority'. The doctrine is to some extent anomalous and the courts seems keen to keep it in check (*Smith v Henniker-Major & Co* [2002] EWCA Civ 762, [2002] Ch 182 at [61], per Robert Walker LJ).

Ratification may be express or implied from the principal's unequivocal conduct. In *Hogan v London Irish Rugby Football Trading Ltd* (20 December 1999, unreported), the defendants were held to have ratified oral agreements made by A, their chief coach and director of rugby, with the players, by allowing them to represent the Club and turn up for training, and by continuing to pay them at the rate agreed with A. If ratification is to be implied from the principal's conduct, he must usually be shown to have had full knowledge of the agent's unauthorised acts and a real choice as to whether or not he wished to adopt them (*The Bonita; The Charlotte* (1861) 1 Lush 252). This means that the principal must have had knowledge of what the agent has done; it does not mean that he needs to know that the agent lacked authority to do it (*ING Re (UK) Ltd v R & V Versicherung AG* [2006] EWHC 1544 (Comm), [2006] 2 All ER (Comm) 870 at [155]-[157]). Ignorance of the law will not allow the principal to avoid the effect of an act that, objectively viewed, exposes him to liability to third parties (*AMB Generali Holdings AB v SEB Trygg Liv Holding AB* [2005] EWCA Civ 1237, [2006] 1 Lloyd's Rep 318 at [43]). However, a principal with incomplete knowledge may be held to have ratified the unauthorised acts of his agent if it can be shown that he took a risk as to how the circumstances might turn out (*Marsh v Joseph* [1897] 1 Ch 213). Silence or inactivity alone will not amount to ratification as it does not provide clear and unequivocal evidence of the principal's approval and adoption of his agent's actions (*Crampsey v Deveney* (1969) 2 DLR (3d) 161 at 164, per Judson J; *713860 Ontario Ltd v Royal Trust Corpn of Canada* (22 January 1996, unreported), per Wilson J, an Ontario case cited in *Markesinis and Munday* at p 82, and since upheld on appeal, unreported, 1 March 1999). But silence or inactivity may amount to ratification where it is coupled with other factors: for example, where the principal is aware of all the material facts and appreciates that he is regarded as having accepted the position of principal, and he takes no steps to disown that character within a reasonable time, or adopts no means of asserting his rights at the earliest possible time (*Suncorp Insurance and Finance v Milano Assicurazioni SpA* [1993] 2 Lloyd's Rep 225 at 234–235, per Waller J; *Yona International Ltd v La Réunion Française Société Anonyme D'Assurances et de Réassurances* [1996] 2 Lloyd's Rep 84 at 103, per Moore-Bick J). A party wishing to ratify a transaction must adopt it in its entirely, but adoption of part of a transaction may be held to amount to ratification of the whole (*Smith v Henniker-Major & Co*, above, at [56], per Robert Walker LJ).

The principal can only ratify acts which the agent purported to do on the principal's behalf. As the next case illustrates, if the agent purports to act on his own behalf the principal cannot ratify.

Keighley, Maxsted & Co v Durant

[1901] AC 240, House of Lords

Keighley, Maxstead & Co (KM) instructed Roberts, a corn merchant, to buy wheat at a certain price on the joint account of themselves and Roberts. Roberts could not buy at this price, but he agreed to purchase wheat from Durant at a higher price. Although Roberts intended to buy the wheat on behalf of himself and KM, he bought it in his own name without informing Durant that he was also acting for KM. KM then purported to ratify the agreement. The price was not paid to Durant who claimed to hold KM liable on the contract. Day J dismissed the action, but he was reversed by the Court of Appeal. The House of Lords allowed an appeal from the Court of Appeal's decision.

Lord Macnaghten: As a general rule, only persons who are parties to a contract, acting either by themselves or by an authorized agent, can sue or be sued on the contract. A stranger cannot enforce the contract, nor can it be enforced against a stranger. That is the rule; but there are exceptions. The most remarkable exception, I think, results from the doctrine of ratification as established in English law. That doctrine is thus stated by Tindal CJ in *Wilson v Tumman* ((1843) 6 Man & G 236 at 242): 'That an act done, *for another*, by a person, not assuming to act for himself, but for such other person, though without any precedent authority whatever, becomes the act of the principal, if subsequently ratified by him, is the known and well-established rule of law. In that case the principal is bound by the act, whether it be for his detriment or his advantage, and whether it be founded on a tort or on a contract, to the same effect as by, and with all the consequences which follow from, the same act done by his *previous* authority.' And so by a wholesome and convenient fiction, a person ratifying the act of another, who, without authority, has made a contract openly and avowedly on his behalf, is deemed to be, though in fact he was not, a party to the contract. Does the fiction cover the case of a person who makes no avowal at all, but assumes to act for himself and for no one else? If Tindal CJ's statement of the law is accurate, it would seem to exclude the case of a person who may intend to act for another, but at the same time keeps his intention locked up in his own breast; for it cannot be said that a person who so conducts himself does assume to act for anybody but himself. But ought the doctrine of ratification to be extended to such a case? On principle I should say certainly not. It is, I think, a well-established principle in English law that civil obligations are not to be created by, or founded upon, undisclosed intentions. That is a very old principle. Lord Blackburn, enforcing it in the case of *Brogden v Metropolitan Rly Co* ((1877) 2 App Cas 666 at 692), traces it back to the year-books of Edward IV (17 Edw 4,2, pi 2) and to a quaint judgment of Brian CJ: 'It is common learning,' said that Chief Justice, who was a great authority in those days, 'that the thought of a man is not triable, for the Devil has not knowledge of man's thoughts.'

Sir E Fry quotes the same observation in his work on Specific Performance, s 295, p 133, 3rd edn. It is, I think, a sound maxim—at least, in its legal aspect: and in my opinion it is not to be put aside or disregarded merely because it may be that, in a case like the present, no injustice might be done to the actual parties to the contract by giving effect to the undisclosed intentions of a would-be agent.

Lord Shand: The question which arises on this state of the facts is whether, where a person who has avowedly made a contract for himself (1) without a suggestion that he is acting to any extent for another (an undisclosed principal), and (2) without any authority to act for another, can effectually bind a third party as principal, or as a joint obligant with himself, to the person with whom he contracted, by the fact that in his own mind merely he made a contract in the hope and expectation that his contract would be ratified or shared by the person as to whom he entertained that hope and expectation. I am clearly of opinion, with all respect to the majority of the Court of Appeal, that he cannot. The only contract actually made is by the person himself and for himself, and it seems to me to be conclusive against the argument for the respondents, that if their reasoning were sound it would be in his power, on an averment of what was passing in his own mind, to make the contract afterwards either one for himself only, as in fact it was, or one affecting or binding on another as a contracting party, even although he had no authority for this. The result would be to give one of two contracting parties in his option, merely from what was passing in his own mind and not disclosed, the power of saying the contract was his alone, or a contract in which others were bound with him. That, I think, he certainly cannot do in any case where he had no authority, when he made the contract, to bind any one but himself.

Lord Davey: The argument seems to be that as the law permits an undisclosed principal, on whose behalf a contract has been made, to sue and be sued on the contract, and as the effect of ratification is equivalent to a previous mandate, a person who ratifies a contract intended but not expressed to be made on his behalf is in the same position as any other undisclosed principal. Further, it is said that whether the intention of the contractor be expressed or not, its existence is mere matter of evidence, and once it is proved the conclusion ought to follow. Romer LJ held that on principle it ought to be held that ratification (in the case before the Court) is possible, and that to hold the contrary would be to establish an anomaly in the law, and moreover a useless one. My Lords, I cannot agree. There is a wide difference between an agency existing at the date of the contract which is susceptible of proof, and a repudiation of which by the agent would be fraudulent, and an intention locked up in the mind of the contractor, which he may either abandon or act on at his own pleasure, and the ascertainment of which involves an inquiry into the state of his mind at the date of the contract. Where the intention to contract on behalf of another is expressed in the contract, it passes from the region of speculation into that of fact, and becomes irrevocable. In what sense, it may be asked, does a man contract for another, when it depends on his own will whether he will give that other the benefit of the contract or not? In the next place, the rule which permits an undisclosed principal to sue and be sued on a contract to which he is not a party, though well settled, is itself an anomaly, and to extend it to the case of a person who accepts the benefit of an undisclosed intention of a party to the contract would, in my opinion, be adding another anomaly to the law, and not correcting an anomaly.

Lord Lindley: That ratification when it exists is equivalent to a previous authority is true enough (subject to some exceptions which need not be referred to). But, before the one expression can be substituted for the other, care must be taken that ratification is established.

It was strongly contended that there was no reason why the doctrine of ratification should not apply to undisclosed principals in general, and that no one could be injured by it if it were so applied. I am not convinced of this. But in this case there is no evidence in existence that, at the time when Roberts made his contract, he was in fact acting, as distinguished from intending to act, for the defendants as possible principals, and the decision appealed from, if affirmed, would introduce a very dangerous doctrine. It would enable one person to make a contract between two others by creating a principal and saying what his own undisclosed intentions were, and these could not be tested.

[The Earl of Halsbury LC, and Lords James of Hereford, Brampton and Robertson delivered concurring opinions.]

NOTES

1. The decision of the House of Lords in *Keighley, Maxsted & Co v Durant* has been described as 'peremptory and short-sighted' (I Brown [2004] JBL 391, 394). Can you think why? For criticism of the rule precluding ratification of an undisclosed principal, see A Rochvarg (1989) 34 McGill LJ 286. The rule has been abandoned in the third edition of the US *Restatement of the Law of Agency* (para 4.03 and Comment b). But the rule is well established in English law and unlikely to be altered in the near future: in *Welsh Development Agency v Export Finance Co Ltd* [1992] BCLC 148 at 158, Dillon LJ described it as 'clear law'.

2. In *Keighley, Maxsted & Co v Durant* the undisclosed principal evaded liability. But in *Spiro v Lintern* (discussed above at p 127), where *Keighley, Maxsted & Co v Durant* was followed and applied, the undisclosed principal was held liable to the third party, even though the agent had acted beyond her actual authority. How did this liability arise?

3. As a general rule, an undisclosed principal may sue and be sued on a contract made by an agent acting *within* the scope of his actual authority (see below, p 180).

(i) Other requirements for ratification

(1) The principal must be in existence at the time of the agent's act. Thus a newly incorporated company cannot ratify a prior contract made by its promoters (*Kelner v Baxter* (1866) LR 2 CP 174), although the contract will normally take effect as one between the third party and the promoter allowing both parties to sue and be sued on it (Companies Act 2006, s 51(1); *Braymist Ltd v Wise Finance Co Ltd* [2002] EWCA Civ 127, [2002] Ch 273, applying the identically worded Companies Act 1985, s 36C(1)). The Contracts (Rights of Third Parties) Act 1999 (below, p 151) does not change this requirement even though s 1(3) provides that a 'third party' may enforce a term of a contract to which he is not a party despite the fact that he is not in existence when the contract is entered into. The disclosed principal should not be regarded as a 'third party' for these purposes as he is a party to the contract and able to enforce it as promisee. The way round the problem would be for the agent to be made a party to a contract that included provision for a third party beneficiary, ie the non-existent principal (E Peel, *Treitel's Law of*

Contract (12th edn, 2007), para 16–061). Alternatively, a novation (see below, p 939) could take place once the principal has come into existence. Neither solution involves ratification.

(2) According to Willes J in *Watson v Swann* (1862) 11 CBNS 756 at 771:

To entitle a person to sue upon a contract, it must clearly be shown that he himself made it, or that it was made on his behalf by an agent authorised to act for him. The law obviously requires that the person for whom the agent professes to act must be a person capable of being ascertained at the time. It is not necessary that he should be named; but there must be such a description of him as shall amount to a reasonable designation of the person intended to be bound by the contract.

In that case, an agent was instructed to effect a general policy of insurance on goods for a principal. The agent was unable to do this, so he declared the goods on the back of a general policy of insurance which he had previously effected for himself. Later, when the goods had been lost, the principal sued on the policy. It was held that the principal could not recover on the policy because it was not made on his behalf. At the time the policy was effected by the agent the principal was not even known to him.

The narrow scope of Willes J's dicta has been criticised (see, eg *Bowstead and Reynolds,* para 2–065; *Markesinis and Munday,* p 69). In fact policies of marine insurance may be taken out 'for and on behalf of any person interested' and such persons can ratify even though not named on the policy (*Hagedorn v Oliverson* (1814) 2 M & S 485). The reasoning underlying this broader approach was set out by Coleman J in *National Oilwell (UK) Ltd v Davy Offshore Ltd* [1993] 2 Lloyd's Rep 582 at 596–597 (a non-marine insurance case):

Where at the time when the contract of insurance was made the principal assured or other contracting party had no actual authority to bind the other party to the contract of insurance, but the policy is expressed to insure not only the principal assured but also a class of others who are not identified in that policy, a party who at the time when the policy was effected could have been ascertained to qualify as a member of that class can ratify and sue on the policy as co-assured if at that time it was intended by the principal assured or other contracting party to create privity of contract with the insurer on behalf of that party.

Evidence as to whether in any particular case the principal assured or other contracting party did have the requisite intention may be provided by the terms of the policy itself, by the terms of any contract between the principal assured or other contracting party and the alleged co-assured and by any other admissible material showing what was subjectively intended by the principal assured.

There seems no good reason to restrict the application of Coleman J's propositions to insurance law. As the distinguished editor of *Markesinis and Munday* observes (at p 70): 'If third parties (eg underwriters) are willing to contract under such terms and if principals are prepared to ratify such contracts, there seems no reason why the law should refuse to give effect to the parties' collective wishes, not least because it serves an obvious commercial convenience'. See also F Reynolds 'Some Agency Problems in Insurance Law', Ch 4 in FD Rose (ed) *Consensus Ad Idem* (1996), pp 82–83.

(3) The principal must have been competent at the time when the act was done by the agent, eg a principal who was an enemy alien at the time of the agent's act could not ratify: *Boston Deep Sea Fishing and Ice Co Ltd v Farnham (Inspector of Taxes)* [1957] 1 WLR 1051. The principal must also have capacity at the date of the purported ratification, eg a principal cannot ratify if he is an enemy alien at the date of purported ratification, even though he was not one at the time the act was done.

(4) An act which is void *ab initio* (eg on grounds of illegality or because it is a nullity) cannot be ratified. In the leading case of *Brook v Hook* (1871) LR 6 Exch 89 a distinction was drawn between voidable acts, which can be ratified, and void acts, which cannot. However, as unauthorised acts cannot properly be described as voidable (if anything, they could be described as void), such a general distinction seems unsatisfactory. *Brook v Hook* involved forgery of the principal's signature on a promissory note by his agent. It was held that the principal could not ratify the agent's act as the signature was a nullity. It is submitted that the case is better explained as one where by forging the principal's signature the agent did not purport to act on behalf of the principal; quite the contrary, the agent purported to be the principal himself (E Peel, *Treitel's Law of Contract* (12th edn, 2007), para 16–045). Furthermore, a principal cannot ratify an unauthorised contract which is prohibited by statute (*Bedford Insurance Co Ltd v Instituto de Resseguros do Brasil* [1985] QB 966 at 986), but otherwise a principal can ratify an unlawful act.

(ii) Effect of ratification

Bolton Partners v Lambert
(1889) 41 Ch D 295

Lambert made an offer to Scratchley, an agent of Bolton Partners, to take the lease of certain properties. The offer was accepted by Scratchley on behalf of Bolton Partners, though he had no authority to do so. Lambert withdrew the offer before Bolton Partners ratified Scratchley's acceptance. Bolton Partners claimed specific performance of the contract. Affirming the decision of Kekewich J, the Court of Appeal held that Bolton Partners were entitled to specific performance of the contract.

Cotton LJ: But then it is said that on the 13th of January, 1887, the Defendant entirely withdrew the offer he had made. Of course the withdrawal could not be effective, if it were made after the contract had become complete. As soon as an offer has been accepted the contract is complete. But it is said that there could be a withdrawal by the Defendant on the 13th of January on this ground, that the offer of the Defendant had been accepted by *Scratchley,* a director of the Plaintiff company, who was not authorized to bind the company by acceptance of the offer, and therefore that until the company ratified *Scratchley's* act there was no acceptance on behalf of the company binding on the company, and therefore the Defendant could withdraw his offer. Is that so? The rule as to ratification by a principal of acts done by an assumed agent is that the ratification is thrown back to the date of the act done, and that the agent is put in the same position as if he had had authority to do the act at the time the act was done by him. Various cases have been referred to as laying down this principle, but there is no case exactly like the present one. The case of *Hagedorn v Oliverson* ((1814) 2 M & S 485) is a strong case of the application of the principle. It was there pointed out how favourable the rule was to the principal, because till ratification he was not bound, and he had an option to adopt or not to adopt what had been done. In that case the plaintiff had effected an insurance on a ship in which another person was interested, and it was held that long after the ship had been lost the other person might adopt the act of the plaintiff, though done without authority, so as to enable the plaintiff to sue upon the policy. Again, in *Ancona v Marks* ((1862) 7 H & N 686), where a bill was indorsed to and sued on in the name of *Ancona,* who had given no authority for that purpose, yet it was held that *Ancona* could, after the action had been brought, ratify what had been done, and that the subsequent ratification was equivalent to a prior authority so as to entitle *Ancona* to sue upon the bill. It was said by Mr *Brice* that in that case there was a previously existing liability of the defendant towards some person; but the liability of the defendant to *Ancona* was established by *Ancona*'s authorizing and ratifying the act of the agent, and a previously existing liability to others did not affect the principle laid down.

The rule as to ratification is of course subject to some exceptions. An estate once vested cannot be divested, nor can an act lawful at the time of its performance be rendered unlawful, by the application of the doctrine of ratification. The case of *Walter v James* ((1871) LR 6 Exch 124) was relied on by the Appellant, but in that case there was an agreement between the assumed agent of the defendant and the plaintiff to cancel what had been done before any ratification by the defendant; in the present case there was no agreement made between *Scratchley* and the Defendant that what had been done by *Scratchley* should be considered as null and void.

The case of *Bird v Brown* ((1850) 4 Exch 786), which was also relied on by the Appellant, is distinguishable from this case. There it was held that the ratification could not operate to divest the ownership which had previously vested in the purchaser by the delivery of the goods before the ratification of the alleged *stoppage in transitu*. So also in *Lyell v Kennedy* ((1887) 18 QBD 796) the plaintiff, who represented the lawful heir, desired, after the defendant *Kennedy* had acquired a title to the estate by means of the *Statute of Limitations*, and after the title of the heir was gone, to ratify the act *of Kennedy* as to the receipt of rents, so as to make the estate vest in the heir. In my opinion none of these cases support the Appellant's contention.

I think the proper view is that the acceptance by *Scratchley* did constitute a contract, subject to its being shewn that *Scratchley* had authority to bind the company. If that were not shewn there would be no contract on the part of the company, but when and as soon as authority was given to *Scratchley* to bind the company the authority was thrown back to the time when the act was done by *Scratchley*, and prevented the Defendant withdrawing his offer, because it was then no longer an offer, but a binding contract.

Lindley LJ: The question is what is the consequence of the withdrawal of the offer after acceptance by the assumed agent but before the authority of the agent has been ratified? Is the withdrawal in time? It is said on the one hand that the ordinary principle of law applies, viz, that an offer may be withdrawn before acceptance. That proposition is of course true. But the question is—acceptance by whom? It is not a question whether a mere offer can be withdrawn, but the question is whether, when there has been in fact an acceptance which is in form an acceptance by a principal through his agent, though the person assuming to act as agent has not then been so authorized, there can or cannot be a withdrawal of the offer before the ratification of the acceptance? I can find no authority in the books to warrant the contention that an offer made, and in fact accepted by a principal through an agent or otherwise, can be withdrawn. The true view on the contrary appears to be that the doctrine as to the retrospective action of ratification is applicable.

Lopes LJ: An important point is raised with regard to the withdrawal of the offer before ratification in this case.

If there had been no withdrawal of the offer this case would have been simple. The ratification by the Plaintiffs would have related back to the time of the acceptance of the Defendant's offer by *Scratchley*, and the Plaintiffs would have adopted a contract made on their behalf.

It is said that there was no contract which could be ratified, because *Scratchley* at the time he accepted the Defendant's offer had no authority to act for the Plaintiffs. Directly *Scratchley* on behalf and in the name of the Plaintiffs accepted the Defendant's offer I think there was a contract made by *Scratchley* assuming to act for the Plaintiffs, subject to proof by the Plaintiffs that *Scratchley* had that authority.

The Plaintiffs subsequently did adopt the contract, and thereby recognised the authority of their agent *Scratchley*. Directly they did so the doctrine of ratification applied and gave the same effect to the contract made by *Scratchley* as it would have had if *Scratchley* had been clothed with a precedent authority to make it.

If *Scratchley* had acted under a precedent authority the withdrawal of the offer by the Defendant would have been inoperative, and it is equally inoperative where the Plaintiffs have ratified and adopted the contract of the agent. To hold otherwise would be to deprive the doctrine of ratification of its retrospective effect. To use the words of Baron *Martin* in *Brook v Hook* ((1871) LR 6 Exch 89 at 96), the ratification would not be 'dragged back as it were, and made equipollent to a prior command.'

I have nothing to add with regard to the other points raised. I agree with what has been said on those points. The appeal must be dismissed.

NOTES

1.　The effect of the rule in *Bolton Partners v Lambert* is limited in a number of ways:

(1)　Ratification must take place within a reasonable time after acceptance of the offer by the unauthorised person: *Managers of the Metropolitan Asylums Board v Kingham & Sons* (1890) 6 TLR 217. What is a reasonable time will depend on the facts of the case. The third party offeror may abridge the time within which the ratification must take place by informing the principal of his wish to withdraw from the contract (*Re Portuguese Consolidated Copper Mines Ltd* (1890) 45 Ch D 16). There is dictum by Fry LJ in the *Metropolitan Asylums Board* case that 'reasonable time can never extend after the time at which the contract is to commence'. But this dictum has since been disapproved, and can no longer be considered as valid (see, eg *Bedford Insurance Co Ltd v Instituto de Resseguros do Brasil* [1985] QB 966 at 987, per Parker J). It has long been established that a policy of marine insurance may be ratified after loss (*Williams v North China Insurance Co* (1876) 1 CPD 757), and it has recently been suggested that the same rule applies to non-marine insurance (*National Oilwell (UK) Ltd v Davy Offshore Ltd* [1993] 2 Lloyd's Rep 582, 607–608; cf *Grover & Grover Ltd v Matthews* [1910] 2 KB 401). If ratification after loss is contemplated by the terms of the contract this should be allowed.

(2)　The rule in *Bolton Partners v Lambert* will not apply if the third party's offer was expressly made subject to ratification (*Metropolitan Asylums Board v Kingham,* above, at 218, per Fry LJ), or the third party's acceptance was expressly made subject to ratification (*Watson v Davies* [1931] 1 Ch 455 at 469, per Maugham J), or the '[third] party to the contract has intimation of the limitation of the agent's authority' (*Warehousing and Forwarding Co of East Africa Ltd v Jafferali & Sons Ltd* [1964] AC 1 at 9, per Lord Guest). In all such cases the third party may withdraw his offer at any time before the principal ratifies the agent's unauthorised acceptance.

(3)　It has been stated by Professor Fridman (*Fridman,* at 102) that 'although, following *Bolton Partners v Lambert*, the contract which is ratified is considered to have been in existence from the moment when the agent in fact made it with the third party, none the less it has been held that ratification will not entitle the principal to sue for any breach of contract which may have occurred *before* the time for ratification'. Fridman cites the case of *Kidderminster Corpn v Hardwick* (1873) LR 9 Exch 13. He continues:

> ... if the third party, between the time of the agent's acceptance and the principal's ratification does something which, in effect, makes the contract between the third party and the principal virtually non-existent (eg commencing to work for another employer, after having agreed to work for the principal) then the third party will be able to have all the advantages of revocation or withdrawal of his offer, even though he cannot technically revoke or withdraw it.

Associate Professor C-H Tan finds this difficult to accept (see (2003) 117 LQR 626 at pp 632–634), and of *Kidderminster* he says:

It is clear that it provides no such support. Rather than absolving a third party from liability for breaches prior to ratification, *Kidderminster* suggests more fundamentally that the third party may withdraw from its obligations altogether prior to any ratification by the principal. It therefore challenges the very basis of *Bolton Partners v Lambert* instead of merely limiting its effect.

The two cases are indeed irreconcilable (and it should be noted that *Kidderminster* was not referred to in *Bolton Partners v Lambert*).

(4) The agent and the third party may cancel the unauthorised transaction by mutual consent: *Walter v James* (1871) LR 6 Exch 124.

(5) Ratification is not effective where to permit it would unfairly prejudice a third party, and in particular where (a) it is essential to the validity of an act that it should be done within a certain time, the act cannot be ratified after the expiration of that time, to the prejudice of any third party, and (b) ratification may not be recognised if it will affect proprietary rights which have arisen in favour of the third party or others claiming through him since the act of the unauthorised agent (*Bowstead and Reynolds,* art 19). Thus, in *Bird v Brown* (1850) 4 Exch 786, the agent of a consignor of goods, acting without authority, gave notice of stoppage in transit on his principal's behalf. The goods arrived at their destination and were demanded by the trustee in bankruptcy of the consignee. It was held that the consignor could not later ratify the stoppage in transit and so divest the property in the goods, as this had in the meantime vested in the consignee's trustee in bankruptcy. The decision should be contrasted with *Presentaciones Musicales SA v Secunda* [1994] Ch 271 (noted by I Brown (1994) 110 LQR 531). There a solicitor issued a writ within the limitation period but without his client's authority. The client later purported to ratify the solicitor's action, even though the limitation period had since expired. The Court of Appeal held the ratification to be effective. The court held that as an unauthorised issue of a writ was not a complete nullity, it could be ratified after the expiration of the limitation period. Dillon and Nourse LJJ (at 280–281) distinguished *Bird v Brown* as a case where 'the act done by the self-appointed agent, before the crucial date, had no effect in law unless ratified'. The third member of the court, Roch LJ, simply regarded *Bird v Brown* as authority for the rule that ratification will not be allowed to deprive a third party of any property rights which have vested in him before ratification (see also the explanation of the case given by Cotton LJ in *Bolton Partners v Lambert,* above). The issue is considered further by C-H Tan in (2001) 117 LQR 626. In each case it is important to assess whether there has been unfair prejudice to the third party; even a relatively small amount of prejudice coupled with a long delay before ratification may be unfair (*Smith v Henniker-Major & Co* [2002] EWCA Civ 762, [203] Ch 182 at [82], per Robert Walker LJ, obiter). Moreover, it has recently been held by the Court of Appeal that there is no absolute rule that a contract cannot be ratified if the effect of ratification would be to divest an accrued property right, although the court did go on to accept that in the vast majority of cases it would be unjust to the third party to give effect to a ratification if this was the result (*Owners of the ship 'Borvigilant' v Owners of the ship 'Romina G'* [2003] EWCA Civ 935, [2003] 2 Lloyd's Rep 520 at [70] and [87]).

2. *Bolton Partners v Lambert* has been criticised for putting the third party in a worse position than he would have been in if he had made his offer direct to the principal, for then he could have withdrawn the offer before the principal accepted it (WA Seavey (1920)

29 Yale LJ 859 at p 891). The case was specifically not followed in *Fleming v Bank of New Zealand* [1900] AC 577 (PC), and was disapproved of in the dissenting judgment of Isaacs J in *Davison v Vickery's Motors Ltd* (1925) 37 CLR 1, HC of A. The case has more recently been criticised by the Supreme Court of New South Wales in *NM Superannuation Pty Ltd v Hughes* (1992) 7 ACSR 105 at 115–117, per Cohen J. Furthermore, most jurisdictions in the US allow the third party to withdraw his offer before ratification and the 1983 Geneva Convention on Agency in the International Sale of Goods (above, p 110) allows a third party to withdraw before ratification if, at the time of contracting, he was unaware of the agent's lack of authority (art 15(2)).

Yet *Bolton Partners v Lambert* may not be as prejudicial to the third party as first appears. As we have seen, there are a number of exceptions to the rule. Furthermore, it must be remembered that if the principal ratifies the contract the third party gets what he bargained for, and that if he does not ratify, the third party can sue the agent for breach of warranty of authority. The real prejudice to the third party is the possibility of uncertainty whilst waiting to see whether the principal will ratify the contract or not. However, as we have seen, even this period may be curtailed if the third party serves notice on the principal of his wish to withdraw from the contract (above, p 146).

QUESTIONS

1.   Why should an undisclosed principal be prohibited from ratifying the unauthorised acts of his agent?

2.   Adam contracts with Ted, telling him that he is acting on behalf of Paul. In fact, Adam is acting on his own behalf. Can Paul ratify the contract? See *Re Tiedemann & Ledermann Frères* [1899] 2 QB 66.

CHAPTER 5

RELATIONS WITH THIRD PARTIES

We have seen how an agent has power to affect the legal relations of his principal with regard to third parties (above, p 96). Typically the agent will do this by contracting on behalf of the principal or by disposing of the principal's property. In this chapter we shall concentrate on the effect of contracts made by agents; the unauthorised disposition of property by an agent is considered in Chapter 9.

When considering the rights and liabilities arising under a contract made by an agent, it is important to ascertain whether the agent was acting for a disclosed or undisclosed principal. A *disclosed* principal is one of whose existence the third party is aware at the time of contracting with the agent. If the name of the principal is known to the third party then the principal is described as 'named'. If the third party does not know the principal's name, but knows of his existence, the principal is described as 'unnamed'.[1] Whether named or unnamed the principal remains disclosed. On the other hand, if the third party is unaware of the existence of the principal at the time he contracts with the agent, ie the third party thinks the agent is contracting on his own behalf and not for someone else, the principal is described as *undisclosed*.

1 DISCLOSED AGENCY

(a) Relations between principal and third party

(i) *The general rule*

Montgomerie v United Kingdom Mutual Steamship Association
[1891] 1 QB 370, Queen's Bench Division

Montgomerie was the part-owner of a ship which he insured with the defendant mutual insurance association. The policy of insurance was effected by Perry, Raines & Co who

---

[1] The words 'identified' and 'unidentified' are used in preference to 'named' and 'unnamed' in the third edition of the US *Restatement of the Law of Agency* (2006). Professor Reynolds adopts the terminology in the eighteenth edition (2006) of *Bowstead and Reynolds on Agency,* and notes that the change reflects the fact than an unnamed principal may nevertheless be identified (see para 1–037). Whilst this is undoubtedly true,

acted as Montgomerie's agent. Perry, Raines & Co was a member of the association but Montgomerie was not, and his name did not appear on the policy. When Montgomerie sued the association to recover a loss on the ship, the association claimed that the terms of the policy expressly excluded their liability to anyone other than a member of the association. Wright J gave judgment for the association.

Wright J: There is no doubt whatever as to the general rule as regards an agent, that where a person contracts as agent for a principal the contract is the contract of the principal, and not that of the agent; and, prima facie, at common law the only person who may sue is the principal, and the only person who can be sued is the principal. To that rule there are, of course, many exceptions. First, the agent may be added as the party to the contract if he has so contracted, and is appointed as the party to be sued. Secondly, the principal may be excluded in several other cases. He may be excluded if the contract is made by a deed inter partes, to which the principal is no party. In that case, by ancient rule of common law, it does not matter whether the person made a party is or is not an agent.... Another exception is as regards bills and notes. If a person who is an agent makes himself a party in writing to a bill or note, by the law merchant a principal cannot be added. Another exception is that by usage, which is treated as forming part of the contract or of the law merchant, where there is a foreign principal, generally speaking the agent in England is the party to the contract, and not the foreign principal; but this is subject to certain limitations. Then a principal's liability may be limited, though not excluded. If the other party elects to sue the agent, he cannot afterwards sue the principal. Again, where the principal is an undisclosed principal, he must, if he sues, accept the facts as he finds them at the date of his disclosure, so far as those facts are consistent with reasonable and proper conduct on the part of the other party. Again, if the principal is sued, he is entitled to an allowance for payments which he may have made to his agent if the other party gave credit originally to that agent. Also, and this is very important, in all cases the parties can by their express contract provide that the agent shall be the person liable either concurrently with or to the exclusion of the principal, or that the agent shall be the party to sue either concurrently with or to the exclusion of the principal....

...The question, then, is, Have the parties so contracted that Montgomerie and his co-plaintiffs cannot sue, the alternative being that the action should have been brought in the name of Perry, Raines & Co? I have come to the conclusion that the parties have so contracted. I think that the rules annexed to the policy and the articles of association which are incorporated with the policy shew plainly that it was the intention of the parties that the association should look to the member only for contribution, and should have to deal with and be entitled to say that they would deal with the member only in respect of the settlements of losses.

NOTES

1.   Montgomerie was an undisclosed principal but the statement made by Wright J as to the normal relationship between the principal and the third party applies to disclosed principals generally.

2.   Where the agent acts within the scope of his authority on behalf of a disclosed principal, direct contractual relations are established between the principal and the third party. If the agent acts within the scope of his actual authority (express or implied), or the principal subsequently ratifies the agent's unauthorised acts, the principal may sue and be sued on the contract. But, as we have already seen, where the agent has only apparent authority the principal will be liable on the contract made by his agent but he will not be able to sue upon it himself, unless he ratifies his agent's unauthorised act (above, p 122). The editor of

we shall continue to use the terms 'named' and 'unnamed' principals as this is how the English courts have traditionally referred to them (and how they are described in the extracts from the judgments that appear in this chapter).

Markesinis and Munday submits that the same rule applies when an agent of necessity contracts on behalf of a principal (p 145). But, unlike apparent authority, agency of necessity is not based on estoppel and so it is difficult to see why the principal should be prevented from bringing an action on the contract. Where the agent acts without authority, and there is no ratification, the principal will incur no liability to the third party (eg *Comerford v Britannic Assurance Co Ltd* (1908) 24 TLR 593; *Wiltshire v Sims* (1808) 1 Camp 258).

3.   There are two exceptional cases when a disclosed principal will not be privy to a contract made by his agent acting within the scope of his authority.

First, when the agent contracts by a deed *inter partes* the principal will not be able to sue and be sued on the contract unless he is described in the deed as a party to it and the deed is executed in his name (*Re International Contract Co, Pickering's Claim* (1871) 6 Ch App 525—but where the deed is not *inter partes*, the principal can sue on it if he is a covenantee: *Moody v Condor Insurance Ltd* [2006] EWHC 100 (Ch), [2006] 1 WLR 1847). However, this general rule is itself subject to a number of exceptions:

(1)   if the agent who contracts by deed contracts as trustee for the principal then the principal can sue on the deed (*Harmer v Armstrong* [1934] Ch 65);

(2)   under s 7(1) of the Powers of Attorney Act 1971, as amended by the Law of Property (Miscellaneous Provisions) Act 1989, s 1, Sch 1, para 7(1), if the agent was appointed by a power of attorney, and he acts within the scope of his authority, he may execute the deed in his own name and the principal may sue on it (for detailed consideration of this section, see *Bowstead and Reynolds,* para 8–089; *Fridman,* pp 220–221); and

(3)   under s 56(1) of the Law of Property Act 1925, a principal may acquire an interest in land or other property, or the benefit of any condition, right of entry, covenant or agreement over or respecting land or other property, even though he is not named as a party to the conveyance or instrument (but note that the ambit of this section has been restrictively construed by the courts: see J Beatson *Anson's Law of Contract* (28th edn, 2002), pp 447–448).

(4)   under s 1(1) of the Contracts (Rights of Third Parties) Act 1999, a person who is not a party to a contract may in his own right enforce a term of a contract if (a) the contract expressly provides that he may, or (b) the term purports to confer a benefit on him (unless, in the case of (b), it is apparent from a proper construction of the contract that the parties did not intend to give him enforceable rights: s 1(2)). This provision would allow a disclosed principal to enforce a term of a contract made by deed, which expressly so provides or which confers a benefit on him, even though he is not a party to it and the deed is not executed in his name.

Secondly, a principal cannot be made liable on any negotiable instrument unless his signature appears on it (Bills of Exchange Act 1882, s 23). However, the principal will be liable on the instrument if his signature is written on the document by someone acting by or with his authority (s 91(1) of the 1882 Act). If the agent signs the instrument with the principal's name the principal will be bound. But difficulties can arise when the agent uses a representative signature: see s 26(1) of the 1882 Act; considered below at pp 563–565. A signature by procuration will put the third party on notice that the agent's authority to sign is limited and the principal will only be bound by the signature if the agent was acting within the scope of his actual authority: s 25 of the 1882 Act; considered below at p 563.

4.   There is no longer a presumption that an agent contracting for a foreign principal does so personally and cannot establish privity of contract between the principal and the third party. In *Teheran-Europe Co Ltd v ST Belton (Tractors) Ltd* [1968] 2 QB 545, the Court of Appeal held that modern commercial usage does not raise such a presumption. But the foreign character of the principal is not irrelevant, for as Diplock LJ said (at 558):

...the fact that the principal is a foreigner is one of the circumstances to be taken into account in determining whether or not the other party to the contract was willing, or led the agent to believe that he was willing, to treat as a party to the contract the agent's principal, and, if he was so willing, whether the mutual intention of the other party and the agent was that the agent should be personally entitled to sue and liable to be sued on the contract as well as his principal. But it is only one of many circumstances, and as respects the creation of privity of contract between the other party and the principal its weight may be minimal, particularly in a case such as the present where the terms of payment are cash before delivery and no credit is extended by the other party to the principal. It may have considerably more weight in determining whether the mutual intention of the other party and the agent was that the agent should be personally liable to be sued as well as the principal, particularly if credit has been extended by the other party.

See also FMB Reynolds [1983] CLP 119 at pp 126–127.

5. *Montgomerie v United Mutual Steamship Association* provides an example of a 'commission agent', ie someone who contracts with the third party as principal yet makes the contract on behalf of his own principal (above, p 149).

The dicta of Wright J in *Montgomerie v United Mutual Steamship Association* makes it clear that, as a general rule, where an agent makes a contract on behalf of a disclosed principal he can neither sue or be sued on that contract. The textbook writers usually express this result in the maxim that the agent 'drops out' of the transaction (see, eg *Bowstead and Reynolds*, para 9–002; *Markesinis and Munday*, p 185, *Fridman*, p 122). But the maxim must be treated with caution, especially outside the area of contract (see R Stevens [2005] LMCLQ 101). There is no specific rule of agency law which says the agent will automatically 'drop out' and escape liability. The agent can neither sue nor be sued on the contract because where the agency is disclosed it is objectively apparent to the third party that the other contracting party is the principal and not the agent (the reverse is true where the agency is undisclosed). This is an application of the general law of contract. Furthermore, even though the agent cannot sue or be sued on the contract where the agency is disclosed, the rights and liabilities of the principal and the third party may still be affected by the agent in a number of ways.

(ii) Settlement with the agent

Irvine & Co v Watson & Sons
(1880) 5 QBD 414, Court of Appeal

W & Sons employed C, a broker, to purchase oil for them. C purchased the oil from I & Co with payment to be by 'cash on or before delivery'. At the time of purchase C informed I & Co that he was buying for principals, although he did not reveal the name of his principals. I & Co delivered the oil to C without payment, and W & Sons, not knowing that I & Co had not been paid, in good faith paid C. C did not pay I & Co, who then sued W & Sons for the price. Bowen J gave judgment for I & Co. W & Sons appealed.

Bramwell LJ: I am of opinion that the judgment must be affirmed. The facts of the case are shortly these: The plaintiffs sold certain casks of oil, and on the face of the contract of sale Conning appeared as the purchaser. But the plaintiffs knew that he was only an agent buying for principals, for he told them so at the time of the sale, therefore they knew that they had a right against somebody besides

Conning. On the other hand, the defendants knew that somebody or other had a remedy against them, for they had authorized Conning, who was an ordinary broker, to pledge their credit, and the invoice specified the goods to have been bought 'per John Conning.' Then, that being so, the defendants paid the broker; and the question is whether such payment discharged them from their liability to the plaintiffs. I think it is impossible to say that it discharged them, unless they were misled by some conduct of the plaintiffs into the belief that the broker had already settled with the plaintiffs, and made such payment in consequence of such belief. But it is contended that the plaintiffs here did mislead the defendants into such belief, by parting with the possession of the oil to Conning without getting the money. The terms of the contract were 'cash on or before delivery,' and it is said that the defendants had a right to suppose that the sellers would not deliver unless they received payment of the price at the time of delivery. I do not think, however, that that is a correct view of the case. The plaintiffs had a perfect right to part with the oil to the broker without insisting strictly upon their right to prepayment, and there is, in my opinion, nothing in the facts of the case to justify the defendants in believing that they would so insist. No doubt if there was an invariable custom in the trade to insist on prepayment where the terms of the contract entitled the seller to it, that might alter the matter; and in such case noninsistance on prepayment might discharge the buyer if he paid the broker on the faith of the seller already having been paid. But that is not the case here; the evidence before Bowen J shews that there is no invariable custom to that effect.

Apart from all authorities, then, I am of opinion that the defendants' contention is wrong, and upon looking at the authorities, I do not think that any of them are in direct conflict with that opinion. It is true that in *Thomson v Davenport* ((1829) 9 B & C 78) both Lord Tenterden and Bayley J suggest in the widest terms that a seller is not entitled to sue the undisclosed principal on discovering him, if in the meantime the state of account between the principal and the agent has been altered to the prejudice of the principal. But it is impossible to construe the dicta of those learned judges in that case literally; it would operate most unjustly to the vendor if we did. I think the judges who uttered them did not intend a strictly literal interpretation to be put on their words. But whether they did or no, the opinion of Parke B in *Heald v Kenworthy* ((1855) 10 Exch 739) seems to me preferable; it is this, that 'If the conduct of the seller would make it unjust for him to call upon the buyer for the money, as for example, where the principal is induced by the conduct of the seller to pay his agent the money on the faith that the agent and seller have come to a settlement on the matter, or if any representation to that effect is made by the seller, either by words or conduct, the seller cannot afterwards throw off the mask and sue the principal'. That is in my judgment a much more accurate statement of the law. But then the defendants rely on the case *of Armstrong v Stokes* ((1872) LR 7 QB 598). Now that is a very remarkable case; it seems to have turned in some measure upon the peculiar character filled by Messrs Ryder as commission merchants. The Court seemed to have thought it would be unreasonable to hold that Messrs Ryder had not authority to receive the money. I think upon the facts of that case that the agents would have been entitled to maintain an action for the money against the defendant, for as commission merchants they were not mere agents of the buyer. Moreover the present case is a case, which Blackburn J there expressly declines to decide. He expressly draws a distinction between a case in which, as in *Armstrong v Stokes,* the seller at the time of the sale supposes the agent to be himself a principal, and gives credit to him alone, and one in which, as here, he knows that the person with whom he is dealing has a principal behind, though he does not know who that principal is.

It is to my mind certainly difficult to understand that distinction, or to see how the mere fact of the vendor knowing or not knowing that the agent has a principal behind can affect the liability of that principal. I should certainly have thought that his liability would depend upon what he himself knew, that is to say whether he knew that the vendor had a claim against him and would look to him for payment in the agent's default. But it is sufficient here that the defendants did know that the sellers had a claim against them, unless the broker had already paid for the goods.

Baggallay LJ: ... What then was the effect of that payment? If the dicta in *Thomson v Davenport* are to be taken as strictly correct, they certainly go a long way to support the defendants' contention. But it is to be observed that they were mere dicta, and quite unnecessary to the decision. The largeness of those dicta has since been dissented from by Parke B, in the case of *Heald v Kenworthy,* and with his dissent I entirely agree. He sought to limit the qualification of the general rule to cases, in which the seller by some conduct has misled the buyer into believing that a settlement has been made with the agent. And if that limitation is correct, I am of opinion that there is no such payment here as would discharge the defendants.

But reliance is placed upon the case *of Armstrong v Stokes* as establishing the doctrine that the buyer is released from liability, if he pays the agent at a time at which the seller still gives credit to the agent—and it is contended that as that state of facts existed here, the defendants are accordingly discharged. But I think that is not the true view of the decision in *Armstrong v Stokes.* It must be accepted with reference to the particular circumstances of that case. There at the time of the payment by the principal to the brokers, the sellers still gave credit to the brokers and to the brokers alone. But that is not the case here; the plaintiffs it is true gave credit to Conning, but they did not give him exclusive credit. I do not think I am running counter to any of the decided cases in thinking that this judgment must be affirmed.

Brett LJ considered *Thomson v Davenport* and the limitation placed on the dicta in that case by the judgment of Parke B in *Heald v Kenworthy* and continued:

...But it is suggested that that limitation was overruled in *Armstrong v Stokes.* I think, however, that the Court there did not intend to overrule it, but to treat the case before them as one to which the limitation did not apply. I think they noticed the peculiar character of Manchester commission merchants. Probably their decision means this, that, when the seller deals with the agent as sole principal, and the nature of the agent's business is such that the buyer ought to believe that the seller has so dealt, in such a case it would be unjust to allow the seller to recover from the principal after he paid the agent. Or it may perhaps be that Blackburn J, finding the wider qualification in the very case which lays down the general rule, felt himself bound by the terms of that qualification, and applied them to the case before him.

If the case of *Armstrong v Stokes* arises again, we reserve to ourselves sitting here the right of reconsidering it.

The only other question is whether the present case falls within the qualification as limited by Parke B, whether there was any misleading conduct on the part of the plaintiffs. But the only thing relied on by the defendants on that point was the noninsistence on prepayment by the plaintiffs. And I do not think that that amounted to laches, or was such an act as would justify the defendants in supposing that Conning had already paid the plaintiffs.

NOTES

1.   When the principal is disclosed the estoppel theory is generally accepted as explaining those exceptional cases where the right of the third party is affected by the principal having paid or otherwise settled with the agent (see also *Davison v Donaldson* (1882) 9 QBD 623, CA). Cf when the principal is undisclosed, see below, pp 199–200.

2.   Mere delay by the third party in enforcing his claim against the principal is not usually sufficient to give rise to an estoppel, unless there are other factors which make the delay misleading to the principal (see *Davison v Donaldson,* above).

A disclosed principal is not bound by the *third party* making payment to or settling with the agent, unless the agent had actual or apparent authority to receive the payment or settle on behalf of the principal (*Butwick v Grant* [1924] 2 KB 483; cf when the principal is undisclosed, see below, p 200). The third party will only be discharged if payment is made in the manner which the agent is authorised to accept, eg if the agent is authorised to accept payment in cash, payment by bill of exchange will not discharge the third party (*Hine Bros v*

Steamship Insurance Syndicate Ltd (1895) 72 LT 79). If the agent is not authorised to receive payment but he does so and pays over the money to the principal, the principal will be deemed to have ratified the agent's actions and the third party will be discharged. Exceptionally, if the agent has a lien over the principal's goods for a debt owed to him by the principal, and the agent, acting within his authority, sells the goods to a third party who pays the agent (who has no authority to receive payment), the third party can set off the principal's debt to the agent against the price of the goods which remains owing to the principal (*Hudson v Granger* (1821) 5 B & Ald 27).

(iii) Set-off and other defences available against the agent

The third party is entitled to set up against the disclosed principal all defences which arise out of the contract itself and all defences which are available against the principal himself (eg set-off, the fact that the principal is an enemy alien): *Bowstead and Reynolds,* art 79(1) and commentary thereon. Defences and set-off which the third party may have against the agent personally and which are unconnected with the contract made by the agent are not available against the disclosed principal (unless set-off is authorised by the principal: *Barker v Greenwood* (1837) 2 Y & C Ex 414).

Particular difficulties arise when the third party seeks to rely on the deceit or other misrepresentation of the agent against the principal. If the principal instigates or ratifies the agent's action, he will be held personally liable to the third party. The principal will also be held liable for the agent's deceit or other misrepresentation if the agent was acting within the scope of his actual or apparent authority at the time he made the representation: *Lloyd v Grace, Smith & Co* [1912] AC 716, HL; *Armagas Ltd v Mundogas SA* [1985] 3 All ER 795, CA; affd [1986] AC 717; *Credit Lyonnais Bank Nederland NV v Export Credits Guarantee Department* [2000] 1 AC 486, HL: see above, p 103. In such circumstances, the principal will be liable even if he did not know of the agent's actions (*Refuge Assurance Co Ltd v Kettlewell* [1909] AC 243) and even if the agent was acting for his own benefit and not for the benefit of the principal (*Lloyd v Grace, Smith & Co,* above). There is uncertainty as to whether a principal can exclude liability for his agent's fraud in inducing the making of a contract. What is clear is that the law, on public policy grounds, does not permit a contracting party to exclude liability for his own fraud, and so it is submitted that the contracting party should not be able to exclude liability for his agent's deceit either. The issue did not have to be resolved in *HIH Casualty & General Insurance Ltd v Chase Manhattan Bank* [2003] UKHL 6, [2003] 1 All ER (Comm) 349, where the House of Lords held (at [16]) that a party seeking to exonerate himself from the consequences of his agent's fraud (assuming that is legally possible) must do so 'in clear and unmistakable terms on the face of the contract' and that general words will not be effective. But general words may be effective to cover fraud in the performance (as opposed to the formation) of the contract by an agent (*Frans Mass (UK) Ltd v Samsung (UK) Ltd* [2004] UKHC 1502, [2004] 2 Lloyd's Rep 251 at [152]).

The principal will not be liable in deceit if the agent made an innocent misrepresentation and the principal, who would have known the representation to be false, did not know it had been made (*Armstrong v Strain* [1951] 1 TLR 856; affd [1952] 1 KB 232). However, in such circumstances the principal would be liable to the third party under s 2(1) of the Misrepresentation Act 1967 if the third party had contracted with the principal in reliance upon the agent's misrepresentation (*Gosling v Anderson* (1972) 223 Estates Gazette 1743; although the agent would not be liable to the third party under the statute: *Resolute Maritime Inc v Nippon Kaiji Kyokai* [1983] 2 All ER 1). The principal may also be liable to the third party in negligence on the basis of *Hedley Byrne & Co Ltd v Heller & Partners Ltd* [1964] AC 465, or liable for any negligent misstatement made by the agent when acting within the scope of his authority, if it can be established that the principal and/or the agent owed the third party a duty of care.

Where the third party sues the principal on the contract made through the agent, the principal, whether disclosed or undisclosed, should be able to raise all defences arising out of the transaction with the agent, and defences personal to himself, but not defences personal to the agent: *Bowstead and Reynolds*, art 79(3). For example, the principal could allege the contract is void for mistake or voidable for misrepresentation, but he could not rely on the fact that the agent is a minor.

(iv) Merger and election

Thomson v Davenport

(1829) 9 B & C 78, Court of King's Bench

M'Kune, a 'general Scotch agent' in Liverpool, ordered a quantity of glass and earthenware from Davenport & Co, dealers in Liverpool, for Thomson, who lived in Dumfries. At the time he placed the order M'Kune informed Davenport & Co that he was acting for a principal but he did not reveal the principal's name. The goods were invoiced and debited to M'Kune, but he became bankrupt and Davenport & Co sued Thomson for the price of the goods supplied. The jury of the Borough Court of Liverpool delivered a verdict in favour of Davenport & Co. The Court of King's Bench affirmed that decision.

Lord Tenderden CJ: I am of opinion that the direction give by the learned recorder in this case was right, and that the verdict was also right. I take it to be a general rule, that if a person sells goods (supposing at the time of the contract he is dealing with a principal), but afterwards discovers that the person with whom he has been dealing is not the principal in the transaction, but agent for a third person, though he may in the mean time have debited the agent with it, he may afterwards recover the amount from the real principal; subject, however, to this qualification, that the state of the account between the principal and the agent is not altered to the prejudice of the principal. On the other hand, if at the time of the sale the seller knows, not only that the person who is nominally dealing with him is not principal but agent, and also knows who the principal really is, and, notwithstanding all that knowledge, chooses to make the agent his debtor, dealing with him and him alone, then, according to the cases of *Addison v Gandassequi* ((1812) 4 Taunt 574), and *Paterson v Gandasequi* ((1812) 15 East 62), the seller cannot afterwards, on the failure of the agent, turn round and charge the principal, having once made his election at the time when he had the power of choosing between the one and the other. The present is a middle case. At the time of the dealing for the goods, the plaintiffs were informed that M'Kune, who came to them to buy the goods, was dealing for another, that is, that he was an agent, but they were not informed who the principal was. They had not, therefore, at that time the means of making their election. It is true that they might, perhaps, have obtained those means if they had made further enquiry; but they made no further enquiry. Not knowing who the principal really was, they had not the power at that instant of making their election. That being so, it seems to me that this middle case falls in substance and effect within the first proposition which I have mentioned, the case of a person not known to be an agent; and not within the second, where the buyer is not merely known to be agent, but the name of his principal is also known.

[Bayley J delivered a concurring judgment.]

Littledale J: The general principle of law is, that the seller shall have his remedy against the principal, rather than against any other person. Where goods are bought by an agent, who does not at the time disclose that he is acting as agent; the vendor, although he has debited the agent, may upon discovering the principal, resort to him for payment. But if the principal be known to the seller at the time when he makes the contract, and he, with a full knowledge of the principal, chooses to debit the agent, he thereby makes his election, and cannot afterwards charge the principal. Or if in such case he debits the principal, he cannot afterwards charge the agent. There is a third case; the seller may, in his invoice and bill of parcels, mention both principal and agent: he may debit A as a purchaser for goods bought through B, his agent. In that case, he thereby makes his election to charge the principal, and cannot afterwards resort to the agent. The general principle is, that the seller shall have his remedy against the principal, although he may by electing to take the agent as his debtor, abandon his right against the principal. The present case differs from any of those which I have mentioned. Here the agent purchased the goods in his own name. The name of the principal was not then known to the seller, but it afterwards came to his knowledge. It seems to me to be more consistent with the general principle of law, that the seller shall have his remedy against the principal, rather than against any other person, to hold in this case that the seller, who knew that there was a principal, but did not know who that principal was, may resort to him as soon as he is discovered. Here the agent did not communicate to the seller sufficient information to enable him to debit any other individual. The seller was in the same situation, as if at the time of the contract he had not known that there was any principal besides the person with whom he was dealing, and had afterwards discovered that the goods had been purchased on account of another; and, in that case, it is clear that he might have charged the principal. It is said, that he ought to have ascertained by enquiry of the agent who the principal was, but I think that he was not bound to make such enquiry, and that by debiting the agent with the price of the goods, he has not precluded himself from resorting to the principal, whose name was not disclosed to him . . . . For the reasons already given, I think the plaintiff is entitled to recover.

[Parke J, having been concerned as counsel in the case, gave no opinion.]

Debenham's Ltd v Perkins
(1925) 133 LT 252, King's Bench Division

In March, April and June 1922 Mrs Perkins purchased various items from Debenham's Ltd (the plaintiffs). In May 1922 Mrs Perkins separated from her husband. The plaintiffs obtained judgment against Mrs Perkins for the items purchased after her separation. They then sued her husband for the price of those items sold to Mrs Perkins before her separation alleging that she acted as his agent. The County Court judge entered judgment for the husband on the ground that the plaintiffs had elected to proceed to judgment against the wife. The plaintiffs appealed and Scrutton and Bankes LJJ, sitting as additional judges of the King's Bench Division, allowed the appeal.

Scrutton LJ: When an agent acts for a disclosed principal, it may be that the agent makes himself or herself personally liable as well as the principal. But in such a case the person with whom the contract is made may not get judgment against both. He may get judgment against the principal or he may get judgment against the agent who is liable as principal, but once he has got judgment against either the principal or the agent who has the liability of the principal, he cannot then proceed against the other party who might be liable on the contract if proceedings had been taken against him or her first. This is sometimes explained by the doctrine of election and sometimes by the doctrine that when one has merged a contract in a judgment, one can have only one judgment, and, having merged the contract in the judgment, one cannot use the contract to get a second judgment. It is unnecessary to consider which is right.

In this case the tradesman first of all sued the married woman for nine dated items, claiming for a lump sum the price of the goods sold and delivered. As far as we can surmise what happened at the trial—and I understand that counsel are agreed as to what did happen at the trial in this case—the judge took the view that as to the first four items in date the wife was the agent of a principal, the husband, and not herself personally liable, and therefore judgment could not be entered against her, but he decided that as to the last five items the wife was then living separately and not with her husband, and she was not acting as his agent, but was personally liable. Then comes a very odd fact, that having held that she was not acting as agent for her husband, so that there was no defence and she was personally liable, in some way, which I do not understand, the learned judge, on a third-party procedure, held that the husband was found to indemnify the wife. The learned judge is so experienced a judge that one cannot help thinking that there is something one does not know which must have led him to take that view. Anyhow, as far as the case against the wife was concerned, the result of that procedure was that the tradesman failed to recover anything under the first four items and succeeded in getting a judgment for the amount of the last five items, though they were not specifically set out in the judgment. Whereupon the tradesman, desiring to get his money from somebody, sued the husband for the first three items. Thereupon objection was taken, which I understand can be put in this way: the plaintiff sued for one cause of action, and although it is quite true he did not get what he wanted, he got a judgment for part of that cause of action. Having taken judgment against the one person for the cause of action, he cannot use the cause of action to try to get a judgment against another party. The cause of action, the contract, is merged in the judgment.

But it appears to me that there are really two causes of action, not one, in this case. There is a cause of action against the wife who is liable personally, there is a cause of action against another person supposed to be acting by the agency of the wife, for different items, at different times, resulting in claims of different amounts. It seems to me, therefore, that this claim for one sum as a debt is really the result of two causes of action. If that is so, the fact that the plaintiff has got judgment against the wife on one cause of action does not merge the cause of action on which he has failed to get judgment, and which still remains available against the person against whom that cause of action should properly be brought.

Another way, perhaps, of putting it, though I think it also involves treating the matter as two causes of action, is that a plaintiff does not elect to sue one of two people alternatively liable, because he brings a proceeding against the other which fails, and in which he does not get judgment. He terminates the liability of the person alternatively liable only if he brings an action against his or her alternate and gets judgment, so that having got judgment against the one, the person who is alternatively liable is discharged . . . .

On the best consideration, therefore, that I can give to the matter, it seems to me that the judgment obtained in the first action was for a cause of action different from the one which is now being sued, and that therefore the tradesman ought not to be estopped from continuing to sue the husband for those items not included in the first account. I quite appreciate that the husband says that he has defences which the County Court judge in the first action ought to have appreciated, and which he is going to raise when he is able to put all the facts before the court. We are not, therefore, deciding for the moment who is going to succeed when this action is tried, but only that the judge was premature in stopping the action on the ground either of an election or of *res judicata*.

[Bankes LJ delivered a concurring judgment.]

NOTES

1.   The doctrines of merger and election only become relevant if the agent is personally liable on the main contract he makes with the third party. Remember, in cases of disclosed agency the agent does not normally become personally liable on the contract (above, pp 149–150). But for those exceptional occasions when the agent may contract personally, see below, pp 162–171.

2.   In most cases where an agent has been held to contract personally the courts have held the agent's liability to be in the alternative to that of the principal: eg see *Debenham's Ltd v Perkins*, above, where the assumption of alternative liability underlies Scrutton LJ's

judgment. Yet this approach is open to severe criticism. As the editor of *Markesinis and Munday* astutely observes (p 150):

...even if one is endeavouring to read the intentions of the third party at the time when he concludes his contract with the agent acting for a named or unnamed principal, there is no strong reason to presume that he will always opt for the alternative liability of the agent and the principal rather than for their joint and several liability. After all, joint liability is both more advantageous to the third party and, legally, might appear more conventional. In short, Scrutton LJ's basic assumption in *Debenham's Ltd v Perkins* may be unrealistic and, arguably, contradict the most probable intentions of the parties to the contract.

3.   Merger occurs when the third party obtains judgment against the principal, or the agent, when they are both liable in the alternative. Judgment against one releases the other. This is because there is only a single obligation and two judgments cannot arise out of a single obligation. It used to be the case that judgment against one of two joint debtors released the other, but this is no longer the law (Civil Liability (Contribution) Act 1978, s 3). Similarly, if the principal and agent are jointly and severally liable on the contract, judgment against one will not release the other. It should be noted that the doctrine of merger can apply even if the third party does not know of the existence of the principal (and, *a fortiori,* the principal's identity) at the time he obtained judgment against the agent (*Priestly v Fernie* (1865) 3 H & C 977). In this respect merger differs significantly from election.

4.   When the principal and agent are liable in the alternative on the contract with the third party, the third party may elect to hold one of them exclusively liable and thereby be barred from suing the other. As with merger, election will not apply if the principal and agent are jointly and severally liable or liable on separate causes of action. The election must be clear and unequivocal. Obtaining judgment against the principal or the agent is clearly the best evidence of election (although strictly speaking this will constitute a merger of actions), and it seems that giving exclusive credit to the agent will suffice (see *Thomson v Davenport*). In each case it is a question of fact whether there has been a clear and unequivocal act giving rise to an election (see further below, pp 194–195). Furthermore, as illustrated by *Thomson v Davenport,* the third party must have full knowledge of the facts, including the identity of the principal, before he can be said to have elected.

5.   The doctrines of merger and election raise a number of difficult issues. Professor Reynolds has written an excellent article on the subject in (1970) 86 LQR 318 (developed further in his commentary to article 82 of *Bowstead and Reynolds*). Of particular interest is his view that many of the decisions on election in disclosed agency (including *Thomson v Davenport*) are cases involving contract formation rather than concerning election at all, eg that the disclosed principal was never liable on the contract at all as it was made solely with the agent. There is much to commend this approach, and it may be embraced by the courts at some point in the future. However, for the present, the courts are likely to continue to decide cases according to the familiar and well-entrenched concepts of alternative liability and election.

QUESTION

A bought some goods from T, representing that he was acting on behalf of P Ltd. T charged the price to A's account, but when A became insolvent, T sued P Ltd for the money. Can P Ltd successfully argue that, by debiting A, T made an effective election and can no longer sue P Ltd? Would your answer be different if A, when buying the goods, had made it clear that he was acting for a principal whose identity he refused to disclose?

(b) Relations between agent and third party

(i) *The general rule*

Montgomerie v United Kingdom Mutual Steamship Association

[1891] 1 QB 370, Queen's Bench Division

(See above, pp 149–150.)

Lewis v Nicholson and Parker

(1852) 18 QB 503, Court of Queen's Bench

Lewis was the mortgagee of a bankrupt's property. Nicholson and Parker were solicitors to assignees of the bankrupt. Purporting to act 'on behalf of the assignees' Nicholson and Parker entered into an agreement with Lewis to sell the bankrupt's property and pay Lewis those sums owed to him out of the proceeds of sale. Although the property was sold Lewis was not paid. In fact it turned out that Nicholson and Parker did not have the authority of the assignees to enter into this particular transaction and so Lewis brought an action against the solicitors personally for breach of the agreement.

Lord Campbell CJ: . . . Looking at the two letters which constitute the contract, I think it appears on the face of them, that the defendants did not intend to make themselves personally liable on the contract, but to make a contract between the plaintiff and the assignees. It is quite clear that the plaintiffs solicitor, to whom the letter of 26th August was addressed, was not himself a contracting party, but was acting as agent, making a contract for the plaintiff: and I think that the true construction of the letters is that the defendants also were not contracting parties, but acting as agents for the assignees, making a contract for them, and, as I think, personally contracting that they had authority to make a contract binding the assignees. The letter expresses that, in consideration of the plaintiff consenting to the sale, 'we hereby, on behalf of the assignees, consent.' My brother Shee in effect asks us to read the contract as if the words on behalf of the assignees were not there; but they are there; and the nature of facts shews that they were meant to express a contract by the assignees; for it was the consent of the assignees to pay over the money that was material to the plaintiff. The answer refers to 'the undertaking given by you herein, and contained in your letter.' That however does not shew that it was understood by the writer to be a personal undertaking by the defendants, but merely refers to the undertaking as made in their letter, and by them. I think therefore that, looking at these two letters which form the contract, it appears to have been the intention of both parties that the consent should be that of the assignees, not that of the defendants . . . .

Then the other point is to be considered. I think the facts raise it, as the trade assignee had no authority to make the official assignee personally liable on such a collateral contract. He might give assent, binding on both, to the disposal of the goods or money; but this goes much beyond such authority. So, the principals not being bound, the question arises whether the defendants are liable in this form of action. In the note to *Thomas v Hewes* ((1834) 2 Cr & M 519, 530, note (e), 4 Tyr 335, 338), it is stated to have been said by Bayley B that 'where an agent makes a contract in the name of his principal, and it turns out that the principal is not liable from the want of authority in the agent to make such contract, the agent is personally liable on the contract.' That is a high authority; but I must dissent from it. It is clear that it cannot apply where the contract is peculiarly personal; otherwise this absurdity would follow, that, if A, professing to have but not having authority from B, made a contract that B should marry C, C might sue A for breach of promise of marriage, even though they were of the same sex. . . . I think in no case where it appears that a man did not intend to bind himself, but only to make a contract for a principal, can he be sued as principal, merely because there was no authority. He is liable, if there was any fraud, in an action for deceit, and, in my opinion, as at present advised, on an implied contract that he had authority, whether there was fraud or not. In either way he may be made liable for the damages occasioned by the absence of authority. But I think that to say he is liable as principal is to make a contract, not to construe it. I think therefore that these defendants were liable, but not in this action.

Erle J: The first question is, what is the true construction of this contract. Looking at the terms of the instruments, and the circumstances under which they were written, I think the construction is that the defendants made a contract between the plaintiff and the assignees, and signed it as agents of the assignees....

I also think that the defendants had not the authority of both assignees to make the contract. The question therefore arises, are they liable as principals on the contract, though intending and expressing an intention to act only as agents in making it? I think they are not. I think that, in general, no contract is made by the law contrary to the intention of the parties. The definition of a contract is that it is the mutual intention of the two parties. There is a class of what are called implied contracts, such as the promise to pay money had and received to the plaintiffs use: but, when it is said that such a contract is implied contrary to the intent of the person receiving the money, it is in truth only a technical mode of naming the remedy which the law gives against that wrongdoer. I know of no case in which what is properly called a contract is made by the law contrary to the intent of the parties.

[Wightman and Crompton JJ delivered concurring judgments.]

NOTES

1.   Although the general rule is that the agent 'drops out' of any contract made on behalf of his disclosed principal, the mere fact that a person acts as agent does not prevent him being liable to the third party. As Lord Scarman said in *Yeung Kai Yung v Hong Kong and Shanghai Banking Corpn* [1981] AC 787 at 795 (PC):

It is not the case that, if a principal is liable, his agent cannot be. The true principle of law is that a person is liable for his engagements (as for his torts) even though he acts for another, unless he can show that by the law of agency he is to be held to have expressly or impliedly negatived his personal liability.

2.   The agent may be liable and entitled on the main contract made with the third party (see below) or on a collateral contract (eg in an auction without reserve, there is a collateral contract between the auctioneer and the highest bidder, consisting of an offer by the auctioneer to sell to the highest bidder and an acceptance of that offer when the bid is made: *Barry v Heathcote Ball & Co (Commercial Auctions) Ltd* [2001] 1 All ER 944, CA). Even if not liable on the main contract, the agent may be liable for breach of warranty of authority (as recognised by Lord Campbell CJ in *Lewis v Nicholson and Parker*, also see below, p 173).

3.   The agent may be personally liable in tort (see, generally, *Bowstead and Reynolds*, paras 9-112–9-122; R Stevens [2005] LMCLQ 101, 102ff). As Hobhouse LJ said in *McCullagh v Lane Fox & Partners* (1995) 49 Con LR 124 at 144:

An agent or an employee, owes a duty of care to his principal in relation to the transaction on which he is employed, which can be both contractual and tortious (*Midland Bank Trust Co Ltd v Hett, Stubbs & Kemp* [1979] Ch 384). But, in performing his agency, he may put himself in a position where he owes a duty of care to the person with whom he is dealing on behalf of his principal and be liable to him as well if he makes a careless misrepresentation or does a careless act which causes loss, damage or injury to the third party. Where personal injury is involved, no problem arises. An agent or employee who drives his employer's vehicle on his employer's business carelessly is liable to someone who is injured as a result. The same applies to careless acts causing property damage and can in principle apply to acts causing financial loss.

In *Punjab National Bank v De Boinville* [1992] 1 Lloyd's Rep 7, it was held that employees of an insurance broker engaged by the plaintiffs owed a direct duty of care in tort to the plaintiffs. In *McCullagh v Lane Fox & Partners,* above, the Court of Appeal said that in principle an estate agent employed by the vendor of property could owe a duty of care to the purchaser in respect of statements about the property, although no such duty was owed on the facts. But in *Gran Gelato Ltd v Richcliff (Group) Ltd* [1992] Ch 560, Nicholls V-C declined to impose a duty of care on the vendor's solicitor in answering inquiries before contract—a case which, according to Hobhouse LJ in *McCullagh v Lane Fox & Partners,* above, is probably best restricted to solicitors in conveyancing transactions (see generally C Passmore [1996] NLJ 409). The key question is whether there has been an assumption of responsibility by the agent towards the third party (*Williams v Natural Life Health Foods Ltd* [1998] 2 All ER 577, HL; cf *Merrett v Babb* [2001] EWCA Civ 214, [2001] QB 1174, where a majority of the Court of Appeal distinguished *Williams* on the basis that it was concerned with the liability of a director of a limited company: such a restrictive interpretation was later rejected by Lord Hoffmann in *Standard Chartered Bank v Pakistan National Shipping Corpn (Nos 2 and 4)* [2002] UKHL 43, [2003] 1 AC 959 at [23], who held that *Williams* had nothing to do with company law but was 'an application of the law of principal and agent to the requirement of assumption of responsibility under the *Hedley Byrne* principle'). But this reasoning does not apply in cases of deceit, where liability does not turn on the existence of any assumption of responsibility or special relationship between claimant and defendant. The making by an agent of a knowingly false statement relied on by the person to whom it was made is a tort on the part of the agent (*Noel v Poland* [2001] 2 BCLC 645 at [21], Toulson J). Moreover, agents may be personally liable for deceit notwithstanding the liability of their principals. In *Standard Chartered Bank v Pakistan National Shipping Corp (Nos 2 and 4),* above, a company director, who made a fraudulent misrepresentation within the scope of his employment, was held by the House of Lords to be personally liable in deceit even though his statements were made in a representative capacity (which resulted in the company also being held liable in deceit). The case is noted by Ben Parker [2003] LMCLQ 1 and by Ross Grantham [2003] CLJ 15. See also N Campbell and J Armour [2003] CLJ 290, who put the case (which we support) that questions of a corporate agent's liability do not turn on some special principle of company law but on 'the established rules relating to the particular head of liability, with due regard paid to the defendant's capacity as an agent' (p 291).

(ii) When will the agent be liable on the contract made on behalf of his principal?

Contracts in writing
Universal Steam Navigation Co Ltd v James McKelvie & Co
[1923] AC 492, House of Lords

A charterparty was entered into between TH Seed & Co Ltd, as agents for the owners of the vessel, and 'James McKelvie & Co, Newcastle-on-Tyne, Charterers'. The charterparty was signed: 'or and on behalf of James McKelvie & Co (as agents). JA McKelvie'. When sued for breach of the charterparty, McKelvie & Co claimed to have acted as agents for an Italian company, and denied that they were personally liable on the contract. The Court of Appeal entered judgment for McKelvie & Co. The House of Lords dismissed the owners' appeal from that decision.

Viscount Cave LC: My Lords, apart from authority, I should feel no doubt whatever as to the correctness of the judgment of the Court of Appeal. If the respondents had signed the charterparty without qualification, they would of course have been personally liable to the shipowners; but by adding to their signature the words 'as agents' they indicated clearly that they were signing only as agents for others and had no intention of being personally bound as principals. I can imagine no other purpose for which these words could have been added; and unless they had that meaning, they appear to me to have no sense or meaning at all.

When the cases are examined, it appears that the weight of authority is in favour of the above view.

Lord Shaw of Dunfermline: The first question is in what character Messrs McKelvie signed this document? I see no ground whatsoever for denying effect to the express word 'agents': it was undoubtedly in that character that the contract was signed: there is as little ground for cutting out the express character in which it was signed as for cutting out the signature itself.

The second question is, whether, although thus denominating themselves as 'agents,' Messrs McKelvie were yet signing a contract which by its terms made them principals therein. But its terms do not refer to either 'principals' or 'agents'; the body of the document can be applied to either category. As for the names of the parties, I hold that the names of McKelvie followed by 'Charterers' with nothing said of agency, is definitely stamped with agency by the express affirmation of the signature.

A third view is suggested—namely, that they were ex concessu agents, but yet were principals over and above. This answers itself. Such a confused and unusual situation would require the clearest words to make it intelligible and effective. As at present advised, I have doubts as to whether this could be done....

But I desire to say that in my opinion the appending of the word 'agents' to the signature of a party to a mercantile contract is, in all cases, the dominating factor in the solution of the problem of principal or agent. A highly improbable and conjectural case (in which this dominating factor might be overcome by other parts of the contract) may by an effort of the imagination be figured, but, apart from that, the appending of the word 'agent' to the signature is a conclusive assertion of agency, and a conclusive rejection of the responsibility of a principal, and is and must be accepted in that twofold sense by the other contracting party.

Lord Sumner: ...I agree that for many years past it has, I believe, been generally understood in business, that to add 'as agents' to the signature is all that is necessary to save a party, signing for a principal, from personal liability on the contract, and I agree also that, even as a matter of construction, when a signature so qualified is attached to a general printed form with blanks filled in ad hoc, preponderant importance attaches to the qualification in comparison with printed clauses or even with manuscript insertions in the form. It still, however, remains true, that the qualifying words 'as agents' are a part of the contract and must be construed with the rest of it. They might have been expressed as a separate clause eg 'it is further agreed that the party signing this charter as charterer does so as agent for an undisclosed principal'—and that clause would obviously have to be construed. They are a form of words and not a mere part of the act of signifying assent and closing a negotiation by duly attaching a name. They purport to limit and explain a liability, and not merely to identify the person signing or to justify the inscription of a name by the hand of another person than the owner of it. They are more than the addition of 'junior' or 'Revd.' to the signature, which serves to identify the signatory by distinguishing him from others. They are more than a mere 'per procuration,' which only alleges authority to write another's name....

...It has sometimes been said that when 'agents' is the word added to the signature, it is a mere word of description, and so does not qualify the liability which the act of signing imports. I question this explanation. One's signature is not the place in which to advertise one's calling, nor is 'agent' ordinarily used to describe a trade, as 'tailor' or 'butcher' would be. I have no doubt that, when people add 'agent' to a signature to a contract, they are trying to escape personal liability, but are unaware that the attempt will fail. The result, however, is the same. When words added to a signature in themselves qualify liability, it is because, as words, they can be so construed in conjunction with the contract as a whole.

In construing the words 'as agents,' there is a distinction to be taken. Though it may be somewhat subtle, it has been mentioned in the older cases. Do the words 'as agents' mean 'and as agents,' or 'only as agents'? The positive affirmation, that I sign 'as agent'—that is, for another—is formally consistent with my signing for myself as well. If the act of signing raises a presumption of personal assent and obligation, which has to be sufficiently negatived or qualified by apt words, are the words 'as agent' apt or sufficient to exclude personal liability? For myself, I think that, standing alone, they are. To say 'as agent,' meaning thereby 'also as agent' for some one undisclosed, is substantially useless. If the agent refuses to disclose, the opposite party is no better off. If the statement is true, the rights and liabilities of the principal can be established at any time by proof. The statement only acquires a business efficacy as distinct from a formal content, if it means 'I am not liable but someone else is and he only,' and this is what I think it does mean.

Unless, then, something is to be found to the contrary in the earlier part of this charter, the qualification 'as agents' appears to me to relieve Messrs McKelvie & Co from personal liability on the contract.

Lord Parmoor: ... The words 'as agents' are, in my opinion, clearly words of qualification and not of description. They denote, in unambiguous language, that the respondents did not sign as principals, and did not intend to incur personal liability. The signature applies to the whole contract, and to every term in the contract. I think it would not be admissible to infer an implied term, or implied terms, in the contract inconsistent with the limitation of liability directly expressed in the qualification of the signature, since the effect of such an implication would be to contradict an express term of the contract. It is not impossible that by plain words in the body of the document, persons signing 'as agents,' may expressly undertake some form of personal liability as principals, but I can find no trace of any intention of the respondents to incur any such liability in the charterparty, which is in question in the present appeal....

Different considerations arise when a person signs a contract without qualification, and the question is raised whether he is to be deemed as contracting personally, or as agent only. In such a case the intention of the parties is to be discovered from the contract itself, and the rule laid down in Smith's Leading Cases has been adopted as the rule to be followed. 'That where a person signs a contract in his own name, without qualification, he is prima facie to be deemed to be a person contracting personally, and in order to prevent this liability from attaching, it must be apparent from the other portions of the document that he did not intend to bind himself as principal.' I agree with Atkin LJ that it would tend to confusion to consider these cases in a case in which the signature itself has been expressly qualified.

Atkin LJ, in giving his decision in the present case, says: 'If the words qualify the signature, they qualify the assent, and nothing more matters.' I do not understand Atkin LJ to exclude the possibility that a person, signing 'as agent,' may nevertheless in the same document expressly undertake some form of personal liability. Such a possibility does not, in my opinion, affect the value of the rule as laid down by Atkin LJ, or its acceptance as an accurate guide in the construction of contracts, not regulated by statute, or considerations of a special character. The rule accords with the dictum of Mellish LJ in *Gadd v Houghton* ((1876) 1 Ex D 357 at 360), 'when the signature comes at the end you apply it to everything which occurs throughout the contract.'

In my opinion the appeal should be dismissed with costs.

Bridges & Salmon Ltd v The Swan (Owner), The Swan

[1968] 1 Lloyd's Rep 5, Admiralty Division

The plaintiffs were two firms of boat repairers claiming against the defendant, Mr JD Rodger, for the cost of repairs to the *Swan*. The *Swan* was owned by Mr Rodger but at all material times the vessel had been on hire to JD Rodger Ltd. Mr Rodger was a director of, and shareholder in, JD Rodger Ltd and acted as agent of the company when it ordered repairs to be carried out to the vessel by the plaintiffs. The repairs in question had been ordered partly orally and partly in writing on the company's headed notepaper, signed 'JD Rodger, Director'. At all times the plaintiffs knew that Mr Rodger was the company's agent but they also knew that he was the vessel's owner. The plaintiffs claimed that Mr Rodger was person-ally liable on the repair contracts, the company having become insolvent.

Brandon J: Where A contracts with B on behalf of a disclosed principal C, the question whether both A and C are liable on the contract or only C depends on the intention of the parties. That intention is to be gathered from (1) the nature of the contract, (2) its terms and (3) the surrounding circum-stances...The intention for which the Court looks is not the subjective intention of A or of B. Their subjective intentions may differ. The intention for which the Court looks is an objective intention of both parties, based on what two reasonable businessmen making a contract of that nature, in those terms and in those surrounding circumstances, must be taken to have intended.

Where a contract is wholly in writing, the intention depends on the true construction, having regard to the nature of the contract and the surrounding circumstances, of the document or documents in which the contract is contained. Where, as in the present case, the contract is partly oral and partly in writing, the intention depends on the true effect, having regard again to the nature of the contract and the surrounding circumstances, of the oral and written terms taken together.

Many of the decided cases on questions of this kind relate to contracts wholly in writing. But it seems to me that, in principle, there can be no difference in the approach to the problem, whether the contract concerned is wholly in writing or partly in writing and partly oral. In either case the terms of the contract must be looked at and their true effect ascertained. I therefore think that, although I am here concerned with contracts which are partly oral and partly written, I can nevertheless properly seek guidance from decided cases on contracts wholly in writing.

...[A] distinction has been drawn between cases in which a person contracts expressly as agent and those in which, although he describes himself as an agent, he does not contract expressly as such.

Where it is stated in the contract that a person makes it 'as agent for', or 'on account of', or 'on behalf of', or simply 'for', a principal, or where words of that kind are added after such person's signature, he is not personally liable: *Gadd v Houghton & Co* (1876) 1 Ex D 357; *Universal Steam Navigation Co Ltd v James McKelvie & Co* [1923] AC 492; *Kimber Coal Co Ltd v Stone and Rolfe Ltd* [1926] AC 414, 24 Ll L Rep 429.

Where such words are not used but the person is merely stated to be an agent, or the word 'agent' is just added after his signature, the result is uncertain, because it is not clear whether the word is used as a qualification or merely as a description: see *Gadd v Houghton & Co, supra,* per Lord Justice James at p 359; and *Universal Steam Navigation Co Ltd v James McKelvie & Co, supra,* per Lord Sumner at p 501. In general it would seem that in such a case the person does not avoid personal liability, although there may be exceptions to this general rule depending on the other terms of the contract or the surrounding circumstances.

Where a person contracts as agent for a company and does nothing more than add the word 'director' or 'secretary' after his signature, it seems that he does not avoid personal liability: *Brebner v Henderson* 1925 SC 643. This was a Scottish Appeal to the Court of Session which turned on the construction of s 26 of the Bills of Exchange Act, 1882, but I think the reasoning is applicable to a similar situation at common law.

Bearing in mind the distinctions drawn in the authorities to which I have referred, I return to an analysis of the facts in the present case. It seems to me that the defendant did not ever contract expressly as agent in the sense of saying either orally or in writing that he was acting 'as agent for', or 'on account of, or 'on behalf of, or 'for' the company. What he did was to describe himself to both plaintiffs at an earlier stage as 'Mr Rodger, of J D Rodger Ltd', and later to write the written orders on the company's notepaper and add the word 'Director' to his signature. On the other hand, the plaintiffs' subsequent conduct shows that they understood clearly that the bills for their work were to be sent to the company. It has been argued with force for the defendant that this shows that the plaintiffs understood the defendant to be contracting 'on account of the company and it was to the company alone that they were giving credit. I am not sure, however, that this is the only interpretation to be put on the facts, for it is possible for a person to give credit to a principal without at the same time giving exclusive credit to him.

On this analysis, which takes no account of any special factor arising from the surrounding circumstances, the present case appears to be somewhat near the borderline, with strong arguments available either way. But, as indicated earlier, the surrounding circumstances must also be looked at, and when looked at seem to me to assist considerably in the resolution of the problem.

The main surrounding circumstance, in my view, is that the defendant was at all material times the owner of the *Swan* and that both plaintiffs dealt with him either in the knowledge or on the correct assumption that this was so. The consequence of the defendant being the owner of the *Swan* was that he had a personal interest in the repairs in addition to his interest as director of the company in that the effect of the repairs was to preserve or to improve his own property. In particular, the repairs finally ordered and now sued for were of such an extent and character that they must greatly have increased the value of the vessel. All this was, or must be taken to have been, apparent both to Mr Pearce and to Mr Salmon [the managers of the respective plaintiffs].

The difficulty in the present case seems to me to arise mainly from the fact that the defendant had these two roles, one as director of the company which was operating the *Swan,* and the other as her owner. The defendant claims that, in all his dealings with the first and second plaintiffs in connection with repairs to the *Swan,* he was playing solely the first role. But the question is whether he made it clear to the two managers concerned, by his words oral or written, or his conduct, that this was so, or led them to suppose that he was playing the role of owner as well.

It seems to me that, when a person who is known or correctly assumed to be the owner of a boat, has discussions with a repairing company's manager about repairs to her, it is natural for the manager to assume that, if an order for the repairs is placed, that person will accept personal liability for them as such owner unless he makes the contrary clear beyond doubt. In the present case the defendant did make it clear to both Mr Pearce and Mr Salmon that the accounts for the work should be sent to the company. But the question is whether he made it clear to them at the same time that, although he was the owner of the boat and would therefore derive personal benefit from the repairs, he was nevertheless disowning any personal liability to pay for the work. Unless he did so it seems to me that they were entitled to assume that, while he was placing the order for the company to whom the account was to be sent, he remained also personally liable on the contract.

Approaching the matter in that way I have come to the conclusion that nothing said orally at any time to Mr Pearce, whether by the skipper or engineer of the *Swan* or by the defendant, and nothing contained in the written order to the second plaintiffs dated Oct 14, 1966, did make it clear beyond doubt that the defendant, although owner of the vessel, was disowning personal liability for the cost of the repairs which he was ordering.

I have reached a similar conclusion with regard to the first plaintiffs, although in their case the question of anything significant being said to Mr Salmon by anyone other than the defendant does not arise.

In the result, the decision which I have come to, after considering the nature and terms of the two contracts, and the surrounding circumstances, is that both plaintiffs are entitled to succeed on the second of the three points argued on their behalf, namely, that the defendant, though contracting as agent, did not do so solely as agent but in such a way as to be also personally liable.

NOTES

1. Whether an agent is liable on a contract in writing made on behalf of a disclosed principal depends on the objective intention of the parties, ie of the agent and third party. It is axiomatic to say that each case turns on the construction of the document in question. As Hobhouse J has emphasised: 'each contract has to be construed in its own context and having regard to the whole of its terms' (*Punjab National Bank v De Boinville* [1992] 1 Lloyd's Rep 7 at 12, see also Staughton LJ in the same case at 31). Furthermore, it is important to note that contracts made by deed, bills of exchange, promissory notes and cheques are governed by their own rules (see below, p 170).

2. Whilst generalisations as to the effect of particular words and phrases must be dangerous (*Bowstead and Reynolds,* para 9–037), the following principles offer some general guidance:

(1) If the agent signs the contract in his own name without more, he will be deemed to have contracted personally, unless he can rely on any term of the contract which *plainly* shows he was merely contracting as agent (eg *Gadd v Houghton & Co* (1876) 1 Ex D 357, CA, where brokers signed a contract of sale in their own name without qualification, but were not held personally liable as they were described in the body of the contract as selling 'on account of' someone else; cf *Tudor Marine Ltd v Tradax Export SA, The Virgo* [1976] 2 Lloyd's Rep 135, CA; *Jugoslavenska Linijska Plovidba v Hulsman (t/a Brusse & Sippel Import-Export), The Primorje* [1980] 2 Lloyd's Rep 74; *Seatrade Groningen BV v Geest Industries Ltd, The Frost Express* [1996] 2 Lloyd's Rep 375, CA).

(2) If an agent signs as 'agent', 'broker', 'director' etc, this may amount to no more than a description and not a qualification of his personal liability, unless a contrary intention can be established from the whole of the contract or from the surrounding circumstances (see *Universal Steam Navigation Co v McKelvie,* above, per Lord Sumner; *The Swan,* above).

(3) If the agent clearly indicates by a qualification added to his signature that he is contracting solely as agent, he will not be held personally liable (although see Lord Shaw's reference to a 'highly improbable and conjectural case' in *Universal Steam Navigation Co v McKelvie,* above; see also note 3 below as to the effect of extrinsic evidence of custom or usage).

3. The terms of the written contract indicating that the agent contracted personally cannot be contradicted by parol or other extrinsic evidence (*Higgins v Senior* (1841) 8 M&W 834). However, the agent may have an equitable defence to an action by the third party if he can establish an extrinsic agreement between himself and the third party that he should not be made personally liable (*Wake v Harrop* (1862) 1 H & C 202; *Bowstead and Reynolds,* para 9–040; cf *Fridman,* p 241). But parol evidence of custom or usage may be introduced to show that the agent is personally liable on a contract, when he does not appear otherwise to be so. So long as the parol evidence does not contradict the terms of the written agreement the personal liability of the agent may be established in this way (eg *Hutchinson v Tatham* (1873) LR 8 CP 482, where parol evidence of trade usage was admitted to show that the agent, who signed a charterparty 'as agents to merchants', was liable if the name of the principal was not disclosed in a reasonable time).

4.   When an agent is held personally liable on the contract he makes with the third party, the question arises as to whether he is solely liable or whether he is liable together with his principal. The liability of both principal and agent will often accord with commercial expectations, and there is certainly evidence that the courts have been willing to hold that the agent has undertaken liability as well as the principal (eg see *International Rly Co v Niagara Parks Commission* [1941] AC 328 at 342; *Montgomerie v UK Mutual Steamship Association,* above at p 149; *The Swan,* above at p 165; *Teheran-Europe Co Ltd v ST Belton (Tractors) Ltd,* above at p 152; see also FMB Reynolds (1969) 85 LQR 92). But such cases are probably still to be regarded as exceptional (they are often explained as turning on special trade custom) and it is more likely that the agent will either be held solely liable as principal or not liable at all (see *Universal Steam Navigation Co v McKelvie,* above at p 162, per Lord Shaw; Reynolds, op cit, p 94). There is much that remains uncertain and unsatisfactory in this area (see, in particular, the cases on election: discussed above at pp 156–159). Finally, it should be noted that the terms of the agent's liability is an important issue whenever the agent undertakes personal liability to the third party; it is not an issue restricted to contracts in writing.

5.   See PN Legh-Jones (1969) 32 MLR 325, who argues that *The Swan* was wrongly decided.

Oral contracts

N & J Vlassopulos Ltd v Ney Shipping Ltd, The Santa Carina
[1977] 1 Lloyd's Rep 478, Court of Appeal

The defendants, who were brokers on the Baltic Exchange, telephoned the plaintiffs, who were also brokers there, and asked them to supply bunkers to the vessel *Santa Carina.* Bunkers were supplied but the plaintiffs' invoice remained unpaid. The plaintiffs then brought an action to recover the price from the defendants. The defendants denied liability on the grounds that they were acting merely as agents for their principals, the time charterers of the *Santa Carina,* and that although the plaintiffs did not know the identity of the principals, they did know that the defendants acted as agents. Reversing Mocatta J, the Court of Appeal gave judgment for the defendants.

Lord Denning MR: On the facts I have stated, it is clear that Vlassopulos, the brokers for the suppliers, knew that Ney, the brokers for the time charterers, were ordering the fuel simply as agents. They were agents either for the owners or the time charterers of the vessels. The brokers for the suppliers knew they were agents. They received a telephone message saying: 'Please supply this fuel oil to the vessel'. But they knew it was from the agents as agents.

The Judge held that the brokers who ordered the fuel were personally liable. He was much influenced by the cases where a person gives a written order for goods or signs a written contract when he is known to be acting as an agent. Nevertheless, although he is known to be acting as an agent, he will be liable on that order or liable on that contract if he signs in his own personal name without qualification. That is settled by cases both in this Court and in the House of Lords: see *H O Brandt & Co v H N Morris & Co Ltd* [1917] 2 KB 784 at p 796 per Lord Justice Scrutton, and *Hichens, Harrison, Woolston & Co v Jackson & Sons* [1943] AC 266 at p 273 per Lord Atkin. In order to exclude his liability he has to append to his signature some such words as 'as agent only' or 'for and on behalf of or such exclusion must be apparent elsewhere in the document. That is clear from *Universal Steam Navigation Co v James McKelvie & Co* [1923] AC 492 at pp 505–506.

The Judge thought that those cases on written orders and written contracts should be applied to the present case of an oral contract. He felt that if there is an oral conversation on the telephone, as in this case ordering bunkers, the broker is liable unless he uses some express words so as to show that he is acting as agent only and is not to be held personally liable. He said ([1976] 2 Lloyd's Rep 223 at p 226):

Thus some words must be used to indicate that the agent is not himself undertaking any financial obligation or liability.

I have no doubt that those cases on written orders and written contracts arose out of the old rule of evidence whereby it was not permissible to admit oral evidence to alter or contradict a written contract. Those cases still apply today to written orders and written contracts. But they do not apply to oral orders or oral contracts. At any rate not so rigidly. In many cases if a man, who is an agent for another, orders goods or makes a contract by word of mouth, but does not disclose the name or standing of his principal (so that his credit is unknown to the other contracting party) the agent himself is liable to pay for the goods or to fulfil the contract. It may be that the other contracting party knows that the man is only an agent, but, as he does not know who the principal is, it is to be inferred that he does not rely on the credit of the principal but looks to the agent. That, I think, is the thought underlying the dictum of Mr Justice Salter in *Benton v Campbell, Parker & Co Ltd* [1925] 2 KB 410 at p 414, and the American Restatement on Agency in the comment to para 321. But in other cases that may not be the proper inference. There are cases where, although the man who supplied the goods knows that the other is an agent and does not know his principal, nevertheless he is content to look to the credit of that principal whoever he may be. This is something which Lord Justice Diplock contemplated in the case of *Teheran-Europe Co Ltd v S T Belton (Tractors) Ltd* [1968] 2 Lloyd's Rep 37, [1968] 2 QB 545. He said that

> ... he may be willing to treat as a party to the contract anyone on whose behalf the agent may have been authorised to contract ...

This applies particularly to the case of a broker. As Mr Justice Blackburn said in *Fleet v Murton* (1871) LR 7 QB 126 at p 131.

> ... I take it that there is no doubt at all, in principle, that a broker, as such, merely dealing as broker and not as purchaser of the article, makes a contract from the very nature of things between the buyer and the seller and he is not himself either buyer or seller.

It seems to me that the present case falls into that second category. It was known to both sides that the agents, Ney Shipping Ltd, were only brokers. They were brokers ordering bunkers for a vessel. It was obvious that they were only agents, and they were ordering bunkers for the time charterers or the owners of a vessel. They had often done it before. The accounts for the fuel had always been paid by the principals either directly or through the brokers. It cannot be supposed that the brokers were ever intended to be personally liable. The suppliers would look to the time charterers or the owners, whoever they might be, they being the people to be relied upon. Although they were not named or specified or disclosed, they would be the people to whom the suppliers would look for payment of the oil.

It is just the same, it seems to me, as if the brokers had given a written order for the bunkers and added to their signatures 'as agents only'. In that case they would not have been personally liable. Nor should they be liable in this case when it was done by word of mouth and when the inference from the conduct and the whole of the circumstances was that they were ordering the fuel as agents only.

It can be tested by taking the converse case. Suppose the fuel had been of bad quality and the engines of the ship had been damaged, or the ship delayed, could the brokers Ney Shipping have sued for damages? Or the brokers Vlassopulos have been made liable in damages? Clearly not. It would be for the principals on either side to have sued. So here the brokers Vlassopulos could not sue for the price, nor the brokers Ney be liable for it.

I know that in many trades there is a custom by which the broker is liable. Those cases rest on a custom of the trade. There was no such custom alleged or proved in respect of the brokers on the Baltic Exchange. It seems to me that, in the circumstances of this case, the proper inference is that the agents here were, when they gave the telephone message, giving it as agents only. By their conduct it is to be inferred that it was just the same as if they had given a written order excluding their personal liability and the suppliers looked to the owners or time charterers of the vessel who were the people really liable. It is the unfortunate fact that they have proved insolvent or unable to pay, but it seems to me that that is not a sufficient ground for now making the brokers liable. I would therefore allow the appeal and give judgment for the defendant.

[Roskill and Lawton LJJ delivered concurring judgments.]

NOTES

1.   With oral contracts it is a question of fact in each particular case whether it was intended that the agent should or should not be entitled to sue, and/or held personally liable, on the contract. The agent's failure to name his principal is merely one factor, albeit a significant one, for the court to take into account when assessing whether the agent intended to contract personally.

2.   In *The Santa Carina*, Lord Denning referred to the rule contained in the second edition of the American *Restatement of the Law of Agency* (1958), which provides that when the agent acts for a principal whose existence is known but who is not identified at the time of contracting, the agent is, unless otherwise agreed, a party to the contract. The same rule is now to be found in para 6.02 of the third edition of the *Restatement* (2006). However, the Court of Appeal declined to apply such a general rule to unwritten contracts under English law (and the Supreme Court of Canada has done the same in respect of written contracts: *QNS Paper Co Ltd v Chartwell Shipping Ltd* [1989] 2 SCR 683). *The Santa Carina* has been criticised by Professor Reynolds who argues for a prima facie rule (applicable to both written and unwritten contracts) making the agent liable together with the unnamed principal unless it is absolutely clear that the person concerned acted as agent only. Professor Reynolds submits that because there is no such prima facie rule the courts have caused confusion by wrongly classifying unnamed principal cases as undisclosed principal cases so as to prevent the agent avoiding personal liability. See FMB Reynolds [1983] CLP 119, and also *Bowstead and Reynolds,* para 9-016.

Deeds

If an agent contracts by deed, he will be personally liable so long as he is a party to the deed and has executed it in his own name. In these circumstances, the agent will be liable even if he is described in the deed as acting for and on behalf of a named principal (*Appleton v Binks* (1804) 5 East 148). As to the possible effect of s 7(1) of the Powers of Attorney Act 1971 (as amended) on this rule, see *Fridman,* pp 220–221, 231; *Bowstead and Reynolds,* paras 8-089 and 9-048.

Negotiable instruments

Special rules apply in cases where an agent has signed a bill of exchange, promissory note or cheque. These rules are considered below at pp 563ff.

Agents for foreign principals

See above, p 151.

Agents for fictitious or non-existent principals

(1)   At common law, an agent who purports to act for a non-existent or fictitious principal may be held personally liable on the contract. Whether the agent is liable will turn on the objective construction of the terms of the contract by the court. Even if the parties did

not intend the agent to be liable on the contract, he may still be held liable for breach of warranty of authority, in deceit, or, possibly, for negligent misstatement.

(2) By statute, where a contract purports to be made by or on behalf of a company, at a time when the company has not yet been formed, then subject to any agreement to the contrary, the contract has effect as a contract made with the person purporting to act for the company or as agent for it, and he is personally liable on the contract accordingly: s 51(1) of the Companies Act 2006 (above, p 142). If the agent is to avoid liability under the statute there must be 'a clear exclusion of personal liability': signing the contract 'for and on behalf of X Ltd' would not be enough (*Phonogram Ltd v Lane* [1982] QB 938 at 944, per Lord Denning MR). It has recently been held that s 51(1) also entitles the person or agent purporting to act for the unformed company to enforce the contract against the other party unless such enforcement is otherwise precluded by the ordinary principles governing contractual arrangements (*Braymist Ltd v Wise Finance Co Ltd* [2002] EWCA Civ 127, [2002] Ch 273, applying the identically worded Companies Act 1985, s 36C(1)). See generally A Griffiths (1993) 13 LS 241, and also C Twigg-Flesner (2001) 22 Company Lawyer 274.

(3) Where it turns out that the agent is in fact his own principal, there is authority that the apparent agent can be held personally liable on the contract (*Railton v Hodgson* (1804) 4 Taunt 576n; *Jenkins v Hutchinson* (1849) 13 QB 744; cf *Bowstead and Reynolds* at paras 9-085–9-086, where it is argued that liability on a collateral warranty would be more appropriate).

Statute

A statutory provision may make an agent personally liable on a contract made on behalf of his principal, eg Companies Act 2006, s 51(1) (considered immediately above).

(iii) When will the agent be entitled to sue on the contract made on behalf of his principal?

The agent will be entitled to sue on the contract made on behalf of his disclosed principal in any of the following circumstances:

(1) Where it is the intention of the parties that the agent should have rights as well as liabilities on the contract (eg *Short v Spackman* (1831) 2 B & Ad 962).

(2) Where the agent's right of action arises out of a collateral contract with the third party (although, strictly, this does not allow the agent to sue on the main contract).

(3) Where the agent has some special property in the subject matter of the contract, or possesses a lien over it, or has a beneficial interest in completion of the contract, he may sue the third party. For example, the auctioneer's right to sue the highest bidder for the price stems from his special property in, or lien over, the subject matter of the sale he effects (*Benton v Campbell Parker & Co* [1925] 2 KB 410 at 416, per Salter J); although the right of action actually arises under a collateral contract between the auctioneer and the highest bidder (*Chelmsford Auctions Ltd v Poole* [1973] QB 542 at 548–549, per Lord Denning MR).

(4) Where the agent purports to contract on behalf of a company yet to be formed, the agent may be entitled as well as liable on the contract under s 51(1) of the Companies Act 2006 (as was held to be the case by the Court of Appeal in *Braymist Ltd v Wise Finance Co Ltd* [2002] EWCA Civ 127, [2002] Ch 273: see above).

What if it turns out that the agent is in fact his own principal?

Rayner v Grote

(1846) 15 M & W 359, Court of Exchequer

The plaintiff, purporting to act for a named principal, contracted in writing to sell certain goods to the defendant. After discovering that the plaintiff was in fact the real principal, the defendant accepted delivery and paid for part of the goods. The plaintiff then sued the defendant for non-acceptance of the remainder of the goods. The Court of Exchequer (Pollock CB, Rolfe B and Alderton B) upheld the verdict of the jury in favour of the plaintiff.

Alderton B (delivering the judgment of the Court): …At the time when this contract was made, the plaintiff was himself the real principal in the transaction; and although the contract on the face of it appeared to have been made by him as agent for another party, there was evidence given at the trial, tending strongly to shew, that when the first parcel of the goods was delivered to and accepted by the defendants, the name of the plaintiff as the principal was then fully known to the defendants: and we think that it was then properly left to the jury to infer from the evidence, that the defendants, with the full knowledge of the facts, had received that portion of the goods, and that all parties then treated the contract as one made with the plaintiff as the principal in the transaction. The defendants' counsel, in the argument, contended against this view of the case, and cited the case of *Bickerton v Burrell* as an authority that the plaintiff could not sue in such a case in his own name. That case is indeed in one respect stronger than the present, inasmuch as that was an action for money had and received, whereas this is a case of an executory contract. If, indeed, the contract had been wholly unperformed, and one which the plaintiff, by merely proving himself to be the real principal, was seeking to enforce, the question might admit of some doubt. In many such cases, such as, for instance, the case of contracts in which the skill or solvency of the person who is named as the principal may reasonably be considered as a material ingredient in the contract, it is clear that the agent cannot then shew himself to be the real principal, and sue in his own name; and perhaps it may be fairly urged that this, in all executory contracts, if wholly unperformed, or if partly performed without the knowledge of who is the real principal, may be the general rule. But the facts of this case raise a totally different question, as the jury must be taken to have found, under the learned Judge's direction, that this contract has been in part performed, and that part performance accepted by the defendants with full knowledge that the plaintiff was not the agent, but the real principal. If so, we think the plaintiff may, after that, very properly say that they cannot refuse to complete that contract, by receiving the remainder of the goods, and paying the stipulated price for them. And it may be observed that this case is really distinguishable from *Bickerton v Burrell,* on the very ground on which that case was decided; for here, at all events, before action brought and trial had, the defendants knew that the plaintiff was the principal in the transaction. Perhaps it may be doubted whether that case was well decided on such a distinction, as it may fairly be argued that it would have been quite sufficient to prevent any possible inconvenience or injustice, and more in accordance with former authorities, if the Court had held that a party named as agent, under such circumstances as existed in that case, was entitled, on shewing himself to be the real principal, to maintain the action, the defendant being, however, allowed to make any defence to which he could shew himself to be entitled, either as against the plaintiff or as against the person named as principal by the plaintiff in the contract. It is not, however, necessary for us, in the present case, to question the authority of that decision.

NOTES

1. In *Bickerton v Burrell* (1816) 5 M & S 383, it was held that the plaintiff, having signed a contract as agent for a named principal, could not sue as the real principal, at all events unless he had given notice to the defendant of his true status in advance of bringing the action.

2. It would appear from the dictum of Alderton B in *Rayner v Grote* that an agent who purports to act for a *named* principal may nevertheless sue on the contract as the real principal provided that the agent has informed the third party that he acted on his own behalf, or the third party has otherwise become aware of the true position, *and* the identity of the principal was immaterial to the making of the contract by the third party. The fact that the defendant in *Rayner v Grote,* after discovering that the agent was the real principal, affirmed the contract by accepting delivery and paying for part of the goods, indicated to the court that he did not regard the principal's identity as material. Alderton B also suggested in *Rayner v Grote* that, whenever the contract remained entirely executory, the agent should not be allowed to sue in his own name. However, so long as the identity of the principal is not material to the third party, it is doubtful that there is anything to be gained by preventing the agent from suing on an entirely executory contract once the third party is aware of the true position (see *Markesinis and Munday,* p 201).

3. Alderton B's dictum was cited with approval by Webster J in *Gewa Chartering BV v Remco Shipping Lines Ltd, The Remco* [1984] 2 Lloyd's Rep 205. In that case an agent, purporting to act on behalf of a named principal, entered into a contract for the charter of a ship. Later the agent revealed himself to be the real principal. Webster J held that the agent could not enforce the contract since the other contracting party, the shipowners, regarded the identity of the charterer as material (because the charterer was responsible for payment of freight). It could be shown that the shipowners would not have agreed to the same terms if they had known that the agent was really the principal.

4. There have been a number of cases where an agent, who purports to act for an *unnamed* principal, has been allowed to reveal himself as the real principal and sue on the contract, on the ground that the personal characteristics of the supposed principal cannot have influenced the third party (see *Schmaltz v Avery* (1851) 16 QB 655; *Harper & Co v Vigers Bros* [1909] 2 KB 549; cf *Sharman v Brandt* (1871) LR 6 QB 720). For criticism of this line of authority, see *Bowstead and Reynolds,* paras 9-092–9-093.

QUESTION

Arnold contracts purportedly on behalf of Percy, a noted dog breeder, to buy a valuable prize poodle from Thomas. During the negotiations, Thomas says to Arnold: 'I am surprised that a reputable breeder like Percy is acting through a spiv like you'. Arnold is in fact acting for himself. Two weeks after the conclusion of this contract, Arnold telephones Thomas and admits that he is really the purchaser. At first, Thomas accepts the situation philosophically; but after consulting a lawyer, Daisy, he refuses to deliver up the poodle. Advise Arnold.

(iv) Breach of warranty of authority

Bowstead and Reynolds on Agency
(18th edn, 2006), art 105(1)

Where a person, by words or conduct, represents that he has actual authority to act on behalf of another, and a third party is induced by such representation to act in a manner in which he would not have acted if such representation had not been made, the first-mentioned person is deemed to warrant that the representation is true, and is liable for any loss caused to such third party by a breach of that implied warranty, even if he acted in good faith, under a mistaken belief that he had such authority.

Yonge v Toynbee

[1910] 1 KB 215, Court of Appeal

Solicitors were instructed by Toynbee to defend an action for libel and slander threatened against him by Yonge. Before the action was commenced, and unknown to his solicitors, Toynbee became insane and was certified as being of unsound mind. On commencement of the action the solicitors entered an appearance, delivered a defence and engaged in certain interlocutory proceedings. Subsequently, the solicitors discovered that Toynbee was insane and informed Yonge of that fact. Yonge then applied to have the appearance and all subsequent proceedings struck out and for the solicitors to pay personally his costs of the action, on the ground that they had acted for Toynbee without authority. The Master ordered the appearance and subsequent proceedings to be struck out but refused to make an order that Yonge's costs should be paid by the solicitors personally. The Court of Appeal allowed Yonge's appeal against the Master's refusal to make an order for costs against the solicitors.

Buckley LJ: The interesting and important question in this case is as to the extent to which the principle *of Smout v Ilbery* ((1842) 10 M & W 1) remains good law after the decision in *Collen v Wright* ((1857) 8 E & B 647). In *Smout v Ilbery* Alderson B, in giving the judgment of the Court, dealt with the authorities under three heads: First, the case where the agent made a fraudulent misrepresentation as to his authority with an intention to deceive. In such case the agent is, of course, personally responsible. Secondly, the case where the agent without fraud, but untruly in fact, represented that he had authority when he had none, instancing under this head *Polhill v Walter* ((1832) 3 B & Ad 114). In that case A, having no authority from B to accept a bill on his behalf, did accept it as by his procuration, bona fide believing that B would retrospectively approve that which he was doing. In such case again the agent is personally liable, for he induced the other party to enter into a contract on a misrepresentation of a fact within his own knowledge. The third class is where the agent bona fide believes that he has, but in fact has not, authority. This third class the learned Baron seems to subdivide into two heads—the first where the agent never had authority, but believed that he had (eg when he acted on a forged warrant of attorney which he thought to be genuine), and the second where the agent had in fact full authority originally, but that authority had come to an end without any knowledge, or means of knowledge, on the part of the agent that such was the fact. The latter was the state of facts in *Smout v Ilbery*. I understand *Smout v Ilbery* not to dispute that in the former of these last two cases (that is, where the agent never had authority) he is liable, but to hold that in the latter (namely, where he originally had authority, but that authority has ceased without his having knowledge, or means of knowledge, that it has ceased) he is not liable. The principle is stated in the following words: 'If, then, the true principle derivable from the cases is, that there must be some wrong or omission of right on the part of the agent, in order to make him personally liable on a contract made in the name of his principal, it will follow that the agent is not responsible in such a case as the present. And to this conclusion we have come.' It seems to me that, if that principle be the true principle, then the former of the last two mentioned cases ought to have been resolved in the same way as the latter. I can see no distinction in principle between the case where the agent never had authority and the case where the agent originally had authority, but that authority has ceased without his knowledge or means of knowledge. In the latter case as much as in the former the proposition, I think, is true that without any mala fides he has at the moment of acting represented that he had an authority which in fact he had not. In my opinion he is then liable on an implied contract that he had authority, whether there was fraud or not. That this is the true principle is, I think, shewn by passages which I will quote from judgments in three which I have selected out of the numerous cases upon this subject. In *Collen v Wright* Willes J in giving the judgment of the Court uses the following language: 'I am of opinion that a person who induces another to contract with him, as the agent of a third party, by an unqualified assertion of his being authorized to act as such agent, is answerable to the person who so contracts for any damages which he may sustain by reason of the assertion of authority being untrue.... The fact that the professed agent honestly thinks that he has authority affects the moral character of his act; but his moral innocence, so far as the person whom he has induced to contract is concerned, in no way aids such person or alleviates the inconvenience and damage which he sustains. The obligation arising in such a case is well expressed by saying that a person professing to contract as agent for another, impliedly, if not expressly, undertakes to or promises the person who enters into such contract, upon the faith of the professed agent being duly authorized, that the authority which he professes to have does in point of fact exist.' This language is equally applicable to each of the two classes of cases to which I have referred. The language is not, in my opinion, consistent with maintaining that which *Smout v Ilbery* had laid down as the true principle, that there must be some wrong or omission of right on the part of the agent in order to make him liable. The question is not as to his honesty or bona fides. His liability arises from an implied undertaking or promise made by him that the authority which he professes to have does in point of fact exist. I can see no difference of principle between the case in which the authority never existed at all and the case in which the authority once existed and has ceased to exist. In *Firbank's Executors v Humphreys* ((1886) 18 QBD 54 at 60) the rule is thus stated by Lord Esher: 'The rule to be deduced is that, where a person by asserting that he has the authority of the principal induces another person to enter into any transaction which he would not have entered into but for that assertion, and the assertion turns out to be untrue, to the injury of the person to whom it is made, it must be taken that the person making it undertook that it was true, and he is liable personally for the damage that has occurred.'

Lastly, Lord Davey in *Starkey v Bank of England* ([1903] AC 114 at 119), after stating that the rule extends to every transaction of business into which a third party is induced to enter by a representation that the person with whom he is doing business has the authority of some other person, rejects the argument that the rule in *Collen v Wright* does not extend to cases where the supposed agent did not know that he had no authority, and had not the means of finding out; cites Lord Campbell's language in *Lewis v Nicholson* ((1852) 18 QB 503), that the agent 'is liable, if there was any fraud, in an action for deceit, and, in my opinion, as at present advised, on an implied contract that he had authority, whether there was fraud or not'; and concludes by saying that in his opinion 'it is utterly immaterial for the purpose of the application of this branch of the law whether the supposed agent knew of the defect of his authority or not.'

The result of these judgments, in my opinion, is that the liability of the person who professes to act as agent arises (a) if he has been fraudulent, (b) if he has without fraud untruly represented that he had authority when he had not, and (c) also where he innocently misrepresents that he has authority where the fact is either (1) that he never had authority or (2) that his original authority has ceased by reasons of facts of which he has not knowledge or means of knowledge. Such last-mentioned liability arises from the fact that by professing to act as agent he impliedly contracts that he has authority, and it is immaterial whether he knew of the defect of his authority or not.

This implied contract may, of course, be excluded by the facts of the particular case. If, for instance, the agent proved that at the relevant time he told the party with whom he was contracting that he did not know whether the warrant of attorney under which he was acting was genuine or not, and would not warrant its validity, or that his principal was abroad and he did not know whether he was still living, there will have been no representation upon which the implied contract will arise. This may have been the ratio decidendi in *Smout v Ilbery* as expressed in the passage 'The continuance of the life of the principal was, under these circumstances, a fact equally within the knowledge of both contracting parties'; and this seems to be the ground upon which Story on Agency, s 265a, approves the decision. The husband had left England for China in May, 1839, a time in the history of the world when communication was not what it is now, and the Court seems to have decided upon the ground that the butcher who supplied the goods knew that the facts were such that the wife did not, because she could not, take upon herself to affirm that he was alive. If so, there was no implied contract. The principle, as stated in the words I have quoted, may have been meant to be, but is not in words, rested upon that ground, and, if it is to be understood as it seems to have been understood in *Salton v New Beeston Cycle Co* ([1900] 1 Ch 43), it is not, I think, consistent with *Collen v Wright*. The true principle as deduced from the authorities I have mentioned rests, I think, not upon wrong or omission of right on the part of the agent, but upon implied contract.

The facts here are that the solicitors originally had authority to act for Mr Toynbee; that that authority ceased by reason of his unsoundness of mind; that, subsequently, they on October 30, 1908, undertook to appear, and on November 6 appeared, in the first action, and, after that was discontinued, did on December 21 undertake to appear, and did on December 30 enter an appearance, in the second action; and that they subsequently, on February 22, 1909, delivered a defence pleading privilege, and denying the slander, and did not until April 5 inform the plaintiff that, as the fact was, their client had become of unsound mind. During all this time they were putting the plaintiff to costs, and these costs were incurred upon the faith of their representation that they had authority to act for the defendant. They proved no facts addressed to shew that implied contract was excluded.

It has been pressed upon us that a solicitor is an agent of a special kind with an obligation towards his client to continue to take on his behalf all proper steps in the action. The particular nature of his agency is not, I think, very material. On the other hand it must be borne in mind that after August 21, when the defendant Toynbee wrote to the plaintiffs solicitors, referring them to Messrs Wontner & Sons, the plaintiff could not consistently with professional etiquette communicate personally with the defendant. During the period from August, 1908, to April, 1909, the solicitors had the means of knowing and did not in fact ascertain that the defendant had become of unsound mind. In the interval they did acts which amounted to representations on their part that they were continuing to stand in a position in which they were competent to bind the defendant. This was not the case. They are liable, in my judgment, upon an implied warranty or contract that they had an authority which they had not.

For these reasons I think that the appellent is entitled to succeed and to have an order against the solicitors for damages, and the measure of damage is, no doubt, the amount of the plaintiffs costs thrown away in the action. The appeal, therefore, should be allowed with costs here and below.

Swinfen Eady J: I wish to add that in the conduct of litigation the Court places much reliance upon solicitors, who are its officers; it issues writs at their instance, and accepts appearances for defendants which they enter, as a matter of course, and without questioning their authority; the other parties to the litigation also act upon the same footing, without questioning or investigating the authority of the solicitor on the opposite side; and much confusion and uncertainty would be introduced if a solicitor were not to be under any liability to the opposite party for continuing to act without authority in cases where he originally possessed one…. The manner in which business is ordinarily conducted requires that each party should be able to rely upon the solicitor of the other party having obtained a proper authority before assuming to act. It is always open to a solicitor to communicate as best he can with his own client, and obtain from time to time such authority and instructions as may be necessary. But the solicitor on the other side does not communicate with his opponent's client, and, speaking generally, it is not proper for him to do so, as was pointed out by Kekewich J in *Re Margetson & Jones* ([1897] 2 Ch 314). It is in my opinion essential to the proper conduct of legal business that a solicitor should be held to warrant the authority which he claims of representing the client; if it were not so, no one would be safe in assuming that his opponent's solicitor was duly authorized in what he said or did, and it would be impossible to conduct legal business upon the footing now existing; and, whatever the legal liability may be, the Court, in exercising the authority which it possesses over its own officers, ought to proceed upon the footing that a solicitor assuming to act, in an action, for one of the parties to the action warrants his authority.

[Vaughan Williams LJ delivered a concurring judgment.]

NOTES

1.   Despite the fact that it was held in *Yonge v Toynbee* that the agent's liability to the third party was contractual, debate has continued as to the nature of an agent's liability to a third party when acting without authority. Various alternative theories have been advance, including those based on quasi-contract, negligent misstatement and estoppel, but none

withstand close scrutiny (see *Fridman,* pp 244–247, who concludes that 'the true nature and basis of this anomalous liability is...uncertain and unclear'). In *Farley Health Products Ltd v Babylon Trading Co* (1987) Times, 29 July, Sir Neil Lawson thought that liability for breach of warranty of authority was *sui generis,* not being a claim in contract or tort. However, it is submitted that the best explanation, which reflects the reasoning of Willes J in *Collen v Wright* (1857) 7 E & B 301, and of the Court of Appeal in *Yonge v Toynbee,* is that the agent's liability is based on a collateral contract made with the third party (*AMB Generali Holding AG v SEB Trygg Liv Holding AB* [2005] EWCA Civ 1237, [2006] 1 WLR 2276 at [60], per Buxton LJ). Furthermore, the damages awarded for breach of an agent's warranty of authority will be assessed on normal *Hadley v Baxendale* (1854) 9 Exch 341 principles (see note 5 below), thus reflecting the contractual nature of the liability (although if the agent has been fraudulent or negligent the third party can ask for damages to be assessed on a different basis).

2.   An agent may be liable for breach of warranty of authority whether he is fraudulent, negligent or innocent. Liability is strict and may operate harshly on an agent who is innocently unaware of the initial absence, or subsequent termination, of his authority. However, the harshness of the rule is mitigated in the following respects:

(1)   The agent will not be liable where the third party knew, or ought to have known, that the agent was not warranting his authority (eg *Lilly, Wilson & Co v Smales, Eeles & Co* [1892] 1 QB 456, where it was held that trade custom should have put the third party on notice that the agent was not warranting his authority).

(2)   The agent's representation of authority must be one of fact and not of law (eg *Rashdall v Ford* (1866) LR 2 Eq 750, where directors of a statutory company, with no borrowing powers on a true construction of the incorporating statute, were held to have made a representation of law, and not of fact, when they purported to borrow from a third party). However, it is often difficult to distinguish representations of fact from representations of law, and at least in one area, namely recovery of money paid by mistake, the distinction had been abolished (*Kleinwort Benson Ltd v Lincoln City Council* [1999] 2 AC 349, HL). In the light of this development, which the Court of Appeal has said 'now permeates the law of contract' (*Brennan v Bolt Burden* [2004] EWCA Civ 1017, [2005] QB 303 at [10]), the distinction made between an agent's representation of fact and his representation of law may no longer apply (the distinction has been removed in other areas of contract law, eg it has been held that a contract may be rescinded for a misrepresentation of law: *Pankhania v Hackney London Borough Council* [2002] EWHC 2441 (Ch) at [57]).

(3)   Under s 5(1) of the Powers of Attorney Act 1971, a donee of a power of attorney who acts in pursuance of the power at a time when it has been revoked does not, by reason of the revocation, incur any liability (either to the donor or to any other person) if at the time he did not know that the power had been revoked. The protection afforded by s 5(1) also extends to the donee of a lasting power of attorney (Mental Capacity Act 2005, s 14(5)).

(4)   The agent's warranty is limited. It is that he has authority to make the contract or enter into the transaction, it is not that the contract or transaction will be performed by his principal, or that the principal in solvent (*AMB Generali Holding AG v SEB Trygg Liv Holding AB* [2005] EWCA Civ 1237, [2006] 1 WLR 2276 at [60] ff, per Buxton LJ: held solicitor conducting proceedings only gives a warranty that he has a client who exists and has authorised proceedings; he does not give a warrant as to his client's name, or that he has a good cause of action or is solvent). This means that if the principal is insolvent, the third party cannot recover more from the agent than he could have recovered from the principal, had the agent had authority.

3.   Liability for breach of warranty of authority may extend very widely indeed. Not only may the agent be liable for breach of warranty of his own authority but he may also be liable if he warrants the authority of someone else (*Chapleo v Brunswick Permanent Building Society* (1881) 6 QBD 696). Furthermore, the agent may be held liable to a person unknown to him but who nevertheless relied upon his representation, eg the indorsee of a bill of exchange or a bill of lading (see *Rasnoimport V/O v Guthrie & Co Ltd* [1966] 1 Lloyd's Rep 1, where Mocatta J said at 13 'I can see nothing extravagant or heterodox in holding that the implied warranty of authority... was given by the defendants to all whom they could reasonably foresee would become such indorsees and became actionable by such persons on proof of their having acted in reliance upon the warranty and having suffered damage thereby'—but see FMB Reynolds (1967) 80 LQR 189 for criticism of this decision). The third party need not be induced to transact with the purported principal as a result of the agent's warranty of authority, although this is the paradigm case; he may provide consideration for the agent's warranty by entering into a transaction with someone else. Thus, in *Penn v Bristol and West Building Society* [1997] 3 All ER 470, when a solicitor mistakenly thought he had authority to act for both joint owners of a house, and held himself out as such to another solicitor who, as he was aware, acted for both the prospective purchaser and the building society which was lending money to finance the purchase, the Court of Appeal held that the solicitor's warranty of authority was given to both the purchaser and the building society which acted in reliance on that promise by lending the money to the purchaser.

4.   Will an agent with no actual authority be in breach of his warranty of authority if he has apparent authority or if the principal subsequently ratifies his actions? Professor Treitel submits that the agent would not be liable for breach of his warranty of authority in either of these circumstances (E Peel, *Treitel's Law of Contract* (12th edn, 2007), para 16–081, relying, *inter alia*, on *Rainbow v Howkins* [19041 2 KB 322). We respectfully disagree with this submission. The agent professes that he has authority and this must be taken to mean that he has actual authority. This is because apparent authority is no authority at all but merely a condition which calls into being the power of an 'agent' to alter the legal relations of his 'principal' (see above, pp 121–122). However, the fact that the agent has apparent authority is significant because it avoids loss to the third party which would otherwise result from the agent's breach of warranty of authority. If the third party can hold the principal to the contract or transaction affected by the agent on grounds of the latter's apparent authority, the third party will have suffered no loss by reason of the agent's breach of warranty of authority (see eg *Drew v Nunn* (1879) 4 QBD 661, below at p 258; but the point was not considered in *Yonge v Toynbee*). A similar conclusion can be reached with regard to the principal's ratification of an agent's unauthorised acts. Ratification is not retrospective for all purposes (above, pp 146–147) and so it is better to regard the agent as technically in breach of his warranty of authority, even though the third party's loss will be limited if the principal ratifies the agent's acts (although the third party could still have incurred loss in pursuing the agent before ratification by the principal).

5.   The measure of damages for breach of warranty of authority is the contract measure (see note 1 above). Lord Esher MR put the matter as follows in *Firbank's Executors v Humphreys* (1886) 18 QBD 54 at 60:

The damages under the general rule are arrived at by considering the difference in the position he [the person acting in reliance on the warranty] would have been in had the representation been true and the position he is actually in inconsequence of its being untrue.

This involves a comparison between the position the third party would have been in had the agent had the principal's authority and the position he was actually in, given the absence of that authority. The assessment may not always work in the third party's favour. In *Singh v Sardar Investments Ltd* [2002] EWCA Civ 1706, [2002] NPC 134, the claimants entered into a contract to purchase shop premises from the defendant company. They dealt with one of two brothers who owned the company. It turned out that the brother had no authority to enter into the contract on the company's behalf. The claimants brought an action against him for breach of warranty of authority and claimed damages for loss of bargain, together with the rent they would have received by letting out the upper floors. The Court of Appeal upheld the trial judge's award of only nominal damages. The Court of Appeal held that even if the contract had been authorised the company would have been entitled to rescind it as the claimants were not in a position to fund the purchase at the time of completion.

6.   The prima facie rule is that damages for breach of warranty of authority fall to be assessed at the date of the breach. However, this is not an absolute rule and damages may be assessed at another date if it is more just to do so. The issue arose in *Habton Farms v Nimmo* [2003] EWCA Civ 68, [2004] QB 1. The defendant, a bloodstock agent, purporting to act on behalf of a certain racehorse owner, concluded an agreement with the claimant sellers for the purchase of a horse for £70,000. The agent was unauthorised and the owner refused to take delivery of the horse. The sellers did not accept the owner's 'repudiation' of the purported contract and made no immediate effort to sell the horse. The horse was still in the sellers' possession when, four weeks after the delivery date, it contracted peritonitis and died. The sellers sued the agent for breach of warranty of authority. They claimed damages of £70,000. The agent argued that the damages should be nil as on the day the contract was concluded (ie the date the agent breached his warranty of authority), there was no difference between the contract price and the market price of the horse. The Court of Appeal, by a majority, rejected that submission and held that the correct measure of damages was £70,000. The majority (Clarke and Auld LJ: see, especially, para [127]) held that if the contract had proceeded, the sellers would have divested themselves of the ownership, possession and risk of harm to the horse in return for the price some four weeks before the horse died. Their Lordships held that the sellers should not be put in any worse position than they would have been in if there had been a contract simply because it transpired that they were entitled to damages for the agent's breach of warranty of authority and not to the notional sale price against the owner. The case was to be distinguished from one where a seller accepts the notional buyer's repudiation and sells elsewhere at a lower market price, when the measure of damages would be the contract price less the market value normally identified as that sale price.

2   UNDISCLOSED AGENCY

(a)   Relations between principal and third party

(i)   *The general rule*

Siu Yin Kwan v Eastern Insurance Co Ltd
[1994] 2 AC 199, Privy Council

(The facts appear below at pp 189–190.)

Lord Lloyd delivered the advice of the Privy Council (Lords Templeman, Mustill, Woolf, Lloyd of Berwick and Sir Thomas Eichelbaum): . . . The main features of the law relating to an undisclosed principal have been settled since at least the end of the 18th century. A hundred years later, in 1872, Blackburn J said in *Armstrong v Stokes* (1872) LR 7 QB 598,604 that it had often been doubted whether it was originally right to hold that an undisclosed principal was liable to be sued on the contract made by an agent on his behalf, but added that 'doubts of this kind come now too late'.

For present purposes the law can be summarised shortly. (1) An undisclosed principal may sue and be sued on a contract made by an agent on his behalf, acting within the scope of his actual authority. (2) In entering into the contract, the agent must intend to act on the principal's behalf. (3) The agent of an undisclosed principal may also sue and be sued on the contract. (4) Any defence which the third party may have against the agent is available against his principal. (5) The terms of the contract may, expressly or by implication, exclude the principal's right to sue, and his liability to be sued. The contract itself, or the circumstances surrounding the contract, may show that the agent is the true and only principal.

The origin of, and theoretical justification for, the doctrine of the undisclosed principal has been the subject of much discussion by academic writers. Their Lordships would especially mention the influential article by Goodhart and Hamson 'Undisclosed Principals in Contract' (1932) 4 CLJ 320, commenting on the then recent case of *Collins v Associated Greyhound Racecourses Ltd* [1930] 1 Ch 1. It seems to be generally accepted that, while the development of this branch of the law may have been anomalous, since it runs counter to fundamental principles of privity of contract, it is justified on grounds of commercial convenience.

The present case is concerned with the fifth of the features noted above. The law in that connection was stated by Diplock LJ in *Teheran-Europe Co Ltd v ST Belton (Tractors) Ltd* [1968] 2 QB 545, 555:

> 'Where an agent has … actual authority and enters into a contract with another party intending to do so on behalf of his principal, it matters not whether he discloses to the other party the identity of his principal, or even that he is contracting on behalf of a principal at all, if the other party is willing or leads the agent to believe that he is willing to treat as a party to the contract anyone on whose behalf the agent may have been authorised to contract. In the case of an ordinary commercial contract such willingness of the other party may be assumed by the agent unless either the other party manifests his unwillingness or there are other circumstances which should lead the agent to realise that the other party was not so willing.'

Keighley, Maxsted & Co v Durant
[1901] AC 240, House of Lords

(The facts appear above at p 140.)

Lord Lindley: … as a contract is constituted by the concurrence of two or more persons and by their agreement to the same terms, there is an anomaly in holding one person bound to another of whom he knows nothing and with whom he did not, in fact, intend to contract. But middlemen, through whom contracts are made, are common and useful in business transactions, and in the great mass of contracts it is a matter of indifference to either party whether there is an undisclosed principal or not. If he exists it is, to say the least, extremely convenient that he should be able to sue and be sued as a principal, and he is only allowed to do so upon terms which exclude injustice.

NOTES

1.   The general rule is that an undisclosed principal can sue and be sued on a contract made on his behalf by his agent acting within the scope of his actual authority. This doctrine is widely regarded as anomalous because it gives the undisclosed principal rights, and subjects him to liabilities, that arise under a contract to which he was not originally privy. As Sir Frederick Pollock once commented in (1887) 3 LQR 358 at 359:

The plain truth ought never to be forgotten—that the whole law as to the rights and liabilities of an undisclosed principal is inconsistent with the elementary doctrines of the law of contract. The right of one person to sue another on a contract not really made with the person suing is unknown to every other legal system except that of England and America.

The anomalous nature of the doctrine has also been recognised by other academic commentators (see, eg, OW Holmes 'The History of Agency' in *Selected Essays in Anglo-American Legal History*, Vol 6, p 404; JH Barr (1909) 18 Yale LJ 443) and by the courts (see, eg, *Siu Yin Kwan v Eastern Insurance Co Ltd* [1994] 2 AC 199, at 207, per Lord Lloyd, extract above; *Keighley, Maxsted & Co v Durant* [1901] AC 240, at 261, per Lord Lindley, extract above). However, the undisclosed principal doctrine developed before theories of contract law requiring (objectively determined) consent of the parties became established, and this has led Tan Cheng-Han (2004) 120 LQR 480, to submit (at p 485) that 'it makes no more sense to say that the undisclosed principal doctrine is anomalous when measured by contract principles than it is to say that the doctrine of privity of contract is anomalous because it is inconsistent with the undisclosed principal doctrine'.

2.   Numerous theories have been advanced to explain the doctrine: they are usefully reviewed by A Rochvarg (1989) 34 McGill LJ 286 at pp 298–314. The theories which have received most attention are those based on trust and assignment. It has been argued that the agent is trustee for the undisclosed principal (see Ames, op cit), but it was held by Ungoed-Thomas J in *Pople v Evans* [1969] 2 Ch 255 at 264, in the context of the *res judicata* doctrine, that 'there is no trust relationship between any of the parties which can be recognised as between the third party on the one hand and the principal and agent, or either of them, on the other hand'. The assignment theory was advanced in an influential article written by Goodhart and Hamson, 'Undisclosed Principals in Contract' (1932) 4 CLJ 320, where it was suggested that the contract originally made between the agent (not the principal) and the third party was automatically transferred to the undisclosed principal by 'a primitive and highly restricted form of assignment' (at p 352). However, the analogy is not perfect for, unlike assignment, the undisclosed principal doctrine involves the transfer of liabilities as well as rights and, furthermore, there is no event which can be regarded as an assignment. For further differences between the undisclosed principal doctrine and assignment, see R Powell *The Law of Agency* (2nd edn, 1961), pp 165–166. For these reasons, the assignment theory was firmly rejected by the Privy Council in *Siu Yin Kwan v Eastern Insurance Co Ltd*, above, at 210, per Lord Lloyd. Tan Cheng-Han (2004) 120 LQR 480, has recently advanced (at pp 501–505) a theory based on the existence of an implied contract between third party and undisclosed principal. He relies on a dictum of Diplock LJ in *Teheran-Europe Co Ltd v ST Belton (Tractors) Ltd* [1968] 2 QB 545, 555 (see above, p 180), that ordinarily the third party in a commercial contract is willing to treat as a party to the contract anyone on whose behalf the agent may have been authorised to contract. The idea is that the third party *intends* to contract with the undisclosed principal. But this theory is open to the criticism that, because the third party is unaware of the undisclosed principal's existence, he can have no intention to contract with him. Of course, anyone who enters into a contract could have an undisclosed principal behind him, but that is to imply an intention to contract on the basis of a mere possibility.

3.   The lack of any watertight legal explanation of the undisclosed principal doctrine does not appear to have unduly troubled the courts, which have applied the doctrine in a wide variety of contexts. For example, in *Boyter v Thomson* [1995] 2 AC 628, the House of Lords held that under s 14(5) of the Sale of Goods Act 1979, where a buyer purchases goods from

an agent acting for an undisclosed principal, the buyer was entitled to sue the undisclosed principal for breach of the implied conditions set out under s 14(2) and (3) in respect of the unseaworthiness of a boat that was the subject-matter of the sale. As Lord Jauncey explained (at 632): 'When the subsection applies the normal common law rules of principal and agent also apply'. The courts have been prepared to justify the doctrine simply on grounds of commercial convenience (see *Keighley, Maxsted & Co v Durant,* above, per Lord Lindley; *Teheran-Europe Co Ltd v Belton (Tractors) Ltd* [1968] 2 QB 545 at 552, per Lord Denning MR; *Siu Yin Kwan v Eastern Insurance Co Ltd,* above, at 207, per Lord Lloyd; cf *Freeman & Lockyer v Buckhurst Park Properties (Mangal) Ltd* [1964] 2 QB 480 at 503, per Diplock LJ—above at p 118). This pragmatic approach is to be welcomed, but it has meant that certain aspects of the application of the undisclosed principal doctrine remain unclear, eg the effect of a disposition of goods to the agent of an undisclosed principal (considered by the Court of Appeal of New South Wales in *Maynegrain Pty Ltd v Compafina Bank* [1982] 2 NSWLR 141; reversed on the facts by the Privy Council (1984) 58 ALJR 389, noted by FMB Reynolds (1984) 4 Ox JLS 434).

4.   For an account of the historical development of the undisclosed principal doctrine, see AL Goodhart and CJ Hamson (1932) 4 CLJ 320; SJ Stoljar *The Law of Agency* (1961), pp 204—211. For a comparative treatment of the subject, see W Muller-Freienfels (1953) 16 MLR 299 and (1955) 18 MLR 33.

QUESTIONS

1.   Peter employs Alan to contract with Ted, instructing him to do so in his own name. Ted suspects Alan may be acting for a principal as it is known in the trade that Alan sometimes contracts for himself and sometimes for others. But without making any inquiry as to Alan's status, Ted contracts with him. Peter has now revealed himself to be Alan's principal but Ted wants to hold Alan personally liable on the contract as the agent of an undisclosed principal. Was Peter really an 'undisclosed' principal? See FMB Reynolds [1983] CLP 119 at pp 122–128; *Bowstead and Reynolds,* para 8–075.

2.   The Contracts (Rights of Third Parties) Act 1999 makes it possible for a third party to rely on a term of a contract to which he was not a party (privy). But the Act does not confer rights on an undisclosed principal. Can you see why?

(ii) Exclusion of the undisclosed principal

Look again at Lord Lloyd's fifth principle in the *Siu Yin Kwan v Eastern Insurance Co Ltd* (see extract above, at p 180).

(a) By the terms of the contract

An undisclosed principal is not allowed to intervene where this would be inconsistent with the terms of the contract.

Fred Drughorn Ltd v Rederiaktiebolaget Trans-Atlantic
[1919] AC 203, House of Lords

An undisclosed principal claimed to be entitled to sue on a charterparty signed by its agent as 'charterer'. Affirming the decision of the Court of Appeal, the House of Lords held that evidence was admissible to establish that the agent had contracted on behalf of the principal.

Viscount Haldane: My Lords, by the law of England if B contracts with C prima facie that is a contract between these two only, but if at the time B entered into the contract he was really acting as agent for A, then evidence is generally admissible to show that A was the principal, and A can take advantage of the contract as if it had been actually made between himself and C....

But, my Lords, the principle is limited by [a] consideration, about which . . . there is no doubt, and the applicability of which to the present case is beyond question. In *Humble v Hunter* ((1848) 12 QB 310) it was approved, although it was not necessary to give a decision on the point, and also in *Formby Bros v Formby* ((1910) 102 LT 116) and in other cases. These are authorities for the proposition that evidence of authority of an outside principal is not admissible, if to give such evidence would be to contradict some term in the contract itself. It was held in *Humble v Hunter,* that where a charterer dealt with someone described as the owner, evidence was not admissible to show that some other person was the owner. That is perfectly intelligible. The question is not before us now, but I see no reason to question that where you have the description of a person as the owner of property, and it is a term of the contract that he should contract as owner of that property, you cannot show that another person is the real owner. That is not a question of agency—that is a question of property.

My Lords, in the same way in *Formby Bros v Formby* the term was 'proprietor,' and 'proprietor' was treated in the opinion of the Court of Appeal as on the same footing as the expression 'owner.' But, my Lords, we are not dealing with that case here. The principle remains, but the question is whether the principle applies to a charterparty where the person who says that he signed only as agent describes himself as the charterer.

My Lords, there may be something to be said from the heading of the charterparty in this case, and the reference to the company which claims to have been his principal, for the proposition that, reading the document as a whole, there is evidence that he intended to convey that he was acting as agent for somebody else; but whether that is so or not the term 'charterer' is a very different term from the term 'owner' or the term 'proprietor.' A charterer may be and prima facie is merely entering into a contact. A charterparty is not a lease—it is a chattel that is being dealt with, a chattel that is essentially a mere subject of contract; and although rights of ownership or rights akin to ownership may be given under it prima facie it is a contract for the hiring or use of the vessel. Under these circumstances it is in accordance with ordinary business common- sense and custom that charterers should be able to contract as agents for undisclosed principals who may come in and take the benefit of the charterparty.

But, my Lords, it is said that in this charterparty the terms are such as to exclude that notion. Why is that said to be so? Because the term 'charterer' is used. Well, I have already commented upon that. It is said that the term 'charterer' was meant simply to describe a particular person who is to carry out the nomination of arbitrators and everything else which is contained in the charterparty—to give orders which can only be given by one person, and that for the working out of the charterparty it is essential to treat the person so contracting as designated as a person whose identity cannot be varied or contradicted.

My Lords, the answer is that the principal may take that place, and that the company, in this case acting through its agent, whoever that agent may be, will be in the same position as the charterer contracting originally. There is nothing in that position inconsistent with the stipulations of this charterparty, and therefore it appears to me that the qualifying principle of *Humble v Hunter,* that you shall not contradict the instrument by giving evidence of agency, has no application in this case.

[Lords Shaw of Dunfermline and Wrenbury concurred. Lord Sumner delivered a concurring opinion.]

NOTES

1.   In *Humble v Hunter* (1848) 12 QB 310, a son chartered out a vessel owned by his mother but signed the charterparty as 'CJ Humble Esq, owner of the good ship or vessel called the *Ann*'. It was held that the mother could not enforce the contract as undisclosed principal on the basis that she was in fact the shipowner, since the description of her son as 'owner' was

inconsistent with this. The House of Lords' decision in *Drughorn's* case clearly limits the effect of *Humble v Hunter* (in *Epps v Rothnie* [1945] KB 562 at 565, Scott LJ went so far as to suggest that *Humble v Hunter* had been overruled by *Drughorn's* case). In *Siu Yin Kwan v Eastern Insurance Co Ltd* [1994] 2 AC 199, *Drughorn's* case was relied on by Lord Lloyd (delivering the advice of the Privy Council) when he stated, albeit by way of *obiter dictum,* that the fact that the agent was described in an employer's liability policy as the employer did not exclude the right of the undisclosed principal (the actual employer) to intervene. As Lord Lloyd said (at 209): 'If courts are too ready to construe written contracts as contradicting the right of the undisclosed principal to intervene, it would go far to destroy the beneficial assumption in commercial cases, to which Diplock J referred to in *Teheran- Europe Co Ltd v ST Belton (Tractors) Ltd* [1968] 2 QB 545, 555 [set out above at p 180].' As the editor of *Markesinis and Munday* concludes (at p 160): It will now only be in exceptional cases that the undisclosed principal': intervention will be held inconsistent with the terms of the contract, and possibly only in cases where the agent can be construed see also *Asty Maritime Co Ltd and* to have contracted as the owner of property.' But *Panagiotis Stravelakis v Rocco Giuseppe and Figli SNC, The Astyanax* [1985] 2 Lloyd's Rep 109, where the Court of Appeal held that the description of one party to a charterparty as 'disponent owner' of a vessel was neutral, but that the surrounding circumstances and the course of negotiations were inconsistent with that party contracting as mere agent on behalf of the registered owners of the vessel.

2.   In cases such as those we have just considered, the test which determines whether the undisclosed principal can intervene is whether the agent has impliedly contracted that there is no principal behind him. If the agent has given such an implied undertaking the undisclosed principal may not intervene (AL Goodhart and CJ Hamson (1932) 4 CLJ 320 at p 327 and p 342; *Bowstead and Reynolds,* para 8-080). However, it is always open to exclude the possibility of intervention by an undisclosed principal through an express term that the agent is the real and only principal (*United Kingdom Mutual Steamship Assurance Association v Nevill* (1887) 19 QBD 110).

QUESTION

In *Humble v Hunter,* could the mother have intervened if she had been co-owner of the vessel with her son? See Goodhart and Hamson, op cit, p 327.

(b) Other circumstances

If the third party can show that he wanted to deal with the agent and with no one else, the undisclosed principal cannot intervene. This may be because of some particular attribute of the agent or some reason why he does not wish to deal with the undisclosed principal.

Said v Butt

[1920] 3 KB 497, King's Bench Division

Said wished to attend the first night of a new play to be staged at the Palace Theatre. He knew that the theatre owners would not sell a ticket to him because of an existing dispute with them over allegations Said had made concerning the sale of tickets by the theatre. Said therefore asked his friend Pollock to buy a ticket for him. When Said arrived at the theatre for the performance, Butt (the managing director) refused him admittance. Said sued Butt for wrongfully inducing the owners of the theatre to commit a breach of contract.

McCardie J: ...A first night at the Palace Theatre is, as with other theatres, an event of great importance. The result of a first night may make or mar a play. If the play be good, then word of its success may be spread, not only by the critics, but by members of the audience. The nature and social position and influence of the audience are of obvious importance. First nights have become to a large extent a species of private entertainment given by the theatrical proprietors and management to their friends and acquaintances, and to influential persons, whether critics or otherwise. The boxes, stalls and dress circle are regarded as parts of the theatre which are subject to special allocation by the management. Many tickets for those parts may be given away. The remaining tickets are usually sold by favour only. A first night, therefore, is a special event, with special characteristics. As the plaintiff himself stated in evidence, the management only disposes of first night tickets for the stalls and dress circle to those whom it selects. I may add that it is scarcely likely to choose those who are antagonistic to the management; or who have attacked the character of the theatre officials.... The Palace Theatre officials had no idea that they were selling a ticket to an agent of the plaintiff. If they had known it, they would at once have refused to supply a ticket. I find as a fact that the plaintiff used the name of Mr Pollock in order to disguise that he himself was the purchaser; and I also find that the plaintiff well knew that the Palace Theatre would not have sold him personally a ticket for December 23, 1919. I am satisfied that Mr Pollock himself was aware of the above-mentioned circumstances. I may point out that a theatre stands on a wholly different footing from a public inn, or a public service such as a railway. A public inn, for example, is under a common law duty to supply to all who come provided that accommodation exists; and provided also that the guest is of proper character and behaviour. But a theatre stands upon a wholly different footing. It may sell or refuse to sell tickets at its own option. The public cannot compel a theatre to grant admission.

Under these circumstances, the question is whether the plaintiff, as an undisclosed principal of Mr Pollock, can claim that a binding contract existed between the Palace Theatre, Ltd, and himself.

[His Lordship then considered the authorities dealing with the effect of mistake as to the identity of a contracting party and continued:]

In my opinion the defendant can rightly say, upon the special circumstances of this case, that no contract existed on December 23,1919, upon which the plaintiff could have sued the Palace Theatre. The personal element was here strikingly present. The plaintiff knew that the Palace Theatre would not contract with him for the sale of a seat for December 23. They had expressly refused to do so. He was well aware of their reasons. I hold that by the mere device of utilizing the name and services of Mr Pollock, the plaintiff could not constitute himself a contractor with the Palace Theatre against their knowledge, and contrary to their express refusal. He is disabled from asserting that he was the undisclosed principal of Mr Pollock.

It follows, therefore, that the plaintiff has failed to prove that the defendant caused any breach of a contract between the Palace Theatre, Ltd, and himself.

I realize, however, that the question is one of difficulty....

Dyster v Randall & Sons
[1926] Ch 932, Chancery Division

Dyster knowing that Randall and Sons would not sell certain land to him (because they distrusted him), procured his friend Crossley to purchase the land for him without disclosing that he was acting on Dyster's behalf. When Randall and Sons discovered that Crossley had been acting for Dyster, they sought to resist specific performance of the contract of sale of the land on the grounds that they had been deceived by Dyster.

Lawrence J: ...it is essential to bear in mind that the agreement which the plaintiff seeks to enforce is not one in which any personal qualifications possessed by Crossley formed a material ingredient, but is a simple agreement for sale of land in consideration of a lump sum to be paid on completion. It is an agreement which the defendants would have entered into with any other person. It is well settled that the benefit of such an agreement is assignable and that the assignee can enforce specific performance of it. If Crossley had entered into the agreement on his own behalf (as the defendants believed he had) he could immediately have assigned it to the plaintiff and the defendants would have been bound to convey the plots to the plaintiff. Moreover, as Crossley had not, before signing the agreement, disclosed the fact that he was acting as agent, he was liable under it as principal and the defendants could have compelled him to complete the purchase.

Further, it is to be noted that in this case there was no direct misrepresentation such as there was in *Archer v Stone* ((1898) 78 LT 34). Crossley was not asked by the defendants whether he was buying for the plaintiff and he made no statement to the defendants on the subject. The real question therefore is whether Crossley's silence, in the circumstances, amounted to a misrepresentation which renders the agreement unenforceable in this Court. In my judgment mere non-disclosure as to the person actually entitled to the benefit of a contract for the sale of real estate does not amount to misrepresentation, even though the contracting party knows that, if the disclosure were made, the other party would not enter into the contract; *secus,* if the contract were one in which some personal consideration formed a material ingredient: see *Nash v Dix* ((1898) 78 LT 445) and *Said v Butt* ([1920] 3 KB 497). In *Nash v Dix* North J held that the ostensible purchaser was acting on his own account and not as agent, but it appears to me that the learned judge would have arrived at the same conclusion if the alleged agency had been established. In *Said v Butt* McCardie J relied entirely on the personal consideration which entered into the contract and would obviously have decided otherwise if the personal element had been absent. I therefore hold that the first ground relied upon by the defendants does not afford a good defence to the plaintiffs claim to specific performance.

Greer v Downs Supply Co
[1927] 2 KB 28, Court of Appeal

Downs Supply Co (the respondent) purchased timber from Godwin for £29, it being agreed that the respondent should have the right to set off against the price the sum of £17 owed by Godwin to the respondent. Godwin was in fact acting for an undisclosed principal (the appellant) who sought to intervene on the contract. The Court of Appeal held that the undisclosed principal had no right of action on the contract.

Scrutton LJ: ...The appellant issued a plaint for goods sold and delivered, and the original orders given by the respondent to Godwin were furnished as particulars of the contract of sale. When a plaintiff claims as an undisclosed principal the question sometimes arises whether the contract was made with the agent for reasons personal to the agent which induced the other party to contract with the agent to the exclusion of his principal or any one else. When the learned judge at the trial found that the respondent knew nothing about the appellant and honestly believed he was contracting with Godwin and when it was proved that he was contracting with Godwin because Godwin was his debtor, there was an end of the case for the appellant at the trial.

[Bankes and Lawrence LJJ delivered concurring judgments.]

Rolls-Royce Power Engineering plc v Ricardo Consulting Engineers Ltd
[2003] EWHC 2871, [2004] 2 All ER (Comm) 129, Technology and Construction Court

Allen Power Engineering Ltd (Allen) was a wholly-owned subsidiary of Rolls-Royce Power Engineering plc (RRPE). Under the terms of management agreements controlling the relationship between Allen and RRPE, Allen acted as RRPE's agent in respect of a range of activities. Allen entered into a collaborative agreement with Ricardo Consulting Engineers Ltd (Ricardo) for the development of a new engine (the 'definitive design contract'). The contract followed on from an earlier agreement entered into by the same parties (the 'concept design contract'). An issue arose as to whether Allen entered into the definitive design contract as agent for RRPE, as undisclosed principal, so as to enable RRPE to sue Ricardo on that contract.

Judge Seymour QC (sitting as a judge of the High Court):

[49] It was common ground between Mr Marrin [Counsel for RRPE and Allen] and Mr Fenwick [Counsel for Ricardo] that the principles of law to be applied in answering Issue 1 in the light of my findings of fact relevant to that issue were those summarised by Lord Lloyd of Berwick in giving the advice of the Privy Council in *Siu v Eastern Insurance Co Ltd* [1994] 2 AC 199 at p 207:—

> 'For present purposes the law can be summarised shortly.
>
> (1) An undisclosed principal may sue and be sued on a contract made by an agent on his behalf acting within the scope of his actual authority.
>
> (2) In entering into the contract, the agent must intend to act on the principal's behalf.
>
> (3) The agent of an undisclosed principal may also sue and be sued on the contract.
>
> (4) Any defence which the third party may have against the agent is available against his principal.
>
> (5) The terms of the contract may, expressly or by implication, exclude the principal's right to sue, and his liability to be sued. The contract itself or the circumstances surrounding the contract, may show that the agent is the true and only principal.'

[50] It was in the light of the principles summarised by Lord Lloyd in the passage quoted in the previous paragraph that Mr Fenwick and Mr Sutherland [Counsel for Ricardo] identified as relevant to Issue 1 the question 'In entering into the Definitive Design Contract, did Allen intend to act on RRPE's behalf?'. I accept as accurate the submissions of Mr Fenwick and Mr Sutherland as to the state of the evidence in relation to that question, even following cross-examination. The fact is that there was no evidence that at the time of the making of the Definitive Design Contract anyone at the Allen end gave any thought whatever to the issue on whose behalf Allen was acting in entering into the contract. . . . Thus if it were necessary, in order for a party claiming to be an undisclosed principal to be able to sue on a contract made by his alleged agent, for the agent subjectively at the moment of contracting to have considered that it was acting on behalf of the supposed undisclosed principal, no one within Allen, on the evidence led before me, had that subjective intention in respect of the making of the Definitive Design Contract. That said, at the time the Definitive Design Contract was made the Second Management Agreement was in place. It was a perfectly lawful agreement and there is no obvious reason why effect should not be given to it according to its terms. Thus, if the question were whether, objectively, at the moment at which the Definitive Design Contract was made, arrangements were in place which had the effect that, as between Allen and RRPE, the Definitive Design Contract was to be taken as having been made by Allen on behalf of RRPE, the answer would be affirmative.

[51] My attention was drawn by Mr Marrin, in the context of the question whether the intention of an agent said to have been acting for an undisclosed principal to enter into the relevant contract as agent was to be ascertained objectively or subjectively, to a decision of Colman J, *National Oilwell (UK) Ltd v Davy Offshore Ltd* [1993] 2 Lloyd's Rep 582. A major issue in the case, relevant to the alleged counterclaim of the defendant, was whether the plaintiff and the defendant were co-assured. In the context of that issue it was necessary for Colman J to consider and to analyse various previous decisions relating to co-assurance. In the course of that analysis one question upon which the learned judge had to form a view was as to how intention to enter into a policy of insurance on behalf of other parties might be demonstrated. On that point Colman J said, at p 597:—

> '(3) Evidence as to whether in any particular case the principal assured or other contracting party did have the requisite intention may be provided by the terms of the policy itself by the terms of any contract between the principal assured or other contracting party and the alleged co-assured or by any other admissible material showing what was subjectively intended by the principal assured.'

Mr Marrin accepted that the relevant intention was subjective, as Colman J suggested, but submitted that the Second Management Agreement was, in Colman J's terms 'any contract between the [agent, in this case]...and the alleged [principal]' which demonstrated the requisite intention subjectively.

[52] I agree with Colman J that the relevant intention needs to be proved subjectively. Unless that were so, the second of Lord Lloyd's principles adds nothing to the first, in effect that the contract must have been made by the supposed agent acting within the scope of his actual authority. However, I reject the submission of Mr Marrin that in the present case the terms of the Second Management Agreement provide the requisite proof of the subjective intention of Allen to enter into the Definitive Design Contract on behalf of RRPE. In the passage which I have quoted from his judgment it seems to me that the focus of Colman J's attention was on the need for proof of subjective intention, and he was contemplating that an agreement in appropriate terms made at an appropriate date between the policy holder and the supposed co-assured could provide proof of such subjective intention. That is, in my judgment, a considerable distance from his view having been that, having regard to arrangements previously made which were not present to anyone's mind when the relevant contract were made, the necessary subjective intention was demonstrated. As I have already indicated, in my judgment in the present case Allen has not proved that it consciously intended at the time the Definitive Design Contract was made to enter into it on behalf of RRPE.

[53] There is an even more fundamental objection to a finding that Allen entered into the Definitive Design Contract as agent for RRPE and that depends upon the fifth of Lord Lloyd's principles. He himself went on later on p 207 of his speech to say: –

> The present case is concerned with the fifth of the features noted above. The law in that connection was stated by Diplock LJ in *Teheran-Europe Co. Ltd. v ST Belton (Tractors) Ltd* [1968] 2 QB 545, 555:
>
> > 'Where an agent has...actual authority and enters into a contract with another party intending to do so on behalf of his principal, it matters not whether he discloses to the other party the identity of his principal, or even that he is contracting on behalf of a principal at all, if the other party is willing or leads the agent to believe that he is willing to treat as a party to the contract anyone on whose behalf the agent may have been authorised to contract. In the case of an ordinary commercial contract such willingness of the other party may be assumed unless either the other party manifests his unwillingness or there are other circumstances which should lead the agent to realise that the other party was not so willing.' (see [1994] 1 All ER 213 at 221, [1994] 2 AC 199 at 207)

...

[56] Mr Fenwick and Mr Sutherland submitted, correctly in my judgment, first that the formulation of Diplock LJ approved by the Privy Council in *Siu v Eastern Insurance Co Ltd* did not postulate that unwillingness to treat as a party to the contract anyone on whose behalf the agent may have been authorised to act had to be manifested by means of a term of the contract, and second that the issue was not whether Ricardo would have had an objection to contracting with the party alleged to be the actual undisclosed principal, RRPE, but whether Ricardo was unwilling to take the risk of contracting with anyone whomsoever on whose behalf Allen may have been authorised to act. Their position was, essentially, that the fact that the nature of the services to be provided by Ricardo under the Definitive Design Contract involved employees of Ricardo working in collaboration with employees of Allen in pursuit of a common objective of developing a new engine design for Allen and providing for a transfer of technology made plain that this was not an ordinary commercial contract, but one in respect of which it was inconceivable that the particular identities of the respective contracting parties was not of the greatest significance to the other. A number of witnesses called on behalf of the Claimants spoke of the high reputation of Ricardo and the high regard in which it was held as a result of experience of dealing with it over a number of years. On the Ricardo side Mr Monaghan indicated that it was important to Ricardo to be committing itself to collaborate not with any party which might appear and claim the benefit of the Definitive Design Contract, but with Allen. At para 32 of his witness statement, a passage as to which he was not cross-examined, he said:—

> I have been asked whether it was of any significance to Ricardo that it was contracting with [Allen] rather than anyone else. The answer is that this was of significance. Both the Concept and the Definitive Design contracts were for a collaborative project, in which Ricardo were to work closely with (and to train) the client throughout these design development stages. We agreed to do this (and prepared our budget) on the basis that it was [Allen's] personnel, at [Allen's] premises, who were the client. [Allen] were well known to us and we thought that the intended collaboration was workable on the terms set out in the proposal documents, and was likely to be worthwhile (in the sense that the project was likely to be profitable to Ricardo both financially and in terms of adding to Ricardo's profile and portfolio). Obviously the same would not necessarily be the case with any and every other engineering firm or company.

I accept that evidence.

[57] Moreover, the conclusion of the Definitive Design Contract obviously has to be viewed in the context that it was the successor to and the logical continuation of the work done, apparently successfully, under the Concept Design Contract. It thus was intended to build upon work already done in collaboration between identified individuals who had no doubt developed satisfactory personal relationships in the course of the earlier work. The background of the earlier successful work and the satisfactory working relationships established during the course of it was, as it seems to me, essential to the decision of Ricardo to agree to a continuation. Had the earlier work been fraught with difficulties at a practical level it is impossible sensibly to contemplate that the Definitive Design Contract would have been made. Consequently in my judgment the Definitive Design Contract was manifestly one which was not an ordinary commercial contract and, moreover, was one which was made in circumstances such that, had anyone at Allen given the matter any attention, they would have realised that Ricardo was not willing to, contract with anyone other than Allen.

[58] In the result I find that the answer to Issue 1 as formulated is that Allen did not enter into the Definitive Design Contract as agent for RRPE as undisclosed principal so as to enable RRPE to sue Ricardo on the Definitive Design Contract or Allen to recover damages quantified by reference to the loss allegedly sustained by RRPE.

NOTES

1. The non-assignable nature of a contract normally provides evidence that the parties intended to exclude the intervention of an undisclosed principal, but this is not an absolute rule. In the somewhat unusual case of *Siu Yin Kwan v Eastern Insurance Co Ltd* [1994] 2 AC 199, shipping agents insured in their own name the employers of the crew of a ship, the *Osprey*, against liability. The insurers had dealt with the shipping agents before and knew that they did not own the ship, but it was just about conceivable that they might have employed the crew. (This would have been rare as the owners, not the shipping agents, would have been expected to employ the crew, but the trial judge found that he could not be satisfied that the insurers knew that the agents were not the employers of the crew and this explains why the case was treated as one involving an undisclosed principal and not, as would have been more usual in a case such as this, as one of a disclosed but unnamed principal). The actual employers were the owners of the ship, but they were not mentioned in the proposal form or the policy. Owing to the negligence of the owners, the *Osprey* sank in a typhoon with the loss of two crew members. As the owners were insolvent, the relatives of the dead crew members sued the insurers under the Third Parties (Rights against Insurers) Ordinance of Hong Kong (the UK has similar legislation: see below, p 1192). The success of that action depended on whether the owners could themselves have enforced the policy. The Privy Council held that the owners would have been able to intervene on the contract of insurance as undisclosed principals and that the relatives were entitled to recover against the insurers. Although a non-marine insurance contract (such as an employer's liability policy) is personal in the sense that it is not assignable, the Privy Council held that this did not prevent the intervention of the owners as undisclosed principals in this case because the trial judge had found as a fact that the identity of the actual employer was a matter of indifference to the insurer and not material to the risk. More generally, the Board said (*obiter*) that a contract of insurance was not a personal contract in the sense of a contract to paint a portrait and that an undisclosed principal could intervene on such a contract so long as disclosures relevant to the risk had been made. The case is usefully noted by A Tettenborn [1994] CLJ 223 and also by J Halladay [1994] LMCLQ 174. See further, F Reynolds 'Some Agency Problems in Insurance Law', Ch 4 in FD Rose (ed) *Consensus Ad Idem* (1996), especially pp 89–95.

2.   Whether the undisclosed principal will be prohibited from intervening in cases where the third party would not have dealt with the principal if he had known that the agent was acting for him is a moot point. *Said v Butt* certainly appears to support the exclusion of the undisclosed principal doctrine in these circumstances. In that case there was no express term of the contract excluding the principal's intervention and the contract itself could not be described as a personal contract, unless a ticket for a first night performance is regarded as non-assignable (and even then, as we have just seen, this may not be decisive of the issue). It is submitted that it is best to regard *Said v Butt* as wrongly decided. This task is made somewhat easier by reason of the fact that McCardie J's judgment is based on the erroneous premise that the contract was made between the third party and the undisclosed principal (the correct analysis is that the undisclosed principal intervenes in a contract originally made between the third party and the agent: *Welsh Development Agency v Export Finance Co Ltd* [1992] BCLC 148, 173, 182, CA; see also AL Goodhart and CJ Hamson (1932) 4 CLJ 320, pp 346–352; *Bowstead and Reynolds*, para 8–071; cf Tan Cheng-Han (2004) 120 LQR 480, pp 486–496, who argues that the contract is with the undisclosed principal). Dicta in *Dyster v Randall and Sons* that personality may prevent the undisclosed principal's intervention if it is a 'material ingredient' or 'strikingly present', to use McCardie J's words in *Said v Butt,* should be rejected in so far as they purport to go beyond the circumstances prohibiting intervention as set out under note 1 above (see Goodhart and Hamson, op cit, pp 349–352). Allowing a further exception to the undisclosed principal doctrine merely heaps a further anomaly upon an anomaly (ie the doctrine itself). Furthermore, whatever the dicta in *Dyster v Randall and Sons* the result was clear: the mere fact that the third party would not have dealt with the undisclosed principal was not enough to prevent the principal's intervention.

    However, for a strong defence of *Said v Butt,* see E Peel, *Treitel's Law of Contract* (12th edn, 2007), para 16–059, where it is argued that 'an undisclosed principal should not be allowed to intervene if he knows that the third party does not want to deal with him'; Glanville Williams (1945) 23 Can B Rev 380 at pp 406–412 submits that 'ordinary ideas of fair dealing' lie at the heart of the decision. Professor Reynolds had said that 'this is one of the comparatively few areas in common law where a principle of good faith might provide reasoning not otherwise available' (A Burrows (ed), *English Private Law* (2nd edn, 2007), para 9.76). English law does not recognise a general principle of good faith (see above, p 43).

3. The problem raised by *Said v Butt* will be avoided if it can be shown that the person the third party dealt with was acting as principal and not agent. In *Nash v Dix* (1898) 78 LT 445, the defendants did not wish to sell a Congregational chapel to a committee of Roman Catholics. Instead they sold the chapel to the plaintiff but later refused to complete the transaction when they discovered the plaintiff was going to on-sell it to the Roman Catholic Committee. North J ordered specific performance of the contract of sale on the grounds that the plaintiff was not an agent of the committee but was purchasing the chapel for himself with a view to resale at a profit.

4. If the contract between the agent and the third party was induced by the agent's misrepresentation, the principal cannot enforce it against the third party: *Archer v Stone* (1898) 78 LT 34 (third party asked agent if he was acting for S and he untruthfully denied that he was).

QUESTIONS

1. Why is *Siu Yin Kwan v Eastern Insurance Co Ltd* such an unusual case?

2. What can an insurer do to prevent the intervention of an undisclosed principal on a contract of insurance?

3. If Said had gone to the Palace Theatre to buy a ticket saying it was for a friend, could he have later revealed that his friend was in fact himself? See *The Remco* [1984] 2 Lloyd's Rep 205, above, p 173.

4. Thelma sells her whole crop of strawberries to Agatha. Unknown to Thelma, Agatha is acting as agent for Louise, who Thelma blames for the breakdown of her marriage and has sworn she would never do business with. Before payment, Agatha becomes insolvent and Thelma discovers that Louise is the principal behind her. Thelma now wishes to hold Louise liable for the price. Can Louise successfully resist Thelma's claim on grounds of personality? Contrast *Markesinis and Munday,* p 165, and *Fridman,* pp 263–264, with *Bowstead and Reynolds,* para 8–081.

(c) Deeds, bills of exchange and promissory notes

An undisclosed principal cannot sue or be sued on a deed *inter partes,* nor can he be made liable on any negotiable instrument (see above, p 151).

(iii) Particular aspects of the relationship between undisclosed principal and third party

The rights and liabilities of the undisclosed principal and third party may be affected by the agent in a number of ways.

(a) Merger and election
Clarkson Booker Ltd v Andjel
[1964] 2 QB 775, Court of Appeal

Andjel purchased airline tickets on credit from Clarkson Booker Ltd (the plaintiffs), who were travel agents. In fact Andjel was acting for an undisclosed principal, Peters & Milner Ltd (P & M). Subsequently, on being informed that Andjel was acting for P & M, the plaintiffs wrote to both principal and agent threatening proceedings unless the amount due was paid. Payment was not made and the plaintiffs started proceedings against P & M. However, the plaintiffs were then informed that P & M were insolvent and about to be put into liquidation. The plaintiffs accordingly did not proceed further with their action against the principal, P & M, but started proceedings against the agent, Andjel. Andjel resisted the claim on the ground that the plaintiffs had elected to hold the principal exclusively liable and, therefore, were precluded from proceeding against him, the agent. The County Court judge gave judgment for the plaintiffs. Andjel's appeal from that decision was dismissed by the Court of Appeal.

Willmer LJ: ... the point is taken for the defendant that the plaintiffs, having elected to start proceedings against Peters & Milner Ltd, are now debarred from asserting their claim against the defendant. The contention on behalf of the defendant is that this is a case of true election in that, with full knowledge of the facts, the plaintiffs deliberately and unequivocally chose to pursue their right against the principals, which was a right inconsistent with their right against the defendant as agent. Reliance is placed on a statement contained in Powell on Agency, 2nd edn (1961), p 270, where the following is put forward as proposition (v): 'T (a third party) starts proceedings against P (the principal) or A (the agent). The initiation of proceedings against P or A is strong evidence of election, though not necessarily conclusive. That is so whether T issues a writ or files proof of his debt in bankruptcy proceedings.' This proposition is not accepted by the plaintiffs as a correct statement of the law. It is submitted on their behalf that a plaintiff is barred only if he has sued one or other (ie, principal or agent) to judgment. It is conceded that he cannot then proceed against the other. But that, it is said, is not a true case of election; the remedy is barred because the cause of action has merged in the judgment. It is contended that nothing short of judgment against the principal is sufficient to bar the plaintiffs remedy against the agent. In the present case it is said that there has been nothing amounting either in law or in fact to an election, so as to preclude the present action against the defendant.

The judge, in dealing with this aspect of the case, quoted at some length from the speech of Lord Blackburn in *Scarf v Jardine* ((1882) 7 App Cas 345 at 354–362). I need not quote again the passage from Lord Blackburn. Suffice it to say that he expressed the view that there could be no more unequivocal act than instituting proceedings against one of two possible debtors; this, he thought, amounted to a final election to treat that debtor as liable so as to preclude the plaintiff thereafter from suing the other debtor . . . .

I cannot, of course, do other than attach the greatest possible weight to the decision of the House of Lords in *Scarf v Jardine,* particularly the reasoning of Lord Blackburn. But I do not understand him to mean that where proceedings have once been commenced against one of two possible debtors a plaintiff is necessarily precluded as a matter of law from subsequently taking proceedings against the other. Indeed, Mr Hamilton freely conceded that there must be some cases at least where the mere issue of a writ could not be held to amount to a binding election—for instance, where it is issued for the purpose of preventing limitation time from running out. Similarly, it has been held that an abortive writ issued against a company not yet incorporated at the time when the order for the plaintiffs' services was given did not amount to a binding election so as to preclude a subsequent action against the agents through whom the order was given: see *Longman v Hill* ((1891) 7 TLR 639). But even allowing for such exceptional cases it is clear that the institution of proceedings against either agent or principal is at least strong evidence of an election such as, if not rebutted, will preclude subsequent proceedings against the other. In other words, it raises a prima facie case of election . . . .

Having regard to those authorities, I think that the judge in the present case was plainly right in regarding the question before him as one of fact. But it has been argued that he came to a wrong conclusion on the facts. Since the relevant evidence is all contained in the correspondence, we have been invited to review his findings and to draw our own inferences from the correspondence. In a case such as the present we are clearly entitled to take this course, for we are in as good a position to draw inferences as was the judge.

In the light of the authorities to which I have referred, I approach the question to be decided on the basis that the institution of proceedings against Peters & Milner Ltd affords at least prima facie evidence of an election on the part of the plaintiffs to look only to them for payment of their debt. The question is whether there is any sufficient evidence to rebut the prima facie inference that arises from the institution of those proceedings.

In order to constitute an election which will bar the present proceedings against the defendant, the decision to sue Peters & Milner Ltd must, in the first place, be shown to have been taken with full knowledge of all the relevant facts. In the circumstances of this case I feel no difficulty on this point, for it cannot be suggested that when the plaintiffs made their decision to sue Peters & Milner Ltd they were in any way ignorant of their rights against the defendant.

But, secondly, it must be shown that the decision to institute proceedings against Peters & Milner Ltd was a truly unequivocal act if it is to preclude the plaintiffs from subsequently suing the defendant. This, I think, involves looking closely at the context in which the decision was taken, for any conclusion must be based on a review of all the relevant circumstances. One highly relevant circumstance is the fact that it was the defendant to whom the plaintiffs gave credit, as they had done over previous transactions. The correspondence shows that down to the letters of July 26 the plaintiffs throughout were looking to the defendant for payment of their debt, ie, to the person to whom they had given credit, although they also adumbrated a possible claim against Peters & Milner Ltd. On July 26, as I have already stated, they caused letters to be written to both the defendant and Peters & Milner Ltd, threatening proceedings against each. Clearly, up to that time there was no election to proceed only against the latter.

The whole case for the defendant rests on the fact that on August 8, having taken instructions, the plaintiffs' solicitors wrote to Peters & Milner Ltd announcing their intention 'to obtain judgment' against them. It is true that they did not at that time write any similar letter to the defendant, but they did not then or at any other time ever withdraw their threat to take proceedings against him. There is not, and could not be, any suggestion that the defendant was in any way prejudiced by the course which the plaintiffs took, or that he was in any sense lulled into a false sense of security.

Had the plaintiffs carried out their threat to obtain judgment against Peters & Milner Ltd they would, of course, have been precluded from subsequently taking proceedings against the defendant, for their cause of action would then have been merged in the judgment obtained against Peters & Milner Ltd. But in fact the plaintiffs took no step against Peters & Milner Ltd beyond the issue and service of the writ. Upon being informed of the proposal to put the company into liquidation they took no further action whatsoever against that company. They did not, for instance (as in *Scarf v Jardine* and other cases cited), seek to prove in the liquidation; instead they proceeded to give effect forthwith to their already announced, and never withdrawn, threat to sue the defendant.

On the whole, though I regard the case as being very near the borderline, I find myself unable to disagree with the conclusion arrived at by the judge. I do not think that the plaintiffs, by the mere institution of proceedings against Peters & Milner Ltd, made such an unequivocal election as to debar them from taking the present proceedings against the defendant.

I would accordingly dismiss the appeal.

[Davies LJ concurred.]

Russell LJ: The defendant having contracted as agent for an undisclosed principal, the plaintiffs were entitled to enforce the contract either against the defendant on the footing that he was contracting and liable as principal, or against the principal on the footing that the defendant was not liable, being merely an agent. The plaintiffs could not enforce the contract against both. Their right against the defendant and their right against the principal were inconsistent rights. At some stage the plaintiffs had to elect to avail themselves of one of those inconsistent rights and abandon the other. The question is whether the correct conclusion from the facts of this case is that, prior to the issue of their writ against the defendant, the plaintiffs had so elected. If they had, the election crystallised their rights, and they could not sue the defendant. The judge concluded that they had not so elected.

What were the facts? . . .

Was the judge on those facts wrong in concluding that the plaintiffs had not elected to treat the principal as liable in exoneration of the defendant?

It was reluctantly (although rightly) accepted by counsel for the defendant that the service of a writ against the principal per se does not show an election. Statements by Lord Blackburn in the *Scarf case* [*Scarf v Jardine* (1882) 7 App Cas 345 at 360] cannot be taken as establishing that position in law. It would be in some respects convenient if it were so, as tending to certainty in the application of the law, but even that would not resolve the problems that would arise in the case of a single writ against the principal and agent claiming in the alternative, or in the case of simultaneous or substantially simultaneous writs. The position is that in every case the external acts of the plaintiff must lead to the conclusion, as a matter of fact, that the plaintiff has settled to a choice involving abandonment of his option to enforce his right against one party. I have no doubt that in a given case this may be shown without his proceeding to the length of obtaining a judgment; indeed, if judgment is obtained against either principal or agent, this is more than election, though frequently referred to as election: the judgment supersedes the contractual right against either, and if obtained against the agent precludes action against the principal even if the plaintiff was ignorant of his existence and therefore unable to elect. Further, I have no doubt that, in assessing the facts of a particular case in pursuit of a conclusion on the question of election, the fact of the service of a writ against one and not against the other points significantly towards a decision to exonerate the other. A letter may assert a claim and demand satisfaction, but it is not capable of bearing fruit, even if wholly ignored by the recipient, whereas service of a writ is the first step in actual enforcement of the claim, to be ignored by the recipient at his peril. On the other hand, it is in terms a statement that the plaintiff makes a claim against the defendant. As I have said, it does not necessarily involve abandonment of a similar alternative claim against another possible defendant. It would not do so if there were a simultaneous writ against the other. Nor would it do so if the plaintiff were simultaneously expressly informing the other that the alternative claim was not abandoned. Nor would it do so if simultaneously the plaintiff was maintaining vis-a-vis the other the attitude that he might be looked to for liability on the contract.

What of the present case? It is said for the defendant that the letters of July 26 maintained the alternative claim against each, and that by contrast the writ against one demonstrated the exoneration of the other as a matter of election. I am not on the whole persuaded by this. I do not think that the letter to the principal's solicitors (as such) of August 3 can really be regarded as any less a determination to enforce the right against the principal than the subsequent issue and service of the writ on the principal, but that letter was contemporaneous with correspondence which demonstrates a retention of the right to claim against the defendant. In those circumstances, I am not able to conclude that the facts demonstrate that the plaintiffs finally elected to rely on the liability of the principal under the contract in exoneration of the agent. Consequently, I agree that this appeal fails.

NOTES

1.   In cases of undisclosed agency the third party is able to sue both the agent on the contract made with him and also the principal because of the special rule of law operating in this situation. 'But because the third party has only purported to make one contract with one person, to enter into a single obligation, these two rights of action are commonly said to be alternative': FMB Reynolds (1970) 86 LQR 317 at p 320.

2.   There is clear authority that the doctrine of merger applies to cases of undisclosed agency when the third party proceeds to judgment against the principal or the agent (*Priestly v Fernie* (1865) 3 H & C 977; *Kendall v Hamilton* (1879) 4 App Cas 504 at 514–515, per Lord Cairns LC). For further consideration of the doctrine of merger, see above, p 159.

3.   It is clear from *Clarkson Booker v Andjel* that in cases of undisclosed agency there can be election by means of an unequivocal act short of obtaining judgment against the principal or the agent. What constitutes an election is a question of fact to be decided in the

circumstances of the case. Commencing legal proceedings against one party provides a prima facie case of election, but it is not conclusive (as shown by *Clarkson Booker v Andjel*; applied in *Pyxis Special Shipping Co Ltd v Dritsas & Kaglis Bros Ltd, The Scaplake* [1978] 2 Lloyd's Rep 380; cf *Cyril Lord Carpet Sales Ltd v Browne* (1966) 111 Sol Jo 51, where the Court of Appeal held the commencement of proceedings against the agent was an election barring action against the principal). Debiting one party may also provide evidence of election (*Addison v Gandassequi* (1812) 4 Taunt 574; cf *Thomson v Davenport* (1829) 9 B & C 78, above at p 156).

4.   There is no doubt that in most cases where election is invoked the plea fails. In fact Professor Reynolds submits that in cases of undisclosed agency where the plea has succeeded, and was based on an act short of judgment, the doctrine of estoppel, and not election, may provide the real explanation for those decisions (see (1970) 86 LQR 318, pp 323–328). He submits that:

> . . . it is open to the courts to make articulate the proposition that, short of a judgment, a plaintiff will only lose his right against one party by a representation of fact that the contract is with the other or has been performed by the other, or by a representation of intention not to enforce his right against that one, in either case acted on by that party in such a way that it would be detrimental to him if the plaintiff changed his mind. The clearest case of such detriment would occur when the representation or conduct induced the principal to settle with the agent, but it may be that other cases could arise.

See further his commentary to art 82 of *Bowstead and Reynolds,* and see E Peel, *Treitel's Law of Contract* (12th edn, 2007), para 16–075, who also supports the estoppel theory. A New Zealand judge has stated that 'the doctrine of election is frequently misnamed. Rather, it is to be regarded as being an instance of waiver (or estoppel or release)': *L C Fowler & Sons Ltd v St Stephens College Board of Governors* [1991] 3 NZLR 304 at 308, per Thomas J (noted approvingly by F Reynolds [1994] JBL 149).

(b) Set-off and other defences available against the agent

As a general rule, when an undisclosed principal intervenes on his agent's contract the third party may set up against him any defences, including personal set-off of debts, which would be available to him against the agent as long as those defences accrued before the third party had notice of the principal's existence (*Browning v Provincial Insurance Co of Canada* (1873) LR 5 PC 263 at 272–273; *Rabone v Williams* (1785) 7 Term Rep 360n). However, as the next case illustrates, the third party's rights of set-off appear to be subject to an important restriction.

Cooke & Sons v Eshelby

(1887) 12 App Cas 271, House of Lords

Livesey & Co, a firm of brokers, who were in fact acting on behalf of an undisclosed principal, sold cotton to Cooke & Sons (the appellants). The price not being paid, Eshelby (the respondent), the trustee in bankruptcy of the undisclosed principal, claimed it from Cooke & Sons. Cooke & Sons attempted to set off against the price a debt owed to them by Livesey & Co. Cooke & Sons knew that Livesey & Co were in the habit of dealing both for principals and on their own account but at the time of the sale in question they had no belief whether Livesey & Co were acting as agents or not. Affirming the decision of the Court of Appeal, the House of Lords held there was no right of set-off.

Lord Halsbury LC: My Lords, in this case a merchant in Liverpool effected two sales through his brokers. The brokers effected the sales in their own names. The appellants, the merchants with whom these contracts were made, knew the brokers to be brokers, and that it was their practice to sell in their own names in transactions in which they were acting only as brokers. They also knew that the brokers were in the habit of buying and selling for themselves. The appellants with commendable candour admit that they are unable to say that they believed the brokers to be principals; they knew they might be either one or the other; they say that they dealt with the brokers as principals, but at the same time they admit that they had no belief one way or the other whether they were dealing with principals or brokers.

It appears to me that the principle upon which this case must be decided has been so long established that in such a state of facts as I have recited the legal result cannot be doubtful. The ground upon which all these cases have been decided is that the agent has been permitted by the principal to hold himself out as the principal, and that the person dealing with the agent has believed that the agent was the principal, and has acted on that belief. With reference to both those propositions, namely, first, the permission of the real principal to the agent to assume his character, and with reference to the fact whether those dealing with the supposed principal have in fact acted upon the belief induced by the real principal's conduct, various difficult questions of fact have from time to time arisen; but I do not believe that any doubt has ever been thrown upon the law as decided by a great variety of judges for something more than a century. The cases are all collected in the notes to *George v Clagett* ((1797) 7 Term Rep 359).

In *Baring v Corrie* ((1818) 2 B & Ald 137), in 1818, Lord Tenterden had before him a very similar case to that which is now before your Lordships, and although in that case the Court had to infer what we have here proved by the candid admission of the party, the principle upon which the case was decided is precisely that which appears to me to govern the case now before your Lordships. Lord Tenterden says of the persons who were in that case insisting that they had a right to treat the brokers as principals: 'They knew that Coles & Co acted both as brokers and merchants, and if they meant to deal with them as merchants, and to derive a benefit from so dealing with them, they ought to have inquired whether in this transaction they acted as brokers or not; but they made no inquiry.' And Bayley J says: 'When Coles & Co stood at least in an equivocal situation, the defendants ought in common honesty, if they bought the goods with a view to cover their own debt, to have asked in what character they sold the goods in question. I therefore cannot think that the defendants believed, when they bought the goods, that Coles & Co sold them on their own account. And if so, they can have no defence to the present action.'

I am therefore of opinion that the judgment of the Court of Appeal was right. The selling in his own name by a broker is only one fact, and by no means a conclusive fact, from which, in the absence of other circumstances, it might be inferred that he was selling his own goods. Upon the facts proved or admitted in this case the fact of selling in the broker's name was neither calculated to induce nor did in fact induce that belief.

Lord Watson: . . . According to the practice of the Liverpool cotton market with which the appellants were familiar, brokers in the position of Livesey Sons & Co buy and sell both for themselves and for principals; and in the latter case they transact, sometimes in their own name without disclosing their agency, and at other times in the name of their principal. In their answer to an interrogation by the plaintiff touching their belief that Livesey Sons & Co were acting on behalf of principals in the two transactions in question, the appellants say: 'We had no belief upon the subject. We dealt with Livesey Sons & Co as principals, not knowing whether they were acting as brokers on behalf of principals or on their own account as the principals.'

That is a very candid statement, but I do not think any other answer could have been honestly made by persons who, at the time of the transactions, were cognisant of the practice followed by members of the Liverpool Cotton Association. A sale by a broker in his own name to persons having that knowledge, does not convey to them an assurance that he is selling on his own account; on the contrary it is equivalent to an express intimation that the cotton is either his own property or the property of a principal who has employed him as an agent to sell. A purchaser who is content to buy on these terms cannot, when the real principal comes forward, allege that the broker sold the cotton as his own. If the intending purchaser desires to deal with the broker as a principal and not as an agent in order to secure a right to set-off, he is put upon his inquiry. Should the broker refuse to state whether he is acting for himself or for a principal, the buyer may decline to enter into the transaction. If he chooses to purchase without inquiry, or notwithstanding the broker's refusal to give information, he does so with notice that there may be a principal for whom the broker is acting as agent; and should that ultimately prove to be the fact, he has, in my opinion, no right to set off his indebtedness to the principal against debts owing to him by the agent.

It was argued for the appellants, that in all cases where a broker, having authority to that effect, sells in his own name for an undisclosed principal, the purchaser, at the time when the principal is disclosed, is entitled to be placed in the same position as if the agent had contracted on his own account. That was said to be the rule established by *George v Clagett* ((1797) 7 Term Rep 359), *Sims v Bond* ((1833) 5 B & Ad 389) and subsequent cases. It is clear that Livesey Sons & Co were not mere brokers or middlemen, but were agents within the meaning of these authorities, and if the argument of the appellants were well founded they would be entitled to prevail in this appeal, because in that case their right of set-off had arisen before the 20th of July 1883, when they first had notice that Maximos was the principal.

I do not think it necessary to enter into a minute examination of the authorities, which were fully discussed in the arguments addressed to us. The case *of George v Clagett* ((1797) 7 Term Rep 359) has been commented upon and its principles explained in many subsequent decisions, and notably in *Baring v Corrie* ((1818) 2 B & Ald 137), *Semenza v Brinsley* ((1865) 18 CBNS 467), and *Borries v Imperial Ottoman Bank* ((1873) LR 9 CP 38). These decisions appear to me to establish conclusively that, in order to sustain the defence pleaded by the appellants, it is not enough to shew that the agent sold in his own name. It must be shewn that he sold the goods as his own, or, in other words, that the circumstances attending the sale were calculated to induce, and did induce, in the mind of the purchaser a reasonable belief that the agent was selling on his own account and not for an undisclosed principal; and it must also be shewn that the agent was enabled to appear as the real contracting party by the conduct, or by the authority, express or implied, of the principal. The rule thus explained is intelligible and just; and I agree with Bowen LJ that it rests upon the doctrine of estoppel. It would be inconsistent with fair dealing that a latent principal should by his own act or omission lead a purchaser to rely upon a right of set-off against the agent as the real seller, and should nevertheless be permitted to intervene and deprive the purchaser of that right at the very time when it had become necessary for his protection.

Lord FitzGerald: I concur with my noble and learned friend [Lord Watson] in adopting at once the decision and the reasons of the Court of Appeal. I have, however, some hesitation in accepting the view that the decisions rest on the doctrine of estoppel. Estoppel in pais involves considerations not necessarily applicable to the case before us. There is some danger in professing to state the principle on which a line of decisions rests, and it seems to me to be sufficient to say in the present case that Maximos did not in any way wilfully or otherwise mislead the defendants (Cooke & Sons) or induce them to believe that Livesey & Co were the owners of the goods or authorized to sell them as their own, or practice any imposition on them. The defendants were not in any way misled.

NOTES

1.   Although it has been argued that *Cooke & Sons v Eshelby* might really be a case of an unnamed, as opposed to an undisclosed, principal (because the third party knew there was a risk that the brokers might be acting for a principal), it is generally treated as an undisclosed principal case: see FMB Reynolds (1983) 36 CLP 119 at pp 126 and 133.

2.   In *Cooke & Sons v Eshelby* the House of Lords held that an undisclosed principal would not be bound by the third party's rights of set-off against the agent unless the principal

had misled the third party by allowing the agent to appear as the principal. This estoppel approach may be criticised on two grounds. First, it is difficult to see how the third party can rely on the representation of a person of whose existence he is unaware. Secondly, it could be said that in all cases of undisclosed agency the agent is held out to be the principal.

3.   A preferable approach would be to allow the third party a right of set-off in all cases where he lacks notice of the principal's existence. The undisclosed principal would then intervene on his agent's contract subject to the third party's rights of set-off in much the same way as the assignee of a chose in action takes subject to equities. But what of the case where an undisclosed principal instructs his agent to contract in the principal's name and yet the agent disobeys that instruction and contracts in his own name? On the estoppel theory the principal would not be bound by set-off, whereas under this alternative approach he would be bound. However, it is submitted that this result is not as unjust as it may first appear. It is not the third party's fault that the agent disobeys his instructions, whereas it could be argued that by choosing to deal through an agent the principal takes the risk that the agent may exceed his authority and act as though he is the principal: R Powell *The Law of Agency* (2nd edn, 1961), p 177; SR Derham [1985] CLJ 384 at p 399.

4.   A key element of both the estoppel and subject to equities approaches to set-off is that the third party must not have notice of the existence of a principal at the time he contracted with the agent, or at the time that the debt available for setting off accrued if that was later. On the estoppel approach notice would mean that the third party's prejudice would not have been caused by the principal's conduct. On the subject to equities approach notice would mean that there would not be an equity in favour of the third party. But what is meant by 'notice'? Is it restricted to actual notice? In *Cooke & Sons v Eshelby* Lord Watson referred to the third party's 'reasonable belief that the agent was selling on his own account and not for an undisclosed principal'. Furthermore, there appears to be common law support for the view that the third party will be put on notice of the principal's existence if the circumstances are such as to put the third party on inquiry as to the status of the agent and he fails to make an inquiry (see Derham, op cit, pp 390–395 and the cases cited therein). This common law duty of inquiry should not be confused with the separate equitable doctrine of constructive notice which has no place in commercial transactions (see, eg *Greer v Downs Supply Co* [1927] 2 KB 28; Derham, op cit, p 391: although the statement in the text should be read in conjunction with that appearing above at p 35). On this basis, even if the House of Lords had applied the subject to equities approach to set-off in *Cooke & Sons v Eshelby,* the third party (Cooke & Sons) would probably still have been denied a right of set-off. Cooke & Sons were aware of the risk that the brokers could have been acting for a principal yet they failed to inquire as to what was the true position.

For defences available to the principal against an action brought by the third party, see above, p 156.

QUESTION

Was it really necessary for the Court of Appeal to consider the personal nature of the contract in *Greer v Downs Supply Co* (above, p 186), or could the court have simply held the third party to have a right of set-off against the undisclosed principal?

(c) Settlement with the agent

Armstrong v Stokes

(1872) LR 7 QB 598, Court of Queen's Bench

R & Co were commission merchants who sometimes acted for themselves and sometimes as agents for others. A was a merchant who had dealings with R & Co on a number of occasions but never inquired whether R & Co were acting for themselves or on behalf of others. On one occasion A sold shirts on credit to R & Co when R & Co were acting as agents for S. A delivered the shirts to R & Co who sent them to S. S paid R & Co but R & Co did not pay A. On discovering that R & Co were acting as agents for S, A sued S for the price. The Court of Queen's Bench held that the action failed.

Blackburn J (delivering the judgment of the Court): …[In *Heald v Kenworthy* (1855) 10 Exch 739 at 745] Parke B lays down generally that 'if a person orders an agent to make a purchase for him, he is bound to see that the agent pays the debt; and giving the agent money for that purpose does not amount to payment, unless the agent pays it accordingly.' After commenting on several of the cases already referred to, he concludes: 'I think that there is no authority for saying that a payment made to the agent precludes the seller from recovering from the principal, unless it appears that he has induced the principal to believe that a settlement has been made with the agent.' He states this as generally true wherever a principal has allowed himself to be made a party to a contract, and makes no exception as to the case where the other side made the contract with the agent believing him to be principal, and continued in such belief till after the payment was made. He certainly does not in terms say that there is no qualification of the principle he lays down when applicable to such a case; but recollecting how careful Parke B always was to lay down what he thought to be the law fully and with accuracy, we think the counsel for the plaintiff were justified in arguing that Parke B thought the exception did not exist. And this is, in our opinion, a weighty authority in favour of the plaintiffs contention, more especially as Pollock CB assents in his judgment to the remark thrown out by Parke B during the argument, and afterwards more elaborately stated by him in his judgment. And Alderson B, in his judgment, appears entirely to assent to the judgment of Parke B.

We think that we could not, without straining the evidence, hold in this case that the plaintiff had induced the defendants to believe that he (the plaintiff) had settled with J & O Ryder at the time when the defendants paid them.

This makes it necessary to determine whether we agree in what we think was the opinion of Parke B, acquiesced in by Pollock CB and Alderson B.

We think that, if the rigid rule thus laid down were to be applied to those who were only discovered to be principals after they had fairly paid the price to those whom the vendor believed to be the principals, and to whom alone the vendor gave credit, it would produce intolerable hardship. It may be said, perhaps truly, this is the consequence of that which might originally have been a mistake, in allowing the vendor to have recourse at all against one to whom he never gave credit, and that we ought not to establish an illogical exception in order to cure a fault in a rule. But we find an exception (more or less extensively expressed) always mentioned in the very cases that lay down the rule; and without deciding anything as to the case of a broker, who avowedly acts for a principal (though not necessarily named), and confining ourselves to the present case, which is one in which, to borrow Lord Tenterden's phrase in *Thomson v Davenport* ((1829) 9 B & C 78 at 86), the plaintiff sold the goods to Ryder & Co, 'supposing at the time of the contract he was dealing with a principal,' we think such an exception is established.

We wish to be understood as expressing no opinion as to what would have been the effect of the state of the accounts between the parties if J & O Ryder had been indebted to the defendants on a separate account, so as to give rise to a set-off or mutual credit between them. We confine our decision to the case where the defendants, after the contract was made, and in consequence of it, bona fide and without moral blame, paid J & O Ryder at a time when the plaintiff still gave credit to J & O Ryder, and knew of no one else. We think that after that it was too late for the plaintiff to come upon the defendants.

On this ground we make the rule absolute to enter the verdict for the defendants.

NOTES

1.   Contrast *Armstrong v Stokes* with *Irvine & Co v Watson & Sons* (1880) 5 QBD 414, above at p 152. In *Irvine & Co v Watson & Sons* the principal was disclosed, whereas in *Armstrong v Stokes* the principal was undisclosed. Unlike the case of a disclosed principal, the general rule for an undisclosed principal appears to be that he can avoid liability to the third party if he settles with his own agent. When the principal is disclosed he can only avoid such liability if the third party induced him to settle with the agent. However, if the existence of the principal is unknown to the third party it is difficult to see how he can have induced the principal to settle with the agent.

2.   *Armstrong v Stokes* has been subjected to considerable criticism, eg see *Irvine & Co v Watson*, above at p 153, per Bramwell LJ. The editor of *Markesinis and Munday* goes so far as to state (at 171) that the decision is 'logically indefensible and almost certainly would not be followed by the courts today' (see also *Fridman*, p 267: '*Armstrong v Stokes* . . . is not a good authority today'). But Professor Reynolds is less critical of the rule that an undisclosed principal will be discharged from liability to the third party if he settles with the agent. In (1983) 36 CLP 119, at p 134, he submits that:

. . . for a true undisclosed principal situation this might seem again a reasonable rule. The principal has utilised the services of an intermediary who in the transaction into which he has entered has raised no expectation of the accountability of a principal. Surely the principal's duty is performed by keeping the intermediary in funds: if the third party loses, it is because of his misplaced trust in the intermediary. There is no need to make the principal the insurer.

However, we would agree with Professor Treitel who submits that the argument advanced by Professor Reynolds proves to much. For as Edwin Peel (and Professor Treitel before him) notes: 'whenever an undisclosed principal is sued the third party gets a windfall of this kind' (E Peel, *Treitel's Law of Contract* (12th edn, 2007), para 16–064).

When the third party pays or settles with an agent acting for an undisclosed principal the third party will be discharged from liability to the principal if he was unaware of the principal's existence at the time of payment or settlement (*Coates v Lewes* (1808) 1 Camp 444). However, as in the case of set-off, the third party can only rely on this defence if the principal's conduct induced him to believe that the agent was the principal in the transaction (eg *Ramazotti v Bowring* (1859) 7 CBNS 851). For criticism of this requirement in the context of set-off, see above, p 198.

(b) Relations between the agent and the third party

As the third party contracts in the first instance with the agent and not the undisclosed principal (see above, p 190), it is not surprising to discover that the agent may sue and be sued on that contract (*Sims v Bond* (1833) 5 B & Ad 389 at 393, Denman CJ). Indeed, in *Muldoon v Wood* (1 April 1998, unreported), Sir John Knox, sitting in the Court of Appeal, described the fact that the agent may be sued on the contract as 'elementary law'. If the agent sues the third party on the contract, the third party can set up against him any defence which would have been available against the undisclosed principal, including the fraud of the principal (*Garnac Grain Co Inc v HMF Faure & Fairclough Ltd* [1966] 1 QB 650; revsd on other grounds by the Court of Appeal [1966] 1 QB 650 at 685–668; affd by the House of Lords [1968] AC 1130; however, set-off may not always be available to the third party: see *Fridman,* pp 271–272). But should the undisclosed principal intervene on the contract the agent loses his right of action against the third party (*Atkinson v Cotesworth* (1825) 3 B & C 647; *aliter* if the agent has a lien or other interest over the goods which form the subject matter of the contract).

Even if the principal intervenes on the contract the agent remains liable to the third party until the third party elects whether to hold the principal or the agent liable (above, pp 191–195). In cases of undisclosed agency, the principal and the agent are liable on the contract in the alternative (*Maynegrain Pty Ltd v Compafina Bank* [1982] 2 NS WLR 141 at 150, per Hope JA; revsd on the facts by the Privy Council (1984) 58 ALJR 389).

CHAPTER 6

RELATIONS BETWEEN PRINCIPAL AND AGENT

In most cases the rights and duties of an agent derive either from a contract made between the principal and agent or from the fiduciary nature of their relationship. But they may also derive from other sources, eg tort, statute or the law of restitution. See generally, FE Dowrick (1954) 17 MLR 24.

Most agencies are consensual. But some arise because of the apparent or usual authority of the agent (above, pp 117–128 and pp 128–133), or through necessity (above, pp 133–139). Such agencies are non-consensual and it remains uncertain as to whether they give rise to the normal incidents of a principal-agent relationship. They probably do not (see R Powell *The Law of Agency* (2nd edn, 1961), pp 295–296, fn 4; cf Dowrick, op cit, pp 26–27, fn 15).

1 DUTIES OF THE AGENT

(a) Duty to perform his undertaking and obey instructions

If an agent has entered into a bilateral contract with his principal he must do what he has undertaken to do. For example, in *Turpin v Bilton* (1843) 5 Man & G 455 an agent agreed to insure his principal's ship. He failed to do so, which meant that when the ship was lost the principal was uninsured. It was held that the agent was liable for breach of contract.

When performing his undertaking the agent must obey the lawful and reasonable instructions of his principal, even though he genuinely believes that departing from those instructions would be in his principal's best interests (*The Hermione* [1922] P 162: in the case of a 'commercial agent', defined above at p 160, see the Commercial Agents (Council Directive) Regulations 1993 (SI 1993/3053), reg 3(1), (2), set out below at p 210). But a professional agent, such as a solicitor, may be under a duty to warn and advise the principal of any risks inherent in his instructions. For what happens when the instructions are ambiguous, see above, pp 113–114.

In summary, the agent must follow, and not exceed, the terms of his authority, whether they be express or implied (including those terms implied from custom and usage). But an agent is not obliged to do anything that is illegal, or which, at common law or by statute, is null and void (*Cohen v Kittell* (1889) 22 QBD 680; cf *Fraser v BN Furman (Productions) Ltd* [1967] 1 WLR 898).

On the other hand, if the agent acts under a unilateral contract he is under no duty to do anything at all. Similarly, a gratuitous agent is not bound to do anything, unless his failure to act gives rise to liability in tort. Generally, failure to act does not give rise to tortious liability unless it can be said that there has been an assumption of responsibility to act (see *Henderson v Merrett Syndicates Ltd* [1995] 2 AC 145, and also *Bowstead and Reynolds,* para 6–027). It is arguable, but as yet undecided, that if an agent has agreed to act and then changes his mind, he may be held to have assumed responsibility to the principal to warn him that his intentions have changed (see R Powell *The Law of Agency* (2nd edn, 1961), pp 302–303; R Bradgate *Commercial Law* (2nd edn, 1995), para 6.2.1.1; but contrast *Markesinis and Munday,* p 95; *Fridman,* pp 156–157).

There is some uncertainty as to the nature and extent of the agent's liability to his principal where the agent exceeds his actual authority and, by virtue of his apparent authority, causes the principal to be bound by a disadvantageous contract with a third party. Where there is no contract between principal and agent it is possible that the agent's liability might arise in tort (see *Montrod v Grundkötter Fleischvertriebs GmbH* [2002] EWCA Civ 1954, [2002] 1 WLR 1975). But Lord Hoffmann doubts this, saying that the agent might be liable on an implied contract, but not outside contract (*OGB Ltd v Allan* [2007] UKHL 21, [2007] 2 WLR 920 at [93]; see also P Watts (2007) 123 LQR 519).

(b) Duty of care and skill

A contractually rewarded agent owes a duty to his principal to exercise reasonable care and skill in the performance of his undertaking. The duty can be both contractual and tortious (*Midland Bank Trust Co Ltd v Hett, Stubbs & Kemp* [1979] Ch 384, solicitor held liable to his client in contract and in tort). The availability of a concurrent action in tort has been affirmed by the House of Lords in *Henderson v Merrett Syndicates Ltd* [1995] 2 AC 145 (where the reasoning in *Midland Bank Trust Co Ltd v Hett, Stubbs & Kemp* was approved). Whether the agent complies with the duty is a question of fact. But what is the standard of care which the agent must exercise? Does the same duty and standard of care apply to a gratuitous agent? The next case provides some answers to these questions.

Chaudhry v Prabhakar
[1989] 1 WLR 29, Court of Appeal

Chaudhry (C), who had just passed her driving test, asked Prabhakar (P), a close friend, to find a secondhand car, which had not been involved in an accident, for her to buy. P agreed to do so for no payment. C knew nothing about cars but P, though not a qualified mechanic, did know something about them. P found a car offered for sale by someone who was a car sprayer and panel beater. P noticed that the bonnet of the car had been repaired but he made no enquiries as to whether the car had been involved in an accident. P recommended that C should buy the car and, in answer to C's specific enquiry, informed her that the car had not been involved in an accident. C bought the car. When C later discovered that the car had been involved in an accident and was unroadworthy she sued P for breach of a duty of care. The trial judge gave judgment for C. P appealed but his appeal was dismissed by the Court of Appeal.

Stuart-Smith LJ: Mr Hoyle on behalf of the appellant first defendant accepts that he was under a duty of care to the plaintiff, but he submitted that the judge had imposed too high a standard of care, and when the correct standard was applied the first defendant was not in breach. In the forefront of his argument is the proposition that the first defendant was a gratuitous or unpaid agent and that the duty on such a person is to take such care towards his principal as he would in relation to his own affairs and to exhibit such skill as he actually possesses. He further submitted that this standard is an entirely subjective one. This appears to mean in the context of this case that if the first defendant would have bought the car himself, as he said he would, and is an honest man as the judge found him to be, he cannot be held liable because he has acted up to the standard expected of an unpaid agent.

I cannot accept this; the degree of care and skill owed by a gratuitous agent is stated by *Bowstead on Agency,* 15th edn (1985), art 44(3), p 152 to be:

> ...such skill and care as persons ordinarily exercise in their own affairs or, where the agent has expressly or impliedly held himself out to his principal as possessing skill adequate to the perform-ance of a particular undertaking, such skill and care as would normally be shown by one possessing that skill.

But I am quite satisfied that this is an objective standard and is not simply to be measured by the agent's honest statement that he would have similarly acted if he had been transacting the business on his own account, however foolish that may be. For my part, I would prefer to state an agent's duty of care as that which may reasonably be expected of him in all the circumstances. This was the approach of the Court of Appeal in *Houghland v R R Low (Luxury Coaches) Ltd* [1962] 1 QB 694 on the somewhat analogous case of a gratuitous bailee. Ormerod LJ said, at p 698:

> For my part, I have always found some difficulty in understanding just what was 'gross negligence,' because it appears to me that the standard of care required in a case of bailment, or any other type of case, is the standard demanded by the circumstances of that particular case. It seems to me that to try and put a bailment, for instance, into a watertight compartment—such as gratuitous bailment on the one hand, and bailment for reward on the other—is to overlook the fact that there might well be an infinite variety of cases, which might come into one or the other category. The question that we have to consider in a case of this kind, if it is necessary to consider negligence, is whether in the circumstances of this particular case a sufficient standard of care has been observed by the defendants or their servants.

I have no doubt that one of the relevant circumstances is whether or not the agent is paid. If he is, the relationship is a contractual one and there may be express terms upon which the parties can rely. Moreover, if a paid agent exercised any trade, profession or calling, he is required to exercise the degree of skill and diligence reasonably to be expected of a person exercising such trade, profession or calling, irrespective of the degree of skill he may possess. Where the agent is unpaid, any duty of care arises in tort. Relevant circumstances would be the actual skill and experience that the agent had, though, if he has represented such skill and experience to be greater than it in fact is and the principal has relied on such representation, it seems to me to be reasonable to expect him to show that standard of skill and experience which he claims he possesses. Moreover, the fact that principal and agent are friends does not in my judgment affect the existence of the duty of care, though conceivably it may be a relevant circumstance in considering the degree or standard of care.

Mr Scott on behalf of the plaintiff has submitted that the duty of care arises not only because of the relationship of principal and agent, but also under the doctrine enunciated in *Hedley Byrne & Co Ltd v Heller & Partners Ltd* [1964] AC 465. The House of Lords held that a negligent, though honest, misrepresentation, spoken or written, may give rise to an action for damage for financial loss caused thereby, apart from any contract or fiduciary relationship, since the law will imply a duty of care when a party seeking information from a party possessed of special skill trusts him to exercise care, and that party knew, or ought to have known that reliance was being placed on his skill and judgment.

When considering the question of whether a duty of care arises, the relationship between the parties is material. If they are friends, the true view may be that the advice or representation is made upon a purely social occasion and the circumstances show that there has not been a voluntary assumption of responsibility.

Lord Reid in *Hedley Byrne & Co Ltd v Heller & Partners Ltd* said, at pp 482–483:

> The law ought so far as possible to reflect the standards of the reasonable man, and that is what *Donoghue v Stevenson* [1932] AC 562 sets out to do. The most obvious difference between negligent words and negligent acts is this. Quite careful people often express definite options on social or informal occasions even when they see that others are likely to be influenced by them: and they often do that without taking that care which they would take if asked for their opinion professionally or in a business connection. The appellant agrees that there can be no duty of care on such occasions, and we were referred to American and South African authorities where that is recognised, although their law appears to have gone much further than ours has yet done.

But where, as in this case, the relationship of principal and agent exists, such that a contract comes into existence between the principal and the third party, it seems to me that, at the very least, this relationship is powerful evidence that the occasion is not a purely social one, but, to use Lord Reid's expression, is in a business connection. Indeed the relationship between the parties is one that is equivalent to contract, to use the words of Lord Devlin, at p 530, save only for the absence of consideration.

It seems to me that all the necessary ingredients are here present. The plaintiff clearly relied upon the first defendant's skill and judgment, and, although it may not have been great, it was greater than hers and was quite sufficient for the purpose of asking the appropriate questions of the second defendant. The first defendant also knew that the plaintiff was relying on him; indeed he told her that she did not need to have it inspected by a mechanic and she did not do so on the strength of his recommendation. It was clearly in a business connection, because he knew that she was there and then going to commit herself to buying the car for £4,500 through his agency.

If, as I think, the duty of care in this case can equally be said to arise under the *Hedley Byrne* principle, then logically the standard of care, or the nature and extent of the duty, should be the same as that required of an unpaid agent. And this is an additional reason why I prefer to state the duty as I have, namely, to take such care as is reasonably to be expected of him in all the circumstances.

Stocker LJ: This appeal does not raise any question as to whether or not any duty was owed at all, since it was conceded that the defendant was a gratuitous agent and owed the appropriate duty. On the facts of this particular case I agree that the concession was properly made, though the incidence of the duty may be a matter of dispute.

In many cases in which actionable negligence is claimed in respect of the voluntary giving of advice, the first question that arises is whether any duty of care is owed in respect of such advice where the relationship of the parties is such that no voluntary assumption of legal responsibility was intended or can properly be imputed and where the giving of the advice was motivated solely out of friendship. Thus, in my view, in the absence of other factors giving rise to such a duty, the giving of advice sought in the context of family, domestic or social relationships will not in itself give rise to any duty in respect of such advice. The existence of the duty would depend upon all the circumstances in which the advice was sought or tendered. This problem does not arise in this case because of the concession referred to that the duty of care did exist. Whether the duty arises out of a gratuitous agency or by reason of the extension of the *Donoghue v Stevenson* [1932] AC 562 principle to economic loss sustained as a result of negligent advice as enunciated in *Hedley Byrne & Co Ltd v Heller & Partners Ltd* [1964] AC 465, on the facts of this case, even if the existence of the duty had not been conceded, I should, for my part, have felt bound to conclude that it did exist.

The first defendant accepted the task of finding a motor car suitable for the plaintiff in respect of which a specific characteristic was stipulated—viz that it had not been involved in an accident. The first defendant purported to have done so and stated specifically in answer to the plaintiffs question that it had not been involved in any accident and assured that there was no need to have it examined by a mechanic. He gave her information with regard to its provenance which was incorrect since he did not know the vendor before seeing the car. In making these assertions to the plaintiff he went beyond what was required of him in his capacity as a friend, and it seems to me he owed a duty of care to the plaintiff. The issue arising on this appeal, therefore, relates not to the existence of a duty of care but to its extent.

Mr Hoyle submits that the duty was that of a gratuitous agent which is stated in *Bowstead on Agency,* 15th edn, art 44(3) to be: 'Such skill and care as persons ordinarily exercise in their own affairs.' I doubt whether this is an adequate formulation, at least in the circumstances of this case, when applied to advice given to another. However, even if it be the appropriate duty, the words 'ordinarily exercise[d] in their own affairs' seems to me to postulate an objective and not a subjective standard. If a subjective standard be correct, then in my view the duty so expressed becomes virtually meaningless and would cover circumstances in which no care at all had been taken. Objectively regarded, there was sufficient evidence before the judge from which he could properly conclude that the first defendant did not exercise such care, and the fact that he honestly asserted that he would have been happy to purchase the car himself begs the question rather than resolving it. In my view, the fact that he did not ask the vendor specifically whether or not the car had been involved in any accident did not itself establish a breach provided that he had reasonable grounds for belief that it had not and if he had such reasonable grounds it would not necessarily follow that his assertion to this effect to the plaintiff amounted to actionable negligence. This, however, is to consider this aspect of his advice to her in isolation. He did not, in fact, contrary to his assertion, know the vendor. He did not ask for, or examine, any registration documents, nor make any inquiries as to the previous owner of the car or its provenance. He bought it from a person whose trade was that of a panel beater and observed that the car had a crumpled bon- net. In my view, any purchaser of a car in these circumstances, however naive, would be put on inquiry. Thus, judged even by the standard of care for which Mr Hoyle contends, if objectively considered, the first defendant failed to discharge it.

In my opinion, in the circumstances such as prevailed here, a more appropriate test is that suggested by Ormerod LJ in *Houghland v RR Low (Luxury Coaches) Ltd* [1962] 1 QB 694, 698: 'whether in the circumstances of this particular case a sufficient standard of care has been observed.' On either formu- lation of the duty, in my view, the first defendant failed to discharge the duty and was accordingly liable for actionable negligence as the judge has found.

I have sympathy for the first defendant. He was, as the judge found, acting honestly and without any apparent motive to mislead the plaintiff. Common prudence would indicate that he should have explained the circumstances in which he obtained the car and not voluntarily have accepted a duty which otherwise might well not have been imposed upon him.

May LJ: The real questions in this case, looked at with common sense and avoiding unnecessary legal jargon, were, first, did the friend seeking the car owe the intending purchaser any duty of care in and about his search; secondly, if he did, what was its nature and extent; thirdly, did he commit any breach of that duty causing the plaintiff any damage?

As Stuart-Smith and Stocker LJJ have recorded in their judgments, counsel for the first defendant conceded that his client owed the intending purchaser at least the duty to take such care in and about her business, namely, the search for a suitable car for her, as he would have about his own affairs had he been looking for a car for himself. In the light of the more cautious approach taken in recent cases by the House of Lords and the Privy Council to the question whether a duty of care exists, as expressed by Lord Wilberforce in the familiar passage from his speech in *Anns v Merton London Borough Council* [1978] AC 728, 751–752—see, for instance, the opinion of the Privy Council in *Yuen Kun Yeu v A-G of Hong Kong* [1988] AC 175—I for my part respectfully doubt whether counsel's concession in the instant case was rightly made in law. I do not find the conclusion that one must impose upon a family friend looking out for a first car for a girl of 26 a *Donoghue v Stevenson* duty of care in and about his quest, enforceable with all the formalities of the law of tort, entirely attractive.

Nor do I think, on the facts of this case, that but for the concession one can apply to the young man's answer to the girl's inquiry about the car's history:

... the principle that a duty of care arises where a party is asked for and gives gratuitous advice upon a matter within his particular skill or knowledge and knows or ought to have known that the person asking for the advice will rely upon it and act accordingly

see *Yuen Kun Yeu v A-G of Hong Kong* [1988] AC 175, 192, referring to the effect *of Hedley Byrne & Co Ltd v Heller & Partners Ltd* [1964] AC 465. To do so in this and similar cases will make social relations and responsibilities between friends unnecessarily hazardous.

However the concession was made, and I agree with Stuart-Smith and Stocker LJJ that we must accordingly decide this appeal on that basis. In those circumstances I think that one is driven to the conclusion that the findings by the deputy judge that the plaintiff did ask the first defendant if the car had been involved in an accident, that he had answered that it had not without any direct inquiry to the vendor, whereas in truth it had been involved in a serious accident and been extensively but unskillfully repaired, inevitably led to the conclusion that the first defendant did breach his conceded duty of care and that the plaintiff suffered the damage alleged in consequence.

I too would therefore dismiss this appeal.

NOTES

1.   *Chaudhry v Prabhakar* seems to put paid to the traditional view that there are different standards of care as between gratuitous agents and agents for reward; the Court of Appeal having made it clear that the required standard of any agent is such as is reasonable in all the circumstances. The standard of care will vary with the facts of any particular case and the fact that the agent is acting gratuitously or for reward is simply one of the factors to be taken into account (see Stuart-Smith LJ, above; cf Powell, op cit, p 304). Other factors include whether the agent for reward exercises any trade, profession or calling, and where the agent is unpaid, the skill and experience which he has or represents himself as having (see Stuart-Smith LJ, above).

2.   *Chaudhry v Prabhakar* leaves one important question without a clear answer: when will a gratuitous agent owe a duty of care to his principal? Remember, some doubt was expressed over whether counsel was right to concede the existence of a duty of care in that case (see May LJ, above). See *Markesinis and Munday,* p 97. A further question could be asked: was it really necessary to treat Prabhakar as a gratuitous agent at all? See NE Palmer [1992] SPTL Reporter 35 at p 36, who sees *Chaudhry v Prabhakar* as a straightforward case of liability for negligent advice.

(c) Duties arising from the fiduciary nature of the agency relationship

Agents are normally subject to fiduciary duties. This is because the agent has power to affect the legal relations of his principal and the principal normally places trust and confidence in the agent with regard to the exercise of that power. In these circumstances, equity will intervene and subject the agent to fiduciary duties so as to protect the principal from any abuse of power by the agent.[1] The core duties are those of loyalty and fidelity. As Millett LJ said in *Bristol and West Building Society v Mothew* [1998] Ch 1 at 18:

A fiduciary is someone who has undertaken to act for or on behalf of another in a particular matter in circumstances which give rise to a relationship of trust and confidence. The distinguishing obligation of

---

[1] For a detailed discussion of the nature of fiduciary relationships and the topics considered in this section generally, see R Flannigan [2004] JBL 277; M Conaglen (2005) 121 LQR 452; R Flannigan (2006) 122 LQR 449; R Lee (2007) 27 OxJLS 327.

a fiduciary is the obligation of loyalty. The principal is entitled to the single-minded loyalty of the fiduciary. This core liability has several facets. A fiduciary must act in good faith; he must not make a profit out of his trust; he must not place himself in a position where his duty and his interest may conflict; he may not act for his own benefit or the benefit of a third person without the informed consent of his principal. This is not intended to be an exhaustive list, but it is sufficient to indicate the nature of fiduciary obligations. They are the defining characteristics of the fiduciary.

Fiduciary duties are proscriptive in nature: they tell the fiduciary what he must not do, they do not tell him what he ought to do (*A-G v Blake* [1998] Ch 439 at 455, per Lord Woolf MR; *Breen v Williams* (1996) 186 CLR 71, HC of A, noted by R Nolan (1997) 113 LQR 220). A fiduciary may be subject to positive duties at common law and in equity, eg an agent must act with care and skill, but this is not a fiduciary duty—in the case of a company director, this duty is now codified in the Companies Act 2006 (s 174), which also confirms that it is not a fiduciary duty (s 178(2)). Even the simple duty to account, central though it is, is not a fiduciary duty (*Coulthard v Disco Mix Club Ltd* [2000] 1 WLR 707 at 728, per Sher QC, sitting as a deputy judge; and see also *Compania de Seguros Imperio v Health (REBX) Ltd* [2001] 1 WLR 112, CA). As Millett LJ said in the *Mothew* case (at 16), 'not every breach of a duty by a fiduciary is a breach of fiduciary duty'.

　Despite the fact that most agents are fiduciaries, some are not, and those that are may not act in a fiduciary capacity for all purposes. As Professor Dowrick has noted: 'if P appoints A to be his agent merely to sign a memorandum and places no particular trust in A, the doctrine of fiduciary relations and the incidents of agency which derive from this equitable doctrine would not apply' ((1954) 17 MLR 24 at pp 31–32). However, the term 'non-fiduciary agent' is probably best avoided for, as the distinguished editor of *Bowstead and Reynolds* states (at para 6-036), it seems better to say that where an agent does not act in a fiduciary capacity (eg because he simply carries out specific instructions), this is a reflection of the scope of his duties and the boundaries of the equitable rules'.

　The extent of the fiduciary duties of an agent may vary from case to case ('Fiduciaries are not all required, like the victims of Procrustes, to lie on a bed of the same length': *Brandeis Brokers Ltd v Black* [2001] 2 Lloyd's Rep 359 at 367, per Toulson J). As Lord Upjohn said in *Boardman v Phipps* [1967] 2 AC 46 at 123: 'Rules of equity have to be applied to such a great diversity of circumstances that they can be stated only in the most general terms and applied with particular attention to the exact circumstances of each case.' Lord Browne-Wilkinson made a similar observation in *Kelly v Cooper* [1993] AC 205 at 214–215 (below, pp 213–214), and later in *Henderson v Merrett Syndicates Ltd* [1995] 2 AC 145 at 206 he said:

The phrase 'fiduciary duties' is a dangerous one, giving rise to a mistaken assumption that all fiduciaries owe the same duties in all circumstances. That is not the case. Although, so far as I am aware, every fiduciary is under a duty not to make a profit from his position (unless such profit is authorised), the fiduciary duties owed, for example, by an express trustee are not the same as those owed by an agent. Moreover, and more relevantly, the extent and nature of the fiduciary duties owed in any particular case fall to be determined by reference to any underlying contractual relationship between the parties. Thus, in the case of an agent employed under a contract, the scope of his fiduciary duties is determined by the terms of the underlying contract. Although an agent is, in the absence of contractual provision, in breach of his fiduciary duties if he acts for another who is in competition with his principal, if the contract under which he is acting authorises him to do so, the normal fiduciary duties are modified accordingly: see *Kelly v Cooper* [1993] AC 205, and the cases there cited. The existence of a contract does not exclude the co-existence of concurrent fiduciary duties (indeed, the contract may well be their source); but the contract can and does modify the extent and nature of the general duty that would otherwise arise.

As fiduciary duties of an agent arise in equity, and do not depend upon any contract made between the principal and agent, those duties may apply to both contractual and gratuitous agents alike (contrary dicta of Lord Browne-Wilkinson in *Kelly v Cooper* and *Henderson v Merrett Syndicates,* suggesting that fiduciary duties stem from contract, should be treated with caution). However, the principal and agent may incorporate fiduciary duties into any contract made between them, or, alternatively, exclude or modify those duties from their relationship by the terms of their contract. The exclusion or modification of fiduciary duties is controlled by both common law and statute. At common law, where an agent seeks by a contract term to reserve power to act in a way inconsistent with the agency he must either acknowledge his agency and disclose the potential conflict of interest so as to obtain his principal's consent to it, or he must make it clear that the obligation undertaken is not one of agency at all (see *Bowstead and Reynolds,* para 6-050). In the latter case the clause must give a precise indication of the capacity in which he acts and one that states that he may on occasions change his role is probably ineffective for the purpose (*Brandeis Brokers Ltd v Black,* above, p 369). A contract clause seeking to modify or exclude an agent's fiduciary duties may also be caught by the Unfair Contract Terms Act 1977, and in some cases by the Unfair Terms in Consumer Contracts Regulations 1999 (see below, p 629). For consideration of the special problems raised when directors contract out of their fiduciary duties, see Companies Act 2006, s 232 (provisions protecting directors from liability); *Movitex Ltd v Bulfield* [1988] BCLC 104 (distinction between duties and disabilities of directors); *Gwembe Valley Development Co Ltd v Koshy (No 3)* [2003] EWCA Civ 1478, [2004] 1 BCLC 131 at [104]–[109] (that distinction was 'a needless complication'); and note that the Companies Act 2006, in its statutory statement of director's duties, abandons the distinction between duties and disabilities. As to trustee exemption clauses, see *Armitage v Nurse* [1998] Ch 241 (danger of reducing the obligations of a trustee beyond the 'irreducible core of obligations'); *Citibank NA v MBIA Assurance SA* [2006] EWHC 3215 (Ch), [2007] 1 All ER (Comm) 475 (refusal to recharacterise 'commercial trust' on ground that trustee's obligations had been reduced beyond 'irreducible core'); *Baker v JE Clark & Co (Transport) Ltd* [2006] EWCA Civ 464 (Unfair Contract Terms Act 1977 and Unfair Term in Consumer Contracts Regulations 1999 do not apply to trust instruments because a trust instrument is not a 'contract'); and Law Commission Report No 301, *Trustee Exemption Clauses* (2006) (provisional recommendation to prohibit professional trustees from relying on clauses to exclude or limit liability for breach of trust arising from negligence was abandoned in final report).

Two categories of agent deserve special mention at this stage: company directors and commercial agents.

Company directors: Part 10, Chapter 2, of the Companies Act 2006 codifies the common law and equitable duties applying to company directors. Section 170 sets out the scope and nature of the codified general duties owed by a director of a company to the company. The section makes it clear that the statutory duties described in Ch 2 have been put in place to replace the common law rules and equitable principles from which they are derived (s 170(3)). However, s 170(4) requires the court to have regard to the existing interpretation and the continuing development of the common law rules and equitable principles on which the statutory duties are based when interpreting those duties. Furthermore, s 178 preserves the common law and equitable rules as to remedies for breach of the statutory duties and makes it clear that most of the codified general duties of directors remain fiduciary in character.

There are three general provisions in the 2006 Act designed to reformulate and codify the fiduciary duties owed by directors to their companies. First, s 175 lays down a duty to avoid conflicts of interest so far as third parties are concerned (the 'no-conflict' and 'no-profit' rules—see below—are replaced by a single rule). Secondly, s 176 sets out a duty not to accept benefits from third parties (ie not to accept bribes or secret commission). Thirdly, s 177 requires a director to declare any direct or indirect interest he has in a proposed transaction or arrangement with the company. If the director fails to declare his interest, and the company enters into the impugned transaction, the director is under a new and continuing duty to disclose his interest (s 182).

Commercial Agents: The Commercial Agents (Council Directive) Regulations 1993 lays down duties for commercial agents as defined therein (see above, p 106). Such duties generally reflect those duties which already arise at common law and in equity.[2] By regulation 3(1) a commercial agent must 'in performing his activities look after the interests of his principal and act dutifully and in good faith'. In particular he must (a) make proper efforts to negotiate and, where appropriate, conclude the transactions he is instructed to take care of; (b) communicate to his principal all the necessary information available to him; and (c) comply with reasonable instructions given by his principal (reg 3(2)). The parties may not derogate from these duties (reg 5(1)).

Specific fiduciary duties of an agent

The most important fiduciary duties which may be owed by an agent towards his principal are the following.

(i) Duty not to put himself in a position where his duties as agent conflict with his own interests, or the interests of another principal

Armstrong v Jackson
[1917] 2 KB 822, King's Bench Division

Armstrong instructed Jackson, a stockbroker, to buy shares in a certain company for him. Although Jackson pretended to purchase the shares on the open market, he actually sold his own shares in the company to Armstrong. On discovering the truth some years later, Armstrong claimed to have the transaction set aside. McCardie J upheld the claim and ordered Jackson to repay all sums paid by Armstrong for the shares.

McCardie J: . . . First as to the claim to avoid the transaction. It is obvious that the defendant gravely failed in his duty to the plaintiff. He was instructed to buy shares. But he never carried out his mandate. A broker who is employed to buy shares cannot sell his own shares unless he makes a full and accurate disclosure of the fact to his principal, and the principal, with a full knowledge, gives his assent to the changed position of the broker. The rule is one not merely of law but of obvious morality. As was said by Lord Cairns in *Parker v McKenna* ((1874) 10 Ch App 96 at 118), 'No man can in this Court, acting as an agent, be allowed to put himself into a position in which his interest and his duty will be in conflict.' Now a broker who secretly sells his own shares is in a wholly false position. As vendor it is to his interest to sell his shares at the highest price. As broker it is his clear duty to the principal to buy at the lowest price and to give unbiassed and independent advice (if such be asked) as to the time when and the price at which shares shall be bought, or whether they shall be bought at all. The law has ever required

---

[2] Although attempts to impose fiduciary duties on principals have proved largely unsuccessful (see *Jirna Ltd v Mister Donut of Canada Ltd* (1973) 40 DLR (3d) 303, Sup Ct of Can), the principal of a commercial agent must act 'dutifully and in good faith' towards his agent: Commercial Agents (Council Directive) Regulations 1993, reg 4(1). The parties may not derogate from this regulation: reg 5(1).

a high measure of good faith from an agent. He departs from good faith when he secretly sells his own property to the principal. The rule has long been the same, both at law and equity: see Story on Agency, s 210. It matters not that the broker sells at the market price, or that he acts without intent to defraud: see *Bentley v Craven* ((1853) 18 Beav 75). The prohibition of the law is absolute. It will not allow an agent to place himself in a situation which, under ordinary circumstances, would tempt a man to do that which is not the best for his principal: see per Romilly MR in *Bentley v Craven*. The Court will not enter into discussion as to the propriety of the price charged by the broker, nor is it material to inquire whether the principal has or has not suffered a loss. If the breach of duty by the broker be shown, the Court will set aside the transaction: see *Gillett v Peppercorne* ((1840) 3 Beav 78). The rule was strikingly illustrated in the case of *Rothschild v Brookman* ((1831)5 Bli NS 165 at 197). The facts in that case were not dissimilar to the facts in the present action. The House of Lords (affirming the Court below) set aside transactions in which the agent had secretly acted as principal. In giving his opinion Lord Wynford (formerly Best CJ) used these words: 'If any man who is to be trusted places himself in a condition in which he has an opportunity of taking advantage of his employer, by placing himself in such a situation, whether acting fairly or not, he must suffer the consequence of his situation. Such is the jealousy which the law of England entertains against any such transactions.' . . .

The position of principal and agent gives rise to particular and onerous duties on the part of the agent, and the high standard of conduct required from him springs from the fiduciary relationship between his employer and himself. His position is confidential. It readily lends itself to abuse. A strict and salutary rule is required to meet the special situation. The rules of English law as they now exist spring from the strictness originally required by Courts of Equity in cases where the fiduciary relationship exists. Those requirements are superadded to the common law obligations of diligence and skill: see per Lord Cranworth in *Aberdeen Rly Co v Blaikie Bros* ((1854) 1 Macq 461 at 471 ff) and per Curiam in *Oliver v Court* ((1820) 8 Price 127 at 161).

NOTES

1.   In *Aberdeen Rly Co v Blaikie Bros* (1854) 1 Macq 461 at 471, Lord Cranworth LC provided a classic description of the 'no conflict' rule when he said:

It is a rule of universal application that no one, having [fiduciary] duties to discharge, shall be allowed to enter into engagements in which he has, or can have, a personal interest conflicting, or which may possibly conflict, with the interests of those whom he is bound to protect.

The rule is strictly applied whenever there is an actual conflict of interest and duty or whenever there is 'a real sensible possibility of conflict' (*Boardman v Phipps* [1967] 2 AC 46 at 124, per Lord Upjohn). The fact that the agent has acted in good faith, and produced a benefit for the principal, is irrelevant to the application of the rule (see, eg *Boardman v Phipps*, below at p 216). The rationale behind the rule is that the agent must be deterred from the temptation to place his own interests above those of his principal. However, the agent's duty of loyalty, which stems from the trust and confidence placed in him by his principal, will end on termination of his agency. Thus, in *A-G v Blake* [1998] Ch 439, the Court of Appeal held that a former employee of the Secret Intelligence Service did not owe a continuing duty of loyalty to his employer after he left the service. It further held that the former employee would continue to be subject to a separate fiduciary obligation to maintain the confidentiality of information imparted on him in confidence, as long as the information had not become public knowledge, which it had in this case (there was no appeal on this issue but the House of Lords held the former employee liable to account for profits made in breach of his express undertaking not to divulge any official information gained as a result of his employment: [2001] 1 AC 268). The former agent will also continue to owe fiduciary obligations to his former principal where he continues to have influence over the principal which he exploits for his own benefit. This is a different category of fiduciary relationship than one stemming from either trust and confidence or from confidentiality: it is a relationship of ascendancy and dependency (see Millett LJ, as he then was, writing extra-judicially, in (1998) 114 LQR 214 at pp 219–220).

2.   *Armstrong v Jackson* illustrates one facet of the no conflict rule, ie an agent instructed to purchase property must not sell his own property to the principal. Another facet of the rule is that an agent instructed to sell his principal's property must not buy it himself (*McPherson v Watt* (1877) 3 App Cas 254, where the House of Lords held that the agent had breached the rule when he purchased the property in his brother's name). Where an agent deals with his principal in breach of duty, the principal may rescind the contract (assuming there are no bars to rescission, eg restitution is impossible, intervention of third party rights, affirmation of the contract evidenced by lapse of time after discovering the truth). Alternatively, the principal may affirm the contract and claim an account of any profit made by the agent (*Bentley v Craven* (1853) 18 Beav 75). But special rules apply when the agent sells property to the principal. If the agent sells property which he acquired after the creation of the agency relationship then he must account to the principal for any profit (*Tyrrell v Bank of London* (1862) 10 HL Cas 26). If the agent already owned the property before the agency was created he will not be accountable for any profit but he will have to pay compensation for any loss caused to the principal (*Jacobus Marler Estates Ltd v Marler* (1913) 85 LJPC 167n). See *Bowstead and Reynolds,* para 6-068; see also P Watts [1992] LMCLQ 439.

3.   There will be no breach of duty if the agent makes full disclosure of all material facts to the principal and obtains the principal's consent before placing himself in a position where his interests and duty conflict (*North and South Trust Co v Berkeley* [1971] 1 WLR 470 at 484–485, per Donaldson J). When an agent sells his own property to the principal, or buys the principal's property from him, the agent must also show that the price was fair and that he did not abuse his position in any way (*Gibson v Jeyes* (1801) 6 Ves 266). Furthermore, as we have already seen, the no conflict rule may be excluded by the terms of any contract made between the principal and agent (above, p 208). Exclusion of the duty may be by express or implied terms of the contract (*Kelly v Cooper* [1993] AC 205, below).

So far we have examined the no conflict rule in terms of the agent's duty not to put himself in a position where his duty to his principal conflicts with his own interests. However, the rule also prevents the agent from placing himself in a position where he owes a duty to another person which is inconsistent with his duty to his principal (see *North and South Trust Co v Berkeley* [1971] 1 WLR 470 at 484–485, per Donaldson J; see also the case next cited).

Kelly v Cooper

[1993] AC 205, Privy Council

Kelly instructed Coopers, a firm of estate agents, to sell his house ('Caliban'). Brant, who was the owner of an adjacent house ('Vertigo'), also instructed Coopers to sell his house. Coopers showed Perot, a prospective purchaser, around both houses and Perot made an offer for Vertigo, which was accepted by Brant. Perot then offered to buy Caliban. Coopers did not inform Kelly of the agreement to buy Vertigo. In ignorance of the agreement made between Perot and Brant, Kelly accepted Perot's offer and the sales of both houses were completed. Kelly later brought an action against Coopers claiming that they were in breach of their duties in (1) failing to disclose material information to him and (2) placing themselves in a position where there was a conflict between their duty of disclosure to Kelly and their own interest in ensuring they obtained commission on both houses.

Lord Browne-Wilkinson, delivering the advice of the Privy Council (Lords Keith of Kinkel, Ackner, Browne-Wilkinson, Mustill and Slynn of Hadley), held that Perot's interest in buying both houses was a material factor which could have influenced the negotiations for the price at which Caliban was sold. He continued:

In the view of the Board the resolution of this case depends upon two fundamental propositions: first, agency is a contract made between principal and agent; second, like every other contract, the rights and duties of the principal and agent are dependent upon the terms of the contract between them, whether express or implied. It is not possible to say that all agents owe the same duties to their principals: it is always necessary to have regard to the express or implied terms of the contract....

In a case where a principal instructs as selling agent for his property or goods a person who to his knowledge acts and intends to act for other principals selling property or goods of the same description, the terms to be implied into such agency contract must differ from those to be implied where an agent is not carrying on such general agency business. In the case of estate agents, it is their business to act for numerous principals: where properties are of a similar description, there will be a conflict of interest between the principals each of whom will be concerned to attract potential purchasers to their property rather than that of another. Yet, despite this conflict of interest, estate agents must be free to act for several competing principals otherwise they will be unable to perform their function. Yet it is normally said that it is a breach of an agent's duty to act for competing principals. In the course of acting for each of their principals, estate agents will acquire information confidential to that principal. It cannot be sensibly suggested that an estate agent is contractually bound to disclose to any one of his principals information which is confidential to another of his principals. The position as to confidentiality is even clearer in the case of stockbrokers who cannot be contractually bound to disclose to their private clients inside information disclosed to the brokers in confidence by a company for which they also act. Accordingly in such cases there must be an implied term of the contract with such an agent that he is entitled to act for other principals selling competing properties and to keep confidential the information obtained from each of his principals.

Similar considerations apply to the fiduciary duties of agents. The existence and scope of these duties depends upon the terms on which they are acting. In *New Zealand Netherlands Society Oranje Inc v Kuys* [1973] 1 WLR 1126, 1129–1130, Lord Wilberforce, in giving the judgment of this Board, said:

> The obligation not to profit from a position of trust, or, as it is sometimes relevant to put it, not to allow a conflict to arise between duty and interest, is one of strictness. The strength, and indeed the severity, of the rule has recently been emphasised by the House of Lords: *Boardman v Phipps* [1967] 2 AC 46. It retains its vigour in all jurisdictions where the principles of equity are applied. Naturally it has different applications in different contexts. It applies, in principle, whether the case is one of a trust, express or implied, of partnership, of directorship of a limited company, of principal and agent, or master and servant, but the precise scope of it must be moulded according to the nature of the relationship. As Lord Upjohn said in *Boardman v Phipps* at p 123: 'Rules of equity have to be applied to such a great diversity of circumstances that they can be stated only in the most general terms and applied with particular attention to the exact circumstances of each case.'

In *Hospital Products Ltd v United States Surgical Corpn* (1986) 156 CLR 41, 97, Mason J in the High Court of Australia said:

> That contractual and fiduciary relationships may co-exist between the same parties has never been doubted. Indeed, the existence of a basic contractual relationship has in many situations provided a foundation for the erection of a fiduciary relationship. In these situations it is the contractual foundation which is all important because it is the contract that regulates the basic rights and liabilities of the parties. The fiduciary relationship, if it is to exist at all, must accommodate itself to the terms of the contract so that it is consistent with, and conforms to, them. The fiduciary relationship cannot be superimposed upon the contract in such a way as to alter the operation which the contract was intended to have according to its true construction.

Thus, in the present case, the scope of the fiduciary duties owed by the defendants to the plaintiff (and in particular the alleged duty not to put themselves in a position where their duty and their interest conflicted) are to be defined by the terms of the contract of agency.

Applying those considerations to the present case, their Lordships are of the view that since the plaintiff was well aware that the defendants would be acting also for other vendors of comparable properties and in so doing would receive confidential information from those other vendors, the agency contract between the plaintiff and the defendants cannot have included either a term requiring the defendants to disclose such confidential information to the plaintiff or a term precluding the defendants acting for rival vendors or (c) a term precluding the defendants from seeking to earn commission on the sale of the property of a rival vendor.

Their Lordships are therefore of opinion that the defendants committed no breach of duty, whether contractual or fiduciary, by failing to reveal to the plaintiff Mr Perot's interest in buying Vertigo, since such information was confidential to Mr Brant. Nor did the fact that the defendants had a direct financial interest in securing a sale of Vertigo constitute a breach of fiduciary duty since the contract of agency envisaged that they might have such a conflict of interest.

This decision is consistent with *Lothian v Jenolite Ltd* 1969 SC 111 and does not conflict with any of the other authorities to which their Lordships were referred. The failure of estate agents to communicate material information to their principals which was held to exist in *Keppel v Wheeler* [1927] 1 KB 577 and *Dunton Properties Ltd v Coles, Knapp & Kennedy Ltd* (1959) 174 Estates Gazette 723 related to information received by the estate agents in their capacity as agents of the principal who was complaining and was therefore not subject to any duty of confidentiality owed by the agents to other persons.

North and South Trust Co v Berkeley [1971] 1 WLR 470 raised quite a different problem. The plaintiff was insured under a policy which had been effected by brokers. The insured had made a claim against the insurers. The brokers then accepted instructions from the insurers (ie a person having a contrary interest to that of the insured) to obtain a report from assessors. Having obtained such report, the brokers refused to disclose it to their original principals, the assured. Donaldson J rightly held that this was a breach of duty by the brokers to their principals. In that case, there was nothing in the circumstances to justify the implication of any term in the agency between the assured and the brokers that the brokers should be free to act for the opposing party, the insurers....

As to the defendants' claim for commission, even if a breach of fiduciary duty by the defendants had been proved, they would not thereby have lost their right to commission unless they had acted dishonestly. In *Keppel v Wheeler* [1927] 1 KB 577 the agents admitted an honest breach of fiduciary duty by mistake and yet were entitled to their commission. In the present case the plaintiff did not allege, nor did the judge find, any bad faith by the defendants. Even on the view the judge took therefore there was no ground for depriving the defendants of their commission.

NOTES

1.   *Kelly v Cooper* has its critics. In [1994] JBL 144 at 149, Professor Reynolds writes:

The rather brusque reasoning and the citation of two cases on commercial distributors, seems to deny fiduciary obligations to all and to leave everything to express and even implied terms of the contract. Variable as the degree of fiduciary liability is, such reasoning cannot be appropriate to agency law in general. And it would be most unfortunate if it was taken as a carte blanche for persons acting in potentially inconsistent capacities in the area of financial services.

See also the criticisms of I Brown (1993) 109 LQR 206. However, the contractual approach to the exclusion and modification of fiduciary duties has subsequently been echoed by Lord Jauncey, delivering the advice of the Privy Council, in *Clark Boyce v Mouat* [1994] 1 AC 428, 436, by Lord Browne-Wilkinson in *Henderson v Merrett Syndicates Ltd* [1995] 2 AC 145, 206 (see above, p 208) and by Lord Walker in *Hillier v Barker Booth & Eastwood* [2005] UKHL 8, [2005] 1 WLR 567 at [30]. It has also found favour with the Law Commission (see note 3 below).

2.   *Kelly v Cooper* is a case of unrelated agencies, ie Coopers were not acting as agents for competing principals *in the same transaction*. Implied consent to the agent acting for competing principals was to be derived from the particular business context (an estate agent is known to act for many parties). But in other areas of business activity, for example, where the agent is a solicitor, the normal requirement of undivided loyalty may apply even where the agent acts for two principals in different matters (*Marks & Spencer plc v Freshfields Bruckhaus Deringer* [2004] EWCA Civ 741, [2005] PNLR 4). It is most unlikely that a court will imply a term to enable an agent to act for opposing principals in the same transaction. In such circumstances the agent would have to obtain the fully informed consent *of both* principals to his continuing to act for both of them. For example, in *Clark Boyce v Mouat* [1994] 1 AC 428, the Privy Council held that a solicitor was entitled to act for both parties in a transaction even where their interests might conflict provided he obtained the informed consent of both parties to his so acting. Sometimes, even disclosure will not save the agent when he has put himself in a position 'where he cannot fulfil his obligations to one without failing in his obligations to the other' (*Bristol & West Building Society v Mothew* [1998] Ch 1, 19, per Millett LJ). The agent has only himself to blame for not having refused to act for one of the principals in the first place. For example, in *Hillier v Barker Booth & Eastwood* [2005] UKHL 8, [2005] 1 WLR 567, the House of Lords held a solicitor liable for having put himself in a position where he owed irreconcilable duties to two clients when acting for them in the same transaction: one duty to the claimant to reveal information in his possession that might affect the claimant's interests, and one duty to the other client not to disclose discreditable facts about him without his consent.

3.   The problems facing fiduciaries owing duties to opposing clients are of long standing but they have been highlighted by the growth of multi-function fiduciaries, especially in the financial services industry. With the abolition of single-capacity trading in the mid-1980s following 'Big Bang', it became possible for large firms and banking groups to offer a range of financial services to their customers. This has increased the potential for conflicts of interest. For example, the corporate finance department of a bank may be advising with regard to a rumoured bid from an anonymous bidder, whilst the corporate advisory department of the same bank may be advising the bidder. In these circumstances the bank may be in breach of its duty of confidentiality or its duty to give 'undivided loyalty' to each client, even though it has complied with regulatory rules made pursuant to the Financial Services and Markets Act 2000 (see Ch 17, Section 1). It is by no means certain how far, if at all, such regulatory rules have modified traditional fiduciary duties. The issue was addressed in 1995 by the Law Commission in their report on *Fiduciary Duties and Regulatory Rules* (Report No 236; summarised by H McVea [1997] CfiLR 123). The Law Commission followed the *Kelly v Cooper* line endorsing the use of contractual techniques for modifying the scope of fiduciary duties and general advanced disclosure clauses. The Law Commission also recommended the introduction of a legislative 'safe harbour' which would allow multifunctional fiduciaries in the financial services industry to rely on compliance with regulatory rules as an excuse for deviation from the strict fiduciary obligations imposed by common law. The Government decided against the inclusion of such a provision in the Financial Services and Markets Act 2000 (the more limited protection offered by s 147, which provides for the making of rules relating to the disclosure and use of information, is considered below, p 700). It stated that, in the light of recent case law (in particular, *Prince Jefri Bolkiah v KPMG* [1999] 2 AC 222):

[i]t is the Government's firm belief that the courts would be unlikely to hold that someone could successfully sue an authorised person for breach of fiduciary duties where the authorised person has complied with [Financial Services Authority] rules, which, of course, are made under Parliament's delegated statutory powers.' (*Hansard,* HL, col 1409, 9 May 2000).

This is probably an overly optimistic generalisation, but it is submitted that regulatory rules do offer the courts a guide to the scope of fiduciary obligations in this context.

4.   Although not applicable in *Kelly v Cooper,* the Estate Agents Act 1979, s 21, imposes a duty of disclosure on estate agents who have a personal interest in land about which they negotiate. Failure to disclose such an interest does not render the agent liable to any criminal or civil sanction but it may lead to disqualification under s 3 of the Act.

5.   Lord Browne-Wilkinson said that an agent who was in breach of fiduciary duty would not lose his right to commission unless he acted dishonestly. These *obiter* comments have been criticised for being too narrow in scope (*Stewart Chartering Ltd v Owners of the Ship Peppy* [1997] 2 Lloyd's Rep 722, 729, per D Steel QC, sitting as a deputy High Court judge). Where there is no dishonesty, the real question is whether the agent's breach of duty goes the root of the obligations he has undertaken to his principal. If it does, he loses his right to commission, albeit he acted honestly, unless the agent effects severable transactions (*Hippisley v Knee Bros* [1905] 1 KB 1, CA). For further discussion, see below, p 240.

The no conflict rule is probably the most important of the agent's fiduciary duties. Many of the other fiduciary duties owed by the agent (see below) can be regarded as particular applications of the no conflict rule.

(ii) Duty not to make a secret profit

Unless he makes full disclosure to his principal and obtains his consent, the agent may not use his position as agent, nor his principal's property or confidential information, to make a profit for himself.

The following cases illustrate how the no secret profit rule operates:

(1) *Lamb v Evans* [1893] 1 Ch 218: L, the proprietor of a trades directory, employed canvassers to obtain advertisements from traders to be inserted in the directory. L discovered that some of the canvassers were proposing to assist a rival publication after their agreement with L had come to an end. The Court of Appeal held that the canvassers were 'not entitled to use for the purposes of any other publication the materials which, while in the plaintiff's employment, they had obtained for the purpose of his publication'.

(2) *Hippisley v Knee Bros* [1905] 1 KB 1: H employed KB as agents to sell goods on commission. H also agreed to pay KB's out of pocket expenses. KB sold the goods and charged H with the cost of printing and advertising. KB claimed the full cost even though they had received a discount from those who had provided these services. At all times KB acted honestly and in accordance with trade custom (of which H had no knowledge). The Court of Appeal held that KB were in breach of duty and had to account for the discount as a secret profit. But KB were allowed to keep their commission on the sale because they had acted in good faith and their breach of duty was only incidental to the sale itself.

(3) *Boardman v Phipps* [1967] 2 AC 46: B, a solicitor, and TP, acting together as agents for the trustees of an estate, attended the annual general meeting of a company in which the estate had a minority holding of shares. Later, they obtained information about share prices from the company. They formed the opinion that the company could be made more

profitable and, acting honestly and without concealment (but not having first obtained the 'informed consent' of all the trustees), used their own money to bid for and eventually to acquire a controlling interest in it. Ultimately, they succeeded in making considerable profits for both themselves and the estate from capital distributions on their respective holdings of shares. By a majority of three to two, the House of Lords held that they must account to the trust for the profit that they had made from their own investments: the profit had been made by reason of their fiduciary position as agents and by reason of the opportunity and the knowledge which had come to them while acting in that capacity.

Where the agent breaches his duty not to make a secret profit, he must account to the principal for that profit. A duty to account is a personal liability, but it appears that the agent may also hold his secret profit on constructive trust for the principal (ie the principal has a proprietary remedy). The two key advantages of a proprietary remedy are that it entitles the principal to any enhancement in the value of the secret profit, eg where the agent has used his secret profit to purchase land which has increased in value, and that it gives the principal priority over the agent's unsecured creditors should the agent become insolvent (to the clear detriment of those other creditors). For a long time it appeared that if the agent had used his principal's property to make a secret profit then such profit was held on constructive trust, but if the profit had been made without the use of the principal's property the agent was only personally accountable to the principal (see *Industrial Development Consultants Ltd v Cooley* [1972] 1 WLR 443; *Lister & Co v Stubbs* (1890) 45 Ch D 1). It was always difficult to explain *Boardman v Phipps* on this reasoning. In that case the House of Lords did not distinguish between accountability and constructive trust (in fact there was no need to do so as B, the solicitor, was solvent) and the agents were held liable to account for their profits *and* hold them on constructive trust even though they did not use their principal's property to acquire those profits. The case has often been explained on the ground that confidential information is a special form of trust property (as some of their Lordships thought it was). However, in *A-G for Hong Kong v Reid* [1994] 1 AC 324, the Privy Council held that an agent holds a bribe (which is a secret profit) on constructive trust for his principal. Although Lord Templeman, delivering the advice of the Privy Council, did not specifically address the question of whether a secret profit would normally be held on constructive trust when it was not a bribe, his reasoning, and the fact that he cited *Boardman v Phipps* with approval, suggests that it too would be held on trust by the agent (for criticism of this case, see below, p 223).

If the agent has used confidential information to acquire a benefit, the principal may seek an injunction to restrain the agent making further use of the information and, in the case of a contractual agency, claim damages for breach of contract (which may in an exceptional case include gain-based damages, following *A-G v Blake* [2001] 1 AC 268, HL), or seek an account of profits from the agent (which profits, as we have just seen, the agent would hold on constructive trust: *Boardman v Phipps,* above). It should be noted that the agent's duty not to use confidential information acquired in the course of the agency may extend beyond the termination of the agency relationship, although the duty will not apply once the information enters the public domain (*A-G v Blake*, above).

The no secret profit rule is designed to deter the agent from abusing his position and is strictly applied. For example, in *Boardman v Phipps* the agents were held liable to account for their profits even though they had acted honestly, the trust benefited from their actions, and the trust did not want to buy, and could not have bought, the shares. However, the agents were awarded an equitable allowance for their skill and expenditure in making the profit (cf *Guinness plc v Saunders* [1990] 2 AC 663).

(iii) Duty not to accept bribes

Boston Deep Sea Fishing and Ice Co v Ansell
(1888) 39 Ch D 339, Court of Appeal

Ansell was employed as managing director of the plaintiff company. Acting on behalf of the company, Ansell contracted for the construction of certain fishing-smacks, but, unknown to the company, he took a commission from the shipbuilders on the contract. Ansell also accepted bonuses from two other companies (in which he held shares) with which he had placed orders on behalf of the plaintiff company. Suspecting misconduct, the plaintiff company dismissed Ansell from office and later brought an action against him for an account of the secret commission and bonuses he had received. Reversing Kekewich J, the Court of Appeal held that the receipt of secret commission was a good ground for dismissal. Ansell was also ordered to account for his secret commission and bonuses.

Cotton LJ: . . . If a servant, or a managing director, or any person who is authorized to act, and is acting, for another in the matter of any contract, receives, as regards the contract, any sum, whether by way of percentage or otherwise, from the person with whom he is dealing on behalf of his principal, he is committing a breach of duty. It is not an honest act, and, in my opinion, it is a sufficient act to shew that he cannot be trusted to perform the duties which he has undertaken as servant or agent. He puts himself in such a position that he has a temptation not faithfully to perform his duty to his employer. He has a temptation, especially where he is getting a percentage on expenditure, not to cut down the expenditure, but to let it be increased, so that his percentage may be larger. I do not, however, rely on that, but what I say is this, that where an agent entering into a contract on behalf of his principal, and without the knowledge or assent of that principal, receives money from the person with whom he is dealing, he is doing a wrongful act, he is misconducting himself as regards his agency, and, in my opinion, that gives to his employer, whether a company or an individual, and whether the agent be a servant, or a managing director, power and authority to dismiss him from his employment as a person who by that act is shewn to be incompetent of faithfully discharging his duty to his principal.

Bowen LJ: I will, first of all, deal with what is the cardinal matter of the whole case; whether the Plaintiffs were justified or not in dismissing their managing director as they did. This is an age, I may say, when a large portion of the commercial world makes its livelihood by earning, and by earning honestly, agency commission on sales or other transactions, but it is also a time when a large portion of those who move within the ambit of the commercial world, earn, I am afraid, commission dishonestly by taking commissions not merely from their masters, but from the other parties with whom their master is negotiating, and with whom they are dealing on behalf of their master, and taking such commissions without the knowledge of their master or principal. There never, therefore, was a time in the history of our law when it was more essential that Courts of Justice should draw with precision and firmness the line of demarcation which prevails between commissions which may be honestly received and kept, and commissions taken behind the master's back, and in fraud of the master . . . .

  Now, there can be no question that an agent employed by a principal or master to do business with another, who, unknown to that principal or master, takes from that other person a profit arising out of the business which he is employed to transact, is doing a wrongful act inconsistent with his duty towards his master, and the continuance of confidence between them. He does the wrongful act whether such profit be given to him in return for services which he actually performs for the third party, or whether it be given to him for his supposed influence, or whether it be given to him on any other ground at all; if it is a profit which arises out of the transaction, it belongs to his master, and the agent or servant has no right to take it, or keep it, or bargain for it, or to receive it without bargain, unless his master knows it. It is said if the transaction be one of very old date, that in some way deprives the master of his right to treat it as a breach of faith. As the Lord Justice has pointed out, the age of the fraud may be a reason in the master's mind for not acting on his rights; but it is impossible to say that because a fraud has been concealed for six years, therefore the master has not a right when he discovers it to act upon his discovery, and to put an end to the relation of employer and employed with which such fraud was inconsistent. I, therefore, find it impossible to adopt Mr Justice Kekewich's view, or to come to any other conclusion except that the managing director having been guilty of a fraud on his employers was rightly dismissed by them, and dismissed by them rightly even though they did not discover the fraud until after they had actually pronounced the sentence of dismissal . . . .

That really disposes of the most important part of the dispute between the parties. But I also wish to add one word on the subject of the bonuses which he claims to be entitled to retain as received from the Hull Ice Co and the Hull Fishing Co, otherwise called the Red Cross Co. If that was a profit received by him, as it seems to me to have been, while he was agent, and arising out of the duty which he was employed to do for the company, it falls under the same branch of the law as the profits received in respect of the Shipbuilding Co. I have some little difficulty in following Mr Justice Kekewich's judgment with regard to that. We may perhaps have an inaccurate note of it, but if Mr Justice Kekewich is of opinion that it is the essence of a title to relief in such a case that the principal would have been able to claim as his own money, as between himself and the other party to the business transaction, the money secretly received by his agent, I do not think that is the law. It is true, as Mr Justice Kekewich says, that the money which is sought to be recovered must be money had and received by the agent for the principal's use; but the use which arises in such a case, and the reception to the use of the principal which arises in such a case, does not depend on any privity between the principal and the opposite party with whom the agent is employed to conduct business—it is not that the money ought to have gone into the principal's hands in the first instance; the use arises from the relation between the principal and the agent himself. It is because it is contrary to equity that the agent or the servant should retain money so received without the knowledge of his master. Then the law implies a use, that is to say, there is an implied contract, if you put it as a legal proposition—there is an equitable right, if you treat it as a matter of equity—as between the principal and agent that the agent should pay it over, which renders the agent liable to be sued for money had and received, and there is an equitable right in the master to receive it, and to take it out of the hands of the agent, which gives the principal a right to relief in equity.

[Fry LJ delivered a concurring judgment.]

Industries & General Mortgage Co Ltd v Lewis
[1949] 2 All ER 573, King's Bench Division

Lewis employed an agent to arrange for Industries & General Mortgage Co (IGM) to find someone who could provide him with a short-term loan. IGM arranged the loan and agreed to pay the agent half the fee they would charge Lewis. Lewis was not informed of this payment. Slade J held that although IGM had no dishonest intention to cause the agent to persuade Lewis to accept their rates of commission or to act to his disadvantage, IGM were liable nevertheless to pay Lewis the amount of the bribe as damages or as money had and received.

Slade J: . . . For the purposes of the civil law a bribe means the payment of a secret commission, which only means (i) that the person making the payment makes it to the agent of the other person with whom he is dealing; (ii) that he makes it to that person knowing that that person is acting as the agent of the other person with whom he is dealing; and (iii) that he fails to disclose to the other person with whom he is dealing that he has made that payment to the person whom he knows to be the other person's agent. Those three are the only elements necessary to constitute the payment of a secret commission or bribe for civil purposes. I emphasise 'civil purposes' because the Prevention of Corruption Act 1906, s 1(1), introduces the adverb 'corruptly', and, except in the cases provided for in s 2 of the amending Act of 1916, the onus is put on the prosecution of showing that the payment has been made corruptly. I hold that proof of corruptness or corrupt motive is unnecessary in a civil action, and my authority is the decision of the Court of Appeal in *Hovenden and Sons v Millhoff* (1900) 83 LT 41) where the plaintiffs carried on business as hairdressers' sundrymen and the defendant was a member of a firm of wholesale tobacconists. That firm was dissolved and the defendant carried on the business thereafter alone. For the purpose of purchasing cigars and cigarettes the plaintiffs employed buyers on whose judgment they relied and to whom they paid salaries and bonuses in proportion to their profits, and it was the duty of these buyers to order and to obtain for the plaintiffs the necessary supply of cigars and cigarettes for use in their business on the best trade terms. From 1886 to 1889 the defendant had supplied the plaintiffs with large quantities of cigars and cigarettes for which the plaintiffs had paid upwards of £28,000. In 1889 the plaintiffs discovered that regularly, both at Christmas and Midsummer, during the whole period of their connection with the defendants, he or his firm had made gifts of money in the nature of bribes to the buyers employed by the plaintiffs which were calculated as amounting in all to about 2½ per cent on the invoice price of the goods sold and delivered. On making this discovery, the plaintiffs commenced an action alleging conspiracy between the defendant and the plaintiffs' buyers to defraud the plaintiffs and they also claimed the money which the plaintiffs' buyers had received from the defendant as money had and received to the plaintiffs' use. The jury negatived the allegation of conspiracy, and Grantham J gave judgment for the plaintiffs for one farthing damages. The third answer of the jury was that the payments made to the plaintiffs' buyers by the defendant or his firm had an effect on the minds of the buyers in favour of the defendant. Although the learned judge assessed the damages at one farthing, he formed the conclusion that the action had been substantially one of conspiracy, and as that had been disproved be gave judgment for the defendant and the plaintiffs appealed. The appeal proceeded solely on the cause of action for money had and received. I emphasise that because, conspiracy having been negatived by the jury, the arguments and the *ratio decidendi* of the judgments in the Court of Appeal could have proceeded only on the footing that no charge of fraud had been sustained. Romer LJ, in his judgment, said (83 LT 43):

> It may, therefore, be well to point out what is a bribe in the eyes of the law. Without attempting an exhaustive definition I may say that the following is one statement of what constitutes a bribe. If a gift be made to a confidential agent with the view of inducing the agent to act in favour of the donor in relation to transactions between the donor and the agent's principal and that gift is secret as between the donor and the agent—that is to say, without the knowledge and consent of the principal—then the gift is a bribe in the view of the law.

I emphasise the learned judge's words: 'If a gift be made to a confidential agent with the view of inducing the agent' because counsel for the plaintiffs rightly emphasised those words. Romer LJ proceeds (ibid):

> If a bribe be once established to the court's satisfaction, then certain rules apply. Amongst them the following are now established, and, in my opinion, rightly established, in the interests of morality with the view of discouraging the practice of bribery. First, the court will not inquire into the donor's motive in giving the bribe, nor allow evidence to be gone into as to the motive.

In other words, the learned judge is saying that once the bribe is established, there is an irrebuttable presumption that it was given with an intention to induce the agent to act favourably to the payer and, thereafter, unfavourably to the principal. Romer LJ continues:

Secondly, the court will presume in favour of the principal, and as against the briber and the agent bribed, that the agent was influenced by the bribe; and this presumption is irrebuttable.

That means that the motive of the donor in making the payment to the agent or donee is conclusively presumed against the person who makes the payment, and, secondly, it is conclusively proved against the person making the payment that the donee is affected and influenced by the payment. The Lord Justice goes on:

Thirdly, if the agent be a confidential buyer of goods for his principal from the briber, the court will assume as against the briber that the true price of the goods as between him and the purchaser must be taken to be less than the price paid to, or charged by, the vendor by, at any rate, the amount or value of the bribe.

That is to say, it must be presumed that the price is loaded as against the purchaser at least by the amount of the bribe. Counsel for the plaintiffs says: 'Yes, but earlier the learned judge has said that if a gift be made to a confidential agent with a view to inducing him, it is a bribe, and, therefore, in using the later language and referring to bribes the learned judge is in effect saying: "I am using these later presumptions in cases where a bribe has been established and I have already defined a bribe as being only something which has been established as being paid with a certain motive" '. That, of course, would tear up the whole of the learned judge's observations because he says lower down that the courts will not receive evidence as to what is the motive of the person making the payment. The motive will be conclusively inferred against him. The Court of Appeal allowed the appeal and for the verdict of one farthing they substituted the amount of the bribe....

...[F]or the purposes of a civil action, where you have two parties to a contract introduced by an agent of one of them, once it is established that one of the parties to a contract makes a secret payment to the person whom he knows to be the agent of the other, the law will presume against him that he has acted corruptly, that the agent has been influenced by the payment to the detriment of his principal, and that the principal, the defendant in this case, has suffered damage to at least the amount of the bribe.

NOTES

1.   In *Anangel Atlas Compania Naviera SA v Ishikawajima-Harima Heavy Industries Co Ltd* [1990] 1 Lloyd's Rep 167, 171, Leggatt J proposed the following more succinct definition: 'a bribe consists in a commission or other inducement, which is given by a third party to an agent as such, and which is secret from his principal'. The payment constitutes a bribe even though it does not induce a contract between the principal of the recipient and the donor; it is the making of the payment that gives rise to a conflict of interest on the part of the recipient (*Petrotrade Inc v Smith* [2000] 1 Lloyd's Rep 486 at [16], [17], per David Steel J). The bribe may be given by the third party's agent acting in the course of his authority (*Armagas Ltd v Mundogas SA* [1986] AC 717 at 743, per Robert Goff LJ). It is irrebuttably presumed against the person giving the bribe that his motive was corrupt and against the agent that he was influenced by the bribe (see *Hovenden and Sons v Millhoff*, above; *Donegal International Ltd v Zambia* [2007] EWHC 197 (Comm), [2007] 1 Lloyd's Rep 397 at [275], Andrew Smith J).

2.   In *Shipway v Broadwood* [1899] 1 QB 369, 373, Chitty LJ famously said that 'the real evil is not the payment of money, but the secrecy attending it'. The burden of proving full disclosure of commission paid to an agent by a third party is on the agent. Where there is *no* disclosure the agent will be held to have received a secret commission (bribe). In some cases there may have been partial or inadequate disclosure that is sufficient disclosure to negate secrecy, and so avoid the consequences of the payment being treated as a bribe (see below), but insufficient disclosure to say that the principal's fully informed consent had been obtained, so that the

agent is held to have breached his fiduciary duty by putting himself in a position where he has a conflict of interest. This was held to have been the case in *Hurstanger Ltd v Wilson* [2007] EWCA Civ 299, [2007] 2 All ER (Comm) 1037, where the defendants applied to the claimant through a broker (agent) for a loan to be secured by a charge on the defendants' home. The loan documentation sent to the defendants for signature authorised payment of the broker's fee out of the loan and stated that the defendants 'understand that an amount in the sum of £295 will be debited to the loan balance being the legal costs incurred in this matter'. The claimant paid the agreed arrangement fee to the broker and also a commission of £240. The defendants later fell into arrears and the claimant brought mortgage possession proceedings. The defendants contended that the loan agreement was void or voidable by reason of the payment of the £240 from the claimant to the broker. The Court of Appeal held that this was a 'half-way house case' where there had been sufficient disclosure so that the broker had not received a secret commission, but that the defendants had not given their fully informed consent to the broker's potential conflict of interest. The court refused to order rescission of the loan agreement, on the ground that the remedy would have been unfair and dispropor-tionate, but held instead that the claimant was liable to pay equitable compensation of £240 plus interest to the defendants for procuring the breach of the broker's fiduciary duty.

What remedies are available to the principal if his agent should receive a bribe? See, gener-ally, A Berg [2001] LMCLQ 27 for an excellent, detailed review.

(1)   The agent may be dismissed without notice (*Bulfield v Foamier* (1895) 11 TLR 282).

(2)   The agent will be liable to forfeit his right to commission or remuneration that he would otherwise have received (*Andrews v Ramsay & Co* [1903] 2 KB 635).

(3)   It is clear that the agent must personally account for the bribe, but does he hold it on trust for his principal? For many years, applying the decision of a strong Court of Appeal in *Lister & Co v Stubbs* (1890) 45 Ch D 1, the courts held that the principal's claim to recover the amount of the bribe was personal, not proprietary. This meant that the prin-cipal could not recover any profit made by the agent through investment of the bribe, nor could the principal gain priority over general creditors on the agent's insolvency. But there was much controversy as to whether *Lister & Co v Stubbs* was right or wrong (the arguments on either side are neatly summarised by P Birks in [1993] LMCLQ 30). This controversy has now been resolved by *A-G for Hong Kong v Reid* [1994] 1 AC 324. In that case, the Privy Council held that properties purchased in New Zealand by a Crown servant (the Acting Director of Public Prosecutions for Hong Kong), using mon-ies he had received as bribes, was held by him on constructive trust for the Crown. Lord Templeman, delivering the advice of the Privy Council, said:

When a bribe is offered and accepted in money or in kind, the money or property constituting the bribe belongs in law to the recipient. Money paid to the false fiduciary belongs to him. The legal estate in freehold property conveyed to the false fiduciary by way of bribe vests in him. Equity, however, which acts in personam, insists that it is unconscionable for a fiduciary to obtain and retain a benefit in breach of duty. The provider of a bribe cannot recover it because he committed a criminal offence when he paid the bribe. The false fiduciary who received the bribe in breach of duty must pay and account for the bribe to the person to whom that duty was owed. In the present case, as soon as the first respondent received a bribe in breach of the duties he owed to the Government of Hong Kong, he became a debtor in equity to the Crown for the amount of that bribe. So much is admitted. But if the bribe consists of property which increases in value or if a cash bribe is invested advantageously, the false fiduciary will receive a benefit from his breach of duty unless he is accountable not only for the original amount or value of the bribe but also for the increased value of the property representing the bribe. As soon as the bribe was received it should have been paid or transferred instanter to the person who suffered from the breach of duty. Equity considers as done that which ought to have been done. As soon as the bribe was received, whether in cash or in kind, the false fiduciary held the bribe on a constructive trust for the person injured. Two objections have been raised to this analysis. First it is said that if the fiduciary is in equity a debtor to the person injured, he cannot also be a trustee of the bribe. But there is no reason why equity should not provide two remedies, so long as they do not result in double recovery. If the property representing the bribe exceeds the original bribe in value, the fiduciary cannot retain the benefit of the increase in value which he obtained solely as a result of his breach of duty. Secondly, it is said that if the false fiduciary holds property representing the bribe in trust for the person injured, and if the false fiduciary is or becomes insolvent, the unsecured creditors of the false fiduciary will be deprived of their right to share in the proceeds of that property. But the unsecured creditors cannot be in a better position than their debtor. The authorities show that property acquired by a trustee innocently but in breach of trust and the property from time to time representing the same belong in equity to the cestui que trust and not to the trustee personally whether he is solvent or insolvent. Property acquired by a trustee as a result of a criminal breach of trust and the property from time to time representing the same must also belong in equity to his cestui que trust and not to the trustee whether he is solvent or insolvent.

When a bribe is accepted by a fiduciary in breach of his duty then he holds that bribe in trust for the person to whom the duty was owed. If the property representing the bribe decreases in value the fiduciary must pay the difference between that value and the initial amount of the bribe because he should not have accepted the bribe or incurred the risk of loss. If the property increases in value, the fiduciary is not entitled to any surplus in excess of the initial value of the bribe because he is not allowed by any means to make a profit out of a breach of duty.

Lord Templeman concluded that as *Lister & Co v Stubbs* was inconsistent with this analysis it should not be followed in future.

Although decisions of the Privy Council are not binding on English courts, so that *Lister & Co v Stubbs* remains technically binding on all courts below the House of Lords, Lord Templeman's speech is clearly of great persuasive authority. However, the case has attracted a great deal of hostile criticism (usefully summarised in K Uff 'The Remedies of the Defrauded Principal after *A-G for Hong Kong v Reid*' in D Feldman and F Meisel (eds) *Corporate and Commercial Law: Modern Developments* (1996), Ch 13; but contrast the warm response given to the case by Professor Jones in Goff and Jones *The Law of Restitution* (7th edn, 2007), para 33-025). Leaving aside the strong technical objections to the decision (namely, the inappropriate invocation of the maxim that equity regards as done that which ought to be done), the Privy Council's failure to take proper account of the interests of the insolvent agent's unsecured creditors stands out as a particularly regrettable feature of the case (this aspect of the case has been severely criticised by Professor Goode in his essay 'Proprietary Restitutionary Claims' in WR Cornish et al (eds) *Restitution: Past Present and Future* (1998), Ch 5). The Court of Appeal has since rejected the idea that the proprietary consequences of bribery should be extended to other forms of fraud (*Halifax Building Society v Thomas* [1995] 4 All ER 673, 681, where Peter Gibson LJ distinguished *A-G for Hong Kong v Reid* on the ground that, on the facts before him, there was no fiduciary relationship between the mortgagor and mortgagee 'but merely that of debtor and secured creditor'). The fact that proprietary relief seems only to be available in the context of a breach of fiduciary duty, and not for other wrongs, is 'a distinction which is difficult to justify' (C Rotherham [1997] CfiLR 43at p 44). Nevertheless, in *Daraydan Holdings Ltd v Solland International Ltd* [2004] EWHC 622 (Ch), [2005] Ch 119 at [86], Lawrence Collins J said (obiter) that he preferred *A-G for Hong Kong v Reid* to *Lister & Co v Stubbs,* and continued: 'There are powerful policy reasons for ensuring that a fiduciary does not retain gains acquired in violation of fiduciary duty, and I do not consider that it should make any difference whether the fiduciary is insolvent. There is no injustice to the creditors in their not sharing in an asset for which the fiduciary has not given value, and which the fiduciary should not have had'.

(4) The principal may claim damages in tort for fraud against the agent bribed and the briber (they are jointly and severally liable) for any loss caused as a result of entering into the transaction in respect of which the bribe was given (see *Petrotrade Inc v Smith* [2000] 1 Lloyd's Rep 486, David Steel J; *Fyffes Group Ltd v Templeman* [2000] 2 Lloyd's Rep 643, Toulson J: an additional claim that the briber had dishonestly assisted the agent's breach of fiduciary duty failed in *Petrotrade* but succeeded in *Fyffes*: noted by C Mitchell (2001) 117 LQR 207, 209–210). The defendant cannot reduce his responsibility merely because the principal had the opportunity to investigate or intervene, but failed to take it; there being no defence of contributory negligence, or its equivalent in equity, to a claim based on bribery (*Corporacion Nacional del Cobre de Chile v Sogemin Metals Ltd* [1997] 2 All ER 917, 923, per Carnwath J). In *Mahesan S/O Thambiah v Malaysia Government Officers' Co-operative Housing Society Ltd* [1979] AC 374, the Privy Council held that as against the agent bribed, and the briber, the principal can recover the bribe through an action in restitution, and that the agent and briber are jointly and severally liable in damages for loss caused by the fraud, but that the principal must elect between these two alternative remedies before judgment (per Lord Diplock at 383). Although this decision has been strongly criticised (see A Tettenborn (1979) 95 LQR 68), we believe that the Privy Council were right to put the principal to his election. To allow the principal to recover both the bribe and damages for his loss against a single defendant would allow double recovery and give the principal an undeserved 'windfall' (see C Needham (1979) 95 LQR 536). But there is no reason why the principal cannot recover the bribe from the agent and go on to recover any excess loss in damages from the briber, or vice versa.

(5) The principal may recover the bribe *and* rescind any contract he made with the third party as a consequence of the bribe being paid to his agent (*Logicrose Ltd v Southend United Football Club Ltd* [1988] 1 WLR 1256, noted by G Jones [1989] CLJ 22). The contract made with the third party is considered voidable at the election of the principal (*Hurstanger v Wilson* [2007] EWCA Civ 299, [2007] 2 All ER (Comm) 1037 at [38]). On the other hand, it can be argued that where an agent accepts, or agrees to accept, a bribe he acts contrary to his principal's interests and does not have authority, actual or apparent, of his principal to enter into the contract with the third party, thereby rendering the resultant contract void (*Bowstead and Reynolds*, para 8–218; see also above, p 127). However, the fact that the contract is rendered void for lack of authority may not prevent the principal from being bound by an arbitration agreement contained within it (*Fiona Trust & Holding Corp v Privalov* [2007] UKHL 40, [2007] 2 All ER (Comm) 1053: where the House of Lords held that the principle of separability, enacted in s 7 of the Arbitration Act 1996, required direct impeachment of the arbitration agreement before it could before set aside).

In addition to civil liability, the agent may also be criminally liable. At common law an agent who accepts or agrees to accept a bribe is guilty of conspiracy. Further, under the

Prevention of Corruption Act 1906, s 1, the agent and the person who gave the bribe may each be guilty of an offence if they acted corruptly. Where the payment is made to a public official, a corrupt motive is presumed until the contrary is proved (Prevention of Corruption Act 1916, ss 2, 4). There is also a separate statutory offence of bribery of a public official (Public Bodies Corrupt Practices Act 1889). The criminal law relating to bribery is somewhat complex and confused. In 1998 the Law Commission published a report and draft Bill on Corruption (Law Com No 248). This resulted in the Government publishing a draft Government Bill in 2003. But the draft Bill was heavily criticised by a Joint Parliamentary Committee chaired by Lord Steyn. The Government then published a consultation paper in December 2005. The consultation revealed that there was broad support for reform of the existing law but no consensus as to how it was to be achieved. In March 2007 the Government asked the Law Commission to consider the options for reform. The Law Commission published a consultation paper in November 2007 (LCCP No 185) provisionally recommending a new offence of bribery, which is clearly defined and consistent with the UK's international obligations. In addition, the Law Commission suggests there should be a new offence of bribing a foreign public official. Foreign nationals resident in England and Wales who commit these offences would be subject to the law, irrespective of whether the bribery occurred abroad. The Law Commission intends to publish a final report and draft Bill in autumn 2008.

QUESTIONS

1.   What if an agent accepts a 'bribe' but fails to keep his side of the bargain? Has the agent breached his fiduciary duty? See above and also P Millett [1993] RLR 7 at 13, fn 42.

2.   Where an agent acquires an asset partly with the bribe and partly with the agent's own money, can the principal recover the whole or only part of the value of the asset? See E Peel, *Treitel's Law of Contract* (12th edn, 2007), para 16-097, referring, by analogy, to *Foskett v McKeown* [2001] 1 AC 102, where the wrongdoer was a trustee and not an agent.

(iv) Duty to account

An agent is under a duty to keep the money and property of his principal separate from his own. If the agent fails to keep his principal's property separate from his own, the principal will be entitled to the entire mixed fund, unless the agent can establish any part of it as his own property (*Lupton v White* (1808) 15 Ves 432). This duty only arises where money or property is beneficially owned by the principal, so that the agent is treated as if he were a trustee of it. But in many cases this does not happen because the parties intend that the agent should be free to use the money or property received in his business (see, eg, those reservation of title clause cases considered below at pp 452–470; see, generally, *Bowstead and Reynolds,* para 6-040). In such cases, the agent will not hold money or property *qua* trustee, he will simply be liable to account for it *qua* debtor. However, where the agent is instructed to purchase property for his principal, and does so in his own name, the agent will hold that property on trust for his principal (*Lees v Nuttall* (1829) 1 Russ & M 53).

An agent must also keep accurate accounts of all transactions entered into on behalf of his principal. He must be ready at all times to produce them (*Pearse v Green* (1819) 1 Jac & W 135). Failure to do so means that everything will be presumed against the agent (*Gray v Haig* (1855) 20 Beav 219 at 226, per Romilly MR). The duty to keep and provide records arises out of the fiduciary nature of the principal-agent relationship and independently of any contract between them so that, unless expressly excluded by contract, it survives the termination of the contract of agency (*Yasuda Fire and Marine Insurance Co of Europe Ltd v Orion Marine*

Insurance Underwriting Agency Ltd [1995] QB 174, Coleman J). Further, on the termination of the agency, the principal is entitled to have delivered up to him all documents relating to the agency which have been prepared by the agent for him, eg in *Gibbon v Pease* [1905] 1 KB 810, an architect was ordered to deliver up plans to a house after the work had been completed and paid for. The principal's entitlement to such documents is subject to any right the agent may have to exercise a lien over them (see below, p 243).

(d) Duty not to delegate his authority

De Bussche v Alt

(1878) 8 Ch D 286, Court of Appeal

A shipowner (De Bussche) employed an agent to sell a ship in India, China or Japan at a certain price. The agent was unable to sell the ship himself but, with the shipowner's consent, he employed a sub-agent (Alt) in Japan to do so. In fact, the sub-agent purchased the ship for himself and then resold it to a third party at a handsome profit. Affirming the judgment of Hall V-C, the Court of Appeal held the sub-agent liable to account to the shipowner for his profit.

Thesiger LJ, delivering the judgment of the Court (James, Baggally and Thesiger LJJ): ...As a general rule, no doubt, the maxim *'delegatus non potest delegare'* applies so as to prevent an agent from establishing the relationship of principal and agent between his own principal and a third person; but this maxim when analyzed merely imports that an agent cannot, without authority from his principal, devolve upon another obligations to the principal which he has himself undertaken to personally fulfil; and that, inasmuch as confidence in the particular person employed is at the root of the contract of agency, such authority cannot be implied as an ordinary incident in the contract. But the exigencies of business do from time to time render necessary the carrying out of the instructions of a principal by a person other than the agent originally instructed for the purpose, and where that is the case, the reason of the thing requires that the rule should be relaxed, so as, on the one hand, to enable the agent to appoint what has been termed 'a sub-agent' or 'substitute' (the latter of which designations, although it does not exactly denote the legal relationship of the parties, we adopt for want of a better, and for the sake of brevity); and, on the other hand, to constitute, in the interests and for the protection of the principal, a direct privity of contract between him and such substitute. And we are of opinion that an authority to the effect referred to may and should be implied where, from the conduct of the parties to the original contract of agency, the usage of trade, or the nature of the particular business which is the subject of the agency, it may reasonably be presumed that the parties to the contract of agency originally intended that such authority should exist, or where, in the course of the employment, unforeseen emergencies arise which impose upon the agent the necessity of employing a substitute; and that when such authority exists, and is duly exercised, privity of contract arises between the principal and the substitute, and the latter becomes as responsible to the former for the due discharge of the duties which his employment casts upon him, as if he had been appointed agent by the principal himself. The law upon this point is accurately stated in *Story on Agency*. A case like the present, where a shipowner employs an agent for the purpose of effectuating a sale of a ship at any port where the ship may from time to time in the course of its employment under charter happen to be, is pre-eminently one in which the appointment of substitutes at ports other than those where the agent himself carries on business is a necessity, and must reasonably be presumed to be in the contemplation of the parties; and in the present case, we have, over and above that presumption, what cannot but be looked upon as express authority to appoint a substitute, and a complete ratification of the actual appointment of the Defendant in the letters which passed respectively between *Willis & Son* and the Plaintiff on the one side, and *Gilman & Co* on the other. We are, therefore, of opinion that the relationship of principal and agent was, in respect of the sale of the *Columbine*, for a time at least, constituted between the Plaintiff and the Defendant.

NOTES

1.   An agent cannot delegate his authority to another person, or appoint a sub-agent to do some of the acts which he himself has to do, unless the agent has the express or implied consent of his principal to do so. The rule applies both where the principal places trust and confidence in the agent, and also where the principal relies on the personal skill of the agent.

2.   In *De Bussche v Alt,* Thesiger LJ set out the circumstances when the consent of the principal to delegate will be implied. The performance of purely ministerial acts, which do not involve confidence or discretion, may also be delegated, eg service of a notice to quit by the solicitor of a company which was itself acting as agent (*Allam & Co Ltd v Europa Poster Services Ltd* [1968] 1 WLR 638). For the powers of a trustee to delegate, see the Trustee Delegation Act 1999 and the Trustee Act 2000, ss 11–23, the effects of which are summarised in D Hayton, *Underhill and Hayton Law Relating to Trusts and Trustees* (17th edn, 2007), paras 55.1–55.42.

3.   If the agent makes an unauthorised delegation, the acts of, and payment to, the sub- agent will not bind the principal. But a third party dealing with the sub-agent may be able to rely on the apparent authority of the agent to delegate and thereby hold the principal bound by the sub-agent's acts. Alternatively, the principal will be bound if he ratifies the agent's act of delegation. It should also be noted that where there has been an unauthorised delegation, the principal is not liable to the sub-agent for commission (*Schmaling v Thomlinson* (1815) 6 Taunt 147); the sub-agent has no lien against the principal (*Solly v Rathbone* (1814) 2 M & S 298); the agent will be liable to the principal for wrongful execution of his authority (*Catlin v Bell* (1815) 4 Camp 183) and may be liable for money had and received by the sub-agent (*National Employers' Mutual General Insurance Association Ltd v Elphinstone* [1929] WN 135).

What are the consequences of an authorised delegation of authority by the agent?

Calico Printers' Association Ltd v Barclays Bank Ltd
(1931) 145 LT 51, King's Bench Division

The plaintiffs sold cotton to a consignee in Beirut and sent shipping documents to Barclays Bank Ltd with instructions to insure the goods if the documents were not accepted by the consignee. Barclays Bank did not have an office in Beirut and, with the knowledge of the plaintiffs, instructed the Anglo-Palestine Bank in Beirut to act as their agents. Barclays Bank told the Anglo-Palestine Bank to insure the goods if the documents were not accepted. The Anglo-Palestine Bank did not present the shipping documents for payment and failed to insure the cotton, which was destroyed by fire. The plaintiffs then sued Barclays Bank and the Anglo-Palestine Bank for negligence. Wright J dismissed both claims, holding that the Anglo-Palestine Bank was not liable because there was no privity of contract between them and the plaintiffs, and that Barclays Bank were not liable because they could rely on an exclusion clause in their contract with the plaintiffs.

Wright J: …[T]o leave the goods uninsured was a gross breach of the most elementary business precautions….

On this ground I should hold these defendants liable to the plaintiffs if there were privity between them and the plaintiffs, and this question must now be considered.

To support the argument that there was privity between the plaintiffs and the Anglo-Palestine Bank, reliance was especially placed on a passage from Story on Agency, s 201, as establishing a general principle that where the employment of a sub-agent was authorised either by express terms or by a known course of business, or some unforeseen exigency necessitating such employment, there was privity established between the principal and the sub-agent, so that the sub-agent and not the agent became directly responsible to the principal for any negligence or misconduct in the performance of the mandate. But I do not think the English law has admitted any such general principle, but has in general applied the rule that even where the sub-agent is properly employed, there is still no privity between him and the principal; the latter is entitled to hold the agent liable for breach of the mandate, which he has accepted, and cannot, in general, claim against the sub-agent for negligence or breach of duty. I know of no English case in which a principal has recovered against a sub-agent for negligence. The agent does not as a rule escape liability to the principal merely because employment of the sub-agent is contemplated. To create privity it must be established not only that the principal contemplated that a sub-agent would perform part of the contract, but also that the principal authorised the agent to create privity of contract between the principal and the sub-agent, which is a very different matter requiring precise proof. In general, where a principal employs an agent to carry out a particular employment, the agent undertakes responsibility for the whole transaction, and is responsible for any negligence in carrying it out, even if the negligence be that of the sub-agent properly or necessarily engaged to perform some part, because there is no privity between the principal and the sub-agent.

I think the rule applies to the present case. The defendants, Barclays, by accepting the employment for 74 per cent commission accepted responsibility for the whole service, including that part of it which necessarily involved the employment of a sub-agent or correspondent at Beyrout. The mere fact that he was nominated by the plaintiffs does not in my judgment affect the position; the defendants, Barclays, accepted the nomination and accepted the defendants, the Anglo-Palestine Bank, as their instrument to fulfil their contract. The case is one of most ordinary banking practice, and to accept the contention that the defendants, Barclays, were not responsible for the acts of the defendants, the Anglo-Palestine Bank, their foreign correspondents, or that there was privity between the latter and the plaintiffs, would be in my judgment to go contrary to the whole commercial understanding of a transaction like this.

The case is quite different from that put by Lord Cave LC in the case of *William H Muller and Co (London) Ltd v Lethem* ([1928] AC 34,138 LT 241). In that case the question was whether the appellants were agents in London of a Dutch shipping company so as to be assessable to income tax in respect of business done in this country as such agents. The facts were peculiar, and one view was that the agents were directly appointed by the Dutch shipowners. Lord Cave LC said ([1928] AC at p 47,138 LT at p 250): 'I am disposed to think that in signing both these documents the Dutch firm were acting as directors of the shipping companies, and in that capacity appointed the London firm as direct agents of those companies; but even if that be not so, and if the appointments must be held to have been made by the Dutch firm as shipping-agents for the Dutch companies and not as directors—still it appears to me that they constituted the London firm direct agents of the two companies. In this connection reference may be made to the well-known judgment of Thesiger LJ in De *Bussche v Alt* (38 LT 370, (1878) 8 Ch D 286), where he pointed out that in certain cases, where the exigencies of business require it, an agent must be deemed to have authority to constitute a direct privity of contract between a substitute appointed by him and his principals. In my opinion the present case falls within that category, and the appellants were appointed and became the authorised and regular agents of the two Dutch companies in London.'

For the reasons I have already indicated, I think it should not be held here that the plaintiffs gave any authority to the defendants, Barclays, to constitute a direct privity of contract between them and the Anglo-Palestine Bank; nor is my judgment on this conclusion affected by De Bussche v Alt (sup.) where a bill in equity was filed for an account in respect of secret profits made by a sub-agent for the sale of some ships. The plaintiff, the owner, consigned them for sale to a firm in the East, who appointed the defendant agent for sale in Japan. The plaintiff and the defendant corresponded about the sale; the defendant made large secret profits and was held liable to account. The court there held that the circumstances constituted an express authority to appoint a substitute apart from the complete ratification of the actual appointment, and it was accordingly held that the relationship of principal and agent was constituted as between plaintiff and defendant, at least, pro hac vice. But apart from the specific finding of fact that there was authority to create direct privity, the case turned on equitable principles; the sub-agent was pro tanto in a fiduciary position as regards the secret profits and could not retain them as against the person whom he knew to be entitled, namely, the actual principal. In a later case of a similar character, *Powell and Thomas v Evan Jones and Co* ([1905] 1 KB 11,92 LT 430), the Court of Appeal held that there was evidence to justify the jury in finding there was privity of contract on facts which appear to me very different from those in the present case, but held also that in all the circumstances there was such a fiduciary relationship as between the sub-agent and the principal as placed the former under a personal incapacity to receive any secret reward.

I do not think the three last cited authorities require me to depart from the conclusion that I have arrived at on the facts of this case and the other authorities that I have cited. I accordingly hold that the claim against the defendants, the Anglo-Palestine Bank, fails.

[The decision of Wright J was subsequently affirmed by the Court of Appeal: (1931) 145 LT 51 at 58. There was no appeal against that part of Wright J's judgment set out above.]

NOTES

1. The consequences of authorised delegation depend on whether there is privity of contract between the principal and the sub-agent (criticised by *Bowstead and Reynolds,* para 5–011). The existence of privity of contract turns on whether the agent was clearly authorised to create it, or whether his act in doing so was ratified by the principal. Since *Calico Printers,* the influence of *De Bussche v Alt* has waned on this issue. The general rule is that there is no privity of contract between principal and sub-agent. As Rix J said in *Prentis Donegan & Partners Ltd v Leeds and Leeds Co Inc* [1998] 2 Lloyd's Rep 326,332, 'the authorities show that the *De Bussche v Alt* exception is indeed an exception, and a narrow one, and the burden must be on the defendants to show some special factors . . . to raise an argument that the general rule makes way for the exception'. However, *De Bussche v Alt* was applied in *Velos Group Ltd v Harbour Insurance Services Ltd* [1997] 2 Lloyd's Rep 461, a decision of HHJ Hallgarten QC at the Central London County Court (Business List), where it was held that because it is necessary to use a Lloyd's broker to place insurance in the Lloyd's insurance market, the assured (principal), whose own insurance broker (agent) had used a Lloyd's broker (sub-agent) to place such insurance, could be regarded as in privity of contract with the Lloyd's broker. The correctness of that decision must be in doubt. In *Pangood Ltd v Barclay Brown & Co Ltd* [1999] 1 All ER (Comm) 460, the Court of Appeal, although seemingly without reference to the *Velos* case, rejected the notion that a Lloyd's broker was in privity of contract with the intermediate broker's principal (the assured) where the Lloyd's broker had merely been asked to obtain a quotation and subsequently to effect insurance in accordance with the terms of that quotation.

2. If there is privity of contract between the principal and the sub-agent the appointing agent need only exercise due care and skill in the appointment of the sub-agent; he is not normally liable for the default of the sub-agent (*Aiken v Stewart Wrightson Members Agency Ltd* [1995] 1 WLR 1281). In any event, the agent will usually have included a clause in his contract with the principal excluding liability for the acts and omissions of the sub-agent (but note that such clauses may be subject to review under the Unfair Contract Terms Act 1977 and/or the Unfair Terms in Consumer Contracts Regulations 1999: see below, p 629). Further, if there is privity, the sub-agent becomes the agent of the principal and acquires all the usual rights and duties of an agent.

3.   If there is no privity of contract between the principal and the sub-agent, the sub-agent generally owes no duty to account to the principal (*New Zealand and Australian Land Co v Watson* (1881) 7 QBD 374; cf A Tettenborn (1999) 115 LQR 655, who argues that as the sub-agent purports to act for the principal and has the power to change the principal's position, it is both just and equitable that he should be under a duty to account to him). It has also been held that, in the absence of privity of contract between them, the sub-agent could not be liable to the principal in tort for negligent performance of his work (*Calico Printers' Association v Barclays Bank Ltd,* above). It may be thought that after the landmark decisions of *Donoghue v Stevenson* [1932] AC 562 and *Hedley Byrne & Co Ltd v Heller & Partners Ltd* [1964] AC 465, a sub-agent could now be held liable to the principal for the tort of negligence, irrespective of whether there is privity of contract between them. Indeed, in *Henderson v Merrett Syndicates Ltd* [1995] 2 AC 145, another case involving the Lloyd's insurance market, the House of Lords held that Lloyd's 'managing agents' (sub-agents) owed a duty of care in tort to 'indirect names' (principals), even though there was no privity of contract between them. Despite the facts that the indirect names had employed their own agents (called 'members' agents'), who in turn had entered into sub-agency agreements with the managing agents, the relationship between the indirect names and the managing agents was extremely close. The managing agents held themselves out as having special expertise and thereby assumed responsibility to the indirect names, who placed implicit reliance on that expertise. But this was a 'most unusual' case (per Lord Goff, at 195G). Lord Goff, delivering the main speech in the House, stressed that in other cases the court would not allow an action in tort to short circuit the contractual structure put in place by the parties (citing as an example *Simaan General Contracting Co v Pilkington Glass Ltd (No 2)* [1988] QB 758, a case involving construction sub-contracts: but now contrast *Riyad Bank v Ahli United Arab Bank (UK) plc* [2006] EWCA Civ 780, [2006] 2 Lloyd's Rep 292, where the contractual structure adopted by the parties did not exclude liability in tort to the third party). He continued (at 195H): 'It cannot therefore be inferred from the present case that other sub-agents will be directly liable to the agent's principal in tort.' Lord Goff made it clear that he was dealing with a case of pure economic loss and not physical damage to property. Where an agent negligently causes physical injury to the principal or physical damage to his property, it may be that the principal could sue him in tort even though there was no privity of contract between them (see generally P Cane 'Contract, Tort and the Lloyd's Debacle', Ch 5 in FD Rose (ed) *Consensus Ad Idem* (1996), especially pp 111–118). But in the earlier case of *Balsamo v Medici* [1984] 1 WLR 951, Walton J held that the sub-agent was not liable in tort when he negligently paid over the proceeds of sale of the principal's car to an imposter, which resulted in the principal suffering financial loss.

4.   Even if there is no privity of contract between the principal and the sub-agent, the sub-agent may still be held liable to the principal as a fiduciary for the purposes of disgorging a bribe (*Powell & Thomas v Evan Jones & Co* [1905] 1 KB 11; although, following *A-G for Hong Kong v Reid* [1994] 1 AC 324, that claim would now be proprietary); he may also have a lien against the principal (*Fisher v Smith* (1878) 4 App Cas 1; see below, p 243); and he may be able to rely on the appointing agent's apparent authority to claim remuneration from the principal (*Bowstead and Reynolds,* para 5-015). The principal may also be able to rely on the Contract (Rights of Third Parties) Act 1999 to enforce a term of any contract between the agent and the sub-agent. Under s 1(1) of the Act, the principal may do this if (a) the contract expressly provides that he may, or (b) the term purports to confer a benefit on him, and there is nothing in the contract when read as a whole which indicates that the agent and the sub-agent intended otherwise.

5. It is clear from the *Calico Printers* case that, subject to any express exclusion of liability (which will be subject to statutory control: see note 2 above), if there is no privity of contract between the principal and the sub-agent, the appointing agent will be liable to the principal for the defaults of the sub-agent (see also *Mackersy v Ramsays, Bonars & Co* (1843) 9 Cl & Fin 818; cf *Thomas Cheshire & Co v Vaughan Bros & Co* [1920] 3 KB 240 at 259, where Atkin LJ, *obiter,* suggested that the appointing agent should only be held liable if he did not exercise reasonable care in the selection of the sub-agent). The appointing agent will also be liable to the principal for money had and received by the sub-agent to the use of the principal (*Balsamo v Medici,* above). In these circumstances, the appointing agent must seek redress from the sub-agent.

QUESTIONS

1. Pete employs Sell, It & Fast, a firm of estate agents, to sell his flat. Sell, It & Fast advertise the flat in their own shop window and also in the window of Tomkins, another firm of estate agents, with whom they have a reciprocal advertising arrangement. The advertisement states that all enquiries should be made through Sell, It & Fast. Bob sees the advertisement in Tomkins' window and contacts Sell, It & Fast to arrange to view the flat. Subsequently, Pete agrees to sell the flat to Bob and instructs his parents' solicitor, Conway, to act for him in this matter. Conway agrees to do so but, owing to his ill health, asks his old friend Drabble, a partner in another firm of solicitors, to draw up the documents needed to convey the flat to Bob. The sale of the flat is duly completed and Sell, It & Fast and Conway now claim their agreed fees from Pete. However, Pete has just found out about the involvement of Tomkins and Drabble and seeks your advice as to whether he has to pay Sell, It & Fast's and Conway's fees. See *John McCann & Co v Pow* [1974] 1 WLR 1643; and *Re Becket, Purnell v Paine* [1918] 2 Ch 72.

2. Do the Commercial Agents (Council Directive) Regulations 1993 apply to sub-agencies? See *Light v Ty Europe Ltd* [2003] EWCA Civ 1238, [2004] 1 Lloyd's Rep 693: see above, p 107.

2 RIGHTS OF THE AGENT

(a) Remuneration

(i) A contractual right

With the exception of a 'commercial agent', whose position is now regulated by the Commercial Agents (Council Directive) Regulations 1993 (see below, p 241), an agent will only be entitled to remuneration from his principal for his services if the agency is contractual and there is an express or implied term of the agency contract to that effect (but see also note 4, below at p 234).

Way v Latilla

[1937] 3 All ER 759, House of Lords

An agent, Way, agreed with his principal, Latilla, to send to the principal information concerning gold mines and concessions in West Africa. Although the principal led the agent to believe that he would receive an interest in any concession obtained, no terms as to remuneration were expressly agreed between them. The House of Lords held that the agent was entitled to a reasonable remuneration on an implied contract to pay him a *quantum meruit.*

Lord Atkin: ... The question now is, what are Mr Way's rights to remuneration? He originally claimed that there was a completed agreement to give him an interest in the concession, which, by custom, or on a reasonable basis, the court was asked to define as one-third. The trial judge accepted this view, holding that he was entitled to assess a reasonable share, and he accordingly awarded him £30,000, as being roughly 3 per cent on the sum of about £1,000,000, which he took to represent Mr Latilla's profits in the transaction. The Court of Appeal rejected this view, and, in my opinion, rightly. There certainly was no concluded contract between the parties as to the amount of the share or interest that Mr Way was to receive, and it appears to me impossible for the court to complete the contract for them. If the parties had proceeded on the terms of a written contract, with a material clause that the remuneration was to be a percentage of the gross returns, but with the figure left blank, the court could not supply the figure. The judge relied upon the decision of this House in *Hillas & Co Ltd v Arcos Ltd* ((1932) 147 LT 503). But in that case this House was able to find, in the contract to give an option for the purchase of timber in a future year, an intention to be bound contractually, and all the elements necessary to form a concluded contract. There is no material in the present case upon which any court would decide what was the share which the parties must be taken to have agreed. But, while there is, therefore, no concluded contract as to the remuneration, it is plain that there existed between the parties a contract of employment under which Mr Way was engaged to do work for Mr Latilla in circumstances which clearly indicated that the work was not to be gratuitous. Mr Way, therefore, is entitled to a reasonable remuneration on the implied contract to pay him *quantum meruit.* ...

  Services of this kind are no doubt usually the subject of an express contract as to remuneration, which may take the form of a fee, but may also take the form of a commission, share of profits, or share of proceeds calculated at a percentage, or on some other basis. In the present case, there was no question of fee between the parties from beginning to end. On the contrary, the parties had discussed remuneration on the footing of what may loosely be called a 'participation,' and nothing else. The reference is analogous to the well known distinction between salary and commission. There are many employments the remuneration of which is, by trade usage, invariably fixed on a commission basis. In such cases, if the amount of the commission has not been finally agreed, the quantum meruit would be fixed after taking into account what would be a reasonable commission, in the circumstances, and fixing a sum accordingly. This has been an everyday practice in the courts for years. But, if no trade usage assists the court as to the amount of the commission, it appears to me clear that the court may take into account the bargainings between the parties, not with a view to completing the bargain for them, but as evidence of the value which each of them puts upon the services. If the discussion had ranged between 3 per cent on the one side and 5 per cent on the other, all else being agreed, the court would not be likely to depart from somewhere about those figures, and would be wrong in ignoring them altogether and fixing remuneration on an entirely different basis, upon which, possibly, the services would never have been rendered at all. That, in fixing a salary basis, the court may pay regard to the previous conversation of the parties was decided by the Court of Exchequer in 1869, in *Scarisbrick v Parkinson* ((1869) 20 LT 175), where the terms of an agreement invalid under the Statute of Frauds, were held to be admissible as evidence in a quantum meruit. This seems to me to be good law, and to give effect to a principle which has been adopted regularly by the courts not only in fixing remuneration for services but also in fixing prices, sums due for use and occupation, and, indeed, in all cases where the court has to determine what is a reasonable reward for the consideration given by the claimant. As I have said, the rule applied in fixing the amount of the remuneration necessarily applies to the basis on which the amount is to be fixed, I have therefore no hesitation in saying that the basis of remuneration by fee should, in this case, on the evidence of the parties themselves, be rejected, and that Mr Way is entitled to a sum to be calculated on the basis of some reasonable participation.

What this should be is a task primarily to be undertaken by the trial judge. He did make an alternative award, and arrived at the sum of £5,000. I see no reason to differ from this.

Lord Wright: ...There was, I think, no justification for making for the parties, as Charles J did, a contract which they did not make themselves. It is, however, clear, on the evidence, that the work was done by the appellant and accepted by the respondent on the basis that some remuneration was to be paid to the appellant by the respondent. There was thus an implied promise by the respondent to pay on a *quantum meruit,* that is, to pay what the services were worth. My difference with the Court of Appeal turns on a narrow issue, which is whether the *quantum meruit* should be determined on the footing of a fee as for professional services, or on some other footing. The Court of Appeal took the former view. I cannot, however, with respect, find, on the whole of the evidence in the case, and, in particular, on the discussions between the parties, any sufficient reason for accepting that view. The services of the appellant were, I think, outside the range of his duties as mining engineer, and were those of an agent for purchase, who suggests to his principal a transaction, and negotiates and completes it for him. While it is not unknown that such services should be remunerated by a fee if it is expressly or impliedly so agreed, this is by no means necessarily, and would not generally be, the case. The idea of such a fee being excluded, it follows that the question of the amount to which the appellant is entitled is left at large, and the court must do the best it can to arrive at a figure which seems to it fair and reasonable to both parties, on all the facts of the case. One aspect of the facts to be considered is found in the communings of the parties while the business was going on. Evidence of this nature is admissible to show what the parties had in mind, however indeterminately, with regard to the basis of remuneration. On those facts, the court may be able to infer, or attribute to the parties, an intention that a certain basis of payment should apply. This evidence seems to me to show quite clearly that the appellant was employed on the basis of receiving a remuneration depending on results. If he had been unsuccessful, he would have been entitled to no more than his expenses, but the respondent had led him to believe that, if the concessions he obtained were valuable, his remuneration would be on the basis of some proportion of their value. The realisation of that value was removed from the actual services by the lapse of time (during which large sums of money were expended and adventured), and by many contingencies, and therefore the proper proportion may be comparatively very small, though the fruits of success were very large. The precise figure can be only a rough estimate. If what the court fixes is either too small or too large, the fault must be ascribed to the parties in leaving this important matter in so nebulous a state. But, forming the best judgment I can, I agree with your Lordships that the figure to be awarded to the appellant should be £5,000, which is what Charles J was prepared to adopt if his judgment were reversed.

[Lords Thankerton, Macmillan and Maugham concurred.]

NOTES

1.   Whether a term as to remuneration is to be implied into the agency contract will depend on the normal rules as to the implication of terms into contracts (as set out in the standard contract law textbooks: see, eg E Peel, *Treitel's Law of Contract* (12th edn, 2007), paras 6-028ff). The rules as to implication of terms at common law are strict: a term can only be implied (a) to give business efficacy to the contract, (b) because it is so obviously a stipulation of the agreement that it goes without saying that the parties must have intended it to form part of their contract, (c) as a standard term of a particular type of contractual relationship, eg landlord and tenant, or (d) by trade custom or usage. See also Supply of Goods and Services Act 1982, s 15 (contractual supplier of services to be paid a reasonable sum).

2.   When a professional person is employed as an agent, and there is no express agreement as to remuneration, there is a strong presumption that he is to receive reasonable remuneration for his services (*Miller v Beal* (1879) 27 WR 403). What is reasonable may be assessed according to what is customary in the trade, profession or business in which the agent is employed. But the customary rate must produce a reasonable result if it is to bind the principal (*Wilkie v Scottish Aviation Ltd* 1956 SC 198 at 205, per Lord Clyde). On the remuneration of professional agents generally, see JR Murdoch [1981] Conv 424.

3.   No term may be implied which would be inconsistent with an express term of the agency contract. In *Kofi Sunkersette Obu v A Strauss & Co Ltd* [1951] AC 243, it was an express term of the agency contract that the agent was to receive £50 for expenses and also commission at the discretion of the principal. No commission was paid so, relying on *Way v Latilla,* the agent claimed that he was nevertheless entitled to a reasonable commission by way of a *quantum meruit* for his services. The Privy Council rejected the claim and distinguished *Way v Latilla* on the ground that in the case before them commission was expressly provided for under the agency contract. The agency contract left the basis and rate of commission at the discretion of the principal and the Privy Council would not substitute their own discretion for that of the principal. For a similar case, see *Re Richmond Gate Property Co Ltd* [1965] 1 WLR 335. Cf *Powell v Braun* [1954] 1 WLR 401, CA.

4.   It should also be noted that an agent may be able to claim a reasonable sum on a restitutionary basis if he renders services outside a contract and those services are freely accepted by the principal, with the knowledge that they could not possibly be gratuitous (see, eg *Michael Elliott & Partners Ltd v UK Land plc* [1991] 1 EGLR 39 at 45; cf *Fairvale Ltd v Sabharwal* [1992] 2 EGLR 27 at 28). Some of the leading writers on the law of restitution submit that this theory of free acceptance offers the best explanation of *Way v Lattila* (P Birks *An Introduction to the Law of Restitution* (revised paperback edn, 1989), p 272; Goff and Jones *The Law of Restitution* (7th edn, 2007), para 23-002–23-003, note 9; cf A Burrows *The Law of Restitution* (2nd edn, 2002), p 374).

5.   Where the agent's commission is provided for in the contract between principal and third party, the agent may be entitled to enforce the terms of that contract as a third party beneficiary through the Contract (Rights of Third Parties) Act 1999. In *Nisshin Shipping Co Ltd v Cleaves & Co Ltd* [2003] EWHC 2602, [2004] 1 All ER (Comm) 481, Cleaves, a chartering broker, negotiated a number of charterparties on behalf of Nisshin, a shipowner. In each of the charterparties, Nisshin agreed with the charterers to pay Cleaves its commission. Each charterparty also contained an arbitration clause. Colman J held that Cleaves had the right, as a third party under the 1999 Act, to enforce Nisshin's promise to pay it commission, and that it was entitled (and bound) to do so by arbitration.

(ii)   Effective cause

Unless otherwise agreed, when an agent is to be paid commission on bringing about a particular event, the agent is not entitled to that commission unless he can show that his services were the effective cause of the event.

Millar, Son & Co v Radford
(1903) 19 TLR 575, Court of Appeal

Millar, Son & Co, a firm of estate agents, were instructed by Radford to find a purchaser, or, failing a purchaser, a tenant, for his property. Millars introduced Cook, who took a seven-year lease of the property. Millars were paid their commission. Fifteen months later, without Millars' intervention, Cook purchased the freehold from Radford. Millars then claimed commission on the sale. Upholding the decision of trial judge, the Court of Appeal rejected Millars' claim to further commission.

Collins MR: ...The claim of house agents to be entitled to commission in circumstances like the present is a claim which is often made, and is likely to continue to be made. It is, therefore, important to point out that the right to commission does not arise out of the mere fact that agents have introduced a tenant or a purchaser. It is not sufficient to show that the introduction was a *causa sine qua non*. It is necessary to show that the introduction was an efficient cause in bringing about the letting or the sale. Here the plaintiffs fail to establish what is a condition precedent to their right to commission—viz, that they have brought about the sale. It is open to the defendant in an action like this to say either that, though the plaintiffs effected a sale, they were not his agents, or that, though they were his agents, they had not effected the sale. If the defendant proves either the one or the other, the plaintiffs fail to make out their case.

[Mathew and Cozens-Hardy LJJ delivered concurring judgments.]

NOTES

1.   Today, the equivalent word to 'efficient' is 'effective'. In other words, the agent must be the direct or effective cause of the event upon which his commission is to be paid: there must be no break in the chain of causation. In *County Homesearch Co (Thames & Chilterns) Ltd v Cowham* [2008] EWCA Civ 26, where the Court of Appeal held that the express terms of the agency contract were inconsistent with an implied requirement that the agent be an effective cause of the transaction, Longmore LJ stated (obiter, at [14]) that:

The present day rationale for the implication of a term that the agent should be at least an effective cause of the transaction is thus (mainly at any rate) the need for the client to avoid the risk of having to pay two sets of commission. This is consistent with the older authorities in which the agent was claiming a second commission when his principal, who had already paid a commission for the procuring of a tenant, was asked to pay a second commission on the purchase of the property by the tenant at a later date, see the decision of the House of Lords in *Toulmin v Millar* (1887) 58 LT 96, per Lord Watson, and *Millar v Radford* itself in 1903.

2.   In *Toulmin v Millar* (1887) 58 LT 96, Lord Watson stated that 'in order to found a legal claim for commission there must not only be a causal, there must also be a contractual relation between the introduction and the ultimate transaction of sale'. This means, for example, that an agent instructed to find a tenant will not be entitled to commission if the person he introduces to his principal actually buys the property (*Toulmin v Millar*), and an agent instructed to find a purchaser will not be entitled to commission if he introduces a Government Department which goes on to acquire the property compulsorily (*Hodges & Sons v Hackbridge Park Residential Hotel Ltd* [1940] 1 KB 404). Cf *Rimmer v Knowles* (1874) 30 LT 496, where the agent employed to find a purchaser was held entitled to commission when he introduced a tenant who took a 999 year lease of the property.

3.   In *Nahum v Royal Holloway and Bedford New College* [1999] EMLR 252, the agent, an art dealer, was asked to seek out potential buyers for the principal's paintings, including one by Gainsborough and one by Constable. The principal agreed that the agent would be paid a commission of 2½ per cent of the sale price of any one or more of the paintings sold to a buyer he introduced. The agent introduced a buyer for the Gainsborough and, after a lengthy delay, the same person also purchased the Constable. The agent was paid commission on the first sale but not on the second, as he took no part in the negotiations which led up to the second sale. The Court of Appeal held that he was entitled to commission on both sales. The court held that, subject to there being no express words of the contract requiring a different interpretation, the word 'introduce' carried with it an effective causative element in the bringing in of the purchaser to the transaction. The court stressed that it was doubtful whether it made any difference whether the agent's actions were 'an' or 'the' effective cause except, possibly, where there were two agents both with agreements entitling them to commission on the introduction of a purchaser. What the agent had to show was that it was his actions that really brought about the relation of buyer and seller between the principal and the purchaser (and the Court of Appeal found ample evidence of this in the present case). A test of causation turning on a 'factual inquiry...whether a sale is really brought about by the act of the agent', as suggested in *LJ Hooker Ltd v WJ Adams Estates Pty Ltd* (1977) 138 CLR 52 at 86, HC of A, was adopted by Rix J in *Harding Maughan Hambly Ltd v Cie Europeenne de Courtage d' Assurances et de Reassurances SA* [2000] 1 All ER (Comm) 225 at 251 (in the context of insurance brokers). It would seem, therefore, that it is more important to stress the word 'effective' than either the definite or indefinite article. For a review of the English, Canadian and Australian case law on this issue, see GHL Fridman (2002) 76 ALJ 195.

(iii) Opportunity to earn commission

Luxor (Eastbourne) Ltd v Cooper
[1941] AC108, House of Lords

Luxor (Eastbourne) Ltd and Regal (Hastings) Ltd (the vendors) employed Cooper, an estate agent, to find a purchaser for four of their cinemas. The vendors agreed to pay Cooper a fee of £10,000 on completion of the sale if he introduced a purchaser who bought the cinemas for not less than £185,000. Cooper introduced Burton who made an offer of £185,000 for the cinemas 'subject to contract'. But the vendors withdrew from the negotiations. Cooper sued the vendors for damages, claiming they had broken an implied term of his agency contract by which they undertook to do nothing to prevent his earning commission. Branson J gave judgment for the vendors and, although reversed by the Court of Appeal, his judgment was upheld by the House of Lords.

Lord Russell of Killowen: A few preliminary observations occur to me. (1) Commission contracts are subject to no peculiar rules or principles of their own; the law which governs them is the law which governs all contracts and all questions of agency. (2) No general rule can be laid down by which the rights of the agent or the liability of the principal under commission contracts are to be determined. In each case these must depend upon the exact terms of the contract in question, and upon the true construction of those terms. And (3) contracts by which owners of property, desiring to dispose of it, put it in the hands of agents on commission terms, are not (in default of specific provisions) contracts of employment in the ordinary meaning of those words. No obligation is imposed on the agent to do anything. The contracts are merely promises binding on the principal to pay a sum of money upon the happening of a specified event, which involves the rendering of some service by the agent. There is no real analogy between such contracts, and contracts of employment by which one party binds himself to do certain work, and the other binds himself to pay remuneration for the doing of it....

As to the claim for damages, this rests upon the implication of some provision in the commission contract, the exact terms of which were variously stated in the course of the argument, the object always being to bind the principal not to refuse to complete the sale to the client whom the agent has introduced.

I can find no safe ground on which to base the introduction of any such implied term. Implied terms, as we all know, can only be justified under the compulsion of some necessity. No such compulsion or necessity exists in the case under consideration. The agent is promised a commission if he introduces a purchaser at a specified or minimum price. The owner is desirous of selling. The chances are largely in favour of the deal going through, if a purchaser is introduced. The agent takes the risk in the hope of a substantial remuneration for comparatively small exertion. In the case of the plaintiff his contract was made on September 23, 1935; his client's offer was made on October 2, 1935. A sum of £10,000 (the equivalent of the remuneration of a year's work by a Lord Chancellor) for work done within a period of eight or nine days is no mean reward, and is one well worth a risk. There is no lack of business efficacy in such a contract, even though the principal is free to refuse to sell to the agent's client.

The position will no doubt be different if the matter has proceeded to the stage of a binding contract having been made between the principal and the agent's client. In that case it can be said with truth that a 'purchaser' has been introduced by the agent; in other words the event has happened upon the occurrence of which a right to the promised commission has become vested in the agent. From that moment no act or omission by the principal can deprive the agent of that vested right....

My Lords, in my opinion there is no necessity in these contracts for any implication: and the legal position can be stated thus: If according to the true construction of the contract the event has happened upon the happening of which the agent has acquired a vested right to the commission (by which I mean that it is debitum in praesenti even though only solvendum in futuro), then no act or omission by the principal or anyone else can deprive the agent of that right; but until that event has happened the agent cannot complain if the principal refuses to proceed with, or carry to completion, the transaction with the agent's client.

I have already expressed my view as to the true meaning of a contract to pay a commission for the introduction of a purchaser at a specified or minimum price. It is possible that an owner may be willing to bind himself to pay a commission for the mere introduction of one who offers to purchase at the specified or minimum price; but such a construction of the contract would in my opinion require clear and unequivocal language.

Lord Wright: ...What is in question in all these cases is the interpretation of a particular contract. I deprecate in general the attempt to enunciate decisions on the construction of agreements as if they embodied rules of law. To some extent decisions on one contract may help by way of analogy and illustration in the decision of another contract. But however similar the contracts may appear, the decision as to each must depend on the consideration of the language of the particular contract, read in the light of the material circumstances of the parties in view of which the contract is made. I shall therefore in the first instance examine the particular contract in question in the light of the material facts...It is important to simplify as far as possible the problem of construing commission agency agreements, especially in regard to the sale of houses and land. These are of common occurrence among all classes of the community and it is most undesirable that subtleties and complications of interpretation calculated to lead to disputes should be allowed to confuse what is ex facie a plain and simple agreement...

The case that the suggested term is not properly to be implied becomes, in my opinion, even clearer when account is taken of some of the more general aspects of the course of business in these matters. It is well known that in the ordinary course a property owner intending to sell may put his property on the books of several estate agents with each of whom he makes a contract for payment of commission on a sale. If he effects a sale to the client introduced by one agent, is he to be liable in damages to all the others for preventing them from earning their commission? Common sense and ordinary business understanding clearly give a negative answer. Or suppose that having employed one agent whose client has made an offer, he receives a better offer from a buyer introduced by another agent and concludes the purchase with him. It seems out of the question that he is thereby rendering himself liable in damages to the former agent. Or suppose that owing to changed circumstances he decides that he will not sell at all and breaks off negotiations with the agent's client, is he to be liable for damages to the agent? I can find no justification for such a view. I am assuming a commission contract not containing special terms such as to impose an obligation on the vendor actually to sell through the particular agent to the potential purchaser introduced by that agent. Contracts containing such terms, though not perhaps usual, are possible. But it is said that in the absence of special terms an obligation of that nature can be implied, subject, however, to the qualification that the owner retains his freedom to deal as he likes with his own and to discontinue negotiations, but only so long as in doing so he acts with reasonable excuse or just cause. I find it impossible to define these terms in this connection. If the commission agent has a right to claim commission or damages if the vendor abandons the negotiations and does not complete the sale, his doing so is a breach of contract vis-a-vis the agent and it is immaterial to the agent how sensible or reasonable the vendor's conduct may be from his own point of view. Such a qualified implication seems to me too complicated and artificial. The parties cannot properly be supposed to have intended it, nor can it be taken to be necessary to give business efficacy to the transaction. But I do not discuss this aspect further because, as already explained, I find no basis for the implication, whether general or qualified. And the great difficulty which the Courts have found in defining or applying the idea of 'just cause or reasonable excuse' further goes to show that it is not an implied term necessary to give business efficacy to what the parties must have intended. Nor is the suggested implication made more plausible by expressing it in a negative form as an implied term that the principal will not prevent the agent earning his commission. Such a term must be based upon something which under the contract the principal has agreed to do, of such a nature that failure to do it carries the consequence that the agent cannot earn the commission which would have become due if the principal had done what he had promised. For the purposes of the present problem this promise must be that he would complete the contract. Thus it all comes back to the same issue, namely, that there must be some breach of contract for which damages can be claimed.... It may seem hard that an agent who has introduced a potential purchaser, able and willing to complete, should get nothing for what he has done, if, during the negotiations, the principal decides not to complete, according to his own pleasure and without any reason which quoad the agent is a sufficient excuse. But such is the express contract. And people in ordinary life do not seek the services of commission agents without a good prospect and intention of making use of them. The agent in practice takes what is a business risk. I am assuming that the commission contract is of the type exemplified in this case. The agent may, however, secure a form of contract to which what I have said does not apply. But it is necessary to reserve certain eventualities in which an agent may be entitled to damages where there is a failure to complete even under a contract like the contract in this case. For instance, if the negotiations between the vendor and the purchaser have been duly concluded and a binding executory agreement has been achieved, different considerations may arise. The vendor is then no longer free to dispose of his property. Though the sale is not completed the property in equity has passed from him to the purchaser. If he refuses to complete he would be guilty of a breach of agreement vis-à-vis the purchaser. I think, as at present advised, that it ought then to be held that he is also in breach of his contract with the commission agent, that is, of some term which can properly be implied. But that question and possibly some other questions do not arise in this case and may be reserved. Furthermore, I have been dealing with a contract in regard to the sale of real property and there may be differences where the commission agency is in regard to transactions of a different character. On the whole, however, my opinion is that the contract in question means what it says, that the simple construction is the true construction and that there is no justification for the equitable reconstruction which the Court of Appeal, following authorities which bound it, has applied. I would allow the appeal....

It may be said that…on the view which I have been propounding, the prospect of the agent getting his reward is speculative and may be defeated by the arbitrary will of the principal. That may perhaps be so in some cases. But it is I think clear that under a contract like the present the agent takes a risk in several respects; thus, for instance, the principal may sell independently of the agent to a purchaser other than the purchaser introduced by him, or where the employment is not as sole agent, he may sell through another agent. Why should not the agent take the chance also of the employer changing his mind and deciding not to sell at all? It is said that according to the term which, it is suggested, should be implied he can change his mind if he has a reasonable excuse or just cause. But then why should his freedom to dispose of his property be fettered even in this way? And what is a reasonable excuse or just cause? Is it to be decided from the point of view of the owner or from the point of view of the commission agent? It is just the difficulty of applying these vague phrases which has already led to so much litigation on this question. In my opinion the implied term is unworkable. Even in this case Branson J has taken one view and the Court of Appeal another. If the suggested implied term is discarded, a contract such as the present will be simple and workable. Commission agents may sometimes fail to get the commission that they expected, but they will be relieved from disputes and litigation. And they can always, if they desire, demand what they consider a more favourable form of contract.

[Viscount Simon LC and Lord Romer delivered concurring opinions.
Lord Thankerton concurred with Lord Russell of Killowen's opinion.]

Company law students will be familiar with another aspect of this case, see *Regal (Hastings) Ltd v Gulliver* [1967] 2 AC 134n, [1942] 1 All ER 378, HL.

NOTES

1. Unless there is an express or implied promise to the contrary in the contract of agency, the principal is free to prevent his agent from earning commission. Such a promise may be implied by trade custom, or to give business efficacy to the agency contract, or otherwise to give effect to the intentions of the parties. But as *Luxor (Eastbourne) Ltd v Cooper* illustrates, the courts are generally reluctant to imply such a promise into an agency contract. This is particularly true where, as in *Luxor's* case itself, the implication of such a promise would restrict the principal's freedom to deal with his own property as he wished. For example, in *L French & Co Ltd v Leeston Shipping Co* [1922] 1 AC 451, a shipbroker' s right to commission depended on the continuation of the charterparty he had negotiated for his principal. But the House of Lords refused to imply a term into the shipbroker's agency contract to the effect that his principal, the shipowner, could not sell his ship to the charterer, thereby bringing the charterparty to a premature end. See also *Rhodes v Forwood* (1876) 1 App Cas 256; cf *Turner v Goldsmith* [1891] 1 QB 544 (both cases are considered below at pp 247–248); JF Burrows (1968) 31 MLR 390.

2. In *L French & Co Ltd v Leeston Shipping Co*, the shipbroker (agent) was deprived of commission because the shipowner (principal) and charterer (third party) agreed to terminate the charterparty. No term was to be implied into the agency agreement to prevent this. But a term may well be implied into the agency agreement to the effect that the principal must not break a contract negotiated by the agent with a third party and so deprive the agent of commission due on performance of that contract. In *Alpha Trading Ltd v Dunnshaw-Patten Ltd* [1981] QB 290 such a term was implied. In that case, agents negotiated a contract for the sale of cement by their principal to a third party. The principal breached the sale contract by failing to perform and settled the resulting claim made by the third party. The principal's failure to perform the sale contract prevented the agents earning commission under the terms of their agency contract. The Court of Appeal held that the principal was in breach of an implied term of the agency contract to the effect that he would not breach the sale contract with the third party so as to deprive the agents of their remuneration under the agency contract. *Alpha Trading* was followed in *Martin-Smith v Williams* [1999] EMLR 571, CA, where the principal waived future royalties on which the agent would have earned commission. But contrast *Marcan Shipping (London) Ltd v Polish Steamship Co, The Manifest Lipkowy* [1989] 2 Lloyd's Rep 138, where the Court of Appeal refused to imply a term into a collateral contract made between the agent and third party (the seller) to the effect that the *third party* would not breach a contract for the sale of a ship made between himself and the agent's principal (the buyer), and thereby deprive the agent of commission due under the agency contract made between the principal and agent.

3.   In *Alpha Trading Ltd v Dunnshaw-Pattern Ltd,* Brandon and Templeman LJJ accepted that the observations of Lord Wright in *Luxor (Eastbourne) Ltd v Cooper,* although made in the context of estate agency, were capable of being applied to contracts of agency in general. However, most contracts between estate agents and vendors are unilateral, so it is probably more accurate in such cases to speak in terms of an implied collateral contract, rather than an implied term, that the vendor will not deprive the agent of commission (*Bowstead and Reynolds,* paras 7-016 and 7-035). *Aliter,* where the vendor and agent enter into a 'sole agency' agreement whereby the vendor agrees not to sell his property through another agent. Sole agency agreements are generally regarded as bilateral contracts (*Bowstead and Reynolds,* para 7-036; cf JR Murdoch (1975) 91 LQR 357, pp 374–375). On estate agency agreements generally, see *Fridman,* pp 411–421; *Markesinis and Munday,* pp 125–130; see also JR Murdoch (1975) 91 LQR 357; *The Law of Estate Agency and Auctions* (4th edn, 2003).

(iv) Loss of right to commission

The agent will lose his right to commission if he:

(1) acts outside the scope of his actual authority (*Mason v Clifton* (1863) 3 F & F 899);

(2) acts in a manner which he knows, or ought to have known, to be unlawful (*Josephs v Pebrer* (1825) 3 B & C 639) or is otherwise dishonest (*Kelly v Cooper* [1993] AC 205, 216–217, per Lord Browne-Wilkinson, above, p 214); or

(3) commits a serious breach of his duties as agent (*Boston Deep Sea Fishing and Ice Co Ltd v Ansell* (1888) 39 Ch D 339, above, p 218), unless the agent effects severable transactions, when he will only lose his right to commission on those transactions in respect of which he is in breach of duty (but an honest agent will not lose his right to commission where his breach does not go to the root of the contract of agency: *Hippisley v Knee Bros* [1905] 1 KB 1, above, p 216).

Unless otherwise agreed, an agent is not entitled to commission on transactions which take place after termination of the agency contract (*Crocker Horlock Ltd v B Lang & Co Ltd* [1949] 1 All ER 526). But the agent's right to commission depends upon the construction of the terms of the agency contract. The agency contract may provide that the agent's right to commission accrues before the time when the commission becomes payable. When the right arises before termination, eg when the agent secures the order, commission must be paid, even if it only becomes payable after termination, eg when the order is executed (*Sellers v London Counties Newspapers* [1951] 1 KB 784; *Explora Group plc v Hesco Bastion Ltd* [2005] EWCA Civ 646). Particular difficulties may arise with the construction of terms providing for the payment of commission on 'repeat orders'.

(v) Commercial Agents

Part III of the Commercial Agents (Council Directive) Regulations 1993 deals with the remuneration of commercial agents (as defined in reg 2(1): see above, p 106). Regulation 6(1) provides that:

In the absence of any agreement as to remuneration between the parties, a commercial agent shall be entitled to the remuneration that commercial agents appointed for the goods forming the subject of his agency contract are customarily allowed in the place where he carries on his activities and, if there is no such customary practice, a commercial agent shall be entitled to reasonable remuneration taking into account all the aspects of the transaction.

Although reg 6(3) envisages that a commercial agent need not be remunerated by commission (it provides that regs 7 to 12 do not apply 'where a commercial agent is not remunerated (wholly or in part) by commission'), such agents are typically remunerated by commission. Under reg 7(1) the agent is 'entitled to commission' on 'commercial transactions concluded during the period covered by the agency contract—(a) when the transactions has been concluded as a result of his action; or (b) where the transaction is concluded with a third party whom he has previously acquired as a customer for transactions of the same kind.' It seems that a transaction may be 'concluded as a result of his action' even though the agent was not the effective cause of the transaction—the language of the regulation implies a laxer test (a conclusion reached by the distinguished editor of *Markesinis and Munday,* pp 124–125, who regards *Moore v Piretta PTA Ltd* [1999] 1 All ER 174, a case on the agent's right to an indemnity under reg 17(3), as lending support to this view: there the court held (at 180) that it was enough that the agent was 'instrumental' in winning business for the principal and that 'a small level of involvement is sufficient and it is enough that the agent has merely contributed to bringing the new customer ... the agent must have played an active role'). This interpretation is confirmed by the wording of reg 7(1)(b) and also by reg 8, which deals with the position of the agent's right to commission on business transacted after termination of the agency contract by providing that commission is payable on any transaction *'mainly attributable to his efforts during the period covered by the agency contract'* (emphasis added) which has been entered into within a reasonable period after termination of the contract (for examples of awards of post-termination commission under reg 8, see the decision of Morland J in *Ingmar GB Ltd v Eaton Leonard Inc* [2001] Eu LR 756, and the more fully reasoned judgment of Davis J in *Tigana Ltd v Decoro Ltd* [2003] EWHC 23 (QB), [2003] Eu LR 189). Moreover, the commercial agent is also entitled to commission where the transaction between the principal and third party was concluded in breach of an exclusive agency agreement (reg 7(2)). By reg 10(1) commission becomes due when (a) the principal has executed the transaction; or (b) he should have done so; or (c) the third party has executed the transaction. Regulation 10(2) provides that commission becomes due at the latest when the third party has executed his part of the transaction or should have done so if the principal had executed his part of it (there can be no derogation from this provision: reg 10(4)).

QUESTION

Why do estate agents fall outside the Commercial Agents (Council Directive) Regulations 1993?

(b) Reimbursement and indemnity

An agent has a right against his principal to be reimbursed all expenses and indemnified against all losses and liabilities incurred by him while acting within the scope of his express or implied *actual* authority.

Rhodes v Fielder, Jones and Harrison
(1919) 89 LJKB 159 King's Bench Division

A country solicitor instructed London solicitors to act as his agent in an appeal which was to be heard in the House of Lords. The London solicitors briefed counsel, who went on to win the case. The country solicitor then instructed the London solicitors not to pay counsel's fees, but the London solicitors paid the fees and reimbursed themselves out of monies of the country solicitor in their possession. The country solicitor then brought an action against the London solicitors to recover the monies so retained.

Lush J: …I now come to the second point taken by the plaintiffs, which is this: After the case had been heard in the House of Lords, and after consultations with counsel had been asked for and held, the plaintiff revoked the authority to the defendants to pay these fees, and it was argued that when country solicitors instruct London agents to brief counsel and, in the usual way, the agents have consultations with counsel and incur obligations towards counsel in respect of them which are fully recognized, the country solicitors can revoke their authority to their London agents to pay the counsel's fees. I can only say that to my mind such a proposition is absolutely unsustainable. It is, of course, the fact that the London agents could not be sued for these fees by counsel, but that does not dispose of the question. If they did not pay the fees they would be behaving in a way which would unquestionably place them in a serious position. I think it is right to say this, that a solicitor who has undertaken to pay fees to counsel and refuses to pay them is guilty of misconduct, and therefore it is impossible to say that it was open to the country solicitors in this case to revoke their authority. Authority for this was cited before the Master. The defendants did what they did at the request of the plaintiff, and made themselves responsible as honourable members of their profession for the payment of these fees. I think that the Master was perfectly right, and that the appeal must be dismissed.

Sankey J: As to the second point, I so entirely agree with what has fallen from my brother Lush that I think I should be wasting public time if I said anything further. To my mind it is entirely unarguable.

Appeal dismissed.

NOTES

1.   Where the agency is contractual, the agent's right to reimbursement and indemnity arises as an express or implied term of the contract. However, the right may be expressly excluded by the parties, or by a term implied through the custom of the trade (eg unless otherwise agreed, estate agents are not entitled to claim reimbursement for advertising expenses over and above their commission). The agent's contractual right to reimbursement and indemnity is wide. It covers not only payment of debts which are legally binding on the principal, but also payments which the agent is legally bound to make though the principal is not (*Adams v Morgan & Co* [1924] 1 KB 751) and payments which the agent is under a strong moral obligation to meet (*Rhodes v Fielder, Jones and Harrison*, above).

2.   Where the agency is gratuitous, the agent has only a restitutionary right to reimbursement of payments which he was compelled to make for the benefit of his principal and which

the principal would have been ultimately liable to make himself (see generally Goff and Jones *The Law of Restitution* (7th edn, 2007), Ch 15). However, if a gratuitous agent can rely on an equitable right to indemnity, eg as a trustee or surety, he may be able to obtain a wider indemnity than that which arises under the restitutionary remedy.

3.   The agent has no right to reimbursement for expenses, or to an indemnity for losses and liabilities, incurred in any of the following circumstances:

(1)   when he exceeds his actual authority (*Barron v Fitzgerald* (1840) 6 Bing NC 201), unless his unauthorised acts are subsequently ratified by his principal;

(2)   as a result of the agent's breach of duty, negligence, default, or insolvency (*Lage v Siemens Bros & Co Ltd* (1932) 42 Ll L Rep 252); or

(3)   in the performance of acts which the agent knows, or ought reasonably to know, are unlawful (*Re Parker* (1882) 21 Ch D 408), but the agent may be entitled to a contribution from his principal under the Civil Liability (Contribution) Act 1978.

(c) Lien

To secure his rights of remuneration, reimbursement or indemnity, the agent may be able to exercise a lien over goods belonging to his principal which are in his possession. In general, the lien gives the agent the right to detain his principal's goods until he is paid what he is owed by the principal in respect of those goods, ie it is usually a particular lien (but see below, pp 1111–1113, as to when a general lien may arise). But the agent can only exercise a lien over his principal's goods if he lawfully acquired possession of them in the course of the agency (*Taylor v Robinson* (1818) 2 Moore CP 730), and he holds them in the same capacity as that in which he claims the lien (*Dixon v Stansfeld* (1850) 10 CB 398). Furthermore, an agent's right to exercise a lien may be excluded by the express or implied terms of the agency contract (*Wolstenholm v Sheffield Union Banking Co* (1886) 54 LT 746).

A sub-agent may also be able to exercise a lien over the principal's goods, even though the sub-agent's claims for remuneration, reimbursement and indemnity are against the appointing agent and not the principal. To exercise such a lien the appointment of the sub-agent must have been authorised by the principal (actual or apparent authority of the appointing agent will do): see *Solly v Rathbone* (1814) 2 M & S 298, where it was held that there was no right of lien because the sub-delegation was unauthorised. So long as the sub-delegation is authorised the sub-agent may exercise his lien, even though the appointing agent may have no authority to create privity of contract between the principal and the sub-agent. Where the principal authorises sub-delegation by his agent, but the principal remains undisclosed, the sub-agent may exercise a lien over the principal's goods to secure any claim he may have against the appointing agent, so long as the claim arose before the sub-agent discovered the truth (*Mann v Forrester* (1814) 4 Camp 60). For detailed discussion of the nature of a lien, and also the way it may be acquired and lost, see below, pp 1106ff. See also *Markesinis and Munday,* pp 134–140, for a useful account of the agent's lien.

QUESTION

If an agent is under a fiduciary duty not to place himself in a position where his own interests conflict with those of his principal (above, p 210), how can an agent ever exercise a lien over his principal's goods without being in breach of fiduciary duty? See *Compania Financiera*

Soleada SA v Hamoor Tanker Corpn Inc, The Borag [1980] 1 Lloyd's Rep 111 at 122, per Mustill J, reversed on other grounds [1981] 1 WLR 274.

3 TERMINATION OF AGENCY

(a) Termination of the relationship between principal and agent

Campanari v Woodburn
(1854) 15 CB 400, Court of Common Pleas

P agreed to pay A £100 if A sold P's picture. P died before the picture was sold. Unaware of P's death, A sold the picture and claimed £100 from P's administratrix. Although the administratrix confirmed the sale she refused to pay A his commission. A then sued the administratrix for his commission.

Jervis CJ: I am of opinion that the defendant in this case is entitled to the judgment of the court. As alleged on the face of the declaration, it does not appear that the original contract between the plaintiff and the intestate conferred upon the former an authority which was irrevocable: it simply states that it was agreed between the plaintiff and the intestate that the plaintiff should endeavour to sell a certain picture of the intestate, and that, if the plaintiff succeeded in selling the same, the intestate should pay him £100. So far, therefore, as appears in the declaration, it was a mere employment of the plaintiff to do the act, not carrying with it any irrevocable authority. It is plain that the intestate might in his life-time have revoked the authority, without rendering himself liable to be called upon to pay the £100, though possibly the plaintiff might have had a remedy for a breach of the contract, if the intestate had wrongfully revoked his authority after he had been put to expense in endeavouring to dispose of the picture. In that way, perhaps, the plaintiff might have recovered damages by reason of the revocation. His death, however, was a revocation by the act of God, and the administratrix is not, in my judgment, responsible for anything. It was no fault of hers,—as in *Smout v Ibery* ((1842) 10 M & W 1)—that the contract was not carried out. It must be taken to have been part of the original compact between the plaintiff and the intestate, that, whereas, on the one hand, he would receive a large sum if he succeeded in selling the picture, so, on the other hand, he would take the chance of his authority to sell being revoked by death or otherwise. Mr Maude seems to concede, that, but for what took place subsequently to the death of the intestate, the administratrix would have been liable: but he relies upon the allegation in the declaration, that the plaintiff sold the picture, and that the sale was confirmed by the defendant as administratrix; and contends that therefore she is liable. But it seems to me that that consequence by no means follows. If the defendant as administratrix had, after the death of the intestate, ordered the sale of the picture, no doubt that would have been a new retainer, and she would have been liable to the plaintiff on a quantum meruit. If, with full knowledge of the contract under which the plaintiff was to receive £100 as the stipulated reward for his exertions in selling the picture, the defendant had continued the employment, and it had resulted in a sale, the £100 might have been taken by the jury as the measure of damages. But, without shewing that the defendant had any knowledge whatever of the original contract, the confirmation of the sale is relied on as a confirmation of the original contract. It is enough to say that the averment as to the confirmation of the sale by the defendant does not raise the point which Mr Maude desires to raise. That confirmation, however it might make her liable to an action for a reasonable remuneration for the plaintiff s services, clearly is not sufficient to charge the defendant either personally or in her representative character for the breach of the original contract.

Williams J: I am of the same opinion. It may be convenient to consider what the effect would have been if the declaration had omitted the averment of confirmation of the sale by the defendant. It would then have amounted to a mere statement of an agreement between the plaintiff and the intestate that the plaintiff should endeavour to sell the picture, and, if he succeeded in so doing, the intestate should pay him £100. That clearly would have been revoked by the death. In such a state of things, the mere circumstance of something having been done under the contract, does not make it irrevocable. The contract, after the death of the intestate, was not and could not be confirmed according to its terms. It is perfectly clear, that, if the count had stood without the allegation that the administratrix confirmed the sale, it would have been utterly without foundation. What, then, is the effect of that averment? There is no allegation that the contract was confirmed as between the plaintiff and the deceased; but merely an allegation that the sale was confirmed by the defendant as administratrix. That is manifestly different from an averment that the original contract was confirmed by her, with all its incidents and all its consequences. I do not think it necessary,—though I entertain no doubt on the point,—to give any opinion as to what would have been the effect, if the declaration had contained such an allegation. The utmost that can be said is, that the defendant, as administratrix, might have been liable on a quantum meruit for services performed by the plaintiff as her agent in relation to the sale: but she clearly could not be liable in the way in which she is sought to be charged here.

[Crowder J delivered a concurring judgment.]

Frith v Frith
[1906] AC 254, Privy Council

The appellant had been appointed by a power of attorney to take possession of and manage an estate owned by the respondent. The estate was mortgaged to a third party and the appellant gave a personal guarantee that he would pay the mortgage debt. Neither the mortgage debt nor the guarantee were mentioned in the power of attorney. Later the respondent revoked the appellant's authority and demanded possession of the estate from him. The appellant refused to give up possession on the ground that his authority was coupled with an interest, and was, therefore, irrevocable. The Privy Council held that the appellant's authority was revocable.

Lord Atkinson (delivering the advice of the Privy Council (Earl of Halsbury, Lord Davey, Lord Robertson, Lord Atkinson, and Sir Arthur Wilson)): . . . [I]t cannot be disputed that the general rule of law is that employment of the general character of the appellant's in this case can be terminated at the will of the employer. The proper conduct of the affairs of life necessitates that this should be so. The exception to this rule within which the appellant must bring himself, if he is to succeed, is that where 'an agreement is entered into for sufficient consideration, and either forms part of a security, or is given for the purpose of securing some benefit to the donee of the authority, such authority is irrevocable': Story on Agency, s 476.

It cannot be contended that the ordinary case of an agent or manager employed for pecuniary reward in the shape of a fixed salary comes within this exception, though his employment confers a benefit upon him. And their Lordships are of opinion that the position of the appellant under the instruments appointing him attorney over this estate is in law that of an ordinary agent or manager employed at a salary, and nothing more because the authority which was conferred upon him contains no reference to the special interest in the occupation of his post which his guarantee to Astwood might have given him, was not expressed or intended to be used for the purpose of subserving that interest, and has no connection with it. For these reasons their Lordships think that the authority given to the appellant was revocable. Several cases have been cited by the appellant's counsel in support of his . . . contention. On an examination of them it will be found that the essential distinction between this case and those cited is this, that in each of the latter power and authority were given to a particular individual to do a particular thing, the doing of which conferred a benefit upon him, the authority ceasing when the benefit was reaped, while in this case, as already pointed out, nothing of that kind was ever provided for or contemplated. In *Carmichael's Case* ([1896] 2 Ch 643) the donor of the power, for valuable consideration, conferred upon the donee authority to do a particular thing in which the latter had an interest, namely, to apply for the shares of the company which the donee was promoting for the purpose of purchasing his own property from him, and the donor sought to revoke that authority before the benefit was reaped. In *Spooner v Sandilands* ((1842) 1 Y & C Ch Cas 390) the donor charged his lands with certain debts due and to accrue due to the donees, and put the latter into the possession of those lands and into receipt of the rents and profits of them, for the express purpose of enabling the donees to discharge thereout these same debts; and it was sought to eject the donees before their debts were paid. In *Clerk v Laurie* ((1857) 2 H & N 199) a wife pledged to a bank dividends to which she was entitled to secure advances made to her husband. It was held that while the advances remained unpaid, she could not revoke the bank's authority to receive the dividends. In *Smart v Sandars* ((1848) 5 CB 895) it was decided that the general authority of a factor in whose hands goods were placed for sale, to sell at the best price which could reasonably be obtained, could not be revoked after the factor had made advances on the security of the goods to the owner of them, and while these advances remained unpaid.

NOTES

1.   The principal may terminate his agent's authority by revocation (whether or not this constitutes a breach of contract), so long as the agent has not already fulfilled his obligations. The agent's authority can also be terminated by the following means:

(1)   execution of the agent's commission (*Blackburn v Scholes* (1810) 2 Camp 341);

(2)   if the agent was appointed for a fixed period, expiry of that period (*Dickinson v Lilwal* (1815) 4 Camp 279);

(3)   agreement between the principal and agent;

(4)   destruction of the subject matter of the agency (*Rhodes v Forwood* (1876) 1 App Cas 256; see below, p 247);

(5)   frustration of the agency rendering its performance illegal, impossible or radically different from what the parties originally contemplated (*Marshall v Glanvill* [1917] 2 KB 87);

(6)   the death, insanity or bankruptcy of the principal or the agent, or, where the principal or agent is a company, its winding-up or dissolution (see, eg *Pacific and General Insurance Co Ltd v Hazell* [1997] BCC 400, Moore-Bick J, provisional liquidator placed in control of corporate principal)—but cessation of the agent's business does not automatically terminate the agency relationship (*Triffit Nurseries (a firm) v Salads Etcetera Ltd* [1999] 1 All ER (Comm) 110, 114, Longmore J, affirmed by the Court of Appeal [2000] 1 All ER (Comm) 737, but where doubts are cast on the quesion of revocation of authority by appointment of a receiver): see below, pp 258–261;

(7)   notice of renunciation of the agency given by the agent and accepted by the principal.

2.   *Irrevocable agency*:[3] an agent's authority cannot be revoked by the principal without the agent's consent, or determined by the death, insanity or bankruptcy of the principal, in any of the following circumstances:

---

[3]   See generally F Reynolds 'When is an Agent's Authority Irrevocable?', ch 10 in R Cranston (ed) *Making Commercial Law: Essays in Honour of Roy Goode* (1997).

(1) where the authority of the agent is given by deed, or for valuable consideration, for the purpose of securing or protecting any interest of the agent (*Frith v Frith,* above);

(2) where the agent's authority is given under a power of attorney which is expressed to be irrevocable and is given to secure a proprietary interest of, or the performance of an obligation owed to, the agent (so long as the interest or obligation continues): Powers of Attorney Act 1971, s 4—also note that any lasting power of attorney created under the Mental Capacity Act 2005, and any enduring power of attorney created under the Enduring Power of Attorney Act 1985 (which was repealed by the 2005 Act), is not revoked by the supervening mental incapacity of the donor (MCA 2005, ss 9(1), 13, 66 and Sch 4);

(3) where the agent during the currency of the agency contract has incurred personal liability in the performance of his authority for which the principal must indemnify him (see, eg *Chappell v Bray* (1860) 6 H & N 145; *Read v Anderson* (1884) 13 QBD 779)— although these cases are usually treated as examples of irrevocable authority they are 'better regarded…as examples of circumstances giving rise to the right to be indemnified which in fact rests on wider [contractual, or even restitutionary] principles and which does not depend for its application on continuing authority' (*Pacific and General Insurance Co Ltd v Hazell* [1997] BCC 400, 409–410, per Moore-Bick J, applying *Bowstead and Reynolds,* para 10-010).

3. Termination of the agent's authority is prospective and not retrospective. Both principal and agent will be entitled to sue one another on claims which accrued before termination, eg the principal can sue the agent for the negligent performance of his duties; the agent can sue the principal for remuneration already earned. If the agency is contractual, the very act of termination, whilst effective to end the agent's actual authority, may itself give rise to a claim for breach of contract. This can occur, for example, when the principal revokes the agent's authority without notice. In most cases where the agent is engaged under a bilateral contract (which is not for a fixed term, nor specifies a notice period), the agency will only be terminable on reasonable notice (*Martin-Baker Aircraft Co Ltd v Canadian Flight Equipment Ltd* [1955] 2 QB 556), unless the agent has committed a repudiatory breach of contract so that the principal is entitled to terminate the contract summarily (*Boston Deep Sea Fishing and Ice Co v Ansell* (1888) 39 Ch D 339, see above, p 218). But where the principal has made the agent an offer of a unilateral contract (eg as with an estate agent who is not a sole agent: *Luxor (Eastbourne) Ltd v Cooper* [1941] AC 108; above, p 236) the principal can generally withdraw his offer at will.

4. Some agency agreements are for a fixed period. The question then arises whether the principal will be in breach of the agreement if he goes out of business, or disposes of the subject matter of the agency, before the end of that period and thereby prevents the agent from earning further commission. As the following cases illustrate, the answer depends on the court's construction of the terms of the particular agency agreement in issue.

(1) *Rhodes v Forwood* (1876) 1 App Cas 256: Rhodes, a colliery owner, employed Forwood as sole agent to sell the colliery's coal in Liverpool for seven years. Rhodes sold the colliery and went out of business after four years. Forwood sued Rhodes for breach of the agency contract. The House of Lords rejected Forwood's claim holding that there was no express or implied term of the agency contract that the agreement must continue to seven years. The agency contract had been made subject to the risk that Rhodes might sell the colliery.

(2) *Turner v Goldsmith* [1891] 1 QB 544: Goldsmith, a shirt manufacturer, employed Turner for a period of five years to sell 'the various goods manufactured or sold' by Goldsmith. After two years Goldsmith's shirt factory burnt down and he closed down his business. Turner sued Goldsmith for breach of the agency contract. Reversing the judgment of the trial judge in favour of Goldsmith, the Court of Appeal refused to imply a term making the agency contract subject to the continued existence of the factory. On a true construction of the agency contract, Goldsmith could supply Turner with shirts manufactured by someone else or with other goods altogether.

For further consideration of this issue, see above, pp 239–240.

(b) Commercial agents[4]

The Commercial Agents (Council Directive) Regulations 1993 contain detailed, and in many respects novel, provisions dealing with termination of the agency contract of a commercial agent as defined therein (see above, p 106).

(1) Minimum periods of notice for termination

Where there is an agency contract for a fixed period, and it continues to be performed by both parties after the expiry of the period, reg 14 provides that it 'shall be deemed to be converted' into an agency contract for an indefinite period. Regulations 15 provides that 'where an agency contract is concluded for an indefinite period either party may terminate it by notice'. Regulation 15(2) sets out *minimum* periods of notice (the parties may agree longer periods): one month for the first year of the contract; two months for the second year commenced; and three months for the third year commenced or for the subsequent years. These minimum notice requirements do not prevent immediate termination where the contract is discharged by breach or frustration (reg 16). The breach must be a repudiatory breach (*Crane v Sky In-Home Service Ltd* [2007] EWHC 66 (Ch), [2007] 2 All ER (Comm) 599 at [84], Briggs J).

(2) Indemnity and compensation

Regulation 17(1) provides that on termination of his agency the commercial agent is entitled to be 'indemnified . . . or compensated for damage'. This entitlement results from the idea that an agent may spend money, time and effort establishing a market and goodwill for his principal, but then be deprived of the benefit of his investment through termination of his authority by a principal who seeks to deal directly with customers or employ another agent to do so (*Bowstead and Reynolds,* para 11-038). In effect, the Regulations provide for the agent to be 'bought out' by his principal. The concept of indemnity and compensation have their origins in German and French law respectively. Both concepts are new to English law, which has hitherto only been prepared to award an agent damages on termination of the agency where there has been breach of the agency contract by his principal. By contrast, the availability of an indemnity or compensation payable under the regulations is not based on fault.

Regulation 17(2) provides that 'except where the agency contract otherwise provides, the commercial agent shall be entitled to be compensated rather than indemnified'. In other words, the parties must have opted into the indemnity provisions: compensation is the

---

[4] See, generally, *Bowstead and Reynolds,* Ch 11, and for further detail, Saintier and Scholes, *Commercial Agents and the Law* (2005); Randolph and Davey, *Guide to the Commercial Agents Regulations* (2nd edn, 2003).

default position. According to reg 17(3), the agent is entitled to an indemnity if and to the extent that:

(a) he has brought the principal new customers or has significantly increased the volume of business with existing customers and the principal continues to derive substantial benefits from the business with such customers; and

(b) the payment of this indemnity is equitable having regard to all the circumstances and, in particular, the commission lost by the commercial agent on the business transacted with such customers.

It seems from this provision that an indemnity will only be payable where the principal continues to do business after termination of the agency agreement: in this respect compensation is more advantageous to the agent as it can apply even where the principal has ceased to trade. Furthermore, unlike a claim to compensation, there is a cap on the amount of the indemnity: it must not exceed a figure equivalent to an indemnity for one year calculated from the agent's average annual remuneration over the preceding five years or over the actual length of the agency contract if it was less than five years (reg 17(4)). However, the right to an indemnity does not preclude the agent from seeking damages from his former principal (reg 17(5)).

An agent made a successful claim for an indemnity in *Moore v Piretta PTA Ltd* [1999] 1 All ER 174. The key issue in the case was whether the agent's entitlement should be based on his contribution to the principal's business during the entire term of his agency (seven years) or only during the period of his last written contract (one year). The judge held that the phrase 'agency contract' in reg 17(1) means the agency as a whole rather than the particular contract in place at the date of termination. He further held that an agent brings in new customers for the purposes of reg 17(3)(a) if he is instrumental in obtaining the customer's business: it does not matter that there are other factors at work. Finally, the judge emphasised that purpose of the indemnity is to award the agent a share in the goodwill built up by his efforts: the court is determining the proper value of that goodwill, it is not assessing the agent's 'loss', so mitigation of loss is not a relevant issue.

By reg 17(6) an agent is 'entitled to compensation for the damage he suffers as a result of the termination of his relations with his principal'. For these purposes, damage is deemed to occur particularly when the termination takes place in either or both of the following circumstances, namely circumstances which:

(a) deprive the commercial agent of the commission which proper performance of the agency contract would have procured for him whilst providing his principal with substantial benefits linked to the activities of the commercial agent; or

(b) have not enabled the commercial agent to amortize the costs and expenses that he had incurred in the performance of the agency contract on the advice of his principal.

The rationale behind the post-termination payment of compensation is that the commercial agent, having worked to establish and develop the goodwill of the principal's business, has a quasi-proprietary interest in the agency and should be compensated for the loss of that interest (see C Gardiner [2007] JBL 412, 426 ff). It is the idea of loss to the agent, and not gain to the principal, that is behind the compensation scheme. The method for calculating the compensation payable to the agent was recently clarified by the House of Lords in *Lonsdale v Howard & Hallam Ltd* [2007] UKHL 32, [2007] 1 WLR 2005, where Lord Hoffmann held (at [12]) that 'what has to be valued is the income stream which the agency would have generated' and (at [21]) that compensation should be calculated 'by reference to the value of the agency on the assumption that it continued'. An extended extract from this important decision appears below. There does, however, remain uncertainty as to whether compensation may be claimed in addition to any common law damages due to the agent on termination of the agency. The right to claim damages is expressly preserved by reg 17(5) in respect of an indemnity but the regulations are silent as to the position with regard to compensation. There is nothing in the regulations to suggest that the compensation scheme overrides other remedies for breach of duty (*Lonsdale v Howard & Hallam Ltd* [2006] EWCA Civ 63, [2006] 1 WLR 1281 at [28], Moore-Bick LJ).

Although the indemnity or compensation provisions apply in a wide variety of circumstances (including where termination of the agency contract is due to the agent's death: reg 17(8), and also where the agency contract has expired by effluxion of time: see *Tigana Ltd v Decoro Ltd*, [2003] EWHC 23 (QB), [2003] Eu LR 189 at [79], as approved by the Court of Appeal, obiter, in *Light v Ty Europe Ltd* [2003] EWCA Civ 1238, [2004] 1 Lloyd's Rep 693 at [32], [46] and [53]). There are a few occasions where the entitlement does not arise or is lost. According to reg 18, an indemnity or compensation will not be payable to the commercial agent where: (a) the principal terminates the agency contract because of the agent's repudiatory breach; or (b) the commercial agent himself terminates the agency contract (unless (i) such termination is 'justified by circumstances attributable to the principal', or (ii) on grounds of the age, infirmity or illness of the agent: eg in *Abbott v Condici Ltd* [2005] 2 Lloyd's Rep 450, the agent was held to be entitled to compensation when he reached normal retirement age even though he was healthy and fit); or (c) the commercial agent, with the agreement of the principal, assigns his rights and duties under the agency contract to another person. In *Bell Electric Ltd v Aweco Appliance Systems GmbH & Co KG*, above, at para [54], Elias J considered the meaning of reg 18(a) and 18(b) and stated that:

[I]n my judgment the better view is that reg 18(a) and 18(b)(i) ought to be seen as the reverse sides of the same coin. In other words, the compensation is not payable if the principal terminates in circumstances which would be justifiable at common law because of the agent's conduct; but on the other hand it is payable if the commercial agent terminates in circumstances which are justifiable at common law because of the conduct of the principal. In either case, if the innocent party affirms the contract and precludes the right to rely on the repudiatory breach, the attempt thereafter to terminate the contract, absent some fresh repudiatory breach, will not be justifiable within the meaning of the regulations.

In *Cooper v Pure Fishing (UK) Ltd* [2004] EWCA Civ 375, [2004] 2 Lloyd's Rep 518 at [15], Tuckey LJ stated that reg 18(a) only applies, and an indemnity or compensation is not payable on this ground, where two conditions are met: the principal must 'have terminated' the contract, which means he must have done something unilaterally to bring the contract to an end, and he must do this because of the agent's default. The principal's decision not to renew an agency contract which expired by effluxion of time, even where the decision was based on the agent's default, was held not to fall within reg 18(a) and so compensation was not precluded.

The commercial agent loses his right to an indemnity or compensation if within one year following termination of the agency contract he does not notify his former principal that he intends to pursue his entitlement (reg 17(9)). All the agent need do is give notice of his intention to pursue a claim under reg 17, he does not have to specify whether his claim is to an indemnity or to compensation (*Hackett v Advanced Medical Computer Systems Ltd* [1999] CLC 160, 163).

The parties cannot contract out of regs 17 and 18 'to the detriment of the commercial agent before the agency contract expires' (reg 19). In *Crane v Sky In-Home Service Ltd* [2007]

EWHC 66 (Ch), [2007] 2 All ER (Comm) 599 at [93], Briggs J stated (obiter) that where a contract purported to exclude both indemnity and compensation, the agent would nevertheless be entitled to compensation.

Lonsdale v Howard & Hallam Ltd
[2007] UKHL 32, [2007] 1 WLR 2055, House of Lords

Graham Lonsdale was a commercial agent in the shoe trade. In 1990 Howard & Hallam Ltd, a shoe manufacturer, appointed him as their agent to sell their Elmdale brand in south-east England. A few years later he was appointed by a German manufacturer to sell their Wendel brand in a slightly larger territory. Wendel shoes sold well but Elmdale shoes did not. Sales, and with them Lonsdale's commission income, fell year by year. In 2003 Howard & Hallam ceased trading and duly terminated Lonsdale's agency on the appropriate notice. Lonsdale made a claim for compensation under the 1993 regulations. The trial judge found that the net annual commission was about £8,000 and assessed the appropriate measure of compensation as £5,000. The judge refused to apply the French approach to the 1986 underlying European Directive, whereby the agent was usually awarded two years' gross commission. Both the Court of Appeal and the House of Lords dismissed Lonsdale's appeal.

Lord Hoffmann: [His Lordship set out the terms of art 17 of the 1986 EC Directive on the co-ordination of the laws of the member states relating to self-employed commercial agents, and continued:]

[5]. It will be noticed that although the purpose of the directive is said to be the coordination of the laws of the Member States relating to self-employed commercial agents, article 17 allows Member States to choose between two different rights, one or other of which must be accorded to a commercial agent on the termination of the agency. He must be given a right to either an indemnity in accordance with article 17(2) or compensation in accordance with article 17(3). The English words 'indemnity' and 'compensation' are not very illuminating in marking the distinction between these two rights. They are both ways of dealing with the unfairness which it was thought might arise if the termination of the agency leaves the agent worse off and the principal better off than if the agency had continued. It appears that the right under article 17(2), which the draftsman has chosen to label 'indemnity', is derived from German law and is now contained in section 89b of the *Handelsgesetzbuch*. The right to 'compensation' under article 17(3) is derived from French law and is now contained in article 12 of the *Loi no 91-593 du 25 juin 1991 relative aux rapports entre les agents commerciaux et leurs mandants*. The two systems can plainly lead to different results, so that, on this point at any rate, the extent of the coordination achieved by the directive is modest.

[6]. The United Kingdom chose both systems, in the sense that it allowed the parties to opt for an indemnity under article 17(2) but provided that in default of agreement the agent should be entitled to compensation under article 17(3): see regulation 17(2). In the present case the parties made no choice and Mr Lonsdale is therefore entitled to compensation under article 17(3).

[7]. The question in this appeal is how the compensation should be determined. But for this purpose it is necessary first to decide exactly what the agent should be compensated for. Only then can one proceed to consider how the compensation should be calculated.

[8]. On this first question the directive is explicit. The agent is entitled to be compensated for 'the damage he suffers as a result of the termination of his relations with the principal.' In other words, the agent is treated as having lost something of value as a result of the termination and is entitled to compensation for this loss.

[9]. As this part of the directive is based on French law, I think that one is entitled to look at French law for guidance, or confirmation, as to what it means. Article 12 of the French law says that the agent is entitled to 'une indemnité compensatrice en réparation du préjudice subi'. The French jurisprudence

from which the terms of the article is derived appears to regard the agent as having had a share in the goodwill of the principal's business which he has helped to create. The relationship between principal and agent is treated as having existed for their common benefit. They have co-operated in building up the principal's business: the principal by providing a good product and the agent by his skill and effort in selling. The agent has thereby acquired a share in the goodwill, an asset which the principal retains after the termination of the agency and for which the agent is therefore entitled to compensation: see *Saintier and Scholes*, Commercial Agents and the Law (2005) at pp 175–177.

[10]. This elegant theory explains why the French courts regard the agent as, in principle, entitled to compensation. It does not, however, identify exactly what he is entitled to compensation for. One possibility might have been to value the total goodwill of the principal's business and then to try to attribute some share to the agent. But this would in practice be a hopeless endeavour and the French courts have never tried to do it. Instead, they have settled upon compensating him for what he has lost by being deprived of his business. That is the '*préjudice subi.*' The French case law makes it clear that this ordinarily involves placing a value upon the right to be an agent. That means, primarily, the right to future commissions 'which proper performance of the agency contract would have procured him': see *Saintier and Scholes*, op.cit, pp. 187–188. In my opinion this is the right for which the directive requires the agent to be compensated.

[11]. Having thus determined that the agent is entitled to be compensated for being deprived of the benefit of the agency relationship, the next question is how that loss should be calculated. The value of the agency relationship lies in the prospect of earning commission, the agent's expectation that 'proper performance of the agency contract' will provide him with a future income stream. It is this which must be valued.

[12]. Like any other exercise in valuation, this requires one to say what could reasonably have been obtained, at the date of termination, for the rights which the agent had been enjoying. For this purpose it is obviously necessary to assume that the agency would have continued and the hypothetical purchaser would have been able properly to perform the agency contract. He must be assumed to have been able to take over the agency and (if I may be allowed the metaphor) stand in the shoes of the agent, even if, as a matter of contract, the agency was not assignable or there were in practice no dealings in such agencies: compare *Inland Revenue Commissioners v Crossman* [1937] AC 26. What has to be valued is the income stream which the agency would have generated.

[13]. On the other hand, as at present advised, I see no reason to make any other assumptions contrary to what was the position in the real world at the date of termination. As one is placing a present value upon future income, one must discount future earnings by an appropriate rate of interest. If the agency was by its terms or in fact unassignable, it must be assumed, as I have said, that the hypothetical purchaser would have been entitled to take it over. But there is no basis for assuming that he would then have obtained an assignable asset: compare the Crossman case. Likewise, if the market for the products in which the agent dealt was rising or declining, this would have affected what a hypothetical purchaser would have been willing to give. He would have paid fewer years' purchase for a declining agency than for one in an expanding market. If the agent would have had to incur expense or do work in earning his commission, it cannot be assumed that the hypothetical purchaser would have earned it gross or without having to do anything.

[14]. Mr Philip Moser, who appeared for Mr Lonsdale, objected that this method of calculation was likely to produce less than he would have been awarded by a French court. And it does appear that it is common practice for French courts to value agencies at twice the average annual gross commission over the previous three years. Mr Moser said that in stipulating that agents should receive compensation under article 17(3), the directive was adopting the French practice as Community law. This, he said, was confirmed by the report on the application of article 17 (COM(96) 364 final) which the Commission, pursuant to article 17(6), had issued in 1996. It noted that a body of case law had developed in France concerning the level of compensation. By 'judicial custom', this was fixed as two years' commission, which, they said 'conforms with commercial practice'. However, the courts retained a discretion to

award less when 'the agent's loss was in fact less.' The report said that in France the directive had made no difference: 'pre-existing jurisprudence has continued to be applied.' In England, however, there had been difficulties of interpretation. There was, at that stage, no case law but 'the parties in practice are attempting to apply common law principles'. In particular, it was difficult to see how these principles would enable the courts to reach the figure of twice gross commission which was regularly awarded by French courts. The Commission said that there was 'a need for clarification' of article 17. But nothing has been done about it.

[15]. Mr Moser invited your Lordships to treat the Commission as having indorsed the French method of calculating compensation under article 17(3) as the appropriate interpretation of that article as a Community instrument. It would follow that all Member States which adopt article 17(3) would be bound to treat twice gross commission as the normal compensation for termination of an agency, subject to variation in exceptional cases in which the principal could prove that the actual loss was less or the agent could prove that it was more. If your Lordships did not accept this as the plain and obvious meaning of the directive, he submitted that the question should be referred to the Court of Justice.

[16]. My Lords, I do not accept this submission, to which I think there are at least three answers. First, the Commission report was not indorsing any method of calculation as a true reflection of Community law. That was not its function. The Commission was required by article 17(6) to report on the implementation of the Article, and, if necessary, to submit proposals for amendments. It reported on the basis of information supplied by Member States and noted that the UK position (so far as it could be ascertained in the absence of any judicial pronouncement) was different from the French. But there is no suggestion that either approach would fail to implement the directive.

[17]. Secondly, the provisions of article 17(3) which say what the agent is entitled to be compensated for are perfectly plain. It is the damage which he suffers as a result of the termination. The French domestic law, as I have pointed out, says exactly the same. Where French and English courts differ is in the method by which that damage is calculated. But the Court of Justice has made it clear that the method of calculation is a matter for each Member State to decide. In *Case C-465/04 Honeyvem Informazioni Commerciali Srl v Mariella De Zotti* [2006] ECR I-02879 at paragraphs 34–36 the Court of Justice said:

> 34. …It must be observed that although the system established by article 17 of the Directive is mandatory and prescribes a framework…it does not give any detailed indications as regards the method of calculation of the indemnity for termination of contract.
>
> 35. The Court thus held that, within that framework, the Member States may exercise their discretion as to the choice of methods for calculating the indemnity [Case C-381/98 *Ingmar GB Ltd v Eaton Leonard Technologies Inc* [2000] ECR I-9305 at paragraph 21]
>
> 36. Therefore…within the framework prescribed by article 17(2) of the Directive, the Member States enjoy a margin of discretion which they may exercise…

[18]. Thirdly, it seems that commercial agencies in France operate in market conditions which are different from those prevailing in England. It would appear that in France agencies do change hands and that it is common for the premium charged on such a transaction to be twice the gross commission. Whether the judicial practice of estimating the value of the agency at twice gross commission is based upon this fact of French economic life or whether vendors of agency businesses are able to charge such a premium because the purchaser knows that he will be able to recover that amount, either from the next purchaser or from the principal on termination of the agency, is unclear. *Saintier and Scholes*, op.cit, at p. 187 describe it as a 'chicken-and-egg process'. There does seem to be evidence that some principals demand payment of an estimated twice gross commission in return for the grant of a commercial agency (even if they have to lend the agent the money) because they know that they will have to return this amount to the agent on termination. At any rate, whatever the origins of the practice, it would appear that twice gross commission is often the real value of an agency in France because that is what you could sell it for in the market. As the Commission significantly remarked, the French system

'conforms with commercial practice'. There is no such market in England. It would therefore appear that the difference between French and English practice exists not because their respective courts are applying different rules of law but because they are operating in different markets.

[19]. Mr Moser said that the adoption of anything less favourable to commercial agents than the French method of calculation would not give effect to the purpose of the directive, which is to protect the interests of the commercial agent. No doubt this is one of its purposes: in *Page v Combined Shipping and Trading Co Ltd* [1997] 3 All ER 656, 660 Staughton LJ said, with more than a touch of irony, that the directive appeared to be based upon a belief that 'commercial agents are a downtrodden race, and need and should be afforded protection against their principals.' But these are generalities which do not help one to decide what protection is sufficient to give effect to the policy of the directive. One may however obtain a useful cross-check by considering what an agent could obtain under a system which provided him with an indemnity, since there is no doubt that this too would satisfy the policy of the directive.

[20]. It is a condition of the indemnity that the agent should have 'brought the principal new customers or . . . significantly increased the volume of business with existing customers' and that the principal 'continues to derive substantial benefits from the business with such customers': article 17(2)(a). It follows that in a case such as the present, in which the principal went out of business and therefore derived no benefit from the customers introduced by the agent, no indemnity will be payable: see *Saintier and Scholes*, op.cit, at p. 204. In addition, article 17(2)(b) limits the indemnity to one year's commission. In the face of these provisions which will satisfy the policy of the directive, it is impossible to argue that it requires a payment of twice gross commission whether the principal has derived any benefit from the termination or not.

[21]. In my opinion, therefore, the courts of the United Kingdom would not be acting inconsistently with the directive if they were to calculate the compensation payable under article 17(3) by reference to the value of the agency on the assumption that it continued: the amount which the agent could reasonably expect to receive for the right to stand in his shoes, continue to perform the duties of the agency and receive the commission which he would have received. It remains to consider some of the English and Scottish cases in which the question has been discussed.

[22]. The decision of the Court of Session in *King v Tunnock Ltd* 2000 SC 424 is the only appellate case containing a full discussion of the way compensation should be calculated. Mr King sold cakes and biscuits for Tunnock Ltd. He had taken over the agency from his father in 1962. It was his full time occupation. In 1994 the company closed its bakery and terminated the agency. The evidence was that over the previous two years he had earned gross commission amounting in total to £27,144. The sheriff held that he was not entitled to compensation because the principal, having closed the business, would not enjoy any benefits from the goodwill generated by the agent. But an Extra Division of the Court of Session reversed this interlocutor and awarded compensation in the sum of £27,144.

[23]. I respectfully think that the sheriff was right. In view of the closure of the business, the agency was worth nothing. No one would have given anything for the right to earn future commission on the sales of cakes and biscuits because there would be none to be sold. Nor had the principal retained any goodwill which the agent had helped to build up. The goodwill disappeared when the business closed. The reason why the business closed is not altogether clear but Mr King's low earnings for full time work over the previous two years suggests that it was not doing well. Even if one assumes that commission would have continued at the same rate, it is hard to see why anyone should have paid for the privilege of a full time job which earned him less than he would have been paid as a bus conductor.

[24]. I am bound to say that I do not find the reasoning of the Extra Division, delivered by Lord Caplan, at all convincing. He said that the agency had existed for many years and that it was likely that the agent had good relations with customers. That, no doubt, was true. But Lord Caplan then went on to say:

> In these circumstances we consider it likely that the pursuer would have expected and required a relatively high level of compensation to surrender his successful and long-established agency. The compensation would, of course, require to be tied to the commission he was earning. Thus this is a

case where we can conclude, even on the limited information that is available, that the agent would have expected to receive a capital sum representing at least the total for the last two years of his earnings to be paid before he would voluntarily have given up his agency.

[25]. '[He] would have expected to receive...'. I daresay he might. But would anyone have given it to him? Lord Caplan does not seem to have considered it relevant to ask. It appears that, following *King v Tunnock Ltd*, it is standard practice for the former agent to give evidence of what he would have expected to receive for his agency. In this case, Mr Lonsdale said in a witness statement that he had been advised by an accountant that an established method of valuation was to take the gross profits and multiply them by two and a half. For the last completed accounting year before closure his gross commission was £12,239.34 and he therefore valued the business at £30,598.35.

[26]. Mr Lonsdale at least claimed to have the support of an accountant for his valuation, although he did not call him as a witness. But the Court of Session appears to have arrived at the figure of twice gross commission without any evidence at all. Lord Caplan said that he was 'reassured' that this would be standard compensation in France, but, for the reasons I have explained, the French practice is of no evidential value whatever.

[27]. *King v Tunnock Ltd* was considered by Judge Bowers (sitting as a High Court judge) in *Barrett McKenzie v Escada (UK) Ltd* [2001] EuLR 567. The judge was not attracted by the formulaic approach of the Court of Session but said (at p. 575) that the point on which he agreed with Lord Caplan was that—

> one is valuing the agency and its connections that have been established by the agent at the time at or immediately before termination, and it is really a question of compensating for the notional value of that agency in the open market....

[28]. I agree that this is what compensation in article 17(3) means. My only caution is that one must be careful about the word 'notional'. All that is notional is the assumption that the agency was available to be bought and sold at the relevant date. What it would fetch depends upon circumstances as they existed in the real world at the time: what the earnings prospects of the agency were and what people would have been willing to pay for similar businesses at the time.

[29]. In *Tigana Ltd v Decoro* [2003] EuLR 189 the judge awarded the agent a sum equal to his commission less expenses over the 14 to 15 months during which the agency had subsisted. I would agree that prima facie the value of the agency should be fixed by reference to its net earnings because, as a matter of common sense, that is what will matter to the hypothetical purchaser. Furthermore, in the case of an agent who has more than one agency, the costs must be fairly attributed to each. He cannot simply say, as Mr Lonsdale did in this case, that the marginal cost of the Elmdale agency was little or nothing because he had to see the same customers and go to the same exhibitions for Wendel.

[30]. It may well be that 14 months commission adopted by the judge was a fair valuation. But he seems to have had no evidence that anyone would have paid this figure for a comparable business. Instead, he gave (at p. 221) a non-exhaustive list of 14 factors ((a) to (n)), some of them very wide ranging indeed, which he said would require consideration. The list gives no indication of the weight to be attributed to each factor.

[31]. More recently, in *Smith, Bailey Palmer v Howard & Hallam Ltd* [2006] EuLR 578 Judge Overend (sitting as a High Court judge) dealt with claims by other agents who had worked for the respondent in this case. He noted that the Elmdale brand had been sold to a competitor for £550,000 and that, over the three years before the sale, 42% of the sales and distribution expenses had consisted of agent's commission. On these figures, he considered that it would be right to attribute 42% of the value of the brand to the agents. This seems to me a flawed method of calculation. First, it treats the entire value of the brand, i.e. the goodwill of the Elmdale name, as attributable to sales and marketing. No allowance is made for the possibility that some of the goodwill may have been attributable to the fact that the company made good shoes. Secondly, no allowance is made for the fact that the commission, which is treated as the measure of the proprietary interest of the agents in the assets of the company,

is what the agents were actually paid for their services. On this theory, the advertising agents should have acquired an interest proportionate to what they were paid. Thirdly, the valuation is based entirely on cost rather than what anyone would actually have paid for the agency.

[32]. That brings me to the judgments in the present case. The claim was heard by Judge Harris QC in the Oxford County Court and his judgment was, if I may respectfully say so, a model of clarity and common sense. I shall extract one or two of the most important passages:

'18. If it is kept in mind that the damage for which the agent is to be compensated consists in the loss of the value or goodwill he can be said to have possessed in the agency, then it can be seen that valuation ought to be reasonably straightforward. Small businesses of all kinds are daily being bought and sold, and a major element in the composition of their price will be a valuation of goodwill.

19. But neither side put evidence before the court about how commercial goodwill is convention-ally valued. Nor was I told upon what basis claims of this type are conventionally settled. There was no evidence at all about how commercially to value such assets. It is of course for the claimant, as a seeker of compensation, to prove the value of what he has lost.'

[33]. The judge then found that net commission was running at about £8,000 a year and said:

'20.... The value of that agency, the commercial value is what someone would pay for it; to acquire by assignment a business vehicle with a likely net annual income of £8,000...

22. Commonsense would indicate that few people wanting the opportunity to earn what the claimant was earning would be prepared to pay well over £20,000 for the privilege of doing so, still less would they do so in an industry in remorseless decline, and in which the likely buyers would be men of modest means...

23. Given the absence of evidence about how commercially to value goodwill, or evidence about what price in practice might have been available, the court might be thought to be justified in simply finding that the claimant has failed to prove his case...

30. This was an agency producing a modest and falling income in a steadily deteriorating environ-ment. There is no evidence that anyone would have paid anything to buy it... I am strongly tempted to find that no damage has been established... But perhaps that conclusion, though I regard it as logical, is a little over rigorous given that the defendant has already made a payment. Doing the best I can, I find that the appropriate figure for compensation is one of £5,000.'

[34]. The Court of Appeal approved of this approach. After a thorough review of the authorities, Moore-Bick J quoted paragraph 18 of the judgment (see above) and said that the judge was right in his approach. I agree. Furthermore, I do not think that the judge could have been faulted if he had simply dismissed the claim.

[35]. That is sufficient to dispose of the appeal, but there are three additional comments to be made. First, Mr Moser urged your Lordships not to adopt a principle which required valuation evidence. Valuations, he said, were expensive and most claims were too small to justify the cost. Moore-Bick LJ said (at paragraph 57) that 'in most cases' the court would be likely to benefit from the assistance of an expert witness but that in some cases it might be sufficient to place all the material before the court and invite the judge to act as valuer. It seems to me that once it is firmly understood that the compensation is for the loss of the value of the agency, relatively few cases will go to court. As Judge Harris said, small comparable businesses are bought and sold every day and it should not be difficult for the parties, with the benefit of advice about the going rate for such businesses, to agree on an appropriate valuation. It should not always be necessary for them to obtain a full scale valuation, involving the checking of income and expenditure figures and the application of the going rate to those figures. But I do not see how, if the matter does go to court, the judge can decide the case without some information about the standard methodology for the valuation of such businesses. In this case, the judge was simply invited to pluck a figure out of the air from across the Channel and rightly refused to do so. Nothing is

more likely to cause uncertainty and promote litigation than a lottery system under which judges are invited to choose figures at random.

[36]. It may also be possible, after a period of experience in such valuations, for the court to take judicial notice of what would be the going rate in what I might call the standard case, namely an agency which has continued for some time and in which the net commission figures are fairly stable. It should not be necessary to repeat boilerplate evidence in every case. But the judge must be reasonably confident that he is dealing with the standard case. Adjustments would be needed if, as in this case, the market was in decline or had disappeared altogether.

[37]. Secondly, there is the question raised by the Winemakers' Federation of Australia Inc, who were given leave to intervene and made submissions. They are concerned about the case in which the agent is able to transfer the goodwill he has created with customers to another principal: for example, to persuade the supermarkets to whom he has been selling the produce of one winery to transfer to another. In such a case the former principal would not retain the goodwill which the agent had created and it would be unfair to have to pay compensation on the basis that the agent had gone out of business.

[38]. In my opinion circumstances such as these will be reflected in the process of valuation. The hypothetical purchase of the agency does not involve an assumption that the agent gives a covenant against competition. If the situation in real life is that the hypothetical purchaser would be in competition with the former agent and could not have any assurance that the customers would continue to trade with him, that would affect the amount he was prepared to pay. If it appeared that all the customers were likely to defect to the former agent (or, for that matter, to someone else), he would be unlikely to be prepared to pay much for the agency.

[39]. What matters, of course, is what would have appeared likely at the date of termination and not what actually happened afterwards. But I do not see think that the court is required to shut its eyes to what actually happened. It may provide evidence of what the parties were likely to have expected to happen.

[40]. Thirdly and finally, there is the question of whether a reference should be made to the European Court of Justice. Mr Moser says that the differences in opinion between the Scottish and the English courts and between various English judges show that the law is uncertain. That is true, but what is uncertain is not the meaning of the directive. It is clear that the agent is entitled to compensation for 'the damage he suffers as a result of the termination of his relations with the principal' and that the method by which that damage should be calculated is a discretionary matter for the domestic laws of the Member States. It is the way in which our domestic law should implement that discretion which has been uncertain and the resolution of that uncertainty is the task of this House and not the European Court of Justice.

[41]. I would therfore dismiss the appeal.

[Lords Bingham, Rodger, Carswell and Neuberger agreed.]

Severine Saintier, 'Final guidelines on compensation of commercial agents'
(2008) 124 LQR 31, 36–37

As the first ruling of the House of Lords on the method of calculation of the compensation due, this unanimous decision is of great importance. The recognition of the specificity of the loss the agent suffers on termination and the need for a clear methodology for its assessment is to be welcome. By stating that the loss suffered is that of the agency as an asset to the agent, the court seems to accept that the basis of the payment is the expropriation of the agent's quasi-proprietary interest and not the principal's gain. This analysis, in line with French law, also recognises the different emphasis between compensation and indemnity. However, to take account of the fact that the principal's business is failing as reducing the value of the agency and therefore the value of the compensation blurs the distinction between compensation and indemnity and appears to calculate compensation by reference to existing common law principles. In fact, looking at the state of the principal's business means that in certain cases, in spite of losing the agency, the agent will be left with no compensation. Member States have some discretion in the matter, yet, given the previously mentioned different emphasis between the two options, it is not clear whether this is correct. Although the EU Commission did not consider that calculating compensation by reference to common law principles was a failure to implement the Directive, doing so may nevertheless undermine the specificity of the loss agents suffer on termination, which may be against the protective stance of the implementing text. By emphasising the domestic discretion in the calculation of compensation, their Lordships accentuate the fact that the Directive stipulated a remedy for a loss but left it to Member States to decide how that remedy is to be calculated. If the effect of such a discretion, is that, on similar facts, domestic courts interpret the Directive differently, this raises wider questions as to the effectiveness of this Directive as a tool for harmonisation of European private law, a problem recognised by the European Commission, who, in its Action Plan on a More Coherent European Contract Law (Com (2003) 68 final) criticised the Directive for creating uncertainty (Com (2003) 68 final at para.18).

QUESTIONS

1. What are the key differences between the indemnity scheme and the compensation scheme? Do you think Lord Hoffmann was right to 'cross-check' the basis of his assessment under the compensation scheme with what the commercial agent might have recovered under the indemnity scheme?

2. How far, if at all, do you agree with Saintier's assessment that the House of Lords has taken account of common law principles?

3. Do you agree with Lord Hoffmann's view that 'once it is understood that the compensation is for the loss of the value of the agency, relatively few cases will go to court'? You should bear in mind that, in England, commercial agencies are not bought and sold on a regular basis.

(c) Termination and third parties

Drew v Nunn
(1879) 4 QBD 661, Court of Appeal

Nunn appointed his wife as his agent to purchase goods from Drew. Nunn was present when some of the goods were ordered by his wife and he paid for some of them. Nunn then became insane and was confined to an asylum. But his wife continued to purchase goods on his behalf from Drew, who was unaware of Nunn's insanity. When Nunn regained his sanity he refused to pay for those goods ordered by his wife when he was in the asylum, Mellor J directed the jury that Drew was entitled to recover the price of the goods from Nunn. Nunn appealed.

Brett LJ: This appeal has stood over for a long time, principally on my account, in order to ascertain whether it can be determined upon some clear principle. I have found, however, that the law upon this subject stands upon a very unsatisfactory footing.

[His Lordship then set out the facts of the case. He continued:]

Upon this state of facts two questions arise. Does insanity put an end to the authority of the agent? One would expect to find that this question has been long decided on clear principles; but on looking into Story on Agency, Scotch authorities, Pothier, and other French authorities, I find that no satisfactory

conclusion has been arrived at. If such insanity as existed here did not put an end to the agent's authority, it would be clear that the plaintiff is entitled to succeed; but in my opinion insanity of this kind does
put an end to the agent's authority. It cannot be disputed that some cases of change of status in the
principal put an end to the authority of the agent; thus, the bankruptcy and death of the principal, the
marriage of a female principal, all put an end to the authority of the agent. It may be argued that this
result follows from the circumstance that a different principal is created. Upon bankruptcy the trustee
becomes the principal; upon death the heir or devisee as to realty, the executor or administrator as to
personalty; and upon the marriage of a female principal her husband takes her place. And it has been
argued that by analogy the lunatic continues liable until a fresh principal, namely, his committee, is
appointed. But I cannot think that this is the true ground, for executors are, at least in some instances,
bound to carry out the contracts entered into by their testators. I think that the satisfactory principle to
be adopted is that, where such a change occurs as to the principal that he can no longer act for himself,
the agent whom he has appointed can no longer act for him. In the present case a great change had
occurred in the condition of the principal: he was so far afflicted with insanity as to be disabled from
acting for himself; therefore his wife, who was his agent, could no longer act for him. Upon the ground
which I have pointed out, I think that her authority was terminated. It seems to me that an agent is
liable to be sued by a third person, if he assumes to act on his principal's behalf after he had knowledge
of his principal's incompetency to act. In a case of that kind he is acting wrongfully. The defendant's
wife must be taken to have been aware of her husband's lunacy; and if she had assumed to act on
his behalf with any one to whom he himself had not held her out as his agent, she would have been
acting wrongfully, and, but for the circumstance that she is married, would have been liable in an action
to compensate the person with whom she assumed to act on her husband's behalf. In my opinion,
if a person who has not been held out as agent assumes to act on behalf of a lunatic, the contract is
void against the supposed principal, and the pretended agent is liable to an action for misleading an
innocent person.

The second question then arises, what is the consequence where a principal, who has held out
another as his agent, subsequently becomes insane, and a third person deals with the agent without
notice that the principal is a lunatic? Authority may be given to an agent in two ways. First, it may
be given by some instrument, which of itself asserts that the authority is thereby created, such as a
power of attorney; it is of itself an assertion by the principal that the agent may act for him. Secondly,
an authority may also be created from the principal holding out the agent as entitled to act generally
for him. The agency in the present case was created in the manner last-mentioned. As between the
defendant and his wife, the agency expired upon his becoming to her knowledge insane; but it seems
to me that the person dealing with the agent without knowledge of the principal's insanity has a right
to enter into a contract with him, and the principal, although a lunatic, is bound so that he cannot
repudiate the contract assumed to be made upon his behalf. It is difficult to assign the ground upon
which this doctrine, which however seems to me to be the true principle, exists. It is said that the right
to hold the insane principal liable depends upon contract. I have a difficulty in assenting to this. It has
been said also that the right depends upon estoppel. I cannot see that an estoppel is created. But it has
been said also that the right depends upon representations made by the principal and entitling third
persons to act upon them, until they hear that those representations are withdrawn. The authorities
collected in Story on Agency, ch xviii § 481, p 610 (7th edn), seem to base the right upon the ground
of public policy: it is there said in effect that the existence of the right goes in aid of public business.
It is however a better way of stating the rule to say that the holding out of another person as agent
is a representation upon which, at the time when it was made, third parties had a right to act, and if
no insanity had supervened would still have had a right to act. In this case the wife was held out as
agent, and the plaintiff acted upon the defendant's representation as to her authority without notice
that it had been withdrawn. The defendant cannot escape from the consequences of the representation which he has made; he cannot withdraw the agent's authority as to third persons without giving
them notice of the withdrawal. The principal is bound, although he retracts the agent's authority, if he

has not given notice and the latter wrongfully enters into a contract upon his behalf. The defendant became insane and was unable to withdraw the authority which he had conferred upon his wife: he may be an innocent sufferer by her conduct, but the plaintiff, who dealt with her bona fide, is also innocent, and where one of two persons both innocent must suffer by the wrongful act of a third person, that person making the representation which, as between the two, was the original cause of the mischief, must be the sufferer and must bear the loss. Here it does not lie in the defendant's mouth to say that the plaintiff shall be the sufferer.

A difficulty may arise in the application of a general principle such as this is. Suppose that a person makes a representation which after his death is acted upon by another in ignorance that his death has happened: in my view the estate of the deceased will be bound to make good any loss, which may have occurred through acting upon that representation. It is, however, unnecessary to decide this point to-day.

Upon the grounds above stated I am of opinion that, although the authority of the defendant's wife was put an end to by his insanity, and although she had no authority to deal with the plaintiff, nevertheless the latter is entitled to recover, because the defendant whilst he was sane made representations to the plaintiff, upon which he was entitled to act until he had notice of the defendant's insanity, and he had no notice of the insanity until after he had supplied the goods for the price of which he now sues. The direction of Mellor J was right.

Bramwell LJ: I agree with the judgment just delivered by Brett LJ. It must be taken that the defendant told the plaintiff that his wife had authority to bind him; when that authority had been given, it continued to exist, so far as the plaintiff was concerned, until it was revoked and until he received notice of that revocation. It may be urged that this doctrine does not extend to insanity, which is not an intentional revocation; but I think that insanity forms no exception to the general law as to principal and agent. It may be hard upon an insane principal, if his agent abuses his authority; but, on the other hand, it must be recollected that insanity is not a privilege, it is a misfortune, which must not be allowed to injure innocent persons: it would be productive of mischievous consequences, if insanity annulled every representation made by the person afflicted with it without any notice being given of his malady. If the argument for the defendant were correct, every act done by him or on his behalf after he became insane must be treated as a nullity . . . .

It has been assumed by Brett LJ that the insanity of the defendant was such as to amount to a revocation of his wife's authority. I doubt whether partial mental derangement would have that effect. I think that in order to annul the authority of an agent, insanity must amount to dementia. If a man becomes so far insane as to have no mind, perhaps he ought to be deemed dead for the purpose of contracting. I think that the direction of Mellor J was right.

Brett LJ: I am requested by Cotton LJ to state that he agrees with the conclusion at which we have arrived; but that he does not wish to decide whether the authority of the defendant's wife was terminated, or whether the liability of a contractor lasts until a committee has been appointed. He bases his decision simply upon the ground that the defendant, by holding out his wife as agent, entered into a contract with the plaintiff that she had authority to act upon his behalf, and that until the plaintiff had notice that this authority was revoked he was entitled to act upon the defendant's representations.

I wish to add that if there had been any real question as to the extent of the defendant's insanity, it ought to have been left to the jury; and that as no question was asked of the jury, I must assume that the defendant was insane to the extent which I have mentioned. I may remark that from the mere fact of mental derangement it ought not to be assumed that a person is incompetent to contract; mere weakness of mind or partial derangement is insufficient to exempt a person from responsibility upon the engagements into which he has entered.

NOTES

1. Compare and contrast *Drew v Nunn* and *Yonge v Toynbee* [1910] 1 KB 215 (above, p 174, and see notes at pp 176–179). See R Powell *The Law of Agency* (2nd edn, 1961), pp 405–406; *Bowstead and Reynolds,* para 10-032; and E Peel, *Treitel's Law of Contract* (12th edn, 2007), para 16–109, fn 534, for ways of distinguishing these cases. It should be noted that both the agent and third party may be protected from the normal consequences of the principal's supervening mental incapacity by the Powers of Attorney Act 1971, s 5 (above, p 177) and the Mental Capacity Act 2005, s 14 (the Enduring Powers of Attorney Act 1985, which offered similar protection, has been repealed by the 2005 Act, but existing enduring powers of attorney are unaffected).

2. Despite occasional dicta to the contrary (eg Brett LJ in *Drew v Nunn),* it is probably the case that where the principal dies there can be no apparent authority. For as Lord Ellenborough said in *Watson v King* (1815) 4 Camp 272 at 274: 'How can a valid act be done in the name of a dead man?' Following this reasoning, it is submitted that the personal representatives of a dead principal cannot ratify any contract made on behalf of the deceased after his death (cf *Foster v Bates* (1843) 12 M & W 226; *Campanari v Woodburn,* above, p 244; but neither case is authority against this submission: *Bowstead and Reynolds,* para 10-017; Powell, op cit, p 388, fn 7).

3. There can be no apparent authority when the principal is adjudged bankrupt. This is because when the principal is adjudged bankrupt his estate vests in the trustee in bankruptcy leaving the principal with no capacity to perform the acts which are the subject of the apparent agency. But those dealing with the agent of a bankrupt may have statutory protection under the Insolvency Act 1986, s 284(4), (5). Furthermore, as in cases of death or insanity of the donor of a power of attorney, a third party who deals with the donee of a power of attorney may be able to rely on the Powers of Attorney Act 1971, s 5, to avoid the normal consequences of the donor's supervening bankruptcy.

4. Revocation of the agent's actual authority by the principal does not prevent the principal being bound by the agent's apparent authority, so long as the third party has no notice that the agency has terminated (see *Scarf v Jardine* (1882) 7 App Cas 345 at 356–357, per Lord Blackburn; see also *Curlewis v Birkbeck* (1863) 3 F & F 894). Notice given to the agent is not enough to terminate his apparent authority; notice must be given to the third party. Thus, in *AMB Generali Holding AG v SEB Trygg Liv Holding AB* [2005] EWCA Civ 1237, [2006] 1 WLR 2276, H (the agent) resigned as a director of a company (the principal) but was held to have apparent authority to bind the company to arbitration proceedings after his resignation because of a general representation from his appointment as director that he had all the usual authority of the post, and also from specific representations by the company, the effect of which survived his resignation until the third party was put on notice of it.

QUESTION

An insane principal is bound by the apparent authority of his agent, whereas the estate of a dead principal is not. What policy reasons, if any, justify this distinction?

PART III

DOMESTIC SALES LAW

CHAPTER 7

INTRODUCTION AND DEFINITIONS[1]

1 INTRODUCTION[2]

Prior to 1893, the law governing the sale of goods was almost entirely based on cases decided by the courts at common law. There were a few statutory provisions, but only a few: the two most important were the Factors Acts, discussed below at p 364, and the Statute of Frauds 1677, s 17 (now repealed) which required written evidence for the enforcement of a contract of sale of goods to the value of over £10.

Towards the end of the nineteenth century the subject was much influenced by two leading textbooks, *Blackburn on Sale* and *Benjamin on Sale*. In 1888 the celebrated statutory draftsman, Sir Mackenzie Chalmers, who had already drafted the Bills of Exchange Act 1882 (below, Chapter 16) was commissioned to prepare a Bill for the codification of the law; and this was enacted, with some modifications, as the Sale of Goods Act 1893. Although in more recent times this Act has come in for criticism from some quarters, primarily because it did not, as originally drafted, provide wholly satisfactory remedies for the buyer in consumer contracts, Chalmers' codification has to be seen as a *tour de force*, particularly as a merchants' code—and, since this is a book on commercial law, it is this aspect of the subject with which we shall primarily be concerned. It was not until 1973 (in the Supply of Goods (Implied Terms) Act 1973—an Act mainly concerned with consumer transactions) that significant changes were made to any part of Chalmers' text, and it is a tribute to his skill that it is still in use, virtually unchanged, a century later, as the basis of all commercial sales of goods within the United Kingdom and a very large share of the world's international sales as well.

Following the 1973 amendments and some further changes made by the Unfair Contract Terms Act 1977, the Act of 1893 was consolidated and re-enacted as the Sale of Goods Act 1979, which is now the principal source of the law. All statutory references in this section of the book will be to this Act of 1979 unless otherwise stated: it will usually be referred to simply as 'the Act'. In the consolidation, some minor changes of language were made from the 1893 text, and there was some renumbering of the sections—which calls for a degree of

---

[1] In this and the succeeding chapters dealing with the law of sale of goods, the following abbreviations are used in referring to standard textbooks:

Atiyah: PS Atiyah and JN Adams *The Sale of Goods* (11th edn, 2005)

Benjamin: AG Guest and others (eds) *Benjamin's Sale of Goods* (7th edn, 2006)

Goode: RM Goode *Commercial Law* (3rd edn, 2004).

[2] For an excellent historical survey, see MG Bridge 'The Evolution of Modern Sales Law' [1991] LMCLQ 52.

caution when reading judgments based on the former Act. (However, since *most* sections of the 1893 Act have retained their old numbers in the new Act, cross-references will be given only where this is not the case.) Since its enactment, the 1979 Act has been amended a number of times—in particular by the Sale of Goods (Amendment) Act 1994, the Sale and Supply of Goods Act 1994 and the Sale of Goods (Amendment) Act 1995. In addition, in the area of consumer sales, it has been supplemented by a considerable number of regulations made by statutory instrument, implementing EC directives.

A codifying Act, such as the Sale of Goods Act 1893, is intended to *replace* the previous case law by a fresh statement of what the law is to be; and it is not normally proper to look to the earlier cases for guidance as to the interpretation of such an Act (see the remarks of Lord Herschell in *Bank of England v Vagliano Bros* [1891] AC 107, quoted below, p 531—a case on the Bills of Exchange Act 1882). But in fact this principle has not always been respected, and there are many cases where judges have had regard to the former law. In some circumstances this practice is, perhaps, justified by s 62(2) of the Act, which declares that 'the rules of the common law,...except in so far as they are inconsistent with the provisions of the Act,...apply to contracts for the sale of goods'.

However, there is room for debate as to which 'rules of the common law' are 'inconsistent with the provisions of the Act'. In the leading case of *Re Wait* (below), Atkin LJ not only endorsed the *Vagliano* approach referred to above, saying ([1927] 1 Ch 606 at 631): 'Inasmuch as we are now bound by the plain language of the Code I do not think that decisions in cases before 1893 are of much value', but went on to suggest that some provisions of the Act (which Atkin LJ refers to as 'the Code') were intended to displace general provisions of the common law and equity which might otherwise be thought applicable.

Re Wait
[1927] 1 Ch 606, Court of Appeal

Wait contracted to buy from Balfour, Williamson & Co 1000 tons of wheat which was to arrive at Avonmouth from the United States on the MV *Challenger*. The following day, he agreed to sell 500 tons of this wheat to Humphries & Bobbett, who paid him the price in advance. A few days before the *Challenger* arrived, Wait went bankrupt. By the time that this action was brought, some of the wheat had been disposed of to other buyers, but 530 tons remained which was still in law the property of Wait (or his trustee in bankruptcy) and in his possession. Nothing had been done to identify the 500 tons which was to be used to fulfil Humphries & Bobbett's contract. The Court of Appeal (by a majority, the Chancery judge, Sargant LJ, dissenting) held that Humphries & Bobbett had no claim to any of the wheat, but could only prove in Wait's bankruptcy for the return of the price. In this passage, Atkin LJ rejected an argument that the buyers might be able to assert a claim of a proprietary nature to their share of the wheat based on principles of equity independently of the Act.

Atkin LJ: ...I am of opinion that the claimants fail, and that to grant the relief claimed would violate well established principles of common law and equity. It would also appear to embarrass to a most serious degree the ordinary operations of buying and selling goods, and the banking operations which attend them....

I do not think that at any time here there was an equitable assignment which ever gave the claimants a beneficial interest in these goods. It has been difficult to elicit the moment of time at which the beneficial interest came into existence. At various times in the argument it has been the moment when the 1000 tons were shipped; when they were declared to the debtor by Balfour Williamson & Co; when the bills of lading came into the possession of the bank; when the claimants paid the £5933 5s to the debtor; when the goods were taken up by the trustee [in bankruptcy]; and when the 530 tons came into the possession of the trustee. The difficulty illustrates the danger of seeking to conduct well established principles into territory where they are trespassers. Without deciding the point, I think that much may be said for the proposition that an agreement for the sale of goods does not import any agreement to transfer property other than in accordance with the terms of the Code, that is, the intention of the parties to be derived from the terms of the contract, the conduct of the parties and the circumstances of the case, and, unless a different intention appears, from the rules set out in s 18. The Code was passed at a time when the principles of equity and equitable remedies were recognized and given effect to in all our Courts, and the particular equitable remedy of specific performance is specially referred to in s 52. The total sum of legal relations (meaning by the word 'legal' existing in equity as well as in common law) arising out of the contract for the sale of goods may well be regarded as defined by the Code. It would have been futile in a code intended for commercial men to have created an elaborate structure of rules dealing with rights at law, if at the same time it was intended to leave, subsisting with the legal rights, equitable rights inconsistent with, more extensive, and coming into existence earlier than the rights so carefully set out in the various sections of the Code.

The rules for transfer of property as between seller and buyer, performance of the contract, rights of the unpaid seller against the goods, unpaid sellers' lien, remedies of the seller, remedies of the buyer, appear to be complete and exclusive statements of the legal relations both in law and equity. They have, of course, no relevance when one is considering rights, legal or equitable, which may come into existence dehors the contract for sale. A seller or a purchaser may, of course, create any equity he pleases by way of charge, equitable assignment or any other dealing with or disposition of goods, the subject-matter of sale; and he may, of course, create such an equity as one of the terms expressed in the contract of sale. But the mere sale or agreement to sell or the acts in pursuance of such a contract mentioned in the Code will only produce the legal effects which the Code states.

[Lord Hanworth MR delivered a concurring judgment.
Sargant LJ dissented.]

NOTE

This case would now be decided differently, following the enactment of the Sale of Goods (Amendment) Act 1995, which gives proprietary remedies to a buyer of goods forming part of a larger bulk who has pre-paid the price. The remarks of Atkin LJ, however, are not affected by this statutory change.

The Act applies to contracts for the sale of all types of goods (though in regard to some, eg ships and aircraft, other statutes may be applicable in addition). In general, its provisions govern commercial sales, sales to consumers and transactions between private parties, but in some sections (particularly ss 12–15A, 30, 35 and 35A) a distinction is made between these categories.

2 DEFINITIONS

It is impossible to follow the Act properly without a clear understanding of a few key definitions, which form the basis of its whole structure. The draftsman has used these words and phrases with great precision, and it is clearly important for us also to learn to do so.

(a) 'Contract for the sale of goods'

The Act applies only to 'contracts for the sale of goods'. Such a contract is defined in s 2(1) as 'a contract by which the seller transfers or agrees to transfer the property in goods to the buyer for a money consideration, called the price'. There are a number of transactions closely analogous to sales of goods, as we shall see shortly—some of them governed by rules and principles which are similar, if not identical, to those contained in the Act; but plainly it is legitimate to refer to the Act only when we are concerned with contracts for the sale of goods within the statutory definition. These other transactions are distinguished from contracts for the sale of goods below, at pp 278–293.

(b) 'Sale' and 'agreement to sell'

Where under a contract of sale the 'property' in the goods (a term which we may take as broadly equivalent to 'ownership') is transferred from the seller to the buyer, the contract is called in the Act a 'sale' (s 2(4)). Where the transfer of the property is to take place at a future time or is subject to some condition to be fulfilled later, it is called an 'agreement to sell' (s 2(5)). The term 'contract for the sale of goods' is thus a comprehensive expression, embracing both 'sale' and 'agreement to sell'.

A *sale* may be seen as both a contract and a conveyance: by virtue of the contract itself, the buyer becomes the owner of the goods. An *agreement to sell,* in contrast, is purely a contract: ownership does not pass to the buyer until some later time.

(c) 'Goods'

The term 'goods' is defined in s 61(1) as including 'all personal chattels other than things in action and money, and in Scotland all corporeal moveables except money'; and in particular as including 'emblements, industrial growing crops and things attached to or forming part of the land which are agreed to be severed before sale or under the contract of sale'.

'Personal chattels' (or 'chattels personal') are to be contrasted with 'chattels real', such as leasehold interests in land. The term may be subdivided into 'things in possession' (sometimes referred to as tangibles) and 'things in action' (intangibles, or 'choses in action'). The Act is concerned only with the former.

Apart from chattels real and things in action, it is probably right to assume that the following are not 'goods' for the purposes of the Act (though they may be 'goods', 'things' or 'articles' under other statutory definitions): animals in the wild state; electricity and other forms of energy; human remains, tissue and organs and bodily products (eg blood); the various forms of intellectual property; computer software and other material in digitised form, eg music and images (as distinct from the disk or other object on which it is stored: see *St Albans District Council v International Computers Ltd* [1996] 4 All ER 481 at 493, and S Green and D Saidov [2007] JBL 161); information (and, *a fortiori,* even more nebulous concepts, such as an opportunity). It is perhaps wrong to be too categorical about some of these items: human hair, for instance, is regularly bought by wig-makers, and skeletons by medical students. Money is expressly excluded from the statutory definition, but a coin may be sold as a collector's item and is then regarded as 'goods' (*Moss v Hancock* [1899] 2 QB 111).

On the other hand, the following are all 'goods' capable of being the subject matter of a contract of sale within the Act: ships, aircraft and vehicles; domestic animals, and wild animals which have been reduced into captivity or are dead; water, oil and gases (even air, in the form of compressed air—compare *Britvic Soft Drinks Ltd v Messer UK Ltd* [2002] EWCA Civ 548, [2002] 2 All ER (Comm) 321 (carbon dioxide)).

The dividing line between goods and land (or rather between goods and an interest in land) is very difficult to draw. In fact, there *is* no dividing line. The Act itself declares that 'goods', for the purposes of its provisions, includes crops of every description and things attached to *or forming part* of the land which are agreed to be severed before sale or under the contract of sale. But if this is compared with the definition of 'land' under the Law of Property Act 1925, s 205, we find that 'land' is there defined as including 'land of any tenure, and mines and minerals, . . . buildings or parts of buildings . . . and an easement, right, privilege or benefit in, over, or derived from land'. The only possible conclusion is that some types of transaction may be *both* a contract of sale of goods under the Sale of Goods Act *and* a contract for the sale or transfer of an interest in land under the Law of Property Act. Examples include a contract by a landowner giving another person the right to enter upon his land and fell trees and remove the timber; the right to pick fruit or cut hay; the right to extract minerals or take water; the right to shoot and take away game; and the right to dismantle and remove a building. In land law, these can be seen as easements or *profits à prendre*. In relation to such contracts it may be necessary to look at both statutes and to comply with any mandatory provisions imposed by either (eg the need for writing under the Law of Property (Miscellaneous Provisions) Act 1989, s 2). When it comes to a clash, it is the rules of land law which will ordinarily prevail: so, for instance, if A owns land on which a building is erected and he sells the building to B for removal, any right of B to the building (as 'goods') would be overridden by the claims of a bona fide purchaser of a legal estate in the land who was unaware of the contract with B.

The reference in s 61(1) to 'industrial growing crops' is at first sight puzzling. It reflects the traditional distinction made at common law between *fructus industriales* (produce which was regarded as primarily the end-product of labour, particularly annual or seasonal labour, such as corn, potatoes, etc) and *fructus naturales* (things which were considered part of the natural growth of the soil, for which tilling and cultivating were regarded as unnecessary, or at least not so vital, and which tended to be the product of perennial growth: grass, timber, the fruit from trees). Under the old law, crops in the former category were regarded as goods which could be bought and sold independently of any question of severance: a half-grown crop of potatoes could be sold to a buyer *as goods*. But *fructus naturales* were regarded as part of the land until severance. It is plain that this distinction has not survived the enactment of the Sale of Goods Act. However, even under the Act, severance is essential. In *Saunders v Pilcher* [1949] 2 All ER 1097 a cherry orchard was sold together with its crop of cherries which were ripe and ready to be picked. For tax purposes, the parties purported to make separate sales of the land and the cherries. But the court held that there was only one transaction—a conveyance of the land. The parties did not contemplate that the cherries would be severed *under the contract of sale*, as s 61(1) requires.

The following cases throw light on this issue.

Morgan v Russell & Sons

[1909] 1 KB 357, King's Bench Divisional Court

Morgan was the lessee of land in South Wales on which slag and cinders had been tipped, and adjoining this property was land occupied by other persons on which were two disused cinder-tips, 50 years old. He obtained a licence from these persons to remove this material, and then agreed to sell to Russell & Sons the cinders and slag from all three tips. After a considerable amount of cinders and slag had been removed and paid for, Morgan's lessor and the occupiers of the adjoining properties forbade the removal of any more. Under the law at that time the damages recoverable from Morgan for breach of contract varied, depending upon whether the contract was one for the sale of goods or of an interest in land. (The distinction no longer exists, following the abolition of the rule in *Bain v Fothergill* (1874) LR 7 HL 158 by the Law of Property (Miscellaneous Provisions) Act 1989, s 3.) The court ruled that it was a sale of an interest in land.

Lord Alverstone CJ: The learned judge has found, and we have no power to interfere with that finding, that the cinders and slag had become part of the ground or soil itself, and were not definite or detached heaps resting, so to speak, upon the ground. The learned judge considered that under these circumstances the default, if any, in the carrying out of the agreement arose from a defect in the respondent's title, and that therefore, upon the principle *of Bain v Fothergill,* the appellants were not entitled to recover damages for the loss of their bargain. The case for the appellants was rested upon two grounds: it was first said that this was a contract for the sale of goods within s 62 of the Sale of Goods Act 1893, and therefore the ordinary rule of damages applies; and secondly that, even assuming that the cinders and slag were not goods, the principle of *Bain v Fothergill* would not apply, and the appellants were entitled to general damages. I am clearly of opinion that this was not a contract for the sale of goods. The respondent Morgan did not contract to sell any definite quantity of mineral, nor was it a contract for the sale of a heap of earth which could be said to be a separate thing. In my view the contract was a contract to give free access to certain tips for the purpose of removing cinders and slag which formed part of the soil at the price of *2s 3d* per ton, to include the value of the slag so taken, for so long as the appellants chose to exercise their option to take. The contract appears to me to be exactly analogous to a contract which gives a man a right to enter upon land with liberty to dig from the earth in situ so much gravel or brick earth or coal on payment of a price per ton. The first ground therefore in my opinion is not one upon which the appeal can succeed....

[Walton J delivered a concurring judgment.]

Underwood Ltd v Burgh Castle Brick & Cement Syndicate
[1922] 1 KB 343, King's Bench Division

Underwoods agreed to sell to the Syndicate a large horizontal tandem condensing engine which was a trade fixture on their leasehold premises. As part of the contract, the sellers were to detach the engine from the land and load it on to a railway truck. It was damaged during the loading process and the buyers refused to accept it. They were held entitled to do so, since (for reasons explained below, p 327) the engine was still the seller's property at the time when it was damaged. In his judgment, Rowlatt J assumed throughout that the transaction was governed by the Sale of Goods Act, but his remarks are of interest on the general question of the sale of fixtures.

Rowlatt J: This case raises an important point under the Sale of Goods Act, 1893. This turns on the question whether the property in the engine had passed to the defendants at the time when the accident happened when the engine was being loaded. This engine weighed some thirty tons and was at the time when it was inspected by the defendants affixed to a bed of concrete by means of Lewis bolts and screwed down. By reason of its weight it had sunk into the concrete and become closely united with it, so that the operation of removing it not only involved unfastening it but taking it to pieces....

I think the important point is that the parties were dealing with an article which was a fixture to the premises, and that is different from the case of a loose chattel. The buyers' intention was to buy an article which would be a loose chattel when the processes of detaching and dismantling it were completed, and to convert it into a loose chattel these processes had first to be performed. The case of a tenant's fixtures seems an analogous case. It seems a safe rule to adopt that if a fixture has to be detached so as to make it a chattel again, the act of detaching has to be done before the chattel can be deliverable. The same result is arrived at if the matter be looked at a little more technically. This fixture was not personal property any more than are tenant's fixtures, but was part of the freehold, and what was sold was not personal property but a part of the realty which the sellers had a right to detach and convert into personal property.... In the present case the plaintiffs did not sell their right to sever, but were to sever the fixtures themselves, and when they had done so, and so produced the chattel, they were to deliver it. That was the contract if the matter is analysed. The plaintiffs contended that as between the parties the intention was that the property should pass at the time of the contract and that s 17 of the Sale of Goods Act, 1893, applied. The fallacy of that argument seems to be that it assumes that the sellers had the property in the engine at the time when the contract was made. They had not, although it is true that they had rights which reduced the rights of property of the freeholder in whom the property was to a vanishing quantity. If the property had been mortgaged it would have been no answer to the mortgagees' claim to say that in the Sale of Goods Act, 1893, there is a provision that as between buyer and seller fixtures are goods and chattels. That could not affect the property of the freeholder.

For these reasons I think that the property in this engine did not pass to the defendants at the time when the contract was made, and there must be judgment for them.

NOTE

In *Marshall v Green* (1875) 1 CPD 35, a case decided before the passing of the first Sale of Goods Act in 1893, the court was concerned to decide whether a contract to sell timber which was still standing on the seller's land was a contract to sell the timber as goods, or an interest in land: the court plainly thought that such a contract must be one thing or the other. Grove J said, at 44:

It seems to me that, in determining the question whether there was a contract for an interest in land, we must look to what the parties intended to contract for.... Here the trees were to be cut as soon as possible, but even assuming that they were not to be cut for a month, I think that the test would be whether the parties really looked to their deriving benefit from the land, or merely intended that the land should be in the nature of a warehouse for the trees during that period. Here the parties clearly never contemplated that the purchaser should have anything in the nature of an interest in the land; he was only to have so much timber, which happened to be affixed to the land at the time, but was to be removed as soon as possible, and was to derive no benefit from the soil. If the contract had been for the sale of a young plantation of some rapidly-growing timber, which was not to be cut down until it had become substantially changed and had derived benefit from the land, there might have been an interest in land, but this is not such a case.

This approach may be contrasted with that of the Court of Appeal in *Kursell v Timber Operators & Contractors Ltd* (below, p 273), which was decided many years after the Act of 1893 was passed. The judgments in this later case all treat the issue as a question of sale of goods law, to be decided by reference to the Act.

Part-interests in goods (eg a half or one-third share in a horse, or in a specific heap of grain) pose special problems. To a large extent these will now have been resolved by an amendment made to the definition of 'goods' in s 61(l) by s 2(2) of the Sale of Goods (Amendment) Act 1995, declaring that 'goods' includes an undivided share in goods. It is clear from s 2(2) that a contract to transfer a part-interest in goods, even as between persons who are already part-owners, is to be treated as a contract of sale of goods. However, it is obviously not easy, and in some cases not possible, to apply many of the provisions of the Act literally to a contract for the sale of a part-interest (eg those relating to delivery). The Law Commission (on whose recommendation the amendment to s 61(1) was based) took the view that any problems that might arise would normally be overcome by a finding that it was the express or presumed intention of the parties to disapply the particular statutory provision.

(d) 'Existing goods' and 'future goods'

Section 5 divides 'goods' into two categories: (1) 'existing goods', ie goods owned or possessed by the seller, and (2) 'future goods'—goods to be manufactured or acquired by the seller after the making of the contract of sale. It goes on to make it plain that there cannot be a 'sale' (in the statutory sense, involving an immediate conveyance) of future goods, by declaring that where a seller purports to effect a present sale of future goods, the contract operates as an agreement to sell the goods (s 5(3)).

'Existing' does not mean 'in existence' in an everyday sense. Goods which are in existence, but are not yet owned or possessed by the seller, are 'future goods' for the purposes of the Act. So if S and B are in a supermarket together, and they agree that S will buy a dozen bottles of wine which are at a special discount if bought by the dozen, and that S will then resell six bottles to B, their contract is for 'future goods', even though the bottles are in existence and even if the particular six which B is to take have been identified.

It may be helpful at times to classify 'future goods' into various sub-categories. These will include:

(1) goods to be manufactured by the seller;

(2) goods to be acquired by the seller (by purchase, gift, succession, or otherwise—eg fish which he expects or hopes to catch); goods not yet in existence (eg lambs to be born next spring, fruit or potatoes to be harvested next autumn); and

(3) (possibly) things which do exist, but are not yet 'goods' (eg minerals not yet extracted but still forming part of the seller's land).

The reference in s 5(2) to possession of the goods ('owned *or possessed by* the seller') is, at first sight, puzzling. But some sections of the Act (eg ss 12(3), 22, 24, 25(1) and 48(2)) contemplate a sale being made by a person who has no title or a defective title, and it is probably provisions such as these which the draftsman had in mind when formulating the wording of s 5(2).

The time taken as a reference point for the purpose of s 5(1) is that when the contract of sale is made. This is also the case in relation to the other major classification of goods, into 'specific' and 'unascertained' goods, which is examined next.

(e) 'Specific goods' and 'unascertained goods'

By s 61(1), 'specific goods' means goods identified and agreed on at the time a contract of sale is made. The counterpart expression used in the Act, 'unascertained goods', is curiously not defined anywhere, but must by inference mean goods *not* identified and agreed on at the time the contract of sale is made. For goods to be specific, they must be designated as the unique article or articles that the contract is concerned with, and must be capable of being so designated (and actually so designated) at the time of the contract. It is not necessary that the goods in question should be physically present before the parties at that time, although that would be the most obvious example of 'specific goods': goods can also be specific even though they are identified only by words of description (eg 'the grey horse now in my stable'—there being only one grey horse there). Typically (though not, as we shall see, exclusively), unascertained goods are goods sold 'by description', that is, the goods are commodities of a generic kind such as grain, coal, oil, etc, and the seller undertakes to procure for the buyer the agreed quantity of such goods, with such further characteristics as to quality, etc as may be specified—eg a 'new white 2.0 litre VW Golf GTI car, 5 door', or '100 tonnes of King Edward potatoes, East Anglia grown'.

Unascertained goods fall into three main categories:

(1) generic goods sold by description, as described above;

(2) goods not yet in existence, to be grown or manufactured, such as a suit to be made by a tailor;

(3) a part as yet unidentified out of a specific or identified bulk, eg 10 tonnes out of the 100 tonnes (or out of the unmeasured heap) of potatoes now in my store.

An amendment made to s 61(1) by the Act of 1995 adds a rider to the definition: 'specific goods' now 'includes an undivided share, specified as a fraction or percentage, of goods identified and agreed on as aforesaid'. We must therefore make a distinction between the example just given (10 tonnes out of the identified 100 tonnes of potatoes) and a contract to sell a one-tenth share or a 10 per cent interest in the 100 tonnes. At the completion of the first of these deals, the buyer will own 10 tonnes and the seller the remaining 90, while under the second, the two will become co-owners of the 100 tonnes in the agreed proportions.

The most important reason for distinguishing between specific goods and unascertained goods is to be found in the rule—or at least the basic rule—contained in s 16, which states that it is not possible to transfer the property in unascertained goods to the buyer unless and until the contract goods are ascertained. This basic rule is now subject to an exception contained in s 20A, introduced in 1995 (see below, p 320). But, apart from this one exception, it remains a fundamental proposition which nothing that the parties may agree to or do or say can breach or vary. The leading cases on this point include *Re Wait,* cited above, p 266 which now falls within the exception created by s 20A, and *Kursell v Timber Operators & Contractors Ltd.*

Kursell v Timber Operators & Contractors Ltd
[1927] 1 KB 298, Court of Appeal

The contract between the parties was for the sale of all the merchantable timber growing on a certain date in a forest in Latvia, 'merchantable timber' being defined in the contract as 'all trunks and branches of trees but not seedlings and young trees of less than six inches in diameter at a height of four feet from the ground'. The buyers were to have 15 years to cut the timber. Shortly afterwards, the Latvian government passed a law nationalising the forest. The sellers argued that the property in the timber had passed to the buyers and that accordingly the consequences of the nationalisation decree fell on them. The court held, however, that the timber which was the subject of the contract of sale was not 'specific goods', since the trees answering to the contract measurements had not been identified (and could not, in fact, be identified until the time came to cut them, which could be at any time within the 15-year period); it followed that the timber was still the property of the sellers and the contract was frustrated.

Scrutton LJ: What is the legal result of these facts? In the first place has the property passed? It was said that this was a contract for the sale of specific goods in a deliverable state under s 18, r 1, of the Sale of Goods Act. Specific goods are defined as goods identified and agreed upon at the time a contract of sale is made. It appears to me these goods were neither identified nor agreed upon. Not every tree in the forest passed, but only those complying with a certain measurement not then made. How much of each tree passed depended on where it was cut, how far from the ground. Nor does the timber seem to be in a deliverable state until the buyer has severed it. He cannot under the definition be bound to take delivery of an undetermined part of a tree not yet identified....

For these reasons in my opinion the property had not passed under s 18, r 1, and, therefore, the timber was not at the risk of the purchasers.

[Lord Hanworth MR and Sargant LJ delivered concurring judgments.]

Section 16, and also some other sections (ss 17, 52) use the further expression, 'ascertained goods'. Like 'unascertained goods', this phrase has no statutory definition. But Atkin LJ in *Re Wait* [19271 1 Ch 606 at 630 explained it as meaning goods which at the time of the making of the contract are unascertained but which become identified as the contract goods at some later time. For instance, in *Aldridge v Johnson* (below, p 279), the buyer, who had agreed to buy a quantity of barley, left his own sacks with the seller to be filled with barley from his bulk store. It was held that the barley became 'ascertained' (ie identified as the buyer's) as it was shovelled into his sacks, sackful by sackful, even before the total contract quantity had been measured out.

QUESTIONS

1. Can any category of future goods ever be specific goods in the statutory sense? (Consider the example of the six bottles of wine, above, p 272.)
2. Can goods not yet in existence ever be specific goods in the statutory sense?

(f) 'The property'

The definition of a contract of sale in s 2(1) requires that the seller should transfer or agree to transfer 'the property' in goods to the buyer. In s 61(1) we are told that 'property' means 'the general property in goods, and not merely a special property'. This expression, 'special property', is sometimes used to describe the interest of a pledgee, in order to emphasise the fact that he has something more than mere possession of the goods which have been pledged. (On pledge, see below, p 1091.) A pledgee has title to an interest in the goods which he can deal with, eg by sub-pledge or assignment, and in certain circumstances he has a power of sale. But he does not have *the general property* in the goods, in the statutory sense, and so a transfer of his interest as pledgee cannot be a sale.

In loose terms, we may think of 'the property' as meaning simply 'ownership'. To be more precise, however, 'the property' which a seller transfers or agrees to transfer is his title to *the absolute legal interest* in the goods: see the article by Battersby and Preston of which an extract is cited below. A pledgee has title only to a more limited interest, which is therefore excluded from the statutory definition. For this reason, the Act will not apply to a transfer by an owner of goods to someone else of an interest less than full ownership—eg a contract of hire or some other form of bailment, or which creates a charge over goods. Nor will it apply to the transfer of such an interest by the hirer or bailee or chargee to a third party. And since we are concerned only with the *legal* interest in goods, the Act is not concerned with transfers of beneficial ownership, such as may arise on the creation of a trust.

It does not follow, however, that a seller has to have, or to purport to transfer, a complete or perfect legal title to the goods in order to bring a transaction within the statutory definition of a 'sale of goods'. Sections 21–25 and 48(2) all deal with cases where the seller has no title, or a defective title. And s 12(3) (a provision first inserted by the Supply of Goods (Implied Terms) Act 1973) expressly contemplates that a seller who has only a limited title to goods may contract to sell that title. So, a person who has found an article and has failed to trace its owner may sell his title to it as a finder. The subsection also states that a seller may contract to sell whatever title a third person may have to the goods. This might happen, for instance, when a pawnbroker sells goods as unredeemed pledges: he does not contract to confer on the buyers any better title than the various pledgors may have. This analysis is entirely consistent with the views of Battersby and Preston referred to above: the seller here is contracting to sell such title as he (or the third person) has to an absolute legal interest in the goods, not a title to some more limited interest.

'The Concepts of "Property", "Title" and "Owner" used in the Sale of Goods Act 1893' by G Battersby and AD Preston
(1972) 35 MLR 268, pp 268–272, 288

(Footnotes in the original article are omitted.)

A. THE THREE ELEMENTS INVOLVED IN A TRANSFER OF TANGIBLE PROPERTY

In the transfer of any tangible property, whether land or chattels, three elements are distinguishable, namely, the estate or interest which is transferred, the title to that estate or interest, and the evidence of that title.

(1) Estate or interest transferred

What rights are being transferred and what is their duration? In the context of land, the rights must be, for example, the fee simple, the residue of a 999-year lease, a life estate, or some lesser interest such as a perpetual easement. Similarly, in relation to chattels, although the range of interests recognised by the law is restricted, one needs to distinguish life interests, entailed interests and absolute interests, as well as various kinds of incumbrance. Whether the transfer involves land or chattels, therefore, its nature can be understood only when the estate or interest to be transferred is defined.

(2) Title to that estate or interest

Is there anyone who can show that the transferor's title to the estate or interest is defective? The fundamental rule of the English law of property affecting title is *nemo dat quod non habet*. Its effect is that, although a transfer may comply with the legal formalities required for the transfer of the interest in question, it may yet fail to take effect because the transferor has no title to transfer. It is equally possible, however, that the transferor may have a title, but one which is less than perfect. This follows from the elementary proposition of our law that title to tangible property, whether land or chattels, is relative. The title to such property is protected by the possessory actions, which require only that the plaintiff must have possession or the immediate right to possession. This principle, and the converse rule that, subject to very narrow exceptions, the defendant cannot plead *jus tertii*, mean that mere adverse possession of property confers a title which is good against all the world except a person who can prove a better title, that is to say, a person with a continuing prior title. This notion of relative title permeates our law, and is one of the key concepts in the law of property, though in sale of goods, unlike conveyancing of land, it is frequently forgotten. Given such a concept, the phrase 'owner of property' assumes significance only in relation to a particular issue with a particular person . . . . The concept of absolute ownership, by which is meant an indefeasible title to the absolute interest in the particular property, is as elusive in the realm of chattels as in that of land. True, there are exceptional cases of absolute ownership: a sale of goods in market overt to a purchaser in good faith [was formerly] an exception relating to chattels, and in the case of land one may instance the statutory procedure by which all existing interests may be compulsorily purchased. These exceptional cases, however, in no way derogate from the general principle. In a legal system which guaranteed that all transfers would vest an indefeasible title in the transferee the distinction between title and interest would be unnecessary, but English law, adopting the *nemo dat rule,* does not provide such a guarantee. In any given situation, therefore, the phrase 'transfer of property' needs expanding to 'the transfer of such-and-such a title to such-and-such an interest.'

(3) Evidence of title

By what facts does the transferor of property prove his title? This question assumes great importance in transactions concerning land; in the case of transactions concerning chattels, however, there is normally no investigation of title, the transferor's possession of the chattels apparently as owner affording the only evidence. The reasons for this are not hard to find: it is extremely rare for any documentary title to exist; the transient value of most chattels means that the chain of title will usually be short; there are exceptions to the rule *nemo dat quod non habet* which reduce the risk of bad titles; in any event, the value of chattels must often render investigation of title something of an excess. The question of evidence of title to chattels can accordingly be forgotten.

Our basic submission, therefore, is that the two objects of currency in the English system of property and conveyancing are interests and title, and that what is dealt with in a particular transfer is a particular title to a particular interest in the property in question.

B. THE DEFINITION OF A SALE OF GOODS

With these basic points in mind, we turn to examine in more detail the nature of a sale of goods. The transaction is defined in section 1 [now s 2] of the Sale of Goods Act. Section 1(1) reads:

> A contract of sale of goods is a contract whereby the seller transfers or agrees to transfer the property in goods to the buyer for a money consideration, called the price. There may be a contract of sale between one part owner and another.

This definition is amplified in section 1(3) [now s 2(4), (5)] as follows:

> Where under a contract of sale the property in the goods is transferred from the seller to the buyer the contract is called a sale; but where the transfer of the property in the goods is to take place at a future time or subject to some condition thereafter to be fulfilled the contract is called an agreement to sell.

It will be observed first that the person selling the goods is called 'the seller,' not 'the owner.' The latter term is used at the end of subsection (1) (a 'sale between one part owner and another'), but it is clear from the context that the word 'owner' is not intended to have any flavour different from the word 'seller'; just as 'the seller' is a person who sells or agrees to sell a particular title, so 'the owner' is a person who owns a particular title, and as part owner owns that title concurrently with another. These words and phrases do not, therefore, indicate the use of any concept of absolute ownership.

Secondly, it will be observed that both subsections refer to the transfer of 'property in goods.' What is the concept of 'property' here employed? It is self-evident from the context that the word 'property' is not used in the sense of the physical chattels themselves, for the word 'goods' is used for that purpose. 'Property' therefore refers in some way to the proprietary right which is transferred by the sale. In our submission, 'property' comprises the two elements distinguished earlier as being involved in any transfer of property, namely, interest and title. So far as the interest is concerned, the purpose is to define a sale as involving the transfer of the absolute legal interest in the goods (analogous to the legal fee simple estate in land), as opposed to any lesser interest. This is made clear by the definition of 'property' in section 62 [now s 61] as 'the general property in the goods and not merely a special property.' Clearly, therefore, the creation for value of a bailment, which involves the transfer merely of possession and not of the absolute interest (analogous in many ways to the grant of a lease of land), is not a sale. Equally, in our submission, the transfer for value of a life interest in goods would not be a sale as defined, but would be regarded as an assignment of that life interest. But the concept of 'property' involves also the notion of title, for a sale must involve the transfer of a *particular title* to the absolute interest. In this general definition of sale, however, nothing is said about the *quality* of that title, which may be good, bad or indifferent on the scale of relativity. Nor would one expect anything to be said about the quality of title in the definition of the transaction: it would be logically and linguistically inapposite. What section 1 of the Act really achieves, therefore, is a definition of the nature of the contract of sale of goods, and this definition is expanded into two forms: (i) 'a contract whereby the seller transfers…the property in goods to the buyer' (ii) 'a contract whereby the seller…agrees to transfer the property in goods to the buyer.' These formulations of the definition differ in that the latter separates the stages of contracting to convey and conveyance, while the former telescopes the two stages so that both contract to convey and conveyance occur simultaneously; this telescoping, however, in no way detracts from the point that contract and conveyance are independent notions. More importantly these formulations share the feature that the contract of sale of goods concerns the transfer of a title to the absolute legal interest in the goods. In exactly the same way, one could define a contract for the sale of land as 'a contract for the transfer for value of a title to the fee simple estate' (ie separating the two elements of 'property'); that is merely an explanation of the nature of the transaction, corresponding to the second of the above formulations of the definition of a contract for the sale of goods, and containing within itself no promise as to quality of title, for which the parties are left to provide, if they wish, by appropriate contractual terms. Again, one could define a gift of goods as 'a voluntary transfer of the property in goods,' this merely serving to explain the nature of the transaction, for it is in the last degree unlikely that any undertakings as to the quality of the title will be given. Our point is that in all these cases it is the nature of the transaction that is being defined, and that nature is the transfer of a title to the absolute legal interest. The title which is in fact transferred, unless the case falls within an exception to the *nemo dat* rule, will always be the title vested in the seller at the time of the transfer: if it is poorer than that contracted for, the seller will be liable to the buyer for breach of contract, whilst if it is better than that contracted for, the risk assumed by the buyer will be proportionately less burdensome….

SUMMARY

The above arguments have led to the following principal conclusions:

(1) The notion of relative title is fundamental in English law, and is the main key to understanding the proprietary concepts used in the law of sale of goods.

(2) A distinction must be drawn between title and interest, the law of sale of goods being concerned with the transfer of a title to the absolute legal interest in the goods sold.

(3) The concept of 'property' in the Sale of Goods Act, despite the limited meaning assigned to it by section 62(1), must be expanded to mean 'a title to the absolute legal interest in the goods sold,' which meaning is used consistently throughout the Act.

(4) The concept of 'title,' as used in sections 21–26 of the Act, must be expanded to take in the notion that the transfer relates to the absolute legal interest in the goods sold, with the result that 'title' bears a similar meaning to 'property' in the above sense.

(5) A contract of sale is a contract which involves the transfer of a title to the absolute legal interest, and not necessarily a good title; a transfer which excludes the implied undertakings as to good title is still a sale, and there is no bar to such exclusion as the law now stands.

(6) Care is needed in applying the exceptions to the *nemo dat* rule, because of the ambiguity of expressions such as 'owner' and 'good title.' A few of the exceptions have the effect of generating a new perfect title, but the majority have the much more limited effect of transferring a particular title, which may itself be defeasible, by overriding some prior transaction or interest.

(The whole of this important article is particularly worthy of study.)

NOTES

1.   HL Ho [1997] CLJ 571, makes some further pertinent observations. 'Property', he contends, is 'transaction specific', whereas 'title' is 'entity and time' specific:

'Property must be analysed in the context of a particular transaction and its passing as between the buyer and the seller is not affected by the location of absolute title. Absolute title on the other hand can vest in only one entity at any particular point in time and its location has to be determined by taking into consideration all the relevant transactions.'

The 'relevant transactions' would include, for instance, an event which 'feeds' a defective title so as to perfect it, and a transaction which, under an exception to the *nemo dat* principle (see below, pp 349ff), divests the true owner of title and vests it in a buyer.

2.   Professor Battersby has responded to some criticisms and elaborated some aspects of this article in the light of *National Employers Association Ltd v Jones* (below, p 385): [2001] JBL 1. On relativity of title to goods, see D Fox [2006] CLJ 330 at 340ff.

3 SALE OF GOODS DISTINGUISHED FROM OTHER TRANSACTIONS

There are various types of transaction which in some ways resemble contracts for the sale of goods, but do not fall within the statutory definition. This means that the Act cannot be directly applied to such contracts. However, it may be of indirect relevance, since the Act of 1893 may have codified a rule of the common law which, prior to that date, had an application wider than the sale of goods. The common law rules, in their uncodified form, may be assumed to continue to apply to these other contracts. So it may be that many sale of goods rules are equally applicable to contracts of barter: it is only the dearth of litigated cases on barter that prevents us from knowing how far the parallel extends. Again, in formulating legislation to govern some of these other types of transaction (eg the Supply of Goods and Services Act 1982), the statutory draftsman has often modelled his new law on the Sale of Goods Act and sometimes copied its language verbatim. It would be surprising if a court were to rule that cases decided on the construction of this language in the Sale of Goods Act were not relevant guides to its meaning in the context of the later Act.

(a) Sale distinguished from gift

A gift differs from a sale because there is no consideration for the transfer of the property in the goods. This is usually an obvious matter, but in borderline cases the court may be faced with a very difficult question. Eg in the well-known case *Esso Petroleum Ltd v Customs and Excise Comrs* [1976] 1 All ER 117, motorists were offered a 'free' medallion with each purchase of four gallons of petrol. There was a difference of judicial opinion whether the medallions were the subject of a gift or a sale, or of a contract collateral to the purchase of the petrol which fell into neither of these categories.

(b) Sale distinguished from barter or exchange

The Act stipulates that the consideration in a contract of sale should be in money. If it takes some other form (eg where goods are exchanged for other goods, for services, or for any other thing of value), it is a contract of barter or exchange and not one of sale and the Act will not apply to it. This may not always be important, for it is likely that many of the rules which applied to sales at common law also applied (and continue to apply) to barter. But in the absence of clear precedents we cannot be sure that this is invariably so.

Where goods are exchanged for other goods (and particularly where some money is paid by one of the parties as well), it is not always necessary or appropriate to construe the transaction as one of barter. In *Aldridge v Johnson* (below), the evidence seems to have pointed to an arrangement under which there were reciprocal *sales* of the bullocks and the barley; the prices of each were calculated and then set off against each other, and the balance of £23 was agreed to be paid in cash. In other words, there were two separate contracts of sale, and it is consistent with this analysis that sale of goods principles were applied. In *Dawson v Dutfield,* however (a typical 'trading-in' case), the court preferred to take the view that there was only one contract of sale, namely that by Dawsons to Dutfields of the newer lorries for £475; there was then a subsidiary arrangement that if Dutfields chose to deliver the two older lorries in part exchange, they would be allowed £225 off the price.

Aldridge v Johnson
(1857) 7 E & B 885, Court of Queen's Bench

Aldridge made a deal with Knights to exchange 32 bullocks for 100 quarters of barley, to be measured out of a larger amount lying in Knights' granary which Aldridge had inspected the day before. They valued the bullocks at £6 each (ie £192 in all) and the barley at £215, and agreed that the difference of £23 would be paid in cash. Knights took delivery of the bullocks, and Aldridge sent 200 of his own sacks, each holding half a quarter, to Knights to be filled with barley from the heap in the granary and put on the railway by Knights' men. One hundred and fifty-five of the 200 sacks had been filled when, on Knights' instructions, they were emptied out into the heap again. Aldridge then learned that Knights was about to be declared bankrupt. In this action brought against Johnson, Knights' trustee in bankruptcy, Aldridge claimed the right to 100 quarters out of the barley in the heap; but the court held that only the barley in the 155 sacks had become Aldridge's property. It also held that he had not been divested of it when the sacks were emptied back into the heap. But Aldridge had no claim to the rest of the 100 quarters which had never been put into his sacks.

Lord Campbell CJ: I think that no portion of what remained in bulk ever vested in the plaintiff. We cannot tell what part of that is to vest. No rule of the law of vendor and purchaser is more clear than this: that, until the appropriation and separation of a particular quantity, or signification of assent to the particular quantity, the property is not transferred. Therefore, except as to what was put into the 155 sacks, there must be judgment for the defendant. It is equally clear that, as to what was put into those sacks, there must be judgment for the plaintiff. Looking to all that was done, when the bankrupt put the barley into the sacks *eo instanti* the property in each sack-full vested in the plaintiff. I consider that here was *a priori* an assent by the plaintiff. He had inspected and approved of the barley in bulk. He sent his sacks to be filled out of that bulk. There can be no doubt of his assent to the appropriation of such bulk as should have been put into the sacks. There was also evidence of his subsequent appropriation, by his order that it should be sent on. There remained nothing to be done by the vendor, who had appropriated a part by the direction of the vendee. It is the same as if boxes had been filled and sent on by the bankrupt, in which case it cannot be disputed that the property would pass: and it can make no difference that the plaintiff ordered the sacks to be forwarded by the vendor. As to the question of conversion, the property being in the plaintiff, he has done nothing to divest himself of it. It is not like the case of confusion of goods, where the owner of such articles as oil or wine mixes them with similar articles belonging to another. That is a wrongful act by the owner, for which he is punished by losing his property. Here the plaintiff has done nothing wrong. It was wrong of the bankrupt to mix what had been put into the sacks with the rest of the barley; but no wrong has been done by the plaintiff. That being so, the plaintiffs property comes into the hands of the defendant as the bankrupt's assignee....He claims all the barley, and claims all of it as being the property of the bankrupt. He therefore has converted the plaintiff s property.

[Coleridge, Erle and Crompton JJ delivered concurring judgments.]

NOTES

1.   Like *Re Wait*, this case would now be affected by the new s 20A. Aldridge, as a pre paying buyer, would be able to claim a proprietary interest in the bulk proportionate to 200 notional sackfuls, and not just 155: see below, p 320.

2.   The modern law relating to mixing (or 'confusion') of goods no longer 'punishes' a person who wrongfully mixes his own goods with someone else's by declaring them forfeited to the innocent party. The two become tenants in common of the resulting mix, with any doubts as to either quantity or quality being resolved in the innocent party's favour (*Indian Oil Corpn Ltd v Greenstone Shipping SA (Panama)* [1988] QB 345).

G J Dawson (Clapham) Ltd v H & G Dutfield

[1936] 2 All ER 232, King's Bench Division

Dawsons, dealers in secondhand vehicles, agreed to sell Dutfields two lorries, a Leyland and a Saurer, for a combined price of £475 of which £250 was paid or credited at the time. They also agreed to allow Dutfields £225 as the trade-in price of two Leyland vehicles, which Dutfields were allowed to use while their new purchases were being overhauled, provided that they were delivered to Dawsons within a month. The Saurer turned out to be in a much worse condition than the parties expected and, after arrangements to provide another vehicle in its place had proved abortive, Dawsons sued for the balance of the price of the two lorries. It was held that they could sue for this sum and were not bound to take the other vehicles as trade-ins.

Hilbery J: The first agreement was a complete one and completely executed by the plaintiffs; all that remained to be done was to be done by the defendants. The plaintiffs had discharged their duty. Further the agreement was not a severable one.... There is no evidence of any agreement to put aside the old agreement and treat it as non-existent. There is no more than an expression by the plaintiffs of intention to placate the defendants, an expression of willingness to take back the Saurer and try and find a suitable lorry in order to ease the situation for the defendants. It was the expression of a pious—or I should say business—hope.

Someone must bear the burden of a bad bargain and the loss arising from the fact that the condition of the lorry was so much worse than expected. The thing was sold as it stood, and bought after examination by people who understood that there was much to be done to it. Neither party understood how bad it was. My decision is that the plaintiffs are entitled to the balance of the purchase money in the terms of the claim, owing to the non-delivery of the two Leylands. These had to be delivered within one month and if they had so delivered them, the defendants would have been entitled so to satisfy the purchase price to the extent of £225. They did not do so and there remains £225 as part of the purchase price due to the plaintiffs. The action in such circumstances is not one in detinue, and therefore no demand is necessary. Nor are the plaintiffs bound to claim the lorries. The defendants were merely given the right to satisfy £225 of the purchase price by the delivery of the lorries within one month or thereabouts. Such an arrangement does not deprive the plaintiffs of their right to the purchase price in cash. The defendants have not delivered and there must be judgment for the plaintiffs for the balance of the purchase price.

NOTES

1. In the United States, the price in a contract of sale may be paid in money or otherwise; if it is payable in whole or part in goods, each party is a seller of the goods which he wishes to transfer (Uniform Commercial Code, para 2–304(1)).

2. Some aspects of the contract of barter are now governed by the Supply of Goods and Services Act 1982. This Act provides for statutory terms as to title, quality, etc to be implied into contracts of barter, using much the same language as ss 12–15 of the Sale of Goods Act; but it does not deal with the question—when does the property pass?—which was vital in *Aldridge v Johnson* and might have been answered differently if the transaction had been viewed as one of pure barter.

3. A price is payable in money (and therefore the transaction will be a sale) even where payment is effected by credit card or in some similar way: see the discussion of *Re Charge Card Services Ltd* below, p 818.

QUESTIONS

1. If Dutfields *had* traded in the two older lorries, what would have been the nature of that second transaction—a sale, a barter, or something else? What was the consideration given by Dawsons?

2. In the Irish case *Flynn v Mackin* [1974] IR 101 a motor dealer agreed to supply Father Mackin with a new car in exchange for his old car plus a cash payment of £250. No valuation or price was put by the parties on either vehicle. Was there a sale of (1) the new car, (2) the old car, (3) neither?

(c) Sale of goods distinguished from transfer of an interest in land

There is an overlap between these categories of contract, as has been noted above (p 269). A contract under which a person is to come on to another's land and remove gravel, for instance, may be so drawn as to appear to be a grant of mineral rights, on the one hand, or a sale of the gravel, as goods, on the other. Although it is possible to frame such a contract so as to give it an emphasis either way, it should be borne in mind that more than one statutory regime may be applicable (see above, pp 269–272), and that even though the parties may intend to make a sale of goods, the transaction may be overriden before severance by the claim of a third party with a superior title to the land.

(d) Sale distinguished from bailment

A bailment (see above, p 78) involves the delivery of goods by one person to another for a limited purpose, on terms that the goods will be returned to the bailor or delivered to a third party in accordance with his instructions at the conclusion of the bailment. There is normally no likelihood that a contract of bailment will be confused with one of sale, but the question did arise in *South Australian Insurance Co v Randell* (1869) LR 3 PC 101. In that case, a farmer had delivered corn to a miller and tipped it into a common store, on terms which allowed him to claim at any time either the redelivery of an equivalent quantity of corn or the market price of such corn ruling on the day in which he made his demand. Since the identity of the corn was lost when it was delivered, and there was no obligation on the miller, if redelivery was demanded, to make the redelivery from the same store—or, indeed, from any particular source—it was held that the transaction could not be a bailment but was more in the nature of a sale.

The distinction between sale and bailment may be blurred in some cases involving a manufacturer. For instance, components or part-finished goods may be delivered to a manufacturer, on terms that they will be combined with other goods belonging to the latter and used to make an end-product which is then either redelivered to the original supplier for a charge, or sold on to a third party for a price for which, or out of which, the seller will account to the supplier. The question whether the transaction is a bailment by the supplier of his goods to the manufacturer or one involving a transfer (perhaps a sale) of the property in his goods and a resale back to him (or a sale on to the third party) can be very complex: the answer turns essentially on the terms of the contract, but may also be influenced by such factors as whether one party has supplied the 'principal' goods, and by whether the goods supplied remain identifiable throughout the manufacturing process. Some aspects of this question are discussed below when we examine the *Romalpa* line of cases: see below, p 452.

QUESTIONS

1.   Would the Sale of Goods Act apply to a transaction such as that in *South Australian Insurance Co v Randell*?

2.   Twenty farmers agree to rent a store owned by Bloggs, where they tip their grain into a common bulk when it is harvested in August. It is agreed that Bloggs will sell one-tenth of the total quantity on the first of each month, beginning on 1 October and ending on 1 July, and share out the proceeds (less the rent and a commission) among the farmers on a pro rata basis, proportionate to the total quantity which each has contributed. What is the nature of this arrangement? (See *Mercer v Craven Grain Storage Ltd* [1994] CLC 328, and L Smith (1995) 111 LQR 10.)

3.   A day-old chick costs £1 and the food, etc required to rear it until it is ready to lay costs £2. It can then be sold for £3.50. Consider what different arrangements might be made between A, who hatches chicks, and B, who grows foodstuffs for poultry and has the facilities for rearing them.

A contract of sale should also be distinguished from other forms of bailment, such as a contract to lease or hire goods, and a pledge.

In the commercial world, specialised forms of lease have developed, notably the 'finance lease', under which the position of the lessee is in many respects similar to that of a buyer. The finance lease can be used in relation to plant and vehicles of all sorts, ranging all the way from a photocopier to a jet airliner. In the normal case the term of the lease approximates to that of the expected working life of the goods in question, and the total of the hire charges paid by the lessee over this period is roughly equal to its capital cost plus the lessor's profit from the transaction. The lessee undertakes responsibility for the maintenance and repair of the goods, and to pay the hire charges whether the goods are in working order or not. Thus his position, though different in law, is in practical terms little different from that of a buyer who has agreed to pay the purchase price of the goods by instalments over a similar period, at the end of which they will have come to the end of their useful life. The finance lease may have tax advantages and, as a form of 'off balance-sheet accounting' may be used to enhance the appearance of a firm's financial statements. (See also below, p 927.)

A contract of hire-purchase is a form of bailment, but is sufficiently important to be discussed separately.

(e) Sale distinguished from hire-purchase

In a contract of hire-purchase, goods are hired by their owner to a person for a period, at the end of which he may exercise an option, conferred upon him by the contract, to buy the goods, usually by making a further modest payment. In practical terms (though not in legal form), the position of the hirer under such a contract is very similar to that of a person who has agreed to buy the goods from their owner on the understanding that he is to take immediate delivery, but pay the price by instalments over a period. Such a contract of sale may take two forms. If the property passes to the buyer at once, it is commonly called a 'credit sale'. If the seller retains the property in the goods until the whole of the price is paid, it is termed a 'conditional sale'. Each of these forms of contract of sale differs from a contract of hire-purchase because the buyer is contractually bound to complete the transaction: he has 'agreed to buy'. The hirer under a contract of hire-purchase, in contrast, has only an option to buy, which he is free to exercise or not as he chooses; and he also commonly has the right to terminate the hiring before the expiry of the contemplated period. The effectiveness of hire-purchase—as a transaction which gives possession and use of the goods to the hirer whilst at the same time ensuring that the seller's retention of title gives him maximum protection as regards payment—was established in the leading case *of Helby v Matthews* (below). This may be contrasted with the decision in *Lee v Butler* (below, p 382), where the transaction took the form of a conditional sale agreement, and it was held that the rights of the seller (though protected in the event of the buyer's insolvency) could be defeated by an unauthorised resale of the goods by the buyer to a bona fide third party.

The distinction between hire-purchase and sale can be important. In particular, it should be noted that the two popular forms of 'instalment credit' transaction referred to above—the credit sale and the conditional sale—are in law contracts of sale to which (subject to the consumer credit legislation referred to below) the Sale of Goods Act is applicable, whereas a contract of hire-purchase is wholly outside the scope of the Act, at least until the option to purchase is exercised.

Helby v Matthews
[1895] AC 471, House of Lords

Helby contracted to hire a piano to Brewster for three years at a rental of 10s 6d (52p) a month. The contract included the following provisions:

The owner agrees:

A.   That the hirer may terminate the hiring by delivering up to the owner the said instrument.

B.   If the hirer shall punctually pay the full sum of £18 18s by 10s 6d at date of signing, and by 36 monthly instalments of 10s 6d in advance as aforesaid, the said instrument shall become the sole and absolute property of the hirer.

C.   Unless and until the full sum of £18 18s be paid, the said instrument shall be and continue to be the sole property of the owner.

Brewster, without any authority from Helby, pledged the piano with Matthews, a pawnbroker, as security for a loan. Although Brewster was not the owner of the piano, the pledge would have been effective under the Factors Act 1889, s 9, if the contract had been one of conditional sale (see *Lee v Butler*, below, p 382). The House of Lords, reversing the Court of Appeal, held that it was not a conditional sale, and that Helby was entitled to claim the piano from the pawnbroker.

Lord Herschell LC: My Lords, I cannot, with all respect, concur in the view of the Court of Appeal, that upon the true construction of the agreement Brewster had 'agreed to buy' the piano. An agreement to buy imports a legal obligation to buy. If there was no such legal obligation, there cannot, in my opinion, properly be said to have been an agreement to buy. Where is any such legal obligation to be found? Brewster might buy or not just as he pleased. He did not agree to make thirty-six or any number of monthly payments. All that he undertook was to make the monthly payment of 10s 6d as long as he kept the piano. He had an option no doubt to buy it by continuing the stipulated payments for a sufficient length of time. If he had exercised that option he would have become the purchaser. I cannot see under these circumstances how he can be said either to have bought or agreed to buy the piano. The terms of the contract did not upon its execution bind him to buy, but left him free to do so or not as he pleased, and nothing happened after the contract was made to impose that obligation.

The Master of the Rolls said: 'It is a contract by the seller to sell, and a contract by the purchaser, if he does not change his mind, to buy; and if this agreement goes on to its end, it ends in a purchase. Therefore, it seems to me that the true and proper construction of this instrument, after all, is this: it is an agreement by the one to sell, and an agreement by the other to buy, but with an option on the part of the buyer if he changes his mind to put an end to the contract.' I cannot think that an agreement to buy, 'if he does not change his mind,' is any agreement to buy at all in the eye of the law. If it rests with me to do or not to do a certain thing at a future time, according to the then state of my mind, I cannot be said to have contracted to do it. It appears to me that the contract in question was in reality a contract of hiring, and not in name or pretence only. But for the provision that if the hirer punctually paid the 10s 6d a month for thirty-six months, the piano should be his property, it could not be doubted that it was a mere agreement for its hire, and I cannot see how the fact that this provision was added made it any the less a contract of hiring until that condition had been fulfilled.

I think it very likely that both parties thought it would probably end in a purchase, but this is far from shewing that it was an agreement to buy. The monthly payments were no doubt somewhat higher than they would have been if the agreement had contained no such provision. One can well conceive cases, however, in which a person who had not made up his mind to continue the payments for three years would nevertheless enter into such an agreement. It might be worth his while to make somewhat larger monthly payments for the use of the piano in order that he might enjoy that option if he chose to exercise it. In such a case how could it be said that he had agreed to buy when he had not only come under no obligation to buy, but had not even made up his mind to do so? The agreement is, in its terms, just as applicable to such a case as to one where the hirer had resolved to continue the payments for the three years, and it must be construed upon a consideration of the obligations which its terms create, and not upon a mere speculation as to what was contemplated, or what would probably be done under it.

It was said in the Court of Appeal that there was an agreement by the appellant to sell, and that an agreement to sell connotes an agreement to buy. This is undoubtedly true if the words 'agreement to sell' be used in their strict legal sense; but when a person has, for valuable consideration, bound himself to sell to another on certain terms, if the other chooses to avail himself of the binding offer, he may, in popular language, be said to have agreed to sell, though an agreement to sell in this sense, which is in truth merely an offer which cannot be withdrawn, certainly does not connote an agreement to buy, and it is only in this sense that there can be said to have been an agreement to sell in the present case.

[Lords Watson, Macnaghten and Shand delivered concurring opinions. Lord Morris concurred.]

NOTES

1.   This case established that the owner of the goods which are let out under a hire-purchase agreement cannot lose his title under s 9 of the Factors Act 1889 (or its equivalent, s 25(1) of the Sale of Goods Act 1979). A second ruling of the House of Lords in *McEntire v Crossley Bros Ltd* [1895] AC 457 held that a contract in similar form was not a disguised transaction by way of security and accordingly liable to be held void if not registered as a bill of sale under the Bills of Sale Act (1878) Amendment Act 1882. The two principal difficulties which had arguably stood in the way of the hire-purchase form being fully effective were thus surmounted by these near-contemporaneous decisions; and the way was cleared for it to become the principal instrument for instalment purchases ever since.

2.   In *Forthright Finance Ltd v Carlyle Finance Ltd* [1997] 4 All ER 90, CA Forthright delivered a Ford Cosworth car to Carlyle under a contract, described as a hire-purchase contract, on terms that Carlyle would pay 36 monthly instalments totalling £15,270 and that it would then be deemed to have exercised an option to purchase the car unless it elected not to take title. Since Carlyle was contractually bound to pay all 36 instalments and it was virtually inconceivable that it would elect not to receive title, the Court of Appeal held that the transaction was a conditional sale agreement, 'both in substance and in form'.

3.   Since 1938, there has been legislation designed to protect consumers who fall into difficulties under hire-purchase transactions—whether because the terms of the hiring are onerous or because they have trouble in keeping up the agreed hire payments—and run the risk that the owner will repossess the goods, leaving them little or no redress. The statutory controls have applied for the most part only to transactions coming within prescribed financial and other limits. The legislation currently in force is the Consumer Credit Act 1974 (as amended by the Consumer Credit Act 2006), which regulates transactions where credit is given to individuals (a term which excludes companies and other corporate bodies but is extended to include partnerships with not more than three members). Prior to April, 2007 the Act applied only to transactions where the credit given did not exceed £25,000; but this limit has now been removed so that the Act applies to all consumer credit agreements unless specifically exempted. Two new exemptions, also introduced from April 2007, are where the debtor has a 'high net worth' and agrees to forgo the protection of the Act, and where he is in business and the credit exceeds $25,000: see the 2006 Act, s 3). This legislation applies not only to loans and similar arrangements which involve 'credit' in an everyday sense, but includes hire-purchase contracts and also conditional sales (within similar limits) and some forms of credit-sale. For many purposes, this Act treats hire-purchase and conditional sale contracts as equivalent, thus eroding the distinction between *Lee v Butler* and *Helby v Matthews* which proved so important a hundred years ago. The distinction remains an important one, of course, where the transaction falls outside the statutory limits.

4.   The Supply of Goods (Implied Terms) Act 1973 (which applies to all hire-purchase agreements and not just to 'consumer' transactions) imports into contracts of hire-purchase

implied terms as to title, description, quality, etc which closely parallel those implied into contracts of sale by ss 12–15 of the Sale of Goods Act 1979 (see below, Chapter 10). Moreover, the Unfair Contract Terms Act 1977 treats exemption clauses in the two categories of contract in precisely similar terms.

5.   Notwithstanding the clear fact that in law the supplier of goods under a hire-purchase agreement is and remains their owner and is not merely the holder of a security interest in goods which he has 'sold' to the hirer, there is a strong argument for saying that in economic reality this is the case, and that it would be better if the law recognised it. The legal position is even further divorced from reality if the credit is given, not by the dealer who supplies the goods to his customer, but by a finance company which takes no part in the actual negotiations. If we take the common situation where a customer inspects a car in a dealer's showroom and agrees to take it on hire-purchase, a layman might reasonably think that the dealer was selling the car, the customer buying it, and the finance company lending the buyer the money to pay the price and taking security over the car until this borrowed money was repaid by instalments over time. But in law, what the parties do is quite different: the dealer, who has persuaded his customer to take the car, sells it to the finance company, and the latter then lets it to the customer on hire-purchase. So the 'buyer' is in law a hirer (and a hirer from a faceless institution that he has never met); the dealer is not a seller vis-à-vis his customer—indeed, he is in no direct contractual relationship towards him at all; and the supposed lender on security is a buyer who becomes the owner of the car for so long as any part of the price is outstanding! (For an illustrative case, see *Shogun Finance Ltd v Hudson* (below, p 391).)

In other jurisdictions, such as the United States, Canada and New Zealand, general personal property security laws have been introduced (eg the US Uniform Commercial Code, art 9) which assimilate into one regime all transactions that *in effect* involve the giving of security over personal chattels, regardless of their legal form. This makes unnecessary the elaborate type of legal charade described above which the technicalities of English law impose on similar transactions here. Successive reports (including the report of the Crowther Committee on Consumer Credit (Cmnd 1781, 1962) and the report of Professor Diamond on Security Interests in Property (1989)) have recommended that there should be wholesale reform of this area of English law, along the lines of the transatlantic codes. Since then, successive governments have shown little interest in putting these recommendations into effect, but the question is once again being discussed in the context of a review of company law and change may be on the way: see below, pp 1083, 1122 and 1148.

(f) Sale distinguished from transaction by way of security

Among the forms of security considered later in this book are the pledge, the lien, the mortgage, and the charge: see Chapters 25 and 26. Since neither pledge nor lien involves the transfer of the property in the goods concerned, they are plainly distinguishable from a contract of sale. The same may be said of a charge: the chargor grants an interest in or over his goods in favour of the chargee, which is of a proprietary nature, but he retains the property in his own hands, and the chargee's interest is a defeasible one which is automatically terminated on payment of the debt which it secures. A mortgage resembles a sale rather more closely, in that the legal title to the goods is transferred to the creditor in order to secure the debt: the general property in the goods (to use the wording of the Act) passes to him. But whereas in a sale it passes absolutely, so that the seller has no further interest in the goods, in a mortgage it passes subject to the condition that the mortgagor is entitled to redeem—that is, to have the goods transferred back to him when the debt is paid. The parties remain in a continuing relationship of debtor and creditor, and both retain an interest in the goods during the currency of the mortgage.

Section 62(4) states that the provisions of the Act do not apply to a transaction in the form of a sale which is intended to operate by way of mortgage, pledge, charge or other security. This draws our attention to the possibility that a transaction which is to all appearances a contract of sale may in fact be intended by the parties to do no more than create a security interest in favour of the purported 'buyer': there may be a secret understanding, or an agreement recorded in another document, that the transfer of property in the goods is only conditional and that it will be retransferred when the seller's indebtedness to the buyer has been discharged. Or the sale may be part of a composite transaction (eg a sale followed by a lease-back of the goods to the seller) which, viewed overall, is really meant to be a way of raising money on the security of the goods. In situations falling into these categories, it is not s 62(4) which is likely to pose legal problems, but rather the Bills of Sale Act of 1882 (see below, p 1139); for under this latter Act (which traditionally looks to the substance rather than the form) the transaction, if it *is* held to be a security transaction, risks being declared void for non-compliance with the statute or for want of registration.

This means that the courts may be faced with the difficult task of determining the 'true intention' of the parties in many borderline cases. In older cases, many of which involved consumers dealing with finance companies, transactions were frequently struck down as disguised loans on security (eg *Polsky v S & A Services* [1951] 1 All ER 1062n, CA). The sale and lease-back is, however, a well-established form of transaction, especially in commercial circles, which ought nowadays to be recognised as valid in its own right (see, eg *Eastern Distributors Ltd v Goldring* (below, p 353) and *Mercantile Credit Ltd v Hamblin* (below, p 360)). Even so, surprisingly, we do find an occasional decision (eg *Re Curtain Dream plc* [1990] BCLC 925) ruling that the parties had created a concealed charge which was unenforceable for want of registration.

(g) Sale of goods distinguished from contract for work and materials

There has always been a difficult—indeed an impossible—line to draw here. Suppose that I take my car to a garage to have a new set of tyres fitted. Does the garage sell me the tyres and fit them as something incidental to the sale? Or is it performing a *service,* doing work on the car, and providing the materials ancillary to that service? Is the position different where the work required is a more substantial component in the overall job—fitting new brake linings or replacing a head gasket, say? Does a customer who eats a meal in a hotel or restaurant buy the food, or have it supplied incidentally to the provision of services?

The courts have wavered in their approach to this question. In some early cases, such as *Clay v Yates* (below), what seems to have mattered was the relative importance of the two elements—the labour or the materials. Later, in cases like *Lee v Griffin* (below), they made the issue turn on whether or not there was an end-product in the form of a chattel in which the property was transferred; and most recently, in *Robinson v Graves* (below) the question was said to be determined by the 'substance' of the transaction. However, this is not always a meaningful test—a point which the court may have failed to appreciate—and the decisions which have been reached are far from consistent.

The following have been held to be contracts for work and materials:

— a contract to print a book: *Clay v Yates* (1856) 1 H & N 73;

— a contract to paint a portrait: *Robinson v Graves* [1935] 1 KB 579, CA (below);

— the supply of drugs by a veterinary surgeon when inoculating cattle: *Dodd v Wilson* [1946] 2 All ER 691.

In contrast, the following have been held (or assumed) to be sales of goods:

— a contract to make a set of dentures: *Lee v Griffin* (1861) 1 B & S 272;

— the supply of a meal in a restaurant: *Lockett v Charles Ltd* [1938] 4 All ER 170;

— the supply of a fur jacket made to the customer's order: *J Marcel (Furriers) Ltd v Tapper* [1953] 1 WLR 49;

— the supply and laying of a fitted carpet: *Philip Head & Sons Ltd v Showfronts Ltd* [1970] 1 Lloyd's Rep 140;

— the supply and installation of an animal feed hopper: *H Parsons (Livestock) Ltd v Uttley Ingham & Co Ltd* [1978] QB 791, CA.

It is difficult to resist the conclusion that these decisions have been made on an impressionistic, rather than a logical, basis. Fortunately, the question is less important nowadays than formerly, for two reasons. First, prior to the repeal in 1954 of s 4 of the Sale of Goods Act 1893 (itself traceable back to the Statute of Frauds 1677), a contract for the sale of goods over £10 was not normally enforceable without written evidence, but writing was not required in the case of a contract for services. This distinction has now disappeared (and with it the temptation for judges to make somewhat arbitrary rulings leading to an outcome to meet the justice of the case!). Secondly, in many respects the legal rules applicable are the same whatever classification is given to the transaction: for instance, in relation to the obligation to supply goods or materials of satisfactory quality and suitable for their purpose. In a sale of goods, the relevant rules are to be found in ss 12–15 of the Act; in a contract for work and services, equivalent rules were applied at common law until 1982, and are now set out in statutory form in the Supply of Goods and Services Act 1982, ss 2–5.

However, there are other areas of the law where the two types of transaction may be governed by different legal rules—eg perhaps, in regard to the passing of property and risk; and here the distinction will remain important. Ironically, in a leading case in which this issue might have been crucial, *Hyundai Heavy Industries Co Ltd v Papadopoulos* (below), the House of Lords did not give a clear ruling. This case concerned a contract to build and deliver a ship, and it was held that the contract was of a hybrid nature which, although essentially one of sale, had some characteristics of a contract to do building work: for so long as the ship was unfinished, it was appropriate to apply rules analogous to those of building law, even though the contract would be treated as being one of sale when the work was finished and the ship was ready to deliver.

It should also be noted that it may sometimes be difficult to draw the line between the 'work' and the 'materials' elements in a contract of this kind. This distinction may be important. For instance, under the Supply of Goods and Services Act 1982, s 4, the goods supplied under a contract for the provision of goods must be of satisfactory quality and fit for their purpose (absolute obligations which, in the case of a consumer transaction, cannot be excluded), whereas the supplier of the service, by s 13, undertakes only to use reasonable care and skill in the provision of the service (an implied obligation which can be excluded, subject to the requirement of reasonableness). A veterinary surgeon treating a sick cat will be liable under s 4 if the drug he administers is faulty but he gives the right dose, but under s 13 if the drug is good but the dose is wrong. Moreover, if the treatment is experimental and he agrees with the client that it is to be carried out 'at owner's risk', this disclaimer of liability will be ineffective to exclude s 4 but (if within the reasonableness test) capable of negativing liability under s 13.

Robinson v Graves

[1935] 1 KB 579, Court of Appeal

(The facts appear from the judgment.)

Greer LJ: This appeal raises a very interesting question, which has been well argued and is not free from difficulty, having regard to the fact that there has not yet been any actual decision on the point involved in this case, though there have been in some of the cases dicta tending in one direction and in others dicta tending in the other direction. The question to be decided is this: Whether when a person goes to an artist to have a portrait painted, it may be his own portrait or the portrait of some friend (as for instance his wife), and the commission is accepted by the artist, they are making a bargain for the manufacture of future goods to be delivered when those goods come into existence in circumstances which make it a sale of goods within the meaning of s 4 of the Sale of Goods Act 1893, which has now taken the place of s 17 of the Statute of Frauds relating to the sale of goods.

I propose to look at the question first without dealing with the authorities, because after all we are dealing with the meaning of the English language in the statute and its application to particular facts. I can imagine that nothing would be more surprising to a client going to a portrait painter to have his portrait painted and to the artist who was accepting the commission than to be told that they were making a bargain about the sale of goods. It is, of course, possible that a picture may be ordered in such circumstances as will make it an order for goods to be supplied in the future, but it does not follow that this is the inference to be drawn in every case as between the client and the artist. Looking at the propositions involved from the point of view of interpreting the words in the English language it seems to me that the painting of a portrait in these circumstances would not, in the ordinary use of the English language, be deemed to be the purchase and sale of that which is produced by the artist. It would, on the contrary, be held to be an undertaking by the artist to exercise such skill as he was possessed of in order to produce for reward a thing which would ultimately have to be accepted by the client. If that is so, the contract in this case was not a contract for the sale of goods within the meaning of s 4 of the Sale of Goods Act 1893.

There are only two cases to which I think it is necessary to refer. The first case is *Clay v Yates* ((1856) 1 H & N 73). That case was concerned with the question whether a contract with a printer to print and deliver a book to a customer who desired to have it printed was or was not a sale of goods. In the course of the argument Martin B said this: 'Suppose an artist paints a portrait for 300 guineas, and supplies the canvas for it, which is worth 10s, surely he might recover under a count for work and labour.' I regard that as an expression of opinion by a high authority on all questions of the common law that in those circumstances there would not be any sale of goods, but there would be a contract for work and labour; and in the judgments which follow the learned judges seem to me to agree with that view....

Now it is said that that case is inconsistent with the subsequent case of *Lee v Griffin* ((1861) 1 B & S 272). So far as the facts of that case are concerned it affords no help to the decision of the present case, because it was concerned with the question whether, when a dentist undertakes to make a plate of false teeth—more frequently called a denture—that is or is not a sale of goods. In that case the principal part of that which the parties are dealing with is the chattel which will come into existence when such skill as may be necessary to produce it has been applied by the dentist and those who work for him; but in the course of delivering the judgments in that case Crompton J and Hill J said nothing whatever which would throw any doubt upon the views expressed in the earlier case of *Clay v Yates*. Crompton

J says: 'However, on the point which was made at the trial, whether the plaintiff could not succeed on the count for work, labour, and materials, I am also clearly of opinion against the plaintiff. Whether the cause of action be work and labour, or goods sold and delivered, depends on the particular nature of each individual contract'; and then he refers to the case of *Clay v Yates* as turning upon the peculiar circumstances of the case, and concludes with these words: 'I do not agree with the proposition, that whenever skill is to be exercised in carrying out the contract, that fact makes it a contract for work and labour, and not for the sale of a chattel; it may be the cause of action is for work and labour, when the materials supplied are merely ancillary, as in the case put of an attorney or printer. But in the present case the goods to be furnished, viz, the teeth, are the principal subject-matter; and the case is nearer that of a tailor, who measures for a garment and afterwards supplies the article fitted . . .

If you find, as they did in *Lee v Griffin,* that the substance of the contract was the production of something to be sold by the dentist to the dentist's customer, then that is a sale of goods. But if the substance of the contract, on the other hand, is that skill and labour have to be exercised for the production of the article and that it is only ancillary to that that there will pass from the artist to his client or customer some materials in addition to the skill involved in the production of the portrait, that does not make any difference to the result, because the substance of the contract is the skill and experience of the artist in producing the picture.

For these reasons I am of opinion that in this case the substance of the matter was an agreement for the exercise of skill and it was only incidental that some materials would have to pass from the artist to the gentleman who commissioned the portrait. For these reasons I think that this was not a contract for the sale of goods within the meaning of s 4 of the Sale of Goods Act 1893, but it was a contract for work and labour and materials . . . .

[Slesser and Roche LJJ delivered concurring judgments. Greer LJ added:]

I intended to say and would like to add, that in deciding as we have done we are not deciding anything which is necessarily contrary to the decision of Mathew J in the shortly reported case of *Isaacs v Hardy* ((1884) Cab & El 287), which dealt with a contract of a very different kind—namely, where a picture dealer, whose sole object was to acquire something which he might sell in his business, engaged an artist to paint and deliver to him a picture of a given subject at an agreed price. It must not be taken that we are in any way overruling that case or deciding whether it was right or wrong.

QUESTION

Lee v Griffin was decided in 1861. Whatever the position was at that time, dentistry is nowadays a highly skilled and high-earning profession. Would the same decision be reached today?

Hyundai Heavy Industries Co Ltd v Papadopoulos
[1980] 1 WLR 1129, House of Lords

Hyundai contracted to 'build, launch, equip and complete' a 24,000 ton cargo ship and 'deliver and sell' her to a Liberian company for $14.3m. (Perhaps significantly, the parties were described in the contract respectively as 'the builder' and 'the buyer'.) Payment of the price, which was guaranteed by Papadopoulos, was to be made by five instalments at stated stages of the work. The second instalment fell due on 15 July, but it was still unpaid on 6 September and Hyundai then exercised a contractual right to cancel the contract on the basis of this default. The question for the court to decide was whether the July instalment remained payable notwithstanding the termination of the contract. The House of Lords assumed (although not without some doubt) the correctness of the decision in *Dies v British & International Mining & Finance Corpn Ltd* [1939] 1 KB 724 that, if the contract was one for the sale of goods, the seller had no right to retain or to enforce such a payment. In contrast, if it was a contract for work and materials, there was no doubt that it could be claimed. Their ruling was that, while the ship was in the course of construction, the contract had sufficient of the characteristics of a contract for work and materials for the latter rule to apply.

Viscount Dilhorne: Counsel for the guarantors in the instant case argued that if the buyer in the *Dies* case was entitled to recover an advance which had already been paid, then a fortiori the buyer in the instant case could not be liable to make an advance that was due but unpaid: if he did make it, said counsel, he would be entitled to immediate repayment of it.

I do not accept that argument. In my opinion the *Dies* case and *Palmer* v *Temple* (1839) 9 Ad & El 508 are both distinguishable from the present case because in both these cases the contracts were simply contracts of sale which did not require the vendor to perform any work or incur any expense on the subjects of sale. But the contract in the instant case is not of that comparatively simple character. The obligations of the buyer were not confined to selling the vessel but they included designing and building it and there were special provisions (article 2) that the contract price 'shall include payment for services in the inspection, tests, survey and classification of the vessel' and also 'all costs and expenses for designing and supplying all necessary drawings for the vessel in accordance with the specifications.' Accordingly the builder was obliged to carry out work and to incur expense, starting from the moment that the contract had been signed, including the wages of designers and workmen, fees for inspection and for cost of purchasing materials. It seems very likely that the increasing proportions of the contract price represented by the five instalments bore some relation to the anticipated rate of expenditure, but we have no information on which to make any nice comparison between the amount of expenses that the builder would have to bear from time to time, and the amounts of the instalments payable by the buyer. I do not think that such comparisons are necessary. It is enough that the builder was bound to incur considerable expense in carrying out his part of the contract long before the actual sale could take place. That no doubt is the explanation for the provision in article 10(b) of the shipbuilding contract that:

> ...all payments under the provisions of this article shall not be delayed or withheld by the buyer due to any dispute of whatever nature arising between the builder and the buyer hereto, unless the buyer shall have claimed to cancel the contract under the terms thereof....

The importance evidently attached by the parties to maintaining the cash flow seems to support my view of the contract.

There was no evidence either way as to whether the builders had in fact carried out their obligations to start designing and building the vessel, but in my opinion we must assume, in the absence of evidence or even averment to the contrary, that they had carried out their part of the bargain up till the date of cancellation.

Much of the plausibility of the argument on behalf of the guarantors seemed to me to be derived from the assumption that the *contract* price was simply a *purchase* price. That is not so, and once that misconception has been removed I think it is clear that the shipbuilding contract has little similarity with a contract of sale and much more similarity, so far as the present issues are concerned, with contracts in which the party entitled to be paid had either performed work or provided services for which payment is due by the date of cancellation. In contracts of the latter class, which of course includes building and construction contracts, accrued rights to payment are not (in the absence of express provisions) destroyed by cancellation of the contract....

[Lords Edmund-Davies and Fraser of Tullybelton delivered concurring opinions.
Lords Russell of Killowen and Keith of Kinkel concurred.]

(h) Contract of sale distinguished from agency

As we saw in Chapter 3, there is again sometimes a difficult line to draw between a contract for the sale of goods and one of agency; and the question can arise both between a seller and an agent, on the one hand, and a buyer and an agent, on the other.

Suppose, first, that X is an antiques dealer who travels the country attending auction sales, etc, and Y asks him to look out for a particular kind of table and, if he finds one, to buy it for him. This could be done either on the basis that X would buy as Y's agent, taking remuneration by way of a commission, or by X himself buying the table from its owner and reselling it to Y at a profit. In the former case there is only one contract of sale, with two principal parties; in the latter, two sales and three principal parties. If X and Y have not clearly spelt out the details of their arrangement, the court may be left with a difficult decision.

On the other hand, we may find the converse case. Z may have a showroom in which he displays Ford cars, above which is exhibited the sign 'Sole agent for the sale of Ford cars in the County of Whimshire'. If Z really is an agent, then a customer who agrees to buy a car will actually be buying it from the Ford motor company, and Z is simply a go-between. But it is far more likely that Z is not an agent in the legal sense at all, but a retailer who has bought his stock of cars from Ford and resells each car to the particular customer. Again, there is only one contract of sale in the former case, with one buyer and one seller; in the latter, two contracts of sale, and three principal parties. It is clear that the description which the parties give to their relationship will not be decisive of its true nature in law. The use of the word 'agent' or 'agency' may be a loose, popular usage, obscuring the fact that the person in question is a buyer or a seller.

The courts can have regard to several pointers, none of them in itself conclusive, in reaching a decision in a borderline case. What degree of independence does the 'middle' man have? Is he free to fix his own prices? Is he remunerated by a commission or similar payment, or by taking a profit? Does he have to account to his supplier for the payments he receives, or is he simply invoiced by the supplier for the goods he orders?

The position may be even more complicated. A person may be constituted by the same transaction both someone who has agreed to buy goods and, in addition (eg in some 'retention of title' or *Romalpa* cases (see below, p 452)), the seller's agent to resell the goods. In the world of exporting and importing, it is common for a buyer who is based abroad to be represented in the seller's country by an agent who gives a guarantee to the seller that his principal, the buyer, will pay the price. This, as we saw above, p 104, is called a *del credere* agency; and such an agent has some of the rights given to a seller by the Sale of Goods Act—eg the right to hold the goods under a lien until his principal, the buyer, has reimbursed him for the price (s 38(2)). Again, there is a counterpart: a *confirming agent,* an agent acting for a seller (usually based overseas) who guarantees to the buyer that his principal, the seller, will deliver the goods: see above, p 104.

(i) Sale of goods distinguished from licence to use intellectual property

A contract for the supply of a computer program or other intellectual property may also involve a sale of goods (eg a disk or a hardware system), but a central part of the transaction will be a licence granted by the owner of the copyright in the program, who may or may not be the seller. If the seller is not the owner, there will be a separate contract between the owner and the buyer in which the seller acts as the owner's agent. Of course, there may be no sale of goods at all, as where the program is copied or downloaded directly onto the buyer's computer system.

4   FORMATION OF THE CONTRACT OF SALE

A contract of sale, like any other contract, depends upon establishing an agreement between the parties, which usually follows from the acceptance by one party of an offer made by the other. No special rules apply to sales of goods, except perhaps in regard to the price. As has been noted, the consideration in a contract of sale must consist of money. It may happen that the parties have reached agreement on all aspects of their contract except for fixing the price. In most other types of contract, a failure to agree on the consideration would result in the bargain being incomplete, and void for uncertainty. However, in regard to contracts for the sale of goods, the Act goes some way to fill possible gaps by providing as follows, in s 8:

8. (1) The price in a contract of sale may be fixed by the contract, or may be left to be fixed in a manner agreed by the contract, or may be determined by the course of dealing between the parties.

(2) Where the price is not determined as mentioned in subsection (1) above the buyer must pay a reasonable price.

(3) What is a reasonable price is a question of fact dependent on the circumstances of each particular case.

It is clear from these provisions that the court has power to fix a reasonable price where there has been agreement on all the terms of a contract of sale other than the price. However, if the parties have purposefully left the price open, as something to be negotiated between them in the future, the court may have no option but to declare that there is as yet no binding contract. In *May & Butcher Ltd v R* [1934] 2 KB 17n, HL, an agreement to buy war surplus tentage from the Crown at prices to be agreed upon from time to time between the parties was held not to be a concluded contract. This case may be contrasted with *Hillas & Co Ltd v Arcos Ltd* (1932) 147 LT 503, HL, where the parties had already been in a contractual relationship for the supply of timber in the year 1930, and the buyers sought to exercise an option under that contract to purchase further timber in 1931. The sellers argued that this second contract was not binding because various of its terms were not fully spelt out, but the House of Lords, distinguishing *May & Butcher*, held that the uncertainty could be resolved by reference to the previous course of dealing between the parties.

It may be noted in passing that the Supply of Goods and Services Act 1982, s 15 similarly provides for a reasonable price to be paid in a contract for the supply of a service, where no price has been otherwise fixed.

Section 9 of the Sale of Goods Act deals with the special case where the price is left to be fixed by a valuation made by a third party. Here the contract will not be binding if the third party cannot or does not make the valuation (unless he is prevented from doing so by the fault of one of the parties: s 9(2)); but if the goods have been delivered to the buyer and 'appropriated' by him, he must pay a reasonable price for them (s 9(1)). ('Appropriated' here may be taken as meaning 'dealt with in some way as if he were their owner': elsewhere in the Act, it is used in a rather more technical sense: see below, p 337.)

We should note that in regard to *consumer* sales there is now protective legislation which imposes a statutory 'cooling-off' period, giving the buyer the right to have second thoughts and cancel the contract even though, on ordinary principles, it would be binding on him. Examples of such legislation are the Consumer Protection (Cancellation of Contracts Concluded away from Business Premises) Regulations 1987, SI 1987/2117, implementing Directive 1985/557/EC), aimed at 'doorstep selling', and the Consumer Protection (Distance Selling) Regulations 2000 (SI 2000/ 2334, implementing Directive 1997/7 EC), which applies (inter alia) to mail-order sales and sales concluded over the internet. (For a discussion, see P Hellwege [2004] CLJ 712.) But as this is a book concerned with commercial, rather than consumer, law this topic will not be explored in detail.

CHAPTER 8

PASSING OF THE PROPERTY IN THE GOODS AS BETWEEN SELLER AND BUYER

1 SIGNIFICANCE OF THE PASSING OF PROPERTY

The concept of 'the property' in the goods dominates much of the thinking in English sale of goods law—so much so that Professor Goode calls our preoccupation with the concept 'excessive' (*Commercial Law,* p 216). We saw when discussing s 2(4)–(5) that the Act makes a distinction between a *sale,* where the property is transferred to the buyer under the contract of sale itself, and an *agreement to sell,* where the property is to be transferred some time after the making of the contract. In this chapter, we examine this concept of the passing of the property—the event upon which the seller ceases to be, and the buyer becomes, the owner of the goods (or, in exceptional cases, succeeds to such title as the seller has). This event has significance for many purposes in law, the most important of which are listed below. It should be noted, however, that not all of these are fixed rules of law: some of them may be varied by agreement between the parties, and others state only a provisional or presumptive rule which may in particular situations have to give way to another which in the circumstances has an overriding effect. Subject to these qualifications, which are discussed in more detail below, we may list the following points of distinction.

Where the contract is an *agreement to sell,* and the property remains with the seller:

(1) The contract is still executory.

(2) The buyer has only rights *in personam* against the seller: the seller can exercise proprietary rights in relation to the goods (eg sue a third party in tort if the goods are wrongly detained, stolen or damaged), but the buyer cannot: see *The Aliakmon,* below.

(3) The buyer's remedy against the seller, if he is in breach of contract, is for damages for non-delivery (s 51) (except in the rare case where specific performance is available (s 52: see below, p 485)).

(4) The seller's remedy against the buyer, if he is in breach, is for damages for non-acceptance (s 50); the seller continues to be responsible for the goods (storage charges, disposing of them if perishable, etc).

(5) A seller who has retained the property can in principle sell the goods to a different buyer and give this second buyer a good title, whereas a buyer who has not got title cannot do more than *agree to sell* them to a third party.

(6) The risk of loss is on the seller (s 20).

(7) The contract may be frustrated if the goods perish (s 7).

(8) If the goods are requisitioned, taken as prize, etc, the loss is borne by the seller, and any compensation is payable to the seller.

(9) In the event of the seller's insolvency, the buyer has no right to the goods, but only the right to prove in the insolvency for the return of any part of the price which he has paid, and for damages in respect of any loss that he has suffered: *Re Wait* (above, p 266; but note the effect of the new s 20A, below, p 320).

(10) In the event of the buyer's insolvency, the seller can claim back the goods even though they have been delivered to the buyer: the *Romalpa* case (below, p 452).

(11) Any profits or increase (eg young born to livestock) belong to the seller.

Where the contract is a *sale*, and the property has passed to the buyer:

(1) The contract is executed, ie there is a conveyance as well as a contract.

(2) The buyer has rights *in rem* (proprietary rights) in relation to the goods (eg the right to sue a third party in tort if the goods are wrongly detained, stolen or damaged).

(3) The buyer's remedies against the seller, if he is in breach, are not only for damages for non-delivery (s 51), but also lie in tort.

(4) The seller's remedies against the buyer, if he is in breach, are not only for damages for non-acceptance (s 50), but also for the contract price (s 49(1)); the buyer is left with all responsibility for the goods.

(5) A seller who has parted with title cannot in principle sell the goods to a second buyer, while a buyer to whom the property in goods has passed can sell them on to a third party and give that person a good title.

(6) The risk of loss is on the buyer (s 20).

(7) The contract is not frustrated if the goods perish.

(8) If the goods are requisitioned, taken as prize, etc, the loss is borne by the buyer, and any compensation is payable to the buyer.

(9) In the event of the seller's insolvency, the buyer may claim the goods: *Aldridge v Johnson* (above, p 279).

(10) In the event of the buyer's insolvency, the seller cannot claim back any goods which have been delivered to the buyer, but can only prove in the insolvency for so much of the price as is outstanding, and also for any loss that he has suffered.

(11) Any profits or increase (eg young born to livestock) belong to the buyer.

The distinction between a sale and an agreement to sell may also affect criminal liability—eg if the property has already passed to the buyer he cannot be guilty of theft of the goods (*Edwards v Ddin* [1976] 1 WLR 942, where the accused had driven off without paying for petrol and oil which had been put into his car).

Leigh & Sillavan Ltd v Aliakmon Shipping Co Ltd, The Aliakmon
[1986] AC 785, House of Lords

Leigh & Sillavan Ltd agreed to buy a quantity of steel coils from Kinsho-Mataishi Corpn, to be shipped from Korea to Immingham, Humberside. The contract was on C & F terms (see below, p 506), which meant that at the relevant time the goods were at the buyer's risk; but the property had not passed to them because, under the contract, this was not to take place until payment of the price. The steel was damaged whilst being stowed on the defendants' vessel, the *Aliakmon*, allegedly due to negligence for which the defendants were responsible. The House of Lords held that since the goods were not the buyer's property at the time when the damage was caused, their only claim was for economic loss, in respect of which the defendants owed them no duty of care.

Lord Brandon of Oakbrook: My Lords, this appeal arises in an action in the Commercial Court in which the appellants, who were the c and f buyers of goods carried in the respondents' ship, the *Aliakmon,* claim damages against the latter for damage done to such goods at a time when the risk, but not yet the legal property in them, had passed to the appellants. The main question to be determined is whether, in the circumstances just stated, the respondents owed a duty of care in tort to the appellants in respect of the carriage of such goods....

My Lords, there is a long line of authority for a principle of law that, in order to enable a person to claim in negligence for loss caused to him by reason of loss of or damage to property, he must have had either the legal ownership of or a possessory title to the property concerned at the time when the loss or damage occurred, and it is not enough for him to have only had contractual rights in relation to such property which have been adversely affected by the loss of or damage to it.

[His Lordship examined the authorities, and continued:]

None of these cases concerns a claim by cif or c and f buyers of goods to recover from the owners of the ship in which the goods are carried loss suffered by reason of want of care in the carriage of the goods resulting in their being lost or damaged at a time when the risk in the goods, but not yet the legal property in them, has passed to such buyers. The question whether such a claim would lie, however, came up for decision in *Margarine Union GmbH v Cambay Prince SS Co Ltd (The Wear Breeze)* [1969] 1 QB 219. In that case cif buyers had accepted four delivery orders in respect of as yet undivided portions of a cargo of copra in bulk shipped under two bills of lading. It was common ground that, by doing so, they did not acquire either the legal property in, nor a possessory title to, the portions of copra concerned: they only acquired the legal property later when four portions each of 500 tons were separated from the bulk on or shortly after discharge in Hamburg. The copra having been damaged by want of care by the shipowner's servants or agents in not properly fumigating the holds of the carrying ship before loading, the question arose whether the buyers were entitled to recover from the shipowners in tort for negligence the loss which they had suffered by reason of the copra having been so damaged. Roskill J held that they were not, founding his decision largely on the principle of law established by the line of authority to which I have referred.

[His Lordship then considered and rejected a number of grounds on which it was contended that *The Wear Breeze* had been wrongly decided. He concluded that the plaintiffs had no cause of action in tort.]

[Lords Keith of Kinkel, Brightman, Griffiths and Ackner concurred.]

NOTE

The Carriage of Goods by Sea Act 1992 would now give the buyers the right to sue the carriers in contract on the facts of *The Aliakmon* (see below, p 491), but it remains an authoritative ruling in tort.

As has already been emphasised, some of the differences between a sale and an agreement to sell which have been listed above depend upon rules that are only of *prima facie* application. For instance, s 20, which declares that risk passes with the property in the goods, applies only 'unless otherwise agreed'. Many of the other propositions are qualified by further provisions of the Act—for example, although s 49(2) gives the seller a right to sue for the price once the property has passed, s 28 adds the further condition that, unless otherwise agreed, the seller must also be ready and willing to deliver the goods in exchange for the price: this means that normally no action for the price will lie unless *both* property and possession have passed to the buyer. And it is true that both a seller who has retained possession of the goods can in some circumstances confer a good title on a second buyer even though the property may have passed to the first buyer (s 24), and a buyer who has been given possession has a corresponding power to give a good title to a sub-buyer and so defeat the original seller's title (s 25(1)). For reasons such as this, Professor Lawson (1949) 65 LQR 362 and Professor Atiyah (*Sale of Goods,* Ch 19, but more particularly in earlier editions of his book) have argued that the significance of the concept of property is less than has traditionally been thought: the exceptions and qualifications to the 'rules' listed above are so great as virtually to eat up the rules themselves, so that 'property' should be seen as playing only a marginal, rather than a central, role in our law of sale. In the United States, the law of sale (as contained in the Uniform Commercial Code) has been drafted without using the concept of 'property' at all. This is, of course, perfectly possible, just as it would be possible to draw up the rules for the game of football without using the word 'offside'; but it does have two consequences: first, each of the 'rules' set out above (as to risk, liability to pay the price, etc) has to be separately stated, and stated in more individual and detailed terms because it is not possible to use the word 'property' as a conceptual short-cut; and secondly, there is no convenient 'peg' on which to hang any new rule to cover a situation that the draftsman may not have thought of. (By way of example, the Act contains no rule about goods taken as prize in wartime; but the court was able to use the established concept of 'property' to resolve the issues which arose when the question did come up: see *The Odessa* [1916] 1 AC 145, PC. An American court would have had to resort to more elaborate reasoning.)

The importance of the concept of 'the property' is highlighted when we look at a further question. As a matter of rock-bottom theory, it is the property in the goods which the buyer bargains for when he enters into a contract for the sale of goods—not their possession or use or any of the other aspects of ownership. This is so not simply because that is what the definition in s 2(1) says, but because it is well established by the cases that if the buyer does *not* get the ownership that he has bargained for, he can recover the whole of the price that he has paid, as money paid on a total failure of consideration, despite the fact that he may have had the possession and use of the goods for a considerable time before this fact is discovered: see *Rowland v Divall* (below, p 393). If the buyer in such a case chose instead to frame his claim in damages, he would of course receive a smaller sum, reflecting what he had lost in practical, rather than conceptual, terms.

2 RELATIONSHIP OF PROPERTY TO RISK

The Act in various sections speaks of 'the risk' passing to the buyer, but the term 'risk' is nowhere defined. We may ask: Risk of what? The parties to a contract of sale face many risks: the risk that the market value of the goods in question may go up or down, the risk that perishable goods may deteriorate, and so on. However, we may glean from the decided cases that 'the risk' that the Act is concerned with is the risk that the goods will be wholly or partly destroyed or damaged, for instance by fire or flood or the sinking of the ship on which they are being carried, or lost by theft. It is also clear that we are concerned only with events that are not attributable to the act or fault of either of the parties, or which are dealt with expressly by the terms of the contract (eg by a 'force majeure' clause).

' "Risk" in the Law of Sale' by LS Sealy
[1972B] CLJ 225, pp 226–227

. . . The truth is that risk is a derivative, and essentially negative, concept—an elliptical way of saying that either or both of the primary obligations of one party shall be enforceable, and that those of the other party shall be deemed to have been discharged, even though the normally prerequisite conditions have not been satisfied. That is to say, the legal consequences attaching to 'the risk' fall to be defined purely in terms of the parties' other duties and the corresponding rights and remedies: the seller's right to claim the price, and the buyer's right to resist payment or to demand its return; and the right to claim damages (eg for non-delivery or non-acceptance) or to resist such a claim.

Head v Tattersall may be seen as an illustration of the concept of risk, although the word 'risk' does not appear in any of the judgments.

Head v Tattersall
(1871) LR 7 Exch 7, Court of Exchequer

Head bought from Tattersall, an auctioneer, a horse described in the catalogue as having been hunted with the Bicester and Duke of Grafton's hounds. This information was incorrect. The sale contract contained a condition that 'horses not answering the description must be returned before 5 o'clock on the Wednesday evening next; otherwise the purchaser shall be obliged to keep the lot with all faults'. Head took the horse away and during the time that it was in his custody it was accidentally injured when it took fright and ran against the splinter-bar of a carriage. He returned the horse in its damaged state before the 5 o'clock deadline, on the ground that it had not corresponded with its description. It was held that he was entitled to do so, and to have the whole of his money back.

Cleasby B: The effect of the contract is to give the buyer an option of returning the horse in a particular event and within a specified time; and although it is clear that he might by his conduct have disentitled himself to exercise his option, he has not, in my judgment, done anything so to disentitle himself in the present case. By taking the horse away he did no more than, under his contract, he had a right to do. . . . This being so, the second question remains, whether the right given by the contract was limited, so as only to confer a right to return the horse, provided it remained in the same condition as it was in when sold. It is a sufficient answer to say, that as a time for returning the horse was expressly fixed by the contract, an accident occurring within the time from a cause beyond the plaintiff's control ought not to deprive him of his right, provided he can return the horse in some shape or other . . . . Moreover, the matter may be put thus:—As a general rule, damage from the depreciation of a chattel ought to fall on the person who is the owner of it. Now here the effect of the contract was to vest the property in the buyer subject to a right of rescission in a particular event when it would revest in the seller. I think in such a case that the person who is eventually entitled to the property in the chattel ought to bear any loss arising from any depreciation in its value caused by an accident for which nobody is in fault. Here the defendant is the person in whom the property is revested, and he must therefore bear the loss. The cases cited seem to me to be beside the present question, for here there was an express condition in the contract itself giving to the purchaser an absolute right, under certain circumstances, to return the horse. I think, therefore, the plaintiff is entitled to recover.

[Kelly CB and Bramwell B delivered concurring judgments.]

The prima facie rule relating to risk is contained in s 20(1): unless otherwise agreed, the goods remain at the seller's risk until the property is transferred to the buyer, but from and after the transfer of the property they are at the buyer's risk, whether delivery has been made to him or not. This is, however, only the prima facie rule; and in fact *Head v Tattersall* is a case where such an agreement must, by inference, have been found to exist, for the injury occurred at a time when the property had passed to the buyer and was (at least provisionally) vested in him. *The Aliakmon* (above, p 297) is another example of the parties 'agreeing otherwise'. There, the sale was on 'C & F' terms, which meant under the conventions of international sales law that the goods were at the buyers' risk 'as from shipment' (see below, p 500). However, it was also a term of the contract that the property was not to pass until the price had been paid. So the risk of damage was carried by the buyers even during the time when the goods remained the sellers' property.

Subsections (2) and (3) of s 20 list two further exceptions to the prima facie rule laid down by s 20(1): fault of either party, and liability as a bailee. *Demby Hamilton & Co Ltd v Barden* and *Wiehe v Dennis Bros* respectively provide illustrations of these two exceptions.

Demby Hamilton & Co Ltd v Barden
[1949] 1 All ER 435, King's Bench Division

In November 1945 Barden, a wine merchant, agreed to buy from Demby Hamilton 30 tons of apple juice, to be collected at the rate of one truckload per week by third parties to whom the juice had been sub-sold. The sellers crushed apples sufficient to fulfil this contract (the last apples they had for that season) and put the juice into barrels. If the juice had been collected punctually in accordance with the contract, deliveries would have finished in February 1946, but only two truckloads were collected after 11 December 1945, and eventually, on 7 November 1946, the sellers informed the buyer that the remaining juice had become putrid and had been thrown away. It was held that the loss lay on the buyer, because the delay in taking delivery was due to his fault.

Sellers J: The first requirement of the proviso in question [s 20(2)] is that delivery has been delayed through the fault of the buyer. I am satisfied on the facts in the present case that a good delivery, which would have avoided all loss, was delayed through the fault of the buyer, and that of the third parties. The next requirement of the proviso is that, where delivery has been delayed through the fault of the buyer, the goods are at the risk of the party in fault 'as regards any loss which might not have occurred but for such fault.' The goods referred to there must be the contractual goods which have been assembled by the seller for the purpose of fulfilling his contract and making delivery. The goods may have been defined goods, goods manufactured for the purpose of delivery, or goods which had been acquired by the seller from somebody else for the purpose of fulfilling his contract. It does not seem to me that the Act requires to be construed in any narrow sense. The real question is whether the loss which has accrued was brought about by the delay in delivery, and that must have regard to the goods which were there to be delivered. Different circumstances may arise in different cases. It may be that the seller was in a position to sell the goods elsewhere and acquire other goods for the postponed time of delivery, and if he does not do that and there is some loss in the meantime the responsibility for the loss would be held to fall upon him. Again, there may be cases (and I think this is one of them) where the seller has his goods ready for delivery and has to keep them ready for delivery as and when the buyer proposes to take them. In the present case the position is clear. The casks of apple juice which were not accepted were manufactured at the time of the contract, and the contract required that delivery should be in accordance with sample. It would have been very difficult to have obtained goods which complied with the sample unless the apples had all been crushed at the same time. They would have had to be apples from the same district and the juice from them, when obtained, would have had to be of the same maturity. The condition of apples changes. They may be unripe at one time and too ripe at another. The 30 tons of juice were goods which the sellers rightly and reasonably kept for the fulfilment of their contract. These were the last apples which the sellers had that season for crushing, and, therefore, the goods in question were goods which the sellers had awaiting delivery in fulfilment of their contract with the buyer. I have to ask myself whether this loss might not have occurred but for the fault of the buyer. I am satisfied that it would not have occurred but for his fault. There is, of course, an obligation on a seller to act reasonably, and, if possible, to avoid any loss. As to that, one or two questions arise for consideration. Was there anything the sellers could reasonably do to dispose of these goods when they still had an outstanding obligation to keep them at the disposal of the buyer and when they had to be ready and willing to deliver them when requested? If delivery had been asked for at a later date and they had let these goods go elsewhere they could not have fulfilled their contract. I do not hesitate to find (although to construe this proviso is not easy) that in a practical and business sense this loss has fallen on the sellers by reason of the fact that the buyer refused to take delivery at the proper time and postponed the date of delivery until the goods had deteriorated, and I come to the conclusion that the liability for that loss falls on the buyer....

Wiehe v Dennis Bros
(1913) 29 TLR 250, King's Bench Division

Wiehe in London contracted to buy a Shetland pony called 'Tiny' from Dennis Bros, intended to be presented along with a car and harness to Princess Juliana, daughter of the Queen of the Netherlands. The pony and car were to be delivered in Rotterdam in a month's time. While the pony was in the sellers' custody, a charitable ball was held at Olympia, in the course of which an unauthorised person took the pony out of its stall and led it among the dancers; but it was mishandled and suffered injuries. The sellers were held liable on the basis that they had failed to show that they had taken proper care of it as bailees pending delivery.

Scrutton J: in his Lordship's view one cause of action against the defendants was that they were the bailees of the pony and that the pony was injured without their being able to give any explanation how such injuries were caused. The case therefore fell within *Bullen v Swan Electric Engraving Co* ((1906) 22 TLR 275), where Mr Justice Walton said that there was in the case of a gratuitous bailee an obligation to use such care as a reasonably prudent owner would take of his own property, and also that in an action such as the present it was not sufficient for the defendants, in order to escape liability, merely to prove that the goods were not in their possession because they had been lost, but that they must prove much more than that in order to escape liability.

In this case the defendants did not satisfy the jury as to how the injuries were caused, and they had not satisfied his Lordship that they had used reasonable care. Therefore in his Lordship's opinion the defendants were liable to pay damages for the injuries to the pony which occurred while it was in their custody and as to which no satisfactory explanation had been given as to how they happened. That relieved him from deciding a difficult question of law; namely, whether the property in the pony had passed at the time of the accident, so that it was at the risk of the plaintiff. His Lordship said that he was inclined to think that it had; that the contract was for the sale of a specific object as to which nothing had to be done in order to put it into a deliverable state except to deliver it . . . .

One further point should be made about 'risk'. It is a basic rule in English law that property cannot pass in unascertained goods (s 16: see above, p 273 and below, p 315). But the law does not put a similar obstacle in the way when it comes to the passing of risk. The parties may, by agreement, place the risk of loss on the buyer even before the contract goods have been identified as such. Plainly, this cannot be done in the case of goods sold purely by description, so long as no steps have been taken to appropriate goods to the contract or to identify the source from which they will be appropriated. But in other circumstances it is well established that the risk of loss of goods which are unascertained in the statutory sense may be placed on the buyer. This is illustrated by *Sterns Ltd v Vickers Ltd,* a case concerning a contract to sell an unascertained part out of an identified bulk.

Sterns Ltd v Vickers Ltd
[1923] 1 KB 78, Court of Appeal

The Admiralty sold to Vickers 200,000 gallons of white spirit which was being stored by the London and Thames Haven Oil Wharves Co in 'tank No 78'. Two weeks later, Vickers contracted to sell 120,000 gallons of this spirit to Sterns. Sterns resold the spirit which they had bought to Lazarus. Vickers obtained from the storage company a warrant acknowledging that 120,000 gallons of spirit were being held on Sterns' behalf, and this warrant was indorsed by Sterns to Lazarus. As Lazarus did not want to take immediate delivery of the spirit, he made his own arrangements with the company for further storage and paid them storage rent. Several months later, when Lazarus came to take the spirit, it was found to have been adulterated by being mixed with a spirit of heavier specific gravity. The Court of Appeal held that even though property in the spirit had not passed to the buyers, they had assumed the risk of loss or damage in respect of their share of the bulk spirit from the time when they accepted the storage company's warrant.

Scrutton LJ: I think Mr Thorn Drury is right in saying that as at the material time there had been no severance of the quantity purchased from the larger bulk there were no specific 120,000 gallons in which the property passed. The question as to the effect of such a sale of an undivided portion of a larger bulk has frequently arisen in the Courts, and was much discussed in the well-known case of *Inglis v Stock* ((1885) 10 App Cas 263), where a similar argument to that which was addressed to us here was addressed to the Court for the purpose of showing that a person who had bought a certain number of tons of sugar, part of a larger stock, had no insurable interest in the quantity bought, because no specific bags had been appropriated to the contract and consequently the property in them had not passed. But as Lord Blackburn there pointed out, although the purchaser did not acquire the property in any particular number of tons of sugar he did acquire an undivided interest in the larger bulk and that undivided interest the House of Lords held to be insurable. The acquisition of an undivided interest in a larger bulk clearly will not suffice to pass the property when the appropriation to the contract has to be made by the vendor himself. As Bayley B said in *Gillett v Hill* ((1834) 2 Cr & M 530): 'Where there is a bargain for a certain quantity' of goods 'ex a greater quantity, and there is a power of selection in the vendor to deliver which he thinks fit, then the right to them does not pass to the vendee until the vendor has made his selection, and trover is not maintainable before that is done.' Nor probably will the acquisition of such an undivided interest pass the property, so as to entitle the purchaser to sue for a conversion, in a case where the power of appropriation is, as here, in a third party. But in that latter case, whether the property passes or not, the transfer of the undivided interest carries with it the risk of loss from something happening to the goods, such as a deterioration in their quality, at all events after the vendor has given the purchaser a delivery order upon the party in possession of them, and that party has assented to it. The vendor of a specified quantity out of a bulk in the possession of a third party discharges his obligation to the purchaser as soon as the third party undertakes to the purchaser to deliver him that quantity out of the bulk. In the present case, what happened was that at the date of the contract there was a bulk larger than the quantity sold, and it was of the contract quality according to sample. A delivery warrant was issued by the Thames Haven Company undertaking to deliver that quantity from the bulk which at that time corresponded with the sample. That warrant was accepted by the purchaser and by their sub-purchaser, Lazarus, who proceeded to pay rent for the storage from the date of the warrant. In those circumstances I come clearly to the conclusion that as between the plaintiffs and the defendants the risk was on the plaintiffs the purchasers. The vendors had done all that they undertook to do. The purchasers had the right to go to the storage company and demand delivery, and if they had done so at the time they would have got all that the defendants had undertaken to sell them. What the purchasers here are trying to do is to put the risk after acceptance of the warrant upon persons who had then no control over the goods, for it seems plain that after the acceptance of that warrant the vendors would have had no right to go to the storage company and request them to refuse delivery to the purchaser. For these reasons, treating the matter as a question rather of the transfer of risk than of the passing of property—for strictly I do not think the property passed, but only a right to an undivided share in the bulk to be selected by a third person—I think the view taken by the judge below was erroneous. He seems to have considered the question of transferring the risk, and thought there was no evidence of it. With that view, I cannot agree. I think the only conclusion to be drawn from the evidence is that the risk did pass . . . .

[Bankes LJ delivered a concurring judgment. Eve J concurred.]

QUESTIONS

Sterns v Vickers was, of course, decided before the new s 20A (see below, p 320) was enacted. You may like to consider whether any of the questions which follow would be answered differently if s 20A were in force and Sterns had paid Vickers the full price.

1. Who carried the risk in respect of the other 80,000 gallons?

2. Suppose that when Lazarus came to collect the spirit which he had purchased, there had been no adulteration but 80,000 gallons had been stolen. How much would he be (a) entitled, (b) bound, to take?

3. If other spirit had been mixed with the 200,000 gallons so that the bulk was *improved* in quality, could he have claimed 120,000 gallons of it?

What is the effect, as between the parties, of the passing of the risk? We may summarise the position as follows:

(1) If the risk has passed, the buyer will have to pay the price even though he does not (and will not ever) get the goods, if they have been lost or destroyed; and similarly he must pay the full price even though the goods have been partly lost, or damaged. The buyer, for his part, cannot sue the seller in damages for failing to make delivery, or for delivering less than the contract quantity or damaged goods.

(2) If the risk has not passed at the time when the loss or damage happens, the seller cannot compel the buyer to pay the price, or to take delivery of any remaining goods, or of the goods in their damaged state, or sue him for damages for refusing to do so.

Risk in consumer sales

By an amendment made to the Act in 2002 (Sale and Supply of Goods to Consumers Regulations 2002, SI 2002/3045, reg 4, implementing Directive 1999/44/EC), none of the above rules applies to a contract of sale where the buyer deals as consumer. Instead, a new s 20(4) provides that the goods remain at the seller's risk until they are delivered to the consumer. A 'consumer' for this purpose means a natural person who is acting for purposes outside his trade, business or profession.

3 STATUTORY PROVISIONS RELATING TO PERISHING OF SPECIFIC GOODS

Sections 6 and 7 of the Act contain provisions relating to the 'perishing' of the goods which bear some relationship to the question of risk. They may be seen respectively as particular instances of the contractual doctrines of common mistake and frustration. Each section applies only to contracts for the sale of *specific* goods.

(a) Section 6: specific goods which have perished

Where there is a contract for the sale of specific goods, and the goods without the knowledge of the seller have perished at the time when the contract is made, s 6 of the Act declares that the contract is void.

Section 6 is said by Chalmers himself (*The Sale of Goods* (1st edn, 1890), p 10) to have been based on the well-known House of Lords' decision in *Couturier v Hastie*.

Couturier v Hastie
(1856) 5 HL Cas 673, House of Lords

A cargo of corn was shipped by Couturier in February 1848 for delivery in London. In May Hastie, acting for Couturier on a *del credere* commission (ie as an agent who assumed personal liability for the buyer's obligations: see above, p 104), contracted to sell this cargo to Callander. Unknown to either Hastie or Callander, the cargo had been sold in April by the ship's captain in Tunis, en route to London, because it was overheating. Callander refused to pay for the corn, and so Couturier sued Hastie for the price. Mr Wilde, counsel for Couturier, argued:

The purchase here was not of the cargo absolutely as a thing assumed to be in existence, but merely of the benefit of the expectation of its arrival, and of the securities against the contingency of its loss. The purchaser bought in fact the shipping documents, the rights and interests of the vendor.

In effect, his contention was that the buyer had not bought the cargo of corn, as specific goods, but had contracted to take over the benefit of the voyage, as a venture. (Compare the position of the buyer under a contract made on CIF terms, below, p 498). However, the court held, as a matter of construction, that the subject matter of the contract was the cargo. As it had not been delivered, the seller could not sue for the price.

Lord Cranworth LC: Looking to the contract itself alone, it appears to me clearly that what the parties contemplated, those who bought and those who sold, was that there was an existing something to be sold and bought, and if sold and bought, then the benefit of insurance should go with it. I do not feel pressed by the latter argument, which has been brought forward very ably by Mr Wilde, derived from the subject of insurance. I think the full benefit of the insurance was meant to go as well to losses and damage that occurred previously to the 15th of May, as to losses and damage that occurred subsequently, always assuming that something passed by the contract of the 15th of May. If the contract of the 15th of May had been an operating contract, and there had been a valid sale of a cargo at that time existing, I think the purchaser would have had the benefit of insurance in respect of all damage previously occurring. The contract plainly imports that there was something which was to be sold at the time of the contract, and something to be purchased. No such thing existing, I think the Court of Exchequer Chamber has come to the only reasonable conclusion upon it, and consequently that there must be judgment given by your Lordships for the Defendants. . . .

QUESTION

Is *Couturier* v *Hastie* authority for the proposition stated in s 6?

Some commentators have found the following decision of the Australian High Court difficult to reconcile with the statutory rule laid down by s 6.

McRae v Commonwealth Disposals Commission

(1950) 84 CLR 377, High Court of Australia

The Commission, an agency of the Australian government, advertised for sale 'an oil tanker lying on the Jourmand Reef, which is approximately 100 miles north of Samarai. The vessel is said to contain oil'. McRae agreed to buy the tanker and its contents for £285. He fitted out a salvage expedition at considerable expense and went to the advertised locality, but there was no tanker there—and in fact no reef. No such tanker had ever existed. The High Court held the Commission liable for breach of a contractual promise that there was an oil tanker at the position specified.

Dixon and Fullagar JJ (in a joint judgment): . . . It was not decided in *Couturier v Hastie* ((1856) 5 HL Cas 673) that the contract in that case was void. The question whether it was void or not did not arise. If it had arisen, as in an action by the purchaser for damages, it would have turned on the ulterior question whether the contract was subject to an implied condition precedent. Whatever might then have been held on the facts of *Couturier v Hastie,* it is impossible in this case to imply any such term. The terms of the contract and the surrounding circumstances clearly exclude any such implication. The buyers relied upon, and acted upon, the assertion of the seller that there was a tanker in existence. It is not a case in which the parties can be seen to have proceeded on the basis of a common assumption of fact so as to justify the conclusion that the correctness of the assumption was intended by both parties to be a condition precedent to the creation of contractual obligations. The officers of the Commission made an assumption, but the plaintiffs did not make an assumption in the same sense. They knew nothing except what the Commission had told them. If they had been asked, they would certainly not have said: 'Of course, if there is no tanker, there is no contract.' They would have said: 'We shall have to go and take possession of the tanker. We simply accept the Commission's assurance that there is a tanker and the Commission's promise to give us that tanker.' The only proper construction of the contract is that it included a promise by the Commission that there was a tanker in the position specified. The Commission contracted that there was a tanker there. 'The sale in this case of a ship implies a contract that the subject of the transfer did exist in the character of a ship' (*Barr v Gibson* (1838) 3 M & W 390)). If, on the other hand, the case of *Couturier v Hastie* and this case ought to be treated as cases raising a question of 'mistake', then the Commission cannot in this case rely on any mistake as avoiding the contract, because any mistake was induced by the serious fault of their own servants, who asserted the existence of a tanker recklessly and without any reasonable ground. There *was* a contract, and the Commission contracted that a tanker existed in the position specified. Since there was no such tanker, there has been a breach of contract, and the plaintiffs are entitled to damages for that breach.

Before proceeding to consider the measure of damages, one other matter should be briefly mentioned. The contract was made in Melbourne, and it would seem that its proper law is Victorian law. Section 11 of the Victorian *Goods Act* 1928 corresponds to s 6 of the English *Sale of Goods Act* [1979], and provides that 'where there is a contract for the sale of specific goods, and the goods without the knowledge of the seller have perished at the time when the contract is made the contract is void'. This has been generally supposed to represent the legislature's view of the effect of *Couturier v Hastie*. Whether it correctly represents the effect of the decision in that case or not, it seems clear that the section has no application to the facts of the present case. Here the goods never existed, and the seller ought to have known that they did not exist....

[McTiernan J concurred.]

NOTE

It is possible to explain why s 6 (or rather the Australian equivalent) was not applied in *McRae's* case by reference to the literal wording of the section: the tanker had not 'perished', because no tanker had ever existed. But this is not the *ratio decidendi* of the judgment. The court found that the Commission had contracted to sell a ship and, as a term of that contract, *warranted that they had a ship to sell*. They were held liable to pay damages for breach of this term.

As pointed out by Professor Atiyah (Atiyah, p 104), the parties to a contract on facts similar to *Couturier* v *Hastie* or *McRae's* case are free to make any one of three bargains:

(1) Their contract might be subject to an implied condition precedent that the goods are in existence; if they are not, neither party incurs any liability.

(2) The seller might contract (warrant) that the goods do exist; if they are not, he will be liable in damages to the buyer.

(3) The buyer may agree to take the risk that the goods may have perished prior to the contract—ie, he agrees to pay for the *chance* of getting the goods.

In (1), neither party takes the risk that the goods may not exist; in (2), the seller does; in (3), the buyer does. Where this question of risk is not spelt out clearly, all are possible interpretations of the bargain which the parties have made.

QUESTIONS

1. The decision in *Hedley Byrne & Co Ltd v Heller & Partners Ltd* [1964] AC 465, HL was not even a glimmer on the horizon in 1950, when *McRae* was decided (apart from the long-sighted eyes of Lord Denning!: see *Candler v Crane, Christmas & Co Ltd* [1951] 2 KB 164, CA). If the same facts were to occur in England today, would you advise McRae to rely on *Hedley Byrne* or the Misrepresentation Act 1967, rather than on the *ratio* in that case, and would the outcome be any different?

2. In earlier editions of Cheshire and Fifoot's *Law of Contract* (though not with the same confidence in the current (15th) edition co-authored by Professor Furmston: see p 290), it was suggested that the decision in *McRae* could be better supported on the basis that,

although the contract of sale itself was void under s 6, the Commission had also entered into a *collateral* contract with McRae in which they promised that the ship existed. Consider this suggestion.

3.   McRae, who paid the Commission £285 for the salvage rights to a vessel and its contents worth possibly many thousands of pounds, is reported as having said: 'One often had a couple of hundred pounds on a horse on a Saturday and I might as well have a gamble on this.' Was this not a case, then, of *emptio spei*, the third of Professor Atiyah's possible contracts?

The term 'perish' is not defined in the Act, but the case next cited gives a clear indication that it is to be given a broad interpretation, so as to include (eg) goods which have been stolen, or which have 'perished' in part.

Barrow, Lane & Ballard Ltd v Phillip Phillips & Co

[1929] 1 KB 574, King's Bench Division

On 11 October 1927, Phillips contracted to sell to Ballards a specific lot (or 'parcel') consisting of 700 bags of Chinese ground nuts in shell, held in the stores of a wharf company. Unknown to the parties, 109 of the bags had been stolen before the contract was made; and, after delivery had been made of 150 bags, all the rest were also stolen. Phillips sued Ballards for the price of all 700 bags. It was held that s 6 applied, since the *parcel* of 700 bags had perished when the 109 were stolen.

Wright J: . . . This case raises a . . . problem, which, so far as I know, and so far as learned counsel have been able to ascertain, has never hitherto come before the Court. The problem is this: Where there is a contract for the sale of specific goods, such as the parcel of goods in this case, and some, but not all, of the goods have then ceased to exist for all purposes relevant to the contract because they have been stolen and taken away and cannot be followed or discovered anywhere, what then is the position? Does the case come within s 6 of the Sale of Goods Act, so that it would be the same as if the whole parcel had ceased to exist? In my judgment it does. The contract here was for a parcel of 700 bags, and at the time when it was made there were only 591 bags. A contract for a parcel of 700 bags is something different from a contract for 591 bags, and the position appears to me to be in no way different from what it would have been if the whole 700 bags had ceased to exist. The result is that the parties were contracting about something which, at the date of the contract, without the knowledge or fault of either party, did not exist. To compel the buyer in those circumstances to take 591 bags would be to compel him to take something which he had not contracted to take, and would in my judgment be unjust . . . .

A question of some difficulty arises when the goods are not lost or destroyed, but simply deteriorate in quality. Normally, this question will be determined by considering one or other of the following questions (or perhaps both: see s 33): (1) whether the seller has given any warranty as to the condition which the goods will be in at the material time (see, eg *Mash & Murrell Ltd v JI Emanuel Ltd* (below, p 409)), and (2) which party has the risk. But if the goods have deteriorated beyond the point where they cease to conform to their contract description, or are no longer of any commercial use, there is a case for saying that they have 'perished'. Although this is not borne out by one of the few cases on the point, *Horn v Minister of Food* [1948] 2 All ER 1036 (where potatoes which had rotted to a degree which made them useless even to be fed to cattle were held, obiter, not to have perished), most writers agree that the ruling was wrong, and it was not followed recently in New Zealand: see *Oldfield Asphalts v Grovedale Coolstores (1994) Ltd* [1998] 3 NZLR 479 (portable building seriously damaged by fire). In other contexts, where the question in issue has been essentially the same, there are authoritative decisions the other way. For instance, in

Asfar & Co v Blundell [1896] 1 QB 123, CA a consignment of dates aboard a ship sank in the Thames and was contaminated by sea water and sewage. When salvaged, they were unfit for human consumption (but, surprisingly, still worth a considerable sum for distillation into spirit!). For insurance purposes, however, the cargo was held to be a 'constructive total loss'—surely equivalent to a finding that they had 'perished' had s 6 or s 7 been in issue.

(b) Section 7: specific goods which subsequently perish

In a provision which closely parallels s 6 (above), s 7 states:

Where there is an *agreement to sell* specific goods and subsequently the goods, without any fault on the part of the seller or buyer, perish before the risk passes to the buyer, the agreement is avoided.

Just as a contract lawyer might see s 6 as an instance of common mistake as to the existence of the subject matter (or *res extincta*), so s 7 may be seen as a specific case of the operation of the doctrine of frustration through the destruction of the subject matter of the contract.

The wording of ss 6 and 7 is similar in several places, and it is generally assumed that decisions on the meaning of any common terms are relevant for both.

(c) 'Perishing' of unascertained goods

Both s 6 and s 7, as has been noted, apply only to specific goods. This raises the question whether unascertained goods can ever be said to have perished, and if so what the consequences are in law. It is best to consider the various categories of unascertained goods in sequence.

Generic goods. Goods of this kind which are sold purely by description (the typical 'commodity sale', such as '100 tonnes of King Edward potatoes') are subject to a firm rule, which in principle admits of no exceptions. Such contracts are made on the understanding that the seller undertakes the entire responsibility of ensuring that potatoes answering the contract description will be available for delivery to the buyer on the agreed date, and that he accepts all risks incidental to seeing that they are supplied. The whole point of contracts to buy goods for forward delivery is to hedge the buyer's position against adverse movements in the market, including the risk that supplies may run out. As the extract from the *Intertradex* case (below) shows, this is part of the 'warp and woof of commerce'. The leading case is *Blackburn Bobbin Co Ltd v TW Allen & Sons Ltd*.

Blackburn Bobbin Co Ltd v TW Allen & Sons Ltd
[1918] 2 KB 467, Court of Appeal

Allens contracted to sell to the Blackburn company 70 standards of Finland birch timber [a standard is 165 cubic feet], to be delivered on rail at Hull (where Allens were based) over the period from June to November 1914. Because there had been no sailings from Finnish ports, no timber had been imported from Finland when war broke out in August of that year, and thereafter it became impossible to obtain Finnish timber either directly from Finland or from any other source. It was normal practice for merchants to import all Finnish timber direct from Finland to meet their customers' orders, and stockpiles were not held in England. The Court of Appeal, affirming McCardie J, held that Allens were not excused from their contractual obligations.

Pickford LJ: The defendants contend that the contract was at an end because it was in the contemplation of both parties that the defendants should be able to supply the timber according to the ordinary method of supplying it in the trade, and that when that became impossible both parties were discharged from their obligations. . . .

[His Lordship discussed a number of cases dealing with the doctrine of frustration, and continued:]

In my opinion McCardie J was right in saying that the principle of these cases did not apply to discharge the defendants in this case. He has found that the plaintiffs were unaware at the time of the contract of the circumstance that the timber from Finland was shipped direct from a Finnish port to Hull, and that they did not know whether the transport was or was not partly by rail across Scandinavia, nor did they know that timber merchants in this country did not hold stocks of Finnish birch. I accept the finding that in fact the method of dispatching this timber was not known to the plaintiffs. But there remains the question, Must they be deemed to have contracted on the basis of the continuance of that method although they did not in fact know of it? I see no reason for saying so. Why should a purchaser of goods, not specific goods, be deemed to concern himself with the way in which the seller is going to fulfil his contract by providing the goods he has agreed to sell? The sellers in this case agreed to deliver the timber free on rail at Hull, and it was no concern of the buyers as to how the sellers intended to get the timber there. I can see no reason for saying—and to free the defendants from liability this would have to be said—that the continuance of the normal mode of shipping the timber from Finland was a matter which both parties contemplated as necessary for the fulfilment of the contract. To dissolve the contract the matter relied on must be something which both parties had in their minds when they entered into the contract, such for instance as the existence of the music-hall in *Taylor v Caldwell* ((1863) 3 B & S 826), or the continuance of the vessel in readiness to perform the contract, as in *Jackson v Union Marine Insurance Co* ((1874) LR 10 CP 125). Here there is nothing to show that the plaintiffs contemplated, and there is no reason why they should be deemed to have contemplated, that the sellers should continue to have the ordinary facilities for dispatching the timber from Finland. As I have said, that was a matter which to the plaintiffs was wholly immaterial. It was not a matter forming the basis of the contract they entered into. . . .

For the reasons I have given the defendants have failed on the facts to make out their case that the contract was dissolved. The appeal will be dismissed.

[Bankes and Warrington LJJ delivered concurring judgments.]

Intertradex SA v Lesieur-Tourteaux SARL
[1977] 2 Lloyd's Rep 146, [1978] 2 Lloyd's Rep 509, Queen's Bench Division and Court of Appeal

Intertradex contracted to sell to Lesieur-Tourteaux 800 tonnes of Mali groundnut expellers, CIF Rouen. (On CIF contracts, see below, p 498). The sellers intended to fulfil their obligations from a consignment of 1,000 tonnes which they in turn had contracted to buy from suppliers, 'SEPOM', who (as they, but not the buyers, knew) were the sole crushers and producers of Mali groundnut expellers. The suppliers' factory at Koulikoro was ten days by rail from Abidjan, and four days from Dakar, the only export ports. The suppliers were unable to meet their commitments due to a mechanical breakdown at their factory (for which a replacement part had to be obtained from Germany) and interruptions in the supply by rail of raw materials to their factory. The sellers claimed that they were excused from performance—a view which was upheld by a board of arbitration to which the dispute was referred. Donaldson J, in a judgment affirmed by the Court of Appeal, held that they were not excused.

Donaldson J: That this situation was aggravating or frustrating both for SEPOM and the sellers is not in doubt, but the legal doctrine of frustration is not based upon psychology or emotion . . . .

The sellers' basic obligation was to deliver the goods (or documents covering the goods) in accordance with their contract. The basic risks which they assumed were those of shortage of supply and a rise in price. It was for the assumption of these risks that they would have agreed a price which, hopefully, would have produced a profit. They have qualified this obligation by reference in cll 21 and 22 to a very wide variety of events which might place obstacles in their way. Ingenuity may suggest some concatenation of events to which these clauses do not apply, but which are of so outlandish a nature that the obligation to deliver cannot have been intended to survive in the changed circumstances. But a mere reduction in the supplies available, even from a sole supplier, due to such commonplace events as a breakdown of machinery or the inadequacies of a railway are far removed from this category. They are the warp and woof of industrial and commercial aggravation. Giving the fullest effect to the board's findings of fact and paying the fullest respect to their view of the commercial realities, in my judgment there are no possible grounds for holding the contract between the buyers and sellers to have been frustrated.

Of course, the parties are free to make a contract for the sale of commodities of this kind on other terms; and indeed it is customary in most international sales contracts to incorporate 'force majeure' clauses designed to protect the seller against liability in such events as a failure of supply or a breakdown of transport. In fact, in *Intertradex* itself, there was such a clause, but it was held on the facts that the sellers were not able to rely on it.

In *Re Badische Co Ltd* [1921] 2 Ch 331 Russell J *implied* into a contract, made in England between two English companies, for the supply of dyestuffs (which it was known would come from a German source) a term to the effect that the pre-war commercial conditions prevailing between England and Germany would continue; and he held the sellers excused when this condition could no longer be met. This reasoning, it is submitted, cannot be supported in the light of the strong line of authority to the contrary exemplified by the cases above—a principle summed up in the Latin maxim *genus nunquam perit* ('generic goods can never perish').

It is also possible for the parties to make their contract on altogether different terms, so that it is not a contract of sale at all, but one in which the 'seller' does not commit himself to procure the goods. This was the construction put upon the contract in *Monkland v Jack Barclay Ltd* [1951] 2 KB 252. At that time, new Bentley cars were in short supply and there was a waiting list of over a year. Monkland ordered a Bentley Mark VI from Barclays, but when the expected time for delivery came they refused to let him have one because he was unwilling to comply with a stipulation demanded by the manufacturers that he would not resell the car in the first six months after purchase. The court held that Barclays were under no liability to Monkland because by the terms of their contract they had agreed only to *use their best endeavours* to procure a car for him (an obligation which they had performed), rather than to *sell* him one.

Goods to be manufactured or acquired by the seller. On principle, the same approach should normally govern contracts for the sale of goods which are to be manufactured or otherwise acquired (eg fish to be caught) by the seller. If a tailor agrees to make a suit for a customer or a shipbuilder to build a boat, and the suit or boat is destroyed in a fire when it is 90 per cent finished, the seller has no choice but to obtain a new supply of materials and begin work all over again. And the same would be true if the seller's boatload of fish is swept overboard in a storm on its way back to port. However, the parties may again agree to the contrary, and of course this will be the only possible construction where there is something about the contract which makes the seller's obligation conditional upon the continued availability of the materials which have been lost—for instance, where it has been agreed that the tailor should make a suit from a specific piece of cloth which is later destroyed.

Goods which are to be appropriated from a specific bulk or source. A different rule applies to this class of unascertained goods, since the contract of sale will necessarily be impossible to perform if the source from which the goods are to be appropriated fails. Where, for instance, the parties' contract is not simply one for 100 tonnes of King Edward potatoes, but for 100 tonnes of King Edward potatoes *out of the 200 tonnes now in the seller's store,* the contract will be frustrated if the entire 200 tonnes are destroyed. Similarly, if the 100 tonnes contracted for are to come from the crop to be harvested from a particular field, and bad weather causes the whole crop to fail. The case *of Howell v Coupland* was concerned with a slight variant of these facts.

Howell v Coupland

(1876) 1 QBD 258, Court of Appeal

Coupland, a Lincolnshire farmer, in March 1872 contracted to sell to Howell 200 tons of Regent potatoes to be grown on specified land belonging to Coupland, to be delivered in the following September and October. Coupland planted potatoes on 68 acres of the land—an area sufficient in a normal season to yield over 450 tons; but the crop was struck by an unpreventable disease in August and only 80 tons were produced. Howell took delivery of the 80 tons and paid for them at the contract rate, and sued in this action for damages for Coupland's failure to deliver the balance. It was held that the failure should be excused.

Lord Coleridge CJ: I am of opinion that the judgment ought to be affirmed.... The true ground, as it seems to me, on which the contract should be interpreted, and which is the ground on which, I believe, the Court of Queen's Bench proceeded, is that by the simple and obvious construction of the agreement both parties understood and agreed, that there should be a condition implied that before the time for the performance of the contract the potatoes should be, or should have been, in existence, and should still be existing when the time came for the performance. They had been in existence, and had been destroyed by causes over which the defendant, the contractor, had no control, and it became impossible for him to perform his contract; and, according to the condition which the parties had understood should be in the contract, he was excused from the performance. It was not an absolute contract of delivery under all circumstances, but a contract to deliver so many potatoes, of a particular kind, grown on a specific place, if deliverable from that place. On the facts the condition did arise and the performance was excused. I am, therefore, of opinion that the judgment of the Queen's Bench should be affirmed.

[James and Mellish LJJ, Baggallay JA and Cleasby B delivered concurring judgments.]

QUESTIONS

1. Why would a potato merchant make a contract in March to buy potatoes as yet unplanted which would not be grown until September?

2. If a natural calamity such as frost or disease has struck one farmer's crop, it is likely to have affected others also. What would happen to the market price in such circumstances?

3. If Howell had not wanted the 80 tons, was he bound to take them? (See s 30(1).)

NOTE

There has never been any doubt that *Howell* v *Coupland* is a correct decision, but there has been some debate as to the principle on which it should be regarded as having been based in modern law. Underlying the uncertainty is the note appended by Chalmers to s 7 of the Act, from which it is plain that he considered that that section is illustrated by *Howell* v *Coupland* (see his *Sale of Goods* (1st edn, 1890), p 11). However, s 7 by its terms applies only to contracts for the sale of *specific* goods, and the potatoes in that case were not 'specific' within the statutory definition (as set out in s 61(1)), since no particular 200 tons were identified by the parties at the time when they made their contracts—indeed, the crop had not even been planted then. Mellish LJ in his judgment did, in fact, describe the contract as an agreement to sell 'specific things'; but of course he was speaking many years before the Act was drafted and so this statement is not relevant. The suggestion sometimes made that the words 'specific goods' should be given a meaning outside the statutory definition solely for the purposes of ss 6 and 7 is hard to defend. Nor is it wholly appropriate to explain *Howell v Coupland* as a simple case of common-law frustration, for the consequence of frustration is that the entire contract is avoided, whereas the court in that case ruled that the seller should be excused only in regard to the part of the crop which had failed; and as we shall see shortly from the ruling in *HR & S Sainsbury Ltd v Street* (below), the seller is not excused from his obligation to deliver so much as he has been able to produce.

In *Re Wait* (above, p 266), Atkin LJ made the following comments ([1927] 1 Ch 606 at 631):

An attempt was made to show that the goods were specific goods by citing the decision of *Howell v Coupland,* and arguing that as the goods were called specific there, the term in the Sale of Goods Act, despite the statutory definition, must be used in the same sense. And it was said that in any case s 7 of the Code reproduces the decision in *Howell* v *Coupland,* and as it uses the word 'specific,' the meaning must differ from the statutory definition. These contentions appear to me to ignore the true use of the Code, and to misinterpret *Howell v Coupland.*

[His Lordship stated the facts *of Howell v Coupland,* and continued:]

It was held that on the principle of *Taylor v Caldwell* ((1863) 3 B & S 826) he was relieved from further performance of the contract. Blackburn J says it is a contract for the delivery at a future time of a specific thing so far as this, that it is for the delivery of a portion of a specific thing, in other words the Court implied a condition that a particular thing, the crop, should come into existence or remain in existence. This case had no reference to 'specific or ascertained' for the purpose of passing the property or of specific performance, and I conceive that it would have startled Lord Blackburn if the whole crop had come into existence, to have it contended that 200 tons under the contract had been ascertained before they were both separated and riddled. The case *of Howell* v *Coupland* would now be covered either by s 5, sub-s 2, of the Code or, as is suggested by the learned authors of the last two editions of Benjamin on Sale, by common law principles retained by s 61, sub-s 2 [now s61(2)], of the Code.

Section 5(2) of the Act states that there may be a contract for the sale of goods, the acquisition of which depends upon a contingency which may or may not happen. In *Howell v Coupland*, the contingency was a condition implied by the court that the specified land would yield the amount of potatoes necessary to fulfil the contract. The use of an implied term in this way gives the court more flexibility than the doctrine of frustration would allow, for it makes it possible also to imply an understanding that if there is a shortfall the seller is bound to let the buyer have the smaller amount which has been produced. This was in fact the ruling in *HR & S Sainsbury Ltd v Street*.

HR & S Sainsbury Ltd v Street
[1972] 1 WLR 834, Queen's Bench Division

(The facts appear from the judgment.)

MacKenna J: The plaintiff buyers claim damages against the defendant seller under an alleged contract for the sale of 'about 275 tons' of feed barley for delivery in August or September 1970. The defendant denies the contract. He alleges in the alternative that if he agreed to sell it was a condition precedent of his obligation to deliver that he should in 1970 harvest a crop of at least that tonnage on his farm at East Knoyle, Wiltshire, that he did not harvest such a crop but one of only 140 tons, and that his failure to harvest the larger crop excused him from the obligation to delivery any barley, even the smaller tonnage. He admittedly delivered none. The plaintiffs concede that he harvested only the smaller tonnage and further concede that they are not entitled to damages for his failure to deliver barley which he did not harvest, but assert that they are entitled to recover damages for his failure to deliver the 140 tons harvested. It is agreed that if they are entitled to recover any damages these should be computed at £7.50 per ton.

There are two questions which I must decide. (1) Did the defendant agree to sell 'about 275 tons' of feed barley to the plaintiffs? If he did, (2) was he under any obligation to deliver the 140 tons which he actually harvested? . . .

[His Lordship reviewed the evidence and concluded:]

As to the first question I find that there was a contract between the plaintiffs and the defendant for the purchase of 275 tons of feed barley (5 per cent more or less) to be grown by the defendant on his farm. . . .

As to the second, I am prepared to assume, consistently with the plaintiffs' abandonment of their claim for damages for the tonnage not in fact produced, that it was an implied condition of the contract that if the defendant, through no fault of his, failed to produce the stipulated tonnage of his growing crop, he should not be required to pay damages. It seems a very reasonable condition, considering the risks of agriculture and the fact that the crop was at the contract date still growing. But a condition that he need not deliver any if, through some misfortune, he could not deliver the whole is a very different one, and in my opinion so unreasonable that I would not imply it unless compelled to do so by authority. The way in which the parties chose the more or less conventional figure of one and a half [tons per acre] as the estimated yield of the crop is, I think, an additional reason in this case against the implication. If they had intended that a failure to achieve this optimistic tonnage would mean the end of the contract for both of them, they would have gone about the business of estimating yield in a much more cautious manner.

Mr Rawlins argued that it was reasonable that the defendant should be freed of all his obligations under the contract if without his fault he failed to produce the whole tonnage. 275 tons (5 per cent more or less) set an upper limit to the quantity which the plaintiffs could be compelled to take. It was reasonable, he said, that there should be a lower limit to the amount which the defendant could be compelled to deliver. In a year when the latter's yield was high, market prices would probably be low, and it would be a benefit to the plaintiffs not to be required to take more than an agreed tonnage at the contract price fixed in advance. In a year when the yield was low, as in the present case, it would be a benefit to the defendant if he were free to disregard his contract and to sell his crop to some other buyer at the higher market price. The contract should, if possible, be construed as giving him this freedom. I am not persuaded by the argument. The upper limit of 275 tons might in the circumstances of a particular case be beneficial to both parties. But even if it could be beneficial only to the buyer that is no reason for implying a term that the same figure shall serve as a lower limit to the seller's obligation to deliver, so that his failure to reach that figure, if blameless, would release him from the contract.

[The buyers were accordingly held to be entitled to damages. His Lordship said, in relation to *Howell v Coupland*:]

It is clear from the statement of the facts in the headnote that the case raised no question about the seller's obligation to deliver the potatoes which he had in fact produced, and clear from the last sentence quoted from the judgment of Blackburn J that it gives no support to the view that the bargain was off both as to the 120 tons and the 80. There is nothing in the judgments of the Court of Appeal which touches this question.

After the decision of *Howell v Coupland* the Sale of Goods Act 1893 was passed.

[His Lordship quoted ss 5(2), 6, 7 and 61(2) [now 62(2)] of the Act, and continued:]

The rule of *Howell v Coupland* is, I think, preserved by s 5(2). If I am wrong in that view, because the growing of a crop cannot be considered the 'acquisition' of goods within the meaning of that section, then it is preserved by s 61(2). I do not think that it is preserved by ss 6 or 7. These sections are, in my opinion, dealing with goods existing, and a crop not yet grown does not answer either description.

NOTE

There is one further problem, for which English law does not offer a wholly satisfactory solution. What if Coupland had made a second contract to sell 200 tons of potatoes to another merchant? What would be the rights of the respective parties? Or, to identify the issues more clearly, suppose that S has 20 boxes of champagne in his cellar and in separate contracts he agrees to sell '10 boxes of the champagne in my cellar' to B1 and the same number to B2. Before any boxes have been appropriated to either contract, a thief steals 10 boxes, leaving S in the position where he can perform one or other of his contracts, but not both. Cases in other contexts suggest that in the absence of some provision in the contracts indicating that one of them should be performed first, or that each buyer should take a proportionate share of what goods are available, the seller is not excused for his failure to honour the contract that he chooses not to perform. In the language of the doctrine of frustration, this failure is 'self-induced', resulting from his own election to perform the other: see *Maritime National Fish Ltd v Ocean Trawlers Ltd* [1935] AC 524, PC and *The Super Servant Two* [1990] 1 Lloyd's Rep 1, CA (two cases on the hiring of ships). In the United States, the Uniform Commercial Code, s 2–615 offers a much fairer solution: the seller is allowed to 'prorate' his performance, ie distribute those goods which he does have available *pro rata* amongst the various buyers. (On prorating, see AH Hudson (1968) 31 MLR 535; (1978) 123 Sol Jo 137.) In England this solution is possible only if there is a clause in the contract which permits the seller to take such a way out: as is, in fact, commonly the case in international sales contracts.

4 FRUSTRATION OF SALE OF GOODS CONTRACTS

In the discussion above, we have been concerned with the destruction of the subject matter of the contract which is, of course, one of the grounds upon which a contract can be held to be frustrated at common law. Nothing in the Act prevents the doctrine of frustration from being applied to contracts for the sale of goods where any of the other recognised grounds is relied on, eg supervening illegality, or impossibility caused by such an event as the closing of the port designated by the contract for the shipping of the goods or the sinking of the named ship in which they are to be carried. Many leading 'frustration' cases were concerned with sales of goods: the *Fibrosa* case [1943] AC 32, HL, and the 'Suez' cases such as *Tsakiroglou & Co Ltd v Noblee Thorl GmbH* [1962] AC 93, HL. But we should remember that, as the latter case and the *Intertradex* judgment cited above show, impossibility of performance is not readily inferred in the case of ordinary commodity sales.

Returning to those situations where there has been destruction of the goods which are the subject matter of the contract, we may ask: what is the relation between the concept of 'risk', which we have been examining, and the doctrine of frustration? First, by definition, frustration deals with an *unforeseen* event—something not contemplated by the parties and not provided for by a term of the contract. The rules as to risk *are* terms of the contract, express or implied; and if the parties have agreed that one or the other of them shall carry the risk of accidental loss or damage to the goods, or if the seller has undertaken an *absolute* obligation to see that goods of the contract description will be delivered to the buyer (as in the typical contract to sell generic goods, eg *Blackburn Bobbin Co Ltd v T W Allen & Sons Ltd,* above), there is no scope for the doctrine of frustration to apply in regard to such an event. Second, we should note that there is a difference in the respective *effects* of risk and frustration: the former exposes one party to liability, whereas frustration lets both parties off their obligations. Third, it should be remembered that the Law Reform (Frustrated Contracts) Act 1943, which gives the court some discretionary powers to adjust the losses between the respective parties following a frustrating event, is expressly not made applicable to contracts for the sale of specific goods which, under s 7 or otherwise, are frustrated by reason of the fact that the goods have perished (s 2(5)(c) of the 1943 Act). This is in itself a statutory acknowledgment that there is no room for other solutions to a problem where the concept of risk applies.

5 RULES FOR DETERMINING WHEN THE PROPERTY PASSES

So many issues in our sale of goods law are made to turn on the question whether the property in the goods is still vested in the seller or has passed to the buyer that it is plainly a matter of the greatest importance to identify the point in time when the property passes. The Act deals with this in ss 16–19 by a few basic rules, supplemented by a number of presumptions.

(a) The basic rules

(i) *No property can pass in unascertained goods*

Section 16 has already been referred to more than once. Subject to the exception in s 20A (as to which see below, p 320), where the contract is for unascertained goods, no property in the goods can be transferred to the buyer unless and until the goods have been ascertained. In *Re Wait* (above, p 266), the Court of Appeal (and in particular, Atkin LJ) with considerable emphasis made it plain that there was no room in sale of goods law even for the notion that an *equitable* title might pass or an equitable interest be created, however well established and appropriate such a doctrine might be in relation to the transfer of other types of property such as land or book-debts (*Tailby v Official Receiver* (1888) 13 App Cas 523: see below, p 1029). Perhaps this is to put the point too strongly, for of course the parties to a contract of sale can create an equitable interest in goods *by express agreement* (and may even do so as a term of their sale contract, as in some of the *Romalpa* cases: see below, p 452); but *Re Wait* has eliminated any possibility that such an interest will be held to have arisen by inference or by operation of law. *Re London Wine Co (Shippers) Ltd* [1986] PCC 121 offers a further illustration.

Re London Wine Co (Shippers) Ltd

[1986] PCC 121, Chancery Division

The company had executed a debenture giving a floating charge to its bank secured over all its assets; and the bank, acting under a power conferred by the charge instrument, had appointed a receiver. Certain customers of the company claimed that they had bought wine which was in the possession of the company and that it was their property, either at law or in equity. The bank contended that, since no wine had been appropriated to answer any of the contracts in question, all the wine remained the property of the company and was therefore subject to the charge.

The company had acquired stocks of wine which were held in various warehouses, some of it in bond, some duty paid. These customers had each contracted to buy wine of a particular description from the company (eg '40 cases [of 12 bottles] Volnay Santenots 1969 Domaine Jacques Prieur') and, having paid the price in full, had received from the company a document called a 'Certificate of Title' which described the buyer as the 'sole and beneficial owner' of the wine in question. The company charged the buyer for storage and insurance until he chose to take delivery of the wine or sold it on to someone else. But there was no procedure for identifying or segregating the wine sold to any particular customer. The court considered separately three typical cases:

(1) those (eg that of Mr Strong) where a customer had bought the company's total stock of a particular wine at the date of the purchase;

(2) those (eg that of Mr Button) where two or more customers had bought quantities of a particular wine which, taken together, exhausted the whole of the company's stock of that wine;

(3) those (eg that of Mr Bailey) where the purchase did not exhaust the particular stock, but there had been an acknowledgment that the appropriate quantity of the particular wine was being held to the customer's order. In some of these cases, the customer had pledged his right to the wine as security for a loan—eg a customer called Vinum Ltd had pledged its wine to a finance company called Compass, and a similar acknowledgment had been given to the pledgee.

Oliver J held that in none of these instances had the property, or any other legal or equitable interest of a proprietary nature, passed to the buyer. The bank's security interest therefore prevailed, and the buyers were simply unsecured creditors for the return of the money which they had paid. (Where, however, in case (3), there had been an acknowledgment by the *warehousekeeper* that wine of a particular description was held to the customer's order, it was said that an action for damages based on an estoppel might lie against him, independently of the issue before the court.)

Oliver J: …There, then, are the three categories with which I have to deal and the question which has arisen in each case is whether the wines which have been sold belong to the purchasers and those claiming through or under them or whether on the relevant date they remained the company's property and so became subject to the charge in the debenture which then crystallised. I should perhaps say that there is no question of stocks being insufficient to fulfil all the purchase orders so that there is no competition between purchasers *inter se*…

As regards the case of Mr Strong and Mr Button, Mr Wright's primary submission on their behalf is that the legal title to the goods passed and that, accordingly, the matter ends there. If, however, that is wrong, he submits first that the goods became subject to a valid and effective trust before the relevant date, and, as an alternative to this, that each purchaser had, before the relevant date, a right to specific performance of his contract and that, when the floating charge crystallised, the bank took subject to that right. These two submissions apply equally to the third category and have been adopted and expanded by Mr Stamler on behalf of the respondents Vinum and Compass and since they are, therefore, common to all cases, and, if correct, are conclusive of the whole case, they can conveniently be dealt with first.

As regards the creation of a trust, this is put in this way. On the assumption that no property passed in the goods at law—and it is not argued that this could possibly be the case in the third category represented by Mr Bailey and by Mr Stamler's clients—there was, it is submitted, clearly an intention that the property should pass so far as the company had it in its power to make it do so. One has only to look at the terms of its circulars with their references to *'your* wines,' to the purchaser being 'the beneficial owner' and to the company having a lien. This is reinforced when one looks at the terms of the letters of confirmation which list the quantities and types of wine and confirm that the purchaser is 'the sole beneficial owner of these wines,' and is indeed further reinforced in the case of Compass and Vinum when reference is made to the master agreements with Compass and the company where the company joins in to warrant title to the wine. By issuing these documents, the acknowledged purpose of which was to enable the purchasers to deal with their wines by sale or charge, the company, it is said, evinced the clearest possible intention to declare itself a trustee and once you find such an intention, it matters not that the instrument expressing it fails to do so in unequivocal terms or, indeed, that there is no instrument at all. Reliance is placed upon the recent case of *Re Kayford Ltd* [below, p 1227] where Megarry J said: '...[i]t is well settled that a trust can be created without using the words "trust" or "confidence" or the like: the question is whether in substance a sufficient intention to create a trust has been manifested.'

That, of course, is a proposition with which it is impossible to quarrel but I do not find that case, where the evidence of intention to create a trust was exceptionally clear and where the trust property was from the outset specifically set aside and identified, one which assists me very much in ascertaining whether, in the very different circumstances of the instant case, a trust has been effectively declared. Mr Wright, in his reply, put it rather differently. A trust, he said, may be constituted not merely by direct and express declaration but also by the consequences flowing from the acts of the persons themselves to which consequences the law attaches the label 'trust.' A trust, to put it another way, is the technical description of a legal situation; and where you find (i) an intention to create a beneficial interest in someone else, (ii) an acknowledgment of that intention and (iii) property in the ownership of the person making the acknowledgment which answers the description in the acknowledgment, then there is, at the date of the acknowledgment, an effective and completed trust of all the property of the acknowledger answering to that description. This is, I think, in essence the same submission as that made by Mr Stamler—he submits that where one is dealing with a homogeneous mass there is no problem about certainty. So long as the mass can be identified and there is no uncertainty about the quantitative interest of the beneficiary, the court will find no difficulty in administering the trust if it once finds the necessary intention to create an equitable interest in property of the type comprised in the mass. I think, indeed, that if the case is to be made out at all, it must be put in this way, for the submission itself is based on the premise that there are no specific or ascertained goods in which the beneficiary is interested. Were it otherwise there would be no need to invoke the concept of trust for the title would have passed under the Sale of Goods Act (as, indeed, Mr Wright submits in categories 1 and 2, it did). If trust there be, then it must be a trust of the homogeneous *whole* and the terms of the trust must be that the trustee is to hold that whole upon trust to give effect thereout to the proportionate interest of the beneficiary. Thus if we postulate the case of the company having in warehouse 1,000 cases of a particular wine and selling 100 cases to X the circumstances of this case indicate, it is submitted, that the company created an equitable tenancy in common between itself and X in the whole 1,000 cases in the proportions of 9/10ths and l/10th.

It is with regret that I feel compelled to reject these submissions, for I feel great sympathy with those who paid for their wine and received an assurance that they had title to it. But I find it impossible to spell either out of the acknowledgments signed by the company or out of the circumstances any such trust as is now sought to be set up. Granted that the references to 'beneficial interest' are appropriate words for the creation of a trust; granted, even (although this I think is very difficult to spell out) that that was the company's intention, it seems to me that any such trust must fail on the ground of uncertainty of subject-matter. I appreciate the point taken that the subject-matter is part of a homogeneous mass so that specific identity is of as little importance as it is, for instance, in the case of money. Nevertheless, as it seems to me, to create a trust it must be possible to ascertain with certainty not only what the interest of the beneficiary is to be but to what property it is to attach.

I cannot see how, for instance, a farmer who declares himself to be a trustee of two sheep (without identifying them) can be said to have created a perfect and complete trust whatever rights he may confer by such declaration as a matter of contract. And it would seem to me to be immaterial that at the time he has a flock of sheep out of which he could satisfy the interest. Of course, he could by appropri-ate words, declare himself to be a trustee of a specified proportion of his whole flock and thus create an equitable tenancy in common between himself and the named beneficiary, so that a proprietary inter-est would arise in the beneficiary in an undivided share of all the flock and its produce. But the *mere* declaration that a given number of animals would be held upon trust could not, I should have thought, without very clear words pointing to such an intention, result in the creation of an interest in common in the proportion which that number bears to the number of the whole at the time of the declaration. And where the mass from which the numerical interest is to take effect is not itself ascertainable at the date of the declaration such a conclusion becomes impossible. . . .

I turn now, therefore, to the submissions peculiar to the individual cases. Now in the case of Mr Strong, although the goods were sold by generic description, it happened that at the material time the quantity described was in the company's possession and was the only wine of that description in its possession, although it is not claimed that it could not, without undue difficulty, obtain additional quantities from elsewhere if it required to do so. Mr Wright argues that the result of this was to ascertain the goods and that the property passed; and to make this good he has to rely either upon s 17 or upon an appropriation under s 18, r 5(1) of the Sale of Goods Act. Section 16 states quite clearly that the property is not transferred to the buyer unless and until the goods are ascertained but it is not a necessary corollary of this that the property *does* pass to the buyer when they *are* ascertained. To produce that result one either has had to find an appropriation (from which an intention to pass the property will be inferred) or one has to find an intention manifested in some other way. Mr Wright relies upon what has been referred to as an 'ascertainment by exhaustion' and has drawn my attention to the decision of Roche J in *Wait & James v Midland Bank* ((1926) 31 Com Cas 172).

[His Lordship referred to the facts of that case (below, p 322, and continued:]

The decision in that case was one of obvious common sense because in fact from November 16th onwards there were no goods from which the seller could have fulfilled the contracts except the 850 quarters. They could, no doubt, have delivered 850 quarters of Australian wheat but not 850 quarters of 'ex store Avonmouth ex *Thistleros* [sic].' The instant case seems to me quite different. It is not and cannot be alleged that the sale to Mr Strong was a sale of specific goods. What the company undertook to do was to deliver so many cases and bottles of the specified type of wine 'lying in bond.' This does not in my judgment link the wine sold with any given consignment or warehouse. The fact that the company had at the date of the invoice that amount of wine and that amount only is really irrelevant to the contract. No doubt it could have fulfilled the order from this wine but it could equally have fulfilled it from any other source. It is not contended that there was any act of appropriation and Mr Wright's case is that the property passed under s 17 when the usual title letter mentioning the wine described in the invoice was sent some three months later, by which date, he says, the wine was ascertained. I cannot draw that conclusion from the material before me, for it seems to me clear that the company was, under the contract, at liberty to deliver to the purchaser any bottles of wine which tallied with the description. It never has been, therefore, . . . ascertained what the goods are which are covered by the contract.

The argument in relation to the second category of case is very similar. . . . In my view, the company remained free to fulfil the contracts to its various purchasers from any source, as, for instance, by importing further wine of the same description. That being so, the mere fact that the company sold quantities of wine which in fact exhausted all the stocks which it held cannot, in my judgment, have had the effect of passing a proprietary interest in those stocks to the various purchasers so that they can now claim the goods collectively and ignore the bank's charge.

In the case of the third category of purchaser, represented by Mr Bailey and by Vinum Ltd and their respective pledgees, the case is put rather differently. It is not contended that any proprietary interest passed at law, but what is said is that an interest by estoppel was vested in the purchasers. . . .

In the case of Mr Bailey, the correspondence exhibited shows how, in very many cases, the company, at the instance of the pledgee from the purchaser, invited the warehouseman to issue warehouse receipts acknowledging that he held wine to the account of the pledgee. The case of Compass is even clearer, for here there was a master agreement to which the company was a party and under which it warranted the validity of the warehouse receipts and that the wine was held by it as a custodian for the pledgor.

There is no doubt that the pledgees were intended to and did alter their position on the faith of these representations by advancing money to Mr Bailey and Vinum Ltd respectively.

In these circumstances Mr Wright on behalf of Mr Bailey and Mr Stamler on behalf of Vinum Ltd and its pledgees submit that both the company and the warehouseman are estopped and that there were created in the purchasers and their pledgees proprietary interests by estoppel created before the bank's charge crystallised and so binding upon it.

None of the warehousemen is a party to these proceedings so that nothing that I say would be binding upon them in any event but in fact I cannot see how an estoppel affecting the warehousemen could affect the bank except in so far as such an estoppel created a proprietary interest in the goods in the warehouse subject to which the bank's charge takes effect. But the authorities to which I have referred above make one thing quite clear and that is that no property *actually* passes, although the estoppel operates to enable the plaintiff to prosecute an action in trover in which he can obtain damages from the warehouseman.

I can find here no estoppel which, in my judgment, can affect the bank or preclude it from asserting its real title to the assets of the company at the relevant date. . . .

Accordingly, I have felt compelled, perhaps rather reluctantly, to the conclusion that I must direct: (1) that all three categories of goods described in the schedule to the summons should be dealt with by the receiver as being the property of the company on the relevant date and so subject to the floating charge and (2) that no such goods are subject to any lien or other interest having priority to the floating charge in favour of the respondent purchasers or their respective assigns or mortgagees.

NOTE

A similar decision was reached by the Privy Council in the case of *Re Goldcorp Exchange Ltd* [1995] 1 AC 74, PC, where investors in New Zealand were invited to buy gold from Goldcorp which Goldcorp undertook to store on the customers' behalf. Each buyer received a certificate which purported to verify the fact that he was the owner of the gold he had bought; but in fact no gold was ever appropriated to any particular purchaser. The Privy Council held that no property had ever passed at law and no equitable interest had been created. A more indulgent ruling in favour of the purchasers was reached in *Re Stapylton Fletcher Ltd* [1994] 1 WLR 1181, where (on facts similar to *London Wine*) the sellers had followed up each sale by segregating the relevant quantity of wine from their general trading stock and placing it into separate storage. Although no steps were taken to allocate particular lots of wine to individual sales (so that, for instance, where two customers had bought different quantities of the same wine the company simply transferred the aggregate amount to the other store), it was held that there had been sufficient appropriation for the property to have passed. Where customers' orders had been aggregated, they held the total amount as tenants in common.

In *Customs & Excise Comrs v Everwine Ltd* [2003] EWCA Civ 953 wine belonging to E was held in F's bonded warehouse. Whenever E sold wine to another wine trader he faxed 'release notes' to F specifying the goods that had been sold. It was held that the property had passed to the buyer where the goods specified were the whole of the stock of that description held on that day by F, this being a sufficient appropriation within s 18, r 5; but that there was no appropriation and therefore that no property passed where F held a greater quantity of the stock and no physical separation had taken place.

Just as property cannot be transferred in unascertained goods, so also we may note that there cannot be a valid trust of unidentified property (*Re Wait* (above, p 266); *Re London Wine Co (Shippers) Ltd* (above)); nor can possession be effectively transferred or an attornment made in respect of unascertained goods (*Re London Wine Co*). However, we have seen that the same limitation does not apply to the passing of risk (above, p 302).

In 1993, the Law Commissions made recommendations for the reform of the law so as to meet a number of the criticisms which the inflexible rules established in cases such as *Re Wait* had attracted (*Sale of Goods forming Part of a Bulk,* L Com No 215, 1993). They were prompted to do so partly because of the decision of the Commercial Court in Rotterdam in *The Gosforth,* S en S 1985 Nr 91 (noted in [1986] LMCLQ 4). Here purchasers of goods forming part of a bulk cargo, who had paid for the goods and received delivery orders, found that the goods still belonged to the seller and could be arrested by an unpaid creditor who was suing the seller. The Dutch court in giving judgment referred to s 16 of the UK Sale of Goods Act 1979, under which the court's ruling that the property had not passed would have been the same.

The Commissions' recommendations were implemented by the Sale of Goods (Amendment) Act 1995 and have been incorporated into the 1979 Act as ss 20A and 20B. The result has been to reverse the effect of cases such as *Re Wait,* but only where the contract is for the sale of goods forming part of an identified bulk, and only where the price or part of it has been paid by the buyer. (For the definition of 'bulk' for this purpose, see s 61(1).) The decisions in *London Wine* and *Goldcorp,* where there was no specific bulk from which goods to fulfil the contract were to be obtained, are not affected by this change in the law.

Section 20A provides that where there is a contract for the sale of a specified quantity of unascertained goods which form part of a bulk that is identified either in the contract or by subsequent agreement between the parties, and the buyer has paid all or part of the price, then, unless the parties agree otherwise, property in an undivided share in the bulk is transferred to the buyer and he becomes an owner in common of the bulk. The share which the buyer obtains is proportionate to the amount of the price which he has paid, and not to the quantity which he has contracted to buy. Thus, if S contracts to sell to B 30 tonnes of potatoes out of the 100 tonnes in a particular store and B has paid half of the contract price, he and the seller become co-owners of the 100 tonnes in the proportions 15:85. If a second buyer agrees to buy the remaining 70 tonnes and pays the whole price, the seller and the two buyers become tenants in common in the respective proportions 15:15:70. In so far as a buyer has not paid all or a part of the price, the general rule in s 16 remains applicable: no property can pass in the goods or the corresponding proportion of the goods unless they become ascertained by severance from the bulk.

We should note that the effect of the Act is not to make the buyer the owner of the quantity of the contract goods that he has agreed to buy. In the example above, B does not become the owner of 15 tonnes of potatoes, or of 30 tonnes if he pays the whole price. He becomes a part-owner of the 100 tonnes, not the sole owner of his proportion. A further act of physical separation will be necessary before this comes about.

Section 20A(5) and (6), taken together, state that where a buyer who has paid part only of the price takes delivery of goods from the bulk, he is deemed in the first place to have taken the goods representing his share as a part-owner. So, if B in the example above takes delivery of 10 tonnes of potatoes from the bulk, it is his 15 per cent share which will be proportionately reduced.

Once a buyer has become a part-owner of the bulk, he may transfer his proprietary rights to a sub-buyer. The extended definition of 'goods' in s 61(1) to include an undivided share in goods makes it clear that such a transaction will be a sale of goods—indeed, of specific goods—and not a mere assignment of the first buyer's contractual rights.

Section 20A(4) deals with the possibility that the aggregate of the shares of a number of buyers may exceed the whole of the bulk (eg because the seller has contracted to sell a greater quantity of goods than he actually has, or because part has been lost by (for example) shrinkage or theft): the undivided shares of all the buyers are reduced proportionately.

Section 20B makes a number of consequential provisions. They may be summarised briefly as follows (though the exact wording of the section should be studied in any particular case): (1) each owner in common is deemed to have consented to any delivery of the goods or other dealing with them by another co-owner; (2) no cause of action shall lie against a person who acts in reliance on any such deemed consent; and (3) if there is a shortfall in any goods received by any one buyer, no other buyer is obliged to compensate him. It would follow from this that if each of several buyers takes his contract quantity from the bulk and the last of them finds that there is not enough left to satisfy his contract, his only remedy will be against the seller—unless, of course, the risk has passed to the buyer. In that case, he will not be able to pass on any share of the loss to the other buyers but must stand the whole of it himself.

We should note that the operation of ss 20A and 20B is not confined to the case where a seller is insolvent (as in *Re Wait*), although it will very commonly be in such a situation that the new law will be invoked. A buyer who becomes a co-owner under s 20A will have a right to sue a third party in tort (unlike the unfortunate importers in *The Aliakmon* (above, p 297)) and will be able to resist seizure of the goods by a creditor of the seller (compare *The Gosforth* (above, p 320)).

For commentary on the new law, see T Burns (1996) 59 MLR 260; J Ulph 'The Sale of Goods (Amendment) Act 1995: Co-ownership and the Rogue Seller' [1996] LMCLQ 93; and on the acquisition of *equitable* interests in part of a bulk, S Worthington 'Sorting Out Ownership Interests in a Bulk: Gifts, Sales and Trusts' [1999] JBL 1.

'Ascertainment'

Goods which are unascertained—ie not 'identified and agreed on' at the time when the contract of sale is made (s 61(1))—will become 'ascertained' by being 'identified in accordance with the agreement after the time a contract of sale is made' (per Atkin LJ in *Re Wait* [1927] 1 Ch 606 at 630). Normally this will follow from the act of one or both of the parties or someone designated by them, eg a warehouseman. Sometimes, where the contract goods are capable of prospective identification (eg 'the next calf to be born to my cow "Buttercup"'), ascertainment may happen automatically, when the goods come into existence. Also, occasionally, ascertainment may take place without the act of either party, 'by exhaustion'. This was decided at common law in the case of *Wait & James v Midland Bank* (below), and has now been confirmed by statute (s 18, r 5(3), inserted by the 1995 amending Act on the recommendation of the Law Commissions).

Wait & James v Midland Bank

(1926) 31 Com Cas 172, King's Bench Division

Wait & James (yes, the same Mr Wait as in *Re Wait!*) owned a consignment of wheat which had arrived on the SS *Thistleross* and was placed in a warehouse of the Bristol Dock Authority at Avonmouth. They had entered into contracts to sell various quantities of this wheat to a number of buyers, including contracts respectively for 250, 750 and 250 quarters to a firm called Redlers. Redlers had taken away 400 quarters out of the total of 1,250 quarters due to them, and had pledged the remaining 850 quarters (equal to 6,800 bushels) to the Midland Bank. All the other buyers then took delivery of their wheat, so that exactly 850 quarters remained in the warehouse. Both Wait & James, who had not been paid, and the Bank, claimed to be entitled to this wheat. Roche J held that wheat to satisfy Redlers' contract had been 'ascertained by exhaustion', and that the bank's claim prevailed.

Roche J: It is said, on the other hand, that no property passed to the respondents, because when there purported to be a transfer to them on September 25 in the first case, or at a later date, there was no property in any ascertained goods in Messrs Redlers, the transferors, which was transferred to the bank. The answer to that, I think, is this, that Messrs Wait and James agreed to sell the goods to Messrs Redlers Limited, and that Messrs Redlers Limited, agreed to transfer those goods to the bank. Those goods were in fact transferred to Messrs Redlers Limited, and through Messrs Redlers Limited, to the bank, as soon as they became ascertained on November 16, and then the property passed. That was some 10 or 11 days before Messrs Wait and James sought to exercise their right as unpaid vendors.

The next point which is interposed against the claim of the bank is an objection that this method of ascertainment by exhaustion, as it was usefully expressed by Mr Rayner Goddard, is not a method of ascertainment which does ascertain, but that the only effective way of ascertaining the goods which are in bulk, such as these, and which are sold by weight, is by weighing; and I agree that the most usual and most natural way is to weigh. But I am not prepared to hold that that is the only way of ascertaining the goods dealt with, and that without such weighing there could be no ascertainment. It is not a case such as may arise under s 18[(3)] of the Sale of Goods Act, where weighing is required for the purpose of ascertaining the price; there is no such requirement in this case.... In my judgment, the matter has been dealt with automatically by the facts, and the facts have provided the method of ascertainment in the manner I have already described through the delivery of the rest of the goods to other purchasers. I therefore hold that what remains in the warehouse has been ascertained to be the quantity of goods agreed to be sold by Messrs Wait and James to Messrs Redlers Limited, and to be the goods transferred by Messrs Redlers Limited to the Midland Bank.

In a later case, *Karlshamns Oljefabriker v Eastport Navigation Corpn, The Elafi* [1982] 1 All ER 208, Karlshamns had agreed in two separate contracts to buy two lots of copra, part of a larger cargo aboard the *Elafi* to be delivered at a port in Sweden. All the copra which had been sold to other buyers had been offloaded at Hamburg and Rotterdam, leaving only sufficient to meet the two sales to Karlshamns. Mustill J held that the separate quantities which Karlshamns had agreed to buy could be aggregated and that, the total amount having been ascertained by exhaustion, the property had passed to them.

The rulings in *Wait & James v Midland Bank* and *The Elafi* have now been confirmed by statute, as (respectively) s 18, rr 5(3) and 5(4).

Future goods. Sections 16 and 17 make no mention of future goods; but it is made plain elsewhere in the Act that there cannot be a present sale of future goods—in other words, the parties cannot merely by the terms of their contract cause the property in such goods to pass then and there to the buyer. But such a contract is not without effect. Section 5(3) states that where the seller purports to effect a present sale of future goods, the contract operates as an agreement to sell the goods.

(ii) Section 17: intention of the parties paramount

Subject always to s 16 (above), the primary rule governing the passing of property is contained in s 17: the property in the goods is transferred at such time as the parties intend it to be transferred. Section 17(2) adds, not very helpfully, that for the purpose of ascertaining the intention of the parties, regard is to be had to the terms of the contract, the conduct of the parties and the circumstances of the case.

It follows that the parties are free to express an intention which is the opposite of that which would normally be inferred, and that the court will give effect to such an intention. So, for instance, in *Re Blyth Shipbuilding & Dry Docks Co Ltd* [1926] Ch 494, CA, the parties to a contract to build and deliver a ship, which was to be paid for by instalments, had agreed that on payment of the first instalment of the price the property in the vessel should pass to the buyers. The buyers thus became the owners of the uncompleted vessel, even though in an ordinary case it would plainly have been expected that no property would pass until the ship was finished. Conversely, in the well-known line of *Romalpa* cases (below, p 452), where goods are sold to a manufacturing company in the knowledge that they are to be used in a manufacturing process, the obvious assumption would be that property in the goods should pass to the buyer before they were dealt with in this way, but the courts have on a number of occasions given effect to an express provision in the contract that the seller should retain title until the price has been paid.

However, the parties' expressed intention sometimes has to be overridden by considerations of practicality or by weightier rules of law. Thus, in *Re Blyth Shipbuilding,* the court declined to give effect to a further provision in the contract that 'all materials appropriated' for building the vessel should also become the property of the buyers: this would have made them owners of all the unworked material and the surplus and scrap material that did not end up incorporated into the ship—a result which the parties could not have intended. And in some of the *Romalpa* cases (eg *Borden (UK) Ltd v Scottish Timber Products Ltd* (below, p 462), retention of title clauses have been held ineffective once the goods have lost their identity—eg in that case, resin, once it had been used in the process of manufacturing chipboard.

Section 17 allows the court to give effect to the implied, as well as the express, intention of the parties. In *Re Anchor Line (Henderson Bros) Ltd* [1937] Ch 1, where there was a contract to sell a crane for a deferred purchase price, the court inferred an intention that the property in the crane should remain with the seller from the fact that there was an express clause placing the *risk* on the buyer. It reasoned that since this clause would have been unnecessary if the property had passed when the contract was made, the parties must have intended the opposite.

One important category of contracts where the normal rules may be held to be overridden by the implied intention of the parties is in the area of retail sales, and in particular consumer sales. We shall see shortly that the property in goods is frequently presumed to pass in law at some time earlier than that of delivery and payment—eg at the time when the contract is made (s 18, r 1) or when goods of the contract description are 'appropriated' to the contract (r 5). But in *RV Ward Ltd v Bignall* [1967] 1 QB 534 at 545, CA Diplock LJ said that 'in modern times, very little is needed to give rise to the inference that the property in specific goods is to pass only on delivery or payment'—an observation which, though made in a different context, is clearly appropriate to most retail and consumer sales, including both contracts for the sale of unascertained goods and contracts for specific goods.

(b) Statutory presumptions—s 18

Sections 16 and 17 are the only two *rules of law* relating to the passing of property.

But there are many cases in which s 17 will give no guidance, because the parties to a contract of sale do not normally give any thought to such abstract questions as the transfer of title (and, if they do, they are as like as not to get it wrong!—see *Dennant v Skinner and Collom* (below, p 325)); and there may well be nothing in the express terms of their contract or the surrounding circumstances to throw light on the issue. So the Act, in s 18, sets up a series of *presumptive rules* for ascertaining the intention of the parties which the court can apply. However, we must always bear in mind the opening words of s 18 itself, echoing those of s 17, 'Unless a different intention appears…': the 'rules' in s 18 are no more than prima facie *presumptions as to the intention of the parties* which may be rebutted by evidence to the contrary; they are not to be regarded as rules of law.

(i) *Rule 1: unconditional contracts for the sale of specific goods*

Where there is an *unconditional* contract for the sale of *specific goods* which are *in a deliverable state,* r 1 states the property in the goods passes to the buyer when the contract is made; and that it is immaterial whether the time of payment or the time of delivery, or both, are postponed.

This is a rule which is virtually unique to the common law systems, in contrast to the laws of other jurisdictions which usually link the passing of property with the delivery of possession.

Tarling v Baxter

(1827) 6 B & C 360, Court of King's Bench

On 4 January, the parties agreed on the sale and purchase of a stack of hay, standing on land belonging to the seller's brother. Payment was to be made in a month's time, and no hay was to be cut or taken away until the price had been paid. Before the price was due, the hay was destroyed in a fire. The buyer was held bound to pay the price.

Bayley J: It is quite clear that the loss must fall upon him in whom the property was vested at the time when it was destroyed by fire. And the question is, in whom the property in this hay was vested at that time? By the note of the contract delivered to the plaintiff, the defendant agreed to sell the plaintiff a stack of hay standing in Canonbury Field at the sum of £145, the same to be paid for on the 4th day of February next, and to be allowed to stand on the premises until the first day of May next. Now this was a contract for an immediate, not a prospective sale. Then the question is, in whom did the property vest by virtue of this contract? The right of property and the right of possession are distinct from each other; the right of possession may be in one person, the right of property in another. A vendor may have a qualified right to retain the goods unless payment is duly made, and yet the property in these goods may be in the vendee. The fact in this case, that the hay was not to be paid for until a future period, and that it was not to be cut until it was paid for, makes no difference, provided it was the intention of the parties that the vendee should, by the contract, immediately acquire a right of property in the goods, and the vendor a right of property in the price. The rule of law is, that where there is an immediate sale, and nothing remains to be done by the vendor as between him and the vendee, the property in the thing sold vests in the vendee, and then all the consequences resulting from the vesting of the property follow, one of which is, that if it be destroyed, the loss falls upon the vendee. The note of the buyer imports also an immediate, perfect, absolute agreement of sale. It seems to me that the true construction of the contract is, that the parties intended an immediate sale, and if that be so, the property vested in the vendee, and the loss must fall upon him.

[Holroyd and Littledale JJ delivered concurring judgments.]

Dennant v Skinner and Collom

[1948] 2 KB 164, King's Bench Division

At an auction of cars held by Dennant, a Standard car was knocked down for £345 to a man calling himself King, who also bought five other vehicles. King falsely said that he was the son of a reputable motor dealer and, in reliance on this statement, Dennant allowed him to pay with an uncleared cheque and take the Standard car away, after signing a document acknowledging that the ownership of the vehicles would not pass to him until payment had been received under the cheque. The cheque was dishonoured on presentation. The car was later sold to Collom who resold to Skinner. Dennant claimed the return of the car, as his property; but Hallett J held that property had passed to King on the fall of the hammer, and that the subsequent purported reservation of ownership by Dennant was ineffective.

Hallett J (after dealing with a point based on larceny): I come now to consider the second point on which the plaintiff relies, which I understand is this; that the property in the circumstances of this case did not pass until the price was paid by the cheque being in order or cash substituted for it. The circumstances in regard to that I have already stated, and it remains only to consider the law. In the first place, as I have said, I think that a contract of sale is concluded at an auction sale on the fall of the hammer. The Sale of Goods Act 1893, s 18, r 1, provides: 'Where there is an unconditional contract for the sale of specific goods, in a deliverable state, the property in the goods passes to the buyer when the contract is made, and it is immaterial whether the time of payment or the time of delivery, or both, be postponed.' Accordingly, upon the fall of the hammer the property of this car passed to King unless that prima facie rule is excluded from applying because of a different intention appearing or because there was some condition in the contract which prevented the rule from applying. In my view, this was clearly an unconditional contract of sale, and I can see nothing whatever to make a different intention appear. The only evidence upon which it was ever suggested to exist was the printed conditions, but I can see nothing in those conditions to negative an intention that the property should pass on the fall of the hammer. I think the conditions are entirely consistent with such an intention. By the Sale of Goods Act, s 28: 'Unless otherwise agreed, delivery of the goods and payment of the price are concurrent conditions,' and finally, by yet another section of the Act, namely, s 39(1)(a), an unpaid seller of goods has a lien on the goods or right to retain them for the price while he is in possession of them, and he also has a right of re-sale as limited by the Act. Passing of the property and right to possession are two different things: here the property had passed upon the fall of the hammer, but still Mr Dennant had a right to retain possession of the goods until payment was made. If, when he was ready to deliver the goods, payment was not made, he could have sued for the price, or he could have exercised powers of re-sale, and he could have secured himself by way of lien on the goods for the price, but once he chose, for reasons good, bad, or indifferent as a result of statements fraudulent or honest, to part with the possession of the vehicle by giving delivery of it, he then lost his seller's lien and no longer had a right to possession of the vehicle....

In my view, therefore, the second contention for the plaintiff also fails. However, there was a third aspect of the matter and that arises out of the document which I have already read. Now the document in its terms contemplates that the ownership of the vehicle has not passed to the bidder, but, as

I have already said, in my judgment it had passed upon the fall of the hammer, and if subsequently the bidder executed the document acknowledging that ownership of the vehicle would not pass to him, that could not have any effect on what had already taken place. Can it be said that this document and the transaction it records as regards payment had the effect of divesting the property from King and re-vesting it in Mr Dennant, the seller? That is the only way in which Mr Brundrit has been able to suggest it that the document assists the plaintiff. I have considered that aspect of the matter, but I do not think that such a view of the document is sound. In my view the property had passed on the fall of the hammer; the right to possession had passed when Mr Dennant, persuaded and misled by King's lies, parted with his seller's lien, and there was nothing left upon which Mr Dennant could found a claim in detinue against some third person, in this case Mr Skinner, who was thus in possession of the vehicle.

The result seems to me to be that here the sufferer from the lies of King and from the reliance which Mr Dennant unfortunately placed on him must be Mr Dennant himself and not the innocent parties who are represented by the defendant and the third party in this action. Accordingly there must be judgment for the defendant and the third party.

In order for r 1 to apply, all three of the conditions indicated by the phrases italicised on p 324 above must be met. 'Specific goods' is a term which has already been discussed (above, p 272); we proceed now to consider the concepts of 'unconditional' contract and 'deliverable state'.

Unconditional 'Unconditional' obviously means 'not subject to any conditions', but this is not very helpful, since the term 'condition' is itself notorious for the many different meanings or shades of meaning which it may have in the law of contract. (Professor Stoljar once identified 12!—see (1953) 69 LQR 485.) In two early cases, *Varley v Whipp* [1900] 1 QB 513 and *Ollett v Jordan* [1918] 2 KB 41, contracts were held to be 'conditional' in the present context because the conditions implied by the Act as to conformity with description (s 13) and merchantable quality (the former s 14(2)) remained unfulfilled. This construction would lead to absurd conclusions: if 'unconditional' in r 1 means 'containing no conditions (in the sense of a major or vital term) unfulfilled by the seller', then it would not be possible to ascertain whether the property had passed until the goods had been delivered and inspected and found to be in order. However, these cases are considered not to represent the true position in modern law (see, eg *Benjamin,* para 5–019); instead, the preferred view is that 'unconditional' means 'not subject to any condition upon the fulfilment of which the passing of the property depends'. Although this leaves us with a rather cyclic or question-begging piece of reasoning—the property passes if the contract is unconditional; the contract is unconditional if there is nothing to prevent the property from passing—it will not be the only legal definition that is subject to this criticism.

We can see the concept well illustrated by the *Romalpa* line of cases (below, p 452), where the passing of the property in the goods is made conditional on payment of the price. In contracts for the sale of things attached to or forming part of the soil, there will usually (and in some cases necessarily) be an implied condition that property in the goods will not pass until they have been severed from the freehold. However, as the cases of *Kursell v Timber Operators & Contractors Ltd* and *Underwood v Burgh Castle Cement* (see below) show, there may be other grounds in such circumstances for holding that the property has not passed.

NOTE

It is probably not appreciated by most of today's lawyers that the use of the word 'condition' to mean 'vital term', in contrast with 'warranty', is not a practice of long standing and might well not have been used or understood in this sense by Chalmers himself. In the first edition of his *Sale of Goods* (1890) he included a substantial appendix on the construction of 'terms and conditions' in which the word 'condition' is used only to refer to a contingency, or in the neutral sense of 'term'. Moreover, in his original draft of the Bill, only the implied terms that goods sold by description should correspond with their description (s 13) and that where goods are sold by sample the buyer should have an opportunity of comparing the bulk with the sample (the former s 15(2)(b)) were characterised as conditions: all the other statutorily implied terms were called warranties.

Deliverable state. There is a statutory definition of 'deliverable state'. Section 61(5) provides that goods are in a deliverable state when they are in such a state that the buyer would under the contract be bound to take delivery of them. And in turn, we are told that 'delivery' means 'the voluntary transfer of possession from one person to another' (s 61(1)). (This does not necessarily mean physical delivery—see above, p 104, and below, p 423.) Again, there are problems with this definition. If the goods do not answer their description or are not of satisfactory quality, the buyer has the right to reject them for breach of condition (see ss 11(3), 13, 14(2) and below, p 471). So it might be inferred that the property could never pass in goods which were defective in any respect such as this. But to accept this reasoning is in effect to revive the discredited arguments in *Varley v Whipp* and *Ollett v Jordan* referred to above. Although the question has not been the subject of any direct judicial ruling, writers are generally in agreement that 'deliverable state' in s 18 must be given a more restrictive interpretation so as to avoid this consequence. Professor Goode, for instance, suggests that r 1 should be read as applying 'where, *on the assumption that the goods are what they purport to be,* the seller has not, by the terms of the contract, undertaken to do anything to them as a prerequisite of the buyer's acceptance of delivery' (*Commercial Law,* p 232). This may, in its turn, be too narrow, for it is not obvious that the rule should apply only where the acts in question are to be performed by the seller: the acts could be those of a third party, for instance. (As regards acts to be performed by the buyer, see below, p 331.) Such cases as have been reported on the meaning of 'deliverable state' have been concerned with more straightforward issues.

Kursell v Timber Operators & Contractors Ltd
[1927] 1 KB 298, Court of Appeal

(See the extract from the judgment of Scrutton LJ quoted above, p 273.)

Underwood Ltd v Burgh Castle Brick & Cement Syndicate Ltd
[1922] 1 KB 123, King's Bench Division

(For the facts, see above, p 270.)

Rowlatt J: The sale was that of a specific chattel to be delivered by the plaintiffs, but the fact that it was to be delivered by them is not the test whether the property passed. The test is whether anything remained to be done to the engine by the sellers to put it into a deliverable state; and by that I under-stand a state in which the thing will be the article contracted for by the buyer; I do not mean deliverable in the sense that it is properly packed or anything of that kind. It must have everything done to it that the sellers had to do to it as an article. I do not think therefore that the fact by itself that the sellers had to take the engine to pieces would postpone the time when the property passed. Many chattels have to be taken to pieces before they can be delivered—eg a sideboard or a billiard table; nevertheless the property in these passes on the sale and is not postponed until the article is actually taken to pieces and delivered. I do not, therefore, lay any stress on the fact of the engine having to be taken to pieces. I think the important point is that the parties were dealing with an article which was a fixture to the premises, and that is different from the case of a loose chattel. The buyers' intention was to buy an article which would be a loose chattel when the processes of detaching and dismantling it were completed, and to convert it into a loose chattel these processes had first to be performed. The case of a tenant's fixtures seems an analogous case. It seems a safe rule to adopt that if a fixture has to be detached so as to make it a chattel again, the act of detaching has to be done before the chattel can be deliverable.

Philip Head & Sons Ltd v Showfronts Ltd

[1970] 1 Lloyd's Rep 140, Queen's Bench Division

Showfronts contracted with Heads to supply and lay fitted carpeting for a number of rooms in an office block which they were refurbishing. The carpet for the largest room, a showroom measuring about 40 ft × 20 ft, had to be made from several lengths stitched together: it was very unwieldy and took up to six men to lift it. After being assembled, it was left on the premises on a Friday afternoon and was stolen in the course of the weekend. The court held that it was not in a 'deliverable state' until it had been satisfactorily laid, and so it was the sellers' property and at their risk when it was stolen.

Mocatta J: The problem here is, I think, however, whether it can be said that carpeting in a deliverable state was unconditionally appropriated to the contract. That phrase is defined in s 62(4) of the statute as follows:

> Goods are in a 'deliverable state' within the meaning of this Act when they are in such a state that the buyer would under the contract be bound to take delivery of them.

There is not much assistance in the authorities as to the meaning of this phrase. It is, however, both interesting and, I think, helpful to read a passage from an opinion of Lord Blackburn in *Seath & Co v Moore* (1886) 11 App Cas 350, in which many of the points subsequently codified in the Sale of Goods Act 1893, including some of the problems which I have to deal with here, are discussed. It is true that that case was one dealing with problems arising out of a shipbuilding contract, but in this particular passage Lord Blackburn is purporting to state the relevant principles of English law in general terms. He stated in relation to the passing of property (ibid, at p 370):

> It is essential that the article should be specific and ascertained in a manner binding on both parties, for unless that be so it cannot be construed as a contract to pass the property in that article. And in general, if there are things remaining to be done by the seller to the article before it is in the state in which it is to be finally delivered to the purchaser, the contract will not be construed to be one to pass the property till those things are done....

I find that passage to give valuable guidance here.

I have described as best I can the state of the carpeting subsequently stolen at the time that it came back to these premises after having been stitched up; it was plainly a heavy bundle, very difficult to move. Although I have determined that this was a contract to which the Sale of Goods Act, 1893, applied, nevertheless an important feature of it was undoubtedly the laying of the carpeting following on the planning. It seems to me that one has to consider—in each case it is a case of fact—where there is work to be done in relation to the article sold before the contractual obligations of the sellers are completed, what is the relevant importance of that work in relation to the contract when deciding whether the property has passed and in particular whether the article or goods in question is or are at a particular moment of time in a deliverable state under s 18, r 5(1). I think one is entitled to apply everyday common sense to the matter; a householder, for example, purchasing carpeting under a contract providing that it should be delivered and laid in his house would be very surprised to be told that carpeting, which was in bales which he could hardly move deposited by his contractor in his garage, was then in a deliverable state and his property.

I take the view because of the condition of this carpeting at the time it was stolen and the importance of the last stage in the obligations to be performed by the plaintiffs under this contract, that at the moment when this carpeting was stolen it had not been unconditionally appropriated to the contract in a deliverable state, and accordingly, in my judgment, the property had not passed at the moment that the carpeting was stolen. In those circumstances the plaintiffs' case must fail....

(ii) Rule 2: specific goods to be put into a deliverable state by the seller

Where there is a contract for the sale of *specific goods* and the seller is bound to do something to the goods for the purpose of putting them into a *deliverable state*, r 2 states as a presumption that the property will not pass until the seller has done that thing and the buyer has notice that it has been done. The operation of the rule may be illustrated by two cases which have already been mentioned.

Underwood Ltd v Burgh Castle Brick & Cement Syndicate

(See above, p 327.)

Philip Head & Sons Ltd v Showfronts Ltd

(See above, p 328.)

In most respects, r 2 seems straightforward enough. The terms 'specific goods' and 'deliverable state' have been discussed above, at pp 272, 327. It should be observed that it is necessary not only that the goods should be put into a deliverable state, but that the buyer must also have notice of this before the property will pass. The one point which may cause some surprise is that the wording of the rule is restricted to acts to be performed *by the seller*. This leaves the position unresolved where the act of putting the goods into a deliverable state is to be performed by the buyer, or by some third party. The only inference which we can draw from the fact that the Act is silent on this point is that there is no presumption either way in such a case. Of course, in many situations it will be possible—and perhaps even necessary— for the court to imply a condition into the contract of sale to the effect that the property is not to pass until the goods have been put into a deliverable state. For instance, if there is a contract to sell a second-hand car if it passes the test for an MOT certificate, the car will not be in a 'deliverable state' (within the definition contained in s 61(5)) until it has passed the test, and it will be immaterial whether it is for the seller or the buyer to arrange the test under the contract. Again, if we suppose that in *Underwood Ltd v Burgh Castle Brick & Cement Syndicate* (above) it was the buyer who had to detach the engine from the land, it is hardly conceivable that a court would consider the goods to have been in a 'deliverable state' until this had been done. The same would be true of a sale of standing timber: in the famous words used in *Liford's Case* (1614) 11 Co Rep 46b at 50a: 'Timber trees cannot be felled with a goose quill'. But it will not always be necessary to draw such an inference, particularly if we bear in mind that under s 61(5), 'deliverable' is not restricted in its meaning to 'physically deliverable'. Fruit ready for picking (and, *a fortiori*, crops in the category *fructus industrials*, such as potatoes, ready to be harvested) can surely be 'in such a state that the buyer would under the contract be bound to take delivery of them' even though they are still attached to the land. And the analogy with cases decided under r 3 (such as *Nanka-Bruce v Commonwealth Trust Ltd* (below)) suggests that the courts may be less ready than might at first be supposed to treat contracts not falling strictly within r 2 as conditional.

(iii) Rule 3: specific goods to be weighed or measured, etc by the seller for the purpose of ascertaining the price

Where there is a contract for the sale of *specific goods* in a *deliverable state,* but the seller is bound to weigh, measure, test or do some other act or thing to the goods for the purpose of ascertaining the price, r 3 lays down a presumption that the property in the goods will not pass until the act or thing has been done and the buyer has notice that it has been done.

Turley v Bates
(1863) 2 H & C 200, Court of Exchequer

Turley contracted to sell Bates a heap of fireclay lying on Turley's land at the price of 2s (10p) per ton, to be carted away by Bates and weighed at his own expense. Bates had taken away about 270 tons of clay and paid for it. This action was brought for the price of the remaining clay, estimated to have a value of £110 10s 6d. Bates argued that the property in the heap had not passed to him, so that he was liable only for damages which, in the absence of evidence that the clay had fallen in value, should be nominal damages only. The court held that the property had passed and that he was liable for the price.

The judgment of the court (Channell and Bramwell BB) was delivered by **Channell B:** . . . For the plaintiff it was contended, that where full authority was given to the buyer to remove the clay sold, and all that the seller had to do according to the contract was complete, and where everything that remained to be done was to be done by the buyer at his own expense, viz, as in this case, to cart away and have the clay weighed at his own expense, it must be taken as if there had been such a bargain and sale as to pass the property though the clay had not been removed and weighed, and that the contract price might be recoverable on the count for goods bargained and sold.

For the defendant it was contended, that taking the case on the plaintiff's evidence, and as found by the jury, that there had been a removal and weighing of part of the clay, yet no property passed in any clay until the clay had been weighed at Johnson's machine and the quantity and price thus ascertained, so as to entitle the plaintiff to recover on the count for goods bargained and sold.

In the course of the argument for the defendant we were referred to several cases decided in our Courts which were said to govern the question, and to a passage from my brother Blackburn's Treatise on Contract of Sale, part 2, chap 2, p 152. It was argued that the rule reducible from these authorities was, that so long as a price had been agreed upon according to quantity, to be ascertained by weighing, that until the goods had been weighed and the price so ascertained the contract was incomplete. . . .

It is very doubtful whether in stating the rule to be that where anything remains to be done to the goods for ascertaining the price as weighing, etc, the performance was a condition precedent to the transfer of the property, it was meant by the learned author to include a case where all that remained to be done was to be done by the buyer with full authority from the seller to do the act.

[Channell B referred to a number of cases, and continued:]

From a consideration of these cases, it appears that the principle involved in the rule above quoted is, that something remains to be done by the seller. It is, therefore, very doubtful, as before stated, whether the present case comes within the principle of the rule. But, however that may be, it is clear that this rule does not apply if the parties have made it sufficiently clear whether or not they intend that the property shall pass at once, and that their intention must be looked at in every case. . . .

In the present case the jury have, in effect, adopted the plaintiffs version of the bargain, by their finding that it was for the whole heap. And taking that view of the case, it seems to us clear that the intention of the parties was that the property in the whole heap should pass, notwithstanding the clay was to be weighed at Johnson's machine; and we, therefore, think that the rule to reduce the damages must be discharged.

Most of the comments made in relation to r 2 apply also to r 3. The following case underlines the fact that the presumption laid down by r 3 applies only in the case where the act in question is to be performed *by the seller*.

Nanka-Bruce v Commonwealth Trust

[1926] AC 77, Privy Council

(The facts appear from the judgment.)

The opinion of the Privy Council was delivered by **Lord Shaw:** This is an appeal from the judgment of the Full Court of the Gold Coast Colony affirming a judgment of Beatty J without a jury.

The appellant is a planter and shipper of cocoa, carrying on business at Accra. The respondents carry on business at Accra as general exporters and importers.

One, Laing (the co-defendant with the respondents in the action), was an editor of a newspaper in Accra and a buyer and seller of cocoa. He had previously made purchases of cocoa from the appellant.

The claim of the appellant against the respondents is for damages for conversion of 160 bags of cocoa. The history of this cocoa, so far as is material to the present case, and stated neutrally, is as follows: The appellant entered into a general arrangement with Laing, under which Laing was to receive cocoa from the appellant at the price of 59s per load of 60 lbs. It was recognized that Laing would resell the cocoa to other merchants, and that when these other merchants took delivery by a transfer of the consignment notes the goods would be weighed up at their premises and the weights tested there. That operation being completed, the amount payable by Laing on the contract made with the appellant was, of course, ascertained.

On April 24, 1920, the 160 bags of cocoa were despatched by rail by the appellant to Accra under a consignment note made out in favour of Laing. Laing then acted with the goods thus: He sold them to the respondents, and handed to the respondents' representatives the railway consignment note. The respondents took delivery and, against a large debt due to them from Laing, credited him with the price at which they had purchased the goods. Laing's conduct seems unquestionably to have been dishonest conduct. Both Courts have, however, found that the conduct of the respondents was quite honest, and that they purchased the goods for value and without any notice of any objection to, or defect in, the title of Laing, or the contract under which he had acquired the goods. Both Courts have concurrently found that Laing purchased the cocoa from the appellant. The appellant attacked this finding as erroneous in law, alleging that the weighing up of the goods must be treated as having been a condition precedent to an operative sale.

Their Lordships agree that the provision as to the weight of the goods being tested was not a condition precedent to a sale. The goods were transferred, their price was fixed, and the testing was merely to see whether the goods fitted the weights as represented, but this testing was not suspensive of the contract of sale or a condition precedent to it. To effect such suspension or impose such a condition would require a clear contract between vendor and vendee to that effect. In this case there was no contract whatsoever to carry into effect the weighing, which was simply a means to satisfy the purchaser that he had what he had bargained for and that the full price claimed per the contract was therefore due.

[His Lordship referred to *Cundy v Lindsay* (below, p 349), and continued:]

Applying that law their Lordships find no difficulty in affirming that these goods were de facto sold to Laing by the appellant, and that so far as the respondents were concerned they were honestly and for value bought by them from Laing. Suppose it to be the case that the appellant, defrauded by Laing, to whom he had sold the goods, could have treated the transaction as voidable on that account and sued Laing for remission accordingly, that cannot in law form a ground of impeachment as against buyers in good faith and for value from the person, like Laing, thus vested in the goods by a de facto contract.

   This is an end of the case....

QUESTION

Once the property has passed to the buyer, the seller may in principle sue the buyer for the price (see s 49(1)). In *Nanka-Bruce* it would not have been difficult to quantify the amount which the seller could claim, because the cocoa had already been provisionally weighed. But if the buyer is to do the weighing and the goods are destroyed before the weighing has been done, how is the price to be reckoned? The following case (which turned on the fact that *risk*, as distinct from property, had passed to the buyer), gives a clue.

Castle v Playford

(1872) LR 7 Exch 98, Court of Exchequer Chamber

Castle agreed to sell to Playford a cargo of ice, to be shipped to a port in the United Kingdom and paid for on arrival at the rate of £1 per ton 'weighed on board during delivery'. Under the contract, the risk lay with the buyer. The ship and cargo were lost at sea. The court ruled that the buyer was liable to pay the price which, in the circumstances, had to be an estimated price.

Blackburn J: My impression is, if it were necessary to decide it now, that the effect of this contract is that the property passed; but I think it is unnecessary to decide the matter. The parties in this case have agreed, whether the property passed or not, that the purchaser should, from the time he received the bills of lading, take upon himself all risks and dangers of the seas; and, according to Mr Littler's construction, I do not see what risk he took upon himself at all, unless it was this—that he said, 'If the property perishes by the dangers of the seas, I shall take the risk of having lost the property, whether it be mine or not.'

   The difficulty in the court below arose in reference to the alteration of the time of payment. No doubt it was afterwards provided that payment should be made on the ship's arrival and according to what was delivered. Now here, the ship and cargo have gone to the bottom of the sea; but in the cases of *Alexander v Gardner* ((1835) 1 Bing NC 671), and *Fragano v Long* ((1825) 4 B & C 219), it was held, that if the property did perish before the time for payment came, the time being dependent upon delivery, and if the delivery was prevented by the destruction of the property, the purchaser was to pay an equivalent sum. In the present case, when the ship went down there would be so much ice on board, and, in all probability, upon an ordinary voyage so much would have melted; and what the defendant has taken upon himself to pay is the amount which, in all probability, would have been payable for the ice.

[Cockburn CJ delivered a concurring judgment.
Mellor, Brett and Grove JJ concurred.]

NOTE

In *National Coal Board v Gamble* [1959] 1 QB 11 (a case concerned with a sale of *unascertained* goods), coal was loaded on to a lorry pursuant to a bulk contract and taken to a weighbridge on the seller's premises, where the lorry was found to be nearly 4 tons overladen. The driver said that he would take his chance on the overloading, took the weighbridge ticket and left the premises. He was later stopped by the police and his firm convicted of permitting the lorry to be overweight. The Divisional Court held that the Coal Board, as seller, had rightly been convicted of aiding and abetting the driver in the commission of the offence, since until the goods had been weighed (so that the price could be ascertained) and the weighbridge ticket handed to the driver, the property in the coal remained with the seller, whose employee (the weighbridgeman) could have insisted that the excess be unloaded.

(iv) Rule 4: goods delivered on approval or on sale or return

When goods have been delivered to a buyer 'on approval' or on 'sale or return', or other similar terms, r 4 prescribes that the property passes to the buyer:

(1) when he signifies his approval or acceptance to the seller or does any other act adopting or approving the transaction; or

(2) if he does not signify his approval or acceptance but retains the goods without giving notice of rejection, then, if a time has been fixed for the return of the goods, on the expiration of that time and, if no time has been fixed, on the expiration of a reasonable time.

This is the only time that a contract for the sale of goods 'on approval' or 'on sale or return' is mentioned in the Act. These two expressions may be taken to have the same meaning in English law—namely, that the person to whom the goods have been delivered has the option of buying the goods or not as he chooses, and until he has bought them (or is deemed by r 4 to have done so), the property in the goods remains with the seller. Strictly speaking, therefore, there is no 'sale' at all (and not even an agreement to sell or to buy, but only an offer to sell), until the buyer has exercised his option; and the use in the Act of the terms 'seller' and 'buyer' is anomalous. We may note, in contrast, that in the United States the two expressions 'on approval' and 'on sale or return' are given different meanings: there, the former term is used in the same sense as in England, but 'on sale or return' means that there *is* a sale, and the buyer becomes the owner, subject however to a condition that he may return the goods within an agreed or a reasonable time and rescind the transaction. This analysis is similar to that in *Head v Tattersall* (above, p 299), but with the difference that the buyer is free to return the goods for any reason—even because he simply decides that he does not want them.

An example of an act 'adopting the transaction' is where the 'buyer' sells or pledges the goods, as illustrated by the following case.

Kirkham v Attenborough
[1897] 1 QB 201, Court of Appeal

Kirkham, a manufacturing jeweller, delivered to Winter a quantity of jewellery on sale or return. Winter pledged some of the jewellery to Attenborough. In this action, Kirkham claimed that the goods pledged were still his property, but was unsuccessful.

Lopes LJ: The position of a person who has received goods on sale or return is that he has the option of becoming the purchaser of them, and may become so in three different ways. He may pay the price, or he may retain the goods beyond a reasonable time for their return, or he may do an act inconsistent with his being other than a purchaser. The words of the Act are difficult to construe; but it seems to me that if the recipient of the goods retains them for an unreasonable time he does something inconsistent with the exercise of his option to return them, and thereby adopts the transaction. So if he does any other act inconsistent with their return, as if he sells them or pledges them, because if he pledges them he no longer has the free control over them so as to be in a position to return them. In all these cases he brings himself within the words of the section by adopting the transaction, and the property in the goods passes to him. If that is the state of the law, applying it to this case, it is clear that the plaintiff is not entitled to recover from the defendant either the goods or their price, and the judgment in favour of the plaintiff cannot be supported.

[Lord Esher MR delivered a concurring judgment.
Rigby LJ concurred.]

For the buyer to 'adopt' a transaction under r 4(a), there must be some act of election on his part (by words or conduct). It is not sufficient for the seller simply to show that the buyer is unable to return the goods. In *Elphick v Barnes* (1880) 5 CPD 321 a horse which was delivered on eight days' trial died from an illness on the third day. Lord Denman CJ, treating the contract as one of a sale on approval, said (at 326): 'Here, I think, there was no sale at the time of the horse's death, which happened without the fault of either party, and therefore that the action for goods sold and delivered must fail.'

Rule 4, like the other rules in s 18, only lays down a presumption. It is open to the parties to make any other arrangement as regards the passing of the property—for instance, that it shall not pass to the buyer until the price has been paid. *Kirkham v Attenborough* (above) may be contrasted with *Weiner v Gill*.

Weiner v Gill
[1906] 2 KB 574, Court of Appeal

Weiner, a jeweller, delivered a diamond brooch and other articles to another jeweller, Huhn, on the terms: 'On approbation. On sale only for cash or return. . . . Goods had on approbation or on sale or return remain the property of Samuel Weiner until such goods are settled for or charged.' Huhn delivered the articles to Longman who said that he had a customer for them, but in fact he pawned them with Gill.

Sir Gorell Barnes P: The only question which we have to consider is whether the property in these goods had passed from the plaintiff to Huhn. As a general rule a person in the possession of goods cannot convey a better title to them than he himself has. There are exceptions to that rule, examples of which are to be found in the Factors Act 1889, and in s 25 of the Sale of Goods Act 1893. It has been argued that in the present case the defendants are protected by s 25 of the latter Act, but, having regard to the facts of the case, I do not think that that argument can be successfully maintained. In considering the question whether the property passed from the plaintiff to Huhn regard must be had to the terms of s 17 and s 18 of the Sale of Goods Act.

[The President read the sections and continued:]

If the present case were one falling within the terms 'on sale or return' in r 4, then the case of *Kirkham v Attenborough* [above] would no doubt be in point, because, as was said by Wightman J in *Moss v Sweet* ((1851) 16 QB 493), the meaning of a contract of sale or return is 'that the goods were to be taken as sold, unless returned within a reasonable time.' In the present case, however, we are dealing with a contract of an entirely different character, for on the face of the contract there appears a different intention as to when the property shall pass from that laid down in r 4 of s 18. The terms of the contract shew a clear intention that no property in the goods shall vest in Huhn until he has paid for them or been charged by the plaintiff for them. So that no means existed by which the buyer could exercise such an option as was indicated in r 4. The only thing he could do was to pay cash for them or to get the plaintiff to debit him with the price. That was not done, and therefore, in my opinion, the property in the goods never passed to Huhn, and consequently the defendants have no answer to the plaintiff's claim.

[Lord Alverstone CJ and Farwell LJ delivered concurring judgments.]

QUESTION

Gill was in the position of a bona fide purchaser without notice of the special terms of Weiner's contract, and with no possibility of finding out about them. Should the law do more to protect such a person?

Paragraph (b) of r 4, in contrast with paragraph (a), contemplates that the buyer under a contract on sale or return terms may sometimes become the owner of the goods by inaction. This is illustrated by the case which follows.

Poole v Smith's Car Sales (Balham) Ltd
[1962] 1 WLR 744, Court of Appeal

Both parties were car dealers. In August 1960 Poole, who was about to go on holiday, delivered a Vauxhall car to Smiths with authority to sell it, provided that he received £325, Smiths being allowed to retain any sum received in excess of that figure. In October Poole telephoned several times and asked for the return of the car, and eventually wrote a letter on 7 November stating that if it was not returned by 10 November it would be deemed to have been sold to Smiths. The car was not returned until the end of November, when Poole refused to take it back. It had been driven for some 1,600 miles and had been badly damaged as a result of an accident sustained when two of Smiths' employees had, without authority, taken it out on a joyride. In this action Poole sued for the price, alleging that the property had passed, and was successful.

Ormerod LJ: The whole question now is whether, in the circumstances, the plaintiff is entitled to recover from the defendants either the sum of £325 as the price of goods sold and delivered, or such sum as may be proper as damages for detinue.

The plaintiff, in the first place, says that the car was sent to the defendants on sale or return, and the question which first arises to be determined is whether this was a transaction for sale or return. The judge held, that this was not a transaction having the sharply defined qualities of a contract for sale or return as envisaged by the Sale of Goods Act 1893. Mr Chedlow has raised the point that a contract for sale or return in the ordinary way is a contract where the person to whom the chattel is delivered is intending either to purchase the chattel or to send it back, whereas this was a contract where the defendants might expect to sell the car to one of their customers and if they could not sell it, then to return it, and, in those circumstances, it was not a contract for sale or return. So far as I am concerned, I am afraid I do not understand that distinction. I know of no authority for it, and in the absence of authority which is binding on this court, for my part, I would not make it. . . .

If that was the contract then the questions which arise are when and how did the property pass? It appears that we must be governed either by the express or implied intentions of the parties, or, failing those intentions, by the provisions of s 18 of the Act of 1893, and the rules there laid down. It has been contended on behalf of the plaintiff that the rule which applies here is r 4.

[His Lordship read the rule, and continued:]

The question next arises whether that particular rule which I have read applies; that is to say, whether the property has passed. Mr Chedlow has argued that that rule cannot apply, and the reason why it cannot apply is because of the first words of s 18 of the Sale of Goods Act 1893, which reads: 'Unless a different intention appears.' It was argued that on the evidence in this case it was clear that a different intention appeared, and that it was not the intention that the property should pass in the manner indicated by r 4. I think I need only say here, in dealing with Mr Chedlow's argument, that I can see nothing which warrants the conclusion that any different intention is to be discovered from the circumstances of the case.

So we are thrown back on r 4. By that rule if the parties have fixed a time for the property to pass, then the property will pass at that time. In this case there is no suggestion that any time had been fixed. Failing that, and it is a question of fact, the time for the property to pass is at the expiry of a reasonable time, and the question which arises is what is a reasonable time. . . .

It is a well-known fact that people go on holidays in the months of July, August and September. It has become obvious, I think, in recent years that when people go on holidays, they like to take their cars with them. It may be that many people, when the holidays are over, like to sell those cars and, therefore, it may be a well-recognised fact, and I think it is, that the sellers' market for secondhand motor-cars in October and November is not so good as it is before the holiday season begins or is still in its early stages. In any event, I see no reason why in these days a court should not take judicial notice of the way the market in secondhand cars is carried on and come to a conclusion as to what is a reasonable time.

For my part I am fully satisfied, both on the knowledge which has come to me in the ordinary course of life and through sitting in these courts, and from the evidence before the court in this case, that a reasonable time had expired, certainly in November, for the return of this car; and if that reasonable time had expired, it is clear by reason of the operation of s 18 of the Act of 1893 that the property in the car had passed from the plaintiff to the defendants . . . .

The position remains, therefore, that here was a car delivered on sale or return, that a reasonable time expired without the car being returned and, therefore, there must have been or must be deemed to have been a sale of the car. That being so, the defendants become liable for the purchase price.

[Willmer LJ delivered a concurring judgment.
Danckwerts LJ concurred.]

QUESTION

Suppose that the car had been damaged as a result of Smiths' negligence before the expiry of a reasonable time: what would the legal position be?

NOTE

The case of *Atari Corpn (UK) Ltd v Electronics Boutique Stores (UK) Ltd* [1998] QB 539, CA clarified one or two further points relating to sale or return contracts. Electronics, who were retailers, contracted with Atari for the supply of 'Jaguar' computer games on the terms 'Full sale or return until 31 January 1996'. The games did not sell well and on 19 January 1996 Electronics wrote to Atari saying that they had decided to cease stocking the goods and that the unsold goods would be placed in their central warehouse so that a detailed list could be prepared. (Electronics had a chain of retail outlets in various parts of the country and it would take some time for them to be returned to the warehouse.) It was held that the notice rejecting the unsold goods was effective (so that Electronics was not deemed to have bought them). Neither the fact that the actual quantity and identity of the unsold goods was specified in the notice, nor the fact that the goods were not physically capable of collection when the notice was issued, prevented the notice from being a valid rejection of the goods.

(v) Rule 5: unascertained goods

Rules 1–4 of s 18 are all concerned with specific goods. The only rule dealing with *unascertained* goods is r 5. It states:

(1) Where there is a contract for the sale of unascertained or future goods by description, and goods of that description and in a deliverable state are unconditionally appropriated to the contract, either by the seller with the assent of the buyer or by the buyer with the assent of the seller, the property in the goods then passes to the buyer; and the assent may be given either before or after the appropriation is made.

(2) Where, in pursuance of the contract, the seller delivers the goods to the buyer or to a carrier or other bailee ... (whether named by the buyer or not) for the purpose of transmission to the buyer, and does not reserve the right of disposal, he is to be taken to have unconditionally appropriated the goods to the contract.

We have already met some of the terms used in this rule. As well as *unascertained goods* (see above, p 272) and *future goods* (above, p 272), which were dealt with in Chapter 7, the expression *deliverable state* occurs in rr 1 and 2 and has been discussed above (p 327). *Unconditionally* in this context is probably analogous with 'unconditional contract', as used in r 1 (see above, p 326), but in the present context, where it refers to 'appropriation', it has been the subject of special judicial consideration on a number of occasions, as will be seen in the cases which follow. Of the new expressions, it is best to start with the term 'appropriation'.

'Appropriation' literally means 'taking or dealing with as one's property'—in which sense it is used in s 9(1); but in r 5 it has the rather different connotation of a selecting or setting aside. But even within the broad idea of a setting aside, the word can have a range of meanings. Suppose that a wine merchant who has an order for one dozen bottles of a particular wine for a customer selects a box containing 12 bottles of the wine from a larger quantity in his cellar with the intention of using it to fulfil that order: we may say that he has 'appropriated' the box in question to the contract. But, of course, there is nothing at this stage to stop him changing his mind: if a second customer wants wine of the same description, he could sell him that box without infringing any commitment to the first buyer, and then select (or even procure from elsewhere) another dozen bottles to meet the original order. Nothing that the merchant has done by this 'appropriation' affects his ownership of the wine in question, or his ability to sell it to anyone he may choose. No subjective decision on his part, or unilateral or private act of setting aside, gives the first customer any claim to that box. Nor would an act by the merchant such as putting the goods in his delivery van to be taken to the customer's address, or even writing the customer's name and address on the box: these acts are all reversible or revocable, and the second customer, especially if he is in a hurry, might not mind at all being given a box with writing on it. 'Appropriation', for the purpose of r 5, must mean something more than this.

A second use of the word goes somewhat further, but still does not bring r 5 into play. It may be a term of the contract that at some stage the seller will earmark goods of the particular description for the purpose of meeting his obligations, so that from then onwards he is bound under the contract to deliver those goods and those goods only, but *without* any understanding that the property in the goods is to pass at that stage. So, for example, in a typical CIF contract (see below, p 498), an importer may agree to buy goods of a particular description to be delivered at a specified port in his own country—eg a Dutch merchant may contract to buy 2,000 tonnes of soya bean meal of US origin to be delivered to him at Rotterdam. The seller may very likely have no identified goods in mind at the time of the contract. But it will normally be a term of the contract that, once he has located a suitable consignment, he will give the buyer a 'notice of appropriation' of the goods which he has chosen. This is a contractually binding act, obliging him to use those goods, and those goods only, in fulfilment of the contract. But it will not necessarily follow that such an act of appropriation, even when notified to the buyer, has the added consequence of passing the property in the goods to the buyer—indeed, this would be most unusual for, as we shall see, the normal understanding in a contract on CIF terms is that property will only pass when the shipping documents relating to the goods are handed over in exchange for the purchase price. 'Appropriation', for the purposes of r 5, has to be more than an act of selection, and more than a purely contractual earmarking of goods to answer the contract: it must be an act which is intended and agreed, in terms of the contract, to transfer ownership to the buyer.

Wait v Baker

(1848) 2 Exch 1, Court of Exchequer Chamber

(The facts are immaterial.)

Parke B: …It is admitted by the learned counsel for the defendant, that the property does not pass, unless there is a subsequent appropriation of the goods. The word appropriation may be understood in different senses. It may mean a selection on the part of the vendor, where he has the right to choose the article which he has to supply in performance of his contract; and the contract will shew when the word is used in that sense. Or the word may mean, that both parties have agreed that a certain article shall be delivered in pursuance of the contract, and yet the property may not pass in either case. For the purpose of illustrating this position, suppose a carriage is ordered to be built at a coachmaker's, he may make any one he pleases, and, if it agree with the order, the party is bound to accept it. Now suppose that, at some period subsequent to the order, a further bargain is entered into between this party and the coachbuilder, by which it is agreed that a particular carriage shall be delivered. It would depend upon circumstances whether the property passes, or whether merely the original contract is altered from one which would have been satisfied by the delivery of any carriage answering the terms of the contract, into another contract to supply the particular carriage—which, in the Roman law, was called obligatio certi corporis, where a person is bound to deliver a particular chattel, but where the property does not pass, as it never did by the Roman law, until actual delivery; although the property, after the contract, remained at the risk of the vendee, and if lost without any fault in the vendor, the vendee, and not the vendor, was the sufferer. The law of England is different: here, property does not pass until there is a bargain with respect to a specific article, and everything is done which, according to the intention of the parties to the bargain, was necessary to transfer the property in it. 'Appropriation' may also be used in another sense, and is the one in which Mr Butt uses it on the present occasion; viz where both parties agree upon the specific article in which the property is to pass, and nothing remains to be done in order to pass it.…

The application of the presumption contained in r 5 is illustrated by the following cases (some of which have already been discussed):

Aldridge v Johnson

(See above, p 279.)

Philip Head & Sons Ltd v Showfronts Ltd

(See above, p 328.)

Rohde v Thwaites
(1827) 6 B & C 388, Court of King's Bench

Thwaites had contracted to buy 20 hogsheads (casks) of sugar out of the bulk held by Rohde in his warehouse. Rohde filled 20 hogsheads, of which four were delivered to Thwaites and accepted by him; but he refused to collect the remaining 16. In this action it was held that Rohde could sue for the price of all twenty hogsheads.

Holroyd J: The sugars agreed to be sold being part of a larger parcel, the vendors were to select twenty hogsheads for the vendee. That selection was made by the plaintiffs, and they notified it to the defendant, and the latter then promised to take them away. That is equivalent to an actual acceptance of the sixteen hogsheads by the defendant. That acceptance made the goods his own, subject to the vendor's lien as to the price. If the sugars had afterwards been destroyed by fire, the loss must have fallen on the defendant. I am of opinion that the selection of the sixteen hogsheads by the plaintiffs, and the adoption of that act by the defendants, converted that which before was a mere agreement to sell into an actual sale, and that the property in the sugars thereby passed to the defendant; and, consequently, that [the vendors were] entitled to recover to the value of the whole under the count for goods bargained and sold.

[Bayley J delivered a concurring judgment.
Littledale J concurred.]

Langton v Higgins
(1859) 4 H & N 402, Court of Exchequer

Carter, a Cambridgeshire farmer who owed money to Mrs Langton, agreed to sell her all the oil of peppermint to be distilled from the crop to be grown on his farm in 1858. Mrs Langton sent him the necessary bottles and his wife filled them with the oil; but Carter then sold them to Higgins and shortly afterwards disappeared. It was held that Mrs Langton could sue Higgins in detinue, since the property in the oil had passed to her when the bottles were filled.

Bramwell B: . . . The contract is to sell the whole of the vendor's crop of oil of peppermint grown in a certain year. I do not think that when the oil was made the property passed,—possibly there may have been an obligatio certi corporis; but it appears to me that when the oil was put into the plaintiff's bottles the property in it vested in her. . . . It may be that the vendor would be bound to shew some act of delivery before he could sue for the price; but however that may be, I am of opinion that the property vested in the plaintiff when the oil was put into her bottles. Looking at the principle, there ought to be no doubt. A person agrees to buy a certain article, and sends his bottles to the seller to put the article into. The seller puts the article into the buyer's bottles, then is there any rule to say that the property does not pass? The buyer in effect says, 'I will trust you to deliver into my bottles, and by that means to appropriate to me, the article which I have bought of you.' On the other hand the seller must be taken to say, 'You have sent your bottles and I will put the article in them for you.' In all reason, when a vendee sends his ship, or cart, or cask, or bottle to the vendor, and he puts the article sold into it, that is a delivery to the vendee. If we could suppose the case of a metal vessel filled with a commodity which rendered the vessel useless for subsequent purposes, it would be monstrous if the vendor could say I have destroyed your vessel by putting into it the article you purchased, but still the property in the article never passed to you.' Or suppose a vendor was to deliver a ton of coals into the vendee's cellar, could he say 'I have put the coals in your cellar, but I have a right to take them away again?' But, independently of reason, there is an authority on the subject.

[His Lordship referred to *Blackburn on Sale,* and continued:]

Can there be more complete evidence of intention to pass the property than when the vendee sends her bottles to be filled with the article purchased, and the vendor puts it into the bottles? Therefore, both upon principle and authority, I think that the property in the oil passed to the plaintiff when it was put into the bottles.

[Pollock CB and Martin B delivered concurring judgments.]

Mucklow v Mangles
(1808) 1 Taunt 318, Court of Common Pleas

Royland contracted to build a barge for Pocock. The whole of the agreed price was paid as the work progressed. When it was nearly finished, Pocock's name was painted on the stern. Two days after it had been completed, it was seized by Mangles, a sheriff's officer, who was executing a judgment against Royland. Royland was later adjudicated bankrupt. The question before the court was whether the sheriff had rightly seized the barge, or whether it had become Pocock's property. It was held that the property had not passed to Pocock.

Mansfield CJ: The only effect of the payment, is, that the bankrupt was under a contract to finish the barge: that is quite a different thing from a contract of sale, and until the barge was finished we cannot say that it was so far Pocock's property, that he could have taken it away. It was not finished at the time when Royland committed the act of bankruptcy: it was finished only two days before the execution....

Heath J: ...A tradesman often finishes goods, which he is making in pursuance of an order given by one person, and sells them to another. If the first customer has other goods made for him within the stipulated time, he has no right to complain; he could not bring trover against the purchaser for the goods so sold. The painting of the name on the stern in this case makes no difference. If the thing be in existence at the time of the order, the property of it passes by the contract, but not so, where the subject is to be made.

[Lawrence J concurred.]

NOTE

We really need to know more facts than are stated in the report of this case. Under the law then in force, the 'commencement' of Royland's bankruptcy would have been back-dated to some 'act of bankruptcy' (which is referred to by Mansfield CJ), which plainly took place between the painting of the name and the completion of the work. The title of the trustee in bankruptcy would be deemed to have vested on the date of that act of bankruptcy.

Noblett v Hopkinson

[1905] 2 KB 214, King's Bench Divisional Court

The licensee of a public house was charged with unlawfully opening his premises for the sale of intoxicating liquor on a Sunday, in the circumstances described by Lord Alverstone CJ. The justices had dismissed the charge on the ground that there had been an 'appropriation' of the liquor on the Saturday evening, and consequently no 'sale' on the Sunday. The decision of the justices was reversed on appeal and a conviction entered.

Lord Alverstone CJ: It appears that two men went to the respondent's public-house on Saturday and asked for half a gallon of beer, and asked if it could be sent down to them on Sunday morning; the inference that I think may properly be drawn from this is that they would not have ordered the beer if they could not have had it sent to them on the Sunday. They then paid for the beer, which was drawn and put into a bottle; then, as the case states, the bottle was corked and put on the bar counter, whence it was taken to the brewhouse stable (which was within the curtilage) and remained there till the Sunday morning, when it was given to the barman behind the counter to hand to the two men when they called for it; as a matter of fact the barman seems to have taken if off the premises himself and gone with it to the place where the two men were, where he was stopped by the constable. There was in my opinion no evidence that what was done with the beer on the Saturday evening was done under the licence or by the authority of the purchaser; the evidence seems to shew that it was done by the vendor on his own responsibility, and, if the bottle of beer had been broken during the Saturday night, other beer would have had to be supplied to the men on the Sunday morning. I think therefore that there was not sufficient evidence on which it could properly be found that there was an appropriation of the beer on the Saturday night—I mean of an appropriation made by the respondent as the agent of the purchasers. The statement in the case does not of necessity mean that the beer was put aside in the way described with the consent of the purchasers, and in my opinion, when the justices speak of appropriation, they mean simply an appropriation by the publican.

That is enough for the decision of this case. . . .

[Kennedy and Ridley JJ delivered concurring judgments.]

It should be noted that r 5 requires an appropriation by or under the authority of one party with the *assent* of the other. This assent may be given before or after the appropriation, and will sometimes be inferred (eg from the fact that the seller's appropriation is made by filling containers supplied by the buyer). Rules 2 and 3, in contrast, require only that the buyer should have *notice* that the seller has performed the outstanding act. It is clear that mere notice to the other party will not necessarily give rise to an inference of assent. But the following case shows that such an inference may sometimes be drawn.

Pignataro v Gilroy

[1919] 1 KB 459, King's Bench Divisional Court

The defendants contracted to sell by sample to the plaintiff 140 bags of rice, then unascertained, and in due course notified the buyer that 125 bags were available for collection at one address and 15 at another. Despite two reminders by letter, the plaintiff did not send to collect the 15 bags for nearly a month, by which time they had been stolen. It was held that the property had passed to the plaintiff and that the risk of loss therefore lay on him.

The judgment of the court (Lawrence and Rowlatt JJ) was delivered by **Rowlatt J:** Under the above contract it would be the duty of the sellers to appropriate the goods to the contract; and if such appropriation were assented to, expressly or impliedly, by the buyer the property would have passed. When they received the cheque for the goods and were asked for a delivery order it was right and proper for them to appropriate and place at the disposal of the buyer the goods for which he thus paid in order to effectuate a delivery or its equivalent concurrently with the receipt of the money. They did send a delivery order for the goods at Chambers' Wharf, and as to the 15 bags, told the plaintiff that they were ready, and asked that they should be taken away. It might well be contended that not only as regards the goods covered by the delivery order, but also as regards the goods at the defendants' own premises which they thus told the plaintiff were ready to be taken away in response to the plaintiff's request for a delivery order, there was an appropriation to which by asking for the delivery order the plaintiff had assented in advance. We do not think it necessary to decide this, because we think there was what amounted to an assent subsequent. If the plaintiff had replied saying that he would remove the goods the case would be precisely the same as *Rohde v Thwaites* [above, p 339]. The plaintiff, however, did nothing for a month, and the question is what is the effect of that? If the goods were of the required quality it is difficult to see how the plaintiff could have dissented from the appropriation. He could not object to the place from which he was required to fetch them, because he had inspected rice lying at those premises at the time and for the purposes of this very contract. For the same reason it is not easy to see how he could have objected to their quality unless there happened to be some bags inferior to those which he had inspected. At any rate, he made no objection at all. Now it is obvious that if he made any objection he ought to do so promptly, because he could not place upon the vendors the risk involved in the continued possession of these goods, nor prolong the encumbrance of the vendors' premises. As he chose merely to say nothing for a whole month in response to an appropriation made in consequence of his own letter, we think that comes to precisely the same thing as if he had written saying he would remove them and did not. The learned judge said that there was no evidence of an appropriation with the assent of the buyer. He could only say this if he was looking for an express assent. As the assent may be implied we think that there was not only evidence of it but that it is the only inference possible upon the facts. For these reasons the appeal must be allowed, and judgment entered for the defendants....

Carlos Federspiel & Co SA v Charles Twigg & Co Ltd

[1957] 1 Lloyd's Rep 240, Queen's Bench Division

Federspiels in Costa Rica agreed to buy a number of cycles from Twiggs in England and paid them the price. Under the contract, the goods were to be loaded aboard the SS *Britannica* at Liverpool. Cycles were manufactured to answer the contract and packed in crates marked with the buyers' name, and steps were taken to send the crates to Liverpool for shipment. But the sellers went into receivership before shipment took place. The buyers argued unsuccessfully that the property in the cycles had passed to them.

Pearson J: This is a case in which the contract is for the sale of unascertained goods by description, for the sale of future goods probably still to be manufactured. Afterwards certain goods were manufactured, and the sellers at one time apparently expected to use them in fulfilment of the contract. The question is whether there was an appropriation of those goods to the contract by the sellers with the assent of the buyers within the meaning of Rule 5 of s 18.

I think it is convenient just, in effect, to lay a foundation for the understanding of the exact meaning and effect of s 18 by reading a short passage from an old case, *Mirabita v Imperial Ottoman Bank* (1878) 3 Ex D 164. The relevant passage is from the judgment of Lord Justice Cotton, at p 172, where he says:

> Under a contract for sale of chattels not specific the property does not pass to the purchaser unless there is afterwards an appropriation of the specific chattels to pass under the contract, that is, unless both parties agree as to the specific chattels in which the property is to pass, and nothing remains to be done in order to pass it.

[His Lordship referred to a number of other cases, including *Wait v Baker* (above, p 338) and *Pignataro v Gilroy* (above, p 341), and continued:]

On those authorities, what are the principles emerging? I think one can distinguish these principles. First, r 5 of s 18 of the Act is one of the rules for ascertaining the intention of the parties as to the time at which the property in the goods is to pass to the buyer unless a different intention appears. Therefore the element of common intention has always to be borne in mind. A mere setting apart or selection by the seller of the goods which he expects to use in performance of the contract is not enough. If that is all, he can change his mind and use those goods in performance of some other contract and use some other goods in performance of this contract. To constitute an appropriation of the goods to the contract, the parties must have had, or be reasonably supposed to have had, an intention to attach the contract irrevocably to those goods, so that those goods and no others are the subject of the sale and become the property of the buyer.

Secondly, it is by agreement of the parties that the appropriation, involving a change of ownership, is made, although in some cases the buyer's assent to an appropriation by the seller is conferred in advance by the contract itself or otherwise.

Thirdly, an appropriation by the seller, with the assent of the buyer, may be said always to involve an actual or constructive delivery. If the seller retains possession, he does so as bailee for the buyer. There is a passage in Chalmers' Sale of Goods Act, 12th edn, at p 75, where it is said:

> In the second place, if the decisions be carefully examined, it will be found that in every case where the property has been held to pass, there has been an actual or constructive delivery of the goods to the buyer.

I think that is right, subject only to this possible qualification, that there may be after such constructive delivery an actual delivery still to be made by the seller under the contract. Of course, that is quite possible, because delivery is the transfer of possession, whereas appropriation transfers ownership. So there may be first an appropriation, constructive delivery, whereby the seller becomes bailee for the buyer, and then a subsequent actual delivery involving actual possession, and when I say that I have in mind in particular the two cases cited, namely, *Aldridge v Johnson* [above, p 279], and *Langton v Higgins* [above, p 339].

Fourthly, one has to remember s 20 of the Sale of Goods Act, whereby the ownership and the risk are normally associated. Therefore as it appears that there is reason for thinking, on the construction of the relevant documents, that the goods were, at all material times, still at the seller's risk, that is *prima facie* an indication that the property had not passed to the buyer.

Fifthly, usually but not necessarily, the appropriating act is the last act to be performed by the seller. For instance, if delivery is to be taken by the buyer at the seller's premises and the seller has completed his part of the contract and has appropriated the goods when he has made the goods ready and has identified them and placed them in position to be taken by the buyer and has so informed the buyer, and if the buyer agrees to come and take them, that is the assent to the appropriation. But if there is a further act, an important and decisive act to be done by the seller, then there is *prima facie* evidence that probably the property does not pass until the final act is done.

Applying those principles to the present case I would say this. Firstly, the intention was that the ownership should pass on shipment (or possibly at some later date) because the emphasis is throughout on shipment as the decisive act to be done by the seller in performance of the contract. Secondly, it is impossible to find in this correspondence an agreement to a change of ownership before the time of shipment. The letters, especially those of Aug 27 and Sept 14, which are particularly relied on by the plaintiff, do not contain any provision or implication of any earlier change of ownership. Thirdly, there is no actual or constructive delivery; no suggestion of the seller becoming a bailee for the buyer. Fourthly, there is no suggestion of the goods being at the buyer's risk at any time before shipment; no suggestion that the buyer should insist on the seller arranging insurance for them. Fifthly, the last two acts to be performed by the seller, namely, sending the goods to Liverpool and having the goods shipped on board, were not performed.

Therefore, my decision that the *prima facie* inference which one would have drawn from the contract is that the property was not to pass at any time before shipment, is in my view not displaced by the subsequent correspondence between the parties. It follows, therefore, that there was no appropriation of these goods and therefore the action fails.

An act of appropriation sufficient to pass the property in goods may be performed by a third party, eg a warehouseman. In such a case, the third party may be regarded as the agent of one (or possibly both) of the parties for the purpose.

Wardar's (Import & Export) Co Ltd v W Norwood & Sons Ltd
[1968] 2 QB 663, Court of Appeal

Wardar's agreed to buy from Norwoods 600 cartons of frozen ox kidneys out of a consignment of 1,500 cartons which had been imported from Argentina and were lying in a cold store in Smithfield. A driver, McBeath, employed by a firm of carriers, arrived at 8 am on an October morning to pick up the goods on behalf of Wardar's and take them to Scotland. He had a refrigerated lorry but had forgotten to turn on the refrigerating machinery. When he arrived, 600 cartons had been taken out of the store by the storage firm and placed on the pavement. McBeath handed over a delivery order and the Smithfield porters began to load the van. Loading took until noon (in part because the porters took a one-hour tea-break), by which time the day was warm and some of the cartons were leaking, and the refrigeration in the van was still not fully effective. The kidneys were unfit for consumption when they arrived in Scotland. The Court of Appeal held that the loss fell on the buyers, since property and risk had passed at 8 am and the deterioration had occurred after that time.

Salmon LJ: When McBeath arrived at the cold store at 8 am on October 14, the frozen kidneys which he was to take to Scotland were there on the pavement waiting for him. There is no doubt that they had been in the cold store the day before and, indeed, had then been examined by the buyers soon after they made their oral contract of purchase. As far as the evidence goes, there was absolutely nothing the matter with the kidneys on October 13. There is no evidence as to when these 600 cartons were taken out of the cold store. It seems unlikely that they would have been left on the pavement overnight. Had they been left on the pavement overnight, it is perhaps even more unlikely that they would all have been there in the morning. The natural inference, I think, is that they must have been taken out of the cold store at some time on the morning of October 14 prior to 8 am.

These 600 cartons were part of a consignment of 1500 cartons of frozen kidneys that had been stored in the cold store. The evidence called at the trial showed that the rest of the cartons—that is, 900 of the cartons—had also been sold, and no complaint was made in respect of them. At the time of the sale it was a sale of unascertained goods: 600 cartons were bought out of a total of 1500 cartons. This case really turns upon the question as to when the property passed to the buyers. It is plain that as a rule the goods remain at the sellers' risk until the property does pass to the buyers. After the property passes, the goods are at the buyers' risk: s 20 of the Act of 1893. There are special circumstances (of which *Sterns Ltd v Vickers Ltd* [above, p 302] is an example) when the risk may pass to the buyers even before the property has passed to them; but there are no such special circumstances here. The case depends entirely upon when the property passed.

Under r 5 of s 18, the property passes to the buyers in the case of unascertained goods, such as these, when the goods are unconditionally appropriated to the contract. At 8 am the carrier arrived; and the carrier was the buyers' agent. There were the goods, which had been left on the pavement by the sellers' agent for the purpose of fulfilling the contract. The carrier handed over the delivery note, with the clear intention that those goods should be accepted for loading; and the loading commenced.

It is unnecessary to decide the point whether there was an unconditional appropriation to the contract at the moment when the goods were put onto the pavement, which is perhaps fortunate, because we do not know precisely when that was; but, in my view, there can be no doubt that there was a clear, unconditional appropriation when the delivery order was handed over in respect of the goods which had been deposited on the pavement for loading. There is certainly no evidence that they were not then of merchantable quality. It would seem from the evidence of Mr McBeath, the driver of the lorry, that at some stage the porters wished to take a tea-break. The driver was apparently concerned at the goods being left standing on the pavement, but he was told, according to his evidence, that the tea-break would take only five minutes. It appears that it took about an hour; and it was after the tea-break, according to Mr McBeath, that he first noticed that some of the cartons were dripping, which would be a strong indication that the goods had by then started to deteriorate. Meantime, however, a good many of the cartons had already been loaded into the lorry. Since, however, the goods were appropriated to the contract when the delivery order was handed over and accepted in respect of the goods standing on the pavement, any deterioration that occurred thereafter was at the risk of the buyers. We know that when the goods arrived at their destination the vast bulk of them were not of merchantable quality. We also know from the driver of the lorry that he did not turn on the refrigeration, so he said, until the tea-break was taken. At any rate, the refrigeration did not become effective until 1 pm. It may not be very material, but it does not seem to me to be at all unlikely, if the goods were left in a stuffy lorry, as they were, for some hours, that the deterioration may have occurred during that time. The driver said that this was a hot day. Unless it was a very exceptional day for October 14 in this country, I cannot think that the sun had much strength in it by 8 am. In any event, none of this, I think, matters, because at 8 am these goods were appropriated to the contract and the risk of deterioration then fell on the buyers; and there is no evidence that there was any deterioration before that time . . . .

[Harman LJ delivered a concurring judgment.
Phillimore J concurred.]

Paragraph (2) of r 5 deems goods to have been unconditionally appropriated to the contract when the seller has delivered them to a carrier or other bailee for the purpose of transmission to the buyer. It was unsuccessfully argued in *Wardar's* case that there had been no 'delivery' under this provision until the cartons had actually been put on the lorry; but it is plain that the court considered that delivery had taken place at the time when the delivery order was handed over by McBeath to the cold store firm and accepted. Paragraph (2) also refers to a *reservation of the right of disposal* by the buyer—an expression which is also used, and its meaning elaborated, in s 19(1) and (2). These are perhaps rather superfluous provisions, because it is plain from the whole tenor of ss 17 and 18 that no property can pass under the contract so long as some condition remains to be fulfilled, and that an appropriation to be effective must also be unconditional; and obviously if the seller makes a stipulation that he is reserving a right of disposal even after delivery to the buyer or the carrier, the appropriation will not be unconditional. However, it does no harm for the details in question to be spelt out in the Act, and it is helpful to have it clearly stated as a prima facie rule that where goods are loaded on to a ship for the purposes of transmission to the buyer, and the seller takes the bill of lading in his own name, intending to transfer it to the buyer at some later stage (normally against payment of the price), the property is not to be taken to have passed (s 19(2)). On this question, see further below, p 494.

Finally, before leaving r 5, we should note the two new paragraphs (3) and (4), introduced by the amending Act of 1995, which deal with 'ascertainment by exhaustion'. These paragraphs, and the cases at common law on which they are based, have been discussed above, pp 322ff. However, it should be observed that whereas the rulings at common law were primarily on the issue of *ascertainment,* the new provisions go further, and add a presumption that the goods are not only ascertained by the process of exhaustion, but *appropriated* to the contract.

(c) Acceptance and rejection

Before we leave the topic of the passing of property, it may be appropriate to ask: what is the *latest* time at which property can pass under a contract of sale? The answer would appear to be found in s 35: that is, when the buyer has *accepted* the goods, as explained in that section. (On acceptance, see below, pp 426, 473.) This is the point at which the buyer loses, or abandons, any right which he may have to reject the goods (eg because they are not of the contract description or quality), after which his remedy, if any, is confined to a damages claim.

It is sometimes possible for a buyer to reject goods even *after* the property has passed to him. In such a case, the effect of rejection is that the buyer divests himself of his ownership and causes it to revest in the seller. *Head v Tattersall* (above, p 299) is perhaps an early example of this: the risk, as well as the property, being deemed to have revested in the seller with retrospective effect. Two more modern cases illustrate the same principle.

Kwei Tek Chao v British Traders & Shippers Ltd
[1954] 2 QB 459, Queen's Bench Division

Buyers in Hong Kong contracted to buy from sellers in London a chemical of Swedish origin known as 'Rongalite C'. Under the contract, property passed to the buyers when the price was paid in exchange for the shipping documents: this happened on 12 November. By the time that the goods arrived in Hong Kong on 17 December, the buyers had ascertained that the goods had been shipped outside the contractual period for shipment and that the shipping documents had been forged (by a third party) to conceal this fact. Devlin J held that the buyers could reject the goods for this reason, and that they could do so even though the property had already passed to them: it must be regarded as having passed defeasibly, ie subject to a condition subsequent that in an event such as that which had happened, it could be revested in the sellers by the buyers properly exercising a right of rejection. It followed that the buyers, who had pledged the documents to their bank, had not dealt with the goods in a manner inconsistent with the sellers' ownership so as to lose their right of rejection under s 35 of the Act.

Devlin J: In *Hardy & Co v Hillerns and Fowler* [below, p 474] the question which arose for decision was whether the buyers had accepted the goods under s 35. The goods had arrived, and the case showed that the time during which he had the right to examine them was still running. During that time the buyer delivered some of the goods to a sub-buyer. That was an act which was inconsistent with the ownership of the seller. . . . The court held that, notwithstanding that his time for examination was still open, the buyer could, if he chose to commit an act under s 35 such as intimating that he accepted the goods, accept them.

Mr Roskill has argued that when the goods are delivered to the buyer and he does any act in relation to them which is inconsistent with the ownership of the seller the word 'delivered' there means physical delivery of the goods from the ship. If that is so, no dealing with the documents would be within the meaning of the clause, because it would all have been done before the goods had been delivered. I cannot take that view of it. 'Delivery' as defined by the Act means a voluntary transfer of possession, and I think that it means, therefore, transfer of possession under the contract of sale. In a cif contract the goods are delivered, so far as they are physically delivered, when they are put on board a ship at the port of shipment. The documents are delivered when they are tendered. A buyer who takes delivery from the ship at the port of destination is not taking delivery of the goods under the contract of sale, but merely taking delivery out of his own warehouse, as it were, by the presentation of the document of title to the goods, the master of the ship having been his bailee ever since he became entitled to the bill of lading.

I think that the true answer may be found rather differently. Atkin LJ, in the course of his judgment in *Hardy & Co v Hillerns and Fowler,* dealt with the situation which is always a little puzzling under the cif contract: if the property passes when the documents are handed over, by what legal machinery does the buyer retain a right, as he undoubtedly does, to examine the goods when they arrive, and to reject them if they are not in conformity with the contract? Atkin LJ put forward two views for consideration. One was that the property in the goods, notwithstanding the tendering of the documents, did not pass until the goods had been examined or until an opportunity for examination had been given. The other was that it passed at the time of the tendering of the documents, but only conditionally and could be revested if the buyer properly rejected the goods. Mr Roskill argues (and I think rightly) that for the first possible view indicated by Atkin LJ no other authority can be found, and it would clearly create considerable complications. If there is no property in the goods, how can the buyer pledge them? It would provide a simple answer to the point had it arisen in this case, since there could not be a pledge. I think that the true view is that what the buyer obtains, when the title under the documents is given to him, is the property in the goods, subject to the condition that they revest if upon examination he finds them to be not in accordance with the contract. That means that he gets only conditional property in the goods, the condition being a condition subsequent. All his dealings with the documents are dealings only with that conditional property in the goods. It follows, therefore, that there can be no dealing which is inconsistent with the seller's ownership unless he deals with something more than the conditional property. If the property passes altogether, not being subject to any condition, there is no ownership left in the seller with which any inconsistent act under s 35 could be committed. If the property passes conditionally the only ownership left in the seller is the reversionary interest in the property in the event of the condition subsequent operating to restore it to him. It is that reversionary interest with which the buyer must not, save with the penalty of accepting the goods, commit an inconsistent act. So long as he is merely dealing with the documents he is not purporting to do anything more than pledge the conditional property which he has. Similarly, if he sells the documents of title he sells the conditional property. But if, as was done in *Hardy & Co v Hillerns and Fowler,* when the goods have been landed, he physically deals with the goods and delivers them to his sub-buyer, he is doing an act which is inconsistent with the seller's reversionary interest. The seller's reversionary interest entitles him, immediately upon the operation of the condition subsequent, that is, as soon as opportunity for examination has been given, to have the goods physically returned to him in the place where the examination has taken place without their being dispatched to third parties. The dispatch to a third party is an act, therefore, which interferes with the reversionary interest. A pledge or a transfer of documents such as that which takes place on the ordinary string contract does not....

McDougall v Aeromarine of Emsworth Ltd
[1958] 1 WLR 1126, Queen's Bench Division

Aeromarine contracted to build for McDougall a four-ton cruiser-racer yacht for use in the 1957 yachting season. Payment of the price was to be made by five instalments. The contract contained a term (clause 8) similar to that in *Re Blyth Shipbuilding Co Ltd* (see above, p 323) by virtue of which the property in the uncompleted vessel passed to the buyer on payment of the first instalment. The yacht had defects rendering it unseaworthy when it was launched in June 1957, and these defects had not been remedied several months later when Aeromarine offered to finish the work on varied terms which McDougall was not prepared to accept. Diplock J held that the buyer was justified in rejecting the yacht and that, although the property may have passed pursuant to clause 8, it had passed only defeasibly, and had been revested in Aeromarine when McDougall rightly exercised his right to reject.

Diplock J: The defendants' failure to tender the yacht for delivery in accordance with the contract by September 5 was itself, I think, a breach of condition which the plaintiff was entitled to treat as rescinding the contract. Their intimation, for that was what their offer amounted to, that they could not complete it before the end of the 1957 yachting season was a fortiori, in my opinion, a wrongful repudiation of the contract by the defendants, as was their intimation that they would only complete the contract upon terms different from those of the original contract. The plaintiff by his letter of September 19 elected to treat the defendants' wrongful repudiation of the contract as rescinding it.

I hold that, in all the circumstances of the case, he was entitled to do so; but even if he were not, the defendants cannot rely on the plaintiff's purported rescission of the contract of September 19 as a wrongful repudiation on his part of the contract, thus relieving them from any further obligation to perform it, because they did not accept his repudiation but continued to hold him to the contract; and on October 30 they informed the plaintiff that they would insist either on completing the vessel on terms inconsistent with and less favourable to the plaintiff than those in the original contract, or those that they had offered in their letter of September 5, or upon delivering the vessel in its defective state with an allowance of 50 guineas off the contract price. This was, I think, yet another wrongful repudiation by the defendants of the contract, which the plaintiff was entitled to and did accept. Such part of the property, if any, in the vessel or any portion thereof as had previously vested in him under clause 8 of the contract accordingly revested then in the defendants.

NOTES

1.   See also *JH Ritchie Ltd v Lloyd Ltd* (below, p 475), which deals with the situation where a buyer of defective goods agrees to allow the seller to attempt to repair the defect. The property in the goods will pass to the buyer (and may already have done so) in accordance with the normal rules, but if he later lawfully exercises his right to reject them the property will revert to the seller.

2.   It should not be assumed that the conclusion reached in *Head v Tattersall* (above, p 299)—that the seller bore the risk during the period when the property had provisionally passed to the buyer—would necessarily be the same in other cases with similar facts. Where non-conforming goods are delivered or tendered by the seller, the question whether the buyer has lost the right of rejection is often determined without reference to the issue of risk, and much may depend on the terms of the particular contract, the degree of non-conformity and the nature of the event which prevents return of the goods. On this question, see AH Hudson 'Conformity of Goods on Passing of Risk' in D Feldman and F Meisel (eds) *Corporate and Commercial Law: Modern Developments* (1996), Ch 11.

CHAPTER 9
TRANSFER OF TITLE

1 THE RULE *NEMO DAT QUOD NON HABET*

In most contexts, it would be reasonable to regard the expressions 'Transfer of property as between seller and buyer' and 'Transfer of title' as meaning much the same thing. It therefore comes as something of a surprise to find that the Sale of Goods Act 1979 uses these terms to refer to quite different topics. The 'Transfer of property as between seller and buyer', dealt with in ss 16–19, does indeed have the fairly obvious meaning, ie the process by which ownership passes from the one party to the other. In contrast, under 'Transfer of title', the concern is with a number of situations in which a seller who is a *non-owner,* or a person with a *defective title,* can nevertheless confer a good title on his buyer, and in doing so defeat the claims of the true owner or of a person with a superior title. Of course, these are exceptional situations—as s 21, which sets out the basic rule, makes clear. This rule (summed up in the ancient maxim *nemo dat quod non habet*—or, for short, *nemo dat*), states that, subject to the Act,

where goods are sold by a person who is not their owner, and who does not sell them under the authority or with the consent of the owner, the buyer acquires no better title to the goods than the seller had.

The same, or a similar, basic rule applies (unless there are statutory or common law exceptions) to sales of land and other forms of property, to gifts, to bailments such as hire and pledge, and to the assignment of choses in action; and its importance cannot be over-emphasised—especially since the rule itself can be stated in a few lines, and the bulk of the discussion which is to follow will go into the exceptions at length and in some detail! Two well-known cases illustrate the *nemo dat* rule.

Cundy v Lindsay
(1878) 3 App Cas 459, House of Lords

A rogue called Blenkarn, impersonating a well-known firm named Blenkiron which carried on business in the same street, ordered a quantity of linen by post from Lindsay & Co in Belfast. When the linen arrived, Blenkarn sold part of it to Messrs Cundy, who bought in good faith and without knowledge of Blenkarn's fraud. The first contract was held to be void (in modern terms, on the ground of mistake of identity), so that no title in the linen passed to Blenkarn. It followed that he could not confer any title on Cundy, who were consequently liable to Lindsay & Co in conversion.

Lord Cairns LC: My Lords, you have in this case to discharge a duty which is always a disagreeable one for any Court, namely, to determine as between two parties, both of whom are perfectly innocent, upon which of the two the consequences of a fraud practised upon both of them must fall. My Lords, in discharging that duty your Lordships can do no more than apply, rigorously, the settled and well known rules of law. Now, with regard to the title to personal property, the settled and well known rules of the law may, I take it, be thus expressed: by the law of our country the purchaser of a chattel takes the chattel as a general rule subject to what may turn out to be certain infirmities in the title. If . . . it turns out that the chattel has been found by the person who professed to sell it, the purchaser will not obtain a title good as against the real owner. If it turns out that the chattel has been stolen by the person who has professed to sell it, the purchaser will not obtain a title. If it turns out that the chattel has come into the hands of the person who professed to sell it, by a *de facto* [voidable] contract, that is to say, a contract which has purported to pass the property to him from the owner of the property, there the purchaser will obtain a good title, even although afterwards it should appear that there were circumstances connected with that contract, which would enable the original owner of the goods to reduce it, and to set it aside, because these circumstances so enabling the original owner of the goods, or of the chattel, to reduce the contract and to set it aside, will not be allowed to interfere with a title for valuable consideration obtained by some third party during the interval while the contract remained unreduced.

My Lords, the question, therefore, in the present case, as your Lordships will observe, really becomes the very short and simple one which I am about to state. Was there any contract which, with regard to the goods in question in this case, had passed the property in the goods from the Messrs Lindsay to Alfred Blenkarn? If there was any contract passing that property, even although, as I have said, that contract might afterwards be open to a process of reduction, upon the ground of fraud, still, in the meantime, Blenkarn might have conveyed a good title for valuable consideration to the present Appellants . . . .

Now, my Lords, . . . what the jurors have found is in substance this: it is not necessary to spell out the words, because the substance of it is beyond all doubt. They have found that by the form of the signatures to the letters which were written by Blenkarn, by the mode in which his letters and his applications to the Respondents were made out, and by the way in which he left uncorrected the mode and form in which, in turn, he was addressed by the Respondents; that by all those means he led, and intended to lead, the Respondents to believe, and they did believe, that the person with whom they were communicating was not Blenkarn, the dishonest and irresponsible man, but was a well known and solvent house of Blenkiron & Co, doing business in the same street. My Lords, those things are found as matters of fact, and they are placed beyond the range of dispute and controversy in the case.

If that is so, what is the consequence? It is that Blenkarn—the dishonest man, as I call him—was acting here just in the same way as if he had forged the signature of Blenkiron & Co, the respectable firm, to the applications for goods, and as if, when, in return, the goods were forwarded and letters were sent, accompanying them, he had intercepted the goods and intercepted the letters, and had taken possession of the goods, and of the letters which were addressed to, and intended for, not himself but, the firm of Blenkiron & Co. Now, my Lords, stating the matter shortly in that way, I ask the question, how is it possible to imagine that in that state of things any contract could have arisen between the Respondents and Blenkarn, the dishonest man? Of him they knew nothing, and of him they never thought. With him they never intended to deal. Their minds never, even for an instant of time rested upon him, and as between him and them there was no *consensus* of mind which could lead to any agreement or any contract whatever. As between him and them there was merely the one side to a contract, where, in order to produce a contract, two sides would be required. With the firm of Blenkiron & Co of course there was no contract, for as to them the matter was entirely unknown, and therefore the pretence of a contract was a failure.

The result, therefore, my Lords, is this, that your Lordships have not here to deal with one of those cases in which there is *de facto* a contract made which may afterwards be impeached and set aside, on the ground of fraud; but you have to deal with a case which ranges itself under a completely different chapter of law, the case namely in which a contract never comes into existence. My Lords, that being so, it is idle to talk of the property passing. The property remained, as it originally had been, the property of the Respondents, and the title which was attempted to be given to the Appellants was a title which could not be given to them....

[Lords Hatherley and Penzance delivered concurring opinions.]

Jerome v Bentley & Co

[1952] 2 All ER 114, Queen's Bench Division

Jerome entrusted a stranger, Major Tatham, with a diamond ring on terms that if he could sell it for more than £550 he could keep any surplus for himself, and that if he had not sold it within seven days he was to return it. Twelve days later, Tatham sold the ring for £175 to Bentleys, who bought in good faith thinking that he was the owner. After Bentleys had resold the ring, Jerome sued them in conversion and succeeded, on the ground that Tatham had had no authority to sell the ring to them.

Donovan J: Major Tatham belonged to no...well-known class of agent. He was simply a private individual, carrying on, so far as I know, no calling at all, to whom a ring had been entrusted for sale.... When Major Tatham sold the ring he was not the plaintiff's agent at all except, perhaps, for the purpose of safe custody of the ring. Major Tatham did more than exceed an authority to sell—he usurped it....

It is said here that the plaintiff gave Major Tatham the ring to sell, and if he put limitations on the authority, such as a period of seven days, he should have communicated that fact to any interested third party. I cannot help wondering how the plaintiff was to do this, for he did not know to whom out of the whole population Major Tatham would offer the ring.

[His Lordship referred to a number of cases, and continued:]

That brings me to the circumstances in which Major Tatham sold the ring, the subject of the present dispute. On Jan 11, 1947, his sole duty was to hand the ring back to the plaintiff, and he had no authority to deal with it in any way except for the purpose of its safe custody. He has admitted that he stole the ring as a bailee. In other words, when he entered the shop he intended fraudulently to convert the ring to his own use, and he accomplished that purpose. He then became a thief of the ring.... No one represented Major Tatham to the defendants as the plaintiff's agent with authority to sell the ring. The defendants knew nothing of the plaintiff. In fact, they made Major Tatham show his identity card and sign a declaration that the ring was his. So they dealt with him on the footing of a principal selling his own property.

It is said that, even on the footing that Major Tatham was a thief, the defendants are entitled to succeed on the dictum of Ashhurst J, in *Lickbarrow v Mason* [below, p 352]. Everything, however, depends on the construction to be put on the word 'enabled' in this passage. If I carelessly leave my front door unlocked so that a thief walks in and steals my silver, I have, in a sense, enabled him to steal it by not locking my door, but that does not prevent my recovering it from some innocent purchaser from the thief.... 'Enabled' in this context means the doing of something by one of the innocent parties which in fact misled the other. This is clearly to be deduced from Lord Lindley's speech in *Farquharson Bros & Co v King & Co* [below, p 356]. The plaintiff here did nothing which misled the defendants. In the circumstances I hold that no property in this ring passed to the defendants, and there is nothing to prevent the plaintiff from setting up his title as against them. Therefore, I decide in his favour.

Many of the exceptions to the *nemo dat* rule reflect a concern for the bona fide purchaser in a commercial transaction which is well put by Lord Denning in the following passage.

Bishopsgate Motor Finance Corpn Ltd v Transport Brakes Ltd

[1949] 1 KB 322, Court of Appeal

(The facts are immaterial.)

Denning LJ: In the development of our law, two principles have striven for mastery. The first is for the protection of property: no one can give a better title than he himself possesses. The second is for the protection of commercial transactions: the person who takes in good faith and for value without notice should get a good title. The first principle has held sway for a long time, but it has been modified by the common law itself and by statute so as to meet the needs of our own times.

2 FIRST EXCEPTION: ESTOPPEL

At the beginning of this discussion, only part of s 21(1) was quoted. In full, the subsection reads as follows:

Subject to this Act, where goods are sold by a person who is not their owner, and who does not sell them under the authority or with the consent of the owner, the buyer acquires no better title to the goods than the seller had, unless the owner of the goods is by his conduct precluded from denying the seller's authority to sell.

The word 'precluded' is more or less equivalent to 'estopped', which is perhaps a more familiar term for English lawyers. (Laymen and Scottish lawyers, however, will no doubt feel more at home with the word which the statute actually uses.) There are various ways in which the owner of goods might find himself 'precluded' from denying that he has given another person authority to sell them, but in essence this will be based either on (1) a representation to the buyer (or to the world at large) that that person (the person whom the Act calls 'the seller') is the owner's *agent* to sell the goods, or (2) a similar representation that the 'seller' is the *owner* of the goods. Most of the reported cases turn on the representation of an agency; and so there will necessarily be some overlap between the discussion in the present section and that in Chapter 5. There is also, at least in theory, the possibility that the owner may be in some way 'precluded' by his own negligence from denying the seller's authority to sell, but (as we shall see) this is largely an illusory concept.

At the outset, it is perhaps prudent to refer to the ancient dictum of Ashhurst J in *Lickbarrow v Mason* (1787) 2 Term Rep 63 at 70, which it is customary to cite in the present context. Ashhurst J said:

We may lay it down as a broad general principle that, wherever one of two innocent persons must suffer by the acts of a third, he who has enabled such third person to occasion the loss must sustain it.

This statement is notorious as having been frequently cited (not least in examination questions!), and rarely, if ever, applied: indeed, on the one occasion when it was followed without proper analysis (*Commonwealth Trust v Akotey*, below), the court almost certainly came to the wrong answer. The word 'enabled', if broadly construed, would allow a third party to defeat the claims of the true owner of goods in far too wide a range of circumstances. For instance, if A lent a book to B and B then dishonestly sold it to C, it would be hard to deny that A had 'enabled' B to deceive C into buying the book; but it is unthinkable that the law would allow the proprietary rights of A to be defeated in such circumstances. Similar considerations would apply in the case where A forgot to lock the door of his house and so made it easier for B to steal the book and then sell it to C (see *Jerome v Bentley*, above). So the dictum of Ashhurst J (which was in fact quite appropriate in the special context in which it was used) is nowadays cited largely for the purpose of discrediting it.

Commonwealth Trust v Akotey

[1926] AC 72, Privy Council

Akotey sent 1,050 bags of cocoa by rail to Laing, and sent him the consignment notes. He had previously sold cocoa to Laing, but on this occasion no agreement to sell had been concluded, Laing's offer of £2.50 a ton having been rejected as too low. Laing sold the cocoa to Commonwealth Trust, who bought in good faith. He handed over the consignment notes and was paid the price. Akotey claimed that the cocoa was still his, and sued Commonwealth Trust in conversion. The Privy Council, applying the dictum of Ashhurst J cited above, held that Akotey was estopped by his conduct from setting up his title.

The advice of the Privy Council was delivered by **Lord Shaw:**...It was further argued before their Lordships that although the property in the cocoa had not passed from the respondent, yet that the respondent had so acted as to estop him from setting up his title in answer to the claim of the appellants. Reliance was placed on the well-known statement of Ashhurst J in *Lickbarrow v Mason* [above], 'that wherever one of two innocent persons must suffer by the acts of a third, he who has enabled such third person to occasion the loss must sustain it.' Their Lordships are clearly of opinion that the present is a plain case for the application of that principle. There is no kind of specialty in this case such as occurred in *Farquharson Bros & Co v King & Co* [below, p 356], the parallel to which would be that the goods were delivered to Laing by the fraudulent act of respondent's agent: the goods were in fact delivered over to Laing by the direct act of the respondent himself.

To permit goods to go into the possession of another, with all the insignia of possession thereof and of apparent title, and to leave it open to go behind that possession so given and accompanied, and upset a purchase of the goods made for full value and in good faith, would bring confusion into mercantile transactions, and would be inconsistent with law and with the principles so frequently affirmed, following *Lickbarrow v Mason*.

QUESTION

Was there any significant respect in which the facts of this case were different from those in *Jerome v Bentley* (above)? If not, which decision better represents the law?

The owner of goods will lose his title to a third party (called in s 21(1) the 'buyer') if he has in some way *represented* (or 'held out') the truth of a fact or state of affairs which has led the buyer to believe that the seller is the owner of the goods or is authorised to deal with them on the owner's behalf, and the buyer has relied on this representation. Such a representation may be made by words or by conduct. A well-known case on estoppel by representation is *Eastern Distributors Ltd v Goldring*.

Eastern Distributors Ltd v Goldring

[1957] 2 QB 600, Court of Appeal

(The facts appear from the judgment.)

The judgment of the court (Lord Goddard CJ, Romer LJ and Devlin J) was read by **Devlin J:**...In 1955 the third party, Murphy, was in business, which he describes as that of a mobile greengrocer, and he owned a Bedford utility van which he used in the business and which is the subject-matter of this action. He wanted to buy a Chrysler car from a motor dealer called Coker, but he had no money to pay for it—not even enough for a deposit under a hire-purchase contract, so Coker suggested that he should raise the deposit on the security of the Bedford van by means of a hire-purchase contract on it. If the money was simply borrowed on the security of the van, the necessary instrument would be a bill of sale and would have to be registered as such. But there is nothing to prevent the owner of a vehicle from selling it to a hire-purchase company, pocketing the price and paying it back by instalments; and provided the sale is a genuine one and not a sham, effect will be given to it as a hire-purchase contract. Murphy would then be in a position to buy the Chrysler on hire-purchase terms, using the price of the Bedford to cover the deposit.

Coker was in touch with the plaintiffs, who are a hire-purchase company. The simplest way of carrying out the scheme, so far as it affected the Bedford, would have been for Murphy to have dealt direct with the plaintiffs, but Coker—perhaps because he wanted the deposit for the Chrysler to go straight to him or possibly for some other reason—suggested a different arrangement, and Murphy acquiesced in it. This was, that Coker should pretend to the plaintiffs that he was selling to Murphy the Bedford as well as the Chrysler. This involved also the pretence that Murphy had paid the deposit on both vehicles. Coker would then collect from the plaintiffs the balance of the price of both cars, which would in effect be the money for which he was selling the Chrysler to Murphy; and by paying off the instalments on both cars Murphy would pay the price of the Chrysler. In order to accomplish this plan, Murphy on May 5,1955, signed in blank four hire-purchase documents—namely, the proposal forms and the memoranda of agreement for the Chrysler and the Bedford respectively. He left these for Coker to fill in. He signed also on the same day a delivery note stating that he had taken delivery of the Bedford.

What happened afterwards is uncertain. Coker, whom the judge has found not to be fraudulent, was not available to give evidence. The records of the plaintiffs were in confusion owing to a change of ownership. The judge has found that the proposal for the Chrysler did not go through. Nevertheless, Coker proceeded with the proposal for the Bedford. He did this without Murphy's authority, for the essence of the scheme was that the Bedford transaction was only ancillary to the purchase of the Chrysler. The judge has found that the plaintiffs accepted the Bedford proposal as a genuine hire-purchase transaction and dealt with it accordingly. On May 10, 1955, the plaintiffs bought the Bedford from Coker, as recorded in a sales note, for £180 less an initial payment of £60. The memorandum of hire-purchase agreement was completed on May 19, and the counterpart signed by the plaintiffs was sent to Murphy the same day. Coker let Murphy have the Chrysler for a bit, but then it was taken away and Coker appears to have told Murphy that the whole transaction was cancelled. Murphy says that he regarded himself as the lawful owner of the Bedford. He advertised his greengrocery business for sale and on June 24, 1955, he sold it, including the Bedford, to the defendant for £200. It is not disputed that the defendant bought in good faith and without any knowledge of Murphy's dealings with the Bedford.

Murphy paid no instalments under the hire-purchase contract. On August 22, 1955, the plaintiffs notified him that they would take possession of the Bedford. Later they ascertained that the defendant had it, and in January, 1956, they claimed it from him. He refused to give it up and they issued proceedings against him in the St Albans County Court claiming the vehicle or £180 as its value. The defendant joined Murphy as third party. On January 31, 1957, judgment was given for the plaintiffs against the defendant and for the defendant against the third party. The defendant says that his judgment against the third party is worthless, and the plaintiffs have not even bothered to sue him. So the case raises the familiar question of which of two innocent parties, the plaintiffs or the defendant, shall suffer for the misconduct of a third; and it is necessary to determine which of the two is in law entitled to the Bedford van.

The plaintiffs depend for their title upon the transaction with Coker. If Coker had sold the van on behalf of Murphy and with his authority, that would dispose of the matter. So it would if Murphy had actually transferred the property to Coker so as to give him something which he could sell in his own name. But in fact Murphy never transferred the van to Coker; and although he gave a general author-ization to Coker to act in the way in which he did, he put, as the judge has found, a specific limitation upon Coker's authority and one which indeed followed from the nature of the transaction contem-plated: this was that the two proposals should go forward together. Coker, the judge has found, had no authority to deal with the Bedford separately from the Chrysler. So the plaintiffs cannot claim that they bought the van from the owner or from one who had his actual authority to sell.

But equally it is clear that as against Murphy the plaintiffs acquired a good title to the Bedford. Coker represented that the car was his, and Murphy was privy to that representation being made; so neither can be heard to say that Coker had not a good title to transfer to the plaintiffs. Or, if the matter be looked at as one of principal and agent, the plaintiffs, being ignorant of the limitation placed on Coker's authority, are not affected by it . . . .

[On the relationship between s 21 and the doctrine of estoppel, his Lordship said:]

Of course, there are many cases of sale of goods where an agent has been held out or represented to have an authority to sell which he has not in fact got, and the solution of the difficulty so created might no doubt have been found by the application of the doctrine of estoppel, but in fact the courts of common law approached the problem of the unauthorized sale from a different angle.

They began with the principle that no one could pass a better title than that which he had: nemo dat quod non habet. To this general principle they admitted a number of exceptions, simply on the ground of mercantile convenience. The best known relate to transfers of currency and negotiable instruments. Sales in market overt afford another example. In these cases, as is well known, a transferee may acquire a better title than that of his transferor. In the same way, and for the same reason of mercantile conveni-ence, the courts of common law allowed a good title to a buyer who bought in good faith from a man who apparently had been given by the true owner the right to dispose of the goods. Such a buyer did not merely acquire a title by estoppel, based on the implied representation by the owner that there was a right of disposition and vulnerable at the suit of anyone who was not bound by that representation. He acquired in the same way as the transferee of a negotiable instrument or the buyer in market overt a good title against all the world. . . .

[His Lordship quoted s 21(1), and continued:]

This section expresses the old principle that apparent authority to sell is an exception to the maxim nemo dat quod non habet; and it is plain from the wording that if the owner of the goods is precluded from denying authority, the buyer will in fact acquire a better title than the seller.

We doubt whether this principle, which is sometimes referred to—for example, by Wright J in *Lowther v Harris* [below, p 365]—as common law estoppel, ought really to be regarded as part of the law of es-toppel. At any rate it differs from what is sometimes called 'equitable estoppel' in this vital respect, that the effect of its application is to transfer a real title and not merely a metaphorical title by estoppel. It is unnecessary to determine in this case whether it covers the exercise of every sort of apparent authority in relation to the sale of goods or whether it is confined to apparent authority to sell. . . .

It is sufficient to say that, whatever the limits of the doctrine, it clearly applies to the facts of this case. Coker was armed by Murphy with documents which enabled him to represent to the plaintiffs that he was the owner of the Bedford car and had the right to sell it. The result is that Murphy is, in the words of s 21, precluded from denying Coker's authority to sell, and consequently the plaintiffs acquired the title to the goods which Murphy himself had and Murphy had no title left to pass to the defendant. . . .

NOTES

1. In this case, and also in *Farquharson Bros v King* (below), there is a reference to 'sales in market overt'. This ancient exception to the *nemo dat* principle has now been abolished: see below, p 375.

2.　This case may be contrasted with *Debs v Sibec Developments Ltd* [1990] RTR 91, where a Mercedes car had been stolen from Debs in the course of an armed robbery and he had been forced at gunpoint to sign a document purporting to show that he had sold the car to one of the robbers, Adnam, for cash. On the strength of this document the car was bought by an innocent third party and resold to Sibec. The court held that (a) no title could pass through Adnam, a thief (the *nemo dat* principle), and (b) the exception in s 21 did not apply because Debs had not 'represented' that Adnam had authority to sell the car (since only a representation voluntarily made would bring the matter within s 21), and he had not been negligent.

Very often, the estoppel which brings the exception to the *nemo dat* rule into play will be based on a representation (express or implied) that the 'seller' has the owner's *authority* to sell the goods as his *agent*.

Henderson & Co v Williams

[1895] 1 QB 521, Court of Appeal

(The facts appear from the judgment.)

Lindley LJ: In this case a Liverpool sugar merchant named Grey had 150 bags of sugar belonging to him warehoused in his name in the defendant's warehouse at Goole. On June 6, 1894, Grey was induced by the fraud of one Fletcher to authorize the defendant to hold these bags of sugar according to Fletcher's order. On the same day Fletcher agreed to sell them to the plaintiffs; but before the plaintiffs paid him for them they insisted on having them transferred into their own name. This was done on June 7, and the defendant informed the plaintiffs that he held the sugar at the plaintiffs' order and disposal. Thereupon the plaintiffs paid Fletcher for the goods. Grey afterwards discovered that he had been defrauded, and he gave notice to the defendant not to part with the bags of sugar. The defendant, being indemnified by Grey, has refused to deliver them to the plaintiffs, whereupon they bring this action to recover their value. The defendant defends this action for and on behalf of Grey....

　He contends—(1) that he is not estopped from setting up Grey's title; and (2) that his title is better than that of the plaintiffs. I am of opinion that the defendant is wrong upon the first point, even if he is right on the second. The distinct attornment by the defendant to the plaintiffs on June 7, 1894, clearly, in my opinion, estopped the defendant from denying the plaintiffs' title....

[Lord Halsbury LC and AL Smith LJ delivered concurring judgments.]

Henderson v Williams may be contrasted with *Farquharson Bros v King* (below). In the former, the representation as to Fletcher's authority was made directly by the owner of the sugar, Grey, to the warehouseman (his bailee), and pursuant to this the warehouseman was empowered by his attornment (see above, p 75) to inform the plaintiffs that the sugar was held at their disposal. But in the latter, there was no communication at all between Farquharsons and King & Co, either directly or through the dock company as intermediaries: indeed, King & Co thought that the timber they were buying belonged not to Farquharsons but to another firm called Bayley.

Farquharson Bros & Co v C King & Co

[1902] AC 325, House of Lords

Farquharsons were timber merchants who warehoused in the Surrey Commercial Docks timber which they imported from abroad. They employed a confidential clerk, Capon, who was authorised to sign delivery orders addressed to the dock company, on the strength of which timber would be released to Farquharsons' customers. In 1896, Capon began a series of frauds. Using the name Brown, and working from an address in Battersea, he entered into contracts to sell timber to the respondents, King & Co, representing that 'Brown' was acting as the agent of someone called Bayley. He then issued delivery orders to the dock company directing it to transfer the appropriate quantity of Farquharsons' timber to 'Brown' or deliver it to Brown's order. As 'Brown', he sent further orders to the dock company authorising it to deliver this timber to King & Co. After the frauds had been discovered, Farquharsons sued King & Co in conversion. The House of Lords held that nothing which Farquharsons had done precluded them from denying that Capon had had authority to sell their timber.

Lord Lindley: Capon sold the plaintiffs' timber without their authority, and sold it to the defendants. The defendants honestly bought the timber, and they had no notice that Capon had no right to sell it; but there was no sale in market overt, and the Factors Acts do not apply. The mere fact, therefore, that the defendants acted honestly does not confer upon them a good title as against the plaintiffs, the real owners of the timber. The plaintiffs are entitled to recover the timber or its value, unless they are precluded by their conduct from denying Capon's authority to sell. (Sale of Goods Act 1893, s 21, and see s [62].) Capon sold under the name of Brown, representing himself to be an agent of some persons named Bayley, who were well known in the timber trade. The defendants bought on the faith of his being what he pretended to be. What have the plaintiffs done which precludes them from denying, as against the defendants, Capon's right to do what he pretended he was entitled to do? Putting the question in another form: What have the plaintiffs done to preclude them from denying, as against the defendants, Capon's right to sell to them? To answer those questions it is necessary to consider what the plaintiffs did.

Capon was the plaintiffs' confidential clerk; they gave him a limited power of sale to certain customers, and a general written authority to sign delivery orders on their behalf; and the plaintiffs sent that written authority to the dock company which stored the plaintiffs' timber. This authority would, of course, protect the dock company in delivering timber as ordered by Capon, however fraudulently he might be acting, if the dock company had no notice of anything wrong. By abusing his authority Capon made timber belonging to the plaintiffs deliverable by the dock company to himself under the name of Brown. In that name he sold it, and procured it to be delivered to the defendants. What is there here which precludes the plaintiffs from denying Capon's right to sell to the defendants?

What have the plaintiffs done to mislead the defendants and to induce them to trust Capon? Absolutely nothing. The question for decision ought to be narrowed in this way, for it is in my opinion clear that, when s 21 of the Sale of Goods Act has to be applied to a particular case, the inquiry which has to be made is not a general inquiry as to the authority to sell, apart from all reference to the particular case, but an inquiry into the real or apparent authority of the seller to do that which the defendants say induced them to buy.

It was pointed out by Parke J, afterwards Lord Wensleydale, in *Dickson v Valpy* ((1829) 10 B & C 128, 140), that 'holding out to the world' is a loose expression; the 'holding out' must be to the particular individual who says he relied on it, or under such circumstances of publicity as to justify the inference that he knew of it and acted upon it. The same principle must be borne in mind in dealing with cases like the present. I do not myself see upon what ground a person can be precluded from denying as against another an authority which has never been given in fact, and which the other has never supposed to exist.

It was argued that the dock company were led by the plaintiffs to obey Capon's orders and to deliver to Brown, and that the defendants were induced by the dock company to deal with Brown, or at all events to pay him on the faith of his being entitled to the timber; so that in fact the plaintiffs, through the dock company, misled the defendants. This is ingenious but unsound. Except that delivery orders were sent in the name of Brown to the defendants, and were acted on by the dock company, there is no evidence connecting the dock company with the defendants in these transactions; and the answer to the contention is that the defendants were misled, not by what the plaintiffs did nor by what the plaintiffs authorized the dock company to do, but by Capon's frauds.

It is, of course, true that by employing Capon and trusting him as they did the plaintiffs enabled him to transfer the timber to any one; in other words, the plaintiffs in one sense enabled him to cheat both themselves and others. In that sense, every one who has a servant enables him to steal whatever is within his reach. But if the word 'enable' is used in this wide sense, it is clearly untrue to say, as Ashhurst J said in *Lickbarrow v Mason* [above, p 352], 'that wherever one of two innocent persons must suffer by the acts of a third, he who has enabled such third person to occasion the loss must sustain it.' Such a doctrine is far too wide; and the cases referred to in the argument . . . shew that it cannot be relied upon without considerable qualification. . . .

In the present case, in my view of it, Capon simply stole the plaintiff's goods and sold them to the defendants, and the defendants' title is not improved by the circumstance that the theft was the result of an ingenious fraud on the plaintiffs and on the defendants alike. The defendants were not in any way misled by any act of the plaintiffs on which they placed reliance; and the plaintiffs are not, therefore, precluded from denying Capon's authority to sell . . . .

[The Earl of Halsbury LC and Lords Macnaghten, Shand and Robertson delivered concurring opinions.]

In all of the cases discussed so far, there has been a representation, express or implied, on the part of the owner on which the alleged estoppel was based. It is usual to make a distinction between an *estoppel by representation* and an *estoppel by conduct,* although nothing in law appears to turn on this. Although s 21(1) itself uses the word 'conduct', it tells us nothing about the kinds of conduct (other than a representation) which might 'preclude' an owner from denying the 'seller's' authority to sell his goods. However, one point is well established. This is that for an owner merely to allow another person to have *possession* of his goods carries with it no implication that that person has any authority to sell them, even if the possession is given with a view to the person trying to find a buyer. This point is clearly illustrated by the case of *Jerome v Bentley* (above, p 351). In *Central Newbury Car Auctions Ltd v Unity Finance Ltd* (below), the same principle was applied in a case where the owner of a car had allowed a person to have possession not only of the car, but also of its registration certificate. It was held that the fact that the owner was allowed to arm himself with this document, as well as the car, made no difference, and that even though the owner might have acted negligently in not checking the identity and credentials of this person (see below, p 360), the position would be the same. Another case, *Mercantile Bank of India Ltd v Central Bank of India Ltd* [1938] AC 287, PC, confirms that to entrust another with possession of the *documents of title* to goods (in that case, railway receipts, which in Indian practice were treated as documents of title) can no more be relied on for the purposes of an estoppel than entrusting him with the goods themselves.

Central Newbury Car Auctions Ltd v Unity Finance Ltd
[1957] 1 QB 371, Court of Appeal

Central Newbury bought a Morris car at auction and put it on display in their showroom. Its registration book (now called a registration certificate) was in the name of a previous owner, Ashley. A distinguished-looking person calling himself Cullis agreed to take the car on hire-purchase and was allowed to take it away, together with the registration book. Three days later, a man calling himself Ashley (no doubt the same swindler who had previously called himself Cullis) sold the car to Mercury Motors, signing the transfer of ownership form on the registration book with the name of Ashley. Mercury Motors later sold the car to Unity Finance, who resisted a claim by Central Newbury to have it back. It was held that Mercury Motors were not precluded from denying the swindler's authority to sell.

Morris LJ: …Now it is clear that the person who purported to sell the Morris car to Mercury Motors was not the owner of the car and he did not sell it under the authority or with the consent of the owner. The suggestion is therefore that if possession of a car and of its registration book is given to someone who has no authority to sell, but who wrongly purports to sell, the true owner may lose his ownership. Perhaps, however, the suggestion is more limited and should be stated as being that if an owner negligently gives possession of a car and of its registration book to someone who has no authority to sell but who wrongly purports to sell, the true owner may lose his ownership. But the element of negligence so introduced involves and implies a duty to take care and to be circumspect in regard to one's own property. That in turn raises the question as to whom the duty is owed. So as to cover every potential purchaser it must therefore be asserted that the owner owes a duty to the whole world.

What is said in the present case is that the plaintiffs gave Cullis possession both of the car and of the registration book and were negligent in so doing: it is said, therefore, that because of their conduct in being negligent they are precluded from denying that Cullis had any authority to sell. In other words, it is said that they cannot be heard to say to the defendants that Cullis had no right to sell. Why? Not because they were deceived by Cullis into letting him have the car—but because they also let him have the registration book. This must involve that if A gives to B possession of A's car with its registration book, A cannot be heard to say that he has not given to B an 'authority to sell.' This proposition seems to me to be far-reaching and to involve giving to a registration book a significance which it does not possess.

When Cullis presented himself at Birkenhead he was a complete stranger to Mercury Motors. They accepted what he said to them. They believed that he was Mr Ashley, who was selling his own car. They, of course, did not know that the car belonged to the plaintiffs and had no sort of thought of the plaintiffs in their mind. There was no question of any kind of representation from the plaintiffs. Mercury Motors proceeded to buy because they were duped by Cullis. Cullis would not have had the registration book but for the decision of the plaintiffs to allow him to have it, but, so far as Mercury Motors were concerned, they merely had what Cullis said to them, coupled with the fact of his physical possession of the car and the registration book. If the plaintiffs are to be precluded from denying Cullis's authority to sell, it seems to me that it must be because of the mere circumstance that they gave possession of the book as well as the car to Cullis. If they had given the car and book to Cullis in circumstances which involved no criticism upon them and without any carelessness, the situation would have been exactly the same so far as Mercury Motors are concerned. Therefore, it seems to me that the plaintiffs should only lose their ownership or be precluded from asserting it if it can be said that by parting with their car and its registration book they endowed the possessor of these with an apparent authority to sell. The proposition must be that though no apparent authority to sell can be assumed from mere possession of a car, nor from mere possession of a car registration book, the possession of a car with its book carries an apparent authority to sell. If Mercury Motors can assume that Cullis had a right to sell because Cullis had the car and its book, then it seems immaterial whether the plaintiffs put Cullis into possession because they were deceived without any carelessness on their part or because they were deceived and were in some ways careless. It cannot be that ownership is lost on the basis of enduring punishment for carelessness. The improvident householder who has left a window open at night which gives easy access for a thief is not in a worse position in asserting ownership of stolen articles than is the cautious householder who has checked the secure closing of his house.

It is doubtless true that criticism, particularly when available in the light of after events and after acquired knowledge, can be levelled against the plaintiffs. But it hardly seems entirely appropriate that the criticism should come from the Birkenhead purchasers. Are the plaintiffs to be estopped by negligence while the purchasers may be negligent with impunity? Nor does it seem fitting to weigh in the balance the respective criticisms of the actions of the parties and to see in which direction the scales are tipped.…

[Denning and Hodson LJJ delivered concurring judgments.]

NOTE

The rogue in this case had agreed to take the car on hire-purchase; in other words, he was merely a hirer and had not agreed to buy it. In this latter case, a special statutory exception to the *nemo dat* rule could now be invoked (but only if the buyer is a 'private purchaser' (see below, p 390).

There are suggestions in a number of cases that, in addition to estoppel by representation and estoppel by conduct, it may be possible for an owner of goods to be precluded by his *negligence* from asserting his title against a third party. The concept of estoppel by negligence is not unknown in other parts of the law. For instance, in relation to negotiable instruments: a person who carelessly draws a cheque leaving spaces which allow the amount to be altered by a rogue from 'two pounds' to 'two hundred pounds' may be liable to a holder of the cheque for the latter amount. But—despite the many dicta—it is difficult to find any case which gives support to the view that this concept of estoppel by negligence has any really significant role to play in the law of sale of goods. In *Central Newbury Car Auctions Ltd v Unity Finance Ltd* (above), we saw that Morris LJ said: 'It cannot be that ownership is lost on the basis of enduring punishment for carelessness.'

It is clear from this and other cases (eg *Jerome v Bentley* (above, p 351)) that the courts are not prepared to find that an owner of goods owes a duty of care to the world in general which would be broken merely by entrusting possession of his goods to another, even if the circumstances are somewhat dubious. Recent trends in the law of tort in relation to liability for negligently caused economic loss give no encouragement to the view that we are likely to see much relaxation in this attitude.

And even where it is possible to argue that the owner owed a duty of care to a specific claimant, rather than to all the world, it seems that the courts show the same reluctance to hold that the owner's negligence should cause him to lose the title to his goods. There are still two further hurdles for the claimant to overcome: he must persuade the court (1) that the duty of care was broken, on the facts of the case, and (2) that this breach of duty was the effective cause of the claimant's action in entering into the transaction by which he claims to have acquired the goods. In the cases which are next cited, one or more of these arguments failed.

Mercantile Credit Co Ltd v Hamblin
[1965] 2 QB 242, Court of Appeal

The facts are somewhat similar to *Eastern Distributors Ltd v Goldring* (above, p 353). Mrs Hamblin wished to raise money on the security of her Jaguar car, and a car dealer called Phelan said that he could arrange for her to do this by selling the car to a finance company, Mercantile Credit, and taking it back from the company on hire purchase. He persuaded her to sign blank forms of a hire-purchase agreement with Mercantile Credit and other documents on the understanding that he would find out how much money could be raised and would report back to her before proceeding. In breach of the arrangement and without any authority from her he completed the blank forms and put the deal through and was paid £800 by the finance company. The Court of Appeal held that she was not estopped by negligence from claiming that the car still belonged to her.

Pearson LJ: In order to establish an estoppel by negligence, the finance company has to show (i) that the defendant owed it a duty to be careful, (ii) that in breach of that duty she was negligent, (iii) that her negligence was the proximate or real cause of it being induced to part with the £800 to the dealer.

A great many cases were cited in the argument, but to my mind the principal task is to find what situations or relationships may give rise to the duty to be careful....

In the present case, at the time when the defendant signed the documents in blank she was not then making a contract, but she was contemplating and contingently intending that she would eventually enter into a contract with some persons who would provide her with money on the security of the car. In fact the documents identified those persons as the finance company, but she had not read the documents: consequently, she did not have the finance company in contemplation, but she did contemplate that there would or might be some such persons with whom she would contract. She intended to make such a contract if and when the conditions were fulfilled, ie, if and when the amount and terms obtainable were reported to and agreed by her. She signed in blank the documents which would, if the conditions were fulfilled, constitute her offer to be accepted by the providers of the money, whoever they might be. She entrusted the documents to a dealer, who would be able, if so minded, to fill them in and present them to the providers of the money and secure their acceptance. She was arming the dealer with the means to make a contract ostensibly on her behalf. In my judgment, there was a sufficient relationship of proximity between the defendant and any persons who might contract to provide her with the money that she was seeking, to impose upon her a duty of care with regard to the preparation and custody of the contractual documents. The duty was owing to those persons, whoever they might eventually be found to be. They were in fact the finance company.

The next question is whether she committed any breach of duty, that is to say, whether she was negligent. On the peculiar facts of this case I think that there should not be a finding of negligence against her. She was well acquainted with the dealer, who was apparently respectable, solvent and prosperous, and the blank cheque which he gave her would naturally give her confidence that she could rely on his due performance of the arrangement which they had made.

Suppose, however, that she was negligent. There is then the question whether her negligence was the proximate or real cause of the finance company being induced to part with the money. In my judgment, the proximate or real cause was the fraud of the dealer. She gave him the means to commit his fraud, but his fraud was not, in the situation as it reasonably appeared to her, a natural or foreseeable consequence of what she did, and she should not be held responsible for it. I agree with the judge's finding on this point.

It follows that there is no estoppel by negligence, and no ostensible authority or holding out; the alleged hire-purchase agreement was invalid and not binding on the defendant; she has retained her ownership of the car; the finance company's claim fails, and the appeal should be dismissed....

Salmon LJ: No doubt as a general rule the doctrine of estoppel by negligence applies only to negotiable instruments. I am not, however, by any means persuaded that there are no exceptions to this rule.

If the defendant had known that the dealer was a rogue likely to obtain money by fraud on the strength of the documents, then, in my judgment, she would have owed a duty to the world, of whom the finance company was a part, not to leave the signed documents in the dealer's possession. Her negligence in doing so would have precluded her from denying the truth of any representations the documents contained and on which the finance company had acted to its detriment....

In the special circumstances of this case I do not consider that the defendant was careless in entrusting the dealer with the documents which she had signed in blank. After all, he was one of the most reputable car dealers in Nottingham and in a very large way of business. She could not reasonably foresee that he might use the documents for an improper purpose. She had every reason to trust him and none to doubt him. She left the forms which she had signed in blank with him, so that if she approved on the telephone of the terms and the amount of the loan he could obtain for her, he could immediately close the transaction for her without waiting for her to make the journey to his business premises in order to sign the documents. No doubt it is usually highly imprudent to sign documents in blank but it is not always so, and in the special circumstances of this case the defendant ought not to be blamed. This seems to me to dispose of the case against her....

[Sellers LJ delivered a concurring judgment.]

Moorgate Mercantile Co Ltd v Twitchings

[1977] AC 890, House of Lords

HP Information Ltd (HPI) maintained a register on which car dealers and finance companies recorded all motor-vehicle hire-purchase agreements that were notified to it by its members. At the time of the case, 98 per cent of all such hire-purchase agreements were on this record. The appellants and the respondents were both members of HPI. Moorgate had let a car on hire purchase to a man named McLorg, who then dishonestly sold it to Twitchings. By some error or oversight, Moorgate had failed to notify HPI that the car was on hire-purchase, and so when Twitchings made an inquiry HPI informed him that no hire-purchase agreement was recorded in respect of the car. Moorgate sued Twitchings claiming damages for conversion. Twitchings pleaded in reply that Moorgate were estopped by their negligence in having failed to notify the existence of the hire-purchase agreement; and alternatively they claimed to be entitled to set off the value of the car by way of damages in negligence. The House of Lords, by a majority, held that there was no estoppel, and no liability based on negligence.

Lord Fraser of Tullybelton: The conduct of Moorgate, by which it is said to be estopped from denying McLorg's authority to sell, is its omission to register with HPI its hire purchase agreement with him. That omission is said to have been negligent and is also the basis for the counterclaim of damages for negligence. So there is no practical difference as regards this case between the defence of estoppel by conduct and the counterclaim for damages; both depend upon establishing that Moorgate's omission to register the agreement was negligent. Negative conduct or omission will of course only be negligent, in the sense of wrongful, if there was a duty to act. If Twitchings are to succeed under either head they must therefore show (a) that Moorgate owed a duty to them to take reasonable care to register the agreement, (b) that Moorgate negligently failed to perform that duty, and (c) that their negligence was the proximate or real cause of Twitchings's loss. . . .

   The first question then is whether Moorgate was under such a duty to Twitchings. The mere fact that registering hire purchase agreements was a usual practice in the business of finance houses such as Moorgate will not by itself give rise to a duty on the part of Moorgate towards Twitchings to register its agreements: see *Mercantile Bank of India Ltd v Central Bank of India Ltd* [1938] AC 287, 304. The reason why it is said that the duty was owed is that both parties were members of, or subscribers to, the registration scheme operated through HPI Moorgate, as a finance house, was a full member of HPI and Twitchings, as dealers, was an affiliated member. At an earlier stage of the case it was contended on behalf of Twitchings that there had been a multi-lateral contract to which Moorgate and themselves had been parties, but that contention was not maintained in this House. The proposition here was that their common membership of the scheme created a relationship or propinquity between them which made them 'neighbours' in the sense of *Donoghue v Stevenson* [1932] AC 562, as extended by *Hedley Byrne & Co Ltd v Heller & Partners Ltd* [1964] AC 465, and so gave rise to the duty. If that proposition is right, it means that a finance house, by joining the registration scheme operated by HPI, subjected itself to a duty to other members including affiliated members, and perhaps to all users of the scheme, to take reasonable care to register all its hire purchase agreements with HPI.

[His Lordship examined the 'aims and objects' of HPI, and concluded:]

The primary purpose of the HPI scheme is, in my opinion, to provide protection to finance houses. But finance houses which are members of the scheme are under no obligation to anyone else to protect their own property by using the facilities of HPI. The owner of property is entitled to be careless with it if he likes, and even extreme carelessness with his own property will not preclude him from recovering it from a person who has bought it from someone who dishonestly purported to sell it: see *Farquharson*

Bros & Co v King & Co [above, p 356], and *Swan v North British Australasian Co Ltd* (1863) 2 H & C 175. In my opinion Moorgate's conduct in not registering the hire purchase agreement with McLorg was, at worst, careless in respect of Moorgate's own property, and it was not in breach of any duty to other parties. It was quite different from the kind of conduct considered in *Eastern Distributors Ltd v Goldring* [above, p 353], where the owner of a motor vehicle who had in effect armed a dishonest person with documents enabling him to represent himself as owner was held to be estopped from denying his authority to sell, and see also *Mercantile Credit Co Ltd v Hamblin* [above, p 360]. When Moorgate gave possession of its vehicle to McLorg on hire purchase terms, it was not doing anything of that sort. It is notorious that the person in possession of a motor vehicle is often not the owner of it, and the vehicle log book contains a warning that it is not proof of ownership of the vehicle. The very fact that dealers like Twitchings check with HPI before buying a vehicle from a stranger shows that they are well aware that possession and ownership may be separate. Accordingly, I am of opinion that when Moorgate, having given possession of their vehicle to McLorg under a hire purchase agreement, did not register the agreement with HPI, they were not in breach of any duty owed by them to Twitchings. Twitchings therefore fail to show the first of the three things that they have to establish if their defence is to be upheld. . . .

[Lords Edmund-Davies and Russell of Killowen delivered concurring opinions. Lords Wilberforce and Salmon dissented.]

NOTES

1. As appears from the remarks of Devlin J in *Eastern Distributors Ltd v Goldring*, quoted above, it is perhaps a misnomer to speak of the title conferred upon the buyer under the exception to s 21(1) as being based on an estoppel. Normally, the effect of an estoppel is limited to the two parties in question, and it is binding only on the person making the representation. But the title which the buyer acquires under this exception is a title good against third parties and not just against the representor—for example, he may sue a third party in tort for wrongful interference with the goods.

2. A curious point of construction was raised in *Shaw v Metropolitan Police Comr* [1987] 1 WLR 1332. It will be noted that s 21(1) uses the phrase 'where goods are *sold* . . .', and not some wider expression such as 'where there has been a contract to sell . . .'. The Court of Appeal held that the word 'sold' had to be read literally and that the 'estoppel' exception did not apply where there had been only an agreement to sell. Here an overseas student who was about to leave Britain for his home country had entrusted a rogue (calling himself 'Mr London') with possession of his Porsche car, and had signed papers which were certainly sufficient to preclude him from denying London's authority to sell. London delivered the car to the plaintiff, Shaw, pursuant to an agreement to sell it to him, and disappeared. Shaw claimed to be entitled to keep the car under the exception to s 21(1), but the Court of Appeal held that this was not the case because there had been no *sale* to him—only an agreement to sell.

3. A third kind of estoppel, 'estoppel by judgment', was in issue in *Powell v Wiltshire* [2004] EWCA Civ 534, [2005] QB 117. A person claiming to be the owner of goods may be precluded from denying another person's right to sell those goods (within s 21) if a court has already held, in separate proceedings, that the latter has the better title: he is not allowed to re-open the question of ownership. However, in the case itself the buyer had bought the goods (a light aircraft) *before* judgment was given in another case declaring that his seller was not the owner, and so the estoppel exception did not apply.

3 SECOND EXCEPTION: SALE UNDER THE FACTORS ACT 1889, s 2

The second exception to the *nemo dat* rule is alluded to in s 21(2)(a) of the Sale of Goods Act 1979, which declares that 'nothing in this Act affects the provisions of the Factors Acts or any enactment enabling the apparent owner of goods to dispose of them as if he were their true owner'.

There have been Factors Acts going as far back as 1823; the latest is the Factors Act 1889. One of the oddest things about these Acts is the word 'factor' itself, which has survived in the statutory title even though the term is not used in the Act itself and (in this sense) has dropped out of commercial usage. In modern business, the expression 'factoring' is used in a wholly unrelated technical sense (the assignment or discounting of book-debts) which is described in Chapter 21. There is also a fairly common practice of describing dealers in certain components or spare parts as 'factors'—eg 'motor factors', or 'electrical factors'. The Factors Acts, however, refer to the type of commercial agent described in Chapter 3, who typically handles the goods of his client (or alternatively documents of title relating to such goods) in the course of finding a buyer or seller for them: one everyday example is an auctioneer selling furniture or similar goods which are displayed prior to the sale in his showroom. (In this sense, the expression 'factor' is to be contrasted with 'broker', who is an agent who buys or sells without, as a rule, physically handling the property or documents: see above, p 104.) The statute uses the term 'mercantile agent' instead of the obsolete 'factor', and defines it as follows (Factors Act 1889, s 1(1)):

For the purposes of this Act the expression 'mercantile agent' shall mean a mercantile agent having in the customary course of his business as such agent authority either to sell goods or to consign goods for the purpose of sale, or to buy goods, or to raise money on the security of goods.

We can infer from this not very helpful definition that a mercantile agent must be someone who has a business, and who in the course of that business buys or sells goods for other people.

A more complete picture may be gained if we look also at s 2(1), which is the section of the Factors Act that contains the second of our exceptions to the *nemo dat* rule:

Where a mercantile agent is, with the consent of the owner, in possession of goods or of the documents of title to goods, any sale, pledge, or other disposition of the goods, made by him when acting in the ordinary course of business of a mercantile agent, shall, subject to the provisions of this Act, be as valid as if he were expressly authorised by the owner of the goods to make the same; provided that the person taking under the disposition acts in good faith, and has not at the time of the disposition notice that the person making the disposition has not authority to make the same.

It will thus be seen that the exception applies, broadly, where the mercantile agent has in the course of his business possession of the owner's goods for the purposes of sale, consistently with the traditional but now obsolete meaning of the word 'factor'.

The effect of the exception set out in s 2 is that in the special case where goods are in the possession of a mercantile agent, the ruling laid down in such cases as *Jerome v Bentley* (above, p 351) is reversed. Normally, as we have seen, the mere fact that S has possession of O's goods gives rise to no inference that S has O's authority to sell them to B, and if S has purported to make such a sale, O is not estopped from denying that S has such authority. The same rule applies where S has documents of title relating to the goods (*Mercantile Bank of India v Central Bank of India*, above, p 358). But if S is a *mercantile agent* and the other conditions of s 2(1) are satisfied, B is entitled to infer that S is acting with O's authority, and B will get a good title as against O. An example is *Weiner v Harris*.

Weiner v Harris

[1910] 1 KB 285, Court of Appeal

Weiner, a manufacturing jeweller, entrusted goods to Fisher as his agent for the purposes of sale. Fisher had a shop in Harrogate from which he sold jewellery, and he also travelled the country selling jewellery for other people. The case concerned certain items which Fisher had without Weiner's authority pledged with Harris, a Cardiff pawnbroker.

Cozens-Hardy MR: ... Then it is said that ... this case is not within the Factors Act. It is necessary for that purpose to refer only to ss 1 and 2. Section 1, sub-s 1, says 'For the purposes of this Act the expression "mercantile agent" shall mean a mercantile agent having in the customary course of his business as such agent authority either to sell goods'—that is the only part which is material. Then s 2, sub-s 1, says this: 'Where a mercantile agent is, with the consent of the owner, in possession of goods or of documents of title to goods, any sale, pledge, or other disposition of the goods, made by him when acting in the ordinary course of business of a mercantile agent, shall ... be valid.' Apply that first section. Many thousand pounds' worth of goods were handed over by Weiner to be dealt with on the footing of this letter. I am bound to say I cannot imagine a mercantile agent within the meaning of this section if Fisher was not. He was sent all over the country by Weiner for the very purpose of disposing of the goods upon the footing of the letter, and to say that his business was that of a shopkeeper is altogether irrelevant to any question we have to decide here.... In my opinion ... the defendant, having regard to the provisions of the Factors Act, has a perfectly good title to this pledge.

[Fletcher Moulton and Farwell LJJ delivered concurring judgments.]

A mercantile agent must, as we have seen, have a business. What sort of business? How much of a business? Is it possible to be a mercantile agent on a single occasion? After all, everyone intending to set up in business as a mercantile agent has to begin with his first transaction! The next two cases give an indication of the courts' approach to this question.

Lowther v Harris

[1927] 1 KB 393, King's Bench Division

Colonel Lowther kept furniture and antiques (including two valuable tapestries) stored in a house in Chelsea. Prior had a shop nearby from which he sold mainly glass and china. Lowther engaged Prior to seek buyers for the stored articles, but Prior was not authorised to sell anything without obtaining Lowther's approval. Customers were brought to the house to see the tapestries, and after one such visit Prior obtained Lowther's consent to remove one of the tapestries by falsely telling Lowther that he had sold it to Woodhall for £525. In fact, he had not sold the tapestry to anyone; but he later sold it to Harris for £250. Wright J held that Prior had been entrusted with possession of this tapestry as a mercantile agent, with the consequence that Harris obtained a good title under the Factors Act. (A claim in respect of the second tapestry which Prior had simply stolen and then sold to Harris failed, because it was held that Prior had never had possession of it with Lowther's consent.)

Wright J: ... Unless the defendant has a defence under the Factors Act 1889, or on the ground of common law estoppel, it is clear that he is liable in damages for conversion, which damages, if recoverable by the plaintiff, I fix at £350 in the case of the Aubusson tapestry, and at £270 in the case of the Leopard tapestry. The circumstances relating to the two pieces of tapestry are different and require separate consideration. I shall first deal with the Aubusson tapestry, and shall first consider the defence based on the Factors Act 1889, in order to ascertain if the conditions of the Act are fulfilled. The first question is whether Prior was a mercantile agent—that is, an agent doing a business in buying or selling, or both, having in the customary course of his business such authority to sell goods. I hold that he was. Various objections have been raised. It was contended that Prior was a mere servant or shopman, and had no independent status such as is essential to constitute a mercantile agent. It was held under the earlier Acts that the agent must not be a mere servant or shopman: *Cole v North Western Bank* ((1875) LR 10 CP 354, 372); *Lamb v Attenborough* ((1862) 1 B & S 831); *Hyman v Flewker* ((1863) 13 CBNS 519). I think this is still law under the present Act. In my opinion Prior, who had his own shops, and who gave receipts and took cheques in his own registered business name and earned commissions, was not a mere servant but an agent, even though his discretionary authority was limited. It is also contended that even if he were an agent he was acting as such for one principal only, the plaintiff, and that the Factors Act 1889, requires a general occupation as agent. This, I think, is erroneous. The contrary was decided under the old Acts in *Hyman v Flewker*, and I think the same is the law under the present Act. . . .

The next question is whether Prior was in possession of the Aubusson tapestry, and, if so, with the consent of the plaintiff, and, if he had such possession, whether it was in his capacity as mercantile agent. I add the last consideration because I think that, just as such a condition was imported in the old Factors Acts (see *Cole v North Western Bank* and cases there cited), the same condition must be satisfied under the Factors Act of 1889.

[His Lordship held that the tapestry had been in the possession of Lowther, and not Prior, while it was in the house. He continued:]

But I do hold that Prior became in possession of the Aubusson tapestry when he was allowed to take it away in the van after the plaintiff had sanctioned a sale to Woodhall. It is true that no such sale had in fact been made or was intended to be made, and that the possession was obtained by the fraud of Prior. Possession, however, was in fact obtained by Prior, and obtained by him in his capacity as mercantile agent. For the plaintiff it was contended that Prior obtained the tapestry under colour of an actually completed sale, and merely for purpose of delivery and as a sort of carrier between vendor and vendee. I think that is erroneous. Prior's functions as a mercantile agent were not completed even if a bargain had been concluded, but extended to the delivery of the goods, the collecting of the price, and the giving of a receipt and a subsequent accounting to the plaintiff. Delivery of possession to Prior was a necessary step to enable him to complete his office.

I accordingly hold that Prior obtained possession of the Aubusson tapestry in his capacity as a mercantile agent and with the consent of the plaintiff; having such possession, he made (as I have found above), in the ordinary course of business of a mercantile agent, a sale to the defendant, who, it is not contested, acted in good faith and with no notice of Prior's want of authority. I hold that the defendant establishes his defence as regards the Aubusson tapestry under the Factors Act 1889.

[His Lordship then dealt with the sale of the Leopard tapestry, and held that as to this the defence under the Factors Act 1889, failed, because Prior never had possession of it with the consent of the plaintiff, and therefore the conditions of the Act were not fulfilled. He held that as to this tapestry the plaintiff was entitled to recover.]

Budberg v Jerwood

(1934) 51 TLR 99, King's Bench Division

The Baroness Marie de Budberg had escaped from Russia in 1921, bringing with her a pearl necklace worth £600 which she had smuggled out of the country by concealing it in her mouth. In London she decided to sell it, and entrusted it to Dr Thadee de Wittchinsky, an eminent Russian lawyer who since the revolution had acted as a legal adviser to Russian refugees in England. Dr de Wittchinsky pawned the necklace for £50 without telling the Baroness, and kept the money. Later, he redeemed the pledge and sold the necklace to Jerwood, who bought in good faith. After the death of Dr de Wittchinsky, the true facts were discovered and the Baroness sued to recover her necklace. A plea that Dr de Wittchinsky had acted as a mercantile agent failed.

Macnaghten J in his judgment stated that: . . . a mercantile agent was a person who in the ordinary course of his business as such agent had authority to sell goods. Now, Dr de Wittchinsky was a doctor of laws, who, towards the end of his life, had a permanent residence in London and there carried on business as a lawyer advising Russians living in this country. None of the witnesses had treated him as having any other business than that of a lawyer. But it was suggested that he acted as a mercantile agent in this transaction. It was said that it was possible that a man could be a mercantile agent although he had only one customer. In support of that proposition the defendants cited *Lowther v Harris* (above). He accepted that proposition, but it was qualified to this extent, that the alleged agent must be acting in the particular transaction in a business capacity. Here it was clear that the relationship between the plaintiff and Dr de Wittchinsky was not a business relationship. There was no suggestion of remuneration, and he was acting merely as a friend. In those circumstances the Factors Act did not apply. . . .

For s 2(1) to apply, all the conditions specified in the section must, of course, be satisfied. It is best to take the key phrases one by one, since many of them have been the subject of judicial consideration.

(a) 'Where a mercantile agent is, *with the consent of the owner,* in possession of goods . . .'

This requirement of consent is amplified by sub-ss (2) and (3) of s 2. These provisions state respectively that (1) where the owner has once given consent to the mercantile agent having possession, that consent is deemed to continue even although it has been determined, unless the person dealing with the agent has notice of the determination; and (2) a consent to possession of goods carries with it a deemed consent to the possession of any documents of title relating to the goods which the agent has obtained by reason of his having or having had possession of the goods.

The cases establish that it is not sufficient that the owner should have consented to the agent having possession: he must consent to his having possession *in his capacity as mercantile agent.* The older Factors Acts used the word 'intrusted'; and the essential idea is that this 'intrusting' should be with a view to a sale, or a possible sale, by the agent—that is, for a purpose connected with his business as a selling agent. However, the courts have taken a fairly broad approach to this question, as Denning LJ explained in the following extract:

Pearson v Rose & Young Ltd

[1951] 1 KB 275, Court of Appeal

(The facts are irrelevant.)

Denning LJ: In the early days of the common law the governing principle of our law of property was that no person could give a better title than he himself had. But the needs of commerce have led to a progressive modification of this principle so as to protect innocent purchasers. We have had cases in this court quite recently about sales in market overt and sales by a sheriff; and now we have the present case about sales by a mercantile agent. The cases show how difficult it is to strike the right balance between the claims of true owners and the claims of innocent purchasers. The way that Parliament has done it in the case of mercantile agents is this: Parliament has protected the true owner by making it clear that he does not lose his right to goods when they are taken from him without his consent, as for instance when they have been stolen from his house by a burglar who has handed them over to a mercantile agent. The true owner can in that case claim them back from any person into whose hands they came, even from an innocent purchaser who has bought from a mercantile agent. But Parliament has not protected the true owner, if he has himself consented to a mercantile agent having possession of them: because, by leaving them in the agent's possession, he has clothed the agent with apparent authority to sell them; and he should not therefore be allowed to claim them back from an innocent purchaser.

   The critical question, therefore, in every case is whether the true owner consented to the mercantile agent having possession of the goods. This is often a very difficult question to decide....

   If the true owner consents to the mercantile agent having the goods for repair but not for sale, is that a consent which enables the Factors Act to operate? The answer would seem at first sight to be 'Yes', because it is undoubtedly a consent to the agent having possession. But this needs testing. Suppose, for instance, that the owner of furniture leaves it with a repairer for repair, and that the repairer happens to be a dealer as well, does that mean that the repairer can deprive the true owner of his goods by selling them to a buyer? Clearly not, if the owner did not know the repairer to be a dealer; and even if he did, why should that incidental knowledge deprive the true owner of his goods? Such considerations have led the courts to the conclusion that the consent, which is to enable the Factors Act 1889, to operate, must be a consent to the possession of the goods by a mercantile agent as mercantile agent That means that the owner must consent to the agent having them for a purpose which is in some way or other connected with his business as a mercantile agent. It may not actually be for sale. It may be for display or to get offers, or merely to put in his showroom; but there must be a consent to something of that kind before the owner can be deprived of his goods.

[Somervell LJ and Vaisey J delivered concurring judgments.]

This point, which was also emphasised in *Lowther v Harris* (above), is confirmed by the following cases.

Staffs Motor Guarantee Ltd v British Wagon Co Ltd

[1934] 2 KB 305, King's Bench Division

Heap was a mercantile agent who dealt in second-hand lorries. He had in his possession a six-ton Commer lorry which he had once owned, but had sold to British Wagon and then taken back on hire-purchase. Without authority from British Wagon, he later sold it to Staffs Motor. When Heap failed to keep up his hire-purchase payments, British Wagon repossessed the lorry. Staffs Motor in this action claimed that this action was a violation of their rights as owners, arguing that their purchase from Heap had given them a good title under s 2 of the Factors Act 1889. The Court of Appeal rejected this claim, on the ground that Heap's possession had been qua hirer under the hire-purchase agreement, and not qua mercantile agent.

MacKinnon J: ...The plaintiffs say that the defendants entrusted the possession of the lorry to Heap, who was a mercantile agent for the sale of second-hand lorries, and that they, the plaintiffs, in good faith and without any notice of his want of authority, entered into a contract with him for the purchase of the lorry, and, therefore, they claim that they have a good title to the lorry as against the defendants pursuant to the provisions of that section. There was no doubt some evidence that Heap did deal in second-hand motor vehicles as an ordinary seller of them. I will suppose that, if an ordinary owner of a motor-car had brought his car to Heap and asked him to sell it for him and Heap had sold it to some one at a lower price than that authorized by the true owner or otherwise not in accordance with his instructions, the purchaser from Heap would be entitled under the section which I have quoted to claim as against the true owner. I think, however, that it has rightly been pointed out on behalf of the defendants that there would be this difficulty in the way of the plaintiffs' assertion of that claim, that if the transaction between the defendants and Heap was a genuine transaction—and the plaintiffs' claim in this respect arises on that basis—then the lorry had been sold by Heap to the defendants and had been entrusted by the defendants to Heap not as a mercantile agent dealing in or selling motor vehicles, but to Heap as a hirer of the [lorry] and therefore as its bailee. In these circumstances I do not think that it is open to the plaintiffs to say that the defendants entrusted the [lorry] to Heap as a mercantile agent....

Because one happens to entrust his goods to a man who is in other respects a mercantile agent, but with whom he is dealing not as a mercantile agent but in a different capacity, I do not think that it is open to a third party who buys the goods from that man to say that they were in his possession as a mercantile agent and that therefore he had power to sell them to a purchaser and so give him a good title to them. The claimant must be able to assert not only that the goods were in the man's possession as a mercantile agent, but also that they were entrusted by the owner to him as a mercantile agent....

[MacKinnon J also thought that similar reasoning applied to a claim based on s 25(1) of the Sale of Goods Act 1893 [SGA 1979, s 24], but on this point his judgment has since been overruled: see below, p 378.]

Astley Industrial Trust Ltd v Miller

[1968] 2 All ER 36, Queen's Bench Division

This decision is primarily of importance because it confirmed the authority of the above line of cases even although another ground of decision in the *Staffs Motor* case had since been overruled, as mentioned above. A firm called Droylesden had two businesses: hiring out cars, and dealing in cars. It did not own its hire cars, but took them on hire-purchase from Astley through a dealer called Lomas. Droylesden acquired a new Vauxhall car on hire-purchase from Astley to put into its rental fleet, and the following day, without authority from Astley, sold it to Miller, who bought in good faith. It was held that since Droylesden had possession of the car qua hire-purchaser and not qua motor dealer, s 2 of the Factors Act 1889 did not apply to the transaction, and in consequence Miller was bound to return the car to Astley or pay its value.

Chapman J: ...It is plain on the facts as I have found them: (a) that at the material time the car in question was in the possession of Droylesden, who were not then the true owners; (b) that this possession by Droylesden was with the consent of the true owner, Lomas; (c) that Droylesden were persons who were, albeit as a sideline and as a subsidiary to their main business of hire car operators, trading as motor dealers in the sense that they bought and sold cars, at any rate on the second-hand market.

Counsel for the defendant has contended that, if these three conditions are satisfied, the situation is that a person who is in fact a mercantile agent, and who has in fact possession of someone else's property with the consent of that someone else, is clothed with ostensible or apparent authority to make any sale, pledge or other disposition of it which may appeal to his lust for pecuniary gain or his urge to perpetrate a fraud. Counsel for the plaintiffs, on the other hand, has contended that there is inherent in the statutory language a fourth condition, namely, that the goods must have been entrusted by the true owner or with his permission to the mercantile agent in his capacity as a mercantile agent; unless this is so, there is, he contends, no basis for saying that the true owner has clothed the mercantile agent with authority to act in that capacity. Counsel for the defendant has disputed this interpretation of the statute on the basis that it involves reading into the statute words which are not there.

Of course, one must always construe the words of an Act of Parliament strictly; that is, with precision. This is particularly true when questions of title are concerned and especially when the title is that of a completely honest, respectable and blameless person. The meaning of words, however, does not always end at the minimal dictionary content of each word taken as a separate entity, and this is as true of words in a section of an Act of Parliament as of words in a passage of verse or poetry. Counsel for the defendant's construction would, for example, lead to this result: if I take my car into the local garage to have a puncture repaired, or to be greased, or to have a general check-up before going on holiday, I would be at the risk of the garage not only purporting to sell it, but actually passing good title if, besides carrying out repairs and servicing for customers, they professed the business of buying and selling motor cars (whether second-hand or new). This would seem a startling conclusion. Or to go further to extremes: if my next-door neighbour (being in fact a motor dealer) came to me and said, 'My car has to go into dock for a fortnight. You are going on a cruise for your holidays. Would you, as a friend, lend me your car while you are away?' If, as one neighbour to another, I yielded to his importunity, I would, according to counsel's argument, be at risk of losing my car, merely because he happened to be a motor dealer, if he decided to flog it to some fly-by-night. At such a conclusion one's commonsense revolts.

The authorities seem to be all one way on this point, namely, in favour of counsel for the plaintiffs' argument and against counsel for the defendant.

[His Lordship referred to a number of cases, and continued:]

Counsel for the defendant has contended that this formidable body of authority has all been swept away by *Pacific Motor Auctions Pty Ltd v Motor Credits (Hire Finance) Ltd* (below, p 379). That case dealt with s 28(1) of the Sale of Goods Act 1923–1953, of New South Wales, which covers cases where a person, having sold goods, continues in possession of the goods. That is the equivalent of s 25(1) of our Sale of Goods Act 1893 [now s 24 of the Act of 1979]. The Privy Council, in a judgment delivered by Lord Pearce, held that the continuity of possession required by the section was continuity of a physical possession, and that it did not matter if, by a private transaction, there was a change in the legal nature of the possession, eg from possession of a seller, paid or unpaid, to possession of a bailee under a hire-purchase agreement. In so holding, the Privy Council expressly dissented from the view expressed by MacKinnon J, in *Staffs Motor Guarantee Ltd v British Wagon Co Ltd* [above]. . . . But this view of MacKinnon J, as to the effect of s 25(1) of the Sale of Goods Act 1893, is entirely separate and distinct from the view expressed by the same judge in the same case on the effect of s 2(1) of the Factors Act 1889. On the Sale of Goods Act point, the learned judge has been overruled, but I find nothing in the *Pacific Motor Auctions* case to suggest that the learned judge's point of view on the Factors Act point has been in any way eroded. . . .

Accordingly, I take it to be well settled and unchallenged law that the statutory power to pass title which is vested in a mercantile agent depends on his having possession in his capacity as a mercantile agent and on the true owner having consented to his having possession in that capacity. In the present case, on the facts as I have found them, Droylesden did not have possession of the Vauxhall in their capacity as mercantile agents, nor did Lomas consent to their having possession in that capacity. Droylesden, therefore, had no power to pass title to anybody.

The consent of the owner for the purposes of applying s 2 is regarded as having been given even though it has been obtained by deception.

Folkes v King
[1923] 1 KB 282, Court of Appeal

Folkes entrusted his Austin touring car to Hudson, a mercantile agent, with a view to sale, but on the express understanding that the car would not be sold for less than £575 without Folkes's permission. Hudson dishonestly sold the car at once to Alvarez, who bought in good faith, for £340 and, after several further sales, it was eventually bought by King. Folkes sued King for the return of the car, but his claim was held barred by s 2 of the Factors Act 1889. The main issue in the case turned on the now-obsolete distinction in the criminal law between 'obtaining by false pretences' and 'larceny by a trick'. Older cases had held that there was 'consent' for the purposes of s 2 in the former case, but no 'consent' in the latter. In this case, the Court of Appeal ruled that the distinction was immaterial, and that there was 'consent' in both situations.

Scrutton LJ: ...First on the question whether to prove larceny by a trick is a defence to the Factors Act as excluding consent of the true owner. I can understand that where by a trick there is error in the person there is no true consent and the Factors Act is excluded. But where there is agreement on the person and the true owner intends to give him possession, it does not seem to me that the fact that the person apparently agreeing to accept an agency really means to disregard the agency, and act for his own benefit, destroys the consent of the true owner under the Factors Act. That Act intended to protect a purchaser in good faith carrying out an ordinary mercantile transaction with a person in the position of a mercantile agent. It does not do so completely, for it requires the purchaser to prove that the goods were in possession of the mercantile agent 'with the consent of the owner.' But it does not require the purchaser in addition to prove that the mercantile agent agreed both openly and secretly, ostensibly and really, to the terms on which the owner transferred possession to the mercantile agent. It appears to me to be enough to show that the true owner did intentionally deposit in the hands of the mercantile agent the goods in question. It is admitted that if he was induced to deposit the goods by a fraudulent misrepresentation as to external facts, he has yet consented to give possession, and the Factors Act applies, but it is argued that if he deposits the goods in the possession of an agent who secretly intends to break his contract of agency the Factors Act does not apply. I do not think Parliament had any intention of applying the artificial distinctions of the criminal law to a commercial transaction, defeating it if there were larceny by a trick, but not if there were only larceny by a bailee, or possession obtained by false pretences.

[Bankes LJ and Eve J delivered concurring judgments.]

NOTES

1.   Compare *Lowther v Harris* (above), and also *Du Jardin v Beadman Bros Ltd* [1952] 2 QB 712, where a similar interpretation was given to the expression 'consent of the seller' in s 25(1) of the Sale of Goods Act 1979 (discussed below, p 381).

2.   It is still conceivable that a court would hold that a consent obtained by fraud might amount to no consent at all, if the circumstances were such as to make the owner the victim

of a material mistake of identity, as in such contract cases as *Cundy* v *Lindsay* (above, p 349) and *Ingram* v *Little* [1961] 1 QB 31, CA. In *Folkes* v *King* (above), Scrutton LJ said ([1923] 1 KB 282 at 305): 'I can understand that where by a trick there is error in the person there is no true consent and the Factors Act is excluded.' Compare *Shogun Finance Ltd* v *Hudson* (below, p 391) and *Debs* v *Sibec Developments Ltd* (above, p 356) (duress).

3.   In *Beverley Acceptances Ltd* v *Oakley* [1982] RTR 417, CA it was held that the 'possession' and the 'disposition' referred to in s 2(1) had to be contemporaneous: it was not sufficient that the person in question had once had possession qua mercantile agent but had lost it prior to the purported disposition.

4.   In two cases, the court seems to have put a rather strained interpretation on the wording of s 2 out of indulgence for a car-owner who had been defrauded by a dishonest dealer. In each case the car had been delivered to a dealer with instructions to obtain offers, but with no authority to sell. The dealer had, however, sold the car to a purchaser in circumstances which would have been covered by s 2 but for the fact that the dealer had got possession of the car's registration certificate without the owner's consent. In the first, *Pearson* v *Rose & Young Ltd* [1951] 1 KB 275, CA the registration certificate had been unintentionally left with the dealer when the owner was called away on an errand of mercy; in the second, *Stadium Finance Ltd* v *Robbins* [1962] 2 QB 664, CA the owner had retained the ignition key, but the dealer had used a duplicate key and opened the glove-box where the registration certificate had been locked away. The court in each case seized on the fact that there was no consent to the dealer having possession of the registration certificate and found for the owner, in *Pearson* on the ground that 'the goods' in s 2 meant the car *with* its registration certificate, and the owner had not consented to the dealer having possession of the latter; in *Stadium Finance* on the rather narrower ground that the sale of the car having been made (to a finance company with a view to letting it to a customer on hire-purchase) without either the ignition key or the registration certificate, was not a sale 'in the ordinary course of business'.

QUESTION

Mary entrusts her car to Jock, a back-street car dealer, with instructions not to sell it for less than £4,000. Jock has induced Mary to do so by telling her that he is Jake, a well-known and reputable dealer with showrooms in the High Street. Jock at once sells the car for £3,000 to Lucy, who buys in good faith. Advise Mary.

(b) 'When acting in the ordinary course of business as a mercantile agent'

This phrase was explained by Buckley LJ in *Oppenheimer* v *Attenborough & Son* [1908] 1 KB 221 at 230–231 as follows:

I think it means, 'acting in such a way as a mercantile agent acting in the ordinary course of business of a mercantile agent would act'; that is to say, within business hours, at a proper place of business, and in other respects in the ordinary way in which a mercantile agent would act, so that there is nothing to lead the [buyer] to suppose that anything wrong is being done, or to give him notice that the disposition is one which the mercantile agent had no authority to make.

In *Stadium Finance Ltd* v *Robbins* (above), we saw that the sale of a vehicle without an ignition key or registration certificate might be regarded as not being within the ordinary course of business. This would, of course, depend upon the circumstances: a car might quite properly be sold at a time when the registration certificate had been sent to the authorities (eg to have a change of address recorded).

NOTE

Oppenheimer v *Attenborough & Son* (above) was, in fact, a case where the mercantile agent had *pledged* the goods, and in the extract which has been quoted the word 'pledgee' occurs where we have substituted the word 'buyer'. This case serves as a timely reminder that s 2 of the Factors Act 1889 does, in fact, apply to pledges and other dispositions of goods by a mercantile agent, as well as to sales; and we may note also that it is sufficient that the mercantile agent has possession of the *documents of title* to the goods, and not necessarily of the goods themselves.

QUESTIONS

1. In *Pearson v Rose & Young Ltd* (above), Vaisey J expressed the view that the sale by a mercantile agent of a car with only three wheels would not be a sale in the ordinary course of business. Do you agree?

2. Consider the facts of *Pacific Motor Auctions Pty Ltd v Motor Credits (Hire Finance) Ltd* (below, p 379). Could the buyers in that case have relied on s 2 of the Factors Act (or its Australian equivalent)?

(c) 'Provided that the person taking under the disposition acts in good faith, and has not at the time of the disposition notice that the person making the disposition has not authority to make the same'

The onus of proof on these issues lies upon the buyer: *Heap* v *Motorists' Advisory Agency Ltd* (below). The requirement that the buyer should act in good faith and without notice of any irregularity is closely tied up with the 'ordinary course of business' point which we have just discussed, for any departure from the ordinary course of business may well put the buyer on notice that the circumstances are suspicious.

Heap v Motorists' Advisory Agency Ltd
[1923] 1 KB 577, King's Bench Division

A rogue called North (who was assumed for the purpose of the present question to have been a mercantile agent) obtained possession of Heap's Citroen car, which was worth about £210, and sold it without Heap's authority to the defendants for the very low price of £110. North did not effect the sale himself, but ('apparently for reasons of prudence') used a friend, Cory, to do so. Lush J held that the onus was on the defendants to prove that they had acted in good faith and without notice of the want of authority, and that they had failed to do so, so that s 2 did not protect the defendants.

Lush J: Under s 2 of the Factors Act 1889, however, the buyer gets no title apart from the section. He is allowed to get what I may call a statutory title provided he complies with the terms of the section.

In order to acquire a title which he would not otherwise have, the buyer has to prove all these things that I have mentioned: that the owner consented to the mercantile agent having possession, that the agent acted in the ordinary course of business, and also, I think, that the buyer acted in good faith and had no notice.

If the onus is on the defendants, they have certainly failed to satisfy me that they had no notice that the person selling the car, that is North, had no authority to sell. Indeed, I think that, for this purpose, wherever the onus rests, the defendants must be taken to have had notice. To begin with, the car appears to have been bought considerably under value, though I do not say that the undervalue was so great as to show actual dishonesty. The defendants have endeavoured to prove that it would have cost them £50 or £60 to put it right, and that must no doubt be taken into account; but to my mind it would not have cost them more than £10 or £12, an outlay which would have left the car a remarkably cheap one for the defendants. Another peculiar circumstance was that North did not himself come to the defendants about the car, but got Cory to sell it to them. The defendants admit that they were a little suspicious, and made a point of not buying the car from North but from Cory, whom they knew. Neither North nor Cory produced the registration book, and the defendant never asked for it, though the whole object of registration is to facilitate transfers of cars and enable people to know who owns the car. Another circumstance which I cannot overlook is that after the defendants had given a crossed cheque to Cory he came back and asked for an open cheque because, according to him, North had no banking account near at hand and he wanted the money at once, and the defendants then allowed their cashier to cancel the crossed cheque and give an open cheque. All these circumstances were, in my opinion, enough to put the defendants on their guard and to fix them with notice. I do not say that they wickedly shut their eyes to an obvious fraud, but I do say that they did not do what any reasonable man would have done in this case—namely, decline to buy this car without knowing more about it. They thought it was a good bargain and made up their minds too easily to buy the car. I think they must be taken to have had notice of some want of authority in those who purported to sell it to them. Their manager told me in evidence that he felt rather uncomfortable and suspicious about the sale. In my view the defendants ought not in the circumstances to have bought the car.

The result is that all the defences fail, and I therefore give judgment for the plaintiff for the return of the car or its value with costs.

4 THIRD EXCEPTION: SALE UNDER POWER OF SALE OR COURT ORDER

Section 21(2)(b) of the Sale of Goods Act states that the provisions of the Act do not affect the validity of any contract of sale under any special common law or statutory power of sale or under the order of a court of competent jurisdiction.

It is not necessary to list at length the various situations where a sale of goods may be effected without the authority of the owner under the powers referred to in this provision. It is sufficient to cite a few examples.

Goods may be sold under common law powers by a pledgee: *Re Hardwick, ex p Hubbard* (see below, p 1103) and by an agent of necessity (see above, p 133).

There are many statutory provisions which confer a power of sale, eg upon an unpaid seller of goods (below, p 446), a bailee of uncollected goods (below, p 1118), a landlord who has distrained upon his tenant's goods, and a sheriff who has seized goods under a writ of execution.

In addition, the court may order a sale of goods, either under its inherent powers (eg to enforce a charge) or pursuant to the rules of court (eg to dispose of goods which are perishable or likely to deteriorate); and it may do this even against the wishes of the owner: *Larner v Fawcett* [1950] 2 All ER 727.

5 FOURTH EXCEPTION: SALE IN MARKET OVERT (NOW REPEALED)

Section 22 formerly provided another exception to the *nemo dat* rule: that where goods were sold in 'market overt', according to the usage of the market, a buyer who took in good faith and without notice of any defect or want of title on the part of the seller acquired a good title to the goods. This exception applied only where the market in question was an open, established public market constituted by law or custom—a limitation which excluded many well-known markets. The market overt rule had come to be regarded as archaic and quaint (as indicated by the fact that the leading case was decided in 1596!), and had attracted criticism because it facilitated, and perhaps even encouraged, trafficking in stolen goods. It was abolished by the Sale of Goods (Amendment) Act 1994.

6 FIFTH EXCEPTION: SALE UNDER A VOIDABLE TITLE

Section 23 of the Act confirms the well-known common law rule that where the seller of goods has a voidable title to them, and the title has not been avoided at the time of the sale, the buyer acquires a good title provided that he buys in good faith and without notice of the seller's defect of title. A similar rule applies to pledges of goods.

The commonest case in which a seller will have a voidable title is where he has obtained the goods under a contract induced by misrepresentation (whether fraudulent or innocent). But a contract may also be voidable on other grounds, such as undue influence, duress, and drunkenness.

A voidable transaction must be distinguished from one which is wholly void, eg on the ground of mistake of identity: contrast *Cundy* v *Lindsay* (above, p 349) with *Lewis* v *Averay*, below.

Lewis v Averay
[1972] 1 QB 198, Court of Appeal

Lewis, in Bristol, advertised his Austin Cooper car for sale in a newspaper and agreed to sell it for £450 to a man calling himself Greene, who claimed to be a well-known actor, Richard Greene, and showed a Pinewood Studio pass as evidence of this identity. The rogue 'Greene' was allowed to take the car away in exchange for a cheque which later proved to be worthless. Three days later the rogue sold the car for £200 to Averay, a music student living in London, who bought in good faith. The Court of Appeal held that the first sale was voidable for fraud, but not void for mistake of identity, with the result that Averay got a good title.

Phillimore LJ: . . . I think the law was conveniently stated by Pearce LJ in the course of his judgment in *Ingram v Little* [1961] 1 QB 31 to which reference has already been made. He said, at p 61:

> Each case must be decided on its own facts. The question in such cases is this. Has it been suffi-
> ciently shown in the particular circumstances that, contrary to the prima facie presumption—and I
> would emphasise those words—a party was not contracting with the physical person to whom he
> uttered the offer, but with another individual whom (as the other party ought to have understood)
> he believed to be the physical person present. The answer to that question is a finding of fact.

Now, in that particular case the Court of Appeal, by a majority and in the very special and unusual facts of the case, decided that it had been sufficiently shown in the particular circumstances that, contrary to the prima facie presumption, the lady who was selling the motor car was not dealing with the person actually present. But in the present case I am bound to say that I do not think there was anything which could displace the prima facie presumption that Mr Lewis was dealing with the gentleman present there in the flat—the rogue. It seems to me that when, at the conclusion of the transaction, the car was handed over, the logbook was handed over, the cheque was accepted, and the receipts were given, it is really impossible to say that a contract had not been made. I think this case really is on all fours with *Phillips* v *Brooks* ([1919] 2 KB 243), which has been good law for over 50 years. True, the contract was induced by fraud, and Mr Lewis, when he discovered that he had been defrauded, was entitled to avoid it; but in the meanwhile the rogue had parted with the property in this motor car which he had obtained to Mr Averay, who bought it bona fide without any notice of the fraud, and accordingly he thereby, as I think, acquired a good title.

[Lord Denning MR and Megaw LJ delivered concurring judgments.]

The claim of a buyer who relies on s 23 will be defeated if, before he makes his purchase, the original owner has validly exercised his right to avoid the first transaction. This is normally done by giving notice to the other party, or by retaking possession of the goods. However, in *Car & Universal Finance Co Ltd v Caldwell* it was held that, at least in exceptional circumstances such as occurred in that case, some other action on the owner's part might be sufficient to evince an intention to rescind.

Car & Universal Finance Co Ltd v Caldwell
[1965] 1 QB 525, Court of Appeal

Caldwell was induced to sell his Jaguar car to Norris by fraud. Norris took the car away and sold it to a company called Motobella. After passing through several hands, it was eventually sold several months later to the plaintiffs, who bought in good faith. When Caldwell discovered the fraud, he had at once notified the police and the Automobile Association, but he was unable to communicate with Norris, who had disappeared. The Court of Appeal held that the first contract of sale had been effectively avoided before the car was sold to Motobella, so that Caldwell had the right to claim the car.

Upjohn LJ: On the footing that on January 13 the defendant did everything he reasonably could to avoid the contract of sale, short of communicating his intention so to do to Norris, the whole question is whether such acts of avoidance were effective in law to avoid the contract on that day, or whether communication to Norris of intention to avoid the contract was necessary in law.

Where one party to a contract has an option unilaterally to rescind or disaffirm it by reason of the fraud or misrepresentation of the other party, he must elect to do so within a reasonable time, and cannot do so after he has done anything to affirm the contract with knowledge of the facts giving rise to the option to rescind. In principle and on authority, however, he must, in my judgment, in the ordinary course communicate his intention to rescind to the other party. This must be so because the other party is entitled to treat the contractual nexus as continuing until he is made aware of the intention of the other to exercise his option to rescind. So the intention must be communicated and an uncommunicated intention, for example, by speaking to a third party or making a private note, will be ineffective. The textbooks to which we were referred are unanimous on the subject. 'If a party elects to rescind he must within a reasonable time manifest that election by communicating to the other party his intention to rescind the transaction and claim no interest under it. The communication need not be formal provided it is a distinct and positive repudiation of the transaction': Kerr on Fraud and Mistake, 7th edn (1952), p 530.

Such in my view must be the general principle. Does it admit of any exception? Mr Caplan concedes that there is one: where the subject-matter of the contract is a transfer of property, then the party entitled to do so may disaffirm the contract by retaking possession of the property. Mr Caplan, however, submits this is really a method of communication, though for my part I do not see how that can be true of every case that could be suggested. Is there any other exception? Mr Caplan submits not and that, apart from recaption, there should be a universal rule of law that communication is essential to break the nexus. On the facts of this case, it is clear that Norris intended quite deliberately to disappear and render it impossible for the defendant to communicate with him or to recover the car. While I appreciate Mr Caplan's argument that this point can only arise in cases between the vendor and a third party, I agree with Sellers LJ that this problem must be solved by consideration of the rights between the two contracting parties. Admittedly one of two innocent parties must suffer for the fraud of a third, but that cannot be helped and does not assist to solve the problem.... It is indeed strange that there is no authority in point.

If one party, by absconding, deliberately puts it out of the power of the other to communicate his intention to rescind which he knows the other will almost certainly want to do, I do not think he can any longer insist on his right to be made aware of the election to determine the contract. In these circumstances communication is a useless formality. I think that the law must allow the innocent party to exercise his right of rescission otherwise than by communication or repossession. To hold otherwise would be to allow a fraudulent contracting party by his very fraud to prevent the innocent party from exercising his undoubted right. I would hold that in circumstances such as these the innocent party may evince his intention to disaffirm the contract by overt means falling short of communication or repossession.

We heard much interesting argument on the position where one party makes an innocent misrepresentation which entitles the other to elect to rescind and then innocently so acts that the other cannot find him to communicate his election to him. I say nothing about that case and would leave it to be decided if and when it arises. I am solely concerned with the fraudulent rogue who deliberately makes it impossible for the other to communicate with him or to retake the property.

[Sellers and Davies LJJ delivered concurring judgments.]

For another case where the same issue arose, see *Newtons of Wembley Ltd v Williams* (below, p 383).

7 SIXTH EXCEPTION: SALE BY SELLER CONTINUING IN POSSESSION

The exception which we are about to discuss is, anomalously, governed by two overlapping statutory provisions—the Sale of Goods Act 1979, s 24 and s 8 of the Factors Act 1889. There is a similar overlap between s 25(1) and s 9 (respectively) of these two Acts, which contain the seventh of our exceptions to the *nemo dat* rule. The explanation usually put forward is that when the Sale of Goods Bill 1893 was drafted, it was intended to repeal ss 8 and 9 of the Factors Act, but that this was overlooked when that Act was passed. (Just to add further to the confusion, in the Act of 1893, the present ss 24 and 25(1) were numbered respectively ss 25(1) and 25(2)!) The wording of the two sets of provisions is very nearly the same, and it will be sufficient for most purposes to refer simply to ss 24 and 25(1). Occasionally, however, it may be necessary to draw attention to the differences (see below, p 389).

Section 24 reads as follows:

Where a person having sold goods continues or is in possession of the goods, or of the goods or documents of title to the goods, the delivery or transfer by that person, or by a mercantile agent acting for him, of the goods or documents of title under any sale, pledge, or other disposition thereof, to any person receiving the same in good faith and without notice of the previous sale, has the same effect as if the person making the delivery or transfer were expressly authorised by the owner of the goods to make the same.

Section 8 of the Factors Act 1889 differs from s 24 only in that the words 'or under any agreement for the sale, pledge or other disposition thereof' are inserted before 'to any person'.

A number of detailed points call for discussion.

First, it is not sufficient that the seller should simply resell the goods: there must also be a *delivery of possession* of the goods or documents of title to the second buyer. However, it is now settled that physical delivery of the goods is not necessary—a constructive delivery will suffice. In *Michael Gerson (Leasing) Ltd v Wilkinson* [2001] QB 514, CA a company, E Ltd, sold plant and machinery to Gerson and leased it back, and then later entered into a similar sale and lease-back agreement of the same plant and machinery to S plc. The goods remained in the physical possession of E throughout. It was held that the second sale to S defeated Gerson's title by virtue of s 24, since in order for S to be able to grant a lease-back to E there must have been a prior moment in which possession had been constructively delivered to S as buyer.

Secondly, it will be recalled that in the case of *Staffs Motor Guarantee Ltd v British Wagon Co Ltd* (above, p 368), MacKinnon J held that the possession of a mercantile agent, for the purposes of s 2 of the Factors Act 1889, had to be possession *in his capacity as mercantile agent*, and that because Heap, the seller, had possession of the lorry in that case qua hirer or bailee and not qua mercantile agent, the section did not apply. As it happened, Heap was not only a mercantile agent, but also a person who had previously sold the lorry to another buyer and had continued in possession of it, and so a second argument was advanced that title to the lorry had passed to the second buyer, Staffs Motor, by virtue of the provision which is now s 24. However, once again, the point was taken that Heap's continuing possession was qua hirer and not qua seller (under the former sale), and MacKinnon J held that this was also fatal to Staff Motors' claim.

But on this second point the *Staffs Motor* case has been overruled. The 'qua seller' gloss is not to be put on the phrase 'continues or is in possession' in s 24, at least where the seller has remained in unbroken possession throughout. The new construction was first put forward in the *Pacific Motor Auctions* case (below) which, being a Privy Council decision, did not technically overrule *Staffs Motor,* but the Court of Appeal in *Worcester Works Finance Ltd v Cooden Engineering Co Ltd* [1972] 1 QB 210, CA has since adopted the same approach, as has a later Court of Appeal in *Michael Gerson (Leasing) Ltd v Wilkinson* (above), and so *Staffs Motor* can now be regarded as having been formally overruled, so far as concerns the construction of s 24.

Pacific Motor Auctions Pty Ltd v Motor Credits (Hire Finance) Ltd
[1965] AC 867, Privy Council

A car retailing firm in Sydney called Motordom held its stock of used cars under an arrangement which is sometimes called a 'display' or 'stocking' agreement and sometimes a 'floor plan'. When it bought a car, it would pay the seller in cash (or credit him with the price, if the car was taken as a trade-in) and then immediately resell it to Motor Credits at a discounted price equal to 90 per cent of the price which it had paid. In that way, it kept itself in funds to finance its future trading. The car would not leave Motordom's premises, but remained there on display for the purposes of sale. Motordom thus was in possession of the car as bailee for Motor Credits as owners; it was also a seller who had 'continued in possession' of the car after selling it. Sales of the cars, when effected, were made by Motordom as agents for Motor Credits. Motordom got into financial difficulties, and Motor Credits revoked its authority to sell any further cars. Pacific Auctions, a creditor of Motordom, was owed a substantial amount of money, and its manager called in the evening on that same day to demand payment. When payment was not forthcoming he bought a total of 29 cars at prices which added up to approximately the amount owed, and took them away. Motor Credits demand the return of these cars from Pacific Auctions.

The advice of the Privy Council was delivered by **Lord Pearce:** ..., The point under s 28(1) [of the Sale of Goods Act 1923 (NSW), equivalent to s 24 (UK)] turns on the construction of the words 'where a person having sold goods continues or is in possession of the goods.' Are those words to be construed in their full sense so that wherever a person is found to be in possession of goods which he has previously sold he can, whatever be the capacity in which he has possession, pass a good title? Or is some, and if so what, limitation to be placed on them by considering the quality and title of the seller's possession at the time when he sells them again to an innocent purchaser? ...

The first reported question that arose about the construction of those same words is to be found in *Mitchell v Jones* ((1905) 24 NZLR 932), a case under the New Zealand Sale of Goods Act 1895. There the owner of a horse sold it to a buyer and some days later obtained it back from him on lease. Then, having possession of the horse in the capacity of lessee, he sold it a second time to an innocent purchaser. The full court held that the innocent purchaser was not protected.

Stout CJ said:

> In this case the person who sold the goods gave up possession of them, and gave delivery of them to the buyer. The relationship, therefore, of buyer and seller between them was at an end. It is true that the seller got possession of the goods again, but not as a seller. He got the goods the second time as the bailee of the buyer, and as the bailee he had no warrant, in my opinion, to sell the goods again, nor could he make a good title to them to even a bona fide purchaser.'

And Williams J said that the section 'does not ... apply where a sale has been absolutely final by delivery, and possession has been obtained by the vendee.' It has not been doubted in argument nor do their Lordships doubt that that case was rightly decided.

In 1934, however, Mackinnon J, founding on that case, put a further gloss on the statutory provision in *Staffs Motor Guarantee Ltd v British Wagon Co* [above]. In April one Heap agreed with a finance company to sell his lorry to it and then to hire it from the company on hire-purchase terms. He filled up a proposal form which was accepted, and a hire-purchase agreement dated May 2 was signed. During the term of the hiring he sold it to an innocent purchaser. It seems that there was an interval between the agreement to sell and the hire-purchase agreement, but it does not appear from the report that there was any physical delivery or interruption of Heap's physical possession. Mackinnon J held that 'Heap's possession of the lorry' (at the time of the second sale) 'was not the possession of a seller who had not yet delivered the article sold to the buyer, but was the possession of a bailee under the hire-purchase agreement....' Although the sale had not been completed by physical delivery nor had there been interruption of the seller's physical possession, he held that the case was covered by the principle in *Mitchell v Jones*.

[His Lordship discussed certain other cases, including *Eastern Distributors Ltd v Goldring* (above, p 353), and continued:]

It is plainly right to read the section as inapplicable to cases where there has been a break in the continuity of the physical possession. On this point their Lordships accept the observations of the judges in *Mitchell v Jones* .... But what is the justification for saying that a person does not continue in possession where his physical possession does continue although the title under or by virtue of which he is in possession has changed? The fact that a person having sold goods is described as *continuing* in possession would seem to indicate that the section is not contemplating as relevant a change in the legal title under which he possesses. For the legal title by which he is in possession *cannot* continue. Before the sale he is in possession as an owner, whereas after the sale he is in possession as a bailee holding goods for the new owner. The possession continues unchanged but the title under which he possesses has changed. One may, perhaps, say in loose terms that a person having sold goods continues in possession as long as he is holding because of and only because of the sale; but what justification is there for imposing such an elaborate and artificial construction on the natural meaning of the words? The object of the section is to protect an innocent purchaser who is deceived by the vendor's physical possession of goods or documents and who is inevitably unaware of legal rights which fetter the apparent power to dispose. Where a vendor retains uninterrupted physical possession of the goods why should an unknown arrangement, which substitutes a bailment for ownership, disentitle the innocent purchaser to protection from a danger which is just as great as that from which the section is admittedly intended to protect him?

[His Lordship discussed the history of s 24 and its relation to various provisions in the earlier Factors Acts. He concluded:]

There is therefore the strongest reason for supposing that the words 'continues in possession' were intended to refer to the continuity of physical possession regardless of any private transactions between the seller and purchaser which might alter the legal title under which the possession was held....

It seems to their Lordships that *Staff Motor Guarantee Ltd v British Wagon Co* (and *Eastern Distributors Ltd v Goldring* in so far as it followed it), was wrongly decided...

Documents of title. Section 24 refers not only to the case where the seller is in possession of the *goods*, but also where he is in possession of the *documents of title* to the goods. This expression also occurs in s 2 of the Factors Act 1889 (above, p 364). It is time to examine this concept of a 'document of title' more closely.

The first comment to make is that the term 'document of title' is misleading, because in most cases the documents concerned have nothing to do with the title to the goods. (The bill of lading is an exception.) What the documents do have in common is that they give or evidence a person's right to the *possession* of goods, so that whoever has the document can demand that they be delivered to him or to his order. The statutory definition (Factors Act 1889, s 1(4), adopted by the Sale of Goods Act 1979, s 61(1)), is as follows:

The expression 'document of title' shall include any bill of lading, dock warrant, warehouse-keeper's certificate, and warrant or order for the delivery of goods, and any other document used in the ordinary course of business as proof of the possession or control of goods, or authorising or purporting to authorise, either by indorsement or delivery, the possessor of the document to transfer or receive goods thereby represented.

In practical terms, documents of title fall into two classes.

The first category is an *acknowledgment,* signed by a person who has physical possession of the goods (usually a bailee, such as a warehouseman or a carrier) that he is holding them on a particular person's behalf, and available for delivery to that person. (This latter person may or may not be the owner of the goods: what matters is that he has the right to demand possession from the former.) A seller of goods who holds them as bailee for his buyer may issue such a 'document of title' in favour of the latter. Typically, an acknowledgment of this kind is called a *warrant* (eg a dock warrant, warehouseman's warrant, railway warrant: for an example, see *Sterns Ltd v Vickers Ltd* (above, p 302)). The category also includes a bill of lading, ie a document issued by a sea carrier which acknowledges that the goods in question have been received on board, and which also contains the terms of the contract of carriage: see below, p 490.

The second type of document of title is an *order,* signed by the owner of goods or other person entitled to possession of them, addressed to the warehouseman, carrier or other bailee in whose custody they are, instructing him to deliver the goods to a named person or to his order. Such a document is usually called a *delivery order.*

Although (with the exception of the bill of lading) these documents do not confer rights of ownership on their holders or serve to evidence such rights, they do operate to *protect* an owner's title, because they give the holder the power to control the right of disposal of the goods which they represent. So, for instance, the owner of goods stored in a warehouse can give security over the goods (eg to a bank) by pledging the warehouseman's warrant with the bank. And the use of documents of title is facilitated by the commercial practice of treating the rights evidenced by such documents as being transferable by the physical delivery of the document, usually accompanied by an endorsement written on the document itself.

When we turn to look at the provisions of s 24 relating to documents of title, we see that in this context they do have a bearing on questions of ownership. For this purpose, it is not the document itself or the issuing of such a document which confers rights of ownership; it is the *transfer* to a second buyer of a document of title *which is already in the possession of the seller,* and which he has not parted with under the first contract of sale, that defeats the claims of the first buyer. So, a person who has sold goods to buyer B1, but has kept possession of either the goods themselves or a document of title relating to the goods, has the power to defeat B1's title and confer a good title on buyer B2, by delivering the goods or the document of title to B2. But under s 24 (and also, we shall see, under s 25(1)), actual delivery of one or the other is essential: the mere fact that he has purportedly sold the goods to B2 will give B2 no proprietary rights. In contrast, delivery of the goods or document of title is not necessary to bring a transaction within the exception created by s 2 of the Factors Act 1889 (sale by a mercantile agent).

Of course, in many circumstances any such action by a seller in reselling the goods will be a breach of his contract with the first buyer, and also constitute the tort of conversion or wrongful interference with the goods. The question whether the seller will be liable under these heads is discussed later (see below, p 446).

8 SEVENTH EXCEPTION: SALE BY BUYER IN POSSESSION

Section 25(1) of the Sale of Goods Act 1979 (which is similar to the Factors Act 1889, s 9) is the counterpart of s 24. It reads:

Where a person having bought or agreed to buy goods obtains, with the consent of the seller, possession of the goods or the documents of title to the goods, the delivery or transfer by that person, or by a mercantile agent acting for him, of the goods or documents of title, under any sale, pledge or other disposition thereof, to any person receiving the same in good faith and without notice of any lien or other right of the seller in respect of the goods, has the same effect as if the person making the delivery or transfer were a mercantile agent in possession of the goods or documents of title with the consent of the owner.

Once again, the Factors Act 1889, s 9 differs from this wording only by the inclusion of the phrase 'or under any agreement for the sale, pledge or other disposition thereof before the words 'to any person'.

Care is needed in reading cases decided before 1979, since in the Act of 1893 the present s 25(1) was numbered s 25(2).

Here we can see another situation where the principle *of Jerome v Bentley* (above, p 351) does not apply: although the fact that an owner has let another person have possession of his goods carries no implication or representation that that person has authority to sell them, this latter person may, exceptionally, be deemed to have the power to do so when he is someone who has contracted to buy the goods.

A leading case on this section (or rather on s 9 of the Factors Act 1889, since the Sale of Goods Act 1893 had not then been enacted) is *Lee v Butler,* which marked an important step in the evolution of the hire-purchase agreement.

Lee v Butler

[1893] 2 QB 318, Court of Appeal

Mrs Lloyd agreed to take on 'hire' certain furniture from Hardy under the terms of an agreement, called a 'hire and purchase agreement', paying over a period of three months sums described as 'rent' which totalled £97 4s. It was declared that the furniture should remain the property of Hardy throughout, but that when the full £97 4s had been paid, the furniture would become the sole and absolute property of Mrs Lloyd. Mrs Lloyd, before all the instalments had been paid under the agreement, sold the furniture to Butler. Lee, who had taken an assignment of Hardy's rights under the agreement, claimed to be entitled to the goods, but the court found for Butler under s 9 of the Factors Act 1889 (SGA, s 25(1)).

Lord Esher MR: This is a very plain case, and the construction of the statute is very clear. It deals with 'Dispositions by mercantile agents' in one set of sections, and with 'Dispositions by sellers and buyers of goods' in another set of sections, in which s 9 is included. The case is clearly within that section. [His Lordship read s 9.] Mrs Lloyd had agreed by this hire and purchase agreement to buy the goods, and they were put into her possession with the consent of the owner. Mrs Lloyd sold the goods to the defendant without notice that they were not hers, and he, acting in good faith and with no notice of the plaintiff's rights, received them. Section 9 was passed to meet this very kind of case. I am of opinion that the judgment of Wright J was right, and this appeal should be dismissed.

[Kay LJ delivered a concurring judgment.
Bowen LJ concurred.]

NOTE

The key point in *Lee v Butler* is that Mrs Lloyd, though described as a 'hirer', was *bound* to complete the purchase of the goods. In other words, this was a *conditional sale* agreement, under which the seller retained the property in the goods until the whole of the agreed price had been paid. In a true hire-purchase agreement, the hirer has only an *option* to buy the goods, which he exercises by paying all the hire instalments (and sometimes also a further 'option fee'); and he is free at any time to discontinue the hiring. In the test case of *Helby* v *Matthews* (above, p 283), the House of Lords held that a purported sale of the goods by the hirer under such a contract to a third person did not come within s 25(1), and so an owner in the position of Hardy would be protected against unauthorised sales by the hirer. This ruling has been the basis of the hire-purchase agreement ever since.

Paradoxically, the Consumer Credit Act 1974 now declares that conditional sale agreements coming within the protection of the Act are to be treated for many purposes as hire-purchase agreements, so as to give consumers who buy under conditional sale agreements the statutory protection conferred by that Act; and s 25(2) of the Sale of Goods Act 1979 expressly reverses *Lee v Butler* in relation to agreements falling within the statutory limits: see above, p 285.

The wording of s 25(1) has some curious features.

First, for a long time the words '*bought* or agreed to buy' were regarded as puzzling, because it was thought that if a person had *bought* goods he would have a good title anyway, which would enable him to sell to a sub-buyer without any need to invoke s 25(1). But in *Newtons of Wembley Ltd v Williams* it was demonstrated that the draftsman of the section had truly remarkable foresight, and that there is indeed a role for the word 'bought'.

Newtons of Wembley Ltd v Williams

[1965] 1 QB 560, Court of Appeal

On 16 June 1962 Newtons sold a Sunbeam Rapier car to Andrew and allowed him to take it away. Andrew's purchase was fraudulent, because he paid for the car with a worthless cheque. Newtons were unable to trace Andrew, but they informed the police and Hire Purchase Information Ltd (see above, p 362), and sent out two men to try and trace and seize the car. About a month later Andrew sold the car to Biss at a streetside market in Warren Street, London, Biss paying Andrew the whole price in £5 notes. Biss resold the car to Williams, who refused to give it up to Newtons after it had been traced.

Sellers LJ followed *Car & Universal Finance Co Ltd v Caldwell* (above, p 376) in holding that Newtons had effectively avoided the sale to Andrew by informing the police etc, and continued: The title the defendant seeks to advance is the title of Biss, when Biss was the buyer, or the purported buyer, of the car from Andrew in the Warren Street market on or about July 6, 1962.

Quite clearly, at common law, Andrew at that date had no title to give, and at common law Biss obtained no title. It was submitted before us that at that stage Andrew was a complete stranger in this matter, that the case is clear, and that possession should be given to the plaintiffs, or damages in lieu thereof. But in fact Andrew was not a complete stranger. Andrew had in fact the possession of the car, which had been given to him or which he had obtained when he acquired the car on the handing over of the cheque on June 15.

In those circumstances, notwithstanding the position at common law—or because of it—the defendant has relied on the Factors Act, 1889; and the question which arises in this case is whether the transaction between Andrew and Biss can be brought within the provisions of that Act.

I turn first to s 9. It is one of two sections, ss 8 and 9, dealing with dispositions by sellers and buyers of goods, s 8 dealing with the disposition by a seller remaining in possession, s 9 with disposition by a buyer obtaining possession.

[His Lordship read s 9 and continued:]

Andrew had bought the goods and obtained them with the consent of the plaintiffs. He had subsequently delivered them on a sale to Biss and, if Biss was a person receiving the same in good faith and without notice of any lien or other right of the original seller, then this section provides that the transaction shall have the same effect as if the person making the delivery, ie, Andrew, were a mercantile agent in possession of the goods or documents of title with the consent of the owner. So the first part of s 9 is complied with on the facts of this case, and the question arises whether the second part, the receiving of the goods in good faith (and it is not suggested that Biss had notice of any lien or other right of the original seller), has been complied with, and whether, treating Andrew as a mercantile agent, the requirements of s 9 in that respect have been complied with.

[Other parts of the judgment of Sellers LJ are set out below.]
[Pearson LJ delivered a concurring judgment. Diplock LJ concurred.]

The second puzzle arising from the wording of s 25(1) is concerned with the concluding words:

> has the same effect as if the person making the delivery or transfer were a mercantile agent in possession of the goods or documents of title with the consent of the owner.

It will be noticed that this wording differs markedly from the concluding words of s 24:

> has the same effect as if the person making the delivery or transfer were expressly authorised by the owner of the goods to make the same.

No case prior to *Newtons of Wembley*, at least in England, had ever considered the meaning of these words, which cannot be given full effect without invoking s 2 of the Factors Act 1889 and all the accumulated learning relating to that section. Taken literally, it would appear that s 25(1) could not be successfully invoked unless the first buyer had access to a place of business and conducted the second sale 'in the ordinary course of business of a mercantile agent'. This would seem to rule out most private buyers, and would suggest that the seminal case of *Lee v Butler* (above, p 382) was decided *per incuriam*. In *Newtons of Wembley* itself, the court was able to reach a fairly easy answer on the rather fortuitous facts of the case, but the basic question remains unresolved.

Newtons of Wembley Ltd v Williams

[1965] 1 QB 560, Court of Appeal

(The facts are given above.)

Sellers LJ: The only other question which arises is how far s 9, on its true construction, takes the ultimate sub-buyer (the defendant in the present case), relying, as he does, on what happened between Andrew and Biss. The judge treated s 9 as placing Andrew in the position of a mercantile agent, but with the obligation on the defendant of establishing not only that Biss took in good faith (I leave out the other requirement of no notice of the plaintiff's rights; nothing arose on that), but also that in the transaction between Andrew and Biss (Andrew being treated as a mercantile agent in accordance with s 9), Andrew was 'acting in the ordinary course of business of a mercantile agent.' . . .

Before one takes too favourable a view for the sub-buyer and too harsh a view against the true owner of the goods as to the cases where s 9 can be invoked, one must remember that it is taking away the right which would have existed at common law, and for myself I should not be prepared to enlarge it more than the words clearly permitted and required. It seems to me that all that s 9 can be said clearly to do is to place the buyer in possession in the position of a mercantile agent when he has in fact in his possession the goods of somebody else, and it does no more than clothe him with that fictitious or notional position on any disposition of those goods. Section 2(1) makes it clear that the sub-buyer from a mercantile agent, to whom that section applies, has in order to obtain the full advantage of the sub-section, to establish that the mercantile agent was acting in the ordinary course of business. . . . Counsel for the plaintiffs sought to establish that a transaction taking place in this somewhat unusual market, the street kerb in Warren Street, was, on the face of it, something which was not an ordinary business transaction in any way, by a mercantile agent or anybody else, but was to some extent suspect. But the judge had evidence about this and he said, and I think it is within the knowledge of the court, that there had been an established market in secondhand cars in this area on this very site for a long time. Although he said that he had some doubt at one time about the sale to Biss being in the ordinary course of business, for, as he pointed out, there were no business premises, the sale was in the street, and it was for cash, yet he came to the conclusion, which I think cannot be challenged, that there was in Warren Street and its neighbourhood an established street market for cash dealing in cars. When one looks at what took place in that area and finds the prospective buyer coming up and getting into contact with the prospective seller in regard to a car, with an offer and an acceptance, trial of the car and a looking over it and some questions asked and a delivery—I do not find anything to indicate that it was not in the ordinary course of business of a mercantile agent. It seems to me that the defendant has established that essential fact.

NOTE

LA Rutherford and IA Todd [1979] CLJ 346 draw attention to the fact that s 25(1) deems the *delivery or transfer* of the goods or documents to have been expressly authorised, and not the 'sale, pledge or other disposition'. In the light of this, they argue that the scope of the subsection may be more limited than has generally been assumed.

The final conundrum concerning s 25(1) focuses on its very last word: 'with the consent of the *owner*'. In the earlier parts of the subsection, all the relevant references are to the 'seller'. At least at first sight, this would suggest that the 'owner' mentioned at the end is a different person from the seller; and it could very readily be taken to mean 'the true owner'. From this it would follow that if S agreed to sell goods to B1 and gave him possession, and B1 then sold them to B2, B2 would get a good title even against a true owner, O, from whom the goods had been stolen before they were acquired by S. Although not an impossible construction, this would be surprising, for none of the other exceptions to the *nemo dat* rule (apart from the now repealed market overt exception) has ever been understood to allow title to be conferred through a thief. Some commentators therefore concluded that the word 'owner' in the section had to be read as a slip for 'seller'. The question has now been resolved more happily by the House of Lords, which favoured a still different approach.

National Employers' Mutual General Insurance Association Ltd v Jones
[1990] 1 AC 24, House of Lords

Miss Hopkin owned a Ford Fiesta car which was stolen in 1983 and, after passing through several hands, was bought by a firm called Autochoice, which sold it to Mid-Glamorgan Motors, who resold it to Jones. When Miss Hopkin's insurers (who had been subrogated to her rights: see below, p 1205) claimed the car from Jones, he sought the protection of s 25(1). All the courts found for the insurers. The trial judge and a majority of the Court of Appeal took the view that the word 'owner' in s 25(1) had to be read as 'seller'. The House of Lords upheld the finding on a different construction: the section was to be taken as referring to a *notional* sale by a *notional* mercantile agent in possession of the goods with the consent of their *notional* owner.

Lord Goff of Chieveley outlined the history of the Factors Acts prior to 1889, and continued: Such are the statutory precursors of the Factors Act 1889. . . . [The] relevant sections are ss 2, 8 and 9. Section 2 is concerned to provide for the validity of sales, pledges and other dispositions of goods by mercantile agents who are, 'with the consent of the owner,' in possession of the goods or of documents of title to the goods; such transactions, it is provided, shall be as valid as if the mercantile agents were expressly authorised 'by the owner of the goods to make the same.' Plainly, the owner of the goods here referred to is the owner with whose consent the agent is in possession of them. The section cannot be read as having the effect of adversely affecting the title of any person, other than the person who had entrusted the goods or documents of title to the mercantile agents; it cannot adversely affect the title of one from whom the goods had been stolen, whose goods have come into possession of the mercantile agent from the thief, or from a person deriving the title from the thief. . . .

I come therefore to ss 8 and 9. I will, for the sake of clarity set out the two sections again, in order to identify with initials the relevant actors in the drama. In s 8, I have identified the vendor as A; the first purchaser, who has allowed A to remain in possession of the goods or documents of title, I shall hereafter refer to as B1; and the second purchaser, to whom A has sold, pledged or otherwise disposed of the goods or documents of title, I have identified as B2. In s 9, I have identified the seller referred to in line 2 of the section as A; the person who bought or agreed to buy the goods from A, and who obtained possession of the goods or documents of title with A's consent, I have identified as B; and the person to whom B delivers or transfers the goods or documents of title under a sale, pledge or other disposal, or an agreement for the same, I have identified as C. Interpolating these initials, the sections read:

> **8.** Where a person (A), having sold goods, continues, or is, in possession of the goods or of the documents of title to the goods, the delivery or transfer by that person (A), or by a mercantile agent acting for him, of the goods or documents of title under any sale, pledge, or other disposition thereof, or under any agreement for sale, pledge, or other disposition thereof, to any person (B2) receiving the same in good faith and without notice of the previous sale, shall have the same effect as if the person making the delivery or transfer were expressly authorised by the owner of the goods to make the same.
>
> **9.** Where a person (B), having bought or agreed to buy goods, obtains with the consent of the seller (A) possession of the goods or the documents of title to the goods, the delivery or transfer, by that person (B) or by a mercantile agent acting for him, of the goods or documents of title, under any sale, pledge, or other disposition thereof, or under any agreement for sale, pledge, or other disposition thereof, to any person (C) receiving the same in good faith and without notice of any lien or other right of the original seller (A) in respect of the goods, shall have the same effect as if the person (B) making the delivery or transfer were a mercantile agent in possession of the goods or documents of title with the consent of the owner.

These two sections, of course, go slightly further than ss 3 and 4 of the Factors Act 1877, in that they take effect not only when the relevant person ((A) in s 8, and (B) in s 9) is allowed to be in possession of the documents of title to the goods, but also when he is allowed to be in possession of the goods themselves. It is relevant to observe also that, whereas the statutory hypothesis at the end of ss 3 and 4 of the Factors Act 1877 refers to the transaction taking effect as if the person making the delivery or transfer was a person entrusted by the *vendee* with the goods or documents, or entrusted by the *vendor* with the documents, as the case may be, we now see, in ss 8 and 9 of the Factors Act 1889, a different phraseology, referring not to the vendee (B1) or the vendor (A), but just to the 'owner of the goods' or 'the owner.' It is upon the slender foundation of this change of phraseology that the appellant, in the present case, has sought to build his argument that s 9 has the effect of adversely affecting the title, not only of a person (A) who has allowed another person (B) to be in possession of the relevant goods or documents, but also of anybody from whom the goods have been stolen, and whose goods have come into the possession of another who sells them.

For s 9 to have any such effect would constitute a change in policy of a fundamental kind, of which there is no evidence whatsoever in the remainder of the Act of 1889. . . .

For the reasons I have set out, the statutory context provides overwhelming evidence that the legislature never intended, either in s 9 of the Factors Act 1889, or in s 25(2) of the Sale of Goods Act 1893 (or its successor, s 25(1) of the Sale of Goods Act 1979) to achieve the result contended for by the appellant. But there is further internal evidence, in the Act of 1889, that such a result can never have been intended.

Let me concentrate for a moment, not on s 9, but on s 8, of the Factors Act 1889. The submission for the appellant has to be that, when A has sold goods to B1, and B1 allows A to remain in possession of the goods after the sale, a subsequent sale by A to B2 will be effective to divest the title of a person from whom the goods have previously been stolen before they came into the hands of A. It is obvious that this can never have been the intention of the legislature. If it was, what was the relevance of the sale to B1, and the fact that B1 has allowed A to remain in possession? Assuming B1 to have acted in good faith, why should not A, whom I will assume to be the thief, give as good a title to B1 as to B2? Each is relying equally upon the possession of A of the goods. In truth, the whole section proceeds upon the assumption that the relevant owner of the goods, who is deemed to have authorised their delivery and transfer, is B1—the person to whom the goods have been sold by A, and who has allowed A to remain in possession of them. And exactly the same point can be made in relation to s 9 itself. What is the relevance of the fact that B is in possession of the goods or documents of title with the permission of A? Again, there seems to be no good reason why C should get a good title, but that B (whom I assume to be acting in good faith) should not; each is simply relying, in good faith, upon the possession of his vendor.

Furthermore, if the construction of s 9 (and, by implication, s 8) urged by the appellant is correct, then we find a startling contrast between the policy underlying those two sections, and that underlying s 2. For s 2 goes no further than to divest the title of a person who has entrusted the mercantile agent with the possession of the relevant goods or documents of title; if ss 8 and 9 were to have the effect of divesting the title of a person from whom the goods have been stolen, and who has not entrusted them to the person who has purported to sell them to the purchaser, it is difficult to see why s 2 should have been so limited in its effect.

As a matter of construction of the relevant statutory provisions, therefore, I have reached the conclusion that the submission advanced by the appellant cannot be sustained. In my opinion, s 9 of the Factors Act 1889 must be read as providing that the delivery or transfer glven by the intermediate transferor (B) shall have the same effect as if he was a mercantile agent in possession of the goods or documents of title with the consent of the owner who entrusted them to him (A). Such a construction is, in my opinion, to be derived from the terms of s 2(1) of the Act, to which s 9 evidently refers, and also from the legislative context which 1 have already discussed. The same construction must, of course, be placed upon s 25(1) of the Sale of Goods Act 1979.

[Lords Bridge of Harwich, Lowry, Brandon of Oakbrook and Griffiths concurred.]

The following case is also of relevance, and raised some interesting incidental points.

DF Mount Ltd v Jay & Jay (Provisions) Co Ltd
[1960] 1QB 159, Queen's Bench Division

Jays agreed to sell to Merrick 250 cartons of Australian canned peaches, part of a larger consignment owned by them and lying in the warehouse of Delta Storage Ltd, Greenwich. Merrick made it plain that he would pay the price from the moneys which he would receive from his own customers when the goods had been resold. Jays made out two delivery orders addressed to Delta in favour of Merrick, one for 150 cartons and another for 100. Merrick sent the delivery orders to Delta endorsed with the words 'Please transfer to our sub-order'. Merrick then agreed to resell the 250 cartons to Mount, and received the price from Mount in exchange for a delivery order addressed to Delta and signed by Merrick. Jays were never paid by Merrick. Both Jays and Mount claimed to be entitled to the peaches, which were still in the hands of Delta. Judgment was given in favour of Mount on the ground that Jays had 'assented' to the resale under s 47(1) (see below, p 442); but the case also contains a discussion of two points relevant to the present *nemo dat* exception: does it matter that the contract goods are not identified, but unascertained? And is it necessary under s 25(1) for the sub-buyer to receive the *same* delivery order that the buyer received from the original seller?

Salmon J held that Jays had 'assented' to the sub-sale by Mount under s 47(1), and continued: The sale of the 250 cartons was a sale of unascertained goods. In my judgment, however, there is no reason why s 47 should not apply to unascertained goods, although I respectfully agree with Pickford J that an inference can in some circumstances more readily be drawn against the seller in the case of a sale of specific goods than in the case of a sale of unascertained goods. I hold that the defendants assented to the sale of the cartons by Merrick within the meaning of s 47.

This is enough to dispose of the case, but I will deal briefly with some of the other points which have been canvassed. Mr Silkin argues that even had there been no sufficient assent by the defendants, he would be entitled to succeed under the proviso to s 47 [now s 47(2)].

[His Lordship read the proviso and continued:]

It is conceded that the plaintiffs took that delivery order in good faith and for valuable consideration. Mr Noakes argues, however, that there has been no transfer by Merrick within the meaning of the proviso. The material words to consider are: '... where a document of title to goods has been lawfully transferred to any person as buyer, ... and that person transfers the document to a person. ...'

It seems to me that these words confine the proviso to cases where a document is transferred to the buyer and the same document is then transferred by him to the person who takes in good faith and for valuable consideration. If Merrick had indorsed the delivery orders he received from the defendants and transferred them to the plaintiffs, the proviso would, in my judgment, have applied; but he did not do so. He sent those delivery orders to the wharf, and made out a fresh delivery order in favour of the plaintiffs.

It is strange that there appears to be no authority on this point. It is clear that the person who transfers the document of title to the buyer may originate it himself and need not have received it from some third party in order to 'transfer' it within the meaning of the proviso: *see Ant Jurgens Margarine Fabrieken v Louis Dreyfus & Co* ([1914] 3 KB 40). In my judgment, however, on the plain language of the section, it must be that very document which is transferred by the buyer for the proviso to operate. I am conscious that this construction leads to a very artificial result, but I cannot avoid it without doing violence to the plain language of the section.

Mr Silkin, however, also relies on s 25(2) of the Sale of Goods Act 1893 [now s 25(1)].

[His Lordship read the subsection and continued:]

It seems to me that the language of this subsection is less rigorous than that of the proviso to s 47 and does not compel me to hold that the subsection applies only in those cases where the buyer transfers the same document as that of which he is in possession with the consent of the seller. I would observe that there seems to be no authority on this point.

The object of the subsection is to protect an innocent person in his dealings with a buyer who appears to have the right to deal with the goods in that he has been allowed by the seller to be in possession of the goods or documents of title relating to them. In such a case the subsection provides that any transfer of the goods or documents of title by the buyer to a person acting in good faith and without notice of any want of authority on the part of the buyer shall be as valid as if expressly authorised by the seller.

In the present case the defendants sent the documents of title to Merrick with the intention that they should enable him to obtain money from his customers. With the help of these documents, which he sent to the wharf so that the wharfingers would give a reassuring reply to any inquiry that the plaintiffs might make, or at least not query any delivery order they received from the plaintiffs, Merrick managed to obtain a substantial sum of money from the plaintiffs.

In my view, the transfer by Merrick of the delivery order…was, by virtue of s 25(2), as valid as if expressly authorised by the defendants.

NOTES

1. While the judgment of Salmon J does refer to the fact that the goods were unascertained, the discussion is perfunctory and refers only to s 47, and not also to s 25(1). Section 25(1) in fact uses the phrase 'sale, pledge or other disposition thereof', which would appear to exclude a mere agreement to sell. However, if this point had been taken, it might have been resolved by invoking s 9 of the Factors Act 1889 instead of s 25(1). The wording of these two sections is almost the same, but s 9 crucially adds the words 'or under any *agreement for sale*, pledge or other disposition thereof'. This appears to be one of the few cases in the reports where the difference in wording between s 25(1) and s 9 might have been significant. There is a similar variation, as we have seen, between s 24 and s 8 of the 1889 Act.

But the difficulties do not stop at this point. On Salmon J's reasoning, Mount became the owner of 'the 250 cartons' of peaches. But (assuming that there had been no appropriation by exhaustion and ignoring the complications that have since been introduced by s 20A), this ruling runs counter to the basic principle that no property can be transferred until the contract goods have been ascertained (s 16). In the event of Jays' insolvency, all the difficulties exemplified by *Re Wait* (above, p 266) would have to be faced. It is difficult to resist the conclusion that on this issue *Mount v Jay* is open to reconsideration. This is borne out by *Re Highway Foods International Ltd* [1995] 1 BCLC 209, where goods were sold by A to B and subsold by B to C, in each case on terms that the seller retained title to the goods until his price had been paid. The transactions were thus, strictly speaking, agreements to sell and not sales. Neither price was paid. It was held that s 9 of the Factors Act 1889 did not have the effect of depriving A of his title and vesting it in C, since no title would have passed to C under the notional transaction (involving a mercantile agent) which s 9 contemplates unless A had been paid his price. However, since in this case the goods *were* ascertained, the judge stated that a *sale* by B to C, accompanied by delivery, would have conferred a good title on C.

2. This case draws our attention to the significance of the slight differences in wording between s 25(2), s 47 and s 9 of the Factors Act 1889—the significant point being that s 25(2) and s 9 omit the word 'the' before the second reference to 'documents of title', which was considered vital in the construction of s 47. It surely cannot have been the intention of the legislature to say nearly the same thing in three different ways. It is a matter for regret that the opportunity was not taken to clarify the position (and also that involving s 24 and s 8) when the legislation was consolidated in 1979.

3. As is the case with s 24, it is essential for s 25(1) to apply that the person claiming the benefit of this exception should have taken delivery of the goods from the original buyer, or had a document of title transferred to him. Such delivery may be actual or constructive (see *Michael Gerson (Leasing) Ltd v Wilkinson* (above, p 378)), but the mere fact of a sale without such delivery or transfer is not sufficient. (But note also (as Salmon J confirms) that the *issue* of a delivery order by the seller or buyer is treated as equivalent to the 'transfer' of a similar document which has emanated from a third party.)

4.   It should be noted that the section uses the phrase 'under any sale, pledge, *or other disposition thereof*' (as also does s 24). These two exceptions to the *nemo dat* rule are therefore not confined to the case of a second sale or pledge. Where, for instance, a builder who has agreed to buy materials on terms that title remains in the seller uses these materials in constructing a house for a customer, there is a 'disposition' within s 25(1): the customer would get a good title and could not be sued in conversion by the original seller. However, a 'disposition' probably requires some voluntary act on the part of the first buyer: see *The Saetta* (below, p 468), where the owners of the chartered ship simply took over the fuel oil on board when they resumed possession of her: the court, without ruling whether there had been a 'disposition' by the charterers, held that in the absence of any voluntary act there had been no 'delivery' by them of the oil, and that s 25(1) did not apply.

5.   In *Four Point Garage Ltd v Carter* [1985] 3 All ER 12, the goods in question were delivered by the seller directly to the sub-purchaser. Simon Brown J held that s 25(1) applied, because the buyer was deemed to have taken constructive delivery of the goods and the seller to have acted as the buyer's agent in making delivery to the sub-purchaser.

6.   The onus is on the person receiving the goods to prove that he received them without notice of any claim of the original seller: *Fairfax Gerrard Holdings Ltd v Capital Bank plc* [2006] EWHC Civ 3439, [2007] 1 Lloyd's Rep 171.

9 EIGHTH EXCEPTION: SALE BY UNPAID SELLER UNDER SGA 1979, s 48

This exception to the *nemo dat* rule overlaps to some extent with the sixth (sale by seller in possession), but there are important points of difference. It is discussed with the other seller's remedies below, at p 446.

10 NINTH EXCEPTION: PRIVATE PURCHASE OF MOTOR VEHICLE HELD ON HIRE PURCHASE

Most of the Hire-Purchase Act 1964 has long since been repealed, but Part III remains in force (in the form of a revised text which incorporates some amendments made by the Consumer Credit Act 1974). This part of the Act is concerned to protect *private purchasers* acting in good faith who buy *motor vehicles* which have been let out on hire purchase without notice of the existence of the hire-purchase agreement. It will be recalled that *Helby v Matthews* (above, p 283) confirmed that a person who has taken goods on hire purchase is merely a hirer and not someone who has 'bought or agreed to buy' the goods, and so he cannot give a good title to under s 25(1) to someone who buys the goods from him. When the Hire-Purchase Act 1964 was enacted, this special exception to the *nemo dat* rule was introduced as a result of a concession made by the motor trade. (The alternative proposed by the government was to set up a registration system for the ownership of vehicles which would have been very costly to administer.)

The details of Part III are quite complex. The most important points are as follows:

(1) It applies only to 'motor vehicles'—mechanically propelled vehicles intended or adapted for use on public roads (s 29(1))—a definition which would include cars, motor-cycles, motorised caravans and lorries, but not caravans, trailers and boats. Agricultural machines such as combine harvesters could pose a problem of construction.

(2) 'Private purchaser' has a special meaning: someone who is not a 'trade or finance purchaser' (s 29(2)). This excludes all motor dealers and finance companies, but not other forms of business purchaser (eg a butcher who buys a van). However, in *GE Capital Bank Ltd v Rushton* [2005] EWCA Civ 1556, [2006] 1 WLR 899 a person who had not previously had any dealings in the motor trade bought 13 vehicles with a view to selling them on as a business venture. He was held not to be a 'private purchaser' within s 29(2).

(3) The Act applies to vehicles which have been acquired under conditional sale contracts (such as the contract in *Lee v Butler,* above, p 382) as well as under hire-purchase agreements (s 27(1)). There is no financial or other statutory limitation on the scope of the Act (in contrast with most other hire-purchase legislation, which is confined to *consumer* transactions).

(4) Only the *first* private purchaser from the hirer (or 'debtor', as he is termed in the Act) is protected. Thus, if the debtor sells the vehicle to X, who has notice of the hire-purchase agreement, X will not get a good title, and neither will Y, if X sells on to Y, even if Y is a bona fide purchaser without notice. (This is surely an oversight on the part of the draftsman.) However, if a vehicle which is on hire purchase is disposed of to a trade or finance purchaser, the first private purchaser from that trade or finance purchaser is protected (s 27(2)–(5)).

(5) A private purchaser will not be protected under Part III if the 'hire-purchase' transaction is a legal nullity. In *Shogun Finance Ltd v Hudson* [2003] UKHL 62, [2004] 1 AC 919 a rogue calling himself Patel, and purporting to identify himself by producing genuine documents which had been stolen from a real Mr Patel, obtained a Mitsubishi Shogun vehicle from a dealer by signing hire-purchase documents naming Shogun Finance as owners and Patel as the hirer. The rogue then 'sold' the vehicle to the defendant, Hudson, a private purchaser. It was held that the hire-purchase contract was void on the ground of mistake of identity (compare *Cundy v Lindsay* (above, p 349)) and that Shogun Finance had not lost their title to the vehicle.

Reform of the law. On 20 January 1994 the Department of Trade and Industry published a Consultation Document containing proposals for the reform of some of the exceptions to the *nemo dat* rule and extending Part III of the Hire-Purchase Act 1964 to cover all goods on hire-purchase and similar contracts. More controversially, it also proposed that anyone who is in possession of goods with the owner's consent should have power to confer a good title on an innocent purchaser. It is a reasonably safe prediction that this last suggestion, with its potentially far-reaching consequences, will never gain support: see the criticism of BJ Davenport (1994) 110 LQR 165.

CHAPTER 10
STATUTORY IMPLIED TERMS

1 INTRODUCTION

Sections 12–15 contain the statutory rules governing the seller's obligations to give a good title, to ensure that the buyer enjoys quiet possession, etc and to deliver goods of the description and quality that the contract specifies. These are set out in the form of *implied terms*. In principle (and certainly in the Act as originally enacted), the parties are free to exclude or vary these implied terms, since s 55(1) states that 'where a right, duty or liability would arise under a contract of sale of goods by implication of law, it may … be negatived or varied by express agreement, or by the course of dealing between the parties, or by such usage as binds both parties to the contract'. But the parties' freedom to do this has, since 1977, been considerably limited by the Unfair Contract Terms Act 1977, which expressly makes s 55(1) subject to its provisions. The Unfair Terms in Consumer Contracts Regulations 1999, SI 1999/2083, also make inroads upon this general principle. These statutory restrictions on freedom of contract are more severe in the case of consumer sales than other contracts of sale; in contrast, in regard to international sales (called in the 1977 Act 'international supply contracts'), they do not apply at all. We shall note the effect of these restrictions later in this chapter.

In relation to England and Wales the statutory implied terms are classified by the Sale of Goods Act as *conditions* or *warranties*. The Act does not contemplate the possibility that there may also be 'innominate' terms of the kind recognised in *Hong Kong Fir Shipping Co Ltd v Kawasaki Kisen Kaisha Ltd* [1962] 2 QB 26, CA—that is, terms where the remedy for breach is made to depend on the seriousness of the breach. However, there is clearly nothing to prevent a court from categorising an *express* term in a contract of sale of goods as innominate; and, in fact, the Court of Appeal did so in *Cehave NV v Bremer Handelsgesellschaft mbH, The Hansa Nord* [1976] QB 44, CA, in relation to the term 'shipment to be made in good condition'. Where this construction is put upon an obligation to be fulfilled by the seller, the buyer will have a right to reject the goods only if the breach is such as to go to the root of the contract; failing this, he will be confined to a remedy in damages.

Section 11 sets out in statutory form the definition of a condition (and, by implication, of a warranty), and the conventional rules of the general law of contract relating to the breach of such terms.

The division of contractual terms into conditions, warranties and innominate terms is peculiar to the law of England and Wales, and the Act makes different provision for Scotland.

Since the amending Act of 1994, this has been done by using the neutral expression 'term' in the subsection where the basic rule is set out, and then in a later subsection stating that, in regard to England and Wales, the term is to be a condition or a warranty. Previously, the basic rule had simply stated: 'there is an implied condition that...' or 'there is an implied warranty that...' In the present chapter only the position in England and Wales will be considered.

The new s 15A, inserted by the amending Act of 1994, qualifies the rights which the buyer would normally have for a breach of condition by the seller, in the case of the statutory conditions implied by ss 13, 14(2) and (3) and 15 (but only where the buyer does not 'deal as consumer'. (For the meaning of this expression, see below, p 420.) If the breach is so slight that it would be unreasonable for him to reject the goods, it is to be treated only as a breach of warranty, unless a contrary intention appears in or is to be implied from the contract.

2 THE IMPLIED CONDITION AS TO TITLE (s 12(1))

Subject to one statutory exception (s 12(3), discussed below), in every contract of sale there is an implied condition on the part of the seller that in the case of a sale he has a right to sell the goods, and in the case of an agreement to sell he will have such a right at the time when the property is to pass (s 12(1)). So, if goods are sold which turn out to have been stolen, the buyer is entitled to the return of the whole of the purchase price.

Rowland v Divall
[1923] 2 KB 500, Court of Appeal

(The facts appear from the judgment.)

Scrutton LJ: The plaintiff purchased a car from the defendant for £334. He drove it from Brighton, where he bought it, to the place where he had a garage, painted it and kept it there for about two months. He then sold it to a third person who had it in his possession for another two months. Then came the police, who claimed it as the stolen car for which they had been looking. It appears that it had been stolen before the defendant became possessed of it, and consequently he had no title that he could convey to the plaintiff. In these circumstances the plaintiff sued the defendant for the price he paid for the car as on a total failure of consideration. Now before the passing of the Sale of Goods Act there was a good deal of confusion in the authorities as to the exact nature of the vendor's contract with respect to his title to sell. It was originally said that a vendor did not warrant his title. But gradually a number of exceptions crept in, till at last the exceptions became the rule, the rule being that the vendor warranted that he had title to what he purported to sell, except in certain special cases, such as that of a sale by a sheriff, who does not so warrant. Then came the Sale of Goods Act, which re-enacted that rule, but did so with this alteration: it re-enacted it as a condition, not as a warranty. Section 12 says in express terms that there shall be 'An implied condition on the part of the seller that...he has a right to sell the goods.' It being now a condition, wherever that condition is broken the contract can be rescinded, and with the rescission the buyer can demand a return of the purchase money, unless he has, with knowledge of the facts, held on to the bargain so as to waive the condition. But Mr Doughty argues that there can never be a rescission where a restitutio in integrum is impossible, and that here the plaintiff cannot rescind because he cannot return the car. To that the buyer's answer is that the reason of his inability to return it—namely, the fact that the defendant had no title to it—is the very thing of which he is complaining, and that it does not lie in the defendant's mouth to set up as a defence to the action his own breach of the implied condition that he had a right to sell. In my opinion that answer is well founded, and it would, I think, be absurd to apply the rule as to restitutio in integrum to such a state of facts. No doubt the general rule is that a buyer cannot rescind a contract of sale and get back the purchase money unless he can restore the subject matter. There are a large number of cases on the subject, some of which are not very easy to reconcile with others. Some of them make it highly probable that a certain degree of deterioration of the goods is not sufficient to take away the right to recover the purchase money. However I do not think it necessary to refer to them. It certainly seems to me that, in a case of rescission for the breach of the condition that the seller had a right to sell the goods, it cannot be that the buyer is deprived of his right to get back the purchase money because he cannot restore the goods which, from the nature of the transaction, are not the goods of the seller at all, and which the seller therefore has no right to under any circumstances. For these reasons I think that the plaintiff is entitled to recover the whole of the purchase money as for a total failure of consideration, and that the appeal must be allowed.

Atkin LJ: I agree. It seems to me that in this case there has been a total failure of consideration, that is to say that the buyer has not got any part of that for which he paid the purchase money. He paid the money in order that he might get the property, and he has not got it. It is true that the seller delivered to him the de facto possession, but the seller had not got the right to possession and consequently could not give it to the buyer. Therefore the buyer, during the time that he had the car in his actual possession had no right to it, and was at all times liable to the true owner for its conversion. Now there is no doubt that what the buyer had a right to get was the property in the car, for the Sale of Goods Act expressly provides that in every contract of sale there is an implied condition that the seller has a right to sell.... The whole object of a sale is to transfer property from one person to another....

It seems to me that in this case there must be a right to reject, and also a right to sue for the price paid as money had and received on failure of the consideration, and further that there is no obligation on the part of the buyer to return the car, for ex hypothesi the seller had no right to receive it. Under these circumstances can it make any difference that the buyer has used the car before he found out that there was a breach of the condition? To my mind it makes no difference at all. The buyer accepted the car on the representation of the seller that he had a right to sell it, and inasmuch as the seller had no such right he is not entitled to say that the buyer has enjoyed a benefit under the contract. In fact the buyer has not received any part of that which he contracted to receive—namely, the property and right to possession—and, that being so, there has been a total failure of consideration. The plaintiff is entitled to recover the £334 which he paid.

[Bankes LJ delivered a concurring judgment.]

NOTE

This rule can work considerable injustice, as is shown by the later case of *Butterworth v Kingsway Motors* [1954] 1 WLR 1286, where a car which was owned by a finance company and let on hire-purchase was wrongfully sold by the hirer and passed through several hands before being bought by the plaintiff, who used it for nearly a whole year before it was reclaimed by the finance company. (The Hire-Purchase Act 1964, Part III (above, p 390) was not yet in force.) It was held, following *Rowland v Divall*, that the plaintiff could recover all of his purchase price (£1725) from his immediate seller because of the breach of the condition implied by s 12(1), even though he had had the use of the car for almost a year, and the far smaller sum of £175 would have been sufficient to pay off the finance company's interest in the car. Had the plaintiff been restricted to a remedy in damages, he would of course have been entitled to be paid much less.

The Law Reform Committee, in its Twelfth Report (*Transfer of Title to Chattels*, Cmnd 2958, 1967), para 36, recommended that a buyer in these circumstances should be entitled to recover no more than his actual loss, giving credit for any benefit he may have had from the goods while they were in his possession, but no action has ever been taken to implement this proposal.

The following case shows that s 12(1) (which uses the phrase 'a right to sell the goods') is wider in its scope than might be inferred from the label 'implied condition as to title' which is commonly applied to it.

Niblett Ltd v Confectioners' Materials Co Ltd

[1921] 3 KB 387, Court of Appeal

(The facts appear from the judgment.)

Bankes LJ: In August 1919, the parties entered into a contract for the sale of 3000 cases of condensed milk. The contract was originally made at an interview, but it was subsequently confirmed by writing in the form of a sold note dated August 18 sent by the respondents to the appellants with a request that they would sign a counterpart, that is to say, a bought note, in the same terms, which the appellants did. The contract appears to be wholly embodied in the writing. Notwithstanding this both parties seem to have treated the contract as partly oral and partly in writing, and to have adduced parol evidence as to its terms, and counsel for the respondents have contended that it was agreed that one or more of three brands of condensed milk, including the 'Nissly' brand, might be delivered in fulfilment of the contract, and Bailhache J appears to have dealt with the case on that footing. Two thousand cases were delivered, and give rise to no question. One thousand arrived bearing labels with the word 'Nissly' upon them. It came to the knowledge of the Nestle and Anglo-Swiss Co that parcels of condensed milk were being imported with this label upon them, and they took up the position that these 1000 cases infringed their registered trade mark. They objected to these goods being dealt with in any way. The justice of their objection was admitted by the respondents, who gave an undertaking not to sell, offer for sale, or dispose of any condensed milk under the title of 'Nissly.' The appellants did their best to sell, exchange, or export the goods, but found that the only possible way of dealing with them was to strip them of their labels and sell them without marks or labels.

Bailhache J came to the clear conclusion that if s 12 of the Sale of Goods Act 1893 is to be construed literally the respondents had no right to sell the goods as they were, and that the appellants were not enjoying and never had enjoyed quiet possession of the goods; that they could never get them from the Commissioners of Customs, and that if they had got them they were never in a position to deal with them, because of the Nestle Co's threat. But he felt himself bound by the judgment of Lord Russell CJ in *Monforts v Marsden* ((1895)12 RPC 266) to give to s 12 a meaning and effect which he would not have attributed to it but for that case. With the greatest respect to Lord Russell CJ I think the doubts cast by Bailhache J upon that decision are justified. The case was heard and decided by Lord Russell CJ on circuit. He took the view that s 12 was to be read with qualifications like those which limit the implied covenant for quiet enjoyment in a conveyance of real property by a grantor who conveys as beneficial owner under s 7 of the Conveyancing Act 1881, and he imposed upon the implied obligations in s 12 of the Sale of Goods Act 1893, a restriction limiting their operation to acts and omissions of the vendor and those acting by his authority. I cannot agree with the view thus expressed by Lord Russell. I think s 12 has a much wider effect, and that the language does not warrant the limitation imposed by Lord Russell. The goods tendered must still be goods which the vendor has a right to sell. Therefore in my opinion the appellants have established a right of action under s 12, sub-s 1, of the Act.

It is not necessary to consider whether there is also a good cause of action under s 12, sub-s 2, and I say nothing upon that point....

[Scrutton and Atkin LJJ delivered concurring judgments.]

NOTE

Section 12 does not say that the seller undertakes that the buyer will get a good title, but rather that he himself has a right to sell the goods. So the seller may be in breach of the section even if (because the transaction comes within an exception to the *nemo dat* rule) he is able to confer a good title on the buyer: see *Barber v NWS Bank plc* [1996] 1 WLR 641, CA. In this case the buyer could have acquired a good title under Part III of the Hire Purchase Act 1964 (see above, p 390), but the court decreed that he could nevertheless rescind the transaction following *Rowland v Divall*. See also on this issue I Brown (1992) 108 LQR 221, discussing *R v Wheeler* (1990) 92 Cr App Rep 279.

3 SALE OF A LIMITED TITLE

Prior to 1973, there was considerable academic debate over the question whether the implied condition as to title could be excluded by an express stipulation in the contract (and, if so, whether the resulting transaction was a contract of sale of goods at all). However, the issue is now resolved by s 12(3), a provision which was first introduced by the Supply of Goods (Implied Terms) Act 1973. This subsection allows a person to contract to sell such title to goods as he (or another person) may have—so that a person who has found a watch and cannot trace the owner can sell his 'finder's title', and a landlord distraining on his tenant's goods or a sheriff who has seized goods in execution to satisfy a judgment debt can sell them on the understanding that the buyer shall get whatever title to them the tenant or debtor may have had. But, apart from this special provision, the condition implied by s 12(1) cannot be excluded or modified in any way by the operation of an exemption clause (Unfair Contract Terms Act 1977, s 6(1)(a))—unless the contract is of a kind to which that Act does not apply at all, such as an international sale contract.

4 THE IMPLIED WARRANTIES AS TO FREEDOM FROM ENCUMBRANCES AND QUIET POSSESSION (s 12(2)(a), (b))

Section 12 goes on to supplement the implied condition as to title by providing for two implied *warranties:* first, that the goods are, and will remain, free from any undisclosed encumbrances (s 12(2)(a)) and, secondly, that the buyer will enjoy quiet and undisturbed possession (s 12(2)(b)). These are the only statutory implied terms that are characterised as warranties and not conditions. It follows that if either of these implied terms is broken, the buyer will have only a remedy in damages and will not be able to reject the goods.

Where there has been a breach of s 12(1) (title), there will normally be a breach of s 12(2)(b) (quiet possession) also. In *Niblett v Confectioners' Materials Ltd* (above), Atkin LJ in the Court of Appeal held that there had also been a breach of s 12(2)(b). In *Mason v Burningham* [1949] 2 KB 545, CA, where the plaintiff bought a secondhand typewriter which turned out to have been stolen and had to be returned to its rightful owner, she could plainly have sued under s 12(1) (as in *Rowland v Divall* (above)), but chose instead to rely only on s 12(2)(b). She was awarded by way of damages not only a refund of the purchase price, but also a sum which she had reasonably (in the view of the court) paid to have the typewriter overhauled and put into first-class condition following the purchase.

Microbeads AC v Vinhurst Road Markings Ltd [1975] 1 WLR 218, CA, is a case which closely parallels *Niblett v Confectioners' Materials Ltd* (above): here the road-marking machines which were the subject of the contract turned out two years later to infringe the patent of a third party, who threatened to institute proceedings against the buyer. Since the patent was not granted to the third party until after the date of the contract of sale, there had been no breach of the condition as to title at the time when the property in the goods passed to the buyer, and so it was not possible to invoke s 12(1). But the court held that a remedy lay under s 12(2)(b).

The scope of s 12(2)(b) has never been fully explored. From the above cases, it is plain that there will be a breach of the statutory warranty if the buyer's possession is disturbed by the lawful act of a third person who asserts a superior title or a right which impairs the buyer's title or his freedom to possess and use the goods. On the other hand, it is plain that the seller will not be in breach of his undertaking if a stranger who has no connection with the seller (eg a trespasser or a vandal) simply commits a tort which interferes with the buyer's rights. However, a tort committed by the seller himself or his agent will cause him to incur liability under s 12(2)(b). In *Empresa Exportadora de Azucar v Industria Azucarera Nacional SA, The Playa Larga* [1983] 2 Lloyd's Rep 171 the seller, the Cuban state sugar trading agency, had sold sugar to a buyer in Chile and had sent a cargo of sugar aboard the *Playa Larga* to Valparaiso in part fulfilment of its obligations. When the Allende regime in Chile was over-thrown and replaced by a right-wing military dictatorship, the Cuban government ordered the seller to break off all trading relations with its Chilean buyer, and the seller ordered the ship not to unload the sugar. This action was held to amount to a breach of s 12(2)(b), and the seller was obliged to pay damages.

Subsections (4) and (5) of s 12 apply to the case where a contract of sale is made under s 12(3)—that is, where the seller contracts to transfer a limited title. Under these subsections, modified forms of the warranties as to freedom from encumbrances and quiet possession are implied in such a contract.

QUESTION

Why do you think that the Act characterises the implied terms in s 12(2) and 12(3) as warranties rather than conditions?

5 THE IMPLIED CONDITION THAT THE GOODS WILL CORRESPOND WITH THEIR DESCRIPTION (s 13)

Where there is a contract for the sale of goods by description, there is an implied condition that the goods will correspond with the description (s 13(1)). Section 13(2) goes on to say that if the sale is by sample as well as by description, the goods must comply with both the sample and their description.

This provision has been regarded as curious by some commentators, who have expressed surprise that the Act should bother to include such a rule at all, and thought it even more odd that the obligation should be described as an *implied* condition when there is surely an *express* obligation to deliver goods of the description by which they were sold.

The explanation has to be sought in the earlier history of the law of sale, some time before the codifying Act. In many of the older cases, a distinction was made between a sale of specific goods, on the one hand, and a sale of goods 'by description' on the other. An identified horse or vehicle may be regarded as typical of the former: the buyer could inspect it, have his own experts look at it, and was expected to rely on his own judgment in order to satisfy himself that he was getting what he wanted: *caveat emptor*. Alternatively, he could ask the seller for an express warranty (eg as to a horse's soundness) if he wanted to have the seller accept responsibility in some particular respect. Where, however, the sale was for generic goods which had no identity (eg '100 tons of King Edward potatoes'), the qualities of the goods which the buyer was bargaining to have could be ascertained only by reference to the contractual description by which they were sold (and, in commercial contracts, a further term, implied by law, that they should be of 'merchantable' quality under that description (now Sale of Goods Act 1979 (SGA 1979), s 14(2)); but in the modern version of this subsection the term used is 'satisfactory' quality and references to the contractual description have been eliminated). It was thus vital that, in the case of goods sold by description, the seller should be required to deliver goods conforming exactly to the description that the contract specified, and that the law should allow the buyer to reject the goods if they did not. Hence, in Chalmers' original draft, the implied term as to conformity with description was one of only two implied terms which he made *conditions* (the other, for similar reasons, being what is now part of s 34(2), relating to sales by sample). All the other statutory implied terms— even the implied term as to title—were characterised merely as warranties, it being left to the buyer to stipulate expressly that compliance with any particular term should be a 'condition' for his benefit if he thought it sufficiently important.

In the event, the law took a quite different turn soon after the Act of 1893 was passed. Chalmers did not clearly incorporate into this part of his Bill the distinction between sales of specific goods and sales by description that is explained above, and his Bill was altered during its passage through Parliament so as to make most of the statutory implied terms conditions, and not merely warranties. (At much the same time, lawyers allowed the meaning of the word 'condition' to slip from that of 'pure' condition to its modern connotation, 'term of vital importance'.) In *Varley v Whipp* [1900] 1 QB 513 the term 'sale by description' was interpreted as including a second-hand reaping machine (ie specific goods) which the buyer had not seen, and since then it has been extended to goods which the buyer has seen and inspected (*Grant v Australian Knitting Mills Ltd* [1936] AC 85, PC (woollen underpants bought in a retail shop); *Beale v Taylor* [1967] 1 WLR 1193, CA (a secondhand car advertised for sale in a newspaper)). These cases have led to the term 'sale by description' being given a meaning so attenuated as to give rise to speculation whether any contract of sale will be regarded as *not* being made 'by description': in *Grant* Lord Wright said ([1936] AC 85 at 100):

...there is a sale by description even though the buyer is buying something displayed before him on the counter: a thing is sold by description, though it is specific, so long as it is sold not merely as the specific thing but as a thing corresponding to a description, eg woollen under-garments.

Section 13(3), a new provision inserted by an amendment made in 1973, puts this matter even further beyond doubt by providing:

A sale of goods is not prevented from being a sale by description by reason only that, being exposed for sale or hire, they are selected by the buyer.

The main explanation for this extraordinary widening of the meaning of the term 'sale by description' is to be found in relation not to s 13, but to s 14(2), where the phrase was, prior to 1973, a precondition for the statutory implication of a duty to supply goods of 'merchantable quality'. The reason for implying such a term in a *mercantile* context has been explained above; but in more recent times s 14(2) came to be pressed more and more into service for the purpose of giving the buyer in a *consumer* sale a remedy where he had been sold defective goods. The customer who bought the underpants in *Grant v Australian Knitting Mills Ltd* suffered severe dermatitis because there were excess sulphites, a chemical irritant, in the pants which had not been washed out in the process of manufacture; he could not, in 1936, have been given a remedy under s 14(2) without a preliminary finding that the goods had been sold to him 'by description'—a hurdle which the Privy Council simply took in cavalier fashion without any great concern.

When we move out of the consumer sphere and back into the world of merchants with which this book is primarily concerned, we see that the implied condition as to correspondence with description has an important role to play, particularly in 'commodity' sales—contracts for the sale of generic goods—where the buyer has only the contract description to rely on in order to ensure that the goods he gets are the goods that he wants. This is illustrated by the two cases next cited, which may be regarded as 'classic' decisions on this issue—even though, paradoxically, amendments made by the 1994 Act (see below, p 471) make it likely that they would now be decided the other way!

Re Moore & Co Ltd and Landauer & Co's Arbitration
[1921] 2 KB 519, Court of Appeal

Moore & Co contracted to sell to Landauer & Co a quantity of Australian canned fruits, described as being packed in cases containing 30 cans each. When the ship containing the goods arrived in London, it was found that only about half of the consignment was packed in cases of 30, the rest being in cases of 24. The buyers rejected the goods without giving any reason; and were held by the Court of Appeal to have been entitled to do so under s 13.

Atkin LJ: It appears to me to be clear that the stipulation in the contract that there shall be 2½ dozen tins in a case is part of the description of the goods. There is, therefore, an implied condition that the goods when tendered shall correspond with the description. That condition was broken, and there was a right to reject. It appears to me also to be plain that by reason of s 30, sub-s 3, of the Sale of Goods Act 1893, the sellers were not entitled to insist upon the buyers accepting so much of the goods tendered as happened to correspond with the description. I think the buyers were entitled to reject the whole.

[Bankes and Scrutton LJJ delivered concurring judgments.]

Arcos Ltd v EA Ronaasen & Son
[1933] AC 470, House of Lords

This was a contract for the sale of Russian timber cut into staves for the purpose of making cement barrels. The contract specified that the staves should be ½ inch in thickness. The buyers claimed to be entitled to reject the timber because most of the staves were thicker than half an inch, although a large proportion were not more than $^9/_{16}$ of an inch. It was found that the staves were fit for making cement barrels and merchantable under the contract specification. Even so, the House of Lords upheld the buyers' right to reject for non-conformity with the contract description.

Lord Atkin: The decisions of the learned judge and of the Court of Appeal appear to me to have been unquestionably right. On the facts as stated by the umpire as of the time of inspection only about 5 per cent of the goods corresponded with the description: and the umpire finds it impossible to say what proportion conformed at the time of shipment.

It was contended that in all commercial contracts the question was whether there was a 'substantial' compliance with the contract: there always must be some margin: and it is for the tribunal of fact to determine whether the margin is exceeded or not. I cannot agree. If the written contract specifies conditions of weight, measurement and the like, those conditions must be complied with. A ton does not mean about a ton, or a yard about a yard. Still less when you descend to minute measurements does ½ inch mean about ½ inch. If the seller wants a margin he must and in my experience does stipulate for it. Of course by recognized trade usage particular figures may be given a different meaning, as in a baker's dozen; or there may be even incorporated a definite margin more or less: but there is no evidence or finding of such a usage in the present case.

No doubt there may be microscopic deviations which business men and therefore lawyers will ignore. And in this respect it is necessary to remember that description and quantity are not necessarily the same: and that the legal rights in respect of them are regulated by different sections of the code, description by s 13, quantity, by s 30. It will be found that most of the cases that admit any deviation from the contract are cases where there has been an excess or deficiency in quantity which the Court has considered negligible. But apart from this consideration the right view is that the conditions of the contract must be strictly performed. If a condition is not performed the buyer has a right to reject.

[Lords Buckmaster and Warrington of Clyffe delivered concurring opinions.
Lords Blanesburgh and Macmillan concurred.]

NOTE

These two decisions have been heavily criticised by some commentators, who have drawn attention to the fact that the goods delivered were apparently in each case perfectly suitable for the buyers' purpose, and that the buyers' undenied reason for wanting to reject them was that the market price for such goods had fallen and they wanted to get out of an unprofitable bargain. But there are important arguments which fully justify the court's strict approach to the requirement of conformity with description, *in the commercial context in which these cases were decided.* First, merchants put a high premium on certainty: a firm rule means that they know where they stand, whereas much delay would be caused if every case had to go to court in order to ascertain whether the deviation from the contract was significant, or what the real motives of the parties were. Secondly, more often than not, the buyers of commodities are not merchants who intend to use the goods themselves, but dealers who have bought to sell on, and who may well already have resold the goods to sub-buyers; and in such a case they will usually have resold the goods by the same description. There could well be a long chain of further sub-contracts. If there is a dispute over conformity with description under the first sale, the court is not to know what use for the goods the ultimate buyer may have in mind, or whether it is such as would entitle him to reject them. Thirdly, as we shall see (below, p 511) the completion of these contracts of sale is very often carried out not by the parties themselves, but by others on their behalf (such as their respective banks) by payment of the price in exchange for the shipping documents relating to the goods—possibly in a foreign country. These representatives will not be in a position to know whether goods which do not fully comply with the contract description will nevertheless be suitable for their clients' purpose (still less, their clients' sub-purchasers' purpose), and so the only workable rule has to be one calling for strict conformity.

Against the background of this discussion, we are in a better position to look a little more closely at the concept of 'sale by description', and in particular to ask which out of the many words used in reference to the goods being sold are part of their contract 'description'.

The approach of the courts will depend upon the context. In the commercial context of commodity sales, we have seen from *Re Moore and Landauer* and *Arcos v Ronaasen* (above) that words regarding the packing of the goods and their dimensions may be part of their description. The same may be true of references to the origin of the goods, their analysis, etc: the parties can make any element or item part of the description and, if the court concludes that that was their intention, the buyer is entitled to stipulate that that, and that alone, is what he shall get. In contrast, particularly when the case is concerned with specific or identifiable goods, it is open to the court to hold that, although descriptive words were used, the goods were not 'sold by' that description. This is clear from *Reardon Smith Line Ltd v Yngvar Hansen-Tangen* (where a contract to charter a ship raised analogous questions) and even more so, in the somewhat specialist world of the art market, from *Harlingdon & Leinster Enterprises Ltd v Christopher Hull Fine Art Ltd.* The issue for the court is then to decide whether the parties attached sufficient weight to the particular words as to warrant their being treated as part of the contractual description.

Reardon Smith Line Ltd v Yngvar Hansen-Tangen
[1976] 1 WLR 989, House of Lords

In 1972 Sanko, a Japanese shipbuilding company, contracted to charter to Hansen-Tangen a new 80,000-ton tanker, to be delivered when construction was completed in 1974. Since at the time when the contract was entered into construction had not begun, it was provided that Sanko would declare the yard where the vessel was to be built and its hull number at a later date. In fulfilment of this requirement, Sanko notified Hansen-Tangen that the vessel was to be built by the Osaka company and 'known as Hull No 354 until named'. Osaka's own yard was not large enough to build an 80,000-ton ship, and so it arranged for the work to be done by a subsidiary company, Oshima, 300 miles away, and Oshima gave the proposed vessel its own hull number, 004, though it continued to be shown in Osaka's own books as No 354. Hansan-Tangen later contracted to sub-charter the tanker to Reardon Smith, describing it as 'newbuilding motor tank vessel called Yard No 354 at Osaka'. When the ship was ready for delivery the market had collapsed owing to the oil crisis of 1974, and the charterers sought to reject it on the ground that it did not correspond with the contractual description.

Lord Wilberforce stated the facts and continued: These being the background facts, the whole case…turns, in my opinion, upon the long italicised passage in the sub-charter set out above which, for convenience of reference I repeat:

> (the good) Japanese flag (subject to Clause 41) Newbuilding motor tank vessel called Yard No 354 at Osaka Zosen.

I shall refer to this as the 'box' since it appears enclosed in a typed box on the document….

I ask what was the commercial purpose of these charterparties and what was the factual background against which they were made? The purpose is clear: it was to make available to (1) Hansen-Tangen and

(2) to Reardon Smith a medium-sized tanker suitable for use as such, this tanker not being in existence, or even under construction at the date of either charter, and, at the date of the intermediate charter not even the subject of contracts made by the supplying company. The vessel was to be constructed in a Japanese yard and made available on charter to Sanko as part of a programme. At the date of the sub-charter the vessel was identified in contracts for its construction in Japan and had a serial number. In order to ensure that the tanker was suitable for its purpose a detailed specification was drawn up—by way of a warranted description with which of course the vessel must strictly comply.

In addition, since at the time of either charterparty the vessel was not in existence or under construction, some means had to be agreed upon for identifying the particular vessel—one out of a programme—which would form the subject matter of the charters. This was indispensable so as to enable those committing themselves to hire the vessel, to sub-hire it, if they wished, and if necessary to arrange finance. This necessary identification was to be effected by nomination, by Sanko in the first place and then by Hansen-Tangen.

The text of the charterparties confirms beyond doubt that this was what was intended and done. The preamble, in the Shelltime 3 form, provides for the insertion of a name—'being owners of the good…tank vessel called….' The box insertion in the subcharter was made in this place—'called Yard No 354 at Osaka Zosen.' The intermediate charter, entered into before Sanko had nominated any vessel, provided in its preamble—instead of 'called…' for declaration by the owners together with the Hull number, and the addendum, entered into after Sanko had nominated, provided 'to be built by Osaka Shipbuilding Co Ltd and known as Hull No 354 until named'. What is vital about each of these insertions is that they were simple substitutes for a name, serving no purpose but to provide a means whereby the charterers could identify the ship. At the dates when these insertions were made no importance could have been attached to the matters now said to be so significant—they were not a matter of negotiation, but of unilateral declaration. What is now sought is to elevate them into strict contractual terms in the nature of 'conditions.'

The appellants sought, necessarily, to give to the box and the corresponding provision in the intermediate charter contractual effect. They argued that these words formed part of the 'description' of the future goods contracted to be provided that, by analogy with contracts for the sale of goods, any departure from the description entitled the other party to reject, that there were departures in that the vessel was not built by Osaka Shipbuilding Co Ltd and was not Hull No 354. I shall attempt to deal with each of these contentions.

In the first place, I am not prepared to accept that authorities as to 'description' in sale of goods cases are to be extended, or applied, to such a contract as we have here. Some of these cases either in themselves (*Re Moore and Co and Landauer and Co* [above, p 399] or as they have been interpreted (eg *Behn v Burness* (1863) 3 B & S 751) I find to be excessively technical and due for fresh examination in this House. Even if a strict and technical view must be taken as regards the description of unascertained future goods (eg commodities) as to which each detail of the description must be assumed to be vital, it may be, and in my opinion is, right to treat other contracts of sale of goods in a similar manner to other contracts generally so as to ask whether a particular item in a description constitutes a substantial ingredient of the 'identity' of the thing sold, and only if it does to treat it as a condition (see *Couchman v Hill* [1947] KB 554, 559, per Scott LJ). I would respectfully endorse what was recently said by Roskill LJ in *Cehave NV v Bremer Handelsgesellschaft mbH* [1976] QB 44, 71:

> In principle it is not easy to see why the law relating to contracts for the sale of goods should be different from the law relating to the performance of other contractual obligations, whether charterparties or other types of contract. Sale of goods law is but one branch of the general law of contract. It is desirable that the same legal principles should apply to the law of contract as a whole and that different legal principles should not apply to different branches of that law….

The general law of contract has developed, along much more rational lines (eg *Hong Kong Fir Shipping Co Ltd v Kawasaki Kisen Kaisha Ltd* [1962] 2 QB 26), in attending to the nature and gravity of a breach or departure rather than in accepting rigid categories which do or do not automatically give a right to rescind, and if the choice were between extending cases under the Sale of Goods Act 1893 into other fields, or allowing more modern doctrine to infect those cases, my preference would be clear. The importance of this line of argument is that Mocatta J and Lord Denning MR used it in the present case so as to reject the appellants' argument on 'description' and I agree with them. But in case it does not appeal to this House, I am also satisfied that the appellants fail to bring the present case within the strictest rules as to 'description.'

In my opinion that fatal defect in their argument consists in their use of the words 'identity' or 'identification' to bridge two meanings. It is one thing to say of given words that their purpose is to state (identify) an essential part of the description of the goods. It is another to say that they provide one party with a specific indication (identification) of the goods so that he can find them and if he wishes sub-dispose of them. The appellants wish to say of words which 'identify' the goods in the second sense, that they describe them in the first. I have already given reasons why I can only read the words in the second sense.

The difference is vital. If the words are read in the first sense, then, unless I am right in the legal argument above, each element in them has to be given contractual force. The vessel must, as a matter of contract, and as an essential term, be built by Osaka and must bear their Yard No 354—if not the description is not complied with and the vessel tendered is not that contracted for.

If in the second sense, the only question is whether the words provide a means of identifying the vessel. If they fairly do this, they have fulfilled their function. It follows that if the second sense is correct, the words used can be construed much more liberally than they would have to be construed if they were providing essential elements of the description....

So the question becomes simply whether, as a matter of fact, it can fairly be said that—as a means of identification—the vessel was Yard No 354 at Osaka Zosen or 'built by Osaka Shipping Co Ltd and known as Hull No 354 until named.' To answer this, regard may be had to the actual arrangements for building the vessel and numbering it before named.

My Lords, I have no doubt, for the reasons given by the Court of Appeal, that an affirmative answer must be given. I shall not set out the evidence which clearly makes this good. The fact is that the vessel always was Osaka Hull No 354—though also Oshima No 4—and equally it can fairly be said to have been 'built' by Osaka Shipbuilding Co Ltd as the company which planned, organised and directed the building and contractually engaged with Sculptor to build it, though also it could be said to have been built by Oshima Shipbuilding Co Ltd. For the purpose of the identificatory clause, the words used are quite sufficient to cover the facts. No other vessel could be referred to: the reference fits the vessel in question.

[Viscount Dilhorne and Lord Russell of Killowen delivered concurring opinions. Lords Simon of Glaisdale and Kilbrandon concurred.]

Harlingdon & Leinster Enterprises Ltd v Christopher Hull Fine Art Ltd
[1991] 1 QB 564, Court of Appeal

This contract concerned the sale for £6000 of a painting described as being the work of Gabriele Münter, a painter of the German expressionist school. The parties were both art dealers, the buyers (but not the sellers) being specialists in this area of the art market. The painting was a forgery worth £50 to £100. The Court of Appeal held that although the seller had used the words 'by Münter' in describing the painting, it had not been *sold by* that description—the buyer having relied on his own judgment in regard to this question of attribution. Accordingly, he was not liable to the buyer for breach of s 13.

Nourse LJ: The judge [Judge Oddie] found that both at the time when the agreement was made and subsequently when the invoice was made out both Mr Hull and Mr Runkel [the representatives respectively of the sellers and the buyers] believed that the painting was by Münter and that, if either had not believed that, the deal would not have been made. He made the following further findings:

> In my judgment Runkel must have known and accepted that Hull was disclaiming any judgment, knowledge or private information which would or could have grounded the latter's earlier statement to Braasch that he had two paintings by Gabriele Münter for sale . . . I think the only conclusion which can be drawn from the unusual facts of this case is that it was Runkel's exercise of his own judgment as to the quality of the pictures, including the factor of the identity of their painter, which induced him to enter into the agreement he made with Hull. However, I am not satisfied that without the attribution, given what followed in the circumstances in which it was made, Runkel would not have purchased the painting. If it had never been made, Runkel would never have gone to see the paintings. But when he did go and examine the painting, he considered whether it was a Münter or not; he did agree to buy it, regardless of the attribution, because he relied on his own judgment. . . . It was reliance on his own assessment and not upon anything said by a man who had gone out of his way to stress his ignorance of the paintings which led Runkel astray.

Thus did the judge find as fact that the plaintiffs did not rely on the description of the painting as one by Gabriele Münter. They relied only on their own assessment. . . . Section 13(1) of the Sale of Goods Act 1979 is in these terms:

> Where there is a contract for the sale of goods by description, there is an implied condition that the goods will correspond with the description.

The sales to which the subsection is expressed to apply are sales 'by description.' Authority apart, those words would suggest that the description must be influential in the sale, not necessarily alone, but so as to become an essential term, ie a condition, of the contract. Without such influence a description cannot be said to be one *by* which the contract for the sale of the goods is made.

I think that the authorities to which we were referred are consistent with this view of s 13(1).

[Slade LJ delivered a concurring judgment.
Stuart-Smith LJ dissented.]

We may contrast the cases above with *Beale v Taylor* [1967] 1 WLR 1193, CA, where a car was advertised for sale in a newspaper as a 'Herald convertible, white, 1961, twin carbs', and was bought after the buyer had inspected it. It was in fact a hybrid made up of the back half of a 1961 Triumph Herald convertible welded to the front half of an older model. The Court of Appeal held that the date, 1961, was part of the contract description and that the buyer could reject under s 13. It is plain that the court has considerable discretion in the scope which it may give to the concept of a sale 'by description' where the sale is of a specific article.

NOTE

Where goods have deteriorated or been adulterated, there will come a point where it is arguable that they are not simply different in *quality* from what might have been expected, but are not goods answering to the contract 'description' at all—for instance, cement which has been allowed to become wet so as to be commercially useless. The question must be resolved as a matter of degree. In *Pinnock Bros v Lewis & Peat Ltd* [1923] 1 KB 690 copra cake intended to be fed to livestock which had been adulterated with castor beans and rendered poisonous was described by Roche J as something 'which could not properly be described as copra cake at all'. In contrast, in *Ashington Piggeries Ltd v Christopher Hill Ltd* [1972] AC 441, HL, herring meal mixed into a feeding compound for mink which had become toxic through reaction to a preservative was held still to answer the description 'herring meal': it was not shown to be toxic to other animals, and remained suitable for other commercial purposes, such as a fertiliser. (Compare the cases discussed above, p 307, in relation to ss 6 and 7 of the Act.)

6 IMPLIED TERMS AS TO QUALITY AND FITNESS

(a) No general rule

The Sale of Goods Act 1979, s 14, contains provisions by which undertakings on the part of the seller as to the quality of the goods and their fitness for a particular purpose are implied into certain contracts of sale. However, it is most important to note that these provisions constitute *exceptions* to the general rule, and that the basic rule denies that a seller is deemed to give any such undertakings. In other words, the traditional broad principal of *caveat emptor* governs this aspect of the law of sale, as so many others. Section 14(1) confirms this:

Except as provided by this section and s 15 below and subject to any other enactment, there is no implied term about the quality or fitness for any particular purpose of goods supplied under a contract of sale.

However, apart from statute, a term about quality or fitness may be implied by usage (s 14(4)).

(b) Statutory exceptions: 'where the seller sells goods in the course of a business'

The two exceptions contained in s 14(2) and 14(3) apply only 'where the seller sells goods in the course of a business'. These subsections have established an important code for the protection of people who buy as consumers from a retailer or manufacturer; but their scope is much wider than consumer protection measures; and, indeed, they were not originally conceived as primarily intended for this purpose. The exceptions apply also to transactions between one merchant and another, whether they are manufacturers, wholesalers, importers, retailers or any other kind of dealer. The provisions also apply where a sale is made by a person who in the course of a business is acting as agent for another (including an undisclosed principal: see *Boyter v Thomson* [1995] 2 AC 628, HL), except where the fact that the seller (the agent's principal) is not selling in the course of a business is known to the buyer or reasonable steps have been taken to bring this fact to the buyer's notice (s 14(5)). But where a private person sells to a business buyer or to another private person, it will be a case of *caveat emptor*.

A question which remained unresolved for a considerable time after the enactment of these sections in their modern form (in 1973) was this: whether a person sells 'in the course of a business' where his business does not normally include that of selling goods, or of selling goods of the type in question—eg a solicitor who sells off a surplus desk or computer. The issue has now been resolved by the ruling of the Court of Appeal in *Stevenson v Rogers* [1999] 1 All ER 613, CA where Stevenson, who had been in business as a fisherman for 20 years, sold his fishing boat, the *Jelle,* and bought another as a replacement. Even though this was a one-off venture and was merely incidental to the business which Stevenson carried on, it was held that the sale *was* made 'in the course of' that business so as to bring the transaction within the scope of s 14 and render the seller potentially liable under the terms as to quality and fitness implied by that section.

NOTE

The question whether a person sells or buys 'in the course of a business' arises in a number of contexts, and the similar expression 'in the ordinary course of his business' in yet others. The construction of these phrases necessarily depends on their context, and so care should be taken in comparing one with another. Currently, commentators have thought that there may be inconsistency between the rulings in *Stevenson v Rogers* and in a number of cases concerned with the definition of 'dealing as a consumer' in the Unfair Contract Terms Act 1977, s 12 and other consumer-protection legislation. Under this provision a buyer will not be regarded as dealing 'as a consumer' if he—or it (for a company is not excluded)—does so 'in the course of a business' (see below, p 419). In *R & B Customs Brokers Co Ltd v United Dominion Trust Ltd* [1988] 1 WLR 321 R & B, a company in the business of shipping brokers, bought a car for one of its directors to use in that business. This was a one-off transaction: R & B had no connection with the motor trade. It was held not to have bought 'in the course of a business' and so was entitled to protection as a consumer. *R & B* has been followed by the Court of Appeal in *Feldaroll Foundry plc v Hermes Leasing (London) Ltd* [2004] EWCA Civ 747 (noted by C Twigg-Flesner, (2005) 121 LQR 41). The contrasting cases remain authorities, each in its own context,—as does the hire-purchase case *GE Capital Bank Ltd v Rushton* (above, p 391).

(c) Implied condition that the goods are of satisfactory quality

Where a seller sells goods in the course of a business, there is a condition implied by statute that the goods supplied under the contract are of satisfactory quality. There is, however, no such condition (1) as regards defects specifically drawn to the buyer's attention before the contract is made, or (2) if the buyer examines the goods before the contract is made, as regards defects which that examination ought to reveal, or (3) in the case of a sale by sample, in regard to any matter which would have been apparent on a reasonable examination of the sample (s 14(2C)).

This provision is new, dating only from the amending Act of 1995. It replaces earlier formulations of a similar rule going back to the 1893 Act (in which it was numbered s 14(1)) that used the term 'merchantable quality'. The concept of 'merchantable quality' was not given any statutory definition in the Act of 1893. This was, no doubt, understandable in an Act which at the time was thought of primarily as a merchants' code: whether a consignment of goods was of 'merchantable' quality under its contract description was a question which could be resolved by bringing in as evidence the opinion of other merchants who dealt in such goods, or by referring the question to an arbitrator or umpire who was expert in the particular trade. But more recently problems have arisen where s 14(2) has been invoked in a consumer context—eg in relation to such questions as whether a car which had a mechanical fault or damaged bodywork or upholstery was 'merchantable', and whether it made a difference that the car was sold as new or second-hand.

These problems were not made any easier because there was little agreement among the judges as to the meaning of the term 'merchantable', even when it was used in the context of a transaction between merchants. Some early cases (eg *Jackson v Rotax Motor & Cycle Co* [1910] 2 KB 937, CA) seem to have construed it as equivalent to 'saleable' or 'resaleable' or 'saleable under that description'. A second set of judicial definitions turned primarily on the notion of what a reasonable buyer would accept in performance of a contract of sale of goods under that description (*Bristol Tramways etc Carriage Co Ltd v Fiat Motors Ltd* (below, p 412)) which were sold at or about the contract price (*BS Brown & Sons v Craiks Ltd* [1970] 1 WLR 752, HL). A third approach focused on the purpose for which the goods were required: not the buyer's specific purpose (which is a distinct question dealt with by s 14(3)), but the usual or normal purpose for which such goods are bought, or at least one such purpose. In *Henry Kendall & Sons v William Lillico & Sons Ltd* [1969] 2 AC 31, HL (a case sometimes referred to as *Hardwick Game Farm Ltd v SAPPA*) a groundnut extraction imported from Brazil was used as an ingredient in a compound poultry meal and fed by farmers to pheasants. The extraction contained a substance which made it toxic to poultry, but it was perfectly suitable for cattle, pigs and other livestock. A majority of the House of Lords held that it was merchantable.

In 1973, a statutory definition of 'merchantable quality' was introduced in an endeavour to give guidance on this question; but it did little more than bring together the various elements listed above. It read:

Goods of any kind are of merchantable quality . . . if they are as fit for the purpose or purposes for which goods of that kind are commonly bought as it is reasonable to expect having regard to any description applied to them, the price (if relevant) and all the other relevant circumstances.

But this reform achieved little. There was a difference of opinion on the question whether the new provision simply restated the common law or was intended to replace it; there was also controversy as to whether the goods had to be fit for *all* the usual purposes or only some or most of them; and, above all, it did not address many of the problems that commonly arose in the context of consumer sales. So it was a case of 'back to the drawing board'; and the Law Commissions in due course recommended wholesale changes which involved abandoning altogether the concept of 'merchantable quality'. In their report ('Sale and Supply of Goods', L Com No 160, Scot L Com No 104, Cd 137 (1987)) they proposed the new term 'acceptable quality'; but when eventually the reforms reached the statute book in the Sale and Supply of Goods Act 1994, the expression 'satisfactory quality' was preferred.

The new definition is now incorporated in the Sale of Goods Act and reads (s 14(2A), (2B)):

(2A) For the purposes of this Act, goods are of satisfactory quality if they meet the standard that a reasonable person would regard as satisfactory, taking account of any description of the goods, the price (if relevant) and all the other relevant circumstances.

(2B) For the purposes of this Act, the quality of the goods includes their state and condition and the following (among others) are in appropriate cases aspects of the quality of the goods—

  (a) fitness for all the purposes for which goods of the kind in question are commonly supplied,

  (b) appearance and finish,

  (c) freedom from minor defects,

  (d) safety, and

  (e) durability.

The principal focus is thus now on 'acceptability', judged by the standards of the reasonable person. It will be seen that some features have been brought forward from the former definitions (description, price, state and condition) and that 'fitness for purpose' has been, in a sense, demoted from part of the definition to being merely an 'aspect' of quality in an appropriate case. (However, there is now a clear statement that regard is to be had to *all* the purposes for which such goods are commonly supplied, so that *Kendall v Lillico* (above) might well not now be followed.) Subparagraphs (b) to (e) go a considerable way to signal a new departure, away from considerations which might influence a merchant and towards those which would matter to a consumer. It remains to be seen how well the new definition will work, especially in a mercantile context.

A further gloss has been put on the definition of 'satisfactory quality' by an amendment made to the Act in 2002 (Sale and Supply of Goods to Consumers Regulations 2002, SI 2002/3045, reg 3, implementing Directive 1999/44/EC). This applies only to a contract of sale where the buyer deals as a consumer (defined as 'any natural person who is acting for purposes outside his trade, business or profession'). A new s 14(2D) states that the 'relevant circumstances' mentioned in s 14(2A) are to include 'any public statements on the specific characteristics of the goods made about them by the seller, the producer or his representative, particularly in advertising or on labelling'. ('Producer' means the manufacturer, the importer of the goods into the European Economic Area or anyone else who purports to be a producer by placing his name, trade mark or other distinctive sign on the goods: reg 6(1)). So a seller may be held liable for statements made about the goods by the manufacturer or other producer; but he will escape liability if: (1) he was not, and could not reasonably have been, aware of the statement; (2) the statement had been publicly withdrawn or corrected before the contract was made; or (3) the buyer's decision to buy the goods could not have been influenced by the statement (s 14(2E)).

Two other points may be noted arising out of the statutory language.

First, 'quality', in relation to goods, includes their state or condition (s 61(1)). So, in *Niblett v Confectioners' Materials Ltd* (above, p 395), the tinned milk with labels which infringed the Nestle trade mark were held not to be of merchantable quality, with the result that there was a breach of s 14(2) as well as of s 12(1). Secondly, s 14(2) states that the implied term is that the goods *supplied under the contract of sale* are of satisfactory quality, and not just 'the goods sold'. This more general phrase has been construed as including the container in which the goods were supplied. In *Geddling v Marsh* [1920] 1 KB 668 mineral water was sold to the plaintiff in a 'returnable' bottle which was bailed and not sold to her: the bottle burst and injured her. The court ruled that the bottle was 'supplied under a contract of sale' and that she could recover damages under s 14(2).

The time factor. The new statutory definition makes specific reference to 'durability', a term which is obviously appropriate in the context of sales (especially to consumers) of cars, refrigerators, etc but not, in the nature of things, to goods which are of a perishable nature or liable to deteriorate. This can give rise to problems in commercial sales, and in particular 'export' transactions. Suppose, for instance, that goods are sold and delivered by S to B which, to the knowledge of S, B intends to transport to a distant place. Must the goods be of satisfactory quality *both* at the time when they are delivered *and* at the time when they arrive at that place, or is it sufficient that they are satisfactory at the former time? Or is there some other test? In relation to the former requirement of 'merchantable quality', the courts resolved this issue with something of a compromise formulation. It was settled that the relevant time was the time of delivery (*Cordova Land Co Ltd v Victor Bros Inc* [1966] 1 WLR 793, where skins sold to be shipped from the United States to Hull were found to be damaged on arrival at Hull: held, there could be no breach of any implied term in the absence of evidence that the goods were defective at the time when they were shipped). But where it was contemplated by the parties that the goods were to undergo a journey, they would not be regarded as being of merchantable quality unless, at the time they were delivered, they were in a fit state to endure a normal journey of that kind and be in a merchantable state when they arrived. It is likely that this will continue to be the rule with regard to 'satisfactory' quality.

Mash & Murrell Ltd v Joseph I Emanuel Ltd
[1961] 1 WLR 862, Queen's Bench Division (reversed by the Court of Appeal on other grounds, [1962] 1 WLR 16n)

The contract was for the sale of Cyprus spring crop potatoes, C & F Liverpool, to be shipped on the SS *Ionian* from a port in Cyprus (Limassol). (On C & F contracts, see below, p 506.) When the potatoes arrived in Liverpool they were rotten and unfit for human consumption.

Diplock J found on the evidence that the potatoes when loaded at Limassol were not fit to travel to Liverpool, and said:...These goods being bought c & f Liverpool, the warranty as to merchantability was a warranty that they should remain merchantable for a reasonable time, the time reasonable in all the circumstances, which means a time for the normal transit to the destination, Liverpool, and for disposal after. That warranty was, in my view, broken.

[The Court of Appeal ([1962] 1 WLR 16n) reversed this decision on the facts, finding that the potatoes had suffered from excess heat and lack of ventilation on the voyage. For the purpose of this finding, it assumed that the view of Diplock J correctly expressed the law.]

Before leaving s 14(2), mention should be made of the three statutory exceptions in s 14(2C):

Defects specifically drawn to the buyer's attention. In *Bartlett v Sidney Marcus Ltd* [1965] 1 WLR 1013 the buyer could not be heard to complain of a defective clutch in a secondhand car which he had been told about before entering into the contract.

Defects which an examination made by the buyer ought to have revealed. This proviso was altered in 1973: previously, it appeared from the decided cases that a buyer who had only been able to make a cursory examination might be debarred from a remedy if a more thorough examination would have revealed the defect in question. This was based on the former wording of the proviso ('as regards defects which *such* examination ought to have revealed'). The revised wording ('as regards defects which *that* examination ought to reveal') makes it fairly clear that the exception will apply only if the buyer has examined the goods and the defect ought to have been revealed by such an examination as he actually did make.

Defects which ought to have been apparent on a reasonable examination of the sample. This provision (which is new) applies only in the case of a contract for sale by sample, and complements s 15(2)(c). Under the latter subsection, the seller undertakes responsibility for any defect making the quality of the goods unsatisfactory which would not be apparent on reasonable examination of the sample. Under the present provision, responsibility for any defect which would be so apparent lies with the buyer. In contrast with s 14(2C)(b), discussed in the preceding paragraph, this exception applies whether or not the buyer has actually made an examination.

NOTE

Many textbooks on the law of sale of goods contain detailed discussions of cases such as *Bartlett v Sidney Marcus Ltd* (above) which were concerned with consumers who complained that the cars which they had been sold were not as good as they had expected. The statutory implied term as to merchantable quality under the former law did not always provide an acceptable remedy in such cases. For instance, in *Business Application Specialists*

Ltd v Nationwide Credit Corpn Ltd [1988] RTR 332 a secondhand Mercedes sold for nearly £15,000 was found to need repairs costing £635: it was nevertheless held to be merchantable. And in *Rogers v Parish (Scarborough) Ltd* [1987] QB 933, CA, there was a difference of opinion between the trial judge and the Court of Appeal whether a car with leaking oil seals which was driven 5000 miles before being repaired (and was in fact repaired by the seller at no cost to the buyer) was merchantable. In contrast, in *Bartlett v Sydney Marcus Ltd* (above) a secondhand car, known when sold to have a defective clutch, cost rather more to repair than the buyer expected: it was held to be merchantable. The new concept of satisfactory quality is likely to prove more favourable to buyers in this type of case, especially if it is read in conjunction with s 48A(3), (4) (see below, p 486), which establishes a presumption in consumer sales that goods which are not of satisfactory quality at any time within the period of six months after delivery were subject to the same defect at the date of delivery.

Some further examples

Cases decided since the 1995 Act introduced the concept of 'satisfactory quality' include the following—some in a commercial, and some in a consumer, context. (For further examples, see WCH Ervine [2004] JBL 617.)

Britvic Soft Drinks Ltd v Messer UK Ltd [2002] EWCA Civ 548, [2002] 2 All ER (Comm) 321. Carbon dioxide was supplied to be used in the manufacture of sparkling drinks. It was contaminated with benzene, a carcinogenic. Although the gas did not infringe the relevant British Standard and, in the quantities used in the drinks, would pose no threat to health for consumers, it was held not to be of satisfactory quality because it was commercially necessary for the buyer to recall all the drinks from sale for fear of adverse publicity.

Clegg v Andersson [2003] EWCA Civ 320, [2003] 1 All ER (Comm) 721. Andersson sold Mr and Mrs Clegg a new yacht for £236,000. It was delivered with a keel that was some 800kg overweight, requiring remedial work estimated to cost about £1,680. The yacht was held not to be of satisfactory quality. Hale LJ said that in the case of a high-priced quality product (such as a 'brand-new boat') 'the customer may be entitled to expect that it is free from even minor defects, in other words perfect or nearly so'.

Jewson Ltd v Boyhan [2003] EWCA Civ 1030, [2004] 1 Lloyd's Rep 505. Kelly, who was converting a former school building into flats, bought 13 electric boilers to install in them. The boilers worked perfectly well, but it was discovered that they had the effect of giving the flats low 'home energy ratings' under a government assessment procedure. This was likely to put off potential purchasers of the flats and make it more difficult for them to get a mortgage. The Court of Appeal held that the boilers were of satisfactory quality.

Bramhill v Edwards [2004] EWCA Civ 403, [2004] 2 Lloyd's Rep 653. Bramhill bought a large motor home from Edwards, who had imported it from the United States. It turned out to be two inches wider than the legal limit in this country, but there was evidence that a significant number of similar over-width motor homes were in use in the UK and that the authorities were turning a blind eye to this breach of the law. The Court of Appeal held that the buyer had no remedy under s 14(2).

Balmoral Group Ltd v Borealis (UK) Ltd [2006] EWHC 1900 (Comm), [2006] 2 Lloyd's Rep 629. Polyethylene which included a novel component was supplied for the manufacture of oil tanks, but many of the tanks became brittle and fractured. The court ruled that the test of satisfactory quality did not require that where a material had a very wide range of possible uses the 'fit for all purposes' test should mean 'fit for every conceivable purpose'. A manufacturer who switched to a new type of polyethylene could be expected to review its processing operations so that the tanks which it produced were of acceptable standard.

(d) Implied condition as to fitness for purpose (s 14(3))

We have seen that the definition of 'satisfactory quality' under s 14(2) carries within it the notion that the goods sold should be fit for all the purposes for which goods of that description are commonly used. If the buyer wants the goods for a *particular* purpose, his case will be stronger if he can bring it within the wording of s 14(3)—which, confusingly, was numbered as s 14(1) in the Act of 1893. This reads as follows:

Where the seller sells goods in the course of a business and the buyer, expressly or by implication, makes known...to the seller...any particular purpose for which the goods are being bought, there is an implied [condition] that the goods supplied under the contract are reasonably fit for that purpose, whether or not that is a purpose for which such goods are commonly supplied, except where the circumstances show that the buyer does not rely, or that it is unreasonable for him to rely, on the skill or judgment of the seller....

It will be noted that s 14(3) contains a number of phrases which are used also in s 14(2) and have been discussed above in relation to that provision. These include 'where the seller sells goods in the course of a business' and 'the goods supplied under the contract'.

Again, we should bear in mind that the condition implied by s 14(3) is the *exception*, and not the rule: the basic rule is *caveat emptor*, as set out in s 14(1).

The words 'particular purpose' have always been given a very broad interpretation. It would be natural to assume that they were intended to be construed in a restrictive sense, and confined to the situation where the goods in question have a potentially wide range of purposes and the buyer wants them for just one such purpose—eg perhaps, where he buys paint and makes it known to the seller that he wishes to use it to paint metal that is exposed outdoors. (Compare the *Cammell Laird* case (below), where a propeller was ordered for the special purpose of being fitted to a particular ship.) But this is not the approach which the courts have adopted. Where goods have only one purpose, or one obvious purpose, this has been regarded as the 'particular' purpose—and, indeed, if it is the obvious purpose the courts will take it for granted that this purpose was made known to the seller, so that the case will be very readily deemed to fall within the section. So, for instance, food will be taken to have been bought for the 'particular' purpose of being eaten (*Wallis v Russell* [1902] 2 IR 585), milk to be drunk (*Frost v Aylesbury Dairy Co* [1905] 1 KB 608, CA) and a hot-water bottle for filling with hot water to warm a bed (*Priest v Last* [1903] 2 KB 148, CA). This construction is given added support by the inclusion in the section of the words 'whether or not that is a purpose for which such goods are commonly supplied'. The main reason why the courts have adopted this generous interpretation of the statutory language is, once again, to broaden the scope of the remedies available to a buyer in a consumer sale: if, for some reason, s 14(2) can not be invoked, he has a second-string argument under s 14(3). In a very large number of cases, both s 14(2) and s 14(3) will be held to have been broken on the same facts.

The key issue in regard to s 14(3) is that of *reliance*: there must have been something said or done to bring home to the seller the fact that he was being relied upon to supply goods fit for the buyer's particular purpose. This onus will be an easy one to discharge where the purpose is a natural or likely one (eg that food is fit to eat). The section in its current form (the wording was revised in 1973) helps the court in determining this question of reliance by laying down a presumption that once a particular purpose has been made known to the seller, it is assumed that the buyer will have relied on the seller to provide goods fit for that purpose; but, even so, it must be found that such reliance was reasonable on the facts. The cases cited below illustrate the courts' approach to the questions of 'particular purpose' and reliance.

Bristol Tramways etc Carriage Co Ltd v Fiat Motors Ltd

[1910] 2 KB 831, Court of Appeal

The plaintiffs successfully claimed damages in respect of seven omnibuses sold to them by the defendants (as the trial judge found) for the purpose 'of conveying passengers in and near Bristol, a heavy traffic in a hilly district'. The omnibuses were not sufficiently robust for this work, and had to be reconstructed. The sellers were held to be in breach of the condition implied under s 14(1) of the 1893 Act (now s 14(3)) that they would fit for this purpose.

Cozens-Hardy MR: This is an action in which the plaintiffs claim damages in respect of seven Fiat motor omnibuses sold by the defendants to the plaintiffs. The learned judge, Lawrance J, who tried this case without a jury, has held that the omnibuses as delivered were not fit to perform the duty required of them, and that the plaintiffs made fully known to the defendants the particular purpose for which the omnibuses were required, and that they relied upon the defendants' skill and judgment in the matter.

The case really turns upon s 14 of the Sale of Goods Act, 1893....

Turning to s 14, it is plain that the defendants were told that the omnibuses were required for heavy passenger traffic at Bristol. I am disposed to think that such a statement of purpose suffices to shew that the buyer relied upon the seller's skill or judgment without any further evidence on the point, but, however that may be, I think there was in the present case ample evidence that the plaintiffs did rely upon the defendants' skill or judgment. This being so, there was an implied condition that the omnibuses should be reasonably fit for the declared purpose....

[Farwell and Kennedy LJJ delivered concurring judgments.]

Cammell Laird & Co Ltd v Manganese Bronze & Brass Co Ltd

[1934] AC 402, House of Lords

Cammell Laird had agreed to build two ships for the United Molasses Company, and had contracted with Manganese Bronze to have propellers made for these ships to designs which specified the general dimensions of the propellers but not the thickness and shaping of the blades, which it was left to Manganese Bronze, as specialist suppliers, to determine. Four propellers had to be made before two were produced which performed satisfactorily. Cammell Laird claimed damages for the delay in finishing their work caused by the fact that the first propellers supplied were defective, alleging a breach of s 14(3) [s 14(1) of the 1893 Act], The House of Lords held that the defects in the propellers lay in those areas of the design where Cammell Laird had relied on Manganese Bronze's specialist skill and judgment, and upheld the claim.

Lord Macmillan: The appellants also contended that they were entitled to succeed under s 14, sub-s 1, of the Sale of Good Act 1893 [1979 Act, s 14(3)]. [His Lordship quoted the subsection and continued:]

Now there is no question that it is in the course of the respondents' business to supply ships' propellers. But there is room for argument as to whether the appellants made known to the respondents 'the particular purpose' for which the propeller was wanted. On the one hand it was contended that no particular purpose was expressed or implied which the propeller was to serve, and that if any purpose was implied it was merely the ordinary and general purpose which all ships' propellers serve—namely, as the word itself connotes, the purpose of propulsion. On the other hand it was contended that the contract disclosed that the propeller was wanted for a particular purpose—the purpose, namely, of being fitted to and working in association with the ship and engines No 972 which the appellants were building. Having regard to the decision and the reasoning in the case of *Manchester Liners Ltd v Rea Ltd* ([1922] 2 AC 74), I am of opinion that there was in the present instance sufficient disclosure of a particular purpose within the statutory meaning.

But that is not enough. To get the benefit of s 14, sub-s 1, the particular purpose must be so made known as to show that the buyer relies on the seller's skill or judgment. The respondents' argument was that the appellants by their detailed specification so tied the respondents' hands as to negative the idea that anything was left or intended to be left to their skill or judgment, except mere matters of material and workmanship, as to which there was no suggestion of failure on their part. That there was an important margin within which the respondents' skill and judgment had scope for exercise is best demonstrated by the fact already mentioned that while all the three propellers which they made for this ship were in conformity with the specification, it was only at the third attempt that the respondents succeeded in supplying a propeller that would work.

The defect, whatever it was, which existed in the first two propellers as well as the remedying of that defect achieved in the third propeller, thus lay in the region within which the respondents were free, so far as the specification went, to exercise their skill and judgment. I therefore reach the conclusion that there was room here for the exercise of the respondents' skill and judgment and I hold that the particular purpose for which the propeller was wanted was so made known to the respondents as to show that the appellants relied on their skill and judgment.

The appellants are thus entitled, in my opinion, to succeed . . . .

[Lords Tomlin, Warrington of Clyffe, Russell of Killowen and Wright delivered concurring opinions.]

Teheran-Europe Co Ltd v ST Belton (Tractors) Ltd
[1968] 2 QB 545, Court of Appeal

Belton, an English company, contracted to sell mobile air compressors which they had acquired as government surplus to Teheran-Europe Ltd, a company incorporated in Iran (then known as Persia) and carrying on business in Teheran. The buyers made known to the sellers that the compressors were required for resale as 'new and unused' machines in Iran. An action under s 14(3) [then s 14(1)] failed because, although this 'particular purpose' had been made known to the sellers, the circumstances were not such as to show that the buyers had relied on their skill and judgment.

Lord Denning MR: Now, as I read this contract, it was a contract for the sale of goods by description. These were air compressors, described as new and unused—described in the catalogue and in the correspondence. There was clearly an implied term that they should comply with the description as set out in s 13(1) of the Sale of Goods Act.

So far as s 14(1) is concerned, it is quite clear that the buyers made known to the sellers that they were required for resale in Persia. In the letter of August 10, 1967, Richards Marketing Ltd wrote to S T Belton (Tractors) Ltd: 'We have now received provisional estimates for packing these units singly suitable for shipment to Khorranshahr, and cross-country transit.' Khorranshahr, as far as I understand it, is in Persia. And then in the letter of August 9, 1957, they said: 'Our clients are asking for a liberal supply of descriptive literature for advertising purposes in Iran.' So that it is quite clear that the buyers made known to the sellers that they required them for resale in Persia.

But the section of the statute contains a further requirement before a condition is implied . . . . The particular purpose must be made known 'so as to show that the buyer relies on the seller's skill or judgment.' That means that the buyer makes the particular purpose known to the seller in such a way that the seller knows that he is being relied upon. That cannot be said here. The sellers here did not know they were being relied on for resale in Persia. They knew nothing of conditions in Persia. The buyers knew all about those conditions. The buyers saw the machine here. They read its description.

They relied upon their own skill and judgment to see that it was suitable for resale in Persia, and not on the seller's. At all events, they did not make the purpose known to the seller in such circumstances as to show him that they relied on the seller's skill and judgment. So I do not think there was an implied term that they should be fit for the purpose of being resold in Persia.

[Diplock and Sachs LJJ delivered concurring judgments.]

NOTES

1. The two cases cited above were decided under the former law, which in effect required the buyer to prove that the circumstances were such as to show that he relied on the seller's skill and judgment. Section 14(3) now reverses the position, leaving it to the seller to show that the buyer did not rely on his skill and judgment, or that it was unreasonable for him to do so. However, it is likely that the same result would now be reached in each case under the revised wording.

2. In *Britvic Soft Drinks Ltd v Messer UK Ltd* (above, p 410) it was held sufficient for the purposes of s 14(3) that the buyer should rely on the skill and judgment of a person from whom his seller had acquired the goods. In that case carbon dioxide was bought by Britvic from Messer for the purpose of carbonating soft drinks. It was contaminated with benzene through the fault of its manufacturer, Terra, who had supplied the gas to Messer. Messer was held to be in breach of s 14(3) because Britvic had relied on the skill and judgment of Terra not to permit their product to be contaminated.

3. The question of reliance was also in issue in two of the other cases discussed on p 410, where liability under s 14(3) was alleged as well as breach of the condition of satisfactory quality. In both *Jewson v Boyhan* and *Bramhill v Edwards* it was held that the buyer had not relied on the seller to supply goods fit for his particular purpose, so that he also failed on this alternative ground.

Henry Kendall & Sons v William Lillico & Sons Ltd (also sometimes known as Hardwick Garm Farm v SAPPA) [1969] 2 AC 31,
House of Lords

(This case also raised questions under s 14(2): see above, p 407. Although that part of the decision may now be open to question, in view of the fact that the definition of 'satisfactory quality' requires the goods to be fit for *all* their common purposes, the concept of a 'particular purpose', which is the subject of the extract which follows, remains unchanged.)

Lord Pearce: ...My Lords, young pheasants on the Hardwick Game Farm were killed or stunted through eating food which was compounded and supplied by Suffolk Agricultural and Poultry Producers Association Ltd ('SAPPA'). Nobody has doubted that the Hardwick Garm Farm had a good cause of action or that SAPPA were right in admitting it. The question is, how far that loss can be handed on to the various merchants up the line of supply. ...

The damage came from a latent toxin in Brazilian groundnut meal which SAPPA used as an ingredient in their compound food. They had bought the meal from Grimsdale...Grimsdale have been held liable under s 14(1) of the Sale of Goods Act 1893 [1979 Act, s 14(3)], in that the meal was not reasonably fit for the purpose, but not liable under s 14(2) since the meal was held to be merchantable. Grimsdale bought the meal from Kendall who have likewise been held liable under s 14[(3)] but not under s 14(2). Kendall appeal against this liability.

When Grimsdale orally sold to SAPPA, it was in the course of Grimsdale's business to sell cattle and poultry feeding stuffs to the manufacturers of compound feeding stuffs. Grimsdale knew that the meal was 'liable to be used in the manufacture of compound feeding stuffs for cattle or poultry.' They were further aware that SAPPA 'only compounded feeding stuffs for poultry, pheasants and pigs' and 'did not compound feeding stuffs for cattle.' It was held that the particular purpose was made known so as to show that SAPPA relied on Grimsdale's skill and judgment. It has been held unanimously by the trial judge and the Court of Appeal that the condition of fitness implied by s 14[(3)] has been proved and that the meal was not fit for the purpose for which it was supplied. In my opinion, that view is right. And it is clear that the injury to the pheasants was well within the range of damages recoverable. Therefore, whether or not Grimsdale can hand on their liability to Kendall, they cannot avoid liability themselves....

The more difficult question is whether Grimsdale's purchase from Kendall contained under s 14[(3)] or 14(2) conditions which were broken....

When Kendall sold to Grimsdale they were aware that the purpose of Grimsdale was 'to resell in smaller quantities to be compounded into food for cattle and poultry' .... If, therefore, a condition resulted under s 14[(3)] from that knowledge, the food must be fit for cattle and poultry. Fitness for one coupled with unfitness for the other would not suffice.

The judge and the Court of Appeal held that the purpose of Grimsdale was 'a particular purpose' within s 14[(3)]. It was argued that such a purpose was too wide and had not enough particularity to constitute a particular purpose. I do not accept this contention. Almost every purpose is capable of some sub-division, some further and better particulars.... In general it would be wrong to say, as was suggested in argument, that a wide purpose is unfair to the seller because it purports to require fitness for every conceivable subdivision of purpose within the main purpose.

I would expect a tribunal of fact to decide that a car sold in this country was reasonably fit for touring even though it was not well adapted for conditions in a heat wave; but not, if it could not cope adequately with rain. If, however, it developed some lethal or dangerous trick in very hot weather, I would expect it to be found unfit. In deciding the question of fact the rarity of the unsuitability would be weighed against the gravity of its consequences. Again, if food was merely unpalatable or useless on rare occasions, it might well be reasonably suitable for food. But I should certainly not expect it to be held reasonably suitable if even on very rare occasions it killed the consumer. The question for the tribunal of fact is simply 'were these goods reasonably fit for the specified purpose?'

'To resell in smaller quantities to be compounded into food for cattle and poultry' was, therefore, a particular purpose within s 14[(3)]. If a particular purpose is made known, that is sufficient to raise the inference that the buyer relies on the seller's skill and judgment unless there is something to displace the inference. There is no need for a buyer formally to 'make known' that which is already known.... The reliance need not be exclusive. Partial reliance will suffice....

It is argued that the width of the purpose should prevent one from inferring that there was reliance. I do not think so. The compounders of food for cattle and poultry need healthy ingredients, as the sellers knew. The parties were not considering what admixture of healthy groundnut meal would be good for particular animals or birds, but whether assuming a certain quantity of groundnut meal would be a fit ingredient, the goods delivered would be healthy or harmful groundnut meal. It was reasonable that the buyer should rely on the seller to deliver groundnut meal which would, as groundnut meal, be a healthy and not a harmful ingredient in a compound.

In my opinion, there was on the circumstances of this case sufficient to establish reliance by Grimsdale on Kendall and a resulting condition.

The condition did not mean that the food was fit, however strange or unsuitable the proportions of the compound might prove to be. It meant that the food was fit if compounded reasonably and competently according to current standards. Goods are not fit if they have hidden limitations requiring special precautions unknown to the buyer or seller. The groundnut meal delivered was plainly not fit for the purpose of reselling in small lots to compounders of food for cattle and poultry. It was highly toxic. It is beside the point that Kendalls were unaware of the proportions in which it was to be compounded. It was unfit for use in the normal range of proportions....

Kendall are therefore liable in breach of the condition under s 14[(3)]....

[Lords Reid, Morris of Borth-y-Gest, Guest and Wilberforce delivered opinions concurring on this issue. Lord Guest dissented on another point.]

In *Ashington Piggeries Ltd v Christopher Hill Ltd* [1972] AC 441, HL (see above, p 404), similar questions arose in relation to a feeding compound, mixed by the sellers to the buyers' formula, which contained herring meal that was contaminated by a toxic preservative and proved fatal when fed to the buyers' mink. The herring meal had in turn been bought by the sellers from Norwegian suppliers who had no knowledge of the precise use to which it was to be put, but knew that the herring meal was to be used in compounding animal foodstuffs, and it was held that they ought reasonably to have foreseen that it might be fed to mink. The toxin affected different species of animals in varying degrees, but it was especially harmful to mink. Although only the buyers had any expertise relating to mink, it was held that both the sellers and their Norwegian suppliers were in breach of s 14(3), because they had been relied on to supply goods which were reasonably fit for feeding to animals generally (not limited specifically to mink).

NOTES

1. In *Aswan Engineering Establishment Co v Lupdine Ltd* [1987] 1 WLR 1, CA, the buyers had made known to the sellers that the plastic pails for which they were contracting were wanted 'for export'. (In fact, they were to be filled with a liquid waterproofing compound and exported to Kuwait, where they collapsed in temperatures which reached 70°C.) Lloyd LJ said that 'for export' was a purpose that 'could hardly be wider', and that the wider the purpose, the greater would be the dilution of the sellers' responsibility under s 14(3). But in any event it was held that the buyers (who had been sent a sample pail before placing their order) had not relied on the sellers' skill or judgment in any sense relevant to s 14(3). The pails were also held to be of merchantable quality under s 14(2), as formerly worded.

2. In *Slater v Finning Ltd* [1997] AC 473, HL a replacement camshaft was supplied by Finnings to be fitted to a marine diesel engine owned by Slater. The camshaft was of a type which worked satisfactorily in other engines but not when fitted to Slater's: there was excessive noise and considerable wear, which was attributable to some factors external to the camshaft and engine—probably the design of the boat in which it was installed. The buyer's claim under s 14(3) was unsuccessful. Lord Keith of Kinkel said, at p 483:

There is no breach of the implied condition of fitness where the failure of the goods to meet the intended purpose arises from an abnormal feature or idiosyncrasy, not made known to the seller by the buyer, in the buyer or in the circumstances of the use of the goods by the buyer. That is the case whether or not the buyer is himself aware of the abnormal feature or idiosyncrasy.

This decision followed *Griffiths v Peter Conway Ltd* [1939] 1 All ER 685, where a lady who bought a Harris tweed coat suffered dermatitis, not because the coat was unsuitable for normal wear but because she had an unusually sensitive skin.

3. In *Wormell v RHM Agriculture (East) Ltd* [1987] 1 WLR 1091, CA it was held that instructions supplied with the goods (in that case, a herbicide) have to be taken into account in considering whether goods are fit for their purpose. In other cases a failure to supply information about the goods has been held to be a breach of the implied term as to description (s 13): see SW Hedley [2001] JBL 114. And in consumer sales, statements made in advertisements or on labelling are relevant in determining whether the goods are of satisfactory quality (s 14(2)): above, p 408.

4. The passages which, in the interests of simplification, were omitted when quoting s 14(3) (above, p 411) contain references to a mysterious figure called a 'credit-broker'. This more elaborate wording is intended to bring within the scope of s 14(3) the 'triangular' transaction where (for example) a vehicle is bought on conditional-sale or credit-sale terms from a finance company after the customer has chosen it from the stock of a motor dealer. The finance company will be bound to supply a vehicle fit for the buyer's particular purpose if the buyer has made that purpose known to the dealer (the 'credit-broker'). A similar provision (s 10(3) of the Supply of Goods (Implied Terms) Act 1973) governs transactions where the customer takes the goods on hire purchase.

7 TERMS IMPLIED IN SALES OF GOODS BY SAMPLE (s 15)

Section 15 deals with goods which are sold by sample. There are two implied conditions, set out in s 15(2):

(1) that the bulk will correspond with the sample in quality (s 15(2)(a));

(2) that the goods will be free from any defect, making their quality unsatisfactory, which would not be apparent on reasonable examination of the sample (s 15(2)(c)).

These provisions are in themselves more or less self-explanatory. The only likely surprise lies in the concept of a 'sale by sample' itself, and its legal function. The term is defined, not very helpfully, in s 15(1):

A contract of sale is a contract for sale by sample where there is an express or implied term to that effect in the contract.

This makes it plain that it is not sufficient that the buyer should merely have seen a specimen of the goods in question; the parties must have agreed that the sale shall be a sale *by reference to* that sample.

The cases show that the function of a sample is very similar to that of a contractual description, or perhaps to supplement that contractual description. In *Drummond v Van Ingen* (1887) 12 App Cas 284 at 297, HL, Lord Macnaghten explained this function as follows:

The office of a sample is to present to the eye the real meaning and intention of the parties with regard to the subject matter of the contract which, owing to the imperfection of language, it may be difficult or impossible to express in words. The sample speaks for itself. But it cannot be treated as saying more than such a sample would tell a merchant of the class to which the buyer belongs, using due care and diligence, and appealing to it in the ordinary way and with the knowledge possessed by merchants of that class at the time. No doubt the sample might be made to say a great deal more. Pulled to pieces and examined by unusual tests which curiosity or suspicion might suggest, it would doubtless reveal every secret of its construction. But that is not the way in which business is done in this country.

From this statement we can infer that a seller in a sale by sample does not guarantee that the bulk will comply with the sample in every possible respect: but only that it will be as like the sample as an ordinary comparison or inspection would reveal. Over and above this, the buyer must rely on the implied terms contained in s 14(2) and (3), or stipulate for an express warranty. However, there is limited further protection conferred by s 15(2)(c), which implies a condition that the goods will be free from any latent defect which makes their quality unsatisfactory. The case next cited confirms the restricted scope both of the function of a 'sale by sample' and of this latter condition.

Steels & Busks Ltd v Bleecker Bik & Co Ltd

[1956] 1 Lloyd's Rep 228, Queen's Bench Division

Steels & Busks contracted to buy from Bleecker Bik five tons of pale crepe rubber, 'quality as previously delivered'. The court construed this as a sale by sample, the 'sample' being the rubber delivered under previous contracts. Steels & Busks used the rubber to manufacture corsets, but it turned out (unlike the earlier deliveries) to contain an invisible preservative, PNP, which stained the fabric of the corsets. Sellers J held that there had been no breach of the condition implied by s 15(2)(a): the rubber was in accordance with the sample on any visual test. Nor had there been a breach of the condition as to merchantability (now satisfactory quality) implied by s 15(2)(c): this rubber was perfectly useful for commercial purposes once the staining chemical had been washed out or neutralised.

Sellers J: In assessing the quality of the goods and their state and condition on delivery, the [arbitration] Appeal Committee have applied the normal market standard and applied the normal tests. Para 8 of the award deals with the arbitrators' views:

> As understood in the market, quality is determined by visual inspection of samples drawn in the wharves after rubber has been landed; such inspection extends to colour, texture, and the possibility of impurities such as specks of bark, sand, bits of cotton, and deterioration. The kind of chemical used in the preparation of rubber has never been regarded as entering into the quality of rubber. If the quality of pale crepe were to depend on the chemical preservative used, there might be as many qualities as there are preservatives; no such idea is known to the trade. 'PNP' is not a defect in rubber nor is it an adulterant or impurity. It is a preservative used, though less frequently in pale crepe than in other types of rubber, and its presence does not affect quality. We have not overlooked the statutory definition of 'quality of goods' in s 62(1) of the Sale of Goods Act [see now s 14(2B)], but we do not regard the presence of 'PNP' as a matter affecting state or condition....

If the buyers are to succeed in their claim, it must, I think, only be on the ground that the 21 bales did not comply with the sample, that is, the first delivery. In one respect the bales complained of did not so comply. They contained 'PNP,' whereas the sample did not, and it was submitted that s 15(2)(a) of the Sale of Goods Act had not been complied with as the bulk did not correspond with the sample in quality.

[His Lordship quoted the section, and continued:]

Section 15(2) is not inconsistent with the view that where there is (as here) a defect not apparent on reasonable examination of the sample, the buyers' rights arise, if at all, under sub-s (2)(c) and not under sub-s (2)(a), but it is not, I think, conclusive as a matter of construction....

   Drummond v Van Ingen (1887) 12 App Cas 284, is the case upon which s 15 is largely based....

   In that case, the contract expressly provided that quality and weight should be equal to certain numbered samples; and the Earl of Selborne LC, at p 288, said this about its construction;

> I think that the word 'quality' as used in the contracts, ought to be restricted to those qualities which were patent, or discoverable from such examination and inspection of the samples as, under the circumstances, the respondents might reasonably be expected to make.

In *Drummond v Van Ingen* the House of Lords was able, by giving the sample clause a restricted meaning, to hold that its terms did not exclude an implied warranty covering latent defects. It is of the essence of this reasoning that a clause of this sort does not cover latent qualities or defects at all. In that case it was the seller's argument that was defeated by this construction. But, by the same token, it is not open to a buyer to submit a sample to an analysis unusual in the trade so as to reveal in it certain attributes or qualities hitherto unsuspected, and then to require, by virtue of the sample clause alone, that the bulk should contain the same qualities. If, for example, a buyer, to use the words of Lord Macnaghten, pulls a sample of cloth to pieces and discovers by means of analysis that the dye contains a certain proportion of a certain chemical, he cannot by virtue of the same clause require that the dye in the bulk shall contain the same proportion of the same chemical. He may, of course, complain that if it does not contain that proportion, it would be unmerchantable or would fail to satisfy some other express or implied condition as to quality; but he cannot say that it breaks the condition that the bulk shall correspond with the sample in quality, for that condition is dealing only with apparent quality....

I am in complete agreement with that construction of s 15(2)(a), and I am grateful for that passage, which I adopt and apply here....

The extent to which a sample may be held to 'speak' must depend on the contract and what is contemplated by the parties in regard to it. A sample may be analysed, X-rayed—tested to destruction. In the present case the parties were content, in accordance with the normal practice of the trade, to rely on a visual examination. Neither 'PNP' nor, I think, any other chemical in general use for coagulation and preservation or either is detectable by visual examination, and therefore the presence or absence of the chemical cannot in itself be a breach of the sample clause....

The buyers had in fact used the first delivery and found it satisfactory and that no doubt resulted in the repeat orders. The crude rubber had received treatment and processing by them and revealed no defect. Such circumstances would not enlarge the liability of the sellers, as the contract remained, as far as the compliance with a sample was concerned, a contract which called for compliance in those matters revealed by visual examination and those matters only....

8 EXCLUSION OF SELLER'S LIABILITY

The Unfair Contract Terms Act 1977 (UCTA), s 6, restricts the ability of a seller to negative or vary the terms implied by ss 12–15 of the Sale of Goods Act 1979.

Two preliminary points must be made. First, the Act of 1977 does not apply at all to 'international supply contracts'—a term which includes contracts for the sale of goods where the seller and buyer are based in different jurisdictions *and* one of three additional conditions applies:

(1) the goods are to be carried from one state to another;

(2) the acts constituting the offer and acceptance have been done in different territories; or

(3) the goods are to be delivered to a territory other than that in which the offer and acceptance took place (UCTA, s 26).

Secondly, s 6 (unlike the rest of UCTA) is not restricted in its application to 'business liability' (as defined in s 1(3)). So, for instance, liability for breach of s 12 of the Sale of Goods Act (the condition as to title, etc) cannot be excluded even in a contract of sale made between two private persons.

Section 12 of UCTA makes a distinction between contracts in which a person (in the present context, the buyer) 'deals as consumer', and other contracts of sale.

The definition of a person who 'deals as consumer' is now extraordinarily complex, as a result of an amendment made to s 12 in 2002 by the Sale and Supply of Goods to Consumers

Regulations 2002, SI 2002/3045 implementing Directive 1999/44/EC. The section now reads as follows.

12 'Dealing as consumer'

(1) A party to a contract 'deals as consumer' in relation to another party if—

    (a) he neither makes the contract in the course of a business nor holds himself out as doing so; and

    (b) the other party does make the contract in the course of a business; and

    (c) in the case of a contract governed by the law of sale of goods or hire-purchase, or by section 7 of this Act, the goods passing under or in pursuance of the contract are of a type ordinarily supplied for private use or consumption.

(1A) But if the party first mentioned in subsection (1) is an individual paragraph (c) of that subsection must be ignored.

(2) But the buyer is not in any circumstances to be regarded as dealing as consumer—

    (a) if he is an individual and the goods are second hand goods sold at public auction at which individuals have the opportunity of attending the sale in person;

    (b) if he is not an individual and the goods are sold by auction or by competitive tender.

NOTES

1.   This section is so appallingly drafted because the 1999 Directive was brought into force by statutory instrument under the European Communities Act 1972. This procedure allows amendments to be made to primary legislation (such as UCTA) only to the limited extent necessary to implement the relevant directive. The result is an unhappy marriage between the original wording of the 1977 Act (eg s 12(2) (a) and (b)) and that of the Directive (eg sub-s (2)(a)).

2.   Section 7 of UCTA deals in similar terms with contracts such as those for work and materials and barter.

Section 6 of UCTA makes the following rules regarding clauses purporting to exempt a seller from liability under ss 12–15 of the Sale of Goods Act:

(1) Liability under s 12 (undertakings as to title, etc) cannot be excluded or restricted at all. (Note, however, that s 12 itself makes provision for the case where a seller purports to sell only a limited title: see s 12(3) (above, p 396.)

(2) Liability under ss 13 (conformity with description), 14(2) (satisfactory quality), 14(3) (fitness for purpose) and 15 (conformity with sample) *cannot* be excluded or restricted *as against a person dealing as consumer,* and, as against any other buyer, can be excluded or restricted only in so far as the term satisfies the 'requirement of reasonableness'.

The 'requirement of reasonableness' is defined for the purposes of the Act generally as 'that the term shall have been a fair and reasonable one to be included having regard to the circumstances which were, or ought reasonably to have been, known to or in the contemplation of the parties when the contract was made' (UCTA, s 11(1)). More particularly, in regard to contracts for the sale of goods, the court is directed to have regard to a number of guidelines which are set out in Sch 2 to UCTA (s 11(2)). These include such matters as the relative bargaining strength of the parties, the amount of choice available to the buyer, and whether the goods were specially made or adapted to his order.

    Of course, the exemption clauses in a contract for the sale of goods will not necessarily be confined to those which purport to exclude or restrict liability under ss 12–15 of the Sale of Goods Act. In the case of other exemption clauses (eg terms seeking to restrict the buyer's remedies in the case of a late delivery or short delivery) it will be necessary to have regard to other provisions of UCTA to see whether they apply—eg s 2 (terms excluding liability for negligence), s 3 (liability arising in contract, where one of the parties deals as consumer or on the other's written standard terms of business)—and in these circumstances the 'business liability' restriction imposed by s 1(3) will apply.

By way of illustration, we may instance two cases on the issue of 'unreasonableness'. In *Knight Machinery (Holdings) Ltd v Rennie* 1995 SLT 166, the inclusion of a term requiring the buyer of a printing machine to give written notice of rejection within seven days of delivery was held to be unreasonable; the machine took several days to install and defects might not be discovered until after a much longer trial period. And in *St Albans City Council v International Computers Ltd* [1996] 4 All ER 481, CA a multinational company which had supplied a computer system could not enforce a provision limiting its liability to £100,000: it was insured for £50 million.

Some reported cases dealing with exemption clauses in contracts for the sale of goods were decided under earlier legislation—eg *George Mitchell (Chesterhall) Ltd v Finney Lock Seeds Ltd* [1983] 2 AC 803, HL, and *R W Green Ltd v Cade Bros Farms* [1978] 1 Lloyd's Rep 602. These rulings should be treated with caution, because the wording of the previous legislation was different: in particular, in applying the test of 'reasonableness', the court was formerly empowered to have regard to events occurring *after* the formation of the contract—something which UCTA does not allow (sees 11(1)).

The Unfair Terms in Consumer Contracts Regulations 1999, SI 1999/2083, replacing earlier regulations enacted in 1994 (SI 1994/3159) adds another layer to this area of the law. Regrettably, no attempt was made when these Regulations were enacted to synthesise or reconcile them with those parts of UCCA which cover the same ground, and so in some cases it may be necessary to check against both sets of provisions. Apart from a number of variations in detail, there are two important differences of general application between UCTA and the Regulations. First, the Regulations apply only in *consumer* contracts for the sale of goods or services (and, annoyingly, the definition of 'consumer' is not the same: see reg 3(1)) and, secondly, they apply to any contractual term, and not just to terms which seek to restrict or avoid liability. There is also a different list of types of contract to which the Regulations do not apply (see reg 4)—and, since the focus is on consumer contracts, most sales made in a commercial context will not be affected. The main effect of the Regulations is that any term which 'contrary to the requirement of good faith...causes a significant imbalance in the parties' rights to the detriment of the consumer' shall not be binding on him (reg 5, as elaborated by Sch 2.).

9 PRODUCT LIABILITY

In 1985, after much debate, the EC Council adopted a Directive (85/374/EEC) which required member states to introduce legislation making manufacturers and other 'producers' strictly liable for damage caused by their products. The Directive was implemented in this country by Part I of the Consumer Protection Act 1987. The liability established by this statute will not, of course, apply primarily as between a seller and a buyer of goods, since the buyer will already have remedies under the contract of sale which are likely to be rather more extensive; but it may provide a direct remedy for a buyer against the original 'producer' of the goods, or (if the seller is himself their 'producer') give a cause of action to consumers of the goods and other parties who are not themselves buyers.

Under the 1987 Act, where damage is caused by a defect in a product, the producer is liable to the victim without the need for proof of fault. 'Damage' is defined as meaning death or personal injury or damage to property—but only property which is of a type ordinarily intended for private use or consumption. Accordingly, economic loss is excluded, as is damage to commercial and public property. It should be noted also that no claim lies in respect of the defective product itself. Other points to note are:

(1) primary agricultural products were originally excluded, if unprocessed, but this exception has since been removed;

(2) 'producer' includes an importer, and also a supplier where the original producer cannot be identified; and

(3) the law allows a 'state of the art' defence—ie a plea that the product met technical or scientific standards which were regarded as acceptable at the relevant time.

Other legislation, backed by criminal sanctions, confers wide powers on 'enforcement authorities' to maintain safety standards in supplying products for use by consumers, eg the General Product Safety Regulations 2005 (SI 2005/1803).

10   CONSUMER GUARANTEES

In 1999 the Parliament and Council of the EC adopted a Directive (commonly referred to as the 'Consumer Guarantees Directive' (1999/44/EC)) which has been implemented into UK law by the Sale and Supply of Goods to Consumers Regulations 2002, SI 2002/3045. The Regulations apply to any transaction by which goods are sold or otherwise supplied to a consumer (defined as any natural person who, in the contracts covered by the Regulations, is acting for purposes which are outside his trade, business or profession). The Directive does not require that a guarantee should be given to the consumer, but states that if a guarantee is given, it is to be legally binding. This is provided for by reg 15(1): 'the guarantee takes effect at the time the goods are delivered as a contractual obligation owed by the guarantor under the conditions set out in the guarantee statement and the associated advertising'—so eliminating any possibility that the guarantee might be declared unenforceable for want of consideration. A consumer guarantee is defined as 'any undertaking to a consumer by a person acting in the course of his business, given without extra charge, to reimburse the price paid or to replace, repair or handle consumer goods in any way if they do not meet the specifications set out in the guarantee statement or the relevant advertising'. Other subparagraphs of reg 15 require details of the guarantee to be set out in plain language and in English, and empower the Director General of Fair Trading and local weights and measures authorities to apply for an injunction to secure compliance by a guarantor with his obligations.

CHAPTER 11

PERFORMANCE OF THE CONTRACT

The Act sets out in ss 27–37 a number of rules about the parties' respective obligations in regard to the payment of the price and the delivery of the goods. The selection of only these rules and their grouping into a separate Part is somewhat arbitrary. The terms implied into contracts of sale by ss 12–15, for instance, could very well have been expressed by the draftsman as 'duties of the seller'—a duty to pass a good title to the buyer, a duty to deliver goods of the contract description, etc. We shall, however, follow the lead given by the Act.

1 DUTIES OF THE SELLER

(a) To deliver the goods

Sections 27ff of the Act spell out the duties of the seller in regard to delivery, in terms which are more or less self-explanatory. It is the duty of the seller to deliver the goods in accordance with the terms of the contract of sale (s 27). Unless otherwise agreed, he must be ready and willing to give possession of the goods to the buyer in exchange for the price (s 28).

The meaning of 'delivery'. The term 'delivery' may be the source of some confusion, as we saw in relation to the term 'deliverable state' (above, p 327). 'Delivery', in the statutory sense, means 'voluntary transfer of possession from one person to another'. Thus, it does not necessarily mean *physical* delivery, still less 'delivery' in the popular sense of sending the goods in a vehicle to the buyer's premises. In fact, the Act says that, in the absence of some express or implied provision in the contract, the place of delivery is the seller's place of business, if he has one, and if not, his residence; except that, if the contract is for specific goods, which are known when the contract is made to be in some other place, then that place is the place of delivery (s 29(2)).

Under the statutory definition, the term 'delivery' is dependent upon the common law concept of possession, whose meaning (as we saw in Chapter 2) is rather elusive. Three forms of delivery are particularly relevant for present purposes:

(1) actual, or physical delivery: this means the handing over of the goods themselves, whether to a buyer, a carrier or other person;

(2) symbolic delivery: handing over something which symbolises the goods; in particular, a bill of lading relating to goods which are at sea, and possibly the ignition key of a vehicle or the key of a locked building in which the goods are stored;

(3) constructive delivery: this refers to a transfer of the *right* to possession of goods which are in the physical custody of a third party, and is effected by a procedure known as *attornment*, which has been described above, p 75.

Attornment, it will be recalled, involves all three parties: (1) the seller (S) must instruct the third party (T) to hold the goods to the order of the buyer (B); and (2) T must acknowledge to B that he is now holding the goods on B's behalf. Most commonly, this will be done by the issue of a *delivery order* by S addressed to T, and handed to B or sent directly to T; T will then either make acknowledgment of the new state of affairs by some form of endorsement on the delivery order, or by issuing a *warrant* made out in favour of B (see above, p 380). Either way, the attornment will then be complete: the right to possession which was formerly vested in S will have been transferred to B, and T becomes a bailee of the goods for B. There will, however, be no effective transfer of possession in this sense without step (2) above: neither an agreement solely between S and B, nor any arrangement between S and T alone, is sufficient. This is confirmed by s 29(4) of the Act.

Delivery and payment Section 28 makes delivery and payment 'concurrent conditions', in the absence of any agreement to the contrary: that is to say (in the words of the Act) the seller must be ready and willing to give possession of the goods to the buyer in exchange for the price, and the buyer must be ready and willing to pay the price in exchange for possession of the goods. This provision raises some conceptual difficulties, since in theory (as we have seen: above, p 298) it is the *property* in the goods which the buyer bargains for in exchange for the price, and not possession. But s 28 says, in effect, that (unless otherwise agreed) a buyer can withhold payment if he does not get possession, and a seller can withhold delivery unless he gets payment; and so as a *practical* matter, it is often more realistic to think of delivery and payment as given in exchange for each other, rather than in abstract terms of property.

Time of delivery. Stipulations as to the time of performance of a contractual obligation may be made 'of the essence' of the contract or not (ie may be made either conditions or warranties), as determined by the parties' agreement. Section 10(2) confirms this in relation to contracts for the sale of goods, adding a presumptive rule (s 10(1)) that stipulations as to the time of payment are *not* of the essence. It is therefore up to the parties to settle whether a term relating to the time of delivery is to be regarded as a condition. However, in many mercantile transactions, it is well established by case law that stipulations as to the time of delivery will be so construed—particularly where the goods are to travel by sea transport. Thus, in *Bowes v Shand* (1877) 2 App Cas 455, HL, rice which was to be shipped 'during the months of March and/or April' was in fact loaded in February; the buyer was held entitled to reject. (Compare *Kwei Tek Chao v British Traders & Shippers NV* (above, p 346).)

Section 29(3) states that where, under the contract of sale, the seller is to send the goods to the buyer, but no time for doing so is fixed, he is bound to send them within a reasonable time. What is a reasonable time is a question of fact (s 59). It is also provided that a demand or tender of delivery may be treated as ineffectual unless made at a reasonable hour—again, a question of fact (s 29(5)).

Other rules about delivery. As we have seen, there is no rule of law which obliges the seller to 'deliver' the goods to the buyer, in the sense of taking or sending them to the buyer: whether it is for him to do this or for the buyer to take possession of the goods is a question that depends on the terms of the contract, express or implied (s 29(1)). But since, apart from any such contractual provision, the place of delivery will, prima facie, be the seller's place of business or his residence—or, in the case of specific goods, the place where they are known to be (s 29(2))—it will normally be for the buyer to make arrangements to take delivery at that place. Unless otherwise agreed, the expenses of and incidental to putting the goods into a deliverable state must be borne by the seller (s 29(6)).

Subject to some minor qualifications introduced in 1994 (see below, p 471), the seller must deliver the exact contract quantity—neither more nor less (s 30); and he cannot require the buyer to accept delivery by instalments (s 31). Nor, in fact, can the buyer require the seller to make delivery by instalments—although the Act does not mention this. These rules are examined in more detail below, pp 426 and 471.

If the contract provides that the seller may, or must, send the goods to the buyer, delivery of the goods to a carrier (whether named by the buyer or not) for the purpose of transmission to the buyer is prima facie deemed to be a delivery of goods to the buyer (s 32(1)). 'Carrier', for this purpose, of course includes a ship. Section 32 goes on to provide that the seller must make a contract with the carrier on reasonable terms and, if it involves sea transit, give adequate notice to the buyer to enable him to insure them during their sea transit (s 32(3)). Any risk of deterioration in the goods necessarily incidental to the course of transit is to be borne by the buyer (s 33).

Note that by an amendment made to the Act in 2002 (Sale and Supply of Goods to Consumers Regulations 2002, SI 2002/3045, reg 4(3), implementing Directive 1999/44/EC), s 32(1)—(3) is disapplied in the case of a sale to a consumer, and it is provided instead that if pursuant to the contract the seller is authorised or required to send the goods to the buyer, delivery to a carrier is not delivery to the buyer. A 'consumer' for this purpose means a natural person who is acting for purposes which are outside his trade, business or profession. The scope of this new provision (s 32(4)), and in particular its relationship to s 18, rule 5(2) (on the passing of property: above, p 345) is not at all clear. The better view is probably that s 32(4) is concerned only with the question whether the consumer buyer has accepted the goods, and does not qualify s 18, r 5(2) in any way (see Benjamin, para 5–098).

2 DUTIES OF THE BUYER

The statutory duties of the buyer are: to take delivery (ss 27, 28, 37(1)); to accept the goods (s 27); and to pay the price (ss 27, 28).

(a) To take delivery

The basic rules regarding the place, time, etc of delivery have already been discussed (above, p 423). If the seller is ready and willing to deliver the goods and requests the buyer to take delivery, and the buyer does not within a reasonable time after such a request take delivery of the goods, the buyer will be liable in damages to the seller (s 37(1)). Where the seller makes a defective tender, the buyer is not bound to take delivery of the goods tendered but has the choice of remedies set out in s 30, discussed below, p 471.

(b) To accept the goods

The meaning of the term 'acceptance' in this context is explained in s 35. The buyer is deemed to have accepted the goods (1) by intimating that fact to the seller, (2) by dealing with the goods as owner (but see below, p 474), or (3) by retaining the goods beyond a reasonable time.

(c) To pay the price

The buyer is bound to pay the price in accordance with the terms of the contract of sale (s 27). But unless otherwise agreed, he is not required to make payment unless the seller is ready and willing to give him possession of the goods in exchange for the price (s 28).

A payment by cheque or any other form of negotiable instrument is normally regarded as only a conditional payment; and if it is not met or is dishonoured the seller's right to sue for the price, and his statutory rights as an unpaid seller, are revived (s 38(1)(b)). Exceptionally, the seller may agree to accept payment in this form in satisfaction of the buyer's obligation to pay the price. In this case, if the cheque is not met, his only remedy is on the instrument itself. On payment by credit cards, etc, see below, Chapter 20.

The contract may provide for payment in a foreign currency, and in this case the court has power to give its judgment in that currency: *Miliangos v George Frank (Textiles) Ltd* [1976] AC 443, HL.

3   INSTALMENT CONTRACTS

(a) Introduction

A contract of sale may provide for delivery of the goods, or payment of the price, or both, to be made by instalments. In general, such contracts will be governed by the ordinary rules of the law of contract. It may be crucial, for instance, to determine whether the contract (or, more accurately, the seller's obligation) is 'entire' or 'divisible'. An example of the former might be the sale by a mail-order company of an encyclopedia set, to be delivered to the buyer by posting one volume every month; and of the latter, the sale of 100 tonnes of coal to be delivered at the rate of 10 tonnes on the Monday of each week. The failure by the seller to deliver one volume of the encyclopedia would justify a claim by the buyer to be entitled to reject all the volumes so far received and have his money back. But a similar failure to deliver one instalment of the coal would, at the most, entitle the buyer to terminate the contract as regards *future* deliveries: there would be no question of a right to *restitutio in integrum* with retrospective effect. It is important to appreciate that the Act deals with only some points relating to instalment contracts, and leaves others (such as the distinction just made between entire and divisible obligations) to be decided by reference to the general law.

(b) Buyer not bound to accept delivery by instalments (s 31(1))

Section 31(1) declares that, unless otherwise agreed, the buyer of goods is not bound to accept delivery by instalments. It is also a rule (although not stated in the Act) that the buyer is not entitled to *require* delivery to be made by instalments (*Honck v Muller* (1881) 7 QBD 92, CA, especially at 99).

Behrend & Co v Produce Brokers' Co
[1920] 3 KB 530, King's Bench Division

(The facts appear from the judgment.)

Bailhache J: In this case the sellers, by two contracts of sale...bound themselves to the buyers to deliver in London, ex the steamship *Port Inglis,* to the buyers' craft alongside, two separate parcels of cotton seed, one of 176 tons and the other of 400 tons. The buyers on their part had to pay for these parcels against shipping documents and to send craft to receive the goods. The buyers fulfilled both these obligations and received from the *Port Inglis* some fifteen tons of one parcel and twenty-two tons of the other. When these had been delivered it was discovered that the rest of the seed was lying under cargo for Hull, and the *Port Inglis* stopped delivery and left for that port, promising to return and deliver the rest of the seed. She returned in about a fortnight's time and the seed was tendered to the buyers, but the buyers had meantime informed the sellers that they regarded the departure of the *Port Inglis* with the remainder of the seed on board as a failure to deliver and a breach of contract. They kept so much of the seed as had been delivered to them and demanded repayment of so much of the contract price as represented the seed undelivered.

The umpire has decided in the buyers' favour and I am asked to say whether he was right. Everything depends upon whether the departure of the *Port Inglis* for Hull with the greater part of both parcels of seed on board was a failure to deliver, notwithstanding the promise to return and complete delivery. Both contracts between the parties are in the same terms and neither has any express provision on the subject. In my opinion, the buyer under such a contract, and where each parcel of goods is indivisible, as here, has the right to have delivery on the arrival of the steamship, not necessarily immediately or continuously; he must take his turn or the goods may be so stowed that other goods have to be discharged before the whole of the buyers' parcel can be got out. To such delays and others which may occur in the course of unloading the buyer must submit, but in the absence of any stipulation to the contrary the buyer, being ready with his craft, is entitled to delivery of the whole of an indivisible parcel of goods sold to him for delivery from a vessel which has begun delivery to him before she leaves the port to deliver goods elsewhere. If this is so the rest of the case is covered by s 30 of the Sale of Goods Act, and the buyer can either reject the whole of the goods, including those actually delivered, in which case he can recover the whole of his money; or he may keep the goods actually delivered and reject the rest, in which case he must pay for the goods kept at the contract price, and he can recover the price paid for the undelivered portion....I think that the award is right.

(c) Breach in respect of one or more instalments (s 31(2))

Section 31(2) makes provision for one particular type of instalment contract. It states:

Where there is a contract for the sale of goods to be delivered by stated instalments, which are to be separately paid for, and the seller makes defective deliveries in respect of one or more instalments, or the buyer neglects or refuses to take delivery of or pay for one or more instalments, it is a question in each case depending on the terms of the contract and the circumstances of the case whether the breach of the contract is a repudiation of the whole contract or whether it is a severable breach giving rise to a claim for compensation but not to a right to treat the whole contract as repudiated.

It is likely that the rules stated in this subsection reflect propositions of the common law which have a wider application: for instance, similar rules would surely govern a contract for the sale of goods to be delivered by instalments which are not to be separately paid for but, perhaps, paid for in some other way. The operation of s 31(2) in practice is illustrated by the following cases.

Maple Flock Co Ltd v Universal Furniture Products (Wembley) Ltd
[1934] 1 KB 148, Court of Appeal

Maple contracted to sell to Universal 100 tons of rag flock 'to be delivered three loads per week as required'. The weekly deliveries were to be separately paid for. After 18 loads, each of one and a half tons, had been delivered, the buyers wrote purporting to cancel the remainder of the contract on the ground that an analysis of the sixteenth load had shown that its chlorine content was over eight times the government standard. The court held that this single breach did not justify termination of the contract as a whole.

Lord Hewart CJ delivered the judgment of the court (Lord Hewart CJ, Lord Wright and Slesser LJ): The decision of this case depends on the true construction and application of s 31, sub-s 2, of the Sale of Goods Act 1893 . . . That sub-section was based on decisions before the Act, and has been the subject of decisions since the Act. A contract for the sale of goods by instalments is a single contract, not a complex of as many contracts as there are instalments under it. The law might have been determined in the sense that any breach of condition in respect of any one or more instalments would entitle the party aggrieved to claim that the contract has been repudiated as a whole; or on the other hand the law as established might have been that any breach, however, serious, in respect of one or more instalments should not have consequences extending beyond the particular instalment or instalments or affecting the contract as a whole. The sub-section, however, which deals equally with breaches either by the buyer or the seller, requires the Court to decide on the merits of the particular case what effect, if any, the breach or breaches should have on the contract as a whole.

[His Lordship referred to a number of decided cases, and continued:]

With the help of these authorities we deduce that the main tests to be considered in applying the sub-section to the present case are, first, the ratio quantitatively which the breach bears to the contract as a whole, and secondly the degree of probability or improbability that such a breach will be repeated. On the first point, the delivery complained of amounts to no more than 1½ tons out of a contract for 100 tons. On the second point, our conclusion is that the chance of the breach being repeated is practically negligible. We assume that the sample found defective fairly represents the bulk; but bearing in mind the judge's finding that the breach was extraordinary and that the appellant's business was carefully conducted, bearing in mind also that the appellants were warned, and bearing in mind that the delivery complained of was an isolated instance out of 20 satisfactory deliveries actually made both before and after the instalment objected to, we hold that it cannot reasonably be inferred that similar breaches would occur in regard to subsequent deliveries. Indeed, we do not understand that the learned Judge came to any different conclusion. He seems, however, to have decided against the appellants on a third and separate ground, that is, that a delivery not satisfying the Government requirements would or might lead to the respondents being prosecuted. . . . Though we think he exaggerates the likelihood of the respondents in such a case being held responsible, we do not wish to underrate the gravity to the respondents of their being even prosecuted. But we cannot follow the Judge's reasoning that the bare possibility, however remote, of this happening would justify the respondents in rescinding in this case. There may indeed be such cases, as also cases where the consequences of a single breach of contract may be so serious as to involve a frustration of the contract and justify rescission, or furthermore, the contract might contain an express condition that a breach would justify rescission, in which case effect would be given to such a condition by the Court. But none of these circumstances can be predicated of this case. We think the deciding factor here is the extreme improbability of the breach being repeated, and on that ground, and on the isolated and limited character of the breach complained of, there was, in our judgment, no sufficient justification to entitle the respondents to refuse further deliveries as they did.

The appeal must accordingly be allowed and judgment entered for the appellants, with costs here and below, for damages for their breach of contract in refusing further deliveries.

Withers v Reynolds

(1831) 2 B & Ad 882, Court of King's Bench

Withers, a stable-keeper, contracted to buy wheat straw from Reynolds, to be delivered at the rate of three loads per fortnight, and paid for on delivery. After about ten weeks, Withers insisted on paying for the straw one delivery in arrear. The court ruled that this was a repudiation which justified Reynolds in refusing all further performance.

Parke J: The substance of the agreement was, that the straw should be paid for on delivery. The defendant clearly did not contemplate giving credit. When, therefore, the plaintiff said that he would not pay on delivery, (as he did, in substance, when he insisted on keeping one load on hand), the defendant was not obliged to go on supplying him.

Patteson J: If the plaintiff had merely failed to pay for any particular load, that, of itself, might not have been an excuse to the defendant for delivering no more straw: but the plaintiff here expressly refuses to pay for the loads as delivered; the defendant, therefore, is not liable for ceasing to perform his part of the contract.

[Lord Tenterden CJ and Taunton J delivered concurring judgments.]

Warinco AG v Samor SpA

[1977] 2 Lloyd's Rep 582, [1979] 1 Lloyd's Rep 450,
Queen's Bench Division and Court of Appeal

(The facts are immaterial.)

Donaldson J: It is a popular myth, which lawyers do little to dispel, that the law is a highly technical matter with mysterious rules leading to results which are contrary to commonsense. Nothing could be further from the truth, both in general and in the particular instance of the law relating to the repudiation of contracts.

If a buyer under a contract calling for delivery by instalments commits a breach of that contract before all the deliveries have been made and that breach is so serious as to go to the root of the contract—in other words, to destroy the basis of the contract—commonsense suggests that the seller should not be expected to go to the trouble and expense of tendering later instalments if he does not want to. The law so provides.

Again, if it becomes clear that the buyer will be unable to accept or to pay for later instalments, commonsense suggests that the seller should, if he wishes, be discharged from any obligation further to perform his part of the contract. The law so provides.

Finally, if a buyer acts or speaks in a manner which declares in clear terms that he will not in future perform his part of the contract, the seller should, in common sense and fairness, have the option of being discharged from further obligation under the contract. And that is the law.

But common sense also suggests that there can be borderline cases in which it is not quite so clear what should happen. The law is at a disadvantage here in that it must draw a line. The line which it draws is indicated by the question: 'Has the buyer evinced an intention to abandon or to refuse to perform the contract?'. In answering this question, the law has regard to such factors as the degree to which the delivery of one instalment is linked with another, the proportion of the contract which has been affected by the allegedly repudiatory breach and the probability that the breach will be repeated. However, these are merely part of the raw material for answering the question. They cannot be conclusive in themselves.

Two other cases may be mentioned:

(1) *Robert A Munro & Co Ltd v Meyer* [1930] 2 KB 312, where there was a contract to supply 1500 tons of meat-and-bone meal by instalments of 125 tons per month. After 631 tons had been delivered, it was discovered that all the meal delivered so far had been deliberately adulterated with cocoa husk, so that it failed to conform to its description. Wright J granted a declaration that the buyers were not bound to take delivery of any further instalments.

(2) *Regent ORG Aisenstadt und Barig v Francesco of Jermyn Street Ltd* [1981] 3 All ER 327: Regent, a firm of German clothing manufacturers, agreed to sell 62 suits to Francesco, retailers of menswear. Delivery was to be by instalments, the number and size to be at Regent's discretion. Francesco told Regent that they wished to cancel the order, but Regent insisted on continuing to make deliveries because the suits were already in production. Francesco then purported to cancel the contract on the ground that one delivery had been one suit short, relying on s 30(1) of the Act (see below, p 471), which entitles a buyer who is tendered short delivery to reject all the contract goods. Mustill J ruled that where the contract provided for delivery to be made by instalments, s 31(2) applied to the exclusion of s 30(1), and the repudiation was wrongful in the circumstances.

NOTES

1. The statement of the law in the *Maple Flock* case may be regarded as an instance of the 'innominate term' approach to the question of breach of contract favoured by the Court of Appeal in *Hong Kong Fir Shipping Co Ltd v Kawasaki Kisen Kaisha Ltd* [1962] 2 QB 26.

2. The delivery of only one suit short in the *Regent* case (above) would, in any case, probably not now fall within s 30(1): see s 30(2A), which (in non-consumer contracts) applies a 'reasonableness' test where a shortfall in delivery is 'slight'.

CHAPTER 12
REMEDIES OF THE SELLER

1 ACTION FOR THE PRICE

The seller's right to bring an action for the price is described in s 49 of the Act in rather surprisingly restrictive terms. Section 49 states that he is entitled to do so only in two specified situations:

(1) where, under the contract of sale, the property in the goods has passed to the buyer, and he wrongfully neglects or refuses to pay for the goods according to the terms of the contract (s 49(1));

(2) where, under the contract, the price is payable on a day certain irrespective of delivery, and the buyer wrongfully neglects or refuses to pay the price (s 49(2)).

However, there are some other situations where the seller may sue for the price (see paragraph (c) below); so s 49 cannot be regarded as a complete statement of the law.

(a) Where the property has passed to the buyer (s 49(1))

For the seller to be able to sue for the price under this subsection, it is not sufficient that the property has passed to the buyer. The buyer must also have wrongfully neglected or refused to pay the price; and this neglect or refusal will not be 'wrongful' if the price is not yet due under the terms of the contract (eg where the seller has agreed to give credit), or if the seller is in breach of certain obligations on his part (eg where s 28 applies, to be ready and willing to give possession of the goods to the buyer in exchange for the price).

(b) Where the price is payable on a day certain irrespective of delivery (s 49(2))

If the contract stipulates a fixed date for payment, or a date that can be calculated by reference to some objective fact (eg 'seven days after arrival of ship'), irrespective of delivery, the seller can sue for the price even though the property has not passed, and even though no goods have yet been appropriated to the contract. Again, however, the buyer must have wrongfully neglected or refused to pay for the goods. The meaning of the phrase 'a day certain irrespective of delivery' was discussed in *Workman Clark & Co Ltd v Lloyd Brazileño* (below, p 435).

(c) Where the risk has passed

The draftsman appears to have overlooked the fact that there are some other situations, not covered by s 49, where the seller may sue for the price. The most obvious is where the risk has passed to the buyer before the property has passed and the goods are destroyed or lost in an event covered by the concept of 'risk': see *Castle v Playford* (above, p 332) and *Manbre Saccharine Co Ltd v Corn Products Co Ltd* (below, p 501).

(d) Other situations

However, in other situations where it might with justice have been held that the price was payable even though neither of the s 49 requirements had been complied with, the courts have held that the seller has only an action for damages for non-acceptance of the goods under s 50. The unsatisfactory consequence may then be, not only that the seller is kept out of his money for a long time, but that he is left with the goods on his hands and the burden of seeing to their disposal. These are cases where the buyer by his own wrongful act has prevented the price from becoming due and payable, such as the two following.

Stein, Forbes & Co v County Tailoring Co
(1916) 86 LJKB 448, King's Bench Division

Stein Forbes contracted to sell sheepskins on CIF terms (see below, p 498) to County Tailoring, 'Payment: Net cash against documents on arrival of the steamer'. The steamer arrived, but County Tailoring wrongfully refused to take up the documents or to pay the price. Atkin J held them liable in damages but not bound to pay the price.

Atkin J held that the defendants had been guilty of breach of contract, and continued: The material question that remains is as to the plaintiffs' remedy. The plaintiffs have sued only for the price of the goods. Their counsel contended that they were entitled to the price, even though the property in the goods had not passed to the defendants, on the ground that here was a sum certain payable at a fixed time, and that, as the defendants had prevented delivery, they could not rely upon non-delivery. I do not think, however, that the plaintiffs can establish their claim on that footing. This is not the case of a day being appointed for payment of money, and the day happening before the thing which is the consideration for the payment. In such a case, which falls within one of the well known rules in the notes to *Pordage v Cole* [1669] 1 Wms Saund (1871 ed), 548 at 551, the money can be claimed before performance. Such a case is provided for by the Sale of Goods Act 1893, s 49, sub-s 2. But this is not a case where the price is payable on a day certain irrespective of delivery. On the contrary, it is payable expressly against delivery.

Counsel for the plaintiffs further said that the property had in fact passed to the defendants, and that, upon the plaintiffs being willing to transfer possession, they were entitled to the price. I think that there are many objections to this view. At what time property passes under a contract of sale depends upon the intention of the parties.

[His Lordship read ss 16 and 17, sub-s 1 of the Sale of Goods Act 1893, and continued:]

The Act provides certain rules for ascertaining the intention of the parties unless a different intention appears. Counsel for the plaintiffs contends that, as soon as the goods are unconditionally appropriated to the contract and the seller holds the documents at the disposal of the buyer, the property passes. The value of that proposition depends on the meaning of 'unconditionally.' I doubt whether goods are appropriated unconditionally if the seller does not mean the buyer to have them unless he pays for them. But it seems to me impossible to lay down a general rule applicable to all cif contracts. The overruling question is, 'Does the intention of the parties appear in the course of the making and the fulfilment of the contract?'

[His Lordship read s 19 of the Sale of Goods Act 1893, and continued:]

In the present case the goods were shipped at New York on behalf of the plaintiffs, and the bill of lading was taken to the order of the banking firm which financed the transaction for the plaintiffs. On arrival of the ship the plaintiffs had to take up the bill of lading from the bankers, and, as the defendants would not take up the documents, the plaintiffs had to take delivery of the goods from the ship. It seems quite plain that the seller or his banker reserved the *jus disponendi*. It was said that the property passed to the buyer on shipment, and the seller only received his unpaid vendor's lien. That view seems to me inconsistent with s 19 of the Sale of Goods Act 1893, and with every business probability.

Then it is said that, whatever the original intention may be, at any rate the property passes when there is an appropriation of specific goods, as by the invoice in this case and a tender or willingness to tender. It would be a remarkable intention in a commercial man to keep the property on shipment in order to secure payment, but yet in taking the necessary steps to procure payment by appropriation and tender to part with the property before payment is in fact made. I think that in such cases the ordinary inference to be drawn is that the seller does not intend to part with the property except against payment. It seems to me that this view is confirmed by the provision of s 19, sub-s 3 of the Act.

Unless the property has passed, I do not think that in this case the plaintiffs can sue for the price, and in my opinion it has not passed. The plaintiffs' claim is, therefore, for damages.

Colley v Overseas Exporters Ltd
[1921] 3 KB 302, King's Bench Division

Colley agreed to sell leather belting to the defendant company on FOB terms (see below, p 494). The contract obliged the buyers to nominate a ship on to which the seller was to make arrangements to load the goods, and provided that the price was to be paid when delivery was made to the ship. The buyers failed to nominate a ship, despite five abortive attempts, and the goods lay on the docks. It was held that the seller could not sue for the price, even though it was due to the buyer's own default that the event which would have made the price payable under the contract had not occurred.

McCardie J: This action is brought...to recover the sum of £985 17s 4d alleged to be due from the defendants to the plaintiff as the price of goods. The only question is whether that liquidated sum is due. No question arises as yet as to damages against the defendants. The case raises a point of legal interest and practical utility as to the circumstances under which the purchase price of goods can be sued for....

The defendants committed no deliberate breach of contract; they suffered a series of misfortunes. They failed however to name an effective ship. The plaintiff on his part did all he could to carry out his obligations. Under these circumstances the plaintiff seeks to recover the price of the goods in question. The able argument of Mr Willes for the plaintiff rested on two well-known passages in the judgment of Lord Blackburn in *Mackay v Dick* ((1881) 6 App Cas 251). The first passage is this: 'I think I may safely say, as a general rule, that where in a written contract it appears that both parties have agreed that something shall be done, which cannot effectually be done unless both concur in doing it, the construction of the contract is that each agrees to do all that is necessary to be done on his part for the carrying out of that thing, though there may be no express words to that effect.' The second passage is this: 'It would follow in point of law that the defender having had the machine delivered to him, was by his contract to keep it, unless on a fair test according to the contract it failed to do the stipulated quantity of work, in which case he would be entitled to call on the pursuers to remove it. And *by his own default* he can now never be in a position to call upon the pursuers to take back the machine, on the ground that the test had not been satisfied, he must, as far as regards that, keep, and consequently pay for it.' I will consider later on the facts in *Mackay v Dick*. The contention of Mr Willes before me was that inasmuch as the defendants' own fault had here prevented the goods from being put on board they were disabled from saying that the price, which would have been payable if and when the goods had actually been put on board, was not now due to the plaintiff. This is a novel and interesting submission ...

The circumstances ... under which a claim to the price may be made (as distinguished from a claim of damages for breach of contract) are indicated in s 49 of [the Sale of Goods] Act.

[His Lordship read the section, and continued:]

Here sub-s 2 of s 49 does not apply, as it apparently did in *Workman, Clark & Co v Lloyd Brazileño* ([1908] 1 KB 968), where the price was payable by stated instalments on stated dates. The parties before me here made no special agreement as to the payment of the price. Nor can it be said that sub-s 1 of s 49 applies here, for the property in the goods has not in fact and law passed to the buyer ... Unless therefore the principle involved in the words of Lord Blackburn in the second passage cited from *Mackay v Dick* applies here the plaintiff will fail. Does the principle go to the extent submitted by Mr Willes? It is well to consider *Mackay v Dick*. The headnote says: 'If, in the case of a contract of sale and delivery, which makes acceptance of the thing sold and payment of the price conditional on a certain thing being done by the seller, the buyer prevents the possibility of the seller fulfilling the condition, the contract is to be taken as satisfied.' If this headnote be given its full apparent effect then the principle it suggests would be most far reaching and the results extraordinary. The facts in *Mackay v Dick* must be remembered. Concisely put they were these. By a contract in two letters the seller agreed to sell and deliver at the buyer's works a digging machine. The price of £1125 was payable after the machine had satisfactorily performed certain tests. If it failed to perform them the buyer was to remove the machine. The machine was actually delivered into the buyer's possession. Owing however to the buyer's own default it did not perform the tests. He refused to pay the price, and the seller thereupon brought his action for the £1125. The plaintiff succeeded on the principle stated by Lord Blackburn. It is to be clearly noted that a specific machine was fully deliverable by the seller to the buyer. Apparently the property in the machine actually passed to the buyer. ... Hence I think that the sale and delivery of the machine must in *Mackay v Dick* be deemed to have been complete, and payment of the price was therefore subject only to the 'resolutive condition' imposed by the clause as to the test: see Chalmers' Sale of Goods, 8th ed, pp 6,7, and the cases there cited as to resolutive conditions. Default by the buyer as to the test was proved, and thus the seller got his judgment for the price. The actual decision in *Mackay v Dick* does not therefore aid the plaintiff here. The real question is as to the extent to which the principle indicated by Lord Blackburn in the second passage I have quoted operates to make a price payable which, apart from that principle, would not be payable ... In my opinion ... no action will lie for the price of goods until the property has passed, save only in the special cases provided for by s 49, sub-s 2. This seems plain both on the code and on common law principle. I have searched in vain for authority to the contrary. A clear distinction exists between cases where the default of the buyer has occurred after the property has passed and cases where that default has been before the property has passed. To the former cases *Mackay v Dick* may be applied on appropriate facts. To the latter cases *Mackay v Dick* does not apply so as to enable the buyer to recover the price as distinguished from damages for breach of contract. To hold that *Mackay v Dick* applies where the property has not passed would lead to extraordinary results. Here the substantial allegation against the defendants is that their default prevented the plaintiff from passing the property and so entitling him to the price. Just the same default however would, in substance, have been committed if the defendants had repudiated the contract before the goods had been sent from Sheffield. So too every buyer who refuses to take delivery of unascertained goods and thereby prevents the transference of property in them from the seller commits a similar default. If the ingenious contention of Mr Willes were correct it would be difficult to imagine a case of sale of goods, even though unascertained, to which *Mackay v Dick* would not apply....

It follows therefore for the reasons given that the plaintiff is not entitled to recover the price of the goods in question. If he desires to claim damages he must amend his writ. On the record at present before me he cannot ask for judgment.

Where by the terms of a contract of sale the price is to be paid by instalments, each payable 'on a day certain', each instalment of the price may be sued for as it becomes due: *Workman, Clark & Co Ltd v Lloyd Brazileño* [1908] 1 KB 968, CA—a case like *Re Blyth Shipbuilding & Dry Docks Co Ltd* (above, p 323), where the price of a ship to be built for the buyer was to be paid for by five instalments as the work progressed. In a case like this, we can see again the advantage of an action for the price, in comparison with a mere claim for damages: if the seller cannot sue for instalments of the price, when due, his position will be particularly onerous, as he will be left with an uncompleted ship and no source to look to to maintain his cash-flow.

(e) The right to interest on the price

Section 54 preserves any right that the seller may have, apart from the Act, to claim interest on the price. At common law, interest is payable only if the contract so provides; but the courts now have a wide statutory discretion to award interest in many cases, eg under the Supreme Court Act 1981, s 35A. In practice, interest is regularly awarded in commercial claims for debt. There is now also a statutory entitlement to interest under the Late Payment of Commercial Debts (Interest) Act 1998.

(f) Buyer's right to reduction of price in consumer contracts

Under s 48C (introduced by the Sale and Supply of Goods to Consumers Regulations 2002, SI 2002/3045, implementing Directive 1999/44/EC) a buyer who is a consumer may require the seller to reduce the price by an appropriate amount where goods have been delivered which do not conform to the contract and either it is not possible or practicable to replace or repair the goods or the seller has failed to replace or repair them after being required to do so: see below, p 486.

2 ACTION FOR DAMAGES FOR NON-ACCEPTANCE

The seller may bring an action against the buyer for damages for non-acceptance when the buyer has wrongfully neglected to accept and pay for the goods (s 50(1)). The buyer has a counterpart claim against the seller for damages for non-delivery (s 51(1)). Both sections then go on to state in similar terms the rule as to remoteness of damage which contract lawyers will recognise as the 'first rule' in *Hadley v Baxendale* (1854) 9 Exch 341: that the measure of damages is the estimated loss directly and naturally resulting, in the ordinary course of events, from the defendant party's breach of contract (ss 50(2), 51(2)); and they then continue with a statement of another well-known formula for the assessment of damages, the 'market price' rule (ss 50(3), 51(3)). For the action for damages for non-acceptance, this reads as follows:

Where there is an available market for the goods in question the measure of damages is prima facie to be ascertained by the difference between the contract price and the market or current price at the time or times when the goods ought to have been accepted or (if no time was fixed for acceptance) at the time of the refusal to accept (s 50(3)).

Thus, the statutory rules restate principles which are part of the normal damages rules in the law of contract. But they go only so far: they do not, for instance, mention the 'second rule' in *Hadley v Baxendale,* which deals with claims for 'unusual' losses for which the buyer is deemed to have assumed liability by reason of special facts known to the parties at the time when the contract was entered into. In such cases, we must fall back on the common law.

The 'market price' rule is closely connected with the general principle that a party seeking damages is under an obligation to take steps to mitigate his loss. If, when the buyer refuses to accept the goods, there is a market where other buyers are ready to take them off the seller's hands and to pay the going price for them, he will have discharged his duty to mitigate if he disposes of the goods promptly to such a buyer. Looking at it the other way, if the seller does not do this and he is later able to obtain only a smaller price for the goods—perhaps because they have deteriorated, or because demand has fallen off—the buyer will rightly be able to argue that he should not be liable for the whole of the seller's loss because the opportunity to mitigate was not taken.

Section 50(3) will apply only if there is an 'available market' for the goods in question. (On the concept of a 'market', see RM Goode [1991] LMCLQ 177.) There have been various judicial definitions of this term. It is sufficient to quote one, from the judgment of Jenkins LJ in *Charter v Sullivan* [1957] 2 QB 117 at 128, CA:

I . . . will content myself with the negative proposition that I doubt if there can be an available market for particular goods in any sense relevant to s 50(3) of the Sale of Goods Act [1979] unless those goods are available for sale in the market at the market or current price in the sense of the price, whatever it may be, fixed by reference to supply and demand as the price at which a purchaser for the goods in question can be found, be it greater than or less than or equal to the contract price.

In that case, the contract was for the sale of a new Hillman car, at a time when the retail price of all such cars was fixed by the manufacturers. The court held that in these circumstances s 50(3) should not be applied, since the price of Hillman cars was not free to fluctuate in response to supply and demand. Since demand for such cars then exceeded the supply available, and the seller had been able to resell the car for the same price within a few days, he had suffered no loss and was held entitled only to nominal damages. This case may be contrasted with *W L Thompson Ltd v Robinson (Gunmakers) Ltd* [1955] Ch 177, where once again the retail price of the car (a 'Vanguard') was fixed by the manufacturers, but at that time the supply of Vanguard cars exceeded the demand. This meant that when the buyer refused to accept the car the seller lost the profit on a sale, and he was awarded this sum as damages for loss of bargain. In *Lazenby Garages Ltd v Wright* [1976] 1 WLR 459, CA, it was held that there is no 'available market' for secondhand cars: the court took the rather surprising view that every secondhand car is a unique article, so that the measure of the seller's loss if the buyer refuses to accept is not reckoned by reference to a market price, but by the actual loss (if any) which the seller has sustained.

Section 50(3) states that the relevant market price is that available at the *time* of the failure or refusal to accept. It is also established by the cases that a similar test applies in regard to the *place* of the relevant market: the court asks whether a market existed for goods of the contract description at the place where the buyer ought to have taken delivery, and uses as a yardstick the price prevailing on that market.

More complicated questions may arise where there is an *anticipatory* repudiation by the buyer which is accepted by the seller: although, once again, damages are prima facie to be assessed by reference to the market price at the time when the goods ought to have been accepted—ie the time fixed for delivery by the contract (s 50(3)), the seller's duty to mitigate his loss may well place him under an obligation to resell the goods as soon as possible after he has accepted the buyer's repudiation, if this takes place against the background of a falling market. (If the seller does not accept the repudiation, of course, he is under no duty to mitigate until an actual breach occurs: *Tredegar Iron & Coal Co Ltd v Hawthorn Bros & Co* (1902) 18 TLR 716.)

Further difficult issues may be encountered in the case of an international sale, where the buyer's breach takes place after the goods have been shipped. If there is an available market for such goods 'afloat', to which the seller can have recourse, the price on this market will be appropriate; but if there is not, the first possible place where he will be able to dispose of them will be the port of arrival. (Section 50(3) is, after all, only a prima facie rule.) Thus, in *Muller, MacLean & Co v Leslie & Anderson* (1921) 8 Ll L Rep 328, the contract was for a consignment of padlocks FOB New York, to be shipped to India. The buyers wrongly refused to accept the shipping documents after the goods had been shipped. Damages were awarded to the sellers based on the market price in India at the time of the ship's arrival.

Where, because there is no available market, s 50(3) does not apply, the court must fall back on the ordinary rules of the law of contract as to the assessment of damages, estimating the seller's loss as best it can. If he has lost a profit on a retail sale, as in *Thompson v Robinson* (above), he can claim the amount of that profit. If he has resold to a substitute buyer at a lower price, the resale price will be at least prima facie evidence by which his loss can be calculated.

The seller will also be able to claim as damages the reasonable costs of reselling the goods and any incidental expenses, eg for storage, transport, etc. This is confirmed by s 37(1).

For a critical examination of the market price rule, see JN Adams 'Damages in Sale of Goods' [2002] JBL 553. We must remember also that the 'market price' formula is only a prima facie rule, which may not always be appropriate. In *Bem Dis A Turk Ticaret S/A TR v International Agri Trade Co Ltd* [1999] All ER (Comm) 619 a consignment of tapioca was to be shipped from Thailand to Turkey but importation was banned by the Turkish government, and the buyers told the sellers not to load the ship which they had chartered. The sellers successfully sued for the cost of cancelling the hire of the ship. The Court of Appeal rejected an argument that the market price rule should be applied.

3 SELLER'S RIGHT TO TERMINATE CONTRACT UPON BREACH OR REPUDIATION BY BUYER

If the buyer wrongfully fails or refuses to perform one or more of his obligations under the contract, this may be a breach or repudiation of the contract which will allow the seller to terminate the contract and treat himself as discharged from further performance. Whether he can do so or not falls to be determined by normal contract principles. Thus, in *Bunge Corpn v Tradax SA* [1981] 1 WLR 711, HL, the buyers were required by a term of the contract to provide a vessel and to give the sellers at least 15 days' notice of the readiness of the vessel to load. They were four days late in doing so. It was held that this provision as to time was a condition, breach of which entitled the sellers to treat the contract as repudiated. A similar consequence would follow where the buyer is held to have been in breach of an intermediate or innominate term and the breach is regarded as serious.

4   REMEDIES OF AN UNPAID SELLER

(a) Introduction

In addition to the remedies described above, which are simply applications to the law of sale of ordinary principles of the law of contract, the Act confers additional remedies upon a seller who is *unpaid*. These are set out in s 39(2) as follows:

(1) a *lien* on the goods or right to retain them for the price while he is in possession of them;

(2) in the case of the insolvency of the buyer, a right of *stopping the goods in transit* after he has parted with the possession of them; and

(3) a *right of resale*, as limited by the Act.

Section 39(2) states that an unpaid seller who is still the owner of the goods (ie where the property has not passed to the buyer) has rights analogous to the right of lien and stoppage in transit set out in s 39(1). This confirms that the rights of the seller in such a case are no less than they would be if the property had passed. It is arguable that he would in many circumstances be able to assert such rights anyway, by virtue of the fact that he is the owner of the goods; but the Act removes any doubts which there might be on the point.

The rights described in s 39(1) and elaborated in the rest of Part V of the Act are described as 'rights against the goods'. In contrast with the seller's rights to sue for the price and for damages, which are rights to proceed *in personam* against the buyer by way of a money claim in the courts, these rights give the seller powers, in the nature of self-help remedies, which he can exercise directly against the goods. For this reason, they are sometimes referred to as the seller's 'real' remedies.

A seller is an 'unpaid seller' for the purposes of s 39 in the circumstances set out in s 38(1). This will be the case:

(1) when the whole of the price has not been paid or tendered; or

(2) when a bill of exchange or other negotiable instrument has been received by the seller as conditional payment, and the condition on which it was received has not been fulfilled by reason of the dishonour of the instrument or otherwise.

By s 38(2), certain other persons are given the same rights as the seller—an agent of the seller to whom a bill of lading respecting the goods has been indorsed, and a consignor or agent who has himself paid or is directly responsible to the buyer for the price.

The question whether a seller is 'unpaid' turns simply upon the *fact* whether payment has been made (or tendered) or not: it is not concerned with the rights and wrongs of the situation, such as whether payment is actually due. A seller who has agreed to allow his buyer credit is thus an unpaid seller, even during the time when the period for credit is still running. Note also (1) that a seller is 'unpaid' so long as *any part* of the price is outstanding, and (2) that if payment has been *tendered,* this is treated as equivalent to payment, so that a seller who has refused to accept payment when tendered will lose his unpaid seller's remedies.

Where the seller has accepted a cheque or other negotiable instrument in payment of the price, the normal understanding is that he receives it as a conditional payment, rather than in satisfaction of the buyer's obligations. In this case, his remedies as an unpaid seller are suspended while the instrument is current, but revive if the instrument is dishonoured, or if the buyer becomes insolvent.

(b) Unpaid seller's lien

The unpaid seller's right of *lien* is his right, if he is in possession of the goods, to retain possession of them until the price is paid or tendered (s 41(1)). A lien is thus a form of possessory security. As discussed more fully in Chapter 23, it is a right to *retain* goods which are already in the party's possession (in contrast with a pledge, which is based on a *delivery* of possession). Not every unpaid seller may claim a lien. The right arises in the following cases (s 41(1)):

(1) where the goods have been sold without any stipulation as to credit;

(2) where the goods have been sold on credit but the term of credit has expired;

(3) where the buyer becomes insolvent.

The seller may assert his lien even though he is in possession as the buyer's bailee or agent (s 41(2)).

A seller has a right of lien even though part only of the price is unpaid (s 38(l)(a)); and he may exercise his lien (for the whole price, if appropriate) against part only of the goods, if he has already delivered the rest to the buyer, unless he is held to have waived his lien (s 42).

An unpaid seller loses his lien in three circumstances (s 43(1)):

(1) when he delivers the goods to a carrier or other bailee for the purpose of transmission to the buyer without reserving the right of disposal of the goods;

(2) when the buyer or his agent lawfully obtains possession of the goods;

(3) by waiver.

In addition, of course, he will lose his lien if the price is paid or tendered to him; but not by reason only that he obtains a judgment for the price (s 43(2)).

Section 43(1) underlines the essential nature of the lien as a right to *retain* possession: if the unpaid seller parts with the goods, he cannot reassert his lien even if he gets back possession: *Valpy v Gibson,* below. He may also lose his lien by delivering the goods to a carrier for the purpose of transmission to the buyer, unless he 'reserves the right of disposal'—a phrase which, as we saw in relation to s 19 (above, p 345), most often refers to a seller who ships goods and takes the bill of lading in his own name.

Valpy v Gibson

(1847) 4 CB 837, Court of Common Pleas

Brown, a merchant in Birmingham, bought cloth from Gibson. Gibson sent the cloth to Leech, Harrison & Co, shipping agents, at Liverpool, in four cases marked for shipment to

Valparaiso, requesting Leech & Co to put them on board as directed by Brown. After the goods had been loaded on to a ship, Brown's agent, Alison, ordered them to be returned to Gibson to be repacked in eight cases instead of four. Gibson was still in possession of the goods, and unpaid, when Brown was declared bankrupt. It was held that it was too late for Gibson to claim an unpaid seller's lien.

The judgment of the court (Wilde CJ, Coltman, Maule and Cresswell JJ) was delivered by **Wilde CJ:** The right which it was contended the defendants had, as vendors in the actual and lawful possession of the goods, on the insolvency of the vendee, cannot, we think, be sustained. The goods being sold on credit, and the complete property and possession having vested in Brown, they became his absolutely, without any lien or right of the vendors attaching to them, any more than on any other property of Brown; and their delivery to the defendants to be re-packed, could not have the effect of creating a lien for the price, without an agreement to that effect. We therefore think there must be judgment for the plaintiffs.

Section 43(1) has to be read in conjunction with s 47, which describes other situations in which an unpaid seller will lose his right of lien. (Section 47 also applies to the unpaid seller's right of stoppage in transit (below, p 443).) There is a further overlap: s 47 links in also with s 25(1) and the almost identical Factors Act 1889, s 9 (concerning sales by a buyer in possession), which we discussed as an exception to the *nemo dat* rule (see above, p 381). Section 47 is concerned with the effect on the unpaid seller's real remedies of a sub-sale or other disposition of the goods made by the buyer. It reads:

(1) Subject to this Act, the unpaid seller's right of lien or retention or stoppage in transit is not affected by any sale or other disposition of the goods which the buyer may have made, unless the seller has assented to it.

(2) Where a document of title to goods has been lawfully transferred to any person as buyer or owner of the goods, and that person transfers the document to a person who takes it in good faith and for valuable consideration, then

(a) if the last-mentioned transfer was by way of sale, the unpaid seller's right of lien or retention or stoppage in transit is defeated; and

(b) if the last-mentioned transfer was made by way of pledge or other disposition for value, the unpaid seller's right of lien or retention or stoppage in transit can only be exercised subject to the rights of the transferee.

Note that in the Act of 1893, s 47 was not divided into subsections; instead, what is now s 47(2) appeared as a proviso to the general rule now stated in s 47(1).

Section 47(2) deals with the position when the seller has delivered or transferred a 'document of title' to the buyer. (For the definition of this term, see above, p 380.) It is important to note that the mere fact that the seller has handed a document of title to the buyer will not of itself affect the seller's rights of lien and stoppage: there must be *two* 'transfers' of the document before s 47(2) can apply.

Mordaunt Bros v British Oil and Cake Mills Ltd illustrates the general proposition stated in s 47(1), while *Mount v Jay* throws light on the two exceptions referred to in s 47: assent of the seller (s 47(1)), and the transfer of a document of title (s 47(2)(a)); however, on the special facts of the case, the wording of s 25(1) proved to be more appropriate than that of s 47(2) (a).

Mordaunt Bros v British Oil and Cake Mills Ltd
[1910] 2 KB 502, King's Bench Division

BOCM contracted to sell various lots of boiled linseed oil to Crichton Bros, who resold it to Mordaunts. Mordaunts had paid Crichtons all or most of the price of their purchases. Possession remained with BOCM, who had not been paid by Crichtons. Delivery orders had been sent by Crichtons to BOCM, directing BOCM to deliver to Mordaunts an amount of oil appropriate to each contract, which BOCM usually acknowledged and recorded in its books. It was held that these acts did not constitute an 'assent' by BOCM to the resale for the purposes of s 47(1).

Pickford J: It was next argued that the plaintiffs were entitled to succeed by virtue of s 47 of the Sale of Goods Act 1893, on the ground that the defendants had assented to the sales by Crichton Brothers to the plaintiffs. Several cases were cited in which it was held that unpaid vendors had assented to sub-sales so as to preclude themselves from asserting their right of lien. As a matter of fact all those cases related to sub-sales of specific goods. I am not, however, going to decide that s 47 has no application to unascertained goods; but I wish to point out that such acts as presenting to an unpaid vendor delivery orders in favour of sub-purchasers and the entry accordingly of the names of the sub-purchasers in the books of the unpaid vendor may have a different effect according as the goods are specific or unascertained. In the former case it may be more readily inferred that the unpaid vendor has assumed the position of an agent or bailee holding the goods for and on behalf of the sub-purchaser or holder of the delivery order, and the acceptance of the delivery order and entry of the holder's name in the books by the unpaid vendor might in the case of specific goods justify the inference that the unpaid vendor had accepted that position. No such inference could be drawn if the goods were not in existence, and it does not follow that because the inference may be drawn in the case of specific goods it will also be drawn in the case of goods in existence but unascertained. In my opinion the assent which affects the unpaid seller's right of lien must be such an assent as in the circumstances shews that the seller intends to renounce his rights against the goods. It is not enough to shew that the fact of a sub-contract has been brought to his notice and that he has assented to it merely in the sense of acknowledging the receipt of the information. His assent to the sub-contract in that sense would simply mean that he acknowledged the right of the purchaser under the sub-contract to have the goods subject to his own paramount right under the contract with his original purchaser to hold the goods until he is paid the purchase-money. Such an assent would imply no intention of making delivery to a sub-purchaser until payment was made under the original contract. The assent contemplated by s 47 of the Sale of Goods Act 1893, means something more than that; it means an assent given in such circumstances as shew that the unpaid seller intends that the sub-contract shall be carried out irrespective of the terms of the original contract.

   Now in the circumstances of this case what was the effect of the inquiry by the plaintiffs whether the delivery orders of Crichton Brothers were 'in order' and the defendants' reply that they were? I think some light is thrown on the nature and purpose of this inquiry by the fact that the plaintiffs parted with their money before making the inquiry. Neither party regarded those inquiries as directed to the questions whether the defendants were to hold the oil as agents for the plaintiffs, renouncing any rights they might have to hold the goods till they were paid for by Crichton Brothers, and whether they were prepared to deliver to the plaintiffs and look elsewhere than to the goods themselves for any rights they might have in respect of them. Whatever might have been the effect of such an inquiry and answer in a case where specific goods were in question, I think in the present case where the goods were unascertained the inquiry and answer amounted to no more than this—that the defendants were ready to carry out the contract between themselves and Crichton Brothers with this modification, that delivery should be made to the plaintiffs instead of to Crichton Brothers, but that the delivery should be subject to all the other terms and incidents of the contract with Crichton Brothers.

DF Mount Ltd v Jay & Jay (Provisions) Co Ltd
[1960] 1 QB 159, Queen's Bench Division

(For the facts and another part of the decision, see above, p 387. This part of Salmon J's judgment is concerned with the question of 'assent'.)

Salmon J: The case raises the familiar problem—which of two innocent persons, the plaintiffs or the defendants, shall suffer for the trickery of a rogue.

The plaintiffs rely first on s 47 of the Sale of Goods Act 1893.

[His Lordship read s 47, and continued:]

There is a proviso to the section, with which I shall deal in a moment. The plaintiffs contend that the defendants assented to the sale or disposition of the 250 cartons by Merrick to the plaintiffs, and thereby lost their right as unpaid sellers to the lien which they would otherwise have had upon the cartons. The defendants contend that if they assented to the sub-sale by Merrick, their assent was not an assent within the meaning of s 47, and rely upon *Mordaunt Bros v British Oil and Cake Mills Ltd* [above]. It is clear from Pickford J's judgment in that case that the assent contemplated by s 47 means 'an assent given in such circumstances as show that the unpaid seller intends that the sub-contract shall be carried out irrespective of the terms of the original contract' and must be 'such an assent as in the circumstances shows that the seller intends to renounce his rights against the goods.' Pickford J held that there had been no such assent on the part of the sellers.

The facts of that case are, however, very different from those of the present case. There the sellers had at no time any reason to doubt the buyer's ability to pay, and were not informed of the sub-sale until after the sale was effected. Pickford J held that the sellers had assented to the sub-sale merely in the sense that they acknowledged its existence and the right of the sub-buyer to have the goods subject to their own paramount rights under the contract with the original buyer to hold the goods until paid the purchase price.

In the present case the defendants were anxious to get rid of the goods on a falling market. They knew that Merrick could only pay for them out of the money he obtained from his customers, and that he could only obtain the money from his customers against delivery orders in favour of those customers. In my view, the true inference is that the defendants assented to Merrick reselling the goods, in the sense that they intended to renounce their rights against the goods and to take the risk of Merrick's honesty. The defendants are reputable merchants and I am sure that it was not their intention to get rid of their goods on a falling market through Merrick on the basis that, if he defaulted, they could hold the goods against the customers from whom he obtained the money out of which they were to be paid. . . .

[His Lordship then expressed the view that it was immaterial that the goods were unascertained: see above, p 388.]

[Salmon J also upheld a second argument that Mount was entitled to succeed under s 25(1) (see above, p 387), since Merrick, the first buyer, had received a document of title from Jays and had delivered a second document of title to Mount. It would not have been possible for Mount to rely on the similar provision in s 47(2), however, because the language of s 47(2) is clearly restricted to the case where the *same* document of title is transferred to the sub-buyer.]

QUESTIONS

1.   Is it reasonable to suppose that the draftsman of the Act intended s 25(1) to be construed differently from s 47(2)?

2. Both the cases cited above accept that s 47(2) can apply to a sale of unascertained goods, which have at no stage been appropriated to the contract. Section 39(2) may give some support to this view. But could not Jays have responded to Mount's demand simply by saying that whatever peaches were still in their hands were their own property, to do what they liked with? Is the decision in *Mount v Jay* consistent with s 16? (On this point, see the contrasting arguments of AGL Nicol (1979) 42 MLR 129 and RM Goode *Proprietary Rights and Insolvency in Sales Transactions* (2nd edn, 1989), pp 64–68.)

3. What would have been the position if Jays had become insolvent after Merrick had subsold to Mount and the goods had remained unascertained?

(c) Seller's right to stop the goods in transit

Sections 44–46 set out the second of the unpaid seller's 'real' remedies: to stop the goods if they are still in transit to the buyer, before they have actually reached him. For this remedy to be available, it is not sufficient that the seller should be 'unpaid'; the buyer must also have become insolvent. (For the definition of 'insolvent', see s 61(4), which makes it plain that it is 'commercial' or 'cash-flow' insolvency that matters, and not the buyer's asset position. On insolvency generally, see below, Chapter 27.)

In the Act of 1893, the Latin phrase 'in transitu' was used. The anglicised version was introduced in 1979.

When a seller delivers possession of the goods to a carrier for transmission to the buyer and does not reserve the right of disposal, he loses his lien (s 43(1)(a)). The right of stoppage enables him to resume possession of the goods, at any time during the period that they are in transit, thus allowing him to exercise rights similar to those that he would have under a lien. Once again, s 39(2) confirms that it is immaterial whether the property in the goods has passed to the buyer or not.

The function of the 'carrier' may involve any form of transport: ship, rail, road, air, or a combination of methods.

Section 45 sets out the rules which define the duration of the transit and defines the events in which it will terminate and put an end to the seller's right of stoppage. These events are:

(1) delivery of the goods by the carrier to the buyer or his agent, whether after they have arrived or before they have reached the appointed destination (s 45(1), (2));

(2) attornment by the carrier to the buyer or his agent after they have reached the appointed destination (s 45(3));

(3) a wrongful refusal by the carrier to deliver the goods to the buyer or his agent (s45(6)).

A delivery of part of the goods does not prevent the seller from exercising his right of stoppage against the remainder, unless the part delivery indicates an agreement to give up possession of the whole of the goods (s 45(7)).

If the buyer rejects the goods and they remain in the possession of the carrier, the transit is deemed to continue, even though the seller has refused to take them back (s45(4)).

Section 46 describes how the right of stoppage is effected, and defines the obligations of the carrier and the seller in the circumstances. The seller must either take actual possession of the goods, or give notice of his claim to the carrier or other person who has possession of the goods, either directly to that person or to his principal (s 46(l)–(3)). The carrier must then redeliver the goods to the seller at the latter's expense (s 46(4)).

The seller's right of stoppage is not affected by any subsale which the buyer may have made, unless a document of title has been transferred to the buyer and from him to the subpurchaser, in circumstances which bring into play the provisions of s 47(2) (which has been discussed above, p 440 in the context of the unpaid seller's lien). The following cases illustrate the exercise of the seller's right of stoppage.

The Tigress

(1863) 32 LJPM & A 97, Court of Admiralty

Lucy & Son had sold Bushe wheat which was at sea aboard the *Tigress*, and had endorsed one copy of the bill of lading to Bushe, although they had not been paid. Bushe had become bankrupt while the wheat was still on board. Lucy & Son, purportedly exercising their right of stoppage, directed the master to deliver the wheat to themselves, and tendered payment of the freight. The ship's master refused to deliver the wheat to Lucy & Co without proof that the wheat belonged to them. It was held that he was wrong to do so: he had to assume that the seller was acting within his rights.

Dr Lushington: ...All that is necessary is for the vendor to assert his claim as vendor and owner. Were it otherwise, were the vendor obliged formally to prove his title to exercise the right of stoppage *in transitu,* that right would be worthless; for the validity of a stoppage *in transitu* depends upon several conditions. First, the vendor must be unpaid; secondly, the vendee must be insolvent; thirdly, the vendee must not have indorsed over for value. But the proof that these conditions have been fulfilled would always be difficult for the vendor—often impossible; for instance, whether the vendor is or is not unpaid may depend upon the balance of a current account; whether the vendee is insolvent may not transpire till afterwards, when the bill of exchange for the goods becomes due.... And, lastly, whether the vendee has or has not indorsed the bill of lading over, is a matter not within the cognizance of the vendor. He exercises his right of stoppage *in transitu* at his own peril, and it is incumbent upon the master to give effect to a claim as soon as he is satisfied it is made by the vendor, unless he is aware of a legal defeasance of the vendor's claim. Such, according to my opinion, is the law as laid down by Lord Campbell, in *Gurney v Behrend* ((1854) 3 E & B 622). Lord Campbell uses these words: '*Prima facie* the defendants had a right to stop the wheat, for it was still *in transitu,* and they were unpaid vendors. The onus is on the plaintiffs to prove that they had become the owners, and that the right to stop *in transitu* was gone.' Moreover, I find that the indemnity set out as an exhibit to the petition, and stated in the petition to have been presented to the master, recites that Bushe is the holder of the bill of lading, and claims the wheat under it. So that, in fact, the master had full knowledge of all the circumstances at the time. The defendant then further objects thus: assuming the plaintiffs had a right to stop *in transitu,* and duly asserted that right, yet the master was guilty of no breach of duty in refusing to deliver; he simply is retaining the custody of the wheat for the right owner, as soon as the claim shall be established. Now to this argument I cannot accede; for I think there are cases without number to shew that the right to stop means the right not only to countermand delivery to the vendee, but to order delivery to the vendor. Were it otherwise, the right to stop would be useless, and trade would be impeded. The refusal of the master to deliver upon demand is, in cases like the present, sufficient evidence of conversion—*Wilson v Anderton* ((1830) 1 B & Ad 450). The master may indeed sometimes suffer for an innocent mistake; but he can always protect himself from liability by filing a bill of interpleader in Chancery. For these reasons, I am satisfied that this petition sufficiently shews a *prima facie* case of such breach of duty as renders the vessel liable in this Court, and therefore the objections must be overruled.

Taylor v Great Eastern Rly Co
(1901) 17 TLR 394, King's Bench Division

Barnard Brothers sold a quantity of barley to Sanders and consigned it to Elsenham station, where the railway company acknowledged that it was holding the grain to Sanders' order. Later, when Sanders became insolvent, Barnard Brothers purported to exercise a right of stoppage. But it was held that they could not do so, because the transit had determined when the acknowledgment was issued.

Bigham J: The first question is whether Barnard Brothers were on November 30 entitled to stop the goods as being still *in transitu*. I am of opinion that they were not. The *transitus* was over as soon as a reasonable time had elapsed for Sanders to elect whether he would take the goods away or leave them in the defendants' depot on rent. Such a reasonable time had elapsed, and, having regard to the fact that it was the practice of the defendants to hold goods for Sanders as warehousekeepers at rent when they were not removed after arrival at the stations, I find that, by agreement between Sanders and the defendants, the goods were at the time when Barnards took them away in the possession of the defendants as warehousekeepers for Sanders. I should have been of the same opinion even if there had been no course of business, for I do not think that after service of a notice such as that used in this case it is competent for a consignee by silence indefinitely to fix upon a railway company the onerous responsibilities of common carriers. I am satisfied that, if the defendants had sued Sanders for rent, Sanders could not have successfully resisted the claim. It was argued that the words in the advice note 'the grain is now held at owner's sole risk and subject to the usual warehouse charges' meant that the goods were held by the defendants on account of whom it might concern, and that 'owner's' did not necessarily mean Sanders, but might mean Barnards or any one else who should turn out to be the owners. I do not think there is anything in this point. The advice note is addressed to Sanders for the purpose of affecting him, not for the purpose of affecting any one else, and, moreover, Sanders was the owner of the goods; a right in the vendor to stop *in transitu* does not prevent the buyer from being the owner of the goods; in fact, it necessarily supposes him to be the owner.

Reddall v Union Castle Mail Steamship Co Ltd
(1914) 84 LJKB 360, King's Bench Division

Rutherfords sold a bale of goods to Snow, knowing that he was buying for someone in South Africa. Snow instructed Rutherfords to send the goods to the Union Co's ship *Armadale Castle* at Southampton, to be marked for shipment to Algoa Bay in South Africa. Rutherfords consigned the bale by rail to Southampton as instructed, where Snow, 'in anticipation of in-solvency' told the Union Co to 'stop all shipments'. In consequence, the bale did not leave with the ship, but was kept in storage at Snow's expense until it was handed to Rutherfords in response to a claim to stop in transit. Reddall, Snow's trustee in bankruptcy, sued the Union Co in conversion, and was successful: the court ruled that the transit had ceased when the buyers intercepted the goods before they had been loaded.

Bailhache J: I think, upon these facts, the original transit was to Algoa Bay. The cases upon stoppage *in transitu* are very numerous, and, where the transit is made in stages, difficult to reconcile. I think, however, that it is true to say that, where goods are delivered by the seller or his agent to a carrier, and pass at each successive stage of the transit from the hands of one carrier to another, without the intervention of a forwarding agent, to the destination indicated by the buyer to the seller, the transit continues until that destination is reached. It makes no difference in such a case whether an intermediate carrier receives his instructions direct from the buyer or from the seller, provided that those instructions are given to facilitate the transit of the goods upon the journey originally intended and communicated to the buyer . . . .

This does not dispose of the case, because the goods were intercepted at Southampton and the journey to Algoa Bay was stopped. The buyers, not having contracted with the sellers that the goods should go to Algoa Bay, were within their rights in doing this. . . . The defendants thereafter held the goods at rent at the buyers' disposal, and would not and could not have sent them forward to Algoa Bay, or to any other destination, without fresh instructions from the buyers. I think, therefore, that, although the original transit was to Algoa Bay, that transit had been ended at Southampton, and that under the circumstances the pretended stoppage *in transitu* was too late, and the defendants were wrong in delivering the goods to the sellers. Where the original *transitus* is interrupted by the buyers, I think the test is whether the goods will be set in motion again without further orders from the buyers; if not, the transit is ended and the right to stop lost.

There will be judgment, therefore, for the plaintiff in this case.

If, when he receives notice of stoppage, the carrier has a lien on the goods for unpaid freight, the seller is liable to pay the freight, and also the costs of redelivery: *Booth Steamship Co Ltd v Cargo Fleet Iron Co Ltd* [1916] 2 KB 570, CA.

(d) Rescission and resale by the seller

No automatic rescission. Section 48(1) states that, except as provided later in s 48, a contract of sale is not rescinded by the mere fact that an unpaid seller has exercised his right of lien or stoppage. The contract continues on foot, so that if the buyer (or his trustee in bankruptcy) tenders the price and any other moneys owing, he can require that the goods be delivered to him. If the property in the goods has passed to the buyer, it will remain with him notwithstanding the fact that the seller has exercised his right of lien or stoppage. The seller must take some further step in order to terminate the contract and revest the property in himself or vest it in a new buyer.

Section 48 confusingly runs together various issues which are not necessarily related. Subsections (1), (2) and (3) refer to an *unpaid* seller, but sub-s (4) applies to all sellers; sub-ss (1) and (4) and (it has been held, by implication, also sub-s (3)), are concerned with the question of 'rescission' of the contract of sale—but not sub-s (2); while sub-ss (3) and (4) deal with a seller's *right* of resale (as explained below), whereas in contrast sub-s (2) is concerned with the *effect* of a resale, whether rightful or not! We shall do our best to disentangle these questions in the discussion that follows.

When the seller has a right of resale. Section 48(3), (4) sets out the circumstances in which a seller has a right of resale, and the consequences of such a resale. The use of the word 'right' is important. We saw earlier that a seller who continues or is in possession of the goods has the power in certain circumstances to confer a good title upon a second buyer if he resells the goods (s 24; Factors Act 1889, s 8: above, p 377. But those provisions give the seller nothing more than the *power* to pass a good title: a seller who relies on s 24 or s 8 without more will, at least prima facie, be acting in breach of his contract with the first buyer and liable to him in damages accordingly. If the property has passed to the buyer, he may also be liable to him in tort. However, if the seller resells in exercise of a *right* to do so, he will not be so liable. In fact, it is only s 48(4) which expressly states that the contract of sale is rescinded when the seller exercises his right of resale, but this was held to be also implicit in s 48(3) in *R V Ward Ltd v Bignall* (below). The three situations in which s 48 confers such a right are:

(1) where the *unpaid* seller gives *notice* to the buyer of his intention to resell, and the buyer does not within a reasonable time pay or tender the price (s 48(3));

(2) where the seller is *unpaid* and the goods are *perishable* (s 48(3));

(3) where the seller *expressly reserves* the right of resale in case the buyer should make default (s 48(4)).

RV Ward Ltd v Bignall

[1967] 1 QB 534, Court of Appeal

On 6 May Bignall contracted to buy from Wards two cars, a Vanguard estate and a Ford Zodiac, for a total price of £850, paying a deposit of £25. Later in the same day, he refused to pay the balance or take delivery of either car. Wards the next day gave notice to him through their solicitors that if he did not complete the purchase by 11 May they would dispose of the cars. The Vanguard was later sold for £350, but the Zodiac remained unsold. In this action Wards sued Bignall, claiming (before the Court of Appeal) the balance of the contract price less the amount received for the Vanguard, together with certain expenses. The court held that by reselling the Vanguard, Wards had rescinded the whole contract, so that their only claim was for damages for non-acceptance, obliging them to bring into account the market value of the unsold Zodiac, which remained their property. The trial judge had calculated the damages at £497 10s, but on appeal this was reduced to £47 10s.

Sellers LJ: The question on this part of the appeal is whether, [on the assumption that] the property passed on the sale, the Zodiac car which has not been [resold] remains the buyer's property so that the action of the plaintiffs is for the price, or whether by the sale of the Vanguard the plaintiffs have rescinded the whole contract on the buyer's breach of it so that the ownership of the Zodiac reverted back to the plaintiffs and their remedy is in damages under the statute, or, in effect, damages for non-acceptance, giving credit for what they have received from the sale of the goods or part thereof.

Subsections (1) and (2) of s 48 speak clearly. Subsection (4) expressly provides: 'the original contract of sale is thereby rescinded.' That was necessary because, where the seller 'expressly reserves a right of re-sale in case the buyer should make default,' a seller who re-sold under such a contract would be applying and affirming the contract, and his action would be consistent with it. Under subs (3) no such provision of rescission is necessary, for, if an unpaid seller re-sells, he puts it out of his power to perform his contract and his action is inconsistent with a subsisting sale to the original buyer. Once there is a re-sale in accordance with s 48 by an unpaid seller in possession of the contractual goods the contract of sale is rescinded, whether the re-sale be of the whole of the goods or of part of them, and in this respect subss (3) and (4) fall into line.

As the property in the goods reverts on such a re-sale, the seller retains the proceeds of sale whether they be greater or less than the contractual price. The probability in normal trade is that the price would be less, giving rise to a claim for damages, as for non-acceptance of the goods....

Subsection (4) makes the resale operate as a rescission and leaves the remedy, if any loss ensues, in damages. That brings it into harmony with subs (3), which also gives a claim for damages for any loss occasioned by the original buyer's breach of contract. If the unpaid seller resells the goods, he puts it out of his power to perform his obligation under the original contract, that is, to deliver the contractual goods to the buyer. By the notice to the buyer, the seller makes payment of the price 'of the essence of the contract,' as it is sometimes put. It requires the buyer to pay the price or tender it within a reasonable time.

If he fails to do so, the seller in possession of the goods may treat the bargain as rescinded and resell the goods. The suit for damages becomes comparable to a claim for damages for non-acceptance of the goods where the property never has passed. The property has reverted on the resale, and the second buyer gets a good title. The seller resells as owner. Subsection (2) expressly gives the buyer a good title thereto as against the original buyer.

On this view of the law the plaintiffs cannot recover the price of the Zodiac, which is in the circumstances their property. They can, however, recover any loss which they have sustained by the buyer's default. The parties have sensibly agreed that the value of the Zodiac in May, 1965, was £450. The total contract price was £850, against which the plaintiffs have received £25 in cash and £350 in respect of the Vanguard, and have to give credit for £450 for the Zodiac. To the loss of £25 must be added the sum for advertising, which was admittedly reasonably incurred—£22 10s. The plaintiffs' loss was, therefore, £47 10s.

I would allow the appeal and enter judgment for £47 10s in favour of the plaintiffs in substitution for the award of the deputy judge.

Diplock LJ: Whether or not the property had passed on May 6,1965, the seller was only liable to deliver upon payment or tender of the balance of the purchase price (see the Sale of Goods Act, s 28) and was entitled until then to retain possession, either by virtue of his lien as an unpaid seller if the property had passed (Sale of Goods Act, s 39(1)), or by virtue of his right to withhold delivery if the property had not passed (subs (2) of the same section). In either case, the unpaid seller has a right to resell the goods if he gives notice of his intention to do so and the buyer does not within a reasonable time pay or tender the price (Sale of Goods Act, s 48(3))... This subsection enables a seller in possession of the goods to make time of payment of the purchase price of the essence of the contract whether the property has passed or not. The seller cannot have greater rights of resale if the property has already passed to the buyer than those which he would have if the property had remained in him.

In this court it has been contended on behalf of the seller that, when an unpaid seller who retains possession of goods the property in which has passed to the buyer exercises his statutory right of resale under s 48(3) of the Sale of Goods Act, he does not thereby elect to treat the contract as rescinded, but remains entitled to recover the purchase price from the buyer although he must give credit for the net proceeds of sale of any of the goods which he has sold. Authority for this proposition is to be found in the judgment of Finnemore J in *Gallagher v Shilcock* ([1949] 2 KB 765), and the question in this appeal is whether that judgment is right or not.

Finnemore J based his conclusion on his view as to the construction of s 48 of the Sale of Goods Act, and in particular upon the contrast between the express reference in subs (4) of s 48 to the contract being rescinded when goods are resold under an express right of resale and the absence of any reference to rescission in subs (3) of s 48. With great respect, however, I think that that disregards basic principles of the law of contract, and that there is another explanation for the contrast between the two subsections.

Rescission of a contract discharges both parties from any further liability to perform their respective primary obligations under the contract, that is to say, to do thereafter those things which by their contract they had stipulated they would do. Where rescission occurs as a result of one party exercising his right to treat a breach by the other party of a stipulation in the contract as a repudiation of the contract, this gives rise to a secondary obligation of the party in breach to compensate the other party for the loss occasioned to him as a consequence of the rescission, and this secondary obligation is enforceable in an action for damages. Until, however, there is rescission by acceptance of the repudiation, the liability of both parties to perform their primary obligations under the contract continues. Thus, under a contract for the sale of goods which has not been rescinded, the seller remains liable to transfer the property in the goods to the buyer and to deliver possession of them to him until he has discharged those obligations by performing them, and the buyer remains correspondingly liable to pay for the goods and to accept possession of them.

The election by a party not in default to exercise his right of rescission by treating the contract as repudiated may be evinced by words or by conduct. Any act which puts it out of his power to perform thereafter his primary obligations under the contract, if it is an act which he is entitled to do without notice to the party in default, must amount to an election to rescind the contract. If it is an act which he is not entitled to do, it will amount to a wrongful repudiation of the contract on his part which the other party can in turn elect to treat as rescinding the contract.

Part IV of the Sale of Goods Act, ss 38 to 48, deals with the rights of an unpaid seller both before the property in the goods has passed to the buyer and after it has passed. The mere fact that a seller is unpaid does not necessarily mean that the buyer is in breach of the contract, or, if he is, that his breach is one which entitles the seller to exercise his right to treat the contract as repudiated.

[His Lordship referred to ss 39 and 48, and continued:]

If the contract provided for delivery upon a specified date, the seller's conduct in failing to deliver on that date would put it out of his power to perform one of his primary obligations under the contract if time were of the essence of the contract. It was, therefore, necessary, or at least prudent, to provide expressly that if his failure to deliver were in the mere exercise of a lien or right of stoppage in transitu it did not discharge his liability to deliver the goods upon tender of the contract price, or the buyer's liability to accept the goods and to pay for them.

Subsection (2) deals with a different topic, videlicet, the title of a new buyer to whom the goods are resold by the seller. If the property in the goods at the time of the resale remained in the seller, the new buyer would obtain a good title at common law and would require no statutory protection. The subsection is, therefore, limited to cases where the property in the goods at the time of resale had already passed to the original buyer, and provides that, where the seller is in possession of the goods in the exercise of his unpaid seller's lien or right of stoppage in transitu, the new buyer shall acquire a good title, and this is so whether or not the seller had a right of resale as against the original buyer.

Subsection (3)...is the provision of the Act which confers 'a right of resale as limited by this Act,' referred to in s 39(1)(c). The right dealt with in this subsection is a right as against the original buyer. As a stipulation as to time of payment is not deemed to be of the essence of a contract of sale unless a different intention appears from the terms of the contract (Sale of Goods Act, s 10(1)), failure by the buyer to pay on the stipulated date is not conduct by him which entitles the unpaid seller to treat the contract as repudiated. He remains liable to deliver the goods to the buyer upon tender of the contract price (Sale of Goods Act, s 28). Apart from this subsection, if the unpaid seller resold the goods before or after the property had passed to the original buyer, he would remain liable to the original buyer for damages for non-delivery if the original buyer tendered the purchase price after the resale, and if the property had already passed to the original buyer at the time of the resale he would be liable to an alternative action by the original buyer for damages for conversion. The purpose of the subsection is to make time of payment of the essence of the contract whenever the goods are of a perishable nature, and to enable an unpaid seller, whatever the nature of the goods, to make payment within a reasonable time after notice of the essence of the contract. As already pointed out, an unpaid seller who resells the goods before the property has passed puts it out of his power to perform his primary obligation to the buyer to transfer the property in the goods to the buyer and, whether or not the property has already passed, to deliver up possession of the goods to the buyer. By making the act of resale one which the unpaid seller is entitled to perform, the subsection empowers the seller by his conduct in doing that act to exercise his right to treat the contract as repudiated by the buyer, that is, as rescinded, with the consequence that the buyer is discharged from any further liability to perform his primary obligation to pay the purchase price, and becomes subject to the secondary obligation to pay damages for non-acceptance of the goods. If the contract were not rescinded by the resale the seller would still be entitled to bring an action against the buyer for the price of the goods although, no doubt, he would have to credit the buyer with the proceeds of the resale. If that were the intention of the subsection one would have expected it to provide this in express terms. That it was not the intention is, however, apparent from the words used to define the remedy of the unpaid seller who has exercised his right of resale, videlicet, to 'recover from the original buyer damages for any loss occasioned by his breach of contract.' It is, of course, well-established that where a contract for the sale of goods is rescinded after the property in the goods has passed to the buyer the rescission divests the buyer of his property in the goods.

Subsection (4) deals with the consequences of a resale by a seller, not necessarily an 'unpaid seller' as defined in s 38, made in the exercise of an express right of resale reserved in the contract on the buyer making default. If such an express right were exercisable after the property in the goods had passed to the buyer, its exercise might, on one view, be regarded as an alternative mode of performance of the seller's primary obligations under the contract, and the resale as being made by the seller as agent for the buyer. It was, therefore, necessary to provide expressly that the exercise of an express power of resale should rescind the original contract of sale. That is, in my view, the explanation of the express reference to rescission in subs (4). The absence of a similar express reference to rescission in subs (3) is no sufficient ground for ascribing to subs (3) a meaning which the actual words of the subsection would appear to contradict and which would, in my view, conflict with the general principles of the law of contract.

In the present case the unpaid seller only resold part of the goods which he had contracted to sell to the original buyer. This makes no difference, however. His primary duty under the contract was to deliver both cars to the buyer. If he delivered only one, the buyer would be entitled to reject it (Sale of Goods Act, s 30(1)). By his conduct in selling the Vanguard on May 24, 1965, the unpaid seller put it out of his power to perform his primary obligation under the contract. He thereby elected to treat the contract as rescinded. The property in the Zodiac thereupon reverted to him, and his only remedy against the buyer after May 24, 1965, was for damages for non-acceptance of the two cars, of which the prima facie measure is the difference between the contract price and their market value on May 24, 1965.

I, too, would allow this appeal, and enter judgment for the plaintiffs for £47 10s instead of £497 10s.

[Russell LJ concurred.]

NOTES

1.   The word 'rescind' is used in varying senses in different textbooks on the law of contract. In many contexts, it is helpful to distinguish between (1) 'terminating' a contract for breach, which discharges the parties from further performance of such primary obligations as are outstanding, but leaves open to the party not in breach his remedy in damages, and (2) 'rescinding' a contract (eg for misrepresentation), which has the effect of restoring the parties to their original positions (rescission *'ab initio'*). In s 48 and the judgments in *Ward v Bignall* the word 'rescind' is used as equivalent to 'terminate for breach', so far as the *contractual* position is concerned, but is preferred to 'terminate' because the focus is on the destination of the *property* in the goods. It is made clear that, when a seller validly exercises a right of resale, there is a 'rescission' in the sense that the property is revested in him before passing to the new buyer. It follows that if the resale is made for a higher price, the seller may keep it all (*Commission Car Sales (Hastings) Ltd v Saul* [1957] NZLR 144).

2.   We may infer from the judgments in this case the following additional points:

(1)   A resale of *part* of the goods operates to rescind the whole contract.

(2)   An unpaid seller's right of resale is said to be 'as limited by this Act' (s 39(1)(c)). But this should not be taken to mean that the right of resale is limited to those cases where he has exercised his right of lien or stoppage in transit. There could, for instance, be a right of resale reserved by the terms of the contract of sale in specified events, as in some of the *Romalpa* cases (see below, p 452). Alternatively, the buyer could be in breach of his obligation to pay the price on the agreed date, in a case where time has been made of the

essence of the contract. Section 48 does not have the effect of excluding or restricting any right of resale which the seller may have at common law.

(3) Section 48(4) applies whether the seller is an unpaid seller or not.

(e) Effect of resale by an unpaid seller

Section 48(2) states that where an unpaid seller *who has exercised his right of lien or retention or stoppage in transit* resells the goods, the second buyer acquires a good title to them as against the original buyer. There is a degree of overlap between this provision and s 24 (sale by seller in possession, broadly equivalent to s 8 of the Factors Act 1889: above, p 377), but there are also important differences, which we may list as follows:

(1) Section 24 applies whether the seller is an unpaid seller or not; for s 48(2) to apply, he must be unpaid.

(2) Section 24 applies where the seller 'continues or is in possession of the goods, or of the documents of title to the goods'; s 48(2) applies where an unpaid seller 'has exercised his right of lien or retention or stoppage in transit'. There are plainly circumstances when one only of these requirements will have been met.

(3) Section 24 applies only where the goods or document of title are *delivered* to the second buyer; there is no such requirement in s 48(2).

(4) Section 24 operates only in favour of a bona fide purchaser who takes without notice; again, there is no such requirement in s 48(2).

(5) Section 24 is expressed to operate for the benefit not only of a sub-buyer, but also someone who takes under a pledge or other disposition of the goods (and, under s 8 of the Factors Act, also someone who has *agreed* to buy or take under a pledge or other disposition); s 48 applies only to a resale.

NOTE

In the opinion of Lord Diplock in *Ward v Bignall,* s 48(2) applies—and is needed—only where the property in the goods has passed to the buyer. Where a seller who has *retained* the property resells the goods, he can confer a good title on the second buyer by virtue of his ownership, and there is no need to invoke s 48(2). The seller may, however, still be liable to the first buyer for breach of contract. Since s 24 also speaks only of a person who has *sold* goods, we may infer that a person who has retained title to the goods (ie, only agreed to sell them) can confer a good title on a second purchaser by virtue of his ownership and does not need to invoke the provisions of that section.

QUESTION

S agrees to sell to B1 goods which are stored in W s warehouse. S retains the property in the goods but gives B1 a delivery order addressed to W. Not having been paid by B1, S resells the goods to B2, telling him that he has been let down by a previous buyer, B1. S gives B2 a delivery order. The following day, B1 contracts to sell the goods to X, and endorses his delivery order over to X. Who is entitled to the goods (1) before any delivery order is presented to W; (2) if B2 presents his delivery order to W before X; (3) if X presents his delivery order to W before B2?

(f) Retention of title clauses

It is of course axiomatic that a clause in a contract of sale may stipulate that the seller shall retain the title to the goods until a stated event has happened, and in particular until he has been paid the price; and this may be done even though possession of the goods is given to the buyer: see ss 2(3) and 19(3). The case of *Lee v Butler* (above, p 382) is an example. The term 'retention of title clause' has, however, come to have a special connotation in a commercial context as a result of the landmark decision in the *Romalpa* case (below). In a typical 'retention of title' contract, the buyer is likely to be either a company engaged in the manufacturing or construction industry which buys raw materials or components for the purposes of it business, or a company which acquires the goods with a view to reselling them or letting them on hire or lease to its own customers. (An individual may also buy goods subject to a retention of title—as, indeed, was the case in *Lee v Butler*—but we shall assume that the buyer is a company, since it is in relation to company buyers that the most interesting (and most complex!) issues arise.) Another point of distinction, in practice, is that cases like *Lee v Butler* (and similarly in the hire-purchase cases) the goods are normally durables of some type which are to be paid for by instalments; and one of the main risks which the seller wishes to guard against is that the buyer will resell the goods before he has paid the whole of the price: in contrast, the *Romalpa* cases are concerned with goods—often of a consumable kind—which both parties contemplate may be used up or disposed of in some way before the price is paid, and the main risk for the seller is the buyer's insolvency.

Aluminium Industrie Vaassen BV v Romalpa Aluminium Ltd
[1976] 1 WLR 676, Queen's Bench Division and Court of Appeal

The plaintiffs (AIV), a Dutch company, supplied aluminium foil to Romalpa in England on AIV's standard terms of trading, parts of which are quoted in the judgment of Mocatta J. Romalpa went into receivership owing AIV £122,239. The receiver had in his possession unprocessed aluminium foil worth £50,000 and £35,152 representing the proceeds of subsales of foil which had been made by Romalpa. It was held (1) that AIV's claim to the unprocessed foil prevailed over that of the receiver, because AIV had effectively retained title to it; and (2) that AIV was entitled to the money representing the proceeds of subsales on the basis of the doctrine of tracing established in *Re Hallett's Estate* (1880) 13 Ch D 696, CA.

Mocatta J: The first major issue in this case turns on whether clause 13, in what the plaintiffs say are their general selling terms and conditions for aluminium foil, applied to the transactions done between the plaintiffs and the defendants, in respect of which £122,239 is owing. That clause began with this important reservation of title. The first sentence of the clause reads as follows:

> The ownership of the material to be delivered by AIV (that is the plaintiffs) will only be transferred to purchaser when he has met all that is owing to AIV, no matter on what grounds.

I read the remainder of the clause in view of its somewhat elaborate nature and of subsequent issues arising:

> Until the date of payment, purchaser, if AIV so desires, is required to store this material in such a way that it is clearly the property of AIV. AIV and purchaser agree that, if purchaser should make (a) new object(s) from the material, mix this material with (an)other object(s) or if this material in any way whatsoever becomes a constituent of (an)other object(s) AIV will be given the ownership of this

(these) new object(s) as surety of the full payment of what purchaser owes AIV. To this end AIV and purchaser now agree that the ownership of the article(s) in question, whether finished or not, are to be transferred to AIV and that this transfer of ownership will be considered to have taken place through and at the moment of the single operation or event by which the material is converted into (a) new object(s), or is mixed with or becomes a constituent or (an)other object(s). Until the moment of full payment of what purchaser owes AIV purchaser shall keep the object(s) in question for AIV in his capacity of fiduciary owner and, if required, shall store this (these) object(s) in such a way that it (they) can be recognized as such. Nevertheless, purchaser will be entitled to sell these objects to a third party within the framework of the normal carrying on of his business and to deliver them on condition that—if AIV so requires—purchaser, as long as he has not fully discharged his debt to AIV shall hand over to AIV the claims he has against the buyer emanating from this transaction.

If the plaintiffs can establish that clause 13 does apply, as between themselves and the defendants, they are admittedly entitled to succeed on their second claim, the goods in question in the possession of the defendants still being their property. But their first claim, namely, the right to trace, is disputed. I must therefore deal first with the hotly contested point whether clause 13 did apply between the plaintiffs and the defendants.

[His Lordship referred to the course of dealing between the parties, and answered this question in the affirmative. He continued:]

Having decided that clause 13 did apply to the many transactions between the plaintiffs and defendants after September 1, 1973, when the defendants took over the aluminium foil business that the partnership had previously conducted with the plaintiffs, I now have to deal with the consequences of that decision as applying to the claims in the action.

In the first place, it is admitted that the plaintiffs are the owners of the remaining unsold aluminium foil held by the receiver, and that they are entitled to an order for its delivery up to them. The real contest arose in relation to the plaintiffs' right to a charge on the receiver's account with the [bank] to the extent of £35,152.66 representing, as certified by the receiver, the sum recovered by him from customers of the defendants as a result of AIV materials supplied to the defendants by the plaintiffs. This right the plaintiffs claim on the basis of the principle established in *Re Hallett 's Estate* (1880) 13 Ch D 696 entitling them to trace the proceeds of the sale of their property sold by the plaintiffs into the receiver's bank account. It is common ground that the effect of clause 13 is that, while money was owing by the defendants to the plaintiffs, any aluminium foil delivered by the plaintiffs to the defendants, while still in their possession, was held by them as bailees.

It is further common ground that the clause must be read subject to the necessary implication that the defendants were entitled to sell the foil to sub-purchasers. It is curious that this is not said about sales of unmixed foil whilst it is said in the last sentence of the clause about foil mixed with other material. In respect of this, it is to be noted that the defendants were, if required, to assign to the plaintiffs' their rights against sub-purchasers in respect of the mixed materials sold to them. Notwithstanding the generally far-reaching and somewhat elaborate provisions in clause 13, reserving the plaintiffs' right of ownership in the goods until nothing was owing from the purchasers, and the admission that the clause had the effect of making the defendants bailees of the goods while in their possession until all money owing had been paid, the argument for the defendants was that once foil had been sold to bona fide purchasers, the relationship between the plaintiffs and the defendants was purely one of debtor and creditor. As against this, the plaintiffs argued that a fiduciary relationship stemming from the bailment continued after sales to third parties, and that in consequence equitable remedies applied, including the right to trace proceeds of the sub-sales. It was not necessary, said the plaintiffs, to find as a prerequisite to the right to trace an express or constructive trust. The equitable proprietary remedy followed as a consequence of the finding that the defendants were bailees.

Having indicated the general nature of the competing arguments, I can go straight to the judgment of Sir George Jessel MR in *Re Hallett's Estate* (1880) 13 Ch D 696. Although in that case there had been breaches of express trust, it is clear from the passages I am about to read that the reasoning was not founded on this, and that the principle stated applied to much wider circumstances. It is necessary to make certain fairly extensive quotations. Sir George Jessel MR said, at p 708:

> The modern doctrine of equity as regards property disposed of by persons in a fiduciary position is a very clear and well-established doctrine. You can, if the sale was rightful, take the proceeds of the sale, if you can identify them. If the sale was wrongful, you can still take the proceeds of the sale, in a sense adopting the sale for the purpose of taking the proceeds, if you can identify them. There is no distinction, therefore, between a rightful and a wrongful disposition of the property, so far as regards the right of the beneficial owner to follow the proceeds....

Pausing there for a moment, it is not, of course, suggested here that there was a wrongful disposition of the plaintiffs' property when the defendants sold the foil to bona fide sub-purchasers....

There then follows this passage showing the width of the application of the principle:

> Has it ever been suggested, until very recently, that there is any distinction between an express trustee, or an agent, or a bailee, or a collector of rents, or anybody else in a fiduciary position? I have never heard, until quite recently, such a distinction suggested....It can have no foundation in principle, because the beneficial ownership is the same, wherever the legal ownership may be.

There is the following short passage, at p 710:

> Now that being the established doctrine of equity on this point, I will take the case of the pure bailee. If the bailee sells the goods bailed, the bailor can in equity follow the proceeds, and can follow the proceeds wherever they can be distinguished, either being actually kept separate, or being mixed up with other moneys.

These passages are clearly most apposite, since they refer to the position of a mere bailee, and were strongly relied upon by Mr Lincoln. Mr Pickering sought to avoid them by saying that they were obiter or had in some way been modified in *Re Diplock* [1948] Ch 465 and that it was necessary that there should be some express or constructive trust before the equitable doctrine could apply. My attention was not drawn to any passage in *Re Diplock* criticising or modifying, in any way, the statements of principle which I have quoted. Although I fully recognise that in considering this problem I find myself in a most unfamiliar field, I feel it my duty to follow and apply those statements. Mr Pickering drew my attention to two authorities as illustrating the simple debtor/creditor relationship, namely, *King v Hutton* [1900] 2 QB 504 and *Henry v Hammond* [1913] 2 KB 515. It is unnecessary to refer to these in detail, save to say that the former makes it clear that the special facts of each case are crucial in determining whether there is a simple debtor/creditor relationship, although the intention of the parties as ascertained from the terms of their contract shows that some kind of fiduciary relationship exists. The preservation of ownership clause contains unusual and fairly elaborate provisions departing substantially from the debtor/creditor relationship and shows, in my view, the intention to create a fiduciary relationship to which the principle stated in *Re Hallett's Estate* applies. A further point made by Mr Pickering was that if the plaintiffs were to succeed in their tracing claim this would, in effect, be a method available against a liquidator to a creditor of avoiding the provisions establishing the need to register charges on book debts: see s 95(1), (2)(e) of the Companies Act 1948 [Companies Act 2006, s 860(7)(f)]. He used this only as an argument against the effect of clause 13 contended for by Mr Lincoln. As to this, I think Mr Lincoln's answer was well founded, namely, that if property in the foil never passed to the defendants with the result that the proceeds of sub-sales belonged in equity to the plaintiffs, s 95(1) had no application.

The plaintiffs accordingly succeed....

[The defendants appealed.]

Roskill LJ: ...Are the plaintiffs entitled to the proceeds of sales to sub-purchasers now held by the receiver? We were told both by Mr Price and by Mr Lincoln that the receiver received these moneys after he had entered into his receivership from sales made by the defendants to sub-purchasers before that date. The receiver, properly if I may say so, kept those moneys separate; as we were told that there is no complication arising of those moneys having become mixed with other moneys, because they were always kept separate. There was no suggestion that the sub-sales in question were other than authorised by the plaintiffs or that the sub-purchasers concerned did not acquire a valid title to the several quantities of foil which each of them bought. The sole question is whether, on the facts and on the true construction of the bargain, including the general conditions, between the plaintiffs and the defendants, the plaintiffs are entitled to trace and recover those proceeds of the sub-sales, upon the well-known principles laid down in the judgment of Sir George Jessel MR in *Re Hallett's Estate*. . . .

The critical question is whether there was a fiduciary relationship between the plaintiffs and the defendants which entitles the plaintiffs successfully to claim these moneys in the way and upon the footing which I have just described. Mr Price strenuously argued that the bargain between the parties was a perfectly ordinary bargain, creating the ordinary contractual relationship of seller and buyer, with the consequence that if the buyers—that is to say the defendants—became insolvent before payment for the goods was made by them to the sellers,—that is, the plaintiffs—the sellers were left with their ordinary contractual or, as he put it, personal remedy as unsecured creditors of the buyers, and that there was no additional proprietary remedy (again to borrow his language) available to them justifying their seeking to trace and recover the proceeds of the sub-sales which had come from the sub-purchasers into the hands of the receiver.

It seems to me clear that, but for the provisions of clause 13—which have to be read in conjunction with the other relevant clauses I have mentioned—this would be the position. The individual contracts were for delivery ex the plaintiffs' works in Holland, and, apart from special provisions, in English law at least—as already stated, there is no evidence of Dutch law and therefore we must apply English law to these contracts—both property and risk would have passed to the defendants upon such delivery.

But clause 13 plainly provides otherwise. The defendants as sellers were to retain the property in the goods until all—and I underline '*all*'—that was owing to them had been paid. . . . It is obvious, to my mind, that the business purpose of the whole of this clause, read in its context in the general conditions, was to secure the plaintiffs, so far as possible, against the risks of non-payment after they had parted with possession of the goods delivered, whether or not those goods retained their identity after delivery. I unhesitatingly accept that part of Mr Lincoln's submission. In the case of unmanufactured goods this was to be achieved by the plaintiffs retaining the property until all payments due had been made, to which were added the special rights given by clause 25. In the case of mixed or manufactured goods, more elaborate provisions were made and indeed were obviously required if the avowed object of clause 13 were to be achieved in the case of the latter class of goods. The plaintiffs were to be given the ownership of these mixed or manufactured goods as 'surety' for 'full payment.' 'Surety' I think in this context must mean, as Mr Lincoln contended yesterday, 'security.' This is as between the defendants and the plaintiffs, and it is not necessary to consider how far this provision would protect the plaintiffs against adverse claims, at any rate in this country, by third parties. Further, the clause later provides that until 'full payment' is made the defendants shall keep the mixed goods for the plaintiffs as 'fiduciary owners'—not perhaps the happiest of phrases but one which suggests, at least to an English lawyer, that in relation to mixed or manufactured goods there was produced what in English law would be called a fiduciary relationship in this respect. The clause goes on to give to the defendants an express power of sale of such goods, and the right to deliver them; and adds an obligation upon the defendants, if required by the plaintiffs so to do, to assign (to use English legal language) to the plaintiffs the benefit of any claim against a sub-purchaser so long as the defendants have not fully discharged all their indebtedness to the plaintiffs. . . .

The burden of Mr Lincoln's argument was, first, that all goods dealt with in pursuance of clause 13 were, until *all* debts were discharged, the plaintiffs' goods which the defendants were authorised to sell on the plaintiffs' behalf and for the plaintiffs' account but only within the framework of clause 13. Since the goods were the plaintiffs', the defendants remained accountable to the plaintiffs for them or for their proceeds of sale, so long as any indebtedness whatever remained outstanding from the defendants to the plaintiffs. Hence the creation of the fiduciary relationship upon which Mr Lincoln sought to rely. The burden of Mr Price's argument was, as already stated, that the clause created in the first part no more than the ordinary debtor/creditor, buyer/seller, relationship, and that nothing in the second part justified placing additional fiduciary obligations upon the defendants in respect of unmanufactured goods, referred to in the first part of the clause.

[His Lordship held that clause 13 impliedly authorised Romalpa to sell the unmanufactured, as well as the manufactured, goods, on terms that they were accountable to AIV for the proceeds of sale. He continued:]

I see no difficulty in the contractual concept that, as between the defendants and their sub-purchasers, the defendants sold as principals, but that, as between themselves and the plaintiffs, those goods which they were selling as principals within their implied authority from the plaintiffs were the plaintiffs' goods which they were selling as agents for the plaintiffs to whom they remained fully accountable. If an agent lawfully sells his principal's goods, he stands in a fiduciary relationship to his principal and remains accountable to his principal for those goods and their proceeds. A bailee is in like position in relation to his bailor's goods. What, then, is there here to relieve the defendants from their obligation to account to the plaintiffs for those goods of the plaintiffs which they lawfully sell to sub-purchasers? The fact that they so sold them as principals does not, as I think, affect their relationship with the plaintiffs; nor (as at present advised) do I think—contrary to Mr Price's argument—that the sub-purchasers could on this analysis have sued the plaintiffs upon the sub-contracts as undisclosed principals for, say, breach of warranty of quality.

It seems to me clear...that to give effect to what I regard as the obvious purpose of clause 13 one must imply into the first part of the clause not only the power to sell but also the obligation to account in accordance with the normal fiduciary relationship of principal and agent, bailor and bailee. Accordingly, like the judge I find no difficulty in holding that the principles in *Hallett's* case are of immediate application, and I think that the plaintiffs are entitled to trace these proceeds of sale and to recover them, as Mocatta J has held by his judgment.

It is ironic that the starting point for this major modern commercial development was not a high-powered collaboration between the best brains in the City and the Temple, but a rather poor translation into English of a document drafted by a Dutch lawyer! It is perhaps also significant, with hindsight, that this seminal case came before a commercial court in which some key issues of an equitable nature were not argued. The same cannot be said of the second leading case in the series, *Re Bond Worth Ltd* (below), where the hearing lasted for 15 full days and over 90 authorities were cited in argument. But before looking at *Re Bond Worth*, it is necessary to understand something of the way in which companies normally finance their operations. Most companies depend upon some degree of borrowing in order to maintain their cash-flow. When a company borrows money, and more particularly when it borrows it on overdraft from a bank, it is usually required to give security in the form of a general *floating charge* to the bank. Such a charge (as is explained more fully below, p 1132) allows the company to carry on its business without interference from the bank, unless and until it defaults on the terms of its loan. If that does happen (for instance, if the company's overdraft is run up beyond the agreed limit), the bank can move in immediately and take possession of all of the company's assets, traditionally by the appointment of a receiver—an insolvency practitioner whose role it is to enforce the bank's security, if necessary by selling up these assets. (More recently, in consequence of a change in the law which came into effect in 2003, he will probably appoint an administrator rather than a receiver for this purpose: see below, p 1215.) If we take the case of B, a company manufacturing furniture, which has given a floating charge to its bank, and suppose that S is a timber firm which is asked to supply timber to B on credit, it is easy to see that if S simply sells the wood to B and is not paid, and then the bank intervenes by appointing a receiver or administrator (or some other insolvency procedure, such as liquidation, ensues), the bank is in a position to claim the timber as part of B's assets while S, who has supplied the timber which has gone to swell the assets, is a mere unsecured creditor whose debt will rank after that of the bank. The obvious answer to S's predicament is for him to supply the timber to B on terms that it will remain S's property until it has been paid for—ie, to insert a 'retention of title' clause into the contract of sale. The *Romalpa* case, and several other cases since, have upheld the validity of such a clause—at least where the goods in question remain identifiable as the contract goods, or part of them: *Clough Mill Ltd v Martin* (below), or where they have been used in a manufacturing process which is reversible (eg motors fitted to air compressors but which can be detached simply by unbolting them: *Hendy Lennox (Industrial Engines) Ltd v Grahame Puttick Ltd* [1984] 1 WLR 485).

But the position becomes more complicated in a number of situations:

(1) where the goods have been used in an irreversible manufacturing process (eg resin, in the manufacture of chipboard), so that the original goods have lost their identity: *Borden (UK) Ltd v Scottish Timber Products Ltd* (below);

(2) where the goods have been mixed with other goods, so that, again, it is impossible to determine which are the goods that were sold under the contract in question: *Re Andrabell Ltd* (below);

(3) Where the goods have been affixed to other property of the buyer (eg joinery built into his house, or a new gasket fitted to his motor) so as to become his by accretion;

(4) where the goods have ceased to be the property of either seller or buyer, eg by being resold to a customer of B.

In an attempt to meet some of these problems, the draftsmen have endeavoured to make their retention of title clauses more elaborate. A variety of ancillary clauses have been developed. These include:

(1) a provision which requires the buyer (B) to keep the goods separate from other goods, perhaps also stipulating that he shall hold the goods as bailee for the seller (S);

(2) a provision which seeks to confer upon S proprietary rights in relation to the proceeds of any sale of the goods made by B to a third party; such a provision may be reinforced by other terms which require B to keep such proceeds separate from other moneys, to hold them on a fiduciary basis, to pay them into a special account, etc;

(3) a provision which seeks to extend S's proprietary rights into any goods which may be manufactured by B and which incorporate the goods which S has sold;

(4) (a combination of (2) and (3)): a provision which declares that S shall have a proprietary interest in the proceeds of any sale made by B of goods which are the product of such a manufacturing process;

(5) (an 'all moneys' clause): a stipulation that S shall retain the property in the goods sold (and possibly have some or all of the other rights listed in (2), (3) and (4) above) until S has been paid not only the price of those goods, but all other debts which are outstanding between S and B.

The ingenuity of the draftsman will not necessarily stop there. He will, for instance, almost certainly include a power for S or his agents to enter B's premises and seize the sale goods, and any other goods in which by virtue of the contract S has acquired a proprietary interest.

Unhappily for many sellers, the precedent set in the *Romalpa* case ran into difficulties in the very next reported case, *Re Bond Worth Ltd* (below). Many of the devices suggested above have since encountered similar problems in subsequent test cases. These difficulties stem from the fact that there is a very fine line between a true 'retention of title' clause and a provision which creates a *charge*.

A *charge* is a proprietary right created by a debtor in favour of another person empowering the latter to look to specified property of the debtor for satisfaction of the debt. (For a full discussion of this concept, see below, p 1131.) Where, under a contract of sale of goods, the seller reserves to himself the entire property in the goods until the price is paid, there is no charge, since the buyer has never owned the property over which the supposed charge could have been created. Where, however, the property first passes to the buyer and he in turn purports to *revest* it in the seller, or to confer some interest in it on the seller, until the price is paid, all the elements of a charge are likely to be present. It was held in *Re Bond Worth Ltd* (below) that if the seller purports to reserve to himself an *equitable* interest in the goods until the price is paid, and meantime to transfer only a bare legal title to the buyer, this may also constitute a charge. And it is almost inevitable, in the nature of things, that where the contract seeks to confer upon the seller a right to look for satisfaction of the price to property which is worth more than that amount (or to a sum of money which exceeds the price which he is owed), the courts will construe the transaction as one involving a charge. So it is likely that this construction will be placed on any contract which attempts to vest in the seller the property in the *product* resulting from work done by the buyer on the goods, or from some manufacturing process to which they have been subjected, until the price is paid, for it is hardly credible that the parties would have intended that the buyer should abandon to the seller the value which he has added to the original sale goods. In the same way, any claim asserted by the seller against the *proceeds of sale* of the goods or their product to a subpurchaser will be regarded as a charge. Had an argument along these lines been fully explored in the *Romalpa* case itself, the outcome (at least as regards the proceeds of sale of the foil) might well have been different.

In principle, there can be no objection to the creation of a charge, as such, in any of these circumstances. But there is a clear practical reason why the parties will not wish to do so. Where the buyer is a company which has already given a floating charge over all of its assets, present and future, to its bank, that charge will almost always include a term which prohibits the company from creating any other charge ranking ahead of that of the bank. If the seller has actual or constructive notice of this term (which under the rules of company law and current practice he will almost certainly be deemed to have), of course any attempt on his part to create a prior charge in his own favour is doomed to fail. And so he will avoid at all costs making any concession that the contract of sale involves a charge. And in so doing, he falls into a second trap; for if the court does hold that there is a charge, it will be void because it has not been registered under the Companies Act. The cases which follow show many examples where a purported reservation of title has been construed as falling on the wrong side of this critical line, and struck down as an unregistered charge.

Re Bond Worth Ltd

[1980] Ch 228, Chancery Division

'Acrilan' fibre was supplied by Monsanto to Bond Worth for use in the manufacture of carpets. The contract of sale provided that 'equitable and beneficial ownership' of the Acrilan should remain in the sellers until the price had been paid, or until prior resale, in which case Monsanto's beneficial ownership was to attach to the proceeds of the resale. It was also stipulated that Monsanto should have the equitable and beneficial ownership in any products made out of the fibre. Slade J held that these provisions were consistent only with the creation of a floating charge, and that the transaction was void for non-registration as a charge under the Companies Act.

Slade J: I turn to consider the relevant contracts. In my judgment at least the following points are fairly clear:

(1) They were absolute contracts for the sale of goods within the meaning of s 1(2) of the Sale of Goods Act 1893, though this is not to say that they did not comprise other features in addition.

(2) The legal title or property in the Acrilan fibre comprised in any one of the contracts passed to Bond Worth when the fibre was delivered to Bond Worth: see s 18, rule 1 of the Sale of Goods Act 1893. In using the term 'property' in this context I refer to the general property in the goods (which is the definition given to the word in s 62(1) of that Act) and not merely a special property, such as that possessed by a bailee.

(3) The risk in the goods likewise passed to Bond Worth on delivery. This followed not only from s 20 of the Sale of Goods Act 1893, but also from the opening words of sub-clause (a) of the retention of title clause. Thus if, after delivery, the goods had been stolen or destroyed before Bond Worth had had the opportunity to use them in any way, Bond Worth would nevertheless have had to pay the full purchase price for them.

(4) Though sub-clause (a) of the retention of title clause provided that 'equitable and beneficial own-ership' in the goods would remain with Monsanto until full payment for the whole amount of the relevant order had been received or until prior resale, it was manifestly not the intention to confer on or reserve to Monsanto all the rights which would normally be enjoyed by a sui juris person, having the sole beneficial title to property, as against the trustee holding the legal title. Mr Sears, on behalf of Monsanto, expressly conceded and affirmed that Monsanto would not, by virtue of its so called 'equitable and beneficial ownership,' have had the right to call for re-delivery of the goods, at any rate so long as Bond Worth was not in default under its payments. Bond Worth, on the other hand, was to have far-reaching rights even before payment to deal with the goods, which would not normally be possessed by a trustee holding the legal title therein on behalf of one sole, sui juris beneficiary.

(5) Even during the period before full payment had been received by Monsanto and notwithstanding the provisions relating to 'equitable and beneficial ownership,' Bond Worth were to be at liberty to sell all or any part of the goods and to transfer the property therein to a purchaser. The words 'until prior resale,' in sub-clause (a) of the retention of title clause, render the implication of such authority to resell inevitable. They go far beyond the provisions of s 25(1) of the Sale of Goods Act 1893 which empower a buyer of goods in possession after sale in some circumstances, even without the authority of his vendor, to resell and pass a good title to a purchaser on a resale, but confer no authority on him to effect such resale, as between him and his vendor.

(6) The parties nevertheless intended that if Bond Worth were to resell all or any part of the goods at a time when Monsanto had not yet been paid the full price due under the order, Monsanto's 'equitable and beneficial ownership,' whatever that meant, would attach to the proceeds of sale or to the claim for such proceeds.

(7) Even during the period before full payment had been received by Monsanto and notwithstanding the provisions relating to 'equitable and beneficial ownership,' Bond Worth were to be at liberty to use the goods for the purposes of manufacture....

(8) The parties nevertheless intended that if, by virtue of such last-mentioned use, the goods should become constituents of or be converted into other products, the retention of title clause should attach to such other products as if they had been the original subject matter of the sale....

Thus far, the position would seem to me reasonably clear. The real difficulty arises concerning the meaning and legal effect, if any, of the provisions in the retention of title clause concerning 'equitable and beneficial ownership.' If the contracts embody something more than a mere sale, what is this additional feature? What is the nature of the relationship beyond a mere vendor-purchaser relationship between Monsanto and Bond Worth that comes into existence by virtue of the provisions relating to 'equitable and beneficial ownership'?

In *Aluminium Industrie Vaassen BV v Romalpa Aluminium Ltd* [above, p 452], to which I shall have to refer in greater detail later, it was expressly admitted that the retention of title clause had the effect of making the defendants *bailees* of the relevant goods while in their possession until all money owing had been paid, . . . On the different facts of the present case, however, there can be no question of a bailor-bailee relationship, since it is common ground that the property in the Acrilan fibre passed to Bond Worth at latest when it was delivered, while it is of the essence of a bailment that the general property in the goods concerned remains in the bailor, while only a special property passes to the bailee, which entitles him to exercise certain possessory remedies. Nor can the relationship be one of agency, since the documents contain no suggestion that Bond Worth is to be regarded as an agent and the rights which by necessary implication are given to it deal with the goods on its own behalf are quite inconsistent with a principal-agent relationship.

In these circumstances, I think it plain that, if the retention of title clause operated to create any effective rights at all for the benefit of Monsanto, such rights can only have been rights either (i) by way of a trust under which Monsanto was the sole beneficiary or (ii) by way of a trust under which Monsanto had a charge in equity over the relevant assets to secure payment of the unpaid purchase price. No possible third alternative has occurred to me.

[His Lordship examined the authorities, and continued:]

The implicit authority and freedom of Bond Worth to employ the relevant raw materials, products and other moneys as it pleased and for its own purposes during the subsistence of the operation of the retention of title clause were in my judgment quite incompatible with the existence of a relationship of Bond Worth as trustee and Monsanto as beneficiary solely and absolutely entitled to such assets, which is the relationship asserted.

I have, however, already indicated that this is not my own view of the effect, if any, of the retention of title clause when properly construed, but that such effect, if any, is a declaration of trust by Bond Worth in respect of the relevant assets by way of equitable charge to secure repayment of the moneys from time to time owing in respect of the relevant order. Does the authority and freedom of Bond Worth, to which I have last referred, by itself negative the existence of a valid trust by way of equitable charge? In my judgment, in so far as it might be suggested that the clause operated to create in this manner an immediate *specific* charge, the answer to this question must be 'yes.' It is in my judgment quite incompatible with the existence of an effective trust by way of specific charge in equity over specific assets that the alleged trustee should be free to use them as he pleases for his own benefit in the course of his own business.

There is, however, one type of charge (and I think one type only) which, by its very nature, leaves a company at liberty to deal with the assets charged in the ordinary course of its business, without regard to the charge, until stopped by a winding up or by the appointment of a receiver or the happening of some other agreed event. I refer to what is commonly known as a 'floating charge' . . . Such a charge remains unattached to any particular property and leaves the company with a licence to deal with, and even sell, the assets falling within its ambit in the ordinary course of business, as if the charge had not been given, until it is stopped by one or other of the events to which I have referred, when it is said to 'crystallise'; it then becomes effectively fixed to the assets within its scope.

Romer LJ in *Re Yorkshire Woolcombers' Association Ltd* [1903] 2 Ch 384 gave the following description of a floating charge:

> I certainly do not intend to attempt to give an exact definition of the term 'floating charge' nor am I prepared to say that there will not be a floating charge within the meaning of the Act, which does

not contain all of the three characteristics that I am about to mention, but I certainly think that if a charge has the three characteristics that I am about to mention, it is a floating charge. (1) If it is a charge on a class of assets of a company present and future; (2) if that class is one which, in the ordinary course of the business of the company, would be changing from time to time; and (3) if you find that by the charge it is contemplated that, until some future step is taken by or on behalf of those interested in the charge, the company may carry on its business in the ordinary way as far as concerns the particular class of assets I am dealing with.

This description of a floating charge shows that it need not extend to all the assets of the company. It may cover assets merely of a specified category or categories. The third characteristic mentioned by Romer LJ is clearly present in relation to each of the four categories of charged assets in the present case; it was clearly contemplated that until some future step was taken by or on behalf of Monsanto, Bond Worth might carry on its business in the ordinary way in relation to each of these four categories. The second characteristic mentioned by him is likewise clearly present at least in relation to each of the second, third and fourth categories of charged assets; these are ex hypothesi classes of assets which in the ordinary course of business will be changing from time to time.

This much could be said against the existence of floating charges in the present case. As regards the first characteristic mentioned by Romer LJ, the charge on the first category of charged assets is exclusively a charge on present assets of the company, while the charges on the other three categories of charged assets are exclusively charges on future assets of the company. If the charges are looked at separately, they do not comprise classes of mixed present and future assets. Furthermore, the second characteristic mentioned by him is present in relation to the first category of charged assets (the raw fibre) only in the sense that the assets comprised in this category may diminish by being used for the purposes of manufacture or sale; they cannot be increased. I do not, however, think that these points of possible distinction prevent all or any of the four relevant charges from being floating charges within the ordinary meaning of legal terminology. Romer LJ himself disclaimed any intention of saying that there could not be a floating charge within the meaning of the Companies Act which did not contain all the three characteristics that he mentioned.

The critical distinction in my judgment is that between a specific charge on the one hand and a floating charge on the other. Vaughan Williams LJ pointed out in the *Woolcombers* case that it is quite inconsistent with the nature of a specific charge, though not of a floating charge, that the mortgagor is at liberty to deal with the relevant property as he pleases. He said, at p 294:

> I do not think that for a 'specific security' you need have a security of a subject matter which is then in existence. I mean by 'then' at the time of the execution of the security; but what you do require to make a specific security is that the security whenever it has once come into existence, and been identified or appropriated as a security, shall never thereafter at the will of the mortgagor cease to be a security. If at the will of the mortgagor he can dispose of it and prevent its being any longer a security, although something else may be substituted more or less for it, that is not a 'specific security'.

When that case went on appeal to the House of Lords, under the name *Illingworth v Houldsworth* [1904] AC 355, Lord Macnaghten drew the distinction between a specific charge and a floating charge in the following terms:

> A specific charge, I think, is one that without more fastens on ascertained and definite property or property capable of being ascertained and defined; a floating charge, on the other hand, is ambulatory and shifting in its nature, hovering over and so to speak floating with the property which it is intended to affect until some event occurs or some act is done which causes it to settle and fasten on the subject of the charge within its reach and grasp.

In the present case, in my judgment, the respective charges on each of the four categories of charged assets were ambulatory and shifting in their nature, and were intended to hover over them until the happening of an event which caused them to crystallise. The assets comprised in each of the four categories were of a fluctuating class, albeit in the case of the first category liable to fluctuate only by diminution. Until a crystallising event occurred, it was clearly not intended that any restriction should be placed on Bond Worth to deal with them in the ordinary course of its business.

Accordingly in the end I answer [the] question by saying that in my judgment the effect of the retention of title clause was to create floating equitable charges over the four categories of charged assets, for the purpose of securing payment of the purchase prices due under the relevant orders, and to constitute Bond Worth a trustee of such assets for the purpose of such security, but for no other purpose....

[Since no particulars of this charge had been registered, it was held void under what is now Part 25 of the Companies Act 2006.]

NOTES

1.　In the course of his judgment, Slade J said ([1980] Ch 228 at 248):

In my judgment, any contract which, by way of security for the payment of a debt, confers an interest in property defeasible or destructible upon payment of such debt, or appropriates such property for the discharge of the debt, must necessarily be regarded as creating a mortgage or charge, as the case may be. The existence of the equity of redemption is quite inconsistent with the existence of a bare trustee-beneficiary relationship.

This passage has been frequently quoted in later cases.

2.　Although Monsanto, by the terms of the contracts, purported to *retain* equitable and beneficial ownership in the goods, Slade J held that the contract had to be construed as taking effect in two steps: there was first a *sale* of the entire property in the fibre to Bond Worth, which was then 'followed by a security, *eo instanti*, given back by Bond Worth to the vendor, Monsanto'. Bond Worth had therefore *created* a charge, which brought the transaction within the registration requirements of the Companies Act. Commentators (eg R Gregory (1990) 106 LQR 551) have since queried whether this vital link in Slade J's reasoning has survived the rejection by the House of Lords of the '*scintilla temporis*' fiction in the conveyancing case of *Abbey National Building Society v Cann* [1991] 1 AC 56, HL; but *Bond Worth* was later followed on this point in *Stroud Architectural Systems Ltd v John Laing Construction Ltd* [1994] BCC 18.

Borden (UK) Ltd v Scottish Timber Products Ltd
[1981] Ch 25, Court of Appeal

Bordens sold resin to Scottish Timber, on terms that the property in the resin was not to pass to the buyers until payment had been made for all goods supplied to them by Bordens. The resin was bought to be mixed with hardeners and wood chippings and made into chipboard (an irreversible process), and was normally used within two days. Bordens were owed over £300,000 when the buyers went into receivership. They claimed to be entitled to trace their proprietary interest in the resin into the finished chipboard and the proceeds of sale of the chipboard. The Court of Appeal held, however, that the resin ceased to exist as such once it was used in making the chipboard, and that the sellers lost their title to it in consequence.

Buckley LJ: It is common ground that it was the common intention of the parties that the defendants should be at liberty to use the resin in the manufacture of chipboard. After they had so used the resin there could, in my opinion, be no property in the resin distinct from the property in the chipboard produced by the process. The manufacture had amalgamated the resin and the other ingredients into a new product by an irreversible process and the resin, as resin, could not be recovered for any purpose; for all practical purposes it had ceased to exist and the ownership in that resin must also have ceased to exist.

The [retention of title] condition does not expressly deal with any property in the chipboard, or create any equitable charge upon the chipboard, produced by the manufacture. If any term is to be implied, that must be a term which is necessary to give the contract business efficacy, but it must also be a term which the court can see unambiguously to be a term which the parties would have inserted into their contract had they thought it appropriate to express it. If no such term can be identified, then the court may have to conclude that the contract was inept to achieve any valuable, practical result in that respect.

Is it possible here to imply any term giving the plaintiffs a proprietary interest in the chipboard manufactured by the defendants, or giving the plaintiffs an equitable charge upon that chipboard?

Common ownership of the chipboard at law is not asserted by the defendants; so the plaintiffs must either have the entire ownership of the chipboard, which is not suggested, or they must have some equitable interest in the chipboard or an equitable charge of some kind upon the chipboard. For my part, I find it quite impossible to spell out of this condition any provision properly to be implied to that effect.

It was impossible for the plaintiffs to reserve any property in the manufactured chipboard, because they never had any property in it; the property in that product originates in the defendants when the chipboard is manufactured. Any interest which the plaintiffs might have had in the chipboard must have arisen either by transfer of ownership or by some constructive trust or equitable charge, and, as I say, I find it impossible to spell out of this condition anything of that nature.

Mr Mowbray, in a very valiant argument, has contended that he can achieve his end by relying upon the doctrine of tracing. But in my judgment it is a fundamental feature of the doctrine of tracing that the property to be traced can be identified at every stage of its journey through life, and that it can be identified as property to which a fiduciary obligation still attaches in favour of the person who traces it.

In the present case, in the circumstances that I have described of the resin losing its identity in the chipboard, I find it impossible to hold that the resin can be traced into the chipboard, or to any other form of property into which the chipboard might at any time be converted. Accordingly, it seems to me that the doctrine of tracing is inapplicable to a case such as this....

[Bridge and Templeman LJJ delivered concurring judgments.]

Re Peachdart Ltd
[1984] Ch 131, Chancery Division

Leather was supplied by Freudenbergs to Peachdart to be made into handbags, on terms that until payment of the price the sellers retained ownership in the leather and the right to trace their interest into any proceeds of sale of the leather or of goods made out of it, by virtue of a fiduciary relationship created between the buyer and sellers. Vinelott J held, however, that the sellers' interest was lost once the leather had been appropriated in the handbag-making process.

Vinelott J: Turning to the partly or wholly manufactured handbags and the proceeds of sale of those sold before the receiver was appointed, Mr Littman's submission was shortly as follows. It was said that under the terms of the bailment of each parcel of leather supplied by Freudenbergs pending payment in full of the price for that parcel the company as bailee was entitled to use the leather in the manufacture of handbags, a process which involved cutting and shaping and sewing a piece of leather and attaching to it hinges, handles, clasps and the like, in the course of which the piece of leather would remain identifiable throughout. The thread and attachments which were, it was said (and I do not think it is disputed) of comparatively minor value, then became the property of Freudenbergs as accessories to the leather. Thus the company remained a bailee of the handbags throughout the process of manufacture, and when the company sold the handbag it sold it (as in *Romalpa*) as agent for Freudenbergs, and was accordingly accountable to Freudenbergs as owner for the entire proceeds of sale. Freudenbergs was not entitled to a mere charge. Mr Littman instanced as an analogy a sportsman who having shot a rare animal takes the skin to a leather worker and instructs him to make it into a game bag. There the property in the skin would remain with the sportsman notwithstanding that the skin would undergo many operations and would have thread and other material added to it. He distinguished the *Borden* case on the ground that in that case the resin was inevitably consumed and destroyed as a separate substance when used in the manufacture of chipboard. The title retention clause accordingly did not purport to vest the property in the chipboard in the vendor, and if it had done so the vesting could only have been by way of equitable transfer of something not in existence when the resin was sold.

To my mind it is impossible to suppose that in the instant case, even assuming in Freudenbergs' favour that the company became a bailee of the leather when it was first delivered to it, the parties intended that until a parcel of leather had been fully paid for the company would remain a bailee of each piece of leather comprised in the parcel throughout the whole process of manufacture, that Freudenbergs should have the right until the parcel had been fully paid for, to enter the company's premises and identify and take away any partly or completely manufactured handbag derived from it, and that on the sale of a completed handbag the company would be under an obligation to pay the proceeds of sale into a separate interest bearing account and to keep them apart from their other moneys and not employ them in the trade.

It may be that, as Mr Littman asserts, an expert in the leather trade could identify each handbag whether partly or completely manufactured as made from a skin comprised in a particular parcel of leather. But after a handbag had been sold it would be impossible to do so. There is nothing in the conditions of sale which requires the company to keep a record of handbags sold so as to identify those of which it was a bailee and agent of Freudenbergs. No such records were in fact kept and there is nothing in the evidence which suggests that the parties contemplated that they would be. Indeed on the facts of this case it would be impossible for Freudenbergs now to prove that the handbags sold by the company but not paid for when the receiver was appointed were in fact made out of leather comprised in any of the parcels to which the unpaid invoices relied on by Freudenbergs relate. It seems to me that the parties must have intended that at least after a piece of leather had been appropriated to be manufactured into a handbag and work had started on it (when the leather would cease to have any significant value as raw material) the leather would cease to be the exclusive property of Freudenbergs (whether as bailor or as unpaid vendor) and that Freudenbergs would thereafter have a charge on handbags in the course of manufacture and on the distinctive products which would come into existence at the end of the process of manufacture (the value of which would be derived for the most part from Mr Launer's reputation and skill in design and the skill in his workforce). The charge would in due course shift to the proceeds of sale. That I accept does some violence to the language of clause 11(b) in so far as that clause provides that, 'The property in the whole or such other goods shall be *and remain* with the seller' (my emphasis). I do not think that those words compel the conclusion that the company was to be a mere bailee throughout the whole process of manufacture until the purchase price of the relevant parcel had been paid, and that on a sale before that time it would be no more than an agent for Freudenbergs. The language is, I think, consistent with the view that once the process of manufacture had started so that in the course of manufacture work and materials provided by the company would result in the leather being converted into (that is incorporated in or used as material for) other goods of a distinctive character the property in those other goods would vest in Freudenbergs only as security for any outstanding balance of the price of the relevant parcel of leather. What the draftsman has done is to elide and I think confuse two quite different relationships, that of bailor and bailee, with a superimposed contract of sale (or of vendor and purchaser) on the one hand and that of chargor and chargee on the other hand.

Mr Littman conceded, and I think he must concede, that if Freudenbergs had no more than a charge on the partly completed and completed handbags the charge was void for non-registration. It was also void as regards the book debts against the bank, which under the debenture had a prior fixed charge....

NOTES

1.　NE Palmer *Bailment* (2nd edn, 1991), pp 166–168 suggests that Vinelott J perhaps too readily (given the clear wording of the contract) rejected the argument that the leather would remain the sellers' property after it had been made into handbags. Unlike the resin in the *Borden* case (above, p 462), which ceased to exist, the leather here was still the dominant constituent in the end-product. However, in the more recent case of *Modelboard Ltd v Outer Box Ltd* [1993] BCLC 623, it was held that cardboard which had been made into cardboard boxes had ceased to be 'the goods' (ie the cardboard) which had been the subject of the original sale, and so it is not likely that this argument would have prevailed. (The *result* in *Peachdart* can, however, be justified on other grounds, for there was no provision in the contract requiring either that the handbags made from Freudenberg's leather should be kept separate from other handbags or that the proceeds of sale of such handbags should similarly be kept separate.)

2.　In *Chaigley Farms Ltd v Crawford, Kaye & Grayshire Ltd* [1996] BCC 957 it was held that livestock which had been delivered by a farmer to an abattoir for slaughter on terms that they should remain the farmer's property until paid for lost their identity as the contract 'goods' when the living animals became carcasses of meat. The case was decided simply on this point: there was no difficulty in identifying the carcasses as those to which the contract related. The judge conceded that he was probably not giving effect to the intention of the parties, but said that there was 'an inescapable difference between a live animal and a dead one, particularly a dead one minus hide or skin, offal, etc not sold on as butcher's meat'. This may be contrasted with a New Zealand decision where the opposite conclusion was reached at first instance on similar facts: *Re Weddell New Zealand Ltd* (1996) 5 NZBLC 104,055. (On appeal, however, the decision was reversed on other grounds: see [1997] 2 NZLR 455.) In another New Zealand decision, *Pongakawa Sawmill Ltd v New Zealand Forest Products Ltd* [1992] 3 NZLR 304, logs sold to a sawmilling company were held not to have lost their identity and to have remained the seller's property even after they had been sawn into timber.

Hendy Lennox (Industrial Engines) Ltd v Grahame Puttick Ltd
[1984] 1 WLR 485, Queen's Bench Division

Lennox had supplied Puttick with diesel engines under contracts which reserved their title as sellers until full payment of the price. The engines were incorporated into generating sets which would then be sold to Puttick's customers; but each engine remained identifiable by its serial number and could easily be unbolted from the generating set. Puttick went into receivership at a time when three generating sets were in its possession. Two sets were in a deliverable state and Staughton J held that the property in them had passed to Puttick's customers, so that Lennox's claim to the two engines concerned was lost; but since the third set was not in a deliverable state (although its engine had been affixed) he held that Lennox could assert a proprietary claim to retake that engine.

Staughton J: I am aware that until very recently the radio and radar apparatus on a ship was commonly hired by the shipowner rather than bought by him. No doubt it was attached to the ship; but I do not suppose that it thereby became the property of the shipowner or his mortgagee. Nor in my judgment would an engine which was the property of A become the property of B merely because B incorporated it in a generator set otherwise composed of his own materials.

Those reflections and the facts of this case persuade me that the proprietary rights of the sellers in the engines were not affected when the engines were wholly or partially incorporated into generator sets. They were not like the Acrilan which became yarn and then carpet (the *Bond Worth* case), or the resin which became chipboard (*Borden's* case), or the leather which became handbags (the *Peachdart* case).... They just remained engines, albeit connected to other things.

Clough Mill Ltd v Martin
[1985] 1 WLR 111, Court of Appeal

Clough Mill, spinners of yarn, sold yarn to Heatherdale, a manufacturer of fabrics, on terms which included the following (as the first and fourth sentences respectively of condition 12):

However, the ownership of the material shall remain with the seller, which reserves the right to dispose of the material until payment in full for all the material has been received by it in accordance with the terms of this contract or until such time as the buyer sells the material to its customers by way of bona fide sale at full market value....

If any of the material is incorporated in or used as material for other goods before such payment the property in the whole of such goods shall be and remain with the seller until such payment has been made, or the other goods have been sold as aforesaid, and all the seller's rights hereunder in the material shall extend to those other goods.

The Court of Appeal held that Clough Mill could claim to be the owner of unused yarn which was in Heatherdale's possession when it went into receivership.

Sir John Donaldson MR: ... Section 95 of the Companies Act 1948 [cf Companies Act 2006, s 874(1)] provides:

> (1)...every charge created...by a company...shall, so far as any security on the company's property...is conferred thereby, be void against the liquidator and any creditor of the company [unless registered]...

Accordingly s 95 can only apply if (a) the company creates a charge, and (b) that charge *confers* a security on *the company's property.*

The plaintiff's demands upon the defendant related solely to unused and unsold yarn and it is quite clear that if the first sentence of condition 12 had stood alone, s 95 would have had no application. The agreement between the plaintiff and the buyer involved the plaintiff *retaining* property in the goods. It did not involve the buyer *conferring* a charge on any property, but still less on its own property.

The argument that the object of the exercise was to give the plaintiff security for the price of the yarn does not of itself advance the matter. Just as it is possible to increase the amount of cash available to a business by borrowing, buying on hire-purchase or credit sale terms, factoring book debts or raising additional share capital, all with different legal incidents, so it is possible to achieve security for an unpaid purchase price in different ways, with different legal consequences. The parties have chosen not to use the charging method in relation to unused yarn.

Fortunately we do not have to decide whether the fourth sentence of condition 12 creates a charge to which s 95 of the Act of 1948 would apply. I say 'fortunately,' because this seems to me to be a difficult question. If the incorporation of the yarn in, or its use as material for, other goods leaves the yarn in a separate and identifiable state, I see no reason why the plaintiff should not retain property in it and thereby avoid the application of s 95. However, in that situation I should have though that the buyer was clearly purporting to create a charge on the 'other goods' which would never have been the plaintiffs goods. I say 'purporting,' because those goods might themselves remain the property of another supplier in consequence of the inclusion of the equivalent of the first sentence of condition 12 in the relevant sale contract. If, on the other hand, the incorporation of the yarn created a situation in which it ceased to be identifiable and a new product was created consisting of the yarn and the other material, it would be necessary to determine who owned that product. If, and to the extent that, the answer was the buyer, it seems to me that the fourth sentence would create a charge.

For present purposes I am content to assume that in some circumstances the fourth sentence of condition 12 would indeed give rise to a charge to which s 95 of the Act of 1948 would apply, but they are not the circumstances which exist in the instant appeal and I see no reason to distort the plain language of the first sentence on the false assumption that the parties must be deemed to have intended that the same legal framework should apply both before and after the yarn was made up into other goods.

There remains one other aspect which creates problems, but again is not, I think, determinative of this appeal. The first sentence of condition 12 retains property in all the material to which the contract relates until the price of that material has been paid in full. Thus if three-quarters of the yarn had been paid for, the plaintiffs would retain ownership of, and have a right to resell, all the material. Such a resale would be likely to realise more than was owed by the buyer. What happens then? I am inclined to think that the word 'until' in the phrase 'reserves the right to dispose of the material until payment in full for all the material has been received' connotes not only a temporal, but also a quantitative limitation.

In other words, the plaintiff can go on selling hank by hank until they have been paid in full, but if thereafter they continue to sell, they are accountable to the buyer for having sold goods which, upon full payment having been achieved, became the buyer's goods.

Other cases concerned with retention of title clauses include the following:

(1) *Re Andrabell Ltd* [1984] 3 All ER 407: In a number of contracts of sale Airborne Accessories Ltd supplied travel bags to Andrabell, a retailer, on terms that ownership should not pass to Andrabell until it had paid Airborne the 'total purchase price'. When Andrabell went into liquidation, Airborne claimed to be entitled to certain bags which were in its possession and to moneys, allegedly representing the proceeds of sale of bags, which Airborne had paid into its general bank account. In view of the following facts, Peter Gibson J held that no fiduciary relationship had been created:

   (a) the passing of the property in the bags was postponed only until full payment was made for the particular consignment, rather than Andrabell's total indebtedness;

   (b) there was no provision requiring the bags to be stored separately;

   (c) there was no express acknowledgment of a fiduciary relationship, and no provision that Airborne should have the benefit of the sub-sales;

   (d) Andrabell was not constituted Airborne's agent to resell;

   (e) there was no obligation to keep the proceeds of sale separate from other moneys;

   (f) the contracts provided for a 45-day period of credit, during which time Andrabell was free to use the proceeds of any subsales in any way that it liked.

   In the absence of a fiduciary relationship, he said, the parties had to be treated simply as creditor and debtor, and there was no duty to account. Nor could Airborne claim any of the bags.

QUESTION

Assuming that all the bags in Andrabell's possession were identifiable as having been supplied by Airborne, why did the claim for return of the bags fail? Could Airborne have succeeded if the contract had been differently worded?

(2) *Specialist Plant Services Ltd v Braithwaite Ltd* [1987] BCLC 1, CA: The plaintiff company supplied parts and materials for the purposes of repairing a machine owned by Braithwaite. The contract contained a provision that the supplier should be given ownership of the machine 'as surety for the full payment' of what the customer owed. This was held to create a charge.

(3) *E Pfeiffer Weinkellerei-Weineinkauf GmbH & Co v Arbuthnot Factors Ltd* [1988] 1 WLR 150 and *Compaq Computer Ltd v Abercorn Group Ltd* [1991] BCC 484: In each of these cases goods (respectively wines and computing equipment) were supplied on retention of title terms to a retailer who sold or leased them to customers. The supplier purported to reserve title to the goods, and also a proprietary interest in the moneys representing the proceeds of the subsales and leases, until the price of the goods was paid; and its claim in each case was against these moneys. Since the suppliers' claim was only in respect of so much of the proceeds as was necessary to satisfy the outstanding price, the court held that the contracts amounted to an equitable assignment of the proceeds by way of charge, which was inconsistent with the fiduciary relationship on which a proprietary claim would be based; and because no charge had been registered, the suppliers could not succeed. (The suppliers also failed on a second ground, namely that the proceeds had been assigned to a factoring house which was held to have priority: see below, p 1010.)

(4) *Tatung (UK) Ltd v Galex Telesure Ltd* (1988) 5 BCC 325: This case concerned television and video equipment which was sold to a retailer on terms which authorised the goods to be resold or let on hire to customers, but which purported to reserve title in the goods to the suppliers and to confer on them rights to the proceeds of sale or hire of the goods until the purchase price and any other sums owing to the suppliers had been paid. Since the suppliers' interest in the proceeds was defeasible upon payment of whatever the retailers owed to the suppliers, it was held that the contract created rights by way of security rather than an absolute interest.

(5) *Armour v Thyssen Edelstahlwerke AG* [1991] 2 AC 339, HL: Here German sellers successfully claimed to have retained title to steel sold and delivered to a Scottish company. It was held that a retention of title clause in standard form was effective (in regard to the original goods, which were identifiable) in Scots law.

(6) *Forsythe International (UK) Ltd v Silver Shipping Co Ltd, The Saetta* [1993] 2 Lloyd's Rep 268: The *Saetta* was owned by Silver and chartered to Petroglobe. Forsythe sold fuel oil to Petroglobe which was delivered into the ship's bunkers. The sale contract reserved title in the oil to the sellers. When Petroglobe failed to pay the hire charges on time Silver repossessed the ship under a power conferred by a clause in the charterparty, which also provided that any fuel oil on board thereupon became the property of Silver. Clarke J held that the oil still belonged to Forsythe and that in consequence Silver's act amounted to the tort of conversion as against Forsythe. (He also held that the taking of possession by Silver was not a 'delivery' by Petroglobe which would give Silver a good title under s 25(1) (see above, p 390): 'delivery' required a conscious, voluntary act on the part of the party making delivery.)

(7) *Re Highway Foods International Ltd* [1995] 1 BCLC 209. Meat was sold by A to B and resold by B to C. Each contract reserved title to the seller until the price was paid. It was held that the subsale (since, strictly speaking, it was only an agreement to sell) did not confer a good title on C under the Factors Act 1889, s 9: see above, p 389.

(8) In *Associated Alloys Pty Ltd v CAN 001 452 106 Pty Ltd* (2000) 202 CLR 558 the Australian High Court upheld the effectiveness of a 'proceeds subclause' and ruled that it did not involve the creation of a charge. The clause in question provided that if the buyer should use the goods that were subject to a retention of title provision in a manufacturing or similar process, the buyer should hold 'such part of the proceeds of such process as relates to the goods' in trust for the seller, the 'part' in question being equal in dollar terms to the amount owing by the buyer to the seller at the time of the receipt of the proceeds. In other words (assuming that no part of the price had been paid), the proceeds of any sale of the product should be held on trust for the seller and the buyer in proportions which reflected the value of their respective inputs. Doubts have been expressed whether an English court would reach a similar conclusion.

NOTE

Retention of title provisions are in widespread use, but in practice they provide sellers with rather less protection that might be expected—not because many cases are taken to court and the provision struck down as an unregistered charge, but for more down-to-earth reasons. Among the major obstacles standing in the way of a seller seeking to assert his title we may list: the difficulty in proving that the retention of title provision was incorporated into the contract of sale; problems of obtaining access to the buyer's premises or other place where the goods are believed to be in order to identify them; the question of distinguishing the seller's goods from those supplied by others, or those that have been paid for from those that have not; and the risk that the goods may have lost their identity, eg through being used in a manufacturing process, or that they may have been sold. See on these issues Professor S Wheeler *Retention of Title Clauses: Impact and Implications* (1991).

Reform of the law. It is clear from the cases that the theoretical basis of many of the customary *Romalpa* terms—at least the more elaborate ones—is unclear, and that much uncertainty would be avoided if this topic were made the subject of clarifying legislation. But views differ as to the best course to be taken.

There are some who argue that the law should be changed so that, regardless of contractual form, all retention of title clauses should be deemed to create a charge and require registration. This would, of course, suit the banks, who would almost always be able to enforce their own charges in priority.

There is a counter-argument which stresses the commercial importance and utility of *Romalpa* terms, and expresses concern that already much of the protection which sellers have sought to secure for themselves has been whittled away by successive judgments: a simple business need, it is contended, is being thwarted by over-elaborate legal niceties.

It is probably true to say that there is this commercial need, and that it would be wrong to ignore it. Moreover, there is a working 'retention of title' regime in many other EU countries (as evidenced by the fact that German and Dutch plaintiffs feature prominently in the list of English cases cited above), and with the progressive removal of barriers to trade within the Community, it makes little sense for the United Kingdom to be the odd one out.

It would be wrong to say that the government—or, rather, successive governments—have not recognised the need for reform. There have been numerous official reports and consultation papers published in which the topic has received attention, including the reports of the Crowther Committee (1971) and the Cork Committee (1982), the Diamond Report (1989), and the Law Commission's *Final Report on Company Security Interests* (2005). All have stressed the need for change, and a variety of solutions have been proposed. But there has been no legislative action, not even for a more limited reform dealing only with buyers who are companies: see the discussion below, at pp 1083, 1122 and 1148. The subject seems doomed to languish indefinitely in a 'too difficult' tray on a desk somewhere in the DBERR.

QUESTION

In *Borden (UK) Ltd v Scottish Timber Products Ltd*, Templeman LJ said ([1981] Ch 25 at 42):

Unsecured creditors rank after preferential creditors, mortgagees and the holders of floating charges and they receive a raw deal: see *Business Computers Ltd v Anglo-African Leasing Ltd* [1977] 1 WLR 578, 580. It is not therefore surprising that this court looked with sympathy on an invention designed to provide some protection for one class of unsecured creditors, namely unpaid sellers of goods: see *Aluminium Industrie Vaassen BV v Romalpa Aluminium Ltd* [1976] 1 WLR 676, although there is no logical reason why this class of creditor should be favoured as against other creditors such as the suppliers of consumables and services.

Do you agree that there is 'no logical reason' for this distinction? If so, what attitude should the law take?

CHAPTER 13
REMEDIES OF THE BUYER

1 INTRODUCTION

This topic, which is of course the counterpart of 'Duties of the seller' (above, p 423), was, until recently, relatively straightforward, largely restating principles of the general law of contract. But amendments made by the Sale and Supply of Goods Act 1994 have made the law rather more complicated.

2 TO REJECT THE GOODS

If the seller delivers or tenders goods which are not of the contract description, whether as regards quantity or quality, the first and most obvious remedy of the buyer will be to reject them. As we saw earlier, the right to reject may be exercised even after the property has passed to the buyer, provided that he has not 'accepted' the goods within the meaning of s 35 (*Kwei Tek Chao v British Traders & Shippers Ltd; McDougall v Aeromarine of Emsworth Ltd* (above, pp 346–347)).

Where the seller has delivered the wrong *quantity* of goods, the buyer has the choice of remedies set out in s 30:

(1) in the case of a short delivery, to reject the goods or to accept them and pay at the contract rate;

(2) in the case of an excessive delivery, to reject the goods, to accept the contract quantity and reject the rest, or to accept all the goods and pay for the excess at the contract rate.

Superimposed upon these basic rules, we now have a qualification to the buyer's right to reject the goods where the shortfall or excess is 'slight' as a result of new subsections (2A) to (2B), introduced by the Sale and Supply of Goods Act 1994. The law has, in fact, always been prepared to overlook a disparity in measurement which is commercially insignificant (the *de minimis* exception). In *Shipton, Anderson & Co v Weil Bros & Co* [1912] 1 KB 574, this principle was applied: there, a cargo of 4950 tons of wheat was overweight by 55 lbs (a difference in price of 20p in £40,000, which the sellers did not claim). But, apart from this, the seller's obligation to deliver the quantity of goods contracted for has traditionally been interpreted strictly.

The law now provides that a buyer *who does not deal as consumer* may not reject the whole of the goods delivered if the shortfall or excess is *so slight that it would be unreasonable for him to do so* (s 30(2A)). The onus of proof is on the seller (s 30(2B)).

A similar resctriction now applies to the buyer's right to reject for conformity with the contract description or sample, or breach of the implied terms as to quality and fitness for purpose (s 15A)—but again, only where the buyer is not a consumer: see above. (For the meaning of 'deal as consumer', we must refer to the Unfair Contract Terms Act 1977, as amended in 2002: see s 61(5A) and above, p 419.)

Section 30 used also to provide for the case where the seller delivered the goods he contracted to sell mixed with goods of a different description. This is now catered for by the new s 35A: see below, p 474.

The rules set out in s 30 may be excluded by any usage of trade, course of dealing or (subject to the legislation on unfair terms) special agreement between the parties: s 30(5).

It should be noted that s 30 deals only with the *contractual* aspects of a wrong delivery. The question whether, and if so at what point, *property* passes from seller to buyer remains to be determined by ss 16ff: see J Ulph [1998] LCMLQ 4.

The right to reject will also lie if the seller has broken a condition of the contract, or has committed a serious breach of an innominate term. The most common breaches of terms as to *quality* will be breaches of the statutory conditions implied by ss 12–15 of the Act, although of course there may be express conditions as well. An example of a breach of an innominate term is *Cehave NV v Bremer Handelsgesellschaft mbH, The Hansa Nord* [1976] QB 44, CA, where the seller of a cargo of citrus pulp pellets was in breach of an express term, 'shipment to be made in good condition', but not in the view of the Court of Appeal to a degree which went to the root of the contract. Accordingly, the buyer was entitled to damages only, and not to reject the goods. The same approach is also appropriate where there has been a breach of a contract to be performed by instalments (where s 31 (2) applies, to the exclusion of s 30: see above, p 430).

A seller normally has the right to cure a defective tender of goods, if this can be done within the time allowed by the contract and is not otherwise inconsistent with the contract.

Borrowman, Phillips & Co v Free & Hollis
(1878) 4 QBD 500, Court of Appeal

This case concerned a contract to buy a cargo of American maize, to be shipped between 15 May and 30 June. The sellers offered the buyers a cargo on the *Charles Platt*, but the buyers rejected this offer (it was held, by an arbitrator, rightly) because the sellers had no shipping documents. The sellers then, within the period specified by the contract, offered a second cargo on the *Maria D*, which the buyers also rejected. The sellers had to resell the cargo of the *Maria D* at a loss, and sued the buyers for damages for non-acceptance. The trial judge (Denman J) ruled that the buyers were not bound to accept the second tender once the sellers had appropriated the first cargo to the contract; but the Court of Appeal reversed this decision.

Brett LJ: I now pass to the point, upon which the judgment of Denman J was given. It has been argued by the defendants' counsel that the plaintiffs could not lawfully tender the cargo of the *Maria D*, because they had already tendered that of the *Charles Platt,* and had insisted upon that tender. The doctrine of election was relied upon, and it was urged that, even if the offer of the *Charles Platt* was not of itself a sufficient election, the plaintiffs were ousted of their right to sue in this action by referring the matter to arbitration. It may be that that if the plaintiffs had recovered damages in an action for not accepting the cargo of the *Charles Platt* they could not maintain this suit; but in the present case there were no trial and judgment, it was only a reference to arbitration, whether the plaintiffs could according to mercantile usage tender the cargo of the *Charles Platt*. The question comes down to the narrow point, whether the plaintiffs are barred by the doctrine of election. For the defendants reliance has been placed upon a passage in Blackburn on Contract of Sale, pp 128, 129, to the effect that when in pursuance of a contract to sell unspecified goods the vendor has appropriated certain goods, he has made an election which is irrevocable; but I think that passage has nothing to do with the principle to be applied in the present case. It may be that, where goods which fulfil the terms of a contract are appropriated for sale in performance thereof, there is an election by the vendor which is irrevocable; but here the contention for the defendants is that the cargo of the *Charles Platt* was not in accordance with the contract....

I have only to add that a different rule might have been applied, if the defendants had accepted the cargo of the *Charles Platt*; it is possible that the tender of the plaintiffs could not in that case have been withdrawn. I wish it however to be understood, that this is a point upon which I express no opinion.

[Bramwell and Cotton LJJ delivered concurring judgments.]

The decision in *Borrowman v Free* was approved by the House of Lords in *The Kanchenjunga* [1990] 1 Lloyd's Rep 391, HL. See generally on this topic A Apps 'The Right to Cure Defective Performance' [1994] LMCLQ 525.

The buyer loses the right to reject the goods when he 'accepts' the goods (or is deemed to have accepted them) in the circumstances set out in s 35. (On acceptance, see also above, p 426). The loss of the right to reject does not affect his right to claim damages in respect of any shortfall or defect in the delivery (s 11(4)). The rules governing acceptance (and the related rules as to the buyer's right to examine the goods) were extensively revised by the Sale and Supply of Goods Act 1994. The new provisions include a right of 'partial rejection'—ie allow the buyer to accept some of the goods without losing his right to reject the rest on the ground that they are not in conformity with the contract.

Section 34 states that, unless otherwise agreed, when the seller tenders delivery of the goods to the buyer, he is bound on request to afford the buyer a reasonable opportunity of examining the goods to see if they are in conformity with the contract and, in the case of a sale by sample, of comparing the bulk with the sample. The buyer will not be deemed to have accepted the goods if he has not been given this opportunity—unless he has previously examined them (s 35(2)).

Subject to this, a buyer is deemed to have accepted the goods (s 35(1), (4)):

(a) when he intimates to the seller that he has accepted them;

(b) when the goods have been delivered to him and he does any act in relation to them which is inconsistent with the ownership of the seller;

(c) when after the lapse of a reasonable time he retains the goods without intimating to the seller that he has rejected them.

Section 35(2) states that where goods are delivered to the buyer and he has not previously examined them, he is not deemed to have accepted them unless he has had a reasonable opportunity of examining them in order to see whether they are in conformity with the contract (and, where appropriate, with a sample). This factor is also relevant in determining whether the buyer has kept the goods for more than a reasonable time under (c) above. A consumer buyer cannot waive his rights under sub-s (2): s 35(3).

If a buyer is entitled to reject the goods, he may do so for any reason he likes: he is not required to act reasonably in choosing rejection rather than some other remedy. The only question is whether he has lost that right by accepting the goods (*Clegg v Olle Andersson* [2003] EWCA Civ 320, [2003] 1 All ER (Comm) 721).

Subsection (6) of s 35 (which was introduced in 1994) removes or clarifies certain doubts which had arisen under the earlier legislation. A buyer is not deemed to have accepted the goods merely because he has asked for, or agreed to, their repair by the seller or under an arrangement with him, or because the goods are delivered to another person under a sub-sale or other disposition. Prior to this, it had been held that an act of this kind was 'an act in relation to the goods which is inconsistent with the ownership of the seller' and therefore deemed to be an acceptance under s 35(1)(b). So, if a car is delivered to a buyer in a defective state and he agrees to allow the seller (or the manufacturer or some other person) to have the fault attended to, this will not in itself prevent him from exercising his right to reject on this or some other ground. In *Clegg v Anderson* (above) a yacht was sold with an overweight keel which rendered it unsatisfactory unless remedial work was done. Negotiations about this possible work took several months. It was held that the buyer had not lost his right to reject during this time. (See also the ruling of the House of Lords in *JH Ritchie Ltd v Lloyd Ltd*, below.)

Nor will it be a bar to his right to reject that the buyer has resold the goods to a sub-purchaser or that the goods have been delivered to such a person. The position at common law was quite different. In the old case of *Perkins v Bell* [1893] 1 QB 193, CA Perkins, a farmer, had contracted to sell barley to Bell and to deliver it in sacks at his local railway station. Bell resold the barley to brewers in another county and directed the stationmaster to send it on to them. The sub-buyers rejected the barley as being of inferior quality. It was held that Bell had lost the right to reject vis-à-vis Perkins by dealing with the barley in this way. Perhaps the decision in this case was not unreasonable, for Bell could have examined the barley at the station and satisfied himself as to its quality before sending it on. But in the later case of *Hardy & Co v Hillerns & Fowler* [1923] 2 KB 490, CA it was held that the act of reselling was in itself an act inconsistent with the ownership of the sellers—a decision which would create insuperable difficulties for a buyer of, say, goods in sealed containers, when there would be no opportunity to examine the goods until after the sub-buyer had received them. These problems were largely resolved by an amendment to the law made in 1967, which postponed 'acceptance' until the buyer had had a reasonable opportunity of examining the goods. The current Act incorporates these reforms in its revised wording.

Another change to s 35 effected in 1994 introduces the concept of a 'commercial unit', the significance of which will be apparent when we come to examine the new s 35A, below, as well as s 35 itself. A 'commercial unit' means a unit 'division of which would materially impair the value of the goods or the character of the unit' (s 35(7)). Fairly obviously, shoes are sold in pairs and so a commercial unit would be a pair and not a single shoe; and the same would be true of a three-piece suit or a 12-volume encyclopedia. But where bagged cement is sold by the tonne (consisting of twenty 50-kilo bags), any unbroken bag (rather than a tonne) would be a commercial unit. Section 35(7) states that where a contract is for the sale of goods making one or more commercial units, a buyer accepting any goods included in a unit is deemed to have accepted all the goods making the unit. So a buyer who has written his name in volume 1 of the encyclopedia set is bound to take the remaining volumes, but a builder who has opened (say) two bags out of a delivery of a tonne of cement may be able to reject all the unbroken bags, but not those two.

The new s 35 A clarifies the buyer's rights to reject part of the goods whilst retaining the rest. It deals not only where part only of the goods delivered are good (ie of the contract quality or description) and the rest are not, but also where the whole consignment is defective but the buyer chooses to retain some of them or is unable to return them. The section provides that, subject to any agreement to the contrary, if the buyer has a right to reject the goods by reason of a breach on the part of the seller that affects some or all of them but accepts some only of the goods, he does not by accepting them lose his right to reject the rest. However, to the extent that some of the goods delivered are in conformity with the contract, he is deemed to accept the whole of that part. So, if we suppose that the contract is for 12 bottles of brandy, and the seller delivers eight bottles of brandy and four of whisky, or eight bottles of brandy which are of acceptable quality and four which are adulterated, the buyer must take all the eight bottles of brandy that conform to the contract if he accepts any brandy at all; but he is not deemed to have accepted any of the whisky or of the inferior brandy by reason of the fact that he has accepted the good brandy, or to have accepted the whole of the whisky or the inferior brandy because he has accepted part of it.

Where the contract is for a sale by instalments, these rules apply to the right to reject each instalment as if it were a separate contract of sale (s 35A(3)).

If a buyer has rightly rejected the goods, he is not bound to return them to the seller. It is sufficient if he informs the seller that he refuses to accept them (s 36). It is then up to the seller to make arrangements for them to be collected or disposed of.

If a buyer who has rejected goods has paid all or part of the price and the seller does not make an effective substituted delivery, he may of course claim restitution of the money that he has paid. He may also claim damages for any incidental or consequential losses, provided that they are not too remote.

Note that the statutory rules about acceptance discussed above apply only to sales of goods. There are no corresponding sections in related Acts, such as the Supply of Goods and Services Act 1982. In cases falling within the latter the common law doctrines of affirmation and waiver will apply (R Bradgate (2004) 120 QR 558).

The statutory provision dealing with the position where the seller offers to repair defective goods was discussed by the House of Lords in the following case.

JH Ritchie Ltd v Lloyd Ltd
[2007] UKHL 9, [2007] 1 WLR 670 (House of Lords)

Richies, a farming company based in Paisley, bought a combination seed drill and power harrow from Lloyds. Within two days of starting to use it a they had to stop work because it had developed serious vibrations. They agreed to allow the seller to take back the machine in order that it could be inspected and, if possible, repaired, and they completed their sowing operations for that season using a replacement machine provided by the sellers. It turned out that two bearings to rotors on the harrow were missing, making the equipment unsatisfactory for use. The sellers had the missing parts replaced in the next few weeks and notified Ritchies that the machine had been repaired and was ready for collection. But despite repeated requests, the sellers refused to tell Ritchies what the fault was. The buyers accordingly decided to reject the machine, and asked for the return of the price. It was held by the House of Lords (reversing the Scottish court below) that they were entitled to do so, it being necessary to imply into their agreement to allow the repair work a condition that they would be informed about the fault and what had been done to cure it.

Lord Mance:

[47] Section 35(6)(a) was introduced into the Sale of Goods Act 1979 by the Sale and Supply of Goods Act 1994 to address the risk that a buyer who 'asks for, or agrees to, their repair by or under

an arrangement with the seller' might, merely thereby, lose the right to reject non-compliant goods delivered to him under the contract for sale . . .

[48] However, the Act does not say that such an arrangement has no effect at all. Nor could it, since the nature and effect of any arrangement is a fact-specific matter. At one end of the spectrum, one can take the example of a material, but readily identified, defect, easily curable and with no possible consequential implications (eg an obviously defective or missing part in the case of a machine not yet used). In that event, an arrangement might be made for perhaps costly and time-consuming repair by the seller which would commit the buyer outright to accepting the goods if and when they were satisfactorily repaired and returned. The arrangement would amount not to immediate acceptance (because that is the whole point of s 35(6)(a)), but to acceptance conditional upon satisfactory repair and return.

[49] But that is not the present case, where the source of the problem experienced during three days' use of the harrow was unknown and could not be ascertained on superficial examination even by the seller. In consequence the arrangement actually made on 29 April 1999 did not simply involve asking for or agreeing to repair. Instead, it was arranged that the seller would take the harrow away for inspection and, if possible, repair.

[50] Inspection might have shown that the problem was irreparable or so expensive to cure that the seller was not prepared to undertake any repair. In that case, the buyer could and would no doubt have rejected the harrow and drill, and would have had a claim against the seller for non-performance of the contract for sale. Or it might have shown that the problem was simple and inconsequential, in which case no doubt the harrow would have been repaired, returned and accepted by the buyer, provided of course that the repair was satisfactory. In the present case, the problem proved to be quite serious: the harrow, . . . had not been fitted with bearings which it should ordinarily have had from manufacture. Not unreasonably, as the Sheriff found, the buyer, when it eventually learned this informally, had concerns about the consequential implications for other parts of the harrow having run without these bearings for three days (on 26, 27 and 28 April 1999).

[51] The circumstance giving rise to this case is that the buyer was never given the chance to comment on the seller's findings on inspection of the harrow. The next contact between seller and buyer after 29 April 1999 came only when the seller had obtained and installed new bearings. The seller at that point (on or around 17 May 1999) contacted the buyer and informed it that the harrow had been repaired and was ready for return. So it was only then that the buyer had the chance to air any concerns. The buyer not surprisingly asked what had been wrong with the harrow, but the seller was unwilling to say. Only informally did the buyer receive information from one of the seller's employees that bearings had been missing. The buyer then asked that the seller obtain and present an engineer's report to show that there had been no consequential damage. This was refused. The buyer in these circumstances claimed on 26 May 1999 to reject the drill and harrow and to recover their price.

[52] In my view, the buyer's rejection was justified. The harrow was, after its delivery to the buyer and payment of the price in March 1999, the buyer's property and at the buyer's risk, subject in each case to the buyer's right to reject it as defective. . . . The parties no doubt hoped that satisfactory repair would be possible. But in my view it was a natural implication of the arrangement made that the seller would, at least upon request, inform the buyer of the nature of the problem which required to be remedied. Indeed, I would normally have expected the seller to report such information before any repair, although it is not necessary here to decide whether the implication went so far as to require this.

[53] By failing to report the result of the inspection, and by presenting the buyer with the fait accompli of repaired goods, the seller short-circuited the procedure I would have expected. By refusing to inform the buyer of the cause of the problem on request after repair, the seller was on any view in breach of the implicitly agreed procedure, and also aroused suspicion. By failing to agree to supply an engineer's report, the seller lost the opportunity to persuade the buyer to accept the goods notwithstanding the seller's failure to follow the procedure implicitly agreed.

[54] In my opinion, the failure to disclose the nature of the problem was on any view a material breach of the arrangement made on 29 April 1999. Even assuming that the arrangement made on 29 April 1999 committed the buyer to accept the goods if and when the harrow could be and was satisfactorily repaired and returned, it was implicit that the buyer would be informed of the nature of the problem on request at that stage, if only to enable the buyer to decide when and how to examine or test the harrow in order to determine whether it had been satisfactorily repaired. Assuming, alternatively, that there was a duty to report the nature of the problem to the buyer before any repair, and that the buyer retained a right at that earlier point (by when the seller would have incurred very little if any extra expense) to decide whether to have the harrow repaired or to reject, the failure to disclose was material for even more fundamental reasons. There may be other possible analyses, and it is not material in this case to consider precisely which analysis might apply. All that here matters is that there was a duty to disclose which was not performed. Even though the harrow after repair was (the Sheriff Principal found) in as good as new condition, the seller's failure to follow the procedure implicitly agreed justified the buyer in refusing to accept the goods sold. The buyer was still prepared to accept the goods, if the seller at its expense obtained a clean engineer's report, but the seller refused to do this either. The buyer was in this situation justified on 26 May 1999 in rejecting the goods.

[Lords Hope of Craighead, Rodger of Earlsferry and Brown of Eaton-under-Heywood delivered concurring opinions. Lord Scott of Foscote concurred.]

3 BUYER'S ACTION FOR DAMAGES FOR NON-DELIVERY

The buyer's right to sue the seller for damages for non-delivery closely parallels the seller's action for damages for non-acceptance (s 50: see above, p 435). Section 51 provides:

(1) Where the seller wrongfully neglects or refuses to deliver the goods to the buyer, the buyer may maintain an action against the seller for damages for non-delivery.

(2) The measure of damages is the estimated loss directly or naturally resulting, in the ordinary course of events, from the seller's breach of contract.

(3) Where there is an available market for the goods in question the measure of damages is prima facie to be ascertained by the difference between the contract price and the market or current price of the goods at the time or times when they ought to have been delivered or (if no time was fixed) at the time of the refusal to deliver.

The concept of 'an available market' and the rule that, where there is such a market, the price prevailing there is prima facie to be used to ascertain the measure of damages, have already been discussed in relation to the seller's action for damages for non-acceptance (see above, p 436). The place and time when the delivery ought to have been made will once again, prima facie, be the relevant time and place for the reckoning of the market price; and this will be true whether there is an actual or an anticipatory breach. However, in the case of an anticipatory breach, once the seller's repudiation has been accepted, the buyer's duty to mitigate his loss may oblige him to accept lower damages if he fails to buy against a rising market. These points are illustrated by the following cases.

Melachrino v Nickoll & Knight
[1920] 1 KB 693, King's Bench Division

Melachrino agreed in two separate contracts to sell Egyptian cotton seed to Nickoll & Knight, to be shipped to London on the SS *Asaos*, expected to arrive between 10 January and

10 February 1917. The sellers repudiated the contracts on 14 December 1916, and the buyers accepted their repudiation on the same day. On 14 December the market price of cotton seed was above the contract price; for the whole of the period between 10 January and 10 February it was below it. The court held that the buyer was entitled to only nominal damages.

Bailhache J: Upon these facts the question arises: Are the buyers' damages to be fixed with reference to the market prices on December 14, 1916, or with reference to the prices ruling at the time when the goods might be expected to be delivered? If the former the damages are substantial, if the latter nominal. The arbitrators have assessed the damages as at the date of the anticipatory breach.

There was a market for the goods and in that case the prima facie rules for the measurement of damages as laid down in s 51 of the Sale of Goods Act 1893, vary according to whether there is a fixed time for delivery or not. If there is no fixed time the measure is the difference between the contract price and the market price at the time of refusal to deliver. The first point to determine therefore is whether this was a contract of that kind. In my opinion it was not. The time was not certain but it was fixed by reference to the happening of an event—namely, the arrival of the *Asaos* in the United Kingdom. I take it that when s 51 speaks of no time being fixed for delivery it refers to those contracts in which no mention of time is made and which therefore are to be performed within the indefinite period known as a reasonable time under the circumstances.

In regard to other cases of which this is one the prima facie measure of damages is said to be the difference between the contract price and the market price at the time the goods ought to have been delivered—in this case the period between January 10 and February 10, 1917. In a constantly fluctuating market and if the prices during that period had ruled higher than the contract prices there might have been some difficulty in determining the proper price to be taken, but in this case that point does not arise, as at all times between those dates the market prices were below the contract prices.

Section 51 does not in terms deal with an anticipatory breach, and in the case of a breach by effluxion of time it is clear that it makes no difference to the measure of damages whether a buyer goes into the market or is content to take the difference in price without troubling to buy against the defaulting seller. The question to be decided is whether the same rule applies in the case of an anticipatory breach.

An anticipatory breach occurs when the seller refuses to deliver before the contractual time for delivery has arrived and the buyer accepts his refusal as a breach of contract.

In that case the following rules are well established, subject of course to any express provisions to the contrary in any particular contract.

Immediately upon the anticipatory breach the buyer may bring his action whether he buys against the seller or not.

It is the duty of the buyer to go into the market and buy against the defaulting seller if a reasonable opportunity offers. This is expressed by the phrase 'It is the buyer's duty to mitigate damages.' In that event the damages are assessed with reference to the market price on the date of the repurchase. If the buyer does not perform his duty in this respect the seller is none the less entitled to have damages assessed as at the date when a fresh contract might and ought to have been made.

As a corollary to this rule the buyer may if he pleases go into the market and buy against the seller: as he is bound to do so to mitigate damages, so he is entitled to do so to cover himself against his commitments or to secure the goods. In that case again the damages are assessed with reference to the market price at the date of the repurchase.

It is also settled law that when default is made by the seller by refusal to deliver within the contract time the buyer is under no duty to accept the repudiation and buy against him but may claim the difference between the contract price and the market price at the date when under the contract the goods should have been delivered.

Further, in the case of an anticipatory breach [accepted by the buyer] the contract is at an end and the defaulting seller cannot take advantage of any subsequent circumstances which would have afforded him a justification for non-performance of his contract had his repudiation not been accepted.

In logical strictness it would appear to follow that equally the defaulting seller cannot take advantage of a fall in the market before the due date for delivery to escape liability for damages.

It looks therefore at first sight as though the date at which the difference between the contract price and the market price ought to be taken for the assessment of damages when the buyer does not buy against the seller should follow by analogy the rule adopted where the buyer goes into the market and buys, or where the breach is failure to deliver at the due date and should be at or about the date when the buyer intimates his acceptance of the repudiation though he does not actually go into the market against the seller. If so, in this case, the date would be about December 14, when the buyer claimed arbitration and so the arbitrators have found.

As against this line of reasoning, it must be remembered that the object of damages is to place a person whose contract is broken in as nearly as possible the same position as if it had been performed. This result is secured by measuring damages either at the date of the repurchase, in the case of repurchase on an anticipatory breach, or at the date when the goods ought to have been delivered when there is no anticipatory breach whether there is a repurchase or not. In these cases the buyer gets a new contract as nearly as may be like the broken contract and the defaulting seller pays the extra expense incurred by the buyer in restoring his position.

Where however there is an anticipatory breach but no buying against the defaulting seller, and the price falls below the contract price between the date of the anticipatory breach and the date when the goods ought to have been delivered, the adoption of the date of the anticipatory breach as the date at which the market price ought to be taken would put the buyer in a better position than if his contract had been duly performed. He would if that date were adopted be given a profit and retain his money wherewith to buy the goods if so minded on the fall of the market. It would be in effect, to use a homely phrase, to allow him to eat his cake and have it. Perhaps it is better to avoid figures of speech however picturesque and to say, to make a profit from the anticipatory breach while the contract if duly performed would have shown a loss—a position which is I think irreconcilable with the principles upon which damages are awarded as between buyer and seller.

In my opinion the true rule is that where there is an anticipatory breach by a seller to deliver goods for which there is a market at a fixed date the buyer without buying against the seller may bring his action at once, but that if he does so his damages must be assessed with reference to the market price of the goods at the time when they ought to have been delivered under the contract. If the action comes to trial before the contractual date for delivery has arrived the Court must arrive at that price as best it can.

To this rule there is one exception for the benefit of the defaulting seller—namely, that if he can show that the buyer acted unreasonably in not buying against him the date to be taken is the date at which the buyer ought to have gone into the market to mitigate damages....

The result in this case is that the damages are nominal.

Tai Hing Cotton Mill Ltd v Kamsing Knitting Factory
[1979] AC 91, Privy Council

Tai Hing contracted to sell 1500 bales of cotton yarn to Kamsing at HK$1335 per bale, delivery to be made as required by the buyers on giving one month's notice. In July 1973, when 424 bales remained undelivered, the sellers wrote to the buyers repudiating the contract. The buyers for some months pressed the sellers to continue to deliver supplies, but eventually on 28 November 1973 they issued a writ claiming damages for breach. The market price of cotton was $3300 per bale in August 1973 but fell steadily from September 1973 onwards. The Privy Council held that the sellers' repudiation was not a 'refusal to deliver' within s 51(3), since they remained bound to deliver until the repudiation was accepted; rather, this was a case of an anticipatory breach which was not accepted until 28 November; that this was the latest date on which the buyers could have given the sellers notice requiring delivery of all the outstanding bales; and that accordingly damages should be assessed by reference to the market price one month after that, ie on 28 December 1973.

The advice of the Privy Council was delivered by **Lord Keith of Kinkel:** The principal question in the appeal is whether the majority of the Full Court were right in holding that damages for the sellers' admitted breach of contract fell to be ascertained as at July 31,1973, the date of the sellers' repudiation of the contract, notwithstanding that the buyers did not accept the repudiation, and rescind the contract, until they issued and served their writ in the present action on November 28, 1973.

The answer to that question turns on the proper construction of s 53 of the Hong Kong Sale of Goods Ordinance [UK, s 51]...

Before this Board it was contended for the sellers that the second limb of subs (3) [ie the expression 'the time of the refusal to deliver'] did not apply to cases of anticipatory breach of contract, that damages fell to be assessed by reference to market price at the time when the goods ought to have been delivered, and that such time was a reasonable period (say, one month) after the last date upon which the buyers might have called for delivery of the balance of the contractual goods. That date was November 28, 1973, being the date upon which the buyers, by issuing and serving their writ, had accepted the sellers' repudiation and rescinded the contract. Thus the damages fell to be ascertained by reference to the market price of comparable goods at December 28, 1973, and since the buyers had led no evidence about market price on that date they had failed to prove any loss and the damages should be nominal...

Mr Gatehouse for the buyers, while accepting that the second limb of s 51 (3) of the Sale of Goods Act 1893 and of s 53(3) of the Hong Kong Ordinance did not apply to cases of anticipatory breach where the contract stipulated a fixed time for delivery, argued that it did apply to such cases where no fixed time was stipulated...

[His Lordship referred to a number of cases, and continued:]

In their Lordships' opinion the cases referred to by Mr Gatehouse are not authoritative upon the point at issue and have in themselves no persuasive effect. The force of Mr Gatehouse's argument resides essentially in the plain terms of the second limb of s 51 (3). Their Lordships are attracted by the consideration that this may have been enacted in order to provide a universal rule of simple application for cases where the contract fixes no time for delivery, as where delivery is to be within a reasonable time or on demand by the purchaser. In such cases there may be great difficulty in determining when the contract ought to have been performed, and there could be much convenience in assessing damages as at the date of repudiation by the seller, assuming the buyer accepts it. Further, if the enactment is not intended to apply to a repudiation in such cases, it is difficult to see what content it can have. It could not apply, in cases where delivery is to be made on demand by the buyer, to a refusal to deliver following on a demand duly made, because the demand, having been made in accordance with the contract, would fix the time for delivery. It might be intended to apply, where delivery is to be made within a reasonable time, to a refusal to deliver intimated at the expiry of the period of reasonable time, but if so nothing significant would have been added to the first limb. It may well be, however, that the enactment was introduced into the subsection without consideration in depth of the juristic position, and that on analysis it proves, exceptionally, to have no content whatever. It would be surprising if the first limb of one and the same subsection were intended to be a specific application of the general principle in the preceding subsection, and the second limb to be a radical departure from it. If Parliament had intended to introduce a new rule of the nature contended for, their Lordships would have expected this to be done by clearer and more specific language than appears in the second limb of subs (3).

Atkin LJ, in the course of that part of his judgment in *Millett v Van Heek & Co* ([1921] 2 KB 369 at 377) which dealt with the question whether the second limb of s 51(3) applied to cases of anticipatory breach, expressed the view that it [would be anomalous if] a plaintiff should not only have the option, but be compelled, to fix his damages in reference to the time when the repudiation takes place. It appears to their Lordships that a plaintiff in such a case is not necessarily so compelled. He is not required to accept the repudiation, and if he does not do so the repudiation has no effect. He may wait until there has been an actual failure by the defendant to perform the contract, either on account of an unmet demand or on account of a reasonable time having elapsed without delivery. In this event the damages would be assessed, not at the date of the unaccepted repudiation, but at the date of the actual failure to perform. A more important consideration, in their Lordships' view, is that if the plaintiff did accept the repudiation, and if the market were to fall substantially up to the time when in the event the contract ought to have been performed, the plaintiff would be placed in a better position than if there had been due performance. This would represent an important inroad on a fundamental principle of assessment of damages, namely, that they should be no more than compensatory....

Their Lordships therefore affirm the principle that the second limb of s 51(3) of the Act of 1893 and of s 53(3) of the Hong Kong Ordinance, does not apply in any case of anticipatory breach of contract.

It follows that the majority of the Full Court in the present case were wrong to assess damages on the basis of the market price of cotton yarn on July 31, 1973.... The buyers did not accept the sellers' repudiation of July 31, and at any time thereafter could have demanded delivery of the balance of yarn on one month's notice. That situation continued until November 28, 1973, when the buyers issued and served their writ, thereby accepting the repudiation and rescinding the contract. November 28 was thus the last day upon which the buyers could have given reasonable notice requiring delivery of the yarn, and in their Lordships' opinion the appropriate date upon which to consider the market price of yarn for the purpose of assessing damages was one month thereafter, namely December 28, 1973.

Where the 'market price' rule applies, it is unnecessary to award the buyer additional damages for any loss of profit which he expected to make from reselling the goods—even if the seller knew, or ought to have foreseen, at the time of making the contract that this was the buyer's intention. For, if there *is* a market available for the purchase of equivalent goods, the buyer can have recourse to it (and may well be bound to do so, to fulfil his duty to mitigate) in order to meet his obligations under the sub-sale. This is so whether the market price is higher or lower than the original sale price, as is shown by the two cases below.

Williams v Reynolds

(1865) 6 B & S 495, Court of Queen's Bench

(The facts appear from the judgment.)

Blackburn J: The plaintiff and the defendants entered into a contract on the 1st April, by which the defendants agreed to sell 500 piculs of China cotton at 16¾d per lb, guaranteed fair, to be delivered in August, so that the defendants had all that month to supply a certain quantity of cotton, answering the description given, at a certain price. At the end of August they had failed to fulfil their contract. And if the case stood there, the measure of damages would have been the difference between the contact price of 16¾d and the market price at the end of August, the latest time for delivery, which was 18¼d.

The question is, whether the plaintiff is entitled to recover a further sum, this being a contract, not for the delivery of specific cotton, but of cotton of a particular description....The additional facts here are that, on the 25th May, nearly two months after the original contract and three months before its completion, the plaintiff made a contract to supply Mayall & Anderson, at Liverpool, with the same quantity and quality of cotton at 19¾d, to be delivered in August. If the defendants had fulfilled their contract the plaintiff would have handed over the cotton to his purchasers, and would have gained a considerable profit by the transaction. It was argued that because this purchase was made on the Liverpool Cotton Exchange, where all persons know that cotton is bought on speculation to sell again, the defendants would be aware that the plaintiff would enter into a fresh contract, relying on the performance by them of their contract, and that the nonfulfilment of it would occasion the breach of the second contract, and so the loss of profit by the resale would be natural consequence of the defendants' breach of contract....I cannot see that loss of profit from a contract subsequently made by the purchaser...follows as a natural consequence from the original seller's breach of contract. Though the purchaser might naturally rely on the seller's contract to enable him to fulfil his own, it is not necessary that he should do so; and if the seller was a slippery customer it would be imprudent to do it: in that case the purchaser would, as a prudent man, go into the market and supply himself from thence. Here the plaintiff had reason to rely on the defendants, but that does not entitle him to throw upon them the loss of the profit he would have made.

[Crompton and Shee JJ delivered concurring judgments.]

Williams Bros v ET Agius Ltd
[1914] AC 510, House of Lords

Agius contracted to sell 4,500 tons of coal to Williams at 16s 3d (81p) per ton, and Williams then contracted to sell coal of the same description of Ghiron at 19s (95p) per ton. Agius failed to deliver. The market price at the time of Agius's breach was 23s 6d (£1.18) per ton. The court awarded Williams damages based on the market price, and held that the subsale was irrelevant.

Lord Moulton: My Lords, the question for the decision of your Lordships in this appeal is set out very plainly in the award, in the form of a special case, which forms the basis of this litigation. It is whether the appellants are right in their contention that the measure of damages put forward by them in respect of the admitted breach by the respondents of the contract to deliver a cargo of coals in November, 1910, is correct. That contention is that the proper measure of damages is the difference between the contract price of 16s 3d per ton and the market price on the date of the breach of contract, which the arbitrator finds to be 23s 6d per ton.

Inasmuch as this is a plain case of a failure to deliver a specified quantity of an article obtainable in the market, the measure of damages is well established. The case comes under the rule laid down in the case of *Rodocanachi v Milburn* ((1886) 18 QBD 67), and regularly and repeatedly followed ever since, and ultimately embodied in the Sale of Goods Act 1893, s 51, sub-s 3. The contention of the appellants is in accordance with that rule, and the question put to the Court in the special case must accordingly be answered in their favour.

This consideration is, in my opinion, sufficient to decide this appeal, but, in deference to the opinions expressed by the majority of the Court of Appeal, I propose to examine the matters which it is suggested make the measure of damages in the present case other than that given by the recognized rule to which I have already referred.

From the facts of the case as found in the award, and the documents therein referred to, we learn that the appellants made a contract to sell a cargo of coal to the Italian firm of P Ghiron, and that they intended to fulfil that contract by the cargo to be delivered by the respondents in November. The price to be paid by the said P Ghiron was 19s per ton, and the respondents contend that it is the difference between 19s per ton and the contract price of 16s 3d per ton which is the true measure of damages.

If these were the only facts of the case the contention of the respondents would be precisely that view of the damages in the case of an article purchasable in the market which was negatived by the decision in *Rodocanachi v Milburn*. That case rests on the sound ground that it is immaterial what the buyer is intending to do with the purchased goods. He is entitled to recover the expenses of putting himself into the position of having those goods, and this he can do by going into the market and purchasing them at the market price. To do so he must pay a sum which is larger than that which he would have had to pay under the contract by the difference between the two prices. This difference is, therefore, the true measure of his loss from the breach, for it is that which it will cost him to put himself in the same position as if the contract had been fulfilled.

[His Lordship then considered and rejected an argument that there had not been a subsale to Ghiron, but an assignment to him of the benefit of the first contract. Damages based on the market price were accordingly awarded.]

[Viscount Haldane LC and Lords Dunedin and Atkinson delivered concurring opinions. Lord Parker of Waddington concurred.]

Where there is no available market for goods of the contract description, the court must make its own assessment of the amount of the buyer's loss. It may, for instance, have regard to price movements in other, comparable markets (eg *The Arpad* [1934] P 189, where there was no available market for 'Roumanian wheat', but the price of wheat generally had fallen), or, if a sub-sale by the buyer was within the reasonable contemplation of the parties, the buyer's lost profit on the resale (*Patrick v Russo-British Grain Export Co Ltd* [1927] 2 KB 535). In *The Alecos M* [1991] 1 Lloyd's Rep 120, CA the contract was for the sale of a secondhand ship 'including spare propeller'; but no spare propeller was delivered. There was no available market for such a propeller and there was evidence that it was no longer customary for new ships to be supplied with a spare propeller. To manufacture a propeller would have cost $121,000. In the absence of proof that the buyers genuinely intended to buy a spare propeller if none was delivered under the contract, the court upheld a ruling that they should not be awarded damages under s 51 equivalent to the replacement cost, but only a notional scrap value of $1,100. There may have been 'rough justice' in this decision, but it is open to criticism: see GH Treitel (1991) 107 LQR 364.

In a sale on CIF terms (see below, p 498), the seller may be in breach either of his duty to deliver the proper documents relating to the goods, or of his duty to deliver the goods at the destination port (or both). In the former case, there may be a difficulty in fixing the time and place by reference to which the existence of an available market is to be determined. Sometimes, it will be possible to buy equivalent goods 'already afloat', and the relevant time will then be that when the proper documents ought to have been delivered. Failing this, the appropriate time may be that when the goods ought to have been delivered at their destination, and this will also then be the relevant place. But the buyer may, by virtue of his duty to mitigate his loss, be obliged to contract to buy comparable goods at the place of destination as soon as he rejects the documents, and this will bring forward the date for fixing the market price: see *C Sharp & Co Ltd v Nosawa & Co* [1917] 2 KB 814.

4 ACTION FOR DAMAGES FOR LATE DELIVERY

The Act contains no provision relating to the assessment of damages when the seller fails to deliver on the due date but the buyer accepts them when they are tendered late. The issue therefore falls to be determined an ordinary contractual principles. If there is an available market for the goods, prima facie the measure of the buyer's loss is the difference in the market price on the two dates: thus, if the market is rising, he will get substantial damages, while if it is falling, he will have suffered no loss. (See, eg the well-known case of *Koufos v C Czarnikow Ltd, The Heron II* [1969] 1 AC 350, HL, where late delivery was made by a carrier.) If there is no available market, ordinary contract principles will still apply: indeed, the equally well-known case of *Victoria Laundry (Windsor) Ltd v Newman Industries Ltd* [1949] 2 KB 528, CA, where the plaintiffs recovered the profits which they had foreseeably lost during the period of the delay, was itself a case of late delivery in a sale of goods contract.

5   ACTION FOR DAMAGES FOR BREACH OF WARRANTY

Section 53 sets out a series of propositions about the buyer's remedies where there has been a breach of warranty by the seller, or where the buyer has elected (or is compelled) to treat a breach of condition as a breach of warranty. His remedy is for damages only: he cannot reject the goods. Alternatively, he may 'set up against the seller the breach of warranty in diminution or extinction of the price' (s 53(1)).

The measure of damages (again, echoing the rule in *Hadley v Baxendale* (1854) 9 Exch 341) is the estimated loss directly and naturally resulting, in the ordinary course of events, from the breach of warranty (s 53(2)). The measure of damages for breach of a warranty of quality is prima facie the difference between the value of the goods at the time they were delivered to the buyer and the value they would have had if they had fulfilled the warranty (s 53(3)). In such a case, the fact that there has been a subsale of the goods is normally irrelevant (*Slater v Hoyle & Smith Ltd* [1920] 2 KB 11, CA). Exceptionally, in *Van Den Hurk v Martens & Co Ltd* [1920] 1 KB 850, where it was known that the goods had been resold to a sub-buyer abroad and that they were to be despatched to him unopened and without any examination, the court substituted the market price at the time and place of the second delivery abroad as being more appropriate for the assessment of damages than the time and place of delivery under the principal contract.

However, it has to be remembered that the 'difference in value' test, like the 'market price' formula, is only a prima facie rule, and the case of *Bence Graphics International Ltd v Fasson UK Ltd* [1998] QB 87 demonstrates that (at least in the present context of defective delivery, as distinct perhaps from non-delivery (s 51) or non-acceptance (s 50)), it may not take a great deal to displace the rule. The plaintiffs here had contracted to buy vinyl film on which they printed words and numbers and which was then sold on to end-users for affixing to sea-borne bulk containers. The film was not up to scratch because the writing soon became illegible. Remarkably, few of the end-users made any complaint or claim. On the assumption that the film, as delivered, had no market value, the plaintiffs could have been awarded damages of over £500,000, but in fact all that they stood to lose was a mere £22,000 plus whatever was needed to compensate the few complaining end-users. The Court of Appeal declined to apply the 'difference in value' yardstick and held that the buyers could recover only their actual loss, in effect applying the basic *Hadley v Baxendale* principles to the exclusion of s 53(3).

Consequential losses for breach of warranty are assessed on ordinary contractual principles: *H Parsons (Livestock) Ltd v Uttley Ingham & Co Ltd* [1978] QB 791, CA—again, a sale of goods case which has a leading place in the contract syllabus.

QUESTION

Some end-users of Bence's product may have chosen not to sue them because they did not want to damage the goodwill which had been built up between them in the course of a long business relationship. Alternatively, some may have taken their future business elsewhere, causing Bence to lose profits. Yet Fasson was paid in full for a worthless product—a half million windfall. Should the law be concerned with these issues? (See GH Treitel (1997) 113 LQR 188 and C Hawes (2005) 121 LQR 389.)

6 BUYER'S REMEDIES AT COMMON LAW

Like the seller (see above, pp 432, 437), the buyer may have remedies at common law for breaches of the contract of sale by the seller which are not specifically dealt with by the Act. So, if the seller under a contract on CIF terms fails to give a notice of appropriation as required by the contract, the buyer may treat this as justification for terminating the contract (*Société Italo-Belge v Palm & Vegetable Oils (Malaysia) Sdn Bhd, The Post Chaser* [1981] 2 Lloyd's Rep 695). Where the breach does not entitle the buyer to terminate, he has of course a remedy in damages for any loss that he has suffered (*Cehave NV v Bremer Handelsgesellschaft mbH, The Hansa Nord* (above, p 392)). Moreover it should be borne in mind that, apart from his remedies in contract, a buyer may in an appropriate case be entitled to relief on grounds such as misrepresentation, negligence, or product liability.

7 SPECIFIC PERFORMANCE

Section 52(1) empowers the court, in an action by a buyer for breach of contract for failure to deliver *specific or ascertained goods,* to order (if it thinks fit) that the contract be performed specifically, without giving the seller the option of retaining the goods on payment of damages.

We saw earlier in *Re Wait* [1927] 1 Ch 606, CA (above, p 266), that a person who has contracted to buy *unascertained* goods cannot invoke this provision, at least for so long as the goods remain unascertained, and that the court will not grant corresponding relief on general equitable principles in such a case. The court has a discretion under s 52, which it will not exercise if the contract is concerned with goods of an ordinary description which the buyer intends to resell (*Cohen v Roche* [1927] 1 KB 169: the 'ordinary' goods were in fact 'eight genuine Hepplewhite chairs'!). An order under s 52 has been made in respect of a ship, of a design especially suited to the buyer's needs (*Behnke v Bede Shipping Co Ltd* [1927] 1 KB 649) and (though not specifically under s 52) of an ornamental door designed by Adam (*Phillips v Lamdin* [1949] 2 KB 33).

Under the new Part 5A which applies in consumer sales (see below), an additional power to order specific performance is conferred by s 48E. The court may make such an order against the seller where he has delivered goods which do not conform to the contract. Although the section uses the word 'may', it is possible that the court's discretion is more limited than it would be under the traditional equitable jurisdiction: see DR Harris (2003) 119 LQR 541.

8 BUYER'S ADDITIONAL REMEDIES IN CONSUMER SALES

A new Part 5A (ss 48A–48F) was introduced into the Act in 2002 by the Sale and Supply of Goods to Consumers Regulations 2002, SI 2002/3045, implementing Directive 1999/44/EC. This confers additional rights on a buyer who is a consumer (defined as 'any natural person who is acting for purposes outside his trade, business or profession'), where the goods do not conform to the contract of sale at the time of delivery. Goods do not conform if there is a breach of an express term or of a term implied by s 13, 14 or 15 (s 48F). There is a (rebuttable) presumption that if the goods do not conform to the contract at any time within the six months after delivery they did not conform at the time when they were delivered, but of course this will not apply if (for example) the goods are perishable (s 48A(3), (4)).

The buyer's additional remedies are, in the first place, to require the seller to repair or replace the goods, although he cannot insist on either of these remedies if this would be impossible, or 'disproportionate', having regard to various factors set out in s 48B(3)–(5). In that event (and also if the seller has failed to repair or replace the goods within a reasonable time), the buyer has the further remedies: (1) to require the seller to reduce the purchase price by an appropriate amount; or (2) to rescind the contract. Sections 48B–48E spell out these rights and the limitations on their exercise in more detail, and empower the court to make orders to give effect to the buyer's rights even if this is not the remedy which the buyer seeks.

Similar changes have been made to the Supply of Goods and Services Act 1982 to deal with contracts by which goods are transferred otherwise than under a contract of sale (eg by barter or under a contract for work and materials) and contracts of hire, and to the Supply of Goods (Implied Terms) Act 1973 to deal with contracts of hire-purchase.

PART IV

INTERNATIONAL SALES

CHAPTER 14

INTERNATIONAL SALES

1 INTRODUCTION

There is more than one way in which a sale of goods contract may have an international element—for example, the seller and buyer may be in different jurisdictions, or the contract may contemplate that the goods are to be carried from one country to another. The Unfair Contract Terms Act 1977 has its own special definition (see above, p 419). We are concerned in this section with contracts that involve the transport of the goods from one country to another. These will not necessarily be the countries in which the seller and buyer are respectively based—indeed, they may be based anywhere, even in the same country. A contract of this kind exposes the parties to greater risks than a purely domestic sale: physical risks associated with transport and the extra handling; financial risks, such as movements in exchange rates; political risks (extending even to the possibility of war, blockades, etc); and legal risks if a foreign system of law is involved, or a judgment or award has to be enforced in a foreign country. Some of these risks can be covered by insurance. Others may be avoided by careful drafting of the sales contract—a choice of law clause, for instance, will normally ensure that the contract is governed by a known set of legal rules. Much uncertainty can be resolved if the parties use one of the standard contract forms of the relevant trade association, which have been tried and tested over the years, eg the GAFTA forms of the Grain and Feed Trade Association, or those of the London Metal Exchange. There are also standard international terms of trade, such as INCOTERMS (the International Rules for the Interpretation of Trade Terms promulgated by the International Chamber of Commerce). These may have customary or even statutory force in some jurisdictions, but will be applied in English law only if chosen by the parties.

Two attempts have been made to establish standard terms of trade on a supra-national basis by international treaty. The first, the Uniform Law on International Sales, based on a Convention signed at The Hague in 1964, failed to gain wide support and has not been a success. The United Kingdom has, in fact, ratified this Convention, but on the basis that it will apply only where the parties have agreed that this will be the case—ie 'opted in' (Uniform Laws on International Sales Act 1967). Since in practice parties have rarely, if ever, done this, the Uniform Law is in effect a dead letter in this country. The second treaty, the United Nations Convention on Contracts for the International Sale of Goods (commonly known as the Vienna Convention), is clearly destined to supersede the Uniform Law, since it has gained wide support. The Convention was adopted at a United Nations conference held in Vienna in 1980 and became operative at the beginning of 1988. It has since been ratified or acceded to by some 70 States. However, since the United Kingdom has not ratified this Convention and has no present plans to do so, we shall not discuss it further in this work. (For further reading, see JO Honnold *Uniform Law for International Sales under the 1980 United Nations Convention International Sale of Goods* (3rd edn, 1999); L D'Arcy (ed), *Schmitthoff's Export Trade* (10th edn, 2000), Ch 14; MG Bridge, The Bifocal World of International Sales' in R Cranston (ed) *Making Commercial Law* (1997); BAK Nicholas (1989) 105 LQR 201.)

For many reasons, it makes best sense to take as our example of an international sale a contract where the goods are to be carried by sea—this being the traditional export-import transaction and so the one for which well-established legal rules have evolved. Because of the time which it takes for goods to travel by sea, it is also particularly necessary in this type of transaction for the parties to be able to make arrangements to finance the deal and for this purpose to give security over the goods to their respective banks. To meet these problems, the *documents* relating to the sale and carriage of the goods have been elevated to a position of special symbolic importance, to the point where for many purposes they are treated in law as representing the goods themselves: for instance, 'delivery' of the goods can be effected by handing over these documents.

The principal documents for this purpose are:

(1) the bill of lading;

(2) the commercial invoice;

(3) the policy of marine insurance.

The bill of lading. The bill of lading is a document with a threefold purpose. (For an illustration, see Form 2 in the Appendix.) It is issued by the carrier (ie the owner or charterer of the ship) to the consignor of the goods, or to someone nominated by him, shortly after the goods have been loaded. First, it acknowledges the fact that the goods have been received, describing them in an itemised list, and evidences the fact that they have been loaded in apparent good order and condition. (If not, the defect is noted—eg that some barrels were leaking—and the bill is then called a 'claused', as distinct from a 'clean', bill.) Secondly, it normally contains the terms of the contract of carriage, identifying the route and destination. Thirdly, it is regarded in law as evidencing the rights of possession and ownership in respect of the goods, so that these rights are deemed (at least prima facie) to be vested in the holder of the bill of lading—the person who is in possession. Delivery of the goods at their destination is normally made by the carrier to the holder against the surrender of the bill. A bill of lading may be made out in different ways, rather like a cheque: to a named person 'or his order'; to a named person 'or bearer'; or to a named person only (usually by a statement that the document is 'not transferable' or 'non-negotiable'). In the first two of these cases the rights evidenced by the bill may be transferred from one holder to another simply by handing over possession of the document, with an indorsement unless it is a bearer bill. In the third case (commonly called a 'straight' bill) no rights can be transferred in this way. But, despite the similarity to a cheque, a bill of lading is not a *negotiable instrument* in the sense discussed in Chapter 15, since in no case can a transferee acquire a better title than that of the preceding holder. A straight bill may or may not be a 'bill of lading' within a particular statutory definition (see *JI MacWilliam Co Inc v Mediterranean Shipping Co SA, The Rafaela S* [2005] UKHL 11, [2005] 2 AC 423). A 'sea waybill' is, like a straight bill of lading, a document made out in favour of a named consignee, but which does not take the form of a traditional bill of lading. For practical purposes the two may be regarded as equivalent.

The commercial invoice. This is an invoice itemising the goods sold and describing them in a way which makes it possible to identify them as the contract goods, or as answering to the description of the contract goods.

The policy of marine insurance. This must be expressed in such a way as to make it clear that it covers the goods specified in the other two documents for the whole of the voyage covered by the bill of lading. When the bill of lading is transferred from one person to another, the policy of insurance will be assigned at the same time.

Other documents which may be required under particular contracts may include: a certificate of origin; a certificate of quality or inspection certificate (important because there usually will be no opportunity for the buyer or any later sub-purchasers to inspect the goods until after they have reached their destination); export and/or import licences.

The Carriage of Goods by Sea Act 1992 (replacing the Bills of Lading Act 1855) overcomes problems which would arise at common law under the doctrine of privity of contract when a bill of lading is transferred from one holder to another. The original parties to a bill are the carrier and (normally) the consignor. Where the goods are the subject of a contract of sale, the consignor may already be the seller of the goods, or he may sell them after shipment. His buyer may, in turn, resell the goods, and this may be repeated so that there is a chain of sub-buyers. Any of these parties who is entitled to the goods at a particular time may have pledged his interest in the goods as security to his bank, and deposited the bill with the bank. Alternatively, the consignor may have had the bill made out in the name of the consignee if he is already the owner of the goods. If the doctrine of privity of contract were applied strictly, the contractual rights and duties evidenced by the bill would be enforceable only as between the consignor and the carrier; and the buyer, the sub-buyer or the consignee in the circumstances described above would be in no contractual relationship with the carrier. The Act of 1992 modifies this position by providing that whoever is the lawful holder of a bill is entitled to sue the carrier on the contract of carriage, and that if anyone who is thus entitled asserts such contractual rights against the carrier, he assumes the corresponding contractual duties—although these liabilities will cease if the bill is transferred to another holder: *Borealis AB v Stargas Ltd* [2001] UKHL 17, [2002] 2 AC 205. (In fact, the Act applies also to certain other documents commonly used in sea transport, such as sea waybills and ship's delivery orders. These documents are not bills of lading in the full sense: they do not contain the terms of the contract of carriage, and they are not regarded as symbolising the goods for the purpose of transferring title. The Act of 1855 did not apply to them, or give rights to the holder as the 1992 Act now does.)

A buyer of goods to whom this package of shipping documents has been effectively transferred can therefore assert:

(1) contractual rights against his immediate seller under the contract of sale;

(2) contractual rights against the carrier under the contract of carriage, by virtue of the Act of 1992: in turn, he will be liable to the carrier for the freight;

(3) his rights, as assignee of the benefit of the insurance policy, against the insurer, if the goods are lost or damaged by an event which the policy covers.

In addition, if the property in the goods has passed to him, he will have rights in tort against anyone who has wrongfully interfered with the goods or refused to deliver them up, or negligently damaged them. However, this will not be so if he does not own the goods, even though they may be at his risk (*The Aliakmon* [1986] AC 785, HL). This gap in the law was not remedied by the Act of 1992: *The Aliakmon* is still an authority as a tort case—although, ironically, the buyers would now have rights in contract against the carrier under the new Act, since they had become holders of the bill of lading.

The Contracts (Rights of Third Parties) Act 1999 has made inroads into the common law doctrine of privity by providing that a person who is not a party to a contract may enforce a term in a contract if the contract so provides or (subject to some qualifications) if the term purports to confer a benefit on him (s 1). However, s 6(5) declares that s 1 confers no rights on a third party in the case of (a) a contract for the carriage of goods by sea or (b) a contract for the carriage of goods by rail, road or air which is subject to the rules of an international transport Convention. The contracts referred to in s 6(5) are defined in more detail in s 6(6) so as to include most, but not quite all, categories of international or inter-state transport; and so it will only be in the exceptional cases where a contract does not fall within s 6(6) that there will be any possibility that the 1999 Act might be invoked. In any case, there is a very important distinction between the two Acts: the 1999 Act only gives the third party the *benefit* of the contractual term or terms in question, without any corresponding obligations, whereas under the 1992 Act he acquires duties as well as rights.

Section 6(5) makes one exception to the general disapplication of the 1999 Act to the contracts of carriage in question: a third party may rely on s 1 to avail himself of an exclusion or limitation of liability in the contract. This will mean that the employees of the carrier, if sufficiently identified as so entitled by the contract, could claim the benefit of such a clause (commonly referred to as a *'Himalaya'* clause).

2　TYPICAL EXPORT TRANSACTIONS

The parties to an international contract of sale are free to make any arrangement they choose as regards delivery, risk and the other incidents of the transaction. In practice, the contract is likely to fall under one or another of a series of recognised heads, which we can set out in a list that covers a whole spectrum of possible arrangements, beginning with the 'ex works' contract (where all the responsibilities connected with transport, etc are assumed by the buyer) and ranging all the way to the contract 'delivered, duty paid' (where the entire burden in these respects is carried by the seller). The main heads are:

Ex works (and variants: ex factory, warehouse, store);

Free carrier;

Free alongside (FAS);

Free on board (FOB);

Cost and freight (C & F);

Cost, insurance, freight (CIF, or CF & I) (variants: CIF & C (commission), CIF & E (exchange), CIF & C & I (commission and interest));

Carriage paid;

Carriage and insurance paid;

Delivered at frontier;

Delivered ex ship (also called 'arrival');

Delivered ex quay;

Delivered duty unpaid;

Delivered duty paid.

Examples of such contracts can be found going back for well over a century, and in some cases for many centuries. More modern methods of transport have led to the introduction of variants, such as FOB airport, where the goods are to be carried by air. The *container trade* (where the goods are stowed in a container before being carried by road, rail or sea or a combination of modes) has spawned a further variety of trade terms:

Full container load (FCL);

Less than full container load (LCL);

Free carrier (broadly equivalent to FOB);

Freight carriage paid (equivalent to C & F);

Freight carriage and insurance paid (equivalent to CIF).

The contracts at the two extremes of the first list above differ very little from domestic sales. Where a seller sells on 'ex works' or similar terms, he has only to make delivery at or near his own place of business, as he might do to a local buyer, and everything else is up to the buyer. The fact that the goods are destined for export, if the seller knows this, may have some bearing on the question whether they are of satisfactory quality (*Mash & Murrell Ltd v Emanuel,* above, p 409), and he may be expected under the terms of the contract to provide a certificate of origin or other documentation (or, alternatively, to co-operate with the buyer in procuring it); but property, possession and risk will normally pass at the point of delivery, and all the problems thereafter are the buyer's. Where a seller undertakes to 'deliver, duty paid', in contrast, it is his business to get the goods all the way to the point of delivery in the buyer's country, and the buyer's position will be little different from that of a buyer under a domestic purchase in that country.

In this book, we shall look in more detail at four of the more common of the traditional standard-form contracts: FAS, FOB, CIF and 'arrival'. For further information, reference may be made to L D'Arcy (ed), *Schmitthoff's Export Trade* (10th edn, 2000).

3   FAS CONTRACTS

'FAS' stands for 'free alongside ship'. Here the first, inland, journey to the port of shipment is the seller's responsibility, but he assumes no obligation beyond that (except, perhaps, obligations in regard to procuring certificates of origin, etc). The contract is really no different in essence from a domestic sale on FOR ('free on rail') terms, or even from one where the seller agrees to deliver the goods at any other place within the seller's own country. Typically, the seller's duties might include the following:

— to supply the goods, with evidence of conformity with the contract;

— to deliver the goods alongside the ship, at the place and at or within the time stipulated by the contract or nominated by the buyer;

— to give the buyer notice of the above;

— to provide a certificate of origin;

— to co-operate with the buyer in obtaining other necessary documentation, eg an export licence.

The buyer, for his part, will have the following duties:

— to procure a ship, or shipping space, and give the seller due notice of the name of the ship and the place and time of loading;

— to pay the price;

— to bear all the costs of loading from alongside ship;

— to bear the costs of procuring all documentation, including the export licence, bill of lading, etc.

Property, possession and risk will normally pass to the buyer on delivery—ie when the goods have been placed alongside the ship so that they can be taken on board by crane, ship's tackle or the equivalent. 'Alongside' may mean (depending upon the custom of the particular port) on the docks, in a lighter, etc.

4 FOB CONTRACTS

The contract on FOB ('free on board') terms is the first of the two 'mainstream' export transactions for which detailed rules have been very fully worked out over the years. There can, of course, be a wide variety of FOB arrangements, but we shall look first at a contract on 'classic' or 'strict' FOB terms. Here, the seller undertakes not just to get the goods *to* the ship, but to see them loaded *on to* the ship, and to bear the cost of loading them; but it is the buyer's business to make all the arrangements regarding the shipping and insurance of the goods. The contract will state, typically: 'FOB, Felixstowe, shipment in August', or, perhaps, 'FOB, East Anglian port'. The understanding then is that the seller must hold himself ready to put the goods on any ship nominated by the buyer at the nominated port at any time during the month of August. The first step in performance will be taken by the buyer, who has the right (and the duty) to find a suitable ship calling at the port of loading within the contract period: he may, for instance, nominate the 'MV *Neptune,* expected ready to load at Felixstowe, 7 August'. This may mean chartering a ship, if the goods are enough to constitute a whole cargo, or booking space on a general cargo ship if what he is buying is less than a shipload. Then the respective duties of the parties unfold in sequence. The seller must have the goods ready to ship at that time and place; then he has to have them loaded on to the ship at his own expense; the buyer must be ready to pay the price on completion of the loading; and so on. At the conclusion of the loading of the goods, the consignor is issued with a document called a 'mate's receipt', which acknowledges receipt of the goods, itemised as to quantity and description, and confirmed to be in apparent good order and condition. In an FOB contract, this will be given to the seller, who receives it on behalf of the buyer; and the price may be payable under the contract in exchange for this document. In that case, the buyer will shortly afterwards surrender the mate's receipt to the carrier and receive in its place the bill of lading, which will of course be made out in the buyer's name. Alternatively, the contract may provide for the seller to procure the bill of lading, in which case he will retain the mate's receipt and have the bill of lading issued in either his own name or that of the buyer (depending upon the provisions of the contract) and receive payment in exchange for the bill itself. If the bill is made out to the seller, he will be a party to the contract of carriage; and he will also have 'reserved the right of disposal' in regard to the goods, which will normally prevent the property from passing to the buyer until the bill is transferred to him (s 18, rule 5(2); s 19(1), (2)).

The critical moment in an FOB contract occurs when the goods 'cross the ship's rail', normally by being swung by a crane or derrick, but sometimes less dramatically (eg in the case of oil or grain) in the course of being pumped or sucked through a pipe from shore to ship. At this point risk normally passes, and possession and property may pass also. But the property will not pass if the seller has 'reserved the right of disposal' (eg by retaining the bill of lading), or the contract goods are unascertained, or the contract provides otherwise. For an example of a case where the seller reserved the right of disposal see *The Ciudad de Pasto* [1989] 1 All ER 951, where the seller of a consignment of prawns destined for Japan had retained the shipping documents until the outstanding balance (20 per cent) of the price was paid.

Under an FOB contract of this traditional type, the seller's and buyer's duties may be listed as follows.

The seller's duties will typically include:

— to supply the goods, with evidence of conformity with contract;
— to deliver the goods on board the ship, at the place and time stipulated by the contract or nominated by the buyer;
— to obtain the export licence;
— to bear all costs up to and including loading (across the ship's rail);
— to provide documents evidencing delivery to the ship, certificate of origin, etc;
— to co-operate with the buyer in procuring the bill of lading and other documentation;
— to give notice to the buyer to enable him to insure the goods during their sea transit (see s 32(3)).

The buyer's duties are as follows:

— to procure a suitable ship or shipping space and give the seller due notice of the ship and place and time of loading;
— to pay the price;
— to bear all costs subsequent to the goods passing the ship's rail;
— to bear the costs of procuring all documentation, including the bill of lading and certificate of origin.

Variations on the 'classic' FOB contract are very common. In the 'extended' FOB contract, the seller takes on the additional responsibilities of making the shipping and insurance arrangements. It may be more convenient for the seller to do this, especially where the goods sold do not amount to a complete cargo. The seller is often better placed to deal with exporting agencies in his own country—or he may be in the exporting business himself. Of course, every additional duty which the seller undertakes is likely to be reflected in the price which he charges the buyer.

Some of the cases which have been cited in earlier chapters were concerned with contracts made on FOB terms—eg *Colley v Overseas Exporters Ltd* (above, p 433) and *Carlos Federspiel & Co SA v Charles Twigg & Co Ltd* (above, p 342). The case which follows contains a description of this type of contract, and shows the importance in law of the moment when the goods pass the ship's rail.

Pyrene Co Ltd v Scindia Navigation Co Ltd
[1954] 2 QB 402, Queen's Bench Division

An airport fire tender, which had been sold on FOB terms by Pyrene to the government of India, was dropped and damaged while being loaded for export on to a ship belonging to

Scindia. It had not crossed the ship's rail. Contracts for the carriage of goods by sea were at the material time regulated by an international Convention known as the Hague Rules (now superseded by the Hague-Visby Rules), which limited the liability of the carrier for negligent damage to the goods to £200. But the contract of carriage here had been made between Scindia and the buyers. This action was brought in tort by the sellers (as consignors of the goods in question), claiming £966 damages against Scindia for negligently damaging the tender. The question was whether the limitation of liability under the Hague Rules could be pleaded in defence. It was argued that the doctrine of privity prevented Scindia from relying directly on the contract of carriage. Devlin J held, however, that on the facts the sellers had 'participated' in the contract of carriage sufficiently for them to be bound by the Hague Rules, or that (alternatively) there was a *collateral* contract between the parties, into which the Hague Rules could be incorporated on the basis of usage or custom. In the course of his judgment, he explained some details regarding the nature of FOB contracts and the incidents of their performance.

Devlin J: I come . . . to the question whether the plaintiffs are privy to the contract of carriage.

In this type of case the seller as shipper makes the contract for the benefit of the buyer. . . .

The contract of sale provided for delivery fob London, the price including dock and harbour dues and port rates to be paid by the seller; and further expressly provided that freight was to be engaged by the buyer, who was to give due notice to the seller when and on board what vessel the goods were to be delivered. Payment was to be made twenty-one days after delivery and after receipt of certain documents for which the contract called, such as invoice, inspection certificate, etc, and of the dock company's or mate's receipt. In the special circumstances of this case and because of delay in shipment, payment was in fact made in advance, but on the terms that that should not affect the seller's obligations as to delivery. As I have said, it was agreed that the property did not pass till delivery over the ship's rail.

It is worth noting that the problem which I have to consider does not arise as a matter of course in every fob contract. The fob contract has become a flexible instrument. In what counsel called the classic type as described, for example, in *Wimble, Sons & Co v Rosenberg & Sons* ([1913] 3 KB 743), the buyer's duty is to nominate the ship, and the seller's to put the goods on board for account of the buyer and procure a bill of lading in terms usual in the trade. In such a case the seller is directly a party to the contract of carriage at least until he takes out the bill of lading in the buyer's name. Probably the classic type is based on the assumption that the ship nominated will be willing to load any goods brought down to the berth or at least those of which she is notified. Under present conditions, when space often has to be booked well in advance, the contract of carriage comes into existence at an earlier point of time. Sometimes the seller is asked to make the necessary arrangements; and the contract may then provide for his taking the bill of lading in his own name and obtaining payment against the transfer, as in a cif contract. Sometimes the buyer engages his own forwarding agent at the port of loading to book space and to procure the bill of lading; if freight has to be paid in advance this method may be the most convenient. In such a case the seller discharges his duty by putting the goods on board, getting the mate's receipt and handing it to the forwarding agent to enable him to obtain the bill of lading. The present case belongs to this third type; and it is only in this type, I think, that any doubt can arise about the seller being a party to the contract.

The contract of carriage in this case was made in the office of Bahr Behrend & Co, for they are both agents for ISD and freight brokers for the defendants. An instruction came to Bahr Behrend from ISD to arrange for the shipment of these goods among other cargo, and a note by Bahr Behrend dated March 29, 1951, records that the shipment was booked per the *Jalazed*. The ordinary practice is for ISD to prepare a bill of lading (the defendants have a special form for Government of India shipments) and to send it to Bahr Behrend. Bahr Behrend check the items on it from a return made out by the cargo superintendent after shipment and then sign and issue the bill of lading on behalf of the defendants generally some days after the ship has sailed, dependent on the volume of the cargo to be dealt with.

It is the practice in the Port of London for all loading to be done by the port authority at the ship's expense. The whole charge, therefore, for loading from alongside is paid by the ship and covered by the freight; in this case, it included the cost of lighterage from the dock to the ship's side. On April 7 Bahr Behrend, on behalf of ISD, notified the plaintiffs that space had been engaged, and instructed them to dispatch the goods to arrive alongside the vessel.

The question at once arises: if, as the plaintiffs contend, there is no contractual relationship between them and the defendants, how do they get these goods on board? If the ship sails off without loading the goods the plaintiffs are in breach of their contract of sale. Have they no redress against the ship? Mr Megaw argues that they would have none, and that vis-à-vis the sellers the ship in loading acts as a volunteer. This seems to me to be a position which none of the three parties would have accepted for a moment.

Let me look at the situation first from the standpoint of the shipper, ISD. In the ordinary case, such as I have been considering above, where the shipper takes out a bill of lading or an insurance policy, he has at the time of the contract himself got the property in the goods; the question whether he contracts for the benefit of subsequent owners depends on proof of his intention at the time of contracting. But where, as in this case, he has not got the property at the time of the contract, and does not intend to acquire it before the contract begins to operate, he must act as agent. He cannot intend otherwise; the intention is inherent in the act; he must either profess agency or confess himself a wrongdoer. For if the shipowner lifts the seller's goods from the dock without the seller's authority he is guilty of conversion to which the shipper, by requiring him to do it, makes himself a party.

Let me look at it now from the standpoint of the ship. If the shipowners were sued for conversion they would surely have redress against the shipper. A person who requests a carrier to handle goods must have the right to deal with them or it would not be safe to contract with him. A shipowner cannot be supposed to inquire whether the goods he handles do or do not belong to the shipper who entrusts them to his care; if the goods are not the shipper's there must be implied a warranty of authority by him that he has the right to contract with regard to them.

Then from the standpoint of the seller, if his goods are left behind, and it is said to him: 'You made no contract with the ship; what else did you expect?' he would answer, I think, that he naturally supposed that all the necessary arrangements had been made by the shippers.

In brief, I think the inference irresistible that it was the intention of all three parties that the seller should participate in the contract of affreightment so far as it affected him. If it were intended that he should be a party to the whole of the contract his position would be that of an undisclosed principal and the ordinary law of agency would apply. But that is obviously not intended; he could not, for example, be sued for the freight. This is the sort of situation that is covered by the wider principle; the third party takes those benefits of the contract which appertain to his interest therein, but takes them, of course, subject to whatever qualifications with regard to them the contract imposes. It is argued that it is not reasonable to suppose that the seller would submit to the terms of a contract whose detail he does not know and which might not give him the sort of protection of which he would approve. I do not think that as a matter of business this is so. Most people board a bus or train without considering what protection they will get in the event of an accident. I see nothing unreasonably imprudent in a seller assuming that the buyer, whose stake in the contract is greater than his, would have obtained whatever terms are usual in the trade; if he were legally minded enough to inquire what they were, the answer would be that by statutory requirement the contract was governed by the Hague Rules.

If this conclusion is wrong, there is an alternative way by which, on the facts of this case, the same result would be achieved. By delivering the goods alongside the seller impliedly invited the shipowner to load them, and the shipowner by lifting the goods impliedly accepted that invitation. The implied contract so created must incorporate the shipowner's usual terms; none other could have been contemplated; the shipowner would not contract for the loading of the goods on terms different from those which he offered for the voyage as a whole. This simple solution was the one which Lord Sumner preferred in *Elder, Dempster & Co Ltd v Paterson, Zochonis & Co Ltd* [1924] AC 522, and which was adopted in respect of the stevedores' liability in the cases I have mentioned. But, as I have said, the problem in those cases was a rather different one, and I do not think that the solution fits so well the circumstances of this case. First, it means that if the goods were not lifted there would be no contract; and while that does not arise in this case, a solution that leaves it in the air is not so acceptable as one that covers it. Secondly, I find it difficult to infer that the shipowner by lifting the goods intended to make any new contract; he would not know where the property in the goods lay; I think he must have supposed that he was acting under a contract already made through Bahr Behrend, and on the assumption that Bahr Behrend had authority to make it. Thirdly, I doubt whether the seller intended to make any separate contract when he sent down the goods; I think that he, too, would have supposed that they would be dealt with under the contract of affreightment....

In my judgment the plaintiffs are bound by the Hague Rules as embodied in the contract of carriage and, accordingly, can recover no more than £200. There will be judgment for them for that sum.

NOTES

1.　Devlin J's view that the sellers 'participated' in the contract of carriage is difficult to understand, since it is clear that he did not consider that they were bound by all of its terms—their participation was at best partial, and whatever consideration moved from them was not the promise to pay the freight, but something else, which was unexpressed. It seems that the content of this part-contract, if spelt out, would have been little different from that of the collateral contract which the judge put forward as an alternative; and this alternative reasoning may therefore be easier to accept.

2.　The Contracts (Rights of Third Parties) Act 1999 now allows a third party to enforce a term of a contract that expressly or impliedly confers a *benefit* on him and, to that extent, makes inroads into the traditional doctrine of privity of contract. But the Act does not in any way qualify the privity doctrine in regard to *obligations* or *limitations* which it is sought to impose on someone who is not a party to the contract. It also has no application to contracts for the carriage of goods by sea, or contracts for the carriage of goods by road, rail or air which are covered by an international Convention (see above, p 492). So, in general, the remarks of Devlin J on these facts as regards the doctrine of privity survive the reforms of 1999. However, there is an exception: a third party in these contracts of carriage may avail himself of the benefit of an exclusion or limitation of liability in such a contract. If, therefore, we had a case where a contract for the carriage of goods by sea incorporated the Hague-Visby Rules or included an express limitation of liability, a stevedore who negligently damaged the goods could invoke the protection of the limitation if the other requirements of the 1999 Act were satisfied.

5 CIF CONTRACTS

This is the second of the 'classic' export-sale forms. The letters 'CIF' stand for 'cost, insurance, freight'. In this type of contract the point of delivery is moved further down the sequence, to a time *after* the goods have been shipped; but in reality we are looking at a contract of a wholly different character. In a CIF contract, the buyer looks to the seller to make the whole of the shipping arrangements, including those relating to insurance, and the buyer takes delivery of the goods symbolically, commonly while they are somewhere at sea, by taking over the shipping documents relating to the consignment—including, at least, the bill of lading, commercial invoice and insurance policy. As will become apparent, what the buyer bargains for is not so much to acquire the goods in a physical sense, as to take over the whole commercial *venture*. It has even been suggested on occasion that in a CIF contract the subject matter of the contract is not the goods, but the documents; but this view has no judicial support and there is no doubt that the Sale of Goods Act applies to such contracts.

In contrast with the FOB contract, which specifies the port of loading, a CIF contract specifies the port of arrival: thus, if goods are sold on terms 'CIF Felixstowe', the seller undertakes to provide goods which are destined to arrive at that port. Most contracts for the sale of goods on CIF terms are for commodities of some sort, such as crude oil or sugar or grain—in legal terms, unascertained goods which are sold by description; and it will be no concern of the buyer how the seller finds the goods to meet his contract. In other words, if we suppose a contract for the sale of 2000 tonnes of Missouri wheat sold CIF Rotterdam, the likelihood is not that the seller will be the American farmer who grew the wheat, or even the American merchant who shipped it, but a commodity dealer who has sold wheat of this description 'forward' (perhaps several months previously) and seeks to honour his commitment by finding wheat *already afloat* which answers the contract description. (The buyer may well also be another middleman—a dealer or importer, and not the European farmer who will eventually feed the wheat to his livestock or the miller who will turn it into flour.) So, when we read through the lists of the respective duties of the seller and buyer, we should bear in mind that our notional seller and buyer are pictured as the parties at the very beginning of what may be quite a long chain of successive sales, all made on similar CIF terms, and that not all of these duties will be applicable to parties further down the chain.

The seller's duties will include:

— to ship at the agreed port of shipment goods of the contract description (or procure goods afloat which have been so shipped);
— to procure a contract of sea carriage by which the goods will be delivered to the contract destination;
— to insure the goods under an insurance contract which will be available for the benefit of the buyer;
— to procure a commercial invoice in conformity with the contract;
— to tender these documents to the buyer (or his agent or bank).

The buyer's duties will be:

— to accept the documents, if they are in conformity with the contract, and pay the price;
— to take delivery of the goods at the agreed destination, and pay all unloading costs;
— to pay customs and other duties at the port of arrival;
— to procure any necessary import licence.

In practice, the freight is often deducted from the overall price and left to be paid by the buyer when the ship has reached its destination.

(a) The importance of the shipping documents

The key feature of the CIF contract is the role played by the documents in the performance of the contract. Once the buyer has had these documents delivered to him in a way which effectively transfers or assigns to him the rights which they embody, he is in a position to assert his title to the goods (since property normally passes on delivery of the bill of lading), and with it, the right to possession; he can demand delivery of the goods at the port of arrival, and sue a wrongdoer in tort if the goods are wrongfully damaged or lost or detained; he has contractual rights against the carrier, if the goods are missing or damaged or delayed in delivery; and he has the right to claim on the policy of insurance in the event of accidental loss or damage—say, in a storm at sea. The buyer takes over from the seller the whole *package* of rights and liabilities which make up the commercial venture. This means that he is bound to go through with the deal—to pay the price and take up the documents, when tendered—even though the goods may have been lost (see the *Manbre Saccharine* case, below). However, since he has only the documents to go on, the law rightly says that he is bound to complete by taking up the documents only if the documents tendered are strictly in conformity with the contract. It must be apparent from the documents themselves that everything is in order. The commercial invoice, the bill of lading and the insurance policy must describe the goods in exactly the same terms as the contract description; the quantities must tally; the contract of carriage must also be consistent with the contract, as regards date of shipment, route, etc; and the policy of insurance must accurately reflect the details of the voyage contemplated by the contract and the risks which the contract stipulates that it must guard against. Moreover, the buyer is entitled to insist on 'continuous documentary cover': the contract of carriage must cover the whole of the period during which the goods are in transit; the insurance policy must likewise cover all the normal risks to all the goods continuously for the whole period from shipment to arrival. The buyer may insist on this even though at the time of performance the discrepancy appears to have become irrelevant (eg even if the voyage has been safely completed), for the documentation may turn out to be necessary later if an unforeseen claim should arise.

The buyer under a CIF contract has two rights of rejection (*Kwei Tek Chao v British Traders*, above, p 346): if the documents are not in order, he may refuse to take them up, and treat this as a repudiatory breach by the seller; and even after he has accepted the documents, he has a right to reject the goods if, on arrival, they prove not to be in conformity with the contract. Conversely, if the buyer rejects the documents when they are apparently in order, the seller may elect to treat this as a repudiation on the part of the buyer, and is relieved from the duty of delivering the goods themselves (*Berger v Gill & Duffus*, below, p 504).

In a CIF contract the property in the goods and the right to possession normally pass to the buyer when the documents are handed over. But the *risk* is deemed to have passed retrospectively 'as from' shipment—in other words, the buyer takes over the risk with retrospective effect back to the time of shipment. This may mean that he has to pay the price and take up the documents even though the goods have been lost: *Manbre Saccharine Co Ltd v Corn Products Co Ltd* (below). He will, however, succeed to such rights as the seller may have against the carrier and insurer in such a case.

Ross T Smyth & Co Ltd v TD Bailey, Sons & Co

[1940] 3 All ER 60, House of Lords

(The facts are immaterial.)

Lord Wright: The contract in question here is of a type familiar in commerce, and is described as a cif contract. The initials indicate that the price is to include cost, insurance and freight. It is a type of contract which is more widely and more frequently in use than any other contract used for purposes of sea-borne commerce. An enormous number of transactions, in value amounting to untold sums, are carried out every year under cif contracts. The essential characteristics of this contract have often been described. The seller has to ship or acquire after that shipment the contract goods, as to which, if unascertained, he is generally required to give a notice of appropriation. On or after shipment, he has to obtain proper bills of lading and proper policies of insurance. He fulfils his contract by transferring the bills of lading and the policies to the buyer. As a general rule, he does so only against payment of the price, less the freight, which the buyer has to pay. In the invoice which accompanies the tender of the documents on the 'prompt'—that is, the date fixed for payment—the freight is deducted, for this reason. In this course of business, the general property in the goods remains in the seller until he transfers the bills of lading. These rules, which are simple enough to state in general terms, are of the utmost importance in commercial transactions. I have dwelt upon them perhaps unnecessarily, because the judgment of the Court of Appeal might seem to throw doubt on one of their most essential aspects. The property which the seller retains while he or his agent, or the banker to whom he has pledged the documents, retains the bills of lading is the general property, and not a special property by way of security. In general, however, the importance of the retention of the property is not only to secure payment from the buyer but for purposes of finance. The general course of international commerce involves the practice of raising money on the documents so as to bridge the period between shipment and the time of obtaining payment against documents. These credit facilities, which are of the first importance, would be completely unsettled if the incidence of the property were made a matter of doubt. By mercantile law, the bills of lading are the symbols of the goods. The general property in the goods must be in the seller if he is to be able to pledge them. The whole system of commercial credits depends on the seller's ability to give a charge on the goods and the policies of insurance. A mere unpaid seller's lien would, for obvious reasons, be inadequate and unsatisfactory . . . .

Manbre Saccharine Co Ltd v Corn Products Co Ltd
[1919] 1 KB 198, King's Bench Division

Under two separate contracts, Corn Products sold starch and corn syrup to Manbre Saccharine on terms CIF London. Goods answering the contract description were shipped aboard the SS *Algonquin*, which was sunk by a torpedo or mine on 12 March 1917. The sellers tendered the documents relating to the goods on 14 March, but the buyers refused to take them up or pay the price. It was held that they were bound to do so, and that this was a breach of contract.

McCardie J: The first question arising can be briefly stated as follows: Can a vendor under an ordinary cif contract effectively tender appropriate documents to the buyer in respect of goods shipped on a vessel which at the time of tender the vendor knows to have been totally lost? . . .

I conceive that the essential feature of an ordinary cif contract as compared with an ordinary contract for the sale of goods rests in the fact that performance of the bargain is to be fulfilled by delivery of documents and not by the actual physical delivery of goods by the vendor. All that the buyer can call for is delivery of the customary documents. This represents the measure of the buyer's right and the extent of the vendor's duty. The buyer cannot refuse the documents and ask for the actual goods, nor can the vendor withhold the documents and tender the goods they represent. The position is stated with weight and clearness in the treatise on charterparties by Scrutton LJ, 8th edn, p 167, in the notes to article 59 as follows: 'The best way of approaching the consideration of all questions on cif sales is to realise that this form of the sale of goods is one to be performed by the delivery of documents representing the goods—ie, of documents giving the right to have the goods delivered or the possible right, if they are lost or damaged, of recovering their value from the shipowner or from underwriters. It results from this that various rules in the Sale of Goods Act 1893, which is primarily drafted in relation to the sale and delivery of goods on land, can only be applied to cif sales mutatis mutandis. And there may be cases in which the buyer must pay the full price for delivery of the documents, though he can get nothing out of them, and though in any intelligible sense no property in the goods can ever pass to him—ie, if the goods have been lost by a peril excepted by the bill of lading, and by a peril not insured by the policy, the bill of lading and the policy yet being in the proper commercial form called for by the contract.'

In *Arnhold Karberg &Co v Blythe, Green, Jourdain & Co* [below], Scrutton LJ, when a judge of first instance, described a cif contract as being a sale of documents relating to goods and not a sale of goods. But when the Court of Appeal considered that case Bankes LJ and Warrington LJ commented on the language of Scrutton J and indicated their view that a cif contract is a contract for the sale of goods to be performed by the delivery of documents. But I respectfully venture to think that the difference is one of phrase only. For in reality, as I have said, the obligation of the vendor is to deliver documents rather than goods—to transfer symbols rather than the physical property represented thereby. If the vendor fulfils his contract by shipping the appropriate goods in the appropriate manner under a proper contract of carriage, and if he also obtains the proper documents for tender to the purchaser, I am unable to see how the rights or duties of either party are affected by the loss of ship or goods, or by knowledge of such loss by the vendor, prior to actual tender of the documents. If the ship be lost prior to tender but without the knowledge of the seller it was, I assume, always clear that he could make an effective proffer of the documents to the buyer. In my opinion it is also clear that he can make an effective tender even though he possess at the time of tender actual knowledge of the loss of the ship or goods. For the purchaser in case of loss will get the documents he bargained for, and if the policy be that required by the contract, and if the loss be covered thereby, he will secure the insurance moneys. The contingency of loss is within and not outside the contemplation of the parties to a cif contract. I therefore hold that the plaintiffs were not entitled to reject the tender of documents in the present case upon the ground that the *Algonquin* had, to the knowledge of the defendants, sunk prior to the tender of documents. This view will simplify the performance of cif contracts and prevent delay either through doubts as to the loss of ship or goods or through difficult questions with regard to the knowledge or suspicion of a vendor as to the actual occurrence of a loss.

NOTE

In this case the appropriation took place before the goods were lost, when the seller shipped the particular goods which were to answer the contract. A more difficult question arises where the seller appropriates to the contract goods which have been shipped some time previously and which have since been lost: is the buyer bound to accept the documents? The question is not free from difficulty, but it is generally accepted that, at least in the case where the seller *knows* that the goods are lost, this would not be an effective appropriation.

Arnhold Karberg & Co v Blythe, Green, Jourdain & Co
[1916] 1 KB 495, Court of Appeal

In this case it was held that the documents tendered under a CIF contract must be valid and effective at the time of tender: it is not sufficient that they were valid when issued. Blythe & Co had contracted to buy Chinese horse beans CIF Naples. Beans were duly shipped in July 1914 aboard a German ship, the *Gernis*; but before the documents were due to be tendered war was declared against Germany, with the consequence that the contract of carriage contained in the bill of lading became void for illegality. The Court of Appeal, affirming Scrutton J, held that the buyers were entitled to reject this bill.

Bankes LJ: We have had in this case a very full and interesting discussion on the question of the effect of the outbreak of war upon certain cif contracts entered into before the outbreak of war….In my opinion the answer to the question which the Court has to decide is to be found on the face of the contracts, and upon consideration of what the terms of those contracts provide. The contract on the part of the sellers is a contract for the sale of goods whereby the sellers also undertake, inter alia, to enter into a contract of affreightment to the appointed destination, which contract will be evidenced by the bill of lading, and secondly to take out a policy or policies of insurance upon the terms current in the trade, but which policy or policies were not in this case to include war risks. On the buyers' part they undertook to pay net cash in London in exchange for the bill or bills of lading and policies of insurance, either on arrival of the goods at the port of discharge, or at the expiration of three months from the date of the bills of lading should the goods not sooner arrive, or on the posting of the vessel at Lloyd's as a total loss. In any case, however, the payment is to be in exchange for the bill or bills of lading and policy or policies of insurance. What is the meaning of the buyer's contract thus expressed, that he is to pay in exchange for a bill of lading? In my opinion it means what it says, that in exchange for the price he is to receive a bill of lading which is still a subsisting contract of affreightment of the goods to the port of destination, and a policy or policies of insurance which is, or are still, a subsisting contract, or subsisting contracts, of insurance. It is said that this construction, which seems to me so obviously the natural construction, ignores the fact that in a contract of this kind certain risks fall upon the buyer. I quite accept the contention that certain risks do fall upon the buyer. For instance, in the present cases all war risks fell on the buyer, as the parties have agreed that the seller shall be under no obligation to obtain policies covering war risks. I agree also that the condition of the goods at the time of the tender of the shipping documents is not material, nor is the value of the documents at the time of tender material. In all such matters the risk is on the buyer. He may be obliged to pay for goods although they may be at the bottom of the sea, or although through some unforeseen circumstance they may never arrive, or although they may have been lost owing to some cause not covered by the agreed form of policy. All these risks, however, are risks affecting the goods. In effect the contention of the appellants appears to me to be a contention that one of the risks undertaken by the buyer is a risk affecting his contract, and not the goods the subject-matter of the contract. I cannot agree with this view. It appears to me that the question of the construction of the contract must depend upon the language used, and not upon any such considerations as these. In the present case it is not disputed that the outbreak of war dissolved the contract of affreightment, and that so far as any further prosecution of the voyage was concerned the bill of lading was no longer an effective document. Under those circumstances, in my opinion that bill of lading was not a bill of lading within the meaning of the contract in respect of which the seller was under an obligation to pay cash in exchange.

Scrutton J in his judgment has used one expression with which I do not agree. The expression is the one in which he says that 'the key to many of the difficulties arising in cif contracts is to keep firmly in mind the cardinal distinction that a cif sale is not a sale of goods, but a sale of documents relating to goods.' I am not able to agree with that view of the contract, that it is a sale of documents relating to goods. I prefer to look upon it as a contract for the sale of goods to be performed by the delivery of documents, and what those documents are must depend upon the terms of the contract itself.

[Swinfen Eady and Warrington LJJ delivered concurring judgments.]

Hansson v Hamel & Horley Ltd
[1922] 2 AC 36, House of Lords

Hansson agreed to sell 350 tons of Norwegian cod guano to Hamel & Horley CIF Kobe or Yokohama. Since there were no ships running directly from Norway to these Japanese ports, the guano was sent on a local ship, the *Kiev*, from Braatvag in Norway to Hamburg and there transshipped to the *Atlas Maru* for the ocean voyage to Japan. After the *Atlas Maru* had sailed, the seller tendered to the buyers in purported performance of his contract a bill of lading, which related only to the 'ocean' leg of the transport. The buyers were held entitled to insist on 'continuous documentary cover', ie documentary evidence of a contract or contracts of carriage covering both legs of the journey and the period of transshipment, and to reject this tender.

Lord Sumner: A cf and i [CIF] seller, as has often been pointed out, has to cover the buyer by procuring and tendering documents which will be available for his protection from shipment to destination, and I think that this ocean bill of lading afforded the buyer no protection in regard to the interval of thirteen days which elapsed between the dates of the two bills of lading and presumably between the departure from Braatvag and the arrival at Hamburg....

When documents are to be taken up the buyer is entitled to documents which substantially confer protective rights throughout. He is not buying a litigation, as Lord Trevethin (then A T Lawrence J) says in the *General Trading Co's Case* ((1911)16 Com Cas 95, 101). These documents have to be handled by banks, they have to be taken to be such as can be retendered to sub-purchasers, and it is essential that they should so conform to the accustomed shipping documents as to be reasonably and readily fit to pass current in commerce. I am quite sure that, under the circumstances of this case, this ocean bill of lading does not satisfy these conditions. It bears notice of its insufficiency and ambiguity on its face: for, though called a through bill of lading, it is not really so. It is the contract of the subsequent carrier only, without any complementary promises to bind the prior carriers in the through transit.... As things stood, the buyer was plainly left with a considerable lacuna in the documentary cover to which the contract entitled him....

[Lords Buckmaster, Atkinson, Wrenbury and Carson concurred.]

Kwei Tek Chao v British Traders & Shippers Ltd
[1954] 2 QB 459, Queen's Bench Division

(See the extract cited above, p 346. This case confirms that the buyer has two rights to reject: he may refuse to take up the documents if they are not in conformity with the contract, and he may reject the goods even after having accepted the documents, if he later discovers a breach on the seller's part.)

Berger & Co Inc v Gill & Duffus SA
[1984] AC 382, House of Lords

Bergers contracted to sell to Gill & Duffus 500 tonnes of Argentine bolita beans CIF Le Havre. The contract provided for payment to be made against shipping documents, and also that a certificate given by independent assessors (GSC) as to the quality of the beans at the port of discharge should be final. The ship first unloaded only 445 tonnes at Le Havre, and overcarried the remaining 55 tonnes to Rotterdam. This part of the consignment reached Le Havre some two weeks later. Meantime, the buyers twice rejected the documents, on grounds relating to the certificate of quality as regards the 445 tonnes which the House of Lords held to be unfounded. The buyers were accordingly guilty of a repudiatory breach which, it was held, discharged the sellers from their obligation to deliver the 55 tonnes and debarred the buyers from any right that they might have had to reject the goods. In consequence, the buyers were held liable in damages for non-acceptance in respect of the entire 500 tonnes.

Lord Diplock: In the instant case it has never been contended that the actual shipping documents tendered by the sellers to the buyers on 22 March 1977 and re-tendered on 30 March did not relate to the whole quantity of 500 tonnes or did not upon the face of them conform to the terms of the cif contract of 22 December 1976. That being so it is, in my view, a legal characteristic of a cif contract so well established in English law as to be beyond the realm of controversy that the refusal by the buyer under such a contract to pay to the seller, or to a banker nominated in the contract if the contract so provides, the purchase price upon presentation at the place stipulated in the contract, of shipping documents which on their face conform to those called for by the contract, constitutes a fundamental breach of contract, which the seller is entitled to elect to treat as rescinding the contract and relieving him of any obligation to continue to perform any of his own primary obligations under it; or, to use the terminology of the Sale of Goods Act 1893, 'to treat the contract as repudiated.' So far as concerns the instant case the relevant primary obligation of the sellers of which they were relieved, was any further obligation to deliver to the buyers any of the goods that were the subject matter of the contract.

That a refusal by the buyer to accept the tender of shipping documents which on the face of them conform to the requirements of a cif contract and upon such acceptance to pay the contract price amounts to a breach of condition (in the meaning given to that expression in the Sale of Goods Act 1893) has been taken for granted so universally by English courts as not to have attracted any subsequent positive exposition worthy of citation, ever since Lord Cairns put it thus in *Shepherd v Harrison* (1871) LR 5 HL 116, 132, a case where payment was to be by acceptance of a documentary bill of exchange.

> I hold it to be perfectly clear that when a cargo comes in this way, protected by a bill of lading and a bill of exchange, it is the duty of those to whom the bill of lading and the bill of exchange are transmitted in a letter, *either 'to approbate or to reprobate' entirely and completely, then and there.*

Recognition of the principle so stated (to which I have myself supplied the emphasis) is implicit in all judgments dealing with bankers' confirmed credits as a mode of payment including the most recent judgments of this House....

In the instant case the sellers did elect to treat the contract as repudiated on 1 April 1977. They then ceased to be under any contractual obligation to deliver to the buyers any 'Argentine bolita beans—1974 crop.' The buyers on the other hand became liable to the sellers in damages for breach of contract. Prima facie the measure of such damages would be the difference between the contract price of the 500 tonnes of beans that were the subject matter of the contract and the price obtainable on the market for the documents representing the goods at date of the acceptance of the repudiation. Such prima facie measure might, however, fall to be reduced by any sum which the buyers could establish they would have been entitled to set up in diminution of the contract price by reason of a breach of warranty as to description or quality of the goods represented by the shipping documents that had been actually shipped by the sellers if those goods had in fact been delivered to them....

I turn now to analyse what it was that went wrong with the case in the Court of Appeal. Here it was recognised that the cif contract was a single contract for a consignment of 500 tonnes. What appears to have been wholly overlooked is that the sellers, on 1 April 1977, had in fact elected, as they were entitled to do, to treat the buyers' rejection of the shipping documents as a repudiatory breach that had brought to an end their primary obligation under the contract to deliver any goods at all to the buyers. No mention of this election on the sellers' part is to be found in any of the judgments. Robert Goff LJ, in his dissenting judgment, does say that on rejection of the documents by the buyers 'the sellers became entitled to bring the contract [sc. for the 500 tonnes] to an end,' but there is nothing to indicate that his attention was directed to the fact that the sellers had acted on that entitlement and *had* brought the contract to an end.

My Lords, it is trite law for which I do not find it necessary to refer to any other authority than the judgment of Devlin J in *Kwei Tele Chao v British Traders and Shippers Ltd* [above], that when a buyer under a cif contract accepts shipping documents which transfer the property in the goods to him, the property in the goods that he obtains is subject to the condition subsequent that it will revest in the seller if upon examination of the goods themselves upon arrival the buyer finds them to be not in accordance with the contract in some respect which would entitle him to reject them, and he does in fact reject them. But this is because the cif contract remains on foot; and being a contract for the sale of goods, the buyer has the right under s 35 of the Sale of Goods Act 1893 to reject the goods themselves for non-conformity with the contract and retains this right until he has had a reasonable opportunity of examining the goods after they have been delivered.

My Lords, it is not necessary in the instant case to consider whether a similar right to reject the goods upon delivery is retained by a buyer who, in breach of contract, has refused to accept the shipping documents when duly presented in accordance with the provisions of the contract, and the seller has *not* elected to treat such refusal as a repudiatory breach bringing all further primary obligations on his part under the contract to an end....

Whatever legal problems might be presented by a situation resulting from a seller's failure to treat the buyer's rejection of conforming shipping documents as bringing the contract to an end, it would, in my view, be contrary to the basic concepts of the law of contract that deal with the different remedies for different categories of breach, if a seller of goods who had elected to treat the buyer's breach of a condition of the contract, or a fundamental breach of an innominate term, as bringing to an end his own further primary obligations under the contract (or in the terminology of the Sale of Goods Act 1893 'to treat the contract as repudiated') continued to be under any legal obligation to deliver to the buyer any goods, if the election so to treat the buyer's breach were made before the actual goods had been delivered to him. As already mentioned, if the seller sued the buyer for damages for his failure to pay the price of the goods against tender of conforming shipping documents, the buyer, if he could prove that the seller would not have been able to deliver goods under those shipping documents that conformed with the contract of sale, would be able to displace the prima facie measure of damages by an amount by which the value of the goods was reduced below the contract price by that disconformity; but this goes to a quantum of damages alone....

Given the absence of any suggestion of difference in quality between the 55 tonnes and the 445 [tonnes] that GSC had certified as equal to the sealed sample by reference to which the cif contract was made, the buyers lacked the finding of fact essential to their defence in part to the sellers' claim in damages, that on balance of probabilities GSC would not have issued a similar certificate in respect of the 55 tonnes....

[His Lordship accordingly held that the buyers were liable in damages for non-acceptance of the whole 500 tonnes, reckoned by reference to the market price at the relevant date.]

[Lords Keith of Kinkel, Roskill, Brandon of Oakbrook and Templeman concurred.]

QUESTION

The new ss 15A and 30(2A) of the Act state that a buyer who is not a consumer may not reject the goods on the grounds (respectively) that they do not conform with their contract description or that the wrong quantity has been delivered, where the breach is so slight that it would be unreasonable for him to reject. Suppose that there is such a breach in a CIF contract as regards (a) the goods as described in the documents, or alternatively (b) the goods themselves on arrival at their destination: should the buyer be able to reject the documents or the goods?

(b) Variants of the CIF contract

The basic principles applicable to a CIF contract apply with the necessary modifications to contracts where the buyer agrees to pay, in addition to cost, insurance and freight, for some extra items such as commission, exchange and interest (CIF & C, etc, referred to in the list above, p 492). The same is true of the C & F contract, where it is the buyer rather than the seller who has the responsibility of arranging the insurance cover. (One reason for this may be that the laws of the buyer's country require him to take out insurance with a local insurer, or possibly with a state-owned insurance agency, in order to save foreign exchange.) It is more likely that a C & F contract will be one which contemplates that the seller is an exporter who will procure and despatch the goods, rather than one which can be fulfilled by buying goods already afloat, since in the latter case there will be insurance cover in place which it assumed the buyer will take over.

6 EX SHIP OR 'ARRIVAL' CONTRACTS

Under a contract of this description, the buyer is bound to pay the price only if actual delivery of the goods is made to him at the port of delivery, the seller bearing all costs up to but not including unloading costs and import duties. Property and risk will pass with delivery of possession. It is not sufficient that the seller tenders a valid set of shipping documents: the buyer is entitled to the goods, not just the documents; and if the seller cannot procure the delivery of the goods from the ship, he has not fulfilled his obligations.

Comptoir d'Achat et de Vente du Boerenbond Beige S/A v Luis de Ridder Ltda, The Julia
[1949] AC 293, House of Lords

Rye was sold to a Belgian company under a contract expressed to be on terms 'CIF Antwerp', but which was held to be an 'arrival' contract. While the goods were at sea, the buyer paid the price in exchange for documents which included a delivery order, but the ship was prevented from unloading at Antwerp when the Germans invaded Belgium. The goods were unloaded at Lisbon instead. The buyers claimed their money back, alleging a total failure of consideration; the sellers argued in reply that the delivery of the documents was at least part performance, which was enough to defeat the buyer's claim. It was held that since the contract, as an 'arrival' contract, required actual delivery to be made at Antwerp, the consideration had totally failed.

Lord Porter: My Lords, this is an appeal [from] a judgment of the Court of Appeal affirming by a majority the judgment of Morris J who upheld an award of an umpire stated in the form of a special case under the Arbitration Acts 1889 to 1934. The arbitration arose out of a contract for the sale of rye by the respondents (the sellers) to the appellants (the buyers). The buyers, who were the claimants in the arbitration, asked for the refund of the purchase price paid by them under the contract on the ground that the consideration had wholly failed. The question for your Lordships' consideration is whether there was such a total failure of consideration.

The learned judge in agreement with the umpire, as I understand him, regarded the contract as a cif contract modified to some extent, but not altered in its essential characteristics. The buyers had, in his view, entered into a contract for the purchase of documents or, more accurately, for the purchase of a parcel of rye, the fulfilment of which was to be implemented by the handing over of documents. The documents, he considered, might be varied at the option of the sellers, who would fulfil their contract if they chose to tender a delivery order instead of a bill of lading, and a certificate instead of a policy of insurance. Even the stringency of these obligations he regarded as reduced by the practice of the parties with the result that delivery order meant an instruction to their own agents (countersigned, it is true, by those agents) and a certificate of insurance which was never tendered to or held on behalf or at the disposal of the buyers. The delivery order, Morris J considered, 'doubtless possessed commercial value.' In other words, the buyers were purchasers of documents and had received that for which they stipulated, ie, the usual delivery order and a certificate of insurance which would compel or incite the sellers to recover any loss from underwriters and pay it over to the buyers.

My Lords, the obligations imposed upon a seller under a cif contract are well known, and in the ordinary case include the tender of a bill of lading covering the goods contracted to be sold and no others, coupled with an insurance policy in the normal form and accompanied by an invoice which shows the price and, as in this case, usually contains a deduction of the freight which the buyer pays before delivery at the port of discharge. Against tender of these documents the purchaser must pay the price. In such a case the property may pass either on shipment or on tender, the risk generally passes on shipment or as from shipment, but possession does not pass until the documents which represent the goods are handed over in exchange for the price. In the result the buyer after receipt of the documents can claim against the ship for breach of the contract of carriage and against the underwriter for any loss covered by the policy. The strict form of cif contract may, however, be modified: a provision that a delivery order may be substituted for a bill of lading or a certificate of insurance for a policy would not, I think, make the contract concluded upon something other than cif terms, but in deciding whether it comes within that category or not all the permutations and combinations of provision and circumstance must be taken into consideration. Not every contract which is expressed to be a cif contract is such. . . . In the present case therefore it is not as if a usual form of delivery order had been given and accepted or an insurance certificate covering the parcel was in the hands of Van Bree as agents for the buyers, nor can a solution be found in the mere designation of the contract as cif. . . . The true effect of all its terms must be taken into account, though, of course, the description cif must not be neglected. It is true, no doubt, to say that some steps had been taken towards the performance of this contract, eg, the goods had been shipped, an invoice sent, the customary so-called delivery order had been transmitted and that delivery order amongst its provisions contained a declaration by the sellers' agents, Belgian Grain and Produce Co Ltd that they gave a share of the present delivery order of $4,973 in a certificate of insurance. But the taking of steps towards performance is not necessarily a part performance of a contract. The question is whether the purchaser has got what he is entitled to in return for the price. Of course, if the buyers paid the sum claimed in order to obtain the delivery order and the share purported to be given by it in the certificate of insurance, the contract would have been performed in part at least, but I do not so construe the contract, even when illuminated by the practice adopted by the parties. That practice seems to me rather to show that the payment was not made for the documents but as an advance payment for a contract afterwards to be performed. With all due respect to the learned judge and the Master of the Rolls, I can see no sufficient reason for supposing . . . that the delivery order had some commercial value. . . . There was no evidence of commercial value and the document itself was merely an instruction by one agent of the sellers to another. . . . The document appears to me to be no more than an indication that a promise already made by the sellers would be carried out in due course, but in no way increases their obligations or adds to the security of the buyers.

My Lords, the object and the result of a cif contract is to enable sellers and buyers to deal with cargoes or parcels afloat and to transfer them freely from hand to hand by giving constructive possession of the goods which are being dealt with. Undoubtedly the practice of shipping and insuring produce in bulk is to make the process more difficult, but a ship's delivery order and a certificate of insurance transferred to or held for a buyer still leaves it possible for some, though less satisfactory, dealing with the goods whilst at sea to take place. The practice adopted between buyers and sellers in the present case renders such dealing well nigh impossible. The buyer gets neither property nor possession until the goods are delivered to him at Antwerp, and the certificate of insurance, if it enures to his benefit at all, except on the journey from ship to warehouse, has never been held for or delivered to him. . . .

The vital question in the present case, as I see it, is whether the buyers paid for the documents as representing the goods or for the delivery of the goods themselves. The time and place of payment are elements to be considered but by no means conclusive of the question: such considerations may, on the one hand, indicate a payment in advance or, on the other, they may show a payment postponed until the arrival of the ship, though the property in the goods or the risk have passed to the buyer whilst the goods are still at sea, as in *Castle v Playford* [above, p 332]. But the whole circumstances have to be looked at and where, as, in my opinion, is the case here, no further security beyond that contained in the original contract passed to the buyers as a result of payment, where the property and possession both remained in the sellers until delivery in Antwerp, where the sellers were to pay for deficiency in bill of lading weight, guaranteed condition on arrival and made themselves responsible for all averages, the true view, I think, is that it is not a cif contract even in a modified form but a contract to deliver at Antwerp. Nor do I think it matters that payment is said to be not only on presentation but 'in exchange for' documents. There are many ways of carrying out the contract to which that expression would apply, but in truth whether the payment is described as made on presentation of or in exchange for a document, the document was not a fulfilment or even a partial fulfilment of the contract: it was but a step on the way. What the buyers wanted was delivery of the goods in Antwerp. What the sellers wanted was payment of the price before that date, and the delivery of the documents furnished the date for payment, but had no effect on the property or possession of the goods or the buyers' rights against the sellers. If this be the true view there was plainly a frustration of the adventure—indeed the sellers admit so much in their pleading—and no part performance and the consideration had wholly failed. The buyers are accordingly entitled to recover the money which they have paid. . . .

[Lords Simonds, du Parcq, Normand and MacDermott delivered concurring opinions.]

7 CONTRACTS FOR THE INTERNATIONAL SALE OF GOODS SHIPPED IN BULK

We saw in the classic ruling in *Re Wait* (above, p 266) that under the traditional rules of sale of goods law, as codified in s 16 of the Act, no property in goods could pass until the contract goods had been ascertained. Normally, in an export-sale context, this would be by some act of appropriation: in *Re Wait,* the physical separation of the buyer's grain after the ship had docked in this country. At common law, *possession* also cannot exist in an un-ascertained part of a larger bulk. In consequence, many problems are likely to arise in the case of goods shipped in bulk—eg where a seller ships 10,000 tonnes as a complete cargo and then contracts to sell 1000 tonnes to each of ten separate purchasers. Even if the carrier (as is common) issues multiple bills of lading in respect of the goods (eg ten bills each relating to 1000 tonnes), the delivery of such a bill to a buyer is not effective, in itself, to pass rights of ownership or possession to him. He would have no claim at common law or in equity to the goods in the event of the seller's insolvency (*Re Wait*), no right to sue a third party in tort (*The Aliakmon,* above, p 297), and he had no rights against the carrier either at common law or under the Bills of Lading Act 1855. (However, the Carriage of Goods by Sea Act 1992 now does give him *contractual* rights against the carrier in such a case.) The position is certainly no more favourable if the buyer receives a document of lower standing than a bill of lading, such as a ship's waybill or delivery order (although, once again, the Act of 1992 has given the buyer rights against the carrier which can be exercised by the holder of such a document). It follows that, apart from statute, none of the consequences normally associated with the transfer of a bill of lading (and in particular the passing of property and the right to possession) apply where the goods in question form part of a larger bulk and remain unappropriated. This is so whether the contract of sale is made on FOB, CIF or any other terms.

However, the Sale of Goods (Amendment) Act 1995 has changed the position—but only where the buyer has paid the seller all or part of the contract price. To the extent that he has done this, he now becomes a co-owner with the seller (and/or other buyers) of the entire bulk. So if the first buyer, B1, has paid the whole price of his 1000 tonnes, he becomes a one-tenth part-owner of the cargo, and if B2 has paid half of his contract price, he acquires a one-twentieth share, and so on. Such buyers now have proprietary rights which protect them in the event of the seller's bankruptcy and which entitle them to sue wrongdoers in tort, and their relationship vis-à-vis the seller and other buyers is governed by the new ss 20A and 20B. But in so far as buyers have not paid all or any part of the price, the pre-1995 rules continue to apply.

QUESTION

Suppose that the 1995 amendment had been in force when the events of *The Julia* occurred. Would this have affected (a) the legal position, (b) the decision?

8 CONTRACTS OF SALE INVOLVING ROAD, RAIL, AND/OR AIR TRANSPORT

There is no equivalent to the bill of lading in a contract for the sale of goods involving air transport. The whole procedure happens too quickly for there to be any need to deal with the goods while they are in transit, or for either party's bank to wish to have security of a documentary kind over the goods during this period. Instead, an 'air waybill' is issued, which is usually made out in the name of the buyer as consignee. The usual terms on which the goods are carried are 'FOB airport'. Under such a contract, the seller's responsibilities will cease when the goods are delivered to the air carrier or his agent at the exporting airport. Various international conventions (principally the Warsaw Convention of 1929, as amended) apply to sales involving air transport, and have been given the force of law within the UK by the Carriage by Air Act 1961 and other legislation.

The CIM (*Convention internationale concernant le transport de merchandises par chemin de fer*—part of COTIF, the *Convention Relative aux Transports Internationaux Ferroriaires*) and CMR (*Convention relative au contrat de transport international de merchandises par route*) are international Conventions which deal respectively with the rail and road transport of goods across frontiers. (On the CIM and CMR, see MA Clarke *International Carriage of Goods by Road: CMR* (4th edn, 2000); A Messent and DA Glass, *Hill and Messent CMR: Contracts for the International Carriage of Goods by Road* (3rd edn, 2000).) The United Kingdom is a party to both Conventions (and, in addition, COTIF has become part of the domestic law under the Railways (Convention on International Carriage by Rail) Regulations 2005, SI 2005/2092). These Conventions apply even where the goods are handled by successive carriers. The position is more complicated when multimodal transport is involved, as is common in the container transport business. Here, it is normal for the principal contract of carriage to be made with a single firm called a 'combined transport operator', which assumes overall responsibility and subcontracts to others for all or some of the separate parts of the journey. The contract is evidenced by a 'combined transport document', which necessarily lacks many of the advantages that are accorded to a bill of lading. (For an example, see below, p 1245.) The International Chamber of Commerce has worked out a number of standard forms of contract which are appropriate in a variety of circumstances. (These do not, of course, have the force of law but apply only if contractually adopted by the parties.) As a result, although the practical difficulties associated with multimodal transport have largely been overcome, at least as between the immediate parties, the legal problems arising from questions of privity of contract and the conflict of laws are potentially very complex. The position, especially as regards risk, is likely to be all the worse when a container carries a mixed load (LFL, ie less than a full load), and so cannot be sealed up by the seller before he parts with possession. For a discussion of a number of the problems arising from multi-modal transport, see D Faber [1996] 1 LMCLQ 503.

9 PAYMENT IN INTERNATIONAL SALES TRANSACTIONS

In earlier times, payment in international contracts of sale was commonly effected by bill of exchange: the seller would draw a bill on the buyer for the price and transmit it and the bill of lading to him together (a 'documentary bill': see below, p 847); and the understanding was that the buyer would take up the bill of lading only if he accepted the bill of exchange or honoured it by payment (see Sale of Goods Act 1979, s 19(3)). This method has been superseded by modern practices and is now little used. Instead, it will usually be a term of the contract that the buyer will procure the opening of a confirmed letter of credit in the seller's favour before the goods are shipped (a requirement which has been construed as a condition of the contract: *Trans Trust SPRL v Danubian Trading Co Ltd* [1952] 2 QB 297).

Payment by banker's commercial letter of credit is considered in detail below, in Chapter 21. In practice, the working of the system depends upon two fundamental rules. The first is the doctrine of strict compliance: the bank is entitled to reject the shipping documents if not in strict conformity with the contract: *Equitable Trust Co of New York v Dawson Partners Ltd* (below, p 858); *JHRayner & Co Ltd v Hambro's Bank Ltd* (below, p 859). The second is the autonomy of the credit: the bank must pay against the documents if they are in order, regardless of any later instructions from the buyer, his bankruptcy, suspicions regarding the validity of the underlying sale transaction, etc (*Urquhart Lindsay & Co Ltd v Eastern Bank Ltd* [1922] 1 KB 318; *Hamzeh Malas & Sons v British Imex Industries Ltd* (below, p 865)).

Current trends

The classic export-sale transactions described in this chapter and the legislation and case-law associated with them are ideally suited to contracts dealing with contracts for the sale of bulk commodities, such as grain and minerals, which are to be despatched by sea carriage on a voyage of some distance. They are not always so suitable for various types of sales contract which are in common use today. We have seen for instance, that they are inappropriate to meet the cases where the goods are to be carried by air. Ships, too, are faster than they used to be and distances (eg across the channel) sometimes so short that there is insufficient time to put together all the documentation which a typical sale on CIF terms requires—especially since, with increased government regulation, many more documents are now required for a commercial shipment than was the case a few decades ago. Cargoes often reach their destination well before the bill of lading arrives, even if it is sent by airmail. So, in order to meet these problems and to speed the turnaround of ships, some of the older practices have been discarded. For instance, 'straight' bills of lading or sea waybills (documents made out in the name of the consignee) and freight forwarders' receipts are frequently preferred to bills of lading because, although they offer less legal protection, the consignee can take delivery of the goods simply on proof of identity without having to produce physically the relevant document. (In turn, as we have seen with the Carriage of Goods by Sea Act 1992, legislation in many countries now extends some of the advantages of the bill of lading to these documents.) Again, the containerisation of goods and, with it, the use of multimodal forms of transport means that much of the traditional forms of export-sale contract are inappropriate.

The use of documents like sea waybills rather than bills of lading has the added advantage that they can be transmitted electronically, since nothing turns on the possession of the actual piece of paper—indeed, the waybill may never exist in paper form. Payment by electronic means is, of course, already well established (see Chapter 18). The use of computerised systems and electronic communications facilitates the co-ordination of manufacturing, invoicing, despatch, warehousing, stock control and many other aspects of commerce. And so moves are already under way to eliminate the traditional reliance on paper in international sales. Many countries allow customs declarations to be made by means of electronic messages. The one area of difficulty is in regard to the bill of lading. So far, efforts to give these paperless procedures attributes which match the negotiability of the bill of lading have met with only partial success. In the oil transportation industry, an experimental system (SeaDocs) using a third party as a central depositary-custodian of the original bill and a computerised record of subsequent transactions was introduced in 1986. (The parties identified themselves by codes similar to bank-card pin-numbers.) However, it did not attract enough subscribers and lasted only a short time. A more sophisticated system was approved by the Comité Maritime International (CMI) in 1990. This involved the carrier itself acting as the registry with which transactions relating to the goods were recorded, with each deal being recorded by a coded 'private key'. The most successful venture to date is known by the acronym 'Bolero' (Bill of Lading Electronic Registry Organisation) which, like SeaDocs, uses a central title registry where the terms of the contract of carriage and the rights of consignors, consignees and intermediate parties are securely recorded, and instructions regarding the transfer of ownership, etc are given by the parties concerned using agreed authentication procedures. A 'Bolero bill of lading' in paperless form aims to replicate as nearly as possible the characteristics of a traditional bill of lading. The main obstacle to the use of a system of this sort is that most legislation, and all the relevant international treaties, continue to assume the existence of a bill of lading in paper form, and so the new procedures can only be put in place by private contractual arrangements.

Section 1(5) of the Carriage of Goods by Sea Act 1992 paves the way for an extension of the provisions of that Act to cases where electronic means are used in place of documents of carriage: the Secretary of State is empowered to make regulations adapting the statute accordingly.

On the move towards paperless trading, see B Kozolchyk in R Cranston and RM Goode (eds) *Commercial and Consumer Law* (1993), Ch 9, D Faber [1996] LMCLQ 232; C Pejovic 'Documents of Title in Carriage of Goods by Sea' [2001] JBL 461 and MA Clarke 'Transport documents: their transferability as documents of title; electronic documents' [2002] LMCLQ 356.

PART V

BILLS OF EXCHANGE AND BANKING

CHAPTER 15

NEGOTIABLE INSTRUMENTS

1 INTRODUCTION[1]

As you enter the world of negotiable instruments you could be forgiven for thinking that you are travelling back in time. The modern world is dominated by the microchip and instantaneous telecommunication networks which have allowed the development of electronic payment systems capable of transferring vast sums around the globe at the touch of a button. Negotiable instruments are at the other end of the spectrum. The tangible nature of the instrument (a piece of paper) dominates the intangible right to payment embodied in the instrument. Transfer of the right to payment requires physical delivery of the instrument itself. This can be a slow and cumbersome process. Negotiable instruments seem to be redolent of a bygone age.

However, negotiable instruments merit our attention for two important reasons. First, they are still used to a significant degree as a method of making payment in the commercial world, especially in the area of international trade (see below, Chapter 21). Bills of exchange, one type of negotiable instrument, are frequently used where a seller of goods allows his overseas buyer a period of credit but needs access to funds in the interim. The seller draws a bill of exchange in his own favour on the buyer or, more usually, on a bank that has undertaken to pay under the terms of a documentary credit. As a credit period has been agreed, the bill will be payable at a future date, eg 90 or 180 days after sight. The seller then presents the bill for acceptance by the buyer or, in the case of a documentary credit transaction, by the bank. Once the bill has been accepted, the seller does not have to wait until it matures to receive funds. He can take advantage of the negotiable character of the bill and discount (sell) it to his own bank for an immediate (but reduced) cash payment. The seller's own bank is left to collect payment from the buyer, or other party that has accepted liability, on maturity of the instrument. In certain cases, the seller will obtain an advance on the bill from

---

[1] See generally, J James *Richardson's Guide to Negotiable Instruments* (8th edn, 1991); R Bradgate *Commercial Law* (3rd edn, 2000), Chs 28–30; RM Goode *Commercial Law* (3rd edn, 2004), Part 3. For detailed analysis, see AG Guest *Chalmers and Guest on Bills of Exchange, Cheques and Promissory Notes* (16th edn, 2005); N Elliott, J Odgers and JM Phillips *Byles on Bills of Exchange and Cheques* (28th edn, 2007). J Barnard Byles, who wrote the first edition of his treatise of the law of bills of exchange in 1829, was responsible for what may be the only bills and notes joke. He is said to have named his horse 'Bills' so that as he rode up people could say 'Here comes Byles on Bills'! (see JS Rogers *The Early History of the Law of Bills and Notes* (1995), p 7). For an outstanding comparative treatment of the subject, see EP Ellinger 'Negotiable Instruments', in U Drobnig (ed) *International Encyclopedia of Comparative Law* Vol IX, Ch 4.

his own bank before acceptance and leave it to the bank to present the bill for acceptance and for payment. The second important reason for examining the law relating to negotiable instruments is because it encapsulates many of the fundamental principles and concepts of commercial law in general.

- Mercantile custom and usage has been, and remains, an important influence in this area. It was, after all, the fact that the common law refused to recognise the transferability of a debt that led commercial men to embody the debt in a chattel (a piece of paper) and render the debt transferable through transfer of the chattel.

- Nowhere is certainty more prized than in the law relating to negotiable instruments. In *Carlos v Fancourt* (1794) 5 Term Rep 482 at 486, Ashhurst J stated that '[c]ertainty is a great object in commercial instruments; and unless they carry their own validity on the face of them, they are not negotiable ...'. This requirement ensures that negotiable instruments are freely negotiable and saleable and it lies at the heart of the definition of a bill of exchange contained in s 3(1) of the Bills of Exchange Act 1882.

- Protection of the bona fide purchaser for value is paramount. It is a fundamental principle of the law relating to negotiable instruments that the bona fide holder for value of a negotiable instrument is able to acquire a better title than that of his transferor. Negotiable instruments represent a major exception to the *nemo dat* rule (see above, Chapter 9, Section 1). The marketability of the instrument is enhanced through the protection afforded to the good faith purchaser.

2 DEFINITION OF A NEGOTIABLE INSTRUMENT

There is no statutory definition of the term 'negotiable instrument'. Any definition must be drawn from the common law. To define the term, the concepts of 'instrument' and 'negotiability' require separate consideration.

(a) Instrument

An instrument is a document which physically embodies a payment obligation so that the possessor of the instrument (following any necessary indorsement in his favour) is presumed to be entitled to claim payment of the money it represents. It has been described by Professor Goode as 'a document of title to money' (RM Goode *Commercial Law* (3rd edn, 2004), p 476) and must be distinguished from a document of title to goods, such as a bill of lading. To be a document of title to money an instrument must contain an undertaking to pay a sum of money (eg as in a promissory note) or an order to another to pay a sum of money to the person giving the order or a third person (eg as in a bill of exchange). Alternatively, the undertaking or order may relate to the delivery of a security for money (*Goodwin v Robarts* (1876) 1 App Cas 476). A document which is primarily a receipt for money, even if coupled with a promise to pay it, is not an instrument (*Akbar Khan v Attar Singh* [1936] 2 All ER 545, PC; applied in *Claydon v Bradley* [1987] 1 All ER 522, CA).

If an instrument is made payable to bearer, or if it is made payable to a specified person or his order and it has been indorsed (ie signed on the back) by or with the authority of that person, it is described as being 'in a deliverable state'. The possessor, otherwise known as the 'holder', of an instrument in a deliverable state is presumed to be entitled to payment of the money due under it. This is because the instrument embodies the contractual right to payment and that right is transferable by mere delivery.

'The Nature of the Negotiable Instrument' by A Barak
(1983) 18 Israel LR 49, pp 53–55, 57–58, 60–63, 65

III. THE NEGOTIABLE INSTRUMENT AS A CHATTEL

(a) Rights on and to the negotiable instrument

In discussing the negotiable instrument one refers not only to rights on it, but also to rights in, or to it. While this is not accurate terminology from a strictly juridical point of view, it does reflect the proprietary character of the negotiable instrument. The negotiable instrument is a physically tangible thing, and just as one speaks of ownership of, or title to, a chair or a car, so one can speak of ownership of a negotiable instrument. . . .

(b) Consequences of the proprietary nature of the negotiable instrument

The negotiable instrument is, then, seen to be a chattel. Its owner has the same powers as the owner of any other property. He can retain possession of it, sell it, transfer it, give it away as a gift, destroy it, or alter it. These actions may, of course, affect the very ownership of the instrument or its value. When the owner of the instrument has possession of it, there is a unity of ownership and possession. This, however, is not essential and the two can equally well be in separate hands. For example, an instrument to the order of A is stolen from him. A remains the owner, but the thief has possession. When possession is unlawfully separated from ownership, the law of conversion comes into operation and gives the owner—who is entitled to immediate possession—the right to demand restitution of the instrument or its value. But, of course, possession can also be separated from ownership lawfully when, for example, the owner delivers it into the custody of another person for safekeeping or as a deposit. . . .

(c) The negotiable instrument as a special kind of chattel

It cannot be denied that the negotiable instrument is unlike other chattels. One does not refer to it as a chattel naturally and as a matter of course. Its proprietary nature is not its most important side, for its inherent value as a chattel is negligible. The real value of the negotiable instrument lies in the obligations it embodies. A legal system in which the proprietary nature of the negotiable instrument is hardly stressed at all is conceivable. It is not absolutely essential to dwell on the instrument's proprietary qualities. Reference to it as a chattel in the common law countries is for the purpose of attaining certain results. Just as a chattel can be transferred from hand to hand, so too can a negotiable instrument be transferred, since it is itself a chattel. However, it embodies an obligation and, by transferring the chattel, one transfers the obligation as well. Thus, it was possible to transfer the obligation embodied in a negotiable instrument at a time when ordinary obligations could not, as a rule, be transferred.

> The common law did not recognize the transferability of a debt, but accepted that the owner of a chattel could sell, pledge or deliver it to someone else at will. If the debt be given the outward appearance of a chattel, why should it not be transferable just as a chattel is? Why should such a debt not be subject to the law of property which allows a chattel to be transferred from hand to hand without difficulty? While the law remained steadfast in its refusal to allow the transfer of debts, men of commerce came to grasp that, by giving a debt the qualities of a chattel, the problem of freely transferring it would be solved. [Sussman, *The Law of Bills of Exchange* (6th edn, 1983), p 4.]

Today, reference to the negotiable instrument as a chattel has further consequences—for example, the possibility of resorting to the law of conversion when the instrument is taken from its owner unlawfully. . . .

IV. THE NEGOTIABLE INSTRUMENT AS AN OBLIGATION

(a) The negotiable instrument as a new and independent obligation

In most cases bills are drawn in the course of commercial transactions between the parties. When A draws a bill to the order of B the reason generally is that A owes B money, either on account of a loan which B has given him, or of goods supplied to him by B. In cases of this kind, the instrument is evidence of the existence of A's liability to B. The obligation does not derive from the instrument itself, but from the initial transaction between the two. However, the instrument is not merely a piece of evidence. A's signature on it creates a new and independent obligation, whereby A is liable to B and to any person to whom B transfers the instrument. This obligation is in addition to—and often even in place of—that deriving from the initial transaction. Accordingly, if a bill, given by A to B as a conditional discharge of the initial transaction, is dishonoured, B has two causes of action: one on the initial transaction between him and A; the other on the obligation created by the instrument itself. Insofar as the former is concerned, the instrument is no more than written evidence. As for the latter, the initial transaction constitutes the consideration. Thus, by virtue of the signatures on it, the negotiable instrument creates a new and independent obligation, completely different from the obligation deriving from the initial transaction. Moreover, the instrument does not only give rise to one single obligation; there are as many obligations as there are signatures on it—some of them primary obligations, some secondary.

(b) The negotiable instrument as a contract

The wording of the Bills of Exchange Ordinance clearly indicates that the obligation on a bill is a contract. This contract, however, is—it will be noted—unilateral, not bilateral. There is no mutual exchange of undertakings and only one party is liable on such a contract; the rules of offer and acceptance do not apply to it. True, the contract on a negotiable instrument is not complete until the instrument is delivered 'in order to give effect thereto'; but delivery is not the same as acceptance of an offer in the law of contract.

Frequently, a negotiable instrument is made within the framework of a bilateral contract. For example, A undertakes to sell goods to B and in consideration B gives A a bill. That is a bilateral contract; but the bill has an existence of its own. Once it has been made, an additional contract arises—that on the bill itself. If B fails to pay the bill, A will generally have two contractual remedies—one based on the bilateral contract, the other on the bill. There is, of course, a close connection between the two contracts: payment of the bill discharges the bilateral contract; failure on the part of A to perform his undertaking under the bilateral contract may provide B with a defence to an action brought on the bill. But this connection must not be allowed to blur the material difference between the two or hide the fact that the bill has a separate existence of its own as a unilateral contract.

(c) Consequences of the contractual nature of the negotiable instrument

Subject to the special rules which follow from the negotiability of the instrument, the obligation on it is just like any other contractual obligation to pay a certain sum of money. Thus, capacity to incur liability as a party to a bill is coextensive with capacity to contract. Events which invalidate contracts generally, also invalidate liability on a bill. Defences available under the general law of contract, such as duress, fraud, failure of consideration and so on, are equally a part of the law of negotiable instruments. It is a well-known fact that the plea of *non est factum,* so common in the law of contract, was first raised in a case concerning a negotiable instrument. The contractual nature of the negotiable instrument is similarly reflected in the application of the doctrine of consideration. A number of legal systems, in which consideration is essential for the creation of contractual liability, make consideration a prerequisite of liability on a negotiable instrument too—since that liability is itself a form of contractual liability. On the other hand, systems in which consideration is not one of the elements of the contract, and which require no more than *causa* for example, are found to forgo the need for consideration and make do with *causa* in the case of liability on a negotiable instrument too.

Since the obligations on a negotiable instrument are contractual obligations, there is nothing to prevent the guarantor known to the general law of contract being used in this connection. And, indeed, the ordinary rules applicable to the relations between guarantor and the person to whom he gives the guarantee do apply in the case of negotiable instruments as well. These obligations are, moreover, themselves divisible into principal and secondary obligations, the latter being by way of guarantee for the performance of the former. Accordingly, the relations between the two are governed by the general rules of guarantee.

Again, the fact that the obligations we are considering are contractual obligations, which—by their very nature—are transferable, means that, in principle, there is no reason why they cannot be transferred from one person to another in accordance with the rules of assignment applicable to ordinary contractual obligations. And, in fact, this is the position in English Law....

(d) The negotiable instrument as a special kind of contract

While the obligation on a negotiable instrument is of a contractual nature, what characterises it is the fact that it is 'negotiable'. Accordingly, apart from being transferable under the general law of contract, it can be transferred in the special manner established by the law merchant—namely, by negotiation....

(b) Negotiability

The holder may not be the 'true owner' of the instrument. The true owner is the person entitled to the property in and possession of the instrument against all others. But the true owner may have lost the instrument, or it may have been stolen from him. The 'holder' of the instrument would be the finder or the thief who is in possession of it (assuming the instrument is in a deliverable state). Figure 1 illustrates how one person can be the 'true owner' and another the 'holder' of a stolen instrument (note that the instrument is in a deliverable state because it is made payable to bearer).

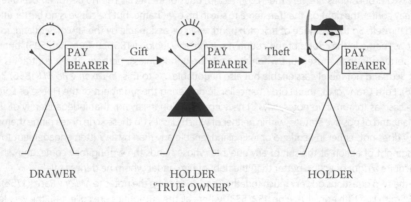

Figure 1 'True owner' and 'holder'

In Figure 1, the true owner has a superior title to the instrument and, relying on the fact that the instrument is a chattel, she can sue the holder in conversion. However, should the instrument reach the hands of a holder who gave value for the instrument, in good faith and without notice of the defect in the title of his transferor, that person takes an indefeasible title to the instrument. The true owner has no claim against him. But the instrument must be a *negotiable* instrument for the bona fide purchaser to take an indefeasible title to it. Figure 2 illustrates how a bona fide purchaser for value (called a 'holder in due course' in the Bills of Exchange Act 1882) may take possession of a stolen instrument and acquire a better title than her transferor.

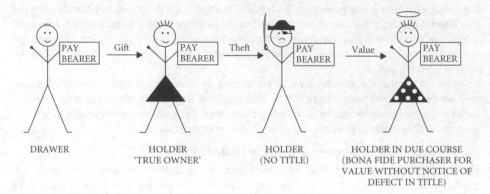

Figure 2 Negotiability

It is its capacity to be acquired free from defects in the title of prior parties which character-ises an instrument as 'negotiable' in the strict sense of the word.

Crouch v Credit Foncier of England
(1873) LR 8 QB 374, Court of Queen's Bench

Blackburn J: In the present case the plaintiff has taken upon himself the burden of establishing both that the property in the debenture passed to him by delivery, and that the right to sue in his own name was transferred to him.

The two propositions are very much connected, but not identical. The holder of an overdue bill or note may confer the right on the transferee to sue in his own name, but he conveys no better title than he had himself. So the assignee of a Scotch bond, which is assignable by the law of Scotland, may sue in his own name in the courts of this country: see *Innes v Dunlop* ((1800) 8 Term Rep 595); but he has not a better title than those from whom he took the bond, unless, perhaps, if the contract is by the law of Scotland not merely assignable but also negotiable. As to this, in *Dixon v Bovill* ((1856) 3 Macq 1 at 16), Lord Cranworth, then Lord Chancellor, in delivering the judgment of the House of Lords in a Scotch case as to iron scrip notes, says, 'I have no hesitation in saying, that independently of the law merchant and of positive statute, within neither of which classes do these scrip notes range themselves, the law does not, either in Scotland or in England, enable any man by a written engagement to give a floating right of action at the suit of any one into whose hands the writing may come, and who may thus acquire a right of action better than the right of him under whom he derives title'.

But the two questions go very much together; and, indeed, in the notes to *Miller v Race* ((1758) 1 Burr 452, 1 Smith LC (13th edn, 1929) pp 452, 533), where all the authorities are collected, the very learned author says: Tt may therefore be laid down as a safe rule that where an instrument is by the custom of trade transferable, like cash, by delivery, and is also capable of being sued upon by the person holding it pro tempore, then it is entitled to the name of a *negotiable instrument,* and the property in it passes to a bona fide transferee for value, though the transfer may not have taken place in market overt. But that if either of the above requisites be wanting, ie, if it be either not accustomably transferable, or, though it be accustomably transferable, yet, if its nature be such as to render it incapable of being put in suit by the party holding it pro tempore, it is not a *negotiable instrument,* nor will delivery of it pass the property of it to a vendee, however bona fide, if the transferor himself have not a good title to it, and the transfer be made out of market overt.'

Bills of exchange and promissory notes, whether payable to order or to bearer, are by the law merchant negotiable in both senses of the word. The person who, by a genuine indorsement, or, where it is payable to bearer, by a delivery, becomes holder, may sue in his own name on the contract, and if he is a bona fide holder for value, he has a good title notwithstanding any defect of title in the party (whether indorser or deliverer) from whom he took it....

NOTES

1.   According to Blackburn J a negotiable instrument has two characteristics, namely: (1) it is 'transferable, like cash, by delivery' (which assumes it is in a deliverable state) so that the transferee can enforce the rights embodied in it in his own name; and (2) the transferee, being a bona fide holder for value, can acquire a better title to it than that of his transferor.

2.   By contrast, a bill of lading in a deliverable state is transferable by delivery and so can be described as 'negotiable' in one sense of the word. But it is not 'negotiable' in the strict sense as it cannot pass a title free from equities of prior parties: *Kum v Wah Tat Bank Ltd* [1971] 1 Lloyd's Rep 439 at 446, per Lord Diplock, PC. Cf C Debattista *Sale of Goods Carried by Sea* (2nd edn, 1998), paras 3–15 to 3–27, who argues that a bill of lading can be described as 'negotiable' in the strict sense of the word because, under the Factors Act 1889 and ss 24 and 25 of the Sale of Goods Act 1979, its transferee may be able to take a better title to the goods it represents than his transferor had. For a comprehensive rebuttal of Debattista's theory, see A Tettenborn [1991] LMCLQ 538, pp 541–542. However, note that under s 47(2) of the Sale of Goods Act 1979 a bona fide transferee for value of a bill of lading may defeat an unpaid seller's right of stoppage in transit even though the right of stoppage may have been valid against his transferor.

3.   The distinction between using the term 'negotiable' to mean 'transferable' and using it in its strict sense was made clear by Bowen LJ in *Simmons v London Joint Stock Bank* [1891] 1 Ch 270 at 294 when he said that:

A negotiable instrument payable to bearer is one which, by the custom of trade, passes from hand to hand by delivery, and the holder of which for the time being, if he is a *bona fide* holder for value without notice, has a good title, notwithstanding any defect of title in the person from whom he took it. A contractual document in other words may be such that, by virtue of its delivery, all the rights of the transferor are transferred to and can be enforced by the transferee against the original contracting party, but it may yet fall short of being a completely negotiable instrument, because the transferee acquires by mere delivery no better title than his transferor.

See s 8(1) of the Bills of Exchange Act 1882 and s 6(2) of the Cheques Act 1957 for examples of when the term 'negotiable' is used only in the sense of 'transferable'.

4.   In its Report on Banking Services Law and Practice (Cm 622, 1989), a Review Committee chaired by Professor Jack recommended a statutory definition of the term 'negotiable', which would apply to all negotiable instruments (Rec 8(3)). This recommendation was rejected by the government in its subsequent White Paper on banking services (Cm 1026, 1990, Annex 6).

(c) A composite definition

In summary, a 'negotiable instrument' is a document of title embodying rights to the payment of money or a security for money, which, by custom or legislation, is (a) transferable by delivery (or by indorsement and delivery) in such a way that the holder *pro tempore* may sue on it in his own name and in his own right, and (b) a *bona fide* transferee for value may acquire a good and complete title to the document and the rights embodied therein, notwithstanding that his predecessor had a defective title or no title at all (adopted from Cowen *The Law of Negotiable Instruments in South Africa* (5th edn, 1985), Vol 1, p 52).

QUESTIONS

1.   Negotiable instruments are one of the most important exceptions to the *nemo dat* rule. Why should they be given such a privileged status? See Chafee (1918) 31 Harvard LR1104, p 1146.

2.   Can the bona fide transferee for value of a non-negotiable instrument ever take the instrument free from defects in the title of his transferor? See *Goodwin v Robarts* (1876) 1 App Cas 476 at 489, HL; *Easton v London Joint Stock Bank* (1886) 34 Ch D 95 at 113–114, CA; *Colonial Bank v Cady and Williams* (1890) 15 App Cas 267 at 285, HL.

3   HOW INSTRUMENTS COME TO BE NEGOTIABLE

There are two ways in which documents may come to be recognised as negotiable instruments: (1) statute; and (2) mercantile usage.

(a) Statute

In most, perhaps all, cases statutory recognition of negotiability merely confirms previous judicial acceptance of a mercantile usage which recognised an instrument as negotiable. For example, bills of exchange and cheques were accepted as negotiable by the courts before they were recognised as such by the Bills of Exchange Act 1882.

There has been some debate as to whether the Promissory Notes Act 1704 made promissory notes negotiable when that had not previously been the case, or whether it was merely declaratory of the law as it stood before Lord Holt's landmark decision in *Clerke v Martin* (1702) 2 Ld Raym 757. In that case Lord Holt held that a promissory note payable to order was not a bill of exchange, and was, therefore, not negotiable. He said:

... that this note could not be a bill of exchange. That the maintaining of these actions upon such notes, were innovations upon the rules of the common law; and that it amounted to the setting up a new sort of specialty, unknown to the common law, and invented in Lombard Street, which attempted in these matters of bills of exchange to give laws to Westminster Hall. That the continuing to declare upon these notes upon the custom of merchants proceeded from obstinacy and opinionativeness, since he had always expressed his opinion against them, and since there was so easy a method, as to declare upon a general indebitatus assumpsit for money lent, etc....

Most commentators have interpreted this decision as wrong and have held the 1704 Act to be declaratory of the case law as it existed prior to *Clerke v Martin* (for a judicial statement to this effect, see *Goodwin v Robarts* (1875) LR 10 Exch 337 at 350, per Cockburn CJ delivering the judgment of the Exchequer Chamber). But Professor Holden has argued that Lord Holt's decision was correct and that promissory notes had not been recognised as negotiable prior to his decision (J Milnes Holden *The History of Negotiable Instruments in English Law* (1955), pp 79–84). If Holden is right then the 1704 Act was constitutive of negotiability.

As to whether the East India Company Bonds Act 1811 actually made bonds of the East India Company negotiable or merely transferable by delivery, see Holden (above), p 245 and Chorley (1932) 48 LQR 51, p 53.

(b) Mercantile usage

Instruments may be regarded as negotiable through judicially recognised mercantile usage.

Goodwin v Robarts

(1875) LR 10 Exch 337, Exchequer Chamber

Through his stockbroker Goodwin purchased certain Russian and Hungarian government scrip. The scrip promised to give the bearer, after all instalments had been paid, a bond for the amount paid, with interest. Goodwin allowed his stockbroker to retain possession of the scrip and the stockbroker fraudulently pledged it with the defendant bankers as security for a loan. The stockbroker went bankrupt and the bankers sold the scrip. Goodwin brought an action against the bankers to recover the amount realised on the sale. The bankers argued that through mercantile usage such scrip had been treated as negotiable by delivery so that Goodwin had lost his title to it. The judgment of the Exchequer Chamber was delivered by Cockburn CJ.

Cockburn CJ: …The substance of [the defendants'] argument is, that, because the scrip does not correspond with any of the forms of the securities for money which have been hitherto held to be negotiable by the law merchant, and does not contain a direct promise to pay money, but only a promise to give security for money, it is not a security to which, by the law merchant, the character of negotiability can attach.

Having given the fullest consideration to this argument, we are of opinion that it cannot prevail. It is founded on the view that the law merchant thus referred to is fixed and stereotyped, and incapable of being expanded and enlarged so as to meet the wants and requirements of trade in the varying circumstances of commerce. It is true that the law merchant is sometimes spoken of as a fixed body of law, forming part of the common law, and as it were coeval with it. But as a matter of legal history, this view is altogether incorrect. The law merchant thus spoken of with reference to bills of exchange and other negotiable securities, though forming part of the general body of the lex mercatoria, is of comparatively recent origin. It is neither more nor less than the usages of merchants and traders in the different departments of trade, ratified by the decisions of Courts of law, which, upon such usages being proved before them, have adopted them as settled law with a view to the interests of trade and the public convenience, the Court proceeding herein on the well-known principle of law that, with reference to transactions in the different departments of trade, Courts of law, in giving effect to the contracts and dealings of the parties, will assume that the latter have dealt with one another on the footing of any custom or usage prevailing generally in the particular department. By this process, what before was usage only, unsanctioned by legal decision, has become engrafted upon, or incorporated into, the common law, and may thus be said to form part of it. 'When a general usage has been judicially ascertained and established,' says Lord Campbell, in *Brandao v Barnett* ((1846) 12 Cl & Fin 787 at 805), 'it becomes a part of the law merchant, which Courts of justice are bound to know and recognise.'

[Cockburn CJ then traced the history of how bills of exchange, promissory notes, bankers' notes, exchequer bills and cheques came to be regarded as negotiable and continued:]

It thus appears that all these instruments which are said to have derived their negotiability from the law merchant had their origin, and that at no very remote period, in mercantile usage, and were adopted into the law by our Courts as being in conformity with the usages of trade; of which, if it were needed, a further confirmation might be found in the fact that, according to the old form of declaring on bills of exchange, the declaration always was founded on the custom of merchants.

Usage, adopted by the Courts, having been thus the origin of the whole of the so-called law merchant as to negotiable securities, what is there to prevent our acting upon the principle acted upon by our predecessors, and followed in the precedents they have left to us? Why is it to be said that a new usage which has sprung up under altered circumstances, is to be less admissible than the usages of past times? Why is the door to be now shut to the admission and adoption of usage in a matter altogether of cognate character, as though the law had been finally stereotyped and settled by some positive and peremptory enactment?

[Cockburn CJ then distinguished several cases relied on by Goodwin and continued:]

We must by no means be understood as saying that mercantile usage, however extensive, should be allowed to prevail if contrary to positive law, including in the latter such usages as, having been made the subject of legal decision, and having been sanctioned and adopted by the Courts, have become, by such adoption, part of the common law. To give effect to a usage which involves a defiance or disregard of the law would be obviously contrary to a fundamental principle. And we quite agree that this would apply quite as strongly to an attempt to set up a new usage against one which has become settled and adopted by the common law as to one in conflict with the more ancient rules of the common law itself....

If we could see our way to the conclusion that, in holding the scrip in question to pass by delivery, and to be available to bearer, we were giving effect to a usage incompatible either with the common law or with the law merchant as incorporated into and embodied in it, our decision would be a very different one from that which we are about to pronounce. But so far from this being the case, we are, on the contrary, in our opinion, only acting on an established principle of that law in giving legal effect to a usage, now become universal, to treat this form of security, being on the face of it expressly made transferable to bearer, as the representative of money, and as such, being made to bearer, as assignable by delivery. This being the conclusion at which we have arrived, the judgment of the Court of Exchequer will be affirmed.

[The House of Lords upheld the judgment of the Court of Exchequer Chamber and approved the ratio decidendi of that decision: (1876) 1 App Cas 476.]

NOTES

1.   Compare the willingness of Cockburn CJ to ratify mercantile usage with the unwillingness of Lord Holt to do the same in *Clerke v Martin* (above, p 522). W S Holdsworth remarked that one of the effects of *Clerke v Martin,* and its statutory reversal in the Promissory Notes Act 1704, was to teach the courts that 'they could not wholly ignore approved mercantile custom; that they must adapt their rules to such customs; that in fact there were cases in which Lombard Street must be allowed to give laws to Westminster Hall' (WS Holdsworth *A History of English Law* Vol VIII, p 176). Chorley went so far as to say that Cockburn CJ's statements on the judicial recognition of mercantile usage 'should be inscribed in letters of gold in every Court handling commercial litigation': (1932) 48 LQR 51, p 55.

2.   Even if the usage is of recent origin the courts will still recognise it (*Bechuanaland Exploration Co v London Trading Bank Ltd* [1898] 2 QB 658). As Bigham J stated in *Edelstein v Schuler & Co* [1902] 2 KB 144 at 154:

...but it is to be remembered that in these days usage is established much more quickly than it was in days gone by; more depends on the number of the transactions which help to create it than on the time over which the transactions are spread....

3. Before a court will recognise an instrument as negotiable through mercantile usage the following conditions must be satisfied:

(1) the usage must be 'reasonable, certain and notorious': *Devonald v Rosser & Sons* [1906] 2 KB 728 at 743, per Farwell LJ, CA;

(2) the usage must be general and not 'a custom or habit which prevails only in a particular market or particular section of the commercial world': *Easton v London Joint Stock Bank* (1886) 34 Ch D 95 at 113, per Bowen LJ, CA; reversed on a different point sub nom *Sheffield (Earl of) v London Joint Stock Bank* (1888) 13 App Cas 333;

(3) the instrument's terms must not be incompatible with negotiability (eg not marked 'non-negotiable') nor stated to be transferable by some method other than delivery: *London and County Banking Co Ltd v London and River Plate Bank Ltd* (1887) 20 QBD 232 at 239, per Manisty J.

QUESTION

Unless recognised as negotiable by statute or mercantile usage, an instrument cannot be made negotiable simply by an express specification to that effect in its terms (*Crouch v Credit Fonder of England* (1873) LR 8 QB 374 at 386, per Blackburn J). Why? What advantage would there be in recognising such an instrument as negotiable?

4 TYPES OF NEGOTIABLE INSTRUMENT

Negotiable instruments include the following documents:

(1) bills of exchange;

(2) cheques;

(3) promissory notes;

(4) bank notes;

(5) treasury bills;

(6) banker's drafts;

(7) dividend warrants;

(8) share warrants;

(9) bearer scrip;

(10) bearer debentures;

(11) bearer bonds;

(12) floating rate notes;

(13) certificates of deposit.

The following documents are not negotiable instruments:

(1) bills of lading;

(2) dock warrants;

(3) delivery orders;

(4) postal or money orders;

(5) registered share certificates;

(6) registered debentures;

(7) insurance policies;

(8) IOUs.

The list is not closed. New instruments may be recognised as negotiable at any time through statute or mercantile usage.

5 ADVANTAGES OF A NEGOTIABLE INSTRUMENT

Before 1874 the assignment of a promise to pay money was not permitted (apart from limited exceptions) at common law. It was the refusal of the common law to allow the transfer of promises to pay money which contributed to the use of negotiable instruments to achieve that end. Only with the enactment of s 25(6) of the Supreme Court of Judicature Act 1873 have promises to pay money been generally assignable at law (since repealed and substantially re-enacted by s 136 of the Law of Property Act 1925: see below, Chapter 22). However, there remain a number of distinct advantages in embodying a payment obligation in a negotiable instrument and transferring it by delivery (or delivery and indorsement) rather than merely assigning the obligation under the 1925 Act. These advantages can be summarised as follows:

(1) the transferee of a negotiable instrument can sue in his own name, even though there has been no assignment in writing, or notice to the obligor or even if the transfer is not absolute, as required for assignments under the statute; and

(2) the transferee of a negotiable instrument who takes it for value and in good faith acquires a good title free from equities, whereas an assignee under the statute always takes subject to equities.

The ease with which a negotiable instrument can be transferred, and the security of title which it can provide, means it can be readily sold to raise cash before the payment obligation on the instrument becomes due.

Even if the payee does not intend to transfer the payment obligation there are advantages in receiving payment by means of a negotiable instrument. As the instrument embodies its own payment obligation divorced from the underlying transaction from which it originates, payment under the instrument, at least in theory, becomes certain, regardless of any breach of that underlying transaction. The principle of autonomy of the payment obligation, central to the marketability of the instrument, will benefit even the original payee. This has led bills of exchange to be treated as cash ensuring that in most cases the courts will give summary judgment on the instrument and refuse to stay execution of that judgment pending trial of any counter-claim.

Cebora SNC v SIP (Industrial Products) Ltd
[1976] 1 Lloyd's Rep 271, Court of Appeal

The plaintiffs entered into a distribution agreement with the defendants whereby the defendants were given the exclusive right to sell the plaintiffs' products in the United Kingdom. In payment of the price of products supplied by the plaintiffs under this agreement the defendants drew five bills of exchange. Following disputes between the parties, the defendants gave instructions that the bills should be dishonoured. The plaintiffs applied for summary judgment on the bills and the defendants counterclaimed for non-delivery of goods, delivery of defective goods and loss of profit. The District Registrar entered judgment for the plaintiffs and refused the defendants' application for a stay of execution pending trial of their counterclaim. May J dismissed the defendants' appeal, as did the Court of Appeal (Buckley and Stephenson LJJ, and Sir Eric Sachs).

Sir Eric Sachs: Any erosion of the certainties of the application by our Courts of the law merchant relating to bills of exchange is likely to work to the detriment of this country, which depends on international trade to a degree that needs no emphasis. For some generations one of those certainties has been that the bona fide holder for value of a bill of exchange is entitled, save in truly exceptional circumstances, on its maturity to have it treated as cash, so that in an action upon it the Court will refuse to regard either as a defence or as grounds for a stay of execution any set off, legal or equitable, or any counterclaim, whether arising on the particular transaction upon which the bill of exchange came into existence, or, a fortiori, arising in any other way. This rule of practice is thus, in effect, pay up on the bill of exchange first and pursue claims later....

In my judgment, the Courts should be really careful not to whittle away the rule of practice by introducing unnecessary exceptions to it under the influence of sympathy-evoking stories, and should have due regard to the maxim that hard cases can make bad law. Indeed, in these days of increasing international interdependence and increasing need to foster liquidity of resources, the rule may be said to be of special import to the business community. Pleas to leave in Court large sums to deteriorate in value while official referee scale proceedings are fought out may well to that community seem rather divorced from business realities, and should perhaps be examined with considerable caution.

Nova (Jersey) Knit Ltd v Kammgarn Spinnerei GmbH
[1977] 2 All ER 463, House of Lords

An English company and a German company set up a partnership in Germany. The English company sold machines to the German company to be used for the partnership and the German company issued bills of exchange for the price. The English company brought an action on the bills. The German company sought to bring a defence and counterclaim for unliquidated damages for mismanagement of the partnership and defects in the machines. The House of Lords (Lord Wilberforce, Viscount Dilhorne, Lords Salmon, Fraser and Russell) held the German company liable to pay the bills in full without set-off or counterclaim. By a majority (Lord Salmon dissenting), their Lordships refused a stay of execution of the judgment based on an arbitration agreement contained in the underlying contract.

Lord Wilberforce: ... When one person buys goods from another, it is often, one would think generally, important for the seller to be sure of his price: he may (as indeed the appellants here) have bought the goods from someone else whom he has to pay. He may demand payment in cash; but if the buyer cannot provide this at once, he may agree to take bills of exchange payable at future dates. These are taken as equivalent to deferred instalments of cash. Unless they are to be treated as unconditionally payable instruments (as in the [Bills of Exchange Act 1882], s 3, says 'an unconditional order in writing'), which the seller can negotiate for cash, the seller might just as well give credit. And it is for this reason that English law (and German law appears to be no different) does not allow cross-claims, or defences, except such limited defences as those based on fraud, invalidity, or failure of consideration, to be made....

Lord Russell of Killowen: ...It is in my opinion well established that a claim for unliquidated damages under a contract for sale is no defence to a claim under a bill of exchange accepted by the purchaser: nor is it available as set-off or counterclaim. This is a deep rooted concept of English commercial law. A vendor and purchaser who agree upon payment by acceptance of bills of exchange do so not simply upon the basis that credit is given to the purchaser so that the vendor must in due course sue for the price under the contract of sale. The bill is itself a contract separate from the contract of sale. Its purpose is not merely to serve as a negotiable instrument, it is also to avoid postponement of the purchaser's liability to the vendor himself, a postponement grounded upon some allegation of failure in some respect by the vendor under the underlying contract, unless it be total or quantified partial failure of consideration....

NOTES

1.   It is clear from *Nova (Jersey) Knit* that cross claims for unliquidated damages cannot be set up in answer to a claim on a bill of exchange. But certain other defences may be available. A total failure of consideration, or a quantified (liquidated) partial failure, may be relied on as a defence against immediate parties and against a subsequent holder who is not a holder for value. A total failure of consideration would arise, for example, where a buyer, who had paid for good by drawing a bill of exchange in favour of the seller, rejected all the goods on delivery because they were not of satisfactory quality and/or fit for their purpose (see Sale of Goods Act 1979, s 14(2), (3)). A quantified (liquidated) partial failure of consideration would arise, for example, where some of the delivered goods were rejected and others were not (see Sale of Goods Act 1979, s 35 A). The defence would operate to the extent of the value of the goods that had been rejected. Another defence that could be raised against an immediate party to the bill, or against a remote party who is not a holder in due course, is where the validity of the instrument can be called into question because, for example, its issue was induced by conspiracy or misrepresentation (*SAFA Ltd v Banque Du Caire* [2000] 2 All ER (Comm) 567, CA; *Solo Industries UK Ltd v Canara Bank* [2001] EWCA Civ 1059, [2001] 2 All ER (Comm) 217). In each case, the availability of a defence depends on the status of the holder claiming to enforce the bill (as to which, see below, Chapter 16, Section 5).

2.   Although treated as the equivalent of cash, a bill of exchange is not legal tender and, subject to any agreement or usage to the contrary, a creditor is only obliged to accept legal tender, ie cash, in payment of a debt (*Gordon v Strange* (1847) 1 Exch 477). If a bill of exchange, promissory note or cheque is accepted in payment of a debt it depends on the intention of the parties as to whether it is taken in absolute or conditional payment of the debt. In *Re Charge Card Services Ltd* [1989] Ch 497 at 511, CA, Browne-Wilkinson V-C stated that:

...It is common ground that where a debt is 'paid' by cheque or bill of exchange, there is a presumption that such payment is conditional on the cheque or bill being honoured. If it is not honoured, the condition is not satisfied and the liability of the purchaser to pay the price remains. Such presumption can be rebutted by showing an express or implied intention that the cheque or bill is taken in total satisfaction of the liability....

For further statements to the same effect, see *Crockfords Club Ltd v Mehta* [1992] 1 WLR 355 at 366, CA; *Homes v Smith* [2000] Lloyd's Rep Bank 139 at [35], CA.

3. In *Re Charge Card Services Ltd* [1989] Ch 497 at 517, the Court of Appeal left open the question whether the presumption of conditional payment would be rebutted merely by the fact that the cheque had been accompanied by a cheque guarantee card. At first instance ([1987] Ch 150 at 166), Millett J had stated (*obiter*) that the presumption would not be rebutted in those circumstances.

QUESTIONS

1. Is there any advantage to a creditor in accepting payment by negotiable instrument as opposed to cash? If so, would this enable a debtor to argue that payment by negotiable instrument provided its own consideration to support the creditor's agreement to accept a lesser sum in settlement of an undisputed debt? See *D &C Builders v Rees* [1966] 2 QB 617, CA. See also McLauchlan (1987) 12 NZULR 259 and *James Cook Hotel Ltd v Caux Corporate Services Ltd* [1989] LRC (Comm) 518 (New Zealand).

2. If a negotiable instrument is used to pay a debt and, when in the creditor's hands, the instrument is accidentally destroyed before its maturity, can the creditor return to the debtor demanding payment of the debt?

CHAPTER 16

BILLS OF EXCHANGE

1 THE USE OF BILLS OF EXCHANGE

'Electronic Funds Transfer as a Deferred Settlement System'
by E P Ellinger in RM Goode (ed) *Electronic Banking,*
the Legal Implications **(1985), pp 40–41**

Bills of exchange are used predominantly in the context of two facilities associated with international trade: the documentary credit (which is used exclusively in this context) and the acceptance credit (which is used in domestic projects as well). In the case of documentary credits, the seller usually draws a bill of exchange on the issuing or confirming bank for the amount of the credit. The bill, which may be payable at 90 or 180 days after sight, will be 'discounted' by the seller's own bank, who thereupon becomes the negotiating bank. This bank arranges for the presentment of the bill for acceptance and for payment, usually by engaging a correspondent.

The arrangement differs in an acceptance credit. Here an industrialist or manufacturer, who requires extra liquidity, may be unable to obtain a loan from his bank. But the bank may be prepared to lend him its credit. To do so, it authorises him to draw on itself bills of exchange for an amount not exceeding a stated ceiling. The bills are, thus, signed by the industrialist as drawer and by the bank as acceptor. The industrialist obtains his required finance by discounting the bill. He is able to arrange for this on the strength of the combined effect of the signatures of the bank and of himself. The instrument may be discounted several times on the bills market. At maturity, it is met by the bank (the acceptor), which seeks reimbursement from the drawer. If the drawer is not in a position to settle, another set of bills is 'rolled over'.

There are, of course, other transactions in which bills of exchange are being used. Thus, a bill accompanies cif documents transmitted by the seller of the goods to the purchaser. But in all the cases involved, the bill serves the same two objects. First, it purports to charge the person on whom it is drawn (the 'drawee'), whose consent to the demand ('acceptance') constitutes a deferred payment undertaking. Secondly, the bill is meant to be discounted. It therefore has to be negotiable . . . .

2 THE BILLS OF EXCHANGE ACT 1882

The primary source of the law of bills of exchange is the Bills of Exchange Act 1882 (the 'BEA'). The Act was drafted by Sir Mackenzie Chalmers, who also drafted the Sale of Goods Act 1893 and the Marine Insurance Act 1906. It is a masterpiece of statutory draftsmanship.

The Preamble to the BEA states that it was intended 'to codify the law relating to Bills of Exchange, Cheques and Promissory Notes' (although it also altered the common law in a number of respects). The way the courts interpret a codification statute of this nature is revealed in the following extract.

Bank of England v Vagliano Bros

[1891] AC 107, House of Lords

(The facts appear below, p 538. The case turned on the meaning of s 7(3) of the BEA. The Court of Appeal had qualified the wording of the subsection by introducing a limitation to be found in the common law.)

Lord Herschell: My Lords, with sincere respect for the learned Judges who have taken this view, I cannot bring myself to think that this is the proper way to deal with such a statute as the Bills of Exchange Act, which was intended to be a code of the law relating to negotiable instruments. I think the proper course is in the first instance to examine the language of the statute and to ask what is its natural meaning, uninfluenced by any considerations derived from the previous state of the law and not to start with inquiring how the law previously stood, and then, assuming that it was probably intended to leave it unaltered, to see if the words of the enactment will bear an interpretation in conformity with this view.

If a statute, intended to embody in a code a particular branch of the law, is to be treated in this fashion, it appears to me that its utility will be almost entirely destroyed, and the very object with which it was enacted will be frustrated. The purpose of such a statute surely was that on any point specifically dealt with by it, the law should be ascertained by interpreting the language used instead of, as before, by roaming over a vast number of authorities in order to discover what the law was, extracting it by a minute critical examination of the prior decisions, dependent upon a knowledge of the exact effect even of an obsolete proceeding such as a demurrer to evidence. I am of course far from asserting that resort may never be had to the previous state of the law for the purpose of aiding in the construction of the provisions of the code. If, for example, a provision be of doubtful import, such resort would be perfectly legitimate. Or, again, if in a code of the law of negotiable instruments words be found which have previously acquired a technical meaning, or been used in a sense other than their ordinary one, in relation to such instruments, the same interpretation might well be put upon them in the code. I give these as examples merely; they, of course, do not exhaust the category. What, however, I am venturing to insist upon is, that the first step taken should be to interpret the language of the statute, and that an appeal to earlier decisions can only be justified on some special ground.

One further remark I have to make before I proceed to consider the language of the statute. The Bills of Exchange Act was certainly not intended to be merely a code of the existing law. It is not open to question that it was intended to alter, and did alter it in certain respects. And I do not think that it is to be presumed that any particular provision was intended to be a statement of the existing law, rather than a substituted enactment.

NOTES

1.   The Act does not, in general, extend to negotiable instruments other than bills of exchange, cheques and promissory notes (although see BEA, s 95 and Cheques Act 1957, s 5).

2.   Lord Herschell gave examples of when it would be legitimate to examine the common law as an aid to construction of the provisions of the BEA. The common law remains relevant in many other ways. This is emphasised by A Barak in the following extract.

'The Nature of the Negotiable Instrument' by A Barak
(1983) 18 Israel LR 49, pp 69–70

...[S]everal different sets of rules apply to the negotiable instrument: since it is a chattel—the general law applicable to chattels (such as sales and torts); since it is an obligation—the general law of obligations (for example the rules as to capacity); and since it is a negotiable paper—the special rules applicable to such instruments. In most countries, the law of negotiable instruments is normally confined to that latter body of rules. Israel's Bills of Exchange Ordinance deals almost entirely with the bill as a negotiable instrument; it makes virtually no reference at all to the bill as a chattel or an obligation. Those aspects of the bill are covered by the general law. Hence, one can draw a distinction between the law of negotiable instruments in the strict sense and the law of negotiable instruments in the broad sense. The former deals with the bill as a negotiable paper and, as said, is usually to be found in special legislation. The latter deals with the bill as a chattel and an obligation and is usually to be found in the general law. The parallel existence of the two has been possible because legislation on negotiable instruments was never intended to provide an exhaustive list of the rules of law dealing with such instruments. From the time of the very earliest legislation in this field it has been clear that, alongside the special rules governing the bill as a negotiable instrument, the ordinary rules relating to it as a chattel and an obligation continue to apply....

NOTES

1.   Israel's Bills of Exchange Ordinance is based on the English BEA and so Barak's comments are equally relevant to the 1882 Act.

2.   Section 97(2) of the BEA provides that: The rules of common law including the law merchant, save in so far as they are inconsistent with the express provisions of this Act, shall continue to apply to bills of exchange, promissory notes, and cheques.'

3.   An example of the general law applicable to chattels relevant to bills is the tort of conversion. This is the remedy usually, but not always, available to the true owner of a stolen bill. An example of the general law of obligations applicable to bills is the doctrine of consideration. In this case the Act expressly imports the common law rules as s 27(1)(a) of the BEA states that valuable consideration for a bill may be constituted by any consideration sufficient to support a simple contract.

QUESTION

Lord Herschell's restrictive method of interpreting a codifying statute has not always been followed by the courts (eg *Ashington Piggeries Ltd v Christopher Hill Ltd* [1972] AC 441). What are its disadvantages?

3 DEFINITION OF A BILL OF EXCHANGE

Section 3 of the BEA defines a bill of exchange as follows:

(1) A bill of exchange is an unconditional order in writing, addressed by one person to another, signed by the person giving it, requiring the person to whom it is addressed to pay

on demand or at a fixed or determinable future time a sum certain in money to or to the order of a specified person, or to bearer.

(2) An instrument which does not comply with these conditions, or which orders any act to be done in addition to the payment of money, is not a bill of exchange.

The person who draws the bill and gives the order to pay is called the 'drawer'. The person upon whom the bill is drawn, and who is thereby ordered to pay, is called the 'drawee'. When the drawee indicates his willingness to pay, he is then called the 'acceptor'. The person identified in the bill as the person to or to whose order the money is to be paid is called the 'payee', or, if the bill is drawn payable to bearer, and he is in possession of the bill, the 'bearer'. A bill payable to order is negotiated (meaning transferred) by the indorsement of the payee (or of a subsequent transferee) completed by delivery. The person indorsing the bill is called the Endorser' and the person to whom it is indorsed, the 'indorsee'. A bill payable to bearer is negotiated by mere delivery. The payee or an indorsee of a bill who is in possession of it, or the bearer, is called the 'holder'.

Figures 1 and 2 are examples of instruments that fall within the statutory definition of a bill of exchange. The accompanying notes should help you identify the relevant parties to the instruments.

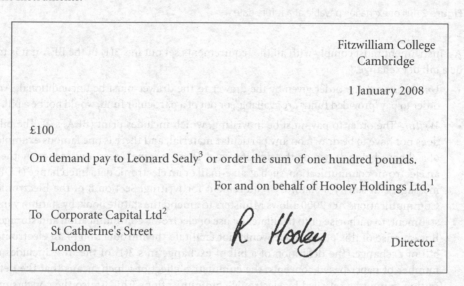

Fitzwilliam College
Cambridge

1 January 2008

£100

On demand pay to Leonard Sealy[3] or order the sum of one hundred pounds.

For and on behalf of Hooley Holdings Ltd,[1]

To   Corporate Capital Ltd[2]
     St Catherine's Street
     London   *R Hooley*   Director

Figure 1 Bill of exchange payable on demand

NOTES

1. The 'drawer'.
2. The 'drawee'.
3. The 'payee' (when the bill is delivered to him he becomes the first 'holder').
4. The 'acceptor' (when the 'drawee' has accepted the bill he is then called the 'acceptor').

Figure 2 Bill of exchange payable at a future date

An instrument must comply with all the requirements set out in s 3(1) of the BEA if it is to be a bill of exchange.

- *Unconditional* The order given by the drawer to the drawee must be unconditional. An order to pay 'provided funds are available', or out of a particular fund, would not be a bill.

- *Writing* The order to pay must be in writing, which includes print (BEA, s 2). The bill does not have to be drawn on any particular material, and there is one famous example of a cheque being drawn on the side of a cow! There is some uncertainty as to whether an electronic communication, such as an e-mail or an electronic data interchange (EDI) message, can satisfy a statutory requirement for writing. Section 8 of the Electronic Communications Act 2000 allows Ministers to amend the statute book, by statutory instrument, to authorise or to facilitate the use of electronic communication and storage. But exercise of this power alone would not facilitate the introduction of an electronic bill of exchange. The definition of a bill of exchange in s 3(1) of the BEA includes a number of paper-based concepts, the cumulative effect of which means that the definition cannot be satisfied by electronic communications (this is also the conclusion of the Law Commission in its Advice to Government, *Electronic Commerce: Formal Requirements in Commercial Transactions,* December 2001, para 9.5). There are other obstacles that would have to be overcome before it was possible to have an electronic bill of exchange. The functions of a bill of exchange could be replicated electronically by way of a series of contractually enforceable promises to pay but those promises would fall outside the Bills of Exchange Act 1882. Such promises would not therefore provide the protection which the Act gives to bona fide purchasers for value, a statutory protection which cannot be created by contract alone (Law Com, above, para 9.6). There would also be the problem of ensuring that the holder could not transfer the same electronic bill of exchange to more than one party (Law Com, above, para 9.7).

- *Addressed by one person to another* If the drawer draws the instrument on himself, it is not a bill of exchange but the holder of such an instrument has the option of treating it either as a bill of exchange or as a promissory note (BEA, s 5(2)). The instrument is a bill of exchange where the drawer names himself as the payee.

• *Signed by the person giving it* The drawer must sign the bill personally or through an agent. A stamped facsimile of a signature is probably sufficient, but a digital signature (on an electronic bill of exchange) may not be (at least until the relevant Minister exercises his powers under s 8 of the Electronic Communication Act 2000 and declares it to be sufficient). If the signature of the drawer is forged or placed on the bill without his authority, the signature is 'wholly inoperative', although certain estoppels may arise as against the drawer (BEA, s 24) and against the acceptor (BEA, s 54(2)(a)) and any indorser (BEA, s 55(2)(b)). It is arguable that where the drawer's signature is forged, then the instrument is not a bill at all.

• *On demand or at a fixed or determinable future time* By s 10(1) of the BEA, a bill is payable on demand: (a) which is expressed to be payable on demand, or at sight, or on presentation; or (b) in which no time for payment is expressed. By s 11 of the BEA, a bill is payable at a fixed or determinable future time: (a) if it is expressed to be payable at a fixed period after date or sight; or (b) on or at a fixed period after the occurrence of a specified event which is certain to happen, though the time of happening may be uncertain. It is vital that the time of payment is certain according to the terms of the bill. This renders the bill saleable. Where time of payment is not certain from the face of the instrument it will not be treated as a bill of exchange. Thus, an instrument drawn payable *by* a specified date does not fall within the statutory definition because the acceptor has the option of paying before that date (*Claydon v Bradley* [1987] 1 All ER 522, CA, following *Williamson v Rider* [1963] 1 QB 89, CA, criticised by AH Hudson (1962) 25 MLR 593, pp 596–596), and an instrument expressed to be payable on a contingency is not a bill, and the happening of the event does not cure the defect (BEA, s 11). However, the courts are prepared to overcome faulty expressions in an instrument where the true meaning is obvious despite the defect. In *Hong Kong & Shanghai Banking Corpn Ltd v GD Trade Co Ltd* [1998] CLC 238, the Court of Appeal inserted a '/' between the words 'acceptance' and 'sight' and held the instrument to be a bill of exchange payable at '90 days after acceptance/sight'. This had the effect of making the bill payable at a fixed period after the date of sight (ie presentation for acceptance), whether it was actually accepted or not (an instrument payable on, or a fixed period after, acceptance is not a bill of exchange because acceptance by the drawee is a contingency: *Korea Exchange Bank v Debenhams (Central Buying) Ltd* [1979] 1 Lloyd's Rep 548, CA). Their Lordships also tentatively suggested (without deciding the issue) that acceptance of a bill not previously negotiated, in terms which unequivocally stated that it was payable on a specified day, cured any uncertainty as to the date of maturity of the bill as originally drawn. Alternatively, it might be possible to treat the terms of the acceptance as turning the instrument into a promissory note (*Novaknit Hellas SA v Kumar Bros International Ltd* [1998] CLC 971, CA).

• *A sum certain in money* 'Money' includes legal tender and foreign currency (including the euro). A sum payable is a sum certain even though required to be paid with interest, or by stated instalments, or according to an indicated rate of exchange or a rate of exchange to be ascertained as directed on the bill (BEA, s 9(1)).

• *To or to the order of a specified person or to bearer* Where a bill is not payable to bearer, the payee must be named or otherwise indicated therein with reasonable certainty (BEA, s 7(1)). Payment to the holder of an office for the time being (eg 'Treasurer of the Cambridge University Law Society') is permissible (BEA, s 7(2)). Where the payee is a fictitious or non-existent person the bill may be treated as payable to bearer (BEA, s 7(3): see below, p 538). An instrument drawn payable to 'cash or order' is not a bill of exchange, as it is not payable to a specified person or to bearer (*Orbit Mining and Trading Co Ltd v Westminster Bank Ltd* [1963] 1 QB 794, CA). But a bill drawn payable to 'cash or bearer' would appear to be a valid bill payable to bearer (*Grant v Vaughan* (1764) 3 Burr 1516), as is a bill payable to 'X or bearer' (*M K International Development Co Ltd v Housing Bank* [1991] 1 Bank LR 74, CA). In *Chamberlain v Young and Tower* [1893] 2 QB 206, an instrument drawn 'pay to…order' was construed as being a valid bill payable 'to my order' so as to give effect to the drawer's clear intention to create a negotiable instrument. It is a moot point whether an instrument drawn 'pay………or order' is a valid bill. The words 'or order' negative any inference that it is payable to bearer (cf *Wookey v Pole* (1820) 4 B & Ald 1). Despite a number of early nineteenth century cases holding that such an instrument was not a bill of exchange (*R v Richards* (1811) Russ & Ry 193; *R v Randall* (1811) Russ & Ry 195), it is generally accepted that an instrument drawn 'pay…….or order' would now be construed as payable 'to myself or order' (see *Chalmers and Guest on Bills of Exchange* (16th edn, 2005), para 2–049; EP Ellinger, E Lomnicka and RJA Hooley *Ellinger's Modern Banking Law* (4th edn, 2006), p 369; cf *Byles on Bills of Exchange and Cheques* (28th edn, 2007), para 3–07). In the Scottish case of *Henderson, Sons & Co Ltd v Wallace and Pennell* (1902) 40 SLR 70, Lord Traynor treated an instrument drawn 'pay…..or order' as a promissory note. However, the issue was left undecided in *Chamberlain v Tower and Young* and in *North and South Insurance Corpn v National Provincial Bank* [1936] 1 KB 328.

An unsigned document cannot be a bill of exchange but a signed document, though failing to comply with all the requirements of s 3(1) of the BEA, may be converted into a bill of exchange where the signatory (the drawer, the acceptor or an indorser) delivers it to another person in order that the missing details may be completed by him. Such a document is an 'inchoate' instrument. The person who takes delivery of an inchoate instrument has prima facie authority to fill it up as a complete bill and to rectify any omission of any material particular, for example the amount or the name of the payee (BEA, s 20(1)). In order that the instrument, when completed, may be enforceable against a person who became a party to it prior to its completion, it must be filled up within a reasonable time and strictly in accordance with the authority given (BEA, s 20(2)). Not surprisingly, given the need to encourage the marketability of bills of exchange, where a completed instrument is negotiated to someone who takes it in good faith and for valuable consideration (ie a holder in due course), that person may enforce the bill against anyone who became a party to it prior to its completion even where it turns out that the bill was not completed within a reasonable time or in accordance with the authority given (BEA, s 20(2)).

Even if the holder of the bill cannot rely on the inchoate instrument provisions set out in s 20 of the BEA, he may be able to argue that the person who signs a negotiable instrument in blank, or while it is otherwise incomplete, is estopped from denying the validity of the completed instrument against him if he has acted to his detriment in reliance upon it (*Lloyds Bank Ltd v Cooke* [1907] 1 KB 794, CA). In *Wilson and Meeson v Pickering* [1946] KB 422, the Court of Appeal emphasised that this type of estoppel was confined to the case of negotiable instruments so that a cheque which had lost its negotiability because it had been crossed 'not negotiable' (see BEA, s 81) fell outside its ambit (cf *Mercantile Credit Co Ltd v Hamblin* [1965] 2 QB 242 at 274–275, 278–279).

4 TRANSFER OF A BILL OF EXCHANGE

We have already seen how the payee of a bill of exchange payable at a future time may discount the bill, ie sell it at a reduced rate, before it matures in order to raise immediate cash (see below, Chapter 15, Section 1 and Chapter 16, Section 1). The payee must 'negotiate' the bill to the purchaser and give him legal title to the sum payable under it. The same bill could, in theory, be negotiated many times down a chain of different people, for example, from A to B, from B to C, from C to D etc.

By s 31(1) of the BEA, 'a bill is negotiated when it is transferred from one person to another in such a manner as to constitute the transferee the holder of the bill'. In this section the word 'negotiated' is used to mean 'transferred', whether or not such transfer is free from equities of prior parties. The actual mode of transfer depends on whether the bill is a bearer bill or payable to order.

(a) Bearer bills

Bearer bills are transferred by delivery, ie through the transfer of possession, whether actual or constructive, from one person to another (BEA, s 31 (2)). A bill of exchange is payable to bearer in any of the following circumstances:

- When it is expressed to be so payable, ie 'Pay bearer' (BEA, s 8(3)).
- When the only or last indorsement is an indorsement in blank (BEA, s 8(3)). An indorsement in blank occurs when the indorser simply signs the bill without specifying an indorsee (BEA, s 34(1)) and is to be contrasted with a special indorsement which occurs when the indorser specifies the person to whom, or to whose order, the bill is to be payable (BEA, s 34(2)). The back of the bill reproduced as Figure 1, above, appears as Figure 3. This shows a special indorsement by the payee (Sealy) and an indorsement in blank by the indorsee (Prichard).

Figure 3 Back of bill of exchange reproduced as Figure 1

NOTES

5. Special endorsement.
6. Indorsement in blank.

- Where the payee is a fictitious or non-existing person the bill may be treated as payable to bearer (BEA, s 7(3)). By virtue of s 34(3) of the BEA, this provision is extended to the case where an indorsee under a special indorsement is a fictitious or non-existent person so that the bill can then be treated as having been indorsed in blank. The next case is the leading authority on whether the payee is fictitious.

Bank of England v Vagliano Bros

[1891] AC 107, House of Lords

Vagliano Brothers regularly accepted bills drawn on them by their foreign correspondent in Odessa, Vucina. Glyka, a clerk employed by Vagliano Brothers, forged Vucina's signature as drawer on a number of such bills. The bills were drawn payable to the order of C Petridi & Co, a firm carrying on business in Constantinople, which had been the payee of some genuine bills previously drawn by Vucina upon Vagliano Brothers. In ignorance of the forgery, Vagliano Brothers accepted these bills payable at the Bank of England. Glyka then forged the indorsement of C Petridi & Co and obtained payment from the Bank of England in the name of a fictitious indorsee. The issue was whether the Bank of England was entitled to treat the bills as payable to bearer and debit Vagliano Brothers' account with the amount of their acceptances. The House of Lords by a majority (Lords Bramwell and Field dissenting) held that the Bank of England had been entitled to do so.

Lord Herschell: ... If I am right in thinking that in the case of a payee who is a fictitious person (whatever be the meaning of that expression) a bill may, as against the acceptor, be treated by a lawful holder as payable to bearer whether the acceptor knew of the fiction or not, why should this right and liability differ according as the name inserted as payee be a creature of the imagination or correspond to that of a real person, the drawer in neither case intending a person so designated to receive payment, and in each case himself indorsing the bill in the name of the nominal payee before putting it into circulation? I am at a loss for any reason why this distinction should exist. It is true that there is this difference between the two cases—that in the one an indorsement by the named payee is physically impossible, whilst in the other it is not. But I do not think this difference affords a sound basis for a distinction between the respective rights and liabilities of the drawer, acceptor, and holder. It seems to me that it would in each case be reasonable, and on the same grounds, that the acceptor should be liable to the holder of the bill, indemnifying himself out of the funds of the drawer or obtaining reimbursement from him....

Do the words, 'where the payee is a fictitious person,' apply only where the payee named never had a real existence? I take it to be clear that by the word 'payee' must be understood the payee named on the face of the bill; for of course by the hypothesis there is no intention that payment should be made to any such person. Where, then, the payee named is so named by way of pretence only, without the intention that he shall be the person to receive payment, is it doing violence to language to say that the payee is a fictitious person? I think not. I do not think that the word 'fictitious' is exclusively used to qualify that which has no real existence. When we speak of a fictitious entry in a book of accounts, we do not mean that the entry has no real existence, but only that it purports to be that which it is not—that it is an entry made for the purpose of pretending that the transaction took place which is represented by it....

I have arrived at the conclusion that, whenever the name inserted as that of the payee is so inserted by way of pretence merely, without any intention that payment shall only be made in conformity therewith, the payee is a fictitious person within the meaning of the statute, whether the name be that of an existing person, or of one who has no existence, and that the bill may, in each case, be treated by a lawful holder as payable to bearer.

I have hitherto been considering the case of a bill drawn by the person whose name is attached to it as drawer, whilst the bills which have given rise to this litigation were not drawn by Vucina, who purported to be the drawer, his name being forged by Glyka. I think it was hardly contended on behalf of the respondents that this made any difference. The bills must, under the circumstances, as against the acceptor, be taken to have been drawn by Vucina, and if they have been made payable to a fictitious person within the meaning of the statute, I do not think it is open to question that they may, as against the acceptor, be treated as payable to bearer, in every case in which they could have been so treated if Vucina had drawn them. If, in the present case, Vucina had himself drawn the bills and inserted the name of C Petridi & Co as payees, as a mere pretence without intending any such persons to receive payment, it follows from what I have said that in my opinion they would have been bills whose payee was a fictitious person, and I do not think they can be regarded as any the less so, in view of the circumstances under which the name of C Petridi & Co was inserted.

Lord Macnaghten: On behalf of the bank, it was pointed out that these pretended bills, being duly accepted and regular and complete on the face of them, were presented for payment apparently in due course; and it was said that although no doubt at the time they were taken to be payable to order, and to be duly indorsed by the payee, yet when it turns out that the payee was a fictitious person, they may be treated as payable to bearer, and so the payment is justified though all the indorsements are inoperative.

On behalf of Vagliano Bros, it was contended that a bill payable to a fictitious person is not payable to bearer unless the acceptor is proved to have been aware of the fiction; and further, it was contended that nothing but a creature of the imagination can properly be described as a fictitious person. I do not think that either of these contentions on behalf of the respondents can be maintained.

Before the Act of 1882, the law seems to have been, as laid down by Lord Ellenborough in *Bennett v Farnell* ((1807) 1 Camp 130 at 180), that 'a bill of exchange made payable to a fictitious person or his order, is neither in effect payable to the order of the drawer nor to bearer, unless it can be shewn that the circumstances of the payee being a fictitious person was known to the acceptor.' The Act of 1882, s 7, sub-s 3, enacts that, 'Where the payee is a fictitious or non-existing person, the bill may be treated as payable to bearer.' As a statement of law before the Act that would have been incomplete and inaccurate. The omission of the qualification required to make it complete and accurate as the law then stood seems to shew that the object of the enactment was to do away with that qualification altogether. The section appears to me to have effected a change in the law in the direction of the more complete negotiability of bills of exchange—a change in accordance, I think, with the tendency of modern views and one in favour of holders in due course, and not, so far as I can see, likely to lead to any hardships or injustice.

Then it was said that the proper meaning of 'fictitious' is 'imaginary.' I do not think so. I think the proper meaning of the word is 'feigned' or 'counterfeit.' It seems to me that the 'C Petridi & Co' named as payees on these pretended bills were, strictly speaking, fictitious persons. When the bills came before Vagliano for acceptance they were fictitious from beginning to end. The drawer was fictitious; the payee was fictitious; the person indicated as agent for presentation was fictitious. One and all they were feigned or counterfeit persons put forward as real persons, each in a several and distinct capacity; whereas, in truth, they were mere make-believes for the persons whose names appeared on the instrument. They were not, I think, the less fictitious because there were in existence real persons for whom these names were intended to pass muster.

[Lord Halsbury LC and Lords Selbourne, Watson and Macnaghten based their opinions mainly on the ground that Vagliano Brothers had misled the Bank of England into making the payments and so the bank was not to be held responsible for them. However, as an additional ground for their opinions Lord Halsbury LC and Lord Watson, together with Lord Morris, held that s 7(3) was to be interpreted as interpreted by Lords Herschell and Macnaghten.]

NOTES

1.   The only genuine signature on these 'bills' was that of Vagliano Brothers as acceptor. The drawer's and payee's signatures were forgeries. As s 3(1) of the BEA requires the drawer's signature to appear on the bill, and Vucina had not signed these bills, they could not fall within the statutory definition of a bill of exchange. This was recognised by Lord Halsbury LC (at 116) and by Lords Watson (at 134), Macnaghten (at 160) and Morris (at 162). As s 7(3) of the BEA states that'... *the bill* may be treated as payable to bearer', the subsection would appear to have little relevance to the 'bills' in the *Vagliano* case. Lords Watson (at 134) and Macnaghten (at 160) stated that as the instruments were not genuine bills of exchange, s 7(3) was not intended to apply to them (see also JR Adams (1891) 7 LQR 295, pp 295–296). Lord Halsbury LC (at 116 and 120) overcame this difficulty by holding that Vagliano Brothers, as acceptor, were estopped from denying that the instrument was a valid bill. Lords Herschell (at 154) and Morris (at 162–163) appear to concur with that view. The estoppel operates at common law and prevents the acceptor from asserting against a bona fide holder for value without notice that the drawer's signature was forged (it is not a statutory estoppel under BEA, s 54(2)(a)—can you see why?). The estoppel will operate against the acceptor so that the instrument, upon which the drawer's signature has been forged, is deemed to be a bill of exchange. Section 7(3) will then treat the bill as payable to bearer if the forger did not intend the named payee to receive payment.

2.   The drawer's intention is, therefore, of utmost importance when deciding whether a payee is fictitious. That this should be so seems anomalous in a case like *Bank of England v Vagliano Bros*. Professor Ellinger observes that whilst such emphasis on the intention of the drawer:

...is supportable in the case of cheques in which the drawer determines the tenor of the bill and is, in effect, the main party to be charged in the event of its dishonour, it is difficult to see that the principle of the *Vagliano* case is appropriate in the case of bills of exchange. In such an instrument, the main obligor is the acceptor and not the drawer. If the acceptor—eg the plaintiffs in the *Vagliano* case—intends the instrument to be payable to a designated payee, such as P & Co, why should the court be guided by the intention of a person whose name does not even appear on the bill, such as the forger G? This argument is reinforced in the case of a bill of exchange because the order to pay the bill is given to the designated bank, the defendants in the *Vagliano* case, by the acceptor! [EP Ellinger, E Lomnicka and RJA Hooley *Ellinger's Modern Banking Law* (4th edn, 2006), p 369]

3.   Focusing on the drawer's intention means that if the drawer does intend the named payee to receive payment that payee is not fictitious, even though the drawer may have been fraudulently induced into drawing the bill in that way. Such a bill falls outside s 7(3) of the BEA and remains payable to order. This was held to have occurred in the following cases.

• In *Vinden v Hughes* [1905] 1 KB 795, a fraudulent clerk made out cheques to certain well known customers and persuaded Vinden, his employer, to sign the cheques even though no money was in fact owing to those customers. The employee then forged the customers' signatures and sold the cheques to Hughes for cash. Hughes passed the cheques through his own bank account, and had the proceeds placed to his credit. Warrington J held that Vinden believed he owed money to his customers when he signed the cheques as drawer and intended those customers to receive their proceeds. So far as Vinden was concerned at that time, the names of the customers/payees had not been inserted as a mere pretence and, therefore, they were not fictitious persons. Vinden could, therefore, recover the proceeds of the cheques from Hughes because the clerk's forged indorsements were wholly ineffective and did not entitle Hughes to receive payment of those proceeds.

- In *North and South Wales Bank v Macbeth* [1908] AC 137, White fraudulently induced Macbeth to draw a cheque in favour of Kerr or order. Kerr was an existing person, and Macbeth, who had been misled by the fraud, intended him to receive the proceeds of the cheque. White then forged Kerr's indorsement and paid the cheque into his account with the appellant bank who received payment of it. Macbeth sued the bank for conversion of the cheque. The House of Lords held that s 7(3) of the BEA did not apply as, although misled, Macbeth intended Kerr or his transferee to receive the proceeds of the cheque. This meant the cheque was payable to order and without Kerr's genuine indorsement the bank was not entitled to receive payment of it.

4.   Who is the drawer for these purposes? In *Vinden v Hughes,* the employer signed the cheques as drawer, the fraudulent clerk merely induced him to do so. But where an employee, with authority to sign cheques, does so with the intention that the named payee should not receive payment, should the employee's intention be attributed to his employer? In *Boma Manufacturing Ltd v Canadian Imperial Bank of Commerce* (1996) 140 DLR (4th) 463 (Supreme Court of Canada), a bookkeeper employed by two associated companies was authorised to sign cheques drawn on the companies' bank accounts. Over a period of time the bookkeeper signed a number of cheques payable to existing employees of the companies, but without the intention that they should receive payment. In fact the bookkeeper forged the indorsement of the named payee on each cheque and paid it into one of her accounts at the defendant (collecting) bank. On discovering the fraud the companies brought an action in conversion against the defendant bank and the issue arose as to whether the bank took the cheques as a holder in due course giving it a complete defence to the claim. The bank could only be a holder in due course if the named payees were fictitious and the cheques deemed payable to bearer under the Canadian equivalent to s 7(3) of the BEA. However, a majority of the Supreme Court held that the payees were not fictitious payees, and the cheques were not payable to bearer, so that the bank had no defence to the action in conversion. Iacobucci J, delivering the judgment of a seven-judge majority, held that it is the intention of the drawer, in the sense of the one from whose account the cheque is drawn, which is significant for the purposes of s 7(3), not the intention of the signatory of the cheque (although in some cases the drawer and the signatory may be one and the same person). In this case the companies were the drawers and it was to be presumed that they intended the named payees to receive the proceeds of the cheques. The intention of the bookkeeper could not be attributed to the companies: she was simply the signatory and, as she was neither a director nor other officer of the companies, she could not be described as the directing mind of the companies. La Forest and McLachlin JJ dissented on the ground that the intention of the signatory should be attributed to the companies. Although the bookkeeper acted beyond the ambit of her actual authority when she prepared and signed the cheques, the dissenting minority held that in the eyes of a third party she would have had apparent authority to sign the cheques as she was an acknowledged signing officer of the companies. The minority judges also justified their decision on policy grounds arguing that by focusing on the intention of the actual signatory there would be a more efficient allocation of risk of loss between the drawer of a fraudulent cheque and the collecting bank, especially where it is an employee of the drawer which perpetrates the fraud, as the employer is in the best position to control fraud within his own organisation and will usually carry insurance to cover the loss. It is submitted that there is much to commend this approach, but it should be noted that similar policy arguments were rejected by the Privy Council in *Tai Hing Cotton Mill Ltd v Liu Chong King Bank Ltd* [1986] AC 80, see below, p 701 (a customer is under no duty to take reasonable precautions in the conduct of his business to prevent forged cheques being presented to the bank

for payment). For strong persuasive criticism of the majority's decision in *Boma,* see B Geva (1997) 28 CBLJ 177, especially pp 192–196.

5.   The intention of the drawer is irrelevant if the payee is non-existing. For example, the drawer may have intended the named payee to receive payment but, unknown to the drawer, that payee may have died before the bill is issued. The problem arose in *Clutton v Attenborough & Son* [1897] AC 90 where a clerk, employed by Clutton, induced his employer to draw cheques payable to one George Brett by falsely representing that a person of that name was entitled to payment for certain work done for Clutton. The clerk obtained possession of the cheques, indorsed them in the name of George Brett and negotiated them to Attenborough & Son who gave value for them in good faith. The House of Lords held that as the cheques fell within s 7(3) of the BEA they were to be treated as payable to bearer and so Attenborough & Son were entitled to receive their proceeds. Lord Halsbury LC noted rather abruptly that 'it has in this case never been suggested that on the face of these instruments the name of George Brett is anything other than the name of a non-existing person'. Despite the possibility that there was at least one person in the world called George Brett when Clutton signed the cheques, the 'George Brett' named as payee did not exist because there was no person of that name who had done work for Clutton. Clutton did not know that George Brett did not exist. However, if the drawer knows that the payee does not exist then he cannot intend payment to be made to him. In these circumstances (eg a cheque drawn payable to 'Ivanhoe'), the payee will be both a fictitious and non-existent person.

6.   There is no practical difference whether the payee is fictitious or non-existent, as s 7(3) of the BEA treats them both in exactly the same way. The subsection is important because it circumvents the effects of s 24 of the BEA. By s 24, a forged or unauthorised signature is treated as wholly inoperative. This means that if the payee's or indorsee's signature is forged any subsequent possessor of the instrument will not be an 'indorsee' and, therefore, not a 'holder' within the definition contained in s 2 of the BEA. However, if the bill is treated as payable to bearer, any forged indorsement is irrelevant because the possessor of a bearer bill will be, in any event, a 'holder' within the statutory definition. A 'holder' who has given value can enforce the bill and an acceptor who pays such a holder gets a good discharge under s 59 of the BEA. Where a bill is payable to order, payment to a person who has acquired it through or under a forged indorsement will not constitute a discharge because payment has not been made to a holder and so has not been made in due course as required by s 59. If the acceptor's bank pays someone who is not capable of giving the acceptor a good discharge then it acts in breach of mandate and may not debit its customer's account. If the acceptor's bank pays a 'holder' then it acts within its mandate (because the acceptor is discharged) and may debit its customer's account. This explains why it was so important in *Bank of England v Vagliano Bros* for the bank to establish that the bills in question were payable to bearer. Given that the payee's signature had been forged, only if the bill was payable to bearer could the acceptor be discharged from his liability and the bank act within its mandate. But see JR Adams (1891) 7 LQR 295 who questions whether the discharge of Vagliano Brothers was a relevant issue given that the drawer's signature was a forgery.

7.   Finally, note that s 7(3) of the BEA is permissive and not peremptory in its wording, ie '…the bill *may* be treated as payable to bearer'. It may be possible, therefore, to draw a bill using words prohibiting its transfer, or indicating an intention that it should not be transferred, which prevent the bill being treated as payable to bearer under s 7(3). For example, a bill drawn 'Pay X only' would not be treated as payable to bearer under s 7(3), even where

X was a fictitious or non existent person, nor would a cheque crossed 'account payee' or 'account payee only', as such a cheque is non-transferable under s 81A(1) of the BEA.

QUESTIONS

1. If a bill of exchange is drawn 'pay cash or order', is it treated as payable to bearer under s 7(3) of the BEA?

2. In *Vinden v Hughes* the clerk used the names of existing customers as payees and s 7(3) of the BEA was held not to apply. The loss occasioned by the clerk's fraud, therefore, fell on the third party, Hughes. If the clerk had simply invented names of non-existing customers then s 7(3) would have applied and the loss would have fallen on the employer, Vinden. Is it reasonable that the third party's rights should depend upon the nature of the misrepresentation made by the person who has induced the drawer to issue the instrument? If not, how should the third party's rights be determined? Should they turn on the fault of the drawer? (see the dissent of Laskin CJC in *Royal Bank of Canada v Concrete Column Clamps (1961) Ltd* (1976) 74 DLR (3d) 26 (Can SC) at 31–32; also the dissent of La Forest and McLachlin JJ in *Boma Manufacturing Ltd v Canadian Imperial Bank of Commerce* (1997) 140 DLR (4th) 463 at 495–496).

(b) Order bills

A bill payable to the order of a specified payee is transferred by indorsement of the payee, or the holder to whom the bill has been specially indorsed, and delivery of it (BEA, s 31(3)). A bill is payable to order in any of the following circumstances:

- When it is expressed to be so payable, eg 'Pay J Smith or order', or when it is payable to a particular person, eg 'Pay J Smith', so long as the bill does not contain words prohibiting transfer or indicating an intention that it should not be transferable (BEA, s 8(4)).

- When the only or last indorsement on the bill is in blank (and, therefore, the bill is payable to bearer) and the holder inserts above the indorsement in blank a direction to pay the bill to or to the order of himself or some other person, ie he converts the indorsement in blank into a special indorsement (BEA, s 34(4)). For example, the bill of exchange appearing in Figures 1 and 3 above, pp 533, 537, could be converted back into an order bill if Prichard delivers it to Hooley and he inserts the words 'Pay R Hooley or order' above Prichard's signature. It seems to follow from the policy behind s 34(4) that a bill originally drawn payable to bearer may also be converted into a order bill by the execution of a special indorsement (EP Ellinger, E Lomnicka and RJA Hooley *Ellinger's Modern Banking Law* (4th edn, 2006), p 368). However, in *Miller Associates (Australia) Pty Ltd v Bennington Pty Ltd* (1975) 7 ALR 144 at 149 (Sup Ct of New South Wales), Sheppard J held that such a bill remains payable to bearer regardless of the 'indorsement'. Sheppard J appeared to be of the opinion that as a bill drawn payable to bearer can be transferred by mere delivery, the signature of a holder of such a bill is irrelevant to its transfer and is not, therefore, an indorsement within the meaning of the Act (cf WJ Chappenden (1981) 55 ALJ 135 at 137). However, the holder's signature will expose him to the same liabilities imposed on an indorser under s 55(2) (see RM Goode *Commercial Law* (3rd edn, 2004), p 491, fn 59). The Report of the Review Committee on Banking Law and Services (Cm 622, 1989) recommended that within a new Negotiable Instruments Act there should be confirmation of the view that a bill drawn payable to bearer remains unaffected by any indorsement

(Rec 8(10); Appendix A, para 20.8 and Appendix N, para 25). As the Government's subsequent White Paper (Cm 1026, 1990) does not envisage a new Act, it did not adopt this recommendation (Annex 6, para 6.11). The issue remains open.

By s 31 (4) of the BEA, where a holder of a bill payable to his order transfers it for value without indorsing it, the transfer gives the transferee such title as the transferor had in the bill, and the transferee in addition acquires the right to have the indorsement of the transferor. In these circumstances the transferee is placed in the position of an assignee of an ordinary chose in action and takes subject to equities of prior parties. If the transferor does indorse the bill he will be liable on it as an indorser but, as the indorsement only takes effect from that time, the transferee will take the instrument subject to any defect of title of which he has become aware between the date of the transfer and the date of the indorsement (see *Whistler v Forster* (1863) 14 CBNS 248).

(c) Destruction of transferability

Under s 8(1) of the BEA, a bill is 'negotiable' (meaning 'transferable' in this section) when drawn, unless it contains words prohibiting transfer, or indicating an intention that it should not be transferable. If the bill is drawn so that it is not transferable then only the original payee can enforce it. However, a non-transferable instrument still appears to fall within the definition of a bill of exchange set out in s 3(1) of the BEA (cf JKMacleod(1997) 113 LQR 133, pp 149–157). It is obvious that if the bill is not transferable then it is not 'negotiable' in the technical sense of the word (ie it cannot be acquired free from defects of title of prior parties). The reverse is not necessarily true. A bill which is not 'negotiable', in the technical sense of the word, can still be transferable.

Hibernian Bank Ltd v Gysin and Hanson
[1939] 1 KB 483, Court of Appeal

The Irish Casing Co Ltd drew a bill of exchange payable three months after date 'to the order of the Irish Casing Co Ltd only the sum of £500 effective value received'. The bill was also crossed 'not negotiable'. After acceptance by the defendants the bill was indorsed by the drawers and transferred to the plaintiffs for value. On presentation for payment by the plaintiffs, as indorsees and holders for value, the bill was dishonoured. The defendants claimed that by its wording the bill was not transferable. Lewis J held that the words 'not negotiable' meant that the bill was not transferable or negotiable and gave judgment for the defendants. The Court of Appeal affirmed his decision.

Slesser LJ: …I am unable to see, construing the document as indicating the intention of the parties, that there was any acceptance of the bill except upon the basis that it was 'not negotiable.' If that be so, then it is difficult to see how the plaintiffs in this case can show any title to sue at all, because it is by reason, and by reason only, of the bill being capable of being transferred in such a manner as to constitute them the holders of the bill that they have any title to sue. If the matter ended there, and the only words for consideration were the words 'not negotiable,' then I think the case would clearly fall within s 8, sub-s 1, of the Act, which provides that 'when a bill contains words prohibiting transfer, or indicating an intention that it should not be transferable, it is valid as between the parties thereto, but is not negotiable.' Section 81 of the Act, defining the words 'not negotiable,' is in terms limited to cheques, and cannot be extended to bills not cheques to alter the natural meaning. But it is said that those words 'not negotiable' must be read subject to the other words, that the bill is payable 'to the order of the Irish Casing Co Ltd, only,' and Mr Murphy [counsel for the plaintiffs] seeks, as I understand him, to reconcile those words by saying that the bill is not negotiable after the order has been given by the Irish Casing Company, and that the absence of negotiability does not exclude the giving of the first order by the Irish Casing Company. I am unable to accept that construction. I think that the words 'not negotiable' are affirmative and govern the whole tenor of the instrument. The matter then comes to this, that either the words 'Not negotiable—Pay to the order of the Irish Casing Company only' make the whole instrument really no bill at all, or some other and more limited meaning must be given to the words 'To the order of the Irish Casing Company only.'

The surrounding circumstances of the case support a view which my brother Clauson has suggested and which has been adopted by Mr Willink [counsel for the defendants], that those words 'To the order of the Irish Casing Co Ltd, only,' are, so to speak, words of convenience, requiring payment to an agent of the Irish Casing Company, but do not, when they are read subject to the words 'not negotiable' amount to constituting the bill a bill payable to order within the meaning of s 8 at all. Fry LJ in *National Bank v Silke* ([1891] 1 QB 435 at 439) says that he is 'inclined to think that s 8 divides bills into three classes—bills not negotiable, bills payable to order, and bills payable to bearer.' In my view, adopting that classification, this is a bill 'not negotiable,' and when Fry LJ goes on to say 'so that a bill payable to order must always be negotiable,' he supports, I think, my conclusion that, in so far as this bill is not negotiable, it is not a bill payable to order within the meaning of the Bills of Exchange Act, and must have some lesser and more conditional effect. I think that that effect may be carried out by limiting it to cases where the order is merely for money to be paid to some one as agent for or for the purposes of the Irish Casing Company, and no more. In that view the instrument does not become irreconcilable or impossible of interpretation. It remains a non-negotiable instrument drawn by the Irish Casing Company Ltd, and accepted by the defendants, but limited as to its effect as between those two parties. It is not transferable; it produces no rights of action in the Hibernian Bank at all....

[Clauson and Du Parcq LJJ concurred.]

NOTES

1.   In *Hibernian Bank v Gysin and Hanson*, the Court of Appeal held that where a bill (not a cheque) is drawn: 'Pay to the order of X only' and is crossed 'not negotiable', it is not transferable. But what if the words 'not negotiable' had been omitted from the bill? Neither the Court of Appeal, nor Lewis J, gave much thought as to whether the word 'only' was effective in itself to override the statement that the bill was to be payable to order. The editors of *Byles on Bills of Exchange and Cheques* (28th edn, 2007), para 8–04, submit that it did do this and that the case could have been decided on the basis of the fact that the bill was drawn in favour of the payee 'only', without involving the question of the effect of the words 'not negotiable'. A bill drawn 'Pay X only' is certainly non-transferable.

2.   What if a bill (not a cheque) is drawn: 'Pay X or order' and crossed 'not negotiable'. Can it be transferred? Professor Guest submits that such words would probably be construed as indicating an intention that the bill should not be transferable within s 8(1) of the BEA, although he accepts the possibility that the words 'not negotiable' might be regarded as an error and have no legal effect (*Chalmers and Guest on Bills of Exchange* (16th edn, 2005), para 14–033). The reasoning of the Court of Appeal, and Lewis J, in the *Hibernian Bank* case strongly supports Professor Guest's submission that the words 'not negotiable' are decisive of the issue. But the issue turns on which words ('Pay X or order' or 'not negotiable') are the best evidence of the drawer's intention.

3.   The holder of a crossed cheque bearing the words 'not negotiable' cannot take a better title than his transferor, although the cheque remains transferable (BEA, s 81). A crossed cheque bearing across its face the words 'account payee' or 'a/c payee', either with or without the word 'only', is non-transferable (BEA, s 81A(1)).

4.   Deletion of the words 'or order' on a printed standard form bill of exchange does not restrict the transferability of the instrument. This is because under s 8(4) of the BEA a bill payable to a particular person is payable to that person's order in any event. The deletion of the words 'or order' would have no practical effect. If the bill was to be made non-transferable the word 'only' should be inserted after the name of the payee.

5.   If a bill is 'negotiable' (meaning 'transferable') when drawn it will remain so until it is restrictively indorsed or discharged by payment or otherwise: see BEA, ss 35, 36(1) and 59.

QUESTIONS

1.   A standard printed form of an uncrossed cheque states 'Pay...or order'. The drawer inserts X's name between the words 'Pay' and 'or order' and adds the words 'not negotiable' to the cheque. Is the cheque transferable? Would your answer be different if the cheque had been drawn in these terms on a blank piece of paper?

2.   If a standard printed form of order cheque is drawn 'Pay X only or order', is it transferable?

5 PERSONS ENTITLED TO THE BENEFIT OF THE OBLIGATION ON THE BILL

The right to enforce payment of a bill lies with its 'holder', defined by s 2 of the BEA as 'the payee or indorsee of a bill or note who is in possession of it, or the bearer thereof. A holder may sue on the bill in his own name (BEA, s 38(1)). Moreover, payment to the holder, within the terms of s 59(1) of the BEA, discharges the bill. Where a bill is stolen, the acceptor is not obliged to pay the thief (as he has no title to the instrument), but a thief in possession of a stolen bearer bill is still a 'holder', and an acceptor who pays the thief gets a good discharge, so long as he does so in good faith and without notice of the defect in title (BEA, s 59(1)). But mere possession is not enough to render a thief the holder of a stolen order bill, and a thief cannot become the holder of a stolen order bill through a forged indorsement (BEA, s 24). Payment made to a thief in possession of a stolen order bill would not discharge the acceptor's liability on the bill.

The BEA recognises three categories of holder: a 'mere holder', a 'holder for value' and a 'holder in due course'. Closely linked to the last category is a holder who derives his title through a holder in due course and who is himself not party to any fraud or illegality affecting the bill. The rights of the holder depend on the category into which he falls. A mere holder is at the bottom of the scale, a holder for value in the middle and a holder in due course at the top.

(a) Mere holder

A mere holder is a holder otherwise than for value, who does not claim title to the bill through a holder in due course. His rights are limited. He can transfer the bill through indorsement and/or delivery, present it for payment, sue on it in his own name and give a good discharge to a drawee or acceptor whose payment is otherwise in due course. But the real weakness of the position of a mere holder who does not himself give consideration for the bill, or is not deemed to have done so (under s 27(2) of the BEA), is that he can be met by the defence of absence or failure of consideration, whether his claim is against an immediate or remote party (these terms are explained at below, p 549).

(b) Holder for value

The liabilities of the drawer, acceptor and indorser of a bill are contractual in nature. Section 21(1) of the BEA specifically refers to their 'contract on the bill'. This means not only that those persons must have the capacity to contract on the bill (BEA, s 22) but also that consideration has been provided for their contractual 'engagement' on the bill (BEA, ss 54(1), 55(1)(a), (2)(a)). The same pre-conditions apply to the maker's contractual engagement on a promissory note (BEA, s 88(1)). That said, every party whose signature appears on a bill is prima facie deemed to have become a party to it for value (BEA, s 30(1)).

Whether 'value' has in fact been given for a bill is determined by s 27 of the BEA. Section 27(1) provides that valuable consideration for a bill may be instituted by: (a) any consideration sufficient to support a simple contract; (b) an antecedent debt or liability, this being deemed valuable consideration whether the bill is payable on demand or at a future time. As the next case illustrates, the antecedent debt or liability in question must be that of the promisor or drawer, maker or negotiator of the instrument, and not of a third party.

Oliver v Davis
[1949] 2 KB 727, Court of Appeal

Davis borrowed £350 from Oliver and gave him a post-dated cheque for £400. Later, he told his fiancee's sister, Miss Woodcock, that he was in difficulty about repaying Oliver, and as a result Miss Woodcock drew a cheque for £400 in favour of Oliver. Before the cheque was presented Miss Woodcock learnt that Davis was already married and stopped her cheque. When sued by Oliver on the cheque, Miss Woodcock contended that there had been no consideration for it. Oliver succeeded before Finnemore J, but Miss Woodcock succeeded on appeal.

Evershed MR: Section 27, sub-s 1 of the Bills of Exchange Act 1882, on which the whole argument turns, is in these terms: 'Valuable consideration for a bill may be constituted by (a) Any consideration sufficient to support a simple contract; (b) An antecedent debt or liability. Such a debt or liability is deemed valuable consideration whether the bill is payable on demand or at a future time.' It is pointed out by Mr Lawson that para (b), referring to an antecedent debt or liability, is on the face of it something distinct in subject-matter from para (a), which refers to considerations sufficient to support a simple contract. I think for myself that the proper construction of the words in (b) 'An antecedent debt or liability' is that they refer to an antecedent debt or liability of the promisor or drawer of the bill and are intended to get over what would otherwise have been prima facie the result that at common law the giving of a cheque for an amount for which you are already indebted imports no consideration, since the obligation is past and has been already incurred. On the facts of this case it may not be strictly necessary to express a concluded view on that matter. But the case in this court of *Crears v Hunter* ((1887) 19 QBD 341) (which, though decided after the date of the Act of 1882, related to the law in regard to bills of exchange which the Act generally codified) including the argument addressed to the court on behalf of the defendant, in my judgment strongly supports the view that 'an antecedent debt or liability' ought so to be construed. This at any rate is plain—that if the antecedent debt or liability of a third party is to be relied upon as supplying 'valuable consideration for a bill,' there must at least be some relationship between the receipt of the bill and the antecedent debt or liability. And for practical purposes it is difficult to see how there can be any distinction between a case in which there is a sufficient relationship for this purpose between the bill and the antecedent debt or liability and a case in which, as a result of that relationship, there is in the ordinary sense a consideration passing from the payee to the drawer of the bill. Otherwise the creditor might recover both on the debt from the third party and on the cheque from the drawer....

Somervell LJ: ...[T]he antecedent debt or liability in s 27, sub-s 1(b) is a debt or liability due from the maker or negotiator of the instrument and not from a third party. That being so, in this case the plaintiff cannot rely on (b). He cannot say: 'Because there was an antecedent debt or liability from the third party, therefore I am entitled to succeed.' *Crears v Hunter,* in my opinion, makes it clear that when dealing with a negotiable instrument given in respect of a debt of a third party, consideration has to be found such as is now referred to in s 27, sub-s 1(a), namely, consideration sufficient to support a simple contract. If that is right, the plaintiff has here to show a consideration sufficient to support a simple contract....

Denning LJ: ...Section 27, sub-s 1(b) of the Act...does not apply to a promise to pay an antecedent debt or liability of a third party. In such a case in order that the promise may be enforced there must be shown a consideration which is sufficient to support a simple contract.

NOTES

1.   What 'consideration sufficient to support a simple contract' could have been provided by Oliver? If he had promised to forbear from suing Davis, or had actually forborne from suing him at the express or implied request of Miss Woodcock, then he would have provided consideration for the cheque (*Alliance Bank v Broom* (1864) 2 Drew & Sm 289; *Fullerton v Provincial Bank of Ireland* [1903] AC 309). This would have provided *present* consideration under s 27(1)(a), not consideration arising out of the antecedent debt or liability of Davis under s 27 (1)(b). On the facts of the case, the Court of Appeal found no evidence of such forbearance. Similarly, in *AEG (UK) Ltd v Lewis* [1993] 2 Bank LR 119, where a daughter drew a cheque to pay a electrical company which had done work for her parents, and gave it on site to the company's employee who had actually executed the work, the Court of Appeal held that the company had not given consideration for the cheque as the antecedent debt or liability was of a third party (the parents) and not of the drawer (the daughter), and that the employee who dealt with the daughter did not have authority from his employer to promise to forbear from enforcing the parents' debt.

2.   Certain dicta of Evershed MR may have gone somewhat further than the opinion expressed by Somervell and Denning LJJ. He stated that the antecedent debt or liability of a third party could be relied on as providing consideration if there was 'some relationship between the receipt of the bill and the antecedent debt or liability'. What did he mean by 'some relationship' ? Could it mean something other than actual forbearance, or a promise to forbear, to sue? In *Bonior v Siery Ltd* [1968] NZLR 254, the payee took a cheque drawn by a company in payment of an antecedent debt owed to him by a director of that company. As a result, the company was entitled to reduce its own indebtedness to the director. Applying the wider dicta of Evershed MR in *Oliver v Davis,* Speight J held (at p 261) that 'there was such a close relationship between payment on behalf of the third party and the affairs of [the company] as constitutes consideration' (but Speight J also held on the facts that there had been a degree of forbearance by the payee). However, there now seems little scope for any application of the wider dicta of Evershed MR by the English courts, which have consistently adopted the orthodox position that the antecedent debt or liability referred

to under s 27(1)(b) cannot be that of a stranger (*Oliver v Davies,* above; *MK International Development Co Ltd v Housing Bank* [1991] 1 Bank LR 74 at 78–79, per Mustill LJ; *AEG (UK) Ltd v Lewis,* above). As Professor Guest submits: 'This may be justified on the ground that, as between immediate parties [see below], consideration—whether present or past—must move from the promisee.' (*Chalmers and Guest on Bills of Exchange* (16th edn, 2004), para 4–023).

3.   Professor Goode argues that, save in relation to a bill taken as security for an existing debt, it is a misconception to regard s 27(1)(b) as an exception to the common law rule as to past consideration (RM Goode, *Commercial Law* (3rd edn, 2004), pp 493–494). This is because it was established by Lush J in *Currie v Misa* (1875) LR 10 Exch 153 at 163–164 that a negotiable instrument is given for value when it is offered, and accepted, as conditional payment of an existing debt. This leaves open the question: why should the same rule not equally apply where the debt is that of a third party?

By s 27(2) of the BEA where value has at any time been given for a bill, the holder is deemed to be a holder for value as regards the acceptor and all parties to the bill who became parties prior to such time. In other words, a holder can be a 'holder for value' despite not having given value himself and, relying on the status afforded to him by s 27(2), he can sue a party to the bill who did not receive value, so long as some other party to the bill in the chain between them gave value. Take Figure 4 as an example.

Figure 4 Holder for value

An order bill payable at a future date is drawn by A on B and accepted by B as payment for goods supplied to him by A. A, who is the named payee, indorses the bill to C for value. C then indorses it to D as a gift. D indorses the bill to E for value. E indorses it to F as a gift. Relying on s 27(2), F (a donee) can sue the acceptor (B) and all parties to the bill who became parties before E gave value, including C who received no value himself.

There are two important limitations on the operation of s 27(2). First, a holder can rely on the subsection to make himself a holder for value as against a remote party but not as against an immediate party. As between immediate parties, consideration must move from the promisee (*Churchill and Sim v Goddard* [1937] 1 KB 92 at 110, per Scott LJ; *Hasan v Willson* [1977] 1 Lloyd's Rep 431 at 442, per Robert Goff J). 'Immediate' parties are those that have dealt directly with each other, eg by an agreement to sell or supply goods or services, or to purchase or discount the instrument. All other parties are 'remote'. For example, in Figure 4, F and D are remote parties, but F and E are immediate parties, which explains why F (a donee) cannot sue E on the bill. Secondly, s 27(2) envisages value being given by a party to the bill and not by a stranger. Nevertheless, these assertions must be considered against the obiter dictum of Danckwerts LJ in the next case.

Diamond v Graham
[1968] 1 WLR 1061, Court of Appeal

To induce Diamond to lend £1,650 to Herman, Graham drew a cheque for £1,665 in favour of Diamond. In return, Herman drew a cheque for £1,665 in favour of Graham and Diamond made the loan to Herman. Later, Graham's cheque in favour of Diamond was dishonoured when presented for payment. When sued on the cheque, Graham argued that Diamond was not a holder for value because no value had passed directly between Diamond and himself, as drawer.

Danckwerts LJ: Prima facie, of course, a bill of exchange is presumed to be for value, and the onus is upon the drawer of the cheque to show that it was not for value, and the discussion which has taken place before us has really revolved round the provisions of s 27(2) of the Bills of Exchange Act, which says:

> Where value has at any time been given for a bill the holder is deemed to be a holder for value as regards the acceptor and all parties to the bill who become parties prior to such time.

The contention of Mr Tibber on behalf of the defendant is that Mr Diamond was not a holder for value because no value had passed directly between him and Mr Graham, the drawer; I think that was the effect of his argument.

There is one thing that I have not mentioned, I think, and that is that when Mr Graham drew the cheque in favour of Mr Diamond, Mr Herman drew his own cheque for the amount and gave it to Mr Graham, but unfortunately Mr Herman's cheque was dishonoured, and I gather that he has since become bankrupt.

It seems to me that in presenting the argument which he did, Mr Tibber was giving a meaning which the words of s 27(2) do not bear, and is not in accordance with the words of that subsection. There is nothing in the subsection which appears to require value to have been given by the holder as long as value has been given for the cheque, and in the present case it seems to me that double value was given for the cheque first of all by Mr Herman, who gave his own cheque to Mr Graham in return for Mr Graham drawing a cheque in favour of Mr Diamond, and as it appears to me further value was given by Mr Diamond when he thereupon released his cheque to Mr Herman, and consequently there was clearly value for the cheque given, and therefore Mr Diamond was a holder for value. It seems to me, therefore, the defence fails, the plaintiff succeeds, and the appeal must be dismissed . . . .

Diplock LJ: . . . . Here there clearly passed between Mr Diamond and Mr Herman 'consideration to support a simple contract.' Was that consideration given for a bill? A bill is defined by s 3(1) in these terms: . . .

Plainly this was a bill, an unconditional order in writing, and it was for the bill that consideration was given to Mr Herman. 'Holder' is defined in s 2: ' "Holder" means the payee or indorsee of a bill or note who is in possession of it.' Mr Diamond was plainly the payee of the bill who acquired possession of it as the result of the consideration which he gave to Mr Herman. It seems to me that clearly he falls within all the requirements of the section.

I should add that Mr Graham became a party to the bill 'prior to such time.' Section 21, which deals with delivery, in sub-s (3) says:

> Where a bill is no longer in the possession of a party who has signed it as drawer . . . a valid and unconditional delivery by him is presumed until the contrary is proved.

Mr Tibber has argued, as my Lord has said, that one must not read the words in their literal meaning, but subject to a qualification that it applies only where the consideration has passed directly between one party to the bill and another party to the bill. I can see nothing in the authorities which requires that qualification, and I can see nothing in common sense or justice which requires that qualification in circumstances (though they must be rare) such as existed in this case.

I too would dismiss the appeal.

Sachs LJ: I agree. Not only has the defendant got nowhere near establishing that he did not become a party for value to this cheque, but upon the evidence it is abundantly clear to my mind that there was valuable consideration given for it within the meaning of s 27(1)(a), and in addition that the value was given for it within the meaning of s 27(2).

Accordingly the appeal must be dismissed.

NOTES

1.   In *Churchill and Sim v Goddard* [1937] 1 KB 92 at 110 Scott LJ held that '…as between immediate parties, the defendant is entitled to prove absence of consideration moving from the plaintiff as a defence to an action on the bill…'. The accuracy of this statement of law was thrown into doubt by Danckwerts LJ's *obiter dictum* in *Diamond v Graham* that there was nothing in s 27(2) 'which appears to require value to have been given by the holder as long as value has been given for the cheque'. However, Danckwerts LJ's interpretation of s 27(2) was subsequently doubted by Roskill LJ in *Pollway Ltd v Abdullah* [1974] 1 WLR 493 at 497 and in *Hasan v Willson* [1977] 1 Lloyd's Rep 431 at 442 Robert Goff J observed that:

…If Lord Justice Danckwerts is to be understood as having stated that, as between immediate parties to a bill, valid consideration may move otherwise than from the promisee, then I have to say, with the greatest respect, that I find it impossible to reconcile this statement with the analysis of the law by the Court of Appeal in *Oliver v Davis*.

See also J Thornley [1968] CLJ 196 and S Scott (1969) 15 McGill LJ 487.

2.   In *Diamond v Graham*, Herman was not a party to the cheque yet this did not stop Danckwerts LJ holding that Diamond was a holder for value under s 27(2). The question arose in *MK International Development Co Ltd v Housing Bank* [1991] 1 Bank LR 74, CA, where, following instructions from one of their customers, the Housing Bank drew a bill of exchange payable to 'MK International or bearer' and debited their customer's account accordingly. The bill was first handed to their customer, who then delivered it to MK International. The Court of Appeal held that as the customer gave value for this bearer bill and held it as bearer, MK International could rely on s 27(2) as holders for value. However, Mustill LJ also considered whether MK International could have relied on s 27(2) if the customer had not been a party to the bill. Mustill LJ (at p 80) expressed a tentative opinion that s 27(2) was:

…not to be read as envisaging value being provided by strangers to the instrument, but rather as a special provision, directed to the position of a holder who wishes to establish that he is a holder for value in good faith without notice and must as a first step show that he is a holder for value; and it relieves him of the necessity to show that he himself gave value. But it does not alter the requirement created by s 27(1) that some party to the instrument must have done so.

Mustill LJ's comments were made at an interlocutory stage of the proceedings. He acknowledged that his remarks on s 27(2) constituted *obiter dicta* and emphasised that he did not want any court seized of the action to regard his decision as foreclosing its decision on this 'new' point.

3.   Section 27(2) states that a holder is deemed to be a holder for value as regards the acceptor 'and all parties to the bill who became parties prior to [the time when value had been given for the bill]'. In *Diamond v Graham* it appears from Danckwerts LJ's judgment that when

Graham drew his cheque in favour of Diamond, Herman simultaneously drew his cheque in favour of Graham. The precise sequence of events is not clear from the report. As Graham's liability as drawer would only be complete and irrevocable when the bill was delivered to Diamond (BEA, s 21(1)), it seems likely that he received Herman's cheque, and hence value, before that time. However, in *MK International Development Co Ltd v Housing Bank* [1991] 1 Bank LR 74, when the issue arose of the simultaneous provision of value for a cheque at the time it was drawn, Staughton LJ held (at p 82) that'... It cannot be right that s 27(2) does not cover the case where a person becomes a party to the bill and receives value simultaneously'.

Rights of a holder for value A holder for value, like any other holder, has the right to sue on the bill in his own name (BEA, s 38(1)). But there is controversy as to the defences that can be raised against him. Two things are certain. First, a holder for value, like a holder in due course, takes the bill subject to 'real' defences, ie those founded on the invalidity of the bill itself (eg forgery of a signature, lack of contractual capacity). Secondly, a holder for value, unlike a holder in due course, takes the bill subject to the defects in title of prior parties (such as fraud, duress, force or illegality connected with the issue, acceptance or negotiation of the bill). In short, a holder in due course may get a better title than his transferor, whereas a holder for value gets no better title (*Arab Bank Ltd v Ross* [1952] 2 QB 216, 229, CA). The uncertainty relates to how far a holder for value takes the bill subject to personal defences of prior parties, ie those defences that are not founded on the bill itself but arise out of the relationship between the parties themselves (eg the defence of total or partial (liquidated) failure of consideration for the bill through non-performance of the underlying transaction; the right to avoid liability on the bill on the ground that its delivery was induced by misrepresentation). A holder in due course takes the bill free from personal defences available to prior parties as between themselves (BEA, s 38(2)), and so it seems to follow that a holder for value, a less protected and privileged category of holder, takes the bill subject to personal defences of prior parties, unless he is also a holder in due course (the BEA is silent on the issue). This is the position whether the holder for value is immediate or remote to the party raising the personal defence, except that a defence based on absence or failure of consideration is only available as between immediate parties and is unavailable against a remote holder for value (but contrast B Geva [1980] CLJ 360).

QUESTION

The Report of the Review Committee on Banking Services Law and Practice (paras 8.14–8.16; rec 8(4)) recommended that the need for consideration as a test of the negotiability of negotiable instruments should be abolished. The Review Committee felt that the requirement produced unnecessary complications when used to distinguish between the various types of holders and was unnecessary evidence of an intention to create legal relations. What 'unnecessary complications' could the Review Committee have been referring to? Other than the need for consideration, what evidence is there to show that a party to a bill intends to enter into legal relations? The government's subsequent White Paper on banking services did not take up this recommendation on consideration (Cm 1026, 1990)).

(c) Holder in due course

A holder in due course is in a protected and privileged position. He holds the bill free from any defects of title of prior parties, and also from mere personal defences available to prior parties amongst themselves (BEA, s 38(2)). Every holder of a bill is prima facie presumed to be a holder in due course (BEA, s 30(2)). To rebut this presumption, the defendant must prove that the requirements for holder in due course status, set out in s 29(1) of the BEA, have not been satisfied. However, if it is shown that the bill was drawn, accepted or negotiated as a result of fraud, duress, force or fear, or illegality, then the claimant can only benefit from the presumption of holder in due course status if he can prove that, following the alleged fraud or illegality, value was given in good faith for the bill (BEA, s 30(2)).

Section 29(1) of the BEA defines a holder in due course as:

a holder who has taken a bill, complete and regular on the face of it, under the following conditions; namely,

(a) That he became the holder of it before it was overdue, and without notice that it had been previously dishonoured, if such was the fact:

(b) That he took the bill in good faith and for value, and that at the time the bill was negotiated to him he had no notice of any defect in the title of the person who negotiated it.

A person seeking enforce a bill as a holder in due course must satisfy each of requirements set out in s 29(1) of the BEA.

(i) He must be a holder of the bill

But a payee cannot be a holder in due course despite the fact that he is listed as a holder in s 2 of the BEA (see above, p 546).

RE Jones Ltd v Waring and Gillow Ltd
[1926] AC 670, House of Lords

A rogue, by fraud, induced the appellants to draw two cheques, one for £2,000 and another for £3,000, payable to the order of the respondents (who were totally innocent of the fraud). The rogue tendered the cheques to the respondents in payment of his existing indebtedness to them. Subsequently, the respondents raised an objection to the signature on the cheques and returned the cheques to the appellants. The appellants then issued the respondents with a new cheque for £5,000. On discovering the fraud the appellants claimed repayment of the proceeds of the cheque from the respondents. By a majority (Viscount Cave LC and Lord Atkinson dissenting), the House of Lords gave judgment for the appellants.

Viscount Cave LC: My Lords, it was contended on behalf of the respondents that they were 'holders in due course' of the cheque for £5000 within the meaning of s 21, sub-s 2, of the Bills of Exchange Act 1882, and entitled on that ground to retain the proceeds of the cheque. I do not think that the expression 'holder in due course' includes the original payee of a cheque. It is true that under the definition clause in the Act (s 2) the word 'holder' includes the payee of a bill unless the context otherwise requires; but it appears from s 29, sub-s 1, that a 'holder in due course' is a person to whom a bill has been 'negotiated,' and from s 31 that a bill is negotiated by being transferred from one person to another and (if payable to order) by indorsement and delivery. In view of these definitions it is difficult to see how the original payee of a cheque can be a 'holder in due course' within the meaning of the Act. Section 21, sub-s 2, which distinguishes immediate from remote parties and includes a holder in due course among the latter, points to the same conclusion. The decision of Lord Russell in *Lewis v Clay* ((1897) 67 LJQB 224) was to the effect that the expression does not include a payee; and the opinion to the contrary expressed by Fletcher Moulton LJ in *Lloyds Bank v Cooke* ([1907] 1 KB 794) does not appear to have been accepted by the other members of the Court of Appeal. This contention therefore fails.

[On the issue of whether the respondents were holders in due course, the majority (Lords Shaw of Dunfermline, Sumner and Carson) delivered opinions concurring with that of the Lord Chancellor. Lord Atkinson concurred.]

NOTES

1. As a payee cannot be a holder in due course, he cannot be deemed to be one under s 30(2) of the BEA. However, the editors of *Byles on Bills of Exchange and Cheques* (28 edn, 2007) state that *R E Jones Ltd v Waring and Gillow* 'did not, specifically, at any rate, reduce the rights of a payee-holder for value below those of a holder in due course. Moreover, it is submitted that the decision did not affect the rights of the payee-holder for value whatever they may be' (para 18–031). It appears that if the issue or acceptance of a bill is affected by the fraud or duress of a third party, that can only be raised as a defence against the original payee who has taken the bill in good faith and for value, if the party sued on the bill can prove that when the payee took it he had notice of the defect (*Talbot v Von Boris* [1911] 1 KB 854, CA; followed by Robert Goff J in *Hasan v Willson* [1977] 1 Lloyd's Rep 431 at 444; as approved and applied in *Dextra Bank & Trust Co Ltd v Bank of Jamaica* [2002] 1 All ER (Comm) 193 at [22], PC). When assessing whether the payee had notice of the third party's fraud etc, the court should take account of the wider circumstances in which the transaction had taken place, including whether there had been previous, similar transactions which the payee knew to be fraudulent (*Abbey National plc v JSF Finance & Currency Exchange Co Ltd* [2006] EWCA Civ 328 at [41]–[44]). Note how the burden of proof rests on the party sued and not the payee, as would be the case if s 30(2) applied (see *Chalmers and Guest on Bills of Exchange* (16th edn, 2005), paras 4–085 and 5–073).

2. The payee can be given the rights of a holder in due course under s 29(3) of the BEA where the bill is negotiated from the payee to an indorsee, who is a holder in due course, and later renegotiated back to the original payee by that indorsee (*Jade International Steel Stahl and Eisen GmbH & Co KG v Robert Nicholas (Steels) Ltd* [1978] QB 917, CA: see below, p 560).

(ii) The bill must be complete and regular on its face (which includes the back of the bill)

The incompleteness or irregularity of the bill stands as a warning to the holder. No matter how honest he is, the holder of such a bill cannot acquire a better title than his transferor.

Incomplete bill

A bill is considered incomplete if any material detail is missing, eg the name of the payee, the amount payable, any necessary indorsements (omission of the date does not render the bill incomplete unless the date is necessary to fix the maturity of the bill).

If the bill is incomplete in a material respect (ie it is an inchoate instrument), the holder has the right to complete it, so long as this is done within a reasonable time and strictly in accordance with the authority given (BEA, s 20: see above, p 536). There is authority to suggest that this enables the holder to convert himself retrospectively into a holder in due course (*Glennie v Bruce Smith* [1908] 1 KB 263 at 268–269, and other cases cited in *Chalmers and Guest on Bills of Exchange* (16th edn, 2005), para 4–052). The bootstraps nature of this approach makes it unattractive. Moreover, it conflicts with the express wording of s 29(1) of the BEA, which requires the holder to have 'taken' a bill that is complete and regular on its face if he is to be a holder in due course. This does not stop a holder completing the bill and then negotiating it to another holder who takes it as a holder in due course, but it would seem to prevent the first holder from elevating himself to that status.

By s 2 of the Cheques Act 1957 if a collecting bank takes for value a cheque payable to order (ie not a non-transferable cheque, such as one crossed 'account payee') without the cheque having been indorsed to it, the cheque will be treated as indorsed in blank and, therefore, payable to bearer. Notwithstanding the omission of the indorsement the cheque is transferable by mere delivery and the bank can take it as a holder in due course (*Midland Bank Ltd v R V Harris Ltd* [1963] 1 WLR 1021 at 1024–1025; *Westminster Bank Ltd v Zang* [1966] AC 182 at 190).

Irregular bill

A bill is considered irregular if it contains a feature that would reasonably put the holder on inquiry. For example, a bill will not be regular on its face if an indorsement is irregular.

Arab Bank Ltd v Ross

[1952] 2 QB 216, Court of Appeal

Ross was the maker of two promissory notes naming a Palestine firm, 'Fathi and Fay sal Nabulsy Company', as payees. One of the partners in that firm indorsed the notes 'Fathi and Fay sal Nabulsy' (the word 'Company' being omitted) and discounted them to the Arab Bank. The issue arose whether the notes were 'complete and regular on [their] face' so that the Arab Bank could succeed with a claim against Ross as holders in due course under s 29. The Court of Appeal held that the indorsements were irregular and that the Arab Bank were not holders in due course. Nevertheless, the bank were held entitled to succeed with their claim on the notes as a holders for value.

Denning LJ: The first question in this case is whether the Arab Bank Ltd were holders in due course of the promissory note, and that depends on whether, at the time they took it, it was 'complete and regular on the face of it' within s 29 of the Bills of Exchange Act 1882. Strangely enough, no one doubts that the 'face' of a bill includes the back of it. I say strangely enough, because people so often insist on the literal interpretation of Acts of Parliament, whereas here everyone agrees that the literal interpretation must be ignored because the meaning is obvious. The meaning is that, looking at the bill, front and back, without the aid of outside evidence, it must be complete and regular in itself.

Regularity is a different thing from validity. The Act itself makes a careful distinction between them. On the one hand an indorsement which is quite invalid may be regular on the face of it. Thus the indorsement may be forged or unauthorized and, therefore, invalid under s 24 of the Act, but nevertheless there may be nothing about it to give rise to any suspicion. The bill is then quite regular on the face of it. Conversely, an indorsement which is quite irregular may nevertheless be valid. Thus, by a misnomer, a payee may be described on the face of the bill by the wrong name, nevertheless, if it is quite plain that the drawer intended him as payee, then an indorsement on the back by the payee in his own true name is valid and sufficient to pass the property in the bill (*Leonard v Wilson* ((1834) 2 Cr & M 589); *Bird & Co v Thomas Cook & Son Ltd* ([1937] 2 All ER 227); *Hadley v Henry* ((1896) 22 VLR 230)), but the difference between front and back makes the indorsement irregular unless the payee adds also the misnomer by which he was described on the front of the bill. This is what he eventually did in *Leonard v Wilson*.

Regularity is also different from liability. The Act makes a distinction between these two also. On the one hand a person who makes an irregular indorsement is liable thereon despite the irregularity. Thus, if a payee, who is wrongly described on the front of the bill, indorses it in his own true name, the indorsement is irregular, but he is liable to any subsequent holder and cannot set up the irregularity as a defence; or, if he is rightly described on the front of the bill, but indorses it in an assumed name, the indorsement is irregular but he is liable thereon as if he had indorsed it in his own name: see s 28(1) and s 55(2) of the Act. Conversely, a regular indorsement will not impose liability if it is forged or unauthorized. Thus, where a firm is the payee, but is described in an unauthorized name which is substantially different from its real name, an indorsement by one partner in that name does not impose liability on the other partners: *Kirk v Blurton* ((1841) 9 M & W 284). It would be otherwise if the name was substantially the same: *Forbes v Marshall* ((1855) 11 Exch 166).

Once regularity is seen to differ both from validity and from liability, the question is when is an indorsement irregular? The answer is, I think, that it is irregular whenever it is such as to give rise to doubt whether it is the indorsement of the named payee. A bill of exchange is like currency. It should be above suspicion. But if it is asked: When does an indorsement give rise to doubt? I would say that that is a practical question which is, as a rule, better answered by a banker than a lawyer. Bankers have to consider the regularity of indorsements every week, and every day of every week, and every hour of every day; whereas the judges sitting in this court have not had to consider it for these last 20 years. So far as I know the last occasion was in *Slingsby's* case ([1932] 1 KB 544).

The Law Merchant is founded on the custom of merchants, and we shall not go far wrong if we follow the custom of bankers of the City of London on this point. They have given evidence that they would not accept the indorsements in this case as a regular indorsement. They said that if a bill is made payable to 'Fathi and Faysal Nabulsy Company' they would not accept an indorsement 'Fathi and Faysal Nabulsy.' I think there is good sense in their view. For aught they know, in Palestine the word 'company' may be of vital significance. It may there signify a different legal entity, just as the word 'limited' does here (*Bank of Montreal v Exhibit and Trading Co* ((1906) 11 Com Cas 250), or it may signify a firm of many partners and not merely two of them. I agree with the bankers that this indorsement does give rise to doubt whether it is the indorsement of the named payee. It was, therefore, irregular…

The truth is, I think, that the bankers adopted this strict attitude both in their own interests and also in the interests of their customers. It would be quite impossible for them to make inquiries to see that all the indorsements on a bill are in fact genuine; but they can at least see that they are regular on the face of them: see *Bank of England v Vagliano* ([1891] AC 107 at 157), per Lord Macnaghten. That is some safeguard against dishonesty. It is a safeguard which the bankers have taken for the past 120 years at least, and I do not think we should throw any doubt today on the correctness of their practice.

I do not stay to discuss the regularity of indorsements by married women or titled folk, except to say that titles and descriptions can often be omitted without impairing the regularity of the indorsement. The word 'company' in this case is not, however, mere description. It is part of the name itself. It was suggested that an indorsement in Arabic letters would be regular. I cannot accept this view. The indorsement should be in the same lettering as the name of the payee; for otherwise it could not be seen on the face of it to be regular. My conclusion is, therefore, that this promissory note, when it was taken by the Arab Bank Ltd, was not complete and regular on the face of it. They were not, therefore, holders in due course.

[Somervell and Romer LJJ delivered concurring judgments.]

(iii) The bill must not be overdue at the time of transfer

A time bill (payable on a particular day) is overdue if not presented for payment on the day it falls due. A demand bill is overdue when it appears on its face to have been in circulation for an unreasonable length of time, which is a question of fact in each case (BEA, s 36(3)).

(iv) The holder must have no notice of previous dishonour

The dishonour may be for non-payment or for non-acceptance. What constitutes 'notice' is considered below.

(v) The holder must have taken the bill without notice and in good faith

Section 29(1) of the BEA contains separate requirements that:

(a) when he takes the bill the holder does not have notice of any previous dishonour for non-acceptance or for non-payment;

(b) at the time the bill was negotiated to him the holder does not have notice of any defect in the title of the person who negotiated it; and

(c) the holder takes the bill in good faith.

The expression 'notice' in s 29(1) means either actual knowledge of a fact or suspicion that something is wrong coupled with a wilful disregard of the means of knowledge. It does not include 'constructive knowledge' (see above, p 35). By s 90 of the BEA, the expression 'good faith' is defined in terms of the holder's honesty and not his negligence. Notice and good faith are linked. Failure to discover a defect in the title of the transferor because of lack of care is not dishonest but deliberately turning a blind eye to suspicious circumstances is.

Jones v Gordon

(1877) 2 App Cas 616, House of Lords

To defraud their creditors, S drew and G accepted a number of bills of exchange. Four of the bills, with an overall face value of £1,727, were purchased by J for £200. J knew that G was in financial difficult, but he refrained from contacting certain people who he knew could give him information as to G's financial affairs. The House of Lords held that J was not a bona fide purchaser who could take the bills free of defects in title as he was deemed to have known of the fraud.

Lord Blackburn: . . . [M]y Lords, I think it is right to say that I consider it to be fully and thoroughly established that if value be given for a bill of exchange, it is not enough to shew that there was carelessness, negligence, or foolishness in not suspecting that the bill was wrong, when there were circumstances which might have led a man to suspect that. All these are matters which tend to shew that there was dishonesty in not doing it, but they do not in themselves make a defence to an action upon a bill of exchange. I take it that in order to make such a defence, whether in the case of a party who is solvent and *sui juris,* or when it is sought to be proved against the estate of a bankrupt, it is necessary to shew that the person who gave value for the bill, whether the value given be great or small, was affected with notice that there was something wrong about it when he took it. I do not think it is necessary that he should have notice of what the particular wrong was. If a man, knowing that a bill was in the hands of a person who had no right to it, should happen to think that perhaps the man had stolen it, when if he had known the real truth he would have found, not that the man had stolen it, but that he had obtained it by false pretences, I think that would not make any difference if he knew that there was something wrong about it and took it. If he takes it in that way he takes it at his peril.

But then I think that such evidence of carelessness or blindness as I have referred to may with other evidence be good evidence upon the question which, I take it, is the real one, whether he did know that there was something wrong in it. If he was (if I may use the phrase) honestly blundering and careless, and so took a bill of exchange or a bank-note when he ought not to have taken it, still he would be entitled to recover. But if the facts and circumstances are such that the jury, or whoever has to try the question, came to the conclusion that he was not honestly blundering and careless, but that he must have had a suspicion that there was something wrong, and that he refrained from asking questions, not because he was an honest blunderer or a stupid man, but because he thought in his own secret mind -1 suspect there is something wrong, and if I ask questions and make farther inquiry, it will no longer be my suspecting it, but my knowing it, and then I shall not be able to recover -1 think that is dishonesty. I think, my Lords, that that is established, not only by good sense and reason, but by the authority of the cases themselves.

[Lords O'Hagan and Gordon delivered concurring judgments.]

NOTE

J paid £200 for bills with a total value of £1,727. This caused Lord Blackburn to note at 631–632 that:

...since the repeal of the Usury Laws we can never inquire into the question as to how much was given for a bill, and if [J's vendor] was in such a position that he could have proved against the estate it would have been no objection at all that he conveyed these bills to another for a nominal amount, that he sold bills nominally amounting to £1,727 for £200. Although I think that could not have been inquired into, yet the amount given in comparison with the apparent value is an important piece of evidence guiding us to a conclusion as to whether or not it was a bona fide transaction.

In *MK International Development Co Ltd v Housing Bank* [1991] 1 Bank LR 74, CA, Mustill LJ (at 79) noted Lord Blackburn's remarks in *Jones v Gordon* and continued:

...It may also be the law that where the bill is given as the price of an indivisible obligation the maker cannot complain even as against an immediate party that the obligation was not worth the amount of the bill, ie that he made a bad bargain: unless perhaps the consideration is so trifling as not to be consideration at all: see *Young v Gordon* (1896) 23 R 419.

(vi) *The holder must take the bill for value*

If a holder is deemed to be a holder for value under s 27(2) of the BEA (see above, p 549), can he establish 'that he took the bill...for value' under s 29(l)(b) and so become a holder in due course? Two cases suggest he can. In *MK International Development Co Ltd v The Housing Bank* [1991] 1 Bank LR 74 at 80, Mustill LJ clearly thought, albeit obiter only, that a holder in due course did not have to provide value himself but that he could rely on s 27(2). In *Clifford Chance v Silver* [1992] 2 Bank LR 11, the Court of Appeal held that a cheque received by the claimant solicitors as stakeholders (ie without themselves giving value for it) was nevertheless held by them as holders in due course because they were deemed to be 'holders for value' pursuant to s 27(2). But in neither case does it appear that the Court of Appeal considered the views of the majority of commentators who believe that it is necessary for a person claiming to be a holder in due course under s 29(1) to have given value personally: see, eg J James *Richardson's Guide to Negotiable Instruments* (8th edn, 1991), p 77; B Geva [1980] CLJ 360, p 364; *Chalmers and Guest on Bills of Exchange* (14th edn, 1991), p 274 (now 16th edn, 2005, para 4–057). It remains strongly arguable that the phrase 'he took the bill in good faith and for value' in s 29(1)(b) implies that a holder in due course must give value personally (see RM Goode *Commercial Law* (3rd edn, 2004), pp 497–498). The issue is considered further by LP Hitchens in [1993] JBL 571. A holder relying on s 27(2) does not give value personally; by contrast, a holder relying on s 27(3) does. Section 27(3) of the BEA deems a person to be a holder for value of a bill over which he has a lien. A holder who is deemed by s 27(3) to be a holder for value will be a holder in due course if the other conditions set out in s 29(1) are also satisfied (*Barclays Bank Ltd v Astley Industrial Trust Ltd* [1970] 2 QB 527 at 539).

Rights of a holder in due course

Cebora SNC v SIP (Industrial Products) Ltd

[1976] 1 Lloyd's Rep 271, Court of Appeal

(See above, p 527.)

NOTES

1.   Under s 38(2) of the BEA, a holder in due course holds the bill free from any defects of title of prior parties, as well as from mere personal defences available to prior parties amongst themselves, and may enforce payment against all parties liable on the bill. Section 29(2) of the BEA provides that 'the title of a person who negotiates a bill is defective when he obtained the bill, or its acceptance, by fraud, duress, or force or fear, or other unlawful means, or for an illegal consideration, or when he negotiates it in breach of faith, or under such circumstances as amount to fraud'. Thus, the title of the person negotiating the bill may be defective as a result of either the circumstances in which he acquired the bill, or those in which he transferred it. In addition, it may be due to a defect in the title of a prior party. The s 29(2) list of 'defects of title' is probably not exhaustive (see Geva [1980] CLJ 360 at 363). The expression 'mere personal defences' is not defined in the BEA and covers defences not founded on the bill itself but arising out of the relationship between the parties themselves. It appears to include matters of set-off or counterclaim and general contractual defences, such as any misrepresentation inducing the contract on the bill. There is some controversy as to whether absence or failure of consideration is a mere personal defence or a defect of title (see above, p 552).

2.   Although the holder in due course is not subject to defects of title or mere personal defences of prior parties, there are 'exceptional circumstances', as referred to by Sir Erich Sachs in the *Ceborra* case, when a bill will not be treated as cash in the hands of such a holder. They are as follows:

(1)   when there are 'real' or 'absolute' defences arising from the invalidity of the bill itself, or the invalidity of the defendant's apparent contract on the bill (eg contractual incapacity, forged or unauthorised signature, *non est factum*): *Chalmers and Guest on Bills of Exchange* (16th edn, 2005), para 5–070;

(2)   when the holder in due course sues as agent or trustee for another person, or when he sues wholly or in part for another person, as any defence or set-off available against that person is available *pro tanto* against the holder: see *Barclays Bank Ltd v Aschaffenburger Zellstoffwerke AG* [1967] 1 Lloyd's Rep 387, CA;

(3)   when the holder in due course does not comply with his duties as to presentment for acceptance and/or payment, or when he fails to comply with the proper procedure on dishonour (see below, Section 8).

3.   In the context of 'regulated' consumer credit and consumer hire agreements (unless they are non-commercial agreements), s 123(1) of the Consumer Credit Act 1974 prohibits the taking of negotiable instruments, other than banknotes or cheques, in discharge of amounts payable by the debtor or hirer or by a surety. Section 123(3) prohibits the taking of any negotiable instrument (including cheques) as a security for an amount payable under such an agreement. Under s 125(1) a person who takes a negotiable instrument in contravention of s 123(1) or (3) is not a holder in due course, and is not entitled to enforce the instrument. However, the transferee of a negotiable instrument from such an owner or creditor can be a holder in due course and is entitled to enforce the instrument (s 125(4)). Even a transferee who is not a holder in due course can enforce such an instrument as the contravention of s 123(1) or (3) is probably not a defect of title within s 29(2) of the 1882 Act (*Chalmers and Guest on Bills of Exchange* (16th edn, 2005), paras 4-070–4-071). In these circumstances the person forced to pay on the instrument is entitled to be indemnified by the owner or creditor (s 125(3)).

QUESTION

Why did Parliament seek to restrict the use of negotiable instruments in the manner set out in ss 123–125 of the Consumer Credit Act 1974? Note that the Consumer Credit (Negotiable Instruments) (Exemption) Order 1984, SI 1984/435, exempts from these restrictions credit transactions financing international trade where credit is provided to the debtor in the course of his business.

(d) Holder in due course by derivation

Section 29(3) of the BEA provides that a holder (whether for value or not) who derives his title to a bill through a holder in due course, and who is not himself a party to any fraud or illegality affecting it, has all the rights of a holder in due course as regards the acceptor and all parties to the bill prior to that holder. It has even been held that a person who draws a bill in his own favour can benefit from s 29(3) where the bill is negotiated from him, as payee, to an indorsee, who is a holder in due course, and later renegotiated back to the original payee by that indorsee.

Jade International Steel Stahl und Eisen GmbH & Co KG v Robert Nicholas (Steels) Ltd
[1978] QB 917, Court of Appeal

Jade drew a bill of exchange, payable to themselves or order, on Nicholas for the price of steel supplied by them to Nicholas. Jade indorsed the bill and discounted it to a German bank (Sparkasse), who discounted it to another German bank, and they, in turn, discounted it to Midland Bank. Each bank took the bill as a holder in due course. Midland Bank presented the bill to Nicholas for acceptance. Nicholas accepted the bill but later dishonoured it when presented for payment owing to a dispute about the quality of the steel supplied by Jade. Midland Bank then indorsed the bill in blank and, as each bank exercised its rights of re-course, the bill was passed back down the line until it reached Jade, whose account Sparkasse had debited with its amount. Jade then brought an action on the bill against Nicholas, who raised the defective quality of the steel as a defence. The issue was whether, under s 29(3) of the BEA, Jade could claim the benefits of holder in due course status enjoyed by the banks. Donaldson J held Jade were entitled to summary judgment on the bill. His decision was upheld on appeal.

Cumming-Bruce LJ: So the short point which is raised as the first point on this appeal is whether in those circumstances the drawer/payee to whom the bill was delivered pursuant to the Midland Bank or Sparkasse's right of recourse is properly to be regarded as a holder who derives his title to the bill through a holder in due course, within the meaning of s 29(3) of the Act.

The submission of Mr Bowsher is that when the plaintiffs recovered the bill pursuant to the Sparkasse Bank's right of recourse they did not thereby derive their title to the bill through the Sparkasse Bank, or through any of the other indorsers, but that it came back to them in their initial capacity as drawer pursuant to their liability as drawer under s 47(2) of the Act. Thus, he submits, that whether or not it is right within the meaning of the subsection to regard the plaintiffs at that stage as holders they were not holders who derived their title through a holder in due course. Initially as drawers they derive title from nobody. When they negotiated the bill in the first instance they then lost their title. All that was left was their liability under s 47(2), the liability to a right of recourse against them in their capacity as drawers. And so the submission is that the words of s 29(3) ought to be read strictly so as to limit the meaning of the words 'derive title to the bill' to those situations in which the bill is negotiated, what I would call on its way upwards, from the original drawer to indorser and subsequent indorsers....

I see the force as a matter of mercantile practice of the submission of Mr Bowsher that there is not any good commercial reason to deprive the defendants of the contractual rights that they initially had before they discounted the bill merely because in the last stages of the story when the bill was being dishonoured it comes back into the drawer's hands pursuant to the right of recourse of a party to whom the bill has been negotiated. The question which in the absence of authority I do not find perfectly straightforward is whether it can be right to place a restricted meaning on the apparently clear words of the subsection so as to exclude these plaintiffs from a capacity which at first sight they have, namely, a holder deriving title to the bill from a holder in due course; and faced with the words of the statute I am persuaded that there is not sufficient reason shown for placing upon those words the restricted meaning for which he contends.

I remain, which may be only a reflection of my inexperience, surprised that in the year 1977, one hundred years almost since this section was placed on the Statute Book, that the point does not appear ever to have come up for decision and is without authority.

For the reasons that I have stated on the first point, which is the only point that has been argued, I would agree that the appeal should be dismissed.

Geoffrey Lane LJ: It seems to me that once the drawers/payees (the plaintiffs in this case) have discounted the bill to the Sparkasse (Sparkasse then becoming the holders in due course), they lose the capacity which they had as immediate parties to the bill as drawers. Then when in the effluxion of time they once again become holders of the bill in the way that I have described, it is in that new fresh capacity of holders via the Sparkasse and the other bank that their situation must be judged. It is unreal as I see it to regard them as having a dual capacity. Indeed, it is something of a logical difficulty to see how they could. I repeat, when they discounted the bill they lost the benefit of their original capacity, and the guise under which they held it on the second occasion becomes the dominating guise for the purpose of deciding whether or not the judge was in a position to consider the question of discretion....

On the first ground I would dismiss this appeal.

[Stephenson LJ delivered a concurring judgment.]

NOTES

1. This decision has the surprising result that a gratuitous payee, who can bring himself within s 29(3), can enforce the bill as though he were a holder in due course (and see the other criticisms of J Thornley [1978] CLJ 236).

2. It is immaterial that the holder in due course by derivation knows of any fraud or illegality when he takes the bill, so long as he is not party to it. Similarly, his knowledge of defects in the title of prior parties is also irrelevant (*Insurance Corpn of Ireland pic v Dunluce Meats Ltd* [1991] NI 286). But s 29(3) only gives the holder in due course by derivation the same rights as the holder in due course through whom he derived his title as against the acceptor and all parties to the bill prior to that holder. This means that if the holder in due course by

derivation took the bill as a gift from the holder in due course he could not sue that holder as he had not provided consideration for the bill (although he could sue the acceptor and prior parties). Further, as certain 'real' defences are available against a holder in due course (eg contractual incapacity, forged or unauthorised signature, *non est factum*), they will also be available against a holder in due course by derivation.

6 LIABILITY ON THE BILL OF EXCHANGE: GENERAL PRINCIPLES

It has already been noted that the liability created by a bill of exchange is contractual (see above, p 547). However, the drawer, acceptor or indorser will only be liable on the bill if:

(a) he has capacity to contract;

(b) his contract on the bill is complete and irrevocable; and

(c) he has signed the instrument as such.

(a) Capacity to contract

By s 22(1) of the BEA, capacity to incur liability as a party to a bill is determined by the general law relating to capacity to contract. If a drawer, acceptor or indorser has no capacity to contract, he is not liable on the bill. With the abolition of the *ultra vires* rule in so far as it affects third parties, a company will rarely be able to plead against a holder of a bill that it does not have capacity to contract (see s 39 of the Companies Act 2006). However, the fact that one party does not have the capacity to contract does not, in itself, release other parties from liability on the bill. Section 5(2) of the BEA provides that where the drawee has no capacity to contract, the holder may treat the instrument, at his option, either as a bill of exchange or as a promissory note.

(b) Complete and irrevocable contract

By s 21(1) of the BEA, every contract on the bill is incomplete and revocable until delivery of the bill. Section 2 of the BEA defines 'delivery' as the transfer of possession, actual or constructive, from one person to another. However, the acceptor's contract can also become complete and irrevocable if he gives notice to, or according to, the directions of the person entitled to the bill that he has accepted it. If the bill is in the hands of a holder in due course a valid delivery of the bill by all parties prior to him, so as to make them liable to him, is conclusively presumed (BEA s 21(2), and see *Clifford Chance v Silver* [1992] 2 Bank LR 11, CA). The same conclusive presumption also applies in favour of a holder in due course by derivation (*Insurance Corpn of Ireland pic v Dunluce Meats Ltd* [1991] NI 286). If the bill is in the hands of a holder, who is not a holder in due course, there is a rebuttable presumption that there was a valid and unconditional delivery by the drawer, acceptor or indorser (BEA, s 21(3)). In such a case, in order to be effectual the delivery must be made either by or under the authority of the party drawing, accepting or indorsing the bill (BEA, s 22(2)(a)). For example, if a drawer draws a bill in favour of a named payee and puts it in his desk, and the bill is later stolen by a thief who hands it to the named payee, the drawer would not be liable since he never authorised delivery at all (remember, the payee cannot be a holder in due course: *RE Jones Ltd v Waring & Gillow Ltd* [1926] AC 670: see above, p 553). By contrast in *Dextra Bank & Trust Co Ltd v Bank of Jamaica* [2001] UKPC 50, [2002] 1 All ER (Comm) 193, the Privy Council held that there had been an effectual delivery where the drawer authorised his agent to deliver the bill to the payee by one method (personal delivery by the agent) but the agent effected physical delivery by another method (agent used an intermediary to effect delivery). Delivery was held to be effectual, even though not made in the prescribed manner, because the payee had given value and did not know of the method of delivery prescribed. The Privy Council stated (at 200) that any other result seemed 'neither just nor consistent with the objective of achieving maximum certainty in mercantile transactions'.

(c) Signature essential to liability

Under s 23 of the BEA, a person is liable as drawer, acceptor or indorser of a bill only if he has signed it as such. Particular issues arise when a bill is signed by an agent.

(i) Liability of the principal

Section 91(1) of the BEA provides that a bill does not have to be signed in a person's own hand 'but it is sufficient if his signature is written thereon by some other person by or under his authority'. The agent will usually sign the bill in his own name and add words to his signature indicating that he signs for and on behalf of a principal, but a simple signature of the principal in the hand of the agent will suffice. In either case the principal will be bound if the agent has his actual (express or implied) or apparent (or ostensible) authority to sign. However, if the agent acts outside the bounds of his actual authority and signs by procuration (eg 'per procurationem', 'per pro' or 'pp'), the principal is not bound by the signature. This is the effect of s 25 of the BEA, which provides that a signature by procuration operates as notice to third parties that the agent's authority is limited so that the principal will only be liable on signatures within the actual limits of the agent's authority. Even a holder in due course will be put on notice by such a signature and will not be able to enforce the bill against the principal if the agent has exceeded his authority (*Morison v London County & Westminster Bank Ltd* [1914] 3 KB 356 at 367, per Lord Reading CJ). Unfortunately, the effect of s 25 means that a principal who has misled a third party, by holding his agent out as having authority, will avoid liability simply because of the form of the agent's signature. This will occur even if the third party has no reasonable opportunity to check the agent's authority. It is not clear whether s 25 extends to all forms of representative signature (eg signatures 'for' or 'on behalf of' the principal). Protection of the third party would suggest that a narrow interpretation of the section is to be preferred.

(ii) Liability of the agent

An agent may be held personally liable on the bill if he signs it in his own name unless he makes it quite clear that he is signing only in his capacity as agent. By s 26(1) of the BEA, where a person signs a bill as drawer, indorser or acceptor, and adds words to his signature, indicating that he signs for or on behalf of a principal, or in a representative capacity, he is not personally liable on the bill, but merely describing himself as an agent, or as filling a representative character, does not exempt him from personal liability. Thus, where an agent signs the bill in his own name and adds words to his signature such as 'per pro', 'for' or 'on behalf of the principal, he will not be personally liable on the bill, but merely adding words to his signature such as 'agent', 'director' or 'secretary', does not exempt him from personal liability. However, the courts are generally reluctant to impose personal liability on agents.

Bondina Ltd v Rollaway Shower Blinds Ltd
[1986] 1 All ER 564, Court of Appeal

Mr Ward, a company director, signed a cheque by placing his signature (without additional words) below the pre-printed name of the company as drawer. At the bottom of the cheque there was a pre-printed line of figures designating the number of the cheque, the branch of the bank and the number of the account which was the company's account. The director denied he was personally liable on the cheque.

Dillon LJ: Counsel for the plaintiffs founds himself on s 26 of the Bills of Exchange Act 1882, which provides by sub-s (1):

> Where a person signs a bill as drawer, indorser, or acceptor, and adds words to his signature, indicating that he signs for or on behalf of a principal, or in a representative character, he is not personally liable thereon; but the mere addition to his signature of words describing him as an agent, or as filling a representative character, does not exempt him from personal liability.

Counsel for the plaintiffs says that Mr Ward has merely signed a printed form of cheque and has not added any relevant words to his signature. As it seems to me, however, when Mr Ward signed the cheque he adopted all the printing and writing on it; not merely the writing designating the payee and the amount for which the cheque was drawn, if that had been written out for him and not by himself, but also the printing of the company's name and the printing of the numbers which designate the company's account. The effect of this is to show that the cheque is drawn on the company's account and not on any other account. It is not a case of a joint liability of several people. It shows plainly, as I construe it, looking no further than the form of the cheque itself, that the drawer of the cheque was the company and not Mr Ward....

[Sir George Waller delivered a concurring judgment.]

If there is doubt as to whether a signature on the bill or note is that of the principal or of the agent, then the construction most favourable to the validity of the instrument is adopted (BEA, s 26(2)).

Rolfe Lubell & Co (a firm) v Keith
[1979] 1 All ER 860, Queen's Bench Division

The plaintiffs would only supply goods to GF Ltd if bills of exchange drawn in payment were personally indorsed by two officers of the company. The bills were accepted by the company and indorsed by the managing director and company secretary who placed their signatures within a rubber-stamped box on the back of the bill, so that it read 'For and on behalf of GF Ltd, X (*signature*) director, Y (*signature*) secretary'. The plaintiffs brought an action against the director claiming he was personally liable on the bills.

Kilner-Brown J: ...In the instant case the form of signature as acceptors on the face of the bill and as indorser on the back of the bill is precisely the same. The two defendants signed for and on behalf of the company and made the company liable on the bill as acceptor. By signing in similar form on the back of the bill they produced what counsel for the plaintiffs described as a mercantile nonsense. An indorsement on the back of a bill amounts to a warrant that the bill will be honoured and imposes in certain circumstances a transfer of liability to the indorser. No one can transfer liability from himself to himself. The only way in which validity can be given to this indorsement is by construing it to bind someone other than the acceptor. As soon therefore as it becomes obvious that the indorsement as worded is meaningless and of no value there is a patent ambiguity which allows evidence to be admitted to give effect to the intentions of the parties....

On the evidence I find as a fact that the first defendant agreed personally to indorse the bills; that his signature is evidence of that agreement and consequently a valid indorsement in a personal capacity and that he is personally liable on the two bills which were dishonoured on presentation. It follows that in my judgment the words 'for and on behalf of the company' are of no significance in so far as the relationship between the plaintiffs and the first defendant are concerned; they do not vary or amend a clear agreement personally to indorse and thereby to warrant and assume liability for the default of the company. The signature is the relevant and significant act.

If the agent signs the bill simply using his principal's name, or if he signs it in his own name but indicating that he accepts no personal liability, then, whether he acts with or without authority, he will not be personally liable on the bill. However, if the agent acts without authority he may be liable in tort for deceit or for breach of warranty of authority.

(iii)   Signatures on company bills, cheques and promissory notes

(a)   Section 51 of the Companies Act 2006

Under s 51(1), where a contract purports to be made by a company, or by a person as agent for a company, at a time when the company has not been formed, then subject to any agreement to the contrary the contract has effect as a contract entered into by the person purporting to act for the company or as agent for it, and he is personally liable on the contract accordingly. Even though the person signing a bill, cheque or promissory note adds words to his signature indicating that he signs for and on behalf of a principal, or in a representative capacity, he will still be personally liable on the instrument if he purports to draw, accept, make or indorse the instrument on behalf of a company which has not been formed (*Phonogram Ltd v Lane* [1982] QB 938, CA).

(b)   Repeal of section 349(4) of the Companies Act 1985

Under s 349(4) of the Companies Act 1985, if a director or other officer of a company signed or authorised to be signed on behalf of the company any bill of exchange, promissory note, cheque or order for money or goods in which its name was not mentioned in legible characters, he was liable to a fine; and he was further personally liable to the holder of the bill etc for the amount of it (unless it was fully paid by the company). The courts applied this sub-section strictly so that directors or other officers of the company were held liable where the company's name was misstated even to a relatively minor degree (see, eg *Fiorentino Comm Giuseppe Srl v Farnesi* [2005] EWHC 160 (Ch), where the company's name was stated as 'Portofino Collections (London)' instead of 'Portofino Collections (London) Ltd' on a cheque), although where the misstatement was attributable to the holder of the bill of exchange etc, that holder was estopped from holding the company's signatory liable (*Durham Fancy Goods Ltd v Michael Jackson (Fancy Goods Ltd)* [1968] 2 QB 839, CA).

Section 349(4) could operate harshly, especially on junior employees of the company, and several commentators, including the authors of this book (see 3rd edn, p 536), called for its repeal. The Company Law Review took the same view in its *Final Report*, which was published in July 2001 (see para 11.57). Section 349(4) of the Companies Act 1985 has been repealed and replaced by s 83 of the Companies Act 2006. Directors and other officers of the company are no longer to be made personally liable for breach of the disclosure requirements relating to a company's name (s 82 empowers the Secretary of State to make provision by regulations for that disclosure). Where a company is seeking to enforce a right arising out of a contract made in the course of a business in respect of which it was in breach of the disclosure requirements, any legal proceedings will be dismissed if the defendant to the proceedings can show that he has a claim against the company which he has been unable to pursue because of the breach or that the company's breach has caused him to suffer financial loss (s 83(1), (2)).

(d) Forged or unauthorised signatures

Section 24 of the BEA provides that where a signature on a bill is forged or placed on it without the authority of the person whose signature it purports to be, the forged or unauthorised signature is wholly inoperative, and no right to retain the bill, discharge it or enforce it can be acquired through or under that signature, unless the party against whom it is sought to retain it or enforce payment of the bill is precluded (ie estopped) from setting up the forgery or want of authority. The section also provides that it does not affect the ratification of an unauthorised signature not amounting to a forgery. But what is a forgery?

Forgery and Counterfeiting Act 1981

1. A person is guilty of forgery if he makes a false instrument, with the intention that he or another shall use it to induce somebody to accept it as genuine, and by reason of so accepting it to do or not to do some act to his own or any other person's prejudice.

9. (1) An instrument is false for the purposes of this Part of the Act—

   . . .

   (d) if it purports to have been made in the terms in which it is made on the authority of a person who did not in fact authorise its making in those terms; . . .

   (2) A person is to be treated for the purposes of this Part of this Act as making a false instrument if he alters an instrument so as to make it false in any respect (whether or not it is false in some other respect apart from that alteration).

NOTE

Section 9(1)(d) of the Forgery and Counterfeiting Act 1981 superseded s 1 of the Forgery Act 1913, which was drafted in similar terms. In *Kreditbank Cassel GmbH v Schenkers Ltd* [1927] 1 KB 826 a branch manager of the defendant company, without authority and fraudulently, drew and indorsed bills on behalf of the company for his own benefit. The Court of Appeal held that the company was not liable on the bills as they were forgeries within the Forgery Act 1913 and the claimants could not rely on the rule in *Turquand's* case ((1856) 6 E & B 327) because that rule did not apply where the bills were forgeries. It would appear, therefore, that a fraudulent unauthorised signature amounts to a forgery and cannot be ratified (*Brook v Hook* (1871) LR 6 Exch 89). Yet this cannot be what was intended by s 24 which distinguishes between unauthorised signatures (which are ratifiable) and forged signatures (which are not ratifiable). The explanation appears to be that when the Bills of Exchange Act 1882 was passed the Forgery Act 1861 was in force and that Act did not treat an unauthorised signature as a forgery (see *Morison v London County and Westminster Bank Ltd* [1914] 3 KB 356 at 366, CA). Consistent with what appears to have been Parliament's intention when the Bills of Exchange Act 1882 was passed, it is submitted by Professor Guest, in *Chalmers and Guest on Bills of Exchange* (16th edn, 2005), para 3–047, that the definition of forgery now contained in the Forgery and Counterfeiting Act 1981 should not be applied to s 24 of the BEA (cf RM Goode *Commercial Law* (3rd edn, 2004), p 517: there is no reason why a signature on behalf of another without his authority should not be ratified even though it is a forgery as defined by the 1981 Act). Yet even if the 1981 Act's definition of forgery is applied to the 1882 Act, it is submitted that, so far as ratification is concerned, the distinction between forged and unauthorised signatures, emphasised by s 24, should be maintained. This is because a true forger does not act, or purport to act, under the authority of the person whose signature he forges and so his signature cannot be ratified; whereas an unauthorised signature can be ratified when the agent purports to act on behalf of a principal.

Greenwood v Martins Bank Ltd
[1933] AC 51, House of Lords

A husband opened an account in his sole name with the respondent bank. His wife forged his signature on various cheques and drew money out of this account. The husband found out about the forgeries but was persuaded by his wife to say nothing. The husband remained silent for eight months and when he finally decided to tell the bank of his wife's action she shot herself. The husband brought an action against the bank to recover the sums paid out of his account on the cheques to which his signature had been forged.

Lord Tomlin: …Now it may be said at once that there can be no question of ratification or of adoption in this case. The necessary elements for ratification were not present, and adoption as understood in English law requires valuable consideration, which is not even suggested here.

The sole question is whether in the circumstances of this case the respondents are entitled to set up an estoppel.

The essential factors giving rise to an estoppel are I think:

(1) A representation or conduct amounting to a representation intended to induce a course of conduct on the part of the person to whom the representation is made.

(2) An act or omission resulting from the representation, whether actual or by conduct, by the person to whom the representation is made.

(3) Detriment to such person as a consequence of the act or omission.

Mere silence cannot amount to a representation, but when there is a duty to disclose deliberate silence may become significant and amount to a representation.

The existence of a duty on the part of the customer of a bank to disclose to the bank his knowledge of such a forgery as the one in question in this case was rightly admitted.

The respondents' case is that the duty ought to have been discharged by the appellant immediately upon his discovery in October, 1929, and that if it had been then discharged they could have sued the appellant's wife in tort and the appellant himself would have been responsible for his wife's tort. They claim that his silence until after his wife's death amounted in these circumstances to a representation that the cheques were not forgeries and deprived the respondents of their remedy.

[Lord Tomlin emphasised that the husband had known of his wife's actions for some months and continued:]

The appellant's silence, therefore, was deliberate and intended to produce the effect which it in fact produced—namely, the leaving of the respondents in ignorance of the true facts so that no action might be taken by them against the appellant's wife. The deliberate abstention from speaking in those circumstances seems to me to amount to a representation to the respondents that the forged cheques were in fact in order, and assuming that detriment to the respondents followed there were, it seems to me, present all the elements essential to estoppel. Further, I do not think that it is any answer to say that if the respondents had not been negligent initially the detriment would not have occurred. The course of conduct relied upon as founding the estoppel was adopted in order to leave the respondents in the condition of ignorance in which the appellant knew they were. It was the duty of the appellant to remove that condition however caused. It is the existence of this duty, coupled with the appellant's deliberate intention to maintain the respondents in their condition of ignorance, that gives its significance to the appellant's silence. What difference can it make that the condition of ignorance was primarily induced by the respondents' own negligence? In my judgment it can make none. For the purposes of the estoppel, which is a procedural matter, the cause of the ignorance is an irrelevant consideration.

[Lords Atkin, Warrington, Thankerton and Macmillan concurred in Lord Tomlin's opinion and the husband's appeal was dismissed.]

NOTES

1.   This was a case of estoppel by representation. Estoppel may also arise by negligence as where a customer of a bank draws a cheque in such a way as to facilitate the fraud or forgery: see *London Joint Stock Bank v Macmillan* [1918] AC 777, HL. *Greenwood v Martins Bank Ltd* was a case where the estoppel prevented the person charged with liability on the bill from relying on the forgery of his own signature. Such a common law estoppel may also prevent a party to the bill from asserting that the signature of another party to the bill is forged or unauthorised: see *Bank of England v Vagliano Bros*, above, p 538.

2.   In a case like *Greenwood v Martins Bank Ltd*, the customer must have actual knowledge of the forgery, or have deliberately turned a bind eye, to be in breach of duty. Constructive knowledge, in the sense that the customer had knowledge of circumstances which would cause a hypothetical reasonable customer to discover the fraud, is not enough (*Price Meats Ltd v Barclays Bank pic* [2000] 2 All ER (Comm) 346; *Patel v Standard Chartered Bank* [2001] Lloyd's Rep Bank 229).

3.   Although a forged signature cannot be ratified, it may be adopted. This would occur, for example, if a customer's signature on a cheque is forged but he subsequently agrees that his bank may debit his account with the cheque. Whether adoption is an example of estoppel by representation or derives from a separate contractual promise, which must be supported by its own consideration, is undecided. In *Greenwood v Martins Bank Ltd*, Lord Tomlin clearly saw it falling into the category of contractual promise. But a forged signature cannot be adopted if the consideration for accepting responsibility for the forged signature is a promise not to prosecute the forger; such consideration is unlawful as being contrary to public policy (*Brook v Hook* (1871) LR 6 Exch 89; *Newell v Royal Bank of Canada* (1997) 147 DLR (4th) 268, NSCA). Whether the adoption of a person's forged indorsement on a bill would give that person rights against prior parties, as opposed to simply making him liable to subsequent parties, has not been addressed by the courts.

A person in possession of an order bill bearing a forged or unauthorised indorsement cannot be a holder in due course (nor any other form of 'holder') of that bill and has no right to enforce it against any person who became a party to the bill prior to the forgery (see above, p 542). However, if after the forged or unauthorised indorsement, the bill is subsequently indorsed, then, under s 55(2)(b) of the BEA the subsequent indorsers will be precluded from denying to a holder in due course the genuineness and regularity in all respects of the previous indorsements. In this context, the term 'holder in due course' must be taken to include a person who would, but for the forged or unauthorised indorsement, have been a holder of the bill. Figure 5 provides an example. An order bill is stolen from C, the first indorsee. The thief forges C's indorsement and delivers the bill to D. D then indorses the bill and delivers it to E, who takes it in good faith for value and without notice of the forgery. E would not be able to hold A, B or C liable on the bill as he is not a holder of the bill as against them (this is the effect of BEA, s 24). But E could hold D liable on the bill relying on the estoppel contained in s 55(2)(b).

Figure 5 Forged indorsements

Similarly, under s 54(2)(a) of the BEA the acceptor will be precluded from denying to a holder in due course the genuineness of the drawer's signature.

(e) Material alteration

Forgery of a signature or an unauthorised signature on the bill must be distinguished from material alteration of the bill. Section 64 of the BEA deals with the situation where a bill is materially altered, eg any alteration of the date, the sum payable, the time of payment, the place of payment, and, where a bill has been accepted generally, the addition of a place of payment without the acceptor's assent. The effect of any material alteration of a bill without the assent of all parties liable thereon, is to avoid the bill, except as against the party who himself made, authorised or assented to the alteration, and subsequent indorsers (BEA, s 64(1)). However, s 64(1) contains the important proviso that where an alteration is not apparent, a holder in due course may avail himself of the bill as if it had not been altered and may enforce payment of it according to its original tenor.

In *Smith v Lloyds TSB Bank plc* [2000] 2 All ER (Comm) 693, the Court of Appeal held that, on a true construction of s 64(1), a cheque (a form of bill of exchange) which had been materially altered by a fraudulent third party was no longer a cheque but, subject to the qualifications in the section, a worthless piece of paper. This was the effect of the word 'avoided' in the section. Thus, there could be no cause of action for damages in conversion for the face value of such an instrument because it no longer represented a chose in action for that amount. The case is considered further below, p 783.

7   LIABILITY ON THE BILL: SPECIFIC PARTIES

(a) Overview

Sections 53–58 of the BEA deal with the liability of specific parties on the bill. Liability on the bill is confined to those who have signed the bill. We have already seen that a person is liable as drawer, acceptor or indorser of a bill only if he has signed it as such (BEA, s 23). The party signing the bill incurs liability to subsequent parties for its payment (and certain statutory estoppels may also be raised against him). This enables the current holder of the bill to claim against any or all of the prior parties to the bill. Where a party liable on the bill has paid the holder, that party can himself recover the amount of the bill from his predecessors (BEA, s 57). Ultimate liability for payment rests with the acceptor (unless the bill is an accommodation bill, when it will lie with the party accommodated: see below, Section 7(c)). In other words, the party primarily liable on the bill is the acceptor and the drawer and indorsers are in a position analogous to that of sureties.

Figure 6 illustrates the flow of rights on a bill of exchange (liabilities are incurred only to subsequent parties and so flow in the opposite direction). In Figure 6, an order bill is drawn by A (the seller of goods) in favour of B (his supplier) and accepted by X (who buys the goods from A). The bill is negotiated (for value) from B to C, from C to D and from D to E, each party indorsing and delivering the bill to the next in the chain. Should X fail to pay the bill on its maturity, the current holder, E, may claim against all prior parties (A, B, C, D and X) or any of them. E may choose to sue D because D is well known to him, but he does not have to do so. D may be insolvent and so E could decide to sue C instead. Once C had paid E, C can similarly choose to bring a claim against all or any of his predecessors (A, B and X). The process goes on with each party, having paid the bill, being entitled to recover against his predecessors. X stands at the end of the chain. He is acceptor and has no one against whom to claim.

Figure 6 Rights on the bill

(b) Liability of the drawee

Section 53(1) of the BEA provides that a bill of exchange, of itself, does not operate as an assignment of funds which the drawer has in the hands of the drawee and that, unless he accepts the bill, the drawee is not liable on the instrument. The drawing of a bill of exchange imposes no obligation upon the drawee to accept or pay the bill (*Credit Lyonnais Bank Nederland NV v Export Credit Guarantee Department* [1998] 1 Lloyd's Rep 19 at 39, per Hobhouse LJ). But this does not prevent the drawee being bound by some extrinsic contractual obligation to accept the bill or pay the sum due on it, for example, where a bank issues a cheque guarantee card it gives an undertaking to any supplier of goods or services to the cardholder that it will honour its customer's cheques (see generally, *First Sport Ltd v Barclays Bank plc* [1993] 1 WLR 1229, CA).

(c) Liability of the acceptor

The acceptor of a bill, by accepting it, engages that he will pay it according to the tenor of his acceptance (BEA, s 54(1)). He is the person primarily liable on the bill. Sometimes the acceptor acts as a surety for another person who may or may not be a party to the bill. In such a case, the bill is called an 'accommodation bill' and the person primarily liable on the bill is the person accommodated and not the acceptor. This is important because with an accommodation bill payment in due course by the person accommodated will discharge the bill (BEA, s 59(3)), whereas the usual rule is that only payment in due course by the drawee or acceptor will discharge the bill (BEA, s 59(1) and (2)).

Various statutory estoppels are raised against the acceptor by virtue of his acceptance. Section 54(2) of the BEA provides that the acceptor is precluded from denying to a holder in due course:

(a) the existence of the drawer, the genuineness of his signature, and his capacity and authority to draw the bill;

(b) in the case of a bill payable to drawer's order, the then capacity of the drawer to indorse, but not the genuineness or validity of his indorsement;

(c) in the case of a bill payable to the order of a third person, the existence of the payee and his then capacity to indorse, but not the genuineness or validity of the indorsement.

(d) Liability of the drawer

By s 55(1) of the BEA, the drawer of a bill by drawing it:

(a) engages that on due presentment it shall be accepted and paid according to its tenor, and that if it be dishonoured he will compensate the holder or any indorser who is compelled to pay it, provided that the requisite proceedings on dishonour be duly taken;

(b) is precluded from denying to a holder in due course the existence of the payee and his then capacity to indorse.

(e) Liability of an indorser

By s 55(2) of the BEA, the indorser of a bill by indorsing it:

(a) engages that on due presentment it shall be accepted and paid according to its tenor, and that if it be dishonoured he will compensate the holder or a subsequent indorser who is compelled to pay it, provided that the requisite proceedings on dishonour be duly taken;

(b) is precluded from denying to a holder in due course the genuineness and regularity in all respects of the drawer's signature and all previous indorsements;

(c) is precluded from denying to his immediate or a subsequent indorsee that the bill was at the time of his indorsement a valid and subsisting bill, and that he had then a good title thereto.

When a bill has been accepted for value, the relationship between the drawer and indorsers on the one hand and the acceptor on the other is analogous, therefore, to that of suretyship. This explains why the drawer and any indorser are discharged from liability if the requisite proceedings on dishonour are not followed (see below, Section 8). It also ensures that they are entitled to the equities of a surety, although in the case of an indorser this will only accrue when the bill has been dishonoured (*Duncan, Fox & Co v North and South Wales Bank* (1880) 6 App Cas 1 at 18–19, HL, per Lord Blackburn).

(f) Liability of a quasi-indorser

Only a holder of a bill can be an indorser. Nevertheless, where a person who is not a holder signs the bill he may incur liabilities. Section 56 of the BEA provides that 'where a person signs a bill otherwise than as drawer or acceptor, he thereby incurs the liabilities of an indorser to a holder in due course'. Thus, the 'quasi-indorser', or 'anomalous indorser', as he is described, will be liable to *subsequent* parties in the event of dishonour by non-acceptance or non-payment. The quasi-indorser usually signs the bill to accommodate or guarantee the liabilities of another party to the bill.

Civil law jurisdictions generally recognise the concept of an *aval,* a form of suretyship undertaken by the indorsement of a bill of exchange which renders the surety liable to subsequent *and prior* holders in the event of default by the party for whose account it is given. But English law does not recognise a guarantee given by way of an *aval* (*G & H Montague GmbH v Irvani* [1990] 2 All ER 225, CA). A quasi-indorser can only be held liable to prior parties in one of two ways. First, through a specific guarantee given in writing by the quasi-indorser which complies with the requirements of s 4 of the Statute of Frauds (1677). Secondly, where the intention to give a guarantee is clear from extrinsic evidence, by enabling a person who is already a party to the bill to take it from the quasi-indorser, insert his own indorsement above that of the quasi-indorser (relying on BEA, s 20: see above, p 536) and then claim on the bill as a 'holder' against the quasi-indorser as an 'indorser' (*Gerald McDonald & Co v Nash & Co* [1924] AC 625, HL). The desire to remedy a perceived injustice has meant that the courts have been prepared to overlook the strict requirement of s 31(3) of the BEA that an indorsement is completed by delivery. As Professor Goode points out, a payee would not have parted with the bill to the quasi-indorser after completing the bill by indorsing it with his own signature above that of the quasi-indorser (RM Goode *Commercial Law* (3rd edn, 2004), p 507, fn 148).

(g) Liability of a transferor of a bearer bill

The holder of a bearer bill who transfers it by mere delivery is not liable on the bill for he has not signed it (BEA, s 58(2)). If he signs the bill he incurs all the liabilities of an indorser. But the transferor of a bearer bill by mere delivery may incur liability *outside* the bill for on transfer he warrants to his immediate transferee (provided the transferee is a holder for value), that the bill is what it purports to be, that he has a right to transfer it and that he is not aware of any fact which renders it valueless (BEA, s 58(3)). The fact that the claim is for breach of warranty arising outside the bill means that (a) it is not for the amount of the bill but for damages or restitution of money paid on a total failure of consideration, and (b) the transferor may be able to meet the claim with a counterclaim on the underlying contract. The holder of a bearer bill who indorses the bill incurs all the liabilities of an indorser.

(h) Exemption and limitation of liability

Under s 16(1) of the BEA, the drawer and any indorser may negative or limit his liability to the holder by an express stipulation on the bill to that effect. The most an acceptor can do to limit his liability is to give a qualified acceptance to the order of the drawer contained in the bill, eg by making his acceptance conditional, or for part only of the amount for which the bill is drawn, or by agreeing to pay only at a particular place (BEA, s 19). If the acceptor purports to exclude his liability completely he would not be deemed to have accepted the bill at all. The holder may reject a qualified acceptance and treat the bill as dishonoured for non-acceptance (BEA, s 44(1)). If the holder takes a qualified acceptance, then, unless the drawer or an indorser has expressly or impliedly authorised the holder to take such an acceptance, the holder must give notice to the drawer and any indorser, who (except in a case of a partial acceptance) may decline to be bound by it and be discharged from his liability on the bill (BEA, s 44(2), (3)).

QUESTION

Barak states that s 58 of the BEA (or rather its Israeli equivalent) 'is no more than a repetition of the general law of sale and its place is there, not in the law of negotiable instruments' (A Barak 'The Nature of the Negotiable Instrument' (1983) 18 Israel LR 49, p 70). Is s 58, therefore, a redundant provision?

8 ENFORCEMENT OF THE BILL

(a) Dishonour by non-acceptance and non-payment

A demand bill is simply presented for payment. The drawee's failure to pay a demand bill duly presented for payment constitutes dishonour by non-payment (BEA, s 47(1)). By contrast, a term bill must first be presented for acceptance if the drawee is to become liable on the bill. The drawee's failure to accept the bill constitutes dishonour by non-acceptance (BEA, s 43(1)). Where a bill has been dishonoured for non-acceptance it is not necessary to go on and present it for payment. The holder has the right (subject to giving notice of dishonour) to proceed immediately against the drawer and any prior indorser (BEA, s 43(2)). Where the bill is accepted by the drawee it must be presented for payment on its maturity. Failure to pay the bill at maturity constitutes dishonour for non-payment (BEA, s 47(1)).

(b) Presentment for acceptance

As a general rule, it is not necessary for the holder to present a bill for acceptance. An acceptor is not an essential party to a bill: the holder of an unaccepted bill may still proceed against the drawer and any prior indorser. On the other hand, the bill must be presented for acceptance when its terms so require, where the bill is drawn payable elsewhere than at the residence or place of business of the drawee, or where presentment is necessary to fix the maturity date of the instrument, for example where the bill is payable 'X days after sight' (BEA, s 39). When a bill payable after sight is negotiated, the holder must either present it for acceptance or negotiate it within a reasonable time; failure to do so discharges the drawer and all indorsers prior to that holder (BEA, s 40).

(c) Presentment for payment

As we have seen, there is no need to present a bill for payment when it has already been dishonoured for non-acceptance. In other cases, unless waived or excused, presentment for payment is essential. If the bill is not duly presented, the drawer and indorsers will be discharged from liability on the bill (BEA, s 45). They are discharged from liability whether or not they have been prejudiced by the omission (although the drawer of a cheque is only discharged to the extent he has suffered actual damage: BEA, s 74). But, where the bill is accepted generally, presentment is not required to preserve the liability of the acceptor on the bill (BEA, s 52(1)). On the other hand, by the terms of a qualified acceptance the acceptor may stipulate that presentment for payment is required, eg at the acceptor's bank.

A bill must be 'duly' presented for payment. Section 45 of the BEA contains detailed rules as to the time and place of presentment. For example, a term bill must be presented for payment on the day it falls due (BEA, s 45, r (1)). As the next case illustrates, presentment the day before or the day after the due date is not due presentment.

Yeoman Credit Ltd v Gregory
[1963] 1 WLR 343, Queen's Bench Division

The plaintiffs drew two bills of exchange on a company called Express Coachcraft Ltd which accepted them, payable at National Provincial Bank Ltd. The defendant was a director of Express Coachcraft Ltd and indorsed the bills as surety. One bill was a 'fixed date' bill payable on 9 December, the other was an 'on demand' bill. Before the plaintiffs presented the bills they were informed by Mr Thornton, a director of Express Coachcraft Ltd, that the bills should be presented at a branch of Midland Bank where there were funds to meet them. The plaintiffs noted this instruction in pencil on the bills. The bills were presented for payment at Midland Bank on 9 December but the bank refused to meet them. They were then presented to National Provincial Bank on 11 December but that bank also dishonoured them.

Megaw J: The two bills which were presented in December were a 'fixed date' bill for £2,000 and an 'on demand' bill for £900. The date for payment of the 'fixed date' bill was December 9, 1959. Section 45, r (1), of the Bills of Exchange Act 1882, provides: 'Where the bill is not payable on demand, presentment must be made on the day it falls due.' Now presentment was made on December 9, the date when this bill fell due, to Midland Bank Ltd, because of the pencil notation on it. In my view, that cannot be treated as being a proper presentment of a bill which was drawn as payable at a different bank at a different place, and I am quite unable to say that that is in any way altered by the fact that, as the result of a telephone conversation, the pencil notation had been made on it and the plaintiffs had been told that it was to be presented at a different place and there, and there only, to be met. Certainly it cannot be a circumstance which could in any way affect the rights or liabilities of the defendant unless it was established that he knew and had consented to those instructions being given to the plaintiffs. What Mr Collins [credit controller of the plaintiffs] quite clearly ought to have done, and what I am sure in retrospect he realises that he ought to have done, was, after that telephone conversation, to have gone to the defendant and to have gone to all indorsers and said: 'I have had this information. Will you please, with our consent, alter the bill so as to put a different place of payment on it, and each of you indicate on the bill your consent to that alteration?' If that had been so, the matter would have been in order. But, whatever may be said about an estoppel in relation to Coachcraft or in relation to Mr Thornton, that cannot apply to the defendant. So far as the defendant is concerned, he was entitled to have the bill presented on December 9 to the named bank, National Provincial Ltd. That was not done. It was presented at the named bank on the following day. That was a bad presentment, and the result of that, under s 45, r (1), of the Act of 1882, is that, without any proof that the defendant was in any way prejudiced by that late presentation, he is excused from liability on the bill. No question arises here—I do not think that any question was sought to be raised by the plaintiffs—under s 46(1) of the Act of 1882 with regard to the excuse of delay in making presentment for payment. If it had been raised, there would, in my view, have been no facts which would have justified any bringing in of that subsection against the defendant. Accordingly, the claim for the bill for £2,000 fails.

With regard to the other bill, for £900, it being a bill payable on demand, that question of time of presentment does not arise. Counsel for the defendant has contended that it was a bad presentment for payment none the less, because of the pencil writing of a different bank on it. In my judgment, that is not a valid contention, and I say no more about it.

NOTES

1. There are some nineteenth century cases which have been interpreted as authority for the proposition that failure to present a bill for payment not only discharges the drawer and indorsers on the bill but also deprives the holder of his right to sue on the underlying contract for which the bill was given (see, for example, *Soward v Palmer* (1818) 8 Taunt 277; *Peacock v Pursell* (1863) 14 CBNS 728; and *Byles on Bills of Exchange & Cheques* (28th edn, 2007), para 12–003). Professor Goode maintains that this line of authority does not support this supposed rule (RM Goode, *Commercial Law* (3rd edn, 2004), p 510, fn 179). In any event it is questionable whether such a draconian rule represents the law today (Goode, above, pp 510–511; *Chalmers and Guest on Bills of Exchange* (16th edn, 2005), para 6–042). Professor Goode submits that the appropriate solution is to treat the drawer as discharged from liability on the underlying contract to the extent that he has suffered prejudice by the non-presentment.

2. By s 45(2) of the BEA, a bill payable on demand must be presented for payment within a reasonable time after its issue in order to render the drawer liable, and within a reasonable time after its indorsement in order to render the indorser liable. But by s 74 of the BEA, where a *cheque* is not presented for payment within a reasonable time of its issue, the drawer is only discharged to the extent of the actual damage suffered by him through the delay (for the special rules relating to the place and method of presentation of cheques, see below, p 774). However, s 45(2) of the BEA continues to apply in relation to an indorser of a cheque, who will be discharged if the cheque was not presented for payment within a reasonable time of its issue even if he was not prejudiced by the delay (cf *King and Boyd v Porter* [1925] NI 107). As to the liability of the maker and indorsers of a promissory note, if it is not duly presented for payment, see BEA, ss 86, 87 and 89.

(d) Notice of dishonour

Where the bill has been dishonoured for non-acceptance or non-payment, the holder must within a reasonable time give notice of dishonour to the drawer and any prior indorser of the bill. Unless notice is excused, failure to give notice of dishonour discharges the drawer and prior indorsers from liability on the bill (BEA, s 48). However, notice given by the holder enures for the benefit of all subsequent holders and also for the benefit of all prior indorsers who have a right of recourse against the party to whom it was given (BEA, s 49, r (3)). For example, where B draws a bill on A payable to C, which C indorses to D, notice given by D (holder) to B (drawer) will enure for the benefit of C (indorser). C can sue B where C is given due notice from D and, in consequence, has a right of recourse against B. Moreover, notice given by or on behalf of an indorser entitled to give notice enures for the benefit of the holder and all indorsers subsequent to the party to whom notice is given (s 49, r (4)). In the example just given, if D gives notice to C (and it is often the case that the holder only gives notice to his immediate indorser), but C gives notice to B, that notice will enure for the benefit of D, and D can sue both B and C.

It is not necessary to give notice of dishonour for non-payment to the acceptor (BEA, s 52(3)); he is, after all, the party who has dishonoured the bill Notice of dishonour is also dispensed with in several other cases (BEA, s 50(2)). As regards the drawer, two situations where notice is dispensed with should be mentioned as they arise reasonably frequently, especially with regard to cheques (BEA, s 50(2)(c)). First, where the drawee or acceptor owes the drawer no duty to accept or pay the bill (eg where the drawer of a cheque has insufficient funds in his account to cover payment and the drawee bank has not agreed to give him an overdraft facility). Secondly, where the drawer has countermanded payment. Finally, it should be noted that the rights of a holder in due course are protected even though a previous holder has failed to give notice of dishonour for non-acceptance (BEA, s 48, r (1)).

(e) Protesting a foreign bill

In the case of a foreign bill, that is a bill that is not or does not on the face of it purport to be both drawn and payable within the British Islands or drawn within the British Islands upon some resident therein, dishonour by non-acceptance or non-payment must be duly protested, ie formally established by a notarial act (BEA, s 51(2)).

9 DISCHARGE OF THE BILL

Discharge of the bill must be distinguished from discharge of a party to the bill. A discharged bill is treated as exhausted so that no party can sue or be sued on the instrument. A party to a bill may be discharged from liability, but others may still remain liable on the instrument. For example, where the bill is paid by an indorser or the drawer, the party making the payment and all subsequent parties are discharged from liability, but the bill is not discharged and may be enforced against prior parties.

A bill may be discharged by any one of the following methods:

- payment in due course, that is to say payment at or after maturity of the bill by or on behalf of the drawee or acceptor to the holder in good faith and without notice that his title to the bill is defective (BEA, s 59(1));

- the acceptor becoming the holder of the bill in his own right at or after maturity of the bill(BEA,s61);

- express waiver by the holder of his rights against the acceptor at or after maturity of the bill (BEA, s 62);

- intentional cancellation of the bill by the holder or his agent when this is apparent from the bill itself (BEA, s 63); and

- in certain circumstances, material alteration of the bill without the assent of the parties liable on it (BEA, s 64: see above, p 569).

When a bill is paid, the person making payment has the right to call on the holder to delivery it up to him immediately (BEA, s 52(4)). Should he not take delivery of the bill, there is a risk that it will remain in circulation and be transferred to a third party. Does the acceptor of a discharged bill, or the maker of a discharged note, incur any liability to the person to whom it has been transferred? The next case addresses the issue.

Glasscock v Balls

(1889) 24 QBD 13, Court of Appeal

As security for a debt, the defendant gave to W a promissory note payable on demand to W's order. On becoming further indebted to W, the defendant executed a mortgage in favour of W to secure all his indebtedness, including the debt already secured by the promissory note. W then transferred the mortgage to H and received from him a sum equal to the amount of the defendant's total indebtedness to W. As security for a debt owed by W to the plaintiff, W indorsed and delivered the promissory note to the plaintiff who took it without knowledge of the previous transactions. The plaintiffs claim on the note against the defendant was upheld by Lord Coleridge CJ. The defendant appealed.

Lord Esher MR: In this case the plaintiff sues the maker of a promissory note payable on demand as indorsee. It was admitted that the plaintiff was indorsee of the note for value without notice of anything that had occurred. The plaintiff cannot be said to have taken the note when overdue, because it was not shewn that payment was ever applied for, and the cases shew that such a note is not to be treated as overdue merely because it is payable on demand and bears date some time back. Under such circumstances prima facie the indorsee for value without notice is entitled to recover on the note. It lies on the defendant to bring the case within some recognised rule which would prevent such an indorsee from recovering upon the note. . . . If a negotiable instrument remains current, even though it has been paid, there is nothing to prevent a person to whom it has been indorsed for value without knowledge that it has been paid from suing . . . [T]he note here has not been paid. Nothing has happened which would prove a plea of payment. Something has happened which would entitle the maker to certain rights as against the payee, but which is not payment of the note. The maker might be entitled to an injunction to prevent the payee from suing on the note, but there has not been a payment of the note. It was said by the defendant's counsel that the note was extinguished. I cannot say I understand the meaning of the term 'extinguished' as used in the argument. I never heard of a plea of extinguishment of a bill or note . . . . No other principle could be suggested by the defendant under which the case could be brought, and therefore it must come under the general principle that the maker of the note, having issued it and allowed it to be in circulation as a negotiable instrument, is liable upon it to an indorsee for value without notice of anything wrong. For these reasons I think the appeal must be dismissed.

[Lindley LJ delivered a concurring judgment.
Lopes LJ concurred.]

NOTES

1. Even though W applied the money received from H in satisfaction of the defendant's indebtedness, the note was not discharged by payment in due course. Payment had not been made by the maker of the note, nor had it been made to the holder as required by s 59(1) of the BEA.

2. Lord Esher's remarks as to the rights of a holder in due course who takes a negotiable instrument after it has been paid are clearly *obiter dicta*. In any event, if a bill, or note, is payable at a fixed date and the holder transfers it after maturity, the transferee could not be a holder in due course as he would take the instrument after it had become overdue (BEA, s 29(1)(a)). The issue seems, therefore, to arise only with regard to a bill, or note, payable on demand which will not be overdue unless it has been in circulation for an unreasonable period of time (BEA, s 36(3)). Even then, the holder of a discharged bill, or note, will probably not be a holder in due course. Section 36(1) of the BEA provides that a bill that has been discharged for payment or otherwise ceases to be negotiable (applied to promissory notes by BEA, s 89(1)). Professor Guest convincingly argues that this seems to rule out the possibility

of such a bill subsequently being 'negotiated' to a holder in due course as required by s 29(1)(b) of the Act (*Chalmers and Guest on Bills of Exchange* (16th edn, 2005), para 8-003; cf L Kadirgamar (1959) 22 MLR 146).

3.   If an order bill is indorsed and transferred after discharge, the indorser will be precluded by s 55(2)(c) of the BEA from denying to his immediate or subsequent indorsee that the bill was at the time of his indorsement a valid and subsisting bill. If a bearer bill is transferred after discharge, the transferor will be liable to his transferee for value for breach of warranty under s 58(3) of the BEA.

10 MISTAKEN PAYMENT

What happens if the drawee or acceptor of an order bill pays someone who has taken the bill under a forged or unauthorised indorsement? As the payee will not be a 'holder' (due to BEA, s 24), the bill is not discharged by payment (subject to the special protection given to bankers, see Chapter 19). The true owner can turn to the drawee/acceptor for payment forcing the latter to attempt to recover their original payment from the erroneous payee as money paid under a mistake of fact. Similar problems arise if a drawee banker pays a cheque after the drawer has countermanded his original order to pay. If the recipient knew of the mistake as to the facts at the time he received the payment he will be ordered to make restitution (*Kendal v Wood* (1870) LR 6 Exch 243). But what if the payment was received in good faith and in ignorance of the mistake?

Barclays Bank Ltd v W J Simms, Son & Cooke (Southern) Ltd
[1980] QB 677, Queen's Bench Division

The first defendants contracted to do certain building works for a housing association. On the issue of an interim certificate of completion of some of the work, the association sent the first defendants a cheque for £24,000 drawn on the plaintiffs. At all times there were sufficient funds in the housing association's account held with the plaintiffs to meet the cheque. The following day the National Westminster Bank, exercising its powers under a debenture, appointed the second defendant as receiver over the property and assets of the first defendants. On hearing of the receiver's appointment, the association instructed the plaintiffs not to pay the cheque. Due to a clerical error, the plaintiffs overlooked the stop order and paid the cheque when presented by the receiver. The plaintiffs demanded repayment of the £24,000 from the defendants.

Robert Goff J: ... This case raises for decision the question whether a bank, which overlooks its customer's instructions to stop payment of a cheque and in consequence pays the cheque on presentation, can recover the money from the payee as having been paid under a mistake of fact. The point is one on which there is no decision in this country; and it is a point, I was told, of considerable importance to bankers, not only because it is an everyday hazard that customers' instructions may be overlooked, but because modern technology, rather than eliminating the risk, has if anything increased it.

[After setting out the facts and reviewing, inter alia, the decisions of the House of Lords in *Kleinwort Sons & Co v Dunlop Rubber Co* (1907) 97 LT 263; *Kerrison v Glyn, Mills, Currie & Co* (1911) 81 LJKB 465 and *R E Jones Ltd v Waring and Gillow Ltd* [1926] AC 670, his Lordship continued:]

From this formidable line of authority certain simple principles can, in my judgment, be deduced: (1) If a person pays money to another under a mistake of fact which causes him to make the payment, he is prima facie entitled to recover it as money paid under a mistake of fact. (2) His claim may however fail if (a) the payer intends that the payee shall have the money at all events, whether the fact be true or false, or is deemed in law so to intend; or (b) the payment is made for good consideration, in particular if the money is paid to discharge, and does discharge, a debt owed to the payee (or a principal on whose behalf he is authorised to receive the payment) by the payer or by a third party by whom he is authorised to discharge the debt; or (c) the payee has changed his position in good faith, or is deemed in law to have done so.

To these simple propositions, I append the following footnotes: (a) *Proposition 1.* This is founded upon the speeches in the three cases in the House of Lords, to which I have referred. It is also consistent with the opinion expressed by Turner J in *Thomas v Houston Corbett & Co* [1969] NZLR 151, 167. Of course, if the money was due under a contract between the payer and the payee, there can be no recovery on this ground unless the contract itself is held void for mistake (as in *Norwich Union Fire Insurance Society Ltd v Wm H Price Ltd* [1934] AC 455) or is rescinded by the plaintiff, (b) *Proposition 2 (a).* This is founded upon the dictum of Parke B in *Kelly v Solari,* 9 M & W 54. I have felt it necessary to add the words 'or is deemed in law so to intend' to accommodate the decision of the Court of Appeal in *Morgan v Ashcroft* [1938] 1 KB 49, a case strongly relied upon by the defendants in the present case, the effect of which I shall have to consider later in this judgment, (c) *Proposition 2 (b).* This is founded upon the decision in *Aiken v Short,* 1 H & N 210, and upon dicta in *Kerrison v Glyn, Mills, Currie & Co* 81 LJKB 465. However, even if the payee has given consideration for the payment, for example by accepting the payment in discharge of a debt owed to him by a third party on whose behalf the payer is authorised to discharge it, that transaction may itself be set aside (and so provide no defence to the claim) if the payer's mistake was induced by the payee, or possibly even where the payee, being aware of the payer's mistake, did not receive the money in good faith: cf. *Ward & Co v Wallis* [1900] 1 QB 675,678–679, *per* Kennedy J (d) *Proposition 2 (c).* This is founded upon the statement of principle of Lord Loreburn LC in *Kleinwort, Sons & Co v Dunlop Rubber Co* 97 LT 263. I have deliberately stated this defence in broad terms, making no reference to the question whether it is dependent upon a breach of duty by the plaintiff or a representation by him independent of the payment, because these matters do not arise for decision in the present case. I have however referred to the possibility that the defendant may be deemed in law to have changed his position, because of a line of authorities concerned with negotiable instruments which I shall have to consider later in this judgment, of which the leading case is *Cocks v Masterman,* 9 B & C 902. (e) I have ignored, in stating the principle of recovery, defences of general application in the law of restitution, for example where public policy precludes restitution, (f) The following propositions are inconsistent with the simple principle of recovery established in the authorities: (i) That to ground recovery, the mistake must have induced the payer to believe that he was liable to pay the money to the payee or his principal, (ii) That to ground recovery, the mistake must have been 'as between' the payer and the payee. Rejection of this test has led to its reformulation (notably by Asquith J in *Weld-Blundell v Synott* [1940] 2 KB 107 and by Windeyer J in *Porter v Latec Finance (Qld) Pty Ltd* (1964) 111 CLR 177,204) in terms which in my judgment mean no more than that the mistake must have caused the payment.

Where a bank pays a cheque drawn upon it by a customer of the bank, in what circumstances may the bank recover the payment from the payee on the ground that it was paid under a mistake of fact?

It is a basic obligation owed by a bank to its customer that it will honour on presentation cheques drawn by the customer on the bank, provided that there are sufficient funds in the customer's account to meet the cheque, or the bank has agreed to provide the customer with overdraft facilities sufficient to meet the cheque. Where the bank honours such a cheque, it acts within its mandate, with the result that the bank is entitled to debit the customer's account with the amount of the cheque, and further that the bank's payment is effective to discharge the obligation of the customer to the payee on the cheque, because the bank has paid the cheque with the authority of the customer.

In other circumstances, the bank is under no obligation to honour its customer's cheques. If however a customer draws a cheque on the bank without funds in his account or agreed overdraft facilities sufficient to meet it, the cheque on presentation constitutes a request to the bank to provide overdraft facilities sufficient to meet the cheque. The bank has an option whether or not to comply with that request. If it declines to do so, it acts entirely within its rights and no legal consequences follow as between the bank and its customer. If however the bank pays the cheque, it accepts the request and the payment has the same legal consequences as if the payment had been made pursuant to previously agreed overdraft facilities; the payment is made within the bank's mandate, and in particular the bank is entitled to debit the customer's account, and the bank's payment discharges the customer's obligation to the payee on the cheque.

In other cases, however, a bank which pays a cheque drawn or purported to be drawn by its customer pays without mandate. A bank does so if, for example, it overlooks or ignores notice of its customer's death, or if it pays a cheque bearing the forged signature of its customer as drawer, but, more important for present purposes, a bank will pay without mandate if it overlooks or ignores notice of countermand of the customer who has drawn the cheque. In such cases the bank, if it pays the cheque, pays without mandate from its customer; and unless the customer is able to and does ratify the payment, the bank cannot debit the customer's account, nor will its payment be effective to discharge the obligation (if any) of the customer on the cheque, because the bank had no authority to discharge such obligation.

It is against the background of these principles, which were not in dispute before me, that I have to consider the position of a bank which pays a cheque under a mistake of fact. In such a case, the crucial question is, in my judgment, whether the payment was with or without mandate. The two typical situations, which exemplify payment with or without mandate, arise first where the bank pays in the mistaken belief that there are sufficient funds or overdraft facilities to meet the cheque, and second where the bank overlooks notice of countermand given by the customer. In each case, there is a mistake by the bank which causes the bank to make the payment. But in the first case, the effect of the bank's payment is to accept the customer's request for overdraft facilities; the payment is therefore within the bank's mandate, with the result that not only is the bank entitled to have recourse to its customer, but the customer's obligation to the payee is discharged. It follows that the payee has given consideration for the payment; with the consequence that, although the payment has been caused by the bank's mistake, the money is irrecoverable from the payee unless the transaction of payment is itself set aside. Although the bank is unable to recover the money, it has a right of recourse to its customer. In the second case, however, the bank's payment is without mandate. The bank has no recourse to its customer; and the debt of the customer to the payee on the cheque is not discharged. Prima facie, the bank is entitled to recover the money from the payee, unless the payee has changed his position in good faith, or is deemed in law to have done so. . . .

If a bank pays a cheque under a mistake of fact, in what circumstances has the payee a good defence to the bank's claim to recover the money, on the principle in Cocks v Masterman *(1829) 9 B&C 902?*

The authorities on this topic have recently been analysed by Kerr J in *National Westminster Bank Ltd v Barclays Bank International Ltd* [1975] QB 654, an analysis which I gratefully adopt and which makes it unnecessary for me to burden this judgment with a full analysis of the authorities. The case before Kerr J was concerned with a claim by the plaintiff bank to recover from the defendant bank a sum paid by it on a forged cheque presented by the defendant bank on behalf of a customer for special collection, which the plaintiff bank had paid to the defendant bank in ignorance of the forgery, and the defendant bank had then credited to its customer's account. A principal question in the case was whether the plaintiff bank was estopped from claiming repayment by a representation, in honouring the cheque, that the cheque was genuine. Kerr J, in holding that the bank made no such representation and was not so estopped, considered the line of cases, commencing with the decision of Lord Mansfield in *Price v Neal* (1762) 3 Burr 1354, in which payments of bills of exchange which contained forged signatures had been held irrecoverable on a number of grounds. The early cases on the topic culminated in the leading case of *Cocks v Masterman* (1829) 9 B & C 902. In that case the plaintiff bankers paid a bill which purported to have been accepted by their customer, in ignorance of the fact that the acceptance was forged—a fact they did not discover until the day after payment. It was held by the Court of King's Bench that they could not recover the money from the defendants, the holders' bankers. Bayley J, who delivered the judgment of the court, said, at pp 908–909:

> ...we are all of opinion that the holder of a bill is entitled to know, on the day when it becomes due, whether it is an honoured or dishonoured bill, and that, if he receive the money and is suffered to retain it during the whole of that day, the parties who paid it cannot recover it back. The holder, indeed, is not bound by law (if the bill be dishonoured by the acceptor) to take any steps against the other parties to the bill till the day after it is dishonoured. But he is entitled so to do, if he thinks fit, and the parties who pay the bill ought not by their negligence to deprive the holder of any right or privilege. If we were to hold that the plaintiffs were entitled to recover, it would be in effect saying that the plaintiffs might deprive the holder of a bill of his right to take steps against the parties to the bill on the day when it becomes due.

The principle to be derived from this case is probably that, if the plaintiff fails to give notice on the day of payment that the bill contained a forged signature and that the money, having been paid in ignorance of that fact, is being claimed back, the defendant is deprived of the opportunity of giving notice of dishonour on the day when the bill falls due, and so is deemed to have changed his position and has a good defence to the claim on that ground. But, whatever the precise basis of the defence, it is clearly founded on the need for the defendant to give notice of dishonour; and it can therefore have no application where notice of dishonour is not required. Thus in *Imperial Bank of Canada v Bank of Hamilton* [1903] AC 49, it was held by the Privy Council that the defence had no application to an unendorsed cheque in which the amount of the cheque had been fraudulently increased by the drawer after it had been certified. The cheque was regarded as a total forgery, and not as a negotiable instrument at all. Lord Lindley, who delivered the advice of the Board, said, at p 58:

> The cheque for the larger amount was a simple forgery; and Bauer, the drawer and forger, was not entitled to any notice of its dishonour by non-payment. There were no indorsers to whom notice of dishonour had to be given. The law as to the necessity of giving notice of dishonour has therefore no application. The rule laid down in *Cocks v Masterman* (1829) 9 B & C 902, and recently reasserted in even wider language by Mathew J in *London and River Plate Bank Ltd v Bank of Liverpool Ltd* [1896] 1 QB 7, has reference to negotiable instruments, on the dishonour of which notice has to be given to some one, namely, to some drawer or indorser, who would be discharged from liability unless such notice were given in proper time. Their Lordships are not aware of any authority for applying so stringent a rule to any other cases. Assuming it to be as stringent as is alleged in such cases as those above described, their Lordships are not prepared to extend it to other cases where notice of the mistake is given in reasonable time, and no loss has been occasioned by the delay in giving it.

Likewise, in *National Westminster Bank Ltd v Barclays Bank International Ltd* [1975] QB 654, Kerr J held that the defence had no application in the case which he had to consider of a wholly forged cheque, which was also not a negotiable instrument at all....

It is therefore a prerequisite of the application of the defence that the defendant should be under a duty to give notice of dishonour. The provisions regarding notice of dishonour in the Bills of Exchange Act 1882 are contained in ss 48 to 50 of the Act. In s 50(2) are set out the circumstances in which notice of dishonour is dispensed with. For present purposes, the relevant provision is contained in s 50(2)(c), which provides (inter alia) that notice of dishonour is dispensed with, as regards the drawer, where the drawer has countermanded payment. It follows that in the case of a simple unendorsed cheque, payment of which is countermanded by the drawer, notice of dishonour is not required; and in such a case the payee cannot invoke the defence established in *Cocks v Masterman* (1829) 9 B & C 902.

It is to be observed that, in *Imperial Bank of Canada v Bank of Hamilton* [1903] AC 49, Lord Lindley described the rule laid down in *Cocks v Masterman* as a stringent rule. It is not merely stringent, but very technical. It is possible that if, in due course, full recognition is accorded to the defence of change of position, there will be no further need for any such stringent rule and the law can be reformulated on a more rational and less technical basis. Whether the law will hereafter develop in this way remains to be seen.

Application of the foregoing principles to the present case
In the light of the above principles, it is plain that in the present case the plaintiff bank is entitled to succeed in its claim. First, it is clear that the mistake of the bank, in overlooking the drawer's instruction to stop payment of the cheque, caused the bank to pay the cheque. Second, since the drawer had in fact countermanded payment, the bank was acting without mandate and so the payment was not effective to discharge the drawer's obligation on the cheque; from this it follows that the payee gave no consideration for the payment, and the claim cannot be defeated on that ground. Third, there is no evidence of any actual change of position on the part of either of the defendants or on the part of the National Westminster Bank; and, since notice of dishonour is not required in a case such as this, the payee is not deemed to have changed his position by reason of lapse of time in notifying them of the plaintiffs error and claiming repayment.

I must confess that I am happy to be able to reach the conclusion that the money is recoverable by the plaintiff bank. If the bank had not failed to overlook its customer's instructions, the cheque would have been returned by it marked 'Orders not to pay,' and there would have followed a perfectly bona fide dispute between the association and the receiver on the question, arising on the terms of the building contract, whether the association was entitled to stop the cheque—which ought to be the real dispute in the case. If the plaintiff bank had been unable to recover the money, not only would that dispute not have been ventilated and resolved on its merits but, in the absence of ratification by the association, the plaintiff bank would have had no recourse to the association. Indeed, if under the terms of the building contract the money had not been due to the defendant company, non-recovery by the plaintiff bank would have meant quite simply a windfall for the preferred creditors of the defendant company at the plaintiff bank's expense. As however I have held that the money is recoverable, the situation is as it should have been; nobody is harmed, and the true dispute between the association and the receiver can be resolved on its merits.

NOTES

1.   The mistaken payer may seek to recover his mistaken payment from the payee by means of a common law action for money had and received. The modern approach is to refer to the action as a 'personal claim in restitution at common law' (*Westdeutsche Landesbank Girozentrale v Islington London Borough Council* [1996] AC 669 at 683, per Lord Goff). The claim is founded on the unjust enrichment of the payee at the expense of the payer. The payer's mistake renders the enrichment of the payee unjust because it vitiates the payer's intention to transfer the benefit to him. Reversal of that unjust enrichment lies at the heart of the claim.

2.   Until recently, English law only allowed a common law action to recover money paid by mistake where the mistake was of fact and not where it was of law (the origin of the mistake of law rule was *Bilbie v Lumley* (1802) 2 East 469). In *Kleinwort Benson Ltd v Lincoln City Council* [1999] 2 AC 349, the House of Lords held (by a 3–2 majority) that the mistake of law rule no longer formed part of English law. It is now settled that a cause of action at common law is available for money paid under a mistake of law (*Deutsche Morgan Grenfell Group plc v Inland Revenue Comrs* [2006] UKHL 449, [2007] 1 AC 558 at [62], per Lord Hope). Following the recent decision of the House of Lords in *Sempra Metals Ltd v Inland Revenue*

Comrs [2007] UKHL 34, [2007] 3 WLR 354, it is also settled that a court has jurisdiction at common law to award compound interest where the claimant seeks a restitutionary remedy for the time value of money paid under a mistake of fact or law.

3.   In *Lloyds Bank plc v Independent Insurance Co Ltd* [2000] QB 110, a customer paid a cheque into his bank and, because he owed a similar sum to a third party, instructed the bank to transfer that sum to the third party as soon as possible. The bank agreed to do this but only on condition that the cheque had first cleared as there were insufficient funds in the account to make the transfer otherwise. However, before the cheque cleared the money was transferred by interbank electronic transfer into the payee's bank account by mistake. On discovering the error the bank sought to recover the payment from the payee. Applying paragraph 2(b) of Goff J's classification in *Barclays Bank v Simms,* the Court of Appeal held that the bank was not entitled to restitution of a transfer of funds which had been made with its customer's authority to discharge a debt owed by that customer to the payee. The payment had been made with the customer's actual authority and, because it discharged his debt to the third party, had been made for good consideration. It was the bank, not its customer, which had imposed the qualification that the transfer was not to be made before the cheque cleared. The bank had acted within its mandate.

4.   As a specific technical defence turning on the holder's prejudice in not being able to give notice of dishonour to prior parties, the rule in *Cocks v Masterman* is flawed. Section 50(1) of the BEA provides that delay in giving notice of dishonour is excused where the delay is caused by circumstances beyond the control of the party giving notice, and is not imputable to his default, misconduct, or negligence. If the holder gives notice of dishonour when informed that the payment was made in mistake of the facts then, under s 50(1), he should not be prejudiced by the delay in giving such notice.

5.   For as long as English law did not recognise any general defence of change of position, the rule in *Cocks v Masterman* had to be based on the technical ground of failure to give notice of dishonour. In *Barclays Bank v Simms,* Robert Goff J recognised that this could all change if full recognition was accorded to the general defence. This came with *Lipkin Gorman v Karpnale Ltd* [1991] 2 AC 548 where the House of Lords finally recognised that a general defence of change of position in good faith is available against restitutionary claims based on unjust enrichment of the defendant. Although their Lordships were at pains to point out that they did not wish to define the scope of the defence in abstract terms, but to let it develop on a case by case basis, Lord Goff did emphasise (at 580) 'that the defence is available to a person whose position has so changed that it would be inequitable in all the circumstances to require him to make restitution, or alternatively to make restitution in full'. This would mean that if the holder, who had been wrongly paid, had actually suffered prejudice because, for example, he had lost an immediate right of recourse against a prior party who had since become insolvent, the defence of change of position would apply. In so far as the rule in *Cocks v Masterman* can be justified on this wider ground it should now be regarded as a specific application of the general defence.

6.   In *Lipkin Gorman* (above) Lord Goff stressed that the mere fact that the recipient has spent the money received, in whole or in part, does not render it inequitable that he should be called upon to repay 'because the expenditure might in any event have been incurred by him in the ordinary course of things' (at 580). If the recipient is to succeed with a defence of change of position he must have incurred expenditure which he would not otherwise have

incurred or have otherwise acted in such a way as to render it unjust that he should now be compelled to refund the payment. Where the recipient has purchased goods or services, the benefit of which he still retains, he might still be held to have been unjustly enriched to their value as a result of the payment. For example, the recipient may have used the mistaken payment to purchase a car that remains in his possession (*Lipkin Gorman*, above, at 560), or shares that have increased in value (*Crédit Suisse (Monaco) SA v Attar* [2004] EWHC 374 (Comm) at [98]), or land that he still retains (*Campden Hill Ltd v Chakrani* [2005] EWHC 911 (Ch) at [87]).

7.   The Court of Appeal had to consider the availability of the defence of change of position in *Scottish Equitable plc v Derby* [2001] EWCA Civ 369, [2001] 2 All ER (Comm) 274. In that case, the claimant life assurance company miscalculated the defendant's pension entitlement, which resulted in him receiving a significant overpayment. The Court of Appeal upheld the trial judge's decision that the claimant was entitled to recover the overpayment, save for a relatively small sum spent by the defendant on making modest improvements to his lifestyle. The Court of Appeal stressed two points with regard to the defence of change of position. First, that for the defence to apply there must be a causal link between the recipient's change of position and the mistaken payment which makes it inequitable for the recipient to be required to make restitution. Moreover, the defence was to be available not only to those who had detrimentally relied on the mistaken payment but also to those who had suffered some other misfortune, for example the innocent recipient of a payment which is later stolen from him, so long as the misfortune could be causally linked to the mistaken receipt. The court appeared to give tacit approval to a 'but for' test of causation. Secondly, it was held that a court should not apply too demanding a standard of proof when an honest recipient says that he has spent an overpayment by improving his lifestyle, but cannot produce any detailed accounting. The defence was not to be limited, as it is in Canada and some of the States of the United States, to specific identifiable items of expenditure.

8.   It was held by Clarke J in *South Tyneside Metropolitan Borough Council v Svenska International plc* [1995] 1 All ER 545 that the defence of change of position was only available where the defendant had changed his position after receipt of the enrichment. In other words, anticipatory change of position was not sufficient to raise the defence. This restrictive interpretation of the defence has been heavily criticised (see, eg A Jones [1995] Conv 490). The requirement that the change of position must follow receipt of the enrichment seems unnecessary. It should be enough that the two are causally linked in some way. It is not surprising, therefore, to find that the Privy Council has since indicated that the defence should extend to anticipatory change of position. In *Dextra Bank & Trust Co Ltd v Bank of Jamaica* [2001] UKPC 50, [2002] 1 All ER (Comm) 193, Lords Bingham and Goff, delivering the advice of the Privy Council in a case where payment was held to be made as a result of a misprediction as to a future event (and so not recoverable) and not as a result of a mistake, stated *obiter* that anticipatory expenditure was enough to raise the defence. Their Lordships reasoned that by the time a claim in unjust enrichment was brought to trial, the defendant would merely want to retain the benefit that *ex hypothesi* he already had received. Moreover, so long as there was a sufficient causal connection between receipt of the enrichment and the expenditure, the injustice of requiring the defendant to make restitution was the same whether the defendant incurred an exceptional expenditure before or after receiving the enrichment. In *Commerzbank AG v Gareth Price-Jones* [2003] EWCA Civ 1663 at [38] and [64], the Court of Appeal followed *Dextra Bank* and held that a change of position in anticipation of an enrichment was to be treated in the same way as one that came afterwards.

9. The change of position defence is only open to someone who has changed his position in good faith. In *Lipkin Gorman* [1991] 2 AC 548 at 580, Lord Goff considered that it was 'plain that the defence is not open to one who has changed his position in bad faith, as where the defendant has paid away the money with knowledge of the facts entitling the plaintiff to restitution; and it is commonly accepted that the defence should not be open to a wrongdoer'. But dishonesty, in the sense of knowledge that one is transgressing ordinary standards of honest behaviour, is not the sole criterion of the right to invoke the defence of change of position. In *Niru Battery Manufacturing Co v Milestone Trading Ltd* [2002] EWHC 1425 (Comm), [2002] 2 All ER (Comm) 705 at [135], Moore Bick J held that lack of good faith was a concept 'capable of embracing a failure to act in a commercially acceptable way and sharp practice of a kind that falls short of outright dishonesty as well as dishonesty itself'. The judge was upheld on appeal, where the Court of Appeal stressed that the key question was whether it would be inequitable or unconscionable to deny restitution ([2003] EWCA Civ 1446, [2004] QB 985 at [148]–[149], [162], [182]–[185], [192]). This approach can be criticised for being too wide and imprecise, moving away from the narrow question of bad faith to the wider one of whether it is inequitable to allow the defence (see Birks (2004) 120 LQR 373, 377; Virgo [2004] CLJ 276, 278). But a more principled approach was restored in *Abou-Rahmah v Abacha* [2006] EWCA Civ 1492, [2007] 1 Lloyd's Rep 115, where Arden and Pill LJJ, at [84] and [102] respectively, focused only on the defendant's conduct at the time of the change of position and not on the general nature of the defendant's conduct (the latter approach being favoured by Rix LJ at [58]). Bad faith does not include negligence (*Dextra Bank*, above, at [45]; *Niru Battery*, above, at [33], CA). On the other hand, where a change of position involves illegality, the change of position will not be taken into account, unless the illegality is very minor (*Barros Mattos Junior v MacDaniels Ltd* [2004] EWHC 1188 (Ch), [2004] 3 All ER 299).

10. Other grounds for denying a restitutionary claim for money paid under a mistake include:

(1) if the payee presented the instrument as agent and, without notice of the claim, has since remitted the proceeds to his principal, the payer can only look to the principal, and not the agent, for repayment (*Buller v Harrison* (1777) 2 Cowp 565 at 568)—but the payee must act as agent and not as principal for the defence to operate (*National Bank of Egypt International Ltd v Oman Housing Bank SAOC* [2002] EWHC 1760 (Comm), [2003] 1 All ER (Comm) 246); and

(2) if the payer is estopped by representation from alleging that he made the payment under a mistake (although mere payment of money cannot in itself constitute a representation which will estop the payer from recovering payment: *Re Jones Ltd v Waring and Gillow Ltd* [1926] AC 670, HL; *Philip Collins Ltd v Davies* [2000] 3 All ER 808 at 825, Ch D).

In *Lipkin Gorman v Karpnale Ltd* [1991] 2 AC 548 at 578, Lord Goff suggested that the defence of an agent who has paid over money might be based on change of position. This seems wrong. Payment over is a separate defence which is well-established with its own rules. It is based on the fact that the agent recipient is a mere conduit pipe for the money, which is treated as paid to the principal, not to the agent, so that the principal, not the agent, is the proper party to be sued (*Portman Building Society v Hamlyn Taylor Neck (a firm)* [1998] 4 All ER 202 at 207, per Millett LJ). The relationship between the two defences is considered further by Elise Bant in 'Payment over and change of position: lessons from agency law' [2007] LMCLQ 225.

The estoppel defence is said to differ from the change of position defence in two respects: (a) it depends on a representation by the person making the payment whereas the change of position defence does not; and (b) it gives a total defence to the claim whereas the change of position defence only provides *a pro tanto* defence. The broad extent of the estoppel defence has recently proved unpopular with the courts and the recipient has only been permitted to retain the amount of his detrimental reliance (*Scottish Equitable plc v Derby* [2001] EWCA Civ 369, [2001] 3 All ER 818; *National Westminster Bank plc v Somer International (UK) Ltd* [2001] EWCA Civ 970, [2002] 1 All ER 198). The future of the defence is uncertain.

11. Professor Goode has been particularly critical of *Barclays Bank v Simms*. In 'The Bank's Right to Recover Money Paid on a Stopped Cheque' (1981) 97 LQR 254, pp 255–256, he writes:

...the defendants ought to have succeeded on two grounds, neither of which appears to have been argued. The first is that whilst the countermand of payment terminated the bank's *actual* authority to pay the cheque, the payee was entitled to rely on the bank's continued *apparent* authority to make payment, so that this was effective to discharge the drawer's liability to the payee on the cheque. The second is that a payee who gives up a cheque on which he has a valid claim in exchange for payment inevitably suffers a change of position, for he no longer has the instrument in his hands, and any claim he wishes to pursue against the drawer will have to be on the original consideration, not on the cheque, so that he loses valuable rights. It will further be argued that if the claim had been dismissed the rights of the parties could then have been adjusted by reference to the principle of subrogation, without unjust enrichment of the drawer or unjust detriment to the bank.

Not everyone agrees with Professor Goode's assessment of the case. In 'Unauthorised Payment and Unjustified Enrichment in Banking Law', Ch 1 of FD Rose (ed) *Restitution and Banking Law* (1998), Justice van Zyl (Judge of the Cape High Court) writes in fairly blunt terms:

There is not the slightest merit in these submissions and it is not surprising that they were not argued. If the bank has no authority to pay out a cheque it certainly cannot have 'apparent' authority to do so, unless the suggestion is that the bank misrepresented that it had authority. Furthermore...payment without authority can under no circumstances discharge the underlying agreement between the drawer and payee or have any legal effect on it whatever. The second argument must likewise be rejected since it is based on the faulty premise that the unauthorised payment discharged the drawer's indebtedness to the payee.

Professor Goode's submissions have also been strongly criticised by Lord Goff and Professor Jones (R Goff and G Jones *The Law of Restitution* (7th edn, 2007), para 4–033). An argument based on the bank's apparent authority to pay was firmly rejected by the Court of Appeal in *Lloyds Bank plc v Independent Insurance Co Ltd* [1999] 1 All ER (Comm) 8, an electronic funds transfer case (see Note 3 above), on the grounds that (a) there was no holding out that the bank had authority to make the payment; and (b) there was no reliance by the payee on the bank having authority to pay.

Nevertheless, there remains strong academic support for the view that a payment made to discharge another's debt and accepted as so doing by the payee creditor should be regarded as discharging the debt irrespective of the consent of the debtor (A Burrows *The Law of Restitution* (2nd edn, 2002), p 141). Further, in *B & H Engineering v First National Bank of SA Ltd* 1995 (2) SA 279 (A), the Appellate Division (now the Supreme Court of Appeal) in South Africa has recently held that payment of a countermanded cheque by the drawee bank discharges the underlying debt between drawer and payee, so that the drawee bank has no claim against the payee for mistaken payment but is left with a restitutionary claim against the drawer based on his unjust enrichment at the bank's expense (the decision is strongly criticised by Justice van Zyl (above), pp 22–26). Similarly, in the United States the Uniform

Commercial Code denies direct recovery by the bank which made the mistaken payment against a payee who took the cheque in good faith and for value: the bank is subrogated to the rights of the payee or holder in due course of the cheque against the drawer, or those of the drawer against the payee, so as to prevent unjust enrichment (Uniform Commercial Code, s 4–407).

The approach taken by the Supreme Court of Appeal in South Africa and by the Uniform Commercial Code in the United States has the superficial attraction of leaving the mistaken bank with a claim for unjust enrichment against its own customer, the drawer, when it is denied recovery against the payee. However, the bank will not necessarily recover all of its mistaken payment from the drawer as the bank is merely subrogated to the payee's claim against him and the drawer may have a defence to some or all of that claim (eg where the drawer stops the cheque because the payee has delivered defective goods). It is submitted that the bank should not be drawn into that dispute but should be allowed to recover its mistaken payment from the payee and withdraw from the scene, leaving the drawer and payee to fight it out amongst themselves (the solution suggested by Professor Birks in 'The Burden on the Bank', Ch 11 of FD Rose (ed) *Restitution and Banking Law* (1998), p 217).

Tracing at common law Sometimes a mistaken payer will first have to trace at common law before he can bring a personal claim for money had and received. Tracing will be necessary in two cases: (1) when making a claim to a substituted asset acquired with the enrichment, and (2) in order to maintain a claim against a remote recipient, ie when the claimant's property was received by the defendant from a third party, rather than having been subtracted directly from the claimant (see PBH Birks 'Overview', Ch 11 in PBH Birks (ed) *Laundering and Tracing* (1995), pp 300–305; LD Smith 'Tracing and Electronic Funds Transfers', Ch 8 in FD Rose (ed) *Restitution and Banking Law* (1998), pp 121–131). In each case tracing merely serves an evidential purpose, identifying the path of value from the claimant to the defendant, and does not give rise to a cause of action or remedy in itself (*Boscawen v Bajwa* [1995] 4 All ER 769 at 776, per Millett LJ; *Foskett v McKeown* [2001] 1 AC 102 at 128, per Lord Millett). As the next case illustrates, difficulties arise where payment is made through the banking system, which entails a series of more or less complex substitutions.

Agip (Africa) Ltd v Jackson
[1991] Ch 547, Court of Appeal

An authorised signatory of the plaintiff (Agip) signed a payment order instructing Agip's Tunisian bankers, Banque du Sud, to transfer US$518,000 to a named payee. Zdiri, Agip's chief accountant, fraudulently altered the name of the payee to Baker Oil Services Ltd, a company controlled by the defendant chartered accountants, which held a US dollar account at Lloyds Bank in London. On receipt of the altered payment order, Banque du Sud debited Agip's account and telexed Lloyds Bank in London to credit Baker Oil's account. Banque du Sud also telexed its correspondent bank, Citibank, in New York and instructed it to credit Lloyds Bank through the New York clearing system. As New York is five hours behind London, Lloyds Bank took a delivery risk and credited Baker Oil's account before being placed in funds through the New York clearing system. Later the money was debited from Baker Oil's account and transferred to an account in the name of the defendants. Acting on their clients' instructions, the defendants transferred all but US$45,000 to unknown parties. At first instance Millett J held that Agip had an equitable proprietary claim to the US$45,000 and was entitled to compensation for the defendants' knowing assistance in a breach of trust; but he rejected Agip's alternative claims based on the receipt of money either at common law (see below) or in equity (because the defendants had received the money as agents and not for their own benefit). The Court of Appeal upheld Millett J's decision on the equitable proprietary claim and the claim for compensation for knowing assistance in a breach of trust. The Court of Appeal dismissed Agip's appeal on the common law action for money had and received. There was no appeal on Millett J's decision to reject the equitable receipt claim.

Fox LJ: …

The right to sue

Agip's claim was for money paid under a mistake of fact. The defendants' contention was that Agip had disclosed no title to sue. The basis of that contention was that the relationship between banker and customer was one of debtor and creditor. When the customer paid money into the bank, the ownership of the money passed to the bank. The bank could do what it liked with it. What the bank undertook to do was to credit the amount of the money to the customer's account, and to honour his drafts or other proper directions in relation to it. Thus, it was said, when Banque du Sud paid Baker Oil it had no authority to do so on behalf of Agip because the order for payment was forged. Further, the Banque du Sud paid with its own money.

In terms of the mechanism of payment, what happened was no different from what would have happened if the order was not forged but genuine. Banque du Sud paid the collecting bank and debited Agip's account at Banque du Sud. In practical terms the Banque du Sud paid with Agip's money in both cases and, indeed, in both cases intended to do so. In both cases the substance of the matter was that money standing to the credit of Agip's account was paid to a third party in accordance with the order or supposed order, as the case may be, of Agip. The direction was to pay from Agip's account. To say that the payment was made out of the Banque du Sud's own funds, while true as far as it goes, only tells half the story. The banker's instruction is to pay from the customer's account. He does so by a payment from his own funds and a corresponding debit. The reality is a payment by the customer, at any rate in a case where the customer has no right to require a re-crediting of his account. Nothing passes in specie. The whole matter is dealt with by accounting transactions partly in the paying bank and partly in the clearing process.

It does not advance the matter to say that the Banque du Sud had no mandate from Agip to make the payment at Agip's expense. What actually happened was that Banque du Sud did so. Moreover, when Agip sued Banque du Sud in the Tunisian courts—and I take it that Tunisian law was the proper law of the banking relationship between Agip and Banque du Sud—to have its account re-credited, it failed to obtain that relief. In those circumstances, to regard Agip as not having paid Baker Oil is highly unreal. Banque du Sud had no intention of paying with its own money. The substance of its intention, which it achieved, was to pay with Agip's money. The order, after all, was an order to pay with Agip's money. I agree, therefore, with the view of Millett J [1990] Ch. 265, 283h that 'the fact remains that the Banque du Sud paid out the plaintiffs' money and not its own'. If Banque du Sud paid away Agip's money, Agip itself must be entitled to pursue such remedies as there may be for its recovery. The money was certainly paid under a mistake of fact.

It was said that the difference between this case and a case where the bank paid with the authority (though given under a mistake of fact) of the customer, was that, in the latter case, the bank paid as agent of the customer and that, accordingly, either the principal or agent could sue. Thus, it was contended that where, as here, there was a claim to recover money paid by mistake of fact, the mistake must be that of the plaintiff or of his agent. That, it was contended, could not be established here. There was no mistake by Agip, which was simply the victim of a fraud. The only mistake was that of Banque du Sud, which paid in the mistaken belief that it had Agip's authority to do so. Banque du Sud, it was said, did not pay as the agent of Agip because it had no authority to pay. In *Westminster Bank Ltd v Hilton* (1926) 43 TLR 124, 126, Lord Atkinson said:

> It is well established that the normal relation between a banker and his customer is that of debtor and creditor, but it is equally well established that quoad the drawing and payment of the customer's

cheques as against money of the customer's in the banker's hands the relation is that of principal and agent. The cheque is an order of the principal's addressed to the agent to pay out of the principal's money in the agent's hands the amount of the cheque to the payee thereof.

The defendants, as I understand it, would accept the proposition as to agency but say that Banque du Sud did not pay as agent of Agip because of lack of authority. The order was forged. It seems to me, however, Banque du Sud plainly intended to pay as agent of Agip. Thus, it paid in accordance with the order as presented to it and debited Agip's account accordingly. There was no reason why it should do anything else. The order as presented to it appeared perfectly regular.

But, accepting the intention, can the Banque du Sud properly be regarded as having paid as agent of Agip? The defendants say the absence of authority concluded the point against Agip. The judge met that by saying that Banque du Sud had general authority from Agip to debit the account in accordance with the instructions. That is correct but it was said that there were no instructions because the order was bad. I do not feel able to accept that. The order emanated from within Agip; it was properly signed and the amount had not been altered. Banque du Sud had no reason at all to doubt its authenticity. The Tunisian court refused to order Banque du Sud to re-credit Agip's account. For practical purposes, therefore, the order was given effect to according to its tenor as if it were a proper order. Everything that was done (i.e. the payments and the debit) stands good so far as the banking transaction is concerned. Agip cannot recover from Banque du Sud. And Banque du Sud does not seek to recover from Baker Oil. It seems to me, therefore, that the order must be regarded as having been paid by Banque du Sud as agent for Agip. That, however, does not alter the circumstance that it was money paid under a mistake of fact. The defendants accepted that a principal could recover where there was either (i) mistaken payment by an authorised agent within his instructions or (ii) mistaken payment in breach of instructions by using money entrusted to the agent by the principal. The present case can be brought within, at any rate, the first of these.

The judge referred to the decision in *Colonial Bank v Exchange Bank of Yarmouth, Nova Scotia* (1885) 11 App Cas 84, 91. In that case it was held that the bank had a sufficient interest to recover the money, if only to obtain relief from the consequences of its liability to its customer. Millett J thought the decision was inconsistent with any suggestion that, far from being the wrong plaintiff, the bank was the only plaintiff. The present point, however, was not before the Privy Council in that case and I think the decision gives only limited assistance.

Looking at the whole matter, however, it seems to me that the judge correctly concluded that Agip's right to sue was made out.

Tracing at common law

The judge held that Agip was not entitled to trace at law. Tracing at law does not depend upon the establishment of an initial fiduciary relationship. Liability depends upon receipt by the defendant of the plaintiffs money and the extent of the liability depends on the amount received. Since liability depends upon receipt the fact that a recipient has not retained the asset is irrelevant. For the same reason dishonesty or lack of inquiry on the part of the recipient are irrelevant. Identification in the defendant's hands of the plaintiff's asset is, however, necessary. It must be shown that the money received by the defendant was the money of the plaintiff. Further, the very limited common law remedies make it difficult to follow at law into mixed funds. The judge's view [1990] Ch 265, 286 of the present case was that the common law remedy was not available. He said:

> The money cannot be followed by treating it as the proceeds of a cheque presented by the collecting bank in exchange for payment by the paying bank. The money was transmitted by telegraphic transfer. There was no cheque or any equivalent. The payment order was not a cheque or its equivalent. It remained throughout in the possession of the Banque du Sud. No copy was sent to Lloyds Bank or Baker Oil or presented to the Banque du Sud in exchange for the money. It was normally the plaintiffs' practice to forward a copy of the payment order to the supplier when paying an invoice but this was for information only. It did not authorise or enable the supplier to obtain payment.

There is no evidence that this practice was followed in the case of forged payment orders and it is exceedingly unlikely that it was. Nothing passed between Tunisia and London but a stream of electrons. It is not possible to treat the money received by Lloyds Bank in London or its correspondent bank in New York as representing the proceeds of the payment order or of any other physical asset previously in its hands and delivered by it in exchange for the money.

Agip relied upon the decision of the Court of Appeal in *Banque Belge pour L'Etranger v Hambrouck* [1921] 1 KB 321. In that case what happened was that Hambrouck was a cashier employed by Pelabon. By fraud he possessed himself of cheques purporting to be drawn by Pelabon but in fact without Pelabon's authority. The cheques (which purported to be drawn to the order of Hambrouck himself or to his order) were crossed so payment had to be made through a bank. Hambrouck, therefore, opened an account with Farrow's Bank at Richmond. He endorsed the cheques and paid them into that account. Farrow's Bank cleared them through the London and South Western Bank which collected the amount of the cheques and placed them to the credit of Hambrouck's account. It seems that no funds were paid into that account other than the amount of the forged cheques: see *per* Atkin LJ at p 331. Hambrouck was living with Mademoiselle Spanoghe to whom he paid various sums of money out of his bank account with Farrow's. Mile Spanoghe paid them into a deposit account of her own in the London Joint City and Midland Bank. No other sums were at any time placed in that deposit account. Certain sums were drawn out for Hambrouck's defence. The balance, £315, was the subject of the action. The Court of Appeal held that Banque Belge was entitled to recover it Bankes LJ at p 328, and Atkin LJ, at p 334, saw no objection to a claim at common law. After having referred to Lord Ellenborough's judgment in *Taylor v Plumer* (1815) 3 M & S 562, Atkin LJ said, at pp 335–336:

> I notice that in *Sinclair v Brougham* [1914] AC 398,419 Lord Haldane LC in dealing with this decision says: 'Lord Ellenborough laid down, as a limit to this proposition, that if the money had become incapable of being traced, as, for instance, when it had been paid into the broker's general account with his banker, the principal had no remedy excepting to prove as a creditor for money had and received,' and proceeds to say 'you can, even at law, follow, but only so long as the relation of debtor and creditor has not superseded the right in rem.' The word above 'as for instance' et seq. do not represent and doubtless do not purport to represent Lord Ellenborough's actual words; and I venture to doubt whether the common law ever so restricted the right as to hold that the money became incapable of being traced, merely because paid into the broker's general account with his banker. The question always was, Had the means of ascertainment failed? But if in 1815 the common law halted outside the bankers' door, by 1879 equity had had the courage to lift the latch, walk in and examine the books: *In re Hallett's Estate* (1879) 13 Ch.D 696. I see no reason why the means of ascertainment so provided should not now be available both for common law and equity proceedings. If, following the principles laid down *In re Hallett's Estate,* it can be ascertained either that the money in the bank, or the commodity which it has bought, is 'the product of, or substitute for, the original thing,' then it still follows 'the nature of the thing itself.' On these principles it would follow that as the money paid into the bank can be identified as the product of the original money, the plaintiffs have the common law right to claim it, and can sue for money had and received. In the present case less difficulty than usual is experienced in tracing the descent of the money, for substantially no other money has ever been mixed with the proceeds of the fraud.

Bankes LJ at p 328, while accepting that tracing at common law was permissible, took a narrower position. He said that there was no difficulty about tracing at law because the money which the bank sought to remove was capable of being traced because the appellant (Mile Spanoghe) never paid any money into the bank except money which was part of the proceeds of Hambrouck's fraud and all the money standing to the credit of the account was now in court. Scrutton LJ at p 330, thought that tracing at common law was probably not permissible because the money had changed its identity when paid into the account at Farrow's. He felt, however, that the Banque Belge could trace in equity and that its claim succeeded.

Now, in the present case, the course of events was as follows. (1) The original payment order was in December signed by an authorised signatory. (2) The name of the payee was then altered to Baker Oil. (3) The altered order was then taken to Banque du Sud who complied with it by debiting the account of Agip with $518,822.92 and then instructing Lloyds Bank to pay Baker Oil. Banque du Sud also instructed Citibank in New York to debit its account with Citibank and credit Lloyds Bank with the amount of the order. (4) Lloyds Bank credited the money to Baker Oil's account on the morning of 7 January. (5) On 8 January, Lloyds Bank in pursuance of instructions from Baker Oil transferred the $518,822.92, which was the only sum standing to the credit of Baker Oil's account, to an account in the name of Jackson & Co. (6) Immediately before the transfer from Baker Oil, Jackson & Co's account was $7,911.80 in credit. In consequence of the transfer it became $526,734.72 in credit.

The inquiry which has to be made is whether the money paid to Jackson & Co's account 'was the product of, or substitute for, the original thing.' In answering that question I do not think that it matters that the order was not a cheque. It was a direction by the account holder to the bank. When Atkin LJ referred in the *Banque Belge* case to the 'original money' he was, I assume, referring to the money credited by Banque Belge (the plaintiff) to Hambrouck's account. Money from that account was the only money in Mile Spanoghe's deposit account. It was not, therefore, difficult to say that the money in issue (ie the residue of Mile Spanoghe's account) could be identified as the product of the original money. There were no complexities of tracing at all. Everything in Mile Spanoghe's account came from Hambrouck's account and everything in Hambrouck's account came from the credit in respect of the fraudulent cheque.

The position in the present case is much more difficult. Banque du Sud can be regarded as having paid with Agip's money but Lloyds Bank, acting as directed by Banque du Sud, paid Baker Oil with its own money. It had no other and, accordingly, took a delivery risk. It was, in the end, put in funds, but it is difficult to see how the origin of those funds can be identified without tracing the money through the New York clearing system. The money in the present case did get mixed on two occasions. The first was in the New York clearing system and the second was in Jackson & Co's own account. The judge held that the latter was of no consequence. I agree. The common law remedy attached to the recipient of the money and its subsequent transposition does not alter his liability. The problem arises at an earlier stage. What did Jackson & Co receive which was the product of Agip's asset? Baker Oil was controlled for present purposes by Jackson & Co but Baker Oil was paid by Lloyds Bank which had not been put in funds from New York. It was subsequently recouped. But it is not possible to show the source from which it was recouped without tracing the money through the New York clearing system. The judge said [1990] Ch 265, 286:

> Unless Lloyds Bank's correspondent bank in New York was also Citibank, this involves tracing the money through the accounts of Citibank and Lloyds Bank's correspondent bank with the Federal Reserve Bank, where it must have been mixed with other money. The money with which Lloyds Bank was reimbursed cannot therefore, without recourse to equity, be identified as being that of the Banque du Sud.

I respectfully agree with that view. Accordingly, it seems to me that the common law remedy is not available.

I should add this. Atkin LJ's approach in the *Banque Belge* case amounts virtually to saying that there is now no difference between the common law and equitable remedies. Indeed, the common law remedy might be wider because of the absence of any requirement of a fiduciary relationship. There may be a good deal to be said for that view but it goes well beyond any other case and well beyond the views of Bankes and Scrutton LJJ. And in the 70 years since the *Banque Belge* decision it has not been applied. Whether, short of the House of Lords, it is now open to the courts to adopt it I need not consider. I would in any event feel difficulty in doing so in the present case where, as I indicate later, it seems to me that the established equitable rules provide an adequate remedy in relation to this action....

[Butler-Sloss and Beldam LJJ concurred.]

NOTES

1.   Did Agip really have title to sue? The Court of Appeal held that 'in practical terms' the bank had paid Baker Oil with Agip's money, but in legal terms payment was with the bank's own money. A bank which pays outside its mandate has no right to debit its customer's account and, if a bank cannot debit its customer's account, it must be paying with its own money and not that of its customer. In the *Agip* case the Court of Appeal appears to have been influenced by the fact that Agip had unsuccessfully brought proceedings against Banque du Sud in Tunisia to have its account re-credited (see E McKendrick [1991] LMCLQ 378, pp 379–381).

2.   It is a well-established rule that it is not possible to trace money at law through a mixed fund (see, eg *Taylor v Plumer* (1815) 3 M & S 562 at 575, per Lord Ellenborough CJ; *Re Diplock* [1948] Ch 465 at 518, per Lord Greene MR; cf LD Smith *The Law of Tracing* (1997), pp 162–174). The common law can only trace though clean substitutions (see, eg *Trustees of the Property of F C Jones & Sons (a firm) v Jones* [1997] Ch 159). This rule prevents common law tracing when money is paid into a bank account which has also received other credits. The rule was fatal to Agip's attempt to trace at common law because the Court of Appeal expressly approved of Millett J's reasoning at first instance that Agip's funds were mixed with other funds during the clearing process in New York (see also *Bank of America v Arnell* [1999] Lloyd's Rep Bank 399 at 405, Aikens J). However, this reasoning seems to misconstrue what happens in a clearing process, where transactions are accounted for individually and the only mixing is in the settlements, which are generally irrelevant (LD Smith *The Law of Tracing* (1997), pp 252–255; see also LD Smith 'Tracing and Electronic Funds Transfer', ch 8 in FD Rose (ed) *Restitution and Banking Law* (1998), pp 131–134, who argues that it is not necessary to trace through a clearing system where the banks involved in the payment process are all acting as agents for one side or the other). The decision in *Agip* is also difficult to reconcile with *Banque Belge pour l'Etranger v Hambrouck* [1921] 1 KB 321 (above), where the plaintiffs were held to be entitled to trace despite the fact that the cheques which Hambrouck had obtained by fraud had been cleared through the clearing system in London (see E McKendrick [1991] LMCLQ 378 at 383–384; cf P Millett (1991) 107 LQR 71, p 73).

3.   Millett J's reasoning at first instance that it is not possible to trace at law where money is transferred using electronic means does not appear to have found favour with the Court of Appeal (see the *obiter* remarks of Fox LJ). However, Millett J was later followed on this point by Tuckey J *in Bank Tejarat v Hong Kong and Shanghai Banking Corpn (CI) Ltd* [1995] 1 Lloyd's Rep 239, and the issue cannot be considered closed. This is unfortunate as there is no good reason why the transfer of funds by electronic means should be treated any differently from the transfer of funds by cheque (ie where there is a tangible asset), where common law tracing is allowed. Distinctions that are made between the electronic transfer of funds and payment by a tangible asset, such as a cheque, fail to appreciate that what is traced is not the physical asset but the value inherent in it (*Foskett v McKeown* [2001] 1 AC 102 at 128, per Lord Millett). There are also sound policy reasons for a uniform approach to this issue. The point is made in EP Ellinger, E Lomnicka and RJA Hooley *Ellinger's Modern Banking Law* (4th edn, 2006), p 279, in the following blunt terms:

Modern banking requires fast and efficient money transmission systems to transfer funds between bank accounts both domestically and internationally. In terms of the value of payments, electronic funds transfer systems are the dominant systems in use. It is unacceptable that the English common law is incapable of operating in this modern environment. The only people to gain from this unsatisfactory state of affairs are criminals and other money launderers who use electronic funds transfer systems to shift their ill-gotten gains around the globe.

Tracing in equity It may benefit a mistaken payer to trace the mistaken payment in equity and assert a proprietary claim against its recipient. This will be of real value to the payer where the recipient is insolvent, as priority may be obtained over his general creditors. The court may enforce the proprietary claim through an equitable charge, lien, constructive trust or by subrogation. Equitable tracing may also be invoked with the aim of seeking a personal equitable remedy based on 'knowing receipt' (see below, p 685). The personal claim, unlike a proprietary one, does not depend upon continued retention of the payment by the defendant.

Generally speaking equitable tracing rules are more flexible than common law tracing rules, and it is possible in equity to trace through a mixed fund (so, eg equitable tracing was possible in *Agip (Africa) Ltd v Jackson* [1991] Ch 547, above). But there are important restrictions on the right to trace in equity. First, it is not possible to trace money which has ceased to exist, eg by being paid into an overdrawn bank account, or an account which has subsequently become overdrawn, even though the account may later return into credit (*Bishopsgate Investment Management Ltd v Homan* [1995] Ch 211, CA). Secondly, the right to trace in equity has been held to be dependent on the establishment of a fiduciary relationship between the claimant and the defendant, or between the claimant and a third party through whose hands the money passes (*Re Diplock* [1948] Ch 465, CA; *Bank of America v Arnell* [1999] Lloyd's Rep Bank 399, Aikens J). This requirement has been widely criticised and seems irrational given that tracing is merely a process of identification and not a right or remedy (see, eg R Goff and G Jones *The Law of Restitution* (7th edn, 2002), paras 2-031–2-033). Recent criticism by Lord Millett in *Foskett v McKeown* [2001] 1 AC 102 at 128–129, indicates that the requirement is likely to be jettisoned when their Lordships next have to address the issue head on.

The requirement of a fiduciary relationship is satisfied, for example, where a payment made by or on behalf of an employer or principal is misapplied by his employee or agent in breach of fiduciary duty (eg as in *Agip (Africa) Ltd v Jackson* [1991] Ch 547, above). In fact dicta of Lord Browne-Wilkinson in *Westdeutsche Landesbank Girozentrale v Islington London Borough Council* [1996] AC 669 at 716, clearly states that when property is obtained by fraud, whether or not in breach of fiduciary duty, equity imposes a constructive trust on the fraudulent recipient so that the property is recoverable and traceable in equity (cf PBH Birks [1996] RLR 3, p 10, who asserts, somewhat optimistically, that this dicta eliminates the requirement of a fiduciary relationship as a prerequisite of equitable tracing). Thus, according to Lord Browne-Wilkinson, money stolen from a bank account can be traced in equity. However, in *Box v Barclays Bank plc* [1998] Lloyd's Rep Bank 185 at 201, Ferris J stated *obiter* that Lord Browne-Wilkinson could not have intended to include all cases of fraud within this principle. Ferris J drew a distinction between transactions which were void, where the principle applied, and those which were merely voidable, where it did not. A similar point was made by Potter LJ in *Twinsectra Ltd v Yardley* [1999] Lloyd's Rep Bank 438 at 461 (the case went on appeal to the House of Lords but this issue was not considered further: see [2002] 2 AC 164). It has recently been suggested by Buxton LJ in *Sinclair Investment Holdings SA v Versailles Trade Finance Ltd* [2005] EWCA Civ 722, [2006] 1 BCLC 60 at [53], that Lord Browne-Wilkinson 'was dealing with the theoretical explanation of the doctrine of tracing' when he said that where property is obtained by fraud equity imposes a constructive trust on the fraudulent recipient. Arden LJ said (at [43]), agreeing with Rimer J in *Shalson v Russo* [2003] EWHC 1637 (Ch), [2005] 2 WLR 1213, that 'the normal position is that title to the stolen moneys does not vest in the thief'.

It has been held that a payment under mistake constituted the recipient a trustee of the money mistakenly paid. In *Chase Manhattan Bank NA v Israel-British Bank (London) Ltd*

[1981] Ch 105, money was paid by mistake by the plaintiff bank to the defendant bank, which subsequently became insolvent and went into liquidation. Goulding J granted a declaration that the defendant bank became trustee for the plaintiff bank of the money mistakenly paid. Goulding J reasoned that 'a person who pays money to another under a factual mistake retains an equitable property in it and the conscience of that other is subjected to a fiduciary duty to respect his proprietary right' (at 119). This reasoning has since been strongly criticised (*obiter*) by Lord Browne-Wilkinson in *Westdeutsche Landesbank Girozentrale v Islington London Borough Council* [1996] AC 669 at 714–715 (a case where money was paid under a void contract) and also by Lord Millett, writing extra-judicially, in 'Restitution and Constructive Trusts', in W Cornish et al (eds) *Restitution—Past, Present and Future* (1998), p 212. *Chase Manhattan* seems no longer to represent good law (Aikens J refused to follow it in *Bank of America v Arnell* [1999] Lloyd's Rep Bank 399, at 406). There is no basis for the contention that, in the ordinary course, a person retains an equitable (or any) interest in money paid away. Nevertheless, Lord Browne-Wilkinson did concede that, despite Goulding J's faulty reasoning, *Chase Manhattan* may well have been rightly decided. The recipient bank had known of the mistake made by the paying bank within two days of the receipt of the money. Lord Browne-Wilkinson concluded (at 715):

> Although the mere receipt of money, in ignorance of the mistake, gives rise to no trust, the retention of the moneys after the recipient bank learned of the mistake may well have given rise to a constructive trust.

Lord Brown-Wilkinson's dicta has since been applied in *Papamichael v National Westminster Bank plc* [2003] 1 Lloyd's Rep 341, 372, and in *Clark v Cutland* [2003] EWCA Civ 810, [2003] 4 All ER 733, 743.

There are a number of defences which may be raised to an equitable claim. In commercial transactions, an equitable claim will often be defeated by the defence of bona fide purchaser (but not change of position: *Foskett v McKeown* [2001] 1 AC 102, 129, per Lord Millett). Other defences include laches (delay) and acquiesence.

QUESTIONS

1. A trustee of a pension fund borrows money from his bank to buy a yacht and later repays the loan using money stolen from the fund. Can the stolen money be traced into the yacht? *Bishopsgate Investment Management Ltd v Homan,* above; *Foskett v McKeown* [1998] Ch 265, CA (although the case went on to the House of Lords, nothing was said there that affected this issue); *Shalson v Russo* [2003] EWHC 1637 (Ch), [2005] 2 WLR 1213 at [141]; see also L Smith [1995] CLJ 290.

2. 'There is no merit in having distinct and different tracing rules at law and in equity, given that tracing is neither a right nor a remedy but merely the process by which the plaintiff establishes what has happened to his property and makes good his claim that the assets which he claims can properly be regarded as representing his property' (*Trustees of the Property of FC Jones & Sons (a firm) v Jones* [1997] Ch 159 at 171–172, per Millett LJ; for similar dicta, see *Foskett v McKeown* [2001] 1 AC 102 at 128–129, per Lord Millett). Is it time to recognise just one tracing regime? See PBH Birks 'The Necessity of a Unitary Law of Tracing', Ch 9 in R Cranston (ed) *Making Commercial Law* (1997).

CHAPTER 17

BANKS AND THEIR CUSTOMERS

In this chapter we will concentrate on the relationship of banker and customer.[1] To place this relationship in its proper context, we will begin with an outline of the way banking activities are controlled in the United Kingdom.

1 BANK REGULATION

(a) An overview

The core business of banking has traditionally encompassed deposit-taking and lending. Deposit-taking and home mortgage lending are regulated by the Financial Services and Markets Act 2000 (FSMA 2000). Section 19 of the Act provides that no person may carry on, or purport to carry on, a regulated activity in the United Kingdom unless authorised or exempt. Deposit-taking and home mortgage lending are included in the list of regulated activities (see FSMA 2000, Sch 2 and the Financial Services and Markets Act 2000 (Regulated Activities) Order 2001, SI 2001/544, as amended). Until mid-1998, the authorisation and supervision of deposit-taking institutions was a function of the Bank of England, the UK's central bank. However, a series of high-profile financial scandals in the 1990s, such as the collapse of the Bank of Credit and Commerce International and that of Barings Bank, raised doubts over whether the Bank of England was an effective supervisor and led the government to introduce legislation transferring the Bank of England's banking supervision function to a new super-regulatory body called the Financial Services Authority (FSA). The transfer was effected by the Bank of England Act 1998, which came into force on 1 June 1998. The functions, responsibilities and powers of the FSA are now contained in the FSMA 2000, which came into force on 1 December 2001.

---

[1] The standard student textbooks are EP Ellinger, E Lomnicka and RJA Hooley *Ellinger's Modern Banking Law* (4th edn, 2006); R Cranston *Principles of Banking Law* (2nd edn, 2002); J Wadsley and GA Penn *The Law Relating to Domestic Banking* (2nd edn, 2000). For reference, see M Hapgood (ed) *Paget's Law of Banking* (13th edn, 2007); P Cresswell, W Blair, G Hill, P Wood, P Phillips and R Hooley *Encyclopaedia of Banking Law* (five volumes with regular updates).

In recent years banks have become multifunctional institutions engaged in a wide range of business activities beyond their traditional core activities of deposit-taking and lending. It is now common for banks to be engaged in activities as diverse as securities (and derivatives) dealing, investment management and insurance. Often these separate activities are carried out by different subsidiary companies within the same banking group. Banks are now able to provide their customers with a wide range of financial services, including unit trusts, life assurance and pension plans. Until recently, the provision of financial services was regulated by the Securities and Investment Board and a series of self-regulatory organisations operating under a scheme established by the Financial Services Act 1986. It is now regulated by the FSA under the FSMA 2000, which repealed and replaced the 1986 Act. The net result of these changes is that the FSA has become the single regulator of the whole of the financial services sector in the UK: banking, insurance and investment business all fall within its domain. The FSA has been described as 'one of the most powerful financial regulators in the world in terms of scope, powers and discretion' (Joint Parliamentary Scrutiny Committee *Draft Financial Services and Markets Bill: First Report* (April 1999)).

The regulatory systems controlling deposit-taking, home mortgage lending and the provision of financial services are creatures of statute. There is also other important legislation, often the result of EU initiatives, which regulates the way that banks deal with their customers. The terms and conditions of bank-customer contracts, which are now usually in writing, must take account of the provisions of the Unfair Contract Term Act 1977 and the Unfair Terms in Consumer Contracts Regulations 1999, SI 1999/2083. The distance marketing of financial services is increasingly common and may even occur on a cross-border basis. Marketing may take place, and contracts concluded, over the telephone or the internet. The Financial Services (Distance Marketing) Regulations 2004, SI 2004/2095, implementing EC Directive 2002/65, requires greater information to be given to consumers prior to the conclusion of any distance contract for the provision of financial services. It also gives consumers a 14-day cooling off period. Certain types of unsolicited services and communications are prohibited. These Regulations compliment the Consumer Protection (Distance Selling) Regulations 2000, SI 2000/2334, implementing EC Directive 97/7, which give protection to consumers in respect of distance contracts for the supply of goods and non-financial services. Banks are already obliged to ensure that their manual and computer-based customer records comply with the Data Protection Act 1998.

The provision of loans and overdrafts to individual (non-corporate) customers is controlled by the Consumer Credit Act 1974. Recent amendments to the Act have abolished the previous £25,000 financial limit so that all credit agreements are prima facie covered irrespective of the amount involved (the amendments are contained within the Consumer Credit Act 2006, ss 1–4). The definition of an 'individual' is narrowed in relation to partnerships so that only those of two or three persons are covered. Further exceptions have been introduced relating to agreements exceeding £25,000 which relate to the debtor's business and to 'high net worth debtors'.

There is no comprehensive statutory regime within the UK governing money transfer operations. The rights and duties of the bank and its customer in relation to bills of exchange, cheques and promissory notes are mainly covered by the Bills of Exchange Act 1882 and the Cheques Act 1957 (see Chapters 16 and 19). Certain types of cross-border credit transfers within the EU are caught by the Cross-Border Credit Transfer Regulations 1999, SI 1999/1876, implementing EC Directive 97/5 (since repealed and replaced by EC Payment Services Directive 2007/64), which lay down the rights and duties of the banks themselves and of their customers. The Cross-Border Payments in Euro Regulations 2003, SI 2003/488, implementing EC Regulation 2560/2001, regulate the charges that may be levied by banks on their customers for making cross-border payments in euro.

Mention must also be made of legislation designed to combat money laundering by serious criminals and the use of the banking system to finance terrorist activities (see the Terrorism Act 2000, as amended by the Anti-terrorism, Crime and Security Act 2001; the Terrorism (United Nations) Measures Order 2001, SI 2001/3365; the Proceeds of Crime Act 2002, Part VII; the Money Laundering Regulations 2007, SI 2007/2157, which implement, in part, the Third EC Money Laundering Directive, EC Directive 2005/60; and the Transfer of Funds (Information on the Payer) Regulations 2007, SI 2007/3298). Legislation designed to combat money laundering and terrorist financing has had a direct impact on the bank-customer relationship as banks are required to know their customers and report their knowledge or suspicions to the relevant authorities. The impact of these developments on the bank's duty to obey its customer's mandate and the duty of confidentiality the bank owes to its customer are considered later in this chapter.

In an attempt to ward off the threat of increased statutory control of banking activities, especially in the retail sector, the banking industry has adopted a series of measures based on self-regulation. The most notable was the introduction in 1992 of a voluntary code of best practice for banks and building societies when dealing with their personal customers in the UK. The code, now called the *Banking Code*, has been reviewed on a number of occasions, the most recent revision being in March 2008. In March 2002 the banking industry introduced the *Business Banking Code*, a voluntary code of best practice for banks when dealing with small business customers, ie non-personal account holders with an annual turnover of less than £1 million or an income of under £1 million in the case of charities and clubs. This code was also last revised in March 2005. The most recent version of this code was also published in March 2008.

(b) The regulation of deposit-taking

Prior to 1979 supervision of the UK banking sector was operated primarily on a non-statutory basis. The Bank of England (the Bank) operated a self-regulatory system based on personal knowledge, mutual trust and co-operation. The system worked reasonably well when the UK banking community was relatively small and homogeneous, but was unsuited to the rapid expansion of the banking sector in the 1960s and 1970s.

The Banking Act 1979 placed the Bank's system of informal regulation on a statutory footing, at least in so far as deposit-taking was concerned. The Act was born out of the secondary banking crisis of the mid-1970s, when unsupervised deposit-taking institutions faced a liquidity crisis, and also out of the first Banking Directive 77/780/EEC, which demanded harmony in controls of credit institutions throughout the Member States of the EEC. The Act prohibited the taking of a deposit in the course of a deposit-taking business unless it was taken by an exempt institution or was an exempt transaction. Under s 2(1) to the Act, exempt institutions were the Bank, recognised banks, licensed institutions (generally known as 'licensed deposit-takers') and certain bodies listed in Sch 1 of the Act, such as the central banks of the EEC countries and building societies. The Bank was given power to 'recognise' banks and 'license' deposit-takers according to criteria laid down in Sch 2 to the Act. The Bank was also given power to supervise an institution's continuing ability to satisfy the conditions for authorisation. However, it was clear from the collapse of Johnson Matthey Bankers (a recognised bank) in 1984 that recognised banks were not subject to as rigorous supervision as licensed deposit-takers.

The collapse of Johnson Matthey Bankers, and the ensuing report of a Committee on the System of Banking Supervision chaired by the Governor of the Bank (Cmnd 9695,1985), led to the Banking Act 1987. The 1987 Act introduced several important changes in the statutory regulation of deposit-taking. First, s 1(1) of the Act clarified the Bank's role by conferring on it 'the duty generally to supervise the institutions authorised by it in the exercise of those powers'. The powers of the Bank to obtain information, require production of documents, carry out investigations and make disclosure of information to third parties were extended. Secondly, the two-tier division between recognised banks and licensed deposit-takers was abolished and replaced by a sole category of 'authorised institutions'. In general terms, the 1987 Act was considerably more detailed than the 1979 Act. This became all the more so when the Second Banking Co-ordination Directive 86/646/EEC of 15 December 1989, introducing the concept of a single banking licence to be recognised throughout the European Community, was brought into effect by the Banking Coordination (Second Council Directive) Regulations 1992, SI 1992/3218, as amended.

The Banking Act 1987 was repealed and replaced by the FSMA 2000 on 1 December 2001. The FSMA 2000 carries forward the need for institutions to be authorised in order to carry on banking in the UK in the sense of 'accepting deposits'. This is done by imposing a 'general prohibition' on anyone carrying on, or purporting to carry on, a regulated activity in the UK unless he is an authorised person or an exempt person (FSMA 2000, s 19(1)). Regulated activities are listed in Sch 2 to the Act and are defined in detail in the Financial Services and Markets Act 2000 (Regulated Activities) Order 2001, SI 2001/544, as amended (the RAO). One such regulated activity is 'accepting deposits' by way of business (RAO, art 5). The extraterritorial scope of the FSMA 2000 means that, although acceptance of the deposit must be in the UK, the deposit-taking business can be based overseas.

Article 5(1) of the RAO defines 'accepting deposits' in terms of two alternative categories of activity. The first is where 'money received by way of deposit is lent to others'. The second is where 'any other activity of the person accepting the deposit is financed wholly or to any material extent, out of the capital or of interest on money received on deposit'. A 'deposit' is defined in art 5(2)–(3) to mean a sum of money paid on the basis that it will be repaid with or without interest or premium either on demand or as agreed. However, it does not include an arrangement for the payment of money on terms which are 'referable to the provision of property (other than currency) or services or the giving of security'. The wide definition of a 'deposit' has led to specific exclusions: eg loans by banks and other institutions engaged in the lending business, loans between companies in the same group and transactions between relatives are all excluded from the definition (RAO, arts 6–9).

Although persons accepting deposits in the UK by way of business generally require authorisation, the FSMA 2000 gives power to the Treasury to exempt institutions from this requirement. Such persons are termed 'exempt persons' and include the Bank of England, other EEA central banks, the EC and related international bodies, certain development banks and also bodies affiliated to government or to local authorities (Financial Services and Markets Act 2000 (Exemption) Order 2001, SI 2001/1201). Unless an exempt person, anyone accepting deposits in the UK by way of business must be an 'authorised person'. This means that they must either be a person who has obtained authorisation from the FSA, or a person authorised in another EEA Member State and entitled, through the application of the single European passport principle, to establish branches or provide cross-border services in the UK (see below, Section 1 (d)).

The FSA is the body to whom an application must be made for permission to carry on a regulated activity. The regime for granting permission is set out in Part IV of the FSMA

2000, as supplemented by the procedures and policies contained in the FSA's Handbook. Schedule 6 to the Act lays down certain 'threshold conditions' which must be met before permission can be granted. Where a bank applies for permission to accept deposits in the UK, the five threshold conditions that must be met are: (1) the bank must either be a body corporate or a partnership; (2) if the bank is a body corporate constituted under the law of any part of the UK its head office and, if it has a registered office, that office, must be in the UK; (3) the FSA must be satisfied that it can supervise the bank effectively; (4) the bank must have adequate resources; and (5) the bank must be 'a fit and proper person having regard to all the circumstances' to carry on the regulated activity. The FSA has power to grant permission without limitation or subject to conditions. There is a right of appeal to the Financial Services and Markets Tribunal for those aggrieved by the FSA's exercise of its powers in relation to permission (FSMA 2000, s 55).

For many years now the UK has had an industry-funded depositor protection scheme (enshrined in both the Banking Act 1979 and the Banking Act 1987). This has ensured that depositors receive (limited) compensation in the event of a bank failing. Depositor compensation is now provided for as part of the Financial Services Compensation Scheme (FSCS) which the FSA was required to establish under the FSMA 2000. The FSCS was created on 1 December 2001 when the Investors Compensation Scheme, the Policyholders' Protection Scheme, the Deposit Protection Scheme (for banks) and the Building Societies Investor Protection Scheme merged into a new single body. The rules for the scheme are to be found in the FSA's Handbook. Following a run on Northern Rock in September 2007 (ie large number of customers demanding repayment of deposits caused by fear of bank insolvency), and amid concern that a general lack of customer confidence might cause a run on other banks, the FSA increased the limit of FSCS cover in October 2007. The previous compensation limit was £31,700 (100% of the first £2,000 and 90% of the next £33,000 of depositors' eligible claims) and this was increased to 100% cover for the first £35,000 of each depositor's claim. The government continues to review compensation arrangements and further proposals for reform are anticipated.[2]

(c) Functions and immunity of the Financial Services Authority

Financial Services and Markets Act 2000, ss 1, 2, and Sch, para 19

1 The Financial Services Authority

(1) The body corporate known as the Financial Services Authority ('the Authority') is to have the functions conferred on it by or under this Act.

(2) The Authority must comply with the requirements as to its constitution set out in Schedule 1.

(3) Schedule 1 also makes provision about the status of the Authority and the exercise of certain of its functions.

---

[2] For an excellent summary of the regulatory regime established by the FSMA 2000 in the context of deposit-taking, see Ch 2 (written by Professor Lomnicka) of EP Ellinger, E Lomnicka and RJA Hooley *Ellinger's Modern Banking Law* (4th edn, 2006). For detailed review, see M Blair et al *Blackstone's Guide to the Financial Services and Markets Act 2000* (2001); W Blair et al *Banking and Financial Services Regulation* (3rd edn, 2002); E Lomnicka and J Powell *Encyclopaedia of Financial Services Law* (looseleaf), Vol 1, Pt 2A.

2 The Authority's general duties

(1) In discharging its general functions the Authority must, so far as is reasonably possible, act in a way—

    (a) which is compatible with the regulatory objectives; and

    (b) which the Authority considers most appropriate for the purpose of meeting those objectives.

(2) The regulatory objectives are—

    (a) market confidence;

    (b) public awareness;

    (c) the protection of consumers; and

    (d) the reduction of financial crime.

(3) In discharging its general functions the Authority must have regard to—

    (a) the need to use its resources in the most efficient and economic way;

    (b) the responsibilities of those who manage the affairs of authorised persons;

    (c) the principle that a burden or restriction which is imposed on a person, or on the carrying on of an activity, should be proportionate to the benefits, considered in general terms, which are expected to result from the imposition of that burden or restriction;

    (d) the desirability of facilitating innovation in connection with regulated activities;

    (e) the international character of financial services and markets and the desirability of maintaining the competitive position of the United Kingdom;

    (f) the need to minimise the adverse effects on competition that may arise from anything done in the discharge of those functions;

    (g) the desirability of facilitating competition between those who are subject to any form of regulation by the Authority.

(4) The Authority's general functions are—

    (a) its function of making rules under this Act (considered as a whole);

    (b) its function of preparing and issuing codes under this Act (considered as a whole);

    (c) its functions in relation to the giving of general guidance (considered as a whole); and

    (d) its function of determining the general policy and principles by reference to which it performs particular functions.

(5) 'General guidance' has the meaning given in section 158(5).

Sch 1, para 19 Exemption from liability in damages

19 (1) Neither the Authority nor any person who is, or is acting as, a member, officer or member of staff of the Authority is to be liable in damages for anything done or omitted in the discharge, or purported discharge, of the Authority's functions.

(2) [Provides for a similar immunity to those investigating complaints against the FSA.]

(3) Neither sub-paragraph (1) nor sub-paragraph (2) applies—

    (a) if the act or omission is shown to have been in bad faith; or

    (b) so as to prevent an award of damages made in respect of an act or omission on the ground that the act or omission was unlawful as a result of section 6(1) of the Human Rights Act 1998.

NOTES

1. The Banking Act 1979 contained no statutory immunity for the Bank of England, the then regulator of deposit-taking in the UK. Statutory immunity only came with the Banking Act 1987 (s 1(4)). However, it has been repeatedly held by the courts that a bank regulator does not owe a duty of care to individual commercial banks (*Minories Finance Ltd v Arthur*

Young (a firm) [1989] 2 All ER 105), nor to their depositors (*Yuen Kun Yeu v A-G of Hong Kong* [1988] AC 175, PC; *Davies v Radcliffe* [1990] 1 WLR 821, PC), when carrying out its regulatory function. As Lord Millett affirmed in *Three Rivers District Council v Bank of England (No 3)* [2001] UKHL 16, [2001] Lloyd's Rep Bank 125 at 169: '[u]nfortunately for the depositors, a regulatory authority cannot be held liable in English law for negligence, however gross, in the exercise of its supervisory functions.'

2. The FSA's statutory immunity is not absolute: it does not apply to acts or omissions shown to have been in bad faith or in breach of the Human Rights Act 1998, nor does it prevent judicial review of the regulator's decisions. The regulator could be liable to depositors for the tort of misfeasance in public office where the necessary elements of the tort are established (*Three Rivers District Council v Bank of England* [2000] 3 All ER 1, where the House of Lords also held that individual depositors were not given rights under relevant European legislation). The tort of misfeasance in public office entails bad faith and so falls outside the statutory immunity. But it will not be easy to prove that the regulator acted or failed to act because of bad faith, as opposed to negligence, and the claim is more likely to be struck out than to succeed (as in *Hall v Bank of England* [2000] Lloyd's Rep Bank 189, CA; although in *Three Rivers District Council v Bank of England (No 3)* [2001] UKHL 16, [2001] Lloyd's Rep Bank 125, the claim was, somewhat surprisingly, allowed to proceed to trial: the action was only abandoned during the course of the trial itself when the Chancellor of the High Court, Sir Andrew Morritt, advised that it was no longer in the best interests of the creditors to continue. In any event, it may also be difficult to show that the acts or omissions of the regulator were the effective cause of the depositors' loss.

3. Does the 'blanket immunity' given to the FSA under the FSMA 2000 contravene art 6 of the European Convention on Human Rights? Article 6 guarantees the right to a fair and public hearing. It could be argued that a depositor is denied that right because the FSA can hide behind its statutory immunity. The immunity will be subject to a proportionality review, but if the courts hold that the FSA does not owe the depositors a duty of care in the first place (see note 1 above), this is not going to help them much.[3]

(d) EC harmonisation measures

A number of changes in UK bank regulation have resulted from the implementation of the EC Single Market in Banking. The Second Banking Co-ordination Directive 89/646/EEC introduced the concept of a single banking licence enabling a bank (or 'credit institution') incorporated in a Member State to enjoy mutual recognition throughout the Community by virtue of recognition in its home country. Once the appropriate licence or authorisation is granted by the home supervisor, the bank can establish and offer certain 'listed' banking services (including deposit-taking, lending and most ordinary types of banking business) in any Community country without first having to obtain host country authorisation. The main burden of the continued supervision of the bank's activities is then placed on the home supervisor and not the host state. Through a series of banking directives, which were later brought together into a single Banking Consolidation Directive 2000/12/EC in May 2000 (this Directive replaced the Second Banking Co-ordination Directive), the EC has ensured similar standards of control across EC Member States. The key directives are now Directive

---

[3] For further analysis of this issue, and also a useful summary of the potential liability of financial regulators in a range of jurisdictions, see C Proctor [2002] BJIBFL 15 and 71, and also M Andenas and D Fairgrieve (2002) 51 ICLQ 757.

2006/48/EC relating to the taking up and pursuit of the business of credit institutions and Directive 2006/49/EC on the capital adequacy of investment firms and credit institutions. These two Directives recast and replace Directives 2000/12/EC (Banking Consolidation Directive) and 93/6/EEC (Capital Adequacy Directive).

The Second Banking Co-ordination Directive was given effect in the UK by the Banking Co-ordination (Second Council Directive) Regulations 1992, SI 1992/3218, as amended, which made substantial amendments to the Banking Act 1987. The Regulations were repealed by a Treasury order made under s 426 of the FSMA 2000. However, the principle of the single European passport has been carried through into the regulatory regime established under the FSMA 2000. Banks authorised to carry on regulated activities in other EEA Member States are granted automatic authorisation to carry on those activities in the UK through branches or the provision of cross-border services, provided they comply with certain formalities (FSMA 2000, s 3 l(l)(b) and Sch 3). These banks, referred to as 'EEA firms' in the FSMA 2000, are subject to regulation as 'authorised persons' by the FSA, but only in a manner that is consistent with EC law which provides for division of responsibility between 'home' (ie other EEA Member State) and 'host' (UK) regulators. UK authorised banks are also entitled to exercise their single European passport rights throughout the EEA (see FSMA 2000, Sch 3, Part III).

(e) The Bank of England

The Bank of England (the Bank) is the UK's central bank. It was incorporated under a Royal Charter in 1694 and functioned as a private joint stock company until it was nationalised and brought under government ownership in 1946. Although the Bank retained a large measure of operational and institutional independence following nationalisation, s 4(1) of the Bank of England Act 1946 (still in force) contains express provision for the Treasury to give directions to the Bank as, after consultation with the Governor of the Bank, it thinks necessary in the public interest (in fact, the Treasury has never given a direction under this power). The Bank of England Act 1998 amends s 4(1) of the 1946 Act to prohibit the Treasury from giving directions in relation to monetary policy.

We have already considered how the Bank lost its banking supervision function to the new FSA under the Bank of England Act 1998 (see Section 1 above). Despite this, it would be a serious mistake to underestimate the critical role the Bank continues to play in the UK's financial sector. A Memorandum of Understanding between the Treasury, the Bank and the FSA (originally signed in October 1997 and revised in March 2006) clearly delineates the respective functions of the three authorities and emphasises that the Bank remains charged with the integrity of the financial system as a whole. Under the terms of the Memorandum of Understanding, the Bank is responsible for (a) the stability of the monetary system—and in this context it should be noted that the Bank of England Act 1998 has given the Bank (qualified) operational independence for monetary policy; (b) the financial system infrastructure, especially payment systems; (c) a broad overview of the financial system as a whole; (d) the ability, in exceptional circumstances, to conduct official financial rescue operations; and (e) the efficiency and effectiveness of the financial sector.

The Bank also remains of central importance to the way banks operate, for it is the banks' bank. There are various aspects to this role. First, in exceptional circumstances, the Bank is the lender of last resort to the banks. The Bank may intervene and rescue a bank which faces financial difficulties—it is more likely to do this where the collapse of one bank could result in a loss of public confidence in the banking system as a whole. Secondly, the leading banks tend to hold their own operational accounts at the Bank—this means that settlement of obligations between banks usually takes place at the Bank, which is particularly important in the context of the operation of the UK's bank payment systems. Thirdly, the Bank has a virtual monopoly on the issue of bank notes in the UK (certain banks in Scotland and Northern Ireland retain a limited right to do so)—the right to issue coins is entrusted to another body, the Mint.

The Bank is also the government's banker. The Bank holds the central account of the government (known as the Exchequer), as well as several other government accounts. Until recently, the Bank also used to manage the government's debt. This involved deciding the pricing and timing of government bond issues, the term structure of the debt and managing the public debt portfolio. However, the Bank of England Act 1998 removed this function from the Bank and transferred it to an executive agency, the Debt Management Office. As the 1998 Act gave the Bank control of operational monetary policy, enabling it to decide on changes in interest rates, it was thought there was a potential conflict of interest between this function and the Bank's continued management of the government's debt (eg a central bank may be reluctant to raise interest rates to control inflationary pressures because this would adversely affect the value of its debt portfolio).

2 WHAT IS A 'BANK'?

A reasonable response to this question would be 'why do you want to know?'. As there is no comprehensive legal definition of the terms 'bank', 'banker' or 'banking', the precise meaning of each term turns on the particular context in which it arises. The most common contexts where the issue becomes important are: (i) the area of bank regulation; (ii) where rights and duties are conferred on banks; and (iii) where there is an attempt to avoid a payment obligation on the ground that it arose on an illegal contract, which is void or unenforceable because it is owed by or to an unlicensed bank (see R Cranston *Principles of Banking Law* (2nd edn, 2002), p 5).

(a) Definition at common law

The common law definition of 'bank', 'banker' or 'banking' remains important for two reasons: (i) under general law certain rights and duties are only conferred on a 'bank' or 'banker', eg the banker's lien and the banker's right of set-off, the banker's duty of confidentiality; and (ii) some statutes use the terms 'bank', 'banker' or 'banking' without further or proper definition (see the following case).

United Dominions Trust Ltd v Kirkwood
[1966] 2 QB 431, Court of Appeal

UDT was a well established finance house with high standing. UDT lent £5,000 to Lonsdale Motors Ltd to enable them to buy cars to put in their showroom to sell. In return Lonsdale Motors Ltd accepted five bills of exchange, each for £1,000, drawn on them by UDT. The defendant was the managing director of Lonsdale Motors Ltd and he indorsed the bills. The bills were not met on presentation and, Lonsdale Motors Ltd having gone into liquidation, UDT sued the defendant as indorsee. The defendant's only defence was that UDT was an unregistered moneylender and that the loan was illegal as it contravened the provisions of the Moneylenders Act 1900. The case turned on whether UDT was 'bona fide carrying on the business of banking' within the meaning of s 6(d) of the Moneylenders Act 1900 so as to exempt it from the provisions of the Act. By a majority (Lord Denning MR and Diplock LJ; Harman LJ dissenting), the Court of Appeal upheld UDT's claim that it was 'bona fide carrying on the business of banking' and allowed it to recover from the defendant.

Lord Denning MR: ...Parliament has conferred many privileges on 'banks' and 'bankers' but it has never defined what is a 'bank' and who is a 'banker'. It has said many times that a banker is a person who carries on 'the business of banking,' but it has never told us what is the business of banking. It has imposed penalties on persons who describe themselves as a 'bank' or 'bankers' when they are not, but it has never told us how to decide whether or not they are bankers.

The characteristics of banking

Seeing that there is no statutory definition of banking, we must do the best we can to find out the usual characteristics which go to make up the business of banking. In the eighteenth century, before cheques came into common use, the principal characteristics were that the banker accepted the money of others on the terms that the persons who deposited it could have it back again from the banker when they asked for it, sometimes on demand, at other times on notice, according to the stipulation made at the time of deposit; and meanwhile the banker was at liberty to make use of the money by lending it out at interest or investing it on mortgage or otherwise. Thus, Dr Johnson in 1755 in his dictionary defined a 'bank' as a 'place where money is laid up to be called for occasionally' and a 'banker' as 'one that traffics in money, one that keeps or manages a bank.' Those characteristics continued for a long time to dominate thought on the subject. Thus, in 1914, Isaacs J in the High Court of Australia said that

> The essential characteristics of the business of banking...may be described as the collection of money by receiving deposits on loan, repayable when and as expressly or impliedly agreed upon, and the utilisation of the money so collected by lending it again in such sums as are required': see *State Savings Bank of Victoria Comrs v Permewan Wright & Co Ltd* ((1915) 19 CLR 457 at 470–471).

You will notice that those characteristics do not mention the use of cheques, or the keeping of current accounts. Accordingly, we find in the courts cases in which a company was held to carry on the business of banking even though it issued no cheques and kept no current accounts but only issued deposit receipts, repayable on notice (see *Re Shields' Estate, Bank of Ireland (Governor & Co) Petitioners)* ([1901] 1 IR 172), or only kept deposit accounts from which the depositors could withdraw their money on demand or on notice, this being on production of a passbook, not by cheque: see *Re Bottomsgate Industrial Co-operative Society* ((1891) 65 LT 712); *State Savings Bank of Victoria Comrs v Permewan Wright & Co Ltd* ((1915) 19 CLR 457). If that were still the law, it would mean that the building societies were all bankers.

The march of time has taken us far beyond those cases of 50 years ago. Money is now paid and received by cheque to such an extent that no person can be considered a banker unless he handles cheques as freely as cash. A customer nowadays who wishes to pay money into his bank takes with him his cash and the cheques, crossed and uncrossed, payable to him. Whereas in the old days it was a characteristic of a banker that he should receive *money* for deposit, it is nowadays a characteristic that he should receive *cheques for collection* on behalf of his customer. How otherwise is the customer to pay his money into the bank? It is the only practicable means, particularly in the case of crossed cheques. Next, when a customer wishes to withdraw the money which he has deposited or to pay his creditors with it, he does it in most cases by drawing a cheque on the bank. Occasionally he does it by a draft on the bank or a written order. Whereas in the old days he might withdraw it on production of a passbook and no cheque, it is nowadays a characteristic of a bank that the customer should be able to withdraw it by cheque, draft or order. This view has gradually gained acceptance: see *Re District Savings Bank Ltd, exp Coe* ((1861) 3 De GF & J 335, at 338), per Turner LJ; *Re Shields' Estate* ([1901] 1 IR 172 at 195), per Lord Ashbourne.

In 1924 Aitkin LJ gave a modern picture of a characteristic banking account in *Joachimson v Swiss Bank Corpn* ([1921] 3 KB 110 at 127):

> The bank undertakes to receive money and collect bills for its customer's account. The proceeds so received are not to be held in trust for the customer, but the bank borrows the proceeds and undertakes to repay them. The promise to repay is to repay at the branch of the bank where the account is kept, and during banking hours. It includes a promise to repay any part of the amount due against the written order of the customer addressed to the bank at the branch . . . bankers never do make a payment to a customer in respect of a current account except on demand.

This was followed in 1948 by the *Bank of Chettinad Ltd of Colombo v IT Comrs, Colombo* ([1948] AC 378 at 383), where the Privy Council accepted the Ceylon description of a 'banking company' as

> a company which carries on as its principal business the accepting of deposits of money on current account or otherwise, subject to withdrawal by cheque, draft or order.

And now the Shorter Oxford Dictionary gives the meaning of a 'bank' in modern use as:

> An establishment for the custody of money received from, or on behalf of, its customers. Its essential duty is to pay their drafts on it: its profits arise from the use of money left unemployed by them.

There are, therefore, two characteristics usually found in bankers today: (i) They accept money from, and collect cheques for, their customers and place them to their credit; (ii) They honour cheques or orders drawn on them by their customers when presented for payment and debit their customers accordingly. These two characteristics carry with them also a third, namely: (iii) They keep current accounts, or something of that nature, in their books in which the credits and debits are entered.

Those three characteristics are much the same as those stated in *Paget's Law of Banking,* 6th edn (1961), p8:

> No-one and nobody, corporate or otherwise, can be a 'banker' who does not (i) take current accounts; (ii) pay cheques drawn on himself; (iii) collect cheques for his customers.

[Lord Denning then reviewed the evidence holding that: (1) whilst UDT did receive money on deposit, these were short-term investments repayable on agreed dates after maturity and were not repayable on notice; and (2) there was no evidence that UDT collected cheques on behalf of customers. He continued:]

Long acceptance as bankers

Thus far the evidence adduced by UDT would not suffice to show that it has the usual characteristics of a banker. But it must be remembered that a recital of *usual* characteristics is not equivalent to a definition. The *usual* characteristics are not the *sole* characteristics. There are other characteristics which go to make a banker. In particular stability, soundness and probity. Parliament would not dream of granting the special privileges of a banker to a ramshackle concern which had no reserves or whose methods were dubious. Like many other beings, a banker is easier to recognise than to define. In case of doubt, it is, I think, permissible to look at the reputation of the firm amongst ordinary intelligent commercial men. If they recognise it as carrying on the business of banking, that should turn the scale. Here it is that UDT comes out well. It has for many years been accepted in the most responsible quarters as being a bank. There was impressive evidence from four of the Big Five Banks that they regarded UDT as a bank; and that UDT was generally regarded in the City of London as a bank. These bankers accorded to UDT all the privileges of being a banker. They paid crossed cheques presented by UDT. They gave it clearance house facilities. They answered references regarding customers, and such like. . . .

Reputation may exclude a person from being a banker: so also it may make him one. Our commercial law has been founded on the opinion of merchants. Lord Mansfield himself used to have his own special jurymen of the City of London who sat regularly with him. He took their opinion as to what was the practice: and laid down the law accordingly—see, for instance, *Lewis v Rucker* 97 ER 769, (1791) 2 Burr 1167 and Campbell, Lives of the Chief Justices, ii, p 407. I would follow his example. In such a matter as this, when Parliament has given no guidance, we cannot do better than look at the reputation of the concern amongst intelligent men of commerce.

This reputation has, moreover, formed the basis of practice which we should not disturb. When merchants have established a course of business which is running smoothly and well with no inconvenience or injustice, it is not for the judges to put a spoke in the wheel and bring it to a halt. Even if someone is able to point to a flaw, the courts should not seize on it so as to invalidate past transactions or produce confusion. So you will find it said from the time of Lord Coke that the law so favours the public good that it will in some cases permit a common error to pass for right: see the 4th Institute, p 240. Communis error facit jus. That is to say, when business has been regulated on the faith of it and the position of parties altered in consequence (Lord Blackburn on several occasions so said): see *R v Sussex Justices* ((1862) 2 B & S 664 at 680); *Davidson v Sinclair* ((1878) 3 App Cas 765 at 788); *Dalton v Angus* ((1881) 6 App Cas 740 at 812). This applies with especial force to commercial practice. When it has grown up and become established, the courts will overlook suggested defects and support it rather than throw it down. Thus it will enforce commercial credits rather than hold them bad for want of consideration. It is a maxim of English law to give effect to everything which appears to have been established for a considerable course of time and to presume that what has been done was done of right, and not in wrong: see *Gibson v Doeg* ((1857) 2 H & N 615 at 623). This maxim is of particular force here where innumerable transactions have been effected on the faith of UDT being a banker, UDT has itself made loans of millions of pounds which are recoverable if its claim to be a banker is correct; but irrecoverable if it is not. Are we to throw all these over? It has described itself on all its documents and cheques as 'bankers' and continues so to do. But if it is not a banker, it is guilty of a criminal offence for each document it so issues. Are we to suggest that it should be prosecuted now? Thousands of its customers have claimed repayment of tax on form R.62 on the basis that it was a banker and the revenue have paid. Has all this been unlawful? Are all its transactions to be thrown into confusion by the suggestion now made for the first time that it is an unregistered moneylender? Rather than come to any such conclusion, we should presume that it has done whatever is necessary to constitute it a banker.

Harman LJ (dissenting): . . . It is notoriously difficult to define the business of banking and no statute has attempted it. Perhaps the best is that stated in the Privy Council case of *Bank of Chettinad Ltd of Colombo v IT Comrs, Colombo* ([1948] AC 378 at 383). The definition there stated as applying in Ceylon is said in the judgment of the board to conflict in no way with the meaning attached to the word 'banking' in England in 1932, which I think has not changed today. The definition is

> a company which carries on as its principal business the accepting of deposits of money on current account or otherwise, subject to withdrawal by cheque, draft or order.

All the witnesses called on UDT's behalf agreed that the keeping of what they called 'current accounts' was an essential part of a banker's business. This involved, according to all the banking witnesses, the collection of customers' cheques.

[Harman LJ then reviewed the evidence and held that UDT did not satisfy this definition of the business of banking. He continued:]

UDT relied also on its reputation and called impressive evidence to show that it was regarded by the Big Five Banks, by the Board of Trade and by the Inland Revenue Commissioners as being a banker. It had a clearing house number and various banker's privileges, for instance, that of compounding for the stamp duty on its cheques. I confess to having been impressed by this evidence: it was said in a dissenting judgment in *Davies v Kennedy* ((1868) 17 WR 305) that a banker is one who is considered in commercial circles to be one, but on the whole I have come to the conclusion that reputation alone is not enough. There must be some performance behind it. The other bankers, seeing UDT's cheques in circulation through the clearing office, did not have any call to inquire into the nature of the business being done as we have had to do and I reluctantly conclude that, on the evidence at present before us, this defence succeeds and that the appeal ought to be allowed accordingly. I regret to find myself unable to subscribe to the views expressed by the Master of the Rolls on this topic. His judgment seems to me to prove that UDT is not a banker.

There remains, however, the fact that UDT is apparently reputed in commercial and financial circles as being a banker. It has for many years enjoyed that reputation and its accompanying privileges and has styled itself bankers. If it is not so, it has been committing a criminal offence and the very large amounts owing to it are all irrecoverable in law. I cannot conceal from myself the serious consequences of my decision on a concern of the highest repute and undoubted probity.

Diplock LJ: …[UDT] asserts that it is bona fide carrying on the business of banking and is therefore not a 'moneylender' within the meaning of the Act. It has been lending money in the course of its business for many years. It has been treated as if it were a banker by government departments and by commercial men, including those who indisputably are themselves bankers. To hold that all these have been mistaken throughout the years it not a decision which a court should reach lightly.

But this, in my view, is not an issue on which communis error jus facere potest. Evidence that a company is generally regarded by commercial men and bankers as being itself a banker is some evidence that it is carrying on the business of banking. If supported by even slight evidence of some banking transactions which it carries out, it may be sufficient proof that in law it is a banker. But if there is actual evidence of the business which it does carry on and relies upon as constituting the business of banking and the court is driven to the conclusion that this, at any rate, is not banking business, the court cannot abdicate its duty so to decide because commercial men and bankers, however numerous or influential, have thought it to be a banker upon whatever information may have been available to them….

What makes a person a banker is not what he does with the money of which he obtains the use, as, for instance, by lending it at interest (as mentioned by Holmes LJ [*Re Shields' Estate, Bank of Ireland (Governor & Co), Petitioners* [1901] 1 IR 172 at 207] and Isaacs J [*State Savings Bank of Victoria Comrs v Permewan, Wright & Co Ltd* (1915) 19 CLR 457 at 471]), by investing it, by discounting bills, etc, but the terms upon which he obtains from other persons, his banking customers, loans of money which he can use as he thinks fit. What I think is common to all modern definitions and essential to the carrying on of the business of banking is that the banker should accept from his customers loans of money on 'deposit,' that is to say, loans for an indefinite period upon running account, repayable as to the whole or any part thereof upon demand by the customer either without notice or upon an agreed period of notice.

Some verbal confusion and perhaps some misunderstanding of the less recent judgments may arise from the fact that an account kept by a banker of his customer's loans made without interest and repayable on demand is nowadays generally called a 'current account,' while the account kept of his customer's loans made at interest and repayable only upon notice is generally known as a 'deposit account.' But accounts of both these types possess the essential characteristics of running accounts of 'deposits' of money by the customer.

Accordingly it is, in my view, essential to the business of banking that a banker should accept money from his customers upon a running account into which sums of money are from time to time paid by the customer and from time to time withdrawn by him by cheque, draft or order. I am inclined to agree with the Master of the Rolls and the author of the current edition of *Paget on Banking*, 6th edn (1961), p 8, that to constitute the business of banking today the banker must also undertake to pay cheques drawn upon himself (the banker) by his customers in favour of third parties up to the amount standing to their credit in their 'current accounts' and to collect cheques for his customers and credit the proceeds to their current accounts. This view of the essential characteristics of the business of banking today is supported by the evidence of the witnesses who were unquestionably bankers who gave expert evidence in the present case....

The...question is whether the evidence in this case is sufficient to satisfy the onus which lies upon UDT of proving that it was at the material time in 1961 a 'person bona fide carrying on the business of banking.'...But the requirement that his carrying on of the business of banking must be bona fide does, I think, involve two requirements. The first is that the banking transactions which he carries out in the course of his business must not be negligible in size and number when compared with the rest of his business. The second is that the transactions relied upon as constituting the accepting of deposits of money from customers on running account must be genuinely of this legal nature and not a mere disguise for transactions of a different legal nature. The court must look to the true nature of the transactions, not merely to their form.

[Diplock LJ then reviewed the evidence and held that UDT carried out a limited banking business in that some customers used 'current accounts' for the payment of cheques drawn in favour of third parties or collection of cheques drawn by third parties. He continued:]

Once one eliminates the kinds of transactions recorded in the 'current accounts' of Lonsdale Motors Ltd as not being in the legal nature of banking transactions at all, the evidence of Mr Garrett in my judgment leaves a complete lacuna as to whether or not the banking transactions which UDT carries out constitute more than a negligible part of their business.

Is that lacuna capable of being filled by evidence of the reputation which UDT enjoys in banking and commercial circles of being 'bankers'? After anxious reflection I think it is, but for reasons which differ from those which have commended themselves to the Master of the Rolls, for which, with great respect, I cannot find sufficient authority in the cases which he cites. Most transactions of the relevant kind would come to the knowledge of bankers, for the cheques would pass through the clearing or would be specially presented and would involve ancillary transactions between such bankers and UDT. Evidence given by bankers that they have regarded UDT as carrying on the business of banking would thus be based upon transactions undertaken by UDT which would be within the general knowledge of the persons giving evidence. Unless the grounds of the witnesses' belief were probed in cross-examination and shown to be mistaken, such evidence in an ordinary case might be sufficient in itself to establish a prima facie case that UDT was bona fide carrying on the business of banking....

[As there had been no cross-examination of the 'banker' witnesses at the trial as to whether the basis of their evidence was mistaken, Diplock LJ was prepared to assume that the grounds of the witnesses' belief were based on the genuine banking transactions undertaken by UDT and were not based on transactions which were later proved not to have been genuine banking transactions, although thought to be so at the time. He concluded:]

For these reasons I agree with the Master of the Rolls that this appeal should be dismissed. My decision is based entirely upon the state in which the evidence was left at the conclusion of this trial. As between UDT and the defendant, the status of UDT as bankers becomes *res judicata*—but between these two parties only. It does not follow that if, in some other case, the evidence were more complete or more closely probed, the result would be the same; but it would at least be more satisfactory.

NOTES

1. Professor Ellinger's comment on *Kirkwood*—to be found on p 72 of EP Ellinger, E Lomnicka and RJA Hooley *Ellinger's Modern Banking Law* (4th edn, 2006)—reads as follows:

It is clear that the three judgments in the *Kirkwood* case take divergent views regarding the importance of reputation for determining whether or not a given institution is a bank. As a rigorous analysis of law, Harman LJ's view is to be preferred. According to the common law definition, a bank is an institution that actually carries on banking business; not an institution which has the reputation of doing so or of being a bank. This definition postulates an objective test. Lord Denning, and to a lesser extent Diplock LJ, propounded a test based on subjective criteria. However, their view derives support from other cases. [See *Stafford v Henry* (1850) Ir 12 Eq 400; *Ex p Coe* (1861) 3 De GF & J 335.]

There must be some doubt as to how much the majority's decision was based on the law and how much it was based on policy. All the merits were with UDT (Kirkwood had no other defence) and the majority were appalled by what would happen if UDT were not recognised as carrying on a banking business. In *Kirkwood* certainty appears to have been the victim of expediency. For further criticism of this case, see M Megrah (1967) 30 MLR 86; and RR Pennington, AH Hudson and JE Mann *Commercial Banking Law* (1978), p 15.

2. The 'usual' or 'essential' characteristics of banking accepted by all three members of the Court of Appeal in *Kirkwood* ties the common law definition of banking to the collection of cheques, the honouring of cheques and the entry of credits and debits in bank ledgers. This was how banks operated when *Kirkwood* was decided back in 1966. Yet in *Kirkwood* itself Lord Denning said ' [t]he march of time has taken us far beyond those cases of 50 years ago' and his observation remains as true today as it was then. We now live in the age of the microchip where cheques are used less and less (the annual volume of personal cheques is less than half of what it was ten years ago) and money is frequently transferred into and out of accounts using electronic means (eg by ATMs and EFTPOS: see below, Chapter 20), with the accounts themselves no longer recorded in ledgers but on a computer database. The *Kirkwood* definition of 'bank' and 'banking' could usefully be reviewed in the light of these modern practices. In any event, it would be better to release the terms 'bank' and 'banking' from the shackles of an overly restrictive common law definition which concentrates too much on the precise mechanisms by which money is paid into and out of bank accounts.

3. Professor Cranston prefers the more generalised analysis of Isaacs J in *State Savings Bank of Victoria Comrs v Permewan Wright & Co Ltd* (1915) 19 CLR 457 at 470–471 (High Court of Australia); although specifically rejected by Lord Denning MR in *Kirkwood,* and there is certainly much to commend this approach (R Cranston *Principles of Banking Law* (2nd edn, 2002), p 5). Isaacs J said:

The essential characteristics of the business of banking are...the collection of money by receiving deposits upon loan, repayable when and as expressly or impliedly agreed upon, and the utilization of the money so collected by lending it again in such sums as are required. These are the essential functions of a bank as an instrument of society. It is, in effect, a financial reservoir receiving streams of currency in every direction, and from which there issue outflowing streams where and as required to sustain and fructify or assist commercial, industrial or other enterprises or adventures...The methods by which the functions of a bank are effected—as by current account, deposit account at call, fixed deposit account, orders, cheques, secured loans, discounting bills, note issue, letters of credit, telegraphic transfers, and any other modes that may be developed by the necessities of business—are merely accidental and auxiliary circumstances, any of which may or may not exist in any particular case.

Nevertheless, money transmission remains an important function of a bank and, although non-banks, eg building societies, now take part in the process, banks remain at the heart of national payment systems (Cruickshank Report *Competition in UK Banking* (March 2000), para 1–14).

4. *Kirkwood* involved an assessment of what was meant by the phrase '*bona fide* carrying on the business of banking'. Diplock LJ thought that an institution would not be carrying on a *bona fide* banking business where its banking business was negligible in size compared with its other business, or its current accounts were operated so as to disguise transactions of a different legal nature, ie loan transactions. Diplock LJ's dictum has since been explained by Lawton LJ in *Re Roe's Legal Charge* [1982] 2 Lloyd's Rep 370. Although Lawton LJ emphasised that he had no intention of defining a bona fide banking business, he did state that an institution could still be regarded as a bank even if:

(1) its banking business was negligible in size compared with that of a clearing bank; and

(2) it carried on business in other fields so long as its banking business was not negligible in size when compared to those other areas of business activity.

5.   The Moneylenders Act 1900 was repealed by the Consumer Credit Act 1974, s 192(4) and Sen 5, Part I, as was s 123 of the Companies Act 1967, which enabled financial institutions like UDT to be listed as bankers for the purpose of exemption under the Moneylenders Acts.

QUESTIONS

1.   How does Lord Denning's judgment differ from that of Lord Justice Diplock in the *Kirkwood* case?

2.   How relevant are the criteria of a banking business set out in the *Kirkwood* case as the use of cheques declines and funds are transferred increasingly by electronic means?

3.   If an institution meets the common law definition of a bank, would you also expect it to be authorised to accept deposits under the FSMA 2000? Does an institution authorised to accept deposits under the FSMA 2000 necessarily meet the common law definition of a bank?

(b) Definition under statute

Some (but relatively few) statutes simply refer to the terms 'bank', 'banker' and 'banking' without further or proper definition. For our purposes, the most important statutes which fall into this category are the Bills of Exchange Act 1882 and the Cheques Act 1957. Section 2 of the Bills of Exchange Act 1882 defines a 'banker' to include a body of persons whether incorporated or not who carry on the 'business of banking'. This definition is also relevant when interpreting the Cheques Act 1957 which, by virtue of s 6(1), is to be construed as one with the Bills of Exchange Act 1882. For each statute the court must turn to the common law for a definition of the 'business of banking' (see Section 2(a) above).

Other statutes contain their own definition of a 'bank': see, for example, s 9(1)(a) of the Bankers' Books Evidence Act 1879; s 5(7) of the Agricultural Credits Act 1928; and s 87(1) of the Solicitors Act 1974. Until recently, the term 'bank' was defined in these statutes as 'an institution authorised under the Banking Act 1987'. As we saw in Section l(b) above, the Banking Act 1987 was repealed and replaced by the FSMA 2000 on 1 December 2001. These statutes have all been amended in similar terms (see the Financial Services and Markets Act 2000 (Consequential Amendments and Repeals) Order 2001, SI 2001/3649). For example, s 9(1)(a) of the Bankers' Books Evidence Act 1879 provides that the expressions 'bank' and 'banker' mean a 'deposit-taker' which, under s 9(1A) of the Act, is defined as:

(a) person who has permission under Part IV of the Financial Services and Markets Act 2000 to accept deposits; or

(b) an EEA firm of the kind mentioned in para 5(b) of Sch 3 to that Act which has permission under para 15 of that Schedule (as a result of qualifying for authorisation under para 12(1) of that Schedule) to accept deposits or other repayable funds from the public, but it does not include a person who has permission to accept deposits only for the purpose of carrying on another regulated activity in accordance with that permission. This means, for example, that a stockbroker, who may accept deposits as part of other regulated activities, would not fall within the definition.

There were tight controls on the use of the terms 'bank' and 'banker' in the Banking Act 1987. Section 67 of the Act provided that, subject to certain exceptions, no person was entitled to use any banking name (ie indicating that the person was a bank or a banker or as carrying on banking business) unless that person was an authorised institution under the Banking Act 1987 which held certain specified amounts of capital. Section 69 of the Act provided that no person was entitled to describe himself or hold himself out as to indicate that he was a bank or a banker or was carrying on a banking business unless authorised (or exempt) under the 1987 Act. These provisions have since been repealed and are not repeated in the FSMA 2000. It seems that the government determined early in its reform process that it was no longer necessary to protect the use of the term 'bank' or 'banker', but to rely on the general principles of misrepresentation and on s 24 of the FSMA 2000, which makes it a criminal offence for anyone who is neither an authorised person nor an exempt person in relation to the regulated activity in question to describe himself as either authorised or exempt or who behaves or otherwise holds himself out as being authorised or exempt under the FSMA 2000 (DA Sabalot [2002] JIBFL 332, p 333). This provision would probably catch an institution that called itself a 'bank' without proper authorisation as this implies such authorisation.

The key term for the purposes of European legislation is not 'bank' or 'banker' but 'credit institution'. Article 4(1)(a) of Directive 2006/48/EC of 14 June 2006, relating to the taking up and pursuit of the business of credit institutions (recast), defines a credit institution as 'an undertaking whose business is to receive deposits or other repayable funds from the public and to grant credits for its own account' (issuers of electronic money are caught by a separate part of the definition). This definition is wider than the definition of a 'bank' under English common law and includes other financial institutions such as building societies and some industrial and provident societies. On the other hand, there is a marked similarity between the definition of a credit institution under EC law and the essential characteristics of banking business as identified by Isaacs J in *State Savings Bank of Victoria Comrs v Permewan Wright & Co Ltd* (1915) 19 CLR 457 at 470–471 (see above, Section 2(a)).

QUESTION

'Seeking to define a "bank" now is rather like trying to define an elephant. Intuitively, you know one when you see one, although you cannot define it' (Sabalot). Is this true? Is it still important under English law to be able to recognise a bank when you see one?

3 WHO IS A 'CUSTOMER'?

There are occasions when it is important to ascertain whether a person is or is not a customer of the bank. First, there are particular incidents which attach to the banker-*customer* relationship at common law (eg the bank's duty to obey its customer's instructions, to exercise reasonable skill and care, and the duty of confidentiality). Secondly, some statutes use the term 'customer' without further definition (see the Bills of Exchange Act 1882, s 75; the Cheques Act 1957, ss 1, 4).

Taxation Comrs v English, Scottish and Australian Bank Ltd
[1920] AC 683, Privy Council

A thief stole a cheque payable to bearer from the Commissioner of Taxation. The thief then opened an account at the respondent bank in the name of 'Stuart Thallon'. The next day 'Thallon' paid the stolen cheque into the account and, after it had been cleared, drew cheques on the proceeds. 'Thallon' then disappeared. The Commissioner brought an action against the bank for conversion of the cheque. In its defence the bank pleaded s 88 of the Bills of Exchange Act 1909 (Commonwealth of Australia), which was similar to s 82 of the Bills of Exchange Act 1882 (now s 4 of the Cheques Act 1957). The Commissioner alleged, *inter alia*, that 'Thallon' was not a customer within the meaning of the section. Upholding the decision of the Supreme Court of New South Wales, the Privy Council (Viscount Haldane, Lords Buckmaster, Dunedin and Atkinson) held that 'Thallon' was a customer and that the bank came within the protection of the Act.

Lord Dunedin (delivering the advice of the Privy Council): . . . Their Lordships are of opinion that the word 'customer' signifies a relationship in which duration is not of the essence. A person whose money has been accepted by a bank on the footing that they undertake to honour cheques up to the amount standing to his credit is, in the view of their Lordships, a customer of the bank in the sense of the statute, irrespective of whether his connection is of short or long standing. The contrast is not between an habitue and a newcomer, but between a person for whom the bank performs a casual service, such as, for instance, cashing a cheque for a person introduced by one of their customers, and a person who has an account of his own at the bank.

NOTES

1. In *Woods v Martins Bank Ltd* [1959] 1 QB 55, the plaintiff wrote to the defendant bank asking it to collect monies he had ordered a building society to pay to the bank, to pay part of the sum received to a particular company and to retain the balance of the proceeds to his order. The bank agreed to comply with the instructions, even though the plaintiff did not have an account with them at the time. Salmon J held that (at 63):

. . . In my view the defendant bank accepted the instructions contained in this letter as the plaintiff's bankers, and at any rate from that date the relationship of banker and customer existed between them.

In *Warren Metals Ltd v Colonial Catering Co Ltd* [1975] 1 NZLR 273 (Supreme Court of New Zealand) McMullin J held that (at 276):

. . . A customer is someone who has an account with a bank or who is in such a relationship with the bank that the relationship of banker and customer exists, even though at that stage he has no account. . . .

2. The opening of an account is the glue that holds the traditional banker-customer relationship together. That relationship turns on the flow of funds into and out of the customer's account and the mechanisms that bring about those movements. But modern banks also offer a wide variety of other services to account and non-account holders alike, eg financial advice, fund management, bank finance. In the broadest sense, those who receive these other services are also 'customers' of the bank. This is recognised by the *Banking Code* (2008 edn), which sets out standards of good banking practice for banks, building societies and other banking service providers in their relations with their personal customers in the UK. The Code indicates that the term 'personal customer' is intended to cover:

Any person who is acting for purposes which are not linked to their trade, business or profession.

By contrast, the term 'business customer' contained in the *Business Banking Code* (2008 edn) is defined exclusively with reference to the account relationship:

A customer who runs a non-personal account and who has a yearly trading turnover of under £1 million (or an income of under £1 million in the case of charities and clubs). For groups of limited companies, the turnover figure relates to the overall group turnover and not individual companies within the group.

3.   It is possible for one bank to become the customer of another bank. This occurs where one bank has an account with another bank, eg the clearing banks maintain accounts at the Bank of England and so there is a banker–customer relationship between them. It also arises where one bank, domestic or foreign, uses another as its agent to gain access to a clearing system (*Importers Co Ltd v Westminster Bank Ltd* [1927] 2 KB 297, CA; *Honourable Society of the Middle Temple v Lloyds Bank plc* [1999] 1 All ER (Comm) 193, Rix J; *Linklaters (a firm) v HSBC Bank plc* [2003] EWHC 1113 (Comm), [2003] 1 Lloyd's Rep 545, Gross J).

Can a person claim to be a customer of the bank when an account is opened in his name, but without his authority?

Stoney Stanton Supplies (Coventry) Ltd v Midland Bank Ltd
[1966] 2 Lloyd's Rep 373, Court of Appeal

As part of a scheme to defraud a third party, F forged the signature of the directors of the plaintiff company on documents requesting the defendant bank to open an account in the plaintiff company's name. The account was opened. The plaintiff company was unaware of this and at no time was F authorised to act on the company's behalf. Money which should have been paid to the third party was paid into the account and, by forging the signature of one of the plaintiff company's directors on various cheques, F drew out £9,000 for his own use. The plaintiff company subsequently went into liquidation and the liquidator sought to recover the £9,000 from the bank alleging, *inter alia*, that the bank was the banker of the plaintiff company and was under a duty to the company to use reasonable care, which it failed to exercise. McNair J found for the bank and the liquidator appealed.

Lord Denning MR: . . . As to the claim against the Bank for breach of duty, that too fails, for the simple reason that there was never any relationship of banker and customer. As far as the opening of the account was concerned, it was not taken out by the company but by Fox, who forged all the documents. The company did not authorize it at all. It is quite impossible to hold that there was any relationship of banker and customer between this company and the Bank. The company never authorized anything at all. It is rather like the case of Mr A in *Robinson v Midland Bank Ltd* (1925) 41 TLR 402. Where a person opens an account in the name of another person without any authority so to do, it is quite plain there is no relationship of banker and customer and so no question of breach of duty arises.

[Danckwerts LJ delivered a concurring judgment.
Winn LJ concurred.]

NOTES

1.   Contrast this case with *Rowlandson v National Westminster Bank Ltd* [1978] 1 WLR 798 where a woman drew a cheque payable at a bank where she was known, but with which she did not have an account, and explained that the proceeds were a gift for her grandchildren. The bank credited the cheque to an account opened in the grandchildren's names and gave their guardians the power to draw on the account. The guardians were not specifically informed of this arrangement and did not expressly approve of it. However, when the guardians eventually learned of the account one of them did draw a cheque on it. It was held by John Mills QC, sitting as a Deputy High Court judge, that the bank was in breach of its duty to the grandchildren by allowing that guardian to draw on the account for his own use. As noted in EP Ellinger, E Lomnicka and RJA Hooley *Ellinger's Modern Banking Law* (4th edn, 2006) at p 121:

[i]t would appear to follow that a contract of banker and customer came into existence between the defendant bank and the grandchildren, presumably as a result of the tacit approval of the opening of the account by the guardians. The case may, undoubtedly, rest on its exceptional facts.

2.   A person may open an account in the name of a nominee and remain the bank's customer. In *Thavorn v Bank of Credit and Commerce International SA* [1985] 1 Lloyd's Rep 259, the plaintiff, an elderly woman, opened an account in her nephew's name but stipulated that during her lifetime she was to be the only person authorised to draw on it. Lloyd J held that the aunt was the customer of the bank and that the nephew was merely her nominee (at 263). But where an account is opened in the name of a company, it is the company and not the sole owner that is the bank's customer (*Diamantides v JP Morgan Chase Bank* [2005] EWHC 263 (Comm), upheld on different grounds [2005] EWCA Civ 1612).

3.   It is important for a bank to know the identity of its customer (the rule is 'KYC' or 'know your customer'). If the bank fails to have appropriate identification procedures in place, it risks committing an offence under legislation designed to combat money laundering. The Money Laundering Regulations 2007, SI 2007/2157, require a bank to apply 'customer due diligence measures' when it establishes a business relationship (eg when opening an account for a new customer), carries out occasional transactions (that is transactions, carried out other than as part of a business relationship, amounting to €15,000 or more), suspects money laundering or terrorist financing, or doubts the accuracy of customer identification information (reg 7). Customer due diligence measures (defined in reg 5) consist of identifying and verifying the identity of the customer and any 'beneficial owner' (defined in reg 6) of the customer, and obtaining information on the purpose and intended nature of the business relationship. A beneficial owner of a customer includes, for example, anyone who ultimately owns or controls 25% of the shares or voting rights in a non-listed company, or who exercises control over the management of a company (reg 6(1)). Banks have to undertake ongoing monitoring of their business relationships (reg 8). The Financial Services Authority also requires the nominated officer within a bank responsible for compliance (commonly known as the MLRO) to manage the risks that are associated with money launderers and terrorist financiers (FSA Handbook, Block 1 High Level Standards: Senior Management Arrangements, Systems and Controls Sourcebook, SYSC3.2.6AR—SYSC3.2.6JG).

QUESTION

In *Stoney Stanton Supplies (Coventry) Ltd v Midland Bank Ltd*:

(i) what was there to prevent the company, through its liquidator, simply ratifying the unauthorised acts of the forger and claiming the account as its own? See *Brook v Hook* (1871) LR 6 Exch 89 (above, p 143); and

(ii) who, if anyone, was the bank's customer? See above, pp 172–173.

4 THE NATURE OF THE BANKER-CUSTOMER RELATIONSHIP

The relationship between bank and customer is contractual and includes the relationship of creditor and debtor with regard to the balance in the customer's bank account.

Libyan Arab Foreign Bank v Bankers Trust Co

[1989] QB 728, Queen's Bench Division

Staughton J: …It is elementary, or hornbook law to use an American expression, that the customer does not own any money in a bank. He has a personal and not a real right. Students are taught at an early stage of their studies in the law that it is incorrect to speak of 'all my money in the bank.' See *Foley v Hill* (1848) 2 HL Cas 28, 36, where Lord Cottenham said:

> Money, when paid into a bank, ceases altogether to be the money of the principal…it is then the money of the banker, who is bound to return an equivalent by paying a similar sum to that deposited with him when he is asked for it….The money placed in the custody of a banker is, to all intents and purposes, the money of the banker, to do with as he pleases….

Naturally the bank does not retain all the money it receives as cash in its vaults; if it did, there would be no point or profit in being a banker. What the bank does is to have available a sufficient sum in cash to meet all demands that are expected to be made on any particular day.

Joachimson v Swiss Bank Corpn

[1921] 3 KB 110, Court of Appeal

On 1 August 1914, one of the partners in the firm of N Joachimson died. As a result, the partnership was dissolved. At the date of dissolution the sum of £2,321 was standing to the credit of the partnership on current account at the defendant bank. At the end of the First World War one of the former partners brought an action in the firm's name to recover that sum. The bank's defence was that, as no demand had been made, no cause of action had accrued to the firm on 1 August 1914 and that, therefore, the action was not maintainable. Roche J found for the firm holding that the debt owing by a banker to his customer could be sued for without any previous demand. The bank appealed.

Bankes LJ: …The question whether there was an accrued cause of action on August 1, 1914, depends upon whether a demand upon a banker is necessary before he comes under an obligation to pay his customer the amount standing to the customer's credit on his current account. This sounds as though it was an important question. In a sense no doubt it is, but it is very rarely that the question will in practice arise. In most of the cases in which the question is likely to arise, even if a demand is necessary to complete the cause of action, a writ is a sufficient demand. It is only therefore in the unlikely case of a banker pleading the Statute of Limitations, or in a case like the present where the facts are very special, that the question becomes important....

In the ordinary case of banker and customer their relations depend either entirely or mainly upon an implied contract....

In [*Foley v Hill* (1848) 2 HL Cas 28] the Law Lords expressed their opinions as to the ordinary relation existing between banker and customer, and those opinions are correctly summarized in the headnote as follows: 'The relation between a banker and customer, who pays money into the bank, is the ordinary relation of debtor and creditor, with a superadded obligation arising out of the custom of bankers to honour the customer's drafts; and that relation is not altered by an agreement by the banker to allow the interest on the balances in the bank.' The point which is raised in the present appeal was not mentioned or discussed, either in the Court below or in the House of Lords, and in my opinion the decision cannot be treated as an exhaustive definition of all the obligations arising out of the relation between banker and customer, or as ruling out the possibility of an implied term of that relation, requiring an express demand of repayment as a condition precedent to the right to sue the banker for the amount standing to the credit of the customer's current account. The recent decision of the House of Lords in *London Joint Stock Bank v Macmillan* ([1918] AC 777), approving *Young v Grote* ((1827) 4 Bing 253), affords one striking instance of an obligation implied in the relation of banker and customer to which no reference was made in *Foley v Hill* ...

Having regard to the peculiarity of that relation there must be, I consider, quite a number of implied superadded obligations beyond the one specifically mentioned in *Foley v Hill* and *Pott v Clegg* ((1847) 16 M & W 321). Unless this were so, the banker, like any ordinary debtor, must seek out his creditor and repay him his loan immediately it becomes due—that is to say, directly after the customer has paid the money into his account—and the customer, like any ordinary creditor, can demand repayment of the loan by his debtor at any time and any place. It is only necessary in the present case to consider the one question whether there is, arising out of the relation of banker and customer, the implied obligation on the part of the customer to make an actual demand for the amount standing to his credit on current account as a condition precedent to a right to sue for that amount.

[Bankes LJ then reviewed a number of cases, including *Foley v Hill,* which contain dicta to the effect that a customer's cause of action against a bank for repayment of money only accrues when demand has been made. He continued:]

These dicta all favour the contention of the present appellants, and they are supported by the very strong body of expert opinion which was given in evidence in the Court below as to the practice of bankers. Applying Lord Esher's test, as laid down in *Hamlyn v Wood* ([1891] 2 QB 488 at 491), to the question whether the term contended for by the appellants must be implied in the contract between banker and customer, I have no hesitation in saying that it must. It seems to me impossible to imagine the relation between banker and customer, as it exists to-day, without the stipulation that, if the customer seeks to withdraw his loan, he must make application to the banker for it.... As no demand for payment in the present case was made on or before August 1, 1914, it follows, in my opinion, that the plaintiffs had no accrued cause of action on that date, and the claim fails on that ground.

Atkin LJ: This case raises the question whether the customer of a bank may sue the banker for the balance standing to the credit of his current account without making a previous demand upon the banker for payment....

The question seems to turn upon the terms of the contract made between banker and customer in ordinary course of business when a current account is opened by the bank. It is said on the one hand that it is a simple contract of loan; it is admitted that there is added, or superadded, an obligation of the bank to honour the customer's drafts to any amount not exceeding the credit balance at any material time; but it is contended that this added obligation does not affect the main contract. The bank has borrowed the money and is under the ordinary obligation of a borrower to repay. The lender can sue for his debt whenever he pleases. I am unable to accept this contention. I think that there is only one contract made between the bank and its customer. The terms of that contract involve obligations on both sides and require careful statement. They appear upon consideration to include the following provisions. The bank undertakes to receive money and to collect bills for its customer's account. The proceeds so received are not to be held in trust for the customer, but the bank borrows the proceeds and undertakes to repay them. The promise to repay is to repay at the branch of the bank where the account is kept, and during banking hours. It includes a promise to repay any part of the amount due against the written order of the customer addressed to the bank at the branch, and as such written orders may be outstanding in the ordinary course of business for two or three days, it is a term of the contract that the bank will not cease to do business with the customer except upon reasonable notice. The customer on his part undertakes to exercise reasonable care in executing his written orders so as not to mislead the bank or to facilitate forgery. I think it is necessarily a term of such contract that the bank is not liable to pay the customer the full amount of his balance until he demands payment from the bank at the branch at which the current account is kept. Whether he must demand it in writing it is not necessary now to determine. The result I have mentioned seems to follow from the ordinary relations of banker and customer, but if it were necessary to fall back upon the course of business and the custom of bankers, I think that it was clearly established by undisputed evidence in this case that bankers never do make a payment to a customer in respect of a current account except upon demand. The contention of the plaintiffs appears to me to ignore the fact that the contract between banker and customer contains special terms, and cannot in its entirety by expressed in the phrasing of an ordinary indebitatus count....

The question appears to me to be in every case, did the parties in fact intend to make the demand a term of the contract? If they did, effect will be given to their contract, whether it be a direct promise to pay or a collateral promise, though in seeking to ascertain their intention the nature of the contract may be material. In the case of such a contract as this, if I have correctly stated the manifold terms of it, it appears to me that the parties must have intended that the money handed to the banker is only payable after a demand. The nature of the contract negatives the duty of the debtor to find out his creditor and pay him his debt. If such a duty existed and were performed, the creditor might be ruined by reason of outstanding cheques being dishonoured. Moreover, payment can only be due, as it appears to me, at the branch where the account is kept, and where the precise liabilities are known. And if this is so, I apprehend that demand at the place where alone the money is payable must be necessary. A decision to the contrary would subvert banking business....

Finally it is perhaps unnecessary to say that the necessity for a demand may be got rid of by special contract or by waiver. A repudiation by a bank of the customer's right to be paid any particular sum would no doubt be a waiver of any demand in respect of such sum.

For these reasons, I am of opinion that the appeal should be allowed, and that judgment should be entered for the defendants on the claim with costs.

[Warrington LJ delivered a concurring judgment.]

NOTES

1.   Atkin LJ saw the banker-customer relationship giving rise to 'one contract'. Bankes LJ differed on this point. He felt the relationship of banker and customer was that of debtor and creditor supplemented with a 'number of implied superadded obligations'. *Paget's Law of Banking* (13th edn, 2007) notes that 'Atkin LJ's concept of a single contract is the more convincing, and it is this concept which has prevailed' (para 7.5). Furthermore, in *Tai Hing Cotton Mill Ltd v Liu Chong Ring Bank Ltd* [1985] 2 All ER 947 at 956, PC, Lord Scarman

described Atkin LJ's judgment in *Joachimson v Swiss Bank Corpn* as '[t]he classic, though not necessarily exhaustive, analysis of the incidents of the contract [between banker and customer]'. As to other incidents of the contract, not referred to by Atkin LJ, see below generally.

2.   Although the banker–customer relationship gives rise to a single contract, that contract may be governed by more than one proper law. The point arose in *Libyan Arab Foreign Bank v Bankers Trust Co* (above, p 615) where a customer had one account in London and another one in New York. Staughton J held that although there was one contract between the bank and its customer it was 'governed in part by the law of England and in part by the law of New York' (at 747). The general rule is that the contract between a bank and its customer is governed by the law of the place where the account is kept (ie the law of the country in which the account-holding branch is situated), unless there is an agreement to the contrary: *Libyan Arab Foreign Bank v Manufacturers Hanover Trust Co* [1988] 2 Lloyd's Rep 494; *Attock Cement Co Ltd v Romanian Bank for Foreign Trade* [1989] 1 WLR 1147, CA and *Libyan Arab Foreign Bank v Manufacturers Hanover Trust Co (No 2)* [1989] 1 Lloyd's Rep 608. The Contracts (Applicable Law) Act 1990, implementing the Rome Convention on the Law Applicable to Contractual Obligations 1980, does not alter this general rule (*Sierra Leone Telecommunications Co Ltd v Barclays Bank plc* [1998] 2 All ER 821 at 827, per Cresswell J).

3.   *Joachimson v Swiss Bank Corpn* was a case concerned with the contract between a bank and its customer arising out of the central account relationship. Once that relationship is established the bank is bound to provide its customer with certain services. But banks also provide their customers with many other services which fall outside the terms of the contract of debtor and creditor. These additional services are provided under specific or 'special contracts' and although banks generally provide them to their customers, they are not bound to do so. Which services are banks bound to provide to their customers (arising under the central debtor-creditor contract) and which are optional (arising out of a specific agreement)? In *Libyan Arab Foreign Bank v Bankers Trust Co* (above, p 615), Staughton J asked a similar question (at 749):

What is the customer entitled to demand? In answering that question one must, I think, distinguish between services which a bank is obliged to provide if asked, and services which many bankers habitually do, but are not bound to, provide. For a private customer with a current account I would include in the first category the delivery of cash in legal tender over the bank's counter and the honouring of cheques drawn by the customer. Other services, such as standing orders, direct debits, banker's drafts, letters of credit, automatic cash tills and foreign currency for travel abroad, may be in the second category of services which the bank is not bound to but usually will supply on demand. I need not decide that point. The answer may depend on the circumstances of a particular case.

4.   It is clear, therefore, that the relationship of debtor and creditor is not the only relationship which may exist between a bank and its customer. Other relationships which may exist between them include, inter alia, those of:

(1) *principal and agent* (which coexists with that of debtor and creditor) for purposes of a customer's instructions to his banker to carry out particular transactions on his account, eg when drawing a cheque or bill of exchange, the customer, as principal, authorises his bank, as agent, to make payment (*Westminster Bank Ltd v Hilton* (1926) 43 TLR 124), and this remains the case even where the account is overdrawn (*Coutts & Co v Stock* [2000] 1 WLR 906 at 909, Lightman J, endorsed by the Court of Appeal (obiter) in *Hollicourt (Contracts) Ltd v Bank of Ireland* [2001] 2 WLR 290 at 296, 300);

(2) *bailor and bailee* if valuables are left with the bank for safe keeping, eg when a bank provides a safe deposit service; and

(3) *beneficiary and trustee* if a bank receives money as a trustee (but not if the bank is appointed a trustee and, exercising an express power in the trust deed, deposits trust money with itself *qua banker,* see *Space Investments Ltd v Canadian Imperial Bank of Commerce Trust Co (Bahamas) Ltd* [1986] 3 All ER 75, where the Privy Council held that in such circumstances the bank held the money absolutely (being a mere debtor) and that the beneficiaries had no proprietary interest in the money so deposited which gave them priority over other unsecured creditors to the assets of the bank on its insolvency; also see *Ross v Lord Advocate* [1986] 1 WLR 1077 at 1094. For a critical analysis of other aspects of Lord Templeman's speech in *Space Investments,* see RM Goode (1987) 103 LQR 433, pp 445–447). For further discussion of those exceptional situations when a bank may become a fiduciary in relation to its customer, see below, pp 656ff.

QUESTIONS

1. How well does the rule that a customer must demand repayment at the branch of his bank that holds his account stand up to modern technology and business practices when customers can now access their accounts remotely, via cash machines and through using EFTPOS debit cards, and where some banks operate over the Internet and through telephone banking services with no branches at all? The courts in one overseas jurisdiction seem prepared to jettison the requirement (*Damayanti Kantilal Doshi v Indian Bank* [1999] 4 SLR 1 at 11, Singapore Court of Appeal). Should we?

2. What is the nature of the relationship between a bank and its customer when the customer's account is overdrawn? See EP Ellinger, E Lomnicka and RJA Hooley *Ellinger's Modern Banking Law* (4th edn, 2006), pp 126–127.

5 TERMS OF THE BANKER-CUSTOMER CONTRACT

(a) Express terms

Banking Services: Law and Practice Report by the Review Committee
(Chairman: Professor RB Jack CBE) 1989, Cm 622

2.07 Statute law relating to banking services is limited, and mostly of venerable age; what exists is largely of a technical character, concerned with the usage of cheques and bills of exchange. Thus, the banker-customer relationship has been largely left to implied contract, whose terms have been elucidated by a patchwork of judicial decisions. Much of this case law is again somewhat ancient, and has changed remarkably little over time. Until fairly recently, there has been scant use of express contractual terms agreed between the parties concerned.

2.08 We shall begin by examining the statutory component of banking services law, move onto common law, and finally look at express contract....

2.13 *Express contract,* the third leg of the legal framework, symbolises the modern trend towards a more arms-length relationship between banker and customer, the reasons for which we shall be examining. For the central account relationship, express contract is so far the exception in this country, although we give at Appendix G [terms and conditions of Midland Bank plc] one instance where the principal terms and conditions of that relationship have been reduced to writing for the bank's personal customers. In this area implied contract still, for the most part, holds sway, and the future is far from clear.

2.14 The situation is different when we turn to more sophisticated banking services, and it is here that express contract has been making inroads, in the last two decades, into the traditional implied basis of the relationship. The use of credit cards, introduced in this country in the late 1960's, has normally been governed by express contract. The same is true of cheque guarantee cards, first introduced about the same time, and of automated teller machines (ATM's, which evolved from cash dispensers in the mid-1970's). The national EFT-POS scheme (Electronic Funds Transfer at Point of Sale) will be underpinned by a network of written contracts between the various parties involved, including a contract between the bank as card issuer and its customer as a user of the EFT-POS system. Express contract has also characterised the various bank-to-bank relationships in the clearing system since the setting up of the Association for Payment Clearing Services (APACS) in 1985.

NOTES

1. In 1987 the Review Committee chaired by Professor Jack (the Jack Committee) was appointed by the government and the Bank of England to examine the need for reform of the law and practice relating to the provision of banking services within the UK. It produced its Report in 1989. When considering proposals for reform, the Jack Committee felt constrained by an overriding need to 'preserve flexibility, so as not to discourage competition and innovation by excessive regulation' (para 4.02). However, within the bounds of this overriding constraint the Jack Committee recognised, *inter alia,* the need to 'achieve fairness and transparency in the banker-customer relationship' (para 4.04). The Jack Committee recommended a self-regulating code of practice governing banker-customer relations (paras 16.10–16.12). In its White Paper *Banking Services Law and Practice* (1990, Cm 1026), the Government accepted the need for a voluntary code of banking practice and welcomed the Jack Committee's recommendations relating to the terms and conditions of the banker-customer contract (Annex 1, paras 1.7–1.9).

2. In response to the Report of the Jack Committee, and in an attempt to stave off legislative intervention, the British Bankers' Association, the Building Societies Association and the Association for Payment Clearing Services drew up a voluntary Code of Good Banking Practice to be observed by banks, building societies and other banking service providers in their dealings with 'personal customers' in the United Kingdom (the Code's definition of a personal customer is set out above, p 613). The first edition of the *Banking Code,* as the code is now called, came into operation in March 1992. It has been through several revisions since then. In 2002, in a move to deflect criticism contained in the Cruickshank Report into *Competition in UK Banking* (2000), and to head off anticipated criticism in a follow-up report of the Competition Commission (Cm 5319, 2002), the banking industry published a new code, the *Business Banking Code,* which sets out standards of best practice for banks when dealing with their (small) 'business customers' (the Code's definition of a business customer is set out above, p 613). Copies of both codes are available via the website of the Banking Code Standards Board (at www.bankingcode.org.uk), an independent body charged with monitoring compliance with the codes and also with their periodic review. The current editions of the *Banking Code* and the *Business Banking Code* came into effect on 31 March 2008.

3. The structure and contents of the *Banking Code* and *Business Banking Code* are similar. Both codes cover the core banking relationship based on current accounts, deposit accounts (and savings accounts in the case of personal customers), payment services, payment cards and personal identification numbers (PINs), and loans and overdrafts. The *Business Banking Code* also extends to merchant services, ie the provision of card acceptance services to businesses (see below, Chapter 20). Some areas of business are excluded from the codes, eg mortgages, investments, insurance and currency accounts. Each code begins with a promise that the bank will act fairly and reasonably in all dealings with the customer by meeting all the commitments and standards in the code. Key commitments are listed as: (1) to supply advertising and promotional literature that is clear and not misleading, (2) to supply clear information on how an account or service works, on terms and conditions and on interest rates, (3) to supply regular statements and inform the customer of changes to terms and conditions and interest rates, (4) to help the customer switch his/her current account between banks that subscribe to the code, (5) to lend responsibly, (6) to deal with things that go wrong quickly and sympathetically, (7) to treat customer information as private and confidential and to operate secure and reliable banking and payment systems, and (8) to publicise the code, have copies available and ensure the bank's staff are trained to put it into practice (section 2 of both codes). Each code then provides detailed guidance on the bank's practices with regard to specific matters: helping the customer to choose products and services (section 3); interest rates (section 4); charges (section 5); terms and conditions (section 6); changing accounts (section 7); advertising and marketing (section 8); running the account (section 9); cards and PINs (section 10); protecting customer information (section 11); preventing misuse of the customer's accounts and the extent of the customer's liability for unauthorised uses of his payment cards (section 12); lending and taking security (section 13); when the customer is in financial difficulty (section 14); complaints (section 15); monitoring compliance with the code (section 16) and sources of further information and advice for the customer (section 17).

4.   The *Banking Code* and the *Business Banking Code* are voluntary codes of practice. Neither code has the force of law, though the courts are likely to have regard to their provisions when considering the extent of a bank's legal liability (as the court did in *Barclays Bank plc v O' Brien* [1994] 1 AC 180). Many of the large number of UK banks that have signed up to the codes have incorporated their terms expressly into their banking contracts. In any event, in so far as the codes are held to evidence trade usage, their provisions will probably be treated as implied terms of the bank-customer contract, unless inconsistent with any express terms. The codes may be given effect in other ways. First, the FSA's 'Principles Handbook (Statements of Principle and Code of Practice for Approved Persons)' requires authorised firms to comply with standards of good practice and the codes are relevant in setting those standards. Secondly, as the codes seek to lay down good banking practice, the Financial Ombudsman is likely to take into account the extent to which a bank has complied with them in deciding what is a 'fair and reasonable' result (see Financial Services and Markets Act 2000, s 228(2): see below, Section 15). Thirdly, the Consumer Protection from Unfair Trading Regulations 2008 prohibit a wide variety of unfair commercial practices, including failure to comply with the 2008 Banking Code (the Office of Fair Trading is the designated enforcing body).

R v Financial Ombudsman Service Ltd, ex parte Norwich and Peterborough Building Society

[2002] EWHC 2379 (Admin), [2003] 1 All ER (Comm) 65, Administrative Court

J had a TESSA account with the Norwich and Peterborough Building Society (N & P). In April 1999, the government substituted a new type of tax free savings account for the TESSA. The new accounts were ISAs. J opened a mini-cash ISA with N & P but, because his TESSA had not matured, he was not eligible under the statutory scheme to open a TESSA Only ISA ('TOISA'). From April 1999, when N & P first offered a mini-cash ISA, until September 2000, when it equalised the rates which it paid on its TESSAs and TOISAs, the rate of interest paid on its TESSAs was always lower than the rate paid on both its TOISAs and on its mini-cash ISAs.

J complained to the Building Societies Ombudsman that he was receiving a lower interest rate on his TESSA than he was on his ISA. The statutory scheme for dealing with complaints against building societies required the Ombudsman to determine the complaint 'by reference to what is, in the adjudicator's opinion, fair in all the circumstances of the case' (Building Societies Act 1986, s 84(2)) and that, in reaching his decision, the Ombudsman was to have regard, *inter alia,* to the provisions of the *Banking Code* (1998 revision) (1986 Act, Sch 12, Part III, para 4). The Ombudsman determined that it was unfair for N & P to pay less interest on its TESSAs than on its TOISAs because the terms of the TOISA, notably as to notice and loss of interest, were less onerous overall than those of the TESSA. He ordered N & P to pay J the difference between the two interest rates for the period from April 1999 to September 2000. The Ombudsman held that, since paras 2.17 and 2.18 of the *Banking Code* required a bank or building society to pay interest on a superseded account which was at least as good as that paid on an account with similar features, where there was no account with similar features a superseded account such as a TESSA should not pay worse interest than any account in the firm's current range with less onerous features. The Ombudsman held that since there was unlikely to be any such comparable account in N & P's range, it should have reminded J that the TESSA could be transferred to another building society or bank and indicated that that could be done without any additional notice period or charge.

N & P challenged the Ombudsman's decision by way of judicial review. It contended, first, that the Ombudsman's finding of unfairness involved a misconstruction of the *Banking Code* and, secondly, that the Ombudsman had applied a test of unfairness (the 'relative onerousness' test), which was itself illogical, in a manner which was irrational.

Ouseley J: ...

[69] The task of interpreting the Banking Code 1998 is in my judgment for the court. The court has to decide its meaning or, as in the *South Yorkshire Transport* case [1993] 1 All ER 289, [1993] 1 WLR 23, the approach or range of considerations permissible in its application. The court undertakes that task using a variety of techniques and materials. It is not confined to those relevant or admissible in the construction of a statute, nor indeed to those more broadly available for the construction of a contract as set out in the *Investors Compensation Scheme* case ([1998] 1 All ER 98: see above, p 22).

[70] The code requires a broad, purposive and commonsense approach. It is to be interpreted according to its spirit and in a non-technical way. The references to the spirit of the code introduced into the 2000 edition merely express what was always necessarily implicit in the nature of the code anyway. However, the obvious need to adopt such an approach does not mean that the task of interpretation is not for the courts. The *Investors Compensation Scheme* case shows that the task for lawyers may be to adopt, not a non-lawyer approach, but an approach which is not driven by grammar, semantics and sophisticated or purist literalism. In *exp Save Our Railways* ([1996] CLC 589) and the *South Yorkshire Transport* case precisely the same approach was adopted; the need to adopt such an approach did not remove the task of interpretation from the court. If any particular expertise is required for the code's interpretation, that can always be provided by way of evidence.

[71] The code, however, is a material consideration for the Ombudsman to take into account. If he misinterprets it, he will have failed to take it into account. It has one meaning. Although people may reasonably differ as to that meaning, it is for the courts to decide what that one meaning is because it is for the courts to decide whether a material consideration has been ignored. The code cannot have as many meanings as reasonable people might attribute to it, all of which have to be considered. The code is to be applied by banks and other deposit-taking institutions; their compliance officers and customers cannot all say that their differing interpretations are right because reasonable. The code has not simply been produced by or for the Ombudsman's use and application. The fact that it will be applied by the Ombudsman in informal adjudications using his expertise does not alter the court's role in determining the code's meaning. The [Banking Code Standards Board] is not the guardian of its meaning; though its views are relevant, it is for the court to consider and weigh those views as to the code's interpretation and not simply to review them in effect for rationality.

[72] Rather, all those factors point instead to the Ombudsman being afforded considerable leeway in the application of the code to the circumstances which he finds.

[His Lordship held that the Ombudsman had been right to find that the code applied to accounts superseded by legislative intervention but that he had erred in his interpretation of the code, in that neither the letter, purpose or spirit of the code required a bank or building society to free its customers of notice or interest penalty and tell them that they could freely transfer their accounts to a competitor. The code envisaged only that if the bank or building society had no similar account, the account holder should be able to transfer freely to the next best dissimilar account which that bank or building society had available. It followed that the Ombudsman had misinterpreted the code and had failed thereby to have regard to it. However, his Lordship held that the Ombudsman's decision would not be quashed because it rested on two separate bases, the other being that N & P had been unfair in its treatment of TESSA interest rates because it paid less interest on the TESSA than on the less onerous TOISA. Nothing in the erroneous interpretation of the code had been imported into the concept or application of the 'relative onerousness' test. The Ombudsman's decision on relative onerousness had not gone beyond the broad concept of 'unfair treatment' of which he was the judge and accordingly the application would be dismissed.]

NOTE

Part XVI of the FSMA 2000 provides for the establishment of an ombudsman scheme for the whole of the financial services industry. The Financial Ombudsman Service (FOS) came into operation on 1 December 2001. It replaces eight previous dispute resolution services, including the Building Societies Ombudsman Scheme and the Banking Ombudsman Scheme. The FOS determines matters 'by reference to what is, in the opinion of the ombudsman, fair and reasonable in all circumstances of the case' (FSMA 2000, s 228(2)). The FOS is considered further in Section 15 below.

(b) Implied terms

It is important to remember that the banker-customer contract is made up of implied terms as well as express ones. In *Joachimson v Swiss Bank Corpn* [1921] 3 KB 110 (above, p 615), the Court of Appeal identified a number (but not necessarily all) of the key terms which are to be implied into the banker-customer contract because of the very nature of that relationship. In the absence of statutory provision the cases in which the courts will imply a term into a contract are strictly limited to those occasions (1) where the term is necessary to give business efficacy to the contract, (2) where the term was so obviously a stipulation in the agreement that it goes without saying that the parties must have intended it to form part of their contract, (3) where the term has become standardised in a particular type of contract and (4) where the term is implied by the custom of a locality or the usage of a particular trade.

In *Hare v Henty* (1861) 10 CBNS 65, Willes J famously stated that a 'man who employs a banker is bound by the usage of bankers' (at 77). The usage becomes binding as an implied term of the banker-customer contract, whether or not the customer is aware of it, so long as it is certain, notorious and reasonable (see above, p 30). Usage which derogates from the customer's substantive rights is deemed to be unreasonable and only binds the customer where he is aware of it (*Barclays Bank plc v Bank of England* [1985] 1 All ER 385 at 394; *Turner v Royal Bank of Scotland plc* [1999] 2 All ER (Comm) 664, CA). The rules of an exchange or clearing house can be usage for this purpose (*Cunliffe-Owen v Teather & Greenwood* [1967] 1 WLR 1421 (Stock Exchange rules); *Shearson Lehman Hutton Inc v MacLaine Watson & Co Ltd* [1989] 2 Lloyd's Rep 570 (London Metal Exchange)). This means, for example, that where a customer instructs his bank to transfer funds to a third party, or effect a transaction on an exchange, the customer may be bound by the rules of the clearing system or exchange used by the bank, even if the customer is unaware of those rules, so long as the rules represent the usage of bankers and that usage is reasonable. Conversely, the customer may be able to invoke the clearing system or exchange rules against his own bank for his own benefit (*Tayeb v HSBC Bank plc* [2004] EWHC 1529 (Comm), [2004] All ER 1024 at [57]). But the doctrine of privity of contract, and the probable express exclusion of the operation of the Contracts (Rights of Third Parties) Act 1999 in the rules of the exchange or clearing house, mean that the customer is unlikely to be able to enforce those rules against any bank other than his own bank (see further below, p 732).

A bank can be expected to have its own standard terms of trading. These may be incorporated into the banker-customer contract either expressly or by implication. The next case illustrates the point.

Emerald Meats (London) Ltd v AIB Group (UK) Ltd
[2002] EWCA Civ 460, Court of Appeal

The claimant customer held a current account with the defendant bank. Most of the time the account was overdrawn. There was an agreed overdraft facility, some of the terms of which were set out in facility letters issued from time to time. The customer complained that it had been overcharged interest on the overdrawn account. The complaint was that when a cheque drawn on a different bank was paid into the overdrawn account, the customer was charged interest on the sum representing the value of the cheque for a day longer than it should have been. The customer pointed to the fact that where, for example, such a cheque was paid into an overdrawn account on a Monday, the cheque would pass through the clearing system and the defendant bank would receive value from the bank upon which the cheque was drawn on the Wednesday. The defendant bank would be credited with the value of the cheque for the whole of the Wednesday, but the balance on the customer's account would not be adjusted 'for interest purposes' until the Thursday.

The customer submitted that as the facility letters did not expressly address, by reference to the clearing cycle, the question of the period in respect of which interest would be charged, there should be a term implied that the defendant bank could only charge interest during the period when money borrowed on an overdraft was outstanding, ie for Monday and Tuesday (but not Wednesday) in the example given. The defendant bank submitted that the customer's argument overlooked the distinction between where a collecting bank received value and where it received payment for a cheque. In the example given, the paying bank gave value to the collecting bank on the Wednesday but, under the clearing system rules, might go on to give notice of dishonour of the cheque to the collecting bank on the following day. If this occurred, the collecting bank would be obliged to repay the value received. On this basis, it was argued, the defendant bank could follow its usual practice and legitimately charge interest on the basis of a three day clearing cycle.

His Honour Judge Stow QC found for the bank. The customer appealed.

Pill LJ ...

[10] The judge decided, in the customer's favour, that neither 'an established usage amongst bankers' nor a 'universal practice of banks' to operate a three day cycle had been made out. An implied term to that effect could not be established on the basis of the custom and practice of the trade. The judge also held that the bank was not doing 'anything unlawful in charging the customer interest' for the third day though I do not understand the reference to 'unlawful' to mean anything other than 'in breach of contract'. The judge held that the bank had not expressly made clear to the customer what its practice was but that neither had it misled the customer as to the three day clearance cycle.

[11] The judge found for the bank on the following basis:

'In my view, when a customer, particularly a business customer, enters into a business relationship with a bank, they must be accepted as doing so on the basis of the bank's standard terms, practices and conditions. If they are not prepared to do so, they can make enquiries as to the position, and they can, if they want to, negotiate different terms or decline to form any relationship with the bank....

I find that when the parties entered into a relationship, they did so on the basis that, in so far as the terms and conditions were not expressly spelt out in the facility letters, they were on the bank's usual terms, conditions and practices, and one of those was the operation of the three day clearance cycle.'

[12] Reliance was placed by the judge on the decision of this Court in *Lloyds Bank plc v Voller* [2000] 2 All ER (Comm) 978. A regular customer with a bank went into overdraft on his personal account. There was no express agreement as to the rate of interest and the customer contended that the appropriate rate was not the standard interest rate but the lower rate which had been applied to his loan account. It was held (Potter LJ and Wall J) that when a customer drew a cheque on his account which caused the account to go into overdraft, the customer had by necessary implication requested the bank to grant an overdraft of the necessary amount on its usual terms as to interest and other charges and, in deciding to honour the cheque, the bank had by implication accepted that offer. Indeed, the Court held that the bank would have been entitled to charge at the unauthorised overdraft rate and not at the lower rate for an authorised overdraft rate it in fact applied.

[13] Mr Hapgood [Counsel for the customer] submits that the principle that the bank could apply its normal practice did not arise in a situation in which there was a facility letter which did not specify the three day cycle and where the term sought to be implied was not obvious and conflicted with the date on which the bank had received value. There should not be an obligation upon a customer to ask about the clearance cycle.

[14] The basis on which a bank may charge for an overdraft is a matter for negotiation, as to the rate of interest, the length of the clearance cycle and any other terms. A bank can however be expected to have standard terms of trading on such matters as the length of the clearance cycle, which apply in the absence of specific negotiation. A customer who seeks and obtains an overdraft facility can be taken to have agreed those standard terms unless a different agreement is made or unless the term so implied is extortionate or contrary to all approved banking practice.

[15] It is necessary to consider the commercial morality of the three day clearing period only to decide whether the term to be implied falls into either or both of these categories. It is clear from the expert evidence that, while there had been a move in banking to a two day cycle, the three day cycle was widely used at the material time. Moreover, on the basis of [the joint experts'] report, with its references to the clearing procedure and its risks, implication of the term cannot be excluded on the basis that it is extortionate or contrary to what is a widely adopted business practice.

[16] In the absence of the agreement of a different term, the judge was in my judgment correct to hold that a term should be implied that the bank's standard terms would apply. The judge was correct to conclude that the customer entering into an arrangement could expect to pay interest on the basis of the standard practice adopted by the bank, that is the three day clearing cycle. In *Voller,* Wall J stated, at 982G:

> The only proper conclusion which can be drawn, in the absence of any evidence that there was a different agreement between Mr Voller and the bank, is that the bank was granting him overdraft facilities at the standard rate for overdrafts.

Voller does, rightly in my view, assert the principle that, in the absence of express agreement, the bank's standard terms as to interest are incorporated into the contract. The length of the clearance cycle was not in issue in *Voller* but, as between two days and three days, the principle that standard terms apply is relevant in the present case. The position would be likely to be different if the term in question was extortionate or contrary to all acknowledged and approved banking practice.

[17] While I do not decide the case on this ground, the customer in the present case cannot have been unaware of the general effect of the clearing cycle. The customer relies on the bank's document entitled 'Business Banking Charges' (May 1992) for its statement to customers that 'when your loan or overdraft has been agreed we will confirm the details of the agreement and the cost of borrowing in writing'. That is clearly a reference to facility letters and the clearing cycle is not specified in those letters. However, the guide does include 'a simple guide to our charges' and the customer is advised to 'remember when you are paying in cheques to your account to allow at least four working days, excluding the date of lodgement, for those cheques to be cleared'. A short explanation is given of the 'clearing cycle'. The guide continues:

> Even though they may appear immediately on your statement, you may incur interest charges and fees if you draw against uncleared cheques.

[18] While I accept that the guidance does not deal precisely with the situation now in question, it does introduce the customer to the concept of the clearing cycle and the incurring of interest charges during that cycle. Moreover, as to acceptance of standard terms, the customer's witness, Mr ID Marshall, when it was put to him that, 'at the time that you opened the account, you were happy to accept the bank's usual service because you didn't ask the bank anything about it', replied in the affirmative.

[19] I would dismiss this appeal.

Longmore LJ: ...

[24] I agree with the judge. Mr Hapgood submitted that the question to be asked was 'What term as to the period for which interest is to be chargeable is the customer to be fairly taken to have agreed?'. He answered that by saying that the customer cannot be taken to have agreed that his bank 'should take an extra day's interest'. He bolstered that submission by saying that the agreement could not have been that the bank could make a profit of its own from the interest charging arrangement since that would be a secret profit.

[25] This latter submission is not to my mind correct. Although Allied Irish Bank acts as the customer's agent to present and collect on its customer's behalf the amounts of the cheques paid to the customer by the customer's clients, that is the limit of its agency. Any secret profit made from that operation would, no doubt, be recoverable by the customer. But arrangements for an overdraft are made between one principal and another and the terms as to accounting or interest charges made between Allied Irish Bank and its own clearing bank are also made between principals. The fact that as between Allied and Barclays, Allied are credited with the value of the cleared cheque for the whole of Wednesday has no legal relevance to the terms of the contract made between Allied Irish Bank and its customer as to its overdraft arrangements. Allied are perfectly entitled to make what profits they can from their own banking arrangements without being accountable to their customers for such profit.

[26] If that conclusion is correct it must also follow that Mr Hapgood's answer to his own question is not the correct one. The bank must be able 'to take an extra day's interest' if that can fairly be part of its own contractual arrangements. The only correct answer to the question 'What term is the customer to be fairly taken to have agreed' is then that interest will be chargeable over such period as conforms to the Bank's usual practice provided such practice is a reasonable one. Since, on the notional example with which we have been working, the customer has borrowed the money for part of Monday, the whole of Tuesday and for that part of Wednesday which occurs before payment is made to Allied via the clearing system, I cannot bring myself to hold that it is unreasonable for the practice to be that interest is charged for 3 days. This is so even though it is the usual practice of bankers to ignore parts of a day. The expert evidence, recited by my Lord, was to the effect that major clearing banks have operated a two day clearance cycle since 1994 and now charge interest on that basis to their customers. But it was also to the effect that a 3-day cycle is still common in some banks for the charging of interest. Undoubtedly, it would be more reasonable to charge interest only for 2 days; but I do not think it can be said, on the evidence, to be an unreasonable practice to charge interest for 3 days. With some reluctance, I would dismiss the appeal.

Sir Martin Nourse: [27] I agree.

NOTES

1. From November 2007, the payee of a UK cheque has been entitled to interest (if the account bears interest) or credit, if overdrawn, on proceeds after a maximum period of two days from deposit of the cheque. See also the *Banking Code* and the *Business Banking Code* (2008 edns), p 31 and p 34 respectively.

2. In *Kitchen v HSBC Bank plc* [2000] 1 All ER (Comm) 787, a 14-year term loan agreement included the term that: 'Interest shall accrue daily and be debited and compounded in accordance with the Bank's current practice from time to time.' The bank compounded the interest by quarterly debits in accordance with its current practice. The customer complained that he had been overcharged. The Court of Appeal noted (at 791) that 'the legal basis of a banker's entitlement to charge his customer compound interest with regular rests (whether annual, half-yearly or, in accordance with modern banking practice, quarterly) was put beyond doubt by the House of Lords in *National Bank of Greece SA v Pinios Shipping Co, The Maira* [1990] 1 AC 637, [1990] 1 All ER 78'. It followed that the bank was entitled to charge interest as it did. However, Sedley LJ (at 795) made the following pertinent observation:

I do, however, associated myself with his remarks about the lack of transparency in this form of loan agreement. Although the issue is settled by the highest authority, it seems to me an unnecessary misfortune that borrowers are not only compelled in practice to accept whatever terms the bank stipulates but that, when the bank stipulates an opaque term which depends for its meaning on how the bank chooses to compute interest, the law fixes the borrower with whatever burden the bank's practices impose.

The law's assumption that people know what bankers know about the latter's practices has, I would respectfully think, only limited reality. For many people, to sign a loan agreement like the present one will be to assume an indeterminate financial burden, and that in my view is not fair, at least unless the potential magnitude of the burden is clearly spelt out to them before they sign.

(c) Unilateral variation clauses

Banking Services: Law and Practice Report by the Review Committee
(Chairman: Professor RB Jack CBE) 1989, Cm 622

6.25 ...Banks' present terms and conditions will often allow them to change those terms and conditions unilaterally overnight, and present their customers with a *fait accompli* which may be to their disadvantage. We see no case for requiring banks to negotiate changes in contract terms with individual customers, which would clearly be unmanageable, as would a similar requirement applying to the original contract. But we do think it fair to expect that customers are given reasonable notice of any proposals for contract variation, to allow them to make any necessary adjustment. The US EFT Act 1978 requires 21 days, and the Australian code of good practice on EFT 30 days, for this purpose. We would not stipulate a precise period ourselves, but would look for a standard of best practice to be established on the matter.

NOTES

1. The *Banking Code* (2008 edn) provides that:

    6.3 When you become a customer, we will tell you how we will let you know about changes to terms and conditions.

    6.4 If the change is to your disadvantage, we will tell you about it personally at least 30 days before we make the change. At any time up to 60 days from the date of the notice you may, without notice, switch your account or close it without having to pay any extra charges or interest for doing this.

    6.5 We may make any other change immediately and tell you about it within 30 days.

    6.6 If we have made a major change or a lot of minor changes in any one year, we will give you a copy of the new terms and conditions or a summary of the changes.

The *Business Banking Code* (2008 edn) contains similar provisions, although special terms apply in the case of merchant services, ie where the bank provides facilities allowing the customer to accept payment by debit and credit cards (see para 6.7 of the code).

2. Clauses which provide for unilateral variation of contract terms and conditions may fall foul of the common law either as being void for uncertainty (*Kabwand Pty Ltd v National Australia Bank* (1989) 11 ATPR 40–950), or because clear words are necessary if a contract is to give one party, power unilaterally to vary its terms (*Lombard Tricity Finance Ltd v Paton* [1989] 1 All ER 918, CA). Moreover, the bank's exercise of its discretion may not be entirely unfettered. In *Paragon Finance plc v Staunton* [2001] EWCA Civ 1466, [2001] 2 All ER (Comm) 1025, where a residential mortgage agreement contained a variable interest clause at the lender's discretion, the Court of Appeal held that a term could be implied into the agreement that the discretion to vary interest rates should not be exercised dishonestly, for an improper purpose, capriciously, arbitrarily or in a way that no reasonable lender acting reasonably would use it. The lender's conduct does not have to be objectively justifiable (*Lymington Marina Ltd v Macnamara* [2007] EWCA Civ 151, [2007] 2 All ER (Comm) 825 at [43], [69]), but the lender does have to act rationally (*Socimer International Bank Ltd v Standard Bank London Ltd* [2008] EWCA Civ 116 at [66]). In *Paragon Finance plc v Pender* [2005] EWCA Civ 760, [2005] 1 WLR 3412 at [120], Jonathan Parker LJ thought it acceptable for a lender to adopt a policy of raising rates to levels at which borrowers in general, or a particular class of borrower, might be expected to turn to another lender at more favourable rates, so long as this was done for a genuine commercial reason. But note that in *Sterling Credit Ltd v Rahman* [2002] EWHC 3008 (Ch), Park J held that the Court of Appeal's decision in *Paragon Finance plc v Staunton* did not require a lender to reduce interest rates from time to time as prevailing market rates fell: this would have imposed a positive obligation on the lender whereas *Paragon Finance* only imposed a negative obligation.

The Consumer Credit Act 1974 has for a long time contained provisions for the setting aside of extortionate interest (ss 137–140). However, these provisions have not resulted in many successful challenges in the courts. There are two reasons for this. First, the threshold is high ('extortionate'). Secondly, the court is not entitled to examine the behaviour of the creditor after the agreement has been concluded. The Consumer Credit Act 2006 addresses these problems. The 2006 Act amends the 1974 Act by replacing ss 137–140 with new ss 140A–140D.

These new provisions give the court power to re-open 'unfair' credit agreements because of any terms of the agreement (or 'related' agreement) and/or the way the creditor has exercised his rights (including enforcement rights) under the agreement or related agreement.

3.   Under the Consumer Credit Act 1974, there already exists a limited statutory control on a creditor's power to vary a 'regulated agreement' (see p 596 above). Section 82 of the 1974 Act provides that where a regulated agreement contains a power of variation, then no variation can take effect before notice of it is given in the manner prescribed in the Consumer Credit (Notice of Variations of Agreements) Regulations 1977, SI 1977/328, as amended. These notice provisions cover overdrafts and credit cards.

4.   Further statutory control over variation clauses is provided by the Unfair Contract Terms Act 1977, s 3(2)(b)(i) (but altering the interest rate on a loan is not a change in 'contractual performance' falling within the subsection: see *Paragon Finance plc v Staunton,* above, at [75]–[77]), and the Unfair Terms in Consumer Contracts Regulations 1999, SI 1999/2083, Sch 2, para l(j) (but note exceptions in Sch 2, para 2, which allow the bank to vary interest rates provided the consumer is quickly informed and is free to dissolve the contract—the same applies to the variation of other charges so long as it is for a valid reason).

(i) Unfair Contract Terms Act 1977

Under the Unfair Contract Terms Act 1977, where the customer is a 'consumer' (which can include a company in appropriate circumstances), or deals on the bank's written standard terms of business, any term in the banker–customer contract which seeks to exclude or limit the liability of the bank for negligence (s 2(2)), or for breach of contract (s 3(2)(a)), or allows the bank to render a contractual performance substantially different from that which was reasonably expected (s 3(2)(b)(i)), or allows the bank to render no performance at all (s 3(2)(b)(ii)), will be ineffective except in so far as it satisfies the requirement of reasonableness (s 11 and Sch 2). Terms in bank contracts with consumer customers are more likely to be declared unreasonable than those in contracts with business customers (see *National Westminster Bank v Utrecht-American Finance Company* [2001] EWCA Civ 658, [2001] 3 All ER 733 at [57]–[62], CA).

(ii) Unfair Terms in Consumer Contracts Regulations 1999, SI 1999/2083

These Regulations, which implement the EC Directive on Unfair Contract Terms (93/13/EEC) and replace an earlier version of the Regulations (SI 1994/3159), apply to unfair terms in contracts between consumers (who must be natural persons) and commercial sellers or suppliers (who may be natural or legal persons, eg a company) (reg 4(1)). A consumer is someone who, in a contract covered by the Regulations, does not act for a purpose related to his trade, business or profession (reg 3(1)). The fact that the transaction in question is of high value does not in itself prevent someone being a consumer (*Standard Bank London Ltd v Apostolakis* [2002] CLC 933). An unfair term is one which has not been individually negotiated and which contrary to the requirement of good faith causes a significant imbalance in the parties' rights and obligations under the contract to the detriment of the consumer (reg 5(1)). The burden of proving that the term has been individually negotiated is on the seller or supplier (reg 5(4)). A contract term will always be regarded as not having been individually negotiated where it has been drafted in advance and the consumer has not been able to influence the substance of the term (reg 5(2)). Furthermore, notwithstanding that a specific term or certain aspects of it in a contract has been individually negotiated, the Regulations will apply to the rest of the contract if an overall assessment of it indicates that it is a pre-formulated standard contract (reg 5(3)). Thus, the Regulations are particularly relevant to the standard form contracts under which banks provide banking services to their consumer customers.

The unfairness of a contractual term is to be assessed by taking into account various matters, including the nature of the goods or services provided under the contract, the surrounding circumstances at the time the contract was made, and all the other terms of the contract or of another contract on which it is dependent (reg 6(1)). However, in so far as it is in plain intelligible language, the assessment of fairness of a term does not relate (a) to the definition of the main subject matter of the contract, or (b) to the adequacy of the price or remuneration, as against goods or services supplied in exchange (reg 6(2)). Schedule 2 contains an indicative and non-exhaustive list of terms which may be regarded as unfair (eg clauses which inappropriately exclude or limit the consumer's right of set-off or counterclaim, forfeiture clauses and penalty clauses).

Where a term is declared to be unfair it will not bind the consumer, but the contract continues to bind the parties if it is capable of continuing in existence without the unfair term (reg 8). The Regulations also provide that the written terms of a contract which falls within the Regulations must be expressed in plain, intelligible language, and if there is any doubt as to the meaning of a written term, the interpretation most favourable to the consumer is to prevail (reg 7).

Schedule 2 to the 1994 version of the Regulations identified four matters to be taken into account when determining whether a term satisfied the requirement of 'good faith': the strength of the bargaining position of the parties, whether the consumer had any inducement to agree to the term, whether the goods or services were sold or supplied to the special order of the consumer, and the extent to which the seller or supplier had dealt fairly and equitably with the consumer. There is no similar guidance as to the meaning of 'good faith' in the 1999 Regulations, although this does not prevent a court taking these matters, as well as others, into account. The concept of 'good faith' was recently explained by Lord Bingham in *Director General of Fair Trading v First National Bank plc* [2001] UKHL 52, [2002] 1 AC 481 at [17], a case decided under the 1994 Regulations, in the following terms:

The requirement of good faith in this context is one of fair and open dealing. Openness requires that the terms should be expressed fully, clearly and legibly, containing no concealed pitfalls or traps. Appropriate prominence should be given to terms which might operate disadvantageously to the customer. Fair dealing requires that a supplier should not, whether deliberately or unconsciously, take advantage of the consumer's necessity, indigence, lack of experience, unfamiliarity with the subject matter of the contract, weak bargaining position or any other factor listed in or analogous to those listed in Sch of the regulations. Good faith in this context is not an artificial or technical concept; nor, since Lord Mansfield was its champion, is it a concept wholly unfamiliar to British lawyers. It looks to good standards of commercial morality and practice. Regulation 4(1) [now reg 5(1) in 1999 Regulations] lays down a composite test, covering both the making and the substance of the contract, and must be applied bearing clearly in mind the objective which the regulations are designed to promote.

In the *Director General of Fair Trading* case, the House of Lords held that a default provision in a loan agreement, which allowed the lender to charge interest at the contract rate until payment, both before and after obtaining judgment against the consumer borrower, was not an unfair term. In other cases, the term may not pass the test of unfairness (see, eg *Standard Bank London Ltd v Apostolakis (No 2)* [2002] CLC 939, exclusive jurisdiction clause in foreign exchange margin trading contract between bank and consumer customer considered, (*obiter*) by Steel J to be unfair; but not all such clauses will be held to be unfair, the main problem in this case was that the existence of the clause came as a surprise to the consumer). It remains to be seen whether failure to comply with the requirements of the *Banking Code* or the *Business Banking Code* will itself be regarded as evidence of lack of good faith. As the Codes have been accepted by the banking industry as setting the standard of best practice, there is every chance that it will be so regarded.[4]

6 BANK'S DUTY TO HONOUR THE CUSTOMER'S MANDATE

When the customer opens his account he will give the bank authority to operate the account in accordance with his instructions. This is the customer's 'mandate'. So long as the bank acts within the terms of the mandate it may debit his account. The mandate should be clear and unambiguous, eg by identifying the person or persons who can draw on the account (but even a customer's irrevocable authority to a bank to accept the written demand of a particular person may later be overridden by the oral instructions of the customer himself: *Morrell v Workers Savings & Loan Bank* [2007] UKPC 3 at [10]). A bank that pays out on a *patently* ambiguous mandate, without first seeking clarification from its customer, runs the risk of being unable to debit the customer's account (*Patel v Standard Chartered Bank* [2001] Lloyd's Rep Bank 229, Toulson J). From time to time the customer will instruct the bank to make payments from his account, and the bank is under a duty to obey those instructions so long as they comply with the terms of the original mandate. In the past most payment instructions were given by the use of cheques but in modern banking practice they are just as likely to be given by electronic means (eg through use of a debit card at a retail outlet, or through use of a telephone banking or an Internet banking service).

Sierra Leone Telecommunications Co Ltd v Barclays Bank plc

[1998] 2 All ER 821, Queen's Bench Division (Commercial Court)

Cresswell J: . . . It is a basic obligation owed by a bank to its customer that the bank will honour on presentation a cheque drawn by the customer on the bank provided that there are sufficient funds in the customer's account to meet the cheque or the bank has agreed to provide the customer with overdraft facilities sufficient to meet the cheque. Where the bank honours such a cheque or other instructions it acts within its mandate, with the result that the bank is entitled to debit the customer's account with the amount of the cheque or other instruction.

Joachimson v Swiss Bank Corpn

[1921] 3 KB 110, Court of Appeal

(See above, p 615.)

NOTES

1.   The bank is obliged to honour its customer's payment instructions only if there are sufficient funds in the customer's account or available by way of agreed overdraft facility (*Bank*

---

[4] For an excellent summary of the regulation of the banking contract through common law, statute and the Banking Codes, see R Cranston *Principles of Banking Law* (2nd edn, 2002), pp 144 ff.

of New South Wales v Laing [1954] AC 135 at 154, PC). Where there are insufficient funds available to cover the full amount of the customer's payment instruction, the bank may ignore it completely. In such circumstances the customer's payment instruction stands as an offer to the bank to extend credit to him on the bank's usual terms as to interest and other charges, unless other terms have been agreed between them (*Emerald Meats (London) Ltd v AIB Group (UK) Ltd* [2002] EWCA Civ 460 at [12], CA, see above, p 624; *Lloyds Bank plc v Voller* [2000] 2 All ER (Comm) 978 at 982, CA; *Barclays Bank Ltd v WJ Simms, Son & Cooke (Southern) Ltd* [1980] QB 677 at 699, see above, p 578). Banks usually levy higher interest and other charges where the customer has not previously agreed an overdraft facility with the bank. These charges have recently been criticised by consumer groups on the ground that they are much greater than the administrative costs incurred by the bank. It is argued that the contractual terms which impose such charges are unenforceable as penalty clauses (under the common law rules against penalty clauses), or because they are unfair under the Unfair Terms in Consumer Contracts Regulations 1999, Sch 2, para 1(e). The banks dispute these contentions. They say that the penalty clause doctrine does not apply because the customer does not breach any term of the bank-customer contract by issuing a cheque which if honoured would cause his account to go overdrawn (a penalty clause is only triggered on breach) and because the charges are part of the price of the service provided by the bank they are exempt from any test of fairness under the 1999 Regulations (see reg 6(2)). In a recent test case, *Office of Fair Trading v Abbey National plc* [2008] EWHC 875 (Comm), Andrew Smith J held (i) that such terms are not exempt from an assessment of fairness under the 1999 Regulations (without ruling on the issue of fairness itself), and (ii) that they are not penalty clauses at common law. It has recently been held that whilst a customer is entitled to recover compound interest on any charges unlawfully debited to his account, the customer is not entitled to the same rate of compound interest on the sum deducted as the bank is entitled to charge the customer for withdrawals in excess of an agreed overdraft facility (*Halliday v HBOS plc* [2007] EWHC 1780 (QB) at [9], Underhill J; but see also *Sempra Metals Ltd v Inland Revenue Comrs* [2007] UKHL 34, [2007] 3 WLR 354, on the right to recover compound interest generally).

2.   In certain circumstances a bank may combine a customer's bank accounts by setting the credit balance on one account off against the debit balance on another to determine the total state of indebtedness between that customer and the bank. This is known as the banker's right of combination. It may allow the bank to refuse to honour a payment instruction received from the customer unless the overall credit balance on the customer's accounts taken together is sufficient to meet the payment. Of course, the bank would only seek to do this where it was doubtful about the customer's solvency. The banker's right of combination should not be confused with the exercise of a banker's lien (*Halesowen Presswork and Assemblies Ltd v National Westminster Bank Ltd* [1911] 1 QB 1 at 46, per Buckley LJ). A lien is a right to retain possession of property that belongs to someone else, and the bank has no lien over funds which, when deposited by the customer, becomes its own property (*R Spectrum Plus Ltd* [2005] UKHL 41, [2005] 2 AC 680 at [60], per Lord Hope). The right of combination is a particular form of contractual set-off (the views of PR Wood, *English and International Set-Off* (1989), pp 92–94 and RM Goode *Legal Problems of Credit and Security* (3rd edn, 2003), paras 7.32 ff, being preferred to those of S McCracken *The Banker's Remedy of Set-Off* (2nd edn, 1998), Ch 1 and R Derham *The Law of Set-Off* (3rd edn, 2003), Ch 15, on this point). It may, therefore, be excluded by express or implied agreement of the bank and customer. The bank may exercise its right of combination without

notice to its customer, unless the bank has previously agreed not to combine accounts. If it were otherwise the bank would run the risk that a customer placed on notice of combination would empty the account in credit and render the right of combination useless. The banker's right of combination is lost if the bank and customer have agreed to keep accounts separate (*Barclays Bank Ltd v Okenarhe* [1966] 2 Lloyd's Rep 87 at 95; contrast the statutory right of set-off on insolvency under s 323 of the Insolvency Act 1986, applied to companies under r 4.90 of the Insolvency Rules 1986, which cannot be overridden by contract: House of Lords in *Halesowen* [1972] AC 785 at 805, 809, 824). Such an agreement may be implied, as is usually the case when a customer opens a loan account (*Bradford Old Bank Ltd v Sutcliffe* [1918] 2 KB 833), or where a deposit account has a fixed maturity date as opposed to being repayable on demand. Combination is also inapplicable where a fund is deposited with the bank for a special purpose of which it has knowledge (*Barclays Bank Ltd v Quistclose Investments Ltd* [1970] AC 567, HL). There is some controversy as to whether the mere fact of maintaining accounts in different currencies or different jurisdictions should itself give rise to an implied agreement not to combine (see, eg McCracken, above, p 32). Further, an account opened by a customer as trustee, agent or nominee of another person, may not be combined with the customer's private account (*Union Bank of Australia v Murray-Aynsley* [1898] AC 693). However, the bank may be able to exercise an equitable right of set-off between a personal account and a 'nominee' account, if there is clear and undisputed evidence that the customer entitled to the funds in both accounts was one and the same person (*SAMA v Dresdner Bank AG* [2004] EWCA Civ 1074, [2005] 1 Lloyd's Rep 12; *Uttamchandani v Central Bank of India* (1989) 133 Sol Jo 262, CA; *Bhogal v Punjab National Bank* [1988] 2 All ER 296,. There is some uncertainty as to the availability of combination between a customer's personal account and a joint account. Dicta in some cases suggests that combination can only occur when the customer is entitled to the entire interest in the joint account (see *Ex p Morier* (1879) 12 Ch D 491 at 496, CA; *Bhogal v Punjab National Bank,* above, 301 at 307, CA). However, it is submitted that combination should be allowed where it can be clearly established that the debtor is solely entitled to a discrete part of the joint account (see *Abbey National plc v McCann* [1997] NIJB 158,172, NICA: noted by D Capper [1999] LMCLQ 21).

3.   A bank is not obliged to combine a customer's accounts held at different branches of the same bank in order to meet a cheque where there are insufficient funds in the account at the branch on which it is drawn (*Garnett v McKewan* (1872) LR 8 Exch 10 at 14). Whether the bank is obliged to combine accounts kept at the same branch remains an open question, but it is submitted that, as the customer could always have transferred funds from one account to the other to meet the cheque, the bank should not have to order the customer's financial affairs for him and be obliged to take the initiative. However, in practice the bank will usually honour the customer's cheque, and hold the credit balances on other accounts as security for the overdraft, combining the accounts if necessary.

4.   If the bank dishonours the customer's cheque without good cause the bank will be liable in damages for breach of contract. For many years the amount of damages recoverable by the customer differed according to whether he was a trader or a non-trader. Where the customer was a trader he could recover substantial damages for injury to his credit and reputation without proof of actual loss (*Wilson v United Counties Bank Ltd* [1920] AC 102 at 112, per Lord Birkenhead), but where he was a non-trader he could only recover nominal damages for breach of contract, unless he proved actual loss (*Gibbons v Westminster Bank* [1939] 2 KB 882; *Rae v Yorkshire Bank plc* [1988] FLR 1, CA). However, the distinction between traders

and non-traders has been swept away by the Court of Appeal in *Kpohraror v Woolwich Building Society* [1996] 4 All ER 119. Evans LJ observed that in modern social conditions it is not only tradesmen for whom the dishonour of a cheque might be obviously injurious. The credit rating of individuals is as important for their personal transactions, including mortgages and hire-purchase and banking facilities, and it is notorious that central registers are kept containing information relevant to credit ratings. Accordingly, the Court of Appeal held that in every case (trader and non-trader alike) there is a presumption of fact that the customer suffers some injury to his credit and reputation when his cheque is wrongfully dishonoured. This development is to be welcomed for it acknowledges the important role of credit in modern consumer society (R Hooley [1996] CLJ 189, p 191; cf N Enonchong (1997) 60 MLR 412). A bank which wrongfully dishonours its customer's cheque may also be liable to its customer, the drawer, in defamation. It is standard banking practice for the drawer's bank to note the reason for dishonour on the cheque, and this statement will be passed back to the collecting bank and the holder of the cheque. Where the drawer's bank implies that the cheque was dishonoured for supposed lack of funds (eg by using the now notorious phrase 'refer to drawer'—held to be potentially defamatory by the jury in *Jayson v Midland Bank Ltd* [1968] 1 Lloyd's Rep 409), the drawer will have an action for defamation against his bank should it turn out that the cheque was wrongfully dishonoured. Dishonour of a cheque without stating a reason is probably not defamatory (*Frost v London Joint Stock Bank Ltd* (1906) 22 TLR 760, CA).

5.   When does the bank have 'good cause' to refuse to honour the customer's payment instructions? The main ground is lack of funds (above) but other grounds include:

(i)   The customer's payment instructions must be unambiguous in form, otherwise the bank may refuse payment (*London Joint Stock Bank Ltd v Macmillan* [1918] AC 777 at 815, per Lord Haldane). Where the instructions are given by cheque, the bank may refuse to pay if the cheque is not properly drawn (*Cunliffe Brooks & Co v Blackburn and District Benefit Building Society* (1884) 9 App Cas 857 at 864, per Lord Blackburn). In the absence of special instructions to the contrary from their customers, it is the practice of banks not to pay cheques which are 'stale'. Usually a cheque is treated as stale if presented for payment six months or more after the date written on it (see *Commissioners of Inland Revenue v Thomas Cook (N) Ltd* [2003] 2 NLR 296 at [31–39], upheld on different grounds [2004] UKPC 53). The practice is so widespread that there is probably a term implied into the banker-customer contract that the bank may refuse to honour a cheque if not presented until an unreasonable time after its date.

(ii)   Where a bank has reasonable grounds for believing that there is a serious or real possibility that a payment instruction has been given without the proper authority of its customer, although it is regular and in accordance with the mandate, the bank is justified in refusing to honour the instruction—in fact the bank would be in breach of duty to its customer if, without inquiry, it did otherwise (*Barclays Bank plc v Quincecare Ltd* [1992] 4 All ER 363 at 375–376, per Steyn J; *Lipkin Gorman (a firm) v Karpnale Ltd* [1992] 4 All ER 409, per May LJ, and at 439, 441, per Parker LJ: see below, pp 645–650). Similarly, where a bank has serious grounds for doubting the continuing authority of those operating the account on behalf of the customer the bank is entitled, and indeed bound, to refuse to honour their payment instructions, at least until the court determines the identity of the authorised signatories or the signatories are able to provide the bank with adequate evidence of continuing authority (*Sierra Leone Telecommunications Co Ltd v Barclays Bank plc* [1998] 2 All ER 821, Cresswell J).

(iii) A bank is entitled, and indeed bound, to refuse to pay a payment instruction where to do so would render it liable as an accessory to misfeasance or breach of trust (*Royal Brunei Airlines Sdn Bhd v Tan* [1995] 2 AC 378, PC—see below, p 683). However, the bank must have positive evidence of misfeasance or breach of trust: mere suspicion is not enough to refuse its customer's instructions (*TTS International v Cantrade Private Bank* (1995) unreported decision of the Royal Court of Jersey, but see (1995) 4 J Int Tr 60).

(iii) A bank must freeze an account where it knows or suspects that the account contains the proceeds of crime (*Squirrell Ltd v National Westminster Bank plc* [2005] EWHC 664 (Ch), [2006] 1 WLR 637, considering s 328 of the Proceeds of Crime Act 2002, which creates an offence of facilitating the acquisition, retention, use or control of criminal property). In practice, the bank cannot give an explanation to its customer for fear of committing a 'tipping-off' offence (POCA 2002, ss 333, 342) unless the relevant authorities (the Serious Organised Crime Agency ('SOCA')) consent or the court so directs (*Bank of Scotland v A Ltd* [2001] EWCA Civ 52, [2001] 1 WLR 751; *Amalgamated Metal Trading Ltd v City of London Police Financial Investigation Unit* [2003] EWHC 703 (Comm), [2003] 1 WLR 2711). The bank does not act in breach of contract by refusing to honour its customer's payment instructions where it is suspicious that the money in the account is criminal property (*K Ltd v National Westminster Bank plc* [2006] EWCA Civ 1039, [2007] 1 WLR 311, where it was held that the bank does not have to adduce evidence to support any such suspicion or even show that there were reasonable grounds for the suspicion). The bank must report its knowledge or suspicion to SOCA (an 'authorised disclosure' under POCA 2002, s 338). If, after an initial period of 7 days to investigate the matter, SOCA refuses to give the bank consent to deal with the suspect account, it remains frozen for a further period of 31 days (POCA 2002, s 335). At any stage the bank, or any other person affected by the freezing of the account, may ask SOCA to look at the matter again (*R (on the application of UMBS Online Ltd) v Serious Organised Crime Agency* [2007] EWCA Civ 406). At the end of the 31 day moratorium, SOCA must apply to the court for an order to prohibit further dealing with the funds in the account (POCA 2002, s 41). Unless such an order has been made, the bank is now bound to act in accordance with its customer's instructions.

(iv) A bank may be prevented from honouring its customer's payment instructions by a third party debt order (formerly called a 'garnishee order') or a freezing injunction (formerly called a *Mareva* injunction). A third party debt order is an order of the court granted to a judgment creditor, which attaches to funds held by a third party (eg a bank) who owes money to the judgment debtor (eg the bank's customer). The procedural rules relating to third party debt orders are to be found in Part 72 of the Civil Procedure Rules 1998 (see also *Alawiye v Mahamood* [2005] EWHC 277 (Ch), [2006] 3 All ER 668, on evidence relating to the state of the judgment debtor's account). The judgment creditor must first obtain an interim third party debt order. Once an interim order is served on the bank, it must not make any payment from its customer's account that reduces the balance below the amount specified in the order. Where the order does not specify a sum (which is rare), the order attaches to the whole of the customer's balance, no matter what the amount of the judgment debt (*Rogers v Whiteley* [1892] AC 118). Following service of the interim order, a hearing takes place which both the bank and the customer may attend to object to the court making a final third party debt order. Should the court make the order final, the bank will be ordered to pay over the amount specified in the order to the judgment creditor. Compliance with the final order discharges the bank's indebtedness to its own customer (but there is no discharge if the bank pays in reliance on only an interim order: *Crantrave Ltd v Lloyds TSB Bank plc* [2000] QB 917, CA). A third party debt order may be made over an account held by the customer as trustee but the order is unlikely to be made final where the account is a trust account (*Plunkett v Barclays Bank Ltd* [1936] 2 KB 107). A joint account is attachable only in respect of a joint debt (*Beasley v Roney* [1891] 1 QB 509 at 512, per Pollock B). The third party must be within the jurisdiction for the court to make a third party debt order, eg where an overseas bank has a branch in the jurisdiction (CPR, r 72.1(1)). However, an English court will not make a third party debt order over a foreign debt, eg where funds are held in an account at an overseas branch of the bank, either because it has no jurisdiction to do so, or as a matter of discretion, or because to do so would be contrary to general principles of international law (*Société Eram Shipping Co Ltd v Compagnie Internationale de Navigation* [2003] UKHL 30, [2004] 1 AC 260; *Kuwait Oil Tanker Co SAK v Qabazard* [2003] UKHL 31 [2004] 1 AC 300). A court will not make a third party debt order final where there is a prior equitable charge or flawed asset arrangement over the account (*Fraser v Oystertec plc* [2004] EWHC 1582 (Ch), [2005] BPIR 381).

(v)   A freezing injunction freezes the customer's assets when there is a danger that the customer will remove assets from the jurisdiction or otherwise dissipate assets to avoid execution of a judgment which may be made or has been made against him. A freezing injunction may be granted over foreign assets and even extend worldwide (when special provisions are included within the terms of the order to protect banks concerned that they may be held liable to the customer in a foreign jurisdiction if they obey the order of the English court: see *Babanaft International Co SA v Bassatne* [1990] Ch 13, CA; *Derby & Co Ltd v Weldon (Nos 3 and 4)* [1990] Ch 65, CA; *Baltic Shipping Co v Translink Shipping Ltd* [1995] 1 Lloyd's Rep 673; *Bank of China v NBM LLC* [2001] EWCA Civ 1933, [2002] 1 All ER 717; *Dadourian Group International Inc v Simms* [2006] EWCA Civ 399, [2006] 2 Lloyd's Rep 354). If the bank has notice of a freezing injunction directed to the customer then this will suspend the bank's duty to honour its customer's mandate (*Z Ltd v A-Z and AA-LL* [1982] QB 558, CA); but a bank given notice of the grant of a freezing injunction does not owe the successful applicant a duty to take reasonable care to comply with its terms: *Customs and Excise Comrs v Barclays Bank plc* [2006] UKHL 28, [2007] 1 AC 181). However, the terms of the injunction may allow payment of trade creditors in the ordinary course of business (*Iraqi Ministry of Defence v Arcepey Shipping Co SA* [1981] QB 65). Further, cheques supported by cheque guarantee cards, and drawn prior to the date the order is served on the bank, fall outside the ambit of the injunction. As the bank is entitled and bound to honour its own collateral obligation to the third party (made via the cheque guarantee card) to pay the cheque, it may debit its customer's account accordingly (*Z Ltd v A-Z and AA-LL*, above, at 592–593, per Kerr LJ). Similarly, freezing injunctions have been held not to affect a bank's duty to make payment under letters of credit, negotiable instruments and documentary collections, save in very exceptional circumstances (*Z Ltd v A-Z and AA-LL*, above; *Lewis & Peat (Produce) Ltd v Almatu Properties Ltd* [1993] 2 Bank LR 45, CA). It should be noted that the courts are most reluctant to grant a freezing injunction against a bank itself as this would affect the bank's ability to pay its creditors their due debts (*Polly Peck International plc v Nadir (No 2)* [1992] 4 All ER 769, CA; *Camdex International Ltd v Bank of Zambia (No 2)* [1997] 1 All ER 728, CA).

(vi) The winding up of a company by the court is deemed to commence at the time of the presentation of the petition for winding up (or, if the company was already in voluntary liquidation, at the time when the resolution for voluntary winding up was passed): see s 129 of the Insolvency Act 1986. By s 127 of the 1986 Act, in a winding up of a company by the court, any disposition of the company's property made after the commencement of the winding up is, unless the court otherwise orders, void. Until recently, all payments into and out of a company's bank account were considered to be dispositions of the company's property and void (*Re Gray's Inn Construction Ltd* [1980] 1 WLR 711, CA). That view has turned out to be too sweeping. Payments into an account in credit have been held not to constitute dispositions of the company's property as the amount standing to the credit of the customer's account is increased (*Re Barn Crown Ltd* [1994] 4 All ER 42, criticised in RM Goode *Principles of Corporate Insolvency Law* (3rd edn, 2005), para 11–128). Payments into an overdrawn account do constitute dispositions of the company's property and are void under s 127 unless validated by the court (*Re Gray's Inn Construction Ltd*, above). Payments made out of a company's bank account, whether the account is in credit or overdrawn, have been held not to constitute a disposition of the company's property to the bank, which merely acts as the company's agent in making a disposition in favour of the third party (*Hollicourt (Contracts) Ltd v Bank of Ireland* [2001] Ch 555, CA, endorsing the ruling of Lightman J in *Coutts & Co v Stock* [2000] 1 WLR 906, and noted by C Hare [2001] CLJ 468). In any event, a bank is well advised to ask the court for a validation order under s 127 before allowing it to continue to operate the account (the principles that govern the validation of a disposition, either prospectively or retrospectively, are set out in *Re Gray's Inn Construction Ltd,* above). If a disposition is made in good faith in the ordinary course of business when the parties are unaware of the presentation of the petition, and it is completed before the winding up order is made, the court is likely to validate it (unless it can be challenged as a preference: as to which, see *Re Tain Construction Ltd* [2003] BPIR 1188). A winding-up order terminates the bank's authority to pay against its customer's payment instructions from the time that the order is made (*National Westminster Bank Ltd v Halesowen Presswork and Assemblies Ltd* [1972] AC 785).

(vii) The bankruptcy of an individual commences with the day on which the bankruptcy order is made (s 278(a) of the Insolvency Act 1986). From that day the bank no longer has authority to pay against the bankrupt customer's payment instructions, whether or not the bank knows that the order has been made. Further, by s 284(1) of the 1986 Act any disposition of property made by the bankrupt between the presentation of the bankruptcy petition and the vesting of the bankrupt's estate in his trustee (ie the day he is appointed) is void, except to the extent that it is made with the consent of, or is ratified by, the court. The wording of s 284(1) is similar to that of s 127 of the 1986 Act, and so s 284(1) should apply to dispositions of the type caught by s 127. The discretion vested in the court under s 284(1) is also likely to be exercised in a way similar to the discretion vested under s 127. If the bank makes a payment which is caught by s 284(1), but does so unaware of the presentation of the petition, the court is likely to ratify the payment. The bank is given further protection by s 284(5) which allows it to maintain a debit if the bank pays against the bankrupt's payment instruction after the making of a bankruptcy order, unless the bank did so with notice of the bankruptcy or it is not reasonably practical to recover the amount from the payee. It would seem that the subsection only applies where the payment is made out of an overdrawn account, because only then has the bankrupt 'incurred a debt to a banker' by reason of the making of the payment (*Paget's Law of Banking* (13th edn, 2007), para 14.48). A bank which receives a payment into the account before the bankruptcy order may be protected by s 284(4).

By sub-s (4), the amount paid into the account is irrecoverable if received before the commencement of the bankruptcy in good faith, for value and without notice of the presentation of the bankruptcy petition.

(viii) When the bank account is closed, either by the bank or by the customer, the bank's duty and authority to honour the customer's mandate terminates (see Section 14 below).

7 BANK'S DUTY TO OBEY THE CUSTOMER'S COUNTERMAND

The converse of the bank's duty to obey the customer's mandate is the bank's obligation to obey his countermand—with regard to cheques, this obligation is defined by statute.

Bills of Exchange Act 1882

75. The duty and authority of a banker to pay a cheque drawn on him by his customer are determined by—

(1) Countermand of payment:

(2) Notice of the customer's death.

Notice of countermand must be clear and unambiguous (*Westminster Bank v Hilton* (1926) 43 TLR 124: see below), and it must be brought to the actual (not constructive) knowledge of the bank (*Curtice v London City and Midland Bank Ltd* [1908] 1 KB 293: see below). Unless otherwise agreed, notice of countermand must be given to the branch of the bank were the account is kept (*London, Provincial and South Western Bank Ltd v Buszard* (1918) 35 TLR 142).

Curtice v London City and Midland Bank Ltd
[1908] 1 KB 293, Court of Appeal

The plaintiff was a customer of the Willesden Green branch of the defendant bank. He drew a cheque on that branch payable to Jones. After business hours on the same day, the plaintiff telegraphed the branch to stop payment of the cheque. The Post Office's telegram messenger, finding the bank closed, placed the telegram in the bank's letter-box at 6.15 pm. By an oversight, the telegram was not taken out of the letter-box and shown to the branch manager until two days later, by which time the cheque had been paid. The plaintiff then drew a cheque for the whole of the balance of his account, including the amount of the cheque which he had drawn in favour of Jones. The defendant bank dishonoured the cheque and the plaintiff then sued for the whole balance as money had and received. The county court judge found for the plaintiff holding that there had been a good countermand of payment and that decision was upheld on appeal to the Divisional Court. The bank further appealed to the Court of Appeal.

Cozens-Hardy MR: …Countermand is really a matter of fact. It means much more than a change of purpose on the part of the customer. It means, in addition, the notification of that change of purpose to the bank. There is no such thing as a constructive countermand in a commercial transaction of this kind.

In my opinion, on the admitted facts of this case, the cheque was not countermanded, although it may well be that it was due to the negligence of the bank that they did not receive notice of the customer's desire to stop the cheque. For such negligence the bank might be liable, but the measure of damage would be by no means the same as in an action for money had and received. I agree with the judgment of AT Lawrence J on this point, and that is sufficient to dispose of the appeal. But as we have had an argument addressed to us as to the effect upon the duty of a bank of the mere receipt of a telegram, I wish to add a few words on that. A telegram may, reasonably and in the ordinary course of business, be acted upon by the bank, at least to the extent of postponing the honouring of the cheque until further inquiry can be made. But I am not satisfied that the bank is bound as a matter of law to accept an unauthenticated telegram as sufficient authority for the serious step of refusing to pay a cheque.

The result is that the appeal is allowed, with costs here and below.

Fletcher Moulton LJ: ...A banker (although so far as his financial relations to his customer are concerned he stands in the position of debtor and creditor) is for such a purpose as this only a particular type of agent; he is in the possession of money of the customer, and his duty is to obey the directions of the customer as to paying that money out. If an order is given to him he has the ordinary rights of any agent with regard to the mode in which that order shall be given to him. I use the word 'mode' in its widest sense. It has long been held that an order must be unambiguous. If a master chooses to give an order to his servant that bears two meanings, he cannot find fault with his servant for having taken the meaning which it was not in fact intended to bear; and that applies to a banker when receiving orders as much as to agents generally.

Now that principle which applies to the duty of conveying the mandate in a form in which the meaning is unambiguous applies, in my opinion, mutatis mutandis to the question of its authenticity. If the mandate is sent in a form in which a servant, acting reasonably, has no security that the mandate comes from his employer, the employer cannot grumble that he did not act upon it. Authenticity and meaning appear to me, in the general law of agency, to stand on the same footing, subject, of course, to the broad difference of circumstances which are due to the difference of nature of the two. In my opinion a telegram which is only an official but unauthenticated copy of a document, in itself unauthenticated, cannot be said to be necessarily and as a matter of law a mandate communicated in such a way that its provenance is unambiguous....

With regard to the second point, as to the doctrine that there may be in law constructive notice of the meaning of a countermand which has not reached the mind of the servant, I agree entirely with what the Master of the Rolls has said.

Farwell LJ: ...There is no contract that the banker will do more than honour the cheque. On that is superadded the statute, which shews that the duty and authority of a banker to pay a cheque drawn on him by his customer may be countermanded on notice being given to him. In my opinion that must be actual notice brought to his attention. On the evidence here it is clear that the banker is simply put on inquiry by the receipt of a telegram, and his duty is not to pay at once, but to make inquiries; and, if the mere receipt of a letter or telegram were sufficient countermand, the position of a banker in large business would be most difficult. Supposing a midday post comes in with so many letters that it takes a quarter of an hour (not an unreasonable time) to open them—it is during bank hours, and just as the post comes in or within five minutes afterwards a number of cheques are presented, is it to be said that the banker must thereupon refuse to cash any of those cheques until he has opened all his letters? On the general question of stopping by telegram I am disposed to think that it would depend a great deal on the custom of the bankers, and the agreement, if any, between the customers and their bankers, that business should be conducted by telegram, and this would depend on the evidence in each case. I therefore agree with the result which has been arrived at.

NOTES

1.   Unless otherwise agreed, no particular form is required for an effective countermand. The countermand may be made orally, in person or by telephone, or by letter, telex, fax, email

or other writing. However, in each case the bank must be able reasonably to satisfy itself that the countermand is that of its customer. The bank is not obliged to accept an unauthenticated message as countermand of its duty and authority to pay in accordance with its customer's mandate, although it may rely on the unauthenticated message to delay payment pending confirmation (see *Curtice v London City and Midland Bank Ltd,* above).

2.   An example of an ambiguous countermand arose in *Westminster Bank Ltd v Hilton* (1926) 43 TLR 124. In that case the customer telegraphed his bank to stop payment of a post-dated cheque, giving the wrong cheque number but otherwise correctly stating the details of the cheque. In fact, a cheque with the number specified by the customer (which the customer had not intended to stop) had already been paid. As the post-dated cheque (which the customer had intended to stop) had a later serial number than the cheque which had already been paid and was dated one day later than the stop order, the bank concluded that the stop order did not apply to the post-dated cheque and duly paid it, believing it to be a replacement for the other cheque. The House of Lords held the bank had not been negligent in paying the post-dated cheque. Lord Shaw emphasised that as this was a post-dated cheque the onus was on the customer to inform the bank of this fact, which he had not done (at 129–130). If a principal's instructions are ambiguous and can be interpreted in different ways, the agent will be excused if he acted bona fide in one way even if it is not the way intended by his principal (*Ireland v Livingston* (1872) LR 5 HL 395; see above, p 113). However, where the ambiguity is *patent,* and the agent has the opportunity to seek clarification from his principal, he will not be absolved from liability if he fails to do so (see *Giordano v Royal Bank of Canada* (1973) 38 DLR (3d) 191; *Remfor Industries Ltd v Bank of Montreal* (1978) 90 DLR (3d) 316; cf *Westminster Bank Ltd v Hilton,* above, at 126; *Shapera v Toronto-Dominion Bank* (1970) 17 DLR (3d) 122).

3.   Up to what stage of the payment process does the customer have the right to countermand his payment instruction? This may be the subject of express agreement between the bank and its customer. In the absence of express agreement, the issue will be determined by prevailing banking practice, including the rules governing the operation of the payment system used to transfer funds. In the case of a paper-based credit transfer, such as a bank giro credit, the payment instruction is irrevocable once the credit voucher is delivered by the sending bank to the receiving bank, and with an electronic funds transfer, the general rule is that the instruction becomes irrevocable once the receiving bank accepts the payment order from the sending bank (see Chapter 18, Section 8, below). The position with regard to cheques (paper-based debit transfers) can be summarised as follows. A countermand made after the bank has paid a cheque across the counter would be too late. Where the drawer and payee maintain accounts at different banks, the cheque will pass through the clearing system. Notwithstanding that settlement takes place between banks at the end of each trading day, as the Clearing House Rules make provision for later dishonour by the branch on which the cheque is drawn, a notice of countermand should be effective if received before the time limited by the Rules has run out (AG Guest *Chalmers and Guest on Bills of Exchange* (16th edn, 2005), para 13–039). If the drawer and payee maintain accounts at the same branch or different branches of the same bank, payment is made, and countermand no longer possible, once the paying branch does an unconditional act indicating its decision to pay the cheque. In some cases this may be done through setting in motion the bank's internal process for crediting the payee's account (*Momm v Barclays Bank International Ltd* [1977] QB 790), although in others the making of entries in the bank's records may not be conclusive proof of payment (*Sutherland and Sutherland v Royal Bank of Scotland plc* [1997] 6 Bank LR 132, Outer House of the Court of Session: a provisional or conditional entry may allow for subsequent reversal). (See generally, below, Chapter 18, Section 9).

4. When a cheque is supported by a cheque guarantee card the bank gives a contractual undertaking to the payee, through the agency of the customer, that the bank will not dishonour the cheque on presentation for want of funds in the account, so that it is obliged if necessary to advance moneys to the customer to meet it (*Re Charge Card Services Ltd* [1987] Ch 150 at 166, affd [1989] Ch 497, CA; *First Sport Ltd v Barclays Bank plc* [1993] 1 WLR 1229, CA). Can a cheque be countermanded when supported by a cheque guarantee card? Usually the terms and conditions on which the card is supplied to the customer include an undertaking by the customer not to countermand payment of any cheque backed by the card. Whether this means that any countermand is ineffective, or alternatively that the countermand is effective but the customer is in breach of contract to the bank, has yet to be judicially determined. Academic opinion supports the view that the countermand would be ineffective as the customer has authorised its agent, the bank, to incur a personal liability to the payee, for which the customer has a contractual duty to indemnify the bank (EP Ellinger, E Lomnicka and RJA Hooley *Ellinger's Modern Banking Law* (4th edn, 2006), p 591; AG Guest *Chalmers and Guest on Bills of Exchange* (16th edn, 2005), para 13–042).

5. Section 75(2) of the Bills of Exchange Act 1882 overcomes the normal rule that the authority of the agent is automatically determined by the principal's death (*Campanari v Woodburn* (1854) 15 CB 400; see above, p 244). The effect of s 75(2) on *donatio mortis causa* and *inter vivos* gifts is summarised by Professor Guest in *Chalmers and Guest on Bills of Exchange* (16th edn, 2005), para 13–046, as follows:

...if a customer draws a cheque and hands it to another in contemplation of death, there will be no valid *donatio mortis causa* if the cheque is not presented to and paid by the banker before he has notice of the death [*Re Beaumont* [1902] 1 Ch 889], unless the gift has in the lifetime of the donor been completed by a dealing with the cheque [*Rolls v Pearce* (1877) 5 Ch D 730]. Nor is there an effective gift *inter vivos* of the amount of the cheque at law or in equity, for equity will not intervene to perfect an imperfect gift [*Re Swinburne* [1926] Ch 38; but the gift of a cheque drawn by a third party, which the donor holds, would appear to be good: *Clement v Cheesman* (1884) 27 Ch D 631].

6. The Bills of Exchange Act 1882 does not deal with the effect of the insanity of the customer on the bank's duty to honour his mandate. Under general agency principles, an agent's authority automatically terminates on his principal's insanity (notice of insanity being irrelevant): *Yonge v Toynbee* [1910] 1 KB 215 (see above, p 174). But as the relationship between customer and bank is not solely that of principal and agent, the better view is that only notice of the customer's insanity terminates the bank's authority to pay cheques (FH Ryder (1934) 55 JIB 14). Where an order is made under the Mental Capacity Act 2005 the position should be clearer.

7. The remedies which may be available to the bank when it pays money in error by overlooking a countermand or notice of the customer's death or insanity are:

(i) recovery of money paid under a mistake by the common law action for money had and received (*Barclays Bank Ltd v WJ Simms, Son & Cooke (Southern) Ltd* [1980] QB 677: see above, p 578);

(ii) tracing in equity so that the bank can claim an equitable proprietary interest in the money in the hands of the recipient (see above, p 593);

(iii) raising a defence to the customer's claim that his account was wrongly debited, by pleading that the payment was made for the benefit of the customer in payment of his debts—this is known as the *Liggett* doctrine, taking its name from the next case.

B Liggett (Liverpool) Ltd v Barclays Bank Ltd

[1928] 1 KB 48, King's Bench Division

In breach of mandate, the defendant bank honoured cheques signed by only one director of its customer, the plaintiff company, when the signatures of two directors were required. The cheques were drawn in favour of the plaintiffs creditors. The plaintiff later tried to recover the amounts debited to its account from the defendant bank. Wright J held that the defendant bank had a good defence to the claim on the ground that the defendant bank was entitled to take over the creditor's former remedies against the plaintiff.

Wright J: ...[I]t is contended by the defendant bank that they are entitled to credit for the amounts so paid—that is to say, for all those cheques—in discharging the debts of the company, and they rely upon the equitable doctrine under which a person who has in fact paid the debts of another without authority is allowed to take advantage of his payment. The question which has been debated, and which is not at all an easy question, is whether on the facts of this case that equity applies. It was said by Sir Walter Greaves-Lord and Mr Goldie that in law the position here would simply be this, that the bank for this purpose is in the position of a stranger who without the authority of the plaintiff company has paid off the debts of the plaintiff company, and that being so, the payment was a purely voluntary payment so far as the company was concerned, and hence the company, even if it took the benefit, could not be in any way made responsible for the payments so made. For that rule of common law, a rule of common law which cannot be questioned, reliance is placed, amongst others, on the authority of *Exall v Partridge* (8 TR 308). But the matter must now be decided in a Court which takes cognizance of principles of both law and equity, and the question is whether the equitable principle does apply to the facts of this case. The equitable principle has been applied beyond question over and over again to cases where an agent not having the authority of his principal has borrowed money as on behalf of his principal. Under those circumstances at common law the principal cannot be sued and cannot be made to repay the amount so borrowed, but in equity it has been held that to the extent that the amount so borrowed has been applied in payment of the debts of the principal, the quasi lender is entitled to recover from the quasi borrower. The rule is very clearly stated by Lord Selborne in the case of *Blackburn Building Society v Cunliffe, Brooks & Co* (22 ChD 61,71). The noble and learned Lord said: 'And I think the consistency of the equity allowed in the *Cork and Youghal Ry. Co's* case ((1869) LT 4 Ch 748) with the general rule of law that persons who have no borrowing powers cannot, by borrowing, contract debts to the lenders, may be shown in this way. The test is: has the transaction really added to the liabilities of the company? If the amount of the company's liabilities remains in substance unchanged, but there is, merely for the convenience of payment, a change of the creditor, there is no substantial borrowing in the result; so far as relates to the position of the company. Regarded in that light, it is consistent with the general principle of equity, that those who pay legitimate demands which they are bound in some way or other to meet, and have had the benefit of other people's money advanced to them for that purpose, shall not retain that benefit so as, in substance, to make those other people pay their debts. I take that to be a principle sufficiently sound in equity; and if the result is that by the transaction which assumes the shape of an advance or loan nothing is really added to the liabilities of the company, there has been no real transgression of the principle on which they are prohibited from borrowing.' That principle is well established in respect of borrowings made without authority, and I may refer to the cases of the *Baroness Wenlock v River Dee Co.* (19 QBD 155) and *Bannatyne v Maclver* ([1906] 1 KB 103), in which latter case the principle was applied to a case where the agent who had purported to borrow without authority was the agent, not of the company, but of a private individual. The ground is sometimes put in this way, that the lender or the quasi lender is subrogated to the rights of the creditor who has been paid off. That, obviously, is not precisely true, because no question of subrogation to securities can arise in such a case. The principle has also been applied in *Reversion Fund* *and Insurance Co v Maison Cosway Ltd* ([1913] 1 KB 364), to the case where the plaintiff, the quasi lending company, actually knew that the quasi borrowing company had no authority to borrow. If this were a case in which the plaintiffs' account was in debit throughout to the defendant bank, then each of the cheques in question when presented would constitute a request for a loan, and the payment of that cheque would constitute the granting of that loan, and as the cheque and the request were unauthorized the case would be precisely within those authorities I have just referred to. There was some evidence in this case that at the relevant dates the position of the plaintiff company's account at the defendant bank was that it was in debit and that there was an overdraft; to the extent that that is so, the position will be, in my judgment, exactly as in the cases I have referred to, and the position will be precisely covered by the authority of those cases. But it is not clear that that was so throughout or, indeed, at all. I have to consider, therefore, what the position would be if when each one of those cheques or any one of these cheques was presented the account was in credit. The position then would be that in paying one of those cheques without authority the defendant bank was taking money which belonged to its customer and paying that away without authority. In other words, the defendant bank would be in possession of a credit balance belonging to the customer, and without the customer's authority it would be misapplying that credit balance. Does the equity which I have referred to extend to a case of that character?

...[I]n principle it seems to me that ought to be so [and] I cannot see why the same result should not apply in a case like the one before me, where the banker does not handle actual cash or notes, chattels capable of conversion, but by reason of the present system of banking facilities everything is done by way of credit or debit balances. In such a case there is obviously no conversion, but there is misapplication, under an honest mistake as to the validity of the authority, of the credits which constitute the medium of exchange in place of cash. Under these circumstances I think that the equity I have been referred to ought to be extended even in the case where the cheque which was paid out of the credit balance, and was not paid by way of overdraft, so that the banker will be entitled to the benefit of that payment if he can show that that payment went to discharge a legal liability of the customer. The customer in such a case is really no worse off, because the legal liability which has to be discharged is discharged, though it is discharged under circumstances which at common law would not entitle the bank to debit the customer.

The result is that I must order an inquiry, because I have not the facts before me sufficiently to come to a conclusion whether the rule of equity which I have stated does apply, and if so to what extent. The inquiry I order will be addressed to some referee who will report to me. I shall retain seisin of the case and shall deal with all questions of costs and make such final order as the report which follows on the inquiry may seem to require. The inquiry will be as to the exact circumstances under which each one of the cheques and bills complained of was paid, that is to say, what was the state of the plaintiff company's account with the defendant bank at the date of each payment? Was it made in respect of goods supplied and was it made in the ordinary course of business?

NOTES

1.   Although Wright J avoided using the language of subrogation (because he wrongly thought that subrogation could only be used to transfer secured rights), *Liggett* is generally regarded as a subrogation case. It stands as authority for the proposition that when a bank (P) pays its customer's (D' s) creditor (X) in the mistaken belief that D has authorised it to do so, D's liability should be treated as automatically discharged, leaving the bank (P) unable to recover from the payee (X), but entitled to recover from its customer (D) by taking over (being subrogated to) X's former remedies against D (ie the discharged liability) (see, eg EP Ellinger and CY Lee [1984] LMCLQ 459; cf A Burrows *The Law of Restitution* (2nd edn, 2003), pp 124–125, who claims that the subrogation reasoning in *Liggett* is an unnecessary complication and that the bank should be allowed a direct claim against D for money

mistakenly paid to D's use). *Liggett* can be explained on restitutionary reasoning as subrogation is used to reverse the unjust enrichment of the customer (D) at the expense of the bank (P), the unjust factor being the bank's mistake.

2.   Whether a bank's unauthorised mistaken payment automatically discharges its customer's debts must be doubted. It is a well-established rule that the unrequested payment of another's debt only discharges that debt automatically where it was paid under legal compulsion or by necessity, otherwise prior authorisation, subsequent ratification or some other form of acceptance of the payment by the debtor is required for a good discharge (*Belshaw v Bush* (1851) 11 CB 191; PBH Birks and J Beatson (1976) 92 LQR 188; cf A Burrows *The Law of Restitution* (2nd edn, 2003), pp 293–302). In *Re Cleadon Trust Ltd* [1939] Ch 286, the majority of the Court of Appeal considered that the decision in *Liggett* could be upheld only on the basis that the bank had been expressly authorised to pay by one of the company's directors, and that the director himself had the company's authority to do this, even though the director was not authorised to draw a cheque on the company's account for that purpose on his signature alone. The majority's reasoning has been applied by the Court of Appeal in *Crantrave Ltd v Lloyds TSB Bank plc* [2000] QB 917, where it was held that the *Liggett* defence arises only where the payment from the account is applied to reduce the customer's debt with the customer's authority, or if the customer has ratified the payment. It should be noted, however, that Pill and May LJJ also considered that the bank might have a defence to a claim for breach of mandate where it could be established on the evidence that the customer had been 'unjustly enriched' by the unauthorised payment ([2000] QB 917 at 924 and 925; see also *Majesty Restaurant Pty Ltd v Commonwealth Bank of Australia Ltd* (1999) 47 NSWLR 593, for a case that might fall within this exceptional category).

3.   The need for prior authorisation, or subsequent ratification, of the payment by the customer helps distinguish *Liggett* from the later case of *Barclays Bank Ltd v W J Simms Son & Cooke (Southern) Ltd* [1980] QB 677 at 700 (see above, p 578), where Robert Goff J held that payment of a countermanded cheque (ie a payment without mandate) did not discharge the drawer's liabilty to the payee, so that the drawee bank could recover the mistaken payment from the payee through an action for money had and received. In *Simms* there was no authority to discharge the debt, whereas in *Liggett,* according to the majority in *Re Cleadon Trust,* there was authority to do so. However, the interpretation of *Liggett* provided by the majority in *Re Cleadon Trust* may well be wrong on the ground that a company director who has no authority to borrow on the company's behalf can have no authority to direct a bank to pay the company's creditors on the company's behalf—if so, there would be no automatic discharge of the company's debts by the bank's mistaken payment to the company's creditors and no ensuing right of subrogation (C Mitchell *The Law of Subrogation* (1994), pp 128–129). The bank would then be left with an action for money had and received against the payee, and no right of action based on subrogation against its customer (the policy aspects of this conclusion are considered further above, pp 586–587).

QUESTION

Clare wants to countermand payment of a cheque she drew earlier that day. She takes a letter to that effect round to the branch which holds her account. As she enters the branch Clare sees Sebastian, who she recognises as the branch manager's secretary. Clare hands the letter to Sebastian who assures her that he will hand it to the branch manager without delay. In fact, Sebastian forgets to do this for a week, by which time Clare's cheque has been paid and the funds debited from her account. Advise Clare.

8 BANK'S DUTY OF CARE

A bank has a duty under its contract with its customer to exercise reasonable care and skill in carrying out its part with regard to operations within its contract with its customer. The duty to exercise reasonable care and skill extends over the whole range of banking business within the contract with the customer. The standard of reasonable care and skill is an objective standard applicable to banks. Whether or not it has been attained in a particular case has to be decided in the light of all the facts, which can vary almost infinitely (*Selangor United Rubber Estates Ltd v Cradock (a bankrupt) (No 3)* [1968] 1 WLR 1555 at 1608, per Ungoed-Thomas J).

The duty to exercise reasonable care and skill is implied into the banker–customer contract as a matter of common law or by s 13 of the Supply of Goods and Services Act 1982 (which implies a term to this effect in contracts for the supply of a service in the course of a business). The duty may also arise concurrently in tort (*Henderson v Merrett Syndicates Ltd* [1995] 2 AC 145, HL). But where the bank provides specialist banking services to financially sophisticated customers under the terms of contractual documentation drafted by specialist lawyers, the court will be slow to find a duty of care in tort going beyond the rights and obligations carefully set out in those documents (*IFE Fund SA v Goldman Sachs International* [2006] EWHC 2887 (Comm), [2007] 1 Lloyd's Rep 264 at [63], per Toulson J, affd [2007] EWCA Civ 811 [2007] 2 Lloyd's Rep 449). In those exceptional cases where a bank and its customer are in a fiduciary relationship, a duty to exercise reasonable skill and care may be imposed as a matter of fiduciary law (see, eg *Lloyd's Bank Ltd v Bundy* [1975] QB 326, CA: below, p 658).

It is an implied term of the contract between the bank and its customer that the bank will observe reasonable skill and care in and about executing its customer's orders to transfer money (*Barclays Bank plc v Quincecare Ltd* [1992] 4 All ER 363 at 376, per Steyn J). However, this can create a conflict between the bank's duty to honour the customer's mandate and its duty to exercise reasonable care and skill in and about the execution of the mandate. It is to the resolution of this conflict of duties that the Court of Appeal's decision in the *Lipkin Gorman* case (below) is directed.

Lipkin Gorman (a firm) v Karpnale Ltd
[1989] 1 WLR 1340, Court of Appeal

Cass was a partner in the plaintiff firm of solicitors and had authority to draw on the solicitors' client account with the defendant bank by his signature alone. Cass was a compulsive gambler and to fund his addiction he wrongfully drew cheques on the client account. The bank honoured the cheques even though its branch manager knew Cass was a gambler and was aware that the method used for drawing and paying the relevant cheques was unusual. The bank did not inform the solicitors that Cass was a gambler or that large sums were being withdrawn from the client account under his authority and made no inquiries as to the propriety of those withdrawals. When the frauds were discovered, the solicitors brought an action against the bank and against the casino where Cass had gambled away the money. The claim against the bank was that it had been in breach of duty to the solicitors and was liable as a constructive trustee of the moneys stolen. The solicitors' claim succeeded before Alliott J and the bank appealed.

May LJ: …I turn to the solicitors' claim against the bank based on contract or negligence. We are here concerned with the general relationship between a banker and his customer in the common case where the latter has a current account with the former which is in credit. The underlying basis of this relationship is that it is one of debtor and creditor. The money deposited with a bank becomes its own. It is prima facie bound to meet its debt when called on to do so. As Lord Atkinson said in *Westminster Bank Ltd v Hilton* (1926) 43 TLR 124 at 126:

> It is well established that the normal relation between a banker and his customer is that of debtor and creditor, but it is equally well established that *quoad* the drawing and payment of the customer's cheques as against money of the customer's in the banker's hands the relation is that of principal and agent. The cheque is an order of the principal's addressed to the agent to pay out of the principal's money in the agent's hands the amount of the cheque to the payee thereof.

Indeed any failure by a bank to honour its customer's instructions may well redound to the serious discredit of the customer himself.

On the authorities it is clear that at least in the last century the terms of a customer's mandate to his banker in respect of his current account were sacrosanct. In *Bodenham v Hoskins* (1852) 21 LJ Eq 864, 869 Kindersley V-C said:

> Let us see, therefore, what was the position of the bankers in the matter. I entirely agree with many of the observations that have been made by … counsel for the defendants, that, as between banker and customer, in a naked case of banker and customer, the banker looks only to the customer, in respect of the account opened in that customer's name, and whatever cheques that customer chooses to draw, the banker is to honour. He is not to inquire for what purpose the customer opened the account; he is not to inquire what the monies are that are paid into that account, and he is not to inquire for what purpose monies are drawn out of that account: that is the plain general rule, as between banker and customer.

In the similar case, *Gray v Johnston* (1868) LR 3 HL 1,11, Lord Cairns LC said:

> I think, fortunately, your Lordships will find that the law on that point is clearly laid down, and may be derived without any hesitation from the authorities which have been cited in the argument at your Lordships' bar, and I apprehend that you will agree with me when I say that the result of those authorities is clearly this: in order to hold a banker justified in refusing to pay a demand of his customer, the customer being an executor, and drawing a cheque as an executor, there must, in the first place, be some misapplication, some breach of trust, intended by the executor, and there must in the second place, as was said by Sir John Leach, in the well known case of *Keane v Robarts* (1819) 4 Madd 332,357, be proof that the bankers are privy to the intent to make this misapplication of the trust funds.

In similar vein Lord Westbury said, at p. 14:

> The relation between banker and customer is somewhat peculiar, and it is most important that the rules which regulate it should be well known and carefully observed. A banker is bound to honour an order of his customer with respect to the money belonging to that customer which is in the hands of the banker; and it is impossible for the banker to set up a jus tertii against the order of the customer, or to refuse to honour his draft, on any other ground than some sufficient one resulting from an act of the customer himself. Supposing, therefore, that the banker becomes incidentally aware that the customer, being in a fiduciary or a representative capacity, meditates a breach of trust, and draws a cheque for that purpose, the banker, not being interested in the transaction, has no right to refuse the payment of the cheque, for if he did so he would be making himself a party to an inquiry as between his customer and third persons. He would be setting up a supposed jus tertii as a reason why he should not perform his own distinct obligation to his customer.

Finally, in *Bank of New South Wales v Goulburn Valley Butter Co Pty Ltd* [1902] AC 543, 550, Lord Davey, in giving the opinion of the Privy Council, said: 'The law is well settled that in the absence of notice of fraud or irregularity a banker is bound to honour his customer's cheque.'

However, in two relatively recent decisions, strongly relied on by counsel for the solicitors, it seems to me that at first instance two judges went appreciably further. These two decisions were *Selangor United Rubber Estates Ltd v Cradock (No 3)* [1968] 1 WLR 1555 and *Karak Rubber Co Ltd v Burden (No 2)* [1972] 1 WLR 602. The facts of each case were complicated and it is unnecessary to set them out in detail. The disputes were concerned with the use of a limited company's moneys to finance the purchase of its own shares. In addition to claims against personal defendants the several banks involved in the relevant transaction were also sued, first, as constructive trustees with the directors of the company's funds in respect of breach of trust, secondly, in negligence in relation to the way the banks paid cheques drawn on them. . . .

When Ungoed-Thomas J turned to consider the claim against the banks in *Selangor United Rubber Estates Ltd v Cradock (No 3)* [1968] 1 WLR 1555 based on negligence, he said, at p1591:

> A further and alternative claim is made against the defendant banks for negligence. This is a claim for damages at common law, as contrasted with a claim for equitable relief against the banks, as well as against other defendants, to replace moneys misapplied as trustees or constructive trustees. Both these equitable and common law claims, as against both defendant banks, involve the allegations that they ought to have made inquiry. Such allegations, though differing in the case of each bank, are identical under both the equitable and common law claim, and it is common ground that any standard of care which puts on inquiry or notice is the same under both claims.

In my opinion, whether it was by concession or not, it was wrong to equate the duty to inquire where there has been fraud and the bank is proved to have known of it with that where all that is being alleged is that the bank had been negligent. Nor was it necessary to rely on any such equivalence in order to decide the issues in the *Selangor* case. It was because of this error I think that both Ungoed-Thomas J in the *Selangor* case, at p 1608, and Brightman J in *Karak Rubber Co Ltd v Burden (No 2)* [1972] 1 WLR 602, 628–629 stated the common law of duty of care on a paying banker in the normal case of a current account in credit too highly [in *Selangor* the duty was said to include a duty of care to ascertain the customer's 'really intended instructions as contrasted with the instructions to act on signatures misused to defeat the customer's real intentions']. The relationship between the parties is contractual. The principal obligation is on the bank to honour its customers' cheques in accordance with its mandate on instructions. There is nothing in such a contract, express or implied, which could require a banker to consider the commercial wisdom or otherwise of the particular transaction. Nor is there normally any express term in the contract requiring the banker to exercise any degree of care in deciding whether to honour a customer's cheque which his instructions require him to pay. In my opinion any implied term requiring the banker to exercise care must be limited. To a substantial extent the banker's obligation under such a contract is largely automatic or mechanical. Presented with a cheque drawn in accordance with the terms of that contract, the banker must honour it save in what I would expect to be exceptional circumstances.

Mr Sumption QC on behalf of the bank accepted that an objective test had to be applied and that accordingly there had to be some limits of the bank's entitlement to treat its mandate as absolute. However, he contended that the circumstances in which this was so would be very limited indeed. He accepted that there would be implied into the mandate a term that it should not be given effect to if the relevant transaction was patently dishonest. In so far as any duty to inquire before paying a cheque drawn in accordance with the mandate was concerned, he submitted that this duty could only arise when the transaction on its face was dishonest, but could have an honest explanation if appropriate inquiry was made. Counsel accepted that if a bank knows of facts which a reasonable bank manager would think were probably dishonest then inquiry would be appropriate.

For my part I would hesitate to try to lay down any detailed rules in this context. In the simple case of a current account in credit the basic obligation on the banker is to pay his customer's cheques in accordance with his mandate. Having in mind the vast numbers of cheques which are presented for payment every day in this country, whether over a bank counter or through the clearing bank, it is, in my opinion, only when the circumstances are such that any reasonable cashier would hesitate to pay a cheque at once and refer it to his or her superior, and when any reasonable superior would hesitate to authorise payment without inquiry, that a cheque should not be paid immediately on presentation and such inquiry made. Further, it would, I think, be only in rare circumstances, and only when any reasonable bank manager would do the same, that a manager should instruct his staff to refer all or some of his customers' cheques to him before they are paid. In this analysis I have respectfully derived substantial assistance from the material parts of the judgment of Steyn J in *Barclays Bank plc v Quincecare Ltd* (1988) [1992] 4 All ER 363.

Parker LJ: ...All the cheques were within the bank's mandate and, there being funds to meet them, the bank's primary obligation was to honour them. Such obligation is however not absolute. It is common ground that in some circumstances a bank would, notwithstanding that it honoured a cheque duly signed by a person whose signature it was authorised and required to honour, nevertheless be acting in breach of contract. An extreme example would be where the bank in fact knows a cheque is being drawn in fraud of the customer or, what amounts to the same, they turn a blind eye to the obvious.

The solicitors' claim against the bank in the present case is based on the alternative grounds that in honouring the cheques the bank acted in breach of contract or rendered itself liable as a constructive trustee....

It is in my view clear that the bank could not have rendered itself liable as constructive trustee unless it was also liable for breach of contract and that if it was not liable for breach of contract it could not be liable as constructive trustee. This is because, stated in broad terms, the bank's duty to pay cheques signed in accordance with its mandate is subject to the qualification that it must be performed without negligence and that (i) negligence may exist where there is no question of the circumstances giving rise to a finding of constructive trusteeship; (ii) if there is no negligence I cannot envisage, at least in this case, any facts which would found liability on the ground of constructive trusteeship....

That a bank has a duty of care to its customer when carrying out its mandate is beyond doubt, but so to state advances matters but little, for in each case the question for decision is whether a bank has failed in that duty and there are very many cases on the subject, a considerable number of which were cited in argument. In my view such cases must be approached with caution, for essentially they are no more than decisions of fact, ie of the application of the law to an endless variety of circumstances. Expressions in them, such as that a paying bank must pay under its mandate save in extreme cases, or that a bank is not obliged to act as an amateur detective, or that suspicion is not enough to justify failing to pay according to the mandate, or other like observations which are to be found in the cases, are no more than comments on particular facts or situations and embody in my view no principles of law. Furthermore what would or might have been held to be a breach of duty at one time may not be a breach of duty at another. As Diplock LJ said in *Marfani & Co Ltd v Midland Bank Ltd* [1968] 1 WLR 956, 972:

> What facts ought to be known to the banker, ie, what inquiries he should make, and what facts are sufficient to cause him reasonably to suspect that the customer is not the true owner, must depend upon current banking practice, and change as that practice changes. Cases decided 30 years ago, when the use by the general public of banking facilities was much less widespread, may not be a reliable guide to what the duty of a careful banker in relation to inquiries, and as to facts which should give rise to suspicion, is today.

In addition, cases relating to a collecting banker being sued in conversion and those relating to a paying banker sued for breach of contract raise different considerations. In the former class of case it is for the banker to establish that he collected without negligence, in the latter the burden is on the customer to prove negligence. The statutory protection is also different in the two types of case, as can be seen from the observation of Greer LJ in *Carpenters' Co v British Mutual Banking Co Ltd* [1938] 1 KB 511, 529:

> In my judgment s 60 of the Bills of Exchange Act 1882 only protects a bank when that bank is merely a paying bank, and is not a bank which receives the cheque for collection.

Finally, it is to be noted that the distinction between liability as a constructive trustee and liability for breach of contract is frequently blurred or unconsidered. For the above reasons it would not in my judgment serve any useful purpose to embark on an analysis of the many authorities cited. In the course of his judgment the judge said [1987] 1 WLR 987, 1006:

> When, as in this case, the alleged constructive trustee is a bank, the court's approach must reflect the established contractual duties of a bank. In this context Mr Sumption made five propositions to me, as follows: (1) the bank is entitled to treat the customer's mandate at its face value, save in extreme cases; (2) the bank is not obliged to question any transaction which is in accordance with the mandate, unless a reasonable banker would have grounds for believing that the authorised signatories are misusing their authority for the purpose of defrauding their principals or otherwise defeating his true intention; (3) it follows that, if a bank does not have reasonable grounds for believing that there is fraud, it must pay; (4) mere suspicion or unease do not constitute reasonable grounds and are not enough to justify a bank in failing to act in accordance with a mandate; and (5) a bank is not required to act as an amateur detective. Those propositions were well supported by authority which it is unnecessary for me to cite, and I accept them. Mr Sumption also conceded that, if the bank had reasonable grounds for believing that Cass was operating the clients' account in fraud of the plaintiffs, it would be the duty of the bank not to honour cheques drawn by Cass even when drawn within the mandate. Again, I approach that concession on the basis that reasonable grounds must be construed in the light of the three types of knowledge I have restricted myself to considering.

So far as breach of contract is concerned the judge's approach was in my judgment more favourable to the bank than was justified if, as appears to be the case, he considered that some want of probity was required even to establish a breach of contract. Mr Sumption [counsel for the bank] had not so submitted, nor did he so submit before us. If a reasonable banker would have had reasonable grounds for believing that Cass was operating the client account in fraud, then, in continuing to pay the cash cheques without inquiry the bank would, in my view, be negligent and thus liable for breach of contract, albeit neither Mr Fox [the branch manager] nor anyone else appreciated that the facts did afford reasonable grounds and was thus innocent of any sort of dishonesty.

In *Nihill v Nihill,* Court of Appeal (Civil Division) Transcript No 276 of 1983. Slade LJ said:

> There is thus a strong expression of opinion of a majority of this court in the *Belmont* case [1979] Ch 250, though without finally deciding the point, that constructive notice will not suffice to render a person liable as constructive trustee under this head, unless he has wilfully shut his eyes to dishonesty, or has wilfully or recklessly failed to make such inquiries as an honest and reasonable man would make. Nevertheless, for present purposes, I for my part would be prepared to assume in favour of the plaintiff, though without deciding the point, that the onus of proof which she would have to satisfy in regard to knowledge on the part of the bank would be less onerous than that. I would be prepared to assume, without so deciding, that if there were facts known to the bank which ought to have alerted it to the *probability* that the first and second defendants were committing fraudulently breaches of trust, this would render the bank liable as constructive trustee, if it had assisted in such breaches by allowing the relevant moneys to be drawn out of the relevant account. I deliberately refer to probability rather than to possibility, because in my opinion on no footing could the bank have become liable as constructive trustee in allowing these moneys to

be drawn out of the trust account merely because it knew of the possibility that breaches of trust were being committed. If mere possibility sufficed to fix a bank with liability as constructive trustee in such circumstances, potential liability would arise in almost any instance where a bank allowed trustees to draw on a trust account.

Slade LJ was there considering a case based on constructive trusteeship, not breach of contract, but to a great extent his observations are in my judgment equally applicable to a claim based on breach of contract. I would not, however, accept that a bank could always properly pay if it had reasonable grounds for a belief falling short of probability. The question must be whether, if a reasonable and honest banker knew of the relevant facts, he would have considered that there was a serious or real possibility, albeit not amounting to a probability, that its customer might be being defrauded, or, in this case, that there was a serious or real possibility that Cass was drawing on the client account and using the funds so obtained for his own and not the solicitors' or beneficiaries' purposes. That, at least, the customer must establish. If it is established, then in my view a reasonable banker would be in breach of duty if he continued to pay cheques without inquiry. He could not simply sit back and ignore the situation. In order so to establish the customer cannot, of course, rely on matters which a meticulous ex post facto examination would have brought to light. Such an examination may well show that it was indeed obvious what Cass was doing, but in the present case the inquiry is simply whether Mr Fox, and therefore the bank, had, on the basis of the facts and banking practices established at the time, reason to believe that there was a serious possibility that Cass was misusing his authority to sign under the mandate in order to obtain and misapply the cash . . . in fraud of the solicitors.

[His Lordship then reviewed the volume of cheque transactions carried out at the branch where the solicitors' client account was held and concluded:]

The overall situation which has therefore to be considered is one in which there were a maximum of 63 fraudulent cash cheques drawn by an authorised signatory on one of some 2,800 current accounts over a period during which there were many thousands of cash transactions and during which the total debit entries on the fraudulently operated account were about seven times the number of fraudulent entries. In order for Mr Fox to have had any reason to believe that there even might be something wrong with the operation of the client account, he would have had to examine the paid cheques and conclude that on the basis of their signatures, amounts and frequency, this was a serious possibility.

  On the evidence I can see no basis on which it could be said that a reasonable banker would either have done so or, had he done so, would have had reason to believe any such thing . . . .

  I do not consider that a case of negligence has been made out, still less a case that the bank was liable as constructive trustee. I would therefore allow the appeal of the bank and dismiss the cross-appeal of the solicitors under this head.

Nicholls LJ: For the reasons given by Parker LJ I would allow the bank's cross-appeal . . . .

Appeal allowed with costs.

[The case was appealed to the House of Lords, but not on the question of the duties of the paying bank: [1991] 2 AC 548.]

NOTES

1.   In *Barclays Bank plc v Quincecare Ltd* [1992] 4 All ER 363 (judgment delivered on 24 February 1988), Steyn J had to consider whether a bank, when executing a payment order given by the chairman of its corporate customer, had been put on inquiry that the chairman was acting for his own benefit, or for an unauthorised purpose. Steyn J held as follows:

Given that the bank owes a legal duty to exercise reasonable care in and about executing a customer's order to transfer money, it is nevertheless a duty which must generally speaking be subordinate to the bank's other conflicting contractual duties. Ex hypothesi one is considering a case where the bank received a valid and proper order which it is prima facie bound to execute promptly on pain of incurring liability for consequential loss to the customer. How are these conflicting duties to be reconciled in a case where the customer suffers loss because it is subsequently established that the order to transfer money was an act of misappropriation of money by the director or officer? If the bank executes the order knowing it to be dishonestly given, shutting its eyes to the obvious fact of the dishonesty, or acting recklessly in failing to make such inquiries as an honest and reasonable man would make, no problem arises: the bank will plainly be liable. But in real life such a stark situation seldom arises. The critical question is: what lesser state of knowledge on the part of the bank will oblige the bank to make inquiries as to the legitimacy of the order? In judging where the line is to be drawn there are counter-vailing policy considerations. The law should not impose too burdensome an obligation on bankers, which hampers the effective transacting of banking business unnecessarily. On the other hand, the law should guard against the facilitation of fraud, and exact a reasonable standard of care in order to com-bat fraud and to protect bank customers and innocent third parties. To hold that a bank is only liable when it has displayed a lack of probity would be much too restrictive an approach. On the other hand, to impose liability whenever speculation might suggest dishonesty would impose wholly impractical standards on bankers. In my judgment the sensible compromise, which strikes a fair balance between competing considerations, is simply to say that a banker must refrain from executing an order if and for as long as the banker is 'put on inquiry' in the sense that he has reasonable grounds (although not necessarily proof) for believing that the order is an attempt to misappropriate the funds of the company (see proposition (3) in *Lipkin Gorman v Karpnale Ltd* (1986) [1992] 4 All ER 331 at 349, [1987] 1 WLR 987 at 1006). And, the external standard of the likely perception of an ordinary prudent banker is the governing one. That in my judgment is not too high a standard....

Having stated what appears to me to be the governing principle, it may be useful to consider briefly how one should approach the problem. Everything will no doubt depend on the particular facts of each case. Factors such as the standing of the corporate customer, the bank's knowledge of the signatory, the amount involved, the need for a prompt transfer, the presence of unusual features, and the scope and means for making reasonable inquiries may be relevant. But there is one particular factor which will often be decisive. That is the consideration that, in the absence of telling indications to the contrary, a banker will usually approach a suggestion that a director of a corporate customer is trying to defraud the company with an initial reaction of instinctive disbelief. In *Sanders Bros v Maclean & Co* (1883) 11 QBD 327 at 343 Bowen LJ observed:

> 'But the practice of merchants, it is never superfluous to remark, is not based on the supposition of possible frauds. The object of mercantile usages is to prevent the risk of insolvency, not of fraud; and any one who attempts to follow and understand the law merchant will soon find himself lost if he begins by assuming that merchants conduct their business on the basis of attempting to insure themselves against fraudulent dealing. The contrary is the case. Credit, not distrust, is the basis of commercial dealings; mercantile genius consists principally in knowing whom to trust and with whom to deal, and commercial intercourse and communication is no more based on the suppos-ition of fraud than it is on the supposition of forgery.'

That was, of course, a very different case, and the relationship between merchants is very different from the relationship between a banker and a customer. But, it is right to say that trust, not distrust, is also the basis of a bank's dealings with its customers. And full weight must be given to this consider-ation before one is entitled, in a given case, to conclude that the banker had reasonable grounds for thinking that the order was part of a fraudulent scheme to defraud the company.

On the facts Steyn J found that there was nothing that should have put the bank on inquiry. The bank knew that the funds (which were in fact misappropriated) were required to purchase a business and expected a large part of them to go to the corporate customer's solicitors. The order in question instructed the bank to transfer the bulk of the funds to those solicitors.

2.   In *Verjee v CIBC Bank & Trust Co (Channel Islands) Ltd* [2001] Lloyd's Rep Bank 279, the drawer signed two blank cheques drawn on the defendant bank and gave them to a business acquaintance who, according to the drawer, dishonestly filled in the cheques with the names of the wrong payees and dates before presenting them for payment. The drawer claimed that the bank was in breach of a duty of care which it owed to him when it honoured the cheques on the ground that it should have realised something was wrong and then have made inquiries. Hart J rejected the claim. His Lordship observed (at 282) that where the signatory on the cheque is not necessarily the account holder, as in *Barclays Bank plc v Quincecare,* or the signatory of the cheque is not the only person who is liable on it, as in the *Lipkin Gorman* case, 'it seems to me necessarily the case that the possibility of fraud is always more likely to be present'. By contrast, where, as in the present case, the apparent signatory of the cheque is himself the account holder, then 'if the bank has no reason not to believe the signatory to be genuine, no question on the face of it can arise of some fraud being committed on the signatory'. Similarly, if one joint account holder is entitled under the mandate to draw on the account in his name alone, and he does so in breach of a private agreement with the other account holders, it is unlikely that the bank would be held to be in breach of a duty of care owed to the other account holders unless the bank has some reason for supposing that the mandate was being abused by the joint account holder (*Royal Bank of Scotland plc v Fielding* [2004] EWCA Civ 64 at [107]–[108]).

3.   In a lengthy series of fraudulent transactions, a number of different cashiers will deal with the cheques in question. It seems clear from *Lipkin Gorman* that it is not possible to 'aggregate' the knowledge of every cashier handling the transactions in order to claim that the bank knew enough to detect a suspicious pattern: a breach of contract will only arise where at least one individual in the bank has sufficient personal knowledge for his or her suspicions to be aroused (see S Fennell (1994) 57 MLR 38 at 46–47). A similar approach is taken in insurance law where it has been held that information provided to an insurance company did not give rise to knowledge on the part of the company unless it was received by a person authorised and able to appreciate its significance (*Malhi v Abbey Life Assurance Co Ltd* [1994] CLC 615, CA).

4.   The bank's duty to exercise reasonable care and skill may also arise when services are provided outside a contractual relationship. Thus a bank may be held liable in tort for negligent advice/misstatements made to customers (*Box v Midland Bank Ltd* [1979] 2 Lloyd's Rep 391) and to non-customers under the *Hedley Byrne* principle (*Hedley Byrne & Co Ltd v Heller & Partners Ltd* [1964] AC 465, HL, where a bank only avoided liability for negligent advice given about a customer's credit-worthiness in a bank reference provided to a third party because of its disclaimer). The House of Lords has held that the *Hedley Byrne* principle extends beyond negligent advice/misstatements so that it can apply to economic loss caused by negligent provision of services, and that the basis of a *Hedley Byrne* claim is an assumption of responsibility by the defendant to the claimant (*Henderson v Merrett Syndicates Ltd* [1995] 2 AC 145, HL; *Williams v Natural Life Health Foods Ltd* [1998] 1 WLR 830, HL; cf *Customs & Excise Comrs v Barclays Bank plc* [2006] UKHL 28, [2007] 1 AC 181, where the House of Lords held that, in cases of pure economic loss, an 'assumption of responsibility' was a sufficient, but not a necessary, condition for the imposition of a duty of care: whether there was a duty of care could also turn on the threefold test of foreseeability, proximity and whether it was fair, just and reasonable to impose the duty). The fact that the bank accepts a request for advice is strong evidence of an assumption of responsibility, although an antecedent request for advice is not necessary where the advice is given within the scope of the bank's business (*Morgan v Lloyds Bank plc* [1998] Lloyd's Bank Rep 73, 80, CA). Where a bank assumes a duty to exercise reasonable care in giving advice and complies with that duty, it does not assume a further continuing obligation to keep the advice under review and, if necessary, correct it in the light of supervening events (*Fennoscandia Ltd v Clarke* [1999] 1 All ER (Comm) 365, CA). Furthermore, a bank will not be liable where information or advice supplied by it to a customer is passed on without the bank's knowledge to third parties who rely on it (*Mann v Coutts & Co* [2003] EWHC 2138 (Comm), [2004] 1 All ER (Comm) 1, applying *Caparo Industries plc v Dickman* [1990] 2 AC 605, HL, the leading case on auditors' negligence; cf *Riyad Bank v Ahli United Bank (UK) plc* [2006] EWCA Civ 780, [2006] 2 Lloyd's Rep 292, where it was held to have been obvious that advice given by the bank would be passed on to a third party who would be likely to act on it).

5. There are limits to the extent of a bank's duty of care.

(i) A bank owes its customer a duty of care to detect and report upon forgeries of the customer's signature on cheques drawn on his account (*Greenwood v Martins Bank Ltd* [1932] 1 KB 371 at 381, per Scrutton LJ). The same duty is owed to an agent of a disclosed principal (the customer) who, under a power of attorney for his principal, is the sole signatory on the account (*Weir v National Westminster Bank plc* [1995] 4 Bank LR 249, Inner House of the Court of Session). However, where the agent also holds his own personal account at the bank, the bank does not owe him a wider duty of care as its customer to detect and report upon forgeries of his signature on cheques drawn on some other account (ie an account which was not the customer's account) whenever such cheques purporting to bear the customer's signature come into the bank's possession (*Weir*).

(ii) A paying bank does not owe a duty of care to the payee of a cheque when deciding whether to honour the cheque when presented for payment (*National Westminster Bank Ltd v Barclays Bank International Ltd* [1975] QB 654 at 662, Kerr J). However, the paying bank may owe the payee of a cheque a duty to act carefully and honestly under the *Hedley Byrne* principle when advising the payee of its reason for dishonouring the cheque (*TE Potterton Ltd v Northern Bank Ltd* [1995] 4 Bank LR 179, Irish HC—criticised by EP Ellinger [1995] JBL 583–585).

(iii) A bank that is the payee of a cheque drawn in payment for shares issued on a floatation does not owe a duty of care to protect the drawee bank from loss caused by the theft and fraudulent alteration of the cheque (*Yorkshire Bank plc v Lloyds Bank plc* [1999] 2 All ER (Comm) 153).

(iv) A bank which receives and acknowledges an irrevocable instruction from its customer to transfer funds owes no tortious duty of care to the intended beneficiary of the payment and will not be liable to him should the bank fail to execute the payment instruction (*Wells v First National Commercial Bank* [1998] PNLR 552, CA, although Evans J opined that if the intended beneficiary communicated directly with the bank, a duty might arise from the relationship thus formed: see below, p 739). Likewise, a bank that receives funds does not owe a duty of care to the payer, who is not its customer and to whom it has undertaken no special responsibility, to pay those funds only to the named beneficiary identified in the payment instructions (*Abou-Rahmah v Abacha* [2005] EWHC 2662 (QB), [2006] 1 Lloyd's Rep 484, affd [2006] EWCA Civ 1492, [2007] 1 Lloyd's Rep 115: instruction to credit account of customer named 'Trust International' but fund credited to account of 'Trusty International' which was controlled by fraudsters).

(v) A bank's duty to take reasonable care in ascertaining, interpreting and acting in accordance with the customer's instructions does not imply a duty to warn against, or advise on, the risks inherent in carrying through those instructions (*Redmond v Allied Irish Banks plc* [1987] 2 FTLR 264 at 266, per Saville J). For example, a bank owes no duty of care to advise or warn its customer of the possible tax implications of paying funds into his account (*Schioler v National Westminster Bank Ltd* [1970] 2 QB 719). Similarly, an English bank acting as agent for collection of a cheque owes no duty to a foreign collecting bank to advise on the effect of the Cheques Act 1992 on the meaning and significance of an 'a/c payee only' crossing (*Honourable Society of the Middle Temple v Lloyds Bank plc* [1999] 1 All ER (Comm) 193; *Linklaters (a firm) v HSBC Bank plc* [2003] EWHC 1113 (Comm), [2003] 2 Lloyd's Rep 545; and see below, pp 797–798).

(vi) A bank is generally under no duty to consider the prudence of lending from the customer's point of view or to advise the customer with reference to it (*Williams and Glyn's Bank Ltd v Barnes* [1981] Com LR 205). As Scott LJ said in *Lloyds Bank plc v Cobb* (18 December 1991, unreported), CA:

> …the ordinary relationship of customer and banker does not place on the bank any contractual or tortious duty to advise the customer on the wisdom of commercial projects for the purpose of which the bank is asked to lend. If the bank is to be placed under such a duty, there must be a request from the customer, accepted by the bank, or some other arrangement between the customer and the bank, under which the advice is to be given.

Where the bank examines a borrowing proposal to decide whether or not it wishes to make a loan, it does this for its own purposes as lender and not for the benefit of the borrower. The conflict of interest which exists between the bank's duty to its shareholders as a commercial lender and the interests of the borrower in securing the loan precludes the existence of a duty of care between the bank and the borrower, or between the bank and any third party known by the bank to have a financial interest in the borrower's affairs (*Chapman v Barclays Bank plc* [1997] 6 Bank LR 315 at 318, per Otton LJ). By the same token, the bank owes no duty to the borrower to assess his capacity to repay.

In an exceptional case the bank might assume the role of the borrower's financial adviser. This occurred, for example, in *Verity and Spindler v Lloyds Bank plc* [1995] CLC 1557, where the plaintiffs approached their bank manager with a business proposal to borrow money and purchase a house, which they planned to refurbish and sell at a profit. The bank manager inspected one house, but thought it would not return a profit. He then made an internal inspection of another house and advised the plaintiffs that it would make a viable project and encouraged them to proceed with it. The loan was made and the house purchased, but the refurbishment work took longer, and cost more, than anticipated and the house was eventually sold, following a fall in the property market, at a loss. The plaintiffs then sought to recover that loss from the bank claiming they would not have purchased the house but for the negligent financial advice given to them by the bank manager. Judge Robert Taylor (sitting as a deputy High Court judge) held that the plaintiffs had specifically sought the advice of the bank manager on the prudence of the transaction and that the bank manager, having assumed the role of financial adviser, had been negligent in the advice he had given in this respect. The judge pointed to a number of factors, which established that financial advice had been requested by the plaintiffs and given by the bank manager, including the plaintiffs' financial naivety in financial matters (which must have been obvious to the bank manager), the business nature of the proposed project, the bank's marketing pamphlet advertising free financial advice, the internal inspection of the property by the bank manager (which was not usual practice), and the fact that the plaintiffs had received a warning from the bank manager about earlier business proposals which they had made. It followed from these facts that the bank owed the plaintiffs a duty of care to advise as to the prudence of the transaction. By contrast, in *Murphy v HSBC Bank plc* [2004] EWHC 467 (Ch), Silber J held that a bank had not assumed any responsibility to borrowers who (a), following the bank's initial recommendation, had appointed their own solicitors and accountants to advise them; (b) had not paid the bank for advice; (c) had greater knowledge than the bank of the project to be financed by the loan; (d) knew other people from whom they could seek relevant advice; (e) saw their role at the start of the negotiations as that of selling themselves and their project to the bank; and (f) had not asked for the bank's advice. For a case that a wider duty of care should be imposed on a lending bank where there is justified reliance on the bank by the borrower, see J Wadsley [2003] LMCLQ 341. Note also that the 2008 revisions of the *Banking Code* and the *Business Banking Code* contain a new commitment to 'lend responsibly' (para 2).

(vii)   No duty of care arises where the bank requires the borrower to act in a certain way as a condition of the loan (*Frost v James Finlay Bank Ltd* [2002] EWCA Civ 667, [2002] Lloyd's Rep IR 503: the borrower's reasonable but erroneous belief that such a condition had been imposed did not give rise to a duty of care).

(viii) The banker–customer relationship is not without more one where duties of disclosure are imposed on a bank as a matter of general law and it is not an implied term of the banker–customer contract that the bank must inform the customer of new banking facilities which are relevant to him (*Suriya & Douglas (a firm) v Midland Bank plc* [1999] 1 All ER (Comm) 612, CA: bank owed no duty to customer to inform him of new interest bearing account—but now see paras 4.6–4.8 of the 2008 edition of both the *Banking Code* and the *Business Banking Code',* and see also *R v Financial Ombudsman Service Ltd, ex p Norwich and Peterborough Building Society* [2002] EWHC 2379 (Admin), [2003] 1 All ER (Comm) 65, above, p 621).

(ix)   In the normal course of events, a bank is under no duty of care to proffer explanations as to the nature and effect of a security document executed by a surety, or to advise the surety to take independent legal advice (*Chetwynd-Talbot v Midland Bank Ltd* (1982) 132 NLJ 901; *O'Hara v Allied Irish Banks Ltd* [1985] BCLC 52—the dicta of Kerr LJ in *Cornish v Midland Bank plc* [1985] 3 All ER 513 at 522–523, suggesting that a bank owes such a duty to sureties who are their own customers, has been rightly rejected in the majority of subsequent cases: see *Westpac Banking Corpn v McCreanor* [1990] 1 NZLR 580; *Shivas v Bank of New Zealand* [1990] 2 NZLR 327; *Barclays Bank plc v Khaira* [1992] 1 WLR 623; *Union Bank of Finland v Lelakis* [1995] CLC 27; *Investors Compensation Scheme Ltd v West Bromwich Building Society* [1999] Lloyd's Rep PN 496; but cf *Shotter v Westpac Banking Corpn* [1988] 2 NZLR 316). However, a duty of care may arise where there are special factors, eg where it is clear that the bank is being looked to for advice or is in some close relationship with the prospective surety of a kind where questions of undue influence might arise (*Barclays Bank plc v Khaira,* above, at 637). In any event, where the relationship between the surety and the principal debtor is non-commercial (eg where a wife or cohabitee gives security for their husband's/partner's debts), the bank must take reasonable steps to bring home to the individual guarantor the risks she is running by standing as surety if it is to ensure the security will not be set aside in equity as a result of the principal debtor's undue influence, misrepresentation or other legal wrong (see *Barclays Bank plc v O'Brien* [1994] 1 AC 180, HL; *Royal Bank of Scotland plc v Etridge (No 2)* [2001] UKHL 44, [2002] 2 AC 773: below, p 660). The bank can elect to explain those risks itself at a private meeting with the surety but it is common practice for banks to rely upon confirmation by a solicitor, acting for the surety, that he has advised the surety appropriately (see *O'Brien* and *Etridge (No 2)*).

In *Cornish v Midland Bank plc* [1985] 3 All ER 513, it was conceded, with the approval of the Court of Appeal, that a bank owes a surety a duty of care to give a full and proper explanation of the security documents when it has undertaken the task of giving an explanation. However, in *Barclays Bank plc v O'Brien* [1993] QB 109 at 140–141, Scott LJ said that where equity required the bank to explain the nature of the security document to the surety, the bank was not to be placed under a duty of care (the point did not arise when the case came before the House of Lords: [1994] 1 AC 180). Scott LJ distinguished between the situation where the surety is a customer of the bank or where the bank voluntarily assumes the role of adviser, when it may be under a duty to advise carefully, and that where the bank explains the security documents and the transaction to the surety to avoid the security being set aside in equity, when a duty of care would not arise.

(x)   A bank is under no duty to ensure that a chattel (a ship), mortgaged to the bank by a customer, is adequately insured (*National Bank of Greece SA v Pinios Shipping Co, The Maira* [1990] 1 AC 637, CA; reversed on other grounds: [1990] 1 AC 637 at 666).

(xi)   A bank need not consider 'all relevant matters' before exercising a power to appoint a receiver (*Shamji v Johnson Matthey Bankers Ltd* [1986] BCLC 278; affd [1991] BCLC 36: see below, p 1219).

(xii)   A bank which gives a status opinion or reference as to the respectability and financial standing of a customer does not thereby assume a duty of care to the enquirer correctly to identify its customer (the subject of the reference) as the person with whom the enquirer is dealing (*Gold Coin Joailliers SA v United Bank of Kuwait plc* [1997] 6 Bank LR 60, CA, where the bank gave a status opinion in respect of one of its customers, M, to an enquirer who was in fact dealing with an imposter pretending to be M).

(xiii)   A bank that is notified by a third party of a freezing injunction granted to the third party against one of the bank's customers, affecting an account held by the customer with the bank, owes no duty to the third party to take reasonable care to comply with the terms of the injunction (*Customs & Excise Comrs v Barclays Bank plc* [2006] UKHL 28, [2007] 1 AC 181).

9 BANK'S FIDUCIARY DUTIES

The courts have continually stressed that 'on the face of it the relationship between a bank and its customer is not a fiduciary relationship' (*Bank of Scotland v A Ltd* [2001] EWCA Civ 52, [2001] Lloyd's Rep Bank 73 at [25], per Lord Woolf CJ). We looked at the nature of a fiduciary relationship in Chapter 6 (above, p 207). At its heart is the concept of 'selflessness', namely that the fiduciary is expected to promote the interests of his beneficiary above his own interests. A fiduciary has a duty of loyalty in addition to the duty of skill and competence expected of contracting parties. The banker-customer relationship does not of itself give rise to a fiduciary relationship between the parties because the bank can usually be expected to further its own commercial interests ahead of those of its customer. But sometimes, as Professor (now Judge) Paul Finn explains in the next extract, this will not apply.

'Fiduciary Law and the Modern Commercial World' by Paul Finn in E McKendrick (ed) *Commercial Aspects of Trust and Fiduciary Obligations* (1992), Ch 1, pp 11–12

It clearly is possible for a bank, because of the manner in which it conducts itself either in its financial[32] dealings with a customer or borrower, or in its dealings with a customer's guarantor, to find itself in a fiduciary relationship[33]. The matter of difficulty lies in ascertaining when, realistically, it could be said that this is so given the bank's known self-interest in the dealing[34], and that a fiduciary responsibility would require the bank to act in the other party's interests. The situation must be uncommon where fiduciary altruism as opposed merely to fair dealing could be expected from an obviously interested party: English courts, for example, have acknowledged that banks 'are not charitable institutions'[35]. I would suggest that it should be most unlikely to be found beyond the following three circumstances which are themselves very distinctive. (1) Where the course of the relationship can found the expectation, not only that advice will be given but that, where necessary, it will be given adversely to the bank's interests.[36] (2) Where the bank has created the expectation that it is advising or will advise in the customer's interest in a matter because its own interest therein is represented to be formal, nominal, or technical—the basis, perhaps, for the influential United States decision, *Stewart v Phoenix National Bank*.[37] And (3) where the bank, though expected to act in its own interest in the actual dealing *inter se,* has created the expectation that it will otherwise advise in the customer's interests, for example, on the wisdom of an investment proposal in respect of which a loan application is made. The Canadian decision, *Haywood v Bank of Novia Scotia*[38] and the recent Australian Federal Court decision of *Smith v Commonwealth Bank of Australia*[39] reflect this eventuality.

The above three situations suggest at least environments in which a fiduciary entitlement could feasibly arise. Reason is there in each case to found an expectation that the bank's interest will not be an operative consideration in the advice expected or given. But without such reason, it is difficult to see how a fiduciary rather than a good faith and fair dealing or reasonable care and skill expectation could exist in the fact of the bank's own manifest interest in the dealing. Not surprisingly, in some number of recent New Zealand and Canadian cases where a fiduciary duty has been imposed on banks in contexts other than the three mentioned, the substance of the duty has nothing whatever to do with loyalty but everything to do with fair dealing.[40]

Footnotes:

32 Excluded from consideration here is the situation in which a bank is providing discrete advisory services to a customer, etc.

33 Or one of undue influence if, as seems to be the case in England, these are not properly to be called 'fiduciary': see *National Westminster Bank plc v Morgan* [1985] AC 686—a decision which, lamentably confuses both the law relating to undue influence and that relating to unconscionable dealing.

34 Cf *Stenberg v Northwestern National Bank of Rochester* 238 NW 2d 218, 219 (1976).

35 *National Westminster Bank plc v Morgan* [1983] 3 All ER 85, at 91 per Dunn, LJ.

36 If *Lloyds Bank Ltd. v Bundy* [1975] QB 326 had anything fiduciary in it as Sachs, LJ suggested, it could only have been sustained on the above basis.

37 64 P 2d 101 (1937).

38 (1984) 45 OR (2d) 542.

39 (11 March 1991, unreported), FC of A, Von Doussa, J; affd (1991) 102 ALR 453.

40 See eg *Pacific Industrial Corpn SA. v Bank of New Zealand* [1991] 1 NZLR 368; for a similar example in the insurance context see *Plaza Fibreglass Manufacturing Ltd v Cardinal Insurance Co* (1990) 68 DLR (4th) 586; and see also *Standard Investments Ltd v Canadian Imperial Bank of Commerce* (1985) 22 DLR (4th) 410.

NOTES

1.   In *Lloyds Bank Ltd v Bundy* [1975] QB 326, an elderly father gave his bank a guarantee of his son's business debts. The father also agreed to charge his home to the bank. Sir Eric Sachs held that the bank owed the father a fiduciary duty of care which it had breached by failing to give him proper advice or suggesting that he should obtain independent legal advice. Accordingly, he held that the guarantee and charge should be set aside (Lord Denning and Cairns LJ agreed but based their decisions on other grounds). Sir Eric Sachs emphasised that such a duty would not normally arise between a bank and a customer who had guaranteed the debts of a third party. However, in this case the duty arose because the father was a long-standing customer of the bank who relied on it for advice. In other words, there was a 'special relationship' between the bank and its customer. As Sir Eric Sachs stated (at 341):

Such cases tend to arise where someone relies on the guidance or advice of another, where the other is aware of that reliance and where the person upon whom reliance is placed obtains, or may well obtain, a benefit from the transaction or has some other interest in it being concluded. In addition, there must, of course, be shown to exist a vital element which in this judgment will for convenience by referred to as confidentiality.

It is by no means certain that a fiduciary duty of care arises between a bank and its customer in the way described by Sir Eric Sachs. The decision of the Court of Appeal in *Lloyds Bank Ltd v Bundy* can be upheld on grounds of undue influence alone, without reliance upon the existence of a fiduciary duty of care. This is how the House of Lords viewed the *Bundy* case in *National Westminster Bank plc v Morgan* [1985] AC 686.

2.   It seems that a bank may be placed in a fiduciary relationship where it takes on the role of financial adviser to its customer, and is in a position where it has a conflict of interest as a result. In *Woods v Martins Bank Ltd* [1959] 1 QB 55, the defendant bank advised the plaintiff to invest in a company which was indebted to the bank. The bank did not disclose this fact to the plaintiff. The plaintiff, who was inexperienced in financial matters, lost the full amount invested in the shares. Salmon J held that even if the plaintiff was not the bank's customer at the relevant time, but only a potential customer, the bank owed him a fiduciary duty of care when it gave him financial advice. The case pre-dates *Hedley Byrne & Co Ltd v Heller & Partners Ltd* [1964] AC 465 (until *Hedley Byrne* there was no remedy in tort for a negligent misstatement or careless advice causing financial loss) and so Salmon J was forced to rely on the presence of a fiduciary relationship for liability to be imposed on the bank for its pre-contractual advice. This clearly came to the judge as something of an afterthought when he realised that there was no orthodox basis for holding the bank liable to the plaintiff. The point is made by Len Sealy in 'Fiduciary Obligations, Forty Years On' (1995) 9 JCL 37 at 42, n 45: '[In] *Woods v Martins Bank Ltd* [1959] 1 QB 55 [a] bank manager gave a potential customer negligent advice, and Salmon J found the bank liable on reasoning which is entirely tort-based: see [1958] 3 All ER 166, [1958] 1 WLR 1018. In the 'edited' judgment, as reported in the Law Reports, the single sentence is interpolated ([1959] 1 QB 55 at 72): "In my judgment, a fiduciary relationship existed between the plaintiff and the defendant."' Should a similar case come before the courts today it is likely that would be decided on the *Hedley*

Byrne principle without resort to the device of a fiduciary relationship. However, the decision has been followed in the leading Canadian case of *Standard Investments Ltd v Canadian Imperial Bank of Commerce* (1985) 22 DLR (4th) 410.

3. The literature on this topic includes MH Ogilvie 'Banks, Advice-Giving and Fiduciary Obligations' (1985) 17 Ottawa L Rev 263; D Waters 'Banks, Fiduciary Obligations and Unconscionable Transactions' (1986) 65 Can Bar Rev 37; K Curtis 'The Fiduciary Controversy: Injection of Fiduciary Principles into the Bank-Depositor and Bank-Borrower Relationships' (1987) 20 Loyola LR 795; J Glover 'Banks and Fiduciary Relationships' (1995) 7 Bond LR 50; J Breslin 'Banks as Fiduciaries' (1998) 5 Comm LP 47.

Bank as trustee: A bank appointed to act as a trustee of an estate or an investment fund will be subject to fiduciary duties. In general the bank must not invest with itself. To do so would breach its fiduciary duty as the bank *qua* trustee must not put itself in a position where its duty to the beneficiaries conflicts with its duty to its shareholders (*Marley v Mutual Security Merchants Bank & Trust Co Ltd* [1995] CLC 261, PC). However, a bank will not be in breach of its fiduciary duty where the trust instrument authorises it to open accounts or make deposits or investments with itself, despite being a trustee (*Space Investments Ltd v Canadian Imperial Bank of Commerce Trust Co (Bahamas) Ltd* [1986] 1 WLR 1072, PC). Nevertheless, the bank *qua* trustee must act at all times with due care (a higher standard of care is expected from a professional trustee than from a lay trustee, see *Bartlett v Barclays Trust Co Ltd* [1980] Ch 515, and see also the Trustee Act 2000, s 1, which introduces a statutory duty of care in relation to specific trustee's powers and duties).

Bank as agent: Where the bank acts as its customer's agent it will be subject to fiduciary duties. The principal-agent relationship is normally a fiduciary one. For example, the bank acts as its customer's agent when making and collecting payments and, when doing so, owes the usual fiduciary duties of an agent to its principal (see above, p 207). But, as Professor Cranston has observed, treating the bank as a fiduciary because it is an agent may add little to the analysis (R Cranston *Principles of Banking Law* (2nd edn, 2002), p 189). The paying or collecting bank may owe its customer a fiduciary duty of care, but it owes the same duty in contract in any event (although the fiduciary nature of the obligation may be relevant when considering ancillary matters such as causation, measure of damages and limitation periods). However, Professor Cranston acknowledges that in some contexts it may be significant that the bank, as its customer's agent, is a fiduciary, eg where the customer instructs the bank to buy certain securities, it cannot buy on its own behalf.

10 BANKS AND UNDUE INFLUENCE

Undue influence is an equitable ground of restitution which applies where the defendant or a third party, who have relationships of influence with the claimant, abuse that relationship to induce the claimant to transfer a benefit to the defendant or are presumed to have abused that relationship to induce the transfer of a benefit (see, generally, G Virgo *The Law of Restitution* (2nd edn, 2006), Ch 10; Lord Goff and G Jones (ed) *The Law of Restitution* (7th edn, 2007), Ch 11). A person who has been induced to enter into a transaction (gift or contract) by the undue influence of another ('the wrongdoer') is entitled to set that transaction aside as against the wrongdoer, ie the transaction is voidable and not void. Banks most commonly come up against the doctrine of undue influence when they seek to enforce third party security. It is rare, but not impossible, for a transaction to be impeached on the ground that it resulted from the exercise of undue influence by the bank itself. The normal banker-customer relationship does not give rise to a presumption of undue influence (*National Westminster Bank plc v Morgan* [1985] AC 686, HL), but it is possible (though not usual) for the relationship to become one to which the principles of undue influence apply if the bank attains a status which is effectively that of the customer's 'man of affairs' and proceeds to advise on the wisdom (as opposed to merely explaining the terms) of a proposed transaction in which the bank's interest conflicts with that of the customer (see, eg *Lloyds Bank Ltd v Bundy* [1975] QB 326—the facts of which appear above at p 658). It is more usual for a person who has given security to the bank to cover the indebtedness of the bank's customer to allege that they did so as a result of the undue influence or misrepresentation of that customer. Whether the bank's security is vulnerable to be set aside by the courts will then depend on whether the bank had actual or constructive notice of the undue influence or misrepresentation. The burden is on the complainant to show that the bank had such notice (*Barclays Bank plc v Boulter* [1999] 4 All ER 513 at 518–519, HL).

Royal Bank of Scotland plc v Etridge (No 2)
[2001] UKHL 44, [2002] 2 AC 773, House of Lords

The House heard eight appeals together. In seven of these appeals, the appellant was a wife who had agreed to subject her property, usually her interest in the matrimonial home, to a charge in favour of the bank in order to provide security for the payment of her husband's debts, or the debts of a company by means of which her husband carried on business. In each case the bank started proceedings for possession of the mortgaged property, but the wife defended the action on the ground that her agreement to grant the charge was brought about by the undue influence or misrepresentation of her husband and that, in the circumstances, the bank should not be allowed to enforce the charge against her. In each case the issue was whether the bank had notice of the husband's impropriety or alleged impropriety. In each case the bank had some reason to believe that a solicitor had acted for the wife in the transaction in question. So the question for their Lordships to decide was the extent to which the solicitor's participation, or believed participation, had absolved the bank of the need to make further inquiries about the circumstances in which the wife was persuaded to agree to grant the charge, or to take any further steps to satisfy itself that her consent was a true and informed consent. The eighth appeal before the House, *Kenyon-Brown v Desmond Banks & Co (a firm)* [2001] UKHL 44, [2002] 2 AC 773, was a case in which the wife had brought a claim against the solicitor who acted for her in this type of transaction alleging breach of duty owed to her by the solicitor. The case raised an issue as to the extent of the duty lying on a solicitor who acts for a wife who is proposing to grant a charge over her property as security for her husband's, or his company's, debts.

Lord Bingham:

[1] My Lords, I have had the great advantage of reading in draft the opinions prepared by each of my noble and learned friends.

[2] The transactions which give rise to these appeals are commonplace but of great social and economic importance. It is important that a wife (or anyone in a like position) should not charge her interest in the matrimonial home to secure the borrowing of her husband (or anyone in a like position) without fully understanding the nature and effect of the proposed transaction and that the decision is hers, to agree or not to agree. It is important that lenders should feel able to advance money, in run-of-the-mill cases with no abnormal features, on the security of the wife's interest in the matrimonial home in

reasonable confidence that, if appropriate procedures have been followed in obtaining the security, it will be enforceable if the need for enforcement arises. The law must afford both parties a measure of protection. It cannot prescribe a code which will be proof against error, misunderstanding or mishap. But it can indicate minimum requirements which, if met, will reduce the risk of error, misunderstanding or mishap to an acceptable level. The paramount need in this important field is that these minimum requirements should be clear, simple and practically operable.

[3] My Lords, in my respectful opinion these minimum requirements are clearly identified in the opinions of my noble and learned friends Lord Nicholls of Birkenhead and Lord Scott of Foscote. If these requirements are met the risk that a wife has been misled by her husband as to the facts of a proposed transaction should be eliminated or virtually so. The risk that a wife has been overborne or coerced by her husband will not be eliminated but will be reduced to a level which makes it proper for the lender to proceed. While the opinions of Lord Nicholls and Lord Scott show some difference of expression and approach, I do not myself discern any significant difference of legal principle applicable to these cases, and I agree with both opinions. But if I am wrong and such differences exist, it is plain that the opinion of Lord Nicholls commands the unqualified support of all members of the House.

[4] In agreement with all members of the House, I would allow the appeals of Mrs Wallace, Mrs Bennett and Desmond Banks & Co and dismiss those of Mrs Etridge and Mrs Gill, in each case for the reasons given by Lord Scott. I would allow the appeal of Mrs Harris, bearing in mind that this is an interlocutory case...I would allow the appeal of Mrs Moore and dismiss that of Mrs Coleman...

Lord Nicholls:

[5] My Lords, before your Lordships' House are appeals in eight cases. Each case arises out of a transaction in which a wife charged her interest in her home in favour of a bank as security for her husband's indebtedness or the indebtedness of a company through which he carried on business. The wife later asserted she signed the charge under the undue influence of her husband. In *Barclays Bank plc v O'Brien* [1993] 4 All ER 417, [1994] 1 AC 180 your Lordships enunciated the principles applicable in this type of case. Since then, many cases have come before the courts, testing the implications of the *O'Brien* decision in a variety of different factual situations. Seven of the present appeals are of this character. In each case the bank sought to enforce the charge signed by the wife. The bank claimed an order for possession of the matrimonial home. The wife raised a defence that the bank was on notice that her concurrence in the transaction had been procured by her husband's undue influence. The eighth appeal concerns a claim by a wife for damages from a solicitor who advised her before she entered into a guarantee obligation of this character.

UNDUE INFLUENCE

[6] The issues raised by these appeals make it necessary to go back to first principles. Undue influence is one of the grounds of relief developed by the courts of equity as a court of conscience. The objective is to ensure that the influence of one person over another is not abused. In everyday life people constantly seek to influence the decisions of others. They seek to persuade those with whom they are dealing to enter into transactions, whether great or small. The law has set limits to the means properly employable for this purpose. To this end the common law developed a principle of duress. Originally this was narrow in its scope, restricted to the more blatant forms of physical coercion, such as personal violence.

[7] Here, as elsewhere in the law, equity supplemented the common law. Equity extended the reach of the law to other unacceptable forms of persuasion. The law will investigate the manner in which the intention to enter into the transaction was secured: 'how the intention was produced', in the oft repeated words of Lord Eldon LC, from as long ago as 1807 (*Huguenin v Basely* (1807) 14 Ves Jun 273 at 300, [1803–13] All ER Rep 1 at 13). If the intention was produced by an unacceptable means, the law will not permit the transaction to stand. The means used is regarded as an exercise of improper or 'undue' influence, and hence unacceptable, whenever the consent thus procured ought not fairly to be treated as the expression of a person's free will. It is impossible to be more precise or definitive. The circumstances in which one person acquires influence over another, and the manner in which influence may be exercised, vary too widely to permit of any more specific criterion.

[8] Equity identified broadly two forms of unacceptable conduct. The first comprises overt acts of improper pressure or coercion such as unlawful threats. Today there is much overlap with the principle of duress as this principle has subsequently developed. The second form arises out of a relationship between two persons where one has acquired over another a measure of influence, or ascendancy, of which the ascendant person then takes unfair advantage. An example from the nineteenth century, when much of this law developed, is a case where an impoverished father prevailed upon his inexperienced children to charge their reversionary interests under their parents' marriage settlement with payment of his mortgage debts (see *Bainbrigge v Browne* (1881) 18 Ch D 188).

[9] In cases of this latter nature the influence one person has over another provides scope for misuse without any specific overt acts of persuasion. The relationship between two individuals may be such that, without more, one of them is disposed to agree a course of action proposed by the other. Typically this occurs when one person places trust in another to look after his affairs and interests, and the latter betrays this trust by preferring his own interests. He abuses the influence he has acquired. In *Allcard v Skinner* (1887) 36 Ch D 145, [1886–90] All ER Rep 90, a case well known to every law student, Lindley LJ ((1887) 36 Ch D 145 at 181, [1886–90] All ER Rep 90 at 98) described this class of cases as those in which it was the duty of one party to advise the other or to manage his property for him. In *Zamet v Hyman* [1961] 3 All ER 933 at 936, [1961] 1 WLR 1442 at 1444–1445 Lord Evershed MR referred to relationships where one party owed the other an obligation of candour and protection.

[10] The law has long recognised the need to prevent abuse of influence in these 'relationship' cases despite the absence of evidence of overt acts of persuasive conduct. The types of relationship, such as parent and child, in which this principle falls to be applied cannot be listed exhaustively. Relationships are infinitely various. Sir Guenter Treitel QC has rightly noted that the question is whether one party has reposed sufficient trust and confidence in the other, rather than whether the relationship between the parties belongs to a particular type (see Treitel, *The Law of Contract* (10th edn, 1999) pp 380–381). For example, the relation of banker and customer will not normally meet this criterion, but exceptionally it may (see *National Westminster Bank plc v Morgan* [1985] 1 All ER 821 at 829–831, [1985] AC 686 at 707–709).

[11] Even this test is not comprehensive. The principle is not confined to cases of abuse of trust and confidence. It also includes, for instance, cases where a vulnerable person has been exploited. Indeed, there is no single touchstone for determining whether the principle is applicable. Several expressions have been used in an endeavour to encapsulate the essence: trust and confidence, reliance, dependence or vulnerability on the one hand and ascendancy, domination or control on the other. None of these descriptions is perfect. None is all embracing. Each has its proper place.

[12] In *CIBC Mortgages plc v Pitt* [1993] 4 All ER 433, [1994] 1 AC 200 your Lordships' House decided that in cases of undue influence disadvantage is not a necessary ingredient of the cause of action. It is not essential that the transaction should be disadvantageous to the pressurised or influenced person, either in financial terms or in any other way. However, in the nature of things, questions of undue influence will not usually arise, and the exercise of undue influence is unlikely to occur, where the transaction is innocuous. The issue is likely to arise only when, in some respect, the transaction was disadvantageous either from the outset or as matters turned out.

BURDEN OF PROOF AND PRESUMPTIONS

[13] Whether a transaction was brought about by the exercise of undue influence is a question of fact. Here, as elsewhere, the general principle is that he who asserts a wrong has been committed must prove it. The burden of proving an allegation of undue influence rests upon the person who claims to have been wronged. This is the general rule. The evidence required to discharge the burden of proof depends on the nature of the alleged undue influence, the personality of the parties, their relationship, the extent to which the transaction cannot readily be accounted for by the ordinary motives of ordinary persons in that relationship, and all the circumstances of the case.

[14] Proof that the complainant placed trust and confidence in the other party in relation to the management of the complainant's financial affairs, coupled with a transaction which calls for explanation, will normally be sufficient, failing satisfactory evidence to the contrary, to discharge the burden of proof. On proof of these two matters the stage is set for the court to infer that, in the absence of a satisfactory explanation, the transaction can only have been procured by undue influence. In other words, proof of these two facts is prima facie evidence that the defendant abused the influence he acquired in the parties' relationship. He preferred his own interests. He did not behave fairly to the other. So the evidential burden then shifts to him. It is for him to produce evidence to counter the inference which otherwise should be drawn.

[15] The case of *Bainbrigge v Browne* (1881) 18 Ch D 188, already mentioned, provides a good illustration of this commonplace type of forensic exercise. Fry J held (at 196) that there was no direct evidence upon which he could rely as proving undue pressure by the father. But there existed circumstances 'from which the court will infer pressure and undue influence'. None of the children were entirely emancipated from their father's control. None seemed conversant with business. These circumstances were such as to cast the burden of proof upon the father. He had made no attempt to discharge that burden. He did not appear in court at all. So the children's claim succeeded. Again, more recently, in *Morgan*'s case [1985] 1 All ER 821 at 829, [1985] AC 686 at 707, Lord Scarman noted that a relationship of banker and customer may become one in which a banker acquires a dominating influence. If he does, and a manifestly disadvantageous transaction is proved, 'there would then be room' for a court to presume that it resulted from the exercise of undue influence.

[16] Generations of equity lawyers have conventionally described this situation as one in which a presumption of undue influence arises. This use of the term 'presumption' is descriptive of a shift in the evidential onus on a question of fact. When a plaintiff succeeds by this route he does so because he has succeeded in establishing a case of undue influence. The court has drawn appropriate inferences of fact upon a balanced consideration of the whole of the evidence at the end of a trial in which the burden of proof rested upon the plaintiff. The use, in the course of the trial, of the forensic tool of a shift in the evidential burden of proof should not be permitted to obscure the overall position. These cases are the equitable counterpart of common law cases where the principle of res ipsa loquitur is invoked. There is a rebuttable evidential presumption of undue influence.

[17] The availability of this forensic tool in cases founded on abuse of influence arising from the parties' relationship has led to this type of case sometimes being labelled 'presumed undue influence'. This is by way of contrast with cases involving actual pressure or the like, which are labelled 'actual undue influence' (see *Bank of Credit and Commerce International SA v Aboody* [1992] 4 All ER 955 at 964, [1990] 1 QB 923 at 953, and *Royal Bank of Scotland plc v Etridge (No 2)* [1998] 4 All ER 705 at 711–712 (paras 5–7)). This usage can be a little confusing. In many cases where a plaintiff has claimed that the defendant abused the influence he acquired in a relationship of trust and confidence the plaintiff has succeeded by recourse to the rebuttable evidential presumption. But this need not be so. Such a plaintiff may succeed even where this presumption is not available to him; for instance, where the impugned transaction was not one which called for an explanation.

[18] The evidential presumption discussed above is to be distinguished sharply from a different form of presumption which arises in some cases. The law has adopted a sternly protective attitude towards certain types of relationship in which one party acquires influence over another who is vulnerable and dependent and where, moreover, substantial gifts by the influenced or vulnerable person are not normally to be expected. Examples of relationships within this special class are parent and child, guardian and ward, trustee and beneficiary, solicitor and client, and medical advisor and patient. In these cases the law presumes, irrebuttably, that one party had influence over the other. The complainant need not prove he actually reposed trust and confidence in the other party. It is sufficient for him to prove the existence of the type of relationship.

[19] It is now well established that husband and wife is not one of the relationships to which this latter principle applies. In *Yerkey v Jones* (1939) 63 CLR 649 at 675 Dixon J explained the reason. The Court of Chancery was not blind to the opportunities of obtaining and unfairly using influence over a wife which a husband often possesses. But there is nothing unusual or strange in a wife, from motives of affection or for other reasons, conferring substantial financial benefits on her husband. Although there is no presumption, the court will nevertheless note, as a matter of fact, the opportunities for abuse which flow from a wife's confidence in her husband. The court will take this into account with all the other evidence in the case. Where there is evidence that a husband has taken unfair advantage of his influence over his wife, or her confidence in him, 'it is not difficult for the wife to establish her title to relief (see *Re Lloyds Bank Ltd, Bomze v Bomze* [1931] 1 Ch 289 at 302, per Maugham J).

INDEPENDENT ADVICE

[20] Proof that the complainant received advice from a third party before entering into the impugned transaction is one of the matters a court takes into account when weighing all the evidence. The weight, or importance, to be attached to such advice depends on all the circumstances. In the normal course, advice from a solicitor or other outside advisor can be expected to bring home to a complainant a proper understanding of what he or she is about to do. But a person may understand fully the implications of a proposed transaction, for instance, a substantial gift, and yet still be acting under the undue influence of another. Proof of outside advice does not, of itself, necessarily show that the subsequent completion of the transaction was free from the exercise of undue influence. Whether it will be proper to infer that outside advice had an emancipating effect, so that the transaction was not brought about by the exercise of undue influence, is a question of fact to be decided having regard to all the evidence in the case.

MANIFEST DISADVANTAGE

[21] As already noted, there are two prerequisites to the evidential shift in the burden of proof from the complainant to the other party. First, that the complainant reposed trust and confidence in the other party, or the other party acquired ascendancy over the complainant. Second, that the transaction is not readily explicable by the relationship of the parties.

[22] Lindley LJ summarised this second prerequisite in the leading authority of *Allcard v Skinner* (1887) 36 Ch D 145, [1886–90] All ER Rep 90, where the donor parted with almost all her property. Lindley LJ pointed out that where a gift of a small amount is made to a person standing in a confidential relationship to the donor, some proof of the exercise of the influence of the donee must be given. The mere existence of the influence is not enough. He continued:

> 'But if the gift is so large as not to be reasonably accounted for on the ground of friendship, relationship, charity, or other ordinary motives on which ordinary men act, the burden is upon the donee to support the gift.' (See (1887) 36 Ch D 145 at 185, [1886–90] All ER Rep 90 at 100–101.)

In *Bank of Montreal v Stuart* [1911] AC 120 at 137 Lord Macnaghten used the phrase 'immoderate and irrational' to describe this concept.

[23] The need for this second prerequisite has recently been questioned: see Nourse LJ in *Barclays Bank plc v Coleman* [2000] 1 All ER 385 at 397–399, [2001] QB 20 at 30–32, one of the cases under appeal before your Lordships' House. Mr Sher QC invited your Lordships to depart from the decision of the House on this point in *Morgan's* case.

[24] My Lords, this is not an invitation I would accept. The second prerequisite, as expressed by Lindley LJ, is good sense. It is a necessary limitation upon the width of the first prerequisite. It would be absurd for the law to presume that every gift by a child to a parent, or every transaction between a client and his solicitor or between a patient and his doctor, was brought about by undue influence unless the contrary is affirmatively proved. Such a presumption would be too far-reaching. The law would be out of touch with everyday life if the presumption were to apply to every Christmas or birthday gift by a child to a parent, or to an agreement whereby a client or patient agrees to be responsible for the reasonable fees of his legal or medical advisor. The law would be rightly open to ridicule, for transactions such as these are unexceptionable. They do not suggest that something may be amiss. So something more is needed before the law reverses the burden of proof, something which calls for an explanation. When that something more is present, the greater the disadvantage to the vulnerable person, the more cogent must be the explanation before the presumption will be regarded as rebutted.

[25] This was the approach adopted by Lord Scarman in *Morgan's* case [1985] 1 All ER 821 at 826–829, [1985] AC 686 at 703–707. He cited Lindley LJ's observations in *Allcard v Skinner* (1887) 36 ChD 145 at 185, [1886–90] All ER Rep 90 at 100, whichI have set out above. He noted that whatever the legal character of the transaction, it must constitute a disadvantage sufficiently serious to require evidence to rebut the presumption that in the circumstances of the parties' relationship, it was procured by the exercise of undue influence. Lord Scarman concluded:

> '...the Court of Appeal erred in law in holding that the presumption of undue influence can arise from the evidence of the relationship of the parties without also evidence that the transaction itself was wrongful in that it constituted *an advantage taken of the person subjected to the influence which, failing proof to the contrary, was explicable only on the basis that undue influence had been exercised to procure it:* (See [1985] 1 All ER 821 at 827, [1985] AC 686 at 704; my emphasis.)

[26] Lord Scarman attached the label 'manifest disadvantage' to this second ingredient necessary to raise the presumption. This label has been causing difficulty. It may be apt enough when applied to straightforward transactions such as a substantial gift or a sale at an undervalue. But experience has now shown that this expression can give rise to misunderstanding. The label is being understood and applied in a way which does not accord with the meaning intended by Lord Scarman, its originator.

[27] The problem has arisen in the context of wives guaranteeing payment of their husband's business debts. In recent years judge after judge has grappled with the baffling question whether a wife's guarantee of her husband's bank overdraft, together with a charge on her share of the matrimonial home, was a transaction manifestly to her disadvantage.

[28] In a narrow sense, such a transaction plainly ('manifestly') is disadvantageous to the wife. She undertakes a serious financial obligation, and in return she personally receives nothing. But that would be to take an unrealistically blinkered view of such a transaction. Unlike the relationship of solicitor and client or medical advisor and patient, in the case of husband and wife there are inherent reasons why such a transaction may well be for her benefit. Ordinarily, the fortunes of husband and wife are bound up together. If the husband's business is the source of the family income, the wife has a lively interest in doing what she can to support the business. A wife's affection and self-interest run hand-in-hand in inclining her to join with her husband in charging the matrimonial home, usually a jointly-owned asset, to obtain the financial facilities needed by the business. The finance may be needed to start a new business, or expand a promising business, or rescue an ailing business.

[29] Which, then, is the correct approach to adopt in deciding whether a transaction is disadvantageous to the wife: the narrow approach, or the wider approach? The answer is neither. The answer lies in discarding a label which gives rise to this sort of ambiguity. The better approach is to adhere more directly to the test outlined by Lindley LJ in *Allcard v Skinner,* and adopted by Lord Scarman in *Morgan's* case, in the passages I have cited.

[30] I return to husband and wife cases. I do not think that, *in the ordinary course,* a guarantee of the character I have mentioned is to be regarded as a transaction which, failing proof to the contrary, is explicable only on the basis that it has been procured by the exercise of undue influence by the husband. Wives frequently enter into such transactions. There are good and sufficient reasons why they are willing to do so, despite the risks involved for them and their families. They may be enthusiastic. They may not. They may be less optimistic than their husbands about the prospects of the husbands' businesses. They may be anxious, perhaps exceedingly so. But this is a far cry from saying that such transactions as a class are to be regarded as prima facie evidence of the exercise of undue influence by husbands.

[31] I have emphasised the phrase 'in the ordinary course'. There will be cases where a wife's signature of a guarantee or a charge of her share in the matrimonial home does call for explanation. Nothing I have said above is directed at such a case.

A CAUTIONARY NOTE

[32] I add a cautionary note, prompted by some of the first instance judgments in the cases currently being considered by the House. It concerns the general approach to be adopted by a court when considering whether a wife's guarantee of her husband's bank overdraft was procured by her husband's undue influence. Undue influence has a connotation of impropriety. In the eye of the law, undue influence means that influence has been misused. Statements or conduct by a husband which do not pass beyond the bounds of what may be expected of a reasonable husband in the circumstances should not, without more, be castigated as undue influence. Similarly, when a husband is forecasting the future of business, and expressing his hopes or fears, a degree of hyperbole may be only natural. Courts should not too readily treat such exaggerations as misstatements.

[33] Inaccurate explanations of a proposed transaction are a different matter. So are cases where a husband, in whom a wife has reposed trust and confidence for the management of their financial affairs, prefers his interests to hers and makes a choice for both of them on that footing. Such a husband abuses the influence he has. He fails to discharge the obligation of candour and fairness he owes a wife who is looking to him to make the major financial decisions.

THE COMPLAINANT AND THIRD PARTIES: SURETYSHIP TRANSACTIONS

[34] The problem considered in *Barclays Bank plc v O'Brien* [1993] 4 All ER 417, [1994] 1 AC 180 and raised by the present appeals is of comparatively recent origin. It arises out of the substantial growth in home ownership over the last 30 or 40 years and, as part of that development, the great increase in the number of homes owned jointly by husbands and wives. More than two-thirds of householders in the United Kingdom now own their own homes. For most home-owning couples, their homes are their most valuable asset. They must surely be free, if they so wish, to use this asset as a means of raising money, whether for the purpose of the husband's business or for any other purpose. Their home is their property. The law should not restrict them in the use they may make of it. Bank finance is in fact by far the most important source of external capital for small businesses with fewer than ten employees. These businesses comprise about 95% of all businesses in the country, responsible for nearly one-third of all employment. Finance raised by second mortgages on the principal's home is a significant source of capital for the start-up of small businesses.

[35] If the freedom of home-owners to make economic use of their homes is not to be frustrated, a bank must be able to have confidence that a wife's signature of the necessary guarantee and charge will be as binding upon her as is the signature of anyone else on documents which he or she may sign. Otherwise banks will not be willing to lend money on the security of a jointly owned house or flat.

[36] At the same time, the high degree of trust and confidence and emotional interdependence which normally characterises a marriage relationship provides scope for abuse. One party may take advantage of the other's vulnerability. Unhappily, such abuse does occur. Further, it is all too easy for a husband, anxious or even desperate for bank finance, to misstate the position in some particular or to mislead the wife, wittingly or unwittingly, in some other way. The law would be seriously defective if it did not recognise these realities.

[37] In *O'Brien's* case this House decided where the balance should be held between these competing interests. On the one side, there is the need to protect a wife against a husband's undue influence. On the other side, there is the need for the bank to be able to have reasonable confidence in the strength of its security. Otherwise it would not provide the required money. The problem lies in finding the course best designed to protect wives in a minority of cases without unreasonably hampering the giving and taking of security. The House produced a practical solution. The House decided what are the steps a bank should take to ensure it is not affected by any claim the wife may have that her signature of the documents was procured by the undue influence or other wrong of her husband. Like every compromise, the outcome falls short of achieving in full the objectives of either of the two competing interests. In particular, the steps required of banks will not guarantee that, in future, wives will not be subjected to undue influence or misled when standing as sureties. Short of prohibiting this type of suretyship transaction altogether, there is no way of achieving that result, desirable although it is. What passes between a husband and wife in this regard in the privacy of their own home is not capable of regulation or investigation as a prelude to the wife entering into a suretyship transaction.

[38] The jurisprudential route by which the House reached its conclusion in *O'Brien's* case has attracted criticism from some commentators. It has been said to involve artificiality and thereby create uncertainty in the law. I must first consider this criticism. In the ordinary course a bank which takes a guarantee security from the wife of its customer will be altogether ignorant of any undue influence the customer may have exercised in order to secure the wife's concurrence. In *O'Brien's* case Lord Browne-Wilkinson prayed in aid the doctrine of constructive notice. In circumstances he identified, a creditor is put on inquiry. When that is so, the creditor 'will have constructive notice of the wife's rights' unless the creditor takes reasonable steps to satisfy himself that the wife's agreement to stand surety has been properly obtained (see [1993] 4 All ER 417 at 429, [1994] 1 AC 180 at 196).

[39] Lord Browne-Wilkinson would be the first to recognise this is not a conventional use of the equitable concept of constructive notice. The traditional use of this concept concerns the circumstances in which a transferee of property who acquires a legal estate from a transferor with a defective title may none the less obtain a good title, that is, a better title than the transferor had. That is not the present case. The bank acquires its charge from the wife, and there is nothing wrong with her title to her share of the matrimonial home. The transferor wife is seeking to resile from the very transaction she entered into with the bank, on the ground that her apparent consent was procured by the undue influence or other misconduct, such as misrepresentation, of a third party (her husband). She is seeking to set aside her contract of guarantee and, with it, the charge she gave to the bank.

[40] The traditional view of equity in this tripartite situation seems to be that a person in the position of the wife will only be relieved of her bargain if the other party to the transaction (the bank, in the present instance) was privy to the conduct which led to the wife's entry into the transaction. Knowledge is required (see *Cobbett v Brock* (1855) 20 Beav 524 at 528, 531, 52 ER 706 at 707, 708, per Romilly MR, *Kempson v Ashbee* (1874) LR 10 Ch App 15 at 21, per James LJ, and *Bainbrigge v Browne* (1881) 18 Ch D 188 at 197, per Fry J). The law imposes no obligation on one party to a transaction to check whether the other party's concurrence was obtained by undue influence. But *O'Brien's* case has introduced into the law the concept that, in certain circumstances, a party to a contract may lose the benefit of his contract, entered into in good faith, if he *ought* to have known that the other's concurrence had been procured by the misconduct of a third party.

[41] There is a further respect in which *O'Brien's* case departed from conventional concepts. Traditionally, a person is *deemed* to have notice (that is, he has 'constructive' notice) of a prior right when he does not actually know of it but would have learned of it had he made the requisite inquiries. A purchaser will be treated as having constructive notice of all that a reasonably prudent purchaser would have discovered. In the present type of case, the steps a bank is required to take, lest it have constructive notice that the wife's concurrence was procured improperly by her husband, do not consist of making inquiries. Rather, *O'Brien's* case envisages that the steps taken by the bank will reduce, or even eliminate, the risk of the wife entering into the transaction under any misapprehension or as a result of undue influence by her husband. The steps are not concerned to discover whether the wife has been wronged by her husband in this way. The steps are concerned to minimise the risk that such a wrong may be committed.

[42] These novelties do not point to the conclusion that the decision of this House in *O'Brien's* case is leading the law astray. Lord Browne-Wilkinson ([1993] 4 All ER 417 at 430, [1994] 1 AC 180 at 197) acknowledged he might be extending the law. Some development was sorely needed. The law had to find a way of giving wives a reasonable measure of protection, without adding unreasonably to the expense involved in entering into guarantee transactions of the type under consideration. The protection had to extend also to any misrepresentations made by a husband to his wife. In a situation where there is a substantial risk the husband may exercise his influence improperly regarding the provision of security for his business debts, there is an increased risk that explanations of the transaction given by him to his wife may be misleadingly incomplete or even inaccurate.

[43] The route selected in *O'Brien's* case ought not to have an unsettling effect on established prin-ciples of contract. *O'Brien's* case concerned suretyship transactions. These are tripartite transactions. They involve the debtor as well as the creditor and the guarantor. The guarantor enters into the trans-action at the request of the debtor. The guarantor assumes obligations. On the face of the transaction the guarantor usually receives no benefit in return, unless the guarantee is being given on a commercial basis. Leaving aside cases where the relationship between the surety and the debtor is commercial, a guarantee transaction is one-sided so far as the guarantor is concerned. The creditor knows this. Thus the decision in *O'Brien's* case is directed at a class of contracts which has special features of its own. That said, I must at a later stage in this speech return to the question of the wider implications of the *O'Brien* decision.

THE THRESHOLD: WHEN THE BANK IS PUT ON INQUIRY

[44] In *O'Brien's* case the House considered the circumstances in which a bank, or other creditor, is 'put on inquiry'. Strictly this is a misnomer. As already noted, a bank is not required to make inquiries. But it will be convenient to use the terminology which has now become accepted in this context. The House set a low level for the threshold which must be crossed before a bank is put on inquiry. For practical reasons the level is set much lower than is required to satisfy a court that, failing contrary evidence, the court may infer that the transaction was procured by undue influence. Lord Browne-Wilkinson said:

> 'Therefore, in my judgment a creditor in put on inquiry when a wife offers to stand surety for her husband's debts by the combination of two factors: (a) the transaction is on its face not to the finan-cial advantage of the wife; and (b) there is a substantial risk in transactions of that kind that, in pro-curing the wife to act as surety, the husband has committed a legal or equitable wrong that entitles the wife to set aside the transaction.' (See [1993] 4 All ER 417 at 429, [1994] 1 AC 180 at 196.)

In my view, this passage, read in context, is to be taken to mean, quite simply, that a bank is put on inquiry whenever a wife offers to stand surety for her husband's debts.

[45] The Court of Appeal, comprising Stuart-Smith, Millett and Morritt LJJ, interpreted this passage more restrictively. The threshold, the court said, is somewhat higher. Where condition (a) is satisfied, the bank is put on inquiry if, but only if, the bank is aware that the parties are cohabiting or that the particular surety places implicit trust and confidence in the principal debtor in relation to her financial affairs (see *Royal Bank of Scotland plc v Etridge (No 2)* [1998] 4 All ER 705 at 719).

[46] I respectfully disagree. I do not read (a) and (b) as factual conditions which must be proved in each case before a bank is put on inquiry. I do not understand Lord Browne-Wilkinson to have been saying that, in husband and wife cases, whether the bank is put on inquiry depends on its state of knowledge of the parties' marriage, or of the degree of trust and confidence the particular wife places in her husband in relation to her financial affairs. That would leave banks in a state of considerable uncertainty in a situation where it is important they should know clearly where they stand. The test should be simple and clear and easy to apply in a wide range of circumstances. I read (a) and (b) as Lord Browne-Wilkinson's broad explanation of the reason why a creditor is put on inquiry when a wife offers to stand surety for her husband's debts. These are the two factors which, taken together, constitute the underlying rationale.

[47] The position is likewise if the husband stands surety for his wife's debts. Similarly, in the case of unmarried couples, whether heterosexual or homosexual, where the bank is aware of the relationship (see *O'Brien's* case [1993] 4 All ER 417 at 431, [1994] 1 AC 180 at 198, per Lord Browne-Wilkinson). Cohabitation is not essential. The Court of Appeal rightly so decided in *Massey v Midland Bank plc* [1995] 1 All ER 929 at 933, per Steyn LJ.

[48] As to the type of transactions where a bank is put on inquiry, the case where a wife becomes surety for her husband's debts is, in this context, a straightforward case. The bank is put on inquiry. On the other side of the line is the case where money is being advanced, or has been advanced, to husband and wife jointly. In such a case the bank is not put on inquiry, unless the bank is aware the loan is being made for the husband's purposes, as distinct from their joint purposes. That was decided in *CIBC Mortgages plc v Pitt* [1993] 4 All ER 433, [1994] 1 AC 200.

[49] Less clear cut is the case where the wife becomes surety for the debts of a company whose shares are held by her and her husband. Her shareholding may be nominal, or she may have a minority shareholding or an equal shareholding with her husband. In my view the bank is put on inquiry in such cases, even when the wife is a director or secretary of the company. Such cases cannot be equated with joint loans. The shareholding interests, and the identity of the directors, are not a reliable guide to the identity of the persons who actually have the conduct of the company's business.

THE STEPS A BANK SHOULD TAKE

[50] The principal area of controversy on these appeals concerns the steps a bank should take when it has been put on inquiry. In *O'Brien's* case Lord Browne-Wilkinson ([1993] 4 All ER 417 at 429–430, [1994] 1 AC 180 at 196–197) said that a bank can reasonably be expected to take steps to bring home to the wife the risk she is running by standing as surety and to advise her to take independent advice. That test is applicable to past transactions. All the cases now before your Lordships' House fall into this category. For the future a bank satisfies these requirements if it insists that the wife attend a private meeting with a representative of the bank at which she is told of the extent of her liability as surety, warned of the risk she is running and urged to take independent legal advice. In exceptional cases the bank, to be safe, has to insist that the wife is separately advised.

[51] The practice of the banks involved in the present cases, and it seems reasonable to assume this is the practice of banks generally, is not to have a private meeting with the wife. Nor do the banks themselves take any other steps to bring home to the wife the risk she is running, This has continued to be the practice since the decision in *O'Brien's* case. Banks consider they would stand to lose more than they would gain by holding a private meeting with the wife. They are, apparently, unwilling to assume the responsibility of advising the wife at such a meeting. Instead, the banking practice remains, as before, that in general the bank requires a wife to seek legal advice. The bank seeks written confirmation from a solicitor that he has explained the nature and effect of the documents to the wife.

[52] Many of the difficulties which have arisen in the present cases stem from serious deficiencies, or alleged deficiencies, in the quality of the legal advice given to the wives. I say 'alleged', because three of the appeals before your Lordships' House have not proceeded beyond the interlocutory stage. The banks successfully applied for summary judgment. In these cases the wife's allegations, made in affidavit form, have not been tested by cross-examination. On behalf of the wives it has been submitted that under the current practice the legal advice is often perfunctory in the extreme and, further, that everyone, including the banks, knows this. Independent legal advice is a fiction. The system is a charade. In practice it provides little or no protection for a wife who is under a misapprehension about the risks involved or who is being coerced into signing. She may not even know the present state of her husband's indebtedness.

[53] My Lords, it is plainly neither desirable nor practicable that banks should be required to attempt to discover for themselves whether a wife's consent is being procured by the exercise of undue influence of her husband. This is not a step the banks should be expected to take. Nor, further, is it desirable or practicable that banks should be expected to insist on confirmation from a solicitor that the solicitor has satisfied himself that the wife's consent has not been procured by undue influence. As already noted, the circumstances in which banks are put on inquiry are extremely wide. They embrace every case where a wife is entering into a suretyship transaction in respect of her husband's debts. Many, if not most, wives would be understandably outraged by having to respond to the sort of questioning which would be appropriate before a responsible solicitor could give such a confirmation. In any event, solicitors are not equipped to carry out such an exercise in any really worthwhile way, and they will usually lack the necessary materials. Moreover, the legal costs involved, which would inevitably fall on the husband who is seeking financial assistance from the bank, would be substantial. To require such an intrusive, inconclusive and expensive exercise in every case would be an altogether disproportionate response to the need to protect those cases, presumably a small minority, where a wife is being wronged.

[54] The furthest a bank can be expected to go is to take reasonable steps to satisfy itself that the wife has had brought home to her, in a meaningful way, the practical implications of the proposed transaction. This does not wholly eliminate the risk of undue influence or misrepresentation. But it does mean that a wife enters into a transaction with her eyes open so far as the basic elements of the transaction are concerned.

[55] This is the point at which, in *O'Brien's* case, the House decided that the balance between the competing interests should be held. A bank may itself provide the necessary information directly to the wife. Indeed, it is best equipped to do so. But banks are not following that course. Ought they to be obliged to do so in every case? I do not think Lord Browne-Wilkinson so stated in *O'Brien's* case. I do not understand him to have said that a personal meeting was the only way a bank could discharge its obligation to bring home to the wife the risks she is running. It seems to me that, provided a suitable alternative is available, banks ought not to be compelled to take this course. Their reasons for not wishing to hold a personal meeting are understandable. Commonly, when a bank seeks to enforce a security provided by a customer, it is met with a defence based on assurances alleged to have been given orally by a branch manager at an earlier stage: that the bank would continue to support the business, that the bank would not call in its loan, and so forth. Lengthy litigation ensues. Sometimes the allegations prove to be well founded, sometimes not. Banks are concerned to avoid the prospect of similar litigation which would arise in guarantee cases if they were to adopt a practice of holding a meeting with a wife at which the bank's representative would explain the proposed guarantee transaction. It is not unreasonable for the banks to prefer that this task should be undertaken by an independent legal advisor.

[56] I shall return later to the steps a bank should take when it follows this course. Suffice to say, these steps, together with advice from a solicitor acting for the wife, ought to provide the substance of the protection which *O'Brien's* case intended a wife should have. Ordinarily it will be reasonable that a bank should be able to rely upon confirmation from a solicitor, acting for the wife, that he has advised the wife appropriately.

[57] The position will be otherwise if the bank knows that the solicitor has not duly advised the wife or, I would add, if the bank knows facts from which it ought to have realised that the wife has not received the appropriate advice. In such circumstances the bank will proceed at its own risk.

THE CONTENT OF THE LEGAL ADVICE

[58] In *Royal Bank of Scotland plc v Etridge (No 2)* [1998] 4 All ER 705 at 715 (para 19), the Court of Appeal set out its views of the duties of a solicitor in this context:

> 'A solicitor who is instructed to advise a person who may be subject to the undue influence of another must bear in mind that [it] is not sufficient that she understands the nature and effect of the transaction if she is so affected by the influence of the other that she cannot make an independent decision of her own. It is not sufficient to explain the documentation and ensure she understands the nature of the transaction and wishes to carry it out: see *Powell v Powell* [1900] 1 Ch 243 at 247, approved in *Wright v Carter* ([1903] 1 Ch 27, [1900–3] All ER Rep 706). His duty is to satisfy himself that his client is free from improper influence, and the first step must be to ascertain whether it is one into which she could sensibly be advised to enter if free from such influence. If he is not so satisfied it is his duty to advise her not to enter into it, and to refuse to act further for her in the implementation of the transaction if she persists. In this event, while the contents of his advice must remain confidential, he should inform the other parties (including the bank) that he has seen his client and given her certain advice, and that as a result he has declined to act for her any further. He must in any event advise her that she is under no obligation to enter into the transaction at all and, if she still wishes to do so, that she is not bound to accept the terms of any document which has been put before her: see *Credit Lyonnais Bank Nederland NV v Burch* [1997] 1 All ER 144.'

[59] I am unable to accept this as an accurate formulation of a solicitor's duties in cases such as those now under consideration. In some respects it goes much too far. The observations of Farwell J in *Powell v Powell* [1900] 1 Ch 243 at 247, should not be pressed unduly widely. *Powell v Powell* was a case where strong moral pressure was applied by a stepmother to a girl who was only just 21. She was regarded as not really capable of dealing irrevocably with her parent or guardian in the matter of a substantial settlement. Farwell J's observations cannot be regarded as of general application in all cases where a solicitor is giving advice to a person who may have been subject to undue influence.

[60] More pertinently, in *Re Coomber, Coomber v Coomber* [1911] 1 Ch 723 at 730, Fletcher Moulton LJ summarised the general rules applicable to cases of persons who are competent to form an opinion of their own:

> 'All that is necessary is that some independent person, free from any taint of the relationship, or of the consideration of interest which would affect the act, should put clearly before the person what are the nature and the consequences of the act. It is for adult persons of competent mind to decide whether they will do an act, and I do not think that independent and competent advice means independent and competent approval. It simply means that the advice shall be removed entirely from the suspected atmosphere; and that from the clear language of an independent mind, they should know precisely what they are doing.'

[61] Thus, in the present type of case it is not for the solicitor to veto the transaction by declining to confirm to the bank that he has explained the documents to the wife and the risks she is taking upon herself. If the solicitor considers the transaction is not in the wife's best interests, he will give reasoned advice to the wife to that effect. But at the end of the day the decision on whether to proceed is the decision of the client, not the solicitor. A wife is not to be precluded from entering into a financially unwise transaction if, for her own reasons, she wishes to do so.

[62] That is the general rule. There may, of course, be exceptional circumstances where it is glaringly obvious that the wife is being grievously wronged. In such a case the solicitor should decline to act further. In *Wright v Carter* [1903] 1 Ch 27 at 57–58, [1900–3] All ER Rep 706 at 717, Stirling LJ approved Farwell J's observations in *Powell v Powell* [1900] 1 Ch 243 at 247. But he did so by reference to the extreme example of a poor man divesting himself of all his property in favour of his solicitor.

[63] In *Etridge's* case ([1998] 4 All ER 705 at 722 (para 49)), the Court of Appeal said that if the transaction is 'one into which no competent solicitor could properly advise the wife to enter', the availability of legal advice is insufficient to avoid the bank being fixed with constructive notice. It follows from the views expressed above that I am unable to agree with the Court of Appeal on this point.

[64] I turn to consider the scope of the responsibilities of a solicitor who is advising the wife. In identifying what are the solicitor's responsibilities the starting point must always be the solicitor's retainer. What has he been retained to do? As a general proposition, the scope of a solicitor's duties is dictated by the terms, whether express or implied, of his retainer. In the type of case now under consideration the relevant retainer stems from the bank's concern to receive confirmation from the solicitor that, in short, the solicitor has brought home to the wife the risks involved in the proposed transaction. As a first step the solicitor will need to explain to the wife the purpose for which he has become involved at all. He should explain that, should it ever become necessary, the bank will rely upon his involvement to counter any suggestion that the wife was overborne by her husband or that she did not properly understand the implications of the transaction. The solicitor will need to obtain confirmation from the wife that she wishes him to act for her in the matter and to advise her on the legal and practical implications of the proposed transaction.

[65] When an instruction to this effect is forthcoming, the content of the advice required from a solicitor before giving the confirmation sought by the bank will, inevitably, depend upon the circumstances of the case. Typically, the advice a solicitor can be expected to give should cover the following matters as the core minimum. (1) He will need to explain the nature of the documents and the practical consequences these will have for the wife if she signs them. She could lose her home if her husband's business does not prosper. Her home may be her only substantial asset, as well as the family's home. She could be made bankrupt. (2) He will need to point out the seriousness of the risks involved. The wife should be told the purpose of the proposed new facility, the amount and principal terms of the new facility, and that the bank might increase the amount of the facility, or change its terms, or grant a new facility, without reference to her. She should be told the amount of her liability under her guarantee. The solicitor should discuss the wife's financial means, including her understanding of the value of the property being charged. The solicitor should discuss whether the wife or her husband has any other assets out of which repayment could be made if the husband's business should fail. These matters are relevant to the seriousness of the risks involved. (3) The solicitor will need to state clearly that the wife has a choice. The decision is hers and hers alone. Explanation of the choice facing the wife will call for some discussion of the present financial position, including the amount of the husband's present indebtedness, and the amount of his current overdraft facility. (4) The solicitor should check whether the wife wishes to proceed. She should be asked whether she is content that the solicitor should write to the bank confirming he has explained to her the nature of the documents and the practical implications they may have for her, or whether, for instance, she would prefer him to negotiate with the bank on the terms of the transaction. Matters for negotiation could include the sequence in which the various securities will be called upon or a specific or lower limit to her liabilities. The solicitor should not give any confirmation to the bank without the wife's authority.

[66] The solicitor's discussion with the wife should take place at a face-to-face meeting, in the absence of the husband. It goes without saying that the solicitor's explanations should be couched in suitably non-technical language. It also goes without saying that the solicitor's task is an important one. It is not a formality.

[67] The solicitor should obtain from the bank any information he needs. If the bank fails for any reason to provide information requested by the solicitor, the solicitor should decline to provide the confirmation sought by the bank.

[68] As already noted, the advice which a solicitor can be expected to give must depend on the particular facts of the case. But I have set out this 'core minimum' in some detail, because the quality of the legal advice is the most disturbing feature of some of the present appeals. The perfunctory nature of the advice may well be largely due to a failure by some solicitors to understand what is required in these cases.

INDEPENDENT ADVICE

[69] I turn next to the much-vexed question whether the solicitor advising the wife must act for the wife alone. Or, at the very least, the solicitor must not act for the husband or the bank in the current transaction save in a wholly ministerial capacity, such as carrying out conveyancing formalities or supervising the execution of documents and witnessing signatures. Commonly, in practice, the solicitor advising the wife will be the solicitor acting also for her husband either in the particular transaction or generally.

[70] The first point to note is that this question cannot be answered by reference to reported decisions. The steps a bank must take once it is put on inquiry, if it is to avoid having constructive notice of the wife's rights, are not the subject of exposition in earlier authority. This is a novel situation, created by the *O'Brien* decision.

[71] Next, a simple and clear rule is needed, preferably of well-nigh universal application. In some cases a bank deals directly with a husband and wife and has to take the initiative in requiring the wife to obtain legal advice. In other cases, a bank may deal throughout with solicitors already acting for the husband and wife. The case of *Bank of Baroda v Rayarel* [1995] 2 FCR 631 is an example of the latter type of case. It would not be satisfactory to attempt to draw a distinction along these lines. Any such distinction would lack a principled base. Inevitably, in practice, the distinction would disintegrate in confusion.

[72] Thirdly, here again, a balancing exercise is called for. Some features point in one direction, others in the opposite direction. Factors favouring the need for the solicitor to act for the wife alone include

the following. Sometimes a wife may be inhibited in discussion with a solicitor who is also acting for the husband or whose main client is the husband. This occurred in *Banco Exterior Internacional v Mann* [1995] 1 All ER 936: see the finding of the judge (at 941). Sometimes a solicitor whose main client is the husband may not, in practice, give the same single-minded attention to the wife's position as would a solicitor acting solely for the wife. Her interests may rank lower in the solicitor's scale of priorities, perhaps unconsciously, than the interests of the husband. Instances of incompetent advice, or worse, which have come before the court might perhaps be less likely to recur if a solicitor were instructed to act for the wife alone and gave advice solely to her. As a matter of general understanding, independent advice would suggest that the solicitor should not be acting in the same transaction for the person who, if there is any undue influence, is the source of that influence.

[73] The contrary view is that the solicitor may also act for the husband or the bank, provided the solicitor is satisfied that this is in the wife's best interests and satisfied also that this will not give rise to any conflicts of duty or interest. The principal factors favouring this approach are as follows. A requirement that a wife should receive advice from a solicitor acting solely for her will frequently add significantly to the legal costs. Sometimes a wife will be happier to be advised by a family solicitor known to her than by a complete stranger. Sometimes a solicitor who knows both husband and wife and their histories will be better placed to advise than a solicitor who is a complete stranger.

[74] In my view, overall the latter factors are more weighty than the former. The advantages attendant upon the employment of a solicitor acting solely for the wife do not justify the additional expense this would involve for the husband. When accepting instructions to advise the wife the solicitor assumes responsibilities directly to her, both at law and professionally. These duties, and this is central to the reasoning on this point, are owed to the wife alone. In advising the wife the solicitor is acting for the wife alone. He is concerned only with her interests. I emphasise, therefore, that in every case the solicitor must consider carefully whether there is any conflict of duty or interest and, more widely, whether it would be in the best interests of the wife for him to accept instructions from her. If he decides to accept instructions, his assumption of legal and professional responsibilities to her ought, in the ordinary course of things, to provide sufficient assurance that he will give the requisite advice fully, carefully and conscientiously. Especially so, now that the nature of the advice called for has been clarified. If at any stage the solicitor becomes concerned that there is a real risk that other interests or duties may inhibit his advice to the wife he must cease to act for her.

AGENCY

[75] No system ever works perfectly. There will always be cases where things go wrong, sometimes seriously wrong. The next question concerns the position when a solicitor has accepted instructions to advise a wife but he fails to do so properly. He fails to give her the advice needed to bring home to her the practical implications of her standing as surety. What then? The wife has a remedy in damages against the negligent solicitor. But what is the position of the bank who proceeded in the belief that the wife had been given the necessary advice?

[76] Mr Sher contended that, depending on the facts, the solicitor should be regarded as the agent of the bank. Commonly, what happens is that the bank asks the solicitor acting for the husband to undertake the conveyancing formalities on behalf of the bank. The bank also asks the solicitor to undertake the further task of explaining the nature and effect of the documents to the wife, and then confirming to the bank that he has done so. In carrying out these requested tasks, it was submitted, the solicitor is acting for the bank. The bank requires the solicitor to advise the wife, not for her benefit, but for the benefit and protection of the bank. Any deficiencies in the advice given to the wife should be attributed to the bank. In this regard, it was submitted, the solicitor's knowledge is to be imputed to the bank. A certificate furnished by the solicitor to the bank should not prejudice the position of the wife when, as happened in several cases, the contents of the certificate are untrue. If the solicitor has not given the wife any advice, her rights should not be diminished by the solicitor telling the bank that she has been fully advised.

[77] I cannot accept this analysis. Confirmation from the solicitor that he has advised the wife is one of the bank's preconditions for completion of the transaction. But it is central to this arrangement that in advising the wife the solicitor is acting for the wife and no one else. The bank does not have, and is intended not to have, any knowledge of or control over the advice the solicitor gives the wife. The solicitor is not accountable to the bank for the advice he gives to the wife. To impute to the bank knowledge of what passed between the solicitor and the wife would contradict this essential feature of the arrangement. The mere fact that, for its own purposes, the bank asked the solicitor to advise the wife does not make the solicitor the bank's agent in giving that advice.

[78] In the ordinary case, therefore, deficiencies in the advice given are a matter between the wife and her solicitor. The bank is entitled to proceed on the assumption that a solicitor advising the wife has done his job properly. I have already mentioned what is the bank's position if it knows this is not so, or if it knows facts from which it ought to have realised this is not so.

OBTAINING THE SOLICITOR'S CONFIRMATION

[79] I now return to the steps a bank should take when it has been put on inquiry and for its protection is looking to the fact that the wife has been advised independently by a solicitor. (1) One of the unsatisfactory features in some of the cases is the late stage at which the wife first became involved in the transaction. In practice she had no opportunity to express a view on the identity of the solicitor who advised her. She did not even know that the purpose for which the solicitor was giving her advice was to enable him to send, on her behalf, the protective confirmation sought by the bank. Usually the solicitor acted for both husband and wife. Since the bank is looking for its protection to legal advice given to the wife by a solicitor who, in this respect, is acting solely for her, I consider the bank should take steps to check *directly with the wife* the name of the solicitor she wishes to act for her. To this end, in future the bank should communicate directly with the wife, informing her that for its own protection it will require written confirmation from a solicitor, acting for her, to the effect that the solicitor has fully explained to her the nature of the documents and the practical implications they will have for her. She should be told that the purpose of this requirement is that thereafter she should not be able to dispute she is legally bound by the documents once she has signed them. She should be asked to nominate a solicitor whom she is willing to instruct to advise her, separately from her husband, and act for her in giving the necessary confirmation to the bank. She should be told that, if she wishes, the solicitor may be the same solicitor as is acting for her husband in the transaction. If a solicitor is already acting for the husband and the wife, she should be asked whether she would prefer that a different solicitor should act for her regarding the bank's requirement for confirmation from a solicitor. The bank should not proceed with the transaction until it has received an appropriate response directly from the wife. (2) Representatives of the bank are likely to have a much better picture of the husband's financial affairs than the solicitor. If the bank is not willing to undertake the task of explanation itself, the bank must provide the solicitor with the financial information he needs for this purpose. Accordingly it should become routine practice for banks, if relying on confirmation from a solicitor for their protection, to send to the solicitor the necessary financial information. What is required must depend on the facts of the case. Ordinarily this will include information on the purpose for which the proposed new facility has been requested, the current amount of the husband's indebtedness, the amount of his current overdraft facility, and the amount and terms of any new facility. If the bank's request for security arose from a written application by the husband for a facility, a copy of the application should be sent to the solicitor. The bank will, of course, need first to obtain the consent of its customer to this circulation of confidential information. If this consent is not forthcoming the transaction will not be able to proceed. (3) Exceptionally there may be a case where the bank believes or suspects that the wife has been misled by her husband or is not entering into the transaction of her own free will. If such a case occurs the bank must inform the wife's solicitors of the facts giving rise to its belief or suspicion. (4) The bank should in every case obtain from the wife's solicitor a written confirmation to the effect mentioned above.

[80] These steps will be applicable to future transactions. In respect of past transactions, the bank will ordinarily be regarded as having discharged its obligations if a solicitor who was acting for the wife in the transaction gave the bank confirmation to the effect that he had brought home to the wife the risks she was running by standing as surety.

THE CREDITOR'S DISCLOSURE OBLIGATION

[81] It is a well-established principle that, stated shortly, a creditor is obliged to disclose to a guarantor any unusual feature of the contract between the creditor and the debtor which makes it materially different in a potentially disadvantageous respect from what the guarantor might naturally expect. The precise ambit of this disclosure obligation remains unclear. A useful summary of the authorities appears in O'Donovan and Phillips *The Modern Contract of Guarantee* (3rd edn, 1996) pp 122–130. It is not necessary to pursue these difficult matters in this case. It is sufficient for me to say that, contrary to submissions made, the need to provide protection for wives who are standing as sureties does not point to a need to revisit the scope of this disclosure principle. Wives require a different form of protection. They need a full and clear explanation of the risks involved. Typically, the risks will be risks any surety would expect. The protection needed by wives differs from, and goes beyond, the disclosure of information. The *O'Brien* principle is intended to provide this protection.

A WIDER PRINCIPLE

[82] Before turning to the particular cases I must make a general comment on the *O 'Brien* principle. As noted by Professor Peter Birks QC, the decision in *O'Brien's* case has to be seen as the progenitor of a wider principle (see 'The Burden on the Bank' in *Restitution and Banking Law,* ed Rose (1998) p 195). This calls for explanation. In *O'Brien's* case the House was concerned with formulating a fair and practical solution to problems occurring when a creditor obtains a security from a guarantor whose sexual relationship with the debtor gives rise to a heightened risk of undue influence. But the law does not regard sexual relationships as standing in some special category of their own so far as undue influence is concerned. Sexual relationships are no more than one type of relationship in which an individual may acquire influence over another individual. The *O'Brien* decision cannot sensibly be regarded as confined to sexual relationships, although these are likely to be its main field of application at present. What is appropriate for sexual relationships ought, in principle, to be appropriate also for other relationships where trust and confidence are likely to exist.

[83] The courts have already recognised this. Further application, or development, of the *O'Brien* principle has already taken place. In *Credit Lyonnais Bank Nederland NV v Burch* [1997] 1 All ER 144 the same principle was applied where the relationship was employer and employee. Miss Burch was a junior employee in a company. She was neither a shareholder nor a director. She provided security to the bank for the company's overdraft. She entered into a guarantee of unlimited amount, and gave the bank a second charge over her flat. Nourse LJ (at 146) said the relationship 'may broadly be said to fall under [*O'Brien's* case]'. The Court of Appeal held that the bank was put on inquiry. It knew the facts from which the existence of a relationship of trust and confidence between Miss Burch and Mr Pelosi, the owner of the company, could be inferred.

[84] The crucially important question raised by this wider application of the *O'Brien* principle concerns the circumstances which will put a bank on inquiry. A bank is put on inquiry whenever a wife stands as surety for her husband's debts. It is sufficient that the bank knows of the husband/wife relationship. That bare fact is enough. The bank must then take reasonable steps to bring home to the wife the risks involved. What, then, of other relationships where there is an increased risk of undue influence, such as parent and child? Is it enough that the bank knows of the relationship? For reasons already discussed in relation to husbands and wives, a bank cannot be expected to probe the emotional relationship between two individuals, whoever they may be. Nor is it desirable that a bank should attempt this. Take the case where a father puts forward his daughter as a surety for his business overdraft. A bank should not be called upon to evaluate highly personal matters such as the degree of trust and confidence existing between the father and his daughter, with the bank put on inquiry in one case and not in another. As with wives, so with daughters, whether a bank is put on inquiry should not depend on the degree of trust and confidence the particular daughter places in her father in relation to financial matters. Moreover, as with wives, so with other relationships, the test of what puts a bank on inquiry should be simple, clear and easy to apply in widely varying circumstances. This suggests that, in the case of a father and daughter, knowledge by the bank of the relationship of father and daughter should suffice to put the bank on inquiry. When the bank knows of the relationship, it must then take reasonable steps to ensure the daughter knows what she is letting herself into.

[85] The relationship of parent and child is one of the relationships where the law irrebuttably presumes the existence of trust and confidence. Rightly, this has already been rejected as the boundary of the *O 'Brien* principle. *O'Brien's* case was a husband/wife case. The responsibilities of creditors were enunciated in a case where the law makes no presumption of the existence of trust and confidence.

[86] But the law cannot stop at this point, with banks on inquiry only in cases where the debtor and guarantor have a sexual relationship or the relationship is one where the law presumes the existence of trust and confidence. That would be an arbitrary boundary, and the law has already moved beyond this, in the decision in the *Credit Lyonnais* case. As noted earlier, the reality of life is that relationships in which undue influence can be exercised are infinitely various. They cannot be exhaustively defined. Nor is it possible to produce a comprehensive list of relationships where there is a substantial risk of the exercise of undue influence, all others being excluded from the ambit of the *O'Brien* principle. Human affairs do not lend themselves to categorisations of this sort. The older generation of a family may exercise undue influence over a younger member, as in parent/child cases such as *Bainbrigge v Browne* (1881) 18 Ch D 188 and *Powell v Powell* [1900] 1 Ch 243. Sometimes it is the other way round, as with a nephew and his elderly aunt in *Inche Noriah v Shaik Allie Bin Omar* [1929] AC 127, [1928] All ER Rep 189. An employer may take advantage of his employee, as in the *Credit Lyonnais* case. But it may be the other way round, with an employee taking advantage of her employer, as happened with the secretary/companion and her elderly employer in *Re Craig (deed)* [1970] 2 All ER 390, [1971] Ch 95. The list could go on.

[87] These considerations point forcibly to the conclusion that there is no rational cut-off point, with certain types of relationship being susceptible to the *O'Brien* principle and others not. Further, if a bank is not to be required to evaluate the extent to which its customer has influence over a proposed guarantor, the only practical way forward is to regard banks as 'put on inquiry' in every case where the relationship between the surety and the debtor is non-commercial. The creditor must always take reasonable steps to bring home to the individual guarantor the risks he is running by standing as surety. As a measure of protection, this is valuable. But, in all conscience, it is a modest burden for banks and other lenders. It is no more than is reasonably to be expected of a creditor who is taking a guarantee from an individual. If the bank or other creditor does not take these steps, it is deemed to have notice of any claim the guarantor may have that the transaction was procured by undue influence or misrepresentation on the part of the debtor.

[88] Different considerations apply where the relationship between the debtor and guarantor is commercial, as where a guarantor is being paid a fee, or a company is guaranteeing the debts of another company in the same group. Those engaged in business can be regarded as capable of looking after themselves and understanding the risks involved in the giving of guarantees.

[89] By the decisions of this House in *O'Brien'* s case and the Court of Appeal in the *Credit Lyonnais* case, English law has taken its first strides in the development of some such general principle. It is a workable principle. It is also simple, coherent and eminently desirable. I venture to think this is the way the law is moving, and should continue to move. Equity, it is said, is not past the age of child-bearing. In the present context the equitable concept of being 'put on inquiry' is the parent of a principle of general application, a principle which imposes no more than a modest obligation on banks and other creditors. The existence of this obligation in all non-commercial cases does not go beyond the reasonable requirements of the present times. In future, banks and other creditors should regulate their affairs accordingly.

[Lords Clyde, Hobhouse and Scott delivered concurring judgments.]

NOTES

1. The case has been noted by M Oldham [2002] CLJ 29; D O'Sullivan (2002) 118 LQR 337; R Bigwood, (2002) 65 MLR 435; A Phang and H Tjio [2002] LMCLQ 337; S Wong [2002] JBL 439; D Capper [2002] RLR 100 and G Andrews (2002) 66 Conv 456.

2. In each of the seven wife v bank appeals before the House of Lords in *Etridge (No 2)*, the transactions pre-dated the *O'Brien* case and the bank did not have the advantage of the guidance provided by Lord Brown-Wilkinson. The question to be asked in each case, therefore, was whether at the time the security was granted to the bank, the bank's perception of the risk that the grant might have been procured by the husband's impropriety was such as to have required the bank to take some additional steps to satisfy itself that the wife understood the nature and effect of the transaction. As such the specific guidance offered to banks and solicitors acting for wives in future transactions was strictly *obiter dicta*.

3. Where a wife (or other surety) successfully raises an *O 'Brien* defence, she is entitled to rescind the transaction with the lender. Where the wife has received benefits under the transaction with the lender, she should be required, as a condition of rescission, to make counter-restitution to the lender of the value of the benefit she has received (see *Dunbar Bank plc v Nadeem* [1998] 3 All ER 876, CA). However, it seems that there is no question of the equitable remedy of rescission being subjected to terms where the wife obtained no benefit for herself from the transaction. In *TSB Bank plc v Camfield* [1995] 1 WLR 430, a wife was induced to stand surety by her husband's innocent misrepresentation that their maximum liability in respect of the loan for his business was £15,000, when in fact it was unlimited. The bank was held to have constructive notice of the misrepresentation and the issue turned on whether the security could be partially enforced up to £15,000. The Court of Appeal held that the security was to be set aside in full. As Nourse LJ said (at 437): 'The wife's right to have the transaction set aside in toto as against her husband is no less enforceable against the mortgagee.' The decision has been rightly criticised on the ground that as the wife was prepared to guarantee payment of £15,000, it was appropriate to impose terms (see G Jones (ed), Lord Goff and G Jones *The Law of Restitution* (7th edn, 2007), paras 11-011–11-012; J Poole and A Keyser (2005) 121 LQR 273; but for opposing arguments, see J O' Sullivan 'Undue Influence and Misrepresentation after *O'Brien*: Making Security Secure', Ch 3 of FD Rose (ed) *Restitution and Banking Law* (1998), pp 64–69, and G Virgo's reply, which appears in Ch 4 of the same book, pp 76–77—in *De Molestina v Ponton* [2002] 1 Lloyd's Rep 271, Colman J also rejected partial rescission). In Australia rescission on terms is accepted (*Vadasz v Pioneer Concrete (SA) Pty Ltd* (1995) 184 CLR 102, H Ct, noted by P Watts [2002] CLJ 301), as it is in New Zealand (*Scales Trading Ltd v Far Eastern Shipping Co Public Ltd* [1999] 3 NZLR 26, CA: the PC, having made a different factual finding, did not need to express an opinion on the issue ([2001] 1 All ER (Comm) 319, [2001] 1 NZLR 513). Of course, in a case of undue influence, where the surety's consent is totally vitiated, it is right that the security be set aside in full (but see *Castle Phillips Finance v Piddington* (1994) 70 P & CR 592, an undue influence case, where the Court of Appeal was able to mitigate the effect of setting aside the charge in full by subrogating the creditor to an earlier, valid charge). However, even in a case of undue influence it may occasionally be possible to sever tainted material from untainted material in an instrument, and to set aside only the former, so long as this does not amount to rewriting the contract (*Barclays Bank plc v Caplan* [1998] 1 FLR 532, Ch D).

4.   In *Yorkshire Bank plc v Tinsley* [2004] EWCA Civ 816, [2004] 1 WLR 2380, the Court of Appeal held that where a mortgage granted by a wife to a bank was voidable against the bank because the bank had constructive notice of undue influence by the husband, a replacement mortgage, which was not executed as a result of undue influence, could also be set aside by the wife, at least where it was executed as a condition of the release of the first mortgage. The key factor was that the second mortgage was 'inseparably connected' with the first mortgage (at [25], [26]). The position would be different if the second mortgage is made with a different lender because that lender could not be deemed to be aware of the matters of which the original lender is deemed to be aware (at [21]). Furthermore, the mortgagor will not be entitled to set aside the second mortgage where she was aware of her right to set aside the first mortgage before she entered into the second mortgage (*Wadlow v Samuel* [2007] EWCA Civ 155).

5.   The High Court of Australia has rejected the doctrine of notice in favour of the theory that equity affords special protection to a guarantor who is the wife of the debtor (*Garcia v National Australia Bank Ltd* (1998) 194 CLR 395). The theory was adopted by the Court of Appeal in *O'Brien* ([1993] QB 109) but later rejected by the House of Lords in the same case, where the doctrine of notice was preferred (see above). See, generally, J Edelman and E Bant (2004) 15 JBFLP 5. *O'Brien* principles have been incorporated into the law of Scotland, but explained in terms of the good faith of the creditor (*Smith v Bank of Scotland* 1997 SC 111, HL). *O'Brien* principles have been adopted in New Zealand, although the Court of Appeal has observed that the 'jurisprudential basis of *O'Brien* remains uncertain' (*Wilkinson v ASP Bank Ltd* [1998] 1 NZLR 674 at 698). The reasoning in *O'Brien* was adopted by the Supreme Court of Ireland (*Bank of Nova Scotia v Hogan* [1996] 3 IR 239); it has also been approved by the Supreme Court of Canada (*Gold v Rosenberg* (1997) 152 DLR (4th) 385, [1997] 3 SCR 767; for detailed analysis of the position in Canada, see M Ogilvie (2005) 42 CBLJ 245).

QUESTION

The *Banking Code* (2008 edn) provides (para 13.4) as follows:

If you want us to accept a guarantee or other security from someone for any amounts you owe, we may ask you for your permission to give confidential information about your finances to the person giving the guarantee or other security, or to their legal adviser. We will also:

- encourage them to take independent legal advice to make sure that they understand their commitment and the possible consequences of their decision (if appropriate, the documents we ask them to sign will clearly show this information);
- tell them that by giving the guarantee or other security they may become liable instead of, or as well as, you; and
- tell them what their liability will be.

    We will not take an unlimited guarantee.

See also the *Business Banking Code* (2008 edn), para 13.8, for a similarly worded provision (but adding that unlimited guarantees will be accepted from companies).

    How far does this provision facilitate the bank's compliance with the *O'Brien/Etridge (No 2)* guidelines? Does it go further than *O'Brien/Etridge (No 2)* requires?

11 BANKS AND FRAUD: LIABILITY 'AS A CONSTRUCTIVE TRUSTEE'

Banks (and other financial institutions) run the risk of being caught up in the fraud of third parties because of their position as the holders and transmitters of funds (see, generally, W Blair (2000) 30 HKLJ 74—an excellent article). A bank becomes the potential object of litigation where it has provided banking services to persons behaving in a fraudulent or improper manner. The claim is that the bank has in some way become implicated in the wrongdoing. The bank's 'deep pockets' make it an attractive defendant.

One or more banks will almost inevitably be involved in every fraud of any size, if only as the means of money transmission. Funds necessarily move through the banking system. This puts banks in the front line. It is a fact recognised by the importance attached to the institutional precautions against money laundering. Banks may also be exposed to liability when providing services that are not related to money transmission, for instance, the provision of corporate advisory services, if by so doing they are seen to have been in some way accessory to or assisted in the fraud (see Blair, above).

A constructive trust claim is often the means by which the defrauded party seeks to hold the bank liable. In theory, other causes of action may be available against a bank, but in practice it is a constructive trust claim that is the most likely to be relied on by the defrauded party. Other causes of action include:

- Where a bank still hold funds that represent the proceeds of fraud, the defrauded party may be able to trace those funds in equity and assert a proprietary claim to them. But such a tracing claim is lost where the funds have been paid into an overdrawn account or have been paid away by the bank.

- Where a paper instrument is collected by a bank for a customer with no title, the bank may be liable in conversion to the true owner of the instrument, although the bank usually has a complete defence to the claim where it can show that it has not been negligent and has followed standard banking practice. Furthermore, the tort of conversion does not apply where money is transferred by electronic means (*OBG Ltd v Allan* [2007] UKHL 21, [2007] 2 WLR 920, HL).

- As between the paying bank and its own customer, it is doubtful that a constructive trust claim will succeed unless the bank was in breach of its contractual duty of care in executing its customer's payment instruction (in which case a separate claim in constructive trust becomes redundant): and a bank is obliged to follow payment instructions unless on notice of fraud (*Lipkin Gorman v Karpnale* [1989] 1 WLR 1340, CA, see above, p 645, a point not raised when the case reached the HL).

- As regards a non-customer, there is a general reluctance to impose a duty of care in tort on a bank receiving funds (*Royal Brunei Airlines v Tan* [1995] 2 AC 378 at 391, PC).

(a) The nature of constructive trust actions

The starting point of any analysis of this area of law is the classic dictum of Lord Selborne LC in *Barnes v Addy* (1874) 9 Ch App 244 at 251:

...strangers are not to be made constructive trustees merely because they act as the agents of trustees in transactions within their legal powers, transactions perhaps of which a Court of Equity may disapprove, unless (i) those agents receive and become chargeable with some part of the trust property, or (ii) unless they assist with knowledge in a dishonest and fraudulent design on the part of the trustees.

Further, his Lordship continued, to ensure that 'the transactions of mankind' can be conducted with safety, it is necessary that 'persons dealing honestly as agents [be] at liberty to rely on the legal power of the trustees, and are not to have the character of trustees constructively imposed upon them'. This qualification is relevant in respect of both branches of the doctrine.

The first type of liability is generally known as liability for 'knowing receipt'. The second type of liability was known as liability for 'knowing assistance' until a change in the law in 1995 made it more appropriate to refer to it as liability for 'dishonest assistance'. In both cases liability is personal and not proprietary (see *Re Montagu's Settlement Trusts* [1987] Ch 264 at 276, per Megarry V-C, dealing with knowing receipt; *Twinsectra Ltd v Yardley* [1999] Lloyd's Rep Bank 438 at 467, per Potter LJ, dealing with dishonest assistance). But there the similarly ends. The two types of liability are fundamentally different. As Lord Nicholls observed in *Royal Brunei Airlines v Tan* [1995] 2 AC 378 at 382:

The first limb of Lord Selborne L.C.'s formulation is concerned with the liability of a person as a *recipient* of trust property or its traceable proceeds. The second limb is concerned with what, for want of a better compendious description, can be called the liability of an *accessory* to a trustee's breach of trust. Liability as an accessory is not dependent upon receipt of trust property. It arises even though no trust property has reached the hands of the accessory. It is a form of secondary liability in the sense that it only arises where there has been a breach of trust.

Lord Nicholls went on to opine (at 386) that whereas 'recipient liability is restitution-based; accessory liability is not'.

The distinction was again recently highlighted by the Court of Appeal in *Grupo Torras SA v Al-Sabah* [2001] Lloyd's Rep Bank 36 in the following terms (para 122):

The basis of liability in a case of knowing receipt is quite different from that in a case of dishonest assistance. One is a receipt-based liability which may on examination prove to be either a vindication of persistent property rights or a personal restitutionary claim based on unjust enrichment by subtraction; the other is a fault-based liability as an accessory to a breach of fiduciary duty.

However, as we shall see, until the issue is authoritatively decided upon by the higher courts, the precise relationship between liability under the receipt category of constructive trusteeship and the law of restitution remains unclear and uncertain under English law. By contrast, following the Privy Council's landmark decision in *Royal Brunei Airlines v Tan*, the requirements for accessory liability can now be stated with more certainty. Accessory liability is 'fault-based'; the 'touchstone of liability' is the accessory's dishonesty.

(b) Dishonest assistance

Liability for dishonest assistance will be imposed on anyone who has dishonestly been accessory to, or assisted in, a disposition of property in breach of trust or other fiduciary obligation. In such a case the accessory or assister is traditionally described as a 'constructive trustee' and said to be 'liable to account as a constructive trustee' (see, eg *Westdeutsche Landesbank Girozentrale v Islington London Borough Council* [1996] AC 669 at 705, per Lord Browne-Wilkinson). However, as the accessory or assister does not have to receive any trust property for this type of liability to arise, it seems misleading to describe him as a trustee at all (*Agip (Africa) Ltd v Jackson* [1990] Ch 265 at 292, per Millett J; *Paragon Finance plc v DB Thakerar & Co (a firm)* [1999] 1 All ER 400 at 409, per Millett LJ; *Dubai Aluminium Co Ltd v Salaam* [2002] UKHL 48, [2003] 2 AC 366 at [141], per Lord Millett). It would be more accurate, and less confusing, to regard dishonest participation in a breach of trust as a species of equitable wrong: 'the equitable counterpart of the economic torts' (*Twinsectra Ltd v Yardley* [2002] UKHL 12, [2002] 2 AC 164 at [127], per Lord Millett), or an 'equitable tort' (*Abou-Rahmah v Abacha* [2006] EWCA Civ 1492, [2007] 1 Lloyd's Rep 115 at [2], per Rix LJ). The remedy for the wrongdoing is compensation for the loss caused by the dishonest assistance (*Sinclair Investment Holdings SA v Versailles Trade Finance Ltd* [2007] EWHC 915 (Ch), [2007] 2 All ER (Comm) 993 at [120]-[125], where Rimer J stressed that the remedy was personal and not proprietary/restitutionary). For further discussion of the remedies available against a dishonest assister, see SB Elliott and C Mitchell (2004) 67 MLR 16; S Baughen [2007] LMCLQ 545, 556–558.

There are four requirements for accessory liability to be imposed. They were neatly, and accurately, summarised by Cresswell J in *Bankgesellschaft Berlin AG v Makris* (22 January 1998, unreported):

(i)   There must have been a trust or other fiduciary relationship.

(ii) There must have been a misfeasance or other breach of trust, though *Tan* establishes that such misfeasance or breach of trust need not itself be dishonest or fraudulent,

(iii) The person upon whom liability is to be imposed must, as a matter of fact, have been accessory to, or assisted in, the misfeasance or breach of trust,

(iv) The accessory must have been dishonest.

(i) *There must have been a trust or other fiduciary relationship*

Although the *Barnes v Addy* doctrine started life as a response to the misapplication of trust funds by express trustees, its coverage has since been extended to include the breach of fiduciary duties by others. The doctrine is now commonly applied in the corporate context where directors and other senior officers of the company are deemed to owe fiduciary duties to the company.

Agip (Africa) Ltd v Jackson
[1990] Ch 265, Millett J, affd [1991] Ch 547, Court of Appeal

A senior officer of the company, its chief accountant, was held to be in breach of fiduciary duty when he misappropriated funds from the company's bank account by fraudulently altering the name of the payee on a payment order addressed to the bank after it had been signed by an authorised signatory of the company. The defendants, a group of accountants based in the Isle of Man, assisted in laundering the misapplied funds and were held liable for knowingly assisting in this breach of fiduciary duty. Millett J noted (at 290) that 'the embezzlement of a company's funds almost inevitably involves a breach of fiduciary duty on the part of one of the company's employees or agents'.

(ii) *There must have been a misfeasance or other breach of trust*

In *Barnes v Addy,* Lord Selborne LC ((1874) 9 Ch App 244 at 252) specifically referred to assistance 'in a dishonest and fraudulent design on the part of the trustees' An attempt by

Ungoed-Thomas J, in *Selangor United Rubber Estates Ltd v Cradock (No 3)* [1968] 1 WLR 1555, to jettison the reference to dishonesty and fraud, was emphatically rejected by the Court of Appeal in *Belmont Finance Corpn Ltd v Williams* [1979] Ch 250, on the ground that to depart from it would introduce an undesirable degree of uncertainty over what degree of unethical conduct would suffice if dishonesty was not to be the criterion. It was not until 1995, when the Privy Council delivered its advice in *Royal Brunei Airlines v Tan* [1995] 2 AC 378, that the need to establish dishonesty or fraud on the part of the trustee or other fiduciary was finally abandoned as a prerequisite to accessory liability. This was the main point at issue in the case.

Royal Brunei Airlines v Tan
[1995] 2 AC 378, Privy Council

The plaintiffs, Royal Brunei Airlines, appointed a company ('BLT') to act as its general travel agent for the sale of passenger and cargo transportation. Under the terms of their agreement, BLT was required to account to the airline for all amounts received from sales of tickets. In fact, BLT was afforded a 30-day credit period before it was required to pay the airline. However, the agreement expressly provided that all amounts received from sales of tickets where to be held by BLT on trust for the airline. In practice, money received by BLT was not paid into a separate account but credited to BLT's current account, where it was used to meet the company's normal business expenditure. All this was done to the knowledge and with the assistance of the defendant, who was the managing director and principal shareholder of BLT. When BLT defaulted on its payments to the airline and became insolvent, the claimants sought to make the defendant personally liable on the basis that he assisted the admitted breach of trust.

The Court of Appeal of Brunei found for the defendant on the ground that accessory liability was dependent on the breach of trust being dishonest, whereas here the admitted breach of trust was the result of bad management and not dishonesty. Lord Nicholls, delivering the advice of the Privy Council, took the opposite view of the law. Liability under the accessory category of constructive trusteeship required a breach of trust or other fiduciary duty, but it did not have to be a dishonest one. His Lordship considered that Lord Selborne LC's dictum (the '*Barnes v Addy* straight-jacket') had too often been interpreted as though it were a statute, and that this had inhibited a proper analysis of underlying concepts. Furthermore, Lord Nicholls could point to authority that pre-dated *Barnes v Addy* where there was no requirement that the breach of trust be dishonest and fraudulent. Lord Nicholls preferred to regard the dishonesty of the accessory, not of the trustee, as the touchstone of liability. If the accessory was dishonest, it did not matter that the trustee was innocent: The alternative view would mean that a dishonest third party is liable if the trustee is dishonest, but if the trustee did not act dishonestly that of itself would excuse a dishonest third party from liability. That would make no sense.'

One further point remains uncertain. Does liability as a constructive trustee extend to a case of dishonest assistance in *any* breach of fiduciary duty or is it restricted to assistance in a breach of trust in relation to property? In *Tan,* Lord Nicholls (at 392) stated that 'a liability in equity to make good resulting loss attaches to a person who dishonestly procures or assists in a breach of trust or fiduciary obligation'. Lord Nicholls' formulation does not require the misapplication of trust property or its proceeds, but as the point was not in issue in that case, where trust property had certainly been misapplied, this cannot be taken as the last word on the subject. The issue has been left open in a number of recent cases (*Brown v Bennett* [1999] 1 BCLC 649; *Fyffes Group Ltd v Templeman* [2000] 2 Lloyd's Rep 643; *Goose v Wilson Sandiford & Co (No 2)* [2000] EWCA Civ 73, [2001] Lloyd's Rep PN 189, para [88]; *Gencor ACP Ltd v Dalby* [2000] 2 BCLC 734, 757); though in others the broader approach has been rejected (*Satnam Investments Ltd v Dunlop Heywood & Co Ltd* [1999] 3 All ER 652 at 651; *Petrotrade Inc v Smith* [2000] 1 Lloyd's Rep 486 at 491–492). It is submitted that the dishonest breach of trust in which the defendant assisted should not have to involve trust property or its proceeds of sale, although often it will do so. If accessory liability is to develop as a species of equitable wrongdoing, analogous to the economic tort of wrongful interference with the performance of a contract, there seems little reason to restrict its application to a breach of trust in respect of property. Dishonest assistance in the breach of any equitable obligation, including an obligation not to misapply trust property, should be enough.

(iii) *The person upon whom liability is to be imposed must a matter of fact have been accessory or assisted in the misfeasance or breach of trust*

In many cases banks will not find it easy to avoid the charge that they were accessory to or assisted in a breach of trust, especially one that involves the fraudulent misapplication of trust funds. The provision of banking services to persons behaving in a fraudulent or improper manner often exposes a bank to potential liability under this head. The misapplied trust funds will usually be held in bank accounts and moved between bank accounts. The banks that hold those accounts, as well as any other bank involved as an intermediary in the funds transfer process, run the risk of being accused of providing assistance to the dishonest fiduciary. For example, payment by a bank on the instructions of fraudulent directors of a company of moneys of the company to another person may be such assistance. See, eg *Selangor United Rubber Estates Ltd v Cradock (No 3)* [1968] 1 WLR 1555; *Karak v Rubber Co Ltd v Burden (No 2)* [1972] 1 WLR 602. More worrying still, at least from the bank's point of view, is that the mere provision of advisory services to the fiduciary can be deemed 'assistance' where there is a sufficient causative link between that advice and the breach of trust (see *Brown v Bennett* [1999] 1 BCLC 649), even though the bank itself never comes into contact with the misapplied funds (and note that in *Casio Computer Co Ltd v Sayo* [2001] EWCA Civ 661 at [15], the Court of Appeal held that loss caused by the breach of fiduciary duty is recoverable from the accessory without the need to show a *precise* causal link between the assistance and the loss). It is because the 'assistance' net can be cast so widely that attention has focused so crucially on the level of mental intent required the person giving assistance for him to be held liable under this head of constructive trusteeship. Banks and other financial institutions involved in millions of money transmission activities on a daily basis, and so particularly vulnerable to the charge of 'assistance', have always argued that the level of mental intent should be high.

(iv) *The accessory must have been dishonest*

It is the presence of the necessary level of mental intent, which, following *Royal Brunei Airlines v Tan* [1995] 2 AC 378, is dishonesty, that is the fourth requirement for accessory liability to be imposed. *Tan* has finally settled an issue that has plagued the English courts for many years. The decision is to be welcomed for bringing a greater degree of certainty to this notoriously difficult area.

Lord Nicholls (at 392), speaking for the Privy Council by way of *obiter dicta*, confirmed that 'dishonesty is a necessary ingredient of accessory liability. It is also a sufficient ingredient'. Lord Nicholls also clarified the meaning of dishonesty in this context. The key passage from his judgment reads as follows (at 389):

Whatever may be the position in some criminal or other context (see, for instance, *Reg v Ghosh* [1982] QB 1053), in the context of the accessory liability principle acting dishonestly, or with a lack of probity, which is synonymous, means simply not acting as an honest person would in the circumstances. This is an objective standard. At first sight this may seem surprising. Honesty has a connotation of subjectivity, as distinct from the objectivity of negligence. Honesty, indeed, does have a strong subjective element in that it is a description of a type of conduct assessed in the light of what a person actually knew at the time, as distinct from what a reasonable person would have known or appreciated. Further, honesty and its counterpart dishonesty are mostly concerned with advertent conduct, not inadvertent conduct. Carelessness is not dishonestly. Thus for the most part dishonesty is to be equated with a conscious impropriety. However, these subjective characteristics of honesty do not mean that individuals are free to set their own standards of honesty in particular circumstances. The standard of what constitutes honest conduct is not subjective. Honesty is not an optional scale, with higher or lower values according to the moral standards of each individual. If a person knowingly appropriates another's property, he will not escape a finding of dishonesty simply because he sees nothing wrong in such behaviour. In most situations there is little difficulty in identifying how an honest person would behave. Honest people do not intentionally deceive others to their detriment. Honest people do not knowingly take others' property. Unless there is a very good and compelling reason, an honest person does not participate in a transaction if he knows it involves a misapplication of trust assets to the detriment of the beneficiaries. Nor does an honest person in such a case deliberately close his eyes and ears, or deliberately not ask questions, lest he learns something he would rather not know, and then proceed regardless.

Lord Nicholls expressly referred to an 'objective standard' of dishonesty. But he also spoke of honesty having 'a strong subjective element' and that, for the most part, 'dishonesty is to be equated with a conscious impropriety'. This has left room for doubt and uncertainty as to the precise test to be adopted when assessing whether or not an accessory has been dishonest.

In *Twinsectra Ltd v Yardley* [2002] UKHL 12, [2002] 2 AC 164, a majority of the House of Lords considered that dishonesty 'is a standard which combines an objective test and a subjective test, and which requires that before there can be a finding of dishonesty it must be established that the defendant's conduct was dishonest by the ordinary standards of reasonable and honest people *and* that he himself realised that by those standards his conduct was dishonest' (at [27], per Lord Hutton, emphasis added). This 'combined test' means that the accessory will not be held liable where he did not realise that he was transgressing ordinary standards of honest behaviour. It is submitted that this goes well beyond what Lord Nicholls actually said in *Tan* and comes close to the criminal law standard of dishonesty laid down in *R v Ghosh* [1982] QB 1053, a test specifically rejected in *Tan* (see R Thornton [2002] CLJ 524, 525–526; C Rickett [2002] RLR 112, 117–120; C Mitchell, Ch 4 in Meredith Lectures 2002, *Dirty Money: Civil and Criminal Aspects*, Quebec, 2003). The Court of Appeal in New Zealand has also expressed reservations about the subjective element of the combined test (*US International Marketing Ltd v National Bank of New Zealand* [2004] 1 NZLR 589 at [8], [62], [78]–[79], noted by TM Yeo (2004) 120 LQR 208).

The Privy Council revisited the issue in *Barlow Clowes International Ltd v Eurotrust International Ltd* [2005] UKPC 37, [2006] 1 All ER (Comm) 478 (noted by Conaglen and Goymour [2006] CLJ 18). Lord Hoffmann delivered the unanimous advice of the Privy Council (which included Lord Nicholls). Ostensibly, Lord Hoffmann (at [15]) purported to clarify the 'combined test' of dishonesty laid down in *Twinsectra*, but in actual fact (at [16]) he altered the test by dropping the requirement that the defendant himself must realise that by the standards of reasonable and honest people his conduct was dishonest. Subjective elements, such as what the defendant actually knew at the time and his level of experience or intelligence, are still relevant, for they must be taken into account when assessing whether ordinary people would objectively consider the defendant's conduct to be dishonest. But what is not required is for the defendant himself to realise that his conduct is dishonest before liability can be imposed. Lord Hoffmann (at [28]) made it clear that there is no need to establish that the defendant had knowledge of the existence of the trust, or of the facts giving rise to the trust, it is enough to show that he knew or suspected (but deliberately chose to make no further enquiries) that he was assisting in the misappropriation of money.

Following *Barlow Clowes*, for a bank to be held liable for *dishonest* assistance, what has to be established is that the bank engaged in commercially unacceptable conduct in the light of all the circumstances known to it. The problem arose in *Abu-Rahmah v Abacha* [2006] EWCA Civ 1492, [2007] 1 Lloyd's Rep 115 (noted by Virgo [2007] CLJ 22), where the defendant bank received two payments made by the victims of a fraud with instructions to credit the account of a customer named 'Trust International'. In fact the bank credited the account of an entity called 'Trusty International', which was controlled by the fraudsters. The victims claimed against the bank alleging, *inter alia*, dishonest assistance in a breach of trust. The Court of Appeal upheld the trial judge's finding that the bank had not been dishonest. Rix and Pill LJ did not find it necessary to decide whether *Barlow Clowes*, a decision of the Privy Council, had the effect of overturning *Twinsectra*, a decision of the House of Lords, on the dishonesty issue, because they held that the bank's conduct was not objectively dishonest, as it had no suspicions about the payments at the time they were made. By contrast, Arden LJ considered that *Barlow Clowes* should be followed but held that the bank's general suspicions about the customer's business dealings when the account was opened were not enough to make it dishonest with regard to the particular payments in question.

(c) Knowing receipt

The liability of a recipient of property disposed of in breach of trust is generally known as liability for knowing receipt. Liability is personal and is to restore the value of any property received in breach of trust (but for the purpose of claiming a contribution from another wrongdoer under the Civil Liability (Contribution) Act 1978, the remedy for knowing receipt is deemed to be 'compensatory': see *Charter plc v City Index Ltd* [2007] EWCA Civ 1382 at [32]).

There are three requirements, all of which must be met, for liability to arise under this category. They were summarised by Hoffmann LJ in *El Ajou v Dollar Land Holdings* [1994] 2 All ER 685 at 700, when he stated that the claimant must show:

[F]irst, a disposal of his assets in beach of fiduciary duty; secondly, the beneficial receipt by the defendant of assets which are traceable as representing the assets of the [claimant]; and thirdly, knowledge on the part of the defendant that the assets he received are traceable to a breach of fiduciary duty.

In *Agip (Africa) Ltd v Jackson* [1990] Ch 265, affd [1991] Ch 547, Millett J identified two main types of 'knowing receipt' as follows:

The first is concerned with that of the person who receives for his own benefit trust property transferred to him in breach of trust. He is liable as a constructive trustee if he receives with notice, actual or constructive, that it was trust property and that the transfer to him was a breach of trust; or if he received it without notice but subsequently discovered the facts. In either case he is liable to account for the property, in the first case as from the time he received the property, and in the second as from the time he acquired notice.

The second and...distinct class of case is that of a person, usually an agent of the trustees, who receives the property lawfully and not for his own benefit but who then either misappropriates it or otherwise deals with it in a manner inconsistent with the trust. He is liable to account as constructive trustee if he received the trust property knowing it to be such, though he will not necessarily be required in all circumstances to have known the exact terms of the trust.

The second class is sometimes referred to as 'liability for inconsistent dealing'. But where the inconsistent dealing is not for the benefit of the agent, there seems to be a good case for saying that liability only arises if there has been dishonest assistance. The point is made by William Blair QC in (2000) 30 HKLJ 74 at 82:

Because beneficial receipt is the essence of the knowing receipt type constructive trust, it may be doubted that the second class of case identified in this passage is properly treated as falling within this category. Where the defendant does not receive the trust property for his own benefit, and the allegation is that he dealt with it in a manner which is inconsistent with the trust, it is submitted that liability must be established in accordance with the principles applicable to knowing assistance.

(i) Beneficial receipt

Liability depends on *beneficial* receipt of the property disposed of in breach of trust or of its traceable product. Agents who receive trust money in a ministerial capacity, ie for the benefit of their principal and not for their own use and benefit, are not to be made liable for 'knowing receipt'.

In *Agip (Africa) Ltd v Jackson* [1990] Ch 265 at 292, Millett J expressed the clear view (obiter) that paying and collecting banks could not normally be brought within the 'knowing receipt' category since they do not generally receive money for their own benefit, acting only as their customer's agent, but that the position would be otherwise if the collecting bank uses the money to reduce or discharge the customer's overdraft, when it would be using the money for its own benefit (implicitly approved on appeal [1991] Ch 547, and applied by the Supreme Court of Canada in *Citadel General Assurance Co v Lloyds Bank Canada* (1997) 152 DLR (4th) 411 at 422–423).

A bank account may fluctuate between credit and debit and so it may not be easy to ascertain whether money received into the account was received beneficially or not. Writing extra-judicially, Lord Millett has emphasised that the mere continuation of a running account should not be sufficient to render the bank liable as a recipient: there must probably be some conscious appropriation of the sum paid into the account in reduction of the overdraft (PJ Millett 'Tracing the Proceeds of Fraud' (1991) 107 LQR 71, p 83, n 46). This provides an important gloss to his Lordship's dictum in *Agip*, although we await a court to adopt it.

On Millett J's reasoning, if a bank receives trust property into an account in credit, knowing that it has been paid in breach of trust, the bank cannot be held liable under the 'knowing receipt' category of constructive trust: it may, however, be held liable under the 'dishonest assistance' category if the necessary elements of that head of liability are all present. Of course, a bank would be considered to have *beneficially* received trust property where it exercised a right of set-off against it once it was credited to the account, or debited its commission, fees or other charges against the trust property. Again, some conscious appropriation by the bank seems necessary. However, it has been strongly argued that a bank receives beneficially *all* money deposited, irrespective of the state of the account, as the bank is entitled to do as it pleases with money received to the credit of a customer provided it pays the customer an equivalent sum on demand (see S Gleeson 'The Involuntary Launderer', Ch 5 in PBH Birks (ed) *Laundering and Tracing* (1995), pp 126–127; M Bryan 'Recovering Misdirected Money from Banks: Ministerial Receipt at Law and in Equity', Ch 10 in FD Rose *Restitution and Banking Law* (1998), pp 180–187; cf C Mitchell, Ch 4 in Meredith Lectures 2002, *Dirty Money: Criminal and Civil Aspects* (2003) pp 199–226, citing the arguments of JP Moore 'Restitution from Banks' (unpublished DPhil dissertation), University of Oxford, 2000, that banks receive money beneficially when deposited by the account holder but only ministerially when deposited by someone else).

In *Trustor AB v Smallbone (No 2)* [2001] 3 All ER 987, Morritt V-C held that a court was entitled to pierce the corporate veil and recognise receipt by a company as receipt by the individuals in control of the company if the company was used as a device or facade to conceal the true facts thereby avoiding or concealing any liability of those individuals.

(ii) Level of knowledge required

The third requirement, identified by Hoffmann LJ in *El Ajou* (above, p 685), for receipt-based liability relates to the knowledge of the recipient. Liability depends on the recipient's knowledge of the breach of trust. But the authorities have been unclear as to what level of knowledge is required.

Some cases support the view that liability only arises in cases of dishonesty or want of probity (see, eg *Nelson v Larholt* [1948] 1 KB 339, as interpreted in *Carl-Zeiss-Stiftung v Herbert Smith & Co (No 2)* [1969] 2 Ch 276; *Re Montagu's Settlement Trusts* [1987] Ch 264). This approach has the superficial attraction of putting the level of knowledge necessary for the receipt category of liability on a par with the need for dishonesty under the assistance category. However, it ignores the fact that a recipient *beneficially* receives trust property, whereas the defendant may have assisted another's breach of trust without necessarily being personally enriched. This fact alone seems to argue in favour of some difference in measure between them. Other cases suggest that dishonesty or want of probity is required in commercial transactions, but that mere negligence (so as to include constructive notice) is enough in non-commercial transactions (see *Eagle Trust plc v SBC Securities Ltd* [1991] 1 BCLC438, although Vinelott J clouded the issue by relying on the concept of 'inferred knowledge'; *Eagle Trust plc v SBC Securities Ltd (No 2)* [1996] 1 BCLC 121; *Cowan de Groot Properties Ltd v Eagle Trust plc* [1992] 4 All ER 700). A third line of cases support the view that negligence is enough to give rise to receipt-based liability whether the transaction is commercial or non-commercial (see *Nelson v Larholt,* above, as interpreted in *Cowan de Groot Properties v Eagle Trust* [1992] 4 All ER 700; *Belmont Finance Corpn Ltd v Williams Furniture Ltd (No 2)* [1980] 1 All ER 393; *International Sales and Agencies Ltd v Marcus* [1982] 3 All ER 551; *Westpac Banking Corpn v Savin* [1985] 2 NZLR 41, NZCA; *Powell v Thompson* [1991] 1 NZLR 597 at 607–610; *Citadel General Assurance Co v Lloyds Bank Canada* (1997) 152 DLR (4th) 411 at 429, Sup Ct, Can).

The next case provides the most authoritative guidance on the issue.

BCCI v Akindele
[2001] Ch 437, Court of Appeal

BCCI's liquidators claimed that A, a Nigerian businessman, was liable to repay the proceeds of an investment agreement that had been executed by BCCI's directors in breach of trust.

The liquidators claimed under both the 'knowing receipt' and 'dishonest assistance' heads of constructive trust. At first instance, both claims failed. There was no appeal on the assistance claim as the liquidators could not prove that A had been dishonest. So only the receipt claim reached the Court of Appeal, where the key questions addressed by the court where: What must be the recipient's state of knowledge? Must he be dishonest?

Nourse LJ, delivering the judgment of the court, held:

- Dishonesty is not a necessary ingredient of liability in knowing receipt.

- Just as there was a single test of dishonesty for knowing assistance (see *Tan,* above), there should be a single test of knowledge for knowing receipt.

- All that is necessary is that the recipient's state of knowledge must be such as to make it unconscionable for him to retain the benefit of the receipt.

- This test, while it could not avoid difficulties of application, ought to avoid the difficulties of definition which have bedevilled other categorisations of the requisite degree of knowledge, such as the *Baden* five point scale ('I have grave doubts about its utility in cases of knowing receipt'.)

- Applying that test to the facts of the case, A's state of knowledge was not such as to have made him liable under the head of knowing receipt.

It is submitted that the rejection of dishonesty as the appropriate fault element for knowing receipt is welcome. It is more appropriate to a cause of action founded on culpable acts: eg procuring or assisting a breach of trust, than it is to passive receipt (see R Nolan [2000] CLJ 447). However, the term 'unconscionable' lacks objectivity and is open to subjective interpretation. This leads to uncertainty. In *Tan,* Lord Nicholls (at 392) was particularly critical of the use of unconscionability as the test of liability for assistance:

[i]f it means no more than dishonesty, then dishonesty is the preferable label. If it means something different, it must be said that it is not clear what that something different is. Either way, the term is best avoided in this context.

There has already been speculation as to what the term 'unconscionable' means in this context (see, eg S Barkehall Thomas (2001) 21 OJLS 239, pp 253–264, who formulates guidelines so as to render the test economically efficient, and also J Stevens [2001] RLR 99, who considers Nourse LJ's analysis to be 'flawed'). In *Papamichael v National Westminster Bank plc* [2003] EWHC 164 (Comm), [2003] 1 Lloyd's Rep 341 at [247], Judge Chambers QC treated actual knowledge as a necessary condition for liability. By contrast, in *Criterion Properties plc v Stratford UK Properties LLC* [2002] EWCA Civ 1883, [2003] 1 WLR 2108 at [38] (affd on different grounds: [2004] UKHL 28, [2004] 1 WLR 1846), the Court of Appeal held that an assessment of unconscionability based merely on whether the recipient had actual knowledge of the circumstances which gave rise to the breach of duty 'was too narrow and one-sided a view of the matter'. The court was to have regard to the recipient's actions and knowledge in the context of the commercial relationship as a whole to determine whether the test of unconscionability was satisfied. This chimes with *Akindele* itself, where Nourse LJ was at pains to emphasise that the new test would enable the courts to give common sense decisions in the commercial context. This seems to mean that the courts will pay equal regard to the need for speed in commercial transactions, which limits the ability to investigate matters, while also recognising that there must be cases where there is no justification on the known facts for allowing a commercial man who has received funds paid in breach of trust to plead the shelter of the exigencies of commercial life (see Butterworths *Corporate Law Update,* 3 August 2000).

It was pointed out above that the English courts are increasingly coming to regard 'knowing receipt' as restitution-based. Certain distinguished judges and scholars argue in favour of a standard of strict liability subject only to the defences of bona fide purchaser without notice and change of position (see Peter Birks 'Receipt', in P Birks & A Pretto (eds) *Breach of Trust* (2002), p 213; Lord Nicholls, writing extra-judicially, in W Cornish et al (eds) *Restitution—Past, Present and Future* (1998), p 231; Lord Walker, 'Dishonesty and Unconscionable Conduct in Commercial Life' (2005) 27 Sydney Law Review 187, 202). Nourse LJ touched on the issue in *BCCI v Akindele.* His Lordship doubted whether strict liability coupled with a change of position defence would be preferable to fault-based liability in many commercial transactions (at 456). Nourse LJ thought it was commercially unworkable, and also contrary to the internal management rule of company law, that simply on proof of an internal misapplication of the company's funds, the burden should shift to the recipient to defend the receipt either by change of position or in some other way. For the moment, the issue must await determination by the House of Lords (and there is increasing dicta from their Lordships' House in favour of strict liability: *Criterion Properties plc v Stratford UK Properties LLC* [2004] UKHL 28, [2004] 1 WLR 1846 at [4], per Lord Nicholls; *Twinsectra Ltd v Yardley* [2002] UKHL 12, [2002] 2 AC 164, 194, per Lord Millett; but contrast *Farah Constructions Pty Ltd v Say-Dee Pty Ltd* [2007] HCA 22 at [131] and [151]–[155], noted with approval by Conaglen and Nolan [2007] CLJ 515, 516, where the High Court of Australia (obiter) preferred fault-based liability over strict liability).

12 BANK'S DUTY OF CONFIDENTIALITY

A bank owes its customer a legal, and not merely a moral, duty of confidentiality, arising out of an implied term of the bank-customer contract.

Tournier v National Provincial and Union Bank of England
[1924] 1 KB 461, Court of Appeal

Tournier was a customer of the bank and his account was overdrawn. A cheque was drawn by another customer of the bank in favour of Tournier who, instead of paying it into his own account, indorsed it over to a third party. When the cheque was presented for payment the bank contacted the indorsee's bank and was informed that the indorsee was a bookmaker. The bank subsequently telephoned Tournier's employer for his address and in the course of that conversation disclosed to the employer that Tournier was indebted to them and was sending money to a bookmaker. As a result of this disclosure Tournier lost his job. Tournier then sued the bank for slander and for breach of an implied term of his banker-customer contract that the bank would not disclose to third persons the state of his account or any transactions relating thereto. Tournier lost at first instance but appealed on the ground that the trial judge had failed to direct the jury as to the circumstances when it would be reasonable and proper for the bank to disclose information about their customer. The Court of Appeal upheld the appeal and ordered a new trial.

Bankes LJ: …At the present day I think it may be asserted with confidence that the duty is a legal one arising out of contract, and that the duty is not absolute but qualified. It is not possible to frame any exhaustive definition of the duty. The most that can be done is to classify the qualification, and to indicate its limits...In my opinion it is necessary in a case like the present to direct the jury what are the limits, and what are the qualifications of the contractual duty of secrecy implied in the relation of banker and customer. There appears to be no authority on the point. On principle I think that the qualifications can be classified under four heads: (a) Where disclosure is under compulsion by law; (b) where there is a duty to the public to disclose; (c) where the interests of the bank require disclosure; (d) where the disclosure is made by the express or implied consent of the customer. An instance of the first class is the duty to obey an order under the Bankers' Books Evidence Act. Many instances of the second class might be given. They may be summed up in the language of Lord Finlay in *Weld-Blundell v Stephens* ([1920] AC 956 at 965), where he speaks of cases where a higher duty than the private duty is involved, as where 'danger to the State or public duty may supersede the duty of the agent to his principal'. A simple instance of the third class is where a bank issues a writ claiming payment of an overdraft stating on the face of the writ the amount of the overdraft. The familiar instance of the last class is where the customer authorizes a reference to his banker. It is more difficult to state what the limits of the duty are, either as to time or as to the nature of the disclosure. I certainly think that the duty does not cease the moment a customer closes his account. Information gained during the currency of the account remains confidential unless released under circumstances bringing the case within one of the classes of qualification I have already referred to. Again the confidence is not confined to the actual state of the customer's account. It extends to information derived from the account itself. A more doubtful question, but one vital to this case, is whether the confidence extends to information in reference to the customer and his affairs derived not from the customer's account but from other sources, as, for instance, from the account of another customer of the customer's bank.... The privilege of non-disclosure to which a client or a customer is entitled may vary according to the exact nature of the relationship between the client or the customer and the person on whom the duty rests. It need not be the same in the case of the counsel, the solicitor, the doctor, and the banker, though the underlying principle may be the same. The case of the banker and his customer appears to me to be one in which the confidential relationship between the parties is very marked. The credit of the customer depends very largely upon the strict observance of that confidence. I cannot think that the duty of non-disclosure is confined to information derived from the customer himself or from his account. To take a simple illustration. A police officer goes to a banker to make an inquiry about a customer of the bank. He goes to the bank, because he knows that the person about whom he wants information is a customer of the bank. The police officer is asked why he wants the information. He replies, because the customer is charged with a series of frauds. Is the banker entitled to publish that information? Surely not. He acquired the information in his character of banker. So in the present case Mr Fennell [the branch manager] was put upon inquiry by a cheque drawn in the plaintiffs favour upon a customer's account. He acquired the information which he is said to have divulged in his character as the plaintiffs banker.

Scrutton LJ: ...I have no doubt that it is an implied term of a banker's contract with his customer that the banker shall not disclose the account, or transactions relating thereto, of his customer except in certain circumstances.... I think it is clear that the bank may disclose the customer's account and affairs to an extent reasonable and proper for its own protection, as in collecting or suing for an overdraft; or to an extent reasonable and proper for carrying on the business of the account, as in giving a reason for declining to honour cheques drawn or bills accepted by the customer, when there are insufficient assets; or when ordered to answer questions in the law Courts; or to prevent frauds or crimes. I doubt whether it is sufficient excuse for disclosure, in the absence of the customer's consent, that it was in the interests of the customer, where the customer can be consulted in reasonable time and his consent or dissent obtained. I think also, in accordance with well-known authorities on the duties and privileges of legal advisers, that the implied legal duty towards the customer to keep secret his affairs does not apply to knowledge which the bank acquires before the relation of banker and customer was in contemplation, or after it ceased; or to knowledge derived from other sources during the continuance of the relation.

Atkin LJ: ...In *Joachimson v Swiss Bank Corpn* ([1921] 3 KB 110) this Court had to consider what were the terms of the contract made between banker and customer in the ordinary course of business when a current account is opened by the bank. All the members of the Court were of opinion that the contract included several implied terms, some of which were then stated, so far as was necessary for the determination of that case, which turned upon the necessity of a demand before the customer could sue the bank for the amount of his credit balance. It is now necessary to consider whether there is any, and if so what, implied term as to an obligation of secrecy on the part of the bank....I come to the conclusion that one of the implied terms of the contract is that the bank enter into a qualified obligation with their customer to abstain from disclosing information as to his affairs without his consent.

...To what information does the obligation of secrecy extend? It clearly goes beyond the state of the account, that is, whether there is a debit or a credit balance, and the amount of the balance. It must extend at least to all the transactions that go through the account, and to the securities, if any, given in respect of the account; and in respect of such matters it must, I think, extend beyond the period when the account is closed, or ceases to be an active account. It seems to me inconceivable that either party would contemplate that once the customer had closed his account the bank was to be at liberty to divulge as it pleased the particular transactions which it had conducted for the customer while he was such. I further think that the obligation extends to information obtained from other sources than the customer's actual account, if the occasion upon which the information was obtained arose out of the banking relations of the bank and its customers—for example, with a view to assisting the bank in conducting the customer's business, or in coming to decisions as to its treatment of its customers....In this case, however, I should not extend the obligation to information as to the customer obtained after he had ceased to be customer. Speaking for myself, I find little assistance from considering the implications that have been found by the Courts to arise from contracts in other occupations and professions, such as those of solicitors or doctors. The limitation of the implied term must vary with the special circumstances peculiar to each class of occupation. On the other hand, it seems to me clear that there must be important limitations upon the obligation of the bank not to divulge such information as I have mentioned. It is plain that there is no privilege from disclosure enforced in the course of legal proceedings. But the bank is entitled to secure itself in respect of liabilities it incurs to the customer, or the customer to it, and in respect of liabilities to third parties in respect of the transactions it conducts for or with the customer. It is difficult to hit upon a formula which will define the maximum of the obligation which must necessarily be implied. But I think it safe to say that the obligation not to disclose information such as I have mentioned is subject to the qualification that the bank have the right to disclose such information when, and to the extent to which it is reasonably necessary for the protection of the bank's interests, either as against their customer or as against third parties in respect of transactions of the bank for or with their customer, or for protecting the bank, or persons interested, or the public, against fraud or crime. I have already stated the obligation as an obligation not to disclose without the customer's consent. It is an implied term, and may, therefore, be varied by express agreement. In any case the consent may be express or implied, and to the extent to which it is given the bank will be justified in acting. A common example of such consent would be where a customer gives a banker's reference. The extent to which he authorizes information to be given on such a reference must be a question to be determined on the facts of each case. I do not desire to express any final opinion on the practice of bankers to give one another information as to the affairs of their respective customers, except to say it appears to me that if it is justified it must be upon the basis of an implied consent of the customer.

NOTES

1. Where a bank discloses information in breach of its duty of confidentiality, the customer may sue for damages and/or for an injunction to restrain a repetition of the disclosure (where the customer fears that the bank is about to breach its duty, an injunction may prevent disclosure being made in the first place). In *Jackson v Royal Bank of Scotland* [2005]

UKHL 3, [2005] 1 All ER (Comm) 337, the customer was awarded damages when the bank inadvertently disclosed its customer's mark-up on imported goods, leading to the loss of repeat business. The customer was awarded damages for loss of the chance to earn profits from the repeat business.

2.   The bank's duty of confidentiality extends to all information gained by virtue of the banking relationship and is not limited to information from or about the account itself (the judgments of Bankes and Atkin LJJ being preferred to that of Scrutton LJ on this point: see, eg *Lipkin Gorman v Karpnale Ltd* [1989] 1 WLR 1340 at 1357, per May LJ). As Lord Donaldson MR stated in *Barclays Bank plc v Taylor* [1989] 3 All ER 563 at 565: The banker-customer relationship imposes upon the bank a duty of confidentiality in relation to information concerning its customer and his affairs which it acquires in the character of his banker.' However, Lord Donaldson MR added (at 568) that '[t]he duty to maintain confidentiality is not all-embracing, subject to exceptions. It does not exist in the four exceptional circumstances [identified by Bankes LJ in *Tournier]*' In other words, '[w]here the case is within one of the qualifications to the duty of confidence, the duty, ex hypothesi, does not exist' (*El Jawhary v Bank of Credit and Commerce International SA* [1993] BCLC 396 at 400, per Sir Donald Nicholls V-C).

3.   The courts take a common sense approach when deciding which information is caught by the duty of confidentiality. In *Christofi v Barclays Bank plc* [1999] 2 All ER (Comm) 417, for example, the bank informed the trustee in bankruptcy of the customer's husband that his caution registered over the couple's home had been warned off (ie cancelled) two year's earlier. Under the statutory regime for registration and cancellation of cautions, cancellation could not have taken place without the cautioner having been put on notice by the land registry. In other words, the trustee must have already known of the information that the bank had revealed to him. The customer brought an action against the bank claiming breach of duty of confidentiality. The Court of Appeal, affirming the decision of L Collins QC, struck out the claim as disclosing no cause of action. It was held that the bank could not have breached its implied duty of confidentiality by revealing information to someone who must be taken to have the information under a statutory scheme. The Court of Appeal added (at 426) that the situation would be otherwise where the bank had expressly undertaken not to reveal the information. It is submitted that *Christofi* leaves open the possibility that the bank would have been in breach of its duty of confidentiality if it had revealed the same information to a different person, ie someone who did not have a statutory right to it.

4.   In a thought-provoking note published in [1989] JBL 269, Professor Goode raised some fundamental questions about the scope of the banker's duty of confidentiality and the ambit of the banker-customer relationship. He wrote (at p 270):

What constitutes confidential information?

It is unfortunate that in literature on banking law more attention is devoted to the exceptions to the duty of confidentiality than to the scope of the duty itself. Yet there remain many uncertainties. It is clear that unless protected by one of the exceptions a bank may not disclose information about the customer's affairs coming to the knowledge of the bank in the course of the banker-customer relationship. But how far does this go? Is a bank in breach of duty if it discloses no more than the fact that X is its customer? If X has a current account he will himself be revealing both the name and address of his bankers and the number of his account every time he draws a cheque. Does this indicate that for such a customer the fact that he keeps an account with the bank in question is not confidential? Not necessarily; he may see no reason to withhold the information from those to whom he gives his cheques but feel extremely aggrieved if, without his agreement or statutory authority, the information is disclosed to the tax authorities, the police or a particular creditor who is seeking to garnishee the account. May a bank disclose the state of a company's account to that company's parent or subsidiary? Does it make any difference if the parent or subsidiary is also a customer of the bank?

What information derives from the banker-customer relationship?

An entirely separate question is the ambit of the banker-customer relationship. This has become much harder to define since banks decided to become providers of universal financial services. If, for example, a bank acquires an unincorporated estate agency, do transactions entered into by its banking customers through the estate agency form part of the banker-customer relationship so as to attract the protection of confidentiality? How are we to distinguish banking transactions which are protected from trading transactions which arguably are not? Or are we to conclude that all transactions entered into by banks with customers fall within the purview of the banker-customer relationship?

5. It has been suggested by Professor Cranston that the questions posed by Professor Goode only can be answered when the banker's duty of confidentiality is located within the general principles governing breach of confidence rather than treated as a discrete area of law (see R Cranston *Principles of Banking Law* (2nd edn, 2002), pp 171–174). The leading English case on breach of confidence is *A-G v Guardian Newspapers Ltd (No 2)* [1990] 1 AC 109, where Lord Goff summarised these general principles as follows (at 281–282):

...a duty of confidence arises when confidential information comes to the knowledge of a person (the confidant) in circumstances where he has notice, or is held to have agreed, that the information is confidential, with the effect that it would be just in all the circumstances that he should be precluded from disclosing the information to others...To this broad general principle there are three limiting principles...The first...is that the principle of confidentiality only applies to information to the extent that it is confidential...The second limiting principle is that the duty of confidence applies neither to useless information, nor to trivia...The third limiting principle...is that, although the basis of the law's protection of confidence is that there is a public interest that confidences should be preserved and protected by the law, nevertheless the public interest may be outweighed by some countervailing public interest which favours disclosure...

This approach has a number of attractive features, not least because it can also be used to protect confidential information revealed to a bank by a customer in a non-banking context (eg when the bank provides investment advice or asset management services) or by a non-customer (eg when presenting a business plan in the hope of securing bank finance). However, the general principles applicable to breach of confidence must be modified in the light of banking practice, and it must be admitted that in some respects the two do not always sit easily together, eg information does not have to be inherently confidential to fall within the banker's duty of confidentiality, whereas the general principle of confidentiality only applies to information which is confidential; and information disclosed in the interests of the bank is not subject to the banker's duty of confidentiality, whereas it will only escape the general principle of confidentiality if disclosed in the public interest (see below, Note 8).

6. In its report entitled *Banking Services: Law and Practice* (1989 Cm 622), the Jack Committee recognised that the principle of confidentiality lay at the heart of the banker-customer relationship and warned of the danger of loss of customer confidence in the banking system if the principle was undermined by uncertainty as to the extent of its application in the light of modern banking practices. The Jack Committee recommended that the principle should be strengthened by statutory codification, but this recommendation was later rejected by the government as unnecessary and likely to introduce new difficulties and confusion (White Paper (1990 Cm 1026, p 4)). However, the *Banking Code* (2008 edn) attempts to bolster the duty of confidentiality by stating that banks, building societies and other banking service providers will observe a strict duty of confidentiality about their customers' (and former customers') personal financial affairs and will not disclose details of customer accounts or their names and addresses to any third party, including other companies in the same group, except in the four exceptional cases set out by Bankes LJ in *Tournier* (para 11.1). The Code further states that banks, building societies and other banking service providers will not use the third *Tournier* qualification to justify the disclosure for marketing purposes of their customers' details to third parties, including other companies within the same group (para 11.1). Except in response to a customer's specific request, or where there has been express consent by the customer, banks, building societies and other banking service providers must not pass the customer's name and address to other companies in the same group for marketing purposes, and the customer will not be asked for their consent in return for standard account services (para 8.3). The *Business Banking Code* (2008 edn) carries virtually identical protection for small business customers, save that the duty of confidentiality extends to the customer's business information as well as his personal information (see paras 8.3 and 11.1).

7.   *Qualification 1: compulsion by law.* In *Parry-Jones v Law Society* [1969] 1 Ch 1 at 9, Diplock LJ stated that:

a [contractual] duty of confidence is subject to, and overridden by, the duty of any party to that contract to comply with the law of the land. If it is the duty of such a party to a contract, whether at common law or under statute, to disclose in defined circumstances confidential information, then he must do so, and any express contract to the contrary would be illegal and void.

In its Report, published in 1989, the Jack Committee identified 19 statutes under which disclosure could be compelled (see Appendix Q). The list continues to lengthen and includes the Banker's Book Evidence Act 1879, s 7 (orders for inspection may be made in civil or criminal proceedings); the Police and Criminal Evidence Act 1984, s 9 (a bank may be ordered to produce documents for the purposes of a criminal investigation); the Insolvency Act 1986, ss 236, 366 (a bank can be compelled to disclose information about the affairs of insolvent customers); and the Financial Services and Markets Act 2000, Part XI (powers to order disclosure of information in connection with the exercise of the Financial Services Authority's functions and to aid investigations). Legislation to combat money laundering and the financing of terrorist activities is particularly draconian. A bank commits an offence if it fails to disclose to the Serious Organised Crime Agency its knowledge or suspicion, or that it has reasonable grounds for knowledge or suspicion, that a customer is engaged in money laundering or terrorist offences (Proceeds of Crime Act 2002, s 330; Terrorism Act 2000, s 21 A, as inserted by the Anti-terrorism, Crime and Security Act 2001, Sch 2, Pt 3). The threshold for suspicion is low: the bank only has to consider that there is a more than fanciful possibility that the relevant facts exist (*K Ltd v National Westminster Bank plc* [2006] EWCA Civ 1039, [2007] 1 WLR 311 at [16]). Subjectively, the bank may itself know or suspect the customer is engaged in money laundering or terrorist offences but, even if it does not, it may objectively have reasonable grounds for such knowledge or suspicion. Such disclosure is a 'protected disclosure', ie it 'is not to be taken to breach any restriction on the disclosure of information (however arising)' (Proceeds of Crime Act 2002, s 337(1); Terrorism Act 2000, s 21B(1), as inserted).

The bank owes no duty to its customer to oppose an application for the disclosure of confidential information made under a relevant statutory power or to inform him that such an application has been made (*Barclays Bank plc v Taylor* [1989] 3 All ER 563, CA, where the police applied for disclosure under s 9 of the Police and Criminal Evidence Act 1984).

The same principle applies after disclosure as before it. In *El Jawhary v Bank of Credit and Commerce International SA* [1993] BCLC 396, Sir Donald Nicholls V-C held that, where a bank disclosed information to a third party in circumstances within one of the qualifications to the duty of confidentiality, there was no basis for implying an obligation on the bank to tell the customer what it had done (*Barclays Bank plc v Taylor* and *El Jawhary v BCCI SA* were cited with approval by Kennedy LJ in *Fennoscandia Ltd v Clarke* [1999] 1 All ER (Comm) 365 at 371.) However, in *Robertson v Canadian Imperial Bank of Commerce* [1994] 1 WLR 1493, where as a result of being served with a subpoena (now called a 'witness summons' under the Civil Procedure Rules) a bank produced its customer's bank statements in court in an action to which the customer was not a party, the Privy Council held that such disclosure fell within the first *Tournier* qualification, but refused to exclude the possibility that, in the context of a particular banker-customer relationship, a bank might owe its customer a duty to inform the court where it has been unable to contact its customer or where the bank statements contain material which is irrelevant to the action (in any event, on the facts of the present case the Board held that the customer had failed to prove he had suffered any loss through this omission). The Board also left open the question whether the bank was under an implied contractual duty to inform its customer of service of the subpoena, although their Lordships opined that such an obligation could not go beyond using best endeavours to contact the customer (cf *Barclays Bank plc v Taylor,* above, which was cited to the Board in argument, but regrettably not referred to in the judgment). It is submitted that whilst it may be courteous and good banking practice for a bank to inform a customer of good standing of service of a subpoena (witness summons), it is not necessary to imply such a term into the banker-customer contract, and necessity, not courtesy or good practice, is the only basis for implying such a term (*Liverpool City Council v Irwin* [1977] AC 239 at 254, per Lord Wilberforce—see below, p 703). There seems no reason to differentiate between a bank given notice of an intention to apply for an order for discovery and a bank served with a subpoena (witness summons) (see, generally, RG Toulson and CM Phipps *Confidentiality* (2nd edn, 2006), para 12–010).

A claimant make seek disclosure against a bank in order to start proceedings against a third party, usually one of the bank's customers. The means by which this is done is for the claimant to ask the court to exercise its *Norwich Pharmacal* jurisdiction. Under principles laid down by the House of Lords in *Norwich Pharmacal Co v Customs & Excise Comrs* [1974] AC 133, especially by Lord Reid at 175, a court may order someone, including a bank, who had become 'mixed up' in the wrongful acts of another, to give full information and identify the wrongdoer. The person ordered to make the disclosure must have 'participated' or been 'involved' in the wrongdoing, which may be a civil wrong or a criminal wrong (*Ashworth Hospital Authority v MGN Ltd* [2002] UKHL 29, [2002] 4 All ER 193, especially Lord Woolf CJ at [34], [35] and [53]). For example, a bank that holds an account through which stolen money has passed will fall within the jurisdiction, even though the bank itself was entirely innocent of the wrongdoing. The remedy is, however, one of last resort and the jurisdiction is only to be exercised by the court where the innocent third party is the only practicable source of the information (*Mitsui & Co Ltd v Nexen Petroleum UK Ltd* [2005] EWHC 625 (Ch), [2005] 3 All ER 511 at [24], per Lightman J).

The *Norwich Pharmacal* jurisdiction was applied by the Court of Appeal in *Bankers Trust Co v Shapira* [1980] 1 WLR 1274, where a bank was ordered to disclosure confidential customer information in order to assist the victim of fraud to trace its funds. A *Shapira* order, as this type of order is called, often accompanies a freezing injunction (previously known as a *Mareva* injunction) preventing the rogue dissipating his assets pending the outcome of the

696 Chapter 17 Banks and their customers

action. In *Arab Monetary Fund v Hashim (No 5)* [1992] 2 All ER 911 at 918, Hoffmann J said that a claimant seeking a *Shapira* order must demonstrate a 'real prospect' that the information sought might lead to the location and preservation of assets to which the claimant might make a proprietary claim. As a general rule the claimant may only use the information disclosed to him to bring a proprietary claim to recover his money or a related personal claim against the person who has misapplied it (*Omar v Omar* [1995] 3 All ER 571). Only exceptionally will the court allow the claimant to disclose such information to a third party, as will be the case where the law of a foreign jurisdiction compels the claimant to make such disclosure (*Bank of Crete SA v Koskotas (No 2)* [1993] 1 All ER 748).

A bank served with a *Shapira* order may face a dilemma. In *C v S* [1999] Lloyd's Rep Bank 26, C alleged that its funds had been misappropriated by various defendants other than the bank. The bank was joined to the action for disclosure purposes only to assist C in tracing its funds. C obtained a freezing injunction against the defendants other than the bank, and a disclosure order against the bank. Unknown to C, the bank had already made money laundering reports relating to one of the defendants to the Economic Crimes Unit of the National Criminal Intelligence Service (NCIS). This put the bank in a difficult situation. It was bound to obey the disclosure order, but by disclosing information to C it ran the risk of prosecution under s 93D of the Criminal Justice Act 1988 (since repealed and replaced by the Proceeds of Crime Act 2002, s 342: see also s 333 of the same Act). Section 93D made it an offence for someone, when knowing or suspecting that the police are or are about to conduct an investigation into money laundering activity relating to the proceeds of serious crime, to disclose to another person information which is likely to prejudice the investigation or proposed investigation (s 342 of the Proceeds of Crime Act 2002 is in similar terms). The NCIS would not give any assurance to the bank that if it complied with the disclosure order it would not be prosecuted for 'tipping off under s 93D. The bank was in a situation of double jeopardy—prosecution for 'tipping off if it complied with the disclosure order, contempt of court if it did not.

The bank applied to the court for directions. By the time the case reached the Court of Appeal it was accepted by the parties that disclosure would not prejudice the investigation. Nevertheless, the Court of Appeal took the opportunity to provide guidelines as to what should happen in future in similar cases. First, as soon as the bank is aware that an order is being sought which might involve disclosure of information which might prejudice an investigation, it should inform the Serious Organised Crime Agency (which incorporates the NCIS together with related agencies and departments of the Home Office and HM Customs & Excise) of the position and of the material required to be disclosed. If a disclosure order has already been obtained, and it is coupled with a 'gagging order' not to disclose the fact that the disclosure order has been made, the approach to the SOCA would be impliedly permitted despite the non-disclosure requirement. Secondly, the burden is then on the SOCA to identify the material it does not wish to be disclosed and indicate how it would prefer the order dealt with. In some cases the SOCA will not be concerned about the applicant knowing of the investigation so that it is enough to make compliance with the order subject to an appropriate undertaking to keep the relevant information confidential. In other cases partial disclosure might be acceptable and can be agreed upon. Thirdly, where restricted disclosure is unacceptable to the applicant the directions of the court would have to be sought (the Court of Appeal considered various 'stratagems' as to how the matter could be brought before the court). Fourthly, the burden would be on the SOCA to persuade the court that, where disclosure is to be made, there would be a real likelihood of the investigation being prejudiced. If the SOCA were not to co-operate with the bank, and any requirements of the court in advancing such a case, the court may presume that no prejudice may occur and make a disclosure order. The Court of Appeal stressed that a court would recognise its responsibility to protect the claimant's interests, especially where the claimant could not be heard; the court 'must have material on which to act if it is to deprive an applicant of his normal rights'. See also *Bank of Scotland v A Ltd* [2001] EWCA Civ 52, [2001] 1 WLR 751 (above, p 635); *Tayeb v HSBC Bank plc* [2004] EWHC 1529 (QB), [2004] 4 All ER 1024.

8.   *Qualification 2: Duty to the public.* Given the serious inroads into the duty of confidentiality made by statute, the Jack Committee found it hard to see a role for the second qualification and recommended its abolition (paras 5.30 and 5.41). The government rejected this recommendation on the basis that the statutory route *requires* information from the banker, whereas the second qualification *permits* him to disclose (White Paper (1990) Cm 1026, p 15). There have been few cases where the courts have had to adjudicate on the propriety of disclosure under the second qualification. In *Libyan Arab Foreign Bank v Bankers Trust Co* [1988] 1 Lloyd's Rep 259, Bankers Trust in New York had discussions with the Federal Reserve Board about the plaintiff s accounts and relied, *inter alia,* on the second *Tournier* qualification to justify this disclosure. Staughton J (at 286) was of the tentative view that the qualification applied, although he did not have to decide the issue.

More recently, the existence of an independent ground of disclosure under the second qualification has been highlighted by Millett J in *Price Waterhouse v BCCI Holdings (Luxembourg) SA* [1992] BCLC 583. The case concerned disclosure of confidential information by Price Waterhouse to the Bingham Inquiry. The information concerned Price Waterhouse's client, the Bank of Credit and Commerce International Group (BCCI). While the case concerned the duty of confidentiality owed by accountants to their client, not a bank to its customer, the principles discussed by Millett J are of general relevance. The Bingham Inquiry was a non-statutory inquiry set up by the Chancellor of the Exchequer and the Governor of the Bank of England to investigate the performance by the Bank of England of its statutory functions in relation to the supervision of BCCI (see above, Section 1 for details of the transfer of the Bank of England's supervisory function to the FSA in June 1998). As a non-statutory inquiry it had no statutory power to order disclosure. However, Price Waterhouse wished to co-operate with the Inquiry and applied to the court for a declaration as to what they could and could not do. Millett J held that the public interest in maintaining confidentiality might be outweighed by some countervailing interest in disclosure and the latter was not limited to the public interest in detecting or preventing wrongdoing (citing *A-G v Guardian Newspapers Ltd (No 2)* [1990] 1 AC 109 at 214, 268, 282, HL). At 601 he stated:

The duty of confidentiality, whether contractual or equitable, is subject to a limiting principle. It is subject to the right, not merely the duty, to disclose information where there is a higher public interest in disclosure than in maintaining confidentiality.

In this case Millett J felt that the public interest in disclosure ought to prevail because there was an important public interest in the effective regulation and supervision of authorised banking institutions and the protection of depositors. He concluded that if it was in the public interest to require confidential information to be disclosed to the Bank of England, the appropriate regulatory body at the time, under statutory powers contained in the Banking Act 1987 (now see Part XI of the Financial Services and Markets Act 2000) to enable it to carry out its supervisory function, there was at least as great a public interest in the disclosure of such information to an inquiry set up to review the Bank's past performance of its statutory functions, provided the dissemination of such information was no wider in the latter case than would be authorised in the former case.

Price Waterhouse v BCCI Holdings (Luxembourg) SA concerned the public interest in disclosure of confidential documents to authorities concerned with the regulation of banking institutions. It has been held by Rattee J in *Pharaon v Bank of Credit and Commerce International SA (in liquidation)* [1998] 4 All ER 455, another case following on from the collapse of BCCI, that the public interest in upholding the duty of confidentiality existing between banker and customer was subject to being overridden by the greater public interest in making confidential documents relating to the alleged fraud of an international bank available to the parties to private foreign proceedings for the purpose of uncovering that fraud.

9. *Qualification 3: Interests of the bank.* In *Sutherland v Barclays Bank Ltd* (1938) 5 Legal Decisions Affecting Bankers 163, the bank dishonoured the plaintiff's cheque because there were insufficient funds in her account. The real reason for dishonour was that the bank knew she was gambling. During the course of a telephone conversation between the plaintiff and the bank the plaintiffs husband interrupted and took up his wife's case. The bank then informed the husband that most of the cheques passing through the account were in favour of bookmakers. The plaintiff sued for breach of the duty of confidentiality. Du Parcq LJ thought that the bank was justified in disclosing the information to protect its own reputation. He also held that as the husband had joined the conversation, the bank had the plaintiff's implied consent to disclosure the information to him. The decision has not escaped criticism. First, Professor Cranston argues that, if the banker's duty of confidentiality is located within the general law relating to breach of confidence, disclose can only be justified if it is in the public interest and not merely because it is in the bank's own private interest (R Cranston *Principles of Banking Law* (2nd edn, 2002), pp 174–176). In an effort to explain the *Sutherland* decision, Cranston submits that it might be in the public interest that potentially damaging statements be immediately refuted by a limited release of information (p 176). However, it would seem premature to write off the 'interests of the bank' qualification, especially when it was considered without criticism by Sir Donald Nicholls V-C in *El Jawhary v BCCI* [1993] BCLC 396, and when Chadwick LJ stated (obiter) in *Christofi v Barclays Bank plc* [1999] 2 All ER (Comm) 417 at 425–426 that the bank's disclosure in that case could have been justified under the qualification (see above, Note 2). Moreover, the Court of Appeal has confirmed the existence of an analogous exception to the duty of confidentiality in arbitration proceedings (*AH Shipping Corpn v Shipyard Trogir* [1998] 2 All ER 136 at 147, CA). But whatever the merits of Cranston's first criticism, his second criticism of the *Sutherland* case has real substance to it, namely that the wife's implied consent only went to disclosure of the balance on her account and not to the fact she had been gambling (Cranston, above, p 175; and see also EP Ellinger, E Lomnicka and RJA Hooley *Ellinger's Modern Banking Law* (4th edn, 2006), p 184).

10. *Qualification 4: Customer's consent.* There is an established trade practice that banks provide each other with credit references relating to their customers. In the past banks justified this practice on the ground that their customers gave their implied consent to it. However, the Court of Appeal has held in *Turner v Royal Bank of Scotland plc* [1999] 2 All ER (Comm) 664, that this practice was not sufficiently 'notorious' (ie known to the bank's customers) to make it an implied term of the banker-customer contract. The *Banking Code* and the *Business Banking Code* (2008 editions) now provide that a banker's reference or status enquiry as to a customer's ability to enter into or repay a financial commitment should only be given with the written permission of the customer concerned (para 11.2 of both Codes).

11. *Other relevant legislation.*

(i) The Data Protection Act 1998, which repealed and replaced the Data Protection Act 1984, gives effect to Council Directive 95/46/EC on the protection of individuals with regard to the processing of personal data and the free movement of such data. It protects information about individuals processed by computer and manual records that are held within 'relevant filing systems'. Any processing of personal data must comply with the eight data protection principles set out in Pt I of Sch 1 to the Act. These include the principles that personal data must be used fairly and lawfully; be obtained for specified purposes and used only in ways compatible with those purposes; be adequate, relevant and not excessive in relations to the purpose for which the data are processed; be accurate and, where necessary, kept up to date; and that appropriate measures are taken against unauthorised or unlawful use of data and its accidental loss or damage. A 'data subject', that is an individual who is the subject of personal data, is also given rights under the Act. These include the right of access to personal data (s 7); the right to prevent processing likely to cause damage and distress (s 10); the right to prevent processing of personal data for the purposes of direct marketing (s 11); the right to compensation where damage is suffered as a result of non-compliance with the Act (s 13); and the right to apply to the courts for correction, blocking, erasure or destruction of inaccurate or excessive data (s 14). In order to constitute 'personal data', and thus fall within the scope of the 1998 Act, data must 'relate to' an identifiable living individual (information about companies or limited liability partnerships is not protected). In *Durrant v Financial Services Authority* [2003] EWCA Civ 1746, [2004] FSR 28, the Court of Appeal gave a narrow interpretation to the meaning of personal data: the information should be 'biographical in a significant sense' and should 'have the putative data subject as its focus'. Moreover, information kept in a non-computerised manual system is only to be treated as 'data' if the filing system is sufficiently structured to allow easy access to information specific to the data subject (*Durrant v FSA*). Unstructured bundles of documents kept in boxes do not fall within the scope of a 'relevant filing system', and do not constitute 'data', even if they could easily be scanned and turned into digital information (*Smith v Lloyds TSB plc* [2005] EWHC 246 (Ch), [2005] IP & T 646).

(ii) The Human Rights Act 1998 incorporates the European Convention for the Protection of Human Rights and Fundamental Freedoms into English law. It does this by three mechanisms. First, by requiring the courts to construe all legislation 'so far as it is possible to do so...in a way which is compatible with the Convention rights' (s 3). Secondly, by making it unlawful for a public authority to act in a way which is incompatible with a Convention right (s 6(1)). Thirdly, by introducing a procedure whereby the courts can declare legislation incompatible with the Convention rights, leaving it to Parliament to amend the legislation should it wish to do so (s 4). The Act provides that 'public authority' includes 'a court or tribunal' (s 6(3)). This means that the Convention will inevitably effect such matters as the exercise of judicial discretion, and the development of the common law. The Act does not give private citizens a direct 'horizontal' right of action against each other based on breach of the Convention rights, but it is inevitable that it will have an indirect horizontal effect in the manner in which courts and tribunals deal with proceedings between private parties. In recent years, English law has adapted the action for breach of confidence to provide a remedy for the unauthorised disclosure of personal information (see *Campbell v Mirror Group Newspapers Ltd* [2004] UKHL 22, [2004] 2 AC 457). This development has been mediated by the analogy of the right to privacy conferred by art 8 of the Convention and has required a balancing of that right against the right to freedom of expression conferred by art 10 (*Douglas v Hello! (No 3)*, appeal conjoined in *OBG Ltd v Allan*, [2007] UKHL 21, [2007] 2 WLR 920 at [118], per Lord Hoffmann). However, in *R v IRC, ex p Banque Internationale à Luxembourg SA* [2000] STC 708, Lightman J held that interference with rights of privacy and confidentiality of the bank and its customers, which were protected by art 8, was justified on the ground that information was required by the Inland Revenue for a legitimate aim and to protect the taxation system and revenue. For the case in favour of bolstering the bank's duty of confidentiality through recourse to human rights principles, see R Stokes 'The Banker's Duty of Confidentiality, Money Laundering and the Human Rights Act ' [2007] JBL 502.

(iii) Banks and their employees must be careful not to fall foul of Part V of the Criminal Justice Act 1993, which came into force on 1 March 1994 (the Company Securities (Insider Dealing) Act 1985 is repealed in its entirety). Under s 52(1) of the 1993 Act an individual who has relevant non-public information as an insider, or tippee from an inside source, is guilty of insider dealing if he deals in the prohibited circumstances, in quoted securities that are price affected securities in relation to the information. Encouraging others to deal, knowing or having reasonable cause to believe that the other person would deal in securities in the circumstances covered by the dealing offence, or disclosing information to others, otherwise than in the proper performance of an employment, office or profession, is also prohibited (s 52(2)). The prohibited circumstances, in which it is an offence to deal, are where the transaction takes place on a regulated market, or where the person dealing relies on a professional intermediary or is himself acting as a professional intermediary (s 52(3)). For example, the mergers and acquisitions section of a bank may obtain information from a client company, which is then passed to its dealing arm, who proceed to trade in the shares on the bank's own account on the strength of that information. To avoid this possibility, and to comply with various regulatory requirements under the Financial Services and Markets Act 2000 and rules made thereunder, banks have set up 'Chinese Walls' between their departments (ie systems designed to prohibit the transfer of information in the manner just described). In *Prince Jefri Bolkiah v KPMG (a firm)* [1999] 2 AC 222, the House of Lords recognised the effectiveness of Chinese walls operating in the financial services industry to restrict the movement of information between different departments of the same firm. Where the bank has confidential information from one customer and it proposes to act for another customer with an interest adverse to his in the matter to which the information is or may be relevant, the burden is on the bank to show that even so there is no risk that the information will come into the possession of those now acting for the other party (*Bolkiah,* above, per Lord Millett). For these purposes the risk of leakage must be a real one and not fanciful or theoretical (*Bolkiah,* above, at 237): the crucial question in each case is 'will the barrier work?' (*Young v Robson Rhodes (a firm)* [1999] 3 All ER 524 at 539, per Laddie J). Chinese Walls which are a well-established part of the organisational structure of the firm are more likely to be seen as effective than ad hoc arrangements (*Bolkiah,* above, at 239; *Young,* at 539). But each case turns on its own facts (*Koch Shipping Inc v Richards Butler (a firm)* [2002] EWCA Civ 1280, [2002] 2 All ER (Comm) 957 at [25], per Clarke LJ). It should also be noted that s 147 of the Financial Services and Markets Act 2000 gives the FSA power to make rules relating to the operation of Chinese walls within multidisciplinary authorised persons and groups. The rules are to be found in the FSA Handbook, Conduct of Business Rules. Compliance with these rules gives the bank a 'safe harbour' against contravention of other FSA rules, the misleading statements and practices offences (FSMA 2000, s 397(4), (5)(c)) and engaging in market abuse (FSMA 2000, s 118(8)). But the Act does not protect the bank from civil liability based on breach of fiduciary duties or the duty of confidentiality. Express protection was recommended by the Law Commission in 1995 but the government decided against it believing that developments in the case law (especially the *Bolkiah* decision) made this unnecessary (*Hansard* HL, 9 May 2000, cols 1405–9). The courts are likely to be reluctant to hold a bank liable where it has complied with current practices embodied in the FSA's rules (see R Cranston *Principles of Banking Law* (2nd edn, 2002), p 24).

QUESTIONS

1. 'In England, banks face an increasingly difficult task in balancing and reconciling their various duties and obligations with regard to information on their customers and its confidentiality. While customers may have greater expectations about the preservation of banking confidentiality (given the Banking Codes and such measures as the Data Protection Act 1998), banks find themselves facing a number of dilemmas, particularly given the statutory erosions to the duty of confidence. Ultimately, the public interest may well result in bank confidentiality being no longer the rule, but the exception, in England' (G Griffiths and S Robert-Tissot, in Ch 11 of G Griffiths (ed), *Neate's Bank Confidentiality* (4th edn, 2006), p 282). Do you agree?

2. Account aggregation allows customers to view on a single web page information about their online accounts held with a range of financial institutions. Various technological and legal issues are raised by the development of this banking service (see, eg J Chuah [2002] JIBL 309; M Jelf [2002] IH Lawyer (July/Aug issue) 35). How might the bank's duty of confidentiality affect the operation of such a service?

3. Is a bank entitled to pass on information about its customers to other companies in the same group? What if the information is passed on to assist group members in the marketing of investments and insurance products? What if the information is passed on to protect group companies by informing them of a customer's default in repayment of indebtedness? See *Bank of Tokyo Ltd v Karoon* [1987] AC 45n at 53, 54 (CA), but does this case really provide the answers to these questions?

13   THE CUSTOMER'S DUTY OF CARE

Tai Hing Cotton Mill Ltd v Liu Chong Hing Bank Ltd
[1986] AC 80, Privy Council

(The facts appear from Lord Scarman's judgment.)

The advice of the Judicial Committee of the Privy Council (Lords Scarman, Roskill, Brandon of Oakbrook, Brightman and Templeman) was delivered by **Lord Scarman**: This is an appeal by a company against a decision of the Court of Appeal in Hong Kong whereby its action to recover from three banks sums of money alleged to have been wrongfully debited against its current account with each was dismissed. The appeal raises a question of general principle in the law governing the relationship of banker and customer. Additionally, the appeal calls for consideration of a number of questions arising from the particular circumstances of the company's business relationship with each of the three banks.

The company was a customer of the banks, and maintained with each of them a current account. The banks honoured by payment on presentation some 300 cheques totalling approximately HK$5.5

million which on their face appeared to have been drawn by the company and to bear the signature of Mr Chen, the company's managing director who was one of the company's authorised signatories to its cheques. The banks in each instance debited the company's current account with the amount of the cheque. These cheques, however, were not the company's cheques. They were forgeries. On each the signature of Mr Chen had been forged by an accounts clerk employed by the company, Leung Wing Ling. The central issue in the appeal is upon whom the loss arising from Leung's forgeries is to fall, the company or the banks. The question of general principle is as to the nature and extent of the duty of care owed by a customer to his bank in the operation of a current account....

The question of general principle

The question can be framed in two ways. If put in terms of the law's development, it is whether two House of Lords' decisions, one in 1918 and the other in 1933, represent the existing law. If put in terms of principle, the question is whether English law recognises today any duty of care owed by the customer to his bank in the operation of a current account beyond, first, a duty to refrain from drawing a cheque in such a manner as may facilitate fraud or forgery, and, secondly, a duty to inform the bank of any forgery of a cheque purportedly drawn on the account as soon as he, the customer, becomes aware of it. The first duty was clearly enunciated by the House of Lords in *London Joint Stock Bank Ltd v Macmillan* [1918] AC 777, and the second was laid down, also by the House of Lords, in *Greenwood v Martins Bank Ltd* [1933] AC 51.

The banks accept, of course, that both duties exist and have been recognised for many years to be part of English law. Their case is that English law recognises today, even if it did not in 1918 or 1933, an altogether wider duty of care. This is, they submit, a duty upon the customer to take reasonable precautions in the management of his business with the bank to prevent forged cheques being presented to it for payment. Further, and whether or not they establish the existence of this wider duty, they contend that the customer owes a duty to take such steps to check his periodic (in this case, monthly) bank statements as a reasonable customer in his position would take to enable him to notify the bank of any debit items in the account which he has not authorised. They submit that, given the relationship of banker and customer and the practice of rendering periodic bank statements, the two duties for which they contend are 'necessary incidents' of the relationship. The source of obligation, they say, is to be found both in the contract law as an implied term of the banking contract and in the tort law as a civil obligation arising from the relationship of banker and customer.

They accept that the reasoning to be found in *Macmillan's* case [1918] AC 777 appears at first sight to negative the existence of both the duties for which they contend: but they offer the explanation that the law of contract and the tort law were significantly different in 1918 from the state of the relevant modern law. In particular, they point to developments in the law relating to the circumstances in which the courts will now imply a term into a contract, and to the changes in tort law both as to the range of relationships giving rise to liability in tort and as to the circumstances in which loss or damage will be held to result from breach of a duty of care. Their implied term point they base on the decision of the House of Lords in *Liverpool City Council v Irwin* [1977] AC 239; and their two tort points on decisions of the Board in *Overseas Tankship (UK) Ltd v Morts Dock and Engineering Co Ltd, The Wagon Mound* [1961] AC 388 and of the House of Lords in *Anns v Merton London Borough Council* [1978] AC 728.

The Court of Appeal accepted the banks' submissions. Cons JA was led 'after a great deal of hesitation' to conclude:

> that, in the world in which we live today, it is a necessary condition of the relation of the banker and customer that the customer should take reasonable care to see that in the operation of the account the bank is not injured.

He, therefore, held that, in the absence of express agreement to the contrary, the duty would be implied into the banking contract as a necessary incident of the relationship between customer and banker....

First, it is necessary to determine what *Macmillan's* case [1918] AC 777 decided. Upon this point their Lordships are in no doubt. The House held that the customer owes his bank a duty in drawing a cheque to take reasonable and ordinary precautions against forgery.

> The duty ... is to draw the cheques with reasonable care to prevent forgery, and if, owing to neglect of this duty, forgery takes place, the customer is liable to the bank for the loss: per Lord Finlay LC at p 793.

In so formulating the duty the House excluded as a necessary incident of the banker-customer relationship any wider duty, though of course it is always open to a banker to refuse to do business save upon express terms including such a duty. Lord Finlay LC expressly excluded any such duty saying, at p 795:

> Of course the negligence must be in the transaction itself, that is, in the manner in which the cheque is drawn. It would be no defence to the banker, if the forgery had been that of a clerk of a customer, that the latter had taken the clerk into his service without sufficient inquiry as to his character.

And the House approved the judgment of Bray J in *Kepitigalla Rubber Estates Ltd v National Bank of India Ltd* [1909] 2 KB 1010. In that case the judge held that, while it is the duty of a customer in issuing his mandates (ie his cheques) to his bank to take reasonable care not to mislead the bank, there is no duty on the part of the customer to take precautions in the general course of carrying on his business to prevent forgeries on the part of his servants. Put in the terms of the banks' submission in this case, Bray J negatived the existence of the two duties for which the banks contend, and the House of Lords in *Macmillan's* case [1918] AC 777 agreed with him ....

Implied term

Their Lordships agree with Cons JA that the test of implication is necessity. As Lord Wilberforce put it in *Liverpool City Council v Irwin* [1977] AC 239, 254:

> such obligation should be read into the contract as the nature of the contract itself implicitly requires, no more, no less: a test, in other words, of necessity.

Cons JA went on to quote an observation by Lord Salmon in the *Liverpool* case to the effect that the term sought to be implied must be one without which the whole transaction would become 'inefficacious, futile and absurd' (p 262).

Their Lordships accept as correct the approach adopted by Cons JA. Their Lordships prefer it to that suggested by Hunter J which was to ask the question: does the law impose the term? Implication is the way in which necessary incidents come to be recognised in the absence of express agreement in a contractual relationship. Imposition is apt to describe a duty arising in tort, but inept to describe the necessary incident arising from a contractual relationship.

Their Lordships, however, part company with Cons JA in his conclusion (reached only after great hesitation, he said) that it is necessary to imply into the contract between banker and customer a wider duty than that formulated in *Macmillan's* case. *Macmillan's* case itself decisively illustrates that it is not a *necessary* incident of the banker-customer relationship that the customer should owe his banker the wider duty of care.

The relationship between banker and customer is a matter of contract. The classic, though not necessarily exhaustive, analysis of the incidents of the contract is to be found in the judgment of Atkin LJ in *Joachimson v Swiss Bank Corpn* [1921] 3 KB 110,127: [see above, pp 616–617]. ...

Atkin LJ clearly felt no difficulty in analysing the relationship upon the basis of the limited duty enunciated in *Macmillan's* case. And in *Macmillan's* case itself the protracted discussion, which is now only of historical interest, as to the true ratio decidendi of *Young v Grote* (1827) 4 Bing 253 reveals vividly that the House was aware of the possibility of a wider duty but rejected it.

The argument for the banks is, when analysed, no more than that the obligations of care placed upon banks in the management of a customer's account which the courts have recognised have become with the development of banking business so burdensome that they should be met by a reciprocal increase of responsibility imposed upon the customer: and they cite *Selangor United Rubber Estates Ltd v Cradock (No 3)* [1968] 1 WLR 1555 (Ungoed-Thomas J) and *Karak Rubber Co Ltd v Burden (No 2)* [1972] 1 WLR 602 (Brightman J). One can fully understand the comment of Cons JA that the banks must today look for protection. So be it. They can increase the severity of their terms of business, and they can use their influence, as they have in the past, to seek to persuade the legislature that they should be granted by statute further protection. But it does not follow that because they may need protection as their business expands the necessary incidents of their relationship with their customer must also change. The business of banking is the business not of the customer but of the bank. They offer a service, which is to honour their customer's cheques when drawn upon an account in credit or within an agreed overdraft limit. If they pay out upon cheques which are not his, they are acting outside their mandate and cannot plead his authority in justification of their debit to his account. This is a risk of the service which it is their business to offer. The limits set to the risk in the *Macmillan* [1918] AC 777 and *Greenwood* [1933] AC 51 cases can be seen to be plainly necessary incidents of the relationship. Offered such a service, a customer must obviously take care in the way he draws his cheque, and must obviously warn his bank as soon as he knows that a forger is operating the account. Counsel for the banks asked rhetorically why, once a duty of care was recognised, should it stop at the *Macmillan* and *Greenwood* limits. They submitted that there was no rational stopping place short of the wider duty for which they contended. With very great respect to the ingenious argument addressed to the Board their Lordships find in certain observations of Bray J in *Kepitigalla's* case [1909] 2 KB 1010 a convincing statement of the formidable difficulties in the way of this submission. Bray J said, at pp 1025–1026:

> I think Mr Scrutton's contention equally fails when it is considered apart from authority. It amounts to a contention on the part of the bank that its customers impliedly agreed to take precautions in the general course of carrying on their business to prevent forgeries on the part of their servants. Upon what is that based? It cannot be said to be necessary to make the contract effective. It cannot be said to have really been in the mind of the customer, or, indeed, of the bank, when the relationship of banker and customer was created. What is to be the standard of the extent or number of the precautions to be taken? Applying it to this case, can it be said to have been in the minds of the directors of the company that they were promising to have the pass-book and the cash-book examined at every board meeting, and to have a sufficient number of board meetings to prevent forgeries, or that the secretary should be supervised or watched by the chairman? If the bank desire that their customers should make these promises they must expressly stipulate that they shall. I am inclined to think that a banker who required such a stipulation would soon lose a number of his customers. The truth is that the number of cases where bankers sustain losses of this kind are infinitesimal in comparison with the large business they do, and the profits of banking are sufficient to compensate them for this very small risk. To the individual customer the loss would often be very serious; to the banker it is negligible.

Their Lordships reject, therefore, the implied term submission.

Tort

Their Lordships do not believe that there is anything to the advantage of the law's development in searching for a liability in tort where the parties are in a contractual relationship. This is particularly so in a commercial relationship. Though it is possible as a matter of legal semantics to conduct an analysis of the rights and duties inherent in some contractual relationships including that of banker and customer either as a matter of contract law when the question will be what, if any, terms are to be implied or as a matter of tort law when the task will be to identify a duty arising from the proximity and character of the relationship between the parties, their Lordships believe it to be correct in principle and necessary for the avoidance of confusion in the law to adhere to the contractual analysis: on principle because it is a relationship in which the parties have, subject to a few exceptions, the right to determine their obligations to each other, and for the avoidance of confusion because different consequences do follow according to whether liability arises from contract or tort, eg in the limitation of action . . . .

Their Lordships do not, therefore, embark on an investigation as to whether in the relationship of banker and customer it is possible to identify tort as well as contract as a source of the obligations owed by the one to the other. Their Lordships do not, however, accept that the parties' mutual obligations in tort can be any greater than those to be found expressly or by necessary implication in their contract. If, therefore, as their Lordships have concluded, no duty wider than that recognised in *Macmillan* [1918] AC 777 and *Greenwood* [1933] AC 51 can be implied into the banking contract in the absence of express terms to that effect, the banks cannot rely on the law of tort to provide them with greater protection than that for which they have contracted.

For these reasons their Lordships answer the general question by accepting the submission of the company that in the absence of express terms to the contrary the customer's duty is in English law as laid down in *Macmillan* and *Greenwood.* The customer's duty in relation to forged cheques is, therefore, twofold: he must exercise due care in drawing his cheques so as not to facilitate fraud or forgery and he must inform his bank at once of any unauthorised cheques of which he becomes aware....

Estoppel

Their Lordships having held that the company was not in breach of any duty owed by it to the banks, it is not possible to establish in this case an estoppel arising from mere silence, omission, or failure to act.

Mere silence or inaction cannot amount to a representation unless there be a duty to disclose or act: *Greenwood's* case [1933] AC 51, 57. And their Lordships would reiterate that unless conduct can be interpreted as amounting to an implied representation, it cannot constitute an estoppel: for the essence of estoppel is a representation (express or implied) intended to induce the person to whom it is made to adopt a course of conduct which results in detriment or loss: *Greenwood' s* case, per Lord Tomlin, at p 57.

Appeal allowed.

NOTES

1. In *Henderson v Merrett Syndicates Ltd* [1995] 2 AC 145, the House of Lords held that English law does not prevent a claimant from suing in contract or in tort, where the substantive rights support such 'concurrence' of claims, especially if the claimant's motive is to take advantage of the practical differences which exist between contractual and tortious claims. It was held that Names at Lloyd's might sue members' agents (with whom they had a contract) for negligence as well as for breach of contract in the management of underwriting business so as to gain the advantage of the longer limitation period under the Latent Damage Act 1986. Following *Henderson v Merrett Syndicates,* it is clear that Lord Scarman was wrong in *Tai Hing* when he said that there was no advantage in searching for liability in tort where the parties are in a contractual relationship. As well as different limitation periods there are other practical differences between contract and tort claims including, for example, the measure of recovery (rules about remoteness of damage in tort are less restrictive than in contract), the relevance of the claimant's contributory negligence (it is generally irrelevant in contract, but relevant in tort) and assignability, since only a contractual claim can generally be assigned (see J Beatson *Anson's Law of Contract* (28th edn, 2002), p 23).

2. Where there is a contract between the parties there is no reason in principle why, in particular circumstances, a tort duty of care could not impose wider obligations than those arising under the contract (*Holt v Payne Skillington and De Groot Collis* (1995) 77 BLR 51 at 73, CA; applied in *Sumitomo Bank Ltd v Banque Bruxelles Lambert SA* [1997] 1 Lloyd's Rep 487 at 513, Langley J; but contrast *IFE Fund SA v Goldman Sachs International* [2006] EWHC 2887 (Comm), [2007] 1 Lloyd's Rep 264 at [63], per Touslon J, affd [2007] EWCA Civ 811, [2007] 2 Lloyd's Rep 449). However, a court will not impose a duty of care in tort (imposed by the general law) which is *inconsistent* with the terms of the contract (representing the common intention of the parties), including where no implied term can be established to the same effect as the proposed tort duty. *Tai Hing* is an example of this principle.

3.   How can banks 'increase the severity of their terms of business'? In *Tai Hing* the banks relied on clauses in their contracts with the plaintiff customer which included a requirement that the customer should notify the bank within a specified time of any errors in the monthly bank statements, which would otherwise be deemed correct. Lord Scarman accepted that these clauses were contractual in effect but went on to hold that (at 709–710):

> . . . in no case do they constitute what has come to be called 'conclusive evidence clauses.' Their terms are not such as to bring home to the customer either 'the intended importance of the inspection he is being expressly or impliedly invited to make,' or that they are intended to have conclusive effect against him if he raises no query, or fails to raise a query in time, upon his bank statements. If banks wish to impose upon their customers an express obligation to examine their monthly statements and to make those statements, in the absence of query, unchallengeable by the customer after expiry of a time limit, the burden of the objection and of the sanction imposed must be brought home to the customer . . . . The test is rigorous because the bankers would have their terms of business so construed as to exclude the rights which the customer would enjoy if they were not excluded by express agreement. It must be borne in mind that, in their Lordships' view, the true nature of the obligations of the customer to his bank where there is not express agreement is limited to the *Macmillan* and *Greenwood* duties. Clear and unambiguous provision is needed if the banks are to introduce into the contract a binding obligation upon the customer who does not query his bank statement to accept the statement as accurately setting out the debit items in the accounts.

4.   The verification clauses in *Tai Hing* failed on grounds of construction (see also *Financial Institutions Services Ltd v Negril Negril Holdings Ltd* [2004] UKPC 40). Such clauses will be strictly construed against the bank, ie the courts will apply the *contra proferentem* rule. However, some doubt has been expressed as to whether the clauses in *Tai Hing* really did fall short of the standard demanded by Lord Scarman (EP Ellinger [1986] LMCLQ 8, p 11) and verification clauses using language similar to that found in *Tai Hing* have been upheld by the Canadian Courts, eg *Arrow Transfer Co Ltd v Royal Bank of Canada* (1972) 27 DLR (3d) 81, Can Sup Ct; *Kelly Funeral Homes Ltd v Canadian Imperial Bank of Commerce* (1990) 72 DLR (4th) 276, Ontario H Ct (although in both cases it was the bank's practice to return cleared cheques to customers with their bank statements—this is not the practice of banks in the UK—see, generally, KW Perrett (1999) 14 BFLR 245). Verification clauses may also fail for other reasons. First, the clause may not have been incorporated into the contract (on failure to incorporate terms, though in a different context, see *Burnett v Westminster Bank Ltd* [1966] 1 QB 742). In *Tai Hing* this was not an issue as the customer had signed the bank's conditions. Secondly, where the customer is a consumer or a non-consumer dealing on the bank's written standard terms of business, the clause may be held to be unreasonable and, therefore, ineffective under the Unfair Contract Terms Act 1977 (see above, p 629). Under s 13(1)(c) of the 1977 Act, clauses which exclude or restrict rules of evidence or procedure are treated in the same way as those which exclude or restrict liability. Thirdly, where the customer is a consumer, the clause may be held to be unfair and, therefore, unenforceable under Unfair Terms in Consumer Contracts Regulations 1999, SI 1999/2083 (see above, p 629). Schedule 2, para 1(q) to the Regulations indicates that a term may be unfair where it has the object and effect of unduly restricting the evidence available to the customer against his bank or imposes a burden of proof on the customer when that burden should, by law, be on the bank.

5.   It is clear from *Tai Hing* that unless an effective verification clause is incorporated into the bank-customer contract, the customer is under no duty to examine his bank statements. The same approach has been adopted in a number of Commonwealth countries, eg Canada (*Canadian Pacific Hotels Ltd v Bank of Montreal* (1987) 40 DLR (4th) 385, Sup Ct); Singapore (*Consmat Singapore (Pte) Ltd v Bank of America National Trust and Savings Association* [1992] 2 SLR 828, H Ct); New Zealand (*BNZ v Auckland Information Bureau (Inc) Ltd* [1996] 1 NZLR 420, CA); and Australia (*National Australia Bank Ltd v Hokit Pty Ltd* [1997] 6 Bank LR 177, NSW CA). By contrast, in the United States the customer is under a duty to check his bank statements or accompanying 'items' (cheques) with reasonable care and promptness, to discover any unauthorised signature or material alteration, and to notify the bank promptly of errors (Uniform Commercial Code, s 4–406). Unless the customer can establish negligence on the part of the bank, failure to comply with this duty precludes the customer from disputing the regularity of the payments made, and even where the bank is negligent the customer's right to dispute a payment is barred after one year from the time when the statements or items are made available to him (s 4–406(f)). In *Wealden Woodlands (Kent) Ltd v National Westminster Bank Ltd* (1983) 133 NLJ 719, McNeill J rejected the suggestion that he should bring English law into line with that operating in the United States. This must be right for it is not the normal practice of English banks to return cheques to customers after they have been cleared.

6.   Three points may be made in support of the Privy Council's decision in *Tai Hing* to restrict the duties owed by a customer to those set out in *Macmillan* (to exercise reasonable care in executing his written orders so as not to mislead the bank by ambiguities or to facilitate fraud or forgery) and *Greenwood* (to notify the bank of a forged payment order as soon as he becomes aware of it, and for these purposes the customer must have *actual* knowledge of the forgery as opposed to constructive knowledge: *Price Meats Ltd v Barclays Bank plc* [2000] 2 All ER (Comm) 346; *Patel v Standard Chartered Bank* [2001] Lloyd's Rep Bank 229). These are that:

(1)   the bank is usually in a far better position to absorb the loss than its customer;

(2)   the present law is clear and certain; and

(3)   the bank can always incorporate a verification clause into the bank-customer contract if it requires protection.

However, the chorus of disapproval against *Tai Hing* has been loud (see, for example, the forceful criticism of the case made by MH Ogilvie in (1986) 11 CBLJ 220). The main complaint against the decision is that it fails to bring the law into line with modern banking practices (EP Ellinger [1986] LMCLQ 8). In its Report on Banking Services Law and Practice (1989, Cm 622), the Jack Committee accepted that there was a case for reform of the law, but rejected the idea that customers should be placed under a statutory duty to examine their bank statements (Report, para 6.13). However, in an effort to protect the bank against 'the most reprehensible negligence on its customer's part', the Jack Committee recommended 'a statutory provision whereby, in an action against a bank in debt or for damages, arising from an unauthorised payment, contributory negligence may be raised as a defence, but only if the court is satisfied that the degree of negligence shown by the plaintiff is sufficiently serious for it to be inequitable that the bank should be liable for the whole amount of the debt or damages' (Report, para 6.14).

7.   In its White Paper on Banking Services Law and Practice ((1990 Cm 1026), p 30), the government agreed that the law at present was unfair to banks and stated that it was disposed to make it more evenly balanced between banks and their customers. However, before proposing any changes in the law in this area the government stated its intention to await the forthcoming Law Commission Report on contributory negligence as a defence in contract. The Law Commission produced its Report in December 1993: 'Contributory Negligence as a Defence in Contract' (Law Com No 219). The Law Commission's main recommendation is that 'apportionment of the plaintiffs damages on the ground of contributory negligence should be available in actions in contract where the defendant is in breach of an express or implied contractual duty to take reasonable care or exercise reasonable skill or both, but not where he is in breach of a contractual term which imposes a higher level of duty' (para 4.1). In the context of banking, the Law Commission notes that:

5.20 Under our recommendations, the customer's contributory negligence could be raised as a defence by a bank where the bank is liable for damages for breach of a contractual duty of care, but not where the bank owed a strict duty to the customer, for example, in an action in debt. Banks are subject to an implied contractual duty to carry out the banking service with reasonable care and skill. The customer's contributory negligence will be relevant where the bank is in breach of that duty. However, for the most part actions against banks concern breach of mandate by the bank, for example, where third party fraud has resulted in an unauthorised payment which the bank has debited against the customer's account. The duty of a bank to adhere to the terms of its mandate is strict. Apportionment on the grounds of the customer's contributory negligence will not be available in respect of breach of this duty.

The Law Commission go on to accept that their recommendations do not deal with the problem of customers sharing in the responsibility for payment under a forged mandate. The Law Commission, like the Privy Council in the *Tai Hing* case, believe that the banks are best placed to protect themselves against the consequences of paying on a forged mandate through the use of contract terms such as verification clauses. We have already considered the limitations of that approach (see above, Note 4).

8.   Many of the common law obligations of the customer exemplified in *Macmillan* are, so far as they relate to the use of plastic cards, now set out in the *Banking Code* and the *Business Banking Code* (2008 edns). The customer's obligation—under para 12.7 of both Codes—to advise the card issuer when the card has been lost or stolen, or when someone else knows his personal identity number (PIN) necessary to use the card, probably falls within the ambit of *Macmillan* (R Lawson (1992) 142 NLJ 346, p 354). Both Codes state that the customer's liability for unauthorised use of the card prior to the card issuer being informed of the loss or theft of the card, or that someone else knows the PIN, is limited to a maximum of £50, provided the customer has not acted fraudulently or without reasonable care (para 12.12). This provision extends the protection given only to users of credit-tokens under ss 83 and 84 of the Consumer Credit Act 1974 to users of every type of card (with the exception of digital cash cards, referred to in both Codes as 'electronic purses', and dealt with separately under paras 12.15–12.17, when the £50 restriction only applies if the electronic purse is credited with unauthorised withdrawals from the account). However, para 12.11 of both Codes goes further and provides that the customer 'will' be liable for all losses if he acted fraudulently, and that he 'may' be held liable for losses caused by his failure to act with reasonable care (which may apply where the customer fails to follow the safeguards set out in paras 12.5 or 12.9, or does not keep to their account's terms and conditions—see below, p 840). The 2008 revision of both Codes extends this to online banking (para 12.13).

9.   What happens if the customer benefits from an incorrect entry on his bank statement through, for example, the bank's error in crediting the customer's account with the same sum twice over? If the bank acts within a reasonable time it can rectify the statement to show

the true facts. If the wrongly credited sum has actually been paid out, the bank can seek to recover it as money paid under a mistake of fact. However, if the customer has innocently relied to his detriment on the erroneous credit, eg by spending more money than he would otherwise have done, and it would be inequitable to require him to effect reimbursement, the bank will be estopped from asserting the mistake and prevented from recovering the sum (*United Overseas Bank v Jiwani* [1976] 1 WLR 964, although here the bank was not estopped from recovering its overpayment because the customer ought to have known that the unduly high balance on his account was incorrect). Alternatively, the customer could raise a defence of change of position against the bank's claim (see above, p 583). Furthermore, a bank is not entitled to dishonour cheques drawn bona fide and without negligence on the faith of an incorrect entry in the customer's bank statement (*Holland v Manchester and Liverpool District Banking Co Ltd* (1909) 25 TLR 386, 14 Com Cas 241).

QUESTIONS

1. A leaves his cheque book with B knowing that B has previously been convicted of forgery. B forges A's signature on the cheques and cashes them at A's bank. Can the bank debit A's account?

2. A employs B as his wages clerk. B presents a cheque for £10,000 to A for his signature. B tells A that the cheque is in payment of B's annual bonus of £1,000 (which B has in fact earned). As A is in a hurry he signs the cheque without noticing the discrepancy. If A's bank honours the cheque, can it debit A's account with £10,000? If B had simply forged A's signature on the cheque would A's bank be entitled to debit A's account with £1,000? See *B Liggett (Liverpool) Ltd v Barclays Bank Ltd* [1928] 1 KB 48 (the facts of the case are set out, and the decision analysed, above, p 642).

3. A employs B as his wages clerk. B forges A's signature on one of A's cheques and cashes it at A's bank. When A sues his bank for wrongful debit to his account, the bank pleads that A is vicariously liable for B's fraud. Will the bank succeed with this defence? The defence was pleaded but not pursued in the *Tai Hing* case. It gains support from dicta of Richmond J in *National Bank of New Zealand Ltd v Walpole and Patterson Ltd* [1975] 2 NZLR 7 at 14, and that of La Forest J (dissenting) in *Boma Manufacturing Ltd v Canadian Imperial Bank of Commerce* (1996) 140 DLR (4th) 463 at 499 (the facts of the case appear above, p 541). It does not matter for these purposes that the employee (or agent) is acting in furtherance of his own interests and not those of his employer (or principal), so long as he is acting within the course of his employment (or within the scope of his actual or apparent authority): *Crédit Lyonnais Bank Nederland NV v Export Credit Guarantee Department* [1999] 1 All ER 929, HL; *Lloyd v Grace, Smith & Co* [1912] AC 716, HL, as explained in *Dubai Aluminium Co Ltd v Salaam* [2002] UKHL 48, [2003] 2 AC 366 at [39], [114]. See also EP Ellinger, E Lomnicka and RJA Hooley, *Ellinger's Modern Banking Law* (4th edn, 2006), pp 448–449.

4. A and B are directors of C Ltd. C Ltd has instructed its bank that A is authorised to draw on the company's account jointly with B. In fact A draws a cheque for £1,000 without obtaining B's signature and this is honoured by the bank. Subsequently, B hears of this and makes an entry into the company's books recording that a loan of £1,000 has been made to A. Six months later the new board of directors of C Ltd resolve to bring an action against the bank for breach of mandate. Advise the bank. See *London Intercontinental Trust Ltd v Barclays Bank Ltd* [1980] 1 Lloyd's Rep 241; *Limpgrange Ltd v BCCISA* [1986] FLR 36; *HJ Symons & Co v Barclays Bank plc* [2003] EWHC 1249 (Comm); *Izodia v Royal Bank of*

Scotland International Ltd (1 August 2006, unreported), Royal Court of Jersey: noted (2007) 3 JIBFL 143.

5.   Despite an instruction printed in his cheque book which states that a line should be drawn after the payee's name, A draws a cheque leaving a space between the payee's name and the printed words 'or order'. A hands the cheque to his friend B for delivery to the payee but B inserts 'per B' in the space after the payee's name, indorses it 'B' and obtains payment from A's bank. Can the bank debit A's account? See *Slingsby v District Bank Ltd* [1931] 2 KB 588; affd [1932] 1 KB 544; cf *Lumsden & Co v London Trustee Savings Bank* [1971] 1 Lloyd's Rep 114 at 121.

14 TERMINATION OF BANKER-CUSTOMER RELATIONSHIP

The banker–customer relationship will continue until terminated by the customer, by the bank or by operation of law. Usually the courts deal with termination of the banker–customer relationship in the context of closure of the customer's account, although it is important to note that some aspects of the relationship may continue beyond then, eg the banker's duty of confidentiality in respect of the customer's account extends beyond the point when the account is closed (*Tournier v National Provincial and Union Bank of England* [1924] 1 KB 461 at 473, CA: see above, p 689), and the customer's claims in respect of unauthorised transactions will, in the absence of an agreement to the contrary, continue to be valid (*Limpgrange Ltd v Bank of Credit and Commerce International SA* [1986] FLR 36). As the banker-customer relationship is contractual, the normal rules as to termination of contracts apply.

Fixed-term deposit accounts will mature at the agreed time so that neither bank nor customer may unilaterally terminate their relationship before then, although in practice the bank will usually allow the customer to close the account prematurely on sufferance of an interest penalty. Customers with current accounts or ordinary deposit accounts may unilaterally terminate the relationship at any time by drawing out the remaining funds *and* asking for the account to be closed. In *Bank of Baroda v ASAA Mahomed* [1999] Lloyd's Rep Bank 14, the customer demanded repayment and closure of his deposit account. The bank ignored the demand and continued to operate the account as normal. Some months later the customer's solicitors wrote a letter to the bank making a further demand for repayment, but this was again ignored. A limitation period issue arose which turned on the time of accrual of the customer's cause of action against the bank: was it at the time of the first demand (outside the relevant limitation period) or of the second demand (within the limitation period)? The Court of Appeal held that the customer's cause of action accrued at the time of the second demand and that his claim was not time-barred. Simon Brown LJ held (at 19) that: '[i]f a customer, having demanded closure and repayment of his account, then changes his mind, he can notify the bank accordingly and, assuming always that the bank is content to continue holding the account, the [banker-customer] contract will in effect start afresh. The cause of action arising from the original demand will have ended and a fresh one will arise upon the making of the demand.' His Lordship interpreted the customer's solicitors' letter as implicitly withdrawing the earlier demand and making a new demand from which time started to run afresh. On the assumption that the customer's first demand, by requiring the account to be closed, also operated as notice of termination of the banker-customer contract (which he was not prepared to decide as the relevant factual issues were not argued on appeal), Mantell LJ agreed with Simon Brown LJ's reasoning. It is submitted that Mantell LJ was correct to focus on whether the first demand had the effect of terminating the banker-customer contract, and that he was also right to state in his judgment that neither a customer's demand for repayment (not closure) of the account, nor the bank's failure to comply with that demand, of itself puts an end to that contract. In fact the third member of the court, Mummery LJ, reasoned that neither the customer's first demand, nor the bank's subsequent actions, resulted in the account being closed and the banker-customer contract being terminated, so that, as there was no express or implied terms of the contract preventing the customer making further demands, he was free to make a fresh demand and create a new cause of action. Mantell LJ was prepared to support Mummery LJ's reasoning if, on a true appraisal of the facts of the case, the contract survived the first demand, but it is respectfully submitted that this reasoning is open to the criticism that it leads to the surprising conclusion that a customer will never be time-barred after he makes a demand for repayment, so long as the account is not closed and there is no term of the contract preventing further demands being made.

The *Banking Code* and the *Business Banking Code* (2008 edns) both provide that the bank will close a current account when requested to do so by its customer and, when transferring the account to another financial institution, the bank will provide the new institution with information on standing orders and direct debits within three working days of receiving the new institution's request to do so (see para 7.3 of the former and para 7.1 of the latter code). Following the transfer of a current account, the transferee bank promises to have the new account up and running within ten working days of approving the application (see para 7.4 of the former and para 7.5 of the latter code). Charges incurred through any mistake or unnecessary delay by the bank will be waived (see para 7.5 of the former and para 7.6 of the latter code). These standards represent measures taken by the banking industry to meet the criticism that banks are slow to allow customers to transfer accounts.

It is an implied term of the banker-customer contract that the bank must give reasonable notice before closing a customer's account and terminating their relationship (*Joachimson v Swiss Bank Corpn* [1921] 3 KB 110 at 125, per Warrington LJ, and at 127, per Atkin LJ: above, p 615). Reasonable notice must be long enough in the circumstances to enable the customer to make alternative banking arrangements (*Prosperity Ltd v Lloyds Bank Ltd* (1923) 39 TLR 372). The *Banking Code* and the *Business Banking Code* (2008 edns) both provide that unless there are exceptional circumstances, eg fraud, the bank will not close an account without giving the customer at least 30 days' notice (para 7.6 of the former and para 7.8 of the latter code). The bank does not terminate the banker-customer relationship by simply demanding repayment of the sum outstanding on the customer's account (*National Bank of Greece SA v Pinios Shipping Co, The Maira* [1990] 1 AC 637, HL).

As the relationship between bank and customer is regarded as a personal one, it will automatically terminate by operation of law on the customer's death, insanity, bankruptcy, dissolution (if a partnership) or liquidation (if a company). However, s 75(2) of the Bills of Exchange Act 1882 provides that it is notice of the customer's death that determines the duty and authority of a banker to pay a cheque drawn on him by his customer, and the same rule probably applies in the case of the customer's insanity (see above, p 638). On liquidation of the bank the relationship terminates and the balance standing to the customer's account becomes payable at once without the need of a demand (*Re Russian Commercial*

& Industrial Bank [1955] Ch 148; cf *Bank of Credit and Commerce International SA v Malik* [1996] BCC 15).

15 DISPUTE RESOLUTION

Litigation can be protracted and expensive. In an effort to reduce the time and cost of dispute resolution, a voluntary Banking Ombudsman Scheme was established in 1986. This was one of a range of ombudsman schemes in place across the financial sector. The Banking Ombudsman Scheme was entirely voluntary (although most banks in the United Kingdom joined), unlike the Building Societies Ombudsman Scheme which was compulsory.

The radical changes to the regulation of financial services that came with the FSMA 2000 extended to the various ombudsman schemes. Part XVI of the FSMA 2000 provides for the establishment of an ombudsman scheme for the whole of the financial services industry. The Financial Ombudsman Service (FOS) came into operation on 1 December 2001. It replaces the eight previous dispute resolution schemes, including the Banking Ombudsman Scheme and the Building Societies Ombudsman Scheme.

The FOS has three types of jurisdiction: 'compulsory jurisdiction' (FSMA 2000, s 226), 'voluntary jurisdiction' (FSMA 2000, s 227), and 'consumer credit jurisdiction' (FSMA 2000, s 226A). Its compulsory jurisdiction covers all 'regulated activities' set out in the Financial Services and Markets Act 2000 (Regulated Activities) Order 2001, SI 2001/544, as amended, which includes the acceptance of deposits, as well as mortgage lending and unsecured lending in the form of overdrafts and loan accounts. Banks that are 'authorised persons' under the FSMA 2000 -see above, Section l(b)—must submit to the FOS's jurisdiction with regard to these matters (subject to a right of judicial review); the customer making the complaint need not do so. However, to invoke the compulsory jurisdiction, the complainant must be 'eligible' (FSMA 2000, s 226(2)(a)): this limits access to the scheme to private individuals and small businesses with a turnover of less than £1 million (see Block Four of the FSA's Handbook).

The FOS determines complaints falling within the compulsory jurisdiction 'by reference to what is, in the opinion of the ombudsman, fair and reasonable in all the circumstances of the case' (FSMA 2000, s 228(2)). The FOS takes into account the relevant law, regulations, regulator's rules, guidelines and standards, the Banking Codes and good industry practice (see *R (on the application of IFG Financial Services Ltd) v Financial Ombudsman Service Ltd* [2005] EWHC 1153 (Admin), [2006] 1 BCLC 534: held ombudsman not bound by strict rules of English law where he considers that would not achieve a fair and reasonable result). The FOS may make an 'award' under the compulsory jurisdiction up to £100,000, and the FOS may *recommend* that compensation be paid above that amount (FSMA 2000, s 229(2)(a), (5)). Banks are bound by the award, which is enforceable in the courts; the complainant is not (FSMA 2000, s 228(5)). The FOS may also make a 'direction' under the compulsory jurisdiction (FSMA 2000, s 229(2)(b)), but it does not have power to do so where the direction would require a firm to make a payment that would exceed the statutory cap (*Bunney v Burns Anderson plc* [2007] EWHC 1240 (Ch) at [68], [2008] 1 BCLC 17).

The 'voluntary jurisdiction' extends to unauthorised (as well as authorised) firms and may extend to any activity which could be regulated under the FSMA 2000 (FSMA 2000, s 227). The scope of this jurisdiction is potentially limitless. The FOS's longer-term strategy is to expand the voluntary jurisdiction to cover all authorised firms' financial services activities not caught by the compulsory jurisdiction (see R James and P Morris [2002] PL 640, p 642).

The 'consumer credit jurisdiction' covers activities of firms licensed under the Consumer Credit Act 1974 (as amended by the Consumer Credit Act 2006) to carry on consumer credit and related businesses. Most of the provisions which are applicable to the 'compulsory jurisdiction' also apply to the consumer credit jurisdiction (see s 59 and Sch 2 of the CCA 2006, inserting a new s 226A and Sch 17, Part 3A into the FSMA 2000).

CHAPTER 18
PAYMENT SYSTEMS[1]

1 INTRODUCTION

Payment is a fundamental aspect of commercial transactions. Payment in the legal sense has been defined as 'a gift or loan of money or an act offered and accepted in performance of a money obligation' (RM Goode *Payment Obligations in Commercial and Financial Transactions* (1983), p 11). Any act accepted by the creditor in performance of a money obligation can constitute payment. Payment may be made by the delivery of physical money (ie coins and bank notes by way of legal tender) from the debtor to the creditor. However, payment by the physical delivery of money can be both risky and expensive, incurring transport and insurance costs, as well as loss of interest during transit. These difficulties have led to the development of various forms of payment mechanisms and payment systems. Professor Benjamin Geva, one of the leading commentators in this area, has defined the concept of payment mechanism and payment system in the following terms (B Geva *The Law of Electronic Funds Transfers* (Matthew Bender, New York, looseleaf), s 1.03[l]; and see also B Geva 'The Concept of Payment Mechanism' (1986) 24 Osgoode Hall LJ 1):

Any machinery facilitating the transmission of money which bypasses the transportation of money and its physical delivery from the payor to the payee is a payment mechanism. A payment mechanism facilitating a standard method of payment through a banking system is frequently referred to as a payment system. Payment over a payment mechanism is initiated by payment instructions, given by the payor or under the payor's authority, and is often referred to as a transfer of funds.

In modern business practices, particularly where large sums are involved, and in international transactions, payment is usually made by the transfer of funds from the bank account of the debtor to that of the creditor. In such cases the creditor agrees to accept a claim against his bank in substitution for his claim against his original debtor.

As the creditor's claim against his bank is subject to a credit risk (even banks can fail), and to the off-setting of the claim with a counter-claim, the creditor must consent to payment in this way if it is to amount to discharge of the original debt. The creditor's consent may be

---

[1] The main student textbooks dealing with this subject are EP Ellinger, E Lomnicka and RJA Hooley *Ellinger's Modern Banking Law* (4th edn, 2006), Ch 13; R Cranston *Principles of Banking Law* (2nd edn, 2002), Chs 8–10; R Goode *Commercial Law* (3rd edn, 2004), Ch 17. For more detailed treatment, see *Paget's Law of Banking* (13th edn, 2007), Ch 17 (contributed by RJA Hooley); P Cresswell et al (eds) *Encyclopaedia of Banking Law* (looseleaf), Division Dl 'Payment and Payment Systems' (ed RJA Hooley). For an international perspective, see B Geva *The Law of Electronic Funds Transfers* (looseleaf), and for an excellent comparative treatment, see B Geva *Bank Collections and Payment Transactions—Comparative Study of Legal Aspects* (2001).

express or implied, eg from the fact that he has provided the debtor with his bank account number on his invoice or stationery. The mere fact that the creditor has a bank account is not in itself to be construed as evidencing his tacit consent to accept payment into that account (*Customs and Excise Comrs v National Westminster Bank plc* [2002] EWHC 2204 (Ch), [2003] 1 All ER (Comm) 327, applying *TSB Bank of Scotland plc v Welwyn Hatfield District Council* [1993] 2 Bank LR 267: see below, p 766). Nevertheless, the courts have shown themselves willing to construe the terms of commercial agreements to allow for payment through the transfer of funds between bank accounts. In *Tenax Steamship Co Ltd v Reinante Transoceanica Navigation SA, The Brimnes* [1973] 1 WLR 386; affd [1975] 1 QB 929, CA, under the terms of a charterparty the debtor agreed to pay the creditor $51,000 'in cash in US currency'. Brandon J held that 'cash must be interpreted against the background of modern commercial practice' and 'cannot mean only payment in dollar bills or other legal tender of the United States'. His Lordship held that, in this context, payment 'in cash' meant 'any commercially recognised method of transferring funds the result of which is to give the transferee the unconditional right to the immediate use of the funds transferred'. Brandon J's formulation was later approved by the House of Lords in *A/S Awilco of Solo v Fulvia SpA di Navigazione of Cagliari, The Chikuma* [1981] 1 WLR 314 with substitution of 'unfettered or unrestricted' for 'unconditional' as the adjective before 'right'. Much depends on the context in which the payment obligation arises. Thus, in the context of a customer withdrawing money from his bank account the court will not imply the customer's agreement to waive his right to payment in cash, however large the amount (*Libyan Arab Foreign Bank v Bankers Trust Co* [1989] QB 728, where Staughton J ordered the bank to pay its customer US $292 million in cash!).

2   THE NATURE OF A FUNDS TRANSFER

Payment by funds transfer involves the adjustment of balances on the accounts of the payer and the payee. The payer's account is debited and the payee's account is credited. Thus, the debt owed to the payer by his bank is extinguished or reduced *pro tanto* (or, where the account is overdrawn, his liability to the bank increased) by the amount of the transfer to the payee, whilst the debt owed to the payee by his own bank is increased (or, where the account is overdrawn, his liability is reduced) by the same amount. Property rights are not transferred between accounts (see the extract below). The receipt of a payment message from the payer, or from the payee acting under the payer's authority, leads to the adjustment of the separate property rights (ie choses in action) of the payer and payee against their own banks.

Regina v Preddy
[1996] AC 815, House of Lords

The defendants were charged with obtaining or attempting to obtain mortgage advances from building societies and other lending institutions by deception contrary to s 15(1) of the Theft Act 1968. The defendants had deliberately given false information when they submitted their mortgage applications. In cases where the advances were approved, they were paid, not in cash, but by the CHAPS electronic transfer of funds from the bank account of the lending institution to the account of the defendant (or his solicitor). In each case payment instructions were transmitted over a computer-to-computer telecommunications link between the bank of the lending institution and the bank of the defendant (or his solicitor), which resulted in a debit entry in the former's bank account and a corresponding credit entry in the latter's bank account. Net settlement between the banks took place at the end of each day over their accounts held at the Bank of England. The key question for the House of Lords was whether this process meant that the defendants had 'obtain[ed] property belonging to another' as required by s 15(1). Reversing the Court of Appeal ([1995] Crim LR 564), the House of Lords held that it did not, which resulted in the defendants' convictions being quashed.

Lord Goff of Chieveley: ...I now turn to the first question which your Lordships have to consider, which is whether the debiting of a bank account and the corresponding crediting of another's bank account brought about by dishonest misrepresentation amount to the obtaining of property within section 15 of the Act of 1968.

Under each count, one of the appellants was charged with dishonestly obtaining, or attempting to obtain, from the relevant lending institution an advance by way of mortgage in a certain sum. In point of fact it appears that, when the sum was paid, it was sometimes paid by cheque, sometimes by telegraphic transfer, and sometimes by the CHAPS (Clearing House Automatic Payment System) system. However in the cases where the sum was paid by cheque the appellants were not charged with dishonestly obtaining the cheque. A useful description of the CHAPS system is to be found in the Law Commission's Report, Criminal Law: Conspiracy to Defraud (1994) (Law Com No 228), p 39, n 83. It involves electronic transfer as between banks, and no distinction need be drawn for present purposes between the CHAPS system and telegraphic transfer, each involving a debit entry in the payer's bank account and a corresponding credit entry in the payee's bank account.

The Court of Appeal in the present case concentrated on payments by the CHAPS system. They considered that the prosecution had to prove that the relevant CHAPS electronic transfer was 'property' within section 15(1) of the Act of 1968. They then referred to the definition of property in section 4(1) of the Act as including 'money and all other property, real or personal, including things in action and other intangible property;' and they concluded, following the judgment of the Court of Appeal in *Reg v Williams (Jacqueline)* (unreported), 30 July 1993, that such a transfer was 'intangible property' and therefore property for the purposes of section 15(1).

The opinion expressed by the Court of Appeal in *Reg v Williams* on this point was in fact obiter. The case related to a mortgage advance, the amount having been paid by electronic transfer. The court however concluded that a sum of money represented by a figure in an account fell within the expression 'other intangible property' in section 4(1), and that the reduction of the sum standing in the lending institution's account, and the corresponding increase in the sum standing to the credit of the mortgagor's solicitor's account, constituted the obtaining of intangible property within section 15(1).

In holding that a sum of money represented by a figure in an account constituted 'other intangible property,' the court relied upon the decision of the Privy Council in *Attorney-General of Hong Kong v Nai-Keung* [1987] 1 WLR 1339, in which an export quota surplus to a particular exporter's requirements, which under the laws of Hong Kong could be bought and sold, was held to constitute 'other intangible property' within section 5(1) of the Hong Kong Theft Ordinance (Laws of Hong Kong, 1980 rev. c. 210) (for present purposes identical to section 4(1) of the English Act of 1968). I feel bound to say that that case, which was concerned with an asset capable of being traded on a market, can on that basis be differentiated from cases such as the present. But in any event, as I understand the position, the Court of Appeal were identifying the sums which were the subject of the relevant charges as being sums standing to the credit of the lending institution in its bank account. Those credit entries would, in my opinion, represent debts owing by the bank to the lending institution which constituted choses in action belonging to the lending institution and as such fell within the definition of property in section 4(1) of the Act of 1968.

My own belief is however that identifying the sum in question as property does not advance the argument very far. The crucial question, as I see it, is whether the defendant obtained (or attempted to obtain) property *belonging to another*. Let it be assumed that the lending institution's bank account is in credit, and that there is therefore no difficulty in identifying a credit balance standing in the account as representing property, ie a chose in action, belonging to the lending institution. The question remains however whether the debiting of the lending institution's bank account, and the corresponding crediting of the bank account of the defendant or his solicitor, constitutes obtaining of that property. The difficulty in the way of that conclusion is simply that, when the bank account of the defendant (or his solicitor) is credited, he does not obtain the lending institution's chose in action. On the contrary that chose in action is extinguished or reduced pro tanto, and a chose in action is brought into existence representing a debt in an equivalent sum owed by a different bank to the defendant or his solicitor. In these circumstances, it is difficult to see how the defendant thereby obtained *property belonging to another,* ie to the lending institution.

Professor Sir John Smith, in his commentary on the decision of the Court of Appeal in the present case [1995] Crim LR 564, 565–566, has suggested that 'Effectively, the victim's property has been changed into another form and now belongs to the defendant. There is the gain and equivalent loss which is characteristic of, and perhaps the substance of, obtaining.' But even if this were right, I do not for myself see how this can properly be described as obtaining property belonging to another. In truth the property which the defendant has obtained is the new chose in action constituted by the debt now owed to him by his bank, and represented by the credit entry in his own bank account. This did not come into existence until the debt so created was owed to him by his bank, and so never belonged to anyone else. True, it corresponded to the debit entered in the lending institution's bank account; but it does not follow that the property which the defendant acquired can be identified with the property which the lending institution lost when its account was debited. In truth, section 15(1) is here being invoked for a purpose for which it was never designed, and for which it does not legislate.

I should add that, throughout the above discussion, I have proceeded on the assumption that the bank accounts of the lending institution and the defendant (or his solicitor) are both sufficiently in credit to allow for choses in action of equivalent value to be extinguished in the once case, and created in the other. But this may well not be the case; and in that event further problems would be created, since it is difficult to see how an increase in borrowing can constitute an extinction of a chose in action owned by the lending institution, or a reduction in borrowing can constitute the creation of a chose in action owned by the defendant. It may be that it could be argued that in such circumstances it was the lending institution's bank whose property was 'obtained' by the defendant' but, quite apart from other problems, that argument would in any event fail for the reasons which I have already given. For these reasons, I would answer the first question in the negative.

Lord Jauncey of Tullichettle: My Lords, these cases turn upon the words 'belonging to another' in section 15(1) of the Theft Act 1968. In applying these words to circumstances such as the present there falls to be drawn a crucial distinction between the creation and extinction of rights on the one hand and the transfer of rights on the other. It is only to the latter situation that the words apply.

It would be tempting to say that the appellants by deception obtained money belonging to the lenders and therefore offences have been committed. That however would be to adopt a simplistic approach ignoring the nature of the precise transactions which are involved. I start with the proposition that the money in a bank account standing at credit does not belong to the account holder. He has merely a chose in action which is the right to demand payment of the relevant sum from the bank. I use the word money for convenience but it is of course simply a sum entered into the books of the bank. When a sum of money leaves A's account his chose in action quoad that sum is extinguished. When an equivalent sum is transferred to B's account there is created in B a fresh chose in action being the right to demand payment of that sum from his bank. Applying these simple propositions to the cases where sums of money are transferred from the lender's account to the account of the borrower or his solicitor either by telegraphic transfer or by CHAPS the lender's property which was his chose in action in respect of the relevant sum is extinguished and a new chose in action is created in the borrower or his solicitor. Thus although the borrower has acquired a chose in action quoad a sum of money of equal value to that which the lender had right, he has not acquired the property of the lender which was the latter's right against his own bank. It follows that section 15(1) has no application to such a situation. The position is, of course, even more obvious if the lender's account is in debit at the time of transfer in which event he has no right to demand payment of the sum transferred.

[Lord Mackay of Clashfern LC, Lord Slynn of Hadley and Lord Hoffmann concurred.]

NOTES

1.   It is something of a misnomer to speak of the 'transfer' of funds as there is no actual transfer of coins or banknotes from the payer to the payee. In *Foskett v McKeown* [2001] 1 AC 102 at 128, Lord Millett stressed that '[n]o money passes from paying bank to receiving bank or through the clearing system (where the money flows may be in the opposite direction). There is simply a series of debits and credits which are causally and transactionally linked'. (See also *Customs and Excise Comrs v FDR Ltd* [2000] STC 672 at [37], CA and *Dovey v Bank of New Zealand* [2000] 3 NZLR 641 at 648, NZ CA.) Moreover, there is no assignment to the payee of any debt that may be owed to the payer by his own bank (*Libyan Arab Foreign Bank v Bankers Trust Co* [1989] QB 728 at 750, Staughton J). *Preddy* involved a credit transfer, but the same principle also applies in the case of a debit transfer (for the distinction between credit and debit transfers, see below). Thus, payment by direct debit does not operate to vest in the payee any rights of the payer against his own bank (*Mercedez-Benz Finance Ltd v Clydesdale Bank plc* [1997] CLC 81, Outer House of the Court of Session) and s 53(1) of the Bills of Exchange Act 1882 expressly provides that a bill of exchange (including a cheque, which is a debit instrument), of itself, does not operate as an assignment of funds in the hands of the drawee bank available for the payment thereof (see also *Deposit Protection Board v Dalia* [1994] 2 AC 367 at 400, HL). In each case it is probably more accurate to speak in terms of the *transfer of value,* rather than the transfer of funds, from payer to payee (see David Fox's useful note on *Preddy* in [1996] LMCLQ 456, p 459).

2.   Some advances were paid by telegraphic transfer, but the House of Lords held that no distinction need be drawn for present purposes between the CHAPS system (details of which are set out below, p 732) and telegraphic transfers (see Lord Goff above). In some cases advances were made by cheque, but the House of Lords were not asked whether as 15(1) offence had been committed in these circumstances. However, Lord Goff stated (*obiter*) that no offence would have been committed under the section because again there had been no obtaining of property belonging to another. As Lord Goff emphasised (at 835–837), when a payee deceives a drawer into drawing a cheque in his favour, the payee does not obtain a chose in action belonging to the drawer against his own bank (for the cheque does not constitute a chose in action in the hands of the drawer), the payee acquires a new chose in action, namely his right of action against the drawer on the cheque. The High Court of Australia has declined to follow *Preddy* on this point (*Parsons v R* (1999) 73 ALJR 270 at 277, 'a cheque has characteristics which render it more than a chose in action held by the payee against the drawer'). See further R Hooley 'Payment in a Cashless Society' in Ch 13 of BAK Rider (ed) *The Realm of Company Law* (1998), pp 240–241, where the issue of theft of the piece of paper constituting the cheque itself, touched on by Lord Goff in *Preddy,* is also considered.

3.   *Preddy* exposed an important lacuna in the criminal law. The Law Commission acted quickly and in its report, *Offences of Dishonesty: Money Transfers* (Law Com No 243), published on 10 October 1996, only three months after *Preddy* was decided, proposed, *inter alia*, a new s 15A of the Theft Act 1968 introducing a specific offence of 'obtaining a money

transfer by deception'. Lord Goff introduced the Law Commission's draft Bill into the House of Lords on 24 October 1996, and it was enacted as the Theft Act (Amendment) Act 1996 on 18 December 1996. In fact, both s 15 and s 15A of the Theft Act 1968 have since been repealed by the Fraud Act 2006, which creates a new offence of 'fraud' (s 1). The new offence includes fraud by false representation (s 2), which does not require the defendant to have obtained 'property belonging to another'.

QUESTION

Would the defendants in *Preddy* have obtained 'property belonging to another' if the building society had paid out the mortgage advance in bank notes?

3 TERMINOLOGY

There had been some attempt to standardise the terminology in this area. This has arisen from the influence of art 4A of the American Uniform Commercial Code (adopted in 1989) and the UNCITRAL Model Law on Credit Transfers (1992). The same terminology was adopted in Directive 97/5/EC on cross-border credit transfers, and has entered English law with the implementation of that Directive through the Cross-Border Credit Transfer Regulations 1999, SI 1999/1876. Although the Regulations only apply to cross-border credit transfers in the currencies of EC Member States (including EEA States) and the euro of up to the equivalent of 50,000 euro, the terminology adopted in those Regulations is likely to have much wider influence. In anticipation of that development, the same terminology is adopted in this Chapter. It is summarised in the Prefatory Note to art 4A of the Uniform Commercial Code (UCC) as follows:[2]

X, a debtor, wants to pay an obligation owed to Y. Instead of delivering to Y a negotiable instrument such as a check or some other writing such as a credit card slip that enables Y to obtain payment from a bank, X transmits an instruction to X's bank to credit a sum of money to the bank account of Y. In most cases X's bank and Y's bank are different banks. X's bank may carry out X's instruction by instructing Y's bank to credit Y's account in the amount that X requested. The instruction that X issues to its bank is a 'payment order'. X is the 'sender' of the payment order and X's bank is the 'receiving bank' with respect to X's order. Y is the 'beneficiary' of X's order. When X's bank issues an instruction to Y's bank to carry out X's payment order, X's bank 'executes' X's order. The instruction of X's bank to Y's bank is also a payment order. With respect to that order, X's bank is the sender, Y's bank is the receiving bank, and Y is the beneficiary. The entire series of transactions by which X pays Y is known as the 'funds transfer'. With respect to the funds transfer, X is the 'originator', X's bank is the 'originator's bank', Y is the 'beneficiary' and Y's bank is the 'beneficiary's bank'. In more complex transactions there are one or more additional banks known as 'intermediary banks' between X's bank and Y's bank. In the funds transfer the instruction contained in the payment order of X to its bank is carried out by a series of payment orders by each bank in the transmission chain to the next bank in the chain until Y's bank receives a payment order to make the credit to Y's account.

It should be noted, however, that art 4A restricts the term 'fund transfer' to credit transfers and excludes debit transfers from its scope. In this chapter, the same terminology is used for both credit and debit transfers.

---

[2] The idea of citing the Prefatory Note for this purpose comes from Professor Sir Roy Goode: see RM Goode *Commercial Law* (3rd edn, 2004), p 466.

4 CREDIT/DEBIT TRANSFERS

Funds transfer operations can be classified as either credit transfers or debit transfers according to the way payment instructions are communicated to the originator's bank.

With a *credit transfer* the originator (payer) instructs his bank to cause the account of the beneficiary (payee), at the same or another bank, to be credited. The originator's instruction may be for an individual credit transfer, eg by bank giro credit (see below, p 732) or CHAPS payment (see below, p 732), or for a recurring transfer of funds under a standing order (standing orders are instructions given by a customer to his bank to make regular payments of a fixed amount to a particular beneficiary). On receipt of the originator's instruction, the originator's bank will debit the originator's account, unless the originator has provided his bank with some other means of reimbursement, and credit the beneficiary's account where it is held at the same bank, or, where the beneficiary's account is held at another bank, forward instructions to the beneficiary's bank, which will credit the beneficiary's account.

With a *debit transfer* the beneficiary (payee) conveys instructions to his bank to collect funds from the originator (payer). These instructions may be initiated by the originator himself and passed on to the beneficiary, for example, as happens with the collection of cheques (see below, p 771); alternatively, they may be initiated by the beneficiary himself pursuant to the originator's authority, as happens with direct debits where the originator signs a mandate authorising his bank to pay amounts demanded by the beneficiary (the beneficiary's failure properly to implement a correctly completed direct debit mandate might constitute a breach of an implied term of the underlying contract between them, or even a breach of

Flows of funds
Direction of credit instructions
Direction of debit instructions
Advice

Figure 1 Credit and debit transfers

a duty of care in tort owed by the beneficiary to the originator: *Weldon v GRE Linked Life Assurance Ltd* [2000] 2 All ER (Comm) 914). On receipt of instructions from the beneficiary, the beneficiary's bank usually provisionally credits the beneficiary's account with the amount to be collected and forwards instructions to the originator's bank, which will debit the originator's account. The credit to the beneficiary's account becomes final when the debit to the originator's account becomes irreversible.

The movement of payment instructions and funds in both credit and debit transfers is illustrated by Figure 1.

The originator's order to his bank to make a credit transfer to the beneficiary (whether by standing order mandate, bank giro credit, CHAPS payment order, letter, facsimile or telex etc) is not a negotiable instrument (*Tenax Steamship Co Ltd v Brimnes (Owners of), The Brimnes* [1915] QB 929 at 949,969, CA: funds transfer order given by telex). There is no mercantile custom that credit transfer orders are capable of being transferred from one person to another by delivery (or indorsement and delivery), or that they give the bona fide purchaser for value a title which is free from the defects of title of prior parties, which are the two essential requirements for a negotiable instrument (*Crouch v Crédit Fonder of England* (1873) LR 8 QB 374 at 381–381, per Blackburn J: see above, p 520). The same applies in the case of debit transfer orders, save where the debit transfer is effected by a cheque, which may be a negotiable instrument (although most cheques issued in the UK are not negotiable instruments because they are crossed 'account payee' and, therefore, not transferable: see below, p 768). Yet despite the fact that credit and debit transfer instructions are not afforded the status of negotiable instruments, the courts nevertheless seem prepared, as a matter of modern commercial practice, to regard payment by at least one form of funds transfer operation, namely by direct debit, as having certain characteristics normally associated with payment by negotiable instrument (see the next case).

Esso Petroleum Co Ltd v Milton
[1997] 2 All ER 593, Court of Appeal

Esso owned two garages operated and managed by Milton under licence. Under the terms of two licence agreements, one for each garage, Milton was obliged to purchase all his petrol supplies from Esso and pay for them on or before delivery by direct debit. Milton was forbidden to sell petrol at prices greater than those notified to him by Esso. Towards the end of 1995 Esso instructed Milton to cut petrol prices in the face of stiff pricing competition and it also increased his site rentals. Milton complained that this made his operations unprofitable and, in order to put pressure on Esso, he cancelled his direct debit mandate when almost £170,000 was owing to Esso for petrol supplied. Esso applied for summary judgment under RSC Ord 14 (now see the Civil Procedure Rules 1998, Part 24). Milton admitted the claim, but alleged that the increasingly stringent financial terms which Esso had imposed amounted to a repudiatory breach of contract, and he counterclaimed damages which he sought to set off in equity in extinction of his debt to Esso. The first instance judge dismissed Esso's application for summary judgment, but Esso successfully appealed on two grounds. The first was that Milton's counterclaim, even if good, would not give rise to an equitable set-off. The second was that no set off or counter-claim is available where payment was made, or agreed to be made, by direct debit.

Simon Brown LJ (dissenting): ...I turn, therefore, to Esso's arguments as to why such a counterclaim, being for an unliquidated sum and, accordingly, available only by way of equitable set-off, is not in the present circumstances available to the respondent. These arguments are, first, that the respondent is in the same position as had he countermanded payment by cheque; a claim following a cancelled direct debit mandate is, Esso submit, equivalent to a claim on a dishonoured cheque to which elementarily a mere right of equitable set-off can never constitute a defence (the direct debit argument). . . .

The direct debit system is increasingly commonly used and its essential nature is well known. Those unfamiliar with the system will find it conveniently described in *Chitty on Contracts* (27th edn, 1994) vol 2, paras 33–302 ff.

Esso submit that the closest analogy with the system would be for the intending purchaser to provide a number of signed blank cheques to be presented by the supplier on delivery of the goods or services contracted for. In neither case, they point out, can the creditor prevent the debtor from countermanding his instruction to the bank and in neither does the bank itself assume a direct payment obligation to the creditor. Thus, the creditor in both cases is exposed to the risk of non-payment through the debtor countermanding his instructions. The central question presently arising is whether under the direct debit scheme the debtor should be entitled to escape the specially restrictive rules as to the stay of judgments and the scope of defences which apply with regard to dishonoured cheques. In submitting not, Mr Hapgood [Counsel for Esso] relies upon the well-known authority of *Nova (Jersey) Knit Ltd v Kammgarn Spinnerei GmbH* [1977] 2 All ER 463, [1977] 1 WLR 713, where the House of Lords by a four to one majority overturned the Court of Appeal's decision, which had allowed a plaintiff's action on a dishonoured bill of exchange to be stayed pending the resolution of the defendant's counterclaim for unliquidated damages (see [1976] 2 Lloyd's Rep 155). Lord Wilberforce said ([1977] 2 All ER 463 at 470, [1977] 1 WLR 713 at 721):

> When one person buys goods from another, it is often, one would think generally, important for the seller to be sure of his price: he may [have] (as indeed the appellants here have) bought the goods from someone else whom he has to pay. He may demand payment in cash; but if the buyer cannot provide this at once, he may agree to take bills of exchange payable at future dates. These are taken as equivalent to deferred instalments of cash. Unless they are to be treated as unconditionally payable instruments (as the Bills of Exchange Act 1882, s 3, says, 'an unconditional order in writing'), which the seller can negotiate for cash, the seller might just as well give credit. And it is for this reason that English law (and German law appears to be no different) does not allow cross-claims, or defences, except such limited defences as those based on fraud, invalidity, or failure of consideration, to be made. I fear that the Court of Appeal's decision, if it had been allowed to stand, would have made a very substantial inroad on the commercial principle on which bills of exchange have always rested.

Mr Hapgood points out that almost no cheques today are in fact negotiable instruments: virtually all are crossed account payee only. The creditor's expectations, he submits, are the same irrespective of whether the debtor is to pay by cheque or, as commercially now is found generally more convenient, by direct debit. The differences between the two means of payment are, he submits, for present purposes, technical and immaterial. Mr Hapgood also refers to a judgment of my own in *Esso Petroleum Co Ltd v Craft* [1996] CA Transcript 47 in which, refusing the defendant's ex parte application in this court for leave to appeal against summary judgment in circumstances not dissimilar to the present (save only that the counterclaim there was for damages for alleged short deliveries in the past rather than future loss of profits), I said:

> Payment for that [the particular delivery giving rise to the claim for £ 16,000-odd] was due under a direct debit arrangement, a liability equivalent to that arising upon a dishonoured cheque which, in turn, is to be treated as akin to cash.

As the first instance judgment in that case records, however, it was 'common ground that the status of a direct debit . . . is similar to a cheque or other bill of exchange'. Whether that was rightly conceded is, of course, the very point at issue on this appeal.

Mr Soole [Counsel for Milton] submits that the position here is quite unlike that arising when a cheque is countermanded. In the first place, Esso's claim here is one for the price of goods sold and delivered, not on a dishonoured cheque. And that is no mere technicality: the respondent in this case gave no specific instruction to his bank to pay for these particular deliveries. It is one thing, Mr Soole submits, to cancel a general direct debit mandate; quite another to countermand payment of a signed cheque. Esso's argument, he submits, overlooks the central distinction between the (debtor's) bank mandate and the (creditor's) request for a payment submitted pursuant to it. The mandate does not constitute a cheque, not least because it is not an instruction to pay 'a sum certain in money' as required by the Bills of Exchange Act 1882. And the request, so far from being a signed instrument equivalent to cash provided by the debtor, is drawn rather by the creditor.

In short, submits Mr Soole, the respondent is really in no different position than had he agreed to pay for deliveries by cash or cheque and then declined to do so. What he did was to dishonour a promise, not a cheque. His termination of the mandate gives Esso no rights independently of the licence agreement.

Before expressing my own conclusions on this important point it is, I think, worth setting out verbatim the final written formulation of Esso's argument:

ESSO'S PROPOSITIONS OF LAW Payment by direct debit is equivalent to payment by cash. Accordingly:

(1) In an action for the recovery of a debit, (a) the defence of set-off is not available to a defendant who has wrongfully countermanded a direct debit instruction to his bank and (b) execution of judgment will not be stayed pending the trial of a counterclaim.

(2) Countermand is wrongful if the defendant has expressly or impliedly promised to pay the debt by direct debit.

(3) The plaintiff must plead and prove (a) the consideration for the debt, (b) the defendant's agreement to pay the debt by direct debit and (c) the dishonour of the direct debit.

(4) As in an action by the payee of a dishonoured cheque against the drawer, it is a good defence for the defendant to prove fraud inducing the issue of the direct debit or its invalidity (for example, on the ground that it was issued without the defendant's authority).

By way of oral elaboration of those propositions, Mr Hapgood doubted whether the word 'wrongfully' was strictly required in para (1) (in which event para (2) would be unnecessary); explained that the reference in para (2) to an implied promise was included to enable a future decision to be reached on whether the opening of a direct debit mandate itself gives rise to a promise to pay by that system (such decision being unnecessary in the present case); accepted a variation suggested by Sir John Balcombe that there be added to para (2) the words 'and the plaintiff had not received notice of countermand of the direct debit at the time when consideration moved from him'; and explained that para (3)(a) reflected his recognition of the fact that, unlike the position with cheques, in direct debit cases there is no presumption of consideration in favour of the plaintiff.

Powerfully argued although Esso's case was on this issue, and commercially convenient although no doubt it would be in many, perhaps most, instances to place direct debt arrangements on the same footing as cheques, I find myself ultimately unpersuaded by the argument.

By no means all direct debit cases are akin to actions on a cheque—that, indeed, is reflected in the very complexity of Esso's final formulation of their argument. Of course there will be occasions when a direct debit arrangement is stipulated and accepted by the supplier, just like a cheque, as an alternative to a demand for cash payment. But that will not invariably be so, and I have no doubt that many direct debit arrangements are nowadays entered into for the settlement of transactions effected on credit rather than in substitution for cash transactions. I may have a charge account at a store which routinely allows its customers 28 days' credit. Were I, for convenience, to enter into an agreement to pay my account by periodic direct debit payments, that surely ought not to deny me my basic credit entitlement, nor limit the scope of such defences as would otherwise be available to me were some purchase to prove unsatisfactory. Similarly with service providers.

   There are, of course, certain obvious similarities between cheques and direct debit arrangements just as there are obvious differences too. I find the similarities insufficient to justify deciding as a matter of policy and principle that for Ord 14 purposes the two are equivalent. Nor indeed does such an extension of the special rule for enforcing claims on dishonoured cheques seem to me commercially necessary—to avoid, as Mr Hapgood sought to submit, the supplier having to insist on payment by cash or cheque before delivery. Instead, a supplier intent on achieving by direct debit a position equivalent to that of the holder of a cheque can do so—as, indeed, by their third argument Esso assert they have—by expressly excluding equitable rights of set-off.

Thorpe LJ: . . . [O]n the direct debit argument, I would hold for the appellant. Whilst I am conscious of difficulties and dangers involved in such an extension, I believe that it is consistent with the principle stated by Lord Wilberforce in *Nova (Jersey) Knit Ltd v Kammgarn Spinneret GmbH* [1977] 2 All ER 463 at 470, [1977] 1 WLR 713 at 721). Where goods are effectively sold for cash, the seller should have the security that cash brings when for mutual convenience, the parties have adopted the banking mechanism in general usage for the transfer of cash from one account to another. Twenty years ago that was still by cheque. Theoretically the tanker driver could demand a signed cheque on arrival for an amount to be written in when ascertained by completion of the fuel delivery. But that is only theory. The defendant's annual petrol purchases under the licence agreements amounted to about £5m, and, as the evidence established, Esso's daily collection through the direct debit system for all petrol sales varies between £9m and £20m. The modern mechanism for handling what are effectively cash sales on that scale is the direct debit system. So, it seems to me, that it is a natural evolution rather than an extension of the *Nova Knit* principle to hold that the seller of goods for cash transferred by the direct debit mechanism should be in no worse position than if he had accepted a cheque on delivery. Mr Hapgood QC's formulation emerged in reply and was then modified in argument. No doubt it requires further consideration and perhaps further modification, but I would accept the fundamental principle for which he contends.

Sir John Balcombe: . . . I agree with Thorpe LJ and would allow the appeal also on the ground of the direct debit argument. This is essentially a question of policy. As the evidence in the case discloses— and it is a fact of which we can take judicial notice—modern commercial practice is to treat a direct debit in the same way as a payment by cheque and, as such, the equivalent of cash. The fact that a cheque is, technically, a negotiable instrument is for this purpose irrelevant; in any case modern practice is to require payment by cheque crossed ' A/C Payee only', which is not negotiable. It is its equivalence to cash which is the essential feature of a direct debit and which makes relevant Lord Wilberforce's explanation for the reason why a defence of set-off is not normally allowed in the case of a claim based on a bill of exchange (see *Nova (Jersey) Knit Ltd v Kammgam Spinnerei GmbH* [1977] 2 All ER 463 at 470, [1977] 1 WLR 713 at 721). I accept that the precise circumstances in which a payment by direct debit will preclude a defence of set-off may require to be worked out as further cases show different combinations of fact but, like Thorpe LJ, I accept the fundamental principle that, in general, a payment by direct debit for goods or services received should preclude a defence of set-off.

NOTE

If the majority (Thorpe LJ and Sir John Balcombe) are right on this point, and there must be considerable doubt that they are (see the extract below), their reasoning could also be applied to payment made, or agreed to be made, by other forms of credit and debit transfer between bank accounts, eg by standing order.

'"Pay Now, Sue Later"—Direct Debits, Set-Off and Commercial Practice' by A Tettenborn

(1997) 113 LQR 374, pp 375–377

With the greatest respect to the majority, it is submitted that the direct debit aspect of the decision is hard to support.

To begin with, there is an issue of legal principle. In seeking to equiparate direct debiting arrangements with cheques and bills of exchange, the majority view takes no account of one crucial juridical difference between them. Where goods or services are paid for by cheque, not one but two contracts are in existence: one on the cheque itself, the other arising out of the underlying transaction. The contracts are discrete, and the payee may sue on either: but, as Pollock CB pointed out in *Warwick v Nairn* (1855) 10 Exch 762 at p. 764, the rule precluding set-off only applies to the former. But this analysis simply cannot apply to payments by direct debit. There is no such thing as an action on a direct debit; there is no separate contact contained in a direct debit apart from the underlying contract of sale—or whatever. As Simon Brown LJ pertinently observed (at p. 601), the plaintiffs in *Esso v Milton* were suing for goods sold and delivered, no more, no less: and if this is so it is difficult to see any legal reason to deny the defendants their ordinary rights of set-off which they would have in any other contract of sale.

Not only is the majority decision hard to justify on principle: it is also difficult to support commercially or as a matter of policy. *Pace* Thorpe LJ it is suggested that the origin of, and justification for, the special rules relating to negotiable instruments do not lie in their use as convenient payment mechanisms to obviate the necessity of transferring cash. They lie instead in the transferability of such instruments as commercial paper (a point which, incidentally, explains why the anti-set-off rule applies equally to promissory notes, which are not really payment mechanisms at all, but are nevertheless transferable in the market). If it is envisaged that the holder of a cheque or bill of exchange may want to transfer or discount it for cash, it makes good commercial sense to make it as effective an instrument as possible by limiting severely the factors which may go to impugn the obligation to pay contained in it. But no such argument can apply to direct debits, which are not, and never were intended to be, readily transferable: they are merely a convenient means of arranging for the transfer of funds to the payee. From which it must follow that there is no need to extend to him the jealous and peculiar protection afforded to the holder of a bill of exchange.

Nor, despite its initial attractiveness, is there (with respect) much in a further argument advanced by Thorpe LJ; that since direct debits are set up as a quick and easy means of payment of regular bills, it would be unfair to deprive the payee of the assurance of prompt and full payment which such arrangements give him. The answer to this is straightforward: if the supplier of goods or services wants such an assurance (as well he may), he can always have it by the simple expedient of stipulating in his contract that payments are to be made without deduction or set-off. (Indeed, Esso argued that they had done just this in *Esso v Milton* by virtue of one of the terms of their contract, but in the event it was held that the relevant clause was not sufficiently explicit to have this effect.) But there is, it is submitted, no demonstrated need to go further and say that such a stipulation is implicit in the nature of direct debits themselves. . . .

It remains to mention one more general issue. As Thorpe LJ pointed out (at p 606), the point that cheques are transferable negotiable instruments, whereas direct debits are not, has one logical weakness. Whatever may have been the position in the nineteenth century, when the rule 'pay now and sue the payee later' grew up, today in practice nearly all cheques are non-transferable because they bear the words 'account payee' on their face (see S.81A of the Bills of Exchange Act 1982). Yet, as his Lordship observed, the 'pay now and sue later' rule still applies to them in full force; and if so, why not equally to non-transferable direct debits?

Now, his Lordship's premise is clearly right: but his conclusion is, it is respectfully submitted, a little perverse. If cheques today are indeed just a convenient (non-transferable) means of switching cash balances from one account to another, the logical answer is surely not to extend the 'pay now, sue later' rule but to restrict it: that is, to make cheques more like other means of payment, and not *vice versa*. If we are to recognise changing commercial practice, as we clearly should, there must now be a powerful case for taking cheques outside the rule entirely, so as to limit it to promissory notes and bills of exchange proper where it belongs. Indeed, one might even go further and question whether cheques should continue to come under the regime of the Bills of Exchange Act at all, since any similarity between a modern-day cheque and a traditional bill of exchange is pretty tenuous. But that raises large issues of banking law and practice well beyond the purview of this note.

5 CLEARING AND SETTLEMENT

(a) Clearing

Payment effected through a payment system is initiated by payment instructions given by the originator (payer), or someone else acting with his authority (beneficiary/ payee), to his own bank. In cases where the payment is not 'in-house' (see below), the originator's instructions will lead to further payment instructions passing between the originator's bank and the beneficiary's bank, sometimes through the intermediation of other banks. The process of exchanging payment instructions between participating banks is known as clearing. Clearing may take place through a series of bilateral exchanges of payment instructions between banks, but in the United Kingdom it is more common for clearing to take place multilaterally through a centralised clearing house.

Payment systems are classified as either paper-based or electronic depending on the medium used for inter-bank communication of payment instructions (B Geva *The Law of Electronic Funds Transfers* (looseleaf), s 1.03 [4]). In a paper-based funds transfer system the paper embodying the payment instruction is physically transferred from one bank to another, eg by direct courier or at a centralised clearing house. The cheque and credit clearing are paper-based funds transfer systems (see below, p 732). By contrast, with an electronic funds transfer system the inter-bank communication of payment instructions is by electronic means, for example by magnetic tape, disc or, more usually, telecommunication link. The major inter-bank electronic funds transfer systems in the United Kingdom are the services operated by BACS Payment Schemes Ltd and Voca Ltd ('BACS') and the payment system run by the CHAPS Clearing Company Ltd ('CHAPS'), which incorporates a facility to make sterling and euro payments (see below, p 732).

(b) Settlement

Where the originator and beneficiary have accounts at the same bank, the transfer of funds between the two accounts will usually involve a simple internal accounting exercise at the bank (known as an 'in-house' transfer). The originator's account is debited and the beneficiary's account is credited. The position will be different where the originator's account and the beneficiary's account are held at different banks (known as an 'inter-bank' transfer). In such cases an inter-bank payment instruction will pass from bank to bank, sometimes from the originator's bank directly to the beneficiary's bank, otherwise via intermediary banks which each issue their own payment instruction to the next bank down the chain, until a payment instruction finally reaches the beneficiary's bank. Each inter-bank payment instruction must be paid by the bank sending the instruction to the bank receiving it. It is this process whereby payment is made between the banks themselves of their obligations *inter se* which is known as settlement.

Settlement can occur on either a bilateral or multilateral basis. Bilateral settlement occurs where the bank sending the payment instruction and the bank receiving it are correspondents, meaning that each holds an account with the other. Settlement is effected through an adjustment of that account. Multilateral settlement involves the settlement of accounts of the sending bank and the receiving bank held at a third bank. The third bank could be a common correspondent of the two banks, ie one where they both have accounts; alternatively, and more typically, the third bank could be a central bank. The fact that settlement is usually effected across accounts held at the central bank means that payments involving a particular currency are usually routed through the country of that currency, eg a transfer of US dollars from an originator in London to a beneficiary in Zurich will usually be settled in New York. But note that with the introduction of the single European currency, the euro in 1999—the UK has yet to join the single currency—the linkage between currency and country is removed for inter-bank payments in euro within the EU (for further details, see P Cresswell et al (eds), *Encyclopaedia of Banking Law* (looseleaf), Division Dl 'Payment and Payment Systems' (ed R Hooley), paras 325ff).

Settlement may be either gross or net. With gross settlement the sending and receiving banks settle each payment order separately without regard to any other payment obligations arising between them (see Figure 2 below). This is usually done on a real-time basis, with settlement across the accounts of participating banks held at the central bank as each payment instruction is processed. With net settlement the mutual payment obligations of the parties are set off against each other and only the net balance paid. This process occurs periodically with net balances being settled either at the end of the day ('same-day' funds) or on the following day ('next-day' funds).

Net settlement may be either bilateral or multilateral. (The text which follows is only concerned with payment netting and not with the netting of contractual commitments, for example as carried out in a variety of contracts such as foreign exchange contracts, repurchase agreements, securities trades and derivatives.) In a bilateral net settlement system a participant's exposure is measured by reference to its net position with regard to each individual counterparty and not by reference to the system as a whole (see Figure 3 below). In a multilateral net settlement system a participant's position is measured by reference to its net position with regard to all other participants in the system as a whole. As a result, each participant with end up as a net net debtor or a net net creditor in relation to all other participants in the system. Multilateral netting may arise through direct determination of multilateral net positions (see Figure 4(a) below) or indirectly by netting the net bilateral positions and thereby obtaining net net positions (see Figure 4(b) below). In each case settlement follows the multilateral netting process (see Figure 5 below).

The process of gross and net settlement is illustrated in the following diagrams (reproduced with kind permission of Mario Giovanoli from his chapter 'Legal Issues Regarding Payment and Netting Systems' in JJ Norton, C Reed and I Walden (eds) *Cross-Border Electronic Banking: Challenges and Opportunities* (1st edn, 1995), Ch 9).

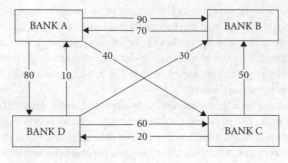

Number of payments: 9
Total volume of transactions: 450

Figure 2 Gross payments without netting

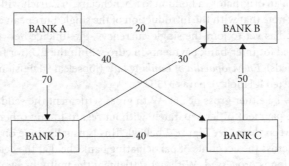

Number of payments: 6
Total volume of transactions: 250

Figure 3 Bilateral netting (bilateral net positions)

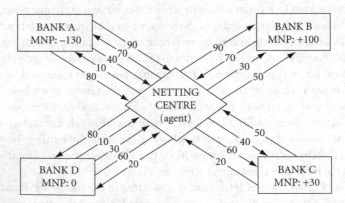

Figure 4 (**a**) Multilateral netting -1. Netting phase (2 systems) Direct multilateral netting: direct determination of multilateral net positions (MNP)

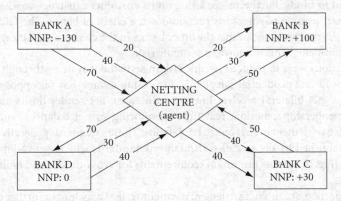

Figure 4(b) Indirect multilateral netting: determination of 'net-net' positions (NNP) by netting the net bilateral positions

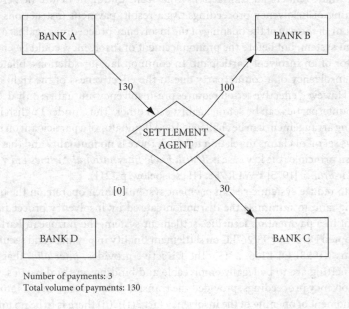

Number of payments: 3
Total volume of payments: 130

Figure 5 Multilateral netting—2. Settlement phase

There are a number of advantages to be gained from net settlement: it reduces the number and value of inter-bank settlement operations, this leads to reduced transaction costs, liquidity is maintained, and it reduces insolvency losses provided netting withstands insolvency. On the other hand, net settlement does result in exposure to several types of risk, including receiver risk (R Sappideen, 'Cross-border electronic funds transfers through large value transfer systems, and the persistence of risk' [2003] JBL 584 at 589 and 593). A bank receiving a payment instruction from another bank participating in a payment system usually makes funds available to its own customer before it has itself been placed in funds on completion of the multilateral net settlement at the end of the day (assuming the receiving bank turns out to be a net creditor). Thus, the receiving bank carries the risk that it might never be placed in funds. Furthermore, acting on its customer's instruction, the receiving bank might itself pass on payment instruction down a chain of banks. The failure of one bank to make payment may mean that the other banks in the chain cannot meet their own payment commitments. This is known as systemic risk.

There are various ways to reduce systemic risk in settlement systems through the introduction of appropriate prudential safeguards, for example same-day (as opposed to next-day) settlement; net bilateral receiver limits (credit caps); net sender limits (debit caps); appropriate membership criterion; real time monitoring of net balances; and schemes which guarantee settlement even if one party defaults. These safeguards generally follow the framework established by the so-called Lamfalussy standards which were adopted by the G-10 central banks in 1990 as minimum requirements for cross-border and multicurrency netting systems.

Failure of a participant in a net settlement payment system may lead to further difficulties under insolvency law. Certain states have rules giving retroactive effect to the pronouncement of insolvency. The zero-hour rule, which applies, for example, in the Netherlands, Austria and Italy, renders all transactions void from midnight before (ie zero hour) the actual opening of insolvency proceedings. As a result, payment instructions introduced after zero hour of the day of the opening of the insolvency proceedings against a participant in a payment system, but before the pronouncement of insolvency, could be challenged by the liquidator of an insolvent participant. In common law jurisdictions, bilateral netting withstands insolvency of a counterparty due to the effectiveness of the right of set-off in insolvency. However, effective set-off requires pre-insolvency mutuality; only debts between the same counterparties can be set-off against each other. Thus, under English law a multi-lateral netting arrangement can be challenged by a liquidator of a participant on the grounds that it allows set off of claims in relation to which there is no mutuality and that it infringes the *paripassu* principle (the key case is *British Eagle International Airlines Ltd v Compagnie Nationale Air France* [1975] 1 WLR 758, HL: see below, p 1211).

In order to reduce systemic risk in payment systems which operate on the basis of payment netting, and to minimise the disruption caused by insolvency proceedings against a participant in a payment or securities settlement system, the European Parliament and Council adopted Directive 98/26/EC on settlement finality in payment and securities settlement systems ([1998] OJ L166, p 45). The Directive provides, *inter alia,* that (i) transfer orders and netting are to be legally enforceable and binding on third parties, even in the event of insolvency proceedings, provided the transfer orders were entered into the system before the moment of opening of the insolvency (art 3(1)); (ii) there is to be no unwinding of a netting because of the operation of national laws or practice which provide for the setting aside of contracts and transactions concluded before the moment of opening of insolvency proceedings (art 3(2)); (iii) a transfer order is not to be revoked by a participant in a system, nor by a third party, from the moment defined by the rules of that system (art 5); and (iv) insolvency proceedings are not to have retrospective effect on the rights and obligations of a participant arising from, or in connection with, its participation in a system earlier than the moment of opening of such proceedings (art 7). The moment of opening of insolvency proceedings is the moment when the relevant judicial or administrative authority handed down its decision (art 6(1)).

The United Kingdom has implemented the Directive through the Financial Markets and Insolvency (Settlement Finality) Regulations 1999, SI 1999/2979 (for an excellent summary, see LS Sealy [2000] CifLR 221). The Regulations apply only to systems which are accorded designation by a 'designating authority'. In its capacity as a designating authority, the Bank of England has granted the CHAPS electronic funds transfer system designated system status. Part III of the Regulations largely displace the rules of insolvency law, giving precedence to the proceedings of the relevant designated system. This reverses the effect of the ruling in *British Eagle* so far as those designated systems are concerned.

Nevertheless, concern about systemic risk in large-value transfer systems led the EU central banks to adopt the principle that Member States should each develop their own real-time gross settlement system for large-value payments. The United Kingdom made CHAPS a real-time gross settlement system in April 1996 (see below, p 732). The various real-time gross settlement systems of Member States of the EU are now connected by TARGET, which is the payment system arrangement allowing high value payments in the new European single currency (the euro) to be made in real-time across borders within the EU. With real-time gross settlement, receiver risk is significantly reduced as no intraday credit is granted to participants in the system. However, lack of credit means that participants must have funds available at the central bank to meet their payment obligation before they can send payment instructions. This reduces liquidity and can lead to gridlock (ie the system cannot get going until participants have received sufficient credits from other participants), although this can be avoided through the central bank offering secured overdraft facilities to participating banks ('daylight overdrafts') or entering into repurchase arrangements. The effectiveness and robustness (whether before insolvency or on insolvency) of arrangements of this nature have been strengthened by the European Parliament and Council Directive 2002/47/EC on financial collateral arrangements ([2002] OJ L168/43), implemented in the UK through the Financial Collateral Arrangements (No 2) Regulations 2003, SI 2003/3226.

6   CLEARING SYSTEMS AND CLEARING RULES

The term 'clearing system' can be used in one of two senses:

In Its narrow sense, 'clearing system' is a mechanism for the calculation of mutual positions within a group of participants ('counterparties') with a view to facilitating the settlement of their mutual obligations on a net basis. In its broad sense, the term further encompasses the settlement of the obligations, that is, the completion of payment discharging them.

[B Geva 'The Clearing House Arrangement' (1991) 19 Can BLJ 138]

A clearing system is operated by an organisation known as a clearing house. The banks which participate in a clearing system (known in the United Kingdom as 'clearing banks') are members of the clearing house. They are bound by the rules of the clearing house through a multilateral contract (although administrative procedures and technical specifications set out in the rules may not be intended to be legally binding). The multilateral contract may arise where the member contracts with the clearing house to conform to the rules; the member is then deemed to have contracted with all other members on the terms of its individual undertaking (on the same principle as applied in *Clarke v Dunraven, The Satanita* [1897] AC 59). Alternatively, the members of the clearing system may agree together to abide by the system rules. The rules must be interpreted against the background of the manner and operation of the particular clearing system. Any interpretation of the rules must also be in accordance with the nature of the rules themselves (see R Cranston *Principles of Banking Law* (2nd edn, 2002), pp 281–282).

A customer of a clearing bank may be bound by, and able to rely on, the clearing house rules against his own bank through an implied term of the banker-customer contract (it is always open for the clearing house rules to be expressly incorporated into a bank's contract with its customer but this is unlikely in practice). The customer is taken to have contracted with reference to the reasonable usage of bankers, including those clearing house rules which represent such reasonable usage (*Hare v Henty* (1861) 10 CBNS 65; *Tayeb v HSBC Bank plc* [2004] EWHC 1529 (Comm), [2004] 4 All ER 1024 at [57]). However, where clearing house rules derogate from the customer's existing rights, the usage codified in the rules will be deemed unreasonable and will not bind the customer without his full knowledge and consent (*Barclays Bank plc v Bank of England* [1985] 1 All ER 385 at 394; see also *Turner v Royal Bank of Scotland plc* [1999] 2 All ER (Comm) 664, CA: above, p 698). In order to rely on the clearing house rules against a member bank other than his own bank, the customer would have to bring himself within the ambit of the Contracts (Rights of Third Parties) Act 1999, which may prove difficult, not least because the member banks may have 'contracted out' of the Act (as occurs, for example, with the CHAPS Rules, Version 1.7, October 2007, r 11.1.1). Agency arguments are likely to prove equally problematical.

There are the four major clearing systems in the United Kingdom; each is run by an independent company operating under the umbrella of the Association for Payment Clearing Services (APACS is the body responsible for money transactions and payment clearing activity generally in the United Kingdom). The main clearing systems are as follows:

(1) the cheque clearing system (operated by the Cheque and Credit Clearing Co Ltd), which is used for the physical exchange of cheques, although see below, p 773 for an assessment of the impact of truncation on cheque clearing (the cheque clearing is considered in detail below at pp 771 et seq);

(2) the credit clearing system (also run by the Cheque and Credit Clearing Co Ltd), which is a paper-based credit transfer system used for the physical exchange of high-volume, low-value, credit collections such as bank giro credits;

(3) BACS (operated by BACS Payment Schemes Ltd and Voca Ltd), which provides a high-volume, low-value, bulk electronic clearing service for credit and debit transfers, including standing orders, direct debits, wages and salaries, pensions and other government benefits;

(4) CHAPS, which is a dual currency system operated by the CHAPS Clearing Co Ltd. It is made up of an electronic sterling credit transfer clearing, normally used for high value transfers, called CHAPS sterling, and an electronic euro credit transfer clearing, called CHAPS euro, that enables euro payments to be made both domestically between member banks and building societies in the United Kingdom and also between those members and members of other realtime gross settlement ('RTGS') systems elsewhere in the EU through TARGET, which is the interlinking network connecting the various RTGS systems operating in individual EU Member States.

Save for CHAPS, which incorporates a facility to make sterling and euro payments and is a real-time gross settlement system, the other clearing systems are multilateral net settlement systems with settlement of balances across the participants' accounts held at the Bank of England at the end of each day.

APACS also oversees the currency clearings, which clear paper-based payment orders drawn in foreign currencies on United Kingdom banks. Following the introduction of the euro, and the subsequent demise of legacy currencies in the euro zone, all currency clearings, apart from US dollar clearing, closed in 2002. A major clearing system available to UK banks, but operating outside the APACS umbrella, is the Euro Banking Association's multilateral cross-border clearing and settlement system providing same-day settlement for euro payments. There are also a number of other payment networks operating outside APACS, such as the Visa and MasterCard networks, which handle various types of payment cards (see below, Chapter 20).

7 DUTIES OF THE BANKS INVOLVED IN A FUNDS TRANSFER

(a) The originator's bank

(i) Relationship with the originator

Where the originator instructs his bank to transfer funds from his account, either to that of a separate beneficiary or to another account of the originator, the originator's bank is under a duty to exercise reasonable care and skill in carrying out those instructions.

Royal Products Ltd v Midland Bank Ltd
[1981] 2 Lloyd's Rep 194, Queen's Bench Division

The plaintiffs ('Royal Products'), a Maltese company, instructed the defendant bank ('Midland') to transfer £13,000 by cable from their current account with Midland in the United Kingdom to their account with the Bank of Industry, Commerce and Agriculture Ltd ('BICAL') in Malta. Midland regularly employed the Bank of Valletta ('National') in Malta as its correspondent and so telexed National instructing it to transfer £13,000 to BICAL. Although National was aware that BICAL was facing liquidity problems at the time, National made the transfer of £13,000 to BICAL and notified BICAL that that amount was to be credited to Royal Products' account. The following day BICAL collapsed and Royal Products failed to receive any of its funds, which had already been debited by Midland from Royal Products' account in the United Kingdom. Royal Products brought an action against Midland claiming the return of £13,000 or damages. Two of Royal Products' main claims were (a) that National were their agents, owing and having broken certain duties and obligations of a fiduciary nature for breach of which Midland were liable, and (b) even if National were not their agents, Midland were vicariously liable for the negligence of National, who acted as Midland's agents (it was not alleged that Midland were in breach of duty themselves). Webster J rejected these claims and gave judgment for Midland.

Webster J: …The question whether [Royal Products] make good any of these claims depends in the first instance on the terms of their instructions to Midland and on the implications of law arising out of those instructions.

The instructions and their implications

Royal Products' instructions were contained in a letter dated Nov 23, 1972, which must have been delivered by hand to Midland on that day. They read:

> *Account No 30039748*
>
> Will you please transfer by full rate cable the sum of £13,000 to our Account No 008516 with the Bank of Industry, Commerce & Agriculture Ltd, Commercial House, South Street, Valetta, Malta. Your cable charges are to be for our account.

The background to these instructions is important. When the instructions were given, Royal Products were, as I have said, a customer of Midland, having a current account with them, and they were also a customer of BICAL, having a current account with that bank also; and they had given similar instructions before. It is also in my view relevant to note that Midland took, as I infer, no fee from the transaction. By letter dated Nov 24,1972, they wrote to Royal Products:

> We have to advise you that in accordance with your request of 23rd instant, we have arranged by cable for the following payment to be effected.
>
> | | |
> |---|---|
> | *Beneficiary* | Yourselves |
> | *Amount* | £13,000 |
> | *Charges* | £10.00 |
>
> *Total amount of* £13,010.00 is being debited to your Company's Account.

When similar instructions had been given on previous occasions Midland had transferred the credit direct, without using the services of National, and this was the first occasion on which they had used those services for this particular purpose in relation to Royal Products. There is no evidence before me as to the manner in which Royal Products contemplated that the transfer would be effected by Midland, but in a letter written on Oct 1, 1979, during the course of these proceedings, in answer to a request by Midland's solicitors, Royal Products' solicitors wrote saying that they admitted that Midland 'were entitled to use the services of the National Bank of Malta as sub agents'. I conclude that Royal Products did not mind how the transfer was effected provided that it was effected, or at least initiated, forthwith, that is to say by a cable sent on the same day, Nov 23. Nor was any evidence adduced as to what Royal Products expected of BICAL if the instructions were implemented and I infer, from the surrounding circumstances which I have mentioned and from the nature of the instructions, that they expected no more than that, when credit or payment was received, the sum should forthwith be credited to Royal Products' current account with BICAL. It was Midland, not Royal Products, who inserted in their instructions to National the words 'for advice credit Royal Products', meaning, as I find, that BICAL were to advise Royal Products of the credit, and, although that fact is consistent with the fact that Royal Products may have expected to be informed when their account was credited, it is not sufficient, in my view, to enable Royal Products' instructions to be read as if they included such a requirement. I return to this point later in this judgment.

What, then, are the legal implications of those instructions? How are they to be regarded, as a matter of law? In my judgment they are to be regarded simply as an authority and instruction, from a customer to its bank, to transfer an amount standing to the credit of that customer with that bank to the credit of its account with another bank, that other bank being impliedly authorized by the customer to accept that credit by virtue of the fact that the customer has a current account with it, no consent to the receipt of the credit being expected from or required of that other bank, by virtue of the same fact. It is, in other words, a banking operation, of a kind which is often carried out internally, that is to say, within the same bank or between two branches of the same bank and which, at least from the point of view of the customer, is no different in nature or quality when, as in the present case, it is carried out between different banks. I use the word 'operation' advisedly, in an attempt to distinguish and exclude a contract, for in my judgment the instructions did not bring into existence, as between Royal Products and Midland, any separate or distinct contract of any kind. In this respect, therefore, the circumstances of this case differ from those of *Calico Printers' Association v Barclays Bank Ltd. and the Anglo-Palestine Co Ltd* (1930) 38 Lloyd's Rep 105; [1930] 36 Com Cas 71, where the defendant bank took ¼ per cent, commission (see Mr Justice Wright at pp 110 and 80), although in other respects to which I will allude later it seems to me that the principle to be derived from the judgment of Mr Justice Wright in that case can be applied to the present one.

Given that this was an ordinary banking operation, as I hold that it was, it follows that in carrying out its part of the transaction Midland owed Royal Products a duty to use reasonable care and skill: see *Selangor United Rubber Estates Ltd v Cradock and Others (No 3),* [1968] 2 Lloyd's Rep 289; [1968] 2 All ER 1073, and *Karak Rubber Co Ltd v Burden and Others (No 2),* [1972] 1 Lloyd's Rep 73; [1972] 1 All ER 1210 and that they would be vicariously liable for the breach of that duty by any servant or agent to whom they delegated the carrying out of the instructions. Midland, therefore, would be liable to Royal Products for National s negligence, if any, in that respect. But in my judgment National owed no duty of any kind direct to Royal Products. Although Midland were entitled, as Royal Products later admitted, to execute the instructions by using the services of National as their correspondents, Royal Products had given Midland no authority which would have had the effect of creating privity of contract between them and National, which was the principle applied by Mr Justice Wright in *Calico Printers* case so as to exclude privity of contract between the plaintiffs and the 'sub-agent' in that case. In my judgment, therefore, National are not to be regarded as having been agents of Royal Products and did not, therefore, owe them any of the duties, including a fiduciary duty, owed by an agent to his principal.

It follows from what I have said that in my view the relevant law is accurately stated in the following passages from the *Law of Banking* by Lord Chorley, 6th edn at p. 374:

> The substantial difference between the branch and the correspondent is that while the former is managed by the servants of the banker acting under his supervision and control, the latter is independently in business and acts only on occasion as an agent and at his discretion. The fact that the correspondent is a legal entity independent of the banker who employs him does not, however, mean that there exists any contractual relationship between him and the banker's customers on whose business he is being employed...As between the customer and his banker, however, the latter is liable for the acts of his correspondent in exactly the same way and within the same limits as for those of his managers and servants, for it is immaterial to the customer whether the banker operates through a branch or through a correspondent, unless, of course, the banker expressly stipulates that he is not to be so liable.

Finally, before turning to the subsequent facts and while still considering the implications of Royal Products' original instructions, it is necessary to decide what had to be done to enable Midland, or National, to contend that those instructions had been fulfilled. Unless there is any authority which compels me to decide otherwise, I would hold that Midland had carried out Royal Products' instructions when it had enabled Royal Products to draw on or otherwise use the amount of credit transferred, which Royal Products would have been able to do once Midland had, in one way or another and either directly or indirectly, made funds available to BICAL to the extent of £13,000 and had notified BICAL that that sum was to be credited to the account of Royal Products. Mr Tugendhat on behalf of Royal Products advanced two arguments in relation to this question which I should mention at this stage. First, in reliance on *Rekstin v Severn Sibirsko and the Bank for Russian Trade,* [1933] 1 KB 47, he submitted that the instructions had not been complied with until BICAL had assented to the receipt of the credit. I reject that submission. In the first place the facts in that case were a long way from the facts in the present case. This is a case of the transfer of a customer's credit from one of his banks to another. *Rekstin's* case was one in which a judgment debtor sought to transfer an amount standing to the credit of its current account at a bank to the current account of another customer of that bank, a customer which enjoyed diplomatic immunity and to which it, the judgment debtor, owed nothing. I respectfully agree with the comment made by Mr Justice Kerr in *Momm and Others v Barclays Bank International Ltd* [1976] 3 All ER 588 at p 597, when he said that in his view that decision should be confined to its special facts.

Secondly he submitted, as a general proposition, that the doctrine of strict compliance was to be applied to the instructions given in this case so that, if they were not strictly complied with, National was precluded from contending that they had been complied with at all. I reject that contention if Mr Tugendhat means (which I suspect that he does not) that there was some duty on Midland or National which required them to do more than comply with Royal Products' instructions as those instructions are to be construed as a matter of law. I reject the submission also if by it he means that in construing those instructions I should, as a matter of law or banking practice, give a legal implication to each detail of them, for it seems to me that the doctrine which would lead to that result has little application to the facts of the present case, having received its first authoritative recognition by Lord Sumner in *Equitable Trust Co of New York v Dawson Partners Ltd* (1926) 27 Lloyd's Rep 49, in the context of confirmed credits. It may be that that doctrine has been or should be applied to all documentary credits; but the transaction in this case is not a 'documentary credit' within the meaning of that expression contained in the Uniform Custom and Practice for Documentary Credits…

I conclude, therefore, that no authority precludes me from holding, as I do, that in order to comply with Royal Products' instructions Midland were required, in the present case by National, their agents, to make funds available to BICAL in one way or another to the extent of £13,000 and to notify BICAL that that sum was to be credited to the account of Royal Products.

[Webster J went on to hold on the facts that Midland had complied with Royal Products' instructions and that National had not been negligent in making the transfer to BICAL when it did.]

NOTES

1.   The duty of a bank to adhere to the terms of its mandate is strict. A bank has no right to debit its customer's account where it acts on a forged or unauthorised mandate. The rule is well established for forged cheques and is premised on banks being 'bound to know the handwriting of their customers' (*Smith v Mercer* (1815) 6 Taunt 76 at 86, per Heath J). However, a bank may also receive funds transfer instructions through the use of an electronic access device, eg via a computer terminal, where the customer uses a password or access code, or through the use of a plastic card in a point of sale terminal or automated teller machine, together with the customer's personal identification number. Whereas a handwritten signature is individual to, and identifies, the signer; the use of an electronic access device does not identify the person who actually gave the instruction: 'it is very much like a door key facilitating entry to the system or, better, a seal affixed to an instrument, authenticating it, but not identifying the one who actually placed it' (B Geva 'Unauthorized Electronic Funds Transfers—Comparative Aspects', Ch 5 in JS Ziegel (ed) *New Developments in International Commercial and Consumer Law* (1998), p 110). A third party may have assumed control of the access device or have been able to bypass it altogether, but from the bank's point of view any technologically effective entry of the access code appears to be a valid authentication. Geva has argued (above) that in an electronic environment the bank's liability should not be strict, but instead premised on its negligence, with a corresponding duty on the customer to exercise reasonable care and diligence to prevent unauthorised electronic funds transfers. Geva continues (pp 110–112):

Typically, such negligence is not individual to a bank employee, as where the latter failed to detect the forgery of a manual signature; rather, in the electronic context, we are concerned with 'systemic negligence', by the bank organization as a whole, on the level of implementing satisfactory computer as well as office procedures…Accordingly, a bank establishing a reasonable security procedure for verifying electronic authentication has discharged its contractual obligation to the customer and may be justified in debiting the customer's account once the procedure has been pursued.

There has been a move towards Geva's approach in the 2008 editions of the *Banking Code* and the *Business Banking Code*, para 12.13 of which state that unless the customer has acted fraudulently or 'without reasonable care' the customer will not be liable for losses which took place through online bank accounts. Online customers are warned, eg, to keep up-to-date anti-virus and spyware software and a personal firewall, and to treat emails claiming to be from a bank 'with caution' (para 12.9).

2.   There are various aspects of the originator's bank's duty to exercise reasonable care and skill. Where the customer does not specify how the transfer is to be made, the bank is free to choose the method of transfer, so long as it exercises reasonable care and skill when making its choice (*Royal Products Ltd v Midland Bank Ltd,* above). Where the customer specifies a particular method of transfer, the bank is not bound to use that method, unless the specification is deemed to be of the essence of the instruction, so long as the alternative method of transfer is at least as secure and as speedy a method of transfer as that specified. In *Dovey v Bank of New Zealand* [2000] 3 NZLR 641, for example, the New Zealand Court of Appeal held that the originator's bank had not breached its contract with the originator when it ignored his instruction to send funds overseas by tested telex and used the faster SWIFT system instead: the specified method was held not to be of the essence of the contract. Where the time of transfer is not specified by the customer, or it cannot be inferred from the method of transfer specified by the customer (eg where the customer instructs his bank to make a CHAPS payment, the inference is that he expects value to be given the same day), the bank must make the payment within a reasonable time (Supply of Goods and Services Act 1982, s 14). Where it is necessary for the originator's bank to employ the services of an intermediary bank it must take reasonable care to engage a reliable intermediary (*Royal Products Ltd v Midland Bank Ltd,* above: although breach of this duty will be hard to establish). The bank must install and maintain a reasonably efficient security system and must exercise reasonable care and skill to ensure that its equipment is operating properly.

3.   It is common practice for the originator's bank to disclaim liability and default of any intermediary bank it employs to execute the fund transfer. Clauses disclaiming liability are usually set out in standard payment instruction forms supplied by the originator's bank for the originator's use. Such a clause may be subject to review under the provisions of the Unfair Contract Terms Act 1977 and the Unfair Terms in Consumer Contracts Regulations 1999, SI 1999/2083 (see above, p 629), but where the payer is a commercial entity the clause is likely to survive such scrutiny (P Cresswell et al *Encyclopaedia of Banking Law* (looseleaf), Division Dl 'Payment and Payment Systems' (ed Hooley), para 853).

Cross-Border Credit Transfer Regulations 1999.[3] In some cases the position of the originator's bank will have to be assessed against the transparency and performance standards imposed by the Cross-Border Credit Transfer Regulations 1999, implementing Directive 97/5/EC on cross-border credit transfers ([1997] OJ L 43/25).[4] These Regulations apply to

---

[3]   SI 1999/1879. For detailed analysis, see R Hooley, 'EU Cross-Border Credit Transfers—The New Regime' [1999] JIBFL 387. The EU also adopted Regulation 2560/2001/EC on 19 December 2001 requiring that bank charges for cross-border payments in euro be the same as for similar national payments ([2001] OJ L 344/13). The Regulation has been implemented in the UK through the Cross-Border Payments in Euro Regulations 2003, SI 2003/488.

[4]   Directive 2007/64/EC on payment services in the internal market, *inter alia,* replaces Directive 97/5/EC. The new Directive has two main objectives. The first objective is to generate more competition in payment markets by removing market entry barriers and guaranteeing market access. The second objective is to provide a simplified and fully harmonised set of rules with regard to information requirements and the rights and obligations linked to the provision and use of payment services. The new Directive will reinforce the

'cross-border credit transfers' which do not exceed 50,000 euro or its equivalent in another EEA currency. A cross-border credit transfer is defined in the reg 2(1) as 'a transaction or series of transactions carried out as a result of instructions given directly by an originator to an institution in one EEA state, the purpose of which is to make funds in an EEA currency available to a beneficiary in another EEA state'. For these purposes, the originator's institution and the beneficiary's institution may be two branches of the same bank located in different EEA states, and the originator and the beneficiary may be one and the same person.

The Regulations alter the position that would otherwise apply at common law. In particular, reg 6 provides for the payment of interest to the originator by the originator's bank where a transfer is not made within the relevant time, unless the delay is attributable to the fault of the originator as the case may be. This gives rise to strict liability on the part of the originator's bank, which is something different from its position at common law where, as we have just seen, liability turns on its failure to exercise reasonable skill and care in and about the execution of the originator's payment order. The originator's bank can recover any compensation paid to the originator from an intermediary bank which may be responsible for the delay. In the absence of agreement to the contrary, the time limit for the originator's bank to ensure money is credited to the beneficiary's bank is the end of the fifth banking day following acceptance of the cross-border transfer order by the originator's bank, so long as the necessary funds were also available to it at that time. Where the originator suffers consequential loss beyond loss of interest, for example, the originator incurs a financial penalty through late payment under the terms of an underlying contract with the beneficiary, any attempt to recover compensation for such loss would fall outside the Regulations. Rights of action in contract and tort, in so far as they may exist, are preserved by reg 15(1), although rules as to remoteness will limit the likelihood of recovery against a bank involved in the funds transfer process.

The Regulations also contain a novel 'money-back guarantee' in the event of a failed transfer. This is to be found in reg 9. Where funds do not reach the beneficiary's bank the originator's first port of call for redress is the originator's bank. Within 14 banking days of the originator's request for a refund, the originator's institution must refund to him the amount of the failed transfer (capped at 12,500 euro or its equivalent in another EEA currency), plus interest and charges. Liability is strict, although certain exceptions apply. Should the failed transfer be for more than 12,500 euro or its equivalent in another EEA currency, or the originator suffers further consequential loss as a result of the failed transfer, he must rely on his common law remedies in contract and tort. Where an originator's bank is liable to refund the originator for a failed transfer, it may pass on that loss to any intermediary bank it instructed, and the loss will then pass down the chain of intermediary banks until it reaches the one responsible for the failed transfer. However, the originator's bank will not be liable to pay a refund if the failed transfer was caused by an error or omission in the instructions given by the originator to the bank or by an intermediate bank nominated by the originator himself. In these circumstances the originator's bank need only exercise all reasonable endeavours to trace and recover the funds. Moreover, in the case of failure through error of an intermediary bank nominated by the beneficiary's bank, the originator has no right to a refund under the

rights and protection of all users of payment services (consumers, retailers, large and small companies and public authorities). But there are limitations to the scope of the new Directive. The new Directive focuses on electronic payments and not payments in cash or by cheque. The new rules will only apply to payments made in an EU currency (whether in euro or in other national currencies used in the EU) where both the payer's payment service provider and the recipient's payment service provider is located in the EU. Member States have until 1 November 2009 to transpose the new Directive into national law.

Regulations. In such a case the EC Directive on cross-border credit transfers provides that the beneficiary's bank is obliged to make funds available to the beneficiary up to a maximum of 12,500 euro (art 8(2)). For credit transfers made from the United Kingdom to another Member State this would be a matter for the law of that other Member State. For credit transfers from another Member State to the United Kingdom, the Regulations provide that where the originator requests a refund under the laws of the other Member State, the beneficiary's bank in the UK must make the amount of the failed transfer available to the beneficiary up to a maximum of 12,500 euro or its equivalent in another EEA currency (reg 11(1), (2)).

The originator's bank will not be liable under the Regulations where the bank's failure to perform its part of the transfer was due to its compliance with relevant money laundering legislation or was due to reasons of *force majeure* (reg 12(1)).

QUESTIONS

1.   Is the relationship between the originator and his bank one of principal and agent?

2.   What of the relationship between the originator's bank and any intermediary bank it employs?

3.   What would be the relationship between the originator's bank and the beneficiary's bank? That of principal/agent, or one of principal/principal?

(ii) Relationship with the beneficiary

The contractual duty of care owed by the originator's bank to the originator does not extend to the beneficiary. There is no contractual link between them, although where the beneficiary is himself a customer of the originator's bank, the bank *in its capacity as the beneficiary's bank* will owe him a contractual duty of care. The Contracts (Rights of Third Parties) Act 1999 is unlikely to assist the beneficiary in this regard. The originator's bank may well have expressly excluded the operation of the Act in the terms agreed with the originator and it is doubtful, even where there is no express exclusion, that within the context of the transaction as a whole the originator and his bank intended to confer an enforceable benefit on the beneficiary (for further reasoning, see *Paget's Law of Banking* (13th edn, 2007), para 17.170). In the normal course of events, the originator's bank will not owe the beneficiary a duty of care in tort (see the next case).

Wells v First National Commercial Bank
[1998] PNLR 552, Court of Appeal

The plaintiff lent money to a Spanish company, secured by a charge on property held by that company in Spain, and by four post-dated bills of exchange issued personally in favour of the plaintiff by U and W, who were owners of the company. The bills of exchange were subsequently dishonoured. The plaintiff commenced proceedings on the bills, those proceedings reaching the stage where either judgment was entered or the plaintiff was entitled to enter judgment. Meanwhile the defendant bank agreed to provide new finance to the company, in return for a first charge on the Spanish property. In order to persuade the plaintiff to release the charge on the property, and in consideration for not entering judgment and/or enforcing judgment in the proceedings on the bills of exchange, the company issued irrevocable instructions to the defendant bank to pay 1 million pesetas to discharge the charge on the property, and to pay a further £275,000 to the plaintiff's solicitors in respect of the sums owing on the bills of exchange. The bank acknowledged receipt of those instructions, knowing that the plaintiff was the intended beneficiary of the payment. There was no direct communication between the bank and the plaintiff. The bank failed to make the transfer. The plaintiff started proceedings against the bank claiming breach of a tortious duty of care. The plaintiff argued that the bank owed him a duty of care because of the irrevocable nature of the payment instructions and the fact that the bank knew that the plaintiff was the intended beneficiary of the transfer. On the bank's application, the judge struck out the plaintiff's claim as disclosing no cause of action. The Court of Appeal dismissed the plaintiff's appeal against that decision.

Evans LJ: ... After noting those preliminary difficulties the judgment proceeds to consider the question whether this was, as counsel had put it, a duty situation as between the plaintiff and the defendants. That is to say, a situation where a person, placed as the bank was after receiving and acknowledging irrevocable instructions from its customer, owed a duty of care to the beneficiary or intended beneficiary of the payment which it was instructed to make.

The learned judge first referred to *Hedley Byrne (Hedley Byrne and Co Ltd v Heller and Partners Ltd* [1964] AC 465). He said that counsel, Mr Pawlak, had not contended before him that the present case could be brought within orthodox *Hedley Byrne* principles. There may have been some misunderstanding and before us Mr Colin Ross-Munro [leading counsel for the plaintiff] has submitted, first, that a claim can be made out under what is called the orthodox *Hedley Byrne* principle. The learned judge then went on to consider what the situation would be if the plaintiffs contentions were correct. He said this, page 8:

> If such a duty of care exists in tort towards the third party, it would have very considerable ramifications for banks. It is a commonplace for banks to be requested by their customers to pay monies to third parties. Indeed, every ordinary cheque drawn on a bank in favour of a named payee is such a request. If the bank wrongly fails to pay the cheque, it may incur a liability to its customer, the drawer. But, I do not believe it has ever been suggested that the bank would also incur a liability to the named payee of an ordinary cheque in the tort of negligence, even if the bank had previously told the customer that it would honour the cheque on presentation.

Mr Ross-Munro submits, first, that the learned judge in that passage failed to record or take account of the distinction between revocable and irrevocable instructions by the customer to the bank. Whilst he is prepared to accept that it might be difficult to establish a duty of care where the instructions were revocable, he submits that it is essential to the plaintiffs argument that in this case the instructions were expressed to be irrevocable.

Mr Ross-Munro, secondly, refers to the passage in the current edition of *Paget's Law of Banking* (11th edn), where there is a passage at page 295 which I should read:

> The relationship with payee
> The paying bank's contractual duty of care and skill does not extend to the payee.... However, it has been suggested that the paying bank owes the payee a tortious duty of care so as to make the bank liable to the payee for its negligence.

That is followed by a reference to recent House of Lords decisions in *Henderson v Merrett Syndicates Ltd* [1995] 2 AC 145 and *White v Jones* [1995] 2 AC 207. The learned editor continues:

> It might be possible to establish such a duty of care under the *Hedley Byrne* principle which was explained in terms of assumption of responsibility by the defendant. It could be argued that the paying banks' assumption of responsibility to its own customer, the payer, should be extended to the intended beneficiary of the payment, the payee. If so this would create a new category of special relationship to which the law attaches a duty of care to prevent economic loss.

Among the footnotes to that passage is the following, No 19:

> Arora, *Electronic Banking and the Law,* (2nd edn 1993), p 149. Although Dr Arora' s reliance on *Anns v Merton London Borough Council* [1978] AC 728 is misplaced as the case was overruled by the House of Lords in *Murphy v Brentwood District Council* [1991] 1 AC 398.

That proposition of law is essentially the one for which Mr Ross-Munro contends in this case. He submits that the burden on the plaintiff is merely to show that the contention is arguable. He enlists of the support of that leading textbook, with the gloss that he emphasises that in the present case the instructions were irrevocable and he goes no further than to submit that a duty of care arises when the instructions are such.

Returning to the judgment, the judge referred to the further House of Lords' decision in *Caparo Industries plc v Dickman* [1990] 2 AC 605 and accurately, as I would say, summarises the effect of that decision in the following passage:

> However, since that decision it is now well-established that for there to be duty to take reasonable care to avoid damage of a particular type (here, pecuniary not physical loss) towards a particular person or category of persons mere foreseeability of damage is not enough. There must also be such a direct and close relationship between the parties as constitutes a relationship of 'proximity' and, in addition, the situation must be one where it is fair, just and reasonable for the law to impose the duty of the scope contended for. In the present case, it is not suggested that there had been any dealing of any sort, or indeed any communication at all, between the Bank and Mr Wells when the Bank received and accepted the letter of instruction of September 29, 1989 from its customer, Granfe.

The learned judge then proceeded to consider the plaintiff's submissions as to *Henderson v Merrett,* on which he commented as follows:

> The *Merrett* case was one where, as Lord Goff put it at page 180G, 'the plaintiff entrusts the defendant with the conduct of his affairs'. I do not believe that the relationship between a Lloyd's managing agent and a Name bears any comparison at all with the situation as it was between the Bank and Mr Wells.

Having referred to *White v Jones* the learned judge said this:

> In my view *White v Jones* is far removed from providing any support, even by analogy, for the [plaintiff's] proposition....

In neither of those passages did the learned judge refer to the distinction between revocable and irrevocable instructions and, again, Mr Ross-Munro submits that by failing to note that distinction the learned judge failed to deal with the plaintiff's essential argument.

The learned judge's final conclusion was this:

> I do not think that either *White v Jones* or the *Merrett* case provide any support for the proposition that, on the facts pleaded, the Bank owed towards Mrs Wells a duty of care to pay the £275,000 as directed in Granfe's letter of instruction of September 29,1989. In my view, it is unarguable that merely by accepting a client's instructions to pay money to a third party a bank incurs a duty in tort towards the third party to comply, or more accurately to take reasonable care to comply, with the client's instructions. A duty of care towards the third party does not arise simply because the bank knows his identity.... If I were to say that there was a duty of care on the present pleaded facts, it would not be an 'incremental' step but, rather, 'a massive extension': cf the observations of Brennan J in the Australian case, *Sutherland Shire Council v Heyman* (1985) 60 ALR 1 at 43 cited with approval by both Lord Bridge and Lord Oliver in *Caparo* [1990] 2 AC 605 at 618D, and 633G–634A.

For my part I must say that I agree entirely both with the learned judge's reasoning and with his conclusion. Mr Ross-Munro's submission that the learned judge failed to take account of the difference between revocable and irrevocable instructions is, of course, a formidable submission. Mr Ross-Munro emphasises that he need show only that the plaintiff's case is arguable, in other words not bound to fail. He emphasises, as already stated, that this is an area of the law which can be said to be in a state of transition, with the narrow 3–2 majority in the House of Lords in *White v Jones*. He submits that the ingredients for establishing a duty of care are all present, whether one adopts the strict *Hedley Byrne* approach or the more general approach shown by *Caparo* and *White v Jones*.

As regards *Hedley Byrne,* he says that there was 'a special relationship' between the bank as payer and the plaintiff as payee. The bank could certainly foresee that the plaintiff as the intended beneficiary of the payment would incur loss if the payment was not made. He emphasises that on a strict application of *Hedley Byrne* no question arises as to whether the imposition of duty of care would be fair, reasonable and just.

However, his second submission, relying upon the more general ground, is that when foreseeability of financial loss is established and, what is more, loss to the individual plaintiff, then there is no reason why it is not fair, just and reasonable for the bank to owe a duty of care to the payee, just as it owes a contractual duty to its customer to make the payment when it becomes due. He submits that the lack of authority is no bar to his submission, referring to the passage in *Paget* which I have already read. He submits, therefore, that the plaintiff's case is clearly arguable and that the plaintiff should be allowed to take the matter to trial.

These are attractive submissions but I do not find them cogent. *Henderson* was a case where there was a commercial situation where the necessary relationship was found to exist. In *White v Jones* the speeches of Lords Goff and Browne-Wilkinson, who with Lord Nolan formed the majority, show that the duty of care was held to exist in that case only because it was an exceptional case. The head note reads as follows:

> …the assumption of responsibility by a solicitor to his client, who had given instructions for the drawing up of a will for execution, extended to an intended beneficiary under the proposed will in circumstances where the solicitor could reasonably foresee that a consequence of his negligence might result in the loss of the intended legacy without either the testator or his estate having a remedy against him; and that, accordingly, in the circumstances the plaintiffs were entitled to the relief sought.

In my view that summary is amply justified by speeches of Lord Goff at page 268, letter C, a passage which I need not read, and Lord Browne-Wilkinson at pages 275–276. I should refer to Lord Nolan's agreement also. In both of those speeches emphasis was laid, first, upon the particular responsibility of a solicitor as a professional man acting in those circumstances on instructions to draw up a will in favour of a third party beneficiary, and, secondly, upon the fact that if the beneficiary had no right to claim and the testator was unable to recover substantial damages for breach of contract or in tort, then it would follow that the solicitor's negligence, which had in fact caused loss to the plaintiff, would not result in his being held liable for that loss. That is not the case here because there was a chain of agreements or contracts on the facts alleged between the plaintiff and the Granfe company and Mr Urquhart and Mr Waddy, under which the plaintiff would seem to have an unanswerable claim.

It seems to me that *White v Jones* can be taken as authority for two propositions which are helpful to Mr Ross-Munro. The first is that the fact that a duty arises under a contract made by the defendant with a party other than the plaintiff does not mean that a duty of care owed to the plaintiff cannot arise. Similarly, and secondly, the fact that there is no relationship between the plaintiff and the defendant is not necessarily a fatal bar to the plaintiffs claim. I should also refer, before leaving *White v Jones,* to a passage in the dissenting speech of Lord Mustill at page 279, letter D, where he said this:

> This is certainly not to deny that where the act or omission complained of occurs between persons who have deliberately involved themselves in a network of commercial or professional contractual relations, such for example as may exist between the numerous parties involved in contracts for large building or engineering works, the contractual framework may be so strong, so complex and so detailed as to exclude the recognition of delictual duties between parties who are not already

connected by contractual links: see for example *Pacific Associates Inc v Baxter* [1990] 1 QB 993. This aspect of the law is far from being fully developed and I need not explore it here.

Lord Browne-Wilkinson who formed a member of the majority at page 274 letter D said this:

(I should add that I agree with my noble and learned friend, Lord Mustill, that this factor should not lead to the conclusion that a duty of care will necessarily be found to exist even where there is a contractual chain of obligations designed by the parties to regulate their dealings.)

The present is not a case of complex or detailed contractual agreements, nevertheless it is a commercial situation where the relationships between the various parties are governed by contracts between themselves.

The question which arises is how to apply these authorities in the present case. The crucial factor, in my view, is that the plaintiff does not allege any dealings or even any communication between himself and the bank. If there was any such communication then he would know about it, therefore the absence of any such allegation in the pleadings can be taken to indicate that no such communication took place. It seems to me that the plaintiff fails under the orthodox *Hedley Byrne* principle because he fails to show that there was any relationship between himself and the bank. The question whether it was a special relationship, or as Lord Devlin put it in *Hedley Byrne,* whether it was a situation 'equivalent to contract' simply does not arise. This is not merely semantic or a play upon words. The fact that there must be some relationship for the *Hedley Byrne* decision to apply goes a long way to explain the difficulties which were faced by the House of Lords in *White v Jones.* Lord Keith of Kinkel and Lord Mustill both found it impossible to hold that the law could recognise or impose a duty of care in the circumstances of that case. The majority did hold that such a duty of care existed on the grounds which have already been referred to.

It seems to me that those grounds clearly were regarded by them as exceptional. The two most significant factors were those to which I have referred: non-availability of any effective remedy either for the beneficiary or for the testator's estate if no duty of care was imposed; and, secondly, the peculiar status of the solicitor when preparing a will. Neither of those factors is present here.

So the question becomes, 'can this also, at least arguably, be regarded as an exceptional case?' It seems to me that almost inevitably the answer must be 'no'. The plaintiff contends for a duty of care which, if it arises here, would arise in the course of an everyday commercial transaction and would go a long way to revolutionise English Banking Law. I agree with the judge's comment that such a duty would not be incremental. I would say that it would be a massive sea change in the regulation of liabilities in a commercial context such as this. The very fact that the facts relied upon are the basic ones to which I have referred, that is to say, a bank is given irrevocable instructions by its customer to make a payment to a third party, prevents the plaintiff from saying that this is an exceptional case. Mr Ross-Munro in my view contends for a duty of care in a case which from both the banking and the legal points of view is common place and certainly no exceptional. It follows from that, in my view, that the plaintiff cannot contend for a duty of care in the present situation in the light of the recent House of Lords authorities to which I have referred. The case is not exceptional, it is a straightforward commercial situation where the duty of care has never been held to exist and where there are no grounds for creating an exception to the basic rule, recognised and established by the House of Lords.

I should add this in deference to Mr Ross-Munro's emphasis upon the fact that the instructions here were 'irrevocable'. It seems to me that even if the instructions were expressed as being irrevocable, nevertheless the bank and its customer could agree to vary that contract. It would be entirely up to them whether to do so or not, unless rights had been acquired by third parties which is the very point in issue in the present case.

Mr Ross-Munro finally submitted that even if the instructions were changed by agreement between the bank and its customer the bank would remain liable to the original intended payee, even though its fresh instructions were to make the payment elsewhere. It seems to me that that exposes the fact that the submission cannot be right. In my judgment the fact that the instructions are expressed as irrevocable does not assist the submission that the bank came under a duty of care.

Finally, I would add this: if the plaintiff had communicated with the bank then it could be, I say no more, a situation which was in Lord Devlin's words 'equivalent to contract'. It may be that in such a situation it would be arguable that a *Hedley Byrne* duty would arise. It would arise from the relationship which in fact was established between them. But here the plaintiff did not have any dealings with the bank, he dealt only with Mr Urquhart and Mr Waddy. He undoubtedly has remedies against them, first, under the bills of exchange and secondly on the pleaded facts for breach of the contract or agreement, if contract there was, between him and them.

Finally, although it may be superfluous, I emphasise that the only allegation made in the present case is the tortious claim for breach of the alleged duty of care. There is no allegation of any contractual claim express or implied. In those circumstances, in my judgment, the conclusion was right and the appeal should be dismissed.

[Hutchison and Mantell LJJ concurred.]

NOTE

In *National Westminster Bank Ltd v Barclays Bank International Ltd* [1975] QB 654 at 662, Kerr J held that a drawee (paying) bank did not owe a duty of care to the payee when deciding whether to honour a cheque presented for payment. However, the drawee bank may owe the payee of a cheque a duty to act carefully and honestly under the *Hedley Byrne* principle when advising the payee of its reasons for dishonouring the cheque (*TE Potterton Ltd v Northern Bank Ltd* [1995] 4 Bank LR 179, Irish High Court: criticised by EP Ellinger [1995] JBL 583–585).

QUESTION

In *White v Jones* [1995] 2 AC 207, where the House of Lords held by a majority that a solicitor who accepts instructions to draft a will owes a duty of care to the intended beneficiary and may be liable to him in tort if he does not implement the testator's instructions within a reasonable time, their Lordships seemed much influenced by the fact that, without the imposition of the duty of care, the intended beneficiary would have suffered a loss without a remedy. Do you think it would have made any difference in *Wells v First National Commercial Bank* if the plaintiff had been left without an alternative remedy? Would the bank have been liable to the company for failing to make the transfer?

(b) The intermediary (correspondent) bank

Where the originator's bank does not have a correspondent relationship with the beneficiary's bank it must employ an intermediary (correspondent) bank to effect the transfer. Intermediary banks may be employed in domestic funds transfers, but they are used more commonly in international funds transfers (as illustrated by the next case). Sometimes both the originator's bank and the beneficiary's bank will each have to employ its own intermediary bank in the same transaction. An intermediary bank employed by the originator's bank acts as its agent, and one employed by the beneficiary's bank acts as that bank's agent. It is often important to ascertain on whose behalf an intermediary bank acts as this may determine such matters as whether the originator can revoke his payment instruction and the time of completion of payment.

Royal Products Ltd v Midland Bank Ltd

See above, p 733.

NOTES

1. The key extract from the judgment of Wright J in *Calico Printers' Association v Barclays Bank Ltd* (1931) 145 LT 51, affd at 58, appears above, p 227, and the relationship between a principal and sub-agent is explored further in the notes which follow the extract. For a contrasting view, see J Vroegop 'The role of correspondent banks in direct funds transfers' [1990] LMCLQ 547.

2. In the United States the intermediary bank has been held liable to the originator for defective performance: see, eg *Silver stein v Chartered Bank of Hong Kong* 392 NYS 2d 296 (1977); *Evra Corpn v Swiss Bank Corpn* 522 F Supp 820 (1981); revsd on other grounds 673 F 2d 951 (1982); *Securities Fund Services Inc v American National Bank & Trust Co* 542 F Supp 323 (1982). See also UNCITRAL's Model Law on International Credit Transfers (25 November, 1992), arts 8 and 17(4).

3. An intermediary bank appointed by the originator's bank owes that bank an implied contractual duty of care and skill. A concurrent duty of care will also arise in tort. In either case an exclusion clause may purport to exclude the duty. Where an intermediary bank incurs liability as a result of carrying out the instructions of the originator's bank, it will usually be entitled to an indemnity or contribution from the originator's bank (*Honourable Society of the Middle Temple v Lloyds Bank plc* [1999] 1 All ER (Comm) 193; *Linklaters (a firm) v HSBC Bank plc* [2003] EWHC 1113 (Comm), [2003] 1 Lloyd's Rep 545). The Cross-Border Credit Transfer Regulations 1999, SI 1999/1876 (see above, p 000) contain their own reimbursement provisions (see regs 6(6) and 10). The intermediary bank may be able to avoid liability by relying on the *force majeure* provision set out in reg 12(1).

(c) The beneficiary's bank

In the case of a debit transfer, such as a payment by direct debit, where the beneficiary (payee) pulls funds from the originator's (payer's) account, the beneficiary's (payee's) bank is acting as an agent of the beneficiary (payee) in the collection process.[5] (Because most cheques are crossed 'account payee', and therefore non-transferable, the collecting bank will now rarely collect a cheque on its own behalf: see below, p 783.) The position is less certain in the case of a credit transfer. The cases suggest that the beneficiary's bank again acts as an agent of the beneficiary.

Mardorf Peach & Co Ltd v Attica Sea Carriers Corporation of Liberia, The Laconia

[1977] AC 850, House of Lords

The Laconia was time chartered by the appellants (the owners) to the respondents (the charterers) on the New York Produce Exchange form, under the terms of which hire was to be paid in cash in US currency semi-monthly in advance 'to the owners...into their bank account

---

[5] It is acknowledged that the language of 'originator' and 'beneficiary', which was developed in the context of credit transfers (see above, p 719), does not apply so readily to debit transfers.

with First National City Bank of New York, 30 Moorgate, London, EC2 to the credit of OFC Account No 705586'. The seventh instalment of hire fell due on 12 April, a Sunday when London banks were closed. At about 3 pm on Monday 13 April the charterers' London bank delivered a payment order for the hire instalment to the owners' bank, where it was accepted and dealt with in the usual way. The bank informed the owners that the payment order had been received, but were instructed to return it at once. When the owners then tried to invoke a forfeiture clause in the charterparty on the grounds of late payment of hire (it was conceded by the charterers that the due date for payment of this instalment was Friday 10 April, as London banks were closed on Saturday and Sunday), the charterers argued that their breach had been waived through acceptance of the late tender by the owners' bank acting as the owners' agents. The House of Lords, reversing a majority decision of the Court of Appeal in favour of the charterers, rejected this contention and gave judgment for the owners.

Lord Wilberforce held that a right of withdrawal had accrued to the owners under the terms of the forfeiture clause in the charterparty and continued: . . .

This leaves the second question, which is whether the right of withdrawal was waived by the owners. The submission of the charterers was that on Monday, April 13, 1970, before the owners purported to withdraw the ship, they accepted the charterers' late payment of the instalment and so affirmed the contract. The arbitrators found that there had not been any waiver, so that the charterers must undertake the task of showing that, upon the facts found, the only possible conclusion must have been there had.

In order to understand the argument, it is necessary to go into the facts in some detail. At about 3 p.m., at which time London banks closed for the day, a messenger from the Midland Bank, acting for the charterers, delivered to the owners' bank, the First National City Bank, 34, Moorgate, London ('FNCB'), a 'payment order' for the amount of the seventh instalment. A payment order is a document issued by one bank to another under a scheme (LCSS) by which banks maintain dollar suspense accounts in which they credit or debit each other with sums in dollars and make periodical settlements. As between banks, a payment order is the equivalent of cash, but a customer cannot draw upon it. The amount must first be credited to his account, but he can, of course, make special arrangements for earlier drawing. At about 3.10 or 3.15 p.m. the payment order was received and stamped in the sorting office of FNCB. It was then taken to the transfer department. There an official called an editor wrote on the face of the order the formula CR ADV & TT Lausanne, an instruction (to be carried out elsewhere in the bank) meaning 'credit advice and telegraphic transfer Lausanne.' Not perhaps quite simultaneously, but at about the same time, another official telephoned to the owners' agents and said that the bank had received a payment order for the amount of the hire: this was in accordance with instructions received by the bank earlier in the day from the owners' agents. This official was immediately told to refuse the money and to return it. Thereupon the editor deleted the annotation he had made on the payment order and wrote on it. 'Beneficiary has refused payment. Advise remitter by phone.' There was no direct evidence that this was done but such may be presumed. The next day FNCB sent to the Midland Bank a payment order for the same amount as that which the Midland Bank had sent the previous day.

My Lords, much ingenuity and effort was used in order to show that this series of actions, or some part of it, constituted acceptance and waiver by the owners of the right to withdraw. But in my opinion it did not approach success. Although the word 'waiver,' like 'estoppel,' covers a variety of situations different in their legal nature, and tends to be indiscriminately used by the courts as a means of relieving parties from bargains or the consequences of bargains which are thought to be harsh or deserving of relief, in the present context what is relied on is clear enough. The charterers had failed to make a punctual payment but it was open to the owners to accept a late payment as if it were punctual, with the consequence that they could not thereafter rely on the default as entitling them to withdraw. All that is needed to establish waiver, in this sense, of the committed breach of contract, is evidence, clear and unequivocal, that such acceptance has taken place, or, after the late payment has been tendered, such a delay in refusing it as might reasonably cause the charterers to believe that it has been accepted.'

My Lords, if this is, as I believe, what would have to be proved in order to establish a waiver in the situation under review, it must be obvious that the facts in the present case do not amount to it. Looked at untechnically, the facts were that the money was sent to the bank, taken into the banking process or machinery, put in course of transmission to the owners, but rejected by the latter as soon as they were informed of its arrival and as soon as they were called upon, or able, to define their position. Put more technically, the bank, though agents of the owners, had a limited authority. It is not necessary to decide whether, in general, and in the absence of specific instructions, bankers in such situations as these have authority to accept late payments—on this matter I regard *The Brimnes* [1975] QB 929 as a special case where an inference to this effect may have been justified on the facts and the observations of the Lords Justices (in particular of Cairns LJ at p 972) as directed to that situation. But here it is clear that the bankers had no such authority and still less any authority to make business decisions as to the continuance or otherwise of the charterparty but that per contra they had express instructions to refer the matter to the owners' agents. On this basis they receive the order (they clearly had no right to reject it out of hand), and, while provisionally starting to process it into the owners' possession, at the same time seek the owners' directions in accordance with the owners' previous instructions. On those directions, they arrest the process and return the money. The acts of the editors—the annotation on the payment order—were internal acts (Brandon J, of a similar situation in *The Brimnes* [1973] 1 WLR 386, 411 called them 'ministerial,' ie acts done without any intention or capacity to affect legal relations with third parties), not irrevocable, but provisional and reversible acts, consistent with an alternative decision of the customer which might be to accept or reject. The customer chose to reject, he did so as rapidly as the circumstances permitted, and he could have given no ground to the charterer for supposing that the payment had been accepted. The charterer did not act upon any such supposition.

The pattern of action is to me so clear that I do not find it necessary to decide the rather technical question whether, as regards the owners, there was payment 'in cash' as required by the charterparty, or not. Whatever it was it was not punctual payment, and not accepted in waiver of the unpunctuality. I think then that there is no basis on which the arbitrators' finding against waiver can be attacked.

Lord Simon of Glaisdale delivered a judgment concurring with Lord Wilberforce.

Lord Salmon: ...Much was sought to be made in argument on behalf of the charterers of the small amount of ministerial work which had been done inside FNCB before the Midland Bank had been informed that the payment was being returned. To my mind none of this even approached a waiver. I doubt whether even if the processing of the payment order had been completed and the owners' account had been credited with the full amount of the payment order before that amount was returned to the Midland Bank on the following day, a finding of waiver could have been justified.

Undoubtedly the owners held out FNCB, indeed they were designated in the charter, as the owners' agents to receive and accept the *punctual* payment of any hire due under the charter.

The charterers had defaulted in payment of the hire due on April 10 when they tendered it to FNCB at about 3 p.m. on Monday, April 13. There is nothing to suggest that that bank was familiar with the terms of the charter or knew whether or not the charterers were in default. Certainly it was not within the banker's express or implied authority to make commercial decisions on behalf of their customers by accepting or rejecting late payments of hire without taking instructions. They did take instructions and were told to reject the payment. They did so and returned it to the charterers on the following day which on any view must have been within a reasonable time. If the bank had kept the payment for an unreasonable time, the charterers might well have been led to believe that the owners had accepted payment. This would have amounted to a waiver of their right to withdraw the vessel. But nothing of the kind happened in the present case.

Clearly if the charterers had paid the hire in US dollar bills on April 10 just before the bank closed, this would have been a punctual cash payment. No doubt a certain amount of processing or paper work has to be done even in relation to a cash payment before it finds its way as a credit into the haven of the customer's account. If the cash is paid into the bank just before it closes on a Friday afternoon it is unlikely, if not impossible, that the customer could have drawn it out before the bank closed for business that afternoon. The customer would probably have had to wait for payment until the following Monday morning. No doubt certain valued customers would be admitted to a bank after banking hours and allowed to cash a cheque even against moneys received on their account but which had not yet passed through the books. There is however no legal obligation on a bank to cash a cheque after banking hours. There has been a great deal of argument as to whether payment of the hire by a payment order just before the bank closed on Friday, April 10 would have amounted to a good payment under the charter. The point does not however arise for decision and I prefer to express no concluded view about it. As at present advised however I am inclined to think that, for the reasons I have indicated, there is no real difference between a payment in dollar bills and a payment by payment orders which in the banking world are generally regarded and accepted as cash.

Lord Fraser of Tullybelton: ...There remains the second question of whether the bank accepted the payment and, by accepting it, operated a waiver of the owners' right. The argument in favour of waiver by acceptance was based on the arbitrators' finding that 'The FNCB began to deal with the order in the usual way by making the relevant entries in their books.' When this finding is analysed in the light of the agreed notes of additional facts, it comes to mean that acceptance occurred after the payment order had been passed from the sorting office in the FNCB, to their transfer department, when an official called an editor marked the payment order 'CR ADV and TT Lausanne' (short for 'credit advice and telegraphic transfer Lausanne'). That was an instruction to other people in the FNCB to transfer the sum in the payment order to a bank in Lausanne as previously instructed by the owners. But about the same time another person in the transfer department telephoned to the owners who instructed that the payment be refused. The marking 'CR ADV and TT Lausanne' was then deleted by the editor who also wrote on the payment order 'Beneficiary had refused payment. Advise remitter by phone.' There is no finding that the Midland Bank was in fact advised by phone. In all probability that would be done about 15.30 hours or soon after but I do not think anything turns on whether it was done or not.

In my opinion, the marking of the payment order in the way I have mentioned, even if accompanied by entries in the books concerning the LCS scheme, cannot have operated to waive the owners' right of withdrawal. I reach that opinion on two grounds. In the first place, the bank was, in my opinion, the agent of the owners only to receive payments for hire but it had no authority, actual or ostensible, to waive the owners' rights. It was the nominated place at which the hire was to be paid; its function in receiving payment was, in the phrase used in *The Brimnes* [1975] QB 929, merely ministerial. It was suggested that the position of the bank was the same as that of the estate agents in *Central Estates (Belgravia) Ltd v Woolgar (No 2)* [1972] 1 WLR 1048, but in my opinion that is wrong because the estate agents had the full authority to manage the property on behalf of the owner. The bank had no such authority. A decision on whether to exercise a right of withdrawing a vessel or to waive the right may be a difficult decision involving consideration of many variable facts, including the state of the freight market and the exact position of the ship at the time, and it would be unreasonable to expect the bank to make the decision. It would also, I think, be unreasonable to expect the owners to instruct the bank in advance before the hire has been received. A reasonable time must be allowed for the bank, after it has received the hire, to take instructions from the owners and a reasonable time for that purpose would certainly extend from 15.00 hours until 18.55 hours. In the second place, the actions of the editor in marking the payment order in the FNCB transfer office were not of a character that could have operated as a waiver of the owners' rights of withdrawal. A waiver would have required an overt action. These were private acts internal to the bank. They were not communicated to the charterers, nor did they have any 'impact' on them, if I may borrow the word used by Russell LJ in *London and County (A & D) Ltd v Wilfred Sportsman Limited* [1971] Ch 764, 782. Moreover, the marking of the payment order did not in my opinion demonstrate a final decision by the editor or by anyone acting for the owners to accept the hire; on the contrary, it was done at about the very time when another person in the same department, who must I think have acted to the knowledge of the editor concerned, was telephoning to the owners for instructions whether to accept the hire or not. I therefore conclude that no waiver occurred at that time.

Lord Russell of Killowen delivered judgment in favour of the owners on the ground that none of the dealings with the payment order constituted an unequivocal act of acceptance on behalf of the owners so as to constitute a waiver.

'The Receiving Bank's Role in Credit Transfer Transactions' by R King
(1982) 45 MLR 369, pp 372–376, 379–383

...The analyses of the facts conducted in *The Laconia* laid great stress on the distinction between receipt of a payment by the bank and acceptance of that payment as fulfilling an obligation owed by the transferor to the bank's customer. Clearly, in cases where the customer has instructed the transferor to make payment to his bank account the bank has no option but to receive the payment. The decision of four of the members of the House in *The Laconia* is that the bank does not have authority to accept such a payment save where it is made pursuant to an existing obligation. However, the decision leaves open the question of whether a payment made in accordance with an existing obligation and accredited to the customer must be regarded as having been accepted, upon receipt by the bank. If this is the case, the bank, since it will not usually be concerned with the way the obligation to pay arises and will not know why the payment is being made, is placed in the position of being able to accept or otherwise a payment without being aware of the rights of the parties. Thus the payment may be made in circumstances where the bank's customer, knowing of a breach of contract by the transferor entitling him to terminate the contract, has not in fact terminated it at the time the payment is made so that an unequivocal acceptance of the payment may amount to a waiver of his right to do so. While it might be objected that on Lord Wilberforce's reasoning such a waiver would require a commercial decision which the bank does not have authority to take, the payment may be made at a time not expected by the customer with the result that he fails to issue the instructions to the bank to return the payment within the reasonable time which Lord Salmon and Bridge LJ consider necessary. Indeed, on Lord Fraser's view it is for the bank to obtain the instructions within a reasonable time of the payment being made. Yet the bank will generally not know whether instructions are required or not.

In the light of the difficulties produced by the analyses in *The Laconia* and the limited nature of the authority with which the bank is said to be clothed it is relevant to consider whether it is necessary to introduce the concept of agency at all. In *Foley v Hill* ((1848) 2 HL Cas 28), the House of Lords held that, in the absence of evidence of a special relationship between a bank and its customer, the relationship is that of debtor and creditor. Thus Lord Cottenham LC said (36–37):

> The money placed in the custody of a banker is, to all intents and purposes, the money of the banker, to do with as he pleases; he is guilty of no breach of trust in employing it; he is not answerable to the principal if he puts it into jeopardy, if he engages in a hazardous speculation; he is not bound to keep it or deal with it or the property of his principal, but he is of course answerable for the amount, because he has contracted, having received that money, to repay to the principal, when demanded, a sum equivalent to that paid into his hands.

Similarly Lord Brougham said (43):

> I am now speaking of the common position of a banker, which consists of the common case of receiving money from his customer on condition of paying it back when asked for, or when drawn

upon, or of receiving from other parties, to the credit of the customer, upon like conditions to be drawn out by the customer, or, in common parlance, the money being repaid when asked for, because the party who receives the money has the use of it as his own, and in the using of which his trade consists, and but for which no banker could exist, especially a banker who pays interest.

These passages suggest that when a bank receives money for the account of its customers it receives the money in its own right and that it makes no difference whether the sum is paid to the bank by the customer himself or by a third party. So, in the same way that it is inappropriate to say that the bank receives money paid by the customer into his own account as agent for the customer it is also inappropriate to say that the bank receives money paid by a third party for the account of the customer as agent for the customer. This point was discussed by the Divisional Court of the Queen's Bench Division in *Midland Bank Ltd v Conway Corporation* ([1965] 1 WLR 1165). Here, the Midland Bank Ltd. received money paid to it for the account of a person resident in Peru in respect of rent payable to that person as freehold owner of demised premises. The Conway Corporation served upon the bank abatement notices in respect of a nuisance upon the premises under the terms of the Public Health Act 1936 upon the basis that the bank was receiving the rent as agent for the freehold owner within the meaning of section 343 (1) of that Act. The court held that in the circumstances the bank was not an agent for the purposes of the Act. The bank gave no receipt for the money, it had no right to refuse acceptance of it and was acting solely under its duty as a banker to receive any money paid in. It was not, therefore, a proper inference that there was a special relationship between the bank and its customer which constituted the bank an agent to receive the rent. Lord Parker CJ and Browne J did not, however, express any view as to whether the bank in receiving money for its customer might be an agent in the more limited sense discussed in *The Laconia* although Browne J recognised that the point 'might give rise to somewhat nice questions'. Sachs J was more forthright (1171): 'Here the money was received by a bank, and prima facie it was received by virtue of the relationship of banker and customer, that is quite a different character from that of an agent.'

Further support for this view is implicit in the judgment of Webster J in *Royal Products Ltd v Midland Bank Ltd* ([1981] 2 Lloyd's Rep 194). [King then sets out the facts of *Royal Products* and an extract from Webster J's judgment (pp 198–199), both of which can be found above, p 733. He continues:]

The following comments may be made. First, that Webster J accepts that it is implicit in the relationship of the customer and the bank that the bank should receive sums paid to it for the account of the customer. There is no question of a 'special relationship' to take the parties outside the principle in *Foley v Hill.* Secondly, completion of the instructions occurs when the customer of the receiving bank is enabled to draw on or otherwise use the sum transferred. This must be distinguished from the time when the sum is credited to the receiving bank which may be prior to completion and the time when the receiving bank has actually credited the sum to the account of the customer which may be after completion. Thirdly, if the bank is to be considered an agent of the customer for receipt of the sum transferred a difficulty arises as to when the bank ceases to hold the money as agent and when it starts to hold the money as debtor. It is clear that Webster J thought that after the customer had been enabled to draw on or otherwise use the sum transferred that his remedy against the bank was as an unsecured creditor and not as an owner of property whose agent had applied it for unauthorised purposes thus indicating that prior to the bank actually crediting the sum to the account of the customer the bank is a debtor and not an agent. Fourthly, Webster J makes no distinction between 'in-house' transactions (that is to say where the transfer is between persons with accounts at the same bank) and 'out-house' transactions (that is to say where the transfer is between persons with accounts at different banks). Fifthly, since the obligations of the customer and the bank regarding receipt of the sum transferred derive from and are implicit in the relationship of banker and customer there is no logical reason why an analysis of the receiving bank's role should vary depending upon whether the transfer is made by the customer himself from another account (as in *Royal Products Ltd v Midland Bank Ltd.*) or whether the transfer is made by a third party. Sixthly, despite the above, Webster J uses the language of agency when he speaks of the 'bank being impliedly authorised by the customer to accept [the] credit.' I will return to this later. . . .

If the above analysis is correct it follows that the decision by the receiving bank to credit its customer's account is not a decision made on behalf of the customer receiving the transfer. Indeed it is more appropriate to say that, if acting under English law, the bank will require receipt of the cover as a condition of carrying out the transferor's bank's instruction. It follows from this that wherever a credit transfer payment of this kind is made, the banks acting in the transaction, including the payee's bank, are the agents or sub-agents of the payer and that the payee's bank in particular is in an analogous position to the payee's bank in *The Brimnes* ([1975] QB 929).

The other two cases mentioned above which deal with transfers made by third parties for the account of a bank's customer are *Momm v Barclays Bank International Ltd.* ([1977] QB 790) and *Rekstin v Severn Sibirsko and The Bank for Russian Trade* ([1933] 1 KB 47). In *Momm v Barclays Bank International Ltd* the plaintiffs and another bank (Herstatt) maintained separate accounts with the defendant bank. The plaintiffs and Herstatt concluded a currency transaction under the terms of which Herstatt were to transfer a sum of money to the plaintiffs' account at the defendant bank valued at June 26, 1974. On June 25 Herstatt instructed the defendants to make the transfer. The defendants did this on receipt of the instruction on June 26. At 4.15 pm on that day Herstatt announced that they were going into liquidation. On June 27, the defendants reversed the entry to the plaintiffs' account as Herstatt's account was in a net deficit position. Kerr J held that the transfer was complete when the defendants would have refused to have accepted countermanding instructions from Herstatt which would have been when the computer processes to credit the plaintiffs' account were set in motion. It made no difference that the defendants had notified neither the plaintiffs nor Herstatt of this prior to their purported revocation of the transfer.

This must be contrasted with the decision of the Court of Appeal in *Rekstin v Severn Sibirsko and The Bank for Russian Trade*. In this case Rekstin obtained a judgment against Severo. In order to avoid execution Severo ordered the Bank for Russian Trade to transfer the sums in its account at the bank to a Russian trade delegation with diplomatic immunity which also had an account at the bank. After a clerk at the bank had made the necessary book entry to close Severo's account, but before the corresponding credit entry in the delegation's account had been made, Rekstin served a garnishee order nisi on the bank. On these facts the Court of Appeal held that the bank still held the sums to the account of Severo and that the garnishee order nisi was effective. In reaching this conclusion the court treated as important the facts that the trade delegation knew nothing of the proposed transfer, that there was no transaction between Severo and the delegation underlying it and that the delegation had never consented to its account being credited with the sum.

Faced with this latter decision, Kerr J in *Momm v Barclays Bank International Ltd* said (801–802): 'In my view this decision should be treated as confined to its special facts. . . I think that it merely decided that payment by means of an in-house transfer has not taken place if the payee has not assented to it, and perhaps also if the transfer has not been completed.' If this is the correct ratio of the *Rekstin* case it seems to follow that in using the words '. . . [the receiving] bank being impliedly authorised by the customer to accept that credit by virtue of the fact that the customer has a current account with it, no consent to the receipt of the credit being expected from or required of [the receiving] bank . . .', Webster J in *Royal Products Ltd v Midland Bank Ltd* (at 197) must not be taken to mean that the receiving bank is 'authorised' in the sense that an agent is given authority by his principal. This is because, if the bank were constituted an agent in this way, there would be no need for any further assent to the receipt of the transfer in cases where the transferee does not know of or contemplate the payment. On the other hand the bank will have a sum of money which it can use for its own purposes subject to an obligation to repay an equivalent sum to the true creditor. In an 'in-house' transaction the sum will be repaid on demand to the intended transferor. In an 'out-house' transaction, as . . . analysis of the transfer in *The Chikuma* ([1981] 1 WLR 314) shows, the sum will be repayable on demand to the transferor's bank or an intermediate bank which provides the 'cover' for the credit to the account of the transferee. It is interesting to note here that in relation to the use of bank accounts to receive payments, Chitty states: 'When the payee prescribes [details of his bank account to the transferor], he manifests willingness to receive payment through giro channels.' The mere fact that a payee has a bank account does not manifest such a willingness and it is not difficult to envisage cases where a person would not wish money to be paid into his account (for example, where the account is overdrawn and the customer knows that the bank will not permit him to draw upon it until the account is in credit). In this respect it is more appropriate to say, not that the customer authorises the bank to receive a credit, but that by virtue of the relationship of banker and customer the bank impliedly permits the customer to arrange for transfers to be made to the bank for the credit of the customer.

If this analysis of the above-mentioned cases is accepted it follows that where parties agree that the liability for payment of one may be discharged by payment made into the bank account of another, the payee agrees not that the bank should receive the payment as agent but that the liability of the payer may be discharged by constituting the bank a debtor of the payee in respect of the sum payable. If the obligation is formulated in this way it is apparent that the mere fact that the payer has constituted the bank a debtor as required cannot affect the actions of the parties in respect of their other rights and liabilities under the contract for the payee has not done any act or made any representation which can amount to a waiver of his rights. Moreover, no issue arises as to whether it is for the bank to obtain instructions about what to do with the transfer or whether the payee should give the bank the necessary instructions, a point which gave rise to a difference of opinion in the House of Lords in *The Laconia*. The payee can only be said to have waived his rights when, knowing of the transfer himself he fails to instruct the bank to return it and he cannot be fixed with the imperfect knowledge of the bank. It is suggested that this is the result which the parties (including the bank) would expect.

One consequence of this analysis relates to the issue of negligence on the part of the payee's bank. The situation contemplated here is a failure by the payee's bank to use reasonable care to credit a payment to the account of the payee whereby the payment is not available to the payee at the critical time. An example of such a failure is to be found in *Afovos Shipping Co SA v R Pagnan and Filli, The Afovos* ([1980] 2 Lloyd's Rep 450). Here the plaintiffs let their vessel to the defendants in consideration for hire payable 'in London to the First National Bank of Chicago [FNBC]:...for the credit of [the plaintiffs]...in cash...in US currency, semi-monthly in advance.' If hire was due and unpaid the plaintiffs had the right to withdraw the vessel provided that they gave two days notice in writing prior to so doing during which time a contractual payment could still be made. The defendants gave instructions to their bank, Credito Italiano, to make payment by credit transfer to FNBC for the account of the plaintiffs. Credito Italiano purported to comply with the instruction by originating a telex transfer. Unfortunately the telex did not arrive at FNBC because the telex number used was not that of FNBC and the telex operator omitted to check that he had received the correct 'answer-back' sign. The telex number had been obtained from the Jaegar & Waldmann telex directory, the most recent edition of which had not been up-dated due to an omission by FNBC. In these circumstances Lloyd J held that FNBC had been negligent in not providing up-to-date information to Jaegar & Waldmann regarding the telex number. However, Lloyd J further held that the effective cause of FNBC s failure to receive the telex was the omission of the employee of Credito Italiano to check the 'answer-back.' Accordingly the non-payment of the hire could not be attributed to the plaintiffs and they were entitled to withdraw the vessel at the expiry of 48 hours from the time of the notice of failure to receive the hire.

If the analysis in this article is correct, even if the negligence of FNBC had been an effective cause of the loss, that negligence could not be ascribed to the plaintiffs, the payees, since FNBC was not their agent for receipt of the telex. The use of the telex transfer was merely a step taken by the defendants (payers) to fulfil their obligation to constitute FNBC a debtor of the plaintiffs for the required sum. The choice of method and time of payment lay with the payer, and it is a legitimate construction of a payment agreement of the type being considered, subject to any express provision to the contrary, that the payer takes the risk of using a method of effecting his payment which may turn out to be inappropriate or of delaying the effecting of his payment until the last minute. There is no reason for the payee to bear this risk simply because he nominates a bank which, in the events that happen, makes a mistake. Support for this view is to be found in *Equitable Trust Company of New York v Dawson Partners Ltd* ((1927) 27 Ll LR 49) where it was held that an issuing bank could not seek reimbursement from a buyer pursuant to a documentary credit transaction where a correspondent bank nominated by the buyer mistakenly paid the seller upon documents which did not comply with the issuing bank's mandate. Moreover, it is open to the parties to provide for a time for payment which apportions the risk differently or alters the consequences of the risk.

In conclusion it may be said that more consideration ought to be given by the courts to the role of banks which receive payments made for the credit of their customers. By assuming that banks receiving such payments are acting as agents for the payee and then stripping the authority conferred by this agency on the banks so as to make their acts largely ministerial the House of Lords in *The Laconia* has not provided for a fully coherent analysis of this role. The time has, perhaps, come for the application in this context of the principle enunciated by the House of Lords in *Foley v Hill*.

NOTES

1. Notwithstanding King's arguments, there are three good reasons why the beneficiary's bank should be deemed to act as the beneficiary's agent in a credit transfer.[6] First, if the beneficiary's bank is not acting as the beneficiary's agent then the originator's bank transfers funds to someone who is not authorised to receive them. The transfer of funds to an unauthorised person would not discharge the originator's underlying indebtedness to the beneficiary (*Customs and Excise Comrs v National Westminster Bank plc* [2002] EWHC 2204 (Ch), [2003] 1 All ER (Comm) 327: see below, p 764). Secondly, treating the beneficiary's bank as the beneficiary's agent is consistent with the rule that payment is complete as between originator and beneficiary on receipt of funds and before a credit is posted to the beneficiary's account. Thirdly, failure to regard the beneficiary's bank as the beneficiary's agent draws an unnecessary distinction between payment by credit transfer and payment by debit transfer so far as completion of payment is concerned.

2. The beneficiary's bank owes a contractual duty of care and skill to its customer, the beneficiary. But does it owe a similar duty to the originator of a funds transfer? There is no privity of contract between the beneficiary's bank and the originator and it is submitted that a contractual claim by the originator based on the Contracts (Rights of Third Parties) Act 1999, s 1(1), is unlikely to succeed as no term of the bank-customer contract between the beneficiary and his own bank purports to confer a benefit on the originator (s 1(1)(b)). Could a duty of care arise in tort? In *Royal Bank of Canada v Stangl* (1992) 32 ACWS (3d) 17, a Canadian decision, the beneficiary's bank was held liable to its sender (a correspondent bank) in negligence for the failure to clarify the contents of a payment order instructing payment into an account that did not belong to the named beneficiary. But English law appears to be different. In *Abou-Rahman v Abacha* [2005] EWHC 2662 (QB), [2006] 1 All ER (Comm) 247, the defendant bank received two payments made by the victims of a fraud with instructions to credit the account of a customer called 'Trust International'. In fact the bank credited the account of an entity called 'Trusty International', which was controlled by the fraudsters. Treacy J, sitting in the English High Court, refused to follow *Stangl* and held that a beneficiary's bank does not owe

---

[6] The first two reasons given in the text are drawn from B Geva *Bank Collections and Payment Transactions—Comparative Study of Legal Aspects* (2001), p 296.

a duty of care to a non-customer originator of a funds transfer to pay money received only to the beneficiary identified in the originator's instructions, or to clarify any discrepancies in those instructions as to the beneficiary's identity with the originator. The judge reminded himself that the case before him was concerned purely with economic loss and that the common law was reluctant to impose a duty of care save in special circumstances. The decision of Treacy J was later upheld by the Court of Appeal, although there was no appeal on this particular issue: [2006] EWCA Civ 1492, [2007] 1 Lloyd's Rep 115.

3.   A different question arises in respect of the liability of the beneficiary's bank to the beneficiary when that bank refuses to accept a transfer of funds into his account. This will turn on the terms of the contract between the beneficiary and his bank. In *Tayeb v HSBC Bank plc* [2004] EWHC 1529 (Comm), [2004] 4 All ER 1024, Colman J held that when a customer opens an account with his bank, which is capable of receiving incoming CHAPS electronic funds transfers, the bank engages that it will accept into his account all CHAPS transfers which comply with the CHAPS Rules and which are otherwise in accordance with the terms of the account (for CHAPS transfers, see p 732 above). In this case, the beneficiary's bank became suspicious of the origin of funds that had been transferred into its customer's account using CHAPS and, without its customer's consent, returned those funds to the originator's bank. Colman J held that the bank was indebted to its customer in the amount of the sum transferred. The judge took account of the CHAPS Rules and held that a CHAPS transfer was ordinarily irreversible once the receiving bank had authenticated the transfer, sent an acknowledgement informing the sending bank that the transfer had been received and credited the funds to its customer's account. However, Colman J added that there was an appropriate analogy with the practice in relation to documentary credits where, at the time of presentation of documents, a bank with cogent evidence of fraud can decline to make payment to the beneficiary (see below, p 867), and that the same exception was likely to apply in respect of illegal transactions (see below, p 880). But mere suspicion as to the origin of the transferred funds did not present the bank with a justifiable reason for returning those funds to the transferor without the customer's consent.

QUESTIONS

1.   If the beneficiary's bank does not act as the beneficiary's agent in a credit transfer operation, does it act as agent for the originator or his bank?

2.   If the beneficiary's bank does act as the beneficiary's agent for the purposes of receiving a credit transfer, how can this be reconciled with their underlying debtor/ creditor relationship?

3.   What remedy does an originator have where the originator's bank has sent accurate payment instructions to the beneficiary's bank but the beneficiary's bank has mistakenly credited funds to the wrong account?

8 COUNTERMAND

The originator's bank is under a duty to obey its customer's countermand. Notice of countermand must be clear and unambiguous (*Westminster Bank Ltd v Hilton* (1926) 136 LT 315), and it must be brought to the actual (not constructive) knowledge of the bank (*Curtice v London City and Midland Bank Ltd* [1908] 1 KB 293: see above, p 638). Unless otherwise agreed, notice of countermand must be given to the branch of the originator's bank where the account is kept (*London, Provincial and South-western Bank Ltd v Buszard* (1918) 35 TLR 142).

As the originator's bank acts as the originator's agent for the purpose of executing his payment instruction, the general rule is that the originator, as principal, may countermand that instruction before it has been executed by the originator's bank, his agent (*Campanari v Woodburn* (1854) 15 CB 400). However, a principal may not revoke his agent's authority after the agent has commenced performance of his mandate and incurred liabilities for which the principal must indemnify him (*Warlow v Harrison* (1859) 1 E & E 309 at 317, Martin B).

The general principles to be applied, in the absence of express contract, when determining the availability of countermand of an originator's payment instruction in a funds transfer operation, have been summarised by Professor Cranston in the following terms:[7]

Firstly, a customer who instructs its bank to hold funds to the disposal of a third party can countermand at least until the time when the funds have been transferred or credit given to the transferee (*Gibson v Minet* (1824) 130 ER 206). Secondly, a customer who instructs its bank to transfer funds to a third party cannot revoke from the moment the bank incurs a commitment to the third party (*Warlow v Harrison* (1859) 1 E & E 309). Thirdly—and this is the typical case—a customer who instructs its bank to pay another bank to the order of a third party cannot revoke once the payee bank has acted on the instructions. This may be a point prior to crediting the payee's account (*Astro Amo Compania Naviera SA v Elf Union SA, The Zographia M* [1976] 2 Lloyd's Rep 382). In all cases, it is irrelevant, from the point of view of revocation, whether the third party has been informed.

Applying these general principles to the typical case where there is an originator's bank and a beneficiary's bank involved in the funds transfer operation, the customer's payment instruction is irrevocable once the beneficiary's bank accepts the payment order from the originator's bank either by returning an acceptance message or by acting on the payment order in some other way, eg by debiting an account of the originator's bank held by the beneficiary's bank or by making a decision unconditionally to credit the beneficiary's account. Where the originator's bank and the beneficiary's bank employ intermediary banks to act on their behalf, as would be the case where neither bank is a member of the relevant clearing system, countermand is no longer possible once the payment order has passed from the originator's side to the beneficiary's side of the payment chain and has been accepted by an intermediary bank acting on behalf of the beneficiary's bank, for example by it sending a further payment order on to the beneficiary's bank or another intermediary bank acting on its behalf.

To avoid uncertainty as to the customer's right of countermand, the originator's bank may include in its contract with the originator an express provision stipulating that the originator may not countermand his payment instruction after a certain point in the payment process. Thus, for example, it is usually made a term of issue of any credit or charge card, debit card or digital cash card (see below, Chapter 20) that the cardholder is prohibited from countermanding payment effected through the use of the card. Similarly, cheque guarantee cards are issued on condition that the customer will not countermand payment of any cheque supported by the card (countermand of a cheque is dealt with above, at p 638).

---

[7] R Cranston 'Law of International Funds Transfers in England' in W Hadding and UH Schneider (eds) *Legal Issues in International Credit Transfers* (1993), p 233.

Alternatively, the originator may be bound by the rules of the payment system used to make the transfer where those rules represent banking usage. It is well established that a 'man who employs a banker is bound by the usage of bankers': the usage becomes an implied term of the bank-customer contract (*Hare v Henty* (1861) 10 CBNS 65, 142 ER 374 at 379). But the customer must know of, and consent to, the usage where it deprives him of a right (*Barclays Bank plc v Bank of England* [1985] 1 All ER 385 at 394; *Turner v Royal Bank of Scotland plc* [1999] 2 All ER (Comm) 664, CA). Revocation of payment instructions will usually be a matter provided for, expressly or by implication, in the rules of the payment system used to effect the transfer (see, eg the CHAPS Rules, Version 1.7, October 2007, r 3.2.1).

9 COMPLETION OF PAYMENT

We are here concerned with completion of payment as between originator (payer) and beneficiary (payee). Determining the time of completion of payment as between originator and beneficiary can be important in certain circumstances, eg where the originator attempts to revoke a payment instruction (although a payment instruction may become irrevocable before payment is made, in theory at least, it cannot be revoked after completion of payment as between the originator and the beneficiary); where the death, liquidation or bankruptcy of the originator terminates the bank's authority to pay; where the contract between originator and beneficiary requires payment to be made strictly on the due date; where it is necessary to determine the time of payment for taxation purposes, or for the calculation of interest; or where there is a failure of one of the banks involved. The issue is considered in detail in J Vroegop 'The time of payment in paper-based and electronic funds transfer systems' [1990] LMCLQ 64, and also by B Geva in his article 'Payment into a Bank Account' [1990] 3 JIBL 108 and in his book *Bank Collections and Payment Transactions—Comparative Study of Legal Aspects* (2001), pp 270–289.

We have seen that payment usually involves the transfer of money, or the performance of some other act, tendered and accepted in discharge of a money obligation (above, p 714). Money means cash, ie coins and bank notes, but the creditor may agree to accept payment by means of a funds transfer into his bank account in fulfilment of an obligation to pay money. In a commercial transaction it should not be difficult to imply the creditor's consent to accept payment by this method, especially where he furnishes the debtor with details of his account to enable to the transfer to take place. By agreeing to payment by funds transfer, the creditor (beneficiary) agrees to accept a right of action against his own bank in lieu of his right of action against his debtor (originator). This substitution of one debtor for another is equivalent to payment by cash and discharges the underlying money obligation between the payer and the payee. Unless the creditor and the debtor have agreed otherwise, completion of payment between them occurs when this substitution takes place.

The precise time of substitution may be difficult to determine. In general, payment by funds transfer will be deemed to be complete when the beneficiary is given an unfettered or unrestricted right against his own bank to the immediate use of the funds transferred (*Tenax Steamship Co Ltd v Reinante Transoceanica Navigation SA, The Brimnes* [1973] 1 WLR 386 at 400, Brandon J; affd [1975] 1 QB 929, CA; *A/S Awilco of Solo v Fulvia SpA di Navigazione of Calgiari, The Chikuma* [1981] 1 WLR 314 at 319, HL: see above, p 715). Various attempts have been made to identify the precise moment at which the beneficiary is given an unfettered or unrestricted right against his own bank to the immediate use of the funds transferred. It is submitted that this occurs, and payment is made between originator and beneficiary, when the beneficiary's bank decides to make an unconditional credit to the beneficiary's account, assuming that the bank has the beneficiary's actual or ostensible authority to accept the transfer on his behalf (the leading case is *Momm (t/a Delbrueck & Co) v Barclays Bank International Ltd* [1977] QB 790, an extract from this case appears below; but see also *Tenax Steamship Co Ltd v Brimnes (Owners), The Brimnes* [1975] QB 929, CA; *Libyan Arab Foreign Bank v Bankers Trust Co* [1989] QB 728, 750; *Libyan Arab Foreign Bank v Manufacturers Hanover Trust Co (No 2)* [1989] 1 Lloyd's Rep 608). It does not matter that the beneficiary's bank has yet to credit the beneficiary's account (*The Brimnes*, above; *Momm*, above; cf *Eyles v Ellis* (1827) 4 Bing 112) or notify him of the transfer (*Eyles v Ellis*, above; *Momm*, above; cf *Rekstin v Severo Sibirsko AO* [1933] 1 KB 47 at 57, 62). Where both originator and beneficiary have accounts at the same bank (an 'in-house' transfer) the bank has the assurance of knowing whether the originator has funds in his account to meet the transfer before it decides to make the unconditional credit to the beneficiary's account. In some cases where the originator and beneficiary have accounts at separate banks (an 'inter-bank' transfer), the beneficiary's bank will require to be put in funds by the originator's bank (or an intermediary bank acting on its behalf) before it will reach a decision to make an unconditional transfer. However, in other cases the beneficiary's bank may be prepared to reach its decision to make an unconditional credit to the beneficiary's account before it is put in funds by the originator's bank, eg where the originator's bank and the beneficiary's bank are correspondents. In each case, once the beneficiary's bank has made its decision to credit the beneficiary's account unconditionally the bank accepts the beneficiary as its creditor for the amount in question and is substituted for the originator as the beneficiary's debtor. Payment has then been made as between the originator and the beneficiary.

Momm and Others (trading as Delbrueck & Co) v Barclays Bank International Ltd
[1977] QB 790, Queen's Bench Division

Herstatt Bank, a German bank, as part of a currency exchange transaction with the plaintiffs, ordered a London branch of the defendants to transfer £120,000 from its account held at that branch to the plaintiffs' account, also held at the same branch, 'value June 26, 1974'. Although Herstatt's account was overdrawn at the time, the defendants decided to make the transfer and set in motion the appropriate computer processes to carry it out. Later that day it was announced that Herstatt Bank had ceased trading and was going into liquidation, but no further action was taken by the defendants that day and processing of the payment from Herstatt to the plaintiffs was completed by the defendants' central computer that night. The following day the defendants reversed the transfer. When the plaintiffs later discovered what had happened they claimed that the transfer was irrevocable and that the defendants had wrongly debited their account. Kerr J gave judgment for the plaintiffs.

Kerr J: ... The issue in the present case is shortly whether the debit in Herstatt's account of £120,000 on June 26, 1974, and a corresponding credit in the plaintiffs' account on the same day, which were processed by the central computer overnight but reversed on the following day, constituted a completed payment on the first day, followed by an unauthorised debit on the second day, or whether no completed payment was ever made. The defendants contend that for either or both of two reasons there was no completed payment. First, because no advice note was sent, or other communication made, to the plaintiffs before the credit on their account was reversed. Secondly, because the defendants maintain that the decision to credit the plaintiffs' account was only provisional on the 26th, and that the final decision against making the payment was made on the 27th by reversing the entries. The latter submission is made in particular in the context of a number of recent shipping cases to which I shall have to return, in which the time of decision was treated as the relevant time.

I must next complete the history. As already mentioned, on June 25,1974, pursuant to their contract, Herstatt instructed the defendants' branch to transfer the sum of £120,000 'value June 26' to the plaintiffs' account at this branch, and also gave instructions for two out-payments on the same day totalling £15,000. This telex was submitted to Mr Bass [assistant manager of the bank's inward sterling transfer department] at about midday on the 26th. The reason for consulting him was that on the morning of the 26th the computerised balance of Herstatt's account at the close of business on the previous day showed a debit of about £4,650. This fact in itself had caused no concern to anyone, since there had been no communication about it between Mr Delf [manager in the bank's International Division], Mr Dunn [manager of the bank's inward sterling transfer department] or Mr Bass. Nor had there been any communication with Herstatt about it, as there had been on previous occasions when they had been overdrawn. This is perhaps not surprising, since there had been considerable movements on Herstatt's account during the previous days without any resulting debit balances. A transfer from the plaintiffs of £150,000 and to the plaintiffs of £160,000 had taken place between these parties on June 24. But since Herstatt's account was overdrawn on the morning of the 26th, though only to a small extent, the telex instructions for further payments totalling £135,000 'value June 26' were referred to Mr Bass. He had to make a decision. He could comply with the instructions or refuse to comply with them wholly or in part, or he could consult Mr Delf. His difficulty was, as on every such occasion, that he could not know whether or to what extent these payments would be covered by credits coming in during the day. In fact, though he did not then know it, £140,000 was received for Herstatt's credit at some unknown time on the same day. However, there were also some smaller further debits, with the result that the opening debit balance of about £4,650 rose to about £15,350 by the end of the day. But in the context of the history of the account as a whole over the last six months, this was by no means alarming, and in itself hardly significant. At any rate, and in all the circumstances not surprisingly, Mr Bass decided to allow the payments to be 'actioned' without reference to higher authority. He accordingly gave instructions that all three payments, the in-house transfer of £120,000 and the two out-house payments of £10,000 and £5,000 respectively, were to be made. Banker's payments for the latter two sums were prepared and despatched. As regards the £120,000, the appropriate computer processes were set in motion to debit Herstatt's account, credit the plaintiffs' account and produce the corresponding advice notes.

Now, Mr Bass said in evidence that he distinguished in his mind between the out-house payments of £15,000 and the in-house transfer of £120,000. He said that he decided to 'action' the latter payment only on a provisional basis. This is where it is necessary to choose one's words with care in determining what Mr Bass's mental process was, in so far as this may be relevant. It was in no way an unusual situation. Mr Bass and Mr Dunn, as well as Mr Delf, were continuously making decisions of this kind several times a day. They were fully conscious of the importance of making payments on the 'value' day. There was nothing unusual or particularly difficult about this decision; indeed, Mr Bass did not even refer it to Mr Delf. I think that his decision to sanction the transfer without reference to Mr Delf may to some extent have been influenced by the thought at the back of his mind that if it should unexpectedly appear from the balance on the following morning that this payment had remained substantially uncovered by credits during the day, and if Herstatt were then unable to provide some satisfactory explanation or promise to remedy the situation quickly, there was always the possibility of reversing the entries on the following day. Mr Bass had this at the back of his mind in relation to all substantial in-house payments which might produce an impermissible overdraft. However, on my impression of the witnesses and of the evidence as a whole, it was only to this very limited extent that Mr Bass, or for that matter

Mr Dunn or Mr Delf, would have regarded the transfer as 'provisional.' Thus, the plaintiffs would have been allowed to draw against it at once. If they had inquired whether the payment had been made, they would have been given an affirmative and not an equivocating answer, and I do not accept the evidence in so far as it suggested otherwise. No instructions would have been accepted from Herstatt to revoke the payment after the computerisation processes had begun. To express the position in legal terms, I do not accept that this was merely a conditional transfer in the sense that whether or not it stood depended on what might or might not happen on the following morning. It was an unconditional transfer, but subject to the remote possibility of the entries being reversed on the following day. This possibility, however remote and indeed unprecedented in the case of a banking customer, merely had the effect that the decision whether or not to make certain in-house payments was somewhat easier than in relation to corresponding out-house payments. But apart from this, the decision-making process itself, and all the physical processes in 'actioning' such payments on the 'value' date, were precisely the same.

However, at about 4.15 p.m. on June 26 it was announced that Herstatt had ceased trading and were going into liquidation. But for this, this action would never have seen the light of day. Mr Delf got to hear about it shortly thereafter by telephone from Germany. His recollection is that he then gave instructions either to Mr Dunn or to Mr Bass that the entries relating to the transfer of £120,000 should be reversed *on that day*. I emphasise these words because he emphasised them in the way in which he gave his evidence, and he clearly recognised the importance of arriving at a final position on the 'value' date itself. However, neither Mr Dunn nor Mr Bass had any recollection of this having happened. I cannot accept the accuracy of Mr Delf s recollection on this point. Both Mr Dunn and Mr Bass only heard about Herstatt's failure when they read about it in the press early the following morning. They then spoke to Mr Delf on the telephone. Even then, as I am satisfied on their evidence, the position remained fluid for some little time while further inquiries were being made. At first the only decision was to hold up the despatch of the advice notes concerning the debit and credit of the £120,000. Shortly thereafter Mr Delf gave instructions for the entries to be reversed, and this was done by instructing the computer to debit the plaintiffs' account and to credit Herstatt's account with £120,000 on June 27. Mr Delf also gave instructions that the relevant pages in the statements of Herstatt and the plaintiffs should be retyped before being sent to them, omitting the original entries and their reversals. In so far as it might be relevant, though in my view it is not, I find that none of this would have happened if Herstatt had not ceased trading and if there had merely been a debit balance of about £15,350 on their account on the morning of the 27th. The reason why it was done was that the defendants did not wish an unauthorised debit balance to appear in Herstatt's account at the time when they went into liquidation.

The subsequent events are of little importance. The plaintiffs made various inquiries directed to ascertain whether or not the £120,000 had been paid. They were told that it had not, 'due to the present position of Herstatt's account.' However, when they asked to see the branch's internal records, the photostat copies of the ledger sheets relating to their account were at once sent to them without any prevarication. These clearly showed the original entries on the 26th and their reversal on the 27th, but for some reason these passed unnoticed. It was only several months later, when the plaintiffs came to see photostat copies of Herstatt's ledger sheets which had apparently equally readily been sent to Herstatt, that they realised what had happened. They then brought this action.

The issue is whether or not a completed payment had been made by the defendants to the plaintiffs on June 26. This is a question of law. If the answer is 'Yes,' it is not contested that the plaintiffs have a good cause of action. If there were no authorities on this point, I think that the reaction, both of a lawyer and a banker, would be to answer this question in the affirmative. I think that both would say two things. First, that in such circumstances a payment has been made if the payee's account is credited with the payment at the close of business on the value date, at any rate if it was credited intentionally and in good faith and not by error or fraud. Secondly, I think that they would say that if a payment requires to be made on a certain day by debiting a pay or customer's account and crediting a payee customer's account, then the position at the end of that day in fact and in law must be that this has either happened or not happened, but that the position cannot be left in the air. In my view both these propositions are correct in law.

The only authorities which are of any assistance are those concerning so-called in-house payments. The oldest of them was decided by the Court of Common Pleas nearly 150 years ago. It is indistinguishable on its facts, unless the process of computerisation has changed the law, which the defendants do not contend. It was an action between payor and payee, but it was rightly not suggested, if there was a completed payment as between them, that the position could be different as between the customers and the bank. In *Eyles v Ellis* (1827) 4 Bing 112, the plaintiff and the defendant had accounts at the same bank. The plaintiff sued the defendant for rent. The defendant contended that he had paid it. What happened was that the defendant instructed his banker to transfer the amount of the rent to the plaintiff's account on a Friday, October 8, the banker having omitted to do so on a previous occasion. The defendant's account was then overdrawn, but the banker complied with the defendant's instructions on that Friday by transferring the amount in his books from the defendant's account to the plaintiffs account. On the same day the defendant wrote to the plaintiff to inform him that the mistake had been rectified, but this letter did not reach the plaintiff until the Sunday. Meanwhile the banker failed on the intervening Saturday. The short judgment of the court was given by Best CJ at pp 113–114, and is worth quoting in full:

> The learned serjeant was right in esteeming this a payment. The plaintiff had made the Maidstone bankers his agents, and had authorised them to receive the money due from the defendant. Was it then paid, or was that done which was equivalent to payment? At first, not; but on the 8th a sum was actually placed to the plaintiffs account; and though no money was transferred in specie, that was an acknowledgment from the bankers that they had received the amount from Ellis. The plaintiff might then have drawn for it, and the bankers could not have refused his draft.

The rest of the court concurred.

Eyles v Ellis has been referred to with apparent approval in a number of subsequent cases, and its correctness has never been questioned: see *per* Lopes LJ in *In re Land Development Association* (1888) 39 ChD 259, 271; *per* Sankey J in *British and North European Bank Ltd v Zalzstein* [1927] 2 KB 92, 96, 98 and *per* Mocatta J in *Zim Israel Navigation Co v Effy Shipping Corpn* [1972] 1 Lloyd's Rep 18, 33. The important feature of the case for present purposes is that the payment was held to be complete when the payee's bank account was credited and before the payee had had any notice that this had happened.

I then turn to a case on which Mr Staughton strongly relied on behalf of the defendants. This was *Rekstin v Severo Sibirsko Gosudarstvennoe Akcionernoe Obschestvo Komseverputj and the Bank for Russian Trade Ltd* [1933] 1 KB 47, a decision of the Divisional Court and the Court of Appeal. The facts were very unusual. I will refer to the first defendants, a Russian trading organisation, as 'Severo' and to the second defendant as 'the bank.' The plaintiffs had obtained a judgment against Severo who had an account at the bank. Severo clearly wished to prevent the plaintiffs from levying execution against the moneys in that account. A Russian trade delegation with diplomatic immunity also had an account at the bank. Severo therefore decided, without the knowledge or consent of the delegation, to close their account and to-transfer all the moneys in it to that of the delegation. Severo so instructed the bank by letter. On receipt of the letter a clerk of the bank made the necessary book entry to close Severo's account and also prepared a slip preparatory to crediting the delegation's account with the equivalent sum. However, the corresponding credit entry in the delegation's account had not been made when the plaintiffs served on the bank a garnishee order nisi in respect of their judgment against Severo. In so far as the headnote of the report suggests that all relevant entries had then been made to credit the delegation's account, it is inaccurate. The following three questions arose. (1) Was the mere notice to the bank to close Severo's account sufficient to bring to an end the relation of banker and customer between Severo and the bank? This was answered in the negative, because the bank continued to owe the moneys in the account to Severo until it had either paid them to Severo or to their order. (2) Was the mandate to the bank to transfer the moneys to the account of the trade delegation still revocable in the circumstances? This was answered in the affirmative and is relevant to the present case. (3) If so, did the garnishee order operate as a revocation? This was also answered in the affirmative and is irrelevant here.

It is not easy to extract from the judgments any clear ratio decidendi underlying the answer to the second issue. Mr Staughton submitted that the ratio was simply that payment to the trade delegation had not been completed, because it had not received any notice of the payment. This was said in *Continental Caoutchou and Gutta Percha Co v Kleinwort Sons & Co* (1903) 8 Com Cas 277, where money was paid to the defendant bank under a mistake by the payor of which the payee was aware. It was held that in those circumstances the payor could recover the money from the bank as money received to the payor's use, a result which might well have followed even after the bank had given notice of the mistaken payment to the payee. However, at any rate in the absence of any mistake, a requirement of notice to the payee would be in direct conflict with *Eyles v Ellis,* 4 Bing 112, which does not appear to have been cited in either of these cases and is not referred to in the judgments. I cannot accept this analysis of the effect of the decision in the *Rekstin* case [1933] 1 KB 47. I think that the majority of the judgments show that the decision was based on either or both of two grounds. First, that there had been no final appropriation of the money to the credit of the trade delegation. Secondly, and evidently of greater importance in the minds of the members of the two courts, the fact that the trade delegation knew nothing of the proposed transfer, that there was no transaction between Severo and the delegation underlying it, and that the delegation had accordingly never assented to its account being credited with these moneys. Both these reasons distinguish the case from the present one. In my view this decision should be treated as confined to its special facts. As Mr Tapp [counsel for the plaintiffs] submitted, I think that it merely decided that payment by means of an in-house transfer has not taken place if the payee has not assented to it, and perhaps also if the transfer has not been completed. I therefore reject Mr Staughton's submission that for present purposes the *Retskin* case decides that there could not have been any completed payment to the plaintiffs unless and until an advice note recording the credit to their account had been despatched to them or had been received by them. Mr Staughton preferred to rely on the time of despatch rather than on the time of receipt, because the evidence showed, as indeed one knows from one's own experience, that in practice some days may elapse before an account holder receives notice of a debit or credit to his account. But in my view the time of despatch would in any event be logically unjustifiable as the relevant time. If notice to the account holder is required, then it seems to me that only the receipt of the notice will do. However, apart from the fact that this would be wholly inconsistent with *Eyles v Ellis,* 4 Bing 112 such a rule would create all sorts of commercial difficulties and would also put a large question-mark against the point of time up to which a payor could countermand his instructions. What would happen, for instance, if he instructed the bank to revoke notice of the payment to the payee by telex or telephone between the despatch of the advice note by post and its receipt? The evidence showed, in my view rightly as a matter of law, that the defendants would not have accepted countermanding instructions from Herstatt once the process of crediting the plaintiffs' account had been set in motion pursuant to Herstatt's telex instructions.

This analysis of the legal position is strongly supported by one of the recent shipping cases to which I have already referred. They all concerned situations in which charterers made or purported to make a late payment of time-charter hire and the shipowners claimed to have validly withdrawn the vessel from the charterers' service before the payment was made. The issue was accordingly always a race between the effective time of payment and the time of withdrawal. The only one of these cases which is of direct assistance for present purposes is *The Brimnes* [1975] QB 929, since this concerned an in-house payment. The relevant facts were as follows. The charterers' bankers, Hambros, were instructed to pay the hire to the shipowners' bankers, MGT in New York, where Hambros also had an account. To pay the hire, Hambros instructed MGT by telex to transfer the appropriate amount from Hambros's account to that of the owners. The position was complicated by the fact that the owners had previously assigned the hire to MGT with the result that there was some difference of opinion in the Court of Appeal whether MGT were acting as payees or as the owners' bankers in receiving the hire, but this is irrelevant for present purposes. All the members of the Court of Appeal clearly considered that payment was complete when MGT decided to credit the shipowners' account and acted on that decision. In a later case, which concerned an out-house payment before a differently constituted Court of Appeal, *Mardorf Peach & Co Ltd v Attica Sea Carriers Corpn of Liberia* [1976] QB 835, this point was taken a little further by making it clear that the time of payment was the time when the bank accepted the payment order and decided to act on it, irrespective of the time which had to elapse before the bank's internal accounting processes had been completed.

Mr Staughton's answer to *The Brimnes* [1975] QB 929 was that it was neither argued nor necessary to argue that the time of payment was later than the time when the bank decided to act on the instructions to credit the shipowners' account and began to act on that decision, and that this point was also not argued in any of the other cases. This is correct. He also relied on a passage in the judgment of Megaw LJ at p 964 where he said that 'the time of payment could not be earlier than the time when MGT made their decision to debit Hambros' account...' But taking the judgments as a whole, it is clear that it never occurred to anyone that notice to the payee was an essential ingredient of a completed payment. Both *Eyles v Ellis,* 4 Bing 112 and the *Rekstin* case [1933] 1 KB 47 were cited in argument, but neither was mentioned in the judgments. The judgments are wholly consistent with *Eyles v Ellis* but do not in any way reflect what Mr Staughton seeks to extract from the *Rekstin* case. I therefore conclude that the authorities clearly support the contention that payment in the present case was complete when Mr Bass decided to accept Herstatt's instructions to credit the plaintiffs' account and the computer processes for doing so were set in motion. Indeed, the present case is a fortiori to *The Brimnes* [1975] QB 929 and *Mardorf Peach & Co Ltd v Attica Sea Carriers Corpn of Liberia* [1976] QB 835, because these processes were in fact completed before the defendants purported to revoke the payment by reversing the entries on the following morning.

This only leaves one further point with which I have to some extent already dealt. The defendants' witnesses said that they acted on the basis that the following morning was to be treated as an extension of the 'value' day, because the final balances for that day are not available from the computer until then, and because they always had in mind the possibility of being able to reverse the entries. I cannot accept this. A day is a day. For banking purposes it ends at the close of working hours, and otherwise at midnight. Commerce requires that it should be clearly ascertainable by the end of the day whether a payment due to be made on that day has been made or not. Whether this has happened or not cannot be held in suspense until the following morning. In this case the payment was made on the due day. What happened on the following morning was that the defendants made an unauthorised reverse payment by the plaintiffs to Herstatt.

The defendants suggest that this result will send their system into disarray. But I do not see why, even if this were relevant. It is no more difficult to decide whether to make an in-house payment than an out-house payment; nor to set the necessary processes in motion if the payment is to be made. The consequences of an affirmative decision should be the same in both cases. The only result will be that the defendants will no longer be able to rely, as against their own payee customers, on the possibility of having second thoughts on the following morning.

It follows that this action succeeds and that there will be judgment for the plaintiffs.

NOTES

1.   Kerr J gave judgment for the plaintiffs on the ground that, as between Herstatt and the plaintiffs, the payment was complete the moment the defendant bank decided to credit the plaintiffs' account and initiated the internal payment process. Kerr J also held, following banking practice, that 'a payment has been made if the payee's account is credited with the payment at the close of business on the value date, at any rate if it was credited intentionally and in good faith and not by error or fraud'. This offers a fall back position where it is not

possible to identify precisely when a 'decision' is made to make payment. However, in some cases the posting of a credit to the beneficiary's account may not be conclusive proof of payment (eg the credit may only be provisional). Where it is difficult to identify a 'decision' to make payment a better approach, particularly suitable where funds are available to the beneficiary's bank, is to apply a 'hypothetical positive response' test (see B Geva 'Payment into a Bank Account' [1990] 3 JIBL 108, 112–115; and see also B Geva *Bank Collections and Payment Transactions* (2001), pp 282–289). Under this test payment is complete as between originator and beneficiary at the first point in time when the beneficiary would have been told, if he had contacted the bank, that his account was to be credited.

2.   In *Momm v Barclays Bank International Ltd,* Kerr J emphasised that the transfer was complete when the bank decided to credit the plaintiffs' account *and initiated the computer process for making the transfer.* However, it is submitted that initiation of the payment process is not essential to completion of the transfer. Initiation of the mechanical accounting process merely provides objective evidence that a decision to credit the beneficiary's account has been made, evidence which may be available from other sources. However, the bank must decide to make an *unconditional* credit to the beneficiary's account for the payment to be complete, as a provisional or conditional credit would allow for its subsequent reversal (see, eg *Sutherland v Sutherland v Royal Bank of Scotland plc* [1997] 6 Bank LR 132; *Holmes v Governor of Brixton Prison* [2004] EWHC 2020 (Admin), [2005] 1 All ER 490). In *Momm,* this did not present a problem as the case involved an in-house transfer at a bank holding the originator's funds, but in other cases the bank may be unsure of being put in funds and so decide to make a provisional credit to the beneficiary's account pending the arrival of funds.

QUESTION

Alan, who owes Bert £100 for work done, provides his own bank (A Bank) with the name of Bert's bank (B Bank) and branch, as well as Bert's bank account number, which Bert had previously given him, and instructs A Bank to transfer £100 from his own account into Bert's account held at B Bank. As A Bank and B Bank are correspondent banks, A Bank sends an e-mail to B Bank in the following terms: 'Please credit £100 immediately to Bert's account, and debit our account with you accordingly.' B Bank's computer is programmed in such a way that whenever it receives a credit transfer request by email from A Bank it automatically generates an email in reply agreeing to do as instructed. Such a reply is automatically sent by B Bank to A Bank in this case. However, B Bank has two customers called Bert, and before it has the chance to check which one is meant to receive the credit, B Bank goes into liquidation. Has Alan made payment to Bert? Would it make any difference if B Bank had mistakenly credited £100 to the wrong account just before going into liquidation?

10   UNWANTED PAYMENTS

Mardorf Peach & Co Ltd v Attica Sea Carriers Corporation of Liberia, The Laconia

See above, p 745.

Customs and Excise Commissioners v National Westminster Bank plc

[2002] EWHC 2204 (Ch), [2003] 1 All ER (Comm) 327, Chancery Division

The claimants, the Commissioners of Customs and Excise (the Customs and Excise), were under a statutory obligation to repay overpaid value added tax (VAT) to the taxpayer, Car Disposals Ltd (CDL). CDL wrote to the Customs and Excise informing them that 'the cheque be paid direct to our solicitors... for them to bank into their client account. The reason [we] make this request is that we are experiencing difficulties with our bank.' Despite this request, the Customs and Excise paid in error a sum representing the amount of overpaid VAT into CDL's account with the defendant bank, National Westminster Bank (NatWest), which duly credited CDL's account with the money, thereby reducing CDL's existing overdraft. On discovering this, CDL complained to the Customs and Excise, which paid CDL a second time by transfer to their solicitors as originally requested. Meanwhile, the Customs and Excise asked Nat West to repay the sum paid to them by mistake. NatWest refused to do so. The Customs and Excise commenced proceedings. NatWest's defence was that the payment had been made for good consideration, which was a recognised defence to recovery of a claim for recovery of a mistaken payment (see above, p 578). NatWest claimed that it was authorised to accept payment on behalf of CDL and, therefore, the payment discharged the Customs and Excise's debt to CDL. The Customs and Excise denied that payment in a manner contrary to CDL's instructions constituted discharge of the debt.

Judge Rich QC (sitting as a judge of the High Court):

...

[6] The mistake alleged in the particulars of claim is:

The claimants, in error, overlooked CDL's letter of instruction, dated 15 October 1998, and acted under a mistaken belief or assumption that CDL had authorised the defendant to accept payment of the VAT refund from the claimants.

If Mr Wolfson [Counsel for NatWest] is right that the defendant was authorised to accept payment, then the mistake alleged was not made, but he accepts that at the least the Customs and Excise were mistaken in believing that they had been authorised to make payment to the bank and counsel are, therefore, agreed that the issue to be determined by the court is as to the authority of the bank and its consequent effect to discharge the claimant's debt to CDL.

[7] In *TSB Bank of Scotland plc v Welwyn Hatfield DC* [1993] 2 Bank LR 267, Hobhouse J made a distinction between what he called the ministerial or physical act of delivery of money and payment of a debt. The case concerns a preliminary issue between Welwyn and Brent, as third party, which the judge (at 271) defined as: 'what suffices to discharge the liability of the recipient of money paid in under an ultra vires contract to make restitution to the payer of the money.'

[8] Brent had paid the capital sum so obtained into Welwyn's bank account. The judge held (at 271): 'what Brent had to show for the purpose of their defence is the same as that necessary to provide a defence to a claim in debt.' Counsel are agreed that the Customs and Excise's statutory duty to repay overpaid VAT is to be treated as a contractual debt. Accordingly, the judgment is precisely in point as to whether the present claimants would, after their payment to the bank, have had a defence to a claim by CDL for the payment which, in fact, they did make to CDL's solicitors.

[9] The judge explained (at 271–272):

To discharge a debt there must have been an accepted payment of that debt, not a mere receipt by the creditor of the sum of money. The late Dr Francis Mann at page 75 of the 'Legal Aspect of Money' [5th edn, 1992], says: 'No creditor is under any legal duty to accept any payment and no debtor can force any payment of any kind upon his creditor without the latter's consent express or implied, precedent or subsequent.' All the debtor can do is make an unconditional tender of the relevant sum to the creditor; if the creditor accepts the sum the liability of the debtor is appropriately discharged or reduced; if the creditor refuses to accept the tender, the debtor may, provided that he remains ready and willing to pay the relevant sum and pays it into court if action is brought against him, raise the defence of tender to the creditor's claim in respect of the debt. The unaccepted tender, therefore, does not discharge the debt but it provides the debtor with a protection in respect of costs and against any award of interest. Brent do not rely upon any defence of tender in this case since they have on a subsequent occasion declined to pay the relevant sum and when sued, instead of paying the sum into court, have disputed their liability altogether. The defence of Brent is a defence of payment before action brought... The physical or ministerial aspect of payment involves the delivery of money by one person to another. Where the two persons meet face to face and the debtor seeks to hand to the creditor legal tender the physical act of delivery (in the absence of some misrepresentation or mistake) will not be achieved without the concurrence of the debtor. Where the relevant contract or the terms of the debt require payment to be made in a particular way, as for example by payment into an identified account at a particular branch of a named bank, the payment will be effected by payment into that account. Prior authority has been given to discharge the debt or other obligation in that way; the debtor has authorised the bank (or other relevant person) to receive and accept the money on his behalf. No further act of concurrence or assent is required from the debtor. The creditor discharges his obligation by making the contractual payment in the contractually stipulated manner.

[10]   In the particular circumstances of that case the judge held that there had been no prior authority for Brent to discharge its liability by payment into Welwyn's bank account, but held that by keeping the money for three weeks and making use of it to earn interest Welwyn had accepted the payment. It does, therefore, in my judgment, constitute authority for the proposition that unsolicited payment to a creditor's bank account will not constitute payment of a debt unless accepted as such. It is no part of the bank's case in this present case that there was any acceptance by CDL.

[11]   Mr Wolfson suggests that the *Welwyn* case could be distinguished on the basis that it was the particular dealings between Brent and Welwyn which made specific authorisation necessary, but realistically accepting the impossibility of such distinction, he invited me to say that the case proceeded on an unwarranted concession, recorded (at 272) as follows:

'Brent accept that they have to show something more than [that the money was paid into an account which was solely under the control of Welwyn] to prove an effective payment which would satisfy the criteria for a common law defence of payment.'

The passages which I have already cited from the judgment of Hobhouse J show that this was not a matter of concession; it was part of the reasoning of the judge which Brent felt bound to accept.

[12]   Mr Wolfson submits that such acceptance is inconsistent with the accepted definition of the scope of a bank's relationship with its customer which Atkin LJ gave in *Joachimson (N) (a firm) v Swiss Bank Corp* [1921] 3 KB 110, [1921] All ER Rep 92 at 100 when he said:

I think that there is only one contract made between the bank and its customer. The terms of that contract involve obligations on both sides and require careful statement. They appear upon consideration to include the following provisions. The bank undertakes to receive money and to collect bills for its customer's account. The proceeds so received are not to be held in trust for the customer, but the bank borrows the proceeds and undertakes to repay them.

I do not need to read any more of the definition. Mr Wolfson says that that undertaking to receive money and collect bills means that the customer must be taken to have authorised a bank so to do. I accept that, but once the distinction between receiving money and collecting bills (the ministerial act) is distinguished from acceptance of payment it can be seen that this dictum is not inconsistent with the requirement to show something more in the form of prior authorisation to prove an effective payment.

[13] Mr Wolfson referred me to a decision of Kerr J in *Momm v Barclays Bank* [1976] 3 All ER 588, [1977] QB 790, but it is not, I think, of assistance because there had been a direction by the creditor to pay into the particular bank account in that case.

[14] In *Royal Products Ltd v Midland Bank Ltd and Bank of Valletta Ltd* [1981] 2 Lloyds Rep 194 at 198, Webster J is recorded as having held that a bank was impliedly authorised by its customer to accept a credit 'by virtue of the fact that the customer had a current account with it', but this was said in the context of an instruction to one bank, of which the plaintiff was a customer, to transfer funds to another bank, of which it was also a customer. It was, as the judge said (at 198):

> ...a banking operation of a kind which is often carried out internally, that is to say, within the same bank or between two branches of the same bank and which, at least from the point of view of the customer, is no different in nature or quality when, as in the present case, it is carried out between different banks.

[15] In my judgment, the judge's analysis of the position in that case cannot justify the conclusion that a bank is impliedly authorised to accept a credit from a third party as payment to its customer, albeit it is its function and duty to accept delivery of funds to have such effect in law as may be determined between the parties. I conclude, therefore, that there is no general rule which enables Mr Wolfson to say that the defendant is, merely by virtue of holding a current account for CDL, authorised to receive payment from the Customs and Excise on CDL's behalf so as to discharge their debt to CDL. No specific authorisation is suggested.

I therefore give judgment to the claimant for £44,454.53 as asked.

NOTES

1.   In *TSB Bank of Scotland plc v Welwyn Hatfield District Council and Council of the London Borough of Brent* [1993] 2 Bank LR 267, Hobhouse J held that a beneficiary (payee) would be deemed to have accepted an unauthorised payment made into his account where he dealt with the transferred funds as his own. In that case the issue before the court was whether an inter-bank transfer of funds by one local authority into the account of another local authority amounted to payment of an underlying restitutionary liability. Hobhouse J held that, despite initial protestations, retention of the money for three weeks, use of the money and eventual return of the money without interest amounted to acceptance of tender by the beneficiary local authority and, therefore, payment.

2.   In *TSB Bank of Scotland plc v Welwyn Hatfield District Council and Council of the London Borough of Brent* (above), the beneficiary local authority was at all times aware that the unauthorised payment had been made into its account. This may not always be the case. In *HMV Fields Properties Ltd v Bracken Self Selection Fabrics Ltd* 1991 SLT 31, a Scottish case, a landlord served the Scottish equivalent of a notice of forfeiture on his tenant for breach of various covenants in the lease. The tenant refused to move out and arbitration proceedings were commenced. Meanwhile, the tenant continued to pay rent by bank giro credit transfer into the landlord's bank account (above, p 732), something which the landlord did not notice for several weeks. When the rent payments eventually came to the landlord's attention it returned them to the tenant, again using the bank giro credit transfer system. On appeal from the arbitration it was held by the First Division of the Inner House of the Court of Session that the landlord was not barred from forfeiture by reason of having accepted rent. It was held that 'acceptance' was a question of fact and, despite the landlord's initial delay of several weeks before returning the rent, there had been no acceptance here. In this case the beneficiary had no knowledge of the payment being made into the account, whereas in the *TSB Bank of Scotland* case the beneficiary was fully aware of the payment.

3. In *Dovey v Bank of New Zealand* [2000] 3 NZLR 641, D instructed his bank (BNZ) in New Zealand to transfer funds to 'my account' at a bank (BCCI) in Luxembourg. In fact D had no account with BCCI. BNZ purported to execute the transfer by instructing its agent bank in London to transfer funds to BCCI's agent bank in London. Payment was made between the agent banks at 10 am on a day about a week later, but at 1 pm on the same day liquidators were appointed to BCCI. In an inadequately pleaded claim against BNZ, D alleged that the bank was in breach of contract because it had not completed his instructions. D alleged that the transaction was incomplete because BCCI had not formally opened an account for him and so had to be treated as holding the funds as agent for BNZ. The New Zealand Court of Appeal showed little hesitation in rejecting that claim. It held that by nominating the bank to which the funds were to be transferred, D gave the bank authority to accept funds on his behalf, even though the bank had yet to open an account for him. There was nothing more BNZ could have done to complete the transaction. Tipping J, delivering the judgment of the Court, added (at [26]) that: '[i]f the receiving bank does not have the payee's authority to receive the money, it is treated as acting pro tanto as the paying bank's agent until that authority is received or the transaction reversed.'

QUESTION

Why would a beneficiary of a funds transfer not want to receive those funds into his bank account?

CHAPTER 19

CHEQUES AND OTHER INSTRUMENTS

1 CHEQUES

A cheque is defined by s 73 of the Bills of Exchange Act 1882 as 'a bill of exchange drawn on a banker payable on demand'. Section 73 also states that except as otherwise provided in the part of the Bills of Exchange Act 1882 relating to cheques (ss 73–82), the provisions of that Act applicable to bills of exchange payable on demand apply to cheques.

All cheques are bills of exchange, and the s 73 definition of a cheque must be read together with that of a bill of exchange set out in s 3 of the Bills of Exchange Act 1882 (above, p 532). However, it has long been recognised that a cheque has, in truth, very different characteristics from those of a bill of exchange (see, eg *Ramchurn Mullick v Luchmeechund Radakissen* (1854) 9 Moo PCC 46 at 69–70, Parke B). First, a cheque, being payable on demand, is intended as an instrument which will immediately be paid, whereas a bill of exchange is frequently drawn payable at a future date and is intended as a credit instrument. Secondly, unlike bills of exchange, cheques are not, and are not intended to be, accepted by the bank on which they are drawn. A bank which refuses or fails to pay a cheque incurs no liability to the payee or other holder of the cheque, whose remedy is to sue the drawer (but where a cheque is supported by a cheque guarantee card the paying bank undertakes to the payee to honour the cheque provided certain conditions are met: see below, p 808). Thirdly, while bills of exchange are often negotiated and the subject of indorsement over to third parties, modern banking law and practice means that cheques are rarely transferred to third parties, beyond the payee. Since the Cheques Act 1992 introduced s 81A into the Bills of Exchange Act 1882, to the effect that crossed cheques marked 'account payee' or 'a/c payee', with or without the word 'only', are not transferable, United Kingdom banks now almost invariably supply their customers with cheque forms which are crossed and pre-printed with the words 'account payee', so that the cheque is valid only as between the parties to it. It follows that the vast majority of cheques issued in the United Kingdom are not negotiable instruments but merely payment orders directing the bank to pay the amount of the cheque to the named payee. This has led one leading commentator to conclude that much of the 'old learning' relating to the negotiability and indorsement of cheques should be jettisoned; that cheques should now be analysed along with other payment methods in the context of the ordinary law governing the banker-customer relationship (the rules as to mandate and countermand are considered above, p 631 and p 638 respectively); and that, at least in the context of the typical account-payee cheque, bills of exchange law should no longer be allowed to dominate the discussion

(R Cranston *Principles of Banking Law* (2nd edn, 2002), p 258). There is much truth in this statement, but it is submitted that it would be premature to ditch all the 'old learning' on negotiability, indorsement and the Bills of Exchange Act 1882, not least because it remains possible for the drawer, before or at the time of issuing a cheque, to delete, and so cancel, the words 'account payee' printed on the cheque, so that the cheque becomes transferable and payable to order or bearer as the case may be. Those payees without bank accounts may well ask the drawer to do this to enable them to transfer the cheque to a friend who has a bank account so that the cheque may be collected through that account (the particular problems facing the 'unbanked' payee of an 'account payee' cheque are explored by JK Macleod in (1997) 113 LQR 133). However, there can be no doubt that modern banking law and practice make it high time for the law of cheques to be severed from the Bills of Exchange Act 1882 and dealt with in separate legislation, as with the Australian Cheques and Payment Orders Act 1986 (in 1998 the Act was amended and renamed the Cheques Act 1986). It should also be noted that the UNCITRAL Convention on Bills of Exchange and Promissory Notes (New York, 1988) specifically excludes cheques.

(a) Crossed cheques

A cheque is crossed when two parallel transverse lines are drawn across its face. This is a general crossing and means that the cheque must be presented for payment through a bank account (Bills of Exchange Act 1882, s 76(1), sometimes the words 'and company', or an abbreviation of those words, are inserted between the parallel lines but this adds nothing). The holder of a crossed cheque cannot present it in person for cash. Sometimes the name of a bank will be written on the face of the cheque. This is a special crossing and means that the cheque must be presented for payment through the named bank (BEA, s 76(2)).

A transferee of a crossed cheque which is also marked 'not negotiable' cannot acquire a better title than his transferor had, although the cheque remains transferable (BEA, s 81). An *uncrossed* cheque marked 'not negotiable' is probably non-transferable (*Hibernian Bank Ltd v Gysin and Hanson* [1939] 1 KB 483; cf *National Bank v Silke* [1891] 1 QB 435, 438; and see AG Guest, *Chalmers and Guest on Bills of Exchange* (16th edn, 2005), para 14–035). Crossed cheques marked 'not negotiable' and uncrossed cheques are hardly ever seen today.

In 1992, following the enactment of the Cheques Act 1992, which introduced s 81A(1) into the BEA, where a cheque is crossed and bears across its face the words 'account payee' or 'a/c payee', either with or without the word 'only', the cheque is non-transferable and is only valid as between the parties to it, ie, the drawer and the payee. Today virtually all cheque forms supplied by UK banks to their customers are crossed and pre-printed 'account payee'. Only the named payee can be the holder of such a cheque. Figure 1 shows a crossed cheque marked 'account payee'.

Who can cross a cheque? By s 77 of the BEA 1882, only the drawer, holder and certain bankers may cross a cheque. A holder may cross an uncrossed cheque or alter a previous crossing by making it more restrictive eg turning a general crossing into a special crossing (BEA, s 77(2), (3) and (4)). A banker to whom a cheque is specially crossed may cross it to another banker for collection (BEA, s 77(5)). If an uncrossed cheque, or a cheque crossed generally, is sent to a banker for collection, he may cross it specially to himself (BEA, s 77(6)). A crossing authorised by the 1882 Act is a material part of the cheque and it is unlawful to obliterate or, except as authorised by the Act, to add to or to alter the crossing (BEA, s 78).

OXBRIDGE BANK   12-34-56
CAMBRIDGE, FENNERS BRANCH

DATE   1 January 2008

PAY   Tom Smith   ONLY

Five hundred and fifty pounds   ACCOUNT PAYEE   £ 550

                                 A.N. OTHER
                                 Andy Other

CHEQUE NO   SORT CODE   ACCOUNT NO
111213   123456   007891011

Figure 1 Cheque crossed 'Account Payee'

Obliteration or unauthorised alteration of the crossing engages s 64 of the Act and voids the cheque except as provided by that section (see above, p 569). However, in those rare cases where a cheque form is not pre-printed with an 'account payee' crossing, the payee of a crossed cheque is probably entitled after issue to add the words 'account payee' to the cheque (making it non-transferable) and this would not be a material alteration or contravene s 78 of the Act (AG Guest *Chalmers and Guest on Bills of Exchange* (16th edn, 2005), para 8–083).

The bank on which a cheque is drawn (ie the bank where the drawer keeps his account) must be careful to pay in accordance with the crossing. The crossing is part of the mandate and failure to adhere to it prevents the bank from debiting the drawer's account (*Bellamy v Majoribanks* (1852) 7 Exch 389, 404; *Bobbett v Pinkett* (1876) 1 Ex D 368, 372). Moreover, s 79(2) of the BEA provides that the bank will be liable to the 'true owner' of the cheque for any loss incurred owing to the cheque having been paid contrary to the crossing, eg where a thief steals a crossed cheque from the payee and the bank allows the thief to present it for payment over the counter. If the true owner is the drawer he will have no claim since he can require the bank to reinstate his account (*Channon v English, Scottish & Australian Bank* (1918) 18 SR (NSW) 30, 38). Section 79(2) goes on to protect the drawer's bank against a claim by the true owner, and allows the bank to debit the drawer's account, where the cheque does not appear (i) to be crossed, or (ii) to have had a crossing which has been obliterated, or (iii) to have a crossing which has been added to or amended in an unauthorised manner, provided that the bank acted in good faith and without negligence.

QUESTIONS

1.   What are the benefits of crossing a cheque?

2.   Are any of the following cheques transferable ? See AG Guest *Chalmers and Guest on Bills of Exchange* (16th edn, 2005), para 14–039.

(1)   An uncrossed cheque marked 'account payee only'.

(2)   A crossed cheque drawn (in handwriting) 'Pay X or order', but bearing the pre printed words 'account payee' across its face.

(3) A crossed cheque drawn (in handwriting) 'Pay Bearer', but bearing the pre-printed words 'account payee' across its face.

(4) A crossed cheque drawn (in handwriting) 'Pay X or bearer', but bearing the pre printed words 'account payee' across its face.

(b) The clearing system

A cheque is a debit instrument. It must be presented for payment to the paying bank, which is the bank on which it is drawn (ie where the drawer keeps his account). The collecting bank is the bank whose customer is the payee or other holder of the cheque and which is entrusted with collection of the amount of the cheque on the customer's behalf and the crediting of it to his account. The cheque clearing system facilitates this process by enabling the bulk presentation of cheques from collecting banks to paying banks in order that they may be paid or dishonoured.

Not all cheques need to be presented for payment through the clearing system. Cheques drawn on the same or a different branch of the payee's bank do not go through the clearing. Where the cheque is uncrossed it need not go through the clearing because it may be presented in person by the payee for payment in cash over the counter of the branch of the paying bank on which it is drawn. Only crossed cheques need be presented for payment through a bank, and even then it is possible for a crossed cheque to be presented for payment without using the clearing system. This applies where the cheque is specially presented by the collecting bank, at the request of the payee, directly to the branch of the paying bank on which it is drawn. However, in practice most cheques are presented for payment through the cheque clearing system.

Barclays Bank plc v Bank of England
[1985] 1 All ER 385, Bingham J sitting as judge-arbitrator

Bingham J: …The origins of the clearing house as it exists today can be traced back to a device adopted by bank employees in the eighteenth century, largely (as it would seem) for their own convenience. During the early years of the eighteenth century the banks employed walk clerks whose task it was to call at other banks in the City and the West End of London to present cheques for payment and obtain cash in exchange. As the use of cheques increased so this task became increasingly laborious. As a result a practice grew whereby, instead of visiting other banks on foot, the clerks would meet at a central point, exchange cheques and settle the difference between the total exchanged. To begin with, the meeting place was unofficial and unrecognised, but the advantages of this central exchange were obvious and in due course a room was hired and, in 1833, a building erected on the present site. The respondent entered the clearing house in 1864…

I start with the case where a customer of a bank (the presenting or collecting bank) delivers to the presenting bank for collection and credit to his account a cheque drawn on another bank (the paying bank) by a person having an account at a branch of the paying bank, the cheque being eligible for handling through the…clearing….The steps which will normally follow are these. (1) The cheque will be stamped (crossed) on receipt by the branch which receives it. The amount will normally be credited to the customer's account forthwith. The customer will not, however, receive value for the cheque on that date: thus the customer cannot without agreement withdraw the sum prior to clearance, he will not earn interest or (if overdrawn) be relieved of his obligation to pay interest and it will not rank as a credit for purposes of calculating bank charges. The credit is provisional in the sense that it will be reversed if the cheque is dishonoured or not satisfactorily cleared and there is in any event a delay before it will become fully effective. (2) The branch which receives the cheque will in most cases encode it, by adding the sum payable under it in magnetisible ink to the cheque number, branch reference number and account number which are already printed on the bottom of it. At the end of the banking day the branch will sort out the cheques received during the day into bundles, one bundle for each bank whose cheques have been received. (3) These bundles will be collected from the branch during the evening of that day or early in the morning of the following day and taken to the clearing department of the pre-senting bank. If the encoding has not for any reason been done at the branch it will be done there, early on the day following receipt of the cheque at the branch. All the bundles received by the presenting bank from all its branches will then be amalgamated and placed in boxes labelled with the name of the bank on which they are drawn, the paying bank. They will also be checked to ensure that the cheques are all facing the same way, have the magnetisable ink characters at the bottom, are free of staples and are unfolded. They will be subject to no other inspection. (4) The cheques so sorted will then be taken in closed boxes to the clearing house, where they are either handed over to employees of the various paying banks or placed in racks reserved for those banks. The boxes are not opened and the cheques themselves are not the subject of consideration or inspection, which would be quite impracticable given that the cheques so handled run to several millions each day. (Sometimes the exchange or delivery may take place not at the clearing house but at the clearing department of the paying bank, but it is not suggested that this variation of practice gives rise to any difference of principle). (5) From the clearing house the cheques will be taken to the clearing department of the paying bank, whose employees then feed all the cheques received for payment into reader-sorter machines. This process performs a number of functions. First, it sorts the cheques received into bundles for each of the paying bank's branches on which cheques have been drawn (and, for some branches, further sorts the cheques according to account number of customer's name). Second, it checks the totals charged against the paying bank in the clearing by the various presenting banks which have delivered cheques for payment, making necessary corrections. Third, it records the magnetisable references on the cheques sorted, so that this information can be transmitted to the computer centre where branch accounts are maintained. From this information a computer projection is (or is in some cases) made showing the state of customer's accounts at the end of the next day if the cheques are paid and no further transactions occur, but no alteration is made to the accounts themselves. No consideration is given to the validity or payability of a cheque at this stage. Thus a cheque obviously defective, for example because unsigned, will not be weeded out but will be treated in the same way as all other cheques. (6) Having been sorted, the cheques drawn on each branch will be delivered to that branch, so as to arrive during the night of the day on which they were received from the presenting bank or early the following morning. On the opening of the branch each cheque received overnight for payment will be inspected and considered by an officer of the branch to determine whether the cheque is technically in order (properly signed and dated, with numbers and figures corresponding, without unsigned alteration, and so on) and whether there is any reason (such as lack of funds, countermand or injunction) why the cheque should not be honoured. In the case of cheques for small amounts, or large and respected customers issuing large numbers of cheques, the process of inspection and consideration may be abbreviated, but the process described is the norm. If the cheque is to be paid, it is cancelled and the drawer's account is debited at the end of that working day. The debit projected by the computer will then take effect. If the cheque is not to be paid, it will be sent by first class post at the end of that working day to the branch at which it was delivered for collection and the computer projection entry will be reversed. Under rules agreed between the banks with seats in the clearing house, to which I must return, this step must be taken on the day the cheque is received at the branch, save in the case of inadvertence, when a delay until the next day is permitted. A telephone call will in that case be made to the branch at which the cheque was received for collection. (7) At the end of each working day the claimants settle between themselves by paying net balances between them. This is done by means of daily transfers to and from accounts maintained by each of them with the respondent [ie the Bank of England]. Such settlements comprise differences established in the…clearing carried out by their clearing departments on the preceding day…, in each case on the assumption that all the cheques received for payment will be honoured. Dishonoured or unpaid cheques are the subject of later adjustment.

NOTES

1.   Since 1985 the cheque clearing system for England and Wales has been run by the Cheque and Credit Clearing Co Ltd, which operates under the supervision of the Association for Payment Clearing Services (the Cheque and Credit Clearing Co is also responsible for the Scottish cheque clearing which takes place in Edinburgh). The cheque clearing takes place in Milton Keynes (having moved there from London in September 2003). It is conducted by the Cheque and Credit Clearing Co on behalf of its settlement members and in accordance with the *Rules for the Conduct of the Cheque Clearing* (but there is also a growing amount of direct exchange of cheques on a bilateral basis at the premises of the collecting or the paying bank). Member banks and building societies are known as settlement members because they must maintain settlement accounts at the Bank of England. Where a non-member bank or building society wishes to use the clearing it must employ the services of a member to act as its agent. A separate town clearing system, for the same day clearing of high value cheques drawn on and paid into City branches of participating banks, was abolished in February 1995. In January 1999 the Cheque and Credit Clearing Co Ltd set up a clearing system for cheques drawn in euros; the system is generally the same as that for the clearing of sterling cheques.

2.   Bingham J describes a 'clearing cycle' that took three banking days after receipt of the cheque. For example, the proceeds of a cheque paid into the payee's account on Monday would not finally be credited to the payee's account, for the purposes of gaining interest or reducing his overdraft, until Thursday. This delay has been criticised and, following the recommendations of the payment systems taskforce set up by the Office of Fair Trading, the banks agreed to reform the clearing process. From November 2007, the payee of a UK cheque has been entitled to interest (if the account bears interest) or credit, if overdrawn, on the proceeds after a maximum of two days from deposit of the cheque, to withdraw the proceeds after a maximum of four days, and to know the fate of the cheque after a maximum of six days. This means that after six working days funds credited to his account cannot be reclaimed, eg, if there are insufficient funds in the drawer's account. These changes are now reflected in the terms of the *Banking Code* and the *Business Banking Code* (2008 editions).

3.   The physical transportation of each cheque from the branch of the collecting bank where it has been deposited for collection, via the clearing house, to the branch of the paying bank on which the cheque is drawn, is a time-consuming and costly process. It requires the daily movement between banks of around 4.9 million cheques (which is the average daily volume of cheques exchanged in England). Cheque truncation short-circuits this process (on cheque truncation generally, see J Vroegop [1990] LMCLQ 244). With a fully truncated system, data from the magnetic ink codeline at the bottom of the cheque is sent electronically from the collecting bank to the paying bank, with the cheque being retained by the collecting bank. (Cheques are issued to customers with the bank and branch number, the account number and the cheque number encoded on them in machine-readable form; and, when the cheque is deposited for collection, the payee's account details and the amount of the cheque are also added in machine-readable form.) The same process applies to a partly truncated system, save that the cheque is not retained by the collecting bank, but kept at the clearing centre of the paying bank.

4.   The collecting bank owes a duty to its customer to present for payment all cheques deposited for collection (*Hare v Henty* (1861) 10 CBNS 65). Presentment is governed by the Bills of Exchange Act 1882, s 45. Section 45 provides that a bill of exchange must be duly presented for payment, and that failure to do so discharges the drawer and indorsers. The bill must be presented 'at the proper place' (BEA, s 45(3)). In the case of a cheque the courts have interpreted this requirement to mean that the cheque must be physically presented for payment at the branch of the bank on which it is drawn and that presentment by electronic means (ie truncation) would not comply with the requirements of s 45 (*Barclays Bank plc v Bank of England* [1985] 1 All ER 385 at 386, Bingham J). However, following an earlier recommendation of the Review Committee on Banking Services Law and Practice (Cm 622, 1989) rec 7(8)), which was accepted by the Government (White Paper (Cm 1026,1990) Annex 5, paras 5.11–5.13), the Bills of Exchange Act 1882 was amended in November 1996 so as to allow for presentment of cheques by electronic means (Deregulation (Bills of Exchange) Order 1996, SI 1996/2993). Section 74B(1) of the 1882 Act permits the collecting bank, as an alternative method of presentment, to notify the paying bank of the cheque's 'essential features' by electronic means or otherwise, instead of presenting the cheque itself. The essential features of the cheque are defined as: (a) its serial number, (b) the paying bank's code, (c) the drawer's account number, and (d) the amount of the cheque as entered by the drawer (BEA, s 74B(6)). However, where a cheque has been presented for payment under s 74B(1) the paying bank may, before close of business on the next business day following presentment, call on the collecting bank to present the cheque itself, and if the paying bank makes such a request, presentment under s 74B(1) is to be disregarded (BEA, s 74B(3)). This provision is important where the paying bank suspects the drawer's signature has been forged or that there has been some other unauthorised alteration of the cheque. In any event it is always open for the banks to agree amongst themselves that certain cheques will still be physically presented for payment, eg high value cheques. Further, s 74A of the 1882 Act enables the paying bank by public notice to specify its clearing centre or head office as the proper place to present the cheque (and this is not limited to presentment by the alternative means allowed by s 74B).

5.   Despite the change in the law allowing for full cheque truncation, this is, in practice, likely to remain some way off. The falling number of cheque transactions (between 1995 and 2005 the number of cheques exchanged between banks has fallen by 60%) due to increased use of payment by direct debit (above, p 720) and by debit card (below, p 809), means that the cost of operating a fully truncated system could be high. The clearing banks have developed an Inter Bank Data Exchange (IBDE) system to allow for the electronic exchange of cheque magnetic codeline information between collecting and paying banks, but this system is currently only used to operate a system of partial truncation with the cheque itself still being physically presented through the clearing system to the paying bank's clearing centre, and retained there, or some other central location in the paying bank, without being sent on to the branch on which it is drawn.

6.   Where a cheque is drawn on the same branch as that of the payee, and the payee pays it into that branch, the cheque does not pass through the clearing (it is a question of fact whether the cheque is presented to the bank in its capacity as drawee or whether it is received by the bank as agent for collection: *Boyd v Emmerson* (1834) 2 Ad & El 184; *Sutherland v Royal Bank of Scotland plc* [1997] 6 Bank LR 132). The branch determines whether or not the cheque is to be paid and, if it is, the accounts of the drawer and the payee held at that branch are adjusted accordingly. Where the cheque is drawn on a different branch of the payee's bank the process is the same as if the drawer and the payee banked at different banks, except that the cheque does not pass through the clearing. The cheque is sent by the collecting branch to the clearing centre of that bank where it is sorted and dispatched to the branch on which it was drawn. Where the payee pays a cheque into a bank other than his own for collection, the collecting bank will send the paying in slip through the clearing house to the clearing department of the payee's bank, which will forward it to the branch to which the proceeds of the cheque are to be paid ('the payee's branch'), and the collecting bank will send the cheque through the clearing house to the clearing department of the drawer's bank, which will forward it to the drawer's branch.

(c) Protection of the paying bank

'Bank's liability for paying fraudulently issued cheques' by EP Ellinger
(1985) 5 Ox JLS 293, pp 293–294

1. Introduction

In recent years there has been an abundance of cases in which dishonest employees have perpetrated frauds by misusing their employer's cheque book. By now some well defined patterns have emerged. There are cases in which the employee obtains a signature executed on a blank or on a partly completed cheque and then fills the instrument in improperly or changes a 'material detail' (within s 64 of the Bills of Exchange Act 1882, the 'BEA') by making the instrument payable to himself or by raising its amount.

Other frauds include the theft of instruments payable to the employer and their payment into the employee's personal account either under a forged indorsement (see, eg *Orbit Mining and Trading Co v Westminster Bank Ltd* [1963] 1 QB 794) or by the imaginative means of opening an account under a suitable fictitious name. By the same token, the employee may steal cheques issued by his employer to a genuine client and pay them to the credit of an account surreptitiously opened by him in the true payee's name. (See, eg *Marfani & Co Ltd v Midland Bank Ltd* [1968] 1 WLR 956; *Lumsden & Co v London Trustee Savings Bank* [1971] 1 Lloyd's Rep 114). The last and most crude type of fraud is the forgery of the employer's signature as drawer by the employee (for a remarkable case in recent years see *National Bank of New Zealand v Walpole & Patterson Ltd* [1975] 2 NZLR 7).

In all three types of case, the drawee bank honours the instrument in breach of its authority. In the first type of case, the cheque is vitiated when the material detail is altered (s 64 BEA). In addition, the bank pays an excessive amount or meets the demand of a person other than the intended payee. In the second case, it pays a cheque under a forged indorsement of the payee, which does not transfer the instrument (*Lacave v Crédit Lyonnais* [1897] 1 QB 148). The bank therefore does not comply with the drawer's instruction to pay the instrument to the 'holder' (given when the cheque is drawn to order: BEA, s 8).

It is clear that bankers are unable to recognize a fraud involving a forged indorsement. The signature of the payee or of the holder is unknown to them. A protection was conferred on them for the first time under s 19 of the Stamp Act 1853, which provided the model for the current provision: s 60 of the BEA. (Section 19 is still in force in respect of instruments which, being outside the scope of the BEA, are not governed by s 60; the bankers' draft—drawn on himself—is an example; *Capital and Counties Bank Ltd v Gordon* [1903] AC 240, 250–1; *Charles v Blackwell* (1877) 2 CPD 151, 159.) In cases of this type, the best advice that can be given to the customer (or 'true owner') is to sue the collecting bank. That bank is liable in conversion, unless it has collected the cheque in good faith, without negligence and for a customer (in which case it is protected by s 4 of the Cheques Act 1957).

In the other two types of fraud, the customer's rights against his own bank depend on common law doctrines. His argument would usually be that the bank paid the cheque without having the mandate to do so. This is particularly so where the customer's signature as drawer was forged. (That the bank's liability is not based on its failure to recognize the customer's signature has been clear since *Cocks v Masterman* (1858) 18 CB 273.) (That he could also sue the collecting bank, see *Chitty on Contracts* (25th edn, 1983) § 2463 and authorities there cited.)

The customer's action against his own bank usually assumes the form of an application for a declaration that the bank is not entitled to debit his account with the forged items. The bank has two possible defences. The one is based on negligence and on estoppel. Fundamentally, it asserts that the frauds or forgeries were occasioned by the customer's own carelessness, which involved a breach of a duty of care owed by him to the bank. It is said that he is, accordingly, precluded from disputing the debits involved. The other, frequently related defence, is based on the customer's failure to detect the frauds through his periodic statements. In some cases these statements include counterfoils which the customer is expected to return to the bank with an indication of any unwarranted debits.

Both defences have been considered by English and Commonwealth authorities. Traditionally, the first defence has been upheld only where the customer's carelessness was directly related to the drawing of the cheque. The second defence has been unsuccessful in England. It has been held consistently that the customer does not owe a contractual duty to peruse his statements or, in earlier days, his passbook. In Canada, where such a duty is undertaken by the customer at the time of the opening of the account, the law has taken a different course.

NOTES

1.   In the circumstances identified by Professor Ellinger the drawee or paying bank (the 'paying bank') cannot debit its customer's account if it honours the cheque. There is no mandate to debit the account. Where the bank does wrongly debit the account, the customer's cause of action against the bank only accrues, and the limitation period starts to run, when he makes a demand for repayment of the amount wrongly debited and such payment is refused (*National Bank of Commerce v National Westminster Bank plc* [1990] 2 Lloyd's Rep 514). If the bank can trace the recipient of the money wrongfully paid, it may have a remedy against him for money paid under a mistake of fact (*National Westminster Bank Ltd v Barclays Bank International Ltd* [1975] QB 654). But the collecting bank will have a defence to the paying bank's restitutionary claim where it has already paid the money over to its customer in ignorance of the paying bank's claim (see above, p 585).

2.   Furthermore, the paying bank may also be liable to the true owner of the cheque in conversion (*Smith v Union Bank of London* (1875) LR 10 QB 291 (affd 1 QBD 31); *Bavins Jnr and Sims v London and South Western Bank Ltd* [1900] 1 QB 270 at 278; cf *Charles v Blackwell* (1877) 2 CPD 151 at 162–163 : see also EP Ellinger, E Lomnicka and RJA Hooley *Ellinger's Modern Banking Law* (4th edn, 2006), pp 438–442). The value of the cheque is deemed to be its face value and the true owner can recover damages of that amount (*Morison v London County and Westminster Bank Ltd* [1914] 3 KB 356, 365, CA; the rule is rightly described as a 'legal fiction' by Lord Nicholls in *OBG Ltd v Allan* [2007] UKHL 21, [2007] 2 WLR 920 at [227]–[228]). However, where the cheque has been materially altered, the measure of damages is not the face value: the cheque is avoided under s 64(1) of the BEA and becomes a worthless piece of paper (*Smith v Lloyds TSB plc* [2000] 2 All ER (Comm) 693, CA: see below,

p 783). The true owner is the person with an immediate right to possession of the cheque (*Marquess of Bute v Barclays Bank Ltd* [1955] 1 QB 202). In cases of misappropriation, the identity of the true owner depends on whether the cheque has been delivered by the drawer to the payee. Problems sometimes arise where a cheque is stolen in the post. Where a cheque is sent by post by a debtor to pay his creditor, the issue turns on whether the creditor expressly or impliedly requested or authorised payment through the post: if he did then he carries the risk of loss in transit and should be treated as the true owner (*Norman v Ricketts* (1886) 3 TLR 182; and see also AG Guest *Chalmers and Guest on Bills of Exchange* (16th edn, 2005), para 2–151). If it is uncertain whether a cheque was misappropriated whilst in the hands of the drawer or the payee, by s 21 (3) of the BEA the payee will be deemed to have received a valid and unconditional delivery of the cheque, and hence be the true owner, until the contrary is proved (*Surrey Asset Finance Ltd v National Westminster Bank plc* (2000) Times, 30 November; permission to appeal refused [2001] EWCA Civ 60).

3.   *Common law defences of the paying bank.* Even if the bank has paid a cheque in the circumstances outlined by Professor Ellinger, it may still debit its customer's account in the following circumstances:

(1)   the customer may be estopped by representation or negligence from relying on a forged or unauthorised signature (see above, pp 566ff, and also B Geva (1998) 114 LQR 251, pp 258ff), or he may be held to have adopted or ratified it (see above, p 568);

(2)   if there is a forged or unauthorised indorsement of a cheque payable to bearer (either because it was drawn payable to bearer, or because it has been indorsed in blank, or because it was drawn payable to a fictitious or non-existent payee) the bank can pay the bearer and debit the customer's account, if payment was made in good faith and without notice of any defect of the bearer's title to the cheque, because payment to the bearer of such a cheque is payment in due course which discharges the instrument (BEA, s 59);

(3)   if the cheque has been materially altered after issue by a person other than the drawer and without his authority or consent, the paying bank cannot take advantage of the proviso to s 64(1) of the Bills of Exchange Act 1882 (see above, p 569) as it is not a holder in due course (*Slingsby v District Bank Ltd* [1931] 2 KB 588 at 600; affd [1932] 1 KB 544); nor is the bank entitled to debit its customer's account when the amount of the cheque has been fraudulently raised on the basis that the customer's mandate is still good for the original amount (BEA, s 64(1) as applied in *Yorkshire Bank plc v Lloyds Bank plc* [1999] 2 All ER (Comm) 153 at 156, and in *Smith v Lloyds TSB plc* [2000] 2 All ER (Comm) 693 at 703, CA: see below, p 783); but the bank may be able to argue that the customer is estopped by his negligence from questioning the debit if the alteration is due to the customer's failure to take usual and reasonable precautions when drawing the cheque (*London Joint Stock Bank Ltd v Macmillan* [1918] AC 777); and

(4)   if the payment discharges the customer's prior indebtedness to the recipient of the payment, the bank may be subrogated to the rights of that recipient and debit its customer's account accordingly (*B Liggett (Liverpool) Ltd v Barclays Bank Ltd* [1928] 1 KB 48; cf *Re Cleadon Trust Ltd* [1939] Ch 286; *Crantrave Ltd v Lloyds TSB Bank plc* [2000] QB 917—the difficult issues raised by the *Liggett* doctrine are considered in detail above, p 642).

4.   *Statutory defences.* There are three statutory defences available to the paying bank:

(1)   Section 60 of the Bills of Exchange Act 1882 provides that a banker who pays in good faith and in the ordinary course of business a cheque (crossed or uncrossed) drawn on

him payable to order on which the indorsement of the payee or any subsequent indorsement is forged or unauthorised is deemed to have paid it in due course. But s 60 cannot apply to cheques crossed 'account payee' as such cheques are non-transferable (s 81A(1) of the 1882 Act) and, therefore, cannot be payable to order as required by the section.

(2) Section 80 of the Bills of Exchange Act 1882 provides that where a banker upon whom a crossed cheque (including a cheque which under s 81A of the 1882 Act or otherwise is not transferable) is drawn pays the cheque to another banker in good faith and without negligence and in accordance with the terms of the crossing, the banker paying the cheque, and, if the cheque has come into the hands of the payee, the drawer, are respectively entitled to the same rights and are placed in the same position as if payment had been made to the true owner thereof. Although s 80 is limited to crossed cheques paid to a banker (s 60 is not), it is not limited to cheques payable to order (s 60 is so limited). Section 80 will apply if the cheque bears a forged or unauthorised indorsement, but it will not protect the paying bank if the drawer's signature has been forged or made without his authority as the instrument is not then a cheque at all, for the signature is wholly inoperative (s 24 of the 1882 Act) so that the instrument does not meet the requirements of a bill of exchange (s 3(1) of the 1882 Act). Neither will the section protect the paying bank where the cheque has been 'materially altered' so as to be caught by s 64(1) of the BEA. The effect of the material alteration is to render the instrument void with the result that it is no longer a cheque but a worthless piece of paper (*Smith v Lloyds TSB Bank plc* [2000] 2 All ER (Comm) 693 at 703, per Pill LJ, see below, p 783). A banker is not to be treated for the purposes of s 80 as having been negligent *by reason only* of his failure to concern himself with any purported indorsement of a cheque which under s 81A(1) of the 1882 Act or otherwise is not transferable (s 81 A(2) of the 1882 Act). In other words, the paying bank can normally ignore any purported indorsement on the cheque, as it is the responsibility of the collecting bank to ensure that a non-transferable cheque is collected only for the account of the named payee. But, as Professor Guest rightly points out, there may be additional circumstances, eg where the paying bank is reliably informed that the cheque has been stolen from the payee (assuming the drawer has not, or has not yet, countermanded payment), in which it might be negligent for a bank to pay a non-transferable cheque bearing a purported indorsement without first satisfying itself that it was in fact being paid to the person entitled to receive it (AG Guest *Chalmers and Guest on Bills of Exchange* (16th edn, 2005), para 14–028). By s 5 of the Cheques Act 1957 the protection offered by s 80 extends to certain other crossed instruments, analogous to cheques, referred to in s 4(2)(b), (c) and (d) of the 1957 Act.

(3) Section 1 of the Cheques Act 1957 provides that where a bank in good faith and in the ordinary course of business pays a cheque drawn on it which is not indorsed or is irregularly indorsed, the bank does not, in doing so, incur any liability by reason only of the absence of, or irregularity in, indorsement, and the bank is deemed to have paid the cheque in due course. (An irregular indorsement is one which on its face does not sufficiently correspond with the payee or named indorsee, eg where a cheque drawn 'Pay D Hooley' is indorsed 'R Hooley'.) However, in its memorandum of 23 September 1957, the Committee of London Clearing Bankers stated that paying banks should require indorsement of cheques cashed over the counter and of cheques with receipt forms attached to them. If a bank pays a cheque without an indorsement as required by the Committee of London Clearing Bankers' memorandum, it would not be acting in the ordinary course of business and would forfeit the protection of s 1 of the Cheques Act 1957.

If the paying bank can bring itself within the protection of any of these statutory provisions it may debit its customer's account with the sum paid. If the bank can rely on s 80 of the 1882 Act or s 1 of the 1957 Act it will also have a defence against any action brought against it by the true owner. Whether the bank will have a defence against an action by the true owner if it can only bring itself within s 60 of the 1882 Act remains unclear (RM Goode, *Commercial Law* (3rd edn, 2004), p 557 and AG Guest *Chalmers and Guest on Bills of Exchange* (16th edn, 2005), para 8–053, recognise the defence; EP Ellinger, E Lomnicka and RJA Hooley *Ellinger's Modern Banking Law* (4th edn, 2006), p 441 and R Bradgate *Commercial Law* (2nd edn, 1995), para 30.2.3, appear to reject the defence).

Carpenters' Co v British Mutual Banking Co Ltd
[1938] 1 KB 511, Court of Appeal

The plaintiffs kept an account with the defendant bank. The plaintiffs' clerk (B) also held an account with the defendant bank. Over a period of time B misappropriated cheques drawn by the plaintiffs payable to the order of various tradesmen who had supplied goods to them. He also procured cheques to be drawn by the plaintiffs in favour of tradesmen who had not supplied goods. In both cases B forged the indorsement of the payees and paid the cheques into his account. The plaintiffs brought an action against the defendant bank for the amount of the cheques. Branson J found as a fact that the defendant bank did not act without negligence and so had lost the protection of s 82 of the Bills of Exchange Act 1882 (now s 4 of the Cheques Act 1957), but that they had paid the cheques in good faith and in the ordinary course of business and, notwithstanding their negligence, they were protected by s 60 of the 1882 Act. The plaintiffs appealed.

Greer LJ: ...In the present case what happened was that when the cheques were presented to the defendant bank they had never ceased to be the property of the drawers, the Carpenters' Company, as they had never in fact been indorsed by the payees. The defendant bank was then asked by Blackborow to receive the cheques, and to place the amounts to the credit of his private account with it. This the bank did, and by so doing it in my judgment converted the cheques to its own use and became liable to the Carpenters' Company, the drawers of the cheques, for the face value of the cheques.

In my judgment s 60 of the Bills of Exchange Act 1882 only protects a bank when that bank is merely a paying bank, and is not a bank which receives the cheque for collection. In my judgment the learned judge was wrong in treating the defendant bank as if the bank had merely been a paying bank, and in failing to apply the law of conversion to the facts proved before him. The sole question which he had to decide was whether the bank was protected by s 82 of the Bills of Exchange Act from its liability for conversion of the cheques. He treated s 82 as applicable to the defendant bank, but decided that it had not proved that it received payment without negligence, but on the contrary he decided that it was negligent....

It remains to say something with reference to the questions discussed in the judgment as to the effect of s 19 of the Stamp Act 1853. I agree with the view to which Slesser LJ called attention in the course of the argument that s 60 of the Bills of Exchange Act 1882 must be treated as inconsistent, so far as cheques are concerned, with the provisions of s 19 of the Stamp Act 1853 and the sole duty of the Court after the passing of the Bills of Exchange Act is to apply s 60 of that Act. The observations of Stirling LJ in *Gordon v London, City & Midland Bank* ([1902] 1 KB 242) were made per incuriam, as they refer to s 19 of the Stamp Act as if it had been part of the Bills of Exchange Act.

I have just referred to the mistake made by Stirling LJ in *Gordon's* case, but the case calls for consideration from another point of view. The cheques in that case belonged to various classes, but they were all crossed cheques. Class No 4 related to crossed cheques drawn on one branch of the defendant bank and handed to another branch for collection. As to these cheques it was held by the Master of the Rolls, Sir Richard Henn Collins, though with some difficulty, that though the defendant bank was a collecting bank as well as a paying bank, it was protected from liability by reason of s 60 of the Bills of Exchange Act. I find it a little difficult to follow the logic of this reasoning, because the bank was no less a collecting bank because it was collecting from one of its branches for the customer and paying the money so collected for the benefit of the fraudulent presenter of the cheque; but, be this as it may, it seems to me that the actual decision does not bind me in the present case inasmuch as there was an express finding of the jury on which the Court of Appeal acted that the bank acted without negligence. It seems to me impossible to say in the present case that the bank acted without negligence. Branson J has expressly found that it acted negligently, and it cannot, therefore, in my judgment, be heard to say when acting negligently that it was acting in the ordinary course of business within the meaning of s 60 of the Bills of Exchange Act 1882. The finding in this case that the bank acted negligently in my judgment distinguishes this case from *Gordon's* case. I note that by para 7 of the statement of claim the action was based alternatively on negligence. I think on this ground the decision in *Gordon's* case is not an authority on which we are bound to decide that the bank having acted negligently is excused by reason of s 60 of the Bills of Exchange Act 1882 from the consequences of its negligence....

For the reasons above stated I am of opinion, though with some hesitation, that the learned judge was wrong in holding that the bank was entitled to the protection of s 60 of the Bills of Exchange Act, and the appeal will be allowed with costs, and judgment entered for the Carpenters' Company for the face value of all the cheques received by the bank and passed to the credit of Blackborow during the six years preceding the issue of the writ.

Slesser LJ: In this case the critical question arises whether or not the defendants have wrongfully received the proceeds of the plaintiffs' cheques and converted them. In so far as they received the plaintiffs' cheques at Blackborow's request and credited their customer Blackborow with the proceeds, which were at all times the property of the plaintiffs, they appear to me to have acted, albeit wrongly, as a receiving bank as well as in the capacity of a paying bank.

As paying banker they may well be protected by s 60 of the Bills of Exchange Act 1882 in so far as they acted in good faith, which is not disputed, and in the ordinary course of business. Branson J has come to the conclusion that in all the facts of this case, which I do not repeat, they did so act in the ordinary course of business. It was argued by Mr Schiller that in so far as the learned judge has held that they failed to show that they acted without negligence within the meaning of s 82 of the Bills of Exchange Act that therefore they cannot be held to have acted in the ordinary course of business. I do not agree; negligence does not necessarily preclude the protection of s 60, a view made clear in the case of the other requirement, of good faith, by s 90 of the same Act, which in terms provides that 'a thing is deemed to be done in good faith, within the meaning of this Act, where it is in fact done honestly, whether it is done negligently or not.' This provision is helpful, I think, in deciding whether an admittedly negligent act can be done in the ordinary course of business. In *Vagliano's* case ([1891] AC 107 at 117) Lord Halsbury LC, speaking of the alleged negligence of bankers evidenced by the pursuit of an unusual course of business, says: 'I should doubt whether...it would be possible to affirm that any particular course was either usual or unusual in the sense that there is some particular course to be pursued when circumstances occur, necessarily giving rise to suspicion.' Branson J points out in his judgment in the present case that there was nothing in the steps taken by the bank which was not in the ordinary course of business, and I agree with him.

Bissell & Co v Fox Bros & Co ((1885) 53 LT 193), which the learned judge cites, was a case decided under s 19 of the Stamp Act 1853, which section has no limitation of reference to payments in the ordinary course of business and therefore is of no assistance on that question in the present case. (See also the dicta of Stirling LJ in *Gordon's* case ([1902] 1 KB 242), which also can only refer to s 19 of the Stamp Act 1853.) That section, I think, is impliedly repealed by s 60 of the Bills of Exchange Act 1882, in the case of bills of exchange and cheques: see Lord Lindley in *Capital & Counties Bank v Gordon* ([1903]

AC 240 at 251). But though I am of opinion that the Stamp Act 1853 is not here applicable, I think that the judge was entitled to hold on the facts that s 60 of the Bills of Exchange Act 1882, applied to this case, and therefore it follows that the bankers as payers are to be deemed to have paid the bill in due course notwithstanding that the indorsement has been forged, and I so treat them.

As receiving bank, however, unless protected by statute, they were guilty of conversion and liable in trover or for money had and received, for they dealt with the cheques which, for the want of a payee, were still the property of the plaintiffs in a manner inconsistent with the plaintiffs' rights as the true owners. See Lord Lindley in *Capital & Counties Bank v Gordon* ([1903] AC 240); Collins MR in the same case ([1902] 1 KB 242); *Morison v London County & Westminster Bank Ltd* ([1914] 3 KB 356 at 365 and 379), per Lord Reading CJ and per Phillimore LJ; *Lloyds Bank Ltd v EB Savory & Co* ([1933] AC 201 at 228), per Lord Wright.

As to the protection of the Bills of Exchange Act 1882, s 82; I think that the judge was entitled as a question of fact to find that the bank had failed to show that they had acted without negligence . . .

I agree with Greer LJ that in so far as Collins MR and the rest of the Court in *Gordon's* case held that s 82 of the Bills of Exchange Act 1882 applied, and that there was no negligence, the observations of the Master of the Rolls and those of Stirling LJ as to the effect of s 60 or s 82 were obiter and are not binding in this case on a finding that there was negligence, and the protection of s 82 cannot be invoked by the bank at all.

It follows, therefore, that, on the finding of the learned judge that the bank have failed to prove that they acted without negligence, they are liable to the true owner in conversion, and that this appeal succeeds.

MacKinnon LJ (dissenting): . . . It is said that in paying them they acted negligently, and for that reason they cannot be said to have paid in the ordinary course of business. I do not agree with that contention. A thing that is done not in the ordinary course of business may be done negligently; but I do not think the converse is necessarily true. A thing may be done negligently and yet be done in the ordinary course of business . . . .

[His Lordship felt bound to follow *Gordon v Capital & Counties Bank* [1902] 1 KB 242 and, therefore, would have dismissed the appeal.]

NOTES

1.   When does the bank pay in the ordinary course of business? The general rule is that the payment must accord with the mode of transacting business which is adopted by the banking community at large (*Australian Mutual Provident Society v Derham* (1979) 39 FLR 165 at 173). For example, if the bank closes at 3.00 pm and yet pays a cheque at 3.05 pm, it still acts in the ordinary course of business, as banks may pay cheques within a reasonable margin of time after their advertised time for closing (*Baines v National Provincial Bank Ltd* (1927) 96 LJKB 801). But payment will not be in the ordinary course of business if, for example, the bank pays a crossed cheque over the counter (*Smith v Union Bank of London* (1875) LR 10 QB 291; affd 1 QBD 31 at 35) or pays an order cheque bearing an irregular indorsement (*Slingsby v District Bank Ltd* [1932] 1 KB 544 at 565–566) although, because of s 1 of the Cheques Act 1957, the irregularity in the indorsement will no longer render the paying bank liable.

2.   Professor Guest prefers the view taken by Slesser and Mackinnon LJJ to that of Greer LJ on the question of whether the bank can pay in the ordinary course of business when it acts negligently (AG Guest *Chalmers and Guest on Bills of Exchange* (16th edn, 2005), para 8-051). The same view has been taken by courts in Australia (*Smith v Commercial Banking Co of Sydney Ltd* (1910) 11 CLR 667 at 677, 688) and in South Africa (*Stapleberg v Barclays Bank* 1963 (3) SA 120). However, the opposite view is taken by Lord Chorley (*Law of Banking* (6th edn, 1974), p 93) and by Professor Holden (*The History of Negotiable Instruments in*

English Law (1955), pp 227–228). Professor Holden even goes so far as to say that 'any sugges-tion that bankers who act negligently are (or can be) acting within "the ordinary course of business" is a gratuitous insult to the very fine body of men and women who are responsible for the day-to-day conduct of British banking' (op cit, p 228)! The Jack Committee have also gone against the view of Slesser and MacKinnon LJJ. Following criticism that the various statutory defences available to the paying banker 'overlap in considerable measure and in some respects their interrelationship is unclear' (R M Goode *Commercial Law* (3rd edn, 2004), p 557), the Jack Committee recommended that these various statutory protections should be brought together and each should be made subject to the condition that the bank has acted 'in good faith and without negligence' (Report, rec 7(5)). The government of the day accepted this recommendation (White Paper (Cm 1026, 1990) Annex 5, para 5.9).

QUESTIONS

1.   How does the protection offered to the paying bank by s 60 of the Bills of Exchange Act 1882 differ, if at all, from that offered by s 80 of the 1882 Act?

2.   A draws a cheque in favour of B. Due to B's carelessness the cheque is stolen from B by C, who fraudulently alters the payee's name to his own. The cheque is duly paid by A's bank when presented for payment by C s bank. Can A's bank debit A's account? Does A's bank have any claim in negligence against B for failing to keep the cheque safe? See *Yorkshire Bank plc v Lloyds Bank plc* [1999] 2 All ER (Comm) 153.

(d)   Protection of the collecting bank

The collecting bank (defined above, p 771) owes its customer a duty to collect the cheque promptly and, once collected, to credit the customer's account with the amount, whether the cheque is payable to the customer himself or to a third party who has indorsed it to the customer. The holder of the cheque is himself obliged to present it for payment within a rea-sonable time of issue or indorsement to him to be sure he can recover in full from the drawer (Bills of Exchange Act 1882, s 74(1)) or indorser (BEA, s 45(2)). In either case, when consider-ing what is a reasonable time regard must be had to the usage of the trade and of bankers (BEA, s 45(2) and s 74(2)). The fact that the vast majority of cheques drawn on one bank and collected by another are presented for payment through the cheque clearing system (above, p 771) means that a court would undoubtedly have regard to all reasonable rules of practice of the clearing system when deciding what was a reasonable time (see RM Goode *Commercial Law* (3rd edn, 2004), p 546).

It is almost invariably the case today that where a cheque is delivered to a bank for collec-tion the bank receives the cheque as agent for the customer for the purposesof collecting it on the customer's behalf (but the proceeds are not held on trust for the customer; the bank merely incurs a commitment to credit the customer's account with an equivalent amount: *Emerald Meats (London) Ltd v AIB Group (UK) Ltd* [2002] EWCA Civ 460). For these pur-poses, the collecting bank's customer may be another domestic or foreign bank using the collecting bank as its agent to gain access to the cheque clearing system (see *Importers Co Ltd v Westminster Bank Ltd* [1927] 2 KB 297; *Honourable Society of the Middle Temple v Lloyds Bank plc* [1999] 1 All ER (Comm) 193; *Linklaters (a firm) v HSBC Bank plc* [2003] EWHC 1113 (Comm), [2003] 2 Lloyd's Rep 545). In theory the collecting bank could give the customer value for the cheque and collect the cheque, to the extent of the value given, on its own behalf as a holder for value, but the fact that UK banks now almost invariably issue cheque forms to their customers which are crossed and preprinted with the words 'account payee', thereby making the cheque non-transferable (BEA, s 81A(1)), means that this is very rare indeed for a collecting bank cannot become the holder of a non-transferable cheque (see R Hooley [1992] CLJ 432).

If the collecting bank collects a cheque for anyone other than the true owner, the bank may be liable to the true owner for conversion of the cheque (for who is the 'true owner' of a cheque, see p 777 above). For the purposes of an action in conversion, the cheque is deemed to have a value equal to the amount for which it is drawn. The fiction in that rule is evident when one considers a cheque drawn by an impecunious customer on an account which is heavily overdrawn (see EP Ellinger, E Lomnicka and RJA Hooley *Ellinger's Modern Banking Law* (4th edn, 2006), pp 618–619; see also *OBG Ltd v Allan* [2007] UKHL 21, [2007] 2 WLR 920 at [227]–[228], Lord Nicholls). The rule has been rejected where the cheque has been materially altered by an unauthorised person: in *Smith v Lloyds TSB Group plc* [2000] 2 All ER (Comm) 693 (see below), the Court of Appeal held that such a cheque is a 'worthless piece of paper'. Alternatively, the amount received for the cheque may be recovered from the bank by the true owner as money had and received. In theory the collecting bank may have a right of indemnity or recourse against its customer, but in practice this may prove worthless (but see *Honourable Society of the Middle Temple v Lloyds Bank plc* (above), where an English clearing bank was held entitled to claim a full indemnity from the overseas bank that had instructed it to act as the collecting agent of the overseas bank, applied in *Linklaters (a firm) v HSBC Bank plc* (above), where Gross J held that the fact the collecting agent was also the paying bank was of no significance to its claim for a complete indemnity and that there was no room for just and equitable apportionment between the two banks under the Civil Liability (Contribution) Act 1978 as this solution was inherently uncertain and carried with it a much increased risk of litigation). As the collecting bank will have a defence to the restitutionary claim for money had and received if it has already paid the proceeds of the cheque over to its customer in good faith and in ignorance of the claim (see above, p 585), the most common form of action brought by the true owner against the bank is an action in conversion.

Smith v Lloyds TSB Bank plc; Harvey Jones Ltd v Woolwich plc

[2000] 2 All ER (Comm) 693, Court of Appeal

These were conjoined appeals. In *Smith*, the Insolvency Service drew a cheque crossed 'A/C Payee Only' in favour of the Inland Revenue. The cheque was issued at the request of the claimants, who were the joint liquidators of a company in creditors' voluntary winding up. The cheque was stolen from the offices of the Inland Revenue and the name of the payee was fraudulently altered to 'Joseph Smitherman' and paid into an account at Lloyds. The cheque was cleared before the fraud was discovered and the claimants sued Lloyds (the collecting bank) for its conversion.

In *Jones*, the claimant company was the payee of a banker's draft issued by Woolwich. The draft was stolen, the name of the payee was fraudulently altered and the draft was paid into an account with the National Westminster Bank. The claimant sued Woolwich (the paying bank) in conversion.

In both cases, it was accepted that the alteration of the payee's name was a 'material alteration' within the meaning of s 64(1) of the Bills of Exchange Act 1882. Conflicting decisions were reached at first instance. In *Smith*, it was held that the claimants were only entitled to nominal damages because the cheque had been avoided by the material alteration. In

Woolwich, it was held that Woolwich was liable for the full face value of the draft. The Court of Appeal held that the claimants in both cases were only entitled to nominal damages.

Pill LJ: These appeals raise questions as to the possible liabilities in conversion of a bank to the true owner of a cheque or banker's draft for the full value of the instrument where the instrument has been fraudulently altered by the deletion of the name of the true payee and substitution of the name of a false payee prior to collection and payment. In *Smith v Lloyds TSB Group plc* (the Lloyds action), the claimants appeal against the decision of Blofeld J, dated 29 June 1999 ([2000] 1 All ER 53), whereby it was ordered, following the hearing of a preliminary issue of law, that the claimant was entitled to no more than nominal damages for the conversion by Lloyds, as the collecting bank, of a cheque which had been fraudulently altered. In the Woolwich action, the bank appeal against a decision of Judge Hallgarten QC, dated 8 June 1999, whereby it was ordered that the true owner of a banker's draft was entitled to damages in conversion for the full face value of a fraudulently altered draft which had been converted by them as paying bank. In each case, the bank relied upon s 64 of the Bills of Exchange Act 1882.

...

The statute

Section 64(1) of the 1882 Act provides:

> Where a bill or acceptance is materially altered without the assent of all parties liable on the bill, the bill is avoided except as against a party who has himself made, authorised, or assented to the alteration, and subsequent endorsers. Provided that, Where a bill has been materially altered, but the alteration is not apparent, and the bill is in the hands of a holder in due course, such holder may avail himself of the bill as if it had not been altered, and may enforce payment of it according to its original tenour...

...

The common ground and the issues

The issues in these appeals are narrowed by the common ground which exists. (1) Authority binding on this court establishes that both a collecting bank and a paying bank may in certain circumstances be liable in the tort of conversion by collecting or paying a cheque for or to someone other than the true owner. (2) In both appeals, the banks accept that they converted the relevant piece of paper. (3) Section 80 of the 1882 Act does not protect a bank which pays on a forged instrument, for example a cheque on which the signature of the drawer has been forged, or an instrument which was once valid but has been avoided by material alteration. The paying bank is not entitled to debit its customer and bears the loss itself. (4) Both the alteration to the name of the payee on the cheque in the Lloyds action and the draft in the Woolwich action were 'material alterations' within the meaning of s 64 of the 1882 Act. (5) In these appeals, no party comes within the exception in or the proviso to s 64(1) of the 1882 Act. (6) Neither alteration was apparent on the face of the document and the failure of the bank to recognise the change in name was not in either case negligent.

In each case, it was alleged that the bank had converted the claimant's cheque. In the Lloyds action, the claim was also based on money had and received. Blofeld J recorded that it was accepted that no separate issue of law arose on that claim. At that stage the claim was kept open on the facts but the complainants now concede that, on the facts of this case, there is no claim for money had and received.

I accept Mr Hapgood's [Counsel for Lloyds] formulation of the main issue in the appeals:

> Where a cheque or banker's draft is fraudulently altered by deleting the name of the true payee and substituting the name of a different payee, and the cheque or draft is then collected and paid, is the paying bank and/or the collecting bank liable in conversion for the full value of the instrument, or is the measure of damage nominal on the ground that the material alteration renders the instrument a nullity by virtue of section 64 of the 1882 Act?

Conversion is an interference with goods inconsistent with the owner's right to possession. Cheques are goods for this purpose. Both defendant banks admit that they converted the relevant piece of paper, the cheque form.

By a legal fiction, a valid cheque is deemed to have a value equal to its face amount. This rule was explained by Scrutton LJ in *Lloyds Bank v Chartered Bank of India, Australia and China* [1929] 1 KB 40 at 55–56, [1928] All ER Rep 285 at 288:

> Conversion primarily is conversion of chattels, and the relation of bank to customer is that of debtor and creditor. As no specific coins in a bank are the property of any specific customer there might appear to be some difficulty in holding that a bank, which paid part of what it owed its customer to some other person not authorized to receive it, had converted its customer's chattels; but a series of decisions...culminating in *Morison's* case ([1914] 3 KB 356, [1914–15] All ER Rep 853) and *Underwood's* case ([1924] 1 KB 775, [1924] All ER Rep 230), have surmounted the difficulty by treating the conversion as of the chattel, the piece of paper, the cheque under which the money was collected, and the value of the chattel converted as the money received under it: see the explanation of Phillimore LJ. in *Morison 's* case.

In *Morison v London County and Westminster Bank Ltd* [1914] 3 KB 356 at 379, [1914–15] All ER Rep 853 at 865, Phillimore LJ stated:

> That the damages for such conversion are (at any rate where the drawer has sufficient funds to his credit and the drawee bank is solvent) the face value of the cheques is...so well established that it is not necessary to inquire into the principle which may underlie the authority. But the principle probably is that, though the plaintiff might at any moment destroy the cheques while they remained in his possession, they are potential instruments whereby the sums they represent may be drawn from his bankers, and, if they get into any other hands than his, he will be the loser to the extent of the sums which they represent. It may be also that any one who has obtained its value by presenting a cheque is estopped from asserting that it has only a nominal value.

...

Slingsby

Each side contends that an authoritative ruling in its favour emerges from the judgment of Scrutton LJ in *Slingsby v District Bank Ltd* [1932] 1 KB 544, [1931] All ER Rep 143. That was the last of three actions by the executors of an estate who wished to invest £5, 000 in war stock and employed a firm of stock-brokers John Prust and Co. The executors drew a cheque on their account at a branch of the District Bank, the payees being expressed to be 'John Prust & Co or order'. It was duly signed by the executors and left with a solicitor Cumberbirch, a partner in the firm, Cumberbirch and Potts. Cumberbirch fraudulently added the words 'per Cumberbirch and Potts' in the space between the words John Prust & Co and the words 'or order'. He then indorsed the cheque 'Cumberbirch and Potts' and paid it into the account, at a branch of Westminster Bank, of a company in which he had an interest. The cheque was dealt with in the usual way in that the account of the company with the Westminster Bank was credited and the account of the executors with the District Bank was debited.

The executors failed in their first action against the Westminster Bank (*Slingsby v Westminster Bank Ltd* [1931] 1 KB 173), which is not material for present purposes, on the ground that the bank was protected by s 82 of the 1882 Act. They failed in a second action against Westminster Bank, the collecting bank, also heard by Finlay J (*Slingsby v Westminster Bank Ltd (No 2)* [1931] 2 KB 583), on the ground that there had been a material alteration by Cumberbirch of the cheque, which had therefore ceased to be a valid cheque and there had been no conversion of any money of the executors. An action against District Bank, the paying bank, succeeded, the Court of Appeal ([1932] 1 KB 544, [1931] All ER Rep 143) upholding a decision of Wright J ([1931] 2 KB 588). The parties are in issue as to the grounds upon which the court found against District Bank and as to the effect of the court's decision upon the judgment of Finlay J in the earlier action.

Finlay J stated that the facts were simple and not really in dispute. Both sides agreed that the alteration to the cheque was a material alteration with the result that, under s 64 of the 1882 Act, the cheque was avoided. The judge accepted the submission that the cheque was by reason of the alteration a mere valueless piece of paper. He stated ([1931] 2 KB 583 at 586):

> I have come to the conclusion that [the bank's] submission is right and ought to prevail. It seems clear that the document, when it came into the hands of the defendant bank, was not a valid cheque at all. It had been avoided by the material alteration made in it. This being so, it seems to me that no action can be brought upon it against the defendants. They have not dealt either with a cheque or the money of the plaintiffs, and on this short ground I think this action must fail.

Miss Simmons [Counsel for the claimants in the Lloyds action] accepts that, if that is a correct statement of the law, the claim against Lloyds fails.

Finlay J twice stated in his judgment that, if that view was correct, the question of negligence did not arise but he none the less considered the conduct of the collecting bank in detail and concluded that there was no negligence and the bank was entitled to the protection of s 82 of the 1882 Act. There was nothing to suggest that further inquiry ought to have been made. It was not disputed that the indorsement was a proper one.

Wright J tried the action against the paying bank in the following year. In *Slingsby v District Bank Ltd* [1931] 2 KB 588 the validity of the indorsement was not admitted. Wright J held that the indorsement was an improper indorsement.

Wright J went on to consider and reject several distinct claims that defences arose. Defences were claimed under s 60 of the 1882 Act, the proviso to s 64(1), s 80, as well as defences by reason of the conduct of the executors and by reason of the liability of Cumberbirch's employers for his fraud. The effect of s 64 does not appear to have been in issue and was stated briefly by the judge. Having held that the alteration was a material alteration within the meaning of s 64(1) Wright J stated (at 599):

> But under the section just cited, the alteration avoids the cheque, subject to the proviso. The defendants cannot charge the plaintiffs with a payment made, however innocently, on a void instrument, or a payment for which they cannot show a mandate from the plaintiffs to pay; the only mandate by the plaintiffs was to pay John Prust & Co. simpliciter, whereas the defendants paid on the simple indorsement of Cumberbirch & Potts, and in any case on an apparent mandate deviating in respect of the description of the payee.

That view of the effect of s 64 is consistent with the view expressed by Finlay J in the earlier case.

Delivering the leading judgment in the Court of Appeal, Scrutton LJ considered three issues, whether Westminster Bank had been negligent, the effect of the indorsement and the effect of s 64. He dealt with them in that order, though it would appear that it was Finlay J who took the logical course of dealing with s 64 first because, if the cheque was a worthless piece of paper, the claim against Westminster Bank was bound to fail and that against District Bank, for debiting its customer's account, was bound to succeed. Scrutton LJ expressed, in strong terms, his disagreement with the finding of Finlay J in the earlier action that Westminster Bank had not been negligent. It was when dealing with the second issue, that is whether the indorsement was a proper one, that Scrutton LJ cited in full the view of Finlay J on the effect of s 64. However, the statement by Finlay J had nothing to do with the point Scrutton LJ was then considering, the propriety of the indorsement. That point had not been in issue before Finlay J. Having cited the passage, Scrutton LJ stated:

> I cannot understand this. There are, of course, difficulties as to how in law you should deal with money claimed by a customer from a bank because the bank has collected it from the customer's bank on a document which does not authorize such collection, but I thought that all those difficulties had been settled by the decision in *Morison's* case, followed by this Court in *Underwood's* case; in the *Lloyds Bank* case; and in *Reckitt* v. *Midland Bank,* lately affirmed in the House of Lords ((1932) 48 TLR 271). *Slingsby* v. *Westminster Bank* is, in my opinion, wrongly decided and should not

be followed by any Court in preference to these decisions of the Court of Appeal.' (See [1932] 1 KB 544 at 558, [1931] All ER Rep 143 at 149.)

Only then did Scrutton LJ consider the effect of s 64. He stated:

> But the legal result of these facts begins earlier than indorsement. This cheque, having been signed by the executors in a form which gave Cumberbirch no rights, was fraudulently altered by Cumberbirch before it was issued and, it was not disputed, altered in a material particular, by the addition of the words 'per Cumberbirch & Potts.' The cheque was thereby avoided under s. 64 of the Bills of Exchange Act. A holder in due course might not be affected by an alteration not apparent, such as this alteration.

But counsel for the District Bank did not contend that the Westminster Bank were holders in due course, and I am clear they were not. They could not therefore justifiably claim on the District Bank, and the cheque when presented to the District Bank was invalid, avoided, a worthless bit of paper, which the District Bank was under no duty to pay. This invalidity comes before any question of indorsement.' (See [1932] 1 KB 544 at 559, [1931] All ER Rep 143 at 149.)

Scrutton LJ went on the repeat his conclusion that the cheque was not properly indorsed and concluded this section of his judgment, stating:

> The protection given by ss. 80 and 82 is excluded in my opinion by the fact that the alteration has made the paper a null and void document, no longer a cheque. (See [1932] 1 KB 544 at 559, [1931] All ER Rep 143 at 150.)

Scrutton LJ concluded his judgment by stating that he might have been content to adopt the careful judgment of Wright J, with which he substantially agreed.

Greer LJ also stated that 'under the provisions of s.64 of the Act the cheque was rendered void except as therein stated' (see [1932] 1 KB 544 at 562, [1931] All ER Rep 143 at 151). The defect in the cheque which rendered it invalid was on the face of the cheque and not merely in the indorsement. Romer LJ listed the six questions which appeared to him to arise from the appeal and expressed his agreement with the conclusions of Wright J. I find it significant that Romer LJ did not identify the effect of s 64 as being an issue in the appeal.

Miss Simmons understandably relies strongly upon the apparent rejection by Scrutton LJ of Finlay J's statement in *Slingsby v District Bank Ltd* of the effect of s 64. However I have come to the conclusion that the apparent disapproval was based upon a wholly uncharacteristic and, with great respect, most unexpected misreading by Scrutton LJ of the judgment of Finlay J in the earlier action. Scrutton LJ expressed in strong terms his disagreement with Finlay J on the negligence issue. He then dealt with the indorsement issue, which had first been raised only in *Slingsby v District Bank Ltd,* but cited from Finlay J's judgment in *Slingsby v Westminster Bank Ltd (No 2)* a passage dealing not with indorsement, but with s 64. That Scrutton LJ was dealing with the indorsement issue at that stage and not s 64 is illustrated by his reference to the *Morison* line of cases which deals with other types of dishonesty and not material alteration which is covered by s 64. When going on to deal specifically with the effect of s 64, Scrutton LJ expressed views entirely consistent with those of Finlay J.

It is submitted that, when stating ([1932] 1 KB 544 at 559, [1931] All ER Rep 143 at 149) that Westminster Bank could not claim against District Bank, Scrutton LJ was distinguishing between the position of the banks as against each other and the position of the customer of the paying bank as against the collecting bank. It is also submitted that Judge Hallgarten QC was right to find that, underlying Scrutton LJ's approach, was the feature that, so far as the claimants in the Woolwich action, as owners, were concerned, the cheque continued to have its face value. In my judgment Scrutton LJ's reasoning upon s 64 is not susceptible to those interpretations.

The effect of s 64 was in my view not seriously in issue in *Slingsby v District Bank Ltd.* Wright J dealt with it briefly and in conformity with the view of Finlay J. All members of the Court of Appeal expressed agreement with Wright J, Greer LJ stating that under the provisions of s 64 the cheque was rendered void and Romer LJ setting out the questions arising upon the appeal without mentioning a question on s 64.

Conclusion

My conclusions can in the event be stated briefly. In my judgment the effect of the presence of the word 'avoided' in s 64(1) of the 1882 Act is that the materially altered cheque or draft is, subject to the qualifications in the section, a worthless piece of paper. The words of Scrutton LJ when dealing with the legal effect of the material alteration of the cheque in that case are to be taken at face value. The piece of paper is no longer a cheque and no action can be brought upon it as a cheque. The cheque is invalidated and no distinction can be drawn between parties who, but for the material alteration, would have had contractual rights based on the cheque. No party can bring an action for damages in conversion for its face value because it no longer represents a chose in action for that amount.

In the case of a cheque, the customer of the paying bank is protected because the bank, which bears the risk, cannot debit the customer's account. In the case of a banker's draft, the customer's account is debited when the draft is issued to him. He has the benefit of a bill drawn by the bank itself, which he may require to satisfy business requirements, but once he has it he assumes the relevant risk as he would assume the risk if he drew bank notes which are stolen. It does not follow from the fact that the paying bank will normally issue a replacement draft, if the invalidity is discovered before the collecting bank credits the wrong account, that the materially altered draft is valid. The paying bank will have suffered no loss and may issue a replacement draft as a matter of good business practice, or possibly contractual obligation. The likelihood of such action does not, however, render valid what s 64 has rendered invalid.

Moreover the consequence of invalidity cannot in my judgment be avoided by alleging an estoppel. The cheque is rendered invalid by s 64 and, by presenting it under normal banking arrangements, the collecting bank was not asserting its validity.

I would dismiss the appeal in the Lloyds action and allow the appeal in the Woolwich action.

[Potter LJ delivered a concurring judgment.
Sir Murray Stuart-Smith concurred.]

QUESTIONS

1.   The cheque in *Smith* was not transferable because it was crossed 'A/C Payee only'. In the case of a transferable cheque, rare though such cheques are these days, the cheque could reach the hands of a holder in due course who could, if the material alteration was not apparent, enforce the cheque according to its original tenour. What is the value of such a cheque?

2.   A collecting bank is usually protected from liability for conversion of a cheque by s 4 of the Cheques Act 1957 where it has acted without negligence (see below, p 792). Does that statutory protection extend to liability for conversion of a cheque which has been materially altered? What if a materially altered cheque has passed through the hands of a holder in due course before it is converted by the collecting bank?

(e) What defences can a collecting bank raise to a claim in conversion?

(i) *Holder in due course*

As UK banks now almost invariably issue their customers with cheque forms which are crossed and pre-printed with the words 'account payee', thereby making the cheque non-transferable (BEA, s 81A(1)), the holder in due course defence will rarely be available to a collecting bank. The collecting bank cannot become a holder in due course, or indeed any other type of holder, of a non-transferable cheque when it is not the named payee (the requirements for holder in due course status are set out in BEA, s 29(1), and are considered in detail above, p 552). In consequence, the holder in due course defence need only be considered in those relatively rare cases where a cheque is uncrossed, or where the words 'account payee' are absent or have been deleted by the drawer of the cheque. Where the collecting bank can establish holder in due course status it acquires an overriding title to the cheque and proceeds.

Westminster Bank Ltd v Zang
[1966] AC 182, House of Lords

Tilley was the managing director and controlling shareholder of Tilley's Autos Ltd. Zang asked him to finance his gambling. Tilley gave Zang £1, 000 in cash, which belonged to the company, and received from Zang a cheque for £1, 000 drawn in favour of 'J Tilley or order'. Without indorsing the cheque, Tilley paid it into the company's account at the bank. The paying-in slip used by Tilley reserved the right of the bank, at its discretion, to postpone payment of cheques drawn against uncleared effects. When presented the cheque was dishonoured. The bank returned the cheque to Tilley who commenced an action on the cheque against Zang but that action was later dismissed for procedural reasons. The cheque was then returned to the bank which commenced its own action for dishonour against Zang. The bank claimed as holder in due course and holder for value. Roskill J gave judgment for the bank but this was reversed by the Court of Appeal. The bank appealed to the House of Lords.

Viscount Dilhorne: ...'Holder' is defined by s 2 of the Bills of Exchange Act 1882, as meaning 'the payee or indorsee of a bill or note who is in possession of it, or the bearer thereof.' As the appellants had received the cheque from Mr Tilley without indorsement by him, they did not become holders of the cheque within the meaning of s 2 of the Bills of Exchange Act 1882.

In 1957 the Cheques Act was passed with the object of reducing the labour involved and the time taken by collecting and paying banks in ensuring not only that each cheque was indorsed but also that the indorsement corresponded with the name of the payee on the face of the cheque. Section 2 deals with the rights of collecting banks in respect of cheques not indorsed by holders and reads as follows:

> A banker who gives value for, or has a lien on, a cheque payable to order which the holder delivers to him for collection without indorsing it, has such (if any) rights as he would have had if, upon delivery, the holder had indorsed it in blank.

The appellants relied upon this section and sought to establish (1) that the holder had delivered the cheque to them, (2) that it had been delivered to them for collection and (3) that they had given value for it or had a lien upon it....

The first question, namely, whether the holder of the cheque had delivered it to the bank, was answered by the Court of Appeal in the affirmative. In my opinion, it is clear that Mr Tilley was, when he delivered the cheque to the bank, the holder of it within the meaning of s 2 of the Bills of Exchange Act 1882.

Much argument was directed to the second question, namely: was the cheque delivered to the bank for collection? It was argued for the respondent that 'collection' in s 2 of the Cheques Act was to be interpreted as meaning collection for payment into the payee's account when the payee is named on the cheque; and that as the appellants had received the cheque unindorsed with the direction that it was to be paid into the account of Tilley's Autos Ltd, they could not rely upon s 2....

Production of a paid cheque indorsed by the payee is very strong evidence of receipt by the payee. By dispensing with the requirement of indorsement on all 'order' cheques, the Cheques Act deprived the drawer of ability to establish receipt by the payee in this way. He might, it is true, be able to secure evidence from the payee's bank if it had been credited to the payee's account, but, if it was credited to the account of some other person, it appears that it would be very difficult, if not impossible, for the drawer to establish into whose account it had gone and that it had been credited to that account on the instructions of the payee. So if 'collection' in s 2 is confined to meaning collection for the payee's account only, the drawer of the cheque not indorsed by the payee may still be able to prove receipt by the payee.

It can safely be assumed that it was not the intention of Parliament, when providing for relief from the need for indorsement, materially to prejudice the position and rights of the collecting and paying banks and of drawers of cheques. Section 1 provides protection for the paying banks. If the prescribed conditions are satisfied, s 2 gives the collecting banks the same rights in respect of an unindorsed cheque as in respect of an indorsed one. Section 4 provides protection for collecting banks and s 3 gives some protection to the drawer. That section provides that an unindorsed cheque which appears to have been paid by the banker on whom it is drawn is evidence of the receipt by the payee of the sum payable by the cheque.

The acceptance of a paid unindorsed cheque as evidence of its receipt by the payee of the sum payable by the cheque does not appear to be as cogent evidence of receipt by the payee as production of a paid cheque indorsed by him. But this is, in my opinion, no ground on which one would be entitled to construe s 2 in the way contended for by the respondent. I regard the language of that section as clear and unambiguous. I can see nothing in the section nor in the other sections of the Act from which it is to be inferred that 'collection' in s 2 means collection only for the payee's account. If that had been the intention of Parliament, it could easily have been expressed. If the protection given to the drawer by s 3 is inadequate, that is a matter for Parliament to rectify.

It is apparently the practice of the banks, which inadvertently was not followed in this case, to require the indorsement of a cheque by the payee when it is to be credited to some account other than that of the payee.

In my view, Mr Tilley handed in the cheque for collection and the appellants received it for collection. To bring themselves within s 2 it is not necessary for the appellants to show that it was after collection to be credited to the payee's account. In my opinion, the second question should be answered in favour of the appellants in the affirmative.

The next question for consideration is whether the appellants gave value for the cheque. They claimed in their statement of claim that by crediting the cheque to the account of Tilley's Autos Ltd, and by reducing the company's overdraft by £1,000 they had done so. Alternatively, they claimed that it was to be implied from the course of dealing between them and Tilley's Autos Ltd, that there was an agreement whereby Tilley's Autos Ltd were entitled to draw against uncleared effects and they alleged that this agreement amounted to their giving value for the cheque.

The claim that they gave value by crediting the cheque to the account of Tilley's Autos Ltd does not appear to have been pursued before Roskill J or in the Court of Appeal. The evidence was to the effect that although the cheque was credited to the account of Tilley's Autos Ltd with the result that the overdraft was reduced by £1,000, nonetheless the bank charged interest on the amount of the uncleared cheque for four days pending its clearance. They thus did not charge interest on £1,000 on the overdraft but charged it on the cheque. In these circumstances, it is hard to see that by crediting it to the account and reducing the overdraft the bank gave value for it....

The account of Tilley's Autos Ltd was described as a 'swinging' account, sometimes substantially in credit and sometimes heavily overdrawn. In 1960 the limit on the overdraft was £2,000. In January, 1962, it was raised to £3,500. Tilley's Autos Ltd were, however, allowed to overdraw considerably in excess of this limit; for instance, the bank statements show that the overdraft on April 5 of £2,978 15s 10d rose to £4,902 15s 9d at the close of business on April 26, and throughout most of April the overdraft was in excess of the limit.

Mr Silburn [the branch manager] was asked whether, if the overdraft was near the limit of £3,500 and a cheque for £1,000 came in drawn by Tilley's Autos Ltd, he would have paid it, if the only thing to meet it was uncleared effects. His answer was that if the account was in bad odour, he would not.

If there had been an agreement of the character alleged, then Mr Silburn would have been bound to meet a cheque for £1,000 drawn by Tilley's Autos Ltd if there was an uncleared cheque of that amount credited to the account, even though the account at the time of the presentation of the cheque drawn by Tilley's Autos Ltd was overdrawn to the limit which Mr Silburn was prepared to allow. The words printed on the paying-in slip also negative the existence of any such implied agreement.

Danckwerts LJ expressed the view that, if the bank did in fact allow the customer to draw against the uncleared cheque for £1,000 before it was cleared, this amounted to giving value for it. Salmon LJ expressed the same opinion. He pointed out that there was no finding that the bank did honour any cheque drawn against the uncleared cheque for £1,000 and said that on the evidence of the bank manager and of the ledger sheet it was difficult to see how any such finding could have been made. Danckwerts LJ said that he felt some doubt as to the right deduction to be made from the accounts....

Evidence was not given that cheques drawn by the company and presented between April 27 and May 2 were only honoured in consequence of the uncleared effects.

In the circumstances, I agree with the opinion of Salmon LJ. In my opinion, the bank did not establish that they had in fact allowed Tilley's Autos Ltd to draw against the cheque for £1,000.

It follows that the bank has failed to establish the facts necessary to support their contentions that they had given value. No such agreement as alleged is to be implied and no cheque was shown to have been honoured in consequence of the payment in of the cheque for £1,000....

For these reasons, in my opinion, the appeal fails and should be dismissed.

[Lord Reid delivered a concurring judgment.
Lords Hodson, Upjohn and Wilberforce concurred.]

NOTES

1. When the case was before the Court of Appeal, Zang successfully argued that by returning the cheque to Tilley the bank had lost both its lien over the cheque, which arose because of an existing overdraft, and also its status as 'holder'. When Tilley returned the cheque to the bank after his abortive attempt to sue Zang, the bank did not take the cheque as a 'holder' as it was not indorsed by Tilley and s 2 of the 1957 Act no longer applied as the bank did not receive the cheque for collection, nor did the bank give value for it, when it took the cheque from Tilley for the second time: [1966] AC 182 at 202–203, 207, 211. This point was not considered by the House of Lords.

2. If the bank collects as agent for its customer, can it ever collect as a holder for value on its own account? The question was answered by Milmo J in *Barclays Bank Ltd v Astley Industrial Trust Ltd* [1970] 2 QB 527 at 538, when he said:

I am unable to accept the contention that a banker cannot at one and the same time be an agent for collection of a cheque and a holder of that cheque for value. It seems to me that the language of s 2 of the Cheques Act 1957 negatives this proposition since it presupposes that a banker who has been given a cheque for collection may nevertheless have given value for it. It is, moreover, a commonplace occurrence for a banker to allow credit to a customer against an uncleared cheque. A banker who permits his customer to draw £5 against an uncleared cheque for £100 has given value for it but is it to be said that in consequence he is no longer the customer's agent for the collection of that cheque? I readily accept that if a banker holds a cheque merely—and I emphasise the word 'merely'—as his customer's agent for collection he cannot be a holder for value and still less a holder in due course; but that is an entirely different proposition.

In this case the bank successfully argued that it had a lien on five cheques paid into the bank because of the payee's existing overdraft. Milmo J held that 'the holder of a cheque who has a lien on it is by virtue of s 27(3) [of the Bills of Exchange Act 1882] deemed to have taken that cheque for value within the meaning of s 29(l)(b) to the extent of the sum for which he has a lien' (at 539). As the bank had acted in good faith and without notice of any defect in the payee's title, it held the cheques as a holder in due course.

3. If the collecting bank can establish itself as a holder for value, or holder in due course, it can sue the drawer in its own name should the cheques be dishonoured on presentation for payment (as happened in *Midland Bank Ltd v R V Harris Ltd* [1963] 1 WLR 1021). But a bank cannot be a holder in due course of a crossed cheque marked 'not negotiable' (s 81 of the 1882 Act). Neither, as we have seen, can it be a holder in due course, nor any other type of holder, of a non-transferable cheque paid in for collection (above, p 788). Furthermore, the bank cannot be a holder in due course if its customer's title depends on a forged signature or indorsement (s 24 of the 1882 Act).

(ii) Cheques Act 1957, s 4

Section 4(1) of the Cheques Act 1957 provides as follows:

Where a banker, in good faith and without negligence—

(a) receives payment for a customer of an instrument to which this section applies; or

(b) having credited a customer's account with the amount of such an instrument, receives payment thereof for himself;

and the customer has no title, or a defective title, to the instrument, the banker does not incur any liability to the true owner of the instrument by reason only of having received payment thereof.

The section applies to a cheque (and also to certain other instruments identified in Note 2 below) and protects the collecting bank from claims for conversion of the cheque and also for money had and received (*Capital and Counties Bank Ltd v Gordon* [1903] AC 240, HL). However, s 4 would not provide a collecting bank with a defence to a claim that by collecting the cheque on behalf of a customer the bank was liable as a constructive trustee, for 'knowing' receipt' or 'dishonest assistance', where it turned out that the customer was acting in breach of trust (for detailed discussion as to how this form of liability might arise, see above, p 679). Nor would s 4 assist a collecting bank where (exceptionally) it paid cash for the cheque instead of crediting the customer's account.

To avail itself of the protection afforded by s 4, the collecting bank must be able to prove that it acted in good faith and without negligence. Often good faith is presumed and negligence is in issue. Negligence is judged against the objective standard of the reasonable banker (*Marfani & Co Ltd v Midland Bank Ltd* [1968] 1 WLR 956, 973, CA; *Linklaters (a firm) v HSBC Bank plc* [2003] EWHC 1113 (Comm), [2003] 2 Lloyd's Rep 545, at [106]). A failure by the bank properly to identify its customer when opening the account is likely to be held to be negligent (and the bank must also have proper procedures for identifying, and verifying the identity of, its customers as required by the Money Laundering Regulations 2007, SI 2007/2157: see above, p 614). Similarly, there may be negligence in the collecting of the cheque itself, eg in the absence of special circumstances, it would generally be negligent to collect payment of an 'account payee' cheque for someone other than the named payee without further inquiry because a such a cheque is non-transferable (BEA, s 81A(1)). In each case the enquiry is fact sensitive and current banking practice is highly relevant to the issue of negligence. Rix LJ makes this point in the next case.

Architects of Wine Ltd v Barclays Bank plc

[2007] EWCA Civ 239, [2007] 2 All ER (Comm) 285, Court of Appeal

The claimant, Architects of Wine Ltd (AoW Ltd), a Cayman Island company, sold a scheme for investing in wine futures into the American market. AoW Ltd was a subsidiary of another Cayman Island company, Paradigm Holdings Ltd. A third company, Architects of Wine UK Ltd (AoW UK), was another subsidiary of Paradigm.

By March 2004, AoW Ltd was facing difficulties with the US regulatory authorities. A number of orders were made against it. Its bankers in the Cayman Islands, and their US correspondents, stopped accepting payments and/or collecting cheques for AoW Ltd from its customers. AoW Ltd then couriered cheques received from its customers to the United Kingdom, where they were paid into AoW UK's sterling and (after June 2004) dollar accounts held at the defendant bank, Barclays Bank plc (the bank). By early September, approximately 400 cheques to the value of US $ 1.3 million had been paid into AoW UK's accounts in this way. None of these cheques were payable to AoW UK and, although the cheques were not printed 'a/c payee only', there was no evidence that they had been indorsed to AoW UK.

In October 2004, AoW Ltd went into liquidation. The liquidators of AoW Ltd commenced proceedings against the bank, alleging strict liability for conversion of the cheques, and applied for summary judgment. The bank relied on s 4 of the Cheques Act 1957 in its defence. David Steele J gave summary judgment in favour of AoW Ltd. He held that the s 4 defence was not open to the bank because it had 'fallen well short of establishing any realistic prospect of success on the issue of negligence'. The bank appealed. It submitted that Mr Penny, an employee of the bank who was an expert on banking practice, had presented unchallenged evidence to the court of current banking practice which showed that a 'sufficient' (not absolute) match of the names of payee and account holder was good compliance and that, in the light of that evidence, the judge had been wrong to say that the bank had no realistic prospect of sustaining the burden of its case that it acted without negligence. The Court of Appeal allowed the bank's appeal.

Rix LJ:

The authorities

[3] We were provided with a substantial selection of relevant authorities on s 4 and its statutory predecessors. Many of them concern the payment by rogues into *personal* accounts of cheques drawn on their company, employers or other principals and which they had stolen or created without authority. Factually, such cases are rather far from the present. Nevertheless, as often in this area of the law, the leading case of *Marfani & Co Ltd v Midland Bank Ltd,* [1968] 1 WLR 956, [1968] 1 Lloyd's Rep 411 is well worth consulting, not for its facts (which concerned a rogue who opened a new account under a false name with the help of an incorrect reference from a valued customer) but for its statements of general principle.

[4] Thus Diplock LJ said this about s 4 (at 972–974):

It is, however, in my view, clear that the intention of the subsection and its statutory predecessors is to substitute for the absolute duty owed at common law by a banker to the true owner of a cheque not to take any steps in the ordinary course of business leading up to an including the receipt of payment of the cheque, and the crediting of the amount of the cheque to the account of his customer, in usurpation of the true owner's title thereto a qualified duty to take reasonable care to refrain from taking any such step which he foresees is, or ought reasonably to have foreseen was, likely to cause loss or damage to the true owner.

The only respect in which this substituted statutory duty differs from a common law cause of action in negligence is that, since it takes the form of a qualified immunity from a strict liability at common law, the onus of showing that he did take such reasonable care lies upon the defendant banker. Granted good faith in the banker (the other condition of the immunity), the usual matter with respect to which the banker must take reasonable care is to satisfy himself that his own customer's title to the cheque delivered to him for collection is not defective, ie, that no other person is the true owner of it. Where the customer is in possession of the cheque at the time of delivery for collection and appears upon the face of it to be the 'holder', ie, the payee or indorsee or the bearer, the banker is, in my view, entitled to assume that the customer is the owner of the cheque unless there are facts which are, or ought to be, known to him which would cause a reasonable banker to suspect that the customer was not the true owner.

What facts ought to be known to the banker, ie, what inquiries he should make, and what facts are sufficient to cause him reasonably to suspect that the customer is not the true owner, must depend upon current banking practice, and change as that practice changes. Cases decided 30 years ago, when the use by the general public of banking facilities was much less widespread, may not be a reliable guide to what the duty of a careful banker in relation to inquiries, and as to facts which should give rise to suspicion, is today [at 972] . . .

What the court has to do is to look at all the circumstances at the time of the acts complained of and to ask itself: were those circumstances such as would cause a reasonable banker possessed of such information about his customer as a reasonable banker would possess, to suspect that his customer was not the true owner of the cheque? [at 973] . . .

In all actions of the kind with which we are here concerned, the banker's customer has in fact turned out to be a fraudulent rogue, and attention is naturally concentrated upon the duty of care which was owed by the banker to the person who has in fact turned out to be the true owner of the cheque. We are always able to be wise after the event, but the banker's duty fell to be performed before it, and the duty which he owed to the true owner ought not to be considered in isolation. At the relevant time, the true owner was entitled to take into consideration the interests of his customer, who, be it remembered, would in all probability turn out to be honest, as most men are, and his own business interests, and to weigh those against the risk of loss or damage to the true owner of the cheque in the unlikely event that he should turn out not to be the customer himself [at 974].

[5] Diplock LJ added this about the evidence of the practice of bankers (at 975):

The only evidence of the practice of bankers was given by the manager and the securities clerk of the branch in question of the defendant bank. No evidence that the general practice of other bankers differed from that adopted by the defendant bank was called by the plaintiff company, although they knew well in advance of the trial, as a result of searching interrogatories, exactly what steps the defendant bank had taken, and what inquiries they had made. It seems a reasonable inference that what the defendants did in the present case was in accordance with current banking practice. Nield J accepted that it was, and Mr Lloyd has not sought to argue the contrary. What he contends is that this court is entitled to examine that practice and to form its own opinion as to whether it does comply with the standard of care which a prudent banker should adopt. That is quite right, but I venture to think that this court should be hesitant before condemning as negligent a practice generally adopted by those engaged in banking business.

[6] One of the tests of what is negligent that has been sounded in the authorities relates to what is out of the ordinary course of business. Thus in *Commissioners of Taxation v English, Scottish and Australian Bank Ltd* [1920] AC 683 (PC) at 688, 89 LJPC 181, 123 LT 34, Lord Dunedin, giving the opinion of the Privy Council, approved (with the addition of the words in italics cited below) the statement of Isaacs J in the High Court of Australia in *Commissioners of State Savings Bank v Permewan, Wright & Co* (1915) 19 CLR 457, 478, [1915] VLR 81 that:

the test of negligence is whether the transaction of paying in any given cheque [*coupled with the circumstances antecedent and present*] was so out of the ordinary course that it ought to have aroused doubts in the bankers' mind, and caused them to make inquiry.

[7] That test was to be applied by 'the standard to be derived from the ordinary practice of bankers, not individuals' (at 689). Isaacs J's test was again approved by this court in *Lloyds Bank Ltd v The Chartered Bank of India, Australia and China* [1929] 1 KB 40, at 59, [1928] All ER Rep 285, 33 Com Cas 306 (Scrutton LJ) and 72 (Sankey LJ). In this connection, we have been reminded, as a counterpoint to what Diplock LJ said in *Marfani* at 974, of what Scrutton LJ said in *A L Underwood Ltd v Bank of Liverpool & Martins* [1924] 1 KB 775 at 793, [1924] All ER Rep 230, 93 LJKB 690 of unusual circumstances:

> If banks, for fear of offending their customers will not make inquiries into unusual circumstances, they must take with the benefit of not annoying their customer the risk of liability because they do not inquire.

[8] For these purposes, it is relevant to consider the nature of the employee of the bank before whom the cheque in question will come for action. If a cheque will only come before a cashier, then the question of negligence has to be applied to the role of a cashier. In *Lloyds Bank v The Chartered Bank* at 72 Sankey LJ also approved of what Bailhache J had said in *Ross v London County Westminster and Parr's Bank* [1919] 1 KB 678, 685, 88 LJKB 927, 35 TLR 315, viz:

> I must attribute to the cashiers and clerks of the defendants the degree of intelligence and care ordinarily required of persons in their position to fit them for the discharge of their duties. It is therefore necessary to consider whether a bank cashier of ordinary intelligence and care on having these cheques presented to him by a private customer of the bank would be informed by the terms of the cheques themselves that it was open to doubt whether the customer had a good title to them.

[9] In many circumstances, however, the conduct of a careful banker's business will mean that the supervision or knowledge of a manager (of some or other level of seniority) will be relevant, for example on the occasion of the opening of an account for a new customer. In this connection consideration may have to be given to the vastness of a modern bank's enterprise. Cheques without number have to be handled by clerical staff or even by wholly automatic processes. What is the bank's duty then in terms of negligence? One answer was given in *Honourable Society of the Middle Temple v Lloyds Bank plc* [1999] 1 All ER (Comm) 193 at 228, [1999] Lloyds Rep Bank 50 (*per* Rix J):

> When, however, the cheque emerges from that multitude and is referred by the clerical staff to management, albeit only as a result of an inquiry after fate, it seems to me that different considerations come into play. The cheque is no longer a mere item following a course in a factory-like process. It no longer becomes impracticable to give it individual attention, or the attention of management. It is referred for just such individual attention, even if the cause of referral is something collateral.

[10] In this connection, Mr Michael Black QC on behalf of the Claimant Respondent, AoW Ltd, now in liquidation, submitted that all aspects of a bank's knowledge about a customer are to be assumed to be accumulated in every employee of the bank, so that a bank cannot rely on any division of knowledge between department and department. For these purposes he relied on a passage in *Lloyds Bank Ltd v E B Savory and Co* [1933] AC 201 at 213, [1932] All ER Rep 106, 102 LJKB 224, *per* Lord Buckmaster. He submitted that a fortiori in the era of computers and information technology, banks could not rely on ignorance as between different departments or officials of a bank. I take the point about computer and information technology. The observations of Lord Buckmaster, however, were dealing with a different problem, viz where the system adopted by the bank made it impossible to achieve what it was acknowledged a proper system of checking the contents of a cheque ought to do. I do not think that it follows that Mr Black's submission is correct, and we have not been referred to an authority which supports it. If it were correct, it would be a very big point. It might be said against it, that it would be liable to make banking impossible. In any event I do not think that such a proposition could be adopted without evidence of current banking practice.

[11] I referred above to Diplock LJ's dictum from *Marfani* of the inappropriateness of simply being wise after the event. That of course is a standard insight in the context of a duty of reasonable care. In this connection we were also referred to what Sankey LJ said in *Lloyds Bank v Chartered Bank* at 73, that:

> a bank cannot be held to be liable for negligence merely because they have not subjected an account to a microscopic examination. It is not to be expected that the officials of banks should also be amateur detectives.

[12] In sum, I would for present purposes underline the following matters as being indicated by these authorities. The s 4 qualified duty does not require an assumption of negligence, just because a bank bears the burden of showing that it took reasonable care. The enquiry is fact sensitive. Current banking practice is highly relevant to the issue of negligence. A bank's evidence about its practice is, especially if unchallenged, relevant evidence of the current practice of bankers. A court is not bound by such evidence, but it will be hesitant to reject it. Notice of what is so out of the ordinary course of events as to arouse doubts in a banker's mind or put him on enquiry is a relevant test of negligence, and may make the proof of the taking of reasonable care very difficult. However, the courts should be wary of hindsight or of imposing on a bank the role of an amateur detective. Ultimately, these principles were not in dispute. I therefore turn to the facts of the case.

...

Discussion and decision

[56] In my judgment there is force in [Counsel for the bank's] criticisms of the judge's decision to give summary judgment against the bank. One issue related to the process by which cashiers at the Regent Street branch and processors at ICO [where cheques were sent by the branch] accepted the cheques as sufficiently matching the name of the customer's account, AoW UK. Although the judge may have been sceptical, he was not I think entitled to reject out of hand, or to disregard, as he appears to have done, the bank's evidence that the current banking practice was that a sufficient match was acceptable and that the names in question did in fact sufficiently match. That evidence was unchallenged. It seems to me to raise an arguable case, a realistic prospect of a defence, based on the absence of negligence at this stage. I agree that it might have been better to have had more detailed evidence about how the practice of a sufficient match operates with respect to company names: Mr Penny's examples, while apposite, related to personal names. The problem of similar corporate names within a group must be a widespread one. All of us, I suspect, know from our own experience about how imprecise we sometimes are about writing exactly the right name on our cheques, and how very frequently we may leave off everything but the trading name itself, eg Marks & Spencer, or Prudential. How is this problem dealt with? How do banks and their customers ensure that the cheques reach the right accounts, especially where there may often be several associate companies which are candidates? In the present case, however, the bank and a fortiori its cashiers knew of only one company, Architects of Wine (UK) Ltd. It did not have to choose between that and its foreign associate, Architects of Wine Ltd. The point that 41 batches totalling some 400 cheques went through without raising a problem is at least double-edged.

[57] The 'sufficient match' issue is primarily for the cashiers and their ICO equivalents. Unless there is something on the face of the cheque which ought to give those employees of the bank notice of a problem which, if they cannot resolve themselves, they ought to bring to the notice of more senior officials, the cheques will pass this check and then enter the numberless queue of cheques being processed.

[58] A second issue, therefore, is whether, despite the similarity of the names, there were aspects of the cheques themselves which ought, at least arguably without further knowledge of the business of the customer, to have alerted the cashiers and ICO of something wrong. The judge relied on the fact that the cheques were all dollar cheques, in sums averaging $3,000, and that about 10% of them gave the payee's address in the Cayman Islands. I certainly understand the argument: but Mr Penny's evidence is again that such matters would not have suggested anything out of the ordinary such as would deprive the bank of its defence. That evidence, as it seems to me, raises a real defence with real prospects. It is plain that English companies do bank foreign currency cheques, and the branches have remittance forms for such foreign currency cheques which can list up to 50 of them on a single form. Once a dollar account is opened, the position changes again: for the operators at ICO would expect a customer with a dollar account to have dollar cheques for collection. It does not seem to me that an average of $3,000 (or even the higher values of some of the cheques) is obviously out of the way for a company dealing with quality wines by mail order. There is no evidence that that is so, or that these values were out of the ordinary course of the value of cheques banked by AoW UK. I note that in 2002 the company had had a banking turnover of £3.3 million, and in 2003 of £2.5 million. Why should not this company have marketed its wines by mail order in the United States? Or have a billing address, a PO Box number it should be noted, in the Cayman Islands? Should cashiers have alerted senior officials simply because of a change of business? Should a proper banking system be designed to throw up, for referral to a more senior official, any such change in the currency of payment? Perhaps so, even though Mr Penny says otherwise. However, that seems to me to be a question for trial.

...

[61] In sum, although AoW Ltd may have a strong case to make at trial, a matter on which I make no comment at all, it is an untested case. At present, the bank's evidence is unchallenged, and I agree with [Counsel for the bank] that the court is not in a position to reject it as raising no realistic prospect of a good defence, even bearing in mind as I do that it is the bank that bears the burden of showing that it acted with reasonable care.

[62] The judge thought otherwise. In this court, I think it is necessary to have considerable respect for the views of an experienced commercial judge that a defendant has not met the test of providing evidence of a defence with a real prospect of success at trial. The commercial court prides itself justifiably on its ability to distinguish the speculative but doomed claim which should be given its quietus sooner rather than later; or to identify the specious if colourable defence, which does not merit a trial. However, I do not regard the bank's defence, on the present state of the evidence, as either speculative or specious. On the contrary, I think that there is some justification in the bank's concern, expressed in submission, that if this summary judgment were to stand, then, on the basis of the judge's judgment that the bank fell 'well short' of raising a proper defence for trial, this bank, and its competitors, would, for reasons which it is not easy to define or restate in advance of a judgment following trial, be required substantially to revisit what are said, expressly in the case of Barclays, and inferentially in the case of its competitors, to be their procedures and current banking practice.

Conclusion

[63] I would therefore allow this appeal.

[Sir Mark Potter P and Wilson LJ agreed.]

NOTES

1. In *Honourable Society of the Middle Temple v Lloyds Bank plc* [1999] 1 All ER (Comm) 193, an English clearing bank collected a stolen account payee cheque as collecting agent for a foreign bank located in Istanbul. Rix J held the English bank to have been negligent and unable to rely on the s 4 defence against the true owner's action for conversion of the cheque. His Lordship distinguished between a bank acting as collecting agent for a domestic bank and one acting on behalf of a foreign bank. Rix J held that a bank acting as collecting agent for a domestic bank was entitled to assume that the domestic bank knew of its responsibilities under the Cheques Act 1992, so that the agent would not be negligent in leaving it to that bank to ensure that the cheque was being collected for the named payee, unless there was something exceptional which brought the cheque to the agent's notice. By contrast, Rix

J held that a bank acting as a collecting agent for a foreign bank was not entitled to make the same assumption, so that the agent would be negligent if it had failed to inform the foreign bank of its responsibilities under the 1992 Act, as Lloyds had failed to do in this case. However, Rix J also held that whilst negligence of the English bank deprived it of a s 4 defence, it did not constitute a breach of duty to the foreign bank because (at 225): 'an English clearing bank has no duty to its foreign correspondent banks to advise them of every aspect of English banking law'. The English agent bank was held to be entitled to a full indemnity from its foreign principal. Gross J applied Rix J's judgment in *Linklaters (a firm) v HSBC Bank plc* [2003] EWHC 1113 (Comm), [2003] 2 Lloyd's Rep 545, holding that it made no difference that, in the case before him, the collecting agent was also the paying bank.

2.   Section 4(2) of the 1957 Act extends the protection afforded by s 4(1) to the collection of cheques and certain other instruments eg conditional orders for payment, instruments drawn payable to 'cash or order', interest and dividend warrants, 'cheques' requiring a receipt, bankers' drafts. Section 3 of the Cheques Act 1992 has amended s 4(2) to include within the definition of 'cheques' those cheques which under s 81A(1) of the Bills of Exchange Act 1882 (see above, p 768) or otherwise are not transferable. However, it appears that an instrument in the form of a cheque to which the drawer's signature is a forgery is not a cheque and is not within s 4. Similarly, an unauthorised material alteration of a cheque avoids the instrument and has the effect of rendering it a worthless piece of paper (*Smith v Lloyds TSB Group plc* [2000] 2 All ER (Comm) 693, CA; see above, p 783). Thus, a materially altered 'cheque' would also fall outside s 4, although the risk to the collecting bank is minimal as the true owner would not be able to recover more than nominal damages for conversion of the instrument.

3.   By s 4(3) of the 1957 Act the collecting bank will not be treated for the purposes of s 4(1) as having been negligent by reason only of its failure to concern itself with absence of, or irregularity in, indorsement of a cheque or other instrument specified in s 4(2). However, a memorandum of the Committee of London Clearing Bankers (23 September 1957) states that indorsement will still be required if (1) the instrument is tendered for an account other than that of the ostensible payee (unless it is specially indorsed to the customer for whose account it is tendered), or if (2) the payee's name is misspelt or he is incorrectly designated and there are circumstances to suggest that the customer is not the person to whom payment is intended to be made, or if (3) an instrument payable to joint payees is tendered for credit of an account to which all are not parties. If a collecting bank does not comply with the memorandum, and that failure is material, it will be unable to establish that it acted without negligence as it will have failed to comply with standard banking practice.

4.   The bank may be both paying and collecting bank, as where both the drawer of a cheque and the person presenting it for payment maintain an account at the same branch or different branches of the drawee bank. In such a case, the bank as paying bank may rely the protection conferred by s 60 or s 80 of the Bills of Exchange Act 1882, but as collecting bank it must rely on s 4 of the Cheques Act 1957 (*Carpenter's Co v British Mutual Banking Co Ltd* [1938] 1 KB 511 (above, p 779). The bank is acting in two capacities and it cannot escape liability incurred in one capacity by setting up what may be a complete defence in the other.

(iii) Banking Act 1979, s 47

Section 47 of the Banking Act 1979 provides as follows:

In any circumstances in which proof of absence of negligence on the part of a banker would be a defence in proceedings by reason of s 4 of the Cheques Act 1957, a defence of contributory negligence shall also be available to the banker notwithstanding the provisions of s 11(1) of the Torts (Interference with Goods) Act 1977.

(iv) Other defences

It is open to the collecting bank to plead in its defence to an action in conversion that (1) the proceeds actually reached the true owner, the payment discharged a debt of the true owner or the true owner benefitted from the payment in some other way (*B Liggett (Liverpool) Ltd v Barclays Bank Ltd* [1928] 1 KB 48); or (2) the true owner ratified the unauthorised transaction or is estopped from alleging the conversion (*Bank of Montreal v Dominion Gresham Guarantee and Casualty Co Ltd* [1930] AC 659 at 666); or (3) the true owner's claim was itself tainted with illegality (*Thackwell v Barclays Bank plc* [1986] 1 All ER 676).

QUESTIONS

1.   Alan banked with the Cambridge branch of NE Bank plc. Using a cheque book supplied by the Cambridge branch, Alan drew a crossed cheque in favour of Bill or order. Bill indorsed the cheque specially to Chris for value. Daniel stole the cheque from Chris, forged Chris's signature on the back and delivered it to Ethel in payment of a debt. Ethel took it to her bank, the Oxford branch of NE Bank plc, who obtained payment of the cheque from Alan's branch and credited Ethel's account with the proceeds. Advise the parties.

2.   What would have been the position in the preceding question if the cheque had been crossed 'account payee'?

3.   Is the term 'negligence', as found in section 4 of the Cheques Act 1957, something of a misnomer? Does the collecting bank owe a duty of care to the true owner of a cheque? Would a collecting bank have acted 'without negligence' for the purposes of s 4 if its carelessness had no causative effect on the loss suffered by the true owner of a stolen cheque? Contrast M Hapgood (ed), *Paget's Law of Banking* (13th edn, 2007), para 24.42, citing, *inter alia, Marfani & Co Ltd v Midland Bank Ltd,* [1968] 1 WLR 956, 976, CA, *Hon Soc of the Middle Temple v Lloyds Bank plc,* [1999] 1 All ER (Comm) 193, 226, with M Brindle and R Cox (eds), *Law of Bank Payments* (3rd edn, 2004), para 7–167, citing, *inter alia, Thackwell v Barclays Bank plc* [1986] 1 All ER 676, 684.

2 PROMISSORY NOTES

The definition of a promissory note is set out in s 83(1) of the Bills of Exchange Act 1882 as follows:

A promissory note is an unconditional promise in writing made by one person to another signed by the maker, engaging to pay, on demand or at a fixed or determinable future time, a sum certain in money, to, or to the order of, a specified person or to bearer.

An example of a promissory note appears as Figure 2.

PROMISSORY NOTE

LAWYERS' COURT
TEMPLE
LONDON EC4

1 JANUARY 2008

£500

THREE MONTHS AFTER DATE I PROMISE TO PAY JOE
BLOGGS THE SUM OF FIVE HUNDRED POUNDS

(SIGNED)   *Tom Smith*

(T V SMITH)

Figure 2 Promissory note

Section 83(1) requires a promissory note to contain a promise to pay. As the next case illustrates, a mere acknowledgment of indebtedness, although it contains an implied promise to pay, is not enough.

Akbar Khan v Attar Singh
[1936] 2 All ER 545, Privy Council

The plaintiff deposited the sum of Rs43,900 with the defendants and received a deposit receipt which stated that 'this amount to be payable after two years. Interest at the rate of Rs5.40 per cent per year to be charged'. The document was stamped as a receipt. The issue before the Privy Council was whether this document was a deposit receipt or a promissory note.

Lord Atkin, delivering the advice of the Board, stated: . . . It is indeed doubtful whether a document can properly be styled a promissory note which does not contain an undertaking to pay, not merely an undertaking which has to be inferred from the words used. It is plain that the implied promise to pay arising from an acknowledgment of a debt will not suffice, for . . . an IOU is not a promissory note, though of the implied promise to pay there can be no doubt . . . .

Their Lordships prefer to decide this point on the broad ground that such a document as this is not and could not be intended to be brought within a definition relating to documents which are to be negotiable instruments. Such documents must come into existence for the purpose only of recording an agreement to pay money and nothing more, though of course they may state the consideration. Receipts and agreements generally are not intended to be negotiable, and serious embarrassment would be caused in commerce if the negotiable net were cast too wide. This document plainly is a receipt for money containing the terms on which it is to be repaid. It is not without significance that the defendants who drew it, and who were experienced moneylenders did not draw it on paper with an impressed stamp as they would have to if the document were a promissory note, and that they affixed a stamp which is sufficient if the document is a simple receipt. Being primarily a receipt even if coupled with a promise to pay it is not a promissory note.

NOTES

1. This ruling of Lord Atkin has been applied by the Court of Appeal in *Claydon v Bradley* [1987] 1 WLR 521 at 526, 528.

2. An IOU is not a promissory note, but merely evidence of indebtedness. Similarly, bankers' negotiable certificates of deposit are not promissory notes as they merely acknowledge receipt of a deposit, but they are negotiable by custom. Floating rate notes are also negotiable by custom, but they are not promissory notes as the sum payable is not certain. By contrast, sterling commercial paper, issued by financial institutions other than banks, usually takes the form of a promissory note payable to bearer (see R MacVicar (1986) 2 JIBFL 40) and Bank of England bank notes are promissory notes payable to bearer on demand (although it is pointless to present bank notes for payment as bank notes are also legal tender and the holder would only receive other bank notes in exchange). Further, by s 5(2) of the Bills of Exchange Act 1882, where in a bill of exchange the drawer and drawee are the same person, or where the drawee is a fictitious person or a person not having capacity to contract, the holder may treat the instrument, at his option, either as a bill of exchange or as a promissory note. For example, the recipient of a banker's draft (an order to pay drawn by a branch of a bank on its head office or another branch of the same bank) may treat the instrument as a promissory note and thereby normally be relieved of the need to present it for payment in order to render the maker liable (BEA, s 87(1)).

3. By s 89(1) of the Bills of Exchange Act 1882, subject to certain qualifications contained in ss 83–89, the provisions of the 1882 Act relating to bills of exchange apply, with the necessary modifications, to promissory notes. By s 89(2) of the Act, the maker of a promissory note is deemed to correspond with the acceptor of a bill, and the first indorser with the drawer of an accepted bill payable to his own order. As the maker is deemed the acceptor, s 89(3) states that the provisions of the Act relating to presentment for acceptance and to acceptance do not apply.

4. What are promissory notes used for? In international trade they are mainly used in forfaiting transactions where the importer will make a promissory note (supported by bank guarantees) which the exporter will indorse (without recourse) to a forfaiter at a discount. The forfaiter bears the credit risk, and economic and political risks, and must obtain payment of the instrument, or rediscount it in the secondary market (see below, p 927). In domestic trade promissory notes serve two functions. First, they provide added security if they are made by a debtor or hirer. They give the creditor or lessor the advantage of being able to bring an action by summary procedure and prevent the maker of the note raising certain defences which would be available if an action was brought on the underlying transaction (a principle affirmed in *Cardinal Financial Investments Corpn v Central Bank of Yemen* [2001] Lloyd's Rep Bank 1 at 3, CA). As this may place the debtor or hirer in a worse position if sued on the note than if sued on the underlying transaction, ss 123 and 124 of the Consumer Credit Act 1974 precludes the taking of promissory notes in respect of regulated consumer credit and consumer hire agreements (see above, p 559). Secondly, as with international trade, they facilitate the refinancing of transactions in that the notes may be discounted to a financial institution. Unlike the assignment of a chose in action which is made subject to equities, the negotiation of a promissory note can pass a title free from any defects in the title of previous parties.

3 BANKER'S DRAFTS

A banker's draft is an order to pay drawn by one branch of a bank on its head office or on another branch of the same bank. It is not a bill of exchange (or a cheque) because it is not drawn by one person on another as required by s 3(1) of the Bills of Exchange Act 1882 (see above, p 532). The instrument is in fact treated as a promissory note made and issued by the bank (*Commercial Banking Co of Sydney v Mann* [1961] AC 1 at 7). However, the holder of a banker's draft has the right to treat it either as a bill of exchange or as a promissory note (BEA, s 5(2)). The bank is protected in the case of such instruments by ss 1 and 4 of the Cheques Act 1957 (ss 1(2)(b), 4(2)(d)) and, in the case of crossed drafts, the provisions of the Bills of Exchange Act 1882 (especially s 80) relating to crossed cheques (Cheques Act 1957, s 5).

  Banker's drafts are often used to make payment in commercial transactions where the supplier of goods or services wants to be sure that he will get paid (eg a car dealer will often demand that his purchaser pays the price, or its balance where a deposit was paid earlier, by bankers' draft before he will release the car to him). A banker's draft is generally treated as equivalent to cash to the extent that the only risk is that of the insolvency of the bank. However, the supplier, who is usually the named payee on the draft (virtually all banker's drafts issued by UK banks are now crossed 'account payee', and so are not transferable because of s 81A(1) of the Bills of Exchange Act 1882), cannot be absolutely certain of payment under a banker's draft as the bank may be able to refuse to pay the draft, or seek to recover money already paid out as money paid by mistake, on the ground that the issue of the draft was obtained by the fraud of its customer (the recipient of the supplier's goods or services), or that the consideration given by its customer for the issue of the draft has failed. English law remains uncertain on these issues, but *RE Jones v Waring & Gillow Ltd* [1926] AC 670 (above, p 553), on the fraud issue, and *Hasan v Willson* [1977] 1 Lloyd's Rep 431 (above, p 551), on the failure of consideration issue, seem to support the bank's case in these circumstances (but for persuasive arguments to the contrary, see A Tettenborn [1998] RLR 63; see also B Geva (1994) 73 Can Bar Rev 21). Exactly the same issues also affect anyone who accepts payment by a building society cheque.

4 TRAVELLERS' CHEQUES

Travellers' cheques are widely used by businessmen and holidaymakers as a means of payment or of acquiring cash when travelling abroad. Travellers' cheques are purchased from banks or their agents. They come in a number of different forms, but in each case the travellers' cheque must be signed by the traveller when issued to him ('the signature') and countersigned by him when he cashes or negotiates the instrument ('the countersignature'). The most common types of travellers' cheque are: (a) where the issuing bank promises to pay a certain amount of money to the payee (whose name is left blank) provided the signature and countersignature correspond; (b) where one or more directors of the issuing bank order the bank to pay a certain amount of money to the payee (whose name is left blank) provided the signature and countersignature correspond; and (c) where the traveller gives an order, as drawer, to the issuing bank to pay to his own order provided the instrument is duly countersigned by him. In each case the travellers' cheque is treated as containing an undertaking by the issuing bank to pay the amount stated in the instrument (normally the undertaking is express). However, as payment is made conditional on the signature and countersigned being by the same person, the instrument in any of the three forms set out above cannot be a bill of exchange, cheque or promissory note within the meaning of ss 3(1), 73 and 83 of the Bills of Exchange Act 1882 (contrast Stassen (1978) 95 SALJ 180, 182–183, who argues that the countersignature is only a means of identification; and also Ottolenghi [1999] JBL 22, p 35). However, there is little doubt that, as a result of modern mercantile custom, travellers' cheques are treated as negotiable instruments throughout the world. This means that the general principles of the law of negotiable instruments apply, with necessary modifications, to travellers' cheques. For a detailed analysis of the law relating to travellers' cheques, see Ellinger (1969) 19 Univ of Toronto LJ 132; Stassen (1978) 95 SALJ 180; Frohlich (1980) 54 ALJ 388; *Chitty on Contracts* (29th edn, 2004), Vol II, paras 34–173ff.

QUESTIONS

1. Adam purchased a number of travellers' cheques from B Bank. He did not sign or countersign the cheques when he collected them as he was in a hurry to get to the airport. At the airport Adam found that his plane had been delayed and so he decided to do some last minute shopping. Despite a number of notices warning passengers not to leave their baggage unattended, Adam left his rucksack on a seat in the departure lounge while he went to browse in a nearby bookshop. Adam spent nearly an hour in the bookshop and on his return to the departure lounge he found that the rucksack had been opened and his travellers' cheques taken. Adam immediately cancelled his holiday and returned to B Bank demanding a refund for the stolen travellers' cheques. B Bank refused to give a refund relying on a clause printed on the inside of the plastic wallet, which had contained his travellers' cheques, which stated that the traveller had a right to a refund so long as he 'properly safeguarded each cheque against loss or theft'. Advise Adam. Compare *Braithwaite v Thomas Cook Travellers Cheques Ltd* [1989] QB 553, with *Fellus v National Westminster Bank plc* (1983) 133 NLJ 766 and *El Awadi v Bank of Credit and Commerce International SA Ltd* [1990] 1 QB 606.

2. In fact it was Chris who had stolen Adam's travellers' cheques. After stealing the cheques, Chris immediately signed them in his own name. He then went to a local department store where he used the cheques to pay for some jewellery. Before tendering the cheques in payment, Chris countersigned them in the presence of the shop assistant. The department store now seeks payment of the cheques from B Bank. Advise the bank. Compare *City National Bank of Galveston v American Express Co* 7 SW 2d 886 (1928); affd 16 SW 2d 278 (1929), with *American Express Co v Anadarko Bank and Trust Co* 67 P 2d 55 (1937). See also *Chitty on Contracts* (29th edn, 2004), Vol II, para 34–174.

CHAPTER 20

PAYMENT CARDS[1]

1 INTRODUCTION

Payment through the use of plastic payment cards continues to increase in popularity. Figures 1, 2 and 3 illustrate recent trends. Payment cards are usually used for relatively small value retail payments. They also account for 80 per cent of cash withdrawals.

	Credit		Charge		Debit		Total payment cards	
Year	Number	% Change	Number	% Change	Number	% Change	Number	% Change
1996	31,336	10.8	2,803	11.8	32,473	14.2	66,611	12.5
1997	35,461	13.2	2,982	6.4	36,646	12.9	75,089	12.7
1998	38,299	8.0	3,270	9.7	42,529	16.1	84,097	12.0
1999	41,424	8.2	3,447	5.4	46,083	8.4	90,953	8.2
2000	47,080	13.7	3,772	9.4	49,730	7.9	100,582	10.6
2001	51,701	9.8	4,426	17.3	54,305	9.2	110,433	9.8
2002	58,794	13.7	4,311	−2.6	59,419	9.4	122,524	10.9
2003	66,825	13.7	4,431	2.8	62,854	5.8	134,110	9.5
2004	69,888	4.6	4,423	−0.2	65,544	4.3	139,855	4.3
2005	69,858	..	4,725	6.8	66,990	2.2	141,573	1.2
2006	69,521	−0.5	4,931	4.4	68,348	2.0	142,800	0.9

Figure 1 Number of UK-issued cards 1996–2006 (thousands)

[1] EP Ellinger, E Lomnicka and RJA Hooley, *Ellinger's Modern Banking Law* (4th edn, 2006), Ch 14; M Smith and P Robertson 'Plastic Money', Ch 4 in M Brindle and R Cox (eds), *Law of Bank Payments* (3rd edn, 2004); P Cresswell et al (eds), *Encyclopaedia of Banking Law* (1982, looseleaf), Division Dl 'Payment and Payment Systems' (ed Hooley), paras 1201 ff; G Stephenson *Credit, Debit & Cheque Cards* (1993).

Year	Payment cards		ATM-only		Cheque guarantee		eurocheque[a]		Total all cards	
	Number	% Change	Number	% Change	Number	% Change	Number	% Change	Number	% Change
1996	66,611	12.5	24,702	−8.0	3,754	−9.4	1,575	−3.6	96,642	5.2
1997	75,089	12.7	24,320	−1.5	3,451	−8.1	1,496	−5.0	104,355	8.0
1998	84,097	12.0	23,747	−2.4	3,041	−11.9	1,392	−6.9	112,277	7.6
1999	90,953	8.2	23,304	−1.9	2,989	−1.7	1,091	−21.6	118,338	5.4
2000	100,582	10.6	23,024	−1.2	2,854	−4.5	834	−23.6	127,294	7.6
2001	110,433	9.8	24,032	4.4	2,369	−17.0			136,833	7.5
2002	122,524	10.9	23,196	−3.5	1,810	−23.6			147,530	7.8
2003	134,110	9.5	24,874	7.2	1,605	−11.3			160,588	8.9
2004	139,855	4.3	24,829	−0.2	831	−48.2			165,515	3.1
2005	141,573	1.2	22,867	−7.9	667	−19.8			165,106	−0.2
2006	142,800	0.9	21,294	−6.9	541	−18.9			164,636	−0.3

[a] eurocheques were withdrawn during 2001 and are no longer issued in the UK.

Figure 1 (*Continued*)

Year	Purchases in the UK						Total purchases in the UK	
	Credit		Charge		Debit			
	Number	% Change	Number	% Change	Number	% Change	Number	% Change
1996	886	11.9	139	19.8	1,270	26.5	2,296	20.1
1997	977	10.2	151	9.0	1,503	18.3	2,631	14.6
1998	1,059	8.4	165	8.7	1,736	15.5	2,960	12.5
1999	1,169	10.4	175	6.2	2,062	18.8	3,406	15.1
2000	1,264	8.1	187	7.2	2,337	13.3	3,789	11.2
2001	1,341	6.1	220	17.6	2,696	15.3	4,258	12.4
2002	1,471	9.7	216	-2.0	2,994	11.1	4,681	9.9
2003	1,598	8.6	224	3.8	3,364	12.4	5,186	10.8
2004	1,727	8.1	222	−1.1	3,690	9.7	5,639	8.7
2005	1,674	−3.1	250	12.9	4,084	10.7	6,008	6.5
2006	1,659	−0.9	271	8.1	4,512	10.5	6,441	7.2

Figure 2 Transaction volumes 1996–2006 (millions)

Year	Purchases in the UK		Cash acquisition in the UK		Total transactions in the UK	
	Number	% Change	Number	% Change	Number	% Change
1996	2,296	20.1	1,560	11.0	3,856	16.2
1997	2,631	14.6	1,642	5.2	4,273	10.8
1998	2,960	12.5	1,763	7.4	4,722	10.5
1999	3,406	15.1	1,854	5.2	5,260	11.4
2000	3,789	11.2	1,915	3.3	5,704	8.4
2001	4,258	12.4	2,128	11.1	6,386	12.0
2002	4,681	9.9	2,263	6.4	6,944	8.7
2003	5,186	10.8	2,354	4.0	7,540	8.6
2004	5,639	8.7	2,430	3.2	8,069	7.0
2005	6,008	6.5	2,621	7.8	8,629	6.9
2006	6,441	7.2	2,703	3.2	9,144	6.0

Year	Transactions in the UK		Transactions outside the UK		Total number of transactions	
	Number	% Change	Number	% Change	Number	% Change
1996	3,856	16.2	82	23.3	3,938	16.4
1997	4,273	10.8	106	29.8	4,380	11.2
1998	4,722	10.5	125	17.5	4,847	10.7
1999	5,260	11.4	137	9.4	5,397	11.3
2000	5,704	8.4	163	19.6	5,867	8.7
2001	6,386	12.0	194	18.5	6,579	12.1
2002	6,944	8.7	212	9.6	7,157	8.8
2003	7,540	8.6	230	8.1	7,770	8.6
2004	8,069	7.0	264	15.1	8,333	7.3
2005	8,629	6.9	279	5.7	8,908	6.9
2006	9,144	6.0	288	3.0	9,432	5.9

Figure 2 (*Continued*)

Year	Purchases in the UK						Total purchases in the UK	
	Credit		Charge		Debit			
	Value	% Change	Value	% Change	Value	% Change	Value	% Change
1996	39,513	17.5	10,818	21.9	37,056	30.2	87,386	23.1
1997	45,633	15.5	12,424	14.8	45,058	21.6	103,115	18.0
1998	51,070	11.9	13,404	7.9	53,720	19.2	118,194	14.6
1999	59,786	17.1	15,854	18.3	64,650	20.3	140,291	18.7
2000	66,122	10.6	18,793	18.5	75,987	17.5	160,903	14.7
2001	71,631	8.3	21,979	17.0	94,919	24.9	188,529	17.2
2002	81,105	13.2	22,006	0.1	107,845	13.6	210,956	11.9
2003	91,368	12.7	22,036	0.1	130,469	21.0	243,874	15.6
2004	99,432	8.8	23,363	6.0	150,152	15.1	272,947	11.9
2005	99,554	0.1	24,497	4.9	170,672	13.7	294,723	8.0
2006	97,937	-1.6	27,966	14.2	194,863	14.2	320,765	8.8

Year	Purchases in the UK		Cash acquisition in the UK		Total transactions in the UK	
	Value	% Change	Value	% Change	Value	% Change
1996	87,386	23.1	82,250	9.8	169,636	16.3
1997	103,115	18.0	91,210	10.9	194,325	14.6
1998	118,194	14.6	101,196	10.9	219,390	12.9
1999	140,291	18.7	107,443	6.2	247,734	12.9
2000	160,903	14.7	117,093	9.0	277,995	12.2
2001	188,529	17.2	139,620	19.2	328,149	18.0
2002	210,956	11.9	149,198	6.9	360,155	9.8
2003	243,874	15.6	157,827	5.8	401,701	11.5
2004	272,947	11.9	170,901	8.3	443,848	10.5
2005	294,723	8.0	183,979	7.7	478,702	7.9
2006	320,765	8.8	198,032	7.6	518,797	8.4

Figure 3 Transaction values 1996–2006 (£ millions)

	Transactions in the UK		Transactions outside the UK		Total value of transactions	
Year	Value	% Change	Value	% Change	Value	% Change
1996	169,636	16.3	5,701	25.1	175,337	16.6
1997	194,325	14.6	6,909	21.2	201,234	14.8
1998	219,390	12.9	8,185	18.5	227,576	13.1
1999	247,734	12.9	9,062	10.7	256,796	12.8
2000	277,995	12.2	12,182	34.4	290,177	13.0
2001	328,149	18.0	14,100	15.7	342,249	17.9
2002	360,155	9.8	16,017	13.6	376,172	9.9
2003	401,701	11.5	18,330	14.4	420,031	11.7
2004	443,848	10.5	20,006	9.1	463,854	10.4
2005	478,702	7.9	20,759	3.8	499,461	7.7
2006	518,797	8.4	22,994	10.8	541,791	8.5

Figure 3 (*Continued*)

[Figures 1, 2 and 3 are taken from the *UK Payment Statistics 2007*, published by the Association for Payment Clearing Services.]

2   TYPES OF PAYMENT CARD

The main types of payment card in general circulation in the United Kingdom are:

(a) **Cheque cards**—which are issued by banks and building societies to their customers for use with cheques drawn by the customer. Through the card the issuing bank undertakes to the payee that payment of the drawer's cheques (drawn up to the limit indicated on the card itself, ie £50, £100 or £250) will be made, regardless of the state of the drawer's account, provided that certain conditions are met. The standard conditions for use of a cheque card, which are set out in the Rules of the UK Domestic Cheque Guarantee Card Community, are that (i) the cheque bears the name and code number, where printed, on the card; (ii) the cheque is dated with the actual date of issue; (iii) the cheque is signed before the expiry of the card in the presence of the payee by the account holder; (iv) the card number is written on the cheque by the payee; and (v) the card has not been altered or defaced. This type of card is often referred to a 'cheque guarantee card', but this is strictly a misnomer because the obligation assumed by the bank is not a secondary obligation dependent on default by the card-holder, but a separate and independent payment obligation (*First Sport Ltd v Barclays Bank plc* [1993] 3 All ER 789, 795, CA).

(b) **Credit (and charge) cards**—which enable the holder to whom such a card is issued to obtain goods and services without payment in cash or by cheque, and to obtain cash. A credit card gives the holder a revolving credit facility with a monthly credit limit. The card-holder does not have to settle his account in full at the end of each month but has the option to take extended credit, subject to an obligation to make a specified minimum payment each month. Amounts outstanding at the end of a set period commencing with the date of the monthly statement sent by the card-issuer to the card-holder attract interest charged on a daily basis. Unlike a credit card, the primary function of a charge card (also called a 'travel and entertainment card') is to facilitate payment, rather than to provide a credit facility. The holder of a charge card must normally settle his account in full within a specified period after the date of a monthly statement sent by the card-issuer to the card-holder. Delinquent accounts may be charged a sum equal to interest, but this is described by the card-issuer as 'liquidated damages' for failure by the card-holder to honour the terms of card membership. Credit and charge cards may be 'two-party' cards, which means the card is issued by shops and stores for the purchase of their own goods and services. Alternatively, they may be 'three-party' cards issued by banks, building societies, credit card and finance companies etc for the purchase of goods and services from participating retailers (in fact a fourth party, the 'merchant acquirer', is also often involved in the transaction: see below, p 823). In the UK most 'three-party' cards operate through the Visa and MasterCard networks (credit cards) and the American Express and Diners Club networks (charge cards).

(c) **Debit cards**—debit card payments are now invariably made using EFTPOS ('electronic funds transfer at point of sale') systems. There are two major EFTPOS debit card schemes in operation in the UK: Visa Delta (owned by Visa), and Switch/Maestro, run by S2 Card Services Ltd using MasterCard's brand Maestro. In a typical retail transaction, the cardholder presents the retailer with a plastic debit card that incorporates a micro-chip which holds information relating to the cardholder's current bank account (but note that in some cases the cardholder may use his debit card to make a purchase over the telephone or via the internet when he will simply provide the retailer with his card details). The card is inserted into a card reader installed at the retailer's point of sale terminal and the retailer enters the amount of the transaction into his terminal (but note that 'contactless' cards are now being developed where the card is simply tapped against, or waived over, a reader). The cardholder is then invited to insert his personal identification number (PIN) into the machine (since 14 February 2006 cardholders have been required to know their PINs). Where the transaction is over a given amount the retailer's terminal will seek authorisation from the authorisation centre of the cardholder's bank to accept the card, although the precise circumstances where authorisation is required will vary according to the rules of each EFTPOS system. The PIN acts as the cardholder's mandate to his bank to debit his account and credit the retailer's account, and a message to this effect is transmitted, via one of the EFTPOS networks, to the cardholder's bank and the retailer's bank. The message may be transmitted either directly to the EFTPOS network or stored at the retailer's terminal for transmission in batch mode at the close of business that day. When the cardholder's bank and the retailer's bank have received their respective debit and credit instructions over the network, the cardholder's and retailer's accounts will be adjusted accordingly. Where an EFTPOS system operates on-line it is technically possible for the transmission of the debit/credit message from the retailer's terminal, and adjustments of accounts at the cardholder's and retailer's banks, to be virtually instantaneous.

Credit card transactions may also be executed using EFTPOS terminals, eg VISA and MasterCard operate such systems. But with most credit (and charge) card schemes a separate card account is opened for the customer with debits made against that account. The cardholder will then make payments into the account from a current account with a bank by cheque, direct debit or sometimes even by standing order. By contrast, a debit card operates directly on the cardholder's current account, to which debits are posted as the card is used to pay for goods and services (or to obtain cash), and a corresponding credit is made to the account of the supplier who has accepted payment by debit card (a debit card may also be used to obtain cash from a supplier who offers a 'cashback facility'). Thus, debit cards perform a similar function to that performed by cheques, and it is not surprising that the increased use of debit cards has contributed, together with the increased use of direct debit payments, to a significant drop in the number of cheque transactions in recent years.

(d) **ATM cards**—which give customers access (when used in conjunction with their personal identification number or 'PIN') to Automated Teller Machines (ATMs). The first ATMs introduced in the UK in 1967 only dispensed cash. ATMs now provide a variety of services. Typically, a customer can use an ATM to withdraw cash from his account, make a balance enquiry, order a bank statement, order a cheque book, change his PIN, pay bills and accept deposits. An ATM card can only be used in the ATMs of the card-issuing bank and the ATMs of other banks with whom the issuing bank has reached a reciprocal agreement. Reciprocal agreements were introduced to provide shared ATM networks giving customers access to their accounts via any ATM within the network. A number of ATM networks were established, namely, the FOUR BANKS, MINT and LINK networks. All UK ATM owners have since joined the LINK network and the FOUR BANKS and MINT networks have closed. There are also a number of international ATM networks, eg the Visa and MasterCard networks.

(e) **Multifunctional cards**—often a single card will have several functions, eg debit cards usually also operate as cheque cards and/or ATM cards. For the purpose of legal analysis, each function must be examined separately.

Banks are also starting to make **digital cash cards** (sometimes called 'electronic purses') available to customers in certain areas. Digital cash, also known as 'electronic money', is designed to mimic the essential features of cash payment, namely that transfer of possession of physical cash transfers ownership of the cash and immediately discharges the debt owed by the transferor to the transferee. Digital cash systems are either smart card systems, where electronic value is stored in a microchip on a smart card, or software based systems where tokens or coins are stored in the memory of a computer. The 'value', 'tokens' or 'coins' take the form of digital information. Digital cash allows payment to be made simply by transferring digital information directly between debtor and creditor so that value is transferred immediately upon delivery. In some systems the recipient of digital cash can immediately use it to pay for other goods or services. Other systems require the token to be deposited in a bank account or with the issuer who will then issue a token of equivalent value or credit the value to an account. *Mondex* is an example of a smart card system. The customer has digital information representing monetary value loaded on to a smart card at Mondex-enabled ATMs (loading from a current or credit card account) or at a special purpose machine (loading from cash). The process merely involves the creation and maintenance of a record of value ('stored value') on the smart card rather than the store of discrete coins. Value can then be transferred from card to card, or from card to a microchip held by a merchant, through the exchange of that digital information. Where the merchant receives payment through the transfer of stored value from a Mondex card, he may himself transfers that value on to a third party, eg his supplier. The merchant does not have to redeem Mondex value for 'real' value at his bank, although that option always remains open to him. Like physical cash, Mondex value is fungible and can be transferred from person to person.

QUESTIONS

1. Digital cash has proved less popular with consumers than originally envisaged. Why do you think that is so?

2. It is estimated that in the UK in 2006 there were some 426 million plastic card payments made over the Internet amounting to over £30 billion (*APACS The Way We Pay 2007: UK Plastic Cards*, p 21). Credit cards accounted for some three-quarters of all Internet payments. What concerns might a consumer have when using a payment card in this way? See S Miller 'Payment in an On-Line World', Ch 4 in L Edwards and C Waelde (eds) *Law and the Internet—A Framework for Electronic Commerce* (2nd edn, 2000), and see also below, pp 838ff.

3 CONTRACTUAL NETWORKS

(a) Cheque cards

First Sport Ltd v Barclays Bank plc
[1993] 3 All ER 789, Court of Appeal

The facts are set out in Evans LJ's judgment.

Evans LJ: The plaintiff is a retailer who supplied goods worth £49.99 to a customer who paid for them by a personal cheque drawn on Barclays Bank, the defendants, supported by a Barclays Connect Card. The account was that of Wasim Najbat Khan and both the cheque book from which the cheque came and the card had been issued to him. But they were stolen from him in Peterborough on 18 September 1991. The plaintiff's customer was the thief or some other person who was dishonestly using the stolen cheque and card and who forged Mr Khan's signature on the cheque.

The defendants, whom I shall call 'the bank', refused payment of the cheque. The plaintiff began proceedings in the Peterborough County Court which came before the district judge. He made an award in their favour, but the bank appealed. Judge Morrell allowed the appeal, and the plaintiff now appeals to this court. . . .

The agreed facts, in so far as they have not been summarised above, were:

> The unknown fraudster presented a cheque from the cheque book, numbered 100038 in the sum of £49·99 and the cheque guarantee card to Mr Farquharson, who was an employee of the plaintiff, at those premises. The district judge decided that in the absence of seeing the cheque guarantee card—for that has never come to light—on the balance of probabilities after that card was stolen the genuine signature had been removed from the card and replaced by the signature of the person who presented the cheque and the card to the plaintiff's employee. It follows from that that the alteration either was or may have been undetectable. That is the finding which the district judge made and to that finding I shall be faithful. Goods to the value of £49·99, or cash, were handed over. In due course the cheque was presented to the appellant Barclays Bank, which refused to honour it because, as was the case, it had not been signed by Mr Khan. Mr Khan's signature had been forged upon it.

The finding that the genuine signature had been removed from the card and replaced by the signature of the person who presented the card to the plaintiff's employee is somewhat mystifying. The cheque, which of course has been produced, bears the forged signature of Mr Khan. It follows that the altered signature on the card must have been the same. Why there should have been this double forgery is not at all clear. But the appeal has been argued on the basis that it is irrelevant whether the card was altered or not. The bank does not suggest that the alteration was apparent, and the issue raised for decision by this court is whether the bank is liable to pay the cheque when the signature on the cheque is forged, although apparently the same as the signature, true or forged, upon the card.

This depends upon the terms of whatever contract came into existence, as a result of the transaction, between the plaintiff and the bank. It is common ground that when a cheque is presented by the account holder, supported by a cheque card, and is accepted by a retailer in accordance with the conditions stated on the card, then a contract comes into existence between the retailer and the bank. That contract is independent of the contract for the sale or supply of goods between the retailer and his customer, who has presented the card, and of the relationship between the account holder and the bank. In *Metropolitan Police Comr v Charles* [1976] 3 All ER 112 at 121, [1977] AC 177 at 191 Lord Edmund-Davies referred to this as 'the all-important contract between payee and bank' and he described the process of contracting as follows:

> ... it is the representation by the drawer's production of the card that he has [the bank's authority to bind it] that creates such contractual relationship and estops the bank from refusing to honour the cheque. By drawing the cheque the accused represented that it would be met, and by producing the card so that the number thereon could be indorsed on the cheque he in effect represented, 'I am authorised by the bank to show this to you and so create a direct contractual relationship between the bank and you that they will honour this cheque'. The production of the card was the badge of the accused's ostensible authority to make such a representation on the bank's behalf.

The issue in the present case is whether the same contractual relationship arises when the card is presented and the cheque signed, not by the account holder but by a person who falsely claims to be and appears to be the person authorised to sign.

The Connect Card presented to the plaintiffs had the same account number as the cheque and the name of the account holder appeared as 'Mr W N Khan'. The same name, without the prefix, was printed on the cheque. The reverse of the card beneath a space for the 'authorised signature' contained the following:

> This Card may only be used by the authorised signatory. It is the property of Barclays Bank PLC and if found should be returned to any branch of Barclays or Barclaycard, Northampton NN1 1SG to whom the loss must immediately be notified—telephone 0604 230230.
>
> Payment of one personal cheque not exceeding £50 issued within the United Kingdom (including the Channel Islands and Isle of Man) during the validity period shown hereon in settlement of any one transaction is guaranteed provided: no other cheque guaranteed by a card issued by Barclays is also used to settle that transaction: the cheque is taken from a Barclays cheque book issued in the United Kingdom: the signature agrees with the specimen hereon and is written in the presence of the payee who must record the Card's number on the reverse of the cheque.

Mr Neville Thomas QC for the bank submits that no contract can come into being when the cheque card is presented by someone other than the authorised signatory and the signature on the cheque is forged. He contends that such a person has no authority, actual or apparent, to make an offer on behalf of the bank, or to make any representation which binds the bank, so that in the absence of any direct communication, which is not alleged here, there cannot be any contractual obligation on the bank. Moreover, under s 24(2) of the Bills of Exchange Act 1882 the cheque form bearing the forged signature is worthless as a cheque or bill of exchange and is no more than a 'sham piece of paper': *National Westminster Bank Ltd v Barclays Bank International Ltd* [1974] 3 All ER 834 at 836, [1975] QB 654 at 656–657 per Kerr J.

Mr Douglas for the plaintiff contends that the cheque card contains an unequivocal undertaking by the bank that it will honour personal cheques when the conditions stated on the card are complied with by the payee of the cheque. These conditions are set out in the second paragraph, and they do not include the first sentence of the first paragraph, which reads: 'This Card may only be used by the authorised signatory.' That, he submits, is addressed only to whoever may be in possession of the card and operates so as to limit the bank's express authority to use the card to the authorised signatory only. He disputes that any question of authority arises, because the card itself, when it comes into the hands of the retailer or other payee of the cheque, conveys the bank's offer to him and no agent is necessary. Alternatively, if the question of agency does arise, then the bearer of the card who can comply with the conditions stated on it has apparent authority to enter into the transaction on behalf of the bank.

The best starting point for consideration of these competing submissions is, in my judgment, the bank's own statement printed on the reverse of the card. There is no reason as a matter of principle why this should not be addressed to the retailer, regardless of the identity of the bearer of the card. Conversely, the words might convey the meaning that the bank would only be bound if the cheque was signed by the authorised signatory, and by no other. The question is, what do the words on their true construction mean? This is a question of law and, although the words should be given their natural and ordinary meaning, the sense in which they were or might be understood by an individual retailer is strictly irrelevant: *Woodhouse AC Israel Cocoa Ltd SA v Nigerian Produce Marketing Co Ltd* [1972] 2 All ER 271, [1972] AC 741.

The express offer contained in the second paragraph, in its essentials, is:

> Payment of one personal cheque . . . is guaranteed provided . . . the cheque is taken from a Barclays cheque book [and] the signature agrees with the specimen hereon and is written in the presence of the payee who must record the Card's number on the reverse of the cheque.

It is common ground that all of the conditions set out in this paragraph were complied with, and in particular that the signature on the cheque agreed with the specimen signature on the card.

The first sentence of the first paragraph informed the retailer, as well as all bearers of the card, that only the authorised signatory was entitled to use the card. If Mr Douglas goes so far as to suggest that the retailer in effect can disregard it, then I cannot accept his submission to that extent. The sentence puts the retailer on notice that he can only deal with the authorised signatory, for the purpose of entering into any transaction with the bank, but this does not answer the question whether he can safely deal with a person whom he reasonably believes is the authorised signatory, but who in fact is not. It goes without saying that the retailer must act in good faith.

If the second paragraph stated in terms that the bank's undertaking was conditional upon the card being presented and the cheque being signed by the account holder, then the answer would be clear. The retailer would know that the bank was not accepting the risks of a forged signature and of the card and cheque being in the wrong hands. But the second paragraph does not say this, and what it does say about signatures is to the contrary effect. It would be unnecessary to require the retailer to compare the cheque signature with that on the card, if the bank was not bound by a forged signature. Moreover, the words 'agrees with the specimen' indicate, as Mr Douglas submitted, that the bank requires the retailer, as a condition of its offer, to concern himself with appearances, so as to minimise the risk of forgery or unauthorised use. If the bank was not bearing the risk, then it is difficult to see what commercial or other purpose was served by imposing that condition on the retailer. In short, if the bank's undertaking was conditional upon the cheque being signed by the authorised signatory and by no other, then the second paragraph could have said so, but it did not.

The question of construction therefore becomes: should the first sentence of the first paragraph be read with the second paragraph so as to import this further condition, which was not otherwise expressed? In my judgment, this is not the meaning conveyed by the card. The first sentence has effect in the way I have stated above: the retailer is put on notice that only the authorised signatory can use the card. The requirement that he should compare the signatures shows that the bank had in mind the possibility that the card might be presented by someone other than the authorised signatory, yet it does not state that the bank will not be liable in these circumstances, as it easily could have done.

The legal analysis in my judgment is as follows. The card conveys to the retailer, or to any other person to whom it is presented, an offer made by the bank which, if accepted, establishes contractual relations between them. This strictly is a unilateral contract and it is unnecessary for the retailer's acceptance to be communicated to the bank: *United Dominions Trust (Commercial) Ltd v Eagle Aircraft Services Ltd, United Dominions Trust (Commercial) Ltd v Eagle Aviation Ltd* [1968] 1 All ER 104, [1968] 1 WLR 74. But the question of authority is not irrelevant, as Mr Douglas submits. The bearer must have authority to convey the offer on behalf of the bank. The authorised signatory has actual authority to do this, and even if this authority has been terminated, or is limited in any way, he will continue to have ostensible authority to convey the bank's offer on its behalf. If the bearer is some other person, even a thief, and provided the retailer had no reason to believe that he is not the authorised signatory and account holder, then in my judgment he too has ostensible authority to this limited extent. If the bank had intended to make it clear to the retailer that such a person would have no authority, actual or apparent, then the statement could have been worded to that effect. Thus, the scope of the bearer's apparent authority depends upon the correct interpretation of the bank's own statement on the card. The retailer in my judgment is entitled to rely upon that statement, on its true construction, and if he complies with the conditions then the bank becomes bound by its undertaking to payees.

Mr Thomas submits that in the absence of actual authority there must be some form of apparent authority, and that this is neither the case of a true agent who exceeds his actual authority whilst remaining within the limits of the usual authority of a person employed by the principal in his position, nor a case where the principal has represented that the agent has the authority which he claims. The self-professed agent cannot create or enlarge his own authority by any representation which he makes to the third party, and so, as Mr Thomas submits, the principal must be shown to be estopped by some representation which he himself has made. In my judgment, however, the necessary representation is established here, in the form of the statement on the card which the bank addressed to retailers or other cheque-payees to whom the card might be produced. The scope of the representation and therefore of the estoppel thus depends upon the terms in which the statement is made.

Other aspects of the legal position can be mentioned briefly. The drawing and acceptance of the cheque imposes no liability on the bank, for two reasons. First, even a valid cheque is no more than an instruction by the drawer to the bank to pay the amount stated to the payee. The bank incurs no obligation to the payee: *R v Kassim* [1991] 3 All ER 713, [1992] 1 AC 9 and see *Chitty on Contracts* (26th edn, 1989) vol 2, para 2831. Secondly, the forged signature means that legally the cheque is unsigned: Bills of Exchange Act 1882, s 24. But this does not mean that the reference to 'cheque' in the bank's statement on the card must be interpreted in this technical sense. The conditions contemplate the possibility of a cheque form being signed by a person other than the authorised signatory, who forges the latter's signature, and such a document is included, in my judgment, in the references to 'cheque' in the second paragraph, giving that word its natural and ordinary meaning in this context.

The bank's undertaking that payment of the cheque is 'guaranteed' does not mean that its contract with the payee, when the offer is accepted, is strictly a contract of guarantee. It is a separate and independent obligation which is not dependent in any way upon default by the customer, whether the authorised signatory or not, in the performance of any obligation which he incurs. To this extent, the commonly used description of such cards as 'cheque guarantee cards' is strictly a misnomer.

It is perhaps surprising that the central issue which arises here has not been decided in any reported case, but it is also noteworthy that in the leading cases of *Metropolitan Police Comr v Charles* [1976] 3 All ER 112, [1977] AC 177 (where the card was presented by the authorised signatory) and *R v Kassim* [1991] 3 All ER 713, [1992] 1 AC 9 the reported facts show that the bank or credit organisation which issued the card had paid the amount due to the payee, and in *R v Beck* [1985] 1 All ER 571, [1985] 1 WLR 22, where fraud was involved, the bank and the credit organisation likewise paid the amounts claimed by the payees, though the transactions were not directly comparable and they did so for commercial reasons without admitting their liability to do so. In *R v Kassim* [1991] 3 All ER 713 at 721, [1992] 1 AC 9 at 19 Lord Ackner pointed out that: 'All [the tradesman] will be concerned with is that the conditions on the card are satisfied' and, referring to *R v Beck,* that the French traders were reimbursed 'because [they] had complied with all the necessary conditions' (see [1991] 3 All ER 713 at 719, [1992] 1 AC 9 at 17). These dicta are helpful to the plaintiffs but they were not directed towards the particular issue that arises here.

The lack of direct authority makes it necessary to approach the issue on the basis of principle. This leads to the true construction of the bank's statement on the card, for the reasons which I have tried to express, and in the present case in my judgment to the conclusion that the plaintiff is entitled to succeed.

Kennedy LJ (dissenting):

The bank's offer

In my judgment the critical words are the first words which appear on the back of the card after the signature, namely 'This Card may only be used by the authorised signatory'. They are not simply, as Mr Douglas for the plaintiffs submitted, words of warning to the authorised signatory (ie the bank's customer to whom the card was issued) or to anyone who might happen to find the card. Those words are also there to advise any supplier of goods or services as to who was entitled to use the card. The card does not say, for example. 'This card may be used by any bearer', although if Mr Douglas is right that is what it should have said.

If the authorised signatory produces the card then, as the agent of the bank, he conveys to the supplier of goods the bank's standing offer, which is that, if the transaction proceeds as set out in the second paragraph of the printed terms, payment of the cheque in the sum not exceeding £50 'is guaranteed'. What is envisaged is not the usual situation giving rise to liability under a contract of guarantee, because as far as the supplier of goods is concerned there will be no initial default by the debtor, but my analysis of the situation thus far seems to be in line with what was said by Lord Diplock in *Metropolitan Police Comr v Charles* [1976] 3 All ER 112 at 114, [1977] AC 177 at 182:

> By exhibiting to the payee a cheque card containing the undertaking by the bank to honour cheques drawn in compliance with the conditions endorsed on the back, and drawing the cheque accordingly, the drawer represents to the payee that he has actual authority from the bank to make a contract with the payee on the bank's behalf that it will honour the cheque on presentment for payment.

And similarly Lord Edmund-Davies said ([1976] 3 All ER 112 at 121, [1977] AC 177 at 191):

> ...in order to make the bank liable to the payee there must be knowledge on the payee's part that the drawer has the bank's authority to bind it, for in the absence of such knowledge the all-important contract between payee and bank is not created; and it is the representation by the drawer's production of the card that he has that authority that creates such contractual relationship and estops the bank from refusing to honour the cheque...

If the producer of the card is a thief who has altered the signature on the card so that he can match it when he signs the cheque then, in my judgment, he cannot have either the actual or even ostensible authority to bind the bank. Clearly he does not have actual authority, and he could only have ostensible authority if the bank had so conducted itself towards the supplier of goods as to be estopped from denying the truth of the representation, and that situation simply does not arise in this case. The bank cannot be estopped from denying the authority of the thief to use the card simply because it issued this card with these words on it to its own customer for his own use....

No valid cheque

By virtue of s 73 of the Bills of Exchange Act 1882 'A cheque is a bill of exchange drawn on a banker payable on demand', and the provisions of that Act apply to a cheque such as that which was signed in the present case. Section 24 of the 1882 Act provides:

> Subject to the provisions of this Act, where a signature on a bill is forged or placed thereon without the authority of the person whose signature it purports to be, the forged or unauthorised signature is wholly inoperative, and no right to retain the bill or to give a discharge therefor or to enforce payment thereof against any party thereto can be acquired through or under that signature, unless the party against whom it is sought to retain or enforce payment of the bill is precluded from setting up the forgery or want of authority.

The effect of that provision is that in law a forged cheque is not a cheque or negotiable instrument but 'a mere sham piece of paper' (per Kerr J in *National Westminster Bank Ltd v Barclays Bank International Ltd* [1974] 3 All ER 834 at 836, [1975] QB 654 at 656–657) and, in the context of the present case, that, says the bank, means that there was no cheque to guarantee. In my judgment that is right, and I do not accept that in order properly to construe the written terms on the back of the card it is necessary to give the word 'cheque' some wide non-legal definition. The supplier of goods has already been warned that the card may only be used by the authorised signatory, and if it is so used his position is not further jeopardised by giving to the word 'cheque' its normal legal meaning. The words printed on the card do not suggest, as they could have done, that the bank agrees to pay the sum of money written on the cheque form. Furthermore, I do not see any reason in the circumstances of this case to conclude that the bank should be regarded as precluded from setting up the forgery or want of authority in any proceedings brought against it to enforce payment of the cheque.

The commercial argument

Mr Douglas argued that at least in 1991 part of the object of the cheque guarantee card was to relieve suppliers of goods of the risk of accepting a forged and therefore worthless cheque. If his other arguments are right then the card certainly had that effect, but a card still had considerable value even if he is mistaken. Given that a cheque was signed by an authorised card holder in accordance with the printed terms, the supplier no longer had to worry about whether the signatory actually had a bank account, or about whether there would be sufficient funds in that account to meet the cheque on presentation. As Lord Ackner said in *R v Kassim* [1991] 3 All ER 713 at 721, [1992] 1 AC 9 at 19:

> . . .the whole object of the card is to relieve the tradesman from concerning himself with the relationship between the customer and his own bank . . .

Conclusion

Accordingly in my judgment, having regard to the cheque guarantee terms in use in 1991 (but which have now been superseded), the bank was entitled to refuse to pay, and I would dismiss this appeal.

Sir Thomas Bingham MR: . . . The payment for goods by cheque, supported by a cheque guarantee card, is a very familiar everyday event. But on legal analysis it may be seen to involve four contractual relationships: that between the buyer and the seller under the contract of sale; that between the buyer as drawer of a bill of exchange and the seller as payee of the bill; that between the buyer as customer and his banker; and that between the buyer's bank and the seller. This appeal turns very largely on the last of these relationships. Both parties agree that such a direct contractual relationship between bank and seller may arise, and that where it does it will be because an offer made by or on behalf of the bank has already been duly accepted by the seller. The parties also agree (I am content to accept rightly) that when the direct contractual relationship does arise the bank assumes a primary liability towards the seller and not a secondary liability dependent on the default of its customer. . . .

It is clear that the dishonest buyer lacked actual authority to bind the bank. By its opening statement on the back of the card (that the card could be used only by the authorised signatory) the bank made that clear. I would read that statement as an instruction to the authorised signatory himself, but if it had been no more than that it need not have appeared on the card itself (where other instructions to the cardholder did not appear). The remainder of that opening paragraph was not addressed solely to the cardholder, and I think the opening statement was also addressed (among others) to sellers to whom the card might be presented.

It is of course elementary that a finding of ostensible authority cannot be based on the false assertion of the purported agent that he has authority which in truth he lacks. Such a finding must be based on a holding out by the alleged principal of the alleged agent as having his authority to act on his behalf in the relevant respect, which authority (after reliance upon it by the third party) the alleged principal is not permitted to deny. The simple justice underlying the rule is obvious: if A induces B to treat C as A's agent with authority to bind him, it would be quite unfair if A were afterwards free to disavow the transaction on the basis that C was never his agent at all, even though in truth he never was.

The central issue in this case is how, if at all, this principle applies to the present facts. The bank says it has no application: it argues that it has done nothing to hold out the thief of this card, or his dishonest associate, as its agent with authority to bind it. First Sport does not agree. The bank could, First Sport argues, have limited its liability to £50 on cheques actually drawn by the authorised signatory of the card. But on that basis conditions (3) and (4) would have been quite unnecessary. Whatever a buyer's actual authority, the bank's conditions (2), (3) and (4) held out as having authority to bind the bank a buyer who presented the card and signed in the seller's presence a cheque taken from a Barclays United Kingdom cheque book in a manner which agreed with the specimen signature on the card.

After considerable hesitation, born of the able arguments on each side and strengthened by Evans and Kennedy LJJ's disagreement, I am persuaded that First Sport is right. My reasons are as much practical as legal. If the bank had made clear that it would in no circumstances accept any liability at all on any cheque not signed by the authorised signatory of the card, then the shop assistants and garage attendants to whom such cards are usually presented would have been put on notice, and it may be that evidence of a buyer's true identity would have been demanded as a matter of routine. But read as a whole the bank's offer (including the conditions) did not make that clear: instead, it encouraged the belief that if the written terms of the offer and the conditions were met the bank would accept liability to the extent specified. Thereby, as it seems to me, it held out anyone able to fulfil all those conditions as having authority to bind it. It may of course be that the bank inserted conditions (3) and (4) to protect itself against the administrative hassle of dealing with invalid claims based on forged cheques, but I do not think that is how the conditions would have been understood by a reasonable retailer to whom the card was presented.

The bank argued that it was not liable since a forged cheque was wholly inoperative by virtue of s 24 of the Bills of Exchange Act 1882. I do not accept this: references to 'cheque' in the bank's offer should not be read as importing complex concepts derived from the Act. I would understand a cheque within the meaning of the bank's terms to be that which a reasonable seller would regard as such. He would not on the present facts have regarded the forged cheque as 'a mere sham piece of paper' and it was not argued that he should have done. Kerr J's observation in *National Westminster Bank Ltd v Barclays Bank International Ltd* [1974] 3 All ER 834 at 866, [1975] QB 654 at 656–657 was made in the context of a dispute between a paying bank and a collecting bank, which was, as I think quite different.

I would accordingly allow the appeal. In doing so, I do not in any way disagree with the learned trial judge. He was, unhappily and through no fault of his own, misled into deciding the case on the basis of conditions which, it is now accepted, were not on the relevant card. We have accordingly heard no argument on those conditions. But we have of course read his judgment, and I would for my part have needed much persuasion that on the terms which he construed his finding for the bank was wrong.

[The Court of Appeal granted leave to appeal to the House of Lords, but an appeal was not pursued.]

NOTES

1. The decision of Court of Appeal turned on the particular wording of the conditions stated on the cheque card in question. The standard wording of cheque card conditions was later changed so as to state that the cheque must be signed 'in the presence of the payee by the person whose signature appears on the card'. In *First Sport*, the trial judge, through no fault of his own, had decided the case in favour of the bank by reference to the wording of this revised condition and not to the actual wording on the card in question. Sir Thomas Bingham MR expressed strong provisional support for the judge's ruling on the effect of the revised condition.

2. The current conditions of use of the UK Domestic Cheque Guarantee Card Scheme—to be found at www.cardwatch.org.uk—provide that the cheque must be signed 'in the presence of the payee by the account holder'. In *First Sport*, Evans LJ said that if the bank's undertaking was conditional upon the card being presented and the cheque being signed by the

account holder then the answer would be clear: 'The retailer would know that the bank was not accepting the risks of a forged signature and of the card and the cheque being in the wrong hands.'

3.   The question whether a cheque supported by a cheque card constitutes absolute or conditional payment is considered above, p 529.

QUESTIONS

1.   What happens where a thief steals a blank cheque card before it is signed by the authorised user, or places a new signature strip on the card, and then inserts his own (or a false) signature on the card and the same signature on the cheque used in the transaction? How, if at all, would your answer differ according to the different wording of the cheque card conditions as set out in Notes 1 and 2 above?

2.   Was Evans LJ right in *First Sport* to say that a thief of a cheque card has ostensible authority to convey the bank's offer on its behalf to the retailer unless the bank makes it clear in the wording of the card that such a person would have no authority, actual or ostensible? How has the bank held out the thief to have ostensible authority in such circumstances?

(b) Credit and charge cards

Re Charge Card Services Ltd
[1989] Ch 497, Court of Appeal

Charge Card Services Ltd ('the company') ran a fuel card scheme for the purchase of petrol and other fuels from approved garages with the use of charge cards issued by the company. The company went into creditors' voluntary liquidation owing substantial sums to garages which had supplied fuel in return for vouchers signed by fuel card holders. There were also substantial sums owing to the company from cardholders who had purchased fuel with the use of their fuel cards before the date of the liquidation. Under a factoring agreement the company had assigned all its receivables to Commercial Credit Services Ltd. A dispute arose between the unpaid garages and the factoring company as to which of them was entitled to the moneys owed to the company by the card-holders. Millett J's first instance decision (at [1987] Ch 150), that the factoring company was entitled to the moneys on the ground that a cardholder's payment obligation to the garage was absolutely, not conditionally, discharged by use of the fuel card, was upheld on appeal.

Sir Nicolas Browne-Wilkinson V-C: …The case raises fundamental questions as to the legal character of credit card sales. It is therefore convenient, before turning to the specific questions argued, to set out what, in my judgment, are the normal features of credit card or charge card transactions, there being no relevant distinction between charge cards and credit cards for present purposes.

1.   The general features of credit card transactions
(A) There is an underlying contractual scheme which predates the individual contracts of sale. Under such scheme, the suppliers have agreed to accept the card in payment of the price of goods purchased: the purchasers are entitled to use the credit card to commit the credit card company to pay the suppliers. (B) That underlying scheme is established by two separate contracts. The first is made between the credit company and the seller: the seller agrees to accept payment by use of the card from anyone holding the card and the credit company agrees to pay to the supplier the price of goods supplied less a discount. The second contract is between the credit company and the cardholder: the cardholder is

provided with a card which enables him to pay the price by its use and in return agrees to pay the credit company the full amount of the price charged by the supplier. (C) The underlying scheme is designed primarily for use in over-the-counter sales, ie sales where the only connection between a particular seller and a particular buyer is one sale. (D) The actual sale and purchase of the commodity is the subject of a third bilateral contract made between buyer and seller. In the majority of cases, this sale contract will be an oral, over-the-counter sale. Tendering and acceptance of the credit card in payment is made on the tacit assumption that the legal consequences will be regulated by the separate underlying contractual obligations between the seller and the credit company and the buyer and the credit company. (E) Because the transactions intended to be covered by the scheme would primarily be over-the-counter sales, the card does not carry the address of the cardholder and the supplier will have no record of his address. Therefore the seller has no obvious means of tracing the purchaser save through the credit company. (F) In the circumstances, credit cards have come to be regarded as substitutes for cash; they are frequently referred to as 'plastic money.' (G) The credit card scheme provides advantages to both seller and purchaser. The seller is able to attract custom by agreeing to accept credit card payment. The purchaser, by using the card, minimises the need to carry cash and obtains at least a period of free credit during the period until payment to the card company is due.

2. The particular features of this scheme

In the present case, the fuel card scheme run by the company contained all those features. The scheme and the contracts in which it is contained draws a distinction between the account holder and the cardholders, the former being the company or person who contracts with the company, the latter being the persons authorised by the account holder to use the card. The distinction is of no significance in the present case and I will refer to both classes as 'the cardholder.' It merely reflects the fact that many account holders were haulage and fleet operators rather than individuals.

The underlying scheme is constituted by two bilateral contracts, viz: (a) The contract between the garage and the company ('the franchise agreement'). By the franchise agreement the garage undertook to honour the company's fuel card. There were two different ways in which the garage could claim payment: nothing turns on the difference between them. The company in effect undertook that on receipt of vouchers signed by the cardholders together with a claim form, payment of the price (less commission) would be made to the garage within five days at the latest, (b) The contract between the cardholder and the company ('the subscriber agreement'). There is a major issue as to the proper construction of the subscriber agreement to which I will have to revert. In essence, the cardholder authorised the company to pay for fuel supplied to the cardholder and to debit the cardholder. The company was to send to the cardholder a monthly statement of the amount debited and the cardholder was bound to pay to the company within 14 days the full amount shown owing in the statement.

In addition there was a third contract ('the forecourt agreement') made between the cardholder and the garage. This contract came into existence when the cardholder bought fuel at the garage. It was necessarily an oral agreement. In the present case, the forecourt agreement has a special feature not to be found in the majority of credit card purchases. At a self-service garage, the petrol is put into the tank by the purchaser/cardholder before there is any contact between him and the staff of the garage. It is common ground that the contract for the sale of the petrol is made at that stage, the garage having made an open offer to sell at pump prices which is accepted by the motorist putting petrol in the tank. Having done so, the motorist then goes to pay for the petrol and produces the fuel card. That is the first time at which the garage knows that payment is to be made not in cash but by using the card. There is a dispute between the parties whether, in those circumstances, the purchaser ever becomes liable to the garage to satisfy the price by payment in cash.

3. The issues

The following principal points were argued, (a) Commercial Credit contended that self-service forecourt sales do not at any stage give rise to a primary obligation on a fuel card holder to pay cash for the petrol. It is said that the garage makes an open offer, by exhibiting the fuel card sign on the forecourt, that it will accept payment either in cash or by means of the card. Therefore, it is said, there is no primary obligation to pay cash which can revive when the company fails to honour the fuel card. The judge rejected this contention [1987] Ch 150, 164. I find it unnecessary to decide the point since, on the view I take of the case, it makes no difference, (b) Is there a general principle of law that whenever a method of payment is adopted which involves a risk of non-payment by a third party there is a presumption that the acceptance of payment through a third party is conditional on the third party making the payment, and that if he does not pay the original obligation of the purchaser remains? (c) If there is no such general principle, was the acceptance of the fuel card by garages merely conditional payment or was it an absolute payment? (d) Mr Potts, for the garages, put forward an alternative argument. He submitted that on the true construction of the subscriber agreement the cardholder was only liable to pay the company if and when the company had paid the garage. On this basis he submitted that since the company had not paid the garages the sums recovered from the cardholders by the liquidator ought either to be applied in paying the garages or alternatively should be returned to the cardholders since the cardholders were never liable to pay either the garages or the company. On the view which I have formed on the construction of the subscriber agreement (see at 5. below) this point does not arise for decision. I will deal with points (b) and (c) in turn.

4. Is there a general presumption of conditional payment?

Mr Potts' argument is founded on the law applicable to cheques, bills of exchange and letters of credit. It is common ground that where a debt is 'paid' by cheque or bill of exchange, there is a presumption that such payment is conditional on the cheque or bill being honoured. If it is not honoured, the condition is not satisfied and the liability of the purchaser to pay the price remains. Such presumption can be rebutted by showing an express or implied intention that the cheque or bill is taken in total satisfaction of the liability: see *Chitty on Contracts,* 25th edn (1983), vol 1, pp 800–802, paras 1436 et seq; *Sayer v Wagstaff* (1844) 14 LJ Ch 116; *In re London, Birmingham and South Staffordshire Banking Co Ltd* (1865) 34 Beav 332; *In re Romer & Haslam* [1893] 2 QB 286; *Allen v Royal Bank of Canada* (1925) 95 LJPC 17 and *Bolt & Nut Co (Tipton) Ltd v Rowlands Nicholls Co Ltd* [1964] 2 QB 10.

There is a similar presumption applicable to payments made by means of letters of credit. If the seller does not receive payment under the letter of credit, it is presumed that the buyer is still liable to pay the price although this presumption can be rebutted by express or implied agreement to the contrary: see *WJ Alan &. Co Ltd v El Nasr Export and Import Co* [1972] 2 QB 189, 212b, *per* Lord Denning MR and, at p 22 1e, *per* Stephenson LJ; *Maran Road Saw Mill v Austin Taylor & Co Ltd* [1975] 1 Lloyd's Rep 156 and *E D & F Man Ltd v Nigerian Sweets & Confectionery Co Ltd* [1977] 2 Lloyd's Rep 50.

Like the judge (see [1987] Ch 150, 166a), I cannot detect from the authorities any such general principle as Mr Potts suggests which is applicable to all cases where payment is to be effected through a third party. The cases on cheques and bills of exchange do not contain any reference to such a principle. They are all cases where there was an obligation to pay a sum of money which predated the tendering of the cheque. The principle applied is that the obligation to discharge the pre-existing debt has not been satisfied unless the creditor has expressly or impliedly agreed to accept the cheque or bill in final satisfaction.

When a similar rule was applied to letters of credit in *WJ Alan & Co Ltd v El Nasr Export and Import Co* [1972] 2 QB 189, Lord Denning MR, with whom Stephenson LJ agreed, did not treat the matter as decided by any existing general principle of law. He described the question as one of construction to be determined in the light of the consequences: see p 209d. He then considered the consequences of treating a letter of credit as being an absolute or a conditional payment in the light of the circumstances affecting the type of commercial transaction in which letters of credit are used. He reached the conclusion that in those circumstances payment by letters of credit should be treated as conditional. Although he referred to the position as being analogous to that applicable to cheques and bills of exchange, he did not treat those cases as establishing any such general principle as Mr Potts relies on.

In my judgment, there is no such general principle. Each method of payment has to be considered in the light of the consequences and other circumstances attending that type of payment. When, as with credit cards, a new form of payment is introduced applicable to new sets of circumstances, it is necessary to consider whether such payment should be treated as absolute or conditional in the light of the consequences and circumstances of such new type of payment, not according to any general principle.

5. Was the acceptance of the fuel card by the garages conditional or absolute payment?

The answer to this question must depend on the terms of the forecourt agreement since this is the only contract made between the garage and the cardholder. The terms on which the garage accepted payment from the cardholder must be determined by the only contract to which they are parties. To determine the terms of the forecourt agreement is not an easy task. Such agreement is at best oral and, in the majority of cases, not even that. The sale contract is made by putting the fuel in the tank before the parties have met: tender of the card and the making out of the signature of the voucher for the sale is often conducted in complete silence. Moreover, although both garage and cardholder are in general aware that some underlying contract exists between the garage and the company and between the cardholder and the company, neither the garage nor the cardholder is aware of the exact terms of the contract to which they are not a party. Therefore the terms of the forecourt agreement have to be inferred from the surrounding circumstances known to the parties.

At the time of the sale, it is almost inconceivable that either party addressed its mind to the question. 'What will be the position if the company does not pay the garage?' At one stage in the argument, both parties were contending that *The Moorcock* test (see *The Moorcock* (1889) 14 PD 64) should be applied to determine what term should be implied in the agreement. If such test were to be applied, one would be looking for a term that any reasonable garage proprietor and cardholder would have agreed should be the result. On such a test, it is most unlikely that any term could properly be implied. But, in my judgment, this is not the right test since in a case such as the present there has to be *some* term regulating the legal effect of the acceptance of the card. The law has to give an answer to the problem. In my judgment, the correct approach in such a case is that the court should seek to infer from the parties' conduct and the surrounding circumstances what is the fair term to imply: this approach became common ground between the parties.

A sale using the fuel card for payment did not, in my judgment, differ in any material respect from an ordinary credit card sale. The one peculiarity of the transaction: viz. that the contract for sale of the petrol took place when the tank was filled and not, as in a supermarket, at the till, does not make any relevant difference. The question remains, on what terms did the supplier accept the card in payment?

Although neither party to the forecourt agreement knew the exact terms of the other party's contract with the company, both parties were aware of the underlying contractual structure. The customer/cardholder knew that, if he signed the voucher, the supplier/garage would be entitled to receive a payment for the petrol which would fully discharge the customer's liability for the price: depending on his sophistication, the customer/cardholder might or might not have known that the company would deduct commission in paying the garage. On the other side, the garage knew that on signing the voucher the cardholder rendered himself liable to the company to pay to the company the price of the petrol. Before entering into the forecourt agreement, both parties had entered into their respective contracts with the company and their underlying assumption must have been that on completion of the sale of the petrol by use of the fuel card, the parties' future rights and obligations would be regulated by those underlying contracts. In the majority of cases, the garage had no record of the address of the customer and no ready means of tracing him.

To my mind, all these factors point clearly to the conclusion that, quite apart from any special features of the fuel card scheme, the transaction was one in which the garage was accepting payment by card in substitution for payment in cash, ie, as an unconditional discharge of the price. The garage was accepting the company's obligation to pay instead of cash from a purchaser of whose address he was totally unaware. One way of looking at the matter is to say that there was a quasi-novation of the purchaser's liability. By the underlying scheme, the company had bound the garage to accept the card and had authorised the cardholder to pledge the company's credit. By the signature of the voucher all parties became bound: the garage was bound to accept the card in payment; the company was bound to pay the garage; and the cardholder was bound to pay the company. The garage, knowing that the cardholder was bound to pay the company and knowing that it was entitled to payment from the company which the garage itself had elected to do business with, must in my judgment be taken to have accepted the company's obligation to pay in place of any liability on the customer to pay the garage direct.

In the present case, there are two additional features which point the same way. First, under the franchise agreement, the company undertook to provide a guarantee of its obligations to the garage. This undertaking unhappily was not honoured. But the inclusion of the term in the franchise agreement provides some support for the view that, in the event of the company being unable to pay, the garage was looking for payment, not to the customer, but to the guarantor lying behind the company.

Secondly, there is a feature of great importance which may or may not be common to all credit card sales. Mr Potts in effect accepted that neither party could have envisaged that the cardholder/ customer would have to pay twice: once to the company and again to the garage. To avoid this result, he submitted that the acceptance of the card by the garage was conditional on *either* the company paying the garage *or* the cardholder paying the company. A condition to that effect is wholly different to that applicable in the case of cheques or letters of credit. I find it an impossible condition to imply. I fully see the force of implying a condition that payment is conditional on the actual discharge of the price by a third party: such condition is based on the fundamental premise that a seller expects to be paid for the goods sold. But I can see no reason for implying a condition that the seller is not to be so paid if the buyer has discharged another obligation to a different party. In truth, the suggestion of this additional condition is merely a forensic device designed to avoid what everyone looking at the transaction feels, viz. that in no circumstances can the result be that the cardholder has to pay both the garage and the company.

[The Vice-Chancellor then examined the particular features of the subscriber agreement in issue and held that they supported his conclusion that payment by credit or charge card is normally to be taken as an absolute, not a conditional, discharge of the card-holder's liability. He continued:]

I do not find the analogy with cheques at all close or helpful. Payments by cheque involve the unilateral act of the buyer and his agent, the bank on which the cheque is drawn. The buyer's basic obligation to pay the price is sought to be discharged through a third party, the bank, which is in no contractual relationship with the seller. Moreover, the seller has had no say in the selection of the bank. It is very far from the position in a credit card sale where the seller has agreed to rely on the credit of the credit card company and there is a pre-existing contractual obligation on the credit card company to pay the supplier quite separate from any obligation of the buyer.

The analogy with letters of credit is much closer. In both, there are three parties to the arrangement and, once the letter of credit is issued, the bank is contractually bound to pay on the presentation of the documents. But the whole commercial context of the two types of transaction is totally different. The letter of credit is primarily an instrument of international trade issued pursuant to an individually negotiated contract of considerable substance made in writing: the credit card is used for small, over-the-counter transactions between strangers there being, at best, an oral agreement and more often an agreement by conduct. In the case of credit card sales, the seller does not even know the address of the purchaser, which makes it hard to infer an intention that he will have a right of recourse against the purchaser. It is normally the buyer, not the seller, who selects the bank issuing the letter of credit: if, unusually, the seller does select the bank, this factor may rebut the presumption of conditional payment by letter of credit: see *WJ Alan & Co Ltd v El Nasr Export and Import Co* [1972] 2 QB 189, 210a. In contrast, in a credit card transaction the seller has decided long before the specific supply contract is made whether or not to accept the cards of the credit card company and has entered into an overall contract with it, under which the seller is obliged to accept the card and the credit card company is bound to pay him. With letters of credit, the issuing bank is the agent of the buyer and not the seller and it is the buyer who pays for the facility: in credit card transactions the credit card company is in a contractual relationship with both but it is the seller who pays for the facility by allowing the deduction of the commission. These differences are, in my judgment, so fundamental that the law affecting letters of credit is not of great assistance in deciding what law should apply to credit card transactions.

Accordingly, I agree with the judge, and broadly for the same reasons, that the cardholder's obligations to the garages were absolutely, not conditionally, discharged by the garage accepting the voucher signed by the cardholder and that accordingly the appeal should be dismissed. I reach this conclusion with satisfaction since I think it reflects the popular perception of the role of credit cards in modern retail trade as 'plastic money.'

The judge expressed certain views as to the effect of payment by use of a cheque supported by the production of a bank card: see [1987] Ch 150, 166d. As the point is not directly material in the present case and there may well be features of such transactions of which I am ignorant, I prefer to express no view on that point.

[Nourse and Stuart-Smith LJJ concurred.]

NOTES

1. *Re Charge Card Services Ltd* involved a simplified card scheme with a single card-issuer. By contrast, numerous banks and other financial institutions issue Visa credit cards and MasterCards in the UK. Each scheme has its own master agreement which operates as a binding contract between the participating banks and other financial institutions. The master agreement provides for such matters as the form of the card, card authorisation procedures and settlement between participating financial institutions. Under the master agreement, participating financial institutions generally become entitled to issue cards in their own name to their customers, and to admit suppliers to the scheme so as to entitle them to accept cards in payment for goods and services supplied by them. A supplier contracts with a 'merchant acquirer', a financial institution giving the supplier admission to the scheme (the merchant acquirer is often the supplier's own bank, so long as it is a participant in the particular scheme). By this contract, the supplier is authorised and obliged to accept all cards issued under the scheme in payment for goods or services, and the merchant acquirer agrees to pay to the supplier the value of the goods or services supplied, less a handling charge, provided the supplier has complied with certain stipulated conditions (eg he has obtained specific transaction authorisation if the price is over a stated ceiling). For each transaction the supplier transmits both card and transaction details to the merchant acquirer over an EFTPOS system (paper-sales vouchers, signed by the card-holder, as now rarely used). The merchant acquirer then pays the supplier as agreed. Under the terms of the master agreement, the merchant acquirer obtains reimbursement from the participating financial institution which issued the card used in the transaction (unless they happen to be one and the same). It may be the case that some or all of the participating financial institutions' services, performed as 'issuer' or 'merchant acquirer' or both, are 'outsourced' to separate companies (for a clear explanation of how outsourcing operates, see *Customs and Excise Comrs v FDR Ltd* [2000] STC 672 at [11]–[19], per Laws LJ).

2. Where a credit or charge card is issued by a store for the purchase of its own goods or services, there may only be one contractual relationship, namely that between the store and the customer; however, in-store cards are often issued by a separate company which is a subsidiary of the retailer.

3. In *Re Charge Card Services Ltd* [1987] Ch 150, Millett J, at first instance, analysed the true nature of the consideration for the goods or services supplied when payment is to

be obtained by the supplier by the use of a credit or charge card. His Lordship stated (at 164) that:

Three possibilities have been canvassed. The first is that the consideration for the supply is not the price (which is to be paid by the card-issuing company, a stranger to the contract of supply) but production of the card and signature of a voucher. I reject this analysis, which is quite unrealistic. Production of the card and signature of a voucher are not the consideration itself but the means of obtaining it. Moreover, a sale of goods requires a monetary consideration: see section 2(1) of the Sale of Goods Act 1979. This analysis would thus lead to the conclusion that, where payment is to be made by credit or charge card, the contract of supply is not a sale of goods, with the result that the statutory conditions and warranties are not implied. The second possibility which has been suggested is that there is a sale of goods, but the contract is a tripartite contract under which the consideration for the supply to the cardholder is the undertaking of the card-issuing company to pay the price to the supplier. I reject this analysis, which confuses the result of all the arrangements made with the legal means employed to achieve it. On the use of the card, there is no tripartite agreement, but three separate bilateral contracts come into operation. In my judgment, the true consideration in the contract of supply is the price, to be satisfied by the cardholder, by means of the card if he wishes.

4. *Re Charge Card Services Ltd* was followed in *Customs and Excise Comrs v Diners Club Ltd* [1989] 2 All ER 385, CA.

(c) Debit card

The debit card schemes which operate in the UK generate the same types of contractual relations as arise with credit and charge card transactions. What is set out above in relation to credit and charge cards can equally be applied to debit cards. Debit card transactions involve four discrete contractual relationships, namely those between: (i) card-holder and supplier (further explained in *Debenhams Retail plc v Customs and Excise Comrs* [2005] EWCA Civ 892, [2005] STC 1155); (ii) card-issuing bank and card-holder (giving the card-holder authority to use the card and the card-issuing bank authority to debit the card-holder's account with the amount of any card transaction entered into); (iii) supplier and merchant acquirer (obliging the supplier to accept all cards issued under the scheme in payment for goods or services and containing the merchant acquirer's undertaking to pay the supplier for the value of good and services supplied); and (iv) the participating banks and financial institutions themselves (covering various matters including, most importantly, the means of transfer of funds from one institution to another).

The general consensus is that payment by debit card should be treated like payment by credit or charge card and constitute absolute, and not conditional, discharge of the underlying indebtedness (see, eg EP Ellinger, E Lomnicka and RJA Hooley, *Ellinger's Modern Banking Law* (4th edn, 2006), p 594; *Paget's Law of Banking* (13th edn, 2007), para 17.220; Cresswell et al (eds), *Encyclopaedia of Banking Law* (1982, looseleaf), Division Dl 'Payment and Payment Systems' (ed R Hooley), para 25). Although debit cards perform a payment function similar to that performed by cheques, which only constitute conditional payment, there is an important distinction between them. Payment by cheque does not give the supplier the benefit of the drawee bank's undertaking to pay (the position where the cheque is supported by a cheque card is considered above), whereas payment by debit card (like credit and charge cards) gives the supplier a direct payment undertaking from the bank or other financial institution which admitted him into the scheme. It is the fact that the card-holder knows that use of the card means that a third party becomes obliged to pay the supplier that prevents the card-holder from countermanding his payment instruction once he has entered his PIN into the supplier's point of sale terminal (in fact the terms of the contract between the card-issuing bank and the card-holder usually expressly preclude countermand from this point in time).

(d) ATM cards

Where an ATM card is used to withdraw cash from an automated teller machine operated by the card-issuing bank there will be only one contractual relationship involved, as the issuer and the supplier of cash is one and the same. However, we have already noted that banks which issue ATM cards are usually members of an ATM network allowing customers to use their cards in any ATM operated by other banks and financial institutions which are members of that network. Until recently, there were three major ATM networks established in the UK, namely, the FOUR BANKS, MINT and LINK networks (international networks are run by such bodies as Visa and MasterCard). However, all UK ATM owners are now members of the LINK network and the FOUR BANKS and MINT networks have closed. The ATM network is held together by a master agreement between the network members.

Where a card-holder uses an ATM card issued by his own bank to withdraw cash from a machine operated by another bank within the same network, there is some uncertainty as to whether the card-holder and the bank whose ATM is used enter into a direct contractual relationship or whether the bank acts merely as the agent of the card-holder's own bank (the relationship between the banks themselves was examined in *Royal Bank of Scotland Group plc v Customs and Excise Comrs* [2002] STC 575, Second Division, Inner House, Court of Session). It is arguable that there is a unilateral contract between the card-holder and the bank whose ATM is used, which comes into existence in a similar way to the unilateral contract which arises when a supplier accepts a cheque card. The distinction becomes important when assessing whether an ATM card is a 'credit-token' for the purposes of the Consumer Credit Act 1974 (see below).

(e) Digital cash cards

R Hooley 'Payment in a Cashless Society', Ch 13 in BAK Rider (ed) *The Realm of Company Law—A Collection of Papers in Honour of Professor Leonard Sealy*
(1998), pp 245–252

The Mondex electronic cash system operates under the umbrella of Mondex International.[78] Mondex International grants franchises to banks in individual countries enabling them to develop the system in that country. Franchises exist in the United States, Canada, New Zealand and Hong Kong. Mondex trials started in the United Kingdom (in Swindon) in 1995 and are due to be completed in July 1997. Trials begin in the Republic of Ireland in 1998.

It is part of the function of the franchisee banks in each country to establish an issuer, or in Mondex terms an 'originator', of electronic cash in that country. The originator fulfils the role of a central bank for electronic cash. In this sense, 'electronic cash' means digital information which represents monetary value, ie coins or bank notes or a credit to a bank account.[79] All electronic cash issued by the originator represents a claim on it for 'real' value. The originator's liability is contingent on being presented with electronic cash, that is, the digital information issued by it. The originator distributes electronic cash to the various banks participating in the scheme. Each bank must pay for the electronic cash issued to it by transferring an equivalent amount of real funds, eg by CHAPS payment, to the originator. The originator then holds a float of real value which stands behind the electronic cash it has issued. The availability of a float to meet the originator's exposure on issued electronic cash is intended to maintain customer confidence in the system.[80] The participating banks issued with electronic cash by the originator may themselves re-issue that cash to consumers for cash payment, or for a debit to the consumer's account. In each case the issuing bank undertakes to redeem such electronic cash as the consumer holds on his Mondex card from time to time in the future. Alternatively, the consumer may redeem his electronic cash at another bank participating in the system.

The originator's liability to redeem electronic cash is a contractual liability. The immediate contracting party to whom the promise is made is the bank to whom the electronic cash is issued. Each participating bank will be in a direct contractual relationship with the originator. However, it is intended that the originator will also be liable to consumers to whom the electronic cash has been re-issued by the participating banks, and also to any other person to whom the electronic cash is further transferred.[81] This further transferee may be a person who has themselves purchased a Mondex card from a participating bank, but equally it could be someone who is given a card, and the electronic cash contained on it, as a gift. In each case the challenge is to establish a contractual relationship between the holder of electronic cash and the originator. The doctrine of privity of contract prevents the participating bank creating legally enforceable rights for third parties in the terms of its contract with the originator.[82] It seems it is intended for each cardholder to enter into an express contract with the bank which issues the card.[83] It may be possible to construe that agreement in such a way that the issuing bank also acts as agent for the originator thereby creating a contractual link between originator and cardholder. The problem remains the donee of a card who has no contract with the issuing bank, and no apparent contract with the originator. Similar problems arise with regard to the relationship between a cardholder and a participating bank which is not the bank which issued the card. It is intended that the cardholder should be able to go to any participating bank and exchange his electronic cash for real value. How does this right arise?

As electronic cash is akin to an electronic 'token', it may be helpful to examine analogous situations where money is exchanged for tokens which may then be used to pay for goods or services or redeemed by the issuer for cash.[84] In *Lipkin Gorman (a firm) v Karpnale Ltd,* [85] Cass, a partner in a firm of solicitors, misappropriated funds from his firm's client account and gambled it away at the Playboy Club. The firm of solicitors sought to recover the money paid to the Club as money had and received. The Club raised various defences to this claim, including that of bona fide purchaser for value.[86] One of the issues which the House of Lords had to decide was whether the Club had given value for the money paid over by the Cass when it had provided him with plastic chips in exchange for cash. The plastic chips could be wagered at the gaming tables, used to pay for refreshments at the Club, or redeemed by the Club for cash. Nevertheless, the House of Lords held that the provision of chips for cash did not constitute consideration for the money paid by Cass. According to Lord Goff, the chips were merely a convenient mechanism for facilitating gambling with that money.[87] Lord Goff drew an analogy with the situation where a customer pays over money to a department store for chips which he can then use to pay for goods in the store.[88] He held that the payment represented a gratuitous deposit of money with the store, with liberty to the customer to draw upon that deposit to pay for goods purchased in the store. Lord Goff preferred this 'common sense' approach to the alternative 'technical' approach which explained the transaction in terms of the store giving consideration for the money in the form of a chose in action created by its promise to repay a like sum, subject to draw down in respect of goods purchased in the store. Lord Goff concluded that 'by receiving the money in these circumstances the store does not for present purposes give valuable consideration for it'.[89]

Professor Treitel submits that it was the desire to protect the victim of the theft (the firm of solicitors) which led the House of Lords to reject the somewhat technical argument the chips constituted consideration for the money.[90] Treitel submits that in other circumstances, e.g. where it was necessary to determine the enforceability of the parties' promises, the court would be less reluctant to hold that there was consideration. After all, earlier in his speech, Lord Goff said:

> 'A contract is made when the customer obtains his chips under which the store agrees that, if goods
> are purchased by the customer, the store will accept chips to the equivalent value of the price, and
> further that it will redeem for cash any chips returned to it before the customer leaves the store. If a
> customer offers to buy a certain item of goods at the store, and the girl behind the counter accepts
> his offer but then refuses to accept the customer's chips, the store will be in breach of contract
> for chips. Likewise if, before he leaves the store, the customer hands in some or all of his chips at
> the cash desk, and the girl at the cash desk refuses to redeem them, the store will be in breach of
> contract for chips.[91]

So, in a different context, the chips may have been held to constitute consideration for the money paid
to the Club by its member, or vice versa. In the context of the enforcement of promises made through
the operation of the Mondex electronic cash system, the originator's issuance of digital information (or
electronic 'tokens') could certainly constitute consideration for the participating banks transfer of funds
to the originator. The problem remains, however, of identifying how the benefit of the originator's
promise to redeem electronic cash for real value may be 'transferred' to a third party who has no direct
contractual link with the originator.

There are a number of possible answers to these problems.[92] The re-issue of electronic cash could
constitute an assignment of the bank's claim against the originator. Adopting an argument similar to
the 'technical' approach rejected by Lord Goff in *Lipkin Gorman,* it could be argued that the originator
makes a promise to repay a like sum to that deposited with it by a participating bank on presentation
of electronic cash. The promise constitutes a chose in action in favour of that bank. The effect of the
re-issue of electronic cash by a participating bank to the customer might then constitute an equitable
assignment to the customer of part of the chose in action owed to the bank by the originator. The
assignment would be equitable because it would normally only be for part of the debt owed to the
bank by the originator,[93] and it would not be in writing as required for a legal assignment.[94] However,
it is submitted that the argument that the bank's chose in action has been assigned to the consumer is
unsustainable. First, it is submitted that, in the context of the Mondex scheme, the exchange of funds
for electronic cash constitutes the purchase of an electronic token rather than the deposit of funds
subject to a promise to repay. Electronic tokens are purchased from the originator, as they are later
purchased from any participating bank, in much the same way that foreign exchange is sold and purchased.[95] Secondly, for there to be an equitable assignment there must be an intention to assign and
this seems to go against the very essence of the way the Mondex system is intended to operate.[96] The
assignment analysis has been rejected for traditional funds transfer systems and it would be strange if
it where to operate for electronic cash which is intended to be more akin to cash payment.

Alternatively, it might be possible to treat electronic cash as a form of negotiable instrument; in other
words, as a form of promissory note. For this approach to get off the ground, the originator's promise
to pay would have to be found in the encrypted digital information issued by it, which is probably not
the case with current electronic cash systems,[97] although it may apply to future ones. The advantage of
this approach is that it partly reflects the intention of the parties to use electronic cash as a substitute
for physical cash. Bank notes are promissory notes issued by the Bank of England payable to bearer on
demand, title to which can pass on mere delivery.[98] Each bank note represents a claim on the Bank of
England, although the bank of England may satisfy that claim by simply paying the holder with other
bank notes.[99] Another analogous instrument would be the bank draft, which is a document drawn by a
branch of a bank on its head office or another branch. A bank draft is equivalent to a promissory note[100]
and the holder may at his option treat the instrument either as a bill of exchange or as a promissory
note.[101] Bank drafts are treated in practice as equivalent to cash.[102]

The private issue of bank notes by commercial banks was severely restricted by the Bank Charter
Act 1844, and the last English private bank entitled to issue bank notes ceased to exist in 1921.[103] The
Bank Charter Act 1844 was enacted in the national interest to prevent the excessive issue of notes by

banks and to facilitate the ultimate transfer of the whole note issue in England and Wales to the Bank of England.[104] Section 11 of the 1844 Act, as amended by the Statute Law Revision Act 1891 and the Currency and Bank Notes Act 1928, provides:

> From and after the passing of this Act it shall not be lawful for any banker[105] to draw, accept, make or issue in England and Wales, any bill of exchange or promissory note or engagement for the repayment of money to bearer on demand, or to borrow, owe, or take up in England or Wales any sums or sum of money on the bills or notes of such banker payable to bearer on demand.

A bank draft payable to bearer on demand would probably infringe section 11.[106] So also might an electronic cash issuer's 'engagement' to repay money to the bearer of electronic cash on demand. If electronic cash is intended to take over the function of physical cash, including bank notes, logic dictates that those who issue electronic cash, thereby performing a central bank function, should be subject to the same restraints on issue as apply to bank notes themselves. Of course, Parliament could never have contemplated the issue of electronic cash in 1844, but the purposes underlying the legislation remain as applicable today as they did then. The old restrictive common law definition of 'banker' and 'the business of banking' set out by the Court of Appeal in *United Dominion Trust v Kirkwood*[107] would probably save an issuer of electronic cash, set up in a similar way to a Mondex originator, from being classified as a 'banker' for the purposes of section 11 of the 1844 Act,[108] but the *UDT v Kirkwood* definition seems singularly unsuited to modern banking practice and will need to be reformulated before too long.

Although electronic cash may serve the same function as a promissory note, it does not constitute such an instrument as currently defined. Section 83(1) of the Bills of Exchange Act 1882 defines a promissory note in terms of 'an unconditional promise *in writing* made by one person to another *signed by* the maker...' (emphasis added). Similarly, section 3(1) of the Bills of Exchange Act 1882 provides that a bill of exchange must be 'an unconditional order *in writing*...*signed* by the person giving it...' (emphasis added). In both cases the written instrument represents the reification or embodiment of the maker's (promissory note) or drawer's (bill of exchange) payment obligation. How can the payment undertaking of an issuer of electronic cash be said to be reified in intangible encrypted digital information? By section 5 of, and Schedule 1 to, the Interpretation Act 1978, in any Act, unless the contrary intention appears, 'writing' includes 'typing, printing, lithography, photography and other modes of representing or reproducing words in a visible form'. Intangible encrypted digital information appears to fall outside that definition.[109] There would also be further difficulties because the promise to pay would not be signed by the issuer.[110] Following the Report of the Review Committee on Banking Services Law and Practice,[111] the Government agreed to introduce legislation to enable the issue and trading of negotiable instruments in purely electronic ('dematerialised') form.[112] Legislation is still awaited. It may be the case that electronic cash could be afforded the status of a negotiable instrument by statute. This would create what has been described by Joanna Benjamin as 'a quantum leap from the existing law merchant' which traditionally regards the basis of 'negotiability' as possession of tangible property and sees the nature of an 'instrument' as tangible.[113]

The remaining, and probably the best, explanation as to why a third party holder of electronic cash has an enforceable right to convert it into real value, turns on treating the Mondex system as a series of standing offers of unilateral contracts.[114] The originator and any bank displaying a Mondex symbol makes a standing offer to the world to convert electronic cash for real value.[115] The offer is accepted by a consumer when he tenders electronic cash for conversion. The tender of electronic cash constitutes both acceptance of the standing offer and consideration for the promise to convert. The fact that the electronic cash, ie the encrypted digital information, is itself worthless should not prevent it constituting consideration for the originator's and the participating banks' promise to convert. In *Chappell & Co Ltd v Nestle Co Ltd,*[116] chocolate manufacturers sold gramophone records for Is 6d plus three wrappers of their bars of chocolate. The House of Lords held that the delivery of the wrappers, which were worthless in themselves, formed part of the consideration. If delivery of the wrappers could form part of the consideration there is no reason why they could not form the entire consideration for a contract. The same could be said of any token, including one in electronic form. Although *Lipkin Gorman (a firm) v Karpnale Ltd*[117] appears to contradict this approach, we have already seen that it may be possible to distinguish the decision in that case according to the particular context in which the question of consideration arose.[118] If *Lipkin Gorman* proved to be an insurmountable obstacle to finding consideration for the originator's or participating banks' promise to convert, the courts could always regard those promises binding without the need for consideration, as already happens in the case of a bank's payment undertaking embodied in an irrevocable letter of credit.[119]

If, under the current law, an electronic cash scheme must rely on contract for legal effect, there is a danger that, were the scheme to be limited only to those who are its members, it would operate in a way which would make it inferior to those instruments which have the advantage of being fully negotiable.[120] In *Lipkin Gorman (a firm) v Karpnale Ltd,* plastic chips circulated between members of the casino, and as between the members and the casino the chips were treated as currency.[121] But bring in an outsider, a non-member, and the position changes. Now it is necessary to draw the outsider into the contractual network, and this, as we have seen, can be a complicated and somewhat artificial process. One answer lies in the statutory recognition of the negotiable character of electronic cash, another is simply to treat electronic cash as currency. Can this be done?

Footnotes

78. This section of the chapter concentrates on the Mondex system because it is more closely analogous to physical cash than other electronic cash systems. For further analysis of the Mondex system, see C Reed and L Davies, *Digital Cash—The Legal Implications,* 1995, pp 7–9; 'Electronic Cash and Payment Schemes: Digitising the Future' *Journal of International Banking and Financial Law,* 1997, p 103 (edited transcript of a round table discussion).

79. In fact the Mondex system does not tokenise the digital information but maintains a counter of value on the consumer's smart card. By contrast DigiCash produces electronic 'coins' for storage on computer.

80. But the float still remains vulnerable to depletion through forgery of electronic cash and bad investment.

81. See the transcript of the round table discussion, n 78 above, p 104.

82. For detailed analysis of the doctrine of privity of contract, see G H Treitel, *The Law of Contract,* 1995, 9th edn, Chapter 15; Cheshire, Fifoot and Furmston *Law of Contract,* 1996, 13th edn, Chapter 14; *Chitty on Contracts,* 1994, 27th edn, Chapter 18. See also Law Commission Report (No 242), *Privity of Contract: Contracts for the Benefit of Third Parties,* 1996.

83. See Reed and Davies, at n 78 above, p 14.

84. An agreement to transfer goods against tokens is not a contract of sale of goods as defined by s 2(1) of the Sale of Goods Act 1979, and therefore falls outside that statute, as the goods are not sold for 'a money consideration', but a sale at a money price to be satisfied by tokens does fall within the statute.

85. [1991] 2 AC 548.

86. R Goff and G Jones, *The Law of Restitution,* 1995, 4th edn, Chapter 41; P Birks, *An Introduction to the Law of Restitution,* 1985, pp 439–447; A Burrows, *The Law of Restitution* 1993, pp 472–475.

87. [1991] 2 AC 548 p 575G–H, citing with approval dicta of Davies LJ in *CRT Ltd v Ward* [1965] 2 QB 63 p 79: The chips are not money or money's worth. They are mere counters or symbols used for the convenience of all concerned in the gaming'.

88. Ibid, pp 576–577.

89. Ibid, p 577A.

90. GH Treitel, *The Law of Contract,* 1995, 9th edn, p 82. See also D Fox, 'The Transfer of Legal Title to Money', RLR, 1996 p 63.

91. [1991] 2 AC 548, p 576B–D.

92. It seems totally unrealistic to regard the participating bank as trustee of the originator's promise, holding the promise on trust for the benefit of the consumer to whom the bank issues electronic cash.

93. Part of a debt cannot be assigned at law under the Law of Property Act 1925, s 136(1) (a point recently confirmed by both the Court of Appeal and the House of Lords in *Deposit Protection Board v Dalia* [1994] 2 AC 367, pp 380–381, per Simon Brown LJ, and p 392, per Lord Browne-Wilkinson).

94. Law of Property Act 1925, s 136(1). On the requirement of writing, see below.

95. C Reed, *Legal Regulation of Internet Banking: A European Perspective,* 1996, p 36. See also RM Goode, *Payment Obligations in Commercial and Financial Transactions,* 1983, pp 3–4.

96. See 'Electronic Cash and Payment Schemes: Digitising the Future', *Journal of International Banking and Financial Law,* 1997', p 103 (edited transcript of a round table discussion).

97. For a brief introduction to the various types of electronic cash products, see T Sabri, *Journal of International Banking and Financial Law,* 1997, p 105.

98. S 3 of the Currency and Bank Notes Act 1954 defines bank notes as 'notes of the Bank of England payable to bearer on demand'. But a bank note 'is not an ordinary commercial contract to pay money. It is in one sense a promissory note in terms, but no one can describe it simply as a promissory note. It is part of the currency of the country': *Suffel v Bank of England* (1882) 9 QBD 555, p 563, per Jessel MR, p 567, per Brett LJ. See also *The Guardian of the Poor of the Lichfield Union v Greene* (1857) 26 LJ Ex 140, per Bramwell B.

99. The right of a holder of a bank note to have the note converted into gold was abolished under the Gold Standard (Amendment) Act 1931. As bank notes also constitute legal tender the holder who presents a bank note to the Bank of England for payment would only receive other bank notes in exchange. In his seminal work, *Commercial Law* 1995, 2nd edn, p 491, Professor RM Goode draws attention to Professor Karl Olivecrona's witty observation: 'Paradoxically enough, the claims on the central bank are always good because they can never be honoured. Payment does not come into question, since there are no media of payment available' (K Olivecrona, *The Problem of the Monetary Unit,* pp 62–63).

100. *Commercial Banking Co of Sydney Ltd v Mann* [1961] AC 1, p 7, PC.

101. Bills of Exchange Act 1882, s 5(2).

102. RR Pennington, AH Hudson and JE Mann, Commercial Banking Law 1978, p 80.

103. JM Holden, The History of Negotiable Instruments in English Law 1955, pp 196–198. The amalgamation in 1921 of Messrs Fox, Fowler & Co of Wellington, Somerset, marked the disappearance of the last private bank in England and Wales with note issuing powers.

104. M Hapgood (ed.) Paget's Law of Banking 1996, 11th edn, p 255.

105. 'Banker' is defined by s. 28 as any person carrying on the business of banking.

106. See Paget, see n 104 above, p 255.

107. [1966] 2 QB 431.

108. See n 105 above.

109. C Reed, Electronic Finance Law 1991, p 115; I Walden, 'Data Security and Document Image Processing: Legal Security for Cross-Border Electronic Banking', J J Norton, C Reed and I Walden (eds), Cross-Border Electronic Banking: Challenges and Opportunities, 1995, pp 43–44; D Faber, 'Electronic Bills of Lading', LMCLQ, 1996, p 235; J Benjamin, The Law of Global Custody, 1996, p 19 (who rightly submits that it would be unsafe to extrapolate a general principle that an instrument can be intangible from cases such as *Alliance and Leicester Building Society v Ghahremani* [19921 NLJR 313 and *Derby & Co Ltd v Weldon (No 9)* [1991] 2 All ER 901, where information stored on a hard disk of a computer was held to be a document for the purposes of an order for discovery under RSC Ord 24). See generally, C Reed, Digital Information Law: Electronic Documents and Requirements of Form, 1996.

110. Chalmers and Guest on Bills of Exchange, Cheques and Promissory Notes 1991, 14th edn, p 24. See also, n 109 above.

111. (1989) Cm 622, rec 8(9).

112. (1990) Cm 1026, Annex 6, paras 6.9–6.10.

113. J Benjamin, The Law of Global Custody, 1996, p 19. See also J Benjamin, 'Computerisation and Negotiability—Part I' Journal of International Banking and Financial Law, 1995, p 253.

114. The classic authority is *Carlill v Carbolic Smoke Ball Co* [1893] 1 QB 256. See also *Bowerman v Association of British Travel Agents* [1995] NLJR 1815. See generally, C Reed and L Davies, Digital Cash—The Legal Implications, 1995, pp 14–15; C Reed, Legal Regulation of Internet Banking—A European Perspective, 1996, pp 35–36.

115. C Reed, Legal Regulation of Internet Banking—A European Perspective, 1996, at p 35, asserts that while a participating bank may be able to withdraw its offer before acceptance, the originator would be unable to do so. Such a restriction on the originator's ability to revoke its offer makes good commercial sense as it would help maintain consumer confidence in the system. However, the precise legal basis for preventing the offeror revoking his offer of a unilateral contract remains somewhat uncertain; see G H Treitel, The Law of Contract, 1995, 9th edn, pp 35–39; Cheshire, Fifoot and Furmston Law of Contract, 1996, 13th edn, pp 59–62; Chitty on Contracts, 1994, 27th edn, paras 2–052 to 2–057.

116. [1960] AC 87.

117. [1991] 2 AC 548.

118. See n 95 above.

119. EP Ellinger, Documentary Letters of Credit—A Comparative Study, 1970, Chapters III-V; HC Gutteridge and M Megrah, Bankers' Commercial Credits, 1984, 7th edn, Chapter 3; RM Goode, 'Abstract Payment Undertakings', P Cane and J Stapleton (eds) Essays for Patrick Atiyah, 1991, Chapter 9.

120. Note the warning given by the Review Committee on Banking Services Law and Practice, 1989 Cm 622, para 8.34.

121. [1991] 2 AC 548, p 561F (Lord Templeman).

NOTES

1. The late Dr FA Mann provided the classic legal definition of money in his seminal work, *The Legal Aspect of Money* (5th edn, 1992), p 8, when he wrote that:

...in law, the quality of money is to be attributed to all chattels which, by authority of the law and denominated with reference to a unit of account, are meant to serve as universal means of exchange in the State of issue.

Dr Mann's definition of money is now to be found in Charles Proctor, *Mann on the Legal Aspect of Money* (6th edn, 2005), paras 1.15ff, where it is the subject of critical evaluation. Digital cash (or 'electronic money') cannot be money under Dr Mann's definition. First, only tangible movables can be money. The contractual rights upon which digital cash is based create intangible rights over money and not money in themselves. Secondly, digital cash is not issued by or under the authority of the State. Digital cash systems operating in the UK are privately run. However, there are regulatory controls on the issue of digital cash in the UK (see the Financial Services and Markets Act 2000 (Regulated Activities) (Amendment) Order 2002, SI 2002/682; the Electronic Money (Miscellaneous Amendments) Regulations 2002, SI 2002/765; and the Financial Services Authority's *Electronic Money Sourcebook*, implementing Directive 2000/46/EC on the taking up, pursuit and prudential supervision of the business of electronic money institutions and EC Directive 2000/28 amending Directive 2000/12 relating to the take up and pursuit of the business of credit institutions). Thirdly, digital cash does not serve as a universal means of exchange. The holder of digital cash can only use his 'cash' at a retailer or bank which is a member of that particular digital cash system and not elsewhere. The fact that digital cash does not constitute money at law means that it cannot be legal tender. Legal tender is such money in the legal sense as is defined by statute (Currency and Bank Notes Act 1954; Coinage Act 1971, as amended by the Currency Act 1983). In other words, all legal tender is money, but not all money is legal tender (*Mann on the Legal Aspect of Money*, above, para 2.25). Unless otherwise agreed, a creditor is not entitled to demand, and is not obliged to accept, anything other than legal tender in discharge of the debt owed to him. It is only the creditor's consent which allows digital cash to function as money. Whether digital cash operates as absolute or conditional discharge of the underlying indebtedness between the debtor and creditor will turn on the intention of the parties. It seems highly probable that it will normally be treated as absolute payment for the same reasons indicated by the Court of Appeal in *Re Charge Card Services Ltd* [1989] Ch 497 (above) when dealing with credit and charge cards. For further reading, see B Crawford (1997) 12 BFLR 399; S Stern [1998] CfiLR 217; S Miller, 'Payment in an On-Line World', Ch 4 in L Edwards and C Waelde (eds) *Law and the Internet—A Framework for Electronic Commerce* (2nd edn, 2000) ; D Kreitszheim (2003) 14 JBFLP 161 and 261.

2.   An alternative approach is to regard digital cash as merely a mechanism whereby an account holder enables a third party to gain access to money held on his account (see T Tether 'Payment Systems for E-Commerce', Ch 7 in Reed et al (eds) *Cross-Border Electronic Banking* (2nd edn, 2000), pp. 192–194; and see also A Tyree 'The legal nature of electronic money' (1999) 10 JBFLP 273). Where the system keeps a record of the issue of digital cash and the unique coding of the money issued, this could be construed as a record of an account held for the customer who has been issued with that money. When that customer transfers digital cash to a third party, this could be construed as giving the third party a means of access to that account. However, the fundamental problem with this approach is that it rests on the premise that there is a debtor-creditor relationship between the issuer (or, in the case of Mondex, the participating bank which issues digital cash to the customer) and the customer. In other words, it assumes that the consumer makes a 'deposit' of funds with the issuer in exchange for digital cash. It is this 'deposit' which would generate a debtor-creditor relationship between them as the deposit would represent a loan repayable to the consumer. It is submitted that this does not accurately represent the relationship between the consumer and the issuer. There is no indebtedness between them until the consumer or his transferee presents digital cash for redemption; if the consumer loses his smart card in the interim he loses the money stored on it. If there was a real debtor-creditor relationship between the consumer and the issuer, losing the means of access to his account would not relieve the bank from its liability to repay him sums held on deposit.

3.   In some cases, depending on the wording of the master agreement between the issuer ('originator') of the digital cash and the participating banks, the problem of creating a contractual right of redemption for the holder of electronic money may now be resolved by the Contracts (Rights of Third Parties) Act 1999. This legislation circumvents the doctrine of privity of contract. By s 1(1), a person who is not a party to a contract (a 'third party') may in his own right enforce a term of the contract if (a) the contract expressly provides that he may, or (b) the term purports to confer a benefit on him (although this does not apply if on a proper construction of the contact it appears that the parties did not intend the term to be enforceable by the third party). The third party must be expressly identified in the contract by name, as a member of a class or as answering a particular description but need not be in existence when the contract is entered into (s 1(3)). This would appear to enable the operators of digital cash systems to provide in the contracts between the issuer and

the participating banks, and also in any master agreement between the participating banks themselves, that third-party holders of digital cash (ie members of a class or as answering a particular description) should have an enforceable right of redemption against the issuer and/or the participating banks.

QUESTION

How would you normally expect a shop to indicate its willingness to accept payment by digital cash?

4 THE REGULATION OF CONTRACTUAL RELATIONSHIPS

Resolution of any dispute between card-holder and card-issuer, card-holder and supplier, supplier and card-issuer (or other financial institution which has admitted him to the scheme) and between the financial institutions which are members of the particular payment card scheme, will normally depend on the terms of the contract governing the relevant contractual relationship in issue. The point can be neatly illustrated by the following case. In *Tony Mekwin MTV & Co v National Westminster Bank plc* [1998] CCLR 22, when the plaintiff attempted to use his National Westminster Business MasterCard at a service station the attendant was not satisfied that the card-holder's signature matched the one on the card and so contacted the relevant MasterCard office which informed him that, although the card had not been reported stolen, if the signature did not match the one on the card then the card was to be retained. In fact the attendant had made a mistake and the plaintiff was offered the return of his card the next day. However, the plaintiff refused to have the card back and instead started proceedings against the defendant card-issuing bank alleging breach of contract in ordering retention of the card. The county court judge found in favour of the bank and the Court of Appeal dismissed the plaintiff's application for leave to appeal from that decision. Aldous LJ examined the card-issuing contract and pointed to the clause which stated: 'All cards are and remain the property of the bank at all times. The business is responsible for recovering and returning all cards issued to it if the bank or its agent so requests.' He held that there was nothing in the agreement which prevented the bank retaining the card if, for some reason, it should be suspicious that the person presenting it was not the person to whom it had been issued. The card was the property of the bank and not of the plaintiff.

(a) The unfair terms legislation

The card-issuing contract and the merchant agreement by which a supplier becomes a member of a particular scheme will generally be on the card-issuer/bank's written standard terms of business and be caught by the Unfair Contract Terms Act 1977. It would certainly be wrong to assume that the 1977 Act can only be of use to a cardholder against the card-issuer, it may also protect a supplier trying to escape the effect of a particularly draconian term in his agreement with the bank or other financial institution which admitted him to the card scheme (eg there is some controversy as to whether the 'charge back' clause in a merchant agreement, which, *inter alia,* makes the supplier liable when goods and services are obtained by a fraudster in a 'card not present' transaction, is invalid as unfair and unreasonable under the Unfair Contract Terms Act 1977: see Brownsword and MacGowan 'Credit Card Fraud' [1997] NLJ 1806; the response by S Ward at [1998] NLJ 7; and Brownsword and MacGowan's reply at [1998] NLJ 133).

The 1977 Act only catches terms which can broadly be described as 'exclusion' or 'limitation' clauses in a contract falling within the ambit of the legislation. The Unfair Terms in Consumer Contracts Regulations 1999, SI 1999/2083, are much broader in scope, catching virtually all terms in a consumer contract where that term has not been individually negotiated. The Regulations will therefore be relevant to the card-issuing contract where the contracting card-holder is a consumer (defined in such a way as to exclude companies), but not where the card-holder is acting in a business capacity. The Regulations do not apply to a merchant agreement between a supplier and the bank or other financial institution which admitted him to the scheme.

The structure of the 1977 Act and the 1999 Regulations are considered above at p 629.

(b) The Consumer Credit Act 1974

The Consumer Credit Act 1974 may be relevant when considering the relationship between card-issuer and card-holder (for an extremely useful review of this area, see M Smith and P Robertson 'Plastic Money', Ch 4 in M Brindle and R Cox (eds), *Law of Bank Payment* (3rd edn, 2004), paras 4–058 et seq). So far as payment cards are concerned, the Consumer Credit Act 1974, where it is applicable (as to which, see below), is relevant in three respects:

(1) The manner in which the card was supplied to the card-holder affects the enforceability of the credit agreement by the creditor. Section 51 of the Act makes it an offence to supply an unsolicited credit-token (although this provision does not apply to replacements for cards already issued). Section 66 of the Act excludes the card-holder from liability under a credit-token agreement for use of a credit-token unless the credit-token has been previously accepted by the card-holder (either by signature of the card itself, or of a receipt for the card, or by first use of the card). Part V of the 1974 Act sets out a number of formal requirements relating to the execution of a regulated consumer credit agreement (which includes a credit-token agreement) which, if ignored, make the agreement unenforceable without leave of the court (see generally RM Goode *Consumer Credit Law and Practice* (looseleaf), paras 1C [30.1]–[30.400]).

(2) The Act imposes limits on the card-holder's liability for unauthorised use of the card by a third party (see below Section 5).

(3) The Act imposes liability on the card-issuer for the supplier's breach of contract or misrepresentation in relation to goods or services paid for with the card (see below, Section 6).

Section 14(1) of the Act defines a credit-token to mean a card, cheque, voucher, coupon, stamp, form, booklet or other document or thing given to an individual (ie not a company) by a person carrying on a consumer credit business, who undertakes:

(a) that on production of it (whether or not some other action is also required) he will supply cash, goods and services (or any of them) on credit, or

(b) that where, on the production of it to a third party (whether or not any other action is required), the third party supplies cash, goods and services (or any of them), he will pay the third party for them (whether or not deducting any discount or commission), in return for payment to him by the individual.

(Where s 14(1)(b) applies a deemed provision of credit arises under s 14(3).)

A consumer credit business means any business so far as it comprises or relates to the provision of credit under regulated consumer credit agreements (s 189(1)). A regulated consumer credit agreement is an agreement between an individual (the debtor) and any other person (the creditor) by which the creditor provides the debtor with credit of any amount, unless it is an exempt agreement under s 16 (s 8). An 'individual' includes a small partnership, and an unincorporated association, but not a company (s 189(1)). A previous financial limit of £25,000 was removed by the Consumer Credit Act 2006, although the Act introduced exemptions relating to agreements exceeding £25,000 which relate to the debtor's business and to 'high net worth' debtors.

A credit-token agreement is defined by s 14(2) as a regulated agreement, which in this context means a regulated consumer credit agreement (ss 8(3), 189(1)), for the provision of credit in connection with the use of a credit-token.

There is some controversy as to which payment cards fall within the definition of a 'credit-token' and which are issued under 'credit-token agreements'. We shall look at each of the main types of payment cards in turn, remembering that each separate function of a multi-function card must be considered in the context of the Consumer Credit Act 1974.

(i) **cheque cards**—it is clear that a cheque card is not a credit-token within the meaning of s 14(1) of the Consumer Credit Act 1974. There is no undertaking by the card-issuer himself to supply cash, goods or services, whether on credit or at all, nor is there an undertaking to pay for cash, goods or services supplied by a third party. The card-issuer does not promise to pay suppliers who trade with the card-holder. It is the card-holder who pays for the goods or services with his cheque; the card-issuer merely gives a separate undertaking not to dishonour the cheque if certain conditions are observed (as to which, see above, p 808). As a cheque card is not a credit-token, it cannot be issued under a credit-token agreement (and so the provisions of the 1974 Act relating to credit-token agreements do not apply), although it seems that a cheque card may still be issued under a consumer credit agreement because the card-holder can draw cheques which the bank is bound to honour at the payee's demand even if the account holder is overdrawn (EP Ellinger, E Lomnicka and RJA Hooley *Ellinger's Modern Banking Law* (4th edn, 2006), pp 602–603, following Consumer Credit Act 1974, Sch 2, Pt 2, Example 21; cf AP Dobson 'The Cheque Card as a Consumer Credit Agreement' [1977] JBL 126).

(ii) **credit cards**—there is no doubt that credit cards fall within the statutory definition of a 'credit-token' whether they be 'two-party' cards (s 14(l)(a)) or 'three-party' cards (s 14(l)(b)). The fact that a supplier may be recruited to a card scheme by a bank or other financial institution which is not the card-issuer does not prevent the card being treated as a 'three-party' card for the purposes of regulation under the Consumer Credit Act 1974. The key undertaking for the purposes of s 14(l)(b) is that given by the card-issuer to the card-holder. However, a credit card can only be issued under a credit-token agreement where the contracting card-holder is an individual (ie not a company).

(iii) **charge cards**—'two-party' and 'three-party' charge card agreements, which enable the card-holder to acquire goods and services, but require him to settle the balance in full at the end of each billing period, are exempt agreements by virtue of art 3(l)(a)(ii) of the Consumer Credit (Exempt Agreements) Order 1989, SI 1989/ 869. As a result of this exemption, the card-issuer does not carry on a 'consumer credit business' and so the card is not a 'credit-token' (and not issued under a credit-token agreement). However, where the charge-card enables the card-holder to obtain cash, it will not be exempt (being a debtor-creditor agreement) and will be a 'credit-token', unless the low cost credit exemption applies (SI 1989/869, art 4) (EP Ellinger, E Lomnicka and RJA Hooley *Ellinger's Modern Banking Law* (4th edn, 2006), p 600).

(iv) **debit cards**—the position with regard to debit cards is much less certain. It has been argued by some commentators that debit cards are not credit-tokens unless issued in connection with an overdraft facility (RM Goode *Consumer Credit Law and Practice* (looseleaf) paras 1C [25.83]—[25.84], who argues, *inter alia*, that a debit card is merely a payment mechanism, like a cheque), and that, even if debit-cards are credit-tokens, they are not issued under credit-token agreements (M Smith and P Robertson 'Plastic Money', in Ch 4 of M Brindle and R Cox (eds) *Law of Bank Payments* (3rd edn, 2004), para 4–070, who argue that there is insufficient connection between the use of a debit card and the provision of credit to satisfy the s 14(2) definition of a credit-token agreement). However, we submit that a debit card falls within the definition of a credit-token set out in s 14(l)(b) of the 1974 Act because the card enables the card-holder to obtain goods or services from suppliers against the card-issuer's undertaking to pay those suppliers by way of debit from the cardholder' s account. The fact that the supplier may have been admitted to the debit card scheme by a bank or other financial institution other than the card-issuing bank does not alter the situation. We further submit that the agreement under which a debit card is issued normally falls within the definition of a credit-token agreement set out in s 14(2); the link between the use of the debit card and the provision of credit being made through the operation of s 14(3) of the Act. Section 14(3) deems credit to have been given to the debit card-holder, which is drawn on whenever the card is used to obtain cash, goods or services from a third party. The issue awaits judicial determination.

Whether or not debit cards are credit-tokens, or the subject of credit-token agreements, s 187(3 A) of the Consumer Credit Act 1974, as amended by s 89 of the Banking Act 1989, makes it clear that EFTPOS debit cards, which effect the electronic transfer of funds from a current account held at a bank or building society, are not within the scope of s 56 or s 75 of the 1974 Act, the key connected lender liability provisions of the legislation (see section 6 below). In so far as a debit card may be used to obtain cash, the agreement may be excepted from the requirements of Part V of the Consumer Credit Act 1974 (being a debtor-creditor agreement entitling the debtor to overdraw on a current account) by a determination of the Director General of Fair Trading under s 74(3), (3 A) of the Act. This exception also applies where an EFTPOS facility operates directly on such a current account (see AG Guest and MG Lloyd *Encyclopedia of Consumer Credit Law* (1975, looseleaf), para 2–015).

(v) **ATM cards**—like debit cards, ATM cards can give rise to some uncertainty. An ATM card issued by a bank for use only in its own ATMs, and which only allows the customer to withdraw cash when his account is in credit, is not a credit-token. However, a card which can be used to make withdrawals against as overdraft facility or other form of credit is a credit-token under s 14(l)(a) of the Consumer Credit Act 1974. Some ATMs function on the basis of the balance at the close of the day preceding the transaction. This may allow the customer to withdraw cash when his account is actually overdrawn. Although it has been argued that an ATM card is a credit-token in these circumstances (by Professor Lomnicka in EP Ellinger, E Lomnicka and RJA Hooley, *Ellinger's Modern Banking Law* (4th edn, 2006), pp 600–601), the bank does not *undertake* to provide credit to the customer and so this conclusion must be doubted (all the more strongly where the terms of issue prohibit using the card when the account is, or will become, overdrawn). Where a bank issues an ATM card which can be used to make withdrawals from the machines of other banks and building societies under a shared ATM scheme, the card is probably a credit-token, unless the cash dispensing bank or building society acts merely as the agent of the card-issuing bank (see above, p 825). But for a strongly argued case the other way, see Professor Lomnicka in *Ellinger's Modern Banking Law* (above), at p 601.

Although an ATM card may constitute a credit-token, it does not automatically follow that the agreement under which the card was issued will be a credit-token agreement. Where an ATM card can be used to withdraw cash from an account in debit, the card will only be issued under a credit-token agreement if there is sufficient connection between the card and the agreement to provide credit. This probably means that there will be no credit-token agreement within the meaning of s 14(2) unless the provision of an overdraft facility was actually a term of the agreement pursuant to which the ATM card was issued (M Smith and P Robertson 'Plastic Money', in Ch 4 of M Brindle and R Cox (eds) *Law of Bank Payments* (3rd edn, 2004), para 4–071). The position may be different where the ATM card can be used to withdraw cash from machines of other banks and building societies under a shared ATM scheme. Unless the cash-dispensing bank or building society is simply regarded as being an agent of the card-issuing bank, the ATM card will be a credit-token under s 14(1)(b) and there will be a deemed provision of credit to the card-holder through the operation of s 14(3) of the 1974 Act. Credit is thereby provided in connection with the use of the ATM card and the agreement under which the card was issued would meet the s 14(2) definition of a credit-token agreement. However, a credit-token agreement which only permits the card-holder to overdraw his current account will normally be exempted from the formalities required by Part V of the Consumer Credit Act 1974 by a determination of the Director General of Fair Trading under s 74(3), (3 A) of the Act. The same exception may also apply where cash is obtained from a current account using machines of banks other than those machines of the card-issuing bank, but this would only occur where the credit-token agreement also enabled the card-holder to overdraw on the current account (s 74(1)(b)).

(vi) digital cash cards—there is likely to be some controversy as to whether this new type of payment card falls within the definition of a credit-token set out in s 14(1) of the Consumer Credit Act 1974. It could be argued that a digital cash card falls within paragraph (b) of s 14(1), because the card enables the card-holder to obtain goods or services from a supplier who is himself entitled to demand conversion of 'digital cash' into real cash (ie into coins and bank notes, or into a credit to the supplier's bank account) by the card-issuer or merchant acquirer who admitted the supplier into the scheme. However, we submit that digital cash cards are more likely to be held to fall outside the statutory definition of a credit-token. There are two reasons for this. First, a digital cash card is a form of pre-payment card, whereby the card-holder pays for the card on issue. In no real sense is credit extended to him. Secondly, the words 'in return for payment to him by the individual' in s 14(1)(b) implies that the card-issuer undertakes to pay the supplier, with a right then to be reimbursed by the card-holder. By contrast, where a digital cash card is used to pay a supplier the card-issuer has already received payment from the card-holder in advance of the transaction. The fact that the card-holder may have used an overdraft facility to purchase the digital cash card in the first place does not affect the status of the card itself. The source of value must be distinguished from the issuance of the card.

5 LIABILITY FOR UNAUTHORISED TRANSACTION[2]

Where a payment card is lost or stolen and made the subject of unauthorised use, the card-issuer may seek to rely on terms of the card-issuing contract (a) to reverse the normal burden of proof, so that the card-holder must prove that the use was unauthorised, or (b) to make the card-holder liable for all use made of the card, whether authorised or not. Such terms were not uncommon before the first edition of what is now called the *Banking Code* came into force in March 1992 (see, eg *McConville v Barclays Bank plc* [1993] 2 Bank LR 211, 212). Now, thankfully, such terms are rarely found in card-issuing contracts where the card-issuer is a UK financial institution. In any event, such terms would be vulnerable to attack under the unfair terms legislation considered above (see, especially, the Unfair Contract Terms Act 1977, s 3(2)(b)(i); the Unfair Terms in Consumer Contracts Regulations 1999, Sch 2, para1(q)).

In certain circumstances the card-holder may be able to argue that his card is a credit-token under the Consumer Credit Act 1974, s 14(1), issued to him under a credit-token agreement (s 14(2)), and that his liability for unauthorised use should be limited under ss 83 and 84 of the Act, in effect, to a maximum of £50 prior to notification to the bank that the card is lost, stolen or otherwise liable to misuse. On the other hand, the card-holder can be held liable for all loss occasioned through use of the card by a person who acquired possession of it with his consent (s 83(3)). However, after the card-issuer has been so notified in accordance with the provisions of s 84, the card-holder will not be liable for further loss arising from use of the card (s 84(3)). Moreover, where the Act applies and the card-holder claims that the use of his card was unauthorised, then under s 171 (4)(b) of the Act it would be for the bank to prove either that the use was authorised, or that the use occurred before the bank had been given notice as stated above. However, the protection offered by the Consumer Credit Act 1974, ss 83, 84, only applies to cards which are the subject of credit-token agreements, as is the case with credit cards, but there is some controversy as to whether debit cards and ATM cards are protected by these provisions (see above, pp 836–837). It seems reasonably certain that cheque cards, charge cards used to acquire goods or services, and digital cash cards are not covered by the protection offered by ss 83, 84. This disparity between the treatment of different types of payment cards was criticised by the Review Committee on Banking Services Law and Practice, which recommended legislation to bring greater consistency in this area (see (1989, Cm 622), rec 10(10)). Although the government of the day stated its intention to introduce legislation along the lines of the Consumer Credit Act 1974, ss 83 and 84, to provide the same protection in respect of all payment cards (see White Paper (1990) Cm 1026, Annex 4, para 4.6), no such legislation is pending.

One recent legislative development has been the enactment of the Consumer Protection (Distance Selling) Regulations 2000, SI 2000/2334 (as amended), implementing EC Directive 97/7 on the protection of consumers in relation to distance contracts. The Regulations apply

---

[2] For a comparative analysis of the rules of common law, US and civil law jurisdictions dealing with unauthorised electronic transfers, see B Geva, 'Unauthorized Electronic Funds Transfers—Comparative Aspects', Ch 5 of JS Ziegel (ed) *New Developments in International Commercial and Consumer Law* (1998); B Geva *Bank Collections and Payment Transactions—Comparative Study of Legal Aspects* (2001), Pt 4C; B Geva, 'Consumer Liability in Unauthorised Electronic Funds Transfers' (2003) 38 CBLJ 207, and JF Dolan's comment at 282. See also, above, p 736.

	Credit		Charge		Debit		ATM-only		Cheque guarantee[a]		eurocheque[b]		Total fraud losses	
	Value	%Change	Value	%Change	Value	%Change	Value	%Change	Value	%Change	Value	%Change	Value	%Change
1996	43.7	14.1	14.2	41.2	25.4	26.8	*		12.8		1.0		97.0	16.4
1997	60.4	38.4	16.6	17.5	33.9	33.8	*		10.4		0.7		122.0	25.8
1998	68.8	13.9	16.1	-3.2	39.6	16.7	*		10.0		0.5		135.0	10.7
1999	99.9	45.2	23.6	46.4	54.9	38.7	0.4		9.1		0.4		188.4	39.5
2000	179.4	79.6	37.1	57.2	90.6	65.1	0.6		9.0		0.3		317.0	68.2
2001	228.3	27.2	45.7	23.2	128.1	41.3	0.8		8.5		0.1		411.5	29.8
2002	218.7	-4.2	48.0	5.1	149.0	16.4	1.2		7.6				424.6	3.2
2003	215.1	-1.6	32.6	-32.1	165.0	10.7	1.7		6.0				420.4	-1.0
2004	229.0	6.4	30.3	-7.1	236.5	43.4	3.9		5.1				504.8	20.1
2005	201.6	-12.0	32.9	8.4	196.0	-17.1	4.9		4.0				439.4	-13.0
2006	193.3	-4.1	30.4	-7.5	195.8	-0.1	4.7		3.6				428.0	-2.6

(a) Losses on cheque guarantee cards include losses on multi-function cards when used to guarantee personal cheques.

(b) eurocheques were withdrawn during 2001 and are no longer issued in the UK.

Figure 4 Fraudulent Transactions on UK-issued cards (values £ millions)

[Figure 4 is taken from the *UK Payment Statistics 2007*, published by the Association for Payment Clearing Services.]

to contracts for goods or non-financial services to be supplied to a consumer where the contract is made exclusively by means of distance communication, eg by telephone, by e-mail or over the internet, as a result of an organised marketing campaign. Regulation 21 provides that a consumer is entitled to cancel payment where fraudulent use has been made of his payment card in connection with distance contracts covered by the Regulations, and that in the event of fraudulent use, the consumer is entitled to be recredited with the sums paid or have them repaid by the card issuer. The term 'payment card' is broadly defined in the Regulations and 'includes credit cards, charge cards, debit cards and store cards' (reg 21(6)). But digital cash cards probably fall outside this definition. Regulation 14 of the Financial Services (Distance Marketing) Regulations 2004, SI 2004/2095, makes similar provision with respect to the fraudulent use of a consumer's payment card in connection with a distance contract for the provision of financial services. Neither reg 21, nor reg 14, apply where the card is a 'credit-token' protected by the Consumer Credit Act 1974 (SI 2001/2334, reg 21(4); SI 2004/2095, reg 14(3)). In such a case s 83(1) of the 1974 Act provides that the debtor is not to be liable for loss arising from use of the credit facility. It is not possible to impose any liability on the card-holder (CCA, s 84(3A)–(3D)).

The *Banking Code* and the *Business Banking Code*—voluntary codes of practice for the banking industry, which are examined in detail above, p 620—take a much more consistent approach to the different types of payment card so far as personal and (small) business customers are concerned. Save for digital cash cards (see below), the Codes do not distinguish between different types of payment card. This makes the Codes particularly relevant to card-holders who have cards which do not fall within the protection offered by ss 83 and 84 of the Consumer Credit Act 1974. Both Codes contain provisions that limit the card-holder's liability for misuse of his card in similar, but not identical, terms to those in ss 83 and 84 of the CCA. The relevant terms of the Codes are usually expressly incorporated into the contract under which the payment card is issued.

Both Codes provide that, unless the card issuer can establish that the customer acted fraudulently or without reasonable care, the customer's liability for misuse of the card is to be limited (2008 edns of both Codes, para 12.12). First, where someone else uses the card before the customer informs the card issuer that it has been lost or stolen or that someone else knows the PIN (personal identification number), the customer's liability is capped at £50. Secondly, where someone else uses card details without the customer's permission, and the card has not been lost or stolen, the customer is not liable at all. Thirdly, where someone else uses card details without the customer's permission for a transaction where the customer does not have to be present (eg on Internet purchase), the customer is not liable at all. Fourthly, the customer is not liable where the card is used before he receives it. Failure to follow the guidance in para 12.5, eg where the card-holder writes his PIN on the back of his card, may show lack of reasonable care (para 12.11).

Both Codes treat digital cash cards, or 'electronic purses' as they are referred to in the Codes, differently. An electronic purse is treated like cash so that if the purse is lost or stolen the card-holder loses the electronic money loaded onto it (para 12.15). However, the Codes recognise that a card-holder requires protection where value can be loaded on to his electronic purse through direct access to his bank account. Both Codes provides that, unless the card-issuer can establish that the card-holder acted fraudulently or without reasonable care, the latter's liability for misuse of his electronic purse will be capped at £50 if the electronic purse is credited by unauthorised withdrawals from his account before he informs the card-issuer that the electronic purse has been lost, stolen or misused (para 12.16). On the other hand, the card-holder will not be liable for any sum transferred from his account to his electronic purse after he has informed the card-issuer that the electronic purse has been lost, stolen or that someone else knows the PIN (para 12.17).

QUESTIONS

1.   A 'phantom withdrawal' refers to the situation where a card-holder allegedly uses a card and personal identification number (PIN) at an ATM, has his account debited by his bank, and later claims that the card and PIN were not used by him or an authorised person. What legal principles would you expect the Financial Services Ombudsman, who took over from the Banking Ombudsman with the coming into force of the Financial Services and Markets Act 2000, to apply when dealing with a card-holder's complaint that he has been the victim of a phantom withdrawal? See C Reed 'Consumer Electronic Banking' [1994] 11 JIBL451.

2.   Is a smart card loaded with digital cash a 'payment card' that falls within reg 21 of the Consumer Protection (Distance Selling) Regulations 2000? See *Paget's Law of Banking* (13th edn, 2007), para 17.267.

6 CONNECTED LENDER LIABILITY[3]

Section 75(1) of the Consumer Credit Act 1974 provides that 'if a debtor under a debtor-creditor-supplier agreement falling within s 12(b) or (c) of the Act has, in relation to a transaction financed by the agreement, any claim against the supplier in respect of a misrepresentation or breach of contract, he shall have a like claim against the creditor, who, with the supplier, shall accordingly be jointly and severally liable to the debtor' In the context of payment cards, this important provision only applies to 'three-party' credit card transactions (card-holder uses card to pay for goods/services from supplier recruited to scheme by card issuer) and, as recently confirmed by the Court of Appeal in *Office of Fair Trading v Lloyds TSB Bank plc* [2006] EWCA Civ 268, [2007] QB 1 (there was no appeal on this point to House of Lords: [2007] UKHL 48, [2008] 1 AC 316 at [24]), 'four-party' credit card transactions (supplier recruited by merchant acquirer who is not the card issuer). It does not apply to purchases made using a 'two-party' credit card (which fall under s 12(a), not s 12(b) or (c), of the Act), or a charge card (which is 'exempt' if the card can only be used to acquire goods or services, and is a debtor-creditor agreement, not a debtor-creditor-supplier agreement, if the card can be used to acquire cash on credit: see above, pp 835–836), or an EFTPOS debit card (which is expressly excluded from the operation of s 75 by s 187(3A) of the Act), or a cheque card (which is not a debtor-creditor-supplier agreement), or an ATM card (again, not a debtor-creditor-supplier agreement), or a digital cash card (again, not a debtor-creditor-supplier agreement). Where s 75 applies, so as to make the credit card-issuer liable to the card-holder who has contracted with the issuer (where an additional non-contracting card-holder uses the card s 75 does not apply), then the card-issuer is entitled to be indemnified by the supplier, subject to any agreement

---

[3] For a comparative analysis of connected lender liability as part of consumer protection law in the UK, N America and the European Union, see EZ Lomnicka 'Connected Lender Liability' in EZ Lomnicka and CGJ Morse (eds) *Contemporary Issues in Commercial Law—Essays in Honour of Professor AG Guest* (1997), pp 93–116.

between them (s 75(2)). The card-holder has a claim against the issuer even if, in entering the transaction with the supplier, he has exceeded his credit limit or otherwise contravened the credit agreement (s 75(4)).

There is an important limitation to the availability of a s 75 claim against a card-issuer. By virtue of s 75(3), s 75(1) does not apply to a claim so far as the claim relates to any single item with a cash price of or under £100 or over £30,000 (the section also does not apply to a claim under a noncommercial agreement, but in practice this will never be the case in respect of a credit card agreement). However, it should be noted that a claim may be made where a credit card is used to make part payment of less than £100 in respect of an item priced over £100. It has been unclear for some time as to whether s 75(1) extends to a claim by a card-holder in respect of a transaction made abroad with a foreign supplier when the supply transaction is governed by a foreign law. In *Office of Fair Trading v Lloyds TSB Bank plc* [2007] UKHL 48, [2008] 1 AC 316, the House of Lords held that s 75(1) does indeed apply to foreign transactions. Their Lordships felt that such an interpretation was consistent with the principles that lay behind the recommendation of the Crowther Committee on Consumer Credit in 1971 that there should be connected lender liability in future consumer credit legislation (which appeared as s 75(1) in the 1974 Act). Lord Mance (at [29]) considered that, in relation to overseas transactions, there was an even greater discrepancy than in domestic transactions between the card-holder's ability to pursue suppliers on the one hand and the ease with which card issuers could obtain redress through contractual and commercial ties which Crowther contemplated would link them together. His Lordship concluded that '[c]ard issuers' ability to bear irrecoverable losses and so "spread the burden" exists in relation to both overseas and domestic transactions'. It remains the case, however, that the card-holder must still be able to prove that he has a valid claim under the foreign law against the foreign supplier in respect of misrepresentation or breach of contract if he is to have a claim against the UK card-issuer under s 75(1).

The other important connected lender liability provision set out in the Consumer Credit Act 1974 is that found in s 56. By virtue of s 56(2), where negotiations ('antecedent negotiations') are conducted with the debtor (ie the card-holder who contracts with the card-issuer) by the supplier in relation to a transaction financed or proposed to be financed by a debtor-creditor-supplier agreement within s 12(b) or (c) (ie by a 'three-party' or 'four-party' credit card), they are deemed to be conducted by the supplier ('the negotiator') in the capacity as agent of the creditor (ie the card-issuer) as well as in his actual capacity. Through this provision the card-issuer may become liable for any pre-contractual misrepresentation by the supplier, quite apart from the provisions of s 75. In fact s 56 appears to be broader in its application than s 75 in at least two respects. First, s 56 is not restricted by any monetary limitations as found in s 75(3). Secondly, whereas s 75 is limited to imposing liability on the creditor for the supplier's breach of contract or misrepresentation, there is no such limitation where the supplier is deemed to have conducted negotiations as the creditor's agent under s 56. Thus, Professor Goode highlights the significance of s 56 where the supplier has delivered, in advance of the transaction being completed or paid for (ie while 'antecedent negotiations' as still taking place), dangerous goods which cause physical damage to the card-holder's property (RM Goode *Consumer Credit Law and Practice* (2000–01, looseleaf), para IC [32.19]).

QUESTION

Joe applies for and obtains a credit card from his bank, Trust Bank Ltd, which he uses to purchase a dishwasher from Eleco Stores at a cost of £500. After two weeks the dishwasher malfunctions, due to a design fault, and floods his kitchen causing considerable damage. When Joe goes round to Eleco Stores to complain, he finds that it has closed down.

Advise Joe as to any remedy he may have against his bank.

How, if at all, would it affect your answer in each of the following alternative scenarios:

(a) Joe paid £450 in cash and £50 using his credit card;

(b) the dishwasher had been purchased by Joe's wife, Sue, using a second credit card issued to her by the bank under the terms of its agreement with Joe;

(c) Joe had applied for his card in the name of his company, JJ Contractors Ltd;

(d) Eleco Stores had not been recruited to the credit card scheme by Trust Bank, but by a different merchant acquirer;

(e) Joe had used his credit card to buy the dishwasher from a store in France.

PART VI

THE FINANCING OF INTERNATIONAL TRADE

CHAPTER 21

THE FINANCING OF INTERNATIONAL TRADE

There are various ways to pay for goods sold under an international sales contract. The method chosen for any particular transaction will greatly depend on the seller's confidence in the integrity and solvency of the overseas buyer, as well as on the bargaining strengths of the respective parties. Where the seller has such confidence in the buyer, he may be prepared to supply goods on open account. Here the seller extends a fixed period of credit to the buyer, say 28 days after shipment, before payment has to be made. It is common and cheap, but there is a clear risk of nonpayment by, or insolvency of, the buyer. Where the seller lacks confidence in the honesty or solvency of the buyer, he may insist that payment is made through the intervention of one or more banks. In fob and cif contracts, payment is usually effected through a bank. This increases the cost of the transaction for the buyer as the bank will usually charge a fee for its services. The two most common methods of payment which involve banks are the collection of documentary bills and payment under documentary credits.

1 DOCUMENTARY BILLS[1]

A 'documentary bill' is a bill of exchange to which the bill of lading (or other document of title) is attached. The seller will send a documentary bill to the buyer to ensure that the buyer does not take up the bill of lading, which gives him a right of disposal of the goods, without first accepting or paying the bill of exchange as previously agreed between the parties. If the buyer fails to accept or pay the bill of exchange (depending on whether it is a term or sight bill), he is bound to return the bill of lading to the seller and, if he wrongfully retains the bill of lading, the property in the goods does not pass to him (Sale of Goods Act 1979, s 19(3)). However, this method of payment does not prevent a buyer, who has dishonoured the bill of exchange, from passing title to the goods to a third party under one of the exceptions to the *nemo dat* rule: in particular, under s 9 of the Factors Act 1889 or s 25 of the Sale of Goods Act 1979 (*Cahn & Mayer v Pockett's Bristol Channel Steam Packet Co Ltd* [1899] 1 QB 643, CA).

---

[1] See, generally, EP Ellinger and H Tjio 'Uniform Rules for Collections' [1996] JBL 382; *Benjamin's Sale of Goods* (7th edn, 2006), paras 22–067 ff.

To avoid the risk of a fraudulent buyer passing title to the goods to a third party, the seller may instruct his own bank (the 'remitting bank') to deliver the bill of lading, and other shipping documents, to the buyer in his own country and, as a precondition to the release of those documents, collect the price from him, ie by acceptance or payment of the bill of exchange. If the remitting bank does not have an office in the buyer's country, it may instruct a local bank (the 'collecting bank') to perform this task as its agent. In this situation, according to general principles of agency law, there is privity of contract between the seller and the remitting bank, and also between the remitting bank and the collecting bank, but not between the seller and the collecting bank, unless the seller contemplates that a sub-agent will be employed *and* authorises the remitting bank to create privity of contract between himself and the collecting bank (*Calico Printers' Association Ltd v Barclays Bank Ltd* (1931) 145 LT 51 (above, p 227), affd on appeal without reference to this point: at 58). Relations between the seller and the remitting bank, and between the remitting bank and the collecting bank, will usually be governed by the International Chamber of Commerce's *Uniform Rules for Collections* (the latest revision is URC 522, published in 1995). The seller is a party to a collection governed by URC 522, but the Rules do not create privity of contract between seller and collecting bank (*Grosvenor Casinos Ltd v National Bank of Abu Dhabi* [2008] EWHC 511 (Comm); cf (*Bastone & Firminger Ltd v Nasima Enterprises (Nigeria) Ltd* [1996] CLC 1902 at 1908, per Rix J, who saw the point as fully arguable). The Rules only apply if incorporated into the contracts by the parties, whether expressly or by course of dealings or simply by the international custom and practice of bankers (*Harlow & Jones Ltd v American Express Bank Ltd* [1990] 2 Lloyd's Rep 343 at 349, per Gatehouse J; *Minories Finance Ltd v Afribank Nigeria Ltd* [1995] 1 Lloyd's Rep 134 at 139, per Longmore J).

In most cases the remitting bank will discount the bill of exchange before acceptance or payment by the buyer. A bill of exchange is discounted when the bank credits the seller's account with the full amount of the bill (less banking charges) or when the bank agrees to advance to the seller a percentage of the face value of the bill but withholds the balance until the bill is paid by the buyer. This has the advantage of releasing funds to the seller at an earlier date than if he waited for the bill of exchange to mature. But the remitting bank will usually retain a right of recourse against the seller: if the buyer dishonours the bill of exchange by non-acceptance or non-payment, the bank can sue the seller on the bill. This highlights the real disadvantage, from the seller's point of view, of payment under a documentary bill which is collected by, or discounted to, a bank: the buyer may accept the bill of exchange so that the bill of lading will be released to him, yet the seller has no assurance that the buyer will pay when the bill matures. Documentary credits provide a solution to this problem.

QUESTIONS

1.   From the buyer's point of view, what are the advantages of payment by means of a documentary bill?

2.   Does the remitting bank become a party to the bill of exchange by discounting it for the seller? What would be the practical significance of the remitting bank becoming a party to the bill? See *Barclays Bank Ltd v Aschaffenburger Zellstoffwerke AG* [1967] 1 Lloyd's Rep 387; *Barclays Bank Ltd v Astley Industrial Trust Ltd* [1970] 2 QB 527 at 538–539.

2 DOCUMENTARY CREDITS[2]

(a) The function and operation of documentary credits

A documentary credit represents a bank's assurance of payment against presentation of specified documents. It is the most common method of payment in international sales. The seller stipulates in the contract of sale that payment is to be by documentary credit. The buyer then gets his bank to issue the credit in favour of the seller, so that the seller has the bank's independent payment undertaking. This has two advantages from the seller's point of view. First, subject to the solvency of the bank, the seller is certain of payment under the credit provided he can present conforming documents to the bank and comply with any other terms of the credit. Secondly, where the credit is transferable, the seller can use it to finance his own acquisition of the goods.

A documentary credit transaction normally operates as follows (assuming the underlying transaction is one of sale):

• The seller and the overseas buyer agree in the contract of sale that payment shall be made under a documentary credit.

• The buyer (acting as the 'applicant' for the credit) requests a bank in his own country (the 'issuing' bank) to open a documentary credit in favour of the seller (the 'beneficiary') on the terms specified by the buyer in his instructions (for an example of a request to open a documentary credit, see Form 3 in the Appendix).

• The issuing bank opens an irrevocable credit (see below, p 855; revocable credits are now rare) and by its terms undertakes to pay the contract price or to incur a deferred payment undertaking and pay at maturity, or to accept a bill of exchange drawn by the beneficiary and pay at maturity, provided that the specified documents (that is to say, the transport document, such as a bill of lading, the policy of insurance, the invoice and other documents specified in the credit, eg certificates of origin, certificates of quality and packing lists) are duly tendered and any other terms and conditions of the credit are complied with.

• The issuing bank may open the credit by sending it direct to the seller; alternatively, as happens in most cases, the issuing bank may arrange for a bank in the seller's country (the 'advising' or 'correspondent' bank) to advise the seller that the credit has been opened.

• The issuing bank may also ask the advising bank to add its 'confirmation' to the credit. If the bank agrees to add its confirmation, and it may be under no obligation to do so, the advising bank (now called the 'confirming' bank) gives the seller a separate payment undertaking in terms similar to that given by the issuing bank and the seller benefits from having the payment obligation localised in his own country.

• The seller ships the goods and tenders the required documents (often through his own bank, which acts as his agent) to the advising bank (acting as the nominated bank[3]) or

---

[2] The leading textbooks on this subject are R Jack, A Malek and D Quest *Documentary Credits* (3rd edn, 2001); R King *Gutteridge and Megrah's Law of Bankers' Commercial Credits* (8th edn, 2001); and *Benjamin's Sale of Goods* (7th edn, 2006), Ch 23. Excellent coverage can also be found in RM Goode *Commercial Law* (3rd edn, 2004), Ch 35; and M Brindle and R Cox (eds) *Law of Bank Payments* (3rd edn, 2004), Ch 8. For excellent comparative studies, see B Kozolchyk 'Letters of Credit' in *International Encyclopedia of Comparative Law*, Vol 9, Ch 5 and EP Ellinger *Documentary Letters of Credit—A Comparative Study* (1970).

[3] 'Nominated bank' means the bank authorised in the credit to honour or negotiate or, in the case of a freely available credit, any bank (UCP 600, arts 2 and 6(a)).

confirming bank. If the documents conform to the terms of the credit, the advising bank (as a nominated bank[4]) or confirming bank will pay the contract price, or incur a deferred payment undertaking and pay at maturity, or accept a bill of exchange and pay at maturity, or negotiate a bill of exchange drawn for the price, and seek reimbursement from the issuing bank.

- Before releasing the documents to the buyer, the issuing bank will in turn seek payment from him. If the buyer is not in a position to pay without first reselling the goods, the issuing bank may release the documents to him under a 'trust receipt', thereby giving the buyer access to the goods on arrival without destroying the bank's security interest in the goods and in the proceeds of sale (see Form 7 in the Appendix).[5]

(b) The contracts arising out of a documentary credit transaction

(i) The contractual network

A documentary credit transaction is held together by a series of interconnected contractual relationships. First, there is the underlying contract of sale between the seller and the buyer. Secondly, when the issuing bank agrees to act on the instructions of the buyer a contract comes into existence between them. Thirdly, when a correspondent bank agrees to act on the instructions of the issuing bank, and advises or confirms the credit, there is a contractual relationship between the issuing bank and its correspondent. Finally, the payment undertakings given to the seller by the issuing and confirming banks in a documentary credit transaction are contractual in nature (despite the fact that they do not readily comply with some of the general principles of contract law: see (ii) below). As Figure 1 illustrates, in relation to a confirmed irrevocable credit, there are five contractual relationships involved (Lord Diplock identified four contractual relationships in *United City Merchants (Investments) Ltd v Royal Bank of Canada, The American Accord* [1983] 1 AC 168 at 181–183 (below, p 868), omitting to refer to the contract between the issuing bank and the seller; but see *Bank of Baroda v Vysya Bank Ltd* [1994] 2 Lloyd's Rep 87 at 90, Mance J; *Bank of Credit & Commerce Hong Kong Ltd (in liquidation) v Sonali Bank* [1995] 1 Lloyd's Rep 227 at 237, Cresswell J).

(ii) The nature of the banks' undertakings

When the credit is irrevocable and confirmed, the issuing and confirming banks each give contractual undertakings to the seller to pay (or pay, accept or negotiate bills of exchange) according to the terms of the credit. Yet it is far from clear as to what, if any, consideration is provided by the seller in support of these payment undertakings. Various attempts have been made to find consideration moving from the seller, or otherwise explain the legal basis of the banks' undertakings. It has been argued, for example, that consideration for the credit is the seller's agreement to present shipping documents to the bank or, alternatively, that

---

[4] Unless a nominated bank is the confirming bank, an authorisation to honour or negotiate does not impose any obligation on that nominated bank to do so, except when expressly agreed to by that nominated bank and so communicated to the beneficiary (UCP 600, art 12(a)). Receipt or examination and forwarding of documents by a nominated bank that is not a confirming bank does not make that nominated bank liable to honour or negotiate (UCP 600, art 12(c)).

[5] But the use of a 'trust receipt' may not give the bank complete protection: see *Lloyds Bank Ltd v Bank of America* [1938] 2 KB 147, noted below at p 0000. See generally EP Ellinger 'Trust Receipt Financing' [2003] JIBLR 305.

the credit becomes binding as a result of the seller's reliance on it, such reliance either constituting acceptance of an offer giving rise to a unilateral contract or making the bank's undertaking binding by estoppel.

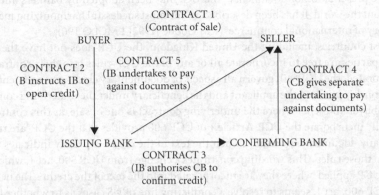

Figure 1 The parties to a confirmed irrevocable credit

None of these theories stands up to rigorous analysis (see RM Goode 'Abstract Payment Undertakings', Ch 9 of P Cane and J Stapleton (eds), *Essays for Patrick Atiyah* (1991), p 218). Of the two theories highlighted, Professor Goode rightly points out that (a) the seller makes no promise to the bank to produce the snipping documents, and (b) the idea that reliance of the seller makes the bank's promise binding is irreconcilable with the commercial understanding of the credit as irrevocable from the moment it is communicated to the seller. The enactment of the Contracts (Rights of Third Parties) Act 1999, which allows third parties (the beneficiary under the credit) to enforce rights conferred on them in other peoples' contracts (the contract between the applicant and the issuing bank), does not take the matter any further forward. Article 4(a) of the UCP 600 (see below) provides that the beneficiary cannot avail himself of the contract between the banks or between the applicant and the issuing bank, and this would be effective to exclude the operation of the Act (Contracts (Rights of Third Parties) Act 1999, s 1(2)).

Probably the best explanation is that the undertakings of the banks are binding through mercantile usage (*Hamzeh Malas & Sons v British Imex Industries Ltd* [1958] 2 QB 127 at 129, per Jenkins LJ (see below, p 865); see also Goode in *Essays for Patrick Atiyah*, above, pp 222–225). It would appear, therefore, that documentary credits are an exception to the doctrine of consideration (as is expressly recognised by the American Uniform Commercial Code (1995 Revision), s 5–105). In any event, whatever the theoretical basis for the binding effect of the bank's undertaking, it is most unlikely in practice that an issuing or confirming bank would attempt to avoid payment under the credit on the technical ground of lack of consideration. The bank's commercial reputation would be irreparably damaged if it tried to take the point.

(c) The Uniform Customs and Practice for Documentary Credits

The Uniform Customs and Practice for Documentary Credits (the 'UCP') is a set of rules governing the use of documentary credits. It was first published by the International

Chamber of Commerce in 1933 and has been revised six times since then. The latest revision is UCP 600, which came into effect on 1 July 2007 (noted by EP Ellinger [2007] LMCLQ 152).[6] UCP 600 replaces the 1993 revision (UCP 500). Unless stated otherwise, all references in this chapter are to UCP 600. A supplement to UCP 600 (called the 'eUCP') deals with the electronic presentation of documents. The UCP has been adopted by bankers and traders throughout the world. It has been described as 'the most successful harmonizing measure in the history of international commerce' (RM Goode [1992] LMCLQ 190).

In most countries, including the United Kingdom, the UCP does not have the force of law. The parties are free to incorporate all or any of the UCP rules into their contracts and, if incorporated, the UCP will govern all aspects of documentary credit arrangements except the relationship between the applicant and the beneficiary under the underlying contract, eg between buyer and seller where the underlying contract is one of sale, as this contract does not usually incorporate the UCP. Article 1 of UCP 600 provides that the UCP 'are rules that apply to any documentary credit... when the text of the credit expressly indicates that it is subject to those rules'. This wording constitutes a change from UCP 500, art 1, which stated that the UCP applied 'where they are incorporated into the text of the credit'. The new wording of UCP 600, art 1, seems to resolve a conflicting line of US cases as to whether the UCP could ever be impliedly incorporated into a documentary credit. In this country, Professor Goode has entered into the debate by suggesting that even in the absence of express incorporation the UCP will probably be incorporated as a matter of business practice because it is so widely used by banks all over the world (R Goode, *Commercial Law* (3rd edn, 2004), p 969, citing, by analogy, *Harlow and Jones Ltd v American Express Bank Ltd* [1990] 2 Lloyd's Rep 343, 349, a case on the Uniform Rules for Collections). The wording of UCP 600, art 1, appears to make express incorporation the only option. The eUCP must also be expressly incorporated into the credit if it is to apply (eUCP, art e1(b)). Incorporation of the eUCP has the effect of incorporating the UCP into the credit without express incorporation of the UCP (eUCP, art e2(a)). Where the eUCP applies, its provisions prevail to the extent that they would produce a result different from the application of the UCP (eUCP, art e2(b)).

The UCP may be expressly modified or excluded by the terms of the credit (UCP 600, art 1). In cases where there is no such express exclusion, the courts will endeavour to construe the express terms of the credit so as to avoid conflict with the rules of the UCP (*Forestal Mimosa Ltd v Oriental Credit Ltd* [1986] 1 WLR 631 at 639, CA). If there is conflict between the express terms of the credit and the UCP, the former will prevail over the latter (*Royal Bank of Scotland plc v Cassa di Risparmio Delle Provincie Lombard* [1992] 1 Bank LR 251 at 256, CA). The UCP will usually be construed in a purposive (not a literal) sense (*Glencore International AG v Bank of China* [1996] 1 Lloyd's Rep 135, CA). This must be right as the UCP does not have its origins in English law but represents international custom and

---

[6] The ICC Commission on Banking Technique and Practice meets regularly to consider problems which arise in relation to the application of the UCP. It has produced a number of booklets containing its opinions on the UCP. These opinions have no legal effect, but give useful guidance to the practical problems which arise in relation to documentary credits. Some opinions issued under UCP 500 may still be relevant under UCP 600 when the wording of a particular article has not changed. However, four Position Papers issued by the ICC Banking Commission in September 1994, with reference to UCP 500, are not to be applied under UCP 600. The ICC Banking Commission's 'Policy Statement' on the determination of an original document has been incorporated into the text of UCP 600 (see below, p 864). In October 1997 the ICC established a swift, non-binding, dispute resolution procedure whereby disputes relating to a documentary credit incorporating the UCP, and the application of the UCP and/or the Uniform Rules for Bank-to-Bank Reimbursement under Documentary Credits (see below, p 000), can be referred to a panel of experts. The dispute resolution procedure is governed by the *DOCDEX Rules—Rules for Documentary Credit Dispute Resolution Expertise* (revised in March 2002: ICC Publication No 811).

practice. The UCP is a prime example of the impact of commercial custom and usage on the development of commercial law.

(d) Definition and types of credits

The terms 'documentary credit', 'banker's commercial credit' and 'commercial letter of credit' are synonymous. But documentary credits are only one type of letter of credit. Letters of credit may also be used in transactions which do not involve payment against the presentation of documents. Such letters of credit are called 'open' or 'clean' credits (see, eg *Re Agra and Masterman's Bank, exp Asiatic Banking Corpn* (1867) 2 Ch App 391). Open credits do not fall within the scope of the UCP and so we shall not be concerned with them in this chapter.

Article 2 of UCP 600 defines a documentary credit ('credit') as 'any arrangement, however named or described, that is irrevocable and thereby constitutes a definite undertaking of the issuing bank to honour a complying presentation'. This marks an important change from UCP 500 which covered both revocable and irrevocable credits. But revocable credits are rare in practice and so the change is not unexpected. Article 2 also contains a definition of 'honour', which means 'to pay at sight if the credit is available by sight payment; to incur a deferred payment undertaking and pay at maturity if the credit is available by deferred payment; to accept a bill of exchange ('draft') drawn by the beneficiary and pay at maturity if the credit is available by acceptance.' Article 2 defines a 'complying presentation' of documents as one 'that is in accordance with the terms and conditions of the credit, the applicable provisions of [the UCP] and international standard banking practice.'

The parties to the underlying contract, which we shall continue to assume to be a contract of sale, should choose whether the credit is to be available by sight payment, by deferred payment, by acceptance, or by negotiation. Their choice will be reflected in the terms of the credit:

- 'payment at sight'—The bank undertakes to pay the seller (the beneficiary under the credit) on presentation of the specified documents. It usually calls on the seller to draw a sight bill of exchange (see above, p 503) on the issuing bank, advising bank or another bank and for him to present it with the documents for immediate payment.

- 'deferred payment'—The bank undertakes to pay the seller at some future date determined in accordance with the terms of the credit, eg '180 days from shipment'. Where a future payment by the bank is to be made other than against an accepted bill of exchange (acceptance credit) the credit is known as a deferred payment credit. A deferred payment credit can be discounted before its maturity date by the discounting bank taking an assignment of the beneficiary's rights under the credit. But under the rules of assignment, defences and cross claims that can be raised against the beneficiary (as assignor) are normally available against the discounting bank (as assignee). In other words, there is a risk when a deferred payment credit is discounted before maturity that the discounting bank's claim to payment on maturity will be defeated by a defence that would have been available against the beneficiary. The risk was highlighted by *Banco Santander v Bayfern Ltd* [2000] 1 All ER (Comm) 776 where a confirming bank discounted its own deferred payment undertaking and fraud in the documents was discovered prior to the maturity date. The Court of Appeal held that the issuing bank was not obliged to reimburse the confirming bank. The *Banco Santander* decision was not popular with the banking community. It placed the risk of fraud in a deferred payment credit on the discounting bank. But UCP 600 has now reversed the result in a case like *Banco Santander*. UCP 600, arts 7(c) and 8(c), establish a definite undertaking by issuing and confirming banks to reimburse on maturity whether or not the nominated bank prepaid or purchased its own acceptance or deferred payment undertaking before maturity. Article 12(b) provides that, by nominating a bank to accept or incur a deferred payment undertaking, an issuing bank gives the nominated bank authority to prepay or purchase a draft accepted or a deferred payment undertaking incurred by that bank. It will be the issuing bank that is now liable where a fraud later comes to light, although the issuing bank can in turn recover from the applicant, who is the real victim of the fraud.

- 'acceptance credit'—The bank undertakes to accept bills of exchange drawn on it by the seller. The bill will usually be a time bill payable at a future date so that by accepting the bill the bank agrees to pay the face value of the bill on maturity to the party presenting it. Between acceptance and maturity the seller may discount the bill to his own bank for cash. Negotiation of the bill of exchange to a bank that is invariably acting in good faith ensures the discounting bank takes free of any defences or cross claims that can be raised by the issuing bank against the beneficiary. The commercial benefits of discounting have made acceptance credits an extremely popular form of credit in international sales.

- 'negotiation credit'—In some credits, known as 'straight credits', the issuing bank's payment undertaking is directed solely to the seller. In other credits, known as 'negotiation credits', the issuing bank's payment undertaking is not confined to the seller but extends to the 'nominated bank' authorised to negotiate (ie purchase) bills of exchange ('drafts') drawn by the seller on another party (often, but not always, the issuing bank) and/or documents under a complying presentation, by advancing or agreeing to advance funds to the beneficiary on or before the banking day on which reimbursement is due to the nominated bank (UCP 600, art 2). Under an open negotiation credit, the undertaking extends to any bank. The bank which has negotiated the drafts and/or documents from the beneficiary can then present them under the credit and receive payment in due course (UCP 600, arts 7(c) and 8(c)). The original beneficiary drops out of the picture and is replaced as beneficiary by the negotiating bank. In other words, the negotiating bank acquires a right to payment under the credit in its own right. Sometimes there are ambiguities in the wording of the credit which make it difficult to decide whether it is a straight credit or a negotiation credit (see, eg *European Asian Bank AG v Punjab and Sind Bank (No 2)* [1983] 1 WLR 642, CA).

(i) Revocable and irrevocable credits

Where the credit is revocable, the issuing bank is free to modify or cancel it at any time without notice to the beneficiary (see, eg *Cape Asbestos Co Ltd v Lloyds Bank Ltd* [1921] WN 274, where the seller shipped goods in ignorance of the prior cancellation of the credit). All the issuing bank is required to do is reimburse any other bank that has already paid the credit. Revocable credits are rare and tend only to be found where the parties are not interested in security (eg they are members of the same group of companies), but where they are concerned to save costs. UCP 600 only applies to irrevocable credits; it does not apply to revocable credits (see above, p 853). If the parties to the underlying contract want to use a revocable credit, they should make the credit subject to UCP 500, an earlier version of the UCP, which does extend to such credits.

A credit that does not indicate whether it is revocable or irrevocable will be deemed to be irrevocable (UCP 600, art 3).

An irrevocable credit constitutes a definite undertaking of the issuing bank that it will honour the credit, provided that there is a complying presentation of the documents specified in the credit (UCP 600, arts 2 and 7(a)). Except as otherwise provided by art 38 of the UCP (transferable credits), an irrevocable credit cannot be modified or cancelled after it has been communicated to the seller (beneficiary) without the consent of the seller, issuing bank and confirming bank (if any) (UCP 600, art 10(a)). If the underlying contract of sale is silent as to whether the credit should be revocable or irrevocable, UCP 600, art 3 cannot be used to argue that the credit must be irrevocable. However, because a revocable credit offers no security to the seller, there is a strong presumption that the parties intend the credit to be irrevocable. Irrevocable credits are the norm (for a specimen, see Form 4 in the Appendix).

(ii) Confirmed and unconfirmed credits

A confirmed credit is one to which the advising bank has added its own definite undertaking to honour or negotiate the credit, provided there is a complying presentation of the documents specified in the credit (UCP 600, arts 2 and 8(a)). The credit is unconfirmed when the advising bank has not provided such an undertaking. The advising bank does not incur any liability to the seller (beneficiary) if the credit is unconfirmed (see UCP 600, arts 12 (a) and (c)). The issuing bank may ask the advising bank to confirm the credit but, subject to prior agreement between them, the advising bank is under no obligation to do so (UCP 600, art 9(a)). To avoid the risk of being held liable to pay the seller, with no right of reimbursement from the issuing bank, an advising bank will, in practice, only confirm an irrevocable credit. If the advising bank, in adding its 'confirmation', reserves a right of recourse against the seller, its undertaking does not constitute a confirmation: *Wahbe Tamari & Sons Ltd v Colprogeca-Sociedada Geral de Fibras, Cafes e Products Colonias Lda* [1969] 2 Lloyd's Rep 18 at 21.

(iii) Revolving credits

A revolving credit allows the seller (beneficiary) to present documents and obtain payment as often as he wants during a credit period, so long as the overall financial limit specified in the credit is not exceeded. As each payment is made, the buyer automatically replenishes the sum that has been drawn down under the credit. A revolving credit is particularly useful when the contract of sale contemplates delivery of goods by instalments.

(iv) Transferable and non-transferable credits

Documentary credits are either transferable or non-transferable. A transferable credit allows the seller (the original beneficiary of the credit) to transfer the rights embodied in the credit to a third party, eg his own supplier. Article 38 of UCP 600 sets out a number of conditions which must be met if the credit is to be transferable. Chief amongst these are the requirements that the transferring bank must expressly consent to the extent and manner of the transfer (art 38(a)), *and* that the credit must be expressly designated as 'transferable' by the issuing bank (art 38(b)). In *Bank Negara Indonesia 1946 v Lariza (Singapore) Pte Ltd* [1988] AC 583, the Privy Council held that, for the purposes of what is now art 38(a), the transferring bank's consent 'has to be an express consent made after the request [for transfer] and it has to cover both the extent and manner of the transfer requested' (at 599, per Lord Brandon). This means that a bank may issue a transferable credit and, if it is a credit where no other bank is involved, later refuse to allow the transfer at will. The decision has been rightly criticised for reducing the usefulness of the transferable credit for financing supply transactions (CM Schmitthoff [1988] JBL 49, 53). Unless otherwise stated in the credit, a transferable credit can be transferred only once (UCP 600, art 38(d)).

The term 'transfer' is somewhat misleading. A documentary credit is not a negotiable instrument which can be transferred from one person to another by indorsement and delivery. In practice what happens when the first beneficiary (the seller) wants to transfer the credit to the second beneficiary (usually the seller's own supplier) is that he returns the credit to the transferring bank, which at the first beneficiary's request issues a new credit to the second beneficiary for the whole or part of the amount of the original credit. Where the first beneficiary transfers only a part of the credit, the balance remains payable to him. Unless otherwise stated in the credit, a transferable credit can be transferred only once (UCP 600, art 38(d)). This means that the second beneficiary is not able to transfer part of the credit in favour of his supplier, but it does not prevent the first beneficiary from transferring part of the credit to several different people, so long as the aggregate of the sums transferred does not exceed the amount of the credit and partial shipments and partial drawings are not prohibited under the credit (UCP 600, art 38(d) and (g)).

When a credit is transferred the second beneficiary is substituted to the rights and obligations of the first beneficiary (the seller) under the credit. This means that the second beneficiary can obtain payment under the credit by tendering the specified documents in his own name (the transferring bank must be careful not to reveal information about the transaction underlying the transfer to the applicant for the credit which could cause loss to the first beneficiary: see *Jackson v Royal Bank of Scotland* [2005] UKHL 3, [2005] 1 All ER (Comm) 337, where the transferring bank was held liable in damages to the first beneficiary for breach of its duty of confidentiality when it inadvertently sent the second beneficiary's invoice to the applicant, thereby revealing the size of first beneficiary's mark-up, and caused the applicant to terminate his business relationship with the first beneficiary; see further, CVM Hare, 'Transferable letters of credit: responsibility, remoteness and loss of a chance' [2005] LMCLQ 350). This distinguishes transfer from assignment (see below, Chapter 22). The proceeds of a credit can be assigned to a third party even though the credit is not stated to be transferable (UCP 600, art 39). But assignment does not transfer the right of performance (see A Ward and G McCormack [2001] JIBL 138). This means that even after assignment of the proceeds of the credit, the seller must still present the specified documents to the bank, or the assignee must do so on the seller's behalf.

(v) Back-to-back credits

Under a back-to-back credit arrangement the seller will use the credit opened in his favour by the buyer as security for the issue of a second credit (the back-to-back credit) in favour of the seller's own supplier. Save for those terms relating to price and time for presentation of documents, the two credits will be identical in their terms. If the seller banks with the bank which advised him of the opening of the buyer's credit, he will usually ask that bank to issue the back-to-back credit in favour of his own supplier.

(vi) Standby credits

See below, p 913.

QUESTIONS

1. Are documentary credits negotiable instruments?

2. From the point of view of both the seller and the buyer, what are the advantages and disadvantages of payment being made through an unconfirmed credit? See CM Schmitthoff [1957] JBL 17, p 18.

3. What are the commercial functions of transferable credits and back-to-back credits? See *Ian Stack Ltd v Baker Bosley Ltd* [1958] 2 QB 130 at 138.

(e) Fundamental principles

(i) Strict compliance

English common law adopts the principle of strict compliance. This requires that tendered documents must strictly comply with the terms of the credit. In the words of Viscount Sumner in *Equitable Trust Co of New York v Dawson Partners Ltd* (1927) 27 Ll L Rep 49 at 52: '[t]here is no room for documents which are almost the same, or which will do just as well.' The principle may be justified on several grounds. First, the banks involved in checking the documents can only be expected to be familiar with banking practices and not the commercial practices and terminology of the parties to the underlying contract which may be reflected in the terms of the credit itself. The bank cannot take on responsibility to decide which documents fulfil the underlying commercial purpose of the parties and which do not. Secondly, the banks act (at least in part) as agents of the applicant and must remain within the terms of their principal's mandate to be sure of reimbursement. In summary, for the protection of the issuing (or confirming) bank and the applicant, the bank is only obliged to pay against strictly conforming documents, and is only entitled to reimbursement if the terms of the credit have been strictly complied with.

The principle of strict compliance applies to all contracts arising out of a documentary credit transaction: the underlying contract (but see below); the contract between the applicant and the issuing bank; the contract between the issuing (and confirming) bank and the beneficiary; and the contract between the issuing and correspondent bank. There is some evidence in other jurisdictions that the degree of strictness varies according to the particular contract in issue (see B Kozolchyk, Ch 5 in *International Encyclopedia of Comparative Law*, Vol 9, pp 82–83). In the United States, for example, some courts have applied a strict compliance standard in respect of the contract between the bank and the beneficiary but only a substantial compliance standard in the contract between the applicant and the issuing bank (*Transamerica Delaval Inc v Citibank NA* 545 F Supp 200 (SDNY 1982) 203–204; *Far Eastern Textile Ltd v City National Bank and Trust* 430 F Supp 193 (SD Ohio 1977) 196). On the other hand, it seems that such a 'bifurcated standard' has not attracted wide acceptance and that 'in the overwhelming majority of US cases…the appropriate standard (has been held to be) the strict compliance standard' (G McLaughlin 'The Standard of Strict Documentary Compliance in Letter of Credit Law: An American Perspective' (1990) 1 JBFLP 81). Critics of the bifurcated approach stress that '[n]othing less than strict compliance appears workable as a standard for document checkers within banks' (R Buckley 'Documentary Compliance in Documentary Credits: Lessons from the UCC and the UCP' (2002) 1 Journal of International Commercial Law 69, 75; cf J Dolan 'Letter of Credit Disputes Between Issuer and Customer'; (1989) 105 Banking LJ 380; 'A Principled Exception to the Strict Compliance Rule in Trilateral Letter of Credit Transactions' (2003) 18 BFLR 245).

Under English law there is little evidence of the courts applying a substantial compliance standard as opposed to a strict compliance standard. Such evidence as there is relates to the underlying contract and not to the various contracts that arise out of the credit itself.

Moralice (London) Ltd v ED and F Man
[1954] 2 Lloyd's Rep 526

The seller tendered documents to the bank showing shipment of 499.7 metric tons of sugar. The credit called for documents showing shipment of 500 metric tons. McNair J held that the bank was entitled to reject the documents as the *de minimis* rule did not apply as between the bank and the beneficiary seller, nor did it apply as between the buyer and his bank. (Note that art 30(b) of UCP 600 now provides for certain tolerances as to the quantity of goods: +/- 5% subject to number of exceptions.)

Bunge Corpn v Vegetable Vitamin Foods (Pte) Ltd
[1985] 1 Lloyd's Rep 613

Neill J held (at 616) that while the *de minimis* rule did not apply as between a bank and a beneficiary of a letter of credit, the rule did apply as between the buyer and the seller (the underlying contract was one of sale). He held that there was no breach of contract by the buyers when there were minor differences between the credit as opened and that stipulated in the contract of sale. There had been 'substantial compliance' with the contract of sale. This reasoning can be justified on the ground that, as between the seller and the buyer, what is involved is not a credit relationship, but simply one based on the underlying contract of sale.

The following cases illustrate how the principle of strict compliance has been applied by the English courts to the various relationships arising out of the credit.

Bank v Applicant
Equitable Trust Co of New York v Dawson Partners Ltd
(1927) 27 Ll L Rep 49

The credit called for payment against certain documents including 'a certificate of quality to be issued by experts'. The seller tendered a certificate of quality issued by a single expert. The seller was paid. When the issuing bank tendered the certificate to the buyers, they refused to pay on grounds of non-compliance with the credit. In fact, the seller had been fraudulent and shipped mainly rubbish to the buyers. The House of Lords (by a majority of 4 to 1) ruled in favour of the buyers. Viscount Sumner stated (at 52) that:

[t]here is no room for documents which are almost the same, or which will do just as well. Business could not proceed securely on any other lines. The bank's branch abroad, which knows nothing offi-cially of the details of the transaction thus financed, cannot take upon itself to decide what will do well enough and what will not. If it does as it is told, it is safe; if it declines to do anything else, it is safe; if it departs from the conditions laid down, it acts at its own risk.

Beneficiary v Bank

JH Rayner & Co Ltd v Hambro's Bank Ltd

[1943] KB 37

The credit referred to the shipment of 'Coromandel groundnuts' but the seller tendered a bill of lading for 'machine-shelled groundnut kernels' and an invoice for 'Coromandel groundnuts'. Although it was well known in the trade that 'Coromandel groundnuts' were the same thing as 'machine-shelled groundnut kernels', the Court of Appeal held the bank entitled to reject the bill of lading for non-compliance with the terms of credit. Mackinnon LJ stated (at 41) that '…it is quite impossible to suggest that a banker is to be affected with knowledge of the customs and customary terms of every one of the thousands of trades for whose dealings he may issue a letter of credit'.

Bank v Bank

Bank Melli Iran v Barclays Bank DCO

[1951] 2 Lloyd's Rep 367

Bank Melli opened an irrevocable credit which was confirmed by Barclays Bank. The credit called for the tender of documents evidencing shipment of 'sixty new Chevrolet trucks'. The documents tendered by the seller included an invoice which described the trucks as 'in new condition', a certificate which described them as 'new, good, Chevrolet…trucks' and a delivery order describing them as 'new (hyphen) good'. Barclays Bank accepted the documents, paid the seller and debited Bank Melli's account accordingly. Bank Melli claimed Barclays were in breach of mandate by paying against non-conforming documents. McNair J held that the descriptions in the tendered documents were inconsistent with each other and that the tender was bad. However, he went on to hold that Bank Melli had subsequently ratified the actions of its agent, Barclays Bank, who were entitled to reimbursement.

The wording of the credit is of paramount importance when determining whether there has been compliance with its terms. Even an apparently trivial discrepancy will justify rejection of the documents if the credit is specific as to that requirement.

Seaconsar Far East Ltd v Bank Markazi Jomhouri Islami Iran

[1993] 1 Lloyd's Rep 236

A confirmed irrevocable credit stipulated that all documents presented to the bank should bear the letter of credit number and the buyer's name. The seller presented documents to the advising bank and claimed payment. The advising bank refused to pay relying on the fact that one of the documents, the list of the goods shipped, did not carry the letter of credit number nor the buyer's name. On the seller's application for leave to serve proceedings on the issuing bank out of the jurisdiction, the Court of Appeal, by a majority, held that the tender was clearly bad and refused leave. Lloyd and Beldam LJJ rejected submissions that the omission was trivial and that, in any event, it could be cured by reference to the other tendered documents which all carried the necessary particulars. Their Lordships emphasised that neither of these arguments could apply when the credit clearly and expressly required each document to contain the necessary particulars. Stuart-Smith LJ, dissenting, thought that the seller's case was not 'unworthy of consideration'. The House of Lords later reversed the Court of Appeal on other grounds and gave the seller leave to serve out of the jurisdiction (see [1994] 1 AC

438). When the case later came back to the Court of Appeal on its merits (see [1999] 1 Lloyd's Rep 36), the fact that there were discrepancies in the tendered documents was admitted. Sir Christopher Staughton, delivering the only reasoned judgment of the court, observed (at 38) that 'the discrepancies in the documents do not appear to be of any great significance. But that is neither here nor there. It is hornbook law for bankers that the documents must appear on their face to be precisely in accordance with the terms and conditions of the credit'.

On the other hand, the courts are willing to overlook a trivial defect in the tendered documents where there is a patent typographical error, or other obvious slip or omission.

Seaconsar Far East Ltd v Bank Markazi Jomhouri Islami Iran
[1993] 1 Lloyd's Rep 236

Lloyd LJ: It would not, I think, help to attempt to define the sort of discrepancy which can properly be regarded as trivial. But one might take, by way of example, *Bankers Trust Co v State Bank of India* [1991] 2 Lloyd's Rep 443, where one of the documents gave the buyer's telex number as 931310 instead of 981310.

(Note that under UCP 600, art 14(j) contact details (fax, telephone, e-mail and the like) stated as part of the beneficiary's and the applicant's address are now to be disregarded unless they are of the applicant and appear as part of the consignee or notify party details on a transport document.)

Hing Yip Hing Fat Co Ltd v Daiwa Bank Ltd
[1991] 2 HKLR 35

The Supreme Court of Hong Kong held that there had been a patent typographical error, and no discrepancy, when a document tendered to the issuing bank by the beneficiary gave the name of the applicant for the credit as 'Cheergoal Industrial Limited', when it should have been 'Cheergoal Industries Limited'.

But where it is not clear whether the departure from the detail set out in the credit was a draftsman's error or not, the discrepancy justifies the rejection of the documents (see, eg *Beyene v Irving Trust Co Ltd* (1985) 762 Fed Rep 2d 4, US CA for the Second Circuit held the bank entitled to reject bill of lading which described the notify party as 'Mohammed Soran' when the credit required 'Mohammed Sofan': there was no evidence before the court that 'Soran' would be recognised as an obvious misspelling of 'Sofan' in the Middle East). It is sometimes difficult to draw a clear line between the two types of cases.

There is evidence that the English courts have moved away from a 'mirror image' approach to strict compliance which had been the favoured approach for many years (see above).

Kredietbank Antwerp v Midland Bank plc
[1999] 1 All ER (Comm) 801

The credit specified 'Draft survey report issued by Griffith Inspectorate at port of loading'. The claimant accepted a draft survey report signed on behalf of Daniel C Griffith (Holland) BV, which was described as a 'member of the worldwide inspectorate group'. The defendant rejected the document on the ground that it was not issued by 'Griffith Inspectorate'. The Court of Appeal held that the document was conforming. Evans LJ began by citing those cases where the courts had drawn a line between 'trivial' discrepancies and those which require the bank to reject the tendered documents (see above). He continued (at 806):

For these reasons, the requirement of strict compliance is not equivalent to a test of exact literal compliance in all circumstances and as regards all documents. To some extent, therefore, the banker must exercise his own judgment whether the requirement is satisfied by the documents presented to him.

The case illustrates that whilst the English courts continue to apply the strict compliance rule, they do not take a mechanical or robotic approach to documentary compliance. Of course, how far a court can move away from strict literal compliance remains governed by the precise wording of the credit. On the other hand, the case in no way implies that the English courts require a bank to exercise its judgment as to whether the tendered document fulfils the same commercial purpose as the document called for in the credit. A bank cannot be expected to know the commercial practices of the parties.

The strict compliance rule is commercially convenient in that it enables banks to make quick decisions about the documents presented to them. In fact, it is estimated that approximately 70% of documents initially presented to banks are discrepant (Introduction to UCP 600, p 11). In many cases discrepancies are easily remedied by the seller and the documents represented to the bank. The seller usually has time do this because the bank must specify all of the discrepancies in a notice of rejection which must be given no later than the close of the fifth banking day following receipt of the documents (UCP 600, art 16(c)(ii) and (d)). In other cases, the discrepancies are waived by the buyer. But this may not always happen. The strict compliance rule allows documents to be rejected for insubstantial discrepancies. This may facilitate or encourage what has been described as 'bad faith rejection of documents'. Although the bank may approach the buyer for waiver of the discrepancy, it may not be in the buyer's wider commercial interests to agree to this, for example, where the market has fallen and he can now obtain the same goods at a lower price. However, in *Glencore International AG v Bank of China* [1996] 1 Lloyd's Rep 135 at 153, Sir Thomas Bingham MR observed:

[t]he judge described the Bank of China's argument as 'very technical' and observed that it might appear to lack merit. Both comments are apt. But a rule of strict compliance gives little scope for recognizing the merits.

A 'mirror image' interpretation of the strict compliance rule is probably unworkable in practice. Rejection of tendered documents becomes the norm. Bankers have recognised this for some time. This has led the ICC to promote a more flexible approach to documentary compliance. There were signs of this in UCP 500 and many of the changes introduced by UCP 600 are designed to move away from 'mirror image' compliance of tendered documents with the credit towards a 'functional standard of documentary verification' that allows the credit to function as a payment instrument, something it cannot do when so many documents are rejected on first tender.

The ICC's philosophy is enshrined in the definition of a 'complying presentation' which can be found in UCP 600, art 2 (see above, p 853). It will be recalled that a complying presentation is one in accordance with, *inter alia*, 'international standard banking practices' (for a similar, though not identical, reference to international standard banking practice, see also UCP 500, art 13(a)). A bank cannot be expected to know the commercial practices of the parties to the underlying contract but it can be expected to be aware of the standards of international banking practice (*Kredietbank Antwerp v Midland Bank plc* [1999] 1 All ER

(Comm) 801 at 804, per Evans LJ: 'The professional expertise of a trading bank includes knowledge of the UCP rules and of their practical application'). 'The real difficulty, however, is to identify the practices that reflect agreed international standards. The ICC resolved to address the issue. In May 2000 it established a task force to document international standard banking practice for the examination of documents presented under documentary credits issued subject to the UCP. The task force consulted widely and, in January 2003, the ICC published the *International Standard Banking Practice (ISBP) for the Examination of Documents under Documentary Letters of Credit* (ICC Publication No 645). A revised version of the *ISBP* (ICC Publication No 681) was published to accompany the issue of UCP 600. The text provides detailed answers to important questions relating to the examination of drafts, multimodal transport documents, insurance documents, certificates of origin and a range of other documents associated with documentary credits. The function of the *ISBP* is explained in its Foreword (p 3) as follows:

The ISBP…is a practical complement to the UCP 600, ICC's universally used rules on documentary credits. The ISBP does not amend the UCP. It explains, in explicit detail, how the rules set out in the UCP are to be applied on a day-to-day basis. As such, it fills a needed gap between the general principles announced in the rules and the daily work of the documentary credit practitioner.

The *ISBP* will be relevant when an issue of banking practice comes before the courts. In *Crédit Industriel et Commercial v China Merchants Bank* [2002] EWHC 973 (Comm), [2002] 2 All ER (Comm) 427 at [62], David Steel J considered that the opinions of the ICC Banking Commission were entitled to considerable weight, and we can add that the same must also be said of the *ISBP*. But the *ISBP* merely represents one source of international standard banking practice: it is not the exclusive source. Expert evidence can still be relied upon by the parties to a dispute to establish a local or regional banking practice which may be at odds with that found in the *ISBP* (see EP Ellinger [2007] LMCLQ 152, 159).

The latest revision of the UCP contains a number of new provisions which are designed to ensure that tendered documents are not rejected for overly technical reasons. Two examples can be taken from UCP 600, art 14:

- Sub-art 14(d) provides that data in a document, when read in context with the credit, the document itself and international standard banking practice, need not be identical to, but must not conflict with, data in that document, any other stipulated document or the credit. Documents need not be mirror images of each other, but merely that they must not be inconsistent.

- Sub-art 14(f) provides that if a credit requires presentation of a document other than a transport document, insurance document or commercial invoice, without stipulating by whom the document is to be issued or its data content, banks will accept the document as presented if its content appears to fulfil the function of the required document and otherwise complies with sub-art 14(d). Sub-article 14(f) seems to take data content out of the equation when there is no stipulation as to what it should be. For example, if the credit calls for an inspection certificate without more, the condition will be satisfied if an inspection certificate is presented even if it does not 'pass' the goods. If the buyer wants tender of an inspection certificate which states that the goods have passed inspection, then he must specify this in his application to the issuing bank to open the credit and the credit must be issued in those terms.

Under English common law if the descriptions of the goods in the documents read as a whole comply with the description in the credit that is sufficient unless the credit specifies otherwise or there are inconsistencies between the tendered documents. Article 18(c) of UCP 600 provides that the description of the goods in the commercial invoice must correspond with the description in the credit. Article 14(e) of UCP 600 provides that in all other documents, the goods may be described in general terms not inconsistent with the description of the goods in the credit. Both requirements were previously to be found in UCP 500, art 37(c). Whether the requirements of art 37(c) had been met was at issue in the following cases.

Glencore International AG v Bank of China
[1996] 1 Lloyd's Rep 135

The issuing bank argued that the description of the goods (aluminium ingots) contained in the commercial invoice ('Origin: Any Western brand—Indonesia (Inalum Brand)') was inconsistent with that in the credit ('Origin: Any Western brand'). The Court of Appeal rejected that argument on the basis that the description in the commercial invoice fell within the broad generic nature of the description in the credit.

Packing lists and other specified documents were tendered by the beneficiary and negotiating bank to the issuing bank, but the issuing bank claimed that the packing lists were discrepant as they did not describe the goods as required by the credit. The Court of Appeal rejected this argument, as it required each document to be examined in isolation, and held that the packing lists and other tendered documents formed a set of documents which should be read and considered together, the linkage between the documents being clear and exact and devoid of discrepancy (but it remains the case that the goods must still be properly *identified* in each document: *Banque de I 'Indochine et de Suez SA v J H Rayner (Mincing Lane) Ltd* [1983] QB 711 at 732, CA).

Crédit Agricole Indosuez v Chailease Finance Corpn
[2000] 1 All ER (Comm) 399

The underlying contract related to the sale of a ship. The bank claimed (a) that the tendered bill of sale and signed acceptance of sale, which stated that delivery had taken place on 21 August 1998, did not comply with the terms of the letter of credit, which required the documents to state a delivery date within 17–20 August, and (b) that, because of the difference in the stated dates of delivery, the description of the vessel in the tendered documents was inconsistent with that in the letter of credit. The Court of Appeal held that the tendered documents were not discrepant. As to (a), the court held that the letter of credit did not state that the documents had to show that the vessel had been delivered within a range of dates. As to (b), the court agreed (obiter) with the trial judge that, on a true construction of the credit, the words 'for delivery … during 17–20 August 1998' were not part of the description of the goods. In any event, the court held that as there was ample descriptive information in the acceptance and the bill of sale which made clear that the vessel delivered and accepted was the vessel the subject of the sale agreement, so that the date of actual delivery stated, ie one day beyond the range of dates, did not render the description of the vessel in the documents inconsistent with the description of the goods in the credit.

The basic rule is that original documents must be tendered to the bank, unless the credit calls for copy documents. But, in a world dominated by the word-processor and the photocopier, there has been uncertainty as to what constitutes an original document, uncertainty that has been reflected in the case law. So far as UCP 500 was concerned, the relevant article was art 20(b):

Unless otherwise stipulated in the credit, banks will also accept as an original document(s), a document(s) produced or appearing to have been produced:

  i. by reprographic, automated or computerized systems;

  ii. as carbon copies;

provided that it is marked as original and, where necessary, appears to be signed. A document may be signed by handwriting, by facsimile signature, by perforated signature, by stamp, by symbol, or by other mechanical or electronic method of authentication.

In *Glencore International AC v Bank of China* [1996] 1 Lloyd's Rep 135, the Court of Appeal held that whilst an original handwritten or originally typed document was acceptable, a signed photocopy of a word processed document was not an 'original' document and could be rejected on presentation unless 'marked as original' as required by art 20(b) of UCP 500. Dicta in *Glencore* even suggested that, on a true interpretation of art 20(b), a word processed document was not an original document and could be rejected unless 'marked as original'. The issue arose in *Kredietbank Antwerp v Midland Bank plc* [1999] 1 All ER (Comm) 801, where the Court of Appeal held that so long as the word processed document was *clearly* an original document—'in the sense that it contains the relevant contract, and which is not itself a copy of some other document'—it should be treated as such. Both decisions were reviewed by Steel J in *Crédit Industriel et Commercial v China Merchants Bank* [2002] EWHC 973 (Comm), [2002] 2 All ER (Comm) 427. In this case it was unclear how the relevant documents had been produced but the judge held that the issuing bank was not entitled to reject them as not being original documents. Steel J held that it was appropriate to apply the ICC's Policy Statement published on 12 July 1999. In essence, the Policy Statement embodied the general principle upheld in the *Kredietbank* case, namely that art 20(b) did not apply to a document which appeared on its face to be an original. For these purposes, an original would include a photocopy if it was hand signed by the issuer, or if it was produced on original stationery rather than blank paper. In *Glencore*, the documents were photocopies produced on blank paper but signed. Under the Policy Statement, these documents would be treated as originals.

This would now also be the position under UCP 600 which addresses the problem in article 17 as follows:

a. At least one original of each document stipulated in the credit must be presented.

b. A bank shall treat as an original any document bearing an apparently original signature, mark, stamp or label of the issuer of the document, unless the document itself indicates that it is not an original.

c. Unless a document indicates otherwise, a bank will also accept a document as an original if it:

  i.   appears to be written, typed, perforated or stamped by the document issuer's hand; or

  ii. appears to be on the document issuer's original stationery; or

  iii. states that it is original, unless the statement appears not to apply to the document presented.

Article 17 goes on to permit the presentation of either originals or copies if a credit requires presentation of copies of documents (UCP 600, art 17 (d)). In addition, if a credit requires presentation of multiple documents by using terms such as 'in duplicate', 'in two fold' or 'in two copies', this can be satisfied by the presentation of at least one original and the remaining number in copies, except when the document itself indicates otherwise (UCP 600, art 17(e)).

QUESTION

Which approach to the doctrine of documentary compliance better promotes commercial certainty: the 'mirror image' approach (evident in the English cases) or the 'functional standard of verification' approach (promoted by the ICC)?

(ii) Autonomy of the credit[7]

A documentary credit is separate from and independent of the underlying contract between the seller and the buyer, and the relationship between the issuing bank and the buyer. In general, therefore, the seller's breach of the underlying contract is no defence to the issuing bank (nor to the confirming bank). It is irrelevant to the performance of the credit that the buyer alleges, for example, that the shipped goods are not of satisfactory quality, nor fit for their purpose or that there has been a shortfall in delivery. By the same token, the issuing bank cannot refuse to honour its undertaking just because of the buyer's failure to put it in funds.

The principle of autonomy of the credit is enshrined in the UCP. Article 4 of UCP 600 provides that 'a credit by its nature is a separate transaction from the sale or other contract on which it may be based. Banks are in no way concerned with or bound by such contract, even if any reference whatsoever to it is included in the credit.' The autonomy rule is also linked to the principle, to be found in art 5, that in credit operations '[b]anks deal with documents and not with goods, services or performance to which the documents may relate'. Similarly, art 34 makes clear that in credit operations banks have no responsibility for anything other than conformity of the documents to the credit.

The English courts have applied the principle of autonomy of the credit on numerous occasions. The following case illustrates the point.

Hamzeh Malas & Sons v British Imex Industries Ltd
[1958] 2 QB 127, Court of Appeal

Jordanian buyers (the plaintiffs) agreed to purchase from British sellers (the defendants) a quantity of steel rods, to be delivered in two instalments. Payment for each instalment was to be by two confirmed letters of credit. The buyers duly opened the two credits with the Midland Bank Ltd. The sellers delivered the first instalment and were paid under the first credit. The buyers then complained that that instalment was defective and sought an injunction to restrain the sellers from drawing on the second credit. Donovan J refused to grant the injunction and the buyers appealed against that order.

Jenkins LJ stated the facts and continued: It appears that when the first consignment of steel rods arrived they were, according to the plaintiffs, by no means up to contract quality and many criticisms

---

[7] See, generally, R Goode 'Abstract Payment Undertakings and the Rules of the International Chamber of Commerce' 39 Saint Louis Univ LJ 725 (1995); also, 'Abstract Payment Undertakings in International Transactions' 22 Brooklyn J Int'l L 1 (1996).

were made on that score. That is a matter in issue between the parties. In the meantime the plaintiffs wish to secure themselves in respect of any damages they may be found to be entitled to when this dispute is ultimately tried out, by preventing the defendants from dealing with this outstanding letter of credit. Mr Gardiner [counsel for the plaintiffs], in effect, treats this as no more than part of the price, a sum earmarked to pay for the goods bought under the contract, which the plaintiffs have become entitled to repudiate; and he says that the defendants ought, accordingly, to be restrained from dealing with the amount of this letter of credit. He points out that he is not seeking any order against the bank, but merely against the defendants.

We have been referred to a number of authorities, and it seems to be plain enough that the opening of a confirmed letter of credit constitutes a bargain between the banker and the vendor of the goods, which imposes upon the banker an absolute obligation to pay, irrespective of any dispute there may be between the parties as to whether the goods are up to contract or not. An elaborate commercial system has been built up on the footing that bankers' confirmed credits are of that character, and, in my judgment, it would be wrong for this court in the present case to interfere with that established practice.

There is this to be remembered too. A vendor of goods selling against a confirmed letter of credit is selling under the assurance that nothing will prevent him from receiving the price. That is of no mean advantage when goods manufactured in one country are being sold in another. It is, furthermore, to be observed that vendors are often reselling goods bought from third parties. When they are doing that, and when they are being paid by a confirmed letter of credit, their practice is—and I think it was followed by the defendants in this case—to finance the payments necessary to be made to their suppliers against the letter of credit. That system of financing these operations, as I see it, would break down completely if a dispute as between the vendor and the purchaser was to have the effect of 'freezing,' if I may use that expression, the sum in respect of which the letter of credit was opened.

I agree with Mr Gardiner that this is not a case where it can be said that the court has no jurisdiction to interfere. The court's jurisdiction to grant injunctions is wide, but, in my judgment, this is not a case in which the court ought, in the exercise of its discretion, to grant an injunction. Accordingly, I think this application should be refused.

Sellers LJ: I agree, but I would repeat what my Lord has said on jurisdiction. I would not like it to be taken that I accept, or that the court accepts, the submission if it was made, as I think it was, that the court has no jurisdiction. There may well be cases where the court would exercise jurisdiction as in a case where there is a fraudulent transaction.

Pearce LJ: I agree.

NOTES

1.   The courts have consistently defended the autonomy principle on the ground that irrevocable documentary credits are 'the life-blood of international commerce' which 'must be allowed to be honoured, free from interference by the courts. Otherwise, trust in international commerce could be irreparably damaged' (*RD Harbottle (Mercantile) Ltd v National Westminster Bank Ltd* [1978] QB 146 at 155–156, per Kerr J: below, p 917). The commercial value of the documentary credit system lies in the fact that payment under the credit is virtually assured. Certainty of payment is of paramount importance to the business community and so irrevocable credits are treated like cash by the courts.

2.   The autonomy rule is not absolute. The most important exception to the rule is where there is fraud on the part of the beneficiary or his agent in relation to the presentation of documents to the bank or in relation to the underlying contract of sale. Nevertheless, even in cases of fraud the bank must pay the holder in due course of a bill of exchange accepted by the bank under the terms of the credit on the ground that the bill creates an autonomous

contract independent of the documentary credit itself (*Discount Records Ltd v Barclays Bank Ltd* [1975] 1 All ER 1071). The fraud exception is considered in greater detail below.

3. In *Sirius International Insurance Corpn (Publ) v FAI General Insurance Co Ltd* [2003] EWCA Civ 470, [2003] 1 All ER (Comm) 865, the Court of Appeal held that the principle of autonomy did not mean that a beneficiary could draw on a letter of credit when it had expressly agreed not to do so unless certain conditions were satisfied and those conditions had not been met. In this case, the restrictions were contained in a separate agreement made between the beneficiary (Sirius) and the applicant (FAI). May LJ held (at [27]) that:

although those restrictions were not terms of the letter of credit, and although the bank would have been obliged and entitled to honour a request to pay which fulfilled its terms, that does not mean that, as between themselves and FAI, Sirius were entitled to draw on the letter of credit if the express conditions of this underlying agreement were not fulfilled. They were not so entitled.

The Court of Appeal were also of the opinion that if draw-down was attempted in these circumstances, a court would be likely to grant an injunction restraining the beneficiary from drawing on the letter of credit in breach of express conditions contained in the separate agreement. It should be noted that fraud was not alleged against Sirius and so the case does not fall within the fraud exception to the autonomy principle considered in the next section. The House of Lords later reversed the Court of Appeal's decision on the ground that the express conditions to draw-down had been satisfied. Their Lordships found it unnecessary to examine arguments about the autonomy principle: [2004] UKHL 54, [2004] 1 WLR 3251.

4. The *Sirius* case raises important questions about the extent of the autonomy principle. There must be some concern as to how far it undermines the principle and its consequential benefits of commercial certainty. However, the English courts have not shown themselves willing to embrace the wider principle of 'unconscionable demand' which has gained judicial support in Australia (see, eg *Olex Focas Pty Ltd Skodaexport Co Ltd* [1998] 3 VR 380, where statute brought the concept into play) and Singapore (see, eg *Samwoh Asphalt Premix v Sum Cheong Piling* [2002] BLR 459). It is not entirely clear what constitutes unconscionablity, although it seems to be something more than unfairness and less than fraud, nor as to the standard of proof required to obtain injunctive relief on this ground (see Ganotaki [2004] LMCLQ 148 at 152). The uncertainty that this creates is obvious. Nevertheless, there have been dicta in recent English cases which suggests that the previous reluctance to apply a concept of 'unconsionability' may not last forever (see, especially, the dicta of Potter LJ in *Montrod Ltd v Grundkötter Fleischvertriebs* [2001] EWCA Civ 1954, [2002] 1 All ER (Comm) 257 at [59], and also that of Judge Thornton QC, sitting as a deputy High Court judge, in *TTI Team Telecom International Ltd v Hutchison 3G UK Ltd* [2003] EWHC 762 (TCC), [2003] 1 All ER (Comm) 914 at [37]).

(iii) Autonomy and the fraud exception[8]

The classic statement of the fraud exception to the autonomy principle is to be found in the judgment of Lord Diplock in *United City Merchants (Investments) Ltd v Royal Bank of Canada* [1983] 1 AC 168 (below). Lord Diplock began by affirming the principle that with credits the parties deal in documents and not in goods, and that a bank is obliged to pay if on their face the documents presented conform to the credit notwithstanding that the bank

---

[8] See R Hooley 'Fraud and Letters of Credit' [2003] JIBFL 91 and 132.

may know of a dispute between the buyer and the seller as to the underlying contract of sale. He continued (at 183):

To this general statement of principle as to the contractual obligations of the confirming bank to the seller, there is one established exception: that is where the seller, for the purposes of drawing on the credit, fraudulently presents to the confirming bank documents that contain, expressly or by implication, material representations of fact that to his knowledge are untrue.

Lord Diplock explained the rationale for the fraud exception in terms of an application of the maxim *ex turpi causa non oritur actio* or, in plain English, 'fraud unravels all'. The courts will not allow their process to be used by a dishonest person to carry out a fraud. In *Czarnikow-Rionda Sugar Trading Inc v Standard Bank London Ltd* [1999] 1 All ER (Comm) 890 at 914, when considering a claim for an injunction against an issuing bank and the need to find a substantive cause of action against the party to be restrained, Rix J said that Lord Diplock's reference to the *ex turpi causa* principle 'may appropriately be viewed as an authoritative expression of the source in law of the implied limitation on a bank's mandate'. More recently, in *Mahonia Ltd v JP Morgan Chase Bank* [2003] EWHC 1927 (Comm), [2003] 2 Lloyd's Rep 911 at [39], Colman J held that the *ex turpi causa* explanation 'accords more comfortably with principle and is therefore to be preferred'.

United City Merchants (Investments) Ltd v Royal Bank of Canada, The American Accord
[1983] 1 AC 168, House of Lords

English sellers sold manufacturing equipment to Peruvian buyers and agreed to invoice for the order at twice the correct price, to enable the buyers to evade Peruvian exchange control regulations. Payment was to be made by confirmed irrevocable credit, and this was issued by the buyers' bank and confirmed by Royal Bank of Canada. The goods were shipped on 16 December 1976. However, the credit specified that the last day for shipment was 15 December 1976 and so the carriers' agent fraudulently issued a bill of lading showing shipment to have been made on 15 December. The sellers knew nothing of this fraud. On presentation of the documents the confirming bank refused to pay on the ground that it had information suggesting that shipment had not taken place on the day stated in the bill of lading. The sellers (strictly, the assignees of their rights under the credit) sued the confirming bank under the credit.

Mocatta J held that, as the sellers were innocent of the fraud of the carriers' agent, the bank was wrong to refuse payment of documents which, on their face, appeared to be in order. But, in a second judgment, he held that, because of the breach of Peruvian exchange control regulations, the credit was rendered unenforceable under the Bretton Woods Agreements Order in Council 1946. The Court of Appeal dismissed the sellers' appeal on the ground that whilst it was possible to divide the credit and allow payment for that half of the invoice price which did not infringe the exchange control regulations, the bank had been entitled to rely on the fraud of the carriers' agent and refuse payment of any sum. The sellers appealed.

Lord Diplock:

The documentary credit point

My Lords, for the proposition upon the documentary credit point, both in the broad form for which counsel for the confirming bank have strenuously argued at all stages of this appeal and in the narrower form or 'halfway house' that commended itself to the Court of Appeal, there is no direct authority to be found either in English or Privy Council cases or among the numerous decisions of courts in the United States of America to which reference is made in the judgments of the Court of Appeal in the instant case. So the point falls to be decided by reference to first principles as to the legal nature of the contractual obligations assumed by the various parties to a transaction consisting of an international sale of goods to be financed by means of a confirmed irrevocable documentary credit. It is trite law that there are four autonomous though interconnected contractual relationships involved. (1) The underlying contract for the sale of goods, to which the only parties are the buyer and the seller; (2) the contract between the buyer and the issuing bank under which the latter agrees to issue the credit and either itself or through a confirming bank to notify the credit to the seller and to make payments to or to the order of the seller (or to pay, accept or negotiate bills of exchange drawn by the seller) against presentation of stipulated documents; and the buyer agrees to reimburse the issuing bank for payments made under the credit. For such reimbursement the stipulated documents, if they include a document of title such as a bill of lading, constitute a security available to the issuing bank; (3) if payment is to be made through a confirming bank the contract between the issuing bank and the confirming bank authorising and requiring the latter to make such payments and to remit the stipulated documents to the issuing bank when they are received, the issuing bank in turn agreeing to reimburse the confirming bank for payments made under the credit; (4) the contract between the confirming bank and the seller under which the confirming bank undertakes to pay to the seller (or to accept or negotiate without recourse to drawer bills of exchange drawn by him) up to the amount of the credit against presentation of the stipulated documents.

Again, it is trite law that in contract (4), with which alone the instant appeal is directly concerned, the parties to it, the seller and the confirming bank, 'deal in documents and not in goods,' as art 8 of the Uniform Customs [1974 Revision; now art 5, UCP 2007 Revision] puts it. If, on their face, the documents presented to the confirming bank by the seller conform with the requirements of the credit as notified to him by the confirming bank, that bank is under a contractual obligation to the seller to honour the credit, notwithstanding that the bank has knowledge that the seller at the time of presentation of the conforming documents is alleged by the buyer to have, and in fact has already, committed a breach of his contract with the buyer for the sale of the goods to which the documents appear on their face to relate, that would have entitled the buyer to treat the contract of sale as rescinded and to reject the goods and refuse to pay the seller the purchase price. The whole commercial purpose for which the system of confirmed irrevocable documentary credits has been developed in international trade is to give to the seller an assured right to be paid before he parts with control of the goods that does not permit of any dispute with the buyer as to the performance of the contract of sale being used as a ground for non-payment or reduction or deferment of payment.

To this general statement of principle as to the contractual obligations of the confirming bank to the seller, there is one established exception: that is, where the seller, for the purpose of drawing on the credit, fraudulently presents to the confirming bank documents that contain, expressly or by implication, material representations of fact that to his knowledge are untrue. Although there does not appear among the English authorities any case in which this exception has been applied, it is well established in the American cases of which the leading or 'landmark' case is *Sztejn v J Henry Schroder Banking Corpn* 31 NYS 2d 631 (1941). This judgment of the New York Court of Appeals was referred to with approval by the English Court of Appeal in *Edward Owen Engineering Ltd v Barclays Bank International Ltd* [1978] QB 159 [below, p 915], though this was actually a case about a performance bond under which a bank assumes obligations to a buyer analogous to those assumed by a confirming bank to the seller under a documentary credit. The exception for fraud on the part of the beneficiary seeking to avail himself of the credit is a clear application of the maxim ex turpi causa non oritur actio or, if plain English is to be preferred, 'fraud unravels all.' The courts will not allow their process to be used by a dishonest person to carry out a fraud.

The instant case, however, does not fall within the fraud exception. Mocatta J found the sellers to have been unaware of the inaccuracy of Mr Baker's notation of the date at which the goods were actually on board *American Accord*. They believed that it was true and that the goods had actually been loaded on or before December 15 1976, as required by the documentary credit.

Faced by this finding, the argument for the confirming bank before Mocatta J was directed to supporting the broad proposition: that a confirming bank is not under any obligation, legally enforceable against it by the seller/beneficiary of a documentary credit, to pay to him the sum stipulated in the credit against presentation of documents, if the documents presented, although conforming on their face with the terms of the credit, nevertheless contain some statement of material fact that is not accurate. This proposition which does not call for knowledge on the part of the seller/beneficiary of the existence of any inaccuracy would embrace the fraud exception and render it superfluous.

My Lords, the more closely this bold proposition is subjected to legal analysis, the more implausible it becomes; to assent to it would, in my view, undermine the whole system of financing international trade by means of documentary credits.

It has, so far as I know, never been disputed that as between confirming bank and issuing bank and as between issuing bank and the buyer the contractual duty of each bank under a confirmed irrevocable credit is to examine with reasonable care all documents presented in order to ascertain that they appear *on their face* to be in accordance with the terms and conditions of the credit, and, if they do so appear, to pay to the seller/beneficiary by whom the documents have been presented the sum stipulated by the credit, or to accept or negotiate without recourse to drawer drafts drawn by the seller/beneficiary if the credit so provides. It is so stated in the latest edition of the Uniform Customs. It is equally clear law, and is so provided by art 9 of the Uniform Customs [1974 Revision; now UCP 2007 Revision, art 34], that confirming banks and issuing banks assume no liability or responsibility to one another or to the buyer 'for the form, sufficiency, accuracy, genuineness, falsification or legal effect of any documents.' This is well illustrated by the Privy Council case of *Gian Singh & Co Ltd v Banque de l'Indochine* [1974] 1 WLR 1234 [below, p 896], where the customer was held liable to reimburse the issuing bank for honouring a documentary credit upon presentation of an apparently conforming document which was an ingenious forgery, a fact that the bank had not been negligent in failing to detect upon examination of the document.

It would be strange from the commercial point of view, although not theoretically impossible in law, if the contractual duty owed by confirming and issuing banks to the buyer to honour the credit on presentation of apparently conforming documents despite the fact that they contain inaccuracies or even are forged, were not matched by a corresponding contractual liability of the confirming bank to the seller/beneficiary (in the absence, of course, of any fraud on his part) to pay the sum stipulated in the credit upon presentation of apparently conforming documents. Yet, as is conceded by counsel for the confirming bank in the instant case, if the broad proposition for which he argues is correct, the contractual duties do not match. As respects the confirming bank's contractual duty to the seller to honour the credit, the bank, it is submitted, is only bound to pay upon presentation of documents which not only appear on their face to be in accordance with the terms and conditions of the credit but also do not in fact contain any material statement that is inaccurate. If this submission be correct, the bank's contractual right to refuse to honour the documentary credit cannot, as a matter of legal analysis, depend upon whether *at the time of the refusal* the bank was virtually certain from information obtained by means other than reasonably careful examination of the documents themselves that they contained some material statement that was inaccurate or whether the bank merely suspected this or even had no suspicion that apparently conforming documents contained any inaccuracies at all. If there be any such right of refusal it must depend upon whether the bank, when sued by the seller/beneficiary for breach of its contract to honour the credit, is able to prove that one of the documents did in fact contain what was a material misstatement.

It is conceded that to justify refusal the misstatement must be 'material' but this invites the query: 'material to what?' The suggested answer to this query was: a misstatement of a fact which if the true fact had been disclosed would have entitled the buyer to reject the goods; date of shipment (as in the instant case) or misdescription of the goods are examples. But this is to destroy the autonomy of the documentary credit which is its raison d'être; it is to make the seller's right to payment by the confirming bank dependent upon the buyer's rights against the seller under the terms of the contract for the sale of goods, of which the confirming bank will have no knowledge.

Counsel sought to evade the difficulties disclosed by an analysis of the legal consequences of his broad proposition by praying in aid the practical consideration that a bank, desirous as it would be of protecting its reputation in the competitive business of providing documentary credits, would never exercise its right against a seller/beneficiary to refuse to honour the credit except in cases where at the time of the refusal it already was in possession of irrefutable evidence of the inaccuracy in the documents presented. I must confess that the argument that a seller should be content to rely upon the exercise by banks of business expediency, unbacked by any legal liability, to ensure prompt payment by a foreign buyer does not impress me; but the assumption that underlies reliance upon expediency does not, in my view, itself stand up to legal analysis. Business expediency would not induce the bank to pay the seller/beneficiary against presentation of documents which it was not legally liable to accept as complying with the documentary credit unless, in doing so, it acquired a right legally enforceable against the buyer, to require him to take up the documents himself and reimburse the bank for the amount paid. So any reliance upon business expediency to make the system work if the broad proposition contended for by counsel is correct, must involve that as against the buyer, the bank, when presented with apparently conforming documents by the seller, is legally entitled to the option, *exercisable at its own discretion and regardless of any instructions to the contrary from the buyer,* either (1) to take up the documents and pay the credit and claim reimbursement from the buyer, notwithstanding that the bank has been provided with information that makes it virtually certain that the existence of such inaccuracies can be proved, or (2) to reject the documents and to refuse to pay the credit.

The legal justification for the existence of such an independently exercisable option, it is suggested, lies in the bank's own interest in the goods to which the documents relate, as security for the advance made by the bank to the buyer, when it pays the seller under the documentary credit. But if this were so, the answer to the question: 'to what must the misstatement in the documents be material?' should be: 'material to the price which the goods to which the documents relate would fetch on sale if, failing reimbursement by the buyer, the bank should be driven to realise its security.' But this would not justify the confirming bank's refusal to honour the credit in the instant case; the realisable value on arrival at Callao of a glass fibre manufacturing plant made to the specification of the buyers could not be in any way affected by its having been loaded on board a ship at Felixstowe on December 16, instead of December 15, 1976 . . .

The proposition accepted by the Court of Appeal as constituting a complete defence available to the confirming bank on the documentary credit point has been referred to as a 'half-way house' because it lies not only halfway between the unqualified liability of the confirming bank to honour a documentary credit on presentation of documents which upon reasonably careful examination appear to conform to the terms and conditions of the credit, and what I have referred to as the fraud exception to this unqualified liability which is available to the confirming bank where the seller/beneficiary presents to the confirming bank documents that contain, expressly or by implication, material representations of fact that to his own knowledge are untrue; but it also lies half way between the fraud exception and the broad proposition favoured by the confirming bank with which I have hitherto been dealing. The half-way house is erected upon the narrower proposition that if any of the documents presented under the credit by the seller/beneficiary contain a material misrepresentation of fact that was *false to the knowledge of the person who issued the document* and intended by him to deceive persons into whose hands the document might come, the confirming bank is under no liability to honour the credit, even though, as in the instant case, the persons whom the issuer of the document intended to, and did, deceive included the seller/beneficiary himself.

My Lords, if the broad proposition for which the confirming bank has argued is unacceptable for the reasons that I have already discussed, what rational ground can there be for drawing any distinction between apparently conforming documents that, unknown to the seller, in fact contain a statement of fact that is inaccurate where the inaccuracy was due to inadvertence by the maker of the document, and the like documents where the same inaccuracy had been inserted by the maker of the document with intent to deceive, among others, the seller/beneficiary himself? Ex hypothesi we are dealing only with a case in which the seller/beneficiary claiming under the credit *has* been deceived, for if he presented documents to the confirming bank with knowledge that this apparent conformity with the terms and conditions of the credit was due to the fact that the documents told a lie, the seller/benefici-ary would himself be a party to the misrepresentation made to the confirming bank by the lie in the documents and the case would come within the fraud exception, as did all the American cases referred to as persuasive authority in the judgments of the Court of Appeal in the instant case.

The American cases refer indifferently to documents that are 'forged or fraudulent,' as does the Uniform Commercial Code that has been adopted in nearly all states of the United States of America. The Court of Appeal reached their half-way house in the instant case by starting from the premiss that a confirming bank could refuse to pay against a document that it knew to be forged, even though the seller/beneficiary had no knowledge of that fact. From this premiss they reasoned that if forgery by a third party relieves the confirming bank of liability to pay the seller/beneficiary, fraud by a third party ought to have the same consequence.

I would not wish to be taken as accepting that the premiss as to forged documents is correct, even where the fact that the document is forged deprives it of all legal effect and makes it a nullity, and so worthless to the confirming bank as security for its advances to the buyer. This is certainly not so under the Uniform Commercial Code as against a person who has taken a draft drawn under the credit in circumstances that would make him a holder in due course, and I see no reason why, and there is noth-ing in the Uniform Commercial Code to suggest that a seller/beneficiary who is ignorant of the forgery should be in any worse position because he has not negotiated the draft before presentation. I would prefer to leave open the question of the rights of an innocent seller/beneficiary against the confirming bank when a document presented by him is a nullity because unknown to him it was forged by some third party; for that question does not arise in the instant case. The bill of lading with the wrong date of loading placed on it by the carrier's agent was far from being a nullity. It was a valid transferable receipt for the goods giving the holder a right to claim them at their destination, Callao, and was evidence of the terms of the contract under which they were being carried.

But even assuming the correctness of the Court of Appeal's premiss as respects forgery by a third party of a kind that makes a document a nullity for which at least a rational case can be made out, to say that this leads to the conclusion that fraud by a third party which does not render the document a nullity has the same consequence appears to me, with respect, to be a non sequitur, and I am not persuaded by the reasoning in any of the judgments of the Court of Appeal that it is not.

Upon the documentary credit point I think that Mocatta J was right in deciding it in favour of the sellers and that the Court of Appeal were wrong in reversing him on this point.

[That part of Lord Diplock's opinion dealing with the Bretton Woods point is set out below, p 880.]

[Lords Fraser of Tullybelton, Russell of Killowen, Scarman and Bridge of Harwich concurred.]

In *United City Merchants*, the bill of lading in question contained a false statement but that did not affect the essential validity of the document. It remained a valid transferable receipt for the goods giving the holder a right to claim them at their destination. But what if an innocent seller tenders a document that is a 'nullity' in the sense that it was forged or executed without the authority of the person by whom it purports to be issued? Although Lord Diplock left the issue open in the *United City Merchants* case, it has recently been addressed by the Court of Appeal.

Montrod Ltd v Grundkötter Fleischvertriebs GmbH
[2001] EWCA Civ 1954, [2002] 1 All ER (Comm) 257, Court of Appeal

The underlying contract was a contract of sale of goods (pork) made between a German seller (GK) and a Russian buyer. The letter of credit, opened by the issuing bank (SBC) in favour of the seller, provided for payment of drafts 45 days after presentation of documents. One of the documents to be presented under the credit was an inspection certificate signed by the applicant for the credit (Montrod), a finance company employed by the buyer to facilitate the purchase. This was a device to ensure that Montrod was put in funds by the buyer before it incurred liability as applicant under the credit. However, the fraudulent buyer informed the seller that it should sign the inspection certificate on behalf of Montrod. The seller, honestly believing that it had Montrod's authority to sign the certificate, did so and presented the duly signed certificate under the credit. The pork was delivered to the buyer in Moscow. Between the date of presentation and the date of payment, it became clear that Montrod had not given its authority for the seller to sign the certificate. Montrod disputed the seller's right to payment and the issuing bank's right to reimbursement on the ground that the certificate was a 'nullity'. The first instance judge (reported at [2001] 1 All ER (Comm) 368) held that the seller, whom he found to be innocent of the fraud, was entitled to payment under the credit, and that the issuing bank was entitled to reimbursement from Montrod. The Court of Appeal upheld the decision.

Potter LJ: ...

[56] I consider that the judge was correct in the decision to which he came. The fraud exception to the autonomy principle recognised in English law has hitherto been restricted to, and it is in my view desirable that it should remain based upon, the fraud or knowledge of fraud on the part of the beneficiary or other party seeking payment under and in accordance with the terms of the letter of credit. It should not be avoided or extended by the argument that a document presented, which conforms on its face with the terms of the letter of the credit, is none the less of a character which disentitles the person making the demand to payment because it is fraudulent *in itself* independently of the knowledge and bona fides of the demanding party. In my view, that is the clear import of Lord Diplock's observations in *Gian Singh* [1974] 1 WLR 1234 (below, p 896) and in the *United City Merchants* case [1983] 1 AC 168 (above), in which all their Lordships concurred. As I understand it, Lord Diplock was of the view that a seller/beneficiary who was ignorant of forgery by a third party of one of the documents presented, or of the fact that the document contained a representation false to the knowledge of the person who created it, should not be in a worse position than someone who has taken a draft drawn under a letter of credit in circumstances which rendered him a holder in due course. While he left open the position in relation to a forged document where the effect of the forgery was to render the document a 'nullity', there is nothing to suggest that he would have recognised any nullity exception as extending to a document which was not forged (ie fraudulently produced) but was signed by the creator in honest error as to his authority; nor do I consider that such an exception should be recognised.

[57] That being so, I do not consider that the fact that in this case it was the seller/beneficiary himself who created the document said to be a nullity should *of itself* disentitle him to payment, assuming (as the judge found) that such creation was devoid of any fraudulent intent and was effected in the belief that GK enjoyed the authority of Montrod, as applicant for the credit, to sign and issue the certificate. Although the circumstances were highly unusual, they may none the less be regarded as no more than an illustration of the wide variety of circumstances in which documents come into existence in a commercial context which do not necessarily reflect the factual situation but which parties may none the less employ as a convenient means of progressing a particular transaction. If, in the circumstances of a multipartite transaction, a seller/beneficiary is indeed led to believe that he has authority to create and present a certificate of inspection for the purpose of triggering payment by letter of credit, I do not see why he should be regarded as any less entitled to payment in accordance with UCP 500 than in a case where he receives from a third party a document regular on its face which has, unknown to him, been created without authority.

[58] In my view there are sound policy reasons for not extending the law by creation of a general nullity exception. Most documentary credits issued in the United Kingdom incorporate the UCP by reference. Various revisions of the UCP have been widely adopted in the USA and by United Kingdom and Commonwealth banks. They are intended to embody international banking practice and to create certainty in an area of law where the need for precision and certainty are paramount. The creation of a general nullity exception, the formulation of which does not seem to me susceptible of precision, involves making undesirable inroads into the principles of autonomy and negotiability universally recognised in relation to letter of credit transactions. In the context of the fraud exception, the courts have made clear how difficult it is to invoke the exception and have been at pains to point out that banks deal in documents and questions of apparent conformity. In that context they have made clear that it is not for a bank to make its own enquiries about allegations of fraud brought to its notice; if a party wishes to establish that a demand is fraudulent it must place before the bank evidence of clear and obvious fraud (see the *Edward Owen Engineering Ltd* case cf *Turkiye Is Bankasi AS v Bank of China* [1996] 2 Lloyd's Rep 611 at 617 per Waller J). If a general nullity exception were to be introduced as part of English law it would place banks in a further dilemma as to the necessity to investigate facts, which they are not competent to do and from which UCP 500 is plainly concerned to exempt them. Further, such an exception would be likely to act unfairly upon beneficiaries participating in a chain of contracts in cases where their good faith is not in question. Such a development would thus undermine the system of financing international trade by means of documentary credits.

[59] I have concluded that there is and should be no general nullity exception based upon the concept of a document being fraudulent *in itself* or devoid of commercial value. I would only add, with reference to Lord Diplock's reservation, that I would not seek to exclude the possibility that, in an individual case, the conduct of a beneficiary in connection with the creation and/or presentation of a document forged by a third party might, though itself not amounting to fraud, be of such character as not to deserve the protection available to a holder in due course. In this connection, I note the reference by Mocatta J in the *United City Merchants* case to 'personal fraud' or 'unscrupulous conduct' on the part of the seller presenting documents for payment, a remark upon which Lord Diplock made no adverse comment when approving the original judgment on the documentary credit point. In this connection, we have had brought to our attention the decision of the High Court of Singapore in *Lambias (Importers and Exporters) Co Pte Ltd v Hong Kong & Shanghai Banking Corp* (1993) 2 SLR 751, in which the defendant bank rejected documents tendered under a letter of credit which included a quality and weight inspection certificate required to be countersigned by a named individual. The court held that the certificate contained discrepancies which entitled the bank to refuse the documents tendered and went on to find that the inspection certificate was in any event a nullity in that, not only did it fail to state the particulars of the goods and their quality and weight, but that, having been issued by the beneficiary instead of the applicant, it had been countersigned by an impostor. Having considered the observations, and in particular the reservation, of Lord Diplock in the *United City Merchants* case and the particular facts before the court in relation to the plaintiffs, who had themselves introduced the countersignatory to the bank as the person named, the court observed:

> 'The law cannot condone actions which, although not amounting to fraud per se, are of such recklessness and haste that the documents produced as a result are clearly not in conformity with the requirements of the credit. The plaintiffs in the present case are not guilty of fraud, but they were unknowingly responsible for having aided in the perpetration of the fraud. In such a case, where the fraud was discovered even before all other documents were tendered, I think it is right and proper that the plaintiffs should not be permitted to claim under the letter of credit.'

[60] While such a finding was not necessary to the outcome of the case, it fell within the reservation of Lord Diplock in the United City Merchants case and has certain attractions. However, it is not necessary for ut to decide in this case whether it is correct. This is a case where the judge found neither recklessness, haste, nor blame in the conduct of GK. Furthermore, in the Lambias case the bank rejected the documents as non-compliant, whereas in this case SCB accepted the documents as compliant, having raised Montrod's observations and reservations with Fibi before it did so. Fibi in turn accepted the documents when sent to them, making clear to Montrod that payment would be made unless a court order to prevent it were obtained.

[61] In those circumstances, I consider that GK were entitled to payment and I would affirm the decision of the judge.

Sir Martin Nourse:

[81] I agree with the judgment of Potter LJ and with the orders proposed by him.

Thorpe LJ:

[82] I agree.

NOTES

1. It seems, therefore, that presentation to the bank of a forged or unauthorised document is to be treated in exactly the same way as presentation of a genuine document containing false information. In both cases the seller is entitled to payment under the credit unless he knew of the fraud at the time of presentation of the document to the bank (*Group Josi Re v Walbrook Insurance Co Ltd* [1996] 1 WLR 1152 at 1161, per Staughton LJ, 'it is the time of presentation that is crucial.'). Nevertheless, it remains a cause of some unease that the seller, however innocent himself, becomes entitled to payment through tender of a document that carries a deliberately false shipping date, when tender of a document giving the true shipping date could have been rejected as discrepant (as in *United City Merchants*), or though tender of a document that was, in effect, a worthless piece of waste paper (as in *Montrod*). Both decisions have been strongly criticised: see R M Goode 'Abstract Payment Undertakings', Ch 9 of P Cane and J Stapleton (eds) *Essays for Patrick Atiyah* (1991), pp 228–233 (on *United City Merchants*) and R Hooley [2002] CLJ 279 (on *Montrod*).

2. A nullity exception has been recognised in Singapore.

Beam Technology (MFG) PTE Ltd v Standard Chartered Bank
[2003] 1 SLR 597, Court of Appeal (Singapore)

The appellant sellers contracted to sell electronic components to buyers who obtained a letter of credit from their bank in favour of the sellers. The respondent bank was the confirming bank of the credit. Under the terms of the credit, a clean air waybill was needed to draw on the credit. The buyers notified the sellers that the air waybill would be issued by their freight forwarders, 'Link Express (S) Pte Ltd'. When the sellers presented the documents required to draw on the credit, the confirming bank rejected the documents on the ground that the air waybill was a forgery because 'Link Express (S) Pte Ltd' did not exist. The bank applied to the court for a determination of the question of law whether it was entitled to refuse to make payment when the air waybill was a forgery known to the bank. For the purposes of the application it was agreed that the sellers were not privy to the forgery.

Chao JA (delivering the judgment of the court):

[31] In summary, the current position of the law would appear to be this. The House of Lords in *United City Merchants* had left open the question whether there is a nullity exception although at the Court of Appeal all the three members of the quorum thought there was. In *Montrod*, the Court of Appeal (of a different quorum) was inclined to the view that, apart from the traditional fraud exception (ie fraud or knowledge of fraud on the part of the beneficiary or other party seeking payment), there was no separate nullity exception. In any case, even if there was such a nullity exception, it held that the certificate issued by the seller in *Montrod* in honest belief that he had the authority of the applicant of the letter of credit could not be a nullity. Perhaps another way of differentiating *Montrod* from the present case is that there the certificate required was not an essential document but one touching on the question as to the quality of the goods sold. In short, there is no definite authority on point, although the views of the Court of Appeal in *United City Merchants* are no doubt highly persuasive.

[32] It seems to us that the issue must be approached on first principles. It is clear that the obligation of the issuing/confirming bank towards the beneficiary is independent and separate from the contractual obligations between the seller and the buyer, and the obligation to pay is absolute irrespective of any dispute that may arise between the seller and the buyer. As far as the confirming or negotiating bank is concerned, their duty is only to verify whether what appears on the documents conforms with what is required by the credit. If there is prima facie compliance, the bank is authorised to pay and may claim reimbursement from the issuing bank notwithstanding that a document tendered may subsequently turn out to be a forgery: *Gian Singh*. This is to protect the bank and to ensure the smooth flow of international trade and the avoidance of delay. But we are unable to see why such a rule should also lead to the result that if the confirming or negotiating bank, from whatever source, is able to establish within the prescribed seven-day limit that a material document tendered is a forgery, being null and void, the bank is, nevertheless, obliged to pay.

[33] While the underlying principle is that the negotiating/confirming bank need not investigate the documents tendered, it is altogether a different proposition to say that the bank should ignore what is clearly a null and void document and proceed nevertheless to pay. Implicit in the requirement of a conforming document is the assumption that the document is true and genuine although under the UCP 500 and common law, and in the interest of international trade, the bank is not required to look beyond what appears on the surface of the documents. But to say that a bank, in the face of a forged null and void document (even though the beneficiary is not privy to that forgery), must still pay on the credit, defies reason and good sense. It amounts to saying that the scheme of things under the UCP 500 is only concerned with commas and full stops or some misdescriptions, and that the question as to the genuineness or otherwise of a material document, which was the cause for the issue of the LC, is of no consequence.

[34] As the judge below observed, UCP 500 does not provide that a bank is obliged to accept a document which is a nullity notwithstanding that the time prescribed under art 14 for the bank to reject the document has not expired. Thus the nullity exception which we postulate is a limited one and would not have given rise to the sort of problems which Potter LJ had expressed concern (at 274):

> If a general nullity exception were to be introduced as part of English law it would place banks in a further dilemma as to the necessity to investigate facts which they are not competent to do and from which UCP 500 is plainly concerned to exempt them.

We are not in any way suggesting that the bank is obliged to investigate into any document tendered. The nullity exception would only permit a bank to refuse payment if it is satisfied that a material document is a nullity.

[35] Here, we would like to refer to the following comments of Professor R M Goode in an article in Centre Point entitled 'Reflections on Letters of Credit–1', where he, in discussing the position of the bona fide plaintiff, said:

> Is a plaintiff who seeks to enforce a letter of credit affected by forgery of the documents or other fraud in the transaction if he himself acted in good faith? There is a remarkable dearth of authority on this question. Let us start with the beneficiary. He himself has a duty to tendering forged documents which are in order, and the fact that he acted in good faith in tendering forged documents is thus irrelevant. This fundamental point appears to have been overlooked by Mr Justice Mocatta in *The American Accord* when he held that the beneficiary was entitled to collect payment despite the insertion of a fraudulent shipping date on the bill of lading, since the fraud had been committed by the loading broker who was the agent of the carrier, not of the seller/beneficiary. But this, with

respect, is not to the point. The beneficiary under a credit is not like a holder in due course of a bill of exchange; he is only entitled to be paid if the documents are in order. A fraudulently completed bill of lading does not become a conforming document merely because the fraud is that of a third party.

[36] It is our opinion that the negotiating/confirming bank is not obliged to pay if it has established within the seven-day period that a material document required under the credit is forged and null and void and notice of it is given within that period. While we recognise that there could be difficulties in determining under what circumstances a document would be considered material or a nullity, such a question can only be answered on the facts of each case. One cannot generalise. It is not possible to define when is a document a nullity. But it is really not that much more difficult to answer such questions than to determine what is reasonable, an exercise which the courts are all too familiar with.

Fraud in the underlying transaction

The fraud in the *United City Merchants* case was documentary fraud, ie fraud in relation to the tendered documents. Does the fraud exception apply where the documents presented are truthful but there is fraud in the underlying transaction? There is no English authority that expressly decides the point (although the much criticised majority decision of the Court of Appeal in *Themehelp Ltd v West* [1996] QB 84 lends support to an extension of the fraud exception to fraud in the underlying transaction). By contrast, s 5–109(a) of revised art 5 of the US Uniform Commercial Code refers to 'material fraud by the beneficiary on the issuer or the applicant' (the phrase 'fraud in the transaction' was expressly used in s 5–114 of the original version of art 5). The Supreme Court of Canada has also endorsed the wider scope of the exception. In *Bank of Nova Scotia v Angelica-Whitewear Ltd* [1987] 1 SCR 59 at 83, Le Dain J expressly referred to dicta of Lord Denning in *Edward Owen Engineering Ltd v Barclays Bank Ltd* [1978] QB 159—'the request for payment is made fraudulently in circumstances when there is no right to payment'—as suggesting that it was not intended to limit the fraud exception to documentary fraud. Extending the fraud exception to fraud in the underlying transaction is consistent with Lord Diplock's view that 'fraud unravels all', ie the court will not permit a beneficiary to obtain payment in reliance on his own wrongdoing. As the authors of one of the leading textbooks on documentary credits observe: 'it would be odd if the bank were obliged to pay an obviously fraudulent beneficiary only because fraud did not manifest itself in false documents' (R Jack, A Malek and D Quest *Documentary Credits* (3rd edn, 2001), para 9.24). On the other hand, Professor Dolan, a leading US commentator, warns against the courts engaging in a wide-ranging fraud inquiry which would undermine the independence of letters of credit (JF Dolan, 'Tethering the Fraud Inquiry in Letter of Credit Law' (2006) 21 BFLR 479, 489–490). He calls on the courts to be sure the applicant's allegations involve the beneficiary's attempt to take the proceeds of a credit when he has no honest belief in his right to them, and refuse to elevate underlying contract disputes into letter of credit fraud disputes (p 502).

Established fraud and the bank's right of reimbursement

Where the fraudulent conduct of the beneficiary or other person presenting the documents is clear and obvious to the bank, then the bank should not pay against the documents and it will not be entitled to reimbursement from the applicant or other instructing party. As Rix J said in *Czarnikow-Rionda Sugar Trading Inc v Standard Bank London Ltd* [1999] 1 All ER (Comm) 890 at 914: 'I do not see how payment in the face of fraud can be a mere matter of discretion by a bank: it must be either within its mandate or not, and either a matter of obligation or not'. If the bank refuses to pay, it must be able to prove at the subsequent trial of the action that there was fraud on the part of the seller at the time of presentation of the documents. It is not enough for the bank to refuse to pay on the ground that it had evidence from which a reasonable banker would think that there had been fraud of the seller, whether or not fraud actually existed in fact (*Society of Lloyd's v Canadian Imperial Bank of Canada* [1993] 2 Lloyd's Rep 579 at 581). Where the bank pays, and the buyer later disputes its right to reimbursement on the ground that the fraud was clear and obvious to the bank, the buyer must prove either that the bank was actually aware of the fraud (eg where the beneficiary admits it), or else reckless, in that the only realistic inference to be drawn by the bank was that the demand was fraudulently made (see *Turkiye Is Bankasi AS v Bank of China* [1996] 2 Lloyd's Rep 611; affd [1998] 1 Lloyd's Rep 250, CA).

Injunctions

Usually the bank when faced with clear evidence of fraud will invite the buyer to apply to the court for an injunction. To maintain the status quo until the trial the buyer will seek an interlocutory injunction. This may be obtained against the bank to restrain it from honouring the credit or against the seller to prohibit presentation of documents for payment or negotiation of the drafts (although where the bank has accepted a draft drawn by the seller, and the draft has already been negotiated to a holder in due course, the bank must pay at maturity: *Discount Records Ltd v Barclays Bank Ltd* [1975] 1 All ER 1071). In practice it is notoriously difficult for a buyer to prevent payment of an irrevocable credit on grounds of fraud as the courts have shown a marked reluctance to interfere with the smooth running of the system of documentary credits. As Sir John Donaldson MR stated in *Bolivinter Oil SA v Chase Manhattan Bank* [1984] 1 Lloyd's Rep 251 at 257:

The wholly exceptional case where an injunction may be granted is where it is proved that the bank knows that any demand for payment already made or which may thereafter be made will clearly be fraudulent. But the evidence must be clear, both as to the fact of fraud and as to the bank's knowledge. It would certainly not normally be sufficient that this rests upon the uncorroborated statement of the customer, for irreparable damage can be done to a bank's credit in the relatively brief time which must elapse between the granting of such an injunction and an application by the bank to have it discharged.

It may be argued that an injunction against the beneficiary prohibiting him from making a call on the credit does not interfere with the operations of international commerce and that, in consequence, a mere allegation of fraud on the part of the beneficiary ought to be enough for the court to grant injunctive relief. Although this approach found favour with a majority of the Court of Appeal in *Themehelp Ltd v West* [1996] QB 84 (a performance bond case), it was soundly condemned by Staughton LJ (*obiter*) in *Group Josi Re v Walbrook Insurance Co Ltd* [1996] 1 WLR 1152 at 1161–1162 and by Rix J in *Czarnikow-Rionda Sugar Trading Inc v Standard Bank London Ltd* [1999] 1 All ER (Comm) 890 at 913). An injunction restraining a beneficiary from making a call on the credit should be granted only to the extent that the facts justify the granting of an injunction against the bank restraining payment (see further, A Mugasha, 'Enjoining the Beneficiary's Claim on a Letter of Credit or Bank Guarantee' [2004] JBL 515).

According to *American Cyanimid v Ethicon Ltd* [1975] AC 396, an applicant for an interlocutory injunction must establish that: (a) he has a seriously arguable claim against the party he is seeking to restrain, and (b) the balance of convenience is in favour of the grant of an injunction. Moreover, by reason of *The Siskina* [1979] AC 210, an injunction can only be granted in aid of a substantive cause of action against the person to be restrained. The buyer seeking to restrain a bank from paying under a documentary credit, or his seller from calling on the credit, will rarely be able to meet all these requirements and his application for an interlocutory injunction will usually fail.

First, the buyer will have to establish a substantive cause of action against the person to be restrained (*Czarnikow-Rionda Sugar Trading Inc v Standard Bank London Ltd* [1999] 1 All ER (Comm) 890 at 914; cf *Group Josi Re v Walbrook Insurance Co Ltd* [1996] 1 WLR 1152 at 1160). The problem is where the bank to be restrained is the confirming bank as there is no contractual relation between the applicant for a credit and the confirming bank, and the chances of establishing a duty of care in tort are slim on the current state of the authorities. By contrast, the applicant has a contract with the issuing bank, and an injunction to restrain the issuing bank from paying by itself or its agents should prevent payment by an advising bank that has not confirm the credit because it acts as the issuing bank's agent. Secondly, the burden of proof of fraud is high, even at the interlocutory stage. The generally accepted test was set out by Ackner LJ in *United Trading Corpn SA v Allied Arab Bank Ltd* [1985] 2 Lloyd's Rep 554n at 561:

We would expect the court to require strong corroborative evidence of the allegation, usually in the form of contemporary documents, particularly those emanating from the buyer. In general, for the evidence of fraud to be clear, we would also expect the buyer to have been given an opportunity to answer the allegation and to have failed to provide any, or any adequate answer in circumstances where one could properly be expected. If the Court considers that on the material before it the only realistic inference to draw is that of fraud, then the seller would have made out a sufficient case of fraud.

Thirdly, in documentary credit disputes the balance of convenience is usually against the granting of an injunction, for if the injunction is granted the bank may suffer damage to its reputation if fraud is not proved at trial, whilst if the injunction is refused, and fraud is later proved at trial, the applicant will suffer no loss as the bank's claim against him for reimbursement will fail. Only in the most exceptional circumstances will the balance of convenience favour the grant of an injunction (*Czarnikow-Rionda Sugar Trading Inc v Standard Bank London Ltd,* above, at 916, per Rix J).

Freezing orders

A buyer unable to prevent payment of the credit on grounds of fraud may still be able to obtain an order to restrain the seller from removing the proceeds of the credit from the jurisdiction or otherwise dealing with them within the jurisdiction (called a freezing order, although formerly referred to as a *Mareva* injunction). The order catches the proceeds of the credit as and when received by the seller. It does not prevent payment under the credit, and so the buyer does not have to bring himself within the fraud exception. In exceptional circumstances, a court may grant a worldwide freezing order, but it is unlikely that an English court would grant an order affecting money paid under a documentary credit by a bank abroad (R Jack, A Malek and D Quest *Documentary Credits* (3rd edn, 2001), para 9.65). In appropriate cases the court may combine a freezing order with an ancillary order requiring the proceeds of the credit to be paid into court (*Themehelp Ltd v West* [1996] QB 84 at 103, per Evans LJ). But where the credit is to be paid abroad, it would be an unjustified interference with the operation of the credit to order the bank to pay the money into an account in England (*Britten Norman Ltd v State Ownership Fund of Romania* [2000] 1 Lloyd's Rep Bank 315).

QUESTIONS

1.   In *Montrod Ltd v Grundkötter Fleischvertriebs GmbH* [2001] EWCA Civ 1954, [2002] 1 All ER (Comm) 257, Potter LJ considered that there were 'sound policy reasons' for rejecting a general nullity exception to the autonomy of the credit. What were those reasons? Are they sound? Do they also undermine Potter LJ's tentative (*obiter*) suggestion that a non-fraudulent

beneficiary might be refused payment on tender of apparently conforming documents where he acts recklessly, in haste or is otherwise blameworthy?

2.   Why is it so difficult for a buyer who suspects fraud on the part of the seller to obtain an injunction to restrain the bank from paying the seller under the terms of a documentary credit?

(iv) Autonomy and illegality

A documentary credit may itself be illegal where its issue is prohibited or because of some supervening prohibition. This does not affect the autonomy principle because the credit is illegal in itself rather than because of illegality in the underlying transaction. There is also a growing body of English case law in favour of an illegality exception to the autonomy principle where there is illegality in the underlying transaction which *taints* the documentary credit transaction. This is a true exception to the autonomy principle because the illegality is in the underlying transaction and not in the documentary credit transaction itself. See generally, N Enonchong, 'The autonomy principle of letters of credit: an illegality exception?' [2006] LMCLQ 404.

United City Merchants (Investments) Ltd v Royal Bank of Canada, The American Accord
[1983] 1 AC 168, House of Lords

[The facts appear above, p 868.]

Lord Diplock: The Bretton Woods point arises out of the agreement between the buyers and the seller collateral to the contract of sale of the goods between the same parties that out of the payments in US dollars received by the sellers under the documentary credit in respect of each instalment of the invoice price of the goods, they would transmit to the account of the buyers in America one half of the US dollars received.

   The Bretton Woods Agreements Order in Council 1946, made under the Bretton Woods Agreements Act 1945, gives the force of law in England to art VIII s 2(b) of the Bretton Woods Agreement, which is in the following terms:

> Exchange contracts which involve the currency of any member and which are contrary to the exchange control regulations of that member maintained or imposed consistently with this agreement shall be unenforceable in the territories of any member...

My Lords, I accept as correct the narrow interpretation that was placed upon the expression 'exchange contracts' in this provision of the Bretton Woods Agreement by the Court of Appeal in *Wilson, Smithett & Cope Ltd v Terruzzi* [1976] QB 683. It is confined to contracts to exchange the currency of one country for the currency of another; it does not include contracts entered into in connection with sales of goods which require the conversion by the buyer of one currency into another in order to enable him to pay the purchase price. As was said by Lord Denning MR in his judgment in the *Terruzzi* case at p 714, the court in considering the application of the provision should look at the substance of the contracts and not at the form. It should not enforce a contract that is a mere 'monetary transaction in disguise.'

   I also accept as accurate what was said by Lord Denning MR in a subsequent case as to the effect that should be given by English courts to the word 'unenforceable.' The case, *Batra v Ebrahim*, is unreported, but the relevant passage from Lord Denning's judgment is helpfully cited by Ackner LJ in his own judgment in the instant case: [1982] QB 208, 241F–242B. If in the course of the hearing of an action the court becomes aware that the contract on which a party is suing is one that this country has accepted an international obligation to treat as unenforceable, the court must take the point itself, even though the defendant has not pleaded it, and must refuse to lend its aid to enforce the contract. But this does not have the effect of making an exchange contract that is contrary to the exchange control regulations of a member state other than the United Kingdom into a contract that is 'illegal' under English law or render acts undertaken in this country in performance of such a contract unlawful. Like a contract of guarantee of which there is no note or memorandum in writing it is unenforceable by the courts and nothing more.

Mocatta J, professing to follow the guidance given in the *Terruzzi* case [1976] QB 683, took the view that the contract of sale between the buyers and the sellers at the inflated invoice price was a monetary transaction in disguise and that despite the autonomous character of the contract between the sellers and the confirming bank under the documentary credit, this too was tarred with the same brush and was a monetary transaction in disguise and therefore one which the court should not enforce. He rejected out of hand what he described as a 'rather remarkable submission' that the sellers could recover that half of the invoice price which represented the true sale price of the goods, even if they could not recover that other half of the invoice price which they would receive as trustees for the buyers on trust to transmit it to the buyer's American company in Florida. He held that it was impossible to sever the contract constituted by the documentary credit; it was either enforceable in full or not at all.

In refusing to treat the sellers' claim under the documentary credit for that part of the invoice price that they were to retain for themselves as the sale price of the goods in a different way from that in which he treated their claim to that part of the invoice price which they would receive as trustees for the buyers, I agree with all three members of the Court of Appeal the learned judge fell into error.

I avoid speaking of 'severability,' for this expression is appropriate where the task upon which the court is engaged is construing the language that the parties have used in a written contract. The question whether and to what extent a contract is unenforceable under the Bretton Woods Agreement Order in Council 1946 because it is a monetary transaction in disguise is *not* a question of construction of the contract, but a question of the substance of the transaction to which enforcement of the contract will give effect. If the matter were to be determined simply as a question of construction, the contract between the sellers and the confirming bank constituted by the documentary credit fell altogether outside the Bretton Woods Agreement; it was not a contract to exchange one currency for another currency but a contract to pay currency for documents which included documents of title to goods. On the contrary, the task on which the court is engaged is to penetrate any disguise presented by the actual words the parties have used, to identify any monetary transaction (in the narrow sense of that expression as used in the *Terruzzi* case [1976] QB 683) which those words were intended to conceal and to refuse to enforce the contract to the extent that to do so would give effect to the monetary transaction.

In the instant case there is no difficulty in identifying the monetary transaction that was sought to be concealed by the actual words used in the documentary credit and in the underlying contract of sale. It was to exchange Peruvian currency provided by the buyers in Peru for US \$331,043 to be made available to them in Florida; and to do this was contrary to the exchange control regulations of Peru. Payment under the documentary credit by the confirming bank to the sellers of that half of the invoice price (viz \$331,043) that the sellers would receive as trustees for the buyers on trust to remit it to the account of the buyer's American company in Florida, was an essential part of that monetary transaction and therefore unenforceable; but payment of the other half of the invoice price and of the freight was not; the sellers would receive that part of the payment under the documentary credit on their own behalf and retain it as the genuine purchase price of goods sold by them to the buyers. I agree with the Court of Appeal that there is nothing in the Bretton Woods Agreements Order in Council 1946 that prevents the payment under the documentary credit being enforceable to this extent.

[Lords Fraser of Tullybelton, Russell of Killowen, Scarman and Bridge of Harwich concurred.]

Group Jose Re v Walbrook Insurance Co Ltd
[1996] 1 WLR 1152, Court of Appeal

The plaintiff reinsurers entered into a number of reinsurance contracts with the defendant insurance companies (referred to as 'the stamp companies'), who acted through their agent ('Weavers'). To ensure that the stamp companies paid all their premiums over to the plaintiffs, and did not retain any part of them as a reserve against claims, the plaintiffs opened letters of credit in favour of the stamp companies, which provided for payment on presentation of debit notes stating that the plaintiffs were liable for the amounts in question under the reinsurance contracts. Later the plaintiffs claimed that the reinsurance contracts were void because of their own illegality in carrying on an insurance business without statutory authorisation and applied for injunctions restraining the stamp companies and their agent from presenting documents for payment under the letters of credit. The Court of Appeal (Staughton, Rose and Saville LJJ) held that performance of the reinsurance contracts by the reinsurers was not illegal and refused to grant the injunctions. Staughton LJ alone considered what would have been the effect of illegality of the reinsurance contracts on the letters of credit.

Staughton LJ:
Can a letter of credit be affected by illegality of the underlying transaction?
The reinsurers put their case in this way: (i) the underlying reinsurance contracts were illegal; (ii) directly or by way of taint, this rendered the letter of credit contracts illegal or at least unenforceable; (iii) therefore it would be fraudulent for the stamp companies and Weavers to claim payment under the letters of credit.

That seems to me unnecessarily complicated. Surely one can stop after stage (ii), without bringing fraud into it. I say that because in my judgment illegality is a separate ground for nonpayment under a letter of credit. That may seem a bold assertion, when Lord Diplock in the *United City Merchants* case [1983] 1 AC 168,183 said that there was *'one* established exception.' But in that very case the House of Lords declined to enforce a letter of credit contract in part for another reason, that is to say the exchange control regulations of Peru as applied by the Bretton Woods Agreements Order in Council 1945 (SR & O 1946 No 36). I agree that the Bretton Woods point may well have been of a kind of its own, and not an indication that illegality generally is a defence under a letter of credit. But it does perhaps show that established fraud is not necessarily the only exception.

It seems to me that there must be cases when illegality can affect a letter of credit. Take for example a contract for the sale of arms to Iraq, at a time when such a sale is illegal. The contract provides for the opening of a letter of credit, to operate on presentation of a bill of lading for 1,000 Kalashnikov rifles to be carried to the port of Basra. I do not suppose that a court would give judgment for the beneficiary against the bank in such a case. Would illegality, like fraud, have to be clearly established and known to the bank before it could operate as a defence, or a ground for restraining payment by the bank? That is not an altogether easy question, but I am inclined to think that it would. If the legality of the payment is merely doubtful, it may be that the bank would not be restrained. But whether in a *United City Merchants* type of case, if illegality were clearly proved at trial, it would be a defence that it was not clear at the time when the documents were presented for payment is even more of a problem.

Turning to the present case, if the reinsurance contracts are illegal, and if the letters of credit are being used as a means of paying sums due under those contracts, and if all that is clearly established, would the court restrain the bank from making payment or the beneficiary from demanding it? In my judgment the court would do so. That would not be because the letter of credit contracts were themselves illegal, but because they were being used to carry out an illegal transaction. I hesitate to enter upon a discussion of what is turpis causa, or what is taint. Since *Tinsley v Milligan* [1994] 1 AC 340 the two categories of turpis causa that I identified and the Court of Appeal upheld in *Euro-Diam Ltd v Bathurst* [1990] 1 QB 1 no longer survive. The public conscience test is gone, and one is left (I suppose) with the *Bowmakers* principle (*Bowmakers Ltd v Barnet Instruments Ltd* [1945] KB 65): the defence succeeds if 'the plaintiff seeks to, or is forced to, found his claim on an illegal contract or to plead its illegality in order to support his claim' (Kerr LJ [1990] 1 QB 1, 35).

That is what the stamp companies and Weavers would have to do in this case, if the contracts of insurance are illegal. In order to operate the letters of credit they must present a debit note to the bank. That debit note must be one 'covering the liability for outstanding loss reserves under your umbrella quota share facilities.' In my opinion, and Mr Rokinson does not dispute this, it must say so in terms. On this hypothesis they would be founding on an illegal contract, that is the contract of reinsurance.

Mr Rokison argues that whatever was due to be paid under the reinsurance contracts has already been paid—by the opening of the letter of credit. In one sense that is true; *WJ Alan & Co Ltd v El Nasr Export and Import Co* [1972] 2 QB 189 decided that the opening of a letter of credit, like the giving of a cheque, was or could be conditional payment of money due under a contract, so that nothing remained due from the debtor unless and until the letter of credit or the cheque failed. But that does nothing whatever to convince me that the obligation of the bank to pay under the letters of credit is altogether free of taint from any obligation of the reinsurers which it superseded.

NOTE

Clarke J, deciding the same case at first instance ([1996] 1 Lloyd's Rep 345), held that the letters of credit were not void or unenforceable. His reasoning ran as follows (p 352): (i) the letter of credit represented a contract separate from the underlying reinsurance contract; (ii) the opening of the letter of credit was conditional payment under the reinsurance contract; (iii) in presenting the documents to the bank the stamp companies would not be carrying on the business of insurance prohibited by the statute and nor would the bank in paying under the letters of credit; and (iv) nor would the stamp companies and the bank be aiding and abetting the carrying on by the reinsurers of unauthorised insurance business. As can be seen from the final paragraph of the extract taken from Court of Appeal's decision, Staughton LJ expressly rejected Clarke J's reasoning. However, Colman J returned to the issue in the next case.

Mahonia Ltd v JP Morgan Chase Bank
[2003] EWHC 1927 (Comm), [2003] 2 Lloyd's Rep 911

Mahonia Ltd ('Mahonia'), JP Morgan Chase Bank ('Chase') and Enron North America Corporation ('ENAC'), a subsidiary of Enron Corporation, entered into three swap transactions. Under these arrangements US$350 million was paid by Chase to Mahonia and the same sum from Mahonia to ENAC. Six months later ENAC was to pay Chase US$355.9 million. The overall effect of the circularity of these three swaps was that ENAC was to receive the use of US$350 million for six months and that Chase was to be paid by ENAC an additional US$5.9 million. In order to secure its exposure, Chase required ENAC to procure the issue of standby letters of credit by way of security. One such credit in the amount of US$165 million was provided by the London branch of West LB AG ('the Bank').

Following ENAC's filing for Chapter 11 (a US insolvency procedure), the swap arrangements fell into default and Chase made demand upon the Bank under the letter of credit. The Bank declined to pay on grounds of illegality. The substance of the Bank's case on illegality was that (1) the swaps were a 'cosmetic' device to provide Enron with a loan of US$350 million from Chase that Enron did not have to record in its accounts as a debt, and (2) the omission to show the loan in Enron's accounts was contrary to US securities law and was intended to defraud. On this basis, so the Bank argued, the letter of credit for US$165 million was rendered illegal and/or was unenforceable on grounds of public policy.

Colman J dismissed the claimant's application to strike out the illegality defence and for summary judgment in respect of that defence. He stated that the letter of credit was created for the purpose of forming part of the basis of transactions (the swaps) which were illegal under US law because they had an illegal purpose. The judge held that it did not make any difference that the purpose was unlawful, not under English law, but under the law of a friendly foreign state. He also held that it made no difference that the illegal purpose was known only to the claimant and not to the Bank until long after the demand for payment had been presented.

Colman J:

[63] In order to investigate the enforceability of the letter of credit it is first necessary to identify what function it had in relation to the assumed illegal purpose of the three swaps. That function was to provide security to Chase in case the planned circulation of funds was interrupted by the failure of ENAC to pay Mahonia, the beneficiary under the letter of credit. If ENAC failed to pay Mahonia, then the money would not get back to Chase and the circularity which was an essential feature of the structure of the overall transaction would be broken, with the source of the funding (Chase) remaining out of its money.

[64] The transaction is therefore similar in many ways to one in which the underlying contract is illegal to the knowledge of both parties and therefore unenforceable by either and where one of the parties to it procures an innocent third party to provide to the other a bond which pays against a certificate that the underlying contract has not been performed. Leaving aside the additional feature of a letter of credit, the authorities.... support the proposition that the innocent third party could rely by way of defence on the underlying illegality. The position would be no different if the underlying contract were legal on its face but entered into for an illegal purpose or if the underlying contract were illegal because it required the carrying out of an act in the United States which was unlawful there or was for the purpose of the carrying out of such an act. Does it make any difference that the security was provided by means of a documentary letter of credit confirmed by a bank innocent of the illegality of the underlying transaction, but which has clear evidence of that illegality at the time when it ought otherwise to pay?

[65] As appears from the authorities discussed earlier in this judgment, the impregnability of letters of credit is a consequence of the need to insulate them from the transaction in relation to which they have been utilized as security. That is because they have a special function in international trade which requires that their integrity and irrevocability should not be interfered with unless an ex turpi causa defence can be clearly proved by the bank, as for example in a case of fraud such as to be found in *Sztejn v. J. Henry Schroder Banking Corporation* (1941) 31 NYS 2d 631. As a matter of public policy the Courts will not permit their process to be used to obtain the benefit of an unlawful act. In such a case the policy of the law in withholding its process from the enforcement of benefits derived from an unlawful act displaces the otherwise impregnable nature of the letter of credit. Does that policy extend to a case like the present where the unlawfulness consists not in a fraud on the bank but in the purpose for which the letter of credit has been procured?

[66] I am bound to say that I have found the reasoning of Mr. Justice Clark in the *Group Josi* case...strongly persuasive resting, as it does, on the insulation of the opening and negotiation of the letter of credit from the unlawful carrying on of insurance business. He was able to distinguish between conduct prohibited by the legislation and conduct collateral to that unlawful conduct. Only the latter would have to be relied upon in order to enforce the letters of credit. In that case however the letters of credit were not an integral part of the unlawful conduct. They were simply a facility provided

subsequently to the entering into of the illegal contracts which assisted performance in a manner not specifically rendered illegal. Where, however, the letter of credit plays from the outset an integral part in the illegal transaction, there is, as I see it, a very different situation, when its comes to enforcement for the Court's process is then deployed for the purpose of giving effect to an essential part of the illegal scheme.

[67] Although in *United City Merchants,* sup, Lord Diplock expressly stated that the underlying sale contract and letters of credit were not rendered *illegal* by the Bretton Woods Order in Council, the underlying sale contract was certainly *prohibited* and thereby rendered unenforceable. However, the conclusion that the letter of credit was also rendered unenforceable was derived from the proper construction of the Order in Council which required the Court to go behind contracts which on their proper construction, when taken in isolation, were not exchange contracts but which were a disguise for a prohibited monetary transaction. Accordingly, that case is an example of a letter of credit which because of its cosmetic purpose was directly rendered unenforceable by legislation. Unlike Lord Justice Staughton I therefore am unable to derive from that case any very significant assistance on this point.

[68] However, there is a real conflict between on the one hand the well-established principle that contracts lawful on their face which are entered into in furtherance of an illegal purpose will be unenforceable at the suit of the party having knowledge of that purpose at the time of contracting and on the other hand the policy of the law reflected in all the letter of credit cases of preserving the impregnability of the letter of credit save where the bank has clear evidence of an ex turpi causa defence such as fraud. This conflict is not, in my judgment, a matter which can be resolved simply by postulating the separate nature of the letter of credit and applying reasoning similar to that in the *Bowmakers* case. Thus, like Lord Justice Staughton in *Group Josi,* I find it almost incredible that a party to an unlawful arms transaction would be permitted to enforce a letter of credit which was an integral part of that transaction even if the relevant legislation did not on its proper construction render ancillary contracts illegal. To take an even more extreme example, I cannot believe that any Court would enforce a letter of credit to secure payment for the sale and purchase of heroin between foreign locations in which such underlying contracts were illegal. On the other hand, there is much to be said for the view that the public policy in superseding the impregnability of letters of credit where there is an unlawful underlying transaction defence may not be engaged where the nature of the underlying illegal purpose is relatively trivial, at least where the purpose is to be accomplished in a foreign jurisdiction. The problems which arise from attempting to reconcile conflicting considerations of public policy may well give rise to uncertain consequences, as illustrated in relation to the finality of New York Convention arbitration awards in *Westacre Investments Inc. v. Jugoimport-SDPR Holding Co.,* [1999] Q.B. 740. It would, however, be wrong in principle to invest letters of credit with a rigid inflexibility in the face of strong countervailing public policy considerations. If a beneficiary should as a matter of public policy (ex turpi causa) be precluded from utilizing a letter of credit to benefit from his own fraud, it is hard to see why he should be permitted to use the courts to enforce part of an underlying transaction which would have been unenforceable on grounds of its illegality if no letter of credit had been involved, however serious the material illegality involved. To prevent him doing so in an appropriately serious case such as one involving international crime could hardly be seen as a threat to the lifeblood of international commerce.

[69] In the present case, I have therefore come to the conclusion that on the assumed facts there is at least a strongly arguable case that the letter of credit cannot be permitted to be enforced against the defendant bank. That represents at the very least a realistic prospect of success for the bank's defence based on this point. Furthermore, the conclusion as to whether enforcement is permissible at least arguably depends on the gravity of the illegality alleged. Although on the pleaded case that appears to be considerable, the uncertainty of this area of law is such that this is an issue which ought to be determined by reference to the evidence before the court at trial and not merely on assumptions derived from the pleaded defence. Moreover, I have also concluded, as I have sought to explain, that the fact that the bank did not have clear evidence of such illegality at the date when payment had to be made would not prevent it having a good defence on that basis if such clear evidence were to hand when the Court was called upon to decide the issue. For this purpose I proceed on the basis that it now has sufficiently clear evidence as expressed in the pleading.

[70] Accordingly, the claimant's application to strike out the illegality defence and for summary judgment in respect of that defence will be dismissed.

NOTES

1.   These proceedings involved an application to strike out a defence and for summary judgment. Due to the interlocutory nature of the application, the court proceeded on the basis that the factual matters asserted by the defendant bank were true. At the full trial of the action, Cooke J held that there was no illegality which affected the transaction ([2004] EWHC 1938 (Comm)). However, Cooke J added (obiter, at [432]), expressly following the reasoning of Colman J, that the autonomy of a documentary credit does not prevent it being tainted with illegality of the underlying transaction.

2.   Charles Proctor considers that the illegal objectives alleged to be at issue in the *Mahonia* case fell within the fraud exception because those activities were designed to mislead the investing public (see 'Enron, Letters of Credit and the Autonomy Principle' [2004] JIBFL 204, 207):

'The *Mahonia* decision does, however, break new ground ... In virtually every case in which the fraud exception had previously been pleaded, the arrangements included either fraud against the issuing bank itself or, more usually, against the seller/applicant for the credit. In contrast, *Mahonia* involved a fraud against the financial and securities markets and the investing public generally.'

Proctor makes the point that the fraud was not committed against ENAC because it was party to the fraud. He also argues that the Bank was only a target of the fraud in a very marginal way. He continues:

'In this respect, it may be argued that *Mahonia* has broadened the fraud exception, in the sense that a fraud may fall within the principle even though it is perpetrated against the public as a whole, rather than merely as against a party to the credit. Nevertheless, the ultimate decision seems to be entirely consistent with ... the principle *"ex turpi causa"*.'

Do you agree?

3.   As well as cases of fraud and (to a lesser extent) illegality, there are other circumstances when the court will allow the bank to withhold payment to the beneficiary under the credit after conforming documents have been tendered. These circumstances arise when:

- the credit is procured by misrepresentation of the beneficiary enabling the bank to rescind the credit *ab initio* (*SAFA Ltd v Banque Du Caire* [2000] 2 All ER (Comm) 567, CA): misrepresentation by the applicant for the credit would not vitiate the credit, but if the misrepresentation was fraudulent, and the beneficiary was an accomplice to that fraud, so that there was a conspiracy between them, the bank can refuse payment (*Solo Industries UK Ltd v Canara Bank* [2001] EWCA Civ 1059, [2001] 2 All ER (Comm) 217);

- there is a fundamental mistake which renders the credit void *ab initio*, eg where the credit is issued to the wrong person who is aware of the mistake;

- the bank's duty to pay is frustrated or suspended through supervening illegality or governmental action;

- the bank may set off against the sum due to the beneficiary a liquidated sum due from the beneficiary to the bank (*Hongkong and Shanghai Banking Corpn v Kloeckner & Co*

AG [1990] 2 QB 514) the bank may also have a right of set-off against an assignee of the proceeds of the credit, so long as the liquidated sum due to the bank from the assignee, which the bank seeks to set off against the proceeds of the credit, accrued before notice of assignment was received by the bank (*Marathon Electrical Manufacturing Corpn v Mashreqbank* PSC [1997] CLC 1090).

These circumstances are considered further by Professor Goode in 'Abstract Payment Undertakings', Ch 9 of P Crane and J Stapleton (eds) *Essays for Patrick Atiyah* (1991), pp 225–234.

(f) The contracts arising out of a documentary credit transaction

Earlier in this chapter we listed the contractual relationships arising out of a confirmed irrevocable documentary credit transaction (see above, p 850). Each contract will now be examined in detail.

(i) *The contract of sale*

The credit to comply with the contract of sale

The buyer must ensure the credit is issued in the form prescribed by the contract of sale.

Garcia v Page & Co Ltd
(1936) 55 Ll L Rep 391, King's Bench Division

By a contract dated 27 May 1935, Page & Co sold 2,000 tons of ammonium sulphate to Garcia in Spain, shipment to be during the first half of September 1935. The contract required Garcia 'to open immediately a confirmed credit in London' in favour of Page & Co. There was considerable delay before the credit was opened. On 22 August Page & Co wrote to Garcia stating that if the credit was not received in London by 24 August the contract would be cancelled. The credit was opened on 24 August but not notified to Page & Co until 26 August. Further, the credit did not comply with that provided for in the contract of sale. Page & Co repudiated the contract. A satisfactory credit was opened on 3 September but Page & Co maintained their repudiation. The dispute came before Porter J on a case stated from the arbitrator.

   During the course of counsels' submissions, Porter J stated that he was satisfied that the provision with regard to the opening of the credit was a condition precedent in the sense that the sellers would not ship unless it was arranged.

Porter J (when giving judgment): …In my view, under the original contract there was a contract by which a confirmed credit in the terms specified was a condition precedent, and it had to be opened immediately. That means that the buyer must have such time as is needed by a person of reasonable diligence to get that credit established. I cannot myself believe that to get that credit established a reasonable time would be from May 27 until Aug 22 or Aug 27—whichever date you like to take. But just as I think that that was a condition precedent, so I think it is open to either of the parties, with the consent of the other, to prolong the time; and once you have put an end to the reasonable or particular time you have to allow another reasonable time from the moment you say: 'Now I demand you to fulfil that condition.'

To me it is clear, as at present advised, that up to Aug 22 the sellers were not demanding that the stipulation with regard to the confirmed credit should be immediately fulfilled. On the other hand, they were constantly urging that the matter should be taken in hand and I think making it quite plain that the step ought to be taken as speedily as possible. Then, on Aug 22, they did demand that the matter should be put in hand by the 24th. Whether Aug 24 was a reasonable time does not matter for this purpose. Starting from Aug 22, the buyer ought to have a reasonable time, having regard to all the circumstances of the case, to fulfil it.

To decide whether he had may involve a certain amount of evidence, which the arbitrator may take, of surrounding facts and circumstances—such as the difficulty Spaniards have in creating credits in this country by a particular date. I am not particularly impressed, though it is a matter for the arbitrator, with the difficulties, because some sort of credit was established by Aug 26. However, that is a matter to be taken into account. I think that is all the arbitrator has to find.

I say that because it has been urged upon me that I should take into consideration the fact that when the proper credit was finally established, three days of the time the sellers had for shipment had already elapsed. That is quite true, but I do not think that that seriously helps the case, because the delay that took place up to Aug 22 was with their consent; and if with their consent there were two or three days lost it would be part of their consent that that delay should take place.

For these reasons, I think the case should go back to the arbitrator in order that he may determine whether after Aug 22 the buyer had a reasonable time; and, as I say, the costs will be reserved.

Glencore Grain Rotterdam B V v Lebanese Organisation for International Commerce

[1997] 4 All ER 514, Court of Appeal

The plaintiff sellers concluded a fob contract for the sale of wheat to the defendant buyers, by which the latter had to make payment by an irrevocable letter of credit. The credit opened, however, required tender of documents including a full set of marine bills of lading marked 'freight pre-paid'. The sellers rejected the credit and refused to load the wheat. The Court of Appeal held that the sellers were entitled to do so as the buyers had breached the contract of sale by failing to open a letter of credit conforming with the sale contract.

Evans LJ: The issue, therefore, is whether the buyers under a sale contract on what are described as normal fob terms are entitled to open a letter of credit which requires the sellers to present 'freight pre-paid' bills of lading if they are to receive payment from the buyers' bank. Absent any special agreement, the sellers are entitled to see a conforming letter of credit in place before they begin shipment of the goods, and then their obligation is to ship the contract goods on board the vessel provided by the buyers, for carriage on whatever terms as to freight and otherwise the buyers have agreed with the shipowner. The sellers are expressly free of any obligation to pay freight (special terms apart, fob is the antithesis of c and f—cost and freight) and in the normal course they cannot be sure before shipment that the shipowner will issue freight pre-paid bills of lading, unless they are prepared if necessary to pay the amount of freight themselves, or unless some other guaranteed payment mechanism is already in place. I would put the matter broadly in that way, because it may be that an undertaking from the shipowner himself, or a third party guarantee of the payment of freight following due shipment of the goods, would suffice. It is unnecessary to consider that aspect further in the present case, because all that was offered by the buyers was their own assurance that the freight would be paid, by them or on their behalf. It is abundantly clear, in my judgment, that the buyers' own assurance cannot be enough to serve as a guarantee to the sellers that 'freight pre-paid' bills of lading will be issued when shipment is complete. That would mean, as the judge pointed out, that the security of a bank guarantee for the payment of the price, which is what the letter of credit mechanism provides, would be destroyed. I therefore agree with the judge's observations that the buyers' contention, that the letter of credit terms were in conformity with the contract, is contrary both to the underlying concept of the fob contract (subject always to what special terms may be agreed in a particular case) and to the essential commercial purpose of the letter of credit machinery.

The buyers' submission is that there were special features which entitled the board to reach the conclusion that the buyers were entitled to require freight pre-paid bills in this case. In my judgment, the board's conclusion that the buyers were so entitled 'provided that they did indeed ensure that such freight was paid by the completion of loading' is open to the objections set out by the judge. More generally, Mr Havelock-Allan [Counsel for the buyers] refers to certain specific facts. The sellers knew that Hoboob, the receivers and sub-buyers, had bought on c and f terms and themselves required freight pre-paid bills. The named vessel was time-chartered to the buyers, and so they were entitled to instruct the master to issue 'freight pre-paid' bills (see *Federal Commerce and Navigation Ltd v Molena Alpha Inc, The Nanfri, The Benfri, The Lorfri* [1979] 1 All ER 307, [1979] AC 757). The buyers gave their assurance (though not until 29 March, after the dispute had arisen) that the freight would be paid before the bills were issued 'without any problem'. But none of this, in my judgment, justifies the implication of a term which, for the reasons stated above, would be wholly at variance with the express terms of the fob sale in fact agreed.

In this context, the buyers referred to the judgment of Robert Goff J in *Ficom SA v Sociedad Cadex Ltda* [1980] 2 Lloyd's Rep 118 at 131, which was quoted by the judge. This judgment distinguishes between implying a term in the sale contract and, on the other hand, establishing what the parties agreed should be the terms of the letter of credit issued or to be issued under that contract. The latter process may result in a letter of credit agreement which supplements or even varies the terms originally agreed. This is demonstrated in the present case by the agreement to vary the shipment date to include the month of April. But I do not consider that it is relevant to the question in issue. The freight pre-paid requirement, unless it was a term of the sale contract itself, was introduced by the buyers and immediately rejected by the sellers. The buyers maintained their requirement on 29 March and it is of the essence of their case that the sellers made no further reference to it before the contract came to an end. The sellers thereafter did not act inconsistently with their previous refusal, and their silence on this matter cannot be regarded as an acceptance of the buyer's demand: *Allied Marine Transport Ltd v Vale do Rio Doce Navegacao SA, The Leonidas D* [1985] 2 All ER 796 at 805, [1985] 1 WLR 925 at 936–937 per Robert Goff LJ. In short, the buyers cannot allege that there was a fresh agreement as regards this term of the letter of credit which had the effect either of supplementing or varying the requirements of the sale contract.

For these reasons, as well as those given more succinctly by Longmore J, in my judgment the buyers were not entitled to require the sellers to procure and produce freight pre-paid bills of lading in order to receive payment under the letter of credit opened by them. It follows that the buyers failed to open a letter of credit conforming with the sale contract and, subject to the question of waiver considered below, they were thereby in breach of contract.

[Nourse LJ and Sir Ralph Gibson concurred.]

NOTES

1. *Garcia v Page & Co Ltd* illustrates that the buyer's obligation to have a documentary credit opened in favour of the seller is usually a condition precedent to the seller's obligation to deliver the goods (cf M Clarke [1974] CLJ 260, pp 264–269). Provision of the documentary credit is a condition precedent to any obligation on the part of the seller to perform any aspect of the loading operation which is the seller's responsibility (*Kronos Worldwide Ltd v Sempra Oil Trading Sarl* [2004] EWCA Civ 3, [2004] CLC 136 at [19], per Mance LJ). But the opening of the credit may be construed as a condition precedent to the contract of sale itself (*Trans Trust SPRL v Danubian Trading Co Ltd* [1952] 2 QB 297 at 304, CA), or the contract of sale may impose an obligation on the seller which is a condition precedent to the opening of the credit (*Knotz v Fairclough Dodd and Jones Ltd* [1952] 1 Lloyd's Rep 226).

2.   If the buyer opens a credit which does not comply with the terms of the contract of sale, he may remedy the defect if there is still time before the credit is required (*Kronman & Co v Steinberger* (1922) 10 Ll L Rep 39 at 40, per Greer J). But if the buyer fails to open the credit in time, or does not remedy a defective credit in time, he commits a repudiatory breach which entitles the seller to treat the contract of sale as discharged (*Dix v Grainger* (1922) 10 Ll L Rep 496 at 496–497, per Bailhache J) and claim damages for breach of contract (on the basis of *Hadley v Baxendale* (1854) 9 Exch 341, 156 ER 145). The seller will be able to claim damages for loss of profit on the transaction if, at the time the contract was made, such loss was within the reasonable contemplation of the parties as the probable consequence of the breach (*Trans Trust SPRL v Danubian Trading Co Ltd,* above; *Ian Stach Ltd v Baker Bosley Ltd* [1958] 2 QB 130 at 145).

3.   The seller may decide to ship the goods despite the buyer's failure to open the credit on the due date or in its specified form. In *Panoutsos v Raymond Hadley Corpn of New York* [1917] 2 KB 473, a series of shipments of flour was to be paid for by confirmed bankers' credit. The buyer opened an unconfirmed credit. The sellers knew of this defect but still made some shipments before repudiating the contract. The Court of Appeal held that the non-conformity of the credit had been waived by the sellers and that the waiver could only be revoked if reasonable notice was given to the buyer (at 477–478). But in other cases the seller may be deemed to have agreed to a variation of the contract thus preventing him from changing his mind, even on reasonable notice. Variation, unlike waiver, will only be valid if supported by consideration. Identifying whether a contractual requirement has been waived or varied may prove difficult and will depend on the circumstances of each case. See, for example, *W J Alan & Co Ltd v El Nasr Export and Import Co* [1972] 2 QB 189, where Lord Denning MR decided the case on grounds of waiver of the seller's strict rights under the contract, whereas Megaw and Stephenson LJJ decided it on grounds of variation of the contract. The case is exhaustively examined by M Clarke [1974] CLJ 260.

The time of opening of the credit

Where the contract of sale provides a date for the opening of the credit, the buyer must open the credit by that date. If the contract of sale stipulates that the credit must be opened 'immediately', the buyer has such time as is needed by a person of reasonable diligence to open such a credit (*Garcia v Page & Co Ltd,* above, p 887). But what if no time is stipulated?

Pavia & Co SpA v Thurmann-Nielsen

[1952] 2 QB 84, Court of Appeal

A cif contract for the sale of shelled Brazilian groundnuts provided for payment by confirmed irrevocable credit and for shipment in the period from 1 February to 30 April 1949 at the sellers' option. The buyers did not open the credit until 22 April. The sellers claimed damages for breach of contract by delay in opening the credit. Affirming the decision of McNair J, the Court of Appeal upheld the sellers' claim.

Somervell LJ: . . . Speaking for myself, I would have no doubt, apart from any question arising with regard to export licences, that under this contract the obligation of the buyers was prima facie to open the credit on February 1 and to have it opened and available as from that date . . . .

The argument, which was very clearly put by Mr Widgery [counsel for the buyers], was on these lines: Normally, delivery and payment are concurrent conditions. You do not really need the credit until you are ready to deliver and have got your bills of lading, when you can go round to the bank and get your money. That is the object of it, to see that the seller can get immediate payment. He read to us, as he read to the learned judge below, certain cases in which Scrutton LJ pointed out (as, of course, I accept) that the main object of the credit system is that the seller may get his money when he has shipped his goods and, at any rate, in some forms of credit the buyer gets an interval of time before he has to meet bills. Whether under this particular form of credit there would be any interval of time between the time of its operation and the time when the buyer had to put his bank in credit I do not know, and to my mind it does not matter. I am quite clear that Scrutton LJ was not addressing himself to the problem which is at present before us. My view is that the contract would be unworkable if, as suggested by Mr Widgery, the buyer under it was under no obligation until a date, which he could not possibly know, and which there is no machinery for his finding out, namely, when the seller actually has the goods down at the port ready to be put on to the ship. There are no words in the contract which would justify us in arriving at that result and there is no reason why we should imply any such term into this contract. I do not think it is a question of implication. I think when a seller is given a right to ship over a period and there is machinery for payment, that machinery must be available over the whole of that period. If the buyer is anxious, as he might be if the period of shipment is a long one, not to have to put the credit machinery in motion until shortly before the seller is likely to want to ship, then he must put in some provision by which the credit shall be provided 14 days after a cable received from the seller, or the like. In the absence of any provision of that kind, I think the answer which the judge gave to the question posed is plainly right, and the appeal should be dismissed.

Denning LJ: The question in this case is this: In a contract which provides for payment by confirmed credit, when must the buyer open the credit? In the absence of express stipulation, I think the credit must be made available to the seller at the beginning of the shipment period. The reason is because the seller is entitled, before he ships the goods, to be assured that, on shipment, he will get paid. The seller is not bound to tell the buyer the precise date when he is going to ship; and whenever he does ship the goods, he must be able to draw on the credit. He may ship on the very first day of the shipment period. If, therefore, the buyer is to fulfil his obligations he must make the credit available to the seller at the very first date when the goods may be lawfully shipped in compliance with the contract. I agree with the answer given by McNair J. The appeal should be dismissed.

[Roxburgh J concurred.]

NOTES

1.   In *Sinason-Teicher Inter-American Grain Corpn v Oilcakes and Oilseeds Trading Co Ltd* [1954] 1 WLR 1394, a cif contract for the sale of barley provided for shipment during October-November 1952. The buyers agreed to give the sellers a guarantee that the bank would take up the shipping documents on first presentation. The contract did not stipulate a time when the buyers should give the guarantee but when the buyers had failed to provide it by 10 September the sellers cancelled the contract. Affirming the decision of Devlin J, the Court of Appeal held that the sellers had been wrong to cancel the contract as the buyers had not been in default at that time. In an *obiter dictum* Denning LJ stated (at 1400):

We were referred to *Pavia & Co SpA v Thurmann-Nielsen*. I agree with what Devlin J said about that case. It does not decide that the buyer can delay right up to the first date for shipment. It only decides that he must provide the letter of credit at latest by that date. The correct view is that, if nothing is said about time in the contract, the buyer must provide the letter of credit within a reasonable time before the first date for shipment. The same applies to a bank guarantee: for it stands on a similar footing.

2.   In *Ian Stach Ltd v Baker Bosley Ltd* [1958] 2 QB 130, an fob contract for the sale of steel plates provided for payment by confirmed irrevocable credit and for shipment during August-September 1956 at the buyers' option. The buyers failed to open the credit by 1 August and Diplock J held them to be in breach of contract. It was argued that as the buyer stipulates the shipping date under a 'classic fob contract' (see above, p 494), the credit need only be opened a reasonable time before the date of shipment fixed by the buyer. Diplock J rejected that argument on grounds of uncertainty and held that the prima facie rule was that credit must be opened at the latest by the earliest shipping date. Diplock J observed (at 141) that Denning LJ's statement in the *Sinason-Teicher* case, that the credit must be provided a reasonable time before the first date for shipment, was *obiter* and that the other Lord Justices in that case did not express any view on the matter. Diplock J did not expressly adopt Denning LJ's formulation, but he did not dissent from it either. In fact there is much to be said in favour of Denning LJ's approach, for a shipper cannot be expected to make instantaneous shipping arrangements, and if he does not receive the credit until the day before the start of the shipment period he is likely to lose the benefit of the first few days of that period (see RM Goode *Commercial Law* (3rd edn, 2004), p 980, n 142).

3.   If the contract of sale specifies a shipment date, and not a period of shipment, the buyer must open the credit a reasonable time before that date (*Plasticmoda SpA v Davidsons (Manchester) Ltd* [1952] 1 Lloyd's Rep 527 at 538, per Denning LJ).

4.   A documentary credit becomes irrevocable upon issue; that is, upon its release from the control of the issuing bank or confirming bank, irrespective of the time that it is delivered to or received by the beneficiary (UCP 600, arts 7(b) and 8(b)). However, for the purpose of determining whether the buyer has complied with its obligations under the contract of sale, the credit may be considered to be 'opened' only when it is communicated to the beneficiary (*Bunge Corpn v Vegetable Vitamin Foods (Private) Ltd* [1985] 1 Lloyd's Rep 613 at 617, Neill J). In each case, it will be a question of construction of the contract concerned (R King, *Gutteridge and Megrah's Law of Bankers' Commercial Credits* (8th edn, 2001), para 4–48, n 132). The buyer will be liable for any delay in opening the credit, even if it was caused by circumstances beyond his control (*AE Lindsay & Co Ltd v Cook* [1953] 1 Lloyd's Rep 328 at 355, per Pilcher J).

QUESTION

Where an fob or cif contract does not specify the date by which the credit must be opened, but does specify a period of shipment, when must the buyer open the credit? Contrast Goode, above, p 980 and R Jack, A Malek and D Quest *Documentary Credits* (3rd edn, 2001), para 3.23.

Expiry date and place for presentation

UCP 600, art 6(d)(i) provides that a credit must state an expiry date for presentation and that an expiry date stated for honour or negotiation will be deemed to be an expiry date for presentation. A presentation by or on behalf of the beneficiary must be made on or before the expiry date (art 6(e)). Article 6(d)(ii) provides that the place of the bank with which the credit is available is the place for presentation (and that the place for presentation under a credit available with any bank is that of any bank). A place for presentation other than that of the issuing bank is in addition to the place of the issuing bank. Further, UCP 600, art 14(c) provides that a presentation including one or more original transport documents must be made by or on behalf of the beneficiary not later than 21 days after the date of shipment (but in any event not later than the expiry date of the credit).

The expiry date of the credit or the last day for presentation of documents may be extended by the operation of UCP 600, art 29, which applies where a time limit would otherwise expire on a day on which the bank to which presentation is to be made is closed (other than for reasons specified in art 36, eg Acts of God, riots, civil commotions etc). Article 29(a) extends the time limit to the next succeeding day on which the bank is open. Under sub-art 29(b), a bank which accepts documents on the next succeeding banking day must provide a statement that the documents were presented within the time limits extended under art 29(a). In *Bayerische Vereinsbank Aktiengesellschaft v National Bank of Pakistan* [1997] 1 Lloyd's Rep 59, a confirming bank, which had accepted documents on the next succeeding banking day, failed to supply the issuing bank with the necessary statement. Mance J held that presentation of the statement was not a condition precedent to the confirming bank's right of reimbursement, but that the confirming bank would be liable to pay damages to the issuing bank if the latter suffered any resultant loss (eg where omission of the statement caused delay in payment of the issuing bank by the buyer).

The credit as payment

Unless otherwise agreed, payment by documentary credit constitutes conditional payment of the price. As Lord Denning MR stated (obiter) in *WJ Alan & Co Ltd v El Nasr Export and Import Co* [1972] 2 QB 189 at 212:

…I am of the opinion that in the ordinary way, when the contract of sale stipulates for payment to be made by confirmed irrevocable letter of credit, then, when the letter of credit is issued and accepted by the seller, it operates as conditional payment of the price. It does not operate as absolute payment.

It is analogous to the case where, under a contract of sale, the buyer gives a bill of exchange or a cheque for the price. It is presumed to be given, not as absolute payment, nor as collateral security, but as conditional payment. If the letter of credit is honoured by the bank when the documents are presented to it, the debt is discharged. If it is not honoured, the debt is not discharged: and the seller has a remedy in damages against both banker and buyer.

For reasons supporting this view, see M Clarke [1974] CLJ 260, pp 274–276. See also *ED & F Man Ltd v Nigerian Sweets & Confectionery Co Ltd* [1977] 2 Lloyd's Rep 50 at 56–57, per Ackner J; *Maran Road Saw Mill v Austin Taylor &. Co Ltd* [1975] 1 Lloyd's Rep 156 at 159–160, per Ackner J (noted (1977) 40 MLR 91); and *Re Charge Card Services Ltd* [1989] Ch 497 at 516 (above, p 818).

When the contract of sale specifies that payment is to be by documentary credit the seller must present the documents to the bank. He cannot 'short-circuit' the credit and present documents directly to the buyer and claim payment from him (*Soproma SpA v Marine & Animal By-Products Corpn* [1966] 1 Lloyd's Rep 367 at 385–386, McNair J). However, if the bank defaults, eg by becoming insolvent, the seller can normally claim payment from the buyer by tendering documents directly to him (*Soproma*, at 386). This stems from the fact that in most cases the credit only operates as conditional payment. As Ackner J said in *ED & F Man Ltd v Nigerian Sweets & Confectionery Co Ltd,* above, at 56: The [buyers'] liability to the sellers was a primary liability. This liability was suspended during the period available to the issuing bank to honour the drafts and was activated when the issuing bank failed.' Alternatively, the seller can sue the buyer for damages for breach of contract.

(ii) The contract between buyer and issuing bank

The issuing bank must adhere strictly to the terms of the buyer's instructions

The buyer will usually sign and complete the issuing bank's standard documentary credit application form, which usually incorporates the UCP. This constitutes an offer of a unilateral contract which the issuing bank accepts when it issues the credit. The application form sets out the buyer's instructions in relation to the credit. The issuing bank must adhere strictly to the terms of the buyer's instructions. This means that the issuing bank must ensure that the credit issued to the seller complies with the instructions set out in the application form and that payment, acceptance or negotiation is effected only on presentation of documents which comply with the terms of the credit. Only then will the issuing bank be entitled to reimbursement from the buyer. Where the buyer's instructions are ambiguous, the issuing bank will be entitled to be reimbursed if it construes them reasonably. The point is illustrated by the next case.

Midland Bank Ltd v Seymour
[1955] 2 Lloyd's Rep 147, Queen's Bench Division

Seymour contracted to purchase a large quantity of feathers from Hong Kong sellers. Payment was to be by confirmed irrevocable credit. The credit was issued by the Midland Bank after receiving instructions from Seymour given on the bank's pro forma application form. Seymour had instructed the bank to make the credit 'available in Hong Kong'. On presentation of the shipping documents, the Midland Bank accepted, and later paid, various bills of exchange drawn by the sellers. But the sellers were fraudulent and had shipped rubbish. Seymour refused to reimburse the bank, raising various defences to the bank's claim for payment. One defence was that the documents tendered did not conform to the credit as the bill of lading did not state the description, quantity and price of the goods (although such information was contained in other tendered documents, eg the invoice, which were consistent with the bill of lading). Another defence was that the bank had not complied with its mandate by issuing a credit which provided for acceptance of drafts in London instead of Hong Kong. Devlin J gave judgment for the bank on its claim.

Devlin J held that the sellers had presented conforming documents as the credit was to be construed as requiring the presentation of a set of documents which were consistent between themselves, and which, when read together, provided a statement of the description, quantity and price of the goods. He held that the credit did not require each individual document to provide such information.

Devlin J continued: But if I had not reached that conclusion . . . I should have arrived at the same result on another ground. In my judgment, no principle is better established than that when a banker or anyone else is given instructions or a mandate of this sort, they must be given to him with reasonable clearness. The banker is obliged to act upon them precisely. He may act at his peril if he disobeys them or does not conform with them. In those circumstances there is a corresponding duty cast on the giver of instructions to see that he puts them in a clear form. Perhaps it is putting it too high for this purpose to say that it is a duty cast upon him. The true view of the matter, I think, is that when an agent acts upon ambiguous instructions he is not in default if he can show that he adopted what was a reasonable meaning. It is not enough to say afterwards that if he had construed the documents properly he would on the whole have arrived at the conclusion that in an ambiguous document the meaning which he did not give to it could be better supported than the meaning which he did give to it. If I am wrong in adopting the construction that Mr Diplock gives to this document, I am quite clear that at the best it is ambiguous. It is impossible to say that the document specifies in reasonably clear terms that the bill of lading has to contain the description and quantity.

That argument is met to some extent by Mr Mocatta when he points out that the form which was filled up is not Mr Seymour's own form but is the bank's form; and he relies upon what I think may be called the *contra proferentes* principle on which a person who prepares a form is responsible for any ambiguities that it contains, or must suffer for it. In my judgment, that principle does not apply in this case. It applies (or would apply) if there were some exception, as for example in one of the conditions or clauses on the back of the document which was inserted for the benefit of the bank. If there were some exception there, no doubt the principle would apply.

But this is not a case of that type. This is a printed document which shows the sort of thing that the bank wants, but it is left to the applicant for the credit to fill it up in what way he wants; and if he thinks there is some ambiguity in it there is no difficulty, so far as I can see, in his filling it up in a way to make it clear. For example, if he wanted plainly to specify that the bill of lading should contain the full description, I cannot see that there would be any difficulty in his doing so, or that the bank could conceivably object if he did so. The bank do not care what the bill of lading is or is not required to contain. It cannot matter to them so long as they are told clearly what it is that they have to look for.

[On the issue whether the bank had exceeded its mandate Devlin J continued:]

I have not to determine whether the Midland Bank is in breach by failing to create facilities in Hongkong. If they did so fail, and if it was in breach, it has caused no damage, because the seller has never tried to make use of that. The point is whether the bank is authorized to pay or accept only in Hongkong. . . . If it was authorized so to pay, then although the place of payment may be commercially immaterial, the bank has exceeded its mandate and cannot recover. It is a hard law sometimes which deprives an agent of the right to reimbursement if he has exceeded his authority, even though the excess does not damage his principal's interests. The corollary, which I have already noted in the judgment I delivered earlier, is that the instruction to the agent must be clear and unambiguous.

The mandate to the bank in this case does not make the place of availability expressly exclusive, and I do not think it ought lightly to be assumed that it was intended to be expressly exclusive. Let me take a simple example, uncomplicated by a letter of credit. A, who does business in London, arranges that his debt to X at Edinburgh will be discharged by his agent B, whose place of business is also in London. If matters were left there, X would, in accordance with the ordinary rule, have to come to London to collect his money. But it might well be that A would tell his agent B that he was to travel to Edinburgh to pay X there. If he did, and if before B went to Edinburgh X happened to come to London and call for the money and B paid it, it would be a strong thing to say that B could not debit A. It would be held in such a case as that, I think, that the naming of Edinburgh was merely an additional convenience made for the benefit of X, if he wanted to take advantage of it. So here I think the naming of Hongkong is additional and not exclusive. If it were not named, the drafts would have to be presented at the Midland Bank's place of business in London. That might not be convenient to the seller, and so there is a request for additional facilities in the place where the seller does business... In my judgment, acceptance in London was within the terms of the mandate to the bank in this case.

NOTES

1. The reason for the rule relating to ambiguous or unclear instructions given by the buyer to his bank is best stated by Lord Diplock in *Commercial Banking Co of Sydney Ltd v Jalsard Pty Ltd* [1973] AC 279 at 286, PC:

The banker is not concerned as to whether the documents for which the buyer has stipulated serve any useful commercial purpose or as to why the customer called for tender of a document of a particular description. Both the issuing banker and his correspondent bank have to make quick decisions as to whether a document which has been tendered by the seller complies with the requirements of a credit at the risk of incurring liability to one or other of the parties to the transaction if the decision is wrong. Delay in deciding may in itself result in a breach of his contractual obligations to the buyer or to the seller. This is the reason for the rule that where the banker's instructions from his customer are ambiguous or unclear he commits no breach of his contract with the buyer if he has construed them in a reasonable sense, even though upon the closer consideration which can be given to questions of construction in an action in a court of law, it is possible to say that some other meaning is to be preferred.

2.   But the rule has its limits. In *European Asian Bank AG v Punjab and Sind Bank (No 2)* [1983] 1 WLR 642 at 656, Goff LJ said that 'a party relying on his own interpretation of the relevant document must have acted reasonably in all the circumstances in so doing. If instructions are given to an agent, it is understandable that he should expect to act on those instructions without more; but if, for example, the ambiguity is patent on the face of the document it may well be right (especially with the facilities of modern communication available to him) to have his instructions clarified by his principal, if time permits, before acting upon them'. See also, above, pp 113–114.

3.   In *European Asian Bank AG v Punjab and Sind Bank (No 2)*, above, Goff LJ pointed out that it was not strictly correct to refer to the issuing bank as the agent of the buyer, as Devlin J had done in *Midland Bank Ltd v Seymour*. Goff LJ was right, for the issuing bank does not contract with the seller on the buyer's behalf: the bank enters into a separate contract with the seller as principal. This does not alter the rule that the issuing bank, like an agent, is entitled to give ambiguous instructions a reasonable construction, but it does mean that it is probably more accurate to refer to the buyer's informed acceptance of an unauthorised act of the issuing bank (eg acceptance of non-conforming documents) as waiver of the bank's breach of mandate rather than as ratification of the act itself. The nature of the relationship between the issuing bank and the confirming bank, and the effect of ambiguous instructions passing between them, is considered below at p 899.

The issuing bank must examine the tendered documents to determine whether they appear on their face to constitute a complying presentation

Uniform Customs and Practice for Documentary Credits
(2007 Revision, ICC Publication No 600)

Article 14

Standard of Examination of Documents

a. A nominated bank acting on its nomination, a confirming bank, if any, and the issuing bank must examine a presentation to determine, on the basis of the documents alone, whether or not the documents appear on their face to constitute a complying presentation.

b. A nominated bank acting on its nomination, a confirming bank, if any, and the issuing bank shall each have a maximum of five banking days following the day of presentation to determine if a presentation is complying. This period is not curtailed or otherwise affected by the occurrence on or after the date of presentation of any expiry date or last day for presentation.

Gian Singh & Co Ltd v Banque de l'Indochine
[1974] 1 WLR 1234, Privy Council

Banque de l'Indochine opened an irrevocable documentary credit on the instructions of Gian Singh & Co Ltd (the customer) to finance the purchase of a fishing vessel. The credit required the tender of a certificate signed by Balwant Singh, holder of Malaysian Passport E-13276, certifying that the vessel had been correctly built and was in a condition to sail. The certificate was tendered but the signature of Balwant Singh was a forgery, as was the passport presented to the bank for inspection. The bank accepted the documents and debited its customer's account with the sum paid to the beneficiary. The customer sued the bank claiming that its account had been wrongly debited. The Court of Appeal in Singapore gave judgment for the bank. The Privy Council dismissed the customer's appeal against that decision.

Lord Diplock delivered the advice of the Privy Council (Lords Wilberforce, Diplock, Cross of Chelsea, and Kilbrandon and Sir Harry Gibbs): The fact that a document presented by the beneficiary under a documentary credit, which otherwise conforms to the requirements of the credit, is in fact a forgery does not, of itself, prevent the issuing bank from recovering from its customer money paid under the credit. The duty of the issuing bank, which it may perform either by itself, or by its agent, the notifying bank, is to examine documents with reasonable care to ascertain that they appear on their face to be in accordance with the terms and conditions of the credit. The express provision to this effect in article 7 of the Uniform Customs and Practice for Documentary Credits [1962 Revision] does no more than re-state the duty of the bank at common law. In business transactions financed by documentary credits banks must be able to act promptly on presentation of the documents. In the ordinary case visual inspection of the actual documents presented is all that is called for. The bank is under no duty to take any further steps to investigate the genuineness of a signature which, on the face of it, purports to be the signature of the person named or described in the letter of credit.

The instant case differs from the ordinary case in that there was a special requirement that the signature on the certificate should be that of a person called Balwant Singh, and that that person should also be the holder of Malaysian passport no. E-13276. This requirement imposed upon the bank the additional duty to take reasonable care to see that the signature on the certificate appeared to correspond with the signature on an additional document presented by the beneficiary which, on the face of it, appeared to be a Malaysian passport No E-13276 issued in the name of Balwant Singh. The evidence was that that is what the notifying bank had done when the certificate was presented. The onus of proving lack of reasonable care in failing to detect the forgery of the certificate lies upon the customer. In their Lordships' view, in agreement with all the members of the Court of Appeal, the customer did not succeed in making out any case of negligence against the issuing bank or the notifying bank which acted as its agent, in failing to detect the forgery.

NOTES

1.   Unlike UCP 500, art 13(a), and unlike art 7 of the 1962 UCP Revision, referred to by Lord Diplock in *Gian Singh*, UCP 600, art 14(a) does not expressly state that the bank must conduct its examination 'with reasonable care'. This omission has led Professor Ellinger to state that 'the code appears to provide for a strict duty rather than a duty to exercise due care' ([2007] LMCLQ 152 at 166). However, we submit that the English courts are likely to maintain a duty of reasonable care which is, according to Lord Diplock in *Gian Singh*, the standard laid down by the common law.

2.   UCP, art 14(a), calls for documents to be examined only 'on their face'. The bank does not have to engage in mathematical calculations in order to check compliance (*Crédit Industriel et Commercial v China Merchants Bank* [2002] EWHC 973 (Comm), [2002] 2 All ER (Comm) 427). The superficial nature of the examination is reinforced by UCP 600, art 34, which provides that 'a bank assumes no liability or responsibility for the form, sufficiency, accuracy, genuineness, falsification or legal effect of any document'.

3.   Related UCP provisions:

•   UCP 600, art 14(b), provides that the issuing bank, confirming bank or nominated bank, each has a maximum of five banking days following the day of presentation of documents to determine if the presentation is complying (see further, below at p 901).

- UCP 600, art 14(g), states that a document presented but not required by the credit is to be disregarded and may be returned to the presenter.

- UCP 600, art 14(h), provides that non-documentary conditions are to be ignored. A non-documentary condition would be where the credit contains a reference to goods being of 'US origin'. This condition will be ignored unless the credit also calls for one of the tendered documents—most likely the certificate of origin—to indicate compliance with that condition.

4.   Where the buyer has been the victim of a fraud of the seller (eg the seller ships rubbish, tenders complying documents and receives payment), the buyer must reimburse the issuing bank and pursue the seller for breach of the contract of sale and/or deceit. The buyer might have a claim against the issuing bank in negligence for failing to advise on the transaction, eg as to the need for an inspection certificate from a reliable third party, but such a claim will only succeed where the facts show that the bank has undertaken a duty to advise, which will be rare, or the bank has actually given misleading advice. In *Midland Bank Ltd v Seymour,* above, p 894, the bank was held liable on Seymour's counterclaim for contractual negligence because it failed to pass on certain adverse information about the Hong Kong sellers after being instructed by Seymour to make inquiries. However, the bank was only ordered to pay nominal damages as Seymour had suffered no loss as a result of this breach. See also *Commercial Banking Co of Sydney Ltd v Jalsard Pty Ltd* [1973] AC 279, PC.

5.   General comments:

(i)   If the issuing bank fails to comply with the buyer's instructions with regard to the opening of the credit or as to the acceptance or rejection of documents presented to it, the buyer is under no obligation to accept the documents from the bank and is not obliged to reimburse the bank for any payment made to the beneficiary (the buyer will then be taken to have 'abandoned' the goods to the issuing bank, in whom they will then vest: see RM Goode *Commercial Law* (3rd edn, 2004), p 982). Further, the bank may be liable to the buyer for any loss sustained by him as a result of the bank's breach of contract.

(ii)   The UCP exonerates the issuing bank from liability for matters beyond its control. UCP 600, art 35 (formerly UCP 500, art 16) protects the bank against liability for the consequences arising out of delay and/or loss in transit of messages and for errors in the translation and/or interpretation of messages. But it is submitted that art 35 does not exempt the issuing bank from liability for its own negligence (R Jack, A Malek and D Quest *Documentary Credits* (3rd edn, 2001), para 4.17). UCP 600, art 36 (formerly UCP 500, art 17) excludes liability for force majeure events. UCP 600, art 37 (formerly UCP 500, art 18) is particularly important because it exonerates the issuing bank from all liability for the errors of any correspondent bank employed by the issuing bank to give effect to the instructions of the buyer (applicant). But again it is submitted that this immunity does not extend to the issuing bank's own negligence (Jack, Malek and Quest, above, para 4.20; see also *Bank Leumi v M G Brin & Sons* [1992] LMLN 342, Israeli Supreme Court, noted [1993] LMCLQ 28). Moreover, art 37 does not require the buyer to accept and pay for documents which failed to comply with his instructions: the sole effect of art 37 is to prevent a buyer holding an issuing bank liable for damage caused to the buyer by the action of the correspondent bank instructed by the issuing bank (*Crédit Agricole Indosuez v Generale Bank (No 2)* [1999] 2 All ER (Comm) 1016 at 1024, Steel J). Nevertheless, art 37 may still prove harsh on the buyer when the correspondent bank employed by the issuing bank (ie the advising bank or the confirming bank) has been negligent, for there is no clear way to make the correspondent bank directly liable to him (there is no privity of contract and no duty of care in tort: although it was suggested in *United Trading Corpn SA v Allied Arab Bank* [1985] 2 Lloyd's Rep 554n, CA, that the correspondent bank owes a duty of care to the buyer, this was later doubted in *GKN Contractors Ltd v Lloyds Bank plc* (1985) 30 BLR 48, CA). Article e12 of the eUCP contains additional disclaimers where documents are tendered electronically.

The issuing bank may include exemption clauses in its contracts which are wider than those included in the UCP. For example, it is common to find exemption clauses in which the applicant agrees to be bound by the issuing bank's determination of the regularity of the documents. Professor Ellinger submits that no attempt be made to discourage the use of such clauses as freedom of contract must be respected (EP Ellinger, 'The UCP 500: Considering a New Revision' [2004] LMCLQ 30, 41). Nevertheless, the English courts can usually subject such clauses to a test of reasonableness as the application form used by the applicant to request the opening of a credit is commonly a *pro forma* supplied by the issuing bank which contains the bank's standard terms and conditions (Unfair Contract Terms Act 1977, s 3).

QUESTION

Does acceptance of conforming documents by the issuing bank preclude the buyer from rejecting the goods if they prove defective on arrival? What if the defect was apparent on the face of the documents? See RM Goode *Commercial Law* (3rd edn, 2004), p 981.

(iii) The contract between the issuing bank and the advising or confirming bank

Bank Melli Iran v Barclays Bank DCO
[1951] 2 Lloyd's Rep 367, King's Bench Division

(The facts appear above, p 859.)

McNair J: In my judgment, both on the construction of the documents under which the credit was established and in principle, the relationship between Bank Melli, the instructing bank, and Barclays Bank, the confirming bank, was that of principal and agent. This relationship was held to exist in substantially similar circumstances in *Equitable Trust Co of New York v Dawson Partners Ltd* ((1927) 27 Ll L Rep 49) (see per Viscount Cave LC at p 52, Lord Sumner at p 53, and Lord Shaw of Dunfermline at p 57), and the existence of this relationship is implicit in the judgments of the Court of Appeal in *J H Rayner & Co Ltd v Hambro's Bank Ltd* ([1943] KB 37). I accept as accurate the statement of Professor Gutteridge KC in his book on Bankers' Commercial Credits, at p 51, that 'as between the issuing banker' (in this case Bank Melli) 'and the correspondent' (in this case Barclays Bank) 'the relationship is, unless otherwise agreed, that of principal and agent...' On the facts of this case I find no agreement to the contrary.

NOTES

1. Where the advising bank is instructed to advise the beneficiary of the opening of the credit and/or receive and inspect the documents, it acts merely as the agent of the issuing bank (*Bank Melli Iran v Barclays Bank DCO*, above). Where the advising bank is instructed to confirm the credit, and does so as a confirming bank, it acts in a dual capacity. The relationship between the issuing bank and the confirming bank is that of principal and agent, and yet the confirming bank gives its own payment undertaking to the beneficiary as principal,

not as agent for the issuing bank (see *Bank of Baroda v Vysya Bank Ltd* [1994] 2 Lloyd's Rep 87 at 90, Mance J). This may explain why, in *Crédit Agricole Indosuez v Muslim Commercial Bank Ltd* [2000] 1 All ER (Comm) 172 at 180, Sir Christopher Staughton, sitting the Court of Appeal, said that:

> there is not *in law* an agency relationship between an issuing bank and a confirming bank .. .But in terms of commerce the confirming bank is the correspondent of the issuing bank, and acts for the issuing bank in order to do what the issuing bank is not present to do for itself. That is in my respectful opinion sufficient to attract the rule that an agent is to be excused for acting on a reasonable, even if ultimately wrong, interpretation of his principal's instructions.

2.   An advising or confirming bank which pays the beneficiary against the tender of conforming documents may claim reimbursement from the issuing bank (UCP 600, art 7(c)).[9] So long as the tendered documents are regular on their face, the advising or confirming bank will be entitled to reimbursement even if the documents turn out to be forged or false (UCP 600, art 34). Payment against obviously discrepant documents does not give the advising or confirming bank a right of reimbursement unless the issuing bank has irrevocably waived its entitlement to insist on payment only against conforming documents (as was held to have occurred in *Habib Bank Ltd v Central Bank of Sudan* [2006] EWHC 1767, [2006] 2 Lloyd's Rep 413 at [49], Field J). The reimbursement obligation may be performed directly by the issuing bank itself or indirectly through an intermediary bank, which is in turn reimbursed by the issuing bank (an intermediary bank will often be a US bank when the currency of the credit is US dollars). Such bank-to-bank reimbursements are regulated by UCP 600, art 13[10] and, when incorporated into the relevant contracts, by the International Chamber of Commerce's Uniform Rules for Bank-to-Bank Reimbursement under Documentary Credits (ICC Publication No 525), which came into force on 1 July 1996 (see HN Bennett [1998] LMCLQ 114; EP Ellinger [2007] JIBLR 507).

3.   The advising or confirming bank must adhere strictly to the issuing bank's instructions if it is to claim its right of reimbursement (the receipt of ambiguous instructions is considered in Note 1 above). Where that bank suspects fraud on the issuing bank it is under a duty to inquire and will commit a breach of duty to the issuing bank, its principal, if it fails to do so (cf *Standard Bank London Ltd v Bank of Tokyo Ltd* [1995] 2 Lloyd's Rep 169 at 176, per Waller J, where Standard Bank London, which was in the position of both advising bank *and beneficiary,* was held to owe no duty to investigate the transaction for the benefit of the issuing bank and to owe no duty to warn the issuing bank of any facts that may be discovered).

4.   Sometimes one bank ('the instructing bank') may ask another bank ('the correspondent issuer') to issue a credit in its own name. In such a case, only the correspondent issuer gives a payment undertaking to the beneficiary; there is no direct relationship between the instructing bank and the beneficiary. The correspondent issuer is entitled to reimbursement from the instructing bank. For cases of this type see *National Bank of Egypt v Hannevig's Bank Ltd* (1919) 1 LI L Rep 69 and *Scandinaviska Akt v Barclays Bank* (1925) 22 LI L Rep 523.

---

[9] The advising bank would pay against tender where it was a 'nominated bank' (UCP 600, art 2).
[10] Should the intermediary bank fail to make reimbursement, the issuing bank remains liable to reimburse the bank which has paid the beneficiary (UCP 600, art 13(b)(iii),(c)).

QUESTION

Intra Bank issues an irrevocable documentary credit in favour of Slicker. The credit is advised through Agro Bank. Agro Bank advises Slicker that payment will be made on the tender of certain documents to Intra Bank. Contrary to Intra Bank's instructions, Agro Bank omits to inform Slicker that the tendered documents must include a certificate of origin of the goods shipped. Slicker tenders documents, but not a certificate of origin, to Intra Bank. Relying on this omission, Intra Bank refuses to pay Slicker. Advise Slicker as to his rights, if any, against Intra Bank. Slicker, hearing that Intra Bank is almost insolvent, also seeks your advice as to any rights he may have against Agro Bank.

(iv) *The contracts between the banks and the seller*

Examination of documents and complying presentations

The issuing bank and the confirming bank each undertake to the seller that payment will be made if conforming documents are duly presented (UCP 600, arts 7(a) and 8(a)). The rights and duties of the banks to examine the documents, the time for starting the settlement process where the tendered documents are in order, and the procedures to be adopted where the tendered documents are defective, are set out in arts 14, 15 and 16 of UCP 600 respectively.

We have already seen that banks must examine all tendered documents to determine, on the basis of the documents alone, whether or not the documents appear on their face to constitute a complying presentation, ie whether they constitute a presentation in accordance with the terms and conditions of the credit, the applicable provisions of the UCP and international standard banking practice (UCP 600, art 14(a): above, p 896).

The issuing bank, the confirming bank and any other nominated bank acting on its nomination (including an advising bank) each has a maximum of five banking days following the day of presentation to determine if the presentation is complying (UCP 600, art 14(b): above, p 897). UCP 500 was differently worded. UCP 500, art 13(b), gave the bank a reasonable time, not to exceed seven banking days, to examine the documents and make the determination. What was a reasonable time could be a matter of some uncertainty, but it could certainly arise in less then seven banking days. In *Bankers Trust Co v State Bank of India* [1991] 2 Lloyd's Rep 443, the Court of Appeal held that what was a reasonable time depended not only on the number and complexity of the documents but also on the level of sophistication in dealing with the documents in the particular country where they were being checked. In *Hing Yip Hing Fat Co Ltd v Daiwa Bank Ltd* [1991] 2 HKLR 35 at 57–59, Kaplan J, sitting in the Supreme Court of Hong Kong, took account of such factors as the smaller size of the bank, and the fact that checkers in Hong Kong did not have English as their mother language, when assessing what was a reasonable time for examination of the documents and determination of the bank's position with regard to them. UCP 600 brings greater certainty with the removal of the reference to a reasonable time and its replacement by a fixed period of five banking days following the date of presentation.

Under UCP 500 there was no precise statement as to when an issuing bank, confirming bank or nominated bank had to start the settlement process. By contrast, UCP 600, art 15(a), provides that the issuing bank must honour the credit when it determines that a presentation is complying. When a confirming bank determines that a presentation is complying, it must honour or negotiate and forward the documents to the issuing bank (art 15(b)). When a nominated bank determines that a presentation is complying and honours or negotiates, it must forward the documents to the confirming bank or issuing bank (art 15(c)).

Some problems of interpretation remain.

C Debattista, 'The New UCP 600—Changes to the Tender of the Seller's Shipping Documents under Letters of Credit'
[2007] JBL 329, 339

Thus, for example, what if a bank decides on the second day that the documents are compliant? Can the seller insist on payment on that second day or must he or she wait until the fifth day for payment? Article 14(b) gives the bank five banking days 'to determine if a presentation is complying'. Article 15(a), however, says that '*when* an issuing bank determines that a presentation is complying, it must honour' (emphasis added) and Art. 15(b) and (c) applies the same rule to confirming and nominated banks. Moreover, Art. 16(d) states that the notice of its refusal to pay must be given:

… by telecommunication or, if that is not possible, by other expeditious means *no later than* the close of the fifth banking day following the day of presentation. (emphasis added)

It is at least arguable that while Art. 14(b) gives each bank five banking days to decide *whether* to pay, Art. 15 says that it must pay immediately it comes to that decision and that Art. 16(d) requires the greatest expedition possible. The consequence would be that a bank proven by the beneficiary to have waited for the fifth day would be in breach of its duty to pay the beneficiary and would be liable towards the beneficiary, for example, for interest on the sum due.

The same issue may cause problems for the buyer. If the bank were to pay on the second day, and if the goods are lost or damaged on the fourth day in a sale contract concluded on a 'delivered' basis, is it open to the buyer to complain that the bank had paid the sum under the credit before it was obliged to—and that therefore the bank should indemnify the buyer for the costs of recovering the price from the seller in a foreign jurisdiction—and possibly for the price itself in case of the seller's default? Again, here, it is at least arguable that Art. 14(b) does not *require* the bank to wait five days: it simply gives it five days to examine the documents *if it needs five days*. The consequence would be that a bank is entitled, as far as the buyer it concerned, to pay on the second day if it rightly decides then that the documents comply—and that the bank is entitled to do so without risk of liability towards the buyer.

Waiver of discrepancies

Where an issuing bank, confirming bank or a nominated bank acting on its nomination determines that a presentation does not comply, it may refuse to honour or negotiate the credit (UCP 600, art 16(a)). On the other hand, the discrepancies in the documents may be minor or immaterial and the applicant, keen to get hold of the goods, may be prepared to waive them. UCP 600, art 16(b), facilitates this process by providing that:

When an issuing bank determines that a presentation does not comply, it may in its sole judgment approach the applicant for a waiver of the discrepancies. This does not, however, extend the period mentioned in sub-art 14(b).

Three points should be noted. First, the decision whether to approach the applicant for a waiver is at the sole discretion of the issuing bank. The applicant has no legal remedy against the issuing bank if it rejects non-compliant documents without having approached him. Secondly, UCP 600, art 16(b), does not permit re-examination of the documents by the applicant with a view to finding further discrepancies. In *Bankers Trust Co v State Bank of India* [1991] 2 Lloyd's Rep 443, the Court of Appeal held that it was for the bank and not the applicant to make the decision as to whether or not the documents were discrepant (see also *Bayerische Vereinsbank Aktiengesellschaft v National Bank of Pakistan* [1997] 1 Lloyd's

Rep 59, 69–70. Mance J). Thirdly, if the applicant is to be approached for a waiver, the whole process must be completed, and the issuing bank must make its decision whether or not to accept the documents, within the maximum period of five banking days following presentation (the position was less certain under the wording of UCP 500, art 13(b) (above, p 901): see R Buckley, 'Documentary Compliance in Documentary Credits: Lessons from the UCC for the UCP' (2002) 1 Journal of International Commercial Law 69, 88–89).

Notice of rejection

UCP 600, art 16(c), states that when the issuing bank, the confirming bank, or a nominated bank acting on its nomination, decides to refuse to honour or negotiate a credit, it must give a single notice to that effect to the presenter (ie the beneficiary, bank or other party that makes a presentation of documents under a credit). UCP 600, art 16(d), says that the rejection notice must be given by telecommunication or, if that is not possible, by other expeditious means no later than the close of the fifth banking day following the day of presentation. This provision is more tightly worded than the equivalent provision in UCP 500. UCP 500, art 14(d)(i) required notice to be given 'without delay but no later than the close of the seventh banking day following the day of receipt of the documents'. Under UCP 600 there can be no arguments as to whether the notice was given 'without delay' (eg in *Bayerische Vereinsbank Aktiengesellschaft v National Bank of Pakistan* [1997] 1 Lloyd's Rep 59 at 70, Mance J held that a bank did not act 'without delay' when sending a notice of rejection by DHL courier, when telex and fax facilities were also available). The net effect of UCP 600, arts 14(b) and 16(d), seems to be that a bank has a maximum of five banking days following presentation of the documents to determine if the presentation is compliant, but that the longer it takes to make its determination, the less time it has available to it to give a notice of rejection to the applicant. If the bank fails to comply with the five (banking) day maximum period, it will not have served a proper notice which satisfies art 16 (d) and, because of the effect of UCP 600, art 16(f) (below), will be precluded from claiming that the documents do not comply with the credit (J Ulph, 'The UCP 600: Documentary Credits in the Twenty-first Century' [2007] JBL 355, 364).

The notice of rejection must state the discrepancies in respect of which the document is being rejected. There has been some doubt as to whether a bank would be estopped from later raising further discrepancies not identified in the original rejection notice. The position at common law is that, absent special circumstances raising a true estoppel, the bank will not be prevented from relying upon discrepancies which were not listed in the original rejection notice (*Kydon Compania Naviera SA v National Westminster Bank Ltd, The Lena* [1981] 1 Lloyd's Rep 68, 79). But the position was thought to be different under the UCP (see *Hing Yip Hing Fat Co Ltd v Daiwa Bank Ltd* [1991] 2 HKLR 35, 45–51). The 1993 revision of the UCP clarified the issue by stating, for the first time, that the notice must specify *all* discrepancies in respect of which the bank refused the documents (UCP 500, art 14(d)(ii)). UCP 600, art 16(c)(ii), retains the requirement, although it does so in slightly different language: the bank must give a 'single notice' of rejection to the presenter and that notice must state 'each discrepancy in respect of which the bank refuses to honour or negotiate'. If the bank fails to comply with this requirement, or any other requirement of art 16, it is precluded from claiming that the documents do not constitute a complying presentation (UCP 600, art 16(f)). This seems to mean the bank may be precluded from raising a new objection when documents are re-tendered by the seller having cured the defects identified in the original notice of rejection (but note that in *Paget's Law of Banking*, 13th edn, 2007, para 37.18, it is submitted that there is no such preclusion in the normal course of events).

Under UCP 500, art 14(d)(i), a bank which refused documents had also to state in its rejection notice whether it was holding the documents at the disposal of, or was returning them to, the presenter. The purpose of this provision was that, as soon as the documents had been rejected, they should be put back in circulation. However, problems arose where a bank served a rejection notice and at the same time approached the applicant for a waiver of the discrepancies, and if such waiver was received released the documents without further notice. In *Crédit Industriel et Commercial v China Merchants Bank* [2002] EWHC 973 (Comm), [2002] 2 All ER (Comm) 427, the issuing bank's notice of rejection was held to be bad where it ended with the words: 'Should the disc[repancy] being accepted by the applicant, we shall release the documents to them without further notice to you unless yr instructions to the contrary received prior to our payment. Documents held at yr risk for yr disposal'. Steel J considered (at [68]) that the conditional nature of the rejection was not saved by the potential for acceptance of contrary instructions prior to payment, particularly where no notice was to be given. The message constituted a continuing threat of conversion of the claimant's documents. However, UCP 600, art 16, contains additional options designed to avoid banks sitting on discrepant documents. Under art 16(c)(iii) the rejection notice must state that the bank:

'(a) holds the documents pending further instructions from the presenter; or
 (b) holds the documents until it receives a waiver from the applicant and agrees to accept it, and receives further instructions from the presenter prior to agreeing to accept a waiver; or
 (c) is returning the documents; or
 (d) is acting in accordance with instructions previously received from the presenter.'

According to UCP 600, art 16(f), if the issuing bank or confirming bank fails to act in accordance with the provisions of art 16, it is precluded from claiming that the documents do not constitute a complying presentation. But the article makes no reference to the position of a nominated bank. However, if a nominated bank is employed by the issuing bank or confirming bank to take up and examine the documents on its behalf, the nominated bank's failure to comply with art 16 will bar the issuing bank or confirming bank from claiming that the documents are not conforming (see EP Ellinger [1997] 3 (No 2) DCI 9).

Payment under reserve
Banque de l'Indochine et de Suez SA v JH Rayner (Mincing Lane) Ltd
[1983] QB 711, Court of Appeal

An irrevocable credit was opened by a Djibouti bank and confirmed by the plaintiff bank (the confirming bank). The defendant sellers tendered documents to the confirming bank but the bank considered them to be defective for various reasons which the sellers were informed of. However, the confirming bank agreed to pay the sellers 'under reserve'. When the issuing bank, on the buyer's instructions, rejected the documents, the confirming bank demanded repayment from the sellers. The Court of Appeal affirmed Parker J's decision that the documents were defective but disagreed with his analysis of the effect of a payment under reserve.

Sir John Donaldson MR: It seems that it is not unusual for a confirming bank to be asked to pay on documents which in its view do not fully comply with the terms of the letter of credit. The bank then has to decide whether (a) to refuse payment, (b) to pay, taking an indemnity from the beneficiary in respect of any loss or damage resulting from the deficiency in the documentation or (c) to pay the beneficiary 'under reserve.' Which course is adopted depends upon the extent and importance of the deficiencies as perceived by the confirming bank, the likelihood of the bank at whose request the credit was opened ('the issuing bank') and that bank's customer refusing to accept the correctness of any payment to the beneficiary and the credit worthiness, and value attached by the paying bank to the goodwill, of the person seeking to draw on the letter of credit. It is a tribute to the standing of JH Rayner (Mincing Lane) Ltd, the defendants, in the City of London that, notwithstanding the bank's conviction that the documents were seriously defective, they paid them 'under reserve.'

The use of the expression 'payment under reserve,' as denoting the character of a payment, is, we were told, widespread and would undoubtedly serve a very useful purpose if it had a defined and generally accepted meaning. Unfortunately it seems that it has not. If this is correct, banks will be most unwise to use it without at the same time stating precisely what they mean by it. In the longer term the International Chamber of Commerce, who are the authors and guardians of the Uniform Customs and Practice for Documentary Credits might like to turn their minds to this problem when undertaking the next revision. Meanwhile we have to determine what the parties meant by the expression when they used it on this occasion.

It is common ground that it relates to the circumstances in which the beneficiary can be called upon to repay the money which he has been paid under the letter of credit. The competing submissions are that (1) the money is repayable on demand if the issuing bank, in reliance upon some or all of the deficiencies alleged by the confirming bank, declines to reimburse the confirming bank or to ratify the payment, the beneficiary then being left to sue the confirming bank; (2) money is repayable if, but only if, the circumstances in (1) exist and the beneficiary accepts that the documentation was defective or this is established in a suit brought by the confirming bank against the beneficiary. If (2) is correct, the only effect of the qualification upon the payment, albeit an important effect, is that the beneficiary cannot resist an order for repayment on the basis that the payment itself had been made under a mistake of law. This was the submission accepted by the judge and his reasons appear in his judgment ante, pp 716D-717E; [1982] 2 Lloyd's Rep 476, 479.

The point is clearly one of difficulty. Mr Saville [counsel for the plaintiffs] characterised the view of the judge as 'a lawyer's view' as contrasted with 'a commercial view' and I think that this is right. It depends for its validity upon the parties having had it well in mind that money payable under a mistake of law is irrecoverable and wishing to do no more than eliminate this defence. This seems to me to be an improbable premise, when the parties are a commercial bank and a commodity merchant. As I see it, the dialogue to be imputed to the parties goes something like this:

Merchant: 'These documents are sufficient to satisfy the terms of the letter of credit and certainly will be accepted by my buyer. I am entitled to the money and need it.'

Bank'. 'If we thought that the documents satisfied the terms of the letter of credit, we would pay you at once. However, we do not think that they do and we cannot risk paying you and not being paid ourselves. We are not sure that your buyer will authorise payment, but we can of course ask.'

Merchant: 'But that will take time and meanwhile we shall have a cash flow problem.'

Bank: 'Well the alternative is for you to sue us and that will also take time.

'*Merchant:* 'What about your paying us without prejudice to whether we are entitled to payment and then your seeing what is the reaction of your correspondent bank and our buyer?'

Bank: 'That is all right, but if we are told that we should not have paid, how do we get our money back?'

Merchant: 'You sue us.'

Bank: 'Oh no, that would leave us out of our money for a substantial time. Furthermore it would involve us in facing in two directions. We should not only have to sue you, but also to sue the issuing bank in order to cover the possibility that you might be right. We cannot afford to pay on those terms.'

Merchant: 'All right. I am quite confident that the issuing bank and my buyer will be content that you should pay, particularly since the documents are in fact in order. You pay me and if the issuing bank refuses to reimburse you for the same reason that you are unwilling to pay, we will repay you on demand and then sue you. But we do not think that this will happen.'

Bank: 'We agree. Here is the money "under reserve." '

Kerr LJ: ... What the parties meant, I think, was that payment was to be made under reserve in the sense that the beneficiary would be bound to repay the money on demand if the issuing bank should reject the documents, whether on its own initiative or on the buyer's instructions. I would regard this as a binding agreement made between the confirming bank and the beneficiary by way of a compromise to resolve the impasse created by the uncertainty of their respective legal obligations and rights. For present purposes it is then unnecessary to go further and decide whether such a demand would only be effective if the grounds of the rejection included at least one of the grounds on which the confirming bank had relied in refusing to pay otherwise than under reserve. But I incline to the view that this should be implied, since the agreement to pay and accept the money under reserve will have been made against the background of these grounds of objection.

In the present case the issuing bank in fact rejected the documents on grounds which included at least one of the grounds of objection which had been raised by the plaintiffs. It therefore follows that the judgment in favour of the plaintiffs must in any event be upheld.

[Sir Sebag Shaw concurred.]

NOTES

1.   What are the seller's rights against an issuing bank or confirming bank which either renounces its obligations before time of performance becomes due, or wrongfully refuses to accept conforming documents, or otherwise fails to honour the credit? It should be borne in mind that any renunciation of performance before time of performance becomes due must be clear and unequivocal. An ambiguous statement or one merely casting doubt, even grave doubt, on the bank's willingness to perform is not enough (see *Jaks (UK) Ltd v Cera Investment Bank SA* [1998] 2 Lloyd's Rep 89, where Moore-Bick J held that the issuing bank's telex to the beneficiary stating the credit was cancelled at the applicant's request, but also asking for the beneficiary's agreement to cancellation, was not sufficiently clear and unambiguous to amount to a renunciation). So long as the seller remains able to tender or retender conforming documents (ie he has not sold the goods or done another act indicating his acceptance of the bank's repudiation), he may bring an action against the bank for the face value of the credit together with interest (*Belgian Grain & Produce Co Ltd v Cox & Co (France) Ltd* (1919) 1 Ll L Rep 256). Alternatively, the seller may accept the bank's repudiation and sue for damages. In *Jaks (UK) Ltd v Cera Investment Bank SA,* above, Moore-Bick J emphasised that where the beneficiary decides to treat the contract as discharged he must communicate his decision to the bank clearly and unequivocally. Moore-Bick J held that inactivity might satisfy the requirements of communication where it relates to failure to carry out an act in relation to the other party to the contract, but in the case before him the seller's failure to ship the goods did not amount to communication to the issuing bank of his acceptance of the bank's repudiation as it related to performance of the underlying contract of sale of goods and not to performance of the letter of credit contract (in any event, his Lordship held that as the credit was payable against documents generated on arrival of the goods and not on shipment, the failure to ship would not have been an act of which the bank would have immediately become aware). As the bank's failure to honour a letter of credit is not merely a failure to pay money, but also an act which interferes with performance of the underlying contract of sale, the court will, in an appropriate case (eg where the seller elects to treat the contract of sale as repudiated), assess damages against the bank on a similar basis to those awarded for breach of the buyer's obligation to accept delivery under the contract of sale (see RM Goode *Commercial Law* (3rd edn, 2004), p 1000, citing *Urquhart, Lindsay & Co Ltd v Eastern Bank Ltd* [1922] 1 KB 318 at 324–325). If the seller sues for damages he is under a duty to mitigate his loss. Where the seller suffers loss because the bank has delayed in making payment, he may recover that loss

from the bank so long as it is not too remote (*Ozalid Group (Export) Ltd v African Continental Bank* [1979] 2 Lloyd's Rep 231 at 233). If the bank fails to honour a bill of exchange which it has previously accepted, the seller will sue the bank on the bill of exchange itself.

2. Where payment is not made 'under reserve', can the bank recover money paid to the seller against non-conforming documents?

(i) *Where there is fraud.* Where the bank has paid against forged or fraudulent documents and is unable to obtain reimbursement from the applicant or other instructing party, eg if the applicant is insolvent or if it is found that the bank should not have paid because the fraud was apparent or the documents were discrepant, it can attempt to recover the payment from the beneficiary. The claim is for restitution of money paid under a mistake of fact (*Bank Russo-Iran v Gordon Woodroffe & Co Ltd* (1912) 116 Sol Jo 921, Browne J, cited with apparent approval by Lord Denning MR in *Edward Owen Engineering Ltd v Barclays Bank International Ltd* [1978] QB 159 at 169–170). Change of position is a recognised defence to a claim for recovery of a mistaken payment (for details, see above, p 583). The scope of the defence is still uncertain but it was made clear by Lord Goff in the leading authority on the subject, *Lipkin Gorman v Karpnale* [1991] 2 AC 548, that the defence would not be available to someone who changed his position in bad faith. This explains why the defence is not available to the fraudulent beneficiary who has paid away the proceeds of the credit. But it will usually be available to any bank that has presented documents and collected payment under the credit for the fraudulent beneficiary and then paid over those proceeds to the fraudster (but not in *Niru Battery Manufacturing Co v Milestone Trading Ltd* [2003] EWCA Civ 1446, [2004] 1 All ER (Comm) 193 (noted by Ellinger (2005) 121 LQR 51), where the bank that had received the proceeds of the credit had grounds for believing that the payment may have been made by mistake but failed to make enquires of the issuing bank that had made the mistaken payment).

The bank will also have a claim for damages in deceit against the beneficiary and any third party who has issued a document knowing that it contains a false statement and that it is to be presented to the bank under the credit (*KBC Bank v Industrial Steels (UK) Ltd* [2001] 1 All ER (Comm) 409; *Komercni Banka AS v Stone and Rolls Ltd* [2002] EWHC 2263 (Comm), [2003] 1 Lloyd's Rep 383). The bank may be able to make a recovery from the beneficiary or third party even where it is itself guilty of fraudulent conduct, provided that it does not have to rely on that conduct in support of its claim (*Standard Chartered Bank v Pakistan National Shipping Corpn (No 2)* [2000] 1 All ER (Comm) 1, CA, where the confirming bank falsely represented to the issuing bank that the documents had been presented in time but was still held entitled to recover damages in deceit from the carrier that had issued a bill of lading falsely stating that the goods had been shipped within the shipping period). There is no defence of contributory negligence in the case of deceit (*Standard Chartered Bank v Pakistan National Shipping Corpn (No 2)* [2002] UKHL 43, [2002] 2 All ER (Comm) 931, HL).

(ii) *Cases not involving fraud.* Where the bank has paid against non-conforming documents because of its own mistake it is unlikely to be able to recover the money so paid. Any restitutionary claim would probably be defeated by defences of change of position or estoppel (at least as against claims made by the issuing or confirming banks: claims by those banks would also be barred by UCP 600, art 16(f)—see above, p 904).

(iii) *Bills of exchange.* If the bank negotiates a bill of exchange drawn by the seller on the buyer, who later dishonours the bill, it might be possible for the bank, as holder or indorser, to claim a right of recourse against the seller under ss 43(2) or 47(2) of the Bills of Exchange

Act 1882. But there is considerable doubt whether such a right of recourse applies to a bill drawn under a credit (compare *Benjamin's Sale of Goods* (7th edn, 2006), para 23–164, with D Sheehan, 'Rights of Recourse in Documentary (and Other) Credit Transactions' [2005] JBL 326). The issue is no longer a live one under UCP 600, as art 6(c) provides that a credit must not be issued available by a draft drawn on the applicant (buyer).

(iv) It should be noted that in the United States a bank may have a right of action against the seller for breach of warranty relating to the fraud or forgery of the tendered documents (s 5–110(a) of the Uniform Commercial Code, 1995 Revision). English law does not appear to recognise such a warranty (R Pennington, A Hudson and J Mann *Commercial Banking Law* (1978), pp 357–358; Benjamin, above, para 23–164, n 52; Jack, Malek and Quest, above, para 5.81; cf RM Goode *Commercial Law* (3rd edn, 2004), p 998 and [1980] JBL 443, pp 445–446).

(g) The governing law of documentary credits

Bank of Baroda v Vysya Bank Ltd
[1994] 2 Lloyd's Rep 87, Queen's Bench Division

Aditya, an Indian importer, agreed to purchase a consignment of pig iron through the London office of Granada, an Irish exporter. Aditya instructed Vysya Bank, its bank in India, to open a documentary credit in favour of Granada. The credit was opened and, though initially advised through National Westminster Bank in London, was later confirmed by Bank of Baroda's City of London office. Bank of Baroda paid Granada against tender of documents, which were sent on to Vysya Bank. The credit provided for reimbursement through Citibank in New York. Vysya Bank informed Bank of Baroda that it had already mailed reimbursement instructions to Citibank and authorised Bank of Baroda to claim reimbursement from that bank. However, Vysya Bank subsequently withdrew this authorisation on the ground that the cargo shipped had been the subject of two different sets of bills of lading. Bank of Baroda commenced proceedings in London against Vysya Bank claiming damages for breach of contract between itself as confirmer and Vysya Bank as the issuing bank. The issue before the Commercial Court was whether Bank of Baroda should be given leave to issue and serve a writ on Vysya Bank out of the jurisdiction on the ground that the contract between the two banks was governed by English law (Rules of the Supreme Court, Ord 11, r (1)(d): see now Civil Procedure Rules, Part 6, which is in similar terms to those rules formerly contained in RSC Ord 11, r 1(1)). Mance J gave leave.

Mance J: . . . I shall start with the issue of the governing law which arises under 0.11, r. 1 (1)(*d*)(iii). This is of some general importance, since it involves the application to international letters of credit of the Rome Convention as enacted by the Contracts (Applicable Law) Act, 1990. It was common ground before me in view of the wide provisions of s. 2(1) of the Act and art. 3(1) of the Rome Convention that the proper law of the present contract, however it was made, must be determined in accordance with the Convention. So it is necessary to examine the provisions of art. 4 which read:

1. To the extent that the law applicable to the contract has not been chosen in accordance with Article 3, the contract shall be governed by the law of the country with which it is most closely connected. Nevertheless, a severable part of the contract which has a closer connection with another country may by way of exception be governed by the law of that other country.

2. Subject to the provisions of paragraph 5 of this Article, it shall be presumed that the contract is most closely connected with the country where the party who is to effect the performance which

is characteristic of the contract has, at the time of conclusion of the contract, his habitual residence, or, in the case of a body corporate or unincorporate, its central administration. However, if the contract is entered into in the course of that party's trade or profession, that country shall be the country in which the principal place of business is situated or, where under the terms of the contract the performance is to be effected through a place of business other than the principal place of business, the country in which that other place of business is situated …

5. Paragraph 2 shall not apply if the characteristic performance cannot be determined, and the presumptions in paragraphs 2, 3 and 4 shall be disregarded if it appears from the circumstances as a whole that the contract is more closely connected with another country.

The relevant presumption is contained in par. 2. It raises the question: what is 'the performance which is characteristic of the contract' made between Vysya and Bank of Baroda? Bank of Baroda says that the answer is the addition of its confirmation to the credit and the honouring of the liability accepted thereby. Vysya says that this fails to distinguish the contract between Vysya and Bank of Baroda as confirming banker and Granada as beneficiary. In Vysya's submission the performance which is characteristic of the contract between Vysya and Bank of Baroda is the former's obligation to pay the latter upon presentation of conforming documents.

There are several different contractual relationships which can be identified in a situation such as the present. Leaving aside the underlying sale contract, there are contracts between (i) the buyer and the issuing bank, (ii) the issuing bank and the confirming bank, (iii) the confirming bank and the seller and (iv) the issuing bank and the seller. The last two relationships co-exist, giving a beneficiary two banks which he may hold responsible for payment. As the Uniform Customs put it in art. 10(b):

When an issuing bank authorizes or requests another bank to confirm its irrevocable credit and the latter has added its confirmation, such confirmation constitutes a definite undertaking of such bank (the confirming bank), in addition to that of the issuing bank, provided that the stipulated documents are presented and that the terms and conditions of the credit are complied with: …

Article 11 (d) provides:

By nominating a bank other than itself, or by allowing for negotiation by any bank, or by authorizing or requesting a bank to add its confirmation, the issuing bank authorizes such bank to pay, accept or negotiate, as the case may be, against documents which appear on their face to be in accordance with the terms and conditions of the credit, and undertakes to reimburse such bank in accordance with the provisions of these articles.

As between issuing bank and confirming bank the relationship is one of agency, although as against the beneficiary the confirming bank commits itself as principal (see Jack on Documentary Credits at pars. 5.33 and 5.53). This is consistent with the language of authorization and request used in these articles, even though it is possible that the confirming bank can also rely on art. 16 of the Uniform Customs as against an issuing bank. That the relationship is one of agency is also shown by the language used in the instant case when Bank of Baroda was instructed, whether one looks at Bank of Baroda's or Vysya's account of the making of the contract. …

Both these accounts of the making of the contract between Vysya and Bank of Baroda identify the confirmation as the object or focus of the contract. They confirm the appropriateness of the general conclusion, at which I would anyway arrive, that under a contract between an issuing bank and a confirming bank the performance which is characteristic of the contract is the adding of its confirmation by the latter and its honouring of the obligations accepted thereby in relation to the beneficiary. The liability on the part of the issuing bank to reimburse or indemnify the confirming bank is consequential on the character of the contract; it does not itself characterize the contract.

The fact that reimbursement was to be claimed and made in New York is doubly insignificant, being probably a mere matter of convenience because this was a dollar credit and in any event unrelated to any country whose law could conceivably govern (*cf European Asian Bank v Punjab and Sind Bank* [1981] 2 Lloyd's Rep. 651, 656 per Mr Justice Robert Goff).

Additional confirmation of these conclusions is provided by the text of the report on the Rome Convention by Professors Giuliano and Lagarde to which reference may be made under s. 3(3) of the Act. The report points out that in bilateral or reciprocal contracts the counter-performance by one of the parties in a modern economy usually takes the form of money. It says:

> This is not, of course, the characteristic performance of the contract. It is the performance for which the payment is due, i.e. depending on the type of contract, the delivery of goods, the granting of the right to make use of an item of property, the provision of a service, transport, insurance, banking operations, security, etc., which usually constitutes the centre of gravity and the socio-economic function of the contractual transaction.

A little later the report goes on:

> Thus, for example, in a banking contract the law of the country of the banking establishment with which the transaction is made will normally govern the contract.... To take another example, in an agency contract concluded in France between a Belgian commercial agent and a French company, the characteristic performance being that of the agent, the contract will be governed by Belgian law if the agent has his place of business in Belgium.
>
> In conclusion, Article 4(2) gives specific form and objectivity to the, in itself, too vague concept of 'closest connection'...
>
> For each category of contract, it is the characteristic performance that is in principle the relevant factor in applying the presumption for determining the applicable law, even in situations peculiar to certain contracts, as for example in the contract of guarantee where the characteristic performance is always that of the guarantor, whether in relation to the principal debtor or the creditor.

In this passage the first sentence contemplates the straightforward situation of a banking contract or transaction with or involving a single branch or office of a bank; in the present case, even if the contract was concluded in India its whole focus was upon Bank of Baroda's City of London branch acting as confirming banker under the credit advised to the beneficiary in London. The reference to an agent instructed to undertake his activity in a particular country is directly relevant. Also of some assistance by way of analogy (though not exact since a confirming bank does not act as guarantor of the issuing bank but assumes separate liabilities in identical terms) is the comment that the performance characteristic of a guarantee is always the guarantor's performance (*i.e.* the giving and honouring of the guarantee) whether one looks at his contract with the creditor or the debtor. The same is in my view true of a confirming bank's performance (the addition and honouring of its confirmation), whether one looks at its contract with the beneficiary or with the issuing bank.

It follows in the present case, looking at the position of Bank of Baroda in relation to the confirmation given to Granada, that the performance characteristic of Bank of Baroda's contract with Vysya, however made, was the addition and honouring of its confirmation of the credit in favour of Granada. That performance was to be effected through Bank of Baroda's City of London office, viz 'a place of business other than [its] principal place of business' and so by the express terms of art. 4(2) the presumption is that English law governs the contract between Vysya and Bank of Baroda. For reasons which will further appear below, any wider examination of the circumstances under art. 4(5) simply confirms the application of English law.

[Mance J then considered what was the governing law of the contract between the beneficiary and the confirming bank, and the governing law of the contract between the beneficiary and the issuing bank where the credit is confirmed (or unconfirmed but advised by an agent bank):]

So far I have focused on the contract between Vysya and Bank of Baroda which is the contract immediately in issue. It is relevant to consider the matter more widely, as the arguments before me did, and in this context to consider the proper laws of other contracts involved in the present situation. Whether one looks at art. 4(2) or at art. 4(5) of the Rome Convention, the contract of confirmation between Bank of Baroda's City of London branch as confirming bank and Granada as beneficiary was clearly governed by English law. Even if one ignores the clear application of the presumption in art. 4(2) to that contract, the reasoning in such cases as *European Bank v Punjab Bank* [1981] 2 Lloyd's Rep 651 at pp 656–657 per Mr Justice Robert Goff is as relevant when determining the closeness of connection with any country under art. 4(5) as it was for the purposes of the similar common law test. A suggestion that English law did not, as between beneficiary and confirming bank, govern a credit confirmed through the London branch of a foreign bank for payment in London would be wholly uncommercial.

Vysya submits however that, although Granada's contract as beneficiary with Bank of Baroda as the confirming bank is subject to English law, Granada's parallel contract with Vysya as the issuing bank falls as a result of the Rome Convention (and contrary to the previous common law position) to be regarded s subject to Indian law. It submits that the contract between the buyer and Vysya in India must also be subject to Indian law. In its submission different legal systems govern different contracts involved in the present situation and there is no particular incongruity in holding that the contract between the two Indian banks is subject to Indian law.

I do not think that I need consider to what law the contract between Atiya and Vysya might, even prima facie be subject, if one were to analyse it under English law by reference to the Contracts (Applicable Law) Act. Not only is there practically no information before the Court at all about that contract, it is on any view quite separate from any contract between the banks or the banks and the beneficiary.

A point of importance is involved in the submission that the contract between Granada as beneficiary and Vysya as issuing bank is subject to Indian law. That would mean that, by force of the Contracts (Applicable Law) Act [1990], one and the same credit is here governed by two different laws, and that the applicable law varies according to the bank against which the beneficiary decides to enforce the credit. If the beneficiary enforces the credit against the Bank of Baroda, English law applies, and presumably (whatever the governing law of the contract between confirming and issuing banks) Bank of Baroda can then claim reimbursement from Vysya in respect of liabilities which it has incurred subject to English law. However if the beneficiary chooses to pursue the issuing bank direct, Indian law applies. Counsel for Vysya contemplated this with equanimity as a necessary result of the Contracts (Applicable Law) Act, but I do not. In my judgment it would involve precisely the same wholly undesirable multiplicity of potentially conflicting laws to which Mr Justice Ackner drew attention in his reasoning in *Offshore International SA v Banco Central SA* [1976] 2 Lloyd's Rep 402 at p. 404, col. 1; [1977] 1 WLR 399 at p 401. He there rejected a suggestion that an unconfirmed credit opened by a Spanish company through a New York bank for payment at that bank in New York was subject to Spanish law. In concluding for the purposes of the common law test that the 'closest and most real connection' was with New York law, Mr Justice Ackner said:

> ...I am satisfied that Mr Yorke was correct in his contention that very great inconvenience would arise, if the law of the issuing bank were to be considered as the proper law. The advising bank would have constantly to be seeking to apply a whole variety of foreign laws. Indeed it is very difficult to follow exactly what would flow from Mr Alexander's submission, if the advising bank was (as was not the case) to confirm the letter or credit.

In the present case Bank of Baroda did confirm the credit (whether it or National Westminster Bank strictly performed the function of 'advising bank' is neither here nor there), and the wholly undesirable difficulties mentioned in the last sentence of Mr Justice Ackner's reasoning would be unavoidable on Vysya's submissions.

As between the beneficiary and Vysya, the position under art. 4(2) is that there is a presumption that Indian law applies. This presumption applies, although the performance which is characteristic of the contract is the issue of the letter of credit in London which was to be and was effected in London through National Westminster, initially at least as advising bank, with Bank of Baroda later adding its confirmation. Although such performance was to take place in London, art. 4(2) refers one back, prima facie, to India as the place of Vysya's central administration.

In my judgment this is a situation where it would be quite wrong to stop at art. 4(2). The basic principle is that the governing law is that of the country with which the contract is most closely connected (art. 4(1)). Art. 4(2) is, as stated in Professors Giuliano and Lagarde's report, intended to give 'specific form and objectivity' to that concept. In the present case the application of art. 4(2) would lead to an irregular and subjective position where the governing law of a letter of credit would vary according to whether one was looking at the position of the confirming or the issuing bank. It is of great importance to both beneficiaries and banks concerned in the issue and operation of international letters of credit that there should be clarity and simplicity in such matters. Article 4(5) provides the answer. The Rome Convention was not intended to confuse legal relationships or to disrupt normal expectations in the way which is implicit in Vysya's submissions. Under art. 4(5) the presumptions in art. 4(2), (3) and (4) are to be

> ...disregarded if it appears from the circumstances as a whole that the contract is more closely connected with another country.

I accept that the presumptions are to be applied unless there is valid reason, looking at the circumstances as a whole, not to do so. But I note and consider that there is force in the comment in *Dicey and Morris on The Conflict of Laws* (12th edn) at pp 1137–1138:

> Inevitably the solution of individual cases will depend on the facts, but in principle it is submitted that the presumption may be most easily rebutted in those cases where the place of performance differs from the place of business of the party whose performance is characteristic of the contract.

The present situation provides in my judgment a classic demonstration of the need for and appropriateness of art. 4(5). I conclude that English law applies to the contract between Vysya and Granada.

The fact that the credit was to be confirmed by Bank of Baroda's City of London branch highlights the need for art. 4(5) and its applicability in this case. But I should not be taken as suggesting that the conclusion would be any different if the credit had been an unconfirmed credit to be opened and advised on Vysya's behalf in London through National Westminster or Bank of Baroda's City branch available for negotiation here. I agree with the editors of *Dicey and Morris* that the application of the law of the place of performance would in such a case still be likely to result, by application of art. 4(5), as it did applying common law principles: *Dicey and Morris* pp 1238–1239 illustration 4; and cf *Offshore International SA v Banco Central* SA, [1976] 2 Lloyd's Rep 402; [1977] 1 WLR 399; where the 'very great inconvenience' of any other conclusion in the case of an unconfirmed credit was the direct subject of Mr Justice Ackner's comments which I have already cited.

I therefore conclude that the letter of credit was governed by English law as between the beneficiary and each of the banks. On this basis, it would be wholly anomalous if English law were not also to govern the contract between Vysya and Bank of Baroda and in my opinion it does. As between Bank of Baroda and Vysya the application of the presumption arising under art. 4(2) accords with good sense and sound policy and there is therefore no reason to depart from it.

It follows that Bank of Baroda has made out its case for saying that the Court had jurisdiction to grant leave to issue and serve the writ out of the jurisdiction under the first head of O. 11, r. 1(1)(d)

[Mance J exercised his general discretion whether or not to permit service out of the jurisdiction in favour of Bank of Baroda on the ground that the facts and the evidence showed England to be the most appropriate forum to resolve the dispute. The principles to be applied when exercising such discretion are set out in *Spiliada Maritime Corp v Cansulex Ltd* [1987] AC 460, HL, as applied in *Lubbe v Cape plc* [2000] 1 WLR 1545.]

NOTES

1.   The EEC Convention on the Law Applicable to Contractual Obligations 1980 (known as the Rome Convention) became part of English law on 1 April 1991 following the passing of the Contracts (Applicable Law) Act 1990. It applies to contracts made after that date. Thus,

choice of law questions arising in relation to documentary credit contracts made after 1 April 1991 are to be considered by applying the Rome Convention. The position as to contracts, including documentary credit contracts, made before that date is determined by common law principles and in particular by asking the question—with which system of law have the contracts their closest and most real connection? (*Bank of Credit & Commerce Hong Kong Ltd (in liquidation) v Sonali Bank* [1995] 1 Lloyd's Rep 227 at 237, per Cresswell J). In fact the governing law will usually be the same whether the issue is decided under the Rome Convention or according to common law principles.

2.   In *Marconi Communications International Ltd v Pt Pan Indonesia Bank* Ltd [2005] EWCA Civ 422, [2005] 2 All ER (Comm) 325, both the issuing bank and the confirming bank were located in Indonesia. The beneficiary was advised of the opening of the credit through a third bank located in London. The Court of Appeal held that there was a good arguable case that the contract between the beneficiary and the confirming bank was governed by English law. There was held to be valid reason and commercial logic why, rather than simply applying the presumption in art 4(2) of the Rome Convention, which would have pointed to Indonesian law as the law of the place of characteristic performance of the contract, art 4(5) of the Convention should be applied to the contracts between the beneficiary and the issuing bank and the confirming bank. Their Lordships (at [66]) relied on the fact that the credit was opened in London through the advising bank and contemplated payment of the beneficiary in sterling in London by the advising bank as negotiating bank authorised to make payment to the beneficiary against tender of conforming documents. Christopher Hare has rightly criticised this decision on the ground that the Court of Appeal gave too little weight to the presumption in art 4(2) (C Hare [2005] LMCLQ 417, 419). He submits (at 420) that the credit was freely negotiable and that the fact the advising bank in London was simply one of any number of banks at whose counters negotiation might have occurred ought not to have been sufficient *per se* to displace the presumption in art 4(2). Moreover, as the Court of Appeal also indicated (at [67]) that the contract between the confirming bank and the issuing bank would have been governed by Indonesian law through the application of art 4(2), the application of art 4(5) to the relationship between beneficiary and issuing/confirming banks led to the commercially undesirable result of different laws being applied to various relationships arising out of the same letter of credit transaction (Hare, at 422–423).

3 STANDBY CREDITS, PERFORMANCE BONDS AND GUARANTEES

Standby credits, performance bonds and guarantees have a different function to that of documentary credits. Whereas the function of documentary credits is to provide payment for goods and services against documents, the function of the instruments considered in this section is to provide security against default in performance of the underlying contract. Although standby credits, performance bonds and demand guarantees may be used to secure the performance of the buyer and (more usually) the seller under an international sale contract (see, eg *State Trading Corpn of India Ltd v M Golodetz Ltd* [1989] 2 Lloyd's Rep 277), they are more often found in international construction contracts where the overseas employer requires financial security from a reputable third party (usually a bank) against the contractor defaulting in his performance of the contract.

(a) Standby credits[11]

A standby letter of credit is similar to an ordinary documentary credit in that it is issued by a bank and embodies an undertaking to make payment to a third party (the beneficiary) or to accept bills of exchange drawn by him, provided the beneficiary tenders conforming documents. But, whereas a documentary credit is a primary payment mechanism for discharge of the payment obligation contained in the underlying contract (ie the issuing or confirming bank is the first port of call for payment), the standby credit is given by way of security with the intention that it should only be drawn on if the party by whom the work should be done, or the goods or services provided, (the principal) defaults in the performance of his contractual obligations to the beneficiary (see RM Goode 'Abstract Payment Undertakings', Ch 9 of P Cane and J Stapleton (eds) *Essays for Patrick Atiyah* (1991), pp 212–213, 220; and also RM Goode [1992] LMCLQ 190, pp 192–193).

The liability of a bank under a standby credit is intended to be secondary to that of the principal (although, technically, the form of the credit makes the bank's liability primary) and the credit performs the same security function as would be provided by a bank guarantee (see RM Goode *Commercial Law* (3rd edn, 2004), p 1017). But, unlike a guarantee, a standby credit may be called upon by tendering any specified documents without the beneficiary having to prove actual default by the principal, eg the specified document may be simply a demand from the beneficiary or a statement from him that the principal is in default. Fraudulent calling on the credit is prohibited but, as we have already seen with regard to documentary credits (above, pp 878–879), this is notoriously difficult to establish.

Standby credits are covered by the UCP (subject to its incorporation by the parties), and the principles of autonomy of the credit and strict compliance apply to standby credits as they do to documentary credits in general. However, the UCP is generally regarded as being ill-suited to the security nature of standby credits, and so the International Chamber of Commerce, in collaboration with the Institute of International Banking Law and Practice, has produced separate Rules on International Standby Practices (ISP 98) (ICC Publication No 590), which came into effect on 1 January 1999. Standby credits can be issued subject to the UCP or ISP 98, depending on the will of the parties.

(b) Performance bonds and guarantees[12]

Although the terms 'performance bond' and 'performance guarantee' may be used to denote a true contract of suretyship,[13] they are now more often used to refer to instruments which are similar in form and function to standby credits (when they are sometimes called 'on demand' performance bonds or demand guarantees—hereafter collectively referred to in this text as 'demand guarantees'). The bank which issues a demand guarantee agrees to make

---

[11] See, generally, KP McGuinness *The Law of Guarantee* (2nd edn, 1996), Ch 12; P Zohrab 'Standby Letters of Credit: Autonomy' [1996] NZLJ 392 and 417.

[12] See, generally, G Andrews and R Millett *Law of Guarantees* (4th edn, 2005), Ch 16; R Bertrams *Bank Guarantees in International Trade* (3rd revised edn, 2004).

[13] See, eg *Wardens and Commonalty of the Mystery of Mercers of the City of London v New Hampshire Insurance Co* [1992] 2 Lloyd's Rep 365, CA; *Trafalgar House Construction (Regions) Ltd v General Surety and Guarantee Co Ltd* [1996] AC 199, HL. Under a contract of suretyship the guarantor's payment obligation is secondary in nature, ie it does not arise until the principal has defaulted. Suretyship bonds or guarantees are usually issued by insurance companies and not banks. The ICC has drawn up rules designed primarily for suretyship bonds issued in international transactions: see the Uniform Rules for Contract Bonds (1993, ICC Publication No 524).

payment on production of a written demand by the beneficiary, or his written declaration that the principal has defaulted. The beneficiary need only demand payment, he does not have to prove that the principal has defaulted in performance of the underlying contract (although sometimes the demand may have to be supported by specific documents, such as a certificate from an independent third party indicating the principal has defaulted or that payment is otherwise due).[14] The demand guarantee may be issued by a bank in the principal's country direct to the beneficiary located overseas (a three-party demand guarantee), or it may be issued by a local bank in the beneficiary's country against the counter-guarantee of the principal's bank (a four-party demand guarantee). In either case the principal's bank will require a counter-indemnity from its customer.

Edward Owen Engineering Ltd v Barclays Bank International Ltd
[1978] QB 159, Court of Appeal

The plaintiffs, English suppliers, contracted with Libyan buyers to supply and erect glass-houses in Libya. The plaintiffs agreed to provide the buyers with a performance bond for 10% of the contract price and the buyers agreed to open a confirmed irrevocable credit in their favour. The plaintiffs instructed an English bank, the defendants, to provide the bond against their counter guarantee. The defendants instructed the Umma Bank in Libya to issue the bond, undertaking to pay the amount 'on demand without proof or conditions'. Umma Bank then issued the bond. But the buyers failed to open a confirmed irrevocable documentary credit as agreed and so the plaintiffs terminated the supply contract. Nevertheless, the buyers went on to claim payment under the performance bond from Umma Bank, who in turn claimed payment from the defendants. The plaintiffs sought an injunction to restrain the defendants from paying. An interim injunction was granted by Boreham J but later discharged by Kerr J. The plaintiffs appealed.

Lord Denning MR: A performance bond is a new creature so far as we are concerned. It has many similarities to a letter of credit, with which of course we are very familiar. It has been long established that when a letter of credit is issued and confirmed by a bank, the bank must pay it if the documents are in order and the terms of the credit are satisfied. Any dispute between buyer and seller must be settled between themselves. The bank must honour the credit. That was clearly stated in *Hamzeh Malas & Sons v British Imex Industries Ltd* [1958] 2 QB 127, Jenkins LJ, giving the judgment of this court, said, at p 129: . . . [see above, p 866].

To this general principle there is an exception in the case of what is called established or obvious fraud to the knowledge of the bank. The most illuminating case is of *Sztejn v J Henry Schroder Banking*

---

[14]   See *Gold Coast Ltd v Caja de Ahorros del Mediterraneo* [2001] EWCA Civ 1086, [2002] 1 All ER (Comm) 142 (refund guarantee held to be first demand guarantee despite fact buyer's bank required to certify that buyer had become entitled to refund). Tuckey LJ said (at [11]): 'The question therefore is simply what is the nature of the refund guarantee in this case. This involves construing the instrument in its factual and contractual context having regard to its commercial purpose', and continued (at [15]) 'the task is to decide the nature of the instrument by looking as it as a whole without any preconceptions as to what it is.' In *Marubeni Hong Kong & South China Ltd v The Government of Mongolia* [2005] EWCA Civ 395, [2005] 2 All ER (Comm) 289 (instrument issued by defendant government undertaking to pay 'upon your simple demand all amounts payable under the Agreement if not paid when the same becomes due' was held to be a contract of suretyship). Carnwath LJ said (at [28]) that cases where documents are issued by banks which are 'described as, or assumed to be, performance bonds . . . provide no useful analogy for interpreting a document which was not issued by a bank and which contains no overt indication of an intention to create a performance bond or anything analogous to it.' For case extract, see below, p 1152.

Corpn 31 NYS 2d 631 (1941) which was heard in the New York Court of Appeals. After citing many cases Shientag J said, at p 633:

> It is well established that a letter of credit is independent of the primary contract of sale between the buyer and the seller. The issuing bank agrees to pay upon presentation of documents, not goods. This rule is necessary to preserve the efficiency of the letter of credit as an instrument for the financing of trade.

He said, at p 634, that in that particular case it was different because:

> on the present motion, it must be assumed that the seller has intentionally failed to ship any goods ordered by the buyer. In such a situation, where the seller's fraud has been called to the bank's attention before the drafts and documents have been presented for payment, the principle of the independence of the bank's obligation under the letter of credit should not be extended to protect the unscrupulous seller.

That case shows that there is this exception to the strict rule: the bank ought not to pay under the credit if it knows that the documents are forged or that the request for payment is made fraudulently in circumstances when there is no right to payment.

I would in this regard quote the words of Browne J in an unreported case when he was sitting at first instance. It is *Bank Russo-Iran v Gordon Woodroffe & Co Ltd* ((1972) 116 Sol Jo 921). He said:

> In my judgment, if the documents are presented by the beneficiary himself, and are forged or fraudulent, the bank is entitled to refuse payment if it finds out before payment, and is entitled to recover the money as paid under a mistake of fact if it finds out after payment.

But as Kerr J said in this present case:

> In cases of obvious fraud to the knowledge of the banks, the courts may prevent banks from fulfilling their obligation to third parties.

Such is the law as to a confirmed letter of credit. How does it stand with regard to a performance bond or a performance guarantee? Seeing that it is a guarantee of performance—that is, a guarantee that the supplier will perform his contracted obligations—one would expect that it would be enforced in such a case as this: suppose the English supplier had been paid for the goods and had delivered them, but that the Libyan customer then discovered that they were defective and not up to contract or that they had been delayed. The Libyan customer could then claim damages for the breach. But instead of coming to England to sue for the breach, his remedy would be to claim payment under the guarantee—of the 10 per cent or the 5 per cent of the price—as liquidated damage, so to speak. He claims payment from the Umma Bank. The Umma Bank pay him 'on first request.' They claim on Barclays Bank International. Then Barclays pay 'on first demand without proof or conditions.' And Barclays claim against the English suppliers, the payment being 'conclusive evidence.'

It is obvious that that course of action can be followed, not only when there are substantial breaches of contract, but also when the breaches are insubstantial or trivial, in which case they bear the colour of a penalty rather than liquidated damages: or even when the breaches are merely allegations by the customer without any proof at all: or even when the breaches are non-existent. The performance guarantee then bears the colour of a discount on the price of 10 per cent or 5 per cent, or as the case may be. The customer can always enforce payment by making a claim on the guarantee and it will then be passed down the line to the English supplier. This possibility is so real that the English supplier, if he is wise, will take it into account when quoting his price for the contract.

Take the case one stage further. The English supplier is not in default at all. He has not shipped the goods because he has not been paid. The Libyan customer has not provided the confirmed letter of credit. It is still open to the Libyan customer to make some allegation of default against the English supplier—as for instance not doing the preliminary work or not being ready and willing—and on that allegation to claim payment under the performance guarantee. On that request being made, payment will be made by the banks down the line: and be made by them 'on demand without proof or conditions.'

So, as one takes instance after instance, these performance guarantees are virtually promissory notes payable on demand. So long as the Libyan customers make an honest demand, the banks are bound to pay: and the banks will rarely, if ever, be in a position to know whether the demand is honest or not. At any rate they will not be able to prove it to be dishonest. So they will have to pay.

All this leads to the conclusion that the performance guarantee stands on a similar footing to a letter of credit. A bank which gives a performance guarantee must honour that guarantee according to its terms. It is not concerned in the least with the relations between the supplier and the customer; nor with the question whether the supplier has performed his contracted obligation or not; nor with the question whether the supplier is in default or not. The bank must pay according to its guarantee, on demand, if so stipulated, without proof or conditions. The only exception is when there is a clear fraud of which the bank has notice.

Such has been the course of decision in all the cases there have been this year in our courts here in England. First of all, there was *RD Harbottle (Mercantile) Ltd v National Westminster Bank Ltd* [1978] QB 146 before Kerr J. The judge considered the position in principle. I would like to adopt a passage from his judgment, p 761E–G.

> It is only in exceptional cases that the courts will interfere with the machinery of irrevocable obligations assumed by banks. They are the life-blood of international commerce. Such obligations are regarded as collateral to the underlying rights and obligations between the merchants at either end of the banking chain. Except possibly in clear cases of fraud of which the banks have notice, the courts will leave the merchants to settle their disputes under the contracts by litigation or arbitration.... The courts are not concerned with their difficulties to enforce such claims; these are risks which the merchants take. In this case the plaintiffs took the risk of the unconditional wording of the guarantees. The machinery and commitments of banks are on a different level. They must be allowed to be honoured, free from interference by the courts. Otherwise, trust in international commerce could be irreparably damaged.

Since that time there has been before Donaldson J and afterwards in this court *Howe Richardson Scale Co Ltd v Polimex-Cekop and National Westminster Bank Ltd* ([1915] 1 Lloyd's Rep 161). In that case Roskill LJ spoke to the same effect. He said [at p 165]:

> Whether the obligation arises under a letter of credit or under a guarantee, the obligation of the bank is to perform that which it is required to perform by that particular contract, and that obligation does not in the ordinary way depend on the correct resolution of a dispute as to the sufficiency of performance by the seller to the buyer or by the buyer to the seller as the case may be under the sale and purchase contract; the bank here is simply concerned to see whether the event has happened upon which its obligation to pay has risen.

So there it is: Barclays Bank International has given its guarantee—I might almost say its promise to pay—to Umma Bank on demand without proof or conditions. They gave that promise, the demand was made. The bank must honour it. This court cannot interfere with the obligations of the bank....
I would therefore dismiss this appeal.

Browne LJ: I agree that this appeal should be dismissed for the reasons given by Lord Denning MR. Kerr J in *Harbottle (Mercantile) Ltd v National Westminster Bank Ltd* [1978] QB 146 and this court in the *Howe Richardson* case ([1978] 1 Lloyd's Rep 161) treated a bank's position under a guarantee or performance bond of the type given by Barclays Bank to the Umma Bank as being very similar to the position of a bank which has opened a confirmed irrevocable credit, and I have no doubt that this is right.

Geoffrey Lane LJ: The law applicable in these circumstances is conveniently set out, as Lord Denning MR and Browne LJ have indicated, by Roskill LJ in the recent decision in *Howe Richardson Scale Co Ltd v Polimex-Cekop and National Westminster Bank Ltd*([1978] 1 Lloyd's Rep 161). The passage already cited by my brethren is followed by these words of Roskill LJ:

> The bank takes the view that that time has come and that it is compelled to pay; in my view it would be quite wrong for the court to interfere with Polimex's apparent right under this guarantee to seek payment from the bank, because to do so would involve putting upon the bank an obligation to inquire whether or not there had been timeous performance of the sellers' obligations under the sale contract.

In the present case Mr Ross-Munro [counsel for the suppliers] submits that, since this document between the two banks is expressed to be a guarantee, the bank is under no liability to pay prima facie unless, first of all, there is a principal debtor and, secondly, some default by the principal debtor in his obligations under his contract with the seller. Since, he submits, no such default on the part of the sellers is suggested, the guarantee does not come into effect. The answer to that appears to me to be this. Although this agreement is expressed to be a guarantee, it is not in truth such a contract. It has much more of the characteristics of a promissory note than the characteristics of a guarantee....

The only circumstances which would justify the bank not complying with a demand made under that agreement would be those which would exonerate them under similar circumstances if they had entered into a letter of credit, and that is this, if it had been clear and obvious to the bank that the buyers had been guilty of fraud. Mr Ross-Munro, conceding that that is the situation, endeavours to show that indeed fraud is clear and obvious here, that the bank knew about it, and accordingly he is entitled to succeed.

The way he seeks to establish fraud is this. He points to the undoubted fact that the buyers in Libya have failed to reply to any of the requests for a proper confirmed letter of credit according, Mr Ross-Munro submits, to the terms of the contract and, moreover, have failed to produce any suggestion of any default or breach of contract on the part of the sellers in England which would possibly justify a demand that the performance guarantee be implemented.

I disagree that that amounts to any proof or evidence of fraud. It may be suspicious, it may indicate the possibility of sharp practice, but there is nothing in those facts remotely approaching true evidence of fraud or anything which makes fraud obvious or clear to the bank. Thus there is nothing, it seems to me, which casts any doubt upon the bank's prima facie obligation to fulfil its duty under the two tests which I have set out.

It may be harsh in the result, but the sellers must have been aware of the dangers involved or, if they were not, they should have been aware of them, and either they should have declined to accept the terms of the performance bond or else they should have allowed for the possibility of the present situation arising by making some adjustment in the price.

I agree that the appeal should be dismissed.

Cargill International SA v Bangladesh Sugar and Food Industries Corp
[1996] 4 All ER 563, Queen's Bench Division

The plaintiff sellers agreed to sell a consignment of sugar to the defendant buyers. The sellers provided the buyers with an unconditional performance bond which was issued by the Dhaka branch of Banque Indosuez (the bank). The underlying contract of sale provided that the performance bond was liable to be forfeited if the sellers failed to fulfil any of the terms and conditions of the contract and also if any loss or damage occurred to the buyers as a result of the fault of the sellers. Shipment was made by the sellers, but rejected by the buyers who alleged, *inter alia*, that delivery was late. The sellers then applied for an injunction restraining the buyers from calling on the bond and a declaration that the buyers were not entitled to make a call on the bond or to retain any money so received on the ground that they had suffered no loss since the market for sugar had fallen and the buyers had replaced the rejected sugar at less than the contract price. On the assumption that the sellers were in breach of the contract of sale, Morison J ordered the trial of certain preliminary issues, including whether the buyers were entitled to make a call for the full amount of the performance bond and, if so, whether they were entitled to retain all the moneys received by them.

Morison J: I start with the commercial purpose of a performance bond. There is a wealth of authority concerned with the question whether and in what circumstances an interlocutory injunction may be granted (1) against the bank which issued the bond to restrain it from paying in accordance with its terms, and (2) against the beneficiary of the bond to prevent it from calling the bond.

The court will not grant an injunction in either case unless there has been a lack of good faith. The justification for this lies in the commercial purpose of the bond. Such bond is, effectively, as valuable as a promissory note and is intended to affect the 'tempo' of parties' obligations; in the sense that when an allegation of breach of contract is made (in good faith), the beneficiary can call the bond and receive its value pending the resolution of the contractual disputes. He does not have to await the final determination of his rights before he receives some moneys. On an application for an injunction, it is, therefore, not pertinent that the beneficiary may be wrong to have called the bond because, after a trial or arbitration, the breach of contract may not be established; otherwise, the court would be frustrating the commercial purpose of the bond. The concept that money must be paid without question, and the rights and wrongs argued about later, is a familiar one in international trade, and substantial building contracts. A performance bond may assume the characteristics of a guarantee, especially, if not exclusively, in building contracts, where the beneficiary must show, as a prerequisite for calling on the bond, that by reason of the contractor's non-performance he has sustained damage (see *Trafalgar House Construction (Regions) Ltd v General Surety and Guarantee Co Ltd* [1995] 3 All ER 737, [1996] AC 199).

However, it seems to me implicit in the nature of a bond, and in the approach of the court to injunction applications, that, in the absence of some clear words to a different effect, when the bond is called, there will, at some stage in the future, be an 'accounting' between the parties in the sense that their rights and obligations will be finally determined at some future date. The bond is not intended to represent an 'estimate' of the amount of damages to which the beneficiary may be entitled for the breach alleged to give rise to the right to call. The bond is a 'guarantee' of due performance. If the amount of the bond is not sufficient to satisfy the beneficiary's claim for damages, he can bring proceedings for his loss. As far as I am aware, and no case was cited to me to suggest otherwise, the performance bond is not intended to supplant the right to sue for damages. Indeed, such a contention would conflict with what I believe to be the commercial purpose of these instruments. Mr Hossain submitted that the buyer's rights were exhausted when the bond was called, but he could give no support for the proposition; and he had, I think, no satisfactory explanation as to why his clients should have wished so to restrict their damages. The bond could be called in any number of circumstances, at least some of which could have caused his clients losses substantially in excess of the bond value. If he were right, then, presumably, the beneficiary would decline to call the bond; yet serious loss caused by a breach of contract was the very event for which the bond was required and given in the first place. I reject, entirely, his submission on this point, both as being without legal foundation and as lacking in commercial good sense.

Therefore, the question arises as to why, if the beneficiary can sue to recover what he has actually lost, the seller (in this case) should not be able to recover any overpayment. It would seem, in principle, correct that if a performance bond does not exhaust one party's rights, it should not exhaust the rights of the other party.

What I perceive to be correct in principle, is fortified by authority. In *State Trading Corp of India Ltd v ED & F Man (Sugar) Ltd* [1981] Com LR 235 Lord Denning MR said (in an injunction case):

> I may say that performance bonds fulfil a most useful role in international trade. If the seller defaults in making delivery, the buyer can operate the bond. He does not have to go to far away countries and sue for damages, or go through a long arbitration. He can get the damages at once which are due to him for breach of contract. The bond is given so that, on notice of default being given, the buyer can have his money in hand to meet his claim for damages for the seller's non-performance of contract. If he receives too much, that can be rectified later at an arbitration. The courts must see that these performance bonds are honoured.

If the court had considered that an 'overpayment' could not be recovered, its approach to the grant of injunctive relief might have been different. Almost all cases where such relief has been sought are ones where the plaintiff is saying that there has been no breach, or that he has the benefit of some exclusion clause, or that the other contracting party has not suffered any loss. None of these contentions will suffice, partly because, I think, the court always recognised that the bonds affected the 'tempo' of the parties' obligations but not their substantive rights.

Support may also be found in two Australian cases. In the first, *Australian Conference Association Ltd v Mainline Constructions Pty Ltd (in liq)* (1978) 141 CLR 335, the question before the court was whether the employer under a building contract made with a builder (Mainline) which subsequently went into liquidation was entitled to pay sub-contractors out of the performance bond moneys which it had called, and been paid by the builder's bank. It was the bank's position, inter alia, that the employer was obliged to account to it for any surplus after the sub-contractors had been paid off. The employer conceded that it was not entitled to retain any surplus, and the court clearly believed that to be correct, as did the other two parties. The court's conclusion was that the issue had to be determined by reference to the contract between the employer and Mainline; it concluded that the surplus should be released to Mainline and not to the bank. In a subsequent building case (an injunction case), *Wood Hall Ltd v Pipeline Authority* (1979) 141 CLR 443, the court held that the beneficiary was entitled to call the bond but that once paid, the 'money must be held as security for the contractor's due and faithful performance of the work' (see 141 CLR 443 at 454 per Gibbs J).

Both these cases lend (limited) support for the proposition that moneys paid under a performance bond are designed to be used in accordance with the provisions of the contract and that any surplus is for the account of the party which provided the bond....

In Benjamin *Sale of Goods* (4th edn, 1992) para 23–218, there is the following passage:

> As the making of an excessive demand is, basically, a breach of the beneficiary's underlying contract, the amount ought to be regarded as repayable to the account party rather than to the bank.

The learned editors assume that the overpayment may be recovered and infer that the only question is whether the account party (the seller) or the bank is entitled to receive the repayment. They rely upon the two Australian cases as supporting the conclusion that it is the account party and not the bank which is entitled to the moneys.

As a matter of general principle, therefore, in the light of the commercial purposes of such bonds, the authorities to which I have referred and the textbook comments, I take the view that if there has been a call on a bond which turns out to exceed the true loss sustained, then the party who provided the bond is entitled to recover the overpayment. It seems to me that the account party may hold the amount recovered in trust for the bank, (where, for example, the bank had not been paid by him) but that does not affect his right to bring the claim in his own name. In the normal course of events, the bank will have required its customer to provide it with appropriate security for the giving of the bond, which would be called upon as soon as the bank was required to pay. On the facts of this case, no question of a trust or agency will arise. In principle, I take the view that the account party is always entitled to receive the overpayment, since his entitlement is founded upon the contract between himself and the beneficiary.

I turn therefore to the contract between the parties. Under cl 13 the bond was 'liable to be forfeited . . . if the SELLER fails to fulfil any of the terms and conditions of this contract . . . and also if any loss/damage occurs to the BUYER due to any fault of the SELLER'. It seems to me that on a proper construction of this clause, there is no indication that it was the parties' intention that the bond would either satisfy the whole of the buyer's damages (see above), or prevent the seller from recovering any overpayment. The word 'forfeit' might be apt to suggest that once called, the bond moneys had 'gone' for good. But if it had been the intention of the parties to produce a result whereby the buyer could both call on the bond and sue for damages, whereas the seller forfeited his right to any overpayment, then much plainer words would have been required to take this case away from the general principles as I perceive them to be. That being so, it seems to me that treating the two parts of the clause disjunctively, and treating the right to forfeit as arising if either there was a breach or if any loss or damage occurred to the buyer due to any fault of the seller (which might not be a breach) would make commercial good sense. The buyer is stipulating clearly that, as between himself and the seller, all he needs to show to be entitled to call on the bond is a breach of contract; he need not show damage (although damage will almost always follow); if, on the other hand, say through a misrepresentation by the seller, damage was caused to the buyer then the right to call the bond was conferred by the second half of the clause. But in either event, there will be an 'accounting' at trial or arbitration to ensure that the buyer has not been underpaid or overpaid. . . .

The basis upon which recovery may be made in respect of an overpayment is, I think, contractual rather than quasi contractual. It seems to me that it is necessary to imply into the contract that moneys paid under the bond which exceeded the buyer's actual loss would be recoverable by the seller. I am content to adopt Mr Males' formulation of the term which is to be implied into the sale contract, as a matter of necessity or on the basis that the implication of such a term was so obvious that its incorporation in the contract went without saying: 'that the buyer will account to the seller for the proceeds of the bond, retaining only the amount of any loss suffered as a result of the seller's breach of contract.'

It is unnecessary to consider the interesting argument advanced on penalty. Had I been persuaded that there was a term of the contract between the parties which enabled the buyer to call on the bond when he had suffered no damage, and to retain the moneys, I would have held the provision to have been penal. In *Workers Trust and Merchant Bank Ltd v Dojap Investments Ltd* [1993] 2 All ER 370 at 376, [1993] AC 573 at 582 Lord Browne-Wilkinson said:

> There is clear authority that in a case of a sum paid by one party to another under the contract as security for the performance of that contract, a provision for its forfeiture in the event of non-performance is a penalty from which the court will give relief by ordering repayment of the sum so paid, less any damage actually proved to have been suffered as a result of non-completion: *Public Works Comr v Hills* [1906] AC 368, [1904–7] All ER Rep 919.

[The decision of Morison J was upheld by the Court of Appeal: [1998] 1 WLR 461. There was no appeal against the judge's reasoning that it is implicit in the nature of a performance bond that in the absence of clear contractual words to a different effect there will be an accounting between the parties at some stage after the bond has been called: Potter LJ noted (at 465) that he had himself approved Morison J's reasoning in *Comdel Commodities Ltd v Siporex Trade SA* [1997] 1 Lloyd's Rep 424 at 431. The issue on appeal was whether the references to forfeiture in the underlying contract of sale indicated that the parties intended to oust the usual implication as to any subsequent accounting between the parties. The Court of Appeal held that it did not and that the reference to forfeiture referred only to the position as between the buyers and the bank, and not as between the buyers and the sellers.]

NOTES

1.　Since the *Edward Owen* case, the courts have continued to treat demand guarantees on a similar footing to documentary credits: see, eg *Intraco Ltd v Notis Shipping Corpn, The Bhoja Trader* [1981] 2 Lloyd's Rep 256; *Bolivinter Oil SA v Chase Manhattan Bank* [1984] 1 WLR 392; *Turkiye Is Bankasi AS v Bank of China* [1998] 1 Lloyd's Rep 250; but contrast *Potton*

Homes Ltd v Coleman Contractors (Overseas) Ltd (1984) 28 BLR 19 at 27–29; and see also C Debattista [1997] JBL 289 and Q Loh & TH Wu [2000] LMCLQ 348 (tracing the divergence of Singapore law from English law on this issue). As Professor RM Goode has stated ([1992] LMCLQ 190, p 192):

Demand guarantees share with documentary credits the characteristic of being abstract payment undertakings, that is to say, they are promises of payment which are considered binding upon communication to the beneficiary without the need for acceptance, consideration, reliance, or solemnity of form, and are separate from and independent of the underlying contract.

The fact that a documentary credit is a primary payment mechanism, whereas a demand guarantee is intended as a secondary obligation, must not, of course, be overlooked (Goode, above, p 193).

2.   The autonomous nature of a demand guarantee[15] makes it vulnerable to abusive calling.[16] Although the fraud exception applies, it is notoriously difficult to establish: see, eg *Harbottle (Mercantile) Ltd v National Westminster Bank* [1978] QB 146; *State Trading Corpn of India Ltd v ED & F Man (Sugar) Ltd* [1981] Com LR 235; *GKN Contractors Ltd v Lloyds Bank plc* (1985) 30 BLR 48; *Turkiye Is Bankasi AS v Bank of China* [1998] 1 Lloyd's Rep 250; and, generally, see above, pp 867–880. Only if the court considers that on the material before it, the only realistic inference to draw is that of fraud, will the principal have made out a sufficient case of fraud to obtain an injunction restraining the bank from making payment under the demand guarantee: see, eg *Kvaerner John Brown Ltd v Midland Bank plc* [1998] CLC 446, where Cresswell J granted an interlocutory injunction restraining the bank from making payment under a standby credit, and also against the beneficiary preventing receipt of payment. The same principles which apply in relation to applications for injunctions against banks also apply where the customer seeks an injunction to restrain the beneficiary from making demand: see the strong *obiter dictum* of Staughton LJ in *Group Josi Re v Walbrook Insurance Co Ltd* [1996] 1 WLR 1152 at 1161–1162, and also that of Rix J in *Czarnikow-Rionda Sugar Trading Inc v Standard Bank London Ltd* [1999] 1 All ER (Comm) 890 at 913, criticising the majority decision of the Court of Appeal in *Themehelp Ltd v West* [1996] QB 84. Again, the starting point is that the court will not grant an interlocutory injunction without clear evidence of fraud or lack of good faith on the part of the beneficiary (*TTI Team Telecom International Ltd v Hutchison 3G UK Ltd* [2003] EWHC 762 (TCC), [2003] 1 All ER (Comm) 914). Nevertheless, the issuing bank will not be obliged to pay on a demand guarantee if it is tainted by illegality (*Group Josi Re v Walbrook Insurance Co Ltd*, above, at 1163–1164, per Staughton LJ; *Mahonia Ltd v JP Morgan Chase Bank* [2003] EWHC 1927 (Comm), [2003] 2 Lloyd's Rep 911 at [68], per Colman J) or some other vitiating factor applies, eg the bank issued the demand guarantee as a result of a conspiracy between, or misrepresentation by, its customer and the beneficiary (*Solo Industries UK Ltd v Canara Bank* [2001] EWCA Civ 1059, [2001] 2 All ER (Comm) 217; see also *SAFA Ltd v Banque Du Caire* [2000] 2 All ER (Comm) 567, CA). In cases of abusive calling, the principal probably stands a better chance of obtaining a freezing injunction (formerly known as a *Mareva* injunction) restraining the beneficiary from using the funds he has received in payment of the demand guarantee, than he does of obtaining an injunction to prevent payment in the first place (*Intraco Ltd v Notis Shipping Corpn, The Bhoja Trader* [1981] 2 Lloyd's Rep 256). In appropriate cases the court may combine a freezing injunction with an ancillary order requiring the proceeds of the demand guarantee to be paid into court

---

[15] Now explicit in the ICC's *Uniform Rules for* Demand *Guarantees* (1992, ICC Publication No 458), art 2(b).

[16] See N Enonchong, 'The problem of abusive calls on demand guarantees' [2007] LMCLQ 83.

(*Themehelp Ltd v West* [1996] QB 84 at 103, per Evans LJ). But where the demand guarantee is to be paid abroad, it would be an unjustified interference with the operation of the instrument to order the bank to pay the money into an account in England (*Britten Norman Ltd v State Ownership Fund of Romania* [2000] 1 Lloyd's Rep Bank 315).

3.   Where a bank has paid the beneficiary under a demand guarantee and claims against the principal on a counter-indemnity, summary judgment will be given in favour of the bank unless the principal can show that there is a real prospect of proving at trial that the beneficiary had not honestly believed that he had the right to make the demand and that the bank had been aware of this (*Banque Saud Fransi v Lear Siegler Services Inc* [2006] EWCA Civ 1130, [2007] 1 All ER (Comm) 67). Arden LJ reasoned (at [18]) that the test was different from the one that applied in the case of a claim against a bank on a demand guarantee or letter of credit (where it had to be shown that there was a real prospect that the 'only realistic inference' was fraud), because the giver of a counter-indemnity, unlike the bank, was unlikely to be in a position to know by the time of the summary judgment application whether the fraud exception applied. The test is therefore lower than that which applies when a summary claim is brought against the bank on a demand guarantee, but Arden LJ (at [20]) still described it as 'a high hurdle to meet', and the principal was held not to have satisfied the test in the instant case.

4.   In four-party demand guarantee transactions, the counter-guarantee is not only independent of the underlying contract, but also independent of the primary guarantee (ICC's *Uniform Rules for Demand Guarantees* (1992, ICC Publication No 458), art 2(c); cf *Wahda Bank v Arab Bank plc* [1996] 1 Lloyd's Rep 470 at 473, per Staughton LJ: the extract from his judgment appears below). R Bertrams [1997] JIBFL 373, p 378–379 argues that recognition of the independent nature of the counter-guarantee in relation to the primary guarantee does not imply that the (non-)fulfilment of the terms of the primary guarantee is without significance: claims under the counter-guarantee should be rejected, and applications for restraining orders granted, if it is established that these terms have not been complied with.

5.   The principle of strict compliance applies to demand guarantees. But there has been uncertainty as to whether it applies with the same rigour to demand guarantees as it does to documentary credits: in *Siporex Trade SA v Banque Indosuez* [1986] 2 Lloyd's Rep 146 at 159, Hirst J thought not, whereas in *IE Contractors Ltd v Lloyds Bank plc* [1989] 2 Lloyd's Rep 205 at 207, Leggatt J thought that it did. The true position would seem to be that outlined by Staughton LJ on appeal in the *IE Contractors* case [1990] 2 Lloyd's Rep 496 at 500–501 (noted by H Bennett [1991] 5 JIBL 207), namely, that while there may be more scope for interpreting the demand guarantee as not requiring the demand to follow any particular form, it is in all cases a question of construction of the terms of the guarantee and that, once construed, the requirements of the instrument must be strictly complied with.

6.   The ICC has promulgated rules designed to provide a fair balance between the competing interests of the principal, beneficiary and those banks involved in the issue of demand guarantees: see the ICC's *Uniform Rules for Demand Guarantees* (1992, ICC Publication No 458) (the 'URDG'), which, in due course, are likely to replace the ICC's *Uniform Rules for Contract Guarantees* (1978, ICC Publication No 325)—for the time being parties can choose between either set of rules. The Uniform Rules only apply if adopted by the parties concerned. See generally, R Goode [1992] LMCLQ 190 and his *Guide to the ICC Uniform Rules for Demand Guarantees* (1992, ICC Publication No 510). A further choice for the parties is offered by the ICC's *Rules on International Standby Practices* (ISP 98) (ICC Publication No 590), which came into effect on 1 January 1999. The ISP Rules have the same scope as the URDG and apply to independent guarantee instruments issued subject to them (the relationship between

the URDG and ISP 98 is examined by BG Affaki in (1999) 1 Documentary Credit Insight 3, p 5). In addition, the United Nations Commission on International Trade Law (UNCITRAL) has recently completed a project on standby credits and demand guarantees. UNCITRAL's work culminated in the adoption in 1995 by the General Assembly of the United Nations Convention on Independent Guarantees and Standby Letters of Credit. The Convention covers much of the same ground as the URDG, although it also deals with the power of courts to grant injunctions restraining presentation or payment, something which falls outside the URDG. The Convention came into force on 1 January 2001, though it has not been widely adopted. The United Kingdom has no plans to ratify or accede to the Convention.

7.   There is an implied term in the contract between the beneficiary and the principal that the beneficiary will account to the principal to the extent of any overpayment that arises as a result of a call on the demand guarantee (*Cargill International SA v Bangladesh Sugar and Food Industries Corpn*, above). The amount is due to the principal as a debt, whether or not the principal has indemnified either the paying bank or the indemnifier of the paying bank (*Tradigrain SA v State Trading Corporation of India* [2005] EWHC 2206 (Comm), [2006] 1 All ER (Comm) 197 at [26], Clarke J). The obligation to account arises when the fact of the overpayment has been established either by agreement or judgment (*per* Clarke J, *obiter*, in *Tradigrain* at [28]). There is no implied term in the demand guarantee itself that there will be repayment of any part of a demand later found to be excessive (*Uzinterimpex JSC v Standard Bank plc* [2007] EWHC 1151 (Comm), [2007] 2 Lloyd's Rep 187 at [158], David Steel J).

Governing law and demand guarantees

Since 1 April 1991 the question of the governing law of a demand guarantee and any counter-guarantee involves the application of the Rome Convention on the Law Applicable to Contractual Obligations as enacted in the UK by the Contracts (Applicable Law) Act 1990. The principles to be applied under the Rome Convention are set out above, p 912. For demand guarantees and counter-guarantees which predate 1 April 1991, the governing law will be ascertained according to common law principles: in the absence of an express choice of law by the parties, the implied intention of the parties governs, failing that the law of the place with which the contract has its closest and most real connection. Application of the Rome Convention usually produces the same governing law as that which would have been chosen by common law principles. The next case is a leading case decided on common law principles.

Wahda Bank v Arab Bank plc
[1996] 1 Lloyd's Rep 470, Court of Appeal

English sellers entered into three sale contracts with Libyan buyers for the supply of air defence equipment. Demand guarantees were issued by the plaintiff bank in favour of the buyers at the request of the defendant bank (the sellers' bank) pursuant to the terms of the underlying contracts of sale. The defendant bank, which had itself received counter-indemnities from the sellers, in turn issued counter-guarantees in favour of the plaintiff bank. The demand guarantees were governed by Libyan law and the counter-indemnities were governed by English law, but the counter-guarantees between the two banks did not contain an express choice of law clause. Clarke J held that the inferred intention of the two banks was for the counter-guarantees to be subject to Libyan law. The plaintiff bank appealed as Libyan law gave the defendant bank a good arguable case to the main action for reimbursement, whereas English law did not.

Staughton LJ: The principle of law applicable to this case is, to my mind, what has been called on a previous occasion in the doctrine of infection (*Ilyssia Compania Naviera SA v Bamaodah*, [1985] 1 Lloyd's Rep 107 at p 112). That appears in a passage from Dicey and Morris, *The Conflict of Laws*, 11th edn (1987). I take it from where it was cited, in *Attock Cement Co Ltd v Romanian Bank For Foreign Trade*, [1989] 1 Lloyd's Rep 572 at p 580, col 1; [1989] 1 WLR 1147 at p 1158:

> The legal or commercial connection between one contract and another may enable a court to say that the parties must be held implicitly to have submitted both contracts to the same law.

For example, I have known the doctrine applied to a case where a charter-party had a term by which the proper law was chosen or, at any rate, had a term as to arbitration which could give rise to that inference; it was held that a bill of lading issued under that charter-party was infected by that same proper law.

The Court of Appeal in *Attock,* of which I was a member, decided that where there is a letter of credit issued in connection with a commercial transaction the letter of credit is not, or at any rate not necessarily, infected with the proper law of the commercial contract. That is a topic which was discussed in my judgment in that case at pp 580–581; pp 1158 to 1159. The point is that, as is agreed, a letter of credit is an autonomous contract. It does not depend in any way on performance or non-performance of the underlying commercial contract. And, as it seems to me, the parties to the commercial contract (the sellers) may well wish to have security for the payment that will become due to them, from a bank in a place and governed by a system of law which will assure them of payment, even if they are not able to obtain that system of law to govern their commercial contract. Therefore it was decided in *Attock* that the letter of credit was not necessarily governed by the same law as the commercial contract. What indeed was said was that as is ordinarily the case with banking transactions, it was governed by the law prevailing at the place where payment ought to be made under it.

I do not for one moment resile, even if I could, from what was decided in the *Attock* case. But the present case is different. The counter guarantees (contract C) are in one sense autonomous contracts. At any rate, by English law they can be operated by a demand on its own without regard to anything else that is going on in the outside world; proof of a demand is sufficient. But they are intimately connected with the guarantees (contract B).

A banker who issues a performance bond for a tiny commission will want to ensure that he takes no greater risk than the solvency of the bank putting up his counter guarantee. He will want to ensure that his right of reimbursement is back-to-back the same as his liability; and a banker who instructs another bank to issue a performance bond ought to, and in my view would, readily agree to that. Hence it is that in the absence of any express choice I can infer without any doubt that the parties intended the counter-guarantee (contract C) to be governed by the same law as governed the guarantees (contract B).

That was the decision of Mr Justice Phillips in a precisely similar case: *Turkiye Is Bankasi AS v Bank of China*, [1993] 1 Lloyd's Rep 132. It was also the view taken by two other Judges in a similar situation relating to letters of credit. When one bank issues a letter of credit and instructs another bank to confirm it, once again the confirming bank will wish to be sure that its right of reimbursement is, back-to-back, the same as its liability. It will wish to ensure that it takes no risk other than the solvency of the bank that is going to reimburse it.

The point has arisen, firstly, in the case of *Bank of Baroda v Vysya Bank*, [1994] 2 Lloyd's Rep 87, where Mr Justice Mance at p 94, said that it would be wholly anomalous if the same system of law were not to govern both the contract between the issuing and confirming bank and the contract between the confirming bank and the beneficiary.

It was said even more explicitly in *Bank of Credit and Commerce Hong Kong Ltd (in liquidation) v Sonali Bank*, [1995] 1 Lloyd's Rep 227 by Mr Justice Cresswell at p 237. Having set out a string of contracts, including:

3. The contract between issuing bank . . . and the confirming bank . . .
4. The contract between the issuing bank . . . and the seller/beneficiary . . .

5. The contract between the confirming bank…and the seller/beneficiary containing the confirming bank's additional undertaking…

Mr Justice Cresswell continued:

…The authorities recognize that there are strong commercial reasons why contracts 3,4 and 5 should be governed by the same system of law.

Finally, we were referred to one other case which was an example of the doctrine of infection in this sort of context. It was the case of *Broken Hill Pty Co Ltd v Xenakis,* [1982] 2 Lloyd's Rep 304. There it was held that a guarantee was, as I would put it, infected with the law of the contract guaranteed. One would expect them to be the same. That was the decision of Mr Justice Bingham.

We were referred to a set of rules propagated by the International Chamber of Commerce. They are called the ICC Uniform Rules For Demand Guarantees, ICC Publication No 458, Copyright 1992. They provide in art 2b:

Guarantees by their nature are separate transactions from the contract(s) or tender conditions on which they may be based, and Guarantors are in no way concerned with or bound by such contract(s), or tender conditions, despite the inclusion of a reference to them in the Guarantee.

They then go on in art 2c to deal with 'counter-guarantees' and say that they:

…are by their nature separate transactions the Guarantees…and Instructing Parties are in no way concerned with or bound by such guarantees…

I would not agree with that at all, I must say. The party who gives the performance bond is vitally concerned, I would say, in the counter-guarantee.

Article 27 of those so-called Uniform Rules provides:

Unless otherwise provided in the Guarantee or Counter-Guarantee, its governing law shall be that of the place of business of the Guarantor or Instructing Party (as the case may be), or, if the Guarantor or Instructing Party has more than one place of business, that of the branch that issued the Guarantee or Counter-Guarantee.

This case shows, to my mind, for the reasons that I have given, that that solution will not be very attractive to bankers. I should not be surprised if they decide to adopt something which is more suitable for their needs. However, that is for another day.

I would dismiss the appeal on this point.

[Henry and Pill LJJ concurred.]

NOTE

The result in this case would have been different if the ICC's *Uniform Rules for Demand Guarantees* (1992, ICC Publication No 458) (the 'URDG') had been incorporated in the counter-guarantees. Article 27 of the URDG provides as follows:

Unless otherwise provided in the Guarantee or Counter-Guarantee, its governing law shall be that of the place of business of the Guarantor or Instructing Party (as the case may be), or, if the Guarantor or Instructing Party has more than one place of business, that of the branch that issued the Guarantee or Counter-Guarantee.

As the counter-guarantees were issued from the London branch of the defendant bank, English law would have applied. Staughton LJ stated that he did not believe that art 27 would prove very attractive to bankers as it does not provide for linkage between the governing law of the guarantee and the counter-guarantee in the absence of choice: [1996] 1 Lloyd's Rep 470 at 474.

4 OTHER FINANCING METHODS

There are a number of other methods of financing international trade. They include the following.

(a) Forfaiting[17]

Forfaiting is a type of non-recourse finance which assists the export seller's cash flow whilst giving the buyer a period of credit. The seller draws a term bill of exchange on the buyer, the bill being drawn 'without recourse' to himself. The bill is accepted by the buyer and backed by the buyer's bank, which may either execute an aval on the bill (see above, p 572) or give a separate guarantee. The seller may then indorse the bill 'without recourse' and discount it to his own bank (the forfaiter). Alternatively, the buyer may make a promissory note which is guaranteed by his bank before being indorsed 'without recourse' by the seller and sold to the forfaiter. The advantage of this form of finance from the seller's point of view is that he receives an immediate payment of the cash value of the bill or note (less the usual charges and a discount fee) without recourse should the buyer default on payment. However, the forfaiter has the aval or guarantee of the buyer's bank to fall back on if the bill or note is dishonoured by non-payment. Usually, the forfaiter will itself sell the bill or note on into the *à forfait* market.

(b) International factoring

See below, pp 1071–1072.

(c) International financial leasing

A financial leasing arrangement is a three-party transaction. The lessee negotiates with a supplier to supply goods (usually capital items such as ships, aircraft or heavy equipment). The lessee also negotiates with a lessor (a bank or finance house) which purchases the goods from the supplier and leases them to the lessee. The lease is for the period of the anticipated working life of the asset and rentals are structured so as to amortise the capital cost of the equipment and give the lessor a return on capital (RM Goode [1987] JBL 318 and 399).

The UNIDROIT Convention on International Financial Leasing (1988), in force in only a limited number of States (and not the United Kingdom), governs certain types of financial leasing arrangements, namely those where:

(1) the lessee selects the goods and the supplier without relying primarily on the skill and judgment of the lessor;

(2) the supplier knows that the equipment is being acquired by the lessor in connection with a leasing arrangement; and

(3) the rentals are calculated to amortise the capital cost of the equipment (art 1(2)).

The Convention applies where the lessor and the lessee have places of business in different States and either all three parties (lessor, lessee and supplier) have places of business in

---

[17] See, generally, A Ripley *Forfaiting for Exporters* (1996); HJ Waterman 'Forfaiting', in J Norton and R Auerbach (eds) *International Finance in the 1990s* (1993), pp 239 ff.

Contracting States, or both the supply contract and the lease arrangement are governed by the law of a Contracting State (art 3(1)). The most important feature of the Convention is that it shifts responsibility for the non-delivery, late delivery or delivery of non-conforming equipment from the lessor to the supplier (see arts 8, 10 and 12(5)). This reflects the fact that the lessor has only a financial interest in the transaction. The 2001 Cape Town Convention on International Interests in Mobile Equipment with its associated aircraft Protocol is also of major importance in the field of leasing. Unlike the UNIDROIT Convention, the Cape Town Convention is not confined to cross-border leasing or to financial leasing agreements. UNIDROIT has also drawn up a draft model law on leasing which is designed for equipment financing in developing countries and countries in transition to a market economy. The draft model law covers operating leases as well as financial leases and domestic as well as cross-border transactions.

For further discussion of the 1988 UNIDROIT Convention and the UNIDROIT draft model law, see R Goode, H Kronke and E McKendrick, *Transactional Commercial Law: Text, Cases and Materials* (2007), Ch 10, and also Ch 12 for coverage of the 2001 Cape Town Convention.

(d) Confirming houses

Where an overseas buyer uses the services of a confirming house in the seller's country, and the confirming house makes itself liable to the seller for the price, the confirming house provides, in effect, non-recourse finance to the seller (see above pp 104–105).

5 EXPORT CREDIT GUARANTEES

The seller may insure himself against loss arising from the overseas buyer's failure to pay the price. He can do this by taking out an export credit guarantee (available from government and private agencies). An export guarantee covers such risks as the buyer's insolvency (commercial risk) and his inability to accept the goods or pay the price due to circumstances beyond his control, eg government orders (political risk). Export guarantees may also assist the seller to secure finance from his bank. For detailed discussion, see *Benjamin's Sale of Goods* (7th edn, 2006), Ch 24.

PART VII

ASSIGNMENT AND RECEIVABLES FINANCING

CHAPTER 22

ASSIGNMENT OF CHOSES IN ACTION

1 INTRODUCTION

(a) Chose in action defined

'The History of the Treatment of Choses in Action by the Common Law' by WS Holdsworth
(1920) 33 Harvard LR 967, pp 967–968

'All personal things are either in possession or action. The law knows no *tertium quid* between the two.'[1] It follows from this that the category of *choses* in action is in English law enormously wide, and that it can only be defined in very general terms. This is clear from the terms of the definition given by Channell J in *Torkington v Magee*,[2] which is generally accepted as correct. It runs as follows: '"Chose in action" is a known legal expression used to describe all personal rights of property which can only be claimed or enforced by action, and not by taking physical possession.' In fact the list of *choses* in action known to English law includes a large number of things which differ widely from one another in their essential characteristics. In its primary sense the term *'chose* in action' includes all rights which are enforceable by action—rights to debts of all kinds, and rights of action on a contract or a right to damages for its breach; rights arising by reason of the commission of tort or other wrong; and rights to recover the ownership or possession of property real or personal. It was extended to cover the documents, such as bonds, which evidenced or proved the existence of such rights of action. This led to the inclusion in this class of things of such instruments as bills, notes, cheques, shares in companies, stock in the public funds, bills of lading, and policies of insurance. But many of these documents were in effect documents of title to what was in substance an incorporeal right of property. Hence it was not difficult to include in this category things which were even more obviously property of an incorporeal type, such as patent rights and copyrights. Further accessions to this long list were made by the peculiar division of English law into common law and equity. Uses, trusts, and other equitable interests in property, though regarded by equity as conferring proprietary rights analogous to the rights recognised by law in hereditaments or in chattels, were regarded by the common law as being merely *choses* in action.

Footnotes

1 *Colonial Bank v Whinney* (1885) 30 Ch D 261,285, per Fry LJ, whose dissenting judgment was upheld by the House of Lords (1886) 11 App Cas 426.
2 [1902] 2 KB 427, 430 (see below, p 941).

NOTES

1.   Choses in action are usually divided into legal choses in action on the one hand and equitable choses in action on the other. Legal choses in action are those which before the coming into force of the Supreme Court of Judicature Act 1873 could be enforced by action at law and equitable choses in action are those which were enforceable only by a suit in equity.

2.   The distinction between legal and equitable choses in action is made in *Snell's Equity* (31st edn, 2005), para 3–01:

A chose may be legal (ie formerly enforceable in a court of law), such as a debt, bill of exchange, policy of insurance, sweepstake ticket or share in a company; or it may be equitable (ie formerly enforceable only by a suit in equity), such as a legacy, a legatee's rights in an unadministered estate, a share in a trust fund, surplus proceeds of sale in the hands of a mortgagee, or a right to relief against forfeiture of a lease for non-payment of rent.

For criticism of this form of classification, see *Halsbury's Laws of England* (4th edn (reissue), 2003), Vol 6, para 5.

3.   Rights and remedies are inextricably linked in English law. As Browne-Wilkinson VC said in *Spain v Christie, Manson & Woods Ltd* [1986] 3 All ER 28 at 35: 'in the pragmatic way in which English law has developed, a man's legal rights are in fact those which are protected by a cause of action. It is not in accordance, as I understand it, with the principles in English law to analyse rights as being something separate from the remedy given to an individual'. Holdsworth adopts a similar approach in his summary of the development of the term 'chose in action'. But this approach has its critics. For example, in his excellent book *Commercial and Personal Property Law* (1997), Simon Fisher writes (para 2.11) of Holdsworth's summary: 'primacy is given to the function of the chose in action as a procedure leading to the vindication of a right, instead of the remedy being incidental to the right. This reflects the pragmatic, if illogical, preoccupation of the English common law with the pursuit of remedies at the expense of a logical and systematic formulation of rights (and by extension, interests).'

4.   In *Investors Compensation Scheme Ltd v West Bromwich Building Society* [1998] 1 All ER 98, the House of Lords confirmed that whilst the existence of a remedy or remedies is an essential condition for the existence of a chose in action, that does not mean that the remedies are property in themselves, capable of assignment separately from the chose. Their Lordships held that a claim to rescission of a mortgage is a right of action, but not a chose in action or part of a chose in action which the owner can assign separately from his property. On the other hand, a right to damages is a chose in action which can be assigned. It followed that there was no objection to a clause in the Investors Compensation Scheme claim form by which investors assigned a right to damages against a building society to the Investors Compensation Scheme Ltd, but which did not assign (because legally impossible) a right to rescission of the investors' mortgages with the building society.

5.   In *Goel v Pick* [2006] EWHC 833 (Ch), [2007] 1 All ER 982, Sir Francis Ferris recently held (at [20]) that a car owner's ability to apply to the Driver and Vehicle Licensing Authority

(DVLA), to ask for the transfer of a vehicle registration mark (a VRM) from one vehicle to another (the car owner can not require the DVLA to do so), could not be described as a chose in action and, even if it could be so described, it was not capable of being 'assigned', as distinct from being exercised in accordance with the relevant regulations made under statute that govern the transfer of VRMs. The VRM was 'an item of property only in a very qualified sense.'

(b) Assignment defined

Norman v Federal Comr of Taxation
(1963) 109 CLR 9, High Court of Australia

By a deed dated 21 December 1956 the taxpayer assigned to his wife as a gift all the interest derived from the sum of £3,000 which was part of a sum deposited by him on loan at interest with a named firm. The loan was not for a fixed term and the firm was free to repay it or any part of it at any time without notice. By the same deed the taxpayer also assigned dividends to which he might be entitled arising from estates in which he had a beneficial interest. In 1957 the trustees of these estates transferred to the taxpayer his proportion of certain shares and he was registered as the shareholder. During the year ending 30 June 1958, £450 was paid by way of interest on the loan of £3,000 and dividends amounting to £460 were paid on the shares. The Commissioner claimed that these sums remained the income of the taxpayer and assessable to tax in his hands. The taxpayer argued that because of the deed of assignment the interest and dividend payments were part of his wife's income and not his own. By a majority (McTiernan and Windeyer JJ dissenting) the High Court of Australia held that the assignment of the interest and the dividend payments was ineffective.

Menzies J: ...It is common ground that the assignment did not operate as a legal assignment of interest or the taxpayer's right to it, and the real question is whether there was an effectual equitable assignment of a right to interest. I do not think there was because what was assigned was not an existing right but was no more than a right which might thereafter come into existence and so could not be effectually assigned in equity without consideration.

In general future property was not assignable at common law: *Lunn v Thornton* ((1845) 1 CB 379) but in equity after-acquired property was assignable for value according to the principles stated by Lord Macnaghten in *Tailby v Official Receiver* ((1888) 13 App Cas 523) but only for value notwithstanding the assignment was by deed: *Re Ellenborough* ([1903] 1 Ch 697). If then interest that may arise under a contract has the character of a future rather than an existing right, the deed, lacking consideration, was not effective to entitle the assignee to the interest in question as and when it became due and payable. I regard interest which may accrue in the future upon an existing loan repayable without notice as having the character of a right to come into existence rather than of a right already in existence and I do not regard *G & T Earle (1925) Ltd v Hemsworth RDS* ((1928) 44 TLR 758), upon which Mr Bright for the taxpayer relied, as any authority to the contrary. In that case no more was decided than that an assignment of a specific fund retained under a building contract which did not become payable until an architect's certificate was given, which happened after the date of the assignment, was a good legal assignment of a chose in action. As Wright J, the learned trial judge, said in a judgment fully approved by the Court of Appeal:— 'I find there was a specific fund...In my judgment the retention moneys represented moneys actually earned at the date of the certificate, though in fact these retention moneys, as their name indicates, were to be held as a sort of security and in any case subject to having set off against them any cross-claims, which would reduce the amount when the final settlement came and the final certificate was issued. The retention moneys, therefore, were only future in the sense that they were not payable until some future date' ((1928) 44 TLR 605 at 609). An accruing debt arising out of contract, though not payable at the date of the assignment, was, it was held, assignable at law. One other observation upon the applicability of that case to the present may be made, that is, it is not to be assumed that every right that can now be assigned at law without consideration pursuant to s 25(6) of the Judicature Act and corresponding legislation can also be assigned in equity voluntarily. Thus if, as seems to be generally accepted, . . . the section extends to future debts and not merely debts not presently payable, in equity as distinct from the Judicature Act, the effectiveness of voluntary assignment remains limited to existing rights and interests. See *Tailby v Official Receiver* ((1888) 13 App Cas 523) and *Re McArdle* ([1951] Ch 669 at 676), per Jenkins LJ.

[For the same reason as that given by Windeyer J (below) and because of a specific provision of Australian tax legislation, Menzies J held that the dividend payments remained assessable to tax in the hands of the taxpayer.]

Windeyer J (dissenting): . . . In *Lampet's Case* ((1612) 10 Co Rep 46b at 48a), Coke spoke of 'the great wisdom and policy of the sages and founders of our law, who have provided that no possibility, right, title, nor thing in action, shall be granted or assigned to strangers, for that would be the occasion of multiplying of contentions and suits'. It was a somewhat unsophisticated view of legal rights that led the common lawyers to classify choses in action and debts with mere possibilities, and to condemn all assignments of them as leading to maintenance.

Assignment means the immediate transfer of an existing proprietary right, vested or contingent, from the assignor to the assignee. Anything that in the eye of the law can be regarded as an existing subject of ownership, whether it be a chose in possession or a chose in action, can to-day be assigned, unless it be excepted from the general rule on some ground of public policy or by statute. But a mere expectancy or possibility of becoming entitled in the future to a proprietary right is not an existing chose in action. It is not assignable, except in the inexact sense into which, again to use Maitland's words, lawyers slipped when it is said to be assignable in equity for value.

The distinction between a chose in action, which is an existing legal right, and a mere expectancy or possibility of a future right is of cardinal importance in this case, as will appear. It does not, in my view, depend on whether or not there is a debt presently recoverable by action because presently due and payable. A legal right to be paid money at a future date is, I consider, a present chose in action, at all events when it depends upon an existing contract on the repudiation of which an action could be brought for anticipatory breach.

The common law doctrine that debts and other choses in action were not assignable never applied to Crown debts; and, by the influence of the law merchant, bills of exchange and promissory notes were outside it. And it was never accepted in equity. 'Courts of equity from the earliest times thought the doctrine too absurd for them to adopt' said Buller J in 1791 in the course of a vigorous condemnation of it: *Master v Miller* ((1791) 4 Term Rep 320 at 340). Furthermore he said that already at common law it had been 'so explained away that it remains only an objection to the form of the action in any case'. Blackstone had said 'this nicety is now disregarded': *Commentaries*, ii, 442. In *Balfour v Sea Fire Life Assurance Co* ((1857) 3 CBNS 300 at 308), Willes J said that the doctrine had long been exploded 'as everyone must know'. What had happened was that the common law rule came to be circumvented in various ways. One was by novation. Another was by the assignor giving a power of attorney to the assignee to sue the debtor at law in the assignor's name, without having to render an account: the history of this has been narrated at length by Mr Bailey in learned articles in the *Law Quarterly Review* vols 47 and 48. And courts of equity would come to the assistance of the assignee if the assignor refused to do whatever was necessary to enable the assignee to get the benefit of the assignment. Thus a recalcitrant assignor would be required, on having an indemnity for his costs, to permit his name to be used in an action to recover the debt; or an assignor would be restrained from receiving the debt for himself, as for example in *L'Estrange v L'Estrange* ((1850) 13 Beav 281). Because the assistance of equity was available, it was generally not needed. The common law courts recognized that an assignee might sue in the assignor's name. So that in 1849 it could be said that 'the courts of law have adopted the doctrines of the court of chancery in regard to assignments of choses in action'; so much so that 'In ordinary cases, where the plaintiff has an easy remedy by suing in the name of the assignor, the court (scil. the Court of Chancery) will not entertain jurisdiction, but leave the party to his remedy at law': *Spence, Equitable Jurisdiction of the Court of Chancery,* vol 2, pp 853, 854; and see *Roxburghe v Cox* ((1881) 17 Ch D 520), Dicey, *Parties to an Action* (1870) pp 66–72. Therefore, as the Chief Justice observed during the hearing of this case, it is somewhat misleading to say, as is often said, that before the Judicature Act the common law would not allow assignments of legal choses in action. Long before 1873 the development of common law processes and the impact of equity had pushed the common law prohibition of the assignment of choses in action back into history. Nevertheless the original doctrine survived, to this extent that, until the Judicature Act 1873, s 25(6), and the corresponding statutory provisions in Australia and elsewhere came into operation, an assignee of a legal debt could not in his own name bring an action against the debtor to recover the debt. The original creditor must be the plaintiff on the record. He remained in law the owner of the chose in action. What the provision of the Judicature Act 1873, did was to render unnecessary the previous circumlocutions. Debts and other legal choses in action were made directly assignable by the statutory method. But this, while it simplified assignments, has not simplified the law surrounding them, as the argument in this case showed....

[I]t was said a thing which is not yet in existence cannot be the subject of an equitable assignment except for consideration. That, as I have said, is undoubtedly so. It is true too that the interest, to the extent of £450, that the deed assigned was not due and payable at the date of the deed. But a contract to pay a sum of money on a future day, call it interest or what you will, calculable in amount according to conditions presently agreed, is in my view a presently existing chose in action. As between the parties to a contract of money lent at interest the borrower is simply a debtor who must pay a sum or sums (called interest) that he has, for good consideration (the forbearance of the creditor) contracted to pay to his creditor at the time or times stipulated. Why should not the creditor before the date when this debt becomes due and payable, assign his right to receive payment on the due date? He could assign the whole under the statute: *Walker v Bradford Old Bank Ltd* ((1884) 12 QBD 511). Why not part in equity? What he assigns is not, it seems to me, a right to arise in the future but a present contractual right to be paid at a future date a sum of money, to be calculated in the agreed manner: cf *Lett v Morris* ((1831) 4 Sim 607). In *Brice v Bannister* ((1878) 3 QBD 569 at 573), Lord Coleridge CJ said 'that a debt to become due is a chose in action, is clear'. Interest on money lent is recoverable by action at law as a debt separate from the principal, as the common indebitatus count for interest shows:...

But it was urged this case is not like a case of a loan for a fixed term. What was owing might, it is pointed out, have been repaid by the partnership, or reduced below £3,000, after the date of the deed of assignment and before 1st July 1957. As a matter of law, no doubt that is so. But it does not, I think, follow that the taxpayer had for that reason no assignable right. He had a present right to be paid interest at a future date on the money he had lent, unless in the meantime the loan was repaid. The taxpayer assigned the benefit of this contract, to the extent of £450 to become due conditionally in 1958, to his wife by the deed of 1956. I consider that the deed was an effectual equitable assignment....

I turn now to the second matter, the sum of £460....

Is a dividend that may become payable in the future upon shares presently held something that can be assigned in equity? Is it a present chose in action or a mere possibility? Is it property in existence, or something not in existence and therefore not capable of being assigned in the absence of consideration? I think it is the latter. The court will not compel directors to declare a dividend: *Bond v Barrow Haematite Steel Co* [1902] 1 Ch 353. A dividend is not a debt until it is declared. Until then it is in the eye of the law a possibility only. When it is declared it becomes a debt for which a shareholder who is on the register at the date of the declaration may sue. The companies paid the dividends to the registered holder of the shares, the taxpayer. They knew nothing of the purported assignment. Depending perhaps in some cases on their articles of association, they might have paid the dividends directly to the taxpayer's wife had they been directed by him to do so. But, in the absence of consideration, such a direction would have been merely a revocable mandate, not an assignment. Dividends that may be declared are to my mind quite unlike the interest that will become due according to an existing contract of loan if the loan be not repaid.

[McTiernan J (dissenting) gave a similar judgment to that of Windeyer J.
Dixon CJ delivered a judgment similar to that of Menzies J.
Owen J concurred with Menzies J.]

NOTES

1.   The following dictum of Windeyer J in *Norman v Federal Comr of Taxation* is often cited to explain the meaning of 'assignment':

Assignment means the immediate transfer of an existing proprietary right, vested or contingent, from the assignor to the assignee. Anything that in the eye of the law can be regarded as an existing subject of ownership, whether it be a chose in possession or a chose in action, can to-day be assigned, unless it be excepted from the general rule on some ground of public policy or by statute.

For example, A purchases goods from B on deferred payment credit. B needs finance. B assign's A's debt to C in return for immediate payment from C. When payment from A falls due, A pays C instead of B. The effect of the assignment is to transfer B's payment entitlement to C. A is the debtor, B the assignor and C the assignee.

2.   Section 25(6) of the Supreme Court of Judicature Act 1873 provided in general terms for the assignment of choses in action at law. It was repealed and substantially re-enacted by s 136 of the Law of Property Act 1925. An assignment under s 136 is called a 'statutory' or 'legal' assignment and it will pass the legal right to the chose in action. If there is a legal assignment of a legal or equitable chose in action the assignee may bring an action to enforce the chose in his own name and he does not have to join the assignor as a party to the action. Exceptionally, assignment at law is also possible in the following cases, namely (1) assignments by and to the Crown, (2) assignment of annuities, (3) assignment of certain negotiable instruments under the law merchant (now mostly regulated by statute), and (4) assignment of particular choses in action in accordance with the provisions of special statutory enactments (eg assignment of shares in a company under the Companies Act 2006, s 544 and Part 21; assignment of policies of life insurance under s 1 of the Policies of Assurance Act 1867; assignment of copyright under s 90 of the Copyright, Designs and Patents Act 1988).

3.   Since the seventeenth century the courts of equity have always permitted and given effect to assignments of choses in action. Such an assignment is called an 'equitable assignment' and it will pass an equitable, though not a legal, right to the chose in action. In the case of an *absolute* equitable assignment of an equitable chose in action the assignee can bring an action to enforce the chose in his own name. However, if the assignor retains an interest in the chose, the equitable assignee of an equitable chose in action must join the assignor to the action. In the case of an equitable assignment of a legal chose in action, the action used to have to be brought in the name of the assignor (see Windeyer J, above, as to how equity would compel the assignor to lend his name to the action); however, modern practice is simply for the assignee to join the assignor to the action as co-claimant if he is willing to co-operate, and as co-defendant if he is not. This rule, generally recognised in the case law to be merely procedural in nature (but see G Tolhurst (2002) 118 LQR 98), is designed to ensure that the debtor is protected from the assignor later disputing the validity of the assignment or bringing separate proceedings based on some retained interest in the chose (*Raiffeisen Zentralbank Osterreich AG v Five Star General Trading LLC* [2001] EWCA Civ 68, [2001] QB 825 at [60]; *Weddell v J A Pearce & Major* [1988] Ch 26 at 40–41). The rule may be

waived where it is not needed, in particular where there is no risk of a separate claim by the assignor (*William Brandt's Sons & Co v Dunlop Rubber Co Ltd* [1905] AC 454 at 462, HL, a case of waiver by the debtor; *Hendry v Chartsearch Ltd* [1998] CLC 1382 at 1390, CA, a case of waiver by the court). Proceedings by the assignee alone are not a nullity and joinder, where necessary, may be sought at any time during their course. A similar rule applies where (most unusually) the equitable assignor of a legal chose decides to sue the debtor: the assignor must join the assignee to the proceedings (*Three Rivers District Council v Governor and Co of the Bank of England* [1996] QB 292, CA: criticised by A Tettenborn [1995] CLJ 499). Today equitable assignments are given effect to in all courts to the same extent and in the same manner as formerly in a court of equity (s 49 of the Supreme Court Act 1981).

4.   Whether at law or in equity, only existing proprietary rights (including existing choses in action) can be assigned. Future choses in action (including a mere expectancy or spes successionis) cannot be assigned, although the purported assignment for value of a future chose in action will be given effect in equity as a contract to assign the chose if and when it comes into existence and comes into the hands of the assignor (*Raiffeisen Zentralbank Osterreich AG v Five Star General Trading LLC*, above, at [80]–[81]). The law is best summarised by Windeyer J in *Norman v Federal Comr of Taxation* when he said that (at 24):

…in equity a would-be present assignment of something to be acquired in the future is, when made for value, construed as an agreement to assign the thing when it is acquired. A court of equity will ensure that the would-be assignor performs this agreement, his conscience being bound by the consideration. The purported assignee thus gets an equitable interest in the property immediately the legal ownership of it is acquired by the assignor, assuming it to have been sufficiently described to be then identifiable. The prospective interest of the assignee is in the meantime protected by equity. These principles, which now govern assignments for value of property to be acquired in the future, have been developed and established by a line of well-known cases, of which *Holroyd v Marshall* (1862) 10 HL Cas 191; *Collyer v Isaacs* (1881) 19 Ch D 342; *Tailby v Official Receiver* (1888) 13 App Cas 523; and *Re Lind, Industrials Finance Syndicate v Lind* [1915] 2 Ch 345, are the most important.

5.   As can be seen from *Norman v Federal Comr of Taxation*, it may be extremely difficult to distinguish between existing and future choses in action. Compare that case with the following cases:

G & T Earle Ltd v Hemsworth RDC
(1928) 44 TLR 758, Court of Appeal

A firm of contractors agreed to build certain cottages for Hemsworth RDC. By the terms of the building contract, as subsequently varied, each month the contractors were to be paid 90 per cent of the value of all work completed by them as certified by the architects. The remaining 10 per cent of the value of the work completed was to be held in a retention fund which was to be paid to the contractors on the issue of the architects' final certificate. During the course of the building work the contractors purported to assign to the plaintiffs 'all moneys now or hereafter to become due to us from the Hemsworth Rural District Council for retention money'. At the time of the assignment all the retention fund had accrued but the architects had not issued their final certificate. The issue before the Court of Appeal was whether the money standing to the credit of the retention fund was an existing chose in action or a mere expectancy at the time of the purported assignment. Affirming the decision of Wright J, the Court of Appeal held that it was an existing chose. In the only reasoned judgment delivered in the Court of Appeal, Scrutton LJ stated that 'where the thing assigned arises out of an existing contract, although it may not become payable until a later date than the assignment, it is a debt or other legal thing in action which can be assigned and sued for without joining the assignor as a party'. As the retention money had already been earned when the assignment took place it represented an existing chose in action, even though the time of actual payment had yet to accrue.

Shepherd v Federal Taxation Comr
(1965) 113 CLR 385, High Court of Australia

The taxpayer was the grantee of certain letters patent relating to castors. He granted to C a licence to manufacture the castors and, in return, C agreed to pay him royalties directly in proportion to the number of castors manufactured. By deed the taxpayer then purported to assign by way of gift absolutely and unconditionally to certain named persons all his 'right title and interest in and to an amount equal to ninety per cent of the income which' might accrue during a period of three years under the licence agreement. The High Court of Australia (Barwick CJ and Kitto J; Owen J dissenting) held that on its true construction the deed constituted a present assignment of an existing chose in action. The majority accepted that the taxpayer had assigned his existing contractual right to future royalties, even though the quantum of the royalties had yet to be ascertained. As Kitto J said (at 396): The tree, though not the fruit, existed at the date of the assignment as a proprietary right of the appellant of which he was competent to dispose; and he assigned ninety per centum of the tree.' The majority distinguished *Norman v Federal Comr of Taxation* as a case where the taxpayer had no existing right to future interest payments because interest would only be payable if the loan remained in existence and the taxpayer had no right to keep it in existence in the future as the debtor firm had the right to repay the loan whenever it wished. By contrast, in *Shepherd's* case there was certainty at the time of the assignment that the contractual relationship between the patentee and the licence was not terminable at the whim of the obligor during the period for which the assignment was to operate (see MC Cullity and HAJ Ford (1966) 30 Conv 286).

6.   In his book *Legal Aspects of Receivables Financing* (1991), Dr Fidelis Oditah summarises the distinction made by English law between existing and future receivables as follows (pp 28–29):

English law draws an arbitrary distinction between existing and future receivables on the one hand, and future receivables and other contingent liabilities, on the other. All contractual rights are vested from the moment when the contract is made, even though they may not be presently enforceable, whether because the promisee must first perform his own part of the bargain, or because some condition independent of the will of either party (such as the elapsing of time) has to be satisfied. The result is that English law treats as existing debts not only those which have been *earned* by the promisee, whether or not presently payable, but also those which are *unearned*. The basis for the inclusion of unearned rights to payment in the category of *existing* receivables even where the contract is wholly executory is that they *grow out of a present obligation*. So it is that for a long time the courts have treated as existing or present receivables a legal right to be paid only at a future date if it depends upon an existing contract on the repudiation of which an action could be brought for an anticipatory breach. The contract is the *tree,* the future debts which *may* arise, the fruits. The unearned debts are *potential* and hence existing. But in so lumping earned (even though not presently payable) debts and unearned, albeit potential, debts, as existing debts, the common law has, in a somewhat extravagant fashion, destroyed the vital distinction between *rights in esse* and *rights in potentia*. Thus, a right to interest under a fixed-term loan, future rent from existing leases, sums payable under an existing construction contract, royalties payable under an existing copyright, freight payable under a signed bill of lading, and sums payable for goods or services not yet delivered or rendered, are all present receivables. Uncertainty as to the amount payable is immaterial. Similarly the fact that under some of these contracts nothing may be earned because the right is conditional on counter-performance is not considered important.

This passage from Dr Oditah's book has been cited with approval by Mance J in *Marathon Electrical Manufacturing Corpn v Mashreqbank PSC* [1997] 2 BCLC 460 at 465–466.

7.   For a detailed history of the law relating to the assignment of choses in action, see SJ Bailey (1931) 47 LQR 516, (1932) 48 LQR 248 and 547. For a useful review of the foundations of assignment, see G McMeel [2004] LMCLQ 483–494.

(c) Assignment distinguished from novation, acknowledgment and power of attorney

(i) *Novation*

Assignment involves the transfer of existing proprietary rights without the consent of the debtor. Contractual liabilities cannot be assigned. As Lord Browne-Wilkinson emphasised in *Linden Gardens Trust Ltd v Lenesta Sludge Disposals Ltd* [1994] 1 AC 85 at 103: 'the burden of a contract can never be assigned without the consent of the other party to the contract in which event such consent will give rise to a novation'. However, in some exceptional cases the discharge of a burden by the assignee may be a condition of the enjoyment of the assigned benefit, and in other (even more exceptional) cases the transfer of a benefit may carry a burden with it, even though the two are independent of each other (what Megarry VC referred to as the 'pure principle of benefit and burden' in *Tito v Waddell (No 2)* [1977] Ch 106 at 302).

Novation involves the substitution of a new contract for an existing contract, either between the same parties, or between different parties. Thus, where there is to be a change of creditor, the debtor, the old creditor and the new creditor must be parties to the new contract. Unlike an assignment, which does not require the debtor's consent, a novation requires the consent of all parties (*Rasbora Ltd v JCL Marine Ltd* [1977] 1 Lloyd's Rep 645). The new contract must be supported by consideration moving from the new promisee (*Tatlock v Harris* (1789) 3 Term Rep 174 at 180). See generally, J Bailey (1999) 14 JCL 189.

(ii) *Acknowledgment*

Since the middle of the nineteenth century, it has been possible for a transferee to bring an action against a fundholder for money had and received if the transferor instructs a person (the fundholder) holding a fund for him to pay it to the transferee and the fundholder agrees to do so (*Griffin v Weatherby* (1868) LR 3 QB 753). The transferee need not provide consideration for the fundholder's promise as his remedy is restitutionary and not contractual. It was always accepted that only a fundholder could attorn in this way; a transferee could only enforce a promise made by a mere debtor (ie not holding a fund) if the transferee had supplied consideration for the promise to pay (*Liversidge v Broadbent* (1859) 4 H & N 603). However, in *Shamia v Joory* [1958] 1 QB 448, Barry J rejected this limitation (*Liversidge v Broadbent* not being cited to him) holding that if a creditor asks his debtor to pay a third party, and the debtor agrees to do so, and informs the third party of his agreement, then the third party is entitled to sue the debtor even though he supplied no consideration for the debtor's promise. The decision has been described as 'unsound' and has been subjected to sustained criticism (see, R Goff and G Jones *The Law of Restitution* (7th edn, 2007), para 28–003; JD Davies (1959) 75 LQR 220, pp 231–233; cf E Peel, *Treitel's Law of Contract* (12th edn, 2007), para 12–004). Even if *Shamia v Joory* is correct, the principle of *acknowledgment* (as it has been called) differs from assignment in that it requires the consent of the debtor.

(iii) Power of Attorney

The creditor may give a third party a power of attorney to sue the debtor in the creditor's name without having to account to the creditor (see, for example, *Gerard v Lewis* (1867) LR 2 CP 305). Unlike an assignment, which is irrevocable, the creditor may generally revoke his power of attorney.

QUESTIONS

1. Why was the common law against the assignment of choses in action? See *Fitzroy v Cave* [1905] 2 KB 364 at 372, CA.

2. 'English law adopts a generous interpretation of "existing receivables"'. True or false?

3. Can all existing choses in action be assigned? See below, pp 967ff.

4. Can a debtor assign his payment obligation to a third party? See *Tolhurst v Associated Portland Cement Manufacturers (1900) Ltd* [1902] 2 KB 660 at 668, CA.

2 STATUTORY ASSIGNMENT

Law of Property Act 1925, s 136(1)

136. (1) Any absolute assignment by writing under the hand of the assignor (not purporting to be by way of charge only) of any debt or other legal thing in action, of which express notice in writing has been given to the debtor, trustee or other person from whom the assignor would have been entitled to claim such debt or thing in action, is effectual in law (subject to equities having priority over the right of the assignee) to pass and transfer from the date of such notice—

  (a) the legal right to such debt or thing in action;

  (b) all legal and other remedies for the same; and

  (c) the power to give a good discharge for the same without the concurrence of the assignor:

Provided that, if the debtor, trustee or other person liable in respect of such debt or thing in action has notice—

  (a) that the assignment is disputed by the assignor or any person claiming under him; or

  (b) of any other opposing or conflicting claims to such debt or thing in action;

he may, if he thinks fit, either call upon the persons making claim thereto to interplead concerning the same, or pay the debt or other thing in action into court under the provisions of the Trustee Act 1925.

Requirements

(i) Legal and equitable choses may be assigned

Torkington v Magee

[1902] 2 KB 427, Divisional Court

Magee contracted with Rayner to sell him a reversionary interest in certain funds under a settlement. Rayner by deed assigned his interest in the contract to Torkington and notice in writing of the assignment was given to Magee. Torkington alleged that Magee had broken the contract and brought an action for damages, as assignee, in his own name. The issue before Channell J was whether the executory contract of purchase of the reversionary interest was assignable under s 25 of the Judicature Act 1873 as a 'legal chose in action' (now a 'legal thing in action' in s 136 of the Law of Property Act 1925).

Channell J: . . . We have, therefore, to consider the meaning of the expression 'other legal chose in action' in sub-s 6 of s 25 of the Judicature Act 1873. In order to arrive at this meaning, I think it necessary to consider what is the object of the Act, and of the particular section of the Act in which the words are to be found. The Act provided for the amalgamation of the then existing superior Courts of Law and Equity with a view to the administration in the new Court of one system of law in place of the two systems previously known as Law and Equity, and the general scope of the Act was to enable a suitor to obtain by one proceeding in one Court the same ultimate result as he would previously have obtained either by having selected the right Court, as to which there frequently was a difficulty, or after having been to two Courts in succession, which in some cases he had to do under the old system. The 25th section provided what was to be the rule in future in cases where previously the two systems differed . . . . 'Chose in action' is a known legal expression used to describe all personal rights of property which can only be claimed or enforced by action, and not by taking physical possession. It is an expression large enough to include rights which it can hardly have been intended should be assignable by virtue of the sub-section in question, as, for instance, shares, which can only be transferred as provided by the Companies Acts. It is probably necessary, therefore, to put some limit upon the generality of the words; . . . I think the words 'debt or other legal chose in action' mean 'debt or right which the common law looks on as not assignable by reason of its being a chose in action, but which a Court of Equity deals with as being assignable.' That is the point of difference or variance between the rules of equity and common law which it is intended to deal with by this sub-section. Further, by the words of the sub-section itself the assignment is to be effectual in law, subject to all the equities which would have been entitled to priority over the rights of the assignee if this Act had not been passed. This seems to mean that the cases dealt with are cases where the assignee had some right before the Act—that is to say, where the right of the assignee had previously been recognised by a Court of Equity . . . . Now, the question we have to consider in the present case is whether an executory contract of purchase under which each party has rights and responsibilities, but of which there had been no breach at the date of the assignment, so that at that date no action could be brought upon the contract, but which, if occasion should ever arise to enforce it, must of necessity be enforced by action, is assignable by this sub-section as a 'legal chose in action.' That it is a legal chose in action, and was so at the date of the assignment, cannot be denied; but the question is whether it is so within the meaning of the words as used in the sub-section. I think it is, because it is a case in which the assignee would, at any rate after giving notice of the assignment, have had rights if the Act had not been passed. The Court of Equity would undoubtedly have recognised his right, and would have treated the assignor as being trustee for his assignee, and they would have given to the assignee all the rights and remedies as against his assignor which they gave to a cestui que trust against his trustee, and would have given to him as against the other party to the contract all the rights and remedies which they gave to a cestui que trust against a third person dealing with his trustee in reference to the subject of the trust after notice of the trust . . . . I may mention, not as an authority, but in explanation of the view I take, that I myself in *Marchant v Morton, Down & Co* ([1901] 2 KB 829 at 832) have held that this sub-section is merely machinery; that it enables an action to be brought by the assignee in his own name in cases where previously he would have sued in the assignor's name, but only where he could so sue. I think that in the present case, where there was a contract of sale which gave the purchaser an equitable interest in the property contracted to be sold, the assignment and notice gave the assignee a legal right to sue, not only for specific performance if he had a case for it, but also for damages if he either was driven or elected to take that remedy. I think, therefore, that the appeal should be allowed, and judgment be entered for the plaintiff for £100. The Chief Justice and Mr Justice Darling concur in this judgment.

[The decision of the Divisional Court was reversed on other grounds by the Court of Appeal in [1903] 1 KB 644.]

NOTES

1.   Although both equitable and legal choses in action can be assigned under s 136, they also remain assignable in equity. As Lord Macnaghten stated in *William Brandt's Sons & Co v Dunlop Rubber Co Ltd* [1905] AC 454 at 461: 'The statute does not forbid or destroy equitable assignments or impair their efficacy in the slightest degree.'

2.   The question whether equitable choses can be assigned under s 136 is a somewhat academic one since *absolute* equitable assignments of equitable choses (which alone fall within s 136) already enabled the assignee to sue in his own without joining the assignor and did not need consideration.

(ii) Absolute assignment

A statutory assignment must be absolute. This means that the assignor must have transferred his entire interest in the chose to the assignee. The debtor is then only concerned with the assignee's rights and can pay the assignee without fear of the assignor later asserting rights in the chose against him. Section 136 expressly contrasts an absolute assignment with an assignment purporting to be by way of charge only.

Durham Bros v Robertson
[1898] 1 QB 765, Court of Appeal

Under the terms of a building contract building contractors agreed to build certain houses for Robertson and take a lease of them. The contract also gave the contractors the option of paying an increased ground rent in consideration of which they were to receive from Robertson a sum of £1,080. Later the contractors purported to assign the £1,080 to the plaintiffs by letter in the following terms: 'In consideration of money advanced from time to time we hereby charge the sum of £1,080, being the agreed price for £60 per annum ground-rent which will become due to us from John Robertson... on the completion of the above buildings as security for the advances, and we hereby assign our interest in the above-named sum until the money with added interest be repaid to you.' The plaintiffs gave notice of the assignment to Robertson and an action was started by them to recover the sum due. Robertson claimed that there had not been a valid assignment under s 25(6) of the Judicature Act 1873 (now s 136 of the Law of Property Act 1925). The Court of Appeal agreed with him.

Chitty LJ: ...To bring a case within the sub-section transferring the legal right to sue for the debt and empowering the assignee to give a good discharge for the debt, there must be (in the language of the sub-section) an absolute assignment not purporting to be by way of charge only. It is requisite that the assignment should be, or at all events purport to be, absolute, but it will not suffice if the assignment purport to be by way of charge only. It is plain that every equitable assignment in the wide sense of the term as used in equity is not within the enactment. As the enactment requires that the assignment should be absolute, the question arose whether a mortgage, in the proper sense of the term, and as now generally understood, was within the enactment. In *Tancred v Delagoa Bay and East Africa Rly Co* ((1889) 23 QBD 239) there was an assignment of the debt to secure advances with a proviso for redemption and reassignment upon repayment. It was there held by the Divisional Court (disapproving of a decision in *National Provincial Bank v Harle* ((1881) 6 QBD 626), that such a mortgage fell within the enactment. It appears to me that the decision of the Divisional Court was quite right. The assignment of the debt was absolute: it purported to pass the entire interest of the assignor in the debt to the mortgagee, and it was not an assignment purporting to be by way of charge only. The mortgagor-assignor had a right to redeem, and on repayment of the advances a right to have the assigned debt reassigned to him. Notice of the reassignment pursuant to the sub-section would be given to the original debtor, and he would thus know with certainty in whom the legal right to sue him was vested. I think that the principle of the decision ought not to be confined to the case where there is an express provision for reassignment. Where there is an absolute assignment of the debt, but by way of security, equity would imply a right to a reassignment on redemption, and the sub-section would apply to the case of such an absolute assignment. In a well-known judgment of the Exchequer Chamber in *Halliday v Holgate* ((1868) LR 3 Exch 299), the late Willes J, in delivering the judgment of the Court, distinguished between lien, pledge, and mortgage, and spoke of a mortgage as passing the property out and out. A mortgage is not mentioned in the enactment; but where there is an absolute assignment of the debt, the limiting words as to a charge only are not sufficient to exclude a mortgage....

The assignment before us complies with all the terms of the enactment save one, which is essential: it is not an absolute but a conditional assignment. The commonest and most familiar instance of a conditional assurance is an assurance until JS shall return from Rome. The repayment of the money advanced is an uncertain event, and makes the assignment conditional. Where the Act applies it does not leave the original debtor in uncertainty as to the person to whom the legal right is transferred; it does not involve him in any question as to the state of the accounts between the mortgagor and the mortgagee. The legal right is transferred, and is vested in the assignee. There is no machinery provided by the Act for the reverter of the legal right to the assignor dependent on the performance of a condition; the only method within the provisions of the Act for revesting in the assignor the legal right is by a retransfer to the assignor followed by a notice in writing to the debtor, as in the case of the first transfer of the right. The question is not one of mere technicality or of form: it is one of substance, relating to the protection of the original debtor and placing him in an assured position.

It is necessary to refer to *Brice v Bannister* ((1878) 3 QBD 569). In that case there was an assignment of £100 out of money due or to become due to the assignor under a contract to build a ship, with an express power to give a good discharge to the debtor. Lord Coleridge CJ held that the assignment was within the 25th section. The Court of Appeal decided the case quite apart from the Act. Cotton LJ expressly decided the case on the ground of equitable assignment. That is shewn by the opening sentence of his judgment, where he says that the letter was a good equitable assignment. Bramwell LJ reluctantly assented to this view. Brett LJ dissented, but on general principles. So soon as it was ascertained that there was a good equitable assignment, with power to give a discharge, it became unnecessary to consider whether it fell within the Act or not. In *Ex p Nichols* ((1883) 22 Ch D 782 at 787) the present Master of the Rolls, referring to this decision, treated the assignment as an equitable assignment. He said that the decision was founded on the principle that the right of an equitable assignment of a debt cannot be defeated by a voluntary payment by the debtor to the assignor. The decision of Lord Coleridge CJ in *Brice v Bannister,* that the case fell within the 25th section, appears to me to be open to question. The assignment purported to be by way of charge only. It was a direction to pay the £100 out of money due or to become due. No doubt it purported to be a charge of an unredeemable sum of £100; but still it was a charge. The section speaks of an absolute assignment of any debt or other chose in action. It does not say 'or any part of a debt or chose in action.' It appears to me as at present advised to be questionable whether an assignment of part of an entire debt is within the enactment. If it be, it would seem to leave it in the power of the original creditor to split up the single legal cause of action for the debt into as many separate legal causes of action as he might think fit. However, it is not necessary to decide the point in the present case, and I leave it open for future consideration.

[AL Smith and Collins LJJ concurred.]

Hughes v Pump House Hotel Co Ltd
[1902] 2 KB 190, Court of Appeal

Hughes, a building contractor, assigned to his bank all moneys due or to become due under a building contract with the defendants. The assignment stated that it was '[i]n consideration of [the bank] continuing a bank account with [Hughes] . . . and by way of continuing security to [the bank] for all moneys due or to become due to [the bank] from [Hughes]'. Notice of the assignment was given to the defendants. Subsequently, Hughes brought an action against the defendants to recover sums due under the building contract. On a preliminary issue, Wright J held that the assignment was not absolute but by way of charge only. The defendants appealed.

Mathew LJ: . . . In every case of this kind, all the terms of the instrument must be considered; and, whatever may be the phraseology adopted in some particular part of it, if, on consideration of the whole instrument, it is clear that the intention was to give a charge only, then the action must be in the name of the assignor; while, on the other hand, if it is clear from the instrument as a whole that the intention was to pass all the rights of the assignor in the debt or chose in action to the assignee, then the case will come within s 25, and the action must be brought in the name of the assignee . . . . What, then, is the effect of the assignment? It seems to me clear from its terms that the intention was to pass to the assignees complete control of all moneys payable under the building contract, and to put them for all purposes in the position of the assignor with regard to those moneys. That being so, I think, unless there be some difficulty created by the decisions on the subject, this instrument may be properly described as an absolute assignment, because it is one under which all the rights of the assignor in respect of the moneys payable under the building contract were intended to pass to the assignees, and not one which purports to be by way of charge only. The learned judge appears to have been of opinion that the assignment was not absolute, but purported to be by way of charge only, because the object was that it should be a continuing security for such amount as might from time to time be due from the assignor to the assignees. But, if that were the true criterion, it might equally well be argued that a mortgage is not an absolute assignment, because under a mortgage it may become necessary to take an account in order to ascertain how much is due; but, though a mortgage is only a security for the amount which may be due, it is nevertheless an absolute assignment because the whole right of the mortgagor in the estate passes to the mortgagee.

Cozens-Hardy LJ: . . . If, on the construction of the document, it appears to be an absolute assignment, though subject to an equity of redemption, express or implied, it cannot in my opinion be material to consider what was the consideration for the assignment, or whether the security was for a fixed and definite sum, or for a current account. In either case the debtor can safely pay the assignee, and he is not concerned to inquire into the state of the accounts between the assignor and the assignee: nor does it matter that the assignee has obtained a power of attorney, and a covenant for further assurance from the assignor. Both these elements were found in *Burlinson v Hall* ((1884) 12 QBD 347). The real question, and, in my opinion, the only question, is this: Does the instrument purport to be by way of charge only? It remains to apply these principles to the document of March 7, 1901. In my opinion that document is an absolute assignment, and does not purport to be by way of charge only. It assigns all moneys due or to become due under the contract. It follows that the plaintiff, Hughes, has no right of action, and that the order of Wright J must be discharged.

NOTES

1.   Where an assignment is not absolute it may still be an effective assignment, but effective only in equity and not under the statute, ie the assignor must be joined as a party to the action to enforce the chose.

2.   Assignment by way of security for a debt can be absolute. In *Burlinson v Hall* (1884) 12 QBD 347, DC, debts were assigned to the plaintiff on trust that he should receive them and out of them pay himself a sum due to him from the assignor, and pay the surplus to the assignor. Day J stated:

I think this is an 'absolute assignment.' It is said that it is an assignment of a security for payment of the debt, and that the moment that purpose is answered the surplus will belong to the assignee. But still the assignment is, in terms, absolute. Not indeed absolute as a sale, but absolute as contradistinguished from conditional, an assignment giving a title there and then. This deed does so. True, if the debt due from the assignor were paid off, the assignor might be entitled to have the subject-matter of the assignment re-assigned to him. But the right of the assignee to whom it is assigned is absolute. No person can control him in dealing as he thinks fit with that which was assigned to him.

The same point was made by the Court of Appeal in *Bovis International Inc v Circle Ltd Partnership* (1995) 49 Con LR 12, where Millett LJ stated at 29: 'an assignment does not cease to be absolute merely because it is given by way of security and is subject to an express or implied obligation to reassign on redemption.'

3.   But an assignment by way of charge is not absolute as the title to the chose in action is not transferred to the assignee. As Denman J stated in *Trancred v Delagoa Bay and East Africa Rly Co* (1889) 23 QBD 239 at 239, DC: '. . . a document given "by way of charge" is not one which absolutely transfers the property with a condition for re-conveyance, but is a document which only gives a right to payment out of a particular fund or particular property, without transferring that fund or property'.

4.   In *Durham Bros v Robertson,* an absolute assignment was distinguished from a conditional assignment. Conditional assignments fall outside s 136 of the Law of Property Act 1925 because the assignor retains an interest of a contingent nature in the chose. To enforce a chose which has been conditionally assigned the assignor and assignee must both be before the court otherwise the debtor would be prejudiced to the extent that he would not know if the contingency had accrued without examining the state of accounts between them.

5.   It is now well established that an assignment of part of a debt falls outside s 136 of the Law of Property Act 1925: *Re Steel Wing Co* [1921] 1 Ch 349 at 354; *Williams v Atlantic Assurance Co* [1933] 1 KB 81 at 100; *Deposit Protection Board v Dalia* [1994] 2 AC 367 at 392; *Raiffeisen Zentralbank Osterreich AG v Five Star General Trading LLC* [2001] EWCA Civ 68, [2001] QB 825 at [60], [75]. This is to avoid prejudice to the debtor as the creditor could split up the debt any number of times thereby exposing the debtor to numerous actions (*Durham Bros v Robertson* [1898] 1 QB 765 at 774), and there could be conflicting decisions if the existence and amount of the debt were in dispute (*Re Steel Wing Co*, above, at 357). Part of a debt can be assigned in equity, but here there is no risk of prejudice to the debtor as the assignee cannot sue for that part of the debt which has been assigned without joining the assignor, nor can the assignor sue for the balance without joining the assignee (*Walter & Sullivan Ltd*

v J Murphy & Sons Ltd [1955] 2 QB 584). Assignment of part of an outstanding debt must be distinguished from assignment of the unpaid balance of a debt, which can be assigned under the statute: *Harding v Harding* (1886) 17 QBD 442.

6. An assignment which is absolute under s 136 of the Law of Property Act 1925 may nevertheless be registrable as a charge under Part 25 of the Companies Act 2006. See below, p 1044.

(iii) By writing under the hand of the assignor

No particular form of words is necessary. However, note the following:

(1) The assignor himself must sign the assignment; it is not sufficient for someone other than the assignor to sign in the assignor's name even if that other person is the assignor's agent signing with the assignor's authority (*Technocrats International Inc v Fredic Ltd* [2004] EWHC 692 (QB) at [53], Field J: held no assignment under s 136 where assignor's wife signed assignment in his name and with his authority, but there was an equitable assignment as husband's intention to assign was sufficiently manifest). However, a partner who has authority to deal with a chose in action belonging to the firm, when acting in relation to the business of the firm, may bind the firm and all the partners to the assignment of that chose, even though the other partners have not signed the deed of assignment and are unaware that the assignment has been executed (*Re Briggs & Co, exp Wright* [1906] 2 KB 209).

(2) In *Curran v Newpark Cinemas Ltd* [1951] 1 All ER 295, below, p 951, the Court of Appeal appears to have accepted that the written notice to the debtor could also constitute the assignment in writing itself. For another decision to the same effect, see *Cossill v Strangman* [1963] NSWR 1695 (Supreme Court of New South Wales).

(3) It may be necessary to register the assignment. Under s 344 of the Insolvency Act 1986, where a person engaged in any business makes a general assignment of existing or future book debts, or any class of them, and is subsequently adjudged bankrupt, the assignment will be void against the trustee of the bankrupt's estate as regards book debts which were not paid before the presentation of the bankruptcy petition, unless the assignment had been registered under the Bills of Sale Act 1878. As to registration of a charge on the book debts of a company, see below, p 1046.

(4) In the case of the creation of a 'financial collateral arrangement' (see below, p 1048) over 'financial instruments' such as shares and bonds, and 'cash' that is held in a bank account or 'a similar claim for the repayment of money', including money market deposits and sums payable or received under various operations in financial markets (but not a simple debt incurred in other circumstances), s 136 of the Law of Property Act 1925 does not apply to the extent that the assignment is required to be signed by the assignor or on the assignor's authority (Financial Collateral Arrangements (No 2) Regulations 2003, SI 2003/3226, reg 4(3)).

(iv) Notice to the debtor

Written notice of the assignment must be given to the debtor if the assignment is to fall within s 136 of the Law of Property Act 1925. What constitutes effective notice for this purpose?

WF Harrison & Co Ltd v Burke
[1956] 2 All ER 169, Court of Appeal

Mrs Burke entered into a hire-purchase agreement with a finance company whereby she hired a refrigerated counter on immediate payment of £30 and 24 instalments of £8 9s 6d a month, until a total of £233 8s was paid. Only the £30 was paid. By an assignment dated 7 December 1954, the finance company purported to assign to the plaintiffs the sum of £203 8s as 'now legally due and owing' to them from Mrs Burke. On 6 December 1954, the day before the assignment was executed, a letter, purporting to be a notice of assignment, was drawn up by the plaintiffs, dated 6 December 1954 and addressed to Mrs Burke. The letter stated that 'We hereby give you notice that by an indenture dated Dec 6, 1954, the debt amounting to £203 8s owing by you to [the finance company] has been assigned to us absolutely and the debt is now due and owing to us'. The letter was posted on 8 December and received by Mrs Burke on 9 December.

Denning LJ: . . . The question is whether that is a valid notice of assignment such as to transfer to the plaintiffs the legal right to sue for the debt. The sum owing at Dec 7, 1954, was not £203 8s, as stated in the assignment, but only the instalments which had then accrued due—£33 18s, and, therefore, the notice of assignment did not give the right figure for the debt. Further, it gave the wrong date of the assignment; it said that the indenture was dated Dec 6, 1954, whereas the only assignment produced to the court is one dated Dec 7, 1954. The question is whether that error in giving the date of the assignment makes the notice bad.

In *Stanley v English Fibres Industries Ltd* ((1899) 68 LJQB 839), it was held by Ridley J that, if the date given for the assignment was bad, the notice did not comply with the requirements of the Supreme Court of Judicature Act 1873, s 25(6). I find myself in agreement with that decision. Section 136(1) of the Law of Property Act 1925, shows that the written notice of the assignment is an essential part of the transfer of title to the debt, and the requirements of the subsection must be strictly complied with. I think that the notice itself must be strictly accurate, in particular, in regard to the date which is given for the assignment. Even though it is only one day out, as in this case, the notice of assignment is bad.

I need not say anything about the amount of the debt, which in this case was put at £203 8s, when it was, in fact, only £33 18s; but, as at present advised, I should have thought that a notice of assignment ought to state the amount of the debt correctly, because it concerns a transfer of title and the statutory requirements must be strictly complied with. I find myself in agreement with the judgment of the county court judge that the plaintiffs did not prove a right or title in themselves to this debt in accordance with s 136(1) of the Act of 1925, and I think that the appeal must fail.

Morris LJ: I agree. A question might be raised in regard to the assignment itself, which is an assignment of the debts or sums of money referred to in the schedule. The schedule refers to a debt of £203 8s owing by the first defendant. At the date of the assignment there was not a debt of £203 8s. But we have not had argument in regard to the validity of the assignment itself, and, therefore, I express no opinion in regard to it. We have been concerned with the question whether there has been a valid notice in writing of the assignment. Section 136(1) of the Law of Property Act 1925, requires express notice in writing and provides that if that is given the assignment

> is effectual in law . . . to pass and transfer from the date of such notice—(a) the legal right to such debt or thing in action . . .

The notice in writing in this case refers to a debt amounting to £203 8s. If this were a good notice, it would seem to be a notice that, as from the date thereof, the plaintiffs had a 'legal right to such debt', namely, a debt of £203 8s. There was no debt of £203 8s, but I do not think it necessary to decide this case on that point. I think that the case can be decided on the question of the date. The notice is dated

Dec 6. Whether the purported assignment was good or not, it was not in existence on Dec 6. It came into existence on Dec 7. It seems to me that s 136(1) of the Act of 1925, must be complied with; and I think that the notice dated Dec 6 which purported to be a notice relating to an assignment dated Dec 6, when there was no such assignment in existence, was not a good notice enabling the assignment which came into existence on the following day to pass the legal right to the debt assigned. I therefore agree that the learned judge came to a correct conclusion.

Parker LJ: I also agree.

Van Lynn Developments Ltd v Pelias Construction Co Ltd
[1969] 1 QB 607, Court of Appeal

The defendants were overdrawn at their bank. The plaintiffs paid off that indebtedness and took an assignment of the debt from the bank. The plaintiffs' solicitors then sent a letter to the defendants in the following terms: 'We have been instructed by our above-named clients to apply to you for the payment of a sum of £5,296 19s 5d outstanding to them following the assignment of the debt to them by National Provincial Bank Ltd. Notice of this assignment has already been given to you....' In fact, no such notice had been given and the question arose whether the solicitors' letter was itself a notice of assignment such as to satisfy the statute.

Lord Denning MR: ...What is a sufficient notice of assignment? There are only two or three cases on the subject. There is the case of *Stanley v English Fibres Industries Ltd* ((1899) 68 LJQB 839), which was accepted and applied by this court in *W F Harrison & Co Ltd v Burke* ([1956] 2 All ER 169). Those cases show that, if a notice of assignment purports to identify the assignment by giving the date of the assignment, and that date is a wrong date, then the notice is bad. The short ground of those decisions was that the notice with a wrong date was a notice of a non-existing document. Assuming those cases to be correct, they leave open the question whether it is necessary to give the date of the assignment. Test it this way: Suppose the mistaken sentence were omitted in this letter so that it ran: 'We have been instructed by our above-named clients to apply to you for the payment of a sum of £5,296 19s 5d outstanding to them following the assignment of the debt to them by the National Provincial Bank Limited.' Would that be a good notice, even though it gives no date for the assignment? I think it would. I think the correct interpretation of this statute was given by Atkin J in *Denney, Gasquet and Metcalfe v Conklin* ([1913] 3 KB 177 at 180). It is quite plain from his judgment that no formal requirements are required for a notice of assignment. It is sufficient if it brings

> to the notice of the debtor with reasonable certainty the fact that the deed does assign the debt due from the debtor so as to bind the debt in his hands and prevent him from paying the debt to the original creditor.

It seems to me to be unnecessary that it should give the date of the assignment so long as it makes it plain that there has in fact been an assignment so that the debtor knows to whom he has to pay the debt in the future. After receiving the notice, the debtor will be entitled, of course, to require a sight of the assignment so as to be satisfied that it is valid, and that the assignee can give him a good discharge. But the notice itself is good, even though it gives no date.

This notice does, however, go on to make an inaccurate statement. It says that, 'Notice of this assignment has already been given to you.' But, as Davies LJ said in the course of the argument, that is merely an inaccurate surplusage. It can be ignored.

Davies LJ: ...[I]t is very interesting to notice...what was the unsuccessful argument by Mr Croom-Johnson for the defendants [in *Denney, Gasquet and Metcalfe v Conlin* [1913] 3 KB 177]. According to the report, he submitted (at 179) that:

> In order to be valid the notice must expressly state (1) that there has been an assignment; (2) the names and addresses of the assignees so that the debtor may be in a position to seek out the new creditors created by the assignment for the purpose of paying the debt; and (3) what has been assigned.

The present document does show all that. It sets out the amount of the debt assigned by the bank to the plaintiffs and claims that that should be paid forthwith. It seems to me that, leaving out of consideration the last sentence of the first paragraph of that letter, it is a perfectly satisfactory notice of assignment in every respect, and that its validity cannot be destroyed by the inaccurate statement in the second sentence of that paragraph.

I agree, for the reasons which my Lord has given, that this appeal should be dismissed.

Widgery LJ: ... The statute only requires that information relative to the assignment shall be conveyed to the debtor, and that it shall be conveyed in writing. That fact is fully demonstrated by the judgment of Atkin J to which reference has already been made. Once it is appreciated that the section requires no more, it becomes obvious that the objection to the notice in this case, that it was not intended as a notice but merely to record the fact that notice had already been given, must fail. The letter of June 27 in my judgment undoubtedly contains the necessary particulars and it matters not in the slightest that the writer did not think when he wrote the letter that he was performing the function of giving notice under the section.

So far as the argument based on failure to give the date of the assignment is concerned, it seems to me it would be very undesirable to attach to this procedure technicalities which are not mentioned in the statute and which are not necessary to give effect to it. The notice is a notice given by the assignee for his own protection. It is given by the assignee in order to prevent the debtor continuing to deal with the assignor. It is clearly necessary that the debtor should be given information which tells him that an assignment has been made, which identifies the debt, and which sufficiently identifies the assignee. I see no reason at all why other and irrelevant information should be required as a feature of the notice. It is said that in some instances the debtor would want to know the date of the assignment. For my part I find it very difficult to visualise a case in which the date would have any relevance at all so far as the debtor was concerned, and I would certainly regard it as a retrograde step to require, as a general rule, that the notice should specify the date of the assignment. I would therefore dismiss this appeal.

NOTES

1.   In *Harrison v Burke,* Morris LJ appears to have adopted a less restrictive interpretation of s 136 than does Denning LJ. Denning LJ considered that any inaccuracy in the notice would vitiate it, whereas Morris LJ's judgment rests on the narrower ground that the notice is only vitiated if the date of the assignment recorded on the notice antedates the actual date of the assignment. In any event, Sir Robert Megarry has commented that '[t]here is something to be said for the view that an error as to date should not be fatal *per se,* but should invalidate the assignment only if it induces uncertainty' ((1956) 72 LQR 321, 322). This seems to be the preferable approach. It is odd that a notice without a date of assignment can be valid, whereas one with an incorrect date (which is superfluous information) is necessarily invalid. The recipient of the former may be just as misled as the recipient of the latter (R Munday (1981) 131 NLJ 607, p 608). Furthermore, holding a notice invalid simply because it specifies the incorrect date of the assignment goes against the analogous principles of construction of unilateral notices served under contractual rights as set down by the House of Lords in *Mannai Investment Co Ltd v Eagle Star Life Assurance Co Ltd* [1997] AC 749 (where a notice served by a tenant on his landlord to exercise a break clause in a commercial

lease specified the wrong date from which it was to operate under the terms of the clause, but was nevertheless held by a majority of the House of Lords to be effective). Lords Steyn, Hoffmann and Clyde (Lords Goff and Jauncey dissenting) held that the issue turned on how a reasonable recipient would have understood the notice, taking into account the relevant objective contextual scene (in *Mannai* it was clear that the reasonable recipient of the notice, knowing the terms of the lease, would have been in no doubt that the tenant wished to determine the lease under the relevant break clause). Applying the same approach to a notice served on a debtor under s 136 of the Law of Property Act 1925, it would seem that where the notice specifies the wrong date of the assignment it may still be valid if the reasonable recipient of such a notice would nevertheless realise that he should stop dealing with the assignor and pay the assignee, for then the notice has achieved its purpose (as specified by Widgery LJ in *Van Lynn Developments Ltd v Pelias Construction Co Ltd* [1969] 1 QB 607 at 615: see above, p 948).

2. The strict rules relating to statutory assignments, epitomised in *Harrison v Burke*, are in marked contrast to the more liberal regime for equitable assignments where any informal notice will secure an equitable assignment provided the fact of the assignment is clearly brought to the attention of the debtor, trustee or fundholder (see, for example, *Whittingstall v King* (1882) 46 LT 520).

3. In *Holt v Heatherfield Trust Ltd* [1942] 2 KB 1 at 6, Atkinson J held that:

… 'such notice' [in s 136] is the date of a notice which has been given to the debtor, and refers back to the express notice in writing mentioned earlier in the section. It is express notice in writing given to the debtor, and, in my judgment, the date of that notice is the date on which it is received by or on behalf of the debtor.

This dictum applies when there is a dispute between assignee and debtor, but there is some doubt as to whether it also applies when the dispute is between successive assignees (see E Peel, *Treitel's Law of Contract* (12th edn, 2007), para 15–020).

(v) Notice to assignee ?

Curran v Newpark Cinemas Ltd
[1951] 1 All ER 295, Court of Appeal

Curran obtained judgment against Newpark Cinemas for a debt and costs. The debt was paid but the costs remained outstanding so Curran procured the issue of a garnishee summons against a debtor of Newpark Cinemas. The debtor opposed the summons claiming that, before being served with the summons, Newpark Cinemas had already given the debtor written notice that '. . . pursuant to the arrangements for valuable consideration which we, Newpark Cinemas Ltd, have made with Barclays Bank Ltd, we give you irrevocable directions, instructions and authority to pay to the said Barclays Bank Ltd … all moneys payable to us. … This authority and instructions can be varied or cancelled only by a document duly signed on behalf of Barclays Bank Ltd …'. No notice of assignment had been given by the bank to the debtor and there was no evidence that the bank had been given notice of the document sent by Newpark Cinemas to the debtor. The county court judge held there had been no valid assignment of the debt to the bank. The debtor appealed to the Court of Appeal (Somervell, Jenkins and Birkett LJJ).

Jenkins LJ read the judgment of the court: … It is, no doubt, true that s 136(1) does not require any particular form of assignment, or that the notice given to the debtor should necessarily have been given by the assignee. The sub-section does, however, clearly postulate that, whatever its form, there should be a document amounting to an absolute assignment by writing under the hand of the assignor. Given such an assignment, and given the requisite notice to the debtor, the assignment (to put it shortly) is to operate as a legal assignment of the debt in question. Section 136(1), however, does not provide that a document which would not, independently of the sub-section or its predecessor (Supreme Court of Judicature Act 1873, s 25(6)), have operated as an absolute assignment at law or in equity is to have the force of an absolute assignment for the purposes of the sub-section. The document here relied on is the direction and authority, which in point of form is not an assignment to the bank of the debt in question but merely a direction to the garnishees to pay the debt in question to the bank. On the footing that there had, in fact, been no prior agreement with the bank to give such a direction, and that the bank had not been notified of the fact that such a direction had been given, we think the result would follow that the direction and authority, though expressed to be irrevocable except with the consent of the bank, could in fact have been revoked by the judgment debtors at any time as amounting to no more than an arrangement between the judgment debtors and the garnishees in which they alone were concerned and which, in the absence of any such agreement or notification, conferred no interest in the debt on the bank. If that is right, then we think that the contention of counsel for the garnishees to the effect that the mere production by the garnishees of the direction and authority, without proof of any agreement with, or notice to, the bank, sufficed in itself to establish an absolute assignment of which express notice had been given to the garnishees, and hence a legal assignment by virtue of s 136(1), necessarily fails.

[The Court of Appeal held that whilst there was no evidence that the bank had not been given notice of the direction and authority, there was prima facie evidence of an assignment in that the notice to the debtor referred to prior arrangements with the bank. The garnishee order was set aside and the case remitted to the County Court with a view to the bank being ordered to appear and state its claim.]

But the requirement of notice to, or consent of, the assignee has been rejected in Australia.

Grey v Australian Motorists & General Insurance Co Pty Ltd
[1976] 1 NSWLR 669, Court of Appeal of New South Wales

Grey was a car repairer. The defendant was an insurance company which indemnified motorists against the costs of having their vehicles repaired. Grey claimed the cost of repair of six vehicles from the defendant. The defendant claimed that Grey was not the proper plaintiff as he had previously assigned the debts in question to a finance company. It was alleged that Grey had assigned the debts by completing a number of standard forms of assignment supplied by the finance company which stated that Grey 'irrevocably directs payment of this account direct to the absolute assignee thereof [the finance company]'. The completed forms had been sent to the defendant to obtain payment but there was no evidence that the finance company had notice of or assented to the assignments. A central issue before the Court of Appeal was whether there could be a statutory assignment under s 136 (or rather its Australian equivalent) when no notice of the assignment had been given to the assignee. The Court of Appeal (Samuels and Mahoney JJA; Glass JA dissenting) held that there had been a statutory assignment of the debts.

Glass JA (dissenting): . . . There is little authority on the question whether the operation of the section depends on the assent of the purported assignee. It is clear that a transfer of property made in proper form vests the title in the transferee at once, notwithstanding his lack of knowledge: *Standing v Bowring* ((1885) 31 Ch D 282). His remedy, if he wishes to reject the gift, is to transfer it back. Accordingly, the absence of consent cannot invalidate the assignment. His Honour ruled, however, that an assignment uncommunicated to the assignee cannot be absolute within the meaning of the section. He relied in this respect upon the following passage in the judgment of Asprey JA in *International Leasing Corpn (Vic) Ltd v Aiken* ((1967) 85 WNNSW 766 at 793): '...there can be no effective *absolute* assignment of a debt as between an assignor and an assignee within the meaning of s 12 unless and until the assignee has had notice of the assignment executed by the assignor and has assented to it (see *Rekstin v Severo Sibirsko etc and Bank of Russian Trade Ltd* ([1933] 1 KB 47); Jenks' *English Civil Law,* 4th edn, vol 2, para 1626, pp 890–892; see also *Curran v Newpark Cinemas Ltd* ([1951] 1 All ER 295), where both the last-mentioned case and *Standing v Bowring* were referred to; and cf *Norman v Federal Comr of Taxation* ((1963) 109 CLR 9 at 29), per Windeyer J. An assignment of a debt uncommunicated to the assignee can only be a conditional assignment, that is to say, predicated upon the condition that if the assignee repudiates it when it is brought to his notice, there would be without more, an automatic revesting of the legal ownership of the debt in the assignor.'

With great respect to his Honour, I cannot agree that his proposition is supported by authority in the general terms in which it is formulated. *Rekstin's* case depends upon the special rules governing the relationship of banker and customer. Jenks quoted *Rekstin's* case; and *Curran's* case, to which I shall later refer, stands upon different ground. An absolute assignment is to be contrasted with a conditional assignment. A conditional assignment is an assignment which becomes operative or ceases to be operative upon the happening of an event: *Durham Bros v Robertson* ([1898] 1 QB 765 at 773). Accordingly, an assignment of a chose in action, until a loan is repaid is conditional: ibid. But an assignment of a debt with a proviso for redemption and reassignment upon repayment of a loan is absolute: *Tonered v Delagoa Bay and East Africa Rly Co* ((1889) 23 QBD 239). A distinction is clearly drawn between a reassignment occurring by force of the original transaction (conditional), and a reassignment which depends upon a further assurance (absolute). These authorities, as well as *Standing v Bowring* and the language of the section, and, in my view, inconsistent with the general proposition that an assignment, otherwise absolute in its terms, must operate conditionally where the assignee, not having been consulted, has the right to reassign....

In *Curran v Newpark Cinemas Ltd* the court had before it a direction to a second party to pay money to a bank which had not been communicated to the bank. It was held that the document relied on failed to establish an absolute assignment to the bank, because the direction to pay recorded in it could have been revoked at any time by the party giving it, in the absence of evidence that the bank had been notified or had agreed to the arrangement. The document before us takes a different form....In *Curran's* case the assignment was subject to a condition subsequent.

[However, Glass JA went on to hold that the assignments were conditional on other grounds and, therefore, outside the statute.]

Samuels JA: ...*Curran's* case is distinguishable from the present one. There, Jenkins LJ, as he then was, emphasized that the document in question was not in form an assignment, but 'merely a direction to the garnishees to pay a third party (ie the bank)...' and could only answer the description of an assignment 'if and when communicated to the bank, as, until so communicated, it was revocable by the judgment debtors at any time and, therefore, not absolute'. The authority referred to is *Rekstin's* case. His Lordship went on to say that, although s 136(1) of the Law of Property Act 1925 (the equivalent of s 12 of the Conveyancing Act) did not require any particular form of assignment, it did however 'clearly postulate that, whatever its form, there should be a document amounting to an absolute assignment by writing under the hand of the assignor. Given such an assignment, and given the requisite notice to the debtor, the assignment (to put it shortly) is to operate as a legal assignment of the debt in question'. Accordingly, I would read that judgment (which was the judgment of the court) as having no application to a case where the document relied on is in form an assignment which would, independently of statute, have operated as an absolute assignment at law or in equity. The distinction relevant for present purposes is really that between an assignment and a mere revocable mandate or authority....

Finally, and perhaps most importantly, s 12 sets out the requirements of an effective statutory assignment. It provides that the assignment must be absolute and in writing and stipulates for express notice to the debtor. But it does not mention notice to the assignee, much less the necessity for his consent; nor are either of these stipulations to be found in s 136 of the Law of Property Act 1925 (Imp.). And they did not appear in s 25(6) of the Judicature Act 1873 (Imp.) which s 136 replaced. According to s 12, the conditions to be satisfied if an assignment is to derive validity from the statute are that it must be absolute, in writing and written notice must be given to the debtor. If, in addition, notice to the assignee were required, one would have expected the statute to prescribe it.

[Mahoney JA decided the case on the basis that Grey had admitted that the debts had been assigned.]

NOTES

1.   If there is no prior agreement between the assignor and the assignee, the assignment must be communicated to the assignee by the assignor, or by someone with his authority. The debtor can act as the assignor's agent for this purpose (*Burn v Carvalho* (1839) 4 My & Cr 690).

2.   It could be argued that notice to the assignee only provides evidence of the assignor's intention to assign the chose, as opposed to giving his debtor a revocable mandate to pay the purported assignee. If so, notice to the assignee would be irrelevant if clear evidence of an intention to assign could be supplied from some other source (eg the assignor had executed a deed of assignment). For alternative explanations as to why the assignor must give notice to the assignee, see E Peel, *Treitel's Law of Contract* (12th edn, 2007), para 15–019.

(vi) Consideration?

Re Westerton, Public Trustee v Gray
[1919] 2 Ch 104, Chancery Division

After Mr Westerton's death there was found in his despatch box an envelope containing (1) a deposit receipt for £500 deposited with his bank; (2) an order in writing signed by Mr Westerton directing his bank to pay Mrs Gray the £500 then on deposit; and (3) a letter to Mrs Gray in which Mr Westerton informed her that he wished to give her the £500 in return for all her kindness to him. The deposit receipt was not indorsed by Mr Westerton and no notice was given to the bank of any assignment until after Mr Westerton's death.

Sargant J: …I now turn to the principal difficulty in the case, and that is the absence of valuable consideration. It seems to me, though I am not sure that it was completely admitted by Mr Gover, that apart from the Judicature Act 1873, s 25, sub-s 6, the want of consideration would have been fatal to Mrs Gray' s claim. Prior to the Judicature Act 1873, a legal chose in action such as this debt could not be transferred at law, and the assignee of the debt could only have sued in the name of the assignor, and in the absence of consent by the assignor or of a binding contract by the assignor to allow the use of his name, the use of the assignor's name could only have been enforced by filing a bill in equity and so obtaining an injunction in personam to allow the use of the name, and equity would not have granted that relief unless the assignment had been for valuable consideration. But to my mind the effect of s 25, sub-s 6, of the Judicature Act 1873, has been to improve the position of the assignee of a chose in action who satisfies the words of the sub-section, that is to say, an assignee under an absolute assignment by writing under the hand of the assignor nor purporting to be by way of charge only, by enabling that assignee to dispense at law with the use of the name of the assignor and so to dispense with the circuitous process of compelling the assignor in equity to allow his name to be used in proceedings by the assignee. The result of the sub-section is that an assignee who takes under such an absolute assignment as is there mentioned can now sue at law in his own name, and I see no reason why in the present case the assignee should not do so.…

It does seem to me that the aim of the sub-section was to reform procedure and to make it unnecessary for an assignee who had an out and out assignment to go through the double process that was formerly necessary in the case of an unwilling assignor. . . . To that extent, as I have said, the position of the assignee as a question of procedure was improved; he could come at once at law, and come not in the name of the assignor but in his own name as assignee. But if that is so and by means of that simplification of procedure the assignee has been relieved from taking preliminary proceedings in equity, there seems to me to be nothing very startling in the further conclusion, that the assignee has also been relieved from the terms which equity imposed as a condition of assisting him in obtaining the legal right, if at law the question of consideration was regarded as wholly immaterial; and I think that it must have been so regarded for this reason, that at law the action was brought in the name of the assignor, so that there was no question at all of any transaction between the assignor and the assignee under which the question of consideration could arise. If that be so and if since the Judicature Act 1873, the assignee can come directly in his own name and sue as effectually as he could have done in the name of the assignor, it appears to me that there is no reason for continuing against the assignee those terms which were imposed by equity as a condition of granting relief. The position of the assignee has in this respect been improved once and for all by the sub-section of the Judicature Act in question, which has conferred on him a legal right to sue, and in my judgment I ought not to consider that legal right as being in any way dependent upon the question whether the assignment was made for valuable consideration or not, provided it complies with the express conditions of that sub-section. In my judgment, therefore, Mrs Gray is entitled to the sum of £500 in question with interest from the date of the death of the testator.

NOTES

1.   The dicta in *Re Westerton* to the effect that consideration is always required for equitable assignment of an existing legal chose in action is wrong (at least where the assignor has done everything which is necessary according to the nature of the property to transfer the title to it: see below, pp 964ff).

2.   In *Re Westerton* notice to the debtor was not given until after the death of the assignor. Sargant J, at 111, held that the mere omission to give notice at the time of the assignment was of no consequence so long as notice was given before the action was brought. However, Sargant J did go on to point out that if, without notice of the assignment, the bank had paid the money to the assignor, the payment would have been good payment as against the donee. Notice may also be given after the assignee's death (*Bateman v Hunt* [1904] 2 KB 530 at 538, CA).

QUESTIONS

1.   Bevin, a builder, who was erecting some houses for Smart, executed a written document addressed to his bankers which stated: 'In consideration of your allowing me an overdraft of £1,000, I hereby assign to you my interest in that amount (ie £1,000) out of the monies which will become due to me from Smart, until my overdraft has been fully repaid'. Advise the bankers:

(1)   of the effect of this document;

(2)   of the steps they should take to secure and enforce their rights.

2.   What is the purpose or function of giving written notice to the debtor as required by s 136 of the Law of Property Act 1925?

3 EQUITABLE ASSIGNMENT

(a) Introduction

An assignment not falling within s 136 may nevertheless be effective as an equitable assignment. This may occur where:

(1) the assignment is not in writing signed by the assignor;

(2) the assignment is not absolute because it is by way of charge, or conditional, or of only part of a debt;

(3) no written notice of the assignment has been received by the debtor; or

(4) the assignment is of future property, expectancies or bare possibilities.

(b) Methods of assignment

Timpson's Executors v Yerbury
[1936] 1 KB 645, Court of Appeal

Romer LJ: ...Now the equitable interest in property in the hands of a trustee can be disposed of by the person entitled to it in favour of a third party in any one of four different ways. The person entitled to it (1) can assign it to the third party directly; (2) can direct the trustees to hold the property in trust for the third party (see per Sargant J in *Re Chrimes* ([1917] 1 Ch 30)); (3) can contract for valuable consideration to assign the equitable interest to him; or (4) can declare himself to be a trustee for him of such interest.... 'For a man to make himself a trustee', said Sir George Jessel MR in *Richards v Delbridge* ((1874) LR 18 Eq 11 at 15), 'there must be an expression of intention to become a trustee.' 'It is true', he had said in an earlier part of his judgment, 'he need not use the words "I declare myself a trustee" but he must do something which is equivalent to it, and use expressions which have that meaning.' In *Milroy v Lord* ((1862) 4 De GF & J 264 at 274) Turner LJ, after referring to two methods of making a voluntary settlement valid, namely, by assignment or declaration of trust, added: 'The cases I think go further to this extent, that if the settlement is intended to be effectuated by one of the modes to which I have referred, the Court will not give effect to it by applying another of those modes. If it is intended to take effect by transfer, the Court will not hold the intended transfer to operate as a declaration of trust, for then every imperfect instrument would be made effectual by being converted into a perfect trust.'

NOTES

1. Method (1) can also be used for the assignment of legal choses in action. In *Elders Pastoral Ltd v Bank of New Zealand (No 2)* [1990] 1 WLR 1478, PC, Lord Templeman emphasised that: '[t]he simplest form of an equitable assignment of a debt is an agreement by a debtor with a creditor that a debt due or to become due to the debtor from a third party shall be paid by the third party to the creditor.'

2. Method (2) only applies if the chose is equitable. It probably operates by way of trust rather than assignment (*Halsbury's Laws of England* (4th edn Reissue, 2003), Vol 6, para 27 fn; *Grey v IRC* [1958] Ch 375 at 381, per Upjohn J; on appeal [1958] Ch 690 at 710–711, CA, per Lord Evershed MR, and at 722, per Ormerod LJ; affd [1960] AC 1 at 16, HL, per Lord Radcliffe). However, a creditor (as legal owner) may instruct his debtor to hold a debt on trust for a third person (*M'Fadden v Jenkyns* (1842) 1 Hare 458; 1 Ph 153 (on appeal); criticised by JC Hall [1959] CLJ 99, pp 108–109).

3.   Method (3) can also apply to legal choses in action. An express contract to assign property then ascertained itself constitutes an equitable assignment (if supported by consideration). A contract to assign will be implied in equity where the assignor purports to transfer the chose direct to the assignee for value. See *Holroyd v Marshall* (1862) 10 HL Cas 191; *Tailby v Official Receiver* (1888) 13 App Cas 523 (see below, pp 1028ff).

4.   If the assignor declares himself trustee of his equitable interest (Method 4) there is some doubt as to whether this method operates as an assignment or the creation of a sub-trust (see PVB (1958) 74 LQR 180 at 182).

5.   The assignor may direct his trustees to transfer the legal title to the chose to a third party assignee (*Vandervell v IRC* [1967] 2 AC 291, HL, where the beneficial owner of shares held on trust absolutely for himself directed trustees to transfer the legal title to the shares to a third party with the intention that the third party should also obtain the full beneficial interest).

6.   It is well established that, for want of certainty of subject-matter, there cannot be a trust of a specified number of goods where those goods have not been segregated from a mass of similar goods (the leading authority is *Re Goldcorp Exchange Ltd* [1995] 1 AC 74, PC: see above, pp 319, for discussion of the case and also the impact the Sale of Goods (Amendment) Act 1995 on this area). But the same rule does not apply to money, shares or other choses in action, at least where there is an identifable fund out of which the trust can be carved (the position would be different where there was no identifiable fund: see *Mac-Jordan Construction Ltd v Brookmount Erostin Ltd* [1992] BCLC 350, CA). The key case is *Hunter v Moss* [1994] 1 WLR 452. M intended to give H 50 of M's 950 shares in a private company. M declared himself trustee of 50 of his shares. The Court of Appeal held that the trust did not fail for want of certainty of subject matter. Professor Hayton is strongly critical of the decision. He argues that the trust should have failed for want of certainty as it was not possible to say to which 50 of the 950 shares the trust related (see D Hayton (1994) 110 LQR 335). Nevertheless, *Hunter v Moss* has since been applied in *Re Harvard Securities Ltd* [1997] 2 BCLC 369 (albeit as a matter of binding precedent) and in *Re CA Pacific Finance Ltd* [2000] 1 BCLC 494 (Hong Kong, Court of First Instance). The distinction between goods and choses in action is usually explained on the ground that while goods in a bulk are not necessarily identical, there is no difference between one pound and another pound, or one share and another share of the same class in the same company (see generally J E Martin *Hanbury and Martin's Modern Equity* (17th edn, 2005), para 3–022). However, Professor Goode has recently questioned the wisdom of that approach, whilst supporting the decision (if not the reasoning) in *Hunter v Moss* itself. According to Professor Goode 'the problem of identification, whether in relation to tangibles or intangibles, arises only where the subject-matter of the transaction is susceptible to division into units capable in law of being separately owned and transferred' (RM Goode *Legal Problems of Credit and Security* (3rd edn, 2003), para 2–06). He continues:

Much of the criticism of the decision of the Court of Appeal in *Hunter v Moss* stems from a failure to appreciate that shares of the same issue are no more than fractions of a single asset, namely the share capital of the issuing company, and that on a sale or trust of the shares it is not possible to segregate the shares of the subject of the sale or trust from an interest in the remainder of the issue. In short, such shares are not fungibles at all, they represent co-ownership of a single, identified asset. The same applies to a credit balance in a bank account. The argument advanced by some writers that an assignment of £100 forming part of a £500 credit balance in the assignor's account is void for want of identification, is misconceived, because there is only one, indivisible asset, the credit balance, and the sole effect of the partial assignment is to make the assignee co-owner of the credit balance with the assignor.

See further, R Goode, 'Are intangible assets fungible?' [2003] LMCLQ 379. Does co-ownership provide a solution to the problem?

7.   In *Don King Productions Inc v Warren* [1998] 2 All ER 608 at 632–633, Lightman J stated that:

A declaration of trust in favour of a third party of the benefit of obligations or the profits obtained from a contract is different in character from an assignment of the benefit of the contract to that third party: see *Devefi Pty Ltd v Mateffy Pearl Nagy Pty Ltd* [1993] RPC 493 at 505. Whether the contract contains a provision prohibiting such a declaration of trust must be determined as a matter of construction of the contract. Such a limitation upon the freedom of the party is not lightly to be inferred and a clause prohibiting assignments is prima facie restricted to assignments of the benefit of the obligation and does not extend to declarations of trust of the benefit…

In that case an express prohibition on assignment contained in the terms of the contract between assignor and debtor, and the personal nature of that contract (a promotion and management contract betweeen a boxer (debtor) and his manager/ promoter (assignor)), prevented assignment of the benefit of the contract: however, Lightman J held that the purported assignor held the benefit of the contract on trust for the purported assignee who acquired an equitable interest in it. Despite the fact that the difference between assigning a right and having someone else own the beneficial interest in it under a trust seems marginal (see A Tettenborn [1998] LMCLQ 498 at 500), Lightman J's decision was upheld on appeal: see [2000] Ch 291 and below, p 982.

(c) Requirements

(i) Intention

William Brandt's Sons & Co v Dunlop Rubber Co Ltd
[1905] AC 454, House of Lords

Merchants agreed with a bank, by whom they were financed, that buyers of goods sold by the merchants should pay the price directly to the bank. When goods had been sold, the bank forwarded to the buyers notice in writing that the merchants had made over to the bank the right to receive the purchase money and requested the buyers to sign an undertaking to remit the purchase-money to the bank. The buyers returned the acknowledgment to the bank but then paid a third party by mistake. The bank sued the buyers and the question arose whether there had been an equitable assignment.

Lord Macnaghten held that even without consideration of the notice sent to the buyers there was clear evidence of an equitable assignment between the merchants and the bank (at 460) and continued: The statute [s 25(6) of the Judicature Act 1873; now s 136 of the Law of Property Act 1925] does not forbid or destroy equitable assignments or impair their efficacy in the slightest degree. Where the rules of equity and the rules of the common law conflict, the rules of equity are to prevail. Before the statute there was a conflict as regards assignments of debts and other choses in action. At law it was considered necessary that the debtor should enter into some engagement with the assignee. That was never the rule in equity. It 'is certainly not the doctrine of this Court,' said Lord Eldon, sitting in Chancery in *Ex p South* ((1818) 3 Swan 392). In certain cases the Judicature Act places the assignee in a better position than he was before. Whether the present case falls within the favoured class may perhaps be doubted. At any rate, it is wholly immaterial for the plaintiffs' success in this action. But, says the Lord Chief Justice, 'the document does not, on the face of it, purport to be an assignment nor use the language of an assignment.' An equitable assignment does not always take that form. It may be addressed to the debtor. It may be couched in the language of command. It may be a courteous request. It may assume the form of mere permission. The language is immaterial if the meaning is plain. All that is necessary is that the debtor should be given to understand that the debt has been made over by the creditor to some third person. If the debtor ignores such a notice, he does so at his peril. If the assignment be for valuable consideration and communicated to the third person, it cannot be revoked by the creditor or safely disregarded by the debtor. I think that the documents which passed between Brandts [the Bank] and the company [the buyers] would of themselves . . . have constituted a good equitable assignment.

[Lord James delivered a concurring judgment.
The Earl of Halsbury LC and Lord Lindley concurred.]

NOTES

1. An assignment must be distinguished from a revocable mandate given by a creditor to a third party authorising him to collect payment from the debtor and also from a revocable mandate to the debtor directing him to pay the third party. For example, a cheque is only a revocable mandate and not the assignment of any money standing to the credit of the drawer in his bank account (Bills of Exchange Act 1882, s 53(1); *Hopkinson v Forster* (1874) LR 19 Eq 74; *Deposit Protection Board v Dalia* [1994] 2 AC 367 at 400). For discussion of when the creditor's mandate will be revocable and when it will be irrevocable, see AP Bell *Modern Law of Personal Property in England and Ireland* (1989), pp 370–371.

2. An intention to assign may be shown by conduct alone. In *Coulter v Chief of Dorset Police* [2003] EWHC 3391 (Ch), [2004] 1 WLR 1425, it was held that the benefit of a judgment had been assigned in equity by a retiring chief constable to his successor. Patten J acknowledged the need for there to be 'a sufficient expression of an intention to assign' and held that the resignation of the existing office holder, and the assumption of office by his successor, was 'a sufficient outward manifestation of an intention that the successor office holder should obtain the benefit held on trust by a predecessor, for there to be an equitable assignment of the benefit of the judgment.' On the other hand, the court will not find an intention to assign out of a failed novation where the terms of the contract containing the right to be transferred gave the transferor alternative and mutually exclusive options of novation or assignment and the transferor clearly opted for novation over assignment (*The Argo Fund Ltd v Essar Steel Ltd* [2006] EWCA Civ 241, [2006] 2 All ER (Comm) 104 at [63]).

(ii) Writing

An equitable assignment of a legal chose in action need not be in writing, nor in any particular form. In *Phelps v Sons-Smith & Co* [2001] BPIR 326 at [34], Whiteman QC, sitting as a deputy High Court judge, recently summarised the position as follows:

It is well established that it is not necessary for an equitable assignment to follow any particular form. What is necessary, however, is that there should be an intention to assign, that the subject-matter of the assignment should be so described as to be capable of being identified at the time of the alleged assignment and that there should be some act by the assignor showing that he is transferring the chose in action to the (alleged) assignee.

The deputy judge called for a 'broad approach' to what constitutes such an 'act' and gave as examples 'a letter or an oral statement'. None the less, he did stress that 'there must be an "act" which establishes clearly the nature of the transaction'.

On the other hand, an equitable assignment of an equitable chose in action must be in writing if it falls within s 53(1)(c) of the Law of Property Act 1925.

Law of Property Act 1925, s 53(1)

53. (1) Subject to the provisions hereinafter contained with respect to the creation of interests in land by parol—...

(c) a disposition of an equitable interest or trust subsisting at the time of the disposition, must be in writing signed by the person disposing of the same, or by his agent thereunto lawfully authorised in writing or by will.

NOTES

1. When is there a 'disposition' under s 53(1)(c)? It occurs (and writing is required) in the following circumstances; namely, when:

(1) A assigns an equitable interest to B;

(2) A assigns his equitable interest to trustees to hold on trust for B;

(3) A directs his own trustees to hold on trust for B (*Grey v IRC* [1960] AC 1, HL);

(4) A declares himself a bare trustee of his equitable interest for B, ie A drops out and the existing trustees hold for B instead of A (D J Hayton *Underhill and Hayton's Law of Trusts and Trustees* (17th edn, 2007), para 12.15; cf B Green (1984) 47 MLR 385 at pp 396–399). But writing is not required if the sub-trust creates a new interest, ie if the declaration of trust splits the benefit between A and B, or if it imposes active duties on A as trustee (see PVB (1958) 74 LQR 180 at p 182).

2. In *Oughtred v IRC* [1960] AC 206, the House of Lords left open the question whether a contract for value to assign an equitable interest is a 'disposition', or whether it creates a constructive trust under s 53(2) of the Law of Property Act 1925, which can be oral. However, the issue was revisited by the Court of Appeal in *Neville v Wilson* [1997] Ch 144 (noted by R Nolan [1996] CLJ 436). There nominees held shares in U Ltd on trust for J Ltd, a family company. The shareholders of J Ltd informally agreed to liquidate the company and to divide its equitable interest in the U Ltd shares amongst themselves in proportion to their existing shareholding (the Court of Appeal seems to have treated the acts of the shareholders as the agreement of J Ltd to transfer one of its assets: see Nolan, p 437). The Court of Appeal, applying the analysis of Lord Radcliffe in his dissent in *Oughtred* (at 227) that a specifically enforceable agreement to assign passes an equitable interest to the assignee, held that the informal liquidation agreement, which was specifically enforceable, constituted J Ltd an implied or constructive trustee of its equitable interest for the shareholders, so that the requirement for writing contained in s 53(1)(c) was dispensed with by s 53(2).

3. Section 53(1)(c) does not apply where the assignor, as absolute beneficial owner, instructs his trustees to transfer the legal title to the chose in action to a third party assignee intending him also to take the equitable interest (*Vandervell v IRC* [1967] 2 AC 291: see above, p 956).

4. Section 53(1)(c) does not apply in the case of the creation of a 'financial collateral arrangement' (see below, p 1048) over 'financial instruments' such as shares and bonds, and 'cash' that is held in a bank account or 'a similar claim for the repayment of money', including money market deposits and sums payable or received under various operations in financial markets (but not a simple debt incurred in other circumstances): see Financial Collateral

Arrangements (No 2) Regulations 2003, SI 2003/3226, reg 4(2). However, a financial collateral arrangement must be 'evidenced in writing' (reg 3).

(iii) Notice to assignee

Notice to, or prior agreement of, the assignee is necessary for an effective equitable assignment of a legal or equitable chose (*Morrell v Wootten* (1852) 16 Beav 197; *Re Hamilton* (1921) 124 LT 737). Without such notice or agreement, the assignment is deemed to be revocable (*Re Hamilton,* above). However, whilst a voluntary transfer by declaration of trust of a legal chose does not require notice to, or prior agreement of, the assignee (*Middleton v Pollock* (1876) 2 Ch D 104), that of an equitable chose appears to require the assignee's knowledge (*Re Hamilton,* above), a distinction criticised by JC Hall [1959] CLJ 99, p 105. Where an assignment is by way of deed (and, therefore, irrevocable) it is difficult to see why notice to the assignee should be necessary (although see E Peel, *Treitel's Law of Contract* (12th edn, 2007), para 15–019). The High Court of Australia has gone even further. In *Comptroller of Stamps (Victoria) v Howard-Smith* (1936) 54 CLR 614 at 622, Dixon J said:

Nor does it appear necessary that the intention to pass the equitable property shall be communicated to the assignee. What is necessary is that there shall be an expression of intention then and there to set over the equitable interest, and, perhaps, it should be communicated to someone who does not receive the communication under confidence or in the capacity only of an agent for the donor.

When notice of the assignment is given to the debtor by letter it is effective only when received by him (*Holt v Heatherfield Trust Ltd* [1942] 2 KB 1). However, it has been held that when notice of the assignment is given to the assignee by letter it is effective when posted (*Alexander v Steinhardt, Walker & Co* [1903] 2 KB 208; but this has been doubted in *Timpson's Executors v Yerbury* [1936] 1 KB 645 at 657–658, per Lord Wright MR).

(iv) Notice to debtor

Notice to the debtor is not essential for a valid equitable assignment.

Gorringe v Irwell India Rubber and Gutta Percha Works
(1886) 34 Ch D 128, Court of Appeal

As the defendants were indebted to H & Co, they wrote to them agreeing to hold a sum due from C & Co to H & Co's disposal until the balance of their indebtedness to H & Co was repaid. Before notice of this equitable assignment was given to C & Co, a petition was presented to wind up the defendants, who were subsequently put into liquidation. The liquidator took out a summons to determine whether the money due from C & Co belonged to the defendants or to H & Co. Bacon V-C held that there had been no assignment to H & Co as there had been no notice given to the debtor before the commencement of the winding up. H & Co appealed to the Court of Appeal which allowed the appeal.

Cotton LJ: . . . It is contended that in order to make an assignment of a *chose in action,* such as a debt, a complete charge, notice must be given to the debtor. It is true that there must be such a notice to enable the title of the assignee to prevail against a subsequent assignee. That is established by *Dearle v Hall* [(1823) 3 Russ 1: below, p 1008], but there is no authority for holding this rule to apply as against the assignor of the debt. Though there is no notice to the debtor the title of the assignee is complete as against the assignor.

[Bowen and Fry LJJ delivered concurring judgments.]

NOTES

1. Notice *should* be given to the debtor (or to the trustee) for the following reasons:

(1) If the debtor pays his original creditor, or gives him a negotiable instrument, before he receives notice of the assignment he will be under no obligation to pay the assignee (*Bence v Shearman* [1898] 2 Ch 582). If the debtor disregards the notice and pays the assignor, he is not discharged and remains liable to pay the assignee (*Brice v Bannister* (1878) 3 QBD 569). This also applies following the equitable assignment of part of a debt. If the debtor ignores the notice and pays the assignor that part of the debt which has been assigned, he is not discharged and will have to make a second payment to the assignee (it is submitted that Simon Brown LJ was wrong when he said, dissenting, in *Deposit Protection Board v Dalia* [1994] 2 AC 367 at 382, that even after notice the debtor remains liable to the equitable assignor: the actual decision of the Court of Appeal was reversed on other grounds [1994] 2 AC 367 at 391).

(2) Notice prevents modification of the agreement between assignor and debtor under which the assigned debt arose (*Brice v Bannister,* above).

(3) Notice prevents further 'equities' arising between the debtor and the assignor which might bind the assignee (see below, p 992).

(4) Notice is necessary to preserve the assignee's priority against subsequent assignees under the rule in *Dearle v Hall* (1823) 3 Russ 1 (see below, p 1008).

(5) Notice, if in writing, may turn the assignment into a statutory assignment.

2. Under a contract to assign future property the assignee cannot give notice of the assignment until he has a vested interest in the property. For the problems that this may cause the assignee, see below, pp 1032–1033.

3. In *Warner Bros Records Inc v Rollgreen Ltd* [1976] QB 430, the Court of Appeal held that an equitable assignee of an option to renew a contract for services (a legal chose), who had not given notice of his assignment to the other contracting party, could not exercise the option. Roskill LJ said (at 443) that the only right that can be created in such circumstances in the equitable assignee is the right against the assignor 'who thenceforth becomes the trustee of the benefit of the option for the assignee'. The decision has been rightly criticised on the ground that it fails to distinguish between substantive rights arising in equity out of assignments and the procedure for their enforcement; or between assignments and agreements to assign (E Peel, *Treitel's Law of Contract* (12th edn, 2007), para 15–022, n 95). Although it has been said that the decision is probably best confined to the equitable assignment of contractual options (see D M Kloss (1975) 39 Conv (NS) 261), a similar approach has been taken where there has been the assignment of a right to arbitrate under a contract (*National Iranian Tanker Co v Van der Vleit Engineering Ltd* [1996] CLC 971, where Mance J held that the equitable assignee of the right had to give notice of the assignment to the other party to the contract before commencing arbitration proceedings). For a survey of Australian and New Zealand cases, see O Chin-Aun (2002) 18 JCL 107.

What constitutes effective notice to the debtor?

James Talcott Ltd v John Lewis & Co Ltd
[1940] 3 All ER 592, Court of Appeal

A creditor (the North American Dress Co Ltd) placed the following notice on its invoices by means of a rubber stamp: 'To facilitate our accountancy and banking arrangements, it has been agreed that this invoice be transferred to and payment in London funds should be made to James Talcott Ltd...'. The defendant debtor ignored the notice and paid the creditor. The plaintiff (as assignee) sued the debtor for payment of the sum alleged to be assigned. Macnaghten J dismissed the claim. The plaintiff appealed but the Court of Appeal, by a majority, dismissed the appeal.

MacKinnon LJ: ...One may have a notice to a debtor from his creditor asking him to pay the money to a third party. The terms of it may be such as to indicate that it is to be paid to that third party because that third party has, by virtue of an assignment, become the person entitled to receive it. On the other hand, it may be a request to pay the debt to a third party, not because that third party has a right to it, but because, as a matter of convenience, the creditor desires that it shall be paid to that third party as his agent to receive it in respect of the right of the creditor still surviving to receive the debt himself. Plainness of meaning is necessary in order that the debtor who has received a notice to pay a third party shall be rendered liable to pay the money over again if he disregards the notice. The language is immaterial if the meaning is plain, but that plain meaning must be that the debt and the right to receive it have been transferred to the third party. It is not merely that I have made some arrangement by which I request another to pay this money to the third party as my agent. The question is whether this stamped clause put upon the invoices did amount to a plain intimation to the first defendants that the right to receive this money had been transferred to the plaintiffs.

First of all, it is not a notice sent by the plaintiffs at all. If it were sent direct by the plaintiffs to the first defendants, the mere fact that it emanated from them would go some little way to indicate that they were doing so pursuant to a right of theirs. I do not say that there is very much in that, but the fact that it is stamped on their own invoice by the North American Dress Co Ltd makes it a communication from them, and not a communication from John Lewis & Co Ltd to the plaintiffs. The words are these:

> To facilitate our accountancy and banking arrangements, it has been agreed that this invoice be transferred to and payment in London funds should be made to James Talcott, Ltd.... Errors in this invoice must be notified to James Talcott, Ltd immediately.

It would have been so simple for James Talcott Ltd to give a correct notice, 'This debt has been assigned to us,' or to insist that the North American Dress Co Ltd should in clear terms give that intimation, that it is a matter of extreme wonder and speculation why this stamp should have been couched in this extremely vague and obscure language.

We have been told (I think that it appears from one of the letters) that the wording of this extraordinary sentence was actually settled by counsel. I can only conceive that it was couched in this obscure language to conceal the fact that the North American Dress Co Ltd were carrying on their business with borrowed money, and had assigned to the plaintiffs the money to which they themselves were entitled.

The words begin—and they are the first words to be read by anybody who did read them—'To facilitate our accountancy and banking arrangements...'. The word 'our' suggests that it is still a debt due to the North American Dress Co Ltd and that it is only a matter of their internal business arrangements. It is true that the words go on 'it has been agreed,' and it is suggested that that must mean an agreement between the North American Dress Co Ltd and the plaintiffs, though I do not know why it should. There is nothing to show that it has been agreed between those parties. There are the vague, uncertain words 'it has been agreed.' Then it goes on to say 'that this invoice be transferred to.' It is suggested that those words in themselves ought to be taken to mean that the debt due upon this invoice shall be assigned, but they do not say so. The invoice is transferred:

> ... and payment in London funds should be made to James Talcott Ltd. ... Errors in this invoice must be notified to James Talcott Ltd immediately.

As I have said, it is not enough to make the debtor liable to pay over again if he has creditors, if he has merely received a notice that he is to pay to some other party merely as agent for his creditor. He is not bound to pay over again unless he has received a sufficiently plain notice that the right to receive the money has been transferred to the third party, so that he will at his peril neglect that notice and neglect the right of the third party. I think that this notice stamped on the invoice was ambiguous. I think that it is equally consistent with being merely a request to pay to the plaintiffs, as agents of the creditor to receive the money, and it does not indicate sufficiently clearly that there has been an assignment of the debt to the plaintiffs so that they should become the real creditors of the first defendants, be the only persons entitled to be paid the money. That was the view taken by Macnaghten J, with the result that he dismissed the claim. I think that his decision was right, and that this appeal fails.

Goddard LJ (dissenting): I have the misfortune to differ from MacKinnon LJ and Macnaghten J. I do so only with great hesitation, but, as I have formed a very clear opinion, assisted, I may say, by the very clear and forcible argument of counsel for the appellants, I think that I must express my opinion of dissent. The law of this country allows a creditor to assign his debt to a third party. If the debtor receives notice of that assignment, he must pay the assignee. If he pays the assignor, he does so at his peril. If the assignor does not account to the assignee for the money, the debtor will have to pay a second time. Notice may be given by the assignor or by the assignee. For myself, I think that the fact that the notice is given by the assignor may strengthen the position, as far as the debtor is concerned, in this way. I should not draw any inference which is adverse by reason of the fact that it is given by the assignor, because, if the debtor gets a notice from B telling him to pay B the money he owes to A, he will naturally want to know if he is safe in doing so, and he will apply to A, the assignor. If he gets a notice from the assignor, then, of course, he can safely pay, because he will be paying in accordance with the directions of his creditor.

   I do not say that this is an easy case, and I think that much clearer words could have been used, but, in my opinion, the words are clear enough to indicate the position to John Lewis & Co Ltd, if they ever thought about it. Probably the reason why they did not pay the plaintiffs was that they ignored the notice and never thought about it. I think that it is enough to tell them that the plaintiffs had a charge on, or were interested in, the money, and, therefore, for my part, I would allow this appeal.

Du Parcq LJ: ... A notice to pay a debt to a third person may be given in words which show that there has been an assignment of the debt. It may be given in words which show that there has not been an assignment of the debt. It may be given in words which leave it in doubt whether or not there has been an assignment of the debt. If those words are in the first category, the plaintiffs succeed. If the words are in either of the other categories, the plaintiffs fail. I say either of the other categories, because it is not enough that the notice should be capable of being understood to mean that the debt is assigned. It must be plain and unambiguous, and not reasonably capable, when read by an intelligent business man, of a contrary construction.

NOTES

1.   In deciding whether a notice is clear and unambiguous the court must construe it in context. In *Colonial Mutual General Insurance Co Ltd v ANZ Banking Group (New Zealand) Ltd* [1995] 1 WLR 1140, a mortgagee asked the insurer of mortgaged property to note its interest in an insurance policy taken out in the mortgagor's name. The Privy Council held (at 1145) that 'in the context of a notice to an insurance company by a mortgagee of the insured

property, the language of the notice was plain and unambiguous' and was effective to give the insurer notice of the assignment of the proceeds of the policy from the mortgagor to the mortgagee. This anticipates the modern approach to the construction of unilateral notices and commercial contracts later set out by the House of Lords in *Mannai Investment Ltd v Eagle Star Life Assurance Co Ltd* [1997] AC 749 (see above, p 949).

2.　In *Herkules Piling Ltd v Tilbury Construction Ltd* (1992) 32 Con LR 112, Hirst J held that the debtor did not receive notice of assignment when he received a copy of the contract of assignment from the assignor on discovery in arbitration proceedings. His Lordship held that in order to constitute notice there must be some kind of formal notification by the assignee, or possibly by the assignor on his behalf. Hirst J rejected as wrong a submission that the debtor must or may pay the assignee where he learns by some other credible means that the money does not or may not belong to the assignor but to the assignee. As to when notice to the debtor becomes effective, see above, p 960.

3.　For a comparison between the more relaxed rules of construction applicable to notice of equitable assignments, as opposed to the stricter rules applicable to notice of statutory assignments, see R Munday (1981) 131 NLJ 607, p 608.

4.　Notice of an equitable assignment may be oral. However, the following statutory provision may make it necessary to give notice in writing.

Law of Property Act 1925, s 137(3)

137 . . . . (3) A notice, otherwise than in writing, given to, or received by, a trustee after the commencement of this Act as respects any dealing with an equitable interest in real or personal property, shall not affect the priority of competing claims of purchasers in that equitable interest.

(v) Consideration?

Snell's Equity (31st edn, 2005), para 3–18

(f) *Value sometimes required.* Whether or not value is required for the assignment depends on the type of chose which is being assigned and on the form of the assignment. It should be noted at the outset that the question of value arises only between the assignor and the assignee; the debtor is not permitted to refuse to pay the assignee on this ground.[89]

Value is necessary for an equitable assignment of rights of property not yet in existence,[90] or for the creation of a mere charge (as distinct from a complete transfer),[91] for such assignments are based on there being a contract that the property in question shall be assigned or stand charged.[92] Value is also required for an agreement to assign an existing chose in action at some time in the future.

But value is not required for other equitable assignments of equitable choses provided the assignor has done everything required to be done by him in order to transfer the chose in action.[93] Although the contrary view has been expressed,[94] it has been established that the value is also not required for other equitable assignments of legal choses in action.[95] Thus an assignment of part of a debt is valid despite the absence of consideration.[96] Also an assignment by declaration of trust is effective since a completely constituted trust is valid without consideration.[97]

The application of the doctrine that the assignor must have done everything required to be done by him to transfer the chose in action gives rise to difficulty in relation to direct assignments of legal choses which are capable of assignment within section 136. It has been held that an assignment of a legal chose in action will be valid in equity notwithstanding that no notice has been given to the debtor under section 136 since the giving of such notice is not something required to be done by the assignor.[98] However, it is not clear whether an assignor will have been treated as having done everything required if the assignment itself is made orally and not in writing.[99]

Footnotes

89 *Walker v Bradford Old Bank* (1884) 12 QBD 511.

90 Below, para 3–28.

91 *Re Earl of Lucan* (1890) 45 Ch D 470.

92 See *Matthews v Goodday* (1861) 31 LJ Ch 282.

93 *Kekewich v Manning* (1851) 1 De GM & G 176; *Voyle v Hughes* (1854) 2 Sm & G 18; *Nanney v Morgan* (1887) 37 Ch D 346; *Re McArdle* [1951] Ch 669; *Re Wale* [1956] 1 WLR 1346.

94 *Glegg v Bromley* [1912] 3 KB 474 at 491 (explained in *German v Yates* (1915) 32 TLR 52 and *Holt v Heatherfield Trust* [1942] 2 KB 1); *Re McArdle* [1951] Ch 669 at 673.

95 *Holt v Heatherfield Trust Ltd* [1942] 2 KB 1; and see *Fortescue v Barnett* (1834) 3 My & K 36; *Blakely v Brady* (1839) 3 Dr & Wai 311; *Pearson v Amicable Assurance Office* (1859) 27 Beav 229; *Re King* (1879) 14 Ch D 179; *Re Patrick* [1891] 1 Ch 82; *Re Griffin* [1899] 1 Ch 408; *Pulley v Public Trustee* [1956] NZLR 771; *Norman v Federal Taxation Comr* (1963) 109 CLR 9; *Shepherd v Federal Comr of Taxation* (1965) 113 CLR 385; *Olsson v Dyson* (1970) 120 CLR 365; *Corin v Patton* (1990) 169 CLR 525; Sheridan, 33 Canadian Bar Review 284; 59 LQR 58, 129, 208; 67 LQR 295; Hall, 59 CLJ 99; Marshall, *The Assignment of Choses in Action* (1950) Ch 4.

96 *Shepherd v Federal Comr of Taxation* above; and see *Re McArdle* above.

97 *Ellison v Ellison* (1802) 6 Ves 656; *M'Fadden v Jenkyns* (1842) 1 Hare 458.

98 *Re Griffin* above; *Holt v Heatherfield Trust Ltd* above; *Pulley v Public Trustee* above; *Magee v UDT Finance Ltd* [1983] NZLR 438.

99 See Trietel, *Law of Contract* [(12th edn, 2007), para 15–035] for the view that an oral assignment is sufficient; and see *German v Yates* (195) 32 TLR 52 where the assignment was not in writing; but cf *Olsson v Dyson* above where an oral assignment was held to be insufficient and see *Corin v Patton* above and Meagher Gummow & Lehane, *Equity Doctrine and Remedies* [(4th edn, 2002), paras 6-075–6-155].

NOTES

1. There has been much debate as to whether failure to comply with the requirements of s 136 of the Law of Property Act 1925 prevents the gratuitous equitable assignment of a legal chose in action (when the chose could be assigned under the section) on the basis that the assignor has not done everything in his power to complete the gift. The issue does not arise with the assignment of part of a debt, which could not be assigned under the statute in any event (see above, p 945).

2. Failure by the assignor to give notice to the debtor does not make a gift imperfect as such notice can always be given by the assignee (see *Holt v Heatherfield Trust Ltd* [1942] 2 KB 1). But what if the assignment is oral? In *Olsson v Dyson* (1969) 120 CLR 365, the High Court of Australia took the view that, if property is assignable in law, equity would not enforce a gift of such property unless *all* the legal requirements laid down for its assignment have been completed. More recently, in *Corin v Patton* (1990) 169 CLR 540, the High Court of Australia has taken a more flexible approach to voluntary assignments of legal choses and stated (*obiter*) that a gift will be effective in equity where the donor has done all those things which the donor, and only the donor, can do. In Australia it seems that a gift of a legal chose which does not comply with all the requirements of a statutory assignment will be enforceable in equity as long as the assignment is in writing and signed by the donor, these being all the steps which the donor, and only the

donor, can take (see D Skapinker 'Equitable Assignments', Ch 13 in P Parkinson (ed) *The Principles of Equity* (2nd edn, 2003), paras 1310–1316; see also RP Meagher, JD Heydon and MJ Leeming *Meagher, Gummow and Lehane's Equity Doctrine and Remedies* (4th edn, 2002), paras 6-075–6-155). What of English law? Treitel, for example, argues that an oral voluntary assignment of a legal chose is valid so long as it is a perfect gift, and that a gift is not imperfect *merely* for want of writing (E Peel, *Treitel's Law of Contract* (12th edn, 2007), para 15-035; cf AP Bell, *Modern Law of Personal Property in England and Ireland* (1989), p 373). The issue remains unresolved, but the English courts are likely to be influenced by *Corin v Patton*.

3.   Consideration is only a relevant issue as between the assignor (or his successors in title) and the assignee. So far as the debtor is concerned he cannot refuse to pay the assignee merely on the ground that there has been no consideration: *Walker v Bradford Old Bank* (1884) 12 QBD 511.

4.   A voluntary promise under seal, though unenforceable in equity, may entitle the assignee to sue the assignor for damages for breach of contract (*Cannon v Hartley* [1949] Ch 213) and may later constitute an irrevocable assignment of any such property to which the promisor does become entitled and which is in fact paid to or vested in the promisee (*Re Bowden, Hulbert v Bowden* [1936] Ch 71; and *Re Adlard* [1954] Ch 29).

5.   For detailed discussion as to how far consideration is necessary for an equitable assignment, see RE Megarry (1943) 59 LQR 58 and 208; Professor Hollond (1943) 59 LQR 129; LA Sheridan (1955) 33 Can Bar Rev 284; and, especially, JC Hall [1959] CLJ 99.

QUESTIONS

1.   A purports to assign shares to B, but uses the wrong transfer form. B gives no consideration but does receive notice of the assignment. Has there been a valid equitable assignment of the shares? See *Milroy v Lord* (1862) 4 De GF & J 264. What if the correct form of transfer is used and delivered to B but A dies before the shares have been registered in B's name? See *Re Rose* [1952] Ch 499. What if the correct form of transfer is delivered to the company's auditors who fail to register the transfer but nevertheless inform B that all is in order? See *Pennington v Waine* [2002] EWCA Civ 227, [2002] 2 BCLC 448 but for the ultimate outcome in this case, see also *Hurst v Crampton Bros (Coopers) Ltd* [2002] EWHC 1375 (Ch), [2003] 1 BCLC 304 (which was decided on a different point entirely). Is there a modern tendency to validate gifts? See H Tijo and TM Yeo [2002] LMCLQ 296.

2.   Under their father's will, A and his brothers and sister were entitled to a house after the death of their mother. A's wife, B, carried out certain improvements to the house. After the improvements were completed, A and his brothers and sister wrote to B promising to pay her £500 from the estate when distributed 'in consideration of you carrying out certain alterations and improvements to the house'. Was there a valid equitable assignment of the £500? See *Re McArdle* [1951] Ch 669; REM (1951) 67 LQR 295.

4 PRINCIPLES APPLICABLE TO BOTH STATUTORY AND EQUITABLE ASSIGNMENTS

(a) Non-assignable choses in action

A chose in action is not assignable if the assignment is tainted by maintenance or champerty. A person is guilty of maintenance if he supports litigation in which he has no legitimate concern without just cause or excuse. Champerty is simply maintenance coupled with an agreement that the maintainer is to share in the recoveries of the litigation. Both are contrary to public policy, which Lord Mustill described in *Giles v Thompson* [1994] 1 AC 142 at 164 as 'a principle of public policy designed to protect the purity of justice and the interests of vulnerable litigants.' As Hobhouse LJ said in *Camdex International Ltd v Bank of Zambia* [1998] QB 22 at 29: 'what is objectionable is the trafficking in litigation', although his Lordship went on to note that, 'the modern approach is not to extend the types of involvement in litigation which are considered objectionable'.

In *Giles v Thompson* (at 153), Lord Mustill stated that, in practice, maintenance and champerty are now to be found in only two areas: (i) as the source of the rule which forbids a solicitor from accepting payment for professional services on behalf of a claimant calculated as a proportion of the sum recovered by the defendant (although Parliament has since accepted the concept of conditional fees for all civil proceedings except family proceedings proceedings: see ss 58 and 58A of the Courts and Legal Services Act 1990, as amended by the Access to Justice Act 1999), and (ii) as the ground for denying recognition to the assignment of a 'bare cause of action'. It is (ii) which concerns us here, an area which Lord Mustill described (at 153) 'as having achieved an independent life of its own'. An assignment of a bare cause of action in contract or tort is not permitted, unless the assignee has an appropriate interest in the litigation (although see YL Tan (1990) 106 LQR 656, pp 664–668 as to whether tort claims may be assigned at all). The next case is the leading one in this area.

Trendtex Trading Corpn v Crédit Suisse
[1982] AC 679, House of Lords

The plaintiffs, Trendtex (T), sold cement to an English company (cif Lagos) with payment to be made under a letter of credit issued by the Central Bank of Nigeria (CBN). CBN failed to honour the letter of credit and T sued them for breach of contract. The defendants, Crédit Suisse (CS), who had provided T with financial assistance in connection with the cement contract, guaranteed T's legal costs of the proceedings against CBN. CS saw the proceedings as providing its only prospect of recovering the money owed to it by T. In return, T assigned to CS by way of security its right of action against CBN. T was successful before the Court of Appeal but CBN obtained leave to appeal to the House of Lords. At this juncture, T (now owing US $1.5m to CS) entered into an agreement with CS whereby T assigned outright to CS any residual interest in its claim against CBN and agreed that CS could re-assign the right of action to a purchaser of its choice (the agreement recited that CS had received an offer from a third party to buy the right of action for US $800,000). Five days later CS re-assigned the right of action to a third party for US $ 1.1m and five weeks after that the third party settled with CBN for US $8m. T was suspicious of these arrangements and claimed that the agreement and assignment were void as they savoured of maintenance and champerty. The Court of Appeal (Lord Denning MR, Bridge and Oliver LJJ) upheld the assignment. T appealed.

Lord Wilberforce: …If no party had been involved in the agreement of January 4,1978, but Trendtex and Crédit Suisse, I think that it would have been difficult to contend that the agreement, even if it involved (as I think it did) an assignment of Trendtex's residual interest in the CBN case, offended against the law of maintenance or champerty. As I have already shown, Crédit Suisse had a genuine and substantial interest in the success of the CBN litigation. It had, and I do not think that the legitimacy of its action was challenged, guaranteed the previous costs. It had by the documents of September 6 and November 26, 1976, taken a security interest in the litigation or its proceeds. To carry this a stage further by a surrender of Trendtex's residual interest (if this was the effect of the agreement of January 4, 1978) would, in my view, have been lawful, though a question might have arisen (and indeed may arise) whether, after Crédit Suisse had been satisfied as creditors, Trendtex could claim the return to it of any surplus. The possibility of this could not invalidate the agreement; it would arise under it, and clearly fall within the exclusive jurisdiction clause.

The vice, if any, of the agreement lies in the introduction of the third party. It appears from the face of the agreement not as an obligation, but as a contemplated possibility, that the cause of action against CBN might be sold by Crédit Suisse to a third party, for a sum of US $800,000. This manifestly involved the possibility, and indeed the likelihood, of a profit being made, either by the third party or possibly also by Crédit Suisse, out of the cause of action. In my opinion this manifestly 'savours of champerty,' since it involves trafficking in litigation—a type of transaction which, under English law, is contrary to public policy.

Lord Roskill: …My Lords, before considering these submissions in any detail it is necessary to recall that the Criminal Law Act 1967 by s 13(1) abolished the crimes of maintenance and champerty and by s 14(1) provided that neither should any longer be actionable as a tort. But s 14(2) further provided that these provisions should not affect any rule of law as to the cases in which a contract was to be treated as contrary to public policy or otherwise illegal. It therefore seems plain that Parliament intended to leave the law as to the effect of maintenance and champerty upon contracts unaffected by the abolition of them as crimes and torts.

My Lords, it is clear, when one looks at the cases upon maintenance in this century and indeed towards the end of the last, that the courts have adopted an infinitely more liberal attitude towards the supporting of litigation by a third party than had previously been the case. One has only to read the classic judgment of Danckwerts J affirmed by the Court of Appeal, in *Martell v Consett Iron Co Ltd* [1955] Ch 363 to see how this branch of the law has developed and how the modern view of sufficiency of interest has come about. My Lords, learned counsel cited to your Lordships many of the cases on maintenance which are there discussed. For my part I think no further review of them is necessary today. I would only emphasise the importance when reading them of distinguishing between the use of the word maintenance to denote *lawful* maintenance and the use of that word to denote what was then both a crime and a tort.

My Lords, one of the reasons why equity would not permit the assignment of what became known as a bare cause of action, whether legal or equitable, was because it savoured of maintenance. If one reads the well known judgment of Parker J in *Glegg v Bromley* [1912] 3 KB 474,490, one can see how the relevant law has developed. Though in general choses in action were assignable, yet causes of action which were essentially personal in their character, such as claims for defamation or personal injury, were incapable of assignment for the reason already given. But even so, no objection was raised to assignments of the proceeds of an action for defamation as in *Glegg v Bromley,* for such an assignment would in no way give the assignee the right to intervene in the action and so be contrary to public policy: see Fletcher Moulton LJ, at pp 488–489.

My Lords, just as the law became more liberal in its approach to what was *lawful* maintenance, so it became more liberal in its approach to the circumstances in which it would recognise the validity of an assignment of a cause of action and not strike down such an assignment as one only of a bare cause of action. Where the assignee has by the assignment acquired a property right and the cause of action was incidental to that right, the assignment was held effective. *Ellis v Torrington* [1920] 1 KB 399 is an example of such a case. Scrutton LJ stated, at pp 412–413, that the assignee was not guilty of maintenance or champerty by reason of the assignment he took because he was buying not in order to obtain a cause of action but in order to protect the property which he had bought. But, my Lords, as I read the cases it was not necessary for the assignee always to show a property right to support his assignment. He could take an assignment to support and enlarge that which he had already acquired as, for example, an underwriter by subrogation: see *Compania Colombiana de Seguros v Pacific Steam Navigation Co* [1965] 1 QB 101. My Lords, I am afraid that, with respect, I cannot agree with the learned Master of the Rolls [1980] QB 629, 657 when he said in the instant case that 'The old saying that you cannot assign a "bare right to litigate" is gone.' I venture to think that that still remains a fundamental principle of our law. But it is today true to say that in English law an assignee who can show that he has a genuine commercial interest in the enforcement of the claim of another and to that extent takes an assignment of that claim to himself is entitled to enforce that assignment unless by the terms of that assignment he falls foul of our law of champerty, which, as has often been said, is a branch of our law of maintenance. For my part I can see no reason in English law why Crédit Suisse should not have taken an assignment to themselves of Trendtex's claim against CBN for the purpose of recouping themselves for their own substantial losses arising out of CBN's repudiation of the letter of credit upon which Crédit Suisse were relying to refinance their financing of the purchases by Trendtex of this cement from their German suppliers.

My Lords, I do not therefore think that Mr Brodie [counsel for Trendtex] is correct in criticising the judgment of Oliver LJ ([1980] QB 629) on the ground that the learned Lord Justice failed to distinguish between the interest necessary to support an assignment of a cause of action and the interest which would justify the maintenance of an action by a third party. I think, with respect, that this submission involves over-analysis of the position. The court should look at the totality of the transaction. If the assignment is of a property right or interest and the cause of action is ancillary to that right or interest, or if the assignee had a genuine commercial interest in taking the assignment and in enforcing it for his own benefit, I see no reason why the assignment should be struck down as an assignment of a bare cause of action or as savouring of maintenance.

But, my Lords, to reach that conclusion and thus to reject a substantial part of Mr Brodie's argument for substantially the same reasons as did Oliver LJ does not mean that at least article 1 of the agreement of January 4,1978, is not objectionable as being champertous, for it is not an assignment designed to enable Crédit Suisse to recoup their own losses by enforcing Trendtex's claim against CBN to the maximum amount recoverable. Though your Lordships do not have the agreement between Crédit Suisse and the anonymous third party, it seems to me obvious, as already stated, that the purpose of article 1 of the agreement of January 4, 1978, was to enable the claim against CBN to be sold on to the anonymous third party for that anonymous third party to obtain what profit he could from it, apart from paying to Crédit Suisse the purchase price of US $1,100,000. In other words, the 'spoils,' whatever they might be, to be got from CBN were in effect being divided, the first US $1,100,000 going to Crédit Suisse and the balance, whatever it might ultimately prove to be, to the anonymous third party. Such an agreement, in my opinion, offends for it was a step towards the sale of a bare cause of action to a third party who had no genuine commercial interest in the claim in return for a division of the spoils, Crédit Suisse taking the fixed amount which I have already mentioned. To this extent I find myself in respectful disagreement with Oliver LJ.

[Lord Fraser of Tullybelton delivered a concurring judgment.
Lords Edmund-Davies and Keith of Kinkel concurred.]

[Their Lordships went on to order the action be stayed. Their Lordships held that as the agreement was governed by Swiss law it was for the Swiss courts to decide what effect the invalidity of the assignment under English law had on the agreement as a whole.]

NOTES

1.   In *Trendtex,* Lord Roskill held that although the assignment from T to CS did not savour of maintenance, because CS had a genuine commercial interest in the enforcement of T's claim, the assignment was champertous, because it facilitated the sale of a bare cause of action to a third party who had no genuine commercial interest in the claim in return for a division of the 'spoils' between CS and the third party. This leaves open the question whether an assignee of a right to sue, who *has* a genuine commercial interest in the claim, may nevertheless profit from the assignment. In *Brownton Ltd v Edward Moore Inbucon Ltd* [1985] 3 All ER 499, the Court of Appeal (Sir John Donaldson MR, Lloyd LJ and Sir John Megaw) held that if the assignee has a genuine commercial interest it was not fatal to the validity of the assignment that he may be better off as a result of it, or that he might make a profit out of it (see also *Massai Aviation Services Ltd v Attorney-General for the Bahamas* [2007] UKPC 12). However, Sir John Megaw (at 506) did consider that an excessive level of profit might indicate that the commercial interest was not genuine (see also *Advanced Technology Structures Ltd v Cray Valley Products Ltd* [1993] BCLC 723, CA). Lloyd LJ (at 509) left open the question whether any profit would be returnable by the assignee to the assignor. In answer to that question, the editors of *Chitty on Contracts* (29th edn, 2004) submit that if the assignment is out and out and not by way of security it is difficult to see why the assignee should return any profit to the assignor (Vol 1, para 16–059 fn). For further comment on *Trendtex,* see J Thornely [1982] CLJ 29. On champerty generally, see YL Tan (1990) 106 LQR 656; A Walters (1996) 112 LQR 560; G McMeel [2004] LMCLQ 483, 494–498.

2.   When does an assignee have a 'genuine commercial interest'? In *Brownton Ltd v Edward Moore Inbucon Ltd,* above, the plaintiff sued the first defendant alleging that it had negligently advised the plaintiff to purchase an unsuitable computer. The second defendant supplied the computer and the plaintiff sued it for breach of contract. The first defendant settled with the plaintiff and took an assignment of the plaintiffs right of action against the second defendant. The Court of Appeal held that the first defendant had a genuine commercial interest in taking the assignment as (1) the contracts between the plaintiff and the first and second defendants arose out of same transaction; and (2) the first and second defendants had been sued in respect of the same damage to the plaintiff so that any sum recovered from the second defendant would have gone to reduce the sum recoverable from the first defendant. But compare this case with *Bourne v Colodense Ltd* [1985] ICR 291 where the Court of Appeal held the defendant had a 'commercial interest' in the enforcement of the plaintiff s rights against his union when those rights did not arise in a trade or commercial context (see YL Tan (1990) 106 LQR 656, p 664). The plaintiff unsuccessfully sued the defendant for personal injuries caused by negligence. As the plaintiff's union had agreed to pay the plaintiffs costs, the trial judge ordered the plaintiff to pay the defendant's costs (the House of Lords has since held in *Aiden Shipping Co Ltd v Interbulk Ltd* [1986] AC 965 that a judge can order a person who finances an unsuccessful claimant to pay the defendant's costs pursuant to the Supreme Court Act 1981, s 51). When the union refused to pay the costs the defendant applied to the court for the appointment of a receiver to take proceedings in the plaintiff s name to realise the plaintiff's claim towards the satisfaction of the costs due to the defendant. The Court of Appeal held that the defendant clearly had a commercial interest in the enforcement of such rights as the plaintiff had against his union, for without the enforcement of those rights the defendant would have had a worthless order for costs. In effect, the Court of Appeal regarded the defendant's 'financial interest' as its 'commercial interest' to satisfy the *Trendtex* test. The courts are usually generous in their interpretation of what constitutes a genuine commercial

interest. This raises the question of whether the requirement serves any useful purpose. It has been argued by Professor Tettenborn, following the US model, that it would be better if all intangible rights were *prima facie* freely assignable, with restrictions on assignment only where there were good substantive or policy-based reasons for imposing them, eg where there was a non-assignment clause in the underlying contract (see below, p 972), or in cases of the assignment of personal injury actions, when the personal injury claimant might not be in the best position to bargain unsupervised (see A Tettenborn, 'Assignment of rights to compensation' [2007] LMCLQ 392).

3.   A claim to a simple debt may be assigned even though the debt is disputed and it is contemplated at the time of the assignment that the assignee will have to sue the debtor to recover it. However, even an assignment of a debt will be contrary to public policy and ineffective where it can be proved independently and distinctly that the object or purpose of the assignment was champertous. The point arose in *Camdex International Ltd v Bank of Zambia* [1998] QB 22, where a financial crisis meant that the defendant bank was unable to repay deposits of Kuwaiti Dinars (KD) 20 million made by its customer, the Central Bank of Kuwait. Anticipating that the debt would not be recovered without litigation, the Central Bank of Kuwait assigned it absolutely to the plaintiff under s 136 of the Law of Property Act 1925 in return for a payment of KD 4 million. The defendant bank did not dispute its indebtedness to the Central Bank of Kuwait, nor the amount of the debt, but disputed the validity of the assignment on the ground that it was tainted by champerty. The Court of Appeal upheld the assignment of the debt as a valid assignment of a species of property, which carried with it the right to prosecute the cause of action closely related to that property. The payment of KD 4 million was held to represent a proper commercial valuation of the debt as the defendant bank was insolvent and unable to pay its debts. Hobhouse LJ summarised the law relating to the assignment of debts as follows (at 39):

An assignment of a debt is not invalid even if the necessity for litigation to recover it is contemplated. Provided that there is a bona fide debt, it does not become unassignable merely because the debtor chooses to dispute it. Suing on an assigned debt is not contrary to public policy even if the assignor retains an interest. What is contrary to public policy and ineffective is an agreement which has maintenance or champerty as its object; such a consequence will not be avoided by dressing up a transaction which has that character and intent as an assignment of a debt. But, because the assignment of a debt itself includes no element of maintenance and is sanctioned by statute, any objectionable element alleged to invalidate the assignment has to be proved independently and distinctly in the same way as any other alleged illegality has to be proved in relation to a contract which is on its face valid.

4.   Although the assignment of a bare cause of action is prohibited, the proceeds of an action may be assigned, at least when the assignee has no right to influence the course of the proceedings (*Glegg v Bromley* [1912] 3 KB 474, CA, wife assigned proceeds of defamation action to husband). The proceeds of the action represent property (*future* property if judgment has not yet been given) which may be assigned, there is no assignment of the cause of action itself.

5.   An assignment of a bare cause of action is valid if made by a trustee in bankruptcy or by the liquidator of a company under their statutory powers of sale: Insolvency Act 1986, s 314(l)(b), Sch 5, Pt II, para 9 (bankruptcy); Insolvency Act 1986, ss 165(3), 167(1)(b), Sch 4, Pt III, para 6 (liquidation). For example, in *Ramsey v Hartley* [1977] 1 WLR 686, the Court of Appeal allowed a trustee in bankruptcy to sell the bankrupt's right of action back to the bankrupt himself. However, in a series of cases examining the scope of a liquidator's statutory powers, it has been held that the statutory exemption does not extend to the assignment

of a cause of action conferred exclusively on the liquidator (*Re Ayala Holdings Ltd (No 2)* [1996] 1 BCLC 467—attempt by liquidator to assign rights under the Companies Act 1985, s 395 (see now the Companies Act 2006, s 874) and the Insolvency Act 1986, s 127) or an assignment of the proceeds of such an action (*Re Oasis Merchandising Services Ltd* [1998] Ch 170, CA—attempt by liquidator to assign proceeds of a wrongful trading action under the Insolvency Act 1986, s 214). In neither case is there a sale of 'the company's property' as required by the terms of the statutory exemption. It has also been held that the statutory exemption does not extend to assignments of the proceeds of litigation *made in return for the assignee agreeing to fund the action* (*Grovewood Holdings plc v James Capel & Co Ltd* [1995] Ch 80, the correctness of which was rightly doubted by the Court of Appeal in *Re Oasis Merchandising* (179–180): if the proceeds of an action can properly be described as an asset of the company, then surely they fall within the blanket immunity given by the statutory exemption). By contrast, in *Norglen Ltd v Reeds Rains Prudential Ltd* [1999] 2 AC 1, the House of Lords held that an assignment of a cause of action by a liquidator under his statutory powers was not invalid even if it (a) enabled the company to benefit indirectly from legal aid which was available to the assignee (an individual) when it was not available to the company (the company benefited indirectly because the assignee had agreed to share the proceeds of the cause of action with it); and (b) deprived the defendant in an action of the right to apply for security for costs against the company.

Other non-assignable choses in action

(1) The benefit of the *performance* of a contract is only assignable in 'cases where it can make no difference to the person on whom the obligation lies to which of two persons he is to discharge it' (*Tolhurst v Associated Portland Cement Manufacturers (1900) Ltd* [1902] 2 KB 660 at 668, per Sir R Collins MR). Therefore, the benefit of the performance of a contract which involves personal skill or confidence cannot be assigned. For example, the right to employ a person under a contract of employment is not assignable (*Nokes v Doncaster Amalgamated Collieries Ltd* [1940] AC 1014, although special employment legislation now allows for novation of employment contracts on transfer of a business by sale, other disposition or by operation of law, eg on insolvency); neither an author nor his publisher may assign the right to performance of the other's obligations under a publishing agreement (*Devefi Pty Ltd v Mateffy Pearl Nagy Pty Ltd* [1993] RPC 493); a boxing promoter and manager may not assign the benefit of promotion and management agreements with a boxer (*Don King Productions Inc v Warren* [1999] 2 All ER 218); if a seller of goods has personal confidence in his buyer's ability to keep his business going and pay the seller for goods sold on credit, the contractual right to the seller's performance cannot be assigned (*Cooper v Micklefield Coal and Lime Co Ltd* (1912) 107 LT 457). This restriction does not prevent the assignment of any benefit *arising under* the contract, eg wages or salary due to an employee are normally (subject to Note 2 below) assignable by him (*Shaw & Co v Moss Empires Ltd and Boston* (1908) 25 TLR 190). As Professor Goode has stated in (1979) 42 MLR 553 at 555: 'What is non-transferable is the duty to perform, not the fruits of performance.'

(2) An assignment may be void on grounds of public policy (other than maintenance and champerty). For example, an assignment of the salary of a public officer, paid from central (not local) funds, is void on this ground (eg *Arbuthnot v Norton* (1846) 5 Moo PCC 219, where it was held that a judge could not assign his salary). See DW Logan (1945) 61 LQR 240 for the policy reasons against the assignment of the salary of public officers.

(3) An assignment may be prohibited by statute, eg social security benefit is not assignable (Social Security Administration Act 1992, s 187); a right to a pension under an occupational pension scheme cannot be assigned other than in favour of a widow, widower or dependant (Pensions Act 1995, s 91).

(4) An assignment may be prohibited by the terms of the contract between assignor and debtor. In such circumstances the assignment is ineffective as between assignee and debtor (*Helstan Securities Ltd v Hertfordshire County Council* [1978] 3 All ER 262), but remains effective as between assignor and assignee (*Linden Gardens Trust Ltd v Lenesta Sludge Disposals Ltd and St Martins Property Corpn Ltd v Sir Robert McAlpine & Sons Ltd* [1994] 1 AC 85, HL: see below).

Linden Gardens Trust Ltd v Lenesta Sludge Disposals Ltd and St Martins Property Corp Ltd v Sir Robert McAlpine & Sons Ltd
[1994] 1 AC 85, House of Lords

These were consolidated appeals heard together by the Court of Appeal (1992) 57 BLR 57 and House of Lords. In the *Linden Gardens* case, Stock Conversion and Investment Trust plc ('Stock Conversion'), the lessee of part of a building, engaged a building contractor to remove asbestos from those premises under a standard JCT building contract, Clause 17 of which stipulated expressly that Stock Conversion, the employer, 'shall not without written consent of the contractor assign this contract.' When executing the work the contractor allegedly committed various breaches of contract. Stock Conversion then sold its leasehold interest in the premises to Linden Gardens Trust Ltd ('Linden Gardens') at full market value, and later purported to assign all its rights of action under the building contract to them, although it did not obtain the contractor's consent before doing so. As the full extent of the contractor's breaches became clear, Linden Gardens spent considerable sums remedying them. Linden Gardens, as assignee, then sought to recover its loss by suing the contractor for breach of the building contact. Stock Conversion, the assignor, was not a party to that action.

The facts of the *St Martins* case were similar. Here a building contractor was engaged by St Martins Property Corporation Ltd ('Corporation'), the lessee of a building site, to build shops, offices and flats on the site under a standard JCT building contract, Clause 17 of which was in the same terms as Clause 17 in the *Linden Gardens* case. Before the contractor started work, Corporation sold its leasehold interest in the site at full market value to an associate company, St Martins Property Investments Ltd ('Investments'), and simultaneously purported to assign the benefit of the building contract to them (although without first obtaining the contractor's consent). Subsequently, the contractor allegedly breached that contract causing loss to the new lessee of the site, Investments. That the contractor's breaches occurred after assignment distinguishes the facts of the *St Martins* case from those of the *Linden Gardens* case, as does the fact that in the *St Martins* case the assignor (Corporation) was a party to the action brought by the assignee (Investments) against the contractor.

In both cases the contractors pleaded that they were not liable in damages to the purported assignees (Linden Gardens and Investments) because Clause 17 made both assignments ineffective. This point is dealt with by Lord Browne-Wilkinson in the extract which immediately follows. In the *St Martins* case, the contractor also pleaded that whilst the original contracting party, Corporation, was entitled to sue, it could not recover any more than nominal damages because it had suffered no loss. This point is dealt with in Note 4 on p 1007.

Lord Browne-Wilkinson: …

(1) Does clause 17 prohibit the assignment of the benefit of building contracts?

Staughton LJ (dissenting on this point) held that on its true construction clause 17 did not prohibit the assignment by the employer of the benefit of the building contract. It was urged before your Lordships on behalf of Linden Gardens and Investments that his views were correct.

The argument runs as follows. On any basis, clause 17 is unhappily drafted in that it refers to an assignment of 'the contract.' It is trite law that it is, in any event, impossible to assign 'the contract' as a whole, ie including both burden and benefit. The burden of a contract can never be assigned without the consent of the other party to the contract in which event such consent will give rise to a novation. Therefore one has to discover what the parties meant by this inelegant phrase. It is said that the intention of the parties in using the words 'assign this contract' is demonstrated by clause 17(2) which prohibits both the assignment of the contract by the contractor without the employer's consent and the sub-letting of any portion of the works without the consent of the architect. In clause 17(2), the contractor is only expressly prevented from subletting 'any *portion* of the works.' Yet it must have been the party's intention to limit the contractor's rights to sublet the *whole* of the works. Accordingly, the words in clause 17(2) 'assign this contract' have to be read as meaning 'sublet the whole of the works.' If that is the meaning of the words 'assign this contract' in clause 17(2) they must bear the same meaning in clause 17(1), which accordingly only prohibits the employer from giving substitute performance and does not prohibit the assignment of the benefit of the contract.

Like the majority of the Court of Appeal, I am unable to accept this argument. Although it is true that the phrase 'assign this contract' is not strictly accurate, lawyers frequently use those words inaccurately to describe an assignment of the benefit of a contract since every lawyer knows that the burden of a contract cannot be assigned: see, for example, *Nokes v Doncaster Amalgamated Collieries Ltd* [1940] AC 1014,1019–1020. The prohibition in clause 17(2) against subletting 'any portion of the works' necessarily produces a prohibition against the subletting of the whole of the works: any subletting of the whole will necessarily include a subletting of a portion and is therefore prohibited. Therefore there is no ground for reading the words 'assign this contract' in clause 17(1) as referring only to subletting the whole. Decisively, both clause 17(1) and (2) clearly distinguish between 'assignment' and 'subletting:' it is therefore impossible to read the word 'assign' as meaning 'sublet.' Finally, I find it difficult to comprehend the concept of an employer 'subletting' the performance of his contractual duties which consist primarily of providing access to the site and paying for the works.

Accordingly, in my view clause 17(1) of the contract prohibited the assignment by the employer of the benefit of the contract. This, by itself, is fatal to the claim by Investments (as assignee) in the *St Martins* case.

(2) Does clause 17(1) prohibit the assignment of accrued rights of action?

The majority in the Court of Appeal drew a distinction between an assignment of the right to require future performance of a contract by the other party on the one hand and an assignment of the benefits arising *under* the contract (eg to receive payment due under it or to enforce accrued rights of action) on the other hand. They held that clause 17 only prohibited the assignment of the right to future performance and did not prohibit the assignment of the benefits arising under the contract, in particular accrued causes of action. Therefore, in the *Linden Gardens* case, where all the relevant breaches of contract by the contractors pre-dated the assignment, an assignment to *Linden Gardens* of the accrued rights of action for breach was not prohibited. In contrast, in the *St Martins* case, where all the breaches of contract occurred after the date of the assignment, the majority of the Court of Appeal held that it was a breach of clause 17 to seek to transfer the right to future performance.

This distinction between assigning the right to future performance of a contract and assigning the benefits arising under a contract was largely founded on a Note entitled 'Inalienable Rights?' by Professor RM Goode (1979) 42 MLR 553 on *Helstan Securities Ltd v Hertfordshire County Council* [1978] 3 All ER 262. In that case a contract contained a clause prohibiting the contractor from assigning the contract 'or any benefit therein or thereunder.' The contractors assigned to the plaintiffs the right to a liquidated sum of money then alleged to be due to the contractors under the contract. Croom-Johnson J held that the plaintiffs, as assignees, could not sue the employers to recover the sum of money.

In his Note, Professor Goode rightly pointed out that where a contract between A and B prohibits assignment of contractual rights by A, the effect of such a prohibition is a question of the construction of the contract. There are at least four possible interpretations, viz, (1) that the term does not invalidate a purported assignment by A to C but gives rise only to a claim by B against A for damages for breach of the prohibition; (2) that the term precludes or invalidates any assignment by A to C (so as to entitle B to pay the debt to A) but not so as to preclude A from agreeing, as between himself and C, that he will account to C for what A receives from B: *In re Turcan* (1888) 40 ChD 5; (3) that A is precluded not only from effectively assigning the contractual rights to C, but also from agreeing to account to C for the fruits of the contract when received by A from B; (4) that a purported assignment by A to C constitutes a repudiatory breach of condition entitling B not merely to refuse to pay C but also to refuse to pay A.

Professor Goode then expressed the view that construction (2) (being the *Helstan* case itself) was permissible and effective but that construction (3) to the extent that it purported to render void not only the assignment as between B and C but also as between A and C was contrary to law.

I am content to accept Professor Goode's classification and conclusions, though I am bound to say that I think cases within categories (1) and (4) are very unlikely to occur. But Professor Goode's classification provides no warrant for the view taken by the majority of the Court of Appeal in the present case: he does not discuss or envisage a case where a contractual prohibition against assignment is to be construed as prohibiting an assignment by A to C of rights of future performance but does not prohibit the assignment by A to C of 'the fruits of performance' eg accrued rights of action or debts. Professor Goode only draws a distinction between the assignment of rights to performance and the assignment of rights under the contract in two connections: first, in dealing with the effect of a prohibited assignment as between the assignor and the assignee (in categories (2) and (3)): secondly, in dealing with contracts for personal services. In the latter, he rightly points out that, although an author who has contracted to write a book for a fee cannot perform the contract by supplying a book written by a third party, if he writes the book himself he can assign the right to the fee—the fruits of performance. He expressly mentions that such right to assign the fruits of performance can be prohibited by the express terms of the contract.

However, although I do not think that Professor Goode's article throws any light on the true construction of clause 17. I accept that it is at least hypothetically possible that there might be a case in which the contractual prohibitory term is so expressed as to render invalid the assignment of rights to future performance but not so as to render invalid assignments of the fruits of performance. The question in each case must turn on the terms of the contract in question.

The question is to what extent does clause 17 on its true construction restrict rights of assignment which would otherwise exist? In the context of a complicated building contract, I find it impossible to construe clause 17 as prohibiting only the assignment of rights to future performance, leaving each party free to assign the fruits of the contract. The reason for including the contractual prohibition viewed from the contractor's point of view must be that the contractor wishes to ensure that he deals, and deals only, with the particular employer with whom he has chosen to enter into a contract. Building contracts are pregnant with disputes: some employers are much more reasonable than others in dealing with such disputes. The disputes frequently arise in the context of the contractor suing for the price and being met by a claim for abatement of the price or cross-claims founded on an allegation that the performance of the contract has been defective. Say that, before the final instalment of the price has been paid, the employer has assigned the benefits under the contract to a third party, there being at the time existing rights of action for defective work. On the Court of Appeal's view, those rights of action would have vested in the assignee. Would the original employer be entitled to an abatement of the price, even though the cross-claims would be vested in the assignee? If so, would the assignee be a necessary party to any settlement or litigation of the claims for defective work, thereby requiring the contractor to deal with two parties (one not of his choice) in order to recover the price for the works from the employer? I cannot believe that the parties ever intended to permit such a confused position to arise.

Again, say that before completion of the works the employers assigned the land, together with the existing causes of action against the contractor, to a third party and shortly thereafter the contractor committed a repudiatory breach? On the construction preferred by the Court of Appeal, the right to insist on further performance, being unassignable, would have remained with the original employers whereas the other causes of action and the land would belong to the assignee. Who could decide whether to accept the repudiation, the assignor or the assignee?

These possibilities of confusion (and many others which could be postulated) persuade me that parties who have specifically contracted to prohibit the assignment of the contract cannot have intended to draw a distinction between the right to performance of the contract and the right to the fruits of the contract. In my view they cannot have contemplated a position in which the right to future performance and the right to benefits accrued under the contract should become vested in two separate people. I say again that that result could have been achieved by careful and intricate drafting, spelling out the parties' intentions if they had them. But in the absence of such a clearly expressed intention, it would be wrong to attribute such a perverse intention to the parties. In my judgment, clause 17 clearly prohibits the assignment of any benefit of or under the contract.

It follows that the purported assignment to Linden Gardens without the consent of the contractors constituted a breach of clause 17. The claim of Linden Gardens as assignee must therefore fail unless it can show that the prohibition in clause 17 was either void as being contrary to public policy or, notwithstanding the breach of clause 17, the assignment was effective to assign the chose in action to Linden Gardens.

(3) Is a prohibition on assignment void as being contrary to public policy?

It was submitted that it is normally unlawful as being contrary to public policy to seek to render property inalienable. Since contractual rights are a species of property, it is said that a prohibition against assigning such rights is void as being illegal.

This submission faces formidable difficulties both on authority and in principle. As to the authorities, in *In re Turcan,* 40 ChD 5, a man effected an insurance policy which contained a term that it should not be assignable in any case whatever. He had previously covenanted with trustees to settle after-acquired property. The Court of Appeal held that although he could not assign the benefit of the policy so as to give the trustees the power to recover the money from the insurance company, he could validly make a declaration of trust of the proceeds which required him to hand over such proceeds to the trustees. This case proceeded, therefore, on the footing that the contractual restriction on assignment was valid. In *Helstan Securities* [1978] 3 All ER 262 Croom-Johnson J enforced such a prohibition. In *Reed Publishing Holdings Ltd v Kings Reach Investments Ltd* (unreported), 25 May 1983; Court of Appeal (Civil Division) Transcript No 231 of 1983, the Court of Appeal had to consider an application to join as a party to an action an assignee of the benefit of a contract which contained a prohibition on such assignment. One of their grounds for refusing the application was that by reason of the prohibition the assignment was of no effect.

In none of these cases was the public policy argument advanced. But they indicate a long-term acceptance of the validity of such a prohibition which is accepted as part of the law in *Chitty on Contracts,* 26th edn (1989), Vol 1, p 883, para 1413. We were referred to a decision of the Supreme Court of South Africa, *Paiges v Van Ryn Gold Mines Estates Ltd* 1920 AD 600 in which it was expressly decided that a term prohibiting a workman from assigning his wages was not contrary to public policy. In Scotland a covenant against assigning a lease of minerals (which was treated simply as a contract) was held not to infringe public policy: *Duke of Portland v Bairdand Co* (1865) 4 Macph 10. We were referred to certain cases in the United States, but they give no unequivocal guidance.

In the face of this authority, the House is being invited to change the law by holding that such a prohibition is void as contrary to public policy. For myself I can see no good reason for so doing. Nothing was urged in argument as showing that such a prohibition was contrary to the public interest beyond the fact that such prohibition renders the chose in action inalienable. Certainly in the context of rights over land the law does not favour restrictions on alienability. But even in relation to land law a prohibition against the assignment of a lease is valid. We were not referred to any English case in which the courts have had to consider restrictions on the alienation of tangible personal property, probably because there are few cases in which there would be any desire to restrict such alienation. In the case of real property there is a defined and limited supply of the commodity, and it has been held contrary to public policy to restrict the free market. But no such reason can apply to contractual rights: there is no public need for a market in choses in action. A party to a building contract, as I have sought to explain, can have a genuine commercial interest in seeking to ensure that he is in contractual relations only with a person whom he has selected as the other party to the contract. In the circumstances, I can see no policy reason why a contractual prohibition on assignment of contractual rights should be held contrary to public policy.

To avoid doubt, I must make it clear that I have been considering only the validity of a restriction which prohibits assignments which have the effect of bringing the assignee into direct contractual relations with the other party to the contract. I have not been considering Professor Goode's category (3), ie an attempt by contractual term to prevent one party making over the fruits of the contract to a third party. Professor Goode expresses the view that if the prohibition seeks to prevent the assignor from binding himself to pay over such fruits to the assignee, such prohibition is pro tanto void. I express no view on that point.

(4) Are the assignments (although prohibited) effective to transfer the causes of action to the assignees?

It was submitted that, even though the assignments were in breach of clause 17, they were effective to vest the causes of action in the assignees, ie Professor Goode's category (1). This argument was founded on two bases: first, the decision in *Tom Shaw and Co v Moss Empires Ltd* (1908) 25 TLR 190; second, the fact that an assignment of a leasehold term in breach of a covenant against assignment is effective to vest the term in the assignee.

In the *Tom Shaw* case an actor, B, was engaged by Moss Empires under a contract which prohibited the assignment of his salary. B assigned 10 per cent, of his salary to his agent, Tom Shaw. Tom Shaw sued Moss Empires for 10 per cent, of the salary joining B as second defendant. Moss Empire agreed to pay the 10 per cent, of the salary to Tom Shaw or B, as the court might decide ie in effect it interpleaded. Darling J held, at p 191, that the prohibition on assignment was ineffective: it could 'no more operate to invalidate the assignment than it could to interfere with the laws of gravitation.' He gave judgment for the plaintiffs against both B and Moss Empires, ordering B to pay the costs but making no order for costs against Moss Empires.

The case is inadequately reported and it is hard to discover exactly what it decides. Given that both B and Moss Empires were parties and Moss Empires was in effect interpleading, it may be that the words I have quoted merely indicate that as between the assignor, B and the assignee Tom Shaw, the prohibition contained in the contract between B and Moss Empires could not invalidate B's liability to account to Tom Shaw for the moneys when received and that, since B was a party, payment direct to Tom Shaw was ordered. This view is supported by the fact that no order for costs was made against Moss Empires. If this is the right view of the case, it is unexceptionable: a prohibition on assignment normally only invalidates the assignment as against the other party to the contract so as to prevent a transfer of the chose in action: in the absence of the clearest words it cannot operate to invalidate the contract as between the assignor and the assignee and even then it may be ineffective on the grounds of public policy. If on the other hand Darling J purported to hold that the contractual prohibition was ineffective to prevent B's contractual rights against Moss Empires being transferred to Tom Shaw, it is inconsistent with authority and was wrongly decided.

In the *Helstan Securities* case [1978] 3 All ER 262 Croom-Johnson J did not follow the *Tom Shaw* case and held that the purported assignment in breach of the contractual provision was ineffective to vest the cause of action in the assignee. That decision was followed and applied by the Court of Appeal in the *Reed Publishing Holdings* case, 25 May 1983: see also *In re Turcan,* 40 ChD 5.

Therefore the existing authorities establish that an attempted assignment of contractual rights in breach of a contractual prohibition is ineffective to transfer such contractual rights. I regard the law as being satisfactorily settled in that sense. If the law were otherwise, it would defeat the legitimate commercial reason for inserting the contractual prohibition, viz., to ensure that the original parties to the contract are not brought into direct contractual relations with third parties.

As to the analogy with leases, I was originally impressed by the fact that an assignment of the term in breach of covenant is effective to vest the term in the assignee: *Williams v Earle* (1868) LR 3 QB 739,750; *Old Grovebury Manor Farm Ltd v W Seymour Plant Sales and Hire Ltd (No 2)* [1979] 1 WLR 1397. However, Mr Kentridge in his reply satisfied me that the analogy is a false one. A lease is a hybrid, part contract, part property. So far as rights of alienation are concerned a lease has been treated as a species of property. Historically the law treated interests in land, both freehold and leasehold, as being capable of disposition and looked askance at any attempt to render them inalienable. However, by the time of Coke covenants against the assignment of leases had been held to be good, because the lessor had a continuing interest in the identity of the person who was his tenant: *Holdsworth, A History of English Law,* 2nd edn, Vol III (1914), p 85 and Vol VII (1937), p 281. The law became settled that an assignment in breach of covenant gave rise to a forfeiture, but pending forfeiture the term was vested in the assignee. In contrast, the development of the law affecting the assignment of contractual rights was wholly different. It started from exactly the opposite position, viz, contractual rights were personal and not assignable. Only gradually did the law permitting assignment develop: *Holdsworth,* Vol VII, pp 520–521 and 531 etc. It is therefore not surprising if the law applicable to assignment of contractual rights differs from that applicable to the assignment of leases.

Therefore in my judgment an assignment of contractual rights in breach of a prohibition against such assignment is ineffective to vest the contractual rights in the assignee. It follows that the claim by Linden Gardens fails and the *Linden Garden* action must be dismissed.

[Lords Keith of Kinkel, Bridge of Harwich, Griffiths and Ackner all agreed with Lord Browne-Wilkinson on this issue.]

NOTES

1.   Debtors often include 'non-assignment' clauses in their contracts restricting or absolutely prohibiting the assignment of their debts (see generally, A Allcock [1983] CLJ 328; G McCormack [2000] JBL 422; G Mc Meel [2004] LMCLQ 483). The reasons are various:

- The debtor values the personal qualities of the other contracting party. In *Don King Productions Inc v Warren* [2000] Ch 291, a case concerning boxing promotion, the identity of the promoter was crucial to the boxer and explained the presence of a non-assignment clause. In *Linden Gardens,* above, Lord Browne-Wilkinson explained that a contractor may wish to deal with a particular employer and no other because 'building contracts are pregnant with disputes: some employers are more reasonable than others in dealing with such disputes'.

- The debtor wishes to retain, up to the very date of the discharge of the debts, rights of set-off and the right of raising counterclaims based on different liabilities (certain new 'equities' may not be set up after notice of assignment).

- The debtor may wish to avoid the risk of making the error of paying twice owing to an oversight of a notice of assignment or having to pay more than one creditor if there is an assignment of part of a debt.

Whilst these considerations favour the validity of non-assignment clauses, there are countervailing arguments which support the principle of free assignability of debts. First, a debt is a form of property and, as such, should be freely alienable, unless there is a clear expression of contrary intention in the underlying contract between the assignor and the debtor (*Barbados Trust Co v Bank of Zambia* [2007] EWCA Civ 148, [2007] 1 Lloyd's Rep 495 at [43], per Waller LJ, and at [88], per Rix LJ). Secondly, from a commercial point of view, non-assignment clauses affect the marketability of debts and therefore the validity of receivables financing. Such considerations have prevailed in the United States, where the Uniform Commercial Code renders non-assignment clauses ineffective (rev art 9–406(d)), and this approach has influenced the drafting of international Conventions (see the UNIDROIT Factoring Convention, Art 6 and the UNCITRAL Convention on Receivables Financing, art 11) and UNIDROIT's statement of principles applicable to international commercial contracts (see UNIDROIT Principles for International Commercial Contracts 2004, art 9.1.9). The Law Commission has even recommended that, in the case of an assignment of receivables, a non-assignment clause should be ineffective against the assignee (Law Com Report No 296, 'Company Security Interests' (2005), appendix A, draft Company Security Regulations, reg 35(5)). For competing views on the freedom to assign debts, see P. Zonneveld (2007) 6 JIBFL 313, and T. Prime (2008) 2 JIBFL 71.

2.   The effectiveness of a non-assignment clause depends on its construction. In *Helstan Securities Ltd v Hertfordshire County Council* [1978] 3 All ER 262, a standard Institution of Civil Engineers building contract contained a stipulation that the contractor was not to 'assign the contract or any part thereof or any benefit or interest therein or thereunder' without the employer's written consent. The contractor's claim, which was assigned to the plaintiff, lay in debt. The plaintiff argued that the clause on its true construction did not apply to debts, as distinct from the assignment of the contract itself or other causes of action arising under it. The argument was rejected by Croom-Johnson J who construed the term 'benefit or interest therein or thereunder' widely so as to cover debts which resulted from the performance of the contract. In *Linden Gardens* the House of Lords adopted a similarly broad approach to the construction of Clause 17 when refusing to distinguish between an assignment of the right to future performance of a contract and an assignment of the benefits arising under the contract, eg accrued rights of action or debts. More recently, in *Barbados Trust Co v Bank of Zambia* [2007] EWCA Civ 148, [2007] 1 Lloyd's Rep 495 (below, p 983), the Court of Appeal held that an assignment of an acknowledged debt due from a borrower under a loan agreement was caught by a clause prohibiting assignment of the lender's 'rights and benefits in respect of the facility' without the borrower's prior consent. However, there has been at least one case since *Linden Gardens* where the clause in question was construed as merely extending to the assignment of 'personal' rights of performance and not to the debts arising. In *Flood v Shand Construction Ltd* (1996) 54 Con LR 125, the clause in question prohibited the assignment by the sub-contractor of the benefit of the sub-contract without the other party's consent, but permitted assignment of 'any sum which is or may become due and payable to him under this Sub-Contract'. The Court of Appeal construed the clause as prohibiting the assignment of the right to claim damages or other sums that were not yet due or payable and needed to be established as due and payable by litigation or arbitration or contractual machinery, but as permitting the assignment of the right to recover sums which were already due, ie essentially debts.

3.   A distinction must be made between absolute prohibitions on assignment and qualified prohibitions where an assignment is permitted in certain circumstances, or subject to the assignor obtaining the debtor's consent. A clause in a contract may prohibit assignment without the debtor's prior consent 'which shall not be unreasonably withheld'. In *Hendry v Chartsearch Ltd* [1998] CLC 1382, there was such a prohibition in the contract between the assignor (a company) and the debtor, yet the assignor went ahead and purported to assign

various causes of action arising under the contract to the assignee (the Chairman and a shareholder of the assignor) without seeking the debtor's consent thereto. The assignee later submitted that this omission did not make the assignment ineffective against the debtor because the debtor's consent to the assignment could have not reasonably been refused. Evans LJ preferred to leave the point open, although he thought it arguable that the debtor could object to the validity of the assignment on the ground that he could have reasonably refused consent in the present case (because the corporate assignor could have been required to give security for costs in an action against the debtor, whereas the assignee, as an individual, could not). His Lordship considered that the non-assignment clause was operative even though the parties' trading relationship had come to an end. This, though, was relevant to the question of whether it was reasonable for the debtor to refuse consent. Evans LJ (at 1392) considered that 'the question whether a particular undertaking "survives" repudiation and acceptance depends always on the true construction of the contract in the particular case' (and for a case where the non-assignment clause was held not to survive termination of the contract, see *ANC Ltd v Clark Goldring & Page Ltd* [2001] BPIR 568, where the Court of Appeal held that the issue turned on construction of the terms of the contract in question).

Henry and Millett LJJ dealt with the assignee's main submission head on. They held that where an assignment of contractual rights is prohibited without the prior written consent of the other party (such consent not to be unreasonably refused) then there could be no valid assignment until after (1) written consent had been granted, or (2) the court had declared that the consent had been unnecessarily refused. According to Henry LJ (at 1393):

> [t]he suggestion that the assignor can validly assign in breach of his contract without ever seeking prior consent by asserting that, as such consent could not reasonably be refused, so it is unnecessary, seems to me to be a recipe to promote uncertainty and speculative litigation.

Millett LJ also held (at 1394) that where an ordinary commercial contract provides that a party should not be entitled to assign the benefit of the agreement without the debtor's prior consent, a purported assignment in the face of that prohibition does not constitute a breach of the assignor's contract with the debtor, let alone a repudiatory breach of contract, so that the assignor could later go back to the debtor for his consent to a new assignment. It should be noted that the non-assignment clause in the *Hendry* case did not expressly state that any attempted or purported assignment constituted a breach of contract, as is sometimes the case with non-assignment clauses. Yet in *Linden Gardens,* above, Lord Browne-Wilkinson made the point (at 104) that the situation where a purported assignment constituted a repudiatory breach of the contract between debtor and assignor, entitling the debtor to refuse to pay both the assignee and the assignor, was 'very unlikely to occur'.

Millett LJ went on to hold that as the contract in question required the assignor to obtain the *prior* consent of the other party; retrospective consent, if given, might operate as a waiver, but could not amount to the consent required by the contract. The proper course was for the assignor to ask for consent to a new assignment and to wait until it was given or unreasonably refused before proceeding to make it. In *Orion Finance Ltd v Crown Management Ltd* [1994] 2 BCLC 607, although the defendant had not given his consent, the assignment was held valid because in the circumstances the defendant was estopped from denying that the assignment was valid (cf *Donald Graham v British Gas plc* (8 October 1999, unreported), where, on the facts, Dyson J rejected arguments based on waiver of consent by, and/or estoppel against, the debtor).

4.   A *prior* agreement between an assignor and assignee to assign a contractual right has been held by the Court of Appeal not to infringe a non-assignment clause in the (subsequent) contract

creating that right. The facts of *Foamcrete (UK) Ltd v Thrust Engineering Ltd* [2002] BCC 221 were these. In 1992, a company, PTE, entered into a debenture granting to the Midland Bank fixed charges over all book debts, goodwill and intellectual property and a floating charge over its undertaking and all its property, both present and future. In June 1994, PTE entered into a joint venture agreement with Thrust and, through a supplementary agreement, agreed to sell to Thrust certain stock and work in progress, the price being payable within six months. In August 1994, PTE went into liquidation. In 1996, the Midland Bank, assuming that PTE's right to recover the price from Thrust had passed to it under its 1992 charge, transferred its rights under the charge to Foamcrete. Payment was not made and so Foamcrete started proceedings against Thrust. Thrust's defence was that any purported assignment (from PTE to the Midland Bank) of the debt was ineffective because it was in breach of a term of the original joint venture agreement with PTE which prohibited assignment of the agreement, or any rights thereunder, without the other party's consent. Thrust contended that Foamcrete could not stand in any better position than the Midland Bank, the original debenture holder.

The Court of Appeal (Mummery and Keene LJJ) gave judgment in favour of Foamcrete. The main reason was that the non-assignment clause in the joint venture agreement between PTE and Thrust had not been incorporated in the contract to sell to Thrust the stock and work in progress. In other words, the assignment was not prohibited. However, Mummery LJ, giving the judgment of the court, went on to consider what would have been the position had there been incorporation of the non-assignment clause. He considered that it would have made no difference even if the contract between PTE and Thrust had contained a term preventing assignment. His reasoning ran as follows. *Linden Gardens* was authority for the proposition, stated by Lord Browne-Wilkinson (at 109), that 'an assignment of contractual rights in breach of a prohibition against such assignment is ineffective to vest the contractual rights in the assignee'. Thus, Mummery LJ concluded, such a clause could only be broken *after* the contract containing it was concluded. He considered that the bank's security rights over the debt due from Thrust to PTE, now vested in Foamcrete, did not derive from any assignment by PTE in breach of the non-assignment clause but that they derived from the antecedent charge. For criticisms of this decision, see A Tettenborn [2001] LMCLQ 472.

5.   What remedy does an assignee have against his assignor where the assignment is ineffective against the debtor because of a non-assignment clause? The relationship between the assignor and an assignee for value remains a contractual one and, save where the terms of their agreement amounts to a declaration of trust in favour of the assignee of the benefit of the assignor's contract with the debtor (see below), the purported assignment does not amount to the legal or equitable transfer of any proprietary interest to the assignee (*R v Chester and North Wales Legal Aid Area Office, ex p Floods of Queensferry Ltd* [1998] 2 BCLC 436 at 442–443, 445, CA—where it was expressly held that the corporate assignor had not declared itself a trustee of its cause of action against the debtor; applied in *Bawejem Ltd v MC Fabrications Ltd* [1999] 1 All ER (Comm) 377, CA). In many cases it will be possible for the assignee to bring a breach of contract claim against the assignor where the assignor has failed to obtain the debtor's consent to the assignment (see *Linden Gardens Trust Ltd v Lenesta Sludge Disposals Ltd* [1994] 1 AC 85 at 109–110, per Lord Browne-Wilkinson. However, where the assignor becomes insolvent after the purported assignment and receives payment from the debtor, the assignee will need to assert a proprietary claim against the assignor in order to take priority over his other creditors. In some cases the assignee may be able to rely on the assignor's conduct as amounting to a declaration of trust of the proceeds of the debt in favour of the assignee (see *Re Turcan* (1888) 40 Ch D 5, cited without disapproval by Lord Browne-Wilkinson in *Linden Gardens* at 106: see above).

Declaration of trust

A prohibition on assignment does not prevent a party declaring a trust of the benefit of the contract, ie a trust of the right to performance of the contract. The issue arose in *Don King Productions Inc v Warren* [2000] Ch 291, where W and K, two boxing promoters, formed a partnership and, as part of their agreement, W purported to assign to the partnership all his promotion and management agreements (PMAs) with a number of boxers. The agreement further provided that if and when it came to an end all assets of the partnership should be purchased by W at market value. Relations between the two promoters later soured, and the partnership was wound up. In the resulting litigation, K alleged that the PMAs were part-nership property and that W was obliged to buy them back at market value. W's case was that on dissolution of the partnership he was entitled to retain the PMAs for his own benefit free of charge. W argued that the purported assignment of the PMAs to the partnership had been of no effect because (1) the PMAs involved personal skill and confidence as between boxer and promoter (applying *Nokes v Doncaster Amalgamated Colleries Ltd* [1940] 3 All ER 549: see above, p 972), and (2) most PMAs specifically prohibited assignment. It followed, according to W, that the PMAs did not form part of the partnership assets so as to be caught by the 'buy-back' clause.

The Court of Appeal (Morritt, Aldous and Hutchison LJJ), upholding the first instance decision of Lightman J, decided the issue in favour of K. The court accepted that the PMAs were non-assignable, but held that this did not prevent them from being held on trust by the purported assignor (W) for the purported assignee (the partnership) as this was the 'evident' or 'manifest' intention of the parties as demonstrated by the terms of their agree-ment (at 236). Their Lordships held the parties' intention that the full benefit of the PMAs should be partnership property, manifest in the assignment provision, was also reflected in other terms of the agreement, and the fact that W was legally unable to assign the benefit of the PMAs meant a trust was the only way the evident intention of the parties could be achieved. There was no argument on appeal as to the scope of the non-assignment clauses in the PMAs. Lightman J, at first instance, held (at 319–320) that a declaration of trust in favour of a third party of the benefit of obligations or the profits obtained from a contract was dif-ferent in character from an assignment of the benefit of the contract to that third party, so that a clause prohibiting assignments is prima facie restricted to assignments of the benefit of the obligation and does not extend to declarations of trust of the benefit. It would seem, therefore, that in future the draftsman of a non-assignment clause must make it absolutely clear that the prohibition applies as much to the creation of a trust or other equitable interest in the benefit of the obligation as to straightforward assignment.

Professor Andrew Tettenborn has been highly critical of the reasoning of both Lightman J, and of the Court of Appeal, in the *Don King* case: see, respectively, [1998] LMCLQ 498 and [1999] LMCLQ 353. He suggests there should be no distinction between an equitable assign-ment and 'other equitable interests'. He also suggests that there is a distinction between a trust of the benefit of a promise and a trust of the fruits of the promise. In the latter the inter-ests of third parties are not involved, whereas in the former he suggests they are because the promise is still to be enforced. See also the criticisms of PG Turner, 'Charges of Unassignable Rights' (2004) 20 JCL 97, who argues that you cannot have a trust of, or charge over, an unassignable right.

A beneficiary of a trust of the benefit of a contract can take the procedural step of joining the trustee as a defendant if he refuses to bring an action against the debtor. The issue arose in the next case.

Barbados Trust Co v Bank of Zambia

[2007] EWCA Civ 148, [2007] 1 Lloyd's Rep 495, Court of Appeal

Bank of Zambia ('BoZ') borrowed a large sum of money from a group of banks. Article 12.01(A) of the loan agreement provided that 'each bank may at any time assign all or part of it rights and benefits…to any one or more banks or other financial institutions…provided that any such assignment may only be effective if…the prior written consent of [BoZ] shall have been obtained…' Part of BoZ's debt was assigned to Bank of America ('BoA'), which then assigned the debt to a third party. Subsequently, the third party assigned the debt to Barbados Trust Co ('BT'). BT wanted to bring proceedings against BoZ to recover the debt but it turned out that the assignments to the third party and to BT were ineffective because neither entity was a 'bank or other financial institution' within art 12.01(A). To get round the problem of title to sue, BoA declared itself a trustee of its interest in the debt in favour of BT. BoA did not itself want to bring proceedings against BoZ and so BT joined BoA to the proceedings as second defendant relying on the procedure, endorsed by Lord Wright in *Vandepitte v Preferred Accident Insurance Corpn of New York* [1933] AC 70 at 79, of the beneficiary suing in its own name, naming the trustee as a defendant, where the trustee refused to sue in its own name.

BoZ admitted the debt, but defended the claim on the following bases: (1) that the assignment to BoA had not been with the prior consent of BoZ, and (2) that BT was not entitled to sue as beneficiary, naming BoA as defendant, on the ground that the declaration of trust was simply a prohibited assignment in another name. Langley J decided issue (1), the prior written consent point, in favour of BT, but issue (2), the declaration of trust point, in favour of BoZ: [2006] 1 Lloyd's Rep 723. BT appealed issue (2), and BoZ appealed issue (1). The Court of Appeal (by a majority) dismissed BT's claim on the ground that the assignment to BoA had not been with the prior consent of BoZ. Then, in a series of *obiter* statements, their Lordships stated that the prohibition on assignment contained in art 12.01(A) did not extend to a declaration of trust. However, there was some disagreement between their Lordships as to whether, if BoA had had title to the debt owed by BoZ, BT, as the beneficiary of the trust declared by BoA, was entitled to bring proceedings against BoZ in its own name, joining BoA as a defendant, under the *Vandepitte* procedure. Waller LJ thought BT could rely on the *Vandepitte* procedure; Hooper LJ thought it could not. Rix LJ thought that 'on balance' the *Vandepitte* procedure was available to BT but felt that further evidence would have been required as to whether the declaration of trust was 'merely a device' to bring before the court a claim which BoA would otherwise have allowed to become time-barred. If a mere 'device', Rix LJ felt that it was doubtful whether equity would enforce the trust.

Waller LJ: …

[28]   The issue that arises in this case can be put in these terms. (1) If BoA had attempted to assign the debt to BT by a legal assignment and BT had sued, BoZ would have been entitled to have refused to pay BT, since it was not a bank or financial institution and since consent had not been obtained. … . (2) If BoA were to declare a trust of the proceeds when received and then sue for the debt in its own name, since BoZ could have no interest in the proceeds once in BoA's hands, BoZ would have no answer to BoA's claim and BoA would have to answer to BT's claim once it had received the proceeds. (3) If, however, BoA declares a trust in the right to the debt in favour of BT, and if BoA does not sue, will the court hold, by virtue of the fact that BT sues in its own name, joining BoA as a Defendant, that the Declaration of Trust is simply an assignment in another name, enabling BoZ to refuse to pay, or will the court hold that,

since BT's only remedy in order to enforce the trust between it and BoA is to sue in its own name joining BoA, the effect is to put BoZ in the same position as if BoA itself had sued?

[29] It is important to bear in mind when considering the above questions that what has for short-hand been referred to as the *Vandepitte* short cut is a matter of *procedure* to enable a beneficiary under a trust to obtain what he is beneficially entitled to in a situation in which the trustee will not sue—will not sue for what the trustee is legally entitled to but which if he succeeds he must hold for the beneficiary. It would be understandable if the court would not allow the procedure to be misused to obtain rights that the beneficiary is not otherwise entitled to, but otherwise if the beneficiary has an unanswerable right under a trust and the trustee has an unanswerable claim, why should the court's procedure not be available to enable the rights to be established or brought to fruition? The focus ultimately has to be on which contract governs the entitlement of the beneficiary and the true construction of that contract.

[30] As my Lord, Rix LJ, pointed out during the argument it is necessary to take matters in stages. To spell out the stages consideration has to be given to the following questions. First what is the proper construction of art 12? Does it seek to prohibit a declaration of trust by the legal owner of a debt, BoA, in favour of BT without the consent of BoZ? Does art 12 seek to prohibit BoA suing BoZ on the debt once the declaration of trust in favour of BT has been entered into ie would BoZ have any answer to a claim by BoA once the declaration of Trust has been entered into? If BoZ would have no answer to a claim by BoA, does art 12 seek to prohibit BT using the *Vandepitte* procedure if BoA refuses to sue? If the declaration of Trust is valid as between BoA and BT is it a term of that declaration of Trust that BoA will not sue in its own name and if so what difference would that make? On the assumption that so far the answers are in favour of BT being able to sue with BoA joined as a Defendant, are the circumstances such that the court will hold that the use of the *Vandepitte* procedure should not be available in this case?

[His Lordship then referred to *Don King Productions Inc v Warren* [2000] Ch 291, and the articles by Tettenborn and Turner (see p 982) criticising that decision, and continued:]

[42] All the above articles are helpful in seeking to answer the questions that have to be considered in this case, but at the end of the day each case must be considered by reference to its own context and by reference to the terms of the agreements or contracts, the subject of the case.

[43] The most important and thus the first question to consider is the true construction of art 12. It seems to me that if an embargo was to be placed on a participating bank declaring a trust in relation to sums due or creating a charge over sums due, words could have been used so as to make that clear, ... As regards Mr Handyside's [Counsel for BoZ] submission that a declaration of trust was in effect an 'equitable assignment', I would for my part accept that if it was it would be caught by the prohibition—the word assignment includes assignments both legal and equitable. But a declaration of trust is not an equitable assignment. An equitable assignment if in writing can be converted into a legal assignment under s 136 of the Law of Property Act and that is simply not true of a declaration of trust. The language of art 12 does not in terms include within the prohibition a declaration of trust, and it seems to me that since one is concerned with the question whether a restriction should be placed on the transfer of a piece of property, an acknowledged debt, the court should be slow to contemplate that the parties ever intended such to be within the prohibition.

[44] If, however, that were wrong, I am not sure it is a complete answer in this case because I cannot see how BoZ would by reference to art 12 have any answer to a claim by BoA simply because they had declared a trust of the right to a debt or the proceeds of the debt in favour of a third party, about the existence of whom BoZ was unaware and to whom thus BoZ had not consented. It would thus still leave open two questions, first whether, despite having no answer to a claim by BoA, art 12 prevents the use of the *Vandepitte* procedure by BT, or, if not, the second question, whether the court should allow use of the *Vandepitte* procedure so as to enable BT to enforce its rights against BoA.

[45] It is said that BoZ has, by art 12, a right to decree by whom it should be sued and that to allow the bringing of an action using the *Vandepitte* procedure on an acknowledged debt would be to allow interference in BoZ's contract with its lenders under the facility. This argument seems to me to be a false one. The procedure is 'procedure' and it simply provides a short cut to prevent litigation under which BoA could be forced to sue followed by an action under which BoA sues. In other words albeit BT is the Claimant, it is as if BoA were Claimant seeking to recover that which is due in law which they will then hold for BT. There is thus no interference by BT. In any event to construe suing on an acknowledged debt as interfering in BoZ's contract with its lenders seems to me far fetched. Thus art 12, on its true construction, does not, in my view, prevent the use of the *Vandepitte* procedure.

[46] What then should be the attitude of the court? In that regard one should first consider the terms of the Declaration of Trust. The Declaration of Trust certainly does not provide in terms for BoA not being prepared to sue in its own name, nor is any assistance to be gained from the letters which preceded the declaration in that regard. The Declaration recognises that BT will sue, but it also seems to recognise that there does exist the very situation in which the *Vandepitte* procedure should be available in normal circumstances.

[47] That brings me to the final question, which is whether, if as I am now assuming, art 12 contains some prohibition on alienability, what attitude should the court take to the use of the *Vandepitte* procedure? In my view procedure is then to enable BT to enforce its rights against BoA. It is not a measure of substantive law which might affect the asset, the subject of the declaration of trust. There is no reason why the court should hold that BoZ should be entitled to a defence which it would not have had if some longer and more tortuous form of procedure, compelling BoA to sue, were used. The court has to recognise that it is concerned in this instance both with the enforcement of the trust declared as between BoA and BT as well as with the contract as between BoA and BoZ. I see no reason for the court not to assist BT or any reason why it should provide BoZ with a defence which BoZ does not have against BoA.

Rix LJ: ...

Issue (3): does article 12 prohibit a declaration of trust in respect of the fruits of the Facility? ...

[75] That is a question of construction, and one on which the judge ultimately came to rule in favour of BoZ. Thus at para 54 of his judgment he expressed the functional and practical view that, if art 12.01(A) did not prohibit a declaration of trust, then its prohibition on assignment:

> would achieve very little. Any Bank could declare itself to be a trustee of the Asset for any third party which could then claim the Asset in, in substance, the same way as if it were an assignee,

(ie by making use of the *Vandepitte* procedure). And at para 73 he concluded, after a review of the authorities, that art 12.01(A) as a matter of construction ('the real key to this claim was the construction and effect of art 12.01(A)') did prohibit declarations of trust as well as assignments. His reasoning at this point is succinct, but his ground, as I understand it, is that as the practical effect of the former was the same as the latter, ie to permit third parties, through the *Vandepitte* procedure, to come into direct relations with the obligor under a contract to which the third parties were strangers, therefore the original parties to the Facility must have intended, by their reference to assignment, to prohibit declarations of trust as well.

[76] In my judgment, however, the question of construction must ultimately be kept separate from the different question of what effect will be given to the contractual term which prohibits an assignment and/or declaration of trust as the case may be. I accept that the practical effects which may (or may not) be achievable through the route of the *Vandepitte* procedure may enter as a background factor into the question of construction, ie the objectively understood intentions of the parties, but the questions are nevertheless distinct.

[77] On the question of construction, then, there is in my judgment good authority for the proposition that a failed assignment may take effect as a declaration of trust between its immediate parties. This is certainly true so far as a declaration of trust which is limited to the *proceeds of a claim (or the*

fruits of a contract) when received. The leading authority for this is *In re Turcan* (1888) 40 Ch D 5, 58 LJ Ch 101, 37 WR 70, as approved in *Linden Gardens* itself, where Lord Browne-Wilkinson said this (at 106F):

> As to the authorities, in *In re Turcan*, 40 ChD 5, a man effected an insurance policy which contained a term that it should not be assignable in any case whatever. He had previously covenanted with trustees to settle after-acquired property. The Court of Appeal held that although he could not assign the benefit of the policy so as to give the trustees the power to recover the money from the insurance company, he could validly make a declaration of trust of the proceeds, which required him to hand over such proceeds to the trustees.

[78] That reflects Lord Browne-Wilkinson's acceptance of the second of Professor Goode's four possible interpretations of a prohibition of assignment, discussed as a 'question of the construction of the contract' at 104E/F, thus:

> (2) that the term precludes or invalidates any assignment by A to C (so as to entitle B to pay the debt to A) but not so as to preclude A from agreeing, as between himself and C, that he will account to C for what A receives from B: *In re Turcan* . . .

[79] Similarly, but perhaps more broadly, Lord Browne-Wilkinson said (at 108D):

> a prohibition on assignment normally only invalidates the assignment as against the other party to the contract so as to prevent a transfer of the chose in action: in the absence of the clearest words it cannot operate to invalidate the contract as between the assignor and the assignee and even then it may be ineffective on the grounds of public policy.

Lord Browne-Wilkinson there appears to be contemplating a declaration of trust relating to a chose of action, and not merely proceeds when received.

[His Lordship noted that this broader approach had been applied by Lightman J, at first instance, in the *Don King* case, and continued:]

[87] In these circumstances, my conclusions under this issue are as follows. The fact that a prohibition on assignment between A and B cannot allow a third party, C, as A's purported assignee, to bring a direct contractual claim against B is not in dispute. It was held in *Linden Gardens* to be the consequence of the contractual prohibition. As Lord Browne-Wilkinson said (at 108F):

> Therefore the existing authorities establish that an attempted assignment of contractual rights in breach of a contractual prohibition is ineffective to transfer such contractual rights. I regard the law as being satisfactorily settled in that sense. If the law were otherwise, it would defeat the legitimate commercial reason for inserting the contractual prohibition, viz, to ensure that the original parties to the contract are not brought into direct contractual relations with third parties.

[88] The ineffectiveness of the assignment in breach of a prohibition on assignment is understandable. It is not merely a matter of contract but of property. Although the would-be assignor has legal title to property in the form of a chose in action, he lacks the power, because of the terms on which the property is held, to transfer that property so as to entitle the transferee to exercise those contractual rights himself against the other party to the contract. However, he does not lack the power to render himself a trustee in equity of the property concerned. He would only do that if the prohibition on assignment extended as far as prohibiting a declaration of trust.

[89] There is, however, nothing in art 12.01(A) to suggest that the limitations on assignment go as far as preventing the contract between would-be assignor and assignee taking effect as between those two as a declaration of trust, and a fortiori nothing to prevent a personal contract between them.

. . .

Issue (5): Does use of the Vandepitte procedure mean that BoA is not to be regarded as a claimant, or is it otherwise ineffective or illegitimate to use that procedure to reduce the debt into possession? . . .

[102] I would therefore consider that the effect of the *Vandepitte* procedure is that, although the trustee is nominally a Defendant, his real role as a party is to ensure that, through his presence, his legal right can be properly before the court for adjudication, just as though he was, as he should be if he is indeed a trustee for the Claimant, a Claimant himself. There is support for that in *Harmer v Armstrong* [1934] Ch 65 (CA) at 88, 103 LJ Ch 1, [1933] All ER Rep 778 where Lawrence LJ said:

> The right of a beneficiary in such a case as the present, however, is to enforce the agreement according to its tenor, that is to say in favour of the Defendant Armstrong, and not in favour of the Plaintiff beneficiaries.

[103] In these circumstances, the ultimate question is whether, in circumstances where there has been a prohibition on assignment, and the legal owner declines himself to claim, the law will permit the beneficiary of a trust to make use of the *Vandepitte* procedure in order to reduce a debt into possession. This it seems to me is not itself a question of construction, but of legal principle.

[104] In *Don King*, which was admittedly a case between trustee and beneficiary and not between the original parties to the contracts containing prohibitions on assignment, Lightman J and this court considered that the mere possibility that a declaration of trust might bring in its train the use or attempted use of the *Vandepitte* procedure against other parties in whose favour those prohibitions had been agreed did not prevent the arrangements between the litigants themselves from having effect. On the other hand the law would not permit the *Vandepitte* procedure to be used to curtail the protection for which the parties to a contract had stipulated by means of a prohibition of assignment.

[105] Lightman J said (at 321C/D):

> (1) If one party wishes to protect himself against the other party declaring himself a trustee, and not merely against an assignment, he should expressly so provide. That has not been done in this case.
>
> (2) The applicable principles of trust law in this situation are the basic principles and those (and only those) whose rationale have application in this commercial context: see *Target Holdings Ltd v Redferns* [1996] AC 421, 436. The courts will accordingly be astute to disallow use of the procedural short-cut sanctioned in the *Vandepitte* case [1933] AC 70 in a commercial context where it has no proper place. A beneficiary cannot be allowed to abrogate the fullest protection that the parties to the contract have secured for themselves under the terms of the contract from intrusion into their contractual relations by third parties.

[106] In this court *Morritt LJ* said (at 335H/336C, para 26):

> In that case [*In re Turcan*], as the House of Lords considered in *Linden Gardens Trust Ltd v Lenesta Sludge Disposals Ltd* [1994] 1 AC 85, 106, the court gave effect to the intention of the parties by means of a declaration of trust. But, it is objected, the existence of such a trust would enable one partner to interfere in the management of the personal contract made by a third party with the other partner. I do not agree. The other partner cannot insist on rendering vicarious performance of the personal obligations arising under the contract. Rules and procedures designed to enable a beneficiary to sue in respect of a contract held in trust for him would not be applied so as to jeopardise the trust property. As Lord Browne-Wilkinson observed in *Target Holdings Ltd v Redferns* [1996] AC 421, 435:
>
> > 'in my judgment it is in any event wrong to lift wholesale the detailed rules developed in the context of traditional trusts and then seek to apply them to trusts of quite a different kind. In the modern world the trust has become a valuable device in commercial and financial dealings. The fundamental principles of equity apply as much to such trusts as they do to the traditional trusts in relation to which those principles were originally formulated. But in my judgment it is

important, if the trust is not to be rendered commercially useless, to distinguish between the basic principles of trust law and those specialist rules developed in relation to traditional trusts which are applicable only to such trusts and the rationale of which has no application to trusts of quite a different kind.'

[107] It is possible to read these passages as saying that the *Vandepitte* procedure has no place in the commercial sphere. That, however, would not accord with my understanding of what Lightman J and Morritt LJ were saying. It would also be inconsistent with established lines of cases in the commercial field, such as the trust found in a charterparty in favour of the shipbroker. I understand these passages as saying that the law would not permit rules and procedures, such as the *Vandepitte* procedure, to be misused in the commercial context where inappropriate. Lightman J appears to have particularly in mind contractual stipulations against intrusion into the business affairs of the original contractual parties, whereas Morritt LJ seems to be focusing on personal obligations. The contracts in *Don King* were of both kinds: many had prohibition of assignment clauses, but all of them were contracts of a personal kind, for they concerned the management of boxers.

[108] An example of the courts being cautious in certain circumstances about the use of the *Vandepitte* procedure may be found in *Harmer v Armstrong* [1934] Ch 65 at 88/89.

...

[112] What is a court to do in such circumstances? It seems to me that there is a tension between (a) the interests of those whose contracts, either because they are of an inherently personal nature or because of agreed restrictions on alienability, should not readily be intruded upon by strangers to them, (b) the interests of those who seek to arrange their affairs on the basis of holding property in trust for others, and (c) the public interest, which is concerned to see that contracts are performed, that the beneficiaries of trusts are protected, and that financial assets are not too readily made inalienable especially where markets regularly provide liquidity for the trading of them. If a prohibition on assignment carried all before it, destroying all alienability whatever the circumstances, even to the extent of making it impossible for beneficial interests to be protected in any circumstances in the absence of the legal owner as a formal Claimant, it seems to me that the public interest in freedom of contract and the freedom of markets could be severely prejudiced.

[113] Some illustrations can be given. In *Linden Gardens* at 107/108 the case of *Tom Shaw and Co v Moss Empires Ltd* (1908) 25 TLR 190 was considered. Lord Browne-Wilkinson said:

> In the *Tom Shaw* case an actor, B, was engaged by Moss Empires under a contract which prohibited the assignment of his salary. B assigned 10% of his salary to his agent, Tom Shaw. Tom Shaw sued Moss Empires for 10% of the salary joining B as Second Defendant. Moss Empires agreed to pay the 10% of the salary to Tom Shaw or B as the court might decide ie in effect it interpleaded. Darling J held, at p 191, that the prohibition on assignment was ineffective: it could 'no more operate to invalidate the assignment than it could interfere with the laws of gravitation'. He gave judgment for the Plaintiffs against both B and Moss Empires, ordering B to pay the costs but making no order for costs against Moss Empires.
>
> The case is inadequately reported and it is hard to discover exactly what it decides. Given that both B and Moss Empires were parties and Moss Empires was in effect interpleading, it may be that the words I have quoted merely indicate that as between the assignor, B, and the assignee Tom Shaw, the prohibition contained in the contract between B and Moss Empires could not invalidate B's liability to account to Tom Shaw for the moneys when received and that, since B was a party, payment direct to Tom Shaw was ordered. This view is supported by the fact that no order for costs was made against Moss Empires. If this is the right view of the case, it is unexceptionable: a prohibition on assignment normally only invalidates the assignment as against the other party to the contract so as to prevent a transfer of the chose in action: in the absence of the clearest words it cannot operate to invalidate the contract as between the assignor and the assignee and even then it may be ineffective on the ground of public policy. If on the other hand Darling J purported to hold that the

contractual prohibition was ineffective to prevent B's contractual rights against Moss Empires being transferred to Tom Shaw, it is inconsistent with authority and was wrongly decided.

I have already cited most of the penultimate sentence of that passage out of its context (at para 31 above).

[114] What is going on here? The contract concerned was certainly a personal one, akin to a contract for the writing of a book, but the salary, like the fee for the book, was something separate, the fruits of the contract. However, there was an express prohibition on assignment of those fruits. There was nevertheless a purported assignment, which took effect only as a declaration of trust to account for the moneys when received. Only the would-be assignee, the beneficiary of that trust, sued, but he adopted the *Vandepitte* procedure and joined the would-be assignor, the actor, as Second Defendant. Moss Empires did not mind whom it paid, and in effect interpleaded. It had no defence in substance, other than the prohibition on assignment. That point was taken by the actor, who presumably wished to receive the assigned salary himself. The case therefore illustrates the operation of the *Vandepitte* procedure, despite a failed assignment, on the basis of a declaration of trust and suit by the beneficiary. Would it have made any difference if Moss Empires had not effectively interpleaded? That is possible, on the ground that Moss Empires thereby waived the prohibition in its favour. However, another way of looking at the matter is that in any event the actor, although Defendant, was treated as a Claimant. It would be very unattractive (in the absence of a prohibition on a declaration of trust) if a party who owed his agent a percentage of his earnings, and made a declaration of trust in his favour as security, could prevent his agent recovering simply by declining to claim.

[115] Another example is illustrated by the two cases considered by the House of Lords under the report in *Linden Gardens*. Both concerned construction contracts containing prohibitions on assignment. In the first case, *Linden Gardens* itself, the would-be assignor was not joined as a Defendant, and the assignee Claimant therefore lost (at 109C). In the second case, *St Martins Property Corporation Ltd v Sir Robert McAlpine Ltd*, both the assignor and the assignee claimed, being sister companies within the same group. There was therefore no problem about the title to sue, which remained in the assignor company (at 109F). The main issue there, however, was whether that company had suffered any more than nominal damages, since the loss had been suffered by the assignee company which, because of the prohibition on assignment, lacked its own cause of action. However, the House of Lords was unwilling for the claim to disappear in this way into a black hole, and found an analysis, based on the concept that the assignor company entered into the contract for the benefit of future third parties to whom the property development had been sold and who might thus suffer from defective performance of the contract, which enabled the assignor to recover substantial damages for the assignee. Justice was done, but, if the case was looked at in an overall way, it could be said that the law permitted the problems of a stranger assignee to intrude into the contractual relationship despite the prohibition of assignment. If therefore a purely functional approach had been adopted, on the basis that the assignor could only recover for its own loss, the claim would have failed despite the presence of the assignor as Claimant. In such circumstances, would it have mattered if the assignor and assignee companies had not been in the same group, but in different enterprises, so that in practical terms the assignee would have been the sole Claimant and the assignor would have been joined under the *Vandepitte* procedure as a Second Defendant? I think not.

[116] A third example is an agency contract under which the agent earns commission. Such a contract is both a personal contract and one in which a non-assignment clause is often found, for good commercial reasons. While the contract is on foot it would be entirely understandable that no stranger to that contract should, through assignment, be permitted to intrude upon it. However, suppose the agent becomes insolvent and as a result the contract is brought to an end. The relationship is over, as is any ongoing performance of the contract. However, there is outstanding commission due to the agent. The liquidator has no interest in pursuing a claim he does not understand. He sells the claim to the former managers of the insolvent agent, who have formed a new company. The assignee brings a claim against the debtor principal, joining the liquidator as Defendant. Can the debtor say that he is to answer only if the liquidator is a Claimant rather than a Defendant? That is most unattractive. See *Explora Group plc v Hesco Bastion Ltd* [2005] EWCA Civ 646.

[117] A fourth example of a somewhat different nature is that of the subrogated insurer who sues in his insured's name. If he sues under a contract containing a non-assignment clause, he will not be affected by it. The claim is that of the insured, and there has been no assignment. However, functionally the insured has been paid and has no interest in the claim, and the litigation is conducted entirely by the underwriter for his own benefit, who thus intrudes on his insured's contract with the Defendant. No one would suggest, however, that the non-assignment clause should be given effect because the law of subrogation functionally achieves a result whereby a stranger to the contract can intrude on it.

[118] A closely related example is that of factored invoices. A non-assignment clause will create difficulties for the factoring company. However, it would be highly undesirable if customers could totally prevent their suppliers from factoring their book debts by the device of a non-assignment clause. If the supplier has no interest in suing and has to be joined as a Defendant, is that case crucially different from the case where the supplier is prevailed upon to sue together with the factoring company?

[119] For these reasons, if I had decided issue (1) in favour of finding that BoA had a good legal title to the debt, I would, on balance, have been in favour of saying that, on the facts of this case as far as they appear and on the submissions we have heard, the *Vandepitte* procedure could be used to recover into BoA's possession, for the benefit of BT, a debt which on that hypothesis would have been an acknowledged debt owed by BoA. As it is, I do not have to make a final decision on this ultimate issue. That is perhaps just as well, as the argument on appeal has both far outstripped the evidence with which the parties had come to court in the first place and at the same time failed to focus on the particular facts before the court. Thus we know little about the real considerations which have affected the relationships in this case. Moreover, there was no immediate relationship between BoA and BT to support the declaration of trust, which does not arise out of a failed assignment directly between BoA and BT. It might therefore have been said that that declaration was merely a device to bring before the court, at the instance of BT, a claim which BoA would otherwise have allowed to become time-barred. On that hypothesis, I would be doubtful that equity would enforce the trust.

Hooper LJ: ...

[129] I start with an example. D enters into a contract with A, giving A certain benefits. D agrees with A that A can assign the benefits to anyone other than C. He distrusts C and wants to have nothing to do with him. Notwithstanding this, A assigns the benefits to C. A declines to sue D. C then invokes the *Vandepitte* procedure and brings an action against A and D. Thus D is facing C across the court— something which D had insisted should not happen. I would find it surprising if English law permits this to happen. I would find it surprising if the only way that D could have prevented this happening was by including a further term in his contract with A. I accept that it might gladden the heart of lawyers if the law is that D could have prevented this happening by the inclusion (on legal advice) of a further term in his contract with A.

[130] This example is not this case, but it has similarities. As Langley J said, it is not hard to fathom the commercial realities of a restricted assignment clause such as that found in art 12. In para 10, he wrote:

> Any covenant against or restrictive of assignment is intended to ensure that the original parties to the contract are not brought into direct contractual relations with third parties save to any extent expressly permitted by the covenant. Any borrower, but particularly a central bank, may be concerned to ensure that its affairs and obligations are known and owed to and only enforceable by established and authorised institutions.

...

[139] Whilst I agree with Rix LJ (para 90) that the art 12.01(A) limitations on assignment do not prevent BoA from creating a declaration of trust in favour of BT (as it purported to do by the documents set out by Waller LJ at paras 22 and following), I disagree with the proposition which finds favour with Waller LJ (and with Rix LJ 'on balance'), that the terms of art 12.01(A) permit BT to bring the claim against BoZ. The clause prevents an assignment to a body such as BT and must therefore be construed so as to prevent BT from enforcing the debt directly against BoZ. The clause cannot be circumvented by the device of a declaration of trust and the use of the *Vandepitte* procedure. To require those who draft contracts of this kind to take steps to avoid the device used by BoA and BT to get round the non-assignment clause would be unduly onerous and, as I have said, would only benefit lawyers.

NOTES

1.   Waller LJ considered what would have been the position had he been wrong and art 12.01(A) had prohibited both an assignment and a declaration of trust. He declared (at [45]) that the *Vandepitte* procedure was merely a procedural shortcut allowing the beneficiary to obtain what he was entitled to when the trustee refused to act, thereby avoiding unnecessary litigation under which the trustee would be forced to sue followed by an action under which the trustee sued. The beneficiary would be the actual claimant but it would be as if the trustee was the claimant seeking to recover that which was due in law and which would then be held by the trustee for the beneficiary. Crucially, his Lordship considered that there would be no interference by the beneficiary, and that the beneficiary would not be given rights to which he was not already entitled (see paras [29] and [45]). Greg Tolhurst, writing in [2007] LMCLQ 278, acknowledges that 'there is doctrinal force in the approach of Waller LJ' but goes on to make the pragmatic observation that 'by recognizing a declaration of trust, which is operational before the fruits of the contract are in the hands of the trustee, then the [debtor] by virtue of the *Vandepitte* procedure becomes, to some extent, subject to the whims of a third party, which is what the prohibition is designed to prevent. The ensuing litigation is not driven by the trustee, even though it may be said that it is the trustee's claim, as it is the legal title holder.' See also PG Turner [2008] CLJ 23.

2.   In *Argo Fund Ltd v Essar Steel Ltd* [2005] EWHC 600 (Comm), [2006] 1 All ER (Comm) 56, Aikens J had taken a narrow view of what constituted an 'other financial institution' in a non-assignment clause contained in a bank loan agreement. This had led BT to concede at trial that it did not fall into that category. However, on appeal in the *Argo Fund* case, the term 'other financial institution' received a broader definition: see [2006] EWCA Civ 241, [2006] 2 All ER (Comm) 104. That appeal decision was published between the trial and the appeal in the *Barbados Trust* case but, because of a lack of relevant evidence before the court and the concession made at first instance, BT was not permitted to ague that it fell within the broader definition.

QUESTIONS

1.   Tettenborn [2001] LMCLQ 472 has described the Court of Appeal's decision in *Foamcrete (UK) Ltd v Thrust Engineering Ltd* (see p 981 above) as 'heterodox and unfortunate'. Why? Is *Foamcrete* likely to be welcomed by banks providing secured medium-to long-term finance? What about by factors purchasing existing receivables (debts)? See M Bridge *Personal Property Law* (3rd edn, 2002), p 162.

2.   Draft a clause that you consider to be wide enough to prohibit both the assignment of, and a declaration of trust over, a chose in action without the debtor's consent.

3.   Would you expect a court always to step in and find a declaration of trust by the assignor of the benefit of the contract where there had been a failed assignment because of the presence of a non-assignment clause in the contract between assignor and debtor? What would you expect the court to require evidence of before recognising the presence of a trust?

4.   Why might a commercial lender that assigns a debt due from a borrower that is a third world central bank not itself wish to sue the borrower? Hint: think Bob Geldof!

(b) Assignee takes subject to equities

(i) *The general rule*

The assignee takes 'subject to equities' having priority over his right, whether the assignment is legal (as provided for in the express wording of s 136(1) of the Law of Property Act 1925) or equitable (*Mangles v Dixon* (1852) 3 HL Cas 702 at 731). The phrase 'subject to equities' is generally used to describe situations where the debtor can raise a right he has against the assignor in defence of an action brought by the assignee. The object of the rule is to ensure that the debtor is not prejudiced by the assignment, and the rule may simply be an application of a basic principle of equity that rights which are the subject of an assignment can only be enforced (or denied) to the extent that it is conscionable to do so (see G Tolhurst [1999] CLJ 546 at 556–557). The authorities are reviewed in the next case.

Business Computers Ltd v Anglo-African Leasing Ltd
[1977] 1 WLR 578, Chancery Division

The plaintiffs sold two computers to the defendants under two separate transactions. At 29 May 1974, £10,587.50 remained owing by the defendants to the plaintiffs under these transactions. By a third transaction, the plaintiffs sold another computer to the defendants and then leased it back from them under a hire purchase agreement. Under the terms of the hire-purchase agreement, the plaintiffs were to pay the defendants monthly instalments payable on the 18th of each month. The 13th instalment due on the 18 May was not paid, nor were any subsequent instalments. On 13 June 1974, debenture holders appointed a receiver over the plaintiffs under the terms of a floating charge. This crystallised the charge which had the effect of assigning the sums owed by the defendants to the debenture holders. Notice of the assignment was given to the defendants on 17 June. The receiver claimed the debt of £10,587.50 from the defendants who tried to set off against it (1) the 13th instalment due on 18 May (which the receiver conceded) and (2) damages of £30,000 under the terms of the hire-purchase agreement which the receiver had repudiated on 31 July and which repudiation was accepted by the defendants on 8 August.

Templeman J: . . . Set off has been allowed against an assignee in a variety of circumstances. In *Biggerstaff v Rowan's Wharf Ltd* [1896] 2 Ch 93 a debtor who became entitled to a liquidated claim against a company before a floating charge crystallised was allowed to set off the liquidated claim against the debt after the debenture crystallised. This decision does not assist the defendants because in the present case no claim liquidated or otherwise for £30,000 arose on or before June 17 when the defendants received notice that the debentures had crystallised.

In *Christie v Taunton, Delmard, Lane and Co* [1893] 2 Ch 175 a debtor was allowed to set off against an assignee a debt from the assignor which accrued due before the date of the assignment but was not payable until after the assignment. In the present case the defendants on June 17, 1974, when they received notice of the assignment completed by the appointment of the receiver did not possess a claim for £30,000 payable then or on any subsequent date. That claim only arose in August 1974.

In *Government of Newfoundland v Newfoundland Rly Co* (1888) 13 App Cas 199 a debtor sued by an assignee for a sum payable pursuant to a contract between the debtor and the assignor was allowed to set off a claim for unliquidated damages made by the debtor against the assignor for breach of the same contract by the assignor. This case also does not assist the defendants because the debt owed by the defendants for £10,587.50 arose under different and separate contracts from the hire purchase agreement under which the defendants' claim for £30,000 has now arisen.

In *Watson v Mid Wales Rly Co* (1867) LR 2 CP 593 a debtor sued on a bond by the assignee of the bond was not allowed to set off arrears of rent which accrued due from the assignor to the debtor after the assignment under a lease made before notice of the assignment. Bovill CJ said, at p 598:

> No case has been cited to us where equity has allowed against the assignee of an equitable chose in action a set off of a debt arising between the original parties subsequently to the notice of assignment, out of matters not connected with the debt claimed, nor in any way referring to it.... In all the cases cited ... some qualification occurred in the original contract, or the two transactions were in some way connected together, so as to lead the court to the conclusion that they were made with reference to one another.

In the present case, the claim of the defendants under the hire purchase agreement for £30,000 arose subsequently to notice of the assignment of the debt of £10,587.50 and the transactions out of which the claim and the debt arose respectively were separate and not connected in any way. Set off is therefore not available by the defendants against the assignees, the debenture holders.

In *Re Pinto Leite and Nephews, exp Visconde des Olivaes* [1929] 1 Ch 221 a debtor owed £100,000 payable in January 1932 and the original creditor, after assigning the debt on March 2,1926, became liable to the debtor for £15,000 as a result of a contract entered into between the debtor and the creditor prior to the assignment. There was no connection between the debt of £100,000 and the contract under which the £15,000 became owing. The debtor was not allowed to set off the £15,000 liability against the debt of £100,000 claimed by the assignee. Clauson J said, at p 233:

> It is, of course, well settled that the assignee of a chose in action. .. takes subject to all rights of set off which were available against the assignor, subject only to the exception that, after notice of an equitable assignment of a chose in action, a debtor cannot set off against the assignee a debt which accrues due subsequently to the date of notice, even though that debt may arise out of a liability which existed at or before the date of the notice; but the debtor may set off as against the assignee a debt which accrues due before notice of the assignment, although it is not payable until after that date:

and, at p 236:

> when the debt assigned is at the date of notice of the assignment payable in future, the debtor can set off against the assignee a debt which becomes payable by the assignor to the debtor after notice of assignment, but before the assigned debt becomes payable, if, but only if, the debt so to be set off was debitum in praesenti at the date of notice of assignment.

In the present case the £30,000 claim did not accrue due until after the date of notice of the assignment and cannot therefore be set off.

I was referred to *Bankes v Jarvis* [1903] 1 KB 549, but that case only decided that a debtor could set off against a trustee for the creditor all claims which at the date of the action could have founded a set off against the creditor beneficiary. See also *Hanak v Green* [1958] 2 QB 9, 24 where the decision in *Bankes v Jarvis* was supported on the ground that 'There was a close relationship between the dealings and transactions which gave rise to the respective claims.' No such close relationship was put forward in the present case.

I was referred to *N W Robbie & Co Ltd v Witney Warehouse Co Ltd* [1963] 1 WLR 1324, but that case only decided that a debtor cannot after notice of an assignment of his debt by his creditor improve his position as regards set off by acquiring debts incurred by the assignor creditor to a third party. I have already referred to *George Barker (Transport) Ltd v Eynon* [1974] 1 WLR 462, but that case only decided that if a receiver after his appointment took the benefit of a contract entered into before his appointment, he could not dispute a lien conferred by that contract but not exercised until after the appointment. The defendants in the present case cannot invoke this principle. The contracts under which the debt of £10,587.50 became payable were completed before the receiver was appointed, apart from the payment now sought against the defendants. I was also referred to *Rother Iron Works Ltd v Canterbury Precision Engineers Ltd* [1974] QB 1. In that case, pursuant to a contract made before the appointment of a receiver, a debtor delivered goods to the company and the goods were accepted by the receiver. The debtor was allowed to set off the price of the goods against his debt to the company because the receiver could not take the benefit of the contract without the burden. He was not entitled to the debt and to the goods and to keep the purchase price. A similar point does not arise in the present case.

The result of the relevant authorities is that a debt which accrues due before notice of an assignment is received, whether or not it is payable before that date, or a debt which arises out of the same contract as that which gives rise to trie assigned debt, or is closely connected with that contract, may be set off against the assignee. But a debt which is neither accrued nor connected may not be set off even though it arises from a contract made before the assignment. In the present case the claim for £30,000 did not accrue before June 17, 1974, when the defendants received notice of the appointment of the receiver and thus notice of the completed assignment of the debt of £10,587.50 to the debenture holders and there was no relevant connection between the transactions which gave rise to the claim and to the debt respectively.

NOTES

1.   Defences which the debtor could have raised against the assignor, and cross-claims arising out of, or closely connected with, the transaction which gave rise to the chose being assigned, can be set up by the debtor against the assignee whether they arise before or after the debtor receives notice of the assignment. Defences include any claim that the original transaction giving rise to the chose has been vitiated by illegality, mistake, fraud, or other misrepresentation (*Graham v Johnson* (1869) LR 8 Eq 36). Such cross-claims may be liquidated or unliquidated but they must be so closely connected with the transaction that gave rise to the assigned chose that it would be inequitable not to allow a set-off (*Bim Kemi AB v Blackburn Chemicals Ltd* [2001] EWCA Civ 457, [2001] 2 Lloyd's Rep 93; *Government of Newfoundland v Newfoundland Rly Co* (1888) 13 App Cas 199, PC). However, it appears that at least one category of tort claim is not to be regarded as closely connected with the transaction giving rise to the chose assigned. In *Stoddart v Union Trust Ltd* [1912] 1 KB 181, the Court of Appeal held that a claim for damages for fraudulently inducing the debtor to enter into the contract with the assignor could not be set up against the assignee unless the debtor rescinded the contract. The decision may be criticised on the ground that it draws an unnecessary distinction between a claim for damages for fraud and a claim for damages for breach of contract (see criticisms of A Tettenborn [1987] Conv 385; F Oditah *Legal Aspects of Receivables Financing* (1991) ('Oditah'), pp 234–235; E Peel, *Treitel's Law of Contract* (12th edn, 2007) ('Treitel'), para 15–041).

2.   A cross-claim arising out of some other transaction which is independent of that which gave rise to the chose being assigned may be set off by the debtor against the assignee only if (1) it is a debt or other liquidated sum, *and* (2) it accrued before notice of assignment is given to the debtor (see, eg *Marathon Electrical Manufacturing Corpn v Mashreqbank PSC* [1997] 2 BCLC 460—Mance J held assignment of proceeds of a letter of credit to be subject

to collecting bank's (debtor's) right of set-off where assignor's indebtedness to the bank accrued before notice of assignment had been received). Unless there is contrary agreement between the assignor and the debtor, there can be no set-off if the claims are unconnected and one or both is unliquidated (see, eg *De Mattos v Saunders* (1872) LR 7CP 750). There is also no set-off where the cross-claim is subject to an arbitration clause (*Glencore Grain Ltd v Argos Trading Co Ltd* [1999] 2 All ER (Comm) 288, CA).

3. The debtor may use his cross-claim to reduce or extinguish the assignee's claim for the sum assigned. Where the cross-claim is for an amount exceeding the sum assigned the debtor cannot recover the excess from the assignee as he himself has committed no wrongdoing (*Young v Kitchin* (1878) 3 Ex D 127). The debtor must look to the assignor for the excess. For similar reasons, a debtor cannot recover back a payment already made to the assignee on the ground that the payment was made for a consideration that had totally failed. For example, in *Pan Ocean Shipping Ltd v Creditcorp Ltd, The Trident Beauty* [1994] 1 All ER 470, the House of Lords held that the assignee of freight payable in advance under the terms of a charterparty was not liable to return hire paid to it by the debtor (the charterer) when the assignor (the shipowner) failed to supply the ship. The liability to repay the unearned hire remained with the assignor. But what if the assignor is insolvent? The injustice of this decision is evident when one considers that had the debtor not paid the assignee in advance he could have relied on the 'subject to equities' rule to set up the assignor's failure to perform as a complete defence to any claim by the assignee for payment. Tolhurst submits that the debtor had a reasonable expectation that the nature of the right assigned, a right to payment conditional on provision of the ship, would be respected by the assignee, so that denial of that reasonable expectation without good cause was unconscionable ([1999] CLJ 546 at 560–561).

4. The 'subject to equities' rule does not apply in the following circumstances: (1) if the assigned debt is created by contract, the contract may provide, by an express or implied term, that the assignee takes free of equities (*Re Blakely Ordnance Co* (1867) 3 Ch App 154 at 159–160); and (2) if the debt is embodied in a negotiable instrument, a person who purchases the instrument in good faith, before its maturity, and without notice of any defect in the title of the holder or of previous dishonour, will take it free from equities (Bills of Exchange Act 1882, ss 29(1) and 38(2)). There is also authority for the view that the assignee is only liable to equities available against the original assignor, not to those available against an intermediate assignee (*The Raven* [1980] 2 Lloyd's Rep 266 at 273, Parker J; *Re Milan Tramways Co* (1884) 25 Ch D 587 at 593, CA). However, it has been convincingly argued that where the claim or defence against the intermediate assignee arose after the first assignment it should be available in a claim by a subsequent assignee (Treitel, para 15–043).

5. Further reading: Oditah, Ch 8; G Tolhurst, *The Assignment of Contractual Rights* (2006), paras 8.49ff; SR Derham *The Law of Set-Off* (3rd edn, 2003), Ch 17 and (1991) 107 LQR 12;, PR Wood *English and International Set-Off* (1989), Ch 16. For a call for review of the law of assignee set-off, see A Tettenborn [2002] LMCLQ485.

QUESTIONS

1. What is a 'liquidated' cross-claim? See *Aectra Refining and Marketing Inc v Exmar NV* [1994] 1 WLR 1634, CA.

2. Under separate contracts Owen owed Piper, a builder and decorator, sums of £1,000 for painting and decorating his house and £400 for installing a boiler. Piper assigned the £1,000

in writing to Rigby for value. Piper also wrote to Owen telling him to pay the £400 to Slate (to whom Piper was indebted), and then told Slate by telephone of his instruction to Owen. Soon afterwards, owing to its defective installation, the boiler burst, causing £500-worth of damage to Owen's house. Piper has since been adjudged bankrupt. Advise Tyler (Piper's trustee in bankruptcy), Owen, Rigby and Slate as to the legal position.

3.   Adam owes money to Bill (debt 1) and also to Cathy (debt 2). Dave owes money to Adam (debt 3). Adam assigns Dave's debt (debt 3) in writing to Eric for value. Before he has notice of the assignment of debt 3 to Eric, Dave takes an assignment of Adam's debt to Bill (debt 1). After he has notice of the assignment of debt 3 to Eric, Dave takes an assignment of Adam's debt to Cathy (debt 2). If Eric sues Dave for debt 3, can he set off debt 1 and/or debt 2 against the claim? See *Bennett v White* [1910] 2 KB 643, CA; *NW Robbie & Co Ltd v Witney Warehouse Co Ltd* [1963] 1 WLR 1324, CA.

(ii) Assignee cannot recover more than assignor

Another aspect of the 'subject to equities' rule is the principle that an assignee cannot recover more from the debtor than the assignor could have done had there been no assignment. The principle is of limited scope. It is designed to ensure that the debtor is no worse off as a result of the assignment; it does not enable the debtor to rely on the fact of the assignment in order to escape liability for his breach of contract. The next case illustrates the point.

Offer-Hoar v Larkstore Ltd (Technotrade Ltd, Part 20 defendants)
[2006] EWCA Civ 1079, [2006] 1 WLR 2926, Court of Appeal

Starglade Ltd commissioned Technotrade Ltd, which offered geo-technical site investigation and engineering services, to produce a soil inspection report on a sloping site in Hythe, Kent that Starglade owned. The report showed that the site was satisfactory for a proposed housing development. Starglade used the report to gain full planning permission. Starglade then sold the site to Larkstore, a property development company. Larkstore engaged contractors to carry out building works on the site. While the building works were being carried out, a landslip occurred causing damage to adjacent properties uphill from the site. The owners of those uphill properties alleged that the landslip was caused by the building works. Extensive stabilisation works had to be undertaken by Larkstore. Larkstore then took a statutory assignment of Technotrade's site inspection report from Starglade 'together with all the benefit and interest and rights of Starglade in and under the report and the right to enforce the same'. The owners of the damaged uphill properties commenced proceedings against Larkstore, which itself started Part 20 proceedings against Technotrade, relying on the assignment of the cause of action as the basis of a contractual claim for damages for breach. A number of preliminary points were raised for determination by Wilcox J, but only one substantial issue survived for determination by the Court of Appeal. The issue was whether Larkstore was able, by virtue of the assignment from Starglade, to recover the loss allegedly suffered by it, even though Starglade had not suffered substantial damage while it was entitled to the benefit of the contract with Technotrade and when the cause of action arose and even though the landslip causing the damage occurred before the assignment to Larkstore. It was assumed for the determination of the preliminary issues that there had been a breach of contract by Technotrade in respect of the soil inspection report. Judge David Wilcox determined the issue in favour of Larkstore: [2005] EWHC 2742 (TCC). Technotrade appealed.

Mummery LJ:

The issue

[1] This appeal is against a ruling on a preliminary issue in Pt 20 proceedings. The litigation arises from a dispute about liability for the substantial physical damage and financial loss resulting from building operations on a residential development site.

[2] The main issue turns on the legal effect of the assignment of a cause of action for breach of contract. Is the assignee of the cause of action entitled to recover from the contract-breaker damages for loss, which occurred after the transfer of the development site by the assignor to the assignee, but before the assignment of the cause of action, in a larger sum than the assignor would have recovered?

[3] One possible answer to this question would produce 'a legal black hole'. The expression cropped up in argument. The whole topic of assignment, including possible 'black holes', is of special interest to practitioners in construction law and their clients. A 'black hole' scenario would occur when loss is suffered in consequence of a breach of contract, but the contract-breaker's position is that no one is legally entitled to recover substantial damages from him.

[4] The question was well put in a note in the Law Quarterly Review ((1994) 110 LQR 42 p 44; Mr I N Duncan Wallace QC):

> whether … a contract-breaker can avoid an otherwise inescapable liability in damages as a result of the accident of the transfer of the property and assignment of the benefit of the relevant … contract to a third party, either by arguing that the original contracting party or assignor, having parted with the property at full value, has suffered no loss and that the assignee cannot be in a better position, or conversely that an assignee, in a case where he alone can sue, has paid a reduced price, equally suffering no loss. In other words, does the accident of transfer and assignment create a 'legal black hole' into which the right to damages disappears, leaving the contract-breaker with an uncovenanted immunity?

[5] It will be necessary to consider the leading authorities on the effect of the assignment of a cause of action for breach of contract on the liability of the contract-breaker to the assignee for damages, notably *Linden Gardens Trust Ltd v Lenesta Sludge Disposals Ltd, St Martins Property Corp Ltd v Sir Robert McAlpine & Sons Ltd* (1993) 36 Con LR 1, [1994] 1 AC 85 and (in the Court of Appeal) (1992) 30 Con LR 1. We have been referred to valuable discussions of the decision in an extended case note in the Law Quarterly Review by Mr I N Duncan Wallace QC ((1994) 110 LQR pp 42–55) and in an article in the Construction Law Journal by Mr John Cartwright ((1993) 9 Const LJ pp 281–296).

[6] The 'black hole' question arises here in the context of the assignment of a contract claim for an allegedly negligent soil inspection report obtained by the original owner of a building site for residential development. After the site ceased to be in the ownership of the company which obtained the report, a landslip occurred in the course of building operations by the contractor, who was engaged by the purchaser of the site from the original owner. The cause of action in respect of the report had not, however, been assigned when the site was sold. It was assigned only after the landslip. The assignment was made nearly five years after the site itself had changed hands.

 …

Assignment point: General principles

[30] The perceived problem of the effect of the assignment on the assignee's right to recover substantial damages is temporal in origin. It arises from the particular order in which the following events occurred: the breach of contract by Technotrade, the transfer of ownership of the site by Starglade to Larkstore, the damage caused by the landslip after the transfer and the assignment of the cause of action by Starglade to Larkstore, which occurred years after the transfer of the site.

[31] There are three relevant points of time.

(1) The time of the breach of contract by Technotrade. The contractual cause of action against Technotrade arose when Starglade was the owner of the site. Starglade was only entitled to

recover nominal damages at that time. No substantial damage could be established until the occurrence of the landslip in October 2001.

(2) The time of the landslip. Larkstore was the owner of the site at the time when the landslip occurred and substantial damage was suffered. Starglade was still entitled to the chose in action, but it was not entitled to recover substantial damages, as it had ceased to own the site. Larkstore owned the site and suffered substantial damage, but was not entitled to recover damages form Technotrade for breach of contract, because it had no contract with Technotrade and, at that time, had no assignment from Starglade of the benefit of its contract, rights of action and remedies for breach of contract.

(3) The time of the assignment. Starglade could not, it was submitted, assign to Larkstore more than it had. It did not have a claim for substantial damages against Technotrade in contract, as it had ceased to own the site before the assignment and before the landslip.

[32] The answer to the perceived problem of a limit on the damages which Larkstore, as assignee, is entitled to recover from Technotrade is to be found, in my judgment, in an analysis of the cause of action itself. In this case the cause of action was the right to sue Technotrade for breach of contract in respect of the preparation of the soil inspection report on the site. The cause of action was complete in December 1998 when Technotrade produced the soil report for Starglade.

[33] It is accepted that the report and the rights of action and remedies in respect of it were assignable and were not personal to Starglade. It is also accepted that, although the damages which Starglade could have recovered at the date when the cause of action was complete would have been no more than nominal damages, Starglade, if it had remained the owner of the site, would have been entitled to claim and, if able to prove, recover substantial damages for the landslip which occurred in October 2001.

[34] The remedy in damages for breach of contract is not limited to the loss that could have been proved at the date when the breach occurred and the cause of action first arose. Subject to factual and legal issues of causation, remoteness, quantum and limitation of actions, there is a remedy in damages against the contract-breaker for loss which occurs after the cause of action has accrued. A cause of action may arise years before any substantial damage occurs, as, for example, in the case of negligent advice on title. There is no legal principle which protects the contract-breaker by excluding his liability for substantial damage that occurs after the initial breach of contract.

[35] What difference, if any, can an assignment of the cause of action make to the remedies available to the assignee against the contract-breaker? A statutory assignment in writing under s 136 of the Law of Property Act 1925, of which express notice has been given, as was done in this case, is effectual in law to pass and transfer from the date of notice the legal right to the thing in action and 'all legal and other remedies for the same'. The statutory assignment is expressly made 'subject to equities having priority over the right of the assignee'.

[36] Mr Friedman QC (who did not appear in the court below) submitted on behalf of Technotrade that the assignment makes a crucial difference. His broad submission was that the only losses that Larkstore is entitled to claim by virtue of the assignment of the cause of action are the losses that Starglade could itself have recovered from Technotrade at the time of the assignment. As the assignment of the cause of action took place after Starglade had parted with the site to Larkstore and the substantial damage occurred before the assignment of the cause of action to Larkstore, Starglade and therefore Larkstore had no right to claim and recover substantial damages for loss resulting from the landslip.

[37] In its defence to the Pt 20 particulars of claim Technotrade pleaded that Starglade's rights of action are of no assistance to Larkstore, as Starglade has suffered no losses (para 31). It is pleaded in para 30:

'(i) The well established principle that an assignee of a chose in action (here Larkstore) cannot recover more than the assignor (here Starglade) has lost, is applicable on the particular facts of this claim, which it is averred does not fit within any of the exceptions to the said principle. Starglade has suffered no loss and Larkstore is not entitled to put itself in any better position than the principal to the contract which it has purported to assign.'

[38] The scope of the principle pleaded is discussed generally in *Chitty on Contracts* (29th edn, 2004) ch 19:

'19–073 Assignee cannot recover more than assignor. A further aspect of the idea that an assignee takes an assignment "subject to equities" is the principle that an assignee cannot recover more from the debtor than the assignor could have done had there been no assignment. For example, in [*Dawson v Great Northern and City Rly Co* [1905] 1 KB 260, [1904–7] All ER Rep 913] the assignment of a statutory claim for compensation for damage to land did not entitle the assignee to recover extra loss suffered by reason of a trade carried on by him, but not the assignor, that the assignor would not have suffered.

19–074 The application of this principle has given rise to particular difficulty in relation to building contracts or tort claims for damage to buildings. Say, for example, a building is sold at full value along with an assignment to the purchaser of claims in contract or tort in relation to the building. The building turns out to need repairs as a result of a breach of the builder's contract with the assignor (whether that breach is prior, or subsequent, to the sale to the assignee) or of a tort (damaging the building prior to the sale). The assignee pays for the repairs. It might be argued that the assignor in that situation has suffered no loss so that, applying the governing principle that the assignee cannot recover more than the assignor, the assignee has no substantial claim. If correct, "...the claim to damages would disappear...into some legal black hole, so that the wrong-doer escaped scot-free." Acceptance of the argument would also nullify the purpose of the governing principle which is to avoid prejudice to the debtor and not to allow the debtor to escape liability.

19–075 Perhaps not surprisingly, therefore, that argument was rejected by the House of Lords in a Scottish delict case. And the problem has been circumvented in England by the courts' recognition that, where a third party is, or will become, owner of a defective or damaged property, there is an exception to the general rule that a contracting party can recover damages for its own loss and not for the loss of a third party. Where the exception applies, the contracting party (the assignor) is entitled to substantial damages for the loss suffered by the third party (the assignee): by the same token, an award of substantial damages to the assignee does not infringe the principle that the assignee cannot recover more than the assignor.'

Application of principles

[39] Applying this concise account of the legal principles to the particular circumstances of this case, it is, in my judgment, fallacious to contend that Larkstore cannot recover substantial damages from Technotrade, even if it can prove that Technotrade was in breach of contract and otherwise liable for them.

[40] The contention is based on the propositions that Starglade (the assignor) had only suffered nominal damages at the date of the assignment, because it no longer owned the site, and that Larkstore (the assignee) could not acquire by assignment from Starglade any greater right than Starglade had against Technotrade.

[41] As I see it, that is not the true legal position. What was assigned by Starglade to Larkstore was a cause of action for breach of contract against Technotrade and the legal remedies for it. It was not an assignment of 'a loss', as Mr Friedman described it in his attempt to persuade the court that the amount of the loss recoverable by Larkstore was limited by what loss had been suffered by Starglade, in this case nil. The assignment included the remedy in damages for the cause of action. The remedy in damages for breach of contract is not, in principle, limited to the loss suffered as at the date of the accrual of the cause of action or as at any particular point of time thereafter.

[42] The principle invoked by Technotrade that the assignee cannot recover more than the assignor does not assist it on the facts of this case. The purpose of the principle is to protect the contract-breaker/debtor from being prejudiced by the assignment in having, for example, to pay damages to the assignee which he would not have had to pay to the assignor, had the assignment never taken place. The principle is not intended to enable the contract-breaker/debtor to rely on the fact of the assignment in order to escape all legal liability for breach of contract.

[43] In this case the assignment of 23 February 2004 did not, in itself, prejudice Technotrade by exposing it to a claim for damages by Larkstore, which Starglade could not have brought against Technotrade. The assignment of the cause of action by Starglade to Larkstore was a delayed consequence of the earlier sale of the site. It completed the transaction. If Starglade had not sold the site to Larkstore, it would not have assigned the cause of action against Technotrade to Larkstore and it could have recovered substantial damages against Technotrade for the landslip. The increased exposure of Technotrade for damages for breach of contract was a consequence of the landslip after the cause of action arose. It was not a consequence of the assignment of the cause of action, which was made to enable Larkstore to step fully into the shoes of Starglade following on the earlier sale of the site.

[44] Indeed, if Mr Friedman's arguments were accepted, far from being prejudiced by the assignment, Technotrade would improve its position as a result of it. Technotrade would escape all potential contractual liability for the damage caused by the landslip. It would have ceased to be liable to Starglade, which no longer owned the site. It would not be liable to Larkstore, which did own the site, but the liability to Larkstore would be subject to the Starglade limit proposed by Mr Friedman, which would cancel any claim against Technotrade for substantial damages. By a legal conjuring trick worthy of Houdini the assignment would free Technotrade from the fetters of contractual liability. The position would be that the contract-breaker would be liable to no one for the substantial loss suffered in consequence of the breach. As a matter of legal principle and good sense, this cannot possibly be the law, and fortunately the authorities cited in argument and discussed below do not compel the court to reach such a result.

[45] Mr Friedman submitted that there was no 'legal black hole' or conjuring trick here. He contended that the parties did not contemplate that any one other than Starglade would or might suffer loss in consequence of a breach of contract by Technotrade in respect of the report. Technotrade's retainer was on the basis that it was Starglade who would be carrying out the development of the site. Losses have been suffered by Larkstore because it chose not to seek any form of warranty from Technotrade, did not engage its own geo-technical advisers and relied on the Technotrade report without obtaining the consent of Technotrade for a purpose for which it had not been written.

[46] In my judgment, these arguments amount to no more than an ingenious attempt to deny what has been correctly conceded, namely that the report and the causes of action in respect of it were assignable by Starglade. There was no express prohibition against assignment. No prohibition can be implied from any special circumstances. It was not argued, for example, that the contract between Starglade and Technotrade was of a personal nature and therefore unassignable.

The authorities

[47] Mr Friedman's submissions on the assignment point are not supported by the authorities cited by him to show that the judge had misunderstood or misapplied the correct legal principles. Although the cases were discussed at length in the skeleton arguments and at the hearing, I propose to deal with them quite briskly.

[48] *Dawson v Great Northern and City Rly Co* [1905] 1 KB 260 at 272–274, [1904–7] All ER Rep 913 at 917–918 per Stirling LJ was cited for the proposition that the assignee was not entitled to recover any greater amount of compensation than the assignor could have recovered. The width of the general proposition has to be read in context. In that case compensation under the Lands Clauses Consolidation Act 1845 was not payable to the assignee for 'damage to [her] trade stock' (as distinct from structural damage to premises requiring reinstatement works which did not increase the burden on the defendants), because that was compensation for an item that could not have been recovered by the assignor from the defendants. The assignor did not trade in the stock in question and could not have made a claim for compensation for that item.

[49] *GUS Property Management Ltd v Littlewoods Mail Order Stores Ltd* 1982 SLT 533 was also cited for Lord Keith of Kinkel's statement (at 537–538) that—

'the basic question at issue is whether in this action the Pursuers are really seeking to pursue against the Defenders a claim or claims which the [assignor] could have pursued at the date of the [assignment]...the only relevant loss which by virtue of the [assignment] the Pursuers could claim title to recover is loss suffered by the [assignor] for which the [assignor] could at the date of the [assignment] have sought reparation.'

[50] The speech of Lord Keith was considered in the *Linden Gardens Trust* case (1993) 36 Con LR 1, [1994] 1 AC 85. We heard very detailed submissions on the speech of Lord Browne-Wilkinson in the House of Lords (with which the other members of the Appellate Committee concurred) and on the judgments in the Court of Appeal.

[51] The judge was criticised by Mr Friedman for relying on the following passage in the judgment of Staughton LJ ((1992) 30 Con LR 1 at 16–17):

'That brings me to the last point to be considered in connection with assignment of choses in action. Where the assignment is of a cause of action for damages, the assignee must of course have a sufficient proprietary right, or a genuine commercial interest, if the assignment is not to be invalid. It is no longer in issue in these appeals that the assignees had such a right in each case; we heard no argument to the contrary from the contractors. But it is said that in such a case the assignee can recover no more as damages than the assignor could have recovered.

That proposition seems to me well-founded. It stems from the principle already discussed, that the debtor is not to be put in any worse position by reason of the assignment. And it is established by *Dawson v Great Northern and City Rly Co* [1905] 1 KB 260, [1904–7] All ER Rep 913; see also *GUS Property Management Ltd v Littlewoods Mail Order Stores Ltd* 1982 SLT 533 at 588 by Lord Keith of Kinkel, cited later in this judgment. But in a case such as the present one must elucidate the proposition slightly: the assignee can recover no more damages than the assignor could have recovered if there had been no assignment, *and if the building had not been transferred to the assignee.*'

[52] As I read the judgments of the other members of the court (Sir Michael Kerr (at 32–33) and Nourse LJ (at 38)), it is reasonably clear that they agreed with what Staughton LJ said on this point in the passage cited and at 27–28.

[53] Although the House of Lords overturned the decision of the Court of Appeal on the issue of the effect of the prohibition against assignment, I do not read the speech of Lord Browne-Wilkinson, which did not directly address the issue, as questioning the ruling of the Court of Appeal on the question whether an assignee could recover no more damages than the assignor could have recovered. It was unnecessary for the House to consider the assignee's remedies for breach of contract in view of its decision that the prohibition against assignment rendered the assignments ineffective.

[54] The judgment of Staughton LJ was rightly relied on by the judge. I am respectfully of the view that the ruling of Staughton LJ on this point is correct as a matter of legal principle and good sense, and ought to be followed by this court in this case. It completely disposes of the argument raised in the defence of Technotrade that Larkstore is not entitled to claim substantial damages from Technotrade, because its assignor, Starglade, had suffered no loss, having parted with the site before the landslip occurred and before the assignment of its cause of action to Larkstore.

[55] I must, however, make it clear that the only point raised in this case at this preliminary stage is whether Larkstore had, by virtue of the assignment, a right to sue Technotrade for substantial damages for breach of contract in respect of loss claimed to have been suffered by it in consequence of the landslip at the site. There is no question before this court, nor was there below, as to the proper measure or quantum of damages, which Larkstore is entitled to recover against Technotrade. We have heard no argument on it and I express no views on that aspect of the case.

...

Conclusion

[62] I would dismiss the appeal on the assignment point.

Rix LJ:

[64] I agree, and I would like to add a few observations about the authorities which have been cited to us, particularly in the context of Mr Friedman QC's submission for Technotrade that to uphold the judgment below ([2005] EWHC 2742 (TCC), [2005] All ER (D) 45 (Dec)) would run counter to fundamental principle in ignoring that Starglade, as assignor, simply had no loss, that is to say none other than a purely nominal loss, to pass on to Larkstore as assignee.

[65] In this connection, Mummery LJ has already cited *Chitty on Contracts* (29th edn, 2004) para 19–075, for the proposition that—

> 'where a third party is, or will become, owner of a defective or damaged property, there is an exception to the general rule that a contracting party can recover damages for its own loss and not for the loss of a third party. Where the exception applies, the contracting party (the assignor) is entitled to substantial damages for the loss suffered by the third party (the assignee): by the same token, an award of substantial damages to the assignee does not infringe the principle that the assignee cannot recover more than the assignor.'

[66] The relevant footnote refers to *Linden Gardens Trust Ltd v Lenesta Sludge Disposals Ltd, St Martins Property Corp Ltd v Sir Robert McAlpine & Sons Ltd* (1993) 36 Con LR 1, [1994] 1 AC 85, *Darlington BC v Wiltshier Northern Ltd* (1994) 41 ConLR 122, [1995] 1 WLR 68 and *Alfred McAlpine Construction Ltd v Panatown Ltd* (2000) 71 ConLR 1, [2001] 1 AC 518.

[67] The authorities in this area demonstrate the courts' striving to ensure that wrongdoers do not escape from their liabilities, by reference to the general principle that a person can only recover for his own loss, because of the happenstance that a cause of action lies in the hands of someone other than the person who has suffered the loss. The courts are concerned to see that justice is done between the parties. The general problem has arisen in a number of different ways.

[68] Thus in *GUS Property Management Ltd v Littlewoods Mail Order Stores Ltd* 1982 SLT 533 the pursuers, GUS, were the transferees from an associate company, Rest, of a building which had suffered damage during works to a neighbouring property. Rest therefore had a claim in tort against the defendants, Littlewoods. After the damage had been caused, Rest transferred their building to GUS, as a matter of group policy designed to concentrate the groups' property assets in a single subsidiary. The transfer was made at book value, without any discount being allowed for the damage suffered, and indeed without any reference to the true value of the building. A few years later, Rest also assigned to GUS their cause of action against Littlewoods. Thus the cause of action and the loss caused by the damage started life in the same hands, viz with Rest, and ended up with their assignees, GUS. However, because of the transfer value obtained by Rest, Littlewoods alleged that Rest had suffered no loss, and that their assignees, GUS, therefore had no claim either. The First Division upheld this defence, but the House of Lords reversed that decision. As Lord Keith of Kinkel said, the price for which Rest had transferred the damaged building to GUS was entirely irrelevant for the purpose of measuring the loss suffered by Rest and was quite incapable of founding an argument that Rest had suffered no loss at all. Lord Keith protested against this attempt to make Rest's loss 'disappear…into some legal black hole, so that the wrongdoer escaped scot-free' (see at 177).

[69] The next argument raised by Littlewoods was that GUS were suing, on their pleadings, for their own loss in repairing the damage, and that that was not a loss suffered by Rest. That argument was also rejected. The cost of repairs was merely one way of evidencing the loss. Another possible way was to take the day one diminution of the value of the building due to the damage caused. In either event, the loss had been suffered by Rest, and it was Rest's loss for which GUS were suing as assignees. The First Division had taken too narrow a view of GUS's pleadings, 'which was not conducive to the aim of doing justice between the parties' (see 1982 SLT 533 at 539).

[70] That was a comparatively simple case, because, upon proper analysis, cause of action and loss had both been suffered by the assignor, prior to the assignment. It demonstrates, however, the defendants' attempt to manipulate legal principle to split cause of action and loss between assignor and assignee. The House of Lords would have none of it.

[71] *Linden Gardens Trust Ltd v Lenesta Sludge Disposals Ltd* (1993) 36 Con LR 1, [1994] 1 AC 85 involved two separate cases, heard together. The other case was *St Martins Property Corp Ltd v Sir Robert McAlpine & Sons Ltd*. I shall call the two cases *Lenesta* and *McAlpine* respectively.

[72] In *Lenesta* the lessee of a building entered into an asbestos removal contract with a contractor who sub-contracted it to Lenesta. Lenesta did a bad job and some time later (in 1985), the lessee had to engage a further contractor to complete the task. This realised a loss of some £22,000. The second contractor also did a bad job, overlooking further asbestos, but at that time that was unknown. Thereafter the lessee assigned his lease to Linden at full market value. Later again, the lessee commenced proceedings against both contractors and Lenesta, for breach of contract and negligence. It was at that point that the lessee also assigned to Linden its pleaded rights of action. Subsequently, Linden had to undertake still further work to remedy the situation and incurred a cost of some £236,000 (in 1987/1988). There was a prohibition on assignment in the contractors' contracts. The Court of Appeal ((1992) 30 Con LR 1) held that the assignment was nevertheless effective and awarded damages to Linden for the accumulated costs of remedying the two contractors' defaults. Some of that cost had been incurred by the lessee (Stock Conversion) and subsequently some of it had been incurred by Linden. Thus, as in the *GUS Property Management* case, the causes of action had arisen in the hands of the assignor, Stock Conversion, but (the majority of) the financial consequences of the breaches had been experienced by the assignee, Linden (aside from that part incurred by Stock Conversion before transfer of the lease). The House of Lords, however, held that the assignment was invalid, because of the prohibition on assignment. Therefore, Linden lost its claim. There was no claim by the assignor, Stock Conversion.

[73] At the Court of Appeal level, however, where the assignment was held to be valid, the defendant contractors submitted that the assignee, Linden, could recover no more than the assignor, Stock Conversion could have done, and that the assignor had suffered no loss because he had sold his lease for full market value. It was also submitted that in any event, Linden could not recover the £236,000 it had incurred itself in respect of loss of rent during the works. These were essentially the same arguments as had been run in the *GUS Property Management* case. They failed again. Staughton LJ showed that the sale of the lease at full market value was res inter alios acta, just as much as the transfer at book value in the earlier case, and did not go in diminution of Stock Conversion's loss ((1992) 30 ConLR 1 at 25–27). As for the £236,000 incurred by Linden itself, it was submitted that there had been no right of action vested in Stock Conversion because no remedial work had been carried out by it, but Staughton LJ said (at 28):

> 'It is immaterial that Linden Gardens Trust subsequently incurred the expense of remedial work and suffered loss of rent while it was carried out, although the cost and loss may assist them in establishing the damages which would, but for the assignment have been recoverable by Stock Conversion . . . in my opinion there was an existing right of action for breach of contract.'

[74] Staughton LJ had previously said (at 16–17):

> 'But it is said that in such a case the assignee can recover no more as damages than the assignor could have recovered. That proposition seems to me to be well-founded. It stems from the principle already discussed, that the debtor is not to be put in any worse position by reason of the assignment. And it is established by *Dawson v Great Northern and City Rly Co* [1905] 1 KB 260, [1904–7] All ER Rep 913; see also *GUS Property Management Ltd v Littlewoods Mail Order Stores Ltd* 1982 1982 SLT 533 at 538 by Lord Keith of Kinkel, cited later in this judgment. But in a case such as the present one must elucidate the proposition slightly: the assignee can recover no more damages than the assignor could have recovered if there had been no assignment, *and if the building had not been transferred to the assignee*.'

[75] Sir Michael Kerr (at 33) wrote in essentially the same terms, saying:

'The next point is then that an assignee can recover damages from the debtor to the same extent as his assignor could have done, but he cannot enforce any new claims, let alone under new heads of damage, which would not have been available to the assignor. However, his right to damages, limited to that extent, is enforceable by him even though he is not accountable to his assignor...Both [the £22,000 and the £236,000 losses] are claims for damages which had vested in Stock Conversion and which were validly assigned to Linden Gardens. The fact that, at the time of the assignment, Stock Conversion were unaware of the full extent of the breaches, and therefore of the extent of their claims for damages, does not appear to me to make any difference to the validity and effect of the assignment to Linden Gardens. The only limitation upon Linden Gardens' rights of recovery is the extent to which the defendants may be able to show that Linden Gardens' claims exceed what would have been recoverable by Stock Conversion if there had been no assignment...But that is merely a question which goes to quantum, like the discussion in the speech of Lord Keith in *GUS* as to what would be the appropriate measure of damages in the circumstances.'

[76] Nourse LJ agreed with the judgments of both Staughton LJ and Sir Michael Kerr. In the House of Lords, their Lordships did not have to reach this issue, because they held the assignment to have been invalid.

[77] For the reasons given by Mummery LJ, it seems to me that these authorities are directly applicable to the present appeal. It is true that in one, admittedly important, respect the present case goes beyond the *GUS Property Management* case and *Lenesta*: whereas in those cases the damage caused by the breaches of contract or negligence had already occurred by the time of the assignments, albeit it had not been experienced as a financial loss until quantified by remedial works instituted by the assignees, and the assignees' loss of rent in the present case, although the breach of contract had already occurred before the assignment, the loss arising from the breach had not been caused until the development work was actually undertaken, by which time the development had been sold to Larkstore and the loss had not been experienced, even in an unquantified form, by the assignor Starglade. However, for the reasons given by Mummery LJ, I agree that this difference is not crucial. Damage arising from a breach of contract is often slow in materialising. The delay in this case may give rise hereafter to arguments about causation or remoteness: I say nothing about those problems. However, it was Starglade who had experienced the breach of contract and owned the cause of action, and, subject to issues of causation and remoteness, it would have been Starglade who, subject to such issues, would have been entitled to have recovered for the financial consequences of that breach if it had not sold the development to Larkstore.

[78] Thus the facts that the damages had only been nominal at the time of the sale of the property, or that the substantial loss only occurred after the sale, or that Larkstore suffered that loss before it had acquired, under the assignment, the right of action to go along with the loss, do not in my judgment prevent recovery by Larkstore. Those complications no doubt mean that the arguments about causation and quantum may be affected by considerations which would not have arisen if Starglade had developed the site itself: see *Dawson v Great Northern and City Rly Co* [1905] 1 KB 260, [1904–7] All ER Rep 913, where the defendant was not liable for that part of the assignee's claim which was premised on 'damage to trade stock' by reason of disturbance to her drapery business, which was a different business from that of the assignor, in whose hands the land in question was simply used for the purpose of letting out ([1905] 1 KB 260 at 273–274, [1904–7] All ER Rep 913 at 918). However, to hold that Larkstore's claim as assignee of Starglade's cause of action for breach of contract against Technotrade simply failed in limine would be to consign it to that black hole about which Lord Keith was concerned in the *GUS Property Management* case and which has been repeatedly alluded to in successive cases which have raised analogous problems.

[79] It seems to me that this conclusion is also supported by the result of the other case reported with *Lenesta*, namely *McAlpine*.

[80] In *McAlpine*, as in *Lenesta*, the assignment again failed because of a prohibition against assignment, but in this case both assignor and assignee were parties to the litigation against McAlpine. The assignor was St Martins Property Corporation (Corporation) and the assignee was St Martins Property Investments (Investments). The assignee's claim necessarily failed, but the assignor's claim succeeded. Corporation was concerned in the development of a property and for these purposes entered into a building contract with McAlpine. It later assigned to Investments, for full value, all its interest in the development and associated contracts, including the McAlpine contract. After development, defects were found in the property, costing £800,000 to remedy, and those defects were due to McAlpine's breach of contract. McAlpine argued that because that loss had been suffered by Investments and not by Corporation, neither party could recover. Investments, as purported assignee, could not recover since the assignment was invalid. Corporation, however, could not recover either, because at the time of McAlpine's breach it had no longer had any proprietary interest in the property and had therefore suffered none but a purely nominal loss. Thus the contract and its breach lay between Corporation and McAlpine but the loss lay between Investments and McAlpine, between whom there was neither an original nor an assigned contract.

[81] Nevertheless, the House of Lords held that Corporation could recover substantial damages for the account of Investments. Lord Browne-Wilkinson described McAlpine's argument as 'formidable, if unmeritorious', formidable because apparently based on principle and supported by authority, viz in *Albacruz (Cargo Owners) v Albazero (Owners), The Albazero* [1976] 3 All ER 129, [1977] AC 774. Nevertheless, Lord Browne-Wilkinson held that the *Dunlop v Lambert* (1839) 6 Cl & Fin 600, 7 ER 824 exception applied, whereby one party may be thought of as entering into a contract for the benefit of all parties who may subsequently acquire an interest in goods, because it was contemplated by both original parties to the contract that the goods may be transferred to another party after its making and before its performance has been completed. Lord Browne-Wilkinson put the matter in this way ((1993) 36 ConLR 1 at 28, [1994] 1 AC 85 at 114–115):

> 'In my judgment the present case falls within the rationale of the exceptions to the general rule that a plaintiff can only recover damages for his own loss. The contract was for a large development of property which, to the knowledge of both Corporation and McAlpine, was going to be occupied, and possibly purchased, by a third party and not by Corporation itself. Therefore it could be foreseen that damage caused by a breach would cause loss to a later owner and not merely to the original contracting party, Corporation. As in contracts for the carriage of goods by land, there would be no automatic vesting in the occupier or owners of the property for the time being who sustained the loss of any right of suit against McAlpine. On the contrary, McAlpine had specifically contracted that the rights of action under the building contract *could not* without McAlpine's consent be transferred to third parties who became owners or occupiers and might suffer loss. In such a case, it seems to me proper, as in the case of carriage of goods by land, to treat the parties as having entered into the contract on the footing that Corporation would be entitled to enforce contractual rights for the benefit of those who suffered from defective performance but who, under the terms of the contract, could not acquire any right to hold McAlpine liable for breach. It is truly a case in which the rule provides "a remedy where no other would be available to a person sustaining loss which under a rational legal system ought to be compensated by the person who has caused it".'

[82] Lord Browne-Wilkinson was not impressed by an argument that 'it would be wrong to distort the law...to meet...an exceptional case', since he regarded the problem as one inherent in a standard form of enterprise ((1993) 36 ConLR 1 at 28, [1994] 1 AC 85 at 115).

[83] In a later case, the same solution was applied, by way of an extension of the *Dunlop v Lambert* exception, even though neither factor stressed by Lord Browne-Wilkinson, namely that the contractual parties contemplated transfer of the property to which the contract related, and that the contract prohibited assignment, applied: see *Darlington BC v Wiltshier Northern Ltd* (1994) 41 ConLR 122, [1995] 1 WLR 68. In *Alfred McAlpine Construction Ltd v Panatown Ltd* (2000) 71 ConLR 1, [2001] 1 AC

518, however, the House of Lords while approving the decision in the *Darlington BC* case was unwilling to extend the *Dunlop v Lambert/McAlpine* exception to a situation where the parties had provided the assignee with his own separate and direct avenue of claim against the contractor. See *Chitty* paras 18–050 to 18–063 for a detailed discussion of these cases.

[84] While *McAlpine* and the cases which have followed do not directly apply to the present case, as was common ground before the judge, since here there is no question of Starglade claiming in respect of Larkstore's loss, nevertheless they illustrate the possibilities that, in order to prevent the loss caused by a defendant's breach disappearing into the proverbial black hole, the courts are nowadays willing to go far to create a working, and developing, analysis which will accommodate a claim for substantial damages. Those cases also demonstrate, in my judgment, that if substantial damages may be claimed by the assignor in such circumstances, then there can be no objection to a claim brought by an assignee of a valid assignment, in whom both cause of action and loss unite in the same party.

[85] Underlying all these cases can be heard the drumbeat of a constant theme, which could possibly be described as ubi ius ibi remedium, the maxim that where there is a right there is a remedy; but it could also be said that the courts are anxious to see, if possible, that where a real loss has been caused by a real breach of contract, then there should if at all possible be a real remedy which directs recovery from the defendant towards the party which has suffered the loss. In the case of property development, where it is readily contemplated that a party which prepares the development will transfer the fruits of his work to one or more partners or successors, there is a particular need for some such solution.

[86] The courts have to work with the analytical tools which are to hand. But the essence of the matter is that the general principles which have been developed to ensure that claims are confined to victims (the rule that a party may only claim in respect of his own loss; the rule in favour of privity of contract) and that a wrongdoer should not be made to pay compensation which goes beyond his breach (the rule that an assignee may not recover more than his assignor could have recovered), rules which as far as they go, are necessary and fundamental to good order and fairness in the litigation of claims, are not, if at all possible, to be allowed to become instruments of maladjustment and injustice. Thus the exception developed long ago in the carriage of goods context to allow a contracting party to recover damages against a carrier on behalf of another party to whom the goods in question are subsequently transferred has been brought into use in a modern situation where there is an equal need to find a solution which matches the commercial situation, and where no other solution had been found to be at hand. Of course, where a solution has been provided by statute, as where a contract of carriage of goods by sea is novated statutorily, as in the case of bills of lading, or where there are other solutions readily to hand (as in *The Albazero* or in *Alfred McAlpine Construction Ltd v Panatown Ltd*), there may be no need, and thus it will be thought to be undesirable, to find an exception to general principle.

[87] In the present case, however, although the problem may arise, on these particular facts, in somewhat unusual circumstances, seeing that the consequences of the breach of contract were delayed until the site was actually developed, I do not think that any true exceptions are being created. The first victim of the breach of contract was Starglade, in whose hands the cause of action for that breach originally arose. That cause of action was intended to be assigned to Larkstore at the time of the transfer of the substance of the development, but through an error was not then assigned. The substantive loss alleged to arise from the breach then occurred. At that point the cause of action and that loss are in separate hands: but following the assignment come together again. The apparent difficulty which is said at this preliminary stage to arise is that the assignee is seeking to recover more than the assignor could have recovered: but that, subject to arguments of causation or remoteness which are reserved, is not, at this stage of the argument, because of any novel intrusion brought into the matter by the assignee, but simply because all the possible losses brought in train by the original breach had been suspended until the site was actually developed. Only the breach itself had so far occurred. However, in principle the assignee is seeking to recover no more than the loss which the assignor would have suffered and been entitled to recover if he had not transferred the development. The rule in *Dawson v Great Northern and City Rly Co* [1905] 1 KB 260, [1904–7] All ER Rep 913 is not designed to allow a defendant to escape liability for his breach, but to ensure that he does not have to meet a bigger liability than he would have been under to the assignor. In other words, the assignee cannot bring to his claim losses which do not follow from the original breach, but which he has separately introduced. Similarly, the rule that a party may only recover in respect of his own loss does not seem to me to create any difficulty in a case where cause of action and loss are, at this point, united in the same party. The cause of action for Technotrade's breach always brought with it potential or inchoate liability for all the losses which would ultimately, subject to matters of causation and remoteness, flow from it.

Peter Smith J:

[88] I also agree.

NOTES

1.   The key reasoning was given by Mummery LJ when he said (at [41]) that '[w]hat was assigned by Starglade to Larkstore was a cause of action for breach of contract against Technotrade and the legal remedies for it. It was not an assignment of "a loss"...' The occurrence of loss or damage is not an essential ingredient of a cause of action for breach of contract. In *Technotrade*, the breach occurred before the sale of the site and the loss occurred after the sale, but before the assignment. In *Linden Gardens Trust Ltd v Lenesta Sludge Disposals Ltd* [1994] 1 AC 85 (see above), the breach and the loss—though not the financial cost of remedying the loss—both occurred before the sale and the assignment. Rix LJ said (at [77]) that 'this difference is not crucial'.

2.   In *Technotrade*, the first instance judge held that the assignment did not enable Larkstore to make a claim in tort for negligence against Technotrade. The cause of action in tort did not arise until the damage had occurred and damage was an essential ingredient of the cause of action in tort. The damage occurred after the sale of the site. There was, therefore, no cause of action in tort for Starglade to assign at the date of the assignment. The Court of Appeal did not address this issue. But, remember, a claim in tort is generally non-assignable (see above, p 967).

3.   Rix LJ was keen to stress that the right to damages arising from the cause of action assigned by Starglade to Larkstore would be subject to the rules of causation and remoteness (see paras [77]–[78] and [87]). For example, on the question of causation, Larkstore might have to demonstrate that the landslip caused by its site development would also have occurred had the site been developed by Starglade, and, on the question of remoteness, it might have to show that the original parties reasonably contemplated that the cause of action might be assigned to an entity such as Larkstore (see Chee Ho Tham [2007] LMCLQ 286, 289–290, from which these examples are taken).

4.   In *Technotrade*, there was no question of Starglade claiming in respect of Larkstore's loss as there was no term of the contract between Starglade and Technotrade that prohibited the assignment to Larkstore. But where there is an effective non-assignment clause, as was the case in *St Martins Property Corp Ltd v Sir Robert McAlpine Ltd* [1994] 1 AC 85, the courts have had to show some ingenuity to allow the assignor to recover substantial damages which represent the assignee's, and not his own, loss (see *Technotrade*, above, at [80]-[83]). The courts have been keen to avoid 'legal black holes', where loss is suffered as a result of a breach of contract, but the contract-breaker's position is that no-one is legally entitled to recover substantial damages from him.

(c) Priorities—the rule in *Dearle v Hall*

Where there are two successive assignments (whether legal or equitable) of the same chose in action, the rule in *Dearle v Hall*, which originally related to competing equitable assignments, regulates priorities. Under this rule an assignee for value who is first to give notice to the debtor, trustee or fundholder takes priority, unless he knew of the earlier assignment when he took his assignment.

Dearle v Hall

(1823) 3 Russ 1, Court of Chancery

Brown, a beneficiary, assigned his interest by way of security first to Dearle and then to Sherring. The trustees were not given notice of the assignments. Some years later Brown assigned his interest to Hall. Before purchasing the interest, Hall made inquiries of the trustees and they indicated that the interest was unencumbered. Hall gave the trustees notice of his assignment. Subsequently, Dearle and Sherring gave the trustees notice of their assignments.

Sir Thomas Plumer MR: . . . The ground of this claim is priority of title. They [Dearle and Sherring] rely upon the known maxim, borrowed from the civil law, which in many cases regulates equities—'*qui prior est in tempore, potior est in jure*' ['first in time, first in right']. If, by the first contract, all the thing is given, there remains nothing to be the subject of the second contract, and priority must decide. But it cannot be contended that priority in time must decide, where the legal estate is outstanding. For the maxim, as an equitable rule, admits of exception, and gives way, when the question does not lie between bare and equal equities. If there appears to be, in respect of any circumstance independent of priority of time, a better title in the *puisne* purchaser to call for the legal estate, than in the purchaser who precedes him in date, the case ceases to be a balance of equal equities, and the preference, which priority of date might otherwise have given, is done away with and counteracted. The question here is,—not which assignment is first in date,—but whether there is not, on the part of Hall, a better title to call for the legal estate than Dearle or Sherring can set up? or rather, the question is, Shall these Plaintiffs now have equitable relief to the injury of Hall?

What title have they shown to call on a court of justice to interpose on their behalf, in order to obviate the consequences of their own misconduct? All that has happened is owing to their negligence (a negligence not accounted for) in forbearing to do what they ought to have done, what would have been attended with no difficulty, and what would have effectually prevented all the mischief which has followed. Is a Plaintiff to be heard in a court of equity, who asks its interposition on his behoof, to indemnify him against the effects of his own negligence at the expense of another who has used all due diligence, and who, if he is to suffer loss, will suffer it by reason of the negligence of the very person who prays relief against him? The question here is not, as in *Evans v Bicknell* ((1801) 6 Ves 174), whether a court of equity is to deprive the Plaintiffs of any right—whether it is to take from them, for instance, a legal estate, or to impose any charge upon them. It is simply, whether they are entitled to relief against their own negligence. They did not perfect their securities; a third party has innocently advanced his money, and has perfected his security as far as the nature of the subject permitted him: is this Court to interfere to postpone him to them?

They say, that they were not bound to give notice to the trustees; for that notice does not form part of the necessary conveyance of an equitable interest. I admit, that, if you mean to rely on contract with the individual, you do not need to give notice; from the moment of the contract, he, with whom you are dealing, is personally bound. But if you mean to go further, and to make your right attach upon the thing which is the subject of the contract, it is necessary to give notice; and, unless notice is given, you do not do that which is essential in all cases of transfer of personal property. The law of England has always been, that personal property passes by delivery of possession; and it is possession which determines the apparent ownership. If, therefore, an individual, who in the way of purchase or mortgage contracts with another for the transfer of his interest, does not divest the vendor or mortgagor of possession, but permits him to remain the ostensible owner as before, he must take the consequences which may ensue from such a mode of dealing. That doctrine was explained in *Ryall v Rowles* ((1750) 1 Ves Sen 348, 1 Atk 165), before Lord Hardwicke and three of the Judges. If you, having the right of possession, do not exercise that right, but leave another in actual possession, you enable that person to gain a false and delusive credit, and put it in his power to obtain money from innocent parties on the hypothesis of his being the owner of that which in fact belongs to you. The principle has been long recognised, even in courts of law. In *Twyne 's* case ((1602) 3 Co Rep 80), one of the badges of fraud was, that the possession had remained in the vendor. Possession must follow right; and if you, who have the right, do not take posession, you do not follow up the title, and are responsible for the consequences.

'When a man,' says Lord Bacon (*Maxims of the Law,* max 16), 'is author and mover to another to commit an unlawful act, then he shall not excuse himself by circumstances not pursued.' It is true that a chose in action does not admit of tangible actual possession, and that neither Zachariah Brown nor any person claiming under him were entitled to possess themselves of the fund which yielded the £93 a year. But in *Ryall v Rowles* the Judges held, that, in the case of a chose in action, you must do every thing towards having possession which the subject admits; you must do that which is tantamount to obtaining possession, by placing every person, who has an equitable or legal interest in the matter, under an obligation to treat it as your property. For this purpose, you must give notice to the legal holder of the fund; in the case of a debt, for instance, notice to the debtor is, for many purposes, tantamount to possession. If you omit to give that notice, you are guilty of the same degree and species of neglect as he who leaves a personal chattel, to which he has acquired a title, in the actual possession, and under the absolute control, of another person.

Is there the least doubt, that, if Zachariah Brown had been a trader, all that was done by Dearle and Sherring would not have been in the least effectual against his assignees; but that, according to the doctrine of *Ryall v Rowles,* his assignees would have taken the fund, because there was no notice to those in whom the legal interest was vested? In that case it was the opinion of all the Judges, that he who contracts for a chose in action, and does not follow up his title by notice, gives personal credit to the individual with whom he deals. Notice, then, is necessary to perfect the title,—to give a complete right *in rem,* and not merely a right as against him who conveys his interest. If you are willing to trust the personal credit of the man, and are satisfied that he will make no improper use of the possession in which you allow him to remain, notice is not necessary; for against him the title is perfect without notice. But if he, availing himself of the possession as a means of obtaining credit, induces third persons to purchase from him as the actual owner, and they part with their money before your pocket-conveyance is notified to them, you must be postponed. In being postponed, your security is not invalidated: you had priority, but that priority has not been followed up; and you have permitted another to acquire a better title to the legal possession. What was done by Dearle and Sherring did not exhaust the thing (to borrow the principle of the civil law) but left it still open to traffic. These are the principles on which I think it to be very old law, that possession, or what is tantamount to possession, is the criterion of perfect title to personal chattels, and that he, who does not obtain such possession, must take his chance.

I do not go through the cases which constitute exceptions to the rule, that priority in time shall prevail. A man may lose that priority by actual fraud or constructive fraud; by being silent, for instance, when he ought to speak; by standing by, and keeping his own security concealed. By such conduct, even the advantage of possessing the legal estate may be lost....

On these grounds, I think that the plaintiffs have not shewn a title to call on a court of equity to interpose in their behalf, and to take the fund from an individual who has used due diligence, in order to give it to those whose negligence has occasioned all the mischief. There is no equality of equities between the defendant Hall, and the plaintiffs....

The bill, therefore, must be dismissed, but, as against Hall, without costs. I do not make the plaintiffs pay costs to Hall, because they may have been losers without any intention to commit a fraud, and I am unwilling to add to their loss. Constructive fraud is the utmost that can be imputed to them.

[On appeal, Lord Lyndhurst LC affirmed the Master of the Rolls' judgment.]

NOTES

1.   Sir Thomas Plumer MR sought to justify his decision on two grounds: the conduct of the competing assignees and the need for notice to perfect an equitable assignment. Today, neither ground can be used to justify the rule in *Dearle v Hall*. In *Foster v Cockerell* (1835) 3 Cl & Fin 456 the House of Lords disregarded the conduct of the competing assignees and gave priority to the assignee who was the first to give notice to the trustees. In *Ward v Duncombe* [1893] AC 369 at 392, Lord Macnaghten stressed that notice was not needed to perfect the title of an equitable assignee. As Lord Macnaghten said in that case (at 391): 'I am not sure that the doctrine rests upon any very satisfactory principle.'

2.   An assignee who has notice (including the constructive notice which comes from being put on inquiry: *Spencer v Clarke* (1878) 9 Ch D 137) of a previous assignment when he took his assignment cannot gain priority over it by being the first to give notice to the debtor, trustee or fundholder. This is often referred to as the second limb to the rule in *Dearle v Hall*. In fact, there is no express reference to this proviso in *Dearle v Hall* itself, but it has been emphasised by the courts on numerous occasions since (see, eg *Re Holmes* (1885) 29 Ch D 786 at 789, per Cotton and Lindley LJJ; *Ward v Duncombe* [1893] AC 369 at 384, per Lord Macnaghten). The proviso has been described as 'a rule of good sense' based on 'the ordinary morality of the matter' (*Rhodes v Allied Dunbar Pension Services* [1987] 1 WLR 1703 at 1708, per Harman J, revsd on appeal at [1989] 1 WLR 800, without affecting this statement; but contrast J de Lacy (1999) 28 Anglo-Am LR 87 and 197, who questions the origins of the proviso and calls for its rejection).

3.   The rule in *Dearle v Hall* is open to numerous criticisms (see F Oditah (1989) 9 OJLS 521, pp 525–527). Two deserve special mention. First, it is an arbitrary rule in that it can be relied on by an assignee who has given value, but not by a volunteer (*Justice v Wynne* (1860) 121 Ch R 289 at 304–305, per Brady LC; *United Bank of Kuwait plc v Sahib* [1997] Ch 107 at 119–120, per Chadwick J, affd on appeal at 130, without comment on this point). Secondly, by ignoring the reasons for failure to give notice, it can cause considerable injustice. Thus, in *Re Dallas* [1904] 2 Ch 385, the Court of Appeal applied the rule even though one of the competing assignees of an expectant interest in a legacy was unable at the relevant time to give notice because no qualified trustee had been appointed to receive it. The courts are usually reluctant to extend the application of the rule (eg it does not apply to successive dealings in company shares: *Macmillan Inc v Bishopsgate Investment Trust plc (No 3)* [1995] 3 All ER 747 at 761–762, per Millett J; affd on other grounds [1996] 1 All ER 585).

4.   By s 137(3) of the Law of Property Act 1925, notice of the assignment of an 'equitable interest' must be in writing to preserve priority (see above, p 964).

Compaq Computer Ltd v Abercorn Group Ltd
[1991] BCC 484, Chancery Division

Compaq, a manufacturer of computers and computer products, appointed Abercorn as an authorised dealer and supplied it with computer products on standard terms which reserved title in the products to Compaq until payment of the price. It was further provided that Abercorn would hold the goods as 'bailee and agent' for Compaq and would strictly account to Compaq for the full proceeds thereof received from third parties and keep a separate account of all such proceeds or monies. Abercorn then entered into a written invoice discounting agreement with Kellock, pursuant to which it assigned to Kellock nearly £400,000 owed by customers under sub-sales of Compaq products. Notice in writing of each of these assignments was given by Kellock to the relevant debtor. On Abercorn's subsequent receivership, a dispute arose between Compaq and Kellock as to which of them was entitled to be paid the proceeds of the sub-sales.

Mummery J held that on its true construction the terms of the agreement between Compaq and Abercorn operated by way of a charge over the proceeds of the sub-sales and that charge was void for non-registration under Part XII of the Companies Act 1985 (similar provisions are now to be found contained in Part 25 of the Companies Act 2006: see below, p 1044). On that ground alone, Kellock were entitled to the proceeds of the sub-sales. However, on the assumption that he was wrong on that issue, his Lordship then considered whether Kellock's rights as assignee took priority over Compaq's equitable interest in the proceeds of the sub-sales.

Mummery J: I deal first with the arguments on the rule in *Dearle v Hall* ((1823) 3 Russ 1; 38 ER 475). It was accepted by Compaq that if the rule did apply, Kellock would enjoy priority. Two arguments were advanced on behalf of Compaq as to why the rule in *Dearle v Hall* did not apply.

The first argument was that the rule did not apply because the subject-matter in question consisted of legal choses in action, ie debts owing to Abercorn by subpurchasers of Compaq products. It was contended that the rule is confined to equitable choses in action and to other equitable interests including, after 1926, equitable interests in land—see s 137(1) of the Law of Property Act 1925....

In brief, Compaq's submission was that it is the equitable nature of the property dealt with and not the equitable nature of the dealing with it—for example, by way of assignment—which attracts the rule.

It is, however, established on the authorities that the rule in *Dearle v Hall* applies to equitable assignments of legal choses in action. In *Pfeiffer [E Pfeiffer Weinkellerei-Weineinkauf GmbH & Co v Arbuthnot Factors Ltd* [1988] 1 WLR 150] at p 163 Phillips J said:

> The rule in *Dearle v Hall* is an exception to the general principle that equitable interests take priority in the order in which they are created. The rule applies to dealings with equitable interests in any property and, in particular, to equitable assignments of legal choses in action.
>
> Under the rule, priority depends upon the order in which notice of the interest created by the dealing is given to the person affected by it, ie, in the case of assignments of a debt, the debtor.

He went on to note that counsel conceded that if the rights asserted by the plaintiff were rights conferred by equitable assignment, the rule in *Dearle v Hall* must apply. The judge applied the rule because he held that such security rights as were conferred upon the plaintiff by the agreement were conferred by equitable assignment.

That passage in the judgment of Phillips J was criticised in argument before me. It was submitted that counsel had wrongly made a concession. I disagree. In my judgment, the view of Phillips J and the concession made by counsel receives full support from earlier authorities, including *Dearle v Hall* itself at p 58; 495.

[His Lordship then referred to the following cases, namely: *Gorringe v Irwell India Rubber & Gutta Percha Works* (1886) 34 Ch D 128 at 132, per Cotton LJ (see above, p 931) and, at 135, per Bowen J; *Ward and Pemberton v Duncombe* [1893] AC 369 at 383ff, per Lord Macnaghten; *Marchant v Morton, Down & Co* [1901] 2 KB 829 at 831, per Channell J; and *BS Lyle Ltd v Rosher* [1959] 1 WLR 8 at 16, per Lord Morton and, at 14, per Viscount Kilmuir LC]

Those formulations of the rule both appear to accept its applicability to an equitable assignment of a legal chose in action, such as a debt. I therefore reject the submission that the rule in *Dearle v Hall* cannot apply to this case because the relevant dealings were with debts.

The second argument advanced on behalf of Compaq against the application of the rule in *Dearle v Hall* was that the rule only applies in the case of successive assignments of equitable interests already created and not to the case of the creation of a new equitable interest—for example, by way of a declaration of trust. For this proposition reliance was placed on *Hill v Peters* [1918] 2 Ch 273 at p 279, where Eve J referred to the observations of Lord Macnaghten [in *Ward and Pemberton v Duncombe* [1893] AC 369 at 383] as to the undesirability of doing anything to extend the doctrine of *Dearle v Hall* to cases which were not already covered by it, and stated:

> The principle on which the rule in *Dearle v Hall* is founded, which regards the giving of notice by the assignee as the nearest approach to the taking of possession, has no application, in my opinion, to the beneficiary who has no right to possession himself, and who can only assert his claim to receive through his trustee.

In *Lyle v Rosher* there was argument about the correctness of the opinion expressed by Eve J on the distinction between a declaration of trust and an equitable assignment. No opinion on that question was expressed by four members of the House of Lords. Lord Reid, however, discussed the point and expressed the view at p 22 that,

> to apply the rule in *Dearle v Hall* to defeat the rights of a cestui que trust would introduce an exception to the general law.

—and he concluded at p 23:

> I think that it would be an innovation in the law of England to require a cestui que trust for his own protection to give notice of the trust in his favour to the person who holds the fund.

On the basis of those observations it was submitted on behalf of Compaq that the rule in *Dearle v Hall* did not apply because, as already submitted in argument on the charge point, Abercorn never became beneficially entitled to the proceeds of sale of Compaq products; by virtue of Abercorn's fiduciary obligations, the beneficial interest in those proceeds vested automatically in Compaq. There was, therefore, no assignment by Abercorn, by way of charge or otherwise, of the proceeds of sale. They were the subject of a trust in favour of Compaq which determined when the price of the Compaq products and other sums owing were paid. There was no equitable assignment of a chose in action to compete with the assignment made by Abercorn in favour of Kellock and, if there was only one assignment, there was no room for the application of *Dearle v Hall*.

In my judgment, assuming that there is a distinction between the creation of a trust and an equitable assignment, Compaq's argument fails on the construction of the terms and conditions of the dealer agreement. No bare trust of the proceeds of sale was created in favour of Compaq. An equitable assignment may be effected by an agreement between a debtor and a creditor that the debt owing shall be paid out of a specific fund coming to the debtor—see the speech of Lord Wilberforce in *Swiss Bank Corpn v Lloyds Bank Ltd* [1982] AC 584 at p 613A–E.

In my view, there was such an agreement in this case. In cl 8.3 and cl 8.3.2 Abercorn and Compaq in substance agreed that the debts owing by Abercorn to Compaq would be paid out of a specific fund coming to Abercorn, namely the proceeds of the subsales of Compaq products to Abercorn's customers. That was an equitable assignment of the proceeds of sale. I have held on the charge point that that assignment was by way of charge, registrable and void for want of registration. If I am wrong on that point and the assignment was not by way of charge, it was nevertheless an equitable assignment to which the rule in *Dearle v Hall* can apply when determining whether or not it enjoys priority over another equitable assignment of the same debt or fund.... Kellock had by virtue of the discounting agreement and assignments made pursuant to it priority over Compaq in respect of the proceeds of sale of the Compaq products supplied on the terms and conditions of the dealer agreement.

I should, however, briefly deal with the other argument advanced by Kellock: that it was a purchaser for value of the legal title to the debts without notice of any prior equitable interest of Compaq and therefore took free of any such interest. Paragraph (3) of the schedule requires me to assume that Kellock did not have notice or knowledge of Compaq's terms and conditions....

Kellock's submission was that it was a bona fide purchaser for value of the debts without notice of Compaq's interest at the time of the purchase and that it therefore enjoyed priority over any interest that Compaq might have by way of retention of title, charge or equitable interest. Reliance was placed on *Pitcher v Rawlins* (1872) 7 Ch App 259 at pp 268–269 where James LJ said:

> ...according to my view of the established law of this Court, such a purchaser's plea of a purchase for valuable consideration without notice is an absolute, unqualified, unanswerable defence, and an unanswerable plea to the jurisdiction of this Court.

Taylor v Blakelock (1886) 32 Ch D 560 was also cited along with *Thorndike v Hunt* (1859) 3 De G & J 563, 44 ER 1386 to demonstrate the strength of the position of a purchaser for value in contrast to the position of a volunteer.

The paramount plea of the bona fide purchaser for value without notice of an equitable interest in a debt or other legal thing in action has to be considered, however, in the context of s 136(1) of the Law of Property Act 1925 which provides:...[see above, p 940]....

The effect of that section was considered by Phillips J in *Pfeiffer* at p 162. He accepted the submission that the effect of s 136(1) and of the earlier section which it replaced (s 25(6) of the Supreme Court of Judicature Act 1873) was that it enabled the assignee to acquire a title which has all the procedural advantages of legal title, but so far as priorities are concerned his position is no better than if the assignment had been effected prior to those Acts. Phillips J said at p 162:

> It follows that, even if the assignment is effected for value without notice of a prior equity, priorities fall to be determined as if the assignment had been effected in equity, not in law.

That view was challenged but the judge held that it was supported by the views expressed by Channell J on s 25(6) of the 1873 Act in *Marchant v Morton, Down & Co* at p 832. No distinction was drawn in that case or in *Pfeiffer* between an assignment for value and a voluntary assignment.

It was submitted on behalf of Kellock that the conclusion of Phillips J on this point was wrong, particularly in not recognising a distinction between an assignee for value and a volunteer. I was referred to *Read v Brown* (1888) 22 QBD 128, a case not cited in *Pfeiffer,* for the proposition that s 25(6) of the 1873 Act gave to the assignee of a debt more than the mere right to sue for it. Lord Esher MR said at 131:

> ...it gives him the debt and the legal right to the debt...

He rejected the contention that the provision only affected procedure and confirmed that the words meant what they said, ie they transferred the legal right to the debt as well as the legal remedies for its recovery. He said at p 132:

> The debt is transferred to the assignee and becomes as though it has been his from the beginning; it is no longer to be the debt of the assignor at all, who cannot sue for it, the right to sue being taken from him; the assignee becomes the assignee of a legal debt and is not merely an assignee in equity, and the debt being his, he can sue for it, and sue in his own name.

It was submitted that if this is correct, the matter of priorities is not as stated by Phillips J in *Pfeiffer.* I was referred to obiter comments of Robert Goff J in *Ellerman Lines Ltd v Lancaster Maritime Co Ltd* [1980] 2 Lloyd's Rep 497 at p 503 that:

> ...a legal assignment...ranks before any equitable interest, even a prior equitable interest, unless the assignee had actual or constructive notice of the equitable interest at the time of the assignment.

I was also referred to obiter remarks of Viscount Finlay in *Performing Right Society Ltd v London Theatre of Varieties Ltd* [1924] AC 1 at p 19 to the effect that:

> There may possibly be cases in which a person who has made an equitable assignment might by a subsequent assignment have transferred the legal interest in the same work to a purchaser for value without notice, whose title would prevail over the merely equitable right, and such a possibility is one reason for the rule of making the legal owner a party.

Those authorities were not cited to Phillips J in *Pfeiffer* but I have not been convinced by the arguments advanced on behalf of Kellock that he came to the wrong conclusion in holding that, even if there is a legal assignment for value without notice of a prior equity, priorities fall to be determined as if the assignment had been effected in equity. Section 136(1) provides that the assignment is 'subject to equities having priority over the right of the assignee'. The effect of those words is to create, in the case of a statutory assignment of a chose in action, an exception to the general rule that an equity will not prevail against a bona fide purchaser of a legal estate for value without notice of the prior equity. If that is so, in the hands of Abercorn, the assignor to Kellock, the rights of action against the subpurchasers which it assigned to Kellock were subject to an earlier equitable assignment of those same rights to Compaq and Kellock therefore took subject to that prior equity. Unless the rule in *Dearle v Hall* were applicable, the result would be determined by the ordinary rule as to priorities, ie the basic rule of the order of creation where the merits are equal. The rule in *Dearle v Hall* apart, Kellock could not put itself in a stronger position than Abercorn as against Compaq by giving notice of the assignment from Abercorn to the subpurchasers and by then seeking to rely on the statutory assignment thereby completed to take in priority to the equity of Compaq.

As I have mentioned, it is not necessary to form a final view on this point in order to answer the points of law raised by way of preliminary issue. As at present advised, however, I would follow the decision of Phillips J in *Pfeiffer*.

NOTES

1.　The case is noted by LS Sealy in [1992] CLJ 19.

2.　For a strongly argued case in favour of the bona fide purchaser rule when there is competition between a statutory assignee and an equitable assignee, see F Oditah (1989) 9 OJLS 521, supported by RP Meagher, JD Heydon and MJ Leeming, *Meagher, Gummow and Lehane's Equity Doctrines and Remedies* (4th edn, 2002), at para 8–100, fn 17. But the arguments raised by Dr Oditah were effectively rejected by Mummery J in *Compaq Computers Ltd v Abercorn Group Ltd,* who followed the decision of Phillips J in *E Pfeiffer Weinkellerei-Weinenkauf GmbH & Co v Arbuthnot Factors Ltd* [1988] 1 WLR 150. For similar rejection of the bona fide purchaser rule in this context, see DW McLauchlan (1980) 96 LQR 90, pp 92–93; J Farrar and G McLay 'The interface of floating charges, Romalpa clauses and credit factoring' in J Prebble (ed) *Dimensions in Business Finance Law* (2nd edn, 1992), Ch 3; RM Goode *Commercial Law* (3rd edn, 2004), pp 751–752.

3.　Assuming that a seller's reservation of title clause gives him an equitable right to trace into the proceeds of sub-sales held by the buyer, is priority between the seller and an assignee of the buyer's book debts governed by the rule in *Dearle v Hall*? There is no clear answer to this question. It has been argued by DW McLauchlan that there is no room for the rule when the buyer holds the proceeds on trust for the seller. He argues that the rule in *Dearle v Hall* is restricted to competing assignments and does not apply in a situation when one of the interests is an equitable tracing right arising by operation of law (above, at 95ff). But Professor Goode counters that argument by stating that as it is the seller who chooses the form of his interest, by imposing an accounting obligation in the sale contract, and as he knows that the buyer may sell the debts arising from sub-sales to a bona fide purchaser, then the seller has no cause to complain if the rule in *Dearle v Hall* is applied against him (above, at 752, fn 69). In *Compaq Computer Ltd v Abercorn Group Ltd*, Mummery J avoided having to answer this difficult question by holding that the accounting obligation in the sale contract gave rise to an equitable assignment and not a bare trust. For a general discussion of reservation of title clauses and priorities, see G McCormack *Reservation of Title* (2nd edn, 1995), Ch 9; and F Oditah *Legal Aspects of Receivables Financing* (1991), pp 149–154.

4. For criticism of the application of the rule in *Dearle v Hall* when determining priority in the context of stock-in-trade and receivables financing, see below, p 1069. Proposals for reform of the priority rules are considered below, p 1071.

QUESTIONS

1. In *Ward and Pemberton v Duncombe* (1893) Lord Macnaghten expressed fears that the rule in *Dearle v Hall* might have been 'established at the expense of principles at least as important as those to which (the rule) has been referred'. Identify and critically examine the principles to which Lord Macnaghten referred.

2. A Ltd is owed money by B Ltd for goods supplied. A Ltd assigns (orally) the debt to C Factors Ltd for value. C Factors Ltd immediately gives notice of the assignment to B Ltd. Two weeks later A Ltd assigns (in writing) the same debt to D Factors Ltd for value. D Factors Ltd, which has no knowledge of the previous assignment, gives notice of its assignment to B Ltd. Which assignee has priority to the debt? Would it make any difference to your answer if D Factors Ltd had actually been paid the debt by B Ltd? See *E Pfeiffer Weinkellerei-Weineinkauf GmbH & Co v Arbuthnot Factors Ltd* [1988] 1 WLR 150 at 163.

CHAPTER 23
RECEIVABLES FINANCING

1 GENERAL INTRODUCTION[*]

(a) 'Receivables financing' defined

Legal Aspects of Receivables Financing by F Oditah (1991), p 2

The expression 'receivables financing' is ambiguous.[1] In this book, however, the expression is used to denote any arrangement by which money is raised on the strength of contractual receivables. Receivables form an integral part of the assets of every trading company. Mortgage and charge debts, car loans, insurance premiums, credit card debts, secured consumer loans, equipment loans, freights (including sub-freights), rentals from real and personal property, debts for goods sold or services rendered, are all receivables. So important is this category of liquid assets that Macleod was compelled to write over a hundred years ago:

> . . . if we were asked—who made the discovery which has most deeply affected the fortunes of the human race? We think, after full consideration we might safely answer—the man who first discovered that a debt is a saleable commodity.[2] When Daniel Webster said that credit has done more a thousand times to enrich nations than all the mines of the world, he meant discovery that a debt is a saleable chattel.[3]

A hundred years on, nothing has diminished the importance of receivables as a basis for raising money. If anything, the indications are to the contrary. In developed economies the bulk of corporate wealth is locked up in debts. The recycling of these valuable assets as well as their utilisation in the provision of working capital is the primary focus of this book. As would be expected both the recycling and utilisation take a variety of forms. Receivables could be, and frequently are, discounted either privately or in the money markets. Also they may be, and often are, assigned or charged as security for a loan, or an overdraft or other revolving credit facility. Between discounting and security lies a third possibility—outright assignment in discharge or reduction of a pre-existing debt, very little known and almost completely ignored in discussions of forms and patterns of receivables financing. There could also be more complex combinations of these. Normative arguments as to which form is better are not useful because there is no absolute, universal objective criterion by reference to which their relative merits may be ascertained. A number of considerations are relevant to the choice of any one form. The technique chosen will normally reflect the desire to give the company a financing package tailored to meet its own particular circumstances and needs.

---

[*] See generally, RM Goode *Commercial Law* (3rd edn, 2004), pp 744–752; RM Goode *Legal Problems of Credit and Security* (3rd edn, 2003), Ch V. For detailed analysis, see F Oditah *Legal Aspects of Receivables Financing* (1991); N Ruddy, S Mills and N Davidson *Salinger on Factoring* (4th edn, 2006).

Footnotes

1 In one sense receivables financing means financing the creation of contractual receivables. This is usually the sense in which the related expression 'stock-in-trade financing' is used. Since every going concern necessarily generates receivables, the financing of receivables would in this sense be the financing of an enterprise. The expression, however, has a narrower meaning, namely, the raising of money on the strength of receivables.

2 Macleod *Principles of Economical Philosophy* (2nd edn, 1872), p 481, cited in I Gilmore *Security Interests in Personal Property* (1965), p 213, n 7.

3 Macleod *Elements of Economics* (1881), p 327, cited in I Gilmore, op cit, p 213, n 7.

NOTES

1. Like Dr Oditah's book, this chapter is concerned with the raising of money on the strength of receivables.

2. The term 'receivable' is not defined in English law. In this chapter it will be used to mean 'account receivable' which is 'the right to payment of a sum of money, whether presently or in the future, for goods supplied, services rendered or facilities made available, being a right not embodied in a negotiable instrument' (RM Goode *Legal Problems of Credit and Security* (3rd edn, 2003), para 3–01). The terms 'receivables' and 'book debts' are often used interchangeably. Unlike 'receivables', the term 'book debts' has been the subject of legal definition (see below, p 1046). However, as Dr Oditah has pointed out, the term 'receivables' is wider than 'book debts' and whilst it includes book debts, it is not limited to them (op cit, p 19).

3. A simple contract debt is a *pure* receivable (or 'account receivable' as we have termed it in the previous note). If the debtor tenders a bill of exchange or promissory note in payment of the debt then the negotiable instrument is a *documentary* receivable. This is because the negotiable instrument contains an independent payment obligation which, at least in a general sense, acts in substitution for the payment obligation arising out of the underlying pure receivable (see above, Chapter 15). In consequence, a security over receivables would cover both pure receivables and negotiable instruments tendered in payment by the obligor (*Siebe Gorman & Co Ltd v Barclays Bank Ltd* [1979] 2 Lloyd's Rep 142). On the other hand, negotiable instruments tendered as *security* for payment, but not as payment, in no sense act as a substitute for the underlying pure receivable and are not to be classified as documentary receivables (see Oditah, above, pp 26–27).

(b) Financing techniques: sale or charge

If a trader wants to convert his receivables into cash he can either sell them or mortgage (or charge) them as security for a loan, overdraft or other form of revolving credit. Outright assignment in discharge or reduction of a pre-existing debt is a species of sale (Oditah, above, p 33). Technically, there is no sale when receivables are assigned in repayment of an advance made under a financing agreement. The advance is not the purchase price of the receivables and does not provide the consideration necessary for a sale (Oditah, above, p 71).

The sale of receivables often takes the form of an assignment of a trader's book debts to the financier ('factor') under a factoring agreement (see below, p 1026). It could also involve the block discounting of hire-purchase or credit sale agreements (see below, p 1033). However, other 'sale' mechanisms may also be used (eg a sale and agency agreement, as used in *Welsh Development Agency v Export Finance Co Ltd* [1992] BCLC 148, see below).

A financier who advances cash to a trader may take a mortgage of, or charge over, the trader's receivables as security. A mortgage of a debt is an assignment (statutory or equitable) of it upon terms, express or implied, that it is to be reassigned to the transferor when the obligation which it secures has been discharged. Before reassignment the mortgagee has a proprietary interest in the debt. A charge on a debt (which can only be an *equitable* charge) is a mere incumbrance giving the chargee a preferential right to, but not ownership of, the debt. However, the default provisions in the charge usually confer on the chargee (1) a power of attorney to convert the charge into a mortgage by executing an assignment in the name of the chargor, and (2) a power to appoint a receiver. According to Dr Oditah, '[t]hese powers diminish to vanishing point, any remaining distinction between a charge and a mortgage' (above, at p 96). For further consideration of the distinction between a mortgage and a charge, see R M Goode [1984] JBL 172; and below, Chapter 26.

Securitisation of receivables has become an important source of finance for institutional investors. It can be contrasted with factoring which is mainly used to provide finance for the manufacturing sector. Securitisation involves raising finance by packaging together pools of receivables (eg home mortgages, finance leases, hire-purchase agreements, conditional sale agreements and trade receivables) and then selling them to a special-purpose company. Typically, the special-purpose company raises the purchase price through loan notes issued in the securities market. The loan notes are secured on the receivables. The difference between the interest rate paid to the noteholders and that paid on the original loan by the borrower represents the transferor's profit margin. As securitisation involves either an outright sale or a sale coupled with a sub-charge, it will not be given separate consideration in this chapter. For further details, see PR Wood, *Project Finance, Securitisations, Subordinated Debt* (2nd edn, 2007), Chs 6–9.

(c) How do you distinguish between a sale and a security transaction?

In determining whether a security has been created the courts look to the substance rather than the form of the transaction.

Welsh Development Agency v Export Finance Co Ltd
[1992] BCLC 148, Court of Appeal

The defendant (Exfinco) provided finance to a company called Parrot Corp Ltd (Parrot) which sold computer floppy disks to overseas buyers. The finance was provided under the terms of a Master Agreement whereby Parrot first sold the floppy disks to Exfmco and then resold the same disks to overseas buyers as Exfinco's agent. The sale to Exfinco was at a discount to the resale price as Exfinco would pay Parrot in advance of receiving payment from the overseas buyers. Later Parrot created a charge over its book debts in favour of the plaintiff (WDA). When Parrot went into receivership WDA claimed that moneys owed by the overseas buyers to Parrot were subject to its charge (which had been duly registered). Exfinco claimed to be entitled to these moneys as payment for the goods which it owned and which had been sold on its behalf by Parrot as its agent. One of the main issues was whether the Master Agreement had created a charge on the assets of Parrot which was void for non-registration under s 395 of the Companies Act 1985 (a similar provision is now to be found in s 874 of the Companies

Act 2006: see below, p 1045). Exfinco claimed that the Agreement effected a sale of goods and not a charge on the goods. Reversing Browne-Wilkinson V-C, the Court of Appeal held the Master Agreement to have effected a sale of goods and gave judgment for Exfinco.

Dillon LJ: I turn then to issue 2: were the transactions under the master agreement by way of sale or secured loan?

It is not suggested that the master agreement was in any sense a sham or that its terms did not represent the true agreement between the parties. Moreover it is not suggested in this case, as it was in *Lloyds & Scottish Finance Ltd v Cyril Lord Carpet Sales Ltd* ([1992] BCLC 609), that in what they actually did the parties had departed from what was provided for by the master agreement, and that therefore they ought to be treated as having made some fresh agreement by conduct in the place of the master agreement.

What is said is that in determining the legal categorisation of an agreement and its legal consequences the court looks at the substance of the transaction and not at the labels which the parties have chosen to put on it.

This is trite law, but it is law which has fallen to be applied in different types of cases where different factors are the relevant factors for consideration. It is therefore not surprising that the words used by eminent judges in different cases in applying the principle do not all fit very harmoniously together.

Thus the task of looking for the substance of the parties' agreement and disregarding the labels they have used may arise in a case where their written agreement is a sham intended to mask their true agreement. The task of the courts there is to discover by extrinsic evidence what their true agreement was and to disregard, if inconsistent with the true agreement, the written words of the sham agreement. This is discussed in the judgments of Diplock and Russell LJJ in *Snook v London and West Riding Investments Ltd* [1961] 1 All ER 518, [1967] 2 QB 786 and is exemplified by some of the cases cited in *Street v Mountford* [1985] 2 All ER 289, [1985] AC 809 and *AG Securities v Vaughan* [1988] 3 All ER 1058, [1990] 1 AC 417 where in an endeavour to set up a licence to occupy, rather than a tenancy of, residential accommodation the landlord had introduced into the agreement terms purportedly reserving to himself a right to introduce further occupants which were plainly inconsistent with the real intention.

But the question can also arise where, without any question of sham, there is some objective criterion in law by which the court can test whether the agreement the parties have made does or does not fall into the legal category in which the parties have sought to place their agreement. One can see that in the comments of Lord Templeman in *Street v Mountford* [1985] 2 All ER 289 at 298, [1985] AC 809 at 824 on the case of *Shell-Mex and BP Ltd v Manchester Garages Ltd* [1971] 1 All ER 841, [1971] 1 WLR 612, where the defendant had been allowed to use a petrol company's filling station for the purposes of selling petrol, and the question was whether the transaction was a licence or a tenancy. Lord Templeman said that the agreement was only personal in its nature and therefore a licence if it did not confer the right to exclusive occupation of the filling station, since no other test for distinguishing between a contractual tenancy and a contractual licence appeared to be understandable or workable.

In the present case Mr Moss QC asserts for WDA that there are, on the authorities, clearly laid down criteria for what is a charge, that all those criteria are present in the present case in the master agreement, and that the master agreement is therefore necessarily as a matter of law a charge, whatever the parties may have called it or thought it was.

He relies in particular on the passage in the judgment of Romer LJ in *Re George Inglefield Ltd* [1933] Ch 1 at 27–28, [1932] All ER Rep 244 at 256–257 where Romer LJ sets out what he regarded as the essential differences between a transaction of sale and a transaction of mortgage or charge. These were three, viz:

[i] In a transaction of sale the vendor is not entitled to get back the subject-matter of the sale by returning to the purchaser the money that has passed between them. In the case of a mortgage or charge, the mortgagor is entitled, until he has been foreclosed, to get back the subject-matter of

the mortgage or charge by returning to the mortgagee the money that has passed between them, [ii]...if the mortgagee realises the subject-matter of the mortgage for a sum more than sufficient to repay him, with interest and the costs, the money that has passed between him and the mortgagor he has to account to the mortgagor for the surplus. If the purchaser sells the subject-matter of the purchase, and realizes a profit, of course he has not got to account to the vendor for the profit, [iii]...if the mortgagee realizes the mortgaged property for a sum that is insufficient to repay him the money that [has been] paid to the mortgagor, together with interest and costs, then the mortgagee is entitled to recover from the mortgagor the balance of the money...If the purchaser were to resell the purchased property at a price which was insufficient to recoup him the money that he had paid to the vendor...he would not be entitled to recover the balance from the vendor.

But these indicia do not have the clarity of the distinction between a tenancy and a licence to occupy, viz that it must be a tenancy if the grantee has been given exclusive occupation of the property in question. In particular it is clear from *Re George Inglefield Ltd,* and the *Lloyds & Scottish* case, (a) that there may be a sale of book debts, and not a charge, even though the purchaser has recourse against the vendor to recover the shortfall if the debtor fails to pay the debt in full and (b) that there may be a sale of book debts, even though the purchaser may have to make adjustments and payments to the vendor after the full amounts of the debts have been got in from the debtors. As to the latter see especially the judgment of Lord Hanworth MR in *Re George Inglefield Ltd* [1933] Ch 1 at 20.

In my judgment there is no one clear touchstone by which it can necessarily and inevitably be said that a document which is not a sham and which is expressed as an agreement for sale must necessarily, as a matter of law, amount to no more than the creation of a mortgage or charge on the property expressed to be sold. It is necessary therefore to look at the provisions in the master agreement as a whole to decide whether in substance it amounts to an agreement for the sale of goods or only to a mortgage or charge on goods and their proceeds.

[Ralph Gibson LJ delivered a similar judgment.]

Staughton LJ:

Sale or charge?

(a) *The test*

We were referred to a bewildering array of authority on this topic, some of it by no means easy to reconcile. The problem is not made any easier by the variety of language that has been used: substance, truth, reality, genuine are good words; disguise, cloak, mask, colourable device, label, form, artificial, sham, stratagem and pretence are 'bad names', to adopt the phrase quoted by Dixon J in *Palette Shoes Pty Ltd v Krohn* (1937) 58 CLR 1 at 28. It is necessary to discover, if one can, the ideas which these words are intended to convey.

One can start from the position that statute law in this country, when it enacts rules to be applied to particular transactions, is in general referring to the legal nature of a transaction and not to its economic effect. The leading authority on this point, albeit in a case from Malaya, is the advice of Lord Devlin in *Chow Yoong Hong v Choong Fah Rubber Manufactory Ltd* [1961] 3 All ER 1163 at 1167, [1962] AC 209 at 216:

There are many ways of raising cash besides borrowing...If in form it is not a loan, it is not to the point to say that its object was to raise money for one of them or that the parties could have produced the same result more conveniently by borrowing and lending money.

See too the *Crowther Committee's Report on Consumer Credit* (Cmnd 4596 (1971)) para 1.3.6, where it was said that the existing law was deficient because:

It lacks any functional basis: distinctions between one type of transaction and another are drawn on the basis of legal abstractions rather than on the basis of commercial reality.

There are in my opinion two routes by which this principle can be overcome. The first, which I will call the external route, is to show that the written document does not represent the agreement of the parties. It may, if one wishes, then be called a sham, a cloak or a device. The second is the internal route, when one looks only at the written agreement, in order to ascertain from its terms whether it amounts to a transaction of the legal nature which the parties ascribe to it. These two routes are described, for example, by Lord Hanworth MR in *Re George Inglefield Ltd* [1933] Ch 1 at 19, 23, [1932] All ER Rep 244 at 252, 254, by Maugham LJ in *Re Lovegrove* [1935] Ch 464 at 496, [1935] All ER Rep 749 at 759, and by Knox J in *Re Curtain Dream plc* [1990] BCLC 925 at 937. (I express no view on the way that Knox J described the second route or the result which he reached; an appeal is pending.)

The Welsh Agency do not rely on the external route in this case. They disclaim any argument that the master agreement was a sham. It is not therefore necessary for me to consider the external route in any detail, except for the purpose of showing what this appeal is *not* about. One can show that the written document does not reflect the agreement of the parties by proving a collateral agreement, or at least a common intention, to that effect. Or there may be proof of a subsequent variation, as was argued in *Lloyds & Scottish Finance Ltd v Cyril Lord Carpets Sales Ltd* ([1992] BCLC 609)…

There was here no sham, no collateral agreement or common intention to be bound by different terms, and no subsequent variation to that effect. So I can leave the external route, and turn to an internal consideration of the master agreement itself. This must be carried out on the basis that the parties intended to be bound by its terms, and by nothing else.

If one part of the agreement purports to create a particular legal transaction, it may happen that other provisions are inconsistent with such a transaction. The task of the court is then to ascertain which is the substance, the truth, the reality. That was plainly the approach of Lord Herschell LC in *McEntire v Crossley Bros Ltd* [1895] AC 457 at 463–466, [1895–99] All ER Rep 829 at 832–833, where there are repeated references to inconsistency. See also the speech of Lord Watson where he said ([1895] AC 457 at 467, [1895–99] All ER Rep 829 at 834):

> The duty of a Court is to examine every part of the agreement, every stipulation which it contains, and to consider their mutual bearing upon each other; but it is entirely beyond the function of a Court to discard the plain meaning of any term in the agreement unless there can be found within its four corners other language and other stipulations which necessarily deprive such term of its primary significance.

Mr Moss argued that the court is free to disregard the label which the parties have attached to a transaction. If by label one means the description which is found on the backsheet, or even in a preamble or a recital, I can see that it should be given little if any weight. A label can also be found elsewhere. Thus in *Street v Mountford* [1985] 2 All ER 289, [1985] AC 809, Mrs Mountford agreed 'to take' a furnished room; the references to 'licence' in the agreement were in truth labels and nothing more. 'Licence' was the name by which the agreement described itself. And in *AG Securities v Vaughan* [1988] 2 All ER 309 at 315, [1990] 1 AC 417 at 444 Bingham LJ said that:

> …the true legal nature of a transaction is not to be altered by the description the parties choose to give it.

In my judgment the correct process, when one is following the internal route, is to look at the operative parts of the document, in order to discover what legal transaction they provide for. If some parts appear to be inconsistent with others in this respect, a decision must be made between the two. This is what I understand by ascertaining the substance of the transaction. The cases on whether an agreement provides for a licence or tenancy—*Street v Mountford, AG Securities v Vaughan* and *Asian v Murphy (Nos 1 and 2)* [1989] 3 All ER 130, [1990] 1 WLR 766—do not in my opinion overturn this well-established doctrine. Nor does the decision of the majority of this court in *Gisborne v Burton* [1988] 3 All ER 760, [1989] QB 390. There it was held, with reference to the Agricultural Holdings Act

1948, that one must look at the scheme of a preordained series of transactions as a whole, instead of concentrating on each pre-ordained step individually. The doctrine of revenue law, derived from *W T Ramsay Ltd v IRC* [1981] 1 All ER 865, [1982] AC 300 and other cases, was thus extended to private transactions. I do not need to consider whether it should also be extended to this case; there is no series of transactions here, but only the one master agreement.

It can be said that Exfinco have adopted their method of business because their customers wished to avoid the registration provisions of the Companies Act, and the appearance of loans in their balance sheets. But one should not, from sympathy for creditors or rather for a debenture holder, overthrow both established law and recognised methods of providing finance for trade and industry.

NOTES

1.   The classic formulation of the sham doctrine is found in *Snook v London and West Riding Investments Ltd* [1967] 2 QB 786, where Diplock LJ said (at 802) that a 'sham':

means acts done or documents executed by the parties to the 'sham' which are intended by them to give to third parties or to the court the appearance of creating between the parties legal rights and obligations different from the actual legal rights and obligations (if any) which the parties intend to create. One thing I think, however, is clear in legal principle, morality and the authorities (see *Yorkshire Railway Wagon Co v Maclure* (1882) 21 Ch D 309 and *Stoneleigh Finance Ltd v Phillips* [1965] 2 QB 537), that for acts or documents to be a 'sham', with whatever legal consequences follow from this, all the parties thereto must have a common intention that the acts or documents are not to create the legal rights and obligations which they give the appearance of creating.

The *Snook* definition of a sham has been cited with approval in many cases (see, eg *IRC v McGuckian* [1997] 1 WLR 991 at 1001, per Lord Steyn; *Norglen Ltd v Reeds Rains Prudential Ltd* [1999] 2 AC 1 at 13, per Lord Hoffmann). However, in *Hitch v Stone* [2001] EWCA Civ 63, [2001] STC 214 at [63], Arden LJ indicated that the *Snook* definition related only to one particular type of sham. She developed the point in *Bankway Properties Ltd v Pensfold-Dunsford* [2001] EWCA Civ 528, [2001] 1 WLR 1369, where there could be no finding of a *Snook*-type sham because the parties (landlord and tenant) had no common intention to disguise the true nature of the transaction. Instead Arden LJ (but not Pill LJ, the other member of the court) relied on a second type of sham that she said did not depend on 'common intention' but operated: (a) where there was legislation that it was impossible to contract out of; and (b) the court inferred from the evidence (i) that a party never intended to exercise or enforce a right given to him by a particular clause in the contract and (ii) that the purpose of the clause was to make it appear that the contract was of a type which was outside the legislation.

2.   It is rare for an agreement or document to be held a sham. In *National Westminster Bank plc v Jones* [2001] 1 BCLC 98 at [59] (affd [2002] 1 BCLC 55 without discussion of the issue), Neuberger J explains why:

In one sense, lawyers find it difficult to grapple with the concept of sham, presumably on the basis that, subject to questions of mistake... there is a very strong presumption indeed that parties intend to be bound by the provisions of agreements into which they enter, and, even more, intend the agreements they enter into to take effect....Because a finding of sham carries with it a finding of dishonesty, because innocent third parties may often rely upon the genuineness of a provision or an agreement, and because the court places great weight on the existence and provisions of a formally signed document, there is a strong and natural presumption against holding a provision or a document a sham.

3. Several comments can be made about the various statements made by Dillon and Staughton LJJ in the *Exfinco* case:

- The statement made by Staughton LJ that statute law usually focuses on the legal nature of a transaction and not to its economic effect must now be considered in the light of the dicta of Lord Hoffmann in *MacNiven v Westmoreland Investments Ltd* [2001] UKHL 6, [2001] 1 All ER 865. In that case, which involved the interpretation of tax legislation, Lord Hoffmann said that a term in legislation must first be construed to see whether it was intended to refer to a legal concept or a commercial concept. There seems no doubt according to what Lord Hoffmann said in *MacNiven* (at [33]) that this distinction between juristic and commercial concepts is not confined to tax legislation. If this approach were adopted generally by the courts, there would be a real risk that title finance arrangements could be recharacterised according to their economic function and not their legal nature for some purposes. Moreover, there would be considerable uncertainty as to whether a term in a statute referred to commercial concepts as opposed to purely legal ones (it does seem, however, that when s 874 of the Companies Act 2006 refers to a 'charge', it refers to a purely legal concept: see *Lloyds & Scottish Finance Ltd v Cyril Lord Carpet Sales Ltd* [1992] BCLC 609 at 616, per Lord Wilberforce). However, the House of Lords has since downplayed Lord Hoffmann's distinction between legal concepts and commercial concepts. In *Barclays Mercantile Business Finance Ltd v Mawson (Inspector of Taxes)* [2004] UKHL 51, [2005] 1 AC 684, another case involving the interpretation of tax legislation, Lord Nicholls delivered the opinion of a Judicial Committee which included Lord Hoffmann himself. The Committee said (at [38]) that they did not think that Lord Hoffmann's distinction between legal concepts and commercial concepts was intended to provide a substitute for a close analysis of what the statute meant. It certainly did not justify the assumption that an answer could be obtained by classifying all concepts *a priori* as either 'commercial' or 'legal' for that 'would be the very negation of purposive construction'.

- The internal route is also sometimes called the 'four corners' approach (see *McEntire v Crossley Bros Ltd* [1895] AC 457 at 467, per Lord Watson). The idea is that in searching for the substance of an agreement the court construes the wording of the agreement as a whole. It does not ignore the plain meaning of a term unless there can be found within the four corners of the agreement other language which necessarily deprives the term of its primary significance. But it is not literally true to say that only the contractual document itself must be examined. The court may, under the internal route, have regard to the surrounding circumstances and other relevant factors outside the document in accordance with the normal rules relating to the construction of contracts generally (see Lord Hoffmann in *Investors Compensation Scheme Ltd v West Bromwich Building Society* [1998] 1 WLR 896 at 912, and also in *BCCI SA v Ali* [2001] UKHL 8, [2002] 1 AC 251 at 269). In *Re Spectrum Plus Ltd (in liquidation)* [2005] UKHL 41, [2005] 2 AC 680, where a clause that purported to create a fixed charge over the chargor's book debts was contained in a standard form bank debenture, the House of Lords adopted a similarly broad approach to contract construction. Lord Walker stated (at [159]) that '[t]he wish to achieve legal certainty by the use of a standard precedent cannot override the need to construe any document in its commercial context.' It seems that even the conduct of the parties after execution of the agreement may be relevant to the issue of characterisation of their agreement (see *Agnew v IRC* [2001] UKPC 28, [2001] 2 AC 710, at [48], per Lord Millett), although, as this runs against a well-established principle of contract interpretation (see, eg *Whitworth Street Estates Ltd v Miller* [1970] AC 583, 603, per Lord Reid), the point is controversial (see *Re Spectrum Plus Ltd*, above, at [160], per Lord Walker; and also S Atherton and RJ Mokal (2005) 26 Company Lawyer 10, 16–18).

- Dillon LJ referred to 'objective criterion in law by which the court can test whether the agreement the parties have made does not fall into the legal category in which the parties have sought to place their agreement'. The objective criterion will vary according to context. In the *Exfinco* case the court had to consider the criterion for distinguishing a sale from a charge. The criterion was not easy to identify as 'there is no one clear touchstone' (per Dillon LJ). Moreover, in *Orion Finance Ltd v Crown Financial Management Ltd* [1996] 2 BCLC 78 at 84–85, Millett LJ stressed that there was no single objective criterion by which it is possible to determine whether a transaction is one of sale and repurchase or of security. In other contexts, the criterion may be easier to identify. The right to exclusive occupation is recognised as the central characteristic of a lease which distinguishes it from a licence (*Street v Mountford* [1985] AC 809, HL). The chargor's right to deal with the charged asset for its own account is recognised as the badge of a floating charge and is inconsistent with a fixed charge (*Agnew v IRC*, above, at [13], per Lord Millett; *Re Spectrum Plus Ltd*, above, at [106]–[107], [111]–[112], per Lord Scott, and at [138]-[140], per Lord Walker).

- In *Agnew v IRC* (above), the Privy Council held that a charge over uncollected book debts, which was expressed to be a fixed charge, was, in law, a floating charge because the charge left the chargor company free to collect the debts and use the proceeds in the ordinary course of its business (see below, p 1053). Lord Millett (at [32]) explained the process of characterisation in the following terms:

> The question is not merely one of construction. In deciding whether a charge is a fixed charge or a floating charge, the court is engaged in a two-stage process. At the first stage it must construe the instrument of charge and seek to gather the intentions of the parties from the language they have used. But the object at this stage of the process is not to discover whether the parties intended to create a fixed or a floating charge. It is to ascertain the nature of the rights and obligations which the parties intended to grant each other in respect of the charged assets. Once these have been ascertained, the court can then embark on the second stage of the process, which is one of categorisation. This is a matter of law. It does not depend on the intention of the parties. If their intention, properly gathered from the language of the instrument, is to grant the company rights in respect of the charged assets which are inconsistent with the nature of a fixed charge, then the charge cannot be a fixed charge however they may have chosen to describe it.

Despite the fact that *Agnew* is a decision of the Privy Council, and so not binding on an English court, the authoritative status of Lord Millett's statement cannot be doubted. In any event, Lord Millett's approach to characterisation was later applied by Lord Hoffmann, when delivering the main judgment for a unanimous House of Lords in *Smith v Bridgend County Borough Council* [2001] UKHL 58, [2002] 1 AC 336 at [42]. *Agnew v IRC* was also cited several times, with evident approval, by the House of Lords in *Re Spectrum Plus Ltd*, above, at [106]–[107], per Lord Scott, and at [141] and [151], per Lord Walker.

- It is submitted that Lord Millett's approach to characterisation in *Agnew* is broadly similar to the internal approach adopted by the Court of Appeal in the *Exfinco* case (for the contrary view, see A Berg [2003] JBL 205). In *Exfinco*, the Court of Appeal held that, absent a sham, the court would ignore the labels used by the parties if the rights and obligations created by the documents were inconsistent with those labels. But how is a court to do this unless it knows what the labels mean? This is why Dillon LJ referred to the need for some objective criterion in law by which the court could test the agreement the parties had made. In essence, in following this approach the court is doing no more than that outlined by Lord Millett in *Agnew*: (a) construing the agreement to ascertain the intention of the parties as to their respective rights and obligations, and (b) measuring those rights and obligations against the objective legal criterion of the type of transaction in issue.

4.   In *Re Curtain Dream plc* [1990] BCLC 925, a company obtained a credit line from a financier. Under the terms of the financing agreement, the company was to sell goods to the financier and then repurchase those goods at an increased price. The financier would pay for the goods as soon as it received a bill of exchange, accepted by the company, which provided for payment of the increased sum at the end of a credit period. Until payment had been made, the financier retained title to the goods under the terms of the resale contract. Knox J held the transaction to be one of loan secured by a charge over the goods and not one of sale and resale with a retention of title clause being part of the resale. He held that the most important factor indicating a charge was that the financier was obliged to retransfer the goods back to the company, as this gave the company an equity of redemption in the goods.

5.   An option to repurchase is treated differently from an equity of redemption. As Millett LJ emphasised in *Orion Finance Ltd v Crown Financial Management Ltd* [1996] 2 BCLC 78 at 84:

The transaction may take the form of a sale with an option to repurchase, and this is not to be equated with a right of redemption merely because the repurchase price is calculated by reference to the original sale price together with interest since the date of sale. On the other hand, the presence of a right of recourse by the transferee against the transferor to recover a shortfall may be inconsistent with a sale, but it is not necessarily so, and its absence is not conclusive.

In factoring and block discounting agreements the vendor is usually placed under an obligation to repurchase a factored or discounted receivable which cannot be recovered from the debtor for any reason, including the insolvency of the debtor, but such repurchase or recourse arrangements do not create an equity of redemption and do not turn a sale of receivables into a secured loan (*Olds Discount Co Ltd v John Playfair Ltd* [1938] 3 All ER 275; *Lloyds and Scottish Finance Ltd v Cyril Lord Carpets Sales Ltd* [1992] BCLC 609, HL). This is because the obligation to repurchase in a factoring or block discounting agreement only arises on the happening of an uncertain future event (non-recovery from the debtor), whereas an absolute obligation to repurchase ought to lead to the conclusion that the purported sale is only a sham masking a mortgage or charge which is in reality the substance of the transaction (F Oditah *Legal Aspects of Receivables Financing* (1991), pp 38–39).

6.   For further discussion of the process of recharacterisation: see A Berg 'Recharacterisation' [2001] JIBFL 346; A Berg 'Recharacterisation after Enron' [2003] JBL 205; R Hooley 'Recharacterisation', Ch 3 in D Neo, TH Wu and M Hor (eds), *Lives in the Law: Essays in Honour of Peter Ellinger, Koh Kheng Lian & Tan Sook Yee* (2007), pp 30–51.

QUESTIONS

1.   If the terms of the financing agreement consistently indicate a sale, and this is not a sham, will the courts take into account that a financier's real function is the lending of money when assessing whether the transaction is really one of loan secured by a charge? See *Olds Discount Co Ltd v Cohen* [1938] 3 All ER 281n.

2.   If the financing agreement provides for the sale of receivables, will the courts hold the agreement to be a sham if it can be shown that the parties operated the agreement in a manner different from that envisaged in it? See *Lloyds and Scottish Finance Ltd v Cyril Lord Carpets Sales Ltd* [1992] BCLC 609, HL.

(d) Why is the distinction important?

See the extract from Romer LJ's judgment in *Re George Inglefield Ltd* [1933] Ch 1, which appears above, p 1020. In addition:

(1) a sale of receivables need not be registered (but see s 344 of the Insolvency Act 1986, below, p 1043); a 'charge' over a company's receivables must generally be registered (above, p 862);

(2) even if registered, a mortgage of, or charge over, a company's receivables may be set aside on the company's administration or liquidation because it is deemed a preference, transaction at an undervalue, extortionate credit bargain, floating charge created during the relevant time, or an attempt to defraud creditors (see Insolvency Act 1986, ss 238, 239, 244, 245, 423–425; considered below, pp 1232ff); a sale is unlikely to be avoided on any of these grounds, save that it could be reopened if the level of 'discount' given to the financier is deemed to be extortionate (see F Oditah *Legal Aspects of Receivables Financing* (1991), p 43);

(3) a sale of receivables is liable to *ad valorem* duty on the instruments by which the sale is effected and VAT; a loan secured by a mortgage or charge is not liable to stamp duty and is exempt from VAT;

(4) the creation of additional debt or security may be prohibited by the terms of an existing debenture but a sale would fall outside such a restriction (although it is now usual for the terms of a prohibition to extend to *all* forms of dealing with the company's receivables).

2 FINANCING BY SALE

(a) Factoring

'Some Aspects of Factoring Law—1: The Acquisition of Rights in the Receivables' by R M Goode
[1982] JBL 240, pp 240–241

STRUCTURE OF A FACTORING TRANSACTION

Factoring is a transaction by which one person (the supplier or 'client') supplying goods or services to trade customers on short-term credit assigns the resulting receivables to another, the factor, upon terms that the assignment is to be notified to the debtors[1] and the factor is to collect in the receivables direct, assume responsibility for the maintenance of the relevant accounts and, within agreed limits, bear the risk of default in payment by customers. Factoring is thus a useful method of improving the supplier's liquidity. This could be done either by selling the receivables outright, or by mortgaging or charging them. Hitherto, factoring has almost invariably been carried out by way of outright sale, thus avoiding the need to register an assignment of receivables as a charge on book debts.[2]

Receivables which the factor is prepared to purchase without recourse are termed 'approved' receivables. These are receivables arising from transactions specifically approved by the factor or falling within an agreed limit authorised to be given to a particular customer. It is usual for factoring to be conducted on a 'whole turnover' basis, that is to say, the client offers or assigns all his receivables to the factor. Those which are not approved (termed 'unapproved' receivables) are purchased on a recourse basis. The factor thus provides a collection and accounting service and, as regards approved receivables, credit protection. In addition, instead of deferring payment for the receivables until the date they mature[3] ('maturity factoring') the factor will normally agree to allow the client to draw up to 80 per cent of the price in advance, charging the client a discount for the period the factor is out of his money.

Relations between the factor and the client are governed by a master agreement, the factoring agreement, which incorporates detailed undertakings and warranties by the client in relation to the receivables and the underlying contracts. Breach of these in relation to any receivable will usually render that receivable unapproved and entitle the factor to debit back the price.

Footnotes

1 Usually by a notice of assignment stamped on the invoice. Notification is what distinguishes full factoring from invoice discounting (or non-notification factoring). The latter is a pure financial facility.
2 Under [ss 860–874] of the Companies Act [2006]. Where the client is a sole trader or partnership firm, the assignment will usually be registrable [under s 344 of the Insolvency Act 1986].
3 Or, in the case of approved receivables, the date of the customer's insolvency, if this occurs before maturity.

NOTES

1.   Assignment lies at the heart of factoring. It is important, therefore, to keep in mind the general law relating to the assignment of choses in action when considering factoring arrangements (see above, Chapter 22). However, when negotiable paper is discounted before maturity, the discounting is by negotiation and not by assignment.

2.   There are two types of agreement commonly used by factors. Factoring may take place under a 'whole turnover' agreement whereby the client agrees to sell, and the factor agrees to buy, all the client's receivables. The receivables vest in the factor as they come into existence. By contrast, factoring can also take place under a 'facultative' agreement which provides for the client to offer receivables for sale to the factor at agreed intervals and for acceptance of each offer by the factor as regards those receivables he is willing to purchase. The factor is under no obligation to purchase such receivables as are offered to him. The facultative agreement simply provides a set of putative terms which will govern specific transactions as and when they are entered into (RM Goode [1982] JBL 240, p 241). Under a facultative agreement, receivables vest in the factor only when he has accepted the client's offer to sell. The whole turnover and facultative agreements just described are valid only as equitable assignments. As such, they convey or transfer property (ie debts) from the client to the factor.

3.   A copy of a master 'factoring agreement' (hereafter referred to as the 'MFA') appears as Form 5 in the Appendix. Is it a 'whole turnover' or a 'facultative' agreement?

Can future receivables be factored?

The common law has long set itself against the idea that the transfer of future property (or after-acquired property) creates proprietary rights even after acquisition of the property by the transferor. The common law usually requires some new act of transfer after acquisition to vest a proprietary interest in the transferee. The position is different in equity. The next case is the landmark decision in this area.

Holroyd v Marshall
(1862) 10 HL Cas 191, House of Lords

T (mortgagor) mortgaged mill machinery to secure his indebtedness to H (mortgagee). The mortgage deed (later registered as a bill of sale) contained a covenant by the mortgagor that all machinery placed in the mill in addition to, or in substitution for, the original machinery should be subject to the mortgage. The mortgagor did sell and exchange some of the original machinery, and introduced new machinery. The issue was whether the mortgagee had an interest in respect of the new machinery purchased and introduced after the date of the deed, which prevailed over subsequent execution creditors of the mortgagor. The House of Lords held that the mortgagee had a prevailing equitable interest in the new machinery.

Lord Westbury LC: My Lords, the question is, whether as to the machinery added and substituted since the date of the mortgage the title of the mortgagees, or that of the judgment creditor, ought to prevail. It is admitted that the judgment creditor has no title as to the machinery originally comprised in the bill of sale; but it is contended that the mortgagees had no specific estate or interest in the future machinery. It is also admitted that if the mortgagees had an equitable estate in the added machinery, the same could not be taken in execution by the judgment creditor.

The question may be easily decided by the application of a few elementary principles long settled in the Courts of Equity. In equity it is not necessary for the alienation of property that there should be a formal deed of conveyance. A contract for valuable consideration, by which it is agreed to make a present transfer of property, passes at once the beneficial interest, provided the contract is one of which a Court of Equity will decree specific performance. In the language of Lord Hardwicke, the vendor becomes a trustee for the vendee; subject, of course, to the contract being one to be specifically performed. And this is true, not only of contracts relating to real estate, but also of contracts relating to personal property, provided that the latter are such as a Court of Equity would direct to be specifically performed....

There can be no doubt, therefore, that if the mortgage deed in the present case had contained nothing but the contract which is involved in the aforesaid covenant of Taylor, the mortgagor, such contract would have amounted to a valid assignment in equity of the whole of the machinery and chattels in question, supposing such machinery to have been in existence and upon the mill at the time of the execution of the deed.

But it is alleged that this is not the effect of the contract, because is relates to machinery not existing at the time, but to be acquired and fixed and placed in the mill at a future time. It is quite true that a deed which professes to convey property which is not in existence at the time is as a conveyance void at law, simply because there is nothing to convey. So in equity a contract which engages to transfer property, which is not in existence, cannot operate as an immediate alienation merely because there is nothing to transfer.

But if a vendor or mortgagor agrees to sell or mortgage property, real or personal, of which he is not possessed at the time, and he receives the consideration for the contract, and afterwards becomes possessed of property answering the description in the contract, there is no doubt that a Court of

Equity would compel him to perform the contract, and that the contract would, in equity, transfer the beneficial interest to the mortgagee or purchaser immediately on the property being acquired. This, of course, assumes that the supposed contract is one of that class of which a Court of Equity would decree the specific performance. If it be so, then immediately on the acquisition of the property described the vendor or mortgagor would hold it in trust for the purchaser or mortgagee, according to the terms of the contract. For if a contract be in other respects good and fit to be performed, and the consideration has been received, incapacity to perform it at the time of its execution will be no answer when the means of doing so are afterwards obtained.

Apply these familiar principles to the present case; it follows that immediately on the new machinery and effects being fixed or placed into the mill, they became subject to the operation of the contract, and passed in equity to the mortgagees, to whom Taylor was bound to make a legal conveyance, and for whom he, in the meantime, was a trustee of the property in question.

There is another criterion to prove that the mortgagee acquired an estate or interest in the added machinery as soon as it was brought into the mill. If afterwards the mortgagor had attempted to remove any part of such machinery, except for the purpose of substitution, the mortgagee would have been entitled to an injunction to restrain such removal, and that because of his estate in the specific property. The result is, that the title of the Appellants is to be preferred to that of the judgment creditor.

[Lord Wensleydale concurred.
Lord Chelmsford delivered a concurring judgment.]

Holroyd v Marshall concerned goods. *Tailby v Official Receiver* extended the principle of *Holroyd v Marshall* to future book debts.

Tailby v Official Receiver

(1888) 13 App Cas 523, House of Lords

I compounded with his creditors. At F's request, T signed promissory notes in favour of those creditors and paid a large sum to them. T took from I a bill of sale as counter-security. The bill of sale assigned (*inter alia*) 'all the book debts due and owing or which may during the continuance of this security become due and owing to the said mortgagor'. The bill also contained a power of attorney and a proviso that if the mortgagor on demand failed to pay the amount due, the mortgagee could take possession and sell the mortgaged property. On I's bankruptcy an issue arose as to whether the assignment of future book debts generally, without any delimitation as to time, place, or amount, was too vague to be upheld. Reversing the judgment of the Court of Appeal, the House of Lords upheld the validity of the assignment.

Lord Watson: . . . The rule of equity which applies to the assignment of future choses in action is, as I understand it, a very simple one. Choses in action do not come within the scope of the Bills of Sale Acts, and though not yet existing, may nevertheless be the subject of present assignment. As soon as they come into existence, assignees who have given valuable consideration will, if the new chose in action is in the disposal of their assignor, take precisely the same right and interest as if it had actually belonged to him, or had been within his disposition and control at the time when the assignment was made. There is but one condition which must be fulfilled in order to make the assignee's right attach to a future chose in action, which is, that, on its coming into existence, it shall answer the description in the assignment or, in other words, that it shall be capable of being identified as the thing, or as one of the very things assigned. When there is no uncertainty as to its identification, the beneficial interest will immediately vest in the assignee. Mere difficulty in ascertaining all the things which are included in a general assignment, whether in esse or in posse, will not affect the assignee's right to those things which are capable of ascertainment or are identified. Lord Eldon said in *Lewis v Madocks* ((1803) 8 Ves

156): 'If the Courts find a solid subject of personal property they would attach it rather than render the contract nugatory.'

In the case of book debts, as in the case of choses in action generally, intimation of the assignee's right must be made to the debtor or obligee in order to make it complete. That is the only possession which he can attain, so long as the debt is unpaid, and is sufficient to take it out of the order and disposition of the assignor. In this case the appellant's right, if otherwise valid, was, in any question with the respondent, duly perfected by his notice to Wilson Brothers & Co before Izon became a bankrupt.

The learned judges of the Appeal Court were unanimously of opinion that the description of book debts in the assignment of Tyrell is 'too vague,' and it is upon that ground only that they have held the assignment to be invalid. The term which they have selected, in order to express what they conceived to be the radical defect of the assignment, is susceptible of at least two different meanings. It may either signify that the description is too wide and comprehensive, without implying that there will be any uncertainty as to the debts which it will include, if and when these come into existence, or it may signify that the language of the description is so obscure that it will be impossible, in the time to come, to determine with any degree of certainty to what particular debts it was intended to apply. In the latter sense the description of future book debts in the mortgage of 1879 does not incur the imputation of vagueness. No one has suggested that the expression 'book debt' is indefinite; and it is, in my opinion, very clear that every debt becoming due and owing to the mortgagor, which belongs to the class of book debts (a fact quite capable of ascertainment), is at once identified with the subject-matter of the assignment.

The ground of decision in the Appeal Court was obviously this: that the description of future debts is 'too vague,' in the sense of being too wide and comprehensive, inasmuch as it embraces debts to become due to the mortgagee in any and every business which he may think fit to carry on. If it had been limited to debts arising in the course of the business of packing-case manufacturer, in which Izon was engaged at the date of the mortgage, the Master of the Rolls was, as then advised, prepared to hold that the description would not have been too vague. Upon that point the other members of the Court express no definite opinion, Lindley LJ merely remarking, 'I do not say that an assignment of future book debts must necessarily be too vague.' All of their Lordships were evidently under the impression that they were deciding the case according to a well-established equitable doctrine, which Lopes LJ traces to *Belding v Read* ((1865) 3 H & C 955).

It is unnecessary for the purposes of this case to consider how far a general assignment of all after-acquired property can receive effect, because the assignment in question relates to one species of property only. I have been unable to discover any principle upon which the decision of the Court of Appeal can be supported, unless it is to be found in *Belding v Read* ((1865) 3 H & C 955). That case arose in a Court of Common Law, and, with all deference to the very learned judges who decided it, I am bound to say that, in my opinion, they misapprehended the doctrine laid down by Lord Westbury in *Holroyd v Marshall* ((1862) 10 HL Cas 191), which was not new doctrine, but, as the noble Lord explicitly stated, was the mere enunciation of elementary principles long settled in Courts of Equity. It is possible that the learned judges were misled by the reference which the noble Lord makes to specific performance, an illustration not selected with his usual felicity. Not a single decision by an Equity Court was cited to us, prior in date to *Belding v Read,* which gives the least support to the opinions expressed in that case, and I venture to doubt whether any such decision exists. It is true that judges on the equity side of the Court have, in one or two instances, deferred to the views expressed in *Belding v Read,* which they assumed to be an authoritative exposition of the law applied by this House in *Holroyd v Marshall,* but these views conflict with the previous cases in equity, to which Lord Westbury referred as establishing a well-known and elementary principle. In *Bennett v Cooper* ((1846) 9 Beav 252), Lord Langdale MR gave effect to an equitable mortgage by a debtor of 'all sums of money then or thereafter to become due to him, and all legacies or bequests which had already or might thereafter be given or bequeathed to him or his wife, by any person whomsoever.' I cannot understand upon what principle an assignment of all legacies which may be bequeathed by any person to the assignor is to stand good, and effect is to be denied to a general assignment of all future book debts. As Cotton LJ said, in *Re*

Clarke ((1887) 36 Ch D 348 at 353): 'Vagueness comes to nothing if the property is definite at the time when the Court is asked to enforce the contract.' A future book debt is quite as capable of being identified as a legacy; and in this case the identity of the debt, with the subjects assigned, is not matter of dispute. When the consideration has been given, and the debt has been clearly identified as one of those in respect of which it was given, a Court of Equity will enforce the covenant of the parties, and will not permit the assignor, or those in his right, to defeat the assignment upon the plea that it is too comprehensive.

I am accordingly of opinion that the order appealed from ought to be reversed, and the judgment of the Divisional Court restored.

Lord Macnaghten: ... The claim of the purchaser was rested on well-known principles. It has long been settled that future property, possibilities and expectancies are assignable in equity for value. The mode or form of assignment is absolutely immaterial provided the intention of the parties is clear. To effectuate the intention an assignment for value, in terms present and immediate, has always been regarded in equity as a contract binding on the conscience of the assignor and so binding the subject-matter of the contract when it comes into existence, if it is of such a nature and so described as to be capable of being ascertained and identified ....

My Lords, I should wish to say a few words about *Holroyd v Marshall* ((1862) 10 HL Cas 191), because I am inclined to think that *Belding v Read* ((1865) 3 H & C 955) is not the only case in which Lord Westbury's observations have been misunderstood. To understand Lord Westbury's judgment aright, I think it is necessary to bear in mind the state of the law at the time, and the point to which his Lordship was addressing himself. *Holroyd v Marshall* laid down no new law, nor did it extend the principles of equity in the slightest degree. Long before *Holroyd v Marshall* was determined it was well settled that an assignment of future property for value operates in equity by way of agreement, binding the conscience of the assignor, and so binding the property from the moment when the contract becomes capable of being performed, on the principle that equity considers as done that which ought to be done, and in accordance with the maxim which Lord Thurlow said he took to be universal, 'that whenever persons agree concerning any particular subject, that, in a Court of Equity, as against the party himself, and any claiming under him, voluntary or with notice, raises a trust:' *Legard v Hodges* ((1792) 1 Ves 477). It had also been determined by the highest tribunals in the country, short of this House—by Lord Lyndhurst as Lord Chancellor in England, and by Sir Edward Sugden as Lord Chancellor in Ireland—that an agreement binding property for valuable consideration had precedence over the claim of a judgment creditor. Some confusion, however, had recently been introduced by a decision of a most eminent judge, who was naturally less familiar with the doctrines of equity than with the principles of common law. In that state of things, in *Holroyd v Marshall,* in a contest between an equitable assignee and an execution creditor, Stuart VC decided in favour of the equitable assignee. His decision was reversed by Lord Campbell LC in a judgment which seemed to strike at the root of all equitable titles. Lord Campbell did not hold that the equitable assignee obtained no interest in the property the subject of the contract when it came into existence. He held that the equitable assignee did obtain an interest in equity. But at the same time he held that the interest was of such a fugitive character, so shadowy, and so precarious, that it could not stand against the legal title of the execution creditor, without the help of some new act to give it substance and strength. It was to this view, I think, that Lord Westbury addressed himself; and by way of shewing how real and substantial were equitable interests springing from agreements based on valuable consideration, he referred to the doctrines of specific performance, illustrating his argument by examples. One of the examples, perhaps, requires some qualification. That, however, does not affect the argument. The argument is clear and convincing; but it must not be wrested from its purpose. It is difficult to suppose that Lord Westbury intended to lay down as a rule to guide or perplex the Court, that considerations applicable to cases of specific performance, properly so-called, where the contract is executory, are to be applied to every case of equitable assignment dealing with future property. Lord Selborne has, I think, done good service in pointing out that confusion is sometimes caused by transferring such considerations to questions which arise as to the propriety of the Court requiring something or other to be done in specie (*Wolverhampton and Walsall Rly Co v London and North Western Rly Co* ((1873) LR 16 Eq 433)). His Lordship observes that there is some fallacy and ambiguity in the way in which in cases of that kind those words 'specific performance,' are very frequently used. Greater confusion still, I think, would be caused by transferring considerations applicable to suits for specific performance—involving, as they do, some of the nicest distinctions and most difficult questions that come before the Court—to cases of equitable assignment or specific lien where nothing remains to be done in order to define the rights of the parties, but the Court is merely asked to protect rights completely defined as between the parties to the contract, or to give effect to such rights either by granting an injunction or by appointing a receiver, or by adjudicating on questions between rival claimants.

The truth is that cases of equitable assignment or specific lien, where the consideration has passed, depend on the real meaning of the agreement between the parties. The difficulty, generally speaking, is to ascertain the true scope and effect of the agreement. When that is ascertained you have only to apply the principle that equity considers that done which ought to be done if that principle is applicable under the circumstances of the case. The doctrines relating to specific performance do not, I think, afford a test or a measure of the rights created.

[Lord Herschell delivered a concurring judgment.
Lord FitzGerald upheld the appeal on different grounds.]

NOTES

1.   Lord Westbury's assertion in *Holroyd v Marshall,* that equity only intervenes where the contract under which the debtor undertook to mortgage or charge future property is capable of specific performance, is misleading. In *Tailby v Official Receiver,* the House of Lords correctly interpreted Lord Westbury's reference to specific performance simply to mean that provided the consideration moving from the creditor is executed and not executory, ie the creditor has actually advanced his money to the debtor, and not merely promised to do so, the creditor is entitled to specific performance once property identifiable as the subject matter of the contract is acquired by the debtor. In other words, specific performance is a consequence (not the test) of enforceability in equity.

2.   In the context of the factoring of receivables, future receivables can only be factored under a whole turnover agreement. Under the terms of such an agreement, the factor is obliged to purchase future receivables and, thereby, provides the consideration necessary to support a contract to assign them. The contract to assign constitutes an equitable assignment from the date the consideration is executed. This will be the date that the factor first makes a credit or payment under the agreement. As Professor Goode has noted: '...a single credit or payment suffices, as this type of factoring agreement is an indivisible contract for the global sale of receivables, not a series of separate transactions' ([1982] JBL 240, p 242).

3.   Future receivables cannot be factored under a facultative agreement. This is because the factor is under no obligation to purchase the receivables offered to him and so provides no consideration to support a valid assignment of future receivables. Only after the receivables have come into existence can the client offer them to the factor. If the factor purchases any receivable offered to him an equitable assignment will take place at that stage.

4.   However, the factor faces a number of disadvantages if future receivables are assigned to him and those receivables have not yet come into existence:

(1)   he cannot intervene in actions concerning the property to which he is not yet entitled;

(2)   he cannot give notice of his assignment to secure his priority against other assignees until there is some debtor to whom effective notice can be given (*Re Dallas* [1904] 2 Ch 385);

(3) he cannot give notice of his assignment to the debtor so as to stop the debtor's equities enforceable against the assignor until the debt has come into existence (Oditah, op cit, pp 239–240; compare Salinger, op cit, paras 9–22 to 9–25);

(4) even if he is the first to give notice to the debtor, he may be defeated by a statutory assignee who has actually been paid the debt on the grounds that the statutory assignee is a bona fide purchaser for value of the legal title in the payments received without notice of the factor's equitable assignment (*E Pfeiffer Weinkellerei-Weineinkauf GmbH & Co v Arbuthnot Factors Ltd* [1988] 1 WLR 150 at 163);

(5) if the receivable comes into existence as a result of post-liquidation performance of an underlying contract by the client or its liquidator, the 'disposition' of the receivable under the terms of a pre-liquidation factoring agreement will be void unless the court orders otherwise (Insolvency Act 1986, s 127).

QUESTION

A whole turnover agreement provides that the client is to sell, and the factor is to purchase, 50 per cent of the client's turnover. Is this agreement capable of constituting an equitable assignment?

(b) Block discounting

Lloyds & Scottish Finance Ltd v Cyril Lord Carpets Sales Ltd
[1992] BCLC 609, House of Lords (the case was decided in 1979)

(The facts are irrelevant.)

Lord Scarman: Block discounting is a well-known service offered by certain finance houses to traders who do a substantial business by way of hire-purchase or credit-sale agreements with their customers. Though there are variations of detail, the essential feature of the service is that in return for an immediate advance the trader sells to the finance house at a discount his interest in the agreements he has with his customers. The trader gives the house his guarantee of due performance by his customers of their obligations. He includes a number, often a very large number, of hire-purchase or credit-sale agreements in each discounting transaction: hence the City's name 'block discounting' for this type of transaction. The service is similar to many other financial services offered in the City of London and elsewhere—an immediate advance of money against documents, which are purchased at a discount. It is an adaptation of the historic business of discounting bills and notes to the particular circumstances of the hire-purchase and credit-sale trade. The finance house looks only to the discount for its profit. Once the trader has met his commitment for the advance and the discount charge (out of the moneys received or receivable from his customers whose debts he has sold), the finance house is content that the trader should keep for himself whatever else is collected from the customers.

Of course the facility offered is money. The finance house advances money in reliance upon obligations which have not yet matured. But is it the lending of money? The question was answered (at first instance) 40 years ago. If the transaction be genuine and not a sham to cover something different, the judges held it to be a sale, not a loan. The three cases in which this answer was given have stood over the years unchallenged—and are, no doubt, the basis of City practice. They are *Re George Inglefield Ltd* [1933] Ch 1, [1932] All ER Rep 244; *Olds Discount Co Ltd v Cohen* [1938] 3 All ER 281n and *Olds Discount Co Ltd v Playfair Ltd* [1938] 3 All ER 275.

NOTES

1.   A copy of a master 'block discounting' agreement appears below as Form 6 in the Appendix (hereafter referred to as the 'MBDA').

2.   A block discounting agreement is essentially facultative. It provides a set of terms upon which blocks of receivables may later be sold by a dealer to the finance company. Each sale constitutes a separate transaction by which blocks of debt are equitably assigned to the finance company. Under the terms of the master agreement the dealer gives the finance company a power of attorney to execute a legal assignment, should this prove necessary.

3.   With a block discounting agreement it is usual not to give notice of the assignment of the debt to the dealer's customers. The dealer collects the debt as agent of the finance company. From the dealer's point of view, this has the advantage of allowing the dealer to retain control over his debts and maintain a relationship with his customers. From the finance company's point of view, block discounting saves it the costs associated with debt collection.

4.   Yet block discounting is inherently more risky for the finance company than notification factoring. The main reasons for this are:

(1)   if a customer pays the dealer he is discharged from his debt whether or not the dealer pays the finance company;

(2)   the dealer is under no obligation to account to the finance company for payments received from his customers, nor is he obliged to segregate such payments from his other resources (although under the terms of the master agreement the dealer will have guaranteed payment by the hirers or credit buyers and will have secured that guarantee by accepting a series of bills of exchange, or issuing promissory notes, payable to the finance company); contrast this with factoring where the client receives the proceeds on trust for the factor (*GE Crane Sales Pty Ltd v Comr of Taxation* (1971) 46 ALJR 15, High Court of Australia) and where the client will be liable for conversion if he misappropriates any cheque, or other negotiable instrument, paid to him (*International Factors Ltd v Rodriguez* [1979] QB 351);

(3)   the finance company is at risk of loss of priority to another assignee who gives notice to the hirer or credit buyer (although under the terms of the master agreement the dealer usually undertakes not to assign, charge or otherwise encumber any receivable assigned to the finance company);

(4)   if the finance company does collect the debt itself, it takes the debt subject to all defences and rights of set-off which have accrued between the customer and the dealer in the period up to when the customer receives notice of the assignment.

(c) The financier's discount is not an interest charge

Welsh Development Agency v Export Finance Co Ltd
[1992] BCLC 148, Court of Appeal

(The facts appear above, p 1018.)

Dillon LJ: The essence of the transaction when a trader raises finance by factoring book debts or block discounting hire-purchase agreements is that the trader sells the book debts to a finance company for a price which is necessarily discounted from the full aggregate face value of the debts. It is discounted, primarily, because the trader will be getting an immediate payment, while the finance company will have to wait for the debts to come in from the debtors and they may well not be presently payable. Indeed with hire-purchase agreements the debt will be payable by the hirer by instalments over what may be a considerable period. The rate of discount will also no doubt take into account the risk the finance company is assuming that the debtor will fail to pay the debts....

It is normal, therefore, that the rate of discount for the finance company will be calculated by reference to the appropriate rate of interest for the period for which the finance company is out of its money. It has been normal for the amount of discount to be calculated once and for all; it will be actually received by the finance company when the finance company receives payment of the book debt from the debtor, or from the vendor under rights of recourse for the finance company against the vendor. If the vendor has guaranteed to the finance company that the debtor will pay the debt punctually, and the debtor does not pay punctually, it may well be that the finance company could claim damages from the vendor, to be measured by a computation of interest over the period for which it has been kept out of its money in excess of the period on which the calculation of the amount of the finance company's discount was based.

The classic exposition by Lord Devlin in *Chow Yoong Hong v Choong Fah Rubber Manufactory Ltd* [1961] 3 All ER 1163 at 1167, [1962] AC 209 at 217, of the difference between interest and discounts is as follows:

> When payment is made before due date at a discount, the amount of the discount is no doubt often calculated by reference to the amount of interest which the payer calculates his money would have earned if he had deferred payment to the due date. But that does not mean that discount is the same as interest. Interest postulates the making of a loan and then it runs from day to day until repayment of the loan, its total depending on the length of the loan. Discount is a deduction from the price *fixed once and for all at the time of payment.* (My emphasis.)

Lord Wilberforce made a statement to the same effect—that discount is fixed and paid once and for all whereas interest accrues from day-to-day—in the *Lloyds & Scottish* case after citing from Lord Devlin's opinion in *Chow Yoong Hong.* Lord Wilberforce also referred to statements in *Willingale (Inspector of Taxes) v International Commercial Bank Ltd* [1978] 1 All ER 754 at 756, 760, [1978] AC 834 at 841, 843 by Lord Salmon and by Lord Fraser of Tullybelton to the effect that, unlike interest, discount is not earned and does not accrue from day-to-day.

NOTES

1. In *Welsh Development Agency* the discount was not fixed but fluctuating. It was closely tied to the average period taken by all overseas buyers to pay. However, Dillon LJ held that this did not convert the discount into interest on a loan and did not negate the transaction as being one of sale and purchase.

2. Factors may also make an 'administration charge' if they provide administrative services such as ledger administration, debt collection and credit protection. However, there is evidence that some factors make this charge even when these additional services are not provided (eg *Re Charge Card Services Ltd* [1987] Ch 150 at 171).

(d) The financier's security

Whether finance is provided under a factoring or block discount agreement, the financier usually obtains one or more of the following types of security against the client/dealer (hereafter collectively referred to as the 'client').

(i) Guarantees and indemnities

These appear in the MFA at clause 15.1, and in the MBDA at clause 9. Dr Oditah has noted that these guarantees and indemnities 'afford personal security to the factor [and block discounter] although when combined with a right to set off damages and loss against the retention fund, could, no doubt, prove powerful' (F Oditah *Legal Aspects of Receivables Financing* (1991) p 51).

(ii) A right of recourse

Such a right appears in the MFA at clause 11.11, and in the MBDA at clause 9. The right of recourse found in a factoring or block discounting agreement does not create an equity of redemption giving rise to a mortgage of, or charge over, a debt (see above, p 1025).

(iii) A right of retention

Such a right appears in the MBDA at clause 3, and in the case next cited.

Re Charge Card Services Ltd
[1987] Ch 150, Chancery Division

Charge Card Services Ltd (the company) entered into an invoice discounting agreement by which it agreed to factor its receivables to Commercial Credit Services Ltd (the factor). The relevant provisions of the agreement were as follows:

— By clause 3(a) the factor could require the company to repurchase any receivable in certain specified circumstances (eg if the debtor disputed liability).

— By clause 3(c) the company guaranteed payment by every debtor and agreed to indemnify the factor against loss caused by the debtor's failure to pay.

— By clause 4 the purchase price payable by the factor to the company was the gross amount payable by the debtor less any discount allowable and less a discount charge calculated in the manner prescribed by standard condition 3.

— By clause 6 the factor's obligation to pay was made subject to the right of debits and right of retention set out in standard condition 3.

— By clause 10 (read with clause 11) the factor had the option of determining the agreement on the company going into insolvent liquidation, whereupon the company was obliged to repurchase at face value so much of any receivable purchased by the factor as then remained outstanding. At the date of the trial the factor had not exercised this option.

— By standard condition 3A the factor had to maintain a current account which would be credited with (*inter alia*) the purchase price of each receivable and which would be debited with (*inter alia*) the amount of any receivables which the factor had required the company to repurchase, *inter alia,* under clause 3(a) (but not under clause 10).

— By standard condition 3B the factor was to remit to the company or its order any balance for the time being standing to the credit of the current account less any amount which the factor in its absolute discretion decided to retain as security for:

(i)   any claims or defences against the company;

(ii)   any risk of non-payment by a debtor; and

(iii) any amount prospectively chargeable to the company as a debit under standard condition 3A.

The company went into insolvent liquidation and a dispute arose between its liquidator and the factor as to the validity of the factor's right of retention under standard condition 3B. Millett J upheld the validity of the factor's right.

Millett J: It was submitted on behalf of the company that the right of retention was expressly reserved by Commercial Credit as security for its prospective rights of set off, and that in consequence it constituted a charge on book debts created by the company which was void against the liquidator for want of registration under s 95 of the Companies Act 1948 (now s 860 of the Companies Act 2006)....

In my judgment, and leaving aside for the moment the possible claim under clause 10, the short answer to these submissions is that Commercial Credit's right of retention under standard condition 3B(iii) in respect of any amount prospectively chargeable to the company as a debit to the current account is a matter not of set off but of account. In *Halesowen Presswork & Assemblies Ltd v National Westminster Bank Ltd* [1971] 1 QB 1, Buckley LJ said, at p 46:

> Where the relationship of the banker and customer is a single relationship such as I have already mentioned, albeit embodied in a number of accounts, the situation is not, in my judgment, a situation of lien at all. A lien postulates property of the debtor in the possession or under the control of the creditor. Nor is it a set-off situation, which postulates mutual but independent obligations between the two parties. It is an accounting situation, in which the existence and amount of one party's liability to the other can only be ascertained by discovering the ultimate balance of their mutual dealings.

Counsel for the company put forward a sophisticated analysis of the various provisions of the agreement to show that, despite the wording of clause 4, the discounting charge was not integral to the ascertainment of the purchase price but, like the administration charge, a true contra item. In my judgment, however, the crucial factor is not the definition of the purchase price, but the extent of Commercial Credit's obligation to pay. This is to be found in clause 6, and it is an obligation to pay, not the purchase price, which is merely a credit in the current account, but the balance shown on the current account subject to the right of retention. The right of retention thus constitutes a contractual limitation on the company's right to require payment of the balance on the current account. It is an essential safeguard against overpayment since, except at the end of the month when the discounting and administration charges are debited, and in the unlikely event of there being no bad debts at all, the balance on the current account can never represent the true amount owing by Commercial Credit. The sum made payable by clause 6, therefore, is in effect a provisional payment only and represents the best estimate that can be made at the time of the true state of account between the parties.

In my judgment, this is not a case of set off at all, for there are no mutual but independent obligations capable of being quantified and set off against each other. There are reciprocal obligations giving rise to credits and debits in a single running account, a single liability to pay the ultimate balance found due on taking the account, and provisions for retention and provisional payment in the meantime.

If this analysis is correct, it also provides an answer to the company's claim that the right of retention in standard condition 3B(iii) constitutes a registrable charge, for there is no relevant property capable of forming the subject matter of the charge. The only asset which the company could charge is its chose in action, ie the right to sue Commercial Credit for the sum due under the agreement, but this already contains within it the liability to suffer a retention. Counsel for the company naturally stressed the fact that the right of retention is expressed to be by way of security, but that is of no avail if, as I hold, it secures Commercial Credit, not against default by the company in the performance of its obligations, but against overpayment by itself.

This still leaves the company's liability to repurchase outstanding receivables at face value if Commercial Credit serves a notice of termination under clause 10. The purchase price payable by the company in this event is not available to be debited to the current account under standard condition

3A(ii), but Commercial Credit has the right to retain money to meet it under standard condition 3B(i). It has been conceded before me that this is a true right of set off. Accordingly, as well as in case I am wrong in my analysis of the other rights of retention, I must deal with the company's contentions that the right of retention in standard condition 3B is a registrable charge on the company's book debts and that in so far as it gives a right of set off in respect of sums only contingently due from the company at the date of liquidation it goes beyond what is permitted by s 31 of the Bankruptcy Act 1914 [now s 323 of the Insolvency Act 1986; and r 4.90 of the Insolvency Rules 1986].

If the right of retention constitutes a charge, there is no doubt that it is a charge on book debts and is a charge created by the company. But is it a charge at all? The sum due from Commercial Credit to the company under the agreement is, of course, a book debt of the company which the company can charge to a third party. In my judgment, however, it cannot be charged in favour of Commercial Credit itself, for the simple reason that a charge in favour of a debtor of his own indebtedness to the chargor is conceptually impossible.

Counsel for the company conceded that a debt cannot be assigned in whole or in part to the debtor, since such an assignment operates wholly or partially as a release. Likewise, it was conceded, it cannot be made the subject of a legal or equitable mortgage in favour of the debtor, since this requires a conveyance or assignment by way of security, and this operates as a conditional release. But, it was submitted, an equitable charge need involve no conveyance or assignment of property, so that any objection on this ground falls away.

[His Lordship then examined the requirements for the creation of an equitable charge as set out in *Palmer v Carey* [1926] AC 703 at 706–707 and in *National Provincial and Union Bank of England v Charnley* [1924] 1 KB 431 at 449–450 and continued:]

Thus the essence of an equitable charge is that, without any conveyance or assignment to the chargee, specific property of the chargor is expressly or constructively appropriated to or made answerable for payment of a debt, and the chargee is given the right to resort to the property for the purpose of having it realised and applied in or towards payment of the debt. The availability of equitable remedies has the effect of giving the chargee a proprietary interest by way of security in the property charged.

It is true, therefore, that no conveyance or assignment is involved in the creation of an equitable charge, but in my judgment the benefit of a debt can no more be appropriated or made available to the debtor than it can be conveyed or assigned to him. The objection to a charge in these circumstances is not to the process by which it is created, but to the result. A debt is a chose in action; it is the right to sue the debtor. This can be assigned or made available to a third party, but not to the debtor, who cannot sue himself. Once any assignment or appropriation to the debtor becomes unconditional, the debt is wholly or partially released. The debtor cannot, and does not need to, resort to the creditor's claim against him in order to obtain the benefit of the security; his own liability to the creditor is automatically discharged or reduced.

In *Halesowen Presswork & Assemblies Ltd v National Westminster Bank Ltd* [1971] 1 QB 1, 46 Buckley LJ, in a passage subsequently approved in the House of Lords [1972] AC 785 by Viscount Dilhorne, at p 802, Lord Simon of Glaisdale at p 808, and Lord Cross of Chelsea, at p 810, stated that he could not understand how it could be said with any kind of accuracy that the bank had a lien upon its own indebtedness to its customer. It is true that this comment was made in relation to a lien rather than a charge, and a lien unlike a charge can only attach to tangible property. But the reason why it was said that the bank did not have a lien on the credit balance in its customer's current account was clearly based on the identity of the parties rather than the particular character of the security given.

Counsel for the company relied on *Ex p Caldicott* (1884) 25 Ch D 716, in which a partner deposited money with a bank by way of security for the indebtedness of his firm. The Court of Appeal held that the bank was not required to value its security before proving for its debt against the firm. It was, however, not necessary to decide whether the deposit created a charge; it was sufficient that it did not create a security on the joint estate.

It does not, of course, follow that an attempt to create an express mortgage or charge of a debt in favour of the debtor would be ineffective to create a security. Equity looks to the substance, not the form; and while in my judgment this would not create a mortgage or charge, it would no doubt give a right of set off which would be effective against the creditor's liquidator or trustee in bankruptcy, provided that it did not purport to go beyond what is permitted by s 31 of the Bankruptcy Act 1914 [now s 323 of the Insolvency Act 1986; and r 4.90 of the Insolvency Rules 1986.]

[Although the case went to the Court of Appeal ([1988] 3 All ER 702), there was no appeal on this part of Millett J's judgment.]

NOTE

The suggestion by Millett J that 'charge-backs' were conceptually impossible came as something of a surprise to the banking world, where it was common practice for banks to take charges over their customers' deposits (which constitute debts owed by the bank to its customer) as security. However, there was some Australian authority in favour of the conceptual impossibility of such a charge (*Broad v Stamp Duties Comr* [1980] 2 NSWLR 40), and Professor Goode has been a consistent advocate of this approach (see RM Goode *Legal Problems of Credit and Security* (1st edn, 1982), pp 86–87, and (2nd edn, 1988), pp 124–129)). In (1989) 15 Mon LR 361, p 368, Professor Goode wrote:

...a debt is a species of property only as between the creditor and a third party taking an assignment or charge. In the relationship between creditor and debtor the debt is merely an obligation. As creditor I do not *own* the debt, I am *owed* it. Accordingly as against the debtor I have nothing to assign or charge back to him.

On the other hand, Millett J's dictum has been subjected to severe criticism from the majority of academic writers: see PR Wood (1987) 8 Co Law 262 and *English and International Set-off* (1989), paras 5–134 to 5–181; DE Allan (1989) 15 Mon LR 337; and F Oditah [1992] JBL 541 at pp 555–562. The critics argue that a debt can be 'property' as between the creditor and the debtor, at least when it is charged back to the creditor as security. They point to cases like *Re Jeavons, ex p Mackay, ex p Brown* (1873) 8 Ch App 643 (better reported in (1873) 42 LJ(NS) Bankruptcy 68), where an argument that a debtor cannot have a charge on royalties due from him was rejected by the Court of Appeal. They reject the argument that a charge-back is conceptually impossible because a debtor cannot sue himself by emphasising that a debt constitutes more than a right to sue and that examples can be found of the courts upholding unenforceable debts (eg *Curwen v Milburn* (1889) 42 Ch D 424). They deal with the argument that a charge-back is impossible because it would involve a merger of the security interest and the liability by pointing out that merger is dependent on the intention of the parties, and that merger would not occur provided it was made clear that it was not intended. In addition, the Legal Risk Review Committee, established in 1991 to examine legal uncertainties affecting the wholesale financial markets in the United Kingdom, recommended that there should be legislation to make it clear that charge-backs are permitted under English law (*Final Report of the Legal Risk Review Committee*, October 1992).

At both first instance and in the Court of Appeal in *Welsh Development Agency v Export Finance Co Ltd* ([1991] BCLC 936, Ch D; revsd [1992] BCLC 148, CA) doubts where expressed about the conceptual impossibility of charge-backs, but that was by way of obiter dictum and the point was only briefly considered. However, in *Re Bank of Credit and Commerce International SA (No 8)* [1996] 2 All ER 121, the Court of Appeal, after giving full consideration to all the arguments and relevant authorities, although again only by way of obiter dictum, fully endorsed Millett J's dictum in *Charge Card* that charge-backs were conceptually impossible (which is probably not surprising as Millett LJ was himself one of the judges who heard the case, although the judgment of the court was delivered by Rose LJ). The House of Lords gave leave to appeal.

Re Bank of Credit and Commerce International SA (No 8)
[1998] AC 214, House of Lords

BCCI, a bank which was now in liquidation, had made a loan to a company. To secure the loan the person controlling the company had deposited funds with BCCI and signed a letter charging the funds with the repayment of the company's debt. The depositor did not guarantee payment of the loan or accept any other form of personal liability. The issue was whether BCCI's liquidators could recover the full amount of the loan from the company, leaving the depositor to prove for his deposit as an unsecured creditor, or whether the deposit could be set off against the company's liability for the loan. The Court of Appeal, upholding Rattee J, held that there could be no set-off because there was no mutuality between the claims sought to be set off (as required by r 4.90 of the Insolvency Rules 1986). The borrowing company owed the amount due *to* BCCI (the loan), but the amount due *from* BCCI (the deposit) was owed to the depositor, who himself owed BCCI nothing since he had not given any personal guarantee. The House of Lords affirmed the decision of the Court of Appeal.

The charge-back point arose because it was argued by the company that although the depositor purported to create a charge over his deposit, this was legally ineffective for this purpose (charge-backs being conceptually impossible), and so the only way in which the letter could operate as an effective security, which was what the parties intended, was if it was construed as imposing personal liability on the depositor for the company's indebtedness.

Lord Hoffmann: ...

(b) In re Charge Card Services Ltd
The Court of Appeal rejected the argument that the letter was ineffective unless construed as imposing personal liability. They accepted Mr McDonnell's [Counsel for the borrowing company and the depositor] submission that, by reason of conceptual impossibility, it could not operate as a charge over the deposit. But they said that it could provide perfectly good security by virtue of the contractual provisions in the third paragraph which limited the right to repayment of the deposit and made it what is sometimes called a 'flawed asset.' I agree and could stop there without commenting on the question of whether a charge is conceptually impossible or not. But the point has been very fully argued and should, I think, be dealt with.

The doctrine of conceptual impossibility was first propounded by Millett J in *In re Charge Card Services Ltd* [1987] Ch 150, 175–176 and affirmed, after more extensive discussion, by the Court of Appeal in this case. It has excited a good deal of heat and controversy in banking circles; the Legal Risk Review Committee, set up in 1991 by the Bank of England to identify areas of obscurity and uncertainty in the law affecting financial markets and propose solutions, said that a very large number of submissions from interested parties expressed disquiet about this ruling. It seems clear that documents purporting to create such charges have been used by banks for many years. The point does not previously appear to have been expressly addressed by any court in this country. Supporters of the doctrine rely on the judgments of Buckley LJ (in the Court of Appeal) and Viscount Dilhorne and Lord Cross of Chelsea (in the House of Lords) in *Halesowen Presswork & Assemblies Ltd v Westminster Bank Ltd* [1971] 1 QB 1; [1972] AC 785. The passages in question certainly say that it is a misuse of language to speak of a bank having a lien over its own indebtedness to a customer. But I think that these observations were directed to the use of the word 'lien,' which is a right to retain possession, rather than to the question of whether the bank could have any kind of proprietary interest. Opponents of the doctrine rely upon some 19th century cases, of which it can at least be said that the possibility of a charge over a debt owed by the chargee caused no judicial surprise.

The reason given by the Court of Appeal [1996] Ch 245, 258 was that 'a man cannot have a proprietary interest in a debt or other obligation which he owes another.' In order to test this proposition, I think one needs to identify the normal characteristics of an equitable charge and then ask to what extent they would be inconsistent with a situation in which the property charged consisted of a debt owed by the beneficiary of the charge. There are several well known descriptions of an equitable charge (see, for example, that of Atkin LJ in *National Provincial and Union Bank of England v Charnley* [1924] 1 KB 431, 449–50) but none of them purports to be exhaustive. Nor do I intend to provide one. An equitable charge is a species of charge, which is a proprietary interest granted by way of security. Proprietary interests confer rights in rem which, subject to questions of registration and the equitable doctrine of purchaser for value without notice, will be binding upon third parties and unaffected by the insolvency of the owner of the property charged. A proprietary interest provided by way of security entitles the holder to resort to the property only for the purpose of satisfying some liability due to him (whether from the person providing the security or a third party) and, whatever the form of the transaction, the owner of the property retains an equity of redemption to have the property restored to him when the liability has been discharged. The method by which the holder of the security will resort to the property will ordinarily involve its sale or, more rarely, the extinction of the equity of redemption by foreclosure. A charge is a security interest created without any transfer of title or possession to the beneficiary. An equitable charge can be created by an informal transaction for value (legal charges may require a deed or registration or both) and over any kind of property (equitable as well as legal) but is subject to the doctrine of purchaser for value without notice applicable to all equitable interests.

The depositor's right to claim payment of his deposit is a chose in action which the law has always recognised as property. There is no dispute that a charge over such a chose in action can validly be granted to a third party. In which respects would the fact that the beneficiary of the charge was the debtor himself be inconsistent with the transaction having some or all of the various features which I have enumerated? The method by which the property would be realised would differ slightly: instead of the beneficiary of the charge having to claim payment from the debtor, the realisation would take the form of a book entry. In no other respect, as it seems to me, would the transaction have any consequences different from those which would attach to a charge given to a third party. It would be a proprietary interest in the sense that, subject to questions of registration and purchaser for value without notice, it would be binding upon assignees and a liquidator or trustee in bankruptcy. The depositor would retain an equity of redemption and all the rights which that implies. There would be no merger of interests because the depositor would retain title to the deposit subject only to the bank's charge. The creation of the charge would be consensual and not require any formal assignment or vesting of title in the bank. If all these features can exist despite the fact that the beneficiary of the charge is the debtor, I cannot see why it cannot properly be said that the debtor has a proprietary interest by way of charge over the debt.

The Court of Appeal said that the bank could obtain effective security in other ways. If the deposit was made by the principal debtor, it could rely upon contractual rights of set-off or combining accounts or rules of bankruptcy set-off under provisions such as rule 4.90. If the deposit was made by a third party, it could enter into contractual arrangements such as the limitation on the right to withdraw the deposit in this case, thereby making the deposit a 'flawed asset.' All this is true. It may well be that the security provided in these ways will in most cases be just as good as that provided by a proprietary interest. But that seems to me no reason for preventing banks and their customers from creating charges over deposits if, for reasons of their own, they want to do so. The submissions to the Legal Risk Review Committee made it clear that they do.

If such charges are granted by companies over their 'book debts' they will be registrable under section 395 and 396(1)(e) of the Companies Act 1985 [now ss 860(7)(f) and 874 of the Companies

Act 2006]. There is a suggestion in the judgment of the Court of Appeal that the banking community has been insufficiently grateful for being spared the necessity of registering such charges. In my view, this is a matter on which banks are entitled to make up their own minds and take their own advice on whether the deposit charged is a 'book debt' or not. I express no view on the point, but the judgment of my noble and learned friend, Lord Hutton, in *Northern Bank Ltd v Ross* [1990] BCC 883 suggests that, in the case of deposits with banks, an obligation to register is unlikely to arise.

Since the decision in *In re Charge Card Services Ltd* [1987] Ch 150 statutes have been passed in several offshore banking jurisdictions to reverse its effect. A typical example is section 15A of the Hong Kong Law Amendment and Reform (Consolidation) Ordinance (c 23), which I have already mentioned. It reads:

> For the avoidance of doubt, it is hereby declared that a person ('the first person') is able to create, and always has been able to create, in favour of another person ('the second person') a legal or equitable charge or mortgage over all or any of the first person's interest in a chose in action enforceable by the first person against the second person, and any charge or mortgage so created shall operate neither to merge the interest thereby created with, nor to extinguish or release, that chose in action.

There is similar legislation in Singapore (section 9A of the Civil Law Act (c 43)); Bermuda (the Charge and Security (Special Provisions) Act 1990 (c 53)) and the Cayman Islands (the Property (Miscellaneous Provisions) Law 1994 (No 7 of 1994)). The striking feature about all these provisions is that none of them amend or repeal any rule of common law which would be inconsistent with the existence of a charge over a debt owed by the chargee. They simply say that such a charge can be granted. If the trick can be done as easily as this, it is hard to see where the conceptual impossibility is to be found.

In a case in which there is no threat to the consistency of the law or objection of public policy, I think that the courts should be very slow to declare a practice of the commercial community to be conceptually impossible. Rules of law must obviously be consistent and not self-contradictory; thus in *Rye v Rye* [1962] AC 496,505, Viscount Simonds demonstrated that the notion of a person granting a lease to himself was inconsistent with every feature of a lease, both as a contract and as an estate in land. But the law is fashioned to suit the practicalities of life and legal concepts like 'proprietary interest' and 'charge' are no more than labels given to clusters of related and self-consistent rules of law. Such concepts do not have a life of their own from which the rules are inexorably derived. It follows that in my view the letter was effective to do what it purported to do, namely to create a charge over the deposit in favour of BCCI. This means that the foundation for Mr McDonnell's argument for implying a personal obligation disappears.

[Lords Goff, Nicholls, Hope and Hutton concurred.]

NOTE

It is not surprising that Lord Hoffmann's (highly persuasive) obiter dictum upholding charge-backs has been welcomed by bankers and their advisers (see, eg R Calnan (1998) 114 LQR 174). However, academic commentators have pointed to various weaknesses in Lord Hoffmann's reasoning, and concluded that 'the decision would appear to be based more on practical and commercial considerations than on strongly held views about legal theory' (J Lipton (1998) 9 JBFLP 101, p 109; see also G McCormack [1998] CfiLR 111; S McCracken *The Banker's Remedy of Set-Off* (2nd edn, 1998), pp 205–206). Professor Goode has maintained his opposition to charge-backs, criticising Lord Hoffmann for undermining so fundamental a concept as the distinction between property and obligation for no good reason—he points to the fact that there are other ways for a bank to take security over its customer's deposits, eg through a flawed asset or contractual set-off (see R Goode (1998) 114 LQR 178). Unfortunately, the distinction between property and obligation was not addressed by Lord Hoffmann. Nevertheless, even Professor Goode is forced to accept that the tide has turned in favour of charge-backs and that conceptual and policy problems 'must yield to business practice and legislative developments designed to accommodate it' (RM Goode *Legal Problems of Credit and Security* (3rd edn, 2003), para 3–12, citing, *inter alia*, art 4 of the EC Directive on financial collateral arrangements (Directive 2002/47/EC dated 5 June 2002) which requires Member States to ensure that on the occurrence of an enforcement event cash collateral may be realised by setting off the amount against or applying it in discharge of the relevant financial obligations).

(e) Registration

Insolvency Act 1986, s 344

344. (1) The following applies where a person engaged in any business makes a general assignment to another person of his existing or future book debts, or any class of them, and is subsequently adjudged bankrupt.

(2) The assignment is void against the trustee of the bankrupt's estate as regards book debts which were not paid before the presentation of the bankruptcy petition, unless the assignment has been registered under the Bills of Sale Act 1878.

(3) For the purposes of subsections (1) and (2)—

(a) 'assignment' includes an assignment by way of security or charge on book debts, and

(b) 'general assignment' does not include—

(i) an assignment of book debts due at the date of the assignment from specified debtors or of debts becoming due under specified contracts or

(ii) an assignment of book debts included either in a transfer of a business made in good faith and for value or in an assignment of assets for the benefit of creditors generally.

(4) For the purposes of registration under the Act of 1878 an assignment of book debts is to be treated as if it were a bill of sale given otherwise than by way of security for the payment of a sum of money; and the provisions of that Act with respect to the registration of bills of sale apply accordingly with such necessary modifications as may be made by rules under that Act.

NOTES

1. What are 'book debts'? See below, p 1046.

2. Section 344 only applies to a general assignment of book debts by a person who is subsequently adjudged bankrupt. It does not apply, therefore, to any such assignment made by a company. A company cannot be adjudged bankrupt!

3. Registration does not constitute notice to the debtor and does not guarantee the priority of the assignment over subsequent interests (RM Goode *Legal Problems of Credit and Security* (3rd edn, 2003), paras 3-31–3-32).

3 FINANCING BY SECURED TRANSACTIONS

(a) Generally

A factor may secure the financing transaction in a number of ways; for example, negotiable paper may be pledged with the factor, title may be retained by the factor in a sale and resale agreement and the factor may even claim a right to trace the proceeds of authorised sub-sales (see above, p 1018), and the client's debtor may even attorn to the factor (see above, p 939). However, the most common forms of security taken by the factor are mortgages and equitable charges (see above, p 1018). Problems related to taking a mortgage of, or equitable charge over, a debt will be considered further in this section.

(b) Registration of 'charges' on a company's property

The regime for registration of charges created by a company over its property is set out in Part 25 of the Companies Act 2006. Not every category of charge is affected, but a charge over book debts (s 860(7)(f)) and all floating charges on the company's property (s 860(7)(g)) are caught by the legislation. The main consequence of non-registration is that the charge-holder will lose his priority in an insolvency (s 874(1)).

Companies Act 2006, ss 860, 861 and 874

860 Charges created by a company

(1) A company that creates a charge to which this section applies must deliver the prescribed particulars of the charge, together with the instrument (if any) by which the charge is created or evidenced, to the registrar for registration before the end of the period allowed for registration.

(2) Registration of a charge to which this section applies may instead be effected on the application of a person interested in it.

(3) Where registration is effected on the application of some person other than the company, that person is entitled to recover from the company the amount of any fees properly paid by him to the registrar on registration.

(4) If a company fails to comply with subsection (1), an offence is committed by—
(a) the company, and
(b) every officer of it who is in default.

(5) A person guilty of an offence under this section is liable—
(a) on conviction on indictment, to a fine;
(b) on summary conviction, to a fine not exceeding the statutory maximum.

(6) Subsection (4) does not apply if registration of the charge has been effected on the application of some other person.

(7) This section applies to the following charges—
(a) a charge on land or any interest in land, other than a charge for any rent or other periodical sum issuing out of land,
(b) a charge created or evidenced by an instrument which, if executed by an individual, would require registration as a bill of sale,
(c) a charge for the purposes of securing any issue of debentures,
(d) a charge on uncalled share capital of the company,
(e) a charge on calls made but not paid,
(f) a charge on book debts of the company,
(g) a floating charge on the company's property or undertaking,
(h) a charge on a ship or aircraft, or any share in a ship,
(i) a charge on goodwill or on any intellectual property.

861 Charges which have to be registered: supplementary

(1) The holding of debentures entitling the holder to a charge on land is not, for the purposes of section 860(7)(a), an interest in the land.

(2) It is immaterial for the purposes of this Chapter where land subject to a charge is situated.

(3) The deposit by way of security of a negotiable instrument given to secure the payment of book debts is not, for the purposes of section 860(7)(f), a charge on those book debts.

(4) For the purposes of section 860(7)(i), 'intellectual property' means—

   (a) any patent, trade mark, registered design, copyright or design right;

   (b) any licence under or in respect of any such right.

(5) In this Chapter—

'charge' includes mortgage, and

'company' means a company registered in England and Wales or in Northern Ireland.

874 Consequence of failure to register charges created by a company

(1) If a company creates a charge to which section 860 applies, the charge is void (so far as any security on the company's property or undertaking is conferred by it) against—

   (a) a liquidator of the company,

   (b) an administrator of the company, and

   (c) a creditor of the company,

unless that section is complied with.

(2) Subsection (1) is subject to the provisions of this Chapter.

(3) Subsection (1) is without prejudice to any contract or obligation for repayment of the money secured by the charge; and when a charge becomes void under this section, the money secured by it immediately becomes payable.

NOTES

1. Part 25 of the Companies Act 2006 has replaced Part XII of the Companies Act 1985. However, the registration regimes set out in both Acts are virtually identical. This means that the new regime retains the imperfections of the old. The old Part XII regime has been the subject of sustained criticism and, in 2005, the Law Commission recommended that it be changed to a US style notice-filing system for company charges (Law Com, *Company Security Interests*, Report No 296, 2005). But the Government felt there was no general consensus of support for the Law Commission's proposals and, not wanting further to delay the passage of the Company Law Bill through Parliament, retained the old regime in the new Act. The Government has said that it will continue to consider reform in this area. Although a proposed general power to make company law reform orders was dropped from the legislation during its passage through Parliament, s 894 of the 2006 Act gives the Secretary of State power to amend Part 25 by regulations.

2. We have already seen in the previous chapter that for an assignment to be effective under s 136 of the Law of Property Act 1925 it must be 'absolute' and 'not purporting to be by way of charge only'. However, an assignment may be absolute for the purposes of s 136 and still operate by way of security for a debt (see *Burlinson v Hall* (1884) 12 QBD 347, per Day J; above, p 945). Whether an assignment is absolute under s 136 turns on whether the assignor has unconditionally transferred to the assignee for the time being the sole right to the debt in question as against the debtor. By contrast, a corporate assignor will have executed a 'charge' over its property for the purposes of Part 25 of the Companies Act 2006 if it retains any interest in the nature of an equity of redemption as against the assignee. Thus, an assignment of a debt to secure advances with a proviso for redemption and reassignment upon repayment (ie a mortgage of the debt) would be absolute under s 136 (see *Tancred v Delagoa Bay and East Africa Rly Co* (1889) 23 QBD 239) but registrable as a 'charge' under the Companies Act 2006 if the assignor is a company.

QUESTION

A deposit of negotiable instruments by way of pledge is exempt from registration (s 861(3) of the Companies Act 2006). What justifies this exemption?

(i) What is a 'book debt'?

Independent Automatic Sales Ltd v Knowles & Foster
[1962] 1 WLR 974, Chancery Division

The plaintiff company carried on a business of manufacturing and dealing in automatic machines. For that purpose it obtained finance from the defendant merchant banking firm whereby it was agreed that bills of exchange and other documents belonging to the plaintiff and deposited with the defendant should be pledged to the defendant as continuing security for the payment of all liabilities of the plaintiff to the defendant. The plaintiff then deposited 53 hire-purchase agreements with the defendant as security for a loan. Each agreement included a provision whereby the hirer, on exercising his option to terminate or return the machine, was liable for not less than one half of the purchase price. On the plaintiff's liquidation, the liquidator claimed delivery of the hire-purchase agreements and an account of all money received under them on the ground that the charge created by the deposit of the agreements was void against him for non-registration under s 95 of the Companies Act 1948 (an earlier version of ss 860, 861 and 874 of the Companies Act 2006), since the debts arising under the agreements were 'book debts' within s 95(2)(e) of the 1948 Act.

Buckley J: In my judgment, the charge constituted by the deposit of one of these agreements was a charge upon each and all of the benefits of the company under that agreement. If those benefits included any rights which can properly be described as 'book-debts' the charge was, in part at least, a charge on book-debts and therefore registrable under the section.

Nearly 100 years ago in *Shipley v Marshall* ((1863) 14 CBNS 566) the Court of Common Pleas considered the meaning of the term 'book-debts' as used in s 137 of the Bankruptcy Act 1861. Erie CJ said (at 570): 'By "book-debts," the legislature doubtless intended to describe debts in some way connected with the trade of the bankrupt: and I am inclined to give the term a wider range. But it is enough to say that this was a debt connected with and growing out of the plaintiff's trade.' Williams J said (at 571): 'The words of s 137 are no doubt as Mr Griffits has pointed out, authorising the assignees to sell the "book-debts due or growing due to the bankrupt, and the books relating thereto." This, it is said, can only mean debts which are actually entered in some book kept by the bankrupt in the course of his trade. I cannot, however, accede to that construction. I think the meaning of the statute is, that the assignees shall dispose of all debts due to the bankrupt in respect of which entries could be made in the ordinary course of his business: otherwise, a debt by accident omitted to be entered would not pass by the assignment.' Byles J said (at 573): 'It is said that "book-debts" must mean debts which are entered in the trade-books of the bankrupt. I agree with my Brother Williams that they must be such debts as are commonly entered in books.' And a little later he said: 'Suppose the trader kept no books, or was blind and could not write, and did not choose to incur the expense of keeping a clerk or book-keeper,—upon the construction contended for by the defendant, there could be no book-debts which could be made the subject of sale and assignment under s 137 of the Bankruptcy Act 1861. That surely would not be a very sensible construction to put upon the statute.'

So far as I am aware, no more precise definition of the meaning of the term 'book-debts' has ever been attempted judicially and I shall not attempt one. *Shipley v Marshall,* I think, establishes that, if it can be said of a debt arising in the course of a business and due or growing due to the proprietor of that business that such a debt would or could in the ordinary course of such a business be entered in well-kept books relating to that business, that debt can properly be called a book-debt whether it is in fact entered in the books of the business or not....

Mr Bagnail [counsel for the defendants] has further argued that any debts which could arise under the agreements could only have come into existence after the date of the deposit. I will assume, as seems probable, that at that date all the amounts payable on the signing of the agreements had been paid and that no instalments of hire rent were in arrear. Mr Bagnall's submission was that in these circumstances there would at the date of the deposit have been no book-debts in existence and that, since he says one cannot charge what does not exist, the deposits did not per se constitute any charge on book-debts, although he conceded that if and when a book-debt came into existence under any of the agreements that book-debt would immediately become charged by reason of the deposit. He contends that s 95 does not on its true construction require a charge on future book-debts to be registered and that 'book-debts' in sub-s (2)(e) means only existing book-debts....

I think that there are two answers to this argument. First, for the reason I have already given, I am of opinion that upon the true interpretation of the form of agreement used in this case the hirer became liable immediately upon the agreement coming into operation to the extent of his minimum liability under it notwithstanding that some part of that liability was to be discharged by future payments and that the debts so constituted were existing book-debts at the date of the deposit. The proposition that when the agreements were deposited there were no book-debts in existence which could be charged is, in my judgment, untenable.

Secondly, in my judgment, a charge on future book-debts of a company is registrable under s 95. That it is competent for anyone to whom book-debts may accrue in the future to create an equitable charge upon those book-debts which will attach to them as soon as they come into existence is not disputed. (See *Tailby v Official Receiver* ((1888) 13 App Cas 523.) That such a charge can accurately be described as a charge on book-debts does not appear to me to be open to question. Such a charge would not, of course, be effective until a book-debt came into existence upon which it could operate. Nevertheless, I think it would be accurate to speak of the charge being created at the date of the instrument, deposit or other act giving rise to it, for no further action on the part of the grantor would be required to bring the charge to life. A charge on book-debts, present and future, is not an unusual form of security in the commercial world, and it would seem to me strange if such a charge were registrable (as it undoubtedly is) and a charge confined to future book-debts were not. I find nothing in the language of s 95 requiring me to read sub-s (2)(e) in so restricted a way as to confine it to a charge on existing book-debts....

Accordingly, in my judgment, the charges created by the deposit of 53 agreements were registrable under s 95, and, not having been registered, they are void as against the plaintiff liquidator. There will be a declaration that the charges are void as against the plaintiff liquidator, and an order for the delivery up of the agreements.

NOTES

1. Does a charge created by a company over its bank account require to be registered under s 860 of the Companies Act 2006 as a charge over a 'book debt'? Probably not, as the debt owed by the bank to the company, its customer, will not have arisen in the company's ordinary course of business, unless the company ran an investment business and the deposit was made by way of investment. However, the cases do not provide any clear guidance on this issue—see *Re Brightlife Ltd* [1987] Ch 200; *Re Permanent Houses (Holdings) Ltd* (1988) 5 BCC 151 at 154; and *Northern Bank Ltd v Ross* [1990] BCC 883, NTCA—although in *Re Bank of Credit and Commerce International SA (No 8)* [1998] AC 214 at 227 (above, p 1040), Lord Hoffmann hinted, without deciding the issue, that a charge over a company's deposits with its bank need not be registered (his reasoning, and the commercial uncertainty created by it, has been strongly criticised by J Upton (1998) 9 JBFLP 101, pp 112–114, and also by G McCormack [1998] CfiLR 111).

2. Regulation 4(4) of the Financial Collateral Arrangements (No 2) Regulations 2003, SI 2003/ 3226, provides that the registration requirement contained in s 860 of the Companies

Act 2006 does not apply (if it would otherwise do so) to a security financial collateral arrangement ('a security FCA'), or any charge created or otherwise arising under a security FCA. Thus, where the Regulations apply, there is no need to register a charge over financial collateral, which includes 'cash' that is held in a bank or other account or 'a similar claim for the repayment of money' (reg 3). To qualify as a security FCA the financial collateral must be 'in the possession or under the control of the collateral-taker' (reg 3). In the case of a charge-back, when the bank is the chargee of an account held with itself, the need for 'control' means that the account must be kept 'blocked', ie the charger is prevented from drawing on the account (see H Beale, M Bridge, L Gullifer and E Lomnicka, *The Law of Personal Property Security* (2007), para 10.46). In the past, where a bank took a charge-back over its customer's account balance as part of a 'triple cocktail' (a charge-back, a flawed asset arrangement and a contractual right of set-off), the normal practice would have been to register. It now appears that, where cash is charged as part of a security FCA, registration is unnecessary where the chargor and the chargee are non-natural persons.

QUESTIONS

1.   Is the need to register its charge over the company's property a benefit or burden to the company's financier?

2.   *Re Charge Card Services Ltd* [1987] Ch 150 (above, p 1036) involved a purported charge-back over a running account between a factor and its client company. There was no bank account involved. In the light of Lord Hoffmann's recognition in *Re Bank of Credit and Commerce International SA (No 8)* [1998] AC 214 (above, p 1040) that charge-backs are not conceptually impossible, would the charge-back in *Charge Card* now be registrable? How consistent is the law in the area of registration?

Paul and Frank Ltd v Discount Bank (Overseas) Ltd

[1967] Ch 348, Chancery Division

The plaintiff company had completed a letter of authority to an export credit guarantee organisation (ECG) authorising it to pay the defendant discount bank any moneys which might become payable under an exchange insurance policy. On the plaintiff's liquidation, the liquidator claimed that the letter of authority was void under s 95 of the Companies Act 1948 (an earlier version of ss 860, 861 and 874 of the Companies Act 2006), as an unregistered charge on a book debt of the company.

After hearing the accountancy evidence Pennycuick J held that even after ECG had accepted liability for a claim and the amount of the claim had been ascertained the right to payment under the ECG policy would not in practice have been entered in the books of the plaintiff company.

Pennycuick J continued: I turn now to s 95 of the Companies Act 1948....

Looking at the matter for a moment apart from authority, I do not think that in ordinary speech one would describe as a 'book-debt' the right under a contingency contract before the contingency happens. By 'contingency contract' in this connection I mean contracts of insurance, guarantee, indemnity and the like. However, this point is not free from authority, and I have been referred to two cases as to what is meant by a 'book-debt.'...

Counsel on both sides have addressed their arguments in great part to the nature of the company's right at the date when the contingency under the policy occurred, or alternatively the date when the liability of ECG was accepted and the amount ascertained. Even if this is the true test, the findings on accountancy practice which I have made would conclude the case in favour of the defendants. But I do not think that this is the true test. Section 95 requires registration of a charge on book-debts within 21 days of creation. It seems to me that, in order to ascertain whether any particular charge is a charge on book-debts within the meaning of the section, one must look at the items of property which form the subject matter of the charge at the date of its creation and consider whether any of those items is a book-debt. In the case of an existing item of property, this question can only be answered by reference to its character at the date of creation. Where the item of property is the benefit of a contract and at the date of the charge the benefit of the contract does not comprehend any book-debt, I do not see how that contract can be brought within the section as being a book-debt merely by reason that the contract may ultimately result in a book-debt. Here the ECG policy admittedly did not comprehend any book-debt at the date of the letter of authority, and that seems to me to be an end of the matter.

Mr Sutcliffe, for the plaintiffs, contended that a contract requires registration under paragraph (e) if at any time it may result in a book-debt. If this were right, the section would be of wide scope and would cover a charge on any possible contract which might produce a money obligation unless it could be shown that the obligation, even when admitted and quantified, was such as would not commonly be entered in the books of a company.

Mr Sutcliffe relied on another principle laid down by Buckley J in *Independent Automatic Sales Ltd v Knowles & Foster* ([1962] 1 WLR 974). After holding that upon the true interpretation of the hire-purchase agreement 'the hirer became immediately liable to the extent of his minimum liability under it notwithstanding that some part of that liability is to be discharged by future payments,' Buckley J went on as follows…

[His Lordship quoted the passage cited above, p 1047, and continued:]

Mr Wheeler, for the first defendant, and Mr Bateson, for the second defendant, unless I misunderstood them, found it difficult to resist Mr Sutcliffe's contention on this point, except by saying that the second proposition of Buckley J is wrong. I confess that I do not share that difficulty. If a charge upon its proper construction covers future debts, in the sense of debts under a future contract which, when that contract comes to be made, will constitute book-debts, eg an ordinary contract for the sale of goods on credit, I see no reason why paragraph (e) should not be fairly applicable to the charge; and that, I think, is all that Buckley J says. It by no means follows, it seems to me, that paragraph (e) applies to an existing contract which does not comprehend a book-debt merely by reason that that contract may result in a book-debt in the future. Nor did Buckley J say so.

I prefer to rest my decision on the ground which I have indicated. But, as I have said, if indeed the test were the character of ECG's obligation when liability is admitted and the amount ascertained, then the plaintiffs' claim would fail on the facts, namely, the evidence of accountancy practice.

NOTES

1. Fixed charges over future book debts are registrable (*Independent Automatic Sales*), whereas fixed charges over contingent debts are not (*Paul and Frank*). This means that a book debt which arises from an existing contract will be non-registrable if the debt is contingent, whereas a book debt arising from a non-existent contract will be registrable if the debt is not contingent. However, this distinction, as drawn by Pennycuick J in *Paul and Frank*, has been the subject of considerable criticism, see F Oditah *Legal Aspects of Receivables Financing* (1991), pp 30–32; E Ferran *Mortgage Securitisation—Legal Aspects* (1992), pp 77–80. Furthermore, in *Contemporary Cottages (NZ) Ltd v Margin Traders Ltd* [1981] 2 NZLR 114 (High Court of New Zealand), Thorp J has held (at 126) that:

There seems to me to be a basic conflict between the proposition that registration may be required in respect of a debt not existing at the time of the charge, and the concept that the test is to be the character of the property assigned and charged at the date of the creation of the charge. I prefer the proposition which lies behind the judgment of Buckley J, ie, that the charge over future book debts is created at the time of the execution of an appropriate assignment pursuant to *Tailby's* case, to distinguishing between book debts which arise from existing contracts and book debts which arise from non-existent contracts on any basis which makes charges over the latter registrable but charges over the former not registrable. That consequence, which is necessarily involved in the proposal by Pennycuick J, is one which seems to me, with respect, to indicate the illogicality of the distinction.

2.   In *Re Brush Aggregates Ltd* [1983] BCLC 320, RAK Wright QC, sitting as a deputy judge, held that a charge on future debts which might arise under a contract already in existence at the date of the charge would be registrable as a fixed charge on book debts. As a matter of construction of the terms of the assignment, the deputy judge distinguished *Paul and Frank* as a case involving the assignment by way of security of a contingent contractual right (non-registrable), as opposed to an assignment by way of security of any money which might become due under that contract (registrable). However, considerable doubt has been expressed as to whether the distinction drawn by the deputy judge has any substance to it (see E Ferran, p 79).

3.   In his report, Professor Diamond recommended that charges on insurance policies should become registrable charges (Diamond Report, para 23.5.4). He had no proposals as regard other contingent debts (para 23.9.24). However, it should be noted that under the existing law a *floating* charge over debts (book debts or otherwise) is registrable and this includes a floating charge taken over contingent debts (s 860(7)(g) of the Companies Act 2006). Whether a floating charge over book debts can be registered under s 860(7)(f) remains in issue. In *The Annangel Glory* [1988] 1 Lloyd's Rep 45, Saville J (at 50) raised the question (with regard to registration under s 396(1)(e) of the Companies Act 1985, which was identical to s 860(7)(f) of the 2006 Act) but did not find it necessary to decide the point.

(ii) Distinguishing between a fixed charge and a floating charge over book debts

In *Re New Bullas Trading Ltd* [1994] 1 BCLC 485, a company granted a charge over book debts which was expressed to be a fixed charge over the uncollected book debts and a floating charge over their proceeds. The Court of Appeal, overruling Knox J, held that there were commercial advantages for both parties to these arrangements and that the parties were free to agree to such terms. Accordingly, it upheld the wording of the charge instrument as having the effect of making the charge over the uncollected debts a fixed charge. However, *New Bullas* was the subject of sustained criticism. Professor Goode, (1994) 110 LQR 592, maintained that it is not possible to create separate security interests over a debt and its proceeds: all that is possible is to have a single, continuous security interest which moves from debt to proceeds. Professor Worthington, (1997) 113 LQR 563, while not supporting the view that a book debt and its proceeds constitute an indivisible asset, considered that the wrong conclusion had been reached in *New Bullas* because the security arrangement had left the chargor free to remove the charged assets from the ambit of the security without recourse to the chargee.

In the event, it is Professor Worthington's view which has been upheld. In order for a charge over book debts to be characterised as fixed, *both* the uncollected book debts *and* their proceeds after collection must be under the control of the charge holder. *New Bullas* was held to have been wrongly decided by the Privy Council in *Agnew v Commissioner of Inland Revenue (Re Brumark Investments Ltd)* [2001] UKPC 28, [2001] 2 AC 710, and overruled by the House of Lords in *National Westminster Bank plc v Spectrum Plus Ltd (Re Spectrum Plus Ltd)* [2005] UKHL 41, [2005] 2 AC 680. These two cases now represent the leading modern authorities on the subject.

Agnew v Commissioner of Inland Revenue (Re Brumark Investments Ltd)

[2001] UKPC 28, [2001] 2 AC 710, Privy Council

Brumark had given security over its book debts to its bank, Westpac, in terms which purported to make the debts subject to a fixed charge so long as they were uncollected but a floating charge over the proceeds once they had been collected and received by the company. (These terms were virtually identical to those in *New Bullas.)* The company was free to collect the debts for its own account and to use the proceeds in its business. It went into receivership and the receivers collected the outstanding debts. Fisher J at first instance held that, as uncollected debts, they were subject to a fixed charge (as the parties had agreed) and, as such, not subject to the claims of the company's preferential creditors. The New Zealand Court of Appeal, declining to follow *New Bullas,* held that the fact that the company was free to collect the debts for its own account (and so remove them from the bank's security) was inconsistent with the charge being a fixed charge. It was accordingly a floating charge and the preferential creditors had a prior claim to the proceeds. This ruling was affirmed by the Privy Council.

The opinion of the Judicial Committee was delivered by **Lord Millett:**

The question in this appeal is whether a charge over the uncollected book debts of a company which leaves the company free to collect the and use the proceedings in the ordinary course of its business is a fixed charge or a floating charge.

[His Lordship set out the facts and the terms of the debenture and continued:]

The question is whether the company's right to collect the debts and deal with their proceeds free from the security means that the charge on the uncollected debts, though described in the debenture as fixed, was nevertheless a floating charge until it crystallised by the appointment of the receivers. This is a question of characterisation. To answer it their Lordships must examine the nature of a floating charge and ascertain the features which distinguish it from a fixed charge....

[His Lordship traced the history of the floating charge, referring to cases from *Re Panama, New Zealand and Australian Royal Mail Co* (1870) 5 Ch App 318, CA, to *Re Cosslett (Contractors) Ltd* [1998] Ch 495, CA (below, pp 1079–1083), emphasising in particular the following passage from the judgment of Vaughan Williams LJ in *Re Yorkshire Woolcombers Association Ltd* [1903] 2 Ch 284 at 295:

> but what you do require to make a specific security is that the security whenever it has once come into existence, and been identified or appropriated as a security, *shall never thereafter at the will of the mortgagor cease to be a security. If at the will of the mortgagor he can dispose of it and prevent its being any longer a security, although something else may be substituted more or less for it, that is not a 'specific security'* (Emphasis added.)]

[His Lordship referred to the wording of the debentures in this case and in *New Bullas* and continued:]

The intended effect of the debenture was the same in each case. Until the charge holder intervened the company could continue to collect the debts, though not to assign or factor them, and the debts once collected would cease to exist. The proceeds which took their place would be a different asset which had never been subject to the fixed charge and would from the outset be subject to the floating charge.

The question in *New Bullas,* as in the present case, was whether the book debts which were uncollected when the receivers were appointed were subject to a fixed charge or a floating charge....

The principal theme of the judgment, however, was that the parties were free to make whatever agreement they liked. The question was therefore simply one of construction; unless unlawful the intention of the parties, to be gathered from the terms of the debenture, must prevail. It was clear from the descriptions which the parties attached to the charges that they had intended to create a fixed charge over the book debts while they were uncollected and a floating charge over the proceeds. It was open to the parties to do so, and freedom of contract prevailed.

Their Lordships consider this approach to be fundamentally mistaken. The question is not merely one of construction. In deciding whether a charge is a fixed charge or a floating charge, the court is engaged in a two-stage process. At the first stage it must construe the instrument of charge and seek to gather the intentions of the parties from the language they have used. But the object at this stage of the process is not to discover whether the parties intended to create a fixed or a floating charge. It is to ascertain the nature of the rights and obligations which the parties intended to grant each other in respect of the charged assets. Once these have been ascertained, the court can then embark on the second stage of the process, which is one of categorisation. This is a matter of law. It does not depend on the intention of the parties. If their intention, properly gathered from the language of the instrument, is to grant the company rights in respect of the charged assets which are inconsistent with the nature of a fixed charge, then the charge cannot be a fixed charge however they may have chosen to describe it....In construing a debenture to see whether it creates a fixed or a floating charge, the only intention which is relevant is the intention that the company should be free to deal with the charged assets and withdraw them from the security without the consent of the holder of the charge; or, to put the question another way, whether the charged assets were intended to be under the control of the company or of the charge holder.

[His Lordship considered and rejected an argument which had been upheld by the Court of Appeal in *New Bullas:* that the book debts did not cease to be subject to the charge at the will of the company but that they ceased to be subject to the charge because that was what the parties had agreed in advance when they entered into the debenture. He also rejected as irrelevant a distinction which Fisher J had drawn between a power on the part of the company to *dispose* of the debts (eg by factoring them) and a power to *consume* them (by realising them). He continued:]

Their Lordships turn finally to the questions which have exercised academic commentators: whether a debt or other receivable can be separated from its proceeds; whether they represent a single security interest or two; and whether a charge on book debts necessarily takes effect as a single indivisible charge on the debts and their proceeds irrespective of the way in which it may be drafted.

Property and its proceeds are clearly different assets. On a sale of goods the seller exchanges one asset for another. Both assets continue to exist, the goods in the hands of the buyer and proceeds of sale in the hands of the seller. If a book debt is assigned, the debt is transferred to the assignee in exchange for money paid to the assignor. The seller's former property right in the subject matter of the sale gives him an equivalent property right in its exchange product. The only difference between realising a debt by assignment and collection is that, on collection, the debt is wholly extinguished. As in the case of alienation, it is replaced in the hands of the creditor by a different asset, viz its proceeds.

The Court of Appeal saw no reason to examine the conceptual problems further. They held that, even if a debt and its proceeds are two different assets, the company was free to realise the uncollected debts, and accordingly the charge on those assets (being the assets whose destination was in dispute) could not be a fixed charge. There was simply no need to look at the proceeds at all...

If the company is free to collect the debts, the nature of the charge on the uncollected debts cannot differ according to whether the proceeds are subject to a floating charge or are not subject to any charge. In each case the commercial effect is the same: the charge holder cannot prevent the company from collecting the debts and having the free use of the proceeds. But is does not follow that the nature of the charge on the uncollected book debts may not differ according to whether the proceeds are subject to a fixed charge or a floating charge; for in the one case the charge holder can prevent the company from having the use of the proceeds and in the other it cannot. The question is not whether the company is free to collect the uncollected debts, but whether it is free to do so for its own benefit....

To constitute a charge on book debts a fixed charge, it is sufficient to prohibit the company from realising the debts itself, whether by assignment or collection. If the company seeks permission to do so in respect of a particular debt, the charge holder can refuse permission or grant permission on terms, and can thus direct the application of the proceeds. But it is not necessary to go this far. As their Lordships have already noted, it is not inconsistent with the fixed nature of a charge on book debts for the holder of the charge to appoint the company its agent to collect the debts for its account and on its behalf. The *Siebe Gorman* case [above, p 1007] merely introduced an alternative mechanism for appropriating the proceeds to the security. The proceeds of the debts collected by the company were no longer to be trust moneys but they were required to be paid into a blocked account with the charge holder. The commercial effect was the same: the proceeds were not at the company's disposal. Such an arrangement is inconsistent with the charge being a floating charge, since the debts are not available to the company as a source of its cash flow. But their Lordships would wish to make it clear that it is not enough to provide in the debenture that the account is a blocked account if it is not operated as one in fact....

Their Lordships consider that the *New Bullas* case was wrongly decided.

National Westminster Bank plc v Spectrum Plus Ltd (Re Spectrum Plus Ltd)

[2005] UKHL 41, [2005] 2 AC 680, House of Lords

Spectrum Plus Ltd ('Spectrum') opened a current account at National Westminster Bank plc ('the bank'), obtained an overdraft facility of £250,000 and, on 30 September 1997, executed a debenture to secure its indebtedness to the bank. The security created by the debenture was expressed to include:

A specific charge [of] all book debts and other debts...now and from time to time due or owing to [Spectrum]' (para 2(v)) and 'A floating security [of] its undertaking and all its property assets and rights whatsoever and wheresoever present and/or future including those from the time being charged by way of specific charge pursuant to the foregoing paragraphs if and to the extent that such charges as aforesaid shall fail as specific charges but without prejudice to any such specific charges as shall continue to be effective (para 2 (vii)).

Paragraph 5 of the debenture supported the grant of the charge over book debts:

With reference to the book debts and other debts hereby specifically charged [Spectrum] shall pay into [Spectrum's] account with the bank all moneys which it may receive in respect of such debts and shall not without the prior consent in writing of the bank sell factor discount or otherwise charge or assign the same in favour of any other person or purport to do so and [Spectrum] shall if called upon to do so by the bank from time to time execute legal assignments of such book debts and other debts to the bank.

After the opening of the current account in September 1997, Spectrum collected book debts, paid them into his current account and drew on the account as it wished for its business purposes. The overdraft limit was never exceeded but the account was never in credit.

Spectrum's business fortunes did not prosper and on 15 October 2001 it went into voluntary liquidation. The issue that came before the courts was whether the charge over book debts was a fixed charge, which it was expressed to be, or merely a floating charge. If it was a floating charge Spectrum's preferential creditors were entitled to have their debts paid out of the proceeds of the book debts in priority to the bank (Insolvency Act 1986, s 175). If it was not a floating charge the preferential creditors had no such priority and the bank would be entitled to the whole of the proceeds.

In *Siebe Gorman & Co Ltd v Barclays Bank* [1979] 2 Lloyd's Rep 142, Slade J had held that a similarly worded debenture created a fixed charge over book debts. Reversing Sir Andrew Morritt V-C at first instance [2004] Ch 337, the Court of Appeal [2004] Ch 337, held that the restrictions imposed by the debenture (and the restrictions imposed by the *Siebe Gorman* debenture) had been sufficient to justify the categorisation of the charge as a fixed charge. The Revenue and Customs Commissioners and the Secretary of State for Trade and Industry, as parties subrogated to the preferential creditors, appealed to the House of Lords.

Lord Hope: ...

Did Spectrum's debenture create a fixed charge?

[53] My noble and learned friend, Lord Scott of Foscote has described the facts of the case and summarised all the relevant authorities. I adopt with gratitude all that he has said about them, and I agree with him that the charge which the company granted by way of what the debenture described as a specific charge over its book debts and other debts then and from time to time owing to the company was in law a floating charge. It was not a fixed charge, so s 175(2)(b) applies to it. The preferential creditors have priority over the bank's claims under the debenture to the sums realisable from the book debts and other debts of the company.

[54] There are, as Professor Sarah Worthington has pointed out, a limited number of ways to ensure that a charge over book debts is fixed: *An 'Unsatisfactory Area of the Law'—Fixed and Floating Charges Yet Again*, (2004) 1 International Corporate Rescue, 175, 182. One is to prevent all dealings with the book debts so that they are preserved for the benefit of the chargee's security. This is the only method which is known to Scots law which, as I have said, insists upon assignation of the book debts to the security holder and its intimation to the company's debtor as the equivalent of their delivery. One can, of course, be confident where this method is used that the book debts will be permanently appropriated to the security which is given to the chargee. But a company that wishes to continue to trade will usually find the commercial consequences of such an arrangement unacceptable. Another is to prevent all dealings with the book debts other than their collection, and to require the proceeds when collected to be paid to the chargee in reduction of the chargor's outstanding debt. But this method too is likely to be unacceptable to a company which wishes to carry on its business as normally as possible by maintaining its cash flow and its working capital. A third is to prevent all dealings with the debts other than their collection, and to require the collected proceeds to be paid into an account with the chargee bank. That account must then be blocked so as to preserve the proceeds for the benefit of the chargee's security. A fourth is to prevent all dealings with the debts other than their collection and to require the collected proceeds to be paid into a separate account with a third party bank. The chargee then takes a fixed charge over that account so as to preserve the sums paid into it for the benefit of its security.

[55] The method that was selected in this case comes closest to the third of these. It was selected, no doubt, because it enabled the company to continue to trade as normally as possible while restricting it, at the same time, to some degree as to what it could do with the book debts. The critical question is whether the restrictions that it imposed went far enough. There is no doubt that their effect was to prevent the company from entering into transactions with any third party in relation to the book debts prior to their collection. The uncollected book debts were to be held exclusively for the benefit of the bank. But everything then depended on the nature of the account with the bank into which the proceeds were to paid under the arrangement described in cl 5 of the debenture. As McCarthy J said in *In re Keenan Bros Ltd* [1986] BCLC 242, 2 BCC 98, 247, one must look, not at the declared intention of the parties alone, but to the effect of the instruments whereby the purported to carry out that intention. Was the account one which allowed the company to continue to use the proceeds of the book debts as a source of its cash flow or was it one which, on the contrary, preserved the proceeds intact for the benefit of the bank's security? Was it, putting the point shortly, a blocked account?

[56] I do not see how this question can be answered without examining the contractual relationship in regard to that account between the bank and its customer. An account from which the customer is entitled to withdraw funds whenever it wishes within the agreed limits of any overdraft is not a blocked account. In *Agnew v Commissioners of Inland Revenue* [2001] UKPC 28, [2001] 2 AC 710, 722, para 22 Lord Millett said that the critical feature which led the Irish Supreme Court in *In re Keenan Bros Ltd* [1986] BCLC 242 to characterise the charge on book debts as a fixed charge was that their proceeds were to be segregated in a blocked account where they would be frozen and unusable by the company without the bank's written consent. I respectfully agree. Elsewhere in his judgment he appears to have assumed that the account into which the proceeds of the book debts were to be paid under the debenture in the *Siebe Gorman case* [1979] 2 Lloyd's Rep 142 was also a blocked account: p 727, para 38; p 730, para 48. In para 38 he said that the company could collect the money but was not free to use it as it saw fit. The question whether he was right when he made that assumption is at the heart of this case.

[57] For the reasons which have been explained much more fully by Lord Scott and Lord Walker, I too would hold that it is impossible to conclude that the debenture in the *Siebe Gorman* case had that effect. As I read the critical passage in Slade J's judgment at pp 158–159, he appears to have reached that conclusion in two stages. First, he said, the effect of the debenture was to create a specific charge on the proceeds of the debts as soon as they were received which prevented the company from disposing of an unencumbered title to them without the mortgagor's consent. Second, he said that the bank would have had the right, if it chose, to assert its lien under the charge on the proceeds of the book debts, even at a time when the account into which they were paid was temporarily in credit.

[58] As to the first point, I would agree that the effect of cl 5(c) of the debenture (the equivalent of cl 5 in our case) was that the company was prevented from doing anything with the proceeds of the book debts when collected other than paying them into its account with the bank. But it seems to me that second point—that the bank could assert a lien over the proceeds—overlooks the fact that the account into which the proceeds were to be paid was the company's current account with the bank which the company was to continue to be free to operate for its own business purposes within the agreed limit of its overdraft.

[59] As May LJ said in *Lipkin Gorman v Karpnale Ltd* [1992] 4 All ER 409, [1989] 1 WLR 1340, 1353, the money which a customer deposits with a bank becomes the bank's money, but the bank is prima facie bound to meet its debt when called upon to do so by the customer. In *Westminster Bank Ltd v Hilton* (1926) 43 TLR 124, 126 Lord Atkinson explained the relationship in this way:

> 'It is well established that the normal relation between a banker and his customer is that of debtor and creditor, but it is equally well established that *quoad* the drawing and payment of the customer's cheques as against money of the customer's in the banker's hands the relation is that of principal and agent. The cheque is an order of the principal's addressed to the agent to pay out of the principal's money in the agent's hands the amount of the cheque to the payee thereof.'

The general rule is that a banker is bound to honour his customer's cheque so long as he has funds in his hands if the account is in credit, or up to the agreed limit of any overdraft. He may determine the contract at any time on giving notice to the customer. But he cannot refuse to honour cheques drawn before the notice of determination is received.

[60] A banker has a general lien over all bills, notes and negotiable instruments belonging to the customer which his customer may have deposited with him in security of the customer's indebtedness to the bank. But a lien is a right to retain possession of property that belongs to someone else, and the banker has no lien over funds which, when deposited in its account by the customer, become his own property. Moreover the relationship is one where, if the account is in credit, the banker is indebted to his customer. So it was a misuse of the word lien to say that the bank could assert a right of that kind over the proceeds: see Buckley LJ in the Court of Appeal in *Halesowen Presswork and Assemblies Ltd v Westminster Bank Ltd* [1971] 1 QB 1, 46, and Viscount Dilhorne and Lord Cross of Chelsea in the same case in the House of Lords [1972] AC 785, [1972] 1 All ER 641; Lord Hoffmann in *In re Bank of Credit and Commerce International S A (No 8)* [1998] AC 214, 226. This is not to say that it is impossible to conceive of the creation of an equitable charge over the proceeds of book debts paid into an account in the name the chargor. But the ordinary relationship of banker and customer does not permit the banker, without notice, to refuse to allow his customer to operate a current account as and whenever he wishes while it is credit or is within the limits of any agreed overdraft. The debenture in the *Siebe Gorman* case, which provided for the payment of the proceeds into an account of that kind, lacked any provision which qualified that relationship.

[61] In the Court of Appeal Lord Phillips of Worth Matravers MR [2004] Ch 337, 383, para 94 said that, in the determination of the question whether the charge over the book debts was fixed, the extent of the customer's contractual right to draw out sums equivalent to the amounts paid in must be disregarded. But the relationship between a bank and its customer is founded in contract. The company's undertaking in cl 5 of the debenture to pay the proceeds of the book debts into its account with the bank has to be seen and understood in that context. This was a current account into which the company paid money drawn from a variety of other sources as well as the proceeds of its book debts. In my opinion the company's continuing contractual right to draw out sums equivalent to the amounts paid in is wholly destructive of the argument that there was fixed charge over the uncollected proceeds because the account into which the proceeds were to be paid was blocked.

Lord Scott: ...

What is a floating charge?

[95] It is helpful in answering this question to bear in mind the juridical history of floating charges and the reasons why a degree of statutory intervention became necessary. By the middle of the 19th century industrial and commercial expansion in this country had led to an increasing need by companies for more capital. Subscription for share capital could not meet this need and loan capital had to be raised. But the lenders required security for their loans. Traditional security, in the form of legal or equitable charges on the borrowers' fixed assets, whether land or goods, could not meet the need. The greater part of most entrepreneurial companies' assets would consist of raw materials, work in progress, stock-in-trade and trade debts. These were circulating assets, replaced in the normal course of business and constantly changing. Assets of this character were not amenable to being the subject of traditional forms of security. Equity, however, intervened. *Holroyd v Marshall* (1862) 10 HLC 191 was a case in which a debtor had purported to grant a mortgage not only over his existing machinery but also over all the machinery which, during the continuance of the security, should be placed in his mill. The question arose whether the equitable title of the chargee in respect of new machinery that had been placed in the mill prevailed over the rights of a judgment creditor of the chargor/debtor. Could the chargee assert an equitable interest in the new machinery? Lord Campbell LC held that he could not. But the House of Lords reversed the decision, holding that

> '...immediately on the new machinery and effects being fixed or placed in the mill, they became subject to the operation of the contract, and passed in equity to the mortgagees' (per Lord Westbury at p 211)

and that

> '...in equity it is not disputed that the moment the property comes into existence, the agreement operates on it' (per Lord Chelmsford at p 220).

[96]   *Holroyd v Marshall* opened the way to the grant by companies of security over any class of circulating assets that the chargor company might possess. Acceptance that it was possible to do this became established by the 1870s. In *In re Panama New Zealand and Australian Royal Mail Co* (1870) 5 Ch App 318 the company simply charged its 'undertaking and all sums of money arising therefrom'. Gifford LJ held, at p 322, that 'undertaking' meant

'. . . all the property of the company, not only which existed at the date of the debenture, but which might afterwards become the property of the company.'

He said also that the word 'undertaking'

'. . . necessarily infers that the company will go on, and that the debenture holder could not interfere until either the interest which was due was unpaid, or until the period had arrived for the payment of his principal, and that principal was unpaid.'

(see also *In re Florence Land and Public Works Co* [1878] 10 Ch D 530, 540).

The two features mentioned by Gifford LJ became the hallmark of the new form of security, namely, (1) a charge on the chargor company's assets, or a specified class of assets, present and future and (2) the right of the chargor company to continue to use the charged assets for the time being owned by it and to dispose of them for its normal business purposes until the occurrence of some particular future event. In *In re Colonial Trusts Corporation* (1879) 15 Ch D 465 Jessel MR referred to this form of security as a 'floating security' (see at pp 468, 469 and 472) and in *Moor v Anglo-Italian Bank* (1879) 10 Ch D 681, 687 he contrasted the new form of security with a 'specific charge' on the property of the company.

[97]   By the last decade of the 19th century this form of security, Jessel MR's 'floating security', had become firmly established and in regular use. This new form of security, the floating charge, did not derive from statute. It had been bred by equity lawyers and judges out of the needs of the commercial and industrial entrepreneurs of the time. But the new form of security, notwithstanding its convenience for both borrowers and lenders, had its drawbacks for others. Those dealing with a company could not tell whether its circulating assets were subject to a charge that, if the company became insolvent or ceased business, would allow a debenture holder to 'step in and sweep off everything' (Lord Macnaghten in *Salomon v Salomon & Co Ltd* [1897] AC 22, 53). And if a debenture holder did 'step in and sweep off everything' there would be nothing left for unsecured creditors including, in particular, the company's employees to whom wages arrears might be owing.

[98]   Statutory intervention began in 1897 with the Preferential Payments in Bankruptcy Amendment Act. Where a company was being wound-up or was in receivership ss 2 and 3 of the 1897 Act gave preferential creditors, a class which included employees as well as Crown creditors, priority over the chargee under a floating charge, so far as payment of debts out of the assets subject to that charge was concerned. Preferential creditors had priority anyway over ordinary creditors and the sections did not disturb the priority over ordinary creditors to which the charge holder was entitled by virtue of the charge. These statutory provisions, with very little alteration, are now to be found in ss 40 (receivership) and 175 (winding-up) of the Insolvency Act 1986. And in 1900 further statutory interventions required floating charges to be registered: (see now ss 395 and 396, Companies Act 1985) and provided for floating charges created by an insolvent company within a short period before the commencement of its winding-up to be invalid except to the extent of new money provided by the chargee (see now s 245 Insolvency Act 1986). The statutes which first introduced these reforms did not attempt any definition of a 'floating charge'. Nor have any of their statutory successors done so. The expression has been taken to be self-explanatory. It bears the meaning attributed to it by judicial decision. But the judicial process over the years whereby the concept of a 'floating charge' has been developed must, in my opinion, keep in mind the mischief that these statutory reforms were intended to meet and, in particular, that on a winding-up or receivership preferential creditors were to have their debts paid out of the circulating assets, sometimes referred to as 'ambulatory' assets, of the debtor company in priority to a debenture holder with a charge over those assets.

[99] The classic and frequently cited definition of a floating charge is that which was given by Romer LJ in the Court of Appeal in the *Yorkshire Woolcombers Association* case [1903] 2Ch 284, 295.

> 'I certainly think that if a charge has the three characteristics that I am about to mention it is a floating charge.
>   (1) If it is a charge on a class of assets of a company present and future; (2) if that class is one which, in the ordinary course of the business of the company, would be changing from time to time; and (3) if you find that by the charge it is contemplated that, until some further step is taken by or on behalf of those interested in the charge, the company may carry on its business in the ordinary way as far as concerns the particular class of assets I am dealing with.'

But it is important to notice that Romer LJ prefaced his definition with a qualification. He said—

> 'I certainly do not intend to attempt to give an exact definition of the term 'floating charge', nor am I prepared to say that there will not be a floating charge within the meaning of the Act, which does not contain all the three characteristics...'

The case came to this House under the name *Illingworth v Houldsworth* [1904] AC 355. In short ex tempore speeches their Lordships upheld the Court of Appeal. Lord Macnaghten described the case as 'clear' and offered the following definition of a floating charge in contrast to a 'specific charge'—

> 'A specific charge, I think, is one that without more fastens on ascertained and definite property or property capable of being ascertained and defined; a floating charge, on the other hand, is ambu-latory and shifting in its nature, hovering over and so to speak floating with the property which it is intended to affect until some event occurs or some act is done which causes it to settle and fasten on the subject of the charge within its reach and grasp'(p 358).

[100] And a few years later Buckley LJ in *Evans v Rival Granite Quarries Ltd* [1910] 2 KB 979, 999 similarly contrasted a 'floating security' with a 'specific security.'

> '[A floating security] is not a specific security; the holder cannot affirm that the assets are specific-ally mortgaged to him. The assets are mortgaged in such a way that the mortgagor can deal with them without the concurrence of the mortgagee. A floating security is not a specific mortgage of the assets, plus a licence to the mortgagor to dispose of them in the course of his business, but is a floating mortgage applying to every item comprised in the security, but not specifically affecting any item until some event occurs or some act on the part of the mortgagee is done which causes it to crystallise into a fixed security.'

[101] It is in the nature of commercial lenders to want the most effective security that they can get. It is in the nature of commercial borrowers to want to be able to carry on the business for the purposes of which they are borrowing money with as much freedom from restrictions imposed by their lenders that negotiation can achieve for them. But the lenders are usually in the stronger bargaining position and able to stipulate the terms to be included in the debenture which will constitute their security. So it is not in the least surprising to find attempts by lenders to obtain fixed charges as security rather than floating charges, thereby avoiding the need, if financial misfortune were to visit their borrowers, to yield priority to preferential creditors and also avoiding possible vulnerability under s 245 of the 1986 Act or its statutory predecessors. And it is not surprising to find borrowers agreeable to co-operate in these attempts provided their ability to carry on business in the normal way were not unduly impeded.

[102] There was never any doubt that it was possible to create a fixed charge over a specific, ascer-tained book debt. And *Tailby v Official Receiver* (1888) 13 App Cas 523 established that an assignment of future book debts would be effective to vest in the assignee an equitable interest in the future debts at the moment they became owing to the assignor. So there was no reason why a deben-ture should not be expressed to assign to the debenture holder, by way of security, the company's future book debts. But the question would still remain whether such an assignment, not being an out-and-out assignment as in *Tailby v Official Receiver* but an assignment by way of security, could be said to constitute a fixed security.

[103] There was nothing much that the lenders could do about the third of the characteristics that Romer LJ had regarded as typical of floating charges. Most commercial borrowers would be unlikely to agree to grant charges over their circulating assets that did not enable them to use those assets for their normal business purposes. So it was natural for the quest for fixed charges to be concentrated on the prominence given by Lord Macnaghten in the *Yorkshire Woolcombers* case to the characteristic of a fixed charge as being a charge on 'ascertained and definite property.' As soon as a book debt is incurred and becomes owing to the chargor it constitutes an item of 'ascertained and definite' property and would qualify as a possible object of a fixed charge. So a debenture expressed to grant a fixed charge over present and future book debts would be capable of creating a fixed charge over all such debts as and when they accrued due to the chargor company. Slade J so held in *Siebe Gorman* and no-one has suggested that in that respect he was wrong.

[104] Moreover, the debenture could fortify the apparently fixed character of the charge by including a provision entitling the chargee to call for a formal written assignment by the chargor of the debts as they accrued. Such an assignment unaccompanied by written notice to the debtor would constitute the chargee equitable proprietor, and not simply equitable chargee, of the debt. The appearance of a fixed security would be fortified. It is not surprising, therefore, to find debentures containing provisions of this sort. The *Siebe Gorman* debenture did so. So did the Bank's debenture in the present case. But the intention of the parties that the charge over book debts created and fortified in this way would be a fixed charge has to take account also of Romer LJ's third characteristic of a floating charge, namely, that until some further step by way of intervention is taken by the chargee the chargor company can use the assets in question for its normal business purposes and, in using them, remove them from the security. The fact that a valid fixed charge over present and future book debts is capable of being created does not answer the essential question whether a fixed charge over assets that remain at the disposal of the chargor can be created.

[105] Slade J in *Siebe Gorman* [1979] 2 Lloyd's Rep 142, 158 inclined to the opinion that if the chargor of book debts, having collected the book debts,

> '...[had] had the unrestricted right to deal with the proceeds of any of the relevant book debts paid into its account, so long as that account remained in credit...the charge on such book debts could be no more than a floating charge.'

Hoffmann J in *In re Brightlife Ltd* [1987] Ch 200, 209, in a passage cited with approval by Lord Millett in *Agnew v Commissioners of Inland Revenue* [2001] 2 AC 710, 723, said that the significant feature of the *Brightlife* debenture was that the company was free to collect its debts and pay the proceeds into its bank account. He went on

> 'Once in the account, they would be outside the charge over debts and at the free disposal of the company. In my judgment a right to deal in this way with the charged assets for its own account is a badge of a floating charge and is inconsistent with a fixed charge.'

Similar conclusions were expressed in *In re Keenan Bros Ltd* [1986] BCLC 242 in the Supreme Court of Ireland and by Tompkins J in the *Supercool Refrigeration* case [1994] 3 NZLR 300, in New Zealand.

[106] The Privy Council in the Agnew case agreed with these decisions. Lord Millett pointed out, in para 13 of the Board's opinion, that Romer LJ's first two characteristics, although typical of a floating charge, were not distinctive of it. They were not necessarily inconsistent with a fixed charge. It was the third characteristic, Lord Millett said, which was the hallmark of a floating charge and distinguished it from a fixed charge.

[107] I respectfully agree. Indeed if a security has Romer LJ's third characteristic I am inclined to think that it qualifies as a floating charge, and cannot be a fixed charge, whatever may be its other characteristics. Suppose, for example, a case where an express assignment of a specific debt by way of security were accompanied by a provision that reserved to the assignor the right, terminable by written notice from the assignee, to collect the debt and to use the proceeds for its (the assignor's) business purposes, ie, a right, terminable on notice, for the assignor to withdraw the proceeds of the debt from the security. This security would, in my opinion, be a floating security notwithstanding the express assignment. The assigned debt would be specific and ascertained but its status as a security would not. Unless and until the right of the assignor to collect and deal with the proceeds were terminated, the security would retain its floating characteristic. Or suppose a case in which the charge were expressed to come into existence on the future occurrence of some event and then to be a fixed charge over whatever assets of a specified description the chargor might own at that time. The contractual rights thereby granted would, in my opinion, be properly categorised as a floating security. There can, in my opinion, be no difference in categorisation between the grant of a fixed charge expressed to come into existence on a future event in relation to a specified class of assets owned by the chargor at that time and the grant of a floating charge over the specified class of assets with crystallisation taking place on the occurrence of that event. I endeavoured to make this point in *In re Cosslett (Contractors) Ltd* [2001] UKHL 58, [2002] 1 AC 336, 357, para 63. Nor, in principle, can there be any difference in categorisation between those grants and the grant of a charge over the specified assets expressed to be a fixed charge but where the chargor is permitted until the occurrence of the specified event to remove the charged assets from the security. In all these cases, and in any other case in which the chargor remains free to remove the charged assets from the security, the charge should, in principle, be categorised as a floating charge. The assets would have the circulating, ambulatory character distinctive of a floating charge.

[108] The debenture in the *New Bullas Trading* case [1994] 1 BCLC 485, [1994] BCC 36 had features which illustrate the ingenuity of equity draftsmen in seeking to produce for their clients fixed charges out of circumstances that would normally be associated with floating charges. The debenture was expressed to grant the chargee a fixed charge over the company's present and future book debts. The chargee was entitled to demand that the debts be assigned to it, but never in fact made any such demand. The chargee was entitled to give the chargor instructions as to how the chargor should deal with its book debts, but apparently never in fact gave any such instructions, at any rate none prior to liquidation. The debenture left the chargor free to collect the debts and required the chargor to pay into a specified bank account all money it received in payment of the debts. The debenture then provided that on payment of the money into the bank account the fixed charge would be released and replaced by a floating charge over the money in the account. The obvious intention of these provisions was that on the occurrence of a crystallisation event, eg liquidation, the uncollected book debts at that time would be subject to the fixed charge notwithstanding that if the debts had been paid prior to the crystallisation event the collected money would have been subject to only a floating charge. The preferential creditors would then enjoy no priority over the debenture holder so far as the uncollected debts were concerned.

[109] Nourse LJ could see no reason in law to prevent the parties from providing for a fixed charge on book debts while uncollected but a floating charge on the money collected. He referred at p 492 to the question and answer posed by Lord Macnaghten in *Tailby v Official Receiver* 13 App Cas 523, 545—

> 'Between men of full age and competent understanding ought there to be any limit to the freedom of contract but that imposed by positive law or dictated by considerations of morality or public policy? The limit proposed is purely arbitrary, and I think meaningless and unreasonable.'

These reservations, he thought, supported the view that it was open to contracting parties, if they wished to do so, to provide for a fixed charge on uncollected book debts but a floating charge on the money received in payment of those debts.

[110] Lord Millett expressed the Board's disagreement with Nourse LJ's reasoning and conclusion. Essentially Lord Millett challenged the notion that the security rights granted over a book debt could be any greater than the rights, if any, granted over the money received in payment of the debts (see

[2001] 2 AC 710, para 46). If a book debt were to be charged as security but with an accompanying provision that any money received from the debtor in payment of the debt would belong to the chargor, the co-called 'charge', whether expressed to be a fixed charge or a floating charge, would not be a security at all. It would not constitute a possible source for the repayment of the allegedly secured debt. As Lord Millett said, it would be worthless. If the accompanying provision were, instead, to say that any money received from the debtor would be subject to a floating charge, that provision would, in my opinion, necessarily describe and limit the nature of the charge over the receivable debt. And if the charge were to be expressed to be a fixed charge as respects the receivable debt but a floating charge as respects the money received from the debtor there would be an internal contradiction in the formulation of the charge. Since the essential value of a book debt as a security lies in the money that can be obtained from the debtor in payment it seems to me that Lord Millett was right in concluding that such a security should be categorised as a floating security and that *New Bullas* [1994] 1 BCLC 485 was wrongly decided.

[111] In my opinion, the essential characteristic of a floating charge, the characteristic that distinguishes it from a fixed charge, is that the asset subject to the charge is not finally appropriated as a security for the payment of the debt until the occurrence of some future event. In the meantime the chargor is left free to use the charged asset and to remove it from the security. On this point I am in respectful agreement with Lord Millett. Moreover, recognition that this is the essential characteristic of a floating charge reflects the mischief that the statutory intervention to which I have referred was intended to meet and should ensure that preferential creditors continue to enjoy the priority that s 175 of the 1986 Act and its statutory predecessors intended them to have.

Did the bank's debenture create a fixed charge or only a floating charge?

[112] If, as I think, the hallmark of a floating charge and a characteristic inconsistent with a fixed charge is that the chargor is left free to use the assets subject to the charge and by doing so to withdraw them from the security, how should the charge over book debts granted by the bank's debenture be categorised? The following features of the debenture and the arrangements regarding the bank account into which the collected debts had to be paid need to be taken into account.

1. The extent of the restrictions imposed by the debenture (para 81 above)
2. The rights retained by Spectrum to deal with its debtors and collect the money owed by them (para 81 above)
3. Spectrum's right to draw on its account with the bank into which the collected debts had to be paid, provided it kept within the overdraft limit (para 82 above)
4. The description 'fixed charge' attributed to the charge by the parties themselves.

[113] Restrictions on Spectrum's right to deal with its uncollected book debts go very little way, in my opinion, in supporting the characterisation of the charge as a fixed charge for the reasons I have given in criticising the *New Bullas* decision. It is restrictions on the use that Spectrum could make of the payments made by its debtors that are important. I have already cited the passage at p 158 from Slade J's judgment in *Siebe Gorman* [1979] 2 Lloyd's Rep 142, 158 (para 105 above) and need not repeat it. It makes the same point.

[114] Moreover, the restrictions on Spectrum's right to deal with its uncollected book debts did not enable the bank to realise its security over those uncollected book debts. The bank could not have sold the book debts without first taking some step or steps that would have given it the power to do so. In effect a crystallisation event would, I think, have had to take place. The value of the uncollected book debts as a security lay always in the money that could be obtained from the debtors in payment of those debts.

[115] The bank's debenture required all payments of book debts received by Spectrum to be paid into its account with the bank. The money once received by the bank would become the bank's money and in return Spectrum's account would be credited with the amount that had been received. Whether the account was for the time being in credit or in debit the result of each payment would be the accrual to Spectrum of the right to withdraw from the account a corresponding amount for its normal business purposes.

[116] An attempt has been made to justify the categorisation of the charge as a fixed charge by looking no further than the receipt by the bank, through the operation of the clearing system, of the proceeds of the cheques from Spectrum's debtors that were paid in by Spectrum. The consequent crediting of Spectrum's account with amounts equal to the proceeds of the cheques and Spectrum's ability to draw on that account for its business purposes is not inconsistent, it is suggested, with the categorisation of the charge over the book debts as a fixed charge. This is the point being made by the Master of the Rolls in para 94 of his judgment (cited in para 93 above). It was a point pressed before your Lordships by Mr Moss QC, counsel for the bank. Your Lordships should not, in my opinion, accept this argument. It seeks to perpetuate what I regard as the *New Bullas* heresy, namely, that the categorisation of a charge over book debts can ignore the rights of the chargor over the money received in payment of those debts. The expression 'floating charge' has never been a term of art but is an expression invented by equity lawyers and judges to describe the nature of a particular type of security arrangement between lenders and borrowers. The categorisation depends upon the commercial nature and substance of the arrangement, not upon a formalistic analysis of how the bank clearing system works. If part of the arrangement is that the chargor is free to collect the book debts but must pay the collected money into a specified bank account, the categorisation must depend, in my opinion, on what, if any, restrictions there are on the use the chargor can make of the credit to the account that reflects each payment in.

[117] The bank's debenture placed no restrictions on the use that Spectrum could make of the balance on the account available to be drawn by Spectrum. Slade J in *Siebe Gorman* [1979] Lloyd's Rep 142, 158 thought it might make a difference whether the account were in credit or in debit. I must respectfully disagree. The critical question, in my opinion, is whether the chargor can draw on the account. If the chargor's bank account were in debit and the chargor had no right to draw on it, the account would have become, and would remain until the drawing rights were restored, a blocked account. The situation would be as it was in *Re Keenan Bros Ltd* [1986] BCLC 242. But so long as the chargor can draw on the account, and whether the account is in credit or debit, the money paid in is not being appropriated to the repayment of the debt owing to the debenture holder but is being made available for drawings on the account by the chargor.

[118] Slade J said that the debenture in the *Siebe Gorman* case

> '...creat[ed] in equity a specific charge on the proceeds of [the book debts] as soon as they are received and consequently prevents the mortgagor from disposing of an unencumbered title to the subject matter of such charge without the mortgagee's consent, even before the mortgagee has taken steps to enforce its security'. (p 159)

But it is very difficult to see what feature of the arrangement between chargor and bank chargee in *Siebe Gorman* justified this conclusion. The debenture was on all fours with the debenture in the present case. There is nothing in the report of the case to suggest that the bank account into which the chargor had to pay the collected book debts was other than, as here, a normal bank current account on which the chargor could draw for its normal business purposes. In considering the cited passage it seems to me worth noting that the issues that Slade J had to decide in the *Siebe Gorman* case did not include the question whether the charge over book debts was a fixed charge or a floating charge. The main issue in the case was one of priority as between the bank chargee on the one hand and a subsequent assignee of the charged book debts on the other. This issue turned on notice. Did the subsequent assignee have notice of the bank's charge and the provision barring subsequent assignments? If the subsequent assignee did have notice, the bank would have priority. If not, the subsequent assignee would have priority. The categorisation of the charge did not matter.

[119] Slade J in *Siebe Gorman*, Nourse LJ in the *New Bullas* case, and Mr Moss QC in his submission on behalf of the bank in the present case, attributed considerable significance to the labels that the

parties to the debenture had chosen to attribute to the charge over book debts. Mr Moss indeed argued that a debenture expressed to grant a fixed charge thereby limited by necessary implication the ability of the chargor to deal with the charged assets. He argued that Spectrum had no right without the consent of the bank to draw on the account into which the cheques received by Spectrum in payment of its book debts had to be paid. This limitation was, he said, an inevitable result of the grant by the debenture of the fixed charge. This argument, my Lords, puts the cart before the horse. The nature of the charge depends on the rights of the chargor and chargee respectively over the assets subject to the charge. The moneys in the bank account were assets subject to the charge. If the account had been treated as a blocked account, so long as it remained overdrawn, it would be easy to infer from a combination of that treatment and the description of the charge as a fixed charge that Spectrum had no right to draw on the account until the debit on the account had been discharged. But the account was never so treated. The overdraft facility was there to be drawn on by Spectrum at will. In the operation of the account there was never a suggestion that Spectrum needed to obtain the bank's consent before writing a cheque. The bank could, by notice, have terminated the overdraft facility, required immediate repayment of the indebtedness and turned the account into a blocked account. Pending such a notice, however, Spectrum was free to draw on the account. Its right to do so was inconsistent with the charge being a fixed charge and the label placed on the charge by the debenture cannot, in my opinion, be prayed-in-aid to detract from that right.

[120] The correct conclusion, in my opinion, is that the debenture, although expressed to grant the bank a fixed charge over Spectrum's book debts, in law granted only a floating charge. I think the Vice-Chancellor, save for the precedent point, was correct in his reasoning and his conclusion.

Lord Walker:

[His Lordship began by outlining some of the problems associated with the development of the floating charge, in particular the fact that third parties might be misled by the chargor's 'false wealth' and that there is no statutory definition of a 'floating charge'. He continued:

Upgrading the security to a fixed charge

[135] These difficulties have not diminished over the years. Sections 2 and 3 of the 1897 Act (now re-enacted, with a refinement as to timing, as ss 175 (2) (b) and 40 (2) respectively of the Insolvency Act 1986) make a floating charge more precarious as a security. Banks and other large commercial lenders have therefore tried, for understandable reasons, to upgrade their security by imposing fixed (and not merely floating) charges on parts of a trading customer's circulating capital, especially book debts. This chapter of commercial history has been described by Professor Sir Roy Goode QC, *Legal Problems of Credit and Security*, 3rd ed. (2003) pp121–123. In practice, most standard forms of debenture make the charge extend not just to book debts but to all present and future 'book debts and other debts', the extent of which expression was considered by Hoffmann J in *In re Brightlife Ltd* [1987] Ch 200, 204–5; but nothing turns on that in this appeal. In considering the practical effect of charges on debts it should be borne in mind that money paid into a trading company's bank account will not necessarily represent the proceeds of debts of any description, especially if the trader is a retailer making a large number of cash sales, either over the counter or on a 'cash with order' basis.

[136] Banks and their advisers have had some success in their efforts to upgrade their security. It is quite clear that a fixed charge on book debts, present and future, is conceptually possible. That was the most important point decided (or at any rate confirmed) by Slade J in *Siebe Gorman & Co Ltd v Barclays Bank Ltd* [1979] 2 Lloyd's Rep 142, and the Crown, the appellant in this appeal, does not seek to cast any doubt on that general proposition. The Crown challenges the decision on a much narrower point, that is the correct construction of the particular form of debenture which was before the Court. But that narrow point is itself of considerable general importance because the Siebe Gorman form has become a precedent and has been widely used, either in precisely the same words or in very similar words, by numerous banks.

[137] In Siebe Gorman, Slade J decided that the form of debenture before him did on its true construction restrict the borrower, R H McDonald Ltd ('McDonald') in making use of the proceeds of collected debts in the ordinary course of its business. Slade J clearly accepted that, in the absence of such a restriction, the charge on debts could not as a matter of law have been more than a floating charge, even though the parties described it as a fixed (or specific) charge. He said at p 158,

'if I had accepted the premise that [McDonald] would have had the unrestricted right to deal with the proceeds of any of the relevant book debts paid into its account, so long as that account remained in credit, I would have been inclined to accept the conclusion that the charge on such book debts could be no more than a floating charge.'

The Crown has little quarrel with that, except perhaps for the adjective 'unrestricted.'

The essential difference

[138] This passage brings us close to the issue of legal principle, that is the essential difference between a fixed charge and a floating charge. Under a fixed charge the assets charged as security are permanently appropriated to the payment of the sum charged, in such a way as to give the chargee a proprietary interest in the assets. So long as the charge remains unredeemed, the assets can be released from the charge only with the active concurrence of the chargee. The chargee may have good commercial reasons for agreeing to a partial release. If for instance a bank has a fixed charge over a large area of land which is being developed in phases as a housing estate (another example of a fixed charge on what might be regarded as trading stock) it might be short-sighted of the bank not to agree to take only a fraction of the proceeds of sale of houses in the first phase, so enabling the remainder of the development to be funded. But under a fixed charge that will be a matter for the chargee to decide for itself.

[139] Under a floating charge, by contrast, the chargee does not have the same power to control the security for its own benefit. The chargee has a proprietary interest, but its interest is in a *fund* of circulating capital, and unless and until the chargee intervenes (on crystallisation of the charge) it is for the trader, and not the bank, to decide how to run its business. There is a detailed and helpful analysis of the matter, with full citation of authority, in Professor Sarah Worthington's *Proprietary Interests in Commercial Transactions* (1996) pp 74–77; see also her incisive comment on this case ('An Unsatisfactory Area of the Law—Fixed and Floating Charges Yet Again') in (2004) 1 International Corporate Rescue 175. So long as the company trades in the ordinary way (a requirement emphasised by Romer LJ in the *Yorkshire Woolcombers case* [1903] Ch 284, 295, and by the Earl of Halsbury on appeal in the same case, [1904] AC 355, 357–8) the constituents of the charged fund are in a state of flux (or circulation). Trading stock is sold and becomes represented by book debts; these are collected and paid into the bank; the trader's overdraft facility enables it to draw cheques in favour of its suppliers to pay for new stock; and so the trading cycle continues.

[140] I have drawn attention to Slade J's reference to an 'unrestricted' right to deal with the proceeds of collected debts. It is clear that not every restriction on a trader's freedom of action is a badge of a fixed charge: see *Brightlife* [1987] Ch 200, 209. A prohibition on factoring or otherwise dealing with uncollected debts does not prevent the trader from collecting the debts itself. But if the terms of the debenture were such as to require the trader to pay all its collected debts into the bank and to prohibit the trader from drawing on the account (so that the account is blocked), a charge on debts, described as a fixed or specific charge, would indeed take effect as such (see *Re Keenan Brothers Ltd* [1986] BCLC 242, a decision of the Supreme Court of Ireland, followed by Morritt J in *William Gaskell Group Ltd v Highley* [1994] 1 BCLC 197, [1993] BCC 200). In those circumstances the chargee would be in control, prior to crystallisation, and the trader would be unable to trade in the ordinary way without the chargee's positive concurrence. In *Agnew*, Lord Millett pointed out ([2001] 2 AC 710, 730, para 48) that it was not enough to provide in the debenture for an account to be blocked, if it was not in fact operated as a blocked account.

[141] Both sides agree that the label of 'fixed' or 'specific' (which I take to be synonymous in this context) cannot be decisive if the rights created by the debenture, properly construed, are inconsistent with that label. There is a fairly close parallel (first drawn, I think, by Hoffmann J in *Brightlife* [1987] Ch 200, 209 and often repeated) with the important distinction, in land law, between a lease and a licence: see the decision of this House in *Street v Mountford* [1985] AC 809, [1985] 2 All ER 289. The distinction is clear in principle although landlords (in framing letting agreements) and banks (in framing debentures) may produce legal documents in a form which makes the principle difficult to apply. Whether or not it is appropriate to describe this by some disparaging term such as camouflage, it is the court's duty to characterise the document according to the true legal effect of its terms, as has been very clearly explained by Lord Millett in *Agnew* [2001] 2 AC 710, 725–726, para 32. In each case there is a public interest which overrides unrestrained freedom of contract. On the lease/licence issue, the public interest is the protection of vulnerable people seeking living accommodation. On the fixed/floating issue, it is ensuring that preferential creditors obtain the measure of protection which Parliament intended them to have. This public interest is unaffected by the changes in the classes of preferential creditors made by s 251 of the Enterprise Act 2002.

[142] In my opinion Slade J did not, in *Siebe Gorman*, make any significant error in stating the general principles which apply. But he did not correctly construe the debenture which was before him in that case, and his decision on its construction has had surprisingly far-reaching consequences.

[His Lordship was critical of the *Siebe Gorman* decision and continued:]

Postscript: draftsmen's precedents and collateral transactions

[156] Judges considering this area of the law have often commented on the convenience (in point of legal certainty) of using standard-form clauses, the meaning of which has already been determined by the court. For instance Knox J observed in *Ex p Copp* [1989] BCLC 13, 25:

> 'this is a type of transaction in respect of which judicial precedent is a particularly valuable guide to the commercial adviser. It is one of the main justifications for the doctrine of precedent that the adviser can, if he can rely on precedent, give reliable advice to his clients, and it is trite law that that is a particularly cogent consideration in regard to property transactions of one sort or another.'

Requirements for particulars of floating charges to be registered publicly, and for a company's register of debentures to be open for inspection, suggest that Parliament intended that the existence and scope of any floating charge should be ascertainable by the general public, at least in theory (doubts as to how the system works in practice were expressed by Lord Hoffmann in the *Cosslett case*, [2001] UKHL 58, [2002] 1 AC 336, 347–8, para 19).

[157] These considerations might be thought to lead to the conclusion that everything relevant to the characterisation of a charge should be apparent on the face of the formal debenture, without further inquiry. That was, as I understand it, one of the reasons why Knox J, in *Ex p Copp*, declined to look at evidence about an agreed overdraft limit, regarding it as a 'collateral arrangement'. Knox J may have been right in his view that it was unnecessary to receive evidence about an overdraft limit (which may change from time to time) but he took the wrong approach as to the effect of the debenture itself, as the Vice-Chancellor rightly concluded ([2004] Ch 337, 355, para 40). The form of debenture showed that the recycling of book debts was 'not only permitted but envisaged' and it contained no relevant restriction on that being done in the ordinary course of business.

[158] In practice banks use printed standard forms of debenture in simple cases, and City solicitors no doubt have more sophisticated forms, suitable for very large transactions, in their word-processing libraries. It is most desirable that any form of secured debenture, whether simple or complicated, should contain all the terms necessary for its correct characterisation, without resort to any side-letters or other less formal documents (as in the Australian case of *Hart v Barnes* (1982) 7 ACLR 310, mentioned in *Agnew* at para 23). But the fact is that when a bank takes a charge there will normally be at least three documents in play: the debenture creating the charge, the bank's facility letter offering a term loan or an overdraft, and the bank's general terms and conditions. Sometimes there will be more documents that are relevant. I would not rule out the possibility that in some (probably rare) cases all this documentation might have to be taken into account, in its proper commercial context, in determining whether a charge 'as created' was a fixed or floating charge.

[159] In one of the earliest cases on floating charges, In *re Florence Land and Public Works Co* (1878) 10 Ch D 530, 537, Sir George Jessel MR said,

> 'The question we have to decide must be decided, like all other questions of the kind, having regard to the surrounding circumstances under which the instrument was executed, and especially the respective positions of the parties who were the contracting parties, to carry out whose agreement that instrument was executed.'

Cozens-Hardy LJ made similar observations in *Yorkshire Woolcombers* [1903] 2 Ch 284, 297. Many of the later cases have emphasised the need for the court to look at the commercial realities of the situation. The wish to achieve legal certainty by use of a standard precedent cannot override the need to construe any document in its commercial context.

[160] It is also necessary to bear in mind Lord Millett's warning in *Agnew* [2001] 2 AC 710, 730, para 48, that formal provision for a blocked account is not enough 'if it is not operated as one in fact.' Lord Millett did not expand on this point, which may raise difficult questions as to what Staughton LJ, in *Welsh Development Agency v Export Finance Co Ltd* [1992] BCLC 148, [1992] BCC 270, 186–7, referred to as 'external' and 'internal' routes to the construction of commercial documents. This point is discussed in an article by Stephen Atherton and Rizwaan Jameel Mokal in (2005) 26 Company Lawyer 10, 16–18. These difficulties suggest to me that the expedient mentioned in the postscript to the judgment of the Master of the Rolls (para 99), although no doubt appropriate and efficacious in some commercial contexts, may not provide a simple solution in every case.

[161] On the topic of overruling long-standing decisions which have been relied on by commercial lenders, and on the further topic of prospective overruling, I am in full and respectful agreement with the opinions of my noble and learned friends, Lord Nicholls of Birkenhead and Lord Hope. I would allow this appeal and hold, without any sort of temporal restriction, that *Siebe Gorman* was wrongly decided on the issue of construction.

[Lord Nicholls, Steyn and Brown and Baroness Hale delivered concurring judgments.]

NOTES

1. *Re Spectrum Plus Ltd* was a test case. The debenture was in the bank's standard form and many other banks and other commercial lenders had taken security over their borrowers' book debts using a similar form of debenture. In *Siebe Gorman*, Slade J had endorsed this form of debenture as creating a fixed charge. Imagine the consternation of the lending community when it was told that this long-standing decision, which had for many years been relied on when formulating and using standard form charges on book debts, had been overruled on this point. In *Re Spectrum Plus* the bank even went so far as to ask the House of Lords to overrule *Siebe Gorman* prospectively, leaving undisturbed charges granted before their decision. Their Lordships refused to do this on the ground that banks and other commercial lenders were sophisticated operators who could not have been lulled into a false sense of security by what was a first instance decision, so that *Siebe Gorman* could not have been regarded as finally and definitively settling the law. Moreover, their Lordships felt that if their decision was given only prospective effect, it would result in preferential creditors in many existing liquidations being deprived of priority which Parliament intended they should have.

2. *Re Spectrum Plus Ltd* has left banks and other commercial lenders with the thorny question of how to prevent borrowers exercising control over the proceeds of the book debts. Requiring the proceeds of the book debts to be paid into a blocked account is an effective way to ensure that the lender retains control (so long as the account is operated as such) but it comes at a price. Borrowers will usually require quick and easy access to those funds for their day-to-day working capital requirements. Lenders will not want to take on the administrative burden of having to consent to each and every withdrawal from the 'blocked account'. In the Court of Appeal, Lord Phillips had said (at [99]) that: 'it would seem beyond dispute that a requirement to pay book debts into a blocked account will be sufficient restriction to render a charge over book debts a fixed charge, even if the chargor is permitted to overdraw on another account, into which from time to time transfers are made from the blocked account.' In the House of Lords, Lord Walker commented (at [160]) that although the expedient would be 'appropriate and efficacious in some commercial contexts', it 'may not provide a simple solution in every case.' This level of uncertainty is commercially undesirable. Perhaps it is time for banks and other lenders to accept that fixed charges over book debts are, in practical terms, a thing of the past. Financiers may find that they have to settle for a floating charge over book debts in most cases.

3. The relevance of the conduct of the parties after the debenture has been executed raises a number of difficult issues. In *Re Brumark* [2001] UKPC 28, [2001] 2 AC 710, Lord Millett (at [48]) thought that 'it is not enough to provide in the debenture that the account is a blocked account if it is not operated as one in fact'. This seems to run against the well-established rule that the meaning and construction of a contract cannot be reconsidered by post-contractual events (*James Miller & Partners Ltd v Whitworth Estates (Manchester) Ltd* [1970] AC 583). The difficulties raised by Lord Millett's dictum were recognised by Lord Walker in *Spectrum Plus* (at [160]). More recently, in *Re Beam Tube Products Ltd* [2006] EWHC 486 (Ch), [2006] BCC 615, Blackburne J had to consider the impact of post-contractual conduct on the characterisation of a charge over book debts when deciding a priority dispute between the charge holder and the preferential creditors of the company chargor. In this case the debenture stipulated that the company chargor was to have free use of the proceeds of the book debts once paid into a collection account. However, due to the parties' mistaken interpretation of what the security documentation required, the collection account was never operated in that way and the chargor was not given free use of the proceeds. Nevertheless, Blackburne J held (at [38]) that the parties' subsequent attempt to operate a blocked account could not put the charge holder in any better position (a fixed charge) than it would have been in if the terms of the debenture had been duly observed (a floating charge). This was because, under the relevant insolvency legislation, the requirement was to pay preferential creditors out of a charge which 'as created was a floating charge'.

4. Numerous casenotes and articles have been written on the *Spectrum Plus* decision. The following are particularly useful: R Nolan [2005] CLJ 554; C Hare [2005] LMCLQ 440; D Capper (2006) 6 JCLS 447. See also J Getzler and J Payne (eds), *Company Charges: Spectrum and Beyond* (2006).

(iii) Fixed and floating charges: why the distinction matters

See below, pp 1135–1137.

4 EQUITIES AFFECTING ASSIGNED RECEIVABLES

Unlike a mortgagee of a debt, a chargee does not own the charged debt. This has led Professor Goode to submit that giving notice of the charge to the debtor does not prevent the debtor's right of set-off building up against the debt ([1984] JBL 172, p 174). Cf F Oditah *Legal Aspects of Receivables Financing* (1991), pp 95–96, 245–246. If Professor Goode is correct, the chargee would be placed in a worse position than that of an assignee, who can stop equities accumulating by giving the debtor notice of assignment (see above, pp 992ff). But in practice this distinction is rarely encountered. This is because a charge over receivables usually contains a power to convert it into a mortgage through execution of an assignment by the chargee in the name of the chargor (see above, p 1018). Therefore, for the purposes of set-off, a charge may be equated with an assignment (RM Goode *Legal Problems of Credit and Security* (3rd edn, 2003), para 3–21).

Business Computers Ltd v Anglo-African Leasing Ltd

(See above, p 992.)

NOTES

1. See notes above, pp 994–995.
2. For non-assignable receivables, see above, pp 972ff.

QUESTION

Can a customer recover payment from his supplier's factor when the customer has prepaid for goods which are never supplied, or which, if delivered, are lawfully rejected by him? See *Pan Ocean Shipping Co Ltd v Creditcorp Ltd* [1994] 1 All ER 470, HL.

5 PRIORITIES[4]

(a) The rule in *Dearle v Hall*

A factor who takes an assignment of his client's debts will want to ensure that he takes priority over others asserting rights and interests in the same debts. Where the client assigns the same debt more than once, the assignee who is first to give notice of his assignment to the debtor takes priority, provided that at the time of the assignment to him he was not aware of any earlier assignment to a competing assignee. This is known as the rule in *Dearle v Hall* (see the next case).

---

[4] See generally, F Oditah *Legal Aspects of Receivables Financing* (1991), Ch 6; N Ruddy, S Mills and N Davidson *Salinger on Factoring* (4th edn, 2006), Ch 8.

Dearle v Hall

(See above, p 1008.)

NOTES

See Notes above, p 1010.

(b) Registration and the rule in *Dearle v Hall*

Registration of an assignment as a charge under Part 25 of the Companies Act 2006 does not constitute notice to the debtor so as to give the assignee priority under the first limb of the rule in *Dearle v Hall* (the debtor cannot be expected to search the register), but it may constitute sufficient notice to trigger the second limb. A charge over a company's book debts is registrable under s 860(7)(f) of the Companies Act 2006, but not a sale of book debts nor a charge or other disposition of other kinds of debts. Registration is notice only to those who could reasonably be expected to search the register (see RM Goode *Legal Problems of Credit and Security* (3rd edn, 2003), para 3–29).

(c) Criticism of the rule in *Dearle v Hall*

The rule in *Dearle v Hall* is generally acknowledged to be an unsatisfactory determinant of priority in the context of receivables financing (see DM McLauchlan (1980) 96 LQR 90 at p 98).

Report of the Committee on Consumer Credit (Chairman: Lord Crowther)
(1971, Cmnd 4596), Vol 2, p 579

It is doubtful whether any system of priorities can be provided which will do justice in all situations. Certainly existing rules of law fall far short of the ideal. For example, if a debt is assigned to A and after-wards the assignor fraudulently assigns the same debt to B who takes in good faith then if B is the first to give notice to the debtor he gains priority under the rule in *Dearle v Hall*. This rule implicitly assumes that notice to the debtor is equivalent to notice to the second assignee. But this will not in fact be the case unless the second assignee, before giving value, makes enquiries of the debtor to see whether he has had notice of a prior assignment. In the financing of receivables such enquiries would be quite impracticable and the second assignee would not give notice to the debtors, or indeed have occasion to communicate with them, until after he had taken his assignment and paid the price. Moreover the rule in *Dearle v Hall* does not provide a secured party with any machinery for protecting a security interest in future receivables due from future debtors.

NOTES

1. The problems associated with the factoring of future receivables are highlighted, above, pp 1032–1033.

2. For further criticism of the use of the rule in *Dearle v Hall* to determine priority in the context of receivables financing, see JS Ziegel (1963) 41 Can Bar Rev 54, pp 109–110; RM Goode (1976) 92 LQR 528, p 566; F Oditah *Legal Aspects of Receivables Financing* (1991), pp 140).

(d) Priority conflicts between factor and chargee

Under the rule in *Dearle v Hall*, the factor takes priority over a prior fixed charge covering the same assets where he advances his money without knowledge of the charge and he is the first to give notice to the debtor. Otherwise, the chargee takes priority.

A company which has given a floating charge over its assets remains at liberty to deal with those assets in the ordinary course of its business. This means that a factor who later purchases the company's receivables takes priority over the earlier floating charge, even though he did so with knowledge of the charge. The position is otherwise where the factor has notice of the prior crystallisation of the charge (see below, p 1137) or of a provision prohibiting the factoring of receivables contained in the charge instrument itself (see below, p 1135). Provisions prohibiting the factoring of receivables are now commonly found in charge instruments and so the prudent factor should secure a waiver from the chargee before entering into the factoring agreement.

Where the factoring agreement precedes the floating charge, priority depends on whether it is a whole turnover agreement (see above, p 1027) or a facultative agreement (see above, p 1027). Where money has been advanced by the factor under a whole turnover agreement, the receivables vest automatically in the factor when they come into existence and are not caught by the floating charge. On the other hand, in the case of a facultative agreement the receivables only vest in the factor once they come into existence and have been offered to and accepted by the factor, ie there is a binding contract for their sale and purchase: until then the factor will be bound by notice of crystallisation of the charge or a prohibition against the factoring of receivables contained in the charge instrument.

(e) Priority conflicts between factor and retention of title seller

Compaq Computer Ltd v Abercorn Group Ltd

(See above, p 1010.)

NOTES

See notes above, pp 1014–1015.

QUESTION

A Bank plc lends money to B Ltd and takes as security a floating charge over the company's existing and future assets, including its receivables. As is usual with such charge instruments, the instrument restricts the company's right to factor or discount its receivables. Prescribed particulars of the charge are duly registered with the Registrar of Companies but these particulars do not include details of the restrictive covenant on factoring or discounting. B Ltd then purports to assign all its existing and future receivables to C Factors Ltd under a whole turnover agreement which contains a warranty from B Ltd that it has the unencumbered right to factor its receivables. Having searched the register C Factors Ltd are at all times aware of the bank's floating charge, but they do not know of the restrictive covenant. Will C Factors Ltd acquire the receivables unencumbered by the bank's charge? See RM Goode *Commercial Law* (3rd edn, 2004), pp 662ff; and *Salinger on Factoring,* op cit, paras 8–15ff.

6 REFORM

As Professor Goode has noted: 'In economic terms, a sale of receivables with recourse is virtually indistinguishable from a loan on the security of the receivables, for in both cases the trader receives money now and has to repay it himself, or ensure payments by debtors, later' (RM Goode *Commercial Law* (3rd edn, 2004), p 744). As we have already seen, a major distinction between a sale and a loan secured on a company's book debts is that only the latter must be registered under Part 25 of the Companies Act 2006 (see above, p 1044). Registration protects any third party who subsequently deals with the company and who would otherwise be unaware that the company's book debts were encumbered. However, if the financing arrangement is structured as a sale with a right of recourse, the finance company is fully secured and yet others dealing with the company are ignorant of the fact. This anomaly has been criticised: see, especially, the Report of the Crowther Committee on Consumer Credit (1971, Cmnd 4596), Chs 4 and 5, and also Professor Diamond's report entitled *A Review of Security Interests in Property* (HMSO, 1989), paras 18.2–18.3. The Law Commission has recently revisited the issue. In 2005 the Law Commission recommended that there should be a scheme of electronic 'notice-filing' for charges created by companies (Law Com Report No 296, 'Company Security Interests', Aug 2005). The Law Commission recommended that the sale of receivables of the kind which factoring and discounting agreements cover should be brought within the 'notice-filing' scheme (LC Report, Part 4). This would mean that sales of receivables by companies would have to be registered to be valid on insolvency (LC Report, para 4.25). Their priority would be determined by the date of filing (LC Report, para 4.18). The Law Commission recommended that provisions in the contract generating the receivable that purport to restrict its assignment were no longer to be effective against the assignee (LC Report, para 4.40). None of these recommendations were taken up in the recent reform of company law through the Companies Act 2006 (see further, pp 1089–1090 below).

7 INTERNATIONAL FACTORING[5]

A factoring agreement is considered as 'international' when the factor's client (as supplier of goods or services) and the person responsible for the payment of goods and services are situated in different States. In these circumstances, factoring is used to finance international trade. A common practice is for the supplier to enter into a factoring agreement with a factor in his own country (the 'export factor'). The export factor then enters into an arrangement with correspondent factors (the 'import factors') in the countries of the supplier's customers. The import factors accept the credit risk of the debtors situated in their own country and are responsible for collection. The export factor sub-assigns the purchased debt to the import factors. At all times, the import factor is responsible to the export factor and the export factor is responsible to the supplier. Rights of recourse may be exercised along that chain. This method of international factoring is known as a 'two factor' system.

---

[5] See generally, N Ruddy, S Mills and N Davidson *Salinger on Factoring* (4th edn, 2006), Chs 6 and 12.

Other methods of international factoring include:

(1) the 'single factor' system, where the export factor does not use an import factor for routine collections but only for the collection of seriously overdue debts or on the debtor's insolvency;

(2) 'direct import factoring', where the supplier simply factors the debt to a factor in the importing country;

(3) 'direct export factoring' where the export factor handles the functions of the import factor using correspondents to assist with collections in the debtor's country.

Reflecting the growing importance of international factoring, the International Institute for the Unification of Private Law (UNIDROIT) adopted a draft Convention on international factoring in May 1988. The Convention, known as 'The Unidroit Convention on International Factoring', aims to 'facilitate international factoring, while maintaining a fair balance of interests between the different parties involved in factoring transactions' (in the words of the Preamble to the Convention). However, the Convention has been criticised for its limited scope.[6] It does not cover domestic factoring arrangements nor does does it deal with the relationship between the factor and the supplier (which is governed by domestic law). It also fails to address the questions of priority of competing claims to receivables and ignores difficult questions of conflict of laws raised by international factoring.[7]

In December 2001 the United Nations General Assembly adopted the text of the UNCITRAL Convention on the Assignment of Receivables in International Trade. The Convention applies to international assignments and the assignment of international receivables. For the Convention to apply, the assignor needs to be located in a State party to the Convention. One of the stated purposes of the Convention is to 'promote the availability of capital and credit at more affordable rates and thus facilitate the development of international trade' (Preamble, para 5). The Convention deals mainly with property issues, including priority upon default or insolvency of any one of the participants. It also deals with some contractual issues by way of default rules that apply in the absence of agreement between the parties. The Convention permits the assignment of future receivables and the assignment of receivables in bulk. The Convention comes into force six months after formal ratification of five states. At the time of writing, this has yet to happen. For detailed and authoritative coverage, see S V Bazinas (2001) 9 Tulane J of Int and Comp Law 259.

---

[6] Salinger, n 5, para 12–34.
[7] Salinger, n 5, paras 12–02ff and M Moshinsky (1992) 108 LQR 591.

PART VIII

COMMERCIAL CREDIT AND SECURITY

CHAPTER 24

INTRODUCTION

1 COMMERCIAL CREDIT

Credit plays an important role in the world of commerce. Let us take the sale of goods as an example. The seller may have to borrow money from his bank to finance the expansion of his business so that he can obtain the buyer's order and supply the goods as required. The bank loan is a form of credit. On the other hand, the buyer may be unwilling or unable to pay for the goods in advance or on delivery and require a period of credit from the seller. The buyer may even need to sell the goods himself before he can pay his supplier. In these circumstances, the seller may provide the credit himself by deferring payment, or he may accept payment by means of a bill of exchange payable at a future date. The extent to which the seller is willing to accommodate the buyer will greatly depend on the bargaining strengths of the parties. But a seller who has accommodated the buyer by allowing him credit may be unwilling or unable to wait until the credit period expires before receiving funds locked up in the debt he is owed. In such circumstances, he may sell the debt to a factoring company, or discount the bill of exchange to a bank or discount house, for immediate cash. Alternatively, he may borrow on the strength of those receivables (see above, Chapter 23).

So far we have considered the means by which the seller provides credit to the buyer. However, the seller may be unwilling to do this. The seller may prefer to sell the goods to a third party, such as a finance house, and leave it to the third party to supply the goods to the buyer on credit terms, eg through hire-purchase, conditional sale, credit sale or finance leasing. Alternatively, the buyer may simply borrow money from a commercial lender and use the loan to pay the seller.

But no matter who provides credit, or how, the creditor will usually require some form of security. For example, the seller may reserve title in the goods or demand that payment is made by irrevocable documentary credit; the bank or factoring company may require security over other property belonging to the borrower; the finance house may ask for a third party guarantee. In all these cases the creditor is trying to ensure that he is not left high and dry should the debtor fail before making payment. In certain cases, the creditor may even insure himself against such loss (see above, p 928).

(a) Credit defined

The term 'credit' is used in many different senses. For example, it may be used to describe someone's financial standing (eg 'his credit is good'); alternatively, it may be used in a legal sense, such as to describe some form of financial accommodation. In this chapter, we shall be concerned with credit in the sense of financial accommodation, that is, 'the provision of a benefit (cash, land, goods, services or facilities) for which payment is to be made by the recipient in money at a later date' (RM Goode *Commercial Law* (3rd edn, 2004), pp 578–579; cf the Consumer Credit Act 1974, s 9(1) which defines credit as including 'a cash loan, and any other form of financial accommodation'; see also *Dimond v Lovell* [2002] 1 AC 384, HL.

(b) The forms of credit

There are two forms of credit: loan credit and sale credit. *Loan credit* is granted where money is lent to the debtor on terms that it must be repaid to the creditor, together with interest, in due course, eg as with a bank loan or overdraft. *Sale credit* is granted where the debtor is allowed to defer payment of the price of goods and services supplied, eg as with conditional sale, hire-purchase, and credit sale agreements. It used to be important to distinguish between loan credit and sale credit because of the different regulatory regimes which applied to each (eg the Moneylenders Acts never applied to instalment selling and hire-purchase). However, in so far as a transaction is now caught by the Consumer Credit Act 1974 the distinction between the two forms of credit has become irrelevant in this context. But the distinction remains relevant in other contexts, eg a company' s borrowing powers may be restricted by its Articles of Association, or it may breach the terms of a debenture given to its bankers by further borrowing, yet in both cases the company remains free to purchase goods and service on sale credit.

A distinction must also be made between *fixed-sum credit* and *revolving credit*. Fixed-sum credit is granted where the debtor receives a fixed amount of credit which must be repaid in a lump sum or by instalments over a period of time. Non-instalment loans, hire-purchase agreements and conditional sale agreements are all examples of fixed-sum credit. By contrast, revolving credit is granted where the debtor is allowed a credit facility which he may draw on as and when he pleases, up to an overall credit limit. The debtor may then restore the facility in whole or in part as he repays the creditor. A bank overdraft provides a good example of revolving credit: as cheques are drawn by the customer and paid by the bank, the available balance of the overdraft decreases; as amounts are paid to the credit of the account, the available balance of the overdraft increases. In strict legal terms, the overdraft facility is a standing offer for a loan made by the bank which the customer accepts each time he draws upon that facility, so that a series of unilateral contracts come into existence. By contrast, where the bank provides the customer with a bank loan of a fixed amount, the customer enters into a single bilateral contract with the bank. Both fixed-sum credit and revolving credit may be purchase-money (eg where a customer purchases a car for cash advanced direct from the finance house to the car dealer and where goods and services are purchased by credit card) or non-purchase money (eg a bank loan for general purposes and an overdraft).

(c) The Consumer Credit Act 1974

The Consumer Credit Act 1974 regulates credit agreements entered into by an 'individual' ('the debtor'), which includes small partnerships (three partners or less) and unincorporated associations but not corporations. All such credit agreements are *prima facie* covered by the Act irrespective of the amount involved (a previous financial limit of £25,000 was removed by the Consumer Credit Act 2006, s 2). However, certain types of credit agreement are exempt from regulation under the 1974 Act, these include those agreements where credit is supplied to a natural person who is a 'high net worth debtor', ie someone with an annual net income of £150,000 or more and/or with net assets (excluding their primary residence and certain other assets) to the value of £500,000 or more (1974 Act, s 16A, inserted by Consumer Credit Act 2006, s 3; see also the Consumer Credit (Exempt Agreements) Order 2007, SI 2007/1168, Sch 2), or where the credit exceeds £25,000 and the agreement is entered into 'wholly or predominantly for the purposes of a business' carried on, or intended to be carried on, by the debtor (1974 Act, s 16B, inserted by Consumer Credit Act 2006, s 4) (but note that even these two types of agreement are not exempt from ss 140A-140C of the 1974 Act which enables debtors to challenge unfair relationships with creditors). Credit agreements between private individuals (called 'non-commercial' agreements: s 189(1)) are also exempt from most of the provisions of the Act.

Where the Consumer Credit Act 1974 applies it regulates such matters as the form, contents, terms and enforcement of the credit agreement. Wherever credit is provided to a small partnership or to an unincorporated trader it will be important to consider the effect of the Act on the transaction. This is particularly so where the credit provided is for more than £25,000, because the business purposes exemption only applies where the credit exceeds that sum (remembering also that where the debtor is a natural person, the 'high net worth' exemption might apply). Nevertheless, despite the significant changes made to the consumer credit regime by the Consumer Credit Act 2006, the 1974 Act is still primarily concerned with *consumer* protection, and so we do not intend to consider its provisions any further at this stage. (For further discussion, see below, pp 1146–1148.)

QUESTIONS

1. List the principal institutions granting commercial credit. See RM Goode *Consumer Credit Law: Law and Practice* (looseleaf), para 1A [2.3].

2. 'The provision of credit for trade and industry stimulates production and encourages enterprise. Credit also tides individuals and companies over difficult times' (F Oditah *Legal Aspects of Receivables Financing* (1991), p 1). Can you think of any other motives for demanding credit? Is the provision of credit always a good thing?

2 SECURITY

(a) The nature and purpose of security

In 1985 Professor Diamond was asked by the Minister for Corporate and Consumer Affairs to examine the need for alteration of the law relating to security over property other than land. His report was published by the Department of Trade and Industry in 1989 and is entitled A *Review of Security Interests in Property*. In the extract which follows, Professor Diamond considers the nature and purpose of security.

A Review of Security Interests in Property by Professor AL Diamond
(1989), paras 3.1–3.3

The nature of security

3.1 There are two types of security. One type is often known as personal security. This is where a person who is not otherwise liable under a contract between the debtor and the creditor enters into a separate contract with the creditor under which he assumes some form of liability to ensure that the creditor does not lose (or loses less than he otherwise might) if the debtor fails to perform his contractual obligations. The debtor's contractual obligations may involve the payment of money, but this is not necessarily the case: they may require the performance of any kind of act. Personal security may take the form of a guarantee, caution or indemnity, or may be known as a performance bond. This report is not concerned with this form of security.

3.2 The other type of security is security over property. This is a right relating to property, the purpose of which is to improve the creditor's chance of getting paid or of receiving whatever else the debtor is required to do by way of performance of the contract. It is this type of security—security over property other than land—which is the subject matter of this report. Such security may be possessory, where the creditor takes possession of the subject matter of the security, or non-possessory.

The purpose of security

3.3 As stated in the last paragraph, the purpose of security is to improve the creditor's chance of obtaining performance of the contract with the debtor. In particular, the taking of security may have any one or more of the following effects:

(a) Coercion

In most situations the last thing the creditor wants is to have to enforce his security. His prime objective is that the contract he has entered into with the debtor should be performed. The debtor's fear that the security may be enforced, or a threat by the creditor to enforce the security, will often be enough to ensure that a debtor who is having difficulty in fulfilling all his contracts will give priority to performance in favour of the secured creditor.

(b) Insolvency

If the debtor is unable to meet all his obligations, the creditor with security will usually be in a better position than unsecured creditors, for he will be able to look to the security which, if it has sufficient value, will enable him to receive money on its disposal. In some situations the agreement creating the right by way of security will enable the creditor to appoint a receiver in specified circumstances.

(c) Execution or diligence

Another creditor may, usually after obtaining a judgment against the debtor, attempt to seize the debtor's property by way of execution or diligence, or a landlord may, without obtaining a judgment, distrain on the debtor's goods or sequestrate the debtor's goods for rent. The holder of security will hope to exercise his rights against the property subject to the security and to prevent seizure by or on behalf of the other creditor.

(d) Sale

If the debtor purports to sell the subject matter of the security interest, the question arises whether the holder of the security interest can assert his rights as against the buyer or whether he can, in the alternative or in addition, lay claim to the proceeds of the sale in the debtor's hands.

(e) General

The above may be summed up in Professor Goode's words: 'All forms of real security...confer on the secured creditor at least two basic real rights: the right of pursuit, and the right of preference. The secured party can follow his asset, and its products and proceeds, into the hands of any third party other than one acquiring an overriding title by virtue of some exception to the *nemo dat* rule; and the secured party is entitled to look to the proceeds of the asset to satisfy the debt due to him in priority to the claims of other creditors.' (RM Goode *Commercial Law,* (now 3rd edn, 2004) p 623.) Professor Goode continues: 'Other real rights are available for the enforcement of the security, depending on the nature of the security interest. These are: the retention or recovery of possession of the asset; sale of the asset; foreclosure; and an order vesting legal title in the secured creditor.'

NOTES

1. A creditor holding personal security has merely a personal claim against the third party guarantor (as well as against the original debtor).[1] The weakness of personal security is that its value depends on the continued solvency of the third party. If the third party is made bankrupt, or goes into liquidation, the creditor is only left with a right to prove for a dividend in competition with other unsecured creditors.

2. By contrast, a creditor holding real security (or 'security over property' as Professor Diamond describes it) can rely on his right of preference to ensure priority over other creditors in the event of the debtor's bankruptcy or liquidation. As Professor DE Allan has observed ((1989) 15 Mon LR 337, p 343):

...the principal value of traditional security is to give the creditor a preferred position in the insolvency or liquidation of the debtor. The major fear of creditors is the insolvency of the debtor and the risk that the creditor will have to line up and share *pari passu* with all other creditors. Security provides a means whereby, in the event of this catastrophe, the secured party can make off with the assets against which he is secured and satisfy his claim in full outside the bankruptcy.

But what benefits a creditor holding real security (hereafter referred to as 'a secured creditor') may hinder the debtor and unsecured creditors generally. Professor Allan continues (at p 343):

This privileged position [ie of the secured creditor]...is at variance with a legal policy manifested in the bankruptcy and winding-up legislation of seeking the rehabilitation of the debtor and, where that is not possible, of providing an even-handed distribution among creditors of all types. It concedes to any secured creditor the right to withdraw the assets against which he is secured and virtually to determine unilaterally that the debtor shall be put into bankruptcy or liquidation without reference to whether the situation of the debtor is salvageable and without regard to the interests of other creditors. The position is particularly acute so far as the unsecured creditors are concerned....

Some of Professor Allan's concerns have been met by statutory intervention. In particular, the Insolvency Act 1986, Sch B1, paras 43(2) and 44, impose restrictions on the secured creditor's right to enforce his security where a petition has been presented for an administration order, or the company has gone into administration, without leave of the court or the administrator's consent (see the landmark decision of the Court of Appeal in *Re Atlantic Computer Systems plc* [1992] Ch 505 for guidance on the principles governing the exercise of the court's discretion). Such intervention evidences a modest shift of balance away from secured creditors and back towards the principle of *pari passu* distribution (MG Bridge [1992] JBL 1, p 17). However, the extent to which insolvency law should generally look to redistribute assets from secured to unsecured creditors, in the interests of equality, raises important policy questions (see F Oditah (1992) 108 LQR 459, p 472; R Goode 'Proprietary Rights and

---

[1] Personal security can also be given by the debtor himself on a collateral underaking by way of security, eg on a bill of exchange.

Unsecured Creditors' in BAK Rider (ed) *The Realm of Company Law: A Collection of Papers in Honour of Professor Leonard Sealy* (1998), pp 183–197).

3.   What justifies placing a secured creditor in such a privileged position? This question has generated a vast body of literature, especially in the United States (see, eg the collection of papers published in (1997) 82 Cornell Law Review 1279–1567). A number of theories have been advanced which seek to justify the privilege on grounds of economic efficiency (see A Schwartz (1981) 10 Journal of Legal Studies 1 for a general review; see also TH Jackson and AT Kronman (1979) 88 Yale LJ 1143). None of them is entirely convincing. Probably the best explanation for the priority given to secured creditors over other creditors is that real security makes credit accessible to many debtors who, in the absence of such security, would be unable to obtain unsecured finance. As Dr Oditah explains (F Oditah *Legal Aspects of Receivables Financing* (1991), p 18):

> ...the law recognises and gives effect to the priority of secured creditors because security makes available funds which may otherwise be employed elsewhere, or made available only on terms which the average debtor can ill afford. This may or may not be perceived as detrimental to unsecured creditors of a common debtor, but it can scarcely be shown to be at their expense. Indeed a secured creditor has already paid for his priority through receipt of a lower return on his investment. On the other hand, unsecured creditors have already been paid for allowing this priority and they receive a higher rate of return because of their lower priority position. Since most creditors are free to select the terms on which they would lend, there is no compelling argument based on considerations of fairness for adopting one legal rule rather than the other.

Nevertheless, recent academic studies in the United Kingdom reveal a growing hostility towards secured credit on grounds of unfairness and inefficiency (see, eg V Finch (1999) 62 MLR 633; and see also RJ Mokal (2002) 22 OJLS 686 for a strongly argued case that the pendulum has swung too far). Moreover, there is the potential for conflict between the interests of secured creditors and a modern corporate 'rescue culture' that seeks to assist companies in times of financial difficulty rather than allow secured creditors to scupper plans for survival through enforcement of their security (see generally, Milman and Mond *Security and Corporate Rescue* (1999)). The Enterprise Act 2002 reflects this rescue culture. Two of its provisions illustrate the point. First, s 250 of the Enterprise Act 2002 (inserting s 72A(1) into the Insolvency Act 1986) provides that, with certain exceptions, a floating charge holder may no longer appoint an administrative receiver over the corporate debtor's assets and thereby undermine the prospect of reorganisation of the company through administration. Secondly, s 252 of the Enterprise Act 2002 (inserting s 176A into the Insolvency Act 1986) revives a recommendation of the Cork Committee (Cmnd 8338, (1982), para 1538 ff) that a prescribed amount of the company's 'net property' (the amount of the company's property that, but for s 176A itself, would have been available for distribution to a floating chargee) must be paid into a fund for unsecured creditors (50% of the first £10,000 of the company's net property, followed by 20% of the remainder, but with the overall distribution to be made from the fund capped at £600,000). The prevailing rescue culture is also manifest in the statutory reversal of *Buchler v Talbot (Re Leyland Daf)* [2004] UKHL 9, [2004] AC 298, where the House of Lords held that general liquidation expenses were not payable out of assets subject to a floating charge (see the Companies Act 2006, s 1282, inserting a new s 176ZA into the Insolvency Act 1986). Administration expenses were not affected by *Buchler v Talbot*, which continued to be paid out of floating charge assets, so that until that decision was reversed secured creditors had an incentive to push for liquidation rather than administration.

Whatever the strengths and weaknesses of the arguments for and against secured credit, there can be little doubt that it is here to stay, at least for the foreseeable future (M Bridge (1992) 12 OJLS 333, p 341). To abolish the system of secured credit would be futile for, as Professors Jackson and Kronman have pointed out (op cit, p 1157), '…if the law denied debtors the power to prefer some creditors over others through a system of security agreements, a similar network of priority relationships could be expected to emerge by consensual arrangement between creditors'. The rights given to secured creditors provide a simpler and more efficient system for organising priorities than would arise out of such a complex web of priority agreements between creditors.

4.   Security can be taken over both tangible and intangible property. In the past security was mainly taken over tangible property, that is land and goods. Security over tangible property remains important as is evidenced by the 2001 Convention on International Interests in Mobile Equipment governing security, retention of title and leasing interests in aircraft, space objects and railway rolling stock (see RM Goode [2000] LMCLQ 161). Security can also be taken over documentary intangibles such as documents of title to goods, negotiable instruments and negotiable securities. Today, however, the greatest wealth is tied up in pure intangible property, including receivables (debts) and investment securities (such as shares and bonds) held in dematerialised form on electronic clearing and settlement systems. The ability to take security over pure intangible property is of paramount importance in the modern business world.

QUESTION

Is a secured creditor always ensured priority over other creditors on the debtor's bankruptcy or liquidation? What if two creditors hold security over the same property?

(b) Real security and security interest

In *Bristol Airport plc v Powdrill* [1990] Ch 744 at 760, Browne-Wilkinson V-C, without claiming it was comprehensive, accepted the following description of (real) security:[2]

Security is created where a person ('the creditor') to whom an obligation is owed by another ('the debtor') by statute or contract, in addition to the personal promise of the debtor to discharge the obligation, obtains rights exercisable against some property In which the debtor has an interest in order to enforce the discharge of the debtor's obligation to the creditor.[3]

The essential feature of real security is that it gives the holder of the security a proprietary claim over assets of the debtor (or a third party) to secure payment of a debt or other obligation. Real security means security in a *res* (or asset). It involves the *grant* to the creditor of an *interest* in one or more assets of the debtor (or a third party) to *secure* the debtor's obligations. The interest conferred may be full legal ownership or some lesser property right in the asset,

---

[2] In *Bristol Airport plc v Powdrill* it was held that the statutory right of an airport under the Civil Aviation Act 1982, s 88, to detain an aircraft for failure to pay outstanding aircraft charges was a 'lien or other security' within s 248(b)(i) of the Insolvency Act 1986. The same description of security in its legal sense was later adopted by Lightman J in *Razzaq v Pala* [1997] 1 WLR 1336, where he held that a landlord's right of re-entry for non-payment of rent did not constitute 'security' within the terms of s 383(2) of the Insolvency Act 1986 (a provision equivalent to s 248, but relating to personal insolvency). The landlord's right of re-entry on forfeiture of a lease of land is not a true security interest: *Christopher Moran Holdings Ltd v Bairstow* [2000] 2 AC 172 at 186, per Lord Millett.

[3] Of course, the property of a third party can also be made available by way of security.

but in all cases it must have been given to secure the discharge of a debt or other obligation of the debtor (or a third party) (*Re Cosslett (Contractors) Ltd* [1998] Ch 495 at 508, per Millett LJ). A creditor granted an interest in such circumstances is described as having a 'security interest' (see generally, RM Goode *Legal Problems of Credit and Security* (3rd edn, 2003), Ch 1).

As a consequence of the grant of his interest the secured creditor acquires those rights which inhere in the asset and which, therefore, can be exercised against third parties generally. Such 'real' rights include the rights of pursuit and preference. However, these real rights must be distinguished from rights of pursuit and preference conferred on the creditor by agreement with the debtor (or third party) independently of the creation of any property interest in the asset. In such circumstances, the rights of pursuit and preference will only bind the parties to the particular agreement and not third parties generally (see RM Goode (1989) 15 Mon LR 361, pp 363–364, replying to the contrary argument presented by DE Allan (1989) 15 Mon LR 337 at p 346). However, equity blurs the distinction between rights *in* an asset (real rights) and rights *to* an asset (personal rights). Because equity treats as done that which ought to be done, most agreements to give security in an asset will be treated as proprietary in nature, ie as if the agreements were actual transfers (RM Goode (1987) 103 LQR 433 at pp 437–438; F Oditah (1992) 108 LQR 459. p 470).

Only four types of consensual security (ie created by agreement between the parties) give a creditor a security interest: pledge, contractual lien, mortgage and charge (*Re Cosslett (Contractors) Ltd* [1998] Ch 495 at 508, per Millett LJ: see also RM Goode *Legal Problems of Credit and Security* (3rd edn, 2003), paras 1-42–1-54; and (1989) 15 Mon LR 361 at p 362; cf F Oditah *Legal Aspects of Receivables Financing* (1991), pp 5–11; DE Allan (1989) 15 Mon LR 337 at p 348). Other types of consensual security are regarded as quasi-security (see below). Furthermore, in certain circumstances real security may arise automatically by operation of law. The main category of real security arising by operation of law is the lien (other than the contractual lien). Pledges, common law liens (including contractual liens) and the principal statutory lien (the unpaid seller's lien) are all possessory securities, ie the creditor takes possession of the subject matter of the security (see below, Chapter 25). Mortgages, charges, equitable liens and maritime liens are non-possessory securities (see below, Chapter 26).

(c) Quasi-security

Real security can be contrasted with quasi-security. Although quasi-security is intended to fulfil a security function, it does not give the creditor a security interest because it does not involve rights *in* an asset which bind third parties generally (RM Goode (1989) 15 Mon LR 361, p 362). Examples of such quasi-security include: contractual set-off, subordination agreements, flawed assets, and negative pledge clauses in unsecured financing (see RM Goode *Legal Problems of Credit and Security* (3rd edn, 2003), para 1–17).

Hire-purchase agreements, conditional sale agreements and retention of title clauses (although again fulfilling security functions) are also regarded as quasi-securities. Although in the case of these security devices the creditor does have a right in the asset, it is a right which he retains and not one which the debtor grants to him. Only real rights created by the debtor (not retained by the creditor) are regarded as rights by way of security. This distinction was established by the House of Lords in *McEntire v Crossley Bros Ltd* [1895] AC 457, and has been restated by their Lordships' House in *Armour v Thyssen Edelstahlwerke AG* [1991] 2 AC 339 (on appeal from the Inner House of the Court of Session (Scotland)). In *Armour v Thyssen*, sellers claimed redelivery of steel supplied under a contract of sale containing an 'all monies' reservation of title clause. Receivers of the buyers resisted the claim arguing that the clause constituted an attempt, ineffective under Scottish law, to create a right of security over corporeal movables without transfer of possession, and that the property in the steel passed to the buyers on delivery. The House of Lords upheld the seller's claim on the ground that the buyers had not created a security over the goods in favour of the seller. Lord Jauncey of Tullichettle stated that '[i]t is of the essence of a right of security that the debtor possesses in relation to the property a right which he can transfer to the creditor, which right must be retransferred to him on payment of the debt'. As the contract of sale reserved property in the seller until payment of all debts due, the buyers 'had no interest of any kind whatsoever in the particular goods…[and]…were never in a position to confer on the [sellers] any subordinate right over the steel…' (per Lord Keith of Kinkel). See also, RM Goode (1989) 15 Mon LR 360, p 362 (who argues that if the debtor has neither an interest in the asset *nor the power to dispose of it* he cannot give it in security); cf F Oditah *Legal Aspects of Receivables Financing* (1991), pp 5–8; and DE Allan (1989) 15 Mon LR 337, pp 348–349).

(d) How is the creation of real security to be determined?

There are a number of reasons why it is important to distinguish real security from quasi-security. In general, quasi-security does not require registration under the Bills of Sale Acts 1878–1891 or under Part 25 of the Companies Act 2006 (but see also Insolvency Act 1986, s 344: above, p 1043), whereas certain types of real security (especially consensual non-possessory real security) must be registered under one or other of these statutes, or possibly under some other Act (eg as with land, shares, ships etc). There are other reasons for making the distinction, eg where an agreement creates a security interest in law the debtor has a right to redeem and an interest in any surplus following repossession and sale by the creditor (see RM Goode *Legal Problems of Credit and Security* (3rd edn, 2003), para 1-03). Should a functionally-based notice-filing system for security over personal property ever be introduced into the UK, many (but not all) types of quasi-security would become registrable. This would eliminate one of the reasons for distinguishing real security from quasi-security but the other reasons for making the distinction would remain important (see G McCormack [2003] LMCLQ 80, 91–92). The Law Commission provisionally proposed such a radical scheme in a consultative report on company security interests published in 2004 (LC CP No 176), but the proposal proved controversial and was omitted from its Final Report published in 2005 (LC Report No 296). The Final Report recommended that for the time being a more limited notice-filing scheme should be adopted for company charges and outright sales of receivables. These recommendations were not incorporated into the Companies Act 2006, although the Government has said that it will continue to consider reform in this area.

When determining whether real security has been created the court must identify an intention to create a security interest coupled with an agreement in a form which brings this intention into effect (RM Goode (1989) 15 Mon LR 360, p 364). It is sometimes difficult to ascertain the precise legal form of an agreement which fulfills a security function, but it is well established that the court must look at the *substance* of the transaction and not the labels the parties have chosen to give it. This is illustrated by the next case.

Welsh Development Agency v Export Finance Co Ltd
[1992] BCLC 148, Court of Appeal

(See above, p 1018.)

NOTE

See notes above, pp 1022–1025.

(e) Attachment, perfection and priorities

The process of creating an effective security interest can be broken down into three stages: attachment, perfection and priorities.[4] You should keep these three stages in mind when reading Chapters 25 and 26 on possessory and non-possessory security.

(i) Attachment

Attachment is the process by which a security interest is created as between the creditor and the debtor. The effect of attachment is that the security interest fastens on the asset offered as security so as to give the creditor rights *in rem* against the debtor personally, though not against third parties.[5]

In order for a security interest to attach to an asset, otherwise than by operation of law, the following conditions must be satisfied:[6]

(a) There must be an agreement to create a security interest. Leaving aside the pledge and contractual lien (see below), a valid agreement is enough to create a security interest in equity (ie a mortgage or charge) so long as the following conditions—as well as those contained in sub-paragraphs (b) to (d) below—are fulfilled. First, the agreement must be valid and enforceable as a contract, so it must be supported by consideration and comply with any necessary formalities. Secondly, the particular requirements for recognition of a security interest by a court of equity must be fulfilled: the agreement must manifest an intention to create a present security (*Palmer v Carey* [1926] AC 703), the creditor must have advanced his money (*Rogers v Challis* (1859) 27 Beav 175), the property must be sufficiently identifiable (*Tailby v Official Receiver* (1888) 13 App Cas 523) and the conditions of attachment expressly or implicitly specified by the agreement itself must be fulfilled (so a floating charge, though a present security, will not attach until crystallisation: see below, p 1137)—but where the specified event is a mere contingency which may or may not occur then unless the contingency is simply the debtor's acquisition of an interest in the asset the agreement will not by itself be enough to create a security interest.[7]

In the case of a legal mortgage there must be actual transfer by way of security and compliance with any statutory requirements as to form (see below, p 1124) but, as Professor Goode notes, 'these are not conditions of attachment of a security interest, merely additional steps needed to convert an equitable security into a legal security' (see RM Goode *Legal Problems of Credit and Security* (3rd edn, 2003), para 2–04). However, a pledge requires delivery of actual or constructive possession to the creditor for attachment to take place. Possession is also essential for a contractual lien, although in this case the lienee retains possession of goods that were delivered to him for some other purpose.

---

[4] This tripartite scheme is advocated by Professor Sir Roy Goode, the leading exponent of English security law: see RM Goode *Commercial Law* (3rd edn, 2004), Chs 23 and 24; RM Goode *Legal Problems of Credit and Security* (3rd edn, 2003), Chap II.

[5] Goode *Legal Problems,* para 2–02; Goode *Commercial Law,* p 624, where Professor Goode acknowledges that the term 'attachment' is derived from Article 9 of the American Uniform Commercial Code.

[6] Taken from Goode *Legal Problems,* paras 2–03–2–10; see also Goode *Commercial Law,* pp 627–633.

[7] Goode *Legal Problems,* paras 2–09 and 2–15; Goode *Commercial Law,* p 629; but contrast T Chen-Han (2002) 2 JCLS 191.

(b) The asset must be identifiable as falling within the scope of the security agreement, either because it has been so identified in the agreement or because it has become identified by being later set aside and appropriated to the agreement by an unconditional act of appropriation made in accordance with the agreement. So a security interest cannot be effective if the asset which is prospectively the secured property has not been identified. In the case of security over tangible property, the process is the same as for the identification of goods which are the subject of a contract of sale (see above, p 315). In the case of security over intangible property, there is greater scope for the identification of an asset that remains part of an undivided fund (see above, p 956). There is no need for precise identification of the asset, it is enough that it is identifiable as falling within the terms of the security agreement, eg a debtor can charge *all* his existing and future book debts (*Tailby v Official Receiver* (1888) 13 App Cas 523) or even *all* his assets (*Re Kelcey* [1899] 2 Ch 530; *Syrett v Egerton* [1957] 3 All ER 331).

(c) The debtor must have either a present interest in the asset or power to dispose of the asset as security by virtue of some exception to the *nemo dat* rule (see above, Chapter 9). The grant of security over 'future property' (see below) creates only an inchoate security interest, but when the debtor acquires an asset falling within the after-acquired property clause the security interest attaches to the asset with effect from the date of the agreement, unless the parties have agreed otherwise (as in the case of a floating charge).

(d) There must be some current obligation of the debtor to the creditor which the asset is designed to secure. If there is no current indebtedness, there can be no attachment. If an advance is made and then repaid, attachment ceases, though it will revive with effect from the date of the security agreement if a new advance is later made pursuant to that agreement.

Attachment occurs when all these conditions are satisfied and, unless otherwise agreed, takes effect retrospectively from the date of the security agreement, regardless of the order in which the conditions were fulfilled.[8]

(ii) Perfection

Perfection of a security interest involves the taking of any additional steps prescribed by law for the giving of notice of the security interest so as to bind third parties.[9] Without perfection an attached security interest will only bind the debtor, but after perfection it will also bind third parties, unless the interest is displaced by a particular priority rule.

In some cases the process of attachment also constitutes perfection. This arises where the debtor is a company and the security interest falls outside the list of security interests prescribed by s 860(7) of the Companies Act 2006, eg a fixed mortgage or charge on goods to be imported, other than a ship or aircraft. It also arises in the case of an oral mortgage or charge on goods by an individual, which takes effect without the need for registration under the Bills of Sale Acts. But for any other security interest, which is not perfected simply by attachment, perfection must take place in one of three ways: by taking actual or constructive possession (see below, Chapter 25), by registration (see below, Chapter 26) and, in the case of security over a debt or interest in a fund, by notice to the debtor or fundholder (see above, Chapters 22 and 23).

---

[8] *Goode Legal Problems,* para 2–11; Goode *Commercial Law,* p 628.
[9] Goode *Legal Problems,* para 2–16; Goode *Commercial Law,* p 624.

(iii) Priorities

Priority rules declare the ranking of the security interest in relation to rival claims over the debtor's assets.[10] These rules have evolved at common law and in equity, and will apply unless restricted by statute. They apply equally to tangible and intangible property. The most important priority rules have been summarised by Professor Goode as follows:[11]

(a) a person cannot in general transfer a better title than he himself possesses, so that, in general, priority among competing interests is determined by the order of their creation; but

(b) a legal estate or interest is preferred to an equitable interest; accordingly,

(c) while as between competing equitable interests the first in time prevails, if the holder of the second interest, having advanced his money without notice of the first, gets in the legal title, he obtains priority;

(d) the priority of successive assignees of a debt or other chose in action is determined by the order in which the assignments are made except that an assignee who takes without prior notice of an earlier assignment and is the first to give notice of assignment to the debtor has priority over the earlier assignee;

(e) both legal and equitable interests acquired for value and without notice prevail over mere equities; and

(f) one whose interest derives from the holder of an indefeasible title can shelter behind that title, even if taking with notice of an earlier title or if taking otherwise than for value, unless he committed or assisted in the wrongdoing by which that earlier title was lost.

These principles are supplemented by the following subsidiary, but none the less important, rules:

(1) Even the holder of a legal estate or interest will lose his priority where:

  (a) he has connived at or participated in a fraud as the result of which the later interest was acquired without notice of the prior legal title; or

  (b) he has held out the debtor, or permitted the debtor to hold himself out, as the unencumbered owner of the asset or as authorized to deal with it free from the security interest; or

  (c) he has by his gross negligence in failing to obtain or, possibly, to retain, the title deeds enabled the debtor to deal with the asset as if it were not encumbered by the security interest.

(2) The holder of a floating charge is postponed to the grantee of a subsequent fixed charge unless this is taken with notice of a negative pledge clause in the floating charge.

(3) Normal priority rules may be displaced by agreement between the competing interests. So a first mortgagee may agree to have his interest subordinated to that of the second mortgagee. Such subordination agreements are not uncommon and do not require the consent of the debtor.

(4) There are special rules governing the ability of a secured party, after the grant of a subsequent encumbrance, to tack advances or further advances ranking in priority to the later encumbrances.

(5) Discharge of a security interest automatically promotes junior security interests. So if Blackacre is mortgaged in first to A, then to B, then to C, and the mortgage in favour of A is discharged, B becomes the first mortgagee, C the second mortgagee.

(f) Security over future property

Future property is property which does not exist or in which the debtor has no proprietary interest at the time of giving the security. It must not be confused with *potential* property

[10] Goode *Commercial Law*, p 624.
[11] Goode *Commercial Law*, pp 654–655 (footnotes omitted). See also Goode *Legal Problems*, Ch V.

which is to grow out of an asset in which the debtor has an interest at the time of giving the security, eg milk from a cow or sums payable in the future under an existing building contract.[12] Potential property is regarded as existing (not future) property (see above, p 938). The grant of security over the potential property is treated as the present assignment of existing property, although the security cannot be asserted until the potential property actually comes into existence.

The common law has long set itself against the idea that an agreement to give security over future property could create proprietary rights. So far as the common law is concerned there must be a new act of transfer, after acquisition of the property by the debtor, for proprietary rights to vest in the creditor. The position is different in equity, which treats as done that which ought to be done. There, so long as the prerequisites for the recognition of a security interest by a court of equity have been satisfied (as to which, see above, p 1084), an agreement to give security over future property is treated as a present, but inchoate, security which fastens on the property as soon as it is acquired by the debtor without the need for a new act of transfer (see the landmark decision of the House of Lords in *Holroyd v Marshall* (1862) 10 HL Cas 191, above p 1028, as interpreted by their Lordships' House in *Tailby v Official Receiver* (1888) 13 App Cas 523, above p 1029). Attachment of the security interest takes effect retrospectively relating back to the time of the security agreement (*Tailby v Offical Receiver*, above; *Re Lind* [1915] 2 Ch 345), unless the parties have agreed otherwise (so crystallisation of a floating charge is not retrospective).

(g) Reform

The law regulates transactions according to their form rather than their substance or function. Real security and quasi-security fulfil the same security function but they are regulated differently because of their form. The problems which the 'form over substance' approach can lead to are highlighted by Professor Diamond in the following extract from his report.

A Review of Security Interests in Property by Professor AL Diamond
(1989), paras 8.2.1–8.2.11

8.2 Defects in the present law

8.2.1 *(a) Obstacles to security.* Having concluded that legal obstacles to the creation of security interests where both parties are contracting in the course of a business should be kept to the minimum necessary, how far does the present law reflect this policy? In England and Wales I can sum up the present position as being one where a security interest can be taken in almost anything, provided an appropriate method is used, but that it is not always clear what the most appropriate method is....

8.2.3 For reasons I am coming to, I think English law is in urgent need of reform....

8.2.4 *(b) The law lacks a functional basis.* The English law of security is divided into rigid compartments, making the law fragmented and incoherent. Transactions essentially similar in nature are treated in very different ways. This has the effect of complicating the legal issues quite unnecessarily....

8.2.5 This can cause problems when an attempt is made to create a security interest, for a method must be chosen appropriate to the property concerned and the effect that is desired. There are, for example, many cases in the law reports where the parties adopted the form of a sale followed by a hire-purchase agreement only to find that, perhaps for reasons of timing, perhaps for other reasons, it

[12] Goode *Commercial Law*, pp 631–632.

totally failed to take effect—in England and Wales because the Bills of Sale Acts had not been complied with . . . .

8.2.6 It can also cause problems at the stage of enforcement, for different forms of security interest may have very different consequences. In England and Wales the difference between the equitable rules governing mortgages and the common law or statutory rules governing hire-purchase agreements, for example, can be striking. If goods subject to a mortgage or charge are seized and sold, and fetch more than the amount owed by the debtor to repay the loan with interest and costs, the excess belongs to the debtor. If the goods were subject to a hire-purchase agreement, however, the creditor can keep the excess.

8.2.7 *(c) Complexity.* The compartmentalisation of the law just referred to inevitably gives rise to a law that is complex and uncertain. In England and Wales the old division between common law and equity, parallel systems administered in separate courts before 1876, still looms large in the field of security law. For example, an innocent purchaser, who buys goods not knowing of any security interest in them, may be in a radically different position according to whether the security interest of which he is unaware was equitable or legal. In a case concerning charterparties (*Re Welsh Irish Ferries Ltd* [1986] Ch 471) the judge had to consider whether a contractual 'lien' was a charge registrable under the Companies Act and for this purpose had to explore the effect in equity of a non-statutory assignment of contractual rights. (See too *The Annangel Glory* [1988] 1 Lloyd's Rep 45.)

8.2.8 The complexity of the law leads to difficulty, and perfectly legitimate business activities are in consequence attended with unnecessary expense and delay. The complications may be disastrous for a party who gets it wrong. What should and could be a routine business activity may involve complicated documentation or uncertainty. Particularly difficult are the rules relating to the secured creditor's right to the proceeds of the subject matter of the security if it is sold.

8.2.9 Because issues are decided by reference to rules that evolved for different purposes, the law is capable of acting unfairly and may fail to hold a just balance as between the parties. In some cases creditors have found that they lose the protection that they intended to obtain, and sometimes debtors are harshly treated because of the failure of the law to recognise their true position as a party who has given security. Although any legal rule is capable of producing the wrong result in a particular fact situation, the present law is notably defective. The rules vary widely according to distinctions which have no commercial or rational significance.

8.2.10 *(d) Priorities.* Because there are so many different ways of achieving similar economic ends, it is difficult to reconcile competing interests. This causes problems in determining priorities and leads to fortuitous differences in insolvency. There is no logical plan for ranking conflicting claims, ... The uncertainty of the effect of some clauses in contracts for the sale of goods seeking to retain title can make it difficult for a receiver or liquidator to discover what are in effect security interests.

8.2.11 *(e) Purchasers.* Particularly unfortunate is that the effect of security interests on purchasers may be difficult to ascertain. I have already referred to the effect of the differences between legal and equitable rules in the law of England and Wales. In addition, there is inadequate protection for the purchaser of property subject to a security interest of which he was unaware, and perhaps could not discover. Such purchasers are put at risk and inadequately protected by the law. It may even be difficult for them to secure speedy legal advice because of the fragmentation of the law and the varieties of security interest that are possible.

NOTES

These criticisms of the current law led Professor Diamond (in Part II of his Report) to recommend the introduction of a functionally-based electronic notice-filing system which would apply to all types of consensual security interests. The new system was to be based closely on art 9 of the American Uniform Commercial Code (revised in 2001) and the Personal Property Security Acts introduced in several Canadian provinces. New Zealand introduced similar reforms through its Personal Property Securities Act 1999 (as amended). Under these proposals the term 'security interests' was to be given a functional definition so as to catch both real security, such as mortgages and charges, and also quasi-security, such as retention of title devices. The new notice-filing system was to replace the bills of sale registers and the registration of charges under the Companies Act. The date of filing a 'financing statement' (with minimum particulars) would be the relevant date for determining the priority of competing security interests (but not for possessory security interests). The first to file would win the priority race. Under this system it would even be possible to file an entry before the security interest was actually created so that, for example, a financing statement could be filed in the course of negotiations for a loan.

Professor Diamond was not the first to call for reform of English personal property security law. Similar proposals were made in Part 5 of the Report of the Crowther Committee on Consumer Credit (1971, Cmnd 4596) and later endorsed by the Cork Committee in its review of insolvency law and practice (1982, Cmnd 8558). Professor Sir Roy Goode advocated reform of personal property security law as part of his proposals for an English Commercial Code to parallel the Uniform Commercial Code of the United States (see his Fullagar Memorial Lecture, reprinted in (1988) 14 Monash LR 135). None of these proposals generated sufficient Government interest to get them onto the statute book. However, in 1998 the Secretary of State for Trade and Industry launched a wide-ranging and fundamental review of company law. This led to the Company Law Review Steering Group publishing a Final Report in 2001 which recommended the adoption of a notice-filing system for company charges. However, as the Steering Group had not had time to consult over the details, it recommended that the matter be referred to the Law Commission. As an alternative to its proposal for notice-filing, the Steering Group recommended a number of changes to the existing registration system.

The Law Commission published a first consultation paper (LC CP No 164) in 2002. This provisionally proposed a notice-filing system for company charges (defined to include mortgages), with associated priority rules, and explained how the scheme might be extended to apply also to quasi-security interests, including retention of title devices and outright sales of receivables. The responses to the consultation paper were mixed and more detail was called for. The Law Commission then published a consultative report (LC CP 176) in 2004, which provisionally proposed a scheme based on the Saskatchewan Personal Property Security Act 1993, together with certain elements of art 9 of the revised Uniform Commercial Code. The proposal proved controversial. The Financial Law Committee of the City of London Law Society, amongst others, was particularly concerned that the Law Commission's provisional proposal to register and recharacterise quasi-security would make the law less flexible and more complex that it is at present, would create greater uncertainty, would provide less information to those dealing with companies, and would place unnecessary restraints on freedom of contract in business transactions, as well as being costly to implement (see R Calnan, 'The Reform of Company Security Interests' [2005] JIBFL 25). This resulted in the Law Commission's Final Report (LC Report No 296) being far less radical. In its Final Report, the Law Commission recommended that an electronic notice-filing system (and associated priority rules) be introduced for company charges and the outright sale of receivables, but that it should not be applied to quasi-security without further study. Furthermore, the Law Commission thought that further work was necessary before even its limited recommendations could be extended to charges created by unincorporated business debtors. For comments on the Report, see R Calnan, 'Reforming Priority Law' [2006] JIBFL 4; A McKnight, 'The Reform of English Law Concerning Secured Transactions' [2006] JIBLR 497 and 587; J Ziegel, 'The travails of English chattel security law reform—a transatlantic view' [2006] LMCLQ 110.

In July 2005 the Department of Trade and Industry published a consultation document based on the Law Commission's proposals. The responses to that consultation showed there was a lack of consensus of support for the Law Commission's proposals. The demands of Parliamentary time meant that the Companies Act 2006 contained no major reform of the law on company charges. Part 25 of the 2006 Act reproduces the substance of Part XII of the Companies Act 1985. The 2006 Act does not even take account of the Company Law Review Steering Group's alternative recommendation for changes to the existing regime. However, the Act does give the Secretary of State power to make orders to amend Part 25 (Companies Act 2006, s 894), and the Minister who introduced the amendment in the House of Lords has stated that the Government intends this power to be used 'to address the many imperfections of the present system' but not to replace it (see Hansard, HL (series X) vol 686, cols 480–81, Nov 2, 2006).

CHAPTER 25

POSSESSORY SECURITY

1 PLEDGE

(a) What is a pledge?

Coggs v Bernard

(1703) 2 Ld Raym 909, Court of King's Bench

Holt CJ (describing various types of bailment): The fourth sort is, when goods or chattels are delivered to another as a pawn, to be a security to him for money borrowed of him by the bailor; and this is called in Latin vadium, and in English a pawn or a pledge....

As to the fourth sort of bailment, viz vadium or a pawn, in this I shall consider two things; first, what property the pawnee has in the pawn or pledge, and secondly for what neglects he shall make satisfaction. As to the first, he has a special property, for the pawn is a securing to the pawnee, that he shall be repaid his debt, and to compel the pawner to pay him. But if the pawn be such as it will be the worse for using, the pawnee cannot use it, as cloaths, etc but if it be such, as will be never the worse, as if jewels for the purpose were pawn'd to a lady, she might use them. But then she must do it at her peril, for whereas, if she keeps them lock'd up in her cabinet, if her cabinet should be broke open, and the jewels taken from thence, she would be excused; if she wears them abroad, and is there robb'd of them, she will be answerable. And the reason is, because the pawn is in the nature of a deposit, and as such is not liable to be used. And to this effect is Ow 123. But if the pawn be of such a nature, as the pawnee is at any charge about the thing pawn'd, to maintain it, as a horse, cow, etc then the pawnee may use the horse in a reasonable manner, or milk the cow, etc in recompense for the meat. As to the second point Bracton 99 b gives you the answer. Creditor, qui pignus accepit, re obligatur, et ad illam restituendam tenetur; et cum hujusmodi res in pignus data sit utriusque gratia, scilicet debitoris, quo magis ei pecunia crederetur, et creditoris quo magis ei in tuto sit creditum, sufficit ad ejus rei custodiam diligentiam exactam adhibere, quam si praestiterit, et rem casu amiserit, securus esse possit, nee impedietur creditum petere. In effect, if a creditor takes a pawn, he is bound to restore it upon the payment of the debt; but yet it is sufficient, if the pawnee use true diligence, and he will be indemnified in so doing, and notwithstanding the loss, yet he shall resort to the pawnor for his debt. Agreeable to this is 29 Ass 28, and *Southcote's* case is. But indeed the reason given in *Southcote's* case is, because the pawnee has a special property in the pawn. But that is not the reason of the case; and there is another reason given for it in the Book of Assize, which is indeed the true reason of all these cases, that the law requires nothing extraordinary of the pawnee, but only that he shall use an ordinary care for restoring the goods. But indeed, if the money for which the goods were pawn'd, be tender'd to the pawnee before they are lost, then the pawnee shall be answerable for them; because the pawnee, by detaining them after the tender of the money, is a wrong doer, and it is a wrongful detainer of the goods, and the special property of the pawnee is determined. And a man that keeps goods by wrong, must be answerable for them at all events, for the detaining of them by him, is the reason of the loss. Upon the same difference as the law is in relation to pawns, it will be found to stand in relation to goods found.

Halliday v Holgate

(1868) LR 3 Exch 299, Exchequer Chamber

Willes J: ...There are three kinds of security: the first, a simple lien; the second, a mortgage, passing the property out and out; the third, a security intermediate between a lien and a mortgage—viz, a pledge—where by contract a deposit of goods is made a security for a debt, and the right to the property vests in the pledgee so far as is necessary to secure the debt. It is true the pledgor has such a property in the article pledged as he can convey to a third person, but he has no right to the goods without paying off the debt, and until the debt is paid off the pledgee has the whole present interest.

NOTES

1.   The essential characteristics of a pledge are that: (a) it is created by contract, (b) possession of the property pledged (or of documents of title thereto) must be delivered (actually or constructively) to the pledgee, (c) the pledgor has a right of redemption on discharge of the debt or obligation secured—the pledgee has no right of foreclosure, and (d) the pledgee is given a 'special property' in the subject matter of the pledge, including a power of sale at common law, which he can assign or sub-pledge. Usually, a pledge secures repayment of a debt but, in principle, there is no reason why it should not secure the performance by the pledgor of some other obligation.

2.   Although the pledgee is given special property in the goods pledged, he does not become the general owner of the goods. This led Lord Mersey in *The Odessa* [1916] 1 AC 145 at 158–159, to question whether it was appropriate to describe the pledgee's 'interest' in the goods as a form of property at all. However, even if the pledgee is described as having merely 'a special interest' in the pledged goods, it is, nevertheless, an interest of proprietary significance. As Professor NE Palmer has observed in his treatise on bailment (*Bailment* (2nd edn, 1991), pp 1382–1383):

The pledgee, eg, has an inherent right of sale; and the interests distributed by the pledge (to wit, the pledgor's reversion and the pledgee's special property) are capable of surviving both a sale of the chattel by the pledgor, and its repledge by the pledgee, respectively. Further, in common with other varieties of bailment, the pledgee's possession entitles him to exercise the proprietary and possessory remedies against a third party wrongdoer, and to recover at common law damages calculated according to the full value of the goods (or the full cost of their depreciation) as if he were the owner.

In *Mathew v TM Sutton Ltd* [1994] 4 All ER 793, Chadwick J held that, in view of the nature of a pledge, a pledgee who sells unredeemed chattels for more than the sum owed by the pledgor holds the surplus as a fiduciary on trust for the pledgor. The judgment implies that the fiduciary relationship existed from the time of the original delivery. It seems to follow from this decision that the pledgee would also hold any surplus as a fiduciary on trust for the pledgor (a) where he sues a third party wrongdoer and recovers, by virtue of his possessory title, a sum greater than the amount secured by the pledge, and (b) where he insures the goods for their full value and recovers from the insurer an amount greater than the secured debt (see All ER Annual Review 1994, pp 26–28).

3.   At common law, the terms 'pledge' and 'pawn' were used interchangeably, although the pledge of a bill of lading was never described as a 'pawn' (*Halsbury's Laws of England* (4th edn, 2007 reissue), Vol 36(1), para ln). Under the Pawnbrokers Acts 1872–1960 (now repealed), the term 'pledge' referred to the goods and 'pawn' to the act of delivery or receipt of the goods. Under s 189(1) of the Consumer Credit Act 1974, the term 'pawn' means any article subject to a pledge and 'pledge' means the pawnee's rights over an article taken in pawn. The 'pawnee' is the recipient of the goods and the 'pawnor' is the person who delivered them to the pawnee.

(b) Delivery

Official Assignee of Madras v Mercantile Bank of India Ltd
[1935] AC 53, Privy Council

A firm of merchants (the merchants) purchased groundnuts and transported them to Madras by rail. For each consignment of groundnuts the merchants obtained a railway receipt from the railway companies. The receipt entitled the named consignee, or indorsee, to obtain delivery of the groundnuts from the railway companies. The merchants then raised loans against the consignments by sending, *inter alia,* the railway receipts, duly indorsed in blank, to the respondent bank. On the insolvency of the merchants, the Official Assignee of Madras, in whom their property vested by reason of the insolvency, disputed whether the bank had taken a valid pledge of the groundnuts. The issue before the Privy Council was whether the pledging of railway receipts was a pledge of the goods represented by them or merely a pledge of the actual documents. The Privy Council held that under the relevant Indian legislation the railway receipts were documents of title to the goods and that the owner of the goods could pledge the goods by pledging the documents of title. The Privy Council affirmed the judgment of the High Court of Madras in favour of the bank. But the Privy Council also emphasised that if the case had been governed by English law the result would have been different.

Lord Wright (delivering the advice of the Privy Council): But the arguments advanced on behalf of the appellant have sought to treat the matter as concluded by the history and present state of the relevant law in England, which will now be briefly summarized. At the common law a pledge could not be created except by a delivery of possession of the thing pledged, either actual or constructive. It involved a bailment. If the pledgor had the actual goods in his physical possession, he could effect the pledge by actual delivery; in other cases he could give possession by some symbolic act, such as handing over the key of the store in which they were. If, however, the goods were in the custody of a third person, who held for the bailor so that in law his possession was that of the bailor, the pledge could be effected by a change of the possession of the third party, that is by an order to him from the pledgor to hold for the pledgee, the change being perfected by the third party attorning to the pledgee, that is acknowledging that he thereupon held for him; there was thus a change of possession and a constructive delivery: the goods in the hands of the third party became by this process in the possession constructively of the pledgee. But where goods were represented by documents the transfer of the documents did not change the possession of the goods, save for one exception, unless the custodier (carrier, warehouseman or such) was notified of the transfer and agreed to hold in future as bailee for the pledgee. The one exception was the case of bills of lading, the transfer of which by the law merchant operated as a transfer of the possession of, as well as the property in, the goods. This exception has been explained on the ground that the goods being at sea the master could not be notified; the true explanation may be that it was a rule of the law merchant, developed in order to facilitate mercantile transactions, whereas the process of pledging goods on land was regulated by the narrower rule of the common law and the matter remained stereotyped in the form which it had taken before the importance of documents of title in mercantile transactions was realized. So things have remained in the English law: a pledge of documents is not in general to be deemed a pledge of the goods; a pledge of the documents (always excepting a bill of lading) is merely a pledge of the ipsa corpora of them; the common law continued to regard them as merely tokens of an authority to receive possession....

The common law rule was stated by the House of Lords in *William McEwan & Sons v Smith* ((1849) 2 HL Cas 309). The position of the English law has been fully explained also more recently in *Inglis v Robertson* ([1898] AC 616) and in *Dublin City Distillery Ltd v Doherty* ([1914] AC 823). But there also grew up that legislation which is compendiously described as the Factors Acts, the first in 1823, then an Act in 1825, then an Act in 1842, then an Act in 1877, and finally, the Act in 1889 now in force. The purpose of these Acts was to protect bankers who made advances to mercantile agents: that purpose was effected by means of an inroad on the common law rule that no one could give a better title to goods than he himself had. The persons to whom the Acts applied were defined as agents who had in the customary course of their business as such authority to sell goods or to consign goods for sale or raise money on the security of goods; in the case of such persons thus intrusted with possession of the goods or the documents of title to the goods, the possession of the goods or documents of title to the goods was treated in effect as evidence of a right to pledge them, so that parties bona fide and without notice of any irregularity advancing money to such mercantile agents on the goods or documents were held entitled to a good pledge, even though such mercantile agents were acting in fraud of the true owner. Section 3 of the Factors Act 1889, provides that 'a pledge of [the] documents] of title to goods shall be deemed to be a pledge of the goods.' It has been held that this section only applies to transactions within the Factors Act: *Inglis v Robertson*.

Thus the curious and anomalous position was established that a mercantile agent, acting it may be in fraud of the true owner, can do that which the real owner cannot do, that is, obtain a loan on the security of a pledge of the goods by a pledge of the documents, without the further process being necessary of giving notice of the pledge to the warehouseman or other custodier and obtaining the latter's attornment to the change of possession. But it is obvious that the ordinary process of financing transactions in goods is much facilitated by ability to pledge the goods by the simple process of pledging the documents of title. It need not be repeated that bills of lading stand apart, nor need it be observed here that some warehousing companies have, by means of private Acts, assimilated their warrants or delivery orders to bills of lading for this purpose.

NOTES

1.   As delivery lies at the heart of a pledge, only chattels which are capable of actual, constructive or symbolic delivery can be pledged. Intangible property, such as information, cannot be pledged (see further N Palmer and A Hudson 'Pledge', Ch 24 in N Palmer and E McKendrick (eds) *Interests in Goods* (2nd edn, 1998), p 635). This means, for example, that bearer bonds (negotiable instruments) may be pledged (*Carter v Wake* (1877) 4 Ch D 605) but not the choses in action (the shares) represented by share certificates (*Harrold v Plenty* [1901] 2 Ch 314). For reasons of public policy, certain other chattels may not be pledged, eg firearms, ammunition, military, naval and airforce equipment, equipment issued to those in the territorial army reserve or Royal Auxiliary Air Force, and Social Security cards or used stamps therefor. In each case the prohibition arises under statute.

2.   Delivery by means of the pledge of a bill of lading amounts to a pledge of the goods themselves so long as the goods are identified in the bill of lading (see Note 4 below). The bill of lading is the only document recognised by the common law as a document of title to goods (see generally MA Bools *The Bill of Lading: A Document of Title to Goods* (1997); S Dromgoole and Y Baatz 'The Bill of Lading as a Document of Title', Ch 22 in N Palmer

and E McKendrick (eds) *Interests in Goods* (2nd edn, 1998)). Documents other than bills of lading may be recognised as documents of title to goods at common law by local mercantile custom. A pledge of other documents relating to goods (not being documents of title at common law) operates as a pledge only of the documents themselves and not the actual goods. This includes documents which are documents of title under s 1(4) of the Factors Act 1889, such as delivery orders, delivery warrants and warehouse receipts. However, where a mercantile agent (but not others) pledges such a document of title, the pledge of the document of title is deemed to be a pledge of the goods (s 3 of the 1889 Act, as interpreted by the House of Lords in *Inglis v Robertson* [1898] AC 616). See H Beale, M Bridge, L Gullifer and E Lomnicka, *The Law of Personal Property Security* (2007), para 3.26.

3.   In *Meyerstein v Barber* ((1866) LR 2 CP 38; affd *sub nom Barber v Meyerstein* (1870) LR 4 HL 317) it was argued that delivery of an exhausted bill of lading (as to which see AH Hudson (1963) 26 MLR 442) only operated as an *agreement* to pledge goods and not as an actual pledge effected by the symbolic delivery of the goods themselves. The Court of Common Pleas held that the bill of lading was not exhausted and so delivery of the goods represented by the document had been made to complete the pledge. However, Willes J stated *obiter* that: '…a mere contract to pledge even specific goods, and even if money is actually advanced upon the faith of the contract, is not sufficient to carry the legal property in the goods … such a transaction amounts only to an authority to take possession of the goods…'. By contrast, in *Hilton v Tucker* (1888) 39 Ch D 669, where money was lent pursuant to an agreement that the borrower would deliver certain goods into the lender's possession but the goods were not delivered until a month after the loan had been made, Kekewich J held that with a pledge of goods it was not essential that the loan and delivery of possession should be contemporaneous. His Lordship held that it was enough if possession was delivered within a reasonable time of the loan in pursuance of the contract to pledge. But if delivery does not take place, Willes J's dictum in *Meyerstein v Barber* would apply.

4.   In *Official Assignee of Madras v Mercantile Bank of India Ltd*, Lord Wright stated that there would be constructive delivery of goods held by a third person on behalf of the pledgor if that third person attorned to the pledgee. Constructive delivery will also take place when the goods are in the possession of the pledgor and he contracts to continue to hold them as bailee for the pledgee and not on his own account as owner (*Meyerstein v Barber* (1866) LR 2 CP 38 at 52, per Willes J). In *Dublin City Distillery Ltd v Doherty* [1914] AC 823 at 852, Lord Parker of Waddington stated that the pledgor's agreement to hold the goods on behalf of the pledgee '…operates as a delivery of the goods to the pledgee and a redelivery of the goods by the pledgee to the pledger (*sic*) as bailee for the purposes mentioned in the agreement'. The delivery/redelivery theory can also be used to explain what happens when a third person attorns to the pledgee. But the theory only works if specific goods are pledged. If the goods are part of an undivided bulk, then according to Hope J A in *Maynegrain Pty Ltd v Compafina Bank* [1982] 2 NSWLR 141 at 149 (reversed on another ground (1984)58ALJR389,PC):

> …an attornment in respect of an undifferentiated portion of a larger quantity of goods does not operate as a delivery of some severed portion of the goods and a redelivery of that portion to the attornor; it operates as if such a delivery and redelivery had been effected, the attornor being estopped from denying the necessary severance and appropriation by virtue of the attornment itself, and no doubt in many cases because the attornee has acted to his prejudice on the basis of the attornment. It is, however, irrelevant that the attornee knows that in fact no severance or appropriation has taken place.

The difference between a pledge effected by a true attornment and one arising through an estoppel is that the former gives the pledgee proprietary rights whereas the latter only gives him personal ones (and does not really constitute a pledge at all). The distinction is of vital importance where third party rights are involved. In *Re London Wine Co (Shippers) Ltd* [1986] PCC 121, a sale of goods case where no property passed, an estoppel argument was raised by the pledgees of various buyers to defeat a bank with a floating charge over the seller's assets. Oliver J held that the buyers obtained no 'title by estoppel' and so there were no proprietary rights that they could pass on themselves to the pledgees. The same principle applies to the 'pledge' of a bill of lading which relates to unascertained goods forming part of a bulk. The pledgee cannot acquire constructive (or symbolic) possession of the goods, or obtain proprietary rights thereto, as the goods are not identified: the 'pledge' only operates as an estoppel against the carrier. However, since the enactment of the Sale of Goods (Amendment) Act 1995, introducing ss 20A and 20B into the Sale of Goods Act 1979, the situation may be different as regards the pledge of a bill of lading by a pre-paying buyer of goods forming part of a bulk. The 1995 Act gives the pre-paying buyer a proprietary interest in an undivided share of the bulk and, although the point is not specifically addressed in the Act, there seem to be no good policy reasons for denying the proprietary effect of a pledge of that interest (see L Gulliver [1999] LMCLQ 93, pp 102–104; cf N Palmer and A Hudson 'Pledge', Ch 24 in N Palmer and E McKendrick *Interests in Goods* (2nd edn, 1998), p 625). Further legislation is probably required to clarify the issue.

Wrightson v McArthur and Hutchisons (1919) Ltd
[1921] 2 KB 807, King's Bench Division

In consideration of the plaintiff allowing the first defendant more time to pay for goods, the second defendant (the company) set aside certain specified goods in two rooms on its premises which were locked up and the keys handed to the plaintiff, no other goods being in those rooms. In a subsequent letter to the plaintiff, the company stated that: The goods to be locked up, the keys in your possession, and you to have the right to remove same as desired.' On the company's liquidation, an issue arose as to whether the letter evidenced a charge. If so, the security, being unregistered, was void against the liquidator. On the other hand, if the security was a pledge completed by delivery of possession of the goods without reference to the letter, then it was valid as not requiring registration (see below, p 1105). Rowlatt J upheld the validity of the security.

Rowlatt J: The point to which this case is now reduced is whether the circumstance that the rooms, the keys of which were delivered, were within the defendants' premises, prevents the delivery of the keys conferring possession of the contents of the rooms. If the keys delivered had been the outside key of the whole warehouse containing these goods I should have felt no difficulty, nor should I have felt any difficulty had the key been of an apartment or receptacle in the premises of a third party as was the case in *Hilton v Tucker* ((1888) 39 Ch D 669). On the other hand if, the rooms being in the defendants' premises, the keys had been given without the licence to go and remove the goods at any time I should have thought it clear that possession of the goods did not pass. It would be merely a case of the goods remaining in the defendants' possession with the security that they should not be interfered with, but without any power of affirmative control at the free will of the plaintiff. It would be like the case of furniture left in a locked room in a house that is let furnished, where the lessor has no right to enter except upon reasonable notice and at reasonable times. The actual question has to be considered in the light of the principle that delivery of a key has effect not as symbolic delivery, but as giving the actual control. This was the view expressed by Lord Hardwicke in *Ward v Turner* ((1752) 2 Ves Sen 431), where he says the key is the means of coming at the possession. The matter was fully discussed in the light of all the cases in *Pollock and Wright on Possession in the Common Law,* p 61 and following pages. In *Hilton v Tucker,* already referred to, in a judgment delivered since the date of that work, Kekewich J observes 'that the delivery of the key in order to make constructive possession must be under such circumstances that it really does pass the full control of the place to which admission is to be gained by means of the key.' If I might criticise that statement my criticism would only be as to the propriety of the use of the word 'constructive' in the connection in question.

I think therefore there can be no doubt as to the true principle, and the difficulty is in its application. There are two cases in which delivery of the key of a box in a house has been held to confer possession of the contents. The first was *Jones v Selby* ((1710) Prec Ch 300), referred to by Lord Hardwicke in *Ward v Turner* above mentioned, the other was *Mustapha v Wedlake* ([1891] WN 201), but in both those cases both parties were living in the house and therefore the person receiving the delivery could not be expected to take away the box, but could hold possession of it in the house. It has never been held, so far as I know, that delivery of the key of a box which the deliverer retains in his own house, where the other party does not live, passes possession of the contents. Upon the whole, however, I think that in the case before me the possession was transferred, having regard to the fact that a licence to come and make the necessary entry to use the key was also conferred, a licence which it seems to me could not be revoked. The door into the building would be open in business hours, and the mere fact that the plaintiff might wrongfully be excluded from the whole building does not, I think, affect the matter. If the key had been given him with the intention to pass to him the possession of the room itself upon a demise of it, I cannot doubt that possession would pass. I see no difference when the key is given to pass possession not of the room, but of the chattels. The key guards both in the same way.

NOTES

1. In *Hilton v Tucker* (1888) 39 Ch D 669, pursuant to an agreement with the pledgee, the pledgor hired a room in a building belonging to a third party and stored certain prints and engravings there. The pledgor then wrote to the pledgee informing him that the third party held the key to the room 'which I place entirely at your disposal'. Kekewich J held that the prints and engravings had been constructively delivered to the pledgee even though the pledgor continued to have access to the room (via a duplicate key). Although the pledgee must usually be given exclusive control of the pledged chattels, Kekewich J stressed that in this case the 'laxity in the control of the room' was irrelevant as the pledgor had only a limited right of access (to clean the room and list the chattels) and at all times had acknowledged that his right was subject to the pledgee's paramount control. The issue appears to turn on whether the deliveror really intends to relinquish possession of the chattels to the deliveree. It should also be noted that the question of whether the pledgee needed the third party's permission to pass through the building (to gain access to the room) was not raised in *Hilton v Tucker.* The question was also ignored by Rowlatt J in *Wrightson v McArthur and Hutchisons (1919) Ltd.* As Andrew Bell has observed: 'In general, a key will not confer possession if the third party has not agreed to grant access to persons other than the deliveror' (AP Bell *Modern Law of Personal Property in England and Ireland* (1989), pp 47–48).

2. In *Dublin City Distillery Ltd v Doherty* [1914] AC 823 whisky was kept in a bonded warehouse over which the distillery company and the Inland Revenue had joint control. In particular, the warehouse had two locks; the distillery company held the key to one lock and the Revenue held the key to the other. The distillery company purported to pledge the whisky to the respondent by entering the transaction into its books and by issuing invoices and warrants to the respondent. The House of Lords held that there had been no constructive delivery of the whisky and, therefore, no pledge. Lord Atkinson held that the warrants issued by the distillery company did not entitle the respondent to delivery of the whisky

without further attornment to him (at 847–848; and Lord Sumner at 862–865; cf Lord Parker of Waddington at 853). When reviewing the law relating to constructive delivery, Lord Atkinson accepted that it could take place by delivery of the key to a store or house but doubted 'whether, owing to the dual control over this whisky exercised by the distillers and the Revenue officer, it would not be necessary in the present case that both keys should be delivered' (at 843–844). Lord Parker of Waddington viewed the question of dual control somewhat differently. He held that dual control meant that the distillery company and the Revenue had joint possession of the whisky so that the respondent could not take delivery from either one of them without the consent of the other (at 857–858).

QUESTIONS

1.   Why was the pledgee's licence to enter the pledgor' s premises held to be irrevocable in *Wrightson v McArthur and Hutchinson (1919) Ltd* (above, p 1096)? See Bell, op cit, pp 48–49.

2.   On the issue of 'exclusive control', how can *Hilton v Tucker* be distinguished from *Dublin City Distillery Ltd v Doherty?*

3.   Does transfer of a key constitute actual, constructive or symbolic delivery of the chattels to which it gives access? Compare ACH Barlow (1956) 19 MLR 394 with Bell, op cit, p 58.

(c) Re-delivery

Reeves v Capper
(1838) 5 Bing NC 136, Court of Common Pleas

W, the master of a ship, pledged his chronometer to C as security for a loan. Pursuant to the terms of the loan agreement, C returned the chronometer to W for use on a specific voyage. After the voyage W pledged the chronometer to R. R claimed that the original pledge had been destroyed when C had parted with possession of the chronometer by redelivering it to W. Tindal CJ held that this redelivery did not destroy the pledge.

Tindal CJ: …[W]e agree entirely with the doctrine laid down in *Ryall v Rolle* ((1750) 1 Atk 165), that in the case of a simple pawn of a personal chattel, if the creditor parts with the possession he loses his property in the pledge: but we think the delivery of the chronometer to Wilson under the terms of the agreement itself was not a parting with the possession, but that the possession of Captain Wilson was still the possession of Messrs Capper. The terms of the agreement were, that 'they would allow him the use of it for the voyage:' words that gave him no interest in the chronometer, but only a licence or permission to use it, for a limited time, whilst he continued as their servant, and employed it for the purpose of navigating their ship. During the continuance of the voyage, and when the voyage terminated, the possession of Captain Wilson was the possession of Messrs Capper; just as the possession of plate by a butler is the possession of the master; and the delivery over to the Plaintiff was, as between Captain Wilson and the Defendants a wrongful act, just as the delivery over of the plate by the butler to a stranger would have been; and could give no more right to the bailee than Captain Wilson had himself. We therefore think the property belonged to the Defendants, and that the rule must be made absolute for entering the verdict for the Defendants.

NOTES

1.   Whether the pledgor holds as owner or as bailee after the goods are redelivered to him turns on the intention of the parties. An agreement to hold the goods for a special purpose

indicates such an intention. This type of agreement is commonly found in international trade finance. After the importing buyer has pledged the bill of lading and other shipping documents as security for an advance from his bank, he may later be allowed to take back those documents to enable him to sell the goods and pay off the bank. To ensure that the bank maintains its constructive possession of the goods represented by the documents, it will only release the documents to the buyer under a letter of trust or a trust receipt (an example of which appears as Form 7 in the Appendix). By the terms of such a letter or receipt, the buyer undertakes that in consideration of the release of the documents to him he will hold them on trust for the bank, will use them to sell the goods as the bank's agent and will hold the goods themselves until sale, and the proceeds after sale, on trust for the bank. The effect of the letter of trust or trust receipt is to preserve the bank's pledge over the documents and goods (*North Western Bank Ltd v John Poynter, Son & Macdonalds* [1895] AC 56, HL). See further EP Ellinger, 'Trust Receipt Financing' [2003] JIBLR 305.

2. The pledge will be preserved if the pledgor takes the goods without permission or obtains redelivery by fraud (*Mocatta v Bell* (1857) 24 Beav 585). However, when redelivery is obtained by fraud the pledgee's rights may be lost against a subsequent pledgee or purchaser who takes the pledged chattels bona fide, for value and without notice. In *Babcock v Lawson* (1880) 5 QBD 284, the pledgors, who were merchants, obtained redelivery of the pledged goods by fraudulently misrepresenting to the pledgees that they had sold the goods and that the pledgees would be paid from the proceeds of sale. Upon redelivery, the pledgors obtained an advance from the defendants and deposited the goods with them. The Court of Appeal held that as the pledgees had parted with their special property in the goods to the pledgors, they could not recover the goods from the defendants who had obtained them bona fide and for good consideration. An important feature of this case was that, because of the fraud, the pledgees intended to divest themselves of their special property in the pledged goods. But what if the goods, or documents of title to the goods, are redelivered to the pledgor for a special purpose other than sale? Should the pledgee be bound by any subsequent sale or pledge, or should the *nemo dat* rule apply?

3. A similar problem to that noted at 2 above arises when the pledgee redelivers goods to the pledgor under the terms of a trust receipt. In *Lloyds Bank Ltd v Bank of America* [1938] 2 KB 147, the pledgee bank returned bills of lading to the pledgor, against a trust receipt, so that the pledgor could sell the goods and pay the bank off out of the proceeds. Instead of selling the goods, the pledgor repledged them to a second bank. It was held that the second bank got a good title as against the first bank by virtue of s 2 of the Factors Act 1889 (see above, p 364). The Court of Appeal held that for the purposes of s 2, the pledgee was deemed the (joint) 'owner' of the goods. But s 2 will only apply if, *inter alia*, the pledgor is a mercantile agent and the goods, or documents of title to the goods, were entrusted to him in that capacity (*Astley Industrial Trust Ltd v Miller* [1968] 2 All ER 36).

4. Both *Babcock v Lawson* and *Lloyds Bank v Bank of America* can be distinguished as cases where the pledgees intended to divest themselves of their special property in the goods and redelivered the goods to the pledgor for that purpose. But where a pledgee intends to retain his special property, and redelivers the goods, or the documents of title to the goods, to the pledgor for a purpose other than disposition, his rights are not to be defeated by an unauthorised disposition by the pledgor, so long as the pledgee has not in some other way lent himself to the transaction, eg through an estoppel by representation (*Mercantile Bank of India Ltd v Central Bank of India Ltd* [1938] AC 287, PC). This may seem harsh on a third party who buys, or takes a pledge, from the pledgor in good faith and without notice.

5.   A pledge of goods (or of a document of title thereto) would not be registrable under the notice-filing scheme for company charges proposed by the Law Commission in its Final Report on Company Security Interests (LC Report No 296) published in 2005 (see above, p 1039). However, under the Law Commission's proposals, where a pledgor is given possession of pledged goods (or document of title) under a trust receipt, the pledge will become registrable unless the goods (or document of title) are returned to the pledgee's possession within 15 business days (see draft reg 22(4) of the draft regulations annexed to the Law Commission's Final Report). The Law Commission's proposals are controversial and are unlikely to be made law for some considerable time, if at all.

QUESTION

Swell agrees to lend £1,000 to Tight, an artist, on the security of some of Tight's pictures, and Tight accordingly places these in an empty shed in his garden, locks the shed, and sends the only key to Swell with a letter stating that Swell can enter and remove the pictures whenever he wishes. Consider the rights of the parties in the following alternative circumstances:

(1)   Tight, pretending that he wishes to show the pictures to an admirer, obtains the key from Swell for an hour. Tight removes a picture and sells it to Swap.

(2)   The roof of the shed springs a leak and Swell, on learning of this, hands Tight the key and asks him to cover up the pictures. Tight takes the opportunity to remove a picture and sell it to Flint.

(3)   Tight had previously stolen the pictures from Otto, who now looks to recover them from Swell. See the Torts (Interference with Goods) Act 1977, s 11(2).

(d) Re-pledge by the pledgee

Donald v Suckling
(1866) LR1QB 585, Court of Queen's Bench

The pledgor deposited debentures with Simpson as security for the payment, at maturity, of a bill of exchange indorsed by the pledgor and discounted by Simpson. Before maturity of the bill, Simpson pledged the debentures to the defendant to secure a loan which exceeded the amount secured by the original pledge. The pledgor sought to recover the debentures from the defendant, by a claim in detinue, without tendering the amount of the original debt. The Court of Queen's Bench (Shee J dissenting) held that he was not entitled to do so.

Mellor J: . . . The question thus raised by this plea is, whether a pawnee of debentures, deposited with him as a security for the due payment of money, at a certain time, does, by repledging such debentures and depositing them with a third person as a security for a larger amount, before any default in payment by the pawnor, make void the contract upon which they were deposited with the pawnee, so as to vest in the pawnor an immediate right to the possession thereof, notwithstanding that the debt due by him to the original pawnee remains unpaid. . . .

In a contract of pledge for securing the payment of money, we have seen that the pawnee may sell and transfer the thing pledged on condition broken; but what implied condition is there that the pledgee shall not in the meantime part with the possession thereof to the extent of his interest? It may be that upon a deposit by way of pledge, the express contract between the parties may operate so as to make a parting with the possession, even to the extent of his interest, before condition broken, so essential a violation of it as to revest the right of possession in the pawnor; but in the absence of such terms, why are they to be implied? There may possibly be cases in which the very nature of the thing deposited might induce a jury to believe and find that it was deposited on the understanding that the possession should not be parted with; but in the case before us we have only to deal with the agreement which is stated in the plea. The object of the deposit is to secure the repayment of a loan, and the effect is to create an interest and a right of property in the pawnee, to the extent of the loan, in the goods deposited; but what is the authority for saying that until condition broken the pawnee has only a personal right to retain the goods in his own possession?

In *Johnson v Stear* ((1863) 15 CBNS 330), one Cumming, a bankrupt, had deposited with the defendant 243 cases of brandy, to be held by him as a security for the payment of an acceptance of the bankrupt for £62 10s, discounted by the defendant, and which would become due January 29,1863, and in case such acceptance was not paid at maturity, the defendant was to be at liberty to sell the brandy and apply the proceeds in payment of the acceptance. On the 28th January, before the acceptance became due, the defendant contracted to sell the brandy to a third person, and on the 29th delivered to him the dock warrant, and on the 30th such third person obtained actual possession of the brandy. In an action of trover, brought by the assignee of the bankrupt, the Court of Common Pleas held that the plaintiff was entitled to recover, on the ground that the defendant wrongfully assumed to be owner, in selling; and although that alone might not be a conversion, yet, by delivering over the dock warrant to the vendee in pursuance of such sale, he 'interfered with the right which the bankrupt had on the 29th if he repaid the loan'; but the majority of the Court (Erie CJ, Byles and Keating JJ) held that the plaintiff was only entitled to nominal damages, on the express ground, 'that the deposit of the goods in question with the defendant to secure repayment of a loan to him on a given day, with a power to sell in case of default on that day, created *"an interest and a right of property in the goods, which was more than a mere lien;* and the wrongful act of the pawnee *did not annihilate the contract between the parties nor the interest of the pawnee in the goods* under that contract." ' From that view of the law, as applied to the circumstances of that case, Mr Justice Williams dissented, on the ground 'that the bailment was terminated by the sale before the stipulated time, and consequently that the title of the plaintiff to the goods became as free as if the bailment had never taken place.' Although the dissent of that most learned judge diminishes the authority of that case as a decision on the point, and although it may be open to doubt whether in an action of trover the defendant ought not to have succeeded on the plea of not possessed, and whether the plaintiffs only remedy for damages was not by action on the contract, I am nevertheless of opinion that the substantial ground upon which the majority of the Court proceeded, viz that the 'act of the pawnee did not annihilate the contract, nor the interest of the pawnee in the goods,' is the more consistent with the nature and incidents of a deposit by way of pledge. I think that when the true distinction between the case of a deposit, by way of pledge, of goods, for securing the payment of money, and all cases of lien, correctly so described, is considered, it will be seen that in the former there is no implication, in general, of a contract by the pledgee to retain the personal possession of the goods deposited; and I think that, although he cannot confer upon any third person a better title or a greater interest than he possesses, yet, if nevertheless he does pledge the goods to a third person for a greater interest than he possesses, such an act does not *annihilate the contract of pledge* between himself and the pawnor; but that the transaction is simply inoperative as against the original pawnor, *who upon tender of the sum secured immediately becomes entitled to the possession of the goods,* and can recover in an action for any special damage which he may have sustained by reason of the act of the pawnee in repledging the goods; and I think that such is the true effect of Lord Holt's definition of a 'vadium or pawn' in *Coggs v Bernard* [above, p 1091]; although he was of opinion that the pawnee could in no case use the pledge if it would thereby be damaged, and must use due diligence in the keeping of it, and says that the creditor is bound to restore the pledge upon payment of the debt, because, by detaining it after the tender of the money, he is a wrongdoer, his special property being determined; yet he nowhere says that the misuse or abuse of the pledge before payment or tender annihilates the contract upon which the deposit took place.

If the true distinction between cases of lien and cases of deposit by way of pledge be kept in mind, it will, I think, suffice to determine this case in favour of the defendant, seeing that no tender of the sum secured by the original deposit is alleged to have been made by the plaintiff; and considering the nature of the things deposited, I think that the plaintiff can have sustained no real damage by the repledging of them, and that he cannot successfully claim the immediate right to the possession of the debentures in question.

I am therefore of opinion that our judgment should be for the defendant.

Blackburn J: ... Now I think that the subpledging of goods, held in security for money, before the money is due, is not in general so inconsistent with the contract, as to amount to a renunciation of that contract. There may be cases in which the pledgor has a special personal confidence in the pawnee, and therefore stipulates that the pledge shall be kept by him alone, but no such terms are stated here, and I do not think that any such term is implied by law. In general all that the pledgor requires is the personal contract of the pledgee that on bringing the money the pawn shall be given up to him, and that in the meantime the pledgee shall be responsible for due care being taken for its safe custody. This may very well be done though there has been a subpledge; at least the plaintiff should try the experiment whether, on bringing the money for which he pledged those debentures to Simpson, he cannot get them. And the assignment of the pawn for the purpose of raising money (so long at least as it purports to transfer no more than the pledgee's interest against the pledgor) is so far from being found in practice to be inconsistent with or repugnant to the contract, that it has been introduced into the Factors Acts, and is in the civil law (and according to *Mores v Conham* ((1610) Owen 123) in our own law also) a regular incident in a pledge. If it is done too soon, or to too great an extent, it is doubtless unlawful, but not so repugnant to the contract as to be justly held equivalent to a renunciation of it.

Cockburn CJ: I think it unnecessary to the decision in the present case to determine whether a party, with whom an article has been pledged as a security for the payment of money, has a right to transfer his interest in the thing pledged (subject to the right of redemption in the pawnor) to a third party. I should certainly hesitate to lay down the affirmative of that proposition. Such a right in the pawnee seems quite inconsistent with the undoubted right of the pledgor to have the thing pledged returned to him immediately on the tender of the amount for which the pledge was given. In some instances it may well be inferred from the nature of the thing pledged,—as in the case of a valuable work of art,—that the pawnor, though perfectly willing that the article should be intrusted to the custody of the pawnee, would not have parted with it on the terms that it should be passed on to others and committed to the custody of strangers. It is not, however, necessary to decide this question in the present case. The question here is, whether the transfer of the pledge is not only a breach of the contract on the part of the pawnee, but operates to put an end to the contract altogether, so as to entitle the pawnor to have back the thing pledged without payment of the debt. I am of opinion that the transfer of the pledge does not put an end to the contract, but amounts only to a breach of contract, upon which the owner may bring an action,—for nominal damages if he has sustained no substantial damage; for substantial damages, if the thing pledged is damaged in the hands of the third party, or the owner is prejudiced by delay in not having the thing delivered to him on tendering the amount for which it was pledged.

NOTES

1.   Subject to Mellor J's caveat that a prohibition on repledge may be imposed by an express term in the contract, or might be implied by virtue of the special character of the goods in exceptional cases, the Court of Queen's Bench held in *Donald v Suckling* that a repledge by the pledgee does not destroy the original pledge, even if made before the pledgor's default and for a sum exceeding that secured by the original pledge. Similarly, the original pledge is not destroyed where the pledgee sells the goods prematurely (*Halliday v Holgate* (1868) LR 3 Exch 299), although deliberate destruction of the goods would destroy it (*Cooke v Haddon* (1862) 3 F & F 229, 176 ER 103, pledgee drank wine). However, premature sale of the pledged goods, or a sub-pledge for an amount greater than that secured by the original pledge, is wrongful and may render the pledgee liable for breach of contract (see dicta of Blackburn J

and Cockburn CJ in *Donald v Suckling* at 616–617 and 618; cf Mellor J at 608, who seems to have proceeded on the basis that the repledge was not a breach). The issue was left open in *Halliday v Holgate,* although a *dictum* of Willes J (at 302) suggests that the pledgor may have a claim for damage to his reversionary interest where he suffers actual loss through wrongful dealing with the pledged chattel before his debt is paid off, eg where the pledgee wrongfully sells goods worth more than the sum owed by the pledgor and the goods are now effectively irrecoverable (see A Tettenborn [19941 CLJ 326, pp 333–334).

2.   If the pledgor tenders payment to the pledgee he may demand the return of the pledged chattel. The pledgee is thereby divested of his special property in the chattel and the pledgor is given an immediate right to possess it. This right allows the pledgor to bring an action in conversion against a sub-pledgee who has taken a sub-pledge for an amount greater than that secured by the original pledge, or the purchaser of a chattel wrongfully sold by the pledgee, should the sub-pledgee or purchaser refuse to return the chattel to the pledgor. In both cases the wrongful nature of the disposition renders it ineffective: the sub-pledgee cannot demand additional payment from the pledgor nor can the purchaser claim ownership. But for so long as the original pledgee has a special property in the pledged chattel the pledgor has no immediate right to possession and so cannot bring an action in conversion (*Halliday v Holgate,* above, at 302–303). This explains why it was so important for the pledgor in *Donald v Suckling,* who had not tendered payment, to establish that the original pledgee had been divested of his special property in the debentures.

3.   If the pledgor sells the goods while they are still subject to the pledge, the buyer can sue the sub-pledgee in conversion if he refuses to deliver up the goods after the buyer has tendered the amount owed, under the original pledge, to the original pledgee (*Franklin v Neate* (1844) 13 M & W 481). The buyer cannot sue the original pledgee for breach of the contract of pledge as he is not privy to that contract.

4.   The modes of terminating the pledge are:

(1)   tender of the amount due;

(2)   pledgee redelivering possession of the chattel to the pledgor without reservation (see above, p 1098);

(3)   pledgee accepting some alternative security or other discharge of the debt;

(4)   'annihilation' of the contract of pledge (see above).

Sale of the subject matter of the pledge on the pledgor's default is also a form of termination.

(e) Realisation

Re Hardwick, ex p Hubbard
(1886) 17 QBD 690, Court of Appeal

(The facts are irrelevant.)

Bowen LJ: …A special property in the goods passes to the pledgee in order that he may be able—if his right to sell arises—to sell them. In all such cases there is at Common Law an authority to the pledgee to sell the goods on the default of the pledgor to repay the money, either at the time originally appointed, or after notice by the pledgee.

The Odessa

[1916] 1 AC 145, Privy Council

(The facts are irrelevant.)

Lord Mersey: . . . If the pledgee sells he does so by virtue and to the extent of the pledgor's ownership, and not with a new title of his own. He must appropriate the proceeds of the sale to the payment of the pledgor's debt, for the money resulting from the sale is the pledgor's money to be so applied. The pledgee must account to the pledgor for any surplus after paying the debt. He must take care that the sale is a provident sale, and if the goods are in bulk he must not sell more than is reasonably sufficient to pay off the debt, for he only holds possession for the purpose of securing himself the advance which he has made. He cannot use the goods as his own. These considerations show that the right of sale is exercisable by virtue of an implied authority from the pledgor and for the benefit of both parties. It creates no jus in re in favour of the pledgee; it gives him no more than a jus in rem such as a lienholder possesses, but with this added incident, that he can sell the property motu proprio and without any assistance from the Court.

NOTES

1.   Unlike a mortgagee, a pledgee has no right of foreclosure (*Carter v Wake* (1877) 4 Ch D 605). Unless contract or statute otherwise provides, the pledgee has no right to become the owner of the pledged goods on default by the pledgor. The pledged goods must either be redeemed or sold.

2.   In *Mathew v TM Sutton Ltd* [1994] 4 All ER 793, Chadwick J held that the pledgee holds any surplus after realisation of the pledged chattel as a fiduciary on trust for the pledgor. There the pledgor of unredeemed silver and jewellery successfully claimed that the pledgee was bound to pay him equitable interest on the surplus proceeds. Chadwick J held that because of the nature of a pledge, whereby ownership of the property remains in the pledgor subject only to the 'special interest' to which the pledgee is entitled for the purpose of protecting and realising his security, there is a fiduciary relationship between pledgor and pledgee and the pledgee holds the surplus 'upon trust' for the pledgor.

3.   As the pledge is only collateral security for the pledgor's debt, if sale of the pledged chattel does not realise the amount lent on it the pledgee may bring an action for the deficit (*Jones v Marshall* (1889) 24 QBD 269, per Lord Coleridge CJ).

4.   If a pledge or pawn is caught by the terms of the Consumer Credit Act 1974, redemption and sale are strictly controlled by the terms of that Act (see below).

QUESTION

If the pledgee holds surplus proceeds of sale of the pledged chattel on trust for the pledgor, what happens to the surplus if the pledgee becomes insolvent before paying it over to the pledgor?

(f) Statutory control

(i) *Consumer Credit Act 1974*

Pawnbroking is regulated under the Consumer Credit Act 1974, which applies to pledges that are regulated agreements under that Act. A regulated agreement is an agreement made between an individual (including an unincorporated association and a small partnership but excluding a company) (the 'debtor') and any other person (the 'creditor') by which the creditor provides the debtor with credit of any amount, which is not exempt under s 16 of the Act (Consumer Credit Act 1974, s 8). Further exemptions were introduced into the 1974 Act by the Consumer Credit Act 2006 for agreements relating to high net worth debtors (s 16A) and agreements for credit exceeding £25,000 which relate to the debtor's business (s 16B). When the 1974 Act applies:

(1) the pawnee must be licensed if he takes pawns ('any article subject to a pledge') by way of business (or else he commits an offence and cannot rely on his rights as pledgee) (ss 21, 39 and 40);

(2) a pawn-receipt must be given in the prescribed form, informing the pawnor of his rights (or else the pawnee commits an offence, but he can still rely on his rights as pledgee) (ss 114(1), 115 and 170);

(3) the pawnee cannot sell the pawn within six months of the pawning (s 116(1)) and even then he must give the pawnor notice of his intention to sell and inform him of the asking price (s 121(1));

(4) ownership of an unredeemed pawn passes to the pawnee automatically at the end of a six months redemption period where the pawn is security for fixed sum credit not exceeding £75, or running account credit on which the credit limit does not exceed £75 (s 120(1)(a)).

For further details of the special procedures for the redemption and sale of a pawn caught by the Consumer Credit Act 1974, see ss 114–122 of that Act. But note that ss 114–122 do not apply to pledges of documents of title to goods, nor to pledges of bearer bonds (s 114(3) (a)). Neither do they apply to non-commercial agreements (s 114(3)(b)). A non-commercial agreement is a consumer credit agreement (or consumer hire agreement) not made by the creditor or owner in the course of a business carried on by him (s 189(1)). Note also that a pawnbroking agreement, as an agreement regulated by the 1974 Act, must also comply with those other requirements of the Act that apply to regulated agreements in general, especially with regard to the form and content and signing of the agreement. Failure to comply renders the agreement and the security unenforceable without a court order (*Wilson v First County Trust Ltd (No 2)* [2003] UKHL 40, [2004] 1 AC 816, although note that s 127(3) of the Act has since been repealed by the Consumer Credit Act 2006, s 15). See generally JK Macleod, 'Pawnbroking: A Regulatory Issue' [1995] JBL 155 for an assessment of the effectiveness of current legislation to regulate pawnbroking and related activities.

(ii) Registration

A pledge which takes effect on delivery of a chattel, or document of title thereto, does not require registration under the Bills of Sale Acts 1878–1891 (*Re Hardwick, ex p Hubbard* (1886) 17 QBD 690) or the Companies Act 2006 (*Wrightson v McArthur and Hutchisons (1919) Ltd* [1921] 2 KB 807). The possessory nature of a pledge means that third parties are put on notice of the pledgee's rights without the need for registration. On the other hand, a mere agreement to make a pledge, without any delivery of the chattel or document of title thereto, is registrable (*Dublin City Distillery Ltd v Doherty* [1914] AC 823 at 854, per Lord Parker of Waddington).

(iii) Insolvency Act 1986

Although there is no case directly on the point, it is submitted that a pledge would fall within the definition of 'security' contained in s 248(b) of the Insolvency Act 1986. This is of particular significance when a pledge is taken over a company's property and that company is subsequently made the subject of an administration order (explained below, p 1214). In these circumstances, no steps could be taken to enforce the pledge except with the consent of the administrator or the leave of the court (Insolvency Act 1986, s 1 l(3)(c); see also s 10(l)(b) of the same Act). For the application of s 11(3)(c) to a possessory lien, see below, p 1118.

2 LIEN

(a) What is a lien?

Hammonds v Barclay

(1802) 2 East 227, Court of King's Bench

Grose J: …A lien is a right in one man to retain that which is in his possession belonging to another, till certain demands of him the person in possession are satisfied.

Tappenden v Artus

[1964] 2 QB 185, Court of Appeal

(The facts appear below, at p 1114.)

Diplock LJ: The common law remedy of a possessory lien, like other primitive remedies such as abatement of nuisance, self-defence or ejection of trespassers to land, is one of self-help. It is a remedy in rem exercisable upon the goods, and its exercise requires no intervention by the courts, for it is exercisable only by an artificer who has actual possession of the goods subject to the lien. Since, however, the remedy is the exercise of a right to continue an existing actual possession of the goods, it necessarily involves a right of possession adverse to the right of the person who, but for the lien, would be entitled to immediate possession of the goods. A common law lien, although not enforceable by action, thus affords a defence to an action for recovery of the goods by a person who, but for the lien, would be entitled to immediate possession.

NOTES

1.   Grose J has provided the classic definition of a common law (or possessory) lien. Like a pledge, a common law lien depends on possession, although a lien depends on the *retention* of possession of goods previously delivered to the lienee in some other capacity, whereas a pledge requires a *delivery* of possession as security (*Re Cosslett (Contractors) Ltd* [1998] Ch 495 at 508, per Millett LJ). Furthermore, unlike a pledge, a common law lien merely gives a personal right of retention to the person (the lienee) in possession of goods belonging to another (the lienor) (*Legg v Evans* (1840) 6 M & W 36 at 42, per Parke B). This means that the lienee, in contrast to the pledgee, cannot dispose of his interest and, at common law, he has no implied right to sell the goods which are the subject matter of the lien (*Donald v Suckling* (1866) LR 1 QB 585 at 604, 610, 612; cf *Halsbury's Laws of England* (4th edn, rev), Vol 28, para 719, where it is argued that common law possessory liens are beginning to be recognised as a limited form of property interest capable of assignment where the secured debt is also assigned; see also N Palmer and A Hudson 'Pledge', Ch 24 in N Palmer and

E McKendrick *Interests in Goods* (2nd edn, 1998), p 636, citing *Vered v Inscorp Holdings Ltd* (1993) 31 NSWLR 290, NSW Sup Ct, where an accountant's lien over his client's papers was assigned to a third party along with the debt).

2. There are four main types of lien: (a) common law; (b) statutory; (c) equitable; and (d) maritime. The most important statutory lien is the unpaid seller's lien (ss 41–43 of the Sale of Goods Act 1979; above, p 439). Like the common law lien, a statutory lien such as the unpaid seller's lien is a possessory lien. (For other examples of statutory liens, see the Consumer Credit Act 1974, ss 70(2), 73(5). Statute may create rights similar to a lien, eg under s 88 of the Civil Aviation Act 1982 an airport has the right to detain an aircraft for unpaid airport charges and aviation fuel supplied: *Bristol Airport plc v Powdrill* [1990] Ch 744.) By contrast, equitable and maritime liens are non-possessory liens. An equitable lien is analogous to an equitable charge (see generally, H Beale, M Bridge, L Gullifer and E Lomnicka, *The Law of Personal Property Security* (2007), paras 4.105ff). The lien of the unpaid vendor of land is the most common example of this type of lien, although it is also possible for an equitable lien to arise in relation to personalty (see, eg *International Finance Corpn v DSNL Offshore Ltd* [2005] EWHC 1844 (Comm), [2007] 2 All ER (Comm) 305: lien of purchaser in contract for work and materials in relation to oil rig equipment). However, unless expressly agreed by the parties, an equitable lien will not arise in relation to a contract for the sale of goods as the Sale of Goods Act provides an exhaustive code as to the legal effects of the contract (*Re Wait* [1927] 1 Ch 606, 639, per Atkin LJ (see above, p 266); *International Finance Corporation v DSNL Offshore Ltd*, above, at [49], per Colman J). A maritime lien is a right of action in rem against a ship and freight for payment due under a contract, for the cost of salvage or for damage caused by a ship (*The Law of Personal Property Security*, above, paras 4.129–4.132).

3. The remainder of this chapter will concentrate on the common law lien. Unless expressly stated otherwise, all references in this chapter to a 'lien' should be read as references to that type of lien.

(b) Possession

Forth v Simpson
(1849) 13 QB 680, Court of Queen's Bench

The owner of race horses stabled them with a trainer to be trained and kept. From time to time the horses, by order of the owner, were sent to run at different races, where the owner selected and paid the rider. The trainer claimed a lien over the horses for the cost of training and keep.

Lord Denman CJ: I have little doubt that the care and skill employed by a trainer upon a race horse are of such a nature as would, on general principles, give a right of lien. But it is essential to a lien that the party claiming it should have had the right of continued possession. In the present case there was no right of continued possession; for the owner of the horses might, at his own pleasure, have sent them to any race, and to be ridden by any jockey of his own selection. The circumstances of this case, therefore, make it like the case of a livery stable keeper; for it is immaterial whether the owner's possession be more or less, if he has a right to assert it at all, and to interrupt the possession of the party claiming the lien.

Coleridge J: I also have no doubt that the skill and labour of a trainer are a good foundation for a lien; because he educates an untaught animal, and otherwise adapts it for a particular purpose, and thereby greatly improves its value. But it is a well established principle that, without the right of continuing possession, there can be no right of lien. Now a good test of the existence of such right of possession is to consider in whose possession the race horse is when it is employed in doing that for which it has been trained. The evidence shewed that the horse, during the race, was in the owner's possession, and in his possession rightfully and according to usage or contract. The horse, before the race, is placed for convenience in the stable of the trainer; but during the race it is in the care of the jockey nominated by the owner. It appears too that, if, on any occasion, the jockey were selected by the trainer, the trainer, pro hac vice, would have only the delegated authority of the owner. I think it is part of the understanding that the owner shall have the possession and control of the horse to run at any race. This is quite inconsistent with the trainer's continuing right of possession.

[Patteson and Erie JJ delivered concurring judgments.]

NOTES

1.   *Forth v Simpson* was followed by Rose J in *Ward v Fielden* [1985] CLY 2000. See also *Hatton v Car Maintenance Co Ltd* [1915] 1 Ch 621 at 624 (below).

2.   In *Forth v Simpson*, Coleridge J stated that it was part of the 'understanding' that the owner was to have possession of the horses. This illustrates that the terms of any agreement between the creditor and the debtor can prevent a lien arising. Another example of the parties' agreement being inconsistent with the existence of a lien is where the creditor extends a period of credit to the debtor (*Wilson v Lombank Ltd* [1963] 1 WLR 1294). In such cases the intention of the parties prevents a lien arising.

3.   For a valid lien to arise there must have been a voluntary delivery of possession by the debtor to the creditor (*Re Cosslett (Contractors) Ltd* [1998] Ch 495 at 508–509, CA—no lien where employer exercised contractual right to take possession of plant and materials against the will of the contractor). Possession must not be obtained by force or other tortious means (*Bernal v Pirn* (1835) 1 Gale 17), nor must it arise as a result of fraud or any other kind of misrepresentation (*Madden v Kempster* (1807) 1 Camp 12). Furthermore, as a general rule no lien will arise from wrongful possession resulting from the act of a debtor who is not the owner of the goods (see below, pp 1114ff, for the rule and its exceptions).

4.   For cases on loss of possession, see below, pp 1119ff.

(c) How does a lien arise?

A common law lien generally arises by operation of law (*Re Bond Worth Ltd* [1980] Ch 228 at 250, per Slade J). Unlike a pledge, it does not depend upon the express or implied agreement of the parties. However, it is also possible to create a common law possessory lien by contract (*Gladstone v Birley* (1817) 2 Mer 401 at 404, Grant MR). A contractual lien supersedes or excludes a lien arising by operation of law, and the rights of the parties are governed purely by the contractual terms (*Fisher v Smith* (1878) 4 App Cas 1, HL). The lienee may also be given a contractual power of sale: this does not convert a contractual lien into an equitable charge (*Trident International Ltd v Barlow* [1999] 2 BCLC 506, CA), nor a pledge (*Marcq v Christie Manson & Woods Ltd (t/a Christies)* [2003] EWCA Civ 731, [2003] 3 All ER 561 at [41]).

This section will concentrate on particular liens arising by operation of law (ie by judicially recognised usage). A particular lien gives the lienee the right to retain a chattel until all charges *incurred in respect of that chattel* have been paid. By contrast, a general lien gives the lienee the right to retain a chattel until all claims against the lienor are satisfied, *whether or not those claims arise in respect of the retained chattel.* General liens are considered below, pp 1111ff.

Hatton v Car Maintenance Co Ltd

[1915] 1 Ch 621, Chancery Division

The owner of a motor car entered into an agreement with the defendant company whereby the company agreed to maintain the vehicle, supply a driver and do any necessary repairs. An amount having become due by the owner under the agreement, the company took possession of the car and claimed a lien on it for the amount due. Sargant J rejected the company's claim.

Sargant J: Now it is clear that the amount to be paid is not merely for the repair of the car, but is for the wages of the chauffeur and the supply of petrol and oil, and that kind of thing, and therefore it is an inclusive lump sum.

It was said by Mr Crossfield [Counsel for the defendant] that whenever an article is repaired, the repairer gets a lien on the article for the amount of his charges. Well, I do not dissent at all from that view of the law, assuming that the repairer gets the article in his shop for the purpose of repair and by that repair improves it, as he would ordinarily do. But certainly I cannot find anything in the authorities which have been cited to me to show that, if what the contractor does is not to improve the article but merely to maintain it in its former condition, he gets a lien for the amount spent upon it for that maintenance. The cases with regard to horses seem to point entirely the other way, because it is clear that a jobmaster has no lien at all for the amount of his bill in respect of feeding and keeping a horse at his stable, whereas, on the other hand, a trainer does get a lien upon a horse for the improvement which he effects to the horse in the course of training it for a race. A case was cited to me by Mr Crossfield with regard to the extent of the lien of an innkeeper, but I do not think that has really any application to the present case. Here all that was to be done by the contractor was for the purpose of maintaining the car in the condition in which it was sent to him, and in my judgment he would have no lien, that is no common law lien, in respect of the amount owing to him for that service.

That really would be sufficient to dispose of the case, but I think I ought also to express my opinion that, on the cases cited to me, even if he had such a lien originally, that lien would be lost by virtue of the arrangement under which the owner was to be at liberty to take the car away, and did take the car away, as and when she pleased. The existence of a lien seems to me to be inconsistent with an arrangement under which the article is from time to time taken entirely out of the possession and control of the contractor, for I cannot think that the fact that the chauffeur was to be deemed to be the servant of the company was intended to have the effect, or had the effect, of leaving the car in the possession of the company. I think that clause was inserted for quite other and fairly obvious reasons.

Re Southern Livestock Producers Ltd

[1964] 1 WLR 24, Chancery Division

By an agreement with a pig company, a farmer agreed to 'care for' a herd of pigs and supervise the breeding of the herd. The company supplied boars for the latter purpose. On the company's liquidation, the farmer claimed a lien over the pigs to cover outstanding sums expended in feeding and caring for the herd. Pennycuick J rejected the farmer's claim.

Pennycuick J: The authorities which I have cited bind me in this court. It is perfectly clear that unless the bailee can establish improvement he has no lien. If this matter were free from authority it would, I think, be tempting to draw the line in rather a different place so as to cover the case where a person by the exercise of labour and skill prevents a chattel from deteriorating in contradistinction to improving it. The obvious example is feeding of animals which would otherwise die; but other examples come to mind. It seems to me to be illogical that a kennel keeper should have a lien for the expense of stripping a dog, but not for that of boarding it. However, it is quite impossible for me at this time of day to introduce that sort of modification into a well-established principle.

Turning now to the facts of the present case, the first step is to look again at the agreement. What the farmer undertakes to do under that agreement is to care for a specified number of pigs and piglets. The word 'care' received a definition in the recital. The word means 'house feed care for and arrange for the proper servicing and farrowing of the sows and gilts concerned, and also the piglets farrowed by the sows and gilts. Mr Figgis, who appears for the liquidator, accepts the position that under that agreement the farmer was required to employ, and did employ, labour and skill . . . . But, says Mr Figgis, the agreement does not provide for any improvement upon the subject-matter of the agreement, namely, the pigs and their litters. I have come to the conclusion that I must accept this argument. The operations comprised in the definition of 'care' add up precisely to 'care' in the ordinary sense of that word and do not seem to me to go in any respect beyond it. It is of great importance to observe in this connection that the company is under obligation to supply the boars for the service of the sows. The position would be different if the farmer had to supply the boars. In that case it appears from *Scarfe v Morgan* ((1838) 4 M & W 270) that the farmer would have a lien in respect of service charge, provided he could identify this item.

Mr Sunnucks, for the farmer, contends that one must look at the herd of pigs as a whole and that the agreement provides for the improvement of the herd as a whole by the production of litters. I agree that one must look at the herd as a whole and not pig by pig, and that is, indeed, accepted by Mr Figgis. But when one does look at the herd as a whole, one finds that the production of litters results from the natural properties of the sows in co-operation with the boars supplied by the company, and I do not think this production of litters could fairly be described as an improvement effected by the farmer. What the farmer does is merely to look after the herd as it increases from other causes.

I say again that I am not altogether attracted by the argument on behalf of the liquidator, and I should be glad if I were able to draw the line in a manner rather more generous to the person claiming a lien. But it seems to me that to do so in the way in which I am asked so to do by Mr Sunnucks would be to make an unjustifiable inroad upon well-established principles. I do not think it is legitimate to say that a person improves a flock or herd of animals merely by supervising its natural increase, however much skill and care is involved in that process.

I would add that, even if there were an element of improvement in this respect—that is, supervising the production of litters—the farmer would find himself in this difficulty because under the terms of the agreement it would be impossible to apportion the sums expended by him between the ordinary upkeep on the one hand and the improvement on the other hand.

NOTES

1.   Where goods are entrusted to a person to do work on them, that person will have a lien for the work done, provided that he improves the goods. The lien is called an improver's (or artificer's) lien and it is a particular lien (although, exceptionally, an improver may be able to assert a lien over a part of a composite chattel, or one of a group of chattels, even though he has not worked on that part or on that particular chattel in the group, eg 'a car repairer could exercise a lien on the spare tyre for work carried out on the engine', per Lloyd J in *The Ijaola* [1979] 1 Lloyd's Rep 103 at 116; much depends on whether the contract was entire: see Palmer, op cit, pp 944 and 955). The lien only arises when the work is complete (*Pinnock v Harrison* (1838) 3 M & W 532). However, if the owner of the goods prevents completion by withdrawing his instructions, the improver is entitled to a lien for his charges in respect of that part which is actually completed (*Lilley v Barnsley* (1844) 1 Car & Kir 344).

2. A particular lien can also arise where a person is under a legal obligation to perform services, eg a common carrier or an innkeeper. A common carrier (not a private carrier) has a lien for his carriage charges as they become due, ie when the goods arrive at their destination. An innkeeper's lien extends over the belongings the guest brings into the inn (which includes a hotel: s 1(1) of the Hotel Proprietors Act 1956) and secures the amount of his bill for food and lodging (*Matsuda v Waldorf Hotel Co Ltd* (1910) 27 TLR 153). However, the lien does not affect the clothes the guest is wearing at any particular moment (*Sunbolf v Alford* (1838) 3 M & W 248), neither does it extend to any vehicle (or any property left therein) or any horse or other live animal or its harness or other equipment (s 2(2) of the Hotel Proprietors Act 1956). See generally, G McBain 'Abolishing the Strict Liability of Hotelkeepers' [2006] JBL 705, esp 739–749.

QUESTIONS

1. Does a warehouseman enjoy a common law lien (general or particular) in respect of his storage charges? See *Gordon v Gordon* [2002] EWCA Civ 1884 (must be a lien arising from contract); see also NE Palmer *Bailment* (2nd edn, 1991), pp 873–877.

2. B agrees to restore A's painting for £100. A delivers the painting to B's studio. Before the restoration is complete A demands the return of his picture. Advise B as to whether (a) he may keep the painting until A pays for the work actually done; and (b) he may ignore the demand, complete the restoration and claim the £100. See *Hounslow London Borough Council v Twickenham Garden Developments Ltd* [1971] Ch 233 at 253; and contrast *Bolwell Fibreglass Pty Ltd v Foley* [1984] VR 97 at 111.

(d) General liens

General liens may arise either by express agreement or as a common law right arising from general usage. As the next case illustrates, general liens are discouraged by the courts.

Rushforth v Hadfield

(1805) 6 East 519, Court of King's Bench

A common carrier retained a bankrupt's goods, after the cost of carriage of those goods had been paid, on the ground that he had a right to retain the goods until the cost of carriage of other goods was paid. The assignee of the estate of the bankrupt brought an action in trover against the carrier to recover the value of his goods. The common carrier claimed a general lien arising from a general usage of the trade. At the trial the jury gave a verdict for the carrier; which was moved to be set aside as a verdict against the law and evidence.

Lawrence J: I agree that there ought to be a new trial. Common carriers are every day attempting to alter the situation in which they have been placed by the law. At common law they are bound to receive and carry the goods of the subject for a reasonable reward, to take due care of them in their passage, and to deliver them in the same condition as when they were received: but they are not bound to deliver them without being paid for the carriage of the particular article, and therefore they have a lien to that extent. Of late years however they have been continually attempting to alter their general character by special notices on the one hand to diminish their liability, and on the other hand by extending their lien. But what evidence have we in this case to say that their common law situation is altered? To do that it must be shewn that both parties have consented to the alteration: the carrier cannot alter his situation by his own act alone. It is said that a general lien is convenient to the parties concerned: I do not say that it may not be so, but it must arise out of the contract of the parties. It may be convenient enough for the customer to say, that in consideration that you, the carrier, will give up your right to stop each particular parcel of goods for the price of the carriage, I will agree that you may stop any one parcel of my goods for the carriage price of all together. But still this must be by contract between them; and usage of trade is evidence of such a contract. And where such a usage is general, and has been long established so as to afford a presumption of its being commonly known, it is fair to conclude that the particular parties contracted with reference to it. Then, if in this case there had been evidence of a usage so uniform and frequent as to warrant an inference that the parties contracted with reference to it, it should have been left to the jury to infer that it was part of their contract.

Le Blanc J: . . . General liens are a great inconvenience to the generality of traders, because they give a particular advantage to certain individuals who claim to themselves a special privilege against the body at large of the creditors instead of coming in with them for an equal share of the insolvent's estate. All these general liens infringe upon the system of the bankrupt laws, the object of which is to distribute the debtor's estate proportionably amongst all the creditors, and they ought not to be encouraged. But I do not mean to say that a usage in trade may not be so general and well established as to induce a jury to believe that the parties acted upon it in their particular agreement; and I cannot say that such an agreement would not be good in law. . . . The instances of detainer by carriers for their general balance which were proved at the trial were very few and recent with a view to found so extensive a claim. .. . Without saying therefore that there may not be such a usage as that insisted on, I am clearly of opinion that there should be a new trial in order to have the case submitted to the jury on its true ground, which it does not appear to have been upon the last trial.

[Lord Ellenborough CJ and Grose J delivered concurring judgments.]

[At the new trial the jury gave a verdict for the plaintiff; which was moved to be set aside.]

Rushforth v Hadfield
(1806) 7 East 224, Court of King's Bench

Lord Ellenborough CJ: It is too much to say that there has been a general acquiescence in this claim of the carriers since 1775, merely because there was a particular instance of it at that time. Other instances were only about 10 or 12 years back, and several of them of very recent date. The question however results to this, what was the particular contract of these parties? And as the evidence is silent as to any express agreement between them, it must be collected either from the mode of dealing before practised between the same parties, or from the general dealings of other persons engaged in the same employment, of such notoriety as that they might fairly be presumed to be known to the bankrupt at the time of his dealing with the defendants, from whence the inference was to be drawn that these parties dealt upon the same footing as all others did, with reference to the known usage of the trade. But at least it must be admitted that the claim now set up by the carriers is against the general law of the land, and the proof of it is therefore to be regarded with jealousy. In many cases it would happen that parties would be glad to pay small sums due for the carriage of former goods, rather than incur the risk of a great loss by the detention of goods of value. Much of the evidence is of that description. Other instances again were in the case of solvent persons, who were at all events liable to answer for their general balance. And little or no stress could be laid on some of the more recent instances not brought home to the knowledge of the bankrupt at the time. Most of the evidence therefore is open to observation. If indeed there had been evidence of prior dealings between these parties upon the footing of such an extended lien, that would have furnished good evidence for the jury to have found that they continued to deal upon the same terms. But the question for the jury here was, whether the evidence of a usage for the carriers to retain for their balance were so general as that the bankrupt must be taken to have known and acted upon it? And they have in effect found either that the bankrupt knew of no such usage as that which was given in evidence, or knowing, did not adopt it. And growing liens are always to be looked at with jealousy, and require stronger proof. They are encroachments upon the common law. If they are encouraged the practice will be continually extending to other traders and other matters. The farrier will be claiming a lien upon a horse sent to him to be shod. Carriages and other things which require frequent repair will be detained on the same claim; and there is no saying where it is to stop. It is not for the convenience of the public that these liens should be extended further than they are already established by law. But if any particular inconvenience arise in the course of trade, the parties may, if they think proper, stipulate with their customers for the introduction of such a lien into their dealings. But in the absence of any evidence of that sort to affect the bankrupt, I think the jury have done right in negativing the lien claimed by the defendants on the score of general usage.

Le Blanc J: This is a case where a jury might well be jealous of a general lien attempted to be set up against the policy of the common law, which has given to carriers only a lien for the carriage price of the particular goods. The party therefore who sets up such a claim ought to make out a very strong case. But upon weighing the evidence which was given at the trial, I do not think that this is a case in which the Court are called upon to hold out any encouragement to the claim set up, by overturning what the jury have done, after having the whole matter properly submitted to them.

[Grose and Lawrence JJ delivered concurring judgments.]

NOTES

1. The following have been held to have general liens as a matter of usage: solicitors (*Ismail v Richards Butler (a firm)* [1996] QB 711; *Bentley v Gaisford* [1997] QB 627, CA); bankers (*Brandao v Barnett* (1846) 3 CB 519); factors (*Baring v Corrie* (1818) 2 B & Ald 137); stockbrokers (*Re London & Globe Finance Corpn* [1902] 2 Ch 416); and insurance brokers (*Hewison v Guthrie* (1836) 2 Bing NC 755; *Eide UK Ltd v Lowndes Lambert Group Ltd* [1998] 1 All ER 946, CA). Accountants only enjoy a particular lien over the books of account, files and papers of their clients (*Woodworth v Conroy* [1976] QB 884, CA, although Lawson LJ suggests at 890, without deciding the point, that they may enjoy a wider lien than this).

2. The right to exercise a lien (general or particular) is not enforceable in all circumstances. Section 246(2) of the Insolvency Act 1986 renders a lien unenforceable to the extent that its enforcement would deny possession of any books, papers or other records to an insolvency office-holder (an administrator, liquidator or provisional liquidator of a company) (see below, Ch 29). There is also authority in relation to solicitors (*Re Capital Fire Insurance Association* (1883) 24 Ch D 408) and accountants (*DTC (CNC) Ltd v Gary Sargeant &. Co (a firm)* [1996] 2 All ER 369) which makes it clear that they are not to exercise a lien over books or documents of a client company which are required by statute or by its articles of association to be kept at a particular place, or to be available for a specific purpose such as inspection.

QUESTIONS

1. Why was there such hostility to general liens in *Rushforth v Hadfield*?

2. How may a general lien be 'convenient to the parties concerned' (per Lawrence J, above)? See Bell, op cit, pp 142–143.

(e) Liens and third parties

Tappenden v Artus
[1964] 2 QB 185, Court of Appeal

T allowed A to use a van pending completion of a hire-purchase agreement between them. It was a condition of the bailment that A should tax and insure the vehicle at his own expense. The van broke down and A took it to the defendants' garage for repair. Shortly afterwards T withdrew his permission for A to use the van and demanded its return. The defendants refused to deliver up the van until paid for their work. At first instance, T succeeded in his action against the defendants for the return of the van and damages for its retention. The defendants appealed to the Court of Appeal (Willmer and Diplock LJJ).

Diplock LJ (delivering the judgment of the court): Since a common law lien is a right to continue an existing actual possession of goods (that is to say, to refuse to put an end to a bailment) it can only be exercised by an artificer if his possession was lawful at the time at which the lien first attached. To entitle him to exercise a right of possession under his common law lien adverse to the owner of the goods, he must thus show that his possession under the original delivery of the goods to him was lawful—*Bowmaker Ltd v Wycombe Motors Ltd* ([1946] KB 505)—and continued to be lawful until some work was done by him upon the goods. Where, therefore, as in the present case, possession of the goods was originally given to the artificer not by the owner himself, but by a bailee of the owner, the test whether the artificer can rely upon his common law lien as a defence in an action for detinue brought against him by the owner is whether the owner authorised (or is estopped as against the artificer from denying that he authorised) the bailee to give possession of the goods to the artificer. This, it seems to us, is the test which, after some vacillation, is laid down by the modern authorities. It is as a result of applying this test that the cases which have been cited to us fall upon one side or other of the line....

These cases, all of which fall upon one side of the line, seem to us to do no more than support the propositions that where no question of ostensible authority arises, (1) the mere fact of delivery of possession of goods by an owner to a bailee does not of itself give the bailee authority to deliver possession of the goods to a third party; and (2) that whether the bailee has such authority depends in each case upon the purpose of the bailment and terms of the contract (if any) under which the goods are bailed to him.

The latter proposition was most clearly stated in the judgment of Collins J in the Divisional Court case of *Singer Manufacturing Co v London & South Western Rly Co* ([1894] 1 QB 833), a case which falls on the other side of the line. This passage, although it was not the ratio decidendi of the other member of the court, has been repeatedly cited with approval, and is the foundation of the modern law on this topic. In that case a man who was in possession under a hire-purchase agreement of a Singer sewing machine placed it in a railway cloakroom during the time that the hiring was in existence and, the hiring having come to an end, the owners of the machine claimed it from the railway company, who set up a warehouseman's lien. In his judgment Collins J said this: 'I think in this case the lien may also be rested on another ground; and that is, that the person who deposited this machine was, as between himself and the owner of it, entitled to the possession of it at the time he deposited it. He was entitled to it under a contract of hire, which gave him the right to use it, I presume, for all reasonable purposes incident to such a contract, and among them, I take it, he acquired the right to take the machine with him if he travelled, and to deposit it in a cloakroom if he required to do so. In the course of that reasonable user of the machine, and before the contract of bailment was determined, he gave rights to the railway company in respect of the custody of it. I think those rights must be good against the owners of the machine, who had not determined the hire-purchase agreement at the time that those rights were acquired by the railway company.'

This, in our view, lays down the correct test for determining what authority is conferred by the owner of goods upon the bailee to part with possession of the goods when the purpose of the bailment is the use of the goods by the bailee. He is entitled to make reasonable use of the goods, and if it is reasonably incidental to such use for the bailee to give possession of them to a third person in circumstances which may result in such person acquiring the common law remedy of lien against the goods, the bailee has the authority of the owner to give lawful possession of the goods to the third person. This is not strictly an 'implied term' in *The Moorcock* ((1889) 14 PD 64) sense of the contract between the bailor and the bailee. The grant of authority to use goods is itself to be construed as authority to do in relation to the goods all things that are reasonably incidental to their reasonable use. If the bailor desires to exclude the right of the bailee to do in relation to the goods some particular thing which is reasonably incidental to their reasonable use, he can, of course, do so, but he must do so expressly.

In the case of a bailment for use, therefore, where there is no express prohibition upon his parting with possession of the goods (and no question of ostensible authority arises), the relevant inquiry is whether the giving of actual possession of the goods by the bailee to the person asserting the common law lien was an act which was reasonably incidental to the bailee's reasonable use of the goods. This was the inquiry in *Williams v Allsup* ((1861) 10 CBNS 417) a ship's mortgage case where there was no express provision requiring the mortgagor to keep the ship in repair. Willes J there said (at 427): 'By the permission of the mortgagees the mortgagor has the use of the vessel. He has, therefore, a right to use her in the way in which vessels are ordinarily used. Upon the facts which appear on this case, this vessel could not be so used unless these repairs had been done to her. The state of things, therefore, seems to involve the right of the mortgagor to get the vessel repaired,—not on the credit of the mortgagees, but upon the ordinary terms, subject to the shipwright's lien. It seems to me that the case is the same as if the mortgagees had been present when the order for the repairs was given. To that extent I think the property of the mortgagees is impliedly modified.' It was also the inquiry in *Keene v Thomas* ([1905] 1 KB 136) a hire-purchase case, in which there was an express provision requiring the hirer to keep a dog-cart in repair, and in *Green v All Motors Ltd* ([1917] 1 KB 625), another hire-purchase case, in which there was a similar obligation on the hirer to keep a car in repair. But Scrutton LJ, citing *Williams v Allsup* and *Singer Manufacturing Co v London & South Western Rly Co,* put the decision upon the broader ground with which we concur (at 633): 'The law is clear. The hirer of a chattel is entitled to have it repaired so as to enable him to use it in the way in which such a chattel is ordinarily used. The hirer was therefore entitled, without any express authority from the owner, to have the motor car repaired so as to enable him to use it as a motor car is ordinarily used.'

Albemarle Supply Co v Hind & Co ([1928] 1 KB 307), which was also cited, is on a different point, namely, the ostensible authority of the bailee. It was another case of a hire-purchase agreement, but the agreement contained a term which expressly excluded the hirer's right to create a lien on the vehicles in respect of repairs. The artificer to whom possession of the vehicles was delivered for the purpose of repair was aware that the vehicles were bailed to the hirer under a hire-purchase agreement, but was not aware of the express exclusion of his right to create a lien. It was held that vis-à-vis the artificer the owner had given the hirer ostensible authority to give possession of the vehicles to the artificer for the purpose of effecting repairs, and could not rely upon a secret limitation upon the terms upon which the hirer was authorised to do so, that is, upon terms excluding the artificer's common law remedy of lien. It was a case where the owner was estopped from denying that he had conferred on his bailee authority to give up possession of the vehicles to the artificer on the ordinary terms, and thus subject to the ordinary remedy of lien.

The actual decision in that case is not germane to the present appeal, for the artificer here relies solely upon the actual authority conferred by the bailor on the bailee, and not upon any ostensible authority in excess of that actual authority....

Finally, there is *Bowmaker Ltd v Wycombe Motors Ltd.* It was another hire purchase case in which, however, the bailment to the hirer had been lawfully determined before he delivered possession of the vehicle to the artificer. Since the hirer's possession of the vehicle was itself unlawful, it followed that he could not then confer any lawful possession upon the artificer upon which the artificer could base his claim to a lien. But there is a passage in the judgment of Goddard LJ which summarises with his usual accuracy and clarity the true ratio decidendi of the cases. He said this ([1946] KB 505 at 509): 'So, too, it has been held in the cases to which our attention has been called, more especially *Green v All Motors Ltd* and *Albemarle Supply Co Ltd v Hind & Co* that in the case of a motor car where it is necessary that the motor car should be kept in running condition and repair during the time the hire-purchase agreement is current and valid, the hirer has a right to take it and get it repaired and, if he does so the repairer can exercise an artificer's lien on it, because at the time when the motor car was left with him he, the hirer, had the right, whether you call it by implied authority or by legitimate authority, to use that car in all reasonable ways, and among those ways was a right to get the car repaired and kept in running order. Therefore he was placing it with the repairer with the implied consent of the owner and the artificer's lien on that account will prevail against the owner. These cases have also held, and quite understandably, that an arrangement between the owner and the hirer that the hirer shall not be entitled to create a lien, does not affect the repairer. A repairer has a lien although the owner has purported to limit the hirer's authority to create a lien in that way. That seems to me to depend upon this: Once an artificer exercises his art upon a chattel, the law gives the artificer a lien upon that chattel which he can exercise against the owner of the chattel if the owner of the chattel has placed it with him or has authorised another person to place it with him. If I send my servant with my chattel to get it repaired, the artificer will get the lien which the law gives him on that chattel although I may have told my servant that he is not to create a lien. The fact is that the lien arises by operation of law because the work has been done on the chattel.'

To this statement of principle we would only add the rider that the latter part of it which deals with ostensible authority should be understood as restricted to cases where the artificer has no express notice of the limit upon the authority of the person to whom the owner has given possession of the chattel.

Mr Forbes [Counsel for the plaintiff] has argued that this principle is limited to bailments under contracts of hire purchase where there is a liability on the hirer to keep the goods in repair. We cannot accept this. *Williams v Allsup* was not a hire purchase case at all; the *Singer Company's* case was concerned with a warehousemen's lien, not with an artificer's lien. We think that Mr Hammerton [Counsel for the defendants] is right in his contention that, at any rate if there is consideration for the bailment, the principle applies to all cases where the purpose of the bailment of goods is their use by the bailee.

In the present case the purpose of the bailment of the Dormobile van was clearly for use on the roads by the bailee. Mr Forbes has submitted that it was a gratuitous bailment, made in anticipation of the bailee's entering into a hire-purchase agreement in respect of the van. We do not think this is right. It was a term of the bailment that the bailee, not the bailor, should license the van at his own expense and insure it upon comprehensive terms. This was in fact done in the bailee's own name although it does not appear whether or not this was a term of the prior arrangement as to licensing and insurance. There was thus good consideration in law for the bailment, and it is unnecessary to consider what the position would have been if the bailment had been purely gratuitous.

It is a statutory offence to use a motor vehicle on the highway which is in an unroadworthy condition. If the van should become unroadworthy during the period of the bailment the bailee could not use it for the purposes of the bailment unless he were to have it repaired. In the ordinary way, save in the case of minor adjustments, a motor vehicle can be repaired only by delivering possession of it to an expert mechanic to effect the repairs; and in our view the giving of actual possession of a motor vehicle to an artificer for the purpose of effecting repairs necessary to render it roadworthy is an act reasonably incidental to the bailee's reasonable use of the vehicle. If the bailor desires to exclude the bailee's authority to do this, he must do so expressly....

Different considerations would apply to repairs which were not necessary to make the van roadworthy, for the execution of such repairs might not be reasonably necessary to the reasonable use of the van by the bailee, which was the purpose of the bailment; but there is no suggestion in the evidence that any of the repairs in respect of which the lien was claimed were not necessary to make the van roadworthy.

We are, therefore, of opinion that the artificer was entitled to a common law lien upon the van in respect of the repairs which he effected, and he is entitled to assert that lien against the bailor because the bailor gave the bailee authority to give lawful possession of the van to the artificer for the purpose of effecting such repairs as were necessary to make the van roadworthy.

For these reasons we allow this appeal.

NOTES

1.   Why did the hire-purchaser have ostensible or apparent authority to bind the owner with a lien in *Albemarle Supply Co Ltd v Hind & Co* [1928] 1 KB 307 (below, p 1119) but not in *Bowmaker Ltd v Wycombe Motors Ltd* [1946] KB 505? Merely allowing the hirer to have possession of the vehicle would not of itself be enough to bring into operation the doctrine of estoppel (see above, p 358). However, in *Albemarle* the hire-purchaser had garaged the vehicles with the defendants over a long period with the apparent sanction of the owner (at least the owner did not interfere with this arrangement). Although not explicit in their Lordships' reasoning, it is probable that the Court of Appeal found the necessary representation in this conduct of the owner (this is how the case was explained by Isaacs and Higgins JJ in *Fisher v Automobile Finance Co of Australia Ltd* (1928) 41 CLR 167 at 177 and 180, High Court of Australia). On the other hand, in the *Bowmaker* case the hire-purchaser took the vehicle to the garage for a one-off repair. There was no representation of authority by the owner.

2.   There are other exceptional cases when wrongful possession resulting from the act of a third party may nevertheless bind the owner:

(1)   A mercantile agent, seller or buyer in possession of goods may by wrongful disposition bind the owner (ss 2, 8 and 9 of the Factors Act 1889, and ss 24 and 25 of the Sale of Goods Act 1979).

(2)   If the person claiming the lien is obliged by law to receive the goods, eg a common carrier or an innkeeper, he is not affected by the wrongful disposition by the depositor, (see, for example, *Marsh v Police Comr* [1945] KB 43, where the Court of Appeal held the Ritz Hotel entitled to exercise a lien over stolen goods brought onto its premises by a guest). Whilst an innkeeper's lien is not affected by the fact that the innkeeper knows the goods are not the property of the guest (*Robins & Co v Gray* [1895] 2 QB 501), it is unlikely that a court would allow an innkeeper to exercise a lien over goods he knew to be stolen.

(3)   The lien is claimed in respect of a negotiable instrument received in good faith and without notice of any dishonour (s 27(3) of the Bills of Exchange Act 1882).

QUESTION

Rook hired a car from Bishop, stole a quantity of jewellery from King's shop and drove off in the car, which he then negligently damaged against a wall. He left the car at Queen's garage for repair, pledged one necklace to Pawn for £60 and took the rest of the stolen jewellery to Castle's hotel, where he stayed until he was arrested three weeks later. Queen, Pawn and Castle now refuse to surrender the car and the jewellery unless they are paid, respectively, £80 for repairing the car, £60 for the necklace and £200 for hotel charges. Advise Bishop and King. What is the position if Bishop had originally bought the car from Queen and still owes Queen £50 of the purchase price?

(f) Enforcement

(i) Generally

We have already established that, as a general rule, a common law lien cannot be enforced by sale (above, p 1106). However, a lienee may be given a power of sale in the following circumstances:

(1) By contract;

(2) by trade usage (see *Re Tate, ex p Moffatt* (1841) 2 Mont D & De G 170);

(3) by statute, eg Innkeepers Act 1878, s 1 (innkeeper's right of sale); Torts (Interference with Goods) Act 1977, ss 12 and 13 (bailee's right of sale of uncollected goods); Sale of Goods Act 1979, s 48 (unpaid seller's right of resale).

Additionally, on the application of any party to a cause or matter, a court has power under the Civil Procedure Rules 1998, r 25. 1(1)(c)(v) to order the sale of any property (including land) which is the subject of a claim or as to which any question may arise on a claim and which is of a perishable nature or which for any other good reason it is desirable to sell quickly. In *Larner v Fawcett* [1950] 2 All ER 727, the court of Appeal exercised this power on the interlocutory application of a race horse trainer claiming a lien over the respondent's horse to cover outstanding charges. The court emphasised that the power of sale under what is now r 25. 1(1)(c)(v) could be exercised even though the common law lienee has no power of sale at law or in equity. The court went on to hold that it was proper to make such an order for sale in this case on the grounds that (1) the horse was 'eating its head off' at the trainer's expense; and (2) the owner had unreasonably delayed in requesting its return. The proceeds of sale were ordered to be paid into court to abide the result of the action.

(ii) Insolvency Act 1986

1.   Section 246(2) of the Insolvency Act 1986 provides that a lien or other right to retain possession of any books, papers or other records of a company is unenforceable to the extent that its enforcement would deny possession of any books, papers or other records to an insolvency office-holder (an administrator, liquidator or provisional liquidator of a company). But the section does not apply where a lien is claimed 'on documents which give a title to property and are held as such' (s 246(3)). Thus, in *Re Carter Commercial Developments Ltd* [2002] BPIR 1053, solicitors owed fees by a corporate client that was later placed into administration were held entitled to assert a lien over title deeds to the client's land.

2.   In *Bristol Airport plc v Powdrill* [1990] Ch 744, the Court of Appeal held (*obiter*) that the exercise of a possessory lien over a company's property was included within the statutory definition of 'security' contained in s 248(b) of the Insolvency Act 1986 and, therefore, was caught by s 11(3)(c) of that Act. When an administration order is made in respect of a company (see below, p 1214), 'no...steps may be taken to enforce any security over the company's property...except with the consent of the administrator or the leave of the court' (Insolvency Act 1986, s 11(3)(c)). This could create a number of practical problems for someone claiming a lien over the company's property when an administrator has been appointed, eg is the lien holder liable to damages in conversion if he refuses to hand over the goods to the administrator pending an application to the court for leave? Woolf LJ attempted to deal with a number of these problems when he said (at 768):

You are not taking steps to enforce a security unless by relying on the security you are preventing the administrator doing something to...[a] chattel in which he has an interest which he would otherwise be entitled to do. Taking first the case of the ordinary repairer who is entitled to retain goods until his charges are paid. Unless and until someone who is entitled to possession of those goods seeks to obtain possession of the goods, the lien holder does not take steps to enforce his lien. The security which is given to the lien holder entitles him to refuse to hand over the possession of the goods, but until he makes an unqualified refusal to hand over the goods he has not in my judgment taken steps to enforce the security for the purposes of s 11(3)(c) of the Act of 1986...I would not regard a person who is otherwise entitled to a lien as enforcing that lien if he does not make an unqualified refusal to hand over the goods to an administrator but instead indicates to the administrator that unless the administrator consents to his exercising his right to detain, he will apply promptly to the court for leave and does so. In my view such conduct would not amount to taking steps to enforce the lien within the meaning of s 11(3)(c) of the Act of 1986.

Browne-Wilkinson V-C agreed with Woolf LJ; Staughton LJ did not express an opinion as to the correctness of Woolf LJ's dicta.

In *London Flight Centre (Stansted) Ltd v Osprey Aviation Ltd* [2002] BPIR 1115, a creditor, who was unsecured at the date the debtor went into administration, asserted a contractual lien over one of the debtor's aircraft that happened to come into its possession after that date. Hart J held that the creditor was not entitled to enforce the lien which it had acquired post-administration and thereby gain priority over unsecured creditors and undermine the purposes for which the administration order was made. Hart J stated (at 1125) that 'a possessory lien which the court will not allow to be enforced is an oxymoron. It is no lien at all'.

(g) Termination of lien

Albemarle Supply Co Ltd v Hind and Co
[1928] 1 KB 307, Court of Appeal

B hired three taxicabs from the plaintiffs under hire-purchase agreements. The agreements required B to keep the cabs and their equipment in good repair but prohibited him from selling, pledging or parting with possession of them without the plaintiffs' consent, and from creating a lien on them in respect of repairs. For a number of years B garaged the cabs, and two other cabs, with the defendants who serviced them and carried out necessary repairs. The defendants knew of the hire-purchase agreements but were not aware of their terms. B's account then fell into arrears, but the defendants allowed him to take the cabs from their garage each day on condition that the cabs continued 'in pawn' and were returned to the garage each night. B then fell into arrear with his hire-purchase instalments and the plaintiffs terminated the agreements and demanded the three cabs from the defendants. The defendants claimed a lien over the three cabs for the balance of their general account for all five cabs due from B. The balance of account included the cost of rent, washing, oil and petrol, which would not be the subject of a repairing lien.

Scrutton LJ: The plaintiffs' first line of attack on the lien claim was a clause in their hire-purchase agreement providing that 'the hirer shall not have or be deemed to have any authority to pledge the credit of the owners for repairs to the vehicle or to create a lien upon the same in respect of such repairs.' This Court in *Green v All Motors Ltd* ([1917] 1 KB 625) has held that the mere knowledge by the repairer that there is a hire-purchase agreement without knowledge of its exact terms relating to the car which he repairs does not deprive him of his lien. The owner leaving the cab in the hands of a man who is entitled to use it gives him an implied authority to have it repaired with the resulting lien for repairs. Rowlatt J had held in a previous case, and the judge below in the present case followed his decision, that a contractual limitation of authority not communicated to the repairer does not limit the implied authority derived from the hirer's being allowed to possess and use the car. I agree with this view; if a man is put in a position which holds him out as having a certain authority, people who act on that holding out are not affected by a secret limitation, of which they are ignorant, of the apparent authority. The owners can easily protect themselves by requiring information as to the garage where the cab is kept, and notifying the garage owner that the hirer has no power to create a lien for repairs. They will thus escape the lien, though they may not get their cab repaired.

The plaintiffs next contended that any lien was lost because the cabs went out of the possession of the garage each day to ply for hire. The defendant proved an agreement with Botfield at a time when the lien existed, that the cabs should go out for hire each day on the terms that they should be returned to the garage each night, the lien continuing while the cabs were in possession of the garage. I do not think any plying for hire under this agreement prevented the lien, if any, from continuing, and in my view repair of a damaged cab, though it may be described as 'maintenance,' gave rise to a repairer's lien.

It was next said that the lien for repairs was lost inasmuch as it was originally claimed for a larger amount and a different cause than the right one. I have considered the numerous authorities cited, and in my view the law stands as follows: A person claiming a lien must either claim it for a definite amount, or give the owner particulars from which he himself can calculate the amount for which a lien is due. The owner must then in the absence of express agreement tender an amount covering the lien really existing. If he does not, unless excused, he has no answer to a claim of lien. He may be excused from tendering (1) if he has no knowledge or means of knowledge of the right amount; (2) if the person claiming the lien for a wrong cause or amount makes it clear that he will not release the goods unless his full claim is satisfied, and that claim is wrongful. The fact that the claim is made for more than the right amount does not matter unless the claimant gives no particulars from which the right amount can be calculated, or makes it clear that he insists on the full amount of the right claimed: see *Scarfe v Morgan* ((1838) 4 M & W 270); *Dirks v Richards* ((1842) 4 Man & G 574); *Huth & Co v Lamport* ((1886) 16 QBD 735 at 736), per Lord Esher; and *Rumsey v North Eastern Rly Co* ((1863) 14 CBNS 641 at 651 and 654), per Erle CJ and Willes J.

In the present case the accounts handed to the plaintiffs show the items relating to the repairs to each cab, and the plaintiffs did not tender because they thought their agreement prevented the creation of a lien, not because they could not ascertain what repairs were done. I do not think the defendants ever pinned themselves definitely to a demand for the whole sum.

[Lord Hanworth MR and Sargant J delivered concurring judgments (although Sargant J did not address the issue of loss of possession).]

NOTES

1.   Professor NE Palmer notes that '[t]he loss of possession is a question of fact but the effect upon the lien itself is one of law . . . the question is whether the change of circumstances, and the intentions accompanying it, are inconsistent with the further continuance of the lien' (*Bailment* (2nd edn, 1991), p 949). In *Albemarle Supply Co Ltd v Hind and Co*, the intention of the parties was expressed in the terms of their agreement for the release of the cabs. An intention to maintain the lien may also be implied (see *Allen v Smith* (1862) 12 CBNS 638, where the lien was not lost when a guest took a horse out of an innkeeper's stable intending to return it). But where there is no evidence of a contrary intention (as in the great majority of cases), loss of possession will terminate the lien (see, for example, *Pennington v Reliance Motor Works Ltd* [1923] 1 KB 127).

2.   In *Pennington v Reliance Motor Works Ltd*, above, E agreed with the plaintiff to rebuild his car. Without the plaintiff's authority, E sub-contracted the work to the defendants. The

defendants completed the work and returned the car to E, who delivered it back to the plaintiff. The defendants were not paid by E. When the plaintiff later delivered his car to the defendants for further repairs the defendants claimed a lien on it for the earlier work done for E. McCardie J held that there was no lien as the plaintiff gave no authority, express or implied, to E to create one and no custom of the trade was proved. He also held, in the alternative, that even if there had been a lien it had been lost when the defendants parted with possession of the car to E. As McCardie J stated: '...the defendants allowed E to take possession of the car not for any limited purpose, but in the belief that he would get payment from [the plaintiff], and would pay them as soon as he could'. But contrast *Euro Commercial Leasing Ltd v Cartwright and Lewis* [1995] 2 BCLC 618, where Evans-Lombe J held that solicitors with a general lien over client's money in a client account lost that lien when the money was transferred to the solicitors' office account without an order of court, contrary to Insolvency Act 1986, s 11(3)(c), but that when the error was discovered, and an equivalent sum repaid into the client's account, a 'fresh general lien' attached to the money in the account so reconstituted (for these purposes the judge assumed that money paid back into the client's account became the client's property, although he expressed some doubt about this). His Lordship considered that cases on loss of innkeepers' liens and improvers' liens through loss of possession of the relevant chattel were not analogous to a case of a solicitor's general lien. As one commentator has observed, 'though the judge did not say so, a ground of distinction seems to have been that the accounts were not choses in possession, as was the case in the old authorities, but debts, choses in action' (A Hudson 'Solicitors' Liens', Ch 25 in N Palmer and E McKendrick (eds) *Interests in Goods* (2nd edn, 1998), p 651). It is well established that a solicitor is allowed a lien over money in his client account (*Loescher v Dean* [1950] Ch 491).

3. Therefore, a lien may be terminated by the following means:

(1) a loss of possession to the lienor (or to a third party, as the lienee then loses his immediate right to possession and will be unable to redeliver to the lienor: *Mulliner v Florence* (1878) 3 QBD 484 at 489; cf s 48(2) of the Sale of Goods Act 1979);

(2) waiver of the necessity of making a tender (as outlined by Scrutton LJ in *Albemarle Supply Co Ltd v Hind and Co* (above, p 1119));

(3) payment or tender of the amount due.

It may also be lost by:

(4) accepting alternative security in substitution for the lien (save that taking bills of exchange as alternative security usually only suspends the lien so that it will revive on dishonour—*Stevenson v Blakelock* (1813) 1 M&S 535);

(5) a wrongful sale (*Mulliner v Florence* (1878) 3 QBD 484) or other act of conversion (eg using the goods subject to the lien: *Rust v McNaught and Co Ltd* (1918) 144 LT Jo 440, CA).

Furthermore, the holder of a general lien will be held to have abandoned it if he agrees to release the goods merely on payment of sums due in respect of those goods alone (*Morley v Hay* (1828) 3 Man & Ry KB 396).

QUESTIONS

1. Distinguish *Forth v Simpson* (above, p 1107) from *Albemarle Supply Co Ltd v Hind and Co*.

2.   Would the decision in *Pennington v Reliance Motor Works Ltd* have been different if (a) E had obtained delivery from the defendants by stating (untruthfully) that he had instructed the plaintiff to pay the defendants directly (see *Wallace v Woodgate* (1824) 1 C & P 575); or, alternatively, (b) when returning the car to E, the defendants had expressly reserved a right to retake the goods? (see Bell, op cit, p 147).

(h) Registration

As a common law lien is a possessory security it does not require registration by virtue of the Bills of Sale Acts 1878–1891 (even 'a written agreement to give a lien is not a bill of sale, for the legal lien does not as a rule arise until possession of the property is obtained': *Halsbury's Laws of England* (4th edn reissue, 1997), Vol 28, para 702), nor by virtue of Part 25 of the Companies Act 2006 (*Trident International Ltd v Barlow* [1999] 2 BCLC 506, CA, where it was held that the fact the lienee had a contractual power of sale did not turn a contractual general lien into a registrable charge; see also *Waitomo Wools (NZ) Ltd v Nelsons (NZ) Ltd* [1974] 1 NZLR 484, NZ CA).

3 REFORM

The Law Commission published its final report on *Company Security Interests* in 2005 (Law Com Report No 296). The Law Commission recommended that there should be a scheme of electronic 'notice-filing' for charges created by companies (for further details, see p 1089 above). However, the Law Commission recommended that, with two exceptions, a 'pledge' (which the Law Commission defined to include a contractual possessory lien) was to fall outside the new notice-filing scheme (LC Report, para 3.17). The reason for this exclusion is that where there is actual possession by the creditor, the existence of the pledge would be evident to third parties, and hence a 'false wealth' risk—where assets that may appear to be owned by the debtor are in fact subject to securities in favour of other parties—would not apply. Similarly, where the creditor has constructive possession of the goods that are in the hands of a third party who has attorned to the creditor, the existence of the pledge would soon be found out. However, the situation is different where the goods are in the hands of the debtor and the debtor attorns to the creditor. It would be difficult for the third party to find out that the debtor's apparent possession was subject to the creditor's security in the absence of any requirement to register. Thus, the Law Commission recommended that such attornments should be registrable under a notice-filing system (LC Report, para 3.21). For similar reasons, the Law Commission also recommended that where the debtor was given possession of the pledged goods under a trust receipt, the pledge would become registrable unless the goods were returned to the creditor's possession within 15 business days (LC Report, para 3.25). Liens arising by operation of law, eg a repairer's lien, would not require registration (LC Report, para 3.27). Recent reform of company law, through the Companies Act 2006, has not incorporated any of these recommendations (see further, p 1090 above).

CHAPTER 26

NON-POSSESSORY SECURITY

1 MORTGAGE

(a) Mortgage defined

Santley v Wilde
[1899] 2 Ch 474, Court of Appeal

Lindley MR: . . . [A] mortgage is a conveyance of land or an assignment of chattels as a security for the payment of a debt or the discharge of some other obligation for which it is given. This is the idea of a mortgage: and the security is redeemable on the payment or discharge of such debt or obligation, any provision to the contrary notwithstanding.

Downsview Nominees Ltd v First City Corpn Ltd
[1993] AC 295, Privy Council

Lord Templeman: A mortgage, whether legal or equitable, is security for repayment of a debt. The security may be constituted by a conveyance, assignment or demise or by a charge on any interest in real or personal property. An equitable mortgage is a contract which creates a charge on property but does not pass a legal estate to the creditor. Its operation is that of an executory assurance, which, as between the parties, and so far as equitable rights and remedies are concerned, is equivalent to an actual assurance, and is enforceable under the equitable jurisdiction of the court. All this is well settled law and is to be found in more detail in the textbooks on the subject. . . .

NOTES

1. A mortgage involves the transfer of ownership of property from the mortgagor (the debtor or a third party) to the mortgagee (the creditor) as security for a debt or other obligation (although this no longer remains true for a legal mortgage of land which, since 1926, must be made either by demise for a term of years or by charge by way of legal mortgage: Law of Property Act 1925, ss 85, 86).[1] A mortgage may be either legal or equitable. It may be of

---

[1] In unregistered land, legal mortgages are created either by the grant of a leasehold interest or the creation of a legal charge. In registered land, the only legal mortgage is a registered legal charge (Land Registration Act 2002, s 23(1)(a)).

real or personal property.[2] As a mortgage does not require the delivery of possession of the mortgaged property, that property can be tangible or intangible (ie choses in action can be mortgaged).

2.   A legal mortgage of personal property is a transfer of legal title to the mortgagee with an express or implied proviso for retransfer on redemption.[3] As future property cannot generally be transferred at common law, a legal mortgage usually involves the present transfer of property to which the transferor holds the legal title at the date of the transfer.

3.   The mode of creating a legal mortgage of personal property varies according to the subject matter of the mortgage (the following summary is based on RM Goode *Legal Problems of Credit and Security* (3rd edn, 2003), para 1–13).

- A legal mortgage of goods may be oral but if in writing and given by an individual it must be made by deed and in accordance with the form and other requirements of the Bills of Sale Acts 1878 and 1882 (see below, pp 1139ff), and if made by a company it is registrable under s 860 the Companies Act 2006 (see below, pp 1141ff). The legal mortgage of certain types of goods must also be in a prescribed form and registered in a specialist register, eg a mortgage of a registered ship must be entered in the register of ship mortgages, a mortgage of a registered aircraft must be entered in the register of aircraft mortgages.

- A legal mortgage of a debt or other chose in action is effected by assignment in writing under the hand of the assignor with written notice of the assignment being given to the debtor (thereby complying with the Law of Property Act 1925, s 136; see above, p 940), or alternatively by novation, and in the case of documentary intangibles there is the option of negotiation by delivery together with any necessary indorsements.

- A legal mortgage of registrable intellectual property rights is effected by entry in the relevant register (ie the register of patents, the register of trade marks or the register of designs: but there is no registration of copyright).

- A legal mortgage of securities, such as shares and bonds, is effected through entry of a transfer on the issuer's register in the case of registered securities and by delivery of possession with intent to transfer ownership in the case of bearer securities.

4.   The nature of an equitable mortgage was considered in the next case.

Swiss Bank Corpn v Lloyds Bank Ltd
[1982] AC 584, Court of Appeal

The plaintiff bank agreed to lend foreign currency to IFT to enable it to buy shares and loan stock in FIBI, an Israeli bank. Under clause 3(b) of the loan agreement, IFT agreed to observe all the conditions attached to the Bank of England consent which had been obtained for the loan under the Exchange Control Act 1947 (since repealed). The conditions were,

---

[2]   As the mortgage of land is dealt with in the casebooks on land law, we shall concentrate on the mortgage of personal property (defined above, p 55).

[3]   A mortgagor is said to have an 'equity of redemption' entitling him to redeem or recover the property even though he has failed to pay at the appointed time. The equity of redemption may be determined by release, lapse of time, sale and foreclosure (Fisher and Lightwood *Law of Mortgages* (11th edn, 2002), para 1.9).

inter alia, that on acquisition the FIBI securities should be held in a separate account and that repayment of the loan was to be made from the proceeds of sale of those securities. The plaintiff bank claimed to be an equitable chargee of the FIBI securities or the proceeds of sale thereof. Browne-Wilkinson J upheld the claim but was reversed on appeal.

Buckley LJ: We are not concerned here with a charge on an equitable interest in property but with an equitable charge upon property in the legal ownership of the party creating the charge.

An equitable charge may, it is said, take the form either of an equitable mortgage or of an equitable charge not by way of mortgage. An equitable mortgage is created when the legal owner of the property constituting the security enters into some instrument or does some act which, though insufficient to confer a legal estate or title in the subject matter upon the mortgagee, nevertheless demonstrates a binding intention to create a security in favour of the mortgagee, or in other words evidences a contract to do so.... From the way in which the judge dealt with the matter in his judgment it is, I think, clear that he was applying his mind to the question whether the circumstances of the case gave rise to an equitable charge by way of mortgage. The argument in this court has also proceeded upon the same lines, but I must not overlook the possibility of the existence of an equitable charge which is not of the nature of a mortgage.

The essence of any transaction by way of mortgage is that a debtor confers upon his creditor a proprietary interest in property of the debtor, or undertakes in a binding manner to do so, by the realisation or appropriation of which the creditor can procure the discharge of the debtor's liability to him, and that the proprietary interest is redeemable, or the obligation to create it is defeasible, in the event of the debtor discharging his liability. If there has been no legal transfer of a proprietary interest but merely a binding undertaking to confer such an interest, that obligation, if specifically enforceable, will confer a proprietary interest in the subject matter in equity. The obligation will be specifically enforceable if it is an obligation for the breach of which damages would be an inadequate remedy. A contract to mortgage property, real or personal, will, normally at least, be specifically enforceable, for a mere claim to damages or repayment is obviously less valuable than a security in the event of the debtor's insolvency. If it is specifically enforceable, the obligation to confer the proprietary interest will give rise to an equitable charge upon the subject matter by way of mortgage.

It follows that whether a particular transaction gives rise to an equitable charge of this nature must depend upon the intention of the parties ascertained from what they have done in the then existing circumstances. The intention may be expressed or it may be inferred. If the debtor undertakes to segregate a particular fund or asset and to pay the debt out of that fund or asset, the inference may be drawn, in the absence of any contra indication, that the parties' intention is that the creditor should have such a proprietary interest in the segregated fund or asset as will enable him to realise out of it the amount owed to him by the debtor: compare *Re Nanwa Gold Mines Ltd* [1955] 1 WLR 1080 and contrast *Moseley v Cressey's Co* (1865) LR 1 Eq 405 where there was no obligation to segregate the deposits. But notwithstanding that the matter depends upon the intention of the parties, if upon the true construction of the relevant documents in the light of any admissible evidence as to surrounding circumstances the parties have entered into a transaction the legal effect of which is to give rise to an equitable charge in favour of one of them over property of the other, the fact that they may not have realised this consequence will not mean that there is no charge. They must be presumed to intend the consequence of their acts.

In the present case the loan agreement contained no express requirement that IFT should charge the FIBI securities or the fruits of the borrowing by way of mortgage to secure repayment of the loan. Such intention must be found, if at all, by implication.

A binding obligation that a particular fund shall be applied in a particular manner may found no more than an injunction to restrain its application in another way, but if the obligation be to pay out of the fund a debt due by one party to the transaction to the other, the fund belonging to or being due to the debtor, this amounts to an equitable assignment pro tanto of the fund: see *Rodick v Gandell* (1852) 1

De GM & G 763, 777 and *Palmer v Carey* [1926] AC 703, 706–707:

> This is but an instance of a familiar doctrine of equity that a contract for valuable consideration to transfer or charge a subject matter passes a beneficial interest by way of property in that subject matter if the contract is one of which a court of equity will decree specific performance.

With this in mind I address myself to the construction and effect of clause 3(b) of the loan agreement. It is said that by that subclause IFT covenanted with the plaintiff that all the requirements of the Bank of England from time to time would be observed by IFT during the continuance of the agreement. Accordingly, it is said that IFT covenanted that the loan should be repaid out of the sale proceeds of the securities in the 'relative loan portfolio' (see condition (vii)) and out of no other source save in so far as those sale proceeds should fall short of being sufficient. So, it is said, the relevant loan portfolio, which by the terms of the Bank of England permission was required to be kept as a separate fund distinct from any other foreign currency securities owned by IFT, should be the primary source for repayment of the loan. Therefore, it is contended, the parties have manifested an intention that the plaintiff should have such a proprietary interest in the FIBI securities or any other fruits of the borrowing into which they might be converted from time to time as would enable the plaintiff to realise out of that property, so far as it should suffice, any amount required to repay the loan.

Mr Parker has conceded that IFT was only obliged by clause 3(b) of the loan agreement to observe such requirements of the Bank of England as might be in force from time to time. The Bank of England could have waived or rescinded condition (vii) at any time. He accepts that the equitable charge which the plaintiff claims was consequently a precarious one. The fact that an equitable charge may be precarious, however, is not in my view necessarily a sufficient ground for holding that there is no such charge. A mortgage of a terminable lease would be a precarious security, vulnerable to determination of the lease by the landlord, but I can see no reason why such a lease should not be capable of being the subject matter of a mortgage, if a mortgagee of it could be found. In the present case, however, it is not the continued existence of the subject matter which is precarious; it is those very terms of the contract which are alleged to give rise to the equitable charge, that is to say, the Bank of England conditions requiring segregation of the fruits of the borrowing and repayment of the loan thereout, which might have been terminated or waived by the Bank of England at any time during the continuance of the agreement. The Bank of England might at any time have permitted repayment of the loan out of some other fund, and in that event the plaintiff could have had no ground of complaint about the loan being so discharged. A security of this kind, if capable of constituting a security at all, would, it seems to me, be so precarious that one would need very clear indications that the parties intended, or must be taken to have intended, to enter into such an arrangement by way of security, particularly where the relevant agreement contains an express charge on another subject matter. In my judgment, however, clause 3(b) of the agreement was incapable, upon its true construction, of constituting any security or creating any equitable charge. So far as it consisted of a covenant, it required IFT to observe the requirements of the Bank of England during the continuance of the agreement. It was directed to ensuring that the loan should not become tainted with any illegality by reason of any failure to comply with those requirements, such as they might be from time to time. In this respect it is, I think, significant that the covenant is linked with the warranty contained in the same sub-clause, which is obviously directed to the legality of the transaction at the date of the agreement. The covenant is, in my opinion, in substance a negative one, viz not to do anything which might invalidate the bargain between the parties; but, although some argument was addressed to us based upon this negative quality, it is not that which weighs with me. What is to my mind important is that there is here no obligation to repay the loan out of the fruits of the borrowing in any event; the covenant merely requires IFT to repay the loan in a manner approved by the Bank of England. No doubt the plaintiff could have objected to repayment in any manner not so approved and could have obtained an injunction restraining such repayment, if this would have served any useful purpose; but the covenant does not, in my judgment, confer upon the plaintiff any specifically enforceable right to have the loan repaid out of the FIBI securities or out of any other fruits of the borrowing. It consequently did not, in my judgment, give rise to an equitable charge by way of mortgage.

[Brandon and Brightman LJJ concurred.]
[The decision of the Court of Appeal was affirmed by the House of Lords [1982] AC 584, 604.]

NOTES

1. An equitable mortgage of personal property is a transfer of an equitable title to the mortgagee, or a declaration of trust in his favour, with an express or implied proviso for retransfer or termination of the trust on redemption.

2. An equitable mortgage can arise as follows:

(1) by a present mortgage of an equitable interest (eg a second mortgage of goods when the first mortgage is legal—the second mortgage will be equitable as the owner divests himself of his legal title by the first mortgage thereby leaving himself only with an equity of redemption); or

(2) by an agreement to give a legal or equitable mortgage, so long as it is supported by consideration and can be specifically enforced (see *Swiss Bank Corpn v Lloyds Bank Ltd*, above, p 1124; *Thames Guaranty Ltd v Campbell* [1985] QB 210 at 218; affd [1985] QB 210, CA)—the agreement may be express or implied and may even be based on the intention to create a legal mortgage which is ineffectual for want of proper form.

3. An agreement to mortgage after-acquired property can only operate as a contract to assign the property when it is acquired. A debtor's agreement to mortgage his after-acquired property will give the creditor an equitable interest in the property as soon as it is acquired by the debtor, so long as the creditor has actually advanced the money (ie the consideration is executed) and the property is described sufficiently to be identifiable when acquired (see the landmark decision of the House of Lords in *Holroyd v Marshall* (1862) 10 HL Cas 191, above, p 1028; as explained in the equally important case of *Tailby v Official Receiver* (1888) 13 App Cas 523, HL, above, p 1029). The consideration must be executed because equity will not decree specific performance of a contract to borrow and lend money (*Roger v Challis* (1859) 27 Beav 175).

4. An equitable mortgage of personal property, not being of an equitable interest in such property (which must be in writing under the Law of Property Act 1925, s 53(l)(c)), can be oral (contrast this with an equitable mortgage of land, which must be in writing signed by or on behalf of the parties: Law of Property (Miscellaneous Provisions) Act 1989, s 2(1 J; an equitable mortgage can no longer be created solely by deposit of the title deeds: *United Bank of Kuwait plc v Sahib* [1997] Ch 107, CA). However, writing will be necessary if a mortgage (or other security) relates to a regulated agreement under the Consumer Credit Act 1974 (see below, p 1146) and the security is not given by the debtor himself (Consumer Credit Act 1974, s 105(6)).

5. In *Palmer v Carey* [1926] AC 703 at 706–707, Lord Wrenbury, delivering the advice of the Privy Council, held that a contractual agreement that a specific fund be applied in a particular way could found an injunction to restrain its application in another way but that for a security interest to arise there must also be a specifically enforceable obligation on the debtor to pay the debt out of the fund. The bank's claim to a security interest failed in *Swiss Bank Corpn v Lloyds Bank Ltd* because the loan agreement did not require the loan to be repaid out of the proceeds of sale of the borrower's securities. Similarly, in *Flightline Ltd v Edwards* [2003] EWCA Civ 63, [2003] 1 WLR 1200, where a creditor agreed to discharge a freezing order on funds being paid on the debtor's behalf into a bank account held in the joint names of the parties' solicitors, the Court of Appeal held that the creditor had no valid charge over the monies standing to the credit of the account because it was not a term of the agreement that any judgment obtained by the creditor had to be satisfied out of the monies in the account. Most recently, in *Re TXU Europe Group plc* [2003] EWHC 1305, [2004] 1 BCLC 519, a company agreed with its senior executives that they would continue to be entitled to final salary pensions, despite the cap on earnings that could be used for such assessments under the Finance Act 1989. The company set up a fund which would match the extent to which the pensions were not funded by the Inland Revenue approved scheme. It was clear that the fund was intended to be the source from which the pension obligations would be met, but it was held that the senior executives had no specifically enforceable rights to look to the fund to satisfy their pension claims and did not have a charge over the fund.

(b) Enforcement

The mortgagee may sue the mortgagor on his personal covenant to pay the debt.[4] In addition the mortgagee has a number of *in rem* remedies where the mortgagor is in default.

(i) Foreclosure

Foreclosure extinguishes the equity of redemption of the mortgagor, and all persons claiming through him, and vests the mortgaged property absolutely in the mortgagee. This gives the mortgagee a windfall where the value of the mortgaged property exceeds the secured debt. But foreclosure also extinguishes the residue of the secured debt so that if, after foreclosure, the secured property turns out to be worth less than the secured debt the mortgagee cannot pursue the mortgagor for the shortfall. Unlike the remedy of sale under a power of sale (see below), foreclosure generally requires a court order. Foreclosure proceedings are usually prolonged, the court being keen to give the mortgagor every opportunity to redeem, and hence are very rare (*Palk v Mortgage Services Funding plc* [1993] Ch 330 at 336, per Sir Donald Nicholls VC).

(ii) Sale

Stubbs v Slater
[1910] 1 Ch 632, Court of Appeal

P, being indebted to the defendant stockbrokers, deposited with them as security a certificate for 390 shares, and signed a blank transfer of the same. After sending P repeated notices that they would have to sell the shares if the debt was not paid, the defendants sold the shares. P sued the defendants for wrongful conversion of the shares, alleging *inter alia* that the sale was bad because the notices demanded more than was owed. The Court of Appeal held that in the circumstances the defendants had reasonably exercised their implied power of sale as mortgagees.

Cozens-Hardy MR referred to his own judgment in *Harrold v Plenty* and continued: . . . This then was a transaction of mortgage and not a transaction of pledge. It was a transaction of mortgage, in which there was no express power of sale given, but which by law involves and implies a right in the

---

[4] Sometimes a person may provide real security for another's debts without undertaking any personal liability himself (as in *Re Conley* [1938] 2 All ER 127).

mortgagee to sell after giving reasonable notice. I need scarcely pause to say that the notice here was reasonable, if ever there was reasonable notice. Then the matter came before the Court of Appeal in 1902 in *Deverges v Sandeman, Clark & Co* ([1902] 1 Ch 579). There it was laid down that in the case of a mortgage by deposit of shares there is an implied power to sell, if no time is fixed, upon giving reasonable notice, and the only point decided in that case was whether or not the notice was reasonable. Nothing else was there decided except that the general principle applicable to transactions of this kind was for the first time laid down by the Court of Appeal. In the course of my judgment, which I refer to only because I see no reason to change the view which I there expressed, I say this: 'Although a mistake as to the amount due may destroy the effect of the notice, as between pledgor and pledgee —*Pigot v Cubley* ((1864) 15 CBNS 701) -I think that is not the law as between mortgagor and mortgagee. In order to restrain a mortgagee from selling in the absence of fraud, it is not sufficient to contest the amount due on the mortgage. The mortgagor must pay into Court, or tender to the mortgagee, the amount claimed to be due.' I there referred to *Pigot v Cubley,* saying that a mistake as to the amount due might destroy the effect of the notice as between pledgor and pledgee. I have looked at that case again and as at present advised I can find nothing in the judgment in the Court which bears out the last sentence in the head-note, which says that 'a notice that he'—ie, the pledgee—'will sell unless an excessive sum be paid immediately, is not such a notice as will justify the sale.' But, however that may be, it seems to me that in a mortgage as distinguished from a pledge that head-note affords no ground for the contention that a mortgagee has not a power of sale after giving reasonable notice unless the notice specifies with precise accuracy the amount due on the mortgage. I see no ground for making any exception from the general law in this particular class of mortgage. There was here alleged to be due on the mortgage the sum of £69 odd. That being so, and there having been abundant applications for payment, I am clearly of opinion that the mortgagee had a perfect right to sell these shares.

[Buckley J delivered a concurring judgment.
Joyce J concurred.]

NOTES

1. By the Law of Property Act 1925, s 101(1), where the mortgage is made by deed, a mortgagee is given a statutory power to sell the mortgaged property when the mortgage money has become due. This power applies to any mortgage of any property made by deed, save those to which the Bills of Sale Acts apply (see AP Bell *Modern Law of Personal Property in England and Ireland* (1989), p 187; and below, p 1139). However, in *Re Morritt, exp Official Receiver* (1886) 18 QBD 222 at 241–242, Lopes LJ held (Lord Esher MR concurring) that a power of sale was to be implied into a mortgage within the Bills of Sale Act (1878) Amendment Act 1882, by virtue of s 7 of that Act.

2. *Stubbs v Slater* is a case where a mortgagee of intangible property was held to have a common law power of sale. Whether a mortgagee of tangible property has such a common law power of sale is not clear. In *Re Morritt, ex p Official Receiver* (1886) 18 QBD 222 at 233, Cotton LJ held that a mortgagee of personal chattels, which are in his possession, had a common law power of sale (Lindley and Bowen LJJ concurred). But in the same case Fry LJ, dissenting, held that a power of sale was not to be implied by law into a mortgage of chattels (at 235). See also *Deverges v Sandeman, Clark & Co* [1902] 1 Ch 579 at 589, where Vaughan Williams LJ questioned whether a mortgagee of personal chattels had a common law power of sale. For contrasting treatment of this issue compare Crossley Vaines *Personal Property* (5th edn, 1973), p 447, with Bell, op cit, p 187.

3. An express power of sale will usually be inserted into a well-drafted mortgage of real or personal property. Even if the mortgagee has no express or implied power of sale, he may apply to the court for an order for sale (Law of Property Act 1925, s 91).

4.   Where the mortgagee sells secured property he owes the mortgagor (and others interested) equitable duties to act in good faith, not to use his rights and powers for improper or ulterior purposes (*Worwood v Leisure Merchandising Services Ltd* [2002] 1 BCLC 249; *Meretz Investments NV v ACP Ltd* [2006] EWHC 74 (Ch), [2006] 3 All ER 1029 at [314]: mixed motives are fine so long as one of which is a genuine purpose of recovering, in whole or in part, the amount secured by the mortgage) and to take reasonable care to obtain a proper price (*Downsview Nominees Ltd v First City Corpn Ltd* [1993] AC 295; *Yorkshire Bank plc v Hall* [1999] 1 All ER 879, 893, CA). However, the mortgagee owes no general duty of care in dealing with the secured property: he is free to exercise his powers as he chooses, ie he has a free choice as to the timing of the sale (*Downsview Nominees Ltd v First City Corpn Ltd*, above; *Silven Properties Ltd v Royal Bank of Scotland plc* [2003] EWCA Civ 1409, [2004] 1 WLR 997 at [14]; *Den Norske Bank ASA v Acemex Management Company Ltd* [2003] EWCA Civ 1559, [2004] 1 Lloyd's Rep 1 at [23]). The mortgagee is under no duty to preserve his security unless and until he takes possession of it (*AIB Finance Ltd v Debtors* [1998] 2 All ER 929, CA, although Nourse LJ said, at 937, that it may be possible to conceive of circumstances in which a mortgagee could come under a duty to co-operate with the mortgagor in procuring a sale of a mortgaged property and business as a going concern at a proper price before taking possession). Any surplus following sale will be held for the mortgagor, but the mortgagor remains liable for any shortfall on his express covenant for payment contained in the mortgage deed (*Bristol & West plc v Bartlett* [2002] EWCA Civ 1181, [2002] 2 All ER (Comm) 1105; held that save for exceptional cases, which could not be envisaged at present, claims for a mortgage debt are governed by s 20 of the Limitation Act 1980, which means that the mortgagee has 12 years from accrual of the cause of action to sue for the principal of the debt but only six years to sue for interest).

(iii) Appointment of a receiver

When a mortgage is made by deed a court has power to appoint a receiver over the mortgaged property (Law of Property Act 1925, ss 101,109). However, in most cases the mortgage contains an express power of appointment. A receiver, like the holder of the security who has appointed him, owes a duty to act in good faith and, if he decides to sell the charged property, a limited duty to take reasonable care to obtain a proper price. In the *Downsview Nominees* case (above) the Privy Council dismissed an argument that a receiver owes a more general duty of care to the chargor or to a guarantor of his debt, but this view has been since qualified by the ruling of the Court of Appeal in *Medforth v Blake,* discussed below, p 1224.

(iv) Possession

A mortgagor who defaults is liable to surrender his right to remain in possession of the mortgaged property. Where a mortgage is a security bill of sale for the purposes of the Bills of Sale Act (1878) Amendment Act 1882, there is an implied right of seizure, which is required by the Act to be exercised within certain limits (see ss 7 and 13: discussed below). Where the Consumer Credit Act 1974 applies the seizure will be subject to the 'default notice' provisions of that Act (ss 87–89: discussed below), and the right of seizure under the 1882 Act will be restricted accordingly (s 7A of the 1882 Act).

2 EQUITABLE CHARGE

(a) Equitable charge defined

Swiss Bank Corpn v Lloyds Bank Ltd
[1982] AC 584, Court of Appeal

Buckley LJ: An equitable charge which is not an equitable mortgage is said to be created when property is expressly or constructively made liable, or specially appropriated, to the discharge of a debt or some other obligation, and confers on the chargee a right of realisation by judicial process, that is to say, by the appointment of a receiver or an order for sale....

Re Cosslett (Contractors) Ltd
[1998] Ch 495, Court of Appeal

Millett LJ: It is of the essence of a charge that a particular asset or class of assets is appropriated to the satisfaction of a debt or other obligation of the chargor or a third party, so that the chargee is entitled to look to the asset and its proceeds for the discharge of the liability.

Re Bank of Credit and Commerce International SA (No 8)
[1998] AC 214, House of Lords

Lord Hoffmann: A charge is a security interest created without any transfer of title or possession to the beneficiary. An equitable charge can be created by an informal transaction for value (legal charges may require a deed or registration or both) and over any kind of property (equitable as well as legal) but is subject to the doctrine of purchaser for value without notice applicable to all equitable interests.

NOTES

1. In *Re Bond Worth Ltd* [1980] Ch 228 at 250, Slade J stated that: 'The technical difference between a "mortgage" or "charge", though in practice the phrases are often used interchangeably, is that a mortgage involves a conveyance of property subject to a right of redemption, whereas a charge conveys nothing and merely gives the chargee certain rights over the property as security for the loan.' As a charge is a mere encumbrance and does not convey ownership of property, it can only arise in equity (and so is called an 'equitable charge') or by statute (as is the case with a charge by way of legal mortgage over land: Law of Property Act 1925, ss 85–87). A charge over personal property must be equitable, it cannot be legal.

2. Since a charge, unlike a mortgage, does not involve a conveyance of a proprietary interest, a chargee cannot foreclose or take possession. The remedy of the chargee is to apply to the court for an order for sale or for the appointment of a receiver. In practice, however, there is little difference between a mortgage and a charge as it is usual for the instrument creating the charge to provide expressly that the chargee has the rights of a mortgagee. Note, however, that if the charge is a floating charge secured over the whole or substantially the whole of the company's property, then the chargee may no longer appoint an administrative receiver (Insolvency Act 1986, s 72A; but subject to certain limited exceptions in IA 86,

ss 72B–G: major capital market and financial market transactions, utility transactions, and public-private finance transactions).

3. In general, a charge must be created by agreement which must be supported by consideration (see above, p 1084). An agreement for value for an equitable charge will be treated as an equitable charge (*Tailby v Official Receiver* (1888) 13 App Cas 523 at 549, per Lord Macnaghten). As a charge creates an equitable interest, and does not transfer such an interest, it falls outside s 53(1)(c) of the Law of Property Act 1925 and so may be oral. If the charge extends to future property it must be given for value (a deed is not enough) and the property must be sufficiently described to be identifiable when acquired (see the important decisions of the House of Lords in *Holroyd v Marshall,* above, p 1028, and *Tailby v Official Receiver,* above, p 1029). It is also possible to create an equitable charge by declaration of trust (see *Re Bond Worth Ltd* [1980] Ch 228 at 250; cf *Carreras Rothman Ltd v Freeman Mathews Treasure Ltd* [1985] Ch 207 at 227).

(b)　Fixed and floating charges

(i)　*The nature of fixed and floating charges*

'A specific charge, I think, is one that without more fastens on ascertained and definite property or property capable of being ascertained and defined; a floating charge, on the other hand, is ambulatory and shifting in its nature, hovering over and so to speak floating with the property which it is intended to affect until some event occurs or some act is done which causes it to settle and fasten on the subject of the charge within its reach and grasp...' (*Illingworth v Holdsworth* [1904] AC 355, 358, *per* Lord Macnaghton)

A fixed (or 'specific') charge is a charge created over identified property which prevents the debtor dealing with the property without first paying off the indebtedness secured by the charge or obtaining the chargee's consent. If the debtor does not do this before transferring the property, the transferee will take the property subject to the charge, unless he is a bona fide purchaser for value without notice. Future property may be made the subject of an agreement to charge, provided the agreement is for value and the future property is sufficiently described as to be identifiable when acquired by the chargor. Once the property is acquired by the chargor it automatically becomes subject to the charge (see the landmark House of Lords' decision *of Holroyd v Marshall* (1862) 10 HL Cas 191, which appears above, p 1028). Until then the security interest is inchoate, but on acquisition of property by the chargor it bites, taking effect retrospectively from the date of the security agreement (see *Tailby v Official Receiver* (1888) 13 App Cas 523, another important House of Lords' decision which appears above, p 1029).[5]

By contrast, a floating charge 'hovers' over a changing fund of assets, including assets acquired by the debtor after the creation of the charge. Under a floating charge the debtor is at liberty to deal with the charged assets in the ordinary course of the debtor's business, and does so free from the charge. Only upon the happening of certain events, such as the appointment of a receiver or insolvency, is the floating charge said to 'crystallise' and become fixed on the assets then comprising the fund or subsequently acquired by the debtor. At that point the debtor has no further right to deal with the charged assets.

---

[5] However, the agreement may evince a contrary intention, as in the case of a floating charge. Crystallisation of a floating charge is not retrospective: only *qua* floating security does the charge relate back to the date of the security agreement (see RM Goode, *Commercial Law* (3rd edn, 2004), p 634 fn).

It is not possible in English law for individual borrowers to give a floating charge over their assets, because to do so would infringe the Bills of Sale Acts of 1878 and 1882 (and in particular it would be impossible to meet the requirement that the goods affected be specifically described in a schedule to the instrument). But the Bills of Sale Acts do not apply to companies, and so it is possible for a company to grant a floating charge over some or all of its assets, both present and future. This allows a company to give security over assets which are continually turned over or consumed and replaced in the ordinary course of business, eg over fluctuating assets such as stock-in-trade, raw materials and book debts. The new form of businesss organisation called a Limited Liability Partnership (LLP), being a body corporate, can also borrow on the security of a floating charge (see the Limited Liability Partnerships Act 2000).

The essential characteristics (if not a complete definition) of the floating charge, and the distinction between a floating charge and a fixed charge, appear from the cases which follow.

Agnew v Commissioner of Inland Revenue (Re Brumark Investments Ltd)

[2001] UKPC 28, [2001] 2 AC 710, Privy Council

(The facts and a longer extract appear on p 1051.)

Lord Millett: The most celebrated, and certainly the most often cited, description of a floating charge is that given by Romer LJ in *Re Yorkshire Woolcombers Association Ltd* [1903] 2 Ch 284, 295:

> I certainly do not intend to attempt to give an exact definition of the term 'floating charge' nor am I prepared to say that there will not be a floating charge within the meaning of the Act , which does not contain all of the three characteristics that I am about to mention, but I certainly think that if a charge has the three characteristics that I am about to mention, it is a floating charge. (1) If it is a charge on a class of assets of a company present and future; (2) if that class is one which, in the ordinary course of business of the company, would be changing from time to time; and (3) if you find that by the charge it is contemplated that, until some future step is taken by or on behalf of those interested in the charge, the company may carry on its business in the ordinary way as far as concerns the particular class of assets I am dealing with.

This was offered as a description and not a definition. The first two characteristics are typical of a floating charge but they are not distinctive of it, since they are not necessarily inconsistent with a fixed charge. It is the third characteristic which is the hallmark of a floating charge and serves to distinguish it from a fixed charge. Since the existence of a fixed charge would make it impossible for the company to carry on business in the ordinary way without the consent of the charge holder, it follows that its ability to [do] so without such consent is inconsistent with the fixed nature of the security.

National Westminster Bank plc v Spectrum Plus Ltd (Re Spectrum Plus Ltd)

[2005] UKHL 41, [2005] 2 AC 680, House of Lords

(The facts and a longer extract appear on p 1053.)

Lord Scott: I respectfully agree. Indeed if a security has Romer LJ's third characteristic I am inclined to think that it qualifies as a floating charge, and cannot be a fixed charge, whatever may be its other characteristics. [...] In my opinion, the essential characteristic of a floating charge, the characteristic that distinguishes it from a fixed charge, it that the asset subject to the charge is not finally appropriated as a security for the payment of the debt until the occurrence of some future event. In the meantime the chargor is left free to use the charged asset and to remove it from the security.

Evans v Rival Quarries Ltd

[1910] 2 KB 979, Court of Appeal

(The facts are irrelevant.)

Buckley LJ: ... A floating charge is not a future security; it is a present security which presently affects all the assets of the company expressed to be included in it. On the other hand, it is not a specific security; the holder cannot affirm that the assets are specifically mortgaged to him. The assets are mortgaged in such a way that the mortgagor can deal with them without the concurrence of the mortgagee. A floating security is not a specific mortgage of the assets, plus a licence to the mortgagor to dispose of them in the course of his business, but is a floating mortgage applying to every item comprised in the security, but not specifically affecting any of item until some event occurs or some act on the part of the mortgagee is done which causes it to crystallize into a fixed security.

NOTES

1.   When determining whether a security is a fixed or floating charge the courts will look to the substance rather than the form of the transaction: the parties' description of the charge as one or the other is not conclusive (*Re Armagh Shoes Ltd* [1984] BCLC 405).

2.   It is the third feature identified by Romer LJ in *Re Yorkshire Woolcombers' Association Ltd* (which appears in *Agnew* extract above)—the ability to deal in the ordinary course of business free from control by the chargee—which has come to be recognised as the most essential characteristic of a floating charge. But freedom is a relative rather than an absolute concept, and some degree of restriction is not incompatible with a charge being a floating charge (see *Re Brightlife Ltd* [1987] Ch 200 at 209, per Hoffmann J). In *Re GE Tunbridge Ltd* [1995] 1 BCLC 34, the charge instrument prohibited the company from disposing of certain chattels without the chargee's consent, but it contained no other restrictions—eg no requirement that if the goods were sold, the proceeds should be paid into a designated account—and so it was held to create a floating charge. By contrast, in *Re Cimex Tissues Ltd* [1994] BCC 626, a charge over plant and machinery was held to be a fixed charge even though it was contemplated that some of these items might be replaced from time to time as they wore out. Note, however, that in order for a charge over book debts to be characterised as fixed, both the uncollected book debts and their proceeds after collection must be under the control of the chargee (*Agnew v Commissioner of Inland Revenue* [2001] UKPC 28, [2001] 2 AC 710, see p 1051 above; *Re Spectrum Plus Ltd* [2005] UKHL 41, [2005] 2 AC 680, see p 1053 above). This requires not just that the chargee has a right to take control of the proceeds, but an actual ongoing control over the collected proceeds (*Agnew v CIR* at [48]; *Spectrum* at [55]–[58], [116]–[119], [140]).

3.   The ability of the chargor company to deal with the charged assets in the ordinary course of its business means that it can create security interests that have priority to the floating charge. The priority rules are such that (a) a subsequent fixed legal or equitable charge takes priority over an earlier floating charge (*Wheatley v Silkstone and Haigh Moor Coal Co* (1885) 29 Ch D 715); (b) a company which has given a floating charge over its assets cannot create a second floating charge over the *same* assets to rank in priority to the original floating charge (*Re Benjamin Cope & Sons Ltd* [1914] 1 Ch 800); and (c) a company which has

given a floating charge over its assets may create a second floating charge over *part* of those assets ranking in priority to the original floating charge, provided the power to create such a charge is reserved in the earlier charge (*Re Automatic Bottle Makers Ltd* [1926] Ch 412, CA). In an attempt to avoid subsequent charges taking priority the floating charge will usually contain a provision that restricts the right of the company to create charges that have priority to or rank equally with the floating charge (called a negative pledge clause). The clause will only be effective to retain priority where the subsequent chargee has actual notice of it, and not merely notice of the charge (*English & Scottish Mercantile Investment Co Ltd v Brunton* [1892] 2 QB 700, CA). Notice of the clause must be actual and not merely constructive (*Siebe Gorman & Co Ltd v Barclays Bank Ltd* [1979] 2 Lloyd's Rep 142, overruled by *Re Spectrum Plus Ltd* [2005] 2 AC 680, but not on this point: see also RM Goode *Legal Problems of Credit and Security* (3rd edn, 2003), para 2–27 for rejection of JH Farrar's theory (1974) 38 Conv NS 315, 319, that inferred knowledge of the clause is enough). Notice subjects the subsequent chargee to a personal equity in favour of the floating chargee and this gives the latter priority even though the subsequent security interest was created before crystallisation of the floating charge. It is submitted that the decision of Morritt J in *Griffiths v Yorkshire Bank Ltd* [1994] 1 WLR 1427, that a negative pledge clause only operates as a matter of contract and not of property, so that a second floating charge has priority if crystallising first even if taken with notice of a negative pledge clause in the first floating charge, must be wrong (Neuberger J refused to follow it in *Re H & K Medway Ltd* [1997] 1 WLR 1422). It is certainly inconsistent with the underlying assumption in *English & Scottish Mercantile Investment Co Ltd v Brunton* (see RM Goode *Commercial Law* (3rd edn, 2004), p 687, fn 74).

QUESTION

To secure further borrowing facilities, X Ltd creates a floating charge over its present and future assets in favour of A Bank. The charge contains a negative pledge clause. Later, wishing to purchase a new factory, X Ltd approaches B Bank for a loan. B Bank agrees to make the loan, subject to it taking a mortgage (ie legal charge) over the factory to rank in priority to any other security. X Ltd agrees to this and the loan is made, factory purchased and mortgage executed all within a couple of days. At all material times B Bank was aware of A Bank's floating charge and had actual knowledge of the negative pledge clause. Shortly afterwards X Ltd went into liquidation and the floating charge 'crystallised'. Advise the liquidator as to whether A Bank's charge or B Bank's mortgage has priority. See *Abbey National Building Society v Cann* [1991] 1 AC 56, HL; noted by R Gregory (1990) 106 LQR 550; J de Lacy [1991] LMCLQ 531; G Goldberg (1992) 108 LQR 380.

(ii) Fixed and floating charges: why the distinction matters

(1) Property subject to a fixed charge cannot be dealt with without the charge-holder's consent; in contrast, the chargor under a floating charge may deal with the charged assets in the ordinary course of business without special authorisation.

(2) A floating charge-holder has a relatively low ranking in the priority order of creditors, and in particular ranks below preferential creditors (now primarily employees since the Enterprise Act 2002 abolished Crown preference) in a receivership or winding up of the chargor company (Insolvency Act 1986, ss 40, 175(2)(b), Sch B1, para 65(2) and Sch 6, paras 8–12); but the holder of a fixed charge may have recourse to his security without regard to any other claims.

(3) A floating charge created in the run-up to the chargor company's liquidation or administration may be subject to avoidance under s 245 of the Insolvency Act 1986; a fixed charge only if it involves a preference (considered below, p 1233).

(4) The chargee's interest in property that is subject to a fixed charge is immune from set-offs, execution, distress and garnishment; but if the charge is a floating charge, it may be vulnerable to such claims because of the chargor's freedom to trade prior to crystallisation (see, eg *Biggerstaff v Rowan's Wharf Ltd* [1896] 2 Ch 93, CA, where it was held that prior to crystallisation the company's unsecured creditors could set off debts due by the company against sums which they owed it).

(5) All floating charges are required to be registered; some fixed charges (eg charges over shares, negotiable instruments) are not (see Companies Act 2006, s 860 and below, pp 1141–1145).

(6) A floating charge is subordinated to the costs and expenses of administration and liquidation (Insolvency Act 1986, Sch B1, paras 70 and 99, and IA 1986, s 176ZA, inserted by the Companies Act 2006, s 1282, reversing *Re Leyland Daf Ltd v Buchler v Talbot* [2004] UKHL 9, [2004] 2 AC 298, which denied priority to liquidation expenses).

(7) For charges created after 15 September 2003, the holder of a qualifying floating charge in respect of a company's property may no longer appoint an administrative receiver of the company (Insolvency Act 1976, s 72A, inserted by s 250 of the Enterprise Act 2002). There are a limited number of exceptions: major capital market and financial market transactions, utility transactions and public-private finance transactions (IA 1986, ss 72B–G). The holder of a fixed charge has never been able to appoint an administrative receiver. The appointment of an administrative receiver prevents the company being put into administration (which brings with it an almost total moratorium on the enforcement of secured and unsecured claims against the company).

(8) On insolvency, a prescribed percentage of floating charge (but not fixed charge) asset realisations must be set aside to pay the company's unsecured creditors (see Insolvency Act s 176A, and SI 2003/2097, art 3 and also below, p 1240).

(9) A company administrator needs court approval to dispose of property subject to a fixed charge, but property subject to a floating charge may be freely disposed of, subject to the chargee's priority being transferred to the proceeds acquired from the disposition of the charged property (Insolvency Act 1986, Sch B1, paras 70–71).

NOTES

1.   Section 251 of the Insolvency Act 1986 defines a 'floating charge' as 'a charge which, as created, was a floating charge'. This definition closes a loophole that existed prior to 1986 (exploited in *Re Brightlife Ltd* [1987] Ch 200). The loophole enabled the holder of a floating charge to evade the statutory rules which cut down the effectiveness of a floating charge by showing that the floating charge had crystallised and become a fixed charge before commencement of the liquidation or other relevant statutory date.

2.   There are fewer distinctions to be made between a floating charge and a fixed charge when the floating charge is created or otherwise arises under a financial collateral arrangement ('FCA'). The Financial Collateral Arrangements (No 2) Regulations 2003 (SI 2003/3226), implementing EC Directive 2002/47, are designed to limit credit risk in financial transactions where dispositions of cash (held in a bank account or similar) and securities (eg shares and bonds) are used as collateral under security and title transfer structures. To qualify as

a security FCA the financial collateral must be 'in the possession or under the control of the collateral-taker' (reg 3), and so not all floating charges will fall within the ambit of the regulations (it is probably necessary for the charge to have crystallised before it comes under the possession or control of the collateral-taker). The regulations are particularly relevant to banks, securities firms and other takers of financial collateral in the banking, derivatives, foreign exchange, securities and commodities trading and repo, prime brokerage and related financial markets. This is a specialist area and, for detailed analysis, students are directed to chapter 10 of H Beale, M Bridge, L Gullifer and E Lomnicka, *The Law of Personal Property Security* (2007). For present purposes, it is enough to note that (a) the regulations provide that the registration requirement contained in s 860 of the Companies Act 2006 does not apply (if it would otherwise do so) to a security FCA, or any charge created or otherwise arising under it (reg 4), and (b) the regulations disapply certain provisions of insolvency law to the enforcement of FCAs, including the moratorium on administration, the avoidance of a floating charge under s 245 of the Insolvency Act 1986, the requirement to pay preferential creditors out of floating charge assets and the requirement to pay a share of floating charge assets to the fund for unsecured creditors (Part 3 of the Regulations).

(iv) Crystallisation of a floating charge[6]

A floating charge will crystallise, and become a fixed charge attaching to the assets of the company at that time, (1) when a receiver is appointed; (2) when the company goes into liquidation (since the licence to deal with the assets in the ordinary course of business will then necessarily terminate); (3) when the company ceases to carry on business (*Re Woodroffes (Musical Instruments) Ltd* [1986] Ch 366) or sells its business (*Re Real Meat Co Ltd* [1996] BCC 254); (4) in the case where the debenture empowers the charge-holder to convert the floating charge into a fixed charge by giving the company 'notice of conversion', and such a notice is given (*Re Woodroffes (Musical Instruments) Ltd,* above); and (5) where an event occurs which under the terms of the debenture causes 'automatic' crystallisation.[7] The last ground depends upon there being a provision in the document creating the charge which states that the charge will crystallise on the happening of some particular event—eg if a creditor of the company levies execution against its property, or if the company should give security over assets covered by the charge to a third party without the charge-holder's consent. There has been much controversy over automatic crystallisation clauses, both as to their legality and as to whether, as a matter of policy, their use should be prohibited or subjected to restrictions by law (see, generally, H Beale, M Bridge, L Gullifer and E Lomnicka, *The Law of Personal Property Security* (2007), para 4.58). Nevertheless, there is clear authority both in England and overseas upholding the effectiveness of an automatic crystallisation clause (for England, see *Re Brightlife Ltd* [1987] Ch 200, 214–215, per Hoffmann J; for Australia, see *Fire Nymph Products Ltd v The Heating Centre Property Ltd* (1992) 7 ACSR 365; for New Zealand, see *Re Manurewa Transport Ltd* [1971] NZLR 909, *DFC Financial Services Ltd v Coffey* [1991] 2 NZLR 513, *Covacich v Riordan* [1994] 2 NZLR 502).

---

[6] Part of this text is taken from LS Sealy and S Worthington *Cases and Materials in Company Law* (8th edn, 2007), pp 476–477.

[7] A majority of the court in *Fire Nymph Products Ltd v Heating Centre Pty Ltd* (1992) 7 ACSR 365 (NSWCA) held that a floating charge also crystallises when the charged assets are dealt with otherwise than in the ordinary course of business. This might well be the case where the assets concerned comprised all or a substantial part of the company's property, or the whole of the assets affected by the charge, but it is doubtful that the dictum would apply to the disposal of individual items.

NOTES

1.   Does the chargee have a proprietary interest in the charged assets before crystallisation of a floating charge? There are at least three alternative theories. First, the chargee may have no proprietary interest at all prior to crystallisation; the floating charge is simply an agreement to grant a charge at some time in the future (ie on crystallisation). This is known as the 'mortgage of future assets theory' and is espoused by Dr Gough (see WJ Gough, *Company Charges* (2nd edn, 1996, Ch 13). The second theory is that the chargee holds some proprietary rights before crystallisation, but these are rights in a 'fund' and not in specific assets (see R Goode, *Commercial Law* (3rd edn, 2004), pp 677–680; *Re Spectrum Plus Ltd* [2005] UKHL 41, [2005] 2 AC 680 at [139], per Lord Walker). The third theory is that the chargee's interest is the same whether it is a fixed charge or an uncrystallised floating charge, although in the case of a floating charge there is a licence to deal with the assets which terminates on crystallisation (see S Worthington, *Proprietary Interests in Commercial Transactions* (1996), pp 82-100). It has been suggested that 'the last [theory] is the simplest, since the courts have come to view that the very essence of the difference between fixed and floating charges is the chargor's ability lawfully to deal with charged assets, not some difference in the interest held by the chargee' (A Burrows (ed), *English Private Law* (2nd edn, 2007), para 5.95).

2.   Crystallisation converts a floating charge into a fixed charge which attaches to all assets subject to the charge (including, if the charge instrument so provides, future assets). From that point in time the company loses its freedom to deal with the assets subject to the charge in the ordinary course of its business. The general rule is that post-crystallisation the floating charge has priority over subsequent interests. But a subsequent purchaser or chargee without notice of crystallisation might still be able to obtain priority ahead of the floating chargeholder by relying on the ostensible authority of the company to deal with its property in the ordinary course of business (see RM Goode *Legal Problems of Credit and Security* (3rd edn, 2003), para 5–50). There are no reported cases on the point.

3.   In *Re Brightlife Ltd* [1987] Ch 200, Hoffmann J regarded crystallisation as being a matter of agreement between the parties. On this reasoning there seems no reason why the parties should not later agree to 'decrystallise' a crystallised charge and enable the chargor to deal with its assets again. Such agreement would only be possible where the chargee remained in control of the chargor company's business, which would not be the case where the company was in receivership or liquidation. The possibility of decrystallisation is recognised by statute in Scotland (Insolvency Act 1986, s 62(6)(b)), and would seem to be an automatic consequence of the vacation of office by an administrative receiver in favour of an administrator (Insolvency Act 1986, s 11(1)(b)). Some commentators argue that a new floating charge is created on decrystallisation (see, eg R Grantham [1997] CfiLR 53), but it is more likely that decrystallisation simply removes the restriction on the chargor's dealing power and that the *same* charge refloats (see, eg RM Goode (1994) 110 LQR 592, 604). The issue is important as a new floating charge would require registration.

3 EQUITABLE LIEN

Unlike a common law lien, an equitable lien is a non-possessory security. It is similar to an equitable charge in that it attaches to property belonging to another until certain specific claims have been satisfied. It gives the holder of the equitable lien the same remedies as a chargee, namely to apply to the court for an order for sale or for the appointment of a receiver. However, unlike a charge, which is created by agreement of the parties, an equitable lien arises by operation of law[8] and, as a result, is not required to be registered under the Bills of Sale Acts 1878 and 1882 or under Part 25 of the Companies Act 2006. The most common examples of an equitable lien are the lien of the unpaid vendor of land to secure the purchase price (*Mackreth v Symmons* (1808) 15 Ves 329, 33 ER 778) and the lien of the purchaser to secure repayment of his deposit if the transaction is not completed (*Rose v Watson* (1864) 10 HL Cas 672). There is some uncertainty as to the scope of the equitable lien.[9] It may be exercised in relation to the sale and purchase of intangible personal property (*Re Stucley* [1906] 1 Ch 67), but not in relation to the sale and purchase of goods (*Re Wait* [1927] 1 Ch 606 at 636 and 639, per Atkin LJ; *Transport & General Credit Co Ltd v Morgan* [1939] Ch 531 at 546, per Simonds J).

4 STATUTORY CONTROL

(a) Protection of third parties

The statutory requirement that non-possessory security interests must be registered provides a prospective creditor (ie a third party) with the opportunity to establish whether the debtor has already encumbered the property in his possession. Without registration the non-possessory security interest would be hidden and the prospective creditor could be misled as to the creditworthiness of the debtor (Diamond Report (1989), para 11.1.3; cf F Oditah [1992] JBL 541, pp 542–543). Furthermore, registration may also benefit a creditor by enabling him to publicise his own non-possessory security interest and so reduce the chances of the encumbered asset being disposed of by the debtor to a bona fide third party purchaser without notice of it, and who might, therefore, take priority over it (RM Goode (1984) 100 LQR 234, pp 238–239).

Non-possessory security interests may be registrable under the Bills of Sale Acts 1878 and 1882 (if given by individuals), or under Part 25 of the Companies Act 2006 (if given by companies). We shall concentrate on registration under these statutes, although it should be noted that registration may also be required for certain types of property (eg ships and aircraft) in other specialised registers.

(i) Bills of Sale Acts

The Bills of Sale Act 1878 and the Bills of Sale Act (1878) Amendment Act 1882 (as amended) require, *inter alia*, the registration of bills of sale. It should be noted at once that any security issued by a company is excluded from the operation of these Acts (s 17 of the 1882 Act; and *Richards v Kidderminster Overseers* [1896] 2 Ch 212).

---

[8] A maritime lien is also a non-possessory security interest arising by operation of law. It is a right of action in rem against a ship and her cargo for the cost of salvage or for damage caused by the ship. For details, see H Beale, M Bridge, L Gullifer and E Lomnicka, *The Law of Personal Property Security* (2007), paras 4.129–4.132.

[9] See generally, H Beale, M Bridge, L Gullifer and E Lomnicka, *The Law of Personal Property Security* (2007), paras 4.105–4.128; J Phillips 'Equitable Liens—A Search for a Unifying Principle' in N Palmer and E McKendrick (eds) *Interests in Goods* (2nd edn, 1998), Ch 39; S Worthington *Proprietary Interests in Commercial Transactions* (1996), Ch 9; S Worthington 'Equitable Liens in Commercial Transactions' [1994] CLJ 263; I Hardingham 'Equitable Liens for the Recovery of Purchase Money' (1985) 15 MULR 65.

According to Lord Esher MR in *Mills v Charlesworth* (1890) 25 QBD 421 at 424: 'A bill of sale, in its ordinary meaning, is the document which is given where the legal property in the goods passes to the person who lends money on them, but the possession does not pass'. This common law description of a bill of sale has been considerably extended by the Bills of Sale Acts 1878 and 1882. For the purposes of the 1878 and 1882 Acts, the term 'bill of sale' is defined to include a much broader class of documents relating to 'personal chattels' than is the case at common law (see s 4 of the 1878 Act, which lists the various documents; also s 3 of the 1882 Act). Those documents falling within the statutory definition divide into three broad categories: (1) instruments transferring legal or beneficial ownership of personal chattels; (2) instruments conferring a right to take possession of personal chattels as security for any debt; and (3) agreements by which a right in equity to any personal chattels, or to any charge or security thereon, is to be conferred. In general, all written mortgages and charges relating to personal chattels fall within the statutory definition of a bill of sale and are caught by the Bills of Sale Acts (but not equitable liens, which arise by operation of law and not by agreement).

As a bill of sale is defined in terms of documents, oral transactions fall outside the definition and are not caught by the Bills of Sale Acts. The same applies to transactions whereby the transferee's rights are completed by delivery without reference to any document, eg a pledge or possessory lien (*Charlesworth v Mills* [1892] AC 231 at 235, HL). Furthermore, s 4 of the 1878 Act excludes certain documents from the definition of 'bill of sale'. In particular, 'transfers of goods in the ordinary course of business of any trade or calling' and bills of lading are excluded from the statutory definition. Intangible property is excluded from the definition of 'personal chattels' (s 4 of the 1878 Act) so that, for example, an assignment of book debts would not be caught by the Bills of Sale Acts (although s 344 of the Insolvency Act 1986 makes a general assignment of book debts by way of security registrable under the 1878 Act; see above, p 103). After-acquired property has been held to constitute personal chattels for the purpose of the Bills of Sale Acts (*Welsh Development Agency v Export Finance Co Ltd* [1991] BCLC 936 at 956, per Browne-Wilkinson V-C (reversed by the Court of Appeal on another ground [1992] BCLC 148), disapproving Lord Macnaghten's dictum to the contrary in *Thomas v Kelly* (1888) 13 App Cas 506 at 521). This means that agreements conferring a right in equity over after-acquired goods, under the rule in *Holroyd v Marshall* (1862) 10 HL Cas 191 (above, p 1028), are caught by the Bills of Sale Acts.

There are two types of bills of sale, namely, those given as security for the payment of money ('security bills') and those which are given otherwise than as security for the payment of money ('absolute bills'). The 1878 Act applies to both absolute and security bills so long as they confer on the holder or grantee a power to seize or take possession of any personal chattels comprised in or made subject to the bill (s 3 of the 1878 Act). However, with regard to security bills, the 1878 Act must be read together with the 1882 Act. The 1882 Act applies only to security bills and provides that any provisions in the 1878 Act which are inconsistent with the 1882 Act are repealed as to such bills of sale (s 15 of the 1882 Act).

The 1878 Act sets out a scheme for the registration of bills of sale of personal chattels which remain in the possession of the grantor. Under this scheme all such bills of sale must be attested and registered within seven days of their execution (s 8 of the 1878 Act). If a security bill is not attested and registered within seven days of its execution (and does not truly state the consideration for which it was given) the bill is rendered 'void in respect of the personal chattels comprised therein' (s 8 of the 1882 Act). This means that the security granted by the bill becomes unenforceable, although any other covenant in the bill remains enforceable, eg the grantor's covenant as to payment (*Heseltine v Simmons* [1892] 2 QB 547 at 553–554, CA). To maintain the registration, it must be renewed every five years (s 11 of the 1878 Act). A transfer or assignment of a registered bill of sale need not be registered (s 10 of the 1878 Act).

Registration is a cumbersome process. It is regulated by the 1878 Act which provides that the bill of sale, with every schedule or inventory thereto annexed or therein referred to, and a true copy of the bill and of every schedule or inventory and of every attestation of the execution of such bill, together with an affidavit containing certain required particulars, must be presented to the registrar (a master of the Supreme Court, Queen's Bench Division); and the copy of the bill of sale and the original affidavit must be filed with him. Every security bill must have annexed to it a schedule containing an inventory of the personal chattels comprised in the bill of sale. To ensure that this schedule of chattels is accurate, and that no creditor consulting the registered copy of the bill of sale is misled, failure to include a specific description of an item in the schedule renders the bill void as regard to it, except as against the grantor himself (s 4 of the 1882 Act). The accuracy of the schedule annexed to a security bill is further maintained by s 5 of the 1882 Act which, in general, renders a bill of sale void, except as against the grantor, in respect of any chattels specifically described in the schedule of which the grantor was not the true owner at the time of the execution of the bill of sale (see *Lewis v Thomas* [1919] 1 KB 319, where a person who held goods on hire-purchase was held not to be their true owner). In practice, s 5 of the 1882 Act prevents an individual giving a floating charge over future property.

Registration does not of itself constitute notice to third parties (*Joseph v Lyons* (1884) 15 QBD 280 at 286, CA). It remains possible for a bona fide purchaser from the grantor, without notice of the prior bill of sale, to acquire a good title and override that of the grantee (although in the case of a security bill this will only be possible if the title acquired by the original grantee is purely equitable or the original grantee is estopped from asserting his legal title). If the subsequent disposition of the goods by the grantor is itself a registrable bill of sale, priority will generally be governed by s 10 of the 1878 Act. Under s 10 of the 1878 Act, the date of registration governs priority between two or more bills of sale comprising, in whole or in part, any of the same chattels. With regard to security bills, this general rule applies in the following cases: (1) as between two registered security bills; and (2) where an absolute bill is granted after the grant of a security bill. If a security bill is granted after an absolute bill (whether registered or not) the security bill will be void, except as against the grantor, under s 5 of the 1882 Act.

(ii) Companies Act 2006

L Sealy and S Worthington, *Cases and Materials in Company Law*
(8th edn, 2007), pp 464-467

STATUTORY REQUIREMENTS

Part 25 of Companies Act 2006 imposes on companies a statutory obligation to register particulars of charges which they have created over their property. This requirement was first imposed by CA 1900. It is not every category of charge which is affected—charges over shares and those over negotiable instruments, for instance, escape the net; but the list, as set out in the Act (s 860), is a fairly comprehensive one. In particular, all floating charges are caught by the legislation. But it should be noted that it is only charges *created by the company* which come within Pt 25: a charge created by operation of law, such as an unpaid vendor's lien over land which is the subject of a contract of sale, is outside the scope of the Act.

For every charge that is within the categories set out in the statutory list, CA 2006 s 860 requires companies to deliver to the registrar for registration the 'prescribed particulars' of the charge, together with a copy of the instrument of charge (if any), and to do so within the period allowed for this (basically 21 days, but see s 870). The charge-holder may also see to the registration, and would be well advised to do so if there is any risk that the company will default: s 860(2).

If a company acquires property which is already subject to a charge, particulars of the charge must similarly be delivered for registration (s 862). Where the charge (eg a charge over land or a ship) requires registration under other legislation, both that legislation and CA 2006 must be complied with.

CERTIFICATE OF REGISTRATION

The registrar's staff checks the accuracy of the particulars before they are entered on the register. On registration, a certificate is issued which is conclusive evidence that the requirements of the Act have been complied with (s 869(6)). This is so even where the certificate is inaccurate (*Re Mechanisations (Eaglescliffe) Ltd* [1966] Ch 20), or the facts on which the certificate is based are untrue (eg where the charge instrument is falsely dated: *Re CL Nye Ltd* [1971] Ch 442), or the charge was registered by mistake (*Ali v Top Marques Car Rental Ltd* [2006] EWHC 109).

The effect is that notwithstanding that the details on the register will be incorrect, and people inspecting the register will be misled, the certificate will be conclusive proof that the statutory requirements have been met. As a consequence, the *actual* charge as created by the company will be deemed to be duly registered, and it will have to be observed by the company's creditors and its liquidator or administrator. Because the certificate is conclusive evidence that the requirements have been met, it is impossible to have proceedings for judicial review of the registrar's decision.

Despite all this, the conclusiveness of the certificate was seen as a crucial benefit of the registration system, and a proposed downgrading of it was in large measure the reason for the unpopularity of proposed 1989 reforms (see below).

EFFECT OF FAILURE TO REGISTER

If particulars are not registered within 21 days of the creation of the charge (s 870), CA 2006 s 874 declares that the *security* is void against the liquidator, administrator and any creditor of the company.[10] There are also criminal penalties for non-compliance (s 860).

The nature of this sanction of 'partial voidness' is curious. First, it should be noted that it is the *security* that is avoided, and not the obligation, which remains good as an unsecured debt. Indeed, s 874(3) strengthens the position of the creditor by providing that the money secured by a charge which is rendered void becomes immediately payable. Second, the charge is void only as against the persons mentioned and not, for instance, *inter partes*, nor against an execution creditor. And the chargee may dispose of the property in exercise of a power of sale and give a good title to the purchaser, even though the charge is 'void'.

---

[10] But see *Smith v Bridgend County Borough Council* [2001] UKHL 58, [2002] AC 336 (the appeal of *Cosslett* [1998] Ch 495). Lord Hoffmann: 'When a winding-up order is made and a liquidator appointed, there is no divesting of the company's assets. The liquidator acquires no interest, whether beneficially or as trustee. The assets continue to belong to the company but the liquidator is able to exercise the company's right to collect them for the purposes of the liquidation … It must in my opinion follow that when [CA 1985] s 395 [now CA 2006 s 874] says that the charge shall be 'void against the liquidator', it means void against a company acting by its liquidator, that is to say, a company in liquidation.' The same analysis applies to administration.

EXTENSION OF THE REGISTRATION PERIOD AND RECTIFICATION OF THE REGISTER

CA 2006 s 873 enables applications to court to extend the 21 day registration period or to make other corrections to the register. The court may make whatever orders it sees as just and expedient provided certain pre-conditions are satisfied (s 873(1)), including that it is just and equitable to grant relief. (See *Barclays Bank plc v Stuart Landon Ltd* [2001] EWCA Civ 140, CA for a discussion of the factors to be considered by the court when dealing with an application for late registration of a charge created by a company which is close to liquidation.)

REGISTRATION, PRIORITY AND CONSTRUCTIVE NOTICE OF REGISTERED CHARGES

Registration does not of itself confer priority or give any protection to a charge-holder, although of course non-registration brings all but fatal consequences for his security. Priority as between different charges over the same property is determined by the ordinary rules of law. Thus, for example, a legal charge will normally have priority over an equitable charge, a fixed charge over a floating charge, and, as between two equitable charges, the earlier in time will prevail. So, if a company were to create a charge in favour of A on the first of the month, and then give an identical charge over the same property to B on the 10th, registering particulars on the 15th, B (who had searched the register on the 10th and found it clear) could in all innocence believe that he has a first charge, only to discover later than A has a charge which ranks ahead of his own, so long as it has been registered within the statutory 21 days. B is deemed to have notice of the earlier charge provided A files for registration within the statutory 21 day period. (This is referred to in the Company Law Review (CLR) as 'the 21-day invisibility problem'. It could be eliminated if 'notice filing' were introduced, although even then there could be a gap between the time when a document is delivered to Companies House and the time when it is recorded on the register.)

The doctrine of constructive notice has not been abolished in regard to particulars of charges held by the registrar, and so everyone dealing with a company is deemed to have notice of those particulars which are required by statute to be registered. These are defined by s 869(4), and include the date of creation of the charge, the amount secured, short particulars of the property charged, and the persons entitled to the charge.

However, a practice has developed of including additional information, and in particular, details of any 'negative pledge' clause contained in the charge instrument, ie a provision by which the company undertakes not to create other charges ranking in priority to or *pari passu* with the charge. It was held in *Siebe Gorman & Co Ltd v Barclays Bank Ltd* [1979] 2 Lloyd's Rep 142 (Ch) (overruled in *Spectrum* [2005] UKHL 41, [2005] 2 AC 680, but not on this issue) that the constructive notice doctrine does not extend to such additional information, but only to those matters which the Act prescribes, and so a searcher will be taken to know of such a clause only if he has *actual* notice of it. The point remains controversial, and there is little persuasive authority or argument.[11]

Section 872 contains provision for entering on the register a 'memorandum' that the debt secured by a charge has been satisfied or some or all of the property charged has been released from the security. But there is no *obligation* to register this information under the existing law.

---

[11] See *Wilson v Kelland* [1910] 2 Ch 306. Also see J de Lacy, 'Constructive notice and company charge registration' [2001] Conv 122.

COMPANY'S OWN REGISTER OF CHARGES

The *company itself* is also required to keep a register of charges, together with a copy of every instrument creating or evidencing a registrable charge over its property, and to make these available for inspection, without cost to any creditor or member of the company, and for cost to anyone else (ss 875–877).

Since the register covers every kind of charge, and not only those of which particulars must be filed with the registrar, its obligations are potentially very burdensome indeed. But neither the validity of the charge nor any question relating to priority is affected by a failure to observe the requirement of this section, and in practice the criminal sanctions prescribed are never invoked.

REFORM OF THE REGISTRATION SYSTEM

The need for some sort of registration system is accepted, but the present system, which has changed little for over a century, has long been thought to be deficient. Indeed, changes were made in CA 1989 that were intended to sweep away the old law and replace it with a completely new regime, containing provisions which would reduce the burden on Companies House but at the same time give rather less protection to persons who relied on the registration system. Those proposed reforms met with such opposition from business and professional circles that the government was dissuaded from bringing the regime into operation. Instead, a consultation process was begun which envisaged retaining the earlier CA 1985 provisions, but introducing some modifications. That idea was in turn overtaken by the decision to set up the CLR, which published its own consultation document seeking views on possible ways forward. Following that, the Law Commission was asked to examine the whole of the law on the registration, perfection and priority of company charges, and to consider the case for a new registration system. It was also asked to consider whether such a system should be extended to quasi-securities (retention of title agreements, etc), and to securities created by individuals as well as companies.

The Law Commission, looking to have changes included in CA 2006, made various recommendations, including adoption of a notice filing system (see below) for company charges (see *Company Security Interests,* Law Com No 296, Cm 6654, 2005). The government then issued a further consultation document (*The Registration of Companies' Security Interests (Company Charges): The Economic Impact of the Law Commissions' Proposals,* 2005). This received a rather negative response, and so all these issues now remain subject to still further discussions and deliberations before any decision will be taken on what ought to be done.

This rocky road to reform might be seen as both surprising and disappointing. Both the Crowther Committee (which was concerned with reform of the law on consumer credit: Cmnd 4596, 1971) and Professor Diamond in his report (*A Review of Security Interests in Property* (HMSO, 1989)) categorically recommended that this country should follow the lead of the United States and Canadian jurisdictions in setting up an entirely new system of registration for all personal property security interests, whether created by individuals or companies, on the model of Art 9 of the American Uniform Commercial Code. This would make a separate regime for company charges unnecessary. The same conclusion was reached independently by reform bodies in other Commonwealth jurisdictions, such as Australia and New Zealand—each of which has taken active steps to implement this major change. But, sadly, there seems to be little enthusiasm for any such reform here.

Article 9 is at the same time a more comprehensive system and yet a simpler and more flexible one: it governs all transactions which *in effect* create a security, whatever their form (including eg hire-purchase agreements and sales on retention of title (*Romalpa* [p 452 above]) terms), and works on the principle of 'notice filing'. Priority as between competing registered securities is governed simply by the time of filing of the notice of such security: the security filed first has priority over all that follow. It gives better protection—first, for security holders, in that registration confers priority over others who may claim interests in the same property; secondly, for those intending to take security who, by filing a notice, can cover their position provisionally until the security is completed or the charge attaches; and thirdly, for those seeking to rely on searches of the register, who can take the record at its face value.

NOTE

Regulation 4(4) of the Financial Collateral Arrangements (No 2) Regulations 2003, SI 2003/ 3226, provides that the registration requirement contained in s 860 of the Companies Act 2006 does not apply (if it would otherwise do so) to a security financial collateral arrangement, or any charge created or otherwise arising under a security financial collateral arangement. Thus, where the regulations apply, there is no need to register a charge over 'financial collateral', which is defined to mean cash held in a bank account (or similar) and securities, eg shares and bonds, (reg 3). For an explanation of the regulations, see above, p 1136.

(iii) Insolvency Act 1986

There are controls in the Insolvency Act to protect third parties in the event of any unlawful preference or transaction at an undervalue (ss 238, 239, 339, 340): see below, pp 1232ff.

(b) Protection of debtors

Where security is given by an individual (usually the principal debtor) there are statutory controls which protect him against harsh and unreasonable terms and oppressive enforcement of the security. Such protection is to be found in the Bills of Sale Act (1878) Amendment Act 1882 (as amended) and the Consumer Credit Act 1974. Neither statute affords protection to companies who are principal debtors or who have given security to secure the debt of another person. Companies are regarded as having sufficient bargaining strength to look after their own interests (although this must be doubted when the company is small and heavily indebted to a lender who demands further security).

(i) Bills of Sale Acts

Unlike the Bills of Sale Act 1878, which is concerned with the protection of creditors, the Bills of Sale Act (1878) Amendment Act 1882 is primarily concerned with the protection of the grantor of a security bill (*Manchester, Sheffield and Lincolnshire Rly Co v North Central Wagon Co* (1888) 13 App Cas 554 at 560, per Lord Herschell). Pursuant to s 9 of the 1882 Act, a bill of sale made or given by way of security for the payment of money by the grantor thereof is rendered void unless made in accordance with the form prescribed by the Act. Every bill of sale made or given in consideration of any sum under £30 is also rendered void (s 12 of the 1882 Act). In both cases the security itself, and any personal covenant contained in the bill, is rendered unenforceable (*Davies v Rees* (1886) 17 QBD 408, CA; contrast this sanction with that for non-registration under s 8 of the 1882 Act). A covenant in the bill for the repayment of principal and interest will be unenforceable but the money lent will be recoverable as money had and received, together with reasonable interest (*Bradford Advance Co Ltd v Ayers* [1924] WN 152).

The 1882 Act also prohibits the grantee of a security bill seizing the chattels to which it relates unless (1) the grantor is in default, or fails to comply with any obligation necessary for maintaining the security; (2) the grantor becomes bankrupt, or suffers the goods to be distrained for rent, rates or taxes; (3) the grantor fraudulently removes or allows the goods to be removed from the premises; (4) the grantor fails to comply with a written request for his last receipts for rents, rates and taxes; (5) execution has been levied against the grantor's goods. Even then the seizure may be made subject to the 'default notice' provisions of the Consumer Credit Act 1974 (s 7 A of the 1882 Act; also see below). The goods may not be removed by the grantee within five days of seizure (s 13 of the 1882 Act) thereby giving the grantor the opportunity to apply to the court for relief (s 7 of the 1882 Act).

(ii) Consumer Credit Act 1974

The Consumer Credit Act 1974 regulates credit agreements entered into by an 'individual' ('the debtor'), which includes small partnerships (three partners or less) and unincorporated associations but not corporations. All such credit agreements are *prima facie* covered by the Act irrespective of the amount involved (a previous financial limit of £25,000 was removed by the Consumer Credit Act 2006, s 2). However, certain types of credit agreement are exempt from regulation under the 1974 Act, these include those agreements where credit is supplied to a natural person who is a 'high net worth debtor', ie someone with an annual net income of £150,000 or more and/or with net assets (excluding their primary residence and certain other assets) to the value of £500,000 or more (1974 Act, s 16A, inserted by Consumer Credit Act 2006, s 3; see also the Consumer Credit (Exempt Agreements) Order 2007, SI 2007/1168, Sch 2), or where the credit exceeds £25,000 and the agreement is entered into 'wholly or predominantly for the purposes of a business' carried on, or intended to be carried on, by the debtor (1974 Act, s 16B, inserted by Consumer Credit Act 2006, s 4) (but note that even these two types of agreement are not exempt from ss 140A–140C of the 1974 Act which enables debtors to challenge unfair relationships with creditors). Credit agreements between private individuals (called 'non-commercial' agreements: s 189(1)) are also exempt from most of the provisions of the Act.

The 1974 Act protects the individual debtor in two ways. First, it regulates the business practices of the credit industry in general (eg by restricting advertising and canvassing). In particular, it requires those operating a consumer credit business to be licensed (s 21). The term 'consumer credit business' is defined so as to include within the licensing requirement not only those whose principal business is the provision of credit but also those who supply credit in the course of some other business carried on by them (s 189(1)). Operating a consumer credit business without a licence is a criminal offence (s 39) and any credit agreement entered into by an unlicensed creditor is unenforceable without an order from the Office of Fair Trading (s 40). Secondly, the Act controls the form, content, terms and enforcement of a regulated consumer credit agreement. The form and content of a regulated agreement is prescribed by regulations made under s 60 of the Act (the Consumer Credit (Agreements) Regulations 1983, SI 1983/1553, as amended). The regulations prescribe that, *inter alia,* the agreement must identify any security provided. Failure to comply with these regulations renders the agreement unenforceable without a court order (s 65). The circumstances which the court is to take into account in determining whether to grant an enforcement order are set out in s 127 of the Act (as amended by the Consumer Credit Act 2006, s 15). Enforcement is further controlled by Part VII of the Act. If a debtor is in breach of any term of a regulated consumer credit agreement, no security can be enforced against the debtor without first serving on him a 'default notice' specifying the nature of the alleged breach and giving the debtor at least seven days to take remedial action or pay compensation as specified in the notice (ss 87–89). Seizure is not permitted under the Bills of Sale Act (1878) Amendment Act 1882 if the period of grace specified in the default notice has not expired or the debtor has taken the action specified in the notice (s 7A of the 1882 Act). If the debtor is not in breach of the agreement and the creditor wishes to exercise a contractual right to seize his goods, he must give the debtor at least seven days' notice of his intention to do so (s 76). The control on enforcement only applies where agreement is specified to be for a fixed period (s 76(2)(a)).

Finally, mention must also be made of the new 'unfair relationship' provisions introduced into the 1974 Act by the Consumer Credit Act 2006. Prior to the introduction of these new provisions, sections 137–140 of the 1974 Act gave a court power to reopen a credit agreement if it considered the credit bargain to be 'extortionate'. A credit bargain was extortionate if it (a) required the debtor (or a relative of his) to make payments which were grossly exorbitant, or (b) otherwise grossly contravened ordinary principles of fair dealing. The court was directed to a number of factors in reaching its decision, including the debtor's age, experience, business capacity, state of health etc, but the most important factor was the cost of credit. However, these provisions proved ineffective as a means of protecting consumers. Since 1977 there have been fewer than 30 cases and only 10 were proven to be extortionate: see, eg *London North Securities v Meadows* [2005] 1 P & CR DG16 (34.6% APR with provisions permitting the lender to charge compound interest at the same rate on arrears, costs and charges); *Battooneh v Asombang* [2003] BPIR 4 (ongoing interest at 100%); *Castle Phillips & Co Ltd v Wilkinson* [1992] CCLR 83 (interest rate 333 per cent higher than a standard building society lending rate). There are a number of reasons why these provisions proved to be so ineffective. Most significantly, the test was too onerous with the courts reluctant to find that a bargain was 'grossly exorbitant' or otherwise 'grossly' contravened ordinary principles of fair dealing. There is also the point that ss 137–140 of the 1974 Act did not permit examination of the behaviour of the creditor *after* the contract was made (see *Paragon Finance plc v Nash and Staunton* [2001] EWCA Civ 1466, [2002] 1 WLR 685 and *Broadwick Financial Services Ltd v Spencer* [2002] EWCA Civ 35, [2002] 1 All ER (Comm) 446, where the Court of Appeal held that it could not have regard to how a creditor operated an interest variation clause after the agreement, once the agreement was concluded).

Sections 19–22 of the Consumer Credit Act 2006 have repealed the extortionate credit bargain provisions of the 1974 Act and, through the insertion of new ss 140A–140D into the 1974 Act, replace them with a new 'unfair relationship' test that applies regardless of the amount of credit extended. Section 140A(1) enables a court to consider whether the relationship between the creditor and debtor arising out of that agreement is 'unfair' to the debtor because of: (a) the terms of the agreement or any related agreement; (b) the way in which the creditor has exercised or enforced any of his rights under the agreement or any related agreement; or (c) any other thing done (or not done) by, or on behalf of, the creditor, either before or after the making of the agreement or any related agreement. The court may take into account all matters it thinks relevant relating to the creditor and debtor in making its assessment (s 140A(2)). However, the 2006 Act provides no guidance on what is meant by an 'unfair relationship'. The omission is deliberate as the government wants the test to be flexible and subject to judicial discretion (a point made clear by the Minister of State responsible for the Bill as it passed through Parliament).

The court is provided with a wide range of remedies under s 140B to address the unfairness. The court may: (a) require the creditor (or any associate) to repay any sum paid by the debtor or surety under the credit agreement or any related agreement; (b) require the creditor (or any associate) to do or not to do (or to cease doing) anything specified in the order in connection with the agreement or any related agreement; (c) reduce or discharge any sum payable by the debtor or any surety; (d) direct the return to a surety of any property provided by him for the purpose of a security; (e) otherwise set aside (in whole or in part) any duty imposed on the debtor or a surety under the credit agreement or any related agreement; (f) alter the terms of the agreement or any related agreement; and (g) direct accounts to be taken between any persons.

Section 140A provides a far wider test than applied under the extortionate credit bargain provisions. First, the unfair relationship test applies to a 'credit agreement' which is defined broadly in s 140C(1) as 'any agreement between an individual (the 'debtor') and any other person (the 'creditor') by which the creditor provides the debtor with credit of any amount.' In other words, the test applies regardless of the amount of the credit extended and also extends to those agreements that are otherwise 'exempt' under s 16 of the 1974 Act—such as lending to high net worth individuals and businesses. There is one important exception—the unfair relationship test does *not* apply to consumer credit agreements secured on land and which are regulated by the Financial Services Authority for the purposes of the Financial Services and Markets Act 2000 (s 140A(5)). Thus, first charges on the debtor's dwelling are exempt from the test but not buy-to-let mortgages and second charges. But the test does extend to 'related agreements' which includes agreements consolidated by the main agreements, linked agreements (transactions financed by the credit agreement) and any security provided. Secondly, the court may take into account *all* matters it thinks relevant relating to the creditor and debtor in making its assessment of unfairness (s 140A(2)). This may include an assessment of the exercise and enforcement of the creditor's rights during the currency of the agreement. Thirdly, the burden of proof is reversed so that if the debtor or surety alleges that the relationship between the creditor and the debtor is unfair to the debtor, it is for the creditor to prove to the contrary (s 140B(9)).

QUESTION

Chattel mortgages are rarely used in granting credit. Why?

5 REFORM

In Chapter 24 we saw that Professor Diamond has recommended wholesale reform of the law relating to security in property (other than land) along the lines of art 9 of the US Commercial Code and the Personal Property Security Acts in force in many Canadian provinces (Diamond Report, HMSO 1989, Part II). The new system of security interests proposed by Professor Diamond would extend to all types of consensual security interests, possessory and non-possessory, created by companies, partnerships, and individuals in the course of their business (Diamond Report, paras 1.9–1.15 for summary). A new register of security interests would be introduced together with a notice filing system. The Bills of Sale Acts would be repealed and charges would no longer be registrable under the Companies Act (save for charges over land).

The floating charge would be absorbed within Professor Diamond's new system of security interests (Diamond Report, Ch 16). The essence of the floating charge would be preserved. A security agreement would allow the debtor to dispose of the property in the ordinary course of business and would attach to after-acquired property which falls within the description of the property in the agreement. But crystallisation would lose all or most of its significance as priority would be determined by the date of filing in the new register of security interests. Furthermore, all business people, whether incorporated or not, would be able to create a security interest which extended to after-acquired property and which gave them the right to dispose of the property in the ordinary course of business.

The Law Commission in its recent report on *Company Security Interests* (Law Com No 296, 2005) recommended the introduction of an electronic notice-filing system for company charges and the outright sale of receivables, which would make priority no longer depend upon the date of creation of the security interest but upon the date and time of filing. The Law Commission recognised that from the point of view of the law of security there was a good case for removing the distinction between fixed and floating charges. However, this would entail some changes of substance, particularly in relation to the priority of preferred creditors and the unsecured creditors' fund introduced by the Enterprise Act 2002. The Law Commission believed that these matters could be resolved but it recognised that 'insolvency law has undergone significant changes in recent years and that there is great unwilling-ness to see further changes in the immediate future' (Law Com Rep, para 3.172). The Law Commission recommended that the distinction between fixed and floating charges should be left in place, but be reconsidered when insolvency law is next reviewed (Law Com Rep, para 3.175). However, the Law Commission did recommend that the priority rules should be altered so that the priority of a floating charge would date from the date of registration of the relevant financing statement (Law Com Rep, para 3.180). This would make it unnecessary to have negative pledge clauses and similar clauses designed to prevent floating charges from losing priority to subsequent security interests. Provisions dealing with priority as against preferred creditors and the unsecured creditors' fund were also recommended (Law Com Rep, para 3.187).

In July 2005 the Department of Trade and Industry published a consultation document based on the Law Commission's proposals. The responses to that consultation showed there was a lack of consensus of support for the Law Commission's proposals. The demands of Parliamentary time meant that the Companies Act 2006 contained no major reform of the law on company charges. Part 25 of the 2006 Act reproduces the substance of Part XII of the Companies Act 1985.

CHAPTER 27

GUARANTEES[1]

1 THE LEGAL NATURE OF A GUARANTEE

(1) A contract of guarantee is a contract whereby the surety (or guarantor) promises the actual or potential creditor of a third person (the principal debtor) to be responsible to him, in addition to the principal debtor, for the due performance by the principal debtor of his existing or future obligations to the creditor, if the principal debtor fails to perform those obligations. It imposes an obligation which is secondary to that of the principal debtor, meaning that the surety's liability depends upon default by the principal debtor. The contract may be constituted by the personal engagement of the surety, or by the surety providing real security without any personal liability, or by both (*Smith v Wood* [1929] 1 Ch 14; *Re Conley* [1938] 2 All ER 127).

(2) Another feature of a guarantee is that it is an accessory contract. This means that for there to be a valid contract of guarantee, between surety and creditor, there has to be a valid principal obligation, between the principal debtor and the creditor. It follows from the accessory nature of the contract of guarantee that there is a general principle that a surety's liability is co-extensive with that of the principal debtor. In other words, the surety is generally only liable to the same extent that the principal debtor is liable to the creditor, and that there is usually no liability on the part of the surety if the underlying obligation is void or unenforceable, or if that obligation ceases to exist. However, this general principle may be modified or displaced by the terms of the guarantee (*Moschi v Lep Air Services Ltd* [1973] AC 331 at 349, per Lord Diplock: below, p 1171). Furthermore, in exceptional cases, the courts may ignore the principle altogether and hold the surety liable notwithstanding that the principal obligation guaranteed never arises or becomes unenforceable or ceases to exist otherwise than by the consent or with the agreement of the creditor (eg see below, p 1178). See generally, RE Mitchell (1947) 63 LQR 355; J Steyn (1974) 90 LQR 246; G Andrews and R Millett *Law of Guarantees* (5th edn, 2008), Ch 6.

---

[1] See *generally*, RM Goode *Commercial Law* (3rd edn, 2004), Ch 30; RM Goode *Legal Problems of Credit and Security* (3rd edn, 2003), Ch VIII. For further detail, see G Andrews and R Millett *Law of Guarantees* (5th edn, 2008), J O'Donovan and J Phillips *The Modern Contract of Guarantee* (English edn, 2003) and *Rowlatt on the Law of Principal and Surety* (5th edn, 2001).

2 GUARANTEE AND INDEMNITY DISTINGUISHED

A contract of indemnity is 'a contract by one party to keep the other harmless against loss' (*Yeoman Credit Ltd v Latter* [1961] 1 WLR 828, 830-831, *per* Holroyd Pearce LJ). The distinction between a contract of guarantee and a contract of indemnity is summarised in J O'Donovan and J Phillips, *The Modern Contract of Guarantee* (English edn, 2003), para 1–88, as follows:

'in a contract of indemnity a primary liability is assumed whether or not a third party makes default whilst…in a contract of guarantee the surety assumes a secondary liability to the creditor for the default of another who remains primary liable to the creditor. The contract of indemnity, therefore, is 'a contract by one party to keep the other harmless against loss' and is not dependent on the continuing liability of the principal debtor. The obligation has no reference in law to the debt of another. In other words, an indemnity imposes a primary obligation which is independent of the continuing obligation of another.'

The distinction between the two types of contract is important for the following reasons:

- contracts of guarantee, but not contracts of indemnity, are prima facie unenforceable if they do not comply with the requirements of s 4 of the Statute of Frauds 1677 (the agreement or a note or memorandum thereof should be in writing and signed by the guarantor or his agent): for a recent example, see *Pitts v Jones* [2007] EWCA Civ 1301 (oral guarantee held unenforceable);

- liability of a guarantor, but not of an indemnifier, is normally co-extensive with the liability of the principal debtor—thus, if the underlying contract is set aside, extinguishing the liabilities between the contracting parties, an indemnifier should still be liable (but if the underlying contract is for an illegal purpose then the indemnity may itself be tainted with illegality and unenforceable as a matter of public policy);

- 'the obligation of a guarantor may be discharged by transactions between the creditor and the principal debtor, for example by giving time, the release of securities or novation of the obligation because any of those transactions may alter the mutual rights and obligations of the guarantor and the principal debtor. As there is no need for a principal obligation in the case of an indemnity its discharge depends on the usual rules of contract' (*Scottish & Newcastle plc v Raguz* [2003] EWCA Civ 1070 at [8], per Morritt V-C).

3 CHARACTERISATION

Whether a contract is one of guarantee or of indemnity is a matter of construction. As Holroyd-Pearce LJ said in *Yeoman Credit Ltd v Latter* [1961] 1 WLR 828, 831: '…we must have regard to its essential nature in order to decide whether or not it is really no more than a guarantee'. It is the substance rather than the form of the agreement that counts (*Motemtronic Ltd v Autocar Equipment Ltd* (20 June 1996, unreported), CA, referred to in *Actionstrength Ltd v International Glass Engineering IN.GL.EN SpA* [2001] EWCA Civ 1477, [2002] 4 All ER 468, CA, upheld on appeal [2003] UKHL 17, [2003] 2 AC 541 (but with no appeal on this point); both citing with approval the dictum to this effect of Vaughan Williams LJ in *Harburg India Rubber Comb Co v Martin* [1902] 1 KB 778 at 784-785). Thus, the fact that a contract states that the guarantor is to be liable 'as principal debtor' does not necessarily turn what is in reality a guarantee into an indemnity (*Heald v O'Connor* [1971] 1 WLR 497 at 503, per Fisher J). But this does not mean that a principal debtor clause is meaningless when incorporated into a contract of guarantee. For example, such a clause may be effective to prevent the surety claiming that he is discharged by release of the principal debtor (*General Produce Co v United Bank Ltd* [1979] 2 Lloyd's Rep 255), or it may absolve the creditor from the usual requirement that he must first demand payment from the guarantor before commencing proceedings against him (*MS Fashion Ltd v Bank of Credit & Commerce International SA* [1993] Ch 425, CA, applied in *TS & S Global Ltd v Fithian-Franks* [2007] EWHC 1401 (Ch), [2007] BPIR 1166 at [26]).

A court may also have to decide whether an instrument is a contract of guarantee as opposed to a 'demand guarantee', 'performance bond' or 'demand bond', where the liability of the issuer of the instrument is primary and not secondary, although the intention is that it should not be enforced except in a case of default by the principal debtor. The next case reveals how the court makes the distinction.

Marubeni Hong Kong and South China Ltd v Mongolian Government
[2005] EWCA Civ 395, [2005] 1 WLR 2497, Court of Appeal

The claimant ('MHK'), a Hong Kong company, entered into a contract with Mongolian buyers to sell machinery, equipment and materials for a cashmere processing plant. Pursuant to the terms of the contract of sale, the Mongolian buyers arranged for the provision of a letter, addressed to MHK, signed by the Mongolian Minister of Finance (the 'MMOF'). By the terms of this letter, the Ministry of Finance unconditionally pledged to pay to MHK 'upon your simple demand' all amounts payable under the contract of sale if not paid when the same became due from the buyers. The proper law of the guarantee letter agreement was English law. On the same date as the guarantee letter, the Deputy Minister of Justice of Mongolia signed a legal opinion addressed to MHK stating that the Ministry of Finance had full power and authority to enter into and perform the terms and conditions of the 'guarantee'.

The Mongolian buyers repeatedly failed to pay instalments due under the contract of sale despite the fact that there had been various rescheduling agreements entered into by MHK and/or its parent company and the buyers. MHK gave formal notice to the Mongolian government, acting through the Ministry of Finance, requiring repayment of nearly US $14 million. No payment was made and proceedings were issued. MHK asserted that, on a true construction, the guarantee letter actually constituted an undertaking of primary liability to the claimant, in the form of a demand bond. The Mongolian government disputed this arguing that it had undertaken secondary liability to MHK, in the form of a contract of guarantee, and not primary liability. The government argued that material variation of the transaction to which the guarantee related, which was brought about by the refinancing arrangements, resulted in its secondary liability under the guarantee being discharged by application of the rule in *Holme v Brunskill* (1878) 3 QBD 495 (guarantor discharged automatically if there is any variation of the arrangements with the principal debtor without his consent which might prejudice his interests: see below, p 1179). Cresswell J held that on a true construction of the letter signed by the MMOF, the government undertook secondary liability as guarantor, and not primary liability, to the claimant. Applying the rule in *Holme v Brunskill*, the judge held that rescheduling arrangements, entered into by the Mongolian buyers and the claimant without the knowledge or consent of the government of Mongolia, constituted material variations of the agreement between the Mongolian buyers and MHK and resulted in the discharge of the entirety of the Mongolian government's obligations under the MMOF letter. The Court of Appeal dismissed MHK's appeal from that decision.

Carnwath LJ:

Discussion

[20] One of the problems in cases of this kind is terminology. In ordinary legal language, a 'guarantee', in contrast with an 'indemnity' imposes a secondary liability:

'The distinction between the two contracts is, in brief, that in a contract of guarantee the surety assumes a secondary liability to answer for the debtor who remains primary liable; whereas in a contract of indemnity the surety assumes a primary liability, either alone or jointly with the principal debtor.' (*Chitty on Contracts* (29th ed) vol 2 para 44.013.)

The obligation of the guarantor:

'...is not an obligation himself to pay a sum of money to the creditor, but an obligation to see to it that another person, the debtor, does something...' (*Moschi v LEP Air Services* [1973] AC 331, 347, per Lord Diplock).

[21] The different usages are referred to by Andrews and Millett, *Law of Guarantees* (4th ed) p 14, in a section headed 'Performance bonds':

'Bonds are simple covenants by one person to pay another, either conditionally or unconditionally. A performance bond, also commonly called a performance guarantee, or (confusingly) a demand guarantee, is a binding contractual undertaking given by a person, usually a bank, to pay a specified amount of money to a named beneficiary on the occurrence of a certain event, which is usually the non-fulfilment of a contractual obligation undertaken by the principal to the beneficiary.'

As I understand it, the terms 'demand bond', as used in the grounds of appeal and 'first demand bond' (as used by the judge—para 137) are intended in the same sense. The same authors refer to the difficulties experienced by the courts in determining whether a particular contract which provides for payment 'on demand' is a performance bond, or '...whether it is a guarantee in the true sense (sometimes referred to in this context as a "see to it" guarantee).' A similar contrast is drawn in Jack, *Documentary Credits*, 3rd ed para 12.4:

'Whatever the undertaking may be called, a distinction must be drawn between what is referred to in this chapter as an independent guarantee (encompassing demand guarantees, demand bonds etc) and a true contract of guarantee (or suretyship). Although the terminology unfortunately overlaps, the legal nature is very different...'

[22] Chitty, *Law of Contracts* (29th ed) vol 2 para 44-014 discusses the development of the law of 'performance guarantees', starting with *Edward Owen Engineering Ltd v Barclays Bank International Ltd* [1978] QB 159, [1978] 1 All ER 976:

'A number of cases have involved discussion of the nature of "performance guarantees" which are, in essence, exceptionally stringent contracts of indemnity. They are contractual undertakings, normally granted by banks, to pay or repay, a specified sum in the event of any default in performance by the principal debtor of some other contract with a third party, the creditor. An unusual feature of several modern cases has been that the bank's liability arises on mere demand by the creditor, notwithstanding that it may appear on the evidence that the principal debtor is not in any way in default, or even that the creditor is in default under the principal contract. Such guarantees are sometimes called "first demand guarantees". It has been held that performance guarantees of this nature are analogous to a bank's letter of credit...'

[23] Those passages provide the context for discussing the cases relied on by Mr Howard [Counsel for MHK]. They show that 'demand bonds' (however described) are a specialised form of irrevocable instrument, developed by the banking world for its commercial customers. They have been accepted by the courts as the equivalent of irrevocable letters of credit. As such, they have been described as part of 'the lifeblood of commerce'; and, in the words of Donaldson LJ:

'Thrombosis will occur if, unless fraud is involved, the courts intervene and thereby disturb the mercantile practice of treating rights thereunder as being the equivalent of cash in hand.' (*Intraco Ltd v Notis Shipping Corporation* [1981] 2 Lloyd's Rep 256, 257.)

It cannot be assumed that cases relating to such banking instruments provide any useful guidance when construing guarantees given outside the banking context. The authorities relied on by Mr Howard must be seen in this light.

[24] In *Esal (Commodities) Ltd v Oriental Credit Ltd* [1985] 2 Lloyd's Rep 546, the instrument was issued by a bank; it was described on its face as a 'performance bond'; and it was for a specified amount, being 10% of the purchase price. The only difficulty arose from the wording:

'We undertake to pay the said amount on your written demand in the event that the supplier fails to execute the contract in perfect performance...'

The question was whether this had the effect that the performance bond was ineffective unless and until a breach of the underlying contract had been established. This reading was rejected as being inconsistent with the commercial purpose of a performance bond, that is, to enable the beneficiary to obtain prompt and certain payment, in a context in which the bank is 'not concerned in the least' with the relations between the supplier and the customer (p 549, per Ackner LJ).

[25] In *Siporex Trade SA v Banque Indosuez* [1986] 2 Lloyd's Rep 146 Hirst J applied the same approach to the interpretation of an instrument issued by a bank pursuant to an obligation in an international trade agreement to provide a performance bond. The instrument was described in correspondence between the parties and with the bank as a performance bond. The judge commented:

'There is in my judgment no real hardship on the bank in imposing this strict liability to pay. A performance bond is a commercial instrument. No bank is obliged to enter into it unless they wish to and no doubt when they do so, they properly exact commercial terms and protect themselves by suitable cross-indemnities, such as were entered into in the present case.' (Page 158.)

[26] In *IE Contractors v Lloyds Bank plc* [1990] 2 Lloyd's Rep 496, the documents again were issued by a bank; were described as (or assumed to be) 'performance bonds' (see issue (1) p 498); and were for damages up to specified amounts. The difficulty arose from the unusual form and language of the documents (see p 501-2), and the wording of the operative clause:

'We undertake to pay you, unconditionally, the said amount on demand, being your claim for damages brought about by the above-named principal.'

It was held that this wording required the demand to contain some reference, express or implicit, to a claim for damages; but that this requirement was satisfied on the facts of the case (p 502).

[27] The judgment of Staughton LJ contains some general discussion of the law relating to performance bonds. He discusses the possibility of different triggering events for payment under a performance bond: at one extreme, a simple demand 'without requiring the presentation of any other document or the assertion of any fact'; and, at the other, a bond 'conditioned upon the existence of facts rather than the production of a document asserting those facts' (p 499). He concludes, following *Esal*:

'...there is a bias or presumption in favour of the construction which holds a performance bond to be conditioned upon documents rather than facts. But I would not hold the presumption to be irrebuttable, if the meaning is plain.' (Page 500.)

The latter observation was not necessary to the decision. There was no argument that the instrument in that case required more than the *assertion* of a claim to damages.

[28] In all these cases the documents were issued by banks, and were described as, or assumed to be, performance bonds. Not surprisingly, the courts interpreted them against the background of the law relating to such instruments. They provide no useful analogy for interpreting a document which was not issued by a bank and which contains no overt indication of an intention to create a performance bond or anything analogous to it.

[29] The most recent authority relied on by Mr Howard, decided since the date of the MMOF Letter, is *Gold Coast Ltd v Caja de Ahorros del Mediterraneo* [2001] EWCA Civ 1086, [2002] 1 All ER (Comm) 142. It concerned the interpretation of a refund guarantee issued by a bank pursuant to an obligation in a shipbuilding contract. Payment of specified amounts was to be made on 'your first written demand', subject (under condition 1) to receipt of a certificate issued by Lloyds Bank that the refund had become due. The Court of Appeal held the instrument 'had all the hallmarks of a first demand guarantee':

'It describes itself as a guarantee, but this is simply a label; it does not use the language of guarantee. Rather, the obligation, which is expressed to be an 'irrevocable and unconditional undertaking', is that the banks "will pay" on a first written demand. The only express condition of payment is contained in condition 1. This requires a certificate but makes no reference to arbitration or underlying liability under the shipbuilding contract. The instrument contains its own dispute resolution provisions.' (Paragraph 21.)

Mr Howard relies on the court's disregard of the term 'guarantee'. However, the other features of the instrument were sufficient to displace the ordinary sense of that term. In particular, the provision for a bank certificate as a trigger for payment was a clear indication that the obligation to pay was independent of any need to establish default under the main contract.

[30] Turning to the MMOF Letter, the starting-point in my view is that it is not a banking instrument, and it is not described, either on its face or in the supporting Legal Opinion letter, in terms appropriate to a demand bond or something having similar legal effect. The Legal Opinion describes it as a guarantee. The terminology is not of course conclusive. However, I agree with Cresswell J that, if MHK had wanted the additional security of a demand bond, one would have expected them to have insisted on appropriate language to describe it, in both the instrument itself, and in the Legal Opinion. The absence of such language, in a transaction outside the banking context, creates in my view a strong presumption against MHK's interpretation....

[31] The question then becomes whether there are sufficient indications in the wording of the instrument to displace that presumption. Mr Howard relies on the words 'unconditionally pledges' and 'simple demand'. However, they are qualified by the following words, which indicate that the obligation only arises if 'the amounts payable under the agreement (are) not paid when the same becomes due'. As Cresswell J said, this is wording appropriate to a secondary obligation, that is one conditional upon default by the buyer. It is true that in *Esal* similar wording was held insufficient to displace the ordinary effect of what was admittedly a performance bond. However, here the starting-point is different, and there is no reason for reading the words in other than their ordinary meaning.

[32] That sense is reinforced by the following pledge of '...the full and timely performance and observance by the buyer of all the terms and conditions of the agreement'. It is not suggested, as I understand it, that this indicates anything other than a secondary obligation. It is true that the letter also contains a primary obligation, in the form of an indemnity against cost or damage resulting from the buyer's default. However, this does not assist MHK in this case, and there is no reason to treat this as qualifying the ordinary meaning of the earlier part of the letter.

[33] Finally, Mr Howard relies on the clause under which the Government waives 'any right' to require MHK to proceed against the buyer, or to pursue any other remedy. He suggests that this indicates the commercial purpose of the instrument, analogous to that of a performance bond, to provide security which is readily and easily realisable. If that was the intention, it seems to me a round-about way of indicating the purpose. In any event, it is at best a neutral indication. In a normal performance bond there would be no need for such a waiver, because there would be no question of the issuing party having any such right. Nor am I impressed by the fact that establishing a default under the main contract may require recourse to Japanese arbitration. Whatever the reasons which led the parties to the respective contracts to choose different systems of law, that by itself cannot in my view be a reason for altering the natural interpretation of the MMOF Letter.

[34] I conclude, therefore, that the judge was correct to reject the submission that the MMOF Letter was to be treated as a demand bond or its equivalent.

Sir Martin Nourse and Waller LJ agreed.

NOTES

1. The presumption identified by Carnwath LJ in *Marubeni* was later applied by Gloster J in *Canmer International Inc v UK Mutual Steamship Assurance Association (Bermuda) Ltd, (The 'Rays')* [2005] 2 Lloyd's Rep 479 at [43]-[50], where a letter of undertaking was issued by a P & I Club to procure the release of a vessel. (P & I Clubs are mutual insurance associations that provide liability cover—protection and indemnity—for shipowners and charterer members against third party liabilities relating to the use and operation of ships.) The issue was whether the letter imposed a form of primary liability similar to that arising under a performance bond given by a bank. Gloster J stated that she could see no reason why the principles applicable to performance bonds (ie the imposition of primary liability) could not apply to letters of undertaking issued by P & I Clubs 'if, and only if, the language of the particular letter in question justifies such a construction'. However, on a construction of the wording of the particular undertaking before her, the judge held that there was nothing to rebut the presumption referred to by Carnwath LJ that, outside the banking context, and in the absence of clear words applicable to a performance bond, the undertaking given by the P & I Club should not be regarded as having been intended to impose primary liability.

2. By contrast, in *Van Der Merwe v IIG Capital LLC* [2007] EWHC 2631 (Ch), [2008] 1 All ER (Comm) 435, where a husband and wife, who were directors of the principal debtor company, had each signed a 'guarantee' agreeing 'as principal obligor' to pay 'upon demand' all monies which were or were expressed to be due, owing or payable from the company to the creditor, Lewison J held that the presumption identified by Carnwath LJ in *Marubeni* had been displaced by sufficient indications in the wording of the instrument and that the liability of the husband and wife was primary and not secondary. His Lordship was influenced by a number of factors including the fact that the guarantee was expressed to be payable on demand, that the promise to pay was introduced by the words 'as principal obligor' and, most importantly, that there was a clause in the contract allowing the creditor to serve a certificate on the husband and wife which was to be 'conclusive and binding' as to both amount and liability.

3. Three points can be made about the *Marubeni* case:

• First, there is the observation made by Alan Berg in (2006) 122 LQR 42 at 44, that had the letter been issued by a bank it would have been construed as a demand bond. Berg continues:

    'The application of *Holme v Brunskill* was made to depend less on the terms of the document, than on the classification of the issuer. There seems little commercial logic in *Holme v Brunskill* not applying if the issuer is a bank, but applying if the issuer is another type of financial institution, such as a ministry of finance or an insurance company... Where credit support is provided by an independent financial institution, the commercial context favours a construction that avoids the institution having to investigate factual (and legal) disputes about the underlying contract.'

- Secondly, because the Court of Appeal held that the letter was not to be treated as a demand bond it was not necessary for it to consider whether the rule in *Holme v Brunskill* applied to instruments creating primary liability. The Mongolian government submitted that it did and this view seems to have gained the support of Cresswell J (*obiter*) at first instance ([2004] EWHC 472 (Comm), [2004] 2 Lloyd's Rep 198 at [142]). Bhattacharyya, Reynolds and White (members of the legal team that represented the Mongolian government) have put the case in favour of extending the rule in *Holme v Brunskill* to primary obligations in an article they published in (2005) 20 JIBLR 488 at 493. In fact they argue that there is even greater reason for the rule in the case of a primary liability instrument 'given the more onerous nature of the instrument on the part of the guarantor'. We would beg to differ. The commercial benefits of the principle of certainty of payment in the case of an abstract payment undertaking such as a letter of credit or demand bond outweighs the application of rules such as that in *Holme v Brunskill* that require examination of the underlying contract and slow down the payment process.

- Thirdly, the apparent willingness of the Court of Appeal to characterise an instrument issued by a non-bank as giving rise to secondary liability highlights the importance of any express term of the contract of guarantee which seeks to exclude the operation of the rule in *Holme v Brunskill* or other defences that are generally available to the guarantor.

QUESTION

What distinguishes a contract of guarantee from a contract of insurance (see below, Chapter 28)?

4 TYPES OF GUARANTEES

There are various types of guarantee. The following are the most important.

Bipartite and tripartite guarantees. In most cases the creditor is made a party to the contract of guarantee. But even if he is not a party to the instrument it may be possible for the creditor to enforce the surety's undertaking by relying either on the Contract (Rights of Third Parties) Act 1999, or by arguing that the contract of guarantee, when by deed, is a deed poll and intended to be enforceable by the creditor (*Moody v Condor Insurance Ltd* [2006] EWHC 100 (Ch), [2006] 1 WLR 1847). It is not necessary for the principal debtor also to be made a party to that contract (although the guarantee must *involve* the principal debtor to the extent that the surety's liability is made accessory to his). In most cases, only the creditor and surety are party to the contract of guarantee (bipartite guarantee). In some cases, the principal debtor may not even know that the surety has entered into the guarantee, eg where a dealer guarantees to a finance company that a hire-purchaser will pay his instalments as they fall due under a hire-purchase agreement. However, sometimes all three parties are joined to the contract (tripartite guarantee).

Discrete and continuing guarantees. A guarantee is discrete where the surety guarantees payment of an identified debt or the discharge of the principal debtor's liability in respect of a specific transaction or transactions, eg where a finance company lets a car on hire-purchase and a surety guarantees that the hirer will pay the instalments as they fall due under the terms of the hire-purchase agreement. By contrast, a continuing guarantee extends over a series of transactions between the principal debtor and the creditor under the terms of a master agreement or facility agreed between them. In such cases, the surety's liability is not fixed but varies according to the principal debtor's outstanding indebtedness to the creditor at any one time, eg where a bank extends a general overdraft facility to a company and one of the company's directors guarantees any indebtedness that may accrue with use of that facility (eg see the guarantee which appears as Form 8 in the Appendix). The distinction between 'discrete' and 'continuing' guarantees was highlighted by Hobhouse LJ in *Bank of Credit and Commerce International SA v Simjee* [1997] CLC 135 at 137–138, in the following terms:

The simplest form of guarantee of a monetary liability of a principal debtor is one which identifies an obligation of the principal and simply states that the surety guarantees that that obligation will be discharged. The subject matter of the guarantee is thus the payment of an identified debt or the discharge of the principal's liability in respect of an identified transaction. The liability of the surety is not, as such, qualified in amount or time: a further term is necessary to do that. The liability of the surety to the creditor accrues and becomes actionable as soon as there is a default by the principal. Any repayments by the principal will reduce or extinguish the obligation the subject of the guarantee and therefore the liability of the surety. If there is a running account, prima facie, the rule in *Clayton's Case* (1816) 1 Mer 572 will apply (*Re Quest CAE* (1985) 1 BCC 99,389 at pp 99, 392–399, 393). The liability of the surety is exhausted once the relevant obligation has been performed and does not cover further advances.

This simple situation is capable of being varied or elaborated in many ways. But still the two elements will be identifiable—the obligation or obligations of the principal the subject matter of the guarantee and the accrual of the liability of the surety to the creditor. Where the creditor and principal have a running account and the creditor, the bank, is from time to time providing the principal debtor with finance, whether by granting him overdrafts or loan facilities or issuing paper on his behalf or discounting negotiable and other instruments or debts for him or in any of the other many ways a banker may provide finance to a business, the only satisfactory form of guarantee will be what is called a continuing guarantee. This has the effect of making the subject matter of the guarantee whatever may be the discharge of the indebtedness (and other monetary obligations) of the principal to the bank at any given time. It is in essence a security with a floating subject matter. Ordinarily such a guarantee will not prudently be given unless the surety has a measure of control over the affairs of the principal.

For the guarantee contract to work satisfactorily it is necessary to have some mechanism whereby the accrual of any liability of the surety under the guarantee can be identified and quantified. In its absence, problems can also arise under the Limitation Acts (*Parr's Banking Co Ltd v Yates* [1898] 2 QB 460). The mechanism ordinarily adopted is to express the guarantee as a demand guarantee. Thus, as does the present document, the guarantee will provide that the obligation of the surety arises when a demand is made upon him by the creditor. That demand provides the moment at which a line is drawn under the account between the principal and the creditor and the surety becomes immediately liable for the discharge of whatever are at that time the obligations of the principal to the creditor.

A continuing guarantee is prima facie open-ended. The surety will normally require some mechanism whereby he can bring this state of affairs to an end. Commercially, there is more than one way in which he can do this. One is by including in the guarantee a provision which enables the surety to give notice of termination of the guarantee contract so that the creditor is given a period of time within which he may if he chooses make a demand upon the surety; if he does not do so, the contract then wholly comes to an end. This was held to be the effect of the guarantee in the *Hardman* case [see below]. Another is by having a provision which enables the surety by the service of a notice to bring to an end the continuing character of the guarantee so that from the expiry of the notice its subject matter becomes the obligations of the principal to the creditor at that time. The judge has held that this is the effect of cl. 3 of the guarantee in the present case.

If the provisions of the guarantee are of the latter kind, the guarantee remains in force but only as a guarantee of the performance of identified obligations. It remains a demand guarantee so that, although the notice crystallises the subject matter of the guarantee, it leaves open whether there will be any liability of the surety under the guarantee. No cause of action against the surety will arise until a demand is made upon him. But the demand can only relate to such of the obligations of the principal at the time of the expiry of the notice as still remain unperformed at the time of the demand on the surety.

In *National Westminster Bank v Hardman* [1988] FLR 302, a continuing demand guarantee provided that it was to 'remain in force... until determined by three months' notice in writing from the guarantor'. The Court of Appeal gave these words their ordinary meaning and held that the guarantee ceased to be in force at the end of the notice period, so that the creditor's failure to make demand of the surety before then meant there was no sum due under the guarantee before it terminated, and no demand could be made after termination (for criticism of the decision, see D Marks [1994] JBL 124). The demand guarantee in *BCCI v Simjee* (above) was similarly, but not identically, worded to that in *Hardman*. Clause 3 of the *Simjee* guarantee provided, 'This guarantee is to be a continuing security to [the creditor]... but may and shall be determined... and the liability hereunder crystallised... at the expiration of three months after receipt by [the creditor] from [the surety] of notice in writing'. The Court of Appeal held that the words 'and the liability hereunder crystallised', which were not present in the *Hardman* guarantee, meant that the obligations of the principal debtor crystallised at the end of the notice period and became the subject matter of the guarantee, but that the contract of guarantee itself remained in force, although it could no longer be characterised as a *continuing* guarantee, and a demand could thereafter be made.

In *Silverburn Finance (UK) Ltd v Salt* [2001] EWCA Civ 279, [2001] 2 All ER (Comm) 438, where there was no provision in a continuing guarantee for termination by notice, the Court of Appeal held that the surety was entitled at any time to revoke the guarantee in respect of future liabilities but that he remained liable for any sums incurred by the principal debtor which were the subject of the guarantee up to the time of revocation. In other words, accrued rights were held not to be affected by the revocation.

Limited guarantees. Guarantees may be limited in duration or in amount, or both. It is important to distinguish between the guarantee of a fixed sum, or of part of an indebtedness, and the guarantee of the entire indebtedness with a fixed limit of liability. In the former case, the guaranteed part of the debt is treated as if it were a separate debt, so that on paying that sum the surety discharges that notional separate debt and, unless otherwise provided in the guarantee, becomes entitled to share rateably in securities held for the full indebtedness (*Goodwin v Gray* (1874) 22 WR 312, applied in *Re Butler's Wharf Ltd* [1995] 2 BCLC 43). If the principal debtor becomes insolvent, the creditor can only prove in the insolvency for the balance of the debt, while the surety can prove for the amount he has paid (*Re Sass* [1896] 2 QB 12). By contrast, where the surety has guaranteed the entire indebtedness with a fixed limit of liability, the guaranteed indebtedness remains indivisible and the surety cannot take over the securities held by the creditor, or prove in the principal debtor's insolvency, unless he pays off the entire indebtedness. Unless the surety discharges the entire indebtedness, the creditor can prove in the debtor's insolvency for the full indebtedness, even though the surety had paid under his guarantee (*Re Sass,* above).

5 THE CONTRACT OF GUARANTEE

(a) Formation

A contract of guarantee must meet the basic requirements necessary for all contracts: agreement between the parties (through offer and acceptance), consideration (unless under seal), certainty as to terms, and intention to create legal relations.

A contract of guarantee may be unilateral or bilateral. If the guarantee is given in return for a promise by the creditor to enter into a transaction with the principal debtor, eg to make a loan to him, then the contract of guarantee will be bilateral and the creditor's promise is consideration for the surety's promise under the guarantee. Neither promise may be withdrawn without the consent of the other party. However, it is more often the case that the surety offers to guarantee the principal debtor's obligations in return for some act or forbearance by the creditor. The creditor does not promise to act or forbear but should the act be done or the forbearance given that in itself will constitute both an acceptance of the surety's offer and also consideration for the surety's promise under the guarantee. In these circumstances, the contract of guarantee will be unilateral in character. Furthermore, unless the surety has received separate consideration to hold his offer of a unilateral contract open, he may withdraw it at any time before it is accepted by the creditor. This explains why a continuing guarantee to secure the balance of a running account at a bank can normally be terminated by the surety in respect of future advances. Each advance is treated as divisible consideration for the continuing guarantee (*Offord v Davies* (1862) 12 CBNS 748; *Coulthart v Clementson* (1879) 5 QBD 42 at 46). So long as the consideration for the guarantee is divisible, not entire and indivisible, the guarantee is treated as a standing offer which is accepted *pro tanto* by part performance of the consideration, but which remains revocable at all times as regards future liabilities (per *Chitty on Contracts* (29th edn, 2004), Vol II, para 44–017).

Again, like all contracts, a contract of guarantee may be void or voidable on grounds of fraud, misrepresentation, mistake of fact (including *non est factum*), undue influence, duress, unconscionable dealing or illegality (see the standard contract textbooks for detailed discussion of these vitiating factors). The wrongdoing may be by the creditor himself, but it is frequently by the principal debtor against the surety and then relied on by the surety against the creditor, a situation considered in detail above at pp 659ff (but see also *Moody v Condor Insurance Ltd* [2006] EWHC 100 (Ch), [2006] 1 WLR 1847, where Park J held that fraud of the principal debtor practiced on a commercial guarantee corporation, and unknown to the creditor, did not affect the validity of the guarantee). A contract of guarantee may be void because it is *ultra vires* the surety (see, eg *Crédit Suisse v Borough Council of Allerdale* [1995] 1 Lloyd's Rep 315; affd [1996] 2 Lloyd's Rep 241, CA). But English law does not recognise any wider relief in equity based on mere expectation of a surety than is afforded by the determination whether or not the guarantee is conditional on some circumstance, eg the execution of a guarantee by a third person (*Capital Bank Cashflow Finance Ltd v Southall* [2004] EWCA Civ 817, [2004] 2 All ER (Comm) 675 at [16]).

A contract of guarantee is not a contract *uberrimae fidei* and does not generally require the creditor to disclose all material facts to the surety (*Seaton v Heath* [1899] 1 QB 782 at 792, per Romer LJ; revsd on the facts [1900] AC 135). However, by way of exception to this general rule, the creditor is under a duty to disclose to the surety unusual features of the transaction with the principal debtor which are unknown to the surety (*Hamilton v Watson* (1845) 12 Cl & Fin 109 at 119, per Lord Campbell). Thus, in *Levett v Barclays Bank plc* [1995] 1 WLR

1260, where the surety had allowed treasury stock to be used as security on the understanding that it would be returned to him unencumbered before the maturity date, and yet the contractual arrangements between the creditor and the principal debtor stipulated that the treasury stock should be used to repay the loan, Michael Burton QC, sitting as a deputy High Court judge, held that the creditor was under a duty to the surety to disclose such contractual arrangements which made the principal contract materially different in a potentially disadvantageous respect from the circumstances which the surety might naturally expect (at 1275). The deputy judge expressly left open what the position would have been if there had been something less than a contractual arrangement between the creditor and the principal debtor (at 1277). Later in *Crédit Lyonnaise Bank Nederland v Export Credit Guarantee Department* [1996] 1 Lloyd's Rep 200 (affd on other grounds, [1998] 1 Lloyd's Rep 19, CA, and [2000] 1 AC 486, HL), Longmore J also accepted the existence of the duty of disclosure, but limited it to cases of unusual features of the *transaction* between the creditor and the principal debtor and held that it did not extend to unusual features of the risk (eg that the creditor knew the principal debtor was an unreliable borrower). Yet in *Royal Bank of Scotland plc v Etridge (No 2)* [2001] UKHL 44, [2002] 2 AC 773, where Mrs Bennett gave the bank a guarantee of the indebtedness of her husband's company, the House of Lords held there had been actionable non-disclosure where the bank had failed to inform her that there was a ranking agreement between the bank and another lender, giving the latter priority over the bank's security from the company. This increased the likelihood that the bank might need to rely on Mrs Bennett's guarantee. But the finding of actionable non-disclosure may be criticised on the ground that a surety would generally be expected to inform herself of facts that affect the chances of the guarantee being called upon (see P Watts (2002) 118 LQR 351). The point would have been better dealt with not as one of actionable non-disclosure but as falling within the material that Mrs Bennett's solicitor needed to know in order to counteract the effect of her husband's undue influence (see above, p 660). Other exceptional circumstances where a creditor must make disclosure to a prospective surety are (1) where the creditor is asked a specific question about any matter material to the contract of suretyship (*Westminster Bank Ltd v Cond* (1940) 46 Com Cas 60); (2) where the creditor misleads the surety by volunteering only part of the truth (*Royal Bank of Scotland v Greenshields* 1914 SC 259); and (3) where the surety makes a statement in the creditor's presence showing that he entirely misunderstands the principal debtor's position (*Royal Bank of Scotland v Greenshields*). Misrepresentation and actionable non-disclosure allow the surety to rescind the contract of guarantee. English courts allow the guarantee to be set aside in full (see above, p 677) but this approach is not universally followed overseas (see P Watts [2002] CLJ 301).

(b) Form

Statute of Frauds 1677, s 4

4. No action against executors, etc, upon a special promise, or upon any agreement, or contract for sale of lands, etc, unless agreement, etc, be in writing, and signed.... noe action shall be brought...whereby to charge the defendant upon any speciall promise to answere for the debt default or miscarriages of another person...unlesse the agreement upon which such action shall be brought or some memorandum or note thereof shall be in writeing and signed by the partie to be charged therewith or some other person thereunto by him lawfully authorized.

Mercantile Law Amendment Act 1856, s 3

3. Written guarantee not to be invalid by reason that the consideration does not appear in writing. No special promise to be made by any person... to answer for the debt, default, or miscarriage of another person, being in writing, and signed by the party to be charged therewith, or some other person by him thereunto lawfully authorised, shall be deemed invalid to support an action, suit, or other proceeding to charge the person by whom such promise shall have been made, by reason only that the consideration for such promise does not appear in writing, or by necessary inference from a written document.

Actionstrength Ltd v International Glass Engineering IN.GL.EN SpA

[2003] UKHL 17, [2003] 2 AC 541, House of Lords

(The facts appear from Lord Bingham's judgment.)

Lord Bingham:

[1] My Lords, section 4 of the Statute of Frauds was enacted in 1677 to address a mischief facilitated, it seems, by the procedural deficiencies of the day (*Holdsworth, A History of English Law,* vol VI, pp 388–390): the calling of perjured evidence to prove spurious agreements said to have been made orally. The solution applied to the five classes of contract specified in section 4 was to require, as a condition of enforceability, some written memorandum or note of the agreement signed by the party to be charged under the agreement or his authorised agent.

[2] It quickly became evident that if the 17th century solution addressed one mischief it was capable of giving rise to another: that a party, making and acting on what was thought to be a binding oral agreement, would find his commercial expectations defeated when the time for enforcement came and the other party successfully relied on the lack of a written memorandum or note of the agreement.

[3] In one of the five specified classes of agreement, relating to contracts for the sale or other disposition of land, this second mischief was mitigated by the doctrine of part performance. Implementation of an agreement (even if partial) could be relied on to prove its existence. This doctrine was expressly preserved by section 40(2) of the Law of Property Act 1925, when section 4 of the Statute of Frauds (in its application to real property) was effectively re-enacted in section 40(1). A majority of the House gave the doctrine of part performance a broad interpretation in *Steadman v Steadman* [1976] AC 536. By section 2 of the Law of Property (Miscellaneous Provisions) Act 1989, following a report by the Law Commission (Transfer of Land: Formalities for Contracts for Sale Etc of Land) HC2), June '987 (Law Com No 264), section 40 of the 1925 Act was superseded by a requirement that contracts for the sale or other disposition of land should be made in writing.

[4] By the Law Reform (Enforcement of Contracts) Act 1954, section 4 of the Statute of Frauds was repealed in its application to three of the five classes originally specified. Section 4 now applies only to the class of agreement which is at issue in this appeal, an agreement under which it is sought 'to charge the defendant upon any special promise to answer for the debt, default or miscarriages of another person'.

[5] The facts assumed to be true for purposes of these proceedings at this stage have been helpfully summarised by Lord Walker of Gestingthorpe, whose summary I gratefully adopt and need not repeat. If tested at trial those facts might or might nor be established. But if, as must be assumed, they are correct, they illustrate the second mischief to which I have referred above. Actionstrength agreed with Inglen to supply labour to enable Inglen (the main contractor chosen by St-Gobain) to build a factory for St-Gobain. Inglen's deficiencies as a contractor led to Actionstrength being drawn, more closely than would be normal for a labour-only subcontractor, into the oversight of Inglen's performance. From an early date Actionstrength had difficulty obtaining payment by Inglen and considerable arrears built

up. Actionstrength was contractually entitled to terminate its contract with Inglen on 30 days' notice if duly approved invoices had not been paid within 30 days and remained unpaid. Such termination would have been seriously prejudicial to St-Gobain, whose interest was to take expeditious possession of a completed factory. Actionstrength threatened to withdraw its labour.

St-Gobain induced it not to do so by promising that, if Inglen did not pay Actionstrength any sums which were or became owing, it (St-Gobain) would do so. On that undertaking Actionstrength forebore to withdraw its labour and continued to supply labour to Inglen, whose indebtedness to Actionstrength increased fivefold over the weeks that followed. St-Gobain received the benefit of the work done by the labour which Actionstrength supplied. When Actionstrength, unable to obtain payment by Inglen, sought to enforce the agreement against St-Gobain, that company relied on the absence of a written memorandum or note of the agreement to defeat Actionstrength's claim.

[6] While section 4 of the Statute of Frauds has been repealed or replaced in its application to the other four classes of contract originally specified, it has been retained in relation to guarantees. In 1937 the Law Revision Committee (in its Sixth Interim Report, Statute of Frauds and the Doctrine of Consideration (Cmd 5449), paragraph 16) recommended the repeal of so much as remained of section 4. But a minority headed by Goddard J dissented in relation to guarantees, on the grounds (1) that there was a real danger of inexperienced people being led into undertaking obligations which they did not fully understand, and that opportunities would be given to the unscrupulous to assert that credit was given on the faith of a guarantee which the alleged surety had had no intention of giving; (2) that a guarantee was a special class of contract, being generally one-sided and disinterested as far as the surety was concerned, and the necessity of writing would give the proposed surety an opportunity for thought; (3) that the requirement of writing would ensure that the terms of the guarantee were settled and recorded; (4) that Parliament had imposed a requirement of writing in other contractual contexts; (5) that judges and juries were not infallible on questions of fact, and in the vast majority of cases the surety was getting nothing out of the bargain; (6) that it was desirable to protect the small man; and (7) that the necessity for guarantees to be in writing was generally understood. No action was taken on the 1937 report. In 1953 the Law Reform Committee (First Report, Statute of Frauds and Section of the Sale of Goods Act 1893 (Cmd 8809)) endorsed the recommendation of its predecessor that section 4 of the Statute of Frauds should be largely repealed but, agreeing with those who had earlier dissented, unanimously recommended that the section should continue to apply to guarantees. Effect was given to this report by enactment of the 1954 Act. Whatever the strength of the reasons given by the dissenting minority for retaining the old rule in relation to conventional consumer guarantees, it will be apparent that those reasons have little bearing on cases where the facts are such as those to be assumed here. It was not a bargain struck between inexperienced people, liable to misunderstand what they were doing. St-Gobain, as surety, had a very clear incentive to keep the Actionstrength workforce on site and, on the assumed facts, had an opportunity to think again. There is assumed to be no issue about the terms of the guarantee. English contract law does not ordinarily require writing as a condition of enforceability. It is not obvious why judges are more fallible when ruling on guarantees than other forms of oral contract. These were not small men in need of paternalist protection. While the familiar form of bank guarantee is well understood, it must be at least doubtful whether those who made the assumed agreement in this case appreciated that it was in law a guarantee. The judge at first instance was doubtful whether it was or not. The Court of Appeal reached the view that it was, but regarded the point as interesting and not entirely easy: [2002] 1 WLR 566,568, para 2. Two members of the court discussed the question at a little length, with detailed reference to authority.

[7] It may be questionable whether, in relation to contracts of guarantee, the mischief at which section 4 was originally aimed, is not now outweighed, at least in some classes of case, by the mischief to which it can give rise in a case such as the present, however unusual such cases may be. But that is not a question for the House in its judicial capacity. Sitting judicially, the House must of course give effect to the law of the land of which (in England and Wales) section 4 is part. As Mr McGhee for Actionstrength correctly recognised, that section is fatal to his client's claim unless St-Gobain can be shown to be estopped from relying on the section.

[8] Neither party suggested, nor could it be suggested, that the ordinary rules of estoppel are inapplicable to guarantees. The well known case of *Amalgamated Investment & Property Co Ltd v Texas Commerce International Bank Ltd* [1982] QB 84 is one in which a party was held to be estopped from disputing the assumed effect of a guarantee. But the same approach should be followed as in other cases. On the facts of this case that involves asking three questions. (1) What is the assumption which Actionstrength made? (2) Did St-Gobain induce or encourage the making of that assumption? (3) Is it in all the circumstances unconscionable for St-Gobain to place reliance on section 4? It would, as Mr Soole for St-Gobain submitted, be wrong in principle to ask the third question before both of the first two.

[9] It is implicit in the assumed facts that Actionstrength believed itself to be the beneficiary of an effective guarantee. Its difficulty, in my view insuperable, arises with the second question. For in seeking to show inducement or encouragement Actionstrength can rely on nothing beyond the oral agreement of St-Gobain which, in the absence of writing, is rendered unenforceable by section 4. There was no representation by St-Gobain that it would honour the agreement despite the absence of writing, or that it was not a contract of guarantee, or that it would confirm the agreement in writing. Nor did St-Gobain make any payment direct to Actionstrength which could arguably be relied on as affirming the oral agreement or inducing Actionstrength to go on supplying labour. If St-Gobain were held to be estopped in this case it is hard to see why any oral guarantor, where credit was extended to a debtor on the strength of a guarantee, would not be similarly estopped. The result would be to render nugatory a provision which, despite its age, Parliament has deliberately chosen to retain.

[10] For these reasons, and those given by Lord Hoffmann, Lord Clyde and Lord Walker of Gestingthorpe, with which I agree, I am of the reluctant but clear opinion that the appeal must be dismissed. I agree with the order which Lord Walker proposes.

Lord Clyde: ...

[34] It does not seem to me necessary to resolve the question whether or not there may be cases where a guarantor may be estopped from invoking section 4 of the Statute of Frauds 1677. I am content to proceed upon the assumption that there may be such a case. As it seems to me, the present case can be resolved on its own circumstances without exploring the wider issues of law. The contract in the present case may be taken to have been constituted by the undertaking given by the second defendant and the actings of the claimant in keeping its workforce on site and continuing to work there. The distinct question arises whether the agreement is enforceable. To that question, in the absence of any writing, the Statute of Frauds gives a negative answer. Without entering into questions of the categorisation of different classes of estoppel, it seems to me that some recognisable structural framework must be established before recourse is had to the underlying idea of unconscionable conduct in the particular circumstances. The framework here should include the following elements: that Actionstrength assumed that St-Gobain would honour the guarantee; that that assumption was induced or encouraged by St-Gobain; and that Actionstrength relied on that assumption.

[35] The short answer to the case in my view is that these factors cannot all be found in the material before us, and in particular in the pleadings. The only assurance given to Actionstrength was the promise itself. In order to be estopped from invoking the Statute there must be something more, such as some additional encouragement, inducement or assurance. In addition to the promise there must be some influence exerted by St-Gobain on Actionstrength to lead it to assume that the promise would be honoured. But there is no suggestion made that St-Gobain said or did anything to lead Actionstrength to assume that St-Gobain would not stand on its rights. Nor is St-Gobain said to have done anything which would foster such an assumption. Further the acts of Actionstrength in keeping the labour force on site and continuing to work do not demonstrate a reliance on some assumption of the enforceability of the guarantee. The acts may have followed upon the giving of the verbal promise and they could operate to support the conclusion of the contract. But they do not necessarily relate to an assumption of the enforceability of that contract. They are essentially no different from the acts which any creditor would normally carry out after a surety has given him some guarantee relating to his provision of credit.

[36] For these reasons I agree that the appeal should be dismissed.

Lord Walker: ...

[47] Mr McGhee made clear in his opening submissions (and confirmed in his reply) that he was not relying on proprietary estoppel, or on the equitable doctrine of part performance. But it is worth noting that the doctrine of part performance was developed not as the enforcement of a contract which Parliament had made unenforceable, but as an action on the equities arising out of what had been done towards performance of the oral contract. Granting relief on the strength of those equities was regarded as involving no inconsistency with the Statute of Frauds. Indeed Lord Simon of Glaisdale said in *Steadman v Steadman* [1976] AC 536, 559, in relation to the famous speech by the Earl of Selborne LC in *Maddison v Alderson* (1883) 8 App Cas 467, 475–476, that it achieved 'a complete reconciliation between the provisions of the Statute and the doctrine of part performance'.

[48] Since part performance of an oral contract for the sale of land was an equitable doctrine, the equitable remedy of specific performance was the only relief available. In this case Actionstrength was claiming a liquidated sum (about £1.3m) and that is no doubt part of the reason why Mr McGhee did not seek to rely on part performance. Another reason may be the difficulty (even with the apparent liberalisation effected by *Steadman v Steadman*) of showing that what Actionstrength did, after 11 February 2000, was referable to its pleaded oral contract with St-Gobain (rather than to its written contract with Inglen).

[49] Instead Mr McGhee relied on the broad general principle as to estoppel stated by Oliver J in *Taylors Fashions Ltd v Liverpool Victoria Trustees Co Ltd (Note)* [1982] QB 133 (and since approved and followed by many higher courts). Mr McGhee submitted that this is not a case (such as those referred to by Viscount Radcliffe in *Kok Hoong v Leong Cheong Kweng Mines Ltd* [1964] AC 993, 1015 -1018) in which a clear public policy underlying a statute (for instance, the need to protect vulnerable persons dealing with moneylenders or landlords) prevents an estoppel arising. That appeared not to be in dispute. But Mr McGhee still had to demonstrate how the estoppel which he contended for could take effect (otherwise than through an equitable doctrine for which he did not contend) in a way which is consistent with the provisions of section 4 and does not deprive the section of any real effect.

[50] Mr McGhee accepted that there appears to be no English case (indeed, so far as his researches have gone, no case in any jurisdiction) in which an oral contract of guarantee has been enforced through the medium of an estoppel. However, your Lordships' attention was drawn to two recent decisions which were put forward as offering some assistance. The first is *Bank of Scotland v Wright* [1991] BCLC 244. In that case a director of two companies (one a subsidiary of the other) had given the bank a written guarantee of the liability of the holding company (only); but under an 'interavailable' facility backed by cross-guarantees (by the companies) the holding company was liable for the subsidiary's indebtedness to the bank. When the bank sued the individual guarantor for the whole of the corporate indebtedness there were two issues, the construction of the guarantee and (if the bank failed on that point) estoppel by convention. Brooke J decided the first point in favour of the bank, and said cautiously on the second, at p 266 (after referring to what Viscount Radcliffe said in *Kok Hoong* and to *Humphries v Humphries* [1910] 2 KB 531):

> 'In the light of these authorities I would not exclude the possibility that circumstances might arise in which a guarantor might have acted in such a way as to create or influence the other party's mistaken belief in the effectiveness of his guarantee so that it would be unconscionable to allow him to rely on the Statute of Frauds. Such a finding would depend very much on the court's views, on the facts of any particular case, of the personalities and attributes of the two parties between whom the alleged estoppel was alleged to have arisen.'

I see no reason to disagree with those observations, but they presuppose some sort of representation by the guarantor, together with unconscionability; not just unconscionability on its own.

[51] The other case is *Shah v Shah* [2002] QB 35. There the Court of Appeal was concerned with section 1 of the Law of Property (Miscellaneous Provisions) Act 1989; relating to the execution of deeds. Section 1(3) requires a deed made by an individual to be signed: '(i) by him in the presence of a witness who attests the signature; or (ii) at his direction and in his presence and the presence of two witnesses who each attest the signature.' The deed in question appeared on its face to comply with these requirements, but the evidence was that the witness to the signatures of two of the defendants had nor signed in their presence (but shortly afterwards, nor in their presence). Pill LJ (with whom Tuckey LJ and Sir Christopher Slade agreed) said, at p 41, para 13: 'The delivery of the document constituted an unambiguous representation of fact that it was a deed.' He saw no reason of policy to exclude the operation of an estoppel. I do nor think that this case helps Actionstrength, any more than *Bank of Scotland v Wright* does. In *Shah v Shah* the delivery of an apparently valid deed constituted an unambiguous representation of its nature. In the present case, by contrast, what passed between the parties (as pleaded by Actionstrength and as set our in Mr Sutcliffe's witness statement) did not amount to an unambiguous representation that there was an enforceable contract, or that St-Gobain would not take any point on section 4 of the Statute of Frauds.

[52] That is the point which Mr Soole (for St-Gobain) rightly put in the forefront of his submissions as what he called the short answer to the appeal. He was willing to concede (in line with what Brooke J said in *Bank of Scotland v Wright*) that an explicit assurance that St-Gobain would not plead the Statute of Frauds (like an explicit assurance not to take a limitation point) could found an estoppel. But it would wholly frustrate the continued operation of section 4 in relation to contracts of guarantee if an oral promise were to be treated, without more, as somehow carrying in itself a representation that the promise would be treated as enforceable.

[53] To treat the very same facts as creating as an unenforceable oral contract and as amounting to a representation (enforceable as soon as relied on) that the contract would be enforceable, despite section 4—and to do so while disavowing any reliance on the doctrine of part performance—would be to subvert the whole force of the section as it remains in operation, by Parliament's considered choice, in relation to contracts of guarantee. It would be comparable (in a non-statutory context) to treating the mere fact of a mistaken payment made by A to B as importing a representation by A that the money was indeed due to B, so as to create an estoppel if B (relying on the implicit assurance) acted to his detriment by spending even part of the money.

[54] Mr Soole's submissions appear to me to be unanswerable, and I do nor think it is necessary to go on to what he called his longer answer to the appeal. I quite see that the pleaded oral contract of guarantee is an unusual one, said to have been entered into by a company whose economic strength is no doubt much greater than that of most guaranrors. St-Gobain does appear (again, on Actionstrength's pleaded case) to have obtained the benefit of about a month's work on its factory which might not otherwise have been performed. But in the absence of any assurance (other than the bare oral promise itself) the degree of detrimental reliance on the part of Actionstrength is irrelevant. I think that Simon Brown LJ was right in describing Actionstrength's case on estoppel as hopeless.

[55] I have had the advantage of reading in draft the speeches prepared by my noble and learned friends, Lord Bingham of Cornhill and Lord Hoffmann. I agree with them, and for the reasons which they give, as well as for those set out above, I would dismiss this appeal. I would order the appellant to pay the respondent's costs before your Lordship's House.

[Lord Hoffmann delivered a concurring judgment.
Lord Woolf concurred.]

NOTES

1.   In *J Pereira Fernandes SA v Mehta* [2006] EWHC 813 (Ch), [2006] 1 WLR 1543, Judge Pelling QC, sitting as a judge of the High Court, held that while an e-mail could be sufficient writing for the purposes of s 4, the automatic inclusion of the sender's return e-mail address

in the header did not constitute a signature sufficient to satisfy the section. However, the judge (at [30]) accepted that: 'if a party or a party's agent sending an e-mail types his or her or his or her principal's name to the extent required or permitted by existing case law in the body of an e-mail, then…that would be a sufficient signature for the purposes of s 4'.

2. Section 4 prescribes two ways of achieving enforceability of a guarantee. Thus, in *Elpis Maritime Co Ltd v Marti Chartering Co Inc, The Maria D* [1992] 1 AC 21, the defendant brokers, who were acting for charterers during the negotiation of a charterparty, orally guaranteed payment of demurrage and freight by the charterers to the plaintiff shipowners. The guarantee was later embodied in the terms of the written charterparty made with the shipowners. The first page of the charterparty was signed by the brokers in such a way that indicated that they were acting as agents for the charterers, but all other pages, including the one containing the guarantee, were signed by them without any indication whether they were signing as the charterers' agents. The House of Lords held that the guarantee was enforceable against the brokers. On the assumption that the brokers signed the page of the charterparty containing the guarantee as a contracting party, the prior oral agreement of guarantee was subsumed in the later written agreement, and the written agreement, being signed by the brokers, complied with the first of the two ways of achieving enforceability prescribed by s 4 of the Statute of Frauds. Alternatively, on the assumption that the brokers signed the relevant page as agents for the charterers, so that they were not a contracting party, the relevant page of the charterparty nevertheless contained a sufficient memorandum or note of the prior oral agreement of guarantee signed by the party to be charged, so as to satisfy the second requirement for achieving enforceability prescribed by s 4. The intention with which, or the capacity in which, the brokers signed the relevant page of the charterparty was wholly irrelevant to the question whether there had been compliance with s 4 (per Lord Brandon, at 32–33). What would have been the result of this case if there had been no prior oral agreement, the brokers' guarantee had been contained solely in the written charterparty, and the brokers had signed the charterparty as agents of the charterers?

3. A subsequent agreement to vary the terms of a contract of guarantee must also comply with s 4 if the variation is to be enforceable. If the variation does not comply with s 4, the original contract of guarantee remains enforceable, assuming it complies with s 4, as if it had not been varied (*Morris v Baron & Co* [1918] AC 1 at 16). But an oral variation may be set up by the surety as a defence to a claim brought on the original contract of guarantee (*Re A Debtor (No 517 of 1991)* (1991) Times, 25 November). Section 4 does not apply to a subsequent agreement to terminate or avoid a contract of guarantee (*Morris v Baron & Co*, above).

4. Section 4 does not apply to a variation of the underlying contract between the creditor and the principal debtor. In *Crédit Suisse v Borough Council of Allerdale* [1995] 1 Lloyd's Rep 315 (affd on other grounds [1996] 2 Lloyd's Rep 241), Coleman J held that where a surety consents to a material variation of the underlying contract, and thereby loses his right to be discharged from liability, no new guarantee is created and there need be no further compliance with s 4 as the creditor sues on the original guarantee (at 370–371). Coleman J also held that where the surety does not consent to a material variation of the underlying contract, s 4 does not preclude reliance on an estoppel which would prevent the surety relying on such a material alteration (at 371–372).

5. Where, as a result of a shared mistake, the written guarantee does not record the common intention of the parties, the court may exercise its equitable jurisdiction to rectify the guarantee to accord with such common intention, and this does not offend against s 4 of the Statute of Frauds because a claim for rectification of a guarantee is not an 'action…

brought…whereby to charge the defendant upon' the guarantee (*GMAC Commercial Credit Development Ltd v Sandhu* [2004] EWHC 716 (Comm), [2006] 1 All ER (Comm) 268 at [58]).

6.　　Section 4 does not apply where the surety is a non-natural person (eg company or unincorporated association) providing financial collateral (meaning cash or financial instruments such as shares) as part of a security or title transfer financial collateral arrangement (Financial Collateral Arrangements (No 2) Regulations 2003, SI 2003/3226, reg 4). But the financial collateral arrangement itself must be evidenced in writing (reg 3). These regulations implement EC Directive 2002/47 on financial collateral arrangements and have important practical implications for banks, securities firms and other takers of financial collateral in the banking, derivatives, foreign exchanges, securities and commodities trading and repo, prime brokerage and related financial markets.

Other statutory requirements

Section 105(1) of the Consumer Credit Act 1974 provides that any security (including a guarantee or indemnity) provided in relation to a consumer credit or consumer hire agreement must be in writing (unless it is provided by the debtor or hirer: sub-s (6)). Any contract of guarantee or indemnity caught by sub-s (1) must contain all the express terms of the contract, be signed by or on behalf of the surety, and be in a readily legible form when it is presented to or sent to the surety for his signature (sub-s (4)). If the creditor fails to comply with any of these requirements he must obtain a court order before he can enforce the security against the surety (sub-s (7)). The form and contents of contracts of guarantee and indemnity caught by s 105(1) are regulated by statutory instrument (see generally, G Andrews and R Millett *Law of Guarantees* (5th edn, 2008), Ch 17).

QUESTION

In *Technology Partnership plc v Afro-Asian Communications (UK) Ltd* (12 October 1998, unreported), the defendant applied to strike out the plaintiff's claim that he had personally guaranteed payment for work done by the plaintiff for the defendant's company. Even if the defendant had given an oral warranty to this effect, which was disputed, the Court of Appeal struck out the claim on the ground that there had been a failure to comply with s 4 of the Statute of Frauds. However, during the course of delivering his judgment, Peter Gibson LJ made the following observation:

It is unfortunate that by reason of section 4 [the defendant] escapes the possibility of being held personally liable for his word. I would, for my part, question whether today it is still necessary to give special protection for those who give guarantees. Lord Blackburn in *Steele v M'Kinlay* [1880] 5 App Cas 754 at 768 gave as the reason for the enactment of section 4:

It was thought by the English Legislature that there was a danger of contracts of particular kinds being established by false evidence, or by evidence of loose talk when it was never really meant to make such a contract.

Take a case, admittedly not the present case on the evidence before us, where there can be no doubt as to the oral agreement or as to its terms. For my part, I cannot see why it should be necessary to have the formality of a written memorandum in addition. It may well be that some protection is required for guarantors, such as the possibility of being able to escape from the guarantee within a limited period. But it does seem to me to be arguable that the sanction contained in section 4 is out of all proportion to the mischief which it was originally intended to combat.

By contrast, Pill LJ took a different view:

For my part, I see a practical purpose in the existence of safeguards for those alleged to be guarantors. I do not condone or support the conduct of [the defendant]. Nevertheless the present case does illustrate the type of misunderstanding which may occur and may occur in the case of a vulnerable person (which [the defendant] was not) when it is sought to make someone a guarantor of the debts of some other party. Safeguards in similar situations are provided in the modern law in a number of ways, including the provision of a cooling-off period in some circumstances, as Peter Gibson LJ has indicated. I am not persuaded by anything in this case that it would in modern conditions be safe or appropriate to permit a contract of guarantee to be established merely by oral evidence.

Is it time to repeal s 4 of the Statute of Frauds?

(c) Construction

It is a well-established rule that contracts of guarantee are strictly construed in favour of the surety (*Blest v Brown* (1862) 4 De GF & J 367 at 376, per Lord Campbell). But will the courts maintain a strict approach to the construction of guarantees in the face of the modern approach to the construction of contracts generally? The modern approach to construction of contracts generally can be found in the speech of Lord Hoffmann in *Investors Compensation Scheme Ltd v West Bromwich Building Society* [1998] 1 WLR 896 at 912-913 (see above, p 22). According to the modern approach:

against the background of the admissible matrix of facts know to or at least reasonably available to the parties, the meaning sought is what the language in question would convey to the reasonable man. In that context, the language used is to be given its natural and ordinary meaning, unless the reasonable man would conclude that something has gone wrong in expressing the parties' intentions.

These are the words of Rix LJ in *Liberty Mutual Insurance Co (UK) Ltd v HSBC Bank plc* [2002] EWCA Civ 691 at [54]. However, in that case the Court of Appeal held that this approach is not inconsistent with the maxim of construction which requires 'strict words' to exclude or limit prevailing rules, since, again in the words of Rix LJ (at [56]), 'the reasonable man does not expect fundamental principles of law, equity and justice, such as rights of set-off or of subrogation to be excluded unless the contract clearly says so'.

The Court of Appeal has confirmed that the modern approach to the construction of contracts, summarised by Lord Hoffmann in *ICS v West Bromwich Building Society*, extends to the construction of guarantees. In *Static Control Components (Europe) Ltd v Egan* [2004] EWCA Civ 392, [2004] 2 Lloyd's Rep 429, the question was whether a guarantee in respect of 'the price of all trade goods that you may supply to [the principal debtor]' applied to past debts in respect of goods supplied as well as future ones. The Court of Appeal held that it did. Their Lordships agreed that the principles of contractual construction set out in *ICS v West Bromwich Building Society* applied to contracts of guarantee, even though there was no ambiguity in the words used in the document. The court examined the background knowledge or matrix of fact, which included the fact the guarantee had been preceded by a guarantee for a lesser amount in respect of existing debts, and held that any reasonable person, informed by the background, would have seen no commercial sense in increasing the limit of the guarantee and yet limiting it only to future sales. Their Lordships rejected the surety's submission that this approach was 'creative' or involved 'rewriting' the guarantee and failed to respect the approach of construing a guarantee strictly. Holman J stated (at [19]) that there had been no creativity or rewriting but simply ascertainment of the meaning of the document by the objective approach described by Lord Hoffmann, and added: 'that being the task, it may be that the concept that a guarantee should be 'strictly construed' now adds nothing.' Arden LJ (at [37]) addressed the surety's submission that the guarantee was to be construed *contra proferentem*, that is against the creditor who produced it for the surety to sign. She noted that the *contra proferentem* rule only applied if a document, properly interpreted, admitted of doubt. In this case, she held that the issue was as to the scope of the guarantee and that that issue could be resolved by reference to the relevant background evidence. In this situation, the *contra proferentem* rule had no place.

By contrast, in *Dumford Trading AG v OAO Atlantrybflot* [2005] EWCA Civ 25, [2005] 1 Lloyd's Rep 289, on an application for summary judgment, a differently constituted Court of Appeal considered that (apart from the doctrines of rectification or misnomer), where an existing person was named as guarantor in the guarantee document, there was a danger that extrinsic evidence from the surrounding matrix of fact could create an ambiguity otherwise not present. Where, therefore, company A in a group of companies was identified by the document of guarantee, the court should not look at extrinsic evidence, such as the postal address of the company, so as to construe this unambiguous reference as being to company B, a very similarly-named company in the same group. However, where there is ambiguity on the face of the guarantee the situation will be treated differently. In *Gastronome (UK) Ltd v Anglo Dutch Meats (UK) Ltd* [2006] EWCA Civ 1233, [2006] 2 Lloyd's Rep 587, the Court of Appeal had recourse to extrinsic evidence to identify the entity which was to have the benefit of a guarantee that was ambiguous on its face. In that case the guarantee was contained in a letter addressed to 'Gastronome', but there was no particular company or legal entity of that name. Nevertheless, when construed against the relevant background, the Court of Appeal held that it was indisputable that the commercial purpose of the guarantee was to ensure that the claimant's invoices would be paid for products it supplied to the surety's subsidiary if the subsidiary failed to do so.

An interesting issue, raised by the application of *ICS v West Bromwich Building Society* principles to contracts of guarantee, is identified by the editors of *Chitty on Contracts* (29th edn, 2004) at para 44-057, fn 277, in the following terms:

In the case of a guarantee (as opposed to an indemnity) there is the additional problem in that s 4 of the Statute of Frauds requires that the written agreement or memorandum contains a statement of its material terms: *quaere* whether this would be the case if a written term did not clearly state the ambit of the liability undertaken. For this reason, at least as regards the material terms of contracts of guarantee, if a court concludes 'that the parties must, for whatever reason, have used the wrong words or syntax' (*ICS v West Bromwich Building Society* at 913, per Lord Hoffmann), then the contract itself may be unenforceable for lack of fulfilment of the formal requirements contained in s 4.

We disagree with this assessment for two reasons. First, in a case such as this the court is doing no more than construing the words of the written agreement; it is not purporting to re-write the agreement for the parties. This does not appear to offend the mischief against which s 4 of the Statute of Frauds (see above, p 1161) was originally aimed, namely 'the calling of perjured evidence to prove spurious agreements said to have been made orally' (*Actionstrength Ltd v International Glass Engineering IN.GL.EN SpA* [2003] UKHL 17, [2003] 2 AC 541 at [1], per Lord Bingham). Secondly, as we have already seen (above, p 1167), it is in any event possible for mistakes as to the words used by the parties to be rectified by the courts without engaging s 4.

6 RELATIONS BETWEEN CREDITOR AND SURETY

(a) The nature and extent of the surety's liability

Moschi v Lep Air Services Ltd
[1973] AC 331, House of Lords

The respondent creditors agreed to give up liens held by them over goods supplied to the principal debtor in consideration of the principal debtor's agreement to pay £40,000 to the creditors by weekly instalments. The appellant guaranteed the performance by the principal debtor of its obligation to make the specified payments. The principal debtor repeatedly failed to pay any of the instalments. The creditors treated these breaches of contract as a repudiation and accepted it. They then sued the guarantor for the full amount of the weekly instalments, ie for those instalments which had become due and those which would have become due if the principal debtor's repudiation had not been accepted. The House of Lords, affirming the decision of the Court of Appeal, upheld the creditors' claim.

Lord Reid: The first contention of the appellant is that he is under no liability to pay anything because his obligation under clause (XIII) was discharged by the action of the respondents in accepting the company's repudiation and so bringing the contract to an end. He supports this startling contention by relying on the principle that if a creditor agrees to a variation of the debtor's contract he thereby discharges a guarantor from liability. He argues that acceptance of a repudiation should be regarded as equivalent to a variation of the contract. I agree with your Lordships that there is no substance in this argument and I reject it.

His next argument is more formidable. He says, look at clause (XIII). It merely guarantees that each instalment of £6,000 shall be duly paid. But by reason of the accepted repudiation the contract was brought to an end before the later instalments became payable. So they never did become payable. All that remained after the contract was terminated was a claim for damages. But I never guaranteed to pay damages. If the creditor chooses to act so that future instalments are not payable by the debtor he cannot recover them from me.

To meet that argument I think that it is necessary to see what in fact the appellant did undertake to do. I would not proceed by saying this is a contract of guarantee and there is a general rule applicable to all guarantees. Parties are free to make any agreement they like and we must I think determine just what this agreement means.

With regard to making good to the creditor payments of instalments by the principal debtor there are at least two possible forms of agreement. A person might undertake no more than that if the principal debtor fails to pay any instalment he will pay it. That would be a conditional agreement. There would be no prestable obligation unless and until the debtor failed to pay. There would then on the debtor's failure arise an obligation to pay. If for any reason the debtor ceased to have any obligation to pay the instalment on the due date then he could not fail to pay it on that date. The condition attached to the undertaking would never be purified and the subsidiary obligation would never arise.

On the other hand, the guarantor's obligation might be of a different kind. He might undertake that the principal debtor will carry out his contract. Then if at any time and for any reason the principal debtor acts or fails to act as required by his contract, he not only breaks his own contract but he also puts the guarantor in breach of his contract of guarantee. Then the creditor can sue the guarantor, not for the unpaid instalment but for damages. His contract being that the principal debtor would carry out the principal contract, the damages payable by the guarantor must then be the loss suffered by the creditor due to the principal debtor having failed to do what the guarantor undertook that he would do.

In my view, the appellant's contract is of the latter type. He 'personally guaranteed the performance' by the company 'of its obligation to make the payments at the rate of £6,000 per week.' The rest of the clause does not alter that obligation. So he was in breach of his contract as soon as the company fell into arrears with its payment of the instalments. The guarantor, the appellant, then became liable to the creditor, the respondents, in damages. Those damages were the loss suffered by the creditor by reason of the company's breach. It is not and could not be suggested that by accepting the company's repudiation the creditor in any way increased his loss. The creditor lost more than the maximum which the appellant guaranteed and it appears to me that the whole loss was caused by the debtor having failed to carry out his contract. That being so, the appellant became liable to pay as damages for his breach of contract of guarantee the whole loss up to the maximum of £40,000.

Lord Diplock: The law of guarantee is part of the law of contract. The law of contract is part of the law of obligations. The English law of obligations is about their sources and the remedies which the court can grant to the obligee for a failure by the obligor to perform his obligation voluntarily. Obligations which are performed voluntarily require no intervention by a court of law. They do not give rise to any cause of action.

English law is thus concerned with contracts as a source of obligations. The basic principle which the law of contract seeks to enforce is that a person who makes a promise to another ought to keep his promise. This basic principle is subject to an historical exception that English law does not give the promisee a remedy for the failure by a promisor to perform his promise unless either the promise was made in a particular form, eg under seal, or the promisee in return promises to do something for the promisor which he would not otherwise be obliged to do, ie, gives consideration for the promise. The contract which gives rise to the instant appeal does not fall within this exception. In return for the guarantor's promise to the creditor the latter promised to extend credit to the debtor and to release his lien upon the debtor's goods.

Each promise that a promisor makes to a promisee by entering into a contract with him creates an obligation to perform it owed by the promisor as obligor to the promisee as obligee. If he does not do so voluntarily there are two kinds of remedies which the court can grant to the promisee. It can compel the obligor to pay to the obligee a sum of money to compensate him for the loss that he has sustained as a result of the obligee's failure to perform his obligation. This is the remedy at common law in damages for breach of contract. But there are some kinds of obligation which the court is able to compel the obligor actually to perform. In some cases, such as obligations to transfer title or possession of property to the obligee or to refrain from doing something to the detriment of the obligee, a remedy to compel performance by a decree of specific performance or by injunction is also available. It was formerly obtainable only in a court of equity. In these cases it was an alternative remedy to that of damages for breach of contract obtainable only in a court of common law. But, since a court of common law could make and enforce orders for payment of a sum of money, where the obligation was itself an obligation to pay a sum of money, even a court of common law could compel the obligor to perform it. Historically this was the only remedy which the court would grant at common law when an obligor failed to perform this kind of obligation. The remedy of damages for non-performance of the obligation was not available as an alternative.

It ceased to be important to identify an obligation which the obligor had failed to perform as being an obligation to pay a sum of money after the Judicature Act of 1875 had abolished the necessity for a plaintiff to select the form of action appropriate to his claim. But before the Common Law Procedure Acts 1852 to 1860 there were important procedural differences between an action brought to compel performance of the obligation arising from a promise to pay a sum of money for which the form of action was indebitatus assumpsit, and an action brought to recover compensation for the loss sustained as a result of the obligor's failure to perform any other kind of obligation arising out of contractual promises—for which the form of action was a special assumpsit.

In the absence of modern authority it becomes necessary to go back a century or more to see whether a contractual promise by the guarantor to guarantee to the creditor that the debtor would perform his own obligations to the creditor to pay a sum of money to him was itself classified as giving rise to an obligation on the part of the guarantor to pay that sum of money to the creditor if the debtor did not do so, or as an obligation to see to it that the debtor did perform his own obligations to the creditor.

In s 4 of the Statute of Frauds 1677 a contract of guarantee is described in the language of the 17th century as 'any special promise to answer for the debt, default or miscarriage of another person.' Translated into modern legal terminology 'to answer for' is 'to accept liability for,' and 'debt, default or miscarriage' is descriptive of failure to perform legal obligations, existing and future, arising from any source, not only from contractual promises but in any other factual situations capable of giving rise to legal obligations such as those resulting from bailment, tort, or unsatisfied judgments. These words were so construed by Abbott CJ in *Kirkham v Marter* (1819) 2 B & Ald 613, 616.

By the beginning of the 19th century it appears to have been taken for granted, without need for any citation of authority, that the contractual promise of a guarantor to guarantee the performance by a debtor of his obligations to a creditor arising out of contract gave rise to an obligation on the part of the guarantor to see to it that the debtor performed his own obligations to the creditor. Statements to this effect are to be found in *Wright v Simpson* (1802) 6 Ves 714, 734, per Lord Eldon and in *Re Lockey* (1845) 1 Ph 509, 511, per Lord Lyndhurst. These are the two cases which are cited as authority for this proposition by Sir Sidney Rowlatt in his authoritative work on *Principal and Surety*. They can be supplemented by other similar statements, including one in your Lordships' House, which confirm that it was taken for granted that this was the legal nature of the guarantor's obligation arising out of a contract of guarantee: *Mactaggart v Watson* (1836) 3 Cl & Fin 525, 540, per Lord Brougham.

It is because the obligation of the guarantor is to see to it that the debtor performed his own obligations to the creditor that the guarantor is not entitled to notice from the creditor of the debtor's failure to perform an obligation which is the subject of the guarantee, and that the creditor's cause of action against the guarantor arises at the moment of the debtor's default and the limitation period then starts to run. It is also why, where the contract of guarantee was entered into by the guarantor at the debtor's request, the guarantor has a right in equity to compel the debtor to perform his own obligation to the creditor if it is of a kind in which a court of equity is able to compel performance: see *Ascherson v Tredegar Dry Dock and Wharf Co Ltd* [1909] 2 Ch 401. It is the existence of this right on the part of the guarantor that accounts for the rule laid down by Lord Eldon in *Samuell v Howarth* (1817) 3 Mer 272, 278 and approved by your Lordships' House in *Creighton v Rankin* (1840) 7 Cl & F 325, 346 that where the creditor, after the guarantee has been entered into, gives a contractual promise to the debtor to allow him time to pay the guaranteed debt, the guarantor is discharged from his obligation to the creditor. This is because the creditor by altering the debtor's obligation to him has deprived the guarantor of his equitable right to compel the debtor to perform his original obligation to the creditor, which was all that the guarantor had guaranteed. In contrast, the guarantor is not discharged by the mere voluntary forbearance of the creditor to take steps to obtain timeous performance by the debtor of the obligation which is the subject of the guarantee; for this does not affect the guarantor's equitable right to compel the debtor to perform it.

It follows from the legal nature of the obligation of the guarantor to which a contract of guarantee gives rise that it is not an obligation himself to pay a sum of money to the creditor, but an obligation to see to it that another person, the debtor, does something; and that the creditor's remedy for the guarantor's failure to perform it lies in damages for breach of contract only. That this was so, even where the debtor's own obligation that was the subject of the guarantee was to pay a sum of money, is clear from the fact that formerly the form of action against the guarantor which was available to the creditor was in special assumpsit and not in indebitatus assumpsit: *Mines v Sculthorpe* (1809) 2 Camp 215.

The legal consequence of this is that whenever the debtor has failed voluntarily to perform an obligation which is the subject of the guarantee the creditor can recover from the guarantor as damages for breach of his contract of guarantee whatever sum the creditor could have recovered from the debtor himself as a consequence of that failure. The debtor's liability to the creditor is also the measure of the guarantor's.

Whether any particular contractual promise is to be classified as a guarantee so as to attract all or any of the legal consequences to which I have referred depends upon the words in which the parties have expressed the promise. Even the use of the word 'guarantee' is not in itself conclusive. It is often used loosely in commercial dealings to mean an ordinary warranty. It is sometimes used to mis-describe what is in law a contract of indemnity and not of guarantee. Where the contractual promise can be correctly classified as a guarantee it is open to the parties expressly to exclude or vary any of their mutual rights or obligations which would otherwise result from its being classifiable as a guarantee. Every case must depend upon the true construction of the actual words in which the promise is expressed.

In the instant appeal, however, the actual words used are simple, unambiguous, and contain no qualification except to impose a limit upon the guarantor's maximum liability under the guarantee.

The particular obligation of the debtor of which performance was guaranteed was to satisfy an existing debt to the creditor by instalments to be paid in the future. It arose from one of a number of inter-related mutual promises made by the debtor to the creditor and by the creditor to the debtor all of which were contained in a single contract; but the guarantor did not guarantee performance by the debtor of any obligations arising from any of his other promises. As between the debtor and the creditor all their obligations to one another to which their mutual promises gave rise, including the particular obligation of which performance was guaranteed by the guarantor, possessed the characteristics which the law ascribes to obligations whose common source is the same contract.

The debtor failed to perform voluntarily many of his obligations under the contract—both the obligation of which performance was guaranteed and other obligations. The cumulative effect of these failures by December 22, 1967, was to deprive the creditor of substantially the whole benefit which it was the intention of the parties that he should obtain from the contract. The creditor accordingly became entitled, although not bound, to treat the contract as rescinded: see *Hongkong Fir Shipping Co v Kawasaki Risen Kaisha Ltd* [1962] 2 QB 26. He elected to do so on that date. It was held by the official referee and by the Court of Appeal, in my view rightly, that the debtor's failures to pay the instalments of the existing debt were in themselves sufficient to deprive the creditor of substantially the whole benefit which it was the intention of the parties that he should obtain from the contract, even if his failures to perform other obligations were left out of account.

My Lords, it has become usual to speak of the exercise by one party to a contract of his right to treat the contract as rescinded in circumstances such as these, as an 'acceptance' of the wrongful repudiation of the contract by the other party as a rescission of the contract. But it would be quite erroneous to suppose that any fresh agreement between the parties or any variation of the terms of the original contract is involved when the party who is not in default elects to exercise his right to treat the contract as rescinded because of a repudiatory breach of the contract by the other party. He is exercising a right conferred upon him by law of which the sole source is the original contract. He is not varying that contract; he is enforcing it.

It is no doubt convenient to speak of a contract as being terminated or coming to an end when the party who is not in default exercises his right to treat it as rescinded. But the law is concerned with the effect of that election upon those obligations of the parties of which the contract was the source, and this depends upon the nature of the particular obligation and upon which party promised to perform it.

Generally speaking, the rescission of the contract puts an end to the primary obligations of the party not in default to perform any of his contractual promises which he has not already performed by the time of the rescission. It deprives him of any right as against the other party to continue to perform them. It does not give rise to any secondary obligation in substitution for a primary obligation which has come to an end. The primary obligations of the party in default to perform any of the promises made by him and remaining unperformed likewise come to an end as does his right to continue to perform them. But for his primary obligations there is substituted by operation of law a secondary obligation to pay to the other party a sum of money to compensate him for the loss he has sustained as a result of the failure to perform the primary obligations. This secondary obligation is just as much an obligation arising from the contract as are the primary obligations that it replaces: see *R V Ward Ltd v Bignall* [1967] 1 QB 534, 548.

Although this is the general rule as to the effect of rescission of the contract upon obligations of which it was the source, there may be exceptional primary obligations which continue to exist notwithstanding that the contract has been rescinded. These are obligations that are ancillary to the main purpose of the contract—which is, of course, that the parties should perform their primary obligations voluntarily. Mutual promises to submit to arbitration disputes arising as to the performance by the parties of their other obligations arising from the contract may be expressed in terms which make it clear that it was the common intention of the parties that their primary obligation to continue to perform these promises should continue notwithstanding that their other primary obligations had come to an end: *Heyman v Darwins Ltd* [1942] AC 356.

But this is the exception. Although in the instant appeal the Court of Appeal came to the right decision, I cannot accept entirely that part of their reasoning in support of it in which they suggest that the primary obligation of the debtor to continue to pay the instalments which he had promised under clause (IX) of the contract was not ended by the rescission of the contract but remained in existence although the law no longer permitted him to pay them. A legal obligation to continue to perform is inconsistent with the withdrawal of any legal right to do so. The better explanation is that which I have already given, viz, that upon rescission of the contract the primary obligation of the debtor to pay the instalments was converted by operation of law into a secondary obligation either to pay damages for failure to perform it; or, as these were instalments of a debt existing at the date of the contract, it may be a revived obligation to pay the balance of the whole debt immediately.

The guarantor's obligation under his contract of guarantee does not, as the Court of Appeal appear to suggest, depend upon the debtor's primary obligation continuing to exist after the contract had been rescinded. Nor is it affected by whether the debtor's secondary obligation which was substituted for it by operation of law is classified as an obligation to pay damages or as an obligation to pay the debt. It was the debtor's failure to perform his primary obligation to pay the instalments in circumstances which put an end to it that constituted a failure by the guarantor to perform his own primary obligation to the creditor to see that the instalments were paid by the debtor, and substituted for it a secondary obligation of the guarantor to pay to the creditor a sum of money for the loss he thereby sustained. It is the guarantor's own secondary obligation, not that of the debtor, that the creditor is enforcing in his claim for damages for breach of his contract of guarantee.

Lord Simon of Glaisdale: . . . I have had the advantage of reading the speeches prepared by my noble and learned friends, Lord Reid and Lord Diplock; and I agree with their comments on the judgment of the Court of Appeal. I also agree with the historical analysis made by my noble and learned friend, Lord Diplock: it is important as showing that the liability of a surety at common law always sounded in damages rather than in debt, even when he was guaranteeing a debt. . . .

The accrued instalments . . .

It was argued for the appellant that the respondents' acceptance of the company's repudiation effected a substantial alteration in the contractual relationship of the parties; that this was clearly prejudicial to the appellant's interest as guarantor; that he should, therefore, have been consulted before, and his consent obtained to, the alteration; and that, since he was not so consulted and never consented, he was discharged from liability.

This seems to me to be, with all respect, an impossible argument. It is only in the jurisprudence of Humpty-Dumpty that the rescission of a contract can be equated with its variation. The acceptance of the repudiation of an agreement does not alter its terms in any way—it merely transmutes the primary obligation of the promisor to perform the terms contractually into a secondary obligation, imposed by law, to pay damages for their breach.

Moreover, the suggested rule would make nonsense of the whole commercial purpose of suretyship: you would lose your guarantor at the very moment you most need him—namely, at the moment of fundamental breach by the principal promisor. Take a usual case giving rise to suretyship—that of a trader with a bank overdraft. The bank forbears to close the account (so as to put the trader into bankruptcy or liquidation) in consideration of the trader finding a guarantor of the overdraft and agreeing to pay it off by instalments. The trader thereafter repudiates his obligation to pay off the overdraft by instalments; whereupon the bank closes the account, so terminating the contractual relationship of banker and customer. It would be absurd to suppose that the guarantor of the overdraft was thereby discharged from his liability as surety.

Finally, if authority were needed *Chatterton v Maclean* [1951] 1 All ER 761 is against the appellant's proposition [see the passage from Parker J's judgment cited below].

The outstanding instalments

It was on this part of the case that counsel for the appellant mounted his most formidable argument. In outline this ran as follows. What the appellant was guaranteeing was that the company would make weekly payments on dates most of which fell after December 22,1967. When, on December 22, the respondents accepted the company's repudiation, the contract was rescinded by agreement between them; and the company had thereafter no duty (or, indeed, right) to make the stipulated payments which the appellant had guaranteed. It follows that the subject-matter of the appellant's guarantee entirely disappeared after December 22, so that he was pro tanto exonerated from all liability in relation thereto. The company admittedly become immediately liable to pay damages for breach of its contract to make payments; but the appellant had guaranteed the later payments, not the immediate damages.

It was argued for the respondents, on the other hand, that the contractual duty assumed by the appellant was to ensure the performance by the company of such of its contractual obligations as were guaranteed; and that, when the company evinced an intention not to perform its guaranteed contractual obligations, and when such repudiation was accepted by the respondents, the appellant became in breach of his own obligation, so as himself to be liable in damages.

In my judgment, the argument for the respondents is the correct legal analysis, for the following reasons:

(1) The contention of the appellant is, in my view, both in principle and in practice impossible to reconcile with the rule in *Hochster v De la Tour* (1853) 2 E & B 678—namely, that if a promisor under a contract, even before the time for its performance has arrived, evinces an intention not to perform it, the promisee may treat this as an immediate breach of contract and bring his action accordingly.... In the instant case, therefore, it was accepted that the respondents could, on December 22, treat the company's conduct as a refusal to perform the executory part of the contract, and sue the company at once for damages for breach of contract, notwithstanding that the company might notionally have changed its mind before the time for performance had arrived and decided to comply with its executory obligations. The measure of damages in such an action would be the totality of the outstanding debt with a discount for accelerated payment: cf *Frost v Knight* (1872) LR 7 Exch 111,117. It would be very strange and hardly workable if the promisee had to wait until the time for the promisor's performance had arrived before having his remedy against the surety. Indeed, it is difficult to see how the promisee would even then have any remedy against the surety unless he had himself in the meantime performed his own obligations under the contract or (if those obligations were still executory) held himself ready and willing to perform them. The instant case provides a striking example of the absurdity of any such requirement. Both conceptually and practically, I find it impossible to reconcile the appellant's proposition with the policy of the law exemplified in the doctrine of what is conveniently though perhaps misleadingly called acceptance of anticipatory breach. If the appellant is right, the promisee is still, vis-à-vis the surety, impaled on that same Morton's fork from which the rule in *Hochster v De la Tour* (1853) 2 E & B 678 enabled him to escape vis-a-vis the principal promisor.

(2) The appellant's contention becomes even more unworkable if the obligation the performance of which is guaranteed is not one to pay money, but to deliver goods or to perform services.

(3) The appellant's argument, again in this part of the case, involves that the promisee would lose the benefit of the guarantee at the very moment he most needs it—namely, on a repudiation by the principal promisor of his obligations under the contract.

(4) The respondents' proposition is supported by the high authority of Rowlatt, *The Law of Principal and Surety,* 3rd edn (1936), p 144. The learned author was discussing the rule that on default of the principal promisor causing damage to the promisee the surety is, apart from special stipulation, immediately liable to the full extent of his obligation, without being entitled to require either notice of the default, or previous recourse against the principal, or simultaneous recourse against co-sureties. 'The reason for the rule,' wrote Rowlatt, 'is that it is the surety's duty to see that the principal pays or performs his duty as the case may be . . . .' No other reason for the rule was proposed in argument before your Lordships, nor was the rule itself questioned; which suggests that Rowlatt's proposed reason is the correct one, which his own high standing would in any case vouch. It is true that the authorities which Rowlatt cited for the proposition: *Wright v Simpson* (1802) 6 Ves 714 and *Re Lockey* (1845) 1 Ph 509 are not direct decisions on the point, in the sense of its being their ratio decidendi. But, more significantly, both Lord Eldon in the former case and Lord Lyndhurst in the latter seem to assume without question that the law is as stated by Rowlatt.

(5) That it is the surety's duty to see that the principal pays, or performs his other duty, as the case may be (so that non-payment or other non-performance by the principal is a breach of the surety's contract, sounding in damages), is further suggested by the wording of s 4 of the Statute of Frauds 1677: 'any special promise to answer for the debt, default or miscarriages of another person.' The teutonic 'answer for' is used here in a sense more accurately connoted in modern English by its romance equivalent 'be responsible for' (see *Oxford English Dictionary,* s.v. *answer,* v. I. 3). A further shade of meaning as indicating the nature of the surety's common law obligation may be seen in Shakespeare's 'Let his neck answer for it, if there be any martial law.'

(6) The point is still further reinforced by the historical analysis of my noble and learned friend, Lord Diplock, which shows that the liability of the surety gave rise to an action of special assumpsit not of indebitatus assumpsit, breach therefore sounding in damages and not in debt, even if it was a debt which was guaranteed . . . . This is only consistent with the surety's obligation, even when guaranteeing a payment, being not to pay a sum of money in default but to ensure performance of the principal promisor's obligation.

(7) Although not a direct decision on the point, *Chatterton v Maclean* [1951] 1 All ER 761 supports the respondents' proposition. Parker J is reported as saying, at pp 764–765:

> Counsel for the defendant urges, first, that the very acceptance, the very treating of the hirer's conduct as a repudiation of the contract, amounts to a new contract. That leads to the rather startling conclusion that a guarantor of the performance of a contract is always released where the creditor does what he is lawfully entitled to do, namely, to treat the principal debtor's breach as a repudiation. It would mean that whenever a creditor exercised his ordinary rights a guarantor was released, not merely in respect of future liabilities, but in respect of accrued liabilities.

Parker J treats it as self-evident that, where the principal creditor lawfully accepts the principal debtor's breach as a repudiation of the contract, the surety is *not* released either in respect of accrued or of future liabilities.

It follows, in my judgment, therefore, that when on December 22, 1967, the respondents accepted the company's fundamental breach of the terms of the contract, including those guaranteed, as a repudiation of the contract, the respondents were entitled to sue the appellant for the total sum guaranteed (except in so far as already satisfied by payment made by the company), and that the measure of damages would be such net sum with an appropriate discount for accelerated payment (though in the instant case there is no question of any discount). I would therefore dismiss the appeal on this ground.

[Lord Kilbrandon delivered a concurring judgment.
Lord Gardiner concurred.]

NOTE

Moschi v Lep Air Services Ltd illustrates the principle of co-extensiveness (above, p 1150). The fact that the payments were to be by instalments did not cause any difficulty because the surety had guaranteed *complete performance* of the contract by the principal debtor. But contrast *Moschi* with *Hyundai Heavy Industries Co Ltd v Papadopoulos* [1980] 1 WLR 1129 (above, p 290), where the surety guaranteed payment of instalments due under a shipbuilding contract. In *Hyundai,* a shipbuilding contract provided for payment of five instalments by the buyer. A clause in the contract permitted the shipbuilders to cancel the contract where the buyers were in default in payment of any instalment. The buyers failed to pay the second instalment. The shipbuilders cancelled the contract and sued the surety for the unpaid instalment. The surety argued that since the first instalment was recoverable on cancellation, and the second instalment would likewise have been recoverable if it had been paid (applying *Dies v British and International Mining and Finance Corpn Ltd* [1939] 1 KB 724, where prepayments were recoverable because there had been a total failure of consideration in relation thereto: as explained by Kerr LJ in *Rover International Ltd v Cannon Film Sales Ltd (No 3)* [1989] 3 All ER 423 at 439–440), there was no claim for the second instalment as against the principal debtor or the surety, even though it was unpaid at the date of cancellation. By a majority of 3:2, the House of Lords held that the cancellation did not destroy the shipbuilders' accrued right to recover the second instalment. The majority distinguished *Dies* by holding in effect that there had not been a total failure of consideration by the shipbuilders (see *Rover v Cannon*, above, at 439). Furthermore, their Lordships emphasised that the commercial purpose of the guarantee was to enable the shipbuilders to recover from the surety when the principal debtor failed to pay.

However, Viscount Dilhorne went on to state (obiter, at 1137) that the surety would have been liable for the accrued but unpaid second instalment even if the cancellation had deprived the shipbuilders of their accrued right to that instalment. In that event, the principal debtor would still be liable to pay damages to the creditor for breach of contract, but his liability in damages may be for less than the surety is liable to pay. If Viscount Dilhorne is right, this provides a major exception to the principle of co-extensiveness. But, save for some *obiter dicta* of Roskill LJ in *Hyundai Shipbuilding and Heavy Industries Co Ltd v Pournaras* [1978] 2 Lloyd's Rep 502 (a case on similar facts), Viscount Dilhorne's dictum has little to support or commend it. As G Andrews and R Millett submit (in their book *Law of Guarantees* (5th edn, 2008) at p 283):

… there can be no justification for creating a situation in which the surety remains liable for the instalments in circumstances in which the principal is not, unless the contract on its true construction is to be regarded as one of indemnity rather than one of guarantee. It is submitted, with the greatest respect, that the suggestion that the surety may be liable for accrued instalments in circumstances in which the principal is not, is plainly wrong and should not be followed.

(b) Discharge of the surety

(i) *Where the guarantee is materially altered by the principal debtor, the surety is discharged*

The rule in *Pigot's Case* (1614) 11 Co Rep 26b is to the effect that any material alteration, not approved by all the parties to the original document, made to a deed or other instrument after the execution of that instrument or deed renders it void. The rule was originally laid down to prevent the mutilation of the seals on deeds, but it remains good law today, and it applies to the alteration of a contract of guarantee by the creditor, or a third party, without the surety's consent. In *Raiffeisen Zentrale Osterreich AG v Crossseas Shipping AG* [2000] 1 WLR 1135, Potter LJ identified two categories of materiality for the purposes of the rule in *Pigot's Case:* the first where there was an alteration which affected the very nature and character of the instrument, and the second where the alteration was 'potentially prejudicial' to the surety's legal rights and obligations. This test was recently applied in *Bank of Scotland v Butcher* [2003] EWCA Civ 67, [2003] 1 BCLC 575, where the Court of Appeal held that altering a guarantee from a general guarantee of any indebtedness of the customer to his bank to a guarantee of indebtedness on only one of his bank accounts was not actually or potentially prejudicial to the surety so that the rule in *Pigot's Case* did not apply. It has been held that where a document consists otherwise of print, type and ink writing, the most natural inference to draw of an amendment to that document in pencil is that it is not, and is not intended to be, an operative and final amendment, with the result that it is not to be treated as an alteration of the document at all (*Co-operative Bank v Tipper* [1996] 4 All ER 366, 372).

(ii) Any material alteration of the terms of the contract between the creditor and the principal debtor will discharge the surety

Holme v Brunskill

(1878) 3 QBD 495, Court of Appeal

Holme let Riggindale farm, and a flock of sheep, to George Brunskill. Robert Brunskill, the defendant, guaranteed redelivery of the farm and the flock in good order and condition at the end of the tenancy. Holme later accepted the surrender of one field from George in return for a reduction in rent, without the knowledge or consent of Robert. At the end of the tenancy the flock was reduced in number and quality and so Holme claimed against Robert under the terms of his guarantee. Although the trial jury found that the variation of the terms of the tenancy agreement had not made a material difference to the tenancy, the Court of Appeal held by a majority that the variation had discharged Robert from his liability on the guarantee.

Cotton LJ: It was contended by the defendant, that even if there was a continuance of the old tenancy the effect of the surrender of the Bog Field was to discharge him as surety from all liability. The Bog Field contained about seven acres, and the jury, in answer to a question left to them, at the trial, found that the new agreement with the tenant had not made any substantial or material difference in the relation between the parties, as regards the tenant's capacity to do the things mentioned in the condition of the bond, and for the breaches of which the action was brought. The plaintiff's contention was that this must be treated as a finding that the alteration was immaterial, and that, except in the case of an agreement to give time to the principal debtor, a surety was not discharged by an agreement between the principals made without his assent, unless it materially varied his liability or altered what was in express terms a condition of the contract.

In my opinion this contention on behalf of the plaintiff cannot be sustained. No doubt, there is a distinction between the cases, which have turned on the creditor agreeing to give time to the principal debtor, and the other cases. Where a creditor does bind himself to give time to the principal debtor, he with an exception hereafter referred to, does deprive the surety of a right which he has, that is to say of the right at once to pay off the debt which he has guaranteed, and to sue the principal debtor, and without inquiry whether the surety has, by being deprived of this right, in fact suffered any loss, the Courts have held that he is discharged. The exception to which I have referred is, where the creditor on making the agreement with the principal debtor expressly reserves his right against the surety, but this reservation is held to preserve to the surety the right above referred to, of which he would be otherwise deprived. The cases as to discharge of a surety by an agreement made by the creditor, to give time to the principal debtor, are only an exemplification of the rule stated by Lord Loughborough in the case of *Rees v Berrington* ((1795) 2 Ves 540): 'It is the clearest and most evident equity not to carry on any transaction without the knowledge of him [the surety], who must necessarily, have a concern in every transaction with the principal debtor. You cannot keep him bound and transact his affairs (for they are as much his as your own) without consulting him.'

The true rule in my opinion is, that if there is any agreement between the principals with reference to the contract guaranteed, the surety ought to be consulted, and that if he has not consented to the alteration, although in cases where it is without inquiry evident that the alteration is unsubstantial, or that it cannot be otherwise than beneficial to the surety, the surety may not be discharged; yet, that if it is not self-evident that the alteration is unsubstantial, or one which cannot be prejudicial to the surety, the Court, will not, in an action against the surety, go into an inquiry as to the effect of the alteration, or allow the question, whether the surety is discharged or not, to be determined by the finding of a jury as to the materiality of the alteration or on the question whether it is to the prejudice of the surety, but will hold that in such a case the surety himself must be the sole judge whether or not he will consent to remain liable notwithstanding the alteration, and that if he has not so consented he will be discharged....

In the present case, although the Bog Field contained seven acres only, yet it cannot be said to be evident that the surrender of it could not prejudicially affect the surety. Some of the witnesses for the plaintiff admitted that it was occasionally used for pasturing, that its loss would be appreciable in the spring, and that it might make a difference of fifteen in the number of the sheep which the farm would carry.

The case may also be considered in another point of view. The bond given by the defendant the surety, was to guarantee the delivery up of the flock of sheep therein referred to at the determination of the tenancy of the Riggindale Farm, which in our opinion, must mean Riggindale Farm as then demised to George Brunskill, and the bond certainly implied that he should continue to hold the farm as then demised till the flock was given up. The contention of the plaintiff, if it could be supported, would make a variation in this contract, as to the materiality of which there is at least a doubt, and would make the defendant liable for a deterioration of the flock during the time when the tenant held a smaller farm than that contemplated by the contract of the surety.

The plaintiff's counsel relied on some observations made by Lord Cottenham in the case of *Hollier v Eyre* ((1840) 9 Cl & Fin 1). But, in fact, those observations are in favour of the defendant and not of the plaintiff. What Lord Cottenham says is, 'the surety will be left to judge for himself between his original undertaking and another substituted for it, but that is not the case where the contract remains the same, though part of the subject-matter is withdrawn from its operation/ In this case, as already pointed out, the original contract of the surety was that the flock should be delivered up in good condition, together with the farm, as then demised to the tenant. No part of that which was guaranteed was ever withdrawn from the operation of the bond. But the plaintiff attempts to substitute for the contract that the flock should be given up in good condition, with the farm, as then demised, a contract that it should be delivered up in like condition with a farm of different extent. In my opinion the surety ought to have been asked to decide whether he would assent to the variation. He never did so assent, and in my opinion was discharged from liability, notwithstanding the finding of the jury, inasmuch as in my opinion the question was not one which ought to have been submitted to them.

[Thesiger LJ concurred in this judgment.
Brett LJ dissented from this judgment, holding that the variation, when not violating a specific condition of the surety's contract, must be proved to be material.]

NOTES

1.   The surety has the benefit of implied rights of indemnity and subrogation against the principal debtor, as well as rights of contribution against his co-sureties (see below, pp 1184 and 1185). It is an implied condition of the contract of guarantee that those rights must be preserved, the surety having accepted the risk of liability under his guarantee on that basis. Anything which alters or extinguishes those rights is a breach of condition, unless the guarantee provides otherwise or the surety consents to the act or omission in question (*Finley v Connell Associates* [1999] Lloyd's Rep PN 895, Richards J). The effect of a breach of condition is to entitle the surety to full discharge from liability, whether or not the surety can show he is prejudiced by the breach. Thus, the surety will be discharged from liability where the creditor releases the principal debtor (*Commercial Bank of Tasmania v Jones* [1893] AC 313) or a co-surety (*Mercantile Bank of Sydney v Taylor* [1893] AC 317), releases a security, wholly or in part (*Pledge v Buss* (1860) John 663), binds himself to give time to the principal debtor without reserving his rights against the surety (*Webb v Hewett* (1857) 3 K & J 438), or otherwise varies the terms of the principal contract without the surety's consent in a manner which is not self-evidently non-prejudicial (*Holme v Brunskill*, above). It has recently been held that a voluntary early payment by the principal debtor to the creditor does not amount to a variation of the contract guaranteed, even if the early payment was made at the creditor's request, but that if the principal debtor has entered into a binding agreement with the creditor, under which the principal debtor was bound to pay early, then the contract guaranteed would have been varied and the surety discharged, unless such an agreement was on the facts obviously incapable of prejudicing him (*ST Microelectronics NV v Condor Insurance Ltd* [2006] EWHC 977 (Comm), [2006] 2 Lloyd's Rep 525 at [36]–[38]).

2.   But contrast the effect of an act or omission by the creditor which is a breach of condition with one that is merely a breach of the creditor's equitable obligation to respect the surety's interests, eg where the creditor causes the surety loss by careless failure to register a security (*Wulff v Jay* (1872) LR 7 QB 756). Where there is a breach of this equitable obligation the surety is only discharged from liability under his guarantee to the extent that he is actually prejudiced by the breach. It has even been suggested that where the creditor causes the surety loss by failing to realise a security at the best price he is in breach of a tortious duty of care owed to the surety (*Standard Chartered Bank Ltd v Walker* [1982] 3 All ER 938 at 942, per Lord Denning MR; followed in *American Express International Banking Corpn v Hurley* [1985] 3 All ER 564). However, in *China and South Sea Bank Ltd v Tan Soon Gin* [1990] 1 AC 536, Lord Templeman, delivering the advice of the Privy Council, held that a creditor owed the surety no duty to exercise his power of sale over mortgaged securities, which meant that the surety was not discharged from liability by a reduction in the value of the securities which resulted from the creditor's delay in selling them (but note that under s 91(2) of the Law of Property Act 1925 a mortgagor may apply to the court for an order directing the sale of mortgaged property notwithstanding the mortgagee's wishes to delay the sale: *Palk v Mortgage Services Funding plc* [1993] Ch 330, CA). Lord Templeman decided the case on the basis of equitable principles holding (at 543–544) that:

...the tort of negligence...does not supplant the principles of equity or contradict contractual rights or complement the remedy of judicial review or supplement statutory rights.

But his Lordship also held that once the creditor does decide to sell he must obtain the current market price. In the light of Lord Templeman's overall emphasis on equitable principles, that obligation must arise in equity rather than in tort (*Cuckmere Brick Co Ltd v Mutual Finance Ltd* [1971] Ch 949, where the Court of Appeal held that a mortgagee who decides to sell must take reasonable care to obtain a proper price, would have to be explained on that basis). Similarly, the Court of Appeal in *Parker-Tweedale v Dunbar Bank plc* [1991] Ch 12 and the Privy Council in *Downsview Nominees Ltd v First City Corpn Ltd* [1993] AC 295 have both held that a mortgagee's duties arise in equity and not in tort (see also *AIB Finance Ltd v Debtors* [1998] 2 All ER 929 at 937, CA; *Yorkshire Bank plc v Hall* [1999] 1 All ER 879 at 893, CA; *Medforth v Blake* [2000] Ch 86, below, p 1224). Considerable doubt must now be cast on the common law approach of Lord Denning in *Standard Chartered Bank v Walker*. Nevertheless, whether the duty arises at common law or in equity, it still remains the case that breach of the creditor's duty to realise the security at the best price reduces *pro tanto* the amount for which the surety is liable (*Skipton Building Society v Stott* [2000] 1 QB 261, CA). The creditor's duty to take reasonable care is owed both to the principal debtor (assuming it is his asset that constitutes the security) and to the surety (*Barclays Bank plc v Kingston* [2006] EWHC 533 (QB), [2006] 2 Lloyd's Rep 59 at [18]).

3.   In most commercial contracts of guarantee the surety's rights to full or *pro tanto* discharge from liability (on any of the grounds set out above) are expressly excluded by the terms of the guarantee. Although there is no doubt that the normal incidents of suretyship can be excluded by the terms of the contract of guarantee, the language used to do so must be clear and unequivocal (*Trafalgar House Construction (Regions) Ltd v General Surety & Guarantee Co Ltd* [1996] AC 199, 208, per Lord Jauncey). In each case the term in question must be construed against the commercial background to the guarantee and it must be decided whether the creditor's conduct falls within the ambit of the term (see *Triodos Bank NV v Dobbs* [2005] EWCA Civ 630, [2005] 2 Lloyd's Rep 588: loan agreement which replaced original loan agreement held to be a new agreement, and not a variation of original loan agreement, so not caught by term giving surety's consent to variation contained in his guarantee: but decision criticised by Berg (2006) 122 LQR 42). It may happen that the guarantee contains a term excluding the surety's right to discharge, but the creditor later enters into an agreement with the surety which has the effect of reinstating the rule in *Holme v Brunskill* (*Lloyds TSB Bank v Hayward* [2005] EWCA Civ 466).

There remains uncertainty as to whether a guarantee given by an individual which contains a term that excludes the surety's right to discharge would be subject to review under the Unfair Terms in Consumer Contracts Regulations 1999. In *Governor and Co of the Bank of Scotland v Singh*, unreported, 17 June 2005, Judge Kershaw QC, sitting in the High Court, held that the 1999 Regulations did not apply to a contract of guarantee made by a company director with a bank. The regulations apply to a contract between a supplier and a consumer (reg 4(1)); and a supplier is defined to be one acting in the course of his business (reg 3(1)). The judge reasoned that where a company director provides a guarantee to cover his company's indebtedness to its bank, the company director, as surety, is the supplier of a service to the bank (not the other way round) but 'he does not himself have a trade, business or profession as a guarantor (or, more broadly, as a provider of assorted financial services)'. However, the better view is that the regulations should apply for the protection of individual sureties against unfair terms where their promises of guarantee are genuinely unconnected with their trade, business or profession (*Chitty on Contracts*, 29th edn, 2004, Vol 2, para 44–133A). Finally, a term in the contract of guarantee that purports to exclude the creditor's liability for loss caused to the surety will be subject to the test of 'reasonableness' under the Unfair Contract Terms Act 1977 where the guarantee is on the creditor's written standard term of business or the surety is dealing as consumer (*Governor and Co of the Bank of Scotland v Singh*, above).

(iii) Other reasons for discharge

Payment by the surety of amounts due under the guarantee discharges both the surety and the principal debtor either wholly or *pro tanto*. The surety may also have rights of set-off against the creditor. Thus, in *MS Fashions Ltd v BCCI (No 2)* [1993] Ch 425, where a surety deposited money with a bank to secure the borrowings of his company and by the terms of the security documentation agreed that his liability should be that of a principal debtor (and not merely that of a guarantor), Hoffmann LJ (at first instance) and the Court of Appeal held that, on the bank's subsequent liquidation, automatic mandatory insolvency set-off of the deposit against the surety's obligation to the bank operated so as to repay the principal debtor's indebtedness to the bank. It made no difference that the bank had not made a demand on the surety as he was himself severally liable for the debt. By contrast, in *Re BCCI (No 8)* [1996] Ch 245, where the surety deposited money and granted the bank a charge over it, but did not give any express covenant or personal guarantee to repay, the Court of Appeal held there was no sum due from the surety before demand and there could be no set-off on the bank's subsequent liquidation (affirmed by the House of Lords on other grounds, [1998] AC 214, see above, p 1040). In this case the bank could sue its customer for the outstanding debt, retain the surety's deposit and leave him to prove for a dividend in the bank's insolvency. At first sight, it might seem paradoxical that an insolvent bank is in a better position if it has not obtained a personal guarantee from the surety than if it has (a point made by Rose LJ in *Re BCCI (No 8)* at 253H and 273C; see also *Tam Wing Chuen v BCCI Hong Kong Ltd* [1996] 2 BCLC 69 at 71–72, per Lord Mustill), and one commentator has even gone so far as to claim that *MS Fashions* produces an 'unpalatable result' (R Millett (1996) 112 LQR 524, p 526), but it is submitted that there is no paradox, and certainly no injustice, in allowing a surety to gain the benefit of set-off after he has been required to take on the liabilities of a principal debtor. After all, banks rarely become insolvent and they are generally able to take advantage of the surety's personal liability as an additional form of security.

Payment or performance by the principal debtor will discharge the surety; part payment or part performance by the principal debtor will discharge the surety *pro tanto*. The surety can also *prima facie* avail himself of any right of set-off possessed by the principal debtor against the creditor (see, eg *BOC Group plc v Centeon LLC* [1999] 1 All ER (Comm) 53 at 67; but the pricise extent of the availability of this right of set-off remains controversial: see J Phillips [2001] LMCLQ 383). Furthermore, where the creditor commits a repudiatory breach of the principal contract, and the principal debtor accepts it, the surety is also discharged (as he would be if the creditor commits a repudiatory breach of the contract of guarantee). Where the creditor commits a non-repudiatory breach of the principal contract the surety will not be discharged unless the breach involves a 'not unsubstantial' departure from the terms of the principal contract which has itself been expressly or by implication incorporated into the guarantee (*National Westminster Bank plc v Riley* [1986] BCLC 268 at 275–276; *The Wardens and Commonality of the Mystery of Mercers of the City of London v New Hampshire Insurance Co* [1992] 2 Lloyd's Rep 365).

7 RELATIONS BETWEEN SURETY AND PRINCIPAL DEBTOR

(a) Indemnity

Where the guarantee was given at the request, express or implied, of the principal debtor, the surety has a right to be indemnified by him for liability incurred and payments made under the guarantee. The surety's right to be indemnified arises from an implied contract between the surety and the debtor, although it may alternatively be said to have a restitutionary basis arising from the fact that the surety has been compelled by law to discharge the debt of the principal debtor (*Re a Debtor* [1937] Ch 156; *Anson v Anson* [1953] 1 QB 636 at 641–643). The surety's right to an indemnity does not usually arise until he has paid the creditor. However, as soon as the surety's liability becomes enforceable, even though not yet discharged, equity allows him to bring an action for a declaration that he is entitled to be indemnified and obtain an order that the principal debtor pay to the creditor what is due to him (*Wolmershausen v Gullick* [1893] 2 Ch 514).

So far we have considered the position where the guarantee was requested by the principal debtor. Where no such request was made, and yet a guarantee was given, it is much harder to establish a firm legal basis for the surety's right of indemnity. Without such a request there can be no contractual right. Furthermore, unless the surety enters into the guarantee under compulsion of law or acts in circumstances of necessity (which is unlikely), there is no clear restitutionary basis for the surety's claim. This is because the Court of Appeal ruled in *Owen v Tate* [1976] QB 402 that the surety has no right of recourse against the principal debtor where he voluntarily assumed his obligations under the guarantee without the prior request of the principal debtor. However, *Owen v Tate* has been the subject of much criticism and it may well have been wrongly decided (see P Birks and J Beatson (1976) 92 LQR 188; A Burrows *The Law of Restitution* (2nd edn, 2002), pp 282–286). Alternatively, it has been argued that the surety's right to an indemnity is not based on restitution and unjust enrichment but on the principle of the fair distribution of liabilities, which ensures that parties who are liable each bear an equitable proportion of the liability (see J Hilliard [2002] CLJ 551, pp 556–556).

The surety may modify or waive his right to an indemnity by the terms of his guarantee. Most guarantees contain a clause which provides that, until the claims of the creditor have been paid in full, the surety may not prove in the estate of the principal debtor in competition with the creditor (a 'non-competition' clause), and that if the surety receives any sums in breach of this obligation, he must hold those sums on trust for, and immediately pay them over to, the creditor (a 'turnover trust' clause). In *Re SSSL Realisations (2002) Ltd (in liquidation)* [2006] EWCA Civ 7, [2006] Ch 610, the Court of Appeal held that a non-competition clause was effective on the insolvency of the principal debtor and could not be disclaimed by the principal debtor's liquidator. Chadwick LJ, delivering the only reasoned judgment of the court, also stated (obiter) that an appropriately drafted turnover trust would not create a charge which would be void on insolvency for non-registration.

(b) Subrogation

Where a surety pays the full amount of the indebtedness to which his guarantee relates, he is entitled to be subrogated to the creditor's rights against the principal debtor and any security held by the creditor, whether that security was taken before or after he gave his guarantee and whether or not he was aware of its existence (*Forbes v Jackson* (1882) 19 Ch D 615). The legal basis for the right of subrogation remains controversial. In *Banque Financière de la Cité v Parc Battersea* [1999] 1 AC 221, the House of Lords held that the basis of subrogation was to be found in the law of unjust enrichment. More recently, in *Halifax plc v Omar* [2002] EWCA Civ 121, [2002] 2 P & CR 377, the Court of Appeal drew a distinction between the ordinary case of subrogation, where the claimant seeks to take over a pre-existing security, and the situation arising where the claimant seeks a personal remedy against a particular third party by way of subrogation (as in the *Banque Financière* case). It was held that unjust enrichment was only relevant in the latter type of case, whereas the former type of case turned on 'well-settled' principles of property law (see also *Eagle Star Insurance v Karasiewicz* [2002] EWCA Civ 940, [2002] All ER (D) 240 (Apr)). (The distinction is explored further by Stephen Midwinter in [2003] LMCLQ 6.) The surety' s right of subrogation does not depend on the debtor having requested the surety to provide the guarantee (see generally, A Burrows *The Law of Restitution* (2nd edn, 2002), pp 113–114; cf G Andrews and R Millett, *Law of Guarantees* (5th edn, 2008), para 11.019).

The surety's right of subrogation is reinforced by s 5 of the Mercantile Law Amendment Act 1856 which provides that the surety is entitled to have assigned to him 'every judgment, specialty or other security which shall be held by the creditor' in respect of the debt.

8   RELATIONS BETWEEN CO-SURETIES

Where a surety pays more than his proportionate share of the indebtedness he has an equitable right to recover the excess from any other surety of the same debt, ie from a co-surety. The principles that apply in such cases were summarised in *Hampton v Minns* [2002] 1 All ER (Comm) 481 at 495, Ch D, as follows:

(a) Where more than one person guarantees to the creditor the payment of the same debt, an equity arises such that if one of them pays more than his due proportion of the debt, he is entitled to a contribution from his co-guarantor or co-guarantors.

(b) As between co-guarantors, equity is equality, that is, each should bear an equal burden under the common demand.

(c) The right of contribution is not dependent upon agreement, express or implied.

(d) These principles are all subject to any contractual terms which may limit or extend the parties' liabilities.

As the right to contribution arises in equity and not in contract, the surety is entitled to contribution from a co-surety even though they were unaware of each other's existence. Equity demands that 'burdens be shared equally' (*Legal & General Assurance Society Ltd v Drake Insurance Co Ltd* [1992] QB 887 at 891–892, per Lloyd LJ; *Royal Brompton Hospital National Health Service Trust v Hammond* [2002] UKHL 14, [2002] 2 All ER 801 at [2], per Lord Bingham MR; and see also J Hilliard [2002] CLJ 551). In *Stimpson v Smith* [1999] Ch 340, the Court of Appeal held that a surety is entitled to contribution from his co-surety where he pays off the guaranteed indebtedness and obtains a release of the guarantee even though no demand had yet been made on him by the creditor, so long as payment is not officious or voluntary. Their Lordships reasoned that a demand is not a precondition of liability under a guarantee but a procedural or evidentiary requirement for the benefit of the surety alone which can be waived by him. Where a surety receives any security from the principal debtor, or takes over security from the creditor on discharging his liability, the security must, as between his co-sureties, be brought into account (*Steel v Dixon* (1881) 17 Ch D 825; *Berridge v Berridge* (1890) 44 Ch D 168). This is known as the principle of hotchpot.

The surety may also have statutory rights to contribution under the Civil Liability (Contribution) Act 1978 where he can bring himself within its requirements. Where the surety guarantees performance of the principal debtor of his payment obligation, the surety is liable in *damages* rather than in debt to the creditor and a right to contribution arises under the 1978 Act. On the other hand, where the surety agrees to pay to the creditor whatever the principal debtor owes to the creditor, the surety is liable in *debt* rather than damages and the 1978 Act does not apply (*Hampton v Minns,* above). This means that in the former case, but not in the latter case, a claim by a surety for contribution will be governed by the two-year limitation period imposed by s 10 of the Limitation Act 1980 (*Hampton v Minns,* above).

QUESTION

Alan, Bert and Chris are directors of Datacare Ltd. Each director provides Datacare's bank with a guarantee of the company's overdraft. The guarantees given by Alan and Bert are without limit, but the one given by Chris is limited to £10,000. Datacare's overdraft increases to £60,000 and the bank demands repayment. When the company fails to make repayment, the bank claims £60,000 from Alan under his guarantee. Alan pays the indebtedness in full and seeks your advice as to what amounts, if anything, he may claim from Bert and Chris by way of contribution. Advise Alan. See *Ellesmere Brewery Co v Cooper* [1896] 1 QB 75.

PART IX

PRINCIPLES OF INSURANCE LAW

CHAPTER 28

INSURANCE

1 INTRODUCTION[1]

Broadly speaking, in a contract of insurance one party undertakes, in return for a consideration paid by the other, to pay a sum of money or provide some equivalent benefit to the other *if* a specified event should happen, or *when* such an event should happen, or to make payments to the other *until* such an event should happen, the essence of the arrangement being that it is either uncertain whether, or uncertain when, the event will occur. The contract is commonly known as a 'policy' (at least if it is in writing), the parties are called respectively 'the insurer' (or 'underwriter') and 'the insured' (or 'assured' or 'policyholder'), and the consideration is referred to as 'the premium'.

Contracts of insurance may be subdivided into two categories: (1) *indemnity insurance*, where the undertaking is to provide the insured with an indemnity against a possible future loss or liability—eg damage to property caused by fire, or a motorist's liability in tort to a third party who may be injured by his driving, and (2) *contingency insurance*, where the promise is to pay a specified sum on the happening of a named event—eg a personal injury policy or a life policy. In the latter case, the insurer contracts to pay a predetermined sum when the person whose life is assured dies, and the sum is payable irrespective of the value of the life that is lost. In the same way, if an insurer in a personal injury policy promises to pay the insured £10,000 if he should lose the sight of an eye, he must pay that sum without regard to the loss to the insured that that injury actually represents. Another form of contingency insurance is a contract of annuity, where the premium is a lump sum paid in advance and the insurer agrees to make regular periodic payments of a fixed amount until the death of the person concerned.

It is of the essence of a contract of insurance that the event insured against must be uncertain, either in the sense that it may or may not occur, or that the time of the occurrence is uncertain. Thus, a policy of insurance on goods will not normally protect the insured against depreciation or fair wear and tear, or against losses arising from some internal or inherent cause, such as the deterioration of perishable goods (commonly referred to technically as 'inherent vice'). Nor will it be construed as covering events brought about by the deliberate act of the insured himself (eg loss caused by fraud or arson on his part). There is, in addition,

---

[1] Specialist textbooks include JR Birds *Modern Insurance Law* (6th edn, 2004); MA Clarke *The Law of Insurance Contracts* (looseleaf); J Lowry and P Rawlings *Insurance Law Doctrines and Principles* (2nd edn, 2005); A McGee *The Modern Law of Insurance* (2nd edn, 2006).

a further reason why an insured is debarred from recovering on an insurance in events such as his own fraud or arson, namely the general constraints of public policy.

Gray v Barr

[1971] 2 QB 554, Court of Appeal

Barr took a loaded shotgun to Gray's house to look for his wife, who had been committing adultery with Gray. During an altercation with Gray the shotgun went off and Gray was killed. His dependants claimed damages from Barr under the Fatal Accidents Acts, and Barr sought an indemnity against the Prudential Assurance Co under an insurance policy which covered him against his legal liability to pay damages in respect of injuries to third parties caused by accidents. It was held that his conduct amounted to manslaughter (although a jury had in fact acquitted him when he was charged with this offence in a criminal trial) and that it would be against public policy to allow him to claim on the policy.

Salmon LJ: ... Is the defendant precluded on grounds of public policy from enforcing the contract of insurance ?

It is well settled that if a man commits murder or committed felo de se in the days when suicide was still a crime, neither he nor his personal representatives could be entitled to reap any financial benefit from such an act: *Re Crippen's Estate* [1911] P 108; *Beresford v Royal Insurance Co Ltd* [1938] AC 586. This was because the law recognised that, in the public interest, such acts should be deterred and moreover that it would shock the public conscience if a man could use the courts to enforce a money claim either under a contract or a will by reason of his having committed such acts.

Crimes of violence, particularly when committed with loaded guns, are amongst the worst curses of this age. It is very much in the public interest that they should be deterred. A man, covered by a 'hearth and home' policy such as the present, walks into a bank with a loaded gun. He intends only to frighten and not to shoot the cashier. He slips and accidentally shoots a customer standing by the counter. It would be strange indeed if he could enforce the policy in respect of his liability to that customer. Once you threaten violence with a loaded gun and it goes off it is so easy to plead accident. Evidently it is very difficult for the prosecution to prove the contrary. Although public policy is rightly regarded as an unruly steed which should be cautiously ridden, I am confident that public policy undoubtedly requires that no one who threatens unlawful violence with a loaded gun should be allowed to enforce a claim for indemnity against any liability he may incur as a result of having so acted. I do not intend to lay down any wider proposition. In particular, I am not deciding that a man who has committed manslaughter would, in any circumstances, be prevented from enforcing a contract of indemnity in respect of any liability he may have incurred for causing death or from inheriting under a will or upon the intestacy of anyone whom he has killed. Manslaughter is a crime which varies infinitely in its seriousness. It may come very near to murder or amount to little more than inadvertence, although in the latter class of case the jury only rarely convicts....

The cases of *Tinline* [1921] 3 KB 327 and *James* [1927] 2 KB 311, in which it was held that persons convicted of manslaughter for reckless and drunken driving could nevertheless recover indemnity from their insurers, were doubted in *Haseldine v Hosken* [1933] 1 KB 822 but approved by this court in *Marles v Philip Trant & Sons Ltd* [1954] 1 QB 29. It seems now to be settled law that a motorist can rely on his policy of insurance to indemnify him in respect of his liability for any injuries which he has caused otherwise than on purpose: *Hardy v Motor Insurers' Bureau* [1964] 2 QB 745. These road traffic cases may be sui generis. In any event, although motor cars have sometimes been called lethal weapons, these cases are not in my view akin to the cases in which injuries are caused in the course of unlawfully threatening a man with a loaded gun. Public policy is not static. Even if the crime of suicide had not been abolished by statute, it may be that today Beresford's case would have been differently decided.

In any event, threatening violence with a loaded gun would, I am sure, now be generally regarded as much more shocking and necessary to be deterred than what the unfortunate Major Rowlandson [the suicide] did in *Beresford's* case. I am confident that, in any civilised society, public policy requires that anyone who inflicts injuries in the course of such an act shall not be allowed to use the courts of justice for the purpose of enforcing any contract of indemnity in respect of his liability in damages for causing injury by accident . . . .

[Lord Denning MR and Phillimore LJ delivered concurring judgments.]

There is one further element which is an essential requirement of a contract of insurance, and which distinguishes it from a wagering contract: the event upon which the insurer's liability depends must be one in which the insured has an *insurable interest*—that is to say, the event must, at least prima facie, be one which is adverse to the insured's interests. I cannot, as a rule, insure a stranger's house against fire, because I do not stand to lose anything if it is burnt down; but if I am a mortgagee of the property, this gives me an insurable interest. In the same way, one person normally cannot take out a life policy on the life of someone else, but he could if the latter is a key employee in his business.

Macaura v Northern Assurance Co
[1925] AC 619, House of Lords

Macaura, who owned an estate in Ireland, sold all the timber on the estate to a newly formed company, Irish Canadian Sawmills Ltd, in which Macaura effectively owned all of the shares. He had insured the timber in his own name with the respondent company. When the timber was destroyed in a fire, it was held that he could not claim on the policy because he had no insurable interest in it.

Lord Sumner: My Lords, this appeal relates to an insurance on goods against loss by fire. It is clear that the appellant had no insurable interest in the timber described. It was not his. It belonged to the Irish Canadian Sawmills, Ltd, of Skibbereen, co. Cork. He had no lien or security over it and, though it lay on his land by his permission, he had no responsibility to its owner for its safety, nor was it there under any contract that enabled him to hold it for his debt. He owned almost all the shares in the company, and the company owed him a good deal of money, but, neither as creditor nor as shareholder, could he insure the company's assets. The debt was not exposed to fire nor were the shares, and the fact that he was virtually the company's only creditor, while the timber was its only asset, seems to me to make no difference. He stood in no 'legal or equitable relation to' the timber at all. He had no 'concern in' the subject insured. His relation was to the company, not to its goods, and after the fire he was directly prejudiced by the paucity of the company's assets, not by the fire.

[Lords Buckmaster and Wrenbury delivered concurring opinions.
Lords Atkinson and Phillimore concurred.]

[Note: The strict approach of the House of Lords in this case has attracted some criticism in recent times and, indeed, it has not been followed in some Commonwealth decisions. In this country, too, there are signs that the courts now take a broader view: if a person has a 'factual expectation' that he may suffer consequential loss following a fire or other insured peril which damages property owned by someone else, he may be regarded as having a sufficient interest to insure against the risk. For example, a sub-contractor in a building contract may have such an interest in the works as a whole because he could lose the opportunity to complete his contract (*Petrofina (UK) Ltd v Magnaload Ltd* [1984] QB 127).]

Parts of the law governing contracts of insurance are governed by statute. Thus, the Life Assurance Act 1774 (which is not in fact confined in its application to life insurance but extends also to some other forms of insurance) defines an insurable interest for some purposes, and the Third Parties (Rights against Insurers) Act 1930 allows claims to be made directly against an insurer (eg by the victim of a motoring accident) where the insured is insolvent. The law of *marine insurance* (ie the insurance of ships and their cargoes and freight) is largely codified by the Marine Insurance Act 1906. But for the purposes of the present study, we shall concentrate on the general principles of insurance law, which are based mainly on the common law.

Persons wishing to carry on business as insurers must be authorised to do so by the Financial Services Authority, under powers delegated to it by the Treasury pursuant to the Financial Services and Markets Act 2002 and regulations made thereunder, or the equivalent authority in some other EU Member State. There is provision also under this legislation for compensating persons who suffer loss as a result of the failure of financial services providers (including those carrying on insurance business) to meet claims, and for the establishment of a Financial Ombudsman Scheme to resolve disputes which may arise between providers and their customers. There has in fact been an Insurance Ombudsman since 1981. The former Insurance Ombudsman Bureau is now incorporated as a division within the Scheme. On the work of the Insurance Ombudsman, see W Merricks 'The Jurisprudence of the Ombudsman' [2001] JBL 532.

In 1977 the insurance industry, through the Association of British Insurers and the General Insurance Standards Council, introduced a measure of self-regulation by the publication of non-statutory codes of practice. These 'Standards of Insurance Practice' obliged insurers to adopt a user-friendly approach and not to rely on some of the more technical points of law in their dealings with private customers. The Ombudsman has regularly applied these standards when dealing with the cases before him. In January 2005 these non-statutory codes were replaced by Conduct of Business Rules and guidance notes issued by the Financial Services Authority. (For a full account of these developments, see G McMeel [2005] LMCLQ 186.) The UK has also implemented the EC Insurance Mediation Directive (EC Directive 2002/92/EC) which confers on the Authority power to regulate insurers and their intermediaries when selling insurance and handling claims. Once again, the Directive draws a distinction between commercial customers and individual customers (including some small businesses) and gives greater protection to the latter.

2 FORMATION OF THE CONTRACT

(a) Insurance a contract *uberrimae fidei*

A contract of insurance is the paradigm case of a contract *uberrimae fidei*—a contract of the utmost good faith. The insurer is unlikely to know anything about the insured or the nature of the risk for which cover is sought, apart from such information as he is given by the insured. Accordingly, the insured is required by law to disclose to the insurer in advance of the contract all material facts known to him. A fact is material for this purpose if it is one which would influence the judgment of a prudent insurer in deciding whether to undertake the risk and, if so, at what premium: *Lambert v Cooperative Insurance Society* [1975] 2 Lloyd's Rep 485, CA; *Pan Atlantic Insurance Co Ltd v Pine Top Insurance Co Ltd* [1995] 1

AC 501, HL. Since even a rumour or suspicion that proves to be unfounded may affect the judgment of a prudent insurer—eg where a person is being questioned by the police in connection with a burglary—this may have to be disclosed. In *North Star Shipping Ltd v Sphere Drake Insurance plc* [2006] EWCA Civ 378, [2006] 2 All ER (Comm) 65 a ship, the *North Star*, had been damaged by an explosion. The loss would have been covered by a 'war risks' policy but the insurers declined liability because the shipowner, when taking out the insurance, had not disclosed the fact that its two controlling shareholders were facing fraud charges in courts in Greece and Panama. The charges were entirely false, but the court accepted expert evidence that the mere fact that they had been brought (even if baseless) would have been considered material by a prudent insurer, so that the non-disclosure justified the insurers in rejecting the claim. And if there is a change of cover during the currency of the policy, all relevant facts must again be disclosed. (The insurer is under similar obligations: *Banque Financière de la Cité SA v Westgate Insurance Co Ltd* [1991] 2 AC 249, HL.) If any material information is withheld, and it is proved or inferred that this induces the insurer to enter into the contract, the contract may be avoided.

Glicksman v Lancashire & General Assurance Co Ltd
[1927] AC 139, House of Lords

Glicksman and his partner had insured the stock of their tailoring business against burglary with the respondent company; but the company declined liability when a burglary happened, on the ground that Glicksman had not disclosed at the time when he applied for the cover that another insurance company had once declined to grant him insurance. An arbitrator found as a fact that this information was material, and in consequence the House of Lords (albeit with reluctance) held that the insurer's refusal to accept liability was justified.

Viscount Dunedin: ...The law has often been stated, but perhaps it is just as well to state it again. A contract of insurance is denominated a contract uberrimae fidei. It is possible for persons to stipulate that answers to certain questions shall be the basis of the insurance, and if that is done then there is no question as to materiality left, because the persons have contracted that there should be materiality in those questions; but quite apart from that, and alongside of that, there is the duty of no concealment of any consideration which would affect the mind of the ordinary prudent man in accepting the risk....

The fact that a question of this sort was put showed that the insurance company thought it was material whether a proposal had been refused or not, and that that was brought to the knowledge of the claimant. My Lords, under the circumstances I have considerable doubts, but then I am not entitled to take any view of my own on that, because that is a fact and the arbitrator has found it as a fact and I cannot get beyond the arbitrator's finding. I think that the reasoning of the learned judges in the Court of Appeal is impeccable. This was brought to the knowledge of the claimant that it was a material fact, and he certainly did not disclose it, and, therefore, the policy is void....

[Lords Atkinson, Shaw of Dunfermline, Wrenbury and Carson concurred.]

Woolcott v Sun Alliance and London Insurance Ltd
[1978] 1 WLR 493, Queen's Bench Division

Woolcott's house, which was insured with the Sun Alliance, was destroyed in a fire. The company refused payment because when he had applied for the insurance cover he had not disclosed the fact that he had convictions for robbery and other offences some 12 years previously.

He did not volunteer this information to the building society through which the insurance was taken out, and he was not asked any question about his character on the application form, although the judge accepted that he would have answered such a question truthfully if he had been asked it. Caulfield J held that the company was entitled to deny liability.

Caulfield J: I come now to the issues in this case. They are these: (1) [Discussion of this issue is omitted]...(2) Was there a duty on the plaintiff to disclose his criminal record to the building society in his application for an advance? (3) As there was no disclosure by the plaintiff, was this non-disclosure material?

These are my findings....

On the second issue in this action I refer to the judgment of MacKenna J in *Lambert v Cooperative Insurance Society Ltd* [1975] 2 Lloyd's Rep 485. This judgment I have found the most comprehensive and the most helpful, and I have followed the principles which are fully explained in it. The relevant passage begins where MacKenna J, giving the first judgment of the Court of Appeal, said, at p 487:

> Everyone agrees that the assured is under a duty of disclosure and that the duty is the same when he is applying for a renewal as it is when he is applying for the original policy. The extent of that duty is the matter in controversy. There are, at least in theory, four possible rules or tests which I shall state. (1) The duty is to disclose such facts only as the particular assured believes to be material. (2) It is to disclose such facts as a reasonable man would believe to be material. (3) It is to disclose such facts as the particular insurer would regard as material. (4) It is to disclose such facts as a reasonable or prudent insurer might have treated as material.

Ultimately, in a most comprehensive judgment, he went on to conclude that the proper test was the fourth test, and the principles which he has explained in that case I have followed in reaching my judgment on this particular issue. The duty, in my judgment, rested on the plaintiff, when he completed his application form for a loan, to disclose his criminal record, for, by that application, he was accepting that the society would effect insurance of his property on his behalf as well as on their own behalf. I do not think the absence of a proposal form for insurance modifies in any degree the duty of disclosure on the plaintiff. The plaintiff knew the society would be effecting a policy of insurance on their own behalf and on his behalf, and accordingly, in my judgment, there was a duty upon the plaintiff to disclose such facts as a reasonable or prudent insurer might have treated as material.

On the third issue, I have accepted the evidence of the underwriters who have given evidence. I accept that the criminal record of an assured can affect the moral hazard which insurers have to assess; indeed this is almost self-evident. I therefore hold that on the particular facts of this case the non-disclosure of a serious criminal offence like robbery by the plaintiff was a material non-disclosure.

For these reasons the defendants, in my judgment, are entitled to avoid the policy in so far as that policy affects the plaintiff's separate interest. There will be judgment accordingly.

Many contracts of insurance are effected on the basis of a proposal form which the insured is required to complete beforehand, and in this he will usually be asked a number—often a considerable number—of questions. The fact that specific questions are put to the insured in this way does not displace his obligation to make disclosure under the doctrine of *uberrima fides*. Thus, in *Glicksman's* case, a question on the proposal form asked whether other insurers had at any time refused to give cover to the insured. No insurer had ever refused cover to the *partnership*, and so it was possible for Glicksman and his partner to answer this question truthfully in the negative; but even so, they remained under their common law duty to disclose the fact that Glicksman himself had once been refused insurance.

The fact that a specific question has been put to the insured in a proposal is usually sufficient to satisfy the court that the matter that it deals with is material.

The obligation to make disclosure of material facts under the doctrine of *uberrima fides* is limited to facts of which the insured is aware. In *Joel v Law Union & Crown Insurance Co*

[1908] 2 KB 863, CA, Miss Morrison had taken out insurance on her life without disclosing that she had suffered from mental illness; but this was a fact of which she was unaware because she believed that she had only had depression following influenza. Fletcher Moulton LJ said (at 884): 'The duty is a duty to disclose, and you cannot disclose what you do not know.' This obligation may be extended, in the case of an insured in a business context, to facts which he ought to know; but there is no similar rule of deemed knowledge as regards a private individual, who is not required to do more than act in good faith, as the case next cited shows.

Economides v Commercial Union Insurance plc
[1998] QB 587, Court of Appeal

Economides, a student aged 21, took out insurance cover with Commercial Union for the contents of his flat, on the basis of a proposal form in which he stated that the full cost of replacing these items was £12,000 and that the total value of valuables did not exceed one-third of the sum insured. He declared on the form that the statements were to the best of his knowledge and belief, true and complete. Subsequently, his parents came to live with him and, at his father's suggestion, the cover was increased to £16,000. Some months later the flat was burgled and jewellery belonging to the parents was stolen which was worth over £30,000. The company sought to avoid liability under the policy on the grounds of misrepresentation and non-disclosure. The Court of Appeal held that the assured under a policy of household insurance was only under an obligation to be honest and that his belief, if made in good faith, should be deemed to be honest. Economides had acted honestly and accordingly the policy could not be avoided on either ground.

Simon Brown LJ: . . . The judge below held that 'commercial reality and common sense' required the plaintiff here as the representor to have objectively reasonable grounds for his belief; honesty alone was not enough.

[His Lordship examined a number of authorities and continued:]

[Counsel for the company] submits that Bowen LJ's dictum in *Smith v Land & House Property Corpn* (1884) 28 Ch D 7 at 15—that 'if the facts are not equally known to both sides, then a statement of opinion by the one who knows the facts best involves very often a statement of a material fact, for he impliedly states that he knows facts which justify his opinion'—can be seen to apply equally in an insurance context as in the general law. . . . I understand her to submit, indeed, that it applies with particular force in an insurance context given that contracts of insurance are based upon the utmost good faith and that the insured will always know far more about the facts than the insurer. Given that inevitable inequality of knowledge, she argues, the defendant insurers here were entitled to assume that the plaintiff had reasonable grounds to support his valuation of the contents and that he was not merely relying, however honestly, on his father's say-so. . . .

[Counsel for the insured] accepts, as inevitably he must, that the plaintiff had to have some basis for his statement of belief in this valuation; he could not simply make a blind guess: one cannot believe to be true that which one has not the least idea about. But, he submits, and this is the heart of the argument, the basis of belief does not have to be an objectively reasonable one. What the plaintiff's father told him here was a sufficient basis for his representation: he was under a duty of honesty, not a duty of care.

In my judgment these submissions are well founded. . . . In my judgment the requirement is . . . solely one of honesty.

There are practical and policy considerations too. What would amount to reasonable grounds for belief in this sort of situation? What must a householder seeking contents insurance do? Must he obtain professional valuations of all his goods and chattels? The judge below held that:

> it would have been necessary for him to make substantially more inquiries than he did make before he could be said to have reasonable grounds for his belief. It is not necessary to specify what those inquiries might have involved.

The problem with not specifying them, however, is that householders are left entirely uncertain of the obligations put upon them and are at risk of having insurers seek to avoid liability under the policies. There would be endless scope for dispute. In my judgment, if insurers wish to place upon their assured an obligation to carry out specific inquiries or otherwise take steps to provide objective justification for their valuations, they must spell out these requirements in the proposal form.

I would hold, therefore, that the sole obligation upon the plaintiff when he represented to the defendants on renewal that he believed the full contents value to be £16,000 was that of honesty. That obligation the judge apparently found him to have satisfied. Certainly, given that the plaintiff was at the time aged 21, given that the figure for the increase in cover was put forward by his father, and given that the father was a retired senior police officer, inevitably better able that the plaintiff himself to put a valuation on the additional contents, there would seem to me every reason to accept the plaintiff's honesty.

[His Lordship accordingly held that the company could not avoid the policy for misrepresentation, and that the same test of honesty applied to the argument based on non-disclosure. Peter Gibson LJ and Sir Iain Glidewell delivered concurring judgments.]

However, the common law doctrine may be supplemented by a provision in the contract of insurance which makes the accuracy of replies to the questions in the proposal form a condition of the validity of the policy. If this is the case, the policy can be avoided if untrue information is given, however honestly, by the insured because he is unaware of the true facts. It can also be avoided if inaccurate information is given on a matter which would not otherwise be regarded as material.

There is a similar duty of disclosure whenever insurance cover is renewed. However, there is no common law rule to the effect that the obligation of the utmost good faith applies throughout the duration of the contract, so that, for example, the insured is required to inform the insurer if the circumstances change materially during the currency of the policy. But many contracts of insurance impose such a duty by an express term.

Dawsons Ltd v Bonnin
[1922] 2 AC 413, House of Lords

Dawsons insured a lorry with Bonnin and others, underwriters at Lloyd's, under a policy which recited that the proposal which Dawsons had completed should be the basis of the contract and be held as incorporated in it. In reply to a question in the proposal, they stated that the lorry would usually be garaged at their ordinary place of business in Glasgow; but in fact it was normally garaged at a farm on the outskirts of the city. The lorry was destroyed by a fire at the latter address. The House of Lords held that, although the misstatement was not material, the insurers were entitled to rely on the 'basis of the contract' provision to avoid liability.

Viscount Cave: My Lords, it is common ground that the proposal for the policy of insurance issued by the respondents to the appellants contained a misstatement as to the place where the lorry to be insured would usually be garaged; and the only question is whether this misstatement avoids the policy.

The policy commences with a recital of the proposal (a full copy of which is annexed to the policy), and proceeds 'which proposal shall be the basis of this contract and be held as incorporated therein.'...

Upon the whole, it appears to me, both on principle and on authority, that the meaning and effect of the 'basis' clause, taken by itself, is that any untrue statement in the proposal, or any breach of its promissory clauses, shall avoid the policy; and if that be the contract of the parties, it is fully established, by decisions of your Lordships' House, that the question of materiality has not to be considered....

In these circumstances it appears to me to be irrelevant to consider the conflicting evidence in the case as to whether a misstatement as to the place of garage is, in the ordinary sense, material or not. The parties have agreed that it shall be deemed material, and that concludes the matter.

I must confess that I have little sympathy with the respondents, who seek to profit by a mistake to which their agent contributed; but the case must be decided according to law, and I think that the law is on their side.

[Viscount Haldane and Lord Dunedin delivered concurring opinions. Viscount Finlay and Lord Wrenbury dissented.]

The above rules, if applied strictly, can operate very harshly, especially where the insured is a lay person. This has caused considerable disquiet, which has led to recommendations for reform of the law on two occasions: first, by the Law Reform Committee in its Fifth Report in 1957 (*Conditions and Exceptions in Insurance Policies*, Cmnd 62, 1957) and more recently by the Law Commission in 1980 (*Insurance Law—Non-disclosure and Breach of Warranty* (L Com No 104, Cmnd 8064, 1980)). However, there has not so far been any legislative reform, but since 1977 policyholders who are private individuals have been given a measure of protection by the Statements of Insurance Practice (now superseded by the FSA's Conduct of Business Rules; see above, p 1192), which require an insurer not to repudiate liability against such an insured on the ground of non-disclosure of a material fact which he could not reasonably be expected to disclose. The Insurance Ombudsman has also intervened in a number of rulings to ensure that the worst effects of the doctrine of non-disclosure are mitigated.

Despite this, there continues to be disquiet over the present state of the law. The Law Commission has, since 2006, undertaken a wide review of insurance law and in particular the connected issues of non-disclosure, misrepresentation and breach of warranty. Among the proposals that have been put forward are a requirement that for consumers the insurer should ask specific questions and that in that case there should be no residual duty of disclosure; and that that different rules should apply depending on whether a misrepresentation (or, for businesses, the non-disclosure of a material fact) was fraudulent, negligent or innocent.

In addition to the special rules of the doctrine of *uberrima fides*, the normal principles of misrepresentation and fraud may, of course, also be invoked to invalidate a contract of insurance.

(b) Agency

A contract of insurance is commonly effected through an insurance broker or other agent, or a salesman employed by the insurer. Difficult questions may arise here if, as is common, the intermediary is in law the agent of the insured but is remunerated by a commission paid by the insurer. In addition to the obvious risk of conflicts of interest, there may be uncertainty as to the scope of the intermediary's authority to make representations and to receive information on behalf of the insurer. For instance, in *Dawsons Ltd v Bonnins* (above), the inaccurate reply to the question on the proposal was written down by an 'insurance agent' who was the insurers' local representative and the mistake was not noticed by the insured when the proposal was signed; but this fact did not bar the insurers from disowning liability under the policy.

3 CONTENT AND INTERPRETATION OF THE CONTRACT

(a) The risk, and exceptions

It is obviously of central importance in any contract of insurance to identify the nature and scope of the risk which the policy covers. Although this is purely a matter of construction of the particular contract, many standard terms have, over time, been the subject of judicial rulings which allow the task of construction to be approached with a reasonable degree of certainty. Thus, the meanings of words such as 'accident', 'all risks', 'damage by fire', 'loss' (and 'consequential loss'), 'natural causes' and 'perils of the seas' have been discussed in many authoritative cases, which are cited in some detail in the leading manuals of insurance law. Even so, such words may admit of different shades of meaning which have to be examined in the particular case: in *Gray v Barr,* for instance (above, p 1190), there was a difference of opinion among the judges on the question whether Gray's death had been caused by an 'accident'. The trial judge thought that it had; a majority of the members of the Court of Appeal that it had not; while Salmon LJ thought that it was caused by accident, but not by the kind of 'accident' intended to be covered by the policy. See also *Dhak v Insurance Co of North America (UK) Ltd* [1996] 1 WLR 936, CA where Mrs Dhak died from asphyxiation after drinking a very large quantity of alcohol. The court held that her death had not been 'caused by accidental means' but was the result of her taking a calculated risk of sustaining injury which such excessive drinking necessarily involved.

One well-known rule of construction which may be of particular relevance in relation to insurance contracts is the *contra proferentem* rule—that any ambiguity in a document is to be construed in the sense least favourable to the person who has drawn it up. This is illustrated by *Houghton v Trafalgar Insurance Co Ltd,* below. Again, in *Lancashire County Council v Municipal Insurance Ltd* [1997] QB 897, CA there was a dispute on the question whether the insurer's liability to indemnify the council's liability to pay compensation to tort victims extended to an award of exemplary damages. The court, applying the rule, held that it did. But the *contra proferentem* presumption will not invariably prevail: in *Gray v Barr* (above), Barr was not given the benefit of the doubt over the meaning of the word 'accident'.

We should also bear in mind when ascertaining the scope of the risk covered by the policy that the courts in recent years have abandoned the traditional 'strict' approach to the construction of written contracts in favour of a 'contextual' approach which allows the court to have regard to the factual background and to accept evidence as to the 'wider' matrix of facts of which knowledge may be attributed to the parties when the contract was drawn up (see the *Investors Compensation Scheme* case, discussed above, p 22). This approach has been adopted in quite a number of recent claims based on contracts of insurance—inevitably at some cost in legal certainty.

Houghton v Trafalgar Insurance Co Ltd

[1954] 1 QB 247, Court of Appeal

Six people were being carried in a car designed to seat five when it was involved in an accident. The insurance policy contained a provision excluding liability for damage 'arising whilst the car is conveying any load in excess of that for which it was constructed'. The insurer sought to deny liability, but the court held that the clause was ambiguous and should be construed as referring only to a weight load.

Somervell LJ: It is said that . . . there is no liability under the policy, and that the car was not covered because of a provision in a group of clauses which are headed 'Exclusions.' The first part of the clause which contains the provision relied on reads, '(d) Loss, damage and/or liability caused or arising whilst any such car is engaged in racing, pace-making, in any reliability trials, speed testing, or is conveying any load in excess of that for which it was constructed.' It is argued that the load here was in excess of that for which the car was constructed, in that one passenger was seated on the knees of another and the seating accommodation was all occupied. The judge decided against that contention, adversely to the defendants, who now appeal.

  If there is any ambiguity, since it is the defendants' clause, the ambiguity will be resolved in favour of the assured. In my opinion, the words relied on, 'any load in excess of that for which it was constructed,' only clearly cover cases where there is a weight load specified in respect of the motor-vehicle, be it lorry or van. I agree that the earlier words in the clause obviously are applicable to an ordinary private car in respect of which there is no such specified weight load. But there was—and I think that it would have been inadmissible—no evidence whether this was a form which was used for lorries as well as for ordinary private motor-cars. I do not think that that matters. We have to construe the words in their ordinary meaning, and I think that those words only clearly cover the case which I have put. If that is right, they cannot avail the insurance company in the present case.

Denning LJ: It would surprise most motor-car owners to be told that if they squeezed in an extra passenger, one more than the ordinary seating capacity, thereby they lost the benefit of the insurance policy. But that is what the insurance company are contending here. They say that by reason of this exclusion clause they are under no liability. If the clause had such an interpretation I would regard it almost as a trap. I am glad to find that the clause does not bear that extended interpretation. It is only applicable to cases where there is a specified weight which must not be exceeded, as in the case of lorries. I agree that the appeal should be dismissed.

[Romer LJ delivered a concurring judgment.]

The risk may be defined both affirmatively by words such as 'fire' or 'accident' which specifically describe it, and also by words of exception or limitation which exclude liability in particular cases. The provision in *Houghton's* case is an example of such an exception.

(b) Conditions and warranties

The law of insurance, anomalously, has traditionally used the term 'warranty' in a sense rather different from its use in the general law of contract. A warranty in this sense is an undertaking given by the insured which forms the very basis of the contract, one the breach of which releases the insurer from liability, rather than merely giving rise to a claim in damages. In other words, it is used in a way which to some extent resembles the term 'condition' in other branches of the law. However, the decision of the House of Lords in *Bank of Nova Scotia v Hellenic Mutual War Risks Association (Bermuda) Ltd, The Good Luck* [1992] 1 AC

233, HL has pointed up a subtle but important distinction: the breach of a condition in the general law of contract does not of itself avoid or terminate the contract, but merely gives the party who is not in breach the right to determine it if he so elects; in contrast, in insurance law, if the insured gives a warranty and this is broken, the insurer is *automatically* discharged from liability unless the insurer decides to waive the breach. So if an insured warrants the accuracy of a statement in the proposal, and it proves not to have been true, the insurer is discharged from liability under the policy ab initio. Alternatively, if circumstances change *during* the currency of the policy which cause the warranty to be breached, the insurer is discharged from liability under the policy from that time onwards.

However, the word 'condition' also has a role to play in insurance contracts. Thus, the policy may make it a condition of the insurer's liability in respect of a particular loss that he is given notice of the relevant event within 14 days of its occurrence. In a context such as this, the term 'condition' is used in much the same way (or ways!) as in the general law of contract.

Where a warranty is not complied with, the insurer can avoid liability even though the breach of warranty has no connection with the loss which has occurred, as the following case shows.

Conn v Westminster Motor Insurance Association Ltd

[1966] 1 Lloyd's Rep 407, Court of Appeal

Conn's nine-year-old taxi was badly damaged when it ran off the road as he was driving it at 2 am—probably because he had fallen asleep at the wheel. The defendant insurance company declined liability on the ground that he had failed to comply with a term of the policy which required him to take reasonable steps to maintain the vehicle in an efficient condition. In particular, the taxi's two front tyres were entirely bald—the canvas was showing through in places—and there was also some evidence that the brakes were defective. However, the defective state of the vehicle had not caused or contributed to the accident. The Court of Appeal, reversing the trial judge, held that the company could disown liability.

Willmer LJ: . . . The [trial judge] went on to point out that when the accident happened it was not associated with the smoothness of either of the front tyres or with their condition in combination with the brakes. With all respect, as I have already stated, and as I think is accepted by both sides, that is an entirely irrelevant consideration. We are not concerned with the question whether any breach of the condition (if there was one) caused or contributed to the accident. The only question is whether there was in fact a breach of the condition in the policy . . . .

[Davies and Salmon LJJ delivered concurring judgments.]

The strict legal position in regard to warranties is mitigated for insured persons who are private individuals by non-statutory codes of practice (see above, p 1192). By virtue of these, (1) statements in proposal forms may not be elevated to the status of warranties in relation to matters not material to the risk, and (2) insurers will not normally (in the absence of fraud) repudiate liability on the grounds of breach of warranty where the circumstances of the loss are unconnected with the breach.

It is often a difficult question of construction for the court to determine whether a term in a policy which is expressed to be a warranty is to be given its full technical meaning (ie a promissory warranty on the accuracy or fulfilment of which the validity of the contract depends), or is to be read simply as defining the risk which is covered. The distinction is important, for in the former case a breach will invalidate the contract and allow the insurer to disclaim liability even in respect of a risk which is not affected by the breach, while a breach in the second case will excuse the insurer only if it is causally connected with the loss which is the basis of the claim. This point is illustrated by the following case.

Farr v Motor Traders' Mutual Insurance Society
[1920] 3 KB 669, Court of Appeal

Farr owned two taxis, which he insured with the defendant company, on the basis of a proposal in which he stated that the vehicles were to be driven in only one shift per 24 hours. Six months later, one of the taxis was driven for two shifts in 24 hours for one or two days in August while the other was being repaired. Thereafter each cab was once again used for only one shift per day. When a claim was made in respect of an accident in November to the former of these taxis, the insurer claimed that its use on a double-shift basis during August was a breach of warranty which discharged it from liability. The court held that the statement was not a warranty but was merely descriptive of the risk, and that the insurer was liable.

Bankes LJ: The question in this appeal relates to the construction of a contract of insurance into which the parties have entered. The assured answered certain questions in a proposal form, and those questions and the answers thereto were made the basis of the contract and were incorporated therein. The only question for decision by the learned judge, and by us, is whether the answer to one of the questions constitutes a warranty by the assured. If, as a matter of construction, it can properly be held that the question and answer amount to a warranty, then, however absurd it may appear, the parties have made a bargain to that effect, and if the warranty is broken, the policy comes to an end.

The position is very clearly and accurately put in *Macgillivray on Insurance Law,* p 360, to which Scrutton LJ has called my attention. In the section dealing with representations and warranties in fire policies he says: 'It is a little doubtful how much is to be inferred from the mere description in a fire or burglary policy of the premises or goods insured. It may be put in three ways: (i) that the description is a representation of the state of the premises or goods; (ii) that the description is a definition of risk; (iii) that the description is a warranty that the premises or goods shall correspond thereto.' In this case the question which we have to decide is whether the particular statement in the proposal form is a definition of the risk or a warranty. Then he says: 'But if the description is embodied in the policy'—which is the case here—'whether actually or by reference, it has at least the force of a limitation of the risk to be run. In this view the premises or goods will be covered by the policy so long, but only so long, as they comply with the description, and if the description is considered merely as a limitation of the risk and not a warranty the insurer will not be wholly discharged, but the policy will merely cease to attach until the property once more corresponds to the description.' In the present case the proposal form contains the following: 'Is the vehicle driven solely by the proposer?'—'No.' 'If not, state whether driven in one or more shifts per 24 hours.'—'Just one.' That was a true statement at the time it was made, and it remained a true description of the risk down to August. In that month one of the two taxi-cabs which the assured owned required some repairs, and it was sent away for that purpose. When it was away the assured gave the driver of that cab permission to take out the other cab, as the assured said, in order to earn a few shillings. As a consequence that taxi-cab was for a day or a little longer driven in more than one shift each 24 hours; but apparently that took place for a very short time. Then the practice of driving these two cabs separately by separate drivers in one shift per day each was resumed, and continued down to and including the date when the second accident happened.

The question is whether we are to construe the question and answer, as the defendants contend, as a warranty, the effect of which would be that in August, when the cab was driven in two shifts per day, the policy came to an end; or whether we are to construe them, as Rowlatt J has construed them, as words descriptive of the risk, indicating that whilst the cab is driven in one shift per 24 hours the risk will be covered, but that if in any one day of 24 hours the cab is driven in more than one shift, the risk will no longer be covered and will cease to attach until the owner resumes the practice of driving the cab in one shift only. In my opinion, having regard to the nature of the question, it is impossible to construe the answer thereto as a warranty.

On these short grounds I think that the view taken by Rowlatt J upon the construction of this contract is the correct one, and that the appeal fails.

[Warrington and Scrutton LJJ concurred.]

Another difficult question which has arisen in many cases is whether the insured warrants only that a state of facts is true at the time he makes it, or that it *will continue to be true* throughout the currency of the cover. Again, this is basically a question of construction, but the task of the court is made easier by the existence of a wealth of relevant precedents.

(c) Consumer protection

Contracts of insurance were specifically exempted from the application of the Unfair Contract Terms Act 1977—indeed, the insurance industry obtained this concession in return for their agreement to introduce the Statements of Insurance Practice. However, there is no similar exemption from the Unfair Terms in Consumer Contracts Regulations 1999, SI 1999/2083, and so a term which is held to be unfair will, under those Regulations, not be binding on an insured who is a consumer (reg 8(1)). However, the scope of the Regulations in an insurance context is limited by the fact that this provision has no application to a term which defines the main subject matter of the contract, provided that it is in plain and intelligible language (reg 6(2)); and it is arguable that every term in an insurance contract which serves to define or limit the risk is part of its 'main subject matter'. It is likely, therefore, that (apart from the 'plain language' requirement), the Regulations can only be invoked in relation to (for example) a term requiring notice of a claim to be given within a specified time, and not to any of the warranties, exceptions and limitations which are discussed above. More importantly, perhaps, the Director General of Fair Trading and various consumer protection bodies are given powers to monitor the use of unfair terms and to obtain undertakings or injunctions to control or prevent their use (regs 10–16).

4 LIABILITY OF THE INSURER

(a) Notice

In principle, the insured is entitled to payment of the sum assured on the happening of the event that has been insured against. But in practice most policies stipulate that he should give notice of the event and details of his loss within a specified time, and (depending upon the construction of the contract) it may be a condition precedent to the insurer's liability that this requirement is strictly adhered to.

(b) The onus of proof

The burden of proving that the event which has occurred is covered by the policy and, in a policy of indemnity, that he has suffered loss or damage is on the insured; but where the insurer seeks to avoid liability on the ground that the claim is covered by an exception the onus is normally shifted to him. This will be the case also where he claims to be entitled to avoid liability on the ground that the insured caused the loss deliberately, or that the claim is fraudulent.

The standard of proof is the civil one of the balance of probabilities. The insured is required to show that the event was the 'proximate' or 'operative' cause of his loss—often a difficult issue, but of course one which is not confined to this branch of the law. The court is sometimes willing to take a broad approach: thus, where loss or damage is caused to goods by water as a result of action taken to prevent a fire from spreading, the loss has been treated as caused by the fire (*Symington & Co v Union Insurance Society of Canton* (1928) 97 LJKB 646, CA). In contrast, in *Winicofsky v Army & Navy General Assurance Association Ltd* (1919) 88 LJKB 1111, where goods were stolen during an air raid, it was held that it was not the air raid but the theft which was the cause of the loss—the air raid had merely facilitated it.

In indemnity insurance, the onus is also on the insured to prove the quantum of his loss, except where the parties have agreed the value of the insured property under the terms of the policy. It may also be agreed as a term of the contract that the insurer will pay only for any loss in excess of a specified sum; or that the insured will bear a proportionate part of the loss if the property is insured for less than its full value (sometimes called an 'average' clause—a term which is implied by law in contracts of marine insurance); or that a person who has insured the same risk with more than one insurer will claim only a rateable proportion of his loss.

A claim under a contract of indemnity insurance is, by definition, limited to the amount of the insured's actual loss.

Castellain v Preston

(1883) 11 QBD 380, Court of Appeal

In July 1878 Preston and others, who owned certain land and buildings in Liverpool, contracted to sell the property to their tenants, Rayners. Two weeks later part of the buildings was damaged by a fire. The owners claimed for their loss from their insurers and, after negotiation, were paid a sum of £330. They also completed the sale of the land and received the full purchase price from the buyers. In this action the court held that, since the owners had sustained no loss, they were bound to repay the £330 to their insurers.

Cotton LJ: In this case the appellant's company insured a house belonging to the defendants, and before there was any loss by fire the defendants sold the house to certain purchasers. Afterwards there was a fire, and an agreed sum was paid by the insurance office to the defendants in respect of the loss....

The company seek to obtain the benefit either wholly or partly of the amount paid by them out of the purchase-money which the defendants have received since the fire from the purchasers. In my opinion, the plaintiff is right in that contention. I think that the question turns on the consideration of what a policy of insurance against fire is, and on that the right of the plaintiff depends. The policy is really a contract to indemnify the person insured for the loss which he has sustained in consequence of the peril insured against which has happened, and from that it follows, of course, that as it is only a contract of indemnity, it is only to pay that loss which the assured may have sustained by reason of the fire which has occurred. In order to ascertain what that loss is, everything must be taken into account which is received by and comes to the hand of the assured, and which diminishes that loss. It is only the amount of the loss, when it is considered as a contract of indemnity, which is to be paid after taking into account and estimating those benefits or sums of money which the assured may have received in diminution of the loss....

Brett LJ: ...The very foundation, in my opinion, of every rule which has been applied to insurance law is this, namely, that the contract of insurance contained in a marine or fire policy is a contract of indemnity, and of indemnity only, and that this contract means that the assured, in case of a loss against which the policy has been made, shall be fully indemnified, but shall never be more than fully indemnified. That is the fundamental principle of insurance, and if ever a proposition is brought forward which is at variance with it, that is to say, which either will prevent the assured from obtaining a full indemnity, or which will give to the assured more than a full indemnity, that proposition must certainly be wrong.

[Bowen LJ delivered a concurring judgment.]

(c) Reinstatement

Although the insurer's liability is normally to pay the insured a sum of money to reimburse him for his loss, the contract may give the insurer the option of reinstating the property. Thus, if a building is wholly or partly destroyed by fire, the insurer may have it rebuilt or repaired instead of paying the value of the loss. If the insurer does so elect, he must then reinstate the property whether the cost to him is greater or less than the sum insured. Under the old Fires Prevention (Metropolis) Act 1774, s 83—which, incidentally, is not confined in its application to 'the metropolis'—an insured or other interested person is entitled to *require* an insurance company to apply the policy monies towards reinstating an insured building which is destroyed or damaged by fire, but this statutory obligation extends only to expending the amount of the policy monies and no more.

(d) Insurer's liability to third parties

A policy may be expressed in terms that the insurer agrees to indemnify parties other than the policy holder (eg a policy taken out by a building company which extends to employees and sub-contractors for liabilities incurred by them in carrying out a construction contract). Prior to the enactment of the Contracts (Rights of Third Parties) Act 1999, the doctrine of privity of contract created difficulties if such a party sought to enforce the contract directly against the insurer. But this Act now gives such a party the right to do so, provided that the contract purports to confer a benefit on him and he is expressly identified in the contract by name, as a member of a class, or as answering to a particular description.

Where a policy covers an insured against his liability to third parties (as in motor vehicle and employer's liability insurance), problems may arise if the insured is insolvent or is for some reason unable to enforce the policy—eg if it is a company which has been wound up and dissolved. In such circumstances the third party, such as the victim of a motor accident caused by the insured's negligence, may be prejudiced. In the case of an insolvency, he would rank as an ordinary unsecured creditor and any money claimed under the policy would go into the general pool of assets, while if the insured company has been dissolved he would succeed only if he was able to have the company reinstated by court order. The Third Parties (Rights against Insurers) Act 1930 was passed in order to deal with this sort of problem: as its name suggests, it gives the victim a right to proceed directly against the insurer. But that Act deals mainly with insolvency situations and is not comprehensive, and so the Law Commissions have recommended that the law should be reformed: see their Report, *Third Parties—Rights against Insurers* (L Com No 272, Scot L Com No 184, 2001).

5 RIGHTS OF THE INSURER

An insurer who has reimbursed the insured for his loss under an indemnity policy has three rights: of salvage, of subrogation and of contribution.

(a) Salvage

Where an insurer has compensated an insured for the total loss of the insured property, all rights to the property are ceded by operation of law to the insurer, who thereby becomes their owner. So, if a car or ship is so damaged that it is uneconomic to repair it (a 'constructive total loss') and the insurer pays its owner its full value, the insurer can exercise this right of salvage in respect of the wrecked property and sell it for what it will fetch. In *Holmes v Payne* [1930] 2 KB 301, Mrs Payne lost a pearl necklace which she had insured for an agreed value of £600. The insurers agreed to settle her claim by allowing her to buy other articles of jewellery to a total value of £600. After this, when she had bought only £264 worth of replacement jewellery, the necklace was found. Roche J held that the agreement was equivalent to the payment of a full indemnity, with the consequence that the insurers had become the owners of the necklace and were bound to allow her to buy the other £336 worth of jewellery.

(b) Subrogation

The doctrine of subrogation has its basis in the principle of unjust enrichment. It has two aspects. One, illustrated by the case of *Castellain v Preston* (above, p 1203) is the rule that an insured cannot ever receive more than a full indemnity for his loss, and if he does receive more, he is accountable to the insurer for it. The second is that an insurer who has indemnified his assured is entitled to succeed to all the rights of the latter—as it is commonly put, to 'stand in his shoes'—and so he may, for instance, sue any third party who is liable to the insured for the loss in an action of tort or contract. For this purpose, he may use the insured's name in the litigation. In the well-known case of *Lister v Romford Ice & Cold Storage Co Ltd* [1957] AC 555, HL, Lister, a lorry driver employed by the Romford Ice Company, had negligently injured his father when reversing his lorry. The company's insurers paid damages to the father and then brought this action in the company's name to recoup the money from Lister. It was held that the insurers were entitled to do so for, standing in the company's shoes, they could (1) allege that he was in breach of a term in his contract of employment that he would drive with reasonable care and skill, and (2) alternatively, claim contribution from him as a joint tortfeasor under what is now the Civil Liability (Contribution) Act 1978.

The insured, for his part, may not do anything which prejudices the insurer's right of subrogation, eg grant a release to a tortfeasor or compromise his claim without the insurer's consent.

(c) Contribution

Where an insured has taken out more than one policy of indemnity insurance in respect of the same risk, any one insurer who has met a claim for the loss in full is entitled to claim contribution in equity on a rateable basis from the other insurers.

6 MARINE INSURANCE

The law of insurance has its origins in the early days of seafaring, and most of its principles were worked out first in relation to the risks associated with ships and their cargoes and the loss of freight which the carrier would sustain if a ship should fail to complete its voyage. The law governing contracts of marine insurance was codified by statute in the Marine Insurance Act 1906—the last of the great codification exercises carried out by Sir Mackenzie Chalmers, following his successful work with the Bills of Exchange Act 1882 and the Sale of Goods Act 1893. In some special respects, marine insurance law has developed its own rules; but, broadly speaking, its principles are indicative of those of insurance law generally, and judges in non-marine cases do quite often refer to marine insurance decisions and even to the Act itself for guidance. In this chapter, no special attention has been paid to those topics where marine insurance law has different rules—eg that a contract of marine insurance must be recorded in writing. It is thought sufficient in a work of this nature to deal with the subject of insurance generally, and to add the warning that if an issue of marine insurance is involved, a specialist work should be consulted.

PART X

INSOLVENCY LAW

CHAPTER 29
INSOLVENCY

1 INTRODUCTION

The law relating to the bankruptcy of individuals goes back to a statute of Henry VIII in 1542. The concern of this early legislation (which applied only to persons engaged in trade) was to establish a procedure for the realisation and orderly distribution of the debtor's property among his creditors generally: the fate of the person himself—and still less the question of his rehabilitation into the world of commerce—was not thought to be important. We do not need to look further than the pages of Dickens to discover that in as late as Victorian times people who could not pay their debts were treated little better than criminals, even when their insolvency was due purely to misfortune. There were, it is true, major steps taken to ameliorate the position by the Bankruptcy Acts of 1883 and 1914, but the regime remained a fairly harsh one and the 'stigma of bankruptcy' something that it was never easy to shake off.

Corporate insolvency law, by comparison, dates only from the first companies legislation of 1844. And in stark contrast with the position in bankruptcy, the individuals concerned have usually been able to escape with relative impunity by taking advantage of the principle of limited liability.

Until the reforms of 1985–86 there was separate legislation for bankruptcies and corporate insolvencies, although some of the principles of bankruptcy law were extended to companies by the operation of a general 'incorporation' provision in the Companies Act.

The initiative for change came from the report of the Review Committee on Insolvency Law and Practice (Cmnd 8558, 1982), commonly known as the 'Cork Committee' after its chairman, Sir Kenneth Cork. This committee recommended that the law should be streamlined and modernised and that bankruptcy law and corporate insolvency law should be integrated and brought rather more into line. This would involve a relaxation of the harsher aspects of bankruptcy law, with a much greater emphasis on the restoration of the debtor to a normal role in the community, and at the same time a tightening up in those areas of corporate insolvency law which had formerly lent themselves to abuse. These recommendations were largely implemented by the Insolvency Act 1985; but very little of this Act was brought into force. Instead, it was almost immediately superseded by the Insolvency Act 1986—a consolidating measure which brought together the new legislation of 1985 and large parts of the Companies Act. In the remainder of this chapter, the Insolvency Act 1986 is referred to as 'IA 1986' and section numbers refer to that Act.

The 1986 Act has since been amended, mainly by the Insolvency Act 2000 and the Enterprise Act 2002. The latter Act made significant changes to both bankruptcy law and the law governing corporate insolvencies. A sharper distinction was made between bankruptcies which were due to misfortune (and in particular consumer cases) and those resulting from irresponsible or fraudulent conduct. On the one hand, it was made easier for a non-culpable debtor to obtain an early discharge and resume a normal life, while on the other a guilty bankrupt could be subjected to restrictions on his activities for up to 15 years. In the corporate sphere, secured creditors holding a floating charge over all or substantially all of a company's assets were no longer permitted to enforce their charge by appointing a receiver but were required instead to use the administration regime, and at the same time it was made possible to put a company into administration by a simpler procedure which did not require an application to court. In addition, the longstanding rule which gave priority to Crown debts in an insolvency was abolished.

Two other measures introduced a degree of order into the administration of insolvencies which contain a cross-border element—eg where the debtor (individual or corporate) has assets or creditors in more than one country. The first, the EC Regulation on Insolvency Proceedings 2000, applies throughout the EU (except for Denmark, which has an opt-out). The Regulation requires the insolvency to be administered primarily by main proceedings in the Member State where the debtor has his (or its) principal base, and by ancillary proceedings in other States, and co-ordinates and regulates the relationship between the two. At the same time it provides that the proceedings in every jurisdiction, and the authority of the liquidator or other office-holder in the proceeding, be recognised without any formality throughout the EU. The second is a piece of purely domestic legislation, the Cross-Border Insolvency Regulations 2006, which provides for recognition of the validity of foreign insolvency proceedings instituted anywhere in the world, and the authority of their office-holders, without the need for formal court proceedings. The Regulations are based on the Model Law on Cross-Border Insolvency which was adopted by the UN Commission on International Trade Law (UNCITRAL) in 1997. The enactment of the Regulations was, of course, a unilateral step: a more general international regime will only come into place as other countries follow suit.

2 THE BASIC OBJECTIVES OF INSOLVENCY LAW

We may summarise the basic objectives of insolvency law as follows.
   In the bankruptcy of individuals:

(1) to protect the insolvent from harassment by his creditors;

(2) to enable him to make a fresh start, especially in less blameworthy cases;

(3) to have him reduce his indebtedness by making such contribution from his present resources and future earnings as is just, taking into account his personal circumstances and the claims and needs of his family.

In corporate insolvency:

(1) where possible, to preserve the business, or the viable parts of it (but not necessarily the *company*);

(2) where it is considered that the principle of limited liability has been abused, to impose personal liability and other sanctions on those responsible.

In both forms of insolvency:

(1) to ensure that all creditors participate *pari passu* (ie on an equal footing) in the estate, except in so far as they may have priority as secured creditors or a statutory right to preference;

(2) to ensure that secured creditors deal fairly in realising and enforcing their security, vis-à-vis both the debtor and the other creditors;

(3) to investigate impartially the reasons for failure and to see that such disabilities and penalties as are appropriate are imposed, in the interests of society;

(4) where the assets of the insolvent have been improperly dealt with prior to the onset of insolvency (eg so as to remove them from the estate, or give a preference to some creditors at the expense of others), to recoup the assets for the benefit of the general estate.

The importance of the *pari passu* principle is shown by the following case.

British Eagle International Airlines Ltd v Cie Nationale Air France
[1975] 1 WLR 758, House of Lords

Many of the world's airlines are members of IATA (the International Air Transport Association). A 'clearing house' scheme was set up under which the debts and credits between one airline and another arising from carrying each other's passengers and cargo were not settled directly but were pooled through IATA. A balance was struck each month and the net sum due was then paid by IATA to each airline or vice versa, as appropriate. British Eagle went into liquidation at a time when it was a net debtor to the scheme as a whole, but if the scheme was ignored it was a net creditor as between itself and Air France. The House of Lords, by a majority, held that the clearing house arrangement was contrary to public policy, in that the parties to it were contracting out of the statutory regime which would apply in a liquidation.

Lord Cross of Chelsea: …What the respondents are saying here is that the parties to the 'clearing house' arrangements by agreeing that simple contract debts are to be satisfied in a particular way have succeeded in 'contracting out' of the provisions contained in [Insolvency Act 1986 s 107] for the payment of unsecured debts 'pari passu.' In such a context it is to my mind irrelevant that the parties to the 'clearing house' arrangements had good business reasons for entering into them and did not direct their minds to the question how the arrangements might be affected by the insolvency of one or more of the parties. Such a 'contracting out' must, to my mind, be contrary to public policy. The question is, in essence, whether what was called in argument the 'mini liquidation' flowing from the clearing house arrangements is to yield to or to prevail over the general liquidation. I cannot doubt that on principle the rules of the general liquidation should prevail. I would therefore hold that notwithstanding the clearing house arrangements, British Eagle on its liquidation became entitled to recover payment of the sums payable to it by other airlines for services rendered by it during that period and that airlines which had rendered services to it during that period became on the liquidation entitled to prove for the sums payable to them….

[Lords Diplock and Edmund-Davies concurred.
Lords Morris of Borth-y-Gest and Simon of Glaisdale dissented.]

NOTE

Although the *British Eagle* ruling remains authoritative for the purposes of the general law, it has been recognised that in practice, in the interests of expediency, such 'clearing house' and 'pooling' arrangements perform a useful function in the financial, banking and securities settlement markets. Accordingly, legislation has been passed directing that contracts of this nature made between the participants on these markets are to have effect, to the exclusion of the normal rules of insolvency law: see, eg the Companies Act 1989, Part VII, the Financial Markets and Insolvency Regulations 1991, SI 1991/880 and the Financial Markets and Insolvency (Settlement Finality) Regulations 1999, SI 1999/2979.

3 THE VARIOUS DEFINITIONS OF INSOLVENCY

There is no single meaning of the term 'insolvent'. It is important to distinguish between three different definitions of this unhappy state—or, rather, at least three, since these are broad-brush distinctions and any one of them may have variations on points of detail.

'Balance-sheet' insolvency. The first test of insolvency has regard to the person's assets and liabilities, and looks to see whether there is, overall, a net surplus or a deficit. If there is a deficit, that person is insolvent. A company with investments which have fallen in value may become 'insolvent' within this definition, even though it is currently trading satisfactorily and paying its way.

'Commercial' insolvency. This test is not concerned with the asset position, but with liquidity. It is sometimes also called 'practical' insolvency or insolvency on a 'cash-flow' basis. The person concerned may have substantial assets, but is unable to pay his debts as they fall due. This could be so of a company, for instance, which has its wealth tied up in property that is not readily realisable (eg in out-of-season stock, or half-finished products), or which has over-spent on research and development for a new project which is still on the drawing-board.

'Ultimate' insolvency. Here we are concerned with the final outcome of events. The debtor's assets have been sold for what they will fetch—perhaps in a forced sale, on a break-up basis—and the costs of realisation and of administering the estate are brought into account. If his creditors have received less than 100p in the pound, we can say that the estate was insolvent. Many a person who could very reasonably have claimed to be solvent if his assets were valued on a going-concern basis may prove, in the event, to be insolvent in this sense if the worst happens.

Insolvency, as such, has very few legal consequences. So, for instance, the fact that a person who is a party to a contract becomes insolvent does not amount to a repudiation of the contract or entitle the other party to terminate it, unless the contract so provides. Occasionally, however, rights may be affected by *statute* because a party has become insolvent—eg in a sale of goods, an unpaid seller is given the right to stop the goods in transit if the buyer has become insolvent (see above, p 443). But it is usually only as a consequence of some *insolvency procedure* that the legal position changes—eg when an individual has been declared bankrupt, or a company has gone into liquidation, administration or receivership.

Where 'insolvency' is a precondition for the operation of a provision in a statute or a contract or other document, it is obviously important to determine in which of the various senses the term is to be construed. Thus, in the Sale of Goods Act 1979, a person is deemed to be insolvent 'if he has either ceased to pay his debts in the ordinary course of business or he cannot pay his debts as they become due' (s 61(4)); and so the seller's right of stoppage in transit referred to above will arise if the buyer is 'insolvent' in a 'commercial' sense. In contrast, the question whether a director can be held liable for 'wrongful trading' (see below, p 1237) depends in part on whether there was a 'reasonable prospect that the company would avoid going into insolvent liquidation'; and for this purpose IA 1986 prescribes a 'balance sheet' test (s 214(6)). Plainly, the relevant definition must be examined closely in each case.

4 INSOLVENCY PROCEDURES

(a) Individual insolvency

When an individual becomes insolvent, a choice of statutory procedures is available.

County court administration order made under the County Courts Act 1984, Part VI. (These orders should not be confused with administration orders made in relation to insolvent companies under Part II of the Insolvency Act 1986 (see below, p 1214).) An order may be made against a person who cannot pay the whole of a judgment debt and whose total indebtedness is not more than £5,000. A moratorium comes into effect and an officer of the court supervises the payment of the debts of such creditors as are known by instalments out of the debtor's income.

Individual voluntary arrangement (IVA) (IA 1986, Part VIII). This is a scheme of voluntary arrangement of a fairly informal kind, supervised by a professional insolvency practitioner. A moratorium can be sought from the court, staying all enforcement proceedings while the supervisor of the scheme and the creditors consider proposals to resolve the position, eg by a compromise, which can be made binding on all creditors if supported by a sufficient majority.

Bankruptcy order (IA 1986, Part IX). A bankruptcy order may be made against a person on his own petition, or that of one or more creditors whose debts total at least £750, on the ground that he is unable to pay his debts (or, in the case of a creditor's petition, that he 'appears to be' unable to pay his debts or to have no reasonable prospect' of paying his debts). A 'commercial' rather than a 'balance-sheet' test of insolvency is thus applied. A debtor will be deemed unable to pay his debts if he has failed to pay a debt within three weeks after being served with a statutory demand for payment, or if execution has been issued against him and has been returned unsatisfied. An order will not be made on the basis of a debt which is the subject of a bona fide dispute; nor will the court resolve such a dispute in the bankruptcy proceedings—the parties must litigate the matter elsewhere in the normal way.

The Official Receiver (a government officer attached to the court) takes charge of the bankrupt's assets until an independent insolvency practitioner is appointed trustee. On his appointment, the bankrupt's assets vest in the trustee. He has the responsibility of administering the bankrupt's estate, realising the available assets and applying them, so far as they will go, towards satisfying the creditors. Certain creditors are entitled to be paid in priority: primarily employees, for up to £800 unpaid wages. (For full details, see IA 1986, Sch 6.) (Until recently, the Crown was also entitled to priority, up to certain limits, for unpaid PAYE taxes, VAT and NIC contributions, but this was abolished by the Enterprise Act 2002.) The rules in this respect are identical, or nearly so, to those which apply in a company liquidation, as are those relating to transactions at an undervalue, preferences and transactions defrauding creditors which are discussed below, at pp 1230–1237. The bankrupt is entitled to keep tools, books, vehicles, etc necessary for his employment and furniture, clothing and household equipment necessary for use by him and his family.

During the currency of a bankruptcy order, the bankrupt is subject to a number of disabilities—eg he may not be a company director—and there are restrictions upon his obtaining credit. But it is now the policy of the law that this situation should not continue for any long period: unless there has been some impropriety, or the person has been bankrupt more than once, a *discharge in bankruptcy* becomes effective automatically after one year (at least in most cases). Once a bankrupt is discharged, all his pre-bankruptcy debts are deemed to have been satisfied, and he is free to live a normal life again. Until the Enterprise Act 2002 came into force in 2004, the normal duration of a bankruptcy had been three years, but that Act introduced a distinction between debtors who had been guilty of culpable wrongdoing and those who had not, and reduced the period for the latter.

This reflected a general policy which recognises that many bankruptcies (and particularly those involving consumers or persons in a small way of business) are the consequence of bad luck or poor judgment rather than anything seriously blameworthy, and which seeks to give such debtors a 'fresh start'. In contrast, there is now a power for the court to make a 'bankruptcy restrictions order', similar to a director disqualification order (see the Company Directors Disqualification Act 1986), where fraudulent or irresponsible conduct by the debtor has caused him to become insolvent. Such an order can last after his discharge from bankruptcy and will prevent him from acting as a company director, impose restrictions on obtaining credit, etc for up to 15 years. As an alternative to a court order, he may give a bankruptcy restrictions undertaking to the Secretary of State, which has the same effect.

For further reading, see IF Fletcher *The Law of Insolvency* (3rd edn, 2002); C Berry, E Bailey and SS Miller *Personal Insolvency, Law and Practice* (3rd edn, 2002).

(b) Corporate insolvency

Again, a range of procedures is available.

Company voluntary arrangement (CVA) (IA 1986, Part I). This is a new procedure introduced by the Act of 1986. It is similar in many respects to the individual voluntary arrangement. Once again, a qualified insolvency practitioner is brought in to put proposals to a meeting of the company's creditors and, if they agree to its terms, to supervise the scheme. In contrast with an IVA, there was no provision in IA 1986 as originally enacted enabling a moratorium to be put in place while the proposal for a CVA was being put together and considered by the company's creditors. This was a weakness in the law and was the main reason why the CVA was relatively little used in practice. However, since 1 January 2003, s 1 of and Sch A1 to IA 2000 have been in force—provisions (in quite astonishing detail) which now allow the directors of a company who propose a CVA to take steps to obtain a moratorium while the arrangement is being formulated and put before the creditors for approval. This protection is restricted to 'small' private companies (as defined by the Companies Act 1985, s 247(3)), and is not available for certain categories of company (eg banks and insurance companies), for companies which are already subject to some other insolvency procedure and for a company which has had the benefit of a similar moratorium in the previous 12 months. In practice, the administration procedure (below) is commonly preferred since it is less formal and more flexible.

Administration (IA 1986, Part II). This is another innovation dating from the 1986 reforms. As with a CVA, the affairs of the company are placed under the control of an insolvency practitioner, without putting it into liquidation, but instead of pursuing a plan agreed at a meeting of the company's creditors, the administrator's role and the objectives which he must seek to achieve are primarily laid down by statute. Under Part II as originally enacted, a company could only be put into administration by an order of the court, and the procedure was formal and relatively slow and expensive. In consequence, it was not used as often as might have been expected. One reason was that the law allowed the holder of a floating charge over the company's general assets to veto an administration and put the company into receivership instead—more accurately, into 'administrative' receivership (see below). Since this could be done very speedily and the receiver could normally carry out his functions independently of the court, it was naturally more likely to be preferred.

But with the enactment of the Enterprise Act 2002, everything was stood on its head. Part II was replaced and a new administration regime introduced which in most cases did not require the participation of the court (and the associated formality, delay and expense). At the same time a new s 72A was inserted into the Insolvency Act 1986 which (with a few exceptions) prohibited the holder of a floating charge from appointing an administrative receiver. So if a charge holder wishes to enforce his security against the company's property, he must now normally use the administration procedure. However, the whole process of putting a company into administration has been simplified and streamlined, and the statutory purposes of an administration have been redefined so as to include 'realising property in order to make a distribution to one or more secured or preferential creditors', so that in many ways the disadvantages of administration when compared with receivership have been eliminated or reduced.

The thinking that prompted this change in the law was that, whereas administration is a procedure designed to take into account the interests of all parties—shareholders, creditors and everyone else concerned in the business and its possible survival—the principal function of a receiver is to look after the interests of the creditor who has appointed him, usually by realising sufficient assets to pay off the secured debt. As we shall see, a receiver owes only very limited duties to have regard to the interests of the company itself or any of its other stakeholders. The object of the reforms contained in the Enterprise Act 2002 was to promote more of a 'rescue' culture, making the survival of the company's business, so far as that could be achieved, a primary objective, and it was believed that this could best be done by making greater use of the administration procedure. In addition, the statutory purposes of an administration were reformulated so as to give greater emphasis—indeed, priority—to the survival of the company's business while at the same time making suitable provision, as noted above, to ensure that the security rights of floating changes were respected in the administration.

The new Part II is to be found in Schedule B1 to the Enterprise Act 2002. A company may be put into administration by an out-of-court procedure by (a) the company itself or its directors, or (b) the holder of a floating charge secured over all or substantially all of the company's assets. This is done simply by filing a notice of appointment of the administrator and other prescribed documents with the court: it is not involved in any judicial capacity (although it is given some back-up and supervisory powers). Other persons (eg an unsecured creditor) are still able to have a company put into administration, but only by obtaining a court order. Although the charge holder no longer has the power to block an administration, various rules ensure that he is kept informed of steps taken by other parties and can, for instance, have an insolvency practitioner of his own choosing appointed to act instead of or in addition to some other nominee. But all administrators are now required to perform their functions with the same objectives, ranked in priority as follows:

(a) rescuing the company as a going concern,

(b) achieving a better result for the company's creditors as a whole than would be likely if the company were wound up,

(c) realising property in order to make a distribution to secured or preferential creditors.

So even if it is a charge holder who has made the appointment, his interests now have to be subordinated to objects (a) and (b) if either of them is thought to be achievable.

An administrator has wide statutory powers, which are set out in IA 1986, Sch 1. In addition he may, with the leave of the court, dispose of assets which are in the company's possession but which are owned by others (eg machines which the company has on lease or hire-purchase, or goods which it has contracted to buy on 'retention of title' terms) or which are subject to security interests in favour of other parties (IA 1986, s 15). This provision plainly makes it easier for an administrator to sell the business on a going-concern basis, and prevents the owner or security-holder from being obstructive if such a sale is proposed. Any order which the court makes under s 15 will, of course, include provision for the person concerned to be paid the value of his interest out of the proceeds of sale of the property.

It is unlikely that, in the great majority of cases, the first statutory objective of rescuing the company as a going concern will be regarded as achievable—still less achieved, particularly since it is a prerequisite to an appointment that the company should be insolvent (or, where it is a charge-holder who initiates the procedure, that the security should have become enforceable). However, the appointment of an administrator brings about a moratorium binding on all creditors which will allow a breathing space for him to try to find additional or alternative finance or in some other way restore vitality to the enterprise so that control can be handed back to the directors. A more likely outcome is that the company's *business* or the profitable parts of it will be sold for a better sum than would be likely in a liquidation, so achieving the second statutory purpose. It is only when neither of these objectives is considered likely to be fulfilled that the administrator may proceed to enforce a charge-holder's security.

On his appointment, the administrator calls for a 'statement of affairs' of the company to be prepared by one or more of its officers, and on the strength of this information it is his duty to formulate proposals for achieving the purpose of the administration and to summon meetings of the creditors to consider them with a view to their approval. If they are approved, it is then his duty to seek to carry them out. He is empowered to take custody or control of the company's property and to do anything necessary for the management of its business and property.

But in all too many cases there will be no future for the enterprise and the only option will be to close it down. The Act spells out a straightforward procedure enabling the administration to proceed seamlessly to a liquidation (usually with the same insolvency practitioner becoming liquidator) or, in the worst case, where the company is hopelessly insolvent, empowering the administrator to have it dissolved without further formality.

One advantage that administration has over receivership is that, since it is a 'collective' procedure intended to look after the interests of all the insolvent company's creditors, and since it has the backing of the court, it is much more likely to be recognised by a foreign court, in any jurisdiction where the institution of receivership is unknown.

The case of *Re Cavco Floors Ltd* is an early illustration of the operation of the administration procedure in practice: it also shows the remarkable willingness of the judges in the Companies Court to make the new procedure a workable one, even to the point of bending the rules to accommodate a deserving case.

Re Cavco Floors Ltd
[1990] BCLC 940, Chancery Division

(The facts appear from the judgment.)

Harman J: In this matter counsel (Mr Dicker) appears before me, on the instructions of well-known solicitors in the matter of an intended petition. He offers me an undertaking by the solicitors to present a petition forthwith (whether tonight or tomorrow morning is not important, but very very speedily) and he invites me to make an order now on that intended petition. The petition is the petition of Cavco Floors Ltd (the company) for the making of an administration order in respect of the company; the purposes are for the more advantageous realisation of the company's assets than would be effected on a winding up.

The evidence, which is impressively marshalled in the affidavit of Mrs Harvey, a director and substantial shareholder in the company, sets out the company's business, shows that for the year to July 1989, on what appear to be very well-compiled accounts, the company was trading profitably and had a credit balance on its profit-and-loss account, deposes to the well-known fact that the building trade is currently undergoing severe cash-flow difficulties and finally avers that the company is, on the basis that it is unable to pay its debts as they fall due, insolvent. All that I find impressive and I accept that evidence completely.

Mrs Harvey goes on to depose that there are none the less substantial assets of the company in current contracts which are profitable, a statement which appears to be well warranted by the material before the court, and that if an administrator is appointed who can carry on the business over the next comparatively short time there are various offers for the assets and goodwill of the company which may realise substantially better sums than could conceivably be expected if the company has to go into creditors' voluntary liquidation. She also shows that there is a creditor who has obtained a judgment against the company, although the company has a very substantial claim by way of offset against that creditor, that that creditor has served a statutory demand and may be in a position to present a winding-up petition at any time in the course of this week.

Further, she shows that the National Westminster Bank plc, as the company's bankers, are in a position to appoint an administrative receiver, have a comparatively small secured debt, some £13,000-odd, but have refused the directors' request so to appoint. Quite why they have chosen to take that course I do not understand, since it was advised by the licensed insolvency practitioner now proposed to be appointed as administrator. The bank has, however, written a letter, which it is undertaken will be put in evidence. That letter was written this morning by the insolvency and debt recovery department of the bank to the solicitors acting for the company. It sets out very clearly that the bank has had the draft petition, the affidavit of Mrs Harvey and the draft report of the proposed administrator. By the letter the bank consents to the abridgment of time between presentation of the petition and the hearing and to an administration order to be made forthwith. The bank by that letter therefore entirely accedes to the petition and presumably waives any possibility of objection by the bank as the person entitled to appoint an administrative receiver.

I have been concerned whether it is right for the court to appoint an administrator in this pell-mell way, it being clear that the whole design of ss 8, 9, 10 and 11 of the Insolvency Act 1986 is that Parliament expected that petitions would be presented, notice given of the presentation and the petition should then come on for hearing after a short interim, during which s 10 is designed to assure that nothing whatever can happen to the assets or business of the company. The Insolvency Rules 1986, SI 1986/1925, provide in r 2.1 for the procedure on the making of an administration order. By r 2.2 a report is required, which is satisfied by the report in this case of Mr David Gilbert, the insolvency practitioner, and other procedural requirements are set out. It is quite plain that r 2.5 expects that the petition and affidavits shall be filed, that copies for service shall be provided and that the petition is to be served on various people including the proposed administrator. In this case Mr Gilbert consents to the waiver of that requirement, which I can waive. The 1986 rules provide further by r 2.7(1) that the service of the petition shall be not less than five days before the date fixed for hearing. Again, it is plain that the whole of the rules proceed on a basis that there will be an interval between presentation and hearing.

However, in this case the directors (having been warned of the dangers of trading while insolvent) have said that they are not prepared to carry on the business of the company even for some two or three days during which, the evidence of Mrs Harvey makes it plain, it is vital that the company continue to perform its building contracts, that the bank has withdrawn support and will not finance the business for that short time, and therefore that unless an administrator is appointed forthwith there is a serious risk that the company will suffer the substantial difficulties that arise in the building trade, which it is notorious are quick to be snatched by prime contractors when a sub-contractor fails to perform according to his contract.

I have vacillated for some time whether it is right to abridge the time quite so drastically, but in the end I have concluded under counsel's persuasion that this is a case where the preparation of the petition, the affidavit in support and the r 2.2 statement give me such confidence that the only possible result after hearing representations must be that the court would make an administration order and that no injustice can possibly be caused to any person by my abridging time, not permitting any notice to be given to the creditor who has presented a statutory demand and not giving any time to the bank to have second thoughts on the consent which it gave this morning.

It is, in my view, an undesirable procedure for the court to act before presentation in this way, but it is a procedure which may need to be adopted in some cases and I am convinced by the evidence I have had that it is appropriate in this case. I shall therefore make an administration order and appoint Mr Gilbert as the administrator for the purposes set out in the petition.

Re Cavco Floors was decided under the original Part II, where a court order had to be obtained in all cases. Now that most administrators are appointed out of court, it is not surprising that relatively few cases are reported, mainly on points of statutory interpretation. But it appears that the judges continue to favour a creative and purposive approach, smoothing out the difficulties rather than allowing technical points to hinder the development of a workable new regime.

Receivership, and in particular administrative receivership (IA 1986, Part III). The term *receiver* is a word that is used in a number of contexts, some of which have no necessary connection with insolvency. The court, for instance, has an inherent jurisdiction to appoint a person to act as a receiver in order to protect and preserve property which is the subject of litigation—eg in relation to partnership property pending the resolution of a partnership dispute. It may also appoint a receiver to enforce a charge or other security by taking control of the charged assets and, if appropriate, selling them.

We shall not be concerned in this section with the special rules that apply to receivers appointed by the court, but will look only at the type of receiver who is appointed *out of court,* by the holder of a charge, to enforce the security by taking control of the charged assets on behalf of the charge-holder and, in most cases, to realise the assets and pay off the charge with the proceeds. It has been customary for a century or more for the instrument which creates a charge to include among its terms a power for the charge-holder to appoint a receiver in this way. The power will normally be exercisable if there is some default on the part of the debtor or if an event occurs which puts the security in jeopardy. A receiver may be appointed to enforce either a fixed charge or a floating charge—or, for that matter, a security which combines both; but our interest will be centred mainly on the receiver who is appointed to enforce a floating charge which has been granted by a company over its undertaking and all of its assets, present and future.

Shamji v Johnson Matthey Bankers Ltd shows that the holder of a charge is entitled to have regard to his own interests in deciding whether to appoint a receiver: he owes no duty of care to the chargor or any guarantors.

Shamji v Johnson Matthey Bankers Ltd
[1986] BCLC 278, [1991] BCLC 36, Chancery Division and Court of Appeal

A group of companies owed the defendant bank (JMB) £21m, secured by mortgage debentures. JMB was pressing for the loan to be repaid, but had allowed the group 21 days to try to obtain alternative finance, and had agreed to extend this period by a further 14 days if it was satisfied that the refinancing negotiations were proceeding in a proper and expeditious manner. JMB appointed receivers within this 14-day period. The plaintiff alleged that JMB in taking this step had been in breach of a duty of care towards the group and its guarantors, but the court held that no such duty was recognised in law.

Hoffmann J: Counsel for the defendants said under the terms of the security documents as pleaded in the statement of claim, JMB had a contractual right to appoint a receiver at any time after demanding payment. In the absence of bad faith, the bank could not owe the mortgagors or guarantors a duty of care in deciding whether to exercise that right. It might owe some duty in the way in which the right was exercised (eg it might owe a duty to take reasonable care not to appoint an incompetent) but not as to whether it was exercised or not.

[His Lordship referred to a number of cases, and continued:]

It is clear, however, that in the case of a conflict between the interests of the mortgagor and mortgagee, any duty of care which the mortgagee owes to the mortgagor is subordinated to his right to act in the protection of his own interests. As Salmon LJ said in the *Cuckmere Brick Co* case ([1971] 2 All ER 633 at 643, [1971] Ch 949 at 965):

> If the mortgagee's interests, as he sees them, conflict with those of the mortgagor, the mortgagee can give preference to his own interests....

The appointment of a receiver seems to me to involve an inherent conflict of interest. The purpose of the power is to enable the mortgagee to take the management of the company's property out of the hands of the directors and entrust it to a person of the mortgagee's choice. That power is granted to the mortgagee by the security documents in completely unqualified terms. It seems to me that a decision by the mortgagee to exercise the power cannot be challenged except perhaps on grounds of bad faith. There is no room for the implication of a term that the mortgagee shall be under a duty to the mortgagor to 'consider all relevant matters' before exercising the power. If no such qualification can be read into the security documents, I do not think that a wider duty can exist in tort....

[The Court of Appeal affirmed this judgment, [1991] BCLC 36.]

The term 'receiver' was originally used to describe a person appointed to receive the *income* (eg rents) yielded by the property in question—hence the name. When the receiver's function was extended to include taking charge of the property itself, and perhaps selling it, the name was not changed. But where the property included a business which it was important to keep on foot as a going concern, it was necessary to ensure also that there was continuity of management while the receiver was in office; and so (whether the appointment was made by the court or by the charge-holder) in these cases a *manager* as well as a receiver would be appointed—or, more commonly, the same individual would be appointed as a *receiver and manager.* It is evident that such an appointment will invariably be appropriate where the charge extends to the whole or part of the debtor company's undertaking. In practice, most receivers' powers include a power to manage; and the Insolvency Act 1986, s 29(1) reflects this by stating that a 'receiver' includes a receiver or manager of the property of a company, and also a receiver or manager of part of the property of a company. (Section 29(2) goes on to define a particular category of receiver—an 'administrative receiver'—who is given special statutory powers and duties, which we shall examine later. But the Enterprise Act 2002 has now imposed a ban on the appointment of an administrative receiver (apart from a few exceptions), and a charge holder is obliged to appoint an administrator instead.)

Apart from the special case of administrative receivership, there is little legislation governing receivers: the Insolvency Act 1986 prohibits a body corporate or an undischarged bankrupt from acting as a receiver (ss 30, 31), and parts of the Law of Property Act 1925 dealing with mortgages may be relevant in some cases; but otherwise everything is left to the common law. A receiver usually has extensive powers conferred by the charge document under which he has been appointed and the instrument of appointment itself. It will be provided that in the exercise of these powers he shall be deemed to act as the agent of the company (and not of the charge holder who has appointed him) although this deemed agency will cease if the company should go into liquidation.

This is, however, an anomalous form of 'agency'. It does have the effect of ensuring that liabilities incurred by the receiver are met from the company's assets and not from those of the security-holder, but the company has few, if any, of the normal rights and powers of a principal—eg the power to give directions to the agent, or to remove him from office.

The receiver's responsibilities are focused primarily on the interests of the charge-holder whom he represents. His function may be simply to sell up some or all of the company's assets and apply them towards clearing the charge-holder's debt, with little or no regard to the consequences for the other creditors, employees, shareholders and, indeed, the business itself. But he may, alternatively, be appointed with the responsibility of managing the business for a time, in the hope that the company will trade its way out of a bad patch, or will find a new source of finance, or at the very least that its undertaking can be sold on a going-concern rather than a break-up basis, in whole or in part, and so fetch a better price. Whatever his function, however, the interests of the charge-holder who has appointed him come first, as the following cases illustrate.

Gomba Holdings UK Ltd v Homan

[1986] 1 WLR 1301, Chancery Division

This case was a sequel to *Shamji v Johnson Matthey Bankers Ltd* (above, p 1219). After the receivers had sold assets realising some £11 million, and while negotiations were taking place to make further sales, Shamji claimed to have entered into an agreement with an undisclosed third party which would provide funds to pay off the remainder of the debt owed by his group of companies to the bank. In these proceedings, the companies sought an order requiring the receivers not to dispose of further assets without first giving the companies five days' notice, and a further order compelling the receivers to disclose information about actual and pending sales. Hoffmann J refused both orders.

Hoffmann J: ... I shall consider first motion 3 to restrain the receivers from entering into any commitments to dispose of assets unless they have first given the plaintiffs five working days' written notice of the details of any such proposed commitment. Mr Cullen submitted that pending the proposed redemption, the balance of convenience favoured such an order because the sale of an asset without notice to the plaintiffs might upset the arrangements with the unknown third party. This may be true, although I think there are other matters which also enter into the balance of convenience. But the primary difficulty is that I can see no arguable cause of action which could entitle the plaintiffs to such relief. The security documents give the receivers an unrestricted right to sell at any time. Until actual redemption or at least a valid tender of the redemption price, these powers continue to exist. The fact that the plaintiffs claim that they will shortly be able to redeem cannot give them a right in law to restrict the powers granted to the receivers.

Even if there were a cause of action, I do not think that the balance of convenience would favour an injunction. The receivers are entitled to take the view that they should continue with realisations on the assumption that redemption may not take place. No doubt the receivers will exercise a commercial judgment in the matter. But an enforced delay of five working days or even the need to reveal the proposed transaction to the plaintiffs may cause the loss of an advantageous sale. As against this possibility of loss, the plaintiffs are unable to offer anything in support of a cross-undertaking in damages. I therefore dismiss motion 3.

Most of the three-day hearing of these motions was taken up with discussion of motion 1 for information. The cases do not provide very much guidance on the extent of the duty of a receiver and manager of the property of a company to provide information to the directors during the currency of the receivership. A receiver is an agent of the company and an agent ordinarily has a duty to be ready with his accounts and to provide his principal with information relating to the conduct of his agency. But these generalisations are of limited assistance because a receiver and manager is no ordinary agent. Although nominally the agent of the company, his primary duty is to realise the assets in the interests of the debenture holder and his powers of management are really ancillary to that duty: *Re B Johnson & Co (Builders) Ltd* [1955] Ch 634, 644–645 . . . .

There are, I think, certain principles which can be deduced from what the parties may be supposed to have contemplated as the commercial purpose of the power to appoint a receiver and manager. The first is that the receiver and manager should have the power to carry on the day to day process of realisation and management of the company's property without interference from the board. As Lord Atkinson said in *Moss SS Co Ltd v Whinney* [1912] AC 254, 263, the appointment of a receiver:

> entirely supersedes the company in the conduct of its business, deprives it of all power to enter into contracts in relation to that business, or to sell, pledge, or otherwise dispose of the property put into the possession, or under the control of the receiver and manager. Its powers in these respects are entirely in abeyance.

This relationship between the receivers and the company would suggest that the board may be entitled to periodic accounts but cannot, merely because it is the board and the receivers are agents of the company, demand current information about the conduct of the business . . . .

The second principle which can be deduced from the nature of receivership is that, in the absence of express contrary provision made by statute or the terms of the debenture, any right which the company may have to be supplied with information must be qualified by the receiver's primary duty to the debenture holder. If the receiver considers that disclosure of information would be contrary to the interests of the debenture holder in realising the security, I think he must be entitled to withhold it and probably owes a duty to the debenture holder to do so. The company may be able to challenge the receiver's decision on the ground of bad faith or possibly that it was a decision which no reasonable receiver could have made, but otherwise I think that the receiver is the best judge of the commercial consequences of disclosing information about his activities.

[His Lordship discussed the evidence, and concluded:]

The history of this case, both before and after the appointment of the receivers, is a chronicle of unfulfilled assurances by Mr Shamji that someone was just about to provide the money to pay his debts to the bank. In my judgment the receivers were under no obligation to provide any information until they had firmer evidence that there was a realistic prospect of redemption....

Downsview Nominees Ltd v First City Corpn Ltd
[1993] AC 295, Privy Council

Glen Eden Motors Ltd (GEM) had executed a debenture creating a first charge in favour of the Westpac bank and a debenture creating a second charge to First City Corporation (FCC). GEM had been trading at a loss when the debt due to FCC became payable, and FCC appointed receivers, who decided that it was necessary to sell GEM's assets. They removed Pedersen, the manager of GEM, from office. Pedersen consulted Russell, who controlled Downsview, a finance company, and as a result (1) Downsview took an assignment of the Westpac debenture, (2) it appointed Russell receiver under that debenture, (3) Russell then took control of GEM's assets, displacing the FCC receivers, and (4) Pedersen was reinstated as manager. Russell announced that it was his intention that GEM should trade its way out of its difficulties. FCC and its receivers warned Russell that in their view this course was likely to result in further losses, which would damage the company and FCC as the lower-ranking debentureholder, and they offered to pay off the whole of the money owed under the Westpac debenture. But Downsview refused this offer, and Russell and Pedersen continued to run the company, which lost a further $500,000. The Privy Council held Downsview and Russell liable in damages for breaches of their duty to use their powers as chargee and receiver for proper purposes; but they also confirmed two important points: (1) that a receiver's duties are owed primarily, if not exclusively, to the security holder who has appointed him, and this is inconsistent with the existence of a duty of care in law owed to the company or other creditors; and also (2) that his powers are conferred upon him solely for the purpose of securing the repayment of his appointor's debt, so that if either the company or any other interested party offers to pay off the debt, he must accept that offer and discharge this, his only, function.

The opinion of the Privy Council was delivered by **Lord Templeman,** who dealt with a number of points and continued:

The nature of the duties owed by a receiver and manager appointed by a debenture holder were authoritatively defined by Jenkins LJ in a characteristically learned and comprehensive judgment in *Re B Johnson & Co (Builders) Ltd* [1955] Ch 634, 661–663. Jenkins LJ said:

> ...The primary duty of the receiver is to the debenture holders and not to the company. He is receiver and manager of the property of the company for the debenture holders, not manager of the company. The company is entitled to any surplus of assets remaining after the debenture debt has been discharged, and is entitled to proper accounts. But the whole purpose of the receiver and manager's appointment would obviously be stultified if the company could claim that a receiver and manager owes it any duty comparable to the duty owed to a company by its own directors or managers.
>
> In determining whether a receiver and manager for the debenture holders of a company has broken any duty owed by him to the company, regard must be had to the fact that he is a receiver and manager—that is to say, a receiver, with ancillary powers of management—for the debenture holders, and not simply a person appointed to manage the company's affairs for the benefit of the company.... The duties of a receiver and manager for debenture holders are widely different from those of a manager of the company. He is under no obligation to carry on the company's business at the expense of the debenture holders. Therefore he commits no breach of duty to the company

by refusing to do so, even though his discontinuance of the business may be detrimental from the company's point of view. Again, his power of sale is, in effect, that of a mortgagee, and he therefore commits no breach of duty to the company by a bona fide sale, even though he might have obtained a higher price and even though, from the point of view of the company, as distinct from the debenture holders, the terms might be regarded as disadvantageous.

In a word, in the absence of fraud or mala fides...the company cannot complain of any act or omission of the receiver and manager, provided that he does nothing that he is not empowered to do, and omits nothing that he is enjoined to do by the terms of his appointment....

In the present case the evidence of the second defendant himself and the clear emphatic findings of Gault J [1989] 3 NZLR 710, 749, which have already been cited, show that the second defendant [Russell] accepted appointment and acted as receiver and manager

not for the purpose of enforcing the security under the Westpac debenture but for the purpose of preventing the enforcement by the plaintiffs of the [FCC] debenture.

This and other findings to similar effect establish that, ab initio and throughout his receivership, the second defendant did not exercise his powers for proper purposes. He was at all times in breach of the duty, which was pleaded against him, to exercise his powers in good faith for proper purposes.

Gault J rested his judgment not on breach of a duty to act in good faith for proper purposes but on negligence. He said, at pp 744, 747:

on an application of negligence principles, a receiver owes a duty to the debenture holders to take reasonable care in dealing with the assets of the company...[The first defendant's] position is merely a specific example of the duty a mortgagee has to subsequent chargeholders to exercise its powers with reasonable care...

Richardson J, delivering the judgment of the Court of Appeal [1990] 3 NZLR 265, 278–280, agreed that duties of care in negligence as defined by Gault J were owed by the second defendant as receiver and manager and by the first defendant as first debenture holder to the plaintiffs as second debenture holders....

The general duty of care said to be owed by a mortgagee to subsequent encumbrancers and the mortgagor in negligence is inconsistent with the right of the mortgagee and the duties which the courts applying equitable principles have imposed on the mortgagee. If a mortgagee enters into possession he is liable to account for rent on the basis of wilful default; he must keep mortgage premises in repair; he is liable for waste. Those duties were imposed to ensure that a mortgagee is diligent in discharging his mortgage and returning the property to the mortgagor. If a mortgagee exercises his power of sale in good faith for the purpose of protecting his security, he is not liable to the mortgagor even though he might have obtained a higher price and even though the terms might be regarded as disadvantageous to the mortgagor. *Cuckmere Brick Co Ltd v Mutual Finance Ltd* [1971] Ch 949 is Court of Appeal authority for the proposition that, if the mortgagee decides to sell, he must take reasonable care to obtain a proper price but is no authority for any wider proposition. A receiver exercising his power of sale also owes the same specific duties as the mortgagee. But that apart, the general duty of a receiver and manager appointed by a debenture holder, as defined by Jenkins LJ in *Re B Johnson & Co (Builders) Ltd,* leaves no room for the imposition of a general duty to use reasonable care in dealing with the assets of the company. The duties imposed by equity on a mortgagee and on a receiver and manager would be quite unnecessary if there existed a general duty in negligence to take reasonable care in the exercise of powers and to take reasonable care in dealing with the assets of the mortgagor company....

The liability of the second defendant in the present case is firmly based not on negligence but on the breach of duty. There was overwhelming evidence that the receivership of the second defendant was inspired by him for improper purposes and carried on in bad faith, ultimately verging on fraud. The liability of the first defendant does not arise under negligence but as a result of the first defendant's breach of duty in failing to transfer the Westpac debenture to the first plaintiff at the end of March 1987. It is well settled that the mortgagor and all persons having any interest in the property subject to the mortgage or liable to pay the mortgage debt can redeem. It is now conceded that the first plaintiff was entitled to require the first defendant to assign the Westpac debenture to the first plaintiff on payment of all moneys due to the first defendant under the Westpac debenture....

The first defendant was from the end of March 1987 in breach of its duty to assign the Westpac debenture to the first plaintiff. If that debenture had been assigned, the second defendant would have ceased to be the receiver and manager and none of the avoidable losses caused by the second defendant would have been sustained....

NOTE

Prior to the ruling in this case, it had been accepted as a result of several decisions that a secured creditor and any receiver acting on his behalf was under a duty of care towards the debtor and others interested (eg a guarantor of the debt) when exercising a power of sale, and perhaps more generally: *Cuckmere Brick Co Ltd v Mutual Finance Ltd* [1971] Ch 949, CA; *Standard Chartered Bank Ltd v Walker* [1982] 1 WLR 1410, CA. It is clear that in the *Downsview* ruling the Privy Council wished emphatically to deny that any such duty of care was recognised by the law, except in the very limited case of the actual conduct of the sale of the charged property. However, in the case next cited, the Court of Appeal seems to have been just as anxious to keep open the possibility of finding a duty of care in other circumstances—more particularly in the management of the debtor company's business.

Medforth v Blake

[2000] Ch 86, [1999] 3 All ER 97, Court of Appeal

Medforth was a pig farmer on a very large scale: his annual turnover was over £2m. He ran into financial difficulties and his bank appointed receivers, who ran the business for four and a half years, until Medforth was able to find funding elsewhere and pay off the bank. Although he had repeatedly told the receivers that they could claim large discounts from the suppliers of feedstuffs, amounting to some £1,000 a week, they failed to do so. The court held that the receivers owed a duty (subject to their primary duty to the bank) to manage the business with due diligence, and that for breach of this duty they were liable to compensate Medforth.

Sir Richard Scott, V-C:
    ...As a Privy Council case, the *Downsview Nominees* case is not binding but, as Mr. Smith submitted, it is a persuasive authority of great weight. But what did it decide as to the duties owed by a receiver/manager to a mortgagor? It decided that the duty lies in equity, not in tort. It decided that there is no general duty of care in negligence. It held that the receiver/manager owes the same specific duties when exercising the power of sale as are owed by a mortgagee when exercising the power of sale. Lord Templeman cited with approval the *Cuckmere Brick* case [1971] Ch 949 test, namely, that the mortgagee must take reasonable care to obtain a proper price....

The *Cuckmere Brick* case test can impose liability on a mortgagee notwithstanding the absence of fraud or mala fides. It follows from the *Downsview Nominees* case and *Yorkshire Bank plc v Hall* [1999] 1 WLR 1713 that a receiver/manager who sells but fails to take reasonable care to obtain a proper price may incur liability notwithstanding the absence of fraud or mala fides. Why should the approach be any different if what is under review is not the conduct of a sale but conduct in carrying on a business? If a receiver exercises this power, why does not a specific duty, corresponding to the duty to take reasonable steps to obtain a proper price, arise? If the business is being carried on by a mortgagee, the mortgagee will be liable, as a mortgagee in possession, for loss caused by his failure to do so with due diligence. Why should not the receiver/manager, who, as Lord Templeman held, owes the same specific duties as the mortgagee when selling, owe comparable specific duties when conducting the mortgaged business? It may be that the particularly onerous duties constructed by courts of equity for mortgagee in possession would not be appropriate to apply to a receiver. But, no duties at all save a duty of good faith? That does not seem to me to make commercial sense nor, more importantly, to correspond with the principles expressed in the bulk of the authorities....

I do not accept that there is any difference between the answer that would be given by the common law to the question what duties are owed by a receiver managing a mortgaged property to those interested in the equity of redemption and the answer that would be given by equity to that question. I do not, for my part, think it matters one jot whether the duty is expressed as a common law duty or as a duty in equity. The result is the same. The origin of the receiver's duty, like the mortgagee's duty, lies, however, in equity and we might as well continue to refer to it as a duty in equity.

In my judgment, in principle and on the authorities, the following propositions can be stated. (1) A receiver managing mortgaged property owes duties to the mortgagor and anyone else with an interest in the equity of redemption. (2) The duties include, but are not necessarily confined to, a duty of good faith. (3) The extent and scope of any duty additional to that of good faith will depend on the facts and circumstances of the particular case. (4) In exercising his powers of management the primary duty of the receiver is to try and bring about a situation in which interest on the secured debt can be paid and the debt itself repaid. (5) Subject to that primary duty, the receiver owes a duty to manage the property with due diligence. (6) Due diligence does not oblige the receiver to continue to carry on a business on the mortgaged premises previously carried on by the mortgagor. (7) If the receiver does carry on a business on the mortgaged premises, due diligence requires reasonable steps to be taken in order to try to do so profitably....

[His Lordship accordingly ruled that the trial judge had rightly held the receivers liable for breach of duty.]

[Swinton Thomas and Tuckey LJJ concurred.]

The above cases emphasise the essential difference between a receivership and other forms of insolvency procedure, such as administration or liquidation. An administrator or liquidator is appointed to act in the interests of all the parties who are concerned in the insolvency, and to hold the balance between the various competing interests. A receiver, in contrast, is concerned only with the enforcement of his appointor's security. It is not his role to see to the payment of any other creditors—indeed, if there is a surplus in his hands after realising the security he must hand it over to the company (*Re GL Saunders Ltd* [1986] 1 WLR 215). This, at least, is the traditional position, and it remains true for all receivers except those appointed to enforce a *floating* charge. Here, statute has made some exceptions. First, s 40 of IA 1986 requires that where a receiver is appointed to enforce a floating charge, certain debts which would be entitled to preference in a liquidation (eg some debts owed to employees—and, until this privilege was abolished by the Enterprise Act 2002, various debts owed to the Crown) must be paid in priority to the claims of the charge-holder. A receiver who fails to do so is personally liable to the creditors concerned (*IRC v Goldblatt* [1972] Ch 498). Secondly, under IA 1986, s 176A where a company has gone into receivership (or into liquidation or administration) and its property is subject to a floating charge, the receiver or other office-holder is obliged to set aside a 'prescribed part' of the proceeds of realisation of that property for the benefit of the company's unsecured creditors, and prohibited from distributing anything from that fund to the charge-holder unless the unsecured creditors have been paid in full. This innovation also was one of the changes made by the 2002 Act.

Before leaving the topic of receivership, we should look briefly at *administrative receivership*, a statutory subcategory introduced by IA 1986 but (since the 2002 Act) now banned except for a few special cases, such as electricity and other utility companies. An administrative receiver is a receiver appointed by the holder of a floating charge secured over all, or substantially all, of a company's assets (s 29(2)). The Act requires such a receiver to be a qualified insolvency practitioner, and confers on him an extensive range of powers but at the same time imposes a number of duties (eg to give information and make reports to the company and its creditors).

Taken together, the changes to the law made by the Enterprise Act 2002 have radically transformed the practice in regard to the enforcement of floating charges by the banks and other commercial lenders. Under the law as it formerly stood, the holder of an all-assets charge could enforce his security with little regard for the interest of anyone else, except for those unsecured creditors entitled to priority, of which the most substantial was usually the Crown. In practice, this often meant that the Crown's claims and the secured debt swallowed up everything that there was of the company's assets, with nothing for its general creditors. A charge holder now has to use the administration procedure, where the satisfaction of his debt ranks last among the objectives that the administrator is required to try to achieve. The Crown has lost its preferential status, but this is balanced by the priority given to the unsecured creditors as a whole in respect of the 'prescribed part' of the realisations. But there have been some gains, and not just for charge holders. The legislators realised that the administration procedure established by the 1986 Act was too and slow and cumbersome to be used for the enforcement of an all-assets security, where speedy and decisive action is often required, and so a more streamlined out-of-court procedure was devised to meet this need; and in the event the same procedure was made available for the company itself and its directors. As a result administration is now the most popular insolvency procedure, displacing not only receivership but also the less flexible CVA and even, to some degree, creditors' voluntary liquidations.

Winding up (IA 1986, Part IV). Winding up, or liquidation, is a procedure which anticipates the dissolution of a company—its ceasing to exist as a corporate entity. An insolvency practitioner is appointed to act as *liquidator,* with the task of closing down or selling off the company's business, realising all of its assets, paying off its creditors and, if there is a surplus remaining, distributing it amongst those who are entitled to it under the company's constitution. It is possible that he may keep the business going for a while, but he will do this only with a view to its ultimate sale—rehabilitation is not within a liquidator's terms of reference! The company need not, of course, be insolvent, but the legislation treats every liquidation as a form of insolvency procedure and deals with the whole subject in the Insolvency Act. There are two ways of bringing a liquidation about: by resolution of the company itself (called a 'voluntary' liquidation), and by court order (a 'compulsory' liquidation). We shall deal with each of these in turn.

A *voluntary winding up* may take two forms. If the directors of the company are able to certify that all of its creditors will be paid in full, the liquidation proceeds under the control of the members and is called a 'members' voluntary winding up'. If they cannot do this, control of the liquidation passes to the creditors and it is known as a 'creditors' voluntary winding up'. Either way, a qualified insolvency practitioner is appointed liquidator to administer the winding up. He has very wide powers, which are set out in IA 1986, Sch 4. The court is not normally involved, but it does have advisory and back-up powers which can be invoked if necessary. When he has completed his administration and distributed all the moneys in his hands, the liquidator makes his final account to the members or the creditors, and sends a return to the Registrar of Companies. The company is automatically dissolved three months later.

A *winding up by the court,* or 'compulsory' winding up, results from a court order, which is normally made on the petition of the company itself or one or more of its members or creditors. One of the grounds on which an order may be made is that the company is unable to pay its debts (IA 1986, s 122(l)(f)). For this purpose, a 'commercial' test of insolvency is prima facie the appropriate one, but the Act provides, alternatively, that a company may be deemed to be unable to pay its debts if it is insolvent on a 'balance-sheet' basis (s 123(2)). A company will also be deemed insolvent (as is the case in bankruptcy) if it has failed to comply with a statutory demand for payment of a debt of £750 or more, or if execution against it has been returned unsatisfied (s 123(1)). The Official Receiver takes charge of the company's assets and affairs and either he or an insolvency practitioner agreed on by the members and/or the creditors acts as liquidator, and the administration then proceeds on a basis largely similar to a voluntary liquidation, except that the liquidator is responsible to the court and more immediately under its control.

Assets in the liquidation. In contrast with the position in bankruptcy, the assets in a liquidation are not vested in the liquidator but remain vested in the company. But all control passes from the directors and shareholders to the liquidator.

The assets available to the liquidator include all the property which is beneficially owned by the company at the time when it goes into liquidation. This will exclude assets in the possession of the company which belong to someone else (eg goods which have been supplied to it on 'retention of title' terms: see above, p 452). It will also exclude property which the company holds on trust for another person. Rather surprisingly, the courts have, on occasion, found a trust to exist in circumstances which would ordinarily be regarded as having created a debtor-creditor relationship and not a trust. We look at two examples in the cases which follow.

Re Kayford Ltd

[1975] 1 WLR 279, Chancery Division

Kayfords carried on a mail-order business. Its directors were worried about the financial position of its principal supplier, and consulted the company's accountants. They advised the directors to open a separate bank account and to pay all prepayments made by Kayfords' customers from then on into this new account, and to draw money from it only as the relevant goods were delivered to the customer. When the suppliers became insolvent Kayfords' own financial position became impossible and it also went into liquidation. The court held that the money in the account did not belong to the company but was held on trust for Kayfords' customers.

Megarry J: ...The question for me is whether the money in the bank account...is held on trust for those who paid it, or whether it forms part of the general assets of the company. Mr Heyman appears for the joint liquidators, ...and he has contended that there is no trust, so that the money forms part of the general assets of the company and thus will be available for the creditors generally. On the other hand, Mr Kennedy appears for a Mr Joels, who on December 12 paid the company £32.20 for goods which have not been delivered; and a representation order is sought on behalf of all others whose moneys have been paid into the bank account, some 700 or 800 in number. I make that order. Mr Kennedy, of course, argued for the existence of an effective trust. I may say at the outset that on the facts of the case Mr Heyman was unable to contend that any question of a fraudulent preference arose. If one leaves on one side any case in which an insolvent company seeks to declare a trust in favour of creditors, one is concerned here with the question not of preferring creditors but of preventing those who pay money from becoming creditors, by making them beneficiaries under a trust....

Now there are clearly some loose ends in the case. Nevertheless, despite the loose ends, when I take as a whole the affidavits of Mr Wainwright, Mr Kay and Mr Hall (the bank manager) I feel no doubt that the intention was that there should be a trust. There are no formal difficulties. The property concerned is pure personalty, and so writing, though desirable, is not an essential. There is no doubt about the so-called 'three certainties' of a trust. The subject-matter to be held on trust is clear, and so are the beneficial interests therein, as well as the beneficiaries. As for the requisite certainty of words, it is well settled that a trust can be created without using the words 'trust' or 'confidence' or the like: the question is whether in substance a sufficient intention to create a trust has been manifested.

In *Re Nanwa Gold Mines Ltd* [1955] 1 WLR 1080 the money was sent on the faith of a promise to keep it in a separate account, but there is nothing in that case or in any other authority that I know of to suggest that this is essential. I feel no doubt that here a trust was created. From the outset the advice (which was accepted) was to establish a trust account at the bank. The whole purpose of what was done was to ensure that the moneys remained in the beneficial ownership of those who sent them, and a trust is the obvious means of achieving this. No doubt the general rule is that if you send money to a company for goods which are not delivered, you are merely a creditor of the company unless a trust has been created. The sender may create a trust by using appropriate words when he sends the money (though I wonder how many do this, even if they are equity lawyers), or the company may do it by taking suitable steps on or before receiving the money. If either is done, the obligations in respect of the money are transformed from contract to property, from debt to trust. Payment into a separate bank account is a useful (though by no means conclusive) indication of an intention to create a trust, but of course there is nothing to prevent the company from binding itself by a trust even if there are no effective banking arrangements.

Accordingly, of the alternative declarations sought by the summons, the second, to the effect that the money is held in trust for those who paid it, is in my judgment the declaration that should be made....I should, however, add one thing. Different considerations may perhaps arise in relation to trade creditors; but here I am concerned only with members of the public, some of whom can ill afford to exchange their money for a claim to a dividend in the liquidation, and all of whom are likely to be anxious to avoid this. In cases concerning the public, it seems to me that where money in advance is being paid to a company in return for the future supply of goods or services, it is an entirely proper and honourable thing for a company to do what this company did, upon skilled advice, namely, to start to pay the money into a trust account as soon as there begin to be doubts as to the company's ability to fulfil its obligations to deliver the goods or provide the services. I wish that, sitting in this court, I had heard of this occurring more frequently; and I can only hope that I shall hear more of it in the future.

NOTE

In this case, Megarry J accepted that there was no question of a fraudulent preference, under the law as it then stood. This was undoubtedly correct, for fraudulent preference required proof of a *dishonest* intention on the part of the company that the creditor or creditors concerned would have an advantage in a subsequent liquidation. Under IA 1986, s 239 however, the concept of 'fraudulent preference' has been replaced by 'preference', and the requirement to show dishonesty has been eliminated: see below, p 1237. It is likely that this point would need reconsideration under the new law if the facts of *Re Kayford Ltd* were to occur again.

Barclays Bank Ltd v Quistclose Investments Ltd

[1970] AC 567, House of Lords

Rolls Razor Ltd was in serious financial difficulties. It had declared a dividend on its ordinary shares, but did not have the funds to pay it. With the knowledge of its bank, it agreed to borrow some £209,000 from Quistclose (the respondents) on the understanding that the money would be used only for the purpose of paying the dividend. The loan was made and the money paid in to the bank, but before the shareholders had been paid their dividend Rolls Razor went into liquidation. The House of Lords held that the bank held the £209,000 on a resulting trust for Quistclose.

Lord Wilberforce: …Two questions arise, both of which must be answered favourably to the respondents if they are to recover the money from the bank. The first is whether as between the respondents and Rolls Razor Ltd the terms upon which the loan was made were such as to impress upon the sum of £209,719 8s 6d a trust in their favour in the event of the dividend not being paid. The second is whether, in that event, the bank had such notice of the trust or of the circumstances giving rise to it as to make the trust binding upon them.

It is not difficult to establish precisely upon what terms the money was advanced by the respondents to Rolls Razor Ltd. There is no doubt that the loan was made specifically in order to enable Rolls Razor Ltd to pay the dividend. There is equally, in my opinion, no doubt that the loan was made only so as to enable Rolls Razor Ltd to pay the dividend and for no other purpose. This follows quite clearly from the terms of the letter of Rolls Razor Ltd to the bank of July 15, 1964, which letter, before transmission to the bank, was sent to the respondents under open cover in order that the cheque might be (as it was) enclosed in it. The mutual intention of the respondents and of Rolls Razor Ltd, and the essence of the bargain, was that the sum advanced should not become part of the assets of Rolls Razor Ltd, but should be used exclusively for payment of a particular class of its creditors, namely, those entitled to the dividend. A necessary consequence from this, by process simply of interpretation, must be that if, for any reason, the dividend could not be paid, the money was to be returned to the respondents: the word 'only' or 'exclusively' can have no other meaning or effect.

That arrangements of this character for the payment of a person's creditors by a third person, give rise to a relationship of a fiduciary character or trust, in favour, as a primary trust, of the creditors, and secondarily, if the primary trust fails, of the third person, has been recognised in a series of cases over some 150 years.

[His Lordship referred to a number of authorities and continued:]

The second, and main, argument for the appellant was of a more sophisticated character. The transaction, it was said, between the respondents and Rolls Razor Ltd, was one of loan, giving rise to a legal action of debt. This necessarily excluded the implication of any trust, enforceable in equity, in the respondents' favour: a transaction may attract one action or the other, it could not admit of both.

My Lords, I must say that I find this argument unattractive. Let us see what it involves. It means that the law does not permit an arrangement to be made by which one person agrees to advance money to another, on terms that the money is to be used exclusively to pay debts of the latter, and if, and so far as not so used, rather than becoming a general asset of the latter available to his creditors at large, is to be returned to the lender. The lender is obliged, in such a case, because he is a lender, to accept, whatever the mutual wishes of lender and borrower may be, that the money he was willing to make available for one purpose only shall be freely available for others of the borrower's creditors for whom he has not the slightest desire to provide.

I should be surprised if an argument of this kind—so conceptualist in character—had ever been accepted. In truth it has plainly been rejected by the eminent judges who from 1819 onwards have permitted arrangements of this type to be enforced, and have approved them as being for the benefit of creditors and all concerned. There is surely no difficulty in recognising the coexistence in one trans-action of legal and equitable rights and remedies: when the money is advanced, the lender acquires an equitable right to see that it is applied for the primary designated purpose (see *Re Rogers* (1891) 8 Morr 243 where both Lindley LJ and Kay LJ recognised this): when the purpose has been carried out (ie the debt paid) the lender has his remedy against the borrower in debt: if the primary purpose cannot be carried out, the question arises if a secondary purpose (ie, repayment to the lender) has been agreed, expressly or by implication: it if has, the remedies of equity may be invoked to give effect to it, if it has not (and the money is intended to fall within the general fund of the debtor's assets) then there is the appropriate remedy for recovery of a loan. I can appreciate no reason why the flexible interplay of law and equity cannot let in these practical arrangements, and other variations if desired: it would be to the discredit of both systems if they could not. In the present case the intention to create a secondary trust for the benefit of the lender, to arise if the primary trust, to pay the dividend, could not be carried out, is clear and I can find no reason why the law should not give effect to it.

[Lords Reid, Morris of Borth-y-Gest, Guest and Pearce concurred.]

Other cases in which a relationship was held not to be that of debtor and creditor but to involve a trust include *Carreras Rothmans Ltd v Freeman Mathews Treasure Ltd* [1985] Ch 207; *Chase Manhattan Bank NA v Israel-British Bank (London) Ltd* [1981] Ch 105; *Neste Oy v Lloyds Bank plc* [1983] 2 Lloyd's Rep 658; and *Twinsectra Ltd v Yardley* [2002] UKHL 12, [2002] 2 AC 164; contrast *Swiss Bank Corpn v Lloyds Bank Ltd* [1982] AC 584, HL, where the opposite conclusion was reached.

The liquidator may *disclaim* any asset which is unsaleable or fettered with onerous liabil-ities, and any unprofitable contract (IA 1986, ss 178ff). A person who is disadvantaged by a disclaimer is left to prove for his losses as a creditor in the liquidation.

Avoidance of antecedent transactions. The assets available for distribution by the liquidator may be augmented as a result of the operation of a number of special statutory provisions (sometimes referred to as 'claw-backs'), under which transactions that have taken place in the period immediately prior to the liquidation may be set aside. The language of each of these provisions is complex and calls for careful study; in the present chapter we can only describe them in outline.

First, s 127 of IA 1986 provides that, in a winding up by the court, any disposition of the company's property made after the commencement of the winding up is void, unless the court otherwise orders. This means that if a company has paid off a debt, given security over its property to a creditor, or sold an asset (even for full value) during this 'twilight' period before it goes into liquidation, it is automatically avoided unless the court agrees that it should be upheld. The leading case of *Re Gray's Inn Construction Co Ltd* (below) sets out some of the factors which the court will take into account in deciding whether to exercise this discretion. It also held, perhaps surprisingly, that both payments by a company *into* its bank account and drawings made by the company *out* of its account were 'dispositions' within the meaning of the section.

In a similar provision, executions issued against the property of a company after the com-mencement of the winding up are declared to be void by IA 1986, s 128.

Re Gray's Inn Construction Co Ltd
[1980] 1 WLR 711, Court of Appeal

An order was made to wind up the company on 9 October 1972, on the basis of a petition which had been presented on 3 August. The bank allowed the company to continue to use its bank account while the hearing of the petition was pending. The court, varying the judgment of Templeman J in the court below, ruled (1) that both payments into and payments out of the account were 'dispositions' of the company's property within s 127 and (2) that the bank ought to have become aware of the fact that a petition had been presented at some date before 15 August. In the exercise of its discretion, it allowed transactions made before that date to stand, but declined to validate those which had been effected later. The extract cited below indicates the factors which the court is likely to take into account in exercising its discretion under the statute.

Buckley LJ: ...It is a basic concept of our law governing the liquidation of insolvent estates, whether in bankruptcy or under the Companies Acts, that the free assets of the insolvent at the commencement of the liquidation shall be distributed rateably amongst the insolvent's unsecured creditors as at that date.... In a company's compulsory winding up [this] is achieved by s 227 [of the Companies Act 1948, equivalent to IA 1986, s 127]. There may be occasions, however, when it would be beneficial, not only for the company but also for its unsecured creditors, that the company should be enabled to dispose of some of its property during the period after the petition has been presented but before a winding up order has been made. An obvious example is if the company has an opportunity by acting speedily to dispose of some piece of property at an exceptionally good price. Many applications for validation under the section relate to specific transactions of this kind or analogous kinds. It may sometimes be beneficial to the company and its creditors that the company should be enabled to complete a particular contract or project, or to continue to carry on its business generally in its ordinary course with a view to a sale of the business as a going concern. In any such case the court has power under s 227 of the Companies Act 1948 to validate the particular transaction, or the completion of the particular contract or project, or the continuance of the company's business in its ordinary course, as the case may be. In considering whether to make a validating order the court must always, in my opinion, do its best to ensure that the interests of the unsecured creditors will not be prejudiced. Where the application relates to a specific transaction this may be susceptible of positive proof. In a case of completion of a contract or project the proof may perhaps be less positive but nevertheless be cogent enough to satisfy the court that in the interests of the creditors the company should be enabled to proceed, or at any rate that proceeding in the manner proposed would not prejudice them in any respect. The desirability of the company being enabled to carry on its business generally is likely to be more speculative and will be likely to depend on whether a sale of the business as a going concern will probably be more beneficial than a break-up realisation of the company's assets. In each case, I think, the court must necessarily carry out a balancing exercise.... Each case must depend upon its own particular facts.

Since the policy of the law is to procure so far as practicable rateable payments of the unsecured creditors' claims, it is, in my opinion, clear that the court should not validate any transaction or series of transactions which might result in one or more pre-liquidation creditors being paid in full at the expense of other creditors, who will only receive a dividend, in the absence of special circumstances making such a course desirable in the interests of the unsecured creditors as a body. If, for example, it were in the interests of the creditors generally that the company's business should be carried on, and this could only be achieved by paying for goods already supplied to the company when the petition is presented but not yet paid for, the court might think fit in the exercise of its discretion to validate payment for those goods.

Where a third party proposes to enter into a transaction with a company which is liable to be invalidated under s 227 of the Companies Act 1948, the third party can decline to do so until the company has obtained a validating order, or it might itself seek a validating order, or it can enter into the transaction in anticipation of the court making a retroactive validating order at a later date. In the present case the bank adopted the last course. A third party who does that takes the risk of the court refusing to make the order.

It may not always be feasible, or desirable, that a validating order should be sought before the transaction in question is carried out. The parties may be unaware at the time when the transaction is entered into that a petition has been presented; or the need for speedy action may be such as to preclude an anticipatory application; or the beneficial character of the transaction may be so obvious that there is no real prospect of a liquidator seeking to set it aside, so that an application to the court would waste time, money and effort. But in any case in which the transaction is carried out without an anticipatory validating order the disponee is at risk of the court declining to validate the transaction. It follows, in my view, that the parties when entering into the transaction, if they are aware that it is liable to be invalidated by the section, should have in mind the sort of considerations which would influence the court's decision.

A disposition carried out in good faith in the ordinary course of business at a time when the parties are unaware that a petition has been presented may, it seems, normally be validated by the court ... unless there is any ground for thinking that the transaction may involve an attempt to prefer the disponee, in which case the transaction would probably not be validated. In a number of cases reference has been made to the relevance of the policy of ensuring rateable distribution of the assets....

But although that policy might disincline the court to ratify any transaction which involved preferring a pre-liquidation creditor, it has no relevance to a transaction which is entirely post-liquidation, as for instance a sale of an asset at its full market value after presentation of a petition. Such a transaction involves no dissipation of the company's assets, for it does not reduce the value of those assets. It cannot harm the creditors and there would seem to be no reason why the court should not in the exercise of its discretion validate it. A fortiori, the court would be inclined to validate a transaction which would increase or has increased, the value of the company's assets, or which would preserve, or has preserved, the value of the company's assets from harm which would result from the company's business being paralysed....

[Goff LJ and Sir David Cairns concurred.]

NOTE

Not all of the observations in this case have gone without criticism. Professor Goode has argued, convincingly, that a payment made by a company which is debited to an account with its bank which is already overdrawn does not, without more, involve any disposition of *the company's* property (*Principles of Corporate Insolvency Law* (3rd edn, 2005), para 11–125). And in *Re Barn Crown Ltd* [1994] 2 BCLC 186 it was held that there is no 'disposition', but only an adjustment of entries in the statements recording the accounts between customer and banker, when cheques belonging to the company are paid into an account which is already in credit. This decision, also, has been criticised by Professor Goode (para 11–128): if the bank were to become insolvent, the money would be lost, and so there must have been a 'disposition'. More recently, in *Hollicourt (Contracts) Ltd v Bank of Ireland* [2001] Ch 555, [2001] 1 All ER 289, CA it has been held that where a bank meets a cheque drawn by its customer (whether the account is in credit or overdrawn) it does so merely as the customer's agent, so that, while there is clearly a disposition by the customer in favour of the payee, there is no disposition to the bank itself—as had been assumed in *Gray's* case.

It should be noted that ss 127 and 128 are applicable in all compulsory liquidations, whether or not the company is insolvent.

A second set of statutory provisions (which apply in liquidations of all types) allows the court to order the avoidance of transactions which have taken place prior to the commencement of the winding up—that is, even before the petition is presented or the resolution for winding up is passed. Some of these provisions apply also in an administration. They include:

— *Transactions at an undervalue* (IA 1986, s 238). Where a company has made a gift of property or has parted with property for an inadequate consideration, within two years of the commencement of the winding up, at a time when the company was unable to pay its debts, the court may make an order annulling the transaction.

— *Preferences* (IA 1986, s 239). Where a company has given a preference to a particular creditor (that is, paid his debt or done some other act which would put him in a better position in the event of the company's insolvency) within six months (or, in certain cases, two years) prior to the commencement of the liquidation, at a time when the company was unable to pay its debts, the court may order that it be struck down. It is necessary to show that the company was influenced by a desire to prefer the creditor.

— *Transactions defrauding creditors* (IA 1986, s 423). If a company has entered into a transaction at an undervalue *at any time* for the purpose of putting assets beyond the reach of a creditor or potential creditor, it may be avoided by order of the court.

— *Extortionate credit transactions* (IA 1986, s 244). A transaction involving the giving of credit to the company which was entered into within three years prior to the winding up may be set aside or varied by the court if its terms are deemed extortionate.

— *Floating charges* (IA 1986, s 245). No order of the court is required in this case. A floating charge created by a company within the period of twelve months (or, where the chargee is a person 'connected with' the company, such as a director or another company in the same group, two years) prior to the commencement of its winding up is declared by this section to be invalid, unless (1) 'new value', in the form of money paid or goods or services supplied, was given to the company in consideration of the charge or (2) where the chargee is not a 'connected person', the company was solvent at the relevant time. In other words, where the statutory conditions apply, a *floating* charge may not be taken during the period immediately prior to an insolvent liquidation to secure an *existing* debt. A fixed charge is not caught by s 245, although it may be struck down as a preference if the requirements of s 239 are satisfied. (For the definition of 'connected person'—which is relevant also for the purposes of some of the other sections referred to above—see IA 1986, ss 249, 435.)

The operation of some of these provisions is illustrated by the cases which follow.

Re MC Bacon Ltd

[1990] BCLC 324, Chancery Division

The company had carried on business profitably as an importer and wholesaler of bacon until it lost its main customer. Its fortunes then rapidly dwindled and it soon had to be wound up. This action was brought to challenge a debenture which had been given to its bank on the alternative grounds that it was a transaction at an undervalue (IA 1986, s 238), or a preference (s 239); but Millett J held that it was neither. It was not a transaction at an undervalue because the giving of security had neither depleted the company's assets nor diminished their value, and it was not a preference because the directors' motive in giving the charge had not been to prefer the bank but to keep the company trading.

Millett J: …

Voidable preference

So far as I am aware, this is the first case under the section and its meaning has been the subject of some debate before me. I shall therefore attempt to provide some guidance.

The section replaces s 44(1) of the Bankruptcy Act 1914, which in certain circumstances deemed fraudulent and avoided payments made and other transactions entered into in favour of a creditor 'with a view of giving such creditor...a preference over the other creditors'. Section 44(1) and its predecessors had been construed by the courts as requiring the person seeking to avoid the payment or other transaction to establish that it had been made 'with the dominant intention to prefer' the creditor.

Section 44(1) has been replaced [by IA 1986, s 239] and its language has been entirely recast. Every single word of significance, whether in the form of statutory definition or in its judicial expression, has been jettisoned. 'View', 'dominant', 'intention' and even 'to prefer' have all been discarded. These are replaced by 'influenced', 'desire', and 'to produce in relation to that person the effect mentioned in sub-s (4)(b)'.

I therefore emphatically protest against the citation of cases decided under the old law. They cannot be of any assistance when the language of the statute has been so completely and deliberately changed. It may be that many of the cases which will come before the courts in future will be decided in the same way that they would have been decided under the old law. That may be so, but the grounds of decision will be different. What the court has to do is to interpret the language of the statute and apply it. It will no longer inquire whether there was 'a dominant intention to prefer' the creditor, but whether the company's decision was 'influenced by a desire to produce the effect mentioned in sub-s (4)(b)'.

This is a completely different test. It involves at least two radical departures from the old law. It is no longer necessary to establish a *dominant* intention to prefer. It is sufficient that the decision was *influenced* by the requisite desire. That is the first change. The second is that it is no longer sufficient to establish an *intention* to prefer. There must be a *desire* to produce the effect mentioned in the subsection.

This second change is made necessary by the first, for without it it would be virtually impossible to uphold the validity of a security taken in exchange for the injection of fresh funds into a company in financial difficulties. A man is taken to intend the necessary consequences of his actions, so that an intention to grant a security to a creditor necessarily involves an intention to prefer that creditor in the event of insolvency. The need to establish that such intention was dominant was essential under the old law to prevent perfectly proper transactions from being struck down. With the abolition of that requirement intention could not remain the relevant test. Desire has been substituted. That is a very different matter. Intention is objective, desire is subjective. A man can choose the lesser of two evils without desiring either.

It is not, however, sufficient to establish a desire to make the payment or grant the security which it is sought to avoid. There must have been a desire to produce the effect mentioned in the subsection, that is to say, to improve the creditor's position in the event of an insolvent liquidation. A man is not to be taken as *desiring* all the necessary consequences of his actions. Some consequences may be of advantage to him and be desired by him; others may not affect him and be matters of indifference to him; while still others may be positively disadvantageous to him and not be desired by him, but be regarded by him as the unavoidable price of obtaining the desired advantages. It will still be possible to provide assistance to a company in financial difficulties provided that the company is actuated only by proper commercial considerations. Under the new regime a transaction will not be set aside as a voidable preference unless the company positively wished to improve the creditor's position in the event of its own insolvent liquidation.

There is, of course, no need for there to be direct evidence of the requisite desire. Its existence may be inferred from the circumstances of the case just as the dominant intention could be inferred under the old law. But the mere presence of the requisite desire will not be sufficient by itself. It must have influenced the decision to enter into the transaction. It was submitted on behalf of the bank that it must have been the factor which 'tipped the scales'. I disagree. That is not what sub-s (5) says; it requires only that the desire should have influenced the decision. That requirement is satisfied if it was one of the factors which operated on the minds of those who made the decision. It need not have been the only factor or even the decisive one. In my judgment, it is not necessary to prove that, if the requisite desire had not been present, the company would not have entered into the transaction. That would be too high a test.

It was also submitted that the relevant time was the time when the debenture was created. That cannot be right. The relevant time was the time when the decision to grant it was made. In the present case that is not known with certainty. . . . But it does not matter. If the requisite desire was operating at all, it was operating throughout.

[His Lordship then ruled that the directors' motive had not been a desire to prefer the bank in the event of a liquidation, but to keep the company trading. He continued:]

Transaction at an undervalue

Section 238 of the 1986 Act is concerned with the depletion of a company's assets by transactions at an undervalue.

[His Lordship read s 238(4) and continued:]

The granting of the debenture was not a gift, nor was it without consideration. The consideration consisted of the bank's forbearance from calling in the overdraft and its honouring of cheques and making of fresh advances to the company during the continuance of the facility. The applicant relies therefore on para (b).

To come within that paragraph the transaction must be (i) entered into by the company; (ii) for a consideration; (iii) the value of which measured in money or money's worth; (iv) is significantly less than the value; (v) also measured in money or money's worth; (vi) of the consideration provided by the company. It requires a comparison to be made between the value obtained by the company for the transaction and the value of consideration provided by the company. Both values must be measurable in money or money's worth and both must be considered from the company's point of view.

In my judgment, the applicant's claim to characterise the granting of the bank's debenture as a transaction at an undervalue is misconceived. The mere creation of a security over a company's assets does not deplete them and does not come within the paragraph. By charging its assets the company appropriates them to meet the liabilities due to the secured creditor and adversely affects the rights of other creditors in the event of insolvency. But it does not deplete its assets or diminish their value. It retains the right to redeem and the right to sell or remortgage the charged assets. All it loses is the ability to apply the proceeds otherwise than in satisfaction of the secured debt. That is not something capable of valuation in monetary terms and is not customarily disposed of for value.

In the present case the company did not suffer that loss by reason of the grant of the debenture. Once the bank had demanded a debenture the company could not have sold or charged its assets without applying the proceeds in reduction of the overdraft; had it attempted to do so, the bank would at once have called in the overdraft. By granting the debenture the company parted with nothing of value, and the value of the consideration which it received in return was incapable of being measured in money or money's worth.

Counsel for the applicant (Mr Vos) submitted that the consideration which the company received was, with hindsight, of no value. It merely granted time and with it the opportunity to lose more money. But he could not and did not claim that the company ought to have received a fee or other capital sum in return for the debenture. That gives the game away. The applicant's real complaint is not that the company entered into the transaction at an undervalue but that it entered into it at all.

In my judgment, the transaction does not fall within sub-s (4), and it is unnecessary to consider the application of sub-s (5) which provides a defence to the claim in certain circumstances.

Conclusion

In my judgment, the granting of the debenture to the bank was neither a voidable preference nor a transaction at an undervalue and I dismiss the application.

Re Yeovil Glove Co Ltd
[1965] Ch 148, Court of Appeal

The company had given its bank security by way of a floating charge less than 12 months before going into liquidation. At the time, it had an overdraft of £65,000. In the period between the creation of the charge and the liquidation the bank had met cheques drawn by the company totalling £110,000 and had received about the same sum in credits paid into the account by the company. It owed £67,000 to the bank and had other debts of some £94,000 when it went into liquidation. The Court of Appeal, applying the rule in *Clayton's* case (1816) 1 Mer 572, held that the whole of the £67,000 was cash advanced to the company subsequently to creation of the charge, so that the security was not caught by s 322 of the Companies Act 1948 (equivalent to IA 1986, s 245).

Harman LJ: . . . The only question which arises is whether there was cash paid to the company at the time of or subsequently to the creation of, and in consideration for, the charge. It was admittedly created within 12 months of the winding up at a time when the company was insolvent. It is further agreed that so far as the overdraft was incurred before the date of the floating charge, the charge would not be a valid security for it. The liquidator's claim is a simple one, namely, that as neither cash nor a covenant to pay cash was made at the time of the execution of the document, there was no consideration for it in the legal sense of that term except the bank's immediate forbearance. This seemed to me, I confess, an attractive argument. . . .

It was argued that consideration in law is a well-known term and ought to receive its ordinary meaning, and that subsequent payments provided by the bank to defray the company's day-today outgoings or wages or salaries or indebtedness to its suppliers by cheque would not be consideration in law for the execution of a charge bearing an earlier date unless those payments were made in pursuance of a promise contained in, or made at or before the date of, the charge itself. It was, however, pointed out that such subsequent payments would in fact not be made in consideration for the charge, but in consideration for the promise.

Now it is apparent on the face of the section that cash subsequently paid to the company may be within the exception if so paid in consideration for the anterior charge, and the argument is that the words 'in consideration for' in this section cannot, therefore, be used in the technical sense, but mean 'by reason of or 'having regard to the existence of the charge. Oddly enough, there is no reported decision on these words, nor are they discussed in any of the well-known textbooks. There has, however, come to light a decision of Lord Romer, when a judge of first instance, in *Re Thomas Mortimer Ltd* ([1965] Ch 186n) in 1925, a decision on the corresponding section of the Companies (Consolidation) Act 1908, which was in the same terms as the present section except that the period was three instead of 12 months. A transcript of this judgment was before us. The facts of that case were, I think, indistinguishable from those of the present, and Romer J held that payments by the bank after the date of the charge were made in consideration for the charge. . . .

That decision, if right, is enough to cover the present question, and Plowman J so held. . . .

In the instant case some £111,000, representing its trading receipts, was paid into the No 1 account by the company between the date of the charge and the appointment of the receiver, and the bank paid out during the same period about £110,000. Those payments were either made directly to or to the order of the company, or were transfers to the No 3 or No 4 accounts against advances previously made to the company to defray wages or salaries. All the company's accounts were at all times overdrawn, so that every payment was a provision of new money by means of which, on the figures, it is overwhelmingly probable that all the creditors existing at the date of the charge were in fact paid off.

There arises at this point the consideration which has given me most trouble in this case, namely, that as the No 1 account was carried on after as well as before the charge in precisely the same way, the bank would be entitled in accordance with the rule in *Clayton's Case* ((1816) 1 Mer 572), to treat payments in as being in satisfaction of the earliest advances made. The result is startling, for thus the bank pays itself out of moneys received subsequent to the charge for the whole of the company's indebtedness to it prior to the charge, and which was admittedly not covered by it. The result is that the whole of the pre-charge indebtedness is treated as paid off, and the bank is left bound to set off against its post-charge advances only the excess received after satisfying the company's pre-charge indebtedness. This would seem largely to nullify the effect of the section in the case of a company having at the date of the charge a largely overdrawn account with its bank, and which continues to trade subsequently. Of course, if at the date of the charge a line were drawn in the bank's books and a new account opened, then the company could successfully argue that payments out by the bank subsequent to the charge were, within a few hundred pounds, wholly repaid by the company from its trading receipts, with the result that no substantial sum would be due on the charge. It was, however, held by Romer J in *Re Thomas Mortimer Ltd* that *Clayton's Case* applied with the result stated, and I can see no escape from it, nor in spite of frequent pressing by the court did the appellant's counsel put forward any alternative....

It follows, if the decision in *Re Thomas Mortimer Ltd* be right, that there is admittedly nothing left for the unsecured creditors. In my judgment Romer J's decision was right, and was rightly followed by Plowman J in the present case.

The fallacy in the appellant's argument lies, in my opinion, in the theory that, because the company's payments in to the bank after the date of the charge were more or less equal to the payments out by the bank during the same period, no 'new money' was provided by the bank. This is not the fact. Every such payment was in fact new money having regard to the state of the company's accounts, and it was in fact used to pay the company's creditors. That the indebtedness remained approximately at the same level was due to the fact that this was the limit set by the bank to the company's overdraft. I can find no reason to compel the bank to treat all payments in after the charge as devoted to post-charge indebtedness. The law is in fact the other way....

[Willmer and Russell LJJ delivered concurring judgments.]

The third broad head under which the company's assets may be augmented in a liquidation is by making personal claims against the company's former officers and others for compensation for breach of duty or for contribution on some other ground. The relevant sections of IA 1986 are s 212 (misfeasance), s 213 (fraudulent trading) and s 214 (wrongful trading).

— *Misfeasance* (IA 1986, s 212). This provision does not create a new head of liability but simply provides a summary procedure by which the liquidator may recover property or claim compensation from the company's former officers on the grounds of accountability, misfeasance or breach of duty.

— *Fraudulent trading* (IA 1986, s 213). If, in the course of winding up, it is found that any business of the company has been carried on with intent to defraud creditors or for any fraudulent purpose, the court may order that those who were knowingly parties to this wrongdoing should contribute such sums as it thinks proper to the company's assets. For the purposes of this provision, actual dishonesty must be shown (*Re Patrick & Lyon Ltd* [1933] Ch 786).

— *Wrongful trading* (IA 1986, s 214). A director or former director of a company in insolvent liquidation may be ordered to contribute personally to the assets in the hands of the liquidator if he knew, or ought to have concluded, that there was no reasonable prospect that it would avoid going into insolvent liquidation and failed to take every step with a view to minimising the potential loss to the company's creditors that he ought to have taken. The case next cited illustrates the working of this section.

Re Produce Marketing Consortium Ltd (No 2)

[1989] BCLC 520, Chancery Division

The company (PMC) was in the business of fruit importers and distributors. Its directors, David and Murphy, had continued to run the business when they ought to have known that it was insolvent and heading inevitably towards liquidation. They were ordered to make a payment of £75,000 to the liquidator.

Knox J: ...Section 214 of the 1986 Act...reads, so far as is material, as follows:

(1) Subject to subsection (3) below, if in the course of the winding up of a company it appears that subsection (2) of this section applies in relation to a person who is or has been a director of the company, the court, on the application of the liquidator, may declare that the person is to be liable to make such contribution (if any) to the company's assets as the court thinks proper.

(2) This subsection applies in relation to a person if- (a) the company has gone into insolvent liquidation, (b) at some time before the commencement of the winding up of the company, that person knew or ought to have concluded that there was no reasonable prospect that the company would avoid going into insolvent liquidation, and (c) that person was a director of the company at that time....

(3) The court shall not make a declaration under this section with respect to any person if it is satisfied that after the condition specified in subsection (2)(b) was first satisfied in relation to him that person took every step with a view to minimising the potential loss to the company's creditors as (assuming him to have known that there was no reasonable prospect that the company would avoid going into insolvent liquidation) he ought to have taken.

(4) For the purposes of subsections (2) and (3), the facts which a director of a company ought to know or ascertain, the conclusions which he ought to reach and the steps which he ought to take are those which would be known or ascertained, or reached or taken, by a reasonably diligent person having both—(a) the general knowledge, skill and experience that may reasonably be expected of a person carrying out the same functions as are carried out by that director in relation to the company, and (b) the general knowledge, skill and experience that that director has.

(5) The reference in subsection (4) to the functions carried out in relation to a company by a director of the company includes any functions which he does not carry out but which have been entrusted to him...

The first question is whether it appears that sub-s (2) applies to Mr David and Mr Murphy. There is no question but that they were directors at all material times and that PMC has gone into insolvent liquidation. The issue is whether at some time after 27 April 1986 and before 2 October 1987, when it went into insolvent liquidation, they knew or ought to have concluded that there was no reasonable prospect that PMC would avoid going into insolvent liquidation. It was inevitably conceded by counsel for the first respondent that this question has to be answered by the standards postulated by sub-s (4), so that the facts which Mr David and Mr Murphy ought to have known or ascertained and the conclusions that they ought to have reached are not limited to those which they themselves showing reasonable diligence and having the general knowledge, skill and experience which they respectively had, would have known, ascertained or reached but also those that a person with the general knowledge, skill and experience of someone carrying out their functions would have known, ascertained or reached.

The 1986 Act now has two separate provisions; s 213 dealing with fraudulent trading...and s 214 which deals with what the sidenote calls 'wrongful trading'. It is evident that Parliament intended to widen the scope of the legislation under which directors who trade on when the company is insolvent may, in appropriate circumstances, be required to make a contribution to the assets of the company which, in practical terms, means its creditors.

Two steps in particular were taken in the legislative enlargement of the court's jurisdiction. First, the requirement for an intent to defraud and fraudulent purpose was not retained as an essential....

I pause here to observe that at no stage before me has it been suggested that either Mr David or Mr Murphy fell into this category.

The second enlargement is that the test to be applied by the court has become one under which the director in question is to be judged by the standards of what can reasonably be expected of a person fulfilling his functions, and showing reasonable diligence in doing so. I accept the submission of counsel for the first respondent in this connection, that the requirement to have regard to the functions to be carried out by the director in question, in relation to the company in question, involves having regard to the particular company and its business. It follows that the general knowledge, skill and experience postulated will be much less extensive in a small company in a modest way of business, with simple accounting procedures and equipment, than it will be in a large company with sophisticated procedures.

Nevertheless, certain minimum standards are to be assumed to be attained. Notably there is an obligation laid on companies to cause accounting records to be kept which are such as to disclose with reasonable accuracy at any time the financial position of the company at that time: see the Companies Act 1985, s 221(1) and (2)(a)....

As I have already mentioned, the liquidator gave evidence that the accounting records of PMC were adequate for the purposes of its business. The preparation of accounts was woefully late, more especially in relation to those dealing with the year ending 30 September 1985 which should have been laid and delivered by the end of July 1986.

The knowledge to be imputed in testing whether or not directors knew or ought to have concluded that there was no reasonable prospect of the company avoiding insolvent liquidation is not limited to the documentary material actually available at the given time. This appears from s 214(4) which includes a reference to facts which a director of a company ought not only to know but those which he ought to ascertain, a word which does not appear in sub-s (2)(b). In my judgment this indicates that there is to be included by way of factual information not only what was actually there but what, given reasonable diligence and an appropriate level of general knowledge, skill and experience, was ascertainable. This leads me to the conclusion in this case that I should assume, for the purposes of applying the test in s 214(2), that the financial results for the year ending 30 September 1985 were known at the end of July 1986 at least to the extent of the size of the deficiency of assets over liabilities.

Mr David and Mr Murphy, although they did not have the accounts in their hands until January 1987, did, I find, know that the previous trading year had been a very bad one. They had a close and intimate knowledge of the business and they had a shrewd idea whether the turnover was up or down. In fact it was badly down in that year to £526,459 and although I have no doubt that they did not know in July 1986 that it was that precise figure, I have no doubt that they had a good rough idea of what it was and in particular that it was well down on the previous year. A major drop in turnover meant almost as night follows day that there was a substantial loss incurred, as indeed there was. That in turn meant again, as surely as night follows day, a substantial increase in the deficit of assets over liabilities.

That deals with their actual knowledge but in addition I have to have regard to what they have to be treated as having known or ascertained and that includes the actual deficit of assets over liabilities of £132,870. This was £80,000 over Mr David's personal guarantee. It was a deficit that, for an indefinite period in the future could not be made good even if the optimistic prognostications of level of turnover entertained by Mr David and Mr Murphy were achieved.

Counsel for the first respondent was not able to advance any particular calculation as constituting a basis for concluding that there was a prospect of insolvent liquidation being avoided. He is not to be criticised for that for in my judgment there was none available. Once the loss in the year ending 30 September 1985 was incurred PMC was in irreversible decline, assuming (as I must) that the respondents had no plans for altering the company's business and proposed to go on drawing the level of reasonable remuneration that they were currently receiving....

The next question which arises is whether there is a case under s 214(3) for saying that after the end of July 1986 the respondents took every step with a view to minimising the potential loss to the creditors of PMC as, assuming them to have known that there was no reasonable prospect of PMC avoiding insolvent liquidation, they ought to have taken. This clearly has to be answered No, since they went on trading for another year . . . .

I am therefore driven to the conclusion that the court's discretion arises under s 214(1) . . . .

In my judgment the jurisdiction under s 214 is primarily compensatory rather than penal. Prima facie the appropriate amount that a director is declared to be liable to contribute is the amount by which the company's assets can be discerned to have been depleted by the director's conduct which caused the discretion under sub-s (1) to arise. But Parliament has indeed chosen very wide words of discretion and it would be undesirable to seek to spell out limits on that discretion.

[His Lordship reviewed the facts, and ordered David and Murphy to make a contribution of £75,000.]

Administration of the estate. The company's creditors 'prove' for their debts in the liquidation by submitting a claim in a prescribed form to the liquidator, which he may admit in whole or in part or reject, subject to an appeal to the court. Contingent and future liabilities are admitted at an estimated or discounted value. A creditor who is also indebted to the company normally has the right to *set off* his indebtedness against his claim and either prove for the balance or account for it to the liquidator: thus, to the extent that he can exercise this right, his claim is paid off in full. The House of Lords, in *National Westminster Bank Ltd v Halesowen Presswork & Assemblies Ltd* [1972] AC 785, HL held that the right of set-off is a mandatory feature of insolvency law which is not capable of being waived or varied by contract.

A *secured creditor* may exercise his right to have recourse to the security independently of the liquidation. If there is a surplus after realising the security, he must account for it to the liquidator; if a shortfall, he may prove for the outstanding balance. Alternatively, he may elect to surrender his security and prove for the whole of his debt as an unsecured creditor.

The Act provides that certain debts shall be paid in priority those of other creditors (and to those of the holder of any floating—but not fixed—charge) in the winding up (IA 1986, ss 175, 386 and Sch 6). The list of preferential debts is the same as applies in bankruptcy, administration and receivership. It is now much shorter because the preferential position of the Crown was abolished by s 176A: see above, p 1226. Those entitled include employees, for arrears of wages and other entitlements up to a limit of four months or £800—a sum which is overdue for an increase to reflect over two decades' inflation. Secondly, a 'prescribed part' of the net proceeds of realisation of the company must be set aside for the benefit of its unsecured creditors, in priority to any floating charge holder. (The amount prescribed is 50% of the first £10,000, plus a further 20% of the remainder, up to a maximum prescribed part of £600,000.)

The *order of application of assets* is as follows: (1) expenses of the liquidation, (2) preferential debts, (3) the prescribed part, (4) debts secured by a floating charge, (5) unsecured debts, (6) debts payable to members of the company in their capacity as members (eg unpaid dividends): IA 1986, s 74(2)(f). Any surplus remaining after satisfaction of all the company's liabilities is payable to the members in accordance with their respective rights and liabilities. If the assets are insufficient to pay the debts of any category of creditor in full, the claims of all those in that category abate proportionately.

FORMS

The forms which follow are reproduced by permission of the persons and bodies mentioned on pp xvii–xix, to whom acknowledgment is again made.

These documents are intended to be used solely by students and teachers for the purposes of instruction. They should not be used as precedents or relied on in any other way without the benefit of proper legal advice. The companies and firms concerned and the authors and publishers do not accept any responsibility to any person should they be so used or relied upon.

Forms

1. Commercial invoice
2. Combined transport bill of lading
3. Application to open irrevocable documentary credit
4. Irrevocable documentary credit
5. Factoring agreement
6. Master block discounting agreement
7. Trust receipt
8. 'All monies' continuing bank guarantee

1 Commercial invoice

INVOICE TO

M/S BONGAH TOSE MACHINALET KESHAVAR/I
TEHRAN
I.R.O. IRAN.

DELIVER TO

INVOICE   FS No. 1484/4

STANDEN ENGINEERING LIMITED
HEREWARD WORKS,
STATION ROAD, ELY,
CAMBRIDGESHIRE CB7 4BP
ENGLAND

Telephone: 0353 661111   Telex: 81486
Fax: 0353 662370

DATE	ORDER NO.	DATE DESPATCHED
5.6.91		

QTY.	DESCRIPTION	AMOUNT
		PDS.
	AS PER L/C NO 69/005/002983	
168 PAIRS	CONSISTING OF PART SHIPMENT OF:	
	1000 PAIRS OF NARROW WHEELS TO FIT UNIVERSAL 650 M.	
	AT PDS.679/77 PER PAIR COST	114201/36
	AT PDS. 78/75 PER PAIR FREIGHT	13230/00
	AT PDS.115/6743 PER PAIR USANCE	19433/28
	TOTAL C & F TEHRAN	146864/64

WE HEREBY STATE THAT THE MERCHANDISE IS AS PER PROFORMA
INVOICE NO. 1375 DD 8.11.89

IRANIAN CUSTOMS TARIFF NO. 87/06 85

WE CERTIFY THIS INVOICE TO BE TRUE AND CORRECT AND IN
ACCORDANCE WITH OUR BOOKS, ALSO THAT THE GOODS ARE OF
ENGLAND ORIGIN.

WE HEREBY CERTIFY THAT THE PRICES STATED IN THIS INVOICE
ARE THE CURRENT EXPORT MARKET PRICES FOR THE MERCHANDISE
DESCRIBED THEREIN AND WE ACCEPT FULL RESPONSIBILITY FOR
ANY INACCURACIES OR ERRORS THEREIN.

TOTAL NETT AND GROSS WEIGHT 53760 KGS

FOR AND ON BEHALF OF STANDEN ENGINEERING LIMITED

K. J. T. LINCOLN, SALES MANAGER

C & F TEHRAN	TOTAL	PDS. 146864/64

NOTES

1. This invoice relates to the same transaction as the combined transport bill of lading which appears as Form 2, below. Accompanying it also were a certificate of origin, signed by the local Chamber of Commerce, and an international inspection certificate, confirming that the goods shipped complied strictly in quality and quantity with the specification of the goods in this invoice. These documents were all listed in the letter of credit as required to be produced as conditions of payment.

2. The contract was on C&F terms, and so the sellers were not obliged to make arrangements regarding insurance, or to produce a policy or certificate of insurance.

3. 'Usance' is here used by the parties to refer to the cost of obtaining the letter of credit and other banking charges. In its more usual meaning, 'usance' is the period of time allowed for the payment of a bill of exchange, especially a foreign bill (see the Bills of Exchange Act 1882, s 4). It would normally be the buyer's obligation to arrange for the letter of credit directly with his own bank.

2 Combined transport bill of lading

Consignor M/S STANDEN ENGINEERING LIMITED HEREWARD WORKS. STATION ROAD ELY CAMBRIDGESHIRE CB7 4BP ENGLAND TEL: 0353 661111.	**FBL** FBL No. **844** Customs Reference/Status **G B** Shipper's Reference **B I F A** Forwarder's Reference 6 16 9106 844 01
Consigned to order of TO THE ORDER OF BANK SADERAT IRAN	NEGOTIABLE FIATA COMBINED TRANSPORT BILL OF LADING issued subject to ICC Uniform Rules for a Combined Transport Document (ICC publication 298) **ICC**
Notify address "NOTIFY PARTY" APPLICANT M/S BONGAH TOSE MACHINALET KESHAVARZI TEHRAN I.R.O. IRAN.	**TRANS CARGO** Link House, 62/66 High Street, Billericay, Essex CM12 9BS Phone: 0277 633 666 Fax No: 0277 626643 Tlx: 995878 TCARGO

Place of Receipt		
Ocean Vessel TRUCK	**Port of Loading** ELY, ENGLAND	
Port of Discharge TEHRAN	**Place of Delivery** TEHRAN	

Marks and Numbers	Number and Kind of Packages	Description of Goods	Gross Weight	Measurement
	168 (ONE HUNDRED AND SIXTY EIGHT) PAIRS - S.T.B. ------------------------------------ 168 PAIRS CONSISTING OF PART SHIPMENT OF: 1000 PAIRS OF NARROW WHEELS TO FIT UNIVERSAL 650 M. MERCHANDISE IS AS PER PROFORMA INVOICE NO.1375 DD 8.11.89.		GRS WT. 53760 KGS NET WT. 53760 KGS	

GOODS EN ROUTE
FREIGHT PREPAID
IRANIAN CUSTOMS TARIFF NO. 87/06 B5
SHIPMENT:FROM ENGLAND TO TEHRAN BY TRUCK
INSURANCE EFFECTED IN IRAN
IRAN INSURANCE CO, TLX NO.214154
BANK SADERAT IRAN, MEIDAN ESTEGHLAL BRANCH, L/C NO. 69/005/002983
BANK SADERAT IRAN, LONDON -REF. DC 41175

according to the declaration of the consignor.

The goods and instructions are accepted and dealt with subject to the Standard Conditions printed overleaf.

COPY

Taken in charge in apparent good order and condition, unless otherwise noted herein, at the place of receipt for transport and delivery as mentioned above.

One of these Combined Transport Bills of Lading must be surrendered duly endorsed in exchange for the goods. In Witness whereof the original Combined Transport Bills of Lading all of this tenor and date have been signed in the number stated below, one of which being accomplished the other(s) to be void.

Freight Amount £13230.00	Freight Payable at BILLERICAY	Place and date of issue; Stamp and signature BILLERICAY, 28.06.1991.
Cargo Insurance through the undersigned ☐ not covered ☐ Covered according to attached Policy	Number of Original FBL's THREE (3).	**TRANSCARGO** International UK Ltd., Link House,
For delivery of goods please apply to TIZPAR INTERNATIONAL TRANSPORT (PRIVATE CO LTD) NO. 447 SAADI AVENUE, TEHRAN-11, IRAN. PHONE: 021 304931/5 - TELEX: 212464		62-66 High Street, BILLERICAY, ESSEX, CM12 9BS

Standard Conditions (1992) governing the FIATA MULTIMODAL TRANSPORT BILL OF LADING

Definitions

— 'Freight Forwarder' means the Multimodal Transport Operator who issues this FBL and is named on the face of it and assumes liability for the performance of the multimodal transport contract as a carrier.

— 'Merchant' means and includes the Shipper, the Consignor, the Consignee, the Holder of this FBL, the Receiver and the Owner of the Goods.

— 'Consignor' means the person who concludes the multimodal transport contract with the Freight Forwarder.

— 'Consignee' means the person entitled to receive the goods from the Freight Forwarder.

— 'Taken in charge' means that the goods have been handed over to and accepted for carriage by the Freight Forwarder at the place of receipt evidenced in this FBL.

— 'Goods' means any property including live animals as well as containers, pallets or similar articles of transport or packaging not supplied by the Freight Forwarder, irrespective of whether such property is to be or is carried on or under deck.

1. **Applicability**

    Notwithstanding the heading 'FIATA Multimodal Transport Bill of Lading (FBL)' these conditions shall also apply if only one mode of transport is used,

2. **Issuance of this FBL**

2.1. By issuance of this FBL the Freight Forwarder

   a) undertakes to perform and/or in his own name to procure the performance of the entire transport, from the place at which the goods are taken in charge place of receipt evidenced in this FBL) to the place of delivery designated in this FBL,

   b) assumes liability as set out in these conditions.

2.2. Subject to the conditions of this FBL the Freight Forwarder shall be responsible for the acts and omissions of his servants or agents acting within the scope of their employment, or any other person of whose services he makes use for the performance of the contract evidenced by this FBL, as if such acts and omissions were his own.

3. **Negotiability and title to the goods**

3.1. This FBL is issued in a negotiable form unless it is marked 'non negotiable'. It shall constitute title to the goods and the holder, by endorsement of this FBL, shall be entitled to receive or to transfer the goods herein mentioned.

3.2. The information in this FBL shall be prime facie evidence of the taking in charge by the Freight Forwarder of the goods as described by such information unless a contrary indication, such as 'shipper's weight load and count' 'shipper-packed container' or similar expressions, has been made in the printed text or superimposed on this FBL. However, proof to the contrary shall not be admissible when the FBL has been transferred to the consignee for valuable consideration who in good faith has relied and acted thereon.

4. **Dangerous Goods and Indemnity**

4.1. The Merchant shall comply with rules which are mandatory according to the national law or by reason of International Convention, relating to the carriage of goods of a dangerous nature, and shall in any case inform the Freight Forwarder in writing of the exact nature of the danger, before goods of a dangerous nature are taken in charge by the Freight Forwarder and indicate to him, if need be, the precautions to be taken.

4.2. If the Merchant fails to provide such information and the Freight Forwarder is unaware of the dangerous nature of the goods and the necessary precautions to be taken and if, at any time, they are deemed to be a hazard to life or property, they may at any place be unloaded, destroyed or rendered harmless, as circumstances may require, without compensation. The Merchant shall indemnify the Freight Forwarder against all loss, damage, liability, or expense arising out of their being taken in charge, or their carriage, or of any service incidental thereto.

The burden of proving that the Freight Forwarder knew the exact nature of the danger constituted by the carriage of the said goods shall rest on the Merchant.

4.3. If any goods shall become a danger to life or property, they may in like manner be unloaded or landed at any place or destroyed or rendered harmless. If such danger was not caused by the fault and neglect of the Freight Forwarder he shall have no liability and the Merchant shall indemnify him against all loss, damage, liability and expense arising therefrom.

5. Description of Goods and Merchant's Packing and Inspection

5.1. The Consignor shall be deemed to have guaranteed to the Freight Forwarder the accuracy, at the time the goods were taken in charge by the Freight Forwarder, of all particulars relating to the general nature of the goods, their marks, number, weight, volume and quantity and, if applicable, to the dangerous character of the goods, as furnished by him or on his behalf for insertion on the FBL.

The Consignor shall indemnify the Freight Forwarder against all loss, damage and expense resulting from any inaccuracy or inadequacy of such particulars.

The Consignor shall remain liable even if the FBL has been transferred by him.

The right of the Freight Forwarder to such an indemnity shall in no way limit his liability under this FBL to any person other than the Consignor.

5.2. The Freight Forwarder shall not be liable for any loss, damage or expense caused by defective or insufficient packing of goods or by inadequate loading or packing within containers or other transport units when such loading or packing has been performed by the Merchant or on his behalf by a person other than the Freight Forwarder, or by the defect or unsuitability of the containers or other transport units supplied by the Merchant, or if supplied by the Freight Forwarder if a defect or unsuitability of the containers or other transport units would have been apparent upon reasonable inspection by the Merchant. The Merchant shall indemnify the Freight Forwarder against all loss, damage, liability and expense so caused.

6. Freight Forwarder's Liability

6.1. The responsibility of the Freight Forwarder for the goods under these conditions covers the period from the time the Freight Forwarder has taken the goods in his charge to the time of their delivery.

6.2. The Freight Forwarder shall be liable for loss of or damage to the goods as well as for delay in delivery if the occurrence which caused the loss, damage or delay in delivery took place while the goods were in his charge as defined in Clause 2.1.a, unless the Freight Forwarder proves that no fault or neglect of his own, his servants or agents or any other person referred to in Clause 2.2 has caused or contributed to such loss, damage or delay. However, the Freight Forwarder shall only be liable for loss following from delay in delivery if the Consignor has made a declaration of interest in timely delivery which has been accepted by the Freight Forwarder and stated in this FBL.

6.3.   Arrival times are not guaranteed by the Freight Forwarder. However, delay in delivery occurs when the goods have not been delivered within the time expressly agreed upon or, in the absence of such agreement, within the time which would be reasonable to require of a diligent Freight Forwarder, having regard to the circumstances of the case.

6.4.   If the goods have not been delivered within ninety consecutive days following such date of delivery as determined in Clause 6.3, the claimant may, in the absence of evidence to the contrary, treat the goods as lost.

6.5.   When the Freight Forwarder establishes that, in the circumstances of the case, the loss or damage could be attributed to one or more causes or events, specified in a–e of the present clause, it shall be presumed that it was so caused, always provided, however, that the claimant shall be entitled to prove that the loss or damage was not, in fact, caused wholly or partly by one or more of such causes or events.

a)   an act or omission of the Merchant or person other than the Freight Forwarder acting on behalf of the Merchant or from whom the Freight Forwarder took the goods in charge;

b)   insufficiency or defective condition of the packaging or marks and/or numbers;

c)   handling loading, stowage or unloading of the goods by the Merchant or any person acting on behalf of the Merchant;

d)   inherent vice of the goods;

e)   strike, lockout, stoppage or restraint of labour.

6.6.   **Defences for carriage by sea or inland waterways**
Notwithstanding Clauses 6.2, 6.3 and 6.4, the Freight Forwarder shall not be liable for loss, damage or delay in delivery with respect to goods carried by sea or inland waterways when such loss, damage or delay during such carriage has been caused by:

a)   act, neglect, or default of the master, mariner, pilot or the servants of the carrier in the navigation or in the management of the ship,

b)   fire, unless caused by the actual fault or privity of the carrier, however, always provided that whenever loss or damage has resulted from unseaworthiness of the ship, the Freight Forwarder can prove that due diligence has been exercised to make the ship seaworthy at the commencement of the voyage.

7.   **Paramount Clauses**

7.1.   The conditions shall only take effect to the extent that they are not contrary to the mandatory provisions of International Conventions or national law applicable to the contract evidenced by this FBL.

7.2.   The Hague Rules contained in the International Convention for the unification of certain rules relating to Bills of Lading, dated Brussels 25th August 1924, or in those countries where they are already in force the Hague-Visby Rules contained in the Protocol of Brussels, dated 23rd February 1968, as enacted in the Country of Shipment, shall apply to all carriage of goods by sea and also to the carriage of goods by inland waterways, and such provisions shall apply to all goods whether carried on deck or under deck.

7.3. The Carriage of Goods by Sea Act of the United States of America (COGSA) shall apply to the carriage of goods by sea, whether on deck or under deck, if compulsorily applicable to this FBL or would be applicable but for the goods being carried on deck in accordance with a statement on this FBL.

8.   Limitation of Freight Forwarder's Liability

8.1. Assessment of compensation for loss of or damage to the goods shall be made by reference to the value of such goods at the place and time they are delivered to the consignee or at the place and time when, in accordance with this FBL, they should have been so delivered.

8.2. The value of the goods shall be determined according to the current commodity exchange price or, if there is no such price, according to the current market price or, if there are no such prices, by reference to the normal value of goods of the same name and quality.

8.3. Subject to the provisions of subclauses 8.4 to 8.9 inclusive, the Freight Forwarder shall in no event be or become liable for any loss of or damage to the goods in an amount exceeding the equivalent of 666,67 SDR per package or unit or 2 SDR per kilogramme of gross weight of the goods lost or damaged, whichever is the higher, unless the nature and value of the goods shall have been declared by the Consignor and accepted by the Freight Forwarder before the goods have been taken in his charge, or the ad valorem freight rate paid, and such value is stated in the FBL by him, then such declared value shall be the limit.

8.4. Where a container, pallet or similar article of transport is loaded with more than one package or unit, the packages or other shipping units enumerated in the FBL as packed in such article of transport are deemed packages or shipping units. Except as aforesaid, such article of transport shall be considered the package or unit.

8.5. Notwithstanding the above mentioned provisions, if the multimodal transport does not, according to the contract, include carriage of goods by sea or by inland waterways, the liability of the Freight Forwarder shall be limited to an amount not exceeding 8.33 SDR per kilogramme of gross weight of the goods lost or damaged.

8.6. a) When the loss of or damage to the goods occurred during one particular stage of the multimodal transport, in respect of which an applicable international convention or mandatory national law would have provided another limit of liability if a separate contract of carriage had been made for that particular stage of transport, then the limit of the Freight Forwarder's liability for such loss or damage shall be determined by reference to the provisions of such convention or mandatory national law.

b) Unless the nature and value of the goods shall have been declared by the Merchant and inserted in this FBL, and the ad valorem freight rate paid, the liability of the Freight Forwarder under COGSA, where applicable, shall not exceed US$ 500 per package or in the case of goods not shipped in packages, per customary freight unit.

8.7. If the Freight Forwarder is liable in respect of loss following from delay in delivery, or consequential loss or damage other than loss of or damage to the goods, the liability of the Freight Forwarder shall be limited to an amount not exceeding the equivalent of twice the freight under the multimodal contract for the multimodal transport under this FBL.

8.8. The aggregate liability of Freight Forwarder shall not exceed the limits of liability for total loss of the goods.

8.9. The Freight Forwarder is not entitled to the benefit of the limitation of liability if it is proved that the loss, damage or delay in delivery resulted from a personal act or omission of the Freight Forwarder done with the intent to cause such loss, damage or delay or recklessly and with knowledge that such loss, damage or delay would probably result.

9.   Applicability to Actions in Tort

These conditions apply to all claims against the Freight Forwarder relating to the performance of the contract evidenced by this FBL, whether the claim be founded in contract or in tort.

10.   Liability of Servants and other Persons

10.1. These conditions apply whenever claims relating to the performance of the contract evidenced by this FBL are made against any servant, agent or other person (including any independent contractor) whose services have been used in order to perform the contract, whether such claims are founded in contract or in tort, and the aggregate liability of the Freight Forwarder and of such servants, agents or other persons shall not exceed the limits in Clause 8.

10.2. In entering into this contract as evidenced by this FBL, the Freight Forwarder, to the extent of these provisions, does not only act on his own behalf, but also as agent or trustee for such persons, and such persons shall to this extent be or be deemed to he parties to this contract.

10.3. However, if it is proved that the loss of or such loss or damage to the goods resulted from a personal act or omission of such a person referred to in Clause 10.1 done with intent to cause damage, or recklessly and with knowledge that damage would probably result, such person shall not be entitled to benefit of limitation of liability provided for in Clause 8.

10.4. The aggregate of the amounts recoverable from the Freight Forwarder and the persons referred to in Clauses 2.2 and 10.1 shall not exceed the limits provided for in these conditions.

11.   Method and Route of Transportation

Without notice to the Merchant, the Freight Forwarder has the liberty to carry the goods on or under deck and to choose or substitute the means, route and procedure to be followed in the handling, stowage, storage and transportation of the goods.

12.   Delivery

12.1. Goods shall be deemed to be delivered when they have been handed over or placed at the disposal of the Consignee or his agent in accordance with this FBL or when the goods have been handed over to any authority or other party to whom, pursuant to the law or regulation applicable at the place of delivery, the goods must be handed over, or such other place at which the Freight Forwarder is entitled to call upon the Merchant to take delivery.

12.2. The Freight Forwarder shall also be entitled to store the goods at the sole risk of the Merchant, and the Freight Forwarder's liability shall cease, and the cost of such storage shall be paid upon demand, by the Merchant to the Freight Forwarder.

12.3. If at any time the carriage under this FBL is or is likely to be affected by any hindrance or risk of any kind (including the condition of the goods) not arising from any fault or neglect of the Freight Forwarder or a person referred to in Clause 2.2 and which cannot be avoided by the exercise of reasonable endeavours the Freight Forwarder may:

> abandon the carriage of the goods under this FBL and, where reasonably possible, place the goods or any part of them at the Merchant's disposal at any place which the Freight Forwarder may deem safe and convenient, whereupon delivery shall be deemed to have been made, and the responsibility of the Freight Forwarder in respect of such goods shall cease.

In any event the Freight Forwarder shall be entitled to full freight under this FBL and the Merchant shall pay any additional costs resulting from the above mentioned circumstances.

13. Freight and Charges

13.1. Freight shall be paid in cash, without any reduction or deferment on account of any claim, counterclaim or set-off, whether prepaid or payable at destination.

Freight shall be considered as earned by the Freight Forwarder at the moment when the goods have been taken in his charge, and not to be returned in any event.

13.2. Freight and all other amounts mentioned in this FBL are to be paid in the currency named in this FBL or at the Freight Forwarder's option, in the currency of the country of dispatch or destination at the highest rate of exchange for bankers' sight bills current for prepaid freight on the day of dispatch and for freight payable at destination on the day when the Merchant is notified on arrival of the goods there or on the date of withdrawal of the delivery order, whichever rate is the higher, or at the option of the Freight Forwarder on the date of this FBL.

13.3. All dues, taxes and charges or other expenses in connection with the goods shall be paid by the Merchant.

Where equipment is supplied by the Freight Forwarder, the Merchant shall pay all demurrage and charges which are not due to a fault or neglect of the Freight Forwarder.

13.4. The Merchant shall reimburse the Freight Forwarder in proportion to the amount of freight for any costs for deviation or delay or any other increase of costs of whatever nature caused by war, warlike operations, epidemics, strikes, government directions or force majeure.

13.5. The Merchant warrants the correctness of the declaration of contents, insurance, weight, measurements of value of the goods but the Freight Forwarder has the liberty to have the contents inspected and the weight, measurements or value verified. If on such inspection it is found that the declaration is not correct it is agreed that a sum equal either to five times the difference between the correct figure and the freight charged, or to double the correct freight less the freight charged, whichever sum is the smaller, shall be payable as liquidated damages to the Freight Forwarder for his inspection costs and losses of freight on other goods notwithstanding any other sum having been stated on this FBL as freight payable.

13.6. Despite the acceptance by the Freight Forwarder of instructions to collect freight, charges or other expenses from any other person in respect of the transport under this FBL, the Merchant shall remain responsible for such monies on receipt of evidence of demand and the absence of payment for whatever reason.

14. Lien

The Freight Forwarder shall have a lien on the goods and any documents relating thereto for any amount due at any time to the Freight Forwarder from the Merchant including storage fees and the cost of recovering same, and may enforce such lien in any reasonable manner which he may think fit.

15.   **General Average**

The Merchant shall indemnify the Freight Forwarder in respect of any claims of a General Average nature which may be made on him and shall provide such security as may be required by the Freight Forwarder in this connection.

16.   **Notice**

16.1. Unless notice of loss of or damage to the goods, specifying the general nature of such loss or damage, is given in writing by the consignee to the Freight Forwarder when the goods are delivered to the consignee in accordance with Clause 12, such handing over is prima facie evidence of the delivery by the Freight Forwarder of the goods as described in this FBL.

16.2. Where the loss or damage is not apparent, the same prima facie effect shall apply if notice in writing is not given within 6 consecutive days after the day when the goods were delivered to the consignee in accordance with Clause 12.

17.   **Time bar**

The Freight Forwarder shall, unless otherwise expressly agreed, be discharged of all liability under these conditions unless suit is brought within 9 months after the delivery of the goods, or the date when the goods should have been delivered, or the date when in accordance with clause 6.4 failure to deliver the goods would give the consignee the right to treat the goods as lost.

18.   **Partial invalidity**

If any clause or a part thereof is held to be invalid, the validity of this FBL and the remaining clauses or a part thereof shall not be affected.

19.   **Jurisdiction and applicable law**

Actions against the Freight Forwarder may be instituted only in the place where the Freight Forwarder has his place of business as stated on the reverse of this FBL and shall be decided according to the law of the country in which that place of business is situated.

The ICC logo denotes that this document has been deemed by the ICC to be in conformity with the UNCTAD/ICC Rules for Multimodal Transport Documents. The ICC logo does not imply ICC endorsement of the document nor does it in any way make the ICC party to any possible legal action resulting from the use of this document.

3 Application to open irrevocable documentary credit

HSBC ◆

To: HSBC Bank plc (Bank) ___LONDON_____ Trade Services Centre

APPLICATION FOR IRREVOCABLE DOCUMENTARY CREDIT

Transferable?	☒ No ☐ Yes	D.C Number DC LDI 719379	Date of application 9/2/08

Applicant (name and full address) ABC plc GEORGE HOUSE GEORGES STREET CRAWLEY, WEST SUSSEX	Beneficiary Name and Address (and telephone no, Fax no. Contact name within company, if known) AITCH CORPORATION LX-M SECTION 2-1 COMO STREET, COMO KU TOKYO 100-0400 JAPAN
Applicant's reference	Expiry Date 30/4/08 Place of Expiry JAPAN

Amount: Currency USD .... Figures 93,500·00
Words NINETY THREE THOUSAND FIVE HUNDRED DOLLARS
Acceptable variance in quantity of goods*/DC amount*: +/-...................% (*Delete as appropriate)

Partial Shipment ☒ allowed ☐ not allowed	Transhipment ☒ allowed ☐ not allowed
Latest Shipment Date...... 20/4/08	Shipment/Despatch/Taking in charge From ...ANY JAPANESE PORT To ...FELIXSTOWE, UK

Method of Advice: ☒ Full teletransmission   ☐ Airmail   ☐ Courier

☒ Drafts required drawn on Issuing Bank for full invoice value of the goods: ☒ At Sight: ☐ ....days after Sight

☐ ....days after B/L, AWB, CMR; ☐ ....days after Invoice Date: ☐ Other ....

Advising Bank/Routing Bank (if applicable) HSBC TOKYO *(If left blank, DC will normally be advised through an HSBC Group Office)*	Instruct Advising Bank to add their confirmation ☐ Yes ☒ No If Yes, confirmation charges payable by ☐ Applicant ☐ Beneficiary

Documents to be presented within ...10...days after the date of ☒ Shipment ☐ Receipt but within validity of the documentary credit

Trade term ...FOB............ Place ANY JAPANESE PORT
(e.g. FOB, FCA, CFR, CPT, CIF, CIP, EXW, DDU, DDP)

Goods (brief description including quantity without excessive detail)

FENDERS IN ACCORDANCE WITH PURCHASE
ORDER NUMBER 008224

1016-8A (05/07 - UOI - 1PK x 25)

Documents Required:

Original Invoice(s) signed plus ....2.............. copies

For shipment by sea, full set of original clean "on board" ☑ bills of lading / ☐ multimodal or combined transport documents.

    ☑ made out to the shipper's order, blank endorsed and marked ☐ freight prepaid ☑ freight collect
    and notify ....

    ☐ made out to order of .... and marked ☐ freight prepaid ☐ freight collect
    and notify ....

☐ Air waybill, marked "for the consignor/shipper", marked ☐ freight prepaid ☐ freight collect
and notify..bearing reference to this documentary credit number, showing actual date of despatch of goods including flight number and evidencing despatch of goods to ....

☐ Original CMR/Truck waybill marked ☐ freight prepaid ☐ freight collect ☐ evidencing goods consigned to............

☐ Other transport documents (please specify).................................

☐ If CIF/CIP: Insurance policy/certificate for full CIF/CIP value plus ☐ 10% ☐ ....% blank endorsed, covering institute cargo clauses 'A'/war/strike/other (please specify if required)...........................clauses

☐ If FOB etc: Insurance covered by applicant/buyer

Additional Documents 3

☑ Packing list in ....copies ☐ Export licence/certificate in...........copies ☐ Weight list in...........copies

☐ GSP certificate form A in ....copies ☑ Certificate of...........origin in 3 copies ☐ Other (please specify)

Special Instructions

BILLS OF LADING TO BE ISSUED BY SEA FREIGHT SERVICES LTD AND MUST SHOW A SEPARATE "ON BOARD" NOTATION

Documents to be delivered in one lot unless otherwise specified to the Issuing Bank by ☐ Courier ☐ Registered Airmail
☐ Other (please specify).................

DC charges   Applicant   Beneficiary *(see condition 13 below)*   ☐ On receipt of documents in order, please debit our

Within UK ☑ ☐   Account number ....
Outside UK ☐ ☑   Sort code   40-............-............
   Utilising Forward Contract No/Spot Rate...........

Please debit DC opening commission, advising expenses to our

Account number ....
Sort code   40-............-............

We request you to issue your irrevocable Documentary Credit for our account in accordance with the above instructions and subject to the conditions printed below: ✗   ✗   Signature verified

signed on behalf of applicant in accordance with our mandate held by the Bank

In case of query, please telephone ✗ .... and ask for ✗ ....

Conditions

1. Except so far as otherwise expressly stated, this Documentary Credit is subject to Uniform Customs and Practice for Documentary Credits (2007 Revision), International Chamber of Commerce Publication No. 600.
2. We agree to take out in the manner and to the extent required by the Bank all insurance necessary for the full protection of the Bank's interest in the goods shipped under this Credit, and on behalf of the Bank and subject to its instructions to prosecute or to ensure the prosecution of any claim that may arise under any insurance and to pay the proceeds thereof to the Bank and to provide evidence of insurance if called upon to do so.
3. If this Credit is to be advised through an agency or correspondent bank in USA, you are authorised to accept at your sole discretion and under our responsibility American Institute clauses insurance policies.
4. You are authorised to make any additions to the documents specified under this Credit which you may consider necessary to ensure compliance with government regulations but you are not obliged to do so.
5. We certify that the import of goods described above is not prohibited or restricted and that we hold and undertake to exhibit to you a valid import licence where such licence is required.
6. The words "we", "our" and "us" shall be read as "I", "my" and "me" if this application is signed by or on behalf of an individual.
7. You are authorised at your sole discretion and without obligation to do so whenever you consider it advisable, customary or appropriate to waive or delete the following from the instructions contained on this form (whether completed by me/us or not), namely: "Drafts required at sight/at .... days drawn on issuing bank for full invoice value of goods"
8. In the absence of any instructions to the contrary specified in "Special Instructions" above, you are authorised to instruct any bank or branch concerned to despatch any draft(s) and/or any documents by one or more mails or other method of conveyance at your sole discretion.
9. We undertake on demand to reimburse you in respect of all payments and to

indemnify you in respect of all liabilities, including legal costs, on a full indemnity basis and to discharge all liabilities which you may make or incur for us at our request or as a result of your allowing any drawer and or negotiating/confirming bank to obtain reimbursement before you have had the opportunity to inspect any documents in connection with this Credit and to pay interest from the date of the same having been made or incurred until repayment both before and after my demand made at the stipulated rate by you.
10. We are aware of the implications of article 34 of UCP 600 and acknowledge that where a bank claims to have paid/accepted (honoured) or negotiated under this Credit, its good faith and the fact of payment/acceptance (honour) or negotiation thereof shall be presumed in the absence of evidence to the contrary.
11. As continuing security for the payment of all sums for which we may from time to time be actually or contingently indebted or liable to you for any reason and on any account:
(a) we hereby pledge and agree to pledge to you with full title guarantee firstly all bills, documents of title, transportation documents, insurance policies and other documents representing or relating to the goods shipped under this credit which goods and/or documents are in or come into your or your agent's actual or constructive possession or control and secondly, the goods represented thereby, and we warrant that such documents and goods shall not be subject to any lien, charge or other encumbrance in favour of any other person; and
(b) we agree to ensure that all such documents are properly endorsed and delivered to you and you are hereby authorised to demand the same from any party on your behalf.
12. We furthermore agree that this Credit and any drawing(s) or advance(s) relating thereto shall be subject to the terms of any separate pledge (being in addition to that contained in Condition 11 above) where given to you.
13. Where charges are for the account of the beneficiary and are unpaid for any reason we undertake to reimburse you in full.

4 Irrevocable documentary credit

```
&1008C          20080213    111536    SWT 700  PP09  TOCL  957915  DC LDI719379

        SENDER                      MIDLGB22
        RECEIVER                    HSBCJPJT
        DESTINATION                 HK+SHANGHAI BANKING CORPORATION LTD
                                    TOKYO
                                    CPO BOX 336
                                    HSBC BLDG 11-1 NIHONBASHI 3-CHOME
                                    CHUO-KU TOKYO 103-0027 JAPAN
        MESSAGE TYPE                700 ISSUE OF A DOCUMENTARY CREDIT
        -------------------------------------------------------------------
        FLD.     TEXT                       CONTENTS
        -------------------------------------------------------------------
        27:      SEQUENCE OF TOTAL:         1/1
        40A:     FORM OF DC:                IRREVOCABLE
        20:      DC NO:                     DC LDI719379
        31C:     DATE OF ISSUE:             080213
        40E:     APPLICABLE RULES:          UCP LATEST VERSION
        31D:     EXPIRY DATE AND PLACE:     080430IN COUNTRY OF BENEFICIARY
        50:      APPLICANT:                 ABC PLC
                                            GEORGE HOUSE
                                            GEORGE STREET
                                            CRAWLEY, WEST SUSSEX
        59:      BENEFICIARY:               AITCHO CORPORATION
                                            LX-M SECTION
                                            2-1 COMO STREET
                                            COMO KU TOKYO 100-0400 JAPAN
        32B:     DC AMT:                    USD93500,00
        39B:     MAXIMUM CR AMT:            NOT EXCEEDING
        41D:     AVAILABLE WITH/BY:         ANY BANK
                                            BY NEGOTIATION
*       42C:     DRAFTS AT:                 AT SIGHT
        42D:     DRAWEE:                    ISSUING BANK
        43P:     PARTIAL SHIPMENTS:         ALLOWED
        43T:     TRANSHIPMENT:              ALLOWED
        44E:     LOADING PORT/DEPART AIRPORT:
                 ANY JAPANESE PORT
        44F:     DISCHARGE PORT/DEST AIRPORT:
                 FELIXSTOWE, UNITED KINGDOM
        44C:     LATEST DATE OF SHIPMENT:   080420
        45A:     GOODS:
                 FOB ANY JAPANESE PORT
*                FENDERS IN ACCORDANCE WITH PURCHASE ORDER NUMBERS 008224
        46A:     DOCUMENTS REQUIRED:
*                ORIGINAL INVOICES IN 3 COPIES.
*                FULL SET OF ORIGINAL CLEAN ON BOARD MARINE BILLS OF LADING MADE
                 OUT TO SHIPPERS ORDER, ENDORSED IN BLANK, MARKED FREIGHT
                 COLLECT.
*                ORIGINAL CERTIFICATE OF ORIGIN PLUS 2 COPIES.
                 ORIGINAL PACKING LIST IN 3 COPIES.
        47A:     ADDITIONAL CONDITIONS:
I01 600          ALL PRESENTATIONS CONTAINING DISCREPANCIES WILL ATTRACT A
                 DISCREPANCY FEE OF GBP50.00 PLUS TELEX AND HOLDING CHARGES, IF
                 ANY. THIS CHARGE WILL BE LEVIED WHETHER OR NOT WE ELECT TO
                 CONSULT THE APPLICANT FOR A WAIVER IN ACCORDANCE WITH UCP600
                 ARTICLE 16. THESE CHARGES WILL ALWAYS BE FOR THE ACCOUNT OF THE

                                              611-068784-000.02-     -0
```

20080213   111536   SWT 700 PP09 TOCL 957915 DC LDI719379

BENEFICIARY. IN ACCORDANCE WITH PROVISIONS OF ARTICLE 16C III B
OF UCP600, IF WE GIVE NOTICE OF REFUSAL OF DOCUMENTS PRESENTED
UNDER THIS CREDIT WE SHALL HOWEVER RETAIN THE RIGHT TO ACCEPT A
WAIVER OF DISCREPANCIES FROM THE APPLICANT AND, SUBJECT TO SUCH
WAIVER BEING ACCEPTABLE TO US,

I02 600   TO RELEASE THE DOCUMENTS AGAINST THAT WAIVER WITHOUT REFERENCE TO
THE PRESENTER PROVIDED THAT NO WRITTEN INSTRUCTIONS TO THE
CONTRARY HAVE BEEN RECEIVED BY US FROM THE PRESENTER BEFORE THE
RELEASE OF THE DOCUMENTS.ANY SUCH RELEASE PRIOR TO THE RECEIPT
OF CONTRARY INSTRUCTIONS SHALL NOT CONSTITUTE A FAILURE ON OUR
PART TO HOLD DOCUMENTS AT THE PRESENTERS RISK AND DISPOSAL, AND
WE SHALL HAVE NO LIABILITY TO THE PRESENTER IN RESPECT OF ANY
SUCH RELEASE. UNLESS OTHERWISE EXPRESSLY STATED, ALL DOCUMENTS
MUST BE IN ENGLISH.

I03 600   EXCEPT SO FAR AS OTHERWISE EXPRESSLY STATED, THIS DOCUMENTARY
CREDIT IS SUBJECT TO UNIFORM CUSTOMS AND PRACTICE FOR
DOCUMENTARY CREDIT ICC PUBLICATION NO. 600.
ANY PROCEEDS OF PRESENTATIONS UNDER THIS DC WILL BE SETTLED BY
TELETRANSMISSION AND A CHARGE OF GBP40.00 (OR CURRENCY
EQUIVALENT) WILL BE DEDUCTED.
WHERE ORIGINAL DOCUMENTS OR SIGNATURES ARE REQUIRED
FACSIMILE/PHOTOCOPIES OF DOCUMENTS OR SIGNATURES ARE NOT
ACCEPTABLE.

IOB   IF AN ONBOARD NOTATION HAS BEEN ADDED TO THE BILL OF LADING THIS
 *   MUST BE DATED AND SIGNED BY A FULL SIGNATORY OF THE
 *   CARRIER/MASTER OR NAMED AGENT ON BEHALF OF THE CARRIER/MASTER
 *   TOGETHER WITH THE APPROPRIATE STAMP.
 *   BILLS OF LADING TO BE ISSUED BY SEA FREIGHT SERVICES LTD AND
       MUST SHOW A SEPERATE ON BOARD NOTATION.

    71B: DETAILS OF CHARGES: ALL CHGS OUTSIDE COUNTRY OF ISSUE
                                     FOR ACCOUNT OF BENEFICIARY/EXPORTER
                                     TRANSIT INTEREST CHARGES ARE
                                     PAYABLE BY BENEFICIARY/EXPORTER
    48:    PERIOD OF PRESENTATION: WITHIN 10 DAYS AFTER THE DATE OF
                                     SHIPMENT BUT WITHIN THE VALIDITY OF
                                     THE CREDIT
    49:    CONFIRMATION INSTRUCTIONS: WITHOUT
    78:    INFO TO PRESENTING BK:
ISU *   ON RECEIPT OF DOCUMENTS CONFORMING TO THE TERMS OF THIS
     *   DOCUMENTARY CREDIT, WE UNDERTAKE TO REIMBURSE YOU IN THE
     *   CURRENCY OF THE CREDIT IN ACCORDANCE WITH YOUR INSTRUCTIONS,
     *   WHICH SHOULD
     *   INCLUDE YOUR UID NUMBER AND THE ABA CODE OF THE RECEIVING BANK.
 *   72:   BK TO BK INFO: DOCUMENTS TO BE DESPATCHED BY
                                     COURIER SERVICE IN ONE LOT TO HSBC
                                     BANK PLC, TRADE SERVICES CENTRE
                                     LEVEL 3, 62-76 PARK STREET LONDON
                                     SE1 9RN

611-068784-000.02-   -0

Page 2

20080213   111536   SWT 700 PP09 TOCL 957915 DC LDI719379

611-068784-000.02-   -0

5 Factoring agreement

THIS FACTORING AGREEMENT is made…BETWEEN

(1) *(name of company)* a company registered in England and Wales (Company registration number …) the registered office of which is at *(address)* ('the Company'); and

(2) *(factoring bank)* a company registered in England and Wales (Company registration number …) the registered office of which is at *(address)* acting for the purposes of this agreement through its branch at *(address)* ('the Factor').

WHEREAS

(1) The Company enters into commercial contracts with its Customers (as defined below) pursuant to which the Company sells its products and services to its Customers.

(2) The Company wishes to receive the proceeds of sale resulting from the sale of its products and services before the expiry of the period of credit which it gives to its Customers.

(3) The Factor has agreed to provide finance to the Company against the security of the Debts (as defined below) on the terms of this agreement.

NOW IT IS AGREED AS FOLLOWS

1   Definitions and interpretation

1.1   Definitions

In this agreement:

1.1.1 'an Approved Debt' means any Purchased Debt in respect of which a Purchase Instalment has been paid or is payable and which, at the time in question, has not been disapproved by the Factor pursuant to clause 4 or which, if previously disapproved, has at the time in question been re-approved;

1.1.2 'Customer' means any person to whom the Company supplies goods or for whom the Company carries out work or performs services;

1.1.3 'Debt' means an amount, whether or not presently payable, which is due to the Company at the time of the Offer for goods supplied, work done or services performed, calculated at gross book value before taking into consideration any reduction that may be agreed between the Company and its Customer and any discount a Customer may be entitled to deduct upon prompt payment;

1.1.4 'a Disapproved Debt' means any Purchased Debt that at the time in question is not an Approved Debt;

1.1.5 'the Due Date' means the last day of the third month following the month in which a Debt is incurred, or such other day as the Bank and the Company may together agree;

1.1.6 'the Factoring Charge' means, in relation to each Debt, … % of that Debt;

1.1.7 'the Minimum Annual Factoring Charge' means £…;

1.1.8 'the Minimum Factoring Charge' means £…;

1.1.9 'Offer' means an offer of Debts made by the Company to the Factor in accordance with clause 2;

1.1.10 'Purchase Instalment' means… % of the gross book value of an Approved Debt less the Factoring Charge paid by the Factor to the Company;

1.1.11 'Purchased Debt' means any Debt offered to the Factor and purchased by the Factor whether approved or not;

1.2   Construction

In this agreement:

1.2.1 the contents page and clause headings are included for convenience only and do not affect the construction of this agreement;

1.2.2 words denoting the singular include the plural and vice versa; and

1.2.3 words denoting one gender include all genders.

1.3   Interpretation

In this agreement, unless the context otherwise requires or unless otherwise expressly provided, references to:

1.3.1 persons include references to natural persons, firms, partnerships, companies, corporations, associations, organisations, and trusts, in each case whether or not having a separate legal personality;

1.3.2 documents, instruments and agreements, including, without limitation, this agreement and any document referred to in this agreement, are references to such documents, instruments and agreements as modified, amended, varied, supplemented or novated from time to time;

1.3.3 an authorisation include references to an authorisation, consent, approval, resolution, licence, exemption, filing and registration;

1.3.4 the Factor shall be deemed to be a reference to or to include, as appropriate, its successors or assigns;

1.3.5 clauses are references to clauses of this agreement;

1.3.6 statutory provisions are construed as references to those provisions as respectively amended, consolidated, extended or re-enacted from time to time, and to any orders, regulations, instruments or other subordinate legislation made under the relevant statute;

1.3.7 'a company' include references to any company, corporation or other body corporate, wherever and however incorporated or established;

1.3.8 'the Debts' shall be references to all the Debt and to each and every Debt and references to any other defined term or noun in the plural number or the collective plural shall be interpreted mutates mutandis in the same manner;

1.3.9 'assets' shall be construed so as to include property, income and rights of every kind, present, future and contingent, including uncalled share capital, and every kind of interest in an asset; and

1.3.10 'indebtedness' shall be construed so as to include any obligation, whether incurred as principal or as surety, for the payment or repayment of money, whether present or future, actual or contingent.

2   Offers

2.1   Existing Debts

The Company shall offer to sell to the Factor at their face invoice value all Debts owed to the Company at the date of this agreement.

2.2   Future Debts

The Company shall complete and deliver to the Factor at least once during each [month], or during such other period as may from time to time be agreed by the Company and the

Factor, an offer of all outstanding Debts not previously offered in such form as the Factor may from time to time require.

2.3   No obligation

The Factor shall not be obliged to purchase the Debts referred to in clauses 2.1. and 2.2.

2.4   Contents of Offer

Every Offer shall:

2.4.1   offer to sell to the Factor every Debt not previously offered to the Factor;

2.4.2   be accompanied by the original and one copy of each invoice relating to each Debt which is the subject of the Offer together with such evidence as the Factor may require of the delivery of the goods, the carrying out of the work or the performance of the services in respect of which each Debt has been incurred;

2.4.3   be accompanied by particulars of credits granted to a Customer and not previously notified to the Factor and the original and one copy of every credit note issued in respect of those credits; and

2.4.4   be on the terms and conditions of this agreement.

3   Acceptance

3.1   Method of acceptance

In relation to any Debt offered to the Factor acceptance shall take effect either upon the Factor crediting the account of the Company with the Purchase Instalment or at the close of business on the second working day after the date of receipt by the Factor of the relevant Offer unless the Factor has by then despatched to the Company a notice of non-purchase relating to such Debt.

3.2   Transfer of rights

Upon acceptance by the Factor of the Offer of a Debt all the interest of the Company in the Debt and all subsisting rights and all remedies for enforcing the Debt shall vest in the Factor.

4   Disapproval and re-approval

4.1   Disapproval

The Factor may, at the time of or at any time after the acceptance of an Offer, disapprove in whole or in part any Debt that constitutes part of that Offer.

4.2   Reasons for disapproval

Disapproval may be for reasons of the age of the credit or a credit limit dispute or otherwise and shall be notified to the Company in writing, such notice taking effect on posting.

4.3   Effect of disapproval

Upon disapproval of a Debt, the amount by which the aggregate of any Purchase Instalment and the Factoring Charge exceeds the amount paid to the Factor by the Customer shall become immediately payable by the Company to the Factor.

4.4   Deemed approval of Debt

Unless or until such notice is sent to the Company a Debt will be deemed approved.

4.5   Re-approval of Debt

The Factor may in its absolute discretion subsequently re-approve any Disapproved Debt.

5 Payments to the company

5.1 Purchase Instalments
The Factor shall pay the Purchase Instalment to the Company forthwith upon the acceptance by the Factor of the Company's Offer in respect of an Approved Debt or upon any subsequent approval of a Disapproved Debt by the Factor.

5.2 Suspension of obligation to pay
The Factor shall not be obliged to make any payment to the Company while the Company is in breach of this agreement.

6 Costs of factoring

6.1 Factoring Charge on Debts
The Factor shall be entitled to the Factoring Charge on all Debts purchased by the Factor immediately upon such purchase.

6.2 Minimum Annual Factoring Charge
If in any period of twelve months expiring on an anniversary of the date of this agreement, the aggregate of all Factoring Charges payable has not amounted to the Minimum Annual Factoring Charge, the Factor shall be entitled immediately to a sum equal to the deficiency.

6.3 Termination payment
If upon termination of this agreement for any reason other than default of the Factor the aggregate of all such Factoring Charges either:

6.3.1 has not amounted to the Minimum Factoring Charge, or

6.3.2 since the most recent anniversary of the date of this agreement has not amounted to the Minimum Annual Factoring Charge,

whichever is the greater, the Factor shall be entitled immediately to a sum equal to the deficiency.

6.4 Overdue amounts
The Factor shall be entitled to interest at the rate of ... % a year over the base rate of *(bank)* for the time being prevailing upon any balance from time to time due to the Factor from the Company under this agreement.

6.5 Cost and expenses
The Company shall reimburse the Factor for all costs, charges and expenses incurred by the Factor in connection with entering into this agreement and enforcing its provisions, all stamp duties and penalties payable on assignments and reassignments of Debts, all costs, charges and expenses howsoever arising incurred by the Factor in recovering money owing in respect of Debts and all other monies otherwise payable under this agreement.

6.6 Time for payment
Any amount payable to the Factor under this agreement shall be due and payable on demand unless otherwise provided in this agreement.

7 Notice of assignment to Customers

The Company shall ensure that all invoices and other notices requiring payment of a Debt that is purchased by the Factor be clearly endorsed with a notice in the following form:

'The Debt arising under this invoice has been assigned to .... Payment should only be made to ... Telephone: ... Fax: .... Payment to any other party will not constitute a valid discharge of the Debt and if this invoice is incorrect in any respect,...must be notified immediately.'

8 Collection from customers

8.1 Collection
The Factor shall have the sole and exclusive right of collecting and enforcing payment of every Purchased Debt and the Company shall not, unless so requested by the Factor, be concerned in the collection or enforcement of any Purchased Debt.

8.2 Assistance
The Company shall, if so requested by the Factor, co-operate to procure the collection and enforcement of each Purchased Debt and for such purpose the Factor may institute and conduct legal proceedings in the Company's name over which the Factor shall have full control, but before instituting them the Factor shall give written notice to the Company of its intention to do so.

8.3 Invoices
The Company shall deliver all original or copy invoices, credit notes or receipts in relation to any Debt offered to the Factor direct to the Factor unless otherwise authorised in writing by the Factor.

8.4 Receipt of payments by the Company
The Company shall immediately deliver to the Factor any payment, whether in cash or by cheque or other negotiable instrument, that the Company receives from a Customer in or towards payment of any Purchased Debt and the Company shall not deal with, mark, endorse or otherwise interfere with any such negotiable instrument, and until delivered to the Factor the Company shall hold in trust for the Factor any such payment received in respect of a Purchased Debt.

8.5 Negative undertaking
The Company shall not discount any bill of exchange or other negotiable instrument with any third party.

8.6 Appropriations of mixed payments
If a Customer makes either to the Factor or the Company a general payment on account of indebtedness whether or not arising under this agreement and makes no appropriation of such payment, such payment shall be appropriated:

8.6.1 towards the indebtedness in respect of Purchased Debts, and

8.6.2 towards the discharge of financial liability, if any, on the Company's part arising from obligations incurred by the Company under this agreement,

and the balance, if any, will be appropriated in such manner as the Company may determine.

8.7 Refund of excess mixed payment
The Company shall immediately deliver any general payment to the Factor and if this payment exceeds the amount so appropriated by the Factor, the Factor shall immediately pay the excess to the Company.

8.8 Credit notes
If a Customer becomes entitled to a credit or customer discount in respect of any Purchased Debt, whether approved or otherwise, the Company shall forthwith deliver to the Factor a

credit note in respect of it together with all documents and information relating to it that the Factor may require and the Factor may deliver such credit note to the Customer or may refuse to deliver that credit note in its absolute discretion, but such delivery of a credit note by the Factor shall be without prejudice to any right that the Factor may have as a result of the breach of any warranty contained in clause 14.

9   Accounts

9.1   Maintenance
The Factor shall maintain such accounts as it may consider appropriate and convenient to record the transactions referred to in this agreement.

9.2   Statements of account
Within 15 days after the last day of each month, the Factor shall send to the Company a statement of account which shall constitute conclusive evidence of the state of the account of the Company at the date thereof, unless, within a period of 10 days from receipt of any such statement, the Company notifies the Factor in writing that the Company questions all or any part of that statement.

10   Set-off
Without prejudice to clause 16, the Factor may at any time set-off any amount due to the Factor from the Company against any amount due from the Factor to the Company.

11   Records, information and disclosure

11.1   Corporate records
The Company shall keep all books required by law, and all proper accounts and minute books and shall permit the Factor at all reasonable times to inspect these, and the Company shall deliver to the Factor, at its own expense, copies of such accounts and books when requested by the Factor.

11.2   Annual audited accounts
The Company shall cause a proper audit of its books of account to be completed in relation to each of its financial years which, together with a report of the Company's directors, it shall deliver to the Factor not later than [three] months after the end of that financial year.

11.3   Quarterly financial statements
The Company shall supply the Factor quarterly financial statements relating to its business in such form and at such times as the Factor may reasonably require.

11.4   Other information
The Company shall disclose to the Factor at all times all matters of fact and opinion known to or held by the Company concerning the credit-worthiness of Customers and the validity of the Debt, and shall assist the Factor in every way to safeguard its interest.

11.5   Notification of matters to the Factor
The Company shall notify the Factor in writing immediately or in advance of:

11.5.1 any change in the terms upon which the Company contracts for the supply of goods, the carrying on of work or the performance of services;

11.5.2 any change in the nature of the Company's business;

11.5.3   any bank account opened or closed by the Company or any change in any of the Company's bank accounts;

11.5.4   any financial obligation, conditional or otherwise, the Company enters into;

11.5.5   the names of any business, firm or company in which any of the Company's directors, or any shareholders owning more than 5% of the Company's equity capital, has any interest;

11.5.6   any of the Company's shareholders owning more than 5% of the Company's equity capital at any time in the future;

11.5.7   all future appointments to the Company's board of directors;

11.5.8   transfers of shares where such transfer results in a shareholder owning more than 5% of the Company's equity capital;

11.5.9   any event tending to affect the warranty contained in clause 14.1; and

11.5.10 any event described in Clause 17.2.

11.6   Disputes

The Company shall, immediately upon learning of them, report to the Factor details of reclaimed, repossessed or returned merchandise, Customers' claims and disputes and any other matter affecting Purchased Debts.

11.7   Signatories

The Company shall provide the Factor with specimen signatures of all persons authorised to sign Offers and other documents relating to this agreement on behalf of the Company.

11.8   Confirmation of no security

The Company shall confirm to the Factor in writing before making an Offer under clause 2 that the Company has no fixed or floating charges outstanding on any part of its assets or undertakings and that the Company is not a party to any documentary credit or other arrangement whereby Debts purchased by the Factor are or could become subject to letters of trust or trust receipts.

11.9   Bank letter

The Company shall deliver to the Factor upon the execution of this agreement and upon the opening subsequently of any account with any bank a letter in a form specified by the Factor in respect of each such account duly completed and signed on the Company's behalf.

11.10   Breach of warranty

If, in relation to any Purchased Debt, there is any breach of clause 14 or the full amount owing has not been paid by the Customer by the Due Date, the Factor may disapprove the Debt and/or give written notice requiring the Company to repurchase such Debt forthwith and on the repurchase of such Debt all subsisting rights in respect of the same shall be deemed to have been assigned to the Company.

11.11   Reassignment

The Factor shall be entitled to give notice of such re-assignment to the Customer and on such re-assignment all the Factor's rights and obligations under this agreement in relation to such Debt shall cease. If such Debt has been formally assigned to the Factor pursuant to clause 13, the Factor shall, at the Company's expense, execute a formal reassignment thereof to the Company.

11.12   Payment by Customer

The Company shall procure that each Customer shall pay the full amount payable in respect of each Debt by its Due Date.

12   Negative undertakings

12.1   Security

The Company shall not create any fixed or floating charge or establish any other arrangement in respect of its assets or undertakings pursuant to which the Debts purchased by the Factor are or could become subject.

12.2   Variations to contracts

The Company shall not, without the prior written consent of the Factor, agree with a Customer any extension of time for payment of any Debt, or any waiver or modification of the terms of contract with a Customer.

13   Legal assignments

The Company shall, when requested by the Factor so to do, forthwith at its own cost, execute, stamp and deliver to the Factor a deed in a form approved by the Factor pursuant to which any Purchased Debt together with the benefit of all guarantees or other securities for or in respect of the same is assigned to the Factor absolutely, and, without prejudice to clause 7, the Company shall, if requested by the Factor, forthwith give notice in writing of such assignment to the Customer whose Debt is thereby assigned.

14   Representations and warranties

14.1   Initial

The Company represents and warrants that, in respect of all Debts offered to the Factor by the Company, that:

14.1.1   the Factor shall obtain a title valid binding and enforceable in all respects for the gross book value of such Debts under the normal terms of sale for the Company's business or under such other terms as may be mutually agreed by the Factor and the Company;

14.1.2   before the date of the Offer, the Company shall have fully performed all the obligations required in respect of such Debts;

14.1.3   the Purchased Debt arises in the ordinary course of the Company's business;

14.1.4   the amount payable by the Customer in respect of the Purchased Debt is not less than the gross invoice value, subject only to early settlement discount;

14.1.5   the Customer is not and will not be entitled to any counter-claim, set-off, defence or other equity against the Company in respect of the Debt and that the Company does not know, and could not on reasonable enquiry know, of any facts likely to lead to any such counter-claim, set-off, defence or other equity;

14.1.6   the Factor shall obtain a good unencumbered title to the Debt and the benefit of all related guarantees, indemnities, insurances and securities subject to no prior sale, assignment, transfer or encumbrance;

14.1.7   the Customer from whom the Debt is owing is not in breach of and has not sought to repudiate or rescind, the contract or any other contract with the Company;

14.1.8   the Company has not agreed with a Customer to any extension of time for payment of any Debt or for any waiver or modification of the terms of contract with a Customer except as provided for in this agreement; and

14.1.9   all information, reports and other papers and data furnished to the Factor are accurate, correct and complete in all material respects.

14.2   Repetition

The representations and warranties in clause 14.1 shall be deemed repeated on each day during the currency of this agreement by reference to the facts and circumstances subsisting on each such day.

15   General

15.1   Indemnity

The Company shall indemnify the Factor and keep it indemnified against any claim of whatsoever nature by a Customer against the Company or the Factor.

15.2   Insurance

Where the Debts are credit insured the Company shall not do any thing that could in any way prejudice the continuation in full force and effect of such insurance.

15.3   Security

The Company shall, on request by the Factor, execute a first fixed charge in favour of the Factor on all book and other Debts in such form as the Factor shall require as security for the payment of all sums due from the Company to the Factor under this agreement.

15.4   Assignments of insurances

The Company shall on request by the Factor deliver assignments in such form as the Factor shall require of all insurance policies which relate to Debts purchased by the Factor from the Company.

15.5   Exclusive rights

The Company grants the Factor the sole and exclusive right to factor the Debts and, while this agreement continues, the Company shall not, without the Factor's prior written consent, sell, encumber, assign, factor or transfer any Debt to any other person.

16   Retention on termination

16.1   Retention

If this agreement is terminated by either party hereto under clause 17.1 or if the Factor becomes entitled to terminate this agreement pursuant to clause 17.2, whether or not the agreement is so terminated:

16.1.1   the Factor may retain any amount received by it in respect of any Purchased Debt as security for the satisfaction of any financial liability on the Company's part, whether accrued or not, arising under this agreement or under any contract for the purchase of Debts by the Factor; and

16.1.2   the amounts so retained shall become payable to the Company only after all the amounts due from the Company to the Factor under this agreement have been paid.

16.2   No security interest

Clause 16.1 creates a contractual right of retention only and does not create any equitable charge or other security interest over any amount to which reference is made in that clause.

17 Duration

17.1 Initial period

This agreement shall continue for an initial period of…months and, subject to clause 17.2, until the expiry of not less than [3] months' written notice served by either party upon the other.

17.2 Termination events

The Factor may, upon giving to the Company written notice, terminate this agreement forthwith if:

17.2.1   the Company commits a breach of this agreement or of any contract arising from acceptance of any Offer; or

17.2.2   the Company is in breach of any obligation not referred to in clause 17.2.1; or

17.2.3   a petition for the Company's winding-up is presented or a resolution proposed for the Company's liquidation, whether voluntary or compulsory, or the Company commits any act of bankruptcy, draws a cheque that is dishonoured, calls a meeting of creditors, makes an arrangement or composition with creditors, or permits a judgment to remain unsatisfied for seven days; or

17.2.4   a receiver of any of the Company's assets is appointed; or

17.2.5   a petition is presented for the appointment of any administrative receiver of the Company's assets; or

17.2.6   any distress or execution is levied upon any of the Company's goods or premises; or

17.2.7   the Factor obtains judgment against the Company; or

17.2.8   the Company uses any payment made by the Factor to the Company otherwise than in the ordinary course of its business; or

17.2.9   the Company ceases to be under the same control as at the date of this agreement; or

17.2.10   the whole or part of the Company's business is sold, the Company ceases to carry on business, or the Company, in the Factor's opinion, substantially alters the nature of the its business.

17.3 Accrued rights and obligations

Termination of this agreement shall not affect any rights or obligations of either the Factor or the Company in relation to any Debt purchased prior to such termination and this agreement shall continue to the binding on the Factor and the Company.

18 Power of attorney

The Company, by way of security, irrevocably appoints the Factor as its attorney both before and after the termination of this agreement in the Company's name and on the Company's behalf:

18.1.1   to execute all documents and do all things required in order to give effect to this agreement including, but without limiting the generality of the foregoing, the endorsement on its behalf of any negotiable instrument and the execution of legal assignments of the Debts that may from time to time be sold by the Company to the Factor pursuant to this agreement; and

18.1.2   to appoint and remove at pleasure any substitute or agent for the Factor in respect of such matters.

19 Notices

Any demand, notice or other communication given under this agreement by a party to it shall be in writing and may be delivered to the other party or sent by first class prepaid letter at its address specified in this agreement or to its e-mail address or fax number at that address or to any other address, e-mail address or fax number as may be notified by the relevant party to the other party for that purpose, and shall be deemed to have been given or made and delivered, if by letter, 24 hours after posting, if by delivery, when left at the address, or if by e-mail or fax, transmitted

20 Applicable law

This agreement shall be governed by English Law.

21 Communication with the Company's bank

The Company irrevocably authorises the Factor:

21.1   to furnish its bank with information the Company's bank may require in relation to the state of the Company's accounts with the Factor; and

21.2   to obtain from its bank information the Factor may require as to the state of the Company's account with its bank.

22 Miscellaneous

22.1 Headings
The headings to the clauses in this agreement are intended for ease of reference only and shall not affect the meaning of the clauses.

22.2 No assignment of rights etc
The Company may not assign charge or in any manner dispose of or restrict its rights or obligations under this agreement without the prior written consent of the Factor.

22.3 Waiver
The Factor's rights under this agreement may be exercised as often as necessary, are cumulative and not exclusive of its rights under general law and may be waived only in writing and specifically. Delay in exercising or non-exercising of any such right is not a waiver of that right.

22.4 Severability
If any provision of this agreement is or becomes illegal, invalid or unenforceable that shall not affect the validity or enforceability of the other provisions of this agreement.

22.5 Entire agreement
This agreement is the entire understanding between the Factor and the Company and shall supersede any previous understanding, arrangement or agreement relating to the factoring of Debts by the Factor.

22.6 Counterparts
This agreement may be executed in any number of counterparts and this has the same effect as if the signatures on the separate counterparts were on a single copy of this agreement.

IN WITNESS etc

(signatures (or common seals) of the parties)
(signatures of witnesses)

6   Master block agreement between finance company and dealer providing for the block discounting of hire-purchase and credit sale agreements

THIS AGREEMENT is made the....day of...........

BETWEEN:

(1) *(name of finance company)* whose registered office is at *(address)* Company registration no ... ('the Company') and

(2) *(name of dealer)* [of *(address) or* whose registered office is at *(address)*] [Company Registration no ...] ('the Dealer').

IT IS AGREED as follows:

1   Discounting of Agreements

The Company will at the request of the Dealer and if the Company thinks fit purchase from the Dealer the rights of the Dealer ('the Contract Rights') under the hire-purchase and credit sale agreements ('the Agreements') entered into by the Dealer as owner or seller with the hirers or buyers named in the Agreements together with the goods comprised in such of the Agreements as are hire-purchase agreements.

2   Documents to accompany request to purchase

When submitting requests to purchase to the Company [(which requests shall be submitted at [weekly *or* monthly] intervals and shall relate to not less than ... agreements at a time)] the Dealer shall forward to the Company the following documents:

2.1   A schedule of the Agreements to which the request relates such schedule being in the Company's standard form for the time being or in such other form as may be approved by the Company;

2.2   The original agreements referred to in the schedule;

2.3   A satisfaction note signed by the hirer or buyer under each of the Agreements recording the acknowledgement of the hirer or buyer that he received the goods in proper condition.

3   Payment to Dealer

If the Company accepts the Dealer's request to purchase it shall notify the Dealer accordingly and then the Contract Rights and in the case of hire-purchase agreements the property in the goods comprised in those agreements shall vest in the Company which shall pay to the Dealer a sum representing the total balances outstanding under the Agreements ('the Collection Value') less:

3.1   a retention of...% of the Collection Value by way of security for performance of the Dealer's obligations under this agreement;

3.2   a discount charge of...% (or such other percentage as may from time to time be agreed) of the difference between the Collection Value and the retention.

4   Release of retention

[The retention referred to in clause 3.1 above shall be released to the Dealer after the Company has received from the Dealer and/or the hirers or buyers under the Agreements the Collection Value of the Agreements provided that if the Dealer has incurred any liability to the Company whether under this agreement or under any other agreement or in any manner whatsoever and whether such liability shall be by way of debt or damages the Company may apply in discharge of the Dealer's liability so much of the retention as shall be necessary for that purpose.

or

So long as the Dealer is not in default under this agreement and none of the hirers or buyers is in default under any of the Agreements the Company will release to the Dealer every [month] or with the written consent of the Company the Dealer may every [month] deduct from the instalments collected by him an aliquot portion of the retention spread over the period (or if there are differing periods the average period) for which the sums representing the Collection Value of the discounted agreements are payable. If any hirer or buyer under any of the Agreements is in default or if the Dealer has incurred any liability to the Company whether under this agreement or under any other agreement or in any manner whatsoever and whether such liability shall be by way of debt or damages the Company may apply in discharge of the Dealer's liability so much of the retention as shall be necessary for that purpose.]

5   Duties of Dealer

The Dealer undertakes at his own expense:

5.1   Agreement to assign
To execute an assignment of all or any of the Contract Rights in the form required by the Company and until such assignment to hold the Contract Rights and the Agreements as trustee for the Company.

5.2   Legal charges and stamp duty
To pay to the Company the amount of all legal charges and all stamp duties paid or incurred by the Company on any such assignment the Company being at liberty to recoup itself for such charges and duties out of the retention referred to in clause 3 above.

5.3   Dealer to keep accounts
To maintain proper accounts on behalf of the Company in the names of the hirers and buyers showing the amounts paid by and due from the hirers and buyers both before and after purchase of the Agreements by the Company under this agreement and to permit the Company and its agents full facilities to inspect and audit such accounts and take copies of and extracts from them whenever the Company shall require.

5.4   Dealings with other companies
To notify the Company of all dealings of the Dealer with any other person firm or company with whom the Dealer has an agreement or arrangement to discount hire-purchase credit sale or hiring agreements or rentals or to sell goods to be let by such person firm or company under hire-purchase or credit sale agreements and the Dealer shall at the request of the Company supply full details of all transactions entered into by the Dealer with such person firm or company.

5.5 Dealer's accounts

To provide the Company on request with audited and other accounts and balance sheets relating to the Dealer's business.

5.6 Bills of exchange and notes

By way of collateral security for the due performance of the Dealer's obligations under this agreement to accept or indorse such bills of exchange and make or indorse such promissory notes as may from time to time be required by the Company for sums not exceeding in the aggregate the total balances remaining due from the hirers or buyers under the Agreements. The Company shall have the right to transfer or negotiate any such bills or notes whether or not the Dealer is in default under the terms of this agreement and any transferee or holder of such bills or notes shall take them as a holder in due course free from any equities or defences of the Dealer.

5.7 Collection of instalments as agent

To collect punctually as agent for the Company all sums due under the Agreements and remit such sums without any deduction save as authorised by clause 4 above to the Company at such intervals as the Company may require holding them meanwhile on trust for the Company and if the Company so requires paying such sums into a bank account to be opened in the name of the Company or as the Company shall direct provided that the Company may at any time terminate the Dealer's authority and agency to collect sums from hirers or buyers under the Agreements and the Dealer shall then cease to collect or engage in collecting them.

5.8 Repossess goods on request

At the Dealer's own expense to repossess any goods comprised in any of the Agreements if required so to do but not otherwise provided that the Dealer shall not repossess any goods contrary to law or in an illegal manner and shall indemnify the Company against all claims arising from repossession and shall hold all repossessed goods on trust for the Company and deal with them as the Company shall direct.

6 Waiver of presentment and notice of dishonour

In respect of any bills of exchange or promissory notes taken by the Company from the Dealer pursuant to the provisions of this agreement the Dealer shall be deemed to have waived presentment for acceptance or payment and notice of dishonour and such waiver shall operate in favour of the Company and all other parties to whom the Company shall negotiate or otherwise transfer such bills or notes.

7 Power of attorney

The Dealer irrevocably appoints the Company the Dealer's attorney for the execution of any assignment required to be executed by the Dealer in favour of the Company under the provisions of this agreement and for the purpose of executing all other documents necessary to vest title in the Company to any of the Agreements or any goods comprised in the Agreements and further irrevocably appoints the Company the attorney of the Dealer for the purpose of accepting and indorsing all bills of exchange and making and indorsing all promissory notes which the Dealer is obliged to accept make or indorse pursuant to the provisions of this agreement.

8   Representations by Dealer

Every request to purchase sent by the Dealer to the Company pursuant to the provisions of this agreement shall be deemed to incorporate representations by the Dealer that:

8.1   the deposit shown in each of the Agreements as paid has in fact been paid in the manner stated and that any allowance given to the hirer or buyer for goods taken in part exchange is reasonable in relation to the value of such goods;

8.2   the Dealer is the owner of the goods specified in such of the Agreements as are hire-purchase agreements and that such goods are free from charges or incumbrances;

8.3   the details of the hirer or buyer and the particulars of the goods and other information set out in the Agreements are correct in every respect;

8.4   none of the goods comprised in any of the hire-purchase agreements was previously the property of the hirer or was previously held by the hirer under any other hire-purchase agreement except as stated in the hire-purchase agreement submitted by the Dealer;

8.5   the goods described in each of the Agreements are in existence and have been duly delivered to the hirer or buyer named in that agreement;

8.6   all the requirements of the Consumer Credit Act 1974 any regulations made under that Act and all other relevant Acts and regulations have been complied with in relation to each of the Agreements and that in particular such agreements comply with the formal requirements of the Consumer Credit Act 1974 and regulations made under that Act and the hirers or buyers have been supplied with all requisite copies of the Agreements;

8.7   the provisions of any of the Agreements excluding conditions of fitness or merchantable quality in relation to the goods were brought to the notice of the hirer or buyer and their effect made clear to him;

8.8   no right of action is vested in any hirer or buyer in respect of any representation breach of condition breach of warranty or other express or implied term relating to the goods comprised in any of the Agreements;

8.9   the goods specified in the Agreements are in good order repair and condition and comply in all respects with the requirements of the law and with all terms of the Agreements express or implied;

8.10   all the Agreements are fully valid and enforceable against and are not disputed or subject to cancellation or rescission by the hirers and buyers named in the Agreements and all contracts of guarantee or indemnity given in connection with the Agreements are fully valid enforceable and undisputed and the Dealer has no knowledge of any fact which would or might invalidate any such agreement or contract or affect any right to enforce them.

In the event of any of the above representations being false (whether the falsity was known to the Dealer or not) a loss to the Company shall be deemed to have occurred for the purpose of clause 9 below on the date upon which the company purchased the contract Rights under the Agreement or Agreements in respect of which such representations have been made and the Company may then avail itself of any or all of the remedies provided by clause 9 below.

9 Recourse provisions

9.1 The Dealer shall on demand indemnify the Company against all loss or damage which the Company may sustain as a result of purchasing from the Dealer any contract rights or any goods comprised in any of the Agreements whether or not such loss or damage results from the commission of any breach by the hirer or buyer under such agreement and whether or not the Company has any legal right to claim against such hirer or buyer or against any guarantor or indemnifier in respect of any associated contract of guarantee or indemnity for such loss or damage or has availed itself of its legal remedies against such hirer buyer guarantor or indemnifier or against the goods and the Dealer shall be liable to pay the amount of such loss or damage to the Company immediately it occurs.

9.2 For the purpose of this agreement the Company's loss in relation to any hire-purchase or credit sale agreement shall be deemed to have occurred as provided by clause 8 above or upon termination of the hire-purchase or credit sale agreement or of the hiring of the goods comprised in any such hire-purchase agreement or upon the hirer or buyer making default for 14 days in payment of any sum due under the agreement whichever of the above events shall first occur. Such loss shall be computed as:

    9.2.1 the unpaid balance of the total price or total purchase price payable under the hire-purchase or credit sale agreement including interest on overdue instalments payments made by the Company to third parties pursuant to powers contained in the agreement all legal and other expenses incurred by the Company in relation to the agreement and all other sums for which the hirer or buyer is liable under the hire-purchase or credit sale agreement (or would be liable if the hire-purchase or credit sale agreement were binding on him) and has not paid to the Company **less**

    9.2.2 such rebate for the acceleration of payment as the Company would have been obliged to allow the hirer or buyer under the terms of the hire-purchase or credit sale agreement if the hirer or the buyer had completed his payments on the date of the deemed loss;

provided that where in the case of a hire-purchase agreement the Company has repossessed and sold the goods comprised in the agreement credit shall be given for the net proceeds of sale (after deducting the costs and expenses of repossession storage insurance and sale) in computing such loss.

9.3 Where the Dealer has indemnified the Company as provided in this agreement (and in the case of a hire-purchase agreement the goods have not been sold by the Company) the Company shall at the Dealer's request and at his expense reassign to the Dealer the benefit of the hire-purchase or credit sale agreement (if such agreement is still subsisting and the rights of the owner under that agreement were assigned to the Company and are still vested in the Company) together with the Company's interest in the goods provided that:

    9.3.1 the Company shall not be under any liability to the Dealer to deliver to him the goods comprised in any such hire-purchase agreement or to take any steps for the recovery of such goods nor shall the Company incur any liability to the Dealer if the goods are no longer in existence or available to be repossessed or are in a defective damaged or useless state;

9.3.2 where the Dealer has incurred other liabilities to the Company whether under this agreement or otherwise the Company shall be entitled to dispose of the goods and to assign its rights under the hire-purchase or credit sale agreement and any associated contract of guarantee or indemnity as it thinks fit and to apply the proceeds of sale and of the assignment in reduction of such liabilities of the Dealer.

10   Interest on overdue payments

In the event of the Dealer failing to pay on demand the sums due under clause 9 above the Dealer shall be liable to pay interest on such sums at the rate of … % per year from the date of demand for payment to the date when payment is made. Such interest shall accrue from day to day and shall run after as well as before any judgment obtained against the Dealer.

11   Rights under the Sale of Goods Act 1979

The terms and conditions in favour of the Company under this agreement shall be in addition to and not in substitution for any terms conditions or warranties implied in favour of a purchaser of goods under the Sale of Goods Act 1979.

12   No waiver

The liability of the Dealer under this agreement shall not be discharged diminished or affected by the granting of any time or indulgence to the Dealer or any hirer buyer guarantor or indemnifier or by the effecting of any compromise with or any agreement not to sue any hirer buyer guarantor or indemnifier or by any variation of the terms of any of the Agreements or by the failure of the Company to institute or pursue any legal proceedings against any hirer buyer guarantor or indemnifier or to take any steps of any kind for recovery of the goods or to take hold unimpaired or enforce any security or securities for payment from any hirer buyer guarantor or indemnifier and no waiver by the Company for any branch of the Dealer's obligations under this agreement shall operate as a waiver of any future or continuing breach.

13   Dealer not agent

Save as expressly provided by this agreement the Dealer is not the agent of nor shall be deemed to have authority from the Company for any purpose and in particular he is not the agent of and shall not be deemed to have authority from the Company to vary terminate or accept notice of termination of any of the Agreements or to accept the return of any goods by any hirer or buyer under any such agreement or to institute any legal proceedings against any hirer buyer guarantor or indemnifier and if the Dealer collects any instalment from any hirer buyer after the Dealer's authority to collect such instalments has been terminated pursuant to the provisions of clause 5.7 above the sum so collected shall be held in trust for the Company.

14   Right of set-off

Where the Dealer has incurred any liability to the Company whether under this agreement or otherwise and whether such liability is liquidated or unliquidated the Company may set off the amount of such liability against any such that would otherwise be due to the Dealer under this agreement.

15   Notices

All notices demands and statements required or permitted to be given to the Dealer under the provisions of this agreement shall be validly given if served personally on the Dealer or sent by prepaid post to or left at the address of the Dealer stated in this agreement or at the Dealer's present or last known business or private address or where the Dealer is a registered company to or at its registered office or any present or the last known business address. Any such notice demand or statement sent to the Dealer by post shall be conclusively deemed to have been received by the Dealer within 48 hours after the time of posting.

16   Termination of agreement

This agreement may be terminated by either party by [one month's] notice in writing given at any time but such termination shall be without prejudice to the liabilities of either party accrued before the date of termination.

17   Third party rights

The parties confirm that they do not intend any third party to have the right to enforce any provision of this agreement under the Contracts (Rights of Third Parties) Act 1999 or otherwise.

18   Entire agreement

This agreement, together with any documents referred to in clauses 2 and 3, represents the entire agreement between the parties in relation to its subject matter and supersedes all other written or oral agreements made by or on behalf of the Company and the Dealer in relation to it. It may be changed only by agreement in writing between the parties.

19   Law and jurisdiction

This agreement shall be governed by, and construed in accordance with, English law and the parties shall submit to the exclusive jurisdiction of the courts of England and Wales.

AS WITNESS etc
(signatures of both parties)

7 Trust receipt

To *(name of bank)*
of *(address)*

(date)

1   Acknowledgement of receipt

[I *or* We] acknowledge that [I *or* we] have received from you, upon and subject to the terms and conditions set out below, the documents of title described in the schedule below ('the Documents' relating to the goods described in it ('the Goods'), which are now pledged to you as security upon the terms of *(specify details of memorandum of pledge, letter of hypothecation etc as appropriate)*.

2   Documents etc to be held as trustee

[I *or* We] acknowledge that [I *or* we] have received the Documents and will hold them, the Goods, the proceeds of any sale of the Goods and all insurance money arising from them, as trustee[s] for you.

3   Purpose and terms

[I *or* We] hold the Documents and will deal with them only for the following purpose and on the following terms that is to say in order to obtain delivery of and to warehouse the Goods. The Goods will be warehoused in your name or otherwise as directed by you but at [my *or* our] expense, and [I *or* we] undertake to keep the Goods duly covered by insurance as agreed between us pursuant to *(specify details as above)* and in case of loss to pay the insurance money immediately and specifically to you without any deduction *[or* in order to deliver the Goods to the buyer[s] named in the schedule below. [I *or* We] agree to pay to you immediately and specifically on receipt the whole proceeds of sale and each part of the proceeds (whatever form they may take) without any deduction. Pending the sale, [I *or* we] undertake to keep the Goods duly covered by insurance as agreed between us in *(specify details as above)* and in case of loss to pay the insurance money immediately and specifically to you without any deduction. [I *or* We] confirm that [I am *or* we are] not indebted to the buyer[s].

4   Transaction to be kept separate

[I *or* We] undertake that this transaction will be kept separate from any other transaction and that the Documents, the Goods, the proceeds of any sale and all insurance money shall be kept separate and distinct from any other documents, goods, proceeds of sale or insurance money relating to or arising from any other transaction.

5   Documents returnable on demand

[I *or* We] undertake to return to you immediately on demand at any time (whether or not the purpose set out above shall have been completed) the Documents and/or any other documents received by us in exchange or substitution for them and to comply promptly and fully with any instructions which you may give as to the manner of dealing with the Goods or any of them or the removal of them to, or storage of them at, any place.

6   Governing law and jurisdiction

[Details omitted.]

SCHEDULE

Reference Number: ....

Particulars of the Documents: ....

Description of the Goods: ....

Marks and Numbers: ....

Vessel: ....`

Name[s] of buyer[s]: ....

Invoice price: ....

(signature(s) ofcustomer(s))

8 'All monies' continuing bank guarantee

To *(name of bank)* of *(address)*

(date)

[I *(or)* We] *(name(s) of guarantor(s))* of *(address(es))* ([together called] ('the Guarantor;) in consideration of your from time to time making or continuing loans or advances to or coming under liabilities or discounting bills for or otherwise giving credit or granting banking facilities or accommodation or granting time to or on account of *(name of the principal)* of *(address)* ('the Principal') unconditionally guarantee to and agree with you as follows:

1   Guarantor to pay on demand

The Guarantor shall pay to you on demand:

1.1   all money that is now or shall at any time or times after this date be due or owing or payable to you from or by the Principal under or in respect of any dealing, transaction or engagement either solely or jointly with any other person, firm or company, whether as principal or surety, and whether upon current account or other banking account or otherwise or in respect of bills, drafts, notes or other negotiable instruments made, drawn, accepted, advised, endorsed or paid by you or on your account for the Principal, either solely or jointly as stated above, or that you may from time to time become liable to pay in respect of any bills, drafts, notes, letters of credit or any other dealing, transaction or engagement on account of or for the benefit or accommodation of the Principal, either solely or jointly as stated above, together with

1.2   all interest, costs, commissions and other banking charges and expenses you may in the course of your business as bankers charge against the Principal and all legal and other costs, charges and expenses you may incur in enforcing or obtaining payment of any such money from the Principal, or attempting so to do,

provided that the total amount recoverable from the Guarantor under this guarantee shall not exceed £...together with a further sum for the interest, costs, commissions and other costs, charges and expenses as stated above that have accrued or shall accrue due to you at any time before or at any time after the date of the demand as stated above, provided that if the amount is not completed and this proviso is not deleted, the guarantee will be interpreted as unlimited.

2   Continuing security

This guarantee shall be a continuing security, subject only to such notice as is mentioned below, and shall not be satisfied, discharged or affected by any intermediate payment or settlement of account.

3   Effect of death of guarantor

This guarantee shall not be determined or affected by the death of the Guarantor or of any one or more of the persons constituting the Guarantor.

4   Notice to determine guarantee

The Guarantor or any one or more of the persons constituting the Guarantor or any survivor or survivors of such persons or the personal representatives of the Guarantor or of any one or more of such persons who are dead may at any time give you notice in writing to determine this guarantee at a date ('the Cessation Date') not less than 3 calendar months after receipt by you of such notice and this guarantee shall cease with respect to transactions after the Cessation Date, provided that the Guarantor shall remain liable under this guarantee:

4.1   in respect of all obligations of the Principal to you outstanding at the Cessation Date, with interest on such obligations until actual payment at the rate charged by you against the Principal, and

4.2   in respect of all money, interest, costs, commissions and other banking charges and expenses that will or may become due to you from the Principal under or in respect of any dealing, transaction or engagement effected or entered into either before, on or after the Cessation Date pursuant to any commitment, express or implied, assumed or undertaken by you to the Principal before the Cessation Date, and

4.3   for all legal and other costs, charges and expenses you may incur as stated above.

5   Payment

The obligations of the Guarantor under this guarantee shall be to make payment to you[, in the currency in which the applicable obligation ought to have been or ought to be discharged by the Principal,] strictly in accordance with the terms and provisions of any agreement, express or implied, between you and the Principal applicable to each respective obligation of the Principal, regardless of any law, regulation or decree, now or after this date in effect, which affects or might in any manner affect any of such terms or provisions or your rights as against the Principal.

6   New account

It shall be lawful for you at any time after notice to determine this guarantee has been given or after payment of the money guaranteed hereby has been demanded of the Guarantor to continue any existing or to open any new account with the Principal and no money subsequently paid into such account shall be appropriated in discharge of any money guaranteed hereby unless it has been expressly directed by the person paying the same at the time of such payment to be so appropriated.

[...]

9   Effect of other guarantees etc

This guarantee and your rights under it shall be in addition to and shall not be in any way prejudiced or affected by any one or more other securities or guarantees for the Principal that you may now or subsequently hold whether from the Guarantor or any of the persons constituting the Guarantor or from any other person.

10   Indulgence

You may, at any time and without reference to the Guarantor, refuse further credit to the Principal. The liability of the Guarantor under this guarantee shall be unaffected by any arrangement you may make with the Principal or with any other person that, but for this provision, might operate to diminish or discharge the liability of or otherwise provide a defence to a surety. Without prejudice to the generality of the above you may, at any time and without reference to the Guarantor, give time for payment or grant any other indulgence and give up, deal with, vary, exchange or abstain from perfecting or enforcing any other securities or guarantees held by you at any time and may discharge any party to them and may release or realise such securities or guarantees or any of them, as you think fit and may compound with, accept compositions from and make any other arrangements with the Principal or any person liable on bills, notes or other securities or guarantees held or to be held by you without affecting the Guarantor's liability under this guarantee.

11   Resorting to other means of payment

You are to be at liberty but not bound to resort for your own benefit to any other means of payment at any time and in any order you think fit without in consequence diminishing the liability of the Guarantor and you may enforce this guarantee either for the payment of the ultimate balance after resorting to other means of payment or for the balance due at any time notwithstanding that other means of payment have not been resorted to and in the latter case without entitling the Guarantor to any benefit from such other means of payment so long as any money remains due or owing or payable, whether actually or contingently, from or by the Principal to you.

12   No proof in competition with bank

12.1 This guarantee shall take effect as a guarantee of the whole and every part of the money due or owing or payable and to become due or owing or payable as stated above ('the Money Due') and accordingly the Guarantor shall not be entitled as against you:

  12.1.1 to any right of proof in the bankruptcy, liquidation or insolvency of the Principal or any other surety, or

  12.1.2 to any other right of a surety, including any right of contribution from any other surety, discharging, in whole or in part, his liability in respect of the principal debt, or

  12.1.3 to share in any security held or money received by you on account of the obligations of the Principal or any other sure, or

  12.1.4 to have or exercise any rights as surety, including any such right of contribution as stated above, in competition with you

unless and until the whole of the Money Due has been completely discharged and satisfied.

12.2 Until the Money Due has been discharged and satisfied in full the Guarantor shall not, if any money has become payable or has been paid by the Guarantor under this guarantee, take any step to enforce repayment or to exercise any other rights, claims or remedies of any kind that may accrue howsoever to the Guarantor in respect of:

  12.2.1 the amount so payable or so paid, including any such right of contribution as stated above, or

  12.2.2 any other money for the time being due to the Guarantor from the Principal or any other surety, provided that in the event of the bankruptcy, liquidation or insolvency of the Principal or any other surety, the Guarantor shall, if so directed by you but not otherwise, prove for the whole or any part of the money due to the Guarantor from the Principal or any other surety as stated above on terms that the benefit of such proof and of all money to be received by the Guarantor in respect of it shall be held in trust for you and applied in discharging the obligations of the Guarantor to you under this guarantee.

12.3   To enable you to sue the Principal or any other surety or prove in the bankruptcy, liquidation or insolvency of the Principal or any other surety for the whole of the Money Due, or to preserve intact the liability of any other party, you may at any time place and keep, for such time as you think prudent, any money received, or realised under this guarantee or under any other guarantee or security to the credit, either of the Guarantor, or such other person or transaction, if any, as you think fit, without any intermediate obligation on your part to apply it or any part of it in or towards the discharge of the Money Due, or any intermediate right on the part of the Guarantor to sue the Principal or any other surety or to prove in the bankruptcy, liquidation or insolvency of the Principal or any other surety in competition with or so as to diminish any dividend or other advantage that would or might come to you, or to treat the liability of the Principal or any other surety as diminished.

12.4   As used in this clause and clause 15 of this guarantee the expression 'any other surety' includes any other person constituting the Guarantor and any party or person referred to in clause 10 above.

13   Evidence of amount due

For all purposes including any legal proceedings a copy of any account of the Principal in your books signed by any of your officers shall be accepted by the Guarantor as conclusive evidence of the state of that account.

14   Change in constitution of principal or guarantor

If the Principal or the Guarantor is a partnership or a company, this guarantee shall remain in full force and effect notwithstanding any change in the constitution of the Principal or the Guarantor.

15   No security received by guarantor

It is declared by the Guarantor that no security has been received by the Guarantor from the Principal or any other surety for the giving of this guarantee and it is agreed by the Guarantor that the Guarantor shall not, as long as this guarantee remains in force, take any security in respect of the Guarantor's liability under this guarantee without first obtaining your written consent.

16   Money not recoverable on footing of guarantee

As a separate and independent stipulation it is agreed by the Guarantor that any money mentioned in clause 1 above that may not be recoverable on the footing of a guarantee, whether by reason of any legal limitation, disability or incapacity on or of the Principal or any other fact or circumstance, and whether known to you or the Guarantor or not, shall nevertheless be recoverable from the Guarantor as sole or principal debtor in respect of it and shall be paid by the Guarantor on demand.

17   Change in bank's constitution or its amalgamation etc

This guarantee shall continue to bind the Guarantor notwithstanding any amalgamation or merger that may be effected by you with any other company and notwithstanding any reconstruction by you involving the formation of and transfer of the whole or any part of your undertaking and assets to a new company and notwithstanding the sale or transfer of the whole or any part of your undertaking and assets to another company, whether the company with which you amalgamate or merge or the company to which you transfer the whole or any part of your undertaking and assets, either on a reconstruction or sale or transfer as stated above, does or does not differ from you in its objects, character or constitution, it being the intent of the Guarantor that this guarantee shall remain valid and effectual in all respects in favour of, against and with reference to, and that the benefit of this guarantee and all rights conferred upon you by this guarantee may be assigned to and enforced by, any such company and proceeded on in the same manner to all intents and purposes as if that company had been named in this guarantee instead of and/or in addition to you.

[18   Other currency

If, at the time any demand is made under this guarantee, any amount is due or owing or payable to you from the Principal in any currency or currencies other than that in which any limit contained in the proviso in clause 1 above is expressed, then:

18.1   the obligation of the Guarantor shall be to make payment in that currency, but you may, at your discretion, require payment either in that currency or in the currency of that limit, or partly in one way and partly in the other, and

18.2   that limit shall be treated as a limit expressed in the other currency or, if more than one other currency is involved, as a limit in the aggregate expressed in the other currencies. For this purpose the limit shall be deemed to have been expressed in the other currency or currencies converted at the rate of respective rates of exchange to be determined in good faith by you to be effective at the date of payment, or each respective payment, by the Guarantor]

[19   Payments by guarantor

19.1   Each payment to be made by the Guarantor under this guarantee shall be made to you, in the appropriate currency in accordance with the terms of this guarantee, to the credit of your account with whichever bank or banks located in the country of that currency, as is designated by you.

19.2   All such payments shall be made in full without set-off or counterclaim and free and clear of and without deduction of or withholding for or on account of any tax of any nature now or subsequently imposed by any country or any subdivision or taxing authority of or in such country or any federation or organisation of which such country is a member unless required by law.

19.3   If any such payment is subject to any such tax or if the Guarantor is required to make any such deduction or withholding, the Guarantor shall pay such tax, shall ensure that the payment, deduction or withholding shall not exceed the minimum legal liability for it and shall simultaneously pay to you such additional amount as may be necessary to enable you to receive, after all such payments, deductions and withholdings, a net amount equal to the full amount payable under this guarantee.

19.4   If the Guarantor makes any such payment, deduction or withholding the Guarantor shall within 30 days forward to you an official receipt or other official documentation evidencing the payment or payment of the deduction or withholding.

19.5   As used in this clause, the term 'tax' includes all levies, imposts, duties, charges, fees, deductions, withholdings, turnover tax, transaction tax, stamp tax and any restrictions or conditions resulting in a charge.]

[20   Currency indemnity

It is further agreed by the Guarantor that if any judgment or order is given or made for the payment of any amount due under this guarantee and is expressed in a currency other than that in which that amount is payable by the Guarantor under this guarantee, the Guarantor shall indemnify you against any loss incurred by you as a result of any variation having occurred in rates of exchange between the date as at which that amount is converted into the other currency for the purpose of the judgment or order and the date of actual payment pursuant to it. This indemnity shall constitute a separate and independent obligation of the Guarantor and shall apply irrespective of any indulgence granted to the Guarantor from time to time and shall continue in full force and effect notwithstanding any such judgment or order as stated above.]

21   No waiver of rights under guarantee

No delay or omission on your part in exercising any right, power, privilege or remedy in respect of this guarantee shall impair such right, power, privilege or remedy or be construed as a waiver of it nor shall any single or partial exercise of any such right, power, privilege or remedy preclude any further exercise of it or the exercise of any other right, power, privilege or remedy. The rights, powers, privileges and remedies provided in this guarantee are cumulative and not exclusive of any rights, powers, privileges or remedies provided by law.

22   Joint and several liability

Where this guarantee is signed by or on behalf of more than one person as guarantor or is signed by one person for himself and on behalf of other persons, whether such person is signing on behalf of a partnership or otherwise, the expression 'the Guarantor' shall include all such persons as stated above and the liability of the Guarantor under this guarantee shall be the joint and several liability of such persons and any demand for payment made by you to any one or more of the persons so jointly and severally liable shall be deemed to be a demand made to all such persons. You may release or discharge any one or more of such persons from liability under this guarantee or compound with, accept compositions from, or make any other arrangements with, any of such persons without in consequence releasing or discharging any other party to this guarantee or otherwise prejudicing or affecting your rights and remedies against any such other party.

23   Joint signatories

If this guarantee is signed by or on behalf of more than one person and any one or more of them is not bound by the provisions of this guarantee., whether by reason of his or their lack of capacity or improper execution of this guarantee or for any other reason, the remaining signatory or signatories shall continue to be bound by the provisions of this guarantee as if the other signatory or signatories had never been party to it.

24   Demands

Any demand under this guarantee shall be given by first class prepaid post or fax addressed to the Guarantor or to the person to or upon whom the demand is to be made at the registered or principal office or last known place of abode of the Guarantor or of that person, as the case may be. A demand so made shall be deemed to have been duly made, if left at that address, on the day it was so left or, if sent by first class prepaid post, 2 weekdays after the time when the demand was put in the post and in proving delivery it shall be sufficient to prove that the demand was properly addressed and put in the post. Any such demand sent by fax shall be deemed to have been duly made at the time of dispatch.

25   Interpretation

In this guarantee, where the context permits, the singular includes the plural and vice versa, and references to persons include references to companies.

26   Governing law and jurisdiction

(insert clause as appropriate)

27   Property in the guarantee to belong to the bank

The paper on which this guarantee is written shall remain at all times the property of the Bank

[AS *(or)* IN] WITNESS etc

(signature(s) or signature(s) and seal(s) of guarantor)
(signatures of witnesses)

[I *(or)* We] acknowledge receipt of a copy of the above guarantee

(signature(s) of guarantor)

INDEX